KU-270-333

The HUTCHINSON ALMANAC 2000

The HUTCHINSON ALMANAC 2000

Helicon

Published annually since 1998
Second edition published 1999

Helicon Publishing Ltd
42 Hythe Bridge Street
Oxford OX1 2EP

e-mail: admin@helicon.co.uk
Web site: http://www.helicon.co.uk

Typesetting and Layout
TechType, Abingdon, Oxon

Printed and bound in Italy by
De Agostini, Novara

ISBN 1–85986–301–9

British Cataloguing in Publication Data

A catalogue record of this book is available from the British Library

Contents

Feature Essays

Chronologies

NOTE TO THE READER

Welcome to the second edition of *The Hutchinson Almanac*. The Almanac provides thousands of facts, figures, and statistics about today's world, as well as helpful, practical information, in one accessible and clearly organized volume.

The book is divided into 20 chapters, which together cover all aspects of modern life. The 'Contents' lists the main topics covered in each chapter of the book. Cross-references in the text and a detailed index at the back of the book mean the user can easily locate information they are looking for.

Within each chapter, related items are grouped under appropriate headings, and many are presented in quick reference list, table, or graph form. Throughout the Almanac, key developments and news stories of the year are covered in more depth in 'The Year in Review' at the beginning of each section, in specially commissioned essays written by experts in their respective fields, and in chronologies. A list of useful 'Web sites' appears at the end of most chapters.

In addition to the chapter-specific icons, the following symbols are used throughout the book to denote recurring features:

 Chronology

Glossary

 Directory

New phone codes for six areas of the UK – London, Coventry, Cardiff, Portsmouth, Southampton, and Northern Ireland – will go into use on 22 April 2000 (parallel running began on 1 June 1999). Local numbers in these areas will also change, to become eight-digit numbers, as in the following examples:

London	(0171) 123 4567	→	(020) 7123 4567
London	(0181) 123 4567	→	(020) 8123 4567
Belfast	(01232) 1234567	→	(028) 9012 3456
Cardiff	(01222) 1234567	→	(029) 2012 3456
Coventry	(01203) 1234567	→	(024) 7612 3456
Portsmouth	(01705) 1234567	→	(023) 9212 3456
Southampton	(01703) 1234567	→	(023) 8012 3456

The new codes do not appear in the book.

The information included in the Almanac is derived from the most accurate and up-to-date sources available at the time of compilation. Material in the book covers the period from July 1998 through to the end of June 1999, however, some later updates have been added up to August 1999. Every year all entries in the Almanac are checked and updated by a team of researchers and editors. We welcome reader comments and suggestions on the content of the book. Your feedback is invaluable for the continued improvement of the Almanac, which the editors hope you will enjoy now and for many editions to come.

August 1999

Contributors

Feature Writers

DAPO AKANDE, lecturer in international law at the University of Nottingham

TIM ALLMAN, contributing writer for *Encyclopedia of Technology and Applied Sciences*

PETER BARTLETT, lecturer in anti-discrimination law in the School of Law, University of Nottingham and member of the Ontario bar

DR SUE BERRY, principal lecturer in tourism management in the Faculty of Business, University of Brighton, and a member of the council of the National Trust

PAUL BRAY, freelance journalist specializing in technology

LORD BRIGGS, former vice chancellor of the University of Sussex (1967–76) and provost of Worcester College, Oxford (1976–91), chancellor of the Open University (1978–94), and author of many books on social history

SIMON BUCKBY, journalist with *The Financial Times*, author, and broadcaster

DR IAN J DERBYSHIRE, writer on history, politics, and government; co-author of *Political Systems of the World* and *Politics in Britain: from Callaghan to Thatcher*; and author and editor of the Chambers Political Spotlights series

DR J DENIS DERBYSHIRE, author of *The Business of Government* and *An Introduction to Public Administration*; co-author of *Political Systems of the World* and *Politics in Britain: from Callaghan to Thatcher*

ANNA FARKAS, freelance researcher and writer

DR NICHOLAS J FORD, senior lecturer in geography, University of Exeter, specializing in population and medical geography

BARRY FOX, freelance journalist specializing in communications technology

TIM FURNISS, spaceflight correspondent for the UK aerospace magazine *Flight International*

GEORGE JONES, Chief Political Editor for *The Daily Telegraph*

MAUREEN O'CONNOR, writer on education for *The Independent* and *Times Educational Supplement*; author of *Hackney Downs – the School that Dared to Fight*

DR CHRISTOPHER PARTRIDGE, lecturer in theology and religious studies at University College, Chester

STEPHANIE POWELL, Amnesty International UK Section

BEN RAMOS, freelance writer

SEAN RICKARD, lecturer at Cranfield Management School

PETER ROBINSON, senior economist at the Institute for Public Policy Research, London

DAVID SHUKMAN, BBC World Affairs Correspondent, formerly BBC Defence Correspondent (1987–95), and Europe Correspondent (1995–99)

DR TOM WILKIE, head of biomedical ethics at the Wellcome Trust

---

Researchers
Anne Baker
Alexandra Clayton
Andrew Colquhoun
Malgorzata Colquhoun
Ian Derbyshire
Denis Derbyshire
Anna Farkas
Ramin Gray
Lisa Isenman Sullivan
Sara Jenkins-Jones
Hester Kapur
Myfanwy Lloyd
Richard Martin
Dan McCausland
David Milsted
Sue Purkis
Ben Ramos
Helen Rappaport
Catherine Thompson

Editorial Director
Hilary McGlynn

Managing Editor
Roger Tritton

Co-ordinating Editor
Alysoun Owen

Publishing Systems Manager
Graham Bennett

Database Editor
Claire Lishman

Section Editors
Denise Dresner
Barbara Fraser
Clare Ramos

Editors
Emma Beecham
Clare Collinson
Malgorzata Colquhoun
Tessa Hanford
Mark McGuinness
Rachel Minay
Stephen Pavlovich
Emma Pearse

Permissions Co-ordinator
Connie Hallam

Production Director
Tony Ballsdon

Art and Design Manager
Terence Caven

Picture Research
Elizabeth Loving

QUOTATIONS OF THE YEAR

July 1998

We are not saying that, simply because someone has a past, they can't have a future. We always acknowledge that people have to change.

David Trimble Leader of the Ulster Unionists. Accepting his election as First Minister of the Northern Ireland Assembly; *Daily Telegraph*, 2 July 1998.

One is not amused at that.

Her Majesty the Queen On Sol Campbell's disallowed goal against Argentina; *Daily Telegraph*, 3 July 1998.

Rape isn't actually the worst thing that can happen to a woman if you're safe and alive.

Fay Weldon Novelist. *Independent on Sunday*, 5 July 1998.

Even with my sinuses I could smell the stench coming out of these revelations.

William Hague Leader of the Opposition. Returns from surgery to berate the prime minister on the 'cash-for-access' scandal; *Daily Telegraph*, 9 July 1998.

I'm terribly sorry, but would you mind if my wife and I butted in? The thing is, I've got to go and see the Queen at six o'clock.

Tony Blair Prime Minister. Pulls rank at a parents' evening at the London Oratory school; *Independent*, 11 July 1998.

The honest truth is that if this Government were to propose a massacre of the first-born, it would still have no difficulty in getting it through the Commons.

Diane Abbott Labour MP. On the perils of landslide victories and 'Stepford Backbenchers' (backbenchers with unquestioning allegiance); *Independent on Sunday*, 12 July 1998.

I love you, Spain!

Whitney Houston Singer. Greeting her fans in Portugal; *Independent on Sunday*, 12 July 1998.

We can, if we wish, put our minds to paralyse this country in a matter of hours.

David McNarry Leading member of the Ulster Orange Order. On the stand-off at Drumcree, where troops and police prevented Orangemen from staging a banned march; *Independent on Sunday*, 12 July 1998.

No road is worth a life, let alone the lives of three little boys.

William Bingham Chaplain to the Armagh Lodge of the Orange Order. On the murder in a 'loyalist' firebombing of three young boys in Ballymoney, as members of the Orange Order continued their stand-off with security forces in Drumcree; *Daily Telegraph*, 13 July 1998.

She is not sailing into the dark. The voyage is over and, under the dark escort of Alzheimer's, she has arrived somewhere. So have I.

John Bayley Retired Professor of English. On the illness of his wife, the novelist and philosopher Dame Iris Murdoch, who died on 8 February 1999; *New Yorker*, 20 July 1998.

By burying the remains of innocent victims we want to expiate the sins of our ancestors. Guilty are those who committed this heinous crime and those who have been justifying it for decades – all of us.

Boris Yeltsin President of Russia. At the funeral of Tsar Nicholas II and his family, murdered by the Bolsheviks in 1918; *Daily Telegraph*, 18 July 1998.

If 150 million people fast on Mondays and Thursdays, we would save 3 million tons of rice – the same amount we would otherwise have to import.

B J Habibie President of Indonesia. On his country's food shortages and economic crisis; *Newsweek*, 20 July 1998.

The children crying all night long. Crying, crying, crying. And no one to hear them. That is what I remember.

Lennard Pundi Villager of Warapu, Papua New Guinea. On the tsunami that claimed the life of his infant daughter, and some 4,000 others; *Sunday Telegraph*, 26 July 1998.

We are morally bankrupt in a situation that will bring us to hell.

David Ervin Leader of the Progressive Unionist Party of Northern Ireland. On the murder of three Roman Catholic boys; *Newsweek*, 27 July 1998.

Look what has become of this country. We are one of the world's biggest producers of oil, and we have no fuel. We have more power stations than we need, and no electricity. Madness.

Olusegun Obasanjo President of Nigeria. On his release from prison after three years; *Newsweek*, 27 July 1998.

Did you call in Miss Harman on Monday and say, 'Congratulations on your numerous successes, you're fired'?

William Hague Leader of the Opposition. Questioning the Prime Minister about his cabinet reshuffle; *Daily Telegraph*, 30 July 1998.

August 1998

I'm considered a first-class soldier – I can blow up bridges, ski down mountains, and free-fall from the skies. But in my heart I just want to be a woman.

Joe Rushton Sergeant-Major. On becoming the Army's first transsexual; *Independent on Sunday*, 9 August 1998.

We weren't brought up to throw in the towel. We were brought up to bite bullets and fold towels neatly.

Lord Glenconnor Formerly known as 'King of Mustique' by fellow jetsetters.

On weathering life's misfortunes; *Daily Telegraph*, 11 August 1998.

My biggest mistake was not to include Eileen Drewery in the back-up team for France.

Glenn Hoddle England football manager. Valuing his faith-healer over penalty-taking practice in his World Cup diary; *Sun*, 11 August 1998.

If England win at anything, from the World Cup to tiddlywinks, the people are happy.

Alec Stewart England's cricket captain. After England beat South Africa in the Fifth Test to take the series 2–1, their first home Test series victory since 1985; *Daily Telegraph*, 11 August 1998.

This is for the dead. This is not charity from the Swiss. My father deposited the money. This is my money.

Estelle Sapir Holocaust survivor. On finally receiving some of the money deposited with Crédit Suisse by her father Joseph, who died in the Maideneck concentration camp in 1943; *Daily Telegraph*, 14 August 1998.

The meltdown in Russian markets has reached the terminal phase. The banking system is, to all intents and purposes, pretty well wiped out.

George Soros Currency speculator. Uttering a self-fulfilling prophecy on 13 August, 'Black Thursday' for the Russian economy; *Daily Telegraph*, 14 August 1998.

WHY?

Inscription on a bouquet in Omagh, Co. Armagh. On the killing of 29 people, including 9 children, 14 women, and three generations of a single family, as well as the injuring of over 200 people, after a bomb planted by the 'Real IRA' exploded in the town on 15 August 1998.

This is not a mass grave. These are the bodies of terrorists.

Bozidar Filic Colonel in the Serbian police. On the discovery of some 500 Albanian bodies in a rubbish tip in Kosovo; *Newsweek*, 17 August 1998.

Indeed I did have a relationship with Ms Lewinsky that was not appropriate. In fact, it was wrong.

Bill Clinton President of the USA. Broadcasting to the nation after giving evidence to the grand jury; 17/18 August 1998.

In France we tried to make films like The Full Monty, but they were just boring. It was people on the dole eating soup.

Daniel Auteuil French actor. *Independent*, 22 August 1998.

Botha has been publicly held accountable for his actions in a court of law and he has been afforded every opportunity to defend himself – something which was often denied to his political opponents during the years of his rule.

Alex Boraine Deputy chairman of South Africa's Truth and Reconciliation Commission. After former President P W Botha was fined 10,000 Rand (c. £1,000) for refusing to appear before it; *Daily Telegraph*, 22 August 1998.

Diana benefited a great deal more from her association with the mines issue than the mines issue has benefited in return. The Diana Memorial Fund hasn't given a dime to mine clearance, and she didn't leave it a dime.

Mike Croll Mine clearance expert. *Independent on Sunday*, 23 August 1998.

I am not going anywhere. I am not resigning. To get rid of me would be very difficult and, if you take into account my character, probably impossible.

Boris Yeltsin President of Russia. Broadcasting to the nation as the rouble crashes, and the value of all stocks quoted on the Moscow stock exchange fall below that of Sainsbury's; *Daily Telegraph*, 29 August 1998.

September 1998

Sinn Féin believe the violence we have seen must be for all of us now a thing of the past – over, done with and gone.

Gerry Adams Former IRA commander, president of Sinn Féin, and member of the Northern Ireland Assembly. In a statement – approved by the British, Irish, and American governments – on the eve of President Clinton's visit to Ireland; Radio 5 Live, 1 September 1998.

It is high time to stop the lilt of laughter and language being drowned out by bombs and guns and sirens.

Bill Clinton President of the USA. Addressing 700 relatives of victims of the Omagh bombing at a private meeting in the town; *Daily Telegraph*, 4 September 1998.

I wish I'd been less of a pragmatist when I was young. Mr Blair is a fundamentally decent person, but he doesn't know what he believes in.

Chris Patten Former Conservative MP and former governor of Hong Kong. Interview in the *Daily Telegraph*, 4 September 1998.

If this sale goes through, Murdoch can close his fist round the very heart of British culture and shout triumphantly, 'Gotcha!'.

Sue Mott Sports journalist. On the proposed sale of Manchester United plc to BSkyB for £623 million, later blocked by the Department of Trade and Industry on the recommendation of the Monopolies and Mergers Commission; *Daily Telegraph*, 7 September 1998.

It's unlikely to get worse, because it can't possibly get worse.

Alexander Olson Head of the Public Opinion Foundation. On ceasing to measure President Yeltsin's popularity; *Newsweek*, 7 September 1998.

All Americans, including the President, are entitled to enjoy a private family life, free from public or governmental scrutiny. But ... perjured testimony is an obvious and flagrant affront to the basic concepts of judicial proceedings.

Kenneth Starr Independent counsel. Submitting his report and listing seven grounds for prosecution and possible impeachment of President Clinton; House Judiciary Committee internet site, 11 September 1998.

American morality has been reduced to 'Don't ask, don't tell; can't ask, won't tell'.

James Traficant Ohio member of the House of Representatives (Democrat). Speaking on 10 September as the Starr Report is delivered to Congress in 36 boxes; *Daily Telegraph*, 11 September 1998.

They have let the murderers win.

Ann Finlay A Protestant whose Roman Catholic husband was murdered by a 'loyalist' gunman in 1975. On the release of the first terrorist prisoners from the Maze, in accordance with the Good Friday Agreement; *Daily Telegraph*, 12 September 1998.

A company director who takes a pay rise of £50,000 when the rest of the workforce is getting a few hundred is not part of some 'general trend'. He is a greedy bastard.

John Edmonds Leader of the GMB union. Addressing the Trades Union Congress in Blackpool; Radio 5 Live, 14 September 1998.

I don't really think that the NHS should be financing people waving their potency at a disco.

Frank Dobson Secretary of State for Health. On his refusal, for the time being, to license Viagra for prescription on the NHS; at £4.84 a dose, there were fears that the impotency cure could cost the NHS £1 billion a year; *Daily Telegraph*, 16 September 1998.

It depends upon what the meaning of the word 'is' means. If 'is' means is, and never has been, that's one thing. If it means, there is none, that was a completely true statement.

Bill Clinton President of the USA. Attempting, in his appearance before a grand jury, to explain the true meaning of his earlier assertion: 'There is no sex of any kind, in any manner, shape or form, with Miss Lewinsky'; CNN/House Judiciary Committee videotape transcript, 21 September 1998.

The way the world public with hypocritical lust follows the most private events on the Internet, that – and I use this expression deliberately – makes me puke.

Helmut Kohl Chancellor of Germany. On the Clinton tapes, and allied affairs; *Daily Telegraph*, 22 September 1998.

I would just like to say that no one ever asked me to lie, and I was never promised a job for my silence. And I am sorry. I'm really sorry for everything that's happened. And I hate Linda Tripp.

Monica Lewinsky Former White House aide and presidential inamorata. Concluding her evidence to the grand jury with words that were omitted from the Starr Report; *Daily Telegraph*, 23 September 1998.

Lord make my words sweet and reasonable. For some day I may have to eat them.

Paddy Ashdown Leader of the Liberal Democrats. Addressing his party's conference in Brighton; Radio 5 Live, 24 September 1998.

At Harrow, you could have any boy for a box of Cadbury's milk chocolate. But I didn't want boys.

John Mortimer Novelist and playwright. On his school days; *Daily Telegraph*, 24 September 1998.

The days of 'Scotland the moan' are over. Our Scotland is the Scotland of the good neighbour.

Alex Salmond Leader of the Scottish National Party. Addressing his party's conference in Inverness; Radio 5 Live, 25 September 1998.

If Gordon's strategy goes belly-up, it'll be a much livelier conference next year.

Ken Livingstone Labour MP. Speaking at the Labour Party conference in Blackpool on the economic policy of Chancellor Gordon Brown; *Daily Telegraph*, 29 September 1998.

It will not make a bean of difference to the policy of the party and the direction in which we are going.

Peter Mandelson Secretary of State for Trade and Industry. On the election to Labour's National Executive of four left-wing members; *Daily Telegraph*, 29 September 1998.

October 1998

Blue-collar work is a defence, a disguise. When anyone asks you a question, you can answer, 'More than my job's worth,' or 'Ask the guv'nor, missus.' I like all that.

Magnus Mills Bus driver and novelist, whose first novel, *The Restraint of Beasts*, was shortlisted for the Booker Prize; *Sunday Times*, 4 October 1998.

I could have paid off my debts a lot quicker, but I only did the things I actually believed in myself, like Cranberry Juice Lite.

Sarah Ferguson Duchess of York. On maintaining her integrity in the face of adversity, prior to the launch of her BskyB chat show; *Daily Telegraph*, 5 October 1998.

After a careful reading of the Starr Report, I am impressed by the salacious and voyeuristic nature of your work.

Larry Flynt Publisher of pornographic magazines. In an open letter to Kenneth Starr, offering him a job; *Time*, 5 October 1998.

If the US remains the Great Satan, then Great Britain remains the Great Satan's Father. The British cannot be trusted.

In *Joumhouryieh Islamyieh* ('Islamic Republic'), an Iranian fundamentalist newspaper. Re-asserting the validity of the fatwa against Salman Rushdie, whose security arrangements remained in place despite the Iranian government's disavowal of the death sentence; quoted in *The Week*, 10 October 1998.

With a 17- or 18-year waiting list, I'll probably be dead and buried before I can join my husband.

Rachel Heyhoe-Flint Former England women's cricket captain. On the vote by the MCC to admit women as members; *Time*, 12 October 1998.

The new government's always so keen to try everything new, this is a good chance to try something else.

Ken Livingstone Labour MP. Calling on his supporters to vote for him as a 'write-in' candidate if the London Labour Party fail to short-list him for election as Mayor of London; *BBC Online*, 12 November 1998.

People behave curiously when offered the extremely attractive option of being murdered today or threatened with murder tomorrow.

Viscount Cranborne Conservative leader in the House of Lords. On the introduction of a bill to abolish the voting rights of the hereditary peerage in a reformed second chamber; *Daily Telegraph*, 13 October 1998.

I have been in favour of Lords reform almost since I have been there, because any House which has me in it really needs its head examined.

7th Earl of Onslow Conservative hereditary peer. Who nonetheless opposed the proposal to turn the House of Lords into a 'governmental echo chamber' and vowed to fight it like 'a football hooligan'; *The Times*, 14 October 1998.

Greater Manchester Police has institutionalised racism. We live in a society that has internalised racism and Greater Manchester Police is no exception.

David Wilmot Chief Constable of Greater Manchester. Giving evidence to the Stephen Lawrence inquiry; *Daily Mirror*, 14 October 1998.

It always seemed to me a bit pointless to disapprove of homosexuality. It's like disapproving of rain.

Francis Maude Conservative Treasury spokesman. Whose elder brother, Charles, died of AIDS in 1993; *Daily Telegraph*, 16 November 1998.

I was only an aspirant dictator, not a real one. History teaches you that dictators never end up well.

Augusto Pinochet Former dictator of Chile. Arrested in London on an extradition warrant issued in Spain, in connection with the torture, murder, and disappearance of Spanish citizens during his rule; *The New Yorker*, 16 October 1998.

We don't like violence but we don't mind sex.

Woman pensioner from Essex. Speaking to a researcher into public attitudes to TV wildlife programmes; *Independent*, 17 October 1998.

I have no self-esteem, but the biggest ego in the world.

Mike Tyson Boxer. Successfully pleading for the return of his boxing licence in Las Vegas; *Independent on Sunday*, 18 October 1998.

I've done this, I am sorry, but it's really nothing to do with being a Blue Peter presenter. I'm not Jack the Ripper.

RICHARD BACON Ex-presenter of the children's TV programme *Blue Peter*. On being sacked from the show following an admission that he had taken cocaine; *Daily Telegraph*, 20 October 1998.

A conflict that should never have happened and that we deeply regret.

CARLOS MENEM President of Argentina. Writing on the Falklands War; he afterwards denied it was an apology; *Sun*, 23 October 1998.

The English approach to ideas is not to kill them, but to let them die of neglect.

JEREMY PAXMAN TV journalist and presenter. *Independent*, 24 October 1998.

The British motor industry is really owned by Nazis.

JEREMY CLARKSON TV motoring presenter. Taking part in an informal quiz show at the *Top Gear* stand at the National Motor Show. He also upset people on the Hyundai stand by saying South Koreans were 'too busy eating dogs to design a decent car'; *Daily Telegraph*, 26 October 1998.

It's the missionary position of cooking.

EGON RONAY Chef. On Delia Smith's *How to Cook* TV series, which includes instructions on how to boil water; *Daily Telegraph*, 27 October 1998.

English spinsters made me what I am today.

FRANCO ZEFFIRELLI Film and opera director and Italian senator; *Daily Telegraph*, 27 October 1998.

The Labour Party per contra has after many thirsty years had a cornucopia of luscious psephological fruit emptied over its head.

LORD JENKINS OF HILLHEAD Liberal Democrat peer and former Labour minister. On the vagaries of the first-past-the-post electoral system in Britain; Report of The Independent Commission on the Electoral System, 29 October 1998.

Having looked the past in the eye, having asked for forgiveness and having made amends, let us shut the door on the past – not in order to forget it but in order not to allow it to imprison us.

DESMOND TUTU Former Archbishop of Cape Town. In his foreword to the report of South Africa's Truth and Reconciliation Commission; *Daily Telegraph*, 30 October 1998.

November 1999

I need to be connected with God. I need to live in a high state of spiritual accountability.

BILL CLINTON President of the USA. Quoted by his spiritual counsellor, Baptist minister Tony Campolo; *Independent on Sunday*, 1 November 1998.

We are what we are, the product both of our genes and our experiences.

RON DAVIES Former secretary of state for Wales. In his resignation statement to the House of Commons; *Daily Telegraph*, 3 November 1998.

Mr Tony Benn welcomes compulsory homework for pensioners.

TONY BENN Veteran Labour politician. Making up an example of the sort of standardized New Labour press briefing to which he takes exception; *Sunday Telegraph*, 8 November 1998.

There is more likelihood of Ian Paisley being the next pope, than of me agreeing to a fix or a stitch-up.

RHODRI MORGAN Welsh Labour MP. Refusing to stand down, 'in the interest of party unity', in the election to succeed Ron Davies as Welsh Labour leader. He was subsequently defeated; *Today*, BBC Radio 4, 9 November 1998.

If NASA really wanted to study the effects of space travel on an older American, they should have called on me.

STROM THURMOND 95-year-old US senator. On space pioneer and former congressman John Glenn (77), who was re-launched on a Shuttle mission at the end of October; *Time*, 9 November 1998.

I don't think the public appreciates the magnitude of the problem.

RON ECCLES Director of the Common Cold Centre in Cardiff. Admitting defeat after spending ten years attempting to find a cure for the 200-odd viruses that cause the complaint; *Daily Telegraph*, 10 November 1998.

Tremendously bad things have been done in the name of humanitarian relief.

CLARE SHORT Secretary of State for International Development. On the 'Band-Aid' approach to Third World catastrophe; *Daily Telegraph*, 10 November 1998.

I say what I mean, I mean what I say and I vote accordingly.

DENNIS CANAVAN Labour MP. Who successfully stood as an Independent in the Scottish Assembly elections, having been rejected as a candidate by Scottish New Labour bosses; *The Scotsman*, 12 November 1998.

The difference is that the mice didn't have to work as well.

CAROL VORDERMAN TV presenter and engineering graduate. On research, conducted on pregnant mice, suggesting that pregnancy makes females more intelligent and efficient; *Daily Telegraph*, 12 November 1998.

My immediate response was to go out and score a load of cocaine in rebellion.

EMMA THOMPSON Actress. On the suggestion that she may have been chosen by the government's Women's Unit as a role-model for teenage girls; *Independent on Sunday*, 15 November 1998.

We have no intention of allowing ourselves to be swallowed. We are far too indigestible.

PADDY ASHDOWN Leader of the Liberal Democrats. On his party's cooperation with New Labour; *Independent on Sunday*, 22 November 1998.

There are men walking round Japan in Snowman socks with my signature going up their leg. Bloody dreadful. Stark raving mad.

RAYMOND BRIGGS Creator of *Fungus the Bogeyman* and *The Snowman*. On the oddness of fame; *Daily Telegraph*, 23 November 1998.

If we ditch the pound and join the Euro, that is the end of Great Britain as an independent country. It isn't just a new chapter in our history, it is the closing of the book.

FRANK FIELD Labour MP and former Minister of State at the Department of Social Security. *Daily Telegraph*, 23 November 1998.

It's rather like someone being released from jail after serving two and a half years for a crime he did not commit.

ANTHONY GIBSON Southwest region co-ordinator for the National Farmers' Union. On the promised lifting of the EU ban on exports of British beef; *Daily Telegraph*, 24 November 1998.

Before New Labour, politicians fought elections in order to govern. This administration governs in order to fight elections.

WILLIAM HAGUE Leader of the Opposition. Replying to the Queen's Speech; *Daily Telegraph*, 25 November 1998.

Let us not underestimate how far we have come and let us agree that we have come too far to go back now.

Tony Blair Prime Minister. Addressing the Irish Parliament on the Irish peace progress; Radio 5 Live, 26 November 1998.

Anyone can make a reasonable weather forecast, with 77% accuracy, just by predicting that tomorrow's weather will be the same as today's.

John Thornes of Birmingham University. On research into the accuracy of radio and TV weather forecasters, which found that the best of them, Suzanne Charlton, had an accuracy rate of 46 percent; *Sunday Telegraph*, 29 November 1998.

The man who is tired of London is tired of looking for a parking space.

Paul Theroux Novelist and travel writer who now resides in Hawaii. Interviewed by Michael Shelden, *Daily Telegraph*, 30 November 1998.

December 1998

I have no doubt that, despite the publicity, your puerile conduct will soon be forgotten, although your cause may not be.

Michael Kelly Stipendiary magistrate. Fining Peter Tatchell £18.60 (under the 1860 Ecclesiastical Courts Jurisdiction Act) for disrupting the Archbishop of Canterbury's Easter Sunday sermon as a protest on behalf of gay clergy; *Daily Telegraph*, 2 December 1998.

There are purists who feel it is more honourable to die like James IV at Flodden Field in 1513. But the difficulty about dying is you are dead.

Viscount Cranborne Ex-leader for the Conservative peers. On why he went behind his leader's back in an effort to save, for the time being, a tenth of the hereditary peers in the House of Lords; *Daily Telegraph*, 3 December 1998.

French philosophy aspires to the condition of literature or art. It's about picking up an idea and running with it, possibly over a cliff or into a brick wall.

Ted Honderich Professor, University College, London. Commenting on a poll of philosophers which elected Jacques Derrida 'the thinker whose contribution to the subject has been most overrated'; *Today*, BBC Radio 4, 3 December 1998.

Ramblers are just a bunch of the dirty-mac brigade – the great unwashed.

Nicholas Van Hoogstraten Millionaire property owner. Who blocked a public footpath on his Sussex estate by building a barn on it; *Independent on Sunday*, 6 December 1998.

Everything that has been going on recently undermines trust in presidential authority and authority in general, and that is inadmissible. In present conditions, power should be concentrated in one fist.

Boris Yeltsin President of Russia. Who left hospital, returned to work for three hours to sack his chief of staff, three senior aides, and a security service head, then went back to hospital; *Daily Telegraph*, 8 December 1998.

I am strongly against kiss-and-drop. It is an anomaly and an anachronism, and I would argue very strongly that the idea should be dropped.

Glenda Jackson Former Junior Transport Minister. On outlawing the use of one's car to drop people off at the Millennium Dome, and elsewhere; *Daily Telegraph*, 10 December 1998.

Any further delay will reinforce dark doubts about whether Sinn Féin is drinking from the clear stream of democracy or is still drinking from the dark stream of fascism.

David Trimble Leader of the Ulster Unionists. On the decommissioning of IRA weapons, as he collected his Nobel Peace Prize, won jointly with John Hume of the SDLP. A few days later the IRA reaffirmed its refusal to give up any arms; Radio 5 Live, 10 December 1998.

There is not an anti-English bone in my body. I have forgotten more about English history than most Tory MPs ever learned.

Alex Salmond Leader of the Scottish National Party. *Independent on Sunday*, 13 December 1998.

I think everybody knows who the father is.

Diane Blood The widow who successfully fought a legal battle to be impregnated with her dead husband's sperm. On not having her husband's name on her baby's birth certificate; *Daily Telegraph*, 15 December 1998.

President Saddam is a man to whom a last chance to do right is just a further opportunity to do wrong.

Bill Clinton President of the USA. Addressing the nation after launching missile attacks against Iraq; Radio 5 Live, 16 December 1998.

I only wear them to read with – it's an old-age thing.

Britt Ekland Actress. Explaining why she wore glasses to identify the man who stole her Rolex watch; *Daily Telegraph*, 16 December 1998.

They will fail as they have failed during the Mother of Battles.

Issued by the Revolutionary Command Council of Iraq. In response to the American and British air strikes; *Daily Telegraph*, 17 December 1998.

We were finding that every time we went past Bill Clinton, the zip was undone.

Vicky Brown Employee of Madame Tussaud's. Explaining why the staff had sewn the waxwork's fly shut; *Newsweek*, 21 December 1998.

I dread becoming a therapy bore. I love therapy, and the last thing I want to do is give it a bad name.

Eric Clapton Rock musician and composer. On his recovery from drink and drugs; *Daily Telegraph*, 21 December 1998.

I never wanted anyone's death and I feel sincere pain for all those who lost their lives during those years.

Augusto Pinochet Former dictator of Chile. Letter to his country's National Security Council; *Newsweek*, 21 December 1998.

Wonderful scripts, beautiful characters, truthful acting, and magical twists.

Saeed Jaffrey Actor. On *Coronation Street*, whose cast he joined as corner-shop proprietor Ravi Desai; *Daily Telegraph*, 22 December 1998.

You can trust my word, because I'm a cabinet minister.

Tony Banks Minister for Sport. On England's chances of hosting the 2006 World Cup; Radio 5 Live, 24 December 1998.

Have you tried cannabis? I have heard it's the best thing for it.

Prince of Wales Talking to multiple sclerosis sufferer Karen Drake at the Sue Ryder Home in Cheltenham; *Daily Telegraph*, 24 December 1998.

Peter Mandelson needed his own Peter Mandelson.

Derek Draper Former Labour spin-doctor. On the downfall of his colleague; *Daily Telegraph*, 24 December 1998.

I have not misused my position either as an MP or minister. I have done nothing wrong.

Geoffrey Robinson Former Paymaster-General. Letter of resignation; *Daily Telegraph*, 24 December 1998.

I had hoped you wouldn't ask that question. The answer is no.

Wim Duisenberg Dutch President of the European Central Bank. Asked if he would leave office halfway through his term to make way for a French nominee, as he had originally promised; *Daily Telegraph*, 31 December 1998.

January 1999

From now on, monetary policy, usually an essential part of national sovereignty, will be decided by a truely European institution.

Wim Duisenberg Dutch President of the European Central Bank. Hailing the launch of Europe's single currency; *Daily Telegraph*, 1 January 1999.

It is now up to us to see that we embark on the next stage leading to political unity, which I think is ... the consequence of economic unity.

Jacques Santer President of the European Commission. On the launch of the euro; *Daily Telegraph*, 1 January 1999.

He is known in our house as 'the gentleman who pays the rent'.

Judi Dench Actress. On William Shakespeare; *Daily Telegraph*, 2 January 1999.

That's good. And I'm an alien space baby.

Joe Lockhart White House press secretary. On allegations that President Clinton was the father of an Arkansas prostitute's 13-year-old son. DNA tests proved he wasn't; *Daily Telegraph*, 6 January 1999.

There were worse things I could have put in.

Margaret Cook Ex-wife of Foreign Secretary Robin Cook. On her autobiography, which revealed her ex-husband as a serial adulterer and occasional heavy drinker; *Sunday Telegraph*, 10 January 1999.

Mummy, I've had an accident.

John Park City trader. Breaking the news that he lost £6 million in one ill-advised trade; *Independent on Sunday*, 10 January 1999.

To hell with this stupid show business. Everything was a fake.

Anthony Hopkins Actor. On leaving the profession; *Time*, 11 January 1999.

The people of our community are so horrified they may not want to have anything to do with the Olympics again.

Deeda Seed Salt Lake City councillor. On revelations that the City Fathers procured prostitutes for Olympic officials as part of their successful bid to host the 2002 Winter Games; *Daily Telegraph*, 11 January 1999.

I am a musician, not a businessman or accountant.

Elton John Musician and singer. Issuing a writ against his former manager and accountants Price Waterhouse, alleging that £20 million went missing from his funds; *Daily Telegraph*, 13 January 1999.

They were a gift from God. It was a fight against the enemies of God.

Abu Hassan Yemeni Islamic militant. At his trial, on his gang's kidnapping of 16 Western tourists, four of whom were killed in a shoot-out with troops; *Daily Telegraph*, 14 January 1999.

I end up, as so often when I have tried to get it right, feeling I've slightly made a fool of myself.

Alan Bennett Playwright and actor. On turning down an honorary Oxford doctoral degree in protest at the endowment of the Rupert Murdoch Chair in Language and Communication; *Daily Telegraph*, 15 January 1999.

Mr Clinton does not have the strength of character to be a war criminal.

Henry Kissinger Former US Secretary of State. *Independent*, 16 January 1999.

He had the ability to radiate unusual warmth and charm – when he chose to.

F W de Klerk Former President of South Africa. On his successor, Nelson Mandela; *Independent on Sunday*, 17 January 1999.

I still love Don, he's a great guy. But he's evil, and he steals people's money.

Mike Tyson Heavyweight boxer. On his former promoter, Don King; *Daily Telegraph*, 18 January 1999.

As far as the physical miseries go, I am sure I will cope. I lived at Eton in the 1950s and I know all about life in uncomfortable quarters.

Jonathan Aitken Former Conservative MP and cabinet minister. On the probability of his going to prison for perjury; *Daily Express*, 19 January 1999.

Not just sleepy villages, polite manners, friendly vicars, and the novels of Scott and Austen ... but also the ambitious, the bold, the brassy, the vigorous, the exciting, the leading world nation that we are and can be.

William Hague Leader of the Conservative Party. Outlining his vision of 'the British Way' to the Centre for Policy Studies; *Daily Telegraph*, 19 January 1999.

Too many leaders are carried out or kicked out.

Paddy Ashdown Leader of the Liberal Democrat Party. On announcing his intention to retire at the end of June 1999; Radio 5 Live, 20 January 1999.

Of course he's said it; there's hardly anything he hasn't said.

William Hague Leader of the Conservative Party. On being told that one of his speeches echoed the views of Tony Blair; *Independent on Sunday*, 24 January 1999.

Having come this far, he should do the right thing and marry her.

George Austin Archdeacon of York. On the Prince of Wales and Camilla Parker-Bowles, who 'came out' as a couple, for photographers at a birthday party at the Ritz Hotel; *Daily Telegraph*, 30 January 1999.

You and I have been given two hands and two legs and half-decent brains. Some people have not been born like that for a reason. The karma is working from another lifetime.... What you sow you have to reap.

Glenn Hoddle England football manager. On his belief that people with 'physical deformities' must have 'made mistakes' in a previous incarnation. He was sacked three days later; *The Times*, 30 January 1999.

New Labour is not Labour renewed. It is Labour rejected, renounced. It is a negative. New Labour is, and is meant to be, Not Labour.

Bryan Gould Former Labour MP. *Independent on Sunday*, 31 January 1999.

February 1999

I've had so much pleasure in my life that it doesn't bother me that I'm not going to exist afterwards. I've had heaven already.

Paul Mellon US billionaire philanthropist, art collector, and horse-breeder, who died on 2 February. *Daily Telegraph*, 3 February 1999.

It's complete rubbish that the British film industry is going through a renaissance. The Full Monty isn't a film industry, it's a press release.

Mike Phillips International television director, BBC Worldwide. *Daily Telegraph*, 5 February 1999.

We gave the fans a nine-goal thriller.

Ron Atkinson Manager of Nottingham Forest Football Club. After his team lost 8–1 to Manchester United; Radio 5 Live, 6 February 1999.

The Spanish only understand strength. They are bullfighting. The Foreign Office has been playing cricket.

Andrew Tyrie Conservative MP for Chichester. On the Spanish blockade of Gibraltar; *Hansard*, 11 February 1999.

I got Labour into power and now they are not even thankful enough to let me be Mayor of London.

Mohammed al-Fayed Egyptian citizen and proprietor of Harrods, *Punch*, and Fulham Football Club; *Punch*, 12 February 1999.

I can't speak in sound bites. I refuse to repeat slogans. I hate focus groups. I absolutely hate image consultants.

Kenneth Clarke Former Conservative chancellor; *Independent*, 13 February 1999.

The trouble with fulfilling your ambitions is you think you will be transformed into some sort of archangel and you're not. You still have to wash your socks.

Louis de Bernières Author of the bestselling *Captain Corelli's Mandolin. Independent on Sunday*, 14 February 1999.

A long, cold look has to be taken at the real questions. These are: what happens to these genes if they get into other species, and what about the potential development of antibiotic resistance?

Steve Jones Geneticist. On genetically modified foods; *Daily Telegraph*, 16 February 1999.

There is a genuine prejudice that all things country have to be reactionary and not good for new BBC, new Labour, new Britain, whatever.

Robin Page Presenter of BBC TV's *One Man and His Dog*. On plans to axe the show after 26 years; it was reinstated after a public outcry; *Daily Telegraph*, 18 February 1999.

I used to wonder why the celebrities were so clever and now I know. I am no longer surprised by anything I see on television.

Matthew Parris Writer and broadcaster. Revealing that celebrity contestants on Channel 4's *Countdown* quiz show are 'fed' answers via earphones; Radio 5 Live, 18 February 1999.

It's the worst day for Frinton since the Luftwaffe beat up the town in 1944.

Roy Caddick Secretary of the Residents' Association in Frinton, Essex. After the local authority voted to grant a licence to the town's first pub; *Independent*, 20 February 1999.

The reason I became an actress was to play people infinitely more interesting than I am, and say things infinitely more intelligent and entertaining than anything I could think of myself.

Prunella Scales Actress. *Independent on Sunday*, 21 February 1999.

It's not about precedent, it's about integrity.

David Dein Vice-Chairman of Arsenal Football Club. On his club's insistence on a replay of the FA Cup tie with Sheffield United, which Arsenal won with a legal goal scored in contravention of the 'gentleman's agreement' governing play while a player is injured. Arsenal won the replay; *Daily Telegraph*, 23 February 1999.

Some people seem to find release at the end of it, but I think it's only the release of death. In my other plays, it was the release of deciding to go on living despite the fact that it's terrible.

Sarah Kane Playwright. On her last play, *Crave*, in an interview shortly before her suicide at the age of 28; *Daily Telegraph*, 23 February 1999.

The collective failure of an organization to provide an appropriate and professional service to people because of their colour, culture, or ethnic origin.

William MacPherson Chairman of the Lawrence Inquiry. Providing a definition of 'institutionalized racism'; *Daily Telegraph*, 23 February 1999.

I've been guilty of misusing TV. It's a dangerous medium and is misused all the time.

Oprah Winfrey Television talk show hostess. *Radio Times*, 23 February 1999.

March 1999

We must learn from history, not repeat it, and we must never forget that the destinies of Europe and America are inseparable.

Madeleine Albright US Secretary of State. Speaking at the ceremony at which Hungary, Poland, and the Czech Republic joined NATO; *Newsweek*, March 1999.

It's absolutely delicious. The Secretary of State can vouchsafe for that as well.

Prince of Wales Eating banned beef on the bone at an event to publicize the Welsh Beef and Lamb Co-operative, along with Welsh Secretary Alun Michael MP; Radio 5 Live, 1 March 1999.

This is the punishment for the Anglo-Saxons who sold us out.

Note left on the body of one of the eight tourists, four of them British, hacked to death by Hutu militias in a wildlife reserve on the Rwanda–Uganda border; *Daily Telegraph*, 5 March 1999.

My show is the stupidest show on TV. If you are watching it, get a life. I would not watch my show. My show is a circus. That's all it is.

Jerry Springer Host of an eponymous adversarial talk show. *Independent on Sunday*, 7 March 1999.

I am whiter than white.

Jacques Santer President of the European Commission. On the 'wise persons' report. He and his 19 fellow-commisioners then resigned, and were immediately reappointed on a temporary basis; *Daily Telegraph*, 17 March 1999.

I am going to tell my wife I love her. Then I'm going to have a cup of tea, like any good Englishman.

Brian Jones British balloon pilot. Speaking by radio as his Breitling Orbiter 3 became the first balloon to complete the 26,000-mile nonstop circumnavigation of the world on 20 March; *Independent on Sunday*, 21 March 1999.

Only President Milošević and Serbia stand in the way of peace. Serbia's mounting aggression must be stopped.

Bill Clinton President of the USA. On the failure of talks aimed at halting Serbia's policy of 'ethnic cleansing' in its province of Kosovo; *Daily Telegraph*, 23 March 1999.

For eight minutes on the screen I should only get a little bit of him.

Judi Dench Actress. Accepting the Oscar Award for Best Supporting Actress in *Shakespeare in Love*; CNN, 23 March 1999.

There are strategic interests for the whole of Europe at stake. We cannot contemplate, on the doorstep of the EU, a disintegration into chaos and disorder.

Tony Blair Prime Minister. As NATO leaders order air strikes on Serbia, beginning on 24 March; *Daily Telegraph*, 24 March 1999.

We don't know who to be more angry with, Milošević or NATO.

Belgrade man. As the NATO bombings began on 24 March 1999; *Daily Telegraph*, 25 March 1999.

If responsibility for the humanitarian catastrophe in Kosovo rests on Yugoslavian President Slobodan Milošević, then the spillover is the responsibility of the US and the EU.

Ljubco Georgievski Prime Minister of Macedonia. As the first of some 750,000 refugees expelled from their homes in Kosovo began arriving in Macedonia and Albania; *Daily Telegraph*, 26 March 1999.

They said, 'Ask NATO'.

Nekibe Kelmendi Wife of Kosovan lawyer Bayram Kelmendi. On the reply of Serbian police when she asked them what had happened to her husband, arrested the previous night; *Daily Telegraph*, 26 March 1999.

Tony Blair is the Prime Minister of England. He is very left-wing and is an example of the socialist takeover of Europe.

From a pro-Pinochet Chilean website. *Independent*, 27 March 1999.

Anyone who joins a job where emotionally disturbing experiences are part of their work should get nothing at all for being emotionally disturbed.

Ann Widdecombe Conservative health spokesperson. On the 'compensation culture'; *Independent*, 27 March 1999.

Isn't Kosovo a chain of gas stations?

Woman on a US radio phone-in; *Independent on Sunday*, 28 March 1999.

What has happened to the males? It is quite clear that what is going on in Kosovo is not an improvised affair. A truly horrible situation is unfolding, the likes of which we have not seen since the closing stages of the Second World War.

Jamie Shea NATO spokesman. On the overwhelming preponderance of women and children among the Kosovo refugees; Radio 5 Live, 28 March 1999.

April 1999

This is the one we've all been waiting for. Astronomers' hearts are in their throats.

Stephen Maran Spokesman for the American Astronomical Society. On the discovery of a new galaxy, 14.25 billion years old, by the Hubble telescope; *Newsweek*, April 1999.

Just because we cannot do everything for everyone does not mean we should do nothing for anyone.

Bill Clinton President of the USA. Forestalling demands for the withdrawal of US troops from the Balkans; *MSNBC*, 1 April 1999.

Historically ignorant, politically inept, and internationally illegal.

Peter Tapsell Conservative MP. On British involvement in the NATO bombing of Serbia; *Independent*, 3 April 1999.

It may take time and it won't be easy. But what's ten years?

Aung San Suu Kyi Burmese opposition leader. On her house arrest and persecution by the Burmese regime; *Sunday Telegraph*, 4 April 1999.

The pillars of the nation-state are the sword and the currency, and we have changed that. The euro decision changed the concept of the nation-state and we have to go beyond that.

Romano Prodi President-designate of the European Commission. On the effect and purpose of the single currency; *Daily Telegraph*, 7 April 1999.

There's a fine line between being governor of Texas and making a fool of yourself.

George W Bush Jr Governor of Texas. On the possibility of his presidential candidacy; *Independent*, 10 April 1999.

Do not push us into military action, or there will definitely be a European and possibly a world war.

Boris Yeltsin President of Russia. Warning NATO not to send ground troops into Serbia; reports that Russia had targeted NATO countries with nuclear missiles were later denied; *Daily Telegraph*, 10 April 1999.

Is it fair? Come on, it's politics.

Rudolph Giuliani Mayor of New York City. Defending criticism of First Lady and potential Senate candidate Hillary Clinton on his website, www.HillaryNo.com; *Time*, 12 April 1999.

It ended up being good fun thanks to quite a lot of red wine.

Rosalyn Fawcett Member of the Rylstone and District Women's Institute, and 1 of 11 members, aged 45 to 65, who posed nude for a calendar to raise funds for Leukaemia Research. *Daily Telegraph*, 13 April 1999.

I have received two wonderful graces. First, I have been given time to prepare for a new future. Secondly, I find myself – uncharacteristically – calm and at peace.

Basil Hume Archbishop of Westminster. Informing his priests that he is terminally ill with cancer; *Independent on Sunday*, 18 April 1999.

I've always believed that the race belongs not only to the swift, but also to those who keep on running.

Zoe Koplowitz Multiple sclerosis sufferer who finally completed the 1999 London Marathon in 30 hours 10 minutes. *Daily Telegraph*, 20 April 1999.

It seems that when the immigrants met the locals, they made whoopee, not war.

Erik Trinkaus Anthropologist at Washington University. On the discovery of the 24,500-year-old skeleton of a hybrid Neanderthal–Cro-Magnon child in Portugal, dating from 4,000 years after the migration of Cro-Magnon humans across the Pyrenees; *Daily Telegraph*, 21 April 1999.

This anniversary should be celebrated not only by Sikhs but by all of us who long to live in a saner world where the truth is recognized of Guru Nanak's teaching that 'God's light pervades every creature and every creature is contained in this light'.

Prince of Wales Addressing a celebration in the Albert Hall of the 300th anniversary of the founding of the Sikh Brotherhood; *Daily Telegraph*, 26 April 1999.

I didn't think of myself as an actress, and I didn't think any of you did.

Elizabeth Taylor Actress. Receiving a BAFTA award for lifetime achievement; *Time*, 26 April 1999.

To hear appeals on the news last night, with phone numbers for witnesses and clues, seemed surreal. This was what Jill did – not, surely not, what was being done for Jill.

Nick Ross Co-presenter of BBC TV's *Crimewatch*. On the murder on 26 April 1999 of his colleague Jill Dando; *Daily Telegraph*, 27 April 1999.

May 1999

I think he probably went the way he would have wished.

Glenda Jackson On the actor Oliver Reed, who died on 2 May 1999 after collapsing in a bar in Malta; *Daily Telegraph*, 3 May 1999.

My guess is that they did make the summit. But to me the only way you achieve a summit is to come back alive.

John Mallory Son of the mountaineer George Mallory. On his father, who disappeared, along with Andrew Irvine, while heading for the summit of Mount Everest on 24 June 1924, and whose body was discovered and identified at the end of April; *Daily Telegraph*, 4 May 1999.

We realize this is a number that would really stand out but we decided it is not suitable for release.

Byron Roberts Marketing manager of the Driver and Vehicle Licensing Authority. On banning the combination V14 GRA for use on a licence plate; *Daily Telegraph*, 4 May 1999.

They were clearly very interested in sex in a wide, uncomplicated manner but they had no term for homosexuals. They had different hang-ups from us.

Dyfri Williams Keeper of the Greek and Roman Department at the British Museum. After the British Museum's £1.8 million purchase of the Warren Cup, a Roman silver vessel decorated with scenes of explicit homosexual lovemaking; *Daily Telegraph*, 5 May 1999.

Let us start building the new Scotland – remembering on all sides that civility is not a sign of weakness.

Donald Dewar First Minister of the newly-elected Scottish Parliament. Preparing for coalition talks with the Scottish Liberal Democrats; *Independent on Sunday*, 9 May 1999.

At times it did feel a little silly. The hardest parts were when I was on my own on stage.

John la Bouchardière Assistant director at English National Opera. On miming the part of Jupiter in Handel's Semele in London, before an audience of 2,500, after both star and understudy fell ill; *Daily Telegraph*, 11 May 1999.

My grandmother was utterly convinced that I'd wind up as Archbishop of Canterbury and, to be honest, I've never entirely ruled it out.

Hugh Grant Actor. *Daily Telegraph*, 12 May 1999.

I believe in Methuselah, Frankenstein, alien beings, flying saucers, and the Hand of God. But most of all I believe in on-loan goalkeepers from Swindon Town scoring in the 95th minute.

Michael Knighton Chairman of Third Division Carlisle United Football Club. On the goal that kept his club in the Football League on 8 May 1999; *Daily Telegraph*, 15 May 1999.

I am desperate if I find there are British press on a foreign visit. I know they'll wreck the thing if they possibly can.

Duke of Edinburgh Interviewed in *Sunday Telegraph*, 16 May 1999.

It is the first happy moment since Yitzhak was murdered.

Leah Rabin Widow of Israeli Prime Minister Yitzhak Rabin, murdered by Jewish extremists in 1995. On the election defeat of Israeli Prime Minister Benjamin Netanyahu by Labour Party leader Ehud Barak; *Daily Telegraph*, 19 May 1999.

The fact of the matter is that it is a difficult time in our history for white, straight, middle-aged, middle-class males.

Andrew Motion Poet. On his appointment as Poet Laureate; *Daily Telegraph*, 20 May 1999.

I don't want you to feel that the only way to be loyal to our Labour Government is to accept without question everything that comes from the Front Bench.

Audrey Wise Labour MP for Preston and one of 67 Labour MPs to vote against the government on the Welfare Reform and Pensions Bill. *Hansard*, 20 May 1999.

Everyone has a calling, has to make a living. I'm not trying to kill myself.

Robbie Knievel Stunt rider and son of Evel Knievel. On accomplishing the feat of leaping the Grand Canyon on a 500cc motorbike; *Daily Telegraph*, 22 May 1999.

The current view of the Home Office appears to be that the presumption of innocence is a time-wasting luxury.

John Mortimer Barrister and writer. On government plans to restrict the right to trial by jury; *Independent on Sunday*, 23 May 1999.

By pandering to the whims of these people I appreciate that I made an error in judgement which stems from naivety and foolishness on my part.

Lawrence Dallaglio Former England rugby captain. On the 'sting' in which *News of the World* reporters, posing as executives offering a sponsorship deal, allegedly tricked him into making false claims of having taken and dealt in drugs; Radio 5 Live, 24 May 1999.

Well, what can I say? I don't believe it. Football, I don't know. Bloody hell!

Alex Ferguson Manager of Manchester United Football Club. Seconds after his team scored twice in injury time to beat Bayern Munich 2–1 in the European Champions' Cup Final in Barcelona; the win secured the 'treble' with the Premier League Championship and the FA Cup; ITV, 25 May 1999.

You're looking for topless sheep.

Prince of Wales Addressing tabloid photographers while visiting a hill farm in Wales; *Daily Telegraph*, 28 May 1999.

When we needed to stand up and be counted, we weren't up to it.

David Lloyd England cricket coach. After England's cricketers were knocked out of the World Cup, having lost to South Africa and India; *Daily Telegraph*, 31 May 1999.

June 1999

It is a very painful part of the conflict resolution process.

Gerry Adams President of Sinn Féin and former commander of the IRA in Belfast. On the anguish of relatives of eight of 'the disappeared' (untraced victims of the IRA), as police searched unsuccessfully for their remains after being given vague directions by the IRA; *Daily Telegraph*, 1 June 1999.

The euro has proved itself and will continue to prove itself.

Jacques Santer Caretaker President of the European Commission. As the European currency sank to a new low against the US dollar and the pound, devaluing by 11 percent in 5 months; *Daily Telegraph*, 2 June 1999.

Everything that has happened is a defeat for the policies of Slobodan Milošević, a personal defeat and a defeat for all his allies.

Zoran Zivkovic Leader of Serbia's Democratic Party. On President Milošević's agreement to withdraw troops from Kosovo, following the NATO bombing campaign. *Daily Telegraph*, 5 June 1999.

Yesterday I was at Royal Ascot and today I was at a riot. It's all part of the fun of working in the City.

Banker. On the 'Carnival Against Capitalism' in the City of London on 18 June 199, which degenerated into violence; *Daily Telegraph*, 19 June 1999.

It smells bad and tastes strange, but there is nothing wrong with the product.

Blaming 'bad carbon dioxide' and fungicide on Coca-Cola cans for sickness that affected hundreds of people in Belgium and Luxembourg. Coca-Cola products were withdrawn from sale across continental Europe; Radio 5 Live, 16 June 1999.

I have to ask myself, having looked at that video, if this is the best you can do?

Richard Benson Judge. Discharging two men who had pleaded guilty to publishing obscene material. The judge said he had seen stronger stuff on Channel 5; Radio 5 Live, 9 June 1999.

Good has triumphed over evil. Justice has overcome barbarism, and the values of civilization have prevailed.

Tony Blair Prime Minister. On the agreement of Serbian military leaders to withdraw from Kosovo, a week after Yugoslavia's President Milošević promised they would; Radio 5 Live, 10 June 1999.

No one will believe that a party, Sinn Féin, with a close connection with a paramilitary group could not bring about decommissioning. And if they cannot bring it about, why can they not make it clear that they believe decommissioning should happen? And condemn those who fail to bring it about?

Tony Blair Prime Minister. Speaking in Stranmills, Northern Ireland, after announcing that midnight on 30 June would be the 'absolute deadline' for negotiations; *Daily Telegraph*, 16 June 1999.

The president is rapidly running out of people to blame, although he still has God, the Pope, the President of China and Michael Jackson.

Eric Bloch Zimbabwean political commentator. On President Robert Mugabe of Zimbabwe; *Sunday Telegraph*, 13 June 1999.

1,001 environmental laws wouldn't stop this kind of thing from happening in Belgium. There is no ethics in politics here.

Jurgen Ceder Belgian member of parliament. On the poisoning of animal feed with dioxin, which led to a worldwide ban on Belgian meat, dairy, and egg products; the Belgian government, which knew about it in March, kept the facts secret until the end of May; *Sunday Telegraph*, 13 June 1999.

The Lords' success is down to years of selective in-breeding.

Kenneth Clarke Former Chancellor of the Exchequer. On the peers' victory in the annual Lords v Commons tug-o'-war; *The Independent*, 26 June 1999.

It's entirely their fault, this new racism in Scotland, this anti-Englishness. It was a music-hall joke before, but there is a viciousness to it now that I loathe.

Billy Connolly Comedian and actor. On the Scottish National Party; he also called the Scottish Parliament 'an enormous joke'; *Daily Telegraph*, 28 June 1999.

I was half expecting the coffin to open and David to leap out screaming, 'I fooled you all.' Sadly, it was not to be.

Frank Allen Musician, of The Searchers. On the funeral of Screaming Lord Sutch, singer and leader of the Official Monster Raving Loony Party; *Daily Telegraph*, 29 June 1999.

We knew we were doing the right thing, and we kept our nerve.

Robin Cook Foreign Secretary. Referring to NATO's bombing of Yugoslavia, following Serbia's agreement to withdraw its troops and 'special forces' from Kosovo in return for the cessation of NATO's bombing; *Daily Telegraph*, 5 June 1999.

I don't think I shall subscribe to little William. I think he will go quietly down the tubes on his own.

Julian Critchley Former Conservative MP, expelled from the party for supporting the 'Pro-Euro Conservatives' in the European election. On being asked whether he would still subscribe to party funds; *Today*, Radio Four, 25 June 1999.

We will be left on our own, like we always are.

Serbian soldier. On the outcome of the Kosovo war; *Daily Telegraph*, 5 June 1999.

Do you think Tony Blair can possibly survive after this war? Surely the British will now throw him out?

Zelena Zigon Serbian actress. *Daily Telegraph*, 5 June 1999.

You can judge politicians by how they treat refugees; they do to them what they would like to do to everyone else if they could get away with it.

Ken Livingstone Labour MP. Criticizing the UK government's policy on asylum seekers; *Independent on Sunday*, 13 June 1999.

It is wonderful that God does things so off the wall as this. I think He wants to surprise us out of our rationality.

David Markee Pastor of the Catch The Fire charismatic evangelical church in Ealing, London, UK. On worldwide reports that members of charismatic Christian churches had miraculously acquired gold teeth; *Sunday Telegraph*, 13 June 1999.

If I don't return for good, they will have succeeded. They will have driven us out. But I can see so little hope now.

Hatixe Matluma 65-year-old Kosovo Albanian grandmother. On returning to her home town of Kacanik, which had been destroyed by Serbian occupiers in her absence; *Sunday Telegraph*, 20 June 1999.

No one using the law against others can complain if the law is, in turn, used against them.

Alan Rusbridger Editor of *The Guardian*. On former Conservative minister Jonathan Aitken, sentenced to 18 months' imprisonment for committing perjury in pursuit of his libel case against *The Guardian* and Granada Television; *The Guardian*, 9 June 1999.

We have shown that our army is invincible. Dear citizens, I wish us all a happy peace.

Slobodan Milošević President of Yugoslavia. Broadcasting to his people; CNN, 10 June 1999.

It sometimes seems as it those of us who voted Labour before the 1990s are being accused of poor judgement, or seen as embarrassing elderly relatives at a family get-together.

John Monks General Secretary of the Trades Union Congress. On the apparent abandonment of Labour's 'core support'; *Independent on Sunday*, 20 June 1999.

It's just the way it is, really. That's what you do – you kind of just have champagne.

Kate Moss Model. On her self-confessed 'ten-year drink and drugs binge'; *The Face*, March 1999.

People kept asking if I was going to do a biography of Tony Blair but I wanted to write about a serious politician.

Paul Routledge Biographer of Peter Mandelson. On his plans to write a biography of the Conservative MP Airey Neave, murdered by the IRA in 1979; *Daily Telegraph*, 15 June 1999.

Once the process is set in motion it cannot be slowed down in anything less than a few millennia.

Robert Watson Chairman of the Intergovernmental Panel on Climate Change. On the disappearance beneath the waves of two of the Maldives' 1,196 islands, whose average height above sea level is three feet; *Independent on Sunday*, 13 June 1999.

Calendars and Time

Time Zones and Relative Times in Cities Throughout the World

The surface of the Earth is divided into 24 time zones. Each zone represents 15° of longitude or 1 hour of time. Countries to the east of London and the Greenwich meridian are ahead of Greenwich Mean Time (GMT) and countries to the west are behind. The time indicated in the table below is fixed by law and is called standard time. Use of daylight saving time (such as British Summer Time) varies widely. At 12:00 noon, GMT, the standard time elsewhere around the world is as follows:

City	Time
Abu Dhabi, United Arab Emirates	16:00
Accra, Ghana	12:00
Addis Ababa, Ethiopia	15:00
Adelaide, Australia	21:30
Alexandria, Egypt	14:00
Algiers, Algeria	13:00
Al Manamah (also called Bahrain), Bahrain	15:00
Amman, Jordan	14:00
Amsterdam, Netherlands	13:00
Anchorage (AK), USA	03:00
Ankara, Turkey	14:00
Athens, Greece	14:00
Auckland, New Zealand	24:00
Baghdad, Iraq	15:00
Bahrain	15:00
Bangkok, Thailand	19:00
Barcelona, Spain	13:00
Beijing, China	20:00
Beirut, Lebanon	14:00
Belgrade, Yugoslavia	13:00
Berlin, Germany	13:00
Berne, Switzerland	13:00
Bogota, Colombia	07:00
Bombay, India	17:30
Bonn, Germany	13:00
Brazzaville, Republic of the Congo	13:00
Brisbane, Australia	22:00
Brussels, Belgium	13:00
Bucharest, Romania	14:00
Budapest, Hungary	13:00
Buenos Aires, Argentina	09:00
Cairo, Egypt	14:00
Calcutta, India	17:30
Canberra, Australia	22:00
Cape Town, South Africa	14:00
Caracas, Venezuela	08:00
Casablanca, Morocco	12:00
Chennai (formerly Madras), India	17:30
Chicago (IL), USA	06:00
Cologne, Germany	13:00
Colombo, Sri Lanka	18:00
Copenhagen, Denmark	13:00
Damascus, Syria	14:00
Dar es Salaam, Tanzania	15:00
Darwin, Australia	21:30
Delhi, India	17:30
Denver (CO), USA	05:00
Dhaka, Bangladesh	18:00
Dubai, United Arab Emirates	16:00
Dublin, Republic of Ireland	12:00
Florence, Italy	13:00
Frankfurt, Germany	13:00
Gdansk, Poland	13:00
Geneva, Switzerland	13:00
Gibraltar	13:00
Hague, The, Netherlands	13:00
Harare, Zimbabwe	14:00
Havana, Cuba	07:00
Helsinki, Finland	14:00
Hobart, Australia	22:00
Ho Chi Minh City, Vietnam	19:00
Hong Kong, China	20:00
Istanbul, Turkey	14:00
Jakarta, Indonesia	19:00
Jerusalem, Israel	14:00
Johannesburg, South Africa	14:00
Karachi, Pakistan	17:00
Kiev, Ukraine	14:00
Kuala Lumpur, Malaysia	20:00
Kuwait City, Kuwait	15:00
Kyoto, Japan	21:00
Lagos, Nigeria	13:00
Le Havre, France	13:00
Lima, Peru	07:00
Lisbon, Portugal	12:00
London, England	12:00
Luanda, Angola	13:00
Luxembourg, Luxembourg	13:00
Lyon, France	13:00
Madrid, Spain	13:00
Manila, Philippines	20:00
Marseille, France	13:00
Mecca, Saudi Arabia	15:00
Melbourne, Australia	22:00
Mexico City, Mexico	06:00
Milan, Italy	13:00
Minsk, Belarus	14:00
Monrovia, Liberia	12:00
Montevideo, Uruguay	09:00
Montreal, Canada	07:00
Moscow, Russia	15:00
Munich, Germany	13:00
Nairobi, Kenya	15:00
New Orleans (LA), USA	06:00
New York (NY), USA	07:00
Nicosia, Cyprus	14:00
Oslo, Norway	13:00
Ottawa, Canada	07:00
Panama City, Panama	07:00
Paris, France	13:00
Perth, Australia	20:00
Port Said, Egypt	14:00
Prague, Czech Republic	13:00
Rawalpindi, Pakistan	17:00
Reykjavik, Iceland	12:00
Rio de Janeiro, Brazil	09:00
Riyadh, Saudi Arabia	15:00
Rome, Italy	13:00
San Francisco (CA), USA	04:00
Santiago, Chile	08:00
Seoul, South Korea	21:00
Shanghai, China	20:00
Singapore City, Singapore	20:00
Sofia, Bulgaria	14:00
St Petersburg, Russia	15:00
Stockholm, Sweden	13:00
Sydney, Australia	22:00
Taipei, Taiwan	20:00
Tashkent, Uzbekistan	17:00
Tehran, Iran	15:30
Tel Aviv, Israel	14:00
Tenerife, Canary Islands	12:00
Tokyo, Japan	21:00
Toronto, Canada	07:00
Tripoli, Libya	13:00
Tunis, Tunisia	13:00
Valparaiso, Chile	08:00
Vancouver, Canada	04:00
Vatican City	13:00
Venice, Italy	13:00
Vienna, Austria	13:00
Vladivostok, Russia	22:00
Volgograd, Russia	16:00
Warsaw, Poland	13:00
Wellington, New Zealand	24:00
Yangon (formerly Rangoon), Myanmar	18:30
Yokohama, Japan	21:00
Zagreb, Croatia	13:00
Zürich, Switzerland	13:00

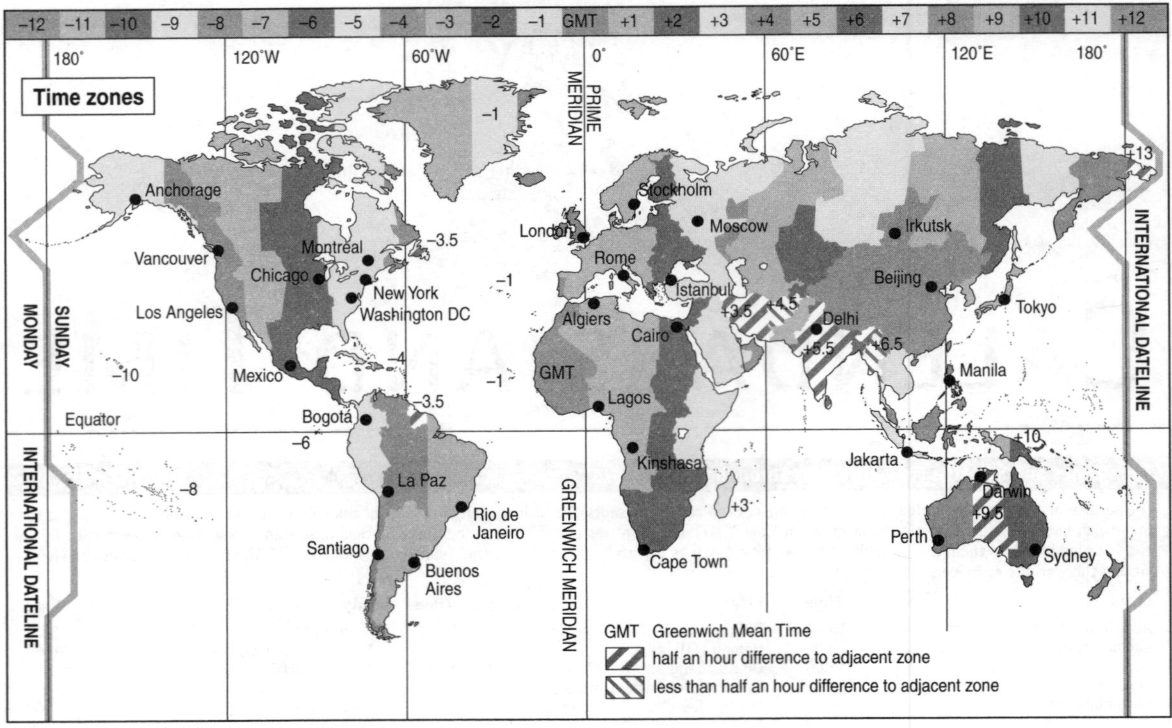

Seasons

2000

Times are in GMT, to the nearest hour.

Vernal (Spring) equinox			Summer solstice			Autumnal equinox			Winter solstice		
Month	**Day**	**Time**	**Month**	**Day**	**Time**	**Month**	**Day**	**Time**	**Month**	**Day**	**Time**
March	20	07:35	June	21	01:48	September	22	17:27	December	21	13:37

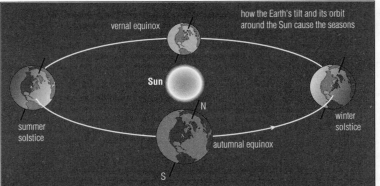

how the Earth's tilt and its orbit around the Sun cause the seasons
vernal equinox
Sun
summer solstice
winter solstice
autumnal equinox
N
S

Seasons *As the Earth orbits the Sun, its axis of rotation always points in the same direction. This means that during the northern hemisphere summer solstice (21 June), the Sun is overhead in the northern hemisphere. At the northern hemisphere winter solstice (usually 22 December), the Sun is overhead in the southern hemisphere.*

Chief Public or Legal Holidays in the UK

(– = not applicable.)

Public holidays[1]	England and Wales	Scotland	Northern Ireland
2000			
New Year	3 January	3, 4 January	3 January
St Patrick's Day	–	–	17 March
Good Friday[2]	21 April	21 April	21 April
Easter Monday	24 April	–	24 April
May Day	1 May	1 May	1 May
Spring	29 May	29 May	29 May
Battle of the Boyne	–	–	12 July
Summer	28 August	7 August	28 August
Christmas[2]	25, 26 December	25, 26 December	25, 26 December

Public holidays[1]	England and Wales	Scotland	Northern Ireland
2001			
New Year	1 January	1, 2 January	1 January
St Patrick's Day	–	–	17 March
Good Friday[2]	13 April	13 April	13 April
Easter Monday	16 April	–	16 April
May Day	7 May	7 May	7 May
Spring	28 May	28 May	28 May
Battle of the Boyne	–	–	12 July
Summer	27 August	6 August	27 August
Christmas[2]	25, 26 December	25, 26 December	25, 26 December

[1] In the Channel Islands, Liberation Day (9 May) is a bank and public holiday.

[2] In England, Wales, and Northern Ireland, Christmas Day and Good Friday are common law holidays.

Civil Calendar

Day	Date
Accession of Queen Elizabeth II	6 February
Duke of York's birthday	19 February
St David's Day	1 March
Commonwealth Day (variable)	2000 – 13 March; 2001 – 12 March; 2002 – 11 March
Prince Edward's birthday	10 March
St Patrick's Day	17 March
Birthday of Queen Elizabeth II	21 April
St George's Day	23 April
Coronation of Queen Elizabeth II	2 June
Duke of Edinburgh's birthday	10 June
Queen's Official Birthday (variable)	usually second Saturday in June
Queen Elizabeth the Queen Mother's birthday	4 August
Princess Royal's birthday	15 August
Princess Margaret's birthday	21 August
Lord Mayor's Day (variable)	2000 – 11 November; 2001 – 10 November; 2002 – 9 November
Remembrance Sunday (variable)	2000 – 12 November; 2001 – 11 November; 2002 – 10 November
Prince of Wales's birthday	14 November
Wedding Day of Queen Elizabeth II	20 November
St Andrew's Day	30 November

The Western Calendar

The calendar is the division of the year into months, weeks, and days, and the method of ordering the years. All early calendars except the ancient Egyptian calendar were lunar. The word 'calendar' comes from the Latin *kalendae* or *calendae,* the first day of the month on which, in ancient Rome, solemn proclamation was made of the appearance of the new moon.

The Western or Gregorian calendar derives from the Julian calendar instituted by Julius Caesar in 46 BC. The Julian calendar was adjusted in 1582 by Pope Gregory XIII, who eliminated error caused by the faulty calculation of the length of a year. The 'New Style' Gregorian calendar was only gradually adopted: Britain and its colonies, including America, adopted it in 1752, when the error amounted to 11 days, so that 3 September 1752 became 14 September 1752, and at the same time the beginning of the year was put back from 25 March to 1 January. Russia did not adopt the Gregorian calendar until after the October Revolution of 1917, so that the event (then 25 October) is currently celebrated on 7 November.

Leap years

From year one in the Western calendar, the assumed date of the birth of Jesus, dates are calculated backwards (BC 'before Christ' or BCE 'before the common era') and forwards (AD Latin Anno Domini, 'in the year of the Lord', or CE 'common era'). The lunar month (the period between one new moon and the next) naturally averages 29.5 days, but the Western calendar uses for convenience a calendar month with a complete number of days, 30 or 31 (February has 28). Since this method leaves six extra hours per year, they are normally added to February as a 29th day every fourth year – a leap year. Leap year numbers are divisible by 4, with the exception of century years, which are leap years only if they are divisible by 400.

Millennia

A millennium is a period of 1,000 years. The question of which year is the first year of the millennium hinges on the date of the first year AD. The sequence of years going from BC to AD does not include the year 0. The sequence of years runs 3 BC, 2 BC, 1 BC, AD 1, AD 2, AD 3, etc. This means that the first year of the first millennium was AD 1. The one thousandth year was AD 1000 and the first day of the second millennium was in AD 1001. It is thus clear that the start of the new millennium will be 1 January 2001. Year AD 2000 will certainly be celebrated, as is natural for a year with such a round number, but accurately speaking we will be celebrating the last year of the millennium, not the start of the new millennium.

Year Equivalents for Gregorian, Jewish, Islamic, and Hindu Calendars

Gregorian equivalents are given and are AD (Anno Domini).

Jewish[1]	(AM)	Islamic[2]	(AH)	Hindu[3]	(SE)
5753	28 September 1992–15 September 1993	1413	2 July 1992–20 June 1993	1914	21 March 1992–21 March 1993
5754	16 September 1993–5 September 1994	1414	21 June 1993–9 June 1994	1915	22 March 1993–21 March 1994
5755	6 September 1994–24 September 1995	1415	10 June 1994–30 May 1995	1916	22 March 1994–21 March 1995
5756	25 September 1995–13 September 1996	1416	31 May 1995–18 May 1996	1917	22 March 1995–20 March 1996
5757	14 September 1996–1 October 1997	1417	19 May 1996–8 May 1997	1918	21 March 1996–21 March 1997
5758	2 October 1997–20 September 1998	1418	8 May 1997–27 April 1998	1919	22 March 1997–21 March 1998
5759	21 September 1998–10 September 1999	1419	27 April 1998–16 April 1999	1920	22 March 1998–21 March 1999
5760	11 September 1999–29 September 2000	1420	17 April 1999–5 April 2000	1921	22 March 1999–21 March 2000
5761	30 September 2000–17 September 2001	1421	6 April 2000–25 March 2001	1922	22 March 2000–21 March 2001
5762	18 September 2001–6 September 2002	1422	26 March 2001–14 March 2002	1923	22 March 2001–21 March 2002

[1] Calculated from 3761 BC, said to be the year after the creation of the world. AM = Anno Mundi. Some say that the Jewish calendar as used today was formulated in AD 358 by Rabbi Hillel II; others that this formulation occurred later. A Jewish year may have 12 or 13 months, each of which normally alternates between 29 and 30 days, and may be one of the following six types: Minimal Common 353 days; Regular Common 354 days; Full Common 355 days; Minimal Leap 383 days; Regular Leap 384 days; Full Leap 385 days.

[2] Calculated from AD 622, the year in which the prophet Mohammed went from Mecca to Medina. AH = Anno Hegirae. The years are purely lunar, and consist of 12 months with alternately 29 or 30 days, plus one extra day at the end of the 12th month in each leap year, of which there are 11 in each cycle of 30 years. The Islamic calendar being lunar, each month begins on the day immediately following the first observation of the new moon in the night sky. Owing to the Earth's axial rotation, the time of this observation varies from place to place. New Year's Day, and the first days of all the months, are therefore also subject to variation.

[3] Calculated from AD 78, the beginning of the Saka Era (SE), used alongside Gregorian dates in Government of India publications since 22 March 1957. Other important Hindu eras include: Vikrama Era (58 BC); Kalacuri Era (AD 248); Gupta Era (AD 320); and Harsa Era (AD 606).

Months of the Year

Month	Derivation of name	Number of days
January	Janus, Roman god of doorways and beginnings	31
February	Februa, Roman festival of purification	28 (29 in a leap year)
March	Mars, Roman god of war	31
April	Latin *aperire*, 'to open'	30
May	Maia, Roman goddess of spring	31
June	Juno, Roman goddess of marriage	30
July	Julius Caesar, Roman general and dictator	31
August	Augustus, Roman emperor	31
September	Latin *septem*, 'seven'; September was the seventh month of the earliest Roman calendar	30
October	Latin *octo*, 'eight'; October was the eighth month of the earliest Roman calendar	31
November	Latin *novem*, 'nine'; November was the ninth month of the earliest Roman calendar	30
December	Latin *decem*, 'ten'; December was the tenth month of the earliest Roman calendar	31

See Also

Major Religious Festivals, pp. 402–405

Month Equivalents for Gregorian, Jewish, Islamic, and Hindu Calendars

Gregorian equivalents to other calendars are given in parentheses; the figures refer to the number of solar days in each month. (– = not applicable.)

Gregorian (Basis: sun)	Jewish (Basis: combination of solar and lunar cycles)	Islamic[1] (Basis: visibility of the new moon)	Hindu (Basis: moon)
January (31)	Tishri (September–October) (30)	Muharram (30)	Caitra (March–April) (29 or 30)
February (28 or 29)	Heshvan (October–November) (29 or 30)	Safar (29)	Vaisakha (April–May) (29 or 30)
March (31)	Kislev (November–December) (29 or 30)	Rabi I (30)	Jaistha (May–June) (29 or 30)
April (30)	Tebet (December–January) (29)	Rabi II (29)	Asadha (June–July) (29 or 30)
May (31)	Shebat (January–February) (30)	Jumada I (30)	Dvitiya Asadha (certain leap years)
June (30)	Adar (February–March) (29 or 30)	Jumada II (29)	Sravana (July–August) (29 or 30)
July (31)	Adar Sheni (leap years only)	Rajab (30)	Dvitiya Sravana (certain leap years)
August (31)	Nisan (March–April) (29)	Shaban (29)	Bhadrapada (August–September) (29 or 30)
September (30)	Iyar (April–May) (30)	Ramadan (30)	Aswin (September–October) (29 or 30)
October (31)	Sivan (May–June) (30)	Shawwal (29)	Kartik (October–November) (29 or 30)
November (30)	Tammuz (June–July) (29)	Dhu al-Qadah (30)	Agra Hayana (November–December) (29 or 30)
December (31)	Av (July–August) (30)	Dhu al-Hijjah (29 or 30)	Paus (December–January) (29 or 30)
–	Elul (August–September) (29)	–	Magh (January–February) (29 or 30)
–	–	–	Phalgun (February–March) (29 or 30)

[1] These are the months of the Islamic calendar. Their equivalents with the Gregorian calendar vary each year.

Days of the Week

The names of the days are based on the seven heavenly bodies used in traditional astrology (the Sun, the Moon, Mars, Mercury, Jupiter, Venus, and Saturn). These bodies were believed at the time (between 1100–1500) to revolve around the Earth and influence its events. The seven-day week became part of the Roman calendar in AD 321.

English	Latin	Saxon	German	French	Italian	Spanish
Sunday	Dies Solis	Sunnandaeg – Sun's Day	Sonntag	dimanche	domenica	domingo
Monday	Dies Lunae	Mōnandaeg – Moon's Day	Montag	lundi	lunedì	lunes
Tuesday	Dies Martis	Tīwesdaeg – Tiw's Day[1]	Dienstag	mardi	martedì	martes
Wednesday	Dies Mercurii	Wōdnesdaeg – Woden's Day[2]	Mittwoch	mercredi	mercoledì	miércoles
Thursday	Dies Jovis	Thunresdaeg – Thor's Day[3]	Donnerstag	jeudi	giovedì	jueves
Friday	Dies Veneris	Frigedaeg – Frigg's Day[4]	Freitag	vendredi	venerdì	viernes
Saturday	Dies Saturni	Saetern-daeg – Saturn's Day	Samstag	samedi	sabato	sábado

[1] Tiw: Anglo-Saxon name for Nordic Tyr, son of Odin and god of war, closest to Mars (Greek Ares), son of Roman god Jupiter (Greek Zeus).
[2] Woden: Anglo-Saxon name for Odin, Nordic dispenser of victory, closest to Mercury (Greek Hermes), Roman messenger of victory.
[3] Thor: Nordic god of thunder, eldest son of Odin, closest to Roman Jupiter (Greek Zeus).
[4] Frigg (or Freyja): wife of Odin, the Nordic goddess of love, equivalent to Venus (Greek Aphrodite).

National Days of Countries Around the World

This list includes the chief days of national celebration for each nation given; it is not exhaustive.

Country	National day
Afghanistan	19 August
Albania	28 November
Algeria	1 November
Andorra	8 September
Angola	11 November
Antigua and Barbuda	1 November
Argentina	25 May
Armenia	21 September
Australia	26 January
Austria	26 October
Azerbaijan	28 May
Bahamas	10 July
Bahrain	16 December
Bangladesh	26 March, 16 December
Barbados	30 November
Belarus	3 July, 27 July
Belgium	21 July
Belize	21 September
Benin	1 August, 30 November
Bhutan	17 December
Bolivia	6 August
Bosnia-Herzegovina	1 March
Botswana	30 September
Brazil	7 September
Brunei	23 February
Bulgaria	3 March
Burkina Faso	4 August, 11 December
Burundi	1 July
Cambodia	9 November
Cameroon	20 May
Canada	1 July
Cape Verde	5 July
Central African Republic	1 December
Chad	13 April, 11 August
Chile	18 September
China	1–2 October
Colombia	20 July
Comoros	6 July
Congo, Democratic Republic of	24 November
Congo, Republic of the	15 August
Costa Rica	15 September
Côte d'Ivoire	7 August, 7 December
Croatia	30 May
Cuba	1 January
Cyprus	1 October
Czech Republic	8 May, 6 July, 28 October
Denmark	16 April, 5 June
Djibouti	27 June
Dominica	3 November
Dominican Republic	27 February
Ecuador	10 August

(continued)

National Days of Countries Around the World (*continued*)

Country	National day
Egypt	23 July
El Salvador	15 September
Equatorial Guinea	12 October
Eritrea	24 May
Estonia	24 February
Ethiopia	2 March, 6 April
Fiji	10 October
Finland	6 December
France	14 July
Gabon	17 August
Gambia	18 February
Georgia	26 May
Germany	3 October
Ghana	6 March
Greece	25 March
Grenada	7 February
Guatemala	15 September
Guinea	2 October
Guinea-Bissau	24 September
Guyana	23 February, 26 May
Haiti	1 January
Honduras	15 September
Hungary	15 March, 20 August, 23 October
Iceland	17 June
India	26 January
Indonesia	17 August
Iran	11 February
Iraq	8 February, 14 July, 17 July, 8 August
Ireland, Republic of	17 March
Israel	–
Italy	2 June
Jamaica	first Monday in August
Japan	23 December
Jordan	25 May
Kazakhstan	25 October
Kenya	12 December
Kiribati	12 July
Korea, North	16 February, 9 September
Korea, South	1 March, 15 August
Kuwait	25 February
Kyrgyzstan	31 August
Laos	2 December
Latvia	18 November
Lebanon	22 November
Lesotho	4 October
Liberia	26 July
Libya	1 September
Liechtenstein	15 August
Lithuania	16 February
Luxembourg	23 June
Macedonia, Former Yugoslav Republic of	2 August, 8 September
Madagascar	26 June
Malawi	6 July
Malaysia	31 August
Maldives	26 July
Mali	22 September
Malta	31 March, 7 June, 8 September, 21 September, 13 December
Marshall Islands	1 May, 21 October
Mauritania	28 November
Mauritius	12 March
Mexico	16 September
Micronesia	–
Moldova	27 August
Monaco	19 November
Mongolia	11 July
Morocco	3 March
Mozambique	25 June
Myanmar	4 January
Namibia	21 March
Nauru	31 January
Nepal	18 February, 28 December
Netherlands	30 April
New Zealand	6 February
Nicaragua	15 September
Niger	18 December
Nigeria	1 October
Norway	17 May
Oman	18 November
Pakistan	23 March, 14 August
Palau	1 October
Panama	3 November
Papua New Guinea	16 September
Paraguay	14–15 May
Peru	28–29 July
Philippines	12 June
Poland	3 May
Portugal	10 June
Qatar	3 September
Romania	1 December
Russia	12 June
Rwanda	1 July
St Kitts and Nevis	19 September
St Lucia	22 February
St Vincent and the Grenadines	27 October
Samoa	1–3 June
San Marino	3 September
São Tomé e Príncipe	12 July
Saudi Arabia	23 September
Senegal	4 April
Seychelles	5 June, 18 June, 29 June
Sierra Leone	27 April
Singapore	9 August
Slovak Republic	1 January, 5 July, 29 August, 1 September
Slovenia	25 June, 26 December
Solomon Islands	7 July
Somalia	1 July
South Africa	27 April
Spain	12 October
Sri Lanka	4 February
Sudan	1 January
Suriname	25 November
Swaziland	6 September
Sweden	6 June
Switzerland	1 August
Syria	17 April
Taiwan	10 October
Tajikistan	9 September
Tanzania	26 April
Thailand	5 December
Togo	13 January
Tonga	4 June
Trinidad and Tobago	31 August, 24 September
Tunisia	20 March
Turkey	29 October
Turkmenistan	27–28 October
Tuvalu	1 October
Uganda	9 October
UK	1 March, 17 March, 23 April, 30 November
Ukraine	24 August
United Arab Emirates	2 December
Uruguay	25 August
USA	4 July
Uzbekistan	1 September, 8 December
Vanuatu	30 July
Vatican City State[1]	22 October
Venezuela	5 July
Vietnam	1–2 September
Yemen	22 May
Yugoslavia (Serbia and Montenegro)	27 April, 29–30 November
Zambia	24 October
Zimbabwe	18 April

[1] The Vatican City State has as its national holiday the date of the current pope's installation; this date is therefore subject to change.

Saints' Days

January

1 Fulgentius
2 Basil and Gregory of Nazianzus, Macarius of Alexandria, Seraphim of Sarov
3 Geneviève
4 Elizabeth Seton
5 Simeon Stylites
6 Balthasar, Caspar and Melchior
7 Lucian of Antioch, Raymond of Peñafort
8 Gudule, Severinus
9 Hadrian the African, Basilissa
10 Agatho, Marcian
11 Theodosius the Cenobiarch
12 Ailred, Benedict Biscop, Arcadius
13 Hilary of Poitiers
14 Kentigern, Sava, Felix
15 Macarius of Egypt, Maurus, Paul of Thebes
16 Honoratus, Priscilla, Juliana
17 Antony of Egypt
18 Prisca
19 Wulfstan
20 Euthymius, Fabian, Sebastian
21 Agnes, Fructuosus, Meinrad
22 Vincent
23 Ildefonsus
24 Babylas, Francis de Sales
25 Paul, Praejectus
26 Paula, Timothy and Titus
27 Angela Merici
28 Thomas Aquinas
29 Gildas
30 Martina, Bathildis
31 John Bosco

February

1 Bridget (or Bride)
2 Joan de Lestonnac
3 Anskar, Blaise, Werburga

(*continued*)

Saints' Days (*continued*)

4 Gilbert of Sempringham, Isidore of Pelusium, Phileas, Andrew Corsini
5 Agatha, Avitus
6 Dorothy, Paul Miki and companions, Vedast
7 Theodore the General
8 Jerome Emiliani
9 Teilo, Apollonia
10 Scholastica
11 Benedict of Aniane, Caedmon, Gregory II
12 Meletius, Julian the Hospitaler
13 Agabus, Catherine dei Ricci
14 Cyril and Methodius, Valentine
15 Sigfrid (patron of Sweden)
16 Juliana
17 Fintan
18 Bernadette (in France), Colman, Flavian, Simeon
19 Conrad
20 Wulfric
21 Peter Damian
22 Margaret of Cortona
23 Polycarp
24 Ethelbert
25 Tarasius, Walburga
26 Alexander, Porphyrius
27 Leander
28 Oswald of York and Worcester

March
1 David
2 Chad, Simplicius
3 Ailred, Cunegund
4 Casimir, Adrian
5 Eusebius of Cremona
6 Chrodegang
7 Perpetua and Felicity
8 Felix, John of God, Pontius
9 Frances of Rome, Gregory of Nyssa, Pacian
10 John Ogilvie, Macarius of Jerusalem, Simplicius
11 Constantine, Oengus, Sophronius
12 Gregory (the Great), Maximilian
13 Nicephorus
14 Matilda
15 Clement Hofbauer, Louise de Marillac
16 Heribert
17 Gertrude, Joseph of Arimathea, Patrick
18 Anselm of Lucca, Cyril of Jerusalem, Edward
19 Joseph
20 Cuthbert, Martin of Braga
21 Serapion of Thmuis, Nicholas of Fluê
22 Basil
23 Turibius de Mongrovejo, Gwinear
24 Catherine of Vadstena
25 Dismas, Alfwold
26 Ludger
27 Rupert of Salzburg
28 Gontran
29 Jonah and Berikjesus
30 John Climacus
31 Acacius

April
1 Hugh of Grenoble, Melito
2 Francis of Paola, Mary of Egypt
3 Richard of Chichester
4 Isidore of Seville
5 Vincent Ferrer
6 William of Eskill
7 Hegesippus, John Baptist de la Salle
8 Perpetuus
9 Madrun
10 Fulbert, Hedda
11 Gemma Galgani, Guthlac, Stanislaus
12 Julius I, Zeno
13 Martin I
14 Caradoc, Tiburtius and Valerian
15 Paternus of Wales, Ruadhan
16 Bernadette, Magnus
17 Stephen Harding
18 Apollonius
19 Alphege, Leo IX
20 Agnes of Montepulciano
21 Anastasius, Anselm, Beuno
22 Alexander and Epipodius
23 George
24 Egbert, Fidelis of Sigmaringen, Mellitus
25 Mark
26 Anacletus, Stephen of Perm
27 Zita
28 Peter Chanel, Vitalis and Valeria
29 Catherine of Siena, Hugh of Cluny, Peter Martyr, Robert
30 Pius V

May
1 Asaph, Joseph the Worker
2 Athanasius
3 Philip and James (the Less)
4 Gotthard, Pelagia, Florian
5 Hilary of Arles
6 Edbert
7 John of Beverley
8 Peter of Tarantaise
9 Pachomius
10 Antoninus, John of Avila
11 Mamertus
12 Epiphanius, Nereus and Achilleus, Pancras
13 Andrew Hubert Fournet
14 Matthias
15 Isidore
16 Brendan, John of Nepomuk, Simon Stock
17 Paschal Baylon
18 John I
19 Dunstan, Ivo, Pudens, Pudentiana
20 Bernadino of Siena
21 Andrew Bobola, Collen, Godric
22 Rita of Cascia
23 Ivo of Chartres, Desiderius
24 Vincent of Lérins, David I of Scotland
25 Bede, Gregory VII, Mary Magdalene de Pazzi
26 Philip Neri, Quadratus
27 Augustine of Canterbury
28 Germain of Paris
29 Theodosia
30 Joan of Arc
31 Petronilla

June
1 Justin Martyr, Pamphilus
2 Erasmus, Marcellinus and Peter, Pothinus
3 Charles Lwanga and companions, Clotilde, Kevin
4 Optatus, Petrock
5 Boniface
6 Norbert
7 Paul of Constantinople, Willibald, Meriadoc
8 William of York
9 Columba, Ephraem
10 Landry of Paris
11 Barnabas
12 Leo III
13 Anthony of Padua
14 Methodius, Dogmael
15 Orsisius, Vitus
16 Cyricus and Julitta
17 Alban, Botulph, Rainerius
18 Gregory Barbarigo
19 Gervasius and Protasius, Romuald
20 Alban
21 Albinus of Mainz, Aloysius Gonzaga
22 John Fisher and Thomas More, Nicetas, Paulinus of Nola
23 Etheldreda
24 Birth of John the Baptist
25 Prosper of Aquitaine, Prosper of Reggio
26 John and Paul
27 Cyril of Alexandria, Ladislaus
28 Irenaeus
29 Peter and Paul
30 First Martyrs of the Church of Rome, Martial, Theobald of Provins

July
1 Oliver Plunket
2 Processus and Martinian
3 Anatolius, Thomas
4 Andrew of Crete, Elizabeth of Portugal, Ulrich
5 Anthony Zaccaria
6 Maria Goretti
7 Palladius, Pantaenus
8 Kilian, Aquila and Prisca (or Priscilla), Procopius
9 Veronica Giuliani
10 Rufina and Secunda, Seven Brothers
11 Benedict
12 John Gualbert, Veronica
13 Mildred, Silas, Henry the Emperor
14 Camillus of Lellis, Deusdedit
15 Bonaventure, Swithin, Vladimir
16 Eustathius, Helier
17 Ennodius, Leo IV, Marcellina, Alexis
18 Arnulf
19 Macrina, Symmachus, Arsenius
20 Aurelius, Margaret
21 Lawrence of Brindisi, Praxedes
22 Mary Magdalene
23 Apollinaris, Bridget of Sweden
24 Christina the Astonishing
25 Christopher, James (the Great)
26 Anne and Joachim
27 Pantaleon
28 Samson
29 Martha, Lupus, Olaf
30 Peter Chrysologus
31 Germanus, Joseph of Arimathea, Ignatius of Loyola

August
1 Alphonsus Liguori, Ethelwold
2 Eusebius of Vercelli, Stephen I
3 Waldef (or Waltheof)
4 Jean-Baptiste Vianney
5 Afra
6 Justus and Pastor
7 Cajetan, Sixtus II and companions
8 Dominic

(*continued*)

Saints' Days (*continued*)

9 Romanus
10 Laurence
11 Clare, Susanna
12 Euplius
13 Maximus, Pontian and Hippolytus, Radegunde
14 Maximilian Kolbe
15 Arnulf, Tarsicius
16 Roch, Stephen of Hungary
17 Hyacinth
18 Helena, Agapitus
19 John Eudes, Sebaldus
20 Bernard, Oswin, Philibert
21 Pius X
22 Symphorianus
23 Rose of Lima
24 Bartholomew, Ouen
25 Joseph Calasanctius, Louis IX, Menas of Constantinople
26 Zephyrinus
27 Caesarius, Monica
28 Augustine of Hippo
29 Sabina
30 Pammachius
31 Aidan, Paulinus of Trier

September

1 Giles
2 William of Roskilde
3 Gregory (the Great)
4 Boniface I, Rosalia
5 Bertin, Laurence Giustiniani
6 Cagnoald
7 Sozon
8 Adrian and Natalia
9 Peter Claver
10 Nicholas of Tolentino
11 Deiniol, Paphnutius
12 Ailbe, Eanswida
13 John Chrysostom
14 Notburga
15 Catherine of Genoa
16 Cornelius, Cyprian of Carthage, Euphemia, Ninian
17 Robert Bellarmine, Hildegard, Lambert, Satyrus
18 Joseph of Copertino
19 Januarius, Theodore of Tarsus
20 Agapetus and Eustace
21 Matthew
22 Maurice and his legion
23 Adamnan
24 Pacificus, Gerard
25 Sergius of Rostov
26 Cosmas and Damian, Cyprian of Carthage, John of Meda
27 Vincent de Paul
28 Exuperius, Wenceslaus
29 Michael (Michaelmas Day), Gabriel and Raphael
30 Jerome

October

1 Remigius, Romanos, Teresa of Lisieux
2 Leodegar (or Leger)
3 Thomas de Cantilupe
4 Ammon, Francis of Assisi, Petronius
5 Placid and Maurus
6 Bruno, Faith
7 Justina
8 Triduana
9 Demetrius of Alexandria, Denis and companions, Dionysius of Paris, John Leonardi
10 Francis Borgia, Paulinus of York
11 Bruno (Bishop of Cologne), Nectarius
12 Wilfrid, Ethelburga of Barking
13 Edward the Confessor
14 Callistus I
15 Teresa of Avila
16 Gall, Hedwig, Lullus, Margaret Mary Alacoque
17 Ignatius of Antioch
18 Luke
19 John de Bréboeuf, Isaac Jogues and companions, Paul of the Cross, Peter of Alcántara
20 Acca
21 Hilarion, Ursula
22 Abercius
23 John of Capistrano
24 Anthony Claret
25 Crispin and Crispinian, Forty Martyrs of England and Wales, Gaudentius
26 Bean, Eata, Cedd
27 Frumentius
28 Simon and Jude
29 Narcissus of Jerusalem
30 Serapion of Antioch
31 Wolfgang

November

1 All Saints, Marcel of Paris, Benignus
2 Victorinus
3 Hubert, Malachy, Martin de Porres, Pirminus, Winifred
4 Charles Borromeo, Vitalis and Agricola, Emeric (or Americus)
5 Elizabeth
6 Illtyd, Leonard
7 Willibrord
8 Willehad
9 Theodore the Recruit
10 Justus, Leo I
11 Martin of Tours, Menas of Egypt, Theodore of Studios
12 Josaphat, Nilus the Ascetic
13 Abbo, Nicholas I
14 Dubricius, Gregory Palamas, Laurence O'Toole
15 Albert the Great, Machutus (or Malo)
16 Edmund of Abingdon, Eucherius, Gertrude (the Great), Margaret of Scotland
17 Elizabeth of Hungary, Gregory Thaumaturgus (the Wonderworker), Gregory of Tours, Hugh of Lincoln
18 Odo, Romanus
19 Nerses
20 Edmund the Martyr
21 Gelasius
22 Cecilia
23 Amphilochius, Clement I, Columban, Felicity, Gregory of Agrigentum
24 Chrysogonus
25 Mercurius, Catherine of Alexandria
26 Siricius, John Berchmans
27 Barlam and Josaphat
28 Simeon Metaphrastes, Catherine Labouré
29 Brendan of Birr
30 Andrew

December

1 Eligius (or Eloi)
2 Chromatius
3 Francis Xavier
4 Barbara, John Damascene, Osmund
5 Sabas
6 Nicholas
7 Ambrose
8 Romaric
9 Leocadia, Peter Fourier
10 Miltiades, Eulalia
11 Damasus, Daniel
12 Jane Frances de Chantal, Vicelin
13 Lucy, Odilia
14 John of the Cross, Spyridon
15 Mary di Rosa, Nino, Valerian
16 Adelaide
17 Begga, Lazarus
18 Winebald, Flannan
20 Dominic of Silos
21 Peter Canisius, Thomas
22 Chaeremon
23 John of Kanty
24 Charbel Makhlouf
25 Anastasia
26 Stephen
27 John the Divine, Fabiola
28 The Holy Innocents
29 Thomas à Becket, Trophimus of Arles (or San Tropez)
30 Anysia
31 Sylvester I

Signs of the Zodiac

Element	Sign	Symbol	Dates	Sign	Symbol	Dates	Sign	Symbol	Dates
Fire	Aries		21 March–20 April	Leo		23 July–23 August	Sagittarius		22 November–22 December
Earth	Taurus		20 April–21 May	Virgo		23 August–23 September	Capricorn		22 December–20 January
Air	Gemini		21 May–21 June	Libra		23 September–23 October	Aquarius		20 January–19 February
Water	Cancer		21 June–23 July	Scorpio		23 October–22 November	Pisces		19 February–21 March

The Chinese Year

The Chinese year is traditionally divided into 12 lunar months, beginning at the second new moon after the winter solstice. As there is a shortfall of approximately 11 days between the lunar and the solar year, an intercalary month is added every two and a half years. The year is also divided into 24 periods of 15–16 days, according to the movement of the Sun. Both the traditional and, from 1911, the Western calendars are in use in China.

Chinese period	English translation	Chinese period	English translation	Chinese period	English translation
Li Chun	Spring Begins	Mang Zhong	Grain in Ear	Han Lu	Cold Dew
Yu Shui	Rain Water	Xia Zhi	Summer Solstice	Shuang Jiang	Frost Descends
Jing Zhe	Insects Waken	Xiao Shu	Slight Heat	Li Dong	Winter Begins
Chun Fen	Vernal Equinox	Da Shu	Great Heat	Xiao Xue	Little Snow
Qing Ming	Clear and Bright	Li Qiu	Autumn Begins	Da Xue	Heavy Snow
Gu Yu	Grain Rains	Chu Shu	Heat Ends	Dong Zhi	Winter Solstice
Li Xia	Summer Begins	Bai Lu	White Dew	Xiao Han	Little Cold
Xiao Man	Grain Fills	Qui Fen	Autumn Equinox	Da Han	Severe Cold

Wedding Anniversaries

In many Western countries, wedding anniversaries have become associated with gifts of different materials. There is variation between countries.

Anniversary	Material	Anniversary	Material	Anniversary	Material
1st	cotton	10th	tin	35th	coral
2nd	paper	11th	steel	40th	ruby
3rd	leather	12th	silk, fine linen	45th	sapphire
4th	fruit, flowers	13th	lace	50th	gold
5th	wood	14th	ivory	55th	emerald
6th	sugar, iron	15th	crystal	60th	diamond
7th	wool	20th	china	70th	platinum
8th	bronze, electrical appliances	25th	silver		
9th	copper, pottery	30th	pearl		

Birth Flowers

Month	Flower
January	carnation, snowdrop
February	primrose, violet
March	jonquil, violet
April	daisy, sweet pea
May	hawthorn, lily of the valley
June	honeysuckle, rose
July	larkspur, water lily
August	gladiolus, poppy
September	aster, morning glory
October	calendula, cosmos
November	chrysanthemum
December	holly, narcissus, poinsettia

Birthstones

Month	Stone	Quality
January	garnet	constancy
February	amethyst	sincerity
March	aquamarine, bloodstone	courage
April	diamond	innocence
May	emerald	love
June	alexandrite, pearl	health and purity
July	ruby	contentment
August	peridot, sardonyx	married happiness
September	sapphire	clear thinking
October	opal, tourmaline	hope
November	topaz	fidelity
December	turquoise, zircon	wealth

The Chinese Zodiac

In the Chinese zodiac, each successive year is named after one of 12 animals. These 12-year cycles are continuously repeated and combined with a sequence of the five elements (water, wood, fire, metal, earth) in a 60-year major cycle.

Dates	Animal	Chinese name
1900–10		
31 January 1900–18 February 1901	Rat	Shu
19 February 1901–7 February 1902	Ox	Niu
8 February 1902–28 January 1903	Tiger	Hu
29 January 1903–15 February 1904	Hare	T'u
16 February 1904–3 February 1905	Dragon	Lung
4 February 1905–24 January 1906	Snake	She
25 January 1906–12 February 1907	Horse	Ma
13 February 1907–1 February 1908	Goat	Yang
2 February 1908–21 January 1909	Monkey	Hou
22 January 1909–9 February 1910	Cockerel	Chi
1910–20		
10 February 1910–29 January 1911	Dog	Kou
30 January 1911–17 February 1912	Pig	Chu
18 February 1912–5 February 1913	Rat	Shu
6 February 1913–15 January 1914	Ox	Niu
16 January 1914–13 February 1915	Tiger	Hu
14 February 1915–2 February 1916	Hare	T'u
3 February 1916–22 January 1917	Dragon	Lung
23 January 1917–10 February 1918	Snake	She
11 February 1918–31 January 1919	Horse	Ma
1 February 1919–19 February 1920	Goat	Yang
1920–30		
20 February 1920–7 February 1921	Monkey	Hou
8 February 1921–27 January 1922	Cockerel	Chi
28 January 1922–15 February 1923	Dog	Kou
16 February 1923–4 February 1924	Pig	Chu
5 February 1924–24 January 1925	Rat	Shu
25 January 1925–12 February 1926	Ox	Niu
13 February 1926–1 February 1927	Tiger	Hu
2 February 1927–22 January 1928	Hare	T'u
23 January 1928–9 February 1929	Dragon	Lung
10 February 1929–29 January 1930	Snake	She
1930–40		
30 January 1930–16 February 1931	Horse	Ma
17 February 1931–5 February 1932	Goat	Yang
6 February 1932–25 January 1933	Monkey	Hou
26 January 1933–13 February 1934	Cockerel	Chi
14 February 1934–3 February 1935	Dog	Kou
4 February 1935–23 January 1936	Pig	Chu
24 January 1936–10 February 1937	Rat	Shu
11 February 1937–30 January 1938	Ox	Niu
31 January 1938–18 February 1939	Tiger	Hu
19 February 1939–7 February 1940	Hare	T'u
1940–50		
8 February 1940–26 January 1941	Dragon	Lung
27 January 1941–14 February 1942	Snake	She
15 February 1942–4 February 1943	Horse	Ma
5 February 1943–24 January 1944	Goat	Yang
25 January 1944–12 February 1945	Monkey	Hou
13 February 1945–1 February 1946	Cockerel	Chi
2 February 1946–21 January 1947	Dog	Kou
22 January 1947–9 February 1948	Pig	Shu
10 February 1948–28 January 1949	Rat	Niu
29 January 1949–16 February 1950	Ox	Hu
1950–60		
17 February 1950–5 February 1951	Tiger	T'u
6 February 1951–26 January 1952	Hare	Lung
27 January 1952–13 February 1953	Dragon	She
14 February 1953–2 February 1954	Snake	Ma
3 February 1954–23 January 1955	Horse	Yang
24 January 1955–11 February 1956	Goat	Hou
12 February 1956–30 January 1957	Monkey	Chi
31 January 1957–17 February 1958	Cockerel	Kou
18 February 1958–7 February 1959	Dog	Chu
8 February 1959–27 January 1960	Pig	Shu
1960–70		
28 January 1960–14 February 1961	Rat	Niu
15 February 1961–4 February 1962	Ox	Hu
5 February 1962–24 January 1963	Tiger	T'u
25 January 1963–12 February 1964	Hare	Lung
13 February 1964–1 February 1965	Dragon	She
2 February 1965–20 January 1966	Snake	Ma
21 January 1966–8 February 1967	Horse	Yang
9 February 1967–29 January 1968	Goat	Hou
30 January 1968–16 February 1969	Monkey	Chi
17 February 1969–5 February 1970	Cockerel	Kou
1970–80		
6 February 1970–26 January 1971	Dog	Chu
27 January 1971–15 January 1972	Pig	Shu
16 January 1972–2 February 1973	Rat	Niu
3 February 1973–22 January 1974	Ox	Hu
23 January 1974–10 February 1975	Tiger	T'u
11 February 1975–30 January 1976	Hare	Lung
31 January 1976–17 February 1977	Dragon	She
18 February 1977–6 February 1978	Snake	Ma
7 February 1978–27 January 1979	Horse	Yang
28 January 1979–15 February 1980	Goat	Hou
1980–90		
16 February 1980–4 February 1981	Monkey	Chi
5 February 1981–24 January 1982	Cockerel	Kou
25 January 1982–12 February 1983	Dog	Chu
13 February 1983–1 February 1984	Pig	Shu
2 February 1984–19 February 1985	Rat	Niu
20 February 1985–8 February 1986	Ox	Hu
9 February 1986–28 January 1987	Tiger	T'u
29 January 1987–16 February 1988	Hare	Lung
17 February 1988–5 February 1989	Dragon	She
6 February 1989–26 January 1990	Snake	Ma
1990–2000		
27 January 1990–14 February 1991	Horse	Yang
15 February 1991–3 February 1992	Goat	Hou
4 February 1992–22 January 1993	Monkey	Chi
23 January 1993–9 February 1994	Cockerel	Kou
10 February 1994–30 January 1995	Dog	Chu
31 January 1995–18 February 1996	Pig	Shu
19 February 1996–7 February 1997	Rat	Niu
8 February 1997–27 January 1998	Ox	Hu
28 January 1998–15 February 1999	Tigers	T'u
16 February 1999–4 February 2000	Hare	Lung
2000–07		
5 February 2000–23 January 2001	Dragon	She
24 January 2001–11 February 2002	Snake	Ma
12 February 2002–31 January 2003	Horse	Yang
1 February 2003–21 January 2004	Goat	Hou
22 January 2004–8 February 2005	Monkey	Chi
9 February 2005–28 January 2006	Cockerel	Kou
29 January 2006–17 February 2007	Dog	Chu
18 February 2007–	Pig	Chu

The Millennium

The Turn of a Millennium: Meaning and Significance

BY ASA BRIGGS

The word 'millennium' – made more familiar than it ever has been as the 20th century reaches its end – has more than one meaning. Derived from the Latin word *mille,* meaning a thousand, it is now used mainly chronologically. With the end of the 20th century the second Christian millennium ends also. Twenty centuries have come and gone since the birth of Christ. A far older use of the word was Christian too. Resting not on chronology but on eschatology – doctrines of first and last things – it referred to a thousand-year future rule of Christ following the Second Coming – his return to earth.

The two meanings, however, have been taken out of their specifically Christian context. The dating system of the Christian calendar, which derived from the Roman calendar, is now widely used throughout the world in non-Christian as well as Christian countries; and the idea of a future state of bliss has long been secularized. The dream of a millennium need not involve belief in the Second Coming of Christ; it can contemplate much more than worship, reconciliation more than adoration.

There are opportunities at the end of a millennium ... for social and cultural historical accounting.

Other religions too must be brought into the picture. Islam shares much with the Judeo-Christian vision, and anthropologists have identified non-Christian religious cults, particularly Melanesian cargo cults in the Pacific, which put their trust in a good time coming ahead – at a date unknown. The South American Tupi-Guarani searched for a 'Land without Evil'. New 20th-century sects and religions such as the Rastafarian movement focus on it.

Behind both meanings of the word 'millennium' there is a sense of the future, although it is a future that can be approached dramatically through apocalypse – divine intervention – or gradually through human action. The word, which for 'New Age' philosophers can lead back into the past, need no longer carry a sense of progress. Moving into a third millennium is often conceived of simply as moving inexorably into the unknown through the passage of time. Yet there are politicians who have looked forward – and still look forward – to a golden age in the same way as religious prophets, some of them promising how to achieve this. The word of hope, 'millenarial', derived from the word millennium, still has more imaginative and emotive content than the word of time, 'millennial'.

The first Christian millennium

At the end of the first Christian millennium there was little contemporary awareness of its chronological significance. Indeed, both the idea of a century as a unit of time and the idea of time as change were unformed. Medieval reckonings of time were different. Even at the end of the 14th century, when there were signs of increased awareness, even of changes of attitudes, the view prevailed that all time was running downhill from the Creation to the Day of Doom (Judgement).

In the centuries following, both the Christian and Judaic traditions saw the rise of religious millenarianism, drawing on the Book of Revelations and the Hebrew prophets. After the Reformation had divided the Christian church, millenarian sects still remained outside religious orthodoxy, but in England came to particular prominence under the Commonwealth in the 17th century. In the 18th century, the Enlightenment pitted reason against revelation, but did not eradicate the questions surrounding the millennium. Increasingly, the fear became revolution rather than apocalypse, but this still looked forward to a future time. Even the challenge of evolutionary ideas in the 19th century was not seen as fundamentally incompatible with Christian thought, although millenarianists were prominent in rejecting the findings of new scientific discoveries about the age of the world.

Fin de siècle

It was at the end of the 19th century, when a self-conscious sense of fin de siècle (end of century) coexisted with enthusiasm for all that was new, that for the first time people argued about just when centuries end, an argument which continued a century after when not only a century but a millennium was ending. The German emperor Wilhelm II (1859–1941), defying arithmetic, settled it when he ordered a salute of 33 guns on 1 January 1900. And when in 1994 Henry Brooke, then British National Heritage Secretary, a post that did not exist a century earlier, announced that the 20th century – and the millennium – would end not on New Year's Eve 1999 but on 31 December 2000, he was immediately challenged and with the help of *The Times* successfully overruled.

Millennial opportunities

As the end of year approaches the fear of the apocalypse has taken new shape. The 'millennium bug' believers predict an untold doom, while religious cults wait for the Day of Judgement. Apart from the long-term value of some of the millennial projects, a number of them based on the local community, there are opportunities at the end of a millennium, as there are at national and international exhibitions, for social and cultural historical accounting.

Lord Briggs was the chancellor of the Open University 1978–94, and is the author of many books on social history

Is This the Right Year?

Debate still simmers over whether 31 December 1999 is the turn of the millennium. 1 January 2001 is officially endorsed as the start of the third millennium by the Greenwich Observatory, the US Naval Observatory, and the *Encyclopedia Britannica*. The problem arises from the institution of the AD (Anno Domini) system in the fifth century, by the Scythian monk, Dionysus Exiguus who, using Roman numerals, dated Christ's birth as AD 1. Accordingly, the end of the first millennium was 31 December 1000, the start of the next was 1 January 1001, and the start of the third millennium should be 1 January 2001. Countries avoiding this dilemma include China, whose calendar is counted in 60-year cycles from 2637 BC, when the calendar was supposedly invented. China is now in the year wu-yin, the 15th year in the 78th cycle, which started on 28 January 1998. Countries abiding by the Islamic calendar will be striding into 1420, and in the Hebrew calendar, years are counted from the creation of the world, which is assumed to have taken place in 3761 BC. The year AD 2000 witnesses the start of Hebrew year AM 5761. However, in Christian countries popular pressure has predominated, and the celebrations take place at the end of 1999.

The Millennium Bug: Write-Off or Rip-Off?

The problem

As the final year of the century draws towards its close, the apocalyptic vision of planes crashing out of the skies, total communications breakdown, and financial crisis is being posited, not by any religious sect, but by the world of computer experts and leaders of industry who claim that the world has reacted too slowly to the prospect of the 'millennium bug'.

Also known as Y2K, the problem is that nearly all computers handle dates using a two-digit shorthand, by excluding the 19 of 1999. When the clocks attempt to flip to the year 2000, computers will instead be presented with the year 00, and will become hopelessly confused. At best they will assume that it is the year 1900; at worst, there will be no way for them to handle the information at all. Predictions of the outcome range from miscalculations on bank accounts, to wholesale disaster as every computer-led object comes to a grinding halt. It is difficult to say which would be worse. If the computers continue to function with the wrong date, they would make hundreds of calculation errors. These would be impossible to trace through the whole financial system and could ruin most investments. If the computers shut down altogether, the fear is that all essential services will be hit, and the world will enter a new stone age.

The believers

The problem was first seriously addressed in the early 1990s, when the banks first began to consider the issue. Since then an entire industry has grown up around the problem, with a massive expansion in the number of computer advisors working to fix the computer clocks before the countdown. An estimated 30,000 computer programmers have been working to fix Y2K in the UK alone, and the bills are reaching astronomical levels, with the cost of reprogramming put at £52 billion. The UK government has set up its own task force to advise on the matter, but a huge number of companies are believed to be ignoring the problem, putting at risk their own business, as well as that of any company they deal with.

Other countries have been slower off the mark, with the Italian government revealing in January that it had just formed a committee to deal with the problem, expressing the hope that Italian enthusiasm and energy could beat the bug in a matter of months. As well as fighting the bug itself, many countries are making other contingency plans. New York has set up a $12 million emergency command centre from which the Mayor would attempt to control the city if chaos breaks out. Other US cities are also taking precautions not seen since the height of the Cold War, and there is believed to be widespread stockpiling of supplies going on in both the UK and USA. Doomsday scenarios include the unplanned launch of missiles by Russia and the USA, who in February agreed to cooperate to avoid unwittingly starting a nuclear war, though Moscow has been slow to respond to the wider problem. The police in the UK admitted in May that they could be hit on the turn of the New Year, as would all emergency services, who rely on computers to handle their control systems.

Those with a fear of flying will no doubt be making sure they are not in the air over the New Year, but so will Virgin Atlantic Airways. None of their fleet will fly between 24 December and late on 1 January 2000, in a move widely believed to be due to the fear of the bug, although the airline claims it is giving its staff a holiday. The reverse is happening in China, where airline bosses promised in January to be airborne over the time change to take the consequences of possible incompetence.

The sceptics

Through the growing panic, increasing numbers of voices have been raised against the over-riding belief in the bug. The sceptics are also predominantly computer-industry insiders. All believe that the Y2K problem exists, but assert that it is more likely to cause minor 'glitches' than a wholesale meltdown. They suggest that the clock re-setting will be simple, and will be a matter of inconvenience for a few hours or at worst a few days. There is increasing criticism of what many see as the profit-led fear-mongering, and the cult-like belief in the worst-case scenarios. Sensible advice is to switch off your computer on New Year's Eve, back up your files, and don't go into a bunker with a computer-controlled time-delay lock.

Distributing Millennium Money

The Millennium Commission

Set up in 1994, the Millennium Commission is chaired by Chris Smith, Secretary of State for Culture, Media, and Sport. Its aim is to help communities and individuals mark the end of the second millennium and celebrate the start of the third. There are five major areas of interest: investing in education; promoting science and technology; supporting communities; encouraging environmental sustainability; and revitalizing the cities. The Commission is responsible for the Millennium Fund, one of the good causes designated by the Government to be funded by money from the National Lottery. The total estimated budget for the fund is £2 billion. After the majority of the projects have been completed the Commission will be reduced to a skeleton organization to oversee the ongoing Millennium Award Scheme.

Capital projects: £1.25 billion

There are 28 major capital projects which include: £46 million for the Millennium Stadium, Cardiff; £35 million for the Glasgow Science Centre; £50 million for the Tate Gallery of Modern Art, London; and £23.25 million for the National Space Centre, Leicester. Smaller projects include grants for IT learning facilities in a Liverpool community centre and the conversion of an ambulance station into a centre for young people in Kingsbridge, Devon.

Festival grants: £100 million

To help people celebrate the millennium, money from the Millennium Fund is directed towards activities in communities throughout the year 2000. The first awards were made up to September 1998 and were for amounts exceeding £5,000. The next round of awards is of grants between £500 and £5,000. The process of application is based on adherence to a set of core principles which stress the widespread appeal of activities, the community benefit, and the lasting value of the events. Awards include £20,000 for a Women's Millennium Festival in Birmingham and £80,000 for The Unique Northumberland Millennium Festival.

Millennium Award schemes: £200 million

These are awards of at least £2,000 made to individuals, enabling thousands of people to undertake activities which fulfil a personal goal as well as benefiting the community. Awards are made through grant-making bodies known as Millennium Award Partners. Out of an initial grant of £200 million, half will be allocated up to the year

2001. The remaining half will form a permanent investment fund which will continue to make grants well into the 21st century. By the year 2004, more than 40,000 people will have participated in one of more than 100 Millennium Award schemes. Awards so far have included £14,380 to Techniquest/Pan Tecnicon in Pontypool, South Wales, to develop a six-month performance and exhibition project involving 50 people, which explores the theme of time. In Leicestershire, Help the Aged Millennium Awards have been given a grant to set up bowling, dancing, and bingo two afternoons per week for an over 60s group.

UK Millennium Dome Exhibition Zones

The interior of the Dome is divided into 15 spaces – a central arena the size of Trafalgar Square, which will be the site of a performance show throughout 2000, and 14 exhibition zones. Each zone has been (or will be) sponsored, as well as receiving money from the National Lottery. As of June 1999.

Exhibition	Description	Sponsorship
Inside the Dome		
Play	Explores how play-time is spent, including an interactive environment	Sponsorship under discussion
Body	An opportunity to experience the body's energy and potential from the inside, promoting health for the new millennium	Boots the Chemists
Learning	Focuses on lifelong learning; includes a modern-day digital 'Domesday Book'	Tesco
Work	Explores the changing world of work and considers how to learn and use new skills	Manpower
Money	Shows how money and finances are changing our lives, and provides a chance to go on a £1 million spending frenzy in the global market	Corporation of London; consortium of financial services institutions
Rest	Invites visitors to let their minds relax in a 'sensory place' and return refreshed	Sponsorship under discussion
Mind	A chance to wonder at the creativity of the human brain	GEC; British Aerospace
Faith	Explores the spiritual and moral dimensions of humankind, including the role of faith in society and belief as shown through the rites of passage	Negotiations with religious groups well advanced
Talk	An opportunity to learn better ways of communicating with each other	BT
Self Portrait	A celebration of all things British, and an opportunity to help decide what being British means for the future	Marks & Spencer
Journey	Reveals how smarter travel solutions will transform journeys in the future	Ford Motor Company
Living Island	Shows how to protect the environment day by day	Sponsorship under discussion
Shared Ground	An opportunity to re-discover pride in local neighbourhoods and learn how to shape communities	Camelot
Home Planet	A chance to experience the spirit of discovery and be amazed at incredible sights, places, and natural phenomena	BA; BAA
Outside the Dome		
SkyScape	Two 2,500-seat cinemas, one of which can be converted into a 3,300-seat performance venue	Sky
Our Town Story	Performance area for stories from towns and cities throughout the UK	McDonald's

How the Millennium Dome Evolved

The Millennium Dome *in Greenwich, UK.*
photo: Sean Aidan

1994 Exhibition in Greenwich is proposed to mark the millennium. The Greenwich Millennium Trust's bid points out that the site bisects the Meridian, and is an area of London in need of renewal.

1996 Mike Davies of the Richard Rogers Partnership begins to design the Dome. The design is unveiled in **November**, backed by the Millennium Commission and Michael Heseltine, who is in charge of the exhibition. Construction costs are estimated at around £350 million, with a further £150 million to fund the exhibition and celebrations.

1997 After criticism of the expense of the Dome and doubts about its future, the new Labour Prime Minister Tony Blair saves the project by a commitment to make it a sustainable site. The official cost of the project in **January** is set at £583 million, though estimates put the real cost closer to £800 million. There is growing concern that transport links to Greenwich may not be completed in time for the opening of the Dome, and that popular support for the exhibition is still low, partly due to uncertainty over what is to be in the exhibition itself. In **October**, the project is visibly taking shape with the erection of the Dome's steel masts.

1998 In **January** Stephen Bayley, the designer responsible for the interior of the Dome, leaves his post. The renamed New Millennium Experience Company insists that the creative thrust of the exhibition would be unveiled within months. When revealed, it includes a giant figure inside the Dome, which visitors will enter and explore. The Dome interior will be divided into 'zones' dealing with all aspects of social and cultural life. Christian organizations complain that the Dome is not a suitable way to mark 2,000 years of Christianity.

1999 In **January** Church leaders threaten to boycott the Dome New Year's Eve celebrations; the Queen and the Prime Minister are already committed to being at the party. In **May** proposals for a church service before the opening of the Dome are put forward. Ministers responsible for the overseeing of the project had suggested that Christian celebrations would be inappropriate, and that the Dome's festivities should represent the whole spectrum of religious belief in the country. The details of the spectacular opening ceremony planned for 31 December are kept secret.

Millennium Dome Vital Statistics

1. It has the biggest roof in the world, covering 80,000 sq m/20 acres.
2. It has the same volume as 1,100 Olympic swimming pools.
3. It could contain 2 Wembley Stadiums or 13 Albert Halls.
4. It covers an area nearly 6 times larger than the Great Pyramid at Giza.
5. The air within the finished Dome will be heavier than the Dome's structure.

Catching the Millennium Dawn

According to the International Meridian Conference, the 'universal day' begins at midnight in the Observatory at Greenwich. Accordingly, the year 2000 has officially arrived when it is midnight on 31 December in Greenwich. However, few people are waiting for midnight at Greenwich to mark the beginning of the year 2000, and the race has been on to see where the sun will rise first in the new dawn of the third millennium. The Pacific islands have been busy claiming priority, with the Republic of Kiribati announcing in 1994 that all its islands would fall within the same date-line, creating a huge shift in the dateline's course. As a result, several of its islands are now expected to be the first to see the dawn on 1 January 2000, including the specially renamed Millennium Island. This is much to the aggravation of the New Zealand islands, most notably Pitt Island, which has also claimed the first dawn. As the dispute goes on the timetable looks like this:

Place	Date (GMT)	GMT	Local
Millennium Island	31 December 1999	15:43	5:43
Flint Island, Kiribati	31 December 1999	15:47	5:47
Antipodes Island	31 December 1999	15:55	3:55
Pitt Island	31 December 1999	16:00	4:45
Kiritimati, Kiribati	31 December 1999	16:31	5:31
Mt Hikurangi, New Zealand	31 December 1999	16:39	4:39

London's Giant Party

London's official millennium celebrations will start at 11 a.m. on 31 December and will continue until the following morning. The highlight of the celebrations is a fireworks display bigger than anything seen before in London. When the chimes of Big Ben ring out on New Year's Eve, the Thames will be turned into a 'river of fire' as 2,000 pyrotechnic candles create a cascading flame, 6 m/20 ft high, that will travel down the river at the speed of sound.

At one minute to midnight the four faces of Big Ben will be lit up as the countdown to the millennium begins, and as the first chime sounds a burst of fireworks will be detonated at Greenwich on the Meridian Line, where the Queen and Tony Blair, the prime minister, will be celebrating in the Millennium Dome. Approximately 18 seconds after the first explosion, the 'Millennium Moment' will arrive at Tower Bridge and the first of the 2,000 pyrotechnic candles will be set off. In 10.8 seconds, the world's biggest-ever sequential firework display will speed down the Thames to Vauxhall Bridge – at the rate at which the earth revolves on our latitude. The river will fall silent after the final chime and a 15-minute firework display – which will be visible from outer space – will immediately follow.

In addition to the fireworks show, there will be a 'global village' celebrating the arrival of the millennium in different parts of the world – dancers, concerts, fairgrounds, trick cyclists, and an 'Elizabethan' street fair near the Globe Theatre featuring ox roasts. The giant street party will be concentrated along both banks of the Thames between Tower Bridge and Vauxhall Bridge. The party-goers will be able to watch live images beamed to them from cities around the world on huge television screens.

The organizers, Big Time, said they were expecting up to 2.5 million people to join in on the capital's festivities.

WEIGHTS, MEASURES, AND NUMBERS

Weights and Measures

Units in the Metric System

Length

1 centimetre	= 10 millimetres	
1 decimetre	= 10 centimetres	= 100 millimetres
1 metre	= 10 decimetres	= 1,000 millimetres
1 decametre	= 10 metres	
1 hectometre	= 10 decametres	= 100 metres
1 kilometre	= 10 hectometres	= 1,000 metres

Area

1 square centimetre	= 100 square millimetres	
1 square metre	= 10,000 square centimetres	= 1,000,000 square millimetres
1 are	= 100 square metres	
1 hectare	= 100 ares	= 10,000 square metres
1 square kilometre	= 100 hectares	= 1,000,000 square metres

Mass (avoirdupois)

1 centigram	= 10 milligrams	
1 decigram	= 10 centigrams	= 100 milligrams
1 gram	= 10 decigrams	= 1,000 milligrams

Mass (avoirdupois)

1 decagram	= 10 grams	
1 hectogram	= 10 decagrams	= 100 grams
1 kilogram	= 10 hectograms	= 1,000 grams
1 metric ton	= 1,000 kilograms	

Volume

1 cubic centimetre	= 1,000 cubic millimetres	
1 cubic decimetre	= 1,000 cubic centimetres	= 1,000,000 cubic millimetres
1 cubic metre	= 1,000 cubic decimetres	= 1,000,000,000 cubic millimetres

Capacity

1 centilitre	= 10 millilitres	
1 decilitre	= 10 centilitres	= 100 millilitres
1 litre	= 10 decilitres	= 1,000 millilitres
1 decalitre	= 10 litres	
1 hectolitre	= 10 decalitres	= 100 litres
1 kilolitre	= 10 hectolitres	= 1,000 litres

Units in the Imperial System

Length

1 foot	= 12 inches
1 yard	= 3 feet
1 rod	= $5\frac{1}{2}$ yards (= $16\frac{1}{2}$ feet)
1 chain	= 4 rods (= 22 yards)
1 furlong	= 10 chains (= 220 yards)
1 mile	= 5,280 feet
1 mile	= 1,760 yards
1 mile	= 8 furlongs

Nautical

1 fathom	= 6 feet
1 cable length	= 120 fathoms
1 nautical mile	= 6,076 feet

Area

1 square foot	= 144 square inches
1 square yard	= 9 square feet
1 square rod	= $30\frac{1}{4}$ square yards
1 acre	= 4 roods
1 acre	= 4,840 square yards
1 square mile	= 640 acres

Volume

1 cubic foot	= 1,728 cubic inches
1 cubic yard	= 27 cubic feet
1 bulk barrel	= 5.8 cubic feet

Shipping

1 register ton	= 100 cubic feet

Capacity

1 fluid ounce	= 8 fluid drams
1 gill	= 5 fluid ounces
1 pint	= 4 gills
1 quart	= 2 pints
1 gallon	= 4 quarts
1 peck	= 2 gallons
1 bushel	= 4 pecks
1 quarter	= 8 bushels
1 bulk barrel	= 36 gallons

Weight (avoirdupois)

1 ounce	= $437\frac{1}{2}$ grains
1 ounce	= 16 drams
1 pound	= 16 ounces
1 stone	= 14 pounds
1 quarter	= 28 pounds
1 hundredweight	= 4 quarters
1 ton	= 20 hundredweight

Imperial and Metric Conversion Factors

To convert from imperial to metric	Multiply by	To convert from metric to imperial	Multiply by
Length			
inches	25.4	millimetres	0.0393701
feet	0.3048	metres	3.28084
yards	0.9144	metres	1.09361
furlongs	0.201168	kilometres	4.97097
miles	1.609344	kilometres	0.621371
Area			
square inches	6.4516	square centimetres	0.1550
square feet	0.092903	square metres	10.7639
square yards	0.836127	square metres	1.19599
square miles	2.589988	square kilometres	0.386102
acres	4046.856422	square metres	0.000247
acres	0.404685	hectares	2.471054
Volume/capacity			
cubic inches	16.387064	cubic centimetres	0.061024
cubic feet	0.028317	cubic metres	35.3147
cubic yards	0.764555	cubic metres	1.30795
cubic miles	4.1682	cubic kilometres	0.239912
fluid ounces (imperial)	28.413063	millilitres	0.035195
fluid ounces (US)	29.5735	millilitres	0.033814
pints (imperial)	0.568261	litres	1.759754
pints (US)	0.473176	litres	2.113377
quarts (imperial)	1.136523	litres	0.879877
quarts (US)	0.946353	litres	1.056688
gallons (imperial)	4.54609	litres	0.219969
gallons (US)	3.785412	litres	0.364172
Mass/weight			
ounces	28.349523	grams	0.035274
pounds	0.453592	kilograms	2.20462
stone (14 lb)	6.350293	kilograms	0.157473
tons (imperial)	1016.046909	kilograms	0.000984
tons (US)	907.18474	kilograms	0.001102
tons (imperial)	1.016047	metric tonnes	0.984207
tons (US)	0.907185	metric tonnes	1.10231

(continued)

Imperial and Metric Conversion Factors (*continued*)

To convert from imperial to metric	Multiply by	To convert from metric to imperial	Multiply by
Speed			
miles per hour	1.609344	kilometres per hour	0.621371
feet per second	0.3048	metres per second	3.28084
Force			
pound-force	4.44822	newton	0.224809
kilogram-force	9.80665	newton	0.101972
Pressure			
pound-force per square inch	6.89476	kilopascals	0.145038
tons-force per square inch (imperial)	15.4443	megapascals	0.064779
atmospheres	10.1325	newtons per square centimetre	0.098692
atmospheres	14.695942	pound-force per square inch	0.068948
Energy			
calorie	4.1868	joule	0.238846
watt hour	3,600	joule	0.000278
Power			
horsepower	0.7457	kilowatts	1.34102
Fuel consumption			
miles per gallon (imperial)	0.3540	kilometres per litre	2.824859
miles per gallon (US)	0.4251	kilometres per litre	2.3521
gallons per mile (imperial)	2.824859	litres per kilometre	0.3540
gallons per mile (US)	2.3521	litres per kilometre	0.4251

Table of Equivalent Temperatures

Celsius and Fahrenheit temperatures can be interconverted as follows:
C = (F – 32) × 100/180; F = (C × 180/100) + 32.

°C	°F	°C	°F	°C	°F	°C	°F	°C	°F	°C	°F	°C	°F	°C	°F
100	212.0	85	185.0	70	158.0	55	131.0	40	104.0	25	77.0	10	50.0	–5	23.0
99	210.2	84	183.2	69	156.2	54	129.2	39	102.2	24	75.2	9	48.2	–6	21.2
98	208.4	83	181.4	68	154.4	53	127.4	38	100.4	23	73.4	8	46.4	–7	19.4
97	206.6	82	179.6	67	152.6	52	125.6	37	98.6	22	71.6	7	44.6	–8	17.6
96	204.8	81	177.8	66	150.8	51	123.8	36	96.8	21	69.8	6	42.8	–9	15.8
95	203.0	80	176.0	65	149.0	50	122.0	35	95.0	20	68.0	5	41.0	–10	14.0
94	201.2	79	174.2	64	147.2	49	120.2	34	93.2	19	66.2	4	39.2	–11	12.2
93	199.4	78	172.4	63	145.4	48	118.4	33	91.4	18	64.4	3	37.4	–12	10.4
92	197.6	77	170.6	62	143.6	47	116.6	32	89.6	17	62.6	2	35.6	–13	8.6
91	195.8	76	168.8	61	141.8	46	114.8	31	87.8	16	60.8	1	33.8	–14	6.8
90	194.0	75	167.0	60	140.0	45	113.0	30	86.0	15	59.0	0	32.0	–15	5.0
89	192.2	74	165.2	59	138.2	44	111.2	29	84.2	14	57.2	–1	30.2	–16	3.2
88	190.4	73	163.4	58	136.4	43	109.4	28	82.4	13	55.4	–2	28.4	–17	1.4
87	188.6	72	161.6	57	134.6	42	107.6	27	80.6	12	53.6	–3	26.6	–18	–0.4
86	186.8	71	159.8	56	132.8	41	105.8	26	78.8	11	51.8	–4	24.8	–19	–2.2

Cooking Conversions

Liquid measures

Imperial: UK	Imperial: US	Metric
$\frac{1}{6}$ fluid ounce	1 teaspoon	5 millilitres
$\frac{1}{2}$ fluid ounce	1 tablespoon	15 millilitres
1 fluid ounce	2 tablespoons	30 millilitres
8 fluid ounces	1 cup	240 millilitres
$\frac{1}{2}$ pint (10 fluid ounces)	$1\frac{1}{4}$ cups	300 millilitres
16 fluid ounces	1 pint (2 cups)	470 millilitres
1 pint (20 fluid ounces)	$2\frac{1}{2}$ cups	600 millilitres
34 fluid ounces	$4\frac{1}{3}$ cups	1 litre
$1\frac{3}{4}$ pints	$4\frac{1}{3}$ cups	1 litre

Oven temperatures

Gas mark	Electric °C	Electric °F	Rating
$\frac{1}{2}$	130	250	very cool
1	140	275	
2	150	300	cool
3	170	325	warm
4	180	350	moderate
5	190	375	fairly hot
6	200	400	
7	220	425	hot
8	230	450	very hot
9	240	475	

Dry measures

Imperial (UK and US)	Metric
1 ounce	28 grams
$3\frac{1}{2}$ ounces	100 grams
4 ounces	113 grams
8 ounces	225 grams
1 pound	450 grams
35 ounces (2.2 pounds)	1 kilogram

International Clothing Sizes

	USA	UK	Europe
Women's dresses	6	8	36
	8	10	38
	10	12	40
	12	14	42
	14	16	44
	16	18	46
	18	20	48
	20	22	50
	22	24	52
Men's suits	36	36	46
	38	38	48
	40	40	50
	42	42	52
	44	44	54
	46	46	56
Men's shirts	14	14	36
	$14\frac{1}{2}$	$14\frac{1}{2}$	37
	15	15	38
	$15\frac{1}{2}$	$15\frac{1}{2}$	39
	16	16	40
	$16\frac{1}{2}$	$16\frac{1}{2}$	41
	17	17	42
	$17\frac{1}{2}$	$17\frac{1}{2}$	43
Men's shoes	$5\frac{1}{2}$	5	38
	6	$5\frac{1}{2}$	38–39
	$6\frac{1}{2}$	6	39
	7	$6\frac{1}{2}$	40
	$7\frac{1}{2}$	7	40–41
	8	$7\frac{1}{2}$	41
	$8\frac{1}{2}$	8	41–42
	9	$8\frac{1}{2}$	42–43
	$9\frac{1}{2}$	9	43
	10	$9\frac{1}{2}$	43–44
	$10\frac{1}{2}$	10	44
	11	$10\frac{1}{2}$	45
	$11\frac{1}{2}$	11	45–46
	12	$11\frac{1}{2}$	46
Women's shoes	$4\frac{1}{2}$	3	36
	5	$3\frac{1}{2}$	36–37
	$5\frac{1}{2}$	4	37
	6	$4\frac{1}{2}$	37–38
	$6\frac{1}{2}$	5	38
	7	$5\frac{1}{2}$	38–39
	$7\frac{1}{2}$	6	39
***Women's shoes** (continued)*	8	$6\frac{1}{2}$	39–40
	$8\frac{1}{2}$	7	40
	9	$7\frac{1}{2}$	40–41
	$9\frac{1}{2}$	8	41
	10	$8\frac{1}{2}$	41–42
	$10\frac{1}{2}$	9	42
	11	$9\frac{1}{2}$	42–43
Children's shoes	0	0	15
	1	1	16–17
	2	2	18
	3	3	19
	4	4	20–21
	5	5	22
	6	6	23
	7	7	24
	8	8	25–26
	9	9	27
	10	10	28
	11	11	29
	12	12	30–31
	13	13	32

International Paper Sizes

Name	Dimensions	Classic series
Classic Series		
large post	419 × 533 mm	$16\frac{1}{2} \times 21$ in
demy	444 × 572 mm	$17\frac{1}{2} \times 22\frac{1}{2}$ in
medium	457 × 584 mm	18 × 23 in
royal	508 × 635 mm	20 × 25 in
double crown	508 × 762 mm	20 × 30 in
A Series (Books, Magazines, Stationery)		
A0	841 × 1189 mm	$33\frac{1}{8} \times 46\frac{3}{4}$ in
A1	594 × 841 mm	$23\frac{3}{8} \times 33\frac{1}{8}$ in
A2	420 × 594 mm	$16\frac{1}{2} \times 23\frac{3}{8}$ in
A3	297 × 420 mm	$11\frac{3}{4} \times 16\frac{1}{2}$ in
A4	210 × 297 mm	$8\frac{1}{4} \times 11\frac{3}{4}$ in
A5	148 × 210 mm	$5\frac{7}{8} \times 8\frac{1}{4}$ in

Name	Dimensions	Classic series
B Series (Posters etc.)		
B0	1,414 × 1,000 mm	$55\frac{5}{8} \times 39\frac{3}{8}$ in
B1	1,000 × 707 mm	$39\frac{3}{8} \times 27\frac{7}{8}$ in
B2	707 × 500 mm	$27\frac{7}{8} \times 19\frac{5}{8}$ in
B3	500 × 353 mm	$19\frac{5}{8} \times 13\frac{7}{8}$ in
B4	353 × 250 mm	$13\frac{7}{8} \times 9\frac{7}{8}$ in
B5	250 × 176 mm	$9\frac{7}{8} \times 7$ in
C Series (Envelopes)		
C4	324 × 229 mm	$12\frac{3}{4} \times 9$ in
C5	229 × 162 mm	$9 \times 6\frac{3}{8}$ in
C6	162 × 114 mm	$6\frac{3}{8} \times 4\frac{1}{2}$ in
DL	220 × 110 mm	$8\frac{5}{8} \times 4\frac{3}{8}$ in

Beaufort Scale

The Beaufort scale is a system of recording wind velocity (speed) devised in 1806 by Francis Beaufort (1774–1857). It is a numerical scale ranging from 0 for calm to 12 for a hurricane.

Number and description	Features	Air speed kph	Air speed mph
0 calm	smoke rises vertically; water smooth	0–2	0–1
1 light air	smoke shows wind direction; water ruffled	2–5	1–3
2 light breeze	leaves rustle; wind felt on face	6–11	4–7
3 gentle breeze	loose paper blows around	12–19	8–12
4 moderate breeze	branches sway	20–29	13–18
5 fresh breeze	small trees sway, leaves blown off	30–39	19–24
6 strong breeze	whistling in telephone wires; sea spray from waves	40–50	25–31
7 near gale	large trees sway	51–61	32–38
8 gale	twigs break from trees	62–74	39–46
9 strong gale	branches break from trees	75–87	47–54
10 storm	trees uprooted; weak buildings collapse	88–101	55–63
11 violent storm	widespread damage	102–117	64–73
12 hurricane	widespread structural damage	above 118	above 74

Decibel Scale

The decibel scale is used primarily to compare sound intensities although it can be used to compare voltages.

Decibels	Typical sound
0	threshold of hearing
10	rustle of leaves in gentle breeze
10	quiet whisper
20	average whisper
20–50	quiet conversation
40–45	theatre (between performances)
50–65	loud conversation
65–70	traffic on busy street
65–90	train
75–80	factory (light/medium work)
90	heavy traffic
90–100	thunder
110–140	jet aircraft at take-off
130	threshold of pain
140–190	space rocket at take-off

Mercalli Scale

The Mercalli scale is a measure of the intensity of an earthquake. It differs from the Richter scale, which measures magnitude. It is named after the Italian seismologist Giuseppe Mercalli (1850–1914). The scale shown here is the Modified Mercalli Intensity Scale, developed in 1931 by US seismologists Harry Wood and Frank Neumann.

Intensity value	Description
I	not felt except by a very few under especially favourable conditions
II	felt only by a few persons at rest, especially on upper floors of buildings
III	felt quite noticeably by persons indoors, especially on upper floors of buildings; many people do not recognize it as an earthquake; standing motor cars may rock slightly; vibrations similar to the passing of a truck; duration estimated
IV	felt indoors by many, outdoors by few during the day; at night, some awakened; dishes, windows, doors disturbed; walls make cracking sound; sensation like heavy truck striking building; standing motor cars rock noticeably
V	felt by nearly everyone; many awakened; some dishes, windows broken; unstable objects overturned; pendulum clocks may stop
VI	felt by all, many frightened; some heavy furniture moved; a few instances of fallen plaster; damage slight
VII	damage negligible in buildings of good design and construction; slight to moderate in well-built ordinary structures; considerable damage in poorly built or badly designed structures; some chimneys broken
VIII	damage slight in specially designed structures; considerable damage in ordinary substantial buildings with partial collapse; damage great in poorly built structures; fall of chimneys, factory stacks, columns, monuments, walls; heavy furniture overturned
IX	damage considerable in specially designed structures; well-designed frame structures thrown out of plumb; damage great in substantial buildings, with partial collapse; buildings shifted off foundations
X	some well-built wooden structures destroyed; most masonry and frame structures destroyed with foundations; rails bent
XI	few, if any (masonry) structures remain standing; bridges destroyed; rails bent greatly
XII	damage total; lines of sight and level are distorted; objects thrown into the air

Richter Scale

The Richter scale is based on measurement of seismic waves, used to determine the magnitude of an earthquake at its epicenter. The magnitude of an earthquake differs from its intensity, measured by the Mercalli scale, which is subjective and varies from place to place for the same earthquake. The Richter scale was named after US seismologist Charles Richter (1900–1985). The relative amount of energy released indicates the ratio of energy between earthquakes of different magnitude.

Magnitude	Relative amount of energy released	Examples	Year
1	1		
2	31		
3	960		
4	30,000	Carlisle, England (4.7)	1979
5	920,000	Wrexham, Wales (5.1)	1990
6	29,000,000	San Fernando (CA) (6.5)	1971
		northern Armenia (6.8)	1988
7	890,000,000	Loma Prieta (CA) (7.1)	1989
		Kobe, Japan (7.2)	1995
		Rasht, Iran (7.7)	1990
		San Francisco (CA) (7.7–7.9)[1]	1906
8	28,000,000,000	Tangshan, China (8.0)	1976
		Gansu, China (8.6)	1920
		Lisbon, Portugal (8.7)	1755
9	850,000,000,000	Prince William Sound (AK) (9.2)	1964

[1] Richter's original estimate of a magnitude of 8.3 has been revised by two recent studies carried out by the California Institute of Technology and the US Geological Survey.

SI Prefixes

Multiple	Prefix	Symbol	Example
1,000,000,000,000,000,000 (10^{18})	exa-	E	Eg (exagram)
1,000,000,000,000,000 (10^{15})	peta-	P	PJ (petajoule)
1,000,000,000,000 (10^{12})	tera-	T	TV (teravolt)
1,000,000,000 (10^{9})	giga-	G	GW (gigawatt)
1,000,000 (10^{6})	mega-	M	MHz (megahertz)
1,000 (10^{3})	kilo-	k	kg (kilogram)
100 (10^{2})	hecto-	h	hm (hectometre)
10 (10^{1})	deca-	da	daN (decanewton)
1/10 (10^{-1})	deci-	d	dC (decicoulomb)
1/100 (10^{-2})	centi-	c	cm (centimetre)
1/1,000 (10^{-3})	milli-	m	mm (millimetre)
1/1,000,000 (10^{-6})	micro-	µ	µF (microfarad)
1/1,000,000,000 (10^{-9})	nano-	n	nm (nanometre)
1/1,000,000,000,000 (10^{-12})	pico-	p	ps (picosecond)
1/1,000,000,000,000,000 (10^{-15})	femto-	f	frad (femtoradian)
1/1,000,000,000,000,000,000 (10^{-18})	atto-	a	aT (attotesla)

SI Units

(French *Système International d'Unités*) A standard system of scientific units used by scientists worldwide. Originally proposed in 1960, it replaces the m.k.s. (metre, kilogram, second), c.g.s. (centimetre, gram, second), and f.p.s. (foot, pound, second) systems. It is based on seven basic units: the metre (m) for length, kilogram (kg) for mass, second (s) for time, ampere (A) for electrical current, kelvin (K) for temperature, mole (mol) for amount of substance, and candela (cd) for luminosity.

Quantity	SI unit	Symbol
absorbed radiation dose	gray	Gy
amount of substance	mole*	mol
electric capacitance	farad	F
electric charge	coulomb	C
electric conductance	siemens	S
electric current	ampere*	A
energy or work	joule	J
force	newton	N
frequency	hertz	Hz
illuminance	lux	lx
inductance	henry	H
length	metre*	m
luminous flux	lumen	lm
luminous intensity	candela*	cd
magnetic flux	weber	Wb
magnetic flux density	tesla	T

Quantity	SI unit	Symbol
mass	kilogram*	kg
plane angle	radian	rad
potential difference	volt	V
power	watt	W
pressure	pascal	Pa
radiation dose equivalent	sievert	Sv
radiation exposure	roentgen	R
radioactivity	becquerel	Bq
resistance	ohm	Ω
solid angle	steradian	sr
sound intensity	decibel	dB
temperature	°Celsius	°C
temperature, thermodynamic	kelvin*	K
time	second*	s

* SI base unit.

Physical Constants

Physical constants, or fundamental constants, are standardized values whose parameters do not change.

Constant	Symbol	Value in SI units
acceleration of free fall	g	9.80665 m s^{-2}
Avogadro's constant	N_A	6.0221367×10^{23} mol^{-1}
Boltzmann's constant	k	1.380658×10^{-23} J K^{-1}
elementary charge	e	$1.60217733 \times 10^{-19}$ C
electronic rest mass	m_e	$9.1093897 \times 10^{-31}$ kg
Faraday's constant	F	9.6485309×10^{4} C mol^{-1}
gas constant	R	8.314510 J K^{-1} mol^{-1}
gravitational constant	G	6.672×10^{-11} N m^{2} kg^{-2}
Loschmidt's number	N_L	2.686763×10^{25} m^{-3}
neutron rest mass	m_n	$1.6749286 \times 10^{-27}$ kg
Planck's constant	h	$6.6260755 \times 10^{-34}$ J s
proton rest mass	m_p	$1.6726231 \times 10^{-27}$ kg
speed of light in a vacuum	c	2.99792458×10^{8} m s^{-1}
standard atmosphere	*atm*	1.01325×10^{5} Pa
Stefan–Boltzmann constant	σ	5.67051×10^{-8} W m^{-2} K^{-4}

Glossary

Miscellaneous Units

Unit	Definition
acoustic ohm	cgs unit of acoustic impedance (the ratio of sound pressure on a surface to sound flux through the surface)
acre	traditional English land measure; 1 acre = 4,480 sq yd (4,047 sq m or 0.4047 ha)
acre-foot	unit sometimes used to measure large volumes of water such as reservoirs; 1 acre-foot = 1,233.5 cu m/43,560 cu ft
astronomical unit	unit (symbol AU) equal to the mean distance of the Earth from the Sun: 149,597,870 km/ 92,955,808 mi
atmosphere	unit of pressure (abbreviation atm); 1 standard atmosphere = 101,325 Pa
barn	unit of area, especially the cross-sectional area of an atomic nucleus; 1 barn = 10^{-28} sq m
barrel	unit of liquid capacity; the volume of a barrel depends on the liquid being measured and the country and state laws. In the USA, 1 barrel of oil = 42 gal (159 l/34.97 imperial gal), but for federal taxing of fermented liquor (such as beer), 1 barrel = 31 gal (117.35 l/25.81 imperial gal). Many states fix a 36-gallon barrel for cistern measurement and federal law uses a 40-gallon barrel to measure 'proof spirits'. 1 barrel of beer in the UK = 163.66 l (43.23 US gal/36 imperial gal)
base box	imperial unit of area used in metal plating; 1 base box = 20.232 sq m/31,360 sq in
baud	unit of electrical signalling speed equal to 1 pulse per second
brewster	unit (symbol B) for measuring reaction of optical materials to stress
British thermal unit	imperial unit of heat (symbol Btu); 1 Btu = approximately 1,055 J
bushel	measure of dry and (in the UK) liquid volume. 1 bushel (struck measure) = 8 dry US gallons (64 dry US pt/35.239 l/2,150.42 cu in). 1 heaped US bushel = 1,278 bushels, struck measure (81.78 dry pt/45.027 l/2,747.715 cu in), often referred to a $1\frac{1}{4}$ bushels, struck measure. In the UK, 1 bushel = 8 imperial gallons (64 imperial pt); 1 UK bushel = 1.03 US bushels

(continued)

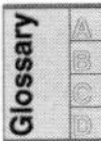

Miscellaneous Units (*continued*)

Unit	Definition
cable	unit of length used on ships, taken as $\frac{1}{10}$ of a nautical mile (185.2 m/607.6 ft)
calorie	cgs unit of heat, now replaced by the joule; 1 calorie = 4.1868 J
carat	unit for measuring mass of precious stones; 1 carat = 0.2 g/0.00705 oz
carat	unit of purity in gold; pure gold is 24-carat
carcel	obsolete unit of luminous intensity
cental	name for the short hundredweight; 1 cental = 45.36 kg/100 lb
chaldron	obsolete unit measuring capacity; 1 chaldron = 1.309 cu m/46.237 cu ft
clausius	in engineering, a unit of entropy; defined as the ratio of energy to temperature above absolute zero
cleanliness unit	unit for measuring air pollution; equal to the number of particles greater than 0.5 μm in diameter per cu ft of air
clo	unit of thermal insulation of clothing; standard clothes have insulation of about 1 clo, the warmest have about 4 clo per 2.5 cm/1 in of thickness
clusec	unit for measuring the power of a vacuum pump
condensation number	in physics, the ratio of the number of molecules condensing on a surface to the number of molecules touching that surface
cord	unit for measuring the volume of wood cut for fuel; 1 cord = 3.62 cu m/128 cu ft, or a stack 2.4 m/8 ft long, 1.2 m/4 ft wide and 1.2 m/4 ft high
crith	unit of mass for weighing gases; 1 crith = the mass of 1 litre of hydrogen gas at standard temperature and pressure
cubit	earliest known unit of length; 1 cubit = approximately 45.7 cm/18 in, the length of the human forearm from the tip of the middle finger to the elbow
curie	former unit of radioactivity (symbol Ci); 1 curie = 3.7×10^{10} becquerels
dalton	international atomic mass unit, equivalent to $\frac{1}{12}$ of the mass of a neutral carbon-12 atom
darcy	cgs unit (symbol D) of permeability, used mainly in geology to describe the permeability of rock
darwin	unit of measurement of evolutionary rate of change
decontamination factor	unit measuring the effectiveness of radiological decontamination; the ratio of original contamination to the radiation remaining
demal	unit measuring concentration; 1 demal = 1 gram-equivalent of solute in 1 cu dm of solvent
denier	unit used to measure the fineness of yarns; 9,000 m of 15 denier nylon weighs 15 g/0.5 oz
dioptre	optical unit measuring the power of a lens; the reciprocal of the focal length in metres
dram	unit of apothecaries' measure; 1 dram = 60 grains/3.888 g
dyne	cgs unit of force; 10^5 dynes = 1 N
einstein unit	unit for measuring photoenergy in atomic physics
eotvos unit	unit (symbol E) for measuring small changes in the intensity of the Earth's gravity with horizontal distance
erg	cgs unit of work; equal to the work done by a force of 1 dyne moving through 1 cm
erlang	unit for measuring telephone traffic intensity; for example, 90 minutes of carried traffic measured over 60 minutes = 1.5 erlangs ('carried traffic' refers to the total duration of completed calls made within a specified period)
fathom	unit of depth measurement in mining and seafaring; 1 fathom = 1.83 m/6 ft
finsen unit	unit (symbol FU) for measuring intensity of ultraviolet light
fluid ounce	measure of capacity; equivalent in the USA to $\frac{1}{16}$ of a pint ($\frac{1}{20}$ of a pint in the UK and Canada)
foot	imperial unit of length (symbol ft), equivalent to 0.3048 m
foot-candle	unit of illuminance, replaced by the lux; 1 foot-candle = 10.76391 lux
foot-pound	imperial unit of energy (symbol ft-lb); 1 ft-lb = 1.356 joule
frigorie	unit (symbol fg) used in refrigeration engineering to measure heat energy, equal to a rate of heat extraction of 1 kilocalorie per hour
furlong	unit of measurement, originating in Anglo-Saxon England, equivalent to 201.168 m/220 yd
galileo	unit (symbol Gal) of acceleration; 1 galileo = 10^{-2} m s^{-2}
gallon	imperial liquid or dry measure subdivided into 4 quarts or 8 pints; 1 US gal = 3.785 l; 1 imperial gal = 4.546 l
gauss	cgs unit (symbol) of magnetic flux density, replaced by the tesla; 1 gauss = 1×10^{-4} tesla
gill	imperial unit of volume for liquid measure; equal to $\frac{1}{4}$ of a pint (in the USA, 4 fl oz/0.118 l; in the UK, 5 fl oz/0.142 l)
grain	smallest unit of mass in the three English systems of measurement (avoirdupois, troy, apothecaries' weights) used in the UK and USA; 1 grain = 0.0648 g
hand	unit used in measuring the height of a horse from front hoof to shoulder (withers); 1 hand = 10.2 cm/4 in
hardness number	unit measuring hardness of materials. There are many different hardness scales: Brinell, Rockwell, and Vickers scales measure the degree of indentation or impression of materials; Mohs' scale measures resistance to scratching against a standard set of minerals
hartree	atomic unit of energy, equivalent to atomic unit of charge divided by atomic unit of length; 1 hartree = 4.850×10^{-18} J
haze factor	unit of visibility in mist or fog; the ratio of brightness of mist compared with that of the object
Hehner number	unit measuring concentration of fatty acids in oils; a Hehner number of 1 = 1 kg of fatty acid in 100 kg of oil or fat
hide	unit of measurement used in the 12th century to measure land; 1 hide = 60–120 acres/25–50 ha
horsepower	imperial unit (abbreviation hp) of power; 1 horsepower = 746 W
hundredweight	imperial unit (abbreviation cwt) of mass; 1 cwt = 45.36 kg/100 lb in the USA and 50.80 kg/112 lb in the UK
inch	imperial unit (abbreviation in) of linear measure, $\frac{1}{12}$ of a ft; 1 in = 2.54 cm
inferno	unit used in astrophysics for describing the temperature inside a star; 1 inferno = 1 billion K (degrees Kelvin)
iodine number	unit measuring the percentage of iodine absorbed in a substance, expressed as grams of iodine absorbed by 100 grams of material

(*continued*)

Glossary

Miscellaneous Units (*continued*)

Unit	Definition
jansky	unit used in radio astronomy to measure radio emissions or flux densities from space; 1 jansky = 10^{-26} W m^{-2} Hz^{-1}. Flux density is the energy in a beam of radiation which passes through an area normal to the beam in a single unit of time. A jansky is a measurement of the energy received from a cosmic radio source per unit area of detector in a single time unit
kayser	unit used in spectroscopy to measure wave number (number of waves in a unit length); a wavelength of 1 cm has a wave number of 1 kayser
knot	unit used in navigation to measure a ship's speed; 1 knot = 1 nautical mile per hour, or about 1.15 miles per hour
league	obsolete imperial unit of length; 1 league = 3 nautical mi/5.56 km or 3 statute mi/4.83 km
light year	unit used in astronomy to measure distance; the distance travelled by light in one year, approximately 9.46×10^{12} km/5.88×10^{12} mi
mache	obsolete unit of radioactive concentration; 1 mache = 3.7×10^{-7} curies of radioactive material per cu m of a medium
maxwell	cgs unit (symbol Mx) of magnetic flux, the strength of a magnetic field in an area multiplied by the area; 1 maxwell = 10^{-8} weber
megaton	measurement of the explosive power of a nuclear weapon; 1 megaton = 1 million tons of trinitrotoluene (TNT)
mil	(a) one-thousandth of a litre; contraction of the word millilitre; (b) imperial measure of length, equal to one-thousandth of an inch; also known as the thou
mile	imperial unit of linear measure; 1 statute mile = 1.60934 km/5,280 ft; 1 international nautical mile = 1.852 km/6,076 ft
millimetre of mercury	unit of pressure (symbol mmHg) used in medicine for measuring blood pressure
morgan	arbitrary unit used in genetics; 1 morgan is the distance along the chromosome in a gene that gives a recombination frequency of 1%
nautical mile	unit of distance used in navigation, equal to the average length of 1 minute of arc on a great circle of the Earth; 1 international nautical mile = 1.852 km/6,076 ft
neper	unit used in telecommunications; gives the attenuation of amplitudes of currents or powers as the natural logarithm of the ratio of the voltage between two points or the current between two points
oersted	cgs unit (symbol Oe) of magnetic field strength, now replaced by amperes per metre (1 Oe = 79.58 amp per m)
ounce	unit of mass, $\frac{1}{16}$ of a pound avoirdupois, equal to 437.5 grains/28.35 g; or 14.6 pound troy, equal to 480 grains/31.10 g
parsec	unit (symbol pc) used in astronomy for distances to stars and galaxies; 1 pc = 3.262 light years, 2.063×10^5 astronomical units, or 3.086×10^{13} km
peck	obsolete unit of dry measure, equal to 8 imperial quarts or 1 quarter bushel (8.1 l in the USA or 9.1 l in the UK)
pennyweight	imperial unit of mass; 1 pennyweight = 24 grains = 1.555×10^{-3} kg
perch	obsolete imperial unit of length; 1 perch = $5\frac{1}{2}$ yards = 5.029 m, also called the rod or pole
pint	imperial unit of liquid or dry measure; in the USA, 1 liquid pint = 16 fl oz/0.473 l, while 1 dry pint = 0.551 l; in the UK, 1 pt = 20 fl oz, $\frac{1}{2}$ quart, $\frac{1}{8}$ gal, or 0.568 l
point	metric unit of mass used in relation to gemstones; 1 point = 0.01 metric carat = 2×10^{-3} g
poise	cgs unit of dynamic viscosity; 1 poise = 1 dyne-second per sq cm
pound	imperial unit (abbreviation lb) of mass; the avoirdupois pound or imperial standard pound = 0.45 kg/7,000 grains, while the pound troy (used for weighing precious metals) = 0.37 kg/5,760 grains
poundal	imperial unit (abbreviation pdl) of force; 1 poundal = 0.1383 newton
quart	imperial liquid or dry measure; in the USA, 1 liquid quart = 0.946 l, while 1 dry quart = 1.101 l; in the UK, 1 quart = 2 pt/1.137 l
rad	unit of absorbed radiation dose, replaced in the SI system by the gray; 1 rad = 0.01 joule of radiation absorbed by 1 kg of matter
relative biological effectiveness	relative damage caused to living tissue by different types of radiation
roentgen	unit (symbol R) of radiation exposure, used for X- and gamma rays
rood	imperial unit of area; 1 rood = $\frac{1}{4}$ acre = 1,011.7 sq m
rydberg	atomic unit of energy; 1 rydberg = 2.425×10^{-18} J
sabin	unit of sound absorption, used in acoustical engineering; 1 sabin = absorption of 1 sq ft (0.093 sq m) of a perfectly absorbing surface
scruple	imperial unit of apothecaries' measure; 1 scruple = 20 grains = 1.3×10^{-3} kg
shackle	unit of length used at sea for measuring cable or chain; 1 shackle = 15 fathoms (90 ft/27 m)
slug	obsolete imperial unit of mass; 1 slug = 14.59 kg/32.17 lb
snellen	unit expressing the visual power of the eye
sone	unit of subjective loudness
standard volume	in physics, the volume occupied by 1 kilogram molecule (molecular mass in kilograms) of any gas at standard temperature and pressure; approximately 22.414 cu m
stokes	cgs unit (symbol St) of kinematic viscosity; 1 stokes = 10^{-4} m^2 s^{-1}
stone	imperial unit (abbreviation st) of mass; 1 stone = 6.35 kg/14 lb
strontium unit	measures concentration of strontium-90 in an organic medium relative to the concentration of calcium
tex	metric unit of line density; 1 tex is the line density of a thread with a mass of 1 gram and a length of 1 kilometre
tog	measure of thermal insulation of a fabric, garment, or quilt; the tog value is equivalent to 10 times the temperature difference (in °C) between the two faces of the article, when the flow of heat across it is equal to 1 W per sq m
tonne	1 unit of mass; the long ton (UK) = 1,016 kg/2,240 lb; 1 short ton (USA) = 907 kg/2,000 lb; 1 metric tonne = 1000 kg/2205 lb
yard	imperial unit (symbol yd) of length, equivalent to 0.9144 m/3 ft

Numbers

Large Numbers

USA and France

Nomenclature for large numbers varies in different countries. In the USA and France, numbers advance by increments of a thousand:

billion	1,000,000,000	1×10^9
trillion	1,000,000,000,000	1×10^{12}
quadrillion	1,000,000,000,000,000	1×10^{15}

UK and Germany

However, in the UK and Germany numbers have traditionally advanced by increments of a million:

million	1,000,000	1×10^6
billion	1,000,000,000,000	1×10^{12}
trillion	1,000,000,000,000,000,000	1×10^{18}
quadrillion	1,000,000,000,000,000,000,000,000	1×10^{24}

This has a certain amount of logic on its side, particularly for classical scholars:

billion = million^2 (bi-)
trillion = million^3 (tri-)
quadrillion = million^4 (quadr-)

Higher numbers

The US usage is becoming prevalent in the UK and Germany, particularly as it is now universally used by economists and statisticians. The higher numbers, in both styles, are as follows:

Number	USA	UK
quintillion	1×10^{18}	1×10^{30}
sextillion	1×10^{21}	1×10^{36}
septillion	1×10^{24}	1×10^{42}
octillion	1×10^{27}	1×10^{48}
nonillion	1×10^{30}	1×10^{54}
decillion	1×10^{33}	1×10^{60}
vigintillion	1×10^{63}	1×10^{120}
centillion	1×10^{303}	1×10^{600}

Roman Numerals

Roman	Arabic	Roman	Arabic	Roman	Arabic
I	1	XIX	19	CM	900
II	2	XX	20	M	1,000
III	3	XXX	30	$\overline{V}$	5,000
IV	4	XL	40	$\overline{X}$	10,000
V	5	L	50	$\overline{L}$	50,000
VI	6	LX	60	$\overline{C}$	100,000
VII	7	XC	90	$\overline{D}$	500,000
VIII	8	C	100	$\overline{M}$	1,000,000
IX	9	CC	200		
X	10	CD	400		
XI	11	D	500		

Prime Numbers

All the prime numbers between 1 and 1,000.

2	97	227	367	509	661	829
3	101	229	373	521	673	839
5	103	233	379	523	677	853
7	107	239	383	541	683	857
11	109	241	389	547	691	859
13	113	251	397	557	701	863
17	127	257	401	563	709	877
19	131	263	409	569	719	881
23	137	269	419	571	727	883
29	139	271	421	577	733	887
31	149	277	431	587	739	907
37	151	281	433	593	743	911
41	157	283	439	599	751	919
43	163	293	443	601	757	929
47	167	307	449	607	761	937
53	173	311	457	613	769	941
59	179	313	461	617	773	947
61	181	317	463	619	787	953
67	191	331	467	631	797	967
71	193	337	479	641	809	971
73	197	347	487	643	811	977
79	199	349	491	647	821	983
83	211	353	499	653	823	991
89	223	359	503	659	827	997

Squares, Cubes, and Roots

Number	Square	Cube	Square root	Cube root
1	1	1	1.000	1.000
2	4	8	1.414	1.260
3	9	27	1.732	1.442
4	16	64	2.000	1.587
5	25	125	2.236	1.710
6	36	216	2.449	1.817
7	49	343	2.646	1.913
8	64	512	2.828	2.000
9	81	729	3.000	2.080
10	100	1,000	3.162	2.154
11	121	1,331	3.317	2.224
12	144	1,728	3.464	2.289
13	169	2,197	3.606	2.351
14	196	2,744	3.742	2.410
15	225	3,375	3.873	2.466
16	256	4,096	4.000	2.520
17	289	4,913	4.123	2.571
18	324	5,832	4.243	2.621
19	361	6,859	4.359	2.668
20	400	8,000	4.472	2.714
25	625	15,625	5.000	2.924
30	900	27,000	5.477	3.107
40	1,600	64,000	6.325	3.420
50	2,500	125,000	7.071	3.684

Multiplication Table

	2	3	4	5	6	7	8	9	10	11	12	13	14	15	16	17	18	19	20	21	22	23	24	25
2	4	6	8	10	12	14	16	18	20	22	24	26	28	30	32	34	36	38	40	42	44	46	48	50
3	6	9	12	15	18	21	24	27	30	33	36	39	42	45	48	51	54	57	60	63	66	69	72	75
4	8	12	16	20	24	28	32	36	40	44	48	52	56	60	64	68	72	76	80	84	88	92	96	100
5	10	15	20	25	30	35	40	45	50	55	60	65	70	75	80	85	90	95	100	105	110	115	120	125
6	12	18	24	30	36	42	48	54	60	66	72	78	84	90	96	102	108	114	120	126	132	138	144	150
7	14	21	28	35	42	49	56	63	70	77	84	91	98	105	112	119	126	133	140	147	154	161	168	175
8	16	24	32	40	48	56	64	72	80	88	96	104	112	120	128	136	144	152	160	168	176	184	192	200
9	18	27	36	45	54	63	72	81	90	99	108	117	126	135	144	153	162	171	180	189	198	207	216	225
10	20	30	40	50	60	70	80	90	100	110	120	130	140	150	160	170	180	190	200	210	220	230	240	250
11	22	33	44	55	66	77	88	99	110	121	132	143	154	165	176	187	198	209	220	231	241	253	264	275
12	24	36	48	60	72	84	96	108	120	132	144	156	168	180	192	204	216	228	240	252	264	276	288	300
13	26	39	52	65	78	91	104	117	130	143	156	169	182	195	208	221	234	247	260	273	286	299	312	325
14	28	42	56	70	84	98	112	126	140	154	168	182	196	210	224	238	252	266	280	294	308	322	336	350
15	30	45	60	75	90	105	120	135	150	165	180	195	210	225	240	255	270	285	300	315	330	345	360	375
16	32	48	64	80	96	112	128	144	160	176	192	208	224	240	256	272	288	304	320	336	352	368	384	400
17	34	51	68	85	102	119	136	153	170	187	204	221	238	255	272	289	306	323	340	357	374	391	408	425
18	36	54	72	90	108	126	144	162	180	198	216	234	252	270	288	306	324	342	360	378	396	414	432	450
19	38	57	76	95	114	133	152	171	190	209	228	247	266	285	304	323	342	361	380	399	418	437	456	475
20	40	60	80	100	120	140	160	180	200	220	240	260	280	300	320	340	360	380	400	420	440	460	480	500
21	42	63	84	105	126	147	168	189	210	231	252	273	294	315	336	357	378	399	420	441	462	483	504	525
22	44	66	88	110	132	154	176	198	220	242	264	286	308	330	352	374	396	418	440	462	484	506	528	550
23	46	69	92	115	138	161	184	207	230	253	276	299	322	345	368	391	414	437	460	483	506	529	552	575
24	48	72	96	120	144	168	192	216	240	264	288	312	336	360	384	408	432	456	480	504	528	552	576	600
25	50	75	100	125	150	175	200	225	250	275	300	325	350	375	400	425	450	475	500	525	550	575	600	625

Fractions as Decimals

Fraction	Decimal	Fraction	Decimal	Fraction	Decimal	Fraction	Decimal	Fraction	Decimal	Fraction	Decimal
$\frac{1}{2}$	0.5000	$\frac{3}{7}$	0.4286	$\frac{8}{9}$	0.8889	$\frac{9}{11}$	0.8182	$\frac{15}{16}$	0.9375	$\frac{9}{32}$	0.2812
$\frac{1}{3}$	0.3333	$\frac{4}{7}$	0.5714	$\frac{1}{10}$	0.1000	$\frac{10}{11}$	0.9091	$\frac{1}{20}$	0.0500	$\frac{11}{32}$	0.3438
$\frac{2}{3}$	0.6667	$\frac{5}{7}$	0.7143	$\frac{3}{10}$	0.3000	$\frac{1}{12}$	0.0833	$\frac{3}{20}$	0.1500	$\frac{13}{32}$	0.4062
$\frac{1}{4}$	0.2500	$\frac{6}{7}$	0.8571	$\frac{7}{10}$	0.7000	$\frac{5}{12}$	0.4167	$\frac{7}{20}$	0.3500	$\frac{15}{32}$	0.4688
$\frac{3}{4}$	0.7500	$\frac{1}{8}$	0.1250	$\frac{9}{10}$	0.9000	$\frac{7}{12}$	0.5833	$\frac{9}{20}$	0.4500	$\frac{17}{32}$	0.5312
$\frac{1}{5}$	0.2000	$\frac{3}{8}$	0.3750	$\frac{1}{11}$	0.0909	$\frac{11}{12}$	0.9167	$\frac{11}{20}$	0.5500	$\frac{19}{32}$	0.5938
$\frac{2}{5}$	0.4000	$\frac{5}{8}$	0.6250	$\frac{2}{11}$	0.1818	$\frac{1}{16}$	0.0625	$\frac{13}{20}$	0.6500	$\frac{21}{32}$	0.6562
$\frac{3}{5}$	0.6000	$\frac{7}{8}$	0.8750	$\frac{3}{11}$	0.2727	$\frac{3}{16}$	0.1875	$\frac{17}{20}$	0.8500	$\frac{23}{32}$	0.7188
$\frac{4}{5}$	0.8000	$\frac{1}{9}$	0.1111	$\frac{4}{11}$	0.3636	$\frac{5}{16}$	0.3125	$\frac{19}{20}$	0.9500	$\frac{25}{32}$	0.7812
$\frac{1}{6}$	0.1667	$\frac{2}{9}$	0.2222	$\frac{5}{11}$	0.4545	$\frac{7}{16}$	0.4375	$\frac{1}{32}$	0.0312	$\frac{27}{32}$	0.8438
$\frac{5}{6}$	0.8333	$\frac{4}{9}$	0.4444	$\frac{6}{11}$	0.5455	$\frac{9}{16}$	0.5625	$\frac{3}{32}$	0.9038	$\frac{29}{32}$	0.9062
$\frac{1}{7}$	0.1429	$\frac{5}{9}$	0.5556	$\frac{7}{11}$	0.6364	$\frac{11}{16}$	0.6875	$\frac{5}{32}$	0.1562	$\frac{31}{32}$	0.9688
$\frac{2}{7}$	0.2857	$\frac{7}{9}$	0.7778	$\frac{8}{11}$	0.7273	$\frac{13}{16}$	0.8125	$\frac{7}{32}$	0.2188		

Percentages as Fractions or Decimals

%	Decimal	Fraction	%	Decimal	Fraction	%	Decimal	Fraction	%	Decimal	Fraction
1	0.01	$\frac{1}{100}$	16	0.16	$\frac{4}{25}$	32	0.32	$\frac{8}{25}$	48	0.48	$\frac{12}{25}$
2	0.02	$\frac{1}{50}$	$16\frac{2}{3}$	0.167	$\frac{1}{6}$	33	0.33	$\frac{33}{100}$	49	0.49	$\frac{49}{100}$
3	0.03	$\frac{3}{100}$	17	0.17	$\frac{17}{100}$	$33\frac{1}{3}$	0.333	$\frac{1}{3}$	50	0.50	$\frac{1}{2}$
4	0.04	$\frac{1}{25}$	18	0.18	$\frac{9}{50}$	34	0.34	$\frac{17}{50}$	55	0.55	$\frac{11}{20}$
5	0.05	$\frac{1}{20}$	19	0.19	$\frac{19}{100}$	35	0.35	$\frac{7}{20}$	60	0.60	$\frac{3}{5}$
6	0.06	$\frac{3}{50}$	20	0.20	$\frac{1}{5}$	36	0.36	$\frac{9}{25}$	65	0.65	$\frac{13}{20}$
7	0.07	$\frac{7}{100}$	21	0.21	$\frac{21}{100}$	37	0.37	$\frac{37}{100}$	66	0.66	$\frac{66}{100}$
8	0.08	$\frac{2}{25}$	22	0.22	$\frac{11}{50}$	38	0.38	$\frac{19}{50}$	$66\frac{2}{3}$	0.667	$\frac{2}{3}$
$8\frac{1}{3}$	0.083	$\frac{1}{12}$	23	0.23	$\frac{23}{100}$	39	0.39	$\frac{39}{100}$	70	0.70	$\frac{7}{10}$
9	0.09	$\frac{9}{100}$	24	0.24	$\frac{6}{25}$	40	0.40	$\frac{2}{5}$	75	0.75	$\frac{3}{4}$
10	0.10	$\frac{1}{10}$	25	0.25	$\frac{1}{4}$	41	0.41	$\frac{41}{100}$	80	0.80	$\frac{4}{5}$
11	0.11	$\frac{11}{100}$	26	0.26	$\frac{13}{50}$	42	0.42	$\frac{21}{50}$	85	0.85	$\frac{17}{20}$
12	0.12	$\frac{3}{25}$	27	0.27	$\frac{27}{100}$	43	0.43	$\frac{43}{100}$	90	0.90	$\frac{9}{10}$
$12\frac{1}{2}$	0.125	$\frac{1}{8}$	28	0.28	$\frac{7}{25}$	44	0.44	$\frac{11}{25}$	95	0.95	$\frac{19}{20}$
13	0.13	$\frac{13}{100}$	29	0.29	$\frac{29}{100}$	45	0.45	$\frac{9}{20}$	100	1.00	1
14	0.14	$\frac{7}{50}$	30	0.30	$\frac{3}{10}$	46	0.46	$\frac{23}{50}$			
15	0.15	$\frac{3}{20}$	31	0.31	$\frac{31}{100}$	47	0.47	$\frac{47}{100}$			

Playing Cards and Dice Chances

Poker

Hand	Number possible	Odds against
royal flush	4	649,739 to 1
straight flush	36	72,192 to 1
four of a kind	624	4,164 to 1
full house	3,744	693 to 1
flush	5,108	508 to 1
straight	10,200	254 to 1
three of a kind	54,912	46 to 1
two pairs	123,552	20 to 1
one pair	1,098,240	1.37 to 1
high card	1,302,540	1 to 1
total	2,598,960	

Bridge

Suit distribution in a hand	Odds against
4-4-3-2	4 to 1
5-4-2-2	8 to 1
6-4-2-1	20 to 1
7-4-1-1	254 to 1
8-4-1-0	2,211 to 1
13-0-0-0	158,753,389,899 to 1

Dice (Chances with two dice and a single throw)

Total count	Odds against
2	35 to 1
3	17 to 1
4	11 to 1
5	8 to 1
6	31 to 5
7	5 to 1
8	31 to 5
9	8 to 1
10	11 to 1
11	17 to 1
12	35 to 1

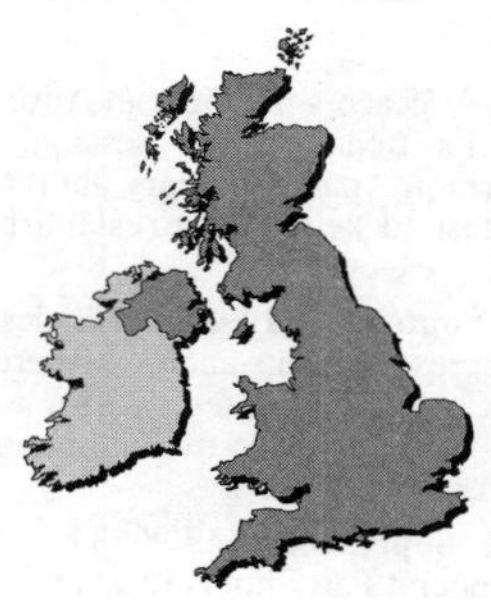

UNITED KINGDOM

The Year in Review

1 July 1998 The Northern Ireland Assembly meets for the first time. David Trimble, leader of the Ulster Unionists, and Seamus Mallon are appointed first and second ministers.

5 July 1998 The National Health Service celebrates its 50th anniversary.

12 July 1998 Three young boys are killed in an arson attack in Ballymoney, Co Antrim, Northern Ireland, as Orangemen protest the re-routing of their Drumcree march. The incident follows eight days of violence. The Orangemen continue their stand-off despite a loss of sympathy created by the deaths.

15 July 1998 The standoff between Orangemen and British and RUC forces at Drumcree ends when security forces forcibly remove the remaining protest-ors in a dawn raid.

22 July 1998 The UK Public Record Office releases documents from World War II that detail plans to assassinate Adolf Hitler. The plan, called Operation Foxley, was conceived in June 1944 but was delayed for months because of disagreement over how it should be carried out. The operation was eventually cancelled in April 1945.

24 July 1998 One of the oldest churches in the UK, built shortly after the Roman legions left in AD 410, is uncovered in the ruins of Vindolanda, on Hadrian's Wall.

27 July 1998 Prime Minister Tony Blair announces his first cabinet reshuffle: he promotes agriculture minister Jack Cunningham to the new position of minister for the cabinet office, heading cabinet activities and serving as a government spokesperson; minister without portfolio Peter Mandelson is promoted to secretary of state for trade and industry; and social security secretary Harriet Harman is sacked, reportedly because of dissatisfaction with reforms in the benefit system.

6 August 1998 Former IRA member Thomas McMahon, who was convicted in 1979 of planting the bomb which killed Lord Mountbatten (a cousin of Queen Elizabeth II), is released from Mountjoy Jail in Dublin, under the Good Friday peace agreement that stipulated the release of IRA prisoners.

15 August 1998 A car bomb explodes in Omagh, County Tyrone, Northern Ireland, killing 28 people, including 15 women and 8 children, in Northern Ireland's worst terrorist act to date. The IRA militant splinter group the Real IRA later admit responsibility.

22 August 1998 Around 40,000 people, including Irish prime minister Bertie Ahern, Irish president Mary MacAleese, British deputy prime minister John Prescott, and Sinn Féin leaders Gerry Adams and Martin McGuinness, attend a memorial service in Omagh, to commemorate the 28 people killed by a terrorist bomb in the town a week before.

31 August 1998 Mourners commemorate the first anniversary of the death of Diana, Princess of Wales, by laying flowers and messages at her home at Kensington Palace, at her burial site at Althorp, and at the site of the fatal car crash in Paris.

1 September 1998 Sinn Féin president Gerry Adams announces that the IRA will permanently cease its violent campaign for a united Ireland and will endeavour instead to achieve its aims by peaceful means. The group is reported to have started decommissioning its arsenal of weapons.

8 September 1998 Sinn Féin president Gerry Adams and Ulster first minister David Trimble hold talks in Northern Ireland, the first meeting between a Sinn Féin leader and an Ulster Unionist leader since 1922.

8 September 1998 The Real IRA, the militant republican group responsible for the bomb that killed 28 people in Omagh on 15 August, announces a complete cease-fire.

14 September 1998 The new Northern Ireland Assembly, created by the Good Friday peace agreement in April, opens for its first working session, at the Stormont parliamentary building in Belfast. Its key task is to establish a governing executive.

14–17 September 1998 The Trades Union Congress holds its annual conference, in Blackpool. Delegates call for a higher and more inclusive minimum wage and lower interest rates.

20–24 September 1998 The Liberal Democrat Party holds its annual conference in Brighton, focusing on changing the electoral system to proportional representation.

23 September 1998 The European Court of Human Rights in Strasbourg, France, rules that a British man who beat his stepson with a bamboo cane in 1993 violated the boy's human rights. The decision means that the UK will have to change its laws on corporal punishment.

27 September 1998–2 October 1998 The Labour Party holds its annual conference in Blackpool, focusing on setting political priorities and pledging domestic reforms in education, the National Health Service, and the benefit system.

6–9 October 1998 The Conservative Party holds its annual conference in Bournemouth. The conference is dominated by debate over joining the European Union's single currency, the euro. Several senior politicians criticize party leader William Hague for his hard-line stance against adopting the currency.

16 October 1998 Northern Ireland first minister David Trimble, leader of the Ulster Unionists, and SDLP leader John Hume share the Nobel Peace Prize for their work in negotiating the Good Friday agreement for peace in Northern Ireland.

21 October 1998 The newly restored Albert Hall, with a re-gilded statue of Prince Albert, is opened in London.

23 October 1998 British pop artist and former Spice Girl Geri Halliwell assumes her role as a United Nations Goodwill Ambassador, focusing on birth control and breast cancer awareness.

27 October 1998 Argentine president Carlos Menem arrives in London for a six-day visit arranged to ease tensions between the two countries resulting from the Falklands War. It is the first visit to the UK by an Argentine leader since 1960.

27 October 1998 Welsh secretary Ron Davies resigns from the cabinet after what he terms an 'error of judgement' led him into a situation in which he was the victim of theft; he reports the incident to the police, but refuses to elaborate on the circumstances. Prime minister Tony Blair accepts his resignation, and Alun Michael succeeds him.

1 November 1998 Renegade loyalist terrorists admit to the murder of Brian Service, a Catholic whom they chose randomly and shot five times in the head on 31 October in Belfast.

2 November 1998 The former Welsh secretary Ron Davies makes a personal statement in the House of Commons, calling for more tolerance of public figures and blasting the media for intrusion into his private life. Newspapers report the involvement of a blackmailer whom Davies had allegedly approached for gay sex on Clapham Common, an incident which left Davies the victim of robbery and led him to resign his post.

10 November 1998 The government announces that it will close the Maze prison near Belfast by 2000, stating that the prison is unsafe for both staff and prisoners.

12–14 November 1998 Prince Charles celebrates his 50th birthday with a banquet at Hampton Court Palace, a reception for 850 guests at Buckingham Palace, and a private party given by Camilla Parker Bowles at Highgrove House, Gloucestershire.

18 November 1998 A European election bill in the UK is defeated for the fifth time by the mainly Conservative House of Lords, but the leader of the Lords, Baroness Jay, promises to invoke the rarely used Parliamentary Act to push the bill through.

18 November 1998 A French court refuses to extradite former MI5 agent David Shayler, who is wanted by the British government for making allegations of corruption and mismanagement in the British security and intelligence services.

24 November 1998 Queen Elizabeth II opens a new session of Parliament. Her speech includes a proposed plan to rescind voting rights of hereditary peers in the House of Lords.

26 November 1998 Tony Blair becomes the first British prime minister to address the Irish parliament in Dublin, as part of an effort to improve relations between the UK and Ireland.

2 December 1998 British Conservative Party leader William Hague sacks House of Lords leader Viscount Cranborne for negotiating with the Labour government a deal whereby the hereditary peers in the House of Lords would keep their seats in exchange for promising not to block proposed legislation.

11 December 1998 In a new obstacle to the peace process, the IRA rejects Unionist demands that they decommission their weapons as a prerequisite for Sinn Féin members to gain seats in the new executive in Northern Ireland.

11 December 1998 The IRA appoints hard-line terrorist Brian Keenan as its new chief of staff in a move to show that it has control over the extremists in the party.

11 December 1998 The Office of National Statistics reports a rise in teenage pregnancies in the UK. The rate is among the highest in Europe – twice that of Germany and three times that of France.

15 December 1998 British social security secretary Alistair Darling announces a government green paper on reforming the country's pension scheme. The new legislation would eliminate the state earnings-related pension scheme (SERPS), and would offer incentives to people to invest in private pensions instead.

18 December 1998 The Loyalist Volunteer Force (LVF) in Northern Ireland becomes the first guerrilla group in the province to surrender arms to the police. The decommissioning of weapons is a major part of the Good Friday peace agreement.

23 December 1998 Around 170 inmates at the Maze prison in Belfast convicted of sectarian violence in Northern Ireland are granted 10 days' leave to celebrate Christmas with their families.

23 December 1998 British trade and industry secretary Peter Mandelson resigns his cabinet post after newspapers report a £373,000 loan for a house from paymaster general Geoffrey Robinson which he failed to declare. Robinson also resigns.

25 December 1998 The Sainsbury supermarket group opens its stores in Headcorn, Kent, and Hammersmith, West London, the company's first Christmas openings in 130 years. The openings are condemned by local residents and church leaders.

4 January 1999 Charlie Whelan, press secretary to the British chancellor of the exchequer Gordon Brown, announces his resignation in response to claims that he had leaked information that caused the loan scandal in which trade secretary Peter Mandelson and paymaster general Geoffrey Robinson resigned in December 1998. Whelan denies allegations that he leaked the information, although he disagreed with Mandelson on several policy issues.

6 January 1999 Prince Edward, the youngest son of Queen Elizabeth, announces his engagement to Sophie Rhys-Jones.

6–8 January 1999 Prime Minister Tony Blair makes his first visit to South Africa since taking office in 1997. He announces a 40 percent increase in British aid to the country.

19 January 1999 Former MP Jonathan Aitken admits to charges of perjury and perverting the course of justice during his failed libel suit against *The Guardian* newspaper and Granada Television, at the Old Bailey in London.

20 January 1999 Liberal Democrat Paddy Ashdown announces his intention to resign as party leader in the summer of 1999, citing family reasons.

25 January 1999 Members of Parliament vote 313–130 to amend the Sexual Offences Bill, lowering the age of consent for gay men to 16, the same as for heterosexuals. However, the House of Lords rejects the Bill, on 13 April.

27 January 1999 Former IRA member Eamon Collins, who turned informer and wrote a book about his terrorist experiences, is killed in Newry, County Armagh, Northern Ireland.

28 January 1999 Prince Charles and his companion Camilla Parker Bowles make their first public appearance together as a couple when they leave a party at the Ritz hotel in London.

4 February 1999 Both republican and loyalist paramilitary groups issue warnings of fresh violence, threatening Northern Ireland peace efforts and the Good Friday agreement. The IRA also reveals that some of its weapons were stolen by republican extremists.

4 February 1999 The British Patent Office rules that the face of Lady Diana cannot be a registered trademark. Her family had applied for the trademark to avoid exploitation of her image.

8 February 1999 The first trial to be held under the 1991 War Crimes Act, which allows the prosecution of World War II criminals living in Britain, opens at the Old Bailey in London. Former Nazi policeman Anthony Sawoniuk is charged with murdering four Jews in Nazi-occupied Belarus. He is convicted of the crime and in April 1999 is given two life sentences.

9 February 1999 The House of Commons foreign affairs committee releases a report condemning Foreign Office officials for their role in a scandal over selling arms to Sierra Leone. The committee claims that foreign office permanent secretary John Kerr and other officials failed to inform their superiors about arms sales to Sierra Leone that were possibly in violation of a United Nations arms embargo.

16 February 1999 The Northern Ireland Assembly approves a plan for the province's new government structure, which would give it control over local issues such as taxation and law enforcement. The Assembly's first minister, David Trimble, insists, however, that no executive for the Assembly can be formed until the IRA starts to decommission its weapons.

17 February 1999 Representatives of the Ulster Unionist Party and Sinn Féin hold bilateral talks for the first time. They meet to resolve the dispute over the decommissioning of IRA weapons, but make no significant progress.

8 March 1999 Northern Ireland secretary Mo Mowlam announces that the deadline for the creation of the Northern Ireland Executive as outlined in the 1998 peace accord is being pushed back from 10 March to 29 March in an effort to resolve the dispute over the decommissioning of IRA weapons.

9 March 1999 Prince Charles lays a wreath at a memorial in Buenos Aires, Argentina, honouring Argentine soldiers who died in the 1982 Falklands War. The gesture is an attempt to further reconciliation between the two countries.

15 March 1999 A car bomb in Lurgan, Northern Ireland, kills prominent Roman Catholic lawyer and human rights advocate Rosemary Nelson. The Red Hand Defenders, an extremist Protestant group that opposes the Northern Ireland peace process, claims responsibility.

17 March 1999 Frankie Currie, a prominent member of the extremist Protestant unionist group the Red Hand Defenders, is shot dead in Belfast, Northern Ireland. Police suspect members of a rival Protestant group of the shooting.

19 March 1999 Labour MP Fiona Jones is sacked for understating her expenses during the 1997 elections. She is the first sitting MP to be sacked for electoral malpractice in 75 years. In April 1999 two High Court judges quash her conviction.

25 March 1999 A jury in Edinburgh acquits Labour MP Mohammed Sarwar of fraud charges. He had been accused of attempting to bribe rival candidates to stand down or curtail their campaigning and had been suspended from his party since June 1997.

26 March 1999 The government announces that starting in 2001, pets from European Union and certain other countries will not have to be quarantined for six months if they have a 'passport' certifying their medical history.

1 April 1999 Prime minister Tony Blair announces that Northern Ireland peace talks will be suspended until 13 April, thereby missing the deadline agreed in April 1998 for establishing the Northern Ireland Executive, the province's new cabinet. The participants in the talks are in a deadlock over the issue of the decommissioning of weapons by the IRA.

17 April 1999 A nail bomb explodes in Brixton Market in London, injuring at least 40 people. A member of the Combat 18 neo-Nazi group, which has been linked to several racist attacks, claims responsibility.

25 April 1999 A nail bomb explodes in the East End of London, in the heart of the city's Bangladeshi community, injuring six people. The incident is linked to the nail bomb explosion in Brixton a week earlier.

26 April 1999 Television presenter Jill Dando is shot dead by an unidentified

gunman outside her home in Fulham, London.

29 April 1999 Prime Minister Tony Blair approves plans for the privatization of the £110 billion benefits system. Under a new scheme, the Single Work-Focused Gateway, people would make one application for all the benefits they are claiming and would receive one cheque.

1 May 1999 A nail bomb explodes in the 'Admiral Duncan', a gay pub in Soho, London, killing 3 people and injuring 73. The incident is linked to similar nail bomb explosions in April in Brixton and the East End.

2 May 1999 British engineer David Copeland is charged with planting the three nail bombs in London that killed three people and injured more than a hundred. He was arrested the previous day at his house in Cove, near Farnborough, Hampshire, where police found bags of nails and explosives.

6 May 1999 Devolution elections are held in Scotland and Wales, and local elections are held in England. The Labour Party is the largest party in the Scottish Parliament and Welsh Assembly, but fails to win an overall majority in either, as the Scottish National Party and Plaid Cymru in Wales, both nationalist parties, gain large numbers of seats.

6 May 1999 Egyptian-born businessman Mohamed Al Fayed is denied British citizenship, based on his failure to pass the 'good character' test set by British home secretary Jack Straw. The decision is said to rest on two issues: his payments to MPs in the 'cash-for-questions' scandal and his failure to report a break-in to a safe deposit box belonging to his business rival Tiny Rowland.

12 May 1999 The new Scottish Parliament comes into existence in Edinburgh. It is Scotland's first parliament for nearly 300 years.

13 May 1999 Scottish secretary Donald Dewar is elected Scotland's new first minister by the Scottish Parliament. His place in the Cabinet is taken by the transport minister John Reid.

14 May 1999 An article published in the *British Medical Journal* reports that British teenagers have the highest incidents in Europe of sexual diseases, pregnancies, and abortions. The article blames poor education and long working hours of parents.

21 May 1999 Family, friends, and colleagues attend the funeral of television presenter Jill Dando in Weston-super-Mare. She was killed 25 days earlier by an unidentified gunman outside her home in west London. A crowd of more than 2,000 gathers around Clarence Park Baptist Church, where the invitation-only service is held.

24 May 1999 The government publishes its draft Freedom of Information Bill, fulfilling Labour's pledge to create the first statutory right for people to access internal government documents. Critics of the bill claim it is a watered-down version of the white paper published in 1998 that proposed an end to government secrecy.

26 May 1999 Queen Elizabeth II officially opens the Welsh Assembly in Cardiff.

26 May 1999 *The Sun* publishes a photograph of Sophie Rhys-Jones, Prince Edward's fiancée, topless. Buckingham Palace lodges a formal complaint with the Press Complaints Commission, claiming it is an invasion of privacy.

8 June 1999 British politician Jonathan Aitken becomes the first former MP this century to be sent to prison, for perjury and perverting the course of justice. He is sentenced to 18 months in an open prison in West Sussex.

10 June 1999 In elections for 87 new Euro-MPs in the UK, voter turnout is only around 25 percent.

11 June 1999 British barrister Cherie Booth, wife of Prime Minister Tony Blair, is appointed as a judge in London, England.

13 June 1999 An estimated 50,000 demonstrators join hands to form a three-mile human chain on the banks of the river Thames in London, as part of the Jubilee 2000 campaign to abolish debt for developing countries.

13 June 1999 The Labour Party loses half of its seats in the European Parliament. Labour MPs blame the proportional representation electoral system for low voter turnout, while the rival Conservative Party claims a resurgence in popularity and a vindication of party leader William Hague's anti-euro policy.

15 June 1999 Conservative Party leader William Hague sacks Peter Lilley, the party's deputy leader, in a cabinet reshuffle. Ann Widdecombe is promoted to shadow home secretary and John Maples replaces Michael Howard as shadow foreign secretary.

16 June 1999 Scottish first minister Donald Dewar announces the initial eight bills for the first Scottish parliament in nearly 300 years. The bills include legislation on education, land reform, reduction of traffic, and the creation of Scotland's first national park, around Loch Lomond.

18 June 1999 A demonstration in the City of London, in which some 3,000 people protest against the arms trade, financial institutions, and third world debt, turns violent. Rioters destroy part of the Futures Exchange, a McDonalds, several cars, and empty flats, and set fire to a bank.

19 June 1999 Prince Edward, the youngest son of Queen Elizabeth, marries Sophie Rhys-Jones at St George's Chapel, Windsor. The Queen gives them the titles Earl and Countess of Wessex.

21 June 1999 On the morning of the summer solstice, hundreds of people invade the 5,000 year-old World Heritage Site of Stonehenge in Wiltshire, tearing down the perimeter fence and climbing the stones, leading to 23 arrests.

22 June 1999 Patrick Magee, known as the 'Brighton bomber', who murdered five people in an attempt to blow up the cabinet of Margaret Thatcher in 1984, is released early from prison as part of the Good Friday peace agreement in Northern Ireland. Unionist leader David Trimble criticizes the release and calls for the sacking of Northern Ireland secretary Mo Mowlam.

24 June 1999 British businessman and director of Manchester United football club Greg Dyke is appointed director general of the BBC. The appointment is fiercely opposed by the Conservative Party and its supporters because he donated £50,000 to the Labour Party.

27 June 1999 British Labour MP for Chesterfield Tony Benn announces that he will stand down at the next election, ending his 50-year career in Parliament.

27 June 1999 The Parades Commission in Northern Ireland bans the Drumcree Orange Order from marching down the Garvaghy Road, through a nationalist part of Portadown.

28 June 1999 Prime Minister Tony Blair and Irish premier Bertie Ahern meet in Northern Ireland to continue negotiations to save the Good Friday peace agreement, which is deadlocked over the IRA's decommissioning of weapons.

30 June 1999 A midnight deadline is set for agreement over the setting up of the power-sharing executive of the Northern Ireland Assembly. British and Irish leaders, as well as President Clinton, work to hammer out an agreement to break the deadlock over the decommissioning of IRA weapons. Sinn Féin agrees to decommission three months after the executive is established. The proposal includes the offer of an IRA statement that the terrorist group fully backs Sinn Féin's position. The midnight deadline passes without full agreement.

Geography

Countries of the UK

(– = not applicable.)

Country	Area		Population (1997 est)	Population density (persons per sq km)	Capital
	sq km	sq mi			
England	130,410	50,351	49,284,000	378	London
Northern Ireland	14,160	5,467	1,675,000	123	Belfast
Scotland	78,789	30,420	5,123,000	66	Edinburgh
Wales	20,758	8,015	2,927,000	141	Cardiff
Total	244,101	94,248	59,009,000	–	–

Highest Points in the UK

Highest point	Region	Height	
		m	ft
England			
Scafell Pike	Cumbria	977	3,206
Sca Fell	Cumbria	963	3,162
Helvellyn	Cumbria	955	3,113
Skiddaw	Cumbria	931	3,054
Bow Fell	Cumbria	902	2,960
Great Gable	Cumbria	898	2,949
Cross Fell	Cumbria	893	2,930
Pillar	Cumbria	892	2,927
Esk Pike	Cumbria	884	2,903
Fairfield	Cumbria	872	2,863
Wales			
Snowdon	Gwynedd	1,085	3,560
Carnedd Llewelyn	Gwynedd/Conwy	1,062	3,484
Carnedd Dafydd	Conwy	1,044	3,426
Glyder Fawr	Gwynedd/Conwy	999	3,279
Glyder Fach	Conwy	994	3,262
Y Garn	Gwynedd/Conwy	946	3,104
Foel-fras	Gwynedd/Conwy	942	3,091
Elidyr-fawr	Gwynedd	923	3,029
Tryfan	Conwy	917	3,010
Aran Fawddwy	Gwynedd	905	2,970
Scotland			
Ben Nevis[1]	Highland	1,344	4,408
Ben Macdhui	Aberdeenshire/Moray	1,309	4,296
Braeriach	Aberdeenshire/Highland	1,296	4,252
Cairn Toul	Aberdeenshire	1,292	4,241
Cairn Gorm	Moray	1,244	4,084
Aonach Beag	Highland	1,236	4,054
Carn Mor Dearg	Highland	1,222	4,012
Aonach Mor	Highland	1,218	3,999
Ben Lawers	Perth and Kinross	1,214	3,984
Beinn a'Bhuird	Aberdeenshire	1,196	3,924
Northern Ireland			
Slieve Donard	Down	852	2,796
Slieve Commedagh	Down	766	2,512
Slieve Bearnagh	Down	730	2,394
Slieve Meelbeg	Down	704	2,310
Slieve Lamagan	Down	703	2,306
Slieve Bingian	Down	685	2,249
Sawel Mountain	Tyrone	683	2,240
Slieve Meelmore	Down	682	2,237
Slieve Muck	Down	670	2,198
Shanlieve	Down	626	2,053

[1] Ben Nevis is the highest point in Scotland and the highest point in the UK.

Highest Points in England, by County

County	High point	Height	
		m	ft
Bedfordshire	Dunstable Down	243	798
Buckinghamshire	Wendover Woods	267	876
Cambridgeshire	Great Chishill	146	478
Cheshire	Shining Tor	559	1,834
Cornwall	Brown Willy	419	1,375
Cumbria	Scafell Pike[1]	977	3,206
Derbyshire	Kinder Scout	636	2,087
Devon	High Willhays	621	2,038
Dorset	Lewesdon Hill	279	917
Durham	Mickle Fell	790	2,591
East Sussex	Ditchling Beacon	248	813
Essex	Oldfield Grove, Langley	147	482
Gloucestershire	Cleeve Cloud	330	1,083
Hampshire	Pilot Hill	286	937
Hertfordshire	Hastoe	244	802
Kent	Westerham Hill	245	805
Lancashire	Gragareth	627	2,057
Leicestershire	Bardon Hill	279	916
Lincolnshire	Normanby-le-Wold	168	551
Norfolk	Roman Camp Beacon, Sheringham	105	344
Northamptonshire	Arbury Hill	224	734
Northumberland	The Cheviot	815	2,674
North Yorkshire	Whernside	736	2,415
Nottinghamshire	Herrod's Hill	202	663
Oxfordshire	Whitehorse Hill	261	856
Shropshire	Brown Clee Hill	540	1,772
Somerset	Dunkery Beacon	520	1,707
Staffordshire	Oliver Hill	513	1,684
Suffolk	Depden	128	419
Surrey	Leith Hill	294	965
Warwickshire	Ilmington Downs	260	854
West Sussex	Black Down Hill	280	919
Wiltshire	Milk Hill and Tan Hill	294	964
Worcestershire	Worcestershire Beacon	425	1,395

[1] Scafell Pike is the highest point in England.

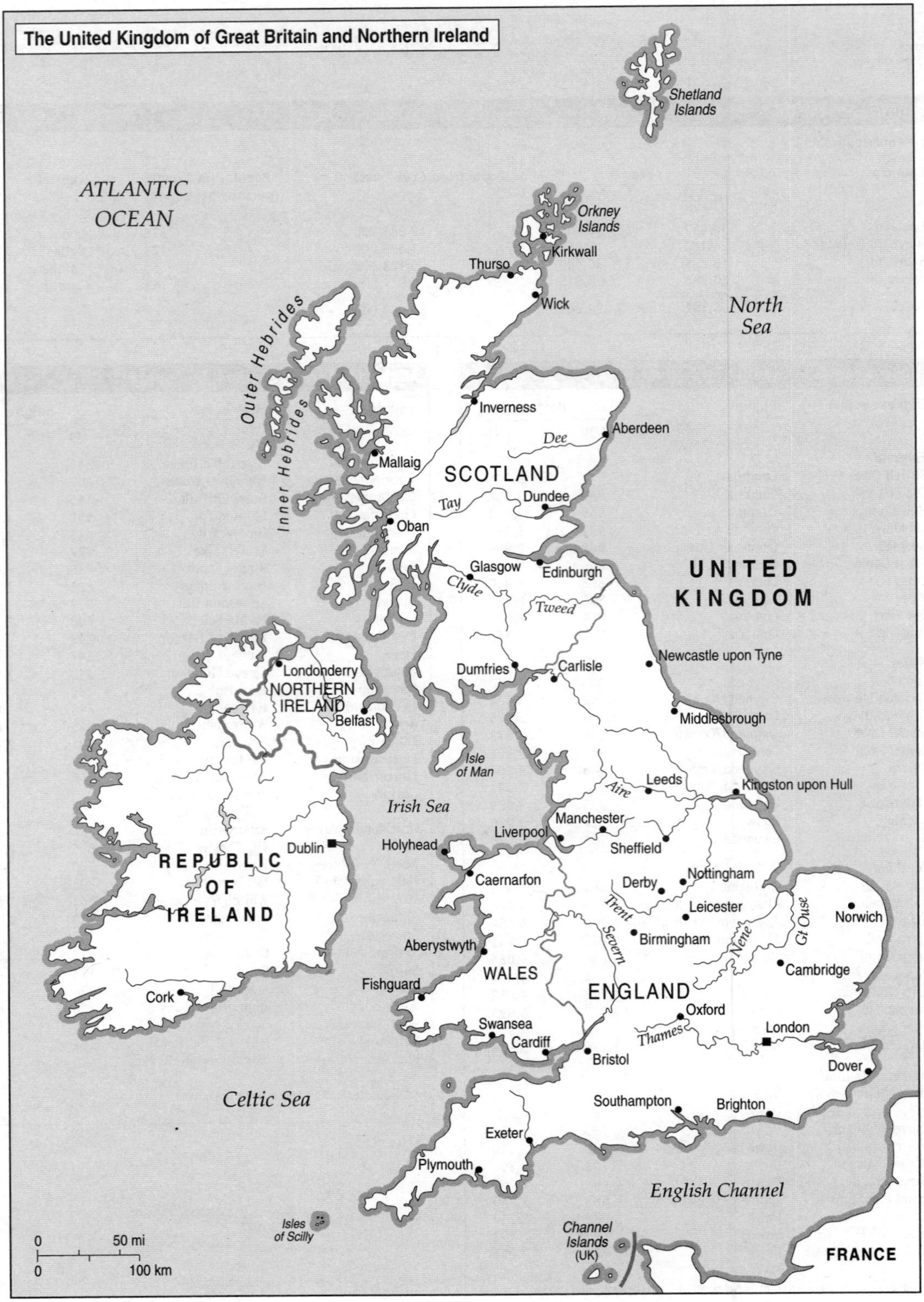
The United Kingdom of Great Britain and Northern Ireland
Shetland Islands
ATLANTIC OCEAN
Orkney Islands
Kirkwall
Thurso
Wick
North Sea
Outer Hebrides
Inner Hebrides
Inverness
Aberdeen
Dee
Mallaig
SCOTLAND
Tay
Dundee
Oban
Glasgow
Edinburgh
Clyde
Tweed
UNITED KINGDOM
Londonderry
NORTHERN IRELAND
Belfast
Dumfries
Carlisle
Newcastle upon Tyne
Middlesbrough
Isle of Man
Aire
Leeds
Kingston upon Hull
Irish Sea
Manchester
Liverpool
Dublin
Holyhead
Sheffield
REPUBLIC OF IRELAND
Caernarfon
Derby
Nottingham
Trent
Leicester
Norwich
Gt Ouse
Severn
Birmingham
Nene
Aberystwyth
Cambridge
WALES
Fishguard
ENGLAND
Cork
Oxford
Swansea
London
Thames
Cardiff
Bristol
Dover
Celtic Sea
Southampton
Brighton
Exeter
Plymouth
English Channel
Isles of Scilly
Channel Islands (UK)
FRANCE
0 50 mi
0 100 km

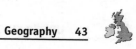

Largest Islands in the UK

Name	Location	Area sq km	Area sq mi	Name	Location	Area sq km	Area sq mi
Lewis with Harris	Outer Hebrides	2,225	859	Rum	Inner Hebrides	110	42
Skye	Inner Hebrides	1,666	643	Sheppey	north coast of Kent	94	36
Mainland, Shetland	Shetland Islands	967	373	Benbecula	Outer Hebrides	93	36
Mull	Inner Hebrides	899	347	Barra	Outer Hebrides	90	35
Anglesey	northwest coast of Wales	714	276	Tiree	Inner Hebrides	75	29
Islay	Inner Hebrides	614	237	Raasay	Inner Hebrides	60	24
Mainland, Orkney	Orkney Islands	536	207	Westray	Orkney Islands	48	19
Arran	Firth of Clyde	435	168	South Ronaldsay	Orkney Islands	46	18
Wight, Isle of	south coast of England	380	147	Sanday	Orkney Islands	40	15
Jura	Inner Hebrides	370	143	Holy Island	northwest coast of Wales	39	15
North Uist	Outer Hebrides	351	136	Fetlar	Shetland Islands	36	14
South Uist	Outer Hebrides	332	128	Stronsay	Orkney Islands	35	14
Yell	Shetland Islands	214	83	Bressay	Shetland Islands	28	11
Hoy	Orkney Islands	137	53	Hayling Island	coast of Hampshire	27	10
Bute	Firth of Clyde	120	46	Shapinsay	Orkney Islands	26	10
Unst	Shetland Islands	120	46	Eigg	Orkney Islands	23	9

Longest Rivers in the UK

Name	Source	Outlet	Length km	Length mi
Severn	Ceredigion/Powys border	Bristol Channel	354	220
Thames	Gloucestershire	North Sea	346	215
Trent	Staffordshire/Cheshire border	Humber estuary	297	185
Great Ouse	Northamptonshire	The Wash	230	143
Wye	Ceredigion	River Severn	215	135
Tay	Highland	Firth of Tay	188	117
Nene	Northamptonshire	The Wash	161	100
Clyde	South Lanarkshire	Firth of Clyde	158	98
Spey	Highland	Moray Firth	157	98
Tweed	Scottish Borders	North Sea	156	97
Dee (Scotland)	Aberdeenshire	North Sea	137	85
Usk	Carmarthenshire/Powys border	Bristol Channel	137	85
Avon (Upper Avon or Warwickshire Avon)	Northamptonshire	River Severn	136	85
Don	Aberdeenshire	North Sea	133	83
Tees	Cumbria	North Sea	130	80
Witham	Leicestershire	The Wash	129	80
Bann	Co Down	Atlantic	122	76
Avon (Bristol Avon)	Gloucestershire	River Severn	121	75
Ribble	North Yorkshire	Irish Sea	120	75
Teifi	Ceredigion	Cardigan Bay	118	73
Dee (Wales)	Bala Lake, Gwynedd	Irish Sea	112	70
Mersey	Stockport, Greater Manchester	Irish Sea	112	70
Nith	East Ayrshire	Solway Firth	112	70
Towy (Welsh Tywi)	Ceredigion/Powys border	Carmarthen Bay	111	69
Welland	Leicestershire	The Wash	110	68
Aire	North Yorkshire	River Ouse	110	68
Wear	Durham	North Sea	107	67
Eden	Cumbria	Solway Firth	104	65
Deveron	Moray	North Sea	100	63
Tamar	Cornwall	Plymouth Sound	97	60
Swale	North Yorkshire	River Ure	97	60

British Dependent Territories

As they do not have permanently resident populations, the dependencies of British Antarctic Territory and British Indian Ocean Territory are not included below.

Anguilla

Topography Anguilla is the most northerly of the Leeward Islands in the eastern Caribbean, a flat and low-lying island of coral and limestone; **Area** 96 sq km/36 sq mi; **Highest point** N/A; **Major towns and cities** The Valley (capital); **Total population** 11,100 (1998 est); **Climate** tropical, moderated by northeast trade winds; average temperature 27°C/80°F; average annual rainfall 89 cm/35 in; **Time** Atlantic Standard Time (Greenwich Mean Time less 4 hours); **Currency** East Caribbean dollar; **Languages** English; **Religion** Christianity; **Head of state** Queen Elizabeth II, represented by Governor Bob Harris; **Head of government** Chief Minister Hubert Hughes; **Major industries** finance; tourism; boat building; fishing; **Agriculture** pigeon peas; corn; sweet potatoes; sheep; goats; pigs; cattle; poultry; **Chamber of Commerce** Chamber of Commerce, PO Box 321, The Valley, Anguilla; phone: (001 264) 497 2701; **Tourist department** Anguilla Tourist Board, Factory Plaza, The Valley, Anguilla, BWI; phone: (001 264) 497 2759; fax: (001 264) 497 3091; e-mail: atbtour@anguillanet.com; Web site: www.abtour @candw.com.ai; **UK office** Anguilla Tourist Board, 3 Epirus Road, London SW6 7UJ; phone: (0171) 937 7725; fax: (0171) 938 4793.

Bermuda

Topography British dependent territory that consists of some 150 islands and islets situated at latitude 32°N and longitude 65 °W in western Atlantic Ocean, off the US (North Carolina) coast. About 20 islands are inhabited. Ten main islands linked by causeways and bridges form a distinctive fishhook-shaped chain. The landscape consists mainly of rolling hills. The coast is dotted with sandy bays, coves, and craggy cliffs. There are no rivers or lakes; **Area** 52 sq km/20 sq mi; **Highest point** 78.9 m/849 ft; **Major towns and cities** Hamilton (capital); St George; **Total population** 62,000 (1998 est); **Climate** sub-tropical, mainly humid; average temperature 21°C/70°F; average annual rainfall 146 cm/57 in; **Time** Greenwich Mean Time less 4 hours; **Currency** Bermudan dollar; **Languages** English; **Religion** Christianity; **Head of state** Queen Elizabeth II, represented by Governor John Thorold Masefield; **Head of government** Premier Jennifer Smith; **Major industries** tourism (70 percent of gross domestic product); offshore insurance; pharmaceutical and paint manufacturing; construction; ship-repairing and boat-building; **Agriculture** bananas; potatoes; tomatoes; carrots; cabbage; citrus fruits; **Chamber of Commerce** Bermuda Chamber of Commerce, 1 Point Pleasant Road, PO Box HM 655, Hamilton HM CX, Bermuda; phone: (001441) 295 4201; fax: (001441) 292 5779; e-mail: bcc@ibl.bm; **Tourist department** Bermuda Department of Tourism, Global House, 43 Church Street, Hamilton HM, Bermuda; phone: (001441) 292 0023; Web site: www.bermudatourism.org; **UK office:** Bermuda Tourism, 1 Battersea Church Road, London SW11 3LY, England; phone: (0171) 771 7001; fax: (0171) 771 7037; e-mail: bermudatourism@ cibgroup. co.uk.

British Virgin Islands

Topography A chain of about 60 islands, islets and cays, 16 inhabited, lying at east end of the Greater Antilles chain, with the Lesser Antilles chain to east and south, in the Caribbean on latitude 18°N and longitude 64°W. The main islands are Tortola, Anegada, Virgin Gorda, and Jost Van Dyke. The landscape consists mainly of steep, thickly wooded hills, with coral reefs, coves, and beaches. There are no rivers; **Area** 150 sq km/58 sq mi; **Highest point** Sage Mountain, 540 m/1,772 ft, on Tortola; **Major towns and cities** Road Town (capital), Tortola Island; East End; Long Look; **Total population** 18,700 (1998 est); **Climate** sub-tropical, temperatures moderated by trade winds, occasional droughts; temperature ranges: winter 22–28°C/71–82°F; summer 26–31°C/79–88°F; erratic rainfall averaging 127 cm/50 in annually; **Time** Greenwich Mean Time less 4 hours; **Currency** US dollar; **Languages** English; **Religion** Christianity; **Head of state** Queen Elizabeth II, represented by Governor Frank Savage; **Head of government** Chief Minister and Minister of Finance Ralph T O'Neal; **Major industries** tourism (75 percent of gross domestic product); financial services; fishing; rum distilling; construction; **Agriculture** livestock (including poultry); fish; fruit; vegetables; **Tourist department**, British Virgin Islands Tourist Board, PO Box 134, Road Town, Tortola, BVI; phone: (001284) 494 3134; fax: (001284) 494 3866; **UK office** British Virgin Islands Tourist Board, 54 Baker Street, London W1M 1DJ; phone: (0171) 240 4259; fax: (0171) 240 4270.

Cayman Islands

Topography Three islands of Grand Cayman, Little Cayman, and Cayman Brac lie in Caribbean Sea northwest of Jamaica at latitude 19.3°N and longitude 81.2°W. Low-lying, 18 m/59 ft above sea level, except in Cayman Brac where the eastern end rises to 42 m/138 ft; rock-bound coasts protected by coral reefs enclosing a few fair anchorages. No rivers; **Area** 260 sq km/100 sq mi; **Highest point** 42 m/140 ft; **Major towns and cities** George Town (capital); West Bay; **Total population** 37,700 (1998 est); **Climate** tropical tempered by trade winds, warm rainy summers (May–October) and cool, relatively dry winters (November–April); average temperature N/A; average annual rainfall 142 cm/56 in; **Time** Greenwich Mean Time less 5 hours; **Currency** Cayman Islands dollars; **Languages** English; **Religion** Christianity; **Head of state** Queen Elizabeth II, represented by Governor Peter John Smith; **Head of government** Governor, who presides over the Executive Council, Peter John Smith; **Major industries** tourism (50 percent of gross domestic product); banking; insurance and finance; real estate and construction; **Agriculture** minor production of vegetables and fruit; livestock; turtle farming; **Chamber of Commerce** Cayman Islands Chamber of Commerce, PO Box 1000 GT, Grand Cayman; phone: (001345) 9498090; fax: (001345) 9490220; e-mail: chamber@ candw.ky; **Tourist department** PO Box 67, George Town, Grand Cayman; phone: (001345) 949 0623; fax: (001345) 949 4053; **UK office** 6 Arlington Street, London SW1A 1RE; phone: (0171) 491 7771; fax: (0171) 409 7773; Web site: www.caymanislands.ky.

Falkland Islands

Topography The Falkland Islands comprise two large islands, East Falkland and West Falkland, and some 700 smaller islands between latitudes 51–53°S and longitudes 57–61°W in the south Atlantic, approximately 770 km/478 mi northeast of Cape Horn, South America. On the main islands deeply indented coastlines afford good anchorages. Generally hilly, the landscape is mainly stony, treeless grassland with no large inland waters; **Area** 12,170 sq km/4,680 sq mi; **Highest point** Mt Usborne on East Falkland, 705 m/2,313 ft; **Major towns and cities** Stanley, on East Falkland (capital); Goose Green; **Total population** 2,800 (1998 est); **Climate** gales in spring, and generally windy, low rainfall evenly distributed throughout the year, with frequent cloud cover, frequent snow which quickly melts; average temperature 5.6°C/42°F; average annual rainfall 62.5 cm/24.6 in; **Time** Greenwich Mean Time less 4 hours; **Currency** Falkland Islands pound; **Languages** English; **Religion** Christianity; **Head of state** Queen Elizabeth II; **Head of government** Richard Ralph; **Major industries** wool processing; fishing; **Agriculture** sheep farming; small dairy herds; fodder crops;

Chamber of Commerce Falkland Islands Development Corporation, PO Box 580, Stanley, Falkland Islands; phone: (010500) 27211; fax: (001500) 27210; **Tourist department** Falkland Islands Tourist Board, Stanley, Falkland Islands, PO Box 580, Stanley, Falkland Islands; **UK office** Falkland House, 14 Broadway, London SW1H 0BH; phone: (0171) 222 2542; fax: (0171) 222 2375.

Gibraltar

Topography Narrow rocky peninsula at latitude 36°N longitude 5°W. Juts out steeply from the adjoining low-lying coast of southwest Spain, at the east end of the Strait of Gibraltar, overlooking the west entrance to the Mediterranean. The Rock of Gibraltar is a long, high mountain with a sandy plain to the north. It has a 2.4 km/1.5 mi knife edge running from a steep north escarpment, then a 1.6 km/1 mi slope to the south, ending in vertical cliffs 30.5 m/100 ft high. The Spanish port of Algeciras lies 8 km/5 mi across the bay to the west, while the coast of Morocco is 21 km/13 mi across the Strait of Gibraltar to the south; **Area** 6.5 sq km/2.5 sq mi; **Highest point** 423 m/1,388 ft; **Major towns and cities** Gibraltar (capital); **Total population** 29,000 (1998 est); **Climate** mild and temperate, snow or frost extremely rare; rainy season September to May; average temperature 17°C/63°F; average annual rainfall 77 cm/30 in; **Time** Greenwich Mean Time plus 1 hour; **Currency** Gibraltar pound; **Languages** English; Spanish; **Religion** Christianity; Islam; **Head of state** Queen Elizabeth II, represented by Governor Sir Richard Luce; **Head of government** Chief Minister Peter Caruana; **Major industries** tourism; banking and finance; construction; commerce; ship repair; support to large UK naval and air base; transit trade and supply depot in the port; light manufacturing of tobacco, roasted coffee, ice, mineral waters, candy, beer, and canned fish; **Chamber of Commerce** Don House, 30/38 Main Street, Gibraltar; phone: (350) 78376; **Tourist department** Gibraltar Tourist Board, Duke of Kent House, Cathedral Square, Gibraltar; phone: (350) 74950; fax: (350) 74943; e-mail: giblondon@aol.com; **UK office** Gibraltar Tourist Board, 179 Strand, London WC2R 1EH; phone: (0171) 836 0777; fax: (0171) 240 6612.

Guernsey

Topography The second-largest of the Channel Islands. Lies at 50°N latitude and 2°W longitude, 130 km/81 mi south of England, 48 km/30 mi west of Normandy, France, and is roughly triangular in shape. In the south, Guernsey rises in a plateau to about 90 m/295 ft, with ragged coastal cliffs. It descends in steps and is drained mainly by streams flowing northward in deeply incised valleys. Northern Guernsey is low-lying, although small outcrops of resistant rock form hills (hougues). The soil on lower ground is of blown sand, raised beach deposits, and the fills of old lagoons. The jurisdiction also covers the smaller islands of Alderney, Herm, and Sark; **Area** 194 sq km/75 sq mi (includes Alderney, Guernsey, Herm, Sark, and some other smaller islands); **Highest point** 90 m/295 ft; **Major towns and cities** St Peter Port (capital); St Sampson; **Total population** 64,500 (1998 est); **Climate** temperate with mild winters and cool summers; about 50 percent of days are overcast; average temperature 11°C/51.8°F; average annual rainfall 75–90 cm/29.5–35.4 in; **Time** British Summer Time in summer; Greenwich Mean Time in winter; **Currency** Guernsey pound; **Languages** English, French; Norman-French dialect spoken in country districts; **Religion** Christianity; **Head of state** Queen Elizabeth II, represented by Lieutenant Governor Sir John Coward; Bailiff de V G Carey; **Major industries** banking; tourism; **Agriculture** tomatoes; flowers (mostly grown in greenhouses); sweet peppers; aubergines; other vegetables and fruit; Guernsey cattle; **Chamber of Commerce** Chamber of Commerce, Suite 3, 16 Glategny Esplanade, St Peter Port; phone: (01481) 727483; fax: (01481) 710755; **Tourist department** States Tourist Board, PO Box 23, Guernsey, CI; phone: (01481) 723552.

The Isle of Man

Topography An island in the Irish Sea, located 109 km/68 mi east of Ireland, 114 km/71 mi west of England, and 24 km/15 mi south of Scotland. It has a rocky, indented coastline and is about 53 km/33 mi long by 10–19 km/6–12 mi wide. The island is well watered, the principal rivers being the Santon, the Silver Burn, the Neb-Rhenass, the Sulby (near Ramsey), the Commo, and the Dhoo and Glass rivers which flow into the River Douglas. Mountains extend nearly the length of the island. Some of the valleys have rich pastures, and livestock is raised extensively; **Area** 588 sq km/227 sq mi; **Highest point** Snaefell, 620 m/2,036 ft; **Major towns and cities** Douglas (capital); Peel; Castletown; Ramsey; **Total population** 74,000 (1995); **Climate** cool summers and mild winters, humid, overcast about half the time; average temperature 8.1°C/46.6°F; average annual rainfall 114.6 cm/45 in; **Time** Greenwich Mean Time in summer; Greenwich Mean Time plus 1 hour in winter; **Currency** Manx pound; **Languages** English; Manx Gaelic; **Religion** Christianity; **Head of state** Queen Elizabeth II, represented by Sir Timothy Daunt; **Head of government** President of the Legislative Council Sir Charles Kerruish. (The parliament of the Isle, Tynwald, is the oldest surviving parliamentary body in the world.); **Major industries** financial services; light manufacturing; tourism; **Agriculture** oats; barley; wheat; turnips; potatoes; cattle; sheep; pigs; poultry; **Chamber of Commerce** Chamber of Commerce, 17 Drinkwater Street, Douglas; phone: (01624) 674941; fax: (01624) 663367; **Tourist department** Department of Tourism and Leisure Headquarters, Sea Terminal, Douglas, Isle of Man IM1 2RG; phone: (01624) 686801; fax: (01624) 686000.

Jersey

Topography The largest and southernmost of the Channel Islands, 19 km/12 mi west of the Cotentin peninsula of France. Situated at 49 °N latitude, 2 °W longitude, Jersey is about 14 km/9 mi across and 8 km/5 mi from north to south and has an area of 137 sq km/45 sq mi. The island is largely a plateau mantled with loess, with deeply incised valleys sloping from north to south. Picturesque cliffs reaching 148 m/486 ft in height line the northern coast; elsewhere, rocky headlands enclose sandy bays bordered by infilled lagoons. Coasts are reef-strewn, but a breakwater in St Aubin's Bay protects St Helier harbour from southwest gales. Blown sand forms dunes at the northern and southern ends of St Ouen's Bay on the western coast; **Area** 137 sq km/45 sq mi; **Highest point** 143 m/496 ft; **Major towns and cities** St Helier (capital); St Saviour; Gorey; St Aubin; **Total population** 89,100 (1998 est); **Climate** temperate, mild winters and cool summers; average temperature 11°C/51.8°F; average annual rainfall 75–90 cm/29.5–35.4 in; **Time** Greenwich Mean Time in summer; Greenwich Mean Time plus 1 hour in winter; **Currency** Jersey pound; **Languages** English; French; Norman-French dialect; **Religion** Christianity; **Head of state** Queen Elizabeth II; **Head of government** Lieutenant Governor General Sir Michael Wilkes; Bailiff Sir Phillip Bailhache; **Major industries** banking and finance; tourism; fishing; granite quarrying; electrical goods; textiles; clothing; **Agriculture** potatoes; cauliflowers; tomatoes; flowers; dairy and cattle farming; **Chamber of Commerce** Chamber of Commerce, 19 Royal Square, St Helier; phone: (001534) 24536; fax: (001534) 34942; **Tourist department** Jersey Tourism, Liberation Square, St Helier, Jersey JE1 1BB; phone: (001534) 500700; fax: (001534) 500899; e-mail: jtourism@itl.net; Web site: www.jtourism.com; **UK office** Jersey Tourism, 7 Lower Grosvenor Place, London SW1W 0EN; phone: (0171) 630 8787; fax: (0171) 630 0747; e-mail: info@jtourismuk.demon.co.uk.

Montserrat

Topography One of the Leeward islands in the eastern Caribbean, at latitude 17°N and longitude 62°W. Volcanic in origin, very mountainous. Comprises three main mountain ranges in the north, centre, and south. Soufriere Hills Volcano erupted on 18 July 1995 and eruptions have been continuing since, causing major devastation to the south and central island and destroying the capital of Plymouth and many other small towns; **Area** 100 sq km/39 sq mi; **Highest**

point Chances Peak, 910 m/2,986 ft; **Major towns and cities** Plymouth Olde Towne (capital); **Total population** 4,000 (1999 est); **Climate** tropical but windy, lies in hurricane zone, September–November rainy, March–June dry; average temperature 28°C/82°F; average annual rainfall 148 cm/58 in; **Time** Greenwich Mean Time less 4 hours; **Currency** Eastern Caribbean dollar; **Languages** English; **Religion** Christianity; **Head of state** Queen Elizabeth II, represented by Governor Frank J Savage; **Head of government** Chief Minister Bertrand Osborne.

Pitcairn Islands

Topography Group of islands in Polynesia, at latitude 25°S, longitude 130°W, 5,300 km/3,300 mi northeast of New Zealand. Rugged volcanic formation; rocky coastline with cliffs. Pitcairn is the main island with smaller Henderson, Ducie, Sandy, and Oeno islands; **Area** 35.5 sq km/13.7 sq mi; **Major towns and cities** Adamstown (capital); **Total population** (Pitcairn Island) 50 (1998 est); **Climate** tropical, hot, humid, modified by southeast trade winds, subject to typhoons, especially in the rainy season (November–March); average temperature 21°C/70°F; average annual rainfall 203 cm/80 in; **Time** Greenwich Mean Time less 9 hours; **Currency** New Zealand dollar; **Languages** English; Tahitian-English dialect; **Religion** Christianity; **Head of state** Queen Elizabeth II, represented by Governor and UK High Commissioner to New Zealand (non-resident) David Joseph Moss; **Head of government** Island Magistrate and Chairman of the Island Council Jay Warren; **Major industries** postage stamp sales; handicrafts; **Agriculture** subsistence fishing and farming; wide variety of fruits and vegetables.

St Helena

Topography Incorporates the islands of St Helena, latitude 16°S longitude 6°W, Ascension, 8°S 14°W, and Tristan da Cunha, 37°S 12°W. St Helena is 1,131 km/703 mi southeast of Ascension, and 1,932 km/1,200 mi from the southwest coast of Africa; Tristan da Cunha is 2,415 km/1,501 mi southwest of St Helena. The islands are volcanic, mountainous, and barren. Tristan da Cunha rises to a volcanic peak, which last erupted in 1961; **Area** St Helena: 122 sq km/47 sq mi; Ascension Island: 88 sq km/34 sq mi; Tristan da Cunha: 110 sq km/42 sq mi; **Highest point** Queen Mary's Peak, 2,060 m/6,758 ft; **Major towns and cities** Jamestown, St Helena (capital); Georgetown, Ascension Island (capital); **Total population** 7,090 (1998 est); **Climate** mild and varies little; average temperature 21°C/70°F; average annual rainfall 32–92 cm/13–36 in; **Time** Greenwich Mean Time; **Currency** St Helena pound; **Languages** English; **Religion** Christianity; **Head of state** Queen Elizabeth II; **Head of government** Governor and Commander in Chief David Smallman; **Major industries** Tristan da Cunha: fishing and fish-freezing; sale of postage stamps; handicrafts; **Agriculture** St Helena: maize; potatoes; sweet potatoes, vegetables; Ascension: fresh meat; vegetables; fruit; Tristan da Cunha: potatoes; apples; peaches.

Turks and Caicos Islands

Topography Two island groups, at latitude 20–22°N and longitude 70–73°W, southeast of the Bahamas in the North Atlantic Ocean. The Turks group consists of two inhabited islands, Grand Turk and Salt Cay, and uninhabited islets, rocks, and reef. The Caicos group comprises the main islands of South Caicos, East Caicos, Middle (or Grand) Caicos, North Caicos, Providenciales, and West Caicos, and other islets. The terrain is flat, arid, and stony; **Area** 430 sq km/166 sq mi; **Highest point** N/A; **Major towns and cities** Cockburn Town, Grand Turk (capital); Cockburn Harbour, South Caicos; **Total population** 16,250 (1998 est); **Climate** tropical, marine, moderated by trade winds, sunny and relatively dry; average temperature 30°C/84°F; average annual rainfall 53.5 cm/21 in; **Time** Greenwich Mean Time less 5 hours; **Currency** US dollar; **Languages** English; **Religion** Christianity; **Head of state** Queen Elizabeth II, represented by Governor John P Kells; **Head of government** Chief Minister Derek Taylor; **Major industries** tourism; offshore financial services; fishing; crawfish and conch processing; **Agriculture** subsistence farming, based on corn and beans; **Chamber of Commerce** Turks and Caicos Chamber of Commerce, PO Box 148, Grand Turk, Turks and Caicos Islands, British West Indies; phone: (001649) 946 2324; fax: (001649) 946 2714; **Tourist department** Tourist Information, Pond Street, Cockburn Town, Grand Turk; phone: (001649) 946 2321.

The British Commonwealth

The British Commonwealth

Association of 54 countries and their dependencies, the majority of which once formed part of the British Empire and are now independent sovereign states. The Commonwealth has no charter or constitution. **Date established** 1931 **Founding members** Anguilla, Australia, Bermuda, British Antarctic Territory, British Virgin Islands, Canada, Cayman Islands, Channel Islands, Cook Islands, Falkland Islands, Falkland Islands Dependency, Gibraltar, Isle of Man, Montserrat, New Zealand, Niue, Norfolk Island, Pitcairn Islands, Tokelau, Turks and Caicos Islands, St Helena, UK **Address** Commonwealth Secretariat, Marlborough House, Pall Mall, London SW1 5HX, UK; phone: (0171) 839 3411; fax: (0171) 930 0827; e-mail: info@commonwealth.int; **Web site** www.thecommonwealth.org/

Country	Capital	Date joined	Area in sq km/sq mi	Constitutional status
In Africa				
Botswana	Gaborone	1966	582,000/224,710	sovereign republic
British Indian Ocean Territory	uninhabited	1965	60/23	British dependent territory
Cameroon	Yaoundé	1995	475,440/183,567	emergent democratic republic
Fiji	Suva	1970, 1997	18,333/7,078	sovereign republic
Gambia	Banjul	1965	10,700/4,131	sovereign republic
Ghana	Accra	1957	238,300/92,007	sovereign republic
Kenya	Nairobi	1963	582,600/224,941	sovereign republic
Lesotho	Maseru	1966	30,400/11,737	sovereign constitutional monarchy
Malawi	Zomba	1964	118,000/45,559	sovereign republic
Mauritius	Port Louis	1968	2,000/772	sovereign republic

(continued)

The British Commonwealth (*continued*)

Country	Capital	Date joined	Area in sq km/sq mi	Constitutional status
Mozambique	Maputo	1995	799,380/308,640	emergent democracy
Namibia	Windhoek	1990	824,000/318,146	sovereign republic
Nigeria	Lagos	1960[1]	924,000/356,756	sovereign republic
St Helena	Jamestown	1931	100/38	British dependent territory[2]
Seychelles	Victoria	1976	450/173	sovereign republic
Sierra Leone	Freetown	1961[3]	73,000/28,185	sovereign republic
South Africa	Pretoria	1910[4]	1,221,000/471,428	sovereign republic
Swaziland	Mbabane	1968	17,400/6,718	sovereign republic
Tanzania	Dodoma	1961	945,000/364,864	sovereign republic
Uganda	Kampala	1962	236,900/91,467	sovereign republic
Zambia	Lusaka	1964	752,600/290,578	sovereign republic
Zimbabwe	Harare	1980	390,300/150,694	sovereign republic
In the Americas				
Anguilla	The Valley	1931	155/59	British dependent territory[2]
Antigua and Barbuda	St John's	1981	400/154	sovereign constitutional monarchy[5]
Bahamas	Nassau	1973	13,900/5,366	sovereign constitutional monarchy[5]
Barbados	Bridgetown	1966	400/154	sovereign constitutional monarchy[5]
Belize	Belmopan	1982	23,000/8,880	sovereign constitutional monarchy[5]
Bermuda	Hamilton	1931	54/20	British dependent territory[2]
British Virgin Islands	Road Town	1931	153/59	British dependent territory[2]
Canada	Ottawa	1931	9,958,400/3,844,938	sovereign constitutional monarchy[5]
Cayman Islands	Georgetown	1931	300/115	British dependent territory[2]
Dominica	Roseau	1978	700/270	sovereign republic
Falkland Islands	Port Stanley	1931	12,100/4,671	British dependent territory[2]
Grenada	St George's	1974	300/115	sovereign constitutional monarchy[5]
Guyana	Georgetown	1966	215,000/83,011	sovereign republic
Jamaica	Kingston	1962	11,400/4,401	sovereign constitutional monarchy[5]
Montserrat	Plymouth	1931	100/38	British dependent territory[2]
St Christopher–Nevis	Basseterre	1983	300/115	sovereign constitutional monarchy[5]
St Lucia	Castries	1979	600/231	sovereign constitutional monarchy[5]
St Vincent and the Grenadines	Kingstown	1979	400/154	sovereign constitutional monarchy[5]
Trinidad and Tobago	Port of Spain	1962	5,100/1,969	sovereign republic
Turks and Caicos Islands	Grand Turk	1931	400/154	British dependent territory[2]
In the Antarctic				
Australian Antarctic Territory	uninhabited	1936	5,403,000/2,086,098	Australian external territory[2]
British Antarctic Territory	uninhabited	1931	390,000/150,579	British dependent territory[2]
Falkland Islands Dependencies	uninhabited	1931	1,600/617	British dependent territories[2]
Ross Dependency	uninhabited	1931	453,000/174,903	New Zealand associated territory[2]
In Asia				
Bangladesh	Dhaka	1972	144,000/55,598	sovereign republic
Brunei	Bandar Seri Begawan	1984	5,800/2,239	sovereign monarchy
India	Delhi	1947	3,166,800/1,222,701	sovereign republic
Malaysia	Kuala Lumpur	1957	329,800/127,335	sovereign constitutional monarchy
Maldives	Malé	1982	300/115	sovereign republic
Pakistan	Islamabad	1947[6]	803,900/310,385	sovereign republic
Singapore	Singapore	1965	600/231	sovereign republic
Sri Lanka	Colombo	1948	66,000/25,482	sovereign republic
In Australasia and the Pacific				
Australia	Canberra	1931	7,682,300/2,966,136	sovereign constitutional monarchy[5]
Cook Islands	Avarua	1931	300/115	New Zealand associated territory[2]
Fiji Islands	Suva	1970[7]	18,274/7,056	sovereign republic
Norfolk Island	Kingston	1931	34/13	Australian external territory[2]
Kiribati	Tawawa	1979	700/270	sovereign republic
Nauru	Yaren	1968	21/8	sovereign republic
New Zealand	Wellington	1931	268,000/103,474	sovereign constitutional monarchy[5]
Niue	Alofi	1931	300/115	New Zealand associated territory[2]
Papua New Guinea	Port Moresby	1975	462,800/178,687	sovereign constitutional monarchy[5]
Pitcairn Islands	Adamstown	1931	5/2	British dependent territory[2]
Solomon Islands	Honiara	1978	27,600/10,656	sovereign constitutional monarchy[5]
Tokelau	Nukunonu	1931	10/3.8	New Zealand associated territory[2]
Tonga	Nuku'alofa	1970	700/270	sovereign monarchy
Tuvalu	Funafuti	1978	24/9	sovereign constitutional monarchy[5]
Vanuatu	Villa	1980	15,000/5,791	sovereign republic
Western Samoa	Apia	1970	2,800/1,081	sovereign republic

(*continued*)

The British Commonwealth (*continued*)

Country	Capital	Date joined	Area in sq km/sq mi	Constitutional status
In Europe				
Channel Islands		1931	200/77	UK crown dependencies[2]
Guernsey	St Peter Port			
Jersey	St Helier			
Cyprus	Nicosia	1961	9,000/3,474	sovereign republic
Gibraltar	Gibraltar	1931	6/2	British dependent territory[2]
Malta	Valletta	1964	300/115	sovereign republic
Isle of Man	Douglas	1931	600/231	UK crown dependency[2]
United Kingdom	London	1931	244,100/94,247	sovereign constitutional monarchy[5]
England	London			
Northern Ireland	Belfast			
Scotland	Edinburgh			
Wales	Cardiff			
Total			34,310,000/13,247,091	

[1] Suspended 1995.
[2] Dependencies of full sovereign Commonwealth members.
[3] Suspended 1997.
[4] Withdrew from membership 1961 and readmitted 1994.
[5] Queen Elizabeth II constitutional monarch and head of state.
[6] Left 1972 and rejoined 1989.
[7] Left 1987 and rejoined 1997.

Constitution and Important Legislation

Constitution of the United Kingdom

The United Kingdom is one of the few countries not to adopt a written constitution; instead it has an accumulation of customs and precedents, together with a body of laws defining certain of its aspects. The most important laws affecting constitutional matters, both current and historic, are described in this section.

Magna Carta, 1215

Essentially a historic document of feudal times, this charter was granted by King John at Runnymede on 15 June 1215. It was originally proposed to the English barons in 1213 by the Archbishop of Canterbury, Stephen Langton, as a reply to the King's demands for excessive feudal dues and attacks on the privileges of the church. The charter defined the barons' obligations to the monarch, confirmed the liberties of the English church, and opposed the arbitrary application of justice. The charter was reissued with changes in 1216, 1217, and 1225. As feudalism declined, the Magna Carta lost its significance, and under the Tudors was almost forgotten. During the 17th century it was rediscovered and reinterpreted by the Parliamentary party as a democratic document. Four original copies exist: one each in Salisbury and Lincoln cathedrals and two in the British Library in London.

Petition of Right, 1628

In British law, the procedure whereby, before the passing of the Crown Proceedings Act 1947, a subject petitioned for legal relief against the crown, for example for money due under a contract, or for property of which the crown had taken possession. The most important example is that drawn up by Edward Coke (former Lord Chief Justice of England) and accepted by Charles I in 1628, declaring illegal: taxation without parliamentary consent, imprisonment without trial, billeting of soldiers on private persons, and use of martial law. When Parliament challenged Charles over military funding in 1629, he dissolved Parliament, imprisoned its leaders, and ruled without parliament until his execution in 1640.

Habeas Corpus, 1679

Writ directed to someone who has custody of a person, ordering them to bring the person before the court issuing the writ, and to justify why the person is detained in custody. Embodied in the English Habeas Corpus Act 1679 by Anthony Ashley Cooper, 1st Earl of Shaftesbury. The main principles were adopted in the US Constitution. The Scottish equivalent is the Wrongous Imprisonment Act 1701.

English Bill of Rights Act, 1689

The Bill of Rights embodied the Declaration of Rights (the statement issued by the Convention Parliament which contained the conditions on which William and Mary were offered the throne). The act made illegal the suspension of laws by royal authority without Parliament's consent; the power to dispense with laws; the establishment of special courts of law; levying money by royal prerogative without Parliament's consent; and the maintenance of a standing army in peacetime without Parliament's consent. It also asserted a right to petition the sovereign, freedom of parliamentary elections, freedom of speech in parliamentary debates, and the necessity of frequent Parliaments.

The Bill of Rights is the nearest approach to a written constitution that the UK possesses. Its provisions, where applicable, were incorporated in the US Constitution ratified in 1788.

Act of Settlement, 1701

A law passed during the reign of King William III to ensure a Protestant succession to the throne by allowing only descendants of Princess Sophia the Electress of Hanover (granddaughter of James I) to succeed. The act excluded the Roman Catholic descendants of James II. Elizabeth II still reigns under this act.

Acts of Union

Several statutes that accomplished the joining of England with Wales (1536), England and Wales with Scotland (1707), and Great Britain with Ireland (1801).

Act of Union of 1536 The Act of Union passed in 1536, during the reign of King Henry VIII, the second English monarch descended from the Welsh House of Tudor. The Act formally united England and Wales. By its terms, the Welsh Marches, estates held for centuries by semi-independent Marcher lords, became several new counties or were added to older counties. Counties and boroughs in Wales were granted representation in the English Parliament.

Act of Union of 1707 The Act of Union passed in 1707 by the parliaments of England and Scotland created the Kingdom of Great Britain. Although Scotland retained its judicial system and its Presbyterian church, its parliament was joined with that of England. The crowns of the two countries had been united in 1603 when James Stuart (James VI of Scotland) succeeded Elizabeth I as James I of England, but the kingdoms otherwise remained separate.

Act of Union of 1801 The Act of Union, which was passed in 1800 and went into effect on 1 January 1801, joined the Kingdom of Great Britain and all of Ireland into the United Kingdom of Great Britain and Ireland. The act was revoked when the Irish Free State was constituted in 1922.

Triennial and Septennial Acts

Acts affecting the length of Parliament and the frequency of its meetings.

1641 Triennial Act required that Parliament should meet every three years, for at least 50 days.
1664 Triennial Act reinstated the act of 1641 which had fallen into abeyance.
1694 Triennial Act stipulated that Parliament should meet at least once every three years and not last more than three years.
1716 Septennial Act extended the term of a Parliament from three to seven years.

Reform Acts

UK acts of Parliament that extended voting rights and redistributed parliamentary seats, also known as Representation of the People Acts.

1832 Reform Act abolished pocket and rotten boroughs (English parliamentary constituencies that returned members to Parliament in spite of having a small numbers of electors, thus leading to an unrepresentative House), redistributed seats on a more equitable basis in the counties, and formed some new boroughs. The franchise was extended to male householders in property worth £10 a year or more in the boroughs and to owners of freehold property worth £2 a year, £10 copyholders, or £50 leaseholders in the counties.
1867 (Second) Reform Act redistributed seats from corrupt and small boroughs to the counties and large urban areas. It also extended the franchise in boroughs to adult male heads of households, and in counties to males who owned, or held on long leases, land worth £5 a year, or who occupied land worth £12 on which they paid poor rates.
1884 (Third) Reform Act extended the franchise to male agricultural labourers.
1918 Representation of The People Act gave the vote to men over the age of 21 and women over the age of 30.
1928 Representation of The People Act extended the vote to women to over the age of 21.
1948 Representation of The People Act abolished the right, held by certain individuals, to have more than one vote.
1969 Representation of The People Act reduced the minimum age of voting to 18.

Parliament Acts

The Parliament Act of 1911 A statute which prohibited the House of Lords from interfering with financial legislation passed by the House of Commons and abolished the power of the Lords to reject other types of legislation passed by the Commons, restricting them to delaying it for up to two years. The law also reduced the maximum life of a parliament from seven years to five. The act was introduced after the Lords rejected Lloyd George's radical People's Budget of 1909. It was fiercely resisted by the Lords and only received their assent when George V agreed to create sufficient Liberal peers to force it through.

The Parliament Act of 1949 This act further limited the period the Lords could delay legislation to one year.

National Government

Prime Ministers of Great Britain and the UK

Term	Name	Party
1721–42	Robert Walpole[1]	Whig
1742–43	Spencer Compton, Earl of Wilmington	Whig
1743–54	Henry Pelham	Whig
1754–56	Thomas Pelham-Holles, 1st Duke of Newcastle	Whig
1756–57	William Cavendish, 4th Duke of Devonshire	Whig
1757–62	Thomas Pelham-Holles, 1st Duke of Newcastle	Whig
1762–63	John Stuart, 3rd Earl of Bute	Tory
1763–65	George Grenville	Whig
1765–66	Charles Watson Wentworth, 2nd Marquess of Rockingham	Whig
1766–68	William Pitt, 1st Earl of Chatham	Tory
1768–70	Augustus Henry Fitzroy, 3rd Duke of Grafton	Whig
1770–82	Frederick North, Lord North[2]	Tory
1782	Charles Watson Wentworth, 2nd Marquess of Rockingham	Whig
1782–83	William Petty-Fitzmaurice, 2nd Earl of Shelburne[3]	Whig
1783	William Henry Cavendish-Bentinck, 3rd Duke of Portland	Whig
1783–1801	William Pitt, The Younger	Tory
1801–04	Henry Addington	Tory
1804–06	William Pitt, The Younger	Tory
1806–07	William Wyndham Grenville, 1st Baron Grenville	Whig
1807–09	William Henry Cavendish-Bentinck, 3rd Duke of Portland	Whig
1809–12	Spencer Perceval	Tory
1812–27	Robert Banks Jenkinson, 2nd Earl of Liverpool	Tory
1827	George Canning	Tory
1827–28	Frederick John Robinson, 1st Viscount Goderich	Tory
1828–30	Arthur Wellesley, 1st Duke of Wellington	Tory
1830–34	Charles Grey, 2nd Earl Grey	Whig
1834	William Lamb, 2nd Viscount Melbourne	Whig
1834	Arthur Wellesley, 1st Duke of Wellington	Tory
1834–35	Sir Robert Peel, 2nd Baronet	Tory
1835–41	William Lamb, 2nd Viscount Melbourne	Whig
1841–46	Sir Robert Peel, 2nd Baronet	Conservative
1846–52	John Russell, Lord Russell	Whig-Liberal
1852	Edward Geoffrey Stanley, 14th Earl of Derby	Conservative

(*continued*)

Prime Ministers of Great Britain and the UK (*continued*)

Term	Name	Party
1852–55	George Hamilton-Gordon, 4th Earl of Aberdeen	Peelite
1855–58	Henry John Temple, 3rd Viscount Palmerston	Liberal
1858–59	Edward Geoffrey Stanley, 14th Earl of Derby	Conservative
1859–65	Henry John Temple, 3rd Viscount Palmerston	Liberal
1865–66	John Russell, 1st Earl Russell	Liberal
1866–68	Edward Geoffrey Stanley, 14th Earl of Derby	Conservative
1868	Benjamin Disraeli	Conservative
1868–74	William Ewart Gladstone	Liberal
1874–80	Benjamin Disraeli[4]	Conservative
1880–85	William Ewart Gladstone	Liberal
1885–86	Robert Cecil, 3rd Marquess of Salisbury	Conservative
1886	William Ewart Gladstone	Liberal
1886–92	Robert Cecil, 3rd Marquess of Salisbury	Conservative
1892–94	William Ewart Gladstone	Liberal
1894–95	Archibald Philip Primrose, 5th Earl of Rosebery	Liberal
1895–1902	Robert Cecil, 3rd Marquess of Salisbury	Conservative
1902–05	Arthur James Balfour	Conservative
1905–08	Sir Henry Campbell-Bannerman	Liberal
1908–16	Herbert Henry Asquith	Liberal
1916–22	David Lloyd George	Liberal
1922–23	Bonar Law	Conservative
1923–24	Stanley Baldwin	Conservative
1924	Ramsay Macdonald	Labour
1924–29	Stanley Baldwin	Conservative
1929–35	Ramsay Macdonald	Labour
1935–37	Stanley Baldwin	Conservative
1937–40	Neville Chamberlain	Conservative
1940–45	Winston Churchill	Conservative
1945–51	Clement Attlee	Labour
1951–55	Winston Churchill[5]	Conservative
1955–57	Sir Anthony Eden	Conservative
1957–63	Harold Macmillan	Conservative
1963–64	Sir Alec Douglas-Home	Conservative
1964–70	Harold Wilson	Labour
1970–74	Edward Heath	Conservative
1974–76	Harold Wilson	Labour
1976–79	James Callaghan	Labour
1979–90	Margaret Thatcher	Conservative
1990–97	John Major	Conservative
1997–	Tony Blair	Labour

[1] From 1725, Sir Robert Walpole.
[2] From 1790, 2nd Earl of Guilford.
[3] From 1784, 1st Marquess of Lansdowne.
[4] From 1876, Earl of Beaconsfield.
[5] From 1953, Sir Winston Churchill.

UK Chancellors of the Exchequer

Date appointed	Name
July 1945	Hugh Dalton
November 1947	Sir Stafford Cripps
October 1950	Hugh Gaitskell
October 1951	'Rab' Butler
December 1955	Harold Macmillan
January 1957	Peter Thorneycroft
January 1958	Derick Heathcoat-Amory
July 1960	Selwyn Lloyd
July 1962	Reginald Maudling
October 1964	James Callaghan
November 1967	Roy Jenkins
June 1970	Iain Macleod
July 1970	Anthony Barber
March 1974	Denis Healey
May 1979	Sir Geoffrey Howe
June 1983	Nigel Lawson
October 1989	John Major
November 1990	Norman Lamont
May 1993	Kenneth Clarke
May 1997	Gordon Brown

UK Leaders of the House of Commons

Date appointed	Name
July 1945	Herbert Morrison
March 1951	Chuter Ede
October 1951	Harry Crookshank
April 1955	'Rab' Butler
October 1961	Iain Macleod
October 1963	Selwyn Lloyd
October 1964	Herbert Bowden
August 1966	Richard Crossman
April 1968	Fred Peart
June 1970	William Whitelaw
April 1972	Robert Carr
November 1972	James Prior
March 1974	Edward Short
April 1976	Michael Foot
May 1979	Norman St John Stevas
January 1981	Francis Pym
April 1982	John Biffen
June 1987	John Wakeham
July 1989	Sir Geoffrey Howe
November 1990	John MacGregor
April 1992	Tony Newton
May 1997	Ann Taylor
July 1998	Margaret Beckett

The Future of Governance in Britain

by George Jones

Tony Blair has redrawn the constitutional map of Britain. When he came to power in May 1997, the United Kingdom was one of the most centralized states in Europe. However, the country enters the new millennium with a Scottish Parliament, a Welsh Assembly, and proportional representation (PR) having established a bridgehead in the British voting system.

The prime minister has described the government's constitutional reforms as the 'biggest programme of change to democracy ever proposed'. Yet most people have still to appreciate the extent of the upheaval in the way they are governed. The changes already implemented by Blair's government – and those still on the drawing board – will have profound implications for the governance of the country. But the consequences of reform will be cumulative and are likely to become apparent gradually over the next decade.

Devolution of power

Westminster is no longer the all-powerful central focus of the British constitution. The House of Commons is being squeezed from above and below. It has already ceded key powers over economic, trade, and industrial decisions to the EU Commission in Brussels and is now transferring responsibilities over domestic issues such as health and education to the Scottish Parliament and Welsh Assembly, while an independent Bank of England takes decisions on interest rates.

Most people have still to appreciate the extent of the upheaval in the way they are governed.

The first result of devolution has been the re-introduction of coalition politics into the country's system of government. The two-party battle between Labour and the Conservatives, which has dominated British political life since the 1920s, has ended. Labour opted to go it alone with a minority administration in Wales but agreed a power-sharing deal with the Liberal Democrats in Scotland. In both Scotland and Wales, the nationalists are the main rivals to Labour – which emerged as the biggest party but without overall control. The Scottish National Party now has a platform on which to step up the campaign for its ultimate goal of Scottish independence.

Growing pains are likely as Westminster's celtic siblings establish themselves. Devolution has already released political forces that had been suppressed under the tight grip of Westminster. Blair, while being generous in devolving power, has shown a desire to maintain control from London. But if devolution is to work he will have to let go.

Reform of the Lords and PR

While the prime minister can claim credit for the speedy delivery of devolution, other elements of his grand constitutional redesign are in trouble. The right of hereditary peers to sit and vote in the House of Lords is being abolished. But there is no clear idea on whether an elected senate, a nominated House of so-called 'government cronies', or a hybrid of both should replace them – or what its powers should be.

Hardly had the dust settled on the outcome of the Scottish and Welsh elections before critics of PR were claiming it was the final nail in the coffin for electoral reform for Westminster. These were the first elections on the British mainland using a form of PR – with a top-up system of seats to reflect the support for the parties. But they gave Blair a sight of a future without a parliamentary majority, ending a Labour dominance in Scotland and Wales that had been taken for granted. PR also paved the way for a Tory revival in both Scotland and Wales, where they had lost all their Westminster seats in 1997. Now they have re-established a presence with MPs in the Scottish Parliament and members in the Welsh Assembly.

Even before Blair had seen PR in action, he had effectively kicked the issue into the long grass because of Cabinet opposition. An independent commission on the voting system headed by Lord Jenkins of Hillhead, the former SDP leader and one of Blair's mentors, recommended replacing the current first-past-the-post system for Westminster elections with Alternative Vote Top-up, designed to reflect voters' party preferences more accurately. But the report admitted that there could be no change until at least 2006 – after the next general election. Meanwhile, Downing Street stressed that there was 'no need to rush' and cast doubt on whether Blair would fulfil Labour's manifesto to hold a referendum on reform before the next election.

But the PR argument is not over – and if the new consensus politics in Scotland proves popular, demand for reform could spread to Westminster.

The Scottish Parliament is already looking at introducing PR for local council elections as a way of reviving interest in town hall polls. If Labour's Commons majority is cut at the next election, interest in PR will be revived as a way of cementing the centre-left alliance and keeping a renewed Tory party out of power for a generation.

A devolved England?

England was hardly mentioned in the devolution legislation. But some Tory MPs are already campaigning for an English parliament and devolution seems certain to highlight a current constitutional – and growing economic – imbalance in favour of Scotland and Wales.

London is to get its own mayor and a 25-strong directly elected assembly in May 2000. Elected mayors are an American-style concept which Labour hopes will help revive interest in local government. The London mayor will have a powerful popular mandate – but limited powers. The mayor will take a 'strategic view' on how London is run, particularly transport, the environment, and tourism, and the assembly will scrutinize his or her actions. There will be no devolution of central government's powers to London. But if London's elected mayor proves a success, other large cities are are likely to get one too.

Ministers have promised that after the next election devolution will be granted to any English region that wants it. But with little public demand so far, the government has adopted an evolutionary approach. Initially, to help foster the regional identity lacking in many parts of the country, the government has created Regional Development Agencies in nine English regions – the North East, North West, Yorkshire and the Humber, West Midlands, East Midlands, Eastern Region, South West, South East, and London – to promote economic development.

Local councils are being encouraged to join together to form voluntary regional chambers. Before directly elected regional government is introduced, there will have to be clear evidence of popular support. First, there must be a plan for devolution drawn up and approved by the regional chamber indicating it is supported by the majority of local authorities in the region; the plan must then be approved by Parliament; and there must be clear evidence of popular suppport, probably including a referendum locally. Regional devolution would almost certainly require further reorganization of local government in England. Regional assemblies would replace the county councils, bringing to an end county government in England.

The new constitutional settlement is likely to be seen as the major achievement of Blair's first term. But there is concern that the changes are being introduced piecemeal. An unwritten constitution that evolved gradually over 600 years is being dismantled at a fast pace – without any overall strategic vision of what Britain's system of government should look like in the 21st century.

George Jones is chief political editor for the Daily Telegraph

UK Secretaries of State for Foreign and Commonwealth Affairs

Known as Secretary of State for Foreign Affairs before 1968.

Date appointed	Name
July 1945	Ernest Bevin
March 1951	Herbert Morrison
October 1951	Sir Anthony Eden
December 1955	Selwyn Lloyd
July 1960	Earl of Home
October 1963	'Rab' Butler
October 1964	Patrick Gordon-Walker
January 1965	Michael Stewart
August 1966	George Brown
March 1968	Michael Stewart
June 1970	Sir Alec Douglas-Home
March 1974	James Callaghan
April 1976	Anthony Crosland
February 1977	David Owen
May 1979	Lord Carrington
April 1982	Francis Pym
June 1983	Sir Geoffrey Howe
June 1989	John Major
October 1989	Douglas Hurd
July 1995	Malcolm Rifkind
May 1997	Robin Cook

UK Secretaries of State for Home Affairs

Date appointed	Name
August 1945	Chuter Ede
October 1951	Sir David Maxwell Fyfe
October 1954	Gwilym Lloyd-George
January 1957	'Rab' Butler
July 1962	Henry Brooke
October 1964	Sir Frank Soskice
December 1965	Roy Jenkins
November 1967	James Callaghan
June 1970	Reginald Maudling
July 1972	Robert Carr
March 1974	Roy Jenkins
September 1976	Merlyn Rees
May 1979	William Whitelaw
June 1983	Leon Brittan
September 1985	Douglas Hurd
October 1989	David Waddington
November 1990	Kenneth Baker
April 1992	Kenneth Clarke
May 1993	Michael Howard
May 1997	Jack Straw

UK Secretaries of State for Defence

Known as Minister of Defence before 1964.

Date appointed	Name	Date appointed	Name	Date appointed	Name
July 1945	Clement Attlee	January 1957	Duncan Sandys	January 1981	John Nott
December 1946	Alan Alexander	October 1959	Harold Watkinson	January 1983	Michael Heseltine
February 1950	Emanuel Shinwell	July 1962	Peter Thorneycroft	January 1986	George Younger
October 1951	Winston Churchill	October 1964	Denis Healey	July 1989	Tom King
March 1952	Earl Alexander of Tunis	June 1970	Lord Carrington	April 1992	Malcolm Rifkind
October 1954	Harold Macmillan	January 1974	Ian Gilmour	July 1995	Michael Portillo
April 1955	Selwyn Lloyd	March 1974	Roy Mason	May 1997	George Robertson
December 1955	Sir Walter Monckton	September 1976	Fred Mulley		
October 1956	Anthony Head	May 1979	Francis Pym		

UK Cabinet Ministers

Position	Cabinet ministers
Prime Minister, First Lord of the Treasury, and Minister for the Civil Service	Tony Blair
Deputy Prime Minister and Secretary of State for the Environment, Transport, and the Regions	John Prescott
Chancellor of the Exchequer	Gordon Brown
Secretary of State for Foreign and Commonwealth Affairs	Robin Cook
Lord Chancellor	Lord Irvine of Lairg
Secretary of State for the Home Department	Jack Straw
Secretary of State for Education and Employment	David Blunkett
President of the Council and Leader of the House of Commons[1]	Margaret Beckett
Minister for the Cabinet Office and Chancellor of the Duchy of Lancaster[2]	Jack Cunningham
Secretary of State for Scotland and First Minister of the Scottish Parliament	John Reid
Secretary of State for Defence	George Robertson
Secretary of State for Health	Frank Dobson
Parliamentary Secretary to the Treasury (Chief Whip)	Ann Taylor
Secretary of State for Culture, Media, and Sport	Chris Smith
Secretary of State for Northern Ireland	Mo (Marjorie) Mowlam
Secretary of State for International Development	Clare Short
Secretary of State for Social Security	Alistair Darling
Secretary of State for Agriculture, Fisheries, and Food	Nick Brown
Leader of the House of Lords, Secretary of State for Women, and Lord Privy Seal[3]	Baroness Jay of Paddington
Secretary of State for Trade and Industry	Stephen Byers
Chief Secretary to the Treasury	Alan Milburn
Secretary of State for Wales	Paul Murphy
Minister of State, Department of the Environment, Transport, and the Regions, with responsibility for Transport[4]	Helen Liddell
Government Chief Whip, House of Lords[4]	The Lord Carter

[1] Also in charge of Millennium Bug preparations.
[2] The Minister is appointed as Chancellor of the Duchy of Lancaster.
[3] The Minister is appointed as Lord Privy Seal.
[4] Not members of the Cabinet, but will attend Cabinet metings.

UK Government Departments

(– = not applicable.)

Department	Address	Responsibilities	Title	Ministers	Executive agencies
Agriculture, Fisheries, and Food (Ministry of)	3–8 Whitehall Place, London SW1A 2HH; phone: (0171) 270 3000	agriculture, horticulture, fisheries, and food; related environmental and rural issues	Minister Ministers of State	Nick Brown Joyce Quin Baroness Hayman	Central Science Laboratory; Intervention Board; Centre for Environment, Fisheries, and Aquaculture Science; Farming and Rural Conservation Agency; Meat Hygiene Service; Pesticides Safety Directorate; Veterinary Laboratories Agency; Veterinary Medicines Directorate

(continued)

UK Government Departments (*continued*)

Department	Address	Responsibilities	Title	Ministers	Executive agencies
Cabinet Office (Office of Public Service)	70 Whitehall, London SW1A 2AS; phone: (0171) 270 3000	key policy areas and issues include: Citizen's Charter; freedom of information; improving the effectiveness and efficiency of central government; machinery of government and standards; Her Majesty's Stationery Office; historical government records and official histories; public bodies and public appointments; quangos; MPs' and MEPs' pay; management of the civil service; Central Office of Information	Minister for the Cabinet Office and Chancellor of the Duchy of Lancaster	Jack Cunningham	The Buying Agency; Central Computer and Telecommunications Agency; Civil Service College; Government Car and Despatch Agency; Property Advisers to the Civil Estate; Security Facilities Executive
			Minister of State	Lord Falconer	
			Lord Privy Seal and Leader of the House of Lords	Baroness Jay	
			Under Secretary of State, Office of Public Service	Ian McCartney	
Culture, Media, and Sport	2–4 Cockspur Street, London SW1Y 5DH; phone: (0171) 211 6000	the arts; public libraries; national museums; tourism; sport; film industry; press regulation; the National Lottery	Secretary of State	Chris Smith	Historic Royal Palaces Agency; Royal Parks Agency
			Minister for Tourism, Film, and Broadcasting	Janet Anderson	
			Minister for Sport	Kate Hoey	
			Minister for the Arts	Alan Howarth	
Defence	Main Building, Whitehall, London SW1A 2HB; phone: (0171) 218 9000	defence policy; control and administration of the armed services	Secretary of State	George Robertson	Armed Forces Personnel Administration Agency; Army Base Repair Organization; Army Base Storage and Distribution Agency; Army Personnel Centre; Army Technical Support Agency; Army Training and Recruitment Agency; Defence Analytical Services Agency; Defence Animal Centre; Defence Bills Agency; Defence Clothing and Textiles Agency; Defence Codification Agency; Defence Communication Services Agency; Defence Dental Agency; Defence Estate Organization; Defence Evaluation and Research Agency; Defence Intelligence and Security Centre; Defence Medical Training Organization; Defence Postal and Courier Services Agency; Defence Secondary Care Agency; Defence Transport and Movements Executive; Defence Vetting Agency; Disposal Sales Agency; Duke of York's Royal Military School; Hydrographic Office; Joint Air Reconnaissance Intelligence Centre Agency; Logistic Information Systems Agency; Medical Supplies Agency; Meteorological Office; Military Survey; Ministry of Defence Police; Naval Aircraft Repair Organization; Naval Bases and Supply Agency; Naval Manning Agency; Naval Recruiting and Training Agency; Pay and Personnel Agency; Queen Victoria School; RAF Logistics Support Service; RAF Maintenance Group; RAF Personnel Management Agency; RAF Signals Engineering Establishment; RAF Training Group; Service Children's Education; Ships Support Agency; Specialist Procurement Services
			Minister for Defence Procurement	Baroness Symons of Vernham Dean	
			Minister for Armed Forces	John Spellar	
			Under Secretary of State	Peter Kilfoyle	

(*continued*)

UK Government Departments (*continued*)

Department	Address	Responsibilities	Title	Ministers	Executive agencies
Education and Employment	Sanctuary Buildings, Great Smith Street, London SW1P 3BT; phone: (0171) 925 5000	school, college, and university education; the Careers Service, Employment Service; youth and adult training policy and programmes; equal opportunities in employment, social policy, and programmes in Europe	Secretary of State	David Blunkett	Employment Service
			Minister for Employment, Welfare to Work, and Equal Opportunites	Andrew Smith	
			Minister for School Standards	Estelle Morris	
			Minister for Education and Employment	Baroness Blackstone	
			Under Secretaries of State	Malcolm Wicks	
				Margaret Hodge	
				Jacqui Smith	
				Michael Wills	
Environment, Transport, and the Regions	2 Marsham Street, London SW1P 3EB; phone: (0171) 890 3000	land use planning; housing; construction industry; environmental protection; water industry; urban and rural regeneration; countryside and wildlife protection; local government finance and structure; land, sea, and air transport; domestic and international civil aviation; shipping and ports; marine pollution; regulation of the road haulage industry; motorways and trunk roads; London Transport; British Rail; Railtrack; Civil Aviation Authority	Deputy Prime Minister and Secretary of State for the Environment, Transport, and the Regions	John Prescott	Coastguard Agency; Driver and Vehicle Licensing Agency; Driving Standards Agency; Highways Agency; Marine Safety Agency; Ordnance Survey; Planning Inspectorate; Queen Elizabeth II Conference Centre; Vehicle Certification Agency; Vehicle Inspectorate
			Minister for the Environment	Michael Meacher	
			Minister for Local Government and Housing	Hilary Armstrong	
			Minister for the Regions, Regeneration, and Planning	Nick Raynsford	
			Minister for Transport	Lord Macdonald of Tradeston	
			Under Secretaries of State	Keith Hill	
				Lord Whitty	
				Chris Mullin	
				Beverley Hughes	
Foreign and Commonwealth Affairs	Whitehall, London SW1A 2AH; phone: (0171) 270 3000	Britain's overseas relations, including relations with overseas governments and international organizations, administration of British Dependent Territories, promoting British trade and exports, protecting British interests, and the welfare of Britons abroad	Secretary of State	Robin Cook	Wilton Park Conference Centre
			Ministers of State	Geoff Hoon (Europe)	
				Peter Hain	
				John Battle	
				Baroness Scotland of Asthal	

(*continued*)

UK Government Departments (*continued*)

Department	Address	Responsibilities	Title	Ministers	Executive agencies
Health	Richmond House, 79 Whitehall, London SW1A 2NS; phone: (0171) 210 3000	National Health Service; local authority social services; public health issues, including the health consequences of environmental and food issues	Secretary of State	Frank Dobson	Medical Devices Agency; Medicines Control Agency; NHS Estates; NHS Pensions Agency
			Minister of State	John Denham	
			Minister for Public Health	Tessa Jowell	
			Under Secretaries of State	Lord Hunt of Kings Heath	
				John Hutton	
				Gisela Stuart	
Home Office	50 Queen Anne's Gate, London SW1H 9AT; phone: (0171) 273 4000	criminal law, probation and prison services; the police; crime prevention; licensing laws; passports, immigration, and nationality; race relations; administration of justice	Secretary of State	Jack Straw	Fire Service College; Forensic Science Service; HM Prison Service; UK Passport Agency
			Ministers of State	Paul Boateng	
				Charles Clarke	
				Barbara Roche	
			Under Secretaries of State	Mike O'Brien	
				Lord Bassam of Brighton	
International Development (formerly the Overseas Development Agency – ODA)	94 Victoria Street, London SW1E 5JL; phone: (0171) 917 7000	Britain's overseas aid to developing countries; global environmental assistance; overseas superannuation	Secretary of State	Clare Short	–
			Under Secretary of State	George Foulkes	
Lord Advocate's Department	Dover House, Whitehall, London SW1A 2AU; phone: (0171) 270 3000; Crown Office, 25 Chambers Street, Edinburgh EH1 1LA; phone: (0131) 226 2626	advises the Scottish Parliament on all issues of Scottish law	Lord Advocate	Lord Hardie	–
			Solicitor General for Scotland	Lynda Clarke	
Lord Chancellor's Department	House of Lords, London SW1A 2AZ; phone: (0171) 210 8500	procedure of civil courts and administration of the Supreme Court, county courts, and tribunals under the Court Service executive agency; legal aid and promotion of general reforms in civil law (England and Wales); Northern Ireland Court Service	Lord Chancellor	Lord Irving of Lairg	Court Service; Public Trust Service. Two further agencies, HM Land Registry and the Public Record Office, report to the Lord Chancellor but are departments in their own right and not part of the Lord Chancellor's Department
			Under Secretaries of State	Keith Vaz	
				David Lock	
Law Officers' Department	9 Buckingham Gate, London SE1E 6JP; phone: (0171) 828 7155	chief legal advisor to the government; all Crown litigation; Law Officers' departments (the Treasury Solicitor's Department, the Crown Prosecution Service, the Serious Fraud Office, and the Legal Secretariat to the Law Officers); aspects of civil and criminal law	Attorney-General	Lord Williams of Mostyn	Treasury Solicitor's Department
			Solicitor-General	Ross Cranston	

(*continued*)

UK Government Departments (*continued*)

Department	Address	Responsibilities	Title	Ministers	Executive agencies
Northern Ireland Office	Stormont Castle, Belfast BT4 3ST; phone: (01232) 763011; Whitehall, London SW1A 2AZ; phone: (0171) 210 3000	constitutional developments; law and order; security and electoral issues	Secretary of State	Marjorie (Mo) Mowlam	The Compensation Agency; Forensic Science Agency of Northern Ireland; Northern Ireland Prison Service
			Minister of State	Adam Ingram	
			Under Secretaries of State	George Howarth	
				John McFall	
				Lord Dubs	
Scottish Office	St Andrew's House, Regent Road, Edinburgh EH1 3DG; phone: (0131) 556 8400; Dover House, Whitehall, London SW1A 2AU; phone: (0171) 270 3000	foreign affairs, defence, taxation, social security, company regulation, economic management; most other areas of responsibility have devolved to the Scottish Parliament	Secretary of State	John Reid	–
			Minister of State	Brian Wilson	–
Social Security	Richmond House, 79 Whitehall, London SW1A 2NS; phone: (0171) 238 0800	the British social security system	Secretary of State for Social Security	Alistair Darling	Benefits Agency; Child Support Agency; Contributions Agency; Information Technology Services Agency; War Pensions Agency
			Minister of State	Jeff Rooker	
			Under Secretaries of State	Hugh Bayley	
				Angela Eagle	
				Baroness Hollis of Heigham	
Trade and Industry	1 Victoria Street, London SW1H 0ET; phone: (0171) 215 5000	industrial and commercial affairs; innovation policy; regional industrial policy; international trade policy; competition policy; small businesses; business and education; industrial relations; employment legislation	Secretary of State for Trade and Industry	Stephen Byers	Companies House; Employment Tribunals Service; Insolvency Service; National Weights and Measures Laboratory; Patent Office; Radiocommunications Agency
			Ministers of State	Helen Liddell	
				Richard Caborn	
				Patricia Hewitt	
			Under Secretaries of State	Kim Howells	
				Alan Johnson	
				Lord Sainsbury of Turville	
HM Treasury	Parliament Street, London SW1P 3AG; phone: (0171) 270 3000	overseeing of Britain's tax and monetary policy; planning and control of public spending; international financial relations; civil service management	Prime Minister, First Lord of the Treasury, and Minister for the Civil Service	Tony Blair	National Savings; Office for National Statistics
			Chancellor of the Exchequer	Gordon Brown	
			Chief Secretary	Alan Milburn	
			Financial Secretary	Stephen Timms	
			Paymaster General	Dawn Primarolo	
			Economic Secretary	Melanie Johnson	

(*continued*)

UK Government Departments (*continued*)

Department	Address	Responsibilities	Title	Ministers	Executive agencies
Welsh Office	New Crown Building, Cathays Park, Cardiff CF1 3NQ; phone: (01222) 825111; Gwydyr House, Whitehall, London SW1A 2ER; phone: (0171) 270 3000	foreign affairs, defence, taxation, social security, broadcasting, overall economic policy; other areas of responsibility have devolved to the Welsh Assembly	Secretary of State and First Secretary to the Welsh Assembly	Paul Murphy	–
			Under Secretary of State	David Hanson	

UK Government Agencies

Agency	Address	Key responsibilities
Central Office of Information	Hercules Road, London SE1 7DU; phone: (0171) 928 2345	offers consultancy and procurement services for publicity material to government departments and agencies and other public-sector bodies; a department in its own right, reporting to the Minister for the Cabinet Office
Crown Prosecution Service	50 Ludgate Hill, London EC4M 7EX; phone: (0171) 273 8000	independently reviews and conducts criminal proceedings begun by the police in England and Wales, except for cases conducted by the Serious Fraud Office; headed by the Director of Public Prosecutions, who is accountable to the Attorney-General
ECGD (Export Credits Guarantee Department)	PO Box 2200, 2 Exchange Tower, Harbour Exchange Square, London E14 9GS; phone: (0171) 512 7000	supports the export of capital and project-related goods and services from the UK; provides insurance to British project and capital goods exporters against not being paid for goods and services; insures new British investment overseas; reports to the Secretary of State for Trade and Industry
Government Offices for the Regions	1/A3 Eland House, Bressenden Place, London SW1E 5DU; phone: (0171) 890 5157	coordinates resources, personnel policy, promoting economic development, and administration for the Government Offices for the Regions (Eastern, East Midlands, London, Merseyside, North-East, North-West, South-East, South-West, West Midlands, Yorkshire and Humberside); reports to the Secretary of State for the Environment, Transport, and the Regions, the President of the Board of Trade, and the Secretary of State for Education and Employment
Her Majesty's Customs and Excise	New King's Beam House, 22 Upper Ground, London SE1 9PJ; phone: (0171) 620 1313	collects and accounts for Customs and Excise revenues; controls imports and exports, compiles trade statistics; polices prohibited goods; reports to the Chancellor of the Exchequer
Her Majesty's Land Registry	Lincoln's Inn Fields, London WC2A 3PH; phone: (0171) 955 0110	registers title to land in England and Wales and records dealings once the property is registered, maintains register of landowners and guarantees their title; provides system for transfer and mortgage of land; executive agency responsible to the Lord Chancellor
Her Majesty's Procurator General and Treasury Solicitor	Queen Anne's Chambers, 28 Broadway, London SW1H 9JS; phone: (0171) 210 3000	provides legal services to many government departments, agencies, and public bodies, including litigation and general legal advice; instructs Parliamentary Counsel on drafting legislation; reports to the Attorney-General
Her Majesty's Stationery Office	St Clements House, 2–16 Colegate, Norwich NR3 1BQ; phone: (01603) 621000	body within the Office of Public Service with responsibilities for printing legislation and government publications; controls and administers Crown copyright and administers parliamentary copyright
Inland Revenue	Somerset House, London WC2R 1LB; phone: (0171) 438 6622	collection and administration of direct taxes in Britain; reports to the Chancellor of the Exchequer
Legal Secretariat to the Law Officers	Attorney General's Chambers, 9 Buckingham Gate, London SW1E 6JP; phone: (0171) 828 7155	supports Law Officers of the Crown in their activities as the Government's main legal advisers
National Savings	Charles House, 375 Kensington High Street, London W14 8SD; phone: (0171) 605 9300	administers and sells a range of investments to personal savers, with the aim of raising funds for the government; an executive agency of the Treasury, reporting to the Chancellor of the Exchequer

(*continued*)

UK Government Agencies (*continued*)

Agency	Address	Key responsibilities
Office for National Statistics	Great George Street, London SW1P 3AQ; phone: (0171) 270 3000	agency created by merger of the Central Statistical Office and the Office of Population, Censuses, and Surveys; responsibilities include collection and interpretation of key national economic and population statistics; administration of marriage laws; local registration of births, deaths, and marriages; accountable to the Chancellor of the Exchequer
Office of Fair Trading	Field House, 15–25 Breams Buildings, London EC4A 1PR; phone: (0171) 211 8000	a non-ministerial department headed by the Director-General of Fair Trading; reviews commercial activities in the UK with the aim of protecting consumers against unfair trading practices
Office of the Data Protection Registrar	Wycliffe House, Water Lane, Wilmslow, Cheshire SK9 5AF; phone: (01625) 545745	reporting directly to Parliament, maintains public register of data users and computer bureaux, enforces data protection legislation, and investigates complaints about breaches of the Data Protection Act; reports directly to Parliament
Office of the Paymaster General	Sutherland House, Russell Way, Crawley, West Sussex RH10 1UH; phone: (01293) 560999	provides banking services for government departments and administers and pays public service pensions
Ordnance Survey	Romsey Road, Southampton SO16 4GU; phone: (01703) 792000	provides official surveying, mapping, and related scientific work in Britain and some foreign countries; reports to the Secretary of State for the Environment
Parliamentary Counsel	36 Whitehall, London SW1A 2AY; phone: (0171) 210 6633	drafts government Bills (except those that relate only to Scotland) and advises departments on parliamentary procedure in England, Wales, and Northern Ireland
Public Record Office	Ruskin Avenue, Kew, Richmond, Surrey TW9 4DU; phone: (0181) 876 3444	supervises the selection and maintenance of records of central government and courts of law, ensures their safety and preservation, and makes them available to the public; a department in its own right, reporting to the Lord Chancellor
Royal Mint	Llantrisant, Pontyclun, Mid Glamorgan CF72 8YT; phone: (01443) 222111	produces and issues coinage for Britain, including circulation coins and commemorative coins and medals
Serious Fraud Office	Elm House, 10–16 Elm Street, London WC1X 0BJ; phone: (0171) 239 7272	investigates and prosecutes serious and complex fraud in England, Wales, and Northern Ireland; reports to the Attorney-General
Treasury Solicitor's Department	Queen Anne's Chambers, 28 Broadway, London SW1H 9JS; phone: (0171) 210 3000	provides legal and litigation services for most government departments, agencies, and public bodies; a department in its own right and an executive agency of the Treasury, reporting to the Attorney-General

UK Parliament

UK Parliamentary Glossary

Term	Description
abstention	refusal by an MP to vote for or against a motion
Act of Parliament	bill passed by the Houses of Parliament (Commons and Lords) and signed by the Queen
address	formal message to the Crown, presented to the Monarch by a Commons whip when the House of Commons wishes to make a point to the Monarch; the message is answered by the Monarch and returned to the Commons by a whip or to the Lords by the Lord Chamberlain
adjournment of the House	request by an MP in the House of Commons to terminate the day's proceedings
admonition	reprimand to an MP who has done something wrong, made by the Speaker of the House of Commons
amendment	alteration proposed in a motion or a bill; amendments can be voted on in order to change what is written in a bill
back bencher	MP who does not hold office in the Government, or any senior position on the leading opposition party
ballot	paper on which an MP registers his/her vote in matters requiring the use of ballots to decide issues in Parliament
Bar of the House	marked by a leather strip, the Bar of the House is the line at the entrance to the House of Commons which non-MPs must not cross
bill	draft of an Act of Parliament, presented to either the House of Commons or the House of Lords, to vote on. If successful, the bill is forwarded for Royal Assent; if granted, it becomes an Act

(*continued*)

UK Parliamentary Glossary (*continued*)

Term	Description
Black Rod	officer of the Royal Household who looks after the doorkeepers and messengers of the House of Lords; Black Rod also issues the orders for entry into the Stranger's Gallery
budget	annual financial statement of the Chancellor of the Exchequer
by-election	election to fill a vacancy in a constituency that arises during the course of a Parliament, usually as a result of the death or resignation of an MP
catching the Speaker's eye	any MP who wishes to speak in the Houses of Commons must stand and wait for the Speaker to see him/her and give them permission to speak
clause	subdivision of an Act or bill
count	if there are less that 40 MPs present in the House of Commons, the Speaker can close the House
crossing the floor	changing allegiance from one political party to another is signified by 'crossing the floor' of the House and taking a seat with an opposing party
dissolution	bringing to an end the Parliament of the Houses of Commons and Lords by the Monarch; it is followed by a general election
father of the House	longest-serving MP in the House of Commons, currently Edward Heath
front benches	benches where members of the Government and senior opposition members sit in the House of Commons; nearest to the centre of the Table of the Commons
galleries	areas in the House of Commons set aside for the public and press to attend sittings
general election	election of a new government by all eligible voters in the country following the dissolution of Parliament
government bill	bill introduced by a Government Minister
Hansard	House of Commons' written reports
Houses of Parliament	Palace housing the House of Commons and the House of Lords
independent member	elected MP who is not a member of any recognized political party. MPs can also leave or be expelled by a political party during a Parliament and sit as independents
maiden speech	first speech in the House of Commons by a new member; traditionally, a new MP standing will be given preference over others by the Speaker
majority government	government formed by the party with the majority of seats in the House of Commons
minority government	government formed by a party that does not hold a majority of seats; it must maintain the confidence of the House in order to remain in government
oath of allegiance	oath of loyalty to the Sovereign that must be made by an MP before he/she can take his/her seat in the House of Commons
order paper	daily timetable of events in the House of Commons and the House of Lords
pairs	if an MP does not wish to vote in the Chamber, he/she has to come to an arrangement with an opposition MP who will not vote either. The overall vote is then reduced by one on each side
parliamentary procedure	rules by which the House of Commons and the House of Lords conduct their business
passage of a bill	process by which a bill obtains Parliamentary approval and becomes law. Once Parliamentary approval has been granted, the bill is forwarded to the Monarch for Royal assent
point of order	a technical or procedural breach of order can be brought to the attention of the Speaker by an MP at any time during a debate or as House business is being conducted; the Speaker decides on the validity of the matter raised and his/her decision is final
portfolio	responsibilities of a Cabinet minister
question time	time when government ministers have to answer questions put by members of the House of Commons and the House of Lords. Prime Ministers' questions are on Wednesdays; other days are rotated among other government departments
recess	period between the end of one Parliament and the start of another
royal assent	approval by the Monarch of a bill passed by the House of Commons and the House of Lords, making it an Act of Parliament
teller	appointed by the Speaker to count the number of ayes and noes in a vote
ten-minute rule	MPs are given ten minutes in which to make their comments or statements. The Speaker keeps time and ends the session at the end of the ten minutes
whip	Member who makes sure that fellow party members vote according to party wishes; they are paid a higher salary than normal back-bench MPs

Acts of Parliament and How a Bill Becomes Law

See also UK Legal System and Judiciary, p. 526.

Statutory law in Britain is provided by Acts of Parliament. Before an act receives the royal assent it is known as a bill; bills are normally proposed by the government. Individual MPs may also propose bills (known as **Private Members Bills**). The right to propose these is selected by ballot. Government departments normally detail proposed legislation in a **Green Paper** which sets out various aspects of a matter on which legislation is contemplated, and invites public discussion and suggestions. This will be followed by a **White Paper** which is the introduction to a bill.

How a Bill Becomes an Act of Parliament

1. First reading of the bill The title is read out in the House of Commons and a minister names a day for the second reading.

2. The bill is officially printed.

3. Second reading A debate on the whole bill in the House of Commons followed by a vote on whether or not the bill should go on to the next stage.

4. Committee stage A committee of MPs considers the bill in detail and makes amendments.

5. Report stage The bill is referred back to the House of Commons which may make further amendments.

6. Third reading The House of Commons votes whether the bill should be sent on to the House of Lords.

7. House of Lords The bill passes through much the same stages in the Lords as in the House of Commons. (Bills may be introduced in the Lords, in which case the House of Commons considers them at this stage.)

8. Last amendments The House of Commons considers any Lords' amendments, and may make further amendments which must usually be agreed by the Lords.

9. Royal assent The Queen gives her formal assent.

10. The bill becomes an act of parliament at royal assent. However, it may not come into force until a day appointed in the act.

Political Parties Represented in Parliament

This table includes parties represented in Parliament. Other political parties which stood in the general election of 1997 were: Albion Party; Alliance Party of Northern Ireland; British National Party; Green Party; Monster Raving Loony Party; National Democrats; Natural Law Party; New Communist Party; Prolife Alliance; Progressive Unionist Party; Referendum Party; Revolutionary Platform of the Socialist Labour Party; Socialist Party; Third Way; UK Independence Party; UK Virtual Party; Ulster Democratic Party.

Party	Headquarters	Leader	Chairperson	Brief history	Political position
Labour	Millbank Tower, Millbank, London SW1P 4GT; phone: (0171) 802 1000; fax: (0171) 802 1234; e-mail: labour-partygeo2.poptel.org.uk; Web site: www.labour.org.uk	Tony Blair	Michael Ancram	Founded in 1900 as the Labour Representation Committee, the party simplified its name to the Labour Party in 1906. It first became the official opposition in 1922. The party's first government (minority) was in 1924, with its first elected majority government in 1945. It is traditionally associated with the Trade Union Movement, who provided much of its funding.	Traditionally a party of the left, its policies include: devolution of power to the regions, reform of the second chamber, and social and educational reform. The party has moved from an ethos of government control (nationalization of industry, strong employment legislation) towards a more free-market ideology, with a subsequent backing from the world of finance and the management of industry.
Conservative and Unionist Party	32 Smith Square, Westminster, London SW1P 3HH; phone: (0171) 222 9000; fax: (0171) 222 1135; e-mail: www.conservative-party.org.uk/email; Web site: www.conservative-party.org.uk	William Hague	Lord Cecil Parkinson	Historically one of the two great parties. Originally known as the Tory Party, the name Conservative was first used in 1830. The current name results from a merger with the Irish Liberal Unionist Party in 1912. The main party in British politics together with the Whigs (Liberal Democrats) until the 20th century, when the Labour party usurped the latter. Produced the first British woman prime minister, Margaret Thatcher.	Traditionally a party of the right, with commitment to maintaining the unity of the nation, low levels of taxation, and low inflation. The present Conservative Party's free-market capitalism is supported by the world of finance and the management of industry.
Liberal Democrats	4 Cowley Street, London SW1P 3NB; phone: (0171) 222 7999; fax: (0171) 799 2170; Web site: www.libdems.org.uk	Charles Kennedy	Baroness Diana Maddock	Historically one of the two great parties. Originally known as the Whigs, the modern Liberal Party began in 1859 and formed its first government in 1868. It last held power in 1919, although the party did forge a 'Lib-Lab' pact with the minority Labour government in 1977. It merged with the breakaway Labour party group, the Social Democratic Party (SDP), in 1988 to become the Social Liberal Democrats (SLD). Became Liberal Democrats in 1989.	Centrist, openly pro-European party, committed to electoral reform and the devolution of power. Advocates increase in taxation to raise money for health and education. Organized on a regional basis with separate headquarters for Welsh and Scottish parties.
Plaid Cymru	18 Park Grove, Caerdydd CF1 3BN; phone: (01222) 646000; Web site: www.plaid-cymru.wales.com	Dafydd Wigley	Marc Phillips	Formed in 1925, and won its first parliamentary seat in 1966. Now the second party in Wales, with four members of parliament.	Welsh nationalist party, committed to a separate socialist Welsh nation, including the promotion of the Welsh language and culture. Forms a joint parliamentary group with the Scottish National Party (SNP).
Scottish National Party (SNP)	6 North Charlotte Street, Edinburgh EH2 4JH; phone: (0131) 226 3661; fax: (0131) 226 7373; Web site: www.snp.org.uk	Winnie Ewing (president); Alex Salmond (national convener)	Alasdair Morgan (national secretary)	Formed in 1934 by the amalgamation of several early nationalist parties. Won its first parliamentary seat in 1945. SNP support was essential to the minority Labour government of 1977. It is the second party in Scotland, with six MPs.	Scottish nationalist party, advocating the separation of Scotland from the UK as an independent state within the European Union. Forms a joint parliamentary group with Plaid Cymru.

(continued)

Political Parties Represented in Parliament *(continued)*

Party	Headquarters	Leader	Chairperson	Brief history	Political position
Ulster Unionist Party (UUP)	3 Glengall Street, Belfast BT12 5AE; phone: (01232) 324601; fax: (01232) 246738; e-mail: uup@uup.org; Web site: www.uup.org	David Trimble	John D Taylor (deputy leader)	Formed in 1905. Formally known as the Ulster Unionist Council, it governed the province between 1921 and 1972. Following the suspension of Home Rule in 1972, the party split in 1973, and other Unionist parties were formed. The Ulster Unionists rejected the Anglo-Irish Agreement of 1985, and joined forces with the Democratic Unionist Party (DUP) to campaign against it. All its MPs resigned their seats. The UUP is in favour of the 1998 Northern Ireland Peace Deal. Currently the largest political party in Northern Ireland, with ten MPs. Its leader David Trimble was elected first minister of the new Northern Ireland Assembly in June 1998.	Protestant party of Northern Ireland. Right-of-centre in orientation, it advocates equality for Northern Ireland within the UK, and opposes union with the Republic of Ireland. The party favours hard-line policies on law and order (advocates the death penalty). Has traditionally voted with the Conservative Party in parliament.
Democratic Unionist Party (DUP)	91 Dundela Avenue, Belfast BT4 3BU; phone: (01232) 471155; e-mail: info@dup.org.uk; Web site: www.dup.org.uk	Dr Ian R K Paisley	James McClure	Formed in 1973 as a breakaway group from the Ulster Unionist Council.	Protestant party, dedicated to maintaining the Constitution of Northern Ireland as an integral part of the UK. Usually supports the Conservative Party.
Social Democratic and Labour Party (SDLP)	611c Lisburn Road, Belfast BT9 7GT; phone: (01232) 247700; Web site: www.indigo.ie/sdlp	John Hume	Jonathan Stephenson	Formed in 1970. It was responsible for setting up the New Ireland Forum in 1983. In 1993 it initiated talks with the leader of Sinn Féin, which prompted a joint UK-Irish peace initiative, and set in motion a Northern Ireland cease-fire (1994–96). Currently has three MPs.	Largely Catholic, left-of-centre party. Aims ultimately at Irish unification, but has distanced itself from violent tactics, adopting a constitutional, conciliatory role. Has traditionally voted with the Labour Party.
Sinn Féin	Sinn Féin, 51/55 Falls Road, Belfast; phone: (01232) 624421; fax: (01232) 622112; Web site: www.sinnfein.ie	Gerry Adams	Martin McGuinness	Irish party founded in 1905. The driving political force behind Irish nationalism between 1916 and 1921. It returned to prominence with the outbreak of 'the Troubles' in Northern Ireland in the late 1960s, when it split into Provisional and Official wings at the same time as the Irish Republican Army (IRA), with which it is closely associated. Currently has two MPs in the UK parliament, and one in the Irish parliament.	Nationalist party. Aims to create a united republican Ireland. The current members do not take their seats, and take no part in the parliamentary process.
UK Unionist (UKUP)	10 Hamilton Road, Bangor, Northern Ireland BT20 4LE; phone: (01232) 521482; fax: (01247) 465037	Robert McCartney	–	Formed in 1997 by Robert McCartney, UUP MP for the North Down constituency. He left the UUP and stood as an independent and then formed his own part in order to take part in talks in the future of Northern Ireland	Aims to preserve the constitutional position of Northern Ireland within the UK. Opposed to the Good Friday Agreement and to any involvement of the Irish government in Northern Ireland affairs.

The Shadow Cabinet

Position	Name	Position	Name
Conservative Party Leader and Leader of the Opposition	William Hague	Shadow Secretary of State for Culture, Media, and Sport	Peter Ainsworth
Shadow Chancellor of the Exchequer	Francis Maude	Shadow Secretary of State for International Development	Gary Streeter
Party Chairman	Michael Ancram	Shadow Minister for Agriculture, Fisheries, and Food	Tim Yeo
Shadow Secretary of State for Home Affairs	Ann Widdecombe	Shadow Secretary of State for Trade and Industry	Angela Browning
Shadow Secretary of State for Foreign and Commonwealth Affairs	John Maples	Shadow Secretary of State for Education and Employment	Theresa May
Shadow Leader of the House of Commons and Constitutional Affairs	George Young	Shadow Minister for the Cabinet Office and Policy Renewal	Andrew Lansley
Shadow Secretary of State for the Environment, Transport, and the Regions	John Redwood	Shadow Minister for Transport	Bernard Jenkin
Shadow Chief Secretary to the Treasury	David Heathcoat-Amory	Opposition Chief Whip (House of Commons)	James Arbuthnot
Shadow Secretary of State for Defence	Iain Duncan Smith	Opposition Chief Whip (House of Lords)	Lord Henley
Shadow Leader of the House of Lords	Lord Strathclyde	Shadow Attorney General[1]	Edward Garnier
Shadow Secretary of State for Northern Ireland	Andrew Mackay		
Shadow Secretary of State for Social Security	David Willetts		
Shadow Secretary of State for Health	Liam Fox		

[1] Not a member of the Shadow Cabinet, but attends all meetings.

Liberal Democrats: Parliamentary Responsibilities

Position	Name	Position	Name
Party Leader	Charles Kennedy	Health Team Leader	Simon Hughes
Deputy Leader in the Commons	Alan Beith	Home and Legal Affairs	Alan Beith
Leader in the Lords	Lord Rodgers of Quarrybank	Northern Ireland	Lembit Öpik
Chief Whip in the Lords	Lord Harris of Greenwich	Local Government and Housing Team Leader	Paul Burstow
Deputy Whip in the Commons	Andrew Stunell	Social Security and Welfare Team Leader	David Rendel
Party President	Baroness Maddock of Christchurch	Trade and Industry Team Leader	David Chidgey
Chief Whip and Shadow Leader of the House	Paul Tyler	Treasury Team Leader	Malcolm Bruce
Agriculture, Fisheries, Food, and Rural Affairs Team Leader[1]	–	Scotland Team Leader	Jim Wallace
Constitution Team Leader	Robert Maclennan	Wales Team Leader	Richard Livsey
Culture, Media, Sport, and Civil Service Team Leader	Robert Maclennan	Women	Jackie Ballard
Education and Employment Team Leader	Don Foster	Young People	Lembit Öpik
Environment and Transport Team Leader	Matthew Taylor	***Additional Responsibilities in the Commons***	
Foreign Affairs, Defence, and Europe Team Leader	Menzies Campbell	Duchy of Lancaster	Robert Maclennan
International Development	Jenny Tonge	Attorney General	John Burnett
		Solicitor General	John Burnett
		Lord Chancellor	John Burnett
		Lord Advocate	Menzies Campbell

[1]Not appointed as of August 1999.

House of Commons

Members of the House of Commons

Con = Conservative; DUP = Democratic Unionist Party; Ind = Independent; Lab = Labour; Lab Coop = Labour Cooperative; LD = Liberal Democrats; PC = Plaid Cymru; SDLP = Social Democratic and Labour Party; SNP = Scottish National Party; SF = Sinn Féin; UKUP = UK Unionist Party; UUP = Ulster Unionist Party

Member	Date of birth	Party	Constituency	Majority at 1997 election	Opponents
Abbott, Diane	27/9/53	Lab	Hackney North and Stoke Newington	15,627	Michael Lavender: Con; Douglas Taylor: LD
Adams, Gerry[1]	6/10/48	SF	Belfast West	7,909	Joe Hendron: SDLP; Fred Parkinson: UUP
Adams, Irene	27/12/47	Lab	Paisley North	12,814	Ian Mackay: SNP; Kenneth Brookes: Con; Alan Jalfs: LD
Ainger, Nick	24/10/49	Lab	Carmarthen West and Pembrokeshire South	9,621	Owen Williams: Con; Daniel Llewellyn: PC
Ainsworth, Bob	19/6/52	Lab	Coventry North East	22,569	Michael Burnett: Con; Geoffrey Sewards: LD
Ainsworth, Peter	16/11/56	Con	Surrey East	15,093	Belinda Ford: LD; David Ross: Lab
Alexander, Douglas	26/10/67	Lab	Paisley South	2,731[2]	Ian Blackford: SNP; Eilen McCartin: LD; Sheila Lawson: Con

(continued)

Members of the House of Commons *(continued)*

Member	Date of birth	Party	Constituency	Majority at 1997 election	Opponents
Allan, Richard	11/2/66	LD	Sheffield Hallam	8,271	Irvine Patnick: Con; Steven Conquest: Lab
Allen, Graham	11/1/53	Lab	Nottingham North	18,801	Gillian Shaw: Con; Rachel Oliver: LD
Amess, David	26/3/52	Con	Southend West	2,615	Nina Stimson: LD; Alan Harley: Lab
Ancram, Michael	7/7/45	Con	Devizes	9,782	Anthony Vickers: LD; Frank Jeffrey: Lab
Anderson, Donald	17/6/39	Lab	Swansea East	25,569	Catherine Dibble: Con; Elwyn Jones: LD
Anderson, Janet	6/12/49	Lab	Rossendale and Darwen	10,949	Patricia Buzzard: Con; Brian Denning LD
Arbuthnot, James	4/8/52	Con	Hampshire North East	14,398	Ian Mann: LD; Peter Dare: Lab
Armstrong, Hilary	30/11/45	Lab	Durham North West	24,754	Louise St John Howe: Con; Anthony Gillings: LD
Ashdown, Paddy	27/2/41	LD	Yeovil	11,403	Nicholas Cambrook: Con; Patrick Conway: Lab
Ashton, Joe	9/10/33	Lab	Bassetlaw	17,348	Martin Cleasby: Con; Mike Kerrigan: LD
Atherton, Candy	17/4/60	Lab	Falmouth and Cambourne	2,688	Sebastian Coe: Con; Terrye Jones: LD
Atkins, Charlotte	24/9/50	Lab	Staffordshire Moorlands	10,049	Andrew Ashworth: Con; Christina Jebb: LD
Atkinson, David	24/3/40	Con	Bournemouth East	4,342	Douglas Eyre: LD; Jessica Stevens: Lab
Atkinson, Peter	19/1/43	Con	Hexham	222	Ian McMinn: Lab; Philip Carr: LD
Austin, John	21/8/44	Lab	Erith and Thamesmead	17,424	Nadhim Zahawi: Con; Alexander Grigg: LD
Baker, Norman	26/7/57	LD	Lewes	1,300	Tim Rathbone: Con; Mark Patton: Lab
Baldry, Antony	10/7/50	Con	Benbury	4,737	Hazel Peperell: Lab; Catherine Bearder: LD
Ballard, Jackie	4/1/53	LD	Taunton	2,452	David Nicholson: Con; Elizabeth Lisgo: Lab
Banks, Tony	8/4/45	Lab	West Ham	19,494	Mark MacGregor: Con; Samantha McDonough: LD
Barnes, Harry	22/7/36	Lab	Derbyshire North East	18,321	Simon Elliott: Con; Stephen Hardy: LD
Barron, Kevin	26/10/46	Lab	Rother Valley	23,485	Steven George Stanbury: Con; Stan Burgess: LD
Battle, John	26/4/51	Lab	Leeds West	19,771	John Whelan: Con; Nigel Amor: LD
Bayley, Hugh	9/1/52	Lab	York, City of	20,523	Simon Mallett: Con; Andrew Waller: LD
Beard, Nigel	10/10/36	Lab	Bexleyheath and Crayford	3,415	David Evennett: Con; Francoise Montford: LD
Beckett, Margaret	15/1/43	Lab	Derby South	16,106	Javed Arain: Con; Jeremy Beckett: LD
Begg, Anne	16/12/55	Lab	Aberdeen South	3,365	Nicol Stephen: LD; Raymond Robertson: Con
Beggs, Roy	20/2/36	UUP	Antrim East	6,389	Sean Neeson: APNI; Jack McKee: DUP
Beith, Alan	20/4/43	LD	Berwick-upon-Tweed	8,042	Paul Brannen: Lab; Nick Herbert: Con
Bell, Martin	31/8/38	Ind	Tatton	11,077	Neil Hamilton: Con; Sam Hill: Ind
Bell, Stuart	16/5/38	Lab	Middlesbrough	25,018	Liam Benham: Con; Alison Charlesworth: LD
Benn, Hilary	26/11/53	Lab	Leeds Central	2,293[3]	Edward Wild: Con; Peter Wild: LD
Benn, Tony	3/4/25	Lab	Chesterfield	5,775	Tony Rogers: LD; Martin Potter: Con
Bennett, Andrew	9/3/39	Lab	Denton and Reddish	20,311	Barbara Nutt: Con; Iain Donaldson: LD
Benton, Joe	28/9/33	Lab	Bootle	28,421	Rupert Matthews: Con; Kiron Reid: LD
Bercow, John	19/1/63	Con	Buckingham	12,386	Robert Lehmann: Lab; Neil Stuart: LD
Beresford, Paul	6/4/46	Con	Mole Valley	10,221	Stephen Cooksey: LD; Christopher Payne: Lab
Bermingham, Gerry	20/8/40	Lab	St Helens South	23,739	Mary Russell: Con; Brian Spencer: LD
Berry, Roger	4/7/48	Lab	Kingswood	14,253	Jonathan Howard: Con; Jeanne Pinkerton: LD
Best, Harold	18/12/37	Lab	Leeds North	3,844	Keith Hampson: Con; Barbara Pearce: LD
Betts, Clive	13/1/50	Lab	Sheffield Attercliffe	21,818	Brendan Peter Doyle: Con; Alice Gail Smith: LD
Blackman, Liz	26/9/49	Lab	Erewash	9,135	Angela Knight: Con; Martin Garnett: LD
Blair, Tony	6/5/53	Lab	Sedgefield	25,143	Elizabeth Pitman: Con; Ronald Beadle: LD
Blears, Hazel	14/5/56	Lab	Salford	17,069	Elliot Bishop: Con; Norman Owen: LD
Blizzard, Bob	31/5/50	Lab	Waveney	12,093	David Porter: Con; Christopher Thomas: LD
Blunkett, David	6/6/47	Lab	Sheffield Brightside	19,954	Francis Butler: LD; Christopher Buckwell: Con
Blunt, Crispin	15/6/60	Con	Reigate	7,741	Andrew Howard: Lab; Peter Samuel: LD
Boateng, Paul	14/6/51	Lab	Brent South	19,691	Stewart Jackson: Con; Julian Brazil: LD
Body, Richard	18/5/27	Con	Boston and Skegness	647	Phil McCauley: Lab; James Dodsworth: LD
Boothroyd, Betty	8/10/29	Speaker	West Bromwich West	15,423	Richard Silvester: Ind Lab; Steve Edwards: Nat Dem
Borrow, David	2/8/52	Lab	Ribble South	5,084	Robert Atkins: Con; Tim Farron: LD
Boswell, Tim	2/12/42	Con	Daventry	7,378	Ken Ritchie: Lab; John Gordon: LD
Bottomley, Peter	30/7/44	Con	Worthing West	7,713	Christopher Hare: LD; John Adams: Lab
Bottomley, Virginia	12/3/48	Con	Surrey South West	2,694	Neil Sherlock: LD; Margaret Leicester: Lab
Bradley, Keith	17/5/50	Lab	Manchester Withington	18,581	Jonathan Smith: Con; Yasmen Zalzala: LD
Bradley, Peter	12/4/53	Lab	Wrekin, The	3,025	Peter Bruinvels: Con; Ian Jenkins: LD
Bradshaw, Ben	30/8/60	Lab	Exeter	11,705	Adrian Rogers: Con; Dennis Brewer: LD
Brady, Graham	20/5/67	Con	Altrincham and Sale West	1,505	Jane Baugh: Lab; Marc Ramsbottom: LD
Brake, Thomas	6/5/62	LD	Carshalton and Wallington	2,267	Nigel Forman: Con; Andrew Theobald: Lab
Brand, Peter	16/5/47	LD	Isle of Wight	6,406	Andrew Turner: Con; Deborah Gardiner: Lab
Brazier, Julian	24/7/53	Con	Canterbury	3,964	Cheryl Hall: Lab; Martin Vye: LD
Breed, Colin	4/5/47	LD	Cornwall South East	6,480	Warwick Lightfoot: Con; Dorothy Kirk: Lab
Brinton, Helen	23/12/54	Lab	Peterborough	7,323	Jacqueline Foster: Con; David Howarth: LD
Brooke, Peter	3/3/34	Con	London and Westminster	4,881	Kate Green: Lab; Michael Dumigan: LD
Brown, Gordon	20/2/51	Lab	Dunfermline East	18,741	John Ramage: SNP; Iain Mitchell: Con
Brown, Nick	13/6/50	Lab	Newcastle upon Tyne East and Wallsend	23,811	Jeremy Middleton: Con; Graham Morgan: LD
Brown, Russell	17/9/51	Lab	Dumfries	9,643	Struan Stevenson: Con; Robert Higgins: SNP

(continued)

Members of the House of Commons *(continued)*

Member	Date of birth	Party	Constituency	Majority at 1997 election	Opponents
Browne, Desmond	22/3/52	Lab	Kilmarnock and Loudoun	7,256	Alex Neil: SNP; Douglas Taylor: Con
Browning, Angela	4/12/46	Con	Tiverton and Honiton	1,653	Jim Barnard: LD; John King: Lab
Bruce, Ian	14/3/47	Con	Dorset South	77	Jim Knight: Lab; Michael Plummer: LD
Bruce, Malcolm	17/11/44	LD	Gordon	6,997	John Porter: Con; Richard Lochhead: SNP
Buck, Karen	30/8/58	Lab	Regent's Park and Kensington North	14,657	Paul McGuinness: Con; Emily Gasson: LD
Burden, Richard	1/9/54	Lab	Birmingham Northfield	11,443	Alan Blumenthal: Con; Michael Ashall: LD
Burgon, Colin	22/4/48	Lab	Elmet	8,779	Spencer Batiste: Con; Brian Jennings: LD
Burnett, John	19/9/45	LD	Devon West and Torridge	1,957	Ian Liddell-Grainger: Con; David Brenton: Lab
Burns, Simon	6/9/52	Con	Chelmsford West	6,691	Martin Bracken: LD; Roy Chad: Lab
Burstow, Paul	13/5/62	LD	Sutton and Cheam	2,097	Olga Maitland: Con; Mark Allison: Lab
Butler, Christine	14/12/43	Lab	Castle Point	1,116	Robert Spink: Con; Michael Baker: LD
Butterfill, John	14/2/41	Con	Bournemouth West	5,710	Janet Dover: LD; Dennis Gritt: Lab
Byers, Stephen	13/4/53	Lab	Tyneside North	26,643	Michael McIntyre: Con; Thomas Malvenna: LD
Cable, Vincent	9/5/43	LD	Twickenham	4,281	Toby Jessel: Con; Eva Tutchell: Lab
Caborn, Richard	6/10/43	Lab	Sheffield Central	16,906	Ali Qadar: LD; Martin Hess: Con
Campbell, Alan	8/7/57	Lab	Tynemouth	11,273	Martin Callanan: Con; Andrew Duffield: LD
Campbell, Anne	6/4/40	Lab	Cambridge	14,137	David Platt: Con; Geoffrey Heathcock: LD
Campbell, Menzies	22/5/41	LD	Fife North East	10,356	Adam Robert Bruce: Con; Colin Welsh: SNP
Campbell, Ronnie	14/8/43	Lab	Blyth Valley	17,736	Andrew Lamb: LD; Barbara Musgrave: Con
Campbell-Savours, Dale	23/8/43	Lab	Workington	19,656	Robert Blunden: Con; Philip Roberts: LD
Canavan, Dennis	8/8/42	Lab	Falkirk West	13,761	David Alexander: SNP; Carol Buchanan: Con
Cann, Jamie	28/6/46	Lab	Ipswich	10,439	Stephen Castle: Con; Nigel Roberts: LD
Caplin, Ivor	8/11/58	Lab	Hove	3,959	Robert Guy: Con; Thomas Pearce: LD
Casale, Roger	22/5/60	Lab	Wimbledon	2,990	Charles Goodson-Wickes: Con; Alison Willott: LD
Cash, William	10/5/40	Con	Stone	3,818	John Wakefield: Lab; Barry Stamp: LD
Caton, Martin	16/6/51	Lab	Gower	13,007	Alan Hugh Cairns: Con; Howard Evans: LD
Cawsey, Ian	14/4/60	Lab	Brigg and Goole	6,389	Donald Stewart: Con; Mary-Rose Hardy: LD
Chapman, Ben	8/7/40	Lab	Wirral South	7,004	Leslie Byrom: Con; Phillip Gilchrist: LD
Chapman, Sydney	17/10/35	Con	Chipping Barnet	1,035	Geoffrey Cooke: Lab; Sean Hooker: LD
Chaytor, David	3/8/49	Lab	Bury North	7,866	Alistair Burt: Con; Neville Kenyon: LD
Chidgey, David	9/7/42	LD	Eastleigh	754	Stephen Reid: Con; Alan Lloyd: Lab
Chisholm, Malcolm	7/3/49	Lab	Edinburgh North and Leith	10,978	Anne Dana: SNP; Ewen Stewart: Con
Chope, Christopher	19/5/47	Con	Christchurch	2,165	Diana Maddock: LD; Charles Mannan: Lab
Church, Judith	19/9/53	Lab	Dagenham	17,054	James Fairrie: Con; Thomas Dobrashian: LD
Clapham, Michael	15/5/43	Lab	Barnsley West and Penistone	17,267	Paul Watkins: Con; Winifred Knight: LD
Clappison, James	14/9/56	Con	Hertsmere	3,075	Beth Kelly: Lab; Ann Gray: LD
Clark, Alan	13/4/28	Con	Kensington and Chelsea	9,519	John Atkinson: Lab; Robert Woodthorpe Brown: LD
Clark, David	19/10/39	Lab	South Shields	22,153	Mark Hoban: Con; David Ord: LD
Clark, Lynda	26/2/49	Lab	Edinburgh Pentlands	4,862	Malcolm Rifkind: Con; Stewart Gibb: SNP
Clark, Michael	8/8/35	Con	Rayleigh	10,684	Raymond Ellis: Lab; Sidney Cumberland: LD
Clark, Paul	29/4/57	Lab	Gillingham	1,980	James Couchman: Con; Robert Sayer: LD
Clark, Tony	6/9/63	Lab	Northampton South	744	Michael Morris: Con; Anthony Worgan: LD
Clarke, Charles	21/9/50	Lab	Norwich South	14,239	Bashir Khanbhai: Con; Andrew Aalders-Dunthorne: LD
Clarke, Eric	9/4/33	Lab	Midlothian	9,870	Lawrence Millar: SNP; Anne Harper: Con
Clarke, Kenneth	2/7/40	Con	Rushcliffe	5,055	Jocelyn Pettitt: Lab; Samuel Boote: LD
Clarke, Tom	10/1/41	Lab	Coatbridge and Chryston	19,295	Brian Nugent: SNP; Piers Wauchope: Con
Clelland, David	27/6/43	Lab	Tyne Bridge	22,906	Adrian Lee: Con; Mary Wallace: LD
Clifton-Brown, Geoffrey	23/3/53	Con	Cotswold	11,965	David Gayler: LD; David Elwell: Lab
Clwyd, Ann	21/3/37	Lab	Cynon Valley	19,755	Alun Davies: PC; Huw Price: LD
Coaker, Vernon	17/6/53	Lab	Gedling	3,802	Andrew Mitchell: Con; Raymond Poynter: LD
Coffey, Ann	31/8/46	Lab	Stockport	18,912	Stephen Fitzsimmons: Con; Sylvia Roberts: LD
Cohen, Harry	10/12/49	Lab	Leyton and Wanstead	15,186	Robert Vaudry: Con; Charles Anglin: LD
Coleman, Iain	18/1/58	Lab	Hammersmith and Fulham	3,842	Matthew Carrington: Con; Alexi Sugden: LD
Collins, Tim	7/5/64	Con	Westmorland and Lonsdale	4,521	Stan Collins: LD; John Harding: Lab
Colman, Anthony	24/7/43	Lab	Putney	2,976	David Mellor: Con; Russell Pyne: LD
Colvin, Michael	27/9/32	Con	Romsey	8,585	Mark Cooper: LD; Joanne Ford: Lab
Connarty, Michael	3/9/47	Lab	Falkirk East	13,385	Keith Brown: SNP; Malcolm Nicol: Con
Cook, Frank	3/11/35	Lab	Stockton North	21,365	Bryan Johnston: Con; Suzanne Fletcher: LD
Cook, Robin	28/2/46	Lab	Livingston	11,747	Peter Johnston: SNP; Hugh Craigie Halkett: Con
Cooper, Yvette	20/3/69	Lab	Pontefract and Castleford	25,725	Adrian Flook: Con; Wesley Paxton: LD
Corbett, Robin	22/12/33	Lab	Birmingham Erdington	12,657	Anthony Tomkins: Con; Ian Garrett: LD
Corbyn, Jeremy	26/5/49	Lab	Islington North	19,955	James Kempton: LD; Simon Fawthrop: Con
Cormack, Patrick	18/5/39	Con	Staffordshire South	7,821	Judith LeMaistre: Lab; Jamie Calder: LD
Corston, Jean	5/5/42	Lab	Bristol East	16,159	Edward Vaizey: Con; Peter Tyzack: LD
Cotter, Brian	24/8/38	LD	Weston-super-Mare	1,274	Margaret Daly: Con; Derek Kraft: Lab
Cousins, Jim	23/2/44	Lab	Newcastle-upon-Tyne Central	16,480	Newmark Brooks: Con; Ruth Berry: LD

(continued)

Members of the House of Commons *(continued)*

Member	Date of birth	Party	Constituency	Majority at 1997 election	Opponents
Cox, Tom	19/1/30	Lab	Tooting	15,011	James Hutchings: Con; Simon James: LD
Cran, James	28/1/44	Con	Beverley and Holderness	811	Norman O'Neill: Lab; John Melling: LD
Cranston, Ross	23/7/48	Lab	Dudley North	9,457	Charles MacNamara: Con; Gerry Lewis: LD
Crausby, David	17/6/46	Lab	Bolton North East	12,669	Robert Wilson: Con; Edmund Critchley: LD
Cryer, Ann	14/12/39	Lab	Keighley	7,132	Gary Waller: Con; Michael Doyle: LD
Cryer, John	11/4/64	Lab	Hornchurch	5,680	Robin Squire: Con; Rabinda Martins: LD
Cummings, John	6/7/43	Lab	Easington	30,012	Jason Hollands: Con; James Heppell: LD
Cunliffe, Lawrence	25/3/29	Lab	Leigh	24,496	Edward Young: Con; Peter Hough: LD
Cunningham, Jack	4/8/39	Lab	Copeland	11,944	Andrew Cumpsty: Con; Roger Putnam: LD
Cunningham, Jim	4/12/41	Lab	Coventry South	10,953	Paul Ivey: Con; Gordon Macdonald: LD
Cunningham, Roseanna	27/7/51	SNP	Perth	3,141	John Godfrey: Con; Douglas Alexander: Lab
Curry, David	13/6/44	Con	Skipton and Ripon	11,620	Thomas Mould: LD; Robert Marchant: Lab
Curtis-Thomas, Clare	30/4/58	Lab	Crosby	7,182	Malcolm Thornton: Con; Paul McVey: LD
Dafis, Cynog	1/4/38	PC	Ceredigion	6,961	Robert Harris: Lab; David Davies: LD
Dalyell, Tam	9/8/32	Lab	Linlithgow	10,838	Kenny MacAskill: SNP; Tom Kerr: Con
Darling, Alistair	28/11/53	Lab	Edinburgh Central	11,070	Michael Scott-Hayward: Con; Fiona Hyslop: SNP
Darvill, Keith	28/5/48	Lab	Upminster	2,770	Nicholas Bonsor: Con; Pamela Peskett: LD
Davey, Edward	25/12/65	LD	Kingston and Surbiton	56	Richard Tracey: Con; Sheila Griffin: Lab
Davey, Valerie	16/4/40	Lab	Bristol West	1,493	William Waldegrave: Con; Charles Boney: LD
Davidson, Ian	8/9/50	Lab	Glasgow Pollock	13,791	David Logan: SNP
Davies, Denzil	9/10/38	Lab	Llanelli	16,039	Marc Phillips: PC; Andrew Hayes: Con
Davies, Geraint	3/5/60	Lab	Croydon Central	3,897	David Congdon: Con; George Schlich: LD
Davies, Quentin	29/5/44	Con	Grantham and Stamford	2,692	Peter Denning: Lab; John Sellick: LD
Davies, Ron	6/8/46	Lab	Caerphilly	25,839	Hugh Harris: Con; Lindsay Whittle: PC
Davis, David	23/12/48	Con	Haltemprice and Howden	7,514	Diana Wallis: LD; George McManus: Lab
Davis, Terry	5/1/38	Lab	Birmingham Hodge Hill	14,200	Edward Grant: Con; Haydn Thomas: LD
Dawson, Hilton	30/9/53	Lab	Lancaster and Wyre	1,295	Keith Mans: Con; John Humberstone: LD
Day, Stephen	30/10/48	Con	Cheadle	3,189	Patsy Calton: LD; Paul Diggett: Lab
Dean, Janet	28/1/49	Lab	Burton	6,330	Ivan Lawrence: Con; David Fletcher: LD
Denham, John	15/7/53	Lab	Southampton Itchen	14,229	Peter Fleet: Con; David Harrison: LD
Dewar, Donald	21/8/37	Lab	Glasgow Anniesland	15,154	William Wilson: SNP; Robert Andrew Palles Brocklehurst: Con
Dismore, Andrew	2/9/54	Lab	Hendon	6,155	John Gorst: Con; Wayne Casey: LD
Dobbin, Jim	26/5/41	Lab	Heywood and Middleton	17,542	Edward Sebastian Grigg: Con; David Clayton: LD
Dobson, Frank	15/3/40	Lab	Holborn and St Pancras	17,903	Julian Smith: Con; Justine McGuinness: LD
Donaldson, Jeffrey	7/12/62	UUP	Lagan Valley	16,925	Edwin Poots: DUP
Donohoe, Brian	10/9/48	Lab	Cunninghame South	14,869	Margaret Burgess: SNP; Pamela Paterson: Con
Doran, Frank	13/4/49	Lab	Aberdeen Central	10,801	Jill Wisely: Con; Brian Topping: SNP
Dorrell, Stephen	25/3/52	Con	Charnwood	5,900	David Knaggs: Lab; Roger Wilson: LD
Dowd, Jim	5/3/51	Lab	Lewisham West	14,317	Clare Whelan: Con; Kathy McGrath: LD
Drew, David	13/4/52	Lab	Stroud	2,910	Roger Knapman: Con; Paul Hodgkinson: LD
Drown, Julia	23/8/62	Lab	Swindon South	5,645	Simon Coombs: Con; Stanley Pajak: LD
Duncan, Alan	31/3/57	Con	Rutland and Melton	8,836	John Meads: Lab; Kim Lee: LD
Duncan Smith, Iain	9/4/54	Con	Chingford and Woodford Green	5,714	Thomas Hutchinson: Lab; Geoffrey Seeff: LD
Dunwoody, Gwyneth	12/12/30	Lab	Crewe and Nantwich	15,798	Michael Loveridge: Con; David Cannon: LD
Eagle, Angela	19/1/61	Lab	Wallasey	19,074	Madeleine Wilcock: Con; Peter Reisdorf: LD
Eagle, Maria	17/2/61	Lab	Liverpool Garston	18,387	Flo Clucas: LD; Nigel Gordon-Johnson: Con
Edwards, Huw	12/4/53	Lab	Monmouth	4,178	Roger Evans: Con; Mark Williams: LD
Efford, Clive	10/7/58	Lab	Eltham	10,182	Clive Blackwood: Con; Amanda Taylor: LD
Ellman, Louise	14/11/45	Lab	Liverpool Riverside	21,799	Beatrice Fraenkel: LD; David Sparrow: Con
Emery, Peter	27/2/26	Con	Devon East	7,489	Rachel Trethewey: LD; Andrew Siantonas: Lab
Ennis, Jeff	13/11/52	Lab	Barnsley East and Mexborough	26,763	Jane Ellison: Con; David Willis: LD
Etherington, William	17/7/41	Lab	Sunderland North	19,697	Andrew Selous: Con; Geoffrey Pryke: LD
Evans, Nigel	10/11/57	Con	Ribble Valley	6,640	Michael Carr: LD; Marcus Johnstone: Lab
Ewing, Margaret	1/9/45	SNP	Moray	5,566	Andrew Findlay: Con; Lewis Macdonald: Lab
Faber, David	7/7/61	Con	Westbury	6,068	John Miller: LD; Kevin Small: Lab
Fabricant, Michael	12/6/50	Con	Lichfield	238	Susan Woodward: Lab; Roger Bennion: LD
Fallon, Michael	14/5/52	Con	Sevenoaks	10,461	John Hayes: Lab; Roger Waslhe: LD
Fearn, Ronnie	6/2/31	LD	Southport	6,170	Matthew Banks: Con; Sarah Norman: Lab
Field, Frank	16/7/42	Lab	Birkenhead	21,845	Albert John Crosby: Con; Roy Wood: LD
Fisher, Mark	29/10/44	Lab	Stoke-on-Trent Central	19,924	David Neil Jones: Con; Edward Fordham: LD
Fitzpatrick, Jim	4/4/52	Lab	Poplar and Canning Town	18,915	Benet Steinberg: Con; Janet Ludlow: LD
Fitzsimons, Lorna	6/8/67	Lab	Rochdale	4,545	Liz Lynne: LD; Mervyn Turnberg: Con
Flight, Howard	16/6/48	Con	Arundel and South Downs	14,035	John Goss: LD; Richard Black: Lab
Flint, Caroline	20/9/61	Lab	Don Valley	14,659	Clare Gledhill: Con; Paul Johnston: LD
Flynn, Paul	9/2/35	Lab	Newport West	14,537	Peter Clarke: Con; Stan Wilson: LD
Follett, Barbara	25/12/42	Lab	Stevenage	11,582	Tim Wood: Con; Alex Wilcock: LD

(continued)

Members of the House of Commons *(continued)*

Member	Date of birth	Party	Constituency	Majority at 1997 election	Opponents
Forsythe, Clifford	24/8/29	UUP	Antrim South	16,611	Donovan McClelland: SDLP
Forth, Eric	9/9/44	Con	Bromley and Chislehurst	11,118	Rob Yeldham: Lab; Paul Booth: LD
Foster, Derek	25/6/37	Lab	Bishop Auckland	21,064	Josephine Fergus: Con; Les Ashworth: LD
Foster, Don	31/3/47	LD	Bath	9,319	Alison McNair: Con; Tim Bush: Lab
Foster, Michael	1/2/46	Lab	Hastings and Rye	2,560	Jacqui Mait: Con; Monroe Palmer: LD
Foster, Michael	14/1/63	Lab	Worcester	7,425	Nicholas Bourne: Con; Paul Chandler: LD
Foulkes, George	21/1/42	Lab	Carrick, Cumnock and Doon Valley	21,062	Alasdair Marshall: Con; Christine Hutchison: SNP
Fowler, Norman	2/2/38	Con	Sutton Coldfield	14,885	Alan York: Lab; James Whorwood: LD
Fox, Liam	22/9/61	Con	Woodspring	7,734	Nanette Kirsen: LD; Debbie Sander: Lab
Fraser, Christopher	19/1/62	Con	Dorset Mid and Poole North	681	Alan Leaman: LD; David Collis: Lab
Fyfe, Maria	25/11/38	Lab	Glasgow Maryhill	14,264	John Wailes: SNP; Elspeth Attwooll: LD
Galbraith, Sam	18/10/45	Lab	Strathkelvin and Bearsden	16,292	David Sharpe: Con; Graeme McCormick: SNP
Gale, Roger	20/8/43	Con	Thanet North	2,766	Iris Johnson: Lab; Paul Kendrick: LD
Galloway, George	16/8/54	Lab	Glasgow Kelvin	9,665	Sandra White: SNP; Elspeth Buchanan: LD
Gapes, Mike	4/9/52	Lab	Ilford South	14,200	Neil Thorne: Con; Aina Khan: LD
Gardiner, Barry	10/3/57	Lab	Brent North	4,019	Rhodes Boyson: Con; Paul Lorber: LD
Garnier, Edward	26/10/52	Con	Harborough	6,524	Mark Cox: LD; Nicholas Holden: Lab
George, Andrew	2/12/58	LD	St Ives	7,170	William Rogers: Con; Christopher Fegan: Lab
George, Bruce	1/6/42	Lab	Walsall	11,312	Leslie Leek: Con; Harry Harris: LD
Gerrard, Neil	3/7/42	Lab	Walthamstow	17,149	Jill Andrew: Con; Jane Jackson: LD
Gibb, Nick	3/9/60	Con	Bognor Regis and Littlehampton	7,321	Roger Nash: Lab; James Walsh: LD
Gibson, Ian	26/9/38	Lab	Norwich North	9,470	Robert Kinghorn: Con; Paul Young: LD
Gill, Christopher	28/10/36	Con	Ludlow	5,909	Ian Huffer: LD; Nuala O'Kane: Lab
Gillan, Cheryl	21/4/52	Con	Chesham and Amersham	13,859	Michael Brand: LD; Christopher Farrelly: Lab
Gilroy, Linda	19/7/49	Lab	Plymouth Sutton	9,440	Andrew Crisp: Con; Steven Melia: LD
Godman, Norman	19/4/38	Lab	Greenock and Inverclyde	13,040	Brian Goodall: SNP; Rodney Ackland: LD
Godsiff, Roger	7/11/46	Lab	Birmingham Sparkbrook and Small Heath	19,526	Kenneth Haredman: Con; Roger Harmer: LD
Goggins, Paul	16/10/53	Lab	Wythenshawe and Sale East	15,019	Paul Fleming: Con; Vanessa Tucker: LD
Golding, Llin	21/3/33	Lab	Newcastle-under-Lyme	17,206	Marcus Hayes: Con; Robin Studd: LD
Goodlad, Alastair	4/7/43	Con	Eddisbury	1,185	Margaret Hanson: Lab; David Reaper: LD
Gordon, Eileen	22/10/46	Lab	Romford	649	Michael Neubert: Con; Nigel Meyer: LD
Gorman, Teresa	30/9/31	Con	Billericay	1,356	Paul Richards: Lab; Geoff Williams: LD
Gorrie, Donald	2/4/33	LD	Edinburgh West	7,253	James Douglas-Hamilton: Con; Lesley Hinds: Lab
Graham, Thomas	5/12/43	Lab	Renfrewshire West	7,979	Colin Campbell: SNP; Charles Cormack: Con
Grant, Bernie	17/2/44	Lab	Tottenham	20,200	Andrew Scantlebury: Con; Neil Hughes: LD
Gray, James	7/11/54	Con	Wiltshire North	3,475	Simon Cordon: LD; Nigel Knowles: Lab
Green, Damian	17/1/56	Con	Ashford	5,345	John Richard Ennals: Lab; John Williams: LD
Greenway, John	19/2/46	Con	Ryedale	5,058	John Keith Orrell: LD; Alison Hiles: Lab
Grieve, Dominic	24/5/56	Con	Beaconsfield	13,987	Peter Mapp: LD; Alastair Hudson: Lab
Griffiths, Jane	17/4/54	Lab	Reading East	3,795	John Watts: Con; Robert Samuel: LD
Griffiths, Nigel	20/5/55	Lab	Edinburgh South	11,452	Elizabeth Smith: Con; Michael Pringle: LD
Griffiths, Win	11/2/43	Lab	Bridgend	15,248	David Davies: Con; Andrew McKinlay: LD
Grocott, Bruce	1/11/40	Lab	Telford	11,290	Bernard Gentry: Con; Nathaniel Green: LD
Grogan, John	24/2/61	Lab	Selby	3,836	Kenneth Hind: Con; Ted Batty: LD
Gummer, John	26/11/39	Con	Suffolk Coastal	3,254	Mark Campbell: Lab; Alexandra Jones: LD
Gunnell, John	1/10/33	Lab	Morley and Rothwell	14,750	Alan Barraclough: Con; Mitchell Galdas: LD
Hague, William	26/3/61	Con	Richmond (Yorks)	10,051	Stephen Merritt: Lab; Jane Harvey: LD
Hain, Peter	16/2/50	Lab	Neath	26,741	David Evans: Con; Trefor Jones: PC
Hall, Mike	20/9/52	Lab	Weaver Vale	13,448	James Byrne: Con; Trevor Griffiths: LD
Hall, Patrick	20/10/51	Lab	Bedford	8,300	Robert John Blackman: Con; Christopher Noyce: LD
Hamilton, Archie	30/12/41	Con	Epsom and Ewell	11,525	Philip Woodford: Lab; John Vincent: LD
Hamilton, Fabian	12/4/55	Lab	Leeds North East	6,959	Tim Kirkhope: Con; Bill Winlow: LD
Hammond, Philip	4/12/55	Con	Runnymede and Weybridge	9,875	Ian Peacock: Lab; Geoffrey Taylor: LD
Hancock, Mike	9/4/46	LD	Portsmouth South	4,327	David Martin: Con; Alan Burnett: Lab
Hanson, David	5/7/57	Lab	Delyn	12,693	Karen Lumley: Con; David Lloyd: LD
Harman, Harriet	30/7/50	Lab	Camberwell and Peckham	16,451	Mark Humphreys: Con; Nigel Williams: LD
Harris, Evan	21/10/65	LD	Oxford West and Abingdon	6,285	Laurence Harris: Con; Susan Brown: Lab
Harvey, Nick	3/8/61	LD	Devon North	6,181	Richard Ashworth: Con; Eithne Brenton: Lab
Haselhurst, Alan	23/6/37	Con	Saffron Walden	10,573	Mervin Caton: LD; Malcolm Fincken: Lab
Hawkins, Nick	27/3/57	Con	Surrey Heath	16,287	David Newman: LD; Susan Jones: Lab
Hayes, John	23/6/58	Con	South Holland and The Deepings	7,991	John Lewis: Lab; Peter Millen: LD
Heal, Sylvia	20/7/42	Lab	Halesowen and Rowley Regis	10,337	John Kennedy: Con; Elaine Todd: LD
Heald, Oliver	15/12/54	Con	Hertfordshire North East	3,088	Ivan Gibbons: Lab; Stephen Jarvis: LD
Healey, John	13/2/60	Lab	Wentworth	23,959	Karl Hamer: Con; James Charters: LD
Heath, David	16/3/54	LD	Somerton and Frome	130	Mark Robinson: Con; Robert Ashford: Lab
Heath, Edward	9/7/16	Con	Old Bexley and Sidcup	3,569	Richard Justham: Lab; Iain King: LD

(continued)

Members of the House of Commons *(continued)*

Member	Date of birth	Party	Constituency	Majority at 1997 election	Opponents
Heathcoat-Amory, David	21/3/49	Con	Wells	528	Peter Gold: LD; Michael Eavis: Lab
Henderson, Doug	9/6/49	Lab	Newcastle-upon-Tyne North	19,332	Gregory White: Con; Peter Allen: LD
Henderson, Ivan	7/6/58	Lab	Harwich	1,216	Iain Sproat: Con; Ann Elvin: LD
Hepburn, Stephen	6/12/59	Lab	Jarrow	21,933	Mark Allatt: Con; Tim Stone: LD
Heppell, John	3/11/48	Lab	Nottingham East	15,419	Andrew Raca: Con; Kevin Mulloy: LD
Heseltine, Michael	21/3/33	Con	Henley	11,167	Timothy Horton: LD; Duncan Enright: Lab
Hesford, Stephen	27/5/57	Lab	Wirral West	2,738	David Hunt: Con; John Thornton: LD
Hewitt, Patricia	2/12/48	Lab	Leicester West	12,864	Richard Thomas: Con; Mark Jones: LD
Hill, Keith	28/7/43	Lab	Streatham	18,423	Ernest Noad: Con; Roger O'Brien: LD
Hinchliffe, David	14/10/48	Lab	Wakefield	14,604	Jonathan Peacock: Con; Douglas Dale: LD
Hodge, Margaret	8/9/44	Lab	Barking	15,896	Keith Langford: Con; Mark Marsh: LD
Hoey, Kate	21/6/46	Lab	Vauxhall	18,660	Keith Kerr: LD; Richard Bacon: Con
Hogg, Douglas	5/2/45	Con	Sleaford and North Hykeham	5,123	Sean Harriss: Lab; John Marriott: LD
Home Robertson, John	5/12/48	Lab	East Lothian	14,221	Murdo Fraser: Con; David McCarthy: SNP
Hood, Jimmy	16/5/48	Lab	Clydesdale	13,809	Andrew Doig: SNP; Mark Andrew Izatt: Con
Hoon, Geoffrey	6/12/53	Lab	Ashfield	22,728	Mark Simmonds: Con; William Smith: LD
Hope, Phil	19/4/55	Lab	Corby	11,860	William Powell: Con; Ian Hankinson: LD
Hopkins, Kelvin	22/8/41	Lab	Luton North	9,626	David Senior: Con; Kathryn Newbound: LD
Horam, John	7/3/39	Con	Orpington	2,952	Christopher Maines: LD; Susan Polydorou: Lab
Howard, Michael	7/7/41	Con	Folkestone and Hythe	6,332	David Laws: LD; Peter Doherty: Lab
Howarth, Alan	11/6/44	Lab	Newport	13,523	David Evans: Con; Alastair Cameron: LD
Howarth, George	29/6/49	Lab	Knowsley North and Sefton East	26,147	Carl Doran: Con; David Bamber: LD
Howarth, Gerald	12/9/47	Con	Aldershot	6,621	Adrian Collett: LD; Terrence Bridgeman: Lab
Howells, Kim	19/1/46	Lab	Pontypridd	23,129	Jonathan Cowen: Con; Gareth Llywelyn: PC
Hoyle, Lindsay	10/6/57	Lab	Chorley	9,870	Den Dover: Con; Simon Jones: LD
Hughes, Beverley	30/3/50	Lab	Stretford and Urmston	13,640	John Gregory: Con; John Bridges: LD
Hughes, Kevin	15/12/52	Lab	Doncaster North	21,937	Peter Kennerley: Con; Michael Cook: LD
Hughes, Simon	17/5/51	LD	Southwark North and Bermondsey	3,387	Jeremy Fraser: Lab; Grant Shapps: Con
Humble, Joan	3/3/51	Lab	Blackpool North and Fleetwood	8,946	Harold Elletson: Con; Beverley Hill: LD
Hume, John	18/1/37	SDLP	Foyle	13,664	Mitchell McLaughlin: SF; William Hay: DUP
Hunter, Andrew	8/1/43	Con	Basingstoke	2,397	Nigel Lickley: Lab; Martin Rimmer: LD
Hurst, Alan	2/9/45	Lab	Braintree	1,451	Tony Newton: Con; Trevor Ellis: LD
Hutton, John	6/5/55	Lab	Barrow and Furness	14,497	Richard Hunt: Con; Aileen Metcalfe: LD
Iddon, Brian	5/7/40	Lab	Bolton South East	21,311	Paul Carter: Con; Frank Harasiwka: LD
Illsley, Eric	9/4/55	Lab	Barnsley Central	24,501	Simon Gutteridge: Con; Darren Finlay: LD
Ingram, Adam	1/2/47	Lab	East Kilbride	17,384	George Gebbie: SNP; Clifford Herbertson: Con
Jack, Michael	17/9/46	Con	Fylde	8,963	John Garrett: Lab; William Greene: LD
Jackson, Glenda	9/5/36	Lab	Hampstead and Highgate	13,289	Elizabeth Gibson: Con; Bridget Fox: LD
Jackson, Helen	19/5/39	Lab	Sheffield Hillsborough	16,451	Arthur Dunworth: LD; David Nuttall: Con
Jackson, Robert	24/9/46	Con	Wantage	6,089	Celia Wilson: Lab; Jenny Riley: LD
Jamieson, David	18/5/47	Lab	Plymouth Devonport	19,127	Anthony Johnson: Con; Richard Cpous: LD
Jenkin, Bernard	9/4/59	Con	Essex North	5,476	Timothy Young: Lab; Andrew Phillips: LD
Jenkins, Brian	19/9/42	Lab	Tamworth	7,496	Ann Lightbown: Con; Jennifer Pinkett: LD
Johnson, Alan	5/9/34	Lab	Hull West and Hessle	15,525	Robert Tress: LD; Cormach Moore: Con
Johnson, Melanie	5/2/55	Lab	Welwyn Hatfield	5,595	David Evans: Con; Rodney Schwartz: LD
Johnson Smith, Geoffrey	16/4/24	Con	Wealden	14,204	Michael Skinner: LD; Nicholas Levine: Lab
Jones, Barry	26/6/38	Lab	Alyn and Deeside	16,403	Timothy Peter Roberts: Con; Eleanor Burnham: LD
Jones, Fiona	27/2/57	Lab	Newark	3,016	Richard Alexander: Con; Peter Harris: LD
Jones, Helen	24/12/54	Lab	Warrington North	19,527	Ray Lacey: Con; Ian Greenhalgh: LD
Jones, Ieuan Wyn	22/5/49	PC	Ynys Mon	2,481	Owen Edwards: Lab; Gwilym Owen: Con
Jones, Jenny	8/2/48	Lab	Wolverhampton South West	5,118	Nicholas Budgen: Con; Matthew Green: LD
Jones, Jon Owen	19/4/54	Lab	Cardiff Central	7,923	Jennifer Randerson: LD; David Melding: Con
Jones, Lynne	26/4/51	Lab	Birmingham Selly Oak	14,088	Graham Green: Con; David Osborne: LD
Jones, Martin	1/3/47	Lab	Clwyd South	13,810	Brosi Johnson: Con; Andrew Chadwick: LD
Jones, Nigel	30/3/48	LD	Cheltenham	6,645	William John Todman: Con; Barry Leach: Lab
Jowell, Tessa	17/9/47	Lab	Dulwich and West Norwood	16,769	Roger Gough: Con; Susan Kramer: LD
Kaufman, Gerald	21/6/30	Lab	Manchester Gorton	17,342	Jackie Pearcey: LD; Guy Senior: Con
Keeble, Sally	13/10/51	Lab	Northampton North	10,000	Tony Marlow: Con; Lesley Dunbar: LD
Keen, Alan	25/11/37	Lab	Feltham and Heston	15,473	Reginald Ground: Con; Colin Penning: LD
Keen, Ann	26/11/48	Lab	Brentford and Isleworth	14,424	Nirj Deva: Con; Gareth Hartwell: LD
Keetch, Paul	21/5/61	LD	Hereford	6,648	Colin Shepherd: Con; Arthur Chappell: Lab
Kelly, Ruth	9/5/68	Lab	Bolton West	7,072	Tom Sackville: Con; Barbara Ronson: LD
Kemp, Fraser	1/9/58	Lab	Houghton and Washington East	26,555	Philip Booth: Con; Keith Miller: LD
Kennedy, Charles	25/11/59	LD	Ross, Skye, and Inverness West	4,019	Donnie Munro: Lab; Margaret Paterson: SNP
Kennedy, Jane	19/1/58	Lab	Liverpool Wavertree	19,701	Richard Kemp: LD; Christopher Malthouse: Con
Key, Robert	22/4/45	Con	Salisbury	6,276	Yvonne Emmerson-Pierce: LD; Richard Rogers: Lab

(continued)

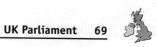

Members of the House of Commons *(continued)*

Member	Date of birth	Party	Constituency	Majority at 1997 election	Opponents
Khabra, Piara	20/11/24	Lab	Ealing Southall	21,423	John Penrose: Con; Nicola Thomson: LD
Kidney, David	21/3/55	Lab	Stafford	4,314	David Cameron: Con; Pamela Hornby: LD
Kilfoyle, Peter	9/6/46	Lab	Liverpool Walton	27,038	Richard Roberts: LD; Mark Kotecha: Con
King, Andrew	14/9/48	Lab	Rugby and Kenilworth	495	James Powsey: Con; Jeremy Roodhouse: LD
King, Oona	22/10/67	Lab	Bethnal Green and Bow	11,285	Kabir Choudhury: Con; Syed Islam: LD
King, Tom	13/6/33	Con	Bridgwater	1,796	Michael Hoban: LD; Roger Lavers: Lab
Kingham, Tess	4/5/63	Lab	Gloucester	8,259	Douglas French: Con; Peter Munisamy: LD
Kirkbride, Julie	5/6/60	Con	Bromsgrove	4,895	Peter McDonald: Lab; Jennette Davy: LD
Kirkwood, Archy	22/4/46	LD	Roxburgh and Berwickshire	7,906	Douglas Younger: Con; Helen Eadie: Lab
Kumar, Ashok	28/5/56	Lab	Middlesbrough South and Cleveland East	10,607	Michael Bates: Con
Ladyman, Stephen	6/11/52	Lab	Thanet South	2,878	Jonathan Aitken: Con; Barbara Hewitt-Silk: LD
Laing, Eleanor	1/2/58	Con	Epping Forest	5,252	Stephen Murray: Lab; Stephen Robinson: LD
Lait, Jackie	16/12/47	Con	Beckenham	1,227[4]	Robert Hughes: Lab; Rosemary Vetterlein: LD
Lansley, Andrew	11/12/56	Con	Cambridgeshire South	8,712	James Quinlan: LD; Tony Gray: Lab
Lawrence, Jackie	9/8/48	Lab	Preseli Pembrokeshire	8,736	Robert Buckland: Con; Jeffrey Clarke: LD
Laxton, Bob	7/9/44	Lab	Derby North	10,615	Greg Knight: Con; Robert Charlesworth: LD
Leigh, Edward	20/7/50	Con	Gainsborough	6,826	Paul Taylor: Lab; Neil Taylor: LD
Lepper, David	15/9/45	Lab	Brighton Pavilion	13,181	Derek Spencer: Con; Ken Blanshard: LD
Leslie, Christopher	28/6/72	Lab	Shipley	2,996	Marcus Fox: Con; John Cole: LD
Letwin, Oliver	19/5/56	Con	Dorset West	1,840	Robin Legg: LD; Robert Bygraves: Lab
Levitt, Tom	10/4/54	Lab	High Peak	8,791	Charles Hendry: Con; Susan Barber: LD
Lewis, Ivan	4/3/67	Lab	Bury South	12,387	David Sumberg: Con; Victor D'Albert: LD
Lewis, Julian	26/9/51	Con	New Forest East	5,215	George Dawson: LD; Alan Goodfellow: Lab
Lewis, Terry	29/12/35	Lab	Worsley	17,741	Damien Garrido: Con; Robert Bleakley: LD
Liddell, Helen	6/12/50	Lab	Airdrie and Shotts	15,412	Keith Robertson: SNP; Nicholas Brook: Con
Lidington, David	30/6/56	Con	Aylesbury	8,419	Sharon Bowles: LD; Robert Langridge: Lab
Lilley, Peter	23/8/43	Con	Hitchen and Harpenden	6,671	Rosemary Sanderson: Lab; Christopher White: LD
Linton, Martin	11/8/44	Lab	Battersea	5,360	John Bowis: Con; Paula Keaveney: LD
Livingstone, Ken	17/6/45	Lab	Brent East	15,882	Mark Gino Francois: Con; Ian Hunter: LD
Livsey, Richard	2/5/35	LD	Brecon and Radnorshire	5,097	Jonathan Evans: Con; Christopher Mann: Lab
Lloyd, Peter	12/11/37	Con	Fareham	10,358	Michael Prior: Lab; Grace Hill: LD
Lloyd, Tony	25/2/50	Lab	Manchester Central	19,682	Alison Firth: LD; Simon McIlwaine: Con
Llywd, Elfyn	26/9/51	PC	Meirionnydd Nant Conwy	6,805	Hefin Rees: Lab; Jeremy Quin: Con
Lock, David	2/5/60	Lab	Wyre Forest	6,946	Anthony Coombs: Con; David Cropp: LD
Lord, Michael	17/10/38	Con	Suffolk Central and Ipswich North	3,538	Carole Jones: Lab; Madeline Goldspink: LD
Loughton, Tim	30/5/62	Con	Worthing East and Shoreham	5,098	Martin Ling: LD; Mark Williams: Lab
Love, Andrew	21/3/49	Lab	Edmonton	13,472	Ian Twinn: Con; Andrew Wiseman: LD
Luff, Peter	18/2/55	Con	Worcestershire Mid	9,412	Diane Smith: Lab; David Barwick: LD
Lyell, Nicholas	6/12/38	Con	Bedfordshire North East	5,883	John Lehall: Lab; Philip Bristow: LD
McAllion, John	13/2/48	Lab	Dundee East	9,961	Shona Robison: SNP; Bruce Mackie: Con
McAvoy, Thomas	14/12/43	Lab	Glasgow Rutherglen	15,007	Ian Gray: SNP; Robert Brown: LD
McCabe, Steve	4/8/55	Lab	Birmingham Hall Green	8,420	Andrew Hargreaves: Con; Charles Dow: LD
McCafferty, Chris	14/10/45	Lab	Calder Valley	6,255	Donald Thompson: Con; Stephen Pearson: LD
McCartney, Ian	25/4/51	Lab	Makerfield	26,177	Michael Winstanley: Con; Bruce Hubbard: LD
McCartney, Robert	24/4/36	UKUP	North Down	1,449	Alan McFarland: UUP
McDonagh, Siobhain	20/2/60	Lab	Mitcham and Morden	13,741	Angela Rumbold: Con; Nicholas Harris: LD
MacDonald, Calum	7/5/56	Lab	Western Isles	3,576	Anne Lorne Gillies: SNP; James McGrigor: Con
McDonnell, John	8/9/51	Lab	Hayes and Harlington	14,289	Andrew Retter: Con; Anthony Little: LD
McFall, John	14/10/44	Lab	Dumbarton	10,883	Bill Mackechnie: SNP; Peter Ramsey: Con
McGrady, Eddie	3/6/35	SDLP	Down South	9,933	Dermott Nesbitt: UUP; Mick Murphy: SF
MacGregor, John	14/2/37	Con	Norfolk South	7,378	Barbara Hacker: LD; Jane Ross: Lab
McGuinness, Martin[1]	23/5/50	SF	Ulster Mid	1,883	William McCrea: DUP; Denis Haughey: SDLP
McGuire, Anne	26/5/49	Lab	Stirling	6,411	Michael Forsyth: Con; Ewan Dow: SNP
McIntosh, Anne	20/9/54	Con	Vale of York	9,721	Matthew Carter: Lab; Charles Hall: LD
McIsaac, Shona	3/4/60	Lab	Cleethorpes	9,176	Michael Brown: Con; Keith Melton: LD
MacKay, Andrew	27/8/49	Con	Bracknell	10,387	Anne Snelgrove: Lab; Alan Hilliar: LD
McKenna, Rosemary	8/5/41	Lab	Cumbernauld and Kilsyth	11,128	Colin Barrie: SNP; Ian Sewell: Con
Mackinlay, Andrew	24/4/49	Lab	Thurrock	17,256	Andrew Rosindell: Con; Joe White: LD
MacLean, David	16/5/53	Con	Penrith and The Border	10,233	Kenneth Walker: LD; Margaret Melling: Lab
McLeish, Henry	15/6/48	Lab	Fife Central	13,713	Tricia Marwick: SNP; Jacob Rees-Mogg: Con
MacLennan, Robert	26/6/36	LD	Caithness, Sutherland, and Easter Ross	2,259	James Hendry: Lab; Evan Harper: SNP
McLoughlin, Patrick	30/11/57	Con	Derbyshire West	4,885	Stephen Clamp: Lab; Christopher Seeley: LD
McNamara, Kevin	5/9/34	Lab	Hull North	19,705	David Lee: Con; David Nolan: LD
McNulty, Tony	3/11/58	Lab	Harrow East	9,737	Hugh Dykes: Con; Baldev Kumar Sharma: LD
MacShane, Denis	21/5/48	Lab	Rotheram	21,469	Simon Gordon: Con; David Wildgoose: LD

(continued)

Members of the House of Commons *(continued)*

Member	Date of birth	Party	Constituency	Majority at 1997 election	Opponents
MacTaggart, Fiona	12/9/53	Lab	Slough	13,071	Peta Jane Buscombe: Con; Chris Bushill: LD
McWalter, Tony	20/3/45	Lab	Hemel Hempstead	3,636	Rob Jones: Con; Patricia Lindsley: LD
McWilliam, John	16/5/41	Lab	Blaydon	16,605	Peter Maughan: LD; Mark Watson: Con
Madel, David	6/8/38	Con	Bedforshire South West	132	Andrew Date: Lab; Stephen Owen: LD
Maginnis, Ken	21/1/38	UUP	Fermanagh and South Tyrone	13,688	Gerry McHugh: SF; Tommy Gallagher: SDLP
Mahon, Alice	28/9/37	Lab	Halifax	11,212	Robert Light: Con; Edgar Waller: LD
Major, John	29/3/43	Con	Huntingdon	18,140	Jason Reece: Lab; Matthew Owen: LD
Malins, Humfrey	31/7/45	Con	Woking	5,678	Philip Goldenberg: LD; Katie Hanson: Lab
Mallaber, Judy	10/7/51	Lab	Amber Valley	11,613	Phillip Oppenheim: Con; Roger Shelley: LD
Mallon, Seamus	17/8/36	SDLP	Newry and Armagh	4,889	Danny Kennedy: UUP; Pat McNamee: SF
Mandelson, Peter	21/10/53	Lab	Hartlepool	17,508	Michael Horsley: Con; Reginald Clark: LD
Maples, John	22/4/43	Con	Stratford-on-Avon	14,106	Susan Juned: LD; Stewart Stacey: Lab
Marek, John	24/12/40	Lab	Wrexham	11,762	Stuart Andrew: Con; Andrew Thomas: LD
Marsden, Gordon	28/11/53	Lab	Blackpool South	11,616	Richard Booth: Con; Doreen Holt: LD
Marsden, Paul	18/3/68	Lab	Shrewsbury and Atcham	1,670	Derek Conway: Con; Anne Woolland: LD
Marshall, David	7/5/41	Lab	Glasgow Shettleston	15,868	Humayan Hanif: SNP; Colin Simpson: Con
Marshall, Jim	13/3/41	Lab	Leicester South	16,493	Christopher Heaton-Harris: Con; Barry Coles: LD
Marshall-Andrews, Robert	10/4/44	Lab	Medway	5,354	Peggy Fenner: Con; Roger Roberts: LD
Martin, Michael	3/7/45	Lab	Glasgow Springburn	17,326	John Brady: SNP; Mark Holdsworth: Con
Martlew, Eric	3/1/49	Lab	Carlisle	12,390	Richard Lawrence: Con; Christopher Mayho: LD
Mates, Michael	9/6/34	Con	Hampshire East	11,590	Robert Booker: LD; Robert Hoyle: Lab
Maude, Francis	4/7/53	Con	Horsham	14,862	Morwen Millson: LD; Maureen Walsh: Lab
Mawhinney, Brian	26/7/40	Con	Cambridgeshire North West	7,754	Lee Steptoe: Lab; Barbara McCoy: LD
Maxton, John	5/5/36	Lab	Glasgow Cathcart	12,965	Maire Whitehead: SNP; Alistair Muir: Con
May, Theresa	1/10/56	Con	Maidenhead	11,981	Andrew Ketteringham: LD; Denise Robson: Lab
Meacher, Michael	4/11/39	Lab	Oldham West and Royton	16,201	Jonathan Lord: Con; Howard Cohen: LD
Meale, Alan	31/7/49	Lab	Mansfield	20,518	Tim Frost: Con; Philip Smith: LD
Merron, Gillian	12/4/59	Lab	Lincoln	11,130	Anthony Brown: Con; Lisa Gabriel: LD
Michael, Alun	22/8/43	Lab	Cardiff South and Penarth	13,881	Caroline Roberts: Con; Simon Wakefield: LD
Michie, Bill	24/11/35	Lab	Sheffield Heeley	17,078	Roger Davison: LD; John Harthman: Con
Michie, Ray	4/2/34	LD	Argyll and Bute	6,081	Neil MacCormick: SNP; Ralph McIlroy Leishman: Con
Milburn, Alan	27/1/58	Lab	Darlington	16,025	Peter Scrope: Con; Les Boxell: LD
Miller, Andrew	23/3/49	Lab	Ellesmere Port and Neston	16,036	Lynn Turnbull: Con; Joanna Pemberton: LD
Mitchell, Austin	19/9/34	Lab	Great Grimsby	16,244	Dean Godson: Con; Andrew De Freitas: LD
Moffatt, Laura	9/4/54	Lab	Crawley	11,707	Jospehine Crabb: Con; Harold De Souza: LD
Moonie, Lewis	25/2/47	Lab	Kirkcaldy	10,710	Stewart Hosie: SNP; Charlotte Black: Con
Moore, Michael	3/6/65	LD	Tweeddale, Ettrick, and Lauderdale	2,290	Keith Gedder: Lab; Alister Jack: Con
Moran, Margaret	19/1/55	Lab	Luton South	11,319	Graham Bright: Con; Keith Fitchett: LD
Morgan, Alasdair	21/4/45	SNP	Galloway and Upper Nithsdale	5,624	Ian Lang: Con; Katy Clark: Lab
Morgan, Julie	2/11/44	Lab	Cardiff North	8,126	Gwilym Jones: Con; Robyn Rowland: LD
Morgan, Rhodri	29/9/39	Lab	Cardiff West	15,628	Simon Hoare: Con; Jacqui Gasson: LD
Morley, Elliott	6/7/52	Lab	Scunthorpe	14,173	Martyn Fisher: Con; Gordon Smith: LD
Morris, Estelle	17/6/52	Lab	Birmingham Yardley	5,315	John Hemming: LD; Anne Jobson: Con
Morris, John	5/11/31	Lab	Aberavon	21,571	Ron McConville: LD; Peter Harper: Con
Moss, Malcolm	6/3/43	Con	Cambridgeshire North East	5,101	Virginia Bucknor: Lab; Andrew Nash: LD
Mountford, Kali	12/1/54	Lab	Colne Valley	4,840	Graham Riddick: Con; Nigel Priestley: LD
Mowlam, Marjorie	18/9/49	Lab	Redcar	21,664	Andrew Isaacs: Con; Joyce Benbow: LD
Mudie, George	6/2/45	Lab	Leeds East	17,466	John Emsley: Con; Madeleine Kirk: LD
Mullin, Chris	12/12/47	Lab	Sunderland South	19,638	Timothy Schofield: Con; John Lennox: LD
Murphy, Denis	2/11/48	Lab	Wansbeck	32,367	Alan Thompson: LD; Paul Green: Con
Murphy, Jim	23/8/67	Lab	Eastwood	3,236	Paul Cullen: Con; Douglas Yates: SNP
Murphy, Paul	25/11/48	Lab	Torfaen	24,536	Neil Parish: Con; Jean Gray: LD
Naysmith, Douglas	1/4/41	Lab	Bristol North West	11,382	Michael Stern: Con; Ian Parry: LD
Nicholls, Patrick	14/11/48	Con	Teignbridge	281	Richard Younger-Ross: LD; Sue Dann: Lab
Norman, Archie	1/5/54	Con	Tunbridge Wells	7,506	Anthony Clayton: LD; Peter Warner: Lab
Norris, Dan	28/1/60	Lab	Wansdyke	4,799	Michael Mark Prisk: Con; Jeff Manning: LD
O'Brien, Brill	25/1/29	Lab	Normanton	15,893	Fiona Bulmer: Con; David Ridgway: LD
O'Brien, Mike	19/1/54	Lab	Warwickshire North	14,767	Stephen Hammond: Con; William Powell: LD
O'Hara, Eddie	1/10/37	Lab	Knowsley South	30,708	Gary Robertson: Con; Clifford Mainey: LD
O'Neill, Martin	6/1/45	Lab	Ochil	4,652	George Reid: SNP; Allan Hogarth: Con
Oaten, Mark	8/3/64	LD	Winchester	21,556[5]	Gerald Malone: Con; Patrick Davies: Lab
Olner, Bill	9/5/42	Lab	Nuneaton	13,540	Richard Blunt: Con; Ron Cockings: LD
Opik, Lembit	2/3/65	LD	Montgomeryshire	6,303	Glyn Davies: Con; Angharad Davies: Lab
Organ, Diana	21/2/52	Lab	Forest of Dean	6,343	Paul Marland: Con; Anthony Lynch: LD
Osborne, Sandra	23/2/56	Lab	Ayr	6,543	Phil Gallie: Con; Ian Blackford: SNP
Ottaway, Richard	24/5/45	Con	Croydon South	11,930	Charles Burling: Lab; Steven Gauge: LD

(continued)

Members of the House of Commons *(continued)*

Member	Date of birth	Party	Constituency	Majority at 1997 election	Opponents
Page, Richard	22/2/41	Con	Hertfordshire South West	10,021	Mark Wilson: Lab; Ann Shaw: LD
Paice, James	24/4/49	Con	Cambridgeshire South East	9,349	Rex Collinson: Lab; Sarah Brinton: LD
Paisley, Ian	6/4/26	DUP	Antrim North	10,574	James Leslie: UUP; Sean Farren: SDLP
Palmer, Nick	5/2/50	Lab	Broxtowe	5,575	Jim Lester: Con; Terrence Miller: LD
Paterson, Owen	24/6/56	Con	Shropshire North	2,195	Ian Lucas: Lab; John Stevens: LD
Pearson, Ian	5/4/59	Lab	Dudley South	13,027	George Simpson: Con; Richard Burt: LD
Pendry, Tom	10/6/34	Lab	Stalybridge and Hyde	14,806	Nicholas de Bois: Con; Martin Cross: LD
Perham, Linda	29/6/47	Lab	Ilford North	3,224	Vivian Bendall: Con; Alan Dean: LD
Pickles, Eric	20/4/52	Con	Brentwood and Ongar	9,690	Elizabeth Bottomley: LD; Marc Young: Lab
Pickthall, Colin	13/9/44	Lab	Lancashire West	17,119	Christopher Varley: Con; Arthur Wood: LD
Pike, Peter	26/6/37	Lab	Burnley	17,062	William Wiggin: Con; Gordon Birtwhistle: LD
Plaskitt, James	23/6/54	Lab	Warwick and Leamington	3,398	Dudley Smith: Con; Nigel Hicks: LD
Pollard, Kerry	27/4/44	Lab	St Albans	4,459	David Rutley: Con; Anthony Rowlands: LD
Pond, Chris	25/9/52	Lab	Gravesham	5,779	Jacques Arnold: Con; Jean Canet: LD
Pope, Greg	29/8/60	Lab	Hyndburn	11,448	Peter Britcliffe: Con; Les Jones: LD
Pound, Stephen	3/7/48	Lab	Ealing North	7,010	Harry Greenway: Con; Anjan Gupta: LD
Powell, Raymond	19/6/28	Lab	Ogmore	24,447	David Unwin: Con; Kirsty Williams: LD
Prentice, Bridget	28/12/52	Lab	Lewisham East	12,127	Philip Hollobone: Con; David Buxton: LD
Prentice, Gordon	28/1/51	Lab	Pendle	10,824	John Midgley: Con; Tony Greaves: LD
Prescott, John	31/5/38	Lab	Hull East	23,318	Angus West: Con; Jim Wastling: LD
Primarolo, Dawn	2/5/54	Lab	Bristol South	19,328	Michael Roe: Con; Stephen Williams: LD
Prior, David	2/12/54	Con	Norfolk North	1,084	Norman Lamb: LD; Michael Cullingham: Lab
Prosser, Gwyn	27/4/43	Lab	Dover	11,739	David Shaw: Con; Mark Corney: LD
Purchase, Ken	8/1/39	Lab	Wolverhampton North East	12,987	David Harvey: Con; Brian Niblett: LD
Quin, Joyce	26/11/44	Lab	Gateshead East and Washington West	24,950	Jacqui Burns: Con; Alan Ord: LD
Quinn, Lawrie	25/12/56	Lab	Scarborough and Whitby	5,124	John Sykes: Con; Martin Allinson: LD
Radice, Giles	4/10/36	Lab	Durham North	26,299	Mark Hardy: Con; Brian Moore: LD
Rammell, Bill	10/10/59	Lab	Harlow	10,514	Jerry Hayes: Con; Lorna Spenceley: LD
Randall, John	5/8/55	Con	Uxbridge	3,766[6]	Andrew Slaughter: Lab; Keith Kerr: LD
Rapson, Syd	17/4/42	Lab	Portsmouth North	4,323	Peter Griffiths: Con; Steve Sollitt: LD
Raynsford, Nick	28/1/45	Lab	Greenwich and Woolwich	18,128	Michael Mitchell: Con; Cherry Luxton: LD
Redwood, John	15/6/51	Con	Wokingham	9,365	Royce Longton: LD; Patricia Colling: Lab
Reed, Andrew	17/9/64	Lab	Loughborough	5,712	Kenneth Andrew: Con; Diana Brass: LD
Reid, John	8/5/47	Lab	Hamilton North and Bellshill	17,067	Michael Matheson: SNP; Gordon McIntosh: Con
Rendel, David	15/4/49	LD	Newbury	8,617	Richard Benyon: Con; Paul Hannon: Lab
Robathan, Andrew	17/7/51	Con	Blaby	6,474	Ross Willmott: Lab; Geoffrey Welsh: LD
Robertson, George	12/4/46	Lab	Hamilton South	15,878	Ian Black: SNP; Robert Dow Kilgour: Con
Robertson, Lawrence	29/3/58	Con	Tewkesbury	9,234	John Sewell: LD; Kelvin Tustin: Lab
Robinson, Geoffrey	25/5/39	Lab	Coventry North West	16,601	Paul Bartlett: Con; Napier Penlington: LD
Robinson, Peter	29/12/48	DUP	Belfast East	6,754	Reg Empey: UUP
Roche, Barbara	13/4/54	Lab	Hornsey and Wood Green	20,499	Helena Hart: Con; Lynne Featherstone: LD
Roe, Marion	15/7/36	Con	Broxbourne	6,653	Ben Coleman: Lab; Julia Davies: LD
Rogers, Allan	24/10/32	Lab	Rhondda	24,931	Leanne Wood: PC; Rodney Berman: LD
Rooker, Jeff	5/6/41	Lab	Birmingham Perry Barr	18,957	Andrew Dunnett: Con; Ray Hassall: LD
Rooney, Terry	11/11/50	Lab	Bradford North	12,770	Rasjid Skinner: Con; Terry Browne: LD
Ross, Ernie	27/7/42	Lab	Dundee West	11,859	John Dorward: SNP; Neil Powrie: Con
Ross, William	4/2/36	UUP	Londonderry East	3,794	Gregory Campbell: DUP; Arthur Docherty: SDLP
Rowe, Andrew	11/99/35	Con	Faversham and Kent Mid	4,173	Alan Stewart: Lab; Bruce Parmenter: LD
Rowlands, Ted	23/1/40	Lab	Merthyr Tydfil and Rhymney	27,086	Duncan Ansty: LD; Jonathan Morgan: Con
Roy, Frank	29/8/58	Lab	Motherwell and Wishaw	12,791	James McGuigan: SNP; Scott Dickson: Con
Ruane, Chris	8/7/58	Lab	Vale of Clwyd	8,955	David Edwards: Con; Daniel Munford: LD
Ruddock, Joan	28/12/43	Lab	Lewisham Deptford	18,878	Irene Kimm: Con; Kofi Appiah: LD
Ruffley, David	18/4/62	Con	Bury St Edmunds	368	Mark Ereira: Lab; David Cooper: LD
Russell, Bob	31/3/46	LD	Colchester	1,551	Stephan Shakespeare: Con; Roderick Green: Lab
Russell, Christine	25/3/45	Lab	Chester, City of	10,553	Gyles Brandreth: Con; David Simpson: LD
Ryan, Joan	8/9/55	Lab	Enfield North	6,812	Mark Field: Con; Michael Hopkins: LD
St Aubyn, Nick	19/11/55	Con	Guildford	4,791	Margaret Sharp: LD; Joseph Burns: Lab
Salmond, Alex	31/12/54	SNP	Banff and Buchan	12,845	William Bell-Frain: Con; Megan Harris: Lab
Salter, Martin	19/4/54	Lab	Reading West	2,997	Nicholas Bennett: Con; Dierdre Tomlin: LD
Sanders, Adrian	25/4/59	LD	Torbay	12	Rupert Allason: Con; Michael Morey: Lab
Sarwar, Mohammad	18/8/52	Lab	Glasgow, Govan	2,914	Nicola Sturgeon: SNP; William Thomas: Con
Savidge, Malcolm	9/5/46	Lab	Aberdeen North	10,010	Brian Adam: SNP; James Gifford: Con
Sawford, Phil	26/6/50	Lab	Kettering	189	Roger Freeman: Con; Roger Aron: LD
Sayeed, Jonathan	20/3/48	Con	Bedfordshire Mid	7,090	Neil Mallett: Lab; Timothy Hill: LD
Sedgemore, Brian	17/3/37	Lab	Hackney South and Shoreditch	14,990	Martin Pantling: LD; Christopher O'Leary: Con
Shaw, Jonathon	3/6/66	Lab	Chatham and Aylesford	2,790	Richard Knox-Johnston: Con; Robin Murray: LD

(continued)

Members of the House of Commons *(continued)*

Member	Date of birth	Party	Constituency	Majority at 1997 election	Opponents
Sheerman, Barry	17/8/40	Lab	Huddersfield	15,848	Bill Forrow: Con; Gordon Beever: LD
Sheldon, Robert	13/9/23	Lab	Ashton-under-Lyne	22,965	Richard Mayson: Con; Timothy Pickstone: LD
Shephard, Gillian	22/1/40	Con	Norfolk South West	2,434	Adrian Heffernan: Lab; David Buckton: LD
Shepherd, Richard	6/12/42	Con	Aldridge-Brownhills	2,526	Janos Toth: Lab; Celia Downie: LD
Shipley, Debra	22/6/57	Lab	Stourbridge	5,645	Warren Hawksley: Con; Chris Bramau: LD
Short, Clare	15/2/46	Lab	Birmingham Ladywood	23,082	Shailesh Vara: Con; Sardul Singh Marwa: LD
Simpson, Alan	20/9/48	Lab	Nottingham South	13,364	Brian Kirsch: Con; Gareth Long: LD
Simpson, Keith	29/3/49	Con	Norfolk Mid	1,336	Daniel Zeichner: Lab; Susan Frary: LD
Singh, Marsha	11/10/54	Lab	Bradford West	3,877	Mohammed Riaz: Con; Helen Wright: LD
Skinner, Dennis	11/2/32	Lab	Bolsover	27,149	Richard Harwood: Con; Ian Cox: LD
Smith, Andrew	1/2/51	Lab	Oxford East	16,665	Jonathan Djanogly: Con; George Kershaw: LD
Smith, Angela	7/1/59	Lab	Basildon	13,280	John Baron: Con; Lindsay Granshaw: LD
Smith, Chris	24/7/51	Lab	Islington South and Finsbury	14,563	Sarah Ludford: LD; David Berens: Con
Smith, Geraldine	29/8/61	Lab	Morecambe and Lunesdale	5,965	Mark Lennox-Boyd: Con; June Greenwell: LD
Smith, Jacqui	3/11/62	Lab	Redditch	6,125	Anthea McIntyre: Con; Malcolm Hall: LD
Smith, John	17/3/51	Lab	Vale of Glamorgan	10,532	Walter Sweeney: Con; Suzanne Campbell: LD
Smith, Llew	16/4/44	Lab	Blaenau Gwent	28,032	Geraldine Layton: LD; Margrit Williams: Con
Smith, Robert	15/4/58	LD	Aberdeenshire West and Kincardine	2,662	George Kynoch: Con; Joy Mowatt: SNP
Smyth, Martin	15/6/31	UUP	Belfast South	4,600	Alasdair McDonald: SDLP
Snape, Peter	12/2/42	Lab	West Bromwich East	13,584	Brian Matsell: Con; Martyn Smith: LD
Soames, Nicholas	12/2/48	Con	Sussex Mid	6,854	Margaret Collins: LD; Mervyn Hamilton: Lab
Soley, Clive	7/5/39	Lab	Ealing Acton and Shepherd's Bush	15,650	Barabara Yerolemou: Con; Andrew Mitchell: LD
Southworth, Helen	13/11/56	Lab	Warrington South	10,807	Christopher Grayling: Con; Peter Walker: LD
Spellar, John	5/8/47	Lab	Warley	15,451	Christopher Pincher: Con; Jeremy Pursehouse: LD
Spelman, Caroline	4/5/58	Con	Meriden	582	Brian Seymour-Smith: Lab; Anthony Dupont: LD
Spicer, Michael	22/1/43	Con	Worcestershire West	3,846	Michael Hadley: LD; Meil Stone: Lab
Spring, Richard	24/9/46	Con	Suffolk West	1,867	Michael Jeffreys: Lab; Adrian Graves: LD
Squire, Rachel	13/7/54	Lab	Dunfermline West	12,354	John Lloyd: SNP; Elizabeth Harris: LD
Stanley, John	19/1/42	Con	Tonbridge and Malling	10,230	Barbara Withstandley: Lab; Keith Brown: LD
Starkey, Phyllis	4/1/47	Lab	Milton Keynes South West	10,092	Barry Legg: Con; Peter Jones: LD
Steen, Anthony	22/7/39	Con	Totnes	877	Rob Chave: LD; Victor Ellery: Lab
Steinberg, Gerry	20/4/45	Lab	Durham, City of	22,504	Richard Chalk: Con; Nigel Martin: LD
Stevenson, George	30/8/38	Lab	Stoke-on-Trent South	18,303	Sheila Scott: Con; Peter Barnett: LD
Stewart, David	5/5/56	Lab	Inverness East, Nairn, and Lochaber	2,339	Fergus Ewing: SNP; Stephen Gallagher: LD
Stewart, Ian	28/8/50	Lab	Eccles	21,916	Gregory Barker: Con; Robert Boyd: LD
Stinchcombe, Paul	25/4/62	Lab	Wellingborough	187	Peter Fry: Con; Peter Smith: LD
Stoate, Howard	14/4/54	Lab	Dartford	4,328	Bob Dunn: Con; Dorothy Webb: LD
Stott, Roger	7/8/43	Lab	Wigan	22,643	Mark Loveday: Con; Trevor Beswick: LD
Strang, Gavin	10/7/43	Lab	Edinburgh East and Musselburgh	14,530	Derrick White: SNP; Kenneth Ward: Con
Straw, Jack	3/8/46	Lab	Blackburn	14,445	Sangeeta Kaur Sidhu: Con; Stephen Fenn: LD
Streeter, Gary	19/1/55	Con	Devon South West	7,433	Chris Mavin: Lab; Keith Baldry: LD
Stringer, Graham	17/2/50	Lab	Manchester Blackley	19,588	Stephen Barclay: Con; Simon Wheale: LD
Stuart, Gisela	26/11/55	Lab	Birmingham Edgbaston	4,842	Andrew Marshall: Con; James Gallagher: LD
Stunnell, Andrew	24/11/42	LD	Hazel Grove	11,814	Brendan Murphy: Con; Jeffrey Lewis: Lab
Sutcliffe, Gerry	13/5/53	Lab	Bradford South	12,936	Anne Hawkesworth: Con; Alexander Wilson-Fletcher: LD
Swayne, Desmond	20/8/56	Con	New Forest West	11,332	Robert Hale: LD; David Griffiths: Lab
Swinney, John	13/4/64	SNP	Tayside North	4,160	Bill Walker: Con; Ian McFatridge: Lab
Syms, Robert	15/8/56	Con	Poole	5,298	Alan Tetlow: LD; Hadyn White: Lab
Tapsell, Peter	1/2/30	Con	Louth and Horncastle	6,900	John Hough: Lab; Fiona Martin: LD
Taylor, Ann	2/7/47	Lab	Dewsbury	8,323	Paul McCormick: Con; Kingsley Hill: LD
Taylor, Dari	13/12/44	Lab	Stockton South	11,585	Tim Devlin: Con; Peter Monck: LD
Taylor, David	22/8/46	Lab	Leicestershire North West	13,219	Robert Goodwill: Con; Stanley Heptinstall: LD
Taylor, Ian	18/4/45	Con	Esher and Walton	14,528	Julie Reay: Lab; Gary Miles: LD
Taylor, John D	24/12/37	UUP	Strangford	5,852	Iris Robinson: DUP
Taylor, John M	19/8/41	Con	Solihull	11,397	Michael Southcombe: LD; Rachel Harris: Lab
Taylor, Matthew	3/1/63	LD	Truro and St Austell	12,501	Neil Badcock: Con; Michael Dooley: Lab
Taylor, Teddy	18/4/37	Con	Rochford and Southend East	4,225	Nigel Smith: Lab; Paula Smith: LD
Temple-Morris, Peter	12/2/38	Con	Leominster	8,835	Terence James: LD; Richard Westwood: Lab
Thomas, Gareth	25/9/54	Lab	Clwyd West	1,848	Rod Richards: Con; Eryl Williams: PC
Thomas, Gareth R	15/7/67	Lab	Harrow West	1,240	Robert Hughes: Con; Pash Nandhra: LD
Thompson, William	26/10/39	UUP	Tyrone West	1,161	Jo Byrne: SDLP; Pat Doherty: SF
Timms, Stephen	29/7/55	Lab	East Ham	19,358	Angela Bray: Con; Imran Khan: SLP
Tipping, Paddy	24/10/49	Lab	Sherwood	16,812	Roland Spencer: Con; Bruce Moult: LD
Todd, Mark	29/12/54	Lab	Derbyshire South	13,967	Edwina Currie: Con; Robert Reynold: LD
Tonge, Jenny	19/2/41	LD	Richmond Park	2,951	Jeremy Hanley: Con; Sue Jenkins: Lab
Touhig, Don	5/12/47	Lab	Islwyn	23,931	Chris Worker: LD; David Walters: Con

(continued)

Members of the House of Commons *(continued)*

Member	Date of birth	Party	Constituency	Majority at 1997 election	Opponents
Townend, John	12/6/34	Con	Yorkshire East	3,337	Ian Male: Lab; David Leadley: LD
Tredinnick, David	19/1/50	Con	Bosworth	1,027	Andrew Furlong: Lab; Jonathan Ellis: LD
Trend, Michael	19/4/52	Con	Windsor	9,917	Christopher Fox: LD; Amanda Williams: Lab
Trickett, Jon	2/7/50	Lab	Hemsworth	23,992	Norman Hazell: Con; Jacqueline Kirby: LD
Trimble, David	15/10/44	UUP	Upper Bann	9,252	Brid Rodgers: SDLP; Bernadette O'Hagan: SF
Truswell, Paul	17/11/55	Lab	Pudsey	6,207	Peter Bone: Con; Jonathan Brown: LD
Turner, Dennis	26/8/42	Lab	Wolverhampton South East	15,182	William Hanbury: Con; Richard Whitehouse: LD
Turner, Desmond	17/7/39	Lab	Brighton Kemptown	3,234	Andrew Bowden: Con; Clive Gray: LD
Turner, George	9/8/40	Lab	Norfolk North West	1,339	Henry Bellingham: Con; Evelyn Knowles: LD
Twigg, Derek	9/7/59	Lab	Halton	23,650	Philip Balmer: Con; Janet Jones: LD
Twigg, Stephen	25/12/66	Lab	Enfield Southgate	1,433	Michael Portillo: Con; Jeremy Browne: LD
Tyler, Paul	29/10/41	LD	Cornwall North	13,847	Nigel Linacre: Con; Anne Lindo: Lab
Tyrie, Andrew	15/1/57	Con	Chichester	9,734	Peter Gardiner: LD; Charlie Smith: Lab
Vaz, Keith	26/11/56	Lab	Leicester East	18,422	Simon Milton: Con; Jay Matabudul: LD
Viggers, Peter	13/3/38	Con	Gosport	6,258	Ivan Gray: Lab; Stephen Hogg: LD
Vis, Rudi	4/4/41	Lab	Finchley and Golders Green	3,189	John Marshall: Con; Jonathan Davies: LD
Walker, Cecil	17/12/24	UUP	Belfast North	13,024	Alban Maginness: SDLP; Gerry Kelly: SF
Wallace, Jim	25/8/54	LD	Orkney and Shetland	6,968	James Paton: Lab; Willie Ross: SNP
Walley, Joan	23/1/49	Lab	Stoke-on-Trent North	17,392	Christopher Day: Con; Henry Jebb: LD
Walter, Robert	3/5/48	Con	Dorset North	2,746	Paula Yates: LD; John Fitzmaurice: Lab
Ward, Claire	9/5/72	Lab	Watford	5,792	Robert Gordon: Con; Andrew Canning: LD
Wardle, Charles	23/8/39	Con	Bexhill and Battle	11,100	Kathryn Field: LD; Robert Beckwith: Lab
Wareing, Robret	20/8/30	Lab	Liverpool West Derby	25,965	Steve Radford: Lib; Anne Hines: LD
Waterson, Nigel	12/10/50	Con	Eastbourne	1,994	Christopher Berry: LD; David Lines: Lab
Watts, Dave	26/8/51	Lab	St Helens North	23,417	Pelham Walker: Con; John Beirne: LD
Webb, Steven	18/7/65	LD	Northavon	2,137	John Cope: Con; Ron Stone: Lab
Wells, Bowen	4/8/35	Con	Hertford and Stortford	6,885	Simon Speller: Lab; Michael Wood: LD
Welsh, Andrew	19/4/44	SNP	Angus	10,189	Sebastian Leslie: Con; Catherine Taylor: Lab
White, Brian	5/5/57	Lab	Milton Keynes North East	240	Peter Butler: Con; Graham Mabbutt: LD
Whitehead, Alan	15/9/50	Lab	Southampton Test	13,684	James Hill: Con; Alan Dowden: LD
Whitney, Raymond	28/11/30	Con	Wycombe	2,370	Christopher Bryant: Lab; Paul Bensilum: LD
Whittingdale, John	16/10/59	Con	Maldon and Chelmsford	10,039	Kevin Freeman: Lab; Graham Pooley: LD
Wicks, Malcolm	1/7/47	Lab	Croydon North	18,398	Ian Martin: Con; Martin Morris: LD
Widdecombe, Ann	4/10/47	Con	Maidstone and The Weald	9,603	John Morgan: Lab; Jane Nelson: LD
Wigley, Dafydd	1/4/43	PC	Caernarfon	7,949	Elwyn Williams: Con; Joan MacQueen: LD
Wilkinson, John	23/9/40	Con	Ruislip Northwood	7,794	Paul Barker: Lab; Chris Edwards: LD
Willetts, David	9/3/56	Con	Havant	3,729	Lynne Armstrong: Lab; Michael Kooner: LD
Williams, Alan	14/10/30	Lab	Swansea West	14,459	Andrew Baker: Con; John Newbury: LD
Williams, Alan Wynne	21/12/45	Lab	Carmarthen East and Dinefwr	3,450	Rhodri Thomas: PC; Edmund Hayward: Con
Williams, Betty	31/7/44	Lab	Conwy	1,596	Roger Roberts: LD; David Jones: Con
Willis, Phil	30/11/41	LD	Harrogate and Knaresborough	6,236	Norman Lamont: Con; Barbara Boyce: Lab
Wills, Michael	20/5/52	Lab	Swindon North	7,688	Guy Opperman: Con; Mike Evemy: LD
Wilshire, David	16/9/43	Con	Spelthorne	3,473	Keith Dibble: Lab; Edward Glynn: LD
Wilson, Brian	13/12/48	Lab	Cunninghame North	11,039	Margaret Mitchell: Con; Kim Nicoll: SNP
Winnick, David	26/6/33	Lab	Walsall North	12,588	Michael Bird: Con; Tracy O'Brien: LD
Winterton, Ann	6/3/41	Con	Congleton	6,130	Joan Walmsley: LD; Freda Scholey: Lab
Winterton, Nicholas	31/3/38	Con	Macclesfield	8,654	Janet Jackson: Lab; Mike Flynn: LD
Winterton, Rosie	10/8/58	Lab	Doncaster Central	17,856	David Turtle: Con; Simon Tarry: LD
Wise, Audrey	4/1/35	Lab	Preston	18,680	Paul Gray: Con; William Chadwick: LD
Wood, Mike	3/3/46	Lab	Batley and Spen	6,141	Elizabeth Peacock: Con; Kath Pinnock: LD
Woodward, Shaun	26/10/58	Con	Witney	7,028	Alexander Hollingsworth: Lab; Angela Lawrence: LD
Woolas, Phil	11/12/59	Lab	Oldham East and Saddleworth	3,389	Chris Davies: LD; John Hudson: Con
Worthington, Tony	11/10/41	Lab	Clydebank and Milngavie	13,320	James Yuill: SNP; Nancy Morgan: Con
Wray, James	28/4/38	Lab	Glasgow Bailliestown	14,840	Patsy Thomson: SNP; Malcolm Gordon Kelly: Con
Wright, Tony	11/3/48	Lab	Cannock Chase	14,478	John Backhouse: Con; Richard Kirby: LD
Wright, Tony	12/8/54	Lab	Great Yarmouth	8,668	Michael Carttiss: Con; Derek Wood: LD
Wyatt, Derek	4/12/49	Lab	Sittingbourne and Sheppey	1,929	Roger Moate: Con; Roger Truelove: LD
Yeo, Tim	20/3/45	Con	Suffolk South	4,175	Paul Bishop: Lab; Anne Pollard: LD
Young, George	16/7/41	Con	Hampshire North West	11,551	Charles Fleming: LD; Michael Mumford: Lab

[1] Do not take their seats.
[2] After a by-election on 6 November 1997 following the death of Gordon McMaster (Lab; majority at the 1997 general election 12,750) on 28 July 1997.
[3] After a by-election on 10 June 1999, following the death of Derek Fatchett (Lab; majority at the 1997 general election 20,689) on 9 May 1999.
[4] After a by-election on 20 November 1997 following the resignation of Piers Merchant (Con; majority at the 1997 general election 4,953) on 21 October 1997.
[5] After a by-election on 20 November 1997 following a successful election petition against the general election result where the majority over the Conservative candidate was 2.
[6] After a by-election on 31 July 1997 following the death of Michael Shersby (Con; majority at the 1997 general election 724) on 8 May 1997.

House of Commons Select Committees

Parliamentary select committees were set up to restore parliamentary control of the executive, improve the quality of legislation, and scrutinize public spending and the work of government departments. Select committees usually consist of 10 to 15 members of all parties, and most are tied to government departments. Select committees represent a major 20th-century parliamentary reform and a possible means – through their all-party membership – of avoiding the repeal of one government's measures by its successor.

Name	Number of members	Chair
Accommodation and Works Committee	9	Sydney Chapman (Con)
Agriculture Committee	11	Peter Luff (Con)
Culture, Media, and Sport Committee	11	Gerald Kaufman (Lab)
Defence Committee	11	Bruce George (Lab)
Deregulation Committee	18	Peter L Pike (Lab)
Education and Employment Committee		
Education Sub-Committee	10	Malcolm Wicks (Lab)
Employment Sub-Committee	9	Derek Foster (Lab)
Environment, Transport, and Regional Affairs Committee		
Environment Sub-Committee	11	Andrew F Bennett (Lab)
Transport Sub-Committee	11	Gwyneth Dunwoody (Lab)
Environmental Audit Committee	16	John Horam (Con)
European Scrutiny Committee	16	Jimmy Hood (Lab)
Food Standards Committee	13	Kevin Barron (Lab)
Foreign Affairs Committee	12	Donald Anderson (Lab)
Health Committee	11	David Hinchliffe (Lab)
Home Affairs Committee	11	Chris Mullin (Lab)
Information Committee	9	Richard Allan (LD)
International Development Committee	11	Bowen Wells (Con)
Liaison Committee	33	Robert Sheldon (Lab)
Modernization Committee	15	Margaret Beckett (Lab)
Northern Ireland Affairs Committee	13	Peter Brooke (Con)
Joint Committee on Parliamentary Privilege	12	Lord Nicholls of Birkenhead (nominated by the House of Lords)
Procedure Committee	14	Nicholas Winterton (Con)
Committee of Public Accounts	16	David Davis (Con)
Select Committee on Public Administration	11	Rhodri Morgan (Lab)
Science and Technology Committee	11	Michael Clark (Con)
Scottish Affairs Committee	11	David Marshall (Lab)
Social Security Committee	11	Archy Kirkwood (LD)
Standards and Privileges Committee	11	Robert Sheldon (Lab)
Trade and Industry Committee	11	Martin O'Neill (Lab)
Treasury Committee	12	Giles Radice (Lab)
Welsh Affairs Committee	11	Martyn Jones (Lab)

Women MPs in the House of Commons

Political party	Number of members	Number of women members	(%) women members
Labour	418	101	24
Conservative	162	14	9
Liberal Democrats	46	3	7
Ulster Unionists	10	0	0
Scottish National Party	6	2	33
Plaid Cymru	4	0	0
Social Democratic and Labour Party	3	0	0
Ulster Democratic Unionist Party	2	0	0
Sinn Féin	2	0	0
United Kingdom Unionist	1	0	0
Independent	1	0	0
The Speaker and three Deputies (do not normally vote)	4	1	25
Total	659	121	18

UK Ministers' Pay

Full ministerial salary entitlement for Ministers in Commons (excluding Parliamentary salary). (In pounds.)

Year	Prime Minister	Cabinet Minister Commons	Cabinet Minister Lords	Minister of State Commons[1]	Minister of State Lords	Parliamentary Under Secretary Commons	Parliamentary Under Secretary Lords
1965	14,000	8,500	8,500	5,625	5,625	3,750	3,750
1972	20,000	13,000	13,000	7,500	7,500	5,500	5,500
1976	20,000	13,000	13,000	7,500	7,500	5,500	5,500
1977	20,000	13,000	13,000	7,500	7,500	5,500	6,020
1978	22,000	14,300	14,300	8,250	8,822	6,050	6,622
1979	33,000	19,650	19,650	12,625	12,911	9,525	9,811
1980	34,650	23,500	23,500	16,250	16,400	12,350	12,500
1981	36,725	27,825	27,825	19,775	23,275	15,100	18,600
1982	38,200	28,950	28,950	20,575	24,200	15,700	19,350
1983	38,987	29,367	30,110	20,867	25,350	15,917	20,390
1984	40,424	30,304	31,680	21,364	26,670	16,154	21,450
1985	41,891	31,271	33,260	21,881	28,000	16,411	22,520
1986	43,328	32,208	34,820	22,378	29,320	16,648	23,580
1987	44,775	33,145	36,390	22,875	30,640	16,885	24,640
1988	45,787	34,157	40,438	23,887	34,688	17,897	28,688
1989	46,109	34,479	41,997	24,209	37,047	18,219	30,647
1990	46,750	35,120	44,591	24,850	39,641	18,860	33,241
1991	50,724	38,105	48,381	26,962	43,010	20,463	36,066
1992	53,007	39,820	50,558	28,175	44,945	21,384	37,689
1994	54,438	40,895	52,260	28,936	46,333	21,961	38,894
1995	57,018	42,834	55,329	30,307	48,835	23,002	41,065
1996	58,557	43,991	57,161	31,125	50,328	23,623	42,361
1996	58,557	43,991	58,876	31,125	51,838	23,623	43,632
1997[2]	100,000	60,000	77,963	31,125	51,838	23,623	43,632
1998	102,750	61,650	80,107	31,981	53,264	24,273	44,832

[1] Until 1980 some Ministers of State received salaries higher than those shown here.
[2] In 1997, the Prime Minister and Cabinet Ministers decided to accept the pre-election salaries of £58,557 (Prime Minister), £43,991 (Cabinet Commons), and £58,876 (Cabinet Lords).

Source: House of Commons Information Office

Members of Parliament: Pay

Year	Salary (£)	Year	Salary (£)	Year	Salary (£)
1911	400	1977	6,270	1989	24,107
1931	360	1978	6,897	1990	26,701
1934	380	1979	9,450	1991	28,970
1935	400	1980	11,750	1992	30,854
1937	600	1981	13,950	1993	30,854
1946	1,000	1982	14,510	1994	31,687
1954[1]	1,250	1983	15,308	1995	33,189
1957	1,750	1984	16,106	1996	34,085
1964	3,250	1985	16,904	1996	43,000
1972	4,500	1986	17,702	1997	43,860
1975	5,750	1987	18,500	1998	45,066
1976	6,062	1988	22,548	1999	47,008

[1] Includes sessional allowance.

Source: House of Commons Information Office

Members of Parliament: Office Cost Allowances

These allowances were first introduced in 1969. These figures represent the maximum that can be claimed.

Year	Allowance (£)	Year	Allowance (£)
1969	500	1986	20,140
1972	1,000	1987	21,302
1974	1,750	1988	22,588
1975	3,200	1989	24,903
1976	3,512	1990	27,166
1977	3,687	1991	28,986
1978	4,200	1992	39,960
1979	4,600	1993	40,380
1980	6,750	1994	41,308
1980	8,000	1995	42,754
1981	8,480	1996 (paid at first)[1]	43,908
1982	8,820	1996 (from July 1996)	46,364
1983	11,364	1997	47,568
1984	12,437	1998	49,232
1985	13,211	1999	50,264

[1] In July 1996 the House decided by resolution that allowances in any one quarter in the year should not exceed £11,591. Increases in subsequent years are to be linked to the Retail Prices Index for March and will apply from April.

Source: House of Commons Information Office

Members of Parliament: Non-Office Cost Allowances

1999 figures. These allowances were first introduced in 1969.

Allowance	Provisions	Amount
Supplementary London Allowance	Members whose constituency is within Inner London can claim a London Supplement payment	£1,436
Additional Costs Allowance	Members with constituencies outside Inner London can claim additional expenses incurred in staying overnight away from home while on Parliamentary duties	annual maximum of £12,984
Motor mileage	for journeys made on Parliamentary business between home, constituency, and Westminster	51.2 pence per mile up to 20,000 miles per annum; 23.6 pence per mile after 20,000 miles per annum
Bicycle allowance	for journeys undertaken by bicycle while on Parliamentary duties in the UK	6.5 pence per mile
Travel warrants	Members receive travel warrants which can be exchanged for tickets to travel by rail, sea, or air on Parliamentary business; journeys cover home, constituency, and Westminster. For journeys outside this triangle, on Parliamentary business, costs can be reimbursed if the Fees Office is notified at least three days in advance (three day rule can be waived in exceptional circumstances)	cost of journey
Parking	Members can use the Parliamentary car park	free
Travel for spouses and children	travel warrants are available for Members' spouses and children under the age of 18, between London and the constituency and/or London and home by rail, sea, or air. Children and spouses can make 15 return journeys per calendar year	cost of journey
Travel to European Community institutions	Members can reclaim their travel costs on Parliamentary business between the UK and the European Community institutions in Brussels, Luxembourg, or Strasbourg. Members are allowed one visit per calendar year	cost of a business class air fare from a London airport and a maximum of two days subsistence at the Civil Service Class A rate
Postage and telephone costs	Members receive free stationery, and free inland telephone and postal services on Parliamentary business	free
Winding-Up Allowance	up to a third of the annual Office Costs Allowance can be paid to reimburse the cost of any work done on Parliamentary business undertaken on behalf of a retiring, defeated, or deceased Member, after the date of cessation.	annual limit £16,755
Resettlement Grant	to assist with the costs of adjusting to 'non-parliamentary life', Members receive this grant if they lose their seat at a general election	amount varies between 50% and 100% of the Member's annual salary at the time of the Dissolution of Parliament, prior to the general election; amount is based on age

Source: House of Commons Information Office

House of Lords

Composition of the House of Lords by Peerage Type

Ten persons who had inherited peerages have disclaimed them for life (three of these now sit in the House by virtue of other titles).

Peerage type	Number
Archbishops and bishops	26
Peers by succession	751 (17 women)
Hereditary peers of first creation	8
Life peers under the Appellate Jurisdiction Act 1876	27
Life peers under the Life Peerages Act 1958	478 (87 women)
Total	1,290
Including	
Lords without Writs of Summons	69 (3 minors)
Peers on leave of absence from the House	58

Source: House of Lords Journal Office, House of Lords, © Crown copyright 1999

Composition of the House of Lords by Rank

Peerage	Number
Prince (of the Blood Royal)	1
Archbishops	2
Dukes and Dukes of Blood Royal	25+3
Marquesses	34
Earls and countesses	169+5
Viscounts	103
Bishops	24
Barons/lords and baronesses and ladies	825+96+3
Total	1,290

Source: House of Lords Journal Office, House of Lords, © Crown copyright 1999

House of Lords Reform

BY DENIS DERBYSHIRE

To those on the left of the political spectrum in the UK the House of Lords, with its built-in Conservative majority of hereditary peers, has always been an anachronism and successive Labour governments have vowed to reform it. But the question always asked was how to do this. The nomination of life peers was a step in that direction but – as life peers are nominated by political parties and not by the people – still not overtly democratic. On the other hand, to have a totally elected chamber, with clearly defined powers in relation to the Commons, as most bicameral (dual chamber) systems are constructed, might produce an upper chamber strong enough to challenge the Commons, and indeed one enjoying greater prestige, as with the US House of Representatives and the Senate.

First steps

The Labour Party decided to institute reform in a gradual way and in its manifesto for the 1997 general election it proposed, initially, to strip hereditary peers of their voting rights. The Conservative Party's response was to set up a committee, under the chairmanship of the former Lord Chancellor, Lord Mackay of Clashfern, to examine the problem and to produce a report in July 1998. After the 1997 Labour general election victory the new Conservative leader, William Hague, threatened to use his party's majority in the Lords to block any legislation to remove hereditary peers' voting rights before the submission of proposals for a comprehensive reform of the House.

A totally elected chamber … might produce an upper chamber strong enough to challenge the Commons.

In October 1998 the Labour leader of the Lords, Baroness Jay, announced that a bill would be introduced to terminate the hereditary component in the House and a royal commission would be set up to consider options for definitive reform. She said that in the period before the royal commission has submitted its report, a 'transitional chamber' of about 530 life peers would legitimize the House. The Conservative Lords' leader, Lord Cranbourne, said that hereditary peers would 'go quietly if an independent chamber is put in place' but legislation would be blocked if only partial reform was attempted. In December 1998 a major constitutional crisis was avoided by the government negotiating with the Conservative Lords' leader a compromise proposal in which 91 hereditary peers would be retained in an interim second chamber, pending full reform.

Lord Cranbourne was summarily dismissed by William Hague for negotiating the agreement without consulting him first. Despite Cranbourne's backing by Conservative peers, Hague upheld the dismissal, writing to him that 'it can never be acceptable for a member of the front bench to seek to bring about a change in the policy of the party without the knowledge or agreement of the party leader or the shadow cabinet'. Lord Cranbourne publicly acknowledged that he had 'behaved quite outrageously' but stood by the agreement. Four front bench Tory peers resigned in protest at Cranbourne's dismissal. Hague maintained that he did not disagree with the agreement, only with the way in which it had been reached.

Royal commission

In February 1999 the government set up a royal commission chaired by the former Conservative cabinet minister Lord Wakeham and asked him to report by the end of the year. Two months later in the House of Commons a Tory backbencher Andrew Tyrie persuaded MPs from all parties to sign an early-day motion calling for an elected upper house. In the same month the former Labour leader in the Lords, Lord Richard, suggested that a reformed House should have power to check the actions of the Commons and act as a parliamentary watchdog.

The Conservative committee, under Lord Mackay, reported, also in April 1999, suggesting two models for a reformed chamber. The first would be a Senate of 480 members, one third elected at each general election to serve for three parliaments, plus 45 members appointed by the prime minister to serve as ministers. The second model was a chamber of 450 members: 150 chosen by an independent appointments commission; 99 chosen by the Scottish parliament and the Welsh assembly; 99 elected, one third at a time from party lists, to serve for three parliaments. The rest would be appointed for life.

In subsequent exchanges it became evident that Prime Minister Tony Blair did not favour even a partly-elected chamber, being obviously concerned about its possible effect on the power of the Commons. The reform of the House of Lords remains in limbo, at least until Lord Wakeham's royal commission makes its report, due at the end of 1999.

Denis Derbyshire is the author of several books on politics

Composition of the House of Lords by Party

Figures are based on those peers who are currently eligible to attend the House of Lords (ie, Peers without Writs of Summons (69) or on leave of absence (58) are excluded).
(– = not applicable.)

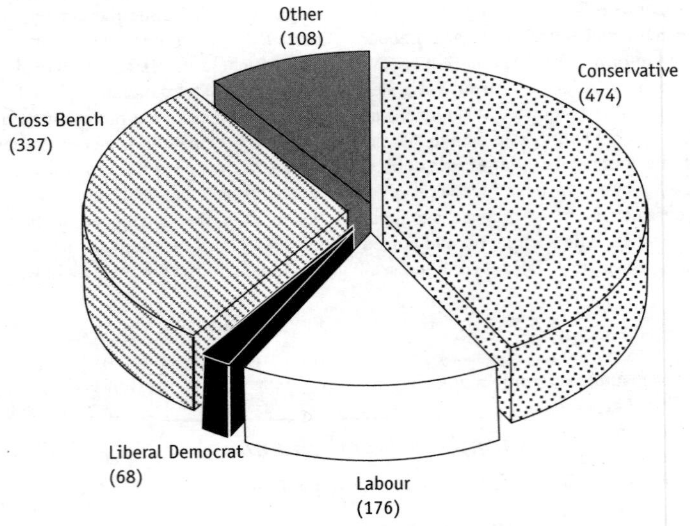

Source: House of Lords Journal Office, House of Lords, © Crown copyright 1999

The House of Lords: Chronology

11th century	Origins of Parliament in the Witans, councils consulted by Saxon Kings and attended by religious leaders, magnates, and the King's own ministers.
13th century	Attendance begins to include representatives of counties, cities, and boroughs.
14th century	Two distinct houses emerge. One, composed of shire and borough representatives, becomes known as the Commons; the other, of religious leaders (Lords Spiritual) and magnates (Lords Temporal) becomes known as the Upper House.
15th century	Membership of Lords Temporal is by now almost entirely hereditary and male; they are known as 'peers'.
16th century	After the suppression of the monasteries in 1539, only bishops attend and the Lords Temporal form the majority for the first time. (Prior to 1539 Lords Spiritual consisted of bishops, abbots, and priors.)
1642	During the Civil War bishops are excluded from the House of Lords, but are returned by the Clergy Act 1661.
17 March 1649	The Rump Parliament officially abolishes the monarchy and two days later, as a result of the House of Lords opposition to the trial of King Charles I, also abolishes the House of Lords. The House ceases to exist but resumes separate sittings in 1660.
13 February 1689	The Bill of Rights is drawn up by the Commons; it establishes the authority of Parliament over the King (enacted July).
1 May 1707 and 28 March 1800	The Acts of Union with Scotland and Ireland entitle Scottish and Irish peers to elect representatives to sit in the Lords.
8 October 1831	The Second Reform Bill to restructure the British parliamentary system is defeated in the House of Lords. Riots flare up in Nottingham and Derby, England, in protest at the defeat of the Bill.
1 November 1876	The Appellate Jurisdictions Act restores the jurisdiction of the House of Lords and of the Judicial Committee of the Privy Council, abolished in 1873. The Act enables the sovereign to create Lords of Appeal in Ordinary (Law Lords) to fulfil the judicial function of the House of Lords. Unlike bishops, retired Law Lords can continue to sit and vote; they are, in effect, the first life peerages.
30 November 1909	The House of Lords rejects the 'People's Budget' by 350 votes to 75. The Liberal government then introduces a bill to end the Lords' power to reject legislation approved by the Commons.
10 August 1911	The Parliament Bill is passed by the House of Lords. Under the Parliament Act 1911 the power of the House of Lords to veto bills is converted into the power to suspend money bills for one month and other bills for a maximum period of two years. The maximum length of a Parliament is reduced from seven to five years (except in an emergency situation).
16 December 1949	The British Parliament Act, amending the original 1911 act, reduces from two years to one the period during which the House of Lords could delay the royal assent to a bill passed by the Commons.
1958	The Life Peerages Act permits the creation of baronies for life, with no limit on numbers. The first life peerages are created on 24 July. At about the same time allowances for peers' out-of-pocket expenses and the system of 'leave of absence' for peers who do not wish to or cannot attend the House for a long period are introduced.
1963	The Peerage Act allows members of the Lords to

(*continued*)

The House of Lords: Chronology *(continued)*

	disclaim their titles (and thus be eligible for membership of the House of Commons); existing peers can disclaim within six months, new peers within one month of succession to a title.
1 November 1968	The Labour government introduces the Parliament (No. 2) Bill, which would create a two-tier House of Lords of created members who could speak and vote and others who could speak but not vote. The bill is abandoned on 17 April 1969.
23 January 1985	The proceedings of the House of Lords are televised for first time.
1997	Reform of the House of Lords is set out in Labour's election manifesto. The newly elected government is committed to abolish the rights of all 750 hereditary peers to sit and vote in the House of Lords.
October 1998	A MORI poll shows that 80 percent of the British public are in favour of the removal of hereditary peers.
24 November 1998	The government sets out its intention to bring forward proposals to reform the House of Lords in the Queen's speech. Labour MPs and peers break with tradition and interrupt the Queen's speech – normally listened to in complete silence – with murmurs of approval as she announces the government's plans.
2 December 1998	Conservative Party leader William Hague sacks Viscount Cranbourne, the Tory leader in the Lords, after it emerges that he helped to negotiate a deal with Labour over reform of the upper house without Hague's knowledge.
20 January 1999	The government sets out proposals to abolish the sitting and voting rights of hereditary peers in the Lords. The House of Lords Bill, the first of the reform's two stages, outlines how the House of Lords will function during the transitional period; sets up an independent committee to appoint or oversee the appointment of new life peers; and establishes a Royal Commission. Hereditary peers and Conservative Lords react angrily to the proposals.
16 March 1999	The House of Lords Bill is passed by the House of Commons and is introduced in the House of Lords the next day.
23 March 1999	More than 130 MPs back cross-party calls for a fully elected chamber to replace the House of Lords.
11 May 1999	Peers overwhelmingly back the compromise Weatherhill amendment, which would retain 92 hereditary peers until lasting reform is completed, signalling first signs of consensus over the contentious legislation. The amendment, put forward by Lord Weatherhill, was the 'deal' that had caused the sacking of Viscount Cranbourne as the Opposition peers' leader in 1998.
12 May 1999	The Royal Commission on the Reform of the House of Lords starts the first of a series of hearings. The commission's report, which will make recommendations concerning the long-term reform of the Lords, is expected to be delivered by 31 December 1999. It will then be considered by a joint committee of both Houses of Parliament.

The Scottish Parliament

The Scottish Parliament was created by the November 1998 Scotland Act, which was passed following the Scottish electorate's overwhelming approval of government proposals in a 11 September 1997 referendum on devolution.

The first elections to the parliament were held on 6 May 1999 and the parliament opened on 12 May 1999. It had last sat in 1707. The Labour Party fell nine short of an overall majority and on 13 May it concluded a pact with the Liberal Democrats to secure Scotland's first coalition government. Labour's leader, Donald Dewar, was elected the country's first minister.

Parliament consists of 129 members, who are elected for four-year terms through a 'semi proportional' electoral system. Seventy-three members are returned on a first-past-the-post basis from single-member constituencies, comprising Scotland's existing 72 Westminster constituencies, with an extra seat created through dividing the Orkney and Shetland constituency into two. An additional 56 members are selected on a proportional basis from party lists in the country's eight electoral regions. These regions are the same as the current European parliamentary boundaries and each elects seven members of the Scottish Parliament (MSPs) through the Additional Member System, a form of proportional representation.

Of the parliament's 129 MSPs, 48 were women, leaving only Sweden and Denmark with more women members of parliament.

The parliament has devolved law-making powers in all areas except defence, foreign affairs, the constitution, social security, company regulation, economic management, and taxation. However, it has the authority to vary, upwards or downwards, the basic rate of income tax in Scotland by up to three pence in the pound, to supplement a block grant equivalent to the current Scottish Office budget of £14.8 billion (in 1998–99). A first minister (equivalent to a Scottish prime minister), with a main office in St Andrew's House, is drawn from the majority grouping within the parliament, and relevant ministers sit with their UK government counterparts at negotiating meetings in Brussels whenever Scottish interests are affected.

The parliament's temporary base is the Church of Scotland General Assembly Hall and City of Edinburgh Council buildings, in the Lawnmarket and on George IV Bridge, in Edinburgh. A permanent home is being built at Holyrood by a design team led by the architect Enric Miralles of Barcelona, with completion planned for the autumn of 2001.

Scottish Devolution: Chronology

31 October 1973 The Kilbrandon Commission on the British Constitution recommends a devolved parliament for Scotland.

27 November 1975 The British government White Paper, 'Our Changing Democracy', proposes devolution for Scotland and Wales.

18 January 1976 The Labour members of parliament Jim Sillars and John Robertson launch the Scottish Labour Party (SLP) to campaign for greater devolution for Scotland.

30 November 1976 The British government publishes a devolution bill for Scotland and Wales.

22 February 1977 The British government is defeated in a motion to stifle debate on the devolution bill; 22 Labour members vote 'no' and 20 others abstain.

25 January 1978 The British government passes an amendment to the Scottish and Welsh devolution bill, requiring the approval of 40 percent of the electorate in a referendum for devolution to take effect.

31 July 1978 Queen Elizabeth II of Britain gives the royal assent to the devolution bill for Scotland and Wales.

1 March 1979 Referenda are held in Britain on devolution. In Scotland it is approved by 51.6 percent of the voters, but this falls short of the required 40 percent of the electorate. Devolution is not on the agenda of the centralizing conservative administrations that hold power for 18 years from May 1979 onwards.

11 September 1997 After gaining power, the Labour Party grants Scotland a devolution referendum, in which 74.3 percent of voters approve the creation of their own parliament, with 63.5 percent voting in favour of giving it tax-raising powers. One week later, Secretary of State for Scotland Donald Dewar announces plans to create a Scottish parliament in Edinburgh. The new parliament is to be granted the power to legislate on education, the environment, health, law enforcement, and transport.

6 May 1999 In the election for the new Scottish Parliament – the first election in Britain to contain an element of proportional representation – Labour is returned as the largest single party, winning 56 of the 129 seats (9 short of an overall majority). The Scottish National Party gains 35 seats, the Conservative Party 18, and the Liberal Democrats 17, while the remaining 3 seats are taken by independents and smaller fringe parties. Only 59 percent of the Scottish electorate exercises its right to vote. On 13 May, Scottish Labour leader Donald Dewar is elected 'first minister'.

1 July 1999 Official opening by Queen Elizabeth II in Edinburgh of the first Scottish parliament to sit for almost 300 years, since the Act of Union of 1707, takes place. Its temporary home is at the Church of Scotland Assembly Hall and City of Edinburgh Council buildings; a new building to be constructed for the parliament in the Holyrood district of the city is not due for completion until late 2001.

The Scottish Parliament Executive

Position	Name
First Minister	Donald Dewar
Deputy First Minister and Minister for Justice	Jim Wallace
Deputy	Angus Mackay
Finance Minister	Jack McConnell
Minister for Health and Community Care	Susan Deacon
Deputy	Iain Gray
Minister for Communities (Local Government, Housing and Social Inclusion)	Wendy Alexander
Deputies	Frank McAveety (Local Government)
	Jackie Baillie (Social Inclusion, Equality and the Voluntary Sector)
Minister for Transport and the Environment (including Land Reform and Water)	Sarah Boyack
Minister for Enterprise and Life-long Learning	Henry McLeish
Deputies	Nicol Stephen
	Alasdair Morrison (Highlands and Islands and Gaelic)
Minister for Rural Affairs	Ross Finnie
Deputy	John Home Robertson (Fisheries)
Minister for Education and Children (Culture, Arts and Sports)	Sam Galbraith
Deputies	Rhona Brankin (Culture and Sport)
	Peter Peacock (Children and Education)
Business Manager and Chief Whip	Tom McCabe
Deputy	Iain Smith
Lord Advocate	Lord Hardie
Deputy	Colin Boyd (Solicitor General)

Members of the Scottish Parliament

Con = Conservative; Ind = Independent; Lab = Labour; LD = Liberal Democrats; SNP = Scottish National Party; SSP = Scottish Socialist Party

Member	Party	Constituency/region
Constituency MSPs		
Alexander, Wendy	Lab	Paisley North
Baillie, Jackie	Lab	Dumbarton
Barrie, Scott	Lab	Dunfermline West
Boyack, Sarah	Lab	Edinburgh Central
Brankin, Rhona	Lab	Midlothian
Canavan, Dennis	Ind	Falkirk West
Chilsholm, Malcolm	Lab	Edinburgh North and Leith
Craigie, Cathie	Lab	Cumbernauld and Kilsyth
Cunningham, Roseanna	SNP	Perth
Curran, Margaret	Lab	Glasgow Ballieston
Deacon, Susan	Lab	Edinburgh East and Musselburgh
Dewar, Donald	Lab	Glasgow Anniesland
Eadie, Helen	Lab	Dunfermline East
Ewing, Fergus	SNP	Inverness East, Nairn, and Lochaber
Ewing, Margaret	SNP	Moray
Ferguson, Patricia	Lab	Glasgow Maryhill
Galbraith, Sam	Lab	Strathkelvin and Bearsden
Gillon, Karen	Lab	Clydesdale
Godman, Trish	Lab	West Renfrewshire
Gray, Iain	Lab	Edinburgh Pentlands
Henry, Hugh	Lab	Paisley South
Hughes, Janis	Lab	Glasgow Rutherglen
Jackson, Gordon	Lab	Glasgow Govan
Jackson, Sylvia	Lab	Stirling
Jamieson, Cathy	Lab	Carrick, Cumnock, and Doon Valley
Jamieson, Margaret	Lab	Kilmarnock and Loudoun
Jenkins, Ian	LD	Tweeddale, Ettrick, and Lauderdale
Kerr, Andy	Lab	East Kilbride
Lamont, Johann	Lab	Glasgow Pollok
Livingstone, Marilyn	Lab	Kirkaldy
Lyon, George	LD	Argyll and Bute
McAllion, John	Lab	Dundee East
McAveety, Frank	Lab	Glasgow Shettleston
McCabe, Tom	Lab	Hamilton South
McConnell, Jack	Lab	Motherwell and Wishaw
Macdonald, Lewis	Lab	Aberdeen Central
Macintosh, Kenneth	Lab	Eastwood
Mackay, Angus	Lab	Edinburgh South
MacLean, Kate	Lab	Dundee West
McLeish, Henry	Lab	Central Fife
McMahon, Michael	Lab	Hamilton North and Bellshill
McNeil, Duncan	Lab	Greenock and Inverclyde
McNeill, Pauline	Lab	Glasgow Kelvin
McNulty, Des	Lab	Clydebank and Milngavie
Martin, Paul	Lab	Glasgow Springburn
Morgan, Alasdair	SNP	Galloway and Upper Nithsdale
Morrison, Alasdair	Lab	Western Isles
Muldoon, Bristow	Lab	Livingston
Mulligan, Mary	Lab	Linlithgow
Munro, John	LD	Ross, Skye, and Inverness West
Murray, Elaine	Lab	Dumfries
Oldfather, Irene	Lab	Cunninghame South
Peattie, Cathy	Lab	Falkirk East
Radcliffe, Nora	LD	Gordon
Robertson, John Home	Lab	East Lothian
Robson, Euan	LD	Roxburgh and Berwickshire
Rumbles, Mike	LD	West Aberdeenshire and Kincardine
Salmond, Alex	SNP	Banff and Buchan
Scott, Tavish	LD	Shetland
Simpson, Richard	Lab	Ochil
Smith, Elaine	Lab	Coatbridge and Chryston
Smith, Iain	LD	North East Fife
Smith, Margaret	LD	Edinburgh West
Stephen, Nicol	LD	Aberdeen South
Stone, Jamie	LD	Caithness, Sutherland, and Easter Ross
Swinney, John	SNP	North Tayside
Thomson, Elaine	Lab	Aberdeen North
Wallace, Jim	LD	Orkney
Watson, Mike	Lab	Glasgow Cathcart
Welsh, Andrew	SNP	Angus
Welsh, Ian	Lab	Ayr
Whitefield, Karen	Lab	Airdrie and Shotts
Wilson, Allan	Lab	Cumminghame North
Regional MSPs		
Adam, Brian	SNP	North East Scotland
Aitken, William	Con	Glasgow
Brown, Robert	LD	Glasgow
Campbell, Colin	SNP	West of Scotland
Crawford, Bruce	SNP	Mid Scotland and Fife
Creech, Christine	SNP	South of Scotland
Davidson, David	Con	North East Scotland
Elder, Dorothy Grace	SNP	Glasgow
Ewing, Winnie	SNP	Highlands and Islands
Fabiani, Linda	SNP	Central Scotland
Fergusson, Alexander	Con	South of Scotland
Finnie, Ross	LD	West of Scotland
Gallie, Phil	Con	South of Scotland
Gibson, Kenneth	SNP	Glasgow
Goldie, Annabel	Con	West of Scotland
Gorrie, Dona	LD	Central Scotland
Grant, Rhoda	Lab	Highlands and Islands
Hamilton, Duncan	SNP	Highlands and Islands
Harding, Keith	Con	Mid Scotland and Fife
Harper, Robin	SNP	Lothians
Hyslop, Fiona	SNP	Lothians
Ingram, Adam	SNP	South of Scotland
Johnston, Nicholas	Con	Mid Scotland and Fife
Johnstone, Alexander	Con	North East Scotland
Lochhead, Richard	SNP	North East Scotland
MacAskill, Kenny	SNP	Lothians
MacDonald, Margo	SNP	Lothians
Marwick, Tricia	SNP	Mid Scotland and Fife
Matheson, Michael	SNP	Central Scotland
McGrigor, Jamie	Con	Highlands and Islands
McGugan, Irene	SNP	North East Scotland
McIntosh, Lindsay	Con	Central Scotland
McLeod, Fiona	SNP	West of Scotland
McLetchie, Davie	Con	Lothians
McMillan, Maureen	Lab	Highlands and Islands
Monteith, Brian	Con	Mid Scotland and Fife
Mundell, David	Con	South of Scotland
Neil, Dona	LD	Central Scotland
Paterson, Gil	SNP	Central Scotland
Peacock, Peter	Lab	Highlands and Islands
Quinan, Lloyd	SNP	West of Scotland
Raffan, Keith	LD	Mid Scotland and Fife
Reid, George	SNP	Mid Scotland and Fife
Robison, Shona	SNP	North East Scotland
Russell, Michael	SNP	South of Scotland
Scanlon, Mary	Con	Highlands and Islands
Selkirk of Douglas, James	Con	Lothians
Sheridan, Tommy	SSP	Glasgow
Steel, Davie	LD	Lothians
Sturgeon, Nicola	SNP	Glasgow
Tosh, Murray	Con	South of Scotland
Ullrich, Kay	SNP	West of Scotland
Wallace, Ben	Con	North East Scotland
White, Sandra	SNP	Glasgow
Wilson, Andrew	SNP	Central Scotland
Young, John	Con	West of Scotland

The Welsh Assembly

The National Assembly for Wales was created by the July 1998 Government of Wales Act, which was passed following the Welsh electorate's narrow approval of government proposals in an 18 September 1997 referendum on devolution.

The Assembly comprises 60 members, who are elected for four-year terms through a 'semi-proportional' electoral system. Forty are returned on a first-past-the-post basis from single-member constituencies, comprising Wales' existing Westminster constituencies. An additional 20 members are selected on a proportional basis from party lists based on Wales' five European Parliament constituencies. The Assembly's first elections were held on 6 May 1999. Labour won 28 seats, three short of a majority in the 60-seat assembly; Plaid Cymru won 17; the Conservatives 9; and the Liberal Democrats 6. Labour's leader, Alun Michael, was elected first secretary.

The first secretary (prif y sgrifennydd y Cynulliad) is elected from within the Assembly, by majority vote, to act as the Assembly's political leader and to appoint a cabinet comprising Assembly secretaries.

The Assembly has taken over virtually all of the functions of the secretary of state for Wales, spending the Welsh Office's £7 billion budget. Foreign affairs, defence, taxation, social security, broadcasting, and overall economic policy remain with the government in London. The Assembly may pass secondary legislation, but, unlike the Scottish Parliament, does not have primary law-making powers, even in areas such as the Welsh language. It implements Westminster legislation and oversees quangos, making them more accountable. The English and Welsh languages are treated equally in the Assembly's work.

The Assembly's temporary base is the Cardiff University Council Chamber and then Crickhowell House on Cardiff Bay. A new building is planned for 2001.

The Cabinet of the Welsh Assembly

Position	Cabinet member
First Secretary	Alun Michael
Economic Development	Rhodri Morgan
Education up to age 16 (the Children and Young People's Minister)	Rosemary Butler
Health and Social Services	Jane Hutt
Post-16 Education and Training	Tom Middlehurst
Agriculture and the Rural Economy	Christine Gwyther
Environment (incorporating Local Government and Planning)	Peter Law
Trefnydd Manager	Andrew Davies

Members of the Welsh Assembly

Con = Conservative; Lab = Labour; LD = Liberal Democrats; PC = Plaid Cymru

Member	Party	Constituency
Constituency Members		
Barrett, Lorraine	Lab	Cardiff South and Penarth
Bates, Mick	LD	Montgomeryshire
Butler, Rosemary	Lab	Newport West
Chapman, Christine	Lab	Cynon Valley
Davidson, Jane	Lab	Pontypridd
Davies, Andrew	Lab	Swansea West
Davies, David	Con	Monmouth
Davies, Geraint	Plaid Cymru	Rhondda
Davies, Ron	Lab	Caerphilly
Edwards, Richard	Lab	Preseli Pembrokeshire
Essex, Sue	Lab	Cardiff North
Feld, Val	Lab	Swansea East
Gibbons, Brian	Lab	Aberavon
Glyn Thomas, Rhodri	Plaid Cymru	Carmarthen East and Dinefwr
Gregory, Janice	Lab	Ogmore
Griffith, John	Lab	Newport East
Gwyther, Christine	Lab	Carmarthen West and South Pembrokeshire
Halford, Alison	Lab	Delyn
Hancock, Brian	Plaid Cymru	Islwyn
Hart, Edwina	Lab	Gower
Hutt, Jane	Lab	Vale of Glamorgan
Jones, Ann	Lab	Vale of Clwyd
Jones, Careth	Plaid Cymru	Conwy
Jones, Carwyn	Lab	Bridgend
Jones, Elin	Plaid Cymru	Ceredigion
Jones, Helen Mary	Plaid Cymru	Llanelli
Law, Peter	Lab	Blaenau Gwent
Lewis, Huw	Lab	Merthyr Tydfil and Rhymney
Marek, John	Lab	Wrexham
Middlehurst, Tom	Lab	Alyn and Deeside
Morgan, Rhodri	Lab	Cardiff West
Neagle, Lynne	Lab	Torfaen
Pugh, Alun	Lab	Clwyd West
Randerson, Jenny	LD	Cardiff Central
Sinclair, Karen	Lab	Clwyd South
Thomas, Dafydd Elis	Plaid Cymru	Meirionnydd Nant Conwy
Thomas, Gwenda	Lab	Neath
Wigley, Dafydd	Plaid Cymru	Caernarfon
Williams, Kirsty	LD	Brecon and Radnor
Wyn Jones, Ieuan	Plaid Cymru	Ynys Môn
Regional Members		
Black, Peter	LD	South Wales West
Bourne, Nicholas	Con	Mid and West Wales
Cairns, Alun	Con	South Wales West
Dafis, Cynog	Plaid Cymru	Mid and West Wales
Davies, Glyn	Con	Mid and West Wales
Davies, Janet	Plaid Cymru	South Wales West
Davies, Jocelyn	Plaid Cymru	South Wales East
German, Michael	LD	South Wales East
Graham, William	Con	South Wales East
Humphreys, Christine	LD	North Wales
Jarman, Pauline	Plaid Cymru	South Wales Central
Lloyd, David	Plaid Cymru	South Wales West
Melding, David	Con	South Wales Central
Michael, Alun	Lab	Mid and West Wales
Morgan, Jonathan	Con	South Wales Central
Richards, Rod	Con	North Wales
Rogers, Peter	Con	North Wales
Ryder, Janet	Plaid Cymru	North Wales
Thomas, Owen John	Plaid Cymru	South Wales Central
Williams, Phil	Plaid Cymru	South Wales East

Welsh Devolution: Chronology

31 October 1973 The Kilbrandon Commission on the British Constitution recommends a devolved parliament for Wales.

1 March 1979 Referenda held in Britain on devolution in Scotland and Wales. It is rejected in Wales by 79.7 percent of the voters, on a 58.8 percent turnout. Devolution is not on the agenda of the centralizing Conservative administrations that come to power for 18 years from May 1979 onwards.

1992 The Labour Party supports devolution for Wales in its election manifesto, but fails to oust the Conservatives at the polls.

22 July 1997 The new Labour government announces plans for partial home rule in Wales, whereby an elected assembly would have some power to govern local affairs and to influence distribution of the annual £7–8 billion government budget for Wales. This assembly is not granted the same tax-raising and legislative powers as its Scottish counterpart.

18 September 1997 Welsh voters narrowly approve the establishment of a representative assembly for Wales (with 50.3 percent in favour). Its Welsh title is Cynulliad Cenedlaethol Cymru.

March 1998 Welsh secretary Ron Davies announces construction of a new waterfront building for the Welsh Assembly, designed by leading British architect Richard Rogers, on the Cardiff Bay redevelopment site. While the new assembly building is being completed, the Assembly will meet at nearby Crickhowell House.

October 1998–1999 The architect of devolution, Ron Davies, resigns after a personal indiscretion. In the ensuing Welsh Labour leadership contest, Alun Michael, regarded by many as the prime minister's preferred choice, defeats the grass-roots populist candidate Rhodri Morgan.

6 May 1999 The Assembly elections, using the same Additional Member System of proportional representation as in Scotland, attract only 40 percent of Welsh voters. Labour emerges as the largest single party, but with no overall majority. The nationalist party Plaid Cymru scores unexpected successes, notably in the former Labour heartland of the South Wales valleys. The final results are: Labour 28 seats, Plaid Cymru 17 seats, Conservatives 9 seats, and the Liberal Democrats 6 seats. On 12 May, Alun Michael is elected 'first minister' for Wales.

26 May 1999 Official opening of Welsh Assembly by Queen Elizabeth II.

1 July 1999 The Welsh Assembly takes over full responsibility for the duties formerly attached to the secretary of state for Wales and the Welsh Office.

The Northern Ireland Assembly

The Northern Ireland Assembly came into being as a result of the 10 April 1998 Good Friday peace agreement, which negotiated the devolution of a range of executive and legislative powers – in areas such as agriculture, economic development, education, the environment, finance, health, and social security – from the secretary of state for Northern Ireland to an elected Assembly. A referendum held on 22 May 1998 resulted in a majority voting in favour of the agreement. Elections were first held on 25 June 1998. The Assembly met for the first time on 1 July 1998, but was not to become fully operational until late in 1999.

Based at the Castle Buildings, Stormont, Belfast, the Assembly comprises 108 members, six from each of the 18 Westminster constituencies in Northern Ireland. Its members are elected by proportional representation, using a system of single transferable votes.

The Assembly has legislative powers and is specifically charged with setting up interconnecting bodies between Northern Ireland and the Republic of Ireland. Important decisions of the Assembly are made by a weighted majority system, which is designed to ensure that minority interests in the Assembly can influence legislation.

The first minister of the Assembly is David Trimble of the Ulster Unionist Party (UUP). His deputy is Seamus Mallon of the Social Democratic and Labour Party (SDLP). The first minister and deputy first minister will sit on an executive committee, which includes up to ten departmental ministers, with posts allocated on the basis of party support.

The Northern Ireland Peace Process Since 1993: Chronology

15 December 1993 The prime ministers of the UK and the Republic of Ireland, John Major and Albert Reynolds, make the 'Downing Street Declaration', stating the basis for talks on peace in Northern Ireland; constitutional change will require the majority agreement of the population of Northern Ireland and the Republic of Ireland.

31 January 1994 Gerry Adams, the president of the Irish republican party Sinn Féin, is granted a visa to visit the USA.

31 August 1994 The Irish Republican Army (IRA) in Northern Ireland announces its complete cessation of violence (the British government lifts it broadcasting ban on representatives of Sinn Féin on 16 September).

22 February 1995 At a press conference in Belfast, the prime ministers of the Republic of Ireland and the UK, John Bruton and John Major, present a framework document for all-party peace negotiations over the future of Northern Ireland.

16 March 1995 The US President Bill Clinton meets Gerry Adams at the White House, Washington, DC, and permits him to raise funds in the USA.

10 May 1995 The British government minister Michael Ancram meets representatives of Sinn Féin, led by Martin McGuinness, in Belfast, the first meeting of a government minister and Sinn Féin since 1973.

24 May 1995 Patrick Mayhew, secretary of state for Northern Ireland, meets Gerry Adams in Washington, DC.

28 November 1995 On the eve of President Bill Clinton's visit to the British Isles, the prime ministers of the UK and the Republic of Ireland, John Major and John Bruton, announce the establishment of a three-person commission to examine the decommissioning of terrorist arms and the aim of holding all-party talks on Northern Ireland by the end of February 1996.

30 November–1 December 1995 President Clinton visits Northern Ireland and Dublin.

9 February 1996 The bombing of South Quay, Canary Wharf, London, breaks the IRA's 17-month cease-fire.

(continued)

The Northern Ireland Peace Process Since 1993: Chronology *(continued)*

10 June 1996 All-party talks on the future of Northern Ireland begin at Stormont Castle, Belfast; Sinn Féin is not admitted because of the IRA's cease-fire violations.

7–13 July 1996 The Royal Ulster Constabulary (RUC) bans a controversial Loyalist apprentice boys' march in Londonderry; the decision is reversed on 11 July and the march takes place; violence continues until 13 July.

21 December 1996 Loyalist terrorists in Northern Ireland break their cease-fire, in force since August 1994, with a car-bomb attack in Belfast.

5 April 1997 The Grand National at Aintree is postponed less than an hour before it is due to start after a coded IRA bomb warning is received.

6 July 1997 Violence flares up at an Orange Order march in Drumcree; the Order subsequently agrees (11 July) to cancel or re-route marches in Londonderry, Belfast, Newry, and Armagh.

20 July 1997 The IRA restores its cease-fire (broken on 9 February 1996) in order to participate in talks on the future of Northern Ireland.

29 August 1997 Britain's Northern Ireland secretary Mo Mowlam invites Sinn Féin to all-party talks.

13 October 1997 Tony Blair meets Gerry Adams at Stormont Castle, Belfast, the first meeting between a British prime minister and a Sinn Féin leader since 1921.

27 December 1997 Billy Wright, a leading member of the Loyalist Volunteer Force (LVF), is shot and killed by two members of the Irish Liberation Army (INLA) at the Maze Prison, near Belfast. The incident escalates concerns for the future of the Northern Ireland peace process.

9 January 1998 Mo Mowlam visits convicted loyalist terrorists in the Maze prison.

10 April 1998 Ireland, Britain, and the political parties in Northern Ireland reach a historic peace agreement over Northern Ireland (known as the Good Friday Agreement) involving the devolution of a wide range of executive and legislative powers to a Northern Ireland Assembly.

25 June 1998 Elections to the Northern Ireland Assembly take place.

13 July 1998 Orangemen throughout Northern Ireland march to celebrate the 308th anniversary of the Battle of the Boyne – despite pressure to abandon the march following the deaths of three Catholic brothers in an arson attack.

15 July 1998 The standoff between Orangemen and British and RUC forces at Drumcree, Northern Ireland, ends when security forces forcibly remove the remaining protestors in a dawn raid.

15 August 1998 A car bomb explodes in Omagh, County Tyrone, Northern Ireland, killing 28 people, including 15 women and 8 children, in Northern Ireland's worst terrorist act to date. The IRA militant splinter group the Real IRA later admit responsibility.

8 September 1998 The Real IRA announces a complete cease-fire.

8 September 1998 Sinn Féin president Gerry Adams and Ulster first minister David Trimble hold talks in Northern Ireland, the first meeting between a Sinn Féin leader and an Ulster Unionist leader since 1922.

16 October 1998 Northern Ireland first minister David Trimble, leader of the Ulster Unionists, and SDLP leader John Hume share the Nobel Peace Prize for their work in negotiating the Good Friday Agreement.

1 November 1998 Renegade loyalist terrorists admit the murder of Brian Service, a Catholic whom they chose randomly and shot five times in the head on 31 October in Belfast, Northern Ireland.

11 December 1998 In a new obstacle to the peace process, the IRA rejects Unionist demands that they decommission their weapons as a prerequisite for Sinn Féin members to gain seats in the new executive in Northern Ireland.

4 February 1999 Both republican and loyalist paramilitary groups issue warnings of fresh violence, threatening Northern Ireland peace efforts and the Good Friday Agreement. The IRA also reveals that some of its weapons were stolen by republican extremists.

16 February 1999 Despite Protestant calls for the unconditional decommissioning of IRA weapons, the Northern Ireland Assembly approves a plan for the province's new government structure, which would give it control over local issues such as taxation and law enforcement.

17 February 1999 Representatives of the Ulster Unionist Party and Sinn Féin hold bilateral talks for the first time. They meet to resolve the dispute over the decommissioning of IRA weapons, but make no significant progress.

8 March 1999 British Northern Ireland secretary Mo Mowlam announces that the deadline for the creation of the Northern Ireland Executive as outlined in the 1998 peace accord is being pushed back from 10 March to 29 March in an effort to resolve the dispute over the decommissioning of IRA weapons.

15 March 1999 A car bomb in Lurgan, Northern Ireland, kills prominent Roman Catholic lawyer and human rights advocate Rosemary Nelson. The Red Hand Defenders, an extremist Protestant group that opposes the Northern Ireland peace process, claims responsibility.

17 March 1999 Frankie Currie, a prominent member of the extremist Protestant unionist group the Red Hand Defenders, is shot dead in Belfast, Northern Ireland. Police suspect members of a rival Protestant group of the shooting.

1 April 1999 Prime minister Tony Blair announces that Northern Ireland peace talks will be suspended until 13 April, thereby missing the deadline agreed in April 1998 for establishing the Northern Ireland executive, the province's new cabinet. The participants in the talks are in a deadlock over the issue of the decommissioning of weapons by the IRA.

20 May 1999 Prime Minister Tony Blair sets a deadline of 30 June 1999 for the formation of the executive, stating that the executive will be suspended if agreement is not reached by that date.

29 June 1999 As talks approach the 30 June deadline, the Ulster Unionists insist that they will not take part in a power-sharing executive with Sinn Féin unless the IRA begins decommissioning.

30 June 1999 Marathon talks at Belfast pass the 30 June deadline without agreement being reached.

2 July 1999 The report of the international decommissiong body chaired by General John de Chastelain states that decommissioning is possible by 22 May 2000.

3 July 1999 Following talks at Stormont, Prime Minister Tony Blair and Taoiseach Bertie Ahern announce a plan to break the deadlock. The executive is to be set up on 15 July and a Devolution Order is to take effect on 18 July. Decommissioning is to begin within days and to be complete by May 2000.

12 July 1999 Drumcree Parade passes off peacefully amid tight security.

13 July 1999 Prime Minister Tony Blair publishes 'fail-safe' emergency legislation aimed at giving Ulster Unionists the guarantees they need to enter into a power-sharing executive with Sinn Féin.

14 July 1999 Ulster Unionists reject the Government's 'fail-safe' proposals.

15 July 1999 Ulster Unionists boycott the Northern Ireland assembly meeting at which ministers for the power-sharing executive were to be nominated. Seamus Mallon resigns as deputy first minister of Northern Ireland.

20 July 1999 Prime Minister Tony Blair and Taoiseach Bertie Ahern meet to plan the review of the Northern Ireland peace process.

Key Players in the Northern Ireland Peace Process

Adams Gerry (1948–) Northern Ireland politician, president of Sinn Féin (the political wing of the Irish Republican Army, IRA) from 1978, and representative of Sinn Féin in the Northern Ireland Assembly since June 1998

Ahern Bertie (1951–) Irish politician, leader of the Fianna Fail (FF) from 1994, and Republic of Ireland prime minister from 1997

Blair Tony (1953–) British politician, leader of the Labour Party from 1994, and UK prime minister from 1997

Bruton John (1947–) Irish politician, leader of Fine Gael (United Ireland Party) from 1990, and Republic of Ireland prime minister 1994–97

De Chastelain General John (1937–) Canadian soldier and chairman of the international commission to oversee the decommissioning of weapons in Northern Ireland from 1997

Democratic Unionist Party (DUP) Northern Ireland political party, which is orientated towards the Protestant Unionist community, opposes union with the Republic of Ireland, and has been led by Ian Paisley since 1971

Hume John (1937–) Northern Ireland politician, leader of the Social Democratic and Labour Party (SDLP) from 1979

McGuinness Martin (1950–) Northern Ireland politician and chief negotiator for Sinn Féin in peace talks

Major John (1943–) British politician and leader of the Conservative Party and UK prime minister 1990–97

Mitchell George (1933–) US politician, Senate majority leader 1989–95, and chairman of the international commission on weapons decommissioning in Northern Ireland 1995–96, brought back in 1999 to revive process

Molyneaux Jim (1920–) Northern Ireland Unionist politician and leader of the Official Ulster Unionist Party (the largest Northern Ireland party) from 1979 until his resignation in 1995

Mowlam Mo (1949–) British Labour politician who was appointed secretary of state for Northern Ireland in 1997

Paisley Ian (1926–) Northern Ireland politician, cleric, and leader of the Democratic Unionist Party (DUP) from 1971

Sinn Féin Irish political party founded in 1905 that aims at creating a united republican Ireland; Gerry Adams has been the party's president since 1978

Social Democratic Labour Party (SDLP) Northern Ireland left-of-centre political party formed in 1970 and led by John Hume; it aims ultimately at Irish unification

Trimble David (1944–) Northern Ireland politician, leader of the Ulster Unionist Party (UUP) from 1995, and Northern Ireland's first minister from 1998

Ulster Unionist Party (UUP) the largest political party in Northern Ireland; it is right-of-centre in orientation and has been led by David Trimble since 1995

Members of the Northern Ireland Assembly

All = The Alliance Party; DUP = Democratic Unionist Party; NIUP = Northern Ireland Unionist Party; NIWC = Northern Ireland Women's Coalition; PUP = Progressive Unionist Party; SDLP = Social Democratic and Labour Party; SF = Sinn Féin; UKUP = UK Unionist Party; UUAP = United Unionist Assembly Party; UUP = Ulster Unionist Party

Member	Party	Constituency
Adams, Gerry	SF	West Belfast
Adamson, Ian	UUP	East Belfast
Agnew, Fraser[1]	UUAP	North Belfast
Lord Alderdice	Speaker	East Belfast
Armitage, Pauline	UUP	East Londonderry
Armstrong, Billy	UUP	Mid Ulster
Attwood, Alex	SDLP	West Belfast
Beggs Jnr, Roy	UUP	East Antrim
Bell, Billy	UUP	Lagan Valley
Bell, Eileen	All	North Down
Benson, Tom	UUP	Strangford
Berry, Paul	DUP	Newry and Armagh
Birnie, Esmond	UUP	South Belfast
Boyd, Norman[2]	NIUP	South Antrim
Bradley, P J	SDLP	South Down
Byrne, Joe	SDLP	West Tyrone
Campbell, Gregory	DUP	East Londonderry
Carrick, Mervyn	DUP	Upper Bann
Carson, Joan	UUP	Fermanagh and South Tyrone
Close, Seamus	All	Lagan Valley
Clyde, Wilson	DUP	South Antrim
Cobain, Fred	UUP	North Belfast
Coulter, Robert	UUP	North Antrim
Dallat, John	SDLP	East Londonderry
Davis, Ivan	UUP	Lagan Valley
De Brun, Bairbre	SF	West Belfast
Dodds, Nigel	DUP	North Belfast
Doherty, Arthur	SDLP	East Londonderry
Doherty, Pat	SF	West Tyrone
Douglas, Boyd[1]	UUAP	East Londonderry
Durkan, Mark	SDLP	Foyle
Empey, Reg	UUP	East Belfast
Ervine, David	PUP	East Belfast
Farren, Sean	SDLP	North Antrim
Fee, John	SDLP	Newry and Armagh
Ford, David	All	South Antrim
Foster, Sam	UUP	Fermanagh and South Tyrone
Gallagher, Tommy	SDLP	Fermanagh and South Tyrone
Gibson, Oliver	DUP	West Tyrone
Gildernew, Michelle	SF	Fermanagh and South Tyrone
Gorman, John	UUP	North Down
Hanna, Carmel	SDLP	South Belfast
Haughey, Dennis	SDLP	Mid Ulster
Hay, William	DUP	Foyle
Hendron, Joe	SDLP	West Belfast
Hilditch, David	DUP	East Antrim
Hume, John	SDLP	Foyle
Hussey, Derek	UUP	West Tyrone
Hutchinson, Billy	PUP	North Belfast
Hutchinson, Roger[2]	NIUP	East Antrim

(continued)

Members of the Northern Ireland Assembly (*continued*)

Member	Party	Constituency
Kane, Gardiner	DUP	North Antrim
Kelly, Gerry	SF	North Belfast
Kelly, John	SF	Mid Ulster
Kennedy, Danny	UUP	Newry and Armagh
Leslie, James	UUP	North Antrim
Lewsley, Patricia	SDLP	Lagan Valley
Maginness, Alban	SDLP	North Belfast
Mallon, Seamus	SDLP	Newry and Armagh
Maskey, Alex	SF	West Belfast
McCarthy, Kieran	All	Strangford
McCartney, Robert	UKUP	North Down
McClarty, David	UUP	East Londonderry
McCrea, William	DUP	Mid Ulster
McCleland, Donovan	SDLP	South Antrim
McDonnell, Alasdair	SDLP	South Belfast
McElduff, Barry	SF	West Tyrone
McFarland, Alan	UUP	North Down
McGimpsey, Michael	UUP	South Belfast
McGrady, Eddie	SDLP	South Down
McGuinness, Martin	SF	Mid Ulster
McHugh, Gerry	SF	Fermanagh and South Tyrone
McLaughlin, Mitchel	SF	Foyle
McMenamin, Eugene	SDLP	West Tyrone
McNamee, Pat	SF	Newry and Armagh
McWilliams, Monica	NIWC	South Belfast
Molloy, Francie	SF	Mid Ulster
Murphy, Conor	SF	Newry and Armagh
Murphy, Mick	SF	South Down
Morrice, Jane	NIWC	North Down
Morrow, Maurice	DUP	Fermanagh and South Tyrone
Neeson, Sean	All	East Antrim
Nelis, Mary	SF	Foyle
Nesbitt, Dermot	UUP	South Down
O'Connor, Danny	SDLP	East Antrim
O'Hagan, Dara	SF	Upper Bann
O'Neill, Eamon	SDLP	South Down
Paisley, Ian	DUP	North Antrim
Paisley Jnr, Ian	DUP	North Antrim
Poots, Edwin	DUP	Lagan Valley
Ramsey, Sue	SF	West Belfast
Robinson, Iris	DUP	Strangford
Robinson, Ken	UUP	East Antrim
Robinson, Mark	DUP	South Belfast
Robinson, Peter	DUP	East Belfast
Roche, Patrick[2]	NIUP	Lagan Valley
Rodgers, Brid	SDLP	Upper Bann
Savage, George	UUP	Upper Bann
Shannon, Jim	DUP	Strangford
Shipley-Dalton, Duncan	UUP	South Antrim
Taylor, John	UUP	Strangford
Tierney, John	SDLP	Foyle
Trimble, David	UUP	Upper Bann
Watson, Denis[1]	UUAP	Upper Bann
Weir, Peter	UUP	North Down
Wells, Jim	DUP	South Down
Wilson, Cedric[2]	NIUP	Strangford
Wilson, Jim	UUP	South Antrim
Wilson, Sammy	DUP	East Belfast

[1] Elected as an Independent candidate and formed the United Unionist Assembly Party (UUAP) with effect from 21 September 1998.
[2] Elected as a UK Unionist candidate and formed the Northern Ireland Unionist Party (NIUP) with effect from 15 January 1999.

Political Composition of the Northern Ireland Assembly

Party	Seats
Ulster Unionist Party (UUP)	28
Social Democratic and Labour Party (SDLP)	24
Democratic Unionist Party (DUP)	20
Sinn Féin (SF)	18
The Alliance Party (All)	6
Northern Ireland Unionist Party (NIUP)[1]	4
Ulster Unionist Assembly Party (UUAP)[2]	3
Northern Ireland Women's Coalition (NIWC)	2
Progressive Unionist Party (PUP)	2
UK Unionist Party (UKUP)	1

[1] Elected as UK Unionist Party, resigned, and formed the Northern Ireland Unionist Party with effect from 15 January 1999.
[2] Elected as independent candidates and formed the United Unionist Assembly Party with effect from 21 September 1998.

Local Government in the UK

Local Government in the United Kingdom

Between 1995 and 1998, far-reaching local government changes took effect in England, Scotland, and Wales.

In England, these changes were based on recommendations of a government commission set up under the Local Government Act 1992. The changes were implemented in stages, and resulted in a combination of the existing two-tier structure, with new single-tier (unitary) authorities. In 1995 and 1996, unitary authorities were introduced for the Isle of Wight, Avon, Cleveland, and Humberside areas (the latter three being abolished as counties); the city of York, formerly in North Yorkshire, also became a unitary authority, while the rest of the county retained the two-tier system. More counties underwent changes in 1997 and 1998, with their main urban centres becoming unitary authorities and the rest of the county keeping the existing two-tier system. The changes were completed in April 1998.

In Scotland,the Local Government (Scotland) Bill 1994 abolished the two-tier system of local government that had been established for the nine Scottish regions in 1975. Since April 1996 there have been 29 mainland unitary authorities, while the 3 island areas (the Orkney Islands, Shetland Islands, and Western Isles) retained their existing single-tier administrative divisions.

In Wales, the Local Government (Wales) Act 1994 abolished the two-tier structure of 8 county and 37 district councils (in existence since 1974) and replaced it with 22 unitary authorities, from April 1996.

English Counties

Bedfordshire

County of south central England (since April 1997 Luton has been a separate unitary authority)

Area 1,192 sq km/460 sq mi; **Towns and cities** Bedford (administrative headquarters), Dunstable; **Physical** the Great Ouse River and its tributary, the Ivel; the county is low lying with the Chiltern Hills in the southwest; **Features** Whipsnade Wild Animal Park, near Dunstable (200 ha/494 acres), belonging to the London Zoological Society; Woburn Abbey, seat of the duke of Bedford; Cranfield Institute of Technology; **Agriculture** cereals (especially wheat and barley); vegetables; **Industries** agricultural machinery; cement manufacture (using local chalk); clay; electrical goods; gravel; motor vehicles and parts; packaging; sand; brickworks at Stewartby; **Population** (1996) 548,800.

Buckinghamshire

County of southeast central England

Area 1,565 sq km/604 sq mi; **Towns** Aylesbury (administrative headquarters), Beaconsfield, Buckingham, High Wycombe, Olney; **Physical** Chiltern Hills; Vale of Aylesbury; **Features** Chequers (country seat of the prime minister); Burnham Beeches; the church of the poet Gray's 'Elegy' at Stoke Poges; Cliveden, a country house designed by Charles Barry (now a hotel; it was once the home of Nancy, Lady Astor); Bletchley Park, home of World War II code-breaking activities, now used as a training post for GCHQ (Britain's electronic surveillance centre); homes of the poets William Cowper at Olney and John Milton at Chalfont St Giles, and of the Tory prime minister Disraeli at Hughenden; grave of William Penn, Quaker founder of Pennsylvania, at Jordans, near Chalfont St Giles; Stowe landscape gardens; **Industries** engineering; furniture (chiefly beech); paper; printing; railway workshops; motor cars; **Agriculture** about 75 percent of the land under cultivation, fertile soil; cereals (barley, wheat, oats); cattle, pigs, poultry, sheep; **Population** (1996) 671,700.

Cambridgeshire

County of eastern England, which has contained the unitary authority Peterborough since April 1998

Area 3,410 sq km/1,316 sq mi; **Towns and cities** Cambridge (administrative headquarters), Ely, Huntingdon, March, Wisbech, St Neots, Whittlesey; **Physical** county is flat with fens, whose soil is very fertile; Bedford Level (a peaty area of the fens); rivers: Nene, Ouse (with tributaries Cam, Lark, and Little Ouse), Welland; **Features** Cambridge University; **Agriculture** the county is one of the chief cereal and sugar-beet producing districts of England; fruit and vegetables are grown; there is also dairy farming and sheep-rearing; **Industries** brewing, paper, electronics, food processing, mechanical engineering; there are scientific and pharmaceutical research establishments; **Population** (1996) 703,100.

Cheshire

County of northwest England, which has contained the unitary authorities Halton and Warrington since April 1998

Area 2,320 sq km/896 sq mi; **Towns and cities** Chester (administrative headquarters), Crewe, Congleton, Macclesfield; **Physical** chiefly a fertile plain, with the Pennines in the east; rivers: Mersey, Dee, Weaver; a sandstone ridge extending south through central Cheshire together with Delamere Forest constitute a woodland and heath landscape; **Features** salt mines and geologically rich former copper workings at Alderley Edge (in use from Roman times until the 1920s); Little Moreton Hall; discovery of Lindow Man, the first 'bogman' to be found in mainland Britain, dating from around 500 BC; Museum of the Chemical Industry on Spike Island; Quarry Bank Mill at Styal is a cotton-industry museum; **Agriculture** arable farming in the north; cheese (at one time produced entirely in farmhouses) and dairy products in the centre and south of the county; **Industries** aerospace industry, chemicals, pharmaceuticals, salt, silk and textiles (at Congleton and Macclesfield), vehicles; **Population** (1996) 980,000.

Cornwall

County in southwest England including the Isles of Scilly (Scillies)

Area (excluding Scillies) 3,550 sq km/1,370 sq mi; **Towns and cities** Truro (administrative headquarters), Camborne, Launceston; Bude, Falmouth, Newquay, Penzance, St Ives (resorts); **Physical** Bodmin Moor (including Brown Willy 419 m/1,375 ft); Land's End peninsula; rivers Camel, Fal, Fowey, Tamar; **Features** St Michael's Mount; Poldhu, site of first transatlantic radio signal (1901); the Stannary or Tinners' Parliament; Tate Gallery, St Ives; the Mineral Tramways Project, which aims to preserve the mining landscape, once the centre of the world's hard-rock mining industry; Eden Project, two 'biomes' (tropical rainforest and Mediterranean) being built in disused china-clay pit near St Austell, scheduled to open in 2000 as a Millennium Commission Landmark Project; the 'Lost' Gardens of Heligan; **Agriculture** crops are early in some places: fruit, oats, and vegetables, including swedes, turnips, and mangolds (a root vegetable used as cattle fodder); spring flowers; cattle and sheep rearing; dairy farming; fishing

England – local government divisions

BA BATH AND NE SOMERSET
BE BEDFORDSHIRE
BR BRACKNELL FOREST
BT BRISTOL
BU BUCKINGHAMSHIRE
DA DARLINGTON
DC DERBY CITY
GR GREATER MANCHESTER
HA HALTON
HE HERTFORDSHIRE
LC LEICESTER CITY
LE LEICESTERSHIRE
LU LUTON
MK MILTON KEYNES
NH NORTHAMPTONSHIRE
NL NORTH LINCOLNSHIRE
NS NORTH SOMERSET
NT NOTTINGHAMSHIRE
PB PETERBOROUGH
PT PORTSMOUTH
R READING
RU RUTLAND
SG SOUTH GLOUCESTERSHIRE
SO SOUTHAMPTON
SS STOCKTON-ON-TEES
ST STOKE-ON-TRENT
TW TELFORD AND WREKIN
WA WARRINGTON
WK WEST BERKSHIRE
WM WEST MIDLANDS
WN WINDSOR AND MAIDENHEAD
WO WOKINGHAM
WR WORCESTERSHIRE

SCOTLAND
NORTHERN IRELAND
NORTHUMBERLAND
TYNE AND WEAR
HARTLEPOOL
DURHAM
REDCAR AND CLEVELAND
DA
SS
MIDDLESBROUGH
CUMBRIA
NORTH YORKSHIRE
North Sea
Isle of Man
YORK
THE EAST RIDING OF YORKSHIRE
LANCASHIRE
BLACKPOOL
WEST YORKSHIRE
KINGSTON UPON HULL
BLACKBURN AND DARWEN
NL
Irish Sea
GR
SOUTH YORKSHIRE
NORTH EAST LINCOLNSHIRE
MERSEYSIDE
WA
HA
LINCOLNSHIRE
REPUBLIC OF IRELAND
CHESHIRE
DERBYSHIRE
NT
ST
NOTTINGHAM CITY
DC
TW
STAFFORDSHIRE
LE
NORFOLK
RU
PB
LC
SHROPSHIRE
WM
ENGLAND
CAMBRIDGESHIRE
SUFFOLK
WALES
WARWICKSHIRE
NH
WR
MK
BE
HEREFORDSHIRE
LU
GLOUCESTERSHIRE
BU
ESSEX
HE
OXFORDSHIRE
SOUTHEND
SLOUGH
GREATER LONDON
THURROCK
SG
SWINDON
R
WN
WK
WO
BR
BT
NS
BA
WILTSHIRE
MEDWAY TOWNS
SURREY
KENT
HAMPSHIRE
SOMERSET
WEST SUSSEX
EAST SUSSEX
SO
PT
POOLE
DEVON
DORSET
BRIGHTON AND HOVE
ISLE OF WIGHT
BOURNEMOUTH
CORNWALL
PLYMOUTH
TORBAY
English Channel
Isles of Scilly
FRANCE

○ unitary authority within another local government area

0 50 mi
0 100 km

(Mevagissey, Newlyn, and St Ives are the principal fishing ports); **Industries** tourism; electronics; kaolin (a white clay used in the manufacture of porcelain; St Austell is the main centre for production); **Population** (1996) 483,300.

Cumbria

County of northwest England, created in 1974 from Cumberland, Westmorland, the Furness district of northwest Lancashire, and the Sedbergh district of northwest Yorkshire

Area 6,810 sq km/2,629 sq mi; **Towns and cities** Carlisle (administrative headquarters), Barrow, Kendal, Penrith, Whitehaven, Workington; **Physical** Scafell Pike (978 m/3,210 ft), the highest mountain in England, Helvellyn (950 m/3,118 ft); Lake Windermere, the largest lake in England (17 km/10.5 mi long, 1.6 km/1 mi wide), and other lakes (Derwentwater, Grasmere, Haweswater, Ullswater); the rivers Eden and Derwent; the M6 motorway runs north to south through the centre of the county; **Features** Lake District National Park; Grizedale Forest sculpture project; Furness peninsula; western part of Hadrian's Wall; **Agriculture** in the north and east there is dairy farming; sheep are also reared; the West Cumberland Farmers is England's largest agricultural cooperative; **Industries** the traditional coal, iron, and steel industries of the coast towns have been replaced by newer industries including chemicals, plastics, marine engineering, electronics, and shipbuilding (at Barrow-in-Furness, nuclear submarines and warships); tourism; salmon fishing; **Population** (1996) 490,600.

Derbyshire

County of north central England (since April 1997 Derby City has been a separate unitary authority)

Area 2,550 sq km/984 sq mi; **Towns and cities** Matlock (administrative headquarters), Buxton, Chesterfield, Glossop, Ilkeston, Long Eaton; **Physical** Peak District National Park (including Kinder Scout 636 m/2,088 ft); rivers Dane, Derwent, Dove, Goyt, Rother, Trent, Wye; Dove Dale; **Features** Chatsworth House, Bakewell (seat of the Duke of Devonshire); Haddon Hall; Hardwick Hall; Kedleston Hall (designed by Robert Adam); well-dressing at Tissington, Wirksworth, Eyam, and other villages; Castleton Caverns; **Agriculture** cereals, root crops, and dairy farming (in the south); sheep farming (in the northern hills); **Industries** heavy engineering; manufacturing (cotton, hosiery, lace, porcelain, textiles); mineral and metal working (barytes, gypsum, lead, zinc); quarrying (marble, sandstone, pipeclay); motor cars; limestone quarrying; **Population** (1996) 962,000.

Devon

County of southwest England; Plymouth and Torbay have been separate unitary authorities since April 1998

Area 6,720 sq km/2,594 sq mi; **Towns and cities** Exeter (administrative headquarters); resorts: Barnstaple, Bideford, Exmouth, Ilfracombe, Sidmouth, Teignmouth, and Tiverton; **Physical** rivers: Dart, Exe, Plym, Tamar, Taw, Teign, Torridge; National Parks: Dartmoor, Exmoor; **Features** Lundy bird sanctuary and marine nature reserve in the Bristol Channel; **Agriculture** sheep and dairy farming, beef cattle; cider and clotted cream; fishing; **Industries** kaolin in the south; lace (at Honiton); Dartington glass; carpets (Axminster); quarrying (granite, limestone, sandstone); minerals (copper, iron, lead, manganese); tourism; **Population** (1996) 1,059,300.

Dorset

County of southwest England (since April 1997 Bournemouth and Poole have been separate unitary authorities)

Area 2,541 sq km/981 sq mi; **Towns and cities** Dorchester (administrative headquarters), Shaftesbury, Sherborne; Lyme Regis, Weymouth, Poole (resorts); **Physical** Chesil Beach, a shingle bank along the coast 19 km/11 mi long, connecting Isle of Portland to the mainland; Dorset Downs (chalk); River Stour, and rivers Frome and Piddle (which flow into Poole Harbour); clay beds in the north and west; Canford Heath, the home of some of Britain's rarest breeding birds and reptiles (including the nightjar, Dartford warbler, sand lizard, and smooth snake); **Features** Isle of Purbeck, a peninsula where china clay and Purbeck 'marble' are quarried, and which includes Corfe Castle and the holiday resort of Swanage; Cranborne Chase; Maiden Castle (prehistoric earthwork); Tank Museum at Royal Armoured Corps Centre, Bovington, where the cottage of the soldier and writer T E Lawrence is a museum; Wimborne Minster; abbey church of Sherborne; **Agriculture** dairy farming; **Industries** Wytch Farm is the largest onshore oilfield in the UK; production at Wareham onshore oilfield started in 1991; quarrying (marble from the Isle of Purbeck, and Portland stone, which has been used for buildings all over the world); manufacturing (rope, twine, and net at Bridport); sand and gravel extraction; tourism; **Population** (1996) 681,900.

Durham

County of northeast England (since April 1997 Darlington has been a separate unitary authority)

Area 2,232 sq km/862 sq mi; **Towns and cities** Durham (administrative headquarters), Newton Aycliffe, Peterlee, Chester-le-Street; **Physical** Pennine Hills; rivers Wear and Tees; **Features** Beamish open-air industrial museum; site of one of Britain's richest coalfields (pits no longer functioning); Bowes Museum; Barnard Castle; Durham Cathedral; University of Durham (1832), housed in Durham Castle; dales in the west of the county; **Agriculture** sheep; dairy produce; hill farming; **Industries** clothing; chemicals; iron and steel processing; light engineering industries; quarrying; cement; pharmaceuticals; **Population** (1996) 608,100.

East Sussex

County of southeast England, created in 1974, formerly part of Sussex (since April 1997 Brighton and Hove has been a separate unitary authority)

Area 1,725 sq km/666 sq mi; **Towns** Lewes (administrative headquarters), Newhaven (cross-channel port), Eastbourne, Rye, Winchelsea; Bexhill-on-Sea, Hastings, St Leonards, Seaford (all coastal resorts); **Physical** Beachy Head, highest headland on the south coast (180 m/590 ft), the eastern end of the South Downs; the Weald (including Ashdown Forest); Friston Forest; rivers Cuckmere, Ouse, and East Rother (which flows into the sea near Rye); Romney Marsh; **Features** the 'Long Man' chalk hill figure at Wilmington, near Eastbourne; prehistoric earthworks; Iron Age hillfort at Mount Caburn, near Lewes; Roman villas; Herstmonceux, with a 15th-century castle (conference and exhibition centre) and adjacent modern buildings, site of the Greenwich Royal Observatory (1958–90); other castles at Hastings, Lewes, Pevensey, and Bodiam; Bayham Abbey; Battle Abbey and the site of the Battle of Hastings; Michelham Priory; Sheffield Park garden; University of Sussex at Falmer, near Brighton, founded in 1961; **Agriculture** cereals; hops; fruit and vegetables; fishing (at Hastings); **Industries** electronics; gypsum; light engineering; timber; **Population** (1996) 734,900.

Essex

County of southeast England, which has contained the unitary authorities Southend and Thurrock since April 1998

Area 3,670 sq km/1,417 sq mi; **Towns and cities** Chelmsford (administrative headquarters), Basildon, Colchester, Harlow, Harwich (port), Clacton-on-Sea (resort); **Physical** flat and marshy near the coast; richly wooded in the southwest; rivers: the Blackwater, Crouch, Colne, Lee, Stour, and Thames; **Features** former royal hunting ground of Epping Forest (2300 ha/5680 acres, controlled from 1882 by the City of London); since 1111 at Little Dunmow (and later at Great Dunmow) the Dunmow flitch (side of cured pork) can be claimed every four years by any couple proving to a jury they have not regretted their marriage within the year (winners are few); Stansted,

London's third airport; new Roman Catholic cathedral at Brentwood (designed by Quinlan Terry) dedicated in 1991; **Agriculture** cereals (wheat), fruit, sugar beet; livestock rearing, dairy products; oysters; **Industries** brewing, cars, cement, engineering (at Dagenham, Chelmsford, and Colchester), food processing, oil products (there are large oil refineries at Shellhaven and Canvey); **Population** (1996) 1,586,100.

Gloucestershire

County of southwest England

Area 2,640 sq km/1,019 sq mi; **Towns and cities** Gloucester (administrative headquarters), Cheltenham, Cirencester, Stroud, Tewkesbury; **Physical** Cotswold Hills; River Severn and tributaries; **Features** Berkeley Castle, where Edward II was murdered; Prinknash Abbey, where pottery is made; Cotswold Farm Park, near Stow-on-the-Wold, which has rare and ancient breeds of farm animals; pre-Norman churches at Cheltenham and Cleeve; Gloucester Cathedral; Tewkesbury Abbey, with early 12th-century nave; **Agriculture** cereals (in the Cotswolds), fruit (apples and pears), cider, dairy products ('double Gloucester' cheese was formerly made here), sheep farming; **Industries** aerospace industry, light engineering, manufacturing (bricks, carpets, furniture, glass, pins, pottery, tiles, watches), plastics, timber; **Population** (1996) 556,300.

Hampshire

County of south England (since April 1997 Portsmouth and Southampton have been separate unitary authorities)

Area 3,679 sq km/1,420 sq mi; **Towns and cities** Winchester (administrative headquarters), Aldershot, Andover, Basingstoke, Eastleigh, Gosport, Romsey, Lymington; **Physical** New Forest (area 373 sq km/144 sq mi), in the southeast of the county, a Saxon royal hunting ground; rivers Avon, Ichen, and Test (which has trout fishing); **Features** Hampshire Basin, where Britain has onshore and offshore oil; Danebury, 2,500-year-old Celtic hillfort; Beaulieu (including National Motor Museum); Broadlands (home of Lord Mountbatten); Highclere castle (home of the Earl of Carnarvon, with gardens by Capability Brown); Hambledon, where the first cricket club was founded in 1750; site of the Roman town of Silchester; Jane Austen's cottage at Chawton (1809–17), now a museum; Twyford Down section of the M3 motorway was completed in 1994 despite protests; **Agriculture** market gardening (watercress); **Industries** aeronautics, brewing, chemicals, electronics, light engineering (at Basingstoke), oil from refineries at Fawley, perfume, pharmaceuticals; **Population** (1996) 1,627,400.

Hertfordshire

County of southeast England

Area 1,630 sq km/629 sq mi; **Towns and cities** Hertford (administrative headquarters), Bishop's Stortford, Hatfield, Hemel Hempstead, Letchworth (the first garden city; followed by Welwyn in 1919), Stevenage (the first new town, designated in 1946), St Albans, Watford, Hitchin; **Physical** rivers Lea, Stort, Colne; part of the Chiltern Hills; **Features** Hatfield House; Knebworth House (home of Lord Lytton); Brocket Hall (home of Palmerston and Melbourne); home of George Bernard Shaw at Ayot St Lawrence; Berkhamsted Castle (Norman); Rothamsted agricultural experimental station; **Agriculture** barley for brewing industry, dairy farming, market gardening, horticulture; **Industries** aircraft, computer electronics, electrical goods, engineering, paper and printing, plastics, pharmaceuticals, tanning; sand and gravel are worked in the south; **Population** (1996) 1,015,800.

Kent

County of southeast England, known as the 'garden of England' (since April 1998 Medway Towns has been a separate unitary authority)

Area 3,730 sq km/1,440 sq mi; **Towns and cities** Maidstone (administrative headquarters), Ashford, Canterbury, Deal, Dover (ferry terminus), Gravesend, Hythe, New Ash Green (a new town), Sevenoaks, Royal Tunbridge Wells; resorts: Folkestone, Margate, Ramsgate; **Physical** the North Downs; White Cliffs of Dover; rivers: Thames, Darent, Medway (traditionally, a 'man of Kent' comes from east of the Medway and a 'Kentish man' from west Kent), Stour; marshes (especially Romney Marsh); the Isles of Grain, Thanet, and Sheppey (on which is the resort of Sheerness, formerly a royal dockyard); the Weald (an agricultural area); Dungeness (peninsula and headland); **Features** Leeds Castle (converted to a palace by Henry VIII); Ightham Mote; Hever Castle (where Henry VIII courted Anne Boleyn); Chartwell (Churchill's country home), Knole, Sissinghurst Castle and gardens; the Brogdale Experimental Horticulture Station at Faversham has the world's finest collection of apple and other fruit trees; the former RAF Manston became Kent International Airport in 1989; Dungeness nuclear power station; **Agriculture** cereals, hops, apples, soft fruit, vegetables; in Kent are found about half the orchards, half the hops, and one fifth of the soft fruit grown in England and Wales; livestock production; **Industries** cement (Gravesend), paper, oil refining, shipbuilding, tourism. The East Kent coalfield ceased production in 1989; **Population** (1996) 1,557,300.

Lancashire

County of northwest England (since April 1998 Blackpool and Blackburn have been separate unitary authorities)

Area 3,040 sq km/1,173 sq mi; **Towns and cities** Preston (administrative headquarters), which forms part of Central Lancashire New Town from 1970 (together with Fulwood, Bamber Bridge, Leyland, and Chorley); Lancaster, Accrington, Burnley; ports Fleetwood and Heysham; seaside resorts Morecambe and Southport; **Features** the River Ribble; the Pennines; the Forest of Bowland (moors and farming valleys); Pendle Hill; **Industries** formerly a world centre of cotton manufacture, now replaced with high-technology aerospace, nuclear fuels, and electronics industries. There is dairy farming and market gardening; **Population** (1996) 1,424,700.

Leicestershire

County of central England (since April 1997 Leicester City and Rutland have been separate unitary authorities)

Area 2,084 sq km/804 sq mi; **Towns and cities** Loughborough, Melton Mowbray, Market Harborough (administrative headquarters at Glenfield, Leicester); **Physical** rivers Soar and Wreake; Charnwood Forest (in the northwest); Vale of Belvoir (under which are large coal deposits); **Features** Belvoir Castle, seat of the dukes of Rutland since the time of Henry VIII, rebuilt by James Wyatt in 1816; Donington Park motor-racing circuit, Castle Donington; Leicestershire has traditionally had several fox-hunts, including the Quorn hunt; **Agriculture** good pasture with horses, cattle, and sheep (especially the New Leicester breed, first bred by Robert Bakewell in the 18th century at Dishley); dairy products (including Stilton cheese at Melton Mowbray); cereals; **Industries** engineering (Loughborough); hosiery (at Earl Shilton, Hinckley, and Loughborough); footwear; bell founding; coal (Asfordby); quarrying of limestone (Barrow-on-Soar, Breedon-on-the-Hill), ironstone (in the northwest), and granite (Enderby, Stoney, and Mountsorrel, known for its paving stones); **Population** (1996) 927,500.

Lincolnshire

County of eastern England

Area 5,890 sq km/2,274 sq mi; **Towns and cities** Lincoln (administrative headquarters), Skegness, Boston, Stamford; **Physical** hills of Lincoln Edge and the Wolds; marshy coastline; the Fens in the southeast; rivers Trent, Welland, Witham; **Features** Belton House, a Restoration mansion; Gibraltar Point National Nature Reserve; **Agriculture** cattle, sheep, horses; cereals (mainly barley); flower bulbs (largest bulb-growing industry in the UK, around Spalding); vegetables; **Population** (1996) 615,900.

Norfolk

County of eastern England

Area 5,360 sq km/2,069 sq mi; **Towns and cities** Norwich (administrative headquarters), King's Lynn, Great Yarmouth (ports); Cromer, Hunstanton (resorts); **Physical** low-lying with the Fens in the west and the Norfolk Broads in the east; rivers Bure, Ouse, Waveney, Yare; **Features** the Broads (a series of lakes famous for fishing and water fowl, and for boating); Halvergate Marshes wildlife area; traditional reed thatching; Grime's Graves (Neolithic flint mines); shrine of Our Lady of Walsingham, a medieval and present-day centre of pilgrimage; Blickling Hall (Jacobean, built 1619–24, situated 14 km/7 mi south of Cromer); residence of Elizabeth II at Sandringham (built 1869–71); **Agriculture** cereals (wheat and barley); fruit and vegetables (beans, sugar beets, swedes, turnips); turkeys, geese, cattle; fishing centred on Great Yarmouth; **Industries** agricultural implements; boots and shoes; brewing and malting; offshore natural gas; tanning; there are flour mills and mustard works; **Population** (1996) 777,000.

North Yorkshire

County of northeast England, created in 1974 from most of the North Riding and parts of the East and West Ridings of Yorkshire (since April 1996 York has been a separate unitary authority)

Area 8,037 sq km/3,102 sq mi; **Towns and cities** Northallerton (administrative headquarters); resorts: Harrogate, Scarborough, Whitby; **Physical** England's largest county; rivers Derwent, Esk, Ouse; includes part of the Pennines; the Vale of York (a vast plain); the Cleveland Hills; North Yorkshire Moors, which form a national park (within which is Fylingdales radar station to give early warning – 4 minutes – of nuclear attack); **Features** Rievaulx Abbey; Yorkshire Dales National Park (including Swaledale, Wensleydale, and Bolton Abbey in Wharfedale); Fountains Abbey near Ripon, with Studley Royal Gardens (a World Heritage site); Castle Howard, designed by Vanbrugh, has Britain's largest collection of 18th–20th-century costume; largest accessible cavern in Britain, the Battlefield Chamber, Ingleton; **Agriculture** cereals, dairy products (Vale of York, Pickering); wool and meat from sheep (North York Moors); **Industries** coal, footwear, clothing, vehicles, plastics, foodstuffs, high technology industries, light industry; **Population** (1996) 734,700.

Northamptonshire

County of central England

Area 2,370 sq km/915 sq mi; **Towns and cities** Northampton (administrative headquarters), Kettering, Corby, Daventry, Wellingborough; **Physical** rivers Avon, Cherwell, Leam, Nene, Ouse, and Welland; **Features** Althorp Park, Spencer family home and burial place of Diana, Princess of Wales; Canons Ashby, Tudor house, home of the Drydens for 400 years; churches with broached spires (an octagonal spire on a square tower); **Agriculture** cereals (wheat and barley), sugar beet, sheep rearing; cattle rearing, especially in the Nene and Welland valleys, where there is rich pasture; **Industries** engineering, food processing, printing, shoemaking; Northampton is the centre of the leather trade in England; **Population** (1996) 604,300.

Northumberland

County of northern England

Area 5,030 sq km/1,942 sq mi; **Towns and cities** Morpeth (administrative headquarters), Berwick-upon-Tweed, Hexham; **Physical** Cheviot Hills; rivers Aln, Coquet, Rede, Till, Tweed, upper Tyne; Northumberland National Park in the west; **Features** Holy Island (Lindisfarne); the Farne island group 8 km/5 mi east of Bamburgh, home to seal and bird colonies; part of Hadrian's Wall (a World Heritage site), including Housesteads Fort; Alnwick and Bamburgh castles; Thomas Bewick museum; Hexham Abbey; the walls of Berwick-upon-Tweed; large moorland areas used for military manoeuvres; Longstone Lighthouse from which Grace Darling rowed to rescue the crew of the *Forfarshire;* wild white cattle of Chillingham; Kielder Water (1982), the largest artificial lake in northern Europe; **Agriculture** sheep, cattle; fishing **Industries** manufacturing of computer monitors (Cramlington); coal was formerly mined at several locations; **Population** (1996) 307,400.

Nottinghamshire

County of central England, which has contained the unitary authority Nottingham City since April 1998

Area 2,160 sq km/834 sq mi; **Towns and cities** West Bridgford (administrative headquarters), Mansfield, Newark, Worksop; **Physical** rivers Erewash, Idle, Soar, Trent; **Features** the remaining areas of Sherwood Forest (home of Robin Hood) are included in the Dukeries, an area of estates; originally 32 km/20 mi long and 12 km/7 mi wide, the forest was formerly a royal hunting ground; Cresswell Crags (remains of prehistoric humans); D H Lawrence commemorative walk from Eastwood (where he lived) to Old Brinsley Colliery; **Agriculture** cereals (barley, wheat), market gardening (potatoes), sugar beet; cattle, sheep; there are many orchards; **Industries** cigarettes, coal mining, engineering, footwear, furniture, gravel, gypsum, ironstone, light engineering, limestone, oil, pharmaceuticals, sandstone, textiles; **Population** (1996) 1,031,800.

Oxfordshire

County of south central England

Area 2,610 sq km/1,007 sq mi; **Towns and cities** Oxford (administrative headquarters), Abingdon, Banbury, Goring, Henley-on-Thames, Wallingford, Witney, Woodstock, Wantage, Chipping Norton, Thame; **Physical** River Thames and tributaries (the Cherwell, Evenlode, Ock, Thame, and Windrush); Cotswold Hills (in the north) and Chiltern Hills (in the southeast); **Features** Vale of the White Horse (with a chalk hill figure 114 m/374 ft, below the hill camp known as Uffington Castle); Oxford University; Blenheim Palace (a World Heritage site), Woodstock (started in 1705 by Vanbrugh with help from Nicholas Hawksmoor, completed in 1722), with landscaped grounds by Capability Brown; early 14th-century Broughton Castle; Rousham Park (1635), Ditchley Park, designed by James Gibbs in 1720; Europe's major fusion project JET (Joint European Torus) at the UK Atomic Energy Authority's fusion laboratories at Culham; the Manor House, Kelmscott (country house of William Morris, leader of the Arts and Crafts movement); Henley Regatta; **Agriculture** cereals, sheep, dairy farming; **Industries** agricultural implements (at Banbury); aluminium (at Banbury); bricks; cars (Cowley); cement; iron ore (in the north); high technology industries; medical electronic equipment; paper; publishing; nuclear research (Harwell); biotechnology; **Population** (1996) 603,100.

Shropshire

County of western England, which has contained the unitary authority of Telford and Wrekin since April 1998. Sometimes abbreviated to **Salop**, Shropshire was officially known by this name from 1974 to 1980

Area 3,490 sq km/1,347 sq mi; **Towns** Shrewsbury (administrative headquarters), Ludlow, Oswestry; **Physical** Shropshire is bisected, on the Welsh border, northwest–southeast by the River Severn; River Teme; Ellesmere (47 ha), the largest of several lakes; the Clee Hills rise to about 610 m/1,800 ft (Brown Clee) in the southwest; **Features** Ironbridge Gorge open-air museum of industrial archaeology, with the Iron Bridge (1779), the world's first cast-iron bridge; Market Drayton is famous for its gingerbread, and Wem for its sweet peas; **Agriculture** cereals (barley, oats, wheat), sugar beet, mangolds (a root vegetable used for cattle feed), vegetables (turnips, swedes), sheep and cattle; dairy farming; forestry; **Industries** brick-making; engineering; limestone; manufacturing: machine tool, agricultural implements (Shrewsbury, Market Drayton, Prees, Whitchurch, Ellesmere), carpets and radio receivers (Bridgnorth), clocks (Whitchurch); Shropshire is the principal iron-producing county of England; **Population** (1996) 421,200.

Somerset

County of southwest England

Area 3,460 sq km/1,336 sq mi; **Towns** Taunton (administrative headquarters); Bridgwater, Frome, Glastonbury, Wells, Yeovil; Burnham-on-Sea, Minehead (coastal resorts); **Physical** rivers Avon, Axe, Brue, Exe, Parret (the principal river), and Yeo; marshy coastline on the Bristol Channel; Mendip Hills; Quantock Hills; Exmoor; Blackdown Hills; **Features** Cheddar Gorge and Wookey Hole, a series of limestone caves where Stone Age flint implements and bones of extinct animals have been found; Glastonbury Tor; **Agriculture** apples; dairy farming; cereals (wheat, barley, oats), vegetables (turnips, mangolds (a root vegetable used as animal feed)); cider; cattle and sheep rearing; willows (withies) for wicker-work; **Industries** agricultural implements; Bath-bricks (manufactured at Bridgwater from the sand of the Parret); chemicals; dairy products (including Cheddar cheese); engineering; food processing; helicopters; leather; mineral working (iron, lead, zinc); stone quarrying (slate); textiles; tourism; **Population** (1996) 482,600.

Staffordshire

County of west central England (since April 1997 Stoke-on-Trent has been a separate unitary authority)

Area 2,720 sq km/1,050 sq mi; **Towns** Stafford (administrative headquarters), Newcastle-under-Lyme, Lichfield, Tamworth, Leek, Uttoxeter; **Physical** largely flat, with hilly regions in the north (part of the Peak district) and southwest; River Trent and its tributaries (the Churnet, Dove, Penk, Sow, and Tame); Cannock Chase (a large open area in the middle of the county); **Features** castles at Chartley, Tamworth, and Tutbury; Lichfield Cathedral; Keele University (1962); Shugborough Hall (17th century), seat of the earls of Lichfield; Staffordshire bull terriers; **Agriculture** dairy farming; **Industries** breweries (Burton-upon-Trent); china and earthenware in the Potteries and the upper Trent basin (including Wedgwood); tractors and agricultural equipment (Uttoxeter); electrical engineering; electronics; **Population** (1996) 555,700.

Suffolk

County of eastern England

Area 3,800 sq km/1,467 sq mi; **Towns** Ipswich (administrative headquarters), Aldeburgh, Beccles, Bury St Edmunds, Felixstowe, Lowestoft, Sudbury, Southwold; **Physical** undulating lowlands in the south and west; flat coastline; rivers Waveney (the boundary with Norfolk), Alde, Deben, Orwell, Stour (the boundary with Essex), Little Ouse; part of the Norfolk Broads; **Features** Minsmere marshland bird reserve, near Aldeburgh; the Sandlings (heathlands and birds); bloodstock rearing and horse racing at Newmarket; Sutton Hoo (7th-century ship burial); Sizewell B, Britain's first pressurized-water nuclear reactor plant; Aldeburgh Festival, held every June at Snape Maltings; **Agriculture** cereals (barley, oats, wheat), sugar beet; cattle, sheep, and pig rearing; fishing (for which Lowestoft is the main centre); **Industries** agricultural machinery; chemicals; coconut matting; electronics; fertilizers; food processing; motor vehicle components; North Sea oil and gas exploration; printing; telecommunications research; silk; timber; brewing; **Population** (1996) 661,600.

Surrey

County of southern England

Area 1,660 sq km/641 sq mi; **Towns** Kingston upon Thames (administrative headquarters), Farnham, Guildford, Leatherhead, Reigate, Woking, Epsom, Dorking; **Physical** rivers Mole, Thames, and Wey; Box Hill (183 m/600 ft), Gibbet Hill (277 m/909 ft), and Leith Hill (299 m/981 ft, 5 km/3 mi south of Dorking, the highest hill in southeast England); North Downs; **Features** Kew Palace and Royal Botanic Gardens, Kew; Yehudi Menuhin School (one of four specialist music schools in England); **Agriculture** vegetables; sheep rearing; dairy farming; horticulture; **Industries** service industries; sand and gravel quarrying; fuller's earth extraction (near Reigate); **Population** (1996) 1,047,100.

Warwickshire

County of central England

Area 1,980 sq km/764 sq mi; **Towns and cities** Warwick (administrative headquarters), Nuneaton, Royal Leamington Spa, Rugby, Stratford-upon-Avon (the birthplace of Shakespeare); **Physical** rivers Avon, Stour, and Tame; remains of the 'Forest of Arden' (portrayed by Shakespeare in *As You Like It*); **Features** Kenilworth and Warwick castles; Edgehill, site of the Battle of Edgehill in 1642, during the English Civil War; annual Royal Agricultural Show held at Stoneleigh; **Agriculture** cereals (oats and wheat); dairy farming; fruit; market gardening; **Industries** cement; engineering; ironstone and lime are worked in the east and south; motor industry; textiles; tourism; **Population** (1996) 500,600.

West Sussex

County of southern England, created in 1974, formerly part of Sussex

Area 1,990 sq km/768 sq mi; **Towns and cities** Chichester (administrative headquarters), Crawley, Horsham, Haywards Heath, Shoreham (port); Bognor Regis, Littlehampton, Worthing (resorts); **Physical** the Weald; South Downs; rivers Adur, Arun, West Rother; **Features** Arundel and Bramber castles; Chichester cathedral; Goodwood House and racecourse; Petworth House (17th century); Wakehurst Place, where the Royal Botanic Gardens, Kew, have additional grounds; Uppark House (1685–90); the Weald and Downland Open Air Museum at Singleton; Fishbourne villa (important Roman site near Chichester); Selsey (reputed landing place of the South Saxons in 447); Gatwick Airport; **Agriculture** cereals (wheat and barley); fruit; market gardening (mainly on the coastal plain); dairy produce; forestry; **Industries** electronics; light engineering; **Population** (1996) 737,300.

Wiltshire

County of southwest England (since April 1997 Swindon has been a separate unitary authority)

Area 3,480 sq km/1,343 sq mi; **Towns and cities** Trowbridge (administrative headquarters), Salisbury, Wilton; Devizes; Chippenham, Warminster; **Physical** Marlborough Downs; Savernake Forest; rivers Kennet, Wylye, Avons (Salisbury and Bristol); Salisbury Plain (32 km/20 mi by 25 km/16 mi, lying at about 120 m/394 ft above sea-level), a military training area used since Napoleonic times; **Features** Longleat House (Marquess of Bath); Wilton House (Earl of Pembroke); Stourhead, with 18th-century gardens; Neolithic Stonehenge, Avebury, Silbury Hill, West Kennet Long Barrow, finest example of a long barrow in Wiltshire, dating from the 3rd millennium BC; Stonehenge, Avebury, and associated sites are a World Heritage site; Salisbury Cathedral, which has the tallest spire in Britain (123 m/404 ft). **Agriculture** cereals (wheat); cattle; dairy-farming (condensed milk, cheese); pig and sheep-farming; **Industries** brewing (Devizes); computing; electronics; engineering (Chippenham); pharmaceuticals; plastics; quarrying (Portland stone); rubber (Bradford-on-Avon, Melksham); tobacco (Devizes); **Population** (1996) 593,300.

Worcestershire

Two-tier county of west central England. Herefordshire and Worcestershire existed as counties until 1974, when they were amalgamated to form the county of Hereford and Worcester; in 1998 this county was divided back into Worcestershire and Herefordshire, which regained their pre-1974 boundaries

Area 1640 sq km/1,020 sq mi; **Towns and cities** Worcester (administrative headquarters), Bewdley, Bromsgrove, Evesham, Kidderminster, Pershore, Stourport, Tenbury Wells; **Physical** Malvern Hills in the southwest (highest point Worcester Beacon 425 m/1394 ft); rivers Severn with tributaries Stour, Teme, and Avon (running through the fertile Vale of Evesham); **Features** Droitwich, once a Victorian spa, reopened its baths in 1985 (the town lies over a subterranean brine reservoir); Three

Choirs Festival at Great Malvern; **Agriculture** cereals (oats, wheat), fruit (apples, pears), hops, vegetables; cider; much of the county is under cultivation, a large part being devoted to permanent pasture, notably for Hereford cattle; **Industries** carpets (Kidderminster), chemicals, engineering, food processing, needles and fishing tackle (Redditch), porcelain (Worcester), salt; **Population** (1996) 535,700.

The Addresses of English County Councils

County	Council offices	Chief executive
Bedfordshire	County Hall, Cauldwell Street, Bedford MK42 9AP; phone: (01234) 363222; fax: (01234) 272982; e-mail: bcclgis@bcclgis.gov.uk	Mr Denis Cleggett
Buckinghamshire	County Hall, Walton Street, Aylesbury, Bucks HP20 1UA; phone: (01296) 395000; fax: (01296) 382481; e-mail: enquiries@buckscc.gov.uk	Mr I Crookhall
Cambridgeshire	Shire Hall, Castle Hill, Cambridge CB3 0AP; phone: (01223) 717111; fax: (01223) 717201; e-mail: alan.barnish@ceu.camcnty.gov.uk; Web site: www.camcnty.gov.uk	Mr Alan Barnish
Cheshire	County Hall, Chester CH1 1SF; phone: (01244) 602424; fax: (01244) 603800	Mr Colin Cheeseman (acting)
Cornwall	New County Hall, Truro, Cornwall TR1 3AY; phone: (01872) 322000; fax: (01872) 270340; e-mail: enquiries@cornwall.gov.uk	Mr John Mills
Cumbria	The Courts, Carlisle CA3 8NA; phone: (01228) 606060; fax: (01228) 606302; e-mail: policy@cumbria/policy.demon.co.uk	Mr Bill Swarbrick
Derbyshire	County Hall, Matlock, Derbyshire DE4 3AG; phone: (01629) 580000; fax: (01629) 585220; e-mail: Derbyshire@usa.net	Mr Nick Hodgson
Devon	County Hall, Topsham Road, Exeter EX2 4QG; phone: (01392) 382000; fax: (01392) 382286; Web site: www.devon-cc.gov.uk	Mr Philip Jenkinson
Dorset	County Hall, Colliton Park, Dorchester, Dorset DT1 1XJ; phone: (01305) 251000; fax: (01305) 224839; Web site: www.dorset-cc.gov.uk	Mr David Jenkins
Durham	County Hall, Durham DH1 5UL; phone: (0191) 386 4411; fax: (0191) 383 3243	Mr K Smith
East Sussex	Pelham House, St Andrew's Lane, Lewes, East Sussex BN7 1UN; phone: (01273) 481000; fax: (01273) 483317	Mrs Cheryl Miller
Essex	County Hall, Chelmsford CM1 1LX; phone: (01245) 492211; fax: (01245) 256731; Web site: www.essexcc.gov.uk	Mr Stuart Ashurst
Gloucestershire	Shire Hall, Westgate Street, Gloucester GL1 2TG; phone: (01452) 425000; fax: (01452) 425876; Web site: www.gloscc.gov.uk	Mr Richard Cockcroft (County Director)
Hampshire	The Castle, Winchester SO23 8UJ; phone: (01962) 841841; fax: (01962) 867273; Web site: www.hants.gov.uk	Mr Peter Robertson
Hertfordshire	County Hall, Peggs Lane, Hertford, Hertfordshire SG13 8DE; phone: (01992) 555555; fax: (01992) 555644; Web site: www.hertscc.gov.uk	Mr Bill Ogley
Kent	Sessions House, County Hall, Maidstone, Kent ME14 1XQ; phone: (01622) 671411; fax: (01622) 694060; e-mail: mick.pitt@kent.gov.uk	Mr Michael Pitt
Lancashire	County Hall, PO Box 100, Preston PR1 0LD; phone: (01772) 254868; fax: (01772) 263506; Web site: www.lancashire.com	Mr G A Johnson
Leicestershire	County Hall, Leicester Road, Glenfield, Leicester LE3 8RA; phone: (0116) 232 3232; fax: (0116) 265 6254; Web site: www.leics.gov.uk	Mr J B Sinnott
Lincolnshire	County Offices, Newland, Lincoln LN1 1YL; phone: (01522) 552000; fax: (01522) 552004	Mr D Bowles (acting)
Norfolk	County Hall, Martineay Lane, Norwich NR1 2DH; phone: (01603) 222222; fax: (01603) 222959; Web site: www.norfolk.gov.uk	Mr Tim Byles
Northamptonshire	George Row, Northampton NN1 1AS; phone: (01604) 236236; fax: (01604) 236223; e-mail: jpicking@northamptonshire.gov.uk	Mr John Picking
Northumberland	County Hall, Morpeth NE61 2EF; phone: (01670) 533000; fax: (01670) 533166; Web site: www.northumberland.gov.uk	Mr Ken Morris
North Yorkshire	County Hall, Race Course Lane, Northallerton, North Yorkshire DL7 8AD; phone: (01609) 780780; fax: (01609) 778199; Web site: www.northyorks.gov.uk	Mr John Ransford
Nottinghamshire	County Hall, West Bridgeford NG2 7QP; phone: (0115) 982 3823; fax: (0115) 977 2419; Web site: www.notscc.gov.uk	Mr Peter Housden
Oxfordshire	County Hall, New Road, Oxford OX1 1ND; phone: (01865) 792422; fax: (01865) 815199; e-mail: oxcis@dial.pipex.com; Web site: www.oxfordshire.gov.uk	Mr John Harwood
Shropshire	The Shire Hall, Abbey Foregate, Shrewsbury, Shropshire SY2 6ND; phone: (01743) 251000; fax: (01743) 252827; Web site: www.shropshire-cc.gov.uk	Mr N Pursey
Somerset	County Hall, Taunton, Somerset TA1 4DY; phone: (01823) 355455; fax: (01823) 355887; Web site: www.somerset.gov.uk	Dr David Radford
Staffordshire	Walton Building, PO Box 11, Martin Street, Stafford ST16 2LH; phone: (01785) 223121; fax: (01785) 215153; Web site: www.staffordshire.gov.uk/	Mr Bernard Price (Clerk and Chief Executive)
Suffolk	County Hall, St Helen Court, Ipswich IP4 2JS; phone: (01473) 583000; fax: (01473) 639002; Web site: www.suffolkcc.gov.uk	Mrs Lin Homer
Surrey	County Hall, Penrhyn Road, Kingston-upon-Thames KT1 2DN; phone: (0181) 541 8800; fax: (0181) 541 8968; Web site: www.surreycc.gov.uk/scc/	Mr Paul Coen
Warwickshire	PO Box 9, Shire Hall, Warwick CV34 4RR; phone: (01926) 410410; fax: (01926) 412479; Web site: www.warwickshire.gov.uk	Mr Ian Caulfield
West Sussex	County Hall, West Street, Chichester PO19 1RO; phone: (01243) 777100; fax: (01243) 777697	Mr Paul Rigg
Wiltshire	County Hall, Bythesea Road, Trowbridge, Wiltshire BA14 8JG; phone: (01225) 713000; fax: (01225) 713092; Web site: www.wiltshire.gov.uk	Dr Keith Robinson
Worcestershire	County Hall, Spetchley Road, Worcester WR5 2NP; phone: (01905) 766333; fax: (01905) 766109; Web site: www.worcestershire.gov.uk	Mr Rob Sykes

The Political Composition of English County Councils

(– = not applicable.)

County	Conservative	Labour	Liberal Democrat	Independent/other	Controlling party	Total councillors
Bedfordshire	25	14	10	0	Conservative	49
Buckinghamshire	38	5	10	1	Conservative	54
Cambridgeshire	33	10	16	0	Conservative	59
Cheshire	19	20	9	0	no overall control	48
Cornwall	8	8	38	25	no overall control	79
Cumbria	23	44	12	4	Labour	83
Derbyshire	12	45	6	1	Labour	64
Devon	14	4	31	5	Liberal Democrat	54
Dorset	15	5	21	1	no overall control	42
Durham	2	53	2	4	Labour	61
East Sussex	21	7	16	0	no overall control	44
Essex	39	24	15	1	no overall control	79
Gloucestershire	21	18	22	2	no overall control	63
Hampshire	42	8	22	2	Conservative	74
Hertfordshire	38	30	9	0	no overall control	77
Kent	46	23	15	0	Conservative	84
Lancashire	23	47	7	1	Labour	78
Leicestershire	25	17	11	1	no overall control	54
Lincolnshire	43	19	11	3	Conservative	76
Norfolk	36	34	13	1	no overall control	84
North Yorkshire	35	12	21	6	no overall control	74
Northamptonshire	27	37	4	0	Labour	68
Northumberland	13	43	8	2	Labour	66
Nottinghamshire	18	41	4	0	Labour	63
Oxfordshire	27	22	19	2	no overall control	70
Shropshire	17	8	13	6	no overall control	44
Somerset	17	3	37	0	Liberal Democrat	57
Staffordshire	20	40	2	0	Labour	62
Suffolk	31	33	15	1	no overall control	80
Surrey	47	6	17	6	Conservative	76
Warwickshire	22	31	8	1	no overall control	62
West Sussex	37	9	24	1	Conservative	71
Wiltshire	23	4	19	1	no overall control	47
Worcestershire	25	22	8	2	no overall control	57
Total	882	746	495	80	–	2,203

Source: Local Government Chronicle Elections Centre, University of Plymouth

English Metropolitan Counties

Manchester, Greater

Metropolitan county of northwest England, created in 1974; in 1986 most of the functions of the former county council were transferred to metropolitan district councils

Area 1,290 sq km/498 sq mi; **Towns and cities** Manchester, Bolton, Bury, Oldham, Rochdale, Salford, Stockport, Tameside, Trafford, Wigan; **Features** Manchester Ship Canal links it with the River Mersey and the sea; Old Trafford cricket ground at Stretford, and the football ground of Manchester United; a second terminal opened at Manchester Airport in 1993; **Industries** engineering, textiles, textile machinery, chemicals, plastics, electrical goods, electronic equipment, paper, printing, rubber, and asbestos; **Population** (1996) 2,575,600.

Merseyside

Metropolitan county of northwest England, created in 1974; in 1986, most of the functions of the former county council were transferred to metropolitan borough councils (The Wirral, Sefton, Liverpool, Knowsley, St Helens)

Area 650 sq km/251 sq mi; **Towns and cities** Liverpool, Bootle, Birkenhead, St Helens, Wallasey, Southport; **Physical** River Mersey; **Features** Merseyside Innovation Centre (MIC), linked with Liverpool and John Moores Universities; Prescot Museum of clock- and watch-making; Speke Hall (Tudor), and Croxteth Hall and Country Park (a working country estate open to the public); **Industries** brewing, chemicals, electrical goods, glassmaking, metal-working, pharmaceutical products, tanning, vehicles; **Population** (1996) 1,420,400.

South Yorkshire

Metropolitan county of northeast England, created in 1974; in 1986, most of the functions of the former county council were transferred to the metropolitan borough councils

Area 1,560 sq km/602 sq mi; **Towns** Barnsley, Doncaster, Rotherham, Sheffield (all administrative centres for the districts of the same name); **Physical** River Don; part of Peak District National Park; a rich diversity of rural landscapes formed between the barren Pennine moors in the southwest and the very low, flat carr-lands (a mixture of marsh and copses) in the east; **Features** The Earth Centre for Environmental Research;

Agriculture sheep; dairy and arable farming; **Industries** metal-work, coal, engineering, iron, and steel; **Population** (1996) 1,304,800.

Tyne and Wear

Metropolitan county of northeast England, created in 1974; in 1986, most of the functions of the former county council were transferred to the metropolitan borough councils

Area 540 sq km/208 sq mi; **Towns and cities** Newcastle upon Tyne, Gateshead, Sunderland (administrative centres for the districts of the same name), South Shields (administrative centre of South Tyneside district), North Shields (administrative centre of North Tyneside district); **Physical** rivers Tyne and Wear; **Features** part of Hadrian's Wall; Newcastle and Gateshead, linked with each other and with the coast on both sides by the Tyne and Wear Metro (a light railway using existing suburban lines, extending 54 km/34 mi); Tyneside International Film Festival; **Industries** once a centre of heavy industry, Tyne and Wear's industry is now being redeveloped and diversified, with car manufacturing on Wearside, electronics, offshore technology (floating production vessels), automobile components, pharmaceuticals, and computers; **Population** (1996) 1,127,300.

West Midlands

Metropolitan county of central England, created in 1974; in 1986, most of the functions of the former county council were transferred to the metropolitan borough councils

Area 900 sq km/347 sq mi; **Towns and cities** Birmingham, Coventry, Dudley, Solihull, Walsall, Wolverhampton (all administrative centres for districts of the same name), Oldbury (administrative centre for Sandwell); **Industries** aircraft components; chemicals; coal mining; engineering; electrical equipment; glass; machine tools; motor vehicles, including Land Rover at Solihull; motor components; **Population** (1996) 2,642,500.

West Yorkshire

Metropolitan county of northeast England, created in 1974; in 1986, most of the functions of the former county council were transferred to the metropolitan borough councils

Area 2,040 sq km/787 sq mi; **Towns and cities** Bradford, Leeds, Wakefield (administrative centres for districts of the same name), Halifax (administrative centre of Calderdale district), Huddersfield (administrative centre of Kirklees district); **Physical** Ilkley Moor, Haworth Moor; high Pennine moorlands in the west, Vale of York to the east; rivers Aire, Calder, Colne, Wharfe; **Features** Haworth Parsonage; part of the Peak District National Park; British Library, Boston Spa (scientific, technical, and business documents); **Industries** woollen textiles, financial services; coal mining in decline; **Population** (1996) 2,109,300.

English Unitary Authorities

Bath and North East Somerset

Unitary authority in southwest England created in 1996 from part of the former county of Avon

Area 351 sq km/136 sq mi; **Towns and cities** Bath (administrative headquarters), Keynsham, Chew Magna, Paulton, Radstock, Peasedown St John, Midsomer Norton; **Features** River Avon and tributaries; Chew Valley Lake; Beckford's Tower (Bath) built in 1827 for William Beckford; Roman baths with hot springs (Bath); Regency architecture including Royal Crescent, The Circus, and Assembly Rooms designed by John Wood (1700–1854) and his son John Wood; Pulteney Bridge, 18th century shop-lined Italianate bridge designed by Robert Adam; Stanton Drew bronze age stone circles including second largest in Great Britain; **Industries** tourism, central government administration, clothing manufacture; **Population** (1996) 158,700.

Blackburn with Darwen

Unitary authority (borough status) in northwest England created in 1998, formerly part of Lancashire

Area 136 sq km2/53 sq mi; **Towns and cities** Blackburn (administrative headquarters), Darwen; **Features** Leeds–Liverpool canal; River Darwen; Darwen Hill and Tower (372 m/1,220 ft); western foothills of Rossendale uplands; Lewis Textile Museum (Blackburn) includes working model of spinning jenny; Blackburn Museum and Art Gallery has largest display of European icons in Britain; **Industries** engineering, brewing, chemicals, high technology industries, textiles, leather, electronics, paint, paper, carpets, compact discs; **Population** (1996) 139,400.

Blackpool

Seaside resort and unitary authority in northwest England, 45 km/28 mi north of Liverpool; part of the county of Lancashire until April 1998

Area 35 sq km/14 sq mi; **Physical** with its neighbours Lytham St Annes to the south and Fleetwood to the north, Blackpool is part of an urban ribbon between the Ribble estuary and Morecambe Bay; **Features** 11 km/7 mi of promenades, known for their autumn 'illuminations' of coloured lights; Blackpool Tower (built in 1894 and modelled on the Eiffel Tower in Paris), 157 m/518 ft high; the Pleasure Beach, an amusement park that includes Europe's largest and fastest roller-coaster, 75 m/235 ft high and 1.5 km/1 mi long (opened in 1994); three 19th-century piers; the Wintergardens, Grand Theatre, and Sealife Centre; a tram, which first operated in 1885, transports visitors along the promenade; **Industries** Blackpool is the largest holiday resort in northern England, and provides important conference business facilities. Other industries include light engineering and the production of confectionery and biscuits; **Population** (1997) 151,200; Blackpool urban area (1991) 261,400.

Bournemouth

Seaside resort and unitary authority in southern England. The town lies on Poole Bay, 40 km/25 mi southwest of Southampton, and was part of the county of Dorset until 1997

Area 46 sq km/18 sq mi; **Features** 10 km/6 mi stretch of sands; parks; winter gardens; two piers; the Russell-Cotes Museum; the Pavilion; the Casa Magni Shelley Museum; Bournemouth University; **Industries** tourism, the provision of insurance, banking, and financial services, and the manufacture of communications systems (Siemens); an International Conference Centre is situated here; **Population** (1997) 161,500.

Bracknell Forest

Unitary authority (borough status) in central south England, created in 1998 from part of the former county of Berkshire

Area 109 sq km/42 sq mi; **Towns** Bracknell (administrative headquarters), Sandhurst, Crowthorne; **Features** Royal Military Academy at Sandhurst (established in 1799 for officer training); the Meteorological Office at Bracknell (one of two global forecasting centres for the world's airlines); Transport Research Laboratory; **Industries** high technology industries, engineering, electronics, manufacture of clothing and furniture, bakery products; **Population** (1997) 109,600.

Brighton and Hove

Unitary authority in southern England, created in 1997

Area 84 sq km/32 sq mi; **Towns** Brighton, Hove (administrative headquarters), Woodingdean, Rottingdean, Portslade-by-Sea; **Features** English Channel; South Downs; Royal Pavilion (Brighton), redesigned and enlarged by John Nash for prince regent in the 19th century; Palace Pier and West Pier (Brighton); Hollingbury Castle fort; Booth Museum of Natural History (Brighton); British Engineerium (Hove); **Industries** financial services (including American Express), tourism, conference facilities, language schools; **Population** (1996) 248,000.

Bristol

Industrial port and unitary authority in southwest England, at the junction of the rivers Avon and Frome; it was part of the former county of Avon to 1996

Area 109 sq km/42 sq mi; **Features** new city centre, with British engineer and inventor Isambard Kingdom Brunel's Temple Meads railway station as its focus; old docks have been redeveloped for housing and industry; there is a 12th-century cathedral and 13th–14th-century St Mary Redcliffe church; National Lifeboat Museum; Clifton Suspension Bridge (completed in 1864), designed by Brunel; aerospace complex in the suburb of Filton; University of Bristol (founded in 1909) and University of the West of England (established in 1992), formerly the Bristol Polytechnic; Ashton Court mansion, which hosts the annual International Balloon Fiesta and North Somerset show; Bristol 2000, a Millennium Commission Landmark Project in the city's harbour area, includes Wildscreen World, the world's first electronic zoo; **Industries** engineering, microelectronics, tobacco, printing, metal refining, banking, insurance, sugar refining, and the manufacture of aircraft engines, chemicals, paper, soap, Bristol 'blue' glass, and chocolate; **Population** (1996) 374,300, urban area (1991) 516,500.

Darlington

Unitary authority (borough status) in northeast England, created in 1997

Area 197 sq km/76 sq mi; **Towns and cities** Darlington (administrative headquarters); villages of Hurworth on Tees, Middleton St George, Heighington, Hurworth Place; **Features** River Skerne flows through Darlington, River Tees forms southern boundary of authority; Darlington Railway Centre and Museum houses English engineer George Stephenson's locomotion engine; **Industries** heavy engineering, iron and steel, vehicle components, bridge building, telecommunications, fitted furniture, textiles, knitting wool, agriculture; **Population** (1996) 100,600.

Derby City

Industrial city and unitary authority in north central England, on the River Derwent, 200 km/124 mi north of London; the city was part of the county of Derbyshire until 1997

Area 87 sq km/30 sq mi; **Features** Derby Cathedral, originally a parish church, was rebuilt in the 18th century but retains its 16th-century tower; the University of Derby was established in 1993; **Industries** cars (Rolls-Royce and Toyota), aero engines (Rolls-Royce), chemicals, paper, textiles, plastics, Royal Crown Derby porcelain (Royal Doulton), and electrical, mining, and engineering equipment; financial services; train repair workshops; **Population** (1996) 218,800.

East Riding of Yorkshire

Unitary authority in northern England created in 1996 from part of the former county of Humberside

Area 2,416 sq km/933 sq mi; **Towns** Beverley (administrative headquarters), Driffield, Goole, Hornsea, Bridlington; **Features** Humber Estuary to south of authority; North Sea to east; Flamborough Head chalk cliffs; Spurn Head – dynamic spit at mouth of estuary; River Hull; River Ouse; Holderness Peninsula; The Wolds; Hornsea Mere; Beverley Minster (13th century); All Saints Tower (34 m/110 ft) at Driffield; Sledmere House – 18th century mansion with grounds laid out by Capability Brown; Rudstone has Britain's tallest standing stone (8 m/25 ft); Sewerby Hall (Bridlington) – Georgian mansion including museum dedicated to the aviator Amy Johnson (1903–1941); Hornsea Pottery; Withernsea Lighthouse (39 m/127 ft) including museum; **Industries** chemicals, pottery, agriculture, agricultural machinery and services, passenger vehicle components, bakery products; **Population** (1996) 310,000.

Halton

Unitary authority in northwest England, created in 1998 from part of Cheshire

Area 74 sq km/29 sq mi; **Towns and cities** Runcorn, Widnes (administrative headquarters), Ditton; **Features** River Mersey divides Runcorn from Widnes and Ditton; Manchester Ship Canal and Bridgewater Canal reach Mersey at Runcorn; St Helen's Canal reaches Mersey via a series of locks at Widnes; Catalyst: the Museum of the Chemical Industry is at Widnes; Norton Priory Museum (Runcorn) is on the site of a 12th-century priory; **Industries** industrial chemicals, pharmaceuticals, plastics manufacturing and coatings, light engineering, scientific instruments; **Population** (1996) 122,300.

Hartlepool

Town, port, and, since 1996, unitary authority in northeast England, formed from part of the county of Cleveland

Area 94 sq km/36 sq mi; **Features** redeveloped dock area including the Museum of Hartlepool (opened in 1995); the Gray Art Gallery and Museum; remains of the medieval town walls; Early English church of St Hilda with a Norman doorway; **Industries** the local economy depends on metal industries, engineering, support services for the oil industry, fishing, and brewing. A nuclear power station is located 5 km/3 mi southeast of the town at Seaton Carew; **Population** (1996) 90,400.

Herefordshire

Unitary authority in west England, created in 1998 from part of the former county of Hereford and Worcester

Area 2,288 sq km/884 sq mi; **Towns and cities** Hereford (administrative headquarters), Leominster, Ross-on-Wye, Ledbury; **Features** River Wye; Herefordshire Beacon (340 m/1,115 ft) Iron Age fort; Hereford Cathedral (11th century) houses the late 13th/early 14th-century Mappa Mundi, and the Chained Library, with over 1,400 chained books and 200 manuscripts dating from the 8th to 12th centuries; Waterworks Museum (Hereford) in restored Victorian pump house; Croft Castle (Leominster); St Mary's Church (Kempley) with medieval wall paintings; The Prospect, a walled clifftop garden in Ross-on-Wye designed by John Kyrle in the 17th century; Norman Church (Kilpeck) with notable carvings; **Industries** agriculture, orchards and cider industry, agricultural services and machinery, precision engineering, light engineering, plastics manufacture; **Population** (1996) 166,100.

Kingston upon Hull

City, port, and unitary authority, created in 1996 from part of the former county of Humberside, situated where the River Hull flows into the north side of the Humber estuary, northeast England

Area 71 sq km/27 sq mi; **Features** 13th-century Holy Trinity Church; restored docklands area; Town Docks Museum; Ferens Art Gallery (1927); University of Hull (1954) and University of Humberside (1992), formerly Humberside Polytechnic; linked with the south bank of the estuary by the Humber Bridge, the world's longest single-span suspension bridge; **Industries** fish processing, flour milling, sawmilling, marine engineering, food processing, and the manufacture of electrical goods, vegetable oils, paint, pharmaceuticals, chemicals, caravans, aircraft, and paper. There are 11 km/7 mi of modern docks located on the Humber estuary. The largest timber port in the UK, it also handles grain, oilseeds, wool, and the export/import of manufactured goods. There are ferries to Rotterdam and Zeebrugge. Following the building of the Queen Elizabeth Dock in 1971, the port's roll-on/roll-off freight traffic has expanded rapidly.; **Population** (1996) 265,000.

Leicester City

Industrial city and unitary authority in central England, on the River Soar. It was part of the county of Leicestershire to 1997

Area 73 sq km/28 sq mi; **Features** 14th-century Guildhall, St Martin's Cathedral, and two universities (University of Leicester, established in 1957, and De Montfort University, formerly Leicester Polytechnic, established in 1992); Bradgate House, the home of Lady Jane Grey, located in Bradgate Park, 10 km/6 mi northwest of Leicester; there is an Eco House in the city; an environment-friendly show home, demonstrating ways in which people can reduce the ecological impact of their homes; **Industries** engineering, food processing, electronics, chemicals, and the manufacture of hosiery, footwear, knitwear, plastics, scientific and medical instruments, electrical products, and construction and woodworking machinery; **Population** (1996) 270,500.

Luton

Industrial town and unitary authority in south-central England, 48 km/30 mi north of London. It was part of the county of Bedfordshire to 1997

Area 43 sq km/17 sq mi; **Features** the Luton Hoo mansion (1767), designed and built by Robert Adam and with a park laid out by Capability Brown, is located south of the town; large church of St Mary (13th–15th centuries) is a cruciform building largely in the Decorated and Perpendicular styles; **Industries** Luton airport is a secondary airport for London. Local industry has traditionally been associated with the manufacture of hats; cars and trucks, chemicals, engineering components, and electrical goods are also produced; **Population** (1996) 181,400.

Medway Towns

Unitary authority in southeast England, created in 1998 by combining the former city council of Rochester upon Medway with Gillingham borough council, both formerly in Kent

Area 194 sq km/75 sq mi; **Towns and cities** Rochester, Chatham, Gillingham, Strood (administrative headquarters); **Features** River Medway flows through Rochester; River Thames forms northern border of authority; reclaimed estuarine mudflats form the Isle of Grain; Charles Dickens Centre (Rochester) is housed in a 16th-century mansion; Royal Naval Dockyard (Chatham); Royal Engineers Museum (Gillingham); Upnor Castle (16th century) at Upper Upnor; **Industries** oil refineries on Isle of Grain, heavy industry, engineering, maritime industries, Thamesport (privately-owned deep-water container port), avionics, financial services, information technology; **Population** (1996) 240,000.

Middlesbrough

Industrial town, port, and unitary authority, on the estuary of the River Tees, northeast England, created in 1996 from part of the former county of Cleveland. The town was the administrative headquarters of the county of Cleveland to 1996. It is the commercial centre of the Teesside industrial area, which also includes Stockton-on-Tees, Redcar, Billingham, Thornaby, and Eston

Area 54 sq km/21 sq mi; **Features** Transporter Bridge (1911) transports cars and passengers across the Tees to Hartlepool in a cable car; Newport Bridge (1934) was the first vertical lift bridge in England; the University of Teesside, formerly Teesside Polytechnic, was established in 1992; the Captain Cook Birthplace Museum commemorates the life of the naval explorer James Cook; the 18th-century National Trust-owned Ormesby Hall is located nearby; **Industries** formerly a centre of heavy industry, it diversified its products in the 1960s; there are constructional, electronics, engineering, and shipbuilding industries, and iron, steel, and chemicals are produced; **Population** (1996) 146,000.

Milton Keynes

Unitary authority in central England, formerly part of Buckinghamshire

Area 311 sq km/120 sq mi; **Towns and cities** Milton Keynes (administrative headquarters), Newport Pagnell, Olney, Bletchley, Stony Stratford, Woburn Sands, Wolverton; **Features** Grand Union Canal; River Great Ouse; River Tove; Open University (established in Milton Keynes in 1971); Milton Keynes National Bowl (venue for outdoor events); National Badminton Centre (Milton Keynes); Bletchley Park, government centre of code-breaking during World War II; Ouse Valley Park with wetland habitats; Peace Pagoda (Milton Keynes), first to be built in northern hemisphere and surrounded by a thousand cherry and cedar trees planted in memory of all war victims; Milton Keynes' famous concrete cows, constructed in 1978 by a community artist and local school children; **Industries** financial services, telecommunications, soft drinks, high technology industries, motor vehicle parts and manufacture (Aston Martin-Lagonda, Mercedes-Benz, Volkswagen-Audi), education (Open University and De Montfort University campuses), vellum and parchment; **Population** (1996) 198,600.

North East Lincolnshire

Unitary authority in eastern England created in 1996 from part of the former county of Humberside

Area 192 sq km/74 sq mi; **Towns and cities** Grimsby (administrative headquarters), Immingham, Cleethorpes, Humberston, New Waltham, Waltham, Healing, Laceby; **Features** Humber Estuary forms east border of authority; River Freshney; Immingham Museum; National Fishing Heritage Centre (Grimsby); **Industries** fishing and associated industries, docks and shipping services at Immingham and Grimsby, chemical manufacture, heavy engineering, marine engineering, oil refining, tourism (Cleethorpes); **Population** (1996) 164,000

North Lincolnshire

Unitary authority in eastern England created in 1996 from part of the former county of Humberside

Area 850 sq km/328 sq mi; **Towns and cities** Scunthorpe (administrative headquarters), Brigg, Barton-upon-Humber, Barrow upon Humber, Epworth; **Features** Humber Estuary forms north border; River Trent; Isle of Axholme; Stainforth and Keadby Canal; River Torne; Humber Bridge southern landfall at Barton upon Humber; Julian's Bower (near Alkborough) – medieval maze cut in turf; wetland nature reserves at Barton Waterside and Blackroft Sands; Sandtoft Transport Centre with 60 trolley buses running on own circuit; Old Rectory (Epworth) where John Wesley, founder of Methodism, was born; **Industries** steelworks and manufacture of steel products, computer equipment and electronics, food processing (Golden Wonder); **Population** (1996) 153,000.

North Somerset

Unitary authority in southwest England created in 1996 from part of the former county of Avon

Area 372 sq km/144 sq mi; **Towns and cities** Weston-Super-Mare (administrative headquarters), Clevedon, Portishead, Yatton, Congresbury; **Features** Severn Estuary forms northwest border of authority; River Yea; River Avon forms northeast border; west end of the Mendips including Bleadon Hill (134 m/440 ft); Clevedon Court – 14th/15th century manor house owned by Elton family; Weston Woods and Worlebury Hill iron age sites (Weston-Super-Mare); International Helicopter Museum (Weston-Super-Mare); **Industries** automotive components, rubber and plastics manufacture; **Population** (1996) 177,000.

Nottingham City

Industrial city and unitary authority in central England, on the River Trent, 200 km/124 mi northwest of London. It was the administrative headquarters of the county of Nottinghamshire to April 1998

Area 74 sq km/29 sq mi; **Features** Nottingham Playhouse (1963), the Theatre Royal (1866), the Royal Concert Hall (1982), and the Castle Museum; University of Nottingham (1881) and Nottingham Trent University (1992), formerly Trent Polytechnic; the Goose Fair, dating from the Middle Ages, is held every October; Nottingham has a racecourse, and test matches are played on the Trent Bridge cricket ground; the Harvey Haddon sports stadium opened in 1964; the National Water Sports Centre is to the east of the city, near the village of Holme Pierrepont; a Tudor mansion, Holme Pierrepont Hall, is also in the village; **Industries** tourism, engineering, and the manufacture of bicycles, textiles, knitwear, pharmaceuticals, tobacco, lace, hosiery, and electronics; **Population** (1996) 285,000.

Peterborough

Unitary authority in eastern England, created in 1998 from part of Cambridgeshire

Area 334 sq km/129 sq mi; **Towns and cities** Peterborough (administrative headquarters), Wittering, Old Fletton, Thorney, Glinton, Northborough, Peakirk; **Features** River Nene; western margins of the Fens; St Peter's Cathedral (Peterborough), 12th century, containing Catherine of Aragon's tomb; Wildfowl and Wetlands Centre at Peakirk; **Industries** aluminium founding and manufacture, electronics, domestic appliances, plastics and rubber manufacture, precision engineering, telecommunications equipment, food manufacture and processing; **Population** (1996) 156,900.

Plymouth

City, seaport, and unitary authority in southwest England, at the mouth of the River Plym; until April 1998 it was part of the county of Devon

Area 79 sq km/31 sq mi; **Features** dockyard and naval base at Devonport; three harbours, Sutton Pool, Catwater (Cattewater), and the Hamoaze, which unite in Plymouth Sound, a bay with a breakwater over 1 km/0.6 mi in length across the entrance; ferry links with France and Spain; Plymouth University, formerly South West Polytechnic, established in 1992; ramparts of a 17th-century citadel, built to guard the harbour soon after the Civil War; Eddystone Rocks lighthouse 22 km/14 mi to the south; the Hoe, an esplanade overlooking Plymouth Sound, with many monuments including a statue of Sir Francis Drake, and Smeaton's Tower, originally erected in 1759 on the Eddystone Rocks and replaced in 1882; Plymouth Dome illustrates the history of the city; aquarium of the Marine Biological Association, which has its headquarters in Plymouth; **Industries** marine and machine tools industries, and clothing, radio equipment, and processed foods are produced; **Population** (1996) 257,000.

Poole

Unitary authority in southwest England, created in 1997 from part of Dorset

Area 64 sq km/25 sq mi; **Towns and cities** Poole (administrative headquarters), Broadstone, Hillbournes, Sandbanks; **Features** River Stour formers northern border of authority; Poole Harbour; Holes Bay; Pergins Island; Maritime Museum (Poole); Compton Acres themed gardens (including water, rock, heather, Japanese, Roman, Italian); Canford Heath, tumuli field; Sandbanks spit guarding entrance to harbour; ferry from Poole to Brownsea Island and the Channel Islands; **Industries** boat building and repair, tourism, electro-mechanical engineering, marine engineering and marine electronics, electrical systems, aeronautical instruments; **Population** (1996) 138,100.

Portsmouth

City, naval port, and unitary authority in southern England, 118 km/73 mi southwest of London, on the peninsula of Portsea Island, opposite the Isle of Wight; it was part of the county of Hampshire until 1997

Area 42 sq km/16 sq mi; **Features** 12th-century cathedral; UK headquarters of IBM (UK) Ltd, Pall Europe Ltd, and Zurich Insurance Group; Portsmouth University, formerly Portsmouth Polytechnic, was established in 1992; the city has won a Millennium Award for a harbour development that will create a maritime leisure complex; Tudor warship *Mary Rose* and Admiral Horatio Nelson's flagship HMS *Victory* are exhibited here; **Industries** high-technology and manufacturing industries, including aircraft engineering, electronics, shipbuilding, and ship maintenance; naval dockyard was closed in 1981, although some naval facilities remain; it is a continental ferry port; **Population** (1996) 189,300.

Reading

Industrial town and unitary authority in southern England, on the River Thames where it meets the Kennet, 61 km/38 mi west of London; it was the administrative headquarters of the county of Berkshire to April 1998

Area 37 sq km/14 sq mi; **Features** remains of a 12th-century Benedictine abbey where Henry I is buried; the Museum of Reading includes Roman and Saxon relics, and a full-size Victorian reproduction of the Bayeaux Tapestry; the Museum of English Rural Life is also here; **Industries** biscuits, brewing, boats, engineering, printing, and electronics; it is an agricultural and horticultural centre with seed-testing grounds, and is a major bulb producer; **Population** (1996) 131,000.

Redcar and Cleveland

Unitary authority in northeast England created in 1996 from part of the former county of Cleveland

Area 240 sq km/93 sq mi; **Towns and cities** Redcar (administrative headquarters), Skelton, Guisborough, Marske-by-the-Sea, Saltburn-by-the-Sea, Brotton, Loftus; **Features** North Sea coast; River Tees forms northwest border; Boulby Cliffs are highest cliffs on England's east coast (203 m/666 ft); 12th-century priory at Guisborough; Cleveland Way long distance path reaches coast at Saltburn; RNLI Zetland Lifeboat Museum (Redcar); Ironstone Mining Museum (Saltburn-by-the-Sea); **Industries** manufacture of steel products (British Steel), engineering, fertilizers and potash products, textiles; **Population** (1996) 144,000.

Rutland

Unitary authority in central England, formerly the smallest English county, which was part of Leicestershire 1974–97

Area 394 sq km/152 sq mi; **Towns and cities** Oakham (administrative headquarters), Uppingham; **Physical** rivers Chater, Eye, Gwash, Welland; **Features** Rutland Water, a large reservoir in the valley of the Gwash at Empingham; **Agriculture** cereals (barley, wheat), sugar beet, potatoes; sheep and cattle are reared, and Stilton cheese is produced; **Industries** clothing, engineering, and plastics; limestone and ironstone are quarried; **Population** (1996) 34,600.

Slough

Industrial town and unitary authority in southern England, near Windsor, 32 km/20 west of London; it was part of the county of Berkshire to April 1998

Area 28 sq km/11 sq mi; **Features** the home of astronomer William Herschel is now a museum; the history of the town is recorded in Slough Museum; **Industries** pharmaceuticals, electronics, engineering, aviation support services, and the manufacture of chocolate, paint, and power tools; a trading estate was developed here in the 1920s, the first of its kind to be established in England; **Population** (1996) 105,000.

Southampton

Industrial city, seaport, and unitary authority in southern England, at the head of Southampton Water, 20 km/12 mi southwest of Winchester; it was part of the county of Hampshire to 1997

Area 52 sq km/20 sq mi; **Features** Southampton University, established in 1952; ferry link to the Isle of Wight; the port is a base for many liners, including P&O's *Oriana;* Southampton City Art Gallery; parts of the medieval town wall survive, including four of the town-wall towers, and Bargate, the elaborate old north gateway to the city; the partly-Norman St Michael's Church has an 18th-century spire 50 m/164 ft high; the 14th-century Wool House now houses a maritime museum; Tudor House

Museum, situated in a half-timbered 15th-century building; the hospital of God's House was originally founded in 1185 for pilgrims going either to the shrine of St Swithin at Winchester, or to Canterbury; 15th-century God's House Tower houses a museum of archaeology; Norman House and Canute's Palace are among the oldest examples of Norman domestic architecture in Britain; a memorial column marks the place of embarkation of the *Mayflower;* the headquarters of the Ordnance Survey are here; **Industries** marine engineering, chemicals, plastics, flour-milling, tobacco, the manufacture of cables and electrical goods, and financial services. It is a major passenger and container port. There is an oil refinery nearby at Fawley; **Population** (1996) 207,100.

Southend

Resort and unitary authority in eastern England, on the Thames estuary, 60 km/37 mi east of London, the nearest seaside resort to London; it was part of the county of Essex to April 1998

Area 42 sq km/16 sq mi; **Features** a pier, 2 km/1.25 mi long, said to be the longest in the world; 11 km/7 mi of seafront, an aquarium, amusement facilities, and many public parks and gardens, including the Cliff Gardens; well known for its flowers, including carpet bedding displays and a Floral Trail Tour; nearly a third of all land in the area is managed for nature conservation, including Belfairs Wood Nature Reserve and Leigh National Nature Reserve on Two Tree Island; **Industries** tourism, financial services, light engineering, and boatbuilding; **Population** (1996) 171,000.

South Gloucestershire

Unitary authority in southwest England created in 1996 from part of the former county of Avon

Area 497 sq km/192 sq mi; **Towns and cities** Thornbury (administrative headquarters), Patchway, Yate, Chipping Sodbury; **Features** River Severn borders northwest; Vale of Berkeley; Severn Road Bridge; Marshfield has one of Britain's longest village streets with 17th century almshouses; 13th century church of St Peter (Dyrham); late 17th century Dyrham Park Mansion; **Industries** agriculture and associated industries; **Population** (1996) 220,000.

Stockton-on-Tees

Unitary authority in northeast England created in 1996 from part of the former county of Cleveland

Area 200 sq km/77 sq mi; **Towns and cities** Stockton-on-Tees (administrative headquarters), Billingham, Yarm, Longnewton; **Features** River Tees forms east border; Tees Barrage; Yarm viaduct; Preston Hall Museum and Park (Stockton); Castlegate Quay (Stockton) includes full-scale replica of *HMS Endeavour;* **Industries** chemicals, polythene film, light and heavy engineering, insulation products, plastics, electronics; **Population** (1996) 176,600.

Stoke-on-Trent

City and unitary authority in central England, on the River Trent, 23 km/14 mi north of Stafford; it was part of the county of Staffordshire to 1997

Area 93 sq km/36 sq mi; **Features** the Gladstone Pottery Museum is a working pottery museum; **Industries** it is the heart of the Potteries, a major ceramic centre, and the largest clayware producer in the world; the ceramics factories of Minton, Wedgwood, Spode, and Royal Doulton are all based here. Other industries include the manufacture of steel, chemicals, engineering machinery, paper, rubber, and tyres. Michelin has its headquarters in the town; **Population** (1996) 254,200.

Swindon

Unitary authority in southwest England, created in 1997 from the former district council of Thamesdown

Area 230 sq km/89 sq mi; **Towns and cities** Swindon (administrative headquarters); villages of Stanton, Fitzwarren, Highworth; **Features** River Thames forms northern border of authority; Barbury Castle, Iron Age hillfort on Marlborough Downs; Great Weatern Railway Museum and National Monuments Records Centre (Swindon); **Industries** insurance, motor vehicle manufacturing, publishing, energy services, high technology industries, information technology; **Population** (1996) 170,000.

Telford and Wrekin

Unitary authority in west England, created in 1998 from part of Shropshire

Area 291 sq km/112 sq mi; **Towns and cities** Telford (administrative headquarters), Newport; **Features** The Wrekin, isolated hill (407 m/1,334 ft); Ironbridge Gorge (World Heritage Site) includes world's first iron bridge, built across River Severn in 1779 by Abraham Darby, and Ironbridge Gorge Museum Trust (seven industrial history museums including Museum of the River, Museum of Iron, Blists Hill Open Air Museum, Coalport China Museum); **Industries** iron founding, agriculture, dairy farming, food processing, confectionery, audio and tape manufacture, electronic tools and equipment, vehicle parts, plastics, clothing manufacture, information technology; **Population** (1996) 144,600.

Thurrock

Unitary authority in eastern England, created in 1998 from part of Essex

Area 163 sq km/63 sq mi; **Towns and cities** Grays (administrative headquarters), Purfleet, Tilbury, Chadwell, St Mary, Stanford-le-Hope, Corringham, South Ockendon; **Features** located on north bank of River Thames; Holehaven Creek forms eastern border of authority; Tilbury Marshes; Mucking Marshes; Dartford Tunnel and Queen Elizabeth II bridge have northern approach through Thurrock; 17th-century Tilbury Fort, with three moats; Alexandra Lake; Lakeside shopping centre; **Industries** oil refineries, power station at west Tilbury Marshes, sand and gravel extraction, cement works, soap, margarine, timber products; **Population** (1996) 130,600.

Torbay

Urban area and unitary authority in southwest England created in April 1998 from part of the county of Devon

Area 627 sq km/242 sq mi; **Towns and cities** Torquay (administrative headquarters), Paignton, Brixham; **Features** Tor Bay; English Channel coast; 23 beaches including Goodrington Sands; Oldway Mansion (Paignton) modelled partly on Versailles; 12th century Torre Abbey (Torquay); replica of Drake's Golden Hind (Brixham); Abbey Mansion (17th/18th century); Paignton Zoo; **Industries** tourism, fishing, electronics, radio equipment, iron founding, horticultural products; **Population** (1996) 128,000.

Warrington

Unitary authority in northwest England, created in 1998 from part of Cheshire

Area 176 sq km/68 sq mi; **Towns and cities** Warrington (administrative headquarters), Lymm, Great Sankey; **Features** River Mersey; Manchester Ship Canal; Warrington Museum and Art Gallery houses over 1,000 paintings; Risley Moss bog and woodland with nature trails and visitors' centre; **Industries** chemicals, food and soft drinks processing, brewing, printing, manufacturing of clothing, leather, metal goods, timber products; **Population** (1996) 151,000.

West Berkshire

Unitary authority in southeast England, created in 1998 from part of the former county of Berkshire

Area 705 sq km/272 sq mi; **Towns and cities** Newbury (administrative headquarters), Hungerford, Lambourn; **Features** River Kennet; River Cambourn; Kennet and Avon Canal; Snelsmore Common Country Park covers 146 acres including wetland habitats; Inkpen Hill (291 m/854 ft) with Stone Age tomb and Walbury Hill (297 m/974 ft) with Iron Age fort are the highest chalk hills in England; Thatcham Moors reedbeds are designated Sites of Special Scientific Interest (SSSI); Greenham Common Women's Peace Camp has been the site of campaigning against nuclear weapons development at Greenham, Burghfield, and Aldermaston since 1981; **Industries** race horse industry, agriculture, dairy cattle, pig farming (including local Berkshire pig); **Population** (1996) 142,600.

Wight, Isle of

Island and unitary authority of southern England

Area area 380 sq km/147 sq mi; **Towns** Newport (administrative headquarters); Ryde, Sandown, Shanklin, and Ventnor (all resorts); **Physical** chalk cliffs and downs, and deep ravines, known locally as 'chines'; the highest point is St Boniface Down (240 m/787 ft); the Needles, a group of pointed chalk rocks up to 30 m/100 ft high in the sea to the west; the Solent, the sea channel between Hampshire and the island; **Features** Benedictine monastery at Quarr Abbey; Parkhurst Prison, just outside Newport; Cowes, venue of Regatta Week and headquarters of the Royal Yacht Squadron; Osborne House, built for Queen Victoria in 1845; **Agriculture** fruit and vegetables grown in south of island; **Industries** aircraft components, electronics, marine engineering; plastics, boatbuilding, sawmills, tourism; **Population** (1996) 130,000.

Windsor and Maidenhead

Unitary authority in southeast England, created in 1998 from part of the former county of Berkshire

Area 198 sq km/76 sq mi; **Towns and cities** Windsor, Maidenhead (administrative headquarters); **Features** River Thames; Windsor Castle, royal residence originally built by William the Conqueror; Windsor Great Park, remnant of royal hunting ground; Eton College, founded by Henry VI in 1440; Household Cavalry Museum (Windsor); Stanley Spencer (1891–1959) Gallery (Cookham on Thames); Ascot Racecourse; **Industries** tourism and service industries, electrical systems and components, chemicals, motor vehicle components, telecommunications, publishing, scientific equipment; **Population** (1996) 140,200.

Wokingham

Unitary authority in southeast England, created in 1998 from part of the former county of Berkshire

Area 179 sq km/69 sq mi; **Towns and cities** Wokingham (administrative headquarters), Twyford; **Features** River Thames forms northern border of authority; Royal Electrical and Mechanical Engineering Corps Museum (Arborfield); Swallowfield Park, house built for 2nd Earl of Clarendon in 1690; National Dairy Museum; Henley Regatta course; large areas of mixed woodland including remnants of old Royal Chase of Windsor Forest and tree-lined avenues; Finchampstead Ridges; **Industries** light engineering, electronics and information technology, telecommunications, computer components and software, plastics; **Population** (1996) 142,000.

York

Unitary authority in northeast England created in 1996 from part of the county of North Yorkshire

Area 271 sq km/105 sq mi; **Towns** York (administrative headquarters); **Features** River Ouse; River Fosse; York Minster –largest medieval cathedral in England, with 15th-century stained glass; York Castle and Museum; National Railway Museum; city walls built by Henry III in 13th century with 4 gates and 39 towers; Jorvik Viking Centre; the Shambles medieval streets; **Industries** agriculture and agricultural services, mechanical engineering, circuit boards, tourism, scientific instruments, confectionery, glass; **Population** (1996) 174,800.

The Addresses of English Unitary Authorities

Authority	Council offices	Chief executive
Bath and North East Somerset	Riverside, Temple Street, Keynsham, Bristol BS3 1LA; phone: (01225) 477793; fax: (01225) 394470; Web site: www.bathnes.gov.uk	Mr John Everitt
Blackburn with Darwen	Town Hall, King William Street, Blackburn BB1 7DY; phone: (01254) 585585; fax: (01254) 697223; Web site: www.blackburn.gov.uk	Mr Philip Watson
Blackpool	Municipal Buildings, Corporation Street, Blackpool FY1 1AD; phone: (01253) 477477; fax: (01253) 477101	Mr G Essex-Crosby
Bournemouth	Town Hall, Bourne Avenue, Bournemouth BH2 6DY; phone: (01202) 451451; fax: (01202) 451000; Web site: www.bournemouth.gov.uk	Mr David Newell
Bracknell	Civic Offices, East Hampstead House, Town Square, Bracknell RG12 1AQ; phone: (01344) 424642; fax: (01344) 352810; Web site: www.bracknell-forest.gov.uk	Mr Gordon Mitchell
Brighton and Hove	Kings House, Grand Avenue, Hove BN3 2LS; phone: (01273) 290000; fax: (01273) 291003; Web site: www.brighton-hove.gov.uk	Mr Glynn Jones
Bristol	The Council House, College Green, Bristol BS1 5TR; phone: (0117) 922 2000; fax: (0117) 922 2024; Web site: www.bristol-city.gov.uk	Ms Lucy de Groot
Darlington	Town Hall, Darlington DL1 5QT; phone: (01325) 380651; fax: (01325) 388018; Web site: www.darlington.org.uk/council/	Mr Barry Keel
Derby	The Council House, Corporation Street, Derby DE1 2FS; phone: (01332) 293111; fax: (01332) 256223	Mr Ray Cowlishaw
East Riding of Yorkshire	County Hall, Beverley, East Riding of Yorkshire HU17 9BA; phone: (01482) 887700; fax: (01482) 884732; Web site: www.east-riding-of-yorkshire.gov.uk	Mr Darryl Stephenson
Halton	Municipal Building, Kingsway, Widnes WA8 7QF; phone: (0151) 424 2061; fax: (0151) 471 7301	Mr Mike Cuff
Hartlepool	Civic Centre, Victoria Road, Hartlepool TS24 8AY; phone: (01429) 266522; fax: (01429) 523856	Mr Brian Dinsdale
Herefordshire	Brockington, 35 Haford Road HR1 1SH; phone: (01432) 260000; fax: (01432) 340189	Mr Neil Pringle
Isle of Wight	County Hall, High Street, Newport, Isle of Wight PO30 1UD; phone: (01983) 823000; fax: (01983) 823138	Mr Bernard Quoroll
Kingston-upon-Hull	Guildhall, Alfred Gelder Street, Kingston-upon-Hull HU1 2AA; phone: (01482) 610610; fax: (01482) 615135; Web site: www.hullcc.gov.uk	Mr Ian Crookham

(continued)

The Addresses of English Unitary Authorities (*continued*)

Authority	Council offices	Chief executive
Leicester	New Walk Centre, Welford Place, Leicester LE1 6ZG; phone: (0116) 254 9922; fax: (0116) 255 3809	Mr Rodney Green
Luton	Town Hall, George Street, Luton LU1 2BQ; phone: (01582) 746000; fax: (01582) 546223; Web site: www.luton.gov.uk	Mrs K Jones
Medway Towns	Civic Centre, High Street, Strood, Rochester ME2 4AU; phone: (01634) 727777; fax: (01634) 732756; Web site: www.intranet.medway.gov.uk	Mrs Judith Armitt
Middlesbrough	PO Box 99A, Municipal Buildings, Russel Street, Middlesbrough TS1 2QQ; phone: (01642) 245432; fax: (01642) 263519; Web site: www.middlesborough.gov.uk	Mr John Foster (Managing Director)
Milton Keynes	Civic Office, 1 Saxon Gate East, Milton Keynes MK9 3EJ; phone: (01908) 691691; fax: (01908) 252769	Mr Howard Miller
Newbury/West Berkshire	Council Offices, Market Street, Newbury RG14 5LD; phone: (01635) 42400; fax: (01635) 519547; Web site: www.westberks.gov.uk	Ms Stella Manzie
North East Lincolnshire	Municipal Offices, Town Hall Square, Grimsby DN31 1HU; phone: (01472) 313131; fax: (01472) 325902; Web site: www.nelincs.gov.uk	Mr Roy Benthan
North Lincolnshire	Pittwood House, Ashby Road, Scunthorpe DN16 1AB; phone: (01724) 296296; fax: (01724) 271617; Web site: www.northlincs.gov.uk	Dr Michael Garnett
North Somerset	Town Hall, Walliscote Grove Road, Weston-super-Mare, BS23 1UJ; phone: (01934) 888888; fax: (01934) 888822	Mr Paul May
Nottingham	The Guildhall, South Sherwood Street, Nottingham NG1 4BT; phone: (0115) 915 5555; fax: (0115) 915 4635; Web site: www.nottinghamcity.gov.uk	Mr Edward Cantle
Peterborough	Town Hall, Bridge Street, Peterborough PE1 1HQ; phone: (01733) 563141; fax: (01733) 452537	Mr W E Samuels
Plymouth	Civic Centre, Armada Way, Plymouth PL1 2EW; phone: (01752) 668000; fax: (01752) 304880	Mrs Alison Stone
Poole	Municipal Buildings, Civic Centre, Poole BH15 2RU; phone: (01202) 633633; fax: (01202) 633899; Web site: www.poole.gov.uk	Mr Jim Brooks
Portsmouth	Civic Offices, Floor 3, Guildhall Square, Portsmouth PO1 2BG; phone: (01705) 822251; fax: (01705) 834571	Mr Nick Gurney
Reading	Civic Centre, Reading RG1 7TD; phone: (0118) 939 0900; fax: (0118) 939 0969; Web site: www.reading.gov.uk	Ms Joyce Markham
Redcar and Cleveland	Town Hall, Fabian Road, South Bank, Middlesbrough, Cleveland TS6 9AR; phone: (01642) 444000; fax: (01642) 444599	Mr Andrew Kilburn
Rutland	Council Offices, Catmose, Oakham, Rutland LE15 6HP; phone: (01572) 722577; fax: (01572) 758307	Dr Janice Morphet
Slough	Town Hall, Bath Road, Slough SL1 3UQ; phone: (01753) 552288; fax: (01753) 692499	Ms Cheryl Coppell
Southampton	Civic Centre, Southampton SO14 7LY; phone: (01703) 223855; fax: (01703) 833232; Web site: www.southampton.gov.uk	Mr John Cairns
Southend on Sea	Civic Centre, Victoria Avenue, Southend on Sea SS2 6ER; phone: (01702) 215000; fax: (01702) 215110; Web site: www.southend.gov.uk	Mr George Krawiec
South Gloucestershire	The Council Office, Castle Street, Thornbury BS35 1HF; phone: (01454) 868686; fax: (01454) 863855	Mr Mike Robinson
Stockton-on-Tees	Municipal Buildings, Church Road, Stockton-on-Tees TS18 1LD; phone: (01642) 393939; fax: (01642) 393002; Web site: www.stockton-bc.gov.uk	Mr George Garlick
Stoke-on-Trent	PO Box 636, Civic Centre, Glebe Street, Stoke on Trent ST4 1RN; phone: (01782) 234567	Mr Brian Smith
Swindon	Civic Offices, Euclid Street, Swindon, Wilts SN1 2JH; phone: (01793) 463000; fax: (01793) 463930; Web site: www.swindon.gov.uk	Mr Paul Doherty
Telford and Wrekin	Civic Office, Telford TF3 4LD; phone: (01952) 202100; fax: (01952) 291060; Web site: www.telford.gov.uk	Mr David Hutchison
Thurrock	Civic Offices, New Road, Grays, Essex RM17 6SL; phone: (01375) 390000; fax: (01375) 652359; Web site: www.thurrock-community.org.uk	Mr Keith Barnes
Torbay	Civic Offices, Castle Circus, Torquay TQ1 3DR; phone: (01803) 201201; fax: (01803) 207006; Web site: www.torbay.gov.uk	Mr Anthony Hodgkiss
Warrington	Town Hall, Sankey Street, Warrington WA1 1UH; phone: (01925) 442140; fax: (01925) 442138; Web site: www.warrington.gov.uk	Mr Steven Broomhead
Windsor and Maidenhead	Town Hall, St Ives Road, Maidenhead, Berks SL6 1RF; phone: (01628) 798888; fax: (01628) 796408	Mr David Lunn
Wokingham	Shute End, Wokingham RG40 1WQ; phone: (0118) 974 6000; fax: (0118) 978 9078; Web site: www.wokingham.gov.uk	Mrs Gillian Norton
York	The Guildhall, St Helen's Square, York YO1 9QN; phone: (01904) 613161; fax: (01904) 551998; Web site: www.york.gov.uk	Mr David Clark

The Political Composition of English Unitary Authorities

(– = not applicable.)

Authority	Labour	Liberal Democrats	Conservative	Independent/other	Controlling party	Total councillors
Bath and North East Somerset	17	30	16	2	no overall control	65
Blackburn with Darwen	43	3	16	0	Labour	62
Blackpool	33	3	8	0	Labour	44
Bournemouth	6	20	25	6	no overall control	57
Bracknell	17	0	23	0	Conservative	40
Brighton and Hove	45	3	27	3	Labour	78
Bristol	37	23	10	0	Labour	70
Darlington	35	2	15	0	Labour	52
Derby	34	4	6	0	Labour	44
East Riding Of Yorkshire	12	22	27	6	no overall control	67
Halton	46	8	1	0	Labour	55
Hartlepool	30	10	6	1	Labour	47
Herefordshire	2	32	8	18	Liberal Democrats	60
Isle of Wight	4	16	15	13	no overall control	48
Kingston-upon-Hull	15	4	1	4	Labour	60
Leicester	30	16	10	0	Labour	56
Luton	36	9	3	0	Labour	48
Medway Towns	39	21	20	0	no overall control	80
Middlesbrough	41	7	4	1	Labour	53
Milton Keynes	27	19	4	1	Labour	51
Newbury/West Berkshire	0	38	15	1	no overall control	54
North East Lincolnshire	22	5	11	4	Labour	42
North Lincolnshire	23	0	19	0	Labour	42
North Somerset	13	11	32	5	Conservative	61
Nottingham	50	2	3	0	Labour	55
Peterborough	25	3	24	5	no overall control	57
Plymouth	47	0	13	0	Labour	60
Poole	3	19	17	0	Liberal Democrats	39
Portsmouth	20	9	10	0	Labour	39
Reading	36	6	3	0	Labour	45
Redcar and Cleveland	32	11	14	2	Labour	59
Rutland	2	4	1	13	no overall control	20
Slough	32	0	6	3	Labour	41
Southampton	27	14	4	0	Labour	45
Southend on Sea	8	12	19	0	no overall control	39
South Gloucestershire	25	37	8	0	Liberal Democrats	70
Stockton-on-Tees	38	5	12	0	Labour	55
Stoke-on-Trent	48	4	2	6	Labour	60
Swindon	39	10	5	0	Labour	54
Telford and Wrekin	38	4	9	3	Labour	54
Thurrock	45	0	4	0	Labour	49
Torbay	2	22	12	0	Liberal Democrats	36
Warrington	45	11	4	0	Labour	60
Windsor and Maidenhead	0	29	22	7	no overall control	58
Wokingham	0	24	30	0	Conservative	54
York	27	22	3	1	Labour	53
Total	1,227	579	529	101	–	2,436

English Metropolitan Borough Councils

The Addresses of English Metropolitan Borough Councils

Borough	Council offices	Chief executive
Barnsley	Town Hall, Church Street, Barnsley S70 2TA; phone: (01226) 770770; fax: (01226) 773305; Web site: www.barnsley.gov.uk	Mr John Edwards
Birmingham	The Council House, Victoria Square, Birmingham B1 1BB; phone: (0121) 303 2000; fax: (0121) 303 1309	Mr Michael Lyons
Bolton	2nd Floor, Town Hall, Civic Centre, Bolton BL1 1RU; phone: (01204) 522311; fax (01204) 381942	Mr Bernard Knight
Bradford	City Hall, Channing Way, Bradford BD1 1HY; phone: (01274) 752111; fax: (01274) 392718; Web site: www.bradford.gov.uk	Mr Ian Stewart
Bury	Town Hall, Knowsley Street, Bury BL9 0SW; phone: (0161) 253 5000; fax: (0161) 253 5108; e-mail: chiefexec@bury.gov.uk; Web site: www.bury.gov.uk	Mr Dennis Taylor
Calderdale	Town Hall, Crossley Street, Halifax HX1 1UJ; phone: (01422) 357257; fax: (01422) 393102	Mr Paul Sheehan
Coventry	Council House, Earl Street, Coventry CV1 5RR; phone: (01203) 833333; fax: (01203) 833680; Web site: www.coventry.gov.uk	Mr Ian Roxburgh
Doncaster	2 Priory Place, Doncaster DN1 1BN; phone: (01302) 734000; fax: (01302) 734040; e-mail: john.leash@doncaster.gov.uk	Mr Alf Taylor
Dudley	The Council House, Priory Road, Dudley DY1 1HF; phone: (01384) 818181; fax (01384) 815226; Web site: www.dudley.gov.uk	Mr A Sparke
Gateshead	Civic Centre, Regent Street, Gateshead NE8 1HH; phone: (0191) 477 1011; fax: (0191) 478 2755	Mr Leslie Elton
Kirklees	PO Box B24, Civic Centre, Huddersfield HD1 1WG; phone: (01484) 221801; fax: (01484) 221777; Web site: www.kirkleesmc.gov.uk	Mr Tony Elson
Knowsley	Municipal Buildings, Archway Road, Huyton L36 9UX; phone: (0151) 489 6000; fax: (0151) 443 3507; Web site: www.knowsley.gov.uk	
Leeds	Civic Hall, Leeds LS1 1UR; phone: (0113) 234 8080; fax: (0113) 247 4870	Mr David Henshaw
Liverpool	Municipal Buildings, Dale Street, Liverpool L69 2DH; phone: (0151) 227 3911; fax: (0151) 225 2017; Web site: www.liverpool.gov.uk	Mr Philip Smith Mr Peter Bounds
Manchester	Town Hall, Manchester M60 2LA; phone: (0161) 234 5000; fax: (0161) 234 3098; Web site: www.manchester.gov.uk	Mr Howard Bernstein
Newcastle-upon-Tyne	Civic Centre, Newcastle-upon-Tyne NE99 2BN; phone: (0191) 232 8520; fax (0191) 230 1107; e-mail: kevin.lavery@newcastle.gov.uk	Mr Kevin Lavery
North Tyneside	Town Hall, High Street East, Wallsend NE28 7RR; phone: (0191) 200 6565; fax: (0191) 200 7272	Mr Gallant, Mr Roberts, Mr Walton, Mr Wright, Mr Jackson (Directors), Mr Doughty (acting)
Oldham	PO Box 160, Civic Centre, West Street, Oldham OL1 1UG; phone: (0161) 911 3000; fax: (0161) 911 4684; Web site: www.oldham.gov.uk	Mr Colin Smith
Rochdale	The Town Hall, The Esplanade, Rochdale OL16 1AB; phone: (01706) 647474; fax (01706) 864755/865450	Mrs Frances Done
Rotherham	Civic Building, Walker Place, Rotherham S65 1UF; phone: (01709) 382121; fax: (01709) 822406; Web site: www.rotherham.gov.uk	Mr Alan Carruthers
St Helens	Town Hall, Victoria Square, Corporation Street, St Helens WA10 1HP; phone: (01744) 456000; fax: (01744) 456889; Web site: www.merseyworld.com/sthelensmbc/	Ms Carol Hudson
Salford	Salford Civic Centre, Chorley Road, Swinton, Salford M27 5FJ; phone: (0161) 794 4711; fax: (0161)728 4290; Web site: www.salford.gov.uk	Mr John Willis
Sandwell	The Sandwell Council House, Oldbury, Warley B69 3DE; phone: (0121) 569 2200; fax: (0121) 569 3100; Web site: www.sandwell.gov.uk	Mr Nigel Summers
Sefton	Town Hall, Lord Street, Southport PR8 1DA; phone: (01704) 533133; fax: (0151) 934 2268; Web site: www.sefton.gov.uk	Mr Graham Haywood
Sheffield	Town Hall, Pinstone Street, Sheffield S1 2HH; phone: (0114) 272 6444; fax: (0114) 273 6844; Web site: www.sheffield.gov.uk	Mr Bob Kerslake
Solihull	PO Box 18, Council House, Solihull B91 3QS; phone: (0121) 704 6000; fax: (0121) 704 6884; e-mail: info@solihull.gov.uk	Dr Norman Perry
South Tyneside	Town Hall and Civic Offices, Westoe Road, South Shields NE33 2RL; phone: (0191) 427 1717; fax (0191) 454 5678; Web site: www.s-tyneside-nbc.gov.uk	Mr Peter Haigh (Director of Corporate Services)
Stockport	Town Hall, Edward Street, Stockport SK1 3XE; phone: (0161) 480 4949; fax: (0161) 480 6773; Web site: www.stockport.gov.uk	Mr John Schultz
Sunderland	Civic Centre, Burdon Road, Sunderland SR2 7DN; phone: (0191) 553 1000; fax: (0191) 553 1188; e-mail: economic.team@sunderland.btinternet.com	Mr Colin Sinclair
Tameside	Wellington Road, Ashton-under-Lyne, Lancashire OL6 6DL; phone: (0161) 342 8355; fax: (0161) 342 3543; e-mail: anne.drinkhill@chiefex.tameside.gov.uk	Mr Michael Greenwood
Trafford	PO Box 10, Trafford Town Hall, Talbot Road, Stretford M32 0YT; phone: (0161) 912 1212; fax: (0161) 912 4184	Mr Allan Lewis
Wakefield	Town Hall, Wood Street, Wakefield WF1 2HQ; phone: (01924) 306090; fax: (01924) 305113	Mr Martin Pullham (Head of Paid Service)
Walsall	Civic Centre, Darwall Street, Walsall WS1 1TP; phone: (01922) 650000; fax: (01922) 720885; Web site: www.walsall.gov.uk	Mr David Winchurch
Wigan	New Town Hall, Library Street, Greater Manchester WN1 1YN; phone: (01942) 244991; fax: (01942) 827451; Web site: www.wiganmbc.gov.uk	Mr Stephen Jones
Wirral	Town Hall, Brighton Street, Wallasey L44 8ED; phone: (0151) 638 7070; fax: (0151) 691 8583	Mr Stephen Maddox
Wolverhampton	Civic Centre, St Peter's Square, Wolverhampton WV1 1SH; phone: (01902) 556556; fax: (01902) 554030; Web site: www.wolverhampton.gov.uk	Mr Derek Anderson

The Political Composition of English Metropolitan Borough Councils

(– = not applicable.)

Borough	Labour	Liberal Democrat	Conservative	Independent/other	Controlling party	Total councillors
Barnsley	59	2	3	2	Labour	66
Birmingham	77	16	20	4	Labour	117
Bolton	41	9	10	0	Labour	60
Bradford	54	10	26	0	Labour	90
Bury	36	3	8	1	Labour	48
Calderdale	20	14	19	1	Labour	54
Coventry	44	0	8	2	Labour	54
Doncaster	37	9	5	12	Labour	63
Dudley	54	10	8	0	Labour	72
Gateshead	49	15	0	2	Labour	66
Kirklees	36	23	10	3	no overall control	72
Knowsley	64	2	0	0	Labour	66
Leeds	71	14	12	2	Labour	99
Liverpool	28	60	0	11	Liberal Democrat	99
Manchester	80	19	0	0	Labour	99
Newcastle-upon-Tyne	64	14	0	0	Labour	78
North Tyneside	38	8	13	1	Labour	60
Oldham	33	26	1	0	Labour	60
Rochdale	35	19	6	0	Labour	60
Rotherham	63	1	2	0	Labour	66
St Helens	37	14	3	0	Labour	54
Salford	56	4	0	0	Labour	60
Sandwell	61	9	2	0	Labour	72
Sefton	30	24	15	0	no overall control	69
Sheffield	39	47	1	0	Liberal Democrat	87
Solihull	15	11	24	1	Liberal Democrat	51
South Tyneside	51	6	0	3	Labour	60
Stockport	26	32	2	3	Liberal Democrat	63
Sunderland	64	3	8	0	Labour	75
Tameside	48	2	4	3	Labour	57
Trafford	33	3	27	0	Labour	63
Wakefield	57	0	3	3	Labour	63
Walsall	31	6	21	2	no overall control	60
Wigan	70	2	0	0	Labour	72
Wirral	39	10	17	0	Labour	66
Wolverhampton	39	3	17	0	Labour	59
Total	1,681	448	295	56	–	2,480

London Borough Councils

The Addresses of London Borough Councils

Borough	Council offices	Chief executive
Barking and Dagenham	Civic Centre, Dagenham RM10 7BN; phone: (0181) 592 4500; fax: (0181) 227 2806; Web site: www.barking-dagenham.gov.uk	Mr W C Smith
Barnet	The Town Hall, The Burroughs, Hendon, London NW4 4BG; phone: (0181) 359 2480; fax: (0181) 359 2480; Web site: www.barnet.gov.uk	Mr Max Caller
Bexley	Bexley Civic Offices, Broadway, Bexleyheath, Kent DA6 7LB; phone: (0181) 303 7777; fax: (0181) 301 2661; Web site: www.bexley.gov.uk	Mr Chris Duffield (Chief Executive and Director of Finance)
Brent	Brent Town Hall, Forty Lane, Wembley HA9 9HD; phone: (0181) 937 1234; fax: (0181) 937 1003	Mr Gareth Daniel
Bromley	Bromley Civic Centre, Stockwell Close, Kentish Way, Bromley BR1 3UH; phone: (0181) 464 3333; fax: (0181) 313 4445	Mr Michael Blanch
Camden	Town Hall, Judd Street, London WC1H 9JE; phone: (0171) 278 4444; fax: (0171) 860 5998	Mr Steve Bundred
Croydon	Taberner House, Park Lane, Croydon CR9 1DH; phone: (0181) 686 4433; fax: (0181) 760 5463; Web site: www.croydon.gov.uk	Mr David Wechsler
Ealing	Town Hall, New Broadway, London W5 2BY; phone: (0181) 579 2424; fax: (0181) 840 5574; Web site: www.ealing.gov.uk	Ms Gillian Guy
Enfield	Civic Centre, Silver Street, Enfield, London EN1 3XA; phone: (0181) 366 6565; fax: (0181) 379 3819; Web site: www.enfield.gov.uk	Mr David Plank
Greenwich	Town Hall, 45–53 Wellington Street, London SE18 6PW; phone: (0181) 854 8888; fax: (0181) 312 5110; Web site: www.greenwich.gov.uk	Mr David Brooks
Hackney	Town Hall, Mare Street, London E8 1EA; phone: (0181) 989 9511	Mr T Elliston
Hammersmith and Fulham	Town Hall, King Street, Hammersmith, London W6 9JU; phone: (0181) 748 3020; fax: (0181) 741 0307; Web site: www.lbhf.gov.uk	Mr Neil Newton (Managing Director)
Haringey	Civic Centre, PO Box 264, High Road, London N22 8LE; phone: (0181) 975 9700	Mr Gurbux Singh
Harrow	Civic Centre, Station Road, Harrow HA1 2XF; phone: (0181) 863 5611; fax: (0181) 420 9683; Web site: www.harrowlb.demon.co.uk	Mr Tony Redmond (Chief Executive and Director of Finance)
Havering	Havering Town Hall, Main Road, Romford RM1 3BD; phone: (01708) 772222; fax: (01708) 772068	Mr Harold Tinworth
Hillingdon	Civic Centre, Uxbridge UB8 1UW; phone: (1895) 250111; fax: (01895) 277047; Web site: www.lbhill.gov.uk	Mr Dorian Leatham
Hounslow	Civic Centre, Lampton Road, Hounslow, London TW3 4DN; phone: (0181) 570 7728; fax: (0181) 862 6093; Web site: www.hounslow.gov.uk	Mr Derek Myers
Islington	Town Hall, Upper Street, London N1 2UD; phone: (0171) 226 1234; fax: (0171) 527 3063; Web site: www.islington.gov.uk	Ms Leisha Fullick
Kensington and Chelsea	Town Hall, Hornton Street, London W8 7NX; phone: (0171) 937 5464; fax: (0171) 938 1445	Mr Alan Taylor
Kingston-upon-Thames	Guildhall, High St, Kingston-upon-Thames KT1 1EU; phone: (0181) 546 2121; fax: (0181) 547 5012; Web site: www.kingston.gov.uk	Mr Bruce McDonald & Mr T Knight (acting)
Lambeth	Town Hall, Brixton Hill, London SW2 1RW; phone: (0171) 926 1000; fax: (0171) 926 2255; e-mail: hrabbatts@lambeth.gov.uk; Web site: www.lambeth.gov.uk	Ms Heather Rabbatts
Lewisham	Town Hall, Catford Road, Catford, London SE6 4IU; phone: (0181) 695 6000	Mr Barry Quirk
Merton	Merton Civic Centre, London Road, Morden SM4 5DX; phone: (0181) 543 2222; fax: (0181) 545 0446 (press office)	Mr Roger Paine (acting)
Newham	Town Hall, Barking Rd, East Ham, London E6 2RP; phone: (0181) 472 1430; fax: (0171) 557 8662	Dr Wendy Thomson
Redbridge	Town Hall, 128–142 High Road, Ilford, Essex IG1 1DD; phone: (0181) 478 3020; fax: (0181) 478 2356; Web site: www.redbridge.gov.uk	Mr Michael Frater
Richmond-upon-Thames	Civic Centre, 44 York Street, Twickenham TW1 3BZ; phone: (0181) 891 1411; fax: (0181) 891 7703; e-mail: press-prrichmond.gov.uk; Web site: www.richmond.gov.uk	Mr Richard Harbord (Chief Executive and Director of Finance)
Southwark	Town Hall, Peckham Road, London SE5 8UB; phone: (0171) 525 7171; fax: (0171) 525 7506; Web site: www.southwark.gov.uk	Mr Robert Coomber
Sutton	Civic Offices, St Nicholas Way, Sutton SM1 1EA; phone: (0181) 770 5000; fax: (0181) 770 5504; Web site: www.sutton.gov.uk	Ms Patricia Hughes
Tower Hamlets	Mulberry Place, 5 Clove Crescent, London E14 2BG; phone: (0171) 364 5000; fax: (0171) 364 4911; Web site: www.towerhamlets.gov.uk	Ms Sylvie Pierce
Waltham Forest	Town Hall, Forest Road, Walthamstow, London E17 4JF; phone: (0181) 527 5544; fax: (0181) 527 8313; Web site: www.lbwf.gov.uk	Mr Alan Tobias
Wandsworth	Town Hall, Wandsworth High Street, London SW18 2PU; phone: (0181) 871 6000; fax: (0181) 871 8181; Web site: www.wandsworth.gov.uk	Mr Gerald Jones
Westminster	City Hall, 64 Victoria Street, London SW1E 6QP; phone: (0171) 641 3438; fax: (0171) 641 3438	Mr William Roots

The Political Composition of London Borough Councils

(– = not applicable.)

Borough	Labour	Conservative	Liberal Democrat	Independent/other	Controlling party	Total councillors
Barking and Dagenham	47	0	1	3	Labour	51
Barnet	26	28	6	0	no overall control	60
Bexley	24	32	6	0	Conservative	62
Brent	43	19	4	0	Labour	66
Bromley	7	28	25	0	no overall control	60
Camden	43	10	6	0	Labour	59
Croydon	38	31	1	0	Labour	70
Ealing	53	15	3	0	Labour	71
Enfield	43	23	0	0	Labour	66
Greenwich	52	8	2	0	Labour	62
Hackney	29	12	17	2	no overall control	60
Hammersmith and Fulham	36	14	0	0	Labour	50
Haringey	54	2	3	0	Labour	59
Harrow	32	20	9	2	Labour	63
Havering	29	14	3	17	no overall control	63
Hillingdon	31	34	4	0	no overall control	69
Hounslow	44	11	4	1	Labour	60
Islington	26	0	26	0	no overall control	52
Kensington and Chelsea	15	39	0	0	Conservative	54
Kingston-upon-Thames	10	21	19	0	no overall control	50
Lambeth	41	5	18	0	Labour	64
Lewisham	61	2	4	0	Labour	67
Merton	39	12	3	3	Labour	57
Newham	60	0	0	0	Labour	60
Redbridge	30	23	9	0	no overall control	62
Richmond-upon-Thames	4	14	34	0	Liberal Democrat	52
Southwark	33	4	27	0	Labour	64
Sutton	5	5	46	0	Liberal Democrat	56
Tower Hamlets	41	0	9	0	Labour	50
Waltham Forest	30	15	12	0	Labour	57
Wandsworth	11	50	0	0	Conservative	61
Westminster	13	47	0	0	Conservative	60
Total	1,050	538	301	28	–	1,917

Source: Local Government Chronicle Elections Centre, University of Plymouth

Scottish Unitary Authorities

Aberdeen City

City and unitary authority in northeast Scotland. The unitary authority was created in 1996 from the district of the same name that was part of Grampian region from 1975; before that it was part of Aberdeenshire. The city of Aberdeen, as well as being the administrative headquarters of the Aberdeen City unitary authority, is the administrative headquarters of Aberdeenshire unitary authority

Area 185 sq km/71 sq mi; **Physical** low-lying coastal area on the banks of the rivers Dee and Don; it has 3 km/2 mi of sandy beaches; **Features** St Andrew's Episcopal Cathedral (consecrated in 1816), King's College (from 1500) and Marischal College (founded in 1593, and housed in one of the world's largest granite buildings constructed in 1836), which together form Aberdeen University, Brig O'Balgownie (1314–18), Municipal Buildings (1867), St Machar Cathedral (from 1370). Aberdeen's granite buildings have given it the name of 'Silver City', although the last granite quarry, in Rubislaw, closed in 1971; **Industries** North Sea oil (it is the main centre in Scotland and Europe for offshore oil exploration and there are shore-based maintenance and service depots for the North Sea oil rigs; an airport and heliport at Dyce, 9.6 km/6 mi northwest of the city, link the mainland to the rigs), oil and gas service industries, paper manufacturing, textiles, engineering, food processing, chemicals, fish processing; **Population** (1996) 219,100.

Aberdeenshire

Unitary authority in northeast Scotland, created in 1996 from three districts within the former Grampian region; its administrative headquarters, Aberdeen, lies outside the authority

Area 6,308 sq km/2,436 sq mi; **Towns** Banff, Fraserburgh, Huntly, Peterhead, Stonehaven, Inverurie; **Physical** area of contrast with mountainous western interior, intensively farmed core, and coastal plain; Cairngorm Mountains; rivers Deveron, Ythan, Don, Dee; **Features** Balmoral Castle; Braemar Games; **Industries** oil and gas, papermaking, whisky distilling, seafood, tourism; **Population** (1996) 226,500.

Angus

Unitary authority on the east coast of Scotland. A former county, it was part of Tayside region 1975–96

Area 2,187 sq km/844 sq mi; **Towns** Forfar (administrative headquarters), Arbroath, Brechin, Carnoustie, Kirriemuir, and Montrose; **Physical** the Grampian Mountains in the north are dissected by the fertile valleys of the rivers Isla, Clova, Prosen, Water of Saughs, and North Esk; the wide Vale of Strathmore separates the Grampian Mountains from the low-lying Sidlaw Hills in the south; **Features** Pictish and Iron Age remains; **Industries** textiles, light engineering (declining), fish processing; **Population** (1996) 111,300.

Argyll and Bute

Unitary authority in western Scotland, created in 1996 from the district of the same name and part of Dumbarton district, which were both parts of Strathclyde region; it includes the islands of Gigha, Bute, Mull, Islay, Jura, Tiree, Coll, Colonsay, Iona, and Staffa

Area 7,016 sq km/2,709 sq mi; **Towns** Lochgilphead (administrative headquarters), Campbeltown, Dunoon, Helensburgh, Inveraray, Oban, Rothesay; **Physical** rural area consisting of mainland and islands; the coast is heavily indented. Inland the area is mountainous; highest peak, Ben Cruachan (1,126 m/3,693 ft). Lochs Fyne and Long are the largest sea lochs; freshwater lochs include Loch Awe and Loch Lomond; Fingal's Cave (Staffa); Corryvrekan Whirlpool (Jura-Scarba); Ben Arthur (The Cobbler), 884 m/2,900 ft; **Features** Bronze, Stone, and Iron Age remains; **Industries** limited manufacture, seaweed processing, fish, timber harvesting; **Population** (1996) 89,300.

Clackmannanshire

Unitary authority in central Scotland, bordering the north side of the Firth of Forth. A former county (until 1974), it was a district of Central region 1975–96

Area 161 sq km/62 sq mi; **Towns** Alloa (administrative headquarters), Tillicoultry; **Physical** compact geographical area comprising the extensive flat flood plain of the River Devon, which rises dramatically at the Ochil Hills to Ben Cleuch (721 m/2,365 ft); **Industries** brewing, distilling, manufacture of bottles and knitwear; **Population** (1996) 47,700.

Dumfries and Galloway

Unitary authority in southern Scotland, formed in 1996 from the regional council of the same name (1975–96)

Area 6,421 sq km/2,479 sq mi; **Towns** Dumfries (administrative headquarters), Annan, Kirkcudbright, Stranraer, Castle Douglas, Newton Stewart; **Physical** area characterized by an indented coastline, including Luce Bay and Wigtown Bay, backed by a low-lying coastal strip of varying width; intensively forested in the Galloways. Much of the inland area is upland: east to west this includes Eskdalemuir (Hart Fell 808 m/2,651 ft), the Lowther Hills (Green Lowther 732 m/2,402 ft), and the Galloway Hills (the Merrick 843 m/2,766 ft); **Features** Wanlockhead (the highest village in Scotland); the oldest working post office in the world at Sanquhar; Glen Trool National Park; Ruthwell Cross, Whithorn archaeological dig; **Industries** timber, chemicals, food processing; **Population** (1996) 147,800.

Dundee City

City and unitary authority in eastern Scotland, on the north side of the Firth of Tay

Area 62 sq km/24 sq mi; **Towns** Dundee (administrative headquarters), Monifieth, Broughty Ferry; **Physical** Firth of Tay; **Features** Tay Bridges; Scott's ship *Discovery;* **Industries** engineering, textiles, electronics, printing, food processing; **Population** (1996) 155,000.

East Ayrshire

Unitary authority in southwest Scotland, created in 1996 from two districts of Strathclyde region

Area 1,269 sq km/490 sq mi; **Towns** Kilmarnock (administrative headquarters), Cumnock, Stewarton, Galston, Crosshouse; **Physical** predominantly low lying and undulating in the north, mountainous toward the south; Loch Doon; rivers Ayr, Irvine; Blackcraig Hill (700 m/2,298 ft); Loudoun Hill; **Features** Burns' House Museum, Mauchline; Loudoun Castle Theme Park; Dunaskin Heritage Museum; **Industries** textiles, light engineering, food and drink, printing; **Population** (1996) 124,000.

East Dunbartonshire

Unitary authority in central Scotland, created in 1996 from two districts of Strathclyde region

Area 175 sq km/67 sq mi; **Towns** Kirkintilloch (administrative headquarters), Bearsden, Milngavie; **Physical** low-lying lands to the south give way dramatically to the Campsie Fells in the north; Earl's Seat (578 m/1,896 ft); River Kelvin; **Features** Forth and Clyde Canal; Antonine Wall; **Population** (1996) 110,000.

East Lothian

Unitary authority in southeast Scotland which was previously a district within Lothian region (1975–96) and a county until 1974

(continued on p. 109)

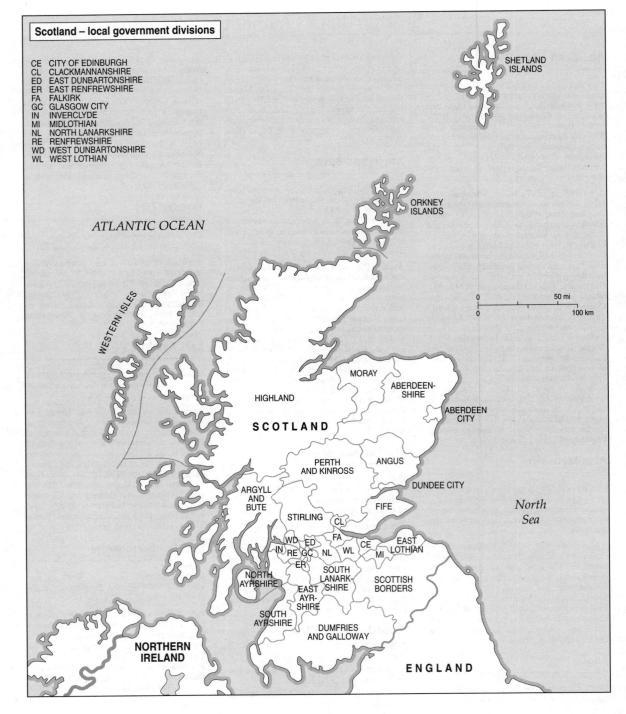

Scotland – local government divisions

CE CITY OF EDINBURGH
CL CLACKMANNANSHIRE
ED EAST DUNBARTONSHIRE
ER EAST RENFREWSHIRE
FA FALKIRK
GC GLASGOW CITY
IN INVERCLYDE
MI MIDLOTHIAN
NL NORTH LANARKSHIRE
RE RENFREWSHIRE
WD WEST DUNBARTONSHIRE
WL WEST LOTHIAN

SHETLAND ISLANDS
ORKNEY ISLANDS
ATLANTIC OCEAN
WESTERN ISLES
0 50 mi
0 100 km
MORAY
ABERDEEN-SHIRE
HIGHLAND
ABERDEEN CITY
SCOTLAND
PERTH AND KINROSS
ANGUS
DUNDEE CITY
ARGYLL AND BUTE
FIFE
North Sea
STIRLING
CL
FA
WD
ED
IN
RE
GC
NL
WL
CE
MI
EAST LOTHIAN
ER
NORTH AYRSHIRE
SOUTH LANARK-SHIRE
SCOTTISH BORDERS
EAST AYR-SHIRE
SOUTH AYRSHIRE
DUMFRIES AND GALLOWAY
NORTHERN IRELAND
ENGLAND

Area 677 sq km/261 sq mi; **Towns** Haddington (administrative headquarters), North Berwick, Dunbar; **Physical** area of contrasts, with coastal plains of cliffs, beaches, and estuarine marines, broad river valley of the Tyne, volcanic outcrops (Bass Rock, Traprain Law), and gentle slopes of the Lammermuir Hills; **Features** Tantallon Castle; Muirfield golf course; Traprain Law fort; **Industries** whisky distilling, agricultural-based; **Population** (1996) 85,500.

East Renfrewshire

Unitary authority in central Scotland, created in 1996 from part of Renfrew district in Strathclyde region

Area 174 sq km/67 sq mi; **Towns** Giffnock (administrative headquarters), Barrhead, Newton Mearns, Clarkston; **Physical** low-lying plateau rising from the plain of the River Clyde; **Industries** engineering, cotton textiles; **Population** (1996) 86,800.

Edinburgh

Capital of Scotland and, as **the City of Edinburgh**, a unitary authority, located near the southern shores of the Firth of Forth

Area 263 sq km/122 sq mi; **Physical** Water of Leith, Salisbury Crags, Arthur's Seat; **Features** Edinburgh Castle; Holyrood House; the Edinburgh Festival; the Royal Scottish Academy; the National Gallery of Scotland; the Royal Mile; the Universities of Edinburgh, Heriot-Watt, and Napier; **Industries** printing, publishing, banking, insurance, chemical manufacture, electronics, distilling, brewing; **Population** (1996) 477,600.

Falkirk

Unitary authority in central Scotland, created from the former district of the same name in 1996 from part of the former Central region

Area 297 sq km/115 sq mi; **Towns** Falkirk (administrative headquarters), Grangemouth; **Physical** centrally located between Edinburgh and Glasgow, this low-lying area borders the southern side of the Firth of Forth; River Avon flows through; **Features** Forth and Clyde and Union canals; Rough Castle; Antonine Wall; **Industries** chemicals and petrochemicals, bus building, soft drinks, toffees; **Population** (1996) 142,500.

Fife

Unitary authority in eastern Scotland, which was formerly a region of three districts (1975–96) and a county until 1974

Area 1,321 sq km/510 sq mi; **Towns** Glenrothes (administrative headquarters), Cupar, Dunfermline, Kirkcaldy, St Andrews; **Physical** coastal area, predominantly low lying, undulating interior with dramatic escarpment at Lomond Hills; rivers Eden and Leven flow through; **Features** Rosyth naval base; Old Course, St Andrews; **Industries** electronics, petrochemicals, light engineering, oil servicing, paper; **Population** (1996) 351,200.

Glasgow

City and unitary authority in west-central Scotland; the unitary authority was formed in 1995 from the majority of land from Glasgow District Council of Strathclyde Region

Area 176 sq km/68 sq mi; **Features** Cathedral of St Mungo; the Gallery of Modern Art; the University of Glasgow; **Industries** engineering, chemicals, printing, whisky blending, brewing, electronics, textiles, light manufacturing; **Population** (1996) 618,400.

Highland

Unitary authority in northern Scotland, created from the region bearing the same name in 1996

Area 26,157 sq km/10,100 sq mi (one-third of Scotland); **Towns** Inverness (administrative headquarters), Thurso, Wick, Fort William, Aviemore; **Physical** mainland Highland consists of a series of glaciated ancient plateau masses dissected by narrow glens and straths (valleys); in the northeast (Caithness), old red sandstone rocks give a softer, lower topography; Ben Nevis (1,343 m/4,406 ft), Cairngorm Mountains; Loch Ness; Cuillin Hills, Skye; includes many of the Inner Hebridean islands; **Features** Caledonian Canal; John O'Groats; Skye Road Bridge; **Industries** winter sports, timber, aluminium smelting, pulp and paper production, whisky distilling, cottage and croft industries; **Population** (1996) 207,500.

Inverclyde

Unitary authority in western Scotland, created in 1996 from Inverclyde district in Strathclyde region

Area 161 sq km/62 sq mi; **Towns** Greenock (administrative headquarters), Port Glasgow, Gourock; **Physical** coastal lowland on the Firth of Clyde estuary, rising sharply to an inland plateau of 305 m/1,000 ft; **Features** Inverkip Marina; **Industries** electronics; **Population** (1996) 90,000.

Midlothian

Unitary authority in southeast Scotland, south of the Firth of Forth, which was previously a district within Lothian region (1975–96) and a county until 1974

Area 363 sq km/140 sq mi; **Towns** Dalkeith (administrative headquarters), Penicuik, Bonnyrigg; **Physical** inland area rising toward the Moorfoot Hills in the south; River Esk; **Features** Crichton Castle, Roslin Castle, Rosslyn Chapel, Newtongrange Mining Museum; **Industries** glass and crystal, coalmining (declining), light manufacturing, food processing; **Population** (1996) 79,900.

Moray

Unitary authority in northeast Scotland, created in 1996 from the Moray district of Grampian region

Area 2,224 sq km/859 sq mi; **Towns** Elgin (administrative headquarters), Forres, Buckie, Lossiemouth; **Physical** the land gradually slopes from the Grampian Mountains in the south (Cairn Gorm 1,245 m/4,085 ft) towards the Moray Firth; extensive coastal lowlands fringe an area of sand-dune formation; part of this land was reclaimed from the sea and is now covered by the Culbin forest. The River Spey reaches the North Sea near Buckie; **Features** Elgin cathedral; Brodie and Duffus castles; Gordonstoun school; **Industries** whisky distilling, food processing; **Population** (1996) 85,00.

North Ayrshire

Unitary authority in western Scotland, created in 1996 from Cunninghame district in Strathclyde region

Area 889 sq km/343 sq mi; **Towns** Irvine (administrative headquarters), Kilwinning, Saltcoats, Largs, Kilbirnie; **Physical** low-lying coastal plain on the mainland, rising inland to a plateau of over 305 m/1,000 ft; the islands of the Firth of Clyde are Arran, Holy Isle, Cumbraes; the rivers Irvine and Garnock reach the sea at Irvine; Goat Fell (874 m/2,867 ft); **Features** Pencil Monument, Largs; Scottish Maritime Museum, Irvine; Hunterston nuclear power station; **Industries** chemicals, electronics, computer manufacturing; **Population** (1996) 139,200.

North Lanarkshire

Unitary authority in central Scotland, created in 1996 from three districts of Strathclyde region

Area 475 sq km/183 sq mi; **Towns** Motherwell (administrative headquarters), Airdrie, Coatbridge, Cumbernauld; **Physical** low-lying, heavily urbanized area; River Clyde; **Industries** paper, pharmaceuticals, engineering, electronics, light manufacturing, food and drink processing; **Population** (1995) 326,700.

Orkney Islands

Island group and unitary authority off the northeast coast of Scotland

Area 1,014 sq km/391 sq mi; **Towns** Kirkwall (administrative headquarters), Stromness, both on Mainland (Pomona); **Physical** there are 90 islands and inlets in the group.

The surface of the islands is irregular and indented by many arms of the sea. Next to Mainland, the most important of the islands are North and South Ronaldsay, Hoy, Rousay, Stronsay, Flotta, Shapinsay, Eday, Sanday, and Westray. The highest peak is Ward Hill in Hoy, which has an elevation of 479 m/1,572 ft. The Old Man of Hoy is an isolated stack of red sandstone 137 m/450 ft high, off Hoy's northwest coast; **Features** Skara Brae Neolithic village, and Maes Howe burial chamber; Scapa Flow; oil terminal on Flotta; **Industries** offshore oil, woollen weaving, wind-powered electricity generation, distilling, boat-building, fish curing; **Population** (1996) 19,600.

Perth and Kinross

Unitary authority in central Scotland, created in 1996 from the district bearing the same name in Tayside region

Area 5,388 sq km/2,080 sq mi; **Towns** Perth (administrative headquarters), Blairgowrie, Crieff, Kinross, Pitlochry, Aberfeldy; **Physical** the geological fault that gives the distinctive character to lowland and highland Scotland passes southwest–northeast through the area. The area is largely centred in the lowlands, along wide fertile valleys such as Strathearn, and the Carse of Gowrie. To the north and west are the Grampians intersected by narrow glens with lochs in their valley floors. Among the highest elevations in the Grampians are Ben Lawers (1,214 m/3,984 ft) and Schiehallion (1,083 m/3,554 ft); in the south are the lower Ochil and Sidlaw Hills; **Features** Highland Games at Pitlochry; Dunkeld Cathedral; Scone Palace; Glenshee Ski Development; **Industries** woollen manufacture, whisky distilling and blending; **Population** (1996) 131,800.

Renfrewshire

Unitary authority in west central Scotland, bordering the Firth of Clyde, which was formed from the northern and western parts of Renfrew district in Strathclyde region (1975–96), which in turn was formed from the former county of Renfrewshire (until 1974)

Area 260 sq km/100 sq mi; **Towns** Paisley (administrative headquarters), Renfrew, Johnstone, Erskine; **Physical** mainly low lying, but hilly in the west, rising to Hill of Stake (525 m/1,723 ft); rivers Clyde, Gryfe, White Cart, Black Cart; **Features** sculptural stones at Inchinnan, near Erskine; Glasgow International Airport; **Industries** engineering, computers, electronics, chemicals; **Population** (1995) 178,300.

Scottish Borders

Unitary authority in southeast Scotland, created in 1996 to replace the former Borders region

Area 4,733 sq km/1,827 sq mi; **Towns** Newtown St Boswells (administrative headquarters), Galashiels, Hawick, Jedburgh, Kelso, Peebles, Selkirk; **Physical** much of the west part of the area is upland (Lammermuir, Moorfoot, and Pentland Hills); Broad Law (840 m/2,756 ft), near Tweedsmuir, is the highest point. The principal river, the Tweed, traverses the region west–east; its tributaries include the River Teviot. The largest loch is St Mary's, and the only substantial area of lowlying agricultural land is the Merse in the southeast, near the English border. The coast is generally precipitous; **Features** Walter Scott's home at Abbotsford; Field Marshal Haig and Walter Scott buried at Dryburgh Abbey; Melrose Abbey (12th century); **Industries** electronics, timber, knitwear, tweed; **Population** (1996) 105,300.

Shetland Islands

Islands and unitary authority off the north coast of Scotland, 80 km/50 mi northeast of the Orkney Islands, an important centre of the North Sea oil industry, and the most northerly part of the UK

Area 1,452 sq km/560 sq mi; **Towns** Lerwick (administrative headquarters), on Mainland, largest of 12 inhabited islands; **Physical** the 100 islands are mostly bleak, hilly, and clad in moorland. The climate is moist, cool, and windy; in summer there is almost perpetual daylight, whilst winter days are very short. On clear winter nights, the *aurora borealis* ('northern lights') can frequently be seen in the sky; **Industries** processed fish, handknits from Fair Isle and Unst, herring fishing, salmon farming, cattle and sheep farming; large oil and gas fields west of Shetland; Europe's largest oil port is Sullom Voe, Mainland; production at Foinaven oilfield, the first to be developed in Atlantic waters; tourism; **Population** (1996) 22,500.

South Ayrshire

Unitary authority in southwest Scotland, created in 1996 from Kyle and Carrick district (1975–96), Strathclyde region

Area 1,245 sq km/480 sq mi; **Towns** Ayr (administrative headquarters), Prestwick, Girvan, Troon, Maybole; **Physical** coastal plain which rises to higher ground inland (500 m/1,640 ft); rivers Ayr, Stinchar, Water of Girvan; Brown Carrick Hill (287 m/942 ft); Ailsa Craig; many beaches interspersed with cliffs and caves; **Features** Glasgow Prestwick Airport; Culzean Castle; Crossraguel Abbey; Royal Troon and Turnberry championship golf courses; Ayr racecourse; **Industries** aerospace, high technology, tourism; **Population** (1996) 114,000.

South Lanarkshire

Unitary authority in south central Scotland, created in 1996 from three districts of Strathclyde region

Area 1,772 sq km/684 sq mi; **Towns** Hamilton (administrative headquarters), Lanark, Rutherglen, East Kilbride, Carluke, Cambuslang; **Physical** area of stark contrast: predominantly rural to the south and urban to the north. The River Clyde flows through the area. Tinto (707 m/2,320 ft) is a key landmark to the south; **Features** Craignethan Castle; Carstairs State Hospital, New Lanark; **Industries** textiles, electronics, engineering; **Population** (1996) 307,100.

Stirling

Unitary authority in central Scotland, created in 1996 from Stirling district, Central region

Area 2,196 sq km/848 sq mi; **Towns** Stirling (administrative headquarters), Dunblane, Aberfoyle; **Physical** mountainous to the north, including the forested Trossachs, and the open moorland north and west of Breadalbane, within the flood plain of the River Forth to the south around Sterling. The area contains many famous Scottish lochs (Tay, Katrine, Lomond) and Scotland's only lake (Lake of Menteith). Peaks include Ben More (1,174 m/3,852 ft) and Ben Venue (727 m/2,385 ft); **Features** Bannockburn Heritage Centre; Stirling Castle (most visited paid attraction in Scotland outside Edinburgh); **Industries** tourism, light engineering; **Population** (1996) 82,000.

West Dunbartonshire

Unitary authority in west central Scotland, created in 1996 from parts of two districts of Strathclyde region

Area 177 sq km/68 sq mi; **Towns** Dumbarton (administrative headquarters), Clydebank, Alexandria; **Physical** Leven valley and coastal land of Firth of Clyde rise toward the upland plateau of the Kilpatrick Hills; **Features** Dumbarton Castle; **Industries** whisky distilling, light manufacturing; **Population** (1996) 97,800.

Western Isles

Island administrative unitary authority area in Scotland, also known as the Outer Hebrides, including the major islands of Lewis, Harris, North and South Uist, Benbecula, and Barra

Area 3,057 sq km/1,180 sq mi; **Towns** Stornoway on Lewis (administrative headquarters), Castlebay, Lochboisdale, Lochmaddy, Tarbert; **Physical** open to the Atlantic Ocean on the west and the stormy Minch to the east, the islands are almost treeless and have extensive peat bogs. There are areas of hills and mountains on all the islands. The only fertile land is the sandy Machair on the west coast. The islands are mainly composed of the oldest rock in Britain, the Lewisian gneiss. Lewis is divided from the mainland by the Minch

channel. The islands south of Lewis are divided from the Inner Hebrides by the Little Minch and the Sea of the Hebrides; uninhabited islands include St Kilda and Rockall; **Features** Callanish monolithic Stone Age circles on Lewis; **Industries** Harris tweed, tourism; **Population** (1996) 27,800.

West Lothian

Unitary authority in central Scotland, south of the Firth of Forth, which was previously a district within Lothian region (1975–96) and a county until 1974

Area 428 sq km/165 sq mi; **Towns** , Livingston (administrative headquarters), Bathgate, Linlithgow; **Physical** low-lying, undulating area through which the River Almond flows; Cairnpapple Hill; **Features** Linlithgow Palace; prehistoric ritual site at Cairnpapple Hill, near Torpichen; **Industries** electronics, engineering, coal-mining, food processing; **Population** (1996) 147,900.

The Addresses of Scottish Unitary Authorities

Authority	Council offices	Chief executive
Aberdeen City	Town House, Broad Street, Aberdeen AB10 1FY; phone: (01224) 522000; fax: (01224) 644346	Mr Douglas Paterson
Aberdeenshire	c/o Woodhill House, Westburn Road, Aberdeen AB16 5GB; phone: (01224) 620981; fax: (01224) 697445; Web site: www.aberdeenshire.gov.uk/	Mr Alan G Campbell
Angus	Angus Council, 7 The Cross, Forfar, Angus DD8 1BX; phone: (01307) 461460; fax: (01307) 461874; e-mail: chiefexec@angus.gov.uk; Web site: www.angus.gov.uk/	Mr Sandy Watson
Argyll and Bute	Kilmory, Lochgilphead, Argyll PA31 8RT; phone: (01546) 602127; fax: (01546) 604138; Web site: www.argyll-bute.gov.uk/	Mr James McLellan
Clackmannanshire	Greenfield, Alloa, Clackmannanshire FK10 2AD; phone: (01259) 452000; fax: (01259) 452010	Mr Bob Allan
Dumfries and Galloway	Council Offices, English Street, Dumfries DG1 2DD; phone: (01387) 260000; fax: (01387) 260034; e-mail: CIS@dumgal.gov.uk; Web site: www.dumgal.gov.uk/	Mr Philip Jones
Dundee City	21 City Square, Dundee DD1 3BY; phone: (01382) 434000; fax: (01382) 434666; Web site: www.dundeecity.gov.uk/	Mr Alex Stephen
East Ayrshire	Council Headquarters, London Road, Kilmarnock KA3 7DG; phone: (01563) 576000; fax: (01563) 576500; Web site: www.east-ayrshire.gov.uk/	Mr David Montgomery
East Dunbartonshire	Tom Johnston House, Civic Way, Kirkintilloch G66 4TJ; phone: (0141) 776 9000; fax: (0141) 777 8576	Mr Con Mallon
East Lothian	Council Buildings, 25 Court Street, Haddington EH41 3HA; phone: (01620) 827200; fax: (01620) 827140	Mr John Lindsay
East Renfrewshire	Council Headquarters, Eastwood Park, Rouken Glen Road, Glasgow G46 6UG; phone: (0141) 577 3000; fax: (0141) 620 0844; Web site: www.eastrenfrewshire.gov.uk/	Mr Peter Daniels
Edinburgh City	City Chambers, High Street, Edinburgh EH1 1YJ; phone: (0131) 200 2000; fax: (0131) 529 7477	Mr Tom Aitchison
Falkirk	Municipal Buildings, West Bridge Street, Falkirk FK1 5RS; phone: (01324) 506070; fax: (01324) 506071; Web site: www.falkirk.electricscotland.com/	Ms Mary Pitcaithly
Fife	Fife House, North Street, Glenrothes KY7 5LT; phone: (01592) 414141; fax: (01592) 414142	Dr John Markland
Glasgow City	City Chambers, George Square, Glasgow G2 1DU; phone: (0141) 287 2000; fax: (0141) 287 5666	Mr James Andrews (acting)
Highland	Regional Buildings, Glenurquhart Road, Inverness IV3 5NX; phone: (01463) 702837; fax: (01463) 702837	Mr Arthur McCourt
Inverclyde	Municipal Buildings, Greenock PA15 1LY; phone: (01475) 724400; fax: (01475) 882777	Mr Robert Cleary
Midlothian	Midlothian House, Buccleuch Street, Dalkeith EH22 1DJ; phone: (0131) 270 7500; fax: (0131) 271 3050; e-mail: info@midlothian.gov.uk; Web site: www.midlothian.gov.uk/	Mr Trevor Muir
Moray	Council Office, High Street, Elgin IV30 1BX; phone: (01343) 543451; fax: (01343) 540183; Web site: www.moray.org/	Ms Karen Williams
North Ayrshire	Cunninghame House, Irvine KA12 8EE; phone: (01294) 324100; fax: (01294) 324144	Mr Bernard Devine
North Lanarkshire	PO Box 14, Civic Centre, Motherwell ML1 1TW; phone: (01698) 302222; fax: (01698) 275125	Mr Andrew Cowe
Orkney	Council Offices, School Place, Kirkwall, Orkney KW15 1NY; phone: (01856) 873535; fax: (01856) 874615	Mr Alastair Buchan
Perth and Kinross	Council Building, 2 High Street, Perth, PH1 5PH; phone: (01738) 475000; fax: (01738) 475005; e-mail: enquiries@pkc.gov.uk; Web site: www.pkc.gov.uk/	Mr Harry Robertson
Renfrewshire	North Building, Cotton Street, Paisley PA1 1WB; phone: (0141) 842 5000; fax: (0141) 848 1450	Mr Thomas Scholes
Scottish Borders	Council Headquarters, Newtown Street, Boswells, Melrose TD6 0SA; phone: (01835) 824000; fax: (01835) 825001	Mr Alastair M Croall
Shetland	Town Hall, Hillhead, Lerwick, Shetland ZE1 0HB; phone: (01595) 693535; fax: (01595) 694349; e-mail: sic@shetland.gov.uk; Web site: www.shetland.gov.uk/	Mr Bill Bennett
South Ayrshire	County Buildings, Wellington Square, Ayr KA7 1DR; phone: (01292) 612000; fax: (01292) 612143; Web site: www.south-ayrshire.gov.uk/	Mr George Thorley
South Lanarkshire	Council Offices, Almada Street, Hamilton ML3 0AA; phone: (01698) 454444; fax: (01698) 454275	Mr Alastair MacNish
Stirling	Council Headquarters, Viewforth, Stirling FK8 2ET; phone: (01786) 443322; fax: (01786) 443078; Web site: www.stirling.gov.uk/	Mr Keith Yates
West Dunbartonshire	Council Offices, Garshake Road, Dumbarton G82 3PU; phone: (01389) 737000; fax: (01389) 737582; e-mail: wdcmgr1@post.almac.co.uk; Web site: www.west-dunbarton.gov.uk/	Mr Michael Watters
Western Isles	Sandwick Road, Stornoway, Isle of Lewes HS1 2BW; phone: (01851) 703773; fax: (01851) 706022; Web site: www.w-isles.gov.uk/	Mr Brian Stewart
West Lothian	West Lothian House, Almondvale Boulevard, Livingston EH54 6QG; phone: (01506) 777000; fax: (01506) 777102	Mr Alex Linkston

The Political Composition of Scottish Unitary Authorities

(– = not applicable.)

Authority	Labour	Independent/ other	Scottish National Party	Liberal Democrat	Conservative	Controlling party	Total councillors
Aberdeen	22	0	3	12	6	Labour	43
Aberdeenshire	0	10	23	28	7	no overall control	68
Angus	1	3	21	2	2	Scottish National Party	29
Argyll and Bute	1	21	5	6	3	Independent	36
Clackmannanshire	8	0	9	0	1	no overall control	18
Dumfries and Galloway	13	15	5	6	8	no overall control	47
Dundee	28	1	3	0	4	Labour	36
East Ayrshire	17	0	14	0	1	Labour	32
East Dunbartonshire	10	0	1	10	3	no overall control	24
East Lothian	17	0	1	0	5	Labour	23
East Renfrewshire	9	1	0	2	8	no overall control	20
Edinburgh	31	0	1	13	13	Labour	58
Falkirk	15	6	9	0	2	no overall control	32
Fife	43	4	9	21	1	Labour	78
Glasgow	74	1	2	1	1	Labour	79
Highlands	10	50	8	12	0	Independent	80
Inverclyde	11	0	0	8	1	Labour	20
Midlothian	17	0	0	1	0	Labour	18
Moray	6	15	2	2	1	no overall control	26
North Ayrshire	25	1	2	0	2	Labour	30
North Lanarkshire	56	2	12	0	0	Labour	70
Orkney	0	21	0	0	0	Independent	21
Perthshire and Kinross	6	2	16	6	11	no overall control	41
Renfrewshire	21	0	15	3	1	Labour	40
Scottish Borders	1	14	4	14	1	Independent	34
Shetland	0	14	0	8	0	Independent	22
South Ayrshire	17	0	0	0	13	Labour	30
South Lanarkshire	54	0	10	1	2	Labour	67
Stirling	11	0	2	0	9	no overall control	22
West Dunbartonshire	14	1	7	0	0	Labour	22
Western Isles	6	22	3	0	0	Independent	31
West Lothian	20	0	11	0	1	Labour	32
Total	564	204	198	156	107	–	1,229

Welsh Unitary Authorities

Anglesey

Island and unitary authority off the north-west coast of Wales

Area 720 sq km/278 sq mi (34 km/21 mi long and 31 km/19 mi broad); **Towns** Llangefni (administrative headquarters), Holyhead, Beaumaris, Amlwch; **Features** separated from the mainland by the Menai Strait, which is crossed by the Britannia tubular railway bridge and Telford's suspension bridge, originally built between 1819 and 1826 but rebuilt since; rich fauna, notably bird life, and flora; many buildings and relics of historic interest; **Industries** manufacture of toys and electrical goods; bromine extraction from the sea; **Population** (1996) 71,100

Blaenau Gwent

Unitary authority in south Wales, created in 1996 from part of the former county of Gwent

Area 109 sq km/42 sq mi; **Towns** Ebbw Vale (administrative headquarters), Tredegar, Abertillery; **Features** Mynydd Carn-y-Cefn (550 m/1,800 ft); rivers Sirhowy and Ebbw; part of the Brecon Beacons National Park is here; **Population** (1996) 73,000.

Bridgend

Unitary authority in south Wales created in 1996 from part of the former county of Mid Glamorgan

Area 40 sq km/15 sq mi; **Towns** Bridgend (administrative headquarters), Porthcawl (resort and residential area), Maesteg; **Physical** most of the authority consists of the western end of a lowland plateau, Bro Morgannwg, a rich agricultural area of mixed farming and large villages; in the north is the Cymer Forest and Mynydd Caerau (556 m/1,824 ft); **Industries** civil engineering; chocolate manufacture; **Population** (1996) 128,300.

Caerphilly

Unitary authority in south Wales, created in 1996 from parts of the former counties of Mid Glamorgan and Gwent

Area 270 sq km/104 sq mi; **Towns** Hengoed (administrative headquarters),

Caerphilly, Bargoed, Newbridge, Rhymney; **Physical** rivers Rhymney and Sirhowy; **Industries** iron and steel production and coal mining have been replaced by a wide range of light industries; **Population** (1996) 172,000.

Cardiff

Unitary authority in south Wales, created in 1996 from part of the former county of South Glamorgan; administrative headquarters is Cardiff

Area 139 sq km/54 sq mi; **Population** (1996) 306,500.

Carmarthenshire

Unitary authority in south Wales; a former county, it was part of Dyfed between 1975 and 1996

Area 2,390 sq km/923 sq mi; **Towns** Carmarthen (administrative headquarters), Llanelli; **Physical** rivers Tywi, Taf, Teifi; Black Mountain range in the east, southern spur of the Cambrian Mountains in the north, including Mynydd Mallaen (459 m/1,1,506 ft); along the coast are extensive sands and marshes. Carmarthenshire is dominated by the Vale of Tywi, but there are numerous grassy hills, mostly under 300 m/1,000 ft; the valleys are fertile and the hillsides afford good pasturage; **Features** Brecon Beacons National Park on the eastern border; Museum of the Woollen Industry at DreFach-Felindre; home of Dylan Thomas in the village of Laugharne, 6 km/3.7 mi southeast of St Clears; **Population** (1996) 68,900.

Ceredigion

Unitary authority in southwest Wales, created in 1996 from part of the former county of Dyfed, of which it was a district

Area 1,793 sq km/ 692 sq mi; **Towns** Aberaeron (administrative headquarters), Aberystwyth, Cardigan, Lampeter, Llandyssul, Tregaron; **Physical** part of the Cambrian Mountains, including Plynlimon Fawr (752 m/2,468 ft); rivers Teifi, Rheidol, Ystwyth, Aeron, Tywi; **Features** remains of Roman roads and military stations, and inscribed stones; ruins of 12th-century Strata Florida Abbey southeast of Aberystwyth; Devil's Bridge) (spanning the Rheidol Falls); **Industries** tourism, woollens production; **Population** (1996) 68,900.

Conwy

Unitary authority in north Wales, created in 1996 from parts of the former counties of Clwyd and Gwynedd

Area 1,107 sq km/427 sq mi; **Towns** Conwy (administrative headquarters), Abergele, Llandudno, Llanrwst; **Physical** rivers Conwy and Elwy; **Features** Snowdonia National Park; coastline of sandy beaches, including the seaside resort of Colwyn Bay; **Industries** tourism; **Population** (1996) 113,000.

Denbighshire

Unitary authority in north Wales. A former county, between 1974 and 1996 it was largely merged, together with Flint and part of Merioneth, into Clwyd; a small area along the western border was included in Gwynedd

Area 844 sq km/326 sq mi; **Towns** Ruthin (administrative headquarters), Denbigh, Llangollen; **Physical** Clwydian range of mountains rises to a height of 555 m/1,820 ft, with Offa's Dyke along the main ridge; rivers Clwyd, Dee, Elwy; **Features** Denbigh and Rhuddlan castles; seaside resorts of Rhyl and Prestatyn; **Industries** agriculture (chiefly dairy), tourism; **Population** (1996) 91,000.

Flintshire

Unitary authority in north Wales. A former county, it was part of Clwyd between 1974 and 1996

Area 437 sq km/167 sq mi; **Towns** Mold (administrative headquarters), Flint, Holywell, Buckley, Connah's Quay; **Physical** bounded by the Irish Sea in the north, the Dee estuary in the east, and the Clwydian Range, which rises to 555 m/1,820 ft, in the southwest; rivers Dee, Alyn; **Industries** artificial silk, chemicals, optical glass; **Population** (1996) 144,000.

Gwynedd

Unitary authority in northwest Wales, created 1996 from part of the former county of Gwynedd

Area 2,546 sq km/983 sq mi; **Towns** Caernarfon (administrative headquarters); **Physical** area includes the highest mountain in Wales, Snowdon (1,085 m/3,560 ft), and the largest Welsh lake, Llyn Tegid (Bala Lake); **Features** Snowdonia National Park, seaside resorts, Bardsey Island; **Industries** gold mining at Dolgellau, textiles, electronics, slate, tourism; **Population** (1996) 116,000.

Merthyr Tydfil

Unitary authority in south Wales, created in 1996 from part of the former county of Mid Glamorgan

Area 111 sq km/43 sq mi; **Towns** Merthyr Tydfil (administrative headquarters); **Features** area includes part of Brecon Beacons National Park; **Industries** light engineering, electrical goods; **Population** (1996) 60,000.

Monmouthshire

Unitary authority in southeast Wales. A former county, between 1974 and 1996 it became (except for a small area on the border with Mid Glamorgan) the county of Gwent

Area 851 sq km/328 sq mi; **Towns** Cwmbran (administrative headquarters), Chepstow; **Physical** rivers Wye and Usk; mountainous in north; **Features** Chepstow and Raglan castles, Tintern Abbey, salmon and trout fishing; peak of Pen-y-Fal or Sugar Loaf (596 m/1,955 ft); **Population** (1996) 80,400.

Neath Port Talbot

Unitary authority in south Wales, created in 1996 from part of the former county of West Glamorgan

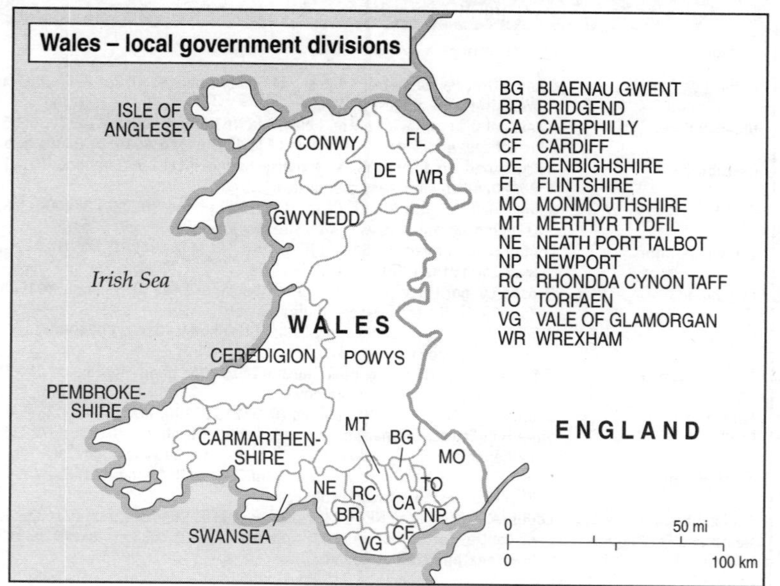

Area 442 sq km/171 sq mi; **Towns** Port Talbot (administrative headquarters); **Physical** the terrain is dominated by the alternation of river valleys and high moorland interfluves; **Features** Roman fort of Nidum is near Neath; **Industries** coal mining, chemicals, various metalworks, variety of light industry; **Population** (1996) 139,400.

Newport

Unitary authority in south Wales, created in 1996 from part of the former county of Gwent

Area 190 sq km/73 sq mi; **Towns** Newport (administrative headquarters); **Physical** rivers Usk Ebbw, Afon Llwyd; **Features** Legionary Museum and Roman amphitheatre at Caerleon; **Industries** steel and aluminium production, engineering, chemicals, fertilizers, electronics; **Population** (1996) 133,300.

Pembrokeshire

Unitary authority in southwest Wales; a former county, from 1974 to 1996 it was part of the county of Dyfed

Area 1,588 sq km/613 sq mi; **Towns** Haverfordwest (administrative headquarters), Milford Haven; **Physical** bounded on the south by the Bristol Channel; valleys and hills inland; rivers East and West Cleddau; **Features** Pembrokeshire Coast National Park; **Industries** oil refinery at Milford Haven, agriculture, fishing, woollen milling; **Population** (1996) 117,700.

Powys

Unitary authority in central Wales, created in 1996 from the former county of Powys

Area 5,179 sq km/1,999 sq mi; **Towns** Llandrindod Wells (administrative headquarters), Brecon, Builth Wells, Newtown, Welshpool; **Physical** mountainous to the north, Black Mountains, rivers Wye and Severn, which both rise on the eastern slopes of Plynlimon; **Features** the Brecon Beacons National Park, Lake Vyrnwy (an artificial reservoir supplying Liverpool and Birmingham), alternative technology centre near Machynlleth; **Industries** agriculture, tourism; **Population** (1996) 123,600.

Rhondda Cynon Taff

Unitary authority in south Wales, created in 1996 from part of the former county of Mid Glamorgan

Area 440 sq km/170 sq mi; **Towns** Clydach Vale (administrative headquarters); **Physical** rivers Rhondda Fawr and Rhondda Fach; **Industries** light industries; **Population** (1996) 232,600.

Swansea

Unitary authority in south Wales, created in 1996 from part of the former county of West Glamorgan

Area 377 sq km/156 sq mi; **Towns** Swansea (administrative headquarters); **Physical** River Tawe; **Features** Gower Peninsula (an area of outstanding natural beauty); **Industries** tinplate manufacture, chemicals, oil refineries; **Population** (1996) 232,000.

Torfaen

Unitary authority in south Wales, created in 1996 from part of the former county of Gwent

Area 98 sq km/38 sq mi; **Towns** Pontypool (administrative headquarters), Cwmbran (the first new town in Wales); **Physical** Coity Mountain in the north, River Afon Llwyd; **Industries** advanced electronics, automotive, engineering; **Population** (1996) 90,700.

Vale of Glamorgan

Unitary authority in south Wales, created in 1996 from parts of the former counties of Mid Glamorgan and South Glamorgan

Area 337 sq km/130 sq mi; **Towns** Barry (administrative headquarters), Penarth; **Physical** lowland area; **Population** (1996) 119,500.

Wrexham

Unitary authority in northeast Wales, created in 1996 from part of the former county of Clywd

Area 500 sq km/193 sq mi; **Towns** Wrexham (administrative headquarters), Holt, Ruabon; **Physical** western side is mountainous, including Ruabon Mountain; River Dee; **Features** Clywedog Valley, with notable countryside and industrial archaeology; **Industries** food manufacture, plastics, pharmaceuticals, high-technology industries; **Population** (1996) 123,50

The Addresses of Welsh Unitary Authorities

Authority	Council offices	Chief executive
Anglesey	Council Offices, Llangefni, Anglesey LL77 7TW; phone: (01248) 752480; fax: (01248) 750839; Web site: www.anglesey.gov.uk/	Mr Lionel Gardener
Blaenau Gwent	Municipal Offices, Civic Centre, Ebbw Vale NP3 6XB; phone: (01495) 350555; fax: (01495) 356111	Mr Roger Leadbeter
Bridgend	Civic Offices, Angel Street, Bridgend CF31 1LX; phone: (01656) 643643; fax: (01656) 643215	Mr Kerry Lewis
Caerphilly	Nelson Road, Tredomen, Ystrad Mynach, Hengoed CF82 7WF; phone: (01443) 815588; fax: (01443) 864202; Web site: www.caerphilly.gov.uk/	Mr Malgwyn Davies
Cardiff	County Hall, Atlantic Wharf, Cardiff CF1 5UW; phone: (01222) 872000; fax: (01222) 872407; e-mail: O.Jenkins@cardiff.gov.uk; Web site: www.cardiff.gov.uk/	Mr Byron Davies
Carmarthenshire	County Hall, Carmarthen SA31 1JP; phone: (01267) 234567; fax: (01267) 222097; Web site: www.carmarthenshire.gov.uk/	Mr Bradley Roynon
Ceredigion	Neuadd Cyngor Ceredigion, Penmorfa, Aberaeron SA46 0PA; phone: (01545) 572000; fax: (01545) 572009; Web site: www.ceredigion.gov.uk/	Mr R Owen Watkin
Conwy	Bodlondeb, Bangor Road, Conwy LL32 8DU; phone: (01492) 574000; fax: (01492) 576003; Web site: www.conwy.gov.uk	Mr Derek Barker
Denbighshire	Council Offices, Wynnstay Road, Ruthin LL15 1YN; phone: (01824) 706000; fax: (01824) 707446; Web site: www.denbighshire.gov.uk/	Mr Huw Vaughan Thomas
Flintshire	County Hall, Mold CH7 6NB; phone: (01352) 702100; fax: (01352) 755910	Mr Philip McGreevy
Gwynedd	Shire Hall Street, Caernarfon, Gwynedd LL55 1SH; phone: (01286) 672255; fax: (01286) 679488; e-mail:enquiries@gwynedd.gov.uk; Web site: www.gwynedd.gov.uk/	Mr Geraint R Jones
Merthyr Tydfil	Civic Centre, Castle Street, Merthyr Tydfil CF47 8AN; phone: (01685) 725000; fax: (01685) 722146; Web site: www.merthyr.gov.uk/	Mr Gary Meredith
Monmouthshire	County Hall, Cwmbran NP44 2XH; phone: (01633) 644644; fax: (01633) 644045	Ms Joyce Redfearn
Neath and Port Talbot	Civic Centre, Port Talbot SA13 1PJ; phone: (01639) 763333; fax: (01639) 763355; Web site: www.neathporttalbot.gov.uk	Mr Ken Sawyers

(continued)

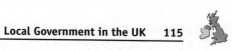

The Addresses of Welsh Unitary Authorities (*continued*)

Authority	Council offices	Chief executive
Newport	Civic Centre, Newport NP9 4UR; phone: (01633) 244491; fax: (01633) 232001; Web site: www.newport.gov.uk/	Mr R D Sandy Blair
Pembrokeshire	Cambria House, Haverfordwest, Pembrokeshire SA61 1TP; phone: (01437) 764551; fax: (01437) 775838; Web site: www.pembrokeshire.gov.uk/	Mr Bryn Parry-Jones
Powys	County Hall, Spa Road, Llandrindod Wells LD1 5LG; phone: (01597) 826368; fax: (01597) 826220; Web site: www.powys.gov.uk/	Miss Jacky Tonge
Rhondda Cynon Taff	The Pavilions, Cambrian Park, Clydach Vale CF40 2XX; phone: (01443) 424000; fax: (01443) 424027; Web site: www.rhondda-cynon-taff.gov.uk/	Mr K Ryley
Swansea	County Hall, Swansea SA1 3SN; phone: (01792) 636000; fax: (01792) 636700; Web site: www.swansea.gov.uk/	Mrs Vivienne Sugar
Torfaen	Civic Centre, Pontypool, Gwent NP4 6YB; phone: (01495) 762200; fax: (01495) 750797	Dr Clive Grace
Vale of Glamorgan	Civic Offices, Holton Road, Barry CF63 4RU; phone: (01446) 700111; fax: (01446) 421479; Web site: www.valeofglamorgan.gov.uk/	Mr David Foster
Wrexham County Borough	Guildhall, Wrexham LL11 1WF; phone: (01978) 292000; fax: (01978) 292106	Mr Derek Griffin

The Political Composition of Welsh Unitary Authorities

(– = not applicable.)

Authority	Labour	Independent/other	Plaid Cymru	Liberal Democrat	Conservative	Controlling party	Total councillors
Anglesey	4	26	9	0	1	Independent	40
Blaenau Gwent	34	7	0	1	0	Labour	42
Bridgend	41	5	2	5	1	Labour	54
Caerphilly	29	3	38	3	0	Labour	73
Cardiff	50	1	1	18	5	Labour	75
Carmarthenshire	28	31	14	1	0	no overall control	74
Ceredigion	1	22	14	7	0	no overall control	44
Conwy	20	13	7	14	5	no overall control	59
Denbighshire	13	23	8	1	2	no overall control	47
Flintshire	42	18	2	7	1	Labour	70
Gwynedd	12	21	44	6	0	Plaid Cymru	83
Merthyr Tydfil	16	13	4	0	0	no overall control	33
Monmouthshire	18	4	0	1	19	no overall control	42
Neath Port Talbot	40	12	10	2	0	Labour	64
Newport	40	2	0	0	5	Labour	47
Pembrokeshire	13	39	2	3	3	Independent	60
Powys	7	58	0	6	1	Independent	72
Rhondda Cynon Taff	26	5	42	2	0	Plaid Cymru	75
Swansea	47	9	2	10	4	Labour	72
Torfaen	39	3	0	1	1	Labour	44
Vale of Glamorgan	19	0	6	0	22	no overall control	47
Wrexham	26	15	0	7	4	no overall control	52
Total	565	330	205	95	74	–	1,269

Northern Ireland Counties and Districts

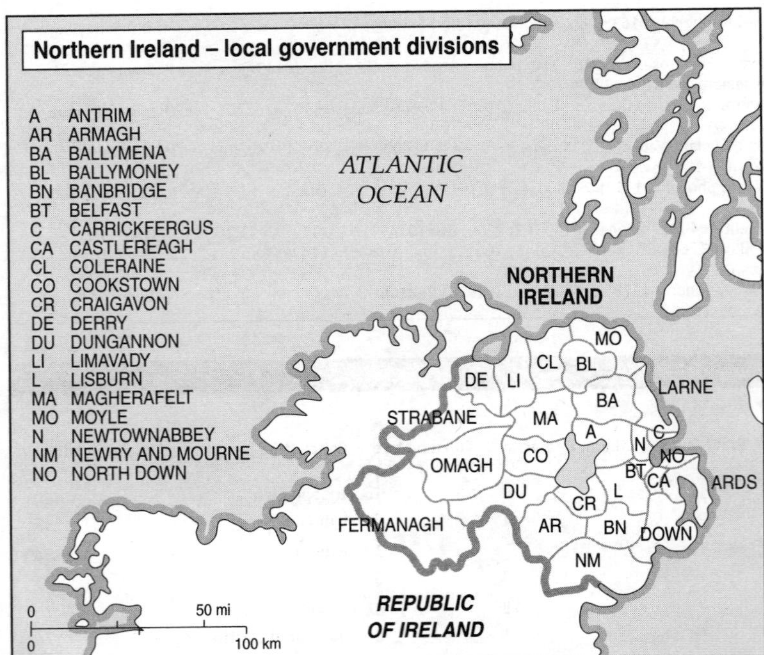

Local Government in Northern Ireland

Northern Ireland has a single-tier system of 26 district councils. Historically there are six counties but these perform no administrative function. Health and Social Services, and Education and Library Services are organized by regional boards.

Antrim

County of Northern Ireland

Area 2,830 sq km/1,092 sq mi; **Towns and cities** Belfast (county town), Larne (port), Antrim, Ballymena, Lisburn, Carrickfergus; **Physical** peat bogs; Antrim borders Lough Neagh, and is separated from Scotland by the North Channel, which is only 21 km/13 mi wide at Torr Head, the narrowest point; the main rivers are the Bann and the Lagan; **Features** Giant's Causeway, a World Heritage Site, consisting of natural hexagonal and pentagonal basalt columns on the coast; Antrim Mountains (highest point Trostan 554 m/1,817 ft) and the Glen of Antrim; Kebble National Nature Reserve, on Rathlin Island, off the coast near Ballycastle; Bushmills Distillery, in the village of Bushmills, has the oldest known licence for distilling whiskey; there are a number of early fortifications, castles, and medieval ecclesiastical remains in the county; the village of Cushendun was built by Clough Williams-Ellis; Gobbins Cliff Path (19th century), to be restored as a millennium project; **Industries** shipbuilding; traditional linen production largely replaced by the manufacture of man-made fibres, whiskey, agriculture (the Bann Valley is particularly fertile); **Population** (1981) 642,000.

Armagh

County of Northern Ireland

Area 1,250 sq km/483 sq mi; **Towns and cities** Armagh (county town), Lurgan and Portadown (merged to form Craigavon), Keady; **Physical** smallest county of Northern Ireland; flat in the north, with many bogs and mounds formed from glacial deposits; low hills in the south, the highest of which is Slieve Gullion (577 m/1,893 ft); principal rivers are the Bann, the Blackwater and its tributary, the Callan; **Industries** linen manufacture (Portadown and Lurgan were the principal centres of the linen industry); milling, light engineering, concrete, potato crisps; **Population** (1981) 119,000.

Down

County of southeastern Northern Ireland

Area 2,470 sq km/953 sq mi; **Towns and cities** Downpatrick (county town), Bangor (seaside resort), Newtownards, Newry, and Banbridge; the northern part lies within the commuter belt for Belfast, and includes part of the city of Belfast, east of the River Lagan; **Physical** Mourne Mountains; Strangford sea lough; **Industries** light manufacturing, plastics, linen, high technology and computer companies, fishing, quarrying; **Population** (1981) 339,200.

Fermanagh

County of Northern Ireland

Area 1,680 sq km/648 sq mi; **Towns** Enniskillen (county town), Lisnaskea, Irvinestown; **Physical** in the centre is a broad trough of low-lying land, in which lie Upper and Lower Lough Erne; **Industries** clothing, tweeds, cotton thread, food processing, light engineering, china, tourism, electronics; **Population** (1991) 50,000.

Londonderry (also known as Derry)

County of Northern Ireland

Area 2,070 sq km/799 sq mi; **Towns and cities** Londonderry (county town), Coleraine, Portstewart, Limavady; **Physical** hilly moorland, coniferous forest; Sperrin Mountains; rivers Foyle, Bann, Roe, Faughan; borders Lough Neagh; **Industries** stone and lime quarrying, food processing, textiles and synthetic fibres, shirt manufacturing, light engineering, chemicals; **Population** (1981) 187,000,

Tyrone

County of Northern Ireland

Area 3,160 sq km/1,220 sq mi; **Towns and cities** Omagh (county town), Dungannon, Strabane, Cookstown; **Features** rivers: Derg, Blackwater, Foyle; Lough Neagh; Sperrin Mountains; **Industries** mainly agricultural: barley, flax, potatoes, turnips, cattle, sheep, brick making, linen, hosiery, shirts; **Population** (1991) 158,500.

Area and Population of Northern Ireland

1996

Board[1] and district		Area	Total population	
			sq km	sq mi
Eastern	Ards	380	17	68,000
	Belfast	110	42	297,000
	Castlereagh	85	33	64,000
	Down	649	251	61,000
	Lisburn	447	173	108,000
	North Down	81	31	74,000
	Total	1,751	676	673,000
Northern	Antrim	421	163	49,000
	Ballymena	630	243	58,000
	Ballymoney	416	161	25,000
	Carrickfergus	81	31	35,000
	Coleraine	486	188	55,000
	Cookstown	514	198	32,000
	Lame	336	130	30,000
	Magherafelt	564	218	38,000
	Moyle	494	191	15,000
	Newtownabbey	151	58	79,000
	Total	4,093	1,580	415,000
Southern	Armagh	671	259	53,000
	Banbridge	451	174	37,000
	Craigavon	282	109	79,000
	Dungannon	772	298	47,000
	Newry and Mourne	898	347	85,000
	Total	3,075	1,187	300,000
Western	Derry	1,699	656	104,000
	Fermanagh	586	226	55,000
	Limavady	381	147	31,000
	Omagh	1,130	436	47,000
	Strabane	862	333	37,000
	Total	4,658	1,798	275,000
Northern Ireland total		13,576	5,242	1,663,000

[1] Health and Social Services Board areas.

Source: *Regional Trends 33*, © Crown copyright 1998

The Addresses of Northern Ireland District Councils

Council	Council offices	Chief executive
Antrim	Council Offices, The Steeple, Antrim BT41 1BJ; phone: (01849) 463113; fax: (01849) 464469; e-mail: contact@antrim.gov.uk; Web site: www.antrim.gov.uk/	Mr Samuel J Magee
Ards	2 Church Street, Newtownards, Co Down BT23 4AP; phone: (01247) 812215; fax: (01247) 819628; e-mail: ards@ards-council.gov.uk; Web site: www.ards-council.gov.uk/	Mr David J Fallows
Armagh	The Palace Demesne, Armagh BT60 4EL; phone: (01861) 529600; fax: (01861) 529601; e-mail: info@armagh.gov.uk; Web site: www.armagh.gov.uk/	Mr Desmond R D Mitchell
Ballymena	'Ardeevin', 80 Galgorm Road, Ballymena, BT42 1AB; phone: (01266) 660300; fax: (01266) 660400; e-mail: townclerk@ballymena.gov.uk; Web site: www.ballymena.gov.uk/	Mr Mervin G Rankin
Ballymoney	Riada House, 14 Charles Street, Ballymoney BT53 6DZ; phone: (012656) 62280; fax: (012656) 65150	Mr John Dempsey
Banbridge	Civic Building, Downshire Road, Banbridge BT32 3JY; phone: (01820) 662991; fax: (01820) 62595/24791	Mr Robert Gilmore
Belfast	City Hall, Belfast, BT1 5GS; phone: (01232) 320202; fax: (01232) 236116; e-mail: webmaster@belfastcity.gov.uk; Web site: www.belfastcity.gov.uk/	Mr Brian Hanna
Carrickfergus	Town Hall, Carrickfergus BT38 7DL; phone: (01960) 351604; fax: (01960) 366676; e-mail: info@carrickfergus.org; Web site: www.carrickfergus.org/	Mr Raymond Boyd
Castlereagh	Borough Offices, 368 Cregagh Road, Belfast BT6 9EZ; phone: (01232) 799021; fax: (01232) 704158; e-mail: chief@castlereagh.gov.uk; Web site: www.castlereagh.gov.uk/	Mr Adrian Donaldson
Coleraine	Cloonavin, 41 Portstewart Road, Coleraine BT52 1EY; phone: (01265) 52181; fax: (01265) 53489	Mr H Wavell T Moore
Cookstown	Council Offices, Burn Road, Cookstown BT80 8DT; phone: (016487) 62205; fax: (016487) 64360	Mr Michael McGuckin
Craigavon	Civic Centre, PO Box 66, Lakeview Road, Craigavon, BT64 1AL; phone: (01762) 341199; fax: (01762) 345514; e-mail: info@craigavon.gov.uk; Web site: www.craigavon.gov.uk/	Mr Trevor E Reaney
Derry	Council Offices, 98 Strand Road, Londonderry BT48 7NN; phone: (01504) 365151; fax: (01504) 368536	Mr John Keanie
Down	24 Strangford Road, Downpatrick, County Down BT30 6SR; phone: (01396) 610800; fax: (01396) 610801; Web site: www.downdc.gov.uk/	Mr Owen P O'Connor
Dungannon	Council Offices, Circular Road, Dungannon BT71 6DT; phone: (01868) 725311; fax: (01868) 720368; e-mail: general@dungannon.gov.uk; Web site: www.dungannon.gov.uk/	Mr William J Beattie
Fermanagh	Townhall, Enniskillen BT74 7BA; phone: (01365) 325050; fax: (01365) 322024; Web site: www.fermanagh.gov.uk/	Mrs Aideen McGinley
Larne	Smiley Buildings, Victoria Road, Larne BT40 1RU; phone: (01574) 272313; fax: (01574) 260660; e-mail: mail@larne-bc.com; Web site: www.larne.com/borough_council/	Mr Colm McGarry
Limavady	7 Connell Street, Limavady, Co Londonderry BT49 0HA; phone: (015047) 22226; fax: (015047) 22010	Mr John K Stevenson
Lisburn	Borough Offices, The Square, Hillsborough BT26 6AH; phone: (01846) 682477; fax: (01846) 689016; e-mail: lisburnbc@compuserve.com; Web site: www.lisburn.gov.uk/	Mr Norman Davidson
Magherafelt	Council Offices, 50 Ballyronan Road, Magherafelt BT45 6EN; phone: (01648) 32151; (01648) 31240	Mr John A McLaughlin
Moyle	Sheskburn House, 7 Mary Street, Ballycastle BT54 6QH; phone: (012657) 62225; fax: (012657) 62515; e-mail: info@moyle-council.org.uk; Web site: www.moyle-council.org/	Mr Richard G Lewis

(continued)

The Addresses of Northern Ireland District Councils (*continued*)

Council	Council offices	Chief executive
Newry and Mourne	O'Hagan House, District Council Offices, Monaghan Row, Newry BT35 8DL; phone: (01693) 65411; fax: (01693) 65313	Mr Kevin O'Neill
Newtownabbey	Headquarters, 1 The Square, Ballyclare BT39 9BA; phone: (01960) 352681; fax: (01960) 340417	Mr Norman Dunn
North Down	Town Hall, The Castle, Bangor BT20 4BT; phone: (01247) 270371; fax: (01247) 271370; e-mail: edo@north-down.gov.uk; Web site: www.north-down.gov.uk/	Mr Adrian McDowell
Omagh	Council Offices, The Grange, Mountjoy Road, Omagh BT79 7BL; phone: (01662) 245321; fax: (01662) 243888; Web site: www.omagh.gov.uk/	Mr John P McKinney
Strabane	District Council Offices, 47 Derry Road, Strabane BT82 8DY; phone: (01504) 382204; fax: (01504) 382264; e-mail: strabanedc@nics.gov.uk; Web site: www.strabanedc.org.uk/	Dr Victor Eakin

The Political Composition of Northern Ireland District Councils

Council	Ulster Unionist	Social Democratic and Labour Party	Democratic Unionist Party	Sinn Féin	Alliance	Independent	Independent Unionist	Progressive Unionist	Ulster Democratic Party	Other	Total
Antrim	9	4	3	1	2	0	0	0	0	0	19
Ards	10	1	5	0	5	0	2	0	0	0	23
Armagh	10	7	2	3	0	0	0	0	0	0	22
Ballymena	11	3	8	0	1	1	0	0	0	0	24
Ballymoney	4	3	6	1	0	2	0	0	0	0	16
Banbridge	9	3	3	0	0	2	0	0	0	0	17
Belfast City	13	7	7	13	6	0	1	3	1	0	51
Carrickfergus	4	0	3	0	5	3	1	0	0	1	17
Castlereagh	5	2	10	0	4	0	1	0	0	1	23
Coleraine	10	3	5	0	3	1	0	0	0	0	22
Cookstown	4	4	2	5	0	0	1	0	0	0	16
Craigavon	11	7	3	2	1	0	0	0	0	2	26
Derry City	3	14	4	8	0	0	1	0	0	0	30
Down	6	12	2	2	0	0	0	0	0	1	23
Dungannon	8	4	3	5	0	0	0	0	0	2	22
Fermanagh	9	4	2	5	0	1	0	0	0	2	23
Larne	0	6	1	3	0	1	1	0	0	3	15
Limavady	7	7	0	1	0	0	0	0	0	0	15
Lisburn	13	2	2	4	3	0	0	0	2	4	30
Magherafelt	2	5	4	5	0	0	0	0	0	0	16
Moyle	3	3	3	1	0	4	0	0	0	1	15
Newry and Mourne	5	12	1	8	0	4	0	0	0	0	30
Newtownabbey	10	1	2	0	3	0	3	1	0	4	24
North Down	6	0	2	0	6	2	1	2	0	6	25
Omagh	3	5	3	6	1	0	0	0	0	3	21
Strabane	3	5	3	4	0	1	0	0	0	0	16
Total	183	119	91	74	41	25	11	6	3	27	580

UK Members of the European Parliament

UK Members of the European Parliament

Con = Conservative; DUP = Democratic Unionist Party; Lab = Labour; LD = Liberal Democrats; Grn = Green; PC = Plaid Cymru; SDLP = Social Democratic and Labour Party; SNP = Scottish National Party; UKIP = UK Independence Party; UUP = Ulster Unionist Party.

Region	1999 election turnout (%)	Member	Party
England			
Eastern	24.74	Beazley, Christopher	Con
		Duff, Andrew	LD
		Howitt, Richard	Lab
		Khanbhai, Bashir	Con
		McNally, Eryl	Lab
		Sturdy, Robert	Con
		Titford, Jeffrey	UKIP
		Van Orden, Geoffrey	Con
East Midlands	22.83	Clegg, Nicholas	LD
		Dunn, William Newton	Con
		Heaton-Harris, Christopher	Con
		Helmer, Roger	Con
		Read, Mel	Lab
		Whitehead, Phillip	Lab
London	23.10	Balfe, Richard	Lab
		Bethell, Nicholas	Con
		Bowis, John	Con
		Evans, Robert	Lab
		Green, Pauline	Lab
		Lambert, Jean	Grn
		Ludford, Sarah	LD
		Moraes, Claude	Lab
		Tannock, Charles	Con
		Villiers, Theresa	Con
North East	19.6	Callanan, Martin	Con
		Donnelly, Alan	Lab
		Hughes, Stephen	Lab
		O'Toole, Mo	Lab
North West	19.67	Atkins, Robert	Con
		Davies, Chris	LD
		Dover, Den	Con
		Foster, Jacqueline	Con
		Inglewood, William Richard	Con
		McCarthy, Arlene	Lab
		Simpson, Brian	Lab
		Sumberg, David	Con
		Titley, Gary	Lab
		Wynn, Terry	Lab
South East	24.95	Deva, Nirj	Con
		Elles, James	Con
		Farage, Nigel	UKIP
		Hannan, Daniel	Con
		Huhne, Christopher	LD
		Lucas, Caroline	Grn
		Nicholson of Winterbourne, Emma	LD
		Perry, Roy	Con
		Provan, James	Con
		Skinner, Peter	Lab
		Watts, Mark	Lab
South West	27.81	Chichester, Giles	Con
		Ford, James Glyn	Lab
		Holmes, Michael	UKIP
		Jackson, Caroline	Con
		Parish, Neil	Con
		Stockton, Alexander	Con
		Watson, Graham	LD
West Midlands	21.21	Bradbourn, Philip	Con
		Bushill-Matthews, Philip	Con
		Cashman, Michael	Lab
		Corrie, John	Con
		Gill, Neena	Lab
		Harbour, Malcolm	Con
		Lynne, Liz	LD
		Murphy, Simon	Lab
Yorkshire and the Humber	19.75	Bowe, David	Lab
		Corbett, Richard	Lab
		Goodwill, Robert	Con
		Kirkhope, Timothy	Con
		McAvan, Linda	Lab
		McMillan-Scott, Edward	Con
		Wallis, Diana	LD
Northern Ireland	48.67	Hume, John	SDLP
		Nicholson, Jim	UUP
		Paisley, Ian	DUP
Scotland	24.83	Attwooll, Elspeth	LD
		Hudghton, Ian	SNP
		MacCormick, Neil	SNP
		Martin, David	Lab
		Miller, William	Lab
		Purvis, John	Con
		Stevenson, Struan	Con
		Taylor, Catherine	Lab
Wales	26.7	Evans, Jillian	PC
		Evans, Jonathan	Con
		Kinnock, Glenys	Lab
		Morgan, Mair Eluned	Lab
		Wyn, Eurig	PC

European Parliament: UK Election Results 1994 and 1999

Party	Number of MEPs 1994	Number of MEPs 1999
Conservative	18	36
Labour	62	29
Liberal Democrats	2	100
UK Independence Party	0	3
Green	0	2
Scottish National Party	2	2
Plaid Cymru	0	2
Pro-Euro Conservative Party	0	0
Others[1]	3	3

[1] All other UK parties including those of Northern Ireland.

European Parliament: UK Election Results Breakdown

Party	Votes received in 1999 election: Number	%	Number of MEPs
Conservative Party	3,578,217	35.77	36
Labour Party	2,803,821	28.03	29
Liberal Democrats	1,266,549	12.66	10
UK Independence Party	696,057	6.96	3
Green Party	625,378	6.25	2
Scottish National Party	268,528	2.68	2
Plaid Cymru	185,235	1.85	2
Pro-Euro Conservative Party	138,097	1.38	0
British National Party	102,647	1.13	0
Liberal Party	93,051	1.93	0
Socialist Labour Party	86,749	0.87	0
Scottish Socialist Party	39,720	0.40	0
MEP Independent Labour Party	36,849	0.37	0
Alternative Labour List	26,963	0.27	0
Natural Law Party	20,329	0.20	0
Socialist Alliance	7,203	0.07	0
Architect, Human Rights Peace in Europe	4,851	0.05	0
EDP English Freedom Party	3,066	0.03	0
Independent Anti-Value Added Tax	2,596	0.03	0
The Humanist Party	2,586	0.03	0
The Hemp Coalition	2,358	0.02	0
Anit-Corruption Pro-Family Christian Alliance	2,251	0.02	0
Independent Open Democracy for Stability	1,857	0.02	0
Weekly Worker	1,724	0.02	0
Socialist Party (Great Britain)	1,510	0.02	0
Independent Making a Profit in Europe	1,400	0.01	0
English Independent Humanist Party	1,049	0.01	0
Accountant for Lower Scottish Taxes	1,632	0.02	0
Northern Ireland: First Preference Votes			
Democratic Unionist Party	192,762	28.40	1
Social Democratic and Labour Party	190,731	28.10	1
Ulster Unionist Party	119,507	17.61	1
Sinn Féin	117,643	17.33	0
Progressive Unionist Party	22,494	3.31	0
UK Unionist Party	20,283	2.99	0
Alliance	14,391	2.12	0
Natural Law Party	998	0.15	0

Cities and Major Towns

The 50 Most Populous Cities and Towns in England

Population figures are based on the 1991 census.

City/town	Population	City/town	Population	City/town	Population
London[1]	7,122,000	Southampton	210,100	Huddersfield	143,700
Birmingham	965,900	Dudley	192,200	Bolton	139,000
Liverpool	481,800	Newcastle-upon-Tyne	189,500	Poole	138,500
Sheffield	431,600	Sunderland	183,300	Peterborough	134,800
Leeds	424,200	Northampton	179,600	Stockport	132,800
Bristol	408,000	Preston	177,700	Ipswich	130,600
Manchester	402,900	Walsall	174,700	Brighton	124,900
Leicester	318,500	Portsmouth	174,700	York	124,600
Kingston-upon-Hull	310,600	Luton	171,700	Rotherham	121,400
Coventry	299,300	Norwich	171,300	Oxford	118,800
Bradford	289,400	Southend-on-Sea	158,500	Gloucester	114,000
Nottingham	270,200	Bournemouth	155,500	Slough	110,700
Stoke-on-Trent	266,200	Middlesbrough	147,400	St Helens	106,300
Wolverhampton	257,900	West Bromwich	146,400	Sutton Coldfield	106,000
Plymouth	245,300	Blackpool	146,300	Blackburn	106,000
Derby	223,800	Oldbury/Smethwick	145,500	Oldham	103,900
Reading	213,500	Swindon	145,200		

[1] 1997

The 10 Most Populous Cities and Towns in Northern Ireland

Population figures are based on the 1991 census.

City/town	Population	City/town	Population
Belfast	279,200	Lisburn	42,100
Londonderry	72,300	Ballymena	28,100
Newtownabbey	56,800	Newtownards	23,900
Bangor	52,400	Carrickfergus	22,800
Coleraine	50,700	Lurgan	21,900

The 20 Most Populous Cities and Towns in Scotland

Population figures are based on the 1991 census.

City/town	Population	City/town	Population
Glasgow	663,000	Ayr	48,000
Edinburgh	401,900	Kirkcaldy	47,200
Aberdeen	189,700	Kilmarnock	44,300
Dundee	159,000	Coatbridge	43,600
Paisley	75,500	Livingston	41,600
East Kilbride	72,400	Perth	41,500
Dunfermline	55,100	Inverness	41,200
Greenock	55,000	Glenrothes	38,650
Hamilton	50,000	Airdrie	37,000
Cumbernauld	48,800	Falkirk	35,600

The 20 Most Populous Cities and Towns in Wales

Population figures are based on the 1991 census.

City/town	Population	City/town	Population
Cardiff	272,100	Bridgend	35,800
Swansea	171,000	Pontypool	35,600
Newport	115,500	Colwyn Bay	29,900
Rhondda	59,900	Aberdare	29,000
Barry	49,900	Pontypridd	28,500
Cwmbran	46,000	Caerphilly	28,500
Llanelli	45,000	Rhyl	24,900
Neath	46,000	Shotton/Hawarden	23,300
Merthyr Tydfil	39,500	Mountain Ash/ Abercynon	21,300
Wrexham	40,600		
Port Talbot	36,600		

Roman Names of English and Welsh Cities and Towns

City/town	Roman settlement
England	
Ancaster	Causennae
Bath	Aquae Sulis
Buxton	Aquae Arnemetiae
Canterbury	Durovernum Cantiacorum
Carlisle	Luguvalium
Castleford	Lagentium
Catterick	Cataractonium
Chelmsford	Caesaromagus
Chester	Deva
Chichester	Noviomagus Regnensium
Cirencester	Corinium Dobunnorum
Colchester	Camulodunum
Dorchester	Durnovaria
Dover	Dubris
Exeter	Isca Dumnoniorum
Gloucester	Glevum
Leicester	Ratae Coritanorum
Lincoln	Lindum
London	Londinium
Manchester	Mancunium
Newcastle-upon-Tyne	Pons Aelius
Rochester-upon-Medway	Durobrivae
Salisbury	Sorbiodonum
Shrewsbury	Viroconium
Tadcaster	Calcaria
Towcester	Lactodorum
Winchester	Venta Belgarum
York	Eboracum
Wales	
Abergavenny	Gobannium
Caerwent	Venta Silurum
Carmarthen	Maridunum

London

London

Capital of England and the United Kingdom, on the River Thames; Greater London, from 1965, comprises the City of London and 32 boroughs. London is the only major European capital without a strategic authority covering the whole area. In a referendum held on 7 May 1998, Londoners voted in favour of the instigation of office of elected mayor.

Area 1,580 sq km/610 sq mi (Greater London); **Population** 7,122,000 (1997 est); **Universities** University of London (Birkbeck College; Goldsmiths College; University College; King's College; Imperial College; Queen Mary & Westfield College; Royal Holloway & Bedford College); City University; Greenwich University; Kingston University; London Guildhall University; London School of Economics and Political Science; Middlesex University; University of East London; University of North London; South Bank University; Thames Valley University; Westminster University; **Airports** Gatwick; Heathrow; Stansted; **Rail** London has an extensive rail network which is linked to the London Underground (tube) at all mainline and several branch railway lines; the Eurostar service to the continent runs from Waterloo Station; **Major railway stations** Euston; Charing Cross; King's Cross; St Pancras; Paddington; Waterloo; Victoria; **Main bus station** Victoria Coach Station **Industries and products** finance (major international centre); newspapers; broadcasting; film; recording; tourism; government; the world's largest office development project is at Canary Wharf; **Places of interest** the National Gallery; The National Portrait Gallery; The British Museum; The Science Museum; The Natural History Museum; The Tate Gallery; The Victoria and Albert Museum; Wallace Collection; Courtauld Institute; The South Bank Complex (Royal Festival Hall; Hayward Gallery; National Theatre; Barbican arts and conference centre); Royal Opera House with the Royal Ballet and Opera Companies; The Royal Albert Hall; many other theatres in the West End; Royal Philharmonic and London Symphony Orchestras; the Tower of London (houses the crown jewels and the royal armouries); Westminster Abbey; The Palace of Westminster (containing the houses of

Parliament); Lambeth Palace; Southwark Cathedral; St James's Palace; Buckingham Palace; Horse Guards Parade; St Paul's Cathedral; Mansion House (residence of the lord mayor); Guildhall (15th century); Trafalgar Square; Nelson's Column; Criminal Court (Old Bailey) and the Inner and Middle Temples; The Royal Parks; **Tourist information centre** London Tourist Board, 26 Grosvenor Gardens, London SW1W 0DU; phone: (0171) 730 3450; fax: (0171) 730 9367; **Chamber of Commerce** London Chamber of Commerce & Industry (LCCI) 33 Queen Street, London EC4R 1AP; phone: (0171) 248 4444.

The Corporation of London

The Corporation of London is the local authority for the City of London, known as the square mile. Its responsibilities extend beyond the City boundaries, and it provides a number of additional facilities. The Corporation of London is unique in operating on a non-party political basis. It is currently engaged in a major review of its electoral arrangements. In response to the Government's Green Paper, *New Leadership for London*, the Corporation is examining ways in which it can improve the City's franchise and work alongside the proposed strategic authority for London. Further information about the review is available from the Town Clerk, Corporation of London, PO Box 270, Guildhall, London EC2P 2EJ.

Committees

Twenty-three committees of elected Members set Corporation policy and oversee the work of departments. These committees are: Barbican Centre; Barbican Residential; Billingsgate and Leadenhall Markets; Board of Governors, City of London Freemen's School; Board of Governors, City of London School; Board of Governors, City of London School for Girls; Board of Governors of the Museum of London; Central Markets; City Lands and Bridge House Estates; City of London Police; Committee of Managers of West Ham Park; Education; Epping Forest and Open Spaces; Establishment; Finance; Hampstead Heath Management; Housing and Sports Development; Libraries, Guildhall Art Gallery, and Archives; Music and Drama; Planning and Transportation; Policy and Resources; Port and City of London Health and Social Services; Spitalfields Market.

Departments

Barbican Centre; Barbican Estate; Billingsgate Market; Chamberlain; City of London Freemen's School; City of London Police; City of London School; City of London School for Girls; City Surveyor; Cleansing; Comptroller and City Solicitor; Education; Environmental Services; Epping Forest; Guildhall School of Music and Drama; Hampstead Heath; Housing and Sports Development; Libraries and Guildhall Art Gallery; London Central Markets; Mansion House; Museum of London; Parks and Gardens; Planning; Remembrancer; Secondary; Social Services; Spitalfields Market; Technical Services; Town Clerk; West Wickham and Coulsdon Commons, Ashtead Common and Burnham Beeches.

The Wards

Within the geographical area covered by the Corporation of London there are 25 wards or voting districts. Each ward elects an alderman and between three and twelve Commoners to represent them in the Court of Common Council, the City of London's 'town council'. All members of the following wards can be contacted via the Corporation of London, PO Box 270, Guildhall, London EC2P 2EJ.

Aldersgate Nicholas Anstee (Alderman), Clifford Green, Peter Leck, Neville Littlestone, Jeremy Mayhew, Joyce Nash (Deputy), Barbara Newman; **Aldgate** John Bowman, Bruce Farthing, Dr Peter Hardwick, John Holland (Deputy), Clive Martin (Alderman), Patrick O'Ferrall; **Bassishaw** Kenneth Ayers, Nigel Branson, David Brewer (Alderman), John Brewster, Peter Martinelli (Deputy); **Billingsgate** William Baverstock Brooks, John Hughesdon (Alderman), Douglas Mobsby (Deputy), Clive Thorp, John Trotter; **Bishopsgate** William Dove, Graham Forbes, Stanley Ginsburg, Anthony Graves, Bernard Morgan (Deputy), Michael Oliver (Alderman), Dorothy Robinson, Esmond Roney (Deputy), Philip Willoughby; **Bread Street** Christopher Davis, Rodney FitzGerald (Deputy), Tom Jackson, Michael Savory (Alderman), John Taylor; **Bridge and Bridge Without** John Bird, Daniel Caspi, Maurice Hart (Deputy), John Owen-Ward, Sir David Rowe-Ham (Alderman); **Broad Street** Sir Christopher Collett (Alderman), Fergus Falk, Archibald Galloway, Brian Harris (Sheriff), David Mizen (Deputy), John Spanner; **Candlewick** Kevin Everett, Stanley Knowles, Sir Richard Nichols (Alderman), Richard Saunders (Deputy), Richard Scriven; **Castle Baynard** Richard Agutter (Alderman), Henry Balls, Sir Colin Cole, Catherine McGuinness, Christopher Mitchell (Deputy); **Cheap** Peter Bull (Alderman), Joseph Byllam-Barnes, Robin Eve, Ann Pembroke (Deputy); **Coleman Street** Hugh Barnes-Yallowley, Michael Cassidy (Deputy), Robert Finch (Alderman), Stuart Fraser, Michael Henderson-Begg, Derek Kemp, Gordon Wixley; **Cordwainer** George Gillon, Sir Brian Jenkins (Alderman), Stephen Sellon, Michael Snyder (Deputy), Reginald Wilmot; **Cornhill** Wilfred Archibald (Deputy), John Haynes, David Howard (Alderman), Keith Sargant, Dr James White; **Cripplegate Within** Lionel Altman, Gavyn Arthur (Alderman and Sheriff), John Barker (Deputy), David Bradshaw, Christopher Punter, Francis Stevenson, Douglas Warner; **Cripplegate Without** Ernest Angell, Gavyn Arthur (Alderman and Sheriff), Stella Currie (Deputy), Roger Daily-Hunt, Rosemary Griffiths, Vivienne Littlechild, Stephen Quilter; **Dowgate** Peter Biroum-Smith, Edwina Coven (Deputy), Alison Gowman (Deputy), Sir Christopher Leaver (Alderman), Michael Sherlock, David Thorp; **Farringdon Within** North Side: Benson Catt, Henry Horlock, Peter Rigby (Deputy), David Shalit; South Side: Anthony Eskenzi (Deputy), Benjamin Hall, Joseph Reed, Richard Regan, Sir Christopher Walford (Alderman); **Farringdon Without** North Side: George Darwin, Sir Peter Gadsden (Alderman), Wendy Mead, John Platts-Mills, Lady Ponsonby (Deputy), Edward Price, Simon Walsh; South Side: John Absalom, Jonathan Charkham, Michael Farrow, Sir Peter Gadsden (Alderman), Gregory Lawrence, Ian Luder, Julian Malins (Deputy); **Langbourn** Frederick Bramwell, George Challis (Deputy), John Henderson, Janet Owen, Sir Alan Traill (Alderman); **Lime Street** Michael Beale (Deputy), Christine Cohen, Dennis Cotgrove, Frederick Everard (Alderman), Ian McNeil; **Portsoken** Roger Brighton, Alfred Dunitz, Geoffrey Lawson, The Rt Hon the Lord Mayor Lord Levene of Portsoken (Alderman), Iris Samuel (Deputy); **Queenhithe** John Fell, Sir Alexander Graham (Alderman), Judith Mayhew, Ivy Sharp (Deputy); **Tower** Roger Chadwick, Sir Roger Cork (Alderman), Maureen Kellett, Anthony Moss, Gerald Pulman (Deputy); **Vintry** Sir John Chalstrey (Alderman), William Fraser, Elizabeth Holliday, Andrew Parmley, Peter Revell-Smith (Deputy); **Walbrook** Martin Farr, Pauline Halliday, Andrew MacLellan (Deputy), Sir Paul Newall (Alderman), Peter Northall-Laurie

The Lord Mayor

The Lord Levene of Portsoken. Born: 8 December 1941; elected Member of the Common Council for the Ward of Candlewick (1983); elected to the Court of Aldermen for Ward of Portsoken (1984); elected Sheriff of the City of London (1995); Life Peer (1997).

The City Guilds (Livery Companies)

The City of London companies, collectively known as the Livery, are surviving members of medieval trade and craft associations, known as guilds. Each livery company is governed by an annually elected court, typically composed as follows: The Master (elected from the Wardens); Upper Warden; Middle Warden; Lower Warden (elected from the Court assistant); between 10 and 20 Court Assistants (elected from the Livery); a Clerk (to keep the records); a Beadle (to keep order).

After years of dispute, an order of precedence for livery companies was settled in 1515, starting with Mercers at number 1 and so on down to number 48. Merchant Taylors and Skinners, however, continued to switch between numbers 6 and 7 in alternate years,

following a compromise reached some 30 years earlier. Numbers 1 to 12 inclusive are known as the Great Twelve. Through choice, the companies of Parish Clerks and Watermen and Lightermen remain City Guilds without grant of livery.

Livery companies in order of precedence
Mercers (general merchants); Grocers; Drapers; Fishmongers; Goldsmiths; Merchant Taylors (tailors); Skinners (fur trade); Haberdashers; Salters; Ironmongers; Vintners; Clothworkers; Dyers; Brewers; Leathersellers; Pewterers; Barbers (also surgeons and dentists); Cutlers; Bakers; Waxchandlers; Tallowchandlers; Armourers and Brasiers (armour-makers and workers in brass); Girdlers (girdles and belts as clothing); Butchers; Saddlers; Carpenters; Cordwainers (workers in fine leather); Painter Stainers; Curriers (dressers of tanned leather); Masons; Plumbers; Innholders; Founders; Poulters; Cooks; Coopers (barrel makers); Tylers and Bricklayers; Bowyers (longbow makers); Fletchers (arrow makers); Blacksmiths; Joiners; Weavers; Woolmen (winders and packers of wool); Scriveners (writers of court letters and legal documents); Fruiterers; Plaisterers (plasterers); Stationers and Newspaper Makers; Broderers (embroiderers); Upholders (upholsterers); Musicians; Turners; Basketmakers; Glaziers; Horners; Farriers (shoers of horses/veterinary surgeons); Paviors (paving, highways); Loriners (stirrups and other harness for horses); Apothecaries (medicine); Shipwrights; Spectaclemakers; Clockmakers; Glovers; Feltmakers (hats); Framework Knitters; Needlemakers; Gardeners; Tinplate Workers; Wheelwrights; Distillers; Pattenmakers (makers of wooden clog-style footwear); Glass Sellers; Coachmakers and Coach Harness Makers; Gunmakers; Gold and Silver Wyre Drawers (gold and silver braid for uniforms); Makers of Playing Cards; Fan Makers; Carmen; Master Mariners; Solicitors; Farmers; Air Pilots and Air Navigators; Tobacco Pipe Makers and Tobacco Blenders; Furniture Makers; Scientific Instrument Makers; Chartered Surveyors; Chartered Accountants; Chartered Secretaries and Administrators; Builders Merchants; Launderers; Marketors; Actuaries; Insurers; Arbitrators; Engineers; Fuellers; Lightmongers; Environmental Cleaners; Chartered Architects; Constructors; Information Technologists.

London Royal Parks

London's royal parks are official public open spaces belonging to the crown. They are managed by the Royal Parks Agency, based in Hyde Park. Phone: (0171) 298 2000; fax: (0171) 298 2005.

Name	Park office	Notes
Brompton Cemetery	The Chapel Office, Brompton Cemetery, Fulham Road, London SW10 9UG; phone: (0171) 352 1201	laid out in 1840 by Benjamin Baud; has a central avenue leading to an octagonal chapel with flanking colonnades; catacombs run under the colonnades and along the west wall; around 205,000 burials have been recorded with an estimated 35,000 headstones; burial record search (small fee includes map and location of grave)
Bushy Park and Longford River	Stockyard Education Centre, Bushy Park, Hampton Court Road, Hampton Hill, Middlesex TW12 2EJ; phone: (0181) 979 1586; fax: (0181) 941 8196	enclosed by Cardinal Wolsey and Henry VIII between 1500 and 1537; Longford River is an artificial waterway created by Charles I in 1639 and running from the River Colne, beyond Heathrow Airport, to the River Thames at Hampton
Greenwich Park	Park Manager, Blackheath Gate, Greenwich Park, London SE10 8QY; phone: (0181) 858 2608; fax: (0181) 293 3782	created in 1433, the first Royal Park to be enclosed; the Old Royal observatory; observatory planetarium (by appointment)
Hyde Park	Park Manager, Rangers Lodge, Hyde Park, London W2 2UH; phone: (0171) 298 2100; fax: (0171) 402 3298	came into existence in 1536; has a tradition of events and public spectacles; gun salutes are fired from the Parade Ground of Knightsbridge barracks on its boundary
Kensington Gardens	Park Manager, Magazine Storeyard, Magazine Gate, Kensington Gardens, London W2 2UH; phone: (0171) 724 2826	formed from land taken from Hyde Park in 1689; Serpentine Gallery
Regent's Park and Primrose Hill	Park Manager, The Store Yard, Inner Circle, Regent's Park, London NW1 4NR; phone: (0171) 486 7905; fax: (0171) 224 1895	royal chase until 1646; the park started to evolve in 1811 with the plans of John Nash, crown architect; also contains the London Zoo; open air theatre
Richmond Park	Superintendent's Office, Holly Lodge, Bog Lodge Yard, Richmond Park, Surrey TW10 5HS; phone: (0181) 948 3209; fax: (0181) 332 2730	enclosed as a hunting park by Charles I in 1637; herds of fallow and red deer roam the park; in 1992 the park was notified as a Site of Special Scientific Interest by English Nature; Pen Ponds
St James's Park and Green Park	Park Manager, The Storeyard, St James's Park, Horse Guards Parade, London SW1A 2BJ; phone (0171) 930 1793; fax: (0171) 839 7639	these two parks lying to the east of Buckingham Palace were acquired by Henry VIII in 1536; provide the backdrop for British ceremonial life with The Mall, the processional route between the Palace and Whitehall and Horse Guards Parade, the venue for major ceremonial occasions

Population and Demography

Population Changes in the UK

Year	Population at start of period[1]	Average annual change				
		Overall annual change (increase)	Births	Deaths[2]	Excess of births over deaths	Net migration and other adjustments[3]
1901–11	38,237,000	385,000	1,091,000	624,000	467,000	–82,000
1911–21	42,082,000	195,000	975,000	689,000	286,000	–92,000
1921–31	44,027,000	201,000	824,000	555,000	268,000	–67,000
1931–51	46,038,000	213,000	793,000	603,000	190,000	22,000
1951–61	50,225,000	258,000	839,000	593,000	246,000	12,000
1961–71	52,807,000	230,000	962,000	638,000	324,000	–14,000
1971–81	55,928,000	42,000	736,000	666,000	69,000	–27,000
1981–91	56,352,000	146,000	757,000	655,000	103,000	43,000
1991–97	57,808,000	200,000	753,000	640,000	114,000	87,000
1997–2001[4]	59,009,000	154,000	719,000	634,000	85,000	69,000
2001–11	59,618,000	131,000	690,000	624,000	66,000	65,000
2011–21	60,929,000	131,000	694,000	628,000	66,000	65,000

[1] Figures give census-enumerated population up to 1951, mid-year estimates of resident population from 1961 to 1996, and mid-1996-based projections of resident population thereafter.

[2] Figures include deaths of non-civilians and merchant seamen who died outside the country. These deaths numbered 577,000 in 1911–21 and 240,000 in 1931–51 for England and Wales; 74,000 in 1911–21, and 34,000 in 1931–51 for Scotland; and 10,000 in 1911–26 for Northern Ireland.

[3] Other adjustments include changes in census visitor balance, in Armed Forces, asylum seekers, etc.

[4] Figures are 1996-based national population projections.

Source: *Annual Abstract of Statistics 1999,* © Crown copyright 1999

Population Summary of the UK

Year	Women	Men	Total
Enumerated Population: Census Figures			
1851	11,404,000	10,855,000	22,259,000
1901	19,745,000	18,492,000	38,237,000
1911	21,725,000	20,357,000	42,082,000
1921	22,994,000	21,033,000	44,027,000
1931	23,978,000	22,060,000	46,038,000
1951	26,107,000	24,118,000	50,225,000
1961	27,228,000	25,481,000	52,709,000
Resident Population: Mid-Year Estimates			
1964	27,800,000	26,191,000	53,991,000
1965	27,982,000	26,368,000	54,350,000
1966	28,132,000	26,511,000	54,643,000
1967	28,286,000	26,673,000	54,214,000
1968	28,429,000	26,784,000	55,214,000
1969	28,553,000	26,908,000	55,461,000
1970	28,641,000	26,992,000	55,632,000
1971	28,761,000	27,167,000	55,928,000
1972	28,837,000	27,259,000	56,709,000
1973	28,891,000	27,332,000	56,223,000
1974	28,887,000	27,349,000	56,236,000
1975	28,865,000	27,361,000	56,226,000
1976	28,856,000	27,360,000	56,216,000
1977	28,845,000	27,345,000	56,190,000
1978	28,849,000	27,330,000	56,178,000
1979	28,867,000	27,373,000	56,240,000
1980	28,919,000	27,411,000	56,330,000
1981	28,943,000	27,409,000	56,352,000
1982	28,927,000	27,391,000	56,318,000
1983	28,948,000	27,429,000	56,377,000
1984	28,995,000	27,511,000	56,506,000
1985	29,074,000	27,611,000	56,685,000
1986	29,153,000	27,698,000	56,852,000
1987	29,220,000	27,789,000	57,009,000
1988	29,282,000	27,876,000	57,158,000
1989	29,368,000	27,989,000	57,358,000
1990	29,443,000	28,118,000	57,561,000
1991	29,562,000	28,246,000	57,808,000
1992	29,645,000	28,362,000	58,006,000
1993	29,718,000	28,474,000	58,191,000
1994	29,803,000	28,592,000	58,395,000
1995	29,878,000	28,727,000	58,606,000
1996	29,946,000	28,856,000	58,801,000
1997	30,019,000	28,990,000	59,009,000
Resident Population: Projections (Mid-Year)[1]			
2001	30,241,000	29,377,000	59,618,000
2006	30,477,000	29,809,000	60,287,000
2011	30,723,000	30,206,000	60,929,000
2021	31,328,000	30,916,000	62,244,000

[1] These projections are 1996-based.

Source: *Annual Abstract of Statistics 1999,* © Crown copyright 1998

Age Distribution in the UK

1997

Age	Male	Female	Total
Under 1	377,000	359,000	736,000
1–4	1,526,000	1,450,000	2,977,000
5–9	2,017,000	1,917,000	3,934,000
10–14	1,915,000	1,716,000	3,731,000
15–19	1,845,000	1,746,000	3,592,000
20–29	4,159,000	3,961,000	8,120,000
30–44	6,663,000	6,501,000	13,165,000
45–59	5,329,000	5,374,000	10,702,000
60–64	1,361,000	1,422,000	2,783,000
65–74	2,299,000	2,707,000	5,006,000
75–84	1,215,000	1,960,000	3,175,000
85 and over	282,000	806,000	1,088,000
School ages (5–15)	4,305,000	4,086,000	8,392,000
Under 18	6,970,000	6,617,000	13,586,000
Pensionable age[1]	3,796,000	6,894,000	10,691,000
All ages	28,990,000	30,019,000	59,009,000

[1] The pensionable age population is that over state retirement age.

Source: *Annual Abstract of Statistics 1999,* © Crown copyright 1999

Ethnic Groups in Great Britain

Average over the period summer 1997 to spring 1998.

Ethnic group		Number
Black		
Caribbean		531,000
African		351,000
other (non-mixed)		127,000
mixed		177,000
Indian		929,000
Pakistani		580,000
Bangladeshi		208,000
Chinese		162,000
Other	Asian (non-mixed)	199,000
	other (non-mixed)	142,000
	mixed	215,000
All ethnic minority groups		3,623,000
White		52,963,000
All ethnic groups[1]		56,602,000

[1] Figure includes ethnic groups not stated.

Source: *Annual Abstract of Statistics 1999,* © Crown copyright 1999

Migration into and out of the UK

Year	Inflow	Outflow	Balance
1985	232,000	174,000	59,000
1986	250,000	213,000	37,000
1987	212,000	210,000	2,000
1988	216,000	237,000	–21,000
1989	250,000	205,000	44,000
1990	267,000	231,000	36,000
1991	267,000	239,000	28,000
1992	216,000	227,000	–11,000
1993	213,000	216,000	–2,000
1994	253,000	191,000	62,000
1995	245,000	192,000	54,000
1996	272,000	216,000	56,000

Source: *Annual Abstract of Statistics 1999,* © Crown copyright 1999

Life Expectancy in the UK

Figures show the average future lifespan that would be lived by a person at the age given in the first column.

Age	Male	Female	Age	Male	Female
0	74.1	79.4	45	31.3	35.8
5	69.7	74.9	50	26.8	31.2
10	64.8	69.9	55	22.4	26.7
15	59.8	65.0	60	18.4	22.4
20	55.0	60.1	65	14.7	18.3
25	50.3	55.1	70	11.5	14.6
30	45.5	50.2	75	8.8	11.3
35	40.7	45.4	80	6.6	8.5
40	36.0	40.5	85	4.9	6.2

Source: *Annual Abstract of Statistics 1998,* © Crown copyright 1998

Death Rates per 1,000 Population in the UK

(N/A = not available.)

Year	0–4	5–9	10–14	15–19	20–24	25–34	35–44	45–54	55–64	65–74	75–84	85 and over	All ages
Men													
1900–02	57.0	4.1	2.4	3.7	5.0	6.6	11.0	18.6	35.0	69.9	143.6	289.6	18.4
1910–12	40.5	3.3	2.0	3.0	3.9	5.0	8.0	14.9	29.8	62.1	133.8	261.5	14.9
1920–22	33.4	2.9	1.8	2.9	3.9	4.5	6.9	11.9	25.3	57.8	131.8	259.1	13.5
1930–32	22.3	2.3	1.5	2.6	3.3	3.5	5.7	11.3	23.7	57.9	134.2	277.0	12.9
1940–42	N/A	N/A	N/A	N/A	N/A	N/A	N/A	N/A	N/A	N/A	N/A	N/A	N/A
1950–52	7.7	0.7	0.5	0.9	1.4	1.6	3.0	8.5	23.2	55.2	127.6	272.0	12.6
1960–62	6.4	0.5	0.4	0.9	1.1	1.1	2.5	7.4	22.2	54.4	123.4	251.0	12.5
1970–72	4.6	0.4	0.4	0.9	1.0	1.0	2.4	7.3	20.9	52.9	116.3	246.1	12.4
1980–82	3.2	0.3	0.3	0.8	0.9	0.9	1.9	6.3	18.2	46.7	107.1	224.9	12.1
1990–92	2.0	0.2	0.2	0.7	0.9	0.9	1.8	4.6	14.3	38.7	92.9	195.7	11.1
1997	1.5	0.1	0.2	0.6	0.9	1.0	1.6	4.1	11.8	33.9	83.4	191.9	10.4

(continued)

Death Rates per 1,000 Population in the UK (*continued*)

Year	0–4	5–9	10–14	15–19	20–24	25–34	35–44	45–54	55–64	65–74	75–84	85 and over	All ages
Women													
1900–02	47.9	4.3	2.6	3.5	4.3	5.8	9.0	14.4	27.9	59.3	127.0	262.6	16.3
1910–12	34.0	3.3	2.1	2.9	3.4	4.4	6.7	11.5	23.1	50.7	113.7	234.0	13.3
1920–22	26.9	2.8	1.9	2.8	3.4	4.1	5.6	9.3	19.2	45.6	111.5	232.4	11.9
1930–32	17.7	2.1	1.5	2.4	2.9	3.3	4.6	8.3	17.6	43.7	110.1	246.3	11.5
1940–42	N/A	N/A	N/A	N/A	N/A	N/A	N/A	N/A	N/A	N/A	N/A	N/A	N/A
1950–52	6.0	0.5	0.4	0.7	1.0	1.4	2.3	5.3	12.9	35.5	98.4	228.8	11.2
1960–62	4.9	0.3	0.3	0.4	0.5	0.8	1.8	4.5	11.0	30.8	87.3	218.5	11.2
1970–72	3.6	0.3	0.2	0.4	0.4	0.6	1.6	4.5	10.5	27.5	76.7	196.1	11.3
1980–82	2.3	0.2	0.2	0.3	0.4	0.5	1.3	3.9	9.9	24.8	67.2	179.5	11.4
1990–92	1.6	0.1	0.2	0.3	0.3	0.4	1.1	2.9	8.4	22.2	58.5	154.6	11.1
1997	1.2	0.1	0.1	0.3	0.3	0.4	1.1	2.7	7.1	20.6	55.2	153.9	11.0

Source: *Annual Abstract of Statistics 1999,* © Crown copyright 1999

Infant and Maternal Mortality in the UK

(Per 1,000 live births.)

Year	Deaths of infants under one year	Maternal deaths in pregnancy and childbirth
1900–02	142	4.71
1910–12	110	3.95
1920–22	82	4.37
1930–32	67	4.54
1940–42	59	3.29
1950–52	30	0.88
1960–62	22	0.36
1970–72	18	0.17
1980–82	12	0.09
1990–92	7	0.07
1997	5.8	0.06

Source: *Annual Abstract of Statistics 1999,* © Crown copyright 1999

Abortions in Great Britain

1997[1]

Age	England and Wales	Scotland
Under 15	1,019	85
15	2,411	204
16–19	29,927	2,428
20–24	44,926	3,434
25–29	40,129	2,643
30–34	28,862	1,852
35–39	16,838	1,090
40–44	5,411	320
45 and over	482	24
All ages	170,005	12,080

[1] Provisional data.

Source: *Annual Abstract of Statistics 1999,* © Crown copyright 1999

Households by Type of Occupancy in Great Britain

A household is defined as a person or group of persons residing at the same address. Figures are expressed as percentages of the total.

Household		1961	1971	1981	1991	1998
One person	under pensionable age	4	6	8	11	14
	over pensionable age	7	12	14	16	14
Two or more unrelated adults		5	4	5	3	3
Single family households[1]	couple, no children	26	27	26	28	28
	couple, one or two dependent children[2]	30	26	25	20	19
	couple, three or more dependent children[2]	8	9	6	5	4
	couple, non-dependent children only	10	8	8	8	7
	lone parent, dependent children[2]	2	3	5	6	7
	lone parent, non-dependent children only	4	4	4	4	3
Multi-family households		3	1	1	1	1
All households[3]		16.3	18.6	20.2	22.4	23.6

[1] Other individuals who were not family members may be included.
[2] May also include non-dependent children.
[3] Includes couples of the same gender in 1998.

Source: *Social Trends 29,* © Crown copyright 1999

See Also  **Birth, Marriage, and Death, pp. 836–842.**

How We Live Now: The Individual in Society

BY SIMON BUCKBY

The dramatic increases in levels of personal education and income over the 20th century have greatly increased life choices for many, but not all, people in the developed world. Unfortunately, this empowerment of the individual and its concomitant consumer culture have spawned a glut of problems. These range from those affecting daily life, such as pollution, to the breakdown of the family- and church-based structure of Western society.

Life and death

Thanks to social reforms, medical advances, and healthier diets, life expectancy is now generally much higher than a century ago, although there is a growing difference in life expectancy between rich and poor. Regardless of social class, children are now usually being educated until they are at least 16, and the numbers entering tertiary education are rising. These years of education are delaying significantly the age at which people start work. Thanks also to the widespread use of contraception since the 1960s, women are choosing to have children later in life, and also to have fewer than previous generations. Rising life expectancy and lower birth rates mean that in industrialized countries the population growth rate is beginning to slow down and even fall, and that the average age of the population is rising dramatically.

These demographic shifts are having a profound impact. For example, governments are becoming increasingly worried about the cost of providing pensions and health care for the elderly. Since young adults have started having fewer children and exploiting their independence, an economically and socially powerful youth culture has emerged.

Greater wealth and equality of opportunity ... will mean even more independence and choice for most.

At work and at home

Equal education, equal opportunities legislation, and the decline in factory work (traditionally a male preserve) coupled with a rise in service industry jobs, mean that about 40 percent of the workforce is now female. This change has transformed the traditional role of women in the family. The family unit has also been affected (in the UK) by changes in the law in the 1960s that made divorce easier. In just one generation, the number of marriages halved, the number of divorces trebled, and the proportion of children born outside marriage quadrupled to a third of all births.

The family is also being revolutionized by the increasing proportion of people becoming single parents (whether through choice or divorce). As recently as 1970, fewer than one in ten families was headed by a single parent, but in some countries that has doubled to more than one in five; in addition, more children are being raised in stepfamilies. Increasingly, adults are living alone, with friends, in same-gender relationships, or with new spouses, and the 'model' family is becoming a thing of the past.

Inner city life

The move towards 'urbanization' is set to continue as people become more mobile, moving to cities, sometimes in other countries, in search of jobs. The bulk of the 50 percent rise in the number of dwellings built in the industrialized world over the last four decades has been concentrated in urban areas. Governments of densely populated countries find themselves with the problem of allowing a sufficient number of new houses to be built without damaging the environment. Growing ethnic diversity has given rise to multicultural understanding in certain quarters and racial tensions in others, the latter worsened through overcrowding. Traffic congestion means that average street speeds are little faster than those in the days of the horse and cart.

Cities are a focus for illegal drugs, and where the poor are at their most visible. Cities also suffer the highest rates of crime: more than half of property crimes affect only one fifth of any community in the developed world, and tend to occur in the poorer parts of urban areas. Although the crime rate rose in all the developed economies by about 5 percent per year from 1920 onwards, it stabilized in the early 1990s and in some cases even started to fall.

Consumer culture

The consumer revolution began when 'white goods', such as washing machines and refrigerators, became more generally available from the 1950s; central heating, telephones, and other home comforts followed. Cheap holidays abroad and television (a rival to the cinema and theatre) have transformed our leisure activities, as have video recorders, satellite dishes, compact disc players, home computers, and Internet access. The number of Internet subscribers and mobile phone users is increasing rapidly. Material possessions account for a rising proportion of people's incomes, although the biggest weekly household bill is still for food and drink.

Yet modern comforts are not available to all. As societies have become wealthier, the gap between the richest and the poorest has grown. In parts of Europe, for instance, the richest 1 percent of adults owns about 20 percent of the total marketable wealth, while the poorest half owns less than 10 percent of the total. Those in the middle third or richest third of the population have seen their incomes grow substantially in the past 20 years; those in the bottom third have not, leaving them relatively worse off. This has led to concern that the homeless, the unemployed, and those dependent on welfare payments are becoming cut off from mainstream society in an 'underclass'.

Life in the third millennium

It seems that the rate of technological and social change will become even faster in the new millennium. Greater wealth and equality of opportunity, together with easier access to education, will mean even more independence and choice for most. Developments in the 20th century brought about a huge and positive increase in individual freedom, yet this is now often in conflict with the institutions that govern society. It is by no means clear how these institutions could be reformed or social stability and moral order maintained without compromising individual freedom. If no solution is found, and if the gap between the richest and the poorest continues to grow as quickly as it has in recent decades, individuals may have a less harmonious relationship with each other than they have had in the past.

Simon Buckby is the director of the Britain in Europe Group and former social affairs correspondent for the Financial Times.

The Richest and Poorest Regions of the UK

Data are for GDP per head at factor cost (excluding taxes on expenditure and subsidies). Figures are index numbers where UK=100.

Region	1986	1996
Northeast	86	85
Northwest and Merseyside	95	91
Yorkshire and the Humber	95	89
East Midlands	98	94
West Midlands	91	94
Eastern	110	109
London	123	123
Southeast	109	114
Southwest	94	95
England	102	102
Wales	86	83
Scotland	95	99
Northern Ireland	79	81

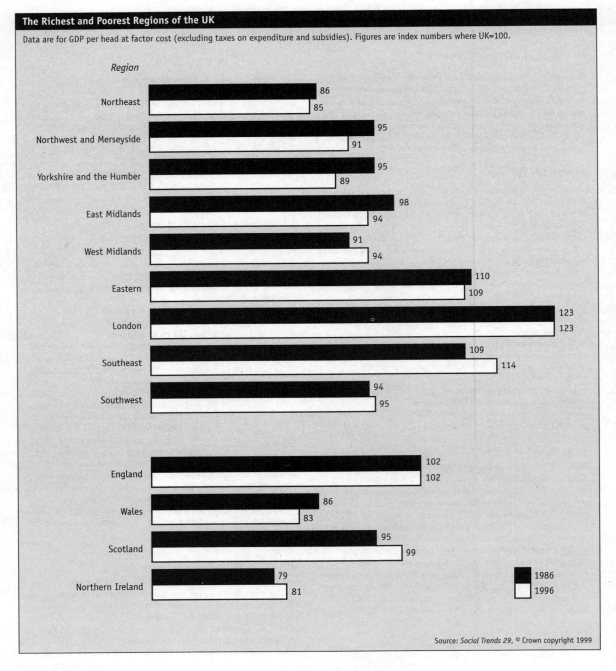

Source: *Social Trends 29*, © Crown copyright 1999

Individual Distribution of Wealth in the UK

Marketable wealth owned by sectors of the population (adults aged 18 and over). Figures are expressed as percentages of the total.

	1976	1981	1986	1991	1994	1995
Most wealthy 1%	21	18	18	17	19	19
Most wealthy 5%	38	36	36	35	38	38
Most wealthy 10%	50	50	50	47	51	50
Most wealthy 25%	71	73	73	71	73	73
Most wealthy 50%	92	92	90	92	93	92

Source: *Social Trends 29*, © Crown copyright 1999

Life in the UK – Yesterday and Today

(– = not applicable.)

	May 1979	May 1989	May 1999
Leaders and Economy			
Government	Conservative	Conservative	Labour
Prime Minister	Margaret Thatcher	Margaret Thatcher	Tony Blair
Chancellor of the Exchequer	Geoffrey Howe	Nigel Lawson	Gordon Brown
Inflation rate	13.4%	7.8%	3.4%
Interest rate	12%	13.75%	5.5%
Unemployment	1.86 million 4.1%	1.81 million 6.1%	1.31 million 4.6%
Women in the workforce	44%	49%	51%
Average income	£5,000	£11,700	£19,000
Average manager's income	£9,000	£25,700	£36,400
What Things Cost			
Average house price in Britain	£19,800	£61,500	£68,300
Price of a loaf of bread	28p	48p	51p
Price of a Mars bar	14p	22p	25p
Price of a pint of beer	38p	91p	£1.73
What We Liked			
Most popular car	Ford Cortina	Ford Fiesta	Ford Focus
Most popular wine	Hirondelle	Piat d'Or	Jacob's Creek
Popular TV programmes	*Blankety Blank, Top of the Pops, Little and Large Show*	*Coronation Street, Neighbours, EastEnders, The Bill*	*EastEnders, Coronation Street, Emmerdale, Stars in their Eyes*
Popular leisure activities	Gardening (59%), dancing (58%), eating out (42%)	Pubs/bars (55%), eating out (47%), DIY (44%)	Pubs/bars (74%), eating out (69%), gardening (52%)
Most popular holiday destination	Spain (visited by 1.9 million)	Spain (visited by 5.7 million)	Spain (visited by 7.7 million)
What We Owned (% of Individuals/Households)			
Cars	60	68	70
Houses	52	66	68
Telephones	75	88	93
Colour televisions	74	95	98
Washing machines	74	87	91
Videos	–	60	82
Home computers	–	19	27
CD players	–	15	58

Source: *The Independent*

Employment and Unemployment

Distribution of the Workforce in the UK

Figures are the number at mid-June of each year.

Category	1992	1993	1994	1995	1996	1997	1998
Workforce[1]	28,483,000	28,279,000	28,404,000	28,356,000	28,471,000	28,368,000	28,368,000
Unemployed[2]	2,734,000	2,919,000	2,644,000	2,308,000	2,146,000	1,598,000	1,361,000
Workforce in employment[3]	25,749,000	25,360,000	25,760,000	26,048,000	26,325,000	26,770,000	27,025,000
HM forces[4]	290,000	271,000	250,000	230,000	221,000	210,000	210,000
Self-employed persons[5]	3,230,000	3,190,000	3,545,000	3,605,000	3,601,000	3,589,000	3,477,000
Employees in employment[6]	21,904,000	21,588,000	21,663,000	21,987,000	22,322,000	22,812,000	23,220,000
Work-related government-supported training programmes[7]	325,000	311,000	302,000	225,000	181,000	159,000	118,000

[1] Data are for workforce in employment plus the claimant unemployed.

[2] Claimant unemployed: those people who were claiming unemployment benefits (Unemployment Benefit, Income Support, or National Insurance Credits) at Employment Service local offices on the day of the monthly count.

[3] Figures include employees in employment, the self-employed, HM forces, and work-related government-supported training programmes.

[4] Data give total number of UK service personnel in HM Regular Forces, wherever serving, and include those on release leave (MoD figures).

[5] Figures include self-employed persons with and without employees and are based on results of the Labour Force Survey. Northern Ireland estimates are not seasonally adjusted.

[6] For all dates, individuals with two jobs as employees of different employers are counted twice.

[7] Figures include all participants on work-related government-supported training programmes who are receiving some work experience on their placement but do not have a contract of employment. The numbers are not subject to seasonal adjustment.

Source: *Annual Abstract of Statistics 1999*, © Crown copyright 1999

Labour Force by Gender and Age in the UK

(In millions.)

Year	16–24	25–44	45–54	55–59	60–64	65 + over	All aged + over
Men							
1971	3.0	6.5	3.2	1.5	1.3	0.6	16.0
1981	3.2	7.1	3.0	1.4	1.0	0.3	16.0
1991	3.1	8.1	3.0	1.1	0.8	0.3	16.4
1997	2.4	8.1	3.4	1.1	0.7	0.3	16.0
2001[1]	2.4	8.2	3.4	1.3	0.7	0.3	16.3
2011[1]	2.8	7.3	3.9	1.3	0.9	0.3	16.5

Year	16–24	25–44	45–54	55–59	60–64	65 + over	All aged + over
Women							
1971	2.3	3.5	2.1	0.9	0.5	0.3	10.0
1981	2.7	4.6	2.1	0.9	0.4	0.2	10.9
1991	2.6	6.1	2.4	0.8	0.3	0.2	12.4
1997	2.0	6.4	2.9	0.8	0.4	0.2	12.7
2001[1]	2.1	6.4	3.0	0.9	0.4	0.2	13.1
2011[1]	2.3	6.2	3.6	1.0	0.7	0.2	14.1

[1] Data for 2001 and 2011 are based on the spring 1996 Labour Force Survey and mid-1996 based population projections.

Source: *Social Trends 29*, © Crown copyright 1999

Employment by Industry and Gender in the UK

As of September 1996. (N = nil or negligible. In percentages unless otherwise indicated.)

Region	Agriculture, hunting, forestry, and fishing	Mining and quarrying (including oil and gas extraction)	Manufacturing	Electricity, gas, and water	Construction	Distribution, hotels and catering, repairs	Transport, storage, and communication	Financial and business services	Public administration and defence	Education, social work, and health services	Other	Whole economy = 100 % (numbers)
Men												
England												
Northeast	1.1	1.1	33.5	0.9	9.5	15.0	7.8	9.4	7.2	10.3	4.1	443,000
Northwest	1.5	0.2	31.8	1.1	6.3	19.6	8.7	13.1	5.3	8.5	3.6	1,046,000
Merseyside	0.4	0.1	23.2	0.7	5.8	21.0	9.5	12.8	8.7	12.9	4.9	201,000

(continued)

Employment by Industry and Gender in the UK (*continued*)

Region	Agriculture, hunting, forestry, and fishing	Mining and quarrying (including oil and gas extraction)	Manufacturing	Electricity, gas, and water	Construction	Distribution, hotels and catering, repairs	Transport, storage, and communication	Financial and business services	Public administration and defence	Education, social work, and health services	Other	Whole economy = 100 % (numbers)
Yorkshire and the Humber	1.9	0.8	32.5	1.0	7.1	18.9	8.1	11.4	5.5	9.1	3.7	922,000
East Midlands	2.5	2.8	35.3	1.1	5.9	18.4	7.2	10.7	4.4	8.5	3.2	807,000
West Midlands	1.8	0.3	38.3	0.8	5.6	18.2	7.2	12.3	4.9	7.6	3.0	1,083,000
Eastern	3.2	0.4	26.1	0.9	5.5	21.2	9.6	16.0	4.8	8.5	3.7	972,000
London	0.1	0.2	10.8	0.4	4.3	20.6	11.7	30.5	7.2	8.2	5.8	1,682,000
Southeast	2.3	0.3	20.5	1.0	5.1	22.6	9.1	19.9	6.3	9.3	3.6	1,533,000
Southwest	3.2	0.6	25.7	1.4	5.2	21.4	7.5	13.9	7.3	9.7	4.0	867,000
England total	1.8	0.6	26.2	0.9	5.7	20.1	8.9	17.0	6.0	8.8	4.0	9,554,000
Wales	3.1	0.8	32.5	1.3	6.2	16.6	6.8	8.3	8.2	11.6	4.5	479,000
Scotland	2.8	2.2	21.9	1.4	9.9	19.7	8.0	12.0	7.1	10.6	4.4	988,000
Northern Ireland	5.8	0.6	24.6	1.4	7.1	18.4	6.0	7.2	12.5	11.6	4.8	286,000
UK TOTAL	2.1	0.8	26.0	1.0	6.1	19.9	8.7	15.9	6.3	9.2	4.1	11,308,000
Women												
England												
Northeast	0.4	0.1	11.7	0.4	1.2	25.5	2.5	13.3	8.7	31.0	5.3	449,000
Northwest	0.5	N	11.9	0.4	1.3	26.0	2.7	15.5	5.8	31.5	4.4	1,061,000
Merseyside	0.1	N	8.5	0.1	0.9	23.8	2.5	16.2	7.9	34.3	5.7	230,000
Yorkshire and the Humber	0.5	0.1	12.3	0.3	1.3	26.7	2.6	16.2	5.9	29.2	4.8	930,000
East Midlands	0.7	0.7	17.0	0.3	1.2	24.3	2.4	14.4	4.8	29.5	4.6	791,000
West Midlands	0.6	N	14.5	0.3	1.0	25.0	2.5	17.3	5.3	28.9	4.6	1,005,000
Eastern	1.0	0.1	10.4	0.3	1.0	26.5	3.3	18.4	4.7	29.4	4.8	955,000
London	0.1	0.1	5.8	0.2	0.8	22.1	4.4	30.8	6.4	23.4	6.0	1,587,000
Southeast	0.8	0.1	7.9	0.3	1.0	26.0	3.6	20.8	5.1	29.6	4.8	1,536,000
Southwest	1.1	N	8.6	0.4	0.9	27.9	2.3	17.1	6.1	30.9	4.6	900,000
England total	0.6	0.1	10.4	0.3	1.1	25.3	3.1	19.5	5.8	28.9	4.9	9,444,000
Wales	1.0	0.1	11.4	0.3	1.3	24.3	1.6	12.0	9.0	33.8	5.1	498,000
Scotland	0.5	0.3	9.7	0.3	1.4	26.0	2.5	15.8	7.0	31.4	4.9	1,007,000
Northern Ireland	0.8	0.1	11.5	0.2	0.8	22.0	1.8	9.2	8.3	41.0	4.3	291,000
UK TOTAL	0.6	0.1	10.4	0.3	1.1	25.3	2.9	18.5	6.1	29.7	4.9	11,239,000

Source: *Regional Trends 33,* © Crown copyright 1998

Economic Activity of Women with Children in the UK

In percentages unless otherwise indicated. As of spring 1998. (– = not applicable).

Status	Age of youngest dependent child: Under 5	5–10	11–15	16–18[1]	No dependent children	All women[2]
Not married/cohabiting[3]						
Working full time	9	18	30	44	47	39
Working part time	18	31	30	30	20	21
Unemployed[4]	9	9	7	–	5	6
Economically inactive	64	41	33	20	28	33
Total (millions)	0.7	0.6	0.3	0.1	4.4	6.1
Married/cohabiting						
Working full time	20	26	36	40	49	37
Working part time	37	48	42	41	26	34
Unemployed[4]	4	3	2	–	2	3
Economically inactive	40	23	20	17	23	26
Total (millions)	2.4	1.6	1.2	0.5	5.2	10.9

[1] Those in full-time education.
[2] Aged 16 to 59.
[3] Includes single, widowed, separated, or divorced.
[4] Based on the International Labour Organization definition.

Source: *Social Trends 29,* © Crown copyright 1999

Average Weekly Earnings by Region and Gender in the UK

As of April 1996. Data relate to full-time employees on adult rates whose pay for the survey pay-period was not affected by absence. (In pounds.)

Region	Average gross weekly earnings					
	Manual male employees	Non-manual male employees	All full-time male employees	Manual female employees	Non-manual female employees	All full time female employees
England						
Northeast	306.3	423.3	360.1	201.2	286.4	269.0
Northwest	311.2	455.7	387.4	198.3	294.3	275.8
Merseyside	318.7	435.9	381.7	205.8	295.1	284.4
Yorkshire and the Humber	305.0	424.6	363.9	189.9	287.7	268.9
East Midlands	311.0	429.1	369.2	191.5	284.4	260.3
West Midlands	311.7	441.4	375.4	193.1	290.3	268.5
Eastern	320.0	463.6	399.5	207.2	313.2	295.9
London	351.0	614.0	541.3	232.6	402.7	386.3
Southeast	320.5	494.1	428.3	215.7	323.0	306.5
Southwest	297.7	450.3	382.4	189.4	293.2	274.8
England average	315.6	489.3	414.0	202.4	321.6	301.3
Wales	312.3	420.2	363.5	196.2	289.5	269.0
Scotland	303.3	449.8	378.0	193.9	293.9	272.4
Northern Ireland	269.2	431.3	355.9	173.3	286.1	265.2
UK AVERAGE	313.1	482.2	407.3	200.2	316.9	296.2

Source: *Regional Trends 33*,

Average Weekly Earnings and Hours in the UK

Data relate to full-time employees on adult rates.

Year	Manufacturing industries: Weekly earnings (£): Including those whose pay was affected by absence	Manufacturing industries: Weekly earnings (£): Excluding those whose pay was affected by absence	Manufacturing industries: Hours[1]	Manufacturing industries: Hourly earnings (£)[1]: Including overtime pay and overtime hours	Manufacturing industries: Hourly earnings (£)[1]: Excluding overtime pay and overtime hours	All industries and services: Weekly earnings (£): Including those whose pay was affected by absence	All industries and services: Weekly earnings (£): Excluding those whose pay was affected by absence	All industries and services: Hours[1]	All industries and services: Hourly earnings (£)[1]: Including overtime pay and overtime hours	All industries and services: Hourly earnings (£)[1]: Excluding overtime pay and overtime hours
Men										
1988	236.3	242.3	43.3	5.50	5.44	240.6	245.8	42.1	5.74	5.73
1989	257.3	264.6	43.6	5.98	5.94	263.5	269.5	42.3	6.28	6.29
1990	282.2	289.2	43.4	6.55	6.50	290.2	295.6	42.2	6.88	6.89
1991	299.5	308.1	42.1	7.20	7.15	312.9	318.9	41.5	7.55	7.57
1992	319.8	328.3	42.3	7.62	7.58	333.6	340.1	41.4	8.07	8.10
1993	334.8	342.7	42.1	7.99	7.95	347.3	353.5	41.3	8.44	8.47
1994	343.0	350.9	42.5	8.16	8.12	355.6	362.1	41.6	8.61	8.65
1995	358.0	364.0	43.0	8.44	8.41	369.0	374.6	41.9	8.91	8.97
1996	373.5	380.0	42.7	8.86	8.81	385.9	391.3	41.7	9.33	9.38
1997	386.7	392.7	42.8	9.17	9.12	403.2	408.7	41.8	9.74	9.82
1998	408.4	416.8	42.6	9.75	9.72	420.3	427.1	41.7	10.20	10.26

(continued)

Average Weekly Earnings and Hours in the UK (*continued*)

Year	Manufacturing industries					All industries and services				
	Weekly earnings (£)		Hours[1]	Hourly earnings (£)[1]		Weekly earnings (£)		Hours[1]	Hourly earnings (£)[1]	
	Including those whose pay was affected by absence	Excluding those whose pay was affected by absence		Including overtime pay and overtime hours	Excluding overtime pay and overtime hours	Including those whose pay was affected by absence	Excluding those whose pay was affected by absence		Including overtime pay and overtime hours	Excluding overtime pay and overtime hours
Women										
1988	138.4	144.3	39.2	3.66	3.62	160.1	164.2	37.6	4.31	4.29
1989	152.7	159.1	39.1	4.04	4.00	178.1	182.3	37.6	4.80	4.78
1990	170.3	177.1	39.1	4.48	4.44	197.0	201.5	37.5	5.30	5.28
1991	184.2	192.9	38.8	4.94	4.91	217.2	222.4	37.4	5.91	5.89
1992	199.3	207.1	38.9	5.28	5.24	235.8	241.1	37.3	6.40	6.38
1993	211.0	220.0	38.9	5.61	5.57	246.9	252.6	37.4	6.70	6.68
1994	218.3	226.8	39.1	5.76	5.72	255.8	261.5	37.6	6.89	6.88
1995	229.2	236.7	39.4	6.01	5.96	264.2	269.8	37.6	7.15	7.14
1996	239.2	246.7	39.3	6.27	6.23	277.9	283.0	37.6	7.51	7.49
1997	251.5	258.8	39.2	6.60	6.56	291.7	297.2	37.6	7.88	7.88
1998	266.4	274.5	39.2	7.01	6.97	303.7	309.6	37.6	8.23	8.22
Average										
1988	212.7	219.4	42.3	5.09	5.02	213.6	218.4	40.6	5.29	5.26
1989	231.7	239.5	42.5	5.55	5.48	234.3	239.7	40.7	5.81	5.79
1990	255.1	262.8	42.4	6.09	6.01	258.0	263.1	40.5	6.37	6.34
1991	271.3	280.7	41.3	6.69	6.62	278.9	284.7	40.0	7.00	6.98
1992	290.7	299.7	41.5	7.09	7.02	298.5	304.6	39.9	7.50	7.49
1993	304.8	313.7	41.3	7.45	7.39	310.9	316.9	39.8	7.84	7.83
1994	312.7	321.6	41.7	7.62	7.55	319.3	325.7	40.1	8.03	8.03
1995	327.1	334.3	42.2	7.92	7.85	330.4	336.3	40.3	8.31	8.32
1996	341.9	349.3	41.9	8.29	8.22	346.0	351.5	40.2	8.70	8.71
1997	354.8	361.7	42.0	8.61	8.53	361.8	367.6	40.3	9.10	9.13
1998	375.4	384.5	41.8	9.17	9.10	377.8	384.5	40.2	9.53	9.54

[1] Excluding those whose pay was affected by absence.

Source: *Annual Abstract of Statistics 1999,* © Crown copyright 1999

Average Weekly Earnings and Hours in Great Britain

Earnings and hours are calculated in April for each year. Data relate to full-time employees on adult rates. (In pounds.)

Worker category		Average weekly earnings[1]		Average hours		Worker category		Average weekly earnings[1]		Average hours	
		1994	1998	1994	1998			1994	1998	1994	1998
Men	manual	280.7	328.5	44.7	45.0	Women	manual	181.9	210.8	40.1	40.2
	non-manual	428.2	506.1	38.9	39.1		non-manual	278.4	330.1	37.0	37.0
All men		362.1	427.1	41.6	41.7	**All women**		261.5	309.6	37.6	37.6
						TOTAL		325.7	384.5	40.1	40.2

[1] Figures exclude those whose pay was affected by absence.

Source: *Annual Abstract of Statistics 1999,* © Crown copyright 1999

Average Earnings Index in the UK

March 1996 = 100. Figures are as of December in the year given.
(n.e.c. = not elsewhere classified; N/A = not available.)

Industry	1996	1997	1998
Agriculture and forestry	N/A	N/A	N/A
Mining and quarrying	102.6	106.1	110.6
Food products, beverages, and tobacco	101.2	105.6	109.9
Textiles	104.1	107.0	108.7
Clothing, leather, and footwear	102.4	105.3	109.8
Wood, wood products, and other manufacturing n.e.c.	103.4	110.0	111.9
Pulp, paper products, printing, and publishing	102.7	106.4	111.1
Chemicals and chemical products	102.3	107.5	114.5
Rubber and plastic products	102.9	107.1	111.7
Other non-metallic mineral products	101.9	107.2	110.5
Basic metals	106.2	109.2	113.4
Fabricated metal products (excluding machinery)	102.5	106.7	108.5
Machinery and equipment n.e.c.	102.1	106.8	110.0
Electrical and optical equipment	102.7	107.1	112.5
Transport equipment	99.0	104.1	107.1
Electricity, gas, and water supply	103.2	102.5	104.5
Construction	100.5	106.0	113.5
Wholesale trade	102.0	106.9	112.5
Retail trade and repairs	94.7	98.2	102.6
Hotels and restaurants	103.6	108.8	112.7
Transport, storage, and communication	101.5	106.3	108.9
Financial intermediation	102.3	108.7	115.4
Real estate renting and business activities	101.2	105.6	111.8
Public administration	99.9	102.9	104.7
Education, health, and social work	102.5	104.8	109.5
Other services	102.4	110.0	117.2

Source: *Monthly Digest of Statistics* May 1999,

Unemployment Rates by Gender and Age in the UK

At spring each year. Unemployment is based on the International Labour Organization definition as a percentage of all economically active persons.
(N/A = not available. In percentages.)

Age	1993	1994	1995	1996	1997	1998
Men						
16–17	18.5	18.8	18.9	21.2	19.3	18.0
18–24	21.1	19.2	17.7	17.1	14.8	13.0
25–44	10.9	10.2	9.0	8.7	7.0	5.8
45–54	9.4	8.6	7.4	6.4	6.1	4.8
55–59	12.3	11.6	10.2	9.9	8.0	6.7
60–64	14.2	11.6	9.9	8.9	7.6	7.0
65 and over	4.6	3.7	N/A	4.1	4.0	N/A
Average	12.4	11.4	10.1	9.7	8.1	6.8
Women						
16–17	15.1	17.0	15.6	15.1	16.0	15.2
18–24	12.9	11.8	11.5	10.2	9.7	9.3
25–44	7.3	7.0	6.7	6.3	5.4	5.2
45–54	5.0	5.0	4.5	4.1	3.8	3.1
55–59	6.0	6.5	4.7	4.2	4.8	3.5
60 and over	3.9	2.9	N/A	N/A	2.0	2.0
Average	7.6	7.3	6.8	6.3	5.8	5.3

Source: *Social Trends 29*,

Unemployment by Region of the UK

Data are the number of unemployment-related benefit claimants as a percentage of the estimated total workforce (the sum of claimants, employees in employment, self-employed, participants on work related government training programmes, and HM Forces) at mid-year. Data are seasonally adjusted and exclude claimants under 18.
(N/A = not available. Annual averages. In percentages.)

Region	1993	1994	1995	1996	1997
Northeast	12.9	12.4	11.6	10.6	8.4
Northwest	9.5	8.7	7.5	6.8	5.1
Merseyside	15.1	14.9	13.6	12.9	10.6
Yorkshire and the Humber	10.2	9.6	8.7	8.0	6.3
East Midlands	9.5	8.7	7.6	6.8	5.0
West Midlands	10.8	9.9	8.3	7.4	5.6
Eastern	9.4	8.1	6.8	6.1	4.3
London	11.6	10.7	9.7	8.9	6.7
Southeast	8.6	7.3	6.1	5.4	3.7
Southwest	9.5	8.1	7.0	6.2	4.4
Average England	10.2	9.2	8.1	7.3	5.4
Scotland	9.7	9.3	8.1	7.9	6.4
Wales	10.3	9.3	8.7	8.2	6.4
Northern Ireland	13.7	12.6	11.4	10.9	8.2
AVERAGE UK	10.3	9.3	8.2	7.5	5.6

Source: *Regional Trends 33*,

Trade Unions of the UK

The following member organizations are listed alphabetically by full union title. Unions' details are based on information given to the Trades Unions Congress (TUC) in late autumn 1998. Membership figures are those filed with the TUC for 1 January 1998. The TUC membership now stands at 78 unions, representing 6.8 million people. (GS = General Secretary; NS = National Secretary; m = male; f = female.)

Abbey National Staff (ANSA) 2nd floor, 16/17 High Street, Tring, Herts HP23 5AH; phone: (01442) 891122; fax: (01442) 891133; e-mail: ansaoffice@compuserve.com; **Membership** m 1,555, f 6,057, total 7,612; **GS** Linda Rolph

Alliance and Leicester Group Union of Staff (ALGUS) Customer Services Centre, Narborough, Leicester LE9 5XX; phone: (0116) 200 2259/3268/2612; fax: (0116) 200 3240; **Membership** total 3,100; **Chair** Clare Clark

Amalgamated Engineering and Electrical Union (AEEU) Hayes Court, West Common Road, Bromley, Kent BR2 7AU; phone: (0181) 462 7755; fax: (0181) 315 8234; Web site: www.aeeu.org.uk; **Membership** m 678,135, f 47,161, total 720,296; **GS** Ken Jackson

Associated Metalworkers Union (AMU) 92 Worsley Road North, Worsley, Manchester M28; phone: (01204) 793245; fax: (01204) 793245; **Membership** total 805; **GS** R Marron

Associated Society of Locomotive Engineers and Firemen (ASLEF) 9 Arkwright Road, Hampstead, London NW3 6AB; phone (0171) 317 8600; fax: (0171) 794 6406; Web site: www.aslef.org.uk; **Membership** m 14,135, f 291, total 14,426; **GS** Mick Rix

Association of First Division Civil Servants (FDA) 2 Caxton Street, London SW1H 0QH; phone: (0171) 343 1111; fax: (0171) 343 1105; e-mail: head-office@fda.org.uk; Web site: www.fda.org.uk; **Membership** total 10,837; **GS** Jonathan Baume

Association of Flight Attendants (AFA) AFA Council 07, United Airlines Cargo Centre, Shoreham Road East, Heathrow Airport, Hounslow, Middlesex TW6 3RD; phone: (0181) 276 6706; fax: (0181) 750 9706; e-mail: 75452.2427@compuserve.com; **Membership** m 127, f 717, total 844; **LEC president** Kevin P Creighan

Association of Magisterial Officers (AMO) 231 Vauxhall Bridge Road, London SW1V 1EG; phone: (0171) 630 5455; fax: (0171) 630 1989; e-mail: helen@amo. org.uk; **Membership** m 1,540, f 4,135, total 5,675; **GS** Rosie Eagleson

Association of Teachers and Lecturers (ATL) 7 Northumberland Street, London WC2N 5DA; phone: (0171) 930 6441; fax: (0171) 930 1359; e-mail: info@atl.org.uk; **Membership** total 112,159; **GS** Peter Smith

Association of University Teachers (AUT) Egmont House, 25–31 Tavistock Place, London WC1H 9UT; phone: (0171) 670 9700; fax: (0171) 670 9799; e-mail: hq@aut.org.uk; Web site: www.aut.org.uk; **Membership** m 28,403, f 12,785, total 41,188; **GS** David Triesman

Bakers, Food and Allied Workers Union (BFAWU) Stanborough House, Great North Road, Stanborough, Welwyn Garden City, Hertfordshire AL8 7TA; phone: (01707) 260150; fax: (01707) 261570; **Membership** m 14,955, f 15,373, total 30,328; **GS** Joe Marino

Banking, Insurance and Finance Union (BIFU) Sheffield House, 1b Amity Grove, London SW20 0LG; phone: (0181) 946 9151; fax: (0181) 879 7916; e-mail: amity@bifu.org.uk; Web site: www.bifu.org.uk; **Membership** m 45,426, f 67,546, total 112,972; **GS** Ed Sweeney

Barclays Bank Union for Financial Staff (UniFI) Oathall House, 68–70 Oathall Road, Haywards Heath, West Sussex RH16 3DG; phone: (01444) 458811; fax: (01444) 416248; e-mail: info@unifi.org.uk; Web site: www.unifi.org.uk; **Membership** m 17,066, f 25,663, total 42,729; **GS** Ed Sweeney

British Actors Equity Association (EQUITY) Guild House, Upper St Martin's Lane, London WC2H 9EG; phone: (0171) 379 6000; fax: (0171) 379 7001; e-mail: info@equity.org.uk; Web site: www.equity.org.uk; **Membership** m 17,216, f 17,286, total 34,502; **GS** Ian McGarry

British Air Line Pilots Association (BALPA) 81 New Road, Harlington, Hayes, Middlesex UB3 5BG; phone: (0181) 476 4000; fax: (0181) 476 4077; e-mail: balpa@balpa.org.uk; Web site: www.balpa.org.uk; **Membership** m 5,849, f 156, total 6,005; **GS** Chris Darke

British Association of Colliery Management Technical, Energy and Administrative Management (BACM-TEAM) 17 South Parade, Doncaster DN1 2DR; phone: (01302) 815551; fax: (01302) 815552; e-mail: bacmteam@aol.com; **Membership** m 4,091, f 222, total 4,313; **GS** Patrick Carragher

British Dietetic Association (BDA) 7th floor, Elizabeth House, 22 Suffolk Street Queensway, Birmingham B1 1LS; phone: (0121) 616 4910; fax: (0121) 616 4901; e-mail: bda@dial.pipex.com; Web site: www.bda.uk.com; **Membership** m 141, f 3,072, total 3,213; **Industrial relations officer** David Wood

British Orthoptic Society (BOS) Tavistock House North, Tavistock Square, London WC1H 9HX; phone: (0171) 387 7992; fax: (0171) 383 2584; e-mail: bos@orthoptics.org.uk; **Membership** m 16, f 848, total 864; **Executive secretary** Sylvia Armour

Broadcasting, Entertainment, Cinematograph and Theatre Union (BECTU) 111 Wardour Street, London W1V 4AY; phone: (0171) 437 8506; fax: (0171) 437 8268; e-mail: bectu@geo2.poptem.org.uk; Web site: www.bectu.org-uk; **Membership** m 18,983, f 10,260, total 29,243; **GS** Roger Bolton

Card Setting Machine Tenters Society (CSMT) 48 Scar End Lane, Staincliffe, Dewsbury, West Yorkshire WF12 4NY; phone: (01924) 400206; **Membership** m 88; f 0, total 88; **GS** Anthony John Moorhouse

Ceramic and Allied Trades Union (CATU) Hillcrest House, Garth Street, Hanley, Stoke-on-Trent ST1 2AB; phone: (01782) 272755; fax: (01782) 284902; **Membership** m 11,905; f 8,573, total 20,478; **GS** Geoff Bagnall

Chartered Society of Physiotherapy (CSP) 14 Bedford Row, London WC1R 4ED; phone: (0171) 306 6666; fax: (0171) 306 6611; **Membership** m 2,748, f 27,548, total 30,296; **Director of industrial relations** Maryan Boroumand

Communication Workers Union (CWU) 150 The Broadway, Wimbledon, London SW19 1RX; phone: (0181) 971 7200; fax: (0181) 971 7300; Web site: www.cwu.org; **Membership** m 217,781, f 56,033, total 273,814; **GS** Derek Hodgson

Community and District Nursing Association (CDNA) 8 University House, Ealing Green, London W5 5ED; phone: (0181) 231 2776; fax: (0181) 231 2782; e-mail: ronan.oconnor@tvu.ac.uk; Web site: www.cdna.org.uk; **Membership** m 115, f 4,880, total 4,995; **Honorary GS** Ann Keen

The Community and Youth Workers' Union (CYWU) Unit 302, The Argent Centre, 60 Frederick Street, Birmingham B1 3HS; phone: (0121) 244 3344; fax: (0121) 244 3345; e-mail: cywu@compuserve.com; Web site: www.ourworld.compuserve.com/homepages/Rod_Norton; **Membership** m 1,320, f 1,612, total 2,932; **GS** Doug Nicholls

Educational Institute of Scotland (EIS) 46 Moray Place, Edinburgh EH3 6BH; phone: (0131) 225 6244; fax: (0131) 220 3151; e-mail: membership@eis.org.uk; Web site: www.eis.org.uk; **Membership** m 14,373, f 36,434, total 50,807; **GS** Ronald A Smith

Engineering and Fastener Trade Union (EFTU) 42 Galton Road, Warley, West Midlands B67 5JU; phone: (0121) 429 2594; fax: (0121) 429 2594; **Membership** total 150; **GS** James Burdis

Engineers and Managers Association (EMA) Flaxman House, Gogmore Lane, Chertsey, Surrey KT16 9JS; phone: (01932) 577007; fax: (01932) 577077; e-mail: hq@ema.org.uk; Web site: www.ema. org.uk; **Membership** m 28,776, f 786, total 29,562; **GS** Tony Cooper

Fire Brigades Union (FBU) Bradley House, 68 Coombe Road, Kingston-upon-Thames, Surrey KT2 7AE; phone: (0181) 541 1765; fax: (0181) 546 5187; e-mail: office@fbu-hot.org.uk; **Membership** m 55,227, f 1,716, total 56,943; **GS** Ken Cameron

General Union of Loom Overlookers (GULO) 9 Wellington Street, St John's, Blackburn BB1 8AF; phone: (01254) 51760; fax: (01254) 51760; **Membership** total 350; **GS** Don Rishton

GMB 22/24 Worple Road, London SW19 4DD; phone: (0181) 947 3131; fax: (0181) 944 6552; e-mail: 100066.3233@compuserve.com; Web site: www.gmb.org.uk; **Membership** m 451,907, f 257,801, total 709,708; **GS and treasurer** John Edmonds

Graphical, Paper and Media Union (GPMU) Keys House, 63–67 Bromham Road, Bedford MK40 2AG; phone: (01234) 351521; fax: (01234) 270580; e-mail: general@gpmu.org.uk; Web site: www.gpmu.org.uk; **Membership** m 170,742, f 34,080, total 204,822; **GS** Tony Dubbins

Guinness Staff Association (GSA) Sun Works Cottage, Park Royal Brewery, Park Royal, London NW10 7RR; phone: (0181) 963 5249; fax: (0181) 963 5184; e-mail: elizabeth.jude@guinness.com; **Membership** m 349, f 213, total 562; **GS** Jim Collins

Hospital Consultants and Specialists Association (HCSA) 1 Kingsclere Road, Overton, Basingstoke, Hampshire RG25 3JA; phone: (01256) 771777; fax: (01256) 770999; e-mail: conspec@hcsa.com; Web site: www.hcsa.com; **Membership** m 2,020, f 248, total 2,268; **Administrative director** Graham Poynton

Independent Union of Halifax Staff (IUHS) Simmons House, 46 Old Bath Road, Charvil, Reading RG10 9QR; phone: (0118) 934 1808; fax: (0118) 932 0208; e-mail: 101670.3051@compuserve.com; **Membership** m 7,039, f 19,178, total 26,217; **GS** Ged Nichols

Institution of Professionals, Managers and Specialists (IPMS) 75–79 York Road, London SE1 7AQ; phone: (0171) 902 6600; fax: (0171) 902 6667; e-mail: ipmshq@ipms.org.uk; Web site: www.ipms.org.uk; **Membership** m 61,381, f 13,203, total 74,584; **GS** Paul Noon

Iron and Steel Trades Confederation (ISTC) Swinton House, 324 Gray's Inn Road, London WC1X 8DD; phone: (0171) 837 6691/2/3; fax: (0171) 278 8378; **Membership** m 47,621, f 2,380; total 50,001; **GS** Michael Leahy

Managerial and Professional Officers (MPO) Terminus House, The High, Harlow, Essex CM20 1TZ; phone: (01279) 434444; fax: (01279) 451176; e-mail: nbmpo@globalnet.co.uk; **Membership** m 8,372, f 1,788, total 10,160; **Chief executive** Rob Newland

Manufacturing Science Finance (MSF) MSF Centre, 33–37 Moreland Street, London EC1V 8HA; phone: (0171) 505 3000; fax: (0171) 505 3030; Web site: www.msf.org.uk; **Membership** m 298,506, f 131,096, total 429,602; **GS** Roger Lyons

Military and Orchestral Musical Instrument Makers Trade Society (MOMIMTS) 2 Whitehouse Avenue, Boreham Wood, Hertfordshire WD6 1HD; **Membership** m 56, f 10, total 66; **GS** F McKenzie

Musicians Union (MU) 60–62 Clapham Road, London SW9 0JJ; phone: (0171) 582 5566; fax: (0171) 582 9805; e-mail: info@musiciansunion.org.uk; Web site: www.musiciansunion.org.uk; **Membership** m 23,620, f 6,860, total 30,480; **GS** Dennis Scard

National Association of Colliery Overmen, Deputies and Shotfirers (NACODS) Simpson House, 48 Nether Hall Road, Doncaster, South Yorkshire DN1 2PZ; phone: (01302) 368015; fax: (01302) 341945; **Membership** m 645, f 0, total 645; **GS** Peter McNestry

National Association of Cooperative Officials (NACO) Coronation House, Arndale Centre, Manchester M4 2HW; phone: (0161) 834 6029; fax: (0161) 832 0671; **Membership** m 2,532, f 637, total 3,169; **GS** Lindsay Ewing

National Association of Probation Officers (NAPO) 4 Chivalry Road, Battersea, London SW11 1HT; phone: (0171) 223 4887; fax: (0171) 223 3503; **Membership** m 2,985, f 3,971, total 6,956; **GS** Judy McKnight

National Association of Schoolmasters, Union of Women Teachers (NASUWT) 5 Wendle Court, 131–137 Wandsworth Road, London SW8 2LH; phone: (0171) 720 5706; fax: (0171) 978 1860; e-mail: nigel.degruchy@nasuwt.org.uk; **Membership** m 68,104, f 104,748, total 172,852; **GS** Nigel de Gruchy

National League of the Blind and Disabled (NLBD) 2 Tenterden Road, London N17 8BE; phone: (0181) 808 6030; fax: (0181) 885 3235; **Membership** m 1,578, f 564, total 2,142; **GS** Joe Mann

National Union of Domestic Appliances and General Operatives (NUDAGO) 7–8 Imperial Buildings, Corporation Street, Rotherham, South Yorkshire S60 1PB; phone: (01709) 382820; fax: (01709) 362826; **Membership** m 1,609; f 641, total 2,250; **GS** Tony McCarthy

National Union of Insurance Workers (NUIW) 27 Old Gloucester Street, London WC1N 3AF; phone: (0171) 405 6798; fax: (0171) 404 8150; e-mail: acorn.house@nuj.org.uk; **Membership** m 8,107, f 1,937, total 10,044; **GS** Ken Perry

National Union of Journalists (NUJ) Acorn House, 314–320 Gray's Inn Road, London WC1X 8DP; phone: (0171) 278 7916; fax: (0171) 837 8143; e-mail: acorn.house@nuj.org.uk; **Membership** m 12,326; f 7,058, total 19,384; **GS** John Foster

National Union of Knitwear, Footwear and Apparel Trades (KFAT) 55 New Walk, Leicester LE1 7EB; phone: (0116) 255 6703; fax: (0116) 255 4406; e-mail: kfat@mcr1.poptel.org.uk; Web site: www.poptel.org.uk/kfat/; **Membership** m 16,279; f 21,796, total 38,075; **GS** Barry Morris

National Union of Lock and Metal Workers (NULMW) Bellamy House, Wilkes Street, Willenhall, West Midlands WV13 2BS; phone: (01902) 366651; fax: (01902) 368035; **Membership** m 2,070, f 2,129, total 4,199; **GS** Ray Ward

National Union of Marine, Aviation and Shipping Transport Officers (NUMAST) Oceanair House, 750–60 High Road, Leytonstone, London E11 3BB; phone: (0181) 989 6677; fax: (0181) 530 1015; **Membership** m 18,311, f 205, total 18,516; **GS** Brian Orrell

National Union of Mineworkers (NUM) Miners' Offices, 2 Huddersfield Road, Barnsley, South Yorkshire S70 2LS; phone: (01226) 215555; fax: (01226) 215561; **Membership** m 5,001, f 0, total 5,001; **President** Arthur Scargill

National Union of Rail, Maritime, and Transport Workers (RMT) Unity House, 205 Euston Road, London NW1 2BL; phone: (0171) 387 4771; fax: (0171) 387 4123; **Membership** m 52,218, f 4,119, total 56,337; **GS** Jimmy Knapp

National Union of Teachers (NUT) Hamilton House, Mabledon Place, London WC1H 9BD; phone: (0171) 388 6191; fax: (0171) 387 8458; Web site: www.teachers.org.uk; **Membership** m 48,226, f 143,602, total 191,828; **GS** Doug McAvoy

Northern Carpet Trades Union (NCTU) 22 Clare Road, Halifax HX1 2HX; phone: (01422) 360492; fax: (01422) 321146; **Membership** m 532, f 123, total 655; **GS** Keith Edmondson

Power Loom Carpet Weavers and Textile Workers Union (PLCWTWU) 148 Hurcott Road, Kidderminster, Worcestershire DY10 2RL; phone: (01562) 823192; fax: (01562) 861469; **Membership** total 1,413; **GS** Gordon Rudd

Prison Officers Association (POA) Cronin House, 245 Church Street, Edmonton, London N9 9HW; phone: (0181) 803 0255; fax: (0181) 803 1761; **Membership** m 24,522, f 4,177, total 28,699; **GS** David Evans

Professional Footballers Association (PFA) 2 Oxford Court, Bishopsgate, Manchester M2 3WQ; phone: (0161) 236 0575; fax: (0161) 228 7229; Web site: www.thepfa.co.uk; **Membership** total 1,473; **Chief executive** Gordon Taylor

Public and Commercial Services Union (PCS) 160 Falcon Road, Clapham Junction, London SW11 2LN; phone: (0171) 924 2727; fax: (0171) 924 1847; Web site: www.pcs.org.uk; **Membership** m 109,146,

f 156,756, total 265,902; **Joint GSs** Barry Reamsbottom, John Sheldon

Scottish Prison Officers' Association (SPOA) 21 Calder Road, Edinburgh EH11 3PF; phone: (0131) 443 8105; fax: (0131) 444 0657; **Membership** m 2,921, f 384, total 3,305; **GS** Derek Turner

Scottish Union of Power-Loom Overlookers (SUPLO) 3 Napier Terrace, Dundee, Tayside DD2 2SL; phone: (01382) 612196; **Membership** total 42; **GS** Jim Reilly

Sheffield Wool Shear Workers Union (SWSWU) 5 Collin Avenue, Sheffield S6 4ES; **Membership** m 9, f 2, total 11; **GS** B Bell

Society of Chiropodists and Podiatrists (SCP) 53 Welbeck Street, London W1M 7HE; phone: (0171) 486 3381; fax: (0171) 935 6359; e-mail: cs@scpod.org; **Membership** m 1,922, f 4,536, total 6,458; **GS** Hilary De Lyon

Society of Radiographers (SoR) 2 Carriage Row, 183 Eversholt Street, London NW1 1BU; phone: (0171) 391 4500; fax: (171) 391 4504; **Membership** m 2,343, f 11,159, total 13,502; **GS and chief executive** Stephen Evans

Society of Telecom Executives (STE) 30 St Georges Road, Wimbledon, London SW19 4BD; phone: (0181) 971 6000; fax: (0181) 971 6002; e-mail: ste@union.org.uk; Web site: www.ste.org.uk; **Membership** m 14,784, f 2,178, total 16,962; **GS** Simon Petch

Transport and General Workers Union (TGWU) Transport House, 16 Palace Street, Victoria, London SW1E 5JD; phone: (0171) 828 7788; fax (0171) 963 4440; e-mail: tgwu@tgwu.org.uk; Web site: www.tgwu.org.uk; **Membership** m 706,851, f 174,506, total 881,357; **GS** Bill Morris

Transport Salaried Staffs Association (TSSA) Walkden House, 10 Melton Street, London NW1 2EJ; phone: (0171) 387 2101; fax: (0171) 383 0656; e-mail: enquiries@ tssa.org.uk; **Membership** m 22,146,
f 8,716, total 31,132; **GS** Richard Rosser

Undeb Cenedlaethol Athrawon Cymru (UCAC) Pen Roc, Rhodfa'r Mor, Aberystwyth SY23 2AZ; phone: (01970) 615577; fax: (01970) 626765; **Membership** m 910, f 2,731, total 3,641; **GS** Edwin Williams

Union for Bradford and Bingley Staff (UBBS) 18d Market Place, Malton, North Yorkshire YO17 7LX; phone: (01653) 697 634; fax: (01653) 695222; **Membership** m 947, f 1,715, total 2,662; **GS** David Matthews

Union of Construction, Allied Trades, and Technicians (UCATT) UCATT House, 177 Abbeville Road, Clapham, London SW4 9RL; phone: (0171) 622 2442; fax: (0171) 720 4081; e-mail: ucatt@ psilink.co.uk; **Membership** m 112,524, f 1,031, total 113,555; **GS** George Brumwell

Union of Shop, Distributive, and Allied Workers (USDAW) Oakley, 188 Wilmslow Road, Fallowfield, Manchester M14 6LJ; phone: (0161) 224 2804; fax: (0161) 257 2566; e-mail: usdaw-co@mcr.poptel.org.uk; Web site: www.poptel.org.uk/usdaw/; **Membership** m 121,010, f 172,460, total 293,470; **GS** Bill Connor

Union of Textile Workers (UTW) Foxlowe, Market Place, Leek, Staffordshire ST13 6AD; phone: (01538) 382068; fax: (01538) 382068; **Membership** m 826, f 733, total 1,559; **GS** Alf Hitchmough

UNISON 1 Mabledon Place, London WC1H 9AJ; phone: (0171) 388 2366; fax: (0171) 387 6692; e-mail: union-mable@unison.org.uk; Web site: www. unison.org.uk/; **Membership** m 364,126, f 936,325, total 1,300,451; **GS** Rodney Bickerstaffe

The University and College Lecturers' Union (NATFHE) 27 Britannia Street, London WC1X 9JP; phone: (0171) 837 3636; fax: (0171) 837 4403; e-mail: hq@natfhe.org.uk; Web site: www.natfhe.org.uk; **Membership** m 35,574, f 29,491, total 65,065; **GS** Paul Mackney

The Writers' Guild of Great Britain (WGGB) (incorporating the Theatre Writers' Union) 430 Edgware Road, London W2 1EH; phone: (0171) 723 8074; fax: (0171) 706 2413; e-mail: postie@wggb.demon.co.uk; Web site: www.writers.org.uk/guild; **Membership** total 1,987; **GS** Alison Gray

The Largest Trade Unions in the UK

Rank	1990		1997	
	Union	Membership	Union	Membership
1	Transport and General Workers Union	1,224,000	UNISON – The Public Service Union	1,300,451
2	GMB	865,000	Transport and General Workers Union	881,357
3	National and Local Government Officers Association	744,000	Amalgamated Engineering and Electrical Union	720,296
4	Amalgamated Engineering Union	702,000	GMB	709,708
5	Manufacturing Science and Finance Union	653,000	Manufacturing Science and Finance Union	416,000
6	National Union of Public Employees	579,000	Royal College of Nursing of the UK	312,141
7	Electrical Electronic Telecommunication and Plumbing Union	367,000	Union of Shop Distributive and Allied Workers	293,470
8	Union of Shop Distributive and Allied Workers	362,000	National Union of Teachers	276,819
9	Royal College of Nursing of the UK	289,000	Communication Workers Union	273,814
10	National Union of Teachers	218,000	National Association of School Masters and Union of Women Teachers	245,932

Source: *Annual Report of the Certification Officer for Trades Unions and Employers' Associations 1998*, © Crown copyright 1998

Trade Union Membership by Type of Job and Length of Service in Great Britain

Figures include all employees, except for those in the armed forces. (N = base too low to provide a reliable estimate. – = not applicable.)

1997

Source: Trades Unions Congress	All (%)	Full time (%)	Part time (%)
All employees	30	34	20
Length of Service			
Less than 1 year	12	14	8
1 to 2 years	17	20	11
2 to 5 years	22	25	15
5 to 10 years	36	38	28
10 to 20 years	47	49	40
20 years or more	58	61	39
Occupational Group			
Managers and administrators	20	21	15
Professional	50	52	43
Associate professional/technical	46	44	53
Clerical and secretarial	25	28	19
Craft and related	34	35	17
Personal and protective	28	38	17
Sales	9	10	9
Plant and machine operatives	38	41	18
Other occupations	26	36	17

	All (%)	Full time (%)	Part time (%)
Managerial Status			
Manager	26	27	20
Foreman or supervisor	39	40	36
No managerial duties	30	35	18
Employment Status			
Permanent	31	35	21
Temporary	19	23	15
Special Working Arrangements			
Flexitime	44	47	29
Job sharing	31	–	29
Term-time working	44	72	24
Annualized hours contract	52	56	38
9-day fortnight/4.5-day week	48	49	N
Work mainly in own home	5	6	4

Source: *Labour Market Trends,*

Political Funds of Trade Unions in the UK

1997

Trade union	Number of members contributing to the political fund[1]	Number of members exempt from contributing to the political fund[1]	Political fund (£) Income	Expenditure	Fund at beginning of year	Fund at end of year
Amalgamated Engineering and Electrical Union	429,421	98,579	931,000	1,829,000	1,267,000	369,000
Associated Society of Locomotive Engineers and Firemen	13,940	315	65,084	96,223	77,668	46,529
Association of Her Majesty's Inspectors of Taxes	2,144	91	6,408	0	51,593	58,001
Association of University Teachers	32,551	0	27,048	21,544	70,805	76,309
Bakers, Food, and Allied Workers Union	28,731	12	60,153	48,843	1,486	12,796
Broadcasting, Entertainment, Cinematograph, and Theatre Union	28,555	95	49,579	34,675	38,489	53,393
Ceramic and Allied Trades Union	20,259	219	95,674	55,623	194,178	234,229
Civil and Public Services Association	0	0	4,368	0	–4,368	0
Communication Managers Association	12,956	630	16,231	22,527	20,449	14,153
Communication Workers Union	231,748	31,005	1,208,272	1,250,741	480,361	437,892
Educational Institute of Scotland	47,812	1,816	82,615	264,241	474,080	292,454
Fire Brigades Union	41,374	10,052	166,412	165,874	187,776	188,314
General Union of Loom Overlookers	225	106	450	721	565	294
GMB	662,446	47,262	2,838,000	2,832,000	72,000	78,000
Graphical, Paper, and Media Union	72,771	132,051	417,878	584,570	739,427	572,735
Institution of Professionals, Managers, and Specialists	63,191	1,302	37,714	9,004	93,513	122,223
Iron and Steel Trades Confederation	26,832	5,647	147,098	147,822	54,381	53,657
Manufacturing, Science, and Finance Union	167,294	248,706	613,000	470,000	396,000	529,000
Midland Area Association of Colliery Officials	317	3	1,699	1,600	3,454	3,553
Musicians Union	27,657	920	34,892	45,174	22,036	11,754
National Association of Colliery Overmen, Deputies, and Shotfirers	781	2	4,144	6,447	33,437	31,134
National Association of Schoolmasters and Union of Women Teachers	136,882	35,970	74,358	126,234	167,919	116,043
National Association of Teachers in Further and Higher Education	53,054	2,864	67,959	73,185	35,327	30,101
National League of the Blind and Disabled	882	1,260	2,713	4,135	8,754	7,332
National Union of Domestic Appliances and General Operatives	2,247	3	1,251	1,190	1,412	1,473

(continued)

Political Funds of Trade Unions in the UK (*continued*)

Trade union	Number of members contributing to the political fund[1]	Number of members exempt from contributing to the political fund[1]	Political fund (£) Income	Expenditure	Fund at beginning of year	Fund at end of year
National Union of Insurance Workers	7,773	2,574	10,985	10,390	84,544	85,139
National Union of Knitwear, Footwear, and Apparel Trades	37,484	591	113,477	86,652	60,031	86,856
National Union of Mineworkers	5,543	392	83,063	97,976	261,450	246,537
National Union of Rail, Maritime, and Transport Workers	55,655	682	225,000	241,000	134,000	118,000
Power Loom Carpet Weavers and Textile Workers Union	1,413	0	1,800	2,575	9,206	8,431
Public Services Tax and Commerce Union	139,788	8,182	258,489	204,830	713,637	767,296
Scottish Carpet Workers Union	620	0	7	0	3,258	3,265
Society of Telecom Executives	9,689	7,273	32,407	82,871	62,162	11,698
Transport and General Workers Union	809,373	24,157	2,405,000	2,469,000	3,895,000	3,831,000
Transport Salaried Staffs Association	27,211	3,912	92,788	135,523	90,149	47,414
Union of Construction, Allied Trades, and Technicians	81,644	9,289	213,000	212,000	7,000	8,000
Union of Democratic Mineworkers	2,387	0	1,692	4,649	11,474	8,517
Union of Shop Distributive and Allied Workers	271,984	21,486	988,009	1,399,223	1,001,902	590,688
Union of Textile Workers	1,547	12	3,203	0	3,247	6,450
Unison: The Public Service Union	1,184,333	93,589	4,660,000	5,148,000	4,407,000	3,919,000
Total for the 40 unions with political funds for 1997	4,740,514	790,869	16,042,920	18,186,062	15,231,802	13,088,660

[1] These columns do not necessarily add up to a union's total membership. This is because, in the case of some trade unions, total membership includes various classes of special category members (for example, honorary, retired, unemployed) who are members under the union's rules but who are neither required to pay the political levy nor to seek formal exemption.

Source: *Annual Report of the Certification Officer for Trade Unions and Employers' Associations 1998*, © Crown copyright 1998

Labour Disputes in the UK

These figures exclude details of stoppages involving fewer than ten workers or lasting less than one day except any in which the aggregate number of working days lost exceeded 100. There may be some under-recording of small or short stoppages. Some stoppages that affected more than one industry group have been counted under each of the industries but only once in the totals. The figures have been rounded and consequently the sum of the constituent items may not agree with the totals. Classifications by size are based on the full duration of stoppages where these continue into the following year. Working days lost per 1,000 employees are based on the latest available mid-year (June) estimates of employees in employment. (N = nil or negligible. In thousands.)

Item	1994	1995	1996	1997
Working Days Lost Through All Stoppages in Progress				
Analysis by industry				
mining, quarrying, electricity, gas, and water	1	1	2	2
manufacturing	58	65	97	86
construction	5	10	8	17
transport, storage, and communication	110	120	884	36
public administration and defence	11	95	158	29
education	70	67	128	28
health and social work	5	16	8	7
other community, social, and personal services	11	23	3	5
all other industries and services	8	16	15	25
Total	278	415	1,303	235
Analysis by number of working days lost in each stoppage				
under 250 days	11	11	14	12
250–499 days	6	10	13	6
500–999 days	24	19	13	17
1,000–4,999 days	53	82	61	72
5,000–24,999 days	68	195	123	101
25,000–49,999 days	N	29	54	26
50,000 days and over	117	68	1,025	N
Working days lost per 1,000 employees, all industries and services	13	19	58	10

(*continued*)

Labour Disputes in the UK (*continued*)

Item	1994	1995	1996	1997
Workers Directly and Indirectly Involved				
Analysis by industry				
mining, quarrying, electricity, gas, and water	N	2	1	N
manufacturing	23	33	34	28
construction	1	2	3	13
transport, storage, and communication	37	54	146	24
public administration and defence	8	28	32	20
education	29	30	122	15
health and social work	2	4	5	5
other community, social, and personal services	2	10	2	1
all other industries and services	5	11	21	23
Total	107	174	364	130
Analysis by duration of stoppage				
not more than 5 days	75	142	208	108
6–10 days	5	11	133	7
11–20 days	1	2	4	14
21–30 days	6	2	3	N
31–50 days	N	10	16	1
51 days and over	20	7	1	N

Source: *Annual Abstract of Statistics 1999*, © Crown copyright 1999

The Royal Family and Peerage

Members of The Royal Family

Senior members of the Royal Family are all related to the three middle sons of King George V: King George VI (1895–1952); Henry, Duke of Gloucester (1900–1974); George, Duke of Kent (1902–1942). The eldest son, the Duke of Windsor (1894–1972), who abdicated from the throne as King Edward VIII in 1936, died childless.

Name and titles	Married	Date of birth	Office	Official residence(s)	Issue
Family of George VI					
The Sovereign: Her Majesty Queen Elizabeth II, of The United Kingdom of Great Britain and Northern Ireland and of her other Realms and Territories, Queen, Head of the Commonwealth, Defender of the Faith	His Royal Highness The Duke of Edinburgh, 20 November 1947	21 April 1926	Buckingham Palace, London SW1A 1AA; phone: (0171) 930 4832	Buckingham Palace, Windsor Castle, Palace of Holyrood House	Prince Charles, Princess Anne, Prince Andrew, Prince Edward
Husband of The Queen: His Royal Highness, The Prince Philip, Duke of Edinburgh, KG, KT, OM, GBE, AC, QSO, PC, Ranger of Windsor Great Park	Her Majesty The Queen, 20 November 1947	10 June 1921			
Mother of The Queen: Her Majesty Queen Elizabeth The Queen Mother, Lady of The Garter, Lady of The Thistle, CI, GCVO, GBE, Dame Grand Cross of the Order of St John, Royal Victorian Chain, Lord Warden and Admiral of the Cinque Ports, Constable of Dover Castle	Prince Albert, Duke of York (later King George VI; died 1952), 26 April 1923	4 August 1900	Clarence House, St James' Palace, London SW1A 1BA; phone: (0171) 930 3141	Clarence House; Royal Lodge, Windsor; Castle of Mey	Queen Elizabeth II, Princess Margaret
Children of The Queen					
His Royal Highness The Prince of Wales (Prince Charles), KG, KT, GCB and Great Master of the Order of the Bath, AK, QSO, PC, ADP (P)	Lady Diana Spencer (later Diana, Princess of Wales; died 1997), 29 July 1981, marriage dissolved 1996	14 November 1948	St James' Palace, London SW1A 1BA; phone: (0171) 930 4832	St James' Palace; Highgrove, Tetbury	His Royal Highness Prince William of Wales (born 21 June 1982), His Royal Highness Prince Henry of Wales (born 15 September 1984)

(*continued*)

Members of The Royal Family (*continued*)

Name and titles	Married	Date of birth	Office	Official residence(s)	Issue
Her Royal Highness The Princess Royal (Princess Anne), KG, GCVO	Captain Mark Phillips, 14 November 1973, marriage dissolved 1992; Captain Timothy Laurence, 12 December 1992	15 August 1950	Buckingham Palace, London SW1A 1AA; phone: (0171) 930 4832	Gatcombe Park, Minchinhampton	Peter Phillips (born 15 November 1977), Zara Phillips (born 15 May 1981)
His Royal Highness The Duke of York (Prince Andrew), CVO, ADC(P)	Sarah Ferguson (now Sarah, Duchess of York), 23 July 1986, marriage dissolved 1996	19 February 1960		Buckingham Palace; Sunninghill Park, Ascot	Princess Beatrice (born 8 August 1988), Princess Eugenie (born 23 March 1990)
His Royal Highness The Prince Edward, CVO, Earl of Wessex	Sophie Rhys-Jones (now the Countess of Wessex), 19 June 1999	10 March 1964		Windsor Castle	none
Sister of The Queen					
Her Royal Highness The Princess Margaret, Countess of Snowdon, CI, GCVO, Royal Victorian Chain, Dame Grand Cross of the Order of St John of Jerusalem	Antony Armstrong-Jones (later Earl of Snowdon), 6 May 1960, marriage dissolved 1978	21 August 1930	Kensington Palace, London W8 4PU; phone: (0171) 930 3141	Kensington Palace	David, Viscount Linley (born 3 November 1961), Lady Sarah Chatto[1] (born 1 May 1964)
Family of Henry, Duke of Gloucester Aunt of The Queen					
Her Royal Highness Princess Alice, Duchess of Gloucester, GCB, CI, GCVO, GBE	Prince Henry, Duke of Gloucester (died 1974), 6 November 1935	25 December 1901	Kensington Palace, London W8 4PU; phone: (0171) 930 6374	Kensington Palace	Prince William (1941–72), Richard, Duke of Gloucester
Cousins of The Queen					
His Royal Highness The Duke of Gloucester (Prince Richard), KG, GCV, Grand Prior of the Order of St John of Jerusalem	Birgitte Eva van Deurs (now HRH The Duchess of Gloucester), 8 July 1972	26 August 1944	Kensington Palace, London W8 4PU; phone: (0171) 930 6374	Kensington Palace	Alexander, Earl of Ulster (born 24 October 1974), Lady Davina Windsor (born 19 November 1977), Lady Rose Windsor (born 1 March 1980)
Family of George, Duke of Kent					
His Royal Highness The Duke of Kent (Prince Edward), KG, GCMG, GCVO, ADC (P)	Katherine Worsley (now HRH The Duchess of Kent), 8 June 1961	9 October 1935	York House, St James' Palace, London SW1 1BQ; phone: (0171) 930 4872	Wren House, London	George, Earl of St Andrews[2] (born 26 June 1962), Lady Helen Taylor[3] (born 28 April 1964), Lord Nicholas Windsor (born 25 July 1970)
Her Royal Highness Princess Alexandra, The Honourable Lady Ogilvy, GCVO	The Right Honourable Sir Angus Ogilvy, 24 April 1963	25 December 1936	Buckingham Palace, London SW1A 1AA; phone: (0171) 930 1860	Thatched House Lodge, Richmond Park, Surrey	James Ogilvy[4] (born 29 February 1964), Marina Mowatt[5] (born 31 July 1966)
His Royal Highness Prince Michael of Kent, KCVO	Baroness Marie-Christine von Reibnitz (now HRH Princess Michael of Kent), 30 June 1978	4 July 1942	Kensington Palace, London W8 4PU; phone: (0171) 930 3519	Kensington Palace; Nether Lypiatt Manor, Stroud	Lord Frederick Windsor (born 6 April 1979), Lady Gabriella Windsor (born 23 April 1981)

[1] Has one son: Samuel Chatto (born 28 July 1996).
[2] Has three children: Lady Marina Windsor (born 30 September 1982), Edward, Baron Downpatrick (born 2 December 1988), Lady Amelia Windsor (born 24 August 1995).
[3] Has two children: Columbus Taylor (born 6 August 1994), Cassius Taylor (born 26 December 1996).
[4] Has two children: Flora Ogilvy (born 15 December 1994), Alexander Ogilvy (born 12 November 1996).
[5] Has two children: Zenouska Mowatt (born 26 May 1990), Christian Mowatt (born 4 June 1993).

The Succession to the Throne

The current succession was determined following the end of the Commonwealth in the 17th century, by the Bill of Rights of 1689. This was amended by the Act of Settlement in 1701 which laid down that only Protestant descendants of Princess Sophia – the Electress of Hanover, granddaughter of James I – can succeed. In February 1998 the government announced that The Queen has agreed that the law should be changed to give females equal rights to succeed to the throne. The Bill which should result from this decision will negate the rule of male primogeniture written into the 1701 Act of Settlement on which royal succession is currently based.

Order of succession	Relationship
The Prince of Wales	Eldest son of Her Majesty The Queen
Prince William of Wales	Eldest son of The Prince of Wales
Prince Henry of Wales	Second son of The Prince of Wales
The Duke of York	Second son of Her Majesty The Queen
Princess Beatrice of York	Eldest daughter of The Duke of York
Princess Eugenie of York	Second daughter of The Duke of York
The Prince Edward	Third son of Her Majesty The Queen
The Princess Royal	Only daughter, second child of Her Majesty The Queen
Peter Phillips	Only son, eldest child, of The Princess Royal
Zara Phillips	Only daughter of The Princess Royal

The Royal Family: the Civil List

Under the Civil List Acts, The Queen Mother and The Duke of Edinburgh receive annual parliamentary allowances to enable them to carry out their public duties. Since 1993, The Queen has repaid to the Treasury the annual parliamentary allowances received by other members of the Royal family. The Queen's income is taxable.

The amounts payable in 1997–98 to members of the Royal Family were as follows:

Parliamentary annuities (not repaid by The Queen)

Her Majesty Queen Elizabeth The Queen Mother £643,000

His Royal Highness The Duke of Edinburgh £359,000

Parliamentary annuities (repaid by The Queen)

His Royal Highness The Duke of York £249,000

His Royal Highness The Prince Edward £96,000

Her Royal Highness The Princess Royal £228,000

Her Royal Highness The Princess Margaret £219,000

Her Royal Highness Princess Alice, Duchess of Gloucester £87,000

Their Royal Highnesses The Duke and Duchess of Gloucester £175,000

Their Royal Highnesses The Duke and Duchess of Kent £236,000

Her Royal Highness Princess Alexandra, Hon Lady Ogilvy £225,000

The Royal Family: Sources of Income

The Queen

The Queen (or officials of the Royal Household acting on her behalf) has four sources of funding:

The Civil List

Set by Parliament as a fixed annual amount of £7.9 million for a period of up to ten years; it is not taxed.

Grants-in-Aid

Paid by the appropriate government departments for expenses incurred.

Property Paid annually by the Department of Culture, Media, and Sport and used for the upkeep of the palaces occupied by members of the Royal Family. These are Buckingham Palace, St James's Palace and Clarence House, Marlborough House Mews, parts of Kensington Palace, Windsor Castle and related buildings, and Hampton Court Mews and Paddocks. Accounts are published and presented to Parliament each year. In 1997–98 the Grant-in-Aid amounted to £19.4 million; it is planned for this to be reduced to £15 million in 1999–2000.

Travel From April 1997, the Royal Household received a Grant-in-Aid from Parliament, through the Department of the Environment, Transport, and the Regions to pay for Royal travel. The Grant-in-Aid for the year to March 1998 amounted to £19.4 million, of which £14.441 million was spent on flying for official engagements by 32 (The Royal) Squadron. It is proposed that the two 32 Squadron Wessex helicopters should be replaced by one Sikorsky S76, with an expected saving of £1.3 million per year.

The Privy Purse

The Privy Purse Office manages the Sovereign's private income from the Duchy of Lancaster. This amounted to £5.7 million before tax for the year to 31 March 1998. The Duchy is a landed estate held in trust for the Sovereign since 1399. The Queen uses the larger part of the Privy Purse to meet official expenses incurred by other Members of the Royal Family. Only the Queen Mother and the Duke of Edinburgh receive payments from Parliament which are not reimbursed by the Queen.

The Queen's Personal Wealth and Income

The Queen's personal income, derived from her personal investment portfolio, is used to meet private expenditure. The Queen owns Balmoral and Sandringham, both inherited from her father. She also owns the stud at Sandringham (with a small amount of land in Hampshire), West Ilsley Stables, and Sunninghill Park, home of the Duke of York. Income derived from public access to Balmoral and Sandringham goes to charity and towards meeting the costs of managing the properties. The Queen owns no property outside the UK.

The Prince of Wales

The Prince of Wales does not receive any money from the state. Instead, he receives the annual net revenues of the Duchy of Cornwall and uses them to meet the costs of all aspects of his public and private commitments and those of his children.

The Duchy of Cornwall

For the year to 31 March 1998, the Duchy's net surplus was £5,955,000. The Duchy is tax exempt because it is a crown body. However, the Prince of Wales has volunteered to pay tax on this amount at the rate of 40 percent.

The Peerage

The peerage comprises holders, in descending order, of the titles of duke, marquess, earl, viscount, and baron. Most hereditary peerages pass on death to the nearest male relative, but some of these titles may be held by a woman in default of a male heir; no title can be passed on to the untitled husband of a woman peer. In the late 19th century, the peerage was augmented by the Lords of Appeal in Ordinary (the nonhereditary life peers) and, from 1958, by a number of specially created life peers of either sex (usually long-standing members of the House of Commons). Since 1963 peers have been able to disclaim their titles, usually to enable them to take a seat in the Commons (where peers are disqualified from membership).

Duke

The title originated in England in 1337, when Edward III created his son Edward, Duke of Cornwall; **Coronet:** eight strawberry leaves; **Title:** His Grace, The Duke of; **Wife's title:** Her Grace, The Duchess of; **Eldest son's title:** takes his father's second title (Marquess, Earl, or Viscount) as a courtesy title; **Younger sons' title:** 'Lord' before forename and family name; **Daughters' title:** 'Lady' before forename and family name.

Marquess

The first English marquess was created in 1385, but the lords of the Scottish and Welsh Marches were known as marchiones before this date; **Coronet:** four strawberry leaves alternating with four silver balls; **Title:** The Most Honourable, The Marquess of; **Wife's title:** The Most Honourable, The Marchioness of; **Eldest son's title:** takes his father's second title (Earl or Viscount) as a courtesy title; **Younger sons' title:** 'Lord' before forename and family name; **Daughters' title:** 'Lady' before forename and family name.

Earl

Earldoms first became hereditary during the Norman period, and the title of earl was the highest hereditary dignity until 1337; **Coronet:** eight silver balls on stalks alternating with eight gold strawberry leaves; **Title:** The Right Honourable, The Earl of; **Wife's title:** The Right Honourable, The Countess of; **Eldest son's title:** takes his father's second title as a courtesy title; **Younger sons' title:** 'The Honourable' before forename and family name; **Daughters' title:** 'Lady' before forename and family name.

Viscount

The title was first granted in England in 1440 to John, Lord Beaumont. Originally the title was given to the deputy sheriff, who acted on behalf of an earl within his estate; **Coronet:** sixteen silver balls; **Title:** The Right Honourable, The Viscount of; **Wife's title:** The Right Honourable, The Viscountess of; **Eldest son's title:** takes his father's second title as a courtesy title; **Younger sons' title:** 'The Honourable' before forename and family name; **Daughters' title:** 'The Honourable' before forename and family name.

Baron

Historically, a baron is any member of the higher nobility, a direct vassal (feudal servant) of the king, not bearing other titles such as duke or count. Life peers, created under the Act of 1958, are always of this rank; **Coronet:** six silver balls; **Title:** The Right Honourable, The Lord; **Wife's title:** The Right Honourable, The Lady; **Eldest son's title:** 'The Honourable' before forename and family name; **Younger sons' title:** 'The Honourable' before forename and family name; **Daughters' title:** 'The Honourable' before forename and family name.

Notes

For Royal Dukes, His Royal Highness and Her Royal Highness are used instead of His or Her Grace. In Scotland, Marquis is used for peers created before the Union with England. In Scotland, 'The Master of' followed by the Viscount's title can be used. The title Baron does not exist in Scotland.

Orders of Chivalry and the Honours List

Modern orders of chivalry are awarded as a mark of royal favour or as a reward for public services. Members of orders are normally created Knights or Dames, titled Sir or Dame; some orders are graded, with the lower grades not being knighted. Honours are awarded by the sovereign and published on New Year's Day, and on the official royal birthday in June. Suggestions for awards are provided by: (1) senior government officials; (2) personal nominations from the Queen; (3) the major political parties, through the Chief Whip; and (4) the prime minister, who can add to, or subtract from, all the above lists.

Order	Created	Ribbon	Motto	Initials	Other
Order of the Garter[1]	1348	blue	*honi soit qui mal y pense* (shame on him who thinks evil of it)	KG	founded by Edward III
Order of the Thistle[2]	1687[3]	green	*nemo me impune lacessit* (no one provokes me with impunity)	KT	ancient Scottish order
Order of the Bath	1725	crimson	*tria juncta in ino* (three joined in one)	GCB, KCB, DCB, CB[4]	founded by Henry IV; divided into civil and military divisions; women became eligible in 1971
Order of Merit[1 5]	1902	blue and crimson	none	OM	founded by Edward VII
Order of the Star of India	1861	light blue with white edges	Heaven's light our guide	GCSI, KCSI, CSI[6]	no new members created since 1947
Order of St Michael and St George	1818	blue with scarlet centre	*auspicium melioris aevi* (token of a better age)	GCMG, KCMG, DCMG, CMG[7]	
Order of the Indian Empire	1868	purple	*imperatricis auspiciis* (under the auspices of the Empress)	GCIE, KCIE, CIE[8]	no new members created since 1947
Imperial Order of the Crown of India[9]	1877	light blue with white edge	none	CI	no new members created since 1947
Royal Victorian Order	1896	blue with red and white edges	Victoria	GCVO, KCVO, DCVO, CVO, LVO, MVO[10]	
Order of the British Empire	1917	pink edged with grey; vertical grey stripe in centre for the military division	for God and the Empire	GBE, KBE, DBE, CBE, OBE, MBE[11]	divided into civil and military divisions in 1918
Companions of Honour[5 12]	1917	carmine with gold edges	none	CH	
Distinguished Service Order	1886	red with blue edges	none	DSO	awarded to members of the armed forces for services in action; a bar may be added for any additional act of service
Imperial Service Order[13]	1902	crimson with blue centre	none	ISO	awarded to members of the Civil Service; no new members created since 1993

1 Only 24 people may hold this order at any one time.
2 Only 16 people may hold this order at any one time.
3 Revived in this year.
4 GCB (Knight/Dame of the Grand Cross); KCB, DCB (Knight/Dame Commander); CB (Companion).
5 Members are not given a knighthood.
6 GCSI (Knight Grand Commander); KCSI (Knight Commander); CSI (Companion).
7 GCMG (Knight/Dame Grand Commander); KCMG, DCMG (Knight/Dame Commander); CMG (Companion).
8 GCIE (Knight/Dame Grand Commander); KCIE (Knight/Dame Commander); CIE (Companion).
9 For women only.
10 GCVO (Knight/Dame of The Grand Cross); KCVO, DCVO (Knight/Dame Commander); LVO (Lieutenant); MVO (Member).
11 GBE/KBE (Knight/Dame Grand Cross); DBE (Knight/Dame Commander); CBE (Commander); OBE (Officer); MBE (Member).
12 Only 65 people may hold this order at any one time.
13 Membership is limited to 1,900 people.

National Anthems and Patriotic Songs

The National Anthem: 'God Save The Queen'

The melody resembles a composition by John Bull and similar words are found from the 16th century. In its present form it was arranged by Dr Thomas Arne, under the title 'Song for Two Voices'. This version was first performed at Drury Lane Theatre in London on 28 September 1745, following the news of the defeat of the army of King George II by the 'Young Pretender' to the British Throne, Prince Charles Edward Stuart, at the battle of Prestonpans. The song immediately became popular as an anti-Jacobite Party song during the 1745 Jacobite Rebellion.

The words below are those sung in 1745, substituting 'Queen' for 'King' where appropriate. On official occasions, only the first verse is usually sung.

God save our gracious Queen, Long live our noble Queen
God save the Queen!
Send her victorious, Happy and Glorious
Long to reign over us
God save the Queen!

O Lord our God arise, Scatter her enemies
And make them fall
Confound their politics,
Frustrate their knavish tricks
On Thee our hopes we fix
Oh, save us all!

Thy choicest gifts in store
On her be pleased to pour
Long may she reign
May she defend our laws,
And ever give us cause
To sing with heart and voice
God save the Queen!

Not in this land alone,
But be God's mercies known
From shore to shore!
Lord make the nations see,
That men should brothers be,
And form one family
The wide world over.

From every latent foe,
From the assassins blow
God save the Queen!
O'er her thine arm extend,
For Britain's sake defend
Our mother, prince, and friend
God save the Queen!

Rule Britannia

Words by James Thomson.

When Britain first, at heaven's command
Arose from out the azure main
This was the charter the charter of the land
And guardian Angels sung this strain:

Rule, Britannia, rule the waves
Britons never will be slaves.

The nations, not so blest as thee
Must, in their turns, to tyrants fall
While thou shalt flourish great and free
The dread and envy of them all.

Still more majestic shalt thou rise
More dreadful, from each foreign stroke
As the loud blast that tears the skies
Serves but to root thy native oak.

Thee haughty tyrants ne'er shall tame
All their attempts to bend thee down
Will but arouse thy generous flame
But work their woe, and thy renown.

To thee belongs the rural reign
Thy cities shall with commerce shine
All thine shall be the subject main
And every shore it circles thine.

The Muses, still with freedom found
Shall to thy happy coast repair
Blest isle! with matchless beauty crowned
And manly hearts to guard the fair.

The Unofficial English National Anthem: 'Land of Hope and Glory'

Although this anthem can identify with the whole of the UK by references to the empire 'wider and still wider, shall thy bounds be set', it is also the unofficial national anthem of England, and is used for the English teams at the Commonwealth Games, although the English national football and rugby teams use 'God Save the Queen'.

Words by A C Benson, music by Sir Edward Elgar from 'Pomp & Circumstance March No. 1'.

Dear Land of Hope, thy hope is crowned.
God make thee mightier yet!
On Sov'ran brows, beloved, renowned,
Once more thy crown is set.
Thine equal laws, by Freedom gained,
Have ruled thee well and long
By Freedom gained, by Truth maintained,
Thine Empire shall be strong.

Land of Hope and Glory, Mother of the Free
How shall we extol thee, who are born of thee?
Wider still and wider shall thy bounds be set
God, who made thee mighty, make thee mightier yet,
God, who made thee mighty, make thee mightier yet.

Thy fame is ancient as the days,
As Ocean large and wide
A pride that dares, and heeds not praise,
A stern and silent pride
Not that false joy that dreams content
With what our sires have won
The blood a hero sire hath spent,
Still nerves a hero son.

The Scottish National Anthem: 'Flower of Scotland'

Although modern, this anthem commemorates the Battle of Bannockburn in 1314 when the Scottish Army under Robert I (the Bruce) King of Scots defeated Edward II, King of England.

O Flower of Scotland,
When will we see Your like again
That fought and died for,
Your wee bit Hill and Glen
And stood against him, Proud Edward's Army
And sent him homeward, Tae think again.

The Hills are bare now, and
Autumn leaves lie thick and still
O'er land that is lost now,
Which those so dearly held
That stood against him,
Proud Edward's Army
And sent him homeward, Tae think again.

Those days are past now,
And in the past they must remain
But we can still rise now,
And be the nation again
That stood against him,
Proud Edward's Army
And sent him homeward, Tae think again.

Flower of Scotland, When will we see Your like again
That fought and died for,
Your wee bit Hill and Glen
And stood against him,
Proud Edward's Army
And sent him homeward, Tae think again.

Scotland The Brave

Hark where the night is falling
Hark hear the pipes a calling
Loudly and proudly calling down thru the glen
There where the hills are sleeping
Now feel the blood a leaping
High as the spirits of the old highland men.

Towering in gallant fame
Scotland my mountain hame
High may your proud standards gloriously wave
Land of my high endeavour
Land of the shining river
Land of my heart forever, Scotland the Brave.

High in the misty mountains
Out by the purple highlands
Brave are the hearts that beat beneath Scottish skies
Wild are the winds to meet you
Staunch are the friends that greet you
Kind as the love that shines from fair maidens eyes.

The Welsh National Anthem: 'Hen Wlad Fy Nhadau'/'Land Of My Fathers'

The words are given in Welsh and English.

Hen Wlad Fy Nhadau

Mae hen wlad fy nhadau yn annwyl i mi
Gwlad beirdd a chantorion, enwogion o fri
Ei gwrol ryfelwyr, gwladgarwyr tra mad
Tros ryddid collasant eu gwaed.

Gwlad, gwlad, pleidiol wyf i'm gwlad
Tra mor yn fur i'r bur hoffbau
O bydded i'r heniaith barhau.

Hen Gymru fynyddig, paradwys y bardd
Pob dyffryn, pob clogwyn i'm golwg sydd hardd
Trwy deimlad gwladgarol, mor swynol yw si
Ei nentydd, afonydd, i mi.

Os treisiodd y gelyn fy ngwlad tan ei droed
Mae hen iaith y Cymry mor fyw ag erioed
Ni luddiwyd yr awen gan erchyll law brad
Na thelyn berseiniol fy ngwlad.

Land of My Fathers

The land of my fathers is dear unto me
Old land where the minstrels are honoured and free
Its warring defenders so gallant and brave
For freedom their life's blood they gave.

Home, home, true am I to home
While seas secure the land so pure
O may the old language endure.

Old land of the mountains, the Eden of bards
Each gorge and each valley a loveliness guards
Through love of my country, charmed voices will be
Its streams, and its rivers, to me.

Though foemen have trampled my land 'neath their feet
The language of Cambria still knows no retreat
The muse is not vanquished by traitor's fell hand.

Web Sites

About the National Trust

http://www.nationaltrust.org.uk/aboutnt.htm

Information about the charity, supported by 2.4 million members, entrusted with the care of large parts of the British countryside and many historic buildings. There is a brief history of the organization, outline of its work, and appeal for assistance.

British Monarchy

http://www.royal.gov.uk/

The official site of the British monarchy includes reviews of its history, its present role and character, and details on the formal order of accession, coronation, and succession that applies to each monarch. There are sections on the royal palaces and parks, the life of Lady Diana, and a guest book for visitors to sign.

Cabinet Office Home Page

http://www.cabinet-office.gov.uk/

Site of the UK cabinet which includes the latest news from Whitehall, access to reports and papers from different departments, and statistics and information about government policy. There is also a full explanation of the 'Government Machine', with links to related sites.

Citizen's Charter Unit

http://www.open.gov.uk/charter/ccuhome.htm

Open government at work. This official explanation of the work of the unit charged with realizing the UK's Citizen's Charter explains the various charters, provides discussion documents, explains how to complain about government services, and invites public feedback.

Countryside Commission

http://www.countryside.gov.uk/

Guide to the work of the Commission and to the attractions of the British countryside. There is information on all of the UK's national parks and officially-designated areas of outstanding beauty. The Commission's work to preserve the countryside is fully explained and there are details of the latest scientific research.

English Heritage

http://www.english-heritage.org.uk/dminterface/dmindex.asp

Site of the public body charged with protecting England's historic environment. The role and structure of English Heritage are described, together with publications and education activities. A clickable map accesses information on historic properties.

FCO Online

http://www.fco.gov.uk/news/

Official statements of British foreign policy. Updated several times daily, this is an invaluable source of information on British policy on a wide range of issues concerning the international community.

Hansard – House of Commons Debates

http://www.parliament.the-stationery-office.co.uk/pa/cm/cmhansrd.htm

The complete proceedings of the House of Commons, posted each day at 12.30 p.m. You can also search archived proceedings going back to 1996.

House of Commons – Members, Ministers, and Committees 1997–1998

http://www.parliament.uk/commons/lib/lists.htm

Regularly updated list of members of the British lower house provided by the House of Commons. MPs are easy to locate as they are listed by their name, by constituency, and by county.

Houses of Parliament Home Page

http://www.parliament.uk/

Site of the UK's House of Commons and House of Lords. There is a guide to visiting, and access to the many government publications and committees.

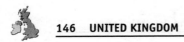

National Assembly for Wales

http://www.assembly.wales.gov.uk/assembly.dbs

Describes the structure and business of the Welsh Assembly, with 'Press notices', 'Who's who in the Assembly', and a 'Record of proceedings'.

NIO Online

http://www.nio.gov.uk/index.htm

Comprehensive information on the administration of criminal justice, security, and the police in Northern Ireland. Frequently updated, this site charts the latest developments in the search for peace and also provides a good introduction to the economy and culture of Ulster.

Northern Ireland Assembly

http://www.ni-assembly.gov.uk/index.htm

Information about the Assembly, its publications and committees, and a 'Register of members' interests'.

Northern Ireland Public Service Web

http://www.nics.gov.uk/

Details of many government services, including the departments of agriculture, economic development, the environment, and health and social services for Northern Ireland.

Northern Ireland Tourist Board

http://www.ni-tourism.com/index.asp

This site covers the needs of anyone planning to visit Northern Ireland, from accommodation to events and attractions. It also features a virtual tour covering history, activities, food and drink, and places to stay.

Oultwood Local Government Web Site Index

http://www.oultwood.com/localgov/

Covering England, Scotland, Wales, Northern Ireland, and Eire, this site provides clickable maps that allow you to find your local council Web site.

Scottish Parliament

http://www.scottish.parliament.uk/

Information about the Scottish Parliament and its activities, including 'The Parliament buildings', 'What's happening', 'Agenda and decisions', and information about the members of the Scottish Parliament.

Select Committees

http://www.parliament.uk/commons/selcom/cmsel.htm

Complete guide to the many select committees of the UK's House of Commons. There is regularly updated news of the sittings of each committee, transcripts of their deliberations, press releases, and details of their members.

10 Downing Street

http://www.number-10.gov.uk/index.html

Official Web site of the British prime minister's residence includes a virtual tour, biographies of recent prime ministers, press releases, and copies of speeches and interviews.

UK Maps

http://www.multimap.com/uk/

This site allows you to search for maps of towns and cities in the UK. You can view the area in a variety of scales, from 1:50,000 to 1:200,000, and also see 'pages' next to your selected street; you can choose between colour or greyscale maps.

United Kingdom

http://www.crwflags.com/fotw/flags/gb.html

Detailed discussion pages with historical information about the Union Jack, its design, and uses.

Visit Britain – British Tourist Authority

http://www.visitbritain.com/frameset.htm

Comprehensive information on tourism in the British Isles, provided by the official tourist promotion agency.

Welcome to CNT

http://www.cnt.org.uk/

Site of the UK Commission for New Towns charged with the management of assets of the UK's new towns. The commission's role to promote relocation of enterprises is well described with a wealth of information and case studies. There are also profiles of the infrastructure, workforce, and advantages of each new town.

Work of the Audit Commission

http://www.audit-commission.gov.uk/

Explanation of the functions of the body charged with ensuring the financial accountability of the British government. There is a history of the external checking of public finances in Britain, an executive summary of the commission reports, and a full description of services offered.

World

The Year in Review

See Also  **Military conflicts of the year, pp 623-625.**

July 1998 By early July approximately one third of the 200,000 Serbs living in the Yugoslav province of Kosovo have left the province, while ethnic Albanians have returned to fight Serbian forces.

7 July 1998 Moshood Abiola, Nigerian opposition leader detained since 1993 by the military dictator, dies from an apparent heart attack in Abuja, Nigeria, at a meeting with US officials trying to negotiate his release. Violence lasting for a week erupts in Lagos at the news.

8 July 1998 The Australian government passes the Native Title Bill, giving greater protection to farmers and miners who fear Aboriginal land claims would destroy their livelihoods. Aboriginal leaders condemn it.

17 July 1998 The last tsar of Russia, Tsar Nicholas II, and his family are buried in St Petersburg, Russia, 80 years after their murder at Yekaterinburg, Russia. Russian president Boris Yeltsin makes a public apology for the murders after initially refusing to attend the ceremony.

29 July 1998 After four days of fighting, Serb forces overrun Kosovo, routing the Kosovo Liberation Army. Over 100,000 ethnic Albanians are displaced.

August 1998 Government forces of the Democratic Republic of Congo lose the Inga hydroelectric dam to rebel forces, who cut power supplies to the capital, Kinshasa.

3 August 1998 Rebel troops in the Democratic Republic of Congo seize several cities in the eastern part of the country, and fight gun battles in the capital, Kinshasa, in their effort to overthrow the government of President Laurent Kabila.

5 August 1998 Iraqi president Saddam Hussein halts cooperation with United Nations weapons inspectors, forbidding them to search suspected nuclear weapons sites, in protest against eight years of trade sanctions by the West.

6 August 1998 Former US White House intern Monica Lewinsky appears before a grand jury to testify about her alleged sexual relationship with US president Bill Clinton, which both she and Clinton had previously denied in the Paula Jones case. After being granted immunity, she reveals that there was a sexual relationship, giving details of several encounters.

7 August 1998 A suicide bomber drives a pick-up truck full of explosives into the car park of the US embassy in Nairobi, Kenya, setting off a bomb that kills 247 people and injures more than 4,000. Another bomb goes off at the US embassy in Dar es Salaam, Tanzania, killing 10 and injuring 74. Saudi multi-

millionaire and Islamic extremist Osama Bin Laden is a key suspect.

17 August 1998 President Clinton testifies before a grand jury about his alleged affair with former White House intern Monica Lewinsky. The grand jury is to determine whether or not Clinton perjured himself in January by denying allegations of sexual relations with Lewinsky and whether or not he tried to obstruct the course of justice by telling her and others to deny the affair. After more than four hours of testimony, Clinton makes a televised speech in which he admits he did have an 'inappropriate' relationship with Lewinsky but denies that he told anyone to lie about it.

20 August 1998 Monica Lewinsky testifies in front of the grand jury for a second time about her relationship with President Clinton. Independent prosecutor Kenneth Starr interrogates her in an effort to find inconsistencies between her testimony and the president's.

23 August 1998 Russian president Boris Yeltsin sacks his entire government for the second time in five months and returns Viktor Chernomyrdin, whom he previously fired and who is widely considered responsible for the country's economic decline, as interim prime minister.

25 August 1998 A bomb at the Planet Hollywood restaurant in Cape Town, South Africa, kills 1 person and injures 27, including 9 Britons. An Islamic fundamentalist group, Muslims Against Global Oppression, claims responsibility. FBI officials investigate possible links with the bombings of the embassies in East Africa earlier in the month.

25 August 1998 Congolese rebels reach Kinshasa, and the government imposes a strict curfew in the capital.

27 August 1998 Two suspects in the bombing of the US embassy in Nairobi, Kenya, earlier in the month – Khalid Salim from Yemen and Mohammed Saddiq Howaidah from Pakistan – are flown to the USA to stand trial.

28 August 1998 President Boris Yeltsin makes an appearance on Russian television. He accepts a major cut in his power but denies that he will resign. Two days later, he rejects a draft accord limiting his constitutional powers and as a result, the parliament does not approve Viktor Chernomyrdin as prime minister, delaying the formation of a new government.

7 September 1998 The Russian parliament rejects president Boris Yeltsin's choice for prime minister, Viktor Chernomyrdin, for a second time, by a vote of 273–138.

8 September 1998 Congolese rebels abandon peace talks with the Congolese government in Victoria Falls, Zimbabwe, after being denied direct communication with Laurent Kabila, the president they are trying to oust.

11 September 1998 The US independent counsel Kenneth Starr releases his report on his case against President Clinton, in which he charges the president with perjury, abuse of power, obstruction of justice, and witness tampering, and recommends impeachment proceedings. Before the report is made public, first to Congress and then via the Internet, Clinton makes a speech in which he expresses contrition for his relationship with former White House intern Monica Lewinsky and for misleading the American people about it.

12 September 1998 The Russian parliament ratifies President Boris Yeltsin's candidate for prime minister, current foreign minister Yevgeny M Primakov.

21 September 1998 The videotape of President Clinton's grand jury testimony on the Monica Lewinsky affair is broadcast on US television. Although the president admits to having an 'inappropriate intimate relationship' with Lewinsky, he refuses to answer detailed questions about their physical relationship, but claims that it does not fall into the definition of sexual relations as outlined in the Paula Jones case.

22 September 1998 South African troops enter Lesotho to try to restore order after a military uprising against the government. The unrest began over the alleged rigging of the 23 May legislative elections.

24 September 1998 The Iranian government announces that it is disavowing the fatwa issued on the life of the writer Salman Rushdie by the Ayatollah Khomeini in 1989.

27 September 1998 Social democrat Gerhard Schroeder unseats Helmut Kohl as German chancellor after Kohl's 16 years in power.

3 October 1998 Australian prime minister John Howard's ruling Liberal Party–National Party coalition narrowly defeats the Australian Labour Party in national elections, but loses seats in parliament.

8 October 1998 The UK, the USA, and their European allies issue a final warning to Serbian president Slobodan Milošević that unless he complies with a six-point ultimatum, NATO countries will respond with air strikes. The ultimatum includes an end to offensive operations, withdrawal of Serbian forces in Kosovo, the withdrawal of heavy weapons, cooperation with the International War Crimes Tribunal, the freedom of safe return for refugees, and a start to peace negotiations.

8 October 1998 The US Congress votes in favour of an impeachment investigation that will enable formal charges to be drawn up against President Clinton in the Monica Lewinsky affair.

13 October 1998 US special envoy Richard Holbrooke brokers a deal with President Milošević that temporarily suspends the threat of NATO air strikes against Serbia, contingent on Serbia upholding the 8 October ultimatum.

14 October 1998 US House of Representatives judiciary committee chairman Henry Hyde announces that the investigation into the allegations against President Clinton in the Monica Lewinsky affair will be limited to three issues: lying under oath, influencing witnesses, and obstructing justice. Previously the committee had planned to investigate 15 charges against the president.

16 October 1998 NATO ambassadors agree to extend to 27 October the deadline for President Milošević to withdraw his forces from Kosovo.

21 October 1998 The Middle East peace summit at the Wye Plantation resort, Maryland, nears crisis point when the chief Israeli spokesman, David Bar-Illan, threatens to walk out of the talks if the Palestinians do not propose stronger resolutions for dealing with terrorism and security.

29 October 1998 South Africa's Truth and Reconciliation Commission, led by Archbishop Desmond Tutu, publishes its report on the country during apartheid. The report condemns all of the main political parties, black and white, for gross human-rights violations.

30 October 1998 A fire at a disco in Gothenburg, Sweden, kills at least 60 teenagers. Fire service officials believe the fire is caused by an electrical fault.

November 1998 The US Anti-Defamation League (ADL) puts Hatefilter on the market. This is a piece of software that blocks access to white supremacist and neo-Nazi Web pages and redirects the user to ADL information about these groups. The software is designed to prevent young Internet surfers from being recruited by hate groups using child-oriented Web sites.

3 November 1998 In US midterm elections, Democrats gain four seats in the House of Representatives, and the balance in the Senate remains the same. Although Congress is still controlled by the Republicans (with a majority of 223–210 in the House and 55–45 in the Senate), it is the first time since 1934 that the party of a sitting president makes midterm gains.

6 November 1998 Two Palestinian suicide bombers set off a blast at Jerusalem's central market, intending to kill Israeli shoppers. Twenty-one people are injured, putting the Middle East peace plan on the brink of collapse.

6 November 1998 US House of Representatives speaker Newt Gingrich resigns as leader of his party and as House speaker, following the Republicans' setbacks in midterm elections.

13 November 1998 Paula Jones, a former employee of President Clinton when he was governor of Arkansas, settles her sexual harassment case against him for $850,000.

13 November 1998 Soldiers in Jakarta, Indonesia, kill seven students and a reporter as they try to stop tens of thousands of protesters from reaching parliament. The protesters are against a parliamentary session

called to repeal authoritarian laws, because they view the members, who were appointed by former dictator Suharto, as attempting to retain the status quo instead of making a commitment to true reform. The following day, at least 14 people are reported killed and hundreds more injured in violent clashes between government security forces and protesters.

16 November 1998 Israeli prime minister Binyamin Netanyahu announces that he is suspending the withdrawal of Israeli troops from the West Bank until PLO leader Yasser Arafat publicly retracts a pledge to declare a Palestinian state next May.

22 November 1998 Muslim mobs in Jakarta, Indonesia, hack at least 7 Christians to death and attack 11 churches after more than a week of political unrest.

8 December 1998 British engineers Darren Hickey, Rudolf Petschi, and Peter Kennedy, and New Zealand engineer Stan Shaw are found decapitated on a roadside outside Grozny, Chechnya. They were taken hostage on 3 October by gunmen who demanded £4 million ransom. Granger Telecom, the British telecom company that employed three of the men, had defied official advice not to send personnel to the lawless republic.

8 December 1998 Impeachment hearings begin against President Clinton, with testimony in front of the judiciary committee of the House of Representatives.

9 December 1998 Interior Minister Ruth Dreifuss is elected president of Switzerland. She is the country's first female and first Jewish president.

12 December 1998 In a referendum, Puerto Ricans vote against becoming a state of the USA, retaining their status as a self-governing commonwealth under US rule.

12 December 1998 The US House of Representatives judiciary committee approves the four articles of impeachment against President Clinton.

13 December 1998 Israel rejects appeals by President Clinton to keep to the timetable of the October Wye agreement that trades 10 percent of the Israeli-occupied West Bank in return for a clampdown on Palestinian extremists.

14 December 1998 President Clinton, on a peace mission to the Middle East, is the first US president to visit Palestinian territory when he meets Palestinian Liberation Organization leader Yasser Arafat on the Gaza Strip.

16 December 1998 Twenty-three Zimbabwean army officers are arrested for plotting to overthrow the government of President Robert Mugabe.

16 December 1998 In Operation Desert Fox, the USA and the UK launch air strikes against Iraq for failing to cooperate with United Nations (UN) weapons inspections. There are four consecutive nights of air strikes.

19 December 1998 The US House of Representatives impeaches President Clinton over allegations of perjury and obstruction of justice in the Monica Lewinsky case. He is only the second president to be impeached in US history, following Andrew Johnson 120 years ago. The case is scheduled to go before the Senate in January 1999.

21 December 1998 The Israeli parliament votes to hold elections in six months time, delaying the peace process.

21 December 1998 President Clinton's approval ratings soar in opinion polls two days after impeachment. A Gallup poll shows an approval rating of 73 percent, up 10 points, and a *New York Times* poll shows 72 percent; 68 percent, and 64 percent respectively said they believed the Senate should not convict Clinton.

29 December 1998 Three British hostages and one Australian are killed in Yemen when government troops storm the hideout of an Islamic kidnap gang. The gang, demanding the release by the government of their leaders, was holding 16 Western tourists hostage.

14 January 1999 The European Parliament votes to place the European Commission on probation and instil wide-ranging reforms in an effort to stem corruption and fraud.

14 January 1999 The impeachment trial of President Clinton opens in the Senate in Washington, DC. It is the first-ever impeachment trial of an elected US president. The president is charged with perjury and obstruction of justice in his testimony about his relationship with former White House intern Monica Lewinsky.

19 January 1999 In his annual State of the Union address, President Clinton emphasizes the country's continuing economic boom and reduction in crime, while the Senate decides whether to prolong his impeachment trial by calling witnesses.

6 February 1999 Video testimony from 1 February by Monica Lewinsky is shown to the Senate in the impeachment trial of President Clinton and is aired on national television. Despite prosecution attempts to use the testimony in their favour, Lewinsky offers no new evidence.

7 February 1999 Serbs and ethnic Albanian leaders from Kosovo meet at Rambouillet, outside Paris, to begin peace talks.

12 February 1999 After a month-long impeachment trial, the US Senate acquits President Clinton of perjury and obstruction of justice, 55–45 and 50–50. The charges would have needed a two-thirds majority to dismiss the president from office.

17 February 1999 Rebels in Congo resume their offensive against the government of Laurent Kabila after efforts fail to revive peace talks.

23 February 1999 On the final day of peace talks at Rambouillet, Serb and ethnic Albanian representatives tentatively agree to an accord to end the conflict in Kosovo. British foreign secretary Robin Cook emphasizes that NATO would be authorized to launch air strikes if the two sides failed to reach a final accord.

27 February 1999 Olusegun Obasanjo of the People's Democratic Party is elected president of Nigeria. He had been the country's military ruler 1976–79. Although the election was held without violent disruption, international observers reported significant irregularities and fraud.

15 March 1999 An independent panel appointed by the European Parliament publishes a report accusing members of the European Commission of corruption and mismanagement. The report is most critical of former French premier Edith Cresson for her failure to stop fraud in programmes under her control and for hiring friends for posts for which they were not qualified.

16 March 1999 All 20 members of the European Commission announce their intention to resign, following the European Parliament's report condemning their performance. Commission president Jacques Santer repeats his denial, however, that the commissioners are guilty of fraud and mismanagement.

18 March 1999 Ethnic Albanian representatives sign a peace agreement in Paris, designed to end the conflict with the Serbian government over the autonomy of Kosovo. Serbian delegates, however, refuse to sign the accord because of its inclusion of a planned NATO peacekeeping force in the region.

23 March 1999 Negotiations between US envoy Richard Holbrooke and Serbian president Milošević fail to draw nearer to a peace agreement on Kosovo, leading to a NATO decision to launch air strikes against Serbia.

24 March 1999 NATO launches air strikes against Serbia, starting off a bombing campaign prompted by President Slobodan Milošević's refusal to sign a peace accord with ethnic Albanians over the area of Kosovo. It is NATO's first assault on a sovereign nation in its 50-year history.

26 March 1999 South African president Nelson Mandela delivers his last parliamentary address before his term ends in June.

30 March 1999 Russian premier Yevgeny Primakov meets with President Milošević in an effort to resolve the conflict in Kosovo. Milošević says that he will only negotiate if NATO stops its bombing campaign, which NATO refuses to do.

4 April 1999 As the refugee crisis of ethnic Albanians fleeing Kosovo worsens, several NATO members agree to plans to airlift up to 110,000 refugees out of the region. More than 400,000 ethnic Albanians have fled the region since NATO began air strikes on 24 March.

8 April 1999 President Milošević declares that peace has been achieved in Kosovo and calls on NATO to cease its bombing campaign against Serb forces. NATO, which rejected Milošević's declaration of a cease-fire two days earlier, claiming continued Serb attacks on ethnic Albanian villages, continues bombing.

9 April 1999 Niger president Ibrahim Barre Mainassara is assassinated by members of his presidential guard at the airport in the capital, Niamey. A military government led by Daouda Wanke, head of the presidential guard, takes power.

12 April 1999 Foreign ministers from NATO's 19 member countries meet for the first time since bombing began in Kosovo. They pledge to continue the bombing campaign until President Milošević withdraws his forces from Kosovo and allows ethnic Albanian refugees to return safely.

13 April 1999 US secretary of state Madeleine Albright meets Russian foreign minister Igor Ivanov in Oslo, Norway, to discuss a political resolution to the conflict in Kosovo. Although they agree that President Milošević must withdraw his forces from Kosovo and allow ethnic Albanian refugees to return, Ivanov says that Russia would not accept an international peacekeeping force in Kosovo unless Milošević agrees to it.

15 April 1999 Abdelaziz Bouteflika, the joint candidate of the National Liberation Front and National Democratic Rally, the ruling military parties, is elected president of Algeria. The other candidates had withdrawn from the race, claiming the election was rigged.

17 April 1999 Indian prime minister Atal Vajpayee, leader of the Hindu nationalist Bharatiya Janata Party, resigns after his government loses a vote of confidence in parliament.

21 April 1999 Colorado legislators withdraw two pending firearms bills that would make it easier to own and carry a handgun, after two students killed 13 people and injured 30 others using guns and bombs at their school in Littleton, Colorado, the previous day.

21 April 1999 Sonia Gandhi, Italian-born leader of India's Congress (I) Party and widow of former prime minister Rajiv Gandhi, declares that her party has enough support in parliament to form a coalition government.

23 April 1999 The heads of 19 NATO countries meet in Washington, DC, for a summit marking the 50th anniversary of the organization. British prime minister Tony Blair announces his resolve to commit ground troops to Yugoslavia in the conflict over the province of Kosovo.

28 April 1999 Vuk Drasković is dismissed as Yugoslav deputy prime minister, after a televised speech in which he claims that the Yugoslav government is ready to accept a peace settlement in the conflict over the province of Kosovo and that NATO could not be defeated.

2 May 1999 US soldiers Steven Gonzales, Andrew Ramirez, and Christopher Stone, who were seized on 31 March by Serbian soldiers on the Yugoslav-Macedonian border and held captive by the Yugoslav government, are released in a deal brokered by US civil-rights activist Jesse Jackson. The three arrive at Ramstein Air Base in Germany and are taken to hospital.

6 May 1999 Russia backs the NATO mandate for a security force in Kosovo under the authority of the United Nations, as well as NATO's demands on President Milošević.

9 May 1999 NATO drops three bombs on the Chinese embassy in Belgrade, Yugoslavia, killing three people. NATO claims that intelligence sources led pilots to believe that it was a Yugoslav government office. Chinese students hurl rocks and bottles at the American embassy in Beijing in protest.

10 May 1999 Israeli prime minister Binyamin Netanyahu orders the closure of the offices of the Palestine Liberation Organization in east Jerusalem. The move, which could cause a bloody confrontation, is seen as a last-ditch strategy by Netanyahu to gain popularity before elections on 17 May.

10 May 1999 The Tanjug news agency in Belgrade announces that Serbia is ready to withdraw some of its forces from the province of Kosovo. NATO dismisses the move as a 'half measure' and says it will continue air strikes.

11 May 1999 China and Russia coordinate their policy on Kosovo and agree to support a United Nations peacekeeping force in the area if NATO ceases its air strikes against Serbia.

11 May 1999 Government forces in Congo drop five bombs on the city of Goma, headquarters of rebel forces, killing 39 people and injuring 47. Doctors report that half of the casualties are children.

12 May 1999 President Yeltsin sacks his prime minister, Yevgeny Primakov, and Primakov's cabinet. The Russian parliament declares that there is no basis for the dismissal and moves for Yeltsin's resignation.

15 May 1999 NATO claims that ethnic Albanian refugees killed in the bombing of the village of Korisa in Kosovo were used as human shields in a Serb military camp.

17 May 1999 Israeli prime minister Binyamin Netanyahu loses to Labour candidate Ehud Barak in national elections. US and Arab leaders welcome the change in government, hoping to rekindle Middle East peace talks, which have been frozen since December.

17 May 1999 The Kuwaiti government approves a law giving women the right to vote and stand for public office from 2003.

18 May 1999 The German and Italian governments announce that they do not support the use of NATO land troops against Serb forces in Kosovo, deepening a rift among the NATO nations.

31 May 1999 The Yugoslav news agency reports that President Milošević has accepted the international peace plan drawn up by the Group of Eight nations. Western leaders react cautiously, waiting to see if Milošević will indeed submit to NATO demands.

2 June 1999 Finnish president Martii Ahtisaari, representing the European Union, and Russian envoy Viktor Chernomyrdin arrive in Belgrade, Yugoslavia, for a meeting with President Milošević to discuss a peace plan to end the conflict over the province of Kosovo.

3 June 1999 South African vice president Thabo Mbeki of the African National Congress (ANC) is elected president of South Africa, replacing Nelson Mandela, who is retiring.

3 June 1999 President Milošević formally accepts a peace plan devised by the European Union and Russia, after 72 days of NATO bombing. NATO plans to continue bombing until Serb forces begin to withdraw from the disputed region of Kosovo.

8 June 1999 The first democratic elections for 44 years are held in Indonesia, amid reports of corruption and irregularities.

9 June 1999 Abdullah II is crowned king of Jordan, inheriting the kingdom from his father, King Hussein, who died in February.

9 June 1999 NATO makes some concessions in its terms for the withdrawal of Yugoslav forces from Kosovo, and (at the Kumanovo air base in Macedonia) Yugoslav military leaders sign the agreement outlining the technicalities of their withdrawal. NATO ceases its bombing campaign.

10 June 1999 As Serb troops start to withdraw from Kosovo, NATO general secretary Javier Solana officially declares an end to the alliance's 78 days of bombing in Yugoslavia, marking an end to the war. NATO makes final preparations for Operation Joint Guardian, the largest peacekeeping force in modern history, which will facilitate the return of up to one million ethnic Albanian refugees to their homes in Kosovo.

14 June 1999 British troops in Kosovo find a police interrogation centre in the capital, Pristina, where torture instruments and identification photographs of ethnic Albanians seem to show evidence of Serb atrocities.

15 June 1999 NATO forces find 20–50 burned bodies in two houses in the village of Velika Krusa, in southern Kosovo. Locals claim that men and boys of the village were separated from their families, shot dead, covered with hay, and burnt

inside the houses. The following day, bodies are discovered in four wells in Vlastion, near Pristina in Kosovo. Local people said that Serb forces killed up to 100 ethnic Albanians shortly before NATO peacekeepers entered Kosovo.

16 June 1999 Ethnic Albanian refugees begin to return in large numbers to their homes in Kosovo, much sooner than United Nations officials expected or planned for. The officials feared loss of life from hidden mines and other dangers.

17 June 1999 Reporters find partially burned bodies and rotting limbs in hastily dug graves near the village of Verboves in Kosovo – new evidence of the systematic killings of ethnic Albanians by Serb troops. The following day, United Nations forensic investigators enter Kosovo to gather evidence of the killings and torture of ethnic Albanians by Serb forces. The British government estimates that 10,000 ethnic Albanians were killed.

24 June 1999 US State Department spokesman James Rubin announces a reward of up to $5 million for information leading to the capture of President Milošević and other leaders charged with war crimes in the province of Kosovo.

29 June 1999 A Turkish court sentences Kurdish rebel leader Abdullah Ocalan to death for treason. The European Union and the Council of Europe both put pressure on the Turkish government to commute the sentence.

Geography

Major Oceans and Seas in the World

Ocean/sea	Area[1]		Average depth	
	sq km	sq mi	m	ft
Pacific Ocean	166,242,000	64,186,000	3,939	12,925
Atlantic Ocean	86,557,000	33,420,000	3,575	11,730
Indian Ocean	73,429,000	28,351,000	3,840	12,598
Arctic Ocean	13,224,000	5,106,000	1,038	3,407
South China Sea	2,975,000	1,149,000	1,464	4,802
Caribbean Sea	2,754,000	1,063,000	2,575	8,448
Mediterranean Sea	2,510,000	969,000	1,501	4,926
Bering Sea	2,261,000	873,000	1,491	4,893
Sea of Okhotsk	1,580,000	610,000	973	3,192
Gulf of Mexico	1,544,000	596,000	1,614	5,297
Sea of Japan	1,013,000	391,000	1,667	5,468
Hudson Bay	730,000	282,000	93	305
East China Sea	665,000	257,000	189	620
Andaman Sea	565,000	218,000	1,118	3,667
Black Sea	461,000	178,000	1,190	3,906
Red Sea	453,000	175,000	538	1,764
North Sea	427,000	165,000	94	308
Baltic Sea	422,000	163,000	55	180
Yellow Sea	294,000	114,000	37	121
Persian Gulf	230,000	89,000	100	328
Gulf of California	153,000	59,000	724	2,375
English Channel	90,000	35,000	54	177
Irish Sea	89,000	34,000	60	197

[1] All figures are approximate, as boundaries of oceans and seas cannot be exactly determined.

Largest Islands in the World

Island	Location	Area	
		sq km	sq mi
Greenland	northern Atlantic	2,175,600	840,000
New Guinea	southwestern Pacific	800,000	309,000
Borneo	southwestern Pacific	744,100	287,300
Madagascar	Indian Ocean	587,041	226,657
Baffin	Canadian Arctic	507,450	195,875
Sumatra	Indian Ocean	424,760	164,000
Honshu	northwestern Pacific	230,966	89,176
Great Britain	northern Atlantic	218,078	84,200
Victoria	Canadian Arctic	217,206	83,896
Ellesmere	Canadian Arctic	196,160	75,767
Sulawesi	Indian Ocean	189,216	73,057
South Island, New Zealand	southwestern Pacific	149,883	57,870
Java	Indian Ocean	126,602	48,900
North Island, New Zealand	southwestern Pacific	114,669	44,274
Cuba	Caribbean Sea	110,860	42,803
Newfoundland	northwestern Atlantic	108,860	42,030
Luzon	western Pacific	104,688	40,420
Iceland	northern Atlantic	103,000	39,768
Mindanao	western Pacific	94,630	36,537
Ireland (Northern Ireland and the Republic of Ireland)	northern Atlantic	84,406	32,590
Hokkaido	northwestern Pacific	83,515	32,245
Sakhalin	northwestern Pacific	76,400	29,500
Hispaniola – Dominican Republic and Haiti	Caribbean Sea	76,192	29,418
Banks	Canadian Arctic	70,028	27,038
Tasmania	southwestern Pacific	67,800	26,171
Sri Lanka	Indian Ocean	65,610	25,332
Devon	Canadian Arctic	55,247	21,331

Longest Rivers in the World

River	Location	Approximate length km	mi
Nile	Africa	6,695	4,160
Amazon	South America	6,570	4,083
Chang Jiang (Yangtze)	China	6,300	3,915
Mississippi–Missouri–Red Rock	USA	6,020	3,741
Huang He (Yellow River)	China	5,464	3,395
Ob–Irtysh	China/Kazakhstan/ Russia	5,410	3,362
Amur–Shilka	Asia	4,416	2,744
Lena	Russia	4,400	2,734
Congo–Zaire	Africa	4,374	2,718
Mackenzie–Peace–Finlay	Canada	4,241	2,635
Mekong	Asia	4,180	2,597
Niger	Africa	4,100	2,548
Yenisei	Russia	4,100	2,548
Paraná	Brazil	3,943	2,450
Mississippi	USA	3,779	2,348
Murray–Darling	Australia	3,751	2,331
Missouri	USA	3,726	2,315
Volga	Russia	3,685	2,290
Madeira	Brazil	3,241	2,014
Purus	Brazil	3,211	1,995
São Francisco	Brazil	3,199	1,988
Yukon	USA/Canada	3,185	1,979
Rio Grande	USA/Mexico	3,058	1,900
Indus	Tibet/Pakistan	2,897	1,800
Danube	central and eastern Europe	2,858	1,776
Japura	Brazil	2,816	1,750
Salween	Myanmar/China	2,800	1,740
Brahmaputra	Asia	2,736	1,700
Euphrates	Iraq	2,736	1,700
Tocantins	Brazil	2,699	1,677
Zambezi	Africa	2,650	1,647
Orinoco	Venezuela	2,559	1,590
Paraguay	Paraguay	2,549	1,584
Amu Darya	Tajikistan/ Turkmenistan/ Uzbekistan	2,540	1,578
Ural	Russia/Kazakhstan	2,535	1,575
Kolyma	Russia	2,513	1,562
Ganges	India/Bangladesh	2,510	1,560
Arkansas	USA	2,344	1,459
Colorado	USA	2,333	1,450
Dnieper	Russia/Belarus/ Ukraine	2,285	1,420
Syr Darya	Asia	2,205	1,370
Irrawaddy	Myanmar	2,152	1,337
Orange	South Africa	2,092	1,300

Largest Deserts in the World

Desert	Location	Area[1] sq km	sq mi
Sahara	northern Africa	9,065,000	3,500,000
Gobi	Mongolia/northeastern China	1,295,000	500,000
Patagonian	Argentina	673,000	260,000
Rub al-Khali	southern Arabian peninsula	647,500	250,000
Kalahari	southwestern Africa	582,800	225,000
Chihuahuan	Mexico/southwestern USA	362,600	140,000
Taklimakan	northern China	362,600	140,000
Great Sandy	northwestern Australia	338,500	130,000
Great Victoria	southwestern Australia	338,500	130,000
Kyzyl Kum	Uzbekistan/Kazakhstan	259,000	100,000
Thar	India/Pakistan	259,000	100,000
Sonoran	Mexico/southwestern USA	181,300	70,000
Simpson	Australia	103,600	40,000
Mojave	southwestern USA	65,000	25,000

[1] Desert areas are very approximate because clear physical boundaries may not occur.

Largest Lakes in the World

Lake	Location	Area sq km	sq mi
Caspian Sea	Azerbaijan/Russia/ Kazakhstan/ Turkmenistan/Iran	370,990	143,239
Superior	USA/Canada	82,071	31,688
Victoria	Tanzania/Kenya/Uganda	69,463	26,820
Aral Sea	Kazakhstan/Uzbekistan	64,500	24,903
Huron	USA/Canada	59,547	22,991
Michigan	USA	57,735	22,291
Tanganyika	Tanzania/Democratic Republic of Congo/ Zambia/Burundi	32,880	12,695
Baikal	Russia	31,499	12,162
Great Bear	Canada	31,316	12,091
Malawi (or Nyasa)	Malawi/Tanzania/ Mozambique	28,867	11,146
Great Slave	Canada	28,560	11,027
Erie	USA/Canada	25,657	9,906
Winnipeg	Canada	25,380	9,799
Ontario	USA/Canada	19,010	7,340
Balkhash	Kazakhstan	18,421	7,112
Ladoga	Russia	17,695	6,832
Chad	Chad/Cameroon/ Nigeria	16,310	6,297
Maracaibo	Venezuela	13,507	5,215

Highest Elevations and Lowest Depressions by Continent

Continent	Highest elevation	Height m	Height ft	Lowest depression	Depth below sea level m	Depth below sea level ft
Africa	Kilimanjaro, Tanzania	5,895	19,337	Lake Assal, Djibouti	153	502
Antarctica	Vinson Massif	5,140	16,863	Lake Vostok[1]	4,000	13,123
Asia	Everest, China–Nepal	8,848	29,028	Dead Sea, Israel/Jordan	400	1,312
Europe	Elbrus, Russia	5,642	18,510	Caspian Sea, Azerbaijan/Russia/Kazakhstan/Turkmenistan/Iran	28	92
North America	McKinley (AK), USA	6,194	20,321	Death Valley (CA), USA	86	282
Oceania	Jaya, New Guinea	5,030	16,502	Lake Eyre, South Australia	16	52
South America	Cerro Aconcagua, Argentina	6,960	22,834	Valdés Peninsula, Argentina	40	131

[1] Discovered by the British Antarctic Survey in 1996, the freshwater Lake Vostok lies beneath the ice sheets and covers an area of 14,000 sq km/5,400 sq mi.

Highest Waterfalls in the World

Waterfall	Location	Total drop m	Total drop ft	Waterfall	Location	Total drop m	Total drop ft
Angel Falls	Venezuela	979	3,212	Skjeggedal	Norway	420	1,378
Yosemite Falls	USA	739	2,425	Glass Falls	Brazil	404	1,325
Mardalsfossen–South	Norway	655	2,149	Krimml	Austria	400	1,312
Tugela Falls	South Africa	614	2,014	Trummelbach Falls	Switzerland	400	1,312
Cuquenan	Venezuela	610	2,000	Takkakaw Falls	Canada	366	1,200
Sutherland	New Zealand	580	1,903	Silver Strand Falls, Yosemite	USA	357	1,170
Ribbon Fall, Yosemite	USA	491	1,612	Wallaman Falls	Australia	346	1,137
Great Karamang River Falls	Guyana	488	1,600	Wollomombi	Australia	335	1,100
Mardalsfossen–North	Norway	468	1,535	Cusiana River Falls	Colombia	300	984
Della Falls	Canada	440	1,443	Giessbach	Switzerland	300	984
Gavarnie Falls	France	422	1,385	Skykkjedalsfossen	Norway	300	984

Highest Mountains in the World by Region

Region/mountain	Location	Height m	Height ft
Africa			
Kilimanjaro	Tanzania	5,895	19,337
Kenya (Batian)	Kenya	5,199	17,057
Ngaliema (formerly Mt Stanley and Margherita Peak)	Democratic Republic of Congo/Uganda	5,110	16,765
Duwoni (formerly Umberto Peak)	Uganda	4,896	16,063
Baker (Edward Peak)	Uganda	4,843	15,889
Alpine Europe			
Mont Blanc	France/Italy	4,807	15,771
Monte Rosa	Switzerland	4,634	15,203
Dom	Switzerland	4,545	14,911
Liskamm	Switzerland/Italy	4,527	14,852
Weisshorn	Switzerland	4,505	14,780
Antarctica			
Vinson Massif		5,140	16,863
Tyree		4,965	16,289
Shinn		4,800	15,748
Gardner		4,690	15,387
Epperley		4,511	14,800
Asia			
Everest	China/Nepal	8,848	29,028
K2	Kashmir/Jammu	8,611	28,251
Kangchenjunga	India/Nepal	8,598	28,208
Lhotse	China/Nepal	8,511	27,923
Yalung Kang	India/Nepal	8,502	27,893

Region/mountain	Location	Height m	Height ft
Australia			
Kosciusko	Snowy Mountains, New South Wales	2,230	7,316
Carpathians			
Gerlachvka	Slovak Republic	2,655	8,711
Moldoveanu	Romania	2,544	8,346
Negoiu	Romania	2,535	8,317
Mindra	Romania	2,518	8,261
Peleaga	Romania	2,509	8,232
Caucasia			
Elbrus, West Peak	Russia	5,642	18,510
Dykh Tau	Russia/Georgia	5,203	17,070
Shkhara	Russia/Georgia	5,201	17,063
Kashtan Tau	Russia/Georgia	5,144	16,876
Dzanghi Tau	Russia	5,049	16,565
New Zealand			
Cook (called Aorongi in Maori)	west coast, South Island	3,754	12,316
North and Central America			
McKinley	Alaska, USA	6,194	20,321
Logan, Yukon	Canada	6,050	19,849
Citlaltépetl (Orizaba)	Mexico	5,610	18,405
St Elias	Alaska, USA/Yukon, Canada	5,489	18,008
Popocatépetl	Mexico	5,452	17,887

(continued)

Highest Mountains in the World by Region (*continued*)

Region/mountain	Location	Height m	Height ft
Oceania[1]			
Jaya	West Irian, Papua New Guinea	5,030	16,502
Daam	West Irian, Papua New Guinea	4,922	16,148
Oost Carstensz (also known as Jayakusumu Timur)	West Irian, Papua New Guinea	4,840	15,879
Trikora	West Irian, Papua New Guinea	4,730	15,518
Enggea	West Irian, Papua New Guinea	4,717	15,476
Polynesia			
Mauna Kea	Hawaii, USA	4,205	13,796
Mauna Loa	Hawaii, USA	4,170	13,681
Pyrenees			
Pico de Aneto	Spain	3,404	11,168
Pico de Posets	Spain	3,371	11,060
Monte Perdido	Spain	3,348	10,984
Pico de la Maladeta	Spain	3,312	10,866
Pic de Vignemale	France/Spain	3,298	10,820
Scandinavia			
Glittertind	Norway	2,472	8,110
Galdhøpiggen	Norway	2,469	8,100
Skagastolstindane	Norway	2,405	7,890
Snohetta	Norway	2,286	7,500
South America			
Cerro Aconcagua	Argentina	6,960	22,834
Ojos del Salado	Argentina/Chile	6,908	22,664
Bonete	Argentina	6,872	22,546
Nevado de Pissis	Argentina/Chile	6,779	22,241
Huascarán Sur	Peru	6,768	22,204

[1] Including all of Papua New Guinea.

Highest Mountains in the World, and First Ascents

Mountain	Location	Height m	Height ft	Year of first ascent	Expedition nationality (leader)
Everest	China/Nepal	8,848	29,028	1953	British/New Zealander (J Hunt)
K2	Kashmir/Jammu	8,611	28,251	1954	Italian (A Desio)
Kangchenjunga	India/Nepal	8,598	28,208	1955	British (C Evans; by the southwest face)
Lhotse	China/Nepal	8,511	27,923	1956	Swiss (E Reiss)
Yalung Kang (formerly Kangchenjunga West Peak)	India/Nepal	8,502	27,893	1973	Japanese (Y Ageta)
Kangchenjunga South Peak	India/Nepal	8,488	27,847	1978	Polish (W Wró)
Makalu I	China/Nepal	8,481	27,824	1955	French (J Couzy)
Kangchenjunga Middle Peak	India/Nepal	8,475	27,805	1973	Polish (W Wró)
Lhotse Shar	China/Nepal	8,383	27,503	1970	Austrian (S Mayerl)
Dhaulagiri	Nepal	8,172	26,811	1960	Swiss/Austrian (K Diemberger)
Manaslu	Nepal	8,156	26,759	1956	Japanese (T Imanishi)
Cho Oyu	China/Nepal	8,153	26,748	1954	Austrian (H Tichy)
Nanga Parbat	Kashmir/Jammu	8,126	26,660	1953	German (K M Herrligkoffer)
Annapurna I	Nepal	8,078	26,502	1950	French (M Herzog)
Gasherbrum I	Kashmir/Jammu	8,068	26,469	1958	US (P K Schoening; by the southwest ridge)
Broad Peak	Kashmir/Jammu	8,047	26,401	1957	Austrian (M Schmuck)
Gasherbrum II	Kashmir/Jammu	8,034	26,358	1956	Austrian (S Larch; by the southwest spur)
Gosainthan	China	8,012	26,286	1964	Chinese (195-strong team; accounts are inconclusive)
Broad Peak (Middle)	Kashmir/Jammu	8,000	26,246	1975	Polish (K Glazek)
Gasherbrum III	Kashmir/Jammu	7,952	26,089	1975	Polish (J Onyszkiewicz)
Annapurna II	Nepal	7,937	26,040	1960	British (C Bonington)
Gasherbrum IV	Kashmir/Jammu	7,923	25,994	1958	Italian (W Bonatti, C Mouri)
Gyachung Kang	Nepal	7,921	25,987	1964	Japanese (Y Kato, K Sakaizqwa)
Disteghil Shar	Kashmir	7,884	25,866	1960	Austrian (G Stärker, D Marchart)
Himalchuli	Nepal	7,864	25,800	1960	Japanese (M Harada, H Tanabe)
Nuptse	Nepal	7,841	25,725	1961	British (D Davis, C Bonington, L Brown)
Manaslu II	Nepal	7,835	25,705	1970	Japanese (H Watanabe, Lhakpa Tsering)
Masherbrum East	Kashmir	7,821	25,659	1960	Pakistani/US (G Bell, W Unsoeld)
Nanda Devi	India	7,817	25,646	1936	British (H W Tilman)
Chomo Lonzo	Nepal	7,815	25,639	1954	French (J Couzy, L Terry)

Major Volcanoes Active in the 20th Century

As of 15 January 1999.

Volcano	Height (m)	Height (ft)	Location	Date of last eruption or activity
Africa				
Cameroon	4,096	13,353	isolated mountain, Cameroon	1986
Nyiragongo	3,470	11,385	Virungu, Democratic Republic of Congo	1994
Nyamuragira	3,056	10,028	Democratic Republic of Congo	1998
Ol Doinyo Lengai	2,886	9,469	Tanzania	1993
Lake Nyos	918	3,011	Cameroon	1986
Erta-Ale	503	1,650	Ethiopia	1995
Antarctica				
Erebus	4,023	13,200	Ross Island, McMurdo Sound	1995
Deception Island	576	1,890	South Shetland Island	1970
Asia				
Kerinci	3,800	12,467	Sumatra, Indonesia	1987
Rindjani	3,726	12,224	Lombok, Indonesia	1966
Semeru	3,676	12,060	Java, Indonesia	1995
Slamet	3,428	11,247	Java, Indonesia	1989
Raung	3,322	10,932	Java, Indonesia	1993
Agung	3,142	10,308	Bali, Indonesia	1964
On-Taka	3,063	10,049	Honshu, Japan	1991
Merapi	2,911	9,551	Java, Indonesia	1998
Marapi	2,891	9,485	Sumatra, Indonesia	1993
Asama	2,530	8,300	Honshu, Japan	1990
Nigata Yake-yama	2,475	8,111	Honshu, Japan	1989
Mayon	2,462	8,084	Luzon, Philippines	1993
Canlaon	2,459	8,070	Negros, Philippines	1993
Chokai	2,225	7,300	Honshu, Japan	1974
Galunggung	2,168	7,113	Java, Indonesia	1984
Azuma	2,042	6,700	Honshu, Japan	1977
Sangeang Api	1,935	6,351	Lesser Sunda Island, Indonesia	1988
Pinatubo	1,759	5,770	Luzon, Philippines	1995
Kelut	1,730	5,679	Java, Indonesia	1990
Unzen	1,360	4,462	Japan	1996
Krakatoa	818	2,685	Sumatra, Indonesia	1996
Taal	300	984	Philippines	1977
Atlantic Ocean				
Pico de Teide	3,716	12,192	Tenerife, Canary Islands, Spain	1909
Fogo	2,835	9,300	Cape Verde Islands	1995
Beerenberg	2,277	7,470	Jan Mayen Island, Norway	1985
Hekla	1,491	4,920	Iceland	1991
Krafla	654	2,145	Iceland	1984
Helgafell	215	706	Iceland	1973
Surtsey	174	570	Iceland	1967
Caribbean				
La Grande Soufrière	1,467	4,813	Basse-Terre, Guadeloupe	1977
Pelée	1,397	4,584	Martinique	1932
La Soufrière St Vincent	1,234	4,048	St Vincent and the Grenadines	1979
Soufriere Hills/ Chances Peak	968	3,176	Montserrat	1999
Central America				
Acatenango	3,960	12,992	Sierra Madre, Guatemala	1972
Fuego	3,835	12,582	Sierra Madre, Guatemala	1991
Tacana	3,780	12,400	Sierra Madre, Guatemala	1988
Santa Maria	3,768	12,362	Sierra Madre, Guatemala	1993
Irazú	3,452	11,325	Cordillera Central, Costa Rica	1992
Turrialba	3,246	10,650	Cordillera Central, Costa Rica	1992
Póas	2,721	8,930	Cordillera Central, Costa Rica	1994
Pacaya	2,543	8,346	Sierra Madre, Guatemala	1998
San Miguel	2,131	6,994	El Salvador	1986
Arenal	1,552	5,092	Costa Rica	1998
Europe				
Kliuchevskoi	4,750	15,584	Kamchatka Peninsula, Russia	1997
Koryakskaya	3,456	11,339	Kamchatka Peninsula, Russia	1957
Sheveluch	3,283	10,771	Kamchatka Peninsula, Russia	1997
Etna	3,236	10,625	Sicily, Italy	1999
Bezymianny	2,882	9,455	Kamchatka Peninsula, Russia	1997
Alaid	2,335	7,662	Kurile Islands, Russia	1986
Tiatia	1,833	6,013	Kurile Islands, Russia	1981
Sarychev Peak	1,512	4,960	Kurile Islands, Russia	1989
Vesuvius	1,289	4,203	Italy	1944
Stromboli	931	3,055	Lipari Islands, Italy	1998
Santorini (Thera)	584	1,960	Cyclades, Greece	1950
Indian Ocean				
Karthala	2,440	8,000	Comoros	1991
Piton de la Fournaise (Le Volcan)	1,823	5,981	Réunion Island, France	1998
Mid-Pacific				
Mauna Loa	4,170	13,681	Hawaii, USA	1984
Kilauea	1,247	4,100	Hawaii, USA	1998
North America				
Popocatépetl	5,452	17,887	Altiplano de México, Mexico	1998
Colima	4,268	14,003	Altiplano de México, Mexico	1999
Spurr	3,374	11,070	Alaska Range (AK) USA	1953
Lassen Peak	3,186	10,453	California, USA	1921
Redoubt	3,108	10,197	Alaska Range (AK) USA	1991
Iliamna	3,052	10,016	Alaska Range (AK) USA	1978
Shishaldin	2,861	9,387	Aleutian Islands (AK) USA	1997
St Helens	2,549	8,364	Washington, USA	1998
Pavlof	2,517	8,261	Alaska Range (AK) USA	1997
Veniaminof	2,507	8,225	Alaska Range (AK) USA	1995
Novarupta (Katmai)	2,298	7,540	Alaska Range (AK) USA	1931
El Chichon	2,225	7,300	Altiplano de México, Mexico	1982
Makushin	2,036	6,680	Aleutian Islands (AK) USA	1987

(continued)

Major Volcanoes Active in the 20th Century *(continued)*

Volcano	Height m	Height ft	Location	Date of last eruption or activity
Oceania				
Ruapehu	2,796	9,175	New Zealand	1997
Ulawun	2,296	7,532	Papua New Guinea	1993
Ngauruhoe	2,290	7,515	New Zealand	1977
Bagana	1,998	6,558	Papua New Guinea	1993
Manam	1,829	6,000	Papua New Guinea	1998
Lamington	1,780	5,844	Papua New Guinea	1956
Karkar	1,499	4,920	Papua New Guinea	1979
Lopevi	1,450	4,755	Vanuatu	1982
Ambrym	1,340	4,376	Vanuatu	1991
Tarawera	1,149	3,770	New Zealand	1973
Langila	1,093	3,586	Papua New Guinea	1996
Rabaul	688	2,257	Papua New Guinea	1997
Pagan	570	1,870	Mariana Islands	1993
White Island	328	1,075	New Zealand	1999
South America				
San Pedro	6,199	20,325	Andes, Chile	1960
Guallatiri	6,060	19,882	Andes, Chile	1993
Lascar	5,990	19,652	Andes, Chile	1995
San José	5,919	19,405	Andes, Chile	1931
Cotopaxi	5,897	19,347	Andes, Ecuador	1975
Tutupaca	5,844	19,160	Andes, Ecuador	1902
Ubinas	5,710	18,720	Andes, Peru	1969
Tupungatito	5,640	18,504	Andes, Chile	1986
Islunga	5,566	18,250	Andes, Chile	1960
Nevado del Ruiz	5,435	17,820	Andes, Colombia	1992
Tolima	5,249	17,210	Andes, Colombia	1943
Sangay	5,230	17,179	Andes, Ecuador	1996

Latitude, Longitude, and Altitude of the World's Major Cities

City	Latitude °	Latitude ′	Longitude °	Longitude ′	Altitude m	Altitude ft
Adelaide, Australia	34	55 S	138	36 E	43	140
Algiers, Algeria	36	50 N	03	00 E	59	194
Almaty, Kazakhstan	43	16 N	76	53 E	775	2,543
Amsterdam, Netherlands	52	22 N	04	53 E	3	10
Ankara, Turkey	39	55 N	32	55 E	862	2,825
Asunción, Paraguay	25	15 S	57	40 W	139	456
Athens, Greece	37	58 N	23	43 E	92	300
Bangkok, Thailand	13	45 N	100	31 E	0	0
Barcelona, Spain	41	23 N	02	09 E	93	305
Beijing, China	39	56 N	116	24 E	183	600
Belfast, Northern Ireland	54	37 N	05	56 W	67	217
Belgrade, Yugoslavia	44	52 N	20	32 E	132	433
Berlin, Germany	52	31 N	13	25 E	34	110
Bogotá, Colombia	04	32 N	74	05 W	2,640	8,660
Bombay, India	18	58 N	72	50 E	8	27
Brussels, Belgium	50	52 N	04	22 E	100	328
Bucharest, Romania	44	25 N	26	07 E	92	302
Budapest, Hungary	47	30 N	19	05 E	139	456
Buenos Aires, Argentina	34	36 S	58	28 W	0	0
Cairo, Egypt	30	03 N	31	15 E	116	381
Cape Town, South Africa	33	55 S	18	22 E	17	56
Caracas, Venezuela	10	28 N	67	02 W	1,042	3,418
Copenhagen, Denmark	55	40 N	12	34 E	9	33
Dakar, Senegal	14	40 N	17	28 W	40	131
Delhi, India	28	35 N	77	12 E	218	714
Detroit (MI), USA	42	19 N	83	02 W	178	585
Djibouti, Djibouti	11	30 N	43	03 E	7	23
Dublin, Republic of Ireland	53	20 N	06	15 W	47	154
Edinburgh, Scotland	55	55 N	03	10 W	134	440
Frankfurt, Germany	50	07 N	08	41 E	103	338
Guatemala City, Guatemala	14	37 N	90	31 W	1,480	4,855
Havana, Cuba	23	08 N	82	23 W	24	80
Helsinki, Finland	60	10 N	25	00 E	46	151
Hong Kong, China	22	18 N	114	10 E	33	109
Istanbul, Turkey	41	06 N	29	03 E	114	374
Jakarta, Indonesia	06	10 S	106	48 E	8	26
Jerusalem, Israel	31	46 N	35	14 E	762	2,500
Johannesburg, South Africa	26	12 S	28	05 E	1,750	5,740
Kabul, Afghanistan	34	30 N	69	13 E	1,827	5,955
Karachi, Pakistan	24	48 N	66	59 E	4	13
Katmandu, Nepal	27	43 S	85	19 E	1,372	4,500
Kiev, Ukraine	50	26 N	30	31 E	179	587
Kinshasa, Democratic Republic of Congo	04	18 S	15	17 E	322	1,066
Lagos, Nigeria	06	27 N	03	24 E	3	10
La Paz, Bolivia	16	27 S	68	22 W	3,658	12,001
Lhasa, Tibet	29	40 N	91	07 E	3,685	12,090
Lima, Peru	12	00 S	77	02 W	120	394
Lisbon, Portugal	38	44 N	09	09 W	77	253
London, UK	51	32 N	00	05 W	75	245
Los Angeles (CA), USA	34	03 N	118	14 W	104	340
Madrid, Spain	40	26 N	03	42 W	660	2,165
Manila, Philippines	14	35 N	120	57 E	14	47
Mecca, Saudi Arabia	21	27 S	39	49 E	2,000	6,562
Melbourne, Australia	37	47 N	144	58 E	35	115
Mexico City, Mexico	19	24 N	99	09 W	2,239	7,347
Milan, Italy	45	27 S	09	10 E	121	397
Montevideo, Uruguay	34	53 N	56	10 W	22	72
Moscow, Russia	55	45 N	37	35 E	120	394
Nagasaki, Japan	32	48 S	129	57 E	133	436
Nairobi, Kenya	01	25 N	36	55 E	1,820	5,971
New Delhi, India	28	36 N	77	12 E	235	770
New York (NY), USA	40	45 N	73	59 W	17	55
Oslo, Norway	59	57 N	10	42 E	94	308
Ottawa, Canada	45	26 N	75	41 W	56	185
Panamá, Panama	08	58 N	79	32 W	0	0
Paris, France	48	52 N	02	20 E	92	300
Prague, Czech Republic	50	05 N	14	26 E	262	860
Quito, Ecuador	0	13 S	78	30 W	2,811	9,222
Reykjavik, Iceland	64	04 N	21	58 W	18	59
Rio de Janeiro, Brazil	22	43 S	43	13 W	9	30
Rome, Italy	41	53 N	12	30 E	29	95
St Petersburg, Russia	59	56 N	30	18 E	4	13
Santiago, Chile	33	27 S	70	40 W	1,500	4,921
Seoul, South Korea	37	34 N	127	00 E	10	34
Shanghai, China	31	10 N	121	28 E	7	23
Singapore	01	14 N	103	55 E	10	33
Sofia, Bulgaria	42	40 N	23	20 E	550	1,805
Stockholm, Sweden	59	17 N	18	03 E	44	144
Sydney, Australia	33	53 S	151	12 E	8	25
Tehran, Iran	35	40 N	51	26 E	1,110	3,937
Tokyo, Japan	35	42 N	139	46 E	9	30
Toronto, Canada	43	39 N	79	23 W	91	300
Tripoli, Libya	32	54 N	13	11 E	0	0
Vancouver, Canada	49	18 N	123	04 W	43	141
Vienna, Austria	48	14 N	16	20 E	203	666
Warsaw, Poland	52	15 N	21	00 E	110	360
Washington, DC, USA	38	53 N	77	00 W	8	25
Wellington, New Zealand	41	18 S	174	47 E	0	0
Zurich, Switzerland	47	21 N	08	31 E	493	1,618

Countries of the World

Afghanistan Republic of

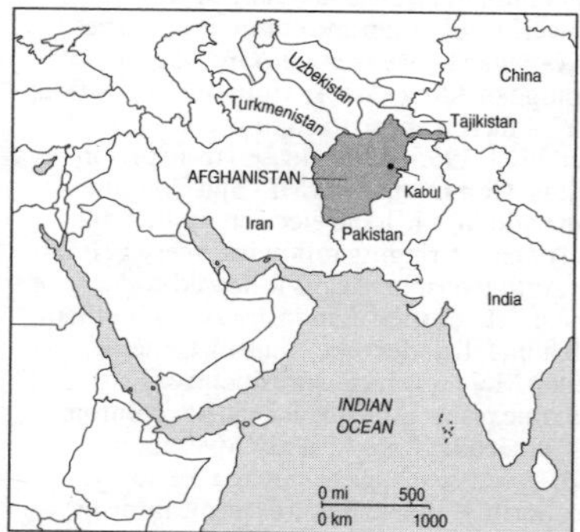

National name: *Islamic Emirate of Afghanistan* **Area:** 652,090 sq km/251,771 sq mi **Capital:** Kabul **Major towns/cities:** Kandahar, Herat, Mazar-i-Sharif, Jalalabad

Government

Head of state and government: Mohammad Rabbani from 1996 **Political system:** transitional **Administrative divisions:** 32 provinces **Political parties:** Hezb-i-Islami, Islamic fundamentalist Mujaheddin, anti-Western; Jamiat-i-Islami, Islamic fundamentalist Mujaheddin; National Liberation Front, moderate Mujaheddin **Armed forces:** approximately 429,000 (1997) **Conscription:** compulsory for four years, with break of three years after second year (since 1992 conscription has been difficult to enforce and desertion is common) **Death penalty:** retains and uses the death penalty for ordinary crimes **Defence spend:** (% GDP) 12.5 (1997) **Education spend:** (% GNP) 2.0 (1992) **Health spend:** (% GDP) 1.6 (1990)

Economy and resources

Currency: afgháni **GDP:** (US$) 12.8 billion (1995 est) **Real GDP growth:** (% change on previous year) N/A **GNP (US$):** N/A **GNP per capita (PPP):** (US$) N/A **Consumer price inflation:** N/A **Foreign debt:** (US$) 9.58 billion (1993) **Major trading partners:** former USSR countries, Japan, Singapore, Germany **Resources:** natural gas, coal, iron ore, barytes, lapis lazuli, salt, talc, copper, chrome, gold, silver, asbestos, small petroleum reserves **Exports:** fruit and nuts, carpets, wool, karakul skins, cotton, natural gas. Principal market: Kyrgyzstan 37.3% (1995) **Imports:** basic manufactured goods and foodstuffs (notably wheat), petroleum products, textiles, fertilizers, vehicles and spare parts. Principal source: Japan 25.6% (1995) **Arable land:** 12.1% (1995)

Population and society

Population: 21,354,000 (1998 est) **Population growth rate:** 5.3% (1995–2000); 2.7% (2000–05) **Population density:** (per sq km) 38.3 (1998 est) **Urban population:** (% of total) 21 (1997) **Age distribution:** (% of total population) 0–14 42.9%, 15–64 54.3%, 65+ 2.7% (1998) **Ethnic groups:** Pathans, or Pushtuns, comprise the largest ethnic group, 54% of the population, followed by the Tajiks (concentrated in the north, 27%), the Uzbeks (8%), and Hazaras (7%) **Language:** Pushtu, Dari (Persian), Uzbek, Turkoman, Kirgiz **Religion:** Muslim (85% Sunni, 15% Shi'ite) **Education:** (compulsory years) 6 **Literacy rate:** 44% (men); 14% (women) (1995 est) **Labour force:** 41% of population: 61% agriculture, 14% industry, 25% services (1992) **Life expectancy:** 45 (men); 46 (women) (1995–2000) **Child mortality rate:** (under 5, per 1,000 live births) 246 (1997) **Physicians:** 1 per 6,730 people (1990 est)

Practical information

Visa requirements: UK: visa required. USA: visa required **Embassy in the UK:** 31 Prince's Gate, London SW7 1QQ. Tel: (0171) 589 8891; fax: (0171) 581 3452 **British embassy:** Karte Parwan, Kabul. Tel: (93) 30511 (the embassy is closed at present) **Chamber of commerce:** Afghan Chamber of Commerce and Industry, Mohd Jah Khan Wat, Kabul. Tel: (93) 26796; telex: 245

Chronology

6th century BC: Part of Persian Empire under Cyrus II and Darius I. **329 BC:** Conquered by Alexander the Great. **323 BC:** Fell to the Seleucids, who ruled from Babylon. **304 BC:** Ruled by Mauryan dynasty in south and independent Bactria in north. **135 BC:** Central Asian tribes established Kusana dynasty. **3rd–7th centuries AD:** Decline of Kusana dynasty. Emergence of Sassanids as ruling power with Hepthalites (central Asian nomads) and western Turks also fighting for control. **642–11th century:** First Muslim invasion followed by a succession of Muslim dynasties, including Mahmud of Ghazni in 998. **1219–14th century:** Mongol invasions led by Genghis Khan and Tamerlane. **16th–18th centuries:** Much of Afghanistan came under the rule of the Mogul Empire under Babur (Zahir) and Nadir Shah. **1747:** Afghanistan became an independent emirate under Dost Muhammad. **1838–42:** First Afghan War, instigated by Britain to counter the threat to British India from expanding Russian influence in Afghanistan. **1878–80:** Second Afghan War. **1919:** Afghanistan recovered full independence following Third Afghan War. **1953:** Lt-Gen Daud Khan became prime minister and introduced social and economic reform programme. **1963:** Daud Khan forced to resign and constitutional monarchy established. **1973:** Monarchy overthrown in coup by Daud Khan. **1978:** Daud Khan assassinated in coup; Muhammad Taraki and the communist People's Democratic Party of Afghanistan (PDPA) took over. Start of Muslim guerrilla (Mujaheddin) resistance. **1979:** Taraki ousted and murdered; replaced by Hafizullah Amin. USSR entered country to prop up government, installing Babrak Karmal in power. **1986:** Replacement of Karmal as PDPA leader by Dr Najibullah Ahmadzai. Partial Soviet troop withdrawal. **1988:** New non-Marxist constitution adopted. **1989:** Withdrawal of Soviet troops; Mujaheddin continued resistance to PDPA regime and civil war intensified. **1991:** US and Soviet military aid withdrawn. Mujaheddin began talks with Russians and Kabul government. **1992:** Najibullah government overthrown. Mujaheddin leader Burhanuddin Rabbani elected president. **1993:** Intensive fighting around Kabul. Peace agreement between Rabbani and dissident Hezb-i-Islami leader Gulbuddin Hekmatyar made Hekmatyar prime minister. **1994:** Continuing rebel attacks on Kabul quelled. Hekmatyar dismissed from office. **1995:** Talibaan Islamic fundamentalist army claimed town of Herat and advanced on Kabul. **1996:** Talibaan controlled two-thirds of country, including Kabul; country split between Talibaan-controlled fundamentalist south and more liberal north; interim council of clerics installed, headed by Mohamad Rabbani; strict Islamic law imposed. **1997:** Talibaan recognized as legitimate government of Afghanistan by Pakistan and Saudi Arabia. **1998:** Two earthquakes in north killed over 8,000 people. August: USA launched missile attack on suspected terrorist site in retaliation for bombings of US embassies in Nairobi and Dar es Salaam. Talibaan extended control in north, massacring 6,000 at Mazar-I-Sharif. **1999:** Fighting resumed in northern Afghanistan after a four-month lull.

Albania Republic of

National name: *Republika e Shqipërisê* **Area:** 28,748 sq km/11,099 sq mi **Capital:** Tiranê (Tirana) **Major towns/cities:** Durrês, Shkodêr, Elbasan, Vlorê, Korçê **Major ports:** Durrês

Government

Head of state: Rexhep Mejdani from 1998 **Head of government:** Pandeli Majko from 1998 **Political system:** emergent democracy **Administrative divisions:** 12 prefectures **Political parties:** Democratic Party of Albania (PDS; formerly the Democratic Party: DP), moderate, market-oriented; Socialist Party of Albania (PSS), ex-communist; Human Rights Union (HMU), Greek minority party **Armed forces:** 54,000 (1997) **Conscription:** compulsory for 15 months **Death penalty:** retains the death penalty for ordinary crimes, but considered abolitionist in practice; committed in 1996 to put into place a moratorium on executions until total abolition **Defence spend:** (% GDP) 6.7 (1997) **Education spend:** (% GDP) 3.4 (1995) **Health spend:** (% GDP) 2.7 (1990–95)

Economy and resources

Currency: lek **GDP:** (US$) 2.3 billion (1997) **Real GDP growth:** (% change on previous year) –8 (1997) **GNP (US$):** (US$) 2.5 billion (1997) **GNP per capita (PPP):** (US$) 2,600 (1997 est) **Consumer price inflation:** 20% (1998) **Unemployment:** 12.1% (1996) **Foreign debt:** (US$) 781 million (1996) **Major trading partners:** Italy, Greece, USA, Germany, Bulgaria **Resources:** chromite (one of world's largest producers), copper, coal, nickel, petroleum and natural gas **Exports:** chromium and chrome products, processed foodstuffs, plant and animal products, bitumen, electricity, tobacco. Principal market: Italy 57.9% (1996) **Imports:** machinery, fuels and minerals, plant and animal raw materials, chemical products. Principal source: Italy 41.7% (1996) **Arable land:** 21% (1995)

Population and society

Population: 3,119,000 (1998 est) **Population growth rate:** 0.6% (1995–2000); 0.8% (2000–05) **Population density:** (per sq km) 121.6 (1998 est) **Urban population:** (% of total) 38 (1997) **Age distribution:** (% of total population) 0–14 33.2%, 15–64 60.9%, 65+ 5.9% (1998) **Ethnic groups:** 90% of Albanian, non-Slavic, descent; 8% ethnic Greek (concentrated in south) **Language:** Albanian, Greek **Religion:** Muslim, Orthodox, Roman Catholic **Education:** (compulsory years) 8 **Literacy rate:** 85% (men); 85% (women) (1994) **Labour force:** 48% of population: 55% agriculture, 23% industry, 22% services (1990) **Life expectancy:** 68 (men); 74 (women) (1995–2000) **Child mortality rate:** (under 5, per 1,000 live births) 49 (1997) **Physicians:** 1 per 530 people (1993 est)

Practical information

Visa requirements: UK: visa not required. USA: visa not required **Embassy in the UK:** 4th Floor, 38 Grosvenor Gardens, London SW1W 0EB. Tel: (0171) 730 5709; fax: (0171) 730 5747 **British embassy:** Office of the British Chargé d'Affaires, c/o French Embassy, Rruga Skënderben 14, Tiranë. Tel: (42) 34250; telex: 2150 **Chamber of commerce:** Chamber of Commerce of the Republic of Albania, Rruga Kavajes 6, Tiranë. Tel/fax: (42) 27997

Chronology

2000 BC: Part of Illyria. **168 BC:** Illyria conquered by Romans. **AD 395:** Became part of Byzantine Empire. **6th–14th centuries:** Byzantine decline exploited by Serbs, Normans, Slavs, Bulgarians, and Venetians. **1381:** Ottoman invasion of Albania followed by years of resistance to Turkish rule. **1468:** Resistance led by national hero Skanderbeg (George Kastrioti) largely collapsed, and Albania passed to Ottoman Empire. **15th–16th centuries:** Thousands fled to southern Italy to escape Ottoman rule; over half of the rest of the population converted to Islam. **1878:** Foundation of Albanian League promoted emergence of nationalism. **1912:** Achieved independence from Turkey as a result of First Balkan War and end of Ottoman Empire in Europe. **1914–20:** Occupied by Italy. **1925:** Declared itself a republic. **1928–39:** Monarchy of King Zog. **1939:** Italian occupation led by Benito Mussolini. **1943–44:** Under German rule following Italian surrender. **1946:** Proclaimed Communist People's Republic of Albania, with Enver Hoxha as premier. **1949:** Developed close links with Joseph Stalin in USSR and entered Comecon (Council for Mutual Economic Assistance). **1961:** Broke with USSR in wake of Nikita Khrushchev's denunciation of Stalin, and withdrew from Comecon. **1978:** Severed diplomatic links with China, choosing isolationism and neutrality. **1982:** Hoxha made Ramiz Alia head of state. **1985:** Death of Hoxha. Alia became head of the Party of Labour of Albania (PLA). **1987:** Normal diplomatic relations restored with Canada, Greece, and West Germany. **1988:** Albania attended conference of Balkan states for the first time since the 1930s. **1990:** One-party system abandoned in face of popular protest; first opposition party formed. **1991:** Communist PLA won first multiparty elections; Alia re-elected president. PLA renamed PSS. **1992:** Presidential elections won by Sali Berisha of the Democratic Party (DP). Alia and other former communist officials charged with corruption and abuse of power. Totalitarian and communist parties banned. **1993:** Open conflict began between ethnic Greeks and Albanians, followed by a purge of ethnic Greeks from senior positions in the civil service and army. Alia sentenced to eight years' imprisonment. DP renamed PDS. **1995:** Alia released from prison following appeal-court ruling. Communist-era MPs and Communist Party officials banned from national and local elections until 2002. **1996:** Ruling PDS accused of ballot-rigging following overwhelming victory in elections. **1997:** Antigovernment riots followed collapse of bogus 'investment' schemes; police killed demonstrators in southern port of Vlorë. Southern Albania fell under rebel control. General election won by PSS; Rexhep Mejdani elected president; ex-communist Fatos Nano became prime minister at head of coalition. Convictions of communist-era leaders overturned. Government signed World Bank and IMF rescue package to salvage economy. **1998:** Sporadic violence in north. Nano resigned as prime minister, replaced by Pandeli Majko. A new constitution was approved in a national referendum.

Algeria Democratic and Popular Republic of

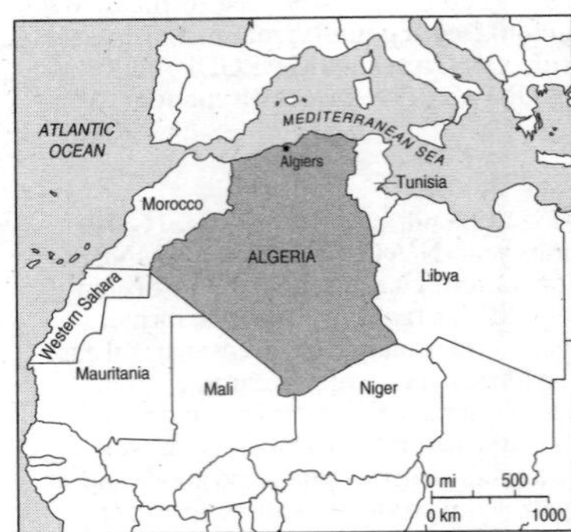

National name: *al-Jumhuriya al-Jazairiya ad-Dimuqratiya ash-Shabiya* **Area:** 2,381,741 sq km/ 919,590 sq mi **Capital:** Algiers (al-Jaza'ir) **Major towns/cities:** Oran, Annaba, Blida, Sétif, Constantine (Qacentina) **Major ports:** Oran (Ouahran), Annaba (Bône

Government

Head of state: Abdel Aziz Bouteflika from 1999 **Head of government:** Ismail Hamdani from 1998 **Political system:** military rule **Administrative divisions:** 48 departments **Political parties:** National Liberation Front (FLN), nationalist, socialist; Socialist Forces Front (FSS), Berber-based, left of centre; Islamic Front for Salvation (FIS), Islamic fundamentalist (banned from 1992); National Democratic Rally (RND), left of centre **Armed forces:** 124,000 (1997) **Conscription:** compulsory for 18 months **Death penalty:** retained and used for ordinary crimes **Defence spend:** (% GDP) 4.6 (1997) **Education spend:** (% GNP) 5.2 (1996) **Health spend:** (% GDP) 3.3 (1990–95)

Economy and resources

Currency: Algerian dinar **GDP:** (US$) 45.9 billion (1997) **Real GDP growth:** (% change on previous year) 3.8 (1997) **GNP (US$):** 45.4 billion (1997) **GNP per capita (PPP):** (US$) 4,600 (1997) **Consumer price inflation:** 12% (1998) **Unemployment:** 25% (1995) **Foreign debt:** (US$) 33.4 billion (1996) **Major trading partners:** France, Italy, Germany, USA, the Netherlands **Resources:** natural gas and petroleum, iron ore, phosphates, lead, zinc, mercury, silver, salt, antimony, copper **Exports:** crude oil, gas, vegetables, tobacco, hides, dates. Principal market: Italy 20.4% (1996) **Imports:** machinery and transportation equipment, food and basic

manufactures. Principal source: France 29.8% (1996) **Arable land:** 3.2% (1995)

Population and society

Population: 30,081,000 (1998 est) **Population growth rate:** 2.3% (1995–2000); 2% (2000–05) **Population density:** (per sq km) 12.8 (1998 est) **Urban population:** (% of total) 57 (1997) **Age distribution:** (% of total population) 0–14 38.2%, 15–64 58.0%, 65+ 3.8% (1998) **Ethnic groups:** 99% of Arab Berber origin, the remainder of European descent, mainly French **Language:** Arabic (official); Berber, French **Religion:** Sunni Muslim (state religion) **Education:** (compulsory years) 9 **Literacy rate:** 64% (men); 45% (women) (1995 est) **Labour force:** 28% of population: 26% agriculture, 31% industry, 43% services (1990) **Life expectancy:** 68 (men); 70 (women) (1995–2000) **Child mortality rate:** (under 5, per 1,000 live births) 52 (1997) **Physicians:** 1 per 1,062 people (1993 est)

Practical information

Visa requirements: UK: visa required. USA visa required **Embassy in the UK:** 54 Holland Park, London W11 3RS. Tel: (0171) 221 7800; fax: (0171) 221 0448 **British embassy:** BP 43, Résidence Cassiopée, Bâtiment B, 7 chemin des Glycines, 16000 Alger-Gare, Algiers. Tel: (2) 622 411; fax: (2) 692 410 **Chamber of commerce:** Chambre Nationale de Commerce (CNC), BP100, Palais Consulaire, rue Amilcar Cabral, Algiers. Tel: (2) 575 555; fax: (2) 629 991

Chronology

9th century BC: Part of Carthaginian Empire, centred on Tunisia to the east, with Annaba, Algiers, and Skikda emerging as important trading posts en route to Spain. **146 BC:** Conquered by Romans, who called the area Numidia. **AD 396:** St Augustine, one of the great early Christian leaders, became Bishop of Hippo, modern Annaba. **6th century:** Part of the Byzantine Empire. **late 7th century:** Conquered by Muslim Arabs, who spread Islam as the basis of a new Berberized Arab-Islamic civilization. **1516:** Ottoman Turks expelled recent Christian Spanish invaders. Under Ottoman rule much influence was left to local Arab tribes, Berbers, Barbary pirates, and deys, administrative officers who were elected for life. **1816:** Anglo-Dutch forces bombarded Algiers as a reprisal against the Barbary pirates' attacks on Mediterranean shipping. **1830–47:** French occupation of Algiers, followed by extension of control to the north, overcoming fierce resistance from Amir Abd al-Qadir, a champion of Arab Algerian nationalism, and from Morocco. **1850–70:** Mountainous inland region, inhabited by the Kabyles, occupied by French. **1871:** Major rebellion against French rule as French settlers began to immigrate and take over the best agricultural land. **1900–09:** Sahara region subdued by France, who kept it under military rule. **1937:** Algerian People's Party (PPA) formed by the charismatic separatist Messali Hadj. **1940:** Following France's defeat by Nazi Germany, Algeria became allied to the pro-Nazi Vichy regime during World War II. **1945:** 8,000 died following the ruthless suppression of an abortive PPA-supported uprising against French rule. **1954–62:** Battle of Algiers: bitter war of independence fought between the National Liberation Front (FLN) and the French colonial army. **1958:** French inability to resolve the escalating civil war in Algeria, where French settlers had risen in favour of integration with France, toppled the Fourth Republic and brought to power, in Paris, Gen Charles de Gaulle, who accepted the principle of national self-determination. **1962:** Independence achieved from France. Republic declared. Ahmed Ben Bella of the FLN elected prime minister; many French settlers fled. **1963:** Ben Bella elected Algeria's first president and one-party state established. **1965:** Ben Bella deposed by military, led by Col Houari Boumédienne (FLN). **1971:** Oil and gas industry nationalized. **1976:** New Islamic-socialist constitution approved. **1978:** Death of Boumédienne. **1979:** Benjedid Chadli (FLN) elected president. Ben Bella freed after 14 years of house arrest. **1981:** Algeria helped secure release of US hostages in Iran. **1988:** Riots in protest at austerity policies; 170 killed. Reform programme introduced. Diplomatic relations restored with Morocco after 12-year break. **1989:** Constitutional changes introduced limited political pluralism. **1991:** Elections cancelled after Islamic fundamentalist Islamic Salvation Front (FIS) won first round of multiparty elections. **1992:** Chadli resigned; military took control of government; Muhammad Boudiaf became president. State of emergency declared and FIS ordered to disband. Boudiaf assassinated, allegedly by fundamentalists; replaced by Ali Kafi. **1993:** Worsening civil strife; assassinations of politicians and other public figures. **1994:** Gen Lamine Zeroual replaced Kafi as president. Fundamentalists' campaign of violence intensified. **1995:** Zeroual won presidential elections. **1996:** Constitution amended to increase president's powers and counter religious fundamentalism. Arabic declared official public language. **1997:** Widespread killing of civilians by Armed Islamic Group (GIA). RND-FLN victory in National Assembly elections. Ahmed Ouyuahia reappointed prime minister. FIS urged 'national conference of reconciliation'. **1998:** Violence continued. President Zeroual announced his retirement, planned for 1999. Prime Minister Ahmed Ouyahia resigned and was replaced by Ismail Hamdani. **1999:** Former Prime Minister Ahmed Ouyahia was elected secretary-general of the ruling National Democratic Rally (RND).

Andorra Principality of

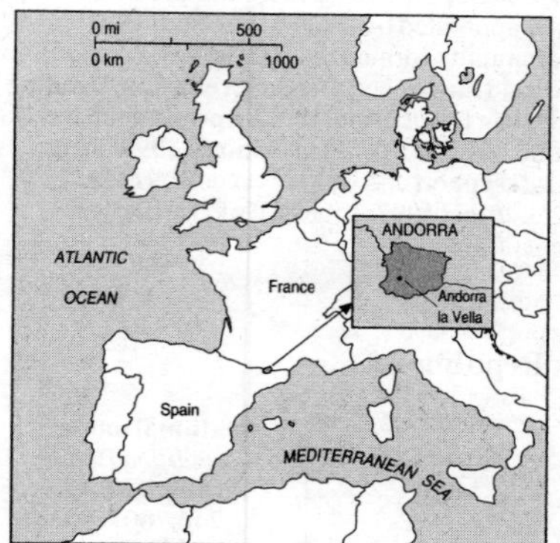

National name: *Principat d'Andorra* **Area:** 468 sq km/181 sq mi **Capital:** Andorra-la-Vella **Major towns/cities:** Les Escaldes, Escaldes-Engordany (suburb of capital)

Government

Heads of state: Joan Marti i Alanis (bishop of Urgel, Spain) and Jacques Chirac (president of France) **Head of government:** Marc Forne from 1994 **Political system:** co-principality **Administrative divisions:** seven parishes **Political parties:** National Democratic Grouping (AND; formerly the Democratic Party of Andorra: PDA) moderate, centrist; National Democratic Initiative (IND), left of centre; New Democracy Party (ND), centrist; National Andorran Coalition (CNA), centrist; Liberal Union (UL), right of centre **Armed forces:** no standing army **Death penalty:** abolished in 1990 (last execution in 1943)

Economy and resources

Currency: French franc and Spanish peseta **GDP:** (US$) 960 million (1995) **Real GDP growth:** (% change on previous year) 3 (1995) **GNP (US$):** 1 billion (1995 est) **GNP per capita (PPP):** (US$) 16,630 (1995 est) **Unemployment:** 0% (1994) **Major trading partners:** France, Spain **Resources:** iron, lead, alum, hydro power **Exports:** cigars and cigarettes, furniture, electricity. Principal market: France 46.7% (1994) **Imports:** foodstuffs, electricity, mineral fuels. Principal source: Spain 38.9% (1994) **Arable land:** 2.2% (1995)

Population and society

Population: 72,000 (1998 est) **Population growth rate:** 5.5% (1990–95) **Population density:** (per sq km) 143.5 (1998 est) **Urban population:** (% of total) 95 (1997) **Age distribution:** (% of total population) 0–14 14.4%, 15–64 73.4%, 65+ 12.3% (1998) **Ethnic groups:** 25% Andorrans, 75% immigrant Spanish workers **Language:** Catalan (official); Spanish, French **Religion:** Roman Catholic **Education:** (compulsory years) 10 **Literacy rate:** 99% (men); 99% (women) (1995 est) **Labour force:** 4% agriculture, 23% industry, 73% services (1992) **Life expectancy:** 70 (men); 73 (women) (1994 est) **Physicians:** 1 per 8 people (1994 est)

Practical information

Visa requirements: UK: visa not required. USA: visa not required **Embassy in the UK:** none; Andorran Trade Delegation, 63 Westover

Road, London SW18 2RF. Tel: (0181) 874 4806 **British embassy:** British Consulate (Barcelona), 13th Floor, Edificio Torre de Barcelona, Avenida Diagonal 477, 08036 Barcelona. Tel: (3) 419 9044; fax: (3) 405 2411 **Chamber of commerce:** Sindicat d'Initiativa de las Valls d'Andorra, Carrer Dr Vilanova, Andorra la Vella. Tel: 820 214; fax: 825 823

Chronology

AD 803: Holy Roman Emperor Charlemagne liberated Andorra from Muslim control. **819:** Louis I, 'the Pious', the son of Charlemagne, granted control over the area to the Spanish bishop of Urgel. **1278:** Treaty signed making Spanish bishop and French count joint rulers of Andorra (through marriage the king of France later inherited the count's right). **1806:** After temporary suspension during the French Revolution, from 1789 the feudal arrangement of dual allegiance to the co-princes (French and Spanish rulers) was re-established by the French emperor Napoleon Bonaparte. **1970:** Extension of franchise to third-generation female and second-generation male Andorrans. **1976:** First political organization, Democratic Party of Andorra, formed. **1977:** Franchise extended to first-generation Andorrans. **1981:** First prime minister appointed by General Council. **1991:** Links with European Community formalized. **1993:** New constitution legalized political parties and introduced first direct elections, leading to coalition government being formed under acting prime minister, Oscar Ribas Reig. Became member of United Nations. **1994:** Reig resigned after coalition lost support and was succeeded by Marc Forne; joined Council of Europe. **1997:** Liberal Union (UL) won assembly majority in general election.

Angola People's Republic of

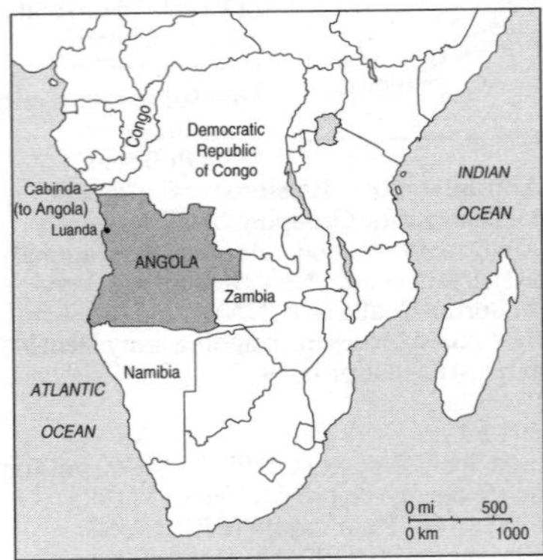

National name: *República Popular de Angola* **Area:** 1,246,700 sq km/ 481,350 sq mi **Capital:** Luanda (and chief port) **Major towns/cities:** Lobito, Benguela, Huambo, Lubango, Malange, Namibe (formerly Moçâmedes) **Major ports:** Huambo, Lubango, Malange

Government

Head of state: José Eduardo dos Santos from 1979 **Head of government:** Fernando Franca van Dunem from 1996 **Political system:** emergent democracy **Administrative divisions:** 18 provinces **Political parties:** People's Movement for the Liberation of Angola–Workers' Party (MPLA–PT), Marxist-Leninist; National Union for the Total Independence of Angola (UNITA); National Front for the Liberation of Angola (FNLA) **Armed forces:** 110,500 (1997); plus a paramilitary force of approximately 15,000 **Conscription:** military service is compulsory for two years **Death penalty:** abolished in 1992 **Defence spend:** (% GDP) 8.8 (1997) **Education spend:** (% GNP) 2.8 (1992); N/A (1993–94) **Health spend:** (% GDP) 4.0 (1990–95)

Economy and resources

Currency: kwanza **GDP:** (US$) 7.39 billion (1997) **Real GDP growth:** (% change on previous year) 7.5 (1997) **GNP (US$):** 3.8 billion (1997) **GNP per capita (PPP):** (US$) 940 (1997) **Consumer price inflation:** 1,200% (1998) **Unemployment:** 15% (1993) **Foreign debt:** (US$) 12.3 billion (1996) **Major trading partners:** Portugal, USA, Germany, France, Japan, Brazil, the Netherlands **Resources:** petroleum, diamonds, granite, iron ore, marble, salt, phosphates, manganese, copper **Exports:** petroleum and petroleum products, diamonds, gas. Principal market: USA 65% (1997) **Imports:** foodstuffs, transport equipment, base metals, electrical equipment. Principal source: Portugal 21.8% (1997) **Arable land:** 2.4% (1995)

Population and society

Population: 12,092,000 (1998 est) **Population growth rate:** 3.3% (1995–2000); 3.1% (2000–05) **Population density:** (per sq km) 8.7 (1998 est) **Urban population:** (% of total) 33 (1997) **Age distribution:** (% of total population) 0–14 44.9%, 15–64 52.4%, 65+ 2.7% (1998) **Ethnic groups:** eight main ethnic groups (Bakonga, Mbunda, Ovimbundu, Lunda-Tchokwe, Nganguela, Nyaneka-Humbe, Hiriro, and Ambo), and about 100 subgroups. A major exodus of Europeans in the 1970s left around 30,000, mainly Portuguese **Language:** Portuguese (official); Bantu dialects **Religion:** Roman Catholic 68%, Protestant 20%, animist 12% **Education:** (compulsory years) 8 **Literacy rate:** 56%(men); 28% (women) (1995 est) **Labour force:** 68.2% agriculture, 10.5% industry, 21.3% services (1991) **Life expectancy:** 45 (men); 48 (women) (1995–2000) **Child mortality rate:** (under 5, per 1,000 live births) 191 (1997) **Physicians:** 1 per 23,725 people (1993 est)

Practical information

Visa requirements: UK: visa required. USA: visa required **Embassy in the UK:** 98 Park Lane, London W1Y 3TA. Tel: (0171) 495 1752; fax: (0171) 495 1635 **British embassy:** CP 1244, Rua Diogo Cão 4, Luanda. Tel: (2) 392 991; fax: (2) 333 331 **Chamber of commerce:** Angolan Chamber of Commerce and Industry, Largo do Kinaxixi 14, 1 ° andar, CP 92, Luanda. Tel: (2) 344 506

Chronology

14th century: Under Wene, the powerful Kongo kingdom extended control over much of northern Angola. **early 16th century:** The Kongo ruler King Afonso I adopted Christianity and sought constructive relations with Portuguese traders. **1575 and 1617:** Portugal secured control over the ports of Luanda and Benguela and began to pentetrate inland, meeting resistance from Queen Nzinga, the Ndonga ruler. **17th–18th centuries:** Inland, the Lunda peoples established powerful kingdoms which stretched into southern Congo; the Portuguese made Angola a key centre for the export of slaves; over 1 million were shipped to Brazil 1580–1680. **1836:** Slave trade officially abolished. **1885–1915:** Military campaigns waged by Portugal to conquer the interior. **1926:** Modern borders delineated. **1951:** Angola became an overseas territory of Portugal. **1956:** Formation of People's Movement for the Liberation of Angola (MPLA), a socialist guerrilla independence movement based in the Congo to the north. **1961:** 50,000 massacred in rebellion on coffee plantations; forced labour abolished, but armed struggle for independence now waged. **1962:** Second nationalist guerrilla movement formed, the National Front for the Liberation of Angola (FNLA), based in north. **1966:** National Union for the Total Independence of Angola (UNITA) formed in southeast Angola as a breakaway from the FNLA. **1975:** Independence achieved from Portugal. MPLA (backed mainly by Cuba) proclaimed People's Republic of Angola under the presidency of Dr Agostinho Neto. FNLA and UNITA (backed by South Africa and the USA) proclaimed People's Democratic Republic of Angola. **1976:** MPLA gained control of most of the country. South African troops withdrew, but Cuban units remained as civil war continued. **1979:** Neto died and was succeeded by José Eduardo dos Santos. **1980:** UNITA guerrillas, aided by South Africa, continued raids against the Luanda government and bases of the Namibian South West Africa People's Organization (SWAPO) in Angola. **1988:** Peace treaty, providing for the withdrawal of all foreign troops, signed with South Africa and Cuba. **1989:** Cease-fire agreed with UNITA broke down and guerrilla activity resumed. **1991:** Peace agreement ended civil war. Amnesty for all political prisoners. New multiparty constitution. **1992:** MPLA general election victory, led by dos Santos, was fiercely disputed by UNITA, and plunged the country into renewed civil war. **1993:** MPLA government recognized by USA. United Nations (UN) sanctions imposed against UNITA. **1994:** Peace treaty signed by government and UNITA representatives. **1995:** UN peacekeepers drafted in. **1996:** UNITA leader Jonas Savimbi rejected offer of vice-presidency. **1997:** Delay in formation of national unity

government. Unity government eventually sworn in but boycotted by Savimbi. **1998:** New agreement leading to the demilitarization of UNITA and its transformation into a political party. UNITA accused of massacres. UNITA ministers suspended and peace process threatened. Government forces clashed with UNITA.

Antigua and Barbuda State of

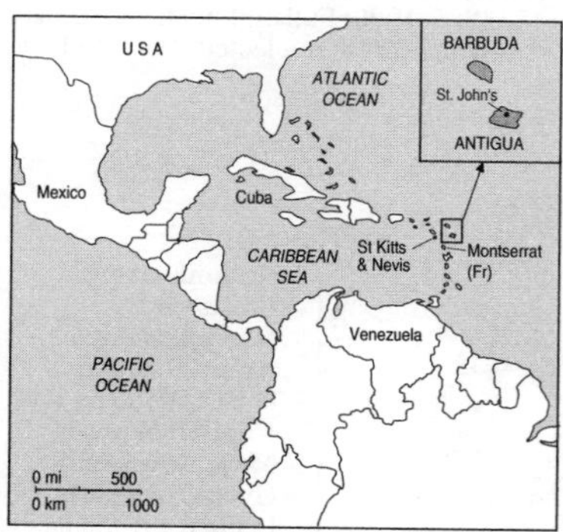

Area: Antigua 280 sq km/108 sq mi, Barbuda 161 sq km/62 sq mi, plus Redonda 1 sq km/0.4 sq mi (440 sq km/169 sq mi altogether) **Capital:** St John's (on Antigua) (and chief port) **Major towns/ cities:** Codrington (on Barbuda)

Government

Head of state: Elizabeth II from 1981, represented by governor general James B Carlisle from 1993 **Head of government:** Lester Bird from 1994 **Political system:** liberal democracy **Administrative divisions:** six parishes **Political parties:** Antigua Labour Party (ALP), moderate left of centre; United Progressive Party (UPP), centrist; Barbuda People's Movement (BPM), left of centre **Armed forces:** 200 (1997); US government leases two military bases on Antigua **Conscription:** military service is voluntary **Death penalty:** retained and used for ordinary crimes **Defence spend:** (% GDP) 0.5% (1997) **Education spend:** (% GNP) 3.7% (1988); N/A (1993–94)

Economy and resources

Currency: Eastern Caribbean dollar **GDP:** (US$) 446 million (1996 est) **Real GDP growth:** (% change on previous year) 4.5 (1997) **GNP (US$):** 489 million (1997) **GNP per capita (PPP):** (US$) 8,720 (1997) **Consumer price inflation:** 3.8% (1997) **Unemployment:** 3.2% (1990) **Foreign debt:** (US$) 435 million (1996) **Major trading partners:** USA, UK, Canada, Trinidad and Tobago, Barbados **Exports:** petroleum products, food, manufactures, machinery and transport equipment. Principal market: USA (mainly re-exports) **Imports:** petroleum, food and live animals, machinery and transport equipment, manufactures, chemicals. Principal source: USA 27% (1994 est) **Arable land:** 18.2% (1995)

Population and society

Population: 67,000 (1998 est) **Population growth rate:** 0.8% (1995–2000) **Population density:** (per sq km) 145.5 (1998 est) **Urban population:** (% of total) 36 (1997) **Age distribution:** (% of total population) 0–14 26.1%, 15–64 68.3%, 65+ 5.6% (1998) **Ethnic groups:** population almost entirely of black African descent **Language:** English **Religion:** Christian (mostly Anglican) **Education:** (compulsory years) 11 **Literacy rate:** 92% (men); 88% (women) (1992) **Labour force:** 11% agriculture, 19.7% industry, 69.3% services (1991) **Life expectancy:** 70 (men); 74 (women) (1994 est) **Child mortality rate:** (under 5, per 1,000 live births) 22 (1995) **Physicians:** 1 per 3,750 people (1990)

Practical information

Visa requirements: UK: visa not required. USA: visa not required **Embassy in the UK:** 15 Thayer Street, London W1M 5LD. Tel: (0171) 486 7073/4/5; fax: (0171) 486 9970 **British embassy:** British High Commission, PO Box 483, Price Waterhouse Centre, 11 Old Parham Road, St John's. Tel: 462 0008/9; fax: 462 2806 **Chamber of commerce:** Antigua and Barbuda Chamber of Commerce and Industry Ltd, Redcliffe Street, POB 774, St John's. Tel: 462 0743; fax: 462 4575

Chronology

1493: Antigua, then peopled by American Indian Caribs, visited by Christopher Columbus; he named it after a painting in the Church of Sante Maria la Antigua, in Seville. **1632:** Antigua colonized by British settlers from St Kitts. **1667:** Treaty of Breda formally ceded Antigua to Britain, ending French claim. **1674:** Christopher Codrington, a sugar planter from Barbados, established sugar plantations and acquired Barbuda island on lease from the British monarch in 1685; Africans brought in as slaves. **1834:** Antigua's slaves were freed. **1860:** Annexation of Barbuda. **1871–1956:** Antigua and Barbuda administered as part of the Leeward Islands federation. **1946:** Antigua Labour Party (ALP) formed by Vere Bird. **1958–62:** Part of West Indies Federation. **1967:** Antigua and Barbuda became an associated state within the Commonwealth, with full internal independence, but Britain responsible for defence and foreign affairs. **1969:** Separatist movement developed on Barbuda. **1971:** Progressive Labour Movement (PLM) won general election, defeating ALP, and George Walter replaced Bird as prime minister. **1976:** PLM called for early independence, but ALP urged caution. ALP, led by Bird, won the general election. **1981:** Independence from Britain achieved. **1983:** Assisted US invasion of Grenada, despite policy on nonalignment. **1991:** Bird remained in power despite calls for his resignation. **1993:** Lester Bird succeeded his father as ALP leader.

Argentina Republic of

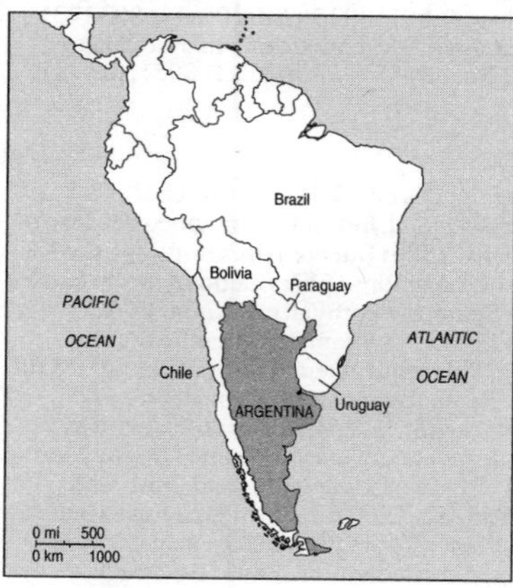

National name: *República Argentina* **Area:** 2,780,092 sq km/1,073,393 sq mi **Capital:** Buenos Aires **Major towns/cities:** Rosario, Córdoba, San Miguel de Tucumán, Mendoza, Santa Fé, La Plata **Major ports:** La Plata and Bahía Blanca **Territories:** claims Falkland Islands (*Islas Malvinas*), South Georgia, the South Sandwich Islands, and part of Antarctica

Government

Head of state and government: Carlos Menem from 1989 **Political system:** democratic federal republic **Administrative divisions:** 23 provinces and one federal district (Buenos Aires) **Political parties:** Radical Civic Union Party (UCR), moderate centrist; Justicialist Party (PJ), right-wing Perónist; Movement for Dignity and Independence (Modin), right-wing; Front for a Country in Solidarity (Frepaso), centre left **Armed forces:** 73,000 plus paramilitary gendarmerie of 31,200 (1997) **Conscription:** abolished in 1995 **Death penalty:** abolished for ordinary crimes in 1984; laws provide for the death penalty for exceptional crimes only **Defence spend:** (% GDP) 1.7 (1997) **Education spend:** (% GNP) 3.5 (1996) **Health spend:** (% GDP) 4.3 (1990–95)

Economy and resources

Currency: peso = 10,000 australs (which it replaced in 1992) **GDP:** (US$) 322.7 billion (1997) **Real GDP growth:** (% change on previous year) 8 (1997) **GNP (US$):** 305.7 billion (1997) **GNP per capita (PPP):** (US$) 9,950 (1997) **Consumer price inflation:** 1.9 (1998) **Unemployment:** 18.4% (1996) **Foreign debt:** (US$) 91.2

billion (1996) **Major trading partners:** USA, Brazil, the Netherlands, Germany, Italy, Uruguay, Chile **Resources:** coal, crude oil, natural gas, iron ore, lead ore, zinc ore, tin, gold, silver, uranium ore, marble, borates, granite **Exports:** meat and meat products, prepared animal fodder, cereals, petroleum and petroleum products, soya beans, vegetable oils and fats. Principal market: Brazil 30.4% (1997) **Imports:** machinery and transport equipment, chemicals and mineral products. Principal sources: Brazil 22.7% (1997) **Arable land:** 9.1% (1995)

Population and society

Population: 36,123,000 (1998 est) **Population growth rate:** 1.3% (1995–2000); 1.1% (2000–05) **Population density:** (per sq km) 13.3 (1998 est) **Urban population:** (% of total) 89 (1997) **Age distribution:** (% of total population) 0–14 27.5%, 15–64 62.4%, 65+ 10.2% (1998) **Ethnic groups:** 85% of European descent, mainly Spanish; 15% mestizo (offspring of Spanish–American and American Indian parents) **Language:** Spanish 95% (official); Italian 3% **Religion:** Roman Catholic (state-supported) **Education:** (compulsory years) 7; age limits 7–16 **Literacy rate:** 95% (men); 95% (women) (1995 est) **Labour force:** 38% of population: 12% agriculture, 32% industry, 55% services **Life expectancy:** 70 (men); 77 (women) (1995–2000) **Child mortality rate:** (under 5, per 1,000 live births) 25 (1997) **Physicians:** 1 per 330 people (1993 est)

Practical information

Visa requirements: UK: visa not required for tourist visits; visa required for business purposes. USA: visa not required for tourist visits; visa required for business purposes **Embassy in the UK:** 53 Hans Place, London SW1X 0LA. Tel: (0171) 584 6494; fax: (0171) 589 3106 **British embassy:** Casilla de Correo 2050, Dr Luis Agote 2412/52, 1425 Buenos Aires. Tel: (1) 803 7070/1; fax: (1) 803 1731 **Chamber of commerce:** Cámara Argentina de Comercio, Avda Leandro N Alem 36, 1003 Buenos Aires. Tel: (1) 331 8051; fax: (1) 331 8055

Chronology

1516: Spanish navigator Juan Diaz de Solis discovered Río de La Plata. **1536:** Buenos Aires founded, but soon abandoned because of attacks by American Indians. **1580:** Buenos Aires re-established as part of Spanish province of Asunción. **1617:** Buenos Aires became a separate province within Spanish viceroyalty of Lima. **1776:** Spanish South American Empire reorganized: Atlantic regions became viceroyalty of La Plata, with Buenos Aires as capital. **1810:** After French conquest of Spain, Buenos Aires junta took over government of viceroyalty. **1816:** Independence proclaimed as United Provinces of Río de La Plata, but Bolivia and Uruguay soon seceded; civil war followed between federalists and those who wanted a unitary state. **1835–52:** Dictatorship of Gen Juan Manuel Rosas. **1853:** Adoption of federal constitution based on US model; Buenos Aires refused to join confederation. **1861:** Buenos Aires incorporated into Argentine confederation by force. **1865–70:** Argentina took part in War of Triple Alliance against Paraguay. **late 19th century:** Large-scale European immigration and rapid economic development; Argentina became a major world supplier of meat and grain. **1880:** Buenos Aires became a special federal district and national capital. **1880–1916:** Government dominated by oligarchy of conservative landowners; each president effectively chose his own successor. **1916:** Following introduction of secret ballot, Radical Party of Hipólito Irigoyen won election victory, beginning a period of 14 years in government. **1930:** Military coup ushered in a series of conservative governments sustained by violence and fraud. **1943:** Group of pro-German army officers seized power; Col Juan Perón emerged as a leading figure. **1946:** Perón won free presidential election; he secured working-class support through welfare measures, trade unionism, and the popularity of his wife, Eva Perón (Evita). **1949:** New constitution abolished federalism and increased powers of president. **1952:** Death of Evita. Support for Perón began to decline. **1955:** Perón overthrown; constitution of 1853 restored. **1966–70:** Dictatorship of Gen Juan Carlos Ongania. **1973:** Perónist Party won free elections; Perón returned from exile in Spain to become president. **1974:** Perón died; succeeded by his third wife, Isabel Perón. **1976:** Coup resulted in rule by military junta headed by Lt-Gen Jorge Videla (until 1978; succeeded by Gen Roberto Viola 1978–81 and Gen Leopoldo Galtieri 1981–82). **1976–83:** Military regime conducted murderous campaign ('Dirty War') against left-wing elements. **1982:** Invasion of Falkland Islands by Argentina. Intervention and defeat by UK; Galtieri replaced by Gen Reynaldo Bignone. **1983:** Return to civilian rule under President Rául Alfonsín; investigation launched into 'disappearance' of more than 8,000 people during 'Dirty War'. **1985:** Economic austerity programme failed to halt hyperinflation. **1989:** Perónist candidate Carlos Menem won presidential election. Annual inflation reached 12,000%. **1990:** Full diplomatic relations with UK restored. **1995:** President Menem re-elected. **1997:** PJ lost its assembly majority.

Armenia Republic of

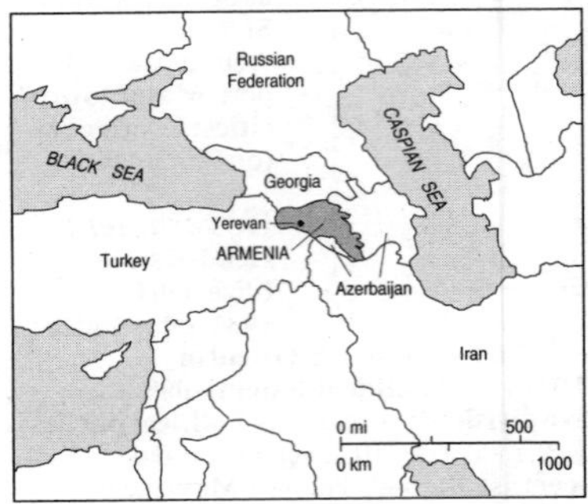

National name: *Haikakan Hanrapetoutioun* **Area:** 29,800 sq km/11,505 sq mi **Capital:** Yerevan **Major towns/cities:** Gyumri (formerly Leninakan), Vanadzor (formerly Kirovakan)

Government

Head of state: Robert Kocharyan from 1998 **Head of government:** Vazgen Sarkisyan from 1999 **Political system:** authoritarian nationalist **Administrative divisions:** 10 regions **Political parties:** Armenian Pan-National Movement (APM), nationalist, left of centre; Armenian Revolutionary Federation (ARF), centrist; Communist Party of Armenia (banned 1991–92); National Unity, opposition coalition **Armed forces:** 60,000 (1997) **Conscription:** compulsory for 18 months **Death penalty:** retained and used for ordinary crimes **Defence spend:** (% GDP) 8.9 (1997) **Education spend:** (% GNP) 2 (1996) **Health spend:** (% GDP) 3.1 (1990–95)

Economy and resources

Currency: dram (replaced Russian rouble in 1993) **GDP:** (US$) 1.6 billion (1997 est) **Real GDP growth:** (% change on previous year) 3 (1997) **GNP (US$):** 2 billion (1997) **GNP per capita (PPP):** (US$) 2,280 (1997) **Consumer price inflation:** 22% (1997) **Unemployment:** 9.1% (1996) **Foreign debt:** (US$) 552 million (1996) **Major trading partners:** Russia, Ukraine, Belarus, Georgia, Kazakhstan, Turkmenistan, USA **Resources:** copper, zinc, molybdenum, iron, silver, marble, granite **Exports:** machinery and metalworking products, chemical and petroleum products. Principal market: Russia 27.1% (1997) **Imports:** light industrial products, petroleum and derivatives, industrial raw materials. Principal source: Russia 22% (1997) **Arable land:** 21.2% (1995)

Population and society

Population: 3,536,000 (1998 est) **Population growth rate:** 0.2% (1995–2000) **Population density:** (per sq km) 114.8 (1998 est) **Urban population:** (% of total) 69 (1997) **Age distribution:** (% of total population) 0–14 26.4 %, 15–64 65.2%, 65+ 8.4% (1998) **Ethnic groups:** 91% of Armenian ethnic descent, 5% Azeri, 2% Russian, and 2% Kurdish **Language:** Armenian **Religion:** Armenian Christian **Education:** (compulsory years) 9 **Literacy rate:** 99% (men); 99% (women) (1995) **Labour force:** 32.2% agriculture, 32.8% industry, 35% services (1993) **Life expectancy:** 67 (men); 74 (women) (1995–2000) **Child mortality rate:** (under 5, per 1,000 live births) 27 (1997) **Physicians:** 1 per 250 people (1994 est)

Practical information

Visa requirements: UK: visa required. USA: visa required **Embassy in the UK:** 25A Cheniston Gardens, London W8 6TG. Tel: (0171) 938 5435; fax: (0171) 938 2595 **British embassy:** Armenia Hotel, 1 Vramshapouh Arka Street, Yerevan 375010. Tel: (2) 151 807; fax: (2) 151 803 **Chamber of commerce:** Chamber of Commerce and Industry of the Republic of Armenia, ulitsa Alevardyan 39, Yerevan. Tel: (2) 565 438; fax: (2) 565 071

Chronology

6th century BC: Armenian peoples moved into the area, which was then part of the Persian Empire. *c.* **94–56 BC:** Under King Tigranes II 'the Great', Armenia reached height of its power, expanding southwards to become the strongest state in the eastern Roman empire, controlling an area from the Caucasus to the Mediterranean. *c.* **AD 300:** Christianity became the state religion when the local ruler was converted by St Gregory the Illuminator. *c.* **AD 390:** Divided between Byzantine Armenia, which became part of Byzantine Empire, and Persarmenia, under Persian control. **886–1045:** Independent under the Bagratid monarchy. **13th century:** After being overrun by the Mongols, a substantially independent Little Armenia survived until 1375. **early 16th century:** Conquered by Muslim Ottoman Turks. **1813–28:** Russia took control of eastern Armenia. **late 19th century:** Revival in Armenian culture and national spirit, provoking Ottoman backlash in western Armenia and international concern at Armenian maltreatment: the 'Armenian Question'. **1894–96:** Massacre of Armenians by Turkish soldiers to suppress unrest. **1915:** Suspected of pro-Russian sympathies, two-thirds of Armenia's population of 2 million were deported to Syria and Palestine. Around 600,000–1 million died en route: the survivors contributed towards an Armenian diaspora in Europe and North America. **1916:** Conquered by tsarist Russia and became part of a brief 'Transcaucasian Alliance' with Georgia and Azerbaijan. **1918:** Became an independent republic. **1920:** Occupied by Red Army of Soviet Union (USSR), but western Armenia remained part of Turkey and northwest Iran. **1936:** Became constituent republic of USSR; rapid industrial development. **late 1980s:** Armenian 'national reawakening', encouraged by *glasnost* (openness) initiative of Soviet leader Mikhail Gorbachev. **1988:** Earthquake – around 20,000 people died. **1989:** Strife-torn Nagorno-Karabakh placed under direct rule from Moscow; civil war erupted with Azerbaijan over Nagorno-Karabakh and Nakhichevan, an Azerbaijani-peopled enclave in Armenia. **1990:** Nationalists secured control of Armenian parliament in elections in May; former dissident Ter-Petrossian indirectly elected president; independence declared, but ignored by Moscow and international community. **1991:** After collapse of USSR, Armenia joined new Commonwealth of Independent States. Ter-Petrossian directly elected president. Nagorno-Karabakh declared its independence. **1992:** Armenia recognized as independent state by USA and admitted into United Nations. **1993:** Armenian forces gained control of more than one-fifth of Azerbaijan, including much of Nagorno-Karabakh. **1994:** Nagorno-Karabakh cease-fire ended conflict. **1995:** Privatization and price-liberalization programme launched. Ruling APM re-elected. **1996:** Ter-Petrossian re-elected president. Hrand Bagratian replaced as prime minister by Armen Sarkissian. **1997:** Sarkissian resigned for health reasons; replaced by Robert Kocharyan. Border fighting with Azerbaijan. Arkady Gukasyan elected president of Nagorno-Karabakh. **1998:** Ter-Petrossian resigned following opposition within his party to his moderate approach to resolving the dispute with Azerbaijan over Nagorno-Karabakh. Prime minister Robert Kocharyan, a hardliner, elected president. Formerly banned ARF brought into cabinet. Commission set up to recommend reductions in president's powers. New election law approved. The deputy defence minister, Vagram Khorkoruni, was shot dead in Yerevan.

Australia Commonwealth of

Area: 7,682,300 sq km/2,966,136 sq mi **Capital:** Canberra **Major towns/cities:** Adelaide, Alice Springs, Brisbane, Darwin, Melbourne, Perth, Sydney, Hobart, Geelong, Newcastle, Townsville, Wollongong

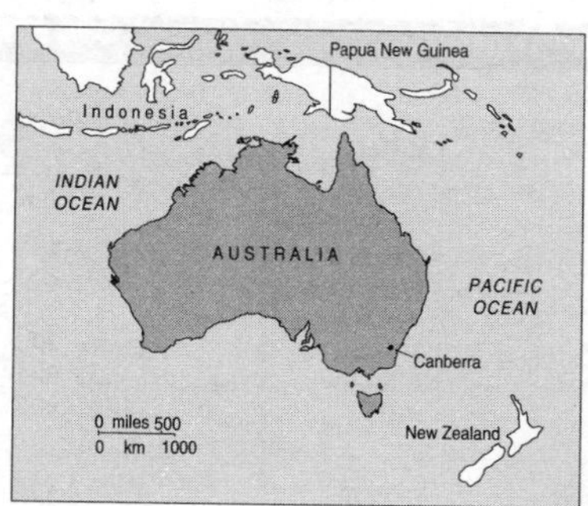

Government

Head of state: Elizabeth II from 1952, represented by governor general William George Hayden from 1989 **Head of government:** John Howard from 1996 **Political system:** federal constitutional monarchy **Administrative divisions:** six states and two territories **Political parties:** Australian Labor Party, moderate left of centre; Liberal Party of Australia, moderate, liberal, free enterprise; National Party of Australia (formerly Country Party), centrist non-metropolitan **Armed forces:** 57,400 (1997) **Conscription:** military service is voluntary **Death penalty:** abolished in 1985 **Defence spend:** (%GDP) 2.2 (1997) **Education spend:** (%GNP) 5.6 (1995) **Health spend:** (%GDP) 6.0 (1990–95)

Economy and resources

Currency: Australian dollar **GDP:** (US$) 394 billion (1997) **Real GDP growth:** (% change on previous year) 2.9 (1997) **GNP (US$):** 380 billion (1997) **GNP per capita (PPP):** (US$) 20,170 (1997) **Consumer price inflation:** 1.8% (1998) **Unemployment:** 8.7% (1997) **Major trading partners:** USA, Japan, UK, New Zealand, Republic of Korea, China, Taiwan, Singapore **Resources:** coal, iron ore (world's third-largest producer), bauxite, copper, zinc (world's second-largest producer), nickel (world's fifth-largest producer), uranium, gold, diamonds **Exports:** major world producer of raw materials: iron ore, aluminium, coal, nickel, zinc, lead, gold, tin, tungsten, uranium, crude oil; wool, meat, cereals, fruit, sugar, wine. Principal markets: Japan 19.5% (1997) **Imports:** processed industrial supplies, transport equipment and parts, road vehicles, petroleum and petroleum products, medicinal and pharmaceutical products, organic chemicals, consumer goods. Principal source: USA 22.6% (1997) **Arable land:** 6.3% (1995)

Population and society

Population: 18,520,000 (1998 est) **Population growth rate:** 1.1% (1995–2000) **Population density:** (per sq km) 2.4 (1998 est) **Urban population:** (% of total) 85 (1997) **Age distribution:** (% of total population) 0–14 21.2%, 15–64 66.4%, 65+ 12.4% (1998) **Ethnic groups:** 99% of European descent; remaining 1% Aborigine or Asian **Language:** English, Aboriginal languages **Religion:** Anglican 26%, other Protestant 17%, Roman Catholic 26% **Education:** (compulsory years) 10 or 11 (states vary) **Literacy rate:** 99% (men); 99% (women) (1995 est) **Labour force:** 50.2% of total population: 5.1% agriculture, 22.5% industry, 72.4% services (1996) **Life expectancy:** 75 (men); 81 (women) (1995–2000) **Child mortality rate:** (under 5, per 1,000 live births) 8 (1997) **Physicians:** 1 per 400 people (1996)

Practical information

Visa requirements: UK: visa required. USA: visa required **Embassy in the UK:** High Commission, Australia House, The Strand, London WC2B 4LA. Tel: (0171) 379 4334; fax: (0171) 240 5333 **British embassy:** British High Commission, Commonwealth Avenue, Yarralumla, Canberra, ACT 2600. Tel: (6) 270 6666; fax: (6)273 3236 **Chamber of commerce:** International Chamber of Commerce, POB E118, Queen Victoria Terrace, Canberra, ACT 2600. Tel: (6) 295 1961; fax: (6) 295 0170. Australian Chamber of Commerce and Industry, POB E14, Queen Victoria Terrace, Canberra ACT 2600. Tel: (6) 273 2311; fax: (6) 273 3196

Chronology

c. **40,000 BC:** Aboriginal immigration from southern India, Sri Lanka, and Southeast Asia. **AD 1606:** First recorded sightings of Australia by Europeans including discovery of Cape York by Dutch explorer Willem Jansz in *Duyfken*. **1770:** Capt James Cook claimed New South

Australia: States and Territories

(– = not applicable.)

State	Capital	Area sq km	Area sq mi	Population (1994)
New South Wales	Sydney	801,600	309,500	6,038,700
Queensland	Brisbane	1,727,200	666,872	3,368,850
South Australia	Adelaide	984,377	380,070	1,427,900
Tasmania	Hobart	67,800	26,177	459,700
Victoria	Melbourne	227,620	87,884	4,373,500
Western Australia	Perth	2,525,500	975,095	1,726,100
Territory				
Australian Capital Territory	Canberra	2,400	926	299,200
Northern Territory	Darwin	1,346,200	519,767	195,100
External Territory				
Ashmore and Cartier Islands	–	5	2	uninhabited
Australian Antarctic Territory	–	6,044,000	2,333,590	uninhabited except for scientific stations
Christmas Island	–	135	52	2,500[1]
Cocos (Keeling) Islands	–	14	5.5	590[2]
Coral Sea Islands	–	[3]	[3]	uninhabited except for scientific stations
Heard Island and McDonald Islands	–	410	158	uninhabited
Norfolk Island	–	40	15.5	1,900[2]

[1] 1994 estimate.
[2] 1993 figure.
[3] Sea area of Coral Sea Islands is 780,000 sq km/301,158 sq mi; land area of the islands is approximately 2.6 sq km/1 sq mi.

Wales for Britain. **1788:** Sydney founded as British penal colony. **late 18th–19th centuries:** Great age of exploration: coastal surveys by George Bass and Matthew Flinders; interior by Charles Sturt, Edward Eyre, Robert Burke and William Wills, John McDouall Stuart, and John Forrest. Overlanders and squatters also opened up new territory, as did bushrangers, including Ned Kelly. **1804:** Castle Hill Rising by Irish convicts in New South Wales. **1813:** Crossing of Blue Mountains removed major barrier to exploration of interior. **1825:** Tasmania seceded from New South Wales. **1829:** Western Australia colonized. **1836:** South Australia colonized. **1840–68:** End of convict transportation. **1850:** British Act of Parliament permitted Australian colonies to draft their own constitutions and achieve virtual self-government. **1851–61:** Gold rushes contributed to exploration and economic growth. **1851:** Victoria seceded from New South Wales. **1855:** Victoria achieved self-government. **1856:** New South Wales, South Australia, and Tasmania achieved self-government. **1859:** Queensland formed from New South Wales and achieved self-government. **1860:** (National) Country Party founded. **1890:** Western Australia achieved self-government. **1891:** Depression gave rise to Australian Labor Party. **1899–1900:** South African War – forces offered by individual colonies. **1901:** Creation of Commonwealth of Australia. **1902:** Immigration Restriction Act introduced language tests for potential settlers; women gained right to vote. **1914–18:** World War I: over 300,000 Australian volunteers fought in Middle East and on western front. **1919:** Australia given mandates over Papua New Guinea and Solomon Islands. **1927:** Seat of federal government moved to Canberra. **1931:** Statute of Westminster confirmed Australian independence. **1933:** Western Australia's vote to secede was overruled. **1939–45:** World War II: Australian troops fought in Greece, North Africa, and the southwest Pacific. **1941:** Curtin's appeal to USA for military help marked shift away from exclusive relationship with Britain. **1944:** Liberal Party founded by Menzies. **1948–75:** Influx of around 2 million new immigrants, chiefly from continental Europe. **1950–53:** Australia contributed troops to United Nations (UN) forces in Korean War. **1951:** Australia joined USA and New Zealand in ANZUS Pacific security alliance. **1965–72:** Australian troops participated in Vietnam War. **1967:** Referendum gave Australian Aborigines full citizenship rights. Australia became a member of the Association of South East Asian Nations (ASEAN). **1973:** Britain entered European Economic Community (EEC), and in 1970s Japan became Australia's chief trading partner. **1974:** 'White Australia' immigration restrictions abolished. **1975:** Constitutional crisis: Governor General John Kerr dismissed Prime Minister Gough Whitlam after senate blocked financial legislation. Papua New Guinea became independent. **1978:** Northern Territory achieved self-government. **1983:** Labor Party returned to power under Bob Hawke. **1986:** Australia Act passed by British Parliament eliminating last vestiges of British legal authority in Australia. **1988:** Free Trade Agreement signed with New Zealand. **1992:** Citizenship Act removed oath of allegiance to British crown. **1993:** Labor Party won record fifth election victory. **1996:** Liberal–National coalition, headed by John Howard, won general election. **1997:** Democrat Party leader switched to Labor Party. **1998:** Howard's Liberal–National coalition government narrowly re-elected.

Austria Republic of

National name: *Republik Österreich* **Area:** 83,500 sq km/32,239 sq mi **Capital:** Vienna **Major towns/cities:** Graz, Linz, Salzburg, Innsbruck, Klagenfurt

Government

Head of state: Thomas Klestil from 1992 **Head of government:** Franz Vranitzky from 1986 **Political system:** democratic federal republic **Administrative divisions:** nine provinces **Political parties:** Social Democratic Party of Austria (SPÖ), democratic socialist; Austrian People's Party (ÖVP), progressive centrist; Freedom (formerly Freedom Party of Austria: FPÖ), right wing; United Green Party of Austria (VGÖ), conservative ecological; Green Alternative Party

Austria: Provinces

Province	Capital	Area sq km	Area sq mi	Population (1996 est)
Burgenland	Eisenstadt	3,965	1,531	275,000
Carinthia	Klagenfurt	9,533	3,681	563,000
Lower Austria	St Pölten	19,174	7,403	1,524,000
Salzburg	Salzburg	7,154	2,762	509,000
Styria	Graz	16,388	6,327	1,207,000
Tyrol	Innsbruck	12,648	4,883	660,000
Upper Austria	Linz	11,980	4,625	1,381,000
Vienna	Vienna	415	160	1,595,000
Vorarlberg	Bregenz	2,601	1,004	344,000

(ALV), radical ecological **Armed forces:** 45,500 (1997) **Conscription:** 6 months **Death penalty:** abolished in 1968 **Defence spend:** (% GDP) 0.8 (1997) **Education spend:** (% GNP) 5.5 (1995) **Health spend:** (% GDP) 5.9 (1990–95)

Economy and resources

Currency: schilling **GDP:** (US$) 206.2 billion (1997) **Real GDP growth:** (% change on previous year) 1.8 (1997) **GNP (US$):** 225.9 billion (1997) **GNP per capita (PPP):** (US$) 21,980 (1997) **Consumer price inflation:** 1.6% (1998) **Unemployment:** 4.4% (1998) **Major trading partners:** EU, Switzerland, USA, Japan **Resources:** lignite, iron, kaolin, gypsum, talcum, magnesite, lead, zinc, forests **Exports:** dairy products, food products, wood and paper products, machinery and transport equipment, metal and metal products, chemical products. Principal market for exports: Germany 35.1% (1997) **Imports:** petroleum and petroleum products, food and live animals, chemicals and related products, textiles, clothing. Principal source: Germany 41.7% (1997) **Arable land:** 17.2% (1995)

Population and society

Population: 8,140,000 (1998 est) **Population growth rate:** 0.6% (1995–2000); 0.2% (2000–05) **Population density:** (per sq km) 98.3 (1998 est) **Urban population:** (% of total) 64 (1997) **Age distribution:** (% of total population) 0–14 17.0%, 15–64 67.5%, 65+ 15.5% (1998) **Ethnic groups:** 98% German, 0.7% Croatian, 0.3% Slovene **Language:** German **Religion:** Roman Catholic 78%, Protestant 5% **Education:** (compulsory years) 9 **Literacy rate:** 99% (men); 99% (women) (1995) **Labour force:** 48.3% of population: 7.2% agriculture, 33.2% industry, 59.6% services (1994) **Life expectancy:** 74 (men); 80 (women) (1995–2000) **Child mortality rate:** (under 5, per 1,000 live births) 7 (1997) **Physicians:** 1 per 253 people (1996)

Practical information

Visa requirements: UK: visa not required. USA: visa not required **Embassy in the UK:** 18 Belgrave Mews West, London SW1X 8HV. Tel: (0171) 235 3731; fax: (0171) 235 8025 **British embassy:** Juarèsgasse 12, 1030 Vienna. Tel: (1) 713 1575; fax: (1) 714 7824 **Chamber of commerce:** Wirtschaftskammer Österreich (Austrian Economic Chamber), Wiedner Haupstrasse 63, 1045 Vienna. Tel: (1) 50105; fax: (1) 50206

Chronology

14 BC: Country south of River Danube conquered by Romans. **5th century AD:** Region occupied by Vandals, Huns, Goths, Lombards, and Avars. **791:** Charlemagne conquered Avars and established East Mark, nucleus of future Austrian Empire. **976:** Holy Roman Emperor Otto II granted East Mark to House of Babenburg, which ruled until 1246. **1156:** Margrave of Austria raised to duke. **1282:** Holy Roman Emperor Rudolf of Habsburg seized Austria and invested his son as its duke; for over 500 years most rulers of Austria were elected Holy Roman emperor. **1453:** Austria became an archduchy. **1519–56:** Emperor Charles V was both archduke of Austria and king of Spain; Habsburgs dominant in Europe. **1526:** Bohemia came under Habsburg rule. **1529:** Vienna besieged by the Ottoman Turks. **1618–48:** Thirty Years' War: Habsburgs weakened by failure to secure control over Germany. **1683:** Polish-Austrian force led by Jan Sobieski defeated the Turks at Vienna. **1699:** Treaty of Karlowitz: Austrians expelled the Turks from Hungary, which came under Habsburg rule. **1713:** By the Treaty of Utrecht, Austria obtained the Spanish Netherlands (Belgium) and political control over most of Italy. **1740–48:** War of Austrian Succession: Prussia (supported by France and Spain) attacked Austria (supported by Holland and England) on the pretext of disputing rights of Maria Theresa; Austria lost Silesia to Prussia. **1772:** Austria joined in partition of Poland, annexing Galicia. **1780–90:** 'Enlightened despotism': Joseph II tried to impose radical reforms. **1792:** Austria went to war with revolutionary France. **1804:** Francis II took the title Emperor of Austria. **1806:** Holy Roman Empire abolished. **1809–48:** Guided by foreign minister Prince Klemens von Metternich, Austria took a leading role in resisting liberalism and nationalism throughout Europe. **1815:** After the Napoleonic Wars, Austria lost its Netherlands but received Lombardy and Venetia. **1848:** Outbreak of liberal-nationalist revolts throughout the Austrian Empire; Ferdinand I abdicated in favour of Franz Joseph; revolutions suppressed with difficulty. **1859:** France and Sardinia expelled Austrians from Lombardy by force. **1866:** Seven Weeks' War: Prussia defeated Austria, which ceded Venetia to Italy. **1867:** Austria conceded equality to Hungary within the dual monarchy of Austria-Hungary. **1878:** Treaty of Berlin: Austria-Hungary occupied Bosnia-Herzegovina; annexed in 1908. **1914:** Archduke Franz Ferdinand, the heir to the throne, assassinated by a Serbian nationalist; Austria-Hungary invaded Serbia, precipitating World War I. **1916:** Death of Franz Joseph; succeeded by Karl I. **1918:** Austria-Hungary collapsed in military defeat; empire dissolved; republic proclaimed. **1919:** Treaty of St Germain reduced Austria to its present boundaries and prohibited union with Germany. **1934:** Political instability culminated in brief civil war; right-wingers defeated socialists. **1938:** The *Anschluss* : Nazi Germany incorporated Austria into the Third Reich. **1945:** Following World War II, the victorious Allies divided Austria into four zones of occupation (US, British, French, and Soviet); Second Republic established under Karl Renner. **1955:** Austrian State Treaty ended occupation; Austria regained independence on condition of neutrality. **1960–70s:** Austria experienced rapid industrialization and prosperity under governments dominated by moderate socialists and centrists. **1986:** Kurt Waldheim elected president, despite allegations of war crimes during World War II. This led to a measure of diplomatic isolation until Waldheim's replacement in 1992. **1995:** Became a full member of European Union (EU). **1998:** NATO membership ruled out. President Klestil reelected.

Azerbaijan Republic of

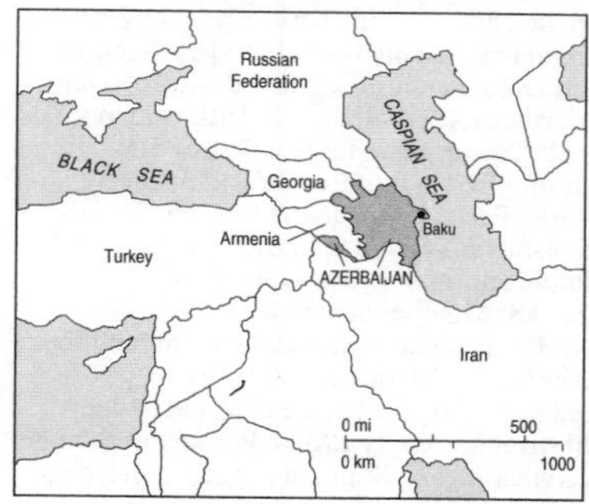

National name: *Azarbaijchan Respublikasy* **Area:** 86,600 sq km/33,436 sq mi **Capital:** Baku **Major towns/cities:** Gyandzha (formerly Kirovabad), Sumgait, Nakhichevan, Stepanakert

Government

Head of state: Geidar Aliyev from 1993 **Head of government:**

Artur Rasizade from 1996 **Political system:** authoritarian nationalist **Administrative divisions:** 54 regions, 11 cities, and one autonomous republic (Nakhchyuan) **Political parties:** Popular Front of Azerbaijan (FPA), democratic nationalist; New Azerbaijan, ex-communist; Communist Party of Azerbaijan (banned 1991–93); Muslim Democratic Party (Musavat), Islamic, pro-Turkic unity **Armed forces:** 66,700 (1997) **Conscription:** military service is for 17 months **Death penalty:** abolished in 1998 **Defence spend:** (% GDP) 4.0 (1997) **Education spend:** (% GNP) 3.3 (1996) **Health spend:** (% GDP) 1.4 (1990–95)

Economy and resources

Currency: manat (left rouble zone in 1993) **GDP:** (US$) 4.39 billion (1997) **Real GDP growth:** (% change on previous year) 5 (1997) **GNP (US$):** 3.9 billion (1997) **GNP per capita (PPP):** (US$) 1,520 (1997) **Consumer price inflation:** 6% (1998) **Unemployment:** 1% (1996) **Foreign debt:** (US$) 435 million (1996) **Major trading partners:** Iran, Turkey, former USSR (principally Russia, Ukraine, and Turkmenistan), Greece **Resources:** petroleum, natural gas, iron ore, aluminium, copper, barytes, cobalt, precious metals, limestone, salt **Exports:** refined petroleum products, machinery, food products, textiles. Principal market: Iran 24.3% (1997) **Imports:** industrial raw materials, processed food, machinery. Principal source: Turkey 22.6% (1997) **Arable land:** 56.7% (1995)

Population and society

Population: 7,669,000 (1998 est) **Population growth rate:** 0.8% (1995–2000) **Population density:** (per sq km) 90.7 (1998 est) **Urban population:** (% of total) 56 (1997) **Age distribution:** (% of total population) 0–14 32.4%, 15–64 61.2%, 65+ 6.4% (1998) **Ethnic groups:** 83% of Azeri descent, 6% Russian, 6% Armenian **Language:** Azeri **Religion:** Shi'ite Muslim 62%, Sunni Muslim 26%, Orthodox Christian 12% **Education:** (compulsory years) 11 **Literacy rate:** 96% (men); 96% (women) (1995 est) **Labour force:** 33.7% agriculture, 24.3% industry, 42% services (1991) **Life expectancy:** 67 (men); 75 (women) (1995–2000) **Child mortality rate:** (under 5, per 1,000 live births) 39 (1997) **Physicians:** 1 per 278 people (1994 est)

Practical information

Visa requirements: UK: visa required. USA: visa required **Embassy in the UK:** 4 Kensington Court, London W8 5DL. Tel: (0171) 938 5482; fax: (0171) 937 1783 **British embassy:** c/o Old Intourist Hotel, Room 214, Baku. Tel: (12) 924 813; fax: (12) (873) 144 6456 **Chamber of commerce:** Chamber of Commerce and Industry, Istiglaliyat Street 31/33, 370001 Baku. Tel: (12) 928 912; fax: (12) 989 324

Chronology

4th century BC: Established as an independent state for the first time by Atrophates, a vassal of Alexander III of Macedon. **7th century:** Spread of Islam. **11th century:** Immigration by Oghuz Seljuk peoples, from the steppes to the northeast. **13th–14th centuries:** Incorporated within Mongol Empire; the Mongol ruler Tamerlane had his capital at Samarkand. **16th century:** Baku besieged and incorporated within Ottoman Empire, before falling under Persian dominance. **1805:** Khanates (chieftaincies), including Karabakh and Shirvan, which had won independence from Persia, gradually became Russian protectorates, being confirmed by the Treaty of Gulistan, which concluded the 1804–13 First Russo-Iranian War. **1828:** Under Treaty of Turkmenchai, which concluded the Second Russo-Iranian War begun in 1826, Persia was granted control over southern and Russia over northern Azerbaijan. **late 19th century:** Petroleum industry developed, resulting in large influx of Slav immigrants to Baku, which supplied half of Russia's oil needs by 1901. **1906:** Himmat ('Effort') Party, linked to the Russian Social-Democrat Labour Party (Bolshevik), founded in Baku. **1912:** Himmat Party banned; Islamic nationalist Musavat ('Equality') Party formed in Baku. **1917–18:** Member of anti-Bolshevik Transcaucasian Federation. **1918:** Became an independent republic. **1920:** Occupied by Red Army and subsequently forcibly secularized. **1922–36:** Became part of the Transcaucasian Federal Republic with Georgia and Armenia. **early 1930s:** Peasant uprisings against agricultural collectivization and Stalinist purges of the local Communist Party. **1936:** Became a constituent republic of the USSR. **late 1980s:** Growth in nationalist sentiment, taking advantage of the *glasnost* initiative of the reformist Soviet leader Mikhail Gorbachev. **1988:** Riots followed the request of Nagorno-Karabakh, an Armenian-peopled enclave within Azerbaijan, for transfer to Armenia. **1989:** Nagorno-Karabakh placed under direct rule from Moscow; civil war broke out with Armenia over Nagorno-Karabakh. **1990:** Soviet troops dispatched to Baku to restore order amid Azeri calls for secession from USSR. **1991:** Independence declared after collapse of anti-Gorbachev coup in Moscow, which had been supported by Azeri communist leadership. Joined new Commonwealth of Independent States (CIS); Nagorno-Karabakh declared independence. **1992:** Admitted into United Nations and accorded diplomatic recognition by the USA; Albulfaz Elchibey, leader of nationalist Popular Front, elected president; renewed campaign to capture Nagorno-Karabakh. **1993:** Elchibey fled military revolt, replaced in a coup by former Communist Party leader Geidar Aliyev, later elected president. Rebel military leader Surat Huseynov appointed prime minister. Nagorno-Karabakh overtaken by Armenian forces. **1994:** Nagorno-Karabakh cease-fire agreed. After coup attempt, Huseynov replaced as premier by Fuad Kuliyev. State of emergency imposed. **1995:** Attempted coup foiled. Pro-Aliyev legislature elected and market-centred economic reform programme introduced. **1996:** Kuliyev replaced by Artur Rasizade. **1997:** Border fighting with Armenia. Arkady Gukasyan elected president of Nagorno-Karabakh. Sharp rise in Caspian Sea oil extraction. Former president Elchibey returned from exile to lead opposition coalition. **1998:** New pro-government grouping, Democratic Azerbaijan, formed. Aliyev re-elected president in disputed October poll. New OSCE peace plan rejected.

Bahamas Commonwealth of the

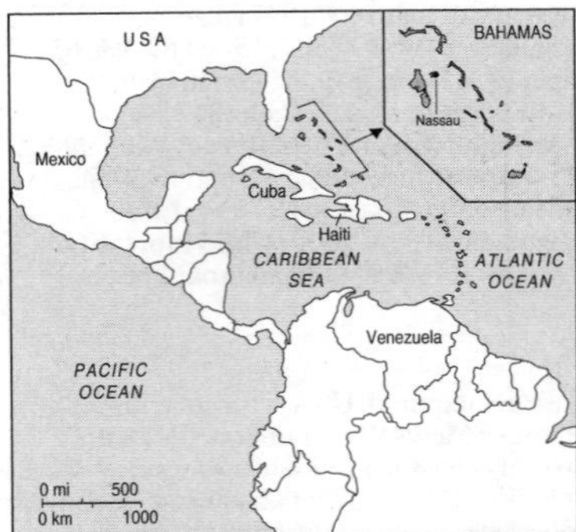

Area: 13,864 sq km/5,352 sq mi **Capital:** Nassau (on New Providence Island) **Major towns/cities:** Freeport (on Grand Bahama) **Principal islands:** Andros, Grand Bahama, Abaco, Eleuthera, New Providence, Berry Islands, Bimini Islands, Great Inagua, Acklins Island, Exuma Islands, Mayguana, Crooked Island, Long Island, Cat Islands, Rum Cay, Watling (San Salvador) Island, Inagua Islands

Government

Head of state: Elizabeth II from 1973, represented by governor general Orville Turnquest from 1995 **Head of government:** Hubert Ingraham from 1992 **Political system:** constitutional monarchy **Administrative divisions:** 21 districts **Political parties:** Progressive Liberal Party (PLP), centrist; Free National Movement (FNM), centre left **Armed forces:** 900 (1997) and 2,300 paramilitary forces **Conscription:** military service is voluntary **Death penalty:** retained and used for ordinary crimes **Defence spend:** (% GDP) 0.6 (1997) **Education spend:** (% GNP) 3.9 (1993–94) **Health spend:** (% GDP) 2.5 (1994)

Economy and resources

Currency: Bahamian dollar **GDP:** (US$) 3.7 billion (1997) **Real GDP growth:** (% change on previous year) 3.7 (1997) **GNP (US$):** 3.28 billion (1997) **GNP per capita (PPP):** (US$) 14,830 (1997 est) **Consumer price inflation:** 1.7% (1997) **Unemployment:** 13% (1994) **Foreign debt:** (US$) 380 million (1996) **Major trading

partners: USA, Aruba, UK, France, Canada **Resources:** aragonite (extracted from seabed), chalk, salt **Exports:** foodstuffs (fish), oil products and transhipments, chemicals, rum, salt. Principal market: USA 24.5% (1997) **Imports:** machinery and transport equipment, basic manufactures, petroleum and products, chemicals. Principal source: USA 34.9% (1997) **Arable land:** 1% (1995)

Population and society

Population: 296,000 (1998 est) **Population growth rate:** 1.2% (1995–2000) **Population density:** (per sq km) 27.8 (1998 est) **Urban population:** (% of total) 88 (1997) **Age distribution:** (% of total population) 0–14 27.9%, 15–64 66.6%, 65+ 5.5% (1998) **Ethnic groups:** about 85% of the population is of African origin, remainder mainly British, American, and Canadian **Language:** English and some Creole **Religion:** Christian 94% (Roman Catholic 26%, Anglican 21%, other Protestant 48%) **Education:** (compulsory years) 10 **Literacy rate:** 98% (men); 95% (women) (1995 est) **Labour force:** 50% of population: 6.5% agriculture, 12.1% industry, 81.4% services (1993) **Life expectancy:** 71 (men); 77 (women) (1995–2000) **Child mortality rate:** (under 5, per 1,000 live births) 17 (1997) **Physicians:** 1 per 800 people (1994 est)

Practical information

Visa requirements: UK: visa not required. USA: visa not required **Embassy in the UK:** 10 Chesterfield St, London W1X 8AH. Tel: (0171) 408 4488; fax: (0171) 499 9937 **British embassy:** British High Commission, PO Box N-7516, 3rd Floor, Bitco Building, East St, Nassau. Tel: 325 7471/2/3; fax: 323 3871 **Chamber of commerce:** Bahamas Chamber of Commerce, Shirley St, POB N-665, Nassau. Tel: 322 2145; fax: 322 4649

Chronology

8th–9th centuries AD: Arawak Indians driven northwards to the islands by the Caribs. **1492:** First visited by Christopher Columbus; Arawaks deported to provide cheap labour for the gold and silver mines of Cuba and Hispaniola (Haiti). **1629:** English king Charles I granted the islands to Robert Heath. **1666:** Colonization of New Providence island began. **1783:** Recovered after brief Spanish occupation and became a British colony, being settled during the American War of Independence by American loyalists, who brought with them black slaves. **1838:** Slaves were emancipated. **1940–45:** The Duke of Windsor, the former King Edward VIII, was governor of Bahamas. **from 1950s:** Major development of the tourist trade, especially from the USA. **1964:** Became internally self-governing. **1967:** First national assembly elections; Lynden Pindling, of the centrist Progressive Liberal Party (PLP), became prime minister. **1973:** Full independence achieved, within the British Commonwealth. **1983:** Allegations of drug trafficking by government ministers. **1984:** Deputy prime minister and two cabinet ministers resigned. Pindling denied any personal involvement and was endorsed as party leader. **1992:** Centre-left Free National Movement (FNM) led by Hubert Ingraham won absolute majority in assembly elections, ending 25 years of rule by Pindling.

Bahrain State of

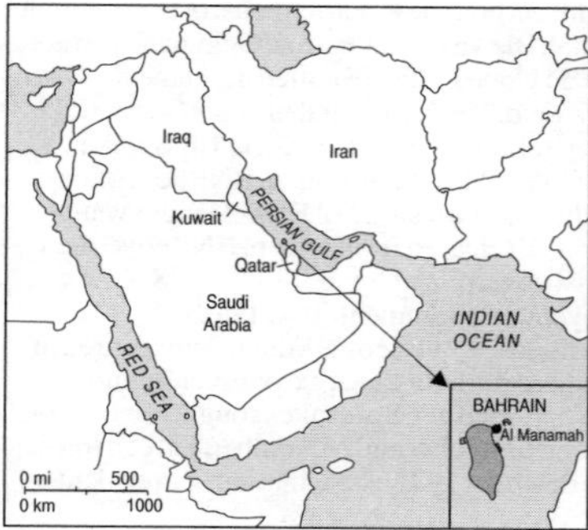

National name: *Dawlat al Bahrayn* **Area:** 688 sq km/266 sq mi **Capital:** Al Manamah on the largest island (also called Bahrain) **Major towns/cities:** Muharraq, Jiddhafs, Isa Town, Hidd, Rifa'a, Sitra **Major ports:** Mina Sulman

Government

Head of state: Sheik Hamad bin Isa al-Khalifa from 1999 **Head of government:** Sheik Khalifa bin Sulman al-Khalifa from 1970 **Political system:** absolute emirate **Administrative divisions:** 12 districts **Political parties:** none **Armed forces:** 11,000 (1997) **Conscription:** military service is voluntary **Death penalty:** retained and used for ordinary crimes **Defence spend:** (% GDP) 6.5 (1997) **Education spend:** (% GNP) 4.8 (1995) **Health spend:** (% GDP) 3.1 (1994)

Economy and resources

Currency: Bahraini dinar **GDP:** (US$) 5.5 billion (1997 est) **Real GDP growth:** (% change on previous year) 1.2 (1997) **GNP (US$):** 4.5 billion (1997) **GNP per capita (PPP):** (US$) 11,500 (1997 est) **Consumer price inflation:** 0.8% (1998) **Unemployment:** 1.8% (1995 official rate; Western diplomats estimate 25–30%) **Foreign debt:** (US$) 2.96 billion (1996) **Major trading partners:** USA, UK, Saudi Arabia, Japan, South Korea, Australia **Resources:** petroleum and natural gas **Exports:** petroleum and petroleum products, aluminium,chemicals (1996). Principal market: India 14% (1997) **Imports:** crude petroleum, machinery and transport equipment, chemicals, basic manufactures. Principal source: Saudi Arabia 40.6% (1997) **Arable land:** 1.4% (1995)

Population and society

Population: 595,000 (1998 est) **Population growth rate:** 2.8% (1990–95); 1.5% (1995–2025) **Population density:** (per sq km) 995.7 (1998) **Urban population:** (% of total) 91 (1997) **Age distribution:** (% of total population) 0–14 30.7%, 15–64 66.5%, 65+ 2.8% (1998) **Ethnic groups:** about 73% Arab and 9% Iranian; Pakistani and Indian minorities **Language:** Arabic (official); Farsi, English, Urdu **Religion:** 85% Muslim (Shi'ite 60%, Sunni 40%), Christian; Islam is the state religion **Education:** (compulsory years) 12 **Literacy rate:** 89% (men); 79% (women) (1995 est) **Labour force:** 45% of population: 2% agriculture, 30% industry, 68% services (1990) **Life expectancy:** 71 (men); 75 (women) (1995–2000) **Child mortality rate:** (under 5, per 1,000 live births) 20 (1997) **Physicians:** 1 per 775 people (1991)

Practical information

Visa requirements: UK: visa not required. USA: visa required **Embassy in the UK:** 98 Gloucester Road, London SW7 4AV. Tel: (0171) 370 5132/3; fax: (0171) 370 7773 **British embassy:** PO Box 114, 21 Government Avenue, Manama, 306. Tel: (973) 534 404; fax: (973) 531 273 **Chamber of commerce:** Bahrain Chamber of Commerce and Industry, PO Box 248, Manama. Tel: (973) 233 913; fax: (973) 241 294

Chronology

4th century AD: Became part of Persian (Iranian) Sassanian Empire. **7th century:** Adopted Islam. **8th century:** Came under Arab Abbasid control. **1521:** Seized by Portugal and held for eight decades, despite local unrest. **1602:** Fell under the control of a Persian Shi'ite dynasty. **1783:** Overthrew Persian rule and became a sheikdom under the Sunni Muslim al-Khalifa dynasty, which originated from the same tribal federation, the Anaza, as the al-Saud family, who now rule Saudi Arabia. **1816–20:** Friendship and peace treaties signed with Britain, which sought to end piracy in the Gulf. **1861:** Became British protectorate, government shared between the ruling sheik (Arab leader) and a British adviser. **1923:** British influence increased when Sheik Isa al-Khalifa was deposed and Charles Belgrave was appointed as the dominating 'adviser' to the new ruler. **1928:** Sovereignty claimed by Persia (Iran). **1930s:** Oil discovered, providing backbone for country's wealth. **1953–56:** Council for National Unity was formed by Arab nationalists, but suppressed after large demonstrations against British participation in the Suez War. **1968:** Britain announced its intention to withdraw its forces. Bahrain formed, with Qatar and the Trucial States of the United Arab Emirates, the Federation of Arab Emirates. **1970:** Iran accepted a United Nations (UN) report showing that Bahrain's inhabitants preferred independence to Iranian control. **1971:** Qatar and the Trucial States withdrew from the federation; Bahrain became an independent state under Sheik Sulman al-Khalifa. **1973:** New constitution adopted, with an elected national assembly dominated by left-nationalist Bahrain National Liberation Front

(BNLF). **1975:** Prime minister Sheik al-Khalifa resigned; national assembly dissolved and political activists driven underground. Emir and his family assumed virtually absolute power. **early 1980s:** Tensions between the Sunni and Shi'ite Muslim communities heightened by Iranian Shi'ite Revolution of 1979. **1986:** Gulf University established in Bahrain. Causeway opened linking the island with Saudi Arabia. **1991:** Bahrain joined UN coalition that ousted Iraq from its occupation of Kuwait; signed defence cooperation agreement with USA. **1994:** Antimonarchy protests by Shi'ite Muslim majority community. **1995:** Sheik al-Khalifa reappointed prime minister. Prodemocracy demonstrations violently suppressed, with 11 deaths. **1999** Sheik al-Khalifa died; succeeded by his son Sheik Hamad.

Bangladesh People's Republic of (formerly East Pakistan)

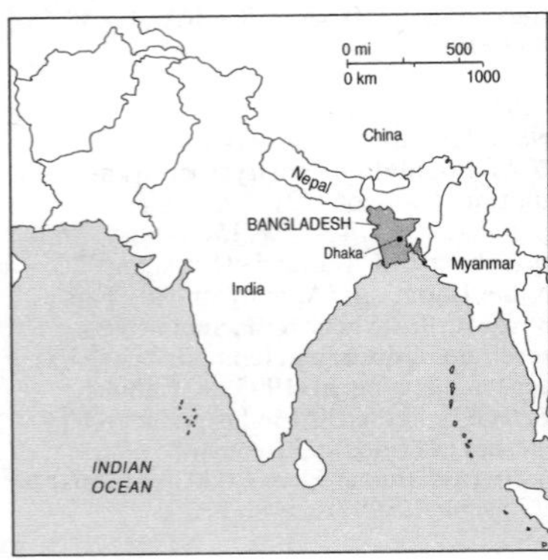

National name: *Gana Prajatantri Bangladesh* **Area:** 144,000 sq km/55,598 sq mi **Capital:** Dhaka (formerly Dacca) **Major towns/cities:** Rajshahi, Khulna, Chittagong, Comilla, Barisal, Sylhet **Major ports:** Chittagong, Khulna

Government

Head of state: Abdur Rahman Biswas from 1991 **Head of government:** Sheikha Hasina Wazed from 1996 **Political system:** emergent democracy **Administrative divisions:** 64 districts within five divisions **Political parties:** Bangladesh Nationalist Party (BNP), Islamic, right of centre; Awami League (AL), secular, moderate socialist; Jatiya Dal (National Party), Islamic nationalist **Armed forces:** 121,000 (1997) **Conscription:** military service is voluntary **Death penalty:** retained and used for ordinary crimes **Defence spend:** (% GDP) 1.9 (1997) **Education spend:** (% GNP) 2.9 (1996) **Health spend:** (% GDP) 1.2 (1990–95)

Economy and resources

Currency: taka **GDP:** (US$) 32.8 billion (1997) **Real GDP growth:** (% change on previous year) 5.7 (1997) **GNP (US$):** 33.2 billion (1997) **GNP per capita (PPP):** (US$) 1,050 (1997) **Consumer price inflation:** 8% (1998) **Unemployment:** 30% (1991 est) **Foreign debt:** (US$) 18.2 billion (1996) **Major trading partners:** USA, Hong Kong, Japan, Singapore, UK **Resources:** natural gas, coal, limestone, china clay, glass sand **Exports:** raw jute and jute goods, tea, clothing, leather and leather products, shrimps and frogs' legs. Principal market: USA 33.3% (1997) **Imports:** wheat, crude petroleum and petroleum products, pharmaceuticals, cement, raw cotton, machinery and transport equipment. Principal source: India 11.6% (1997) **Arable land:** 65% (1995)

Population and society

Population: 124,774,000 (1998 est) **Population growth rate:** 1.6% (1995–2000) **Population density:** (per sq km) 952.6 (1998 est) **Urban population:** (% of total) 20 (1997) **Age distribution:** (% of total population) 0–14 37.4%, 15–64 59.4%, 65+ 3.2% (1998) **Ethnic groups:** 98% of Bengali descent, half a million Bihari, and around 1 million belonging to 'tribal' communities **Language:** Bengali (official); English **Religion:** Sunni Muslim 85%, Hindu 12%; Islam is the state religion **Education:** (compulsory years) 5 **Literacy rate:** 57% (men); 22% (women) (1995 est) **Labour force:** 49% of population: 56.5% agriculture, 9.8% industry, 33.7% services (1993) **Life expectancy:** 58 (men); 58 (women) (1995–2000) **Child mortality rate:** (under 5, per 1,000 live births) 104 (1997) **Physicians:** 1 per 12,884 people (1993 est)

Practical information

Visa requirements: UK: visa required. USA: visa not required for a tourist visit of up to 15 days **Embassy in the UK:** 28 Queen's Gate, London SW7 5JA. Tel: (0171) 584 0081; fax: (0171) 255 2130 **British embassy:** British High Commission, PO Box 6079, United Nations Road, Baridhara, Dhaka 12. Tel: (2) 882 705; fax: (2) 883 437 **Chamber of commerce:** Federation of Bangladesh Chambers of Commerce and Industry, Federation Bhaban, 60 Motijheel C/A, 4th Floor, POB 2079, Dhaka 1000. Tel: (2) 250 566

Chronology

c. **1000 BC:** Arrival of Bang tribe in lower Ganges valley, establishing the kingdom of Banga (Bengal). **8th–12th centuries AD:** Bengal ruled successively by the Buddhist Pala and Hindu Senha dynasties. **1199:** Bengal was invaded and briefly ruled by the Muslim Khiljis from Central Asia. **1517:** Portuguese merchants arrived in Chittagong. **1576:** Bengal conquered by Muslim Mogul emperor Akbar. **1651:** British East India Company established a commercial factory in Bengal. **1757:** Bengal came under de facto British rule after Robert Clive defeated the nawab (ruler) of Bengal at Battle of Plassey. **1905–12:** Bengal briefly partitioned by the British Raj between a Muslim-dominated east and Hindu-dominated west. **1906:** Muslim League (ML) founded in Dhaka. **1947:** Bengal formed into eastern province of Pakistan on partition of British India, with ML administration in power. **1952:** 12 students killed by troops in anti-Urdu and pro-Bengali language riots in Dhaka. **1954:** The opposition United Front, dominated by the Awami League (AL) and campaigning for East Bengal's autonomy, trounced ML in elections. **1955:** East Bengal renamed East Pakistan. **1966:** Sheik Mujibur Rahman of AL announced a Six-Point Programme of autonomy for East Pakistan. **1970:** 500,000 people killed in cyclone. Pro-autonomy AL secured crushing electoral victory in East Pakistan. **1971:** Bangladesh ('land of the Bangla speakers') emerged as independent nation, under leadership of Sheik Mujibur Rahman, after bloody civil war with Indian military intervention on the side of East Pakistan; 10 million refugees fled to India. **1974:** Hundreds of thousands died in famine; state of emergency declared. **1975:** Mujibur Rahman assassinated. Martial law imposed. **1976–77:** Maj-Gen Zia ur-Rahman assumed power as president. **1978–79:** Elections held and civilian rule restored with clear victory for Zia's BNP. **1981:** Maj-Gen Zia assassinated during attempted military coup. Abdul Sattar (BNP) elected president. **1982:** Lt-Gen Hussain Mohammed Ershad assumed power in army coup. Martial law reimposed; market-oriented economic programme adopted. **1986:** Elections held but disputed and boycotted by BNP. Martial law ended. **1987:** State of emergency declared in response to opposition demonstrations and violent strikes. **1988:** Assembly elections boycotted by main opposition parties. State of emergency lifted. Islam made state religion. Monsoon floods left 30 million homeless and thousands dead. **1989:** Power devolved to Chittagong Hill Tracts to end 14-year conflict between local people and army-protected settlers. **1990:** Following mass antigovernment protests, President Ershad resigned; chief justice Shahabuddin Ahmad became interim president. **1991:** Former president Ershad jailed for corruption and illegal possession of arms. Cyclone killed around 139,000 and left up to 10 million homeless. Parliamentary government restored, with Abdur Rahman Biswas president and Begum Khaleda Zia prime minister. **1994–95:** Opposition boycotted parliament, charging government with fraud. **1996:** Zia handed power to neutral caretaker government. General election won by AL, led by Sheika Hasina Wazed, daughter of Sheik Mujibur Rahman. BNP boycotted parliament. Agreement with India on sharing of River Ganges water. **1997:** Former president Ershad released from prison. BNP boycotted parliament in protest against government 'repression'. **1998:** Opposition BNP ended boycott of parliament. Two-thirds of Bangladesh devastated by floods; 1,300 people killed; damages reach $900 million. Corruption charges filed against ex-premier Begum Khaleda Zia. Opposition-supported general strikes sought removal of Sheikh Hasina's government in October and November. Fifteen former army officers sentenced to death for 1975 assassination of President Sheikh Mujibur Rahman.

Barbados

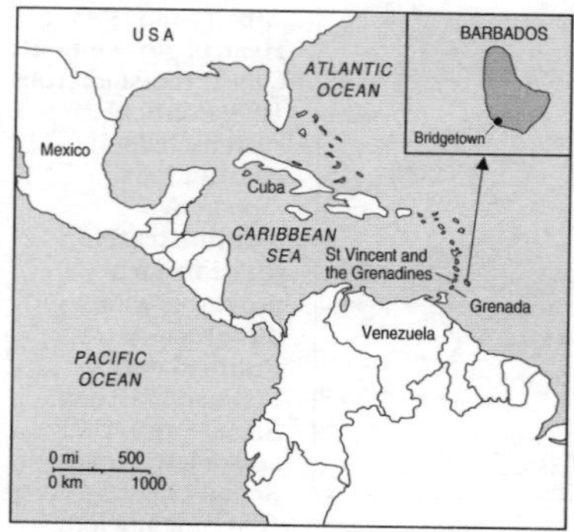

Area: 430 sq km/166 sq mi **Capital:** Bridgetown **Major towns/cities:** Speightstown, Holetown, Oistins

Government

Head of state: Elizabeth II from 1966, represented by Denys Williams from 1995 **Head of government:** Owen Arthur from 1994 **Political system:** constitutional monarchy **Administrative divisions:** 11 parishes **Political parties:** Barbados Labour Party (BLP), moderate left of centre; Democratic Labour Party (DLP), moderate left of centre; National Democratic Party (NDP), centrist **Armed forces:** 600 (1997) **Conscription:** military service is voluntary **Death penalty:** retained and used for ordinary crimes **Defence spend:** (% GDP) 0.6 (1997) **Education spend:** (% GNP) 7.2 (1995) **Health spend:** (% GDP) 10 (1990)

Economy and resources

Currency: Barbados dollar **GDP:** (US$) 2.1 billion (1997 est) **Real GDP growth:** (% change on previous year) 3.5 (1997) **GNP (US$):** 1.74 billion (1997) **GNP per capita (PPP):** (US$) 10,590 (1997 est) **Consumer price inflation:** 2.5% (1998) **Unemployment:** 15.6% (1996) **Foreign debt:** (US$) 590 million (1996) **Major trading partners:** USA, Trinidad and Tobago, Canada, Jamaica, St Lucia **Resources:** petroleum and natural gas **Exports:** sugar, molasses, syrup-rum, chemicals, electrical components. Principal market: USA 17.7% (1997) **Imports:** machinery, foodstuffs, motor cars, construction materials, basic manufactures. Principal source: USA 41.6% (1997) **Arable land:** 37.2% (1995)

Population and society

Population: 259,000 (1998 est) **Population growth rate:** 0.4% (1995–2000) **Population density:** (per sq km) 602.4 (1998 est) **Urban population:** (% of total) 49 (1997) **Age distribution:** (% of total population) 0–14 23.3%, 15–64 66.6%, 65+ 10.1% (1998) **Ethnic groups:** about 80% of African descent, about 16% mixed ethnicity, and 4% of European origin (mostly British) **Language:** English and Bajan (Barbadian English dialect) **Religion:** 33% Anglican, 13% Pentecostalist, 6% Methodist, 4% Roman Catholic **Education:** (compulsory years) 12 **Literacy rate:** 98% (men); 97% (women) (1995 est) **Labour force:** 5.9% agriculture, 18.7% industry, 65% services (1994) **Life expectancy:** 74 (men); 79 (women) (1995–2000) **Child mortality rate:** (under 5, per 1,000 live births) 12 (1997) **Physicians:** 1 per 1,100 people (1993)

Practical information

Visa requirements: UK: visa not required (some visitors will require a business visa). USA: visa not required (some visitors will require a business visa) **Embassy in the UK:** High Commission, 1 Great Russell Street, London WCN 22B 3JY. Tel: (0171) 631 4975; fax: (0171) 323 6872 **British embassy:** British High Commission, PO Box 676, Lower Collymore Rock, St Michael. Tel: 436 6694; fax: 436 5398 **Chamber of commerce:** Barbados Chamber of Commerce Inc, Nemwil House, 1st Floor, Lower Collymore Rock, PO Box 189, St Michael. Tel: 426 2056; fax: 429 2907

Chronology

1536: Visited by Portuguese explorer Pedro a Campos and the name Los Barbados ('The Bearded Ones') given in reference to its 'bearded' fig trees. Indigineous Arawak people were virtually wiped out, via epidemics, after contact with Europeans. **1627:** British colony established; developed as a sugar-plantation economy, initially on basis of black slaves brought in from West Africa. **1639:** Island's first parliament, the House of Assembly, established. **1816:** Last and largest-ever revolt by slaves led by Bussa. **1834:** Slaves freed. **1937:** Outbreak of riots, followed by establishment of the Barbados Labour Party (BLP) by Grantley Adams, and moves towards a more independent political system. **1951:** Universal adult suffrage introduced. BLP won general election. **1954:** Ministerial government established, with BLP leader Adams as first prime minister. **1955:** A group broke away from the BLP and formed the Democratic Labour Party (DLP). **1961:** Independence achieved from Britain. DLP, led by Errol Barrow, in power. **1966:** Barbados achieved full independence within Commonwealth, with Barrow as prime minister. **1967:** Became a member of the United Nations. **1972:** Diplomatic relations with Cuba established. **1976:** BLP, led by Tom Adams, the son of Grantley Adams, returned to power. **1983:** Barbados supported US invasion of Grenada. **1985:** Adams died; Bernard St John became prime minister. **1986:** DLP, led by Barrow, returned to power. **1987:** Barrow died; Erskine Lloyd Sandiford became prime minister. **1994:** BLP, led by Owen Arthur, won decisive election victory. **1999:** BLP gained a landslide victory in the January general elections, securing 26 of the 28 House of Assembly seats.

Belarus Republic of

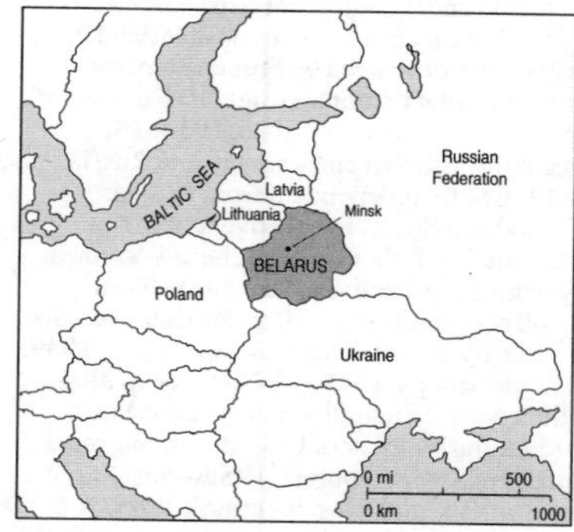

National name: *Respublika Belarus* **Area:** 207,600 sq km/80,154 sq mi **Capital:** Minsk (Mensk) **Major towns/cities:** Gomel, Vitebsk, Mogilev, Bobruisk, Hrodna, Brest

Government

Head of state: Alexandr Lukashenko from 1994 **Head of government:** Syargey Ling from 1996 **Political system:** emergent democracy **Administrative divisions:** six regions (oblasts) **Political parties:** Belarus Communist Party (BCP, banned 1991–92); Belarus Patriotic Movement (BPM), populist; Belarusian Popular Front (BPF; Adradzhenne), moderate nationalist; Christian Democratic Union of Belarus, centrist; Socialist Party of Belarus, left of centre **Armed forces:** 81,800 (1997) **Conscription:** compulsory for 18 months **Death penalty:** retained and used for ordinary crimes **Defence spend:** (% GDP) 2.9 (1997) **Education spend:** (% GNP) 2.9 (1997) **Health spend:** (% GDP) 3.4 (1995)

Economy and resources

Currency: rouble and zaichik **GDP:** (US$) 22.4 billion (1997) **Real GDP growth:** (% change on previous year) 7 (1997) **GNP (US$):** 22.1 billion (1997) **GNP per capita (PPP):** (US$) 4,840 (1997) **Consumer price inflation:** 127% (1998) **Unemployment:** 3.8% (1996) **Foreign debt:** (US$) 1.07 billion (1996) **Major trading partners:** former USSR (principally Russia, Ukraine, and Kazakhstan), Germany, Poland, USA **Resources:** petroleum, natural gas, peat, salt, coal, lignite **Exports:** machinery, chemicals and petrochemicals, iron and steel, light industrial goods. Principal market: Russia 64.7% (1997) **Imports:** petroleum, natural gas, chemicals, machinery, processed foods. Principal source: Russia 53.6% (1997) **Arable land:** 29.3% (1995)

Population and society

Population: 10,315,000 (1998 est) **Population growth rate:** –0.1% (1995–2000); –0.1% (2000–05) **Population density:** (per sq km)

50.1 (1998 est) **Urban population:** (% of total) 73 (1997) **Age distribution:** (% of total population) 0–14 20%, 15–64 66.6%, 65+ 13.4% (1998) **Ethnic groups:** 75% of Belarusian ('eastern Slav') descent, 13% ethnic Russian, 4% Polish, 3% Ukranian, 1% Jewish **Language:** Belarusian (official); Russian, Polish **Religion:** Russian Orthodox, Roman Catholic; Baptist, Muslim, and Jewish minorities **Education:** (compulsory years) 11 **Literacy rate:** 98% (men); 98% (women) (1995 est) **Labour force:** 21.2% agriculture, 34.9% industry, 43.9% services (1994) **Life expectancy:** 64 (men); 75 (women) (1995–2000) **Child mortality rate:** (under 5, per 1,000 live births) 19 (1997) **Physicians:** 1 per 243 people (1995)

Practical information

Visa requirements: UK: visa required. USA: visa required **Embassy in the UK:** 6 Kensington Court, London W8 5DL. Tel: (0171) 937 3288; fax: (0171) 3361 0005 **British embassy:** Zakharova 26, 220034 Minsk. Tel: (172) 368 687; fax: (172) 144 7226 **Chamber of commerce:** Chamber of Commerce and Industry, Masherava 14, 220600 Minsk. Tel: (172) 269 172; fax: (172) 269 860

Chronology

5th–8th centuries: Settled by East Slavic tribes, ancestors of present-day Belarusians. **11th century:** Minsk founded. **12th century:** Part of Kievan Russia, to the south, with independent Belarus state developing around Polotsk, on River Dvina. **14th century:** Incorporated within Slavonic Grand Duchy of Lithuania, to the west. **1569:** Union with Poland. **late 18th century:** Came under control of tsarist Russia as Belarussia ('White Russia'), following three partitions of Poland in 1772, 1793, and 1795. **1812:** Minsk destroyed by French emperor Napoleon Bonaparte during his military campaign against Russia. **1839:** Belarusian Catholic Church forcibly abolished. **1914–18:** Belarus was the site of fierce fighting between Germany and Russia during World War I. **1918–19:** Briefly independent from Russia. **1919–20:** Wars between Poland and Soviet Russia over control of Belarus. **1921:** West Belarus ruled by Poland; East Belarus became a Soviet republic. **1930s:** Agriculture collectivized despite peasant resistance; more than 100,000 people, chiefly writers and intellectuals, shot in mass executions ordered by Soviet dictator Joseph Stalin. **1939:** West Belarus occupied by Soviet troops. **1941–44:** Nazi occupation resulted in death of 1.3 million people, including many Jews; Minsk destroyed. **1945:** Became founding member of United Nations; much of West Belarus incorporated into Soviet republic. **1950s–60s:** Large-scale immigration of ethnic Russians and 'Russification'. **1986:** Fallout from the nearby Chernobyl nuclear reactor in Ukraine rendered 20% of agricultural land unusable. **1989:** Belarusian Popular Front established as national identity revived under *glasnost* initiative of Soviet leader Mikhail Gorbachev. **1990:** Belarusian established as state language and republican sovereignty declared. **1991:** Strikes and unrest in Minsk; BCP suspended following attempted coup against Gorbachev in Moscow; moderate nationalist Stanislav Shushkevich elected president. Independence recognized by USA; Commonwealth of Independent States (CIS) formed in Minsk. **1993:** BCP re-established. **1994:** President Shushkevich ousted; Alexandr Lukashenko, a pro-Russian populist, elected president. **1995:** Friendship and cooperation pact signed with Russia. **1996:** Agreement on economic union with Russia. President's referendum for a new constitution popularly endorsed. Prime Minister Mikhas Chygir replaced by Syargey Ling. **1997:** Observer status in Council of Europe suspended. Treaty with Russia ratified. Council of Republic rejected president's proposals to curb media. Prodemocracy demonstrations. **1998:** Devaluation in Belarus rouble. New left-wing and centrist political coalition created. Food rationing imposed as economy deteriorated. Belarus signed a common policy with Russia on economic, foreign, and military matters.

Belgium Kingdom of

National name: French *Royaume de Belgique,* Flemish *Koninkrijk Belgiê* **Area:** 30,510 sq km/11,779 sq mi **Capital:** Brussels **Major towns/cities:** Antwerp, Ghent, Liège, Charleroi, Bruges, Mons, Namur, Leuven **Major ports:** Antwerp, Ostend, Zeebrugge

Government

Head of state: King Albert from 1993 **Head of government:** Guy Verhofstadt from 1999 **Political system:** federal constitutional monarchy **Administrative divisions:** ten provinces within three regions **Political parties:** Flemish Christian Social Party (CVP), centre left; French Social Christian Party (PSC), centre left; Flemish Socialist Party (SP), left of centre; French Socialist Party (PS), left of centre; Flemish Liberal Party (PVV), moderate centrist; French Liberal Reform Party (PRL), moderate centrist; Flemish People's Party (VU), federalist; Flemish Vlaams Blok, right wing; Flemish Green Party (Agalev); French Green Party (Ecolo) **Armed forces:** 44,500 (1997) **Conscription:** abolished in 1995 **Death penalty:** abolished in 1996 **Defence spend:** (% GDP) 1.6 (1997) **Education spend:** (% GNP) 5.7 (1995) **Health spend:** (% GDP) 7.0 (1990–95)

Economy and resources

Currency: Belgian franc **GDP:** (US$) 242.5 billion (1997) **Real GDP growth:** (% change on previous year) 2.3 (1997) **GNP (US$):** 268.4 billion (1997) **GNP per capita (PPP):** (US$) 22,370 (1997) **Consumer price inflation:** 2.1% (1998) **Unemployment:** 8.8% (1998) **Major trading partners:** Germany, the Netherlands, Belgium, Luxembourg, France, UK, USA **Resources:** coal, coke, natural gas, iron **Exports:** food, livestock and livestock products, gem diamonds, iron and steel manufacturers, machinery and transport equipment, chemicals and related products. Principal market: Germany 19.4% (1997) **Imports:** food and live animals, machinery and transport equipment, precious metals and stones, mineral fuels and lubricants, chemicals and related products. Principal source: Germany 18.8% (1997) **Arable land:** 22% (1995)

Population and society

Population: 10,141,000 (1998 est) **Population growth rate:** 0.3% (1995–2000); 0.1% (2000–05) **Population density:** (per sq km) 336.6 (1998 est) **Urban population:** (% of total) 97 (1997) **Age distribution:** (% of total population) 0–14 17.3%, 15–64 65.9%, 65+ 16.8% (1998) **Ethnic groups:** mainly Flemings in north, Walloons in south **Language:** in the north (Flanders) Flemish (a Dutch dialect, known as *Vlaams*) 55%; in the south (Wallonia) Walloon (a French dialect) 32%; bilingual 11%; German (eastern border) 0.6%. Dutch is official in the north, French in the south; Brussels is officially bilingual **Religion:** Roman Catholic 75%, various Protestant denominations **Education:** (compulsory years) 12 **Literacy rate:** 99% (men); 99% (women) (1995 est) **Labour force:** 42.2% of population: 2.6% agriculture, 27.7% industry, 69.7% services (1992) **Life expectancy:** 74 (men); 81 (women) (1995–2000) **Child mortality rate:** (under 5, per 1,000 live births) 7 (1996) **Physicians:** 1 per 267 people (1995)

Practical information

Visa requirements: UK: visa not required. USA: visa not required **Embassy in the UK:** 103–105 Eaton Square, London SW1W 9AB. Tel: (0171) 470 3700; fax: (0171) 259 6213 **British embassy:** 85 rue d'Arlon, B-1040 Brussels. Tel: (2) 287 6211; fax: (2) 287 6355 **Chamber of commerce:** Kamer van Koophandel en Nijverheid van Antwerpen, 12 Markgravestraat, B-2000 Antwerp. Tel: (3) 232 2219; fax: (3) 233 6442. Chambre de Commerce et d'Industrie de Bruxelles, 500 ave Louise, 1050 Brussels. Tel: (2) 648 5002; fax: (2) 640 9228

Chronology

57 BC: Romans conquered the Belgae (the indigenous Celtic people), and formed province of Belgica. **3rd–4th centuries AD:** Region overrun by Franks and Saxons. **8th–9th centuries:** Part of Frankish Empire; peace and order fostered growth of Ghent, Bruges, and Brussels. **843:** Division of Holy Roman Empire; became part of Lotharingia, but frequent repartitioning followed. **10th–11th centuries:** Seven feudal states emerged: Flanders, Hainaut, Namur, Brabant, Limburg, and Luxembourg, all nominally subject to French king or Holy Roman emperor, but in practice independent. **12th century:** Economy began to flourish: textiles in Bruges, Ghent, and Ypres; copper and tin in Dinant and Liège. **15th century:** One by one, states came under rule of dukes of Burgundy. **1477:** Passed into Habsburg dominions through marriage of Mary of Burgundy to Maximilian, archduke of Austria. **1555:** Division of Habsburg dominions; Low Countries allotted to Spain. **1648:** Independence of Dutch Republic recognized; south retained by Spain. **1713:** Treaty of Utrecht transferred Spanish Netherlands to Austrian rule. **1792–97:** Austrian Netherlands invaded by revolutionary France and finally annexed. **1815:** Congress of Vienna reunited north and south Netherlands as one kingdom under House of Orange. **1830:** Largely French-speaking people in south rebelled against union with Holland and declared Belgian independence. **1831:** Leopold of Saxe-Coburg-Gotha became first king of Belgium. **1839:** Treaty of London recognized independence of Belgium and guaranteed its neutrality. **1847–70:** Government dominated by Liberals; growth of heavy industry. **1870–1914:** Catholic Party predominant. **1914–18:** Invaded and occupied by Germany. Belgian forces under King Albert I fought in conjunction with Allies. **1919:** Acquired Eupen-Malmédy region from Germany. **1940:** Second invasion by Germany; King Leopold III ordered Belgian army to capitulate. **1944–45:** Belgium liberated. **1948:** Belgium formed Benelux customs union with Luxembourg and the Netherlands. **1949:** Belgium was a founding member of North Atlantic Treaty Organization (NATO). **1951:** Leopold III abdicated in favour of his son Baudouin. **1958:** Belgium was a founding member of European Economic Community (EEC), which made Brussels its headquarters. **1967:** NATO made Brussels its headquarters. **1971:** Constitution amended to safeguard cultural rights of Flemish- (in Flanders in north) and French-speaking communities (Walloons in southeast) in an effort to ease linguistic dispute. **1974:** Separate regional councils and ministerial committees established for Flemings and Walloons. **1980:** Open violence over language divisions; regional assemblies for Flanders and Wallonia and three-member executive for Brussels created. **1993:** Federal system adopted, based on Flanders, Wallonia, and Brussels. King Baudouin died, succeeded by his brother Albert. **1995:** Dehaene-led coalition re-elected. **1998:** High-profile campaign to retain the country's unity.

Belize (formerly **British Honduras**)

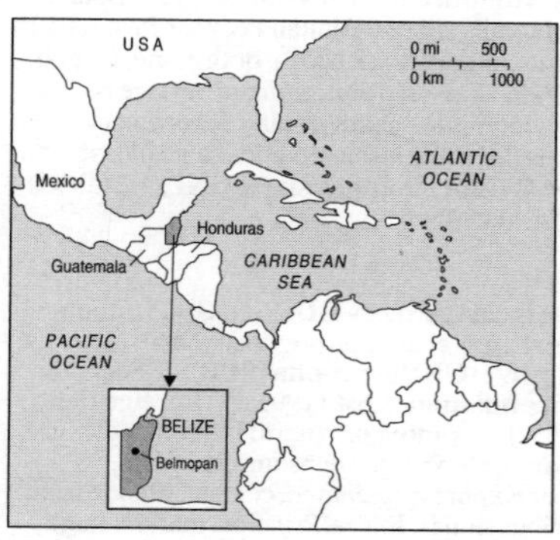

Area: 22,963 sq km/8,866 sq mi **Capital:** Belmopan **Major towns/cities:** Belize City, Dangriga, Orange Walk, Corozal **Major ports:** Belize City, Dangriga, Punta Gorda

Government

Head of state: Elizabeth II from 1981, represented by governor general Dr Norbert Colville Young from 1993 **Head of government:** Manuel Esquivel from 1993 **Political system:** constitutional monarchy **Administrative divisions:** six districts **Political parties:** People's United Party (PUP), left of centre; United Democratic Party (UDP), moderate conservative **Armed forces:** 1,100 (1997); plus 700 militia reserves **Conscription:** military service is voluntary **Death penalty:** retained and used for ordinary crimes **Defence spend:** (% GDP) 2.6 (1997) **Education spend:** (% GNP) 5.0 (1996) **Health spend:** (% GDP) 5.7 (1995)

Economy and resources

Currency: Belize dollar **GDP:** (US$) 651 million (1997 est) **Real GDP growth:** (% change on previous year) 1.8 (1997) **GNP (US$):** 625 million (1997) **GNP per capita (PPP):** (US$) 4,110 (1997) **Consumer price inflation:** 0.8% (1997) **Unemployment:** 13.1% (1994) **Foreign debt:** (US$) 288 million (1996) **Major trading partners:** USA, UK, Mexico, Canada **Exports:** sugar, clothes, citrus products, forestry and fish products, bananas. Principal market: UK 45.5% (1997) **Imports:** foodstuffs, machinery and transport equipment, mineral fuels, chemicals, basic manufactures. Principal source: USA 51.5% (1997) **Arable land:** 2.6% (1995)

Population and society

Population: 230,000 (1998 est) **Population growth rate:** 2.5% (1995–2000); 2.3% (2000–05) **Population density:** (per sq km) 10.1 (1998 est) **Urban population:** (% of total) 47 (1997) **Age distribution:** (% of total population) 0–14 42.2%, 15–64 54.2%, 65+ 3.6% (1998) **Ethnic groups:** Creoles, Mestizos, Caribs, East Indians, Mennonites, Canadians and Europeans, including Spanish and British **Language:** English (official); Spanish (widely spoken), Creole dialects **Religion:** Roman Catholic 60%, Protestant 35% **Education:** (compulsory years) 10 **Literacy rate:** 93% (men); 93% (women) (1994) **Labour force:** 31% of population: 34% agriculture, 19% industry, 48% services (1990) **Life expectancy:** 73 (men); 76 (women) (1995–2000) **Child mortality rate:** (under 5, per 1,000 live births) 36 (1997) **Physicians:** 1 per 2,127 people (1993)

Practical information

Visa requirements: UK: visa not required. USA: visa not required **Embassy in the UK:** 22 Harcourt House, 19 Cavendish Square, London W1M 9AD. Tel: (0171) 499 9728; fax: (0171) 491 4139 **British embassy:** British High Commission, PO Box 91, Embassy Square, Belmopan. Tel: (8) 22146/7; fax: (8) 22761 **Chamber of commerce:** Belize Chamber of Commerce and Industry, 63 Regent Street, POB 291, Belize City. Tel: (2) 75924; fax: (2) 74984

Chronology

325–925 AD: Part of American Indian Maya civilization. **1600s:** Colonized by British buccaneers and log-cutters **1862:** Formally declared a British colony, known as British Honduras. **1893:** Mexico renounced its long-standing claim to the territory. **1954:** Constitution adopted, providing for limited internal self-government. General election won by PUP led by George Price. **1964:** Self-government achieved from the UK. Universal adult suffrage and a two-chamber legislature introduced. **1970:** Capital moved from Belize City to new town of Belmopan. **1973:** Name changed to Belize. **1975:** British troops sent to defend the long-disputed frontier with Guatemala. **1980:** United Nations called for full independence. **1981:** Full independence achieved, with Price as prime minister. **1984:** Price defeated in general election. Manuel Esquivel of the right-of-centre United Democratic Party (UDP) formed government. The UK reaffirmed its undertaking to defend the frontier. **1989:** Price and PUP won general election. **1991:** Diplomatic relations re-established with Guatemala, which finally recognized Belize's sovereignty. **1993:** UDP defeated PUP in general election; Esquivel returned as prime minister. UK announced intention to withdraw troops following resolution of border dispute with Guatemala. **1998:** PUP won sweeping victory in assembly elections.

Benin People's Republic of (formerly known as **Dahomey** 1904–75)

National name: *République Populaire du Bénin* **Area:** 112,622 sq km/ 43,483 sq mi **Capital:** Porto-Novo (official), Cotonou (de facto) **Major towns/cities:** Abomey, Natitingou, Parakou, Kandi, Ouidah, Djougou,

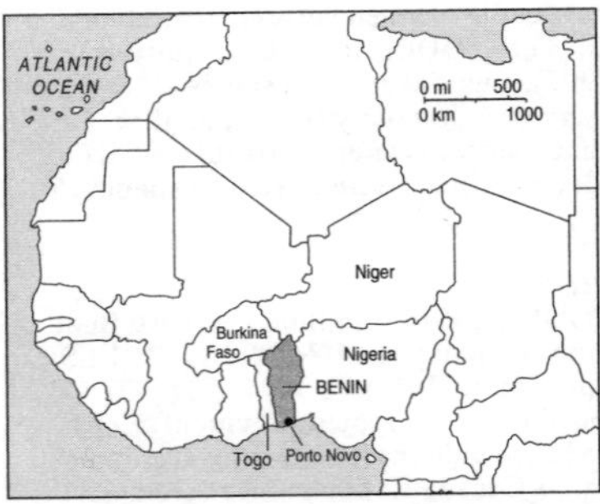

Bohicou **Major ports:** Cotonou t

Government

Head of state: Mathieu Kerekou from 1996 **Head of government:** vacant from 1998 **Political system:** socialist pluralist republic **Administrative divisions:** six provinces **Political parties:** Union for the Triumph of Democratic Renewal (UTDR); National Party for Democracy and Development (PNDD); Party for Democratic Renewal (PRD); Social Democratic Party (PSD); National Union for Solidarity and Progress (UNSP); National Democratic Rally (RND). The general orientation of most parties is left of centre **Armed forces:** 4,800 (1997) **Conscription:** by selective conscription for 18 months **Death penalty:** retained and used for ordinary crimes **Defence spend:** (% GDP) 1.3 (1997) **Education spend:** (% GNP) 3.1 (1995) **Health spend:** (% GDP) 1.7 (1990–95)

Economy and resources

Currency: franc CFA **GDP:** (US$) 2.13 billion (1997) **Real GDP growth:** (% change on previous year) 6.2 (1997 est) **GNP (US$):** 2.2 billion (1997) **GNP per capita (PPP):** (US$) 1,260 (1997) **Consumer price inflation:** 9% (1996) **Foreign debt:** (US$) 1.6 billion (1996) **Major trading partners:** Morocco, France, USA, Portugal, China, Ghana, Nigeria, Thailand, Côte d'Ivoire, Italy **Resources:** petroleum, limestone, marble **Exports:** cotton, crude petroleum, palm oil and other palm products. Principal market: Brazil 18.2% (1997) **Imports:** foodstuffs (particularly cereals), miscellaneous manufactured articles (notably cotton yarn and fabrics), fuels, machinery and transport equipment, chemicals, beverages, tobacco. Principal source: France 21.5% (1997) **Arable land:** 12% (1995)

Population and society

Population: 5,781,000 (1998 est) **Population growth rate:** 2.8% (1995–2000); 2.8% (2000–05) **Population density:** (per sq km) 55.2 (1998 est) **Urban population:** (% of total) 40 (1997) **Age distribution:** (% of total population) 0–14 47.9%, 15–64 49.8%, 65+ 2.3% (1998) **Ethnic groups:** 98% indigenous African, distributed among 42 ethnic groups, the largest being the Fon, Adja, Yoruba, and Braiba; small European (mainly French) community **Language:** French (official); Fon 47% and Yoruba 9% in south; six major tribal languages in north **Religion:** animist 60%, Muslim, Roman Catholic **Education:** (compulsory years) 6 **Literacy rate:** 32% (men); 16% (women) (1995 est) **Labour force:** 46% of population: 64% agriculture, 8% industry, 28% services (1990) **Life expectancy:** 52 (men); 57 (women) (1995–2000) **Child mortality rate:** (under 5, per 1,000 live births) 120 (1997) **Physicians:** 1 per 16,000 people (1994 est)

Practical information

Visa requirements: UK: visa required. USA: visa required **Embassy in the UK:** Dolphin House, 16 The Broadway, Stanmore, Middlesex HA7 4DW. Tel: (0181) 954 8800; fax: (0181) 954 8844 **British embassy:** British Consulate, Lot 24, Patte d'oie, Cotonou. (All staff based in Nigeria.) Tel: 301120 **Chamber of commerce:** Chambre de Commerce, d'Agriculture et d'Industrie de la République du Bénin, ave du Général de Gaulle, BP31, Cotonou. Tel: 313 299

Chronology

12th–13th centuries: Settled by Ewe-speaking people, called the Aja, who mixed with local peoples and gradually formed the Fon ethnic group. **16th century:** Aja kingdom, called Great Ardha, at its peak. **early 17th century:** Kingdom of Dahomey established in south by Fon peoples, who defeated the neighbouring Dan; following contact with European traders, the kingdom became became an intermediary in the slave trade, which was particularly active along the Bight (Bay) of Benin, between Ghana and Nigeria, during the 16th–19th centuries. **1800–50:** King Dezo of Dahomey raised regiments of female soldiers to attack the Yoruba ('land of the big cities') kingdom of eastern Benin and southwest Nigeria to obtain slaves; palm-oil trade developed. **1857:** French base established at Grand-Popo. **1892–94:** War between the French and Dahomey, after which the victorious French established a protectorate. **1899:** Incorporated in federation of French West Africa as Dahomey. **1914:** French troops from Dahomey participated in conquest of German-ruled Togoland to west, during World War I. **1940–44:** Along with the rest of French West Africa, supported the 'Free French' anti-Nazi resistance cause during World War II. **1960:** Independence achieved from France. **1960–72:** Acute political instability, with frequent switches from civilian to military rule, and regional ethnic disputes. **1972:** Military regime established by Major Mathieu Kerekou. **1974:** Kerekou announced that country would follow a path of 'scientific socialism'. **1975:** Name of country changed from Dahomey to Benin. **1977:** Return to civilian rule under new constitution, but with Kerekou as president. **1989:** Army deployed against antigovernment strikers and protesters, inspired by Eastern European revolutions; Marxist-Leninism dropped as official ideology and market-centred economic reform programme adopted. **1990:** Referendum backed establishment of multiparty politics. **1991:** In multiparty elections, President Kerekou was replaced by the leader of the new Benin Renaissance Party (PRB), Nicéphore Soglo, who formed a ten-party coalition government. **1996:** Kerekou defeated Soglo in presidential election run-off despite opposition claims of fraud. **1998:** Prime Minister Adrien Houngbedji resigned; no immediate successor was appointed.

Bhutan Kingdom of

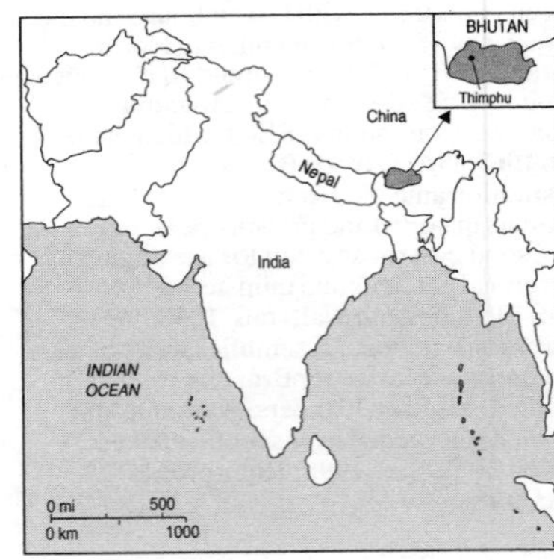

National name: *Druk-yul* **Area:** 46,500 sq km/17,953 sq mi **Capital:** Thimphu (Thimbu) **Major towns/cities:** Paro, Punakha, Mongar, P'sholing, W'phodrang, Bumthang

Government

Head of state: Jigme Singye Wangchuk from 1972 **Head of government:** Lyonpo Jigme Thimley from 1998 **Political system:** absolute monarchy to 1998, when the king conceded political powers to the National Assembly **Administrative divisions:** 20 districts **Political parties:** none officially; illegal Bhutan People's Party (BPP) and Bhutan National Democratic Party (BNDP), both ethnic Nepali **Armed forces:** 6,000 (1996) **Conscription:** military service is voluntary **Death penalty:** retains the death penalty for ordinary crimes but can be considered abolitionist in practice (date of last known execution was 1964) **Education spend:** (% GNP) 4.2 (1995) **Health spend:** (% GDP) 4.1 (1995)

Economy and resources

Currency: ngultrum; also Indian currency **GDP:** (US$) 0.3 billion (1995 est) **Real GDP growth:** (% change on previous year) 6 (1995 est) **GNP (US$):** 296 million (1997) **GNP per capita (PPP):** (US$) 1,180 (1997 est) **Consumer price inflation:** 8.6% (1995 est) **Foreign debt:** (US$) 87 million (1996) **Major trading partners:** India, Middle East, Singapore, Europe **Resources:** limestone, gypsum, coal, slate, dolomite, lead, talc, copper **Exports:** cardamon, cement, timber, fruit, electricity (to India), precious stones, spices. Principal market: India 94% (1994) **Imports:** aircraft, mineral fuels, machinery and transport equipment, rice. Principal source: India 77% (1994) **Arable land:** 2.8% (1995)

Population and society

Population: 2,004,000 (1998 est) **Population growth rate:** 2.8% (1995–2000); 2.3% (2000–05) **Population density:** (per sq km) 40.6 (1998 est) **Urban population:** (% of total) 7 (1997) **Age distribution:** (% of total population) 0–14 40.1%, 15–64 56.0%, 65+ 3.9% (1998) **Ethnic groups:** 54% Bhotia, living principally in north and east; 32% of Tibetan descent; a substantial Nepali minority lives in the south – they are prohibited from moving into the Bhotia-dominated north **Language:** Dzongkha (official, a Tibetan dialect), Sharchop, Bumthap, Nepali, and English **Religion:** 70% Mahayana Buddhist (state religion), 25% Hindu **Education:** not compulsory **Literacy rate:** 51% (men); 25% (women) (1995 est) **Labour force:** 51% of population: 94% agriculture, 1% industry, 5% services (1990) **Life expectancy:** 52 (men); 55 (women) (1995–2000) **Child mortality rate:** (under 5, per 1,000 live births) 142 (1997) **Physicians:** 1 per 6,000 people (1996)

Practical information

Visa requirements: UK: visa required. USA: visa required **Embassy in the UK:** no diplomatic representation **British embassy:** no diplomatic representation **Chamber of commerce:** Bhutan Chamber of Commerce and Industry, POB 147, Thimphu. Tel: (2) 23140; fax: (2) 23936

Chronology

to 8th century: Under effective Indian control. **16th century:** Came under Tibetan rule. **1616–51:** Unified by Ngawang Namgyal, leader of the Drukpa Kagyu (Thunder Dragon) Tibetan Buddhist branch. **1720:** Came under Chinese rule. **1774:** Treaty signed with East India Company. **1865:** Trade treaty with Britain signed after invasion. **1907:** Ugyen Wangchuk, the governor of Tongsa, became Bhutan's first hereditary monarch. **1910:** Anglo-Bhutanese Treaty signed, placing foreign relations under the 'guidance' of the British government in India. **1926:** Jigme Wangchuk succeeded to the throne. **1949:** Indo-Bhutan Treaty of Friendship signed, giving India continued influence over Bhutan's foreign relations, but returning territory annexed in 1865. **1952:** Reformist king Jigme Dorji Wangchuk came to power. **1953:** National assembly (Tshogdu) established. **1958:** Slavery abolished. **1959:** 4,000 Tibetan refugees given asylum after Chinese annexation of Tibet. **1968:** King established first cabinet. **1972:** King died and was succeeded by his Western-educated son Jigme Singye Wangchuk. **1973:** Joined the nonaligned movement. **1979:** Tibetan refugees told to take Bhutanese citizenship or leave; most stayed. **1983:** Bhutan became a founding member of the South Asian Regional Association for Cooperation. **1988:** Buddhist Dzongkha/Drukpa king imposed 'code of conduct' suppressing the customs of the large Hindu-Nepali community in south. **1990:** Hundreds of people allegedly killed during prodemocracy demonstrations. **1993:** Leader of banned Bhutan People's Party (BPP) sentenced to life imprisonment for 'antinational activities'. **1998:** King conceded political powers to the National Assembly. Lyonpo Jigme Thimley became prime minister.

Bolivia Republic of

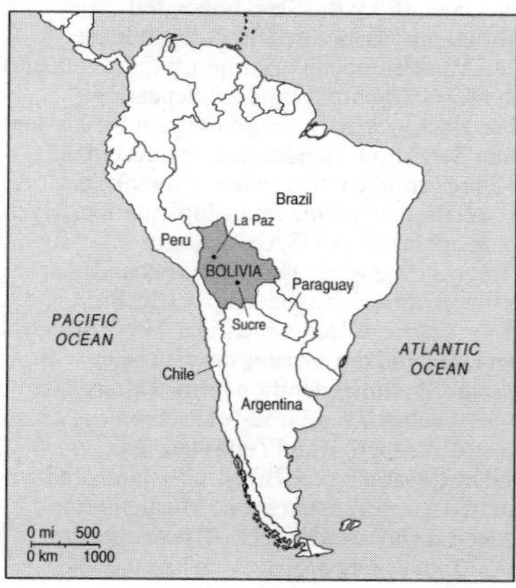

National name: *República de Bolivia* **Area:** 1,098,581 sq km/424,162 sq mi **Capital:** La Paz (seat of government), Sucre (legal capital and seat of judiciary) **Major towns/ cities:** Santa Cruz, Cochabamba, Oruro, El Alto, Potosí ó

Government

Head of state and government: Hugo Banzer Suarez from 1997 **Political system:** emergent democracy **Administrative divisions:** nine departments **Political parties:** National Revolutionary Movement (MNR), centre right; Movement of the Revolutionary Left (MIR), left of centre; Nationalist Democratic Action Party (ADN), right wing; Solidarity and Civic Union (UCS), populist, free market **Armed forces:** 33,500 (1997) **Conscription:** selective conscription for 12 months at the age of 18 **Death penalty:** abolished for ordinary crimes in 1997; laws provide for the death penalty for exceptional crimes only (last execution in 1974) **Defence spend:** (% GDP) 2.0 (1997) **Education spend:** (% GNP) 5.6 (1996) **Health spend:** (% GDP) 2.7 (1990–95)

Economy and resources

Currency: boliviano **GDP:** (US$) 8.1 billion (1997) **Real GDP growth:** (% change on previous year) 5.0 (1997) **GNP (US$):** 7.4 billion (1997) **GNP per capita (PPP):** (US$) 3,280 (1997 est) **Consumer price inflation:** 6.5% (1998) **Unemployment:** 4.2% (1996) **Foreign debt:** (US$) 5.4 billion (1996) **Major trading partners:** USA, Argentina, UK, Brazil, Japan, Belgium **Resources:** petroleum, natural gas, tin (world's fifth-largest producer), zinc, silver, gold, lead, antimony, tungsten, copper **Exports:** metallic minerals, natural gas, jewellery, soya beans, wood. Principal market: USA 21.9% (1997). Illegal trade in coca and its derivatives (mainly cocaine) was worth approximately $600 million in 1990 – almost equal to annual earnings from official exports **Imports:** industrial materials, machinery and transport equipment, consumer goods. Principal source: USA 23.6% (1997) **Arable land:** 2% (1995)

Population and society

Population: 7,957,000 (1998 est) **Population growth rate:** 2.3% (1995–2000); 2.2% (2000–05) **Population density:** (per sq km) 7.2 (1998 est) **Urban population:** (% of total) 63 (1997) **Age distribution:** (% of total population) 0–14 39.4%, 15–64 56.0%, 65+ 4.5% (1998) **Ethnic groups:** 30% Quechua Indians, 25% Aymara Indians, 25–30% mixed, 5–15% of European descent **Language:** Spanish (official); Aymara, Quechua **Religion:** Roman Catholic 95% (state-recognized) **Education:** (compulsory years) 8 **Literacy rate:** 85% (men); 71% (women) (1995 est) **Labour force:** 40% of population: 47% agriculture, 19% industry, 34% services (1993) **Life expectancy:** 60 (men); 63 (women) (1995–2000) **Child mortality rate:** (under 5, per 1,000 live births) 84 (1997) **Physicians:** 1 per 2,348 people (1993 est)

Practical information

Visa requirements: UK: visa not required for a stay of up to 90 days. USA: visa not required for a stay of up to 90 days **Embassy in the UK:** Embassy and Consulate, 106 Eaton Square, London SW1W 9AD. Tel: (0171)235 4248; fax: (0171) 235 1286 **British embassy:** Avenida Arce 2732, Casilla 694, La Paz. Tel: (2) 357 424; fax: (2) 391 063 **Chamber of commerce:** Cámara Nacional de Comercio, Edificio Cámara Nacional de Comercio, Avda Mariscal Santa Cruz 1392, 1 º, Casilla 7, La Paz. Tel: (2) 350 042; fax: (2) 391 004

Chronology

c. **AD 600:** Development of sophisticated civilization at Tiahuanaco, south of Lake Titicaca. *c.* **1200:** Tiahuanaco culture was succeeded by smaller Aymara-speaking kingdoms. **16th century:** Became incorporated within westerly Quechua-speaking Inca civilization, centred in Peru. **1538:** Conquered by Spanish and, known as 'Upper Peru', became part of the Viceroyalty of Peru, whose capital was at Lima (Peru); Charcas (now Sucre) became the local capital. **1545:** Silver discovered at Potosí in the southwest, which developed into chief silver-mining town and most important city in South America in the 17th and 18th centuries. **1776:** Transferred to the Viceroyalty of La Plata, with its capital in Buenos Aires. **late 18th century:** Increasing resistance of American Indians and Mestizos to Spanish rule; silver production slumped. **1825:** Liberated from Spanish rule by the Venezuelan freedom fighter Simón Bolívar, after whom the country was named, and his general, Antonio José de Sucre, after battle of Tumulsa; Sucre became Bolivia's first president. **1836–39:** Part of a federation with Peru, headed by Bolivian president Andres Santa Cruz, but it dissolved following defeat in war with Chile. **1879–84:** Lost coastal territory in the Atacama, containing valuable minerals, after defeat in war with Chile. **1880:** Start of a period of civilian rule which lasted until

1936. **1903:** Lost territory to Brazil. **1932–35:** Lost further territory after defeated by Paraguay in the Chaco War, fought over control of the Chaco Boreal. **1952:** After military regime overthrown by peasants and mineworkers in the Bolivian National Revolution, the formerly exiled Dr Victor Paz Estenssoro of the centrist National Revolutionary Movement (MNR) became president and introduced social and economic reforms, including universal suffrage, nationalization of tin mines, and land redistribution. **1956:** Dr Hernán Siles Zuazo (MNR) became president, defeating Paz. **1960:** Paz returned to power. **1964:** Army coup led by Vice President Gen René Barrientos. **1967:** Peasant uprising, led by Ernesto 'Che' Guevara, put down with US help; Guevara was killed. **1969:** Barrientos killed in plane crash, replaced by Vice President Siles Salinas, who was soon deposed in army coup. **1971:** Col Hugo Banzer Suárez came to power after further military coup. **1974:** Attempted coup prompted Banzer to postpone promised elections and ban political and trade-union activity. **1980:** Inconclusive elections were followed by the country's 189th coup, led by Gen Luis García. Allegations of corruption and drug trafficking led to cancellation of US and European Community (EC) aid. **1981:** García forced to resign. Replaced by Gen Celso Torrelio Villa. **1982:** Torrelio resigned and, with economy worsening, junta handed power over to civilian administration headed by Siles Zuazo. **1983:** US and EC economic aid resumed as austerity measures introduced. **1985:** President Siles resigned after general strike and attempted coup. Election result inconclusive; veteran Dr Paz Estenssoro (MNR) chosen by congress as president. Inflation rate 23,000%. **1989:** Jaime Paz Zamora, of the left-wing Movement of Revolutionary Left (MIR) chosen as president in power-sharing arrangement with Banzer. **1993:** Gonzalo Sanchez de Lozada (MNR) elected president after Banzer withdrew his candidacy. Foreign investment encouraged as inflation fell to single figures. **1997:** Banzer elected president.

Bosnia-Herzegovina Republic of

National name: *Republika Bosna i Hercegovina* **Area:** 51,129 sq km/19,740 sq mi **Capital:** Sarajevo **Major towns/cities:** Banja Luka, Mostar, Prijedor, Tuzla, Zenica

Government

Heads of state: Rotating chairman of the collective presidency, Ante Jelavic from 1999 **Heads of government:** Co-prime ministers Haris Silajdzic (from 1997) and Svetozar Mihajlovic (from 1998) **Political system:** emergent democracy **Political parties:** Party of Democratic Action (PDA), Muslim-oriented; Serbian Renaissance Movement (SPO), Serbian nationalist; Croatian Christian Democratic Union of Bosnia-Herzegovina (CDU), Croatian nationalist; League of Communists (LC) and Socialist Alliance (SA), left wing **Armed forces:** 40,000 (1997) **Death penalty:** abolished for ordinary crimes in 1997; laws provide for the death penalty for exceptional crimes only **Defence spend:** (% GDP) 5.0 (1997)

Economy and resources

Currency: dinar **GDP:** (US$) 1 billion (1995 est) **Real GDP growth:** (% change on previous year) 50 (1996) **GNP (US$):** 2.3 billion (1996) **GNP per capita (PPP):** (US$) 450 (1996 est) **Consumer price inflation:** 40% (1998) **Unemployment:** 28% (1992 est) **Foreign debt:** (US$) 815 million (1996) **Resources:** copper, lead, zinc, iron ore, coal, bauxite, manganese **Exports:** coal, domestic appliances (industrial production and mining remain low). Principal market: Croatia 33.9% (1996) **Imports:** foodstuffs, basic manufactured goods, processed and semiprocessed goods. Principal source: Croatia 32.1% (1996) **Arable land:** 9.8% (1995)

Population and society

Population: 3,675,000 (1998 est) **Population growth rate:** 3.9% (1995–2000) **Population density:** (per sq km) 65.8 (1998 est) **Urban population:** (% of total) 42 (1997) **Age distribution:** (% of total population) 0–14 17.8%, 15–64 70.5%, 65+ 11.7% (1998) **Ethnic groups:** 44% ethnic Muslim, 31% Serb, 17% Croat, 6% 'Yugoslav'. Croats are most thickly settled in southwest Bosnia and western Herzegovina, Serbs in eastern and western Bosnia. Since the start of the civil war in 1992 many Croats and Muslims have fled as refugees to neighbouring states **Language:** Serbian variant of Serbo-Croatian **Religion:** Sunni Muslim, Serbian Orthodox, Roman Catholic **Education:** (compulsory years) 8 **Literacy rate:** 90% (men); 90% (women) (1992) **Labour force:** 2% agriculture, 45% industry, 53% services (1990 est) **Life expectancy:** 71 (men); 76 (women) (1995–2000) **Child mortality rate:** (per 1,000 live births) 20 (1997)

Practical information

Visa requirements: UK: visa not required. USA: visa not required **Embassy in the UK:** 40–41 Conduit Street, London W1R 9FB. Tel: (0171) 734 3758; fax: (0171) 734 3760 **British embassy:** 8 Mustafe Golubica, 71000 Sarajevo. Tel: (71) 444 429; fax: (71) 444 429 **Chamber of commerce:** Chamber of Economy of Bosnia and Herzegovina, Mis. Irbina 13, 71000 Sarajevo. Tel: (71) 211777

Chronology

1st century AD: Part of Roman province of Illyricum. **395:** On division of Roman Empire, stayed in west, along with Croatia and Slovenia, whereas Serbia to the east became part of the Byzantine Empire. **7th century:** Settled by Slav tribes. **12–15th centuries:** Independent state. **1463 and 1482:** Bosnia and Herzegovina, in south, successively conquered by Ottoman Turks; many Slavs were converted to Sunni Islam. **1878:** Became an Austrian protectorate, following Bosnian revolt against Turkish rule in 1875–76. **1908:** Annexed by Austrian Habsburgs in wake of Turkish Revolution. **1914:** Archduke Franz Ferdinand, the Habsburg heir, assassinated in Sarajevo by a Bosnian-Serb extremist, precipitating World War I. **1918:** On collapse of Habsburg Empire, became part of Serb-dominated 'Kingdom of Serbs, Croats, and Slovenes', known as Yugoslavia from 1929. **1941:** Occupied by Nazi Germany and became 'Greater Croatia' fascist puppet state and scene of fierce fighting. **1943–44:** Liberated by the communist Partisans, led by Marshal Tito. **1945:** Became republic within Yugoslav Socialist Federation. **1980:** Upsurge in Islamic nationalism. **1990:** Ethnic violence erupted between Muslims and Serbs. Communists defeated in multiparty elections; coalition formed by Serb, Muslim, and Croatian parties, with a nationalist Muslim, Alija Izetbegovic, as president. **1991:** Serb–Croat civil war in Croatia spread disorder into Bosnia. Fears that Serbia aimed to annex Serb-dominated parts of the republic led to 'sovereignty' declaration by parliament. Serbs within Bosnia established autonomous enclaves. **1992:** In a Serb-boycotted referendum, Bosnian Muslims and Croats voted for independence, which was recognized by USA and European Community; admitted into United Nations (UN). Violent civil war broke out, as independent 'Serbian Republic of Bosnia-Herzegovina', comprising parts of east and west, proclaimed by Bosnian-Serb militia leader Radovan Karadzic, with Serbian backing. UN forces drafted into Sarajevo to break Serb siege of city; Bosnian Serbs accused of 'ethnic cleansing', particularly of Muslims. **1993:** UN–EC peace plan failed. USA began airdrops of food and medical supplies. Six UN 'safe areas' created (Srebrenica, Tuzla, Zepa, Gorazde, Bihac, Sarajevo), intended as havens for Muslim civilians. Croat–Serb partition plan rejected by Muslims. **1994:** Serb siege of Sarajevo lifted after UN–NATO ultimatum and Russian diplomatic intervention. Croat–Muslim federation formed after cease-fire in north. **1995:** Hostilities resumed; 'safe areas' of Srebrenica (where more than 4,000 Muslims were massacred) and Zepa were overrun before the Serbs were halted by Croatians near Bihac. US-sponsored peace accord, providing for two sovereign states (one Muslim–Croat, one Serb) and cease-fire agreed at Dayton, Ohio, USA; peace accord reached; 60,000-strong NATO peacekeeping force deployed. **1996:**

International Criminal Tribunal for Former Yugoslavia began in the Hague. Arms-control accord signed. Three-person presidency elected, consisting of Alija Izetbegovic (Muslim president), Momcilo Krajisnik (Serb), and Kresimir Zubak (Croat). Biljana Plavsic elected president of Serb-controlled Bosnia. Bosnian Serb prime minister Rajko Kasagic dismissed. Full diplomatic relations established with Yugoslavia. New government formed, with Gojko Klickovic as prime minister. NATO-led Stabilization Force replaced Implementation Force. Herceg-Bosna para-state and Bosnian Republic replaced by Muslim–Croat Federation, with Edhem Bicakcic as prime minister. **1997:** Haris Silajdzic (Muslim), and Boro Bosic (Serb), appointed co-chairs of the all-Bosnian Council of Ministers. Serb-dominated part of Bosnia signed joint customs agreement with Yugoslavia. Croat Vladimir Soljic elected president of Muslim–Croat Federation, with Muslim Ejup Ganic as deputy. Municipal elections held; nationalist parties successful. Three-man presidency agreed common passport and citizenship law. **1998:** Moderate, pro-western government formed in Bosnian Serb republic, headed by Milorad Dodik. September polls result in re-election of President Izetbegovic, but success for the extremist candidate, Nikola Poplasen, in the Serb republic. In October Zivko Radisic became the first Bosnian-Serb to hold power as rotating federal president. First Muslims and Croats convicted in The Hague for war crimes during 1992; the moderate Brane Miljus became prime minister of Republika Srpska. Edhem Bicakcic became prime minister of the Bosnian Muslim–Croat statelet, with Ejup Ganic (a Bosnian Muslim) as president; Haris Silajdzic (a Bosnian Muslim) and Svetozar Mihajlovic (a Bosnian Serb moderate) were nominated as co-chairs of the federation.

Botswana Republic of

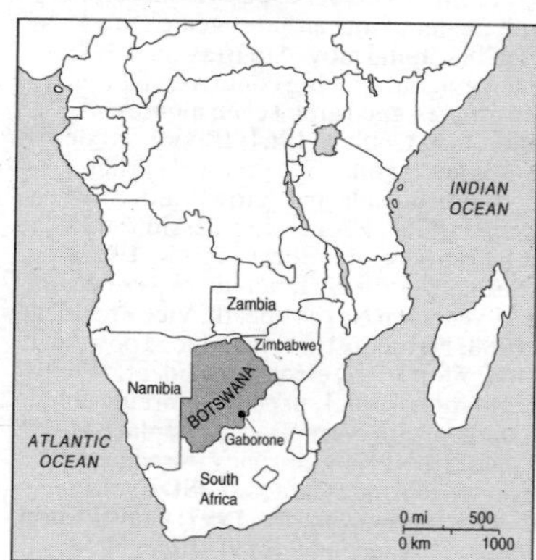

Area: 582,000 sq km/224,710 sq mi **Capital:** Gaborone **Major towns/cities:** Mahalapye, Serowe, Tutume, Bobonong Francistown, Selebi-Phikwe, Lobatse, Molepolol, Kange

Government

Head of state and government: Festus Mogae from 1998 **Political system:** democracy **Administrative divisions:** ten districts and four town councils **Political parties:** Botswana Democratic Party (BDP), moderate centrist; Botswana National Front (BNF), moderate left of centre **Armed forces:** 7,500 (1997) **Conscription:** military service is voluntary **Death penalty:** retained and used for ordinary crimes **Defence spend:** (% GDP) 6.5 (1997) **Education spend:** (% GNP) 10.4 (1996) **Health spend:** (% GDP) 2.2 (1995)

Economy and resources

Currency: franc CFA **GDP:** (US$) 4.93 billion (1997 est) **Real GDP growth:** (% change on previous year) 7.3 (1997) **GNP (US$):** 4.92 billion (1997) **GNP per capita (PPP):** (US$) 8,220 (1997) **Consumer price inflation:** 10% (1998) **Unemployment:** approximately 20% (1995) **Foreign debt:** (US$) 720 million (1996) **Major trading partners:** Lesotho, Namibia, South Africa, Swaziland – all fellow SACU (Southern African Customs Union) members; UK and other European countries, USA **Resources:** diamonds (world's third-largest producer), copper-nickel ore, coal, soda ash, gold, cobalt, salt, plutonium, asbestos, chromite, iron, silver, manganese, talc, uranium **Exports:** diamonds, copper and nickel, beef. Principal market: EU 74% (1996) **Imports:** machinery and transport equipment, food, beverages, tobacco, chemicals and rubber products, textiles and footwear, fuels, wood and paper products. Principal source: SACU 78% (1996) **Arable land:** 0.6% (1995)

Population and society

Population: 1,448,000 (1998 est) **Population growth rate:** 2.2% (1995–2000) **Population density:** (per sq km) 2.5 (1998 est) **Urban population:** (% of total) 67% (1997) **Age distribution:** (% of total population) 0–14 42.3%, 15–64 53.9%, 65+ 3.8% (1998) **Ethnic groups:** about 90% Tswana and 5% Kung and other hunter-gatherer groups; the remainder is European **Language:** English (official), Setswana (national) **Religion:** Christian 50%, animist, Baha'i, Muslim, Hindu **Education:** not compulsory **Literacy rate:** 84% (men); 65% (women) (1995 est) **Labour force:** 44% of population: 46% agriculture, 20% industry, 33% services (1990) **Life expectancy:** 49 (men); 52 (women) (1995–2000) **Child mortality rate:** (under 5, per 1,000 live births) 94 (1997) **Physicians:** 1 per 4,130 people (1994)

Practical information

Visa requirements: UK: visa not required. USA: visa not required **Embassy in the UK:** High Commission, 6 Stratford Place, London W1N 9AE. Tel: (0171) 499 0031; fax: (0171) 495 8595 **British embassy:** British High Commission, Private Bag 0023, Gaborone. Tel: 352 841/2/3; fax: (0171) 356 105 **Chamber of commerce:** Botswana National Chamber of Commerce and Industry, PO Box 20344, Gaborone. Tel: 52677

Chronology

18th century: Formerly inhabited by nomadic hunter-gatherer groups, including the Kung, the area was settled by the Tswana people, from whose eight branches the majority of the people are descended. **1872:** Khama III the Great, a converted Christian, became chief of the Bamangwato, the largest Tswana group. He developed a strong army and greater unity among the Botswana peoples. **1885:** Became the British protectorate of Bechuanaland at the request of Chief Khama, who feared invasion by Boers from the Transvaal (South Africa) following the discovery of gold. **1895:** The southern part of the Bechuanaland Protectorate was annexed by Cape Colony (South Africa). **1960:** New constitution created a legislative council controlled (until 1963) by a British High Commissioner. **1965:** Capital transferred from Mafeking to Gaborone. Internal self-government achieved, with Seretse Khama, the grandson of Khama III and leader of the centrist Democratic Party (BDP), elected head of government. **1966:** Independence achieved from Britain. Name changed to Botswana; Seretse Khama elected president under new presidentialist constitution. **mid-1970s:** The economy grew rapidly as diamond mining expanded. **1980:** Seretse Khama died, and was succeeded by Vice President Quett Masire (BDP). **1985:** South African raid on Gaborone, allegedly in search of African National Congress (ANC) guerrillas. **1993:** Relations with South Africa fully normalized following end of apartheid and establishment of multiracial government. **1997:** Major constitutional changes reduced voting age to 18. **1998:** Festus Mogae (BDP) succeeded President Masire, who retired.

Brazil Federative Republic of

National name: *República Federativa do Brasil* **Area:** 8,511,965 sq km/3,286,469 sq mi **Capital:** Brasília **Major towns/cities:** São Paulo, Belo Horizonte, Nova Iguaçu, Rio de Janeiro, Belém, Recife, Pôrto Alegre, Salvador, Curitiba, Manaus, Fortaleza **Major ports:** Rio de Janeiro, Belém, Recife, Pôrto Alegre, Salvador

Government

Head of state and government: Fernando Henrique Cardoso from 1994 **Political system:** democratic federal republic **Administrative divisions:** 26 states and one federal district **Political parties:** Workers' Party (PT), left of centre; Social Democratic Party (PSDB), moderate, left of centre; Brazilian Democratic Movement Party (PMDB), centre left; Liberal Front Party (PFL), right wing; National Reconstruction Party (PRN), centre right **Armed forces:** 314,700; public security forces under army control 385,600 (1997) **Conscription:** 12 months **Death penalty:** for exceptional crimes only; last execution 1855 **Defence spend:** (% GDP) 2.3 (1997) **Education spend:** (% GNP) 1.3 (1995 est) **Health spend:** (% GDP) 2.7 (1990–95)

Economy and resources

Currency: real **GDP:** (US$) 786.4 billion (1997) **Real GDP growth:** (% change on previous year) 3.2 (1997) **GNP (US$):** 773.4 billion (1997) **GNP per capita (PPP):** (US$) 6,240 (1997) **Consumer price inflation:** 4.2% (1998) **Unemployment:** 4.6% (1996) **Foreign debt:** (US$) 177.8 billion (1996) **Major trading partners:** USA, Germany, Japan, Iran, the Netherlands, France, Argentina, UK **Resources:** iron ore (world's second-largest producer), tin (world's fourth-largest producer), aluminium (world's fourth-largest producer), gold, phosphates, platinum, bauxite, uranium, manganese, coal, copper, petroleum, natural gas, hydroelectric power, forests **Exports:** steel products, transport equipment, coffee, iron ore and concentrates, aluminium, iron, tin, soya beans, orange juice (85% of world's concentrates), tobacco, leather footwear, sugar, beef, textiles. Principal market: USA 17.8% (1997) **Imports:** mineral fuels, machinery and mechanical appliances, chemical products, foodstuffs, coal, wheat, fertilizers, cast iron and steel. Principal source: USA 23.4% (1997) **Arable land:** 6.3% (1995)

Population and society

Population: 165,851,000 (1998 est) **Population growth rate:** 1.2% (1995–2000) **Population density:** (per sq km) 20.1 (1998 est) **Urban population:** (% of total) 80 (1997) **Age distribution:** (% of total population) 0–14 30.2%, 15–64 64.8%, 65+ 5.1% (1998) **Ethnic groups:** wide range of ethnic groups, including 55% of European origin (mainly Portuguese, Italian, and German), 38% of mixed parentage, 6% of African origin, as well as American Indians and Japanese **Language:** Portuguese (official); 120 Indian languages **Religion:** Roman Catholic 89%; Indian faiths **Education:** (compulsory years) 8 **Literacy rate:** 82% (men); 80% (women) (1995 est) **Labour force:** 44% of population: 23% agriculture, 23% industry, 54% services (1990) **Life expectancy:** 63 (men); 71 (women) (1995–2000) **Child mortality rate:** (under 5, per 1,000 live births) 45 (1997) **Physicians:** 1 per 844 people (1993 est)

Practical information

Visa requirements: UK: visa not required for tourist visits. USA: visa required **Embassy in the UK:** 32 Green Street, London W1Y 4AT. Tel: (0171) 499 0877; fax: (0171) 493 5105 **British embassy:** Caixa Postal 07-0586, Setor de Embaixadas Sul, Quadra 801, Conjunto K, 70408-900 Brasília, Distrito Federal. Tel: (61) 225 2710; fax: (61) 225 1777 **Chamber of commerce:** Confederaçao Nacional do Comércio, SCS, Edif. Presidente Dutra, 4 ° andar, Quadra 11, 70327 Brasília, Distrito Federal. Tel: (61) 223 0578

Chronology

1500: Originally inhabited by South American Indians. Portuguese explorer Pedro Alvares Cabral sighted and claimed Brazil for Portugal. **1530:** Start of Portuguese colonization; Portugal monopolized trade but colonial government was decentralized. **1580–1640:** Brazil, with Portugal, came under Spanish rule. **17th century:** Huge sugar-cane plantations established with slave labour in coastal regions, making Brazil world's largest supplier of sugar; cattle ranching developed inland. **1695:** Discovery of gold in central highlands. **1763:** Colonial capital moved from Bahía to Rio de Janeiro. **1770:** Brazil's first coffee plantations established in Rio de Janeiro. **18th century:** Population in 1798 totalled 3.3 million, of which around 1.9 million were slaves, mainly of African origin; significant growth of gold-mining industry. **19th century:** Rapid expansion in coffee growing. **1808:** Following Napoleon's invasion of Portugal, the Portuguese regent, Prince John, arrived in Brazil and established his court at Rio de Janeiro; Brazilian trade opened to foreign merchants. **1815:** United Kingdom of Portugal, Brazil, and Algarve made Brazil co-equal with Portugal and Rio de Janeiro as capital. **1821:** Political disorder in Portugal forced King John VI to return to Europe, leaving government of Brazil to his son, Crown Prince Pedro. **1822:** Pedro defied orders from Portuguese parliament to return to Portugal; he declared Brazil's independence to avoid reversion to colonial status. **1825:** King John VI recognized his son as Emperor Pedro I of Brazil. **1831:** Pedro I abdicated in favour of his infant son, Pedro II; regency (to 1840) dominated by Brazilian politicians. **1847:** First prime minister appointed, but emperor retained wide-ranging powers. **1865–70:** Brazilian efforts to control Uruguay led to War of the Triple Alliance with Paraguay. **1888:** Abolition of slavery in Brazil. **1889:** Monarch overthrown by liberal revolt; federal republic established with central government controlled by coffee planters; by 1902 Brazil produced 65% of world's coffee. **1915–19:** Lack of European imports during World War I led to rapid industrialization, especially in state of São Paulo. **1930:** Revolution against planter oligarchy placed Getúlio Vargas in power; he introduced social reforms and economic planning. **1937:** Vargas established authoritarian corporate state. **1942:** Brazil entered World War II as ally of USA; small fighting force sent to Italy in 1944. **1945:** Vargas ousted by military coup, but Gen Eurico Gaspar Dutra soon forced to abandon free-market policies. **1951:** Vargas elected president; continued to extend state control of economy. **1954:** Vargas committed suicide. **1956–61:** Juscelino Kubitschek became president, pursuing measures geared towards rapid economic growth. **1960:** Capital moved to Brasília. **1961:** Janio Quadros elected president, introducing controversial programme for radical reform; resigned after seven months; succeeded by Vice President João Goulart. **1964:** Bloodless coup established technocratic military regime; free political parties abolished; intense concentration on industrial growth aided by foreign investment and loans. **1970s:** Economic recession and inflation undermined public support for military regime. **1985:** After gradual democratization from 1979, Tancredo Neves became first civilian president in 21 years; on Neves's death, Vice President José Sarney took office. **1988:** New constitution reduced powers of president. **1989:** Fernando Collor (PRN) elected president, promising economic deregulation; Brazil suspended foreign debt payments. **1992:** Collor charged with corruption and replaced by Vice President Itamar Franco. **1994:** New currency introduced (the third in eight years). Fernando Henrique Cardoso (PSDB) elected president. Collor cleared of corruption charges. **1997:** Constitution amended to allow president to seek second term of office. **1998:** Former president Collor acquitted on charges of illegal enrichment. President Cardoso re-elected. IMF rescue package announced.

Brunei State of

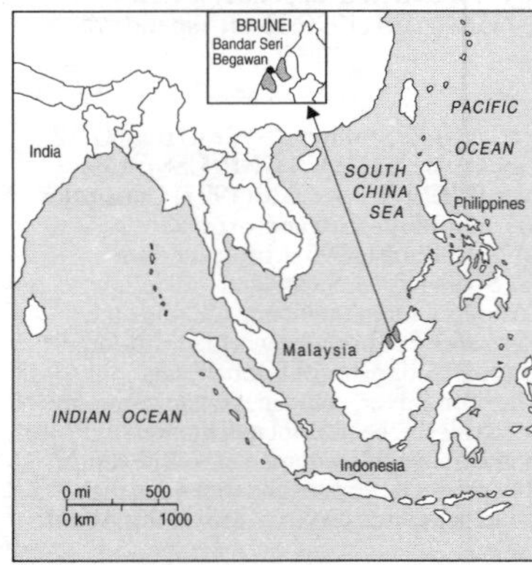

National name: *Negara Brunei Darussalam* **Area:** 5,765 sq km/2,225 sq mi **Capital:** Bandar Seri Begawan **Major towns/cities:** Seria, Kuala Belait, Bangar

Government

Head of state and government: HM Muda Hassanal Bolkiah Mu'izzaddin Waddaulah, Sultan

of Brunei, from 1967 **Political system:** absolute monarchy **Administrative divisions:** four districts **Political parties:** Brunei National Democratic Party (BNDP) and Brunei National United Party (BNUP) (both banned since 1988); Brunei People's Party (BPP) (banned since 1962) **Armed forces:** 5,000 (1997); plus paramilitary forces of 4,100 **Conscription:** military service is voluntary **Death penalty:** retains the death penalty for ordinary crimes but can be considered abolitionist in practice (last execution 1957) **Defence spend:** (% GDP) 6.5 (1996) **Education spend:** (% GNP) 4.5 (1994) **Health spend:** (% GDP) 2.2 (1994)

Economy and resources

Currency: Brunei dollar (ringgit) **GDP:** (US$) 4.9 billion (1995) **Real GDP growth:** (% change on previous year) 2 (1995 est) **GNP (US$):** 7.15 billion (1997) **GNP per capita (PPP):** (US$) 28,000 (1997 est) **Consumer price inflation:** 2.5% (1996) **Unemployment:** 4.8% (1992) **Major trading partners:** Singapore, Japan, USA, EU countries, Malaysia, South Korea, Thailand **Resources:** petroleum, natural gas **Exports:** crude petroleum and natural gas (accounting for 91.7% of total export earnings in 1993). Principal market: Japan 51% (1997) **Imports:** machinery and transport equipment, basic manufactures, food and live animals, chemicals. Principal source: Singapore 41.6% (1997) **Arable land:** 0.6% (1995)

Population and society

Population: 315,000 (1998 est) **Population growth rate:** 2.1% (1990–95) **Population density:** (per sq km) 59.8 (1998 est) **Urban population:** (% of total) 71 (1997) **Age distribution:** (% of total population) 0–14 33.0%, 15–64 62.6%, 65+ 4.4% (1998) **Ethnic groups:** 68% indigenous Malays, predominating in government service and agriculture; more than 20% Chinese, predominating in the commercial sphere **Language:** Malay (official), Chinese (Hokkien), English **Religion:** Muslim 66%, Buddhist 14%, Christian 10% **Education:** (compulsory years) 12 **Literacy rate:** 93% (men); 83% (women) (1995 est) **Labour force:** 41% of population: 2% agriculture, 24% industry, 74% services (1990) **Life expectancy:** 73 (men); 78 (women) (1995–2000) **Child mortality rate:** (under 5, per 1,000 live births) 12 (1997) **Physicians:** 1 per 1,522 people (1994 est)

Practical information

Visa requirements: UK: visa not required for visits of up to 30 days. USA: visa not required **Embassy in the UK:** 19/20 Belgrave Square, London SW1X 8PG. Tel: (0171) 581 0521; fax: (0171) 235 9717 **British embassy:** British High Commission, PO Box 2197, 3rd Floor, Hong Kong Bank Chambers, Jalan Pemancha, Bandar Seri Begawan 2085. Tel: (2) 222 231; fax: (2) 226 002 **Chamber of commerce:** Brunei Darussalem International Chamber of Commerce and Industry, POB 2246, Bandar Seri Begawan 1922. Tel: (2) 236 601; fax: (2) 228 389

Chronology

15th century: Islamic monarchy established, ruling Brunei and north Borneo, including Sabah and Sarawak states of Malaysia. **1841:** Lost control of Sarawak. **1888:** Brunei became a British protectorate. **1906:** Became a dependency when British resident was appointed adviser to the sultan. **1929:** Oil was discovered. **1941–45:** Occupied by Japan. **1950:** Sir Omar became the 28th sultan. **1959:** Written constitution made Britain responsible for defence and external affairs. **1962:** Sultan began rule by decree after plan to join Federation of Malaysia was opposed by a week-long rebellion organized by the Brunei People's Party (BPP). **1967:** Sultan Omar abdicated in favour of his son Hassanal Bolkiah, but remained chief adviser. **1971:** Brunei given full internal self-government. **1975:** United Nations resolution called for independence for Brunei. **1984:** Independence achieved from Britain, with Britain maintaining a small force to protect the oil and gas fields. **1985:** A 'loyal and reliable' political party, the Brunei National Democratic Party (BNDP), legalized. **1986:** Death of former sultan, Omar. Formation of multiethnic Brunei National United Party (BNUP); nonroyals given key cabinet posts for the first time. **1988:** BNDP and BNUP banned. **1991:** Joined nonaligned movement. **1998:** Prince Billah proclaimed heir to the throne.

Bulgaria Republic of

National name: *Republika Bulgaria* **Area:** 110,912 sq km/42,823 sq mi **Capital:** Sofia **Major towns/cities:** Plovdiv, Varna, Ruse, Burgas, Stara Zagora **Major ports:** Black Sea ports Burgas and Varna

Government

Head of state: Petar Stoyanov from 1997 **Head of government:** Ivan Kostov from 1997 **Political system:** emergent democracy **Administrative divisions:** nine regions **Political parties:** Union of Democratic Forces (UDF), right of centre; Bulgarian Socialist Party (BSP), left wing, ex-communist; Movement for Rights and Freedoms (MRF), Turkish-oriented, centrist; Civic Alliances for the Republic (CAR), left of centre; Real Reform Movement (DESIR) **Armed forces:** 101,500 (1997) **Conscription:** compulsory for 12 months **Death penalty:** abolished in 1998 **Defence spend:** (% GDP) 3.4 (1997) **Education spend:** (% GNP) 3.3 (1996) **Health spend:** (% GDP) 4.0 (1990–95)

Economy and resources

Currency: lev **GDP:** (US$) 10 billion (1997) **Real GDP growth:** (% change on previous year) –5.7 (1997) **GNP (US$):** 9.4 billion (1997) **GNP per capita (PPP):** (US$) 3,860 (1997) **Consumer price inflation:** 32% (1998) **Unemployment:** 12.5% (1996) **Foreign debt:** (US$) 9.82 billion (1996) **Major trading partners:** EU countries (principally Germany, Greece, Italy), former USSR (principally Russia), Macedonia, USA **Resources:** coal, iron ore, manganese, lead, zinc, petroleum **Exports:** base metals, chemical and rubber products, processed food, beverages, tobacco, textiles, footwear. Principal market: Italy 11.7% (1997) **Imports:** mineral products and fuels, chemical and rubber products, textiles, footwear, machinery and transport equipment, medicines. Principal source: Russia 28.1% (1997) **Arable land:** 36.2% (1995)

Population and society

Population: 8,336,000 (1998 est) **Population growth rate:** –0.5% (1995–2000) **Population density:** (per sq km) 74.6 (1998 est) **Urban population:** (% of total) 69 (1997) **Age distribution:** (% of total population) 0–14 16.5%, 15–64 67.6%, 65+ 15.9% (1998) **Ethnic groups:** Southern Slavic Bulgarians constitute around 90% of the population; 9% are ethnic Turks, who during the later 1980s were subjected to government pressure to adopt Slavic names and to resettle elsewhere **Language:** Bulgarian, Turkish **Religion:** Eastern Orthodox Christian, Muslim, Roman Catholic, Protestant **Education:** (compulsory years) 8 **Literacy rate:** 93% (men); 93% (women) (1995 est) **Labour force:** 22.1% agriculture, 36.6% industry, 41.3% services (1993) **Life expectancy:** 68 (men); 75 (women) (1995–2000) **Child mortality rate:** (under 5, per 1,000 live births) 18 (1997) **Physicians:** 1 per 298 people (1995)

Practical information

Visa requirements: UK: visa required. USA: visa not required for tourist visits of up to 30 days **Embassy in the UK:** 186–188 Queen's Gate, London SW7 5HL. Tel: (0171) 584 9400; fax: (0171) 584 4948 **British embassy:** Boulevard Vassil Levski 65–67, Sofia 1000. Tel: (2) 885 361/2; fax: (2) 656 022 **Chamber of commerce:** Bulgarian Chamber of Commerce and Industry, 1040 Sofia, Suborna ST 11A. Tel: (2) 872 631; fax: (2) 873 209

Chronology
c. **3500 BC: onwards:** Settlement of semi-nomadic pastoralists from central Asian steppes, who formed the Thracian community. **mid-5th century BC:** Thracian state formed, which was to extend over Bulgaria, northern Greece, and northern Turkey. **4th century BC:** Phillip II and Alexander the Great of Macedonia, to the southwest, waged largely unsuccessful campaigns against Thracian Empire. **AD 50:** Thracians subdued and incorporated within Roman Empire as province of Moesia Inferior. **3rd–6th centuries:** Successively invaded from north and devastated by the Goths, Huns, Bulgars, and Avars. **681:** The Bulgars, an originally Turkic group that had merged with earlier Slav settlers, revolted against the Avars and established, south of River Danube, the first Bulgarian kingdom, with its capital at Pliska, in the Balkans. **864:** Orthodox Christianity adopted by Boris I. **1018:** Subjugated by the Byzantines, whose empire had its capital at Constantinople; led to Bulgarian Church breaking with Rome in 1054. **1185:** Second independent Bulgarian Kingdom formed. **mid-13th century:** Bulgarian state destroyed by Mongol incursions. **1396:** Bulgaria became first European state to be absorbed into Turkish Ottoman Empire; the imposition of harsh feudal system and sacking of monasteries followed. **1859:** Bulgarian Catholic Church re-established links with Rome. **1876:** Bulgarian nationalist revolt against Ottoman rule crushed brutally by Ottomans, with 15,000 massacred at Plovdiv ('Bulgarian Atrocities'). **1878:** At the Congress of Berlin, concluding a Russo-Turkish war in which Bulgarian volunteers had fought alongside the Russians, the area south of the Balkans, Eastern Rumelia, remained an Ottoman province, but the area to the north became the autonomous Principality of Bulgaria, with a liberal constitution and Alexander Battenberg as prince. **1885:** Eastern Rumelia annexed by the Principality; Serbia defeated in war. **1908:** Full independence proclaimed from Turkish rule, with Ferdinand I as tsar. **1913:** Following defeat in the Second Balkan War, King Ferdinand I abdicated and was replaced by his son Boris III. **1919:** Bulgarian Agrarian Union government, led by Alexander Stamboliiski, came to power and redistributed land to poor peasants. **1923:** Agrarian government overthrown in right-wing coup and Stamboliiski murdered. **1934:** Semifascist dictatorship established by King Boris III, who sided with Germany during World War II, but died mysteriously in 1943 after a visit to Adolf Hitler. **1944:** Soviet invasion of German-occupied Bulgaria. **1946:** Monarchy abolished and communist-dominated people's republic proclaimed following plebiscite. **1947:** Gained South Dobruja in the northeast, along the Black Sea, from Romania; Soviet-style constitution established a one-party state; industries and financial institutions nationalized and cooperative farming introduced. **1949:** Death of Georgi Dimitrov, the communist government leader; replaced by Vulko Chervenkov. **1954:** Election of Todor Zhivkov as Bulgarian Communist Party (BCP) general secretary; Bulgaria became a loyal and cautious satellite of the USSR. **1968:** Participated in the Soviet-led invasion of Czechoslovakia. **1971:** Zhivkov became president, under new constitution. **1985–89:** Haphazard administrative and economic reforms, known as *preustroistvo* ('restructuring'), introduced under stimulus of reformist Soviet leader Mikhail Gorbachev. **1989:** Programme of enforced 'Bulgarianization' resulted in mass exodus of ethnic Turks to Turkey. Zhivkov ousted by foreign minister Petar Mladenov. Opposition parties tolerated. **1990:** BCP reformed under new name Bulgarian Socialist Party (BSP). Zhelyu Zhelev of the centre-right Union of Democratic Forces (UDF) indirectly elected president. Following mass demonstrations and general strike, BSP government replaced by coalition. **1991:** New liberal-democratic constitution adopted. UDF beat BSP in general election; formation of first noncommunist, UDF-minority government. **1992:** Zhelev became Bulgaria's first directly elected president. Following industrial unrest, Lyuben Berov became head of a non-party government. Zhivkov sentenced to seven years' imprisonment for corruption while in government. **1993:** Voucher-based 'mass privatization' programme launched. **1994:** Berov resigned; general election won by BSP. **1995:** Zhan Videnov (BSP) became prime minister. **1996:** Radical economic and industrial reforms imposed. Petar Stoyanov replaced Zhelev as president. Mounting inflation and public protest at the state of the economy. **1997:** General strike. Interim government led by Stefan Sofiyanski. UDF leader Ivan Kostov became prime minister. Former communist leader Zhivkov released from house arrest. Bulgarian currency pegged to Deutschmark in return for support from International Monetary Fund. New political group, the Real Reform Movement (DESIR), formed. **1999:** Bulgaria joined the Central European Free Trade Agreement (CEFTA).

Burkina Faso The People's Democratic Republic of (formerly Upper Volta)

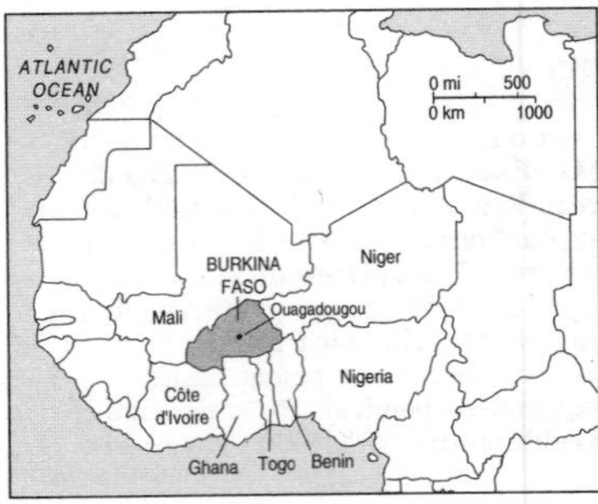

National name: *République Démocratique Populaire de Burkina Faso* **Area:** 274,122 sq km/105,838 sq mi **Capital:** Ouagadougou **Major towns/cities:** Bobo-Dioulasso, Koudougou

Government
Head of state: Blaise Compaoré from 1987 **Head of government:** Kadre Desire Ouedraogo from 1996 **Political system:** emergent democracy **Administrative divisions:** 30 provinces **Political parties:** Popular Front (FP), centre-left coalition grouping; National Convention of Progressive Patriots–Democratic Socialist Party (CNPP–PSD), left of centre **Armed forces:** 5,800 (1997); includes gendarmerie of 4,200 **Conscription:** military service is voluntary **Death penalty:** retained and used for ordinary crimes **Defence spend:** (% GDP) 2.4 (1996) **Education spend:** (% GNP) 1.5 (1996) **Health spend:** (% GDP) 2.3 (1990–95)

Economy and resources
Currency: franc CFA **GDP:** (US$) 2.44 billion (1997) **Real GDP growth:** (% change on previous year) 6.6 (1997) **GNP (US$):** 2.6 billion (1997) **GNP per capita (PPP):** (US$) 990 (1997) **Consumer price inflation:** 3.0% (1997) **Unemployment:** 8.1% (1994 est) **Foreign debt:** (US$) 1.29 billion (1996) **Major trading partners:** France, Côte d'Ivoire, Thailand, Italy, Taiwan, Niger, Nigeria **Resources:** manganese, zinc, limestone, phosphates, diamonds, gold, antimony, marble, silver, lead **Exports:** cotton, gold, livestock and livestock products. Principal market: France 9.3% (1996) **Imports:** machinery and transport equipment, miscellaneous manufactured articles, food products (notably cereals), refined petroleum products, chemicals. Principal source: Côte d'Ivoire 14.2% (1996) **Arable land:** 12.5% (1995)

Population and society
Population: 11,305,000 (1998 est) **Population growth rate:** 2.8% (1995–2000) **Population density:** (per sq km) 41.1 (1998 est) **Urban population:** (% of total) 17% (1997) **Age distribution:** (% of total population) 0–14 48.0%, 15–64 49.0%, 65+ 3.0% (1998) **Ethnic groups:** over 50 ethnic groups, including the nomadic Mossi (48%), Fulani (10%), and Gourma (5%). Settled tribes include: in the north the Lobi-Dagari (7%) and the Mande (7%); in the SE the Bobo (7%); and in the SW the Senoufu (6%) and Gourounsi (5%) **Language:** French (official); about 50 Sudanic languages spoken by 90% of population **Religion:** animist 53%, Sunni Muslim 36%, Roman Catholic 11% **Education:** (compulsory years) 6 **Literacy rate:** 28% (men); 9% (women) (1995 est) **Labour force:** 54% of population: 92% agriculture, 2% industry, 6% services (1990) **Life expectancy:** 45 (men); 47 (women) (1995–2000) **Child mortality rate:** (under 5, per 1,000 live births) 161 (1997) **Physicians:** 1 per 34,804 people (1993 est)

Practical information
Visa requirements: UK: visa required. USA: visa required **Embassy in the UK:** Honorary Consulate, 5 Cinnamon Row, Plantation Wharf, London SW11 3TW. Tel: (0171) 738 1800; fax: (0171) 738 2820 **British embassy:** British Consulate, BP 1918 Ouagadougou. (All

staff based in Abidjan, Côte d'Ivoire.) Tel: (226) 336 363 **Chamber of commerce:** Chambre de Commerce, d'Industrie et d'Artisanat du Burkina, ave Nelson Mandela, 01 BP 502, Ouagadougou 01. Tel: (226) 306 114; fax: (226) 306 116

Chronology

13th–14th centuries: Formerly settled by Bobo, Lobi, and Gurunsi peoples, east and centre were conquered by Mossi and Gurma peoples, who established powerful warrior kingdoms, some of which survived until late 19th century. **1895–1903:** France secured protectorates over the Mossi kingdom of Yatenga and the Gurma region, and annexed the Bobo and Lobi lands, meeting armed resistance. **1904:** The French-controlled region, known as Upper Volta, was attached administratively to French Sudan; tribal chiefs were maintained in their traditional seats and the region was to serve as a labour reservoir for more developed colonies to south. **1919:** Made a separate French colony. **1932:** Partitioned between French Sudan, Ivory Coast, and Niger. **1947:** Became a French overseas territory. **1960:** Independence achieved, with Maurice Yaméogo as the first president. **1966:** Military coup led by Lt-Col Sangoulé Lamizana, and a supreme council of the armed forces established. **1977:** Ban on political activities removed. Referendum approved a new constitution based on civilian rule. **1978:** Lamizana elected president. **1980:** Lamizana overthrown in bloodless coup led by Col Saye Zerbo as economy deteriorated. **1982:** Zerbo ousted in a coup by junior officers: Maj Jean-Baptiste Ouedraogo became president and Capt Thomas Sankara prime minister. **1983:** Sankara seized complete power. **1984:** Upper Volta renamed Burkina Faso ('land of upright men') to signify break with colonial past; literacy and afforestation campaigns by radical Sankara, who established links with Libya, Benin, and Ghana. **1987:** Sankara killed in coup led by Capt Blaise Compaoré. **1991:** New constitution approved. Compaoré re-elected president. **1992:** Multiparty elections won by pro-Compaoré Popular Front (FP), despite opposition claims of ballot-rigging. **1996:** Kadre Desire Ouedraogo appointed prime minister. **1997:** CDP assembly election victory. Ouedraogo reappointed prime minister. **1998:** President Compaoré re-elected.

Burundi Republic of

National name: *Republika y'Uburundi* **Area:** 27,834 sq km/10,746 sq mi **Capital:** Bujumbura **Major towns/cities:** Kitega, Bururi, Ngozi, Muhinga, Muramuya

Government

Head of state: Pierre Buyoya from 1996 **Head of government:** Pascal-Firmin Ndimira from 1996 **Political system:** authoritarian nationalist **Administrative divisions:** 15 provinces **Political parties:** Front for Democracy in Burundi (FRODEBU), left of centre; Union for National Progress (UPRONA), nationalist socialist **Armed forces:** 18,500 (1997); plus paramilitary forces of 3,500 **Conscription:** military service is voluntary **Death penalty:** retained and used for ordinary crimes **Defence spend:** (% GDP) 5.7 (1997) **Education spend:** (% GNP) 3.2 (1996) **Health spend:** (% GDP) 0.9 (1990–95)

Economy and resources

Currency: Burundi franc **GDP:** (US$) 1.24 billion (1997 est) **Real GDP growth:** (% change on previous year) 2.0 (1997) **GNP (US$):** 1.2 billion (1997) **GNP per capita (PPP):** (US$) 590 (1997) **Consumer price inflation:** 20.0% (1997) **Unemployment:** 7.3% (1992) **Foreign debt:** (US$) 1.13 billion (1996) **Major trading partners:** Belgium, Germany, France, Tanzania, Japan, USA **Resources:** nickel, gold, tungsten, phosphates, vanadium, uranium, peat, petroleum deposits have been detected **Exports:** coffee, tea, glass products, hides and skins. Principal market: UK 29.1% (1997) **Imports:** machinery and transport equipment, petroleum and petroleum products, cement, malt (and malt flour). Principal source: Belgium – Luxembourg 18.2% (1997) **Arable land:** 36.2%

Population and society

Population: 6,457,000 (1998 est) **Population growth rate:** 2.8% (1995–2000); 2.6% (2000–05) **Population density:** (per sq km) 215.9 (1998 est) **Urban population:** (% of total) 8% (1997) **Age distribution:** (% of total population) 0–14 47.4%, 15–64 49.6%, 65+ 3.0% (1998) **Ethnic groups:** two main groups: the agriculturalist Hutu, comprising about 85% of the population, and the predominantly pastoralist Tutsi, about 14%. There is a small Pygmy minority, comprising about 1% of the population, and a few Europeans and Asians **Language:** Kirundi (a Bantu language) and French (both official), Kiswahili **Religion:** Roman Catholic 62%, Pentecostalist 5%, Anglican 1%, Muslim 1%, animist **Education:** (compulsory years) 6 **Literacy rate:** 61% (men); 40% (women) (1995 est) **Labour force:** 54% of population: 92% agriculture, 3% industry, 6% services (1990) **Life expectancy:** 46 (men); 49 (women) (1995–2000) **Child mortality rate:** (under 5, per 1,000 live births) 167 (1997) **Physicians:** 1 per 17,153 people (1993 est)

Practical information

Visa requirements: UK: visa required. USA: visa required **Embassy for the UK:** Square Marie Louise 46, 1040 Brussels, Belgium. Tel: (2) 230 4535; fax: (2) 230 7883 **British embassy:** British Consulate, 43 Avenue Bubanza, BP 1344, Bujumbura. (All staff based in Kampala, Uganda.) Tel: (2) 23711 **Chamber of commerce:** Chambre de Commerce et de l'Industrie du Burundi, BP 313, Bujumbura. Tel: (2) 22280

Chronology

10th century: Originally inhabited by the hunter-gatherer Twa Pygmies. Hutu peoples settled in the region and became peasant farmers. **13th century:** Taken over by Banu Hutus. **15th–17th centuries:** The majority Hutu community came under the dominance of the cattle-owning Tutsi peoples, immigrants from the east, who became a semi-aristocracy; the minority Tutsis developed a feudalistic political system, organized around a nominal king, with royal princes in control of local areas. **1890:** Known as Urundi, the Tutsi kingdom, along with neighbouring Rwanda, came under nominal German control as Ruanda-Urundi. **1916:** Occupied by Belgium during World War I. **1923:** Belgium was granted a League of Nations mandate to administer Ruanda-Urundi; it was to rule 'indirectly' through the Tutsi chiefs. **1962:** Separated from Ruanda-Urundi, as Burundi, and given independence as a monarchy under Tutsi King Mwambutsa IV. **1965:** King refused to appoint a Hutu prime minister after an election in which Hutu candidates were victorious; attempted coup by Hutus brutally suppressed. **1966:** King deposed by his teenage son Charles, who became Ntare V; he was in turn deposed by his Tutsi prime minister Col Michel Micombero, who declared Burundi a republic; the Tutsi-dominated Union for National Progress (UPRONA) declared only legal political party. **1972:** Ntare V killed, allegedly by Hutus, provoking a massacre of 150,000 Hutus by Tutsi soldiers; 100,000 Hutus fled to Tanzania. **1976:** Army coup deposed Micombero and appointed the Tutsi Col Jean-Baptiste Bagaza as president, who launched a drive against corruption and a programme of land reforms and economic development. **1987:** Bagaza deposed in coup by the Tutsi Maj Pierre Buyoya. **1988:** About 24,000 Hutus killed by Tutsis and 60,000 fled as refugees to Rwanda. **1992:** New multiparty constitution adopted following referendum. **1993:** Melchior Ndadaye, a Hutu, elected president in first-ever democratic contest but killed in coup by Tutsi-dominated army; 100,000 died in massacres that followed. **1994:** Cyprien Ntaryamira, a Hutu, became president but later killed in air crash along with Rwandan president Juvenal Habyarimana. Ethnic violence; 750,000 Hutus fled to Rwanda. Hutu Sylvestre Ntibantunganya became head of state, serving with a Tutsi prime minister, as part of a four-year power-sharing agreement between main political parties. **1995:** Renewed ethnic violence in the capital, Bujumbura, following

massacre of Hutu refugees. **1996:** Former Tutsi president Pierre Buyoya seized power amid renewed ethnic violence; coup provoked economic sanctions by other African countries. 'Government of national unity' appointed, with Pascal-Firmin Ndimira as premier. Bujumbura shelled by Hutu rebels. **1998:** Renewed fighting between Tutsi-led army and Hutu rebels. Ceasefire agreed between warring political factions.

Cambodia State of (Khmer Republic 1970–76, Democratic Kampuchea 1976–79, People's Republic of Kampuchea 1979–89)

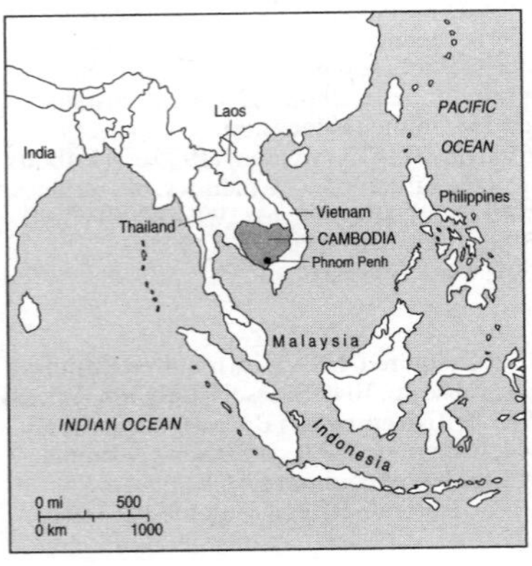

National name: *Roat Kampuchea* **Area:** 181,035 sq km/69,897 sq mi **Capital:** Phnom Penh **Major towns/cities:** Battambang, Kompong Cham **Major ports:** Kompong Cham

Government

Head of state: Prince Norodom Sihanouk from 1991 **Head of government:** joint prime ministers Ung Huot and Hun Sen from 1998 **Political system:** limited constitutional monarchy **Administrative divisions:** 22 provinces **Political parties:** United Front for an Independent, Neutral, Peaceful, and Cooperative Cambodia (FUNCINPEC), nationalist, monarchist; Liberal Democratic Party (BLDP), republican, anticommunist (formerly the Khmer People's National Liberation Front (KPNLF)); Cambodian People's Party (CPP), reform socialist (formerly the communist Kampuchean People's Revolutionary Party (KPRP)); Cambodian National Unity Party (CNUP) (political wing of the Khmer Rouge), ultranationalist communist **Armed forces:** 140,500 (1997) **Conscription:** military service is compulsory for five years between ages 18 and 35 **Death penalty:** abolished in 1989 **Defence spend:** (% GDP) 7.3 (1997) **Education spend:** (% GNP) 2.9 (1996) **Health spend:** (% GDP) 0.7 (1990–95)

Economy and resources

Currency: Cambodian riel **GDP:** (US$) 3.09 billion (1997) **Real GDP growth:** (% change on previous year) 1.0 (1997) **GNP (US$):** 3.2 billion (1997) **GNP per capita (PPP):** (US$) 1,190 (1997 est) **Consumer price inflation:** 14.0% (1997) **Foreign debt:** (US$) 2.11 billion (1996) **Major trading partners:** Singapore, Thailand, Vietnam, Japan, Hong Kong, Indonesia, Taiwan **Resources:** phosphates, iron ore, gemstones, bauxite, silicon, manganese **Exports:** timber, rubber, fishery products. Principal market: Thailand 36.2% (1997) **Imports:** cigarettes, construction materials, petroleum products, motor vehicles, alcoholic beverages, consumer electronics. Principal source: Singapore 35.2% (1995) **Arable land:** 21.6% (1995)

Population and society

Population: 10,716,000 (1998 est) **Population growth rate:** 2.2% (1995–2000) **Population density:** (per sq km) 64.2 (1998 est) **Urban population:** (% of total) 22 (1997) **Age distribution:** (% of total population) 0–14 45.4%, 15–64 51.6%, 65+ 3.0% (1998) **Ethnic groups:** 91% Khmer, 4% Vietnamese, 3% Chinese **Language:** Khmer (official), French **Religion:** Theravāda Buddhist 95%, Muslim, Roman Catholic **Education:** (compulsory years) 6 **Literacy rate:** 48% (men); 65% (women) (1995 est) **Labour force:** 50% of population: 74% agriculture, 8% industry, 19% services (1990) **Life expectancy:** 53 (men); 55 (women) (1995–2000) **Child mortality rate:** (under 5, per 1,000 live births) 131 (1997) **Physicians:** 1 per 9,374 people (1993 est)

Practical information

Visa requirements: UK: visa required. USA: visa required **Embassy in the UK:** no diplomatic representation in the UK **British embassy:** 29 Street 75, Phnom Penh. Tel: (855) 232 7124 **Chamber of commerce:** Council for the Development of Cambodia, Government Palace, quai Sisowath, Wat Phnom, Phnom Penh. Tel: (23) 50428; fax: (23) 61616

Chronology

1st century AD: Part of the kingdom of Hindu-Buddhist Funan (Fou Nan), centred on Mekong delta region. **6th century:** Conquered by the Chenla kingdom. **9th century:** Establishment by Jayavarman II of extensive and sophisticated Khmer Empire, supported by an advanced irrigation system and architectural achievements, with a capital at Angkor in the northwest. **14th century:** Theravāda Buddhism replaced Hinduism. **15th century:** Came under the control of Siam (Thailand), which made Phnom Penh the capital and, later, Champa (Vietnam). **1863:** Became a French protectorate, but traditional political structures left largely intact. **1887:** Became part of French Indo-China Union, which included Laos and Vietnam. **1941:** Prince Norodom Sihanouk was elected king. **1941–45:** Occupied by Japan during World War II. **1946:** Recaptured by France; parliamentary constitution adopted. **1949:** Guerrilla war for independence secured semi-autonomy within the French Union. **1953:** Independence achieved from France as the Kingdom of Cambodia. **1955:** Norodom Sihanouk abdicated as king and became prime minister, representing the Popular Socialist Community mass movement. **1960:** On the death of his father, Norodom Sihanouk became head of state. **later 1960s:** Mounting guerrilla insurgency, led by the communist Khmer Rouge, and civil war in neighbouring Vietnam. **1970:** Sihanouk overthrown by US-backed Lt-Gen Lon Nol in a right-wing coup; name of Khmer Republic adopted; Sihanouk, exiled in China, formed own guerrilla movement. **1975:** Lon Nol overthrown by Khmer Rouge, which was backed by North Vietnam and China; name Kampuchea adopted, with Sihanouk as head of state. **1976–78:** Khmer Rouge, led by Pol Pot, introduced an extreme Maoist communist programme, forcing urban groups into rural areas and resulting in over 2.5 million deaths from famine, disease, and maltreatment; Sihanouk removed from power. **1978–79:** Vietnamese invasion and installation of government headed by Heng Samrin, an anti-Pol Pot communist. **1980–82:** Faced by guerrilla resistance from Pol Pot's Chinese-backed Khmer Rouge and Sihanouk's ASEAN and US-backed nationalists, more than 300,000 Cambodians fled to refugee camps in Thailand and thousands of soldiers were killed. **1985:** Reformist Hun Sen appointed prime minister and more moderate economic and cultural policies pursued. **1987–89:** Vietnamese troop withdrawal. **1989:** Renamed State of Cambodia and Buddhism was re-established as state religion. **1991:** Peace agreement signed in Paris provided for a cease-fire and a United Nations Transitional Authority in Cambodia (UNTAC) to administer country in conjunction with all-party Supreme National Council; communism abandoned. Sihanouk returned as head of state. **1992:** Political prisoners released; refugees resettled; freedom of speech and party formation restored. Khmer Rouge refused to disarm in accordance with peace process. **1993:** Free general elections (boycotted by Khmer Rouge) resulted in win by FUNCINPEC; new constitution adopted. Sihanouk reinstated as constitutional monarch; Prince Norodom Ranariddh, FUNCINPEC leader, appointed executive prime minister, with reform-socialist CPP leader Hun Sen deputy premier. Khmer Rouge continued fighting. **1994:** Antigovernment coup foiled. Surrender of 7,000 guerrillas of outlawed Khmer Rouge in response to government amnesty. **1995:** Prince Norodom Sirivudh, FUNCINPEC leader and half-brother of King Sihanouk, exiled for allegedly plotting to assassinate Hun Sen and topple government. **1996:** Split in Khmer Rouge when deputy leader Ieng Sary formed new Democratic National United Movement (DNUM) and granted amnesty by Sihanouk. Kov Samuth assassinated. Heightened tensions between Hun Sen's CPP and the royalist FUNCINPEC. **1997:** Sixteen people killed in street demonstration; opposition blamed supporters of Hun Sen. Pol Pot sentenced to life imprisonment after trial by Khmer Rouge. FUNCINPEC troops routed by CPP, led by Hun Sen. First prime minister Prince Norodom

Ranariddh deposed and replaced by Ung Huot. King Sihanouk underwent medical treatment in China. Fighting between supporters of Hun Sen and Ranariddh. **1998:** Ranariddh tried in absentia and found guilty of arms smuggling and colluding with Khmer Rouge. However, as part of Japanese-brokered peace deal, he was pardoned by the king and returned home to prepare for July general election. Death of Pol Pot and defection of thousands of Khmer Rouge guerrillas. CPP won National Assembly elections. Political unrest followed the poll. New CPP–FUNCINPEC coalition formed, with Hun Sen as sole prime minister and Prince Norodom Ranariddh as president of the National Assembly. FUNCINPEC troops re-integrated into the government army. Cambodia re-occupied its vacated UN seat.

Cameroon Republic of

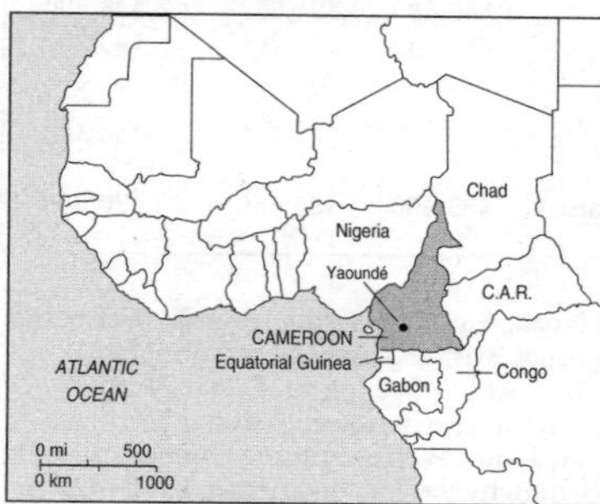

National name: *République du Cameroun* **Area:** 475,440 sq km/183,567 sq mi **Capital:** Yaoundé **Major towns/cities:** Garoua, Douala, Nkongsamba, Maroua, Bamenda, Bafoussam **Major ports:** Douala

Government

Head of state: Paul Biya from 1982 **Head of government:** Simon Achidi Achu from 1992 **Political system:** emergent democracy **Administrative divisions:** ten provinces **Political parties:** Cameroon People's Democratic Movement (RDPC), nationalist, left of centre; Front of Allies for Change (FAC), centre left **Armed forces:** 13,100 (1997); plus 9,000 paramilitary forces **Conscription:** military service is voluntary; paramilitary compulsory training programme in force **Death penalty:** retained and used for ordinary crimes **Defence spend:** (% GDP) 2.9 (1997) **Education spend:** (% GNP) 3.1 (1993–94) **Health spend:** (% GDP) 1 (1990–95)

Economy and resources

Currency: franc CFA **GDP:** (US$) 9.1 billion (1997) **Real GDP growth:** (% change on previous year) 4 (1997) **GNP (US$):** 9.1 billion (1997) **GNP per capita (PPP):** (US$) 1,980 (1997) **Consumer price inflation:** 3% (1998) **Unemployment:** 25% (1990) **Foreign debt:** (US$) 9.5 billion (1996) **Major trading partners:** France, Spain, Italy, Germany, the Netherlands, Belgium, USA **Resources:** petroleum, natural gas, tin ore, limestone, bauxite, iron ore, uranium, gold **Exports:** crude petroleum and petroleum products, timber and timber products, coffee, aluminium, cotton, bananas. Principal market: Italy 25.4% (1997) **Imports:** machinery and transport equipment, basic manufactures, chemicals, fuel. Principal source: France 25% (1997) **Arable land:** 12.8% (1995)

Population and society

Population: 14,305,000 (1998 est) **Population growth rate:** 2.7% (1995–2000) **Population density:** (per sq km) 32.0 (1998 est) **Urban population:** (% of total) 47 (1997) **Age distribution:** (% of total population) 0–14 45.9%, 15–64 50.7%, 65+ 3.3% (1998) **Ethnic groups:** main groups include the Cameroon Highlanders (31%), Equatorial Bantu (19%), Kirdi (11%), Fulani (10%), Northwestern Bantu (8%), and Eastern Nigritic (7%) **Language:** French and English in pidgin variations (official); there has been some discontent with the emphasis on French – there are 163 indigenous peoples with their own African languages (Sudanic languages in north, Bantu languages elsewhere) **Religion:** Roman Catholic 35%, animist 25%, Muslim 22%, Protestant 18% **Education:** (compulsory years) 6 in Eastern Cameroon; 7 in Western Cameroon **Literacy rate:** 66% (men); 43% (women) (1995 est) **Labour force:** 40% of population: 70% agriculture, 9% industry, 21% services (1990) **Life expectancy:** 55 (men); 57 (women) (1995–2000) **Child mortality rate:** (under 5, per 1,000 live births) 104 (1997) **Physicians:** 1 per 11,996 people (1993 est)

Practical information

Visa requirements: UK: visa not required. USA: visa not required **Embassy in the UK:** 84 Holland Park, London W11 3SB. Tel: (0171) 727 0771/3; fax: (0171) 792 9353 **British embassy:** BP 547, Avenue Winston Churchill, Yaoundé. Tel: (237) 220 545/796; fax: (237) 220 148 **Chamber of commerce:** Chambre de Commerce, d'Industrie et des Mines du Cameroun, BP 4011, Place de Gouvernement, Douala. Tel: (237) 423 690; fax: (237) 425 596

Chronology

1472: First visited by the Portuguese, who named it the Rio dos Camaroes ('River of Prawns') after the giant shrimps they found in the Wouri River estuary, and later introduced slave trading. **early 17th century:** The Douala people migrated to the coastal region from the east and came to serve as intermediaries between Portuguese, Dutch, and English traders and interior tribes. **1809–48:** Northern savannas conquered by the Fulani, Muslim pastoral nomads from the southern Sahara, forcing forest and upland peoples southwards. **1856:** Douala chiefs signed a commercial treaty with Britain and invited British protection. **1884:** Treaty signed establishing German rule as the protectorate of Kamerun; cocoa, coffee, and banana plantations developed. **1916:** Captured by Allied forces in World War I. **1919:** Divided under League of Nations' mandates between Britain, which administered the southwest and north, adjoining Nigeria, and France, which administered the east and south (comprising four-fifths of the area), and developed palm oil and cocoa plantations. **1946:** French Cameroon and British Cameroons made UN trust territories. **1955:** French crushed a revolt by the Union of the Cameroon Peoples (UPC), southern-based radical nationalists. **1960:** French Cameroon became the independent Republic of Cameroon, with Ahmadou Ahidjo, a Muslim from the north, elected president; UPC rebellion in southwest crushed, and a state of emergency declared. **1961:** Following a UN plebiscite, northern part of British Cameroons merged with Nigeria and southern part joined the Republic of Cameroon to become the Federal Republic of Cameroon, with French and English as official languages. **1966:** Autocratic one-party regime introduced; government and opposition parties merged to form Cameroon National Union (UNC). **1970s:** Petroleum exports made possible successful investment in education and agriculture. **1972:** New constitution made Cameroon a unitary state. **1982:** President Ahidjo resigned; succeeded by his prime minister Paul Biya, a Christian from the south. **1983:** Biya began to remove the northern Muslim political 'barons' close to Ahidjo, who went into exile in France. **1984:** Biya defeated a plot by Muslim officers from the north to overthrow him. **1985:** UNC adopted the name RDPC. **1990:** Widespread public disorder as living standards declined; Biya granted amnesty to political prisoners. **1992:** Ruling RDPC won first multiparty elections in 28 years. Biya's presidential victory challenged by opposition, who claimed ballot-rigging. **1995:** Cameroon admitted to Commonwealth. **1997:** RDPC assembly election victory; President Biya re-elected.

Canada

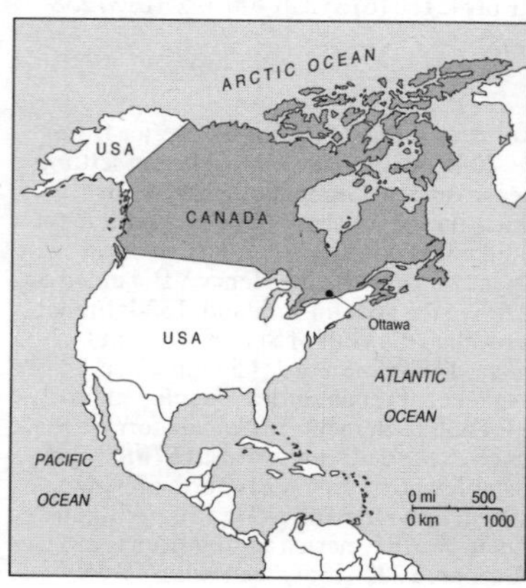

Area: 9,970,610 sq km/3,849,652 sq mi **Capital:** Ottawa **Major towns/cities:** Toronto, Montréal, Vancouver, Edmonton, Calgary, Winnipeg, Québec, Hamilton, Saskatoon, Halifax, Regina, Windsor, Oshawa, London, Kitchener

Government

Head of state: Elizabeth II from 1952, represented by governor general Roméo A LeBlanc

from 1995 **Head of government:** Jean Chrétien from 1993 **Political system:** federal constitutional monarchy **Administrative divisions:** ten provinces and two territories **Political parties:** Liberal Party, nationalist, centrist; Bloc Québécois, Québec-based, separatist; Reform Party, populist, right wing; New Democratic Party (NDP), moderate left of centre; Progressive Conservative Party (PCP), free enterprise, right of centre **Armed forces:** 61,600 (1997) **Conscription:** military service is voluntary **Death penalty:** for exceptional crimes only; last execution 1962 **Defence spend:** (% GDP) 1.3 (1997) **Education spend:** (% GNP) 7.3 (1995) **Health spend:** (% GDP) 6.8 (1990–95)

Economy and resources

Currency: Canadian dollar **GDP:** (US$) 603.1 billion (1997) **Real GDP growth:** (% change on previous year) 3.7 (1997) **GNP (US$):** 583.9 billion (1997) **GNP per capita (PPP):** (US$) 21,860 (1997) **Consumer price inflation:** 2.5% (1998) **Unemployment:** 9.2% (1997) **Major trading partners:** USA, EU countries, Japan, China, Mexico, South Korea **Resources:** petroleum, natural gas, coal, copper (world's third-largest producer), nickel (world's second-largest producer), lead (world's fifth-largest producer), zinc (world's largest producer), iron, gold, uranium, timber **Exports:** motor vehicles and parts, lumber, wood pulp, paper and newsprint, crude petroleum, natural gas, aluminium and alloys, petroleum and coal products. Principal market: USA 81% (1997) **Imports:** motor vehicle parts, passenger vehicles, computers, foodstuffs, telecommunications equipment. Principal source: USA 76.3% (1997) **Arable land:** 4.9% (1995)

Population and society

Population: 30,563,000 (1998 est) **Population growth rate:** 0.9% (1995–2000); 0.9% (2000–05) **Population density:** (per sq km) 3.3 (1998 est) **Urban population:** (% of total) 77% (1997) **Age distribution:** (% of total population) 0–14 19.8%, 15–64 67.8%, 65+ 12.5% (1998) **Ethnic groups:** about 45% of British origin, 29% French, 23% of other European descent, and about 3% American Indians and Inuit **Language:** English, French (both official; 60% English mother tongue, 24% French mother tongue); there are also American Indian languages and the Inuit Inuktitut **Religion:** Roman Catholic, various Protestant denominations **Education:** (compulsory years) 10 **Literacy rate:** 99% (men); 99% (women) (1995 est) **Labour force:** 50.8% of population: 4.1% agriculture, 22.8% industry, 73.1% services (1996) **Life expectancy:** 76 (men); 82 (women) (1995–2000) **Child mortality rate:** (under 5, per 1,000 live births) 7 (1997) **Physicians:** 1 per 476 people (1996)

Practical information

Visa requirements: UK: visa not required. USA: visa not required **Embassy in the UK:** Macdonald House, 1 Grosvenor Square, London W1X 0AB. Tel: (0171) 258 6600; fax: (0171) 258 6333 **British embassy:** British High Commission, 80 Elgin Street, Ottawa KIP 5K7. Tel: (613) 237 1530; fax: (613) 237 7980 **Chamber of commerce:** Canadian Chamber of Commerce, 55 Metcalfe Street, Suite 1160, Ottawa ON KIP 6N4. Tel: (613) 238 400; fax: (613) 238 7643

Chronology

35,000 BC: First evidence of people reaching North America from Asia by way of Beringia. *c.* **2000 BC:** Inuit (Eskimos) began settling Arctic coast from Siberia eastwards to Greenland. *c.* **1000 AD:** Vikings, including Leif Ericsson, established Vinland, a settlement in northeast America that did not survive. **1497:** John Cabot, an Italian navigator in the service of English king Henry VII, landed on Cape Breton Island and claimed the area for England. **1534:** French navigator Jacques Cartier reached the Gulf of St Lawrence and claimed the region for France. **1608:** Samuel de Champlain, a French explorer, founded Québec; French settlers developed fur trade and fisheries. **1663:** French settlements in Canada formed the colony of New France, which expanded southwards. **1670:** Hudson's Bay Company established trading posts north of New France, leading to Anglo-French rivalry. **1689–97:** King William's War: Anglo-French conflict in North America arising from the 'Glorious Revolution' in Europe. **1702–13:** Queen Anne's War: Anglo-French conflict in North America arising from the War of the Spanish Succession in Europe; Britain gained Newfoundland. **1744–48:** King George's War: Anglo-French conflict in North America arising from the War of Austrian Succession in Europe. **1756–63:** Seven Years' War: James Wolfe captured Québec in 1759; France ceded Canada to Britain by the Treaty of Paris. **1775–83:** American Revolution caused influx of 40,000 United Empire Loyalists, who formed New Brunswick in 1784. **1791:** Canada divided into Upper Canada (much of modern Ontario) and Lower Canada (much of modern Québec). **1793:** British explorer Alexander Mackenzie crossed the Rocky Mountains to reach the Pacific coast. **1812–14:** War of 1812 between Britain and USA; US invasions repelled by both provinces. **1820s:** Start of large-scale immigration from British Isles caused resentment among French Canadians. **1837:** Rebellions led by Louis Joseph Papineau in Lower Canada and William Lyon Mackenzie in Upper Canada. **1841:** Upper and Lower Canada united as Province of Canada; achieved internal self-government in 1848. **1867:** British North America Act united Ontario, Québec, Nova Scotia, and New Brunswick in Dominion of Canada. **1869:** Red River Rebellion of Métis (people of mixed French and American Indian descent), led by Louis Riel, against British settlers in Rupert's Land. **1870:** Manitoba (part of Rupert's Land) formed the fifth province of Canada; British Columbia became the sixth in 1871, and Prince Edward Island became the seventh in 1873. **late 19th century:** Growth of large-scale wheat farming, mining, and railways. **1885:** Northwest Rebellion crushed and Riel hanged. Canadian Pacific Railway completed. **1896:** Wilfred Laurier was the first French Canadian to become prime minister. **1905:** Alberta and Saskatchewan formed from Northwest Territories and became provinces of Canada. **1914–18:** Half a million Canadian troops fought for the British Empire on the western front in World War I. **1931:** Statute of Westminster affirmed equality of status between Britain and Dominions. **1939–45:** World War II: Canadian participation in all theatres. **1949:** Newfoundland became the tenth province of Canada; Canada was a founding member of the North Atlantic Treaty Organization (NATO). **1950s:** Postwar boom caused rapid expansion of industry. **1957:** Progressive Conservatives returned to power after 22 years in opposition. **1960:** Québec Liberal Party of Jean Lesage launched 'Quiet Revolution' to re-assert French–Canadian identity. **1970:** Pierre Trudeau invoked War Measures Act to suppress separatist terrorists of the Front de Libération du Québec. **1976:** Parti Québécois won control of Québec provincial government; referendum rejected independence 1980. **1982:** 'Patriation' of constitution removed Britain's last legal control over Canada. **1987:** Meech Lake Accord: constitutional amendment proposed to increase provincial powers (to satisfy Québec); failed to be ratified in 1990. **1989:** Canada and USA agreed to establish free trade by 1999. **1992:** Self-governing homeland for Inuit approved; constitutional reform package, the

Canada: Provinces and Territories

Province	Capital	Area sq km	Area sq mi	Population (1996)
Alberta	Edmonton	661,190	255,285	2,696,800
British Columbia	Victoria	947,800	365,946	3,724,500
Manitoba	Winnipeg	649,950	250,946	1,113,900
New Brunswick	Fredericton	73,440	28,355	738,100
Newfoundland	St John's	405,720	156,648	551,800
Nova Scotia	Halifax	55,490	21,425	909,300
Ontario	Toronto	1,068,580	412,579	10,753,600
Prince Edward Island	Charlottetown	5,660	2,185	134,600
Québec	Québec	1,540,680	594,857	7,138,800
Saskatchewan	Regina	652,330	251,865	990,200
Territory				
Northwest Territories	Yellowknife	3,426,320	1,322,902	64,400
Yukon Territory	Whitehorse	483,450	186,660	30,800

Charlottetown Accord, rejected in national referendum. **1993:** Progressive Conservatives reduced to two seats in crushing election defeat. **1994:** Canada formed the North American Free Trade Area with USA and Mexico. **1995:** Québec referendum narrowly rejected sovereignty proposal. **1997:** Liberals re-elected by narrow margin. **1998:** Supreme court ruling on Quebec's possible secession.

Cape Verde Republic of

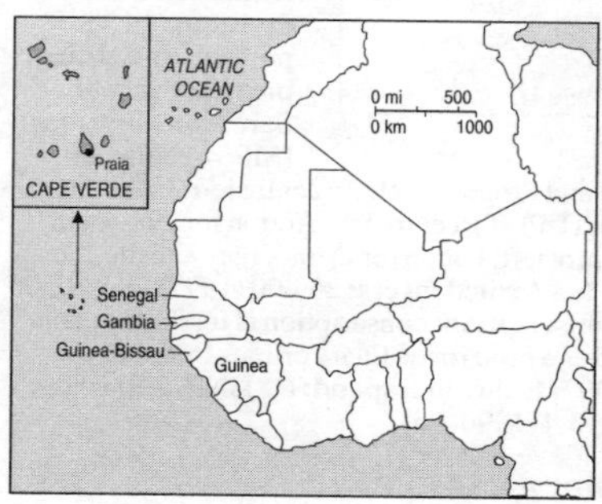

National name: *República de Cabo Verde* **Area:** 4,033 sq km/1,557 sq mi **Capital:** Praia **Major towns/cities:** Mindelo **Major ports:** Mindelo

Government

Head of state: Monteiro Mascarenhas from 1991 **Head of government:** Carlos Viega from 1991 **Political system:** emergent democracy **Administrative divisions:** 14 districts **Political parties:** African Party for the Independence of Cape Verde (PAICV), African nationalist; Movement for Democracy (MPD), moderate, centrist **Armed forces:** 1,100 (1997) **Conscription:** selective conscription **Death penalty:** abolished in 1981 **Defence spend:** (% GDP) 1.7 (1997) **Education spend:** (% GNP) 4.4 (1993–94) **Health spend:** (% GDP) 2 (1993)

Economy and resources

Currency: Cape Verde escudo **GDP:** (US$) 425 million (1997) **Real GDP growth:** (% change on previous year) 5 (1997) **GNP (US$):** 436 million (1997) **GNP per capita (PPP):** (US$) 2,980 (1997) **Consumer price inflation:** 8.0% (1997) **Unemployment:** 25.8% (1990 est) **Foreign debt:** (US$) 210 million (1996) **Major trading partners:** Portugal, the Netherlands, Algeria, Italy, Côte d'Ivoire, Spain, USA, Brazil, Japan **Resources:** salt, pozzolana (volcanic rock), limestone, basalt, kaolin **Exports:** fish, shellfish and fish products, salt, bananas. Principal market: Portugal 50% (1996) **Imports:** food and live animals, machinery and electrical equipment, transport equipment, mineral products, metals. Principal source: Portugal 40.1% (1996) **Arable land:** 9.7% (1995)

Population and society

Population: 408,000 (1998 est) **Population growth rate:** 1.9% (1995–2025) **Population density:** (per sq km) 99.2 (1998 est) **Urban population:** (% of total) 58 (1997) **Age distribution:** (% of total population) 0–14 45.7%, 15–64 48.2%, 65+ 6.1% (1998) **Ethnic groups:** about 60% of mixed descent (Portuguese and African), known as *mestiços* or creoles; the remainder is mainly African. The European population is very small **Language:** Portuguese (official), Creole **Religion:** Roman Catholic 93%, Protestant (Nazarene Church) **Education:** (compulsory years) 6 **Literacy rate:** 80% (men); 60% (women) (1995 est) **Labour force:** 37% of population: 31% agriculture, 30% industry, 40% services (1990) **Life expectancy:** 66 (men); 68 (women) (1995–2000) **Child mortality rate:** (under 5, per 1,000 live births) 57 (1997) **Physicians:** 1 per 5,280 people (1990 est)

Practical information

Visa requirements: UK: visa required. USA: visa required **Embassy for the UK:** 44 Konninginnegracht, 2514 AD, The Hague, the Netherlands. Tel: (70) 346 9623; fax: (70) 346 7702 **British embassy:** British Consulate, c/o Shell Cabo Verde, Sarl Ave, Amílcar Cabral CP4, Sarl Vincente. (All staff based in Dakar, Senegal.) Tel: (238) 314 470; fax: (238) 314 755 **Chamber of commerce:** Associaçao Comercial, Industrial e Agricola de Barlavento, CP 62 Mindelo, São Vicente. Tel: (238) 313 281; fax: (238) 317 110

Chronology

1462: Originally uninhabited; settled by Portuguese, who brought in slave labour from West Africa. **later 19th century:** Decline in prosperity as slave trade ended. **1950s:** Liberation movement developed on the islands and the Portuguese African mainland colony of Guinea-Bissau. **1951:** Became an overseas territory of Portugal. **1975:** Independence achieved. National people's assembly elected, with Aristides of the PAICV as the first executive president; a policy of nonalignment followed. **1981:** Goal of union with Guinea-Bissau abandoned; became one-party state. **1988:** Rising unrest and demand for political reforms. **1991:** In first multiparty elections, new MPD won majority and Monteiro Mascarenhas became president; market-centred economic reforms introduced.

Central African Republic

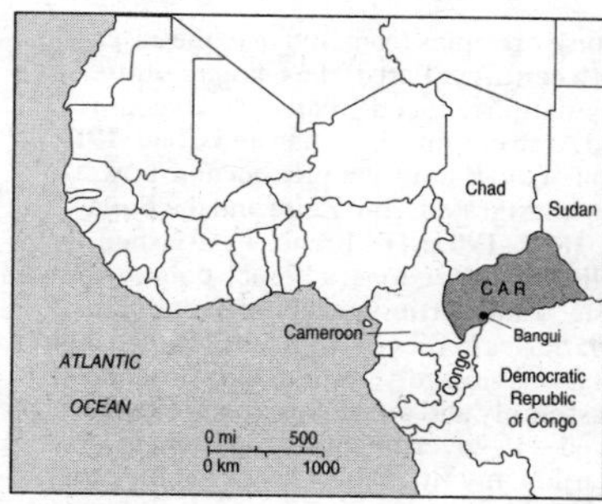

National name: *République Centrafricaine* **Area:** 622,436 sq km/240,322 sq mi **Capital:** Bangui **Major towns/cities:** Berbérati, Bouar, Bambari, Bossangoa, Carnot

Government

Head of state: Anicet Georges Dologuele from 1998 **Head of government:** Gabriel Koyambounou from 1995 **Political system:** emergent democracy **Administrative divisions:** 16 prefectures **Political parties:** Central African People's Liberation Party (MPLC), left of centre; Central African Democratic Rally (RDC), nationalist, right of centre **Armed forces:** 2,700 (1997); plus 2,300 in paramilitary forces **Conscription:** selective national service for two-year period **Death penalty:** retains the death penalty for ordinary crimes but can be considered abolitionist in practice (last execution 1981) **Defence spend:** (% GDP) 4.0 (1997) **Education spend:** (% GNP) 2.8 (1993–94) **Health spend:** (% GDP) 1.9 (1990–95)

Economy and resources

Currency: franc CFA **GDP:** (US$) 978 million (1997 est) **Real GDP growth:** (% change on previous year) 5.8 (1994) **GNP (US$):** 1.1 billion (1997) **GNP per capita (PPP):** (US$) 1,530 (1997) **Consumer price inflation:** 7% (1996) **Unemployment:** 5.6% (1993) **Foreign debt:** (US$) 928 million (1996) **Major trading partners:** France, Belgium, Luxembourg, Cameroon, Germany, Japan, Switzerland, Democratic Republic of Congo **Resources:** gem diamonds and industrial diamonds, gold, uranium, iron ore, manganese, copper **Exports:** diamonds, coffee, timber, cotton. Principal market: Belgium – Luxembourg 36.2% (1997) **Imports:** machinery, road vehicles and parts, basic manufactures, food and chemical products. Principal source: France 30.5% (1997) **Arable land:** 3.1% (1995)

Population and society

Population: 3,485,000 (1998 est) **Population growth rate:** 2.1% (1995–2000) **Population density:** (per sq km) 5.4 (1998 est) **Urban population:** (% of total) 40 (1997) **Age distribution:** (% of total population) 0–14 43.9%, 15–64 52.5%, 65+ 3.6% (1998) **Ethnic groups:** over 80 ethnic groups, but 66% of the population falls into one of three: the Banda (30%), the Baya-Mandjia (29%), and the Mbaka (7%). There are clearly defined ethnic zones; the forest region, inhabited by Bantu groups, the Mbaka, Lissongo, Mbimu, and Babinga; the river banks, populated by the Sango, Yakoma, Baniri, and Buraka; and the savanna region, where the Banda, Sande, Sara, Ndle, and Bizao live. Europeans number fewer than 7,000, the majority being French **Language:** French (official), Sangho (national), Arabic, Hunsa, and Swahili **Religion:** Protestant, Roman Catholic, Muslim, animist **Education:** (compulsory years) 8 **Literacy rate:** 52% (men); 25% (women) (1995 est) **Labour force:** 49% of population: 80% agriculture, 4% industry, 16% services (1990) **Life expectancy:** 46 (men); 51 (women) (1995–2000) **Child mortality rate:** (under 5, per 1,000 live births) 148 (1997) **Physicians:** 1 per 25,920 people (1993 est)

Practical information

Visa requirements: UK: visa required. USA: visa required **Embassy for the UK:** 30 rue des Perchamps, 75016, Paris, France. Tel: (1) 4224 4256; fax: (1) 4288 9895 **British embassy:** British Consulate, PO Box 728, Bangui. (All staff based in Yaoundé, Cameroon.) Tel: (236) 610 300; fax: (236) 615 130 **Chamber of commerce:** Chambre de Commerce, d'Industrie, des Mines et de l'Artisanat, BP 813, Bangui. Tel: (236) 614 255; telex: 5261

Chronology

10th century: Immigration by peoples from Sudan to the east and Cameroon to the west. **16th century:** Part of the Gaoga Empire. **16th–18th centuries:** Population reduced greatly by slave raids both by coastal traders and Arab empires in Sudan and Chad. **19th century:** The Zande nation of the Bandia peoples became powerful in the east. Bantu speakers immigrated from Zaire and the Baya from northern Cameroon. **1889–1903:** The French established control over the area, quelling insurrections; a French colony known as Oubangi-Chari was formed and partitioned among commercial concessionaries. **1920–30:** Series of rebellions against forced labour on coffee and cotton plantations savagely repressed by French. **1946:** Given a territorial assembly and representation in French parliament. **1958:** Achieved self-government within French Equatorial Africa, with Barthélémy Boganda, founder of the pro-independence Movement for the Social Evolution of Black Africa (MESAN) prime minister. **1960:** Achieved independence as Central African Republic; David Dacko, nephew of the late Boganda, elected president. **1962:** The republic made a one-party state, dominated by MESAN and loyal to the French interest. **1965:** Dacko ousted in military coup led by Col Jean-Bedel Bokassa as the economy deteriorated. **1972:** Bokassa, a violent and eccentric autocrat, declared himself president for life. **1977:** Bokassa made himself emperor of the 'Central African Empire'. **1979:** Bokassa deposed by Dacko in French-backed bloodless coup, following violent repressive measures including the massacre of 100 children by the emperor, who went into exile. **1981:** Dacko deposed in a bloodless coup, led by Gen André Kolingba, and military government established. **1983:** Clandestine opposition movement formed. **1984:** Amnesty for all political party leaders announced. President Mitterrand of France paid a state visit. **1988:** Bokassa, who had returned from exile, found guilty of murder and embezzlement; he received death sentence, later commuted to life imprisonment. **1991:** Opposition parties allowed to form. **1992:** Multiparty elections promised, but cancelled with Kolingba in last place. **1993:** Kolingba released thousands of prisoners, including Bokassa. Ange-Félix Patasse of the leftist African People's Labour Party (MLPC) elected president, ending 12 years of military dictatorship. **1996:** Army revolt over pay; Patasse forced into hiding. **1998:** Anicet Georges Dologuele was appointed prime minister.

Chad Republic of

National name: *République du Tchad* **Area:** 1,284,000 sq km/495,752 sq mi **Capital:** N'djaména (formerly Fort Lamy) **Major towns/cities:** Sarh, Moundou, Abéché, Bongor, Doba

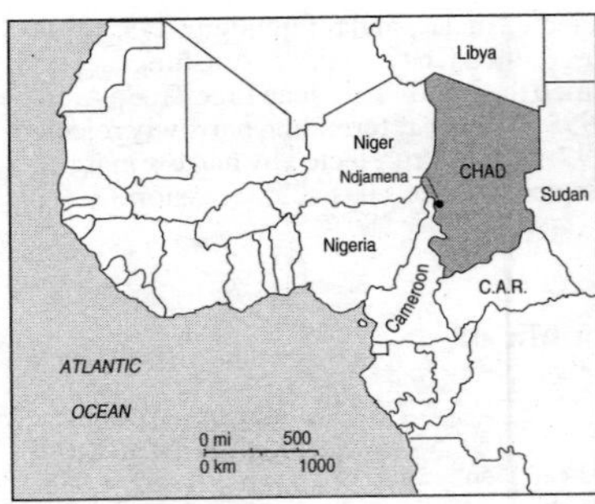

Government

Head of state: Idriss Deby from 1990 **Head of government:** Nassour Ouaidou Guelendouksia from 1997 **Political system:** emergent democracy **Administrative divisions:** 14 prefectures **Political parties:** Patriotic Salvation Movement (MPS), centre left; Alliance for Democracy and Progress (RDP), centre left; Union for Democracy and Progress (UPDT), centre left; Action for Unity and Socialism (ACTUS), centre left; Union for Democracy and the Republic (UDR), centre left **Armed forces:** 25,400 (1997); plus 9,500 in paramilitary forces **Conscription:** conscription is for three years **Death penalty:** retained and used for ordinary crimes **Defence spend:** (% GDP) 4.1 (1997) **Education spend:** (% GNP) 2.9 (1995) **Health spend:** (% GDP) 3.4 (1990–95)

Economy and resources

Currency: franc CFA **GDP:** (US$) 1.6 billion (1997) **Real GDP growth:** (% change on previous year) 5 (1997) **GNP (US$):** 1.6 billion (1997) **GNP per capita (PPP):** (US$) 1,070 (1997) **Consumer price inflation:** 152% (1997) **Foreign debt:** (US$) 997 million (1996) **Major trading partners:** France, Portugal, Nigeria, Cameroon, USA, Belgium, Luxembourg, Italy, Germany **Resources:** petroleum, tungsten, tin ore, bauxite, iron ore, gold, uranium, limestone, kaolin, titanium **Exports:** cotton, live cattle, meat, hides and skins. Principal market: Portugal 29.8% (1997) **Imports:** petroleum and petroleum products, cereals, pharmaceuticals, chemicals, machinery and transport equipment, electrical equipment. Principal source: France 41.3% (1997) **Arable land:** 2.6% (1995)

Population and society

Population: 7,270,000 (1998 est) **Population growth rate:** 2.8% (1995–2000); 2.5% (2000–05) **Population density:** (per sq km) 5.8 (1998 est) **Urban population:** (% of total) 23 (1997) **Age distribution:** (% of total population) 0–14 44.2%, 15–64 52.8%, 65+ 3.0% (1998) **Ethnic groups:** mainly Arabs in the north, and Pagan, or Kirdi, groups in the south. There is no single dominant group in any region, the largest are the Sara, who comprise about a quarter of the total population. Europeans, mainly French, constitute a very small minority **Language:** French, Arabic (both official), over 100 African languages spoken **Religion:** Muslim, Christian, animist **Education:** (compulsory years) 8 **Literacy rate:** 42% (men); 18% (women) (1995 est) **Labour force:** 49% of population: 83% agriculture, 4% industry, 13% services (1990) **Life expectancy:** 46 (men); 49 (women) (1995–2000) **Child mortality rate:** (under 5, per 1,000 live births) 167 (1997) **Physicians:** 1 per 28,570 people (1994 est)

Practical information

Visa requirements: UK: visa required. USA: visa required **Embassy for the UK:** 65 rue des Belles Feuilles, 75116 Paris, France. Tel: (1) 4553 3675; fax: (1) 4553 1609 **British embassy:** British Consulate, BP 877, avenue Charles de Gaulle, N'djaména. (All staff based in Abuja, Nigeria.) Tel: (235) 513 064; telex: 5234 **Chamber of commerce:** Chambre de Commerce, Chambre Consulaire, BP 458, N'djaména. Tel: (235) 515 264

Chronology

7th–9th centuries: Berber pastoral nomads, the Zaghawa, immigrated from north and became ruling aristocracy, dominating the Sao people, sedentary black farmers, and established Kanem state. **9th–19th centuries:** The Zaghawa's Saifi dynasty formed the kingdom of Bornu, which stretched to the west and south of Lake Chad, and converted to Islam in the 11th century. At its height between

the 15th and 18th centuries, it raided the south for slaves, and faced rivalry from the 16th century from the Baguirmi and Ouadai Arab kingdoms. **1820s:** Visited by British explorers. **1890s–1901:** Conquered by France, who ended slave raiding by Arab kingdoms. **1910:** Became a colony in French Equatorial Africa and cotton production expanded in the south. **1944:** The pro-Nazi Vichy government signed agreement giving Libya rights to the Aouzou Strip in northern Chad. **1946:** Became overseas territory of French Republic, with its own territorial assembly and representation in the French parliament. **1960:** Independence achieved, with François Tombalbaye of the Chadian Progressive Party (CPT), dominated by Sara Christians from the south, as president. **1963:** Violent opposition in the Muslim north, led by the Chadian National Liberation Front (Frolinat), backed by Libya following the banning of opposition parties. **1968:** Revolt of northern militias quelled with France's help. **1973:** Africanization campaign launched by Tombalbaye, who changed his first name to Ngarta. **1975:** Tombalbaye killed in military coup led by southerner Gen Félix Malloum. Frolinat continued its resistance. **1978:** Malloum tried to find a political solution by forming a coalition government with former Frolinat leader Hissène Habré, but it soon broke down. **1979:** Malloum forced to leave the country; interim government set up under Gen Goukouni Oueddei (Frolinat). Habré continued his opposition with his Army of the North (FAN), and Libya provided support for Goukouni. **1981–82:** Habré gained control of half the country. Goukouni fled and set up a 'government in exile'. **1983:** Habré's regime recognized by the Organization of African Unity (OAU) and France, but in the north, Goukouni's supporters, with Libya's help, fought on. Eventually a cease-fire was agreed, with latitude 16° north dividing the country. **1987:** Chad, France, and Libya agreed on OAU cease-fire to end the civil war between the Muslim Arab north and Christian and animist black African south. **1988:** Libya relinquished its claims to the Aouzou Strip. **1990:** President Habré ousted after army defeated by Libyan-backed Patriotic Salvation Movement (MPS) rebel troops based in the Sudan and led by Habré's former ally Idriss Deby. **1991–92:** Several antigovernment coups foiled. **1993:** Transitional charter adopted, as prelude to full democracy at a later date. **1997:** Nassour Ouaidou Guelendouksia appointed prime minister. Reconciliation agreement signed with rebel forces.

Chile Republic of

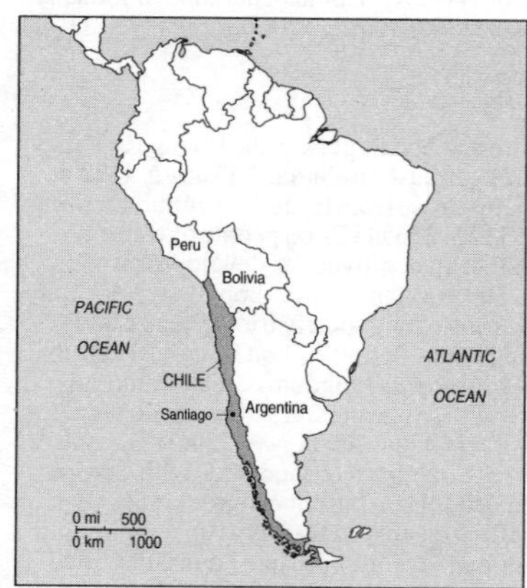

National name: *República de Chile* **Area:** 756,950 sq km/292,258 sq mi **Capital:** Santiago **Major towns/cities:** Concepción, Viña del Mar, Valparaiso, Talcahuano, San Bernardo, Puente Alto, Chillán, Rancagua, Talca, Temuco **Major ports:** Valparaíso, Antofagasta, Arica, Iquique, Punta Arenas **Territories:** Easter Island, Juan Fernández Islands, part of Tierra del Fuego, claim to part of Antarctica

Government

Head of state: Eduardo Frei from 1993 **Head of government:** Dante Cordova from 1995 **Political system:** emergent democracy **Administrative divisions:** 12 regions and one metropolitan area **Political parties:** Christian Democratic Party (PDC), moderate centrist; National Renewal Party (RN), right wing; Socialist Party of Chile (PS), left wing; Independent Democratic Union (UDI), right wing; Party for Democracy (PPD), left of centre; Union of the Centre-Centre (UCC), right wing; Radical Party (PR), left of centre **Armed forces:** 94,300 (1997) **Conscription:** one year (army) or two years (navy and air force) **Death penalty:** retained and used for ordinary crimes **Defence spend:** (% GDP) 2.8 (1997) **Education spend:** (% GNP) 3.1 (1996) **Health spend:** (% GDP) 2.5 (1990–95)

Economy and resources

Currency: Chilean peso **GDP:** (US$) 77.1 billion (1997) **Real GDP growth:** (% change on previous year) 5.8 (1997) **GNP (US$):** 73.3 billion (1997) **GNP per capita (PPP):** (US$) 12,080 (1997) **Consumer price inflation:** 4.7% (1998) **Unemployment:** 6.4% (1996) **Foreign debt:** (US$) 27.4 billion (1996) **Major trading partners:** USA, Japan, Brazil, Germany, Argentina, UK **Resources:** copper (world's largest producer), gold, silver, iron ore, molybdenum, cobalt, iodine, saltpetre, coal, natural gas, petroleum, hydroelectric power **Exports:** copper, fruits, timber products, fishmeal, vegetables, manufactured foodstuffs and beverages. Principal market: USA 17.7% (1997) **Imports:** machinery and transport equipment, wheat, chemical and mineral products, consumer goods, raw materials. Principal source: USA 23.3% (1997) **Arable land:** 5.3% (1995)

Population and society

Population: 14,824,000 (1998 est) **Population growth rate:** 1.4% (1995–2000); 1.2% (2000–05) **Population density:** (per sq km) 19.7 (1998 est) **Urban population:** (% of total) 84 (1997) **Age distribution:** (% of total population) 0–14 25.8%, 15–64 67.6%, 65+ 6.6% (1998) **Ethnic groups:** 65% mestizo (mixed American Indian and Spanish descent), 30% European, remainder mainly American Indian **Language:** Spanish **Religion:** Roman Catholic **Education:** (compulsory years) 8 **Literacy rate:** 93% (men); 93% (women) (1995 est) **Labour force:** 38% of population: 19% agriculture, 25% industry, 56% services (1990) **Life expectancy:** 72 (men); 78 (women) (1995–2000) **Child mortality rate:** (under 5, per 1,000 live births) 15 (1997) **Physicians:** 1 per 942 people (1993 est)

Practical information

Visa requirements: UK: visa not required. USA: visa not required **Embassy in the UK:** 12 Devonshire Street, London W1N 2DS. Tel: (0171) 580 6392; fax: (0171) 436 5204 **British embassy:** Avenida El Bosque Norte (Casilla 16552), Santiago 9. Tel: (2) 231 3737; fax: (2) 231 9771 **Chamber of commerce:** Cámara de Comercio de Santiago de Chile, AG, Santa Lucía 302, 3 º. Casilla 1297, Santiago. Tel: (2) 632 1232; fax: (2) 633 0962

Chronology

1535: First Spanish invasion of Chile abandoned in face of fierce resistance from indigenous Araucanian Indians. **1541:** Pedro de Valdivia began Spanish conquest and founded Santiago. **1553:** Valdivia captured and killed by Araucanian Indians led by Chief Lautaro. **17th century:** Spanish developed small agricultural settlements ruled by government subordinate to viceroy in Lima, Peru. **1778:** King of Spain appointed a separate captain-general to govern Chile. **1810:** Santiago junta proclaimed Chilean autonomy after Napoleon dethroned King of Spain. **1814:** Spanish viceroy regained control of Chile. **1817:** Army of the Andes, led by José de San Martín and Bernardo O'Higgins, defeated the Spanish. **1818:** Achieved independence from Spain with O'Higgins as supreme director. **1823–30:** O'Higgins forced to resign; civil war between conservative centralists and liberal federalists ended with conservative victory. **1833:** Autocratic republican constitution created unitary Roman Catholic state with strong president and limited franchise. **1851–61:** President Manuel Montt bowed to pressure to liberalize constitution and reduce privileges of landowners and church. **1879–84:** Chile defeated Peru and Bolivia in War of the Pacific and increased its territory by a third. **late 19th century:** Mining of nitrate and copper became major industry; large-scale European immigration followed 'pacification' of Araucanian Indians. **1891:** Constitutional dispute between president and congress led to civil war; congressional victory reduced president to figurehead status. **1920:** Election of liberal president Arturo Alessandri Palma; congress blocked his social reform programme. **1925:** New constitution increased presidential powers, separated church and

state, and made primary education compulsory. **1927:** Military coup led to dictatorship of Gen Carlos Ibánez del Campo. **1931:** Sharp fall in price of copper and nitrate caused dramatic economic and political collapse. **1932:** Re-election of President Alessandri, who restored order by harsh measures. **1938:** Popular Front of Radicals, Socialists, and Communists took power under Pedro Aguirre Cedra, who introduced economic policies based on US New Deal. **1947:** Communists organized violent strikes to exploit discontent over high inflation. **1948–58:** Communist Party banned. **1952:** Gen Ibánez elected president on law-and-order platform; austerity policies reduced inflation to 20%. **1958:** Jorge Alessandri (son of former president) succeeded Ibánez as head of Liberal-Conservative coalition. **1964:** Christian Democrat Eduardo Frei Montalva became president; he introduced cautious 'communitarian' social reforms, but failed to combat inflation. **1970:** Salvador Allende, leader of Popular Unity coalition, became world's first democratically elected Marxist president; he embarked on an extensive programme of nationalization and radical social reform. **1973:** Allende killed in CIA-backed military coup; Gen Augusto Pinochet established dictatorship combining severe political repression with free-market economics. **1981:** Pinochet began eight-year term as president under new constitution described as 'transition to democracy'. **1983:** Economic recession provoked growing opposition to regime from all sides. **1988:** Referendum on whether Pinochet should serve a further term resulted in a clear 'No' vote; he agreed to hold elections in following year. **1990:** End of military regime; Christian Democrat Patricio Aylwin became president, with Pinochet as commander in chief of army; investigation into over 2,000 political executions during military regime. **1994:** Eduardo Frei (son of former president) succeeded Aylwin as president. **1995:** Frei introduced measures to reduce military influence in government. **1998:** Pinochet retired from army and was made life senator. State of the economy worsened. Pinochet placed under arrest in the UK; proceedings began to extradite him to Spain on murder charges. **1999:** UK government ruled that Pinochet would be extradited to Spain for crimes including torture.

China People's Republic of

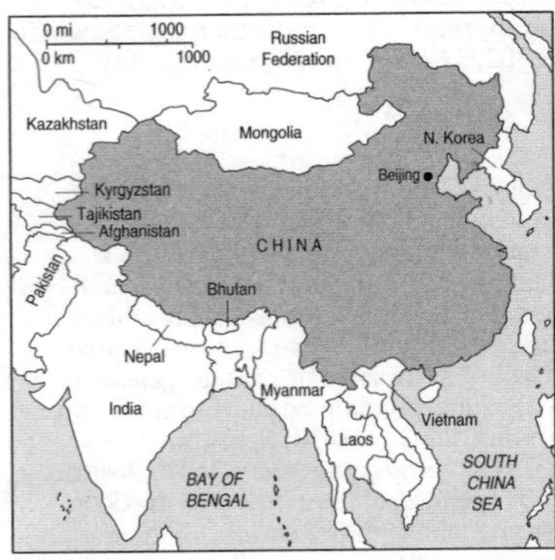

National name: *Zhonghua Renmin Gonghe Guo* **Area:** 9,572,900 sq km/3,696,000 sq mi **Capital:** Beijing (Peking) **Major towns/cities:** Shanghai, Hong Kong, Chongqing (Chungking), Tianjin, Guangzhou (Canton), Shenyang (Mukden), Wuhan, Nanjing (Nanking), Harbin, Chengdu, Xiang, Zibo **Major ports:** Tianjin (Tientsin), Shanghai, Hong Kong, Qingdao (Tsingtao), Guangzhou (Canton)

Government

Head of state: Jiang Zemin from 1993 **Head of government:** Zhu Rongli from 1998 **Political system:** communist republic **Administrative divisions:** 22 provinces, five autonomous regions, and three municipalities **Political party:** Chinese Communist Party (CCP), Marxist-Leninist-Maoist **Armed forces:** 2,840,000; reserves approximately 1.2 million (1997) **Conscription:** selective: 3 years (army and marines), 4 years (air force and navy) **Death penalty:** retained and used for ordinary crimes **Defence spend:** (% GDP) 5.7 (1997) **Education spend:** (% GNP) 2.3 (1995) **Health spend:** (% GDP) 2.1 (1990–95)

Economy and resources

Currency: yuan **GDP:** (US$) 902 billion (1997) **Real GDP growth:** (% change on previous year) 9.3 (1997) **GNP (US$):** 1,055.4 billion (1997) **GNP per capita (PPP):** (US$) 3,570 (1997) **Consumer price inflation:** 7% (1998) **Unemployment:** 2.8% (1994) **Foreign debt:** (US$) 128.8 billion (1996) **Major trading partners:** Japan, USA, Taiwan **Resources:** coal, graphite, tungsten, molybdenum, antimony, tin (world's largest producer), lead (world's fifth-largest producer), mercury, bauxite, phosphate rock, iron ore (world's largest producer), diamonds, gold, manganese, zinc (world's third-largest producer), petroleum, natural gas, fish **Exports:** basic manufactures, miscellaneous manufactured articles (particularly clothing and toys), crude petroleum, machinery and transport equipment, fishery products, cereals, canned food, tea, raw silk, cotton cloth. Principal market: Hong Kong 24% (1997) **Imports:** machinery and transport equipment, basic manufactures, chemicals, wheat, rolled steel, fertilizers. Principal source: Japan 20.4% (1997) **Arable land:** 9.9% (1995)

Population and society

Population: 1,255,698,000 (1998 est) **Population growth rate:** 0.9% (1995–2000) **Population density:** (per sq km) 132.6 (1998 est) **Urban population:** (% of total) 32 (1997) **Age distribution:** (% of total population) 0–14 26.4%, 15–64 67.5%, 65+ 6.1% (1995) **Ethnic groups:** 94% Han Chinese, the remainder being Zhuang, Uygur, Hui (Muslims), Yi, Tibetan, Miao, Manchu, Mongol, Buyi, or Korean; numerous lesser nationalities live mainly in border regions **Language:** Chinese, including Mandarin (official), Cantonese, Wu, and other dialects **Religion:** Taoist, Confucianist, and Buddhist; Muslim 20 million; Catholic 3–6 million (divided between the 'patriotic' church established in 1958 and the 'loyal' church subject to Rome); Protestant 3 million **Education:** (compulsory years) 9 **Literacy rate:** 84% (men); 62% (women) (1995 est) **Labour force:** 59% of population: 72% agriculture, 15% industry, 13% services (1990) **Life expectancy:** 68 (men); 72 (women) (1995–2000) **Child mortality rate:** (under 5, per 1,000 live births) 40 (1997) **Physicians:** 1 per 636 people (1995 est)

Practical information

Visa requirements: UK: visa required. USA: visa required **Embassy in the UK:** 49–51 Portland Place, London W1N 3AH. Tel: (0171) 636 9375/5726; fax: (0171) 636 2981 **British embassy:** 11 Guang Hua Lu, Jian Guo Men Wai, Beijing 100600. Tel: (1) 532 1961/5; fax: (1) 532 1937 **Chamber of commerce:** All-China Federation of Industry and Commerce, 93 Beiheyan Dajie, Beijing 100006. Tel: (1) 513 6677; fax: (1) 512 2631

Chronology

c. **3000 BC:** Yangshao culture reached its peak in the Huang He Valley; displaced by Longshan culture in eastern China. *c.* **1766–** *c.* **1122 BC:** First major dynasty, the Shang, arose from Longshan culture; writing and calendar developed. *c.* **1122–256 BC:** Zhou people of western China overthrew Shang and set up new dynasty; development of money and written laws. *c.* **500 BC:** Confucius expounded philosophy which guided Chinese government and society for the next 2,000 years. **403–221 BC:** 'Warring States Period': Zhou Empire broke up into small kingdoms. **221–206 BC:** Qin kingdom defeated all rivals and established first empire with strong central government; emperor Shi Huangdi built Great Wall of China. **202 BC–AD 220:** Han dynasty expanded empire into central Asia; first overland trade with Europe; art and literature flourished; Buddhism introduced from India. **220–581:** Large-scale rebellion destroyed Han dynasty; empire split into three competing kingdoms; several short-lived dynasties ruled parts of China. **581–618:** Sui dynasty reunified China and repelled Tatar invaders. **618–907:** Tang dynasty enlarged and strengthened the empire; great revival of culture; major rebellion 875–84. **907–60:** 'Five Dynasties and Ten Kingdoms': disintegration of empire amid war and economic decline; development of printing. **960–1279:** Song dynasty reunified China and restored order; civil service examinations introduced; population reached 100 million; Manchurians occupied northern China in 1127. **1279:** Mongols conquered all China, which became part of the vast empire of Kublai Khan, founder of the Yuan dynasty; Venetian traveller Marco Polo visited China 1275–92. **1368:**

China: Provinces

(– = not applicable.)

Province	Alternative transliteration	Capital	Area sq km	Area sq mi	Population (1996 est)
Anhui	Anhwei	Hefei	139,900	54,015	60,700,000
Fujian	Fukien	Fuzhou	123,100	47,528	36,610,000
Gansu	Kansu	Lanzhou	530,000	204,633	24,670,000
Guangdong	Kwantung	Guangzhou	231,400	89,343	69,610,000
Guizhou	Kweichow	Guiyang	174,000	67,181	35,550,000
Hainan		Haikou	34,000	13,127	7,340,000
Hebei	Hopei	Shijiazhuang	202,700	78,262	64,840,000
Heilongjiang	Heilungkiang	Harbin	463,600	178,996	37,280,000
Henan	Honan	Zhengzhou	167,000	64,479	91,720,000
Hubei	Hupei	Wuhan	187,500	72,394	58,250,000
Hunan	–	Changsha	210,500	81,274	64,280,000
Jiangsu	Kiangsu	Nanjing	102,200	39,459	71,100,000
Jiangxi	Kiangsi	Nanchang	164,800	63,629	41,050,000
Jilin	Kirin	Changchun	187,000	72,201	26,100,000
Liaoning	–	Shenyang	151,000	58,301	41,160,000
Qinghai	Tsinghai	Xining	721,000	278,378	4,880,000
Shaanxi	Shensi	Xian	195,800	75,598	35,430,000
Shandong	Shantung	Jinan	153,300	59,189	87,380,000
Shanxi	Shansi	Taiyuan	157,100	60,656	31,090,000
Sichuan	Szechwan	Chengdu	569,000	219,691	114,300,000
Yunnan	–	Kunming	436,200	168,417	40,420,000
Zhejiang	Chekiang	Hangzhou	101,800	39,305	43,430,000
Autonomous Region					
Guangxi Zhuang	Kwangsi Chuang	Nanning	220,400	85,096	45,890,000
Nei Mongol	Inner Mongolia	Hohhot	450,000	173,745	23,070,000
Ningxia Hui	Ninghsia-Hui	Yinchuan	170,000	65,637	5,210,000
Xinjiang Uygur	Sinkiang Uighur	Urumqi	1,646,800	635,829	16,890,000
Xizang	Tibet	Lhasa	1,221,600	471,660	2,440,000
Municipality					
Beijing	Peking	–	17,800	6,873	12,590,000
Shanghai	–	–	5,800	2,239	14,190,000
Tianjin	Tientsin	–	4,000	1,544	9,480,000

Rebellions drove out the Mongols; Ming dynasty expanded empire; architecture flourished in new capital of Beijing; dislike of Mongols led to contempt for all things foreign. **1516:** Portuguese explorers reached Macau; other European traders followed; first Chinese porcelain arrived in Europe 1580. **1644:** Manchurian invasion established the Qing (or Manchu) dynasty; Manchurians assimilated and Chinese trade and culture continued to thrive. **1796–1804:** Anti-Manchu revolt weakened Qing dynasty; population increase in excess of food supplies led to falling living standards and cultural decline. **1839–42:** First Opium War; Britain forced China to cede Hong Kong and open five ports to European trade; Second Opium War extracted further trade concessions 1856–60. **1850–64:** Millions died in Taiping Rebellion; Taipings combined Christian and Chinese beliefs and demanded land reform. **1894–95:** Sino-Japanese War: Chinese driven out of Korea. **1897–98:** Germany, Russia, France, and Britain leased ports in China; conquest by European empires seemed likely. **1898:** Hong Kong was secured by Britain on a 99-year lease. **1900:** Anti-Western Boxer Rebellion crushed by foreign intervention; jealousy between Great Powers prevented partition. **1911:** Revolution broke out; Republic of China proclaimed by Sun Zhong Shan (Sun Yat-sen) of Guomindang (National People's Party). **1912:** Abdication of infant emperor Pu-i; Gen Yuan Shih-K'ai became dictator. **1916:** Power of central government collapsed on death of Yuan Shih-K'ai; northern China dominated by local warlords. **1919:** Beijing students formed 4th May movement to protest at transfer of German possessions in China to Japan. **1921:** Sun Zhong Shan elected president of nominal national government; Chinese Communist Party founded; communists worked with Guomindang to reunite China from 1923. **1925:** Death of Sun Zhong Shan; leadership of Guomindang gradually passed to military commander Jiang Jie Shi (Chiang Kai-shek). **1926–28:** Revolutionary Army of Jiang Jie Shi reunified China; Guomindang broke with communists and tried to suppress them in civil war. **1932:** Japan invaded Manchuria and established puppet state of Manchukuo. **1934–35:** Communists undertook Long March from Jiangxi and Fujian in south to Yan'an in north to escape encirclement by Guomindang. **1937–45:** Japan renewed invasion of China; Chiang Kai-shek received help from USA and Britain from 1941. **1946:** Civil war resumed between Guomindang and communists led by Mao Zedong. **1949:** Victorious communists proclaimed People's Republic of China under Chairman Mao; Guomindang fled to Taiwan. **1950–53:** China intervened heavily in Korean War. **1958:** 'Great Leap Forward': extremist five-year plan to accelerate output severely weakened economy. **1960:** Sino-Soviet split: China accused USSR of betraying communism; USSR withdrew technical advisers; border clashes on Ussuri River in 1969. **1962:** Economic recovery programme under Liu Shaoqi caused divisions between 'rightists' and 'leftists'; brief border war with India. **1966–69:** 'Great Proletarian Cultural Revolution'; leftists overthrew Liu Shaoqi with support of Mao; Red Guards disrupted education, government, and daily life in attempt to enforce revolutionary principles. **1970:** Mao supported efforts of Prime Minister Zhou Enlai to restore order. **1971:** People's Republic of China admitted to United Nations; full diplomatic relations with USA established in 1979. **1976:** Deaths of Zhou Enlai and Mao Zedong led to power struggle between rightists and leftists; Hua Guofeng became leader and arrested leftist 'Gang of Four'. **1977–81:** Rightist Deng Xiaoping emerged as supreme leader; pragmatic economic policies introduced market incentives and encouraged foreign trade. **1987:** Deng Xiaoping retired from Politburo but remained a dominant figure. **1989:** Over 2,000 killed when army crushed prodemocracy student demonstrations in Tiananmen Square, Beijing; international sanctions imposed. **1991:** China and USSR reached agreement on disputed border. **1996:** Reunification with Taiwan declared a priority. **1997:** Deng Xiaoping died aged 92. Border agreement signed with Russia. Hong Kong was returned to Chinese sovereignty. **1998:** Zhu Rongli became new prime minister. The Yangtze in Hubei province flooded, causing widespread devastation. Former Communist leader Chen Xitong sentenced to 16 years' imprisonment. Dissident Xu Wenli jailed for trying to set up an opposition party. **1999:** Jiang Zemin made state visit to USA.

Colombia Republic of

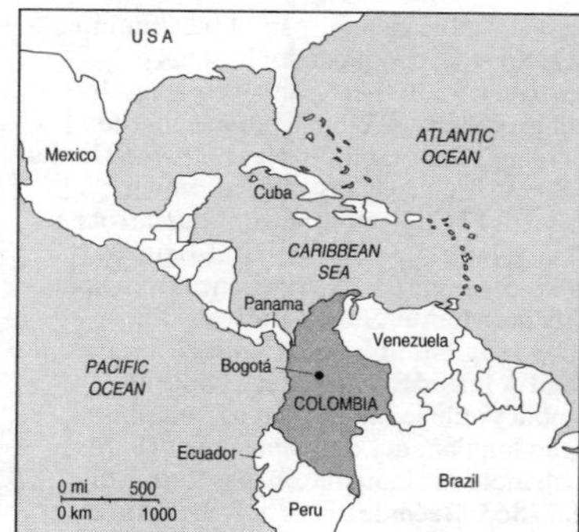

National name: *República de Colombia* **Area:** 1,141,748 sq km/440,828 sq mi **Capital:** Bogotá **Major towns/cities:** Medellín, Cali, Barranquilla, Cartagena, Bucaramanga, Buenaventura **Major ports:** Barranquilla, Cartagena, Buenaventura

Government

Head of state and government: Andres Pastrana from 1998 **Political system:** democracy **Administrative divisions:** 32 departments and one capital district **Political parties:** Liberal Party (PL), centrist; Conservative Party (PSC), right of centre; M-19 Democratic Alliance (ADM-19), left of centre; National Salvation Movement (MSN), right-of-centre coalition grouping **Armed forces:** 146,300 (1997); plus a paramilitary police force of 87,000 **Conscription:** selective conscription for 1–2 years **Death penalty:** abolished in 1910 **Defence spend:** (% GDP) 4.0 (1997) **Education spend:** (% GNP) 4.4 (1996) **Health spend:** (% GDP) 3.0 (1990–95)

Economy and resources

Currency: Colombian peso **GDP:** (US$) 96.4 billion (1997) **Real GDP growth:** (% change on previous year) 2.7 (1997) **GNP (US$):** 86.8 billion (1997) **GNP per capita (PPP):** (US$) 6,720 (1997) **Consumer price inflation:** 18.3% (1998) **Unemployment:** 11.9% (1996) **Foreign debt:** (US$) 28.8 billion (1996) **Major trading partners:** USA, EU countries, Argentina, Brazil, Chile, Mexico, Venezuela, Japan **Resources:** petroleum, natural gas, coal, nickel, emeralds (accounts for about half of world production), gold, manganese, copper, lead, mercury, platinum, limestone, phosphates **Exports:** coffee, petroleum and petroleum products, coal, gold, bananas, cut flowers, cotton, chemicals, textiles, paper. Principal market: USA 37.9% (1997). Illegal trade in cocaine in 1995 it was estimated that approximately $3.5 billion (equivalent to about 4% of GDP) was entering Colombia as the proceeds of drug-trafficking **Imports:** machinery and transport equipment, chemicals, minerals, food, metals. Principal source: USA 41.5% (1997) **Arable land:** 2.3% (1995)

Population and society

Population: 40,803,000 (1998 est) **Population growth rate:** 1.7% (1995–2000); 1.3% (2000–05) **Population density:** (per sq km) 37.1 (1998 est) **Urban population:** (% of total) 74 (1997) **Age distribution:** (% of total population) 0–14 33.2%, 15–64 62.4%, 65+ 4.5% (1998) **Ethnic groups:** main ethnic groups are of mixed Spanish, American Indian, and African descent; Spanish customs and values predominate **Language:** Spanish **Religion:** Roman Catholic **Education:** (compulsory years) 5 **Literacy rate:** 87% (men); 86% (women) (1995 est) **Labour force:** 40% of population: 27% agriculture, 23% industry, 50% services (1990) **Life expectancy:** 68 (men); 74 (women) (1995–2000) **Child mortality rate:** (under 5, per 1,000 live births) 30 (1997) **Physicians:** 1 per 1,105 people (1993 est)

Practical information

Visa requirements: UK: visa not required for a stay of up to 90 days. USA: visa not required for a stay of up to 90 days **Embassy in the UK:** Flat 3A, 3 Hans Crescent, London SW1X 0LN. Tel: (0171) 589 9177; fax: (0171) 581 1829 **British embassy:** Apartado Aéreo 4508, Torre Propaganda Sancho, Calle 98, No. 9–03, Piso 4, Santa Fe de Bogotá DC. Tel: (1) 218 5111; fax: (1) 218 2460 **Chamber of commerce:** Instituto Colombiano de Comercio Exterior, Apartado Aéreo 240193, Calle 28, No. 13-A-15, 5 ° Santa Fe de Bogotá DC. Tel: (1) 283 3284; fax: (1) 281 2560, 283 1953

Chronology

late 15th century: Southern Colombia became part of Inca Empire, whose core lay in Peru. **1522:** Spanish conquistador Pascual de Andagoya reached San Juan River. **1536–38:** Spanish conquest by Jimenez de Quesada overcame powerful Chibcha Indian chiefdom, which had its capital in the uplands at Bogotá and was renowned for its gold crafts; became part of Spanish Viceroyalty of Peru, which covered much of South America. **1717:** Bogotá became capital of new Spanish Viceroyalty of Nueva (New) Granada, which also ruled Ecuador and Venezuela. **1809:** Struggle for independence from Spain began. **1819:** Venezuelan freedom fighter Simón Bolívar, 'The Liberator', who had withdrawn to Colombia 1814, raised a force of 5,000 British mercenaries and defeated Spanish at the battle of Boyaca, establishing Colombia's independence; Gran Colombia formed, also comprising Ecuador, Panama, and Venezuela. **1830:** Became separate state, which included Panama, on dissolution of Republic of Gran Colombia. **1863:** Became major coffee exporter. Federalizing, anti-clerical Liberals came to power, with country divided into nine largely autonomous 'sovereign' states; church disestablished. **1885:** Conservatives came to power, beginning 45 years of political dominance; power was recentralized and church restored to influence. **1899–1903:** Civil war between Liberals and Conservatives, ended with Panama's separation as an independent state. **1930:** Liberals returned to power at the time of the economic depression; social legislation introduced and labour movement encouraged. **1946:** Conservatives returned to power after Liberal vote divided between rival candidates. **1948:** Left-wing mayor of Bogotá assassinated; widespread outcry. **1949:** Start of civil war, 'La Violencia', during which over 250,000 people died. **1957:** Hoping to halt violence, Conservatives and Liberals agreed to form National Front, sharing the presidency. **1970:** National Popular Alliance (ANAPO) formed as left-wing opposition to National Front. **1974:** National Front accord temporarily ended. **1975:** Civil unrest due to disillusionment with government. **1978:** Liberals, under Julio Turbay, revived the accord and began an intensive fight against drug dealers. **1982:** Liberals maintained their control of congress but lost the presidency. Conservative president Belisario Betancur granted guerrillas an amnesty and freed political prisoners. **1984:** Minister of justice assassinated by drug dealers; campaign against them stepped up. **1986:** Virgilio Barco Vargas, Liberal, elected president by record margin. **1989:** Drug cartel assassinated leading presidential candidate; Vargas declared antidrug war; bombing campaign by drug traffickers killed hundreds; police killed José Rodríguez Gacha, one of the most wanted cartel leaders. **1990:** Cesar Gaviria Trujillo elected president. Liberals maintained control of congress. **1991:** New constitution prohibited extradition of Colombians wanted for trial in other countries. Several leading drug traffickers arrested. Many guerrillas abandoned armed struggle, but Colombian Revolutionary Armed Forces (FARC) and National Liberation Army remained active. Liberals won general election. **1993:** Medellín drug-cartel leader Pablo Escobar shot while attempting to avoid arrest. **1994:** Liberals returned to power, with reduced majority. Ernesto Samper Pizano, Liberal, elected president. **1995:** Samper under pressure to resign over corruption allegations; state of emergency declared. Leaders of Cali drug-cartel imprisoned. **1998:** Clashes between army and left-wing guerrillas. Liberal Party secured assembly majority. Andres Pastrama won presidential elections. Peace talks held with rebels.

Comoros Federal Islamic Republic of

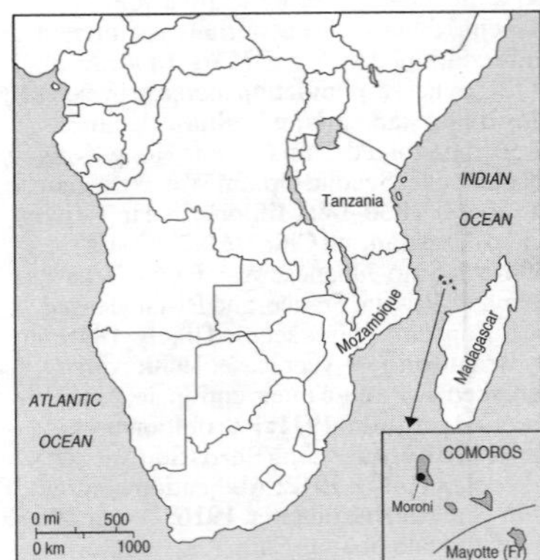

National name: *Jumhurīyat al-Qumur al-Itthādīyah al-Islāmīyah* or *République Fédérale Islamique des Comoros* **Area:** 1,862 sq km/718 sq mi **Capital:** Moroni **Major towns/cities:** Mutsamudu, Domoni, Fomboni, Dzaoudzi

Government

Head of state and government: Azali Assoumani from 1999 **Political system:** transitional **Administrative divisions:** three prefectures (each of the three main islands is a prefecture) **Political parties:** National Union for Democracy in the Comoros (UNDC), Islamic, nationalist; Rally for Democracy and Renewal (RDR), left of centre **Armed forces:** 800 (1995) **Conscription:** military service is voluntary **Death penalty:** retained and used for ordinary crimes **Education spend:** (% GNP) 3.9 (1995) **Health spend:** (% GDP) 3.3 (1990)

Economy and resources

Currency: Comorian franc **GDP:** (US$) 231 million (1996 est) **Real GDP growth:** (% change on previous year) 1.1 (1997) **GNP (US$):** 208 million (1997) **GNP per capita (PPP):** (US$) 1,590 (1997 est) **Consumer price inflation:** 7.5% (1996) **Unemployment:** 16% (1990) **Foreign debt:** (US$) 206 million (1996) **Major trading partners:** France, USA, Bahrain, Kenya, Botswana, Brazil, South Africa **Exports:** vanilla, cloves, ylang-ylang, essences, copra, coffee. Principal market: France 42.9% (1997) **Imports:** rice, petroleum products, transport equipment, meat and dairy products, cement, iron and steel, clothing and footwear. Principal source: France 58.9% (1997) **Arable land:** 35% (1995)

Population and society

Population: 658,000 (1998 est) **Population growth rate:** 2.7% (1995–2025) **Population density:** (per sq km) 251.4 (1998 est) **Urban population:** (% of total) 32 (1997) **Age distribution:** (% of total population) 0–14 42.6%, 15–64 54.5%, 65+ 2.9% (1998) **Ethnic groups:** population of mixed origin, with Africans, Arabs, and Malaysians predominating; the principal ethnic group is the Antalaotra **Language:** Arabic (official), Comorian (Swahili and Arabic dialect), Makua, French **Religion:** Muslim; Islam is the state religion **Education:** (compulsory years) 9 **Literacy rate:** 64% (men); 50% (women) (1995 est) **Labour force:** 44% of population: 77% agriculture, 9% industry, 13% services (1990) **Life expectancy:** 57 (men); 58 (women) (1995–2000) **Child mortality rate:** (under 5, per 1,000 live births) 109 (1997) **Physicians:** 1 per 7,500 people (1990)

Practical information

Visa requirements: UK: visa required. USA: visa required **Embassy for the UK:** 20 rue Marbeau, 75016 Paris, France. Tel: (1) 4067 9054; fax: (1) 4067 7296 **British embassy:** British Consulate, Henri Fraise et Fils 38, Co Océan Indien, PO Box 986, Moroni. Tel: (269) 733 182; fax: (269) 733 182. (All staff based in Madagascar.) **Chamber of commerce:** Chambre de Commerce, d'Industrie et d'Agriculture, BP 763, Moroni. Tel: (269) 610 426

Chronology

5th century AD: First settled by Malay-Polynesian immigrants. **7th century:** Converted to Islam by Arab seafarers and fell under the rule of local sultans. **late 16th century:** First visited by European navigators. **1886:** Moheli island in south became a French protectorate. **1904:** Slave trade abolished, ending influx of Africans. **1912:** Grande Comore and Anjouan, the main islands, joined Moheli to become a French colony, which was attached to Madagascar from 1914. **1947:** Became a French Overseas Territory separate from Madagascar. **1961:** Internal self-government achieved. **1975:** Independence achieved from France, but island of Mayotte to the southeast voted to remain part of France. Joined the United Nations. **1976:** President Ahmed Abdallah overthrown in a coup by Ali Soilih; relations deteriorated with France as a Maoist-Islamic socialist programme was pursued. **1978:** Soilih killed by French mercenaries led by Bob Denard. Federal Islamic republic proclaimed, with exiled Abdallah restored as president; diplomatic relations re-established with France. **1979:** The Comoros became a one-party state; powers of the federal government increased. **1989:** Abdallah killed by French mercenaries who, under French and South African pressure, turned authority over to French administration; Said Muhammad Djohar became president in a multiparty democracy. **1990–92:** Antigovernment coups foiled. **1993:** Djohar's supporters won overall majority in assembly elections. **1995:** Djohar overthrown in coup led by Col Denard, who was persuaded to withdraw by French troops. **1996:** Djohar allowed to return from exile in a nonpolitical capacity and Muhammad Taki Abdoulkarim elected president. National Rally for Development (RND) virtually unopposed in assembly elections. Ahmed Abdou appointed prime minister. **1997:** Secessionist rebels took control of the island of Anjouan. **1999:** Government overthrown by army coup, after government had granted greater autonomy to the islands of Anjouan and Moheli.

Congo, Democratic Republic of (formerly Zaire)

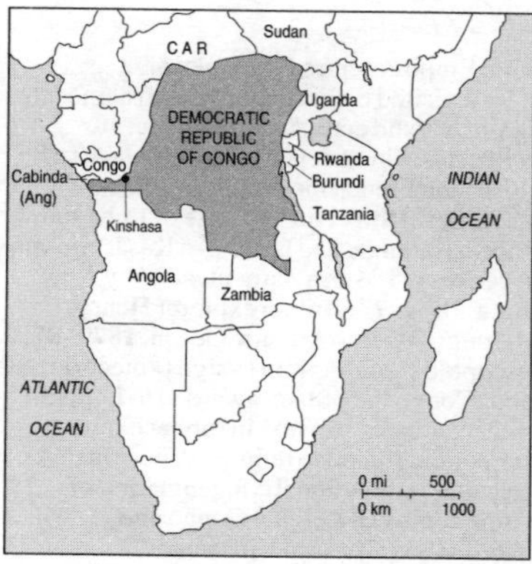

National name: *République Démocratique du Congo* **Area:** 2,344,900 sq km/905,366 sq mi **Capital:** Kinshasa **Major towns/cities:** Lubumbashi, Kananga, Mbuji-Mayi, Kisangani, Bukavu, Kikwit, Matadi **Major ports:** Matadi, Kalemie

Government

Head of state and government: Laurent Kabila from 1997 **Political system:** transitional **Administrative divisions:** ten regions **Political parties:** Popular Movement of the Revolution (MPR), African socialist; Democratic Forces of Congo–Kinshasa (formerly Sacred Union, an alliance of some 130 opposition groups), moderate, centrist; Union for Democracy and Social Progress (UPDS), left of centre; Congolese National Movement–Lumumba (MNC), left of centre **Armed forces:** 40,000 (1997); plus paramilitary forces of 37,000 **Conscription:** military service is compulsory **Death penalty:** retained and used for ordinary crimes **Defence spend:** (% GDP) 5.3 (1997) **Education spend:** (% GNP) 0.9 (1990) **Health spend:** (% GDP) 0.2 (1990–95)

Economy and resources

Currency: zaïre **GDP:** (US$) 5.4 billion (1996 est) **Real GDP growth:** (% change on previous year) 1.5 (1997) **GNP (US$):** 5.1 billion (1997) **GNP per capita (PPP):** (US$) 790 (1997 est) **Consumer price inflation:** 659% (1996) **Unemployment:** 35% (1993 est) **Foreign debt:** (US$) 12.83 billion (1996) **Major trading partners:** Belgium – Luxembourg, USA, France, UK, Germany, South Africa **Resources:** petroleum, copper, cobalt (65% of world's reserves), manganese, zinc, tin, uranium, silver, gold, diamonds (one of the world's largest producers of industrial diamonds) **Exports:** mineral products (mainly copper, cobalt, industrial diamonds, and petroleum), agricultural products (chiefly coffee). Principal market: Belgium – Luxembourg 42.7% (1997) **Imports:** manufactured goods, food and live animals, machinery and transport equipment, chemicals, mineral fuels and lubricants. Principal source: South Africa 21.3% (1997) **Arable land:** 3.2% (1995)

Population and society

Population: 49,139,000 (1998 est) **Population growth rate:** 2.6% (1995–2000) **Population density:** (per sq km) 21.6 (1998 est) **Urban population:** (% of total) 30 (1997) **Age distribution:** (% of total population) 0–14 48.2%, 15–64 49.2%, 65+ 2.6% (1998) **Ethnic groups:** almost entirely of African descent, distributed among over 200 ethnic groups, the most numerous being the Kongo, Luba, Lunda, Mongo, and Zande **Language:** French (official); Swahili, Lingala, Kikongo, and Tshiluba are recognized as national languages; over 200 other languages **Religion:** Roman Catholic, Protestant, Kimbanguist; also half a million Muslims **Education:** (compulsory years) 6 **Literacy rate:** 84% (men); 61% (women) (1995 est) **Labour force:** 43% of population: 68% agriculture, 13% industry, 19% services (1990) **Life expectancy:** 51 (men); 55 (women) (1995–2000) **Child mortality rate:** (under 5, per 1,000 live births) 125 (1997) **Physicians:** 1 per 15,150 people (1993 est)

Practical information

Visa requirements: UK: visa required. USA: visa required **Embassy in the UK:** 26 Chesham Place, London SW1X 8HH. Tel: (0171) 235 6137; fax: (0171) 235 9048 **British embassy:** BP 8049, avenue des Trois Z, Kinshasa-Gombe. Tel: (12) 34775/8 **Chamber of**

commerce: Chambre de Commerce, d'Industrie et d'Agriculture, BP 7247, 10 avenue des Aviateurs, Kinshasa. Tel: (12) 22286; telex: 21071

Chronology

13th century: Rise of Kongo Empire, centred on banks of Zaïre/Congo River. **1483:** First visited by Portuguese, who named the area Zaire (from Zadi, 'big water') and converted local rulers to Christianity. **16th–17th centuries:** Great development of slave trade by Portuguese, Dutch, British, and French merchants, initially supplied by Kongo intermediaries. **18th century:** Rise of Luba state, in southern copper belt of north Katanga, and Lunda, in Kasai region in central south. **mid-19th century:** Eastern Zaire invaded by Arab slave traders from East Africa. **1874–77:** British explorer Henry Morton Stanley navigated Congo River to Atlantic Ocean. **1879–87:** Stanley engaged by King Leopold II of Belgium to sign protection treaties with local chiefs and 'Congo Free State' awarded to Leopold by 1884–85 Berlin Conference; great expansion in rubber export, using forced labour. **1908:** Leopold forced to relinquish personal control of Congo Free State, after international condemnation of human-rights abuses. Became colony of Belgian Congo and important exporter of minerals. **1959:** Riots in Kinshasa (Leopoldville) persuaded Belgium to decolonize rapidly. **1960:** Independence achieved as Republic of the Congo. Civil war broke out between central government based in Kinshasa (Leopoldville) with Joseph Kasavubu as president, and rich mining province of Katanga. **1961:** Former prime minister Patrice Lumumba murdered in Katanga; fighting between mercenaries engaged by Katanga secessionist leader Moise Tshombe, and United Nations troops; Kasai and Kivu provinces also sought (briefly) to secede. **1963:** Katanga secessionist war ended; Tshombe forced into exile. **1964:** Tshombe returned from exile to become prime minister; pro-Marxist groups took control of eastern Zaire. **1965:** Western-backed Col Sese Seko Mobutu seized power in coup, ousting Kasavubu and Tshombe. **1971:** Country renamed Republic of Zaire, with Mobutu as president as *authenticité* (Africanization) policy launched. **1972:** Mobutu's Popular Movement of the Revolution (MPR) became only legal political party. Katanga province renamed Shaba. **1974:** Foreign-owned businesses and plantations seized by Mobutu and given to his political allies. **1977:** Original owners of confiscated properties invited back. Zairean guerrillas, chiefly Lundas, invaded Shaba province from Angola, but were repulsed by Moroccan, French, and Belgian paratroopers. **1980s:** International creditors forced launch of series of austerity programmes, after level of foreign indebtedness had mounted with collapse in world copper prices. **1991:** After antigovernment riots, Mobutu agreed to end ban on multiparty politics and share power with opposition; Etienne Tshisekedi appointed premier, but soon dismissed. **1992:** Tshisekedi reinstated against Mobutu's wishes after renewed rioting. **1993:** Rival pro- and anti-Mobutu governments created. **1994:** Kengo Wa Dondo elected prime minister by interim parliament, with Mobutu's agreement. Influx of Rwandan refugees. **1995:** Secessionist activity in Shaba and Kasai provinces and interethnic warfare in Kivu, adjoining Rwanda in the east. **1996:** Thousands of refugees allowed to return to Rwanda. **1997:** Mobutu ousted by rebel forces of Laurent Kabila, who declared himself president and renamed Zaire the Democratic Republic of Congo. Fighting between army factions. **1998:** Rebellion by Tutsi-led forces, backed by Rwanda and Uganda, against President Kabila; government troops aided by Angola and Zimbabwe in putting down the rebellion. Constituent assembly appointed prior to general election. Peace talks failed.

Congo, Republic of

National name: *République du Congo* **Area:** 342,000 sq km/132,046 sq mi **Capital:** Brazzaville **Major towns/cities:** Pool, Pointe-Noire, Nkayi, Loubomo, Bouenza, Cuvette, Niari, Plateaux **Major ports:** Pointe-Noire

Government

Head of state: Denis Sassou-Nguessou from 1997 **Head of government:** Charles David Ganao from 1996 **Political system:** emergent democracy **Administrative divisions:** nine regions and one capital district **Political parties:** Pan-African Union for Social Democracy (UPADS), moderate, left of centre; Congolese Movement for Democracy and Integral Development (MCDDI), moderate, left of centre; Congolese Labour Party (PCT), left wing **Armed forces:** 10,000 (1997); plus a paramilitary force of 5,000 **Conscription:** national service is voluntary **Death penalty:** retains the death penalty for ordinary crimes but can be considered abolitionist in practice (last execution 1982) **Defence spend:** (% GDP) 2.5 (1997) **Education spend:** (% GNP) 5.9 (1995) **Health spend:** (% GDP) 1.8 (1990–95)

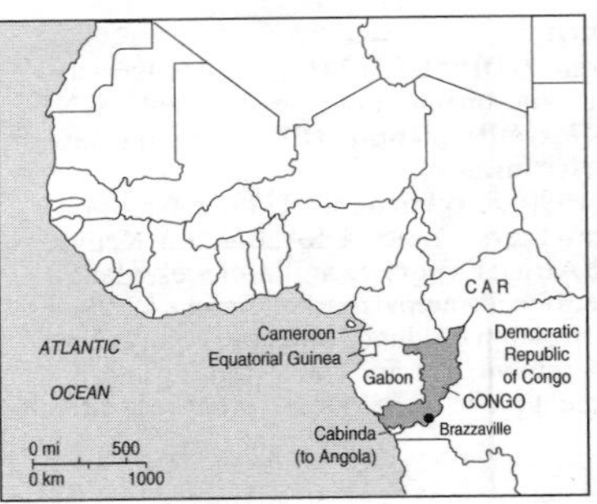

Economy and resources

Currency: franc CFA **GDP:** (US$) 2.29 billion (1997) **Real GDP growth:** (% change on previous year) 1.1 (1997) **GNP (US$):** 1.8 billion (1997) **GNP per capita (PPP):** (US$) 1,380 (1997) **Consumer price inflation:** 7% (1996) **Foreign debt:** (US$) 5.24 billion (1996) **Major trading partners:** France, Belgium, Luxembourg, USA, Italy, Spain, China **Resources:** petroleum, natural gas, lead, zinc, gold, copper, phosphate, iron ore, potash, bauxite **Exports:** petroleum and petroleum products, saw logs and veneer logs, veneer sheets. Principal market: Belgium – Luxembourg 22.7% (1996) **Imports:** machinery, chemical products, iron and steel, transport equipment, foodstuffs. Principal source: France 68.7% (1996) **Arable land:** 0.4% (1995)

Population and society

Population: 2,785,000 (1998 est) **Population growth rate:** 2.8% (1995–2000); 2.6% (2000–05) **Population density:** (per sq km) 7.8 (1998 est) **Urban population:** (% of total) 60 (1997) **Age distribution:** (% of total population) 0–14 42.6%, 15–64 54.0%, 65+ 3.4% (1998) **Ethnic groups:** predominantly Bantu; population comprises 15 main ethnic groups and 75 tribes. The Kongo, or Bakongo, account for about 45% of the population, then come the Bateke, or Teke, at about 20%, and then the Mboshi, or Boubangui, about 16% **Language:** French (official); Kongo languages; local patois Monokutuba and Lingala **Religion:** animist, Christian, Muslim **Education:** (compulsory years) 10 **Literacy rate:** 70% (men); 44% (women) (1995 est) **Labour force:** 42% of population: 49% agriculture, 15% industry, 37% services (1990) **Life expectancy:** 49 (men); 53 (women) (1995–2000) **Child mortality rate:** (under 5, per 1,000 live births) 129 (1997) **Physicians:** 1 per 3,713 people (1993 est)

Practical information

Visa requirements: UK: visa required. USA: visa required **Embassy in the UK:** Honorary Consulate of the Republic of the Congo, Alliance House, 12 Caxton Street, London SW1H 0QS. Tel: (0171) 222 7575; fax: (0171) 233 2087 **British embassy:** British Consulate, Côte de l'Hotel Méridien, rue Lyantey 26, Brazzaville. Tel: (242) 838 527; fax: (242) 837 257 (The embassy closed on 26 July 1991; diplomatic accreditation has been transferred to the British embassy in Kinshasa on a nonresident basis.) **Chamber of commerce:** Chambre Nationale de Commerce, BP 1438, Brazzaville. Tel: (242) 832 956

Chronology

late 15th century: First visited by Portuguese explorers, at which time the Bakongo (a six-state confederation centred south of the Congo River in Angola) and Bateke, both Bantu groups, were the

chief kingdoms. **16th century:** Portuguese, in collaboration with coastal peoples, exported slaves from the interior to plantations in Brazil and São Tomé; missionaries spread Roman Catholicism. **1880:** French explorer Pierre Savorgnan de Brazza established French claims to coastal region, with the makoko (king) of the Bateke accepting French protection. **1905:** International outrage at revelations of the brutalities of forced labour, which decimated the population, as ivory and rubber resources were ruthlessly exploited by private concessionaries. **1910:** As Moyen-Congo, became part of French Equatorial Africa, which also comprised Gabon and the Central African Republic, with the capital at Brazzaville. **1920s:** More than 17,000 were killed as forced labour used to build the Congo-Ocean railroad; first Bakongo political organization founded. **1940–44:** Supported the 'Free French' anti-Nazi resistance cause during World War II, Brazzaville serving as capital for Gen Charles de Gaulle's forces. **1946:** Became autonomous, with a territorial assembly and representation in French parliament. **1960:** Achieved independence from France, with Abbé Fulbert Youlou, a moderate Catholic Bakongo priest, as the first president. **1963:** Youlou forced to resign after labour unrest. Alphonse Massamba-Débat became president with Pascal Lissouba as prime minister, and a single-party state was established under the socialist National Revolutionary Movement (MNR). **1968:** Military coup, led by Capt Marien Ngouabi, ousted Massamba-Débat. **1970:** A Marxist People's Republic declared, with Ngouabi's PCT the only legal party. **1977:** Ngouabi assassinated in a plot by Massamba-Débat, who was executed; Col Joachim Yhombi-Opango became president. **1979:** Yhombi-Opango handed over the presidency to the PCT, who chose Col Denis Sassou-Nguessou as his successor. **early 1980s:** Petroleum production increased fivefold. **1990:** With the collapse of Eastern European communism, the PCT abandoned Marxist-Leninism and promised multiparty politics and market-centred reforms in an economy crippled by foreign debt. **1992:** Multiparty elections gave the coalition dominated by the Pan-African Union for Social Democracy (UPADS) an assembly majority, with Pascal Lissouba elected president. **1993:** Yhombi-Opango appointed prime minister; unrest after opposition disputed election results. **1994:** International panel appointed to investigate election results; UPADS-dominated coalition declared winner. **1995:** New broad-based government formed, including opposition groups; market-centred economic reforms, including privatization. **1996:** Charles David Ganao appointed prime minister. **1997:** Violence between factions continued despite unity government. Sassou-Nguesso took over presidency.

Costa Rica Republic of

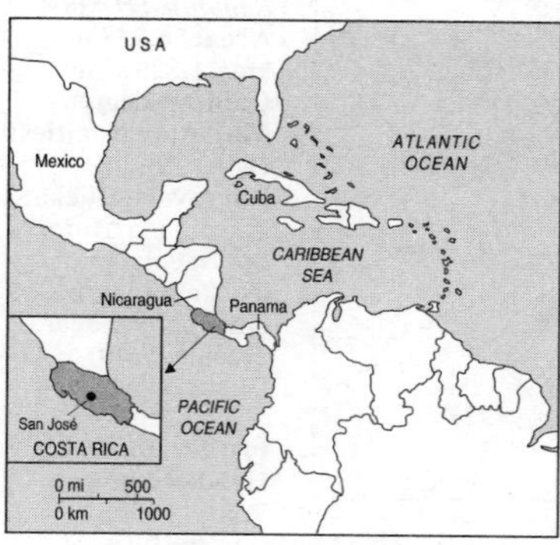

National name: *República de Costa Rica* **Area:** 51,100 sq km/19,729 sq mi **Capital:** San José **Major towns/cities:** Alajuela, Cartago, Limón, Puntarenas **Major ports:** Limón, Puntarenas

Government

Head of state and government: Miguel Angel Rodriguez Echeverria, from 1998 **Political system:** liberal democracy **Administrative divisions:** seven provinces **Political parties:** National Liberation Party (PLN), left of centre; Christian Socialist Unity Party (PUSC), centrist coalition; ten minor parties **Armed forces:** army abolished in 1948; 4,300 civil guards and 3,200 rural guards **Death penalty:** abolished in 1877 **Defence spend:** (% GDP) 0.7 (1997) **Education spend:** (% GNP) 5.3 (1996) **Health spend:** (% GDP) 6.3 (1990–95)

Economy and resources

Currency: colón **GDP:** (US$) 9.35 billion (1997) **Real GDP growth:** (% change on previous year) 2.3 (1997) **GNP (US$):** 9.3 billion (1997) **GNP per capita (PPP):** (US$) 6,410 (1997) **Consumer price inflation:** 15% (1998) **Unemployment:** 5.2% (1995) **Foreign debt:** (US$) 3.45 billion (1996) **Major trading partners:** USA, Japan, Venezuela, Germany, Italy, Guatemala **Resources:** gold, salt, hydro power **Exports:** bananas, coffee, sugar, cocoa, textiles, seafood, meat, tropical fruit. Principal market: USA 44.6% (1997) **Imports:** raw materials for industry and agriculture, consumer goods, machinery and transport equipment, construction materials. Principal source: USA 42.1% (1997) **Arable land:** 5.6% (1995)

Population and society

Population: 3,841,000 (1998 est) **Population growth rate:** 2.1% (1995–2000); 1.8% (2000–05) **Population density:** (per sq km) 71.2 (1998 est) **Urban population:** (% of total) 51 (1997) **Age distribution:** (% of total population) 0–14 33.6%, 15–64 61.4%, 65+ 5.0% (1998) **Ethnic groups:** about 97% of the population is of European descent, mostly Spanish, and about 2% is of African origin **Language:** Spanish (official) **Religion:** Roman Catholic 90% **Education:** (compulsory years) 9 **Literacy rate:** 93% (men); 93% (women) (1995 est) **Labour force:** 38% of population: 26% agriculture, 27% industry, 47% services (1990) **Life expectancy:** 75 (men); 79 (women) (1995–2000) **Child mortality rate:** (under 5, per 1,000 live births) 14 (1997) **Physicians:** 1 per 979 people (1995)

Practical information

Visa requirements: UK: visa not required. USA: visa not required **Embassy in the UK:** Embassy and Consulate, Flat 1, 14 Lancaster Gate, London W2 3LH. Tel: (0171) 706 8844; fax: (0171) 706 8655 **British embassy:** Apartado 815, 11th Floor, Edificio Centro Colón, 1007 San José. Tel (506) 221 5566; fax: (506) 233 9938 **Chamber of commerce:** Cámara de Comercio de Costa Rica, Apartado 1114, Urbanización Tournón, 1000 San José. Tel: (506) 221 0005; fax: (506) 233 7091

Chronology

1502: Visited by Christopher Columbus, who named the area Costa Rica (the rich coast), observing the gold decorations worn by the American Indian Guaymi. **1506:** Colonized by Spain, but fierce guerrilla resistance was mounted by the indigenous population, although many later died from exposure to European diseases. **18th century:** Settlements began to be established in the fertile central highlands, including San José and Alajuela. **1808:** Coffee was introduced from Cuba and soon became the staple crop. **1821:** Independence achieved from Spain, and was joined initially with Mexico. **1824:** Became part of United Provinces (Federation) of Central America, also embracing El Salvador, Guatemala, Honduras, and Nicaragua. **1838:** Became fully independent when it seceded from the Federation. **1849–59:** Under presidency of Juan Rafuel Mora. **1870–82:** Period of military dictatorship. **later 19th century:** Immigration by Europeans to run and work small coffee farms. **1917–19:** Brief dictatorship by Frederico Tinoco. **1940–44:** Liberal reforms, including recognition of workers' rights and minimum wages, introduced by President Rafael Angel Calderón Guradia, founder of the United Christian Socialist Party (PUSC). **1948:** Brief civil war following a disputed presidential election. **1949:** New constitution adopted, giving women and blacks the vote. National army abolished and replaced by civil guard. José Figueres Ferrer, cofounder of the PLN, elected president; he embarked on ambitious socialist programme, nationalizing the banks and introducing a social security system. **1958–73:** Mainly conservative administrations. **1974:** PLN regained the presidency under Daniel Oduber and returned to socialist policies. **1978:** Rodrigo Carazo, conservative, elected president. Sharp deterioration in the state of the economy. **1982:** Luis Alberto Monge (PLN) elected president. Harsh austerity programme introduced. Pressure from the USA to abandon neutral stance and condemn Sandinista regime in Nicaragua. **1985:** Following border clashes with Nicaraguan Sandinista forces, a US-trained antiguerrilla guard formed. **1986:** Oscar Arias Sanchez (PLN) won the presidency on a neutralist platform. **1987:** Arias won Nobel Prize for Peace for devising a Central American peace plan signed by leaders of Nicaragua, El Salvador,

Guatemala, and Honduras. **1990:** Rafael Calderón of the centrist PUSC elected president as economy deteriorated. **1994:** José Maria Figueres Olsen (PLN), son of José Figueres Ferrer, elected president. **1998:** Miguel Angel Rodriguez (PUSC) elected president.

Côte d'Ivoire Republic of

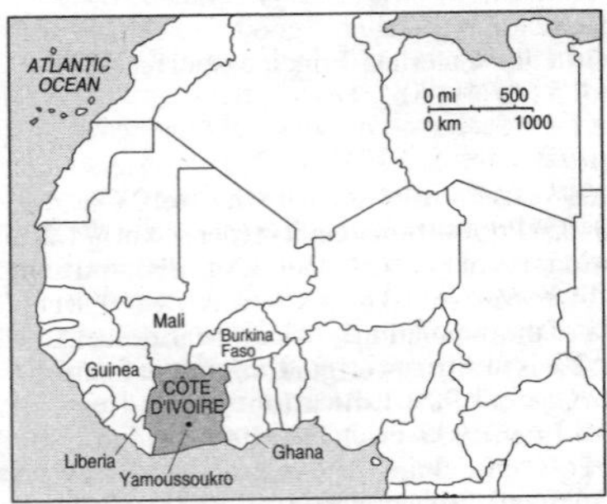

National name: *République de la Côte d'Ivoire* **Area:** 322,463 sq km/ 124,502 sq mi **Capital:** Yamoussoukro **Major towns/cities:** Abidjan, Bouaké, Daloa, Man, Korhogo **Major ports:** Abidjan, San Pedro

Government

Head of state: Henri Konan Bedie from 1993 **Head of government:** Kablan Daniel Duncan from 1993 **Political system:** emergent democracy **Administrative divisions:** 10 regions, comprising 50 departments **Political parties:** Democratic Party of Côte d'Ivoire (PDCI), nationalist, free enterprise; Rally of Republicans (RDR), nationalist; Ivorian Popular Front (FPI), left of centre; Ivorian Labour Party (PIT), left of centre **Armed forces:** 8,400 (1997); plus paramilitary forces numbering 7,000 **Conscription:** selective conscription for six months **Death penalty:** retains the death penalty for ordinary crimes but can be considered abolitionist in practice **Defence spend:** (% GDP) 0.9 (1997) **Education spend:** (% GNP) 5 (1996) **Health spend:** (% GDP) 1.4 (1990–95)

Economy and resources

Currency: franc CFA **GDP:** (US$) 10.25 billion (1997) **Real GDP growth:** (% change on previous year) 6.0 (1997) **GNP (US$):** 10.2 billion (1997) **GNP per capita (PPP):** (US$) 1,640 (1997) **Consumer price inflation:** 3.5% (1998) **Unemployment:** 20% (1992 est) **Foreign debt:** (US$) 19.45 billion (1996) **Major trading partners:** France, Nigeria, Germany, the Netherlands, Italy, USA **Resources:** petroleum, natural gas, diamonds, gold, nickel, reserves of manganese, iron ore, bauxite **Exports:** cocoa beans and products, petroleum products, timber, coffee, cotton, tinned tuna. Principal market: Netherlands 16.6% (1997) **Imports:** crude petroleum, machinery and vehicles, pharmaceuticals, fresh fish, plastics, cereals. Principal source: France 28.5% (1997) **Arable land:** 9.1% (1995)

Population and society

Population: 14,292,000 (1998 est) **Population growth rate:** 2.0% (1995–2000) **Population density:** (per sq km) 48.6 (1998 est) **Urban population:** (% of total) 45 (1997) **Age distribution:** (% of total population) 0–14 46.7%, 15–64 51.1%, 65+ 2.2% (1998) **Ethnic groups:** no single dominant ethnic group; main groups include the Agni, Baoule, Krou, Senoufou, and Mandingo. There are about 2 million Africans who have settled from neighbouring countries, particularly Burkina Faso. Europeans number about 70,000 **Language:** French (official); over 60 local languages **Religion:** animist, Muslim (mainly in north), Christian (mainly Roman Catholic in south) **Education:** (compulsory years) 6 **Literacy rate:** 67% (men); 40% (women) (1995 est) **Labour force:** 37% of population: 60% agriculture, 10% industry, 30% services (1990) **Life expectancy:** 50 (men); 52 (women) (1995–2000) **Child mortality rate:** (under 5, per 1,000 live births) 128 (1997) **Physicians:** 1 per 18,000 people (1994 est)

Practical information

Visa requirements: UK: visa required. USA: visa not required for a stay of less than 90 days **Embassy in the UK:** 2 Upper Belgrave Street, London SW1X 8BJ. Tel: (0171) 235 6991; fax: (0171) 259 5439 **British embassy:** 3rd Floor, Immeuble 'Les Harmonies', Angle boulevard Carde et avenue Dr Jamot, Plateau, Abidjan. Tel: (225) 226850/1/2; fax: (225) 223 221 **Chamber of commerce:** Chambre de Commerce et d'Industrie de Côte d'Ivoire, 01 BP 1399, 6 avenue Joseph Anoma, Abidjan 01. Tel: (225) 331 600; fax: (225) 323 946

Chronology

1460s: Portuguese navigators arrived. **16th century:** Ivory export trade developed by Europeans and slave trade, though to a lesser extent than neighbouring areas; Krou people migrated from Liberia to the west and Senoufo and Lubi from the north. **late 17th century:** French coastal trading posts established at Assini and Grand Bassam. **18th–19th centuries:** Akan peoples, including the Baoulé, immigrated from the east and Malinke from the northwest. **1840s:** French began to conclude commercial treaties with local rulers. **1893:** Colony of Côte d'Ivoire created by French, after war with Mandinkas; Baoulé resistance continued until 1917. **1904:** Became part of French West Africa; cocoa production encouraged. **1940–42:** Under pro-Nazi French Vichy regime. **1946:** Became overseas territory in French Union, with own territorial assembly and representation in French parliament: Felix Houphoüet-Boigny, a Western-educated Baoulé chief who had formed the Democratic Party (PDCI) to campaign for autonomy, was elected to the French assembly. **1947:** A French-controlled area to the north, which had been added to Côte d'Ivoire in 1932, separated to create new state of Upper Volta (now Burkina Faso). **1950–54:** Port of Abidjan constructed. **1958:** Achieved internal self-government. **1960:** Independence secured, with Houphouêt-Boigny as president of a one-party state. **1960s–1980s:** Political stability, close links maintained with France and economic expansion of 10% per annum, as the country became one of the world's largest coffee producers. **1986:** Name changed officially from Ivory Coast to Côte d'Ivoire. **1987–93:** Per capita incomes fell by 25% owing to an austerity programme promoted by the International Monetary Fund. **1990:** Strikes and student unrest. Houphoüet-Boigny re-elected in a contested presidential election, as multiparty politics re-established. **1993:** Houphouêt-Boigny died and was succeeded by parliamentary speaker and Baoulé Henri Konan Bedie. **1995:** Bedie and PDCI re-elected in contest boycotted by opposition.

Croatia Republic of

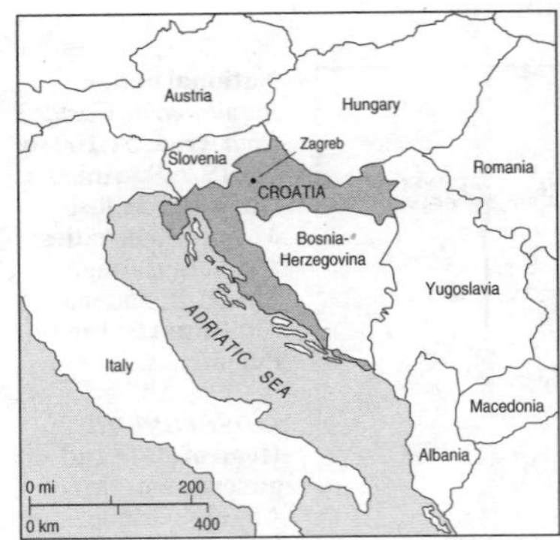

National name: *Republika Hrvatska* **Area:** 56,538 sq km/21,829 sq mi **Capital:** Zagreb **Major towns/cities:** Osijek, Split, Dubrovnik, Rijeka, Zadar, Pula **Major ports:** chief port: Rijeka (Fiume); other ports: Zadar, Sibenik, Split, Dubrovnik

Government

Head of state: Franjo Tudjman from 1990 **Head of government:** Zlatko Matesa from 1995 **Political system:** emergent democracy **Administrative divisions:** 21 counties **Political parties:** Croatian Democratic Union (CDU), Christian Democrat, right of centre, nationalist; Croatian Social-Liberal Party (CSLP), centrist; Social Democratic Party of Change (SDP), reform socialist; Croatian Party of Rights (HSP), Croat-oriented, ultranationalist; Croatian Peasant Party (HSS), rural-based; Serbian National Party (SNS), Serb-oriented **Armed forces:** 58,000 (1997); plus 40,000 in

paramilitary forces **Conscription:** compulsory for ten months **Death penalty:** abolished in 1990 **Defence spend:** (% GDP) 5.7 (1997) **Education spend:** (% GDP) 5.3 (1995) **Health spend:** (% GDP) 8.5 (1990–95)

Economy and resources

Currency: kuna **GDP:** (US$) 19.1 billion (1996) **Real GDP growth:** (% change on previous year) 5.0 (1997) **GNP (US$):** 20.7 billion (1997) **GNP per capita (PPP):** (US$) 4,980 (1997 est) **Consumer price inflation:** 4.3% (1998) **Unemployment:** 15.9% (1996) **Foreign debt:** (US$) 4.7 billion (1996) **Major trading partners:** Germany, Italy, Slovenia, Austria, Iran, former USSR, Bosnia-Herzegovina **Resources:** petroleum, natural gas, coal, lignite, bauxite, iron ore, salt **Exports:** machinery and transport equipment, chemicals, foodstuffs, miscellaneous manufactured items (mainly clothing). Principal market: Italy 17.7% (1998) **Imports:** machinery and transport equipment, basic manufactures, mineral fuels, miscellaneous manufactured articles. Principal source: Germany 19.3% (1998) **Arable land:** 20% (1995)

Population and society

Population: 4,481,000 (1998 est) **Population growth rate:** –0.1% (1995–2000); –0.1% (2000–05) **Population density:** (per sq km) 82.6 (1998 est) **Urban population:** (% of total) 57 (1997) **Age distribution:** (% of total population) 0–14 17.1%, 15–64 68.2%, 65+ 14.7% (1998) **Ethnic groups:** in 1991, 77% of the population were ethnic Croats, 12% were ethnic Serbs, and 1% were Slovenes. The civil war that began in 1992 displaced more than 300,000 Croats from Serbian enclaves within the republic, and created some 500,000 refugees from Bosnia in the republic. Serbs are most thickly settled in areas bordering Bosnia-Herzegovina, and in Slavonia, although more than 150,000 fled from Krajina to Bosnia-Herzegovina and Serbia following the region's recapture by the Croatian army in August 1995. **Language:** Croatian variant of Serbo-Croatian (official); Serbian variant of Serbo-Croatian also widely spoken, particularly in border areas in east **Religion:** Roman Catholic (Croats); Orthodox Christian (Serbs) **Education:** (compulsory years) 8 **Literacy rate:** 97% (men); 97% (women) (1995 est) **Labour force:** 5.3% agriculture, 59.4% industry, 35.3% services (1992) **Life expectancy:** 68 (men); 77 (women) (1995–2000) **Child mortality rate:** (per 1,000 live births) 16 (1997) **Physicians:** 1 per 518 people (1993 est)

Practical information

Visa requirements: UK: visa not required. USA: visa required **Embassy in the UK:** 18–21 Jermyn Street, London SW1Y 6HP. Tel: (0171) 434 2946; fax: (0171) 434 2953 **British embassy:** PO Box 454, 2nd Floor, Astra Tower, Tratinska, 4100 Zagreb. Tel: (1) 334 245; fax: (1) 338 893 **Chamber of commerce:** Croatian Chamber of Commerce, Trg. Ruzveltov 1, 41000 Zagreb. Tel: (1) 453 422; fax: (1) 448 618

Chronology

early centuries AD: Part of Roman region of Pannonia. **AD 395:** On division of Roman Empire, stayed in western half, along with Slovenia and Bosnia. **7th century:** Settled by Carpathian Croats, from northeast; Christianity adopted. **924:** Formed by Tomislav into independent kingdom, which incorporated Bosnia from 10th century. **12th–19th centuries:** Enjoyed autonomy under Hungarian crown, following dynastic union in 1102. **1526–1699:** Slavonia, in east, held by Ottoman Turks, while Serbs were invited by Austria to settle along the border with Ottoman-ruled Bosnia, in Vojna Krajina (military frontier). **1797–1815:** Dalmatia, in west, ruled by France. **19th century:** Part of Austro-Hungarian Habsburg Empire. **1918:** On dissolution of Habsburg Empire, joined Serbia, Slovenia, and Montenegro in 'Kingdom of Serbs, Croats, and Slovenes', under Serbian Karageorgevic dynasty. **1929:** The Kingdom became Yugoslavia. Croatia continued its campaign for autonomy. **1930s:** Ustasa, a Croat terrorist organization, began a campaign against dominance of Yugoslavia by the non-Catholic Serbs. **1941–44:** Following German invasion, a 'Greater Croatia' Nazi puppet state, including most of Bosnia and western Serbia, formed under Ustasa leader, Ante Pavelic; more than half a million Serbs, Jews, and members of the Romany community were massacred in extermination camps. **1945:** Became constituent republic of Yugoslavia Socialist Federation after communist partisans, led by Croat Marshal Tito, overthrew Pavelic. **1970s:** Separatist demands resurfaced, provoking a crackdown. **late 1980s:** Spiralling inflation and a deterioration in living standards sparked industrial unrest and a rise in nationalist sentiment, which affected the local communist party. **1989:** Formation of opposition parties permitted. **1990:** Communists defeated by conservative nationalist CDU led by ex-Partisan Franjo Tudjman in first free election since 1938. Sovereignty declared. **1991:** Serb-dominated region of Krajina in southwest announced secession from Croatia. Croatia declared independence, leading to military conflict with Serbia, and civil war ensued. **1992:** United Nations (UN) peace accord accepted; independence recognized by European Community and USA; Croatia entered UN. UN peacekeeping force stationed in Croatia. Tudjman elected president. **1993:** Government offensive launched to retake parts of Serb-held Krajina, violating the 1992 UN peace accord. **1994:** Accord with Muslims and ethnic Croats within Bosnia, to the east, to link recently formed Muslim–Croat federation with Croatia. **1995:** Serb-held western Slavonia and Krajina captured by government forces; exodus of Croatian Serbs. Offensive extended into Bosnia-Herzegovina to halt Bosnian Serb assault on Bihac in western Bosnia. Serbia agreed to cede control of eastern Slavonia to Croatia over a two-year period. **1996:** Diplomatic relations between Croatia and Yugoslavia restored. Croatia entered Council of Europe. **1997:** Opposition successes in local elections. Tudjman re-elected despite failing health. Serb enclave in eastern Slavonia reintegrated into Croatia. Constitution amended to prevent weakening of Croatia's national sovereignty. **1998:** Croatia resumed control over East Slavonia.

Cuba Republic of

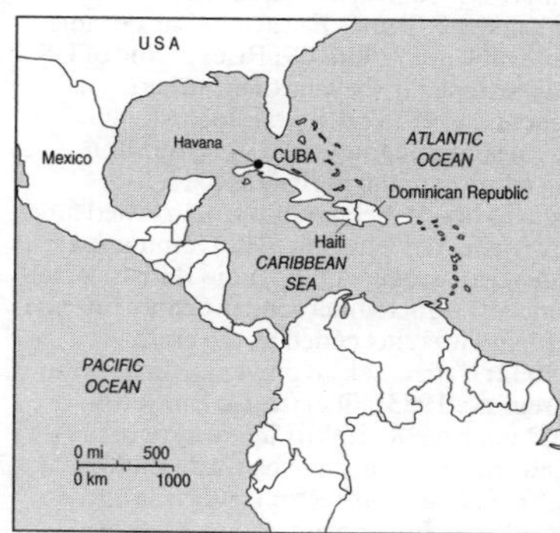

National name: *República de Cuba* **Area:** 110,860 sq km/42,803 sq mi **Capital:** Havana **Major towns/cities:** Santiago de Cuba, Camagüey, Holguín, Guantánamo, Santa Clara, Bayamo, Cienfuegos

Government

Head of state and government: Fidel Castro Ruz from 1959 **Political system:** communist republic **Administrative divisions:** 14 provinces and the special municipality of the Isle of Youth (Isla de la Juventud) **Political party:** Communist Party of Cuba (PCC), Marxist-Leninist **Armed forces:** 60,000 (1997) **Conscription:** compulsory for two years **Death penalty:** retained and used for ordinary crimes **Defence spend:** (% GDP) 5.2 (1997) **Education spend:** (% GNP) 6.6 (1993–94) **Health spend:** (% GDP) 7.9 (1990–95)

Economy and resources

Currency: Cuban peso **GDP:** (US$) 18.8 billion (1997 est) **Real GDP growth:** (% change on previous year) 2.1 (1997) **GNP (US$):** 19.2 billion (1997 est) **GNP per capita (PPP):** (US$) 3,520 (1997 est) **Consumer price inflation:** 8% (1998) **Unemployment:** 17.3% (1994) **Foreign debt:** (US$) 13.6 billion (1996) **Major trading partners:** Canada, Spain, Russia, China, Mexico, Bulgaria **Resources:** iron ore, copper, chromite, gold, manganese, nickel, cobalt, silver, salt **Exports:** sugar, minerals, tobacco, citrus fruits, fish products. Principal market: Russia 17.6% (1997) **Imports:** mineral fuels, machinery and transport equipment, foodstuffs, beverages. Principal source: Spain 13.5% (1997) **Arable land:** 34.2% (1995)

Population and society

Population: 11,116,000 (1998 est) **Population growth rate:** 0.4% (1995–2000) **Population density:** (per sq km) 99.7 (1998 est) **Urban population:** (% of total) 77 (1997) **Age distribution:** (% of total population) 0–14 22.0%, 15–64 68.5%, 65+ 9.5% (1998) **Ethnic groups:** predominantly of mixed Spanish and African or Spanish and American Indian origin **Language:** Spanish **Religion:** Roman Catholic; also Episcopalians and Methodists **Education:** (compulsory years) 6 **Literacy rate:** 95% (men); 93% (women) (1995 est) **Labour force:** 45% of population: 18% agriculture, 30% industry, 51% services (1990) **Life expectancy:** 74 (men); 78 (women) (1995–2000) **Child mortality rate:** (under 5, per 1,000 live births) 11 (1997) **Physicians:** 1 per 212 people (1993 est)

Practical information

Visa requirements: UK: visa required. USA: visa required **Embassy in the UK:** 167 High Holborn, London WC1V 6PA. Tel: (0171) 240 2488; fax: (0171) 836 2602 **British embassy:** Calle 34, 708 Miramar, Havana. Tel: (7) 331 771; fax: (7) 338 104 **Chamber of commerce:** Cámara de Comercio de la República de Cuba, Calle 21, No. 661/701, esq Calle A, Apartado 4237, Vedado, Havana. Tel: (7) 303 356; fax: (7) 333 042

Chronology

3rd century AD: The Ciboney, Cuba's earliest known inhabitants, were dislodged by the immigration of Taino, Arawak Indians from Venezuela. **1492:** Christopher Columbus landed in Cuba and claimed it for Spain. **1511:** Spanish settlement established at Baracoa by Diego Velazquez. **1523:** Decline of American Indian population and rise of sugar plantations led to import of slaves from Africa. **mid-19th century:** Cuba produced one-third of the world's sugar. **1868–78:** Unsuccessful first war for independence from Spain. **1886:** Slavery was abolished. **1895–98:** Further uprising against Spanish rule, led by José Martí, who died in combat; 200,000 soldiers deployed by Spain. **1898:** USA defeated Spain in Spanish-American War; Spain gave up all claims to Cuba, which was ceded to the USA. **1901:** Cuba achieved independence; Tomás Estrada Palma became first president of the Republic of Cuba. **1906–09:** Brief period of US administration after Estrada resigned in the face of an armed rebellion by political opponents. **1909:** The liberal, José Miguel Gomez became president, but soon became tarred by corruption. **1924:** Gerado Machado, an admirer of the Italian fascist leader Benito Mussolini, established a brutal dictatorship which lasted nine years. **1925:** Socialist Party founded, from which the Communist Party later developed. **1933:** Army sergeant Fulgencio Batista seized power. **1934:** USA abandoned its right to intervene in Cuba's internal affairs. **1944:** Batista retired and was succeeded by the civilian Ramon Gray San Martin. **1952:** Batista seized power again to begin an oppressive and corrupt regime. **1953:** Fidel Castro Ruz led an unsuccessful coup against Batista on the 100th anniversary of the birth of Martí. **1956:** Second unsuccessful coup by Castro. **1959:** Batista overthrown by Castro and his 9,000-strong guerrilla army. Constitution of 1940 replaced by a 'Fundamental Law', making Castro prime minister, his brother Raúl Castro his deputy, and Argentine-born Ernesto 'Che' Guevara third in command. **1960:** All US businesses in Cuba appropriated without compensation; USA broke off diplomatic relations. **1961:** USA sponsored an unsuccessful invasion by Cuban exiles at the Bay of Pigs. Castro announced that Cuba had become a communist state, with a Marxist-Leninist programme of economic development, and became allied with the USSR. **1962:** Cuban missile crisis: Cuba was expelled from the Organization of American States. Castro responded by tightening relations with the USSR, which installed nuclear missiles in Cuba (subsequently removed at US insistence). US trade embargo imposed. **1965:** Cuba's sole political party renamed Cuban Communist Party (PCC). With Soviet help, Cuba began to make considerable economic and social progress. **1972:** Cuba became a full member of the Moscow-based Council for Mutual Economic Assistance (COMECON). **1976:** New socialist constitution approved; Castro elected president. **1976–81:** Castro became involved in extensive international commitments, sending troops as Soviet surrogates, particularly to Africa. **1982:** Cuba joined other Latin American countries in giving moral support to Argentina in its dispute with Britain over the Falklands. **1984:** Castro tried to improve US-Cuban relations by discussing exchange of US prisoners in Cuba for Cuban 'undesirables' in the USA. **1988:** Peace accord with South Africa signed, agreeing to withdrawal of Cuban troops from Angola, as part of a reduction in Cuba's overseas military activities. **1991:** Soviet troops withdrawn with the collapse of the USSR. **1993:** US trade embargo tightened; market-oriented reforms introduced in face of deteriorating economy. **1994:** Refugee exodus; US policy on Cuban asylum seekers revised. **1998:** Castro confirmed as president for a further five-year term. UN declined to condemn Cuba's human-rights record.

Cyprus

Greek Republic of Cyprus in south, and Turkish Republic of Northern Cyprus in north

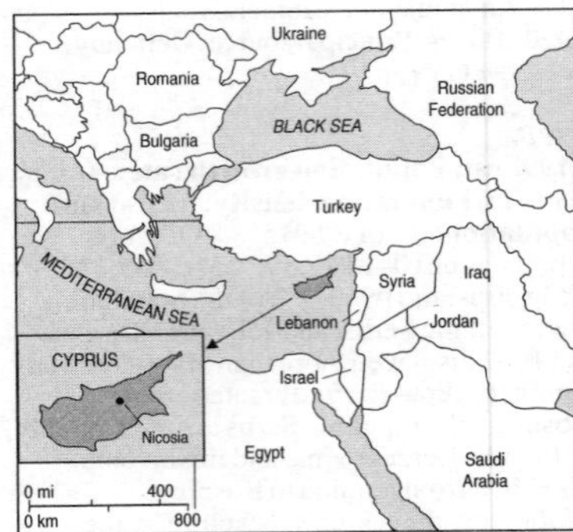

National name: *Kypriakí Dimokratía* (south), and *Kibris Cumhuriyeti* (north) **Area:** 9,251 sq km/ 3,571 sq mi (3,335 sq km/1,287 sq mi is Turkish-occupied) **Capital:** Nicosia (divided between Greek and Turkish Cypriots) **Major towns/cities:** Morphou, Limassol, Larnaca, Famagusta, Paphos **Major ports:** Limassol, Larnaca, and Paphos (Greek); Kyrenia and Famagusta (Turkish)

Government

Head of state and government: Glafkos Clerides (Greek) from 1993, Rauf Denktas (Turkish) from 1976 **Political system:** democratic divided republic **Administrative divisions:** six districts **Political parties:** *Greek zone*: Democratic Party (DEKO), federalist, centre left; Progressive Party of the Working People (AKEL), socialist; Democratic Rally (DISY), centrist; Socialist Party–National Democratic Union of Cyprus (SK–EDEK), socialist; *Turkish zone*: National Unity Party (NUP), Communal Liberation Party (CLP), Republican Turkish Party (RTP), New British Party (NBP) **Armed forces:** National Guard of 10,000 (1997); Turkish Republic of Northern Cyprus (TRNC) 4,000, plus 26,000 reserves (1995) **Conscription:** is for 26 months **Death penalty:** laws provide for the death penalty only for exceptional crimes such as under military law or crimes committed in exceptional circumstances such as wartime; last execution 1962 **Defence spend:** (% GDP) 5.2 (1996) **Education spend:** (% GNP) 4.4 (1995) **Health spend:** (% GDP) 2.1 (1994)

Economy and resources

Currency: Cyprus pound and Turkish lira **GDP:** (US$) 8.5 billion (1997) **Real GDP growth:** (% change on previous year) 2.5 (1997) **GNP (US$):** 10.8 billion (1997) **GNP per capita (PPP):** (US$) 14,090 (1997 est) **Consumer price inflation:** 3.7% (1998) **Unemployment:** government-controlled area: 9.4% (1996) **Foreign debt:** (US$) 2.1 billion (1993) **Major trading partners:** government-controlled area: UK, USA, Arab countries, France, Germany, Greece, Japan, Italy; TRNC area: Turkey, UK, other EU countries **Resources:** copper precipitates, beutonite, umber and other ochres **Exports:** government-controlled area: clothing, potatoes, pharmaceutical products. Principal market: UK 27.1% (1994); TRNC area: citrus fruits, industrial products. Principal market: UK 46.3% (1994); Russia 20.7% (1997) **Imports:** government-controlled area: mineral fuels, textiles, vehicles, metals, foodstuffs, tobacco. Principal source: UK 11.4% (1994); TRNC area: basic manufactures, machinery and transport equipment, food and live animals. Principal source: USA 19% (1997) **Arable land:** 10.8% (1995)

Population and society

Population: 771,000 (1998 est) **Population growth rate:** 0.8% (1995–2025) **Population density:** (per sq km) 81 (1998 est) **Urban population:** (% of total) 55 (1997) **Age distribution:** (% of total population) 0–14 24.5%, 15–64 65.1%, 65+ 10.4% (1998) **Ethnic groups:** about 80% of the population is of Greek origin, while about 18% are of Turkish descent, and live in the northern part of the island within the self-styled Turkish Republic of Northern Cyprus **Language:** Greek and Turkish (official), English **Religion:** Greek Orthodox, Sunni Muslim **Education:** (compulsory years) 9 **Literacy rate:** 94% (men); 94% (women) (1995 est) **Labour force:** 48% of population: 14% agriculture, 30% industry, 56% services (1990) **Life expectancy:** 75 (men); 80 (women) (1995–2000) **Child mortality rate:** (under 5, per 1,000 live births) 8 (1997) **Physicians:** 1 per 1,000 people (1994 est)

Practical information

Visa requirements: UK: visa not required. USA: visa not required **Embassy in the UK:** 93 Park Street, London W1Y 4ET. Tel: (0171) 499 8272; fax: (0171) 491 0691 **British embassy:** British High Commission, PO Box 1978, Alexander Pallis Street, Nicosia. Tel: (2) 473 131/7; fax: (2) 367 198 **Chamber of commerce:** Cyprus Chamber of Commerce and Industry, PO Box 1455, 38 Grivas Dhigenis Avenue, Nicosia. Tel: (2) 449 500; fax: (2) 449 048

Chronology

14th–11th centuries BC: Colonized by Myceneans and Achaeans from Greece. **9th century BC:** Phoenicans settled in Cyprus. **7th century BC:** Several Cypriot kingdoms flourished under Assyrian influence. **414–374 BC:** Under Evagoras of Salamis (in eastern Cyprus) the island's ten city kingdoms were united into one state and Greek culture, including the Greek alphabet, was promoted. **333–58 BC:** Became part of the Greek Hellenistic and then, from 294 BC:, the Egypt-based Ptolemaic empire. **58 BC:** Cyprus was annexed by the Roman Empire. **AD 45:** Christianity introduced. **AD 395:** When the Roman Empire divided, Cyprus was allotted to the Byzantine Empire. **7th–10th centuries:** Byzantines and Muslim Arabs fought for control of Cyprus. **1191:** Richard I of England, 'the Lionheart', conquered Cyprus as a base for Crusades; he later sold it to a French noble, Guy de Lusignan, who established a feudal monarchy which ruled for three centuries. **1498:** Venetian Republic took control of Cyprus. **1571:** Conquered by Ottoman Turks, who introduced Turkish Muslim settlers, but permitted Christianity to continue in rural areas. **1821–33:** Period of unrest, following execution of popular Greek Orthodox Archbishop Kyprianos. **1878:** Anglo-Turkish Convention: Turkey ceded Cyprus to British administration in return for defensive alliance. **1914:** Formally annexed by Britain after Turkey entered World War I as a Central Power. **1915:** Greece rejected an offer of Cyprus in return for entry into World War I on Allied side. **1925:** Cyprus became a crown colony. **1931:** Greek Cypriots rioted in support of demand for union with Greece (*enosis*); legislative council suspended. **1948:** Greek Cypriots rejected new constitution because it did not offer links with Greece. **1951:** Britain rejected Greek proposals for *enosis.* **1955:** National Organization of Cypriot Fighters (EOKA), led by George Grivas, began terrorist campaign for *enosis.* **1956:** British authorities deported Archbishop Makarios, head of the Cypriot Orthodox Church, for encouraging EOKA. **1958:** Britain proposed autonomy for Greek and Turkish Cypriot communities under British sovereignty; plan accepted by Turks, rejected by Greeks; violence increased. **1959:** Britain, Greece, and Turkey agreed to Cypriot independence, with partition and *enosis* both ruled out. **1960:** Cyprus became an independent republic with Archbishop Makarios as president; Britain retained two military bases. **1963:** Makarios proposed major constitutional reforms; Turkish Cypriots withdrew from government and formed separate enclaves; communal fighting broke out. **1964:** United Nations (UN) peacekeeping force installed. **1968:** Intercommunal talks made no progress; Turkish Cypriots demanded federalism; Greek Cypriots insisted on unitary state. **1974:** Coup by Greek officers in Cypriot National Guard installed Nikos Sampson as president; Turkey, fearing *enosis,* invaded northern Cyprus; Greek Cypriot military regime collapsed; President Makarios restored. **1975:** Northern Cyprus declared itself the Turkish Federated State of Cyprus, with Rauf Denktas as president. **1977:** Makarios died; succeeded by Spyros Kyprianou. **1983:** Denktas proclaimed independent Turkish Republic of Cyprus; recognized only by Turkey. **1985:** Summit meeting between Kyprianou and Denktas failed to reach agreement; further peace talks failed in 1989 and 1992. **1988:** Kyprianou succeeded as Greek Cypriot president by Georgios Vassiliou. **1993:** Glafkos Clerides (DISY) replaced Vassiliou. **1994:** European Court of Justice declared trade with northern Cyprus illegal. **1996:** Further peace talks jeopardized by boundary killing of Turkish Cypriot soldier; mounting tension between north and south. **1997:** Decision to purchase Russian anti-aircraft missiles created tension. UN-mediated peace talks between Clerides and Denktascollapsed. **1998:** President Clerides re-elected. Denktas refused to meet British envoy. US mediation failed. Full EU membership negotiations commenced. Greek Cyprus rejected Denktas's confederation proposals.

Czech Republic

National name: *Ceská Republika* **Area:** 78,864 sq km/30,449 sq mi **Capital:** Prague **Major towns/cities:** Brno, Ostrava, Olomouc, Liberec, Plzeň, Ustí nad Labem, Hradec Králové

Government

Head of state: Václav Havel from 1993 **Head of government:** Miloš Zeman from 1998 **Political system:** emergent democracy **Administrative divisions:** eight regions **Political parties:** Civic Democratic Party (CDP), right of centre, free-market; Civic Democratic Alliance (CDA), right of centre, free-market; Civic Movement (CM), liberal, left of centre; Communist Party of Bohemia and Moravia (KSCM), reform socialist; Agrarian Party, centrist, rural-based; Liberal National Social Party (LNSP; formerly the Czech Socialist Party (SP)), reform socialist; Czech Social Democratic Party (CSDP), moderate left of centre; Christian Democratic Union–Czech People's Party (CDU–CPP), centre right; Movement for Autonomous Democracy of Moravia and Silesia (MADMS), Moravian and Silesian-based, separatist; Czech Republican Party, far right **Armed forces:** 61,700 (1997) **Conscription:** compulsory for 12 months **Death penalty:** abolished in 1990 **Defence spend:** (% GDP) 2.2 (1997) **Education spend:** (% GNP) 5.4 (1996) **Health spend:** (% GDP) 7.8 (1990–95)

Economy and resources

Currency: koruna (based on Czechoslovak koruna) **GDP:** (US$) 52 billion (1997) **Real GDP growth:** (% change on previous year) 1.5 (1997) **GNP (US$):** 53.5 billion (1997) **GNP per capita (PPP):** (US$) 11,380 (1997) **Consumer price inflation:** 12.0% (1998) **Unemployment:** 4.4% (1997) **Foreign debt:** (US$) 20.9 billion (1996) **Major trading partners:** EU countries, Slovak Republic, Poland, Russia, USA **Resources:** coal, lignite **Exports:** basic manufactures, machinery and transport equipment, miscellaneous manufactured articles, beer. Principal market: EU 37.4% (1995) **Imports:** machinery and transport equipment, basic manufactures, chemicals and chemical products, mineral fuels. Principal source: EU 34.7% (1995) **Arable land:** 40.7% (1995)

Population and society

Population: 10,282,000 (1998 est) **Population growth rate:** –0.1% (1995–2000); –0.1% (2000–05) **Population density:** (per sq km) 82 (1998 est) **Urban population:** (% of total) 66 (1997) **Age distribution:** (% of total population) 0–14 17.2%, 15–64 69.1%, 65+ 13.7% (1998) **Ethnic groups:** predominantly Western Slav

Czechs; there is also a sizeable Slovak minority and small Polish, German, and Hungarian minorities **Language:** Czech (official) **Religion:** Roman Catholic, Hussite, Presbyterian Evangelical Church of Czech Brethren, Orthodox **Education:** (compulsory years) 9 **Literacy rate:** 99% (men); 99% (women) (1995 est) **Labour force:** 50.2% of population; 6.3% agriculture, 42% industry, 51.7% services (1996) **Life expectancy:** 70 (men); 76 (women) (1995–2000) **Child mortality rate:** (under 5, per 1,000 live births) 9 (1997) **Physicians:** 1 per 345 people (1996)

Practical information

Visa requirements: UK: visa not required. USA: visa not required **Embassy in the UK:** 26–30 Kensington Palace Gardens, London W8 4QY. Tel: (0171) 243 1115; fax: (0171) 727 9654 **British embassy:** Thunovská 14, 11 800 Prague 7. Tel: (2) 2451 0439; fax: (2) 539 927 **Chamber of commerce:** Czech Chamber of Commerce and Industry, Argentinská 38, 170 05 Prague 7. Tel: (2) 6679 4880; fax: (2) 875 348

Chronology

5th century: Settled by West Slavs. **8th century:** Part of Charlemagne's Holy Roman Empire. **9th century:** Kingdom of Greater Moravia, centred around the eastern part of what is now the Czech Republic, founded by the Slavic prince Sviatopluk; Christianity adopted. **906:** Moravia conquered by the Magyars (Hungarians). **995:** Independent state of Bohemia in the northwest, centred around Prague, formed under the Premysl rulers, who had broken away from Moravia; became kingdom in 12th century. **1029:** Moravia became a fief of Bohemia. **1355:** King Charles IV of Bohemia became Holy Roman Emperor. **early 15th century:** Nationalistic Hussite religion, opposed to German and papal influence, founded in Bohemia by John Huss. **1526:** Bohemia came under the control of the Austrian Catholic Habsburgs. **1618:** Hussite revolt precipitated the Thirty Years' War, which resulted in the Bohemians' defeat, more direct rule by the Habsburgs, and re-Catholicization. **1867:** With creation of dual Austro-Hungarian monarchy, Bohemia was reduced to a province of Austria, leading to a growth in national consciousness. **1918:** Austro-Hungarian Empire dismembered; Czechs joined Slovaks in forming Czechoslovakia as independent democratic nation, with Tomas Masaryk president. **1938:** Under the Munich Agreement, Czechoslovakia was forced to surrender the Sudeten German districts in the north to Germany. **1939:** The remainder of Czechoslovakia annexed by Germany, Bohemia-Moravia being administered as a 'protectorate'; President Eduard Beneš set up a government-in-exile in London; liquidation campaigns against intelligentsia. **1945:** Liberated by Soviet and US troops; communist-dominated government of national unity formed under Beneš ; 2 million Sudeten Germans expelled. **1948:** Beneš ousted; communists assumed full control under a Soviet-style single-party constitution. **1950s:** Political opponents purged; nationalization of industries. **1968:** 'Prague Spring' political liberalization programme, instituted by Communist Party leader Alexander Dubš ek, crushed by invasion of Warsaw Pact forces to restore the 'orthodox line'. **1969:** New federal constitution, creating a separate Czech Socialist Republic; Gustáv Husák became Communist Party leader. **1977:** Formation of the 'Charter '77' human-rights group by intellectuals, including the playwright Václav Havel, encouraged a crackdown against dissidents. **1987:** Reformist Miloš Jakeš replaced Husák as communist leader, and introduced a *prestvaba* ('restructuring') reform programme on the Soviet leader Mikhail Gorbachev's *perestroika* model. **1989:** Major prodemocracy demonstrations in Prague; new political parties formed and legalized, including Czech-based Civic Forum under Havel; Communist Party stripped of powers. New 'grand coalition' government formed; Havel appointed state president. Amnesty granted to 22,000 prisoners. **1990:** Multiparty elections won by Civic Forum. **1991:** Civic Forum split into centre-right Civic Democratic Party (CDP) and centre-left Civic Movement (CM), evidence of increasing Czech and Slovak separatism. **1992:** Václav Klaus, leader of Czech-based CDP, became prime minister; Havel resigned as president following nationalist Slovak gains in assembly elections. Creation of separate Czech and Slovak states and a customs union agreed. Market-centred economic-reform programme launched, including mass privatizations. **1993:** Czech Republic became sovereign state within United Nations, with Klaus as prime minister. Havel elected president. **1994:** Joined NATO's 'partnership for peace' programme. Strong economic growth registered. **1996:** Applied for EU membership. Klaus-led coalition lost its parliamentary majority after elections but remained in power. Ruling coalition successful in upper-house elections. **1997:** Former communist leader Miloš Jakeš charged with treason. Ruling coalition survived currency crisis. Czech Republic invited to join NATO and begin EU membership negotiations. Klaus resigned after allegations of misconduct. **1998:** Havel re-elected president. Centre-left Social Democrats won general election and minority government formed by Milos Zeman, including communist ministers and supported from outside by Vaclàv Klaus. Full EU membership negotiations commenced.

Denmark Kingdom of

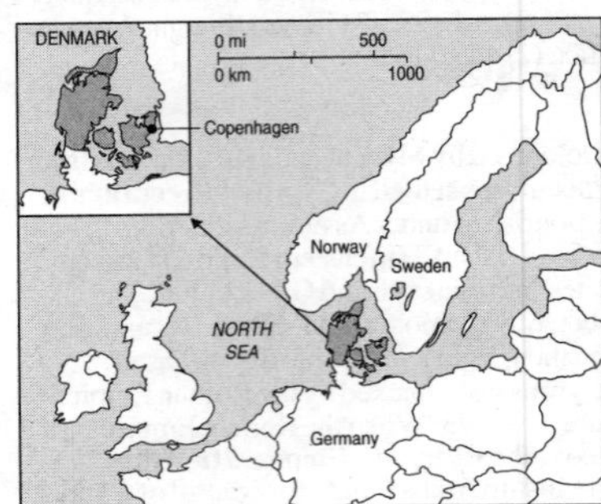

National name: *Kongeriget Danmark* **Area:** 43,075 sq km/16,631 sq mi **Capital:** Copenhagen **Major towns/cities:** Århus, Odense, Ålborg, Esbjerg, Randers **Major ports:** Århus, Odense, Ålborg, Esbjerg **Territories:** the dependencies of Faroe Islands and Greenland

Government

Head of state: Queen Margrethe II from 1972 **Head of government:** Poul Nyrup Rasmussen from 1993 **Political system:** liberal democracy **Administrative divisions:** 14 counties, one city and one borough **Political parties:** Social Democrats (SD), left of centre; Conservative People's Party (KF), moderate centre right; Liberal Party (V), centre left; Socialist People's Party (SF), moderate left wing; Radical Liberals (RV), radical internationalist, left of centre; Centre Democrats (CD), moderate centrist; Progress Party (FP), radical antibureaucratic; Christian People's Party (KrF), interdenominational, family values **Armed forces:** 32,900; 70,400 reservists and volunteer Home Guard of 70,500 (1997) **Conscription:** 9–12 months (27 months for some ranks) **Death penalty:** abolished in 1978 **Defence spend:** (% GDP) 1.7 (1997) **Education spend:** (% GNP) 8.3 (1995) **Health spend:** (% GDP) 5.3 (1990–95)

Economy and resources

Currency: Danish krone **GDP:** (US$) 163 billion (1997) **Real GDP growth:** (% change on previous year) 3.2 (1997) **GNP (US$):** 171.4 billion (1997) **GNP per capita (PPP):** (US$) 22,740 (1997) **Consumer price inflation:** 2.4% (1998) **Unemployment:** 5.1% (1998) **Major trading partners:** EU (principally Germany, Sweden, and UK), Norway, USA **Resources:** crude petroleum, natural gas, salt, limestone **Exports:** pig meat and pork products, other food products, fish, industrial machinery, chemicals, transport equipment. Principal market: Germany 21.4% (1997) **Imports:** food and live animals, machinery, transport equipment, iron, steel, electronics, petroleum, cereals, paper. Principal source: Germany 21.7% (1997) **Arable land:** 54.8% (1995)

Population and society

Population: 5,270,000 (1998 est) **Population growth rate:** 0.2% (1995–2000); 0% (2000–05) **Population density:** (per sq km) 125.9 (1998 est) **Urban population:** (% of total) 85 (1997) **Age distribution:**

(% of total population) 0–14 18.2%, 15–64 66.9%, 65+ 14.9% (1998) **Ethnic groups:** all Danes are part of the Scandinavian ethnic group **Language:** Danish (official); there is a German-speaking minority **Religion:** Lutheran 97% **Education:** (compulsory years) 9 **Literacy rate:** 99% (men); 99% (women) (1995 est) **Labour force:** 53.6% of population: 4% agriculture, 27% industry, 69% services (1996) **Life expectancy:** 73 (men); 78 (women) (1995–2000) **Child mortality rate:** (under 5, per 1,000 live births) 8 (1997) **Physicians:** 1 per 345 people (1994)

Practical information

Visa requirements: UK: visa not required. USA: visa not required **Embassy in the UK:** Royal Danish Embassy, 55 Sloane Street, London SW1X 9SR. Tel: (0171) 333 0200; fax: (0171) 333 0270 **British embassy:** Kastelsvej 36–40, DK-2100 Copenhagen. Tel: (45) 3526 4600; fax: (45) 3332 1501 **Chamber of commerce:** Det Danske Handelskammer, Børsen, DK-1217 Copenhagen K. Tel: (45) 3395 0500; fax: (45) 3332 5216

Chronology

5th–6th centuries: Danes migrated from Sweden. **8th–10th centuries:** Viking raids throughout Europe. *c.* **940–85:** Harald Bluetooth unified Kingdom of Denmark and established Christianity. **1014–35:** King Canute I created empire embracing Denmark, Norway, and England; empire collapsed after his death. **12th century:** Denmark re-emerged as dominant Baltic power. **1340–75:** Valdemar IV restored order after period of civil war and anarchy. **1397:** Union of Kalmar: Denmark, Sweden, and Norway (with Iceland) united under a single monarch. **1449:** Sweden broke away from union. **1460:** Christian I secured duchies of Schleswig and Holstein. **1523:** Denmark recognized Sweden's independence. **1536:** Lutheranism established as official religion of Denmark. **1563–70:** Unsuccessful war to recover Sweden. **1625–29:** Denmark sided with Protestants in Thirty Years' War. **1643–45:** Second attempt to reclaim Sweden ended in failure. **1657–60:** Further failed attempt to reclaim Sweden. **1665:** Frederick III made himself absolute monarch. **1729:** Greenland became Danish province. **1780–81:** Denmark, Russia, and Sweden formed 'Armed Neutrality' coalition to protect neutral shipping during War of American Independence. **1788:** Serfdom abolished. **1800:** France persuaded Denmark to revive Armed Neutrality against British blockade. **1801:** First Battle of Copenhagen: much of Danish fleet destroyed by British navy. **1807:** Second Battle of Copenhagen: British seized rebuilt fleet to pre-empt Danish entry into Napoleonic War on French side. **1814:** Treaty of Kiel: Denmark ceded Norway to Sweden as penalty for supporting France in Napoleonic War; Denmark retained Iceland. **1848–50:** Germans of Schleswig-Holstein revolted with Prussian support. **1849:** Liberal pressure compelled Frederick VII to grant democratic constitution. **1864:** Prussia seized Schleswig-Holstein after short war. **1914–1919:** Denmark neutral during World War I. **1918:** Iceland achieved full self-government. **1919:** Denmark recovered northern Schleswig under peace settlement after World War I. **1929–40:** Welfare state established under left-wing coalition government dominated by Social Democrat Party. **1940–45:** German occupation. **1944:** Iceland declared independence. **1949:** Denmark became a founding member of North Atlantic Treaty Organization (NATO). **1960:** Denmark joined European Free Trade Association (EFTA). **1973:** Withdrew from EFTA and joined European Economic Community (EEC). **1981:** Greenland achieved full self-government. **1992:** Referendum rejected Maastricht Treaty on European union. **1993:** Second referendum approved Maastricht Treaty after government negotiated a series of 'opt-out' clauses. **1996:** Centre Democrats withdrew from governing coalition. **1998:** Government won slim majority in assembly elections. Referendum endorsed Amsterdam EU treaty.

Djibouti Republic of

National name: *Jumhouriyya Djibouti* **Area:** 23,200 sq km/8,957 sq mi **Capital:** Djibouti (and chief port) **Major towns/cities:** Tadjoura, Obock, Dikhil, Ali-Sabieh

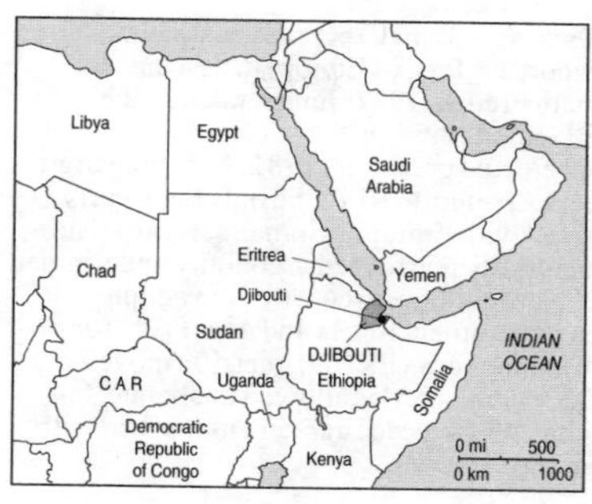

Government

Head of state: Hassan Gouled Aptidon from 1977 **Head of government:** Barkat Gourad from 1981 **Political system:** emergent democracy **Administrative divisions:** five districts **Political parties:** People's Progress Assembly (RPP), nationalist; Democratic Renewal Party (PRD), moderate left of centre **Armed forces:** 9,600 (1997); plus 3,900 French troops **Conscription:** military service is voluntary **Death penalty:** retains the death penalty for ordinary crimes but can be considered abolitionist in practice (no executions since independence) **Defence spend:** (% GDP) 5.0 (1997) **Education spend:** (% GNP) 3.8 (1993–94) **Health spend:** (% GDP) 2.1 (1994)

Economy and resources

Currency: Djibouti franc **GDP:** (US$) 444 million (1996 est) **Real GDP growth:** (% change on previous year) –0.2 (1996 est) **GNP (US$):** 481 million (1994) **GNP per capita (PPP):** (US$) 1,070 (1994 est) **Consumer price inflation:** N/A **Unemployment:** 40% (1995 est) **Foreign debt:** (US$) 241 million (1996) **Major trading partners:** Kenya, Thailand, France, Ethiopia, Somalia **Exports:** hides, cattle, coffee (exports are largely re-exports). Principal market: Somalia 39.5% (1996) **Imports:** vegetable products, foodstuffs, beverages, vinegar, tobacco, machinery and transport equipment, mineral products. Principal source: France 14.7% (1996) **Arable land:** 10% (1995)

Population and society

Population: 623,000 (1998 est) **Population growth rate:** 2.2% (1990–95) **Population density:** (per sq km) 20.1 (1998 est) **Urban population:** (% of total) 83 (1997) **Age distribution:** (% of total population) 0–14 42.8%, 15–64 54.6%, 65+ 2.6% (1998) **Ethnic groups:** population divided mainly into two Hamitic groups; the Issas (Somalis) in the south, and the minority Afars (or Danakil) in the north and west. There are also minorities of Europeans (mostly French), as well as Arabs, Sudanese, and Indians **Language:** French (official), Somali, Afar, Arabic **Religion:** Sunni Muslim **Education:** (compulsory years) 6 **Literacy rate:** 60% (men); 33% (women) (1995 est) **Life expectancy:** 49 (men); 52 (women) (1995–2000) **Child mortality rate:** (under 5, per 1,000 live births) 162 (1997) **Physicians:** 1 per 6,590 people (1993 est)

Practical information

Visa requirements: UK: visa required. USA: visa required **Embassy for the UK:** 26 rue Emile Ménier, 75116 Paris, France. Tel: (1) 4727 4922; fax: (1) 4553 5053 **British embassy:** British Consulate, BP 81 Gellatly Hankey et Cie, Djibouti. Tel: (253) 351 940; fax: (253) 353 294 **Chamber of commerce:** Chambre Internationale de Commerce et d'Industrie, BP 84, Place de Lagarde, Djibouti. Tel: (253) 351 070; fax: (253) 350 096

Chronology

3rd century BC: The north settled by Able immigrants from Arabia, whose descendants are the Afars (Danakil). **early Christian era:** Somali Issas settled in coastal areas and south, ousting Afars. **825:** Islam introduced by missionaries. **16th century:** Portuguese arrived to challenge trading monopoly of Arabs. **1862:** French acquired a port at Obock. **1888:** Annexed by France as part of French Somaliland. **1900s:** Railroad linked Djibouti port with the Ethiopian hinterland. **1946:** Became overseas territory within French Union, with own assembly and representation in French parliament. **1958:** Voted to become overseas territorial member of French Community. **1967:** French Somaliland renamed the French Territory of the Afars

and the Issas. **early 1970s:** Issas (Somali) peoples campaigned for independence, but the minority Afars, of Ethiopian descent, and Europeans sought to remain French. **1977:** Independence achieved as Djibouti, with Hassan Gouled Aptidon, the leader of the independence movement, elected president. **1981:** New constitution made the People's Progress Assembly (RPP) the only legal party. Treaties of friendship signed with Ethiopia, Somalia, Kenya, and Sudan. **1984:** Policy of neutrality reaffirmed. Economy undermined by severe drought. **1992:** New multiparty constitution adopted; fighting erupted between government forces and Afar Front for Restoration of Unity and Democracy (FRUD) guerrilla movement in the northeast. **1993:** Opposition parties allowed to operate, but Gouled re-elected president. **1994:** Peace agreement reached with Afar FRUD militants, ending civil war.

Dominica Commonwealth of

Area: 751 sq km/290 sq mi **Capital:** Roseau, with a deepwater port **Major towns/cities:** Portsmouth, Berekua, Marigot, Rosalie **Major ports:** Roseau, Portsmouth, Berekua, Marigot, Rosaliet

Government

Head of state: Vernon Shaw from 1998 **Head of government:** Edison James from 1995 **Political system:** liberal democracy **Administrative divisions:** ten parishes **Political parties:** Dominica Freedom Party (DFP), centrist; Labour Party of Dominica (LPD), left-of-centre coalition; Dominica United Workers' Party (DUWP), left of centre **Armed forces:** defence force disbanded in 1981; police force of approximately 300 **Death penalty:** retained and used for ordinary crimes **Education spend:** (% GNP) 5.8 (1992); N/A (1993–94)

Economy and resources

Currency: Eastern Caribbean dollar; pound sterling; French franc **GDP:** (US$) 236 million (1997 est) **Real GDP growth:** (% change on previous year) 2.8 (1997) **GNP (US$):** 232 million (1997) **GNP per capita (PPP):** (US$) 4,470 (1997) **Consumer price inflation:** 1.5% (1997) **Unemployment:** 23% (1994) **Foreign debt:** (US$) 110 million (1996) **Major trading partners:** USA, UK, the Netherlands, South Korea, Belgium, Japan, Trinidad and Tobago **Resources:** pumice, limestone, clay **Exports:** bananas, soap, coconuts, grapefruit, galvanized sheets. Principal market: UK 25.3% (1995) **Imports:** food and live animals, basic manufactures, machinery and transport equipment, mineral fuels. Principal source: USA 13% (1995) **Arable land:** 4% (1995)

Population and society

Population: 71,000 (1998 est) **Population growth rate:** 0.5 (1995–2025) **Population density:** (per sq km) 87.6 (1998 est) **Urban population:** (% of total) 70 (1997 est) **Age distribution:** (% of total population) 0–14 27.1%, 15–64 63.4%, 65+ 9.5% (1998) **Ethnic groups:** majority descended from African slaves; a small number of the indigenous Arawaks remain **Language:** English (official), but the Dominican patois reflects earlier periods of French rule **Religion:** Roman Catholic 80% **Education:** (compulsory years) 10 **Literacy rate:** 94% (men); 94% (women) (1994 est) **Labour force:** 25.8% agriculture, 21.2% industry, 53% services (1990) **Life expectancy:** 72 (men); 76 (women) (1994 est) **Child mortality rate:** (under 5, per 1,000 live births) 21 (1995) **Physicians:** 1 per 2,952 people (1993)

Practical information

Visa requirements: UK: visa not required for stays of up to six months. USA: visa not required for stays of up to six months **Embassy in the UK:** High Commisssion, 1 Collingham Gardens, London SW5 0HW. Tel: (0171) 370 5194/5; fax: (0171) 373 8743 **British embassy:** British High Commission, British Consulate, Office of the Honorary British Consul, PO Box 6, Roseau. (All staff based in Bridgetown, Barbados.) Tel: (809) 448 1000; fax: (809) 448 1110 **Chamber of commerce:** Dominica Association of Industry and Commerce, PO Box 85, 111 Bath Road, Roseau. Tel: (809) 448 2874; fax: (809) 448 6868

Chronology

1493: Visited by the explorer Christopher Columbus, who named the island Dominica ('Sunday Island'). **1627:** Presented by the English King Charles I to the Earl of Carlisle, but initial European attempts at colonization were fiercely resisted by the indigenous Carib community. **later 18th century:** Succession of local British and French conflicts over control of the fertile island. **1763:** British given possession of the island by the Treaty of Paris (ending the Seven Years' War), but France continued to challenge this militarily until 1805, when there was formal cession in return for the sum of £12,000. **1834:** Slaves, who had been brought in from Africa, were emancipated. **1870:** Became part of the British Leeward Islands federation. **1940:** Transferred to British Windward Islands federation. **1951:** Universal adult suffrage established. **1958–62:** Part of the West Indies Federation. **1960:** Granted separate, semi-independent status, with a legislative council and chief minister. **1961:** Edward leBlanc, leader of newly formed DLP, became chief minister. **1974:** LeBlanc retired; replaced as chief minister by Patrick John (DLP). **1978:** Independence achieved as a republic within the Commonwealth, with John as prime minister. **1980:** DFP won convincing victory in general election, and Eugenia Charles became Caribbean's first woman prime minister. **1981:** John implicated in plot to overthrow government, but subsequently acquitted. **1983:** Small force participated in US-backed invasion of Grenada. **1985:** John retried, found guilty, and sentenced to 12 years' imprisonment. Regrouping of left-of-centre parties resulted in new Labour Party of Dominica (LPD). **1991:** Windward Islands confederation comprising St Lucia, St Vincent, Grenada, and Dominica proposed. **1993:** Charles resigned DFP leadership, but continued as prime minister. **1995:** DUWP won general election; Edison James appointed prime minister and Eugenia Charles retired from politics. **1998:** Vernon Shaw elected president

Dominican Republic

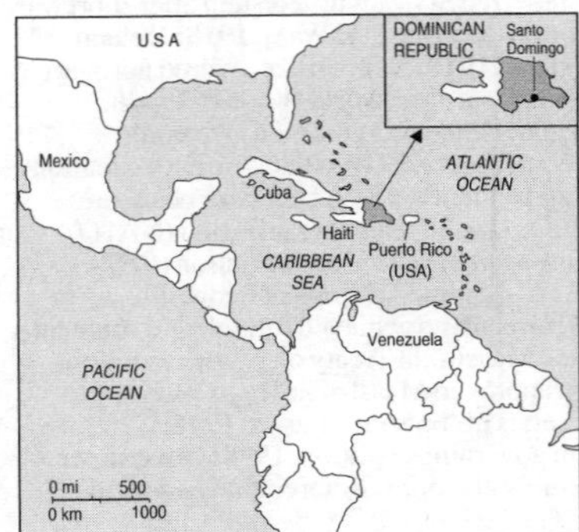

National name: *República Dominicana* **Area:** 48,442 sq km/18,703 sq mi **Capital:** Santo Domingo **Major towns/cities:** Santiago de los Caballeros, La Romana, San Pedro de Macoris, San Francisco de Macoris, Concepcion de la Vega, San Juan

Government

Head of state and government: Leoned Fernandez from 1996 **Political system:** democracy **Administrative divisions:** 29 provinces and a national district (Santo Domingo) **Political parties:** Dominican Revolutionary Party (PRD), moderate, left of centre; Christian Social Reform Party (PRSC), independent socialist; Dominican Liberation Party (PLD), nationalist **Armed forces:** 24,500 (1997); plus a paramilitary force of 15,000 **Conscription:** military service is

voluntary **Death penalty:** abolished in 1966 **Defence spend:** (% GDP) 1.2 (1997) **Education spend:** (% GNP) 2.0 (1996) **Health spend:** (% GDP) 2.0 (1990–95)

Economy and resources

Currency: Dominican Republic peso **GDP:** (US$) 14.93 billion (1997) **Real GDP growth:** (% change on previous year) 6.5 (1997) **GNP (US$):** 13.5 billion (1997) **GNP per capita (PPP):** (US$) 4,540 (1997) **Consumer price inflation:** 8.1% (1998) **Unemployment:** 16.7% (1996) **Foreign debt:** (US$) 4.26 billion (1996) **Major trading partners:** USA, Venezuela, Mexico, Japan, South Korea, the Netherlands, Belgium **Resources:** ferro-nickel, gold, silver **Exports:** raw sugar, molasses, coffee, cocoa, tobacco, ferro-nickel, gold, silver. Principal market: USA 44.7% (1997) **Imports:** petroleum and petroleum products, coal, foodstuffs, wheat, machinery. Principal source: USA 44.1% (1997) **Arable land:** 27.8% (1995)

Population and society

Population: 7,999,000 (1998 est) **Population growth rate:** 1.7% (1995–2000); 1.4% (2000–05) **Population density:** (per sq km) 165.3 (1998 est) **Urban population:** (% of total) 64 (1997) **Age distribution:** (% of total population) 0–14 35.2%, 15–64 60.4%, 65+ 4.4% (1998) **Ethnic groups:** about 73% of the population are mulattos, of mixed European and African descent; about 16% are European; 11% African **Language:** Spanish (official) **Religion:** Roman Catholic **Education:** (compulsory years) 8 **Literacy rate:** 85% (men); 82% (women) (1995 est) **Labour force:** 44% of population: 12.9% agriculture, 23% industry, 64.1% services (1995) **Life expectancy:** 69 (men); 73 (women) (1995–2000) **Child mortality rate:** (under 5, per 1,000 live births) 43 (1997) **Physicians:** 1 per 949 people (1993)

Practical information

Visa requirements: UK: visa not required for stays of up to 90 days. USA: visa not required for stays of up to 60 days **Embassy in the UK:** Honorary Consulate of the Dominican Republic, 6 Queen's Mansions, Brook Green, London W6 7EB. Tel: (0171) 602 1885 **British embassy:** Edificio Corominas Pepin, Ave 27 Febrero No. 233, Santo Domingo. Tel: (809) 472 7111; fax: (809) 472 7574 **Chamber of commerce:** Cámara de Comercio y Produccíon del Distrito Nacional, Apartado Postal 815, Arz. Nouel 206, Santo Domingo. Tel: (809) 682 7206; fax: (809) 685 2228

Chronology

14th century: Settled by Carib Indians, who followed an earlier wave of Arawak Indian immigration. **1492:** Visited by Christopher Columbus, who named it Hispaniola ('Little Spain'). **1496:** At Santo Domingo, the Spanish established the first European settlement in the western hemisphere, which became capital of all Spanish colonies in America. **first half of 16th century:** One-third of a million Arawaks and Caribs died, as a result of enslavement and exposure to European diseases; black African slaves were consequently brought in to work the island's gold and silver mines, which were swiftly exhausted. **1697:** Divided between France, which held the western third (Haiti), and Spain, which held the east (Dominican Republic, or Santo Domingo). **1795:** Santo Domingo was ceded to France. **1808:** Following a revolt by Spanish Creoles, with British support, Santo Domingo was retaken by Spain. **1821:** Became briefly independent after uprising against Spanish rule, and then fell under the control of Haiti. **1844:** Separated from Haiti to form Dominican Republic. **1861–65:** Under Spanish protection. **1904:** The USA took over the near-bankrupt republic's debts. **1916–24:** Temporarily occupied by US forces. **1930:** Military coup established personal dictatorship of Gen Rafael Trujillo Molina after overthrow of president Horacio Vázquez. **1937:** Army massacred 19,000–20,000 Haitians living in the Dominican provinces adjoining the frontier. **1961:** Trujillo assassinated. **1962:** First democratic elections resulted in Juan Bosch, founder of the left-wing Dominican Revolutionary Party (PRD), becoming president. **1963:** Bosch overthrown in military coup. **1965:** 30,000 US marines intervened to restore order and protect foreign nationals after Bosch had attempted to seize power. **1966:** New constitution adopted. Joaquín Balaguer, protégé of Trujillo and leader of the centre-right Christian Social Reform Party (PRSC), became president. **1978:** PRD returned to power, with Silvestre Antonio Guzmán as president. **1982:** PRD re-elected, with Jorge Blanco as president. **1985:** Blanco forced by International Monetary Fund to adopt austerity measures to save economy. **1986:** PRSC returned to power; Balaguer re-elected president. **1990:** Balaguer re-elected by a small majority. **1994:** Balaguer re-elected; election results disputed by opposition but eventually declared valid on condition that Balaguer serve reduced two-year term. **1996:** Leoned Fernandez of the left-wing Dominican Liberation Party (PLD) elected president. **1998:** Dominican Revolutionary Party (PRD) won assembly victory.

Ecuador Republic of

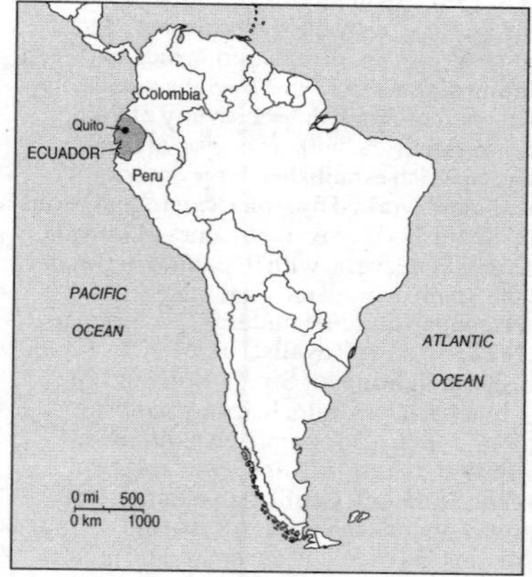

National name: *República del Ecuador* **Area:** 270,670 sq km/104,505 sq mi **Capital:** Quito **Major towns/cities:** Guayaquil, Cuenca, Machala, Portoviejo, Manta, Ambeto, Esmeraldas **Major ports:** Guayaquil

Government

Head of state and government: Jamil Mahuad Witt from 1998 **Political system:** emergent democracy **Administrative divisions:** 21 provinces **Political parties:** Social Christian Party (PSC), right wing; Ecuadorian Roldosist Party (PRE), populist, centre left; Popular Democracy (DP), centre right; Democratic Left (ID), moderate socialist; Conservative Party (PCE), right wing **Armed forces:** 57,100 (1997) **Conscription:** military service is selective for one year **Death penalty:** abolished in 1906 **Defence spend:** (% GDP) 3.5 (1997) **Education spend:** (% GNP) 3.5 (1996) **Health spend:** (% GDP) 2 (1990–95)

Economy and resources

Currency: sucre **GDP:** (US$) 18.88 billion (1997) **Real GDP growth:** (% change on previous year) 3.0 (1997) **GNP (US$):** 19 billion (1997) **GNP per capita (PPP):** (US$) 4,820 (1997) **Consumer price inflation:** 28.1% (1998) **Unemployment:** 8.9% (1993) **Foreign debt:** (US$) 14.49 billion (1996) **Major trading partners:** USA, Colombia, Germany, Chile, Peru, Japan, Italy, Spain **Resources:** petroleum, natural gas, gold, silver, copper, zinc, antimony, iron, uranium, lead, coal **Exports:** petroleum and petroleum products, bananas, shrimps (a major exporter), coffee, seafood products, cocoa beans and products, cut flowers. Principal market: USA 39.2% (1998) **Imports:** machinery and transport equipment, basic manufactures, chemicals, consumer goods. Principal source: USA 29.7% (1998) **Arable land:** 5.7% (1995)

Population and society

Population: 12,175,000 (1998 est) **Population growth rate:** 2.0% (1995–2000); 1.7% (2000–05) **Population density:** (per sq km) 44.6 (1998 est) **Urban population:** (% of total) 61 (1997) **Age distribution:** (% of total population) 0–14 35.9%, 15–64 59.7%, 65+ 4.4% (1998) **Ethnic groups:** about 55% mestizo (of Spanish-American and American Indian parentage), 25% American Indian, 10% Spanish, 10% African **Language:** Spanish (official), Quechua, Jivaro, and other indigenous languages **Religion:** Roman Catholic **Education:** (compulsory years) 6 **Literacy rate:** 88% (men); 84% (women) (1995 est) **Labour force:** 35% of population: 33%

agriculture, 19% industry, 48% services (1990) **Life expectancy:** 67 (men); 73 (women) (1995–2000) **Child mortality rate:** (under 5, per 1,000 live births) 56 (1997) **Physicians:** 1 per 918 people (1993)

Practical information

Visa requirements: UK: visa not required (except for business visits of three–six months). USA: visa not required (except for business visits of three–six months) **Embassy in the UK:** Flat 3B, 3 Hans Crescent, London SW1X 0LS. Tel: (0171) 584 1367; fax: (0171) 823 9701 **British embassy:** Casilla 314, Calle González Suárez 111, Quito. Tel: (2) 560 669; fax: (2) 560 730 **Chamber of commerce:** Federación Nacional de Cámaras de Comercio del Ecuador, Avenida Olmedo 414, Casila y Boyacá, Guayaquil. Tel: (4) 323 130; fax: (4) 323 478

Chronology

1450s: The Caras people, whose kingdom had its capital at Quito, conquered by Incas of Peru. **1531:** Spanish conquistador Francisco Pizarro landed on Ecuadorian coast, en route to Peru, where Incas were defeated. **1534:** Conquered by Spanish. Quito, which had been destroyed by American Indians, was refounded by Sebastian de Belalcazar; the area became part of Spanish Viceroyalty of Peru, which covered much of South America, with its capital at Lima (Peru). **later 16th century:** Spanish established large agrarian estates, owned by Europeans and worked by American Indian peons. **1739:** Became part of new Spanish Viceroyalty of Nueva Granada, which included Colombia and Venezuela, with its capital in Bogotá (Colombia). **1809:** With the Spanish monarchy having been overthrown by Napoleon Bonaparte, creole middle class began to press for independence. **1822:** Spanish Royalists defeated by Field Marshal Antonio José de Sucre, fighting for Simón Bolívar, 'The Liberator', at battle of Pichincha, near Quito; became part of independent Gran Colombia, which also comprised Colombia, Panama, and Venezuela. **1830:** Became fully independent state, after leaving Gran Colombia. **1845–60:** Political instability, with five presidents holding power, increasing tension between conservative Quito and liberal Guayaquil on the coast, and minor wars with Peru and Colombia. **1860–75:** Power held by Gabriel García Moreno, an autocratic theocrat-Conservative who launched education and public-works programmes. **1895–1912:** Dominated by Gen Eloy Alfaro, a radical, anticlerical Liberal from the coastal region, who reduced the power of the church. **1925–48:** Great political instability; no president completed his term of office. **1941:** Lost territory in Amazonia after defeat in war with Peru. **1948–55:** Liberals in power. **1956:** Camilo Ponce became first conservative president in 60 years. **1960:** Liberals in power, with José María Velasco Ibarra returning as president. **1961:** Velasco deposed and replaced by vice president. **1962:** Military junta installed. **1968:** Velasco returned as president. **1970s:** Ecuador emerged as significant oil producer. **1972:** Coup put military back in power. **1979:** New democratic constitution; Liberals in power but opposed by right- and left-wing parties. **1981:** Border dispute with Peru flared up again. **1982:** Deteriorating economy and austerity measures provoked strikes, demonstrations, and state of emergency. **1984–85:** No party with a clear majority in the national congress; León Febres Cordero narrowly won the presidency for the Conservatives. **1988:** Rodrigo Borja Cevallos elected president for moderate left-wing coalition and introduced unpopular austerity measures. **1992:** PUR leader Sixto Duran Ballen elected president; PSC became largest party in congress. Ecuador withdrew from OPEC to enable it to increase its oil exports. **1994:** Mounting opposition to Duran's economic liberalization and privatization programme. **1996:** Abdala Bucaram elected president. **1997:** Bucaram removed from office and replaced by vice-president Rosalia Arteaga, but a national referendum later ratified Fabian Alarcon as interim president. **1998:** Jamil Mahuad Witt elected president. 157-year border dispute settled with Peru.

Egypt **Arab Republic of**

National name: *Jumhuriyat Misr al-Arabiya* **Area:** 1,001,450 sq km/ 386,659 sq mi **Capital:** Cairo **Major towns/cities:** El Gîza, Shubra Al Khayma, Alexandria, Port Said, El-Mahalla el-Koubra, Tauta, El-Mansoura **Major ports:** Alexandria, Port Said, Suez, Damietta, Shubra Al Khayma

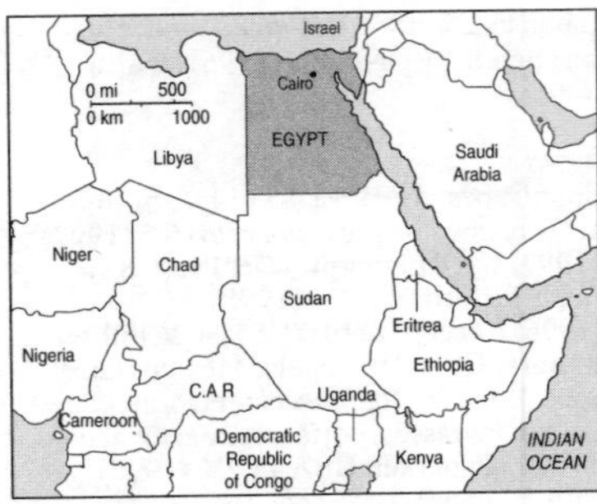

Government

Head of state: Hosni Mubarak from 1981 **Head of government:** Kamal Ahmed Ganzouri from 1996 **Political system:** democracy **Administrative divisions:** 26 governates **Political parties:** National Democratic Party (NDP), moderate, left of centre; Socialist Labour Party (SLP), right of centre; Liberal Socialist Party, free enterprise; New Wafd Party, nationalist; National Progressive Unionist Party, left wing **Armed forces:** 450,000 (1997) **Conscription:** 3 years (selective) **Death penalty:** retained and used for ordinary crimes **Defence spend:** (% GDP) 4.3 (1997) **Education spend:** (% GNP) 5.6 (1995) **Health spend:** (% GDP) 1.6 (1990–95)

Economy and resources

Currency: Egyptian pound **GDP:** (US$) 75.5 billion (1997) **Real GDP growth:** (% change on previous year) 5.0 (1997) **GNP (US$):** 71.2 billion (1997) **GNP per capita (PPP):** (US$) 2,940 (1997) **Consumer price inflation:** 6.2% (1998) **Unemployment:** 13% (1993) **Foreign debt:** (US$) 31.4 billion (1996) **Major trading partners:** USA, Italy, Germany, France **Resources:** petroleum, natural gas, phosphates, manganese, uranium, coal, iron ore, gold **Exports:** petroleum and petroleum products, textiles, clothing, food, live animals. Principal market: EU 34.1% (1997) **Imports:** wheat, maize, dairy products, machinery and transport equipment, wood and wood products, consumer goods. Principal source: EU 41.3% (1997) **Arable land:** 2.8% (1995)

Population and society

Population: 65,978,000 (1998 est) **Population growth rate:** 1.9% (1995–2000) **Population density:** (per sq km) 66.4 (1998 est) **Urban population:** (% of total) 45 (1997) **Age distribution:** (% of total population) 0–14 36.1%, 15–64 60.3%, 65+ 3.7% (1998) **Ethnic groups:** 93% indigenous **Language:** Arabic (official); ancient Egyptian survives to some extent in Coptic; English; French **Religion:** Sunni Muslim 90%, Coptic Christian 7% **Education:** (compulsory years) 5 **Literacy rate:** 63% (men); 34% (women) (1995 est) **Labour force:** 35% of population: 34% agriculture, 21% industry, 45% services (1995) **Life expectancy:** 65 (men); 67 (women) (1995–2000) **Child mortality rate:** (under 5, per 1,000 live births) 66 (1997) **Physicians:** 1 per 1,316 people (1993 est)

Practical information

Visa requirements: UK: visa required. USA: visa required **Embassy in the UK:** 26 South Street, London W1Y 8EL. Tel: (0171) 499 2401; fax: (0171) 355 3568 **British embassy:** 7 Sharia Ahmad Raghab, Garden City, Cairo. Tel: (2) 354 0850; fax: (2) 354 0859 **Chamber of commerce:** Federation of Chambers of Commerce, 4 el-Falaki Square, Cairo. Tel: (2) 355 1164; telex: 92645

Chronology

1st century BC–7th century AD: Conquered by Augustus in AD 30, Egypt passed under rule of Roman, and later Byzantine, governors. **AD 639–42:** Arabs conquered Egypt, introducing Islam and Arabic; succession of Arab dynasties followed. **1250:** Mamelukes seized power. **1517:** Became part of Turkish Ottoman Empire. **1798–1801:** Invasion by Napoleon followed by period of French occupation. **1801:** Control regained by Turks. **1869:** Opening of Suez Canal made Egypt strategically important. **1881–82:** Nationalist revolt resulted in British occupation. **1914:** Egypt became a British protectorate. **1922:** Achieved nominal independence under King

Fuad I. **1936:** Full independence from Britain achieved. King Fuad succeeded by his son Farouk. **1946:** Withdrawal of British troops except from Suez Canal zone. **1952:** Farouk overthrown by army in bloodless coup. **1953:** Egypt declared a republic, with Gen Neguib as president. **1956:** Neguib replaced by Col Gamal Nasser. Nasser announced nationalization of Suez Canal; Egypt attacked by Britain, France, and Israel. Cease-fire agreed following US intervention. **1958:** Short-lived merger of Egypt and Syria as United Arab Republic (UAR). **1967:** Six-Day War with Israel ended in Egypt's defeat and Israeli occupation of Sinai and Gaza Strip. **1970:** Nasser died suddenly; succeeded by Anwar Sadat. **1973:** Attempt to regain territory lost to Israel led to Yom Kippur War; cease-fire arranged by US secretary of state Henry Kissinger. **1978–79:** Camp David talks in USA resulted in a peace treaty between Egypt and Israel. Egypt expelled from Arab League. **1981:** Sadat assassinated by Muslim fundamentalists, succeeded by Hosni Mubarak. **1983:** Improved relations between Egypt and Arab world; only Libya and Syria maintained trade boycott. **1987:** Egypt readmitted to Arab League. **1989:** Improved relations with Libya; diplomatic relations with Syria restored. **1991:** Participation in Gulf War on US-led side. Major force in convening Middle East peace conference in Spain. **1992:** Violence between Muslims and Christians. **1994:** Government crackdown on Islamic militants. **1995:** Abortive attempt to assassinate Mubarak. **1996:** Kamal Ahmed Ganzouri appointed prime minister. **1997:** Islamic extremists killed and injured tourists at Luxor.

El Salvador Republic of

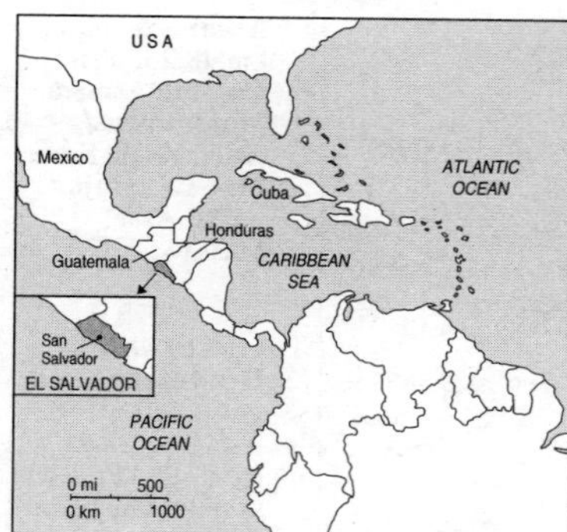

National name: *República de El Salvador* **Area:** 21,393 sq km/8,259 sq mi **Capital:** San Salvador **Major towns/cities:** Soyapango, Santa Ana, San Miguel, Nueva San Salvador, Mejicanos

Government

Head of state and government: Francisco Guillermo Flores Pérez from 1999 **Political system:** emergent democracy **Administrative divisions:** 14 departments **Political parties:** Christian Democrats (PDC), anti-imperialist; Farabundo Martí Liberation Front (FMLN), left wing; National Republican Alliance (ARENA), extreme right wing; National Conciliation Party (PCN), right wing **Armed forces:** 28,400 (1997); plus 12,000 in paramilitary forces **Conscription:** selective conscription for two years **Death penalty:** laws provide for the death penalty only for exceptional crimes such as crimes under military law or crimes committed in exceptional circumstances such as wartime (last known execution in 1973) **Defence spend:** (% GDP) 1.9 (1997) **Education spend:** (% GNP) 2.2 (1995) **Health spend:** (% GDP) 1.2 (1990–95)

Economy and resources

Currency: Salvadorean colón **GDP:** (US$) 8.1 billion (1994) 11.3 billion (1997 est) **Real GDP growth:** (% change on previous year) 3.5 (1997) **GNP (US$):** 10.7 billion (1997) **GNP per capita (PPP):** (US$) 2,810 (1997) **Consumer price inflation:** 7.6% (1998) **Unemployment:** 7.7% (1993) **Foreign debt:** (US$) 2.7 billion (1996) **Major trading partners:** USA, Guatemala, Costa Rica, Honduras, Mexico, Japan, Germany, Venezuela **Resources:** salt, limestone, gypsum **Exports:** coffee, textiles and garments, sugar, shrimp, footwear, pharmaceuticals. Principal market: USA 54.3% (1997) **Imports:** petroleum and other minerals, cereals, chemicals, iron and steel, machinery and transport equipment, consumer goods. Principal source: USA 52.8% (1997) **Arable land:** 26.3% (1995)

Population and society

Population: 6,032,000 (1998 est) **Population growth rate:** 2.2% (1995–2000); 2% (2000–05) **Population density:** (per sq km) 277.6 (1998 est) **Urban population:** (% of total) 46 (1997) **Age distribution:** (% of total population) 0–14 37.0%, 15–64 57.8%, 65+ 5.2% (1998) **Ethnic groups:** about 92% of the population are mestizos, 6% Indians, and 2% of European origin **Language:** Spanish, Nahuatl **Religion:** Roman Catholic, Protestant **Education:** (compulsory years) 9 **Literacy rate:** 76% (men); 70% (women) (1995 est) **Labour force:** 36% of population: 36% agriculture, 21% industry, 43% services (1990) **Life expectancy:** 67 (men); 73 (women) (1995–2000) **Child mortality rate:** (under 5, per 1,000 live births) 48 (1997) **Physicians:** 1 per 1,515 people (1993 est)

Practical information

Visa requirements: UK: visa not required for a stay of up to 90 days. USA: visa required (Tourist Card) **Embassy in the UK:** Tennyson House, 159 Great Portland Street, London W1N 5FD. Tel: (0171) 436 8282; fax: (0171) 436 8181 **British embassy:** PO Box 1591, Paeso General Escalón 4828, San Salvador. Tel: (503) 298 1768/9; fax: (503) 298 3328 **Chamber of commerce:** Cámara de Comercio e Industria de El Salvador, Apartado 1640, 9a Avenida Norte y 5a Calle Poniente, San Salvador. Tel: (503) 771 2055; fax: (503) 771 4461

Chronology

11th century: Pipils, descendants of the Nahuatl-speaking Toltec and Aztec peoples of Mexico, settled in the country and came to dominate El Salvador until the Spanish conquest. **1524:** Conquered by the Spanish adventurer Pedro de Alvarado and made a Spanish colony, with resistance being crushed by 1540. **1821:** Independence achieved from Spain; briefly joined with Mexico. **1823:** Became part of United Provinces (Federation) of Central America, also embracing Costa Rica, Guatemala, Honduras, and Nicaragua. **1833:** Unsuccessful rebellion against Spanish control of land led by Anastasio Aquino. **1840:** Became fully independent when Federation dissolved. **1859–63:** Coffee growing introduced by president Gerardo Barrios. **1932:** Peasant uprising, led by Augustín Farabundo Martí, suppressed by military at a cost of the lives of 30,000, virtually eliminating American Indian Salvadoreans. **1961:** Following a coup, the right-wing National Conciliation Party (PCN) established and in power. **1969:** Brief 'Football War' with Honduras, which El Salvador attacked, at the time of a football competition between the two states, following evictions of thousands of Salvadoran illegal immigrants from Honduras. **1977:** Allegations of human-rights violations; growth of left-wing Farabundo Martí National Liberation Front (FMLN) guerrilla activities. Gen Carlos Romero elected president. **1979:** A coup replaced Romero with a military-civilian junta. **1980:** The archbishop of San Salvador and human-rights champion, Oscar Romero, assassinated; country on verge of civil war. José Napoleón Duarte (PDC) became first civilian president since 1931. **1981:** Mexico and France recognized the FMLN guerrillas as a legitimate political force, but the USA actively assisted the government in its battle against them; 30,000 were killed 1979–81 by right-wing death squads. **1982:** Assembly elections boycotted by left-wing parties. Held amid considerable violence, they were won by far-right National Republican Alliance (ARENA). **1984:** Duarte won presidential election. **1986:** Duarte sought a negotiated settlement with the guerrillas. **1989:** Alfredo Cristiani (ARENA) became president in rigged elections; rebel attacks intensified. **1991:** United Nations-sponsored peace accord signed by representatives of the government and the socialist guerrilla group, the FMLN, which became a political party. **1993:** UN-sponsored commission published report on war atrocities; government amnesty for those implicated; top military leaders officially retired. **1994:** Armando Calderón Sol (ARENA) elected president.

Equatorial Guinea Republic of

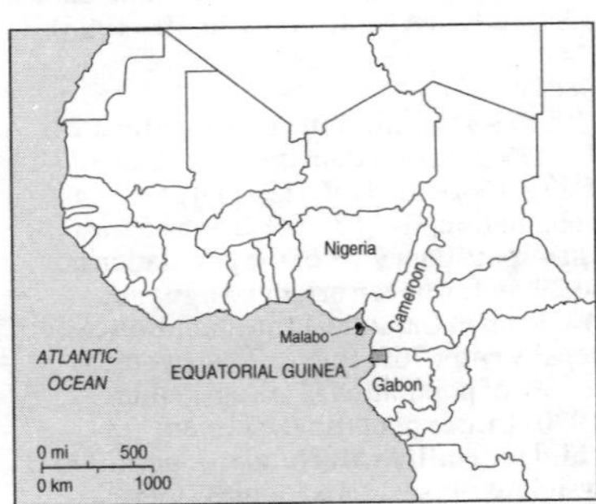

National name: *República de Guinea Ecuatorial* **Area:** 28,051 sq km/10,830 sq mi **Capital:** Malabo **Major towns/cities:** Bata, Evinayong, Ebebiyin, Mongomo

Government

Head of state: Teodoro Obiang Nguema Mbasogo from 1979 **Head of government:** Angel Serafin Seriche Dougan, from 1996 **Political system:** emergent democracy **Administrative divisions:** seven provinces **Political parties:** Democratic Party of Equatorial Guinea (PDGE), nationalist, right of centre, militarily controlled; People's Social Democratic Convention (CSDP), left of centre; Democratic Socialist Union of Equatorial Guinea (UDSGE), left of centre **Armed forces:** 1,320 (1997) **Conscription:** military service is voluntary **Death penalty:** retained and used for ordinary crimes **Defence spend:** (% GDP) 1.3 (1997) **Education spend:** (% GNP) 1.8 (1995)

Economy and resources

Currency: franc CFA **GDP:** (US$) 392 million (1997 est) **Real GDP growth:** (% change on previous year) 52.0 (1997) **GNP (US$):** 444 million (1997) **GNP per capita (PPP):** (US$) 3,600 (1997) **Consumer price inflation:** 7.1% (1997) **Foreign debt:** (US$) 283 million (1996) **Major trading partners:** USA, Spain, Italy, the Netherlands, Liberia, France, Nigeria, Cameroon **Resources:** petroleum, natural gas, gold, uranium, iron ore, tantalum, manganese **Exports:** timber, re-exported ships and boats, textile fibres and waste, cocoa, coffee. Principal market: USA 66% (1997) **Imports:** ships and boats, petroleum and related products, food and live animals, machinery and transport equipment, beverages and tobacco, basic manufactures. Principal source: USA 23% (1997) **Arable land:** 4.6% (1995)

Population and society

Population: 431,000 (1998 est) **Population growth rate:** 2.5% (1995–2000); 2.4% (2000–05) **Population density:** (per sq km) 16.2 (1998 est) **Urban population:** (% of total) 45 (1997) **Age distribution:** (% of total population) 0–14 43.1%, 15–64 53.2%, 65+ 3.8% (1998) **Ethnic groups:** 80–90% of the Fang ethnic group, of Bantu origin; most other groups have been pushed to the coast by Fang expansion **Language:** Spanish (official); pidgin English is widely spoken, and on Annobón (whose people were formerly slaves of the Portuguese) a Portuguese patois; Fang and other African patois spoken on Río Muni **Religion:** Roman Catholic, Protestant, animist **Education:** (compulsory years) 8 **Literacy rate:** 89% (men); 67% (women) (1995 est) **Labour force:** 77% agriculture, 2% industry, 21% services (1990) **Life expectancy:** 48 (men); 52 (women) (1995–2000) **Child mortality rate:** (under 5, per 1,000 live births) 162 (1997) **Physicians:** 1 per 3,520 people (1991)

Practical information

Visa requirements: UK: visa required. USA: visa required **Embassy for the UK:** 6 rue Alfred de Vigny, 75008 Paris, France. Tel: (1) 4766 4433; fax: (1) 4764 9452 **British embassy:** British Consulate, Winston Churchill Avenue, BP 547, Yaoundé, Cameroon. Tel: (237) 220 545; fax: (237) 220 148 (All staff based in Yaoundé, Cameroon.) **Chamber of commerce:** Cámara de Comercio Agrícola y Forestal de Malabo, Apartado 51, Malabo. Tel: (240) 151

Chronology

1472: First visited by Portuguese explorers. **1778:** Bioko (formerly known as Fernando Po) Island ceded to Spain, which established cocoa plantations there in the late 19th century, importing labour from West Africa. **1885:** Mainland territory of Mbini (formerly Rio Muni) came under Spanish rule, the whole colony being known as Spanish Guinea, with the capital at Malabu on Bioko Island. **1920s:** League of Nations special mission sent to investigate the forced, quasi-slave labour conditions on the Bioko cocoa plantations, then the largest in the world. **1959:** Became a Spanish Overseas Province; African population finally granted full citizenship. **early 1960s:** On the mainland, the Fang people spearheaded a nationalist movement directed against Spanish favouritism towards Bioko Island and its controlling Bubi tribe. **1963:** Achieved internal autonomy. **1968:** Independence achieved from Spain. Macias Nguema, a nationalist Fang, became first president, discriminating against the Bubi community. **1970s:** Economy collapsed as Spanish settlers and other minorities fled in the face of intimidation by Nguema's brutal, dictatorial regime, which was marked by the murder, torture, and imprisonment of tens of thousands of political opponents and rivals, as well as the closing of churches. **1979:** Nguema overthrown, tried, and executed. He was replaced by his nephew, Teodoro Obiang Nguema Mbasogo, who established a military regime, but released political prisoners and imposed restrictions on the Catholic church. **1992:** New pluralist constitution approved by referendum. **1993:** Obiang's PDGE won first multiparty elections on low turnout. **1996:** Obiang re-elected amid claims of fraud by opponents. **1998:** Angel Serafin Seriche Dougan re-appointed prime minister.

Eritrea State of

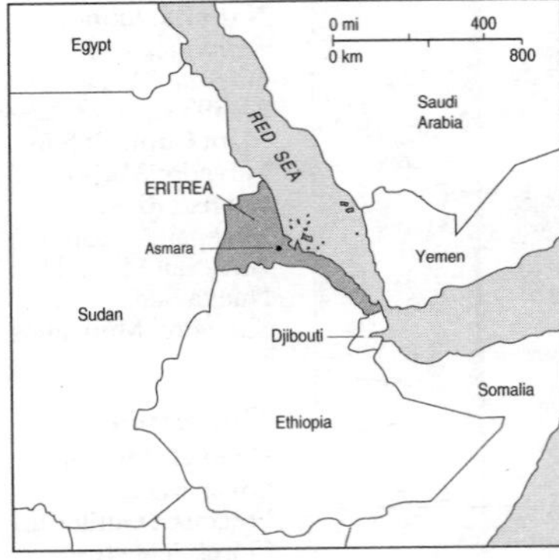

Area: 125,000 sq km/48,262 sq mi **Capital:** Asmara **Major towns/cities:** Asab, Keren, Massawa **Major ports:** Asab, Massawa

Government

Head of state and government: Issaias Afwerki from 1993 **Political system:** emergent democracy **Administrative divisions:** ten provinces **Political parties:** People's Front for Democracy and Justice (PFDJ) (formerly Eritrean People's Liberation Front: EPLF), left of centre; Eritrean National Pact Alliance (ENPA), moderate, centrist **Armed forces:** 46,000 (1997) **Conscription:** compulsory for 18 months **Death penalty:** retained and used for ordinary crimes **Defence spend:** (% GDP) 8.3 (1997) **Education spend:** (% GDP) 1.8 (1996) **Health spend:** (% GDP) 1.1 (1990–95)

Economy and resources

Currency: Ethiopian birr **GDP:** (US$) 714 million (1996) **Real GDP growth:** (% change on previous year) N/A **GNP (US$):** 801 million (1997) **GNP per capita (PPP):** (US$) 1,010 (1997 est) **Consumer price inflation:** 10% (1995 est) **Unemployment:** 50% (1994 est) **Foreign debt:** (US$) 46 million (1996) **Major trading partners:** Ethiopia, Saudi Arabia, Italy, Sudan, United Arab Emirates **Resources:** gold, silver, copper, zinc, sulphur, nickel, chrome, potash, basalt, limestone, marble, sand, silicates **Exports:** textiles, leather and leather products, beverages, petroleum products, basic household goods. Principal market: Ethiopia 65.8% (1996) **Imports:** machinery and transport equipment, petroleum, food and live animals, basic manufactures. Principal source: Saudi Arabia 15.2% (1996) **Arable land:** 4.4% (1995)

Population and society

Population: 3,577,000 (1998 est) **Population growth rate:** 3.7% (1995–2000) **Population density:** (per sq km) 31.7 (1998 est) **Urban population:** (% of total) 18 (1997) **Age distribution:** (% of total population) 0–14 42.8%, 15–64 53.8%, 65+ 3.3% (1998) **Ethnic groups:** several ethnic groups, including the Amhara and the Tigrais **Language:** Tigrinya (official), Arabic (official), Afar, Amharic, Bilen, Hidareb, Kunama, Nara, Rashaida, Saho, and Tigre **Religion:** Sunni Muslim, Coptic Christian **Education:** (compulsory years) 7 **Literacy rate:** 20–25% (men); 5–10% (women) (1995 est) **Life expectancy:** 49 (men); 52 (women) (1995–2000) **Child mortality rate:** (under 5, per 1,000 live births) 143 (1997) **Physicians:** 1 per 45,588 people (1993 est)

Practical information

Visa requirements: UK: visa required. USA: visa required **Embassy in the UK:** Eritrean Consulate, 96 White Lion Street, London N1 9PF. Tel: (0171) 713 0096; fax: (0171) 713 0161 **British embassy:** British Consulate, PO Box 5584, c/o Mitchell Gotts Building, Emperor Yohannes Avenue 5, Asmara. Tel: (1) 120 145; fax: (1) 120 104 **Chamber of commerce:** Asmara Chamber of Commerce, PO Box 856, Asmara. Tel: (1) 21388; fax: (1) 20138

Chronology

4th–7th centuries AD: Part of Ethiopian Aksum kingdom. **8th century:** Islam introduced to coastal areas by Arabs. **12th–16th centuries:** Under influence of Ethiopian Abyssinian kingdoms. **mid-16th century:** Came under control of Turkish Ottoman Empire. **1882:** Occupied by Italy. **1889:** Italian colony of Eritrea created out of Ottoman areas and coastal districts of Ethiopia. **1920s:** Massawa developed into largest port in East Africa. **1935–36:** Used as base for Italy's conquest of Ethiopia and became part of Italian East Africa. **1941:** Became British protectorate after Italy removed from North Africa. **1952:** Federation formed with Ethiopia by United Nations (UN). **1958:** Eritrean People's Liberation Front (EPLF) formed to fight for independence after general strike brutally suppressed by Ethiopian rulers. **1962:** Annexed by Ethiopia, sparking a secessionist rebellion which was to last 30 years and claim 150,000 lives. **1974:** Ethiopian emperor Haile Selassie deposed by military; EPLF continued struggle for independence. **1977–78:** EPLF cleared territory of Ethiopian forces, but position soon reversed by Soviet-backed Marxist Ethiopian government of Col Mengistu Haile Mariam. **mid-1980s:** Severe famine in Eritrea and refugee crisis as Ethiopian government sought forcible resettlement. **1990:** Strategic port of Massawa captured by Eritrean rebel forces. **1991:** Ethiopian president Mengistu overthrown. EPLF secured whole of Eritrea and provisional government formed under Issaias Afwerki. **1993:** Independence approved in regional referendum and recognized by Ethiopia. Transitional government established, with Afwerki elected president; 500,000 refugees outside Eritrea began to return. **1997:** New constitution adopted. **1998:** Border disputes with Ethiopia escalated, with bombing raids from both sides.

Estonia Republic of

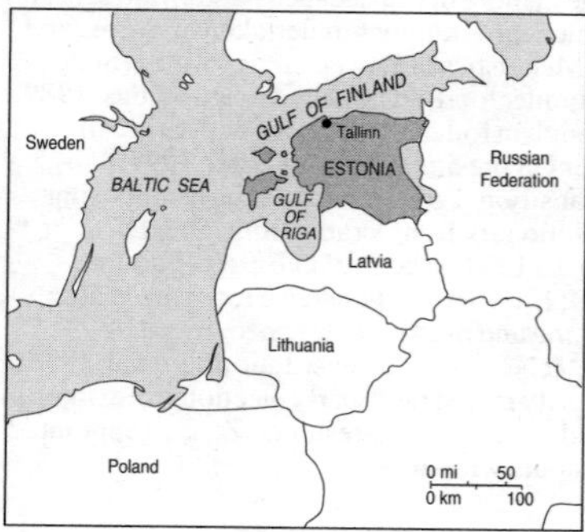

National name: *Eesti Vabariik* **Area:** 45,000 sq km/17,374 sq mi **Capital:** Tallinn **Major towns/cities:** Tartu, Narva, Kohtla-Järve, Pärnu

Government

Head of state: Lennart Meri from 1992 **Head of government:** Mart Siimann from 1997 **Political system:** emergent democracy **Administrative divisions:** 15 counties and six towns **Political parties:** Coalition Party (KMU), ex-communist, left of centre, 'social market'; Isamaa (National Fatherland Party, or Pro Patria), right wing, nationalist, free market; Estonian Reform Party (ERP), freemarket; Centre Party (CP), moderate nationalist (formerly the Estonian Popular Front (EPF; Rahvarinne); Estonian National Independence Party (ENIP), radical nationalist; Communist Party of Estonia (CPE); Our Home is Estonia; Estonian Social Democratic Party (ESDP) (last three draw much of their support from ethnic Russian community) **Armed forces:** 3,500 (1997); plus 14,000 reservists and paramilitary border guard of 2,800 **Conscription:** compulsory for 12 months (men and women) **Death penalty:** abolished in 1998 **Defence spend:** (% GDP) 2.5 (1997) **Education spend:** (% GNP) 7.3 (1996) **Health spend:** (% GDP) 6.3% (1990–95)

Economy and resources

Currency: kroon **GDP:** (US$) 4.6 billion (1997) **Real GDP growth:** (% change on previous year) 5.5 (1997) **GNP (US$):** 4.8 billion (1997) **GNP per capita (PPP):** (US$) 5,010 (1997) **Consumer price inflation:** 9.6% (1998) **Unemployment:** 5.6% (1996) **Foreign debt:** (US$) 405 million (1996) **Major trading partners:** Finland, Russia, Sweden, Germany, Latvia, the Netherlands, Lithuania, UK, Japan **Resources:** oilshale, peat, phosphorite ore, superphosphates **Exports:** foodstuffs, animal products, textiles, timber products, base metals, mineral products, machinery. Principal market: Russia 18.7% (1997) **Imports:** machinery and transport equipment, food products, textiles, mineral products. Principal source: Finland 23.4 (1997) **Arable land:** 26.7% (1995)

Population and society

Population: 1,429,000 (1998 est) **Population growth rate:** –1% (1995–2000) **Population density:** (per sq km) 31.5 (1998 est) **Urban population:** (% of total) 74 (1997) **Age distribution:** (% of total population) 0–14 18.8%, 15–64 66.8%, 65+ 14.3% (1998) **Ethnic groups:** 62% Finno-Ugric ethnic Estonians, 30% Russian, 3% Ukrainian, 2% Belarussian, 1% Finnish **Language:** Estonian (official), Russian **Religion:** Lutheran, Russian Orthodox **Education:** (compulsory years) 9 **Literacy rate:** 99% (men); 99% (women) (1995 est) **Labour force:** 8.7% agriculture, 35.7% industry, 55.6% services (1994) **Life expectancy:** 64 (men); 75 (women) (1995–2000) **Child mortality rate:** (under 5, per 1,000 live births) 18 (1997) **Physicians:** 1 per 312 people (1993)

Practical information

Visa requirements: UK: visa not required. USA: visa not required **Embassy in the UK:** 16 Hyde Park Gate, London SW7 5DG. Tel: (0171) 589 3428; fax: (0171) 589 3430 **British embassy:** Kentmanni 20, EE-0100 Tallinn. Tel: (2) 313 353; fax: (2) 313 354 **Chamber of commerce:** Chamber of Commerce and Industry of the Republic of Estonia, Toom-Kooli Street 17, EE-0001 Tallinn. Tel: (2) 444 929; fax: (2) 443 656

Chronology

1st century AD: First independent state formed. **9th century:** Invaded by Vikings. **13th century:** Tallinn, in the Danish-controlled north, joined Hanseatic League, a northern European union of commercial towns; Livonia, comprising southern Estonia and Latvia, came under control of German Teutonic Knights and was converted to Christianity. **1561:** Sweden took control of northern Estonia. **1629:** Sweden took control of southern Estonia from Poland. **1721:** Sweden ceded the country to tsarist Russia. **late 19th century:** Estonian nationalist movement developed in opposition to Russian political and cultural repression and German economic control. **1914:** Occupied by German troops. **1918–19:** Estonian nationalists, led by Konstantin Pats, proclaimed and achieved independence, despite efforts by the Russian Red Army to regain control. **1920s:** Land reforms and cultural advances under democratic regime. **1934:** Pats overthrew parliamentary democracy in a quasi-fascist coup at a time of economic depression; Baltic Entente mutual defence pact signed with Latvia and Lithuania. **1940:** Estonia incorporated into Soviet Union (USSR); 100,000 Estonians deported to Siberia or killed.

1941–44: German occupation during World War II. **1944:** USSR regained control; 'Sovietization' followed, including agricultural collectivization and immigration of ethnic Russians. **late 1980s:** Beginnings of nationalist dissent, encouraged by *glasnost* initiative of reformist Soviet leader Mikhail Gorbachev. **1988:** Popular Front (EPF) established to campaign for democracy. Sovereignty declaration issued by state assembly rejected by USSR as unconstitutional. **1989:** Estonian replaced Russian as main language. **1990:** CPE monopoly of power abolished; pro-independence candidates secured majority after multiparty elections; coalition government formed with EPF leader Edgar Savisaar as prime minister; Arnold Rüütel became president. Prewar constitution partially restored. **1991:** Independence achieved after attempted anti-Gorbachev coup in Moscow; CPE outlawed. Estonia joined United Nations. **1992:** Savisaar resigned over food and energy shortages; Isamaa leader Lennart Meri became president and free-marketer Mart Laar prime minister. **1993:** Joined Council of Europe; free-trade agreement with Latvia and Lithuania. **1994:** Last Russian troops withdrawn. Radical economic-reform programme introduced; controversial law on 'aliens' passed, requiring non-ethnic Estonians to apply for residency. Laar resigned. **1995:** Former communists won largest number of seats in general election; left-of-centre coalition formed under Tiit Vahi. **1996:** President Meri re-elected. Ruling coalition collapsed; Prime Minister Tiit Vahi continued with a minority government. **1997:** Vahi, accused of corruption, resigned and was replaced by Mart Siimann. Estonia invited to begin European Union membership negotiations. **1998:** The legislature voted to ban electoral alliances in future elections.

Ethiopia Federal Democratic Republic of (formerly known as Abyssinia)

National name: *Hebretesebawit Ityopia* **Area:** 1,096,900 sq km/423,513 sq mi **Capital:** Addis Ababa **Major towns/cities:** Jimma, Dire Dawa, Harar, Nazret, Dessie, Gonder, Mek'elē

Government

Head of state: Negasso Ghidada from 1995 **Head of government:** Meles Zenawi from 1995 **Political system:** transition to democratic federal republic **Administrative divisions:** nine states and one metropolitan area **Political parties:** Ethiopian People's Revolutionary Democratic Front (EPRDF), nationalist, left of centre; Tigré People's Liberation Front (TPLF); Ethiopian People's Democratic Movement (EPDM); United Oromo Liberation Front, Islamic nationalist **Armed forces:** 120,000 (1997) **Conscription:** mlitary service is voluntary **Death penalty:** retained and used for ordinary crimes **Defence spend:** (% GDP) 2.1 (1997) **Education spend:** (% GNP) 4 (1996) **Health spend:** (% GDP) 1.7 (1990–95)

Economy and resources

Currency: Ethiopian birr **GDP:** (US$) 6.3 billion (1997) **Real GDP growth:** (% change on previous year) 6.5 (1996 est) **GNP (US$):** 6.5 billion (1997) **GNP per capita (PPP):** (US$) 510 (1997) **Consumer price inflation:** 6.9% (1996) **Unemployment:** 40.5% (1992 est) **Foreign debt:** (US$) 10.08 billion (1996) **Major trading partners:** Germany, Saudi Arabia, USA, Japan, UK, Italy, France **Resources:** gold, salt, platinum, copper, potash. Reserves of petroleum have not been exploited **Exports:** coffee, hides and skins, petroleum products, fruit and vegetables. Principal market: Germany 26.4% (1996) **Imports:** machinery, aircraft and other vehicles, petroleum and petroleum products, basic manufactures, chemicals and related products. Principal source: Italy 11.6% (1996) **Arable land:** 11.3% (1995)

Population and society

Population: 59,649,000 (1998 est) **Population growth rate:** 3.2% (1995–2000); 2.9% (2000–05) **Population density:** (per sq km) 52.1 (1998 est) **Urban population:** (% of total) 17 (1997) **Age distribution:** (% of total population) 0–14 46.0%, 15–64 51.2%, 65+ 2.8% (1998) **Ethnic groups:** over 70 different ethnic groups, the two main ones are the Galla (mainly in the east and south of the central plateau), who comprise about 40% of the population, and the Amhara and Tigré (largely in the central plateau itself), who constitute about 35% **Language:** Amharic (official), Tigrinya, Orominga, Arabic **Religion:** Sunni Muslim, Christian (Ethiopian Orthodox Church, which has had its own patriarch since 1976) 40%, animist **Education:** (compulsory years) 6 **Literacy rate:** 45% (men); 25% (women) (1995 est) **Labour force:** 88.6% agriculture, 2% industry, 9.4% services (1995) **Life expectancy:** 48 (men); 52 (women) (1995–2000) **Child mortality rate:** (under 5, per 1,000 live births) 166 (1997) **Physicians:** 1 per 32,499 people (1993 est)

Practical information

Visa requirements: UK: visa required. USA: visa required **Embassy in the UK:** 17 Prince's Gate, London SW7 1PZ. Tel: (0171) 589 7212; fax: (0171) 584 7054 **British embassy:** PO Box 858, Fikre Mariam Abatechan Street, Addis Ababa. Tel: (1) 612 354; fax: (1) 610 588 **Chamber of commerce:** Ethiopian Chamber of Commerce, PO Box 517, Mexico Square, Addis Ababa. Tel: (1) 518 240; telex: 21213

Chronology

1st–7th centuries AD: Founded by Semitic immigrants from Saudi Arabia, the kingdom of Aksum and its capital, northwest of Adwa, flourished. It reached its peak in the 4th century when Coptic Christianity was introduced from Egypt. **7th century onwards:** Islam was spread by Arab conquerors. **11th century:** Emergence of independent Ethiopian kingdom of Abyssinia, which was to remain dominant for nine centuries. **late 15th century:** Abyssinia visited by Portuguese explorers. **1889:** Abyssinia reunited by Menelik II. **1896:** Invasion by Italy defeated by Menelik at Adwa, who went on to annex Ogaden in the southeast and areas to the west. **1916:** Haile Selassie became regent. **1930:** Haile Selassie became emperor. **1936:** Conquered by Italy and incorporated in Italian East Africa. **1941:** Return of Emperor Selassie after liberation by the British. **1952:** Ethiopia federated with Eritrea. **1962:** Eritrea annexed by Selassie; Eritrean People's Liberation front (EPLF) resistance movement began, a rebellion that was to continue for 30 years. **1963:** First conference of Selassie-promoted Organization of African Unity (OAU) held in Addis Ababa. **1973–74:** Severe famine in northern Ethiopia; 200,000 died in Wallo province. **1974:** Haile Selassie deposed and replaced by a military government led by Gen Teferi Benti. **1977:** Teferi Benti killed and replaced by Col Mengistu Haile Mariam. Somali forces ejected from the Somali-peopled Ogaden in the southeast. **1977–79:** 'Red Terror' period in which Mengistu's single-party Marxist regime killed thousands of people and promoted collective farming; Tigré People's Liberation Front guerrillas began fighting for regional autonomy in the northern highlands. **1984:** Workers' Party of Ethiopia (WPE) declared the only legal political party. **1985:** Worst famine in more than a decade; Western aid sent and forcible internal resettlement programmes undertaken in Eritrea and Tigré in the north. **1987:** Mengistu Mariam elected president under new constitution. New famine; food aid hindered by guerrillas. **1989:** Coup attempt against Mengistu foiled. Peace talks with Eritrean rebels mediated by former US president Jimmy Carter. **1991:** Mengistu overthrown; transitional government set up by opposing Ethiopian People's Revolutionary Democratic Front (EPRDF), headed by Meles Zenawi. EPLF took control of Eritrea. Famine gripped the country. **1993:** Eritrean independence recognized after referendum; private farming and market sector encouraged by EPRDF government. **1994:** New federal constitution adopted. **1995:** Ruling EPRDF won majority in first multiparty elections to an interim parliament. Negasso Ghidada chosen as president; Zenawi appointed premier. **1998:** Border dispute with Eritrea.

Fiji Islands Republic of

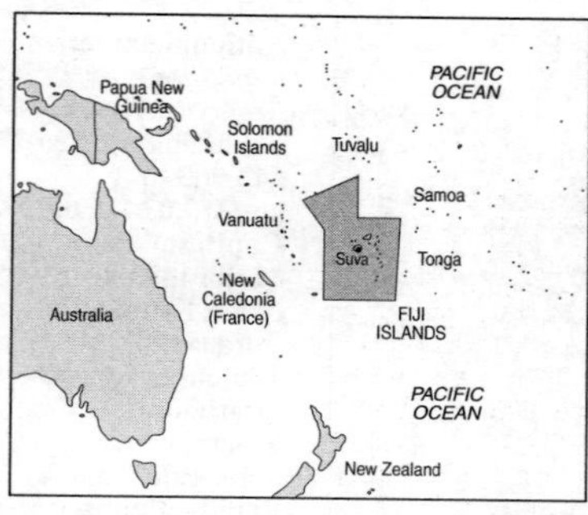

Area: 18,333 sq km/7,078 sq mi **Capital:** Suva **Major towns/cities:** Lautoka, Nadi, Ba, Labasa **Major ports:** Lautoka and Levuka

Government

Head of state: Ratu Sir Kamisese Mara from 1994 **Head of government:** Mahendra Chaudhry from 1999 **Political system:** democracy **Administrative divisions:** 14 provinces **Political parties:** National Federation Party (NFP), moderate left of centre, Indian; Fijian Labour Party (FLP), left of centre, Indian; United Front, Fijian; Fijian Political Party (FPP), Fijian centrist **Armed forces:** 3,600 (1997) **Conscription:** military service is voluntary **Death penalty:** laws provide for the death penalty only for exceptional crimes such as crimes under military law or crimes committed in exceptional cricumstances such as wartime (last execution 1964) **Defence spend:** (% GDP) 2.6 (1997) **Education spend:** (% GNP) 5.4 (1995) **Health spend:** (% GDP) 1.3 (1994)

Economy and resources

Currency: Fiji dollar **GDP:** (US$) 1.8 billion (1997 est) **Real GDP growth:** (% change on previous year) 1.0 (1997) **GNP (US$):** 2 billion (1997) **GNP per capita (PPP):** (US$) 4,040 (1997) **Consumer price inflation:** 2.5% (1996) **Unemployment:** 5.4% (1995) **Foreign debt:** (US$) 217 million (1996) **Major trading partners:** Australia, New Zealand, Japan, UK, USA **Resources:** gold, silver, copper **Exports:** sugar, gold, fish and fish products, clothing, re-exported petroleum products, timber, ginger, molasses. Principal market: Australia 27% (1996) **Imports:** basic manufactured goods, machinery and transport equipment, food, mineral fuels. Principal source: Australia 44.3% (1996) **Arable land:** 10.9% (1995)

Population and society

Population: 796,000 (1998 est) **Population growth rate:** 1.6% (1995–2000) **Population density:** (per sq km) 44 (1998 est) **Urban population:** (% of total) 41 (1997) **Age distribution:** (% of total population) 0–14 34.1%, 15–64 62.7%, 65+ 3.2% (1998) **Ethnic groups:** 48% Fijians (of Melanesian and Polynesian descent), 51% Asians **Language:** English (official), Fijian, Hindi **Religion:** Methodist, Hindu, Muslim, Sikh **Education:** not compulsory **Literacy rate:** 94% (men); 89% (women) (1995 est) **Labour force:** 34% of population: 46% agriculture, 15% industry, 39% services (1990) **Life expectancy:** 71 (men); 75 (women) (1995–2000) **Child mortality rate:** (under 5, per 1,000 live births) 23 (1997) **Physicians:** 1 per 2,011 people (1992)

Practical information

Visa requirements: UK: visa not required. USA: visa not required **Embassy in the UK:** 34 Hyde Park Gate, London SW7 5DN. Tel: (0171) 839 2200; fax: (0171) 839 9050 **British embassy:** PO Box 1355, Victoria House, 47 Gladstone Road, Suva. Tel: (679) 311 033; fax: (679) 301 406 **Chamber of commerce:** Suva Chamber of Commerce, PO Box 337, 2nd Floor, GB Hari Building, 12 Pier Street, Suva. Tel: (679) 303 854; fax: (679) 300 475

Chronology

c. **1500 BC:** Peopled by Polynesian and, later, by Melanesian settlers. **1643:** The islands were visited for the first time by a European, the Dutch navigator Abel Tasman. **1830s:** Arrival of Western Christian missionaries. **1840s–50s:** Western Fiji came under dominance of a Christian convert prince, Cakobau, ruler of Bau islet, who proclaimed himself Tui Viti (King of Fiji), while the east was controlled by Ma'afu, a Christian prince from Tonga. **1857:** British consul appointed, encouraging settlers from Australia and New Zealand to set up cotton farms in Fiji. **1874:** Fiji became a British crown colony after deed of cession signed by King Cakobau. **1875–76:** A third of the Fijian population wiped out by a measles epidemic; rebellion against British suppressed with the assitance of Fijian chiefs. **1877:** Fiji became headquarters of the British Western Pacific High Commission (WPHC), which controlled other British protectorates in the Pacific region. **1879–1916:** Indian labourers brought in, on ten-year indentured contracts, to work sugar plantations. **1904:** Legislative Council formed, with elected Europeans and nominated Fijians, to advise the British governor. **1963:** Legislative Council enlarged; women and Fijians were enfranchised. The predominantly Fijian Alliance Party (AP) formed. **1970:** Independence achieved from Britain; Ratu Sir Kamisese Mara of the AP elected as first prime minister. **1973:** Ratu Sir George Cakobau, great-grandson of the chief who had sworn allegiance to the British in 1874, became governor general. **1985:** FLP formed by Timoci Bavadra, with trade-union backing. **1987:** After general election had brought to power an Indian-dominated coalition led by Bavadra, Lt-Col Sitiveni Rabuka seized power after a military coup, and proclaimed a Fijian-dominated republic outside the Commonwealth. **1990:** New constitution, favouring indigenous (Melanese) Fijians, introduced. Civilian rule re-established, with resignations from cabinet of military officers, but Rabuka remained as home affairs minister, with Mara as prime minister. **1992:** General election produced coalition government with Rabuka of the FPP as prime minister. **1993:** President Ganilau died and was replaced by Ratu Sir Kamisese Mara. **1994:** Rabuka and FPP re-elected. **1997:** Nondiscriminatory constitution introduced. Fiji re-admitted to the Commonwealth. **1998:** New three-party governing coalition formed, led by the Fijian Political Party. **1999:** President Mara's term in office renewed for an additional five years. Mahendra Chaudry became Fiji's first female prime minister.

Finland Republic of

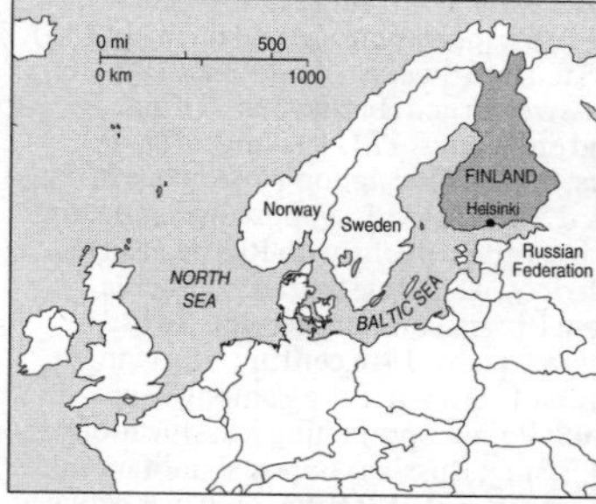

National name: *Suomen Tasavalta* **Area:** 338,145 sq km/130,557 sq mi **Capital:** Helsinki (Helsingfors) **Major towns/cities:** Tampere, Turku, Espoo, Vantaa **Major ports:** Turku, Oulu

Government

Head of state: Martti Ahtisaari from 1994 **Head of government:** Paavo Lipponen from 1995 **Political system:** democracy **Administrative divisions:** 12 provinces **Political parties:** Finnish Social Democratic Party (SSDP), moderate left of centre; National Coalition Party (KOK), moderate right of centre; Finnish Centre Party (KESK), radical centrist, rural-oriented; Swedish People's Party (SFP), independent Swedish-oriented; Finnish Rural Party (SMP), farmers and small businesses; Left-Wing Alliance (VL), left wing **Armed forces:** 31,000 (1997) **Conscription:** up to 11 months, followed by refresher training of 40–100 days (before age 50) **Death penalty:** abolished in 1972 **Defence spend:** (% GDP) 1.7 (1997) **Education spend:** (% GNP) 7.6 (1995) **Health spend:** (% GDP) 5.7 (1990–95)

Economy and resources

Currency: markka **GDP:** (US$) 117.5 billion (1997) **Real GDP growth:** (% change on previous year) 4.1 (1997) **GNP (US$):** 123.8 billion (1997) **GNP per capita (PPP):** (US$) 18,980 (1997) **Consumer price inflation:** 1.5% (1998) **Unemployment:** 11.4% (1998) **Major trading partners:** Germany, Sweden, UK, USA, Russia, Denmark, Norway, the Netherlands **Resources:** copper ore, lead ore, gold, zinc ore, silver, peat, hydro power, forests **Exports:** metal and engineering products, gold, paper and paper products, machinery, ships, wood and pulp, clothing and footwear, chemicals. Principal market: Germany 11% (1997) **Imports:** mineral fuels,

machinery and transport equipment, food and live animals, chemical and related products, textiles, iron and steel. Principal source: Germany 14.5% (1997) **Arable land:** 8.3% (1995)

Population and society

Population: 5,154,000 (1998 est) **Population growth rate:** 0.3% (1995–2000); 0.3% (2000–05) **Population density:** (per sq km) 16.9 (1998 est) **Urban population:** (% of total) 64 (1997) **Age distribution:** (% of total population) 0–14 18.6%, 15–64 66.8%, 65+ 14.6% (1998) **Ethnic groups:** predominantly Finnish; significant Swedish minority; small minorities of native Saami and Russians **Language:** Finnish 93%, Swedish 6% (both official); small Saami- and Russian-speaking minorities **Religion:** Lutheran 90%, Orthodox 1% **Education:** (compulsory years) 9 **Literacy rate:** 100% (men); 100% (women) (1995 est) **Labour force:** 49.4% of population: 7.1% agriculture, 27.6% industry, 65.3% services (1996) **Life expectancy:** 73 (men); 80 (women) (1995–2000) **Child mortality rate:** (under 5, per 1,000 live births) 6 (1997) **Physicians:** 1 per 345 people (1996)

Practical information

Visa requirements: UK: visa not required. USA: visa not required **Embassy in the UK:** 38 Chesham Place, London SW1X 8HW. Tel: (0171) 235 9531; fax: (0171) 235 3680 **British embassy:** Itäinen Puistotie 17, 00140 Helsinki. Tel: (0) 661 293; fax: (0) 661 342 **Chamber of commerce:** Keskuskauppakamari (Central Chamber of Commerce of Finland), PO Box 1000, Fabianinkatu 14, 00101 Helsinki. Tel: (0) 650 133; fax: (0) 650 303

Chronology

1st century: Occupied by Finnic nomads from Asia who drove out native Saami (Lapps) to the far north. **12th–13th centuries:** Series of Swedish crusades conquered Finns and converted them to Christianity. **16th–17th centuries:** Finland was a semi-autonomous Swedish duchy with Swedish landowners ruling Finnish peasants; Finland allowed relative autonomy, becoming a grand duchy in 1581. **1634:** Finland fully incorporated into Swedish kingdom. **1700–21:** Great Northern War between Sweden and Russia; half of Finnish population died in famine and epidemics. **1741–43 and 1788–90:** Further Russo–Swedish wars; much of the fighting took place in Finland. **1808:** Russia invaded Sweden (with support of Napoleon). **1809:** Finland ceded to Russia as grand duchy with Russian tsar as grand duke; Finns retained their own legal system and Lutheran religion and were exempt from Russian military service. **1812:** Helsinki became capital of grand duchy. **19th century:** Growing prosperity was followed by rise of national feeling among new Finnish middle class. **1904–05:** Policies promoting Russification of Finland provoked national uprising; Russians imposed military rule. **1917:** Finland declared independence. **1918:** Bitter civil war between Reds (supported by Russian Bolsheviks) and Whites (supported by Germany); Baron Carl Gustaf Mannerheim led Whites to victory. **1919:** Republican constitution adopted with Kaarlo Juho Ståhlberg as first president. **1927:** Land reform broke up big estates and created many small peasant farms. **1939–40:** Winter War: USSR invaded Finland after demand for military bases was refused. **1940:** Treaty of Moscow: Finland ceded territory to USSR. **1941:** Finland joined German attack on USSR in hope of regaining lost territory. **1944:** Finland agreed separate armistice with USSR; German troops withdrawn. **1947:** Finno-Soviet peace treaty: Finland forced to cede 12% of its total area and to pay $300 million in reparations. **1948:** Finno-Soviet Pact of Friendship, Cooperation, and Mutual Assistance (YYA treaty): Finland pledged to repel any attack on USSR through its territories. **1950s:** Unstable centre-left coalitions excluded communists from government and adopted strict neutrality in foreign affairs. **1955:** Finland joined United Nations (UN) and Nordic Council. **1956:** Urho Kekkonen elected president. General strike as a result of unemployment and inflation. **1973:** Trade agreements signed with European Economic Community (EEC) and Comecon. **1982:** Mauno Koivisto elected president. **1987:** New coalition of Social Democrats and conservatives formed. **1991:** Swing to Centre Party in general election. **1994:** Martti Ahtisaari (SSDP) elected president. **1995:** Finland joined European Union (EU); Social Democrats won general election. **1999:** SSDP narrowly retained power.

France French Republic

National name: *République Française* **Area:** (including Corsica) 543,965 sq km/210,024 sq mi **Capital:** Paris **Major towns/cities:** Lyon, Lille, Bordeaux, Toulouse, Nantes, Strasbourg, Montpellier, Saint-Etienne, Rennes, Reims, Grenoble **Major ports:** Marseille, Nice, Le Havre **Territories:** Guadeloupe, French Guiana, Martinique, Réunion, St Pierre and Miquelon, Southern and Antarctic Territories, New Caledonia, French Polynesia, Wallis and Futuna, Mayotte

Government

Head of state: Jacques Chirac from 1995 **Head of government:** Lionel Jospin from 1997 **Political system:** liberal democracy **Administrative divisions:** 22 regions containing 96 departments, four overseas departments, two territorial collectivities, and four overseas territories **Political parties:** Rally for the Republic (RPR), neo-Gaullist conservative; Union for French Democracy (UDF), centre right; Socialist Party (PS), left of centre; Left Radical Movement (MRG), centre left; French Communist Party (PCF), Marxist-Leninist; National Front, far right; Greens, fundamentalist-ecologist; Génération Ecologie, pragmatic ecologist; Movement for France, right wing, anti-Maastricht **Armed forces:** 380,800; paramilitary gendarmerie 92,300 (1997) **Conscription:** military service is compulsory for 10 months **Death penalty:** abolished in 1981 **Defence spend:** (% GDP) 3.0 (1997) **Education spend:** (% GNP) 5.9 (1995) **Health spend:** (% GDP) 8.0 (1990–95)

Economy and resources

Currency: franc **GDP:** (US$) 1,393.8 billion (1997) **Real GDP growth:** (% change on previous year) 2.4 (1997) **GNP (US$):** 1,526 billion (1997) **GNP per capita (PPP):** (US$) 21,860 (1997) **Consumer price inflation:** 1.6% (1998) **Unemployment:** 11.9% (1998) **Major trading partners:** EU (principally Germany, Italy, Benelux, UK); USA **Resources:** coal, petroleum, natural gas, iron ore, copper, zinc, bauxite **Exports:** machinery and transport equipment, food and live animals, beverages and tobacco, textile yarn, fabrics and other basic manufactures, clothing and accessories, perfumery and cosmetics. Principal market: Germany 15.9% (1997) **Imports:** food and live animals, mineral fuels, machinery and transport equipment, chemicals and chemical products, basic manufactures. Principal source: Germany 16.6% (1997) **Arable land:** 33.3% (1995)

Population and society

Population: 58,683,000 (1998 est) **Population growth rate:** 0.3% (1995–2000); 0.2% (2000–05) **Population density:** (per sq km) 107.8 (1998 est) **Urban population:** (% of total) 75 (1997) **Age distribution:** (% of total population) 0–14 18.9%, 15–64 65.3%, 65+ 15.8% (1998) **Ethnic groups:** predominantly French ethnic, of Celtic and Latin descent; Basque minority in southwest; 7% of the population are immigrants – a third of these are from Algeria and Morocco and live mainly in the Marseille Midi region and in northern cities, 20% originate from Portugal, and 10% each from Italy and Spain **Language:** French (regional languages include Basque, Breton, Catalan, and Provençal) **Religion:** Roman Catholic; also Muslim, Protestant, and Jewish minorities **Education:** (compulsory

France: Regions

Region	Capital	Area sq km	Area sq mi	Population (1996 est)
Alsace	Strasbourg	8,280	3,197	1,701,000
Aquitaine	Bordeaux	41,308	15,949	2,880,000
Auvergne	Clermont-Ferrand	26,013	10,044	1,315,000
Basse-Normandie	Caen	17,589	6,791	1,416,000
Brittany (Bretagne)	Rennes	27,208	10,505	2,861,000
Burgundy (Bourgogne)	Dijon	31,582	12,194	1,625,000
Centre	Orléans	39,151	15,116	2,443,000
Champagne-Ardenne	Châlons-sur-Marne	25,606	9,886	1,353,000
Corsica (Corse)	Ajaccio	8,680	3,351	260,000
Franche-Comté	Besançon	16,202	6,256	1,116,000
Haute-Normandie	Rouen	12,317	4,756	1,782,000
Ile de France	Paris	12,012	4,638	11,027,000
Languedoc-Roussillon	Montpellier	27,376	10,570	2,243,000
Limousin	Limoges	16,942	6,541	718,000
Lorraine	Metz	23,547	9,091	2,312,000
Midi-Pyrénées	Toulouse	45,348	17,509	2,506,000
Nord-Pas-de-Calais	Lille	12,414	4,793	4,001,000
Pays de la Loire	Nantes	32,082	12,387	3,154,000
Picardie	Amiens	19,399	7,490	1,864,000
Poitou-Charentes	Poitiers	25,809	9,965	1,622,000
Provence-Alpes-Côte d'Azur	Marseille	31,400	12,123	4,448,000
Rhône-Alpes	Lyon	43,698	16,872	5,608,000

years) 10 **Literacy rate:** 100% (men); 100% (women) (1995 est) **Labour force:** 44% of population: 5.1% agriculture, 27.7% industry, 67.2% services (1993) **Life expectancy:** 75 (men); 83 (women) (1995–2000) **Child mortality rate:** (under 5, per 1,000 live births) 8 (1997) **Physicians:** 1 per 345 people (1996)

Practical information

Visa requirements: UK: visa not required. USA: visa not required **Embassy in the UK:** 58 Knightsbridge, London SW1X 7JT. Tel: (0171) 201 1000; fax: (0171) 201 1004 **British embassy:** 35 rue du Faubourg St Honoré, 75383 Paris. Tel: (1) 4266 9142; fax: (1) 4266 9590 **Chamber of commerce:** Chambre de Commerce et d'Industrie de Paris, 27 avenue de Friedland, 75382 Paris. Tel: (1) 4289 7000; fax: (1) 4289 7286

Chronology

5th century BC: Celtic peoples invaded the region. **58–51 BC:** Romans conquered Celts and formed province of Gaul. **5th century AD:** Gaul overrun by Franks and other Germanic tribes. **481–511:** Frankish chief Clovis accepted Christianity and formed a kingdom based at Paris; under his successors, the Merovingian dynasty, the kingdom disintegrated. **751–68:** Pepin the Short usurped the Frankish throne, reunified the kingdom, and founded the Carolingian dynasty. **768–814:** Charlemagne conquered much of western Europe and created the Holy Roman Empire. **843:** Treaty of Verdun divided the Holy Roman Empire into three, with the western portion corresponding to modern France. **9th–10th centuries:** Weak central government allowed the great nobles to become virtually independent. **987:** Frankish crown passed to House of Capet; the Capets ruled the district around Paris, but were surrounded by vassals more powerful than themselves. **1180–1223:** Philip II doubled the royal domain and tightened control over the nobles; the power of the Capets gradually extended with support of church and towns. **1328:** When Charles IV died without an heir, Philip VI established the House of Valois. **1337:** Start of the Hundred Years' War: Edward III of England disputed the Valois succession and claimed the throne. English won victories at Crécy in 1346 and Agincourt in 1415. **1429:** Joan of Arc raised the siege of Orléans; Hundred Years' War ended with Charles VII expelling the English 1453. **1483:** France annexed Burgundy and Brittany after Louis XI had restored royal power. **16th–17th centuries:** French kings fought the Habsburgs (of Holy Roman Empire and Spain) for supremacy in western Europe. **1562–98:** Civil wars between nobles were fought under religious slogans, Catholic versus Protestant (or Huguenot). **1589–1610:** Henry IV, first king of Bourbon dynasty, established peace, religious tolerance, and absolute monarchy. **1634–48:** The ministers Richelieu and Mazarin, by intervening in the Thirty Years' War, secured Alsace and made France the leading power in Europe. **1701–14:** War of the Spanish Succession: England, Austria, and allies checked expansionism of France under Louis XIV. **1756–63:** Seven Years' War: France lost most of its colonies in India and Canada to Britain. **1789:** French Revolution abolished absolute monarchy and feudalism; First Republic proclaimed and revolutionary wars began 1792. **1799:** Napoleon Bonaparte seized power in coup; crowned himself emperor in 1804; France conquered much of Europe. **1814:** Defeat of France; restoration of Bourbon monarchy; comeback by Napoleon defeated at Waterloo in 1815. **1830:** Liberal revolution deposed Charles X in favour of his cousin Louis Philippe, the 'Citizen King'. **1848:** Revolution established Second Republic; conflict between liberals and socialists; Louis Napoleon, nephew of Napoleon I, elected president. **1852:** Louis Napoleon proclaimed Second Empire, taking title Napoleon III. **1870–71:** Franco-Prussian War: France lost Alsace-Lorraine; Second Empire abolished; Paris Commune crushed; Third Republic founded. **late 19th century:** France colonized Indochina, much of North Africa, and South Pacific. **1914–18:** France resisted German invasion in World War I; Alsace-Lorraine recovered in 1919. **1936–37:** Left-wing 'Popular Front' government of Léon Blum introduced many social reforms. **1939:** France entered World War II. **1940:** Germany invaded and occupied northern France; Marshal Pétain formed right-wing puppet regime at Vichy; resistance maintained by Maquis and Free French; Germans occupied all France in 1942. **1944:** Allies liberated France; provisional government formed by Gen Charles de Gaulle, leader of Free French. **1946:** Fourth Republic proclaimed. **1949:** Became a member of NATO; withdrew from military command structure in 1966. **1954:** French withdrew from Indochina after eight years of war; start of guerrilla war against French rule in Algeria. **1957:** France was a founder member of the European Economic Community. **1958:** Algerian crisis caused collapse of Fourth Republic; de Gaulle took power, becoming president of the Fifth Republic in 1959. **1962:** Algeria achieved independence. **1968:** 'May events': revolutionary students rioted in Paris; general strike throughout France. **1981:** François Mitterrand elected Fifth Republic's first socialist president. **1986–88:** 'Cohabitation' of socialist president with conservative prime minister; again 1993–95. **1995:** Conservative Jacques Chirac elected president. Widespread condemnation of government's decision to resume nuclear tests in Pacific region. **1996:** End to nuclear testing in South Pacific. Spending cuts agreed to meet European Monetary Union entry criteria. Unemployment at postwar high. **1997:** General election called by President Chirac. Victory for Socialists; Lionel Jospin appointed prime minister. **1998:** Protests by the unemployed.

Gabon Gabonese Republic

National name: *République Gabonaise* **Area:** 267,667 sq km/ 103,346 sq mi **Capital:** Libreville **Major towns/cities:** Port-Gentil, Masuku (Franceville), Lambaréné, Mouanda **Major ports:** Port-Gentil and Owendo

Government

Head of state: Omar Bongo from 1964 **Head of government:** Jean-François Ntoutoume-Emane from 1999 **Political system:** emergent

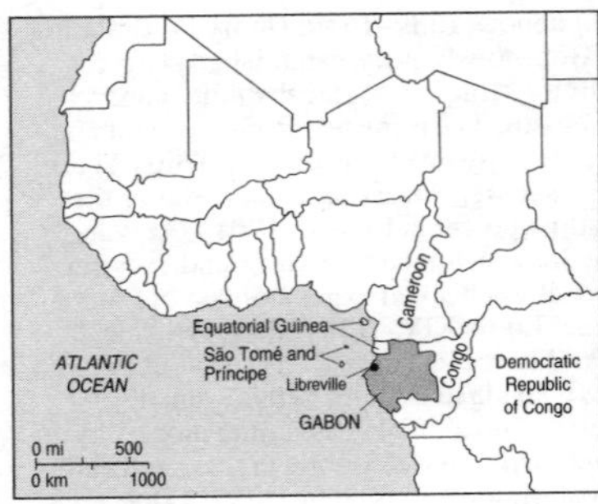

democracy **Administrative divisions:** nine provinces **Political parties:** Gabonese Democratic Party (PDG), nationalist; Gabone Progress Party (PGP), left of centre; National Rally of Woodcutters (RNB), left of centre **Armed forces:** 4,700; plus a paramilitary force of 4,800 (1997) **Conscription:** military service is voluntary **Death penalty:** retained and used for ordinary crimes **Defence spend:** (% GDP) 1.9 (1997) **Education spend:** (% GNP) 3.2 (1993–94) **Health spend:** (% GDP) 0.6 (1990–95)

Economy and resources

Currency: franc CFA **GDP:** (US$) 5.43 billion (1997) **Real GDP growth:** (% change on previous year) 4.0 (1997) **GNP (US$):** 4.9 billion (1997) **GNP per capita (PPP):** (US$) 6,540 (1997) **Consumer price inflation:** 3% (1998) **Foreign debt:** (US$) 4.06 billion (1996) **Major trading partners:** France, USA, Germany, Spain, Japan, the Netherlands **Resources:** petroleum, natural gas, manganese (one of world's foremost producers and exporters), iron ore, uranium, gold, niobium, talc, phosphates **Exports:** petroleum and petroleum products, manganese, timber and wood products, uranium. Principal market: USA 67% (1997) **Imports:** machinery and apparatus, transport equipment, food products, metals and metal products. Principal source: France 38% (1997) **Arable land:** 1.3% (1995)

Population and society

Population: 1,167,000 (1998 est) **Population growth rate:** 2.8% (1995–2000); 2.5% (2000–05) **Population density:** (per sq km) 4.7 (1998 est) **Urban population:** (% of total) 53 (1997) **Age distribution:** (% of total population) 0–14 33.5%, 15–64 61.0%, 65+ 5.5% (1998) **Ethnic groups:** 40 Bantu peoples in four main groupings: the Fang, Eshira, Mbede, and Okande; there are also Pygmies and about 10% Europeans (mainly French) **Language:** French (official), Bantu **Religion:** Roman Catholic, also Muslim, animist **Education:** (compulsory years) 10 **Literacy rate:** 73% (men); 48% (women) (1995 est) **Labour force:** 64.2% agriculture, 10.8% industry, 25% services (1994) **Life expectancy:** 54 (men); 57 (women) (1995–2000) **Child mortality rate:** (under 5, per 1,000 live births) 126 (1997) **Physicians:** 1 per 1,987 people (1993 est)

Practical information

Visa requirements: UK: visa required. USA: visa required **Embassy in the UK:** 27 Elvaston Place, London SW7 5NL. Tel: (0171) 823 9986; fax: (0171) 584 0047 **British embassy:** the British Embassy in Gabon closed in July 1991; all staff based in Yaoundé, Cameroon. The West African Department of the Foreign and Commonwealth Office is currently handling consular and commercial enquiries for Gabon; tel: (0171) 270 2516; fax: (0171) 270 3739 **Chamber of commerce:** Chambre de Commerce, d'Agriculture, d'Industrie et de Mines du Gabon, BP 2234, Libreville. Tel: (241) 722 064; fax: (241) 746 477

Chronology

12th century: Immigration of Bantu speakers into an area previously peopled by Pygmies. **1472:** Gabon Estuary first visited by Portuguese navigators, who named it Gabao ('hooded cloak'), after the shape of the coastal area. **17th–18th centuries:** Fang, from Cameroon in the north, and Omiene peoples colonized the area, attracted by presence in coastal areas of European traders, who developed the ivory and slave trades, which lasted until the mid-19th century. **1839–42:** Mpongwe coastal chiefs agreed to transfer sovereignty to France; Catholic and Protestant missionaries attracted to the area. **1849:** Libreville ('Free Town') formed by slaves from a slave ship liberated by the French. **1889:** Became part of French Congo, with Congo. **1910:** Became part of French Equatorial Africa, which also comprised Congo, Chad, and Central African Republic. **1890s–1920s:** Human and natural resources exploited by private concessionary companies. **1940–44:** Supported the 'Free French' anti-Nazi cause during World War II. **1946:** Became overseas territory within the French Community, with its own assembly. **1960:** Independence achieved; Léon M'ba, a Fang of the pro-French Gabonese Democratic Block (BDG) became the first president. **1964:** Attempted military coup by supporters of rival party foiled with French help. **1967:** M'ba died and was succeeded by his protégé Albert Bernard Bongo, drawn from the Teke community. **1968:** One-party state established, with BDG dissolved and replaced by Gabonese Democratic Party (PDG). **1973:** Bongo converted to Islam and changed his first name to Omar, but continued to follow pro-Western policy course and exploit rich mineral resources to increase prosperity. **1989:** Coup attempt against Bongo defeated as economy deteriorated. **1990:** PDG won first multiparty elections since 1964. French troops sent in to maintain order following antigovernment riots. **1993:** National unity government formed, including some opposition members. **1997:** Paulin Obame-Nguema was reappointed prime minister after ruling Gabonese Democratic Party (PDG) won large assembly majority. **1998:** New party, Rassemblement des Gaullois, recognized. President Bongo reelected. **1999:** Jean-François Ntoutoume-Emane appointed prime minister.

Gambia, The **Republic of**

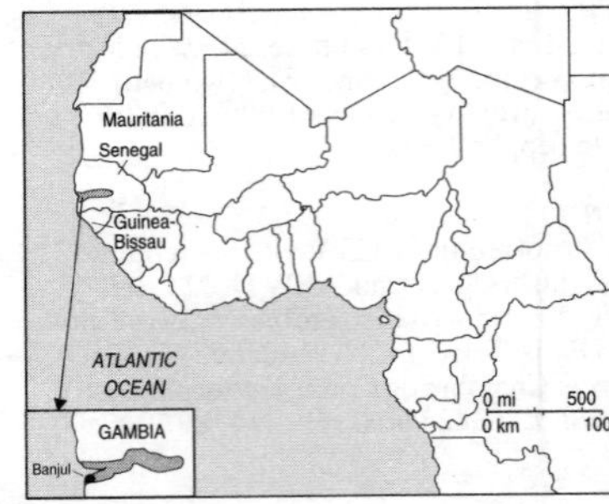

Area: 10,402 sq km/4,016 sq mi **Capital:** Banjul **Major towns/cities:** Serekunda, Birkama, Bakau, Farafenni, Sukuta, Gunjur, Georgetown

Government

Head of state and government: (interim) Yahya Jameh from 1994 **Political system:** transitional **Administrative divisions:** 35 districts, grouped into six Area Councils **Political parties:** Progressive People's Party (PPP), moderate centrist; National Convention Party (NCP), left of centre **Armed forces:** 800 (1997) **Conscription:** military service is mainly voluntary **Death penalty:** retains the death penalty for ordinary crimes but can be considered abolitionist in practice (last execution 1981) **Defence spend:** (% GDP) 3.7 (1997) **Education spend:** (% GNP) 5.5 (1995) **Health spend:** (% GDP) 1.9 (1990–95)

Economy and resources

Currency: dalasi **GDP:** (US$) 385 million (1997 est) **Real GDP growth:** (% change on previous year) 3.2 (1996 est) **GNP (US$):** 409 million (1997) **GNP per capita (PPP):** (US$) 1,340 (1997) **Consumer price inflation:** 5% (1996) **Unemployment:** 26% (1994 est) **Foreign debt:** (US$) 452 million (1996) **Major trading partners:** UK, Belgium, Italy, Hong Kong, China, Japan **Resources:** ilmenite, zircon, rutile, petroleum (well discovered, but not exploited) **Exports:** groundnuts and related products, cotton lint, fish and fish preparations, hides and skins. Principal market: France 36.4% (1996) **Imports:** food and live animals, basic manufactures, machinery and transport equipment, mineral fuels and lubrications, miscellaneous manufactured articles, chemicals. Principal source: UK 14.3% (1996) **Arable land:** 17.5% (1995)

Population and society

Population: 1,229,000 (1998 est) **Population growth rate:** 2.3% (1995–2000) **Population density:** (per sq km) 129.2 (1998 est)

Urban population: (% of total) 31 (1997) **Age distribution:** (% of total population) 0–14 45.8%, 15–64 51.6%, 65+ 2.7% (1998) **Ethnic groups:** wide mix of ethnic groups, the largest is the Mandingo (about 40%); other main groups are the Fula, Wolof, Jola, and Serahuli **Language:** English (official), Mandinka, Fula, and other indigenous tongues **Religion:** Muslim 90%, with animist and Christian minorities **Education:** free, but not compulsory **Literacy rate:** 53% (men); 25% (women) (1995 est) **Labour force:** 50% of population: 79.6% agriculture, 4.2% industry, 16.2% services (1994) **Life expectancy:** 45 (men); 49 (women) (1995–2000) **Child mortality rate:** (under 5, per 1,000 live births) 185 (1997) **Physicians:** 1 per 14,530 people (1991)

Practical information

Visa requirements: UK: visa not required for visits of up to 90 days. USA: visa required **Embassy in the UK:** 57 Kensington Court, London W8 5DG. Tel: (0171) 937 6316/7/8; fax: (0171) 937 9095 **British embassy:** British High Commission, PO Box 507, 48 Atlantic Road, Fajara, Banjul. Tel: (220) 495 133/4; fax: (220) 496 134 **Chamber of commerce:** Gambia Chamber of Commerce and Industry, PO Box 33, 78 Wellington Street, Banjul. Tel: (220) 227 765

Chronology

13th century: Wolof, Malinke (Mandingo), and Fulani tribes settled in the region from east and north. **14th century:** Became part of the great Muslim Mali Empire, which, centred to northeast, also extended across Senegal, Mali, and southern Mauritania. **1455:** Gambia River first sighted by the Portuguese. **1663 and 1681:** British and French established small settlements on the river at Fort James and Albreda. **1843:** The Gambia became a British crown colony, administered with Sierra Leone until 1888. **1965:** Independence achieved as a constitutional monarchy within the Commonwealth, with Dawda K Jawara of the People's Progressive Party (PPP) as prime minister at the head of a multiparty democracy. **1970:** Became a republic, with Jawara as president. **1981:** Attempted coup foiled with the help of Senegal. **1982:** Formed with Senegal the Confederation of Senegambia, which involved integration of military forces, economic and monetary union, and coordinated foreign policy. **1994:** Jawara ousted in military coup, and fled to Senegal; Yahya Jameh named acting head of state. **1995:** Counter-coup attempt failed. **1996:** Civilian constitution adopted.

Georgia Republic of

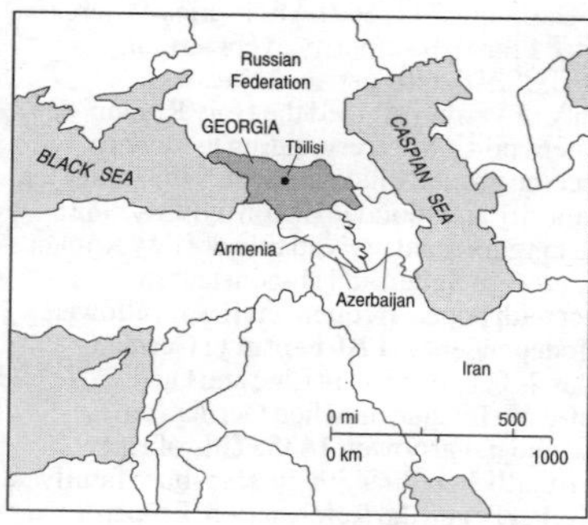

Area: 69,700 sq km/26,911 sq mi **Capital:** Tbilisi **Major towns/cities:** Kutaisi, Rustavi, Batumi, Sukhumi

Government

Head of state: Eduard Shevardnadze from 1992 **Head of government:** Otar Patsatsia from 1993 **Political system:** transitional **Political parties:** Citizens' Union of Georgia (CUG), nationalist, pro-Shevardnadze; National Democratic Party of Georgia (NDPG), nationalist; Round Table/Free Georgia Bloc, nationalist; Georgian Popular Front (GPF), moderate nationalist, prodemocratization; Georgian Communist Party (GCP); National Independence Party (NIP), ultranationalist; Front for the Reinstatement of Legitimate Power in Georgia, strong nationalist **Armed forces:** 33,200 (1997) **Conscription:** compulsory for two years **Death penalty:** abolished in 1997 **Defence spend:** (% GDP) 2.9 (1997) **Education spend:** (% GDP) 5.2% (1995) **Health spend:** (% GDP) 0.8 (1990–95)

Economy and resources

Currency: lari **GDP:** (US$) 4.1 billion (1997 est) **Real GDP growth:** (% change on previous year) 12 (1997) **GNP (US$):** 4.6 billion (1997) **GNP per capita (PPP):** (US$) 1,980 (1997) **Consumer price inflation:** 7% (1998) **Unemployment:** 2% (1993) **Foreign debt:** (US$) 1.36 billion (1996) **Major trading partners:** Russia, Turkey, Turkmenistan, Azerbaijan **Resources:** coal, manganese, barytes, clay, petroleum and natural gas deposits, iron and other ores, gold, agate, marble, alabaster, arsenic, tungsten, mercury **Exports:** metal products, machinery, tea, beverages. Principal market: Russia 27.4% (1997) **Imports:** mineral fuels, chemical and petroleum products, food products (mainly wheat and flour), light industrial products, beverages. Principal source: EU 22% (1997) **Arable land:** 11.1% (1995)

Population and society

Population: 5,059,000 (1998 est) **Population growth rate:** –0.1% (1995–2000) **Population density:** (per sq km) 73.3 (1998 est) **Urban population:** (% of total) 60 (1997) **Age distribution:** (% of total population) 0–14 21.6%, 15–64 66.3%, 65+ 12.1% (1998) **Ethnic groups:** 70% ethnic Georgian, 8% Armenian, 7% ethnic Russian, 5% Azeri, 3% Ossetian, 2% Abkhazian, and 2% Greek **Language:** Georgian **Religion:** Georgian Orthodox, also Muslim **Education:** (compulsory years) 9 **Literacy rate:** 99% (men); 99% (women) (1995 est) **Labour force:** 27.1% agriculture, 19.4% industry, 53.5% services (1991) **Life expectancy:** 69 (men); 77 (women) (1995–2000) **Child mortality rate:** (under 5, per 1,000 live births) 23 (1997) **Physicians:** 1 per 200 people (1994)

Practical information

Visa requirements: UK: visa required. USA: visa required **Embassy in the UK:** 45 Avanmore Road, London W14. Tel/fax: (0171) 603 5325 **British embassy:** Sosiiskaya Naberzehnaya, Moscow 72. Tel: (70095) 231 8511; fax: (70095) 233 3563 **Chamber of commerce:** Chamber of Commerce and Industry of Georgia, Prospekt I, Chavchavadze 11, 380079 Tbilisi. Tel: (32) 230 045; fax: (32) 235 760

Chronology

4th century BC: Georgian kingdom founded. **1st century BC:** Part of Roman Empire. **AD 337:** Christianity adopted. **458:** Tbilisi founded by King Vakhtang Gorgasal. **mid-7th century:** Tbilisi brought under Arab rule and renamed Tiflis. **1121:** Tbilisi liberated by King David II the Builder, of the Gagrationi dynasty, which traced its ancestry to the biblical King David. An empire was established across the Caucasus region, remaining powerful until Mongol onslaughts in the 13th and 14th centuries. **1555:** Western Georgia fell to Turkey and Eastern Georgia to Persia (Iran). **1783:** Treaty of Georgievsk established Russian dominance over Georgia. **1804–13:** First Russo-Iranian war fought largely over Georgia. **late 19th century:** Abolition of serfdom and beginnings of industrialization, but Georgian church suppressed. **1918:** Independence established after Russian Revolution. **1921:** Invaded by Red Army; Soviet republic established. **1922–36:** Linked with Armenia and Azerbaijan as the Transcaucasian Federation. **1930s:** Rapid industrial development, but resistance to agricultural collectivization and violent political purges instituted by the Georgian Soviet dictator Joseph Stalin. **1936:** Became separate republic within the USSR. **early 1940s:** 200,000 Meskhetians deported from southern Georgia to Central Asia on Stalin's orders. **1972:** Drive against endemic corruption launched by new Georgian Communist Party (GCP) leader Eduard Shevardnadze. **1977:** Initiative Group for the Defence of Human Rights formed by Zviad Gamsakhurdia, a nationalist intellectual. **1978:** Violent demonstrations by nationalists in Tbilisi. **1981–88:** Increasing demands for autonomy encouraged from 1986 by the *glasnost* initiative of the reformist Soviet leader Mikhail Gorbachev. **1989:** Formation of nationalist Georgian Popular Front led the minority Abkhazian and Ossetian communities in northwest and central-north Georgia to demand secession, provoking interethnic clashes. State of emergency imposed in Abkhazia; 20 pro-independence demonstrators massacred in Tbilisi by Soviet troops; Georgian sovereignty declared by parliament. **1990:** Nationalist coalition triumphed in elections and Gamsakhurdia became president. GCP seceded from Communist Party of USSR. **1991:** Independence declared. GCP outlawed and all relations with USSR severed. Demonstrations against increasingly dictatorial Gamsakhurdia; state of emergency declared. Georgia failed to join new Commonwealth of Independent States (CIS) as civil war raged. **1992:** Gamsakhurdia fled to Armenia; Shevardnadze, with military backing, appointed interim president. Georgia admitted into United Nations (UN). Clashes continued in South Ossetia and Abkhazia, where independence had been declared. **1993:** Conflict with Abkhazi separatists intensified, forcing Shevardnadze to seek Russian military help. Pro-Gamsakhurdia revolt was put down by government forces and Gamsakhurdia died. **1994:** Georgia joined CIS. Military cooperation pact signed with Russia. Cease-fire agreed with Abkhazi separatists; 2,500 Russian peacekeeping troops deployed in region and paramilitary groups disarmed. Inflation exceeded 5,000% per annum. **1995:** Shevardnadze survived assassination attempt and was re-elected; privatization programme launched. **1996:** Cooperation pact with European Union signed as economic growth resumed and monthly inflation fell to below 3%. Elections to secessionist Abkhazi parliament declared illegal by Georgian government. **1997:** New opposition party, Front for the Reinstatement of Legitimate Power in Georgia, formed. Talks between government and breakaway Abkhazi government. **1998:** Shevardnadze survived another assassination attempt. Outbreak of fighting in Abkhazia.

Germany Federal Republic of

National name: *Bundesrepublik Deutschland* **Area:** 357,041 sq km/ 137,853 sq mi **Capital:** Berlin (government offices moving in phases from Bonn back to Berlin) **Major towns/ cities:** Cologne, Hamburg, Munich, Essen, Frankfurt am Main, Dortmund, Stuttgart, Düsseldorf, Leipzig, Dresden, Bremen, Duisburg, Hannover **Major ports:** Hamburg, Kiel, Bremerhaven, Rostock

Government

Head of state: Johannes Rau from 1999 **Head of government:** Gerhard Schroeder from 1998 **Political system:** liberal democratic federal republic **Administrative divisions:** 16 states **Political parties:** Christian Democratic Union (CDU), right of centre, 'social market'; Christian Social Union (CSU), right of centre; Social Democratic Party (SPD), left of centre; Free Democratic Party (FDP), liberal; Greens, environmentalist; Party of Democratic Socialism (PDS), reform-socialist (formerly Socialist Unity Party: SED); German People's Union (DVU), far-right **Armed forces:** 347,100 (1997) **Conscription:** 10 months **Death penalty:** abolished in the Federal Republic of Germany in 1949 and in the German Democratic Republic in 1987 **Defence spend:** (% GDP) 1.6 (1997) **Education spend:** (% GNP) 4.7 (1995) **Health spend:** (% GDP) 7 (1995)

Economy and resources

Currency: Deutschmark **GDP:** (US$) 2,115.4 billion (1997) **Real GDP growth:** (% change on previous year) 2.5 (1997) **GNP (US$):** 2,319.5 billion (1997) **GNP per capita (PPP):** (US$) 21,300 (1997) **Consumer price inflation:** 1.9% (1998) **Unemployment:** 9.4% (1998) **Major trading partners:** EU (particularly France, the Netherlands, and Ireland), USA, Japan, Switzerland **Resources:** lignite, hard coal, potash salts, crude oil, natural gas, iron ore, copper, timber, nickel, uranium **Exports:** road vehicles, electrical machinery, metals and metal products, textiles, chemicals. Principal market: France 10.7% (1997) **Imports:** road vehicles, electrical machinery, food and live animals, clothing and accessories, crude petroleum and petroleum products. Principal source: France 10.5% (1997) **Arable land:** 33.9% (1995)

Population and society

Population: 82,133,000 (1998 est) **Population growth rate:** 0.3% (1995–2000); –0.1% (2000–05) **Population density:** (per sq km) 234.3 (1998 est) **Urban population:** (% of total) 87 (1997) **Age distribution:** (% of total population) 0–14 15.6%, 15–64 68.5%, 65+ 15.9% (1998) **Ethnic groups:** predominantly Germanic; notable Danish and Slavonic ethnic minorities in the north; significant population of foreigners, including 1.9 million officially recognized *Gastarbeiter* ('guest workers'), predominantly Turks, Greeks, Italians, and Yugoslavs; by 1993 Germany had received more than 200,000 refugees fleeing the Yugoslav civil war **Language:** German **Religion:** Protestant (mainly Lutheran) 43%, Roman Catholic 36% **Education:** (compulsory years) 12 **Literacy rate:** 100% (men); 100% (women) (1995 est) **Labour force:** 48.2% of population: 3.3% agriculture, 37.5% industry, 59.1% services (1996) **Life expectancy:** 73 (men); 80 (women) (1995–2000) **Child mortality rate:** (under 5, per 1,000 live births) 7 (1997) **Physicians:** 1 per 294 people (1996)

Practical information

Visa requirements: UK: visa not required. USA: visa not required **Embassy in the UK:** 23 Belgrave Square, London SW1X 8PZ. Tel: (0171) 824 1300; fax: (0171) 824 1435 **British embassy:** Friedrich-Ebert-Allée 77, 53113 Bonn. Tel: (228) 91670; fax: (228) 9167 331 **Chamber of commerce:** Deutscher Industrie- und Handelstag (Association of German Chambers of Industry and Commerce), Adenauerallée 148, 53113 Bonn. Tel: (228) 1040; fax: (228) 104 158

Chronology

c. **1000 BC:** Germanic tribes from Scandinavia began to settle the region between the rivers Rhine, Elbe, and Danube. **AD 9:** Romans tried and failed to conquer Germanic tribes. **5th century:** Germanic tribes plundered Rome, overran western Europe, and divided it into tribal kingdoms. **496:** Clovis, King of the Franks, conquered the Alemanni tribe of western Germany. **772–804:** After series of fierce wars, Charlemagne extended Frankish authority over Germany, subjugated Saxons, imposed Christianity, and took title of Holy Roman emperor. **843:** Treaty of Verdun divided the Holy Roman Empire into three, with eastern portion corresponding to modern Germany; local princes became virtually independent. **919:** Henry the Fowler restored central authority and founded Saxon dynasty. **962:** Otto the Great enlarged the kingdom and revived title of Holy Roman emperor. **1024–1254:** Emperors of Salian and Hohenstaufen dynasties came into conflict with popes; frequent civil wars allowed German princes to regain independence. **12th century:** German expansion eastwards into lands between rivers Elbe and Oder. **13th–14th centuries:** Hanseatic League of Allied German cities became a great commercial and naval power. **1438:** Title of Holy Roman emperor became virtually hereditary in the Habsburg family of Austria. **1517:** Martin Luther began the Reformation; Emperor Charles V tried to suppress Protestantism; civil war ensued. **1555:** Peace of Augsburg: Charles V forced to accept that each German prince could choose religion of his own lands. **1618–48:** Thirty Years' War: bitter conflict, partly religious, between certain German princes and emperor, with foreign intervention; the war wrecked the German economy and reduced the Holy Roman Empire to a name. **1701:** Frederick I, Elector of Brandenburg, promoted to King of Prussia. **1740:** Frederick the Great of Prussia seized Silesia from Austria and retained it through war of Austrian Succession (1740–48) and Seven

Germany: States

State	Capital	Area sq km	Area sq mi	Population (1995)
Baden-Württemberg	Stuttgart	35,752	13,804	10,319,400
Bavaria	Munich	70,551	27,240	11,993,500
Berlin	Berlin	889	343	3,471,400
Brandenburg	Potsdam	29,479	11,382	2,542,000
Bremen	Bremen	404	156	679,800
Hamburg	Hamburg	755	292	1,705,900
Hessen	Wiesbaden	21,114	8,152	6,009,900
Lower Saxony	Hannover	47,606	18,381	7,780,400
Mecklenburg-West Pomerania	Schwerin	23,170	8,946	1,823,100
North Rhine-Westphalia	Düsseldorf	34,077	13,157	17,893,000
Rhineland-Palatinate	Mainz	19,852	7,665	3,983,300
Saarland	Saarbrücken	2,570	992	1,084,400
Saxony	Dresden	18,412	7,109	4,566,600
Saxony-Anhalt	Magdeburg	20,446	7,894	2,738,900
Schleswig-Holstein	Kiel	15,770	6,089	2,725,500
Thuringia	Erfurt	16,171	6,244	2,503,800

Years' War (1756–63). **1772–95:** Prussia joined Russia and Austria in the partition of Poland. **1792:** Start of French Revolutionary Wars, involving many German states, with much fighting on German soil. **1806:** Holy Roman Empire abolished; France formed puppet Confederation of the Rhine in western Germany and defeated Prussia at Battle of Jena. **1813–15:** National revival enabled Prussia to take part in defeat of Napoleon at Battles of Leipzig and Waterloo. **1814–15:** Congress of Vienna rewarded Prussia with Rhineland, Westphalia, and much of Saxony; loose German Confederation formed by 39 independent states. **1848–49:** Liberal revolutions in many German states; Frankfurt Assembly sought German unity; revolutions suppressed. **1862:** Otto von Bismarck became prime minister of Prussia. **1866:** Seven Weeks' War: Prussia defeated Austria, dissolved German Confederation, and established North German Confederation under Prussian leadership. **1870–71:** Franco-Prussian War; southern German states agreed to German unification; German Empire proclaimed, with King of Prussia as emperor and Bismarck as chancellor. **1890:** Wilhelm II dismissed Bismarck and sought to make Germany a leading power in world politics. **1914:** Germany encouraged Austrian attack on Serbia that started World War I; Germany invaded Belgium and France. **1918:** Germany defeated; revolution overthrew monarchy. **1919:** Treaty of Versailles: Germany lost land to France, Denmark, and Poland; demilitarization and reparations imposed; Weimar Republic proclaimed. **1922–23:** Hyperinflation: in 1922, one dollar was worth 50 marks; in 1923, one dollar was worth 2.5 trillion marks. **1929:** Start of economic slump caused mass unemployment and brought Germany close to revolution. **1933:** Adolf Hitler, leader of Nazi Party, became chancellor. **1934:** Hitler took title of *Führer* (leader), murdered rivals, and created one-party state with militaristic and racist ideology; rearmament reduced unemployment. **1938:** Germany annexed Austria and Sudeten; occupied remainder of Czechoslovakia in 1939. **1939:** German invasion of Poland started World War II; Germany defeated France in 1940, attacked USSR in 1941, and pursued extermination of Jews. **1945:** Germany defeated and deprived of its conquests; eastern lands transferred to Poland; USA, USSR, UK, and France established zones of occupation. **1948–49:** Disputes between Western allies and USSR led to Soviet blockade of West Berlin. **1949:** Partition of Germany: US, French, and British zones in West Germany became Federal Republic of Germany with Konrad Adenauer as chancellor; Soviet zone in East Germany became communist German Democratic Republic led by Walter Ulbricht. **1953:** Uprising in East Berlin suppressed by Soviet troops. **1955:** West Germany became a member of NATO; East Germany joined Warsaw Pact. **1957:** West Germany was a founder member of the European Economic Community. **1960s:** 'Economic miracle': West Germany achieved rapid growth and great prosperity. **1961:** East Germany constructed Berlin Wall to prevent emigration to West Berlin (part of West Germany). **1969:** Willy Brandt, Social Democratic Party chancellor of West Germany, sought better relations with USSR and East Germany. **1971:** Erich Honecker succeeded Ulbricht as Communist Party leader, and became head of state in 1976. **1972:** Basic Treaty established relations between West Germany and East Germany as between foreign states. **1982:** Helmut Kohl (Christian Democratic Union) became West German chancellor. **1989:** Mass exodus of East Germans to West Germany via Hungary; Honecker replaced; East Germany opened frontiers, including Berlin Wall. **1990:** Collapse of communist regime in East Germany; reunification of Germany with Kohl as chancellor. **1991:** Maastricht Treaty: Germany took the lead in pressing for closer European integration. **1995:** Unemployment reached 3.8 million. **1996:** Public-sector labour dispute over welfare reform plans and the worsening economy. Spending cuts agreed to meet European Monetary Union entry criteria. **1997:** Unemployment continued to rise. SPD polled badly in local elections. **1998:** Unemployment reached postwar high of 12.6%. CDU–CSU–FDP coalition defeated in general election and a 'Red–Green' coalition government formed by the SPD and the Greens, with Gerhard Schroeder as chancellor. Kohl replaced as CDU leader by Wolfgang Schäuble. **1999:** Delay announced in the planned phasing out of nuclear power. Johannes Rau elected president.

Ghana Republic of (formerly the **Gold Coast**)

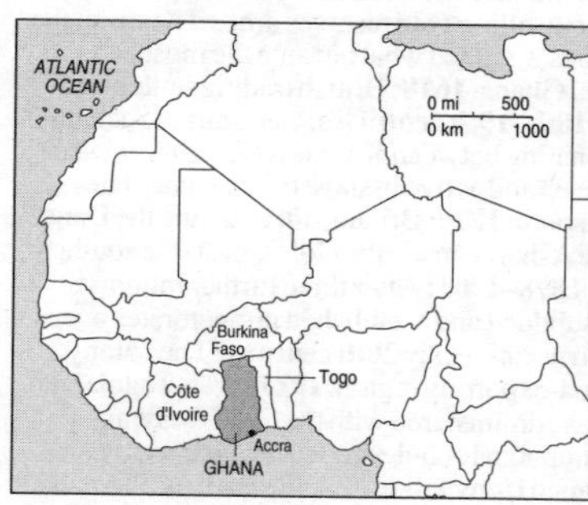

Area: 238,305 sq km/92,009 sq mi **Capital:** Accra **Major towns/cities:** Kumasi, Tamale, Tema, Sekondi-Takoradi, Cape Coast, Sunyani, Koforidua, Ho, Yendi, Tarkwa, Wa, Bolgatanga **Major ports:** Sekondi, Tema

Government

Head of state and government: Jerry Rawlings from 1981 **Political system:** emergent democracy **Administrative divisions:** ten regions **Political parties:** National Democratic Congress (NDC), centrist, progovernment; New Patriotic Party (NPP), left of centre **Armed forces:** 7,000; plus a paramilitary force of 7,500 (1997) **Conscription:** military service is voluntary **Death penalty:** retained and used for ordinary crimes **Defence spend:** (% GDP) 1.5 (1997) **Education spend:** (% GNP) 3.1 (1993–94) **Health spend:** (% GDP) 1.3 (1990–95)

Economy and resources

Currency: cedi **GDP:** (US$) 6.76 billion (1997) **Real GDP growth:** (% change on previous year) 5 (1997) **GNP (US$):** 6.6 billion (1997) **GNP per capita (PPP):** (US$) 1,790 (1997 est) **Consumer price inflation:** 25% (1998) **Unemployment:** 10% (1991) **Foreign debt:** (US$) 6.2 billion (1996) **Major trading partners:** UK, USA, Germany, Nigeria, Japan, France **Resources:** diamonds, gold, manganese, bauxite **Exports:** gold, cocoa and related products, timber. Principal market: Togo 13% (1997) **Imports:** raw materials, machinery and transport equipment, petroleum, food, basic manufactures. Principal source: UK 15% (1997) **Arable land:** 12.3% (1995)

Population and society

Population: 19,162,000 (1998 est) **Population growth rate:** 2.8% (1995–2000); 2.8% (2000–05) **Population density:** (per sq km) 80.4

(1998 est) **Urban population:** (% of total) 37 (1997) **Age distribution:** (% of total population) 0–14 42.9%, 15–64 54.0%, 65+ 3.1% (1998) **Ethnic groups:** over 75 ethnic groups; most significant are the Akan in the south and west (44%), the Mole-Dagbani in the north, the Ewe in the south, the Ga in the region of the capital city, and the Fanti in the coastal area **Language:** English (official) and African languages **Religion:** Christian 62%, Muslim 16%, animist **Education:** (compulsory years) 9 **Literacy rate:** 70% (men); 51% (women) (1995 est) **Labour force:** 47% of population: 47.5% agriculture, 12.8% industry, 39.7% services (1994) **Life expectancy:** 56 (men); 60 (women) (1995–2000) **Child mortality rate:** (under 5, per 1,000 live births) 107 (1997) **Physicians:** 1 per 22,970 people (1993 est)

Practical information

Visa requirements: UK: visa required. USA: visa required **Embassy in the UK:** (education and visas) 104 Highgate Hill, London N6 5HE. Tel: (0181) 342 8686; fax: (0181) 342 8566; (tourist information) 102 Park Street, London W1Y 3RJ. Tel: (0171) 493 4901; fax: (0171) 629 1730 **British embassy:** British High Commission, PO Box 296, Osu Link, off Gamel Abdul Nasser Avenue, Accra. Tel: (21) 221 665; fax: (21) 664 652 **Chamber of commerce:** Ghana National Chamber of Commerce, PO Box 2325, Accra. Tel: (21) 662 427; fax: (21) 662 210

Chronology

5th–12th century: Ghana Empire (from which present-day country's name derives) flourished, with its centre 500 mi/800 km to the northwest, in Mali. **13th century:** In coastal and forest areas Akan peoples founded first states. **15th century:** Gold-seeking Mande traders entered northern Ghana from the northeast, founding Dagomba and Mamprussi states; Portuguese navigators visited coastal region, naming it the 'Gold Coast', building a fort at Elmina, and slave trading began. **17th century:** Gonja kingdom founded in north by Mande speakers; Ga and Ewe states founded in southeast by immigrants from Nigeria; in central Ghana, controlling gold reserves around Kumasi, the Ashanti, a branch of the Akans, founded what became the most powerful state in precolonial Ghana. **1618:** British trading settlement established on Gold Coast. **18th–19th centuries:** Centralized Ashanti kingdom at its height, dominating between Komoe River in the west and Togo Mountains in the east and active in slave trade; Fante state powerful along coast in the south. **1874:** Britain, after ousting the Danes and Dutch and defeating the Ashanti, made the Gold Coast (the southern provinces) a crown colony. **1898–1901:** After three further military campaigns, Britain finally subdued and established protectorates over Ashanti and the northern territories. **early 20th century:** The colony developed into a major cocoa-exporting region. **1917:** West Togoland, formerly German-ruled, was administered with the Gold Coast as British Togoland. **1949:** Campaign for independence launched by Kwame Nkrumah, who formed Convention People's Party (CPP) and became prime minister in 1952. **1957:** Independence achieved, within the Commonwealth, as Ghana, which included British Togoland; Nkrumah became prime minister. Policy of 'African socialism' and nonalignment pursued. **1960:** Became a republic, with Nkrumah as president. **1964:** Ghana became a one-party state, dominated by the CCP, and developed links with communist bloc. **1966:** Nkrumah deposed in military coup and replaced by Gen Joseph Ankrah; political prisoners released. **1969:** Ankrah replaced by Gen Akwasi Afrifa, who initiated a return to civilian government. **1970:** Edward Akufo-Addo elected president. **1972:** Another coup placed Col Ignatius Acheampong at the head of a military government as economy deteriorated. **1978:** Acheampong deposed in a bloodless coup led by Frederick Akuffo; another coup put Flight-Lt Jerry Rawlings, a populist soldier who launched a drive against corruption, in power. **1979:** Return to civilian rule under Hilla Limann. **1981:** Rawlings seized power again. All political parties banned. **1992:** Pluralist constitution approved in referendum, lifting the ban on political parties. Rawlings won presidential elections. **1996:** Rawlings re-elected. New Democratic Congress (NDC) won assembly majority.

Greece Hellenic Republic

National name: *Elliniki Dimokratia* **Area:** 131,957 sq km/50,948 sq mi **Capital:** Athens **Major towns/cities:** Thessaloníki, Piraeus, Patras, Irákleion, Larissa, Volos **Major ports:** Piraeus, Thessaloníki, Patras, Irákleion

Government

Head of state: Costis Stephanopoulos from 1995 **Head of government:** Costis Simitis from 1996 **Political system:** democracy **Administrative divisions:** 13 regions divided into 51 departments **Political parties:** Panhellenic Socialist Movement (PASOK), nationalist, democratic socialist; New Democracy Party (ND), centre right; Democratic Renewal (DIANA), centrist; Communist Party (KJKE), left wing; Political Spring, moderate, left of centre **Armed forces:** 162,300 (1997) **Conscription:** 19–24 months **Death penalty:** abolished in 1993 **Defence spend:** (% GDP) 4.6 (1997) **Education spend:** (% GNP) 3 (1996) **Health spend:** (% GDP) 2.8 (1995)

Economy and resources

Currency: drachma **GDP:** (US$) 119.1 billion (1997) **Real GDP growth:** (% change on previous year) 3.1 (1997) **GNP:** 126.2 billion (1997) **GNP per capita (PPP):** (US$) 13,080 (1997) **Consumer price inflation:** 4% (1998) **Unemployment:** 8.8% (1995) **Major trading partners:** Germany, Italy, France, the Netherlands, USA, UK **Resources:** bauxite, nickel, iron pyrites, magnetite, asbestos, marble, salt, chromite, lignite **Exports:** fruit and vegetables, clothing, mineral fuels and lubricants, textiles, iron and steel, aluminium and aluminium alloys. Principal market: Germany 25.2% (1997) **Imports:** petroleum and petroleum products, machinery and transport equipment, food and live animals, chemicals and chemical products. Principal source: Italy 15.6% (1997) **Arable land:** 18.6% (1995)

Population and society

Population: 10,600,000 (1998 est) **Population growth rate:** 0.3% (1995–2000); 0% (2000–05) **Population density:** (per sq km) 81.5 (1998 est) **Urban population:** (% of total) 60 (1997) **Age distribution:** (% of total population) 0–14 16.1%, 15–64 67.3%, 65+ 16.5% (1998) **Ethnic groups:** predominantly Greek; main minorities are Turks, Slavs, and Albanians **Language:** Greek (official), Macedonian (100,000–200,000 est) **Religion:** Greek Orthodox; also Roman Catholic **Education:** (compulsory years) 9 **Literacy rate:** 98% (men); 89% (women) (1995 est) **Labour force:** 40.6% of population: 20.4% agriculture, 23.2% industry, 56.4% services (1995) **Life expectancy:** 76 (men); 81 (women) (1995–2000) **Child mortality rate:** (under 5, per 1,000 live births) 10 (1997) **Physicians:** 1 per 256 people (1994)

Practical information

Visa requirements: UK: visa not required. USA: visa not required **Embassy in the UK:** Embassy of the Hellenic Republic, 1A Holland Park, London W11 3TP. Tel: (0171) 221 6467; fax: (0171) 243 3202 **British embassy:** Odos Ploutarchon 1, 106 75 Athens. Tel: (1) 723 6211/9; fax: (1) 724 1872 **Chamber of commerce:** Athens Chamber of Commerce, Odos Akademias 7, 106 71 Athens. Tel: (1) 360 2411; fax: (1) 360 7897

Chronology

c. **2000–1200 BC:** Mycenaean civilization flourished. *c.* **1500–1100 BC:** Central Greece and Peloponnese invaded by tribes of Achaeans, Aeolians, Ionians, and Dorians. *c.* **1000–500 BC:** Rise of the Greek city states; Greek colonies established around the shores of the Mediterranean. *c.* **490–404 BC:** Ancient Greek culture reached its zenith in the democratic city state of Athens. **357–338 BC:** Philip II of Macedon won supremacy over Greece; cities fought to regain and

preserve independence. **146 BC:** Roman Empire defeated Macedon and annexed Greece. **476 AD:** Western Roman Empire ended; Eastern Empire continued as Byzantine Empire, based at Constantinople, with essentially Greek culture. **1204:** Crusaders partitioned Byzantine Empire; Athens, Achaea, and Thessaloniki came under Frankish rulers. **late 14th century–1461:** Ottoman Turks conquered mainland Greece and captured Constantinople in 1453; Greek language and culture preserved by Orthodox Church. **1685:** Venetians captured Peloponnese; regained by Turks in 1715. **late 18th century:** Beginnings of Greek nationalism among émigrés and merchant class. **1814:** *Philike Hetairia* ('Friendly Society') formed by revolutionary Greek nationalists in Odessa. **1821:** *Philike Hetairia* raised Peloponnese brigands in revolt against Turks; War of Independence ensued. **1827:** Battle of Navarino: Britain, France, and Russia intervened to destroy Turkish fleet; Count Ioannis Kapodistrias elected president of Greece. **1829:** Treaty of Adrianople: under Russian pressure, Turkey recognized independence of small Greek state. **1832:** Great Powers elected Otto of Bavaria as king of Greece. **1843:** Coup forced King Otto to grant a constitution. **1862:** Mutiny and rebellion led King Otto to abdicate. **1863:** George of Denmark became king of the Hellenes. **1864:** Britain transferred Ionian islands to Greece. **1881:** Following Treaty of Berlin in 1878, Greece was allowed to annex Thessaly and part of Epirus. **late 19th century:** Politics dominated by Kharilaos Trikoupis, who emphasized economic development, and Theodoros Deliyiannis, who emphasized territorial expansion. **1897:** Greco-Turkish War ended in Greek defeat. **1908:** Cretan Assembly led by Eleutherios Venizelos proclaimed union with Greece. **1910:** Venizelos became prime minister and introduced financial, military, and constitutional reforms. **1912–13:** Balkan Wars: Greece annexed a large area of Epirus and Macedonia. **1916:** 'National Schism': Venizelos formed rebel pro-Allied government while royalists remained neutral. **1917–18:** Greek forces fought on Allied side in World War I. **1919–22:** Greek invasion of Asia Minor; after Turkish victory, a million refugees came to Greece. **1924:** Republic declared amid great political instability. **1935:** Greek monarchy restored with George II. **1936:** Gen Ioannia Metaxas established right-wing dictatorship. **1940:** Greece successfully repelled Italian invasion. **1941–44:** German occupation of Greece; rival monarchist and communist resistance groups operated from 1942. **1946–49:** Civil war: communists defeated by monarchists with military aid from Britain and USA. **1952:** Became a member of NATO. **1967:** 'Greek Colonels' seized power under George Papadopoulos; political activity banned; King Constantine II exiled. **1973:** Republic proclaimed with Papadopoulos as president. **1974:** Cyprus crisis caused downfall of military regime; Constantine Karamanlis returned from exile to form Government of National Salvation and restore democracy. **1981:** Andreas Papandreou elected Greece's first socialist prime minister; Greece entered the European Community. **1989–93:** Election defeat of Panhellenic Socialist Movement (PASOK) followed by unstable coalition governments. **1993:** PASOK returned to power. **1996:** Costis Simitis succeeded Papandreou as prime minister. PASOK retained its majority in the general election. **1997:** Direct talks with Turkey resulted in agreement to settle all future disputes peacefully.

Grenada

Area: (including the southern Grenadine Islands, notably Carriacou and Petit Martinique) 344 sq km/133 sq mi **Capital:** St George's **Major towns/cities:** Grenville, Sauteurs, Victoria, Hillsborough (Carriacou)

Government

Head of state: Elizabeth II from 1974, represented by governor general Reginald Palmer from 1992 **Head of government:** Keith Mitchell from 1995 **Political system:** emergent democracy **Administrative divisions:** six parishes **Political parties:** Grenada United Labour Party (GULP), nationalist, left of centre; National Democratic Congress (NDC), centrist; National Party (TNP), centrist

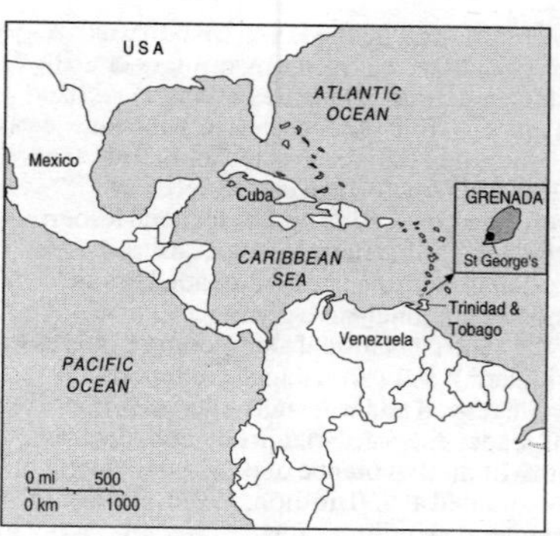

Armed forces: no standing army; 730-strong regional security unit (1997) **Death penalty:** retained and used for ordinary crimes but can be considered abolitionist in practice (last execution in 1978)

Economy and resources

Currency: Eastern Caribbean dollar **GDP:** (US$) 310 million (1997 est) **Real GDP growth:** (% change on previous year) 3.0 (1997) **GNP:** 296 million (1997) **GNP per capita (PPP):** (US$) 4,450 (1997) **Consumer price inflation:** 2.2% (1997) **Unemployment:** 40% (1995 est) **Foreign debt:** (US$) 120 million (1996) **Major trading partners:** USA, UK, Trinidad and Tobago, the Netherlands, Germany **Exports:** cocoa, bananas, cocoa, mace, fresh fruit. Principal market: UK, USA, France 18.5% each (1995) **Imports:** foodstuffs, mineral fuels, machinery and transport equipment, basic manufactures, beverages, tobacco. Principal source: USA 30% (1995) **Arable land:** 11.8% (1995)

Population and society

Population: 93,000 (1998 est) **Population growth rate:** 0.7% (1995–2025) **Population density:** (per sq km) 283.8 (1998 est) **Urban population:** (% of total) 37 (1997 est) **Age distribution:** (% of total population) 0–14 43.1%, 15–64 52.3%, 65+ 4.6% (1998) **Ethnic groups:** majority is of black African descent **Language:** English (official); some French-African patois spoken **Religion:** Roman Catholic 53%, Anglican, Seventh Day Adventist, Pentecostal **Education:** (compulsory years) 11 **Literacy rate:** 85% (1994 est) **Labour force:** 19.8% agriculture, 24.5% industry, 55.7% services (1989) **Life expectancy:** 68 (men); 73 (women) (1996 est) **Child mortality rate:** (under 5, per 1,000 live births) 33 (1995) **Physicians:** 1 per 1,428 people (1991)

Practical information

Visa requirements: UK: visa not required. USA: visa not required **Embassy in the UK:** 1 Collingham Gardens, London SW5 0HW. Tel: (0171) 373 7809; fax: (0171) 370 7040 **British embassy:** British High Commission, 14 Church Street, St George's. Tel: 440 3222; fax: 440 4939 **Chamber of commerce:** Grenada Chamber of Industry and Commerce, PO Box 129, Decaul Building, Mount Gay, St George's. Tel: 440 2937; fax: 440 6627

Chronology

1498: Sighted by the explorer Christopher Columbus; Spanish named it Grenada since its hills were reminiscent of the Andalusian city. **1650:** Colonized by French settlers from Martinique, who faced resistance from the local Carib Indian community armed with poison arrows, before the defeated Caribs performed a mass suicide. **1783:** Ceded to Britain as a colony by the Treaty of Versailles; black African slaves imported to work cotton, sugar, and tobacco plantations. **1795:** Abortive rebellion against British rule led by Julien Fedon, a black planter inspired by the ideas of the French Revolution. **1834:** Slavery abolished. **1950:** Left-wing Grenada United Labour Party (GULP) founded by trade union leader Eric Gairy. **1951:** Universal adult suffrage granted and GULP elected to power in a nonautonomous local assembly. **1958–62:** Part of the Federation of the West Indies. **1967:** Internal self-government achieved. **1974:** Independence achieved within the Commonwealth, with Gairy as prime minister. **1979:** Autocratic Gairy removed in bloodless coup led by left-wing Maurice Bishop of the New Jewel Movement; constitution suspended and a People's Revolutionary Government established. **1982:** Relations with the USA and Britain deteriorated as ties with Cuba and the USSR strengthened. **1983:**

After attempts to improve relations with the USA, Bishop was overthrown by left-wing opponents, precipitating military coup by Gen Hudson Austin. Bishop and three colleagues executed. USA invaded, accompanied by troops from other eastern Caribbean countries; there were 250 fatalities. Austin arrested and 1974 constitution reinstated. **1984:** Newly formed centre-left New National Party (NNP) won general election and its leader, Herbert Blaize, became prime minister. **1989:** Blaize replaced as leader of NNP, but remained as head of government; on his death, he was succeeded by Ben Jones. **1991:** Inconclusive general election; Nicholas Braithwaite of the centrist National Democratic Congress (NDC) became prime minister. Windward Islands confederation proposed. **1995:** Brathwaite retired and was succeeded as prime minister by the new NDC leader, George Brizan. General election won by NNP, led by Keith Mitchell. A plague of pink mealy bugs caused damage to crops estimated at $60 million. **1999:** The ruling NNP gained a sweeping general election victory.

Guatemala Republic of

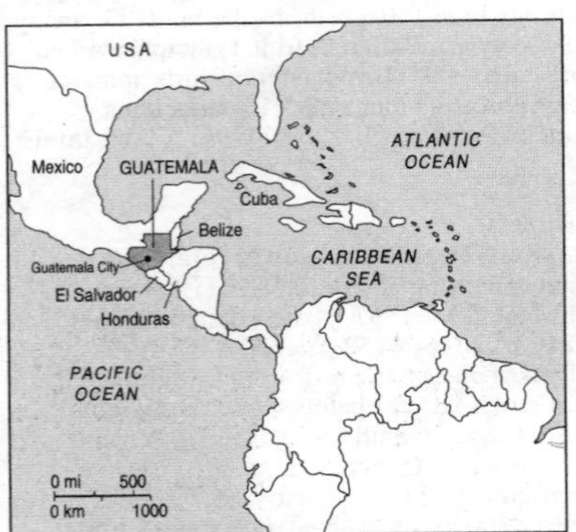

National name: *República de Guatemala* **Area:** 108,889 sq km/42,042 sq mi **Capital:** Guatemala City **Major towns/cities:** Quezaltenango, Escuintla, Puerto Barrios (naval base), Retalhuleu, Chiquimula

Government

Head of state and government: Alvaro Arzú from 1996 **Political system:** democracy **Administrative divisions:** 22 departments **Political parties:** Guatemalan Christian Democratic Party (PDCG), Christian, centre left; Centre Party (UCN), centrist; Revolutionary Party (PR), radical; Movement of National Liberation (MLN), extreme right wing; Democratic Institutional Party (PID), moderate conservative; Solidarity and Action Movement (MAS), right of centre; Guatemalan Republican Front (FRG), right wing; National Advancement Party (PAN), right of centre; Social Democratic Party (PSD), right of centre **Armed forces:** 40,700; plus paramilitary forces of 9,800 (1997) **Conscription:** selective conscription for 30 months **Death penalty:** retained and used for ordinary crimes **Defence spend:** (% GDP) 1.5 (1997) **Education spend:** (% GNP) 1.7 (1995) **Health spend:** (% GDP) 0.9 (1990–95)

Economy and resources

Currency: quetzal **GDP:** (US$) 17.8 billion (1997) **Real GDP growth:** (% change on previous year) 4.2 (1997) **GNP:** 16.8 billion (1997) **GNP per capita (PPP):** (US$) 3,840 (1997) **Consumer price inflation:** 13% (1998) **Unemployment:** 6.1% (1993) **Foreign debt:** (US$) 3.78 billion (1996) **Major trading partners:** USA, El Salvador, Mexico, Costa Rica, Venezuela, Germany, Japan, Honduras **Resources:** petroleum, antimony, gold, silver, nickel, lead, iron, tungsten **Exports:** coffee, bananas, sugar, cardamoms, shellfish, tobacco. Principal market: USA 35.8% (1997) **Imports:** raw materials and intermediate goods for industry, consumer goods, mineral fuels and lubricants. Principal source: USA 41.2% (1997) **Arable land:** 12.5% (1995)

Population and society

Population: 10,801,000 (1998 est) **Population growth rate:** 2.8% (1995–2000); 2.7% (2000–05) **Population density:** (per sq km) 110.7 (1998 est) **Urban population:** (% of total) 40 (1997) **Age distribution:** (% of total population) 0–14 42.9%, 15–64 53.6%, 65+ 3.5% (1998) **Ethnic groups:** two main ethnic groups: American Indians and ladinos (others, including Europeans, black Africans, and mestizos). American Indians are descended from the highland Mayas **Language:** Spanish (official); 45% speak Mayan languages **Religion:** Roman Catholic 70%, Protestant 30% **Education:** (compulsory years) 6 **Literacy rate:** 63% (men); 47% (women) (1995 est) **Labour force:** 35% of population (1990): 48% agriculture, 23% industry, 29% services (1993) **Life expectancy:** 65 (men); 70 (women) (1995–2000) **Child mortality rate:** (under 5, per 1,000 live births) 63 (1997) **Physicians:** 1 per 3,999 people (1993 est)

Practical information

Visa requirements: UK: visa required for business visits and tourist visits of over 90 days. USA: visa not required for a stay of up to 90 days **Embassy in the UK:** 13 Fawcett Street, London SW10 9HN. Tel: (0171) 351 3042; fax: (0171) 376 5708 **British embassy:** British Embassy, 7th Floor, Edificio Centro Financiero, Tower Two, 7a Avenida 5–10, Zona 4, Guatemala City. Tel: (2) 321 601/2/4; fax: (2) 341 904 **Chamber of commerce:** Cámara de Comercio de Guatemala, 10a Calle 3–80, Zona 1, Guatemala City. Tel: (2) 82681; fax: (2) 514 197

Chronology

c. AD **250–900:** Part of culturally advanced Maya civilization. **1524:** Conquered by the Spanish adventurer Pedro de Alvarado and became a Spanish colony. **1821:** Independence achieved from Spain, joining Mexico initially. **1823:** Became part of United Provinces (Federation) of Central America, also embracing Costa Rica, El Salvador, Honduras, and Nicaragua. **1839:** Achieved full independence. **1844–65:** Rafael Carrera held power as president. **1873–85:** The country was modernized on liberal lines by President Justo Rufino Barrios, the army was built up, and coffee growing introduced. **1944:** Juan José Arevalo became president, ending a period of rule by dictators. Socialist programme of reform instituted by Arevalo and his successor, from 1951, Col Jacobo Arbenz Guzman, including establishing a social security system and redistributing land expropriated from large estates to landless peasants. **1954:** Col Carlos Castillo Armas became president in US-backed coup, after United Fruit Company plantations had been nationalized by Arbenz. Land reform halted. **1963:** Castillo assassinated and military coup made Col Enrique Peralta president. **1966:** Cesar Méndez elected president as civilian rule restored. **1970s:** More than 50,000 died in a spate of political violence as the military regime sought to liquidate left-wing dissidents. **1970:** Carlos Araña elected president, with military back in power. **1976:** Earthquake killed 27,000 and left more than 1 million homeless. **1981:** Growth of antigovernment guerrilla movement. Death squads and soldiers killed an estimated 11,000 civilians during the year. **1982:** Right-wing army coup installed Gen Ríos Montt as head of junta and then as president, determined to fight corruption and end violence. **1983:** Montt removed in coup led by Gen Mejía Victores, who declared amnesty for the guerrillas. **1985:** New constitution adopted; PDCG won congressional elections; Marco Vinicio Cerezo Arevalo became civilian president. **1989:** Coup attempt against Cerezo foiled. Over 100,000 people killed and 40,000 reported missing since 1980. **1991:** Jorge Serrano Elías of MAS elected president. Diplomatic relations established with Belize, which Guatemala had long claimed. **1993:** President Serrano deposed after attempting to impose authoritarian regime; Ramiro de Leon Carpio, a human-rights ombudsman, elected president by assembly. **1994:** Peace talks held with Guatemalan Revolutionary National Unity (URNG) rebels. Right-wing parties secured a majority in congress after elections. **1995:** Government criticized by USA and United Nations for widespread human-rights abuses. First cease-fire by rebels in 30 years. **1996:** Alvaro Arzú elected president. Peace agreement ended 36-year war.

Guinea Republic of

National name: *République de Guinée* **Area:** 245,857 sq km/94,925 sq mi **Capital:** Conakry **Major towns/cities:** Labé, Nzérékoré, Kankan, Kindia

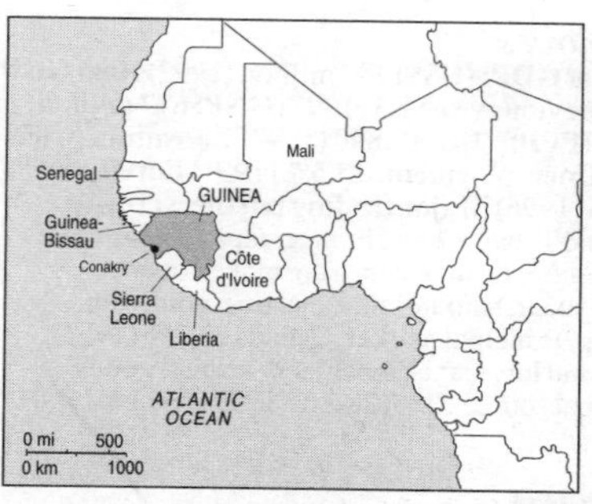

Government

Head of state: Lansana Conté from 1984 **Head of government:** Lamine Sidime from 1999 **Political system:** emergent democracy **Administrative divisions:** 34 provinces (including Conakry) **Political parties:** Party of Unity and Progress (PUP), centrist; Rally of the Guinean People (RPG), left of centre; Union of the New Republic (UNR), left of centre; Party for Renewal and Progress (PRP), left of centre **Armed forces:** 9,700; plus paramilitary forces of 9,600 (1997) **Conscription:** military service is compulsory for two years **Death penalty:** retained and used for ordinary crimes **Defence spend:** (% GDP) 1.6 (1997) **Education spend:** (% GNP) 2.2 (1993) **Health spend:** (% GDP) 1.2 (1990–95)

Economy and resources

Currency: Guinean franc **GDP:** (US$) 4 billion (1997) **Real GDP growth:** (% change on previous year) 4.8 (1997) **GNP:** 3.9 billion (1997) **GNP per capita (PPP):** (US$) 1,850 (1997) **Consumer price inflation:** 10% (1996) **Foreign debt:** (US$) 3.24 billion (1996) **Major trading partners:** France, USA, Belgium, Hong Kong, Spain, Ireland, Côte d'Ivoire **Resources:** bauxite (world's top exporter of bauxite and second-largest producer of bauxite ore), alumina, diamonds, gold, granite, iron ore, uranium, nickel, cobalt, platinum **Exports:** bauxite, alumina, diamonds, coffee. Principal market: Russia 16.7% (1997) **Imports:** foodstuffs, mineral fuels, semi-manufactured goods, consumer goods, textiles and clothing, machinery and transport equipment. Principal source: France 22.4% (1997) **Arable land:** 2.8% (1995)

Population and society

Population: 7,337,000 (1998 est) **Population growth rate:** 1.4% (1995–2000) **Population density:** (per sq km) 30.4 (1998 est) **Urban population:** (% of total) 30 (1995) **Age distribution:** (% of total population) 0–14 43.9%, 15–64 53.5%, 65+ 2.7% (1998) **Ethnic groups:** 24 ethnic groups, including the Malinke, Peul, and Soussou **Language:** French (official), African languages (of which eight are official) **Religion:** Muslim 95%, Christian **Education:** (compulsory years) 6 **Literacy rate:** 35% (men); 13% (women) (1995 est) **Labour force:** 49% of population: 87% agriculture, 2% industry, 11% services (1990) **Life expectancy:** 46 (men); 47 (women) (1995–2000) **Child mortality rate:** (under 5, per 1,000 live births) 190 (1997) **Physicians:** 1 per 7,445 people (1993 est)

Practical information

Visa requirements: UK: visa required. USA: visa required **Embassy for the UK:** 51 rue de la Faisanderie, 75016 Paris, France. Tel: (1) 4704 8148; fax: (1) 4704 5765 **British embassy:** British Consulate, BP 834, Conakry. (All staff based in Dakar, Senegal.) Tel: (224) 442 959; fax: (224) 414 215 **Chamber of commerce:** Chambre de Commerce, d'Industrie et d'Agriculture de Guinée, BP 545, Conakry. Tel: (224) 444 495; telex: 609

Chronology

c. **AD 900:** The Susi people, a community related to the Malinke, immigrated from the northeast, pushing the indigenous Baga towards the Atlantic coast. **13th century:** Susi kingdoms established, extending their influence to the coast; northeast Guinea was part of Muslim Mali Empire, centred to northeast. **mid-15th century:** Portuguese traders visited the coast and later developed trade in slaves and ivory. **1849:** French protectorate established over coastal region around Nunez River, which was administered with Senegal. **1890:** Separate Rivières du Sud colony formed. **1895:** Renamed French Guinea, the colony became part of French West Africa. **1946:** French Guinea became an overseas territory of France. **1958:** Full independence from France achieved as Guinea after referendum rejected remaining within French Community; Sékou Touré of the Democratic Party of Guinea (PDG) elected president. **1960s and 1970s:** Touré established socialist one-party state, leading to deterioration in economy as 200,000 fled abroad. **1979:** Strong opposition to Touré's rigid Marxist policies forced him to accept return to mixed economy and legalize private enterprise. **1984:** Touré died. Bloodless military coup brought Col Lansana Conté to power; PDG outlawed, political prisoners released; market-centred economic reforms. **1985:** Attempted coup against Conté while he was out of the country was foiled by loyal troops. **1991:** Antigovernment general strike and mass protests. **1992:** Constitution amended to allow for multiparty politics. **1993:** Conté narrowly re-elected in first direct presidential election. **1995:** Assembly elections won by Conté's supporters. **1996:** Attempted military coup thwarted. **1998:** President Conté re-elected.

Guinea-Bissau Republic of (formerly Portuguese Guinea)

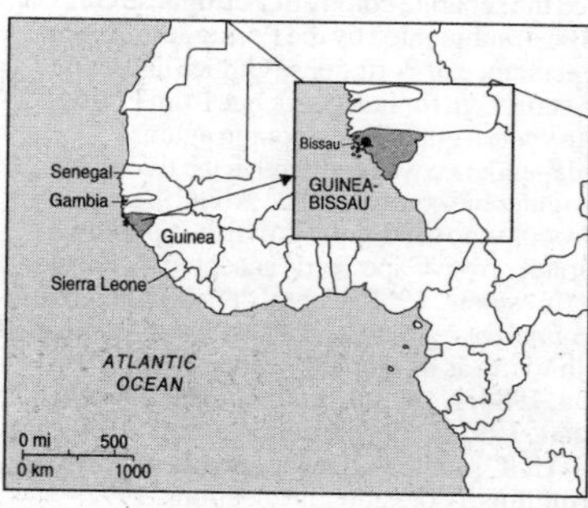

National name: *República da Guiné-Bissau* **Area:** 36,125 sq km/13,947 sq mi **Capital:** Bissau (main port) **Major towns/cities:** Mansôa, São Domingos, Bolama/Bijagós, Catio, Buba, Butata, Farim, Cacine

Government

Head of state: Malan Bacai Sanha from 1999 **Head of government:** Francisco Fadul from 1998 **Political system:** emergent democracy **Administrative divisions:** eight regions **Political parties:** African Party for the Independence of Portuguese Guinea and Cape Verde (PAIGC), nationalist socialist; Party for Social Renovation (PRS), left of centre; Guinea-Bissau Resistance–Bafata Movement (PRGB-MB), centrist **Armed forces:** 7,300; plus paramilitary gendarmerie of 2,000 (1997) **Conscription:** selective conscription **Death penalty:** abolished in 1993 **Defence spend:** (% GDP) 2.6 (1997) **Education spend:** (% GNP) 2.8 (1990) **Health spend:** (% GDP) 1.1 (1990–95)

Economy and resources

Currency: Guinean peso **GDP:** (US$) 265 million (1997) **Real GDP growth:** (% change on previous year) 5.2 (1997) **GNP:** 300 million (1997) **GNP per capita (PPP):** (US$) 1,070 (1997) **Consumer price inflation:** 40% (1996) **Unemployment:** 5.1% (1992) **Foreign debt:** (US$) 937 million (1996) **Major trading partners:** Spain, Thailand, India, Portugal, Côte d'Ivoire, the Netherlands, Japan **Resources:** bauxite, phosphate, petroleum (largely unexploited) **Exports:** cashew nuts, palm kernels, groundnuts, fish and shrimp, timber. Principal market: India 40% (1996) **Imports:** foodstuffs, machinery and transport equipment, fuels, construction materials. Principal source: Portugal 29.2% (1996) **Arable land:** 10.7% (1995)

Population and society

Population: 1,161,000 (1998 est) **Population growth rate:** 2% (1995–2000) **Population density:** (per sq km) 43.1 (1998 est) **Urban population:** (% of total) 23 (1997) **Age distribution:** (% of total population) 0–14 42.4%, 15–64 54.8%, 65+ 2.8% (1998) **Ethnic groups:** majority originated in Africa, and comprises five main ethnic groups: the Balante in the central region, the Fulani in the north, the Malinke in the northern central area, and the Mandyako and Pepel near the coast **Language:** Portuguese (official); Crioulo (Cape Verdean dialect of Portuguese), African languages **Religion:** animist

65%, Muslim 38%, Christian 5% (mainly Roman Catholic) **Education:** (compulsory years) 6 **Literacy rate:** 50% (men); 24% (women) (1995 est) **Labour force:** 48% of population: 85% agriculture, 2% industry, 13% services (1990) **Life expectancy:** 42 (men); 45 (women) (1995–2000) **Child mortality rate:** (under 5, per 1,000 live births) 195 (1997) **Physicians:** 1 per 7,473 person (1991)

Practical information

Visa requirements: UK: visa required. USA: visa required **Embassy in the UK:** Consulate General of the Republic of Guinea-Bissau, 8 Palace Gate, London W8 4RP. Tel: (0171) 589 5253; fax: (0171) 589 9590 **British embassy:** British Consulate, Maregro Int., CP 100, Bissau. (All staff reside at Dakar, Senegal.) Tel: (245) 201 224; fax: (245) 201 265 **Chamber of commerce:** Associacão Comercial e Industrial e Agricola da Guiné-Bissau, Bissau. Tel/fax: (245) 201 602

Chronology

10th century: Known as Gabu, became a tributary kingdom of the Mali Empire to northeast. **1446:** Portuguese arrived, establishing nominal control over coastal areas and capturing slaves to send to Cape Verde. **1546:** Gabu kingdom became independent of Mali and survived until 1867. **1879:** Portugal, which had formerly administered the area with Cape Verde islands, created the separate colony of Portuguese Guinea. **by 1915:** The interior had been subjugated by the Portuguese. **1956:** African Party for the Independence of Portuguese Guinea and Cape Verde (PAIGC) formed to campaign for independence from Portugal. **1961:** The PAIGC began to wage a guerrilla campaign against Portuguese rule. **1973:** Independence was declared in the two-thirds of the country that had fallen under the control of the PAIGC; heavy losses sustained by Portuguese troops who tried to put down the uprising. **1974:** Independence separately from Cape Verde accepted by Portugal, with Luiz Cabral (PAIGC) president. **1980:** Cabral deposed, and João Vieira became chair of a council of revolution. **1981:** PAIGC confirmed as the only legal party, with Vieira as its secretary general; Cape Verde decided not to form a union. **1984:** New constitution made Vieira head of both government and state. **1991:** Other parties legalized in response to public pressure. **1994:** PAIGC secured a clear assembly majority and Vieira narrowly won first multiparty presidential elections. **1997:** Carlos Correia appointed prime minister. **1998:** Peacekeeping troops deployed. Francisco Fadul appointed prime minister. **1999:** Army ousted President Vieira. Malan Bacai Sanha, speaker of the National Assembly, was appointed acting president, pending elections.

Guyana Cooperative Republic of

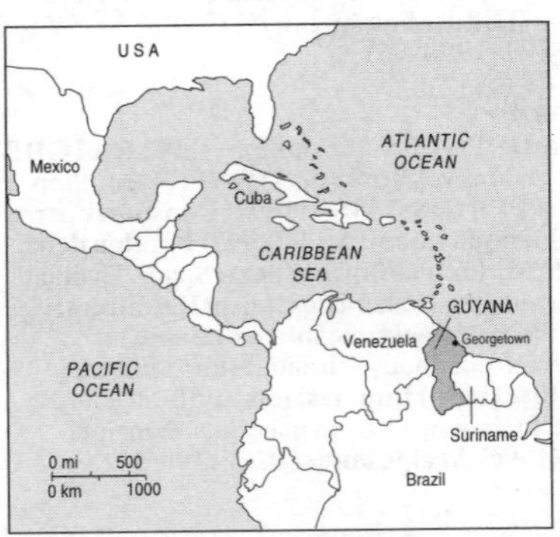

Area: 214,969 sq km/82,999 sq mi **Capital:** Georgetown (and port) **Major towns/cities:** Linden, New Amsterdam, Rose Hall, Corriverton **Major ports:** New Amsterdam

Government

Head of state: Janet Jagan from 1997 **Head of government:** Samuel Hinds from 1992 **Political system:** democracy **Administrative divisions:** ten regions **Political parties:** People's National Congress (PNC), Afro-Guyanan, nationalist socialist; People's Progressive Party (PPP), Indian-based, left wing **Armed forces:** 1,600; plus a paramilitary force of 1,500 (1997) **Conscription:** military service is voluntary **Death penalty:** retained and used for ordinary crimes **Defence spend:** (% GDP) 1 (1997) **Education spend:** (% GNP) 4.9 (1996)

Economy and resources

Currency: Guyana dollar **GDP:** (US$) 740 million (1997) **Real GDP growth:** (% change on previous year) 7.3 (1997) **GNP:** 677 million (1997) **GNP per capita (PPP):** (US$) 2,890 (1997) **Consumer price inflation:** 6.5% (1996) **Unemployment:** 13.5% (1991) **Foreign debt:** (US$) 1.63 billion (1996) **Major trading partners:** USA, Canada, UK, Trinidad and Tobago, Italy, France, Japan **Resources:** gold, diamonds, bauxite, copper, tungsten, iron, nickel, quartz, molybdenum **Exports:** sugar, bauxite, alumina, rice, gold, rum, timber, molasses, shrimp. Principal market: Canada 24.2% (1997) **Imports:** mineral fuels and lubricants, machinery, capital goods, consumer goods. Principal source: USA 28.2% (1997) **Arable land:** 2.4% (1995)

Population and society

Population: 850,000 (1998 est) **Population growth rate:** 1.0% (1995–2000); 1.1% (2000–05) **Population density:** (per sq km) 3.6 (1998 est) **Urban population:** (% of total) 37 (1997) **Age distribution:** (% of total population) 0–14 31.1%, 15–64 64.3%, 65+ 4.6% (1998) **Ethnic groups:** about 51% descended from settlers from the subcontinent of India; about 43% Afro-Indian; small minorities of American Indians, Chinese, and Europeans **Language:** English (official), Hindi, American Indian languages **Religion:** Hindu 54%, Christian 27%, Sunni Muslim 15% **Education:** (compulsory years) 10 **Literacy rate:** 98% (men); 97% (women) (1995 est) **Labour force:** 40% of population (1990): 27% agriculture, 26% industry, 47% services (1993) **Life expectancy:** 61 (men); 68 (women) (1995–2000) **Child mortality rate:** (under 5, per 1,000 live births) 71 (1997) **Physicians:** 1 per 3,360 people (1991)

Practical information

Visa requirements: UK: visa not required. USA: visa not required **Embassy in the UK:** 3 Palace Court, Bayswater Road, London W2 4LP. Tel: (0171) 229 7684; fax: (0171) 727 9809 **British embassy:** British High Commission, PO Box 10849, 44 Main Street, Georgetown. Tel: (2) 65881–4; fax: (2) 53555 **Chamber of commerce:** Georgetown Chamber of Commerce and Industry, PO Box 10110, 156 Waterloo Street, Cumminsburg, Georgetown. Tel: (2) 63519

Chronology

1498: The explorer Christopher Columbus sighted Guyana, whose name, 'land of many waters', was derived from a local American Indian word. *c.* **1620:** Settled by Dutch West India Company, who established armed bases and brought in slaves from Africa. **1814:** After period of French rule, Britain occupied Guyana during the Napoleonic Wars and purchased Demerara, Berbice, and Essequibo. **1831:** Became British colony under name of British Guiana. **1834:** Slavery was abolished, resulting in an influx of indentured labourers from India and China to work on sugar plantations. **1860:** Settlement of the Rupununi Savanna commenced. **1860s:** Gold was discovered. **1899:** International arbitration tribunal found in favour of British Guiana in a long-running dispute with Venezuela over lands west of Essequibo River. **1953:** Assembly elections won by left-wing People's Progressive Party (PPP), drawing most support from the Indian community; Britain suspended constitution and installed interim administration, fearing communist takeover. **1961:** Internal self-government granted; Cheddi Jagan (PPP) became prime minister. **1964:** PNC leader Forbes Burnham led PPP–PNC coalition; racial violence between the Asian- and African-descended communities. **1966:** Independence achieved from Britain as Guyana, with Burnham as prime minister. **1970:** Guyana became a republic within the Commonwealth, with Raymond Arthur Chung as president; Burnham remained as prime minister. **1980:** Burnham became first executive president under new constitution, which ended the three-year boycott of parliament by the PPP. **1985:** Burnham died; succeeded by Desmond Hoyte (PNC), as economy deteriorated. **1992:** PPP had decisive victory in first completely free assembly elections for 20 years; Cheddi Jagan became president; privatization programme launched. **1997:** Samuel Hinds became interim president on the death of Cheddi Jagan. Jagan's wife Janet Jagan elected president. **1998:** Violent antigovernment protests. Government and opposition agreed to independent audit of elections. **1999:** Constitutional reform commission appointed.

Haiti Republic of

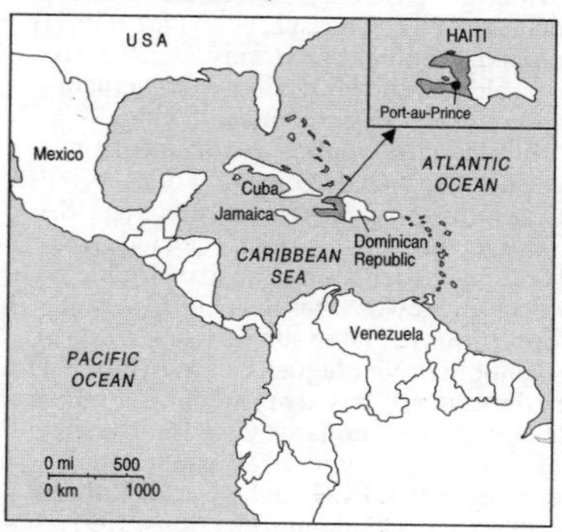

National name: *République d'Haïti* **Area:** 27,750 sq km/10,714 sq mi **Capital:** Port-au-Prince **Major towns/cities:** Cap-Haïtien, Gonaïves, Les Cayes, Port-de-Paix, Jérémie, Jacmée, St Marc

Government

Head of state: René Preval from 1995 **Head of government:** Jacques Edouard Alexis from 1998 **Political system:** transitional **Administrative divisions:** nine departments **Political parties:** National Front for Change and Democracy (FNCD), left of centre; Lavalas Political Organization, populist **Armed forces:** 7,300 (1994); armed forces effectively dissolved in 1995 following restoration of civilian rule in 1994; 5,500 in paramilitary forces (1997) **Conscription:** military service is voluntary **Death penalty:** abolished in 1987 **Defence spend:** (% GDP) 5.2 (1997) **Education spend:** (% GNP) 1.4 (1993–94) **Health spend:** (% GDP) 1.3 (1990–95)

Economy and resources

Currency: gourde **GDP:** (US$) 2.3 billion (1997) **Real GDP growth:** (% change on previous year) 0.8 (1997) **GNP:** 2.5 billion (1997) **GNP per capita (PPP):** (US$) 1,150 (1997 est) **Consumer price inflation:** 17.4% (1997) **Unemployment:** 12.7% (1994) **Foreign debt:** (US$) 897 million (1996) **Major trading partners:** USA, the Netherlands, Antilles, France, Italy, Germany, Japan, UK **Resources:** marble, limestone, calcareous clay, unexploited copper and gold deposits **Exports:** manufactured articles, coffee, essential oils, sisal. Principal market: USA 76.2% (1996) **Imports:** food and live animals, mineral fuels and lubricants, textiles, machinery, chemicals, pharmaceuticals, raw materials, vehicles. Principal source: USA 59.7% (1996) **Arable land:** 20.3% (1995)

Population and society

Population: 7,952,000 (1998 est) **Population growth rate:** 1.9% (1995–95) **Population density:** (per sq km) 246 (1998 est) **Urban population:** (% of total) 33 (1997) **Age distribution:** (% of total population) 0–14 42.6%, 15–64 53.3%, 65+ 4.1% (1998) **Ethnic groups:** about 95% black African descent, the remainder are mulattos or Europeans **Language:** French (official, spoken by literate 10% minority), Creole (official) **Religion:** Christian 95% (of which 80% are Roman Catholic), voodoo 4% **Education:** (compulsory years) 6 **Literacy rate:** 59% (men); 47% (women) (1995 est) **Labour force:** 45% of population: 68% agriculture, 9% industry, 23% services (1990) **Life expectancy:** 53 (men); 56 (women) (1995–2000) **Child mortality rate:** (under 5, per 1,000 live births) 109 (1997) **Physicians:** 1 per 10,855 people (1993)

Practical information

Visa requirements: UK: visa not required. USA: visa not required **Embassy for the UK:** BP 25, 160A avenue Louise, B-1050 Brussels, Belgium. Tel: (2) 649 7381; fax: (2) 640 6080 **British embassy:** British Consulate, PO Box 1302, Hotel Montana, rue F Cardoza, Bourchon, Port-au-Prince. (All staff reside at Kingston, Jamaica.) Tel: (509) 573 969; fax: (509) 574 048 **Chamber of commerce:** Chambre de Commerce et de l'Industrie de Haiti, BP 982, Harry Truman Boulevard, Port-au-Prince. Tel: (509) 222 475; fax: (509) 220 281

Chronology

14th century: Settled by Carib Indians, who followed an earlier wave of Arawak Indian immigration. **1492:** The first landing place of the explorer Christopher Columbus in the New World, who named the island Hispaniola ('Little Spain'). **1496:** At Santo Domingo, now in the Dominican Republic to the east, the Spanish established the first European settlement in the Western hemisphere, which became capital of all Spanish colonies in America. **first half of 16th century:** A third of a million Arawaks and Caribs died, as a result of enslavement and exposure to European diseases; black African slaves were consequently brought in to work the island's gold and silver mines, which were swiftly exhausted. **1697:** Spain ceded western third of Hispaniola to France, which became known as Haiti, but kept the east, which was known as Santo Domingo (the Dominican Republic). **1804:** Independence achieved after uprising against French colonial rule led by the former slave Toussaint l'Ouverture, who died in prison in 1803, and Jean-Jacques Dessalines. **1818–43:** Ruled by Jean-Pierre Boyer, who excluded the blacks from power. **1821:** Santo Domingo fell under the control of Haiti until 1844. **1847–59:** Blacks reasserted themselves under President Faustin Soulouque. **1915:** Haiti invaded by USA as a result of political instability caused by black-mulatto friction; remained under US control until 1934. **1956:** Dr François Duvalier (Papa Doc), a voodoo physician, seized power in military coup and was elected president one year later. **1964:** Duvalier pronounced himself president for life, establishing a dictatorship based around a personal militia, the Tonton Macoutes. **1971:** Duvalier died, succeeded by his son Jean-Claude (Baby Doc); thousands murdered during Duvalier era. **1986:** Duvalier deposed and fled the country; replaced by Lt-Gen Henri Namphy as head of a governing council. **1988:** Leslie Manigat became president, but was ousted in military coup by Brig-Gen Prosper Avril, who installed a civilian government under military control. **1989:** Coup attempt against Avril foiled; US aid resumed. **1990:** Left-wing Catholic priest Jean-Bertrand Aristide elected president. **1991:** Aristide overthrown in military coup led by Brig-Gen Raoul Cedras. Sanctions imposed by Organization of American States (OAS) and USA. **1993:** United Nations (UN) embargo imposed. Aristide's return blocked by military. **1994:** Threat of US invasion led to regime recognizing Aristide as president, under agreement brokered by former US president Jimmy Carter. US troops landed peacefully; Cedras relinquished power and withdrew to Panama; Aristide returned. **1995:** UN peacekeepers drafted in to replace US troops. Assembly elections won by Aristide's supporters. René Preval elected to replace Aristide as president. **1996:** Peaceful handover of power to Preval. **1997:** Prime Minister Smarth resigned, following a series of strikes and protests; he was replaced by Herve Denis. **1998:** Jacques Edouard Alexis nominated prime minister and endorsed by assembly.

Honduras Republic of

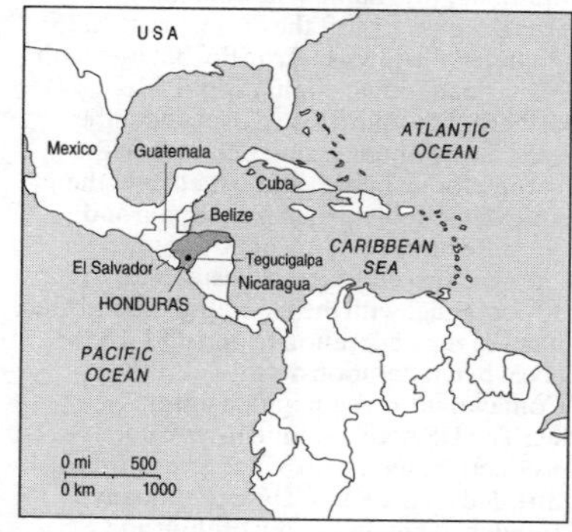

National name: *República de Honduras* **Area:** 112,100 sq km/43,281 sq mi **Capital:** Tegucigalpa **Major towns/cities:** San Pedro Sula, La Ceiba, El Progreso, Choluteca, Juticalpa, Danlí **Major ports:** La Ceiba, Puerto Cortés

Government

Head of state and government: Carlos Flores from 1997 **Political system:** democracy **Administrative divisions:** 18 departments **Political parties:** Liberal Party of Honduras (PLH), centre left; National Party of Honduras (PNH), right wing **Armed forces:** 18,800; plus paramilitary forces numbering 5,500 (1997)

Conscription: military service is voluntary (conscription abolished in 1995) **Death penalty:** abolished in 1956 **Defence spend:** (% GDP) 2.1 (1997) **Education spend:** (% GNP) 3.9 (1995) **Health spend:** (% GDP) 2.8 (1990–95)

Economy and resources

Currency: lempira **GDP:** (US$) 4.5 billion (1997) **Real GDP growth:** (% change on previous year) 4.0 (1997) **GNP:** 4.4 billion (1997) **GNP per capita (PPP):** (US$) 2,200 (1997) **Consumer price inflation:** 19.3% (1998) **Unemployment:** 40% (1994 est) **Foreign debt:** (US$) 4.45 billion (1996) **Major trading partners:** USA, Guatemala, Japan, El Salvador, Germany, Belgium, UK **Resources:** lead, zinc, silver, gold, tin, iron, copper, antimony **Exports:** bananas, lobsters and prawns, zinc, meat. Principal market: USA 73.9% (1997) **Imports:** machinery, appliances and electrical equipment, mineral fuels and lubricants, chemical products, consumer goods. Principal source: USA 61% (1997) **Arable land:** 15.1% (1995)

Population and society

Population: 6,147,000 (1998 est) **Population growth rate:** 2.8% (1995–2000); 2.5% (2000–05) **Population density:** (per sq km) 52.4 (1998 est) **Urban population:** (% of total) 45 (1997) **Age distribution:** (% of total population) 0–14 41.8%, 15–64 54.7%, 65+ 3.4% (1998) **Ethnic groups:** about 90% of mixed American Indian and Spanish descent (known as ladinos or mestizos); there are also Salvadorean, Guatemalan, American, and European minorities **Language:** Spanish (official); English, American Indian languages **Religion:** Roman Catholic **Education:** (compulsory years) 6 **Literacy rate:** 75% (men); 71% (women) (1995 est) **Labour force:** 34% of population: 43.5% agriculture, 19.2% industry, 37.3% services (1994) **Life expectancy:** 68 (men); 72 (women) (1995–2000) **Child mortality rate:** (under 5, per 1,000 live births) 47 (1997) **Physicians:** 1 per 1,266 people (1993 est)

Practical information

Visa requirements: UK: visa not required with full British passport. USA: visa not required **Embassy in the UK:** 115 Gloucester Place, London W1H 3PJ. Tel: (0171) 486 4880; fax: (0171) 486 4550 **British embassy:** Apartado Postal 290, Edificio Palmira, 3 ° Piso, Colonia Palmira, Tegucigalpa. Tel: (504) 325 429; fax: (504) 325 480 **Chamber of commerce:** Federación de Cámaras de Comercio e Industrias de Honduras, Apartado Postal 3393, Edificio Castañito 2 ° Nivel, 6a Avenida, Colonia Los Castaños, Tegucigalpa. Tel: (504) 326 083; fax: (504) 321 870

Chronology

c. AD **250–900:** Part of culturally advanced Maya civilization. **1502:** Visited by Christopher Columbus, who named the country Honduras ('depths') after the deep waters off the north coast. **1525:** Colonized by Spain, who founded the town of Trujillo, but met with fierce resistance from the American Indian population. **17th century onwards:** The northern 'Mosquito Coast' fell under the control of British buccaneers, as the Spanish concentrated on the inland area, with a British protectorate being established over the coast until 1860. **1821:** Achieved independence from Spain and became part of Mexico. **1823:** Became part of United Provinces (Federation) of Central America, also embracing Costa Rica, El Salvador, Guatemala, and Nicaragua, with the Honduran liberal Gen Francisco Morazan, president of the Federation from 1830. **1838:** Achieved full independence when federation dissolved. **1880:** Capital transferred from Comayagua to Tegucigalpa. **later 19th–early 20th centuries:** The USA's economic involvement significant, with banana production, which provided two-thirds of exports in 1913, being controlled by the United Fruit Company; political instability, with frequent changes of constitution and military coups. **1925:** Brief civil war. **1932–49:** Under a right-wing National Party (PNH) dictatorship, led by Gen Tiburcio Carias Andino. **1963–74:** Following a series of military coups, Gen Oswaldo López Arelano held power, before resigning after allegedly accepting bribes from a US company. **1969:** Brief 'Football War' with El Salvador, which attacked Honduras at the time of a football competition between the two states, following evictions of thousands of Salvadoran illegal immigrants from Honduras. **1980:** First civilian government in more than a century elected, with Dr Roberto Suazo of the centrist Liberal Party (PLH) as president, but the commander in chief of the army, Gen Gustavo Alvárez, retained considerable power. **1983:** Close involvement with the USA in providing naval and air bases and allowing Nicaraguan counter-revolutionaries ('Contras') to operate from Honduras. **1984:** Alvarez ousted in coup led by junior officers led by Gen Walter López Reyes, resulting in policy review towards USA and Nicaragua. **1986:** José Azcona del Hoyo (PLH) elected president after electoral law changed, making Suazo ineligible for presidency, and despite receiving fewer votes than his opponent. **1989:** Government and opposition declared support for Central American peace plan to demobilize Nicaraguan Contras (thought to number 55,000 with their dependents) based in Honduras. PNH won assembly elections; its leader, Rafael Leonardo Callejas Romero, elected president. **1992:** Border dispute with El Salvador dating from 1861 was finally resolved. **1993:** PLH, under Carlos Roberto Reina Idiaquez, won assembly and presidential elections. **1997:** Carlos Flores (PLH) elected president.

Hungary Republic of

National name: *Magyar Köztársaság* **Area:** 93,032 sq km/35,919 sq mi **Capital:** Budapest **Major towns/cities:** Miskolc, Debrecen, Szeged, Pécs, Gyor, Nyiregyháza, Székesfehérvár, Kecskemét

Government

Head of state: Arpád Göncz from 1990 **Head of government:** Viktor Orban from 1998 **Political system:** emergent democracy **Administrative divisions:** 19 counties and the capital city (with 22 districts) **Political parties:** over 50, including Hungarian Socialist Party (HSP), reform-socialist; Alliance of Free Democrats (AFD), centrist, radical free market; Hungarian Democratic Forum (MDF), nationalist, centre right; Independent Smallholders Party (ISP), right of centre, agrarian; Christian Democratic People's Party (KDNP), right of centre; Federation of Young Democrats, liberal, anticommunist; Fidesz, right of centre **Armed forces:** 49,100 (1997) **Conscription:** 12 months (men aged 18–23) **Death penalty:** abolished in 1990 **Defence spend:** (% GDP) 1.4 (1997) **Education spend:** (% GNP) 6.0 (1995) **Health spend:** (% GDP) 6.8 (1990–95)

Economy and resources

Currency: forint **GDP:** (US$) 44 billion (1997) **Real GDP growth:** (% change on previous year) 3.5 (1997) **GNP:** 45 billion (1997) **GNP per capita (PPP):** (US$) 7,000 (1997) **Consumer price inflation:** 16% (1998) **Unemployment:** 10.5% (1997) **Foreign debt:** (US$) 26.9 billion (1996) **Major trading partners:** Germany, CIS countries, Italy, Austria, USA **Resources:** lignite, brown coal, natural gas, petroleum, bauxite, hard coal **Exports:** raw materials, semi-finished products, industrial consumer goods, food and agricultural products, transport equipment. Principal market: Germany 37.3% (1997) **Imports:** mineral fuels, raw materials, semi-finished products, transport equipment, food products, consumer goods. Principal source: Germany 26.7% (1997) **Arable land:** 52% (1995)

Population and society

Population: 10,116,000 (1998 est) **Population growth rate:** –0.6%

(1995–2000) **Population density:** (per sq km) 110.5 (1998 est) **Urban population:** (% of total) 66 (1997) **Age distribution:** (% of total population) 0–14 17.5%, 15–64 68.0%, 65+ 14.4% (1998) **Ethnic groups:** 93% indigenous, or Magyar; there is a large Romany community of around 600,000; other ethnic minorities include Germans, Croats, Romanians, Slovaks, Serbs, and Slovenes **Language:** Hungarian (or Magyar), one of the few languages of Europe with non-Indo-European origins; it is grouped with Finnish, Estonian, and others in the Finno-Ugric family **Religion:** Roman Catholic 67%, Calvinist 20%, other Christian denominations, Jewish **Education:** (compulsory years) 10 **Literacy rate:** 99% (men); 99% (women) (1995 est) **Labour force:** 39.7% of population: 8.4% agriculture, 33% industry, 58.6% services (1996) **Life expectancy:** 65 (men); 74 (women) (1995–2000) **Child mortality rate:** (under 5, per 1,000 live births) 16 (1997) **Physicians:** 1 per 238 people (1995)

Practical information

Visa requirements: UK: visa not required. USA: visa not required **Embassy in the UK:** 35 Eaton Place, London SW1X 8BY. Tel: (0171) 235 4048; fax: (0171) 823 1348 **British embassy:** Harmincad Utca 6, 1051 Budapest. Tel: (1) 266 2888; fax: (1) 266 0907 **Chamber of commerce:** Magyar Kereskedelmi és Iparkamara (Hungarian Chamber of Commerce and Industry), PO Box 106, H-1389 Budapest. Tel: (1) 153 3333; fax: (1) 153 1285

Chronology

1st century AD: Region formed part of Roman Empire. **4th century:** Germanic tribes overran central Europe. *c.* **445:** Attila the Hun established a short-lived empire, including Hungarian nomads living far to the east. *c.* **680:** Hungarians settled between the Don and Dniepr rivers under Khazar rule. **9th century:** Hungarians invaded central Europe; ten tribes united under Árpád, chief of the Magyar tribe, who conquered the area corresponding to modern Hungary 896. **10th century:** Hungarians colonized Transylvania and raided their neighbours for plunder and slaves. **955:** Battle of Lech: Germans led by Otto the Great defeated Hungarians. **1001:** St Stephen founded Hungarian kingdom to replace tribal organization and converted Hungarians to Christianity. **12th century:** Hungary became a major power when King Béla III won temporary supremacy over the Balkans. **1308–86:** Angevin dynasty ruled after Arpádian line died out. **1456:** Battle of Belgrade: János Hunyadi defeated Ottoman Turks and saved Hungary from invasion. **1458–90:** Under Mátyás I Corvinus, Hungary enjoyed military success and cultural renaissance. **1526:** Battle of Mohács: Turks under Suleiman the Magnificent decisively defeated Hungarians. **16th century:** Partition of Hungary between Turkey, Austria, and semi-autonomous Transylvania. **1699:** Treaty of Karlowitz: Austrians expelled the Turks from Hungary, which was reunified under Habsburg rule. **1707:** Prince Ferenc Rákóczi II led uprising against Austrians, who promised to respect Hungarian constitution in 1711. **1780–90:** Joseph II's attempts to impose uniform administration throughout Austrian Empire provoked nationalist reaction among Hungarian nobility. **early 19th century:** 'National Revival' movement led by Count Stephen Széchenyi and Lajos Kossuth. **1848:** Hungarian Revolution: nationalists proclaimed self-government; Croat minority resisted Hungarian rule. **1849:** Kossuth repudiated Habsburg monarchy; Austrians crushed revolution with Russian support. **1867:** Austria conceded equality to Hungary within the dual monarchy of Austria-Hungary. **1918:** Austria-Hungary collapsed in military defeat; Count Mihály Károlyi proclaimed Hungarian Republic. **1919:** Communists took power under Béla Kun; Romanians invaded; Admiral Miklós Horthy overthrew Béla Kun. **1920:** Treaty of Trianon: Hungary lost 72% of its territory to Czechoslovakia, Romania, and Yugoslavia; Horthy restored Kingdom of Hungary with himself as regent. **1921:** Count István Bethlen became prime minister of authoritarian aristocratic regime. **1938–41:** Diplomatic collaboration with Germany allowed Hungary to regain territories lost in 1920; Hungary declared war on USSR in alliance with Germany in 1941. **1944:** Germany occupied Hungary and installed Nazi regime. **1945:** USSR 'liberated' Hungary; Smallholders' Party won free elections, but communists led by Mátyás Rákosi took over by stages 1946–49. **1947:** Peace treaty restored 1920 frontiers. **1949:** Hungary became a Soviet-style dictatorship; Rákosi pursued Stalinist policies of collectivization and police terror. **1956:** Hungarian uprising: anti-Soviet demonstrations led prime minister Imre Nagy to propose democratic reforms and neutrality; USSR invaded, crushed dissent, and installed János Kádár as communist leader. **1961:** Kádár began to introduce pragmatic liberal reforms of a limited kind. **1988:** Károly Grosz replaced Kádár and accelerated reform; Hungarian Democratic Forum formed by opposition groups. **1989:** Communist dictatorship dismantled; transitional constitution restored multiparty democracy; opening of border with Austria destroyed the 'Iron Curtain'. **1990:** Elections won by centre–right coalition led by József Antall, who pursued radical free-market reforms. **1991:** Withdrawal of Soviet forces completed. **1994:** Gyula Horn, the leader of the ex-communist Hungarian Socialist Party, became prime minister, pledging to continue reform policies. **1996:** Friendship treaty with Slovak Republic signed. Cooperation treaty with Romania. **1997:** Hungary invited to join NATO and to begin negotiations for membership of the European Union. Referendum gave clear vote in favour of joining NATO. **1998:** Viktor Orban, leader of right-of-centre Fidesz, became prime minister after general election. Full EU membership negotiations commenced. **1999:** Hungary became full member of NATO.

Iceland Republic of

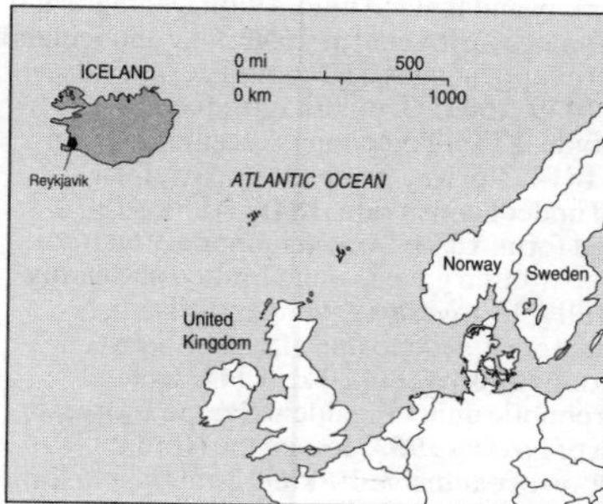

National name: *Lýdveldid Ísland* **Area:** 103,000 sq km/39,768 sq mi **Capital:** Reykjavík **Major towns/cities:** Akureyri, Akranes, Kópavogur, Hafnerfjördur, Vestmannaeyjar

Government

Head of state: Ìlafur Ragnar Grímsson from 1996 **Head of government:** David Oddsson from 1991 **Political system:** democracy **Administrative divisions:** 23 counties within eight districts **Political parties:** Independence Party (IP), right of centre; Progressive Party (PP), radical socialist; People's Alliance (PA), socialist; Social Democratic Party (SDP), moderate, left of centre; Citizens' Party, centrist; Women's Alliance, women- and family-oriented **Armed forces:** no defence forces of its own; US forces under NATO are stationed there: 2,500 military personnel and a 130-strong coastguard (1997) **Death penalty:** abolished in 1928 **Education spend:** (% GNP) 5.4 (1996) **Health spend:** (% GDP) 6.8 (1994)

Economy and resources

Currency: krona **GDP:** (US$) 7.4 billion (1997) **Real GDP growth:** (% change on previous year) 4.6 (1997) **GNP:** 7.5 billion (1997) **GNP per capita (PPP):** (US$) 22,500 (1997) **Consumer price inflation:** 2.2% (1998) **Unemployment:** 3.9% (1997) **Major trading partners:** EU (principally Germany, UK, and Denmark), Norway, USA, Japan **Resources:** aluminium, diatomite, hydroelectric and thermal power, fish **Exports:** fish products, aluminium, ferrosilicon, diatomite, fertilizer, animal products. Principal market: UK 18.9% (1997) **Imports:** machinery and transport equipment, motor vehicles, petroleum and petroleum products, foodstuffs, textiles. Principal source: Germany 11.8% (1997) **Arable land:** 0.1% (1995)

Population and society

Population: 276,000 (1998 est) **Population growth rate:** 1.0% (1995–2000) **Population density:** (per sq km) 2.7 (1998 est) **Urban population:** (% of total) 92 (1997) **Age distribution:** (% of total population) 0–14 23.6%, 15–64 64.7%, 65+ 11.7% (1998) **Ethnic**

groups: most of the population is descended from Norwegians and Celts **Language:** Icelandic, the most archaic Scandinavian language **Religion:** Evangelical Lutheran **Education:** (compulsory years) 9 **Literacy rate:** 99% (men); 99% (women) (1995 est) **Labour force:** 54.6% of population: 9.5% agriculture, 24.2% industry, 66.3% services (1996) **Life expectancy:** 77 (men); 81 (women) (1995–2000) **Child mortality rate:** (under 5, per 1,000 live births) 6 (1997) **Physicians:** 1 per 333 people (1994)

Practical information

Visa requirements: UK: visa not required. USA: visa not required **Embassy in the UK:** 1 Eaton Terrace, London SW1W 8EY. Tel: (0171) 730 5131/2; fax: (0171) 730 1683 **British embassy:** PO Box 460, Laufásvegur 49, 101 Reykjavík. Tel: (354) 551 5883/4; fax: (354) 552 7940 **Chamber of commerce:** Verzlunarrád Islands (Chamber of Commerce), Hús verslunarinnar, 103 Reykjavík. Tel: (354) 588 6666; fax: (354) 568 6564

Chronology

7th century: Iceland discovered by Irish seafarers. **874:** First Norse settler, Ingólfr Arnarson, founded a small colony at Reykjavík. *c.* **900:** Norse settlers came in larger numbers, mainly from Norway. **930:** Settlers established an annual parliament, the Althing, to make laws and resolve disputes. **985:** Eric the Red left Iceland to found a settlement in Greenland. **1000:** Icelanders adopted Christianity. **1263:** Icelanders recognized authority of the king of Norway after brief civil war. **1397:** Norway and Iceland united with Denmark and Sweden under a single monarch. **15th century:** Norway and Iceland were increasingly treated as appendages of Denmark, especially after Sweden seceded in 1449. **1602:** Denmark introduced a monopoly on Icelandic trade. **1783:** Poisonous volcanic eruption caused great loss of life. **1814:** Norway passed to the Swedish crown; Iceland remained under Danish rule. **1845:** Althing re-established in modernized form. **1854:** Danish monopoly on trade abolished. **1874:** New constitution gave Iceland limited autonomy. **1918:** Iceland achieved full self-government under the Danish crown. **1940:** British forces occupied Iceland after Germany invaded Denmark; US troops took over in 1941. **1944:** Iceland became an independent republic under President Sveinn Björnsson. **1949:** Became a member of NATO. **1953:** Joined the Nordic Council. **1958:** Introduction of exclusive 19-km/12-mi fishing limit led to first 'Cod War', when Icelandic patrol boats clashed with British fishing boats. **1972–73:** Iceland extended its fishing limit 80 km/50 mi; renewed confrontation with Britain. **1975–76:** Further extension of fishing limit to 341 km/200 mi caused third 'Cod War' with UK. **1980:** Vigdis Finnbogadóttir became the first woman president of Iceland. **1985:** Iceland declared itself a nuclear-free zone. **1992:** Iceland defied world ban to resume whaling industry. **1996:** Ìlafur Ragnar Grímsson elected president.

India Republic of

National name: Hindi *Bharat* **Area:** 3,166,829 sq km/1,222,713 sq mi **Capital:** Delhi **Major towns/ cities:** Bombay, Calcutta, Chennai (Madras), Bangalore, Hyderabad, Ahmadabad, Kanpur, Pune, Nagpur, Bhopal, Jaipur, Lucknow, Surat **Major ports:** Calcutta, Bombay, Chennai (Madras)

Government

Head of state: Kocheril Raman Narayanan from 1997 **Head of government:** Atal Behari Vajpayee from 1998 **Political system:** liberal democratic federal republic **Administrative divisions:** 25 states and seven centrally administered union territories **Political parties:** All India Congress Committee, or Congress, cross-caste and cross-religion coalition, left of centre; Janata Dal (People's Party), secular, left of centre; Bharatiya Janata Party (BJP), radical right wing, Hindu-chauvinist; Communist Party of India (CPI), Marxist-Leninist; Communist Party of India–Marxist (CPI–M), West Bengal–based moderate socialist **Armed forces:** 1,145,000 (1997) **Conscription:** none, although all citizens are constitutionally obliged to perform national service when called upon **Death penalty:** retained and used for ordinary crimes **Defence spend:** (% GDP) 3.3 (1997) **Education spend:** (% GNP) 3.5 (1995) **Health spend:** (% GDP) 0.7 (1990–95)

Economy and resources

Currency: rupee **GDP:** (US$) 378.6 billion (1997) **Real GDP growth:** (% change on previous year) 5.5 (1997) **GNP:** 373.9 billion (1997) **GNP per capita (PPP):** (US$) 1,650 (1997) **Consumer price inflation:** 7.5% (1998) **Unemployment:** 9.1% **Foreign debt:** (US$) 89.8 billion (1996) **Major trading partners:** USA, CIS, UK, Germany **Resources:** coal, iron ore, copper ore, bauxite, chromite, gold, manganese ore, zinc, lead, limestone, crude oil, natural gas, diamonds **Exports:** tea (world's largest producer), coffee, fish, iron and steel, leather, textiles, clothing, polished diamonds, handmade carpets, engineering goods, chemicals. Principal market: USA 19.3% (1997) **Imports:** nonelectrical machinery, mineral fuels and lubricants, pearls, precious and semiprecious stones, chemicals, transport equipment. Principal source: USA 9.5% (1997) **Arable land:** 55.9% (1995)

Population and society

Population: 982,223,000 (1998 est) **Population growth rate:** 1.6% (1995–2000) **Population density:** (per sq km) 331 (1998 est) **Urban population:** (% of total) 28 (1997) **Age distribution:** (% of total population) 0–14 34.5%, 15–64 60.9%, 65+ 4.6% (1998) **Ethnic groups:** 72% of Indo-Aryan descent; 25% (predominantly in south) Dravidian; 3% Mongoloid **Language:** Hindi, English, and 17 other official languages: Assamese, Bengali, Gujarati, Kannada, Kashmiri, Konkani, Malayalam, Manipur, Marathi, Nepali, Oriya, Punjabi, Sanskrit, Sindhi, Tamil, Telugu, Urdu; more than 1,650 dialects **Religion:** Hindu 83%, Sunni Muslim 11%, Christian 2.5%, Sikh 2% **Education:** (compulsory years) 8 **Literacy rate:** 62% (men); 34% (women) (1995 est) **Labour force:** 43% of population: 64% agriculture, 16% industry, 20% services (1990) **Life expectancy:** 62 (men); 63 (women) (1995–2000) **Child mortality rate:** (under 5, per 1,000 live births) 90 (1997) **Physicians:** 1 per 2,459 people (1993 est)

Practical information

Visa requirements: UK: visa required. USA: visa required **Embassy in the UK:** Office of the High Commissioner for India, India House, Aldwych, London WC2B 4NA. Tel: (0171) 836 8484; fax: (0171) 836 4331 **British embassy:** British High Commission, Shanti Path, Chanakyapuri, New Delhi 110021. Tel: (11) 687 2161; fax: (11) 687 2882 **Chamber of commerce:** India Exchange, 4 India Exchange Place, Calcutta 700001. Tel: (33) 220 3243; fax: (33) 220 4495

Chronology

c. **2500–1500 BC:** The earliest Indian civilization evolved in the Indus Valley with the city states of Harappa and Mohenjo Daro. *c.* **1500–1200 BC:** Aryan peoples from the northwest overran northern India and the Deccan; Brahmanism (a form of Hinduism) developed. **321 BC:** Chandragupta, founder of the Mauryan dynasty, began to unite northern India in a Hindu Empire. **268–232 BC:** Mauryan Empire reached its height under Asoka, who ruled two-thirds of India from his capital Pataliputra. *c.* **180 BC:** Shunga dynasty replaced the Mauryans; Hindu Empire began to break up into smaller kingdoms. **AD 320–480:** Gupta dynasty reunified

India: States and Union Territories

State	Capital	Area		Population
		sq km	sq mi	(1994 est.)
Andhra Pradesh	Hyderabad	275,045	106,195	71,800,000
Arunachal Pradesh	Itanagar	83,743	32,333	965,000
Assam	Dispur	78,438	30,285	24,200,000
Bihar	Patna	173,877	67,134	93,080,000
Goa	Panaji	3,702	1,429	1,235,000
Gujarat	Gandhinagar	196,024	75,685	44,235,000
Haryana	Chandigarh	44,212	17,070	17,925,000
Himachal Pradesh	Shimla	55,673	21,495	5,530,000
Jammu and Kashmir[1]	Srinagar	222,236	85,805	8,435,000
Karnataka	Bangalore	191,791	74,051	48,150,000
Kerala	Trivandrum	38,863	15,005	30,555,000
Madhya Pradesh	Bhopal	443,446	171,215	71,950,000
Maharashtra	Bombay	307,713	118,808	85,565,000
Manipur	Imphal	22,327	8,620	2,010,000
Meghalaya	Shillong	22,429	8,660	1,960,000
Mizoram	Aizawl	21,081	8,139	775,000
Nagaland	Kohima	16,579	6,401	1,410,000
Orissa	Bhubaneshwar	155,707	60,118	33,795,000
Punjab	Chandigarh	5,362	2,070	21,695,000
Rajasthan	Jaipur	342,239	132,138	48,040,000
Sikkim	Gangtok	7096	2,740	444,000
Tamil Nadu	Madras	130,058	50,215	58,840,000
Tripura	Agartala	10,486	4,049	3,055,000
Uttar Pradesh	Lucknow	294,411	113,672	150,695,000
West Bengal	Calcutta	88,752	34,267	73,600,000
Union Territory				
Andaman and 322,000 Islands	Nicobar	Port Blair	8,249	3,185
Chandigarh	Chandigarh	114	44	725,000
Dadra and Nagar Haveli	Silvassa	491	190	153,000
Daman and Diu	Daman	112	43	111,000
Delhi	Delhi	1,483	573	10,865,000
Lakshadweep	Kavaratti	32	12	56,000
Pondicherry	Pondicherry	492	190	894,000

[1] Includes area occupied by Pakistan and China.

northern India. *c.* **500:** Raiding Huns from central Asia destroyed the Gupta dynasty; India reverted to many warring kingdoms. **11th–12th centuries:** Rajput princes of northern India faced repeated Muslim invasions by Arabs, Turks, and Afghans, and in 1206 the first Muslim dynasty was established at Delhi. **14th–16th centuries:** Muslim rule extended over northern India and the Deccan; south remained independent under the Hindu Vijayanagar dynasty. **1498:** Explorer Vasco da Gama reached India, followed by Portuguese, Dutch, French, and English traders. **1526:** Last Muslim invasion: Zahir ud-din Muhammad (Babur) defeated the Sultan of Delhi at Battle of Panipat and established the Mogul Empire, which was consolidated by Akbar the Great (1556–1605). **1600:** East India Company founded by English merchants, who settled in Madras, Bombay, and Calcutta. **17th century:** Mogul Empire reached its zenith under Jahangir (1605–27), Shah Jehan (1628–58), and Aurangzeb (1658–1707). **1739:** Persian king Nadir Shah invaded India and destroyed Mogul prestige; British and French supported rival Indian princes in subsequent internal wars. **1757:** Battle of Plassey: Robert Clive defeated Siraj al-Daulah, nawab of Bengal; Bengal came under control of British East India Company. **1772–85:** Warren Hastings, British governor general of Bengal, raised Indian army and pursued expansionist policies. **early 19th century:** British took control (directly or indirectly) throughout India by defeating powerful Indian states in a series of regional wars. **1858:** 'Indian Mutiny': mutiny in Bengal army erupted into widespread anti-British revolt; rebels sought to restore powers of Mogul emperor. **1858:** British defeated the rebels; East India Company dissolved; India came under the British crown. **1885:** Indian National Congress founded in Bombay as focus for nationalism. **1909:** Morley–Minto Reforms: Indians received right to elect members of Legislative Councils; Hindus and Muslims formed separate electorates. **1919:** British forces killed 379 Indian demonstrators at Amritsar; India Act (Montagu–Chelmsford Reforms) conceded a measure of provincial self-government. **1920–22:** Mohandas Gandhi won control of the Indian National Congress, which launched campaign of civil disobedience in support of demand for complete self-rule. **1935:** India Act provided for Indian control of federal legislature, with defence and external affairs remaining the viceroy's responsibility. **1940:** Muslim League called for India to be partitioned along religious lines. **1947:** British India partitioned into two independent dominions of India (mainly Hindu) and Pakistan (mainly Muslim) amid bloody riots; Jawaharlal Nehru of Congress Party became prime minister. **1950:** India became a republic within the Commonwealth. **1962:** India lost brief border war with China; retained Kashmir in war with Pakistan in 1965. **1966:** Indira Gandhi, daughter of Nehru, became prime minister. **1971:** India defeated Pakistan in war and helped East Pakistan become independent as Bangladesh. **1975:** Found guilty of electoral corruption, Mrs Gandhi declared state of emergency and arrested opponents. **1977–79:** Janata Party formed government under Morarji Desai. **1980:** Mrs Gandhi, heading Congress Party splinter group, Congress (I) ('I' for Indira), returned to power. **1984:** Troops cleared Sikh separatists from the Golden Temple, Amritsar; Mrs Gandhi assassinated by Sikh bodyguards; her son Rajiv Gandhi became prime minister. **1989:** After financial scandals, Congress ('I' was removed after Mrs Gandhi's assassination) lost elections; V P Singh formed Janata Dal minority government. **1990:** Direct rule imposed on Jammu and Kashmir after upsurge in Muslim separatist violence; rising interethnic and religious conflict in Punjab and elsewhere. **1991:** Rajiv Gandhi assassinated during election campaign; P V Narasimha Rao formed minority Congress government. **1992:** Destruction of mosque at Ayodhya, northern India, by Hindu extremists resulted in widespread violence. **1996:** H D Deve Gowda became prime minister of a coalition government. Madras renamed Chennai. Rao resigned as Congress Party president and was replaced by Sitaram Kesri. Direct central rule imposed on Uttar Pradesh after inconclusive assembly elections. **1997:** Deve Gowda's government defeated in confidence vote. United Front government reformed and led by Inder Kumar Gujral. Kocheril Raman Narayanan became first 'untouchable' to be elected president. **1998:** Atal Behari Vajpayee, leader of Bharatiya Janata party, elected prime minister. Sonia Gandhi became leader of Congress Party. Creation of three new states proposed. India carried out five underground nuclear explosions, meeting with international condemnation. Floods in Uttar Pradesh. Congress polled strongly in state elections in northern and central India, reflecting disenchantment with the BJP federal government. **1999:** Indian government renounced further nuclear weapons' testing and promised to sign Comprehensive Test Ban Treaty. Government defeated in confidence vote. Peace talks on Kashmir offered to Pakistan.

Indonesia Republic of

National name: *Republik Indonesia* **Area:** 1,904,569 sq km/735,354 sq mi **Capital:** Jakarta **Major towns/cities:** Surabaya, Bandung, Yogyakarta (Java), Medan, Semarang (Java), Banda Aceh, Palembang (Sumatra), Ujung Pandang (Sulawesi), Denpasar (Bali), Kupang (Timor), Padang, Malang **Major ports:** Tanjung Priok, Surabaya, Semarang (Java), Ujung Pandang (Sulawesi)

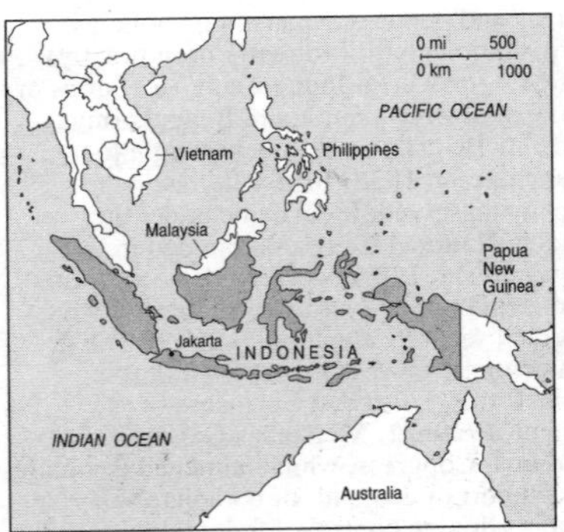

Government
Head of state and government: B J Habibie from 1998 **Political system:** authoritarian nationalist republic **Administrative divisions:** 27 provinces **Political parties:** Sekber Golkar, ruling military-bureaucrat-farmers' party; United Development Party (PPP), moderate Islamic; Indonesian Democratic Party (PDI), nationalist Christian **Armed forces:** 284,000; paramilitary forces 200,000 (1997) **Conscription:** 2 years (selective) **Death penalty:** retained and used for ordinary crimes **Defence spend:** (% GDP) 2.2 (1997) **Education spend:** (% GNP) 1.4 (1996) **Health spend:** (% GDP) 0.7 (1990–95)

Economy and resources
Currency: rupiah **GDP:** (US$) 214.6 billion (1997) **Real GDP growth:** (% change on previous year) 4.1 (1997) **GNP:** 221.9 billion (1997) **GNP per capita (PPP):** (US$) 3,450 (1997) **Consumer price inflation:** 9.8% (1998) **Unemployment:** 10% (1997 est) **Foreign debt:** (US$) 129.03 billion (1996) **Major trading partners:** Japan, Singapore, USA, Hong Kong, Australia, Germany, the Netherlands **Resources:** petroleum (principal producer of petroleum in the Far East), natural gas, bauxite, nickel (world's third-largest producer), copper, tin (world's second-largest producer), gold, coal, forests **Exports:** petroleum and petroleum products, natural and manufactured gas, textiles, rubber, palm oil, wood and wood products, electrical and electronic products, coffee, fishery products, coal, copper, tin, pepper, tea. Principal market: Japan 23.3% (1997) **Imports:** machinery, transport and electrical equipment, manufactured goods, chemical and mineral products. Principal source: Japan 19.8% (1997) **Arable land:** 9.5% (1995)

Population and society
Population: 206,338,000 (1998 est) **Population growth rate:** 1.5% (1995–2000) **Population density:** (per sq km) 116.6 (1998 est) **Urban population:** (% of total) 38% (1997) **Age distribution:** (% of total population) 0–14 30.8%, 15–64 65.2%, 65+ 4.0% (1998) **Ethnic groups:** comprises more than 300 ethnic groups, the majority of which are of Malay descent; important Malay communities include Javanese (about 33% of the population), Sundanese (7%), and Madurese (3%); the largest non-Malay community is the Chinese (2%); substantial numbers of Indians, Melanesians, Micronesians, and Arabs **Language:** Bahasa Indonesia (official), closely related to Malay; there are 583 regional languages and dialects; Javanese is the most widely spoken local language. Dutch is also spoken **Religion:** Muslim 88%, Christian 10%, Buddhist and Hindu 2% (the continued spread of Christianity, together with an Islamic revival, have led to greater religious tensions) **Education:** (compulsory years) 6 **Literacy rate:** 84% (men); 68% (women) (1995 est) **Labour force:** 44% of population: 55% agriculture, 14% industry, 31% services (1990) **Life expectancy:** 63 (men); 67 (women) (1995–2000) **Child mortality rate:** (under 5, per 1,000 live births) 59 (1997) **Physicians:** 1 per 7,028 people (1993 est)

Practical information
Visa requirements: UK: visa not required. USA: visa not required **Embassy in the UK:** 38 Grosvenor Square, London W1X 9AD. Tel: (0171) 499 7661; fax: (0171) 491 4993 **British embassy:** Jalan M H Thamrin 75, Jakarta 10310. Tel: (21) 330 904; fax: (21) 314 1824 **Chamber of commerce:** Indonesian Chamber of Commerce and Industry, 3rd–5th Floors, Chandra Building, Jalan M H Thamrin 20, Jakarta 10350. Tel: (21) 324 000; fax: (21) 310 6098

Chronology
3000–500 BC: Immigrants from southern China displaced original Melanesian population. **6th century AD:** Start of Indian cultural influence; small Hindu and Buddhist kingdoms developed. **8th century:** Buddhist maritime empire of Srivijaya expanded to include all Sumatra and Malay peninsula. **13th century:** Islam introduced to Sumatra by Arab merchants; spread throughout the islands over next 300 years. **14th century:** Eastern Javanese kingdom of Majapahit destroyed Srivijaya and dominated the region. *c.* **1520:** Empire of Majapahit disintegrated; Javanese nobles fled to Bali. **16th century:** Portuguese merchants broke Muslim monopoly of spice trade. **1602:** Dutch East India Company founded; it displaced the Portuguese and monopolized trade with the Spice Islands. **1619:** Dutch East India Company captured port of Jakarta in Java and renamed it Batavia. **17th century:** Dutch introduced coffee plants and established informal control over central Java through divide-and-rule policy among local rulers. **1749:** After frequent military intervention, the Dutch East India Company obtained formal sovereignty over Mataram. **1799:** The Netherlands took over interests of bankrupt Dutch East India Company. **1808:** French forces occupied Java; British expelled them in 1811 and returned Java to the Netherlands in 1816. **1824:** Anglo-Dutch Treaty: Britain recognized entire Indonesian archipelago as Dutch sphere of influence. **1825–30:** Java War: Prince Dipo Negoro led unsuccessful revolt against Dutch rule; further revolt 1894–96. **19th century:** Dutch formalized control over Java and conquered other islands; cultivation of coffee and sugar under tight official control made the Netherlands Indies one of the richest colonies in the world. **1901:** Dutch introduced 'Ethical Policy' supposed to advance local interests. **1908:** Dutch completed conquest of Bali. **1927:** Communist revolts suppressed; Achmed Sukarno founded Indonesian Nationalist Party (PNI) to unite diverse anti-Dutch elements. **1929:** Dutch imprisoned Sukarno and tried to suppress PNI. **1942–45:** Japanese occupation; PNI installed as anti-Western puppet government. **1945:** When Japan surrendered, President Sukarno declared an independent republic, but Dutch set about restoring colonial rule by force. **1947:** Dutch 'police action': all-out attack on Java and Sumatra conquered two-thirds of the republic. **1949:** Under US pressure, Dutch agreed to transfer sovereignty of the Netherlands Indies (except Dutch New Guinea or Irian Jaya) to the Republic of the United States of Indonesia. **1950:** President Sukarno abolished federalism and proclaimed unitary Republic of Indonesia dominated by Java; revolts in Sumatra and South Moluccas. **1959:** To combat severe political instability, Sukarno imposed authoritarian 'guided democracy'. **1963:** The Netherlands ceded Irian Jaya to Indonesia. **1963–66:** Indonesia tried to break up Malaysia by means of blockade and guerrilla attacks. **1965–66:** Clashes between communists and army; Gen Raden Suharto imposed emergency administration and massacred up to 700,000 alleged communists. **1968:** Suharto formally replaced Sukarno as president and proclaimed 'New Order' under strict military rule. **1970s:** Rising oil exports brought significant agricultural and industrial growth. **1975:** Indonesia invaded East Timor when Portuguese rule collapsed; 200,000 died in ensuing war. **1986:** After suppressing revolt on Irian Jaya, Suharto introduced a programme to settle 65,000 Javanese there and on outer islands. **1991:** Democracy Forum launched to promote political dialogue. **1993:** President Suharto re-elected for sixth consecutive term. **1996:** Government crackdown on opponents. **1997:** Hundreds killed in ethnic riots in west Kalimantan province. Drought and famine in Irian Jaya. Forest fires in Borneo and Sumatra blighted large areas of SE Asia with heavy smog and caused catastrophic environmental damage. **1998:** Following mass riots, Suharto stepped down as president and was replaced by Vice President B J Habibie. Partial withdrawal of troops from East Timor and partial autonomy offered. Continuing riots as GDP contracted by 15%. Irian Jaya's status as a military occupation zone ended, following cease-fire agreement with

separatist rebels. Troops killed 16 student demonstrators in Jakarta. Repressive legislation of Suharto era repealed in special legislature session and political parties legalized. Suharto questioned over allegations of corruption. **1999:** Continuing ethnic violence in Borneo, with over 500 people killed in March and April. Government promised a referendum in East Timor on a plan for autonomy, but violent clashes continued; over 25 East Timorese refugees massacred by militia without Indonesian army attempting to stop attack. Peace talks began.

Iran **Islamic Republic of** (formerly **Persia**)

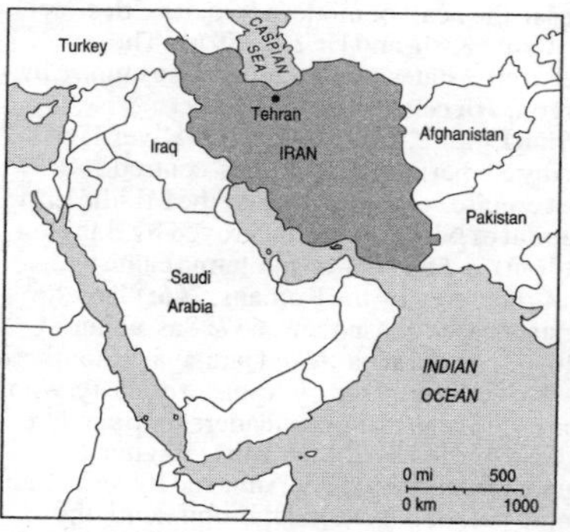

National name: *Jomhori-e-Islami-e-Irân* **Area:** 1,648,000 sq km/636,292 sq mi **Capital:** Tehran **Major towns/cities:** Esfahan, Mashhad, Tabriz, Shiraz, Ahvaz, Bakhtaran, Qom, Kara **Major ports:** Abadan

Government

Head of state and government: Seyyed Mohammad Khatami from 1997 **Leader of the Islamic Revolution:** Seyed Ali Khamenei from 1989 **Political system:** authoritarian Islamic republic **Administrative divisions:** 25 provinces **Political parties:** none officially recognized **Armed forces:** 518,000; plus 350,000 army reserves and 350,000 paramilitary forces (1997) **Conscription:** military service is compulsory for two years **Death penalty:** retained and used for ordinary crimes **Defence spend:** (% GDP) 6.6 (1997) **Education spend:** (% GNP) 4.0 (1995) **Health spend:** (% GDP) 2.8 (1990–95)

Economy and resources

Currency: rial **GDP:** (US$) 93.1 billion (1997 est) **Real GDP growth:** (% change on previous year) 3.5 (1997) **GNP:** 113.5 billion (1997) **GNP per capita (PPP):** (US$) 5,530 (1997) **Consumer price inflation:** 20% (1998) **Unemployment:** 10% (1993 est) **Foreign debt:** (US$) 24.9 billion (1996) **Major trading partners:** Germany, Japan, UK, Italy, United Arab Emirates, Turkey **Resources:** petroleum, natural gas, coal, magnetite, gypsum, iron ore, copper, chromite, salt, bauxite, decorative stone **Exports:** crude petroleum and petroleum products, agricultural goods, metal ores. Principal market: Japan 15.1% (1997) **Imports:** machinery and motor vehicles, paper, textiles, iron and steel and mineral products, chemicals and chemical products. Principal source: Germany 12.8% (1997) **Arable land:** 10.5% (1995)

Population and society

Population: 65,758,000 (1998 est) **Population growth rate:** 2.2% (1995–2000) **Population density:** (per sq km) 42.2 (1998 est) **Urban population:** (% of total) 60 (1997) **Age distribution:** (% of total population) 0–14 43.3%, 15–64 52.6%, 65+ 4.1% (1998) **Ethnic groups:** about 63% of Persian origin, 18% Turkic, 13% other Iranian, 3% Kurdish, and 3% Arabic **Language:** Farsi (official), Kurdish, Turkish, Arabic, English, French **Religion:** Shi'ite Muslim (official) 94%, Sunni Muslim, Zoroastrian, Christian, Jewish, Baha'i **Education:** (compulsory years) 5 **Literacy rate:** 89% (men); 43% (women) (1995 est) **Labour force:** 29% of population: 39% agriculture, 23% industry, 39% services (1990) **Life expectancy:** 69 (men); 70 (women) (1995–2000) **Child mortality rate:** (under 5, per 1,000 live births) 57 (1997) **Physicians:** 1 per 3,142 people (1993 est)

Practical information

Visa requirements: UK: visa required. USA: visa required **Embassy in the UK:** 16 Prince's Gate, London SW7 1PT. Tel: (0171) 584 8101; fax: (0171) 589 4440 **British embassy:** PO Box 11365–4474, 143 Ferdowsi Avenue, Tehran 11344. Tel: (21) 675 011; fax: (21) 678 021 **Chamber of commerce:** Iran Chamber of Commerce, Industries and Mines, 254 Taleghani Avenue, Tehran. Tel: (21) 836 0319; fax: (21) 882 5111

Chronology

c. **2000 BC:** Migration from southern Russia of Aryans, from whom Persians claim descent. **612 BC:** The Medes, from northwest Iran, destroyed Iraq-based Assyrian Empire to the west and established their own empire which extended into central Anatolia (Turkey-in-Asia). **550 BC:** Cyrus the Great overthrew Medes' empire and founded First Persian Empire, the Achaemenid, conquering much of Asia Minor, including Babylonia (Palestine and Syria) in 539 BC:. Expansion continued into Afghanistan under Darius I, who ruled 521–486 BC:. **499–449 BC:** The Persian Wars with Greece ended Persian domination of the ancient world. **330 BC:** Collapse of Achaemenid Empire following defeat by Alexander the Great of Macedon. **AD 224:** Sassanian Persian Empire founded by Ardashir, with its capital at Ctesiphon, in the northeast. **637:** Sassanian Empire destroyed by Muslim Arabs at battle of Qadisiya; Islam replaced Zoroastrianism. **750–1258:** Dominated by the Persianized Abbasid dynasty, who reigned as caliphs (Islamic civil and religious leaders), with a capital in Baghdad (Iraq). **1380s:** Conquered by the Mongol leader, Tamerlane. **1501:** Emergence of Safavids; the arts and architecture flourished, particularly under Abbas I, 'the Great', who ruled 1588–1629. **1736:** The Safavids were deposed by the warrior Nadir Shah Afshar, who ruled until 1747. **1790:** Rise of the Qajars, who transferred the capital from Esfahan in central Iran to Tehran, further north. **19th century:** Increasing influence in the north of tsarist Russia, which took Georgia and much of Armenia 1801–28. Britain exercised influence in the south and east, and fought Iran 1856–57 over claims to Herat (western Afghanistan). **1906:** Parliamentary constitution adopted after a brief revolution. **1925:** Weak and corrupt Qajar dynasty overthrown, with some British official help, in a coup by Col Reza Khan, a nationalist Iranian Cossack military officer, who was crowned shah ('king of kings'), with the title Reza Shah Pahlavi. **1920s onwards:** Economic modernization, Westernization, and secularization programme launched, which proved unpoular with traditionalist elements. **1935:** Name changed from Persia to Iran. **1941:** Owing to his pro-German sentiments, Pahlavi Shah was forced to abdicate during World War II by Allied occupation forces and was succeeded by his son Mohammad Reza Pahlavi, who continued the modernization programme. **1946:** British, US, and Soviet occupation forces left Iran. **1951:** Oilfields nationalized by radical prime minister Muhammad Mossadeq as anti-British and US sentiment increased. **1953:** Mossadeq deposed, the nationalization plan changed, and the US-backed shah, Muhammad Reza Shah Pahlavi, took full control of the government. **1963:** Hundreds of protesters, who demanded the release of the arrested fundamentalist Shi'ite Muslim leader Ayatollah Ruhollah Khomeini, were killed by troops. **1970s:** Spiralling world oil prices brought rapid economic expansion. **1975:** Shah introduced single-party system. **1977:** Mysterious death in An Najaf of Mustafa, eldest son of the exiled Ayatollah Ruhollah Khomeini, sparked demonstrations by theology students, which were suppressed with the loss of six lives. **1978:** Opposition to the Shah organized from France by Ayatollah Ruhollah Khomeini, who demanded a return to the principles of Islam. Hundreds of demonstrators were killed by troops in Jaleh Square, Tehran. **1979:** Amid mounting demonstrations by students and clerics, the shah left the country; Khomeini returned to create a nonparty theocratic Islamic state. Revolutionaries seized 66 US hostages at embassy in Tehran; US economic boycott. **1980:** Iraq invaded Iran, provoking a bitter war; death of exiled shah. **1981:** US hostages released. **1985–87:** Fighting intensified in Iran–Iraq War, with heavy loss of life. **1988:** Cease-fire in the war; talks with Iraq began. **1989:** Khomeini issued a fatwa (public order) for the

death of British writer Salman Rushdie for blasphemy against Islam. On Khomeini's death, Ayatollah Ali Khamenei was elected interim Leader of the Revolution; the speaker of Iranian parliament Hashemi Rafsanjani was elected president. **1990:** Generous peace terms with Iraq accepted to close Iran–Iraq war. **1991:** Nearly 1 million Kurds arrived from northwest Iraq, fleeing persecution by Saddam Hussein after the Gulf War between Iraq and UN forces. **1993:** President Rafsanjani re-elected, but with a smaller margin; free-market economic reforms introduced. **1996:** Rafsanjani supporters won assembly elections. **1997:** Moderate politician Seyyed Mohammad Khatami elected president. **1998:** Signs of rapprochement with the West. Increased tension with Afghanistan, after murder of Iranian civilians by the Talibaan.

Iraq Republic of

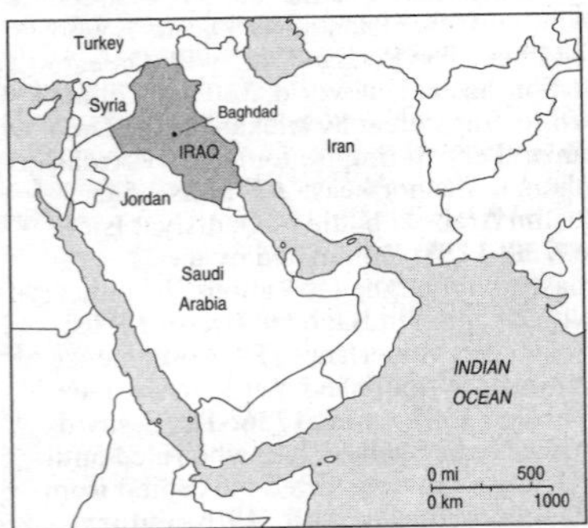

National name: *al Jumhouriya al `Iraqia* **Area:** 434,924 sq km/167,924 sq mi **Capital:** Baghdad **Major towns/cities:** Mosul, Basra, Kirkuk, Hilla, Najaf, Nasiriya **Major ports:** Basra and Um Qass closed from 1980

Government

Head of state and government: Saddam Hussein al-Tikriti from 1979 **Political system:** one-party socialist republic **Administrative divisions:** 18 governates **Political party:** Arab Ba'ath Socialist Party, nationalist socialist **Armed forces:** 387,500; plus 650,000 army reserves (1997) **Conscription:** military service is compulsory for 18–24 months; it is waived on the payment of the equivalent of $800 **Death penalty:** retained and used for ordinary crimes **Defence spend:** (% GDP) 7.4 (1997) **Education spend:** (% GNP) 4.6 (1988)

Economy and resources

Currency: Iraqi dinar **GDP:** (US$) 11.5 billion (1996 est) **Real GDP growth:** (% change on previous year) 0 (1996) **GNP:** N/A **GNP per capita (PPP):** (US$) N/A **Consumer price inflation:** 200% (1997) **Foreign debt:** (US$) 100.4 billion (1996) **Major trading partners:** Jordan, Brazil, Turkey, Japan, the Netherlands, Spain, UK, France **Resources:** petroleum, natural gas, sulphur, phosphates **Exports:** crude petroleum (accounting for more than 98% of total export earnings (1980–89), dates and other dried fruits. Principal market: Jordan 95% (1995) **Imports:** machinery and transport equipment, basic manufactured articles, cereals and other foodstuffs, iron and steel, military goods. Principal source: Jordan 48.7% (1995) **Arable land:** 12.6% (1995)

Population and society

Population: 21,800,000 (1998 est) **Population growth rate:** 2.8% (1995–2000); 2.8% (2000–05) **Population density:** (per sq km) 50.1 (1998 est) **Urban population:** (% of total) 76 (1997) **Age distribution:** (% of total population) 0–14 44.1%, 15–64 52.7%, 65+ 3.2% (1998) **Ethnic groups:** about 79% Arab, 16% Kurdish (mainly in northeast), 3% Persian, 2% Turkish **Language:** Arabic (official); Kurdish, Assyrian, Armenian **Religion:** Shi'ite Muslim 60%, Sunni Muslim 37%, Christian 3% **Education:** (compulsory years) 6 **Literacy rate:** 77% (men); 49% (women) (1995 est) **Labour force:** 26% of population: 16% agriculture, 18% industry, 66% services **Life expectancy:** 61 (men); 64 (women) (1995–2000) **Child mortality rate:** (under 5, per 1,000 live births) 113 (1997) **Physicians:** 1 per 1,659 people (1993 est)

Practical information

Visa requirements: UK: visa required. USA: visa required **Embassy in the UK:** Iraq has no diplomatic representation in the UK. The Embassy of the Hashemite Kingdom of Jordan deals with enquiries relating to Iraq: Iraq Interests Section, 21 Queen's Gate, London SW7 5JG. Tel: (0171) 584 7141/6; fax: (0171) 584 7716 **British embassy:** the UK has no diplomatic representation in Iraq **Chamber of commerce:** Federation of Iraqi Chambers of Commerce, Mustansir Street, Baghdad. Tel: (1) 888 6111

Chronology

c. **3400 BC:** The world's oldest civilization, the Sumerian, arose in the land between the rivers Euphrates and Tigris, known as lower Mesopotamia, which lies in the heart of modern Iraq. Its cities included Lagash, Eridu, Uruk, Kish, and Ur. *c.* **2350 BC:** The confederation of Sumerian city-states was forged into an empire by the Akkadian leader Sargon. **7th century BC:** In northern Mesopotamia, the Assyrian Empire, based around the River Tigris and formerly dominated by Sumeria and Euphrates-centred Babylonia, created a vast empire covering much of the Middle East. **612 BC:** The Assyrian capital of Nineveh was destroyed by Babylon and Mede (in northwest Iran). *c.* **550 BC:** Mesopotamia came under Persian control. **AD 114:** Conquered by the Romans. **266:** Came under the rule of the Persian-based Sassanians. **637:** Sassanian Empire destroyed by Muslim Arabs at battle of Qadisiya, in southern Iraq; Islam spread. **750–1258:** Dominated by Abbasid dynasty, who reigned as caliphs (Islamic civil and religious leaders) in Baghdad. **1258:** Baghdad invaded and burned by Tatars. **1401:** Baghdad destroyed by Mongol ruler Tamerlane. **1533:** Annexed by Suleiman the Magnificent, becoming part of the Ottoman Empire until the 20th century, despite recurrent anti-Ottoman insurrections. **1916:** Occupied by Britain during World War I. **1920:** Iraq became a British League of Nations protectorate. **1921:** Hashemite dynasty established, with Faisal I installed by Britain as king. **1932:** Independence achieved from British protectorate status, with Gen Nuri-el Said as prime minister. **1941–45:** Occupied by Britain during World War II. **1955:** Signed the Baghdad Pact collective security treaty with the UK, Iran, Pakistan, and Turkey. **1958:** Monarchy overthrown in military-led revolution, in which King Faisal was assassinated; Iraq became a republic; joined Jordan in an Arab Federation; withdrew from Baghdad Pact as left-wing military regime assumed power. **1963:** Joint socialist-nationalist Ba'athist-military coup headed by Col Salem Aref and backed by US Central Intelligence Agency; reign of terror launched against the left. **1968:** Ba'athist military coup put Maj-Gen Ahmed Hassan al-Bakr in power. **1979:** Al-Bakr replaced by Saddam Hussein of the Arab Ba'ath Socialist Party. **1980:** War between Iraq and Iran broke out. **1985–87:** Fighting intensified, with heavy loss of life. **1988:** Ceasefire; talks began with Iran. Iraq used chemical weapons against Kurdish rebels seeking greater autonomy in the northwest. **1989:** Unsuccessful coup against President Hussein; Iraq successfully launched ballistic test missile. **1990:** Peace treaty favouring Iran agreed. Iraq invaded and annexed Kuwait in August. US forces massed in Saudi Arabia at request of King Fahd. United Nations (UN) ordered Iraqi withdrawal and imposed total trade ban; further UN resolution sanctioned the use of force. All foreign hostages released. **1991:** US-led Allied forces launched aerial assault on Iraq and destroyed country's infrastructure; land–sea–air offensive to free Kuwait successful. Uprisings of Kurds and Shi'ites brutally suppressed by surviving Iraqi troops. Allied troops established 'safe havens' for Kurds in north prior to withdrawal, and left rapid-reaction force near Turkish border. **1992:** UN imposed 'no-fly zone' over southern Iraq to protect Shi'ites. **1993:** Iraqi incursions into 'no-fly zone' prompted US-led alliance aircraft to bomb strategic targets in Iraq. Continued persecution of Shi'ites in south. **1994:** Iraq renounced claim to Kuwait, but failed to fulfil other conditions required for lifting of UN sanctions. **1995:** Hussein elected (uncontested) in closely monitored presidential election. **1996:** Iraqi-backed attacks on Kurds prompted US retaliation; air strikes destroyed Iraqi military bases in south. **1997:** Iraq continued to resist US and Allied pressure to allow UN weapons inspections.

1998: Iraq expelled UN weapons inspectors, provoking a build-up of US military strength in the Gulf; military conflict averted by agreement secured by UN secretary-general Kofi Annan. April: UN inspectors' report showed that Iraq had failed to meet UN requirements on the destruction of chemical and biological weapons. December: further US and UK air strikes.

Ireland, Republic of

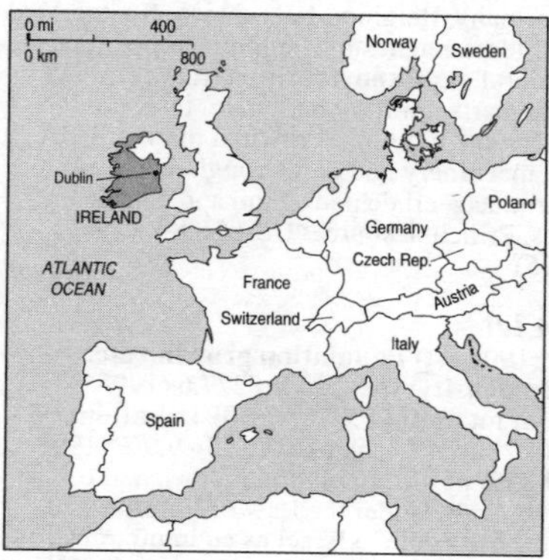

National name: *Eire* **Area:** 70,282 sq km/27,135 sq mi **Capital:** Dublin **Major towns/cities:** Cork, Limerick, Galway, Waterford, Wexford **Major ports:** Cork, Dun Laoghaire, Limerick, Waterford, Galway

Government

Head of state: Mary McAleese from 1997 **Head of government:** Bertie Ahern from 1997 **Political system:** democracy **Administrative divisions:** 26 counties within four provinces **Political parties:** Fianna Fáil (Soldiers of Destiny), moderate centre right; Fine Gael (Irish Tribe or United Ireland Party), moderate centre left; Labour Party, moderate left of centre; Progressive Democrats, radical free-enterprise **Armed forces:** 12,700 (1997) **Conscription:** military service is voluntary **Death penalty:** abolished in 1990 **Defence spend:** (% GDP) 1.0 (1997) **Education spend:** (% GNP) 5.8 (1996) **Health spend:** (% GDP) 5.4 (1990–95)

Economy and resources

Currency: Irish pound (punt Eireannach) **GDP:** (US$) 72.7 billion (1997) **Real GDP growth:** (% change on previous year) 8.0 (1997) **GNP:** 66.4 billion (1997) **GNP per capita (PPP):** (US$) 16,740 (1997) **Consumer price inflation:** 2.5% (1998) **Unemployment:** 7.8% (1998) **Major trading partners:** UK, USA, Germany, France **Resources:** lead, zinc, peat, limestone, gypsum, petroleum, natural gas, copper, silver **Exports:** beef and dairy products, live animals, machinery and transport equipment, electronic goods, chemicals. Principal market: UK 24.3% (1997) **Imports:** petroleum products, machinery and transport equipment, chemicals, foodstuffs, animal feed, textiles and clothing. Principal source: UK 33.7% (1997) **Arable land:** 19.3% (1995)

Population and society

Population: 3,681,000 (1998 est) **Population growth rate:** 0.2% (1995–2000) **Population density:** (per sq km) 52.5 (1998 est) **Urban population:** (% of total) 58 (1997) **Age distribution:** (% of total population) 0–14 21.9%, 15–64 66.8%, 65+ 11.3% (1998) **Ethnic groups:** most of the population has Celtic origins **Language:** Irish Gaelic and English (both official) **Religion:** Roman Catholic 95%, Church of Ireland, other Protestant denominations **Education:** (compulsory years) 9 **Literacy rate:** 99% (men); 99% (women) (1995 est) **Labour force:** 41.3% of population: 10.4% agriculture, 27.2% industry, 62.3% services (1996) **Life expectancy:** 74 (men); 79 (women) (1995–2000) **Child mortality rate:** (under 5, per 1,000 live births) 6 (1997) **Physicians:** 1 per 431 people (1995)

Practical information

Visa requirements: UK: visa not required. USA: visa not required **Embassy in the UK:** 17 Grosvenor Place, London SW1X 7HR. Tel: (0171) 235 2171; fax: (0171) 245 6961 **British embassy:** 31–33 Merrion Road, Dublin 4. Tel: (1) 269 5211; fax: (1) 283 8423 **Chamber of commerce:** Chambers of Commerce of Ireland, 22 Merrion Square, Dublin 2. Tel: (1) 661 2888; fax: (1) 661 2811

Chronology

3rd century BC: The Gaels, a Celtic people, invaded Ireland and formed about 150 small kingdoms. **AD *c.* 432:** St Patrick introduced Christianity. **5th–9th centuries:** Irish Church remained a centre of culture and scholarship. **9th–11th centuries:** The Vikings raided Ireland until defeated by High King Brian Boru at Clontarf in 1014. **12th–13th centuries:** Anglo-Norman adventurers conquered much of Ireland, but no central government was formed and many became assimilated. **14th–15th centuries:** Irish chieftains recovered their lands, restricting English rule to the Pale around Dublin. **1536:** Henry VIII of England made ineffectual efforts to impose the Protestant Reformation on Ireland. **1541:** Irish Parliament recognized Henry VIII as king of Ireland; Henry gave peerages to Irish chieftains. **1579:** English suppressed Desmond rebellion, confiscated rebel lands, and tried to 'plant' them with English settlers. **1610:** James I established plantation of Ulster with Protestant settlers from England and Scotland. **1641:** Catholic Irish rebelled against English rule; Oliver Cromwell brutally reasserted English control 1649–50; Irish landowners evicted and replaced with English landowners. **1689–91:** Williamite War: following the 'Glorious Revolution', the Catholic Irish unsuccessfully supported James II against Protestant William III in civil war. Penal laws barred Catholics from obtaining wealth and power. **1720:** Act passed declaring British Parliament's right to legislate for Ireland. **1739–41:** Famine

Republic of Ireland: Provinces and Counties

Province/county	Administrative headquarters	Area sq km	Area sq mi	Population (1996)
Ulster Province				
Cavan	Cavan	1,890	729	52,900
Donegal	Lifford	4,830	1,864	129,900
Monaghan	Monaghan	1,290	498	51,300
Munster Province				
Clare	Ennis	3,190	1,231	94,000
Cork	Cork	7,460	2,880	420,300
Kerry	Tralee	4,700	1,814	126,100
Limerick	Limerick	2,690	1,038	177,902
Tipperary (North)	Nenagh	2,000	772	58,000
Tipperary (South)	Clonmel	2,260	872	75,500
Waterford	Waterford	1,840	710	94,600
Leinster Province				
Carlow	Carlow	900	347	41,600
Dublin	Dublin	920	355	1,056,700
Kildare	Naas	1,690	652	135,000
Kilkenny	Kilkenny	2,060	795	75,300
Laois (or Laoighis)	Port Laoise	1,720	664	52,900
Longford	Longford	1,040	401	30,200
Louth	Dundalk	820	316	92,200
Meath	Navan	2,340	903	109,700
Offaly	Tullamore	2,000	772	59,100
Westmeath	Mullingar	1,760	679	63,300
Wexford	Wexford	2,350	907	104,400
Wicklow	Wicklow	2,030	783	102,700
Connacht (or Connaught) Province				
Galway	Galway	5,940	2,293	188,600
Leitrim	Carrick-on-Shannon	1,530	590	25,100
Mayo	Castlebar	5,400	2,084	111,500
Roscommon	Roscommon	2,460	949	52,000
Sligo	Sligo	1,800	694	55,800

killed one-third of population of 1.5 million. **1782:** Protestant landlords led by Henry Grattan secured end of restrictions on Irish trade and parliament. **1798:** British suppressed revolt by Society of United Irishmen (with French support) led by Wolfe Tone. **1800:** Act of Union abolished Irish parliament and created United Kingdom of Great Britain and Ireland, effective 1801. **1829:** Daniel O'Connell secured Catholic Emancipation Act, which permitted Catholics to enter parliament. **1846–51:** Potato famine reduced population by 20% through starvation and emigration. **1870:** Land Act increased security for tenants but failed to halt agrarian disorder; Isaac Butt formed political party to campaign for Irish Home Rule (devolution). **1885:** Home Rulers, led by Charles Stewart Parnell, held balance of power in parliament; first Home Rule Bill rejected 1886; second Home Rule Bill defeated in 1893. **1905:** Arthur Griffith founded the nationalist movement Sinn Féin ('Ourselves Alone'). **1914:** Ireland came close to civil war as Ulster prepared to resist implementation of Home Rule Act (postponed because of World War I). **1916:** Easter Rising: nationalists proclaimed a republic in Dublin; British crushed revolt and executed 15 leaders. **1919:** Sinn Féin MPs formed Irish parliament in Dublin in defiance of British government. **1919–21:** Irish Republican Army (IRA) waged guerrilla war against British forces. **1921:** Anglo-Irish Treaty partitioned Ireland; northern Ireland (Ulster) remained part of the United Kingdom; southern Ireland won full internal self-government with dominion status. **1922:** Irish Free State proclaimed; IRA split over Anglo-Irish Treaty led to civil war 1922–23. **1932:** Anti-Treaty party, Fianna Fáil, came to power under Éamonn de Valéra. **1937:** New constitution established Eire (Gaelic name for Ireland) as a sovereign state and refused to acknowledge partition. **1949:** After remaining neutral in World War II, Eire left the Commonwealth and became the Republic of Ireland. **1973:** Ireland joined European Economic Community. **1985:** Anglo-Irish Agreement gave the Republic of Ireland a consultative role, but no powers, in the government of Northern Ireland. **1990:** Mary Robinson became the first woman president of Ireland. **1993:** Downing Street Declaration: joint Anglo-Irish peace proposal for Northern Ireland issued. **1998:** Historic multiparty agreement (the Good Friday Agreement) was reached on the future of Northern Ireland. Subsequent referendum showed large majority in favour of dropping Ireland's claim to the North. Strict legislation against terrorism.

Israel State of

National name: *Medinat Israel* **Area:** 20,800 sq km/8,030 sq mi (as at 1949 armistice) **Capital:** Jerusalem (not recognized by United Nations) **Major towns/cities:** Tel Aviv-Yafo, Haifa, Bat-Yam, Holon, Ramat Gan, Petach Tikva, Rishon Leziyyon, Beersheba **Major ports:** Tel Aviv-Yafo, Haifa, 'Akko (formerly Acre), Eilat

Government

Head of state: Ezer Weizman from 1993 **Head of government:** Ehud Barak from 1999 **Political system:** democracy **Administrative divisions:** six districts **Political parties:** Israel Labour Party, moderate, left of centre; Consolidation Party (Likud), right of centre; Meretz (Vitality), left-of-centre alliance **Armed forces:** 175,000; 430,000 reservists (1997) **Conscription:** voluntary for Christians, Circassians, and Muslims; compulsory for Jews and Druzes (men 36 months, women 21 months) **Death penalty:** exceptional crimes only; last execution in 1962 **Defence spend:** (% GDP) 11.5 (1997) **Education spend:** (% GNP) 6.6 (1995) **Health spend:** (% GDP) 2.1 (1990–95)

Economy and resources

Currency: shekel **GDP:** (US$) 97.9 billion (1997) **Real GDP growth:** (% change on previous year) 2.0 (1997) **GNP:** 87.6 billion (1997) **GNP per capita (PPP):** (US$) 16,960 (1997) **Consumer price inflation:** 8.3% (1998) **Unemployment:** 6.7% (1996) **Foreign debt:** 30.4 billion (1996) **Major trading partners:** USA, UK, Germany, Belgium, Italy, Japan, Switzerland **Resources:** potash, bromides, magnesium, sulphur, copper ore, gold, salt, petroleum, natural gas **Exports:** citrus fruits, worked diamonds, machinery and parts, military hardware, food products, chemical products, textiles and clothing. Principal market: USA 32.1% (1997) **Imports:** machinery and parts, rough diamonds, chemicals and related products, crude petroleum and petroleum products, motor vehicles. Principal source: USA 18.8% (1997) **Arable land:** 17% (1995)

Population and society

Population: 5,984,000 (1998 est) **Population growth rate:** 1.9% (1995–2000) **Population density:** (per sq km) 277.6 (1998 est) **Urban population:** (% of total) 91 (1997) **Age distribution:** (% of total population) 0–14 28.2%, 15–64 62.0%, 65+ 9.9% (1998) **Ethnic groups:** around 85% of the population is Jewish, the majority of the remainder Arab. Under the Law of Return 1950, 'every Jew shall be entitled to come to Israel as an immigrant'; those from the East and Eastern Europe are Ashkenazim, and those from Mediterranean Europe (Spain, Portugal, Italy, France, Greece) and Arab Africa are Sephardim (over 50% of the population is now of Sephardic descent); an Israeli-born Jew is a Sabra **Language:** Hebrew and Arabic (official); English, Yiddish, European and western Asian languages **Religion:** Israel is a secular state, but the predominant faith is Judaism 85%; also Sunni Muslim, Christian, and Druse **Education:** (compulsory years) 11 **Literacy rate:** 97% (men); 93% (women) (1995 est) **Labour force:** 39% of population: 4% agriculture, 29% industry, 67% services (1990) **Life expectancy:** 76 (men); 80 (women) (1995–2000) **Child mortality rate:** (under 5, per 1,000 live births) 9 (1997) **Physicians:** 1 per 350 people (1991)

Practical information

Visa requirements: UK: visa not required. USA: visa not required **Embassy in the UK:** 2 Palace Green, London W8 4QB. Tel: (0171) 957 9500; fax: (0171) 957 9555 **British embassy:** 192 Rehov Hayarkon, Tel Aviv 63405. Tel: (3) 524 9171/8; fax: (3) 524 3313 **Chamber of commerce:** Federation of Israeli Chambers of Commerce, PO Box 20027, 84 Hahashmonaim Street, Tel Aviv 67011. Tel: (3) 563 1010; fax: (3) 561 9025

Chronology

c. **2000 BC:** Abraham, father of the Jewish people, is believed to have come to Palestine from Mesopotamia. *c.* **1225 BC:** Moses led the Jews out of slavery in Egypt towards the promised land of Palestine. **11th century BC:** Saul established a Jewish kingdom in Palestine; developed by kings David and Solomon. **586 BC:** Jews defeated by Babylon and deported; many returned to Palestine 539 BC. **333 BC:** Alexander the Great of Macedonia conquered the entire region. **3rd century BC:** Control of Palestine contested by Ptolemies of Egypt and Seleucids of Syria. **142 BC:** Jewish independence restored after Maccabean revolt. **63 BC:** Palestine fell to Roman Empire. **70 AD:** Romans crushed Zealot rebellion and destroyed Jerusalem; start of dispersion of Jews (diaspora). **614:** Persians took Jerusalem from Byzantine Empire. **637:** Muslim Arabs conquered Palestine. **1099:** First Crusade captured Jerusalem; Christian kingdom lasted a century before falling to sultans of Egypt. **1517:** Palestine conquered by the Ottoman Turks. **1897:** Theodor Herzl organized the First Zionist Congress at Basel to publicize Jewish claims to Palestine. **1917:** The Balfour Declaration: Britain expressed support for the creation of a Jewish National Home in Palestine. **1918:** British forces expelled the Turks from Palestine, which became a British League of Nations

mandate 1920. **1929:** Severe communal violence around Jerusalem caused by Arab alarm at doubling of Jewish population in ten years. **1933:** Jewish riots in protest at British attempts to restrict Jewish immigration. **1937:** The Peel Report, recommending partition, accepted by most Jews but rejected by Arabs; open warfare ensued 1937–38. **1939:** Britain postponed independence plans on account of World War II, and increased military presence. **1946:** Resumption of terrorist violence; Jewish extremists blew up British headquarters in Jerusalem. **1947:** United Nations (UN) voted for partition of Palestine. **1948:** Britain withdrew; Independent State of Israel proclaimed with David Ben-Gurion as prime minister; Israel repulsed invasion by Arab nations; many Palestinian Arabs settled in refugee camps in the Gaza Strip and West Bank. **1952:** Col Gamal Nasser of Egypt stepped up blockade of Israeli ports and support of Arab guerrillas in Gaza. **1956:** War between Israel and Egypt; Israeli invasion of Gaza and Sinai followed by withdrawal in 1957. **1963:** Levi Eshkol succeeded Ben-Gurion as prime minister. **1964:** Palestine Liberation Organization (PLO) founded to unite Palestinian Arabs with the aim of overthrowing the state of Israel. **1967:** Israel defeated Egypt, Syria, and Jordan in the Six-Day War; Gaza, West Bank, east Jerusalem, Sinai, and Golan Heights captured. **1969:** Golda Meir (Labour) elected prime minister; Yassir Arafat became chair of the PLO; escalation of terrorism and border raids. **1973:** Yom Kippur War: Israel repulsed surprise attack by Egypt and Syria. **1974:** Golda Meir succeeded by Yitzhak Rabin. **1977:** Right-wing Likud bloc took office under Menachem Begin; President Anwar Sadat of Egypt began peace initiative. **1979:** Camp David talks ended with signing of peace treaty between Israel and Egypt; Israel withdrew from Sinai. **1980:** United Jerusalem declared capital of Israel. **1982:** Israeli forces invaded southern Lebanon to drive out PLO guerrillas; occupation continued until 1985. **1985:** Labour and Likud formed coalition government led by Shimon Peres 1985–86 and Yitzhak Shamir 1986–90. **1988:** Israeli handling of Palestinian uprising (Intifada) in occupied territories provoked international criticism. **1990:** Shamir headed Likud government following breakup of coalition; PLO formally recognized the state of Israel. **1991:** Iraq launched missile attacks on Israel during Gulf War; Middle East peace talks began in Madrid. **1992:** Labour government elected under Yitzhak Rabin. **1993:** Rabin and Arafat signed peace accord; Israel granted limited autonomy to Gaza Strip and Jericho. **1994:** Arafat became head of autonomous Palestinian authority in Gaza and Jericho; peace agreement between Israel and Jordan. **1995:** Rabin assassinated by Jewish opponent of peace accord; Peres became prime minister. **1996:** Likud government elected under Binyamin Netanyahu, critic of peace accord. Revival of communal violence; peace process threatened. The opening of a 2,000-year-old tunnel near the Al-Aqsa mosque in Jerusalem provoked renewed Palestinian–Israeli conflict. **1997:** Jewish settlement in east Jerusalem widely condemned. Suicide bombs by Hamas in Jerusalem. Partial and limited withdrawal from the West Bank. **1998:** Violence flared on West Bank between Palestinians and Israeli troops. Netanyahu demanded security guarantees from Palestinian authorities; peace process stalled. Bomb explosion in Tel Aviv. Wye Peace Agreement signed with the PLO. Land-for-security deal approved by the Knesset. Promised Israeli withdrawal from the Lebanon subsequently placed in doubt. **1999:** Labour Party candidate Ehud Barak elected prime minister and restarted peace negotiations.

Italy Republic of

National name: *Repubblica Italiana* **Area:** 301,300 sq km/116,331 sq mi **Capital:** Rome **Major towns/cities:** Milan, Naples, Turin, Palermo, Genoa, Bologna **Major ports:** Naples, Genoa, Palermo, Bari, Catania, Trieste

Government

Head of state: Carlo Azeglio Ciampi from 1999 **Head of government:** Massimo d'Alema from 1998 **Political system:** democracy **Administrative divisions:** 94 provinces within 20 regions (of which five have a greater degree of autonomy) **Political parties:** Forza Italia (Go Italy!), free market, right of centre;

Northern League (LN), Milan-based, federalist, right of centre; National Alliance (AN), neofascist; Italian Popular Party (PPI), Catholic, centrist; Italian Renewal Party, centrist; Democratic Party of the Left (PDS), pro-European, moderate left wing (ex-communist); Italian Socialist Party (PSI), moderate socialist; Italian Republican Party (PRI), social democratic, left of centre; Democratic Alliance (AD), moderate left of centre; Christian Democratic Centre (CCD), Christian, centrist; Olive Tree alliance, centre left; Panella List, radical liberal; Union of the Democratic Centre (UDC), right of centre; Pact for Italy, reformist; Communist Refoundation (RC), Marxist; Verdi, environmentalist; La Rete (the Network), anti-Mafia **Armed forces:** 325,200 (1997) **Conscription:** 12 months **Death penalty:** abolished in 1994 **Defence spend:** (% GDP) 1.9 (1997) **Education spend:** (% GNP) 4.9 (1995) **Health spend:** (% GDP) 5.4 (1990–95)

Economy and resources

Currency: lira **GDP:** (US$) 1,146.2 billion (1997) **Real GDP growth:** (% change on previous year) 1.2 (1997) **GNP:** 1,155.4 billion (1997) **GNP per capita (PPP):** (US$) 20,060 (1997) **Consumer price inflation:** 2.4% (1998) **Unemployment:** 12.1% (1997) **Major trading partners:** EU (principally Germany, France, and UK), USA **Resources:** lignite, lead, zinc, mercury, potash, sulphur, fluorspar, bauxite, marble, petroleum, natural gas, fish **Exports:** machinery and transport equipment, textiles, clothing, footwear, wine (leading producer and exporter), metals and metal products, chemicals, wood, paper and rubber goods. Principal market: Germany 16.4% (1997) **Imports:** mineral fuels and lubricants, machinery and transport equipment, chemical products, foodstuffs, metal products. Principal source: Germany 18% (1997) **Arable land:** 27.6% (1995)

Population and society

Population: 57,369,000 (1998 est) **Population growth rate:** 0% (1995–2000); –0.2% (2000–05) **Population density:** (per sq km) 193.1 (1998 est) **Urban population:** (% of total) 67% (1997) **Age distribution:** (% of total population) 0–14 14.4%, 15–64 68.0%, 65+ 17.6% (1998) **Ethnic groups:** mainly Italian; some minorities of German origin **Language:** Italian; German, French, Slovene, and Albanian minorities **Religion:** Roman Catholic 100% (state religion) **Education:** (compulsory years) 8 **Literacy rate:** 98% (men); 96% (women) (1995 est) **Labour force:** 44.6% of the population: 7% agriculture, 32.1% industry, 60.9% services (1996) **Life expectancy:** 75 (men); 81 (women) (1995–2000) **Child mortality rate:** (under 5, per 1,000 live births) 8 (1997) **Physicians:** 1 per 182 people (1996)

Practical information

Visa requirements: UK: visa not required. USA: visa not required **Embassy in the UK:** 14 Three Kings Yard, Davies Street, London W1Y 2EH. Tel: (0171) 312 2200; fax: (0171) 312 2230 **British embassy:** Via XX Settembre 80A, 00187 Rome. Tel: (06) 482 5551; fax: (06) 487 3324 **Chamber of commerce:** Unione Italiana delle Camere di Commercio, Industria, Artigianato e Agricoltura, Piazza Sallustio 21, 00187 Rome. Tel: (06) 47041; telex: 622 327

Chronology

4th and 3rd centuries BC: Italian peninsula united under Roman rule. **AD 476:** End of Western Roman Empire. **568:** Invaded by

Italy: Regions

Region	Capital	Area		Population (1995)
		sq km	sq mi	
Abruzzi	L'Aquila	10,794	4,168	1,267,700
Basilicata	Potenza	9,992	3,858	610,700
Calabria	Catanzaro	15,080	5,822	2,076,100
Campania	Naples	13,595	5,249	5,745,800
Emilia-Romagna	Bologna	22,123	8,542	3,922,600
Friuli-Venezia Giulia[1]	Trieste	7,846	3,029	1,191,200
Lazio	Rome	17,203	6,642	5,193,200
Liguria	Genoa	5,416	2,091	1,663,700
Lombardy	Milan	23,856	9,211	8,910,500
Marche	Ancona	9,694	3,743	1,441,000
Molise	Campobasso	4,438	1,714	332,200
Piedmont	Turin	25,399	9,807	4,298,000
Puglia	Bari	19,347	7,470	4,075,800
Sardinia[1]	Cagliari	24,090	9,301	1,659,500
Sicily[1]	Palermo	25,708	9,926	5,082,700
Trentino-Alto Adige[1]	Trento	13,613	5,256	908,700
Tuscany	Florence	22,992	8,877	3,526,000
Umbria	Perugia	8,456	3,265	822,500
Valle d'Aosta[1]	Aosta	3,262	1,259	118,500
Veneto	Venice	18,364	7,090	4,400,000

[1] Special autonomous region.

Lombards. **756:** Papal States created in central Italy. **800:** Charlemagne united Italy and Germany in Holy Roman Empire. **12th and 13th centuries:** Papacy and Holy Roman Empire contended for political supremacy; papal power reached its peak under Innocent III (1198–1216). **1183:** Cities of Lombard League (founded in 1164) became independent. **14th century:** Beginnings of Renaissance in northern Italy. **15th century:** Most of Italy ruled by five rival states: the city-states of Milan, Florence, and Venice; the Papal States; and the Kingdom of Naples. **1494:** Charles VIII of France invaded Italy. **1529–59:** Spanish Habsburgs secured dominance in Italy. **17th century:** Italy effectively part of Spanish Empire; economic and cultural decline. **1713:** Treaty of Utrecht gave political control of most of Italy to Austrian Habsburgs. **1796–1814:** France conquered Italy, setting up satellite states and introducing principles of French Revolution. **1815:** Old regimes largely restored; Italy divided between Austria, Papal States, Naples, Sardinia, and four duchies. **1831:** Giuseppe Mazzini founded 'Young Italy' movement with aim of creating unified republic. **1848–49:** Liberal revolutions occurred throughout Italy; reversed everywhere except Sardinia, which became centre of nationalism under leadership of Count Camillo di Cavour. **1859:** France and Sardinia forcibly expelled Austrians from Lombardy. **1860:** Sardinia annexed duchies and Papal States (except Rome); Giuseppe Garibaldi overthrew Neapolitan monarchy. **1861:** Victor Emmanuel II of Sardinia proclaimed King of Italy in Turin. **1866:** Italy gained Venetia after defeat of Austria by Prussia. **1870:** Italian forces occupied Rome in defiance of Pope, completing unification of Italy. **1882:** Italy joined Germany and Austria-Hungary in Triple Alliance. **1896:** Attempt to conquer Ethiopia defeated at Battle of Adowa. **1900:** King Umberto I assassinated by an anarchist. **1912:** Annexation of Libya and Dodecanese after Italo-Turkish War. **1915:** Italy entered World War I on side of Allies. **1919:** Peace treaties awarded Trentino, South Tyrol, and Trieste to Italy. **1922:** Mussolini established fascist dictatorship following period of strikes and agrarian revolts. **1935–36:** Conquest of Ethiopia. **1939:** Invasion of Albania. **1940:** Italy entered World War II as ally of Germany. **1943:** Allies invaded southern Italy; Mussolini removed from power; Germans occupied northern and central Italy. **1945:** Allies completed liberation. **1946:** Monarchy replaced by republic. **1947:** Peace treaty stripped Italy of its colonies. **1948:** New constitution adopted; Christian Democrats emerged as main party of government in political system marked by ministerial instability. **1957:** Italy became a founder member of European Economic Community (EEC). **1963:** Creation of first of long series of fragile centre-left coalition governments. **1976:** Communists attempt to join coalition, the 'historic compromise', rejected by Christian Democrats. **1978:** Christian Democrat Aldo Moro, architect of historic compromise, murdered by Red Brigade guerrillas infiltrated by Western intelligence agents. **1983–87:** Bettino Craxi, Italy's first Socialist prime minister, led coalition; economy improved. **1993:** Major political crisis triggered by exposure of government corruption and Mafia links; governing parties discredited; new electoral system replaced proportional representation with 75% majority voting. **1994:** Media tycoon Silvio Berlusconi created new party, Forza Italia, and formed right-wing coalition. **1995:** Lamberto Dini headed nonparty government of 'experts'. **1996:** Olive Tree Alliance won general election; Romano Prodi became prime minister. **1997:** Prodi resigned, 'grand coalition' sought; communist support persuaded Prodi to continue. Berlusconi sentenced for fraud but sentence quashed; Prodi cleared of corruption charges. **1998:** Berlusconi cleared of fraud charges. Prodi's Olive Tree Alliance coalition collapsed as Reformed Communists left. Massimo d'Alema formed a new communist-led coalition. **1999:** Carlo Azeglio Ciampi elected president by special assembly. Former prime minister Prodi became president of the new European Commission.

Jamaica

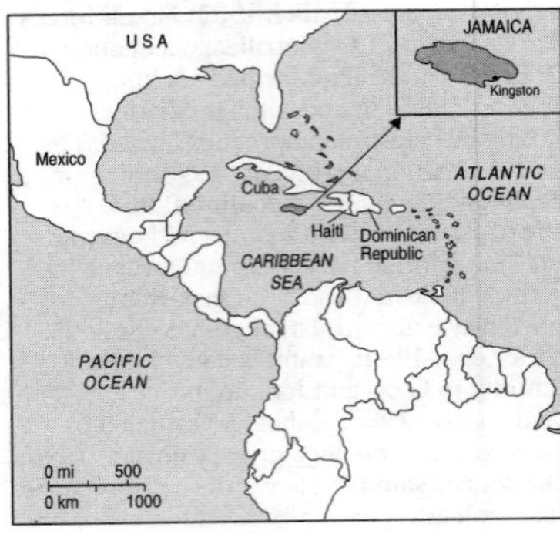

Area: 10,957 sq km/ 4,230 sq mi **Capital:** Kingston **Major towns/ cities:** Montego Bay, Spanish Town, St Andrew, Portmore, May Pen

Government

Head of state: Elizabeth II from 1962, represented by governor general Howard Felix Hanlan Cooke from 1991 **Head of government:** Percival Patterson from 1992 **Political system:** constitutional monarchy **Administrative divisions:** 13 parishes **Political parties:** Jamaica Labour Party (JLP), moderate, centrist; People's National Party (PNP), left of centre; National Democratic Union (NDM), centrist **Armed forces:** 3,320 (1997) **Conscription:** military service is voluntary **Death penalty:** retained and used for ordinary crimes **Defence spend:** (% GDP) 0.6 (1997) **Education spend:** (% GNP) 7.5 (1996) **Health spend:** (% GDP) 3 (1990–95)

Economy and resources

Currency: Jamaican dollar **GDP:** (US$) 5.3 billion (1996) **Real GDP growth:** (% change on previous year) –2.8% (1997) **GNP:** 4.0 billion (1997) **GNP per capita (PPP):** (US$) 3,470 (1997) **Consumer price inflation:** 34.7% (1998) **Unemployment:** 15.7% (1992) **Foreign debt:** (US$) 4.04 billion (1996) **Major trading partners:** USA, UK, Mexico, Venezuela, Germany, Canada, Norway **Resources:** bauxite (one of world's major producers), marble, gypsum, silica, clay **Exports:** bauxite, alumina, gypsum, sugar, bananas, garments, rum. Principal market: USA 33.3% (1997) **Imports:** mineral fuels, machinery and transport equipment, basic manufactures, chemicals, food and live animals, miscellaneous manufactured articles. Principal source: USA 47.7% (1997) **Arable land:** 16.3% (1995)

Population and society

Population: 2,538,000 (1998 est) **Population growth rate:** 0.9% (1995–2000) **Population density:** (per sq km) 243.3 (1998 est)

Urban population: (% of total) 55 (1997) **Age distribution:** (% of total population) 0–14 31.6%, 15–64 61.6%, 65+ 6.8% (1998) **Ethnic groups:** nearly 80% of African descent; about 15% of mixed African-European origin. There are also Chinese, Indian, and European minorities **Language:** English, Jamaican creole **Religion:** Protestant 70%, Rastafarian **Education:** (compulsory years) 6 **Literacy rate:** 98% (men); 99% (women) (1995 est) **Labour force:** 49% of population: 25% agriculture, 23% industry, 52% services (1990) **Life expectancy:** 72 (men); 77 (women) (1995–2000) **Child mortality rate:** (under 5, per 1,000 live births) 20 (1997) **Physicians:** 1 per 6,420 people (1993)

Practical information
Visa requirements: UK: visa not required. USA: visa not required **Embassy in the UK:** 1–2 Prince Consort Road, London SW7 2BZ. Tel: (0171) 823 9911; fax: (0171) 589 5154 **British embassy:** British High Commission, PO Box 575, Trafalgar Road, Kingston 10. Tel: (809) 926 9050; fax: (809) 929 7869 **Chamber of commerce:** PO Box 172, 7–8 East Parade, Kingston. Tel: (809) 922 0150; fax: (809) 924 9056

Chronology
c. **AD 900:** Settled by Arawak Indians, who gave the island the name Jamaica ('well watered'). **1494:** The explorer Christopher Columbus reached Jamaica. **1509:** Occupied by Spanish; much of Arawak community died from exposure to European diseases; black African slaves brought in to work sugar plantations. **1655:** Captured by Britain and became its most valuable Caribbean colony. **1838:** Slavery abolished. **1870:** Banana plantations established as sugar cane industry declined in face of competition from European beet sugar. **1938:** Serious riots during the economic depression and, as a sign of growing political awareness, the People's National Party (PNP) was formed by Norman Manley. **1944:** First constitution adopted. **1958–62:** Part of West Indies Federation. **1959:** Internal self-government granted. **1962:** Independence achieved within the Commonwealth, with Alexander Bustamante of the centre-right Jamaica Labour Party (JLP) as prime minister. **1967:** JLP re-elected under Hugh Shearer. **1972:** Michael Manley of the PNP became prime minister and pursued a policy of economic self-reliance. **1980:** JLP elected, with Edward Seaga as prime minister, following violent election campaign. **1981:** Diplomatic links with Cuba severed; free-market economic programme pursued. **1983:** JLP won all 60 seats in the general election. **1988:** Island badly damaged by Hurricane Gilbert. **1989:** PNP won a landslide victory with a newly moderate Manley returning as prime minister. **1992:** Manley retired; succeeded by Percival Patterson. **1993:** PNP increased its majority in general election. **1998:** Violent crime increased as economy declined.

Japan

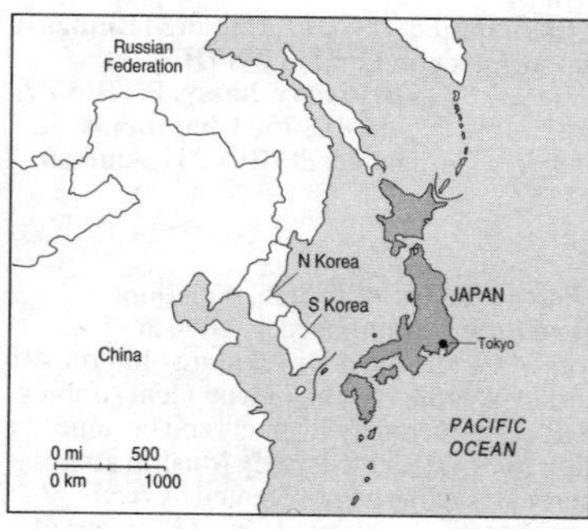

National name: *Nippon* **Area:** 377,535 sq km/145,766 sq mi **Capital:** Tokyo **Major towns/cities:** Yokohama, Osaka, Nagoya, Fukuoka, Kitakyushu, Kyoto, Sapporo, Kobe, Kawasaki, Hiroshima **Major ports:** Osaka, Nagoya, Yokohama, Kobe

Government
Head of state: (figurehead) Emperor Akihito (Heisei) from 1989 **Head of government:** Keizo Obuchi from 1998 **Political system:** liberal democracy **Administrative divisions:** 47 prefectures **Political parties:** Liberal Democratic Party (LDP), right of centre; Shinshinto (New Frontier Party) opposition coalition, centrist reformist; Social Democratic Party of Japan (SDPJ, former Socialist Party), left of centre but moving towards centre; Shinto Sakigake (New Party Harbinger), right of centre; Japanese Communist Party (JCP), socialist; Democratic Party of Japan (DPJ), Sakigake and SDPJ dissidents **Armed forces:** self-defence forces: 235,600; US forces stationed there: 44,800 (1997) **Conscription:** military service is voluntary **Death penalty:** retained and used for ordinary crimes **Defence spend:** (% GDP) 1 (1997) **Education spend:** (% GNP) 3.8 (1995) **Health spend:** (% GDP) 5.7 (1990–95)

Economy and resources
Currency: yen **GDP:** (US$) 4,201.6 billion (1997) **Real GDP growth:** (% change on previous year) 0.9 (1997) **GNP:** 4,772.3 billion (1997) **GNP per capita (PPP):** (US$) 23,400 (1997) **Consumer price inflation:** 1.1% (1998) **Unemployment:** 3.4% (1997) **Major trading partners:** USA, China, Australia, South Korea, Indonesia, Germany, Taiwan, Hong Kong **Resources:** coal, iron, zinc, copper, natural gas, fish **Exports:** motor vehicles, electronic goods and components, chemicals, iron and steel products, scientific and optical equipment. Principal market: USA 30.5% (1998) **Imports:** mineral fuels, foodstuffs, live animals, bauxite, iron ore, copper ore, coking coal, chemicals, textiles, wood. Principal source: USA 23.9% (1998) **Arable land:** 10.5% (1995)

Population and society
Population: 126,281,000 (1998 est) **Population growth rate:** 0.2% (1995–2000); 0.1% (2000–05) **Population density:** (per sq km) 319 (1998 est) **Urban population:** (% of total) 78 (1997) **Age distribution:** (% of total population) 0–14 15.2%, 15–64 68.8%, 65+ 16.0% (1998) **Ethnic groups:** more than 99% of Japanese descent; Ainu (aboriginal people of Japan) in north Japan (Hokkaido, Kuril Islands) **Language:** Japanese; also Ainu **Religion:** Shinto, Buddhist (often combined), Christian **Education:** (compulsory years) 9 **Literacy rate:** 99% (men); 99% (women) (1995 est) **Labour force:** 53.8% of population: 5.5% agriculture, 33.3% industry, 61.2% services (1996) **Life expectancy:** 77 (men); 83 (women) (1995–2000) **Child mortality rate:** (under 5, per 1,000 live births) 6 (1997) **Physicians:** 1 per 542 people (1994)

Practical information
Visa requirements: UK: visa not required. USA: visa not required for a stay of up to 90 days **Embassy in the UK:** 101–104 Piccadilly, London W1V 9FN. Tel: (0171) 465 6500; fax: (0171) 491 9348 **British embassy:** No. 1 Ichiban-cho, Chiyoda-ku, Tokyo 102. Tel: (3) 3265 5511; fax: (3) 5275 3164 **Chamber of commerce:** 2nd Floor, Salisbury House, 29 Finsbury Circus, London EC2M 5QQ. Tel: (0171) 628 0069; fax: (0171) 628 0248. Nippon Shoko Kaigi-sho, 3-2-2, Marunouchi, Chiyoda-ku, Tokyo 10. Tel: (3) 3283 7851

Chronology
660 BC: According to legend, Jimmu Tenno, descendent of the Sun goddess, became the first emperor of Japan. *c.* **400 AD:** The Yamato, one of many warring clans, unified central Japan; Yamato chiefs are the likely ancestors of the imperial family. **5th–6th centuries:** Writing, Confucianism, and Buddhism spread to Japan from China and Korea. **646:** Start of Taika Reform: Emperor Kotoku organized central government on Chinese model. **794:** Heian became imperial capital; later called Kyoto. **858:** Imperial court fell under control of Fujiwara clan, who reduced emperor to figurehead. **11th century:** Central government grew ineffectual; real power exercised by great landowners (daimyo) with private armies of samurai. **1185:** Minamoto clan seized power under Yoritomo, who established military rule. **1192:** Emperor gave Yoritomo the title of shogun (general); the shogun ruled in the name of the emperor. **1274:** Mongol conqueror Kublai Khan attempted to invade Japan, making a second attempt in 1281; on both occasions Japan was saved by a typhoon. **1336:** Warlord Takauji Ashikaga overthrew Minamoto shogunate; emperor recognized Ashikaga shogunate in 1338. **16th century:** Power of Ashikagas declined; constant civil war. **1543:** Portuguese sailors were first Europeans to reach Japan; followed by

Japan: Regions

Region	Chief city	Area sq km	Area sq mi	Population (1995)
Chubu	Nagoya	66,776	25,782	21,400,000
Chugoku	Hiroshima	31,908	12,320	7,775,000
Hokkaido	Sapporo	83,451	32,220	5,692,000
Kanto	Tokyo	32,418	12,517	39,518,000
Kinki	Osaka	33,094	12,778	22,468,000
Kyushu	Fukuoka	42,154	16,276	13,424,000
Okinawa	Naha	2,265	875	1,274,000
Shikoku	Matsuyama	18,798	7,258	4,183,000
Tohuku	Sendai	66,883	25,824	9,834,000

Spanish, Dutch, and English traders. **1549:** Spanish missionary St Francis Xavier began to preach Roman Catholic faith in Japan. **1585–98:** Warlord Hideyoshi took power and attempted to conquer Korea in 1592 and 1597. **1603:** Ieyasu Tokugawa founded new shogunate at Edo, reformed administration, and suppressed Christianity. **1630s:** Japan adopted policy of isolation: all travel forbidden and all foreigners expelled except small colony of Dutch traders in Nagasaki harbour. **1853:** USA sent warships to Edo with demand that Japan open diplomatic and trade relations; Japan conceded in 1854. **1867:** Revolt by isolationist nobles overthrew the Tokugawa shogunate. **1868:** Emperor Mutsuhito assumed full powers, adopted the title *Meiji* ('enlightened rule'), moved imperial capital from Kyoto to Edo (renamed Tokyo), and launched policy of swift Westernization. **1894–95:** Sino-Japanese War: Japan expelled Chinese from Korea. **1902:** Japan entered defensive alliance with Britain; ended in 1921. **1904–05:** Russo-Japanese War: Japan drove Russians from Manchuria and Korea; Korea annexed in 1910. **1914:** Japan entered World War I and occupied German possessions in Far East. **1923:** Earthquake destroyed much of Tokyo and Yokohama. **1931:** Japan invaded Chinese province of Manchuria and created puppet state of Manchukuo; Japanese government came under control of military and extreme nationalists. **1937:** Japan resumed invasion of China. **1940:** After Germany defeated France, Japan occupied French Indo-China. **1941:** Japan attacked US fleet at Pearl Harbor; USA and Britain declared war on Japan. **1942:** Japanese conquered Thailand, Burma, Malaya, Dutch East Indies, Philippines, and northern New Guinea. **1945:** USA dropped atomic bombs on Hiroshima and Nagasaki; Japan surrendered; US general Douglas MacArthur headed Allied occupation administration. **1947:** MacArthur supervised introduction of democratic 'Peace Constitution', accompanied by demilitarization and land reform. **1952:** Occupation ended. **1955:** Liberal Democratic Party (LDP) founded with support of leading business people. **1956:** Japan admitted to United Nations. **1950s–70s:** Rapid economic development; growth of manufacturing exports led to great prosperity. **1993:** Economic recession and financial scandals brought downfall of LDP government in general election. Coalition government formed. **1995:** Earthquake devastated Kobe. **1996:** General election produced inconclusive result; minority LDP government formed, with Ryutaro Hashimoto as prime minister. **1997:** Financial crash after bank failures. **1998:** Hashimoto resigned after LDP polled poorly in upper house elections. Keizo Obuchi, leader of the LDP, became prime minister, with Kiichi Miyazawa as finance minister. The government introduced a new $200 billion economic stimulus package, after GDP contracted 2% in 1998 in the worst recession since World War II. **1999:** The ruling LDP formed a new coalition government with the Liberal Party.

Jordan Hashemite Kingdom of

National name: *Al Mamlaka al Urduniya al Hashemiyah* **Area:** 89,206 sq km/34,442 sq mi (West Bank 5,879 sq km/2,269 sq mi) **Capital:** Amman **Major towns/cities:** Zarqa, Irbid, Saet, Ma'an **Major ports:** Aqaba

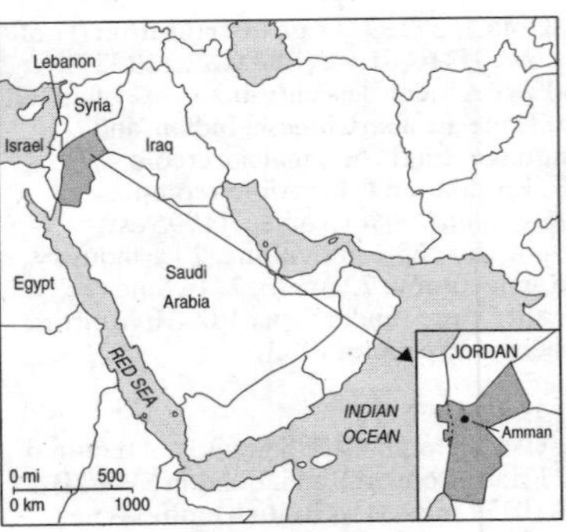

Government

Head of state: King Abdullah ibn Hussein from 1999 **Head of government:** Abdul-Raouf al-Rawabdeh from 1999 **Political system:** constitutional monarchy **Administrative divisions:** eight governates **Political parties:** independent groups loyal to the king predominate; of the 21 parties registered since 1992, the most significant is the Islamic Action Front (IAF), Islamic fundamentalist **Armed forces:** 104,100; plus paramilitary forces of approximately 30,000 (1997) **Conscription:** selective **Death penalty:** retained and used for ordinary crimes **Defence spend:** (% GDP) 6.4 (1997) **Education spend:** (% GNP) 7.3 (1995) **Health spend:** (% GDP) 3.7 (1990–95)

Economy and resources

Currency: Jordanian dinar **GDP:** (US$) 7.9 billion (1997) **Real GDP growth:** (% change on previous year) 5.7 (1997) **GNP:** 7 billion (1997) **GNP per capita (PPP):** (US$) 3,430 (1997) **Consumer price inflation:** 3.4% (1998) **Unemployment:** 25% (1992 est) **Foreign debt:** (US$) 8.1 billion (1996) **Major trading partners:** Iraq, India, Saudi Arabia, Germany, Italy, UK, USA, Japan **Resources:** phosphates, potash, shale **Exports:** phosphate, potash, fertilizers, foodstuffs, pharmaceuticals, fruit and vegetables, cement. Principal market: Iraq 13.3% (1997) **Imports:** food and live animals, basic manufactures, mineral fuels, machinery and transport equipment. Principal source: Iraq 12.5% (1997) **Arable land:** 3.6% (1995)

Population and society

Population: 6,304,000 (1998 est) **Population growth rate:** 3.3% (1995–2000) **Population density:** (per sq km) 48.4 (1998 est) **Urban population:** (% of total) 73 (1997) **Age distribution:** (% of total population) 0–14 43.3%, 15–64 53.8%, 65+ 2.9% (1998) **Ethnic groups:** majority of Arab descent; small Circassian, Armenian, and Kurdish minorities **Language:** Arabic (official), English **Religion:** Sunni Muslim 80%, Christian 8% **Education:** (compulsory years) 10 **Literacy rate:** 75% (men); 70% (women) (1995 est) **Labour force:** 27% of population: 15% agriculture, 23% industry, 61% services (1990) **Life expectancy:** 68 (men); 72 (women) (1995–2000) **Child mortality rate:** (under 5, per 1,000 live births) 36 (1997) **Physicians:** 1 per 825 people (1994)

Practical information

Visa requirements: UK: visa required. USA: visa required **Embassy in the UK:** 6 Upper Phillimore Gardens, London W8 7HB. Tel: (0171) 937 3685; fax: (0171) 937 8795 **British embassy:** PO Box 87, Abdoun, Amman. Tel: (6) 823 100; fax: (6) 813 759 **Chamber of commerce:** Amman Chamber of Commerce, PO Box 287, Amman. Tel: (6) 666 151; telex: 21543

Chronology

13th century BC: Oldest known 'states' of Jordan, including Gideon, Ammon, Moab, and Edom, established. *c.* **1000 BC:** East Jordan was part of kingdom of Israel, under David and Solomon. **4th century BC:** Southeast Jordan occupied by the independent Arabic-speaking Nabataeans. **64 BC:** Conquered by Romans and became part of province of Arabia. **AD 636:** Became largely Muslim after the Byzantine forces of Emperor Heraclius were defeated by Arab armies at battle of Yarmuk, in northern Jordan. **1099–1187:** Part of Latin Kingdom established by Crusaders in Jerusalem. **from early 16th century:** Part of Turkish Ottoman Empire, administered from Damascus. **1920:** Trans-Jordan (the area east of the River Jordan) and Palestine (which includes the West Bank) placed under British

administration by League of Nations mandate. **1923:** Trans-Jordan separated from Palestine and recognized by Britain as a substantially independent state under the rule of Emir Abdullah ibn Hussein, a member of the Hashemite dynasty of Arabia. **1946:** Trans-Jordan achieved independence from Britain, with Abd Allah as king; name changed to Jordan. **1948:** British mandate for Palestine expired, leading to fighting between Arabs and Jews, who each claimed the area. **1950:** Jordan annexed West Bank; 400,000 Palestinian refugees flooded into Jordan, putting pressure on economy. **1951:** King Abdullah assassinated in Jerusalem; succeeded by his son King Talal. **1952:** Partially democratic constitution introduced. **1953:** Hussein ibn Tal Abdulla el Hashim officially became king of Jordan, after his father, King Talal, stepped down. **1958:** Jordan and Iraq formed Arab Federation that ended when Iraqi monarchy was deposed. **1967:** Israel defeated Egypt, Syria, and Jordan in Arab–Israeli Six-Day War, and captured and occupied West Bank, including Arab Jerusalem. Martial law imposed. **1970–71:** Jordanians moved against increasingly radicalized Palestine Liberation Organization (PLO), which had launched guerrilla raids on Israel from Jordanian territory, resulting in bloody civil war, before PLO leadership fled abroad. **1976:** Lower house dissolved, political parties banned, elections postponed until further notice. **1980:** Jordan emerged as important ally of Iraq in its war against Iran, an ally of Syria, with whom Jordan's relations were tense. **1982:** Hussein tried to mediate in Arab–Israeli conflict, following Israeli invasion of Lebanon. **1984:** Women voted for first time; parliament recalled. **1985:** Hussein and PLO leader Yassir Arafat put forward framework for Middle East peace settlement. Secret meeting between Hussein and Israeli prime minister. **1988:** Hussein announced willingness to cease administering West Bank as part of Jordan, passing responsibility to PLO; parliament suspended. **1989:** Prime Minister Zaid al-Rifai resigned; Hussein promised new parliamentary elections. Riots over price increases of up to 50% following fall in oil revenues. First parliamentary elections for 22 years; Muslim Brotherhood won 25 of 80 seats but exiled from government; martial law lifted. **1990:** Hussein unsuccessfully tried to mediate after Iraq's invasion of Kuwait. Huge refugee problems as thousands fled to Jordan from Kuwait and Iraq. **1991:** 24 years of martial law ended; ban on political parties lifted; remained neutral during the Gulf War involving Iraq. **1993:** Candidates loyal to Hussein won majority in parliamentary elections; several leading Islamic fundamentalists lost their seats. **1994:** Economic cooperation pact singed with PLO. Peace treaty signed with Israel, ending 46-year-old state of war. **1996:** Abdul-Karim Kabariti appointed prime minister. **1997:** Success for government supporters in assembly elections. **1998:** Fayez Tarawneh was appointed prime minister. **1999:** King Hussein died; his eldest son, Abdullah, succeeded him. Abdul-Raouf al-Rawabdeh appointed prime minister.

Kazakhstan Republic of

National name: *Kazak Respublikasy* **Area:** 2,717,300 sq km/1,049,150 sq mi **Capital:** Astana (formerly called Akmola) **Major towns/cities:** Karaganda, Pavlodar, Semipalatinsk, Petropavlovsk, Chimkent

Government

Head of state: Nursultan Nazarbayev from 1990 **Head of government:** Nurlan Balgimbayev from 1997 **Political system:** authoritarian nationalist **Administrative divisions:** 19 provinces **Political parties:** Congress of People's Unity of Kazakhstan, moderate, centrist; People's Congress of Kazakhstan, moderate, ethnic; Socialist Party of Kazakhstan (SPK), left wing; Republican Party, right-of-centre coalition **Armed forces:** 35,100 (1997) **Death penalty:** retained and used for ordinary crimes **Defence spend:** (% GDP) 2.3 (1997) **Education spend:** (% GNP) 6.0 (1996) **Health spend:** (% GDP) 2.2 (1990–95)

Economy and resources

Currency: tenge **GDP:** (US$) 22.5 billion (1997) **Real GDP growth:** (% change on previous year) 2.0 (1997) **GNP:** 21.8 billion (1997) **GNP per capita (PPP):** (US$) 3,290 (1997) **Consumer price inflation:** 12.0% (1998) **Unemployment:** 3.5% (1996) **Foreign debt:** (US$) 2.92 billion (1996) **Major trading partners:** Russia and other CIS nations, Germany, the Netherlands, Switzerland, Czech Republic, Italy **Resources:** petroleum, natural gas, coal, bauxite, chromium, copper, iron ore, lead, titanium, magnesium, tungsten, molybdenum, gold, silver, manganese **Exports:** ferrous and non-ferrous metals, mineral products (including petroleum and petroleum products), chemicals. Principal market: Russia 33.9% (1997) **Imports:** energy products and electricity, machinery and transport equipment, chemicals. Principal source: Russia 46% (1997) **Arable land:** 11.9% (1995)

Population and society

Population: 16,319,000 (1998 est) **Population growth rate:** 0.1% (1995–2000) **Population density:** (per sq km) 6.2 (1998 est) **Urban population:** (% of total) 61 (1997) **Age distribution:** (% of total population) 0–14 29.1%, 15–64 63.9%, 65+ 7.0% (1998) **Ethnic groups:** 40% of Kazakh descent, 38% ethnic Russian, 6% German, 5% Ukrainian, 2% Uzbek, and 2% Tatar **Language:** Kazakh (official), related to Turkish; Russian **Religion:** Sunni Muslim **Education:** (compulsory years) 11 **Literacy rate:** 97.5% (men); 97.5% (women) (1995 est) **Labour force:** 24% agriculture, 20.4% industry, 55.6% services (1992) **Life expectancy:** 63 (men); 73 (women) (1995–2000) **Child mortality rate:** (under 5, per 1,000 live births) 39 (1997) **Physicians:** 1 per 254 people (1994)

Practical information

Visa requirements: UK: visa required. USA: visa required **Embassy in the UK:** 3 Warren Mews, London W1P 5DJ. Tel/fax: (0171) 387 1047 **British embassy:** 173 Furmanova Street, Almaty. Tel: (3272) 506 191; fax: (3272) 506 260 **Chamber of commerce:** Chamber of Commerce and Industry of Kazakhstan, pr. Ablaikhana 93/95, 480091 Almaty. Tel: (3272) 621 446; fax: (3272) 620 594

Chronology

early Christian era: Settled by Mongol and Turkic tribes. **8th century:** Spread of Islam. **10th century:** Southward migration into east Kazakhstan of Kazakh tribes, displaced from Mongolia by the Mongols. **13th–14th centuries:** Part of Mongol Empire. **late 15th century:** Kazakhs emerged as distinct ethnic group from Kazakh Orda tribal confederation. **early 17th century:** The nomadic, cattle-breeding Kazakhs split into smaller groups, united in the three Large, Middle, and Lesser Hordes (federations), led by khans (chiefs). **1731–42:** Faced by attacks from the east by Oirot Mongols, protection was sought from the Russian tsars, and Russian control was gradually established. **1822–48:** Conquest by tsarist Russia completed; khans deposed. Large-scale Russian and Ukrainian peasant settlement of the steppes after the abolition of serfdom in Russia in 1861. **1887:** Alma-Alta (now Almaty), established in 1854 as a fortified trading centre and captured by the Russians in 1865, destroyed by earthquake. **1916:** 150,000 killed as anti-Russian rebellion brutally repressed. **1917:** Bolshevik coup in Russia followed by outbreak of civil war in Kazakhstan. **1920:** Autonomous republic in USSR. **early 1930s:** More than 1 million died of starvation during campaign to collectivize agriculture. **1936:** Joined USSR and became a full union republic. **early 1940s:** Volga Germans deported to the republic by Soviet dictator Joseph Stalin. **1954–56:** Part of Soviet leader Nikita Khrushchev's ambitious 'Virgin Lands' agricultural extension programme; large influx of

Russian settlers made Kazakhs a minority in their own republic. **1986:** Nationalist riots in Alma-Alta (now Almaty) after reformist Soviet leader Mikhail Gorbachev ousted local communist leader and installed an ethnic Russian. **1989:** Nursultan Nazarbayev, a reformist and mild nationalist, became leader of Kazakh Communist Party (KCP) and instituted economic and cultural reform programmes, encouraging foreign inward investment. **1990:** Nazarbayev became head of state; economic sovereignty declared. **1991:** Nazarbayev condemned attempted anti-Gorbachev coup in Moscow; KCP abolished. Joined new Commonwealth of Independent States; independence recognized by USA. **1992:** Admitted into United Nations and Conference on Security and Cooperation in Europe (CSCE; now the Organization on Security and Cooperation in Europe, OSCE). **1993:** Presidential power increased by new constitution. Privatization programme launched; Kazakhstan ratified START-1 (disarmament treaty) and Nuclear Non-Proliferation Treaty. **1994:** Economic, social, and military union with Kyrgyzstan and Uzbekistan. **1995:** Economic and military cooperation pact with Russia. Achieved nuclear-free status. Nazarbayev's popular mandate reratified in national referendum. **1997:** Nurlan Balgimbayev appointed prime minister. Major oil agreements with China. Astana (formerly known as Akmola) designated as new capital. **1998:** Opposition united to form People's Front. Constitution amended to end restrictions of presidential terms. A treaty of 'eternal friendship' and a treaty of deepening economic cooperation signed with Uzbekistan. **1999:** Nursultan Nazarbayev re-elected president by a landslide margin, after main rival was barred from standing.

Kenya Republic of

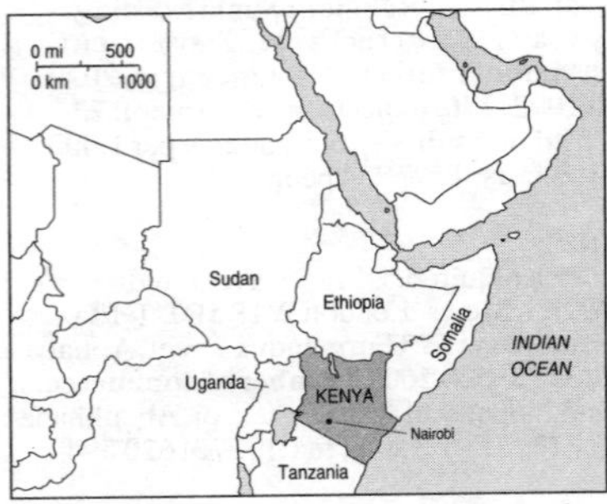

National name: *Jamhuri ya Kenya* **Area:** 582,600 sq km/224,941 sq mi **Capital:** Nairobi **Major towns/cities:** Mombasa, Kisumu, Nakuru, Eldoret, Nyeri **Major ports:** Mombasa

Government

Head of state and government: Daniel arap Moi from 1978 **Political system:** authoritarian nationalist **Administrative divisions:** seven provinces and the Nairobi municipality **Political parties:** Kenya African National Union (KANU), nationalist, centrist; Forum for the Restoration of Democracy–Kenya (FORD–Kenya), left of centre; Forum for the Restoration of Democracy–Asili (FORD–Asili), left of centre; Democratic Party (DP), centrist; Safina, centrist **Armed forces:** 24,200; paramilitary force 5,000 (1997) **Conscription:** military service is voluntary **Death penalty:** retained and used for ordinary crimes **Defence spend:** (% GDP) 2.4 (1997) **Education spend:** (% GNP) 6.6 (1996) **Health spend:** (% GDP) 1.9 (1990–95)

Economy and resources

Currency: Kenya shilling **GDP:** (US$) 9.9 billion (1997) **Real GDP growth:** (% change on previous year) 3.0 (1997) **GNP:** 9.3 billion (1997) **GNP per capita (PPP):** (US$) 1,110 (1997) **Consumer price inflation:** 11.5% (1998) **Unemployment:** 16% (1992 est) **Foreign debt:** (US$) 6.9 billion (1996) **Major trading partners:** Uganda, UK, Tanzania, Germany, Japan, United Arab Emirates **Resources:** soda ash, fluorspar, salt, limestone, rubies, gold, vermiculite, diatonite, garnets **Exports:** coffee, tea, petroleum products, soda ash, horticultural products. Principal market: Uganda 15.1% (1997) **Imports:** crude petroleum, motor vehicles, industrial machinery, iron and steel, chemicals, basic manufactures. Principal source: South Africa 11.4% (1997) **Arable land:** 7% (1995)

Population and society

Population: 29,008,000 (1998 est) **Population growth rate:** 2.2% (1995–2000) **Population density:** (per sq km) 49.8 (1998 est) **Urban population:** (% of total) 31 (1997) **Age distribution:** (% of total population) 0–14 43.6%, 15–64 53.7%, 65+ 2.7% (1998) **Ethnic groups:** main ethnic groups are the Kikuyu (about 21%), the Luhya (14%), the Luo (13%), the Kalenjin (11%), the Kamba (11%), the Kisii (6%), and the Meru (5%); there are also Asian, Arab, and European minorities **Language:** Kiswahili (official), English; there are many local dialects **Religion:** Roman Catholic, Protestant, Muslim, traditional tribal religions **Education:** (years) 8 (not compulsory, but free) **Literacy rate:** 86% (men); 70% (women) (1995 est) **Labour force:** 48% of population: 80% agriculture, 7% industry, 13% services (1990) **Life expectancy:** 52 (men); 56 (women) (1995–2000) **Child mortality rate:** (under 5, per 1,000 live births) 101 (1997) **Physicians:** 1 per 6,430 people (1994)

Practical information

Visa requirements: UK: visa not required. USA: visa required **Embassy in the UK:** 45 Portland Place, London W1N 4AS. Tel: (0171) 636 2371/5; fax: (0171) 323 6717 **British embassy:** British High Commission, PO Box 30465, Bruce House, Standard Street, Nairobi. Tel: (2) 335 944; fax: (2) 333 196 **Chamber of commerce:** Kenya National Chamber of Commerce and Industry, PO Box 47024, Ufanisi House, Hailé Sélassie Avenue, Nairobi. Tel: (2) 334 413

Chronology

8th century: Arab traders began to settle along coast of East Africa. **16th century:** Portuguese defeated coastal states and exerted spasmodic control over them. **18th century:** Sultan of Oman reasserted Arab overlordship of East African coast, making it subordinate to Zanzibar. **19th century:** Europeans, closely followed by Christian missionaries, began to explore inland. **1887:** British East African Company leased area of coastal territory from sultan of Zanzibar. **1895:** Britain claimed large inland region as East African Protectorate. **1903:** Railway from Mombasa to Uganda built using Indian labourers, many of whom settled in the area; British and South African settlers began to farm highlands. **1920:** East African Protectorate became crown colony of Kenya, with legislative council elected by white settlers (and by Indians and Arabs soon afterwards). **1923:** Britain rejected demand for internal self-government by white settlers. **1944:** First African appointment to legislative council; Kenyan African Union (KAU) founded to campaign for African rights. **1947:** Jomo Kenyatta became leader of KAU, which was dominated by Kikuyu tribe. **1952:** Mau Mau (Kikuyu secret society) began terrorist campaign to drive white settlers from tribal lands; Mau Mau largely suppressed by 1954 but state of emergency lasted for eight years. **1953:** Kenyatta charged with management of Mau Mau activities and imprisoned by the British. **1956:** Africans allowed to elect members of legislative council on restricted franchise. **1959:** Kenyatta released from prison, but exiled to northern Kenya. **1960:** Britain announced plans to prepare Kenya for majority African rule. **1961:** Kenyatta allowed to return to help negotiate Kenya's independence. **1963:** Kenya achieved independence with Kenyatta as prime minister. **1964:** Kenya became a republic with Kenyatta as president. **1967:** East African Community (EAC) formed by Kenya, Tanzania, and Uganda to retain customs union inherited from colonial period. **1969:** Kenya became one-party state under Kenyan African National Union (KANU). **1977:** Political and economic disputes led to collapse of EAC. **1978:** Death of President Kenyatta; succeeded by Daniel arap Moi. **1984:** Violent clashes between government troops and ethnic Somali population at Wajir. **1989:** Moi announced release of political prisoners. **1991:** Multiparty system conceded after opposition group was launched. **1997:** Demonstrations calling for democratic reform. Constitutional refoms adopted. **1998:** A bomb exploded at the US embassy in Nairobi, killing over 230 people and injuring 5,000; an anti-American Islamic group claimed responsibility.

Kiribati Republic of (formerly part of the Gilbert and Ellice Islands)

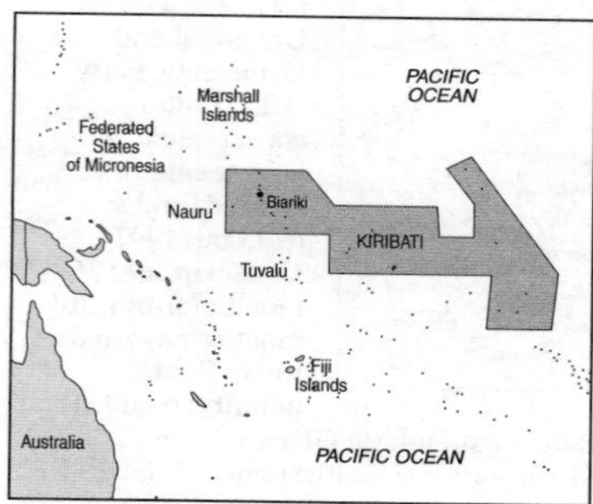

National name: *Ribaberikin Kiribati* **Area:** 717 sq km/277 sq mi **Capital:** Bairiki (on Tarawa Atoll) (and port) **Towns:** pricipal atolls: North Tarawa, Gilbert group, Abaiang, Tabiteuea **Major ports:** Betio (on Tarawa)

Government

Head of state and government: Teburoro Tito from 1994 **Political system:** liberal democracy **Political parties:** Maneaban Te Mauri (MTM), dominant faction; National Progressive Party (NPP), former governing faction 1979–94 **Armed forces:** no standing army **Death penalty:** abolished in 1979 **Education spend:** (% GNP) 11.4 (1996)

Economy and resources

Currency: Australian dollar **GDP:** (US$) 68 million (1995 est) **Real GDP growth:** (% change on previous year) 2.6 (1995 est) **GNP:** 76 million (1997) **GNP per capita (PPP):** (US$) 980 (1997 est) **Consumer price inflation:** 2.9% (1994) **Unemployment:** 2.8% (1990) **Foreign debt:** (US$) 21 million (1993) **Major trading partners:** Australia, Bangladesh, Japan, Fiji Islands, USA, France, New Zealand, China **Resources:** phosphate, salt **Exports:** copra, fish, seaweed, bananas, breadfruit, taro. Principal market: USA (1996) **Imports:** foodstuffs, machinery and transport equipment, mineral fuels, basic manufactures. Principal source: Australia 46% (1996) **Arable land:** 50.7% (1995)

Population and society

Population: 81,000 (1998 est) **Population growth rate:** 1.8% (1995–2000) **Population density:** (per sq km) 117.1 (1998 est) **Urban population:** (% of total) 37 (1997) **Age distribution:** (% of total population) 0–14 38.1%, 15–64 55.9%, 65+ 6% (1992) **Ethnic groups:** predominantly Micronesian, with a Polynesian minority; also European and Chinese minorities **Language:** English (official), Gilbertese **Religion:** Roman Catholic, Protestant (Congregationalist) **Education:** (compulsory years) 9 **Literacy rate:** 90% (men); 90%(women) (1993 est) **Life expectancy:** 51 (men); 56 (women) (1992) **Child mortality rate:** (under 5, per 1,000 live births) 98 (1994) **Physicians:** 1 per 4,685 people (1991)

Practical information

Visa requirements: UK: visa not required for a stay of up to 28 days. USA: visa required **Embassy in the UK:** Consulate of Kiribati, Faith House, 7 Tufton Street, London SW1P 3QN. Tel: (0171) 222 6952; fax: (0171) 976 7180 **British embassy:** the British High Commission in Suva (see Fiji Islands) deals with enquiries relating to Kiribati **Chamber of commerce:** none

Chronology

1st millenium BC: Settled by Austronesian-speaking peoples. **1606:** Visited by Spanish explorers. **late 18th century:** Visited by British naval officers. **1857:** Christian mission established. **1892:** Gilbert (Kiribati) and Ellice (Tuvalu) Islands proclaimed a British protectorate. **1916–39:** Uninhabited Phoenix Islands, Christmas Island, Ocean Island, and Line Island (Banaba) added to colony. **1942–43:** Occupied by Japanese, it was the scene of fierce fighting with US troops. **late 1950s:** UK tested nuclear weapons on Christmas Island (Kiritimati). **1963:** Legislative council established. **1974:** Legislative council replaced by an elected House of Assembly. **1975:** The mainly Melanesian-populated Ellice Islands separated to become Tuvalu. **1977:** The predominantly Micronesian-populated Gilbert Islands granted internal self-government. **1979:** Independence achieved within the Commonwealth, as the Republic of Kiribati, with Ieremia Tabai as president. **1985:** Kiribati's first political party, the opposition Christian Democrats, formed. **1991:** Tabai re-elected but under constitution not allowed to serve further term; Teatao Teannaki won run-off presidential election. **1994:** Government resigned after losing vote of confidence. Ruling National Progressive Party (NPP) defeated in general election. Teburoro Tito elected president. **1998:** In House of Assembly legislative elections the ruling Maneaban Te Mauru (MTM) and the opposition National Progressive Party (NPP) lost seats to independents. President Teburoro Tito, of the MTM, was re-elected for a second term by the House of Assembly.

Korea, North People's Democratic Republic of

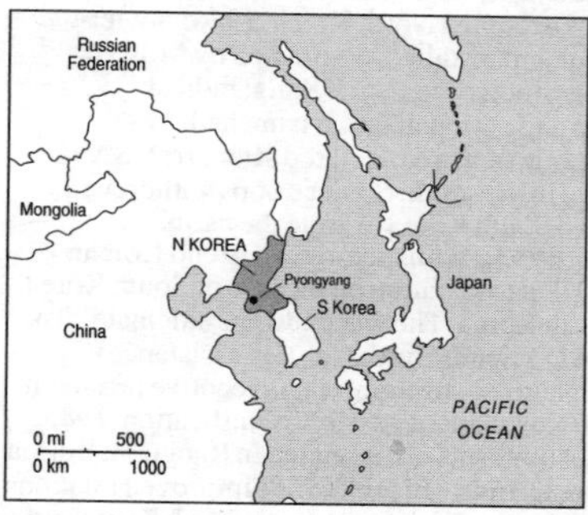

National name: *Chosun Minchu-chui Inmin Konghwa-guk* **Area:** 120,538 sq km/46,539 sq mi **Capital:** Pyongyang **Major towns/cities:** Hamhung, Chongjin, Nampo, Wonsan, Sinuiji

Government

Head of state: Kim Jong Il from 1994 **Head of government:** Hong Song Nam from 1997 **Political system:** communism **Administrative divisions:** three cities and nine provinces **Political parties:** Korean Workers' Party (KWP), Marxist-Leninist (leads Democratic Front for the Reunification of the Fatherland, including Korean Social Democratic Party and Chondoist Chongu Party) **Armed forces:** 1,055,000 (1997) **Conscription:** conscription is selective for 3–10 years **Death penalty:** retained and used for ordinary crimes **Defence spend:** (% GDP) 27% (1997)

Economy and resources

Currency: won **GDP:** (US$) 21.5 billion (1995 est) **Real GDP growth:** (% change on previous year) –5 (1995 est) **GNP:** 21.45 billion (1996) **GNP per capita (PPP):** (US$) 950 (1996 est) **Consumer price inflation:** N/A **Foreign debt:** (US$) 9.8 billion (1994 est) **Major trading partners:** China, Japan, CIS, South Korea, Germany, Italy, Hong Kong, Iran **Resources:** coal, iron, lead, copper, zinc, tin, silver, gold, magnesite (has 40–50% of world's deposits of magnesite) **Exports:** base metals, textiles, vegetable products, machinery and equipment. Principal market: Japan 27.9% (1995 est) **Imports:** petroleum and petroleum products, machinery and equipment, grain, coal, foodstuffs. Principal source: China 32.6% (1995 est) **Arable land:** 14.1% (1995)

Population and society

Population: 23,348,000 (1998 est) **Population growth rate:** 1.6% (1995–2000); 1.3% (2000–05) **Population density:** (per sq km) 176.4 (1998 est) **Urban population:** (% of total) 62 (1997) **Age distribution:** (% of total population) 0–14 25.8%, 15–64 68.3%, 65+ 6.0% (1998) **Ethnic groups:** entirely Korean, with the exception of a 50,000 Chinese minority **Language:** Korean **Religion:** Chondoist, Buddhist, Christian, traditional beliefs **Education:** (compulsory years) 10 **Literacy rate:** 99% (men); 99%(women) (1995 est) **Labour force:** 50% of population: 38% agriculture, 31% industry, 31% services (1990) **Life expectancy:** 69 (men); 75 (women) (1995–2000) **Child mortality rate:** (under 5, per 1,000 live births) 25 (1997) **Physicians:** 1 per 370 people (1993)

Practical information

Visa requirements: UK: visa required. USA: visa required **Embassy for the UK:** General Delegation of the DPRK, 104 boulevard Bineau, 92200 Neuilly-sur-Seine, France. Tel: (1) 4745 1797; fax: (1) 4738 1250 **British embassy:** the UK has no diplomatic representation in North Korea **Chamber of commerce:** DPRK Committee for the Promotion of External Economic Cooperation, Jungsongdong, Central District, Pyongyang. Tel: (2) 33974; fax: (2) 814 498

Chronology

2333 BC: Legendary founding of Korean state by Tangun dynasty. **1122 BC–4th century AD:** Period of Chinese Kija dynasty. **668–1000:** Peninsula unified by Buddhist Shilla kingdom, with capital at Kyongju. **1392–1910:** Period of Chosun, or Yi, dynasty, during which Korea became a vassal of China and Confucianism became dominant intellectual force. **1910:** Korea formally annexed by Japan. **1920s and 1930s:** Heavy industries developed in the coal-rich north, with Koreans forcibly conscripted as low-paid labourers; suppression of Korean culture led to development of resistance movement. **1945:** Russian and US troops entered Korea at the end of World War II, forced surrender of Japanese, and divided the country in two at the 38th parallel. Soviet troops occupied North Korea. **1946:** Soviet-backed provisional government installed, dominated by Moscow-trained Korean communists, including Kim Il Sung; radical programme of land reform and nationalization launched. **1948:** Democratic People's Republic of Korea declared after pro-USA Republic of Korea founded in the south; Soviet troops withdrew. **1950:** North Korea invaded South Korea to unite the nation, beginning the Korean War. **1953:** Armistice agreed to end Korean War, which had involved US participation on the side of South Korea, and Chinese on that of North Korea. The war ended in stalemate, at a cost of 2 million lives. **1961:** Friendship and mutual assistance treaty signed with China. **1972:** New constitution, with executive president, adopted. Talks with South Korea about possible reunification. **1983:** Four South Korean cabinet ministers assassinated in Rangoon, Burma (Myanmar), by North Korean army officers. **1985:** Improved relations with Soviet Union. **1990:** Diplomatic contacts with South Korea and Japan suggested a thaw in North Korea's relations with the rest of the world. **1991:** Became a member of the United Nations. Signed nonaggression agreement with South Korea. **1992:** Signed Nuclear Safeguards Agreement, allowing international inspection of nuclear facilities. Also signed pact with South Korea for mutual inspection of nuclear facilities. **1994:** Kim Il Sung died; succeeded by his son, Kim Jong Il. Agreement to halt nuclear-development programme in return for US aid, resulting in easing of 44-year-old US trade embargo. **1996:** US aid sought in the face of severe famine caused by floods; rice imported from South Korea and food aid provided by UN. **1997:** Kang Song San replaced as prime minister by Hong Song Nam. Grave food shortages revealed. **1998:** UN food-aid operation instituted in effort to avert widespread famine. First direct talks with South Korea since 1994 ended in stalemate. Legislature elections held for first time since 1990. Ballistic missile test fired over Japan. Deceased former leader Kim Il Sung declared 'president for perpetuity'. Relations with the USA deteriorated when the USA demanded access to an underground site in Kumchangri suspected of being part of a renewed nuclear-weapons program. **1999:** Talks on possible reunification suspended.

Korea, South Republic of Korea

National name: *Daehan Min-kuk* **Area:** 98,799 sq km/38,146 sq mi **Capital:** Seoul **Major towns/cities:** Pusan, Taegu, Inchon, Kwangju, Taejon **Major ports:** Pusan, Inchon

Government

Head of state: Kim Dae Jung from 1998 **Head of government:** Kim Jong Pil from 1998 **Political system:** emergent democracy **Administrative divisions:** nine provinces and six cities with provincial status **Political parties:** New Korea Party (NKP, formerly Democratic Liberal Party (DLP)), right of centre; National Congress for New Politics (NCNP), centre left; Democratic Party (DP), left of centre; New Democratic Party (NDP), centrist, pro-private enterprise; United Liberal Democratic Party (ULD), ultra-conservative, pro-private enterprise **Armed forces:** 672,000 (1997) **Conscription:** 26 months (army); 30 months (navy and air force) **Death penalty:** retained and used for ordinary crimes **Defence spend:** (% GDP) 3.3 (1997) **Education spend:** (% GNP) 3.7 (1995) **Health spend:** (% GDP) 1.8 (1990–95)

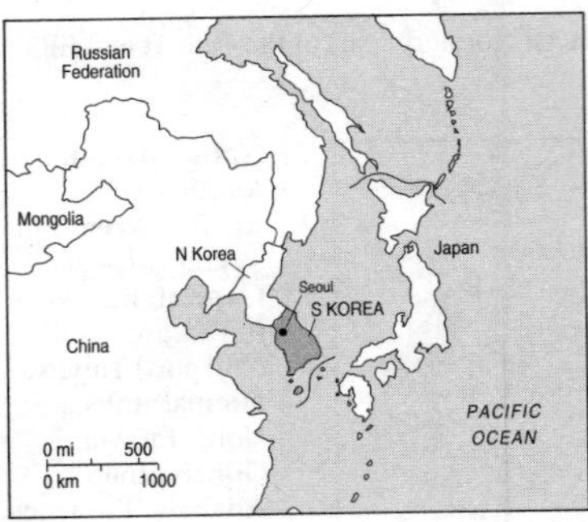

Economy and resources

Currency: won **GDP:** (US$) 438.2 billion (1997) **Real GDP growth:** (% change on previous year) 5.3 (1997) **GNP:** 485.2 billion (1997) **GNP per capita (PPP):** (US$) 13,500 (1997) **Consumer price inflation:** 5.5% (1998) **Unemployment:** 2.6% (1997) **Foreign debt:** (US$) 95.5 billion (1996) **Major trading partners:** USA, Japan, Germany, Saudi Arabia, Australia, Hong Kong, Singapore, China **Resources:** coal, iron ore, tungsten, gold, molybdenum, graphite, fluorite, natural gas, hydroelectric power, fish **Exports:** electrical machinery, textiles, clothing, footwear, telecommunications and sound equipment, chemical products, ships ('invisible export' – overseas construction work). Principal market: USA 15.9% (1997) **Imports:** machinery and transport equipment (especially electrical machinery), petroleum and petroleum products, grain and foodstuffs, steel, chemical products, basic manufactures. Principal source: USA 20.7% (1997) **Arable land:** 18.1% (1995)

Population and society

Population: 46,109,000 (1998 est) **Population growth rate:** 0.9% (1995–2000); 0.8% (2000–05) **Population density:** (per sq km) 472.7 (1998 est) **Urban population:** (% of total) 84 (1997) **Age distribution:** (% of total population) 0–14 22.4%, 15–64 71.2%, 65+ 6.4% (1998) **Ethnic groups:** with the exception of a small Nationalist Chinese minority, the population is almost entirely of Korean descent **Language:** Korean **Religion:** Shamanist, Buddhist, Confucian, Protestant, Roman Catholic **Education:** (compulsory years) 9 **Literacy rate:** 99% (men); 93% (women) (1995 est) **Labour force:** 46.5% of population: 11.6% agriculture, 32.5% industry, 55.9% services (1996) **Life expectancy:** 69 (men); 76 (women) (1995–2000) **Child mortality rate:** (under 5, per 1,000 live births) 12 (1997) **Physicians:** 1 per 909 people (1995)

Practical information

Visa requirements: UK: visa not required for a stay of up to 90 days. USA: visa not required **Embassy in the UK:** 4 Palace Gate, London W8 5NF. Tel: (0171) 581 0247; fax: (0171) 581 8076 **British embassy:** 4 Chung-dong, Chung-ku, Seoul 100. Tel: (2) 735 7341/3; fax: (2) 733 8368 **Chamber of commerce:** Korean Chamber of Commerce and Industry, PO Box 25, 45 4-ka, Namdaemun-no, Chung-ku, Seoul 100.Tel: (2) 316 3114; fax: (2) 757 9475

Chronology

2333 BC: Traditional date of founding of Korean state by Tangun (mythical son from union of bear-woman and god). **1122 BC:** Ancient texts record founding of kingdom in Korea by Chinese nobleman Kija. **194 BC:** Northwest Korea united under warlord, Wiman. **108 BC:** Korea conquered by Chinese. **1st–7th centuries AD:** Three Korean kingdoms – Koguryo, Paekche, and Silla – competed for supremacy. **668:** Korean peninsula unified by Buddhist Silla kingdom; culture combining Chinese and Korean elements flourished. **935:** Silla dynasty overthrown by Wang Kon of Koguryo, who founded Koryo dynasty in its place. **1258:** Korea accepted overlordship of Mongol Yüan Empire. **1392:** Yi dynasty founded by Gen Yi Song-gye, vassal of Chinese Ming

Empire; Confucianism replaced Buddhism as official creed; extreme conservatism characterized Korean society. **1592 and 1597:** Japanese invasions repulsed by Korea. **1636:** Manchu invasion forced Korea to sever ties with Ming dynasty. **18th–19th centuries:** Korea resisted change in political and economic life and rejected contact with Europeans. **1864:** Attempts to reform government and strengthen army by Taewongun (who ruled in name of his son, King Kojong); converts to Christianity persecuted. **1873:** Taewongun forced to cede power to Queen Min; reforms reversed; government authority collapsed. **1882:** Chinese occupied Seoul and installed governor. **1894–95:** Sino-Japanese War: Japan forced China to recognize independence of Korea; Korea fell to Japanese influence. **1896:** Fearing for his life, King Kojong sought protection of Russian legation. **1904–05:** Russo-Japanese War: Japan ended Russian influence in Korea. **1910:** Korea formally annexed by Japan; Japanese settlers introduced modern industry and agriculture; Korean language banned. **1919:** 'Samil' nationalist movement suppressed by Japanese. **1945:** After defeat of Japan in World War II, Russia occupied regions of Korea north of 38th parallel (demarcation line agreed at Yalta Conference) and USA occupied regions south of it. **1948:** USSR refused to permit United Nations (UN) supervision of elections in northern zone; southern zone became independent as Republic of Korea, with Syngman Rhee as president. **1950:** North Korea invaded South Korea; UN forces (mainly from USA) intervened to defend South Korea; China intervened in support of North Korea. **1953:** Korean War ended with armistice which restored 38th parallel; no peace treaty agreed and US troops remained in South Korea. **1960:** President Syngman Rhee forced to resign by student-led protests against corruption and fraudulent elections. **1961:** Military coup placed Gen Park Chung Hee in power; major programme of industrial development began. **1972:** Martial law imposed; presidential powers increased. **1979:** President Park assassinated; interim government of President Choi Kyu-Hah introduced liberalizing reforms. **1979:** Gen Chun Doo Hwan assumed power after anti-government riots; Korea emerged as leading shipbuilding nation and exporter of electronic goods. **1987:** Constitution made more democratic as a result of Liberal pressure; ruling Democratic Justice Party (DJP) candidate Roh Tae Woo elected president amid allegations of fraud. **1988:** Olympic Games held in Seoul. **1991:** Large-scale antigovernment protests forcibly suppressed; South Korea joined UN. **1992:** South Korea established diplomatic relations with China; Kim Young Sam elected president. **1994:** US military presence stepped up in response to perceived threat from North Korea. **1996:** Roh Tae Woo and Chun Doo Hwan charged with treason for alleged role in massacre of demonstrators in 1980. **1997:** South Korea admitted to OECD. Kim Dae Jung, former dissident and political prisoner, became first opposition politician to lead South Korea. **1998:** Kim Dae Jung sworn in as president, with Kim Jong Pil as prime minister. New labour laws ended lifetime employment and financial system opened up. More than 2,000 prisoners released, including 74 political prisoners. Continuing labour unrest as GDP contracted by 5%. **1999:** Talks on possible reunification suspended.

Kuwait State of

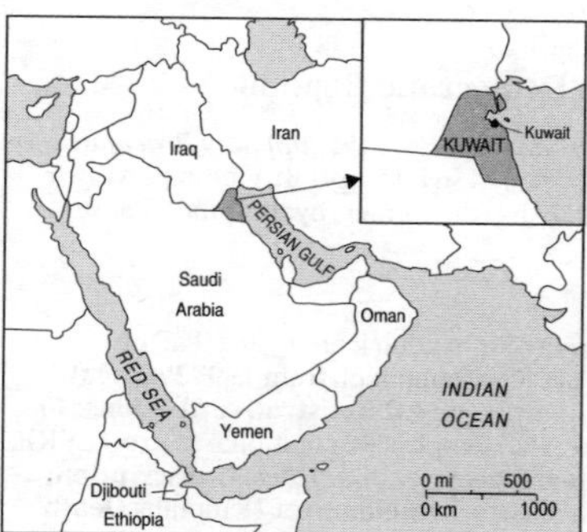

National name: *Dowlat al Kuwait* **Area:** 17,819 sq km/6,879 sq mi **Capital:** Kuwait (also chief port) **Major towns/cities:** as-Salimiya, Hawalli, Faranawiya, Abraq Kheetan, Jahra, Ahmadi, Fahaheel

Government

Head of state: Sheikh Jabir al-Ahmad al-Jabir as-Sabah from 1977 **Head of government:** Crown Prince Sheikh Saad al-Abdullah as-Salinas as-Sabah from 1978 **Political system:** absolute monarchy **Administrative divisions:** five governates **Political parties:** none **Armed forces:** 15,300 (1997) **Conscription:** compulsory for two years **Death penalty:** retained and used for ordinary crimes **Defence spend:** (% GDP) 11.4 (1997) **Education spend:** (% GNP) 5.6 (1995) **Health spend:** (% GDP) 3.6 (1990–95)

Economy and resources

Currency: Kuwaiti dinar **GDP:** (US$) 32.1 billion (1997 est) **Real GDP growth:** (% change on previous year) 3.0 (1997) **GNP:** 35.1 billion (1997) **GNP per capita (PPP):** (US$) 24,270 (1997) **Consumer price inflation:** 4.0% (1998) **Unemployment:** 0.5% (1995 est) **Foreign debt:** (US$) 5.8 billion (1996) **Major trading partners:** USA, Japan, Germany, France, Saudi Arabia, United Arab Emirates, India, UK, Italy **Resources:** petroleum, natural gas, mineral water **Exports:** petroleum and petroleum products (accounted for more than 93% of export revenue in 1994), chemical fertilizer, gas (natural and manufactured), basic manufactures. Principal market: Japan 24.1% (1997) **Imports:** machinery and transport equipment, basic manufactures (especially iron, steel, and textiles) and other manufactured goods, live animals and food. Principal source: USA 22.2% (1997) **Arable land:** 0.3% (1995)

Population and society

Population: 1,811,000 (1998 est) **Population growth rate:** 3.0% (1995–2000) **Population density:** (per sq km) 107.4 (1998 est) **Urban population:** (% of total) 97 (1997) **Age distribution:** (% of total population) 0–14 32.3%, 15–64 65.7%, 65+ 2.0% (1998) **Ethnic groups:** about 42% Kuwaiti, 40% non-Kuwaiti Arab, 5% Indian and Pakistani, 4% Iranian **Language:** Arabic (official) 78%, Kurdish 10%, Farsi 4%, English **Religion:** Sunni Muslim, Shi'ite Muslim, Christian **Education:** (compulsory years) 8 **Literacy rate:** 61% (men); 67% (women) (1995 est) **Labour force:** 42% of population: 1% agriculture, 25% industry, 74% services (1990) **Life expectancy:** 74 (men); 78 (women) (1995–2000) **Child mortality rate:** (under 5, per 1,000 live births) 15 (1997) **Physicians:** 1 per 581 people (1993)

Practical information

Visa requirements: UK: visa required. USA: visa required **Embassy in the UK:** 45–46 Queen's Gate, London SW7 5HR. Tel: (0171) 589 4533; fax: (0171) 589 7183 **British embassy:** PO Box 2, Arabian Gulf Street, 13001 Safat, Kuwait City. Tel: (965) 240 3324/5/6; fax: (965) 240 7395 **Chamber of commerce:** Kuwait Chamber of Commerce and Industry, PO Box 775, Chamber's Building, Ali as-Salem Street, 13008 Safat, Kuwait City. Tel: (965) 243 3864; fax: (965) 240 4110

Chronology

c. **3000 BC:** Archaeological evidence suggests that coastal parts of Kuwait may have been part of a commercial civilization contemporary with the Sumerian, based in Mesopotamia (the Tigris and Euphrates valley area of Iraq). *c.* **323 BC:** Visited by Greek colonists at time of Alexander the Great. **7th century AD:** Islam introduced. **late 16th century:** Fell under nominal control of Turkish Ottoman Empire. **1710:** Control was assumed by the Utab, a member of the Anaza tribal confederation in northern Arabia, and Kuwait city was founded, soon developing from a fishing village into an important port. **1756:** Autonomous sheikdom of Kuwait founded by Abd Rahman of the al-Sabah family, a branch of the Utab. **1776:** British East India Company set up a base in the Gulf. **1899:** Concerned at the potential threat of growing Ottoman and German influence, Britain signed a treaty with Kuwait, establishing a self-governing protectorate in which the Emir received an annual subsidy from Britain in return for agreeing not to alienate any territory to a foreign power. **1914:** Britain recognized Kuwait as an 'independent government under British protection'. **1922–33:** Agreement on frontiers with Iraq, to the north, and Nejd (later Saudi Arabia) to the southwest. **1938:** Oil discovered; large-scale exploitation after World War II transformed the economy. **1961:** Full independence achieved from Britain, with Sheik Abdullah al-Salem al-Sabah as emir. Attempted Iraqi invasion discouraged by dispatch of British troops to the Gulf. **1962:** Constitution introduced, with franchise restricted to 10% of the population. **1965:** Sheik Abdullah died; succeeded by his brother, Sheik Sabah al-Salem al-Sabah. **1977:** Sheik Sabah died; succeeded by Crown Prince Jabir. National Assembly dissolved.

1981: National Assembly was reconstituted. **1983:** Shi'ite guerrillas bombed targets in Kuwait; 17 arrested. **1986:** National assembly dissolved. **1987:** Kuwaiti oil tankers reflagged, received US Navy protection; missile attacks by Iran. **1988:** Aircraft hijacked by pro-Iranian Shi'ites demanding release of convicted guerrillas; Kuwait refused. **1989:** Two of the convicted guerrillas released. **1990:** Prodemocracy demonstrations suppressed. Kuwait annexed by Iraq in August, causing extensive damage to property and environment. Emir set up government in exile in Saudi Arabia. **1991:** US-led coalition forces defeated Iraqi forces in Kuwait in Gulf War. New government omitted any opposition representatives. **1992:** Reconstituted national assembly elected, with opposition nominees, including Islamic candidates, winning majority of seats. **1993:** Incursions by Iraq into Kuwait repelled by US-led air strikes on Iraqi military sites. **1994:** Massing of Iraqi troops on Kuwait border prompted US-led response. Iraqi president Saddam Hussein publicly renounced claim to Kuwait.

Kyrgyzstan Republic of

National name: *Kyrgyz Respublikasy* **Area:** 198,500 sq km/76,640 sq mi **Capital:** Bishkek (formerly Frunze) **Major towns/cities:** Osh, Przhevalsk, Kyzyl-Kiya, Tokmak, Djalal-Abad

Government

Head of state: Askar Akayev from 1990 **Head of government:** Amangeldy Mursadykovich Muraliyev from 1999 **Political system:** emergent democracy **Administrative divisions:** six provinces **Political parties:** Party of Communists of Kyrgyzstan (banned 1991–92); Ata Meken, Kyrgyz-nationalist; Erkin Kyrgyzstan, Kyrgyz-nationalist; Social Democratic Party, nationalist, pro-Akayev; Democratic Movement of Kyrgyzstan, nationalist reformist **Armed forces:** 12,200 (1997) **Conscription:** compulsory for 12–18 months **Death penalty:** retained and used for ordinary crimes **Defence spend:** (% GDP) 2.5 (1997) **Education spend:** (% GNP) 5.7 (1996) **Health spend:** (% GDP) 3.7 (1990–95)

Economy and resources

Currency: som **GDP:** (US$) 1.83 billion (1997) **Real GDP growth:** (% change on previous year) 6.5 (1997) **GNP:** 2 billion (1997) **GNP per capita (PPP):** (US$) 2,040 (1997) **Consumer price inflation:** 22% (1998) **Unemployment:** 4.4% (1996) **Foreign debt:** (US$) 789 million (1996) **Major trading partners:** Russia, Kazakhstan, Uzbekistan, Turkey, China, UK, Cuba, Ukraine **Resources:** petroleum, natural gas, coal, gold, tin, mercury, antimony, zinc, tungsten, uranium **Exports:** wool, cotton yarn, tobacco, electric power, electronic and engineering products, non-ferrous metallurgy, food and beverages. Principal market: Russia 30.4% (1996) **Imports:** petroleum, natural gas, engineering products, food products. Principal source: Russia 19.9% (1996) **Arable land:** 4.3% (1995)

Population and society

Population: 4,643,000 (1998 est) **Population growth rate:** 0.4% (1995–2000) **Population density:** (per sq km) 22.8 (1998 est) **Urban population:** (% of total) 39 (1997) **Age distribution:** (% of total population) 0–14 35.8%, 15–64 58.0%, 65+ 6.2% (1998) **Ethnic groups:** 53% ethnic Kyrgyz, 22% Russian, 13% Uzbek, 3% Ukrainian, and 2% German **Language:** Kyrgyz, a Turkic language **Religion:** Sunni Muslim **Education:** (compulsory years) 9 **Literacy rate:** 97% (men); 97% (women) (1995 est) **Labour force:** 43% agriculture, 21% industry, 36% services (1994) **Life expectancy:** 63 (men); 72 (women) (1995–2000) **Child mortality rate:** (under 5, per 1,000 live births) 46 (1997) **Physicians:** 1 per 337 people (1994)

Practical information

Visa requirements: UK: visa not required. USA: visa not required **Embassy for the UK:** 32 rue de Châtelain, 1050 Brussels, Belgium. Tel: (2) 627 1916; fax: (2) 627 1900 **British embassy:** the British Embassy in Almaty (see Kazakhstan) deals with enquiries relating to Kyrgyzstan **Chamber of commerce:** Kyrgyz Chamber of Commerce and Industry, Kievskaya 107, 720001 Bishkek. Tel: (3312) 210 574; fax: (3312) 210 575

Chronology

8th century: Spread of Islam. **10th century onwards:** Southward migration of Kyrgyz people from upper Yenisey River region to Tian-Shan region; accelerated following rise of Mongol Empire in 13th century. **13th–14th centuries:** Part of Mongol Empire. **1685:** Came under control of Mongol Oirots following centuries of Turkic rule. **1758:** Kyrgyz people became nominal subjects of Chinese Empire, following Oirots' defeat by Chinese rulers, the Manchus. **early 19th century:** Came under suzerainty of Khanate (chieftaincy) of Kokand, to the west. **1864–76:** Incorporated into tsarist Russian Empire. **1916–17:** Many Kyrgyz migrated to China after Russian suppression of rebellion in Central Asia and outbreak of civil war following 1917 October Revolution in Russia, with local armed guerrillas (*basmachi*) resisting Bolshevik Red Army. **1917–1924:** Part of independent Turkestan republic. **1920s:** Land reforms resulted in settlement of many formerly nomadic Kyrgyz; literacy and education improved. **1924:** Became autonomous republic within USSR. **1930s:** Agricultural collectivization programme provoked *basmachi* resistance and local 'nationalist communists' were purged from Kyrgyz Communist Party (KCP). **1936:** Became full union republic within USSR. **1990:** State of emergency imposed in Bishkek after ethnic clashes. Askar Akayev, a reform communist, chosen as president. **1991:** Akayev condemned attempted coup in Moscow against the reformist Mikhail Gorbachev; Kyrgyzstan joined new Commonwealth of Independent States (CIS); independence recognized by USA. **1992:** Joined the United Nations and Conference on Security and Cooperation in Europe (CSCE; now the Organization on Security and Cooperation in Europe, OSCE). Market-centred economic reform programme instituted. **1994:** National referenda overwhelmingly supported Akayev's presidency. Joined Central Asian Union, with Kazakhstan and Uzbekistan. **1995:** Pro-Akayev independents successful in elections to a new bicameral legislature. **1996:** Constitutional amendment increased powers of president. Agreement with Kazakhstan and Uzbekistan to create single economic market. **1997:** Private ownership of land legalized but privatization programme suspended. Agreement on border controls with Russia. **1998:** Kubanychbek Djumaliev became prime minister; he was soon replaced by Jumabek Ibraimov, following sharp depreciation in the currency. A referendum approved private ownership of land.

Laos Lao People's Democratic Republic

National name: *Saathiaranagroat Prachhathippatay Prachhachhon Lao* **Area:** 236,790 sq km/91,424 sq mi **Capital:** Vientiane **Major towns/cities:** Louangphrabang (the former royal capital), Pakse, Savannakhet

Government

Head of state: Gen Khamtay Siphandon from 1998 **Head of government:** Gen Sisavath Keobounphanh from 1998 **Political system:** communist, one-party state **Administrative divisions:** 17 provinces **Political party:** Lao People's Revolutionary Party (LPRP, the only legal party) **Armed forces:** 29,000 (1997) **Conscription:** military service is compulsory for a minimum of 18 months **Death penalty:** retained and used for ordinary crimes **Defence spend:** (% GDP) 3.9 (1997) **Education spend:** (% GNP) 2.5 (1996) **Health spend:** (% GDP) 1.3 (1990–95)

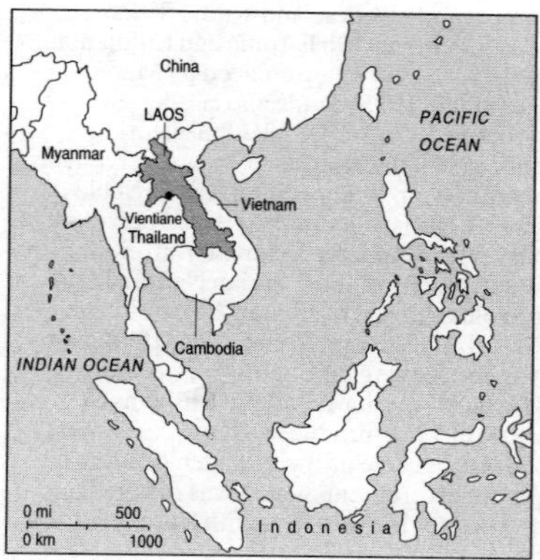

Economy and resources

Currency: new kip **GDP:** (US$) 1.7 billion (1997) **Real GDP growth:** (% change on previous year) 6.0 (1997) **GNP:** 1.9 billion (1997) **GNP per capita (PPP):** (US$) 1,290 (1997) **Consumer price inflation:** 17% (1997) **Unemployment:** 3% (1993) **Foreign debt:** (US$) 2.26 billion (1996) **Major trading partners:** Thailand, Japan, Germany, France, China, Italy **Resources:** coal, tin, gypsum, baryte, lead, zinc, nickel, potash, iron ore; small quantities of gold, silver, and precious stones **Exports:** timber, textiles and garments, motorcycles, electricity, coffee, tin, gypsum. Principal market: Vietnam 42.7% (1997) **Imports:** food (particularly rice and sugar), mineral fuels, machinery and transport equipment, cement, cotton yarn. Principal source: Thailand 56.2% (1997) **Arable land:** 3.8% (1995)

Population and society

Population: 5,163,000 (1998 est) **Population growth rate:** 3.1% (1995–2000), 2.6% (2000–05) **Population density:** (per sq km) 22.8 (1998 est) **Urban population:** (% of total) 22 (1997) **Age distribution:** (% of total population) 0–14 45.2%, 15–64 51.5%, 65+ 3.2% (1998) **Ethnic groups:** 60% Laotian, predominantly Lao Lum, 35% hill dwellers, and 5% Vietnamese and Chinese **Language:** Lao (official), French, English **Religion:** Theravāda Buddhist 85%, animist beliefs among mountain dwellers **Education:** (compulsory years) 5 **Literacy rate:** 92% (men); 76% (women) (1995 est) **Labour force:** 50% of population: 78% agriculture, 6% industry, 16% services (1990) **Life expectancy:** 52 (men); 55 (women) (1995–2000) **Child mortality rate:** (under 5, per 1,000 live births) 140 (1997) **Physicians:** 1 per 4,446 person (1993 est)

Practical information

Visa requirements: UK: visa required. USA: visa required **Embassy for the UK:** 74 avenue Raymond Poincaré, 75116 Paris, France. Tel: (1) 4553 0298; fax: (1) 4727 5789 **British embassy:** the UK has no diplomatic representation in Laos; the British Embassy in Bangkok (see Thailand) deals with enquiries relating to Laos **Chamber of commerce:** Lao National Chamber of Commerce and Industry, BP 4596, rue Phonsay, Vientiane. Tel: (21) 412 392; fax: (21) 414 383

Chronology

c. **2000–500** BC: Early Bronze Age civilizations in central Mekong River and Plain of Jars regions. **5th–8th centuries:** Occupied by immigrants from southern China. **8th century onwards:** Theravāda Buddhism spread by Mon monks. **9th–13th centuries:** Part of the sophisticated Khmer Empire, centred on Angkor in Cambodia. **12th century:** Small independent principalities, notably Louangphrabang, established by Lao invaders from Thailand and Yunnan, southern China; they adopted Buddhism. **14th century:** United by King Fa Ngum; the first independent Laotian state, Lan Xang, formed. It was to dominate for four centuries, broken only by a period of Burmese rule 1574–1637. **17th century:** First visited by Europeans. **1713:** The Lan Xang kingdom split into three separate kingdoms, Louangphrabang, Vientiane, and Champassac, which became tributaries of Siam (Thailand) from the late 18th century. **1893–1945:** Laos was a French protectorate, comprising the three principalities of Louangphrabang, Vientiane, and Champassac. **1945:** Temporarily occupied by Japan. **1946:** Retaken by France, despite opposition by the Chinese-backed Lao Issara (Free Laos) nationalist movement. **1950:** Granted semi-autonomy in French Union, as an associated state under the constitutional monarchy of the king of Louangphrabang. **1954:** Independence achieved from France under the Geneva Agreements, but civil war broke out between a moderate royalist faction of the Lao Issara, led by Prince Souvanna Phouma, and the communist Chinese-backed Pathet Lao (Land of the Lao) led by Prince Souphanouvong (Souvanna's half-brother). **1957:** Coalition government, headed by Souvanna Phouma, established by Vientiane Agreement. **1959:** Savang Vatthana became king. **1960:** Right-wing pro-Western government seized power, headed by Prince Boun Gum. **1962:** Geneva Agreement established new coalition government, led by Souvanna Phouma, but civil war continued, the Pathet Lao receiving backing from the North Vietnamese, and Souvanna Phouma from the USA. **1973:** Vientiane cease-fire agreement divided the country between the communists and the Souvanna Phouma regime and brought the withdrawal of US, Thai, and North Vietnamese forces. **1975:** Communists seized power; republic proclaimed, with Prince Souphanouvong as head of state and the Communist Party leader Kaysone Phomvihane as the controlling prime minister. **1979:** Food shortages and the flight of 250,000 refugees to Thailand led to an easing of the drive towards nationalization and agricultural collectivization. **1985:** Greater economic liberalization received encouragement from the Soviet Union's reformist leader Mikhail Gorbachev. **1989:** First assembly elections since communist takeover; Vietnamese troops withdrawn from the country. **1991:** Kaysone Phomvihane was elected president and the army commander General Khamtay Siphandon became prime minister. Security and cooperation pact signed with Thailand, and agreement reached on phased repatriation of Laotian refugees. **1992:** Phomvihane died; replaced as president by Nouhak Phoumsavan. **1995:** The US lifted its 20-year aid embargo. **1996:** Military tightened its grip on political affairs; but inward investment and private enterprise continued to be encouraged, fuelling economic expansion. **1997:** Membership of Association of South East Asian Nations (ASEAN) announced. **1998:** Khamtay Siphandon became president and was replaced as prime minister by Sisavath Keobounphanh.

Latvia Republic of

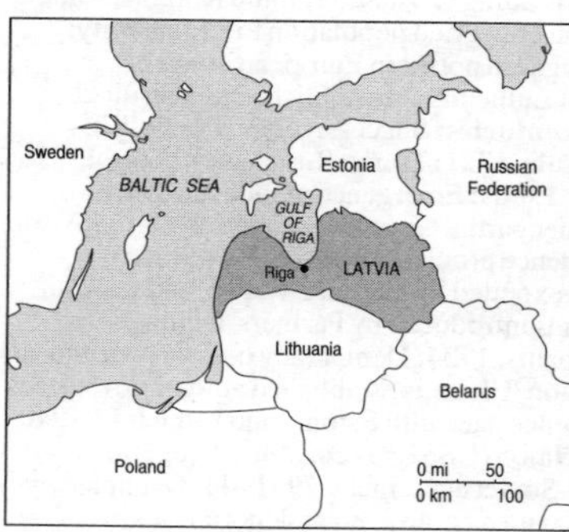

National name: *Latvijas Republika* **Area:** 63,700 sq km/24,594 sq mi **Capital:** Riga **Major towns/cities:** Daugavpils, Leipāja, Jurmala, Jelgava, Ventspils **Major ports:** Ventspils, Leipāja

Government

Head of state: Vaira Vike-Freiberga from 1999 **Head of government:** Vilis Kristopans from 1998 **Political system:** emergent democracy **Administrative divisions:** 26 districts and seven municipalities **Political parties:** Latvian Way, right of centre; Latvian National and Conservative Party (LNNK), right wing, nationalist; Economic-Political Union (formerly known as Harmony for Latvia and Rebirth of the National Economy), centrist; Ravnopravie (Equal Rights), centrist; For the Fatherland and Freedom (FFF), extreme nationalist; Latvian Peasants' Union (LZS), rural based, centre left; Union of Christian Democrats, centre right; Democratic Centre Party, centrist; Movement for Latvia, pro-Russian, populist; Master in Your Own Home (Saimnieks), ex-communist, populist; Latvian National Party of Reforms, right of centre nationalist coalition **Armed forces:** 4,500 (1997) **Conscription:** compulsory for 18 months **Death penalty:** retained and used for ordinary crimes **Defence spend:** (% GDP) 4.6 (1997) **Education spend:** (% GNP) 6.5 (1995) **Health spend:** (% GDP) 4.4 (1990–95)

Economy and resources
Currency: lat **GDP:** (US$) 5.4 billion (1997) **Real GDP growth:** (% change on previous year) 4.0 (1997) **GNP:** 6 billion (1997) **GNP per capita (PPP):** (US$) 3,650 (1997) **Consumer price inflation:** 8.5% (1998) **Unemployment:** 7.2% (1996) **Foreign debt:** (US$) 472 million (1996) **Major trading partners:** Russia, Germany, Lithuania, Finland, Sweden, Estonia **Resources:** peat, gypsum, dolomite, limestone, amber, gravel, sand **Exports:** timber and timber products, textiles, food and agricultural products, machinery and electrical equipment, metal industry products. Principal market: Russia 21% (1997) **Imports:** mineral fuels and products, machinery and electrical equipment, chemical industry products. Principal source: Germany 16% (1997) **Arable land:** 27.6% (1995)

Population and society
Population: 2,424,000 (1998 est) **Population growth rate:** –1.1% (1995–2000) **Population density:** (per sq km) 37 (1998 est) **Urban population:** (% of total) 74 (1997) **Age distribution:** (% of total population) 0–14 18.7%, 15–64 66.4%, 65+ 14.9% (1998) **Ethnic groups:** 53% of Latvian ethnic descent, 34% ethnic Russian, 4% Belarusian, 3% Ukrainian, 2% Polish, 1% Lithuanian **Language:** Latvian **Religion:** Lutheran, Roman Catholic, Russian Orthodox **Education:** (compulsory years) 9 **Literacy rate:** 99% (men); 99% (women) (1995 est) **Labour force:** 19.5% agriculture, 28.5% industry, 52% services (1993) **Life expectancy:** 63 (men); 74 (women) (1995–2000) **Child mortality rate:** (under 5, per 1,000 live births) 21 (1997) **Physicians:** 1 per 293 people (1994)

Practical information
Visa requirements: UK: visa not required. USA: visa required **Embassy in the UK:** 45 Nottingham Place, London W1M 3FE. Tel: (0171) 312 0040; fax: (0171) 312 0042 **British embassy:** Alunana iela 5, LV-1010 Riga. Tel: (371) 782 8126; fax: (371) 733 8132 **Chamber of commerce:** Latvian Chamber of Commerce and Industry, Brivibas bulvaris 21, LV-1849 Riga. Tel: (371) 722 5595; fax: (371) 782 0092

Chronology
9th–10th centuries: Invaded by Vikings and Russians. **13th century:** Conquered by crusading German Teutonic Knights, who named the area Livonia and converted population to Christianity; Riga joined Hanseatic League, a northern European union of commercial towns. **1520s:** Lutheranism established as a result of Reformation. **16th–17th centuries:** Successively under Polish, Lithuanian, and Swedish rule. **1721:** Tsarist Russia took control. **1819:** Serfdom abolished. **1900s:** Emergence of independence movement. **1914–18:** Under partial German occupation during World War I. **1918–19:** Independence proclaimed and achieved after Russian Red Army troops expelled by German, Polish, and Latvian forces. **1920s:** Land reforms introduced by Farmers' Union government of Karlis Ulmanis. **1934:** Democracy overthrown and, at time of economic depression, Ulmanis established autocratic regime; Baltic Entente mutual defence pact with Estonia and Lithuania. **1940:** Incorporated into Soviet Union (USSR) as constituent republic, following secret German–Soviet agreement. **1941–44:** Occupied by Germany. **1944:** USSR regained control; mass deportations of Latvians to Central Asia, followed by immigration of ethnic Russians; agricultural collectivization. **1960s and 1970s:** Extreme repression of Latvian cultural and literary life. **1980s:** Nationalist dissent began to grow, influenced by the Polish Solidarity movement and Mikhail Gorbachev's *glasnost* ('openness') initiative in the USSR. **1988:** Latvian Popular Front established to campaign for independence. Prewar flag readopted; official status given to Latvian language. **1989:** Latvian parliament passed sovereignty declaration. **1990:** Popular Front secured majority in local elections and its leader, Ivan Godmanir, became prime minister. Latvian Communist Party split into pro-independence and pro-Moscow wings. Entered 'transitional period of independence'; Baltic Council reformed. **1991:** Soviet troops briefly seized key installations in Riga. Overwhelming vote for independence in referendum. Full independence achieved following failure of anti-Gorbachev coup attempt in Moscow; Communist Party outlawed. Joined United Nations (UN); market-centred economic reform programme instituted. **1992:** Curbing of rights of noncitizens prompted Russia to request minority protection by UN. **1993:** Right-of-centre Latvian Way won general election, and Valdis Birkavs became premier; free-trade agreement with Estonia and Lithuania. **1994:** Last Russian troops departed. Birkavs replaced by Maris Gailis; economic growth resumed. **1995:** Trade and cooperation agreement signed with European Union (EU). General election produced 'hung parliament', in which extremist parties received most support. Applied for EU membership. Independent Andris Skele became prime minister. **1996:** Guntis Ulmanis re-elected president. Finance minister and deputy prime minister resigned from eight-party coalition. **1997:** New political party formed, Latvian National Party of Reforms. Prime Minister Skele replaced by Guntar Krasts. Former Communist leader Alfreds Rubiks released from prison. **1998:** DPS withdrew from the government, leaving the coalition as a minority. Citizenship laws relaxed to make it easier for ethnic Russians to acquire citizenship. A general election produced a hung parliament; Vilis Kristopans (Latvia's Way) became prime minister, heading a three-party minority coalition government, which was pledged to continued privatization and improving relations with Russia.

Lebanon Republic of

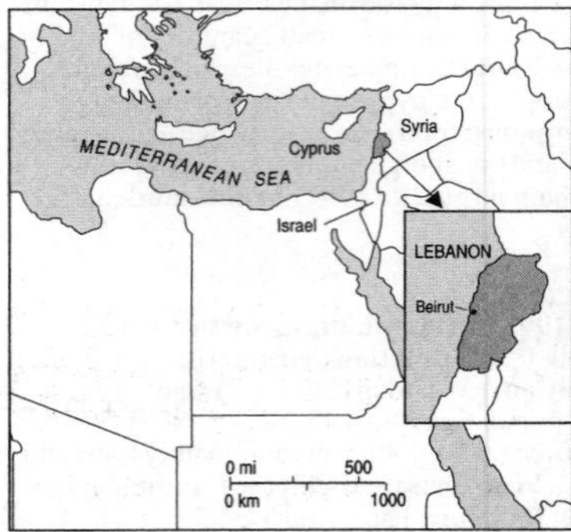

National name: *Jumhouria al-Lubnaniya* **Area:** 10,452 sq km/4,035 sq mi **Capital:** Beirut (and port) **Major towns/cities:** Tripoli, Zahlé, Baabda, Baalbek, Jezzine **Major ports:** Tripoli, Tyre, Sidon, Jounie

Government
Head of state: Emile Lahoud from 1998 **Head of government:** Salim al-Hoss from 1998 **Political system:** emergent democracy **Administrative divisions:** six governates **Political parties:** Phalangist Party, Christian, radical, nationalist; Progressive Socialist Party (PSP), Druse, moderate, socialist; National Liberal Party (NLP), Maronite, centre left; National Bloc, Maronite, moderate; Lebanese Communist Party (PCL), nationalist, communist; Parliamentary Democratic Front, Sunni Muslim, centrist **Armed forces:** 55,100 (1997); in 1995 there were 30,000 Syrian troops and the pro-Israeli South Lebanese army numbered 2,500 **Conscription:** compulsory for 12 months **Death penalty:** retained and used for ordinary crimes **Defence spend:** (% GDP) 4.5 (1997) **Education spend:** (% GNP) 2.5 (1996) **Health spend:** (% GDP) 2.1 (1990–95)

Economy and resources
Currency: Lebanese pound **GDP:** (US$) 14.9 billion (1997) **Real GDP growth:** (% change on previous year) 3.2 (1997) **GNP:** 13.9 billion (1997) **GNP per capita (PPP):** (US$) 5,990 (1997) **Consumer price inflation:** 6.0% (1998) **Unemployment:** 35% (1993 est) **Foreign debt:** (US$) 3.99 billion (1996) **Major trading partners:** United Arab Emirates, Italy, Saudi Arabia, Syria, Germany, USA, France, Kuwait, Jordan **Resources:** there are no commercially viable mineral deposits; small reserves of lignite and iron ore **Exports:** paper products, textiles, fruit and vegetables, jewellery. Principal market: Saudi Arabia 14.1% (1997) **Imports:** electrical equipment, vehicles, petroleum, metals, machinery, consumer goods. Principal source: Italy 13.2% (1997) **Arable land:** 20.7% (1995)

Population and society
Population: 3,191,000 (1998 est) **Population growth rate:** 1.8% (1995–2000) **Population density:** (per sq km) 342.7 (1998 est) **Urban population:** (% of total) 89 (1997) **Age distribution:** (% of total population) 0–14 29.8%, 15–64 63.8%, 65+ 6.4% (1998) **Ethnic groups:** about 90% Arab, with Armenian, Assyrian, Jewish, Turkish,

and Greek minorities **Language:** Arabic (official), French, Armenian, English **Religion:** Muslim 58% (Shiite 35%, Sunni 23%), Christian 27% (mainly Maronite), Druse 3%; other Christian denominations including Orthodox, Armenian, and Roman Catholic **Education:** not compulsory **Literacy rate:** 88% (men); 73% (women) (1995 est) **Labour force:** 31% of population: 7% agriculture, 31% industry, 62% services (1990) **Life expectancy:** 68 (men); 72 (women) (1995–2000) **Child mortality rate:** (under 5, per 1,000 live births) 33 (1997) **Physicians:** 1 per 537 people (1993 est)

Practical information

Visa requirements: UK: visa required. USA: visa required **Embassy in the UK:** 21 Kensington Palace Gardens, London W8 4QH. (0171) 229 7265; fax: (0171) 243 1699 **British embassy:** British Embassy in West Beirut, Shamma Building, Raoucheh, Ras Beirut. Tel: (1) 812 849; telex: 20465 **Chamber of commerce:** Beirut Chamber of Commerce and Industry, PO Box 11-1801, Sanayeh, Beirut. Tel: (1) 349 530; fax: (1) 865 802

Chronology

5th century BC–1st century AD: Part of the eastern Mediterranean Phoenician Empire. **1st century:** Came under Roman rule; Christianity introduced. **635:** Islam introduced by Arab tribes, who settled in southern Lebanon. **11th century:** Druse faith developed by local Muslims. **1516:** Became part of the Turkish Ottoman Empire. **1860:** Massacre of thousands of Christian Maronites by the Muslim Druse led to French intervention. **1920–41:** Administered by French under League of Nations mandate. **1943:** Independence achieved as a republic, with constitution that enshrined Christian and Muslim power-sharing. **1945:** Joined Arab League. **1948–49:** Lebanon joined first Arab war against Israel; Palestinian refugees settled in south. **1958:** Revolt by radical Muslims opposed to pro-Western policies of Christian president, Camille Chamoun. **1964:** Palestine Liberation Organization (PLO) founded in Beirut. **1967:** More Palestinian refugees settled in Lebanon following Arab–Israeli war. **1971:** PLO expelled from Jordan; established headquarters in Lebanon. **1975:** Outbreak of civil war between conservative Christians and leftist Muslims backed by PLO. **1976:** Cease-fire agreed; Syrian-dominated Arab deterrent force formed to keep the peace, but considered by Christians as an occupying force. **1978:** Israel launched limited invasion of southern Lebanon in search of PLO guerrillas. International United Nations peacekeeping force unable to prevent further fighting. **1979:** Part of southern Lebanon declared an 'independent free Lebanon' by right-wing army officer. **1982:** Bachir Gemayel, a Maronite Christian, elected president but assassinated; he was succeeded by his brother Amin Gemayel. Israel again invaded Lebanon. Palestinians withdrew from Beirut under supervision of international peacekeeping force; PLO moved its headquarters to Tunis. **1983:** Agreement reached for withdrawal of Syrian and Israeli troops but abrogated under Syrian pressure; intense fighting between Christian Phalangists and Muslim Druse militias. **1984:** Most of international peacekeeping force withdrawn. Radical Muslim militia took control of west Beirut. **1985:** Lebanon in chaos; many foreigners taken hostage and Israeli troops withdrawn. **1987:** Syrian troops sent into Beirut. **1988:** Agreement on Christian successor to Gemayel failed and Gen Michel Aoun appointed to head caretaker military government; Premier Selim el-Hoss set up rival government; threat of partition hung over country. **1989:** Gen Aoun declared 'war of liberation' against Syrian occupation; Arab League-sponsored talks resulted in cease-fire and revised constitution recognizing Muslim majority; René Mouhawad assassinated after 17 days as president; Maronite Christian Elias Hrawi named as successor; Aoun occupied presidential palace, rejecting constitution. **1990:** Release of Western hostages began. Gen Aoun, crushed by Syrians, surrendered and legitimate government was restored. **1991:** Government extended control to the whole country. Treaty of cooperation with Syria signed. **1992:** Remaining Western hostages released. Pro-Syrian administration re-elected with Rafik al-Hariri as prime minister after many Christians boycotted general election. **1993:** Israel launched attacks against Shia fundamentalist Hezbollah strongholds in southern Lebanon before USA and Syria brokered agreement to avoid use of force. **1996:** Israel launched rocket attack on southern Lebanon in response to Hezbollah activity. USA, Israel, Syria, and Lebanon attempted to broker new cease-fire. **1998:** Army chief, General Emile Lahoud, became president. Salim al-Hoss replaced Rafiq al-Hariri as prime minister. **1999:** Israeli withdrawal from southern Lebanon.

Lesotho Kingdom of

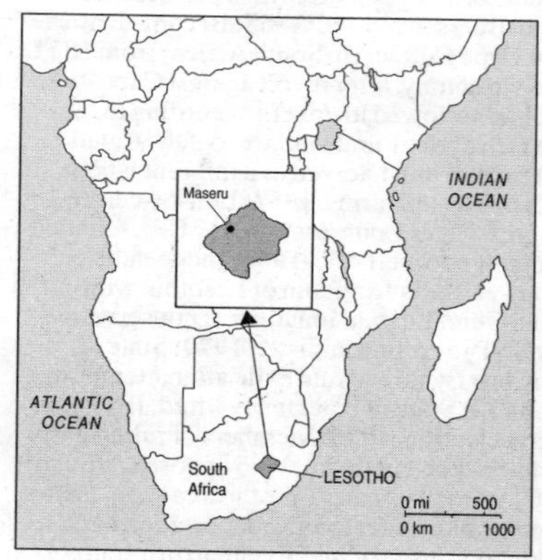

Area: 30,355 sq km/ 11,720 sq mi **Capital:** Maseru **Major towns/cities:** Qacha's Nek, Teyateyaneng, Mafeteng, Hlotse, Roma, Quthing

Government

Head of state: King Letsie III from 1996 **Head of government:** Bethuel Pakulitha Mosisili from 1998 **Political system:** constitutional monarchy **Administrative divisions:** ten districts **Political parties:** Basotho National Party (BNP), traditionalist, nationalist, right of centre; Basutoland Congress Party (BCP), left of centre **Armed forces:** 2,000 (1997) **Conscription:** military service is voluntary **Death penalty:** retained and used for ordinary crimes **Defence spend:** (% GDP) 4.6 (1997) **Education spend:** (% GNP) 5.9 (1995) **Health spend:** (% GDP) 3.5 (1990–95)

Economy and resources

Currency: loti **GDP:** (US$) 950 million (1997) **Real GDP growth:** (% change on previous year) 10.0 (1997) **GNP:** 1.4 billion (1997) **GNP per capita (PPP):** (US$) 2,480 (1997 est) **Consumer price inflation:** 11% (1997) **Unemployment:** 50% (1993 est) **Foreign debt:** (US$) 654 million (1996) **Major trading partners:** SACU (South African Customs Union) members: Lesotho, Botswana, Swaziland, Namibia, and South Africa); Taiwan, Hong Kong, USA, Canada, Italy, and other EU countries **Resources:** diamonds, uranium, lead, iron ore; believed to have petroleum deposits **Exports:** clothing, footwear, furniture, food and live animals (cattle), hides, wool and mohair, baskets. Principal market: SACU 66.3% (1996) **Imports:** food and live animals, machinery and transport equipment, electricity, petroleum products. Principal source: SACU 81.8% (1996) **Arable land:** 10.5% (1995)

Population and society

Population: 2,062,000 (1998 est) **Population growth rate:** 2.5% (1995–2000) **Population density:** (per sq km) 68.9 (1998 est) **Urban population:** (% of total) 26 (1997) **Age distribution:** (% of total population) 0–14 40.2%, 15–64 55.3%, 65+ 4.6% (1998) **Ethnic groups:** almost entirely Bantus (of Southern Sotho) or Basotho **Language:** Sesotho, English (official), Zulu, Xhosa **Religion:** Protestant 42%, Roman Catholic 38%, indigenous beliefs **Education:** (compulsory years) 7 **Literacy rate:** 62% (men); 84% (women) (1995 est) **Labour force:** 76.3% agriculture, 11.1% industry, 12.6% services (1994 est) **Life expectancy:** 57 (men); 60 (women) (1995–2000) **Child mortality rate:** (under 5, per 1,000 live births) 94 (1997) **Physicians:** 1 per 14,306 people (1993)

Practical information

Visa requirements: UK: visa not required for visits of up to 30 days. USA: visa required **Embassy in the UK:** 7 Chesham Place, Belgravia, London SW1 8HN. Tel: (0171) 235 5686; fax: (0171) 235 5023 **British embassy:** British High Commission, PO Box Ms 521, Maseru 100. Tel: (266) 313 961; fax: (266) 310 120 **Chamber of commerce:** Lesotho Chamber of Commerce and Industry, PO Box 79, Maseru 100. Tel: (266) 323 482

Chronology

18th century: Formerly inhabited by nomadic hunter-gatherer San, Zulu-speaking Ngunis, and Sotho-speaking peoples settled in the region. **1820s:** Under the name of Basutoland, Sotho nation founded by Moshoeshoe I, who united the people to repulse Zulu attacks from south. **1843:** Moshoeshoe I negotiated British protection as tension with South African Boers increased. **1868:** Became British territory, administered by Cape Colony (in South Africa) from 1871. **1884:** Became British crown colony, after revolt against Cape Colony control; Basuto chiefs allowed to govern according to custom and tradition, but rich agricultural land west of the Caledon River was lost to South Africa. **1900s:** Served as a migrant labour reserve for South Africa's mines and farms. **1952:** Left-of-centre Basutoland African Congress, later Congress Party (BCP), founded by Ntsu Mokhehle to campaign for self rule. **1966:** Independence achieved within Commonwealth, as Kingdom of Lesotho, with Moshoeshoe II as king and Chief Leabua Jonathan of conservative Basotho National Party (BNP) as prime minister. **1970:** State of emergency declared; king briefly forced into exile after attempting to increase his authority. **1973:** State of emergency lifted; BNP won majority of seats in general election. **1975:** Members of ruling party attacked by South African-backed guerrillas, who opposed African National Congress (ANC) guerrillas using Lesotho as a base. **1986:** South Africa imposed border blockade, forcing deportation of 60 ANC members. Gen Lekhanya ousted Chief Jonathan in a coup. **1990:** Lekhanya replaced in coup by Col Elias Ramaema; Moshoeshoe II dethroned and replaced by son, as King Letsie III. **1993:** Free multiparty elections ended military rule; Ntsu Mokhehle (BCP) became prime minister. **1994:** Fighting between rival army factions ended by peace deal, brokered by Organization of African Unity. **1995:** King Letsie III abdicated to restore King Moshoeshoe II to the throne. **1996:** King Moshoeshoe II killed in car accident; King Letsie III restored to throne. **1998:** LCD general election victory amidst claims of rigged polls; public demonstrations followed. South Africa sent troops to support the government. Government talks with the opposition not progressing. Violent demonstrations in the capital. Interim political authority appointed prior to new elections.

Liberia Republic of

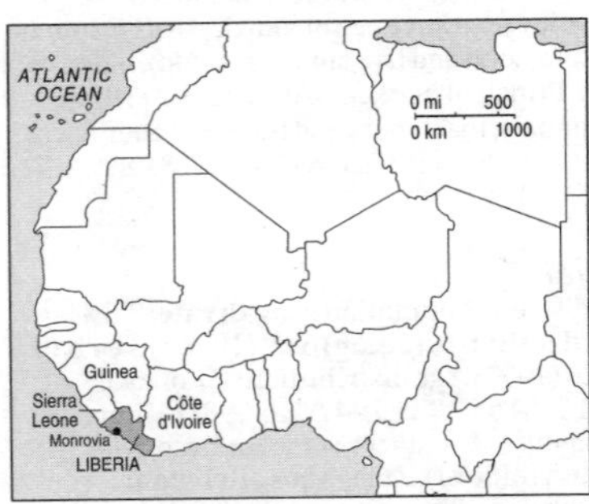

Area: 111,370 sq km/42,999 sq mi **Capital:** Monrovia (and port) **Major towns/cities:** Bensonville, Saniquillie, Gbarnga, Voinjama, Buchanan **Major ports:** Buchanan, Greenville

Government

Head of state and government: Ruth Perry from 1996 **Political system:** emergent democracy **Administrative divisions:** 13 counties **Political parties:** National Democratic Party of Liberia (NDPL), nationalist, left of centre; National Patriotic Front of Liberia (NPFL), left of centre; United Democratic Movement of Liberia for Democracy (Ulimo), left of centre; National Patriotic Party (NPP) **Armed forces:** 22,000 (1997) **Conscription:** military service is voluntary **Death penalty:** retained and used for ordinary crimes **Defence spend:** (% GDP) 3.9 (1997) **Education spend:** (% GNP) 2.7 (1988) **Health spend:** (% GDP) 3.5 (1990)

Economy and resources

Currency: Liberian dollar **GDP:** (US$) 2.4 billion (1995) **Real GDP growth:** (% change on previous year) N/A **GNP:** N/A **GNP per capita (PPP):** (US$) N/A **Consumer price inflation:** 100% (1996) **Unemployment:** 80% (1995 est) **Foreign debt:** (US$) 2.1 billion (1996) **Major trading partners:** Belgium/Luxembourg, Japan, USA, Germany, the Netherlands, Italy, France **Resources:** iron ore, diamonds, gold, barytes, kyanite **Exports:** iron ore, rubber, timber, coffee, cocoa, palm-kernel oil, diamonds, gold. Principal market: Belgium/Luxembourg 36.2% (1997) **Imports:** machinery and transport equipment, mineral fuels, rice, basic manufactures, food and live animals. Principal source: South Korea 38.4% (1997) **Arable land:** 1.3% (1995)

Population and society

Population: 2,666,000 (1998 est) **Population growth rate:** 8.6% (1995–2000) **Population density:** (per sq km) 28.8 (1998 est) **Urban population:** (% of total) 46 (1997) **Age distribution:** (% of total population) 0–14 44.7%, 15–64 51.8%, 65+ 3.5% (1998) **Ethnic groups:** 95% indigenous peoples, including the Kpelle, Bassa, Gio, Kru, Grebo, Mano, Krahn, Gola, Ghandi, Loma, Kissi, Vai, and Bella; 5% descended from repatriated US slaves **Language:** English (official), over 20 Niger-Congo languages **Religion:** animist, Sunni Muslim, Christian **Education:** (compulsory years) 9 **Literacy rate:** 50% (men); 29% (women) (1995 est) **Labour force:** 41% of population: 72% agriculture, 6% industry, 22% services (1990) **Life expectancy:** 50 (men); 53 (women) (1995–2000) **Child mortality rate:** (under 5, per 1,000 live births) 200 (1997)

Practical information

Visa requirements: UK: visa required. USA: visa required **Embassy in the UK:** 2 Pembridge Place, London W2 4XB. Tel: (0171) 221 1036 **British embassy:** the British High Commission in Abidjan (see Ivory Coast) deals with enquiries relating to Liberia **Chamber of commerce:** PO Box 92, Monrovia. Tel: (231) 223 738; telex: 44211

Chronology

1821: Purchased by philanthropic American Colonization Society and turned into settlement for liberated black slaves from southern USA. **1847:** Recognized as an independent republic. **1869:** The True Whig Party founded, which was to dominate politics for more than a century, providing all presidents. **1926:** Large concession sold to Firestone Rubber Company as foreign indebtedness increased. **1944:** William Tubman, descendant of US slaves, elected president. **1971:** Tubman died; succeeded by William Tolbert. **1980:** Tolbert assassinated in military coup led by Sgt Samuel Doe, who banned political parties and launched anticorruption drive. **1984:** New constitution approved in referendum. National Democratic Party (NDPL) founded by Doe as political parties relegalized. **1985:** Doe and the NDPL won decisive victories in allegedly rigged elections. **1990:** Doe killed as bloody civil war broke out, involving Charles Taylor and Gen Hezekiah Bowen, who led rival rebel armies, the National Patriotic Front (NPFL) and the Armed Forces of Liberia (AFL). War left 150,000 dead and 2 million homeless. West African peacekeeping force drafted in. Amos Sawyer, with NPFL backing, became interim head of government. **1992:** Monrovia under siege by Taylor's rebel forces. **1993:** Peace agreement signed, but soon collapsed. **1995:** Ghanaian-backed peace proposals accepted by rebel factions; interim Council of State established, comprising leaders of three main rebel factions and chaired by Wilton Sankawulo. **1996:** Renewed fighting in capital. Peace plan reached in talks convened by the Economic Community of West African States (ECOWAS); Ruth Perry became Liberia's first female head of state. **1997:** National Patriotic Party (NPP), led by Charles Taylor, won majority in assembly elections. **1998:** Fighting in Monrovia between President Taylor's forces and opposition militias.

Libya Great Socialist People's Libyan Arab Republic

National name: *Jamahiriya al-Arabiya al-Libya al-Shabiya al-Ishtirakiya al-Uzma* **Area:** 1,759,540 sq km/679,358 sq mi **Capital:** Tripoli **Towns and cities:** Benghazi, Misurata, Az-Zaiwa, Tobruk, Ajdabiya, Derna **Major ports:** Benghazi, Misurata, Az-Zaiwa, Tobruk, Ajdabiya, Derna

Government

Head of state and government: Moamer al-Khaddhafi from 1969 **Political system:** one-party socialist state **Administrative divisions:** 25 municipalities **Political party:** Arab Socialist Union (ASU), radical, left wing **Armed forces:** 65,000 (1997) **Conscription:** conscription is selective for two years **Death penalty:** retained and used for ordinary crimes **Defence spend:** (% GDP) 4.7 (1997) **Education spend:** (% GNP) 9.6 (1986); N/A (1993–94)

Economy and resources

Currency: Libyan dinar **GDP:** (US$) 29.7 billion (1995) **Real GDP growth:** (% change on previous year) 0.5 (1997) **GNP:** 23.4 billion (1994 est) **GNP per capita (PPP):** (US$) 5,470 (1994 est) **Consumer price inflation:** 30% (1998) **Unemployment:** 30% (1995 est) **Foreign debt:** (US$) 4.2 billion (1996 est) **Major trading partners:** Italy, Germany, Greece, Spain, UK, France, Turkey, Morocco, the Netherlands **Resources:** petroleum, natural gas, iron ore, potassium, magnesium, sulphur, gypsum **Exports:** crude petroleum (accounted for 94% of 1991 export earnings), chemicals and related products. Principal market: Italy 39.8% (1995) **Imports:** machinery and transport equipment, basic manufactures, food and live animals, miscellaneous manufactured articles. Principal source: Italy 21.7% (1995) **Arable land:** 1% (1995)

Population and society

Population: 5,339,000 (1998 est) **Population growth rate:** 3.3% (1995–2000); 3.2% (2000–05) **Population density:** (per sq km) 3.2 (1998 est) **Urban population:** (% of total) 86 (1997) **Age distribution:** (% of total population) 0–14 48.3%, 15–64 48.7%, 65+ 2.9% (1998) **Ethnic groups:** majority are of Berber and Arab origin, with a small number of Tebou and Touareg nomads and semi-nomads, mainly in south **Language:** Arabic **Religion:** Sunni Muslim **Education:** (compulsory years) 9 **Literacy rate:** 75% (men); 50% (women) (1995 est) **Labour force:** 29% of population: 18% agriculture, 31% industry, 51% services (1990) **Life expectancy:** 64 (men); 68 (women) (1995–2000) **Child mortality rate:** (under 5, per 1,000 live births) 75 (1997) **Physicians:** 1 per 957 people (1993 est)

Practical information

Visa requirements: UK: visa required. USA: visa required **Embassy for the UK:** British Interests Section, c/o Embassy of the Italian Republic, PO Box 4206, Sharia Uahran 1, Tripoli. Tel: (21) 333 1191; telex: 20296 (a/b BRITEMB LY) **British embassy:** c/o Permanent Mission of the Socialist People's Libyan Arab Jamahiriya to the United Nations, 309–315 East 48th Street, New York, NY 10017, USA. Tel: (212) 752 5775; fax: (212) 593 4787. Paris Libyan People's Bureau. Tel: (1) 4720 1970 **Chamber of commerce:** Tripoli Chamber of Commerce, Industry and Agriculture, PO Box 2321, Sharia al-Fatah September, Tripoli. Tel: (21) 333 3755; telex: 20181

Chronology

7th century BC: Tripolitania, in western Libya, was settled by Phoenicians, who founded Tripoli; it became an eastern province of Carthaginian kingdom, which was centred on Tunis to the west. **4th century BC:** Cyrenaica, in eastern Libya, colonized by Greeks, who called it Libya. **74 BC:** Became a Roman province, with Tripolitania part of Africa Nova province and Cyrenaica combined with Crete as a province. **19 BC:** The desert region of Fezzan (Phazzania), inhabited by Garmante people, was conquered by Rome. **6th century AD:** Came under control of Byzantine Empire. **7th century:** Conquered by Arabs, who spread Islam: Egypt ruled Cyrenaica and Morrocan Berber Almohads controlled Tripolitania. **mid-16th century:** Became part of Turkish Ottoman Empire, who combined the three ancient regions into one regency in Tripoli. **1711:** Karamanli (Qaramanli) dynasty established virtual independence from Ottomans. **1835:** Ottoman control reasserted. **1911–12:** Conquered by Italy. **1920s:** Resistance to Italian rule by Sanusi order and Umar al-Mukhtar. **1934:** Colony named Libya. **1942:** Italians ousted, and area divided into three provinces: Fezzan (under French control), Cyrenaica, and Tripolitania (under British control). **1951:** Achieved independence as United Kingdom of Libya, under King Idris, former Amir of Cyrenaica and leader of Sanusi order. **1959:** Discovery of oil transformed economy, but also led to unsettling social changes. **1969:** King deposed in military coup led by Col Moamer al-Khaddhafi. Revolution Command Council set up and Arab Socialist Union (ASU) proclaimed the only legal party in a new puritanical Islamic-socialist republic which sought Pan-Arab unity. **1970s:** Economic activity collectivized, oil industry nationalized, opposition suppressed by Khaddhafi's revolutionary regime. **1972:** Proposed federation of Libya, Syria, and Egypt abandoned. **1980:** Proposed merger with Syria abandoned. Libyan troops began fighting in northern Chad. **1986:** US bombed Khaddhafi's headquarters, following allegations of his complicity in terrorist activities. **1988:** Diplomatic relations with Chad restored; political prisoners freed; economy liberalized. **1989:** US navy shot down two Libyan planes; reconciliation with Egypt. **1992:** Khaddhafi under international pressure to extradite suspected Lockerbie and UTA (Union de Transports Aérians) bombers for trial outside Libya. United Nations sanctions imposed; several countries severed diplomatic and air links with Libya. **1995:** Antigovernment campaign of violence by Islamicists. Hundreds of Palestinians and thousands of foreign workers expelled. **1999:** Lockerbie bomb suspects handed over to stand trial by Scottish judges sitting in Holland. Diplomatic relations with UK restored.

Liechtenstein Principality of

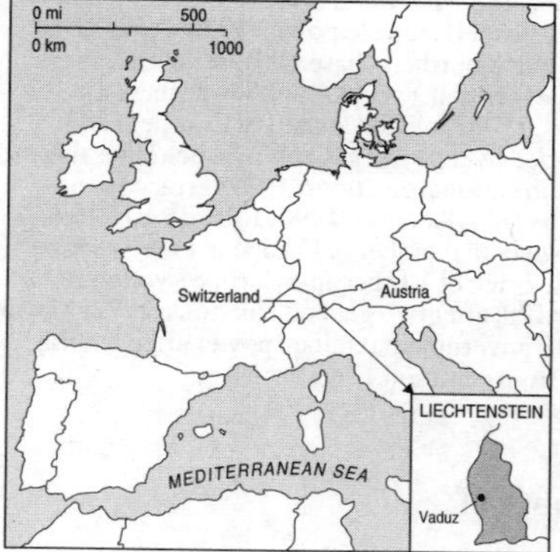

National name: *Fürstentum Liechtenstein* **Area:** 160 sq km/62 sq mi **Capital:** Vaduz **Major towns/cities:** Balzers, Schaan, Ruggell, Triesen, Eschen

Government

Head of state: Prince Hans Adam II from 1989 **Head of government:** Mario Frick from 1993 **Political system:** constitutional monarchy **Administrative divisions:** 11 communes **Political parties:** Patriotic Union (VU), conservative; Progressive Citizens' Party (FBP), conservative **Armed forces:** no standing army since 1868; there is a police force of 59 men and 19 auxiliaries **Conscription:** in an emergency Liechtensteiners under the age of 60 are liable to military service **Death penalty:** abolished in 1987 (last execution in 1785)

Economy and resources

Currency: Swiss franc **GDP:** (US$) 1.3 billion (1995) **Real GDP growth:** (% change on previous year) 0.7 (1995) **GNP:** 1.35 billion (1995 est) **GNP per capita (PPP):** (US$) 25,100 (1995 est) **Consumer price inflation:** 0.8% (1996) **Unemployment:** 1% (1994) **Major trading partners:** Switzerland and other EFTA countries, EU countries **Resources:** hydro power **Exports:** small machinery, artificial teeth and other material for dentistry, stamps, precision instruments, ceramics. Principal market: Switzerland 14% (1994)

Imports: machinery and transport equipment, foodstuffs, textiles, metal goods. Principal source: Switzerland **Arable land:** 25% (1995)

Population and society

Population: 32,000 (1998 est) **Population growth rate:** 1.1% (1995–2000) **Population density:** (per sq km) 197 (1998 est) **Urban population:** (% of total) 21 (1995) **Age distribution:** (% of total population) 0–14 18.9%, 15–64 70.1%, 65+ 11.0% (1998) **Ethnic groups:** indigenous population of Alemannic origin; one-third of the population are foreign-born resident workers **Language:** German (official); an Alemannic dialect is also spoken **Religion:** Roman Catholic (87%), Protestant **Education:** (compulsory years) 8 **Literacy rate:** 99% (men); 99% (women) (1995 est) **Labour force:** 1.7% agriculture, 47.6% industry, 50.7% services (1994) **Life expectancy:** 78 (men); 83 (women) (1995–2000) **Child mortality rate:** (per 1,000 live births) 0.03 (1993)

Practical information

Visa requirements: UK: visa not required. USA: visa not required **Embassy in the UK:** Liechtenstein is generally represented overseas by Switzerland **British embassy:** enquiries relating to Liechtenstein are dealt with by the British Consulate General, Dufourstrasse 56, CH-8008 Zürich, Switzerland. Tel: (1) 261 1520–6; fax: (1) 252 8351 **Chamber of commerce:** Liechtenstein Industrie-und Handeslkammer (Chamber of Industry and Commerce), Postfach 232, Josef Rheinberger-Strasse 11, FL-9490 Vaduz. Tel: (4175) 232 2744; fax: (4175) 233 1503

Chronology

c. AD **500:** Settled by Germanic-speaking Alemanni tribe. **1342:** Became sovereign state. **1434:** Present boundaries established. **1719:** Former independent lordships of Schellenberg and Vaduz were united by Princes of Liechtenstein to form present state. **1815–66:** A member of German Confederation. **1868:** Abolished standing armed forces. **1871:** Liechtenstein was only German principality to stay outside newly formed German Empire. **1918:** Patriotic Union (VU) party founded, drawing most support from the mountainous south. **1919:** Switzerland replaced Austria as foreign representative of Liechtenstein. **1921:** Adopted Swiss currency; constitution created a parliament. **1923:** United with Switzerland in customs and monetary union. **1938:** Prince Franz Josef II came to power. **1970:** After 42 years as main governing party, northern-based Progressive Citizens' Party (FBP) defeated by VU which, except for 1974–78, became dominant force in politics. **1978:** Joined Council of Europe. **1984:** Prince Franz Josef II handed over power to Crown Prince Hans Adam. Vote extended to women in national elections. **1989:** Prince Franz Josef II died; succeeded by Hans Adam II. **1990:** Joined the United Nations. **1991:** Became seventh member of European Free Trade Association. **1993:** Mario Frick of VU became Europe's youngest head of government, aged 28, after two general elections. **1997:** Mario Frick and ruling VU–FBP government retained power after general election. FBP withdrew from coalition.

Lithuania Republic of

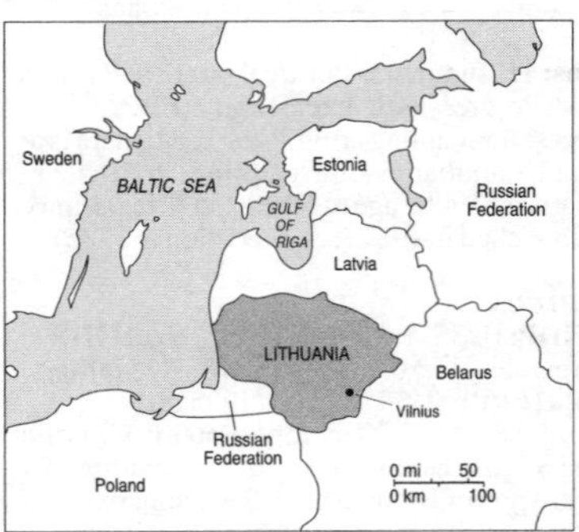

National name: *Lietuvos Respublika* **Area:** 65,200 sq km/25,173 sq mi **Capital:** Vilnius **Major towns/cities:** Kaunas, Klaipeda, Siauliai, Panevezys

Government

Head of state: Valdas Adamkus from 1998 **Head of government:** Rolandas Paksas from 1999 **Political system:** emergent democracy **Administrative divisions:** 12 regions **Political parties:** Lithuanian Democratic Labour Party (LDLP), reform-socialist (ex-communist); Homeland Union–Lithuanian Conservatives (Tevynes Santara), right of centre, nationalist; Christian Democratic Party of Lithuania, centre right; Lithuanian Social Democratic Party, left of centre **Armed forces:** 5,300 (1997) **Conscription:** military service is compulsory for 12 months **Death penalty:** retained and used for ordinary crimes **Defence spend:** (% GDP) 4.4 (1997) **Education spend:** (% GNP) 5.6 (1996) **Health spend:** (% GDP) 5.1 (1990–95)

Economy and resources

Currency: litas **GDP:** (US$) 9.2 billion (1997) **Real GDP growth:** (% change on previous year) 3.8 (1997) **GNP:** 8.3 billion (1997) **GNP per capita (PPP):** (US$) 4,510 (1997) **Consumer price inflation:** 8.0% (1998) **Unemployment:** 6.2% (1996) **Foreign debt:** (US$) 1.28 billion (1996) **Major trading partners:** Russia, Germany, Belarus, Latvia, Ukraine, Poland, Italy, the Netherlands **Resources:** small deposits of petroleum, natural gas, peat, limestone, gravel, clay, sand **Exports:** textiles, machinery and equipment, non-precious metals, animal products, timber. Principal market: Russia 24.5 (1997) **Imports:** petroleum and natural gas products, machinery and transport equipment, chemicals, fertilizers, consumer goods. Principal source: Russia 24.3% (1997) **Arable land:** 45.5% (1995)

Population and society

Population: 3,694,000 (1998 est) **Population growth rate:** –0.3% (1995–2000) **Population density:** (per sq km) 55.2 (1998 est) **Urban population:** (% of total) 73 (1997) **Age distribution:** (% of total population) 0–14 20.5%, 15–64 66.5%, 65+ 13.0% (1998) **Ethnic groups:** 80% Lithuanian ethnic descent, 9% ethnic Russian, 7% Polish, 2% Belarussian, 1% Ukrainian **Language:** Lithuanian (official) **Religion:** predominantly Roman Catholic; Lithuanian Lutheran Church **Education:** (compulsory years) 9 **Literacy rate:** 98% (men); 98% (women) (1995 est) **Labour force:** 19.6% agriculture, 38% industry, 42.4% services (1992) **Life expectancy:** 65 (men); 76 (women) (1995–2000) **Child mortality rate:** (under 5, per 1,000 live births) 16 (1997) **Physicians:** 1 per 247 people (1994)

Practical information

Visa requirements: UK: visa not required for a stay of up to 90 days. USA: visa not required for a stay of up to 90 days **Embassy in the UK:** 17 Essex Villas, London W8 7BP. Tel: (0171) 938 2481; fax: (0171) 938 3329 **British embassy:** PO Box 863, Anta Kalnio 2, 2055 Vilnius. Tel: (2) 222 070; fax: (2) 357 579 **Chamber of commerce:** Association of Lithuanian Chambers of Commerce and Industry, Kudirkos 18, 2600 Vilnius. Tel: (2) 222 630; fax: (2) 222 621

Chronology

late 12th century: Became a separate nation. **1230:** Mindaugas united Lithuanian tribes to resist attempted invasions by German and Livonian Teutonic Knights, and adopted Christianity. **14th century:** Strong Grand Duchy formed by Gediminas, founder of Vilnius and Jogaila dynasty, and his son, Algirdas; absorbing Ruthenian territories to east and south, it stretched from the Baltic to the Black Sea and east, nearly reaching Moscow. **1410:** Led by Duke Vytautas, and in alliance with Poland, the Teutonic Knights were defeated decisively at Battle of Tannenberg. **1569:** Joined Poland in a confederation, under the Union of Lublin, in which Poland had the upper hand and Lithuanian upper classes were Polonized. **1795:** Came under control of Tsarist Russia, following partition of Poland; 'Lithuania Minor' (Kaliningrad) fell to Germany. **1831 and 1863:** Failed revolts for independence. **1880s:** Development of organized nationalist movement. **1914–18:** Occupied by German troops during World War I. **1918–19:** Independence declared and, after uprising against attempted imposition of Soviet Union (USSR) control, was achieved as a democracy. **1920–39:** Province and city of Vilnius occupied by Poles. **1926:** Democracy overthrown in authoritarian coup by Antanas Smetona, who became president. **1934:** Baltic Entente mutual-defence pact signed with Estonia and Latvia. **1939–40:** Secret German–Soviet agreement brought most of Lithuania under Soviet influence as a constituent republic. **1941:**

Lithuania revolted and established own government, but during World War II Germany again occupied the country and 210,000, mainly Jews, were killed. **1944:** USSR resumed rule. **1944–52:** Lithuanian guerrillas fought USSR, which persecuted the Catholic Church, collectivized agriculture, and deported half a million Balts to Siberia. **1972:** Demonstrations against Soviet government. **1980s:** Growth in nationalist dissent, influenced by Polish Solidarity movement and glasnost ('openness') initiative of reformist Soviet leader Mikhail Gorbachev. **1988:** Popular Front, the Sajudis, formed to campaign for increased autonomy; parliament declared Lithuanian the state language and readopted the flag of interwar republic. **1989:** Communist Party split into pro-Moscow and nationalist wings, and lost local monopoly of power; over 1 million took part in nationalist demonstrations. **1990:** Nationalist Sajudis won elections; their leader, Vytautas Landsbergis, became president; unilateral declaration of independence rejected by USSR, who imposed an economic blockade. **1991:** Soviet paratroopers briefly occupied key buildings in Vilnius, killing 13; Communist Party outlawed; independence recognized by USSR and Western nations; admitted into United Nations. **1992:** Ex-communist Democratic Labour Party (LDLP) won majority in parliamentary elections as economic restructuring caused contraction in GDP. **1993:** LDLP leader Algirdas Brazauskas elected president, and Adolfas Slezevicius became prime minister. Free-trade agreement with other Baltic states. Last Russian troops departed. **1994:** Friendship and cooperation treaty with Poland. **1994:** Trade and cooperation agreement with European Union. **1996:** Slezevicius resigned over banking scandal; replaced by Laurynas Stankevicius. New conservative coalition formed, led by Gediminas Vagnorius. **1997:** Border treaty signed with Russia. **1998:** Valdas Adamkus became president.

Luxembourg Grand Duchy of

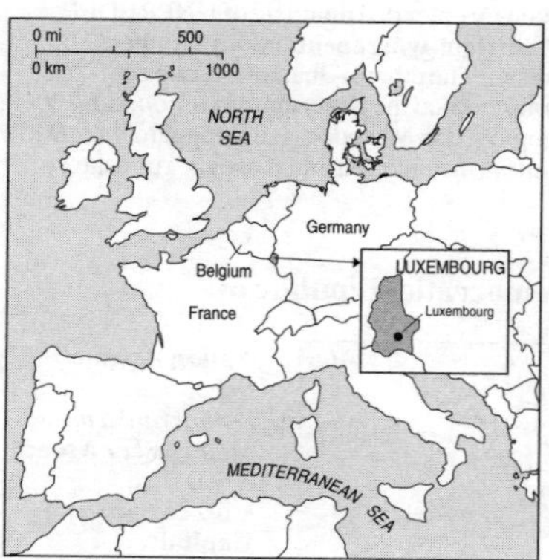

National name: *Grand-Duché de Luxembourg* **Area:** 2,586 sq km/998 sq mi **Capital:** Luxembourg **Major towns/cities:** Esch-Alzette, Differdange, Dudelange, Petange

Government

Head of state: Grand Duke Jean from 1964 **Head of government:** Jean-Claude Juncker from 1995 **Political system:** liberal democracy **Administrative divisions:** 12 cantons **Political parties:** Christian Social Party (PCS), moderate, left of centre; Luxembourg Socialist Workers' Party (POSL), moderate, socialist; Democratic Party (PD), centre left; Communist Party of Luxembourg, pro-European left wing **Armed forces:** 800; gendarmerie 600 (1997) **Conscription:** military service is voluntary **Death penalty:** abolished in 1979 **Defence spend:** (% GDP) 0.8 (1997) **Education spend:** (% GNP) 3.1 (1993–94) **Health spend:** (% GDP) 6.3 (1993)

Economy and resources

Currency: Luxembourg franc **GDP:** (US$) 15.5 billion (1997) **Real GDP growth:** (% change on previous year) 4.1 (1997) **GNP:** 18.8 billion (1997) **GNP per capita (PPP):** (US$) 34,460 (1997) **Consumer price inflation:** 1.6% (1998) **Unemployment:** 2.8% (1998) **Major trading partners:** EU (principally Belgium, Germany, and France) **Resources:** iron ore **Exports:** base metals and manufactures, mechanical and electrical equipment, rubber and related products, plastics, textiles and clothing. Principal market: Germany 28% (1996) **Imports:** machinery and electrical apparatus, transport equipment, mineral products. Principal source: Belgium 38% (1996) **Arable land:** 22%

Population and society

Population: 422,000 (1998 est) **Population growth rate:** 0.5% (1995–2025) **Population density:** (per sq km) 164.4 (1998 est) **Urban population:** (% of total) 90 (1997) **Age distribution:** (% of total population) 0–14 18.2%, 15–64 67.0%, 65+ 14.8% (1998) **Ethnic groups:** majority descended from the Moselle Franks **Language:** French, German, local Letzeburgesch (all official) **Religion:** Roman Catholic **Education:** (compulsory years) 9 **Literacy rate:** 99% (1995 est) **Labour force:** 51.2% of population: 2.6% agriculture, 27.7% industry, 69.7% services (1992) **Life expectancy:** 73 (men); 80 (women) (1995–2000) **Child mortality rate:** (under 5, per 1,000 live births) 7 (1997) **Physicians:** 1 per 455 people (1995)

Practical information

Visa requirements: UK: visa not required. USA: visa not required for a stay of up to 90 days **Embassy in the UK:** 27 Wilton Crescent, London SW1X 8SD. Tel: (0171) 235 6961; fax: (0171) 235 9734 **British embassy:** 14 boulevard Roosevelt, L-2450 Luxembourg-Ville. Tel: (352) 229 864/5/6; fax: (352) 229 867 **Chamber of commerce:** 7 rue Alcide de Gasperi, L-2981 Luxembourg-Kirchberg. Tel: (352) 435 853; fax: (352) 438 326

Chronology

963: Luxembourg became autonomous within Holy Roman Empire under Siegfried, Count of Ardennes. **1060:** Conrad, descendent of Siegfried, took the title Count of Luxembourg. **1354:** Emperor Charles IV promoted Luxembourg to status of duchy. **1441:** Luxembourg ceded to dukes of Burgundy. **1482:** Luxembourg came under Habsburg control. **1555:** Luxembourg became part of Spanish Netherlands on division of Habsburg domains. **1684–97:** Much of Luxembourg occupied by France. **1713:** Treaty of Utrecht transferred Spanish Netherlands to Austria. **1797:** Conquered by revolutionary France. **1815:** Congress of Vienna made Luxembourg a grand duchy, under King William of the Netherlands. **1830:** Most of Luxembourg supported Belgian revolt against the Netherlands. **1839:** Western part of Luxembourg assigned to Belgium. **1842:** Luxembourg entered the Zollverein (German customs union). **1867:** Treaty of London confirmed independence and neutrality of Luxembourg to allay French fears about possible inclusion in a unified Germany. **1870s:** Development of iron and steel industry. **1890:** Link with Dutch crown ended on accession of Queen Wilhelmina, since Luxembourg's law of succession did not permit a woman to rule; Adolphe of Nassau-Weilburg became grand duke. **1912:** Revised law of succession allowed Marie-Adelaide to become grand duchess. **1914–18:** Occupied by Germany. **1919:** Plebiscite overwhelmingly favoured continued independence; Marie-Adelaide abdicated after allegations of collaboration with Germany; succeeded by Grand Duchess Charlotte. **1921:** Entered into close economic links with Belgium. **1940:** Invaded by Germany. **1942–44:** Annexed by Germany. **1948:** Luxembourg formed Benelux customs union with Belgium and the Netherlands. **1949:** Luxembourg became founding member of North Atlantic Treaty Organization (NATO). **1958:** Luxembourg became founding member of European Economic Community (EEC). **1964:** Grand Duchess Charlotte abdicated in favour of her son Jean. **1974–79:** Christian Social Party outside governing coalition for first time since 1919. **1994:** Former premier Jacques Santer became president of European Commission (EC). **1995:** Jean-Claude Juncker became prime minister.

Macedonia Former Yugoslav Republic of (official international name); Republic of Macedon (official internal name)

National name: *Republika Makedonija* **Area:** 25,700 sq km/9,922 sq mi **Capital:** Skopje **Major towns/cities:** Bitolj, Prilep, Kumanovo, Tetovo

Government

Head of state: (acting) Stojan Andov from 1995 **Head of government:** Ljubco Georgievski from 1998 **Political system:** emergent democracy **Administrative divisions:** 34 communes **Political parties:** Socialist Party (SP); Social Democratic Alliance of Macedonia (SM) bloc, left of centre; Party for Democratic Prosperity (PDP), ethnic Albanian, left of centre; Internal Macedonian Revolutionary Organization–Democratic Party for Macedonian National Unity (VMRO–DPMNE), radical nationalist; Democratic Party of Macedonia (DPM), nationalist, free market **Armed forces:** 15,400; plus paramilitary force of 7,500 (1997) **Conscription:** military service is compulsory for nine months **Death penalty:** laws do not provide for the death penalty for any crime **Defence spend:** (% GDP) 10.2 (1997) **Education spend:** (% GNP) 5.6 (1995) **Health spend:** (% GDP) 7.3 (1990–95)

Economy and resources

Currency: Macedonian denar **GDP:** (US$) 2.06 billion (1997) **Real GDP growth:** (% change on previous year) 3.0 (1997) **GNP:** 2.2 billion (1997) **GNP per capita (PPP):** (US$) 4,110 (1997 est) **Consumer price inflation:** 9% (1998) **Unemployment:** 39.8% (1996) **Foreign debt:** (US$) 1.4 billion (1996) **Major trading partners:** Bulgaria, Yugoslavia, Germany, Russia, Italy, Slovenia, Croatia, USA, Turkey, the Netherlands **Resources:** coal, iron, zinc, chromium, manganese, lead, copper, nickel, silver, gold **Exports:** manufactured goods, machinery and transport equipment, miscellaneous manufactured articles, sugar beet, vegetables, cheese, lamb, tobacco. Principal market: Yugoslavia 22.8% (1997) **Imports:** mineral fuels and lubricants, manufactured goods, machinery and transport equipment, food and live animals, chemicals. Principal source: Germany 13.4% (1997) **Arable land:** 23.8% (1995)

Population and society

Population: 1,999,000 (1998 est) **Population growth rate:** 0.7% (1995–2000); 0.7% (2000–05) **Population density:** (per sq km) 78.1 (1998 est) **Urban population:** (% of total) 61 (1997) **Age distribution:** (% of total population) 0–14 23.6%, 15–64 67.0%, 65+ 9.4% (1998) **Ethnic groups:** 66% Macedonian ethnic descent, 22% ethnic Albanian, 5% Turkish, 3% Romanian, 2% Serb, and 2% Muslim, comprising Macedonian Slavs who converted to Islam during the Ottoman era, and are known as Pomaks. This ethnic breakdown is disputed by Macedonia's ethnic Albanian population, who claim that they form 40% of the population, and seek autonomy and by ethnic Serbs, who claim that they form 11.5% **Language:** Macedonian, closely allied to Bulgarian and written in Cyrillic **Religion:** Christian, mainly Orthodox; Muslim 2.5% **Education:** (compulsory years) 8 **Literacy rate:** 94% (1995 est) **Labour force:** 8.6% agriculture, 48.7% industry, 42.7% services (1994) **Life expectancy:** 70 (men); 75 (women) (1995–2000) **Child mortality rate:** (per 1,000 live births) 35 (1997) **Physicians:** 1 per 479 people (1994)

Practical information

Visa requirements: UK: visa not required. USA: visa required **Embassy in the UK:** 10 Harcourt House, 19A Cavendish Square, London W1M 9AD. Tel: (0171) 499 5152; fax (0171) 499 2864 **British embassy:** Office of the British Government Representative, Ul Veljko Vlahovic 26, 91000 Skopje. Tel: (91) 116 772; fax: (91) 117 005 **Chamber of commerce:** Economic Chamber of Macedonia, PO Box 324, Dimitrie Cupovski 13, 91000 Skopje. Tel: (91) 233 215; fax: (91) 116 210

Chronology

4th century BC: Part of ancient great kingdom of Macedonia, which included northern Greece and southwest Bulgaria and, under Alexander the Great, conquered a vast empire; Thessaloniki founded. **146 BC:** Macedonia became a province of the Roman Empire. **395 AD:** On the division of the Roman Empire, came under the control of Byzantine Empire, with its capital at Constantinople. **6th century:** Settled by Slavs, who later converted to Christianity. **9th–14th centuries:** Under successive rule by Bulgars, Byzantium, and Serbia. **1371:** Became part of Islamic Ottoman Empire. **late 19th century:** The 'Internal Macedonian Revolutionary Organization', through terrorism, sought to provoke Great Power intervention against Turks. **1912–13:** After First Balkan War, partitioned between Bulgaria, Greece, and the area that constitutes the current republic of Serbia. **1918:** Serbian part included in what was to become Yugoslavia; Serbian imposed as official language. **1941–44:** Occupied by Bulgaria. **1945:** Created a republic within Yugoslav Socialist Federation. **1967:** The Orthodox Macedonian archbishopric of Skopje, forcibly abolished 200 years earlier by the Turks, was restored. **1980:** Rise of nationalism after death of Yugoslav leader Tito. **1990:** Multiparty elections produced inconclusive result. **1991:** Kiro Gligorov, a pragmatic former communist, became president. Referendum supported independence. **1992:** Independence declared, and accepted by Serbia/Yugoslavia, but international recognition withheld because of Greece's objections to the name. **1993:** Sovereignty recognized by UK and Albania; won United Nations membership under provisional name of Former Yugoslav Republic of Macedonia; Greece blocked full European Union (EU) recognition. **1994:** Independence recognized by USA; trade embargo imposed by Greece, causing severe economic damage. **1995:** Independence recognized by Greece; trade embargo lifted. President Gligorov survived assassination attempt. **1997:** Plans to reduce strength of UN Preventive Deployment Force (UNPREDEP) were abandoned. Government announced compensation for public's losses in failed investment schemes. **1998:** UN extended mandate of UNPREDEP. General election resulted in a right-wing coalition, with Ljubco Georgievski as prime minister. The ethnic Albanian National Democratic Party (NDP) also joined the governing coalition. A 1,700-strong NATO force was deployed in Macedonia to safeguard the 2,000 ceasefire verification monitors in neighbouring Kosovo, Yugoslavia.

Madagascar Democratic Republic of

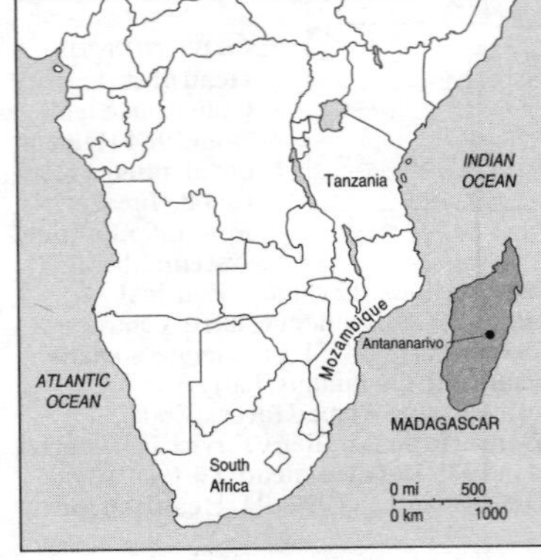

National name: *Repoblika Demokratika n`i Madagaskar* **Area:** 587,041 sq km/226,656 sq mi **Capital:** Antananarivo **Major towns/cities:** Antsirabe, Mahajanga, Fianarantsoa, Toamasina, Ambatondrazaka **Major ports:** Toamasina, Antsiranana, Toliary, Mahajanga

Government

Head of state: Didier Ratsiraka from 1996 **Head of government:** René Tantely Gabrio Andrianarivo from 1998 **Political system:** emergent democracy **Administrative divisions:** six provinces **Political parties:** Vanguard for Economic and Social Recovery (ARES, also known as ARENA), left of centre; One Should Not Be

Judged By One's Works (AVI). left of centre; Rally for Socialism and Democracy (RPSD), left of centre. **Armed forces:** 21,000; plus paramilitary gendarmerie of 7,500 (1997) **Conscription:** military service is compulsory for 18 months **Death penalty:** retains the death penalty for ordinary crimes but can be considered abolitionist in practice (last known execution in 1958) **Defence spend:** (% GDP) 0.8 (1997) **Education spend:** (% GDP) 1.9 (1993–94) **Health spend:** (% GDP) 1.1 (1990–95)

Economy and resources

Currency: Malagasy franc **GDP:** (US$) 3.5 billion (1997) **Real GDP growth:** (% change on previous year) 3.5 (1997) **GNP:** 3.6 billion (1997) **GNP per capita (PPP):** (US$) 910 (1997) **Consumer price inflation:** 8.0% (1998) **Foreign debt:** (US$) 4.17 billion (1996) **Major trading partners:** France, Japan, Germany, USA **Resources:** graphite, chromite, mica, titanium ore, small quantities of precious stones, bauxite and coal deposits, petroleum reserves**Exports:** coffee, shrimps, cloves, vanilla, petroleum products, chromium, cotton fabrics. Principal market: UK 32.1% (1997) **Imports:** minerals (crude petroleum), chemicals, machinery, vehicles and parts, metal products, electrical equipment. Principal source: France 18.6% (1997) **Arable land:** 4.4% (1995)

Population and society

Population: 15,057,000 (1998 est) **Population growth rate:** 3.1% (1995–2000) **Population density:** (per sq km) 24.9 (1998 est) **Urban population:** (% of total) 28 (1997) **Age distribution:** (% of total population) 0–14 44.7%, 15–64 52.0%, 65+ 3.3% (1998) **Ethnic groups:** 18 main Malagasy tribes of Malaysian–Polynesian origin; also French, Chinese, Indians, Pakistanis, and Comorans **Language:** Malagasy (official); French, English **Religion:** traditional beliefs, Roman Catholic, Protestant **Education:** (compulsory years) 5 **Literacy rate:** 88% (men); 73% (women) (1995 est) **Labour force:** 48% of population: 78% agriculture, 7% industry, 15% services (1990) **Life expectancy:** 57 (men); 60 (women) (1995–2000) **Child mortality rate:** (under 5, per 1,000 live births) 103 (1997) **Physicians:** 1 per 8,385 people (1993 est)

Practical information

Visa requirements: UK: visa required. USA: visa required **Embassy in the UK:** Consulate of the Republic of Madagascar, 16 Lanark Mansions, Pennard Road, London W12 8DT. Tel: (0181) 746 0133; fax: (0181) 746 0134 **British embassy:** BP 167, 1er Etage, Immeuble 'Ny Havana', Cité de 67 Ha, 101 Antananarivo. Tel: (2) 27749; fax: (2) 26690 **Chamber of commerce:** Fédération des Chambres de Commerce, d'Industrie et d'Agriculture de Madagascar, BP 166, 20 rue Colbert, 101 Antananarivo. Tel: (2) 21567

Chronology

c. **6th–10th centuries AD:** Settled by migrant Indonesians. **1500:** First visited by European navigators. **17th century:** Development of Merina and Sakalava kingdoms in the central highlands and west coast. **1642–74:** France established a coastal settlement at Fort-Dauphin, which they abandoned after a massacre by local inhabitants. **late 18th–early 19th century:** Merinas, united by their ruler Andrianampoinimerina, became dominant kingdom; court converted to Christianity. **1861:** Ban on Christianity (imposed in 1828) and entry of Europeans lifted by Merina king, Radama II. **1885:** Became French protectorate. **1895:** Merina army defeated by French and became a colony; slavery abolished. **1942–43:** British troops invaded to overthrow French administration allied to the pro-Nazi Germany Vichy regime and install anti-Nazi Free French government. **1947–48:** Nationalist uprising brutally suppressed by French. **1960:** Independence achieved from France, with Philibert Tsiranana, the leader of the Social Democratic Party (PSD), as president. **1972:** Merina-dominated army overthrew Tsiranana's government, dominated by the cotier (coastal tribes), as economy deteriorated. **1975:** Martial law imposed; new one-party state Marxist constitution adopted, with Lt-Commander Didier Ratsiraka as president. **1978:** More than 1,000 people killed in race riots in Majunga city in northwest. **1980:** Ratsiraka abandoned Marxist experiment, which had involved nationalization and severing ties with France. **1983:** Ratsiraka re-elected, despite strong opposition from radical socialist movement under Monja Jaona. **1990:** Political opposition legalized; 36 new parties created. **1991:** Antigovernment demonstrations. Ratsiraka formed new unity government, which included opposition members. **1992:** Constitutional reform approved by referendum. **1993:** Albert Zafy elected president and pro-Zafy left-of-centre coalition won majority in multiparty assembly elections. **1995:** Referendum backed appointment of prime minister by president, rather than assembly. **1996:** Norbert Ratsirahonana became prime minister and then interim president upon parliament's removal of Zafy. Didier Ratsiraka elected president. **1997:** Pascal Rakotomavo appointed prime minister. **1998:** ARES largest party following election. Tantely Andrianarivo appointed prime minister.

Malawi Republic of (formerly Nyasaland)

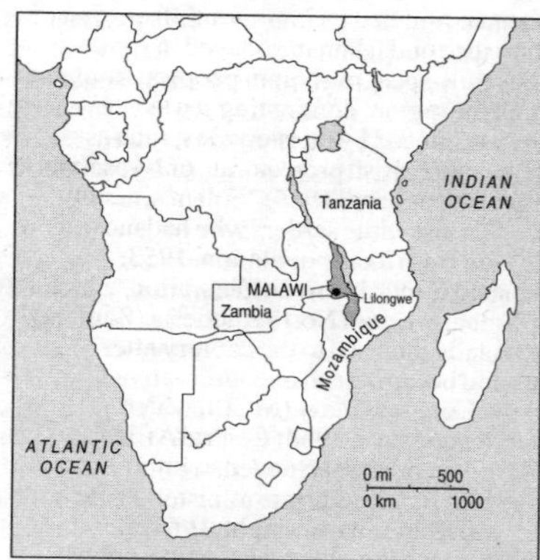

National name: *Malawi* **Area:** 118,000 sq km/ 45,559 sq mi **Capital:** Lilongwe **Major towns/cities:** Blantyre, Lilongwe, Mzuzu, Zomba

Government

Head of state and government: Bakili Muluzi from 1994 **Political system:** emergent democracy **Administrative divisions:** three regions, subdivided into 24 districts **Political parties:** Malawi Congress Party (MCP), multiracial, right wing; United Democratic Front (UDF), left of centre; Alliance for Democracy (AFORD), left of centre **Armed forces:** 5,000 (1997) **Conscription:** military service is voluntary **Death penalty:** retained and used for ordinary crimes **Defence spend:** (% GDP) 1.1 (1997) **Education spend:** (% GNP) 5.7 (1995) **Health spend:** (% GDP) 2.3 (1990–95)

Economy and resources

Currency: Malawi kwacha **GDP:** (US$) 2.4 billion (1997) **Real GDP growth:** (% change on previous year) 6.3 (1997) **GNP:** 2.3 billion (1997) **GNP per capita (PPP):** (US$) 700 (1997) **Consumer price inflation:** 15% (1998) **Unemployment:** 1.3% (1989) **Foreign debt:** (US$) 2.33 billion (1996) **Major trading partners:** South Africa, UK, Japan, Germany, the Netherlands **Resources:** marble, coal, gemstones, bauxite and graphite deposits, reserves of phosphates, uranium, glass sands, asbestos, vermiculite **Exports:** tobacco, tea, sugar, cotton, groundnuts. Principal market: USA 14.3% (1996) **Imports:** petroleum products, fertilizers, coal, machinery and transport equipment, miscellaneous manufactured articles. Principal source: South Africa 35.7% (1996) **Arable land:** 17.8% (1995)

Population and society

Population: 10,346,000 (1998 est) **Population growth rate:** 2.5% (1995–2000); 2% (2000–05) **Population density:** (per sq km) 104.6 (1998 est) **Urban population:** (% of total) 14 (1997) **Age distribution:** (% of total population) 0–14 45.5%, 15–64 51.8%, 65+ 2.7% (1998) **Ethnic groups:** almost all indigenous Africans, divided into numerous ethnic groups, such as the Chewa, Nyanja, Tumbuka, Yao, Lomwe, Sena, Tonga, and Ngoni. There are also Asian and European minorities **Language:** English, Chichewa (both official) **Religion:** Christian 75%, Muslim 20% **Education:** (compulsory years) 8 **Literacy rate:** 52% (men); 31% (women) (1995 est) **Labour force:** 87% agriculture, 5% industry, 8% services (1990) **Life expectancy:** 40 (men); 41 (women) (1995–2000) **Child mortality rate:** (under 5, per 1,000 live births) 221 (1997) **Physicians:** 1 per 44,205 people (1993 est)

Practical information

Visa requirements: UK: visa not required. USA: visa not required **Embassy in the UK:** 33 Grosvenor Street, London W1X 0DE. Tel: (0171) 491 4172/7; fax: (0171) 491 9916 **British embassy:** British High Commission, PO Box 30042, Lingadzi House, Lilongwe 3. Tel: (265) 782 400; fax: (265) 782 657 **Chamber of commerce:** Associated Chambers of Commerce and Industry of Malawi, PO Box 258, Chichiri Trade Fair Grounds, Blantyre. Tel: (265) 671 988; fax: (265) 671 147

Chronology

1st–4th centuries AD: Immigration by Bantu-speaking peoples. **1480:** Foundation of Maravi (Malawi) Confederacy, which covered much of central and southern Malawi and lasted into the 17th century. **1530:** First visited by the Portuguese. **1600:** Ngonde kingdom founded in northern Malawi by immigrants from Tanzania. **18th century:** Chikulamayembe state founded by immigrants from east of Lake Nyasa; slave trade flourished and Islam introduced in some areas. **mid-19th century:** Swahili-speaking Ngoni peoples, from South Africa, and Yao entered the region, dominating settled agriculturalists; Christianity introduced by missionaries, such as David Livingstone. **1891:** Became British protectorate of Nyasaland; cash crops, particularly coffee, introduced. **1915:** Violent uprising, led by Rev John Chilembwe, against white settlers who had moved into the fertile south, taking land from local population. **1953:** Became part of white-dominated Central African Federation, which included South Rhodesia (Zimbabwe) and North Rhodesia (Zambia). **1958:** Dr Hastings Kamuzu Banda returned to the country after working abroad for 40 years and became head of conservative-nationalist Nyasaland/Malawi Congress Party (MCP), which spearheaded campaign for independence. **1963:** Central African Federation dissolved. **1964:** Independence achieved, within Commonwealth, as Malawi, with Banda as prime minister. **1966:** Became one-party republic, with Banda as president. **1967:** Banda became pariah of Black Africa by recognizing racist, white-only republic of South Africa. **1971:** Banda made president for life. **1970s:** Reports of human-rights violations and murder of Banda's opponents. **1980s:** Economy began to deteriorate after nearly two decades of expansion. **1986–89:** Influx of nearly a million refugees from Mozambique. **1992:** Calls for multiparty political system. Countrywide industrial riots caused many fatalities. Western aid suspended over human-rights violations. **1993:** Referendum overwhelmingly supported ending of one-party rule. **1994:** New multiparty constitution adopted. Bakili Muluzi, of the United Democratic Front (UDF), elected president in first free elections for 30 years. Inconclusive assembly elections. **1995:** Banda and former minister of state John Tembo were charged with conspiring to murder four political opponents in 1983, but were cleared.

Malaysia Federation of (FOM)

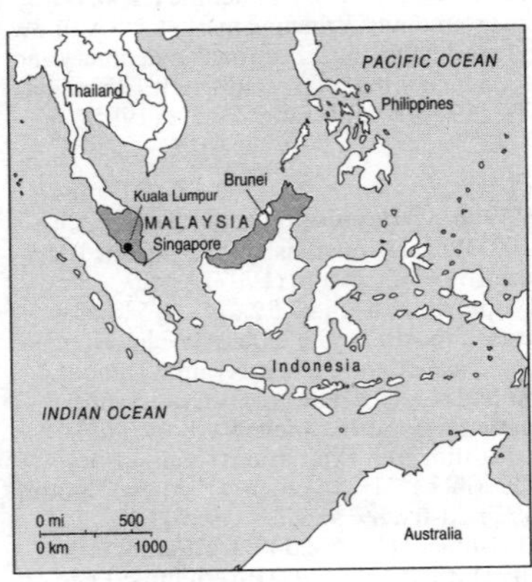

National name: *Persekutuan Tanah Malaysia* **Area:** 329,759 sq km/127,319 sq mi **Capital:** Kuala Lumpur **Major towns/cities:** Johor Baharu, Ipoh, George Town (Penang), Kuala Trengganu, Kuala Baharu, Petalong Jaya, Kelang, Kuching in Sarawak, Kota Kinabalu in Sabah **Major ports:** Kelang

Government

Head of state: Tuanku Salehuddin Abdul Aziz Shan bin al-Marhum Hisamuddin Alam Shah from 1999 **Head of government:** Mahathir bin Mohamed from 1981 **Political system:** liberal democracy **Administrative divisions:** 13 states **Political parties:** New United Malays' National Organization (UMNO Baru), Malay-oriented nationalist; Malaysian Chinese Association (MCA), Chinese-oriented, conservative; Gerakan Party, Chinese-oriented, socialist; Malaysian Indian Congress (MIC), Indian-oriented; Democratic Action Party (DAP), multiracial but Chinese-dominated, left of centre; Pan-Malayan Islamic Party (PAS), Islamic; Semangat '46 (Spirit of 1946), moderate, multiracial **Armed forces:** 111,500; reserve force 37,800; paramilitary force 20,100 (1997) **Conscription:** military service is voluntary **Death penalty:** retained and used for ordinary crimes **Defence spend:** (% GDP) 3.7 (1997) **Education spend:** (% GNP) 5.2 (1996) **Health spend:** (% GDP) 1.4 (1990–95)

Economy and resources

Currency: ringgit **GDP:** (US$) 97.5 billion (1997) **Real GDP growth:** (% change on previous year) 7.0 (1997) **GNP:** 98.2 billion (1997) **GNP per capita (PPP):** (US$) 10,920 (1997) **Consumer price inflation:** 4.5% (1998) **Unemployment:** 2.8% (1995) **Foreign debt:** (US$) 39.7 billion (1996) **Major trading partners:** Japan, USA, Singapore, Taiwan, UK and other EU countries **Resources:** tin, bauxite, copper, iron ore, petroleum, natural gas, forests **Exports:** palm oil, rubber, crude petroleum, machinery and transport equipment, timber, tin, textiles, electronic goods. Principal market: Singapore 20% (1997) **Imports:** machinery and transport equipment, chemicals, foodstuffs, crude petroleum, consumer goods. Principal source: Japan 21.9% (1997) **Arable land:** 5.5% (1995)

Population and society

Population: 21,410,000 (1998 est) **Population growth rate:** 2.0% (1995–2000); 1.7% (2000–05) **Population density:** (per sq km) 63.7 (1998 est) **Urban population:** (% of total) 55 (1997) **Age distribution:** (% of total population) 0–14 35.7%, 15–64 60.4%, 65+ 3.9% (1998) **Ethnic groups:** 58% of the population is Malay, four-fifths of whom live in rural areas; 32% is Chinese, four-fifths of whom are in towns; 9% is Indian, mainly Tamil **Language:** Malay (official), English, Chinese, Tamil, Iban **Religion:** Muslim (official), Buddhist, Hindu, local beliefs **Education:** (compulsory years) 11 **Literacy rate:** 86% (men); 70% (women) (1995 est) **Labour force:** 39% of population: 27% agriculture, 23% industry, 50% services (1990) **Life expectancy:** 70 (men); 74 (women) (1995–2000) **Child mortality rate:** (under 5, per 1,000 live births) 21 (1997) **Physicians:** 1 per 2,441 people (1993 est)

Practical information

Visa requirements: UK: visa not required. USA: visa not required **Embassy in the UK:** 45 Belgrave Square, London SW1X 8QT. Tel: (0171) 235 8033; fax: (0171) 235 5161 **British embassy:** British High Commission, PO Box 11030, 185 Jalan Ampang, 50450 Kuala Lumpur. Tel: (3) 248 2122; fax: (3) 248 0880 **Chamber of commerce:** Malaysian International Chamber of Commerce and Industry, PO Box 12921, Wisma Damansara, 10th Floor, Jalah Semantan, 50792 Kuala Lumpur. Tel: (3) 254 2677; fax: (3) 255 4946

Chronology

1st century AD: Peoples of Malay peninsula influenced by Indian culture and Buddhism. **8th–13th centuries:** Malay peninsula formed part of Buddhist Srivijaya Empire based in Sumatra. **14th century:** Siam (Thailand) expanded to included most of Malay peninsula. **1403:** Muslim traders founded port of Malacca, which became a great commercial centre, encouraging spread of Islam. **1511:** Portuguese attacked and captured Malacca. **1641:** Portuguese ousted from Malacca by Dutch after seven-year blockade. **1786:** British East India Company established a trading post on island of Penang. **1795–1815:** Britain occupied Dutch colonies after France conquered the Netherlands. **1819:** Stamford Raffles of East India Company obtained Singapore from Sultan of Johore. **1824:** Anglo-Dutch Treaty ceded Malacca to Britain in return for territory in Sumatra. **1826:** British possessions of Singapore, Penang, and Malacca formed Straits Settlements, ruled by

governor of Bengal; ports prospered and expanded. **1840:** Sultan of Brunei gave Sarawak to James Brooke, whose family ruled it as an independent state until 1946. **1851:** Responsibility for Straits Settlements assumed by governor general of India. **1858:** British government, through India Office, took over administration of Straits Settlements. **1867:** Straits Settlements became crown colony of British Empire. **1874:** British protectorates established over four Malay states of Perak, Salangor, Pahang, and Negri Sembilan, which federated in 1896. **1888:** Britain declared protectorate over northern Borneo (Sabah). **late 19th century:** Millions of Chinese and thousands of Indians migrated to Malaya to work in tin mines and on rubber plantations. **1909–14:** Britain assumed indirect rule over five northern Malay states after agreement with Siam (Thailand). **1941–45:** Japanese occupation. **1946:** United Malay National Organization (UMNO) founded to oppose British plans for centralized Union of Malaya. **1948:** Britain federated nine Malay states with Penang and Malacca to form single colony of Federation of Malaya. **1948–60:** Malayan emergency: British forces suppressed insurrection by communist guerrillas. **1957:** Federation of Malaya became independent with Prince Abdul Rahman (leader of UMNO) as prime minister. **1963:** Federation of Malaya combined with Singapore, Sarawak, and Sabah to form Federation of Malaysia. **1963–66:** 'The Confrontation' – guerrillas supported by Indonesia opposed federation with intermittent warfare. **1965:** Singapore withdrew from Federation of Malaysia. **1968:** Philippines claimed sovereignty over Sabah. **1969:** Malay resentment of Chinese economic dominance resulted in race riots in Kuala Lumpur. **1971:** *Bumiputra* policies which favoured ethnic Malays in education and employment introduced by Tun Abul Razak of UMNO. **1981:** Mahathir bin Muhammad (UMNO) became prime minister; government increasingly dominated by Muslim Malays. **1987:** Malay–Chinese relations deteriorated; over 100 opposition activists arrested. **1988:** UMNO split over Mahathir's leadership style; his supporters formed UMNO Baru (New UMNO); his critics formed Semangat '46, a new multiracial party in 1989. **1991:** Launch of economic development policy aimed at 7% annual growth. **1996:** Semangat '46 rejoined UMNO Baru, which remained under Mahathir's leadership. **1997:** Currency allowed to float. Parts of Borneo and Sumatra covered by thick smog for several weeks following forest-clearing fires. **1998:** Repatriation of foreign workers commenced. Deputy prime minister Anwar Ibrahim sacked and arrested on personal conduct and corruption charges. Anwar's wife, Wan Azizah Wan Ismail, set up a new opposition group, the Movement for Social Justice. Currency controls introduced as GDP contracted sharply. **1999:** Anwar Ibrahim sentenced to six years in prison on corruption charges.

Maldives Republic of the

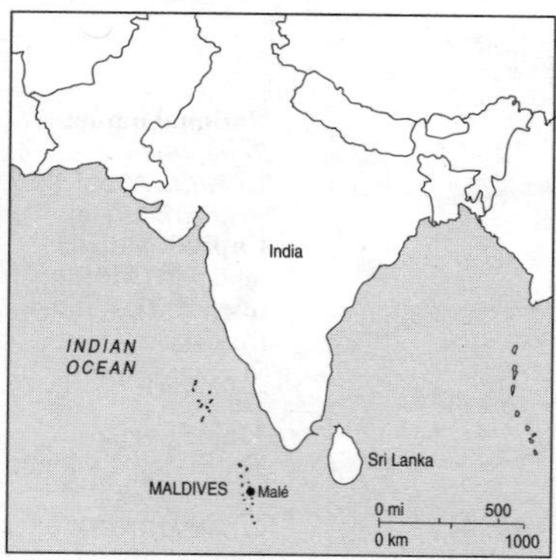

National name: *Divehi Raajjeyge Jumhooriyaa* **Area:** 298 sq km/115 sq mi **Capital:** Malé **Major towns/cities:** Seenu, Kurehdhu, Kunfunadhoo, Dhiggiri, Anthimatha

Government

Head of state and government: Maumoon Abd Gayoom from 1978 **Political system:** authoritarian nationalist **Administrative divisions:** 20 districts **Political parties:** none; candidates elected on basis of personal influence and clan loyalties **Armed forces:** no standing army **Death penalty:** retains the death penalty for ordinary crimes but can be considered abolitionist in practice (last known execution in 1952) **Education spend:** (% GNP) 8.4 (1995) **Health spend:** (% GDP) 5 (1990)

Economy and resources

Currency: rufiya **GDP:** (US$) 274 million (1995) **Real GDP growth:** (% change on previous year) 6.6 (1994) **GNP:** 301 million (1997) **GNP per capita (PPP):** (US$) 3,230 (1997) **Consumer price inflation:** 16.5% (1994) **Unemployment:** 1.6% (1985) **Foreign debt:** (US$) 167 million (1996) **Major trading partners:** UK, Singapore, USA, India, Sri Lanka, Thailand, Germany, Japan **Resources:** coral (mining was banned as a measure against the encroachment of the sea) **Exports:** marine products (tuna bonito ('Maldive Fish'), clothing. Principal market: UK 26% (1995) **Imports:** consumer manufactured goods, petroleum products, food, intermediate and capital goods. Principal source: Singapore 27.4% (1995) **Arable land:** 10% (1995)

Population and society

Population: 271,000 (1998 est) **Population growth rate:** 2.8% (1995–2025) **Population density:** (per sq km) 967.4 (1998 est) **Urban population:** (% of total) 28 (1997) **Age distribution:** (% of total population) 0–14 47.2%, 15–64 49.7%, 65+ 3.1% (1998) **Ethnic groups:** four main groups: Dravidian in the northern islands, Arab in the middle islands, Sinhalese in the southern islands, and African **Language:** Divehi (Sinhalese dialect), English **Religion:** Sunni Muslim **Education:** not compulsory **Literacy rate:** 93% (men); 93% (women) (1995 est) **Labour force:** 41% of population: 32% agriculture, 31% industry, 37% services (1990) **Life expectancy:** 66 (men); 63 (women) (1995–2000) **Child mortality rate:** (under 5, per 1,000 live births) 65 (1997) **Physicians:** 1 per 6,057 people (1992)

Practical information

Visa requirements: UK: visa required. USA: visa required **Embassy in the UK:** Honorary Tourism Representative for the Maldives Republic in the UK, Toni the Maldive Lady, 3 Esher House, 11 Edith Terrace, London SW10 0TH. Tel: (0171) 352 2246; fax: (0171) 351 3382 **British embassy:** the British High Commission in Colombo (see Sri Lanka) deals with enquiries relating to the Maldives **Chamber of commerce:** State Trading Organisation, STO Building, 7 Haveeree Higun, Malé 20-02. Tel: (960) 323 279; fax: (960) 325 218

Chronology

12th century AD: Islam introduced by seafaring Arabs, who displaced the indigenous Dravidian population. **14th century:** Ad-Din sultanate established. **1558–73:** Under Portuguese rule. **1645:** Became a dependency of Ceylon (Sri Lanka), which was ruled by the Dutch until 1796 and then by the British, with Sinhalese and Indian colonies being established. **1887:** Became internally self-governing British protectorate, which remained a dependency of Sri Lanka until 1948. **1932:** Formerly hereditary, the sultanate became an elected position when Maldives' first constitution was introduced. **1953:** Maldive Islands became a republic within the Commonwealth, as the ad-Din sultanate was abolished. **1954:** Sultan restored. **1959–60:** Secessionist rebellion in Suvadiva (Huvadu) and Addu southern atolls. **1965:** Achieved full independence outside Commonwealth. **1968:** Sultan deposed after referendum; republic reinstated with Ibrahim Nasir as president. **1975:** Closure of British airforce staging post on southern island of Gan led to substantial loss in income. **1978:** The autocratic Nasir retired and left the country; replaced by the progressive Maumoon Abd Gayoom. **1980s:** Economic growth boosted by rapid development of tourist industry. **1982:** Rejoined Commonwealth. **1985:** Became founder member of South Asian Association for Regional Cooperation. **1986:** The High Court sentenced exiled Nasir in absentia to 25 years' banishment on charges of embezzlement of public funds, but pardon was granted two years later. **1988:** Coup attempt by Sri Lankan mercenaries, thought to have the backing of former president Nasir, foiled by Indian paratroops. President Gayoom re-elected. **1993:** Gayoom re-elected. **1998:** Gayoom re-elected for a further presidential term.

Mali Republic of

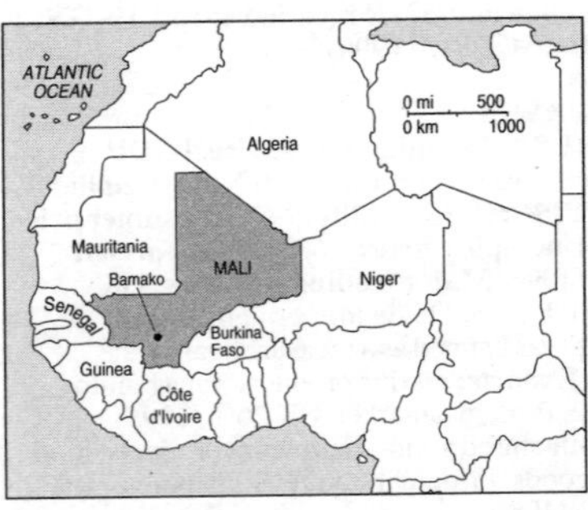

National name: *République du Mali* **Area:** 1,240,142 sq km/478,818 sq mi **Capital:** Bamako **Major towns/cities:** Mopti, Kayes, Ségou, Timbuktu, Sikasso

Government

Head of state: Alpha Oumar Konare from 1992 **Head of government:** Ibrahim Boubaker Keita from 1994 **Political system:** emergent democracy **Administrative divisions:** capital district of Bamako and eight regions **Political parties:** Alliance for Democracy in Mali (ADEMA), left of centre; National Committee for Democratic Initiative (CNID), centre left; Assembly for Democracy and Progress (RDP), left of centre; Civic Society and the Democracy and Progress Party (PDP), left of centre; Malian People's Democratic Union (UDPM), nationalist socialist **Armed forces:** 7,400; plus paramilitary forces of 7,800 (1997) **Conscription:** selective conscription for two years **Death penalty:** retains the death penalty for ordinary crimes but can be considered abolitionist in practice (last execution 1980) **Defence spend:** (% GDP) 1.7 (1997) **Education spend:** (% GNP) 2.2 (1995) **Health spend:** (% GDP) 2.0 (1990–95)

Economy and resources

Currency: franc CFA **GDP:** (US$) 2.5 billion (1997) **Real GDP growth:** (% change on previous year) 5.0 (1997) **GNP:** 2.7 billion (1997) **GNP per capita (PPP):** (US$) 740 (1997) **Consumer price inflation:** 3.0% (1998) **Foreign debt:** (US$) 3.02 billion (1996) **Major trading partners:** Côte d'Ivoire, Thailand, CIS countries, Belgium, France, China, Ireland, Senegal **Resources:** iron ore, uranium, diamonds, bauxite, manganese, copper, lithium, gold **Exports:** cotton, livestock, gold, miscellaneous manufactured articles. Principal market: Thailand 20.3% (1997) **Imports:** machinery and transport equipment, food products, petroleum products, other raw materials, chemicals, miscellaneous manufactured articles. Principal source: Côte d'Ivoire 19% (1997) **Arable land:** 2.8% (1995)

Population and society

Population: 10,694,000 (1998 est) **Population growth rate:** 3.0% (1995–2000); 2.9% (2000–05) **Population density:** (per sq km) 8.3 (1998 est) **Urban population:** (% of total) 28 (1997) **Age distribution:** (% of total population) 0–14 47.4%, 15–64 49.4%, 65+ 3.2% (1998) **Ethnic groups:** around 50% belong to the Mande group, including the Bambara, Malinke, and Sarakole; other significant groups include the Fulani, Minianka, Senutu, Songhai, and the nomadic Tuareg in the north **Language:** French (official), Bambara **Religion:** Sunni Muslim 90%, animist, Christian **Literacy rate:** 41% (men); 24% (women) (1995 est) **Labour force:** 50% of population: 86% agriculture, 2% industry, 12% services (1990) **Life expectancy:** 46 (men); 50 (women) (1995–2000) **Child mortality rate:** (under 5, per 1,000 live births) 178 (1997) **Physicians:** 1 per 18,376 people (1993 est)

Practical information

Visa requirements: UK: visa required. USA: visa required **Embassy for the UK:** 487 avenue Molière, B-1060 Brussels, Belgium. Tel: (2) 345 7432; fax: (2) 344 5700 **British embassy:** British Consulate, BP 1598, Plan International, Bamako. Tel: (223) 230 583; fax: (223) 228 143 **Chamber of commerce:** Chambre de Commerce et d'Industrie de Mali, BP 46, place de la Liberté, Bamako. Tel: (223) 225 036; fax: (223) 222 120

Chronology

5th–13th centuries: Ghana Empire founded by agriculturist Soninke people, based on the Saharan gold trade for which Timbuktu became an important centre. At its height in the 11th century it covered much of the western Sahel, comprising parts of present-day Mali, Senegal, and Mauritania. Wars with Muslim Berber tribes from the north led to its downfall. Its capital was at Kumbi, 125 mi/200 km north of Bamako, in southeast Mauritania. **13th–15th centuries:** Ghana Empire superseded by Muslim Mali Empire of Malinke (Mandingo) people of southwest, from which Mali derives its name. At its peak, under Mansa Musa in the 14th century, it covered parts of Mali, Senegal, Gambia, and southern Mauritania. **15th–16th centuries:** Muslim Songhai Empire, centred around Timbuktu and Gao, superseded Mali Empire. Under Sonni Ali Ber, who ruled 1464–92, it covered Mali, Senegal, Gambia, and parts of Mauritania, Niger, and Nigeria, and included a professional army and civil service. **1591:** Songhai Empire destroyed by Moroccan Berbers, under Ahmad al-Mansur, who launched an invasion to take over western Sudanese gold trade and took control over Timbuktu. **18th–19th centuries:** Niger valley region was divided between the nomadic Tuareg, in the area around Gao in the northeast, and the Fulani and Bambara kingdoms, around Macina and Bambara in the centre and southwest. **late 18th century:** Western Mali visited by Scottish explorer Mungo Park. **mid-19th century:** The Islamic Tukolor, as part of a jihad (holy war) conquered much of western Mali, including Fulani and Bambara kingdoms, while in the south, Samori Ture, a Muslim Malinke (Mandingo) warrior, created a small empire. **1880–95:** Region conquered by French, who overcame Tukolor and Samori resistance to establish colony of French Sudan. **1904:** Became part of federation of French West Africa. **1946:** French Sudan became an overseas territory within the French Union, with its own territorial assembly and representation in the French parliament; the pro-autonomy Sudanese Union and Sudanese Progressive Parties founded in Bamako. **1959:** With Senegal, formed the Federation of Mali. **1960:** Separated from Senegal and became independent Republic of Mali, with Modibo Keita, an authoritarian socialist of the Sudanese Union party, as president. **1968:** Keita replaced in army coup by Lt Moussa Traoré, as economy deteriorated: constitution suspended and political activity banned. **1974:** New constitution made Mali a one-party state, dominated by Traoré's nationalistic socialist Malian People's Democratic Union (UDPM), formed in 1976. **1979:** More than a dozen killed after a student strike was crushed. **1985:** Five-day conflict with Burkina Faso over long-standing border dispute; mediated by International Court of Justice. **late 1980s:** Closer ties developed with the West and free-market economic policies pursued, including privatization, as Soviet influence waned. **1991:** Violent demonstrations and strikes against one-party rule led to 150 deaths; Traoré ousted in a coup led by Lt-Col Amadou Toumani Toure. **1992:** Referendum endorsed new democratic constitution. The opposition Alliance for Democracy in Mali (ADEMA) won multiparty elections; Alpha Oumar Konare elected president. Coalition government formed. Peace pact signed with Tuareg rebels fighting in northern Mali for greater autonomy. **1993–94:** Student unrest forced two changes of prime minister. Ex-president Traoré sentenced to death for his role in suppressing the 1991 riots. **1997:** President Konare re-elected.

Malta Republic of

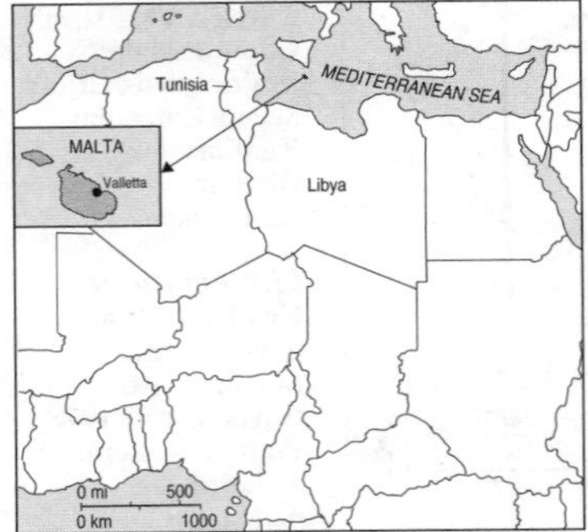

National name: *Repubblika Ta'Malta* **Area:** 320 sq km/124 sq mi **Capital:** Valletta (and port) **Major towns/cities:** Rabat, Birkirkara, Qormi, Sliema, Zetjun, Zabor **Major ports:** Marsaxlokk, Valletta

Government

Head of state: Guido de Marco from 1999 **Head of government:** Edward Fenech Adami from 1998 **Political system:** liberal democracy **Administrative divisions:** 67 local councils **Political parties:** Malta Labour Party (MLP), moderate, left of centre; Nationalist Party (PN), Christian, centrist, pro-European

Armed forces: 2,000 (1997) **Conscription:** military service is voluntary **Death penalty:** laws provide for the death penalty only for exceptional crimes such as crimes under military law or crimes committed in exceptional circumstances such as wartime (last execution 1943) **Defence spend:** (% GDP) 0.9 (1997) **Education spend:** (% GNP) 5.2 (1995)

Economy and resources
Currency: Maltese lira **GDP:** (US$) 3.4 billion (1997 est) **Real GDP growth:** (% change on previous year) 4.0 (1997) **GNP:** 3.2 billion (1997) **GNP per capita (PPP):** (US$) 13,200 (1997 est) **Consumer price inflation:** 3.4% (1998) **Unemployment:** 3.5% (1995) **Foreign debt:** (US$) 953 million (1996) **Major trading partners:** Italy, Germany, UK, USA, France, Libya, the Netherlands **Resources:** stone, sand; offshore petroleum reserves were under exploration 1988–95 **Exports:** machinery and transport equipment, manufactured articles (including clothing), beverages, chemicals, tobacco. Principal market: France 16.5% (1996) **Imports:** machinery and transport equipment, basic manufactures (including textile yarn and fabrics), food and live animals, mineral fuels. Principal source: Italy 19.5% (1996) **Arable land:** 31.3% (1995)

Population and society
Population: 384,000 (1998 est) **Population growth rate:** 0.1% (1995–2000) **Population density:** (per sq km) 1,182.4 (1998 est) **Urban population:** (% of total) 90 (1997) **Age distribution:** (% of total population) 0–14 20.8%, 15–64 67.5%, 65+ 11.6% (1998) **Ethnic groups:** essentially European, supposedly originated from ancient North African kingdom of Carthage **Language:** Maltese, English (both official) **Religion:** Roman Catholic 98% **Education:** (compulsory years) 10 **Literacy rate:** 86% (men); 86% (women) (1995 est) **Labour force:** 2.5% agriculture, 34% industry, 63.5% services (1992) **Life expectancy:** 75 (men); 79 (women) (1995–2000) **Child mortality rate:** (per 1,000 live births) 10 (1997) **Physicians:** 1 per 406 people (1995)

Practical information
Visa requirements: UK: visa not required. USA: visa not required **Embassy in the UK:** Malta House, 36–38 Piccadilly, London W1V 0PP. Tel: (0171) 292 4800; fax: (0171) 734 1832 **British embassy:** British High Commission, PO Box 506, 7 St Anne Street, Floriana, Valetta. Tel: (356) 233 134; fax: (356) 242 001 **Chamber of commerce:** Exchange Building, Republic Street, Valetta VLT 05. Tel: (356) 247 233; fax: (356) 245 223

Chronology
7th century BC: Invaded and subjugated by Carthaginians from North Africa. **218 BC:** Came under Roman control. **AD 60:** Converted to Christianity by the apostle Paul, who was shipwrecked. **395:** On division of Roman Empire, became part of Eastern (Byzantine) portion, dominated by Constantinople. **870:** Came under Arab rule. **1091:** Arabs defeated by Norman Count Roger I of Sicily; Roman Catholic Church re-established. **1530:** Handed over by Holy Roman Emperor Charles V to religious military order, the Hospitallers (Knights of St John of Jerusalem). **1798–1802:** Briefly occupied by French. **1814:** Annexed to Britain by Treaty of Paris on condition that Roman Catholic Church was maintained and Maltese Declaration of Rights honoured. **later 19th century– early 20th century:** Became vital British naval base, with famous dockyard that developed as island's economic mainstay. **1942:** Awarded George Cross for valour in resisting severe Italian aerial attacks during World War II. **1947:** Achieved self-government. **1955:** Dom Mintoff of left-of-centre Malta Labour Party (MLP) became prime minister. **1956:** Referendum approved MLP's proposal for integration with UK. Plebiscite opposed and boycotted by right-of-centre Nationalist Party (PN). **1958:** MLP rejected final British integration proposal. **1962:** PN elected, with Dr Giorgio Borg Olivier as prime minister. **1964:** Independence achieved from Britain, within Commonwealth. Ten-year defence and economic-aid treaty with UK signed. **1971:** Mintoff adopted policy of nonalignment and declared 1964 treaty invalid; negotiations began for leasing NATO base in Malta. **1972:** Seven-year NATO agreement signed. **1974:** Became a republic. **1979:** British military base closed; closer links established with communist and Arab states, including Libya. **1984:** Mintoff retired; replaced by Karmenu Mifsud Bonnici as prime minister and MLP leader. **1987:** Edward Fenech Adami (PN) narrowly elected prime minister; he adopted a more pro-European and pro-American policy stance than preceding administration. **1990:** Formal application made for European Community membership. **1994:** Mifsud Bonnici elected president. **1998:** PN returned to power after snap election.

Marshall Islands Republic of the (RMI)

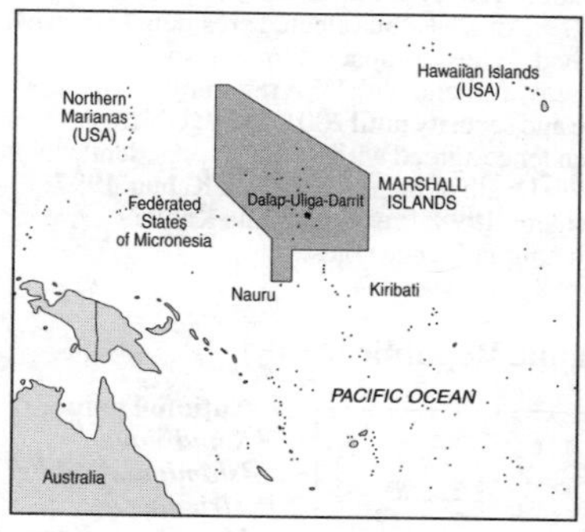

Area: 181 sq km/70 sq mi **Capital:** Dalap-Uliga-Darrit (on Majuro atoll) **Major towns/cities:** Ebeye (the only other town)

Government
Head of state and government: Imata Kabua from 1997 **Political system:** liberal democracy **Political parties:** no organized party system, but in 1991 an opposition grouping, the Ralik Ratak Democratic Party, was founded to oppose the ruling group **Armed forces:** the USA maintains a military presence on the Kwajalein Atoll (the Compact of Free Association gave the USA responsibility for defence in return for US assistance) **Death penalty:** abolished in 1991 **Education spend:** (% GDP) 6 (1994)

Economy and resources
Currency: US dollar **GDP:** (US$) 94 million (1995 est) **Real GDP growth:** (% change on previous year) 1.5 (1995 est) **GNP:** 108 million (1997) **GNP per capita (PPP):** (US$) 1,730 (1997 est) **Consumer price inflation:** 4% (1995 est) **Unemployment:** 16% (1991 est) **Foreign debt:** (US$) 170 million (1994) **Major trading partners:** USA, Japan, Australia **Resources:** phosphates **Exports:** coconut products, trochus shells, copra, handicrafts, fish, live animals. Principal market: USA **Imports:** foodstuffs, beverages and tobacco, building materials, machinery and transport equipment, mineral fuels, chemicals. Principal source: USA

Population and society
Population: 60,000 (1998 est) **Population growth rate:** 3.0% (1995–2025) **Population density:** (per sq km) 348.6 (1998 est) **Urban population:** (% of total) 70.0 (1997) **Age distribution:** (% of total population) 0–14 50.0%, 15–64 47.8%, 65+ 2.3% (1998) **Ethnic groups:** 97% Marshallese, of predominantly Micronesian descent **Language:** Marshallese, English (both official) **Religion:** Christian (mainly Protestant) and Baha'i **Education:** (compulsory years) 8 **Literacy rate:** 91% (men); 90% (women) (1994 est) **Labour force:** 26.1% agriculture, 9.5% industry, 64.4% services (1989) **Life expectancy:** 62 (men); 65 (women) (1995) **Child mortality rate:** (under 5, per 1,000 live births) 48 (1994) **Physicians:** 1 per 2,631 people (1990)

Practical information
Visa requirements: UK: visa required. USA: visa required **Embassy in the UK:** none; enquiries relating to the Marshall Islands are dealt with by the Marshall Islands Visitors Authority, PO Box 1727, Ministry of Resources and Development, Majuro 96960. Tel: (692) 625 3206; fax: (692) 625 3218 **British embassy:** none **Chamber of commerce:** Majuro Chamber of Commerce, Majuro 96960. Tel: (692) 625 3051; fax: (692) 625 3343

Chronology

after *c.* **1000 BC:** Micronesians first settled the islands. **1529:** Visited by Spanish navigator Miguel de Saavedra and thereafter came under Spanish influence. **1875:** Spanish rule formally declared in face of increasing encroachment by German traders. **1885:** German protectorate established. **1914:** Seized by Japan on the outbreak of World War I. **1920–44:** Administered under League of Nations mandate by Japan and vigorously colonized. **1944:** Japanese removed after heavy fighting with US troops during World War II. **1946–63:** Eniwetok and Bikini atolls used for US atom-bomb tests; islanders later demanded rehabilitation and compensation for the damage. **1947:** Became part of United Nations (UN) Pacific Islands Trust Territory, administered by USA. **1979:** Amata Kabua elected president as internal self-government established. **1986:** Compact of Free Association with USA granted islands self-government, with USA retaining responsibility for defence and security until 2001. **1990:** UN trust status terminated. **1991:** Independence agreed with Kabua as president; UN membership granted. **1996:** Death of President Amata Kabua. **1997:** Imata Kabua elected president. **1998:** President Imata Kabua's government survived two no-confidence votes.

Mauritania Islamic Republic of

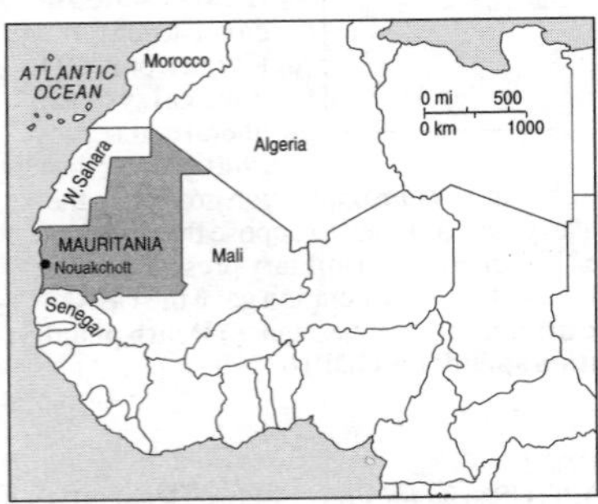

National name: *République Islamique Arabe et Africaine de Mauritanie* **Area:** 1,030,700 sq km/397,953 sq mi **Capital:** Nouakchott (port) **Major towns/ cities:** Nouâdhibou, Kaédi, Zouerate, Kiffa, Rosso, Atar **Major ports:** Nouâdhibou

Government

Head of state: Maaoya Sid'Ahmed Ould Taya from 1984 **Head of government:** Cheik el Avia Ould Muhammad Khouna from 1998 **Political system:** emergent democracy **Administrative divisions:** 12 regions **Political parties:** Democratic and Social Republican Party (PRDS), centre left, militarist; Rally for Democracy and National Unity (RDNU), centrist; Mauritian Renewal Party (MPR), centrist; Umma, Islamic fundamentalist **Armed forces:** 15,700; plus paramilitary force of around 5,000 (1997) **Conscription:** military service is by authorized conscription for two years **Death penalty:** retained and used for ordinary crimes **Defence spend:** (% GDP) 2.2 (1997) **Education spend:** (% GNP) 5.0 (1995) **Health spend:** (% GDP) 1.8 (1990–95)

Economy and resources

Currency: ouguiya **GDP:** (US$) 1.06 billion (1997) **Real GDP growth:** (% change on previous year) 4.9 (1997 est) **GNP:** 1.1 billion (1997) **GNP per capita (PPP):** (US$) 1,870 (1997) **Consumer price inflation:** 5.0% (1997 est) **Unemployment:** 20% (1991 est) **Foreign debt:** (US$) 2.36 billion (1996) **Major trading partners:** Japan, France, Spain, Italy, Belgium, Germany **Resources:** copper, gold, iron ore, gypsum, phosphates, sulphur, peat **Exports:** fish and fish products, iron ore. Principal market: Japan 21.8% (1996) **Imports:** machinery and transport equipment, foodstuffs, consumer goods, building materials, mineral fuels. Principal source: France 29.2% (1996) **Arable land:** 0.2% (1995)

Population and society

Population: 2,529,000 (1998 est) **Population growth rate:** 2.5% (1995–2000); 2.5% (2000–05) **Population density:** (per sq km) 2.4 (1998 est) **Urban population:** (% of total) 54 (1997) **Age distribution:** (% of total population) 0–14 46.5%, 15–64 51.2%, 65+ 2.4% (1998) **Ethnic groups:** over 80% of the population is of Moorish or Moorish-black origin; about 18% is black African (concentrated in the south); there is a small European minority **Language:** French and Hasaniya Arabic (both official), African languages including Pulaar, Soninke, and Wolof **Religion:** Sunni Muslim **Education:** not compulsory **Literacy rate:** 47% (men); 21% (women) (1995 est) **Labour force:** 46% of population: 55% agriculture, 10% industry, 34% services (1990) **Life expectancy:** 52 (men); 55 (women) (1995–2000) **Child mortality rate:** (under 5, per 1,000 live births) 137 (1997) **Physicians:** 1 per 11,316 people (1994)

Practical information

Visa requirements: UK: visa required. USA: visa required **Embassy in the UK:** Honorary Consulate of the Islamic Republic of Mauritania, 140 Bow Common Lane, London E3 4BH. Tel: (0181) 980 4382; fax: (0181) 980 2232 **British embassy:** the British Embassy in Rabat (see Morocco) deals with enquiries relating to Mauritania **Chamber of commerce:** Chambre de Commerce, d'Agriculture, d'Elevage, d'Industrie et des Mines de Mauritanie, BP 215 Nouakchott. Tel: (222) 52214; telex: 581

Chronology

early Christian era: A Roman province with the name Mauritania, after the Mauri, its Berber inhabitants who became active in the long-distance salt trade. **7th–11th centuries:** Eastern Mauritania was incorporated in the larger Ghana Empire, centred on Mali to the east, but with its capital at Kumbi in southeast Mauritania. The Berbers were reduced to vassals and converted to Islam in the 8th century. **11th–12th centuries:** The area's Sanhadja Berber inhabitants, linked to the Morocco-based Almoravid Empire, destroyed the Ghana Empire and spread Islam among neighbouring peoples. **13th–15th centuries:** Southeast Mauritania formed part of Muslim Mali Empire, which extended to east and south. **1441:** Coast visited by Portuguese, who founded port of Arguin and captured Africans to sell as slaves. **15th–16th centuries:** Eastern Mauritania formed part of Muslim Songhai Empire, which spread across western Sahel, and Arab tribes migrated into the area. **1817:** Senegal Treaty recognized coastal region (formerly disputed by European nations) as French sphere of influence. **1903:** Formally became French protectorate. **1920:** Became French colony, within French West Africa. **1960:** Independence achieved, with Moktar Ould Daddah, leader of Mauritanian People's Party (PPM), as president. New capital built at Nouakchott. **1968:** Underlying tensions between agriculturalist black population of south and economically dominant semi-nomadic Arabo-Berber peoples, or Moors, of desert north became more acute after Arabic was made an official language (with French). **1976:** Western Sahara, to the northwest, ceded by Spain to Mauritania and Morocco. Mauritania occupied the southern area and Morocco the mineral-rich north. Polisario Front formed in Sahara to resist this occupation and guerrilla war broke out, with the Polisario receiving backing from Algeria and Libya. **1978:** Daddah deposed in bloodless coup; replaced by Col Mohamed Khouna Ould Haidalla in military government. **1979:** Peace accord signed with Polisario Front in Algiers, in which Mauritania, crippled by cost of military struggle over a largely uninhabited area, renounced claims to southern Western Sahara (Tiris el Gharbia region) and recognized Polisario regime; diplomatic relations restored with Algeria. **1981:** Diplomatic relations with Morocco broken after it annexed southern Western Sahara. **1984:** Haidalla overthrown by Col Maaoya Sid'Ahmed Ould Taya. **1985:** Relations with Morocco restored. **1989:** Violent clashes in Mauritania and Senegal between Moors and black Africans, chiefly of Senegalese origins; over 50,000 Senegalese expelled. **1991:** Amnesty for political prisoners. Calls for resignation of President Taya. Political parties legalized and new multiparty constitution approved in referendum. **1992:** First multiparty elections largely boycotted by opposition; Taya and his Social Democratic Republican Party (DSRP) re-elected. Diplomatic relations with Senegal resumed. **1996:** Cheikh el Avia Ould Muhammad Khouna appointed prime minister.

Mauritius Republic of

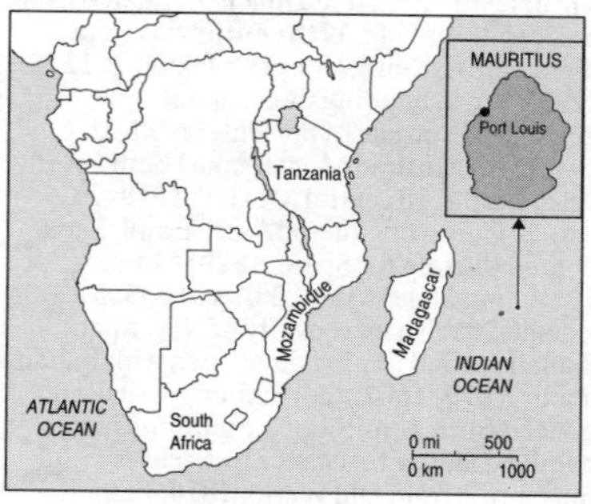

Area: 1,865 sq km/720 sq mi; the island of Rodrigues is part of Mauritius; there are several small island dependencies **Capital:** Port Louis (port) **Major towns/cities:** Beau Bassin-Rose Hill, Curepipe, Quatre Bornes, Vacoas-Phoenix

Government

Head of state: Cassam Uteem from 1992 **Head of government:** Navim Ramgoolam from 1995 **Political system:** liberal democracy **Administrative divisions:** five municipalities and four district councils **Political parties:** Mauritius Socialist Movement (MSM), moderate socialist-republican; Mauritius Labour Party (MLP), democratic socialist, Hindu-oriented; Mauritius Social Democratic Party (PMSD), conservative, Francophile; Mauritius Militant Movement (MMM), Marxist-republican; Organization of Rodriguan People (OPR), left of centre **Armed forces:** no standing defence forces; 1,800-strong police mobile unit (1997) **Death penalty:** abolished in 1985 **Defence spend:** (% GDP) 2.1 (1997) **Education spend:** (% GNP) 4.3 (1995) **Health spend:** (% GDP) 2.2 (1990–95)

Economy and resources

Currency: Mauritian rupee **GDP:** (US$) 4.1 billion (1997) **Real GDP growth:** (% change on previous year) 5.0 (1997) **GNP:** 4.3 billion (1997) **GNP per capita (PPP):** (US$) 9,360 (1997) **Consumer price inflation:** 8.0% (1998) **Unemployment:** 7.1% (1994) **Foreign debt:** (US$) 1.82 billion (1996) **Major trading partners:** UK, France, South Africa, India, Australia, Germany **Exports:** raw sugar, clothing, tea, molasses, jewellery. Principal market: UK 32.1% (1997) **Imports:** textile yarn and fabrics, petroleum products, industrial machinery, motor vehicles, manufactured goods. Principal source: France 18.6% (1997) **Arable land:** 49.3% (1995)

Population and society

Population: 1,141,000 (1998 est) **Population growth rate:** 1.1% (1995–2000); 1.1% (2000–05) **Population density:** (per sq km) 631.8 (1998 est) **Urban population:** (% of total) 41 (1997) **Age distribution:** (% of total population) 0–14 26.4%, 15–64 67.7%, 65+ 5.9% (1998) **Ethnic groups:** five principal ethnic groups: French, black Africans, Indians, Chinese, and Mulattos (or Creoles). Indo-Mauritians predominate, constituting 67% of the population, followed by Creoles (29%), Sino-Mauritians (3.5%), and Europeans (0.5%) **Language:** English (official), French, Creole, Indian languages **Religion:** Hindu, Christian (mainly Roman Catholic), Muslim **Education:** (compulsory years) 7 **Literacy rate:** 87% (men); 78% (women) (1995 est) **Labour force:** 15.7% agriculture, 43.7% industry, 40.6% services (1992) **Life expectancy:** 68 (men); 75 (women) (1995–2000) **Child mortality rate:** (under 5, per 1,000 live births) 16 (1997) **Physicians:** 1 per 1,000 people (1993)

Practical information

Visa requirements: UK: visa not required. USA: visa not required **Embassy in the UK:** 32/33 Elvaston Place, London SW7 5NW. Tel: (0171) 581 0294; fax: (0171) 823 8437 **British embassy:** British High Commission, PO Box 186, Les Cascades Building, Edith Cavell Street, Port Louis. Tel: (230) 211 1361; fax: (230) 211 1369 **Chamber of commerce:** Mauritius Chamber of Commerce and Industry, 3 Royal Street, Port Louis. Tel: (230) 208 3301; fax: (230) 208 0076

Chronology

1598: Previously uninhabited, the island was discovered by the Dutch and named after Prince Morris of Nassau. **1710:** Dutch colonists withdrew. **1721:** Reoccupied by French East India Company, who renamed it Île de France, and established sugar cane and tobacco plantations worked by imported African slaves. **1814:** Ceded to Britain by Treaty of Paris. **1835:** Slavery abolished; indentured Indian and Chinese labourers imported to work the sugar-cane plantations, which were later hit by competition from beet sugar. **1903:** Formerly administered with Seychelles, it became a single colony. **1936:** Mauritius Labour Party (MLP) founded, drawing strong support from sugar workers. **1957:** Internal self-government granted. **1968:** Independence achieved from Britain within Commonwealth, with Seewoosagur Ramgoolam of centrist Indian-dominated MLP as prime minister. **1971:** State of emergency temporarily imposed as a result of industrial unrest. **1982:** Aneerood Jugnauth, of the moderate socialist Mauritius Socialist Movement (MSM) became prime minister, pledging a programme of nonalignment, nationalization, and the creation of a republic. **1992:** Became a republic within the Commonwealth, with Cassam Uteem elected president. **1995:** MLP and cross-community Mauritian Militant Movement (MMM) coalition won election victory; Navim Ramgoolam (MLP) became prime minister.

Mexico United States of

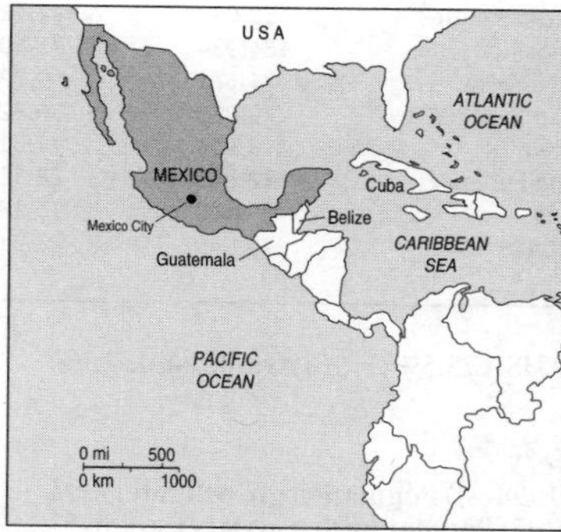

National name: *Estados Unidos Mexicanos* **Area:** 1,958,201 sq km/756,061 sq mi **Capital:** Mexico City **Major towns/cities:** Guadalajara, Monterrey, Puebla, Netzahualcóyotl, Ciudad Juárez, Tijuana **Major ports:** 49 ocean ports

Government

Head of state and government: Ernesto Zedillo Ponce de Leon from 1994 **Political system:** federal democracy **Administrative divisions:** 31 states and a Federal District **Political parties:** Institutional Revolutionary Party (PRI), moderate, left wing; National Action Party (PAN), moderate, Christian, centre right; Party of the Democratic Revolution (PRD), centre left **Armed forces:** 175,000; rural defence militia of 15,000 (1997) **Conscription:** one year, part-time (conscripts selected by lottery) **Death penalty:** only for exceptional crimes; last execution 1937 **Defence spend:** (% GDP) 1 (1997) **Education spend:** (% GNP) 5.3 (1995) **Health spend:** (% GDP) 2.8 (1990–95)

Economy and resources

Currency: Mexican peso **GDP:** (US$) 404.2 billion (1997) **Real GDP growth:** (% change on previous year) 7.6 (1997) **GNP:** 348.6 billion (1997) **GNP per capita (PPP):** (US$) 8,120 (1997) **Consumer price inflation:** 13.1% (1998) **Unemployment:** 3.7% (1997) **Foreign debt:** (US$) 157.1 billion (1996) **Major trading partners:** USA, Japan, Spain, France, Germany, Brazil, Canada **Resources:** petroleum, natural gas, zinc, salt, silver, copper, coal, mercury, manganese, phosphates, uranium, strontium sulphide **Exports:** petroleum and petroleum products, engines and spare parts for motor vehicles, motor vehicles, electrical and electronic goods, fresh and preserved vegetables, coffee, cotton. Principal market: USA 83.9% (1996) **Imports:** motor vehicle chassis, industrial machinery and equipment, iron and steel, telecommunications apparatus, organic chemicals, cereals and cereal preparations, petroleum and petroleum

Mexico: States

State	Capital	Area		Population
		sq km	sq mi	(1995)
Aguascalientes	Aguascalientes	5,589	2,157	862,700
Baja California Norte	Mexicali	70,113	27,071	2,112,100
Baja California Sur	La Paz	73,677	28,447	375,500
Campeche	Campeche	51,833	20,013	642,500
Chiapas	Tuxtla Gutiérrez	73,887	28,528	3,584,800
Chihuahua	Chihuahua	247,087	95,400	2,793,500
Coahuila	Saltillo	151,571	58,522	2,173,800
Colima	Colima	5,455	2,106	488,000
Durango	Victoria de Durango	119,648	46,196	1,431,700
Guanajuato	Guanajuato	30,589	11,810	4,406,600
Guerrero	Chilpancingo	63,794	24,631	2,916,600
Hidalgo	Pachuca de Soto	20,987	8,103	2,112,500
Jalisco	Guadalajara	80,137	30,941	5,991,200
México	Toluca de Lerdo	21,461	8,286	11,708,000
Michoacán	Morelia	59,864	23,113	3,870,600
Morelos	Cuernavaca	4,941	1,908	1,442,700
Nayarit	Tepic	27,621	10,664	896,700
Nuevo León	Monterrey	64,555	24,925	3,550,100
Oaxaca	Oaxaca de Juárez	95,364	36,820	3,228,900
Puebla	Puebla de Zaragoza	33,919	13,096	4,624,400
Querétaro	Querétaro	11,769	4,544	1,250,500
Quintana Roo	Chetumal	50,350	19,440	703,500
San Luis Potosí	San Luis Potosí	62,848	24,266	2,200,800
Sinaloa	Culiacán Rosales	58,092	22,429	2,425,700
Sonora	Hermosillo	184,934	71,403	2,085,500
Tabasco	Villahermosa	24,661	9,522	1,748,800
Tamaulipas	Ciudad Victoria	79,829	30,821	2,527,300
Tlaxcala	Tlaxcala	3,914	1,511	883,900
Veracruz	Jalapa Enríquez	72,815	28,114	6,737,300
Yucatán	Mérida	39,340	15,189	1,556,600
Zacatecas	Zacatecas	75,040	28,973	1,336,500

products. Principal source: USA 75.5% (1996) **Arable land:** 7.5% (1995)

Population and society

Population: 95,831,000 (1998 est) **Population growth rate:** 1.6% (1995–2000); 1.5% (2000–05) **Population density:** (per sq km) 51.2 (1998 est) **Urban population:** (% of total) 74 (1997) **Age distribution:** (% of total population) 0–14 35.6%, 15–64 60.3%, 65+ 4.1% (1998) **Ethnic groups:** around 60% mestizo (mixed American Indian and Spanish descent), 30% American Indians, remainder mainly of European origin **Language:** Spanish (official); Nahuatl, Maya, Zapoteco, Mixteco, Otomi **Religion:** Roman Catholic **Education:** (compulsory years) 6 **Literacy rate:** 89% (men); 85% (women) (1995 est) **Labour force:** 64.4% of population: 23.5% agriculture, 21.7% industry, 54.8% services (1995) **Life expectancy:** 70 (men); 76 (women) (1995–2000) **Child mortality rate:** (under 5, per 1,000 live births) 36 (1997) **Physicians:** 1 per 625 people (1995)

Practical information

Visa requirements: UK: visa (tourist card) required. USA: visa (tourist card) required **Embassy in the UK:** 42 Hertford Street, London W1Y 7TF. Tel: (0171) 499 8586; fax: (0171) 495 4053 **British embassy:** Apartado 96 bis, Rió Lerma 71, Colonia Cuauhtémoc, 06500 Mexico Distrito Federal. Tel: (5) 207 2089; fax: (5) 207 7672 **Chamber of commerce:** Confederacíon de Cámaras Nacionales de Comercio, Servicios y Turismo, Apartado 113 bis, 2° y 3°, Balderas 144, Centro Curuhtémoc, 06079 Mexico Distrito Federal. Tel: (5) 709 1559; fax: (5) 709 1152

Chronology

c. **2600 BC:** Mayan civilization originated in Yucatán peninsula. **1000–500 BC:** Zapotec civilization developed around Monte Albán in southern Mexico. **4th–10th centuries AD:** Mayan Empire at its height. **10th–12th centuries:** Toltecs ruled much of Mexico from their capital at Tula. **12th century:** Aztecs migrated south into valley of Mexico. *c.* **1325:** Aztecs began building their capital Tenochtitlán on site of present-day Mexico City. **15th century:** Montezuma I built up Aztec Empire in central Mexico. **1519–21:** Hernán Cortes conquered Aztec Empire and secured Mexico for Spain. **1520:** Montezuma II, last king of the Aztecs, killed. **1535:** Mexico became Spanish viceroyalty of New Spain; plantations and mining developed with Indian labour. **1519–1607:** Indigenous population reduced from 21 million to 1 million, due mainly to lack of resistance to diseases transported from Old World. **1810:** Father Miguel Hidalgo led unsuccessful revolt against Spanish. **1821:** Independence proclaimed by Augustín de Iturbide with support of Church and landowners. **1822:** Iturbide overthrew provisional government and proclaimed himself Emperor Augustín I. **1824:** Federal republic established amid continuing public disorder. **1824–55:** Military rule of Antonio López de Santa Anna, who imposed stability (he became president in 1833). **1846–48:** Mexican War: Mexico lost California and New Mexico to USA. **1848:** Revolt of Mayan Indians suppressed. **1855:** Benito Juárez aided overthrow of Santa Anna's dictatorship. **1857–60:** Sweeping liberal reforms and anti-clerical legislation introduced by Juárez led to civil war with conservatives. **1861:** Mexico suspended payment on foreign debt leading to French military intervention; Juárez resisted with US support. **1864:** Supported by conservatives, France installed Archduke Maximilian of Austria as emperor of Mexico. **1867:** Maximilian shot by republicans as French troops withdrew; Juárez resumed presidency. **1872:** Death of Juárez. **1876:** Gen Porfirio Diaz established dictatorship; Mexican economy modernized through foreign investment. **1911:** Revolution overthrew Diaz; liberal president Francisco Madero introduced radical land reform and labour legislation but political disorder increased. **1914 and 1916–17:** US military intervened to quell disorder. **1917:** New constitution, designed to ensure permanent democracy, adopted with US encouragement. **1924–35:** Government dominated by anti-clerical Gen Plutarco Calles, who introduced further social reforms. **1929:** Foundation of National Revolutionary Party (PRFN). **1938:** President Lázaro Cárdenas nationalized all foreign-owned oil wells in face of US opposition. **1942:** Mexico declared war on Germany and Japan (and so regained US favour). **1946:** PRFN renamed PRI. **1946–52:** Miguel Alemán first of succession of authoritarian PRI presidents to seek moderation and stability rather than further radical reform. **1960s:** Rapid industrial growth partly financed by borrowing. **1976:** Discovery of huge oil reserves in southeastern state of Chiapas; oil production tripled in six years. **1982:** Falling oil prices caused grave financial crisis; Mexico defaulted on debt. **1985:** Earthquake in Mexico City killed thousands. **1994:** Uprising in Chiapas by Zapatista National Liberation Army (EZLN), seeking rights for Mayan Indian population; Mexico formed North American Free Trade Area with USA and Canada. **1995:** Government agreed to offer greater autonomy to Mayan Indians in Chiapas. **1996:** Short-lived peace talks with EZLN; violent attacks against government by new leftist Popular Revolutionary Army (EPR) increased. **1997:** PRI lost its assembly majority. Civilian counterpart to the Zapatista rebels, the Zapatista National Liberation Front (FZLN), formed. **1998:** Lapsed peace accord with Zapatist rebels reactivated, but talks between the government and the rebels broke down.

Micronesia Federated States of (FSM)

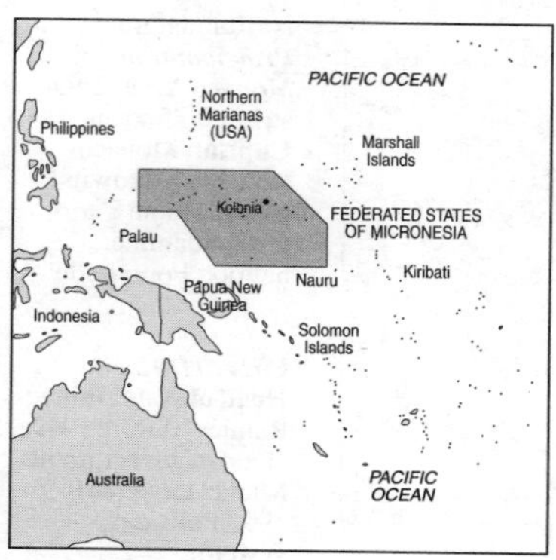

Area: 700 sq km/ 270 sq mi **Capital:** Kolonia, in Pohnpei state **Major towns/ cities:** Weno, in Chuuk state; Lelu, in Kosrae state **Major ports:** Teketik, Lepukos, Okak

Government

Head of state and government: Jacob Nena from 1997 **Political system:** democratic federal state **Administrative divisions:** four states **Political parties:** no formally organized political parties **Armed forces:** USA is responsible for country's defence **Death penalty:** laws do not provide for the death penalty for any crime

Economy and resources

Currency: US dollar **GDP:** (US$) 259 million (1995 est) **Real GDP growth:** (% change on previous year) 1.4 (1994 est) **GNP:** 220 million (1997) **GNP per capita (PPP):** (US$) 1,910 (1997 est) **Consumer price inflation:** 4% (1994 est) **Unemployment:** 13.5% (1990) **Major trading partners:** USA, Japan **Exports:** copra, pepper, fish **Imports:** manufactured goods, machinery and transport equipment, mineral fuels

Population and society

Population: 114,000 (1998 est) **Population growth rate:** 2.4% (1995–2000) **Population density:** (per sq km) 184.7 (1998 est) **Urban population:** (% of total) 29 (1997) **Ethnic groups:** main ethnic groups are the Trukese (41%) and Pohnpeian (26%), both Micronesian **Language:** English (official) and eight local languages **Religion:** Christianity (mainly Roman Catholic in Yap state, Protestant elsewhere) **Education:** (compulsory years) 8 **Literacy rate:** 91% (men); 88% (women) (1980 est) **Labour force:** 48% agriculture, 6% industry, 46% services (1990) **Life expectancy:** 67 (men); 71 (women) (1995–2000) **Child mortality rate:** (under 5, per 1,000 live births) 37 (1994) **Physicians:** 1 per 2,380 people (1993)

Practical information

Visa requirements: UK: visa not required for a stay of up to 30 days. USA: visa not required **Embassy in the UK:** Micronesia has no diplomatic representation in the UK; the Department of Trade and Industry has a Pacific Islands Desk. Tel: (0171) 215 4760; fax: (0171) 215 4398 **British embassy:** the UK has no diplomatic representation in Micronesia **Chamber of commerce:** Resources and Development Department, Pohnpei 96941. Tel: (691) 320 5133. Resources and Development Department, Chuuk 96942. Tel: (691) 330 2552; fax: (691) 330 4194

Chronology

c. **1000 BC:** Micronesians first settled the islands. **1525:** Portuguese navigators first visited Yap and Ulithi islands in the Carolines (Micronesia). **later 16th century:** Fell under Spanish influence. **1874:** Spanish rule formally declared in face of increasing encroachment by German traders. **1885:** Yap seized by German naval forces, but restored to Spain after arbitration by Pope Leo XIII on condition that Germany was allowed freedom of trade. **1899:** Purchased for $4.5 million by Germany from Spain, after the latter's defeat in the Spanish–American War. **1914:** Occupied by Japan on outbreak of World War I. **1919:** Administered under League of Nations mandate by Japan, and vigorously colonized. **1944:** Occupied by USA after Japanese forces defeated in World War II. **1947:** Administered by USA as part of the United Nations (UN) Trust Territory of the Pacific Islands, under the name of the Federated States of Micronesia (FSM). **1979:** Constitution adopted, establishing a federal system for its four constituent states (Yap, Chuuk, Pohnpei, and Kosrae) and internal self-government. **1986:** Compact of Free Association entered into with USA, granting the islands self-government with USA retaining responsibility for defence and security until 2001. **1990:** UN trust status terminated. **1991:** Independence agreed, with Bailey Olter as president. Entered into UN membership.

Moldova Republic of

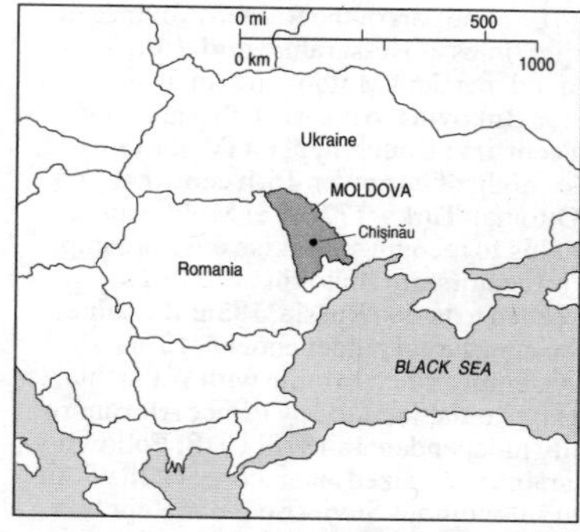

National name: *Republica Moldoveneasca* **Area:** 33,700 sq km/13,011 sq mi **Capital:** Chisinău (Kishinev) **Major towns/cities:** Tiraspol, Beltsy, Bendery

Government

Head of state: Petru Lucinschi from 1997 **Head of government:** Ion Sturza from 1999 **Political system:** emergent democracy **Administrative divisions:** 38 districts, four municipalities, and two autonomous territorial units – Gauguz (Gagauzi Yeri) and Trans-Dniestr (status of latter was under dispute 1996) **Political parties:** Agrarian Democratic Party (ADP), nationalist, centrist; Socialist Party and Yedinstvo/Unity Movement, reform-socialist; Peasants and Intellectuals, Romanian nationalist; Christian Democratic Popular Front (CDPF), Romanian nationalist; Gagauz-Khalky (GKPM; Gagauz People's Movement), Gagauz separatist **Armed forces:** 11,000 (1997) **Conscription:** military service is compulsory for up to 18 months **Death penalty:** abolished in 1995 **Defence spend:** (% GDP) 4.4 (1997) **Education spend:** (% GNP) 9.7 (1996) **Health spend:** (% GDP) 4.9 (1990–95)

Economy and resources

Currency: leu **GDP:** (US$) 2.1 billion (1997) **Real GDP growth:** (% change on previous year) –2.0 (1997) **GNP:** 2.3 billion (1997) **GNP per capita (PPP):** (US$) 2,350 (1997 est) **Consumer price inflation:** 11% (1998) **Unemployment:** 1.5% (1996); 'hidden unemployment' is considerably higher **Foreign debt:** (US$) 834 million (1996) **Major trading partners:** CIS countries (Russia and Ukraine), Romania, Germany, Bulgaria, USA **Resources:** lignite, phosphorites, gypsum, building materials; petroleum and natural gas deposits discovered in the early 1990s were not yet exploited in 1996 **Exports:** food and agricultural products, machinery and equipment, textiles, clothing. Principal market: Russia 58% (1997) **Imports:** mineral fuels, energy and mineral products, mechanical engineering products, foodstuffs, chemicals, textiles, clothing. Principal source: Russia 26% (1997) **Arable land:** 53.8% (1995)

Population and society

Population: 4,378,000 (1998 est) **Population growth rate:** 0.1% (1995–2000) **Population density:** (per sq km) 132.3 (1998 est) **Urban population:** (% of total) 53 (1997) **Age distribution:** (% of total population) 0–14 25.1%, 15–64 65.3%, 65+ 9.7% (1998) **Ethnic groups:** 65% ethnic Moldovan (Romanian), 14% Ukrainian, 13% ethnic Russian, 4% Gagauzi, 2% Bulgarian, 2% Jewish **Language:** Moldovan **Religion:** Russian Orthodox **Education:** (compulsory years) 11 **Literacy rate:** 98.9% (men); 98.9% (women) (1995 est) **Labour force:** 43.3% agriculture, 26% industry, 30.7% services (1992) **Life expectancy:** 64 (men); 72 (women) (1995–2000) **Child mortality rate:** (under 5, per 1,000 live births) 27 (1997) **Physicians:** 1 per 258 people (1994)

Practical information

Visa requirements: UK: visa required. USA: visa required **Embassy in the UK:** 219 Marsh Wall, Isle of Dogs, London E14 9PD. Tel: (0171) 538 8600; fax: (0171) 538 5967 **British embassy:** the British Embassy in Moscow (see Russian Federation) deals with enquiries relating to Moldova **Chamber of commerce:** Chamber of Commerce and Industry of the Republic of Moldova, 28 Emineskou, 277012 Chisinău. Tel: (2) 221 552; fax: (2) 233 810

Chronology

AD 106: The current area covered by Moldova, which lies chiefly between the Prut River, bordering Romania in the west, and the Dniestr River, with Ukraine in the east, was conquered by the Roman Emperor Trajan and became part of the Roman province of Dacia. It was known in earlier times as Bessarabia. **mid-14th century:** Formed part of an independent Moldovan principality, which included areas, such as Bukovina to the west, that are now part of Romania. **late 15th century:** Under Stephen IV 'the Great' the principality reached the height of its power. **16th century:** Became a tributary of the Ottoman Turks. **1774–75:** Moldovan principality, though continuing to recognize Turkish overlordship, was placed under Russian protectorship; Bukovina was lost to Austria. **1812:** Bessarabia ceded to tsarist Russia. **1856:** Remainder of Moldovan principality became largely independent of Turkish control. **1859:** Moldovan Assembly voted to unite with Wallachia, to the southwest, to form state of Romania, ruled by Prince Alexandru Ion Cuza. State became fully independent in 1878. **1918:** Following Russian Revolution, Bessarabia was seized and incorporated within Romania. **1924:** Moldovan autonomous Soviet Socialist Republic (SSR) created, as part of Soviet Union, comprising territory east of Dniestr River. **1940:** Romania returned Bessarabia, east of Prut River, to Soviet Union, which divided it between Moldovan SSR and Ukraine, with Trans-Dniestr region transferred from Ukraine to Moldova. **1941:** Moldovan SSR occupied by Romania and its wartime ally Germany. **1944:** Red Army reconquered Bessarabia. **1946–47:** Widespread famine as agriculture was collectivized; rich farmers and intellectuals liquidated. **1950:** Immigration by settlers from Russia and Ukraine as industries were developed. **late 1980s:** Upsurge in Moldovan nationalism, encouraged by *glasnost* initiative of reformist Soviet leader Mikhail Gorbachev. **1988:** Moldovan Movement in Support of Perestroika (economic restructuring) campaigned for accelerated political reform. **1989:** Nationalist demonstrations in Kishinev (now Chisinău). Moldovan Popular Front (MPF) founded; Moldovan made state language. Campaigns for autonomy among ethnic Russians, strongest in industrialized Trans-Dniestr region, and Turkish-speaking but Orthodox Christian Gagauz minority in southwest. **1990:** MPF polled strongly in parliamentary elections and Mircea Snegur, a reform-nationalist communist, became president. Economic and political sovereignty declared. **1991:** Independence declared and Communist Party outlawed after conservative coup in Moscow against Gorbachev; joined Commonwealth of Independent States (CIS). Insurrection in Trans-Dniestr region. **1992:** Admitted into United Nations and the Conference on Security and Cooperation in Europe; peace agreement signed with Russia to end civil war in Trans-Dniestr, giving special status to the region. MPF-dominated government fell; 'Government of national accord' formed, headed by Andrei Sangheli and dominated by ADP. **1993:** New currency, the leu, introduced. Privatization programme launched and closer ties established with Russia. **1994:** Parliamentary elections won by ADP. Plebiscite rejected nationalist demands for merger with Romania. Russia agreed to withdraw Trans-Dniestr troops by 1997. **1995:** Joined Council of Europe; economic growth resumed. **1996:** Petru Lucinschi elected president. Dniestr region president Igor Smirnov re-elected. **1997:** Ion Cebuc appointed prime minister. New centrist party formed, supporting President Lusinschi. Major party realignments. Cooperation agreement signed with Dniestr region. Law passed providing for elections using proportional representation. **1998:** Communist Party won largest number of seats in parliamentary election, but lacked a majority. **1999:** New coalition led by Ion Sturza.

Monaco Principality of

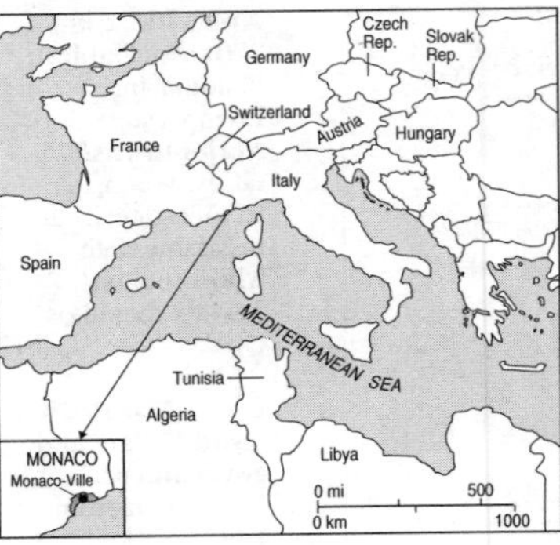

National name: *Principauté de Monaco* **Area:** 1.95 sq km/0.75 sq mi **Capital:** Monaco-Ville **Major towns/ cities:** Monte Carlo, La Condamine; heliport Fontvieille

Government

Head of state: Prince Rainier III from 1949 **Head of government:** Michel Leveque from 1998 **Political system:** constitutional monarchy under French protectorate **Administrative divisions:** four districts **Political parties:** no formal parties, but lists of candidates: Liste Campora, moderate, centrist; Liste Medecin, moderate, centrist **Armed forces:** no standing defence forces; defence is the responsibility of France **Death penalty:** abolished in 1962 **Education spend:** (% GNP) 5.6 (1992)

Economy and resources

Currency: French franc **GDP:** (US$) 847 million (1995) **Real GDP growth:** (% change on previous year) N/A **GNP:** N/A (there are no available data for GNP separate from the figures for France) **GNP per capita (PPP):** (US$) 26,170 (1995 est) **Unemployment:** 2.2% (1994 est) **Major trading partners:** full customs integration with France (for external trade figures, see France) **Imports:** largely dependent on imports from France

Population and society

Population: 33,000 (1998 est) **Population growth rate:** 1.0% (1995–2025) **Population density:** (per sq km) 16,017.5 (1998 est) **Urban population:** (% of total) 100 (1997) **Age distribution:** (% of total population) 0–14 16.8%, 15–64 63.7%, 65+ 19.5% (1998) **Ethnic groups:** 58% French; 19% Monegasque **Language:** French (official); English, Italian **Religion:** Roman Catholic **Education:** (compulsory years) 10 **Literacy rate:** 99% (men); 99% (women) (1995 est) **Life expectancy:** 74 (men); 83 (women) (1995) **Child mortality rate:** (under 5, per 1,000 live births) 7 (1994) **Physicians:** 1 per 254 people (1994)

Practical information

Visa requirements: UK: visa not required. USA: visa not required **Embassy in the UK:** Embassy and Consulate General, 4 Cromwell Place, London SW7 2JE. Tel: (0171) 225 2679; fax: (0171) 581 8161 **British embassy:** British Consulate, BP 265, 33 boulevard Princesse Charlotte, MC-98005, Monaco, Cedex. Tel: 9350 9966; fax: 9350 1447 **Chamber of commerce:** Conseil Economique, 8 rue Louis Notari, MC-98000, Monaco, Cedex. Tel: 9330 2082; fax: 9350 0596

Chronology

1191: The Genoese took control of Monaco, which had formerly been part of the Holy Roman Empire. **1297:** Came under the rule of the Grimaldi dynasty, the current ruling family, who initially allied themselves to the French. **1524–1641:** Came under Spanish protection. **1793:** Annexed by France during French Revolutionary Wars. One member of ruling family was guillotined; the rest imprisoned. **1815:** Placed under protection of Sardinia. **1848:** The towns of Menton and Roquebrune, which had formed the greater part of the principality, seceded and later became part of France. **1861:** Franco-Monegasque treaty restored Monaco's independence under French protection; first casino built. **1865:** Customs union established with France. **1918:** France given veto over succession to throne and established that if reigning prince dies without a male heir, Monaco is to be incorporated into France. **1941–45:** Occupied successively by

Italians and Germans during World War II. **1949:** Prince Rainier III ascended the throne. **1956:** Prince Rainier married US actress Grace Kelly. **1958:** Birth of male heir, Prince Albert. **1959:** Constitution of 1911 suspended and National Council dissolved. **1962:** New, more liberal constitution adopted and National Council restored. **1982:** Princess Grace died in car accident. **1993:** Joined United Nations. **1998:** Michel Leveque reappointed head of government.

Mongolia State of (Outer Mongolia until 1924; People's Republic of Mongolia until 1991)

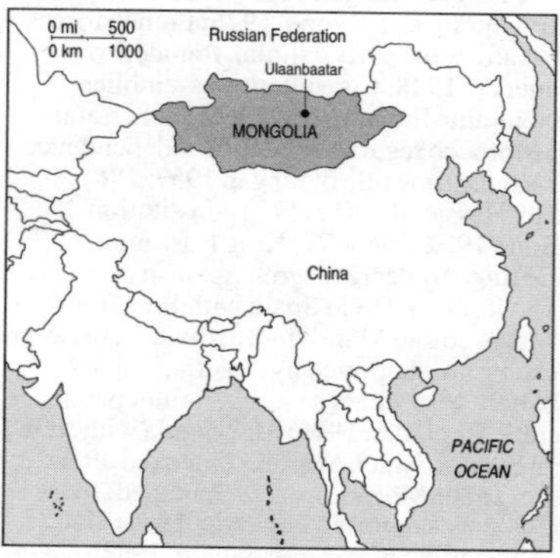

National name: *Mongol Uls* **Area:** 1,565,000 sq km/604,246 sq mi **Capital:** Ulaanbaatar (Ulan Bator) **Major towns/cities:** Darhan, Choybalsan, Erdenet

Government

Head of state: Natsagiyn Bagabandi from 1997 **Head of government:** Janlaviyn Narantsatsralt from 1998 **Political system:** emergent democracy **Administrative divisions:** 18 provinces and three municipalities **Political parties:** Mongolian People's Revolutionary Party (MPRP), reform-socialist (ex-communist); Mongolian National Democratic Party (MNDP), traditionalist, promarket economy; Union Coalition (UC, comprising the MNPD and the Social Democratic Party (SDP)), democratic, promarket economy **Armed forces:** 9,000; plus a paramilitary force of around 5,900 (1997) **Conscription:** military service is compulsory for 12 months **Death penalty:** retained and used for ordinary crimes **Defence spend:** (% GDP) 1.7 (1996) **Education spend:** (% GNP) 6.4 (1996) **Health spend:** (% GDP) 4.8 (1990–95)

Economy and resources

Currency: tugrik **GDP:** (US$) 862 million (1997) **Real GDP growth:** (% change on previous year) 4.0 (1997) **GNP:** 1 billion (1997) **GNP per capita (PPP):** (US$) 4,070 (1997 est) **Consumer price inflation:** 45.8% (1996) **Unemployment:** 8.5% (1994) **Foreign debt:** (US$) 524 million (1996) **Major trading partners:** Russia, China, Japan, Kazakhstan, South Korea, Germany, USA **Resources:** copper, nickel, zinc, molybdenum, phosphorites, tungsten, tin, fluorospar, gold, lead; reserves of petroleum discovered 1994 **Exports:** minerals and metals (primarily copper concentrate), consumer goods, foodstuffs, agricultural products. Principal market: Switzerland 31.5% (1997) **Imports:** engineering goods, mineral fuels and products, industrial consumer goods, foodstuffs. Principal source: Russia 36.2% (1995) **Arable land:** 0.8% (1995)

Population and society

Population: 2,579,000 (1998 est) **Population growth rate:** 2.1% (1995–2000); 1.9% (2000–05) **Population density:** (per sq km) 1.6 (1998 est) **Urban population:** (% of total) 62 (1997) **Age distribution:** (% of total population) 0–14 36.9%, 15–64 59.3%, 65+ 3.7% (1998) **Ethnic groups:** 90% Mongol, 4% Kazakh, 2% Chinese, and 2% Russian **Language:** Khalkha Mongolian (official); Chinese, Russian, and Turkic languages **Religion:** officially none (Tibetan Buddhist Lamaism suppressed in 1930s) **Education:** (compulsory years) 8 **Literacy rate:** 88% (men); 76% (women) (1995 est) **Labour force:** 43% agriculture, 16% industry, 41% services (1995) **Life expectancy:** 64 (men); 67 (women) (1995–2000) **Child mortality rate:** (under 5, per 1,000 live births) 69 (1997) **Physicians:** 1 per 371 people (1993 est)

Practical information

Visa requirements: UK: visa required. USA: visa required **Embassy in the UK:** 7 Kensington Court, London W8 5DL. Tel: (0171) 937 0150; fax: (0171) 937 1117 **British embassy:** PO Box 703, 30 Enkh Taivny Gudammzh, Ulaanbaatar 13. Tel: (1) 358 133; fax: (1) 358 036 **Chamber of commerce:** Mongolian Chamber of Commerce and Industry, Sambuugiyn Gudamj 11, Ulaanbaatar 38. Tel: (1) 324 620; telex: 79336

Chronology

AD 1206: Nomadic Mongol tribes united by Genghis Khan to form nucleus of vast Mongol Empire which, stretching across central Asia, reached its zenith under Genghis Khan's grandson, Kublai Khan. **late 17th century:** Conquered by China to become province of Outer Mongolia. **1911:** Independence proclaimed by Mongolian nationalists after Chinese 'republican revolution'; Tsarist Russia helped Mongolia to secure autonomy, under a traditionalist Buddhist monarchy in the form of a reincarnated lama. **1915:** Chinese sovereignty reasserted. **1921:** Chinese rule overthrown with Soviet help. **1924:** People's Republic proclaimed on death of king, when the monarchy was abolished; defeudalization programme launched, entailing collectivization of agriculture and suppression of Lama Buddhism. **1932:** Armed antigovernment uprising suppressed with Soviet assistance; 100,000 killed in political purges. **1946:** China recognized Mongolia's independence. **1952:** Death of Marshal Horloogiyn Choybalsan, the dominant force in the ruling communist Mongolian People's Revolutionary Party (MPRP) since 1939. **1958:** Yumjaagiyn Tsedenbal became dominant figure in MPRP and country. **1962:** Joined Comecon. **1966:** 20-year friendship, cooperation, and mutual-assistance pact signed with Soviet Union (USSR). Relations with China deteriorated. **1984:** Tsedenbal, the effective leader, retired; replaced by Jambyn Batmunkh. **1987:** Reduction in number of Soviet troops; Mongolia's external contacts broadened. Tolerance of traditional social customs encouraged nationalist revival. **1989:** Further Soviet troop reductions. **1990:** Demonstrations and democratization campaign launched, influenced by events in Eastern Europe; Batmunkh resigned and charged with corruption. Ex-communist MPRP elected in first free multiparty elections; Punsalmaagiyn Ochirbat indirectly elected president. Mongolian script readopted. **1991:** Privatization programme launched. GDP declined by 10%. Ochirbat resigned from MPRP in wake of anti-Gorbachev attempted coup in USSR. **1992:** MPRP returned to power in assembly elections held under new, noncommunist constitution. Economic situation worsened; GDP again declined by 10%. **1993:** Ochirbat won first direct presidential elections. **1996:** Economy showed signs of revival. Union Coalition won assembly elections, defeating MPRP and ending 75 years of communist rule. Defence cooperation agreement signed with USA. Mendsayhany Enhsayhan became prime minister. **1997:** Ex-communist Natsagiyn Bagabandi elected MPRP chairman. Economic shock therapy programme, supervised by IMF and World Bank, created unemployment and made government unpopular. Bagabandi elected president. All taxes and tariffs on trade abolished. **1998:** National Democratic Party (DU) leader Tsakhiagiin Elbegdorj became prime minister. His government toppled after losing a no-confidence vote. Attempts to form a new DU-led government, led by Rinchinnyamiin Amarjargal, failed. Janlaviyn Narantsatsralt, member of the MNDP, became prime minister.

Morocco Kingdom of

National name: *al-Mamlaka al-Maghrebia* **Area:** 458,730 sq km/177,115 sq mi (excluding Western Sahara) **Capital:** Rabat **Major towns/cities:** Casablanca, Marrakesh, Fez, Oujda, Kenitra, Tetouan, Meknès **Major ports:** Casablanca, Tangier, Agadir

Government

Head of state: Hassan II from 1961 **Head of government:** Abderrahmane Youssoufi from 1998 **Political system:** constitutional monarchy **Administrative divisions:** 49 provinces and prefectures with seven economic regions **Political parties:** Constitutional Union (UC), right wing; National Rally of Independents (RNI), royalist;

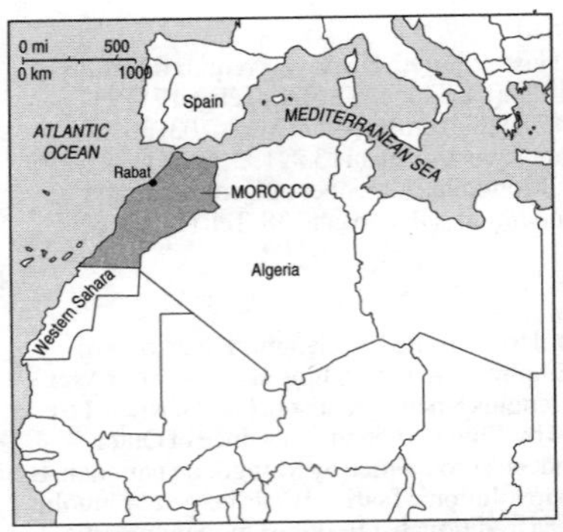

Popular Movement (MP), moderate, centrist; Istiqlal, nationalist, centrist; Socialist Union of Popular Forces (USFP), progressive socialist; National Democratic Party (PND), moderate, nationalist **Armed forces:** 196,300; paramilitary forces of 42,000 (1997) **Conscription:** 18 months **Death penalty:** retained and used for ordinary crimes **Defence spend:** (% GDP) 4.2 (1997) **Education spend:** (% GNP) 5.3 (1996) **Health spend:** (% GDP) 1.6 (1990–95)

Economy and resources

Currency: dirham (DH) **GDP:** (US$) 33.2 billion (1997) **Real GDP growth:** (%) –2.5 (1997) **GNP:** 34.4 billion (1997) **GNP per capita (PPP):** (US$) 3,130 (1997) **Consumer price inflation:** 4.1% (1997) **Unemployment:** 16% (1994) **Foreign debt:** (US$) 21.7 billion (1996) **Major trading partners:** France, Spain, USA, Japan, UK, Italy, Iran **Resources:** phosphate rock and phosphoric acid, coal, iron ore, barytes, lead, copper, manganese, zinc, petroleum, natural gas, fish **Exports:** phosphates and phosphoric acid, mineral products, seafoods and seafood products, citrus fruit, tobacco, clothing, hosiery. Principal market: France 31.7% (1997) **Imports:** crude petroleum, raw materials, wheat, chemicals, sawn wood, consumer goods. Principal source: France 26.6% (1997) **Arable land:** 19.3% (1995)

Population and society

Population: 27,377,000 (1998 est) **Population growth rate:** 1.8% (1995–2000); 1.6% (2000–05) **Population density:** (per sq km) 65.2 (1998 est) **Urban population:** (% of total) 54 (1997) **Age distribution:** (% of total population) 0–14 36.4%, 15–64 59.1%, 65+ 4.5% (1998) **Ethnic groups:** majority indigenous Berbers; sizeable Jewish minority **Language:** Arabic (official) 75%; Berber 25%, French, Spanish **Religion:** Sunni Muslim **Education:** (compulsory years) 6 **Literacy rate:** 61% (men); 38% (women) (1995 est) **Labour force:** 38% of population: 45% agriculture, 25% industry, 31% services (1990) **Life expectancy:** 65 (men); 69 (women) (1995–2000) **Child mortality rate:** (under 5, per 1,000 live births) 64 (1997) **Physicians:** 1 per 3,790 people (1994)

Practical information

Visa requirements: UK: visa not required. USA: visa not required **Embassy in the UK:** 49 Queen's Gate Gardens, London SW7 5NE. Tel: (0171) 581 5001–4; fax: (0171) 225 3862 **British embassy:** BP 45, 17 Boulevard de la Tour Hassan, Rabat. Tel: (7) 720 905/6; fax: (7) 704 531 **Chamber of commerce:** La Fédération des Chambres de Commerce et de l'Industrie du Maroc, 6 rue d'Erfoud, Rabat-Agdal. Tel: (7) 767 078; fax: (7) 767 076

Chronology

10th–3rd centuries BC: Phoenicians from Tyre settled along north coast. **1st century AD:** Northwest Africa became Roman province of Mauritania. **5th–6th centuries:** Invaded by Vandals and Visigoths. **682:** Start of Arab conquest, followed by spread of Islam. **8th century:** King Idris I established small Arab kingdom. **1056–1146:** The Almoravids, a Berber dynasty based at Marrakesh, built an empire embracing Morocco and parts of Algeria and Spain. **1122–1268:** After a civil war, the Almohads, a rival Berber dynasty, overthrew the Almoravids; Almohads extended empire but later lost most of Spain. **1258–1358:** Beni Merin dynasty supplanted Almohads. **14th century:** Moroccan Empire fragmented into separate kingdoms, based in Fez and Marrakesh. **15th century:** Spain and Portugal occupied Moroccan ports; expulsion of Muslims from Spain in 1492. **16th century:** Saadian dynasty restored unity of Morocco and resisted Turkish invasion. **1649:** Foundation of current Alaouite dynasty of sultans; Morocco remained independent and isolated kingdom. **1856:** Under British pressure, sultan opened Morocco to European commerce. **1860:** Spain invaded Morocco, which was forced to cede the southwestern region of Ifni. **1905:** Major international crisis caused by German objections to increasing French influence in Morocco. **1911:** Agadir Crisis: further German objections to French imperialism in Morocco overcome by territorial compensation in central Africa. **1912:** Morocco divided into French and Spanish protectorates; sultan reduced to puppet ruler. **1921:** Moroccan rebels, the Riffs, led by Abd el-Krim, defeated large Spanish force at Anual. **1923:** City of Tangier separated from Spanish Morocco and made a neutral international zone. **1926:** French forces crushed Riff revolt. **1944:** Nationalist party, Istiqlal, founded to campaign for full independence. **1948:** Consultative assemblies introduced. **1953–55:** Serious anti-French riots. **1956:** French and Spanish forces withdrew; Morocco regained effective independence under Sultan Muhammad V, who took title of king in 1957. **1961:** Muhammad V succeeded by Hassan II. **1962:** First constitution adopted; replaced in 1970 and 1972. **1965–77:** King Hassan suspended constitution and ruled by decree. **1969:** Spanish overseas province of Ifni returned to Morocco. **1975:** Spain withdrew from Western Sahara, leaving Morocco and Mauritania to divide it between themselves. **1976:** Polisario Front, supported by Algeria, began guerrilla war in Western Sahara with aim of securing its independence as Sahrahwi Arab Democratic Republic. **1979:** Mauritania withdrew from its portion of Western Sahara, which Morocco annexed after major battles with Polisario. **1984:** Morocco signed mutual defence with Libya, which had previously supported Polisario. **1991:** UN-sponsored cease-fire came into effect in Western Sahara. **1992:** Constitution amended in attempt to increase influence of parliament. **1994:** Abd-al Latif Filali became prime minister. **1996:** New two-chamber assembly approved. **1997:** Assembly elections proved inconclusive. **1998:** Prime Minister Abderrahmane Youssoufi formed centre–left coalition.

Mozambique People's Republic of

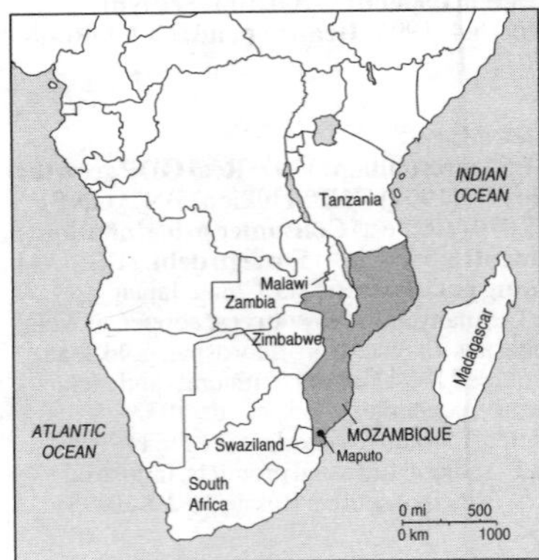

National name: *República Popular de Moçambique* **Area:** 799,380 sq km/ 308,640 sq mi **Capital:** Maputo (and chief port) **Major towns/cities:** Beira, Nampula, Nacala, Chimoio **Major ports:** Beira, Nacala, Quelimane

Government

Head of state: Joaquim Alberto Chissano from 1986 **Head of government:** Pascoal Mocumbi from 1994 **Political system:** emergent democracy **Administrative divisions:** 10 provinces **Political parties:** National Front for the Liberation of Mozambique (Frelimo), free market; Renamo, or Mozambique National Resistance (MNR), former rebel movement, right of centre **Armed forces:** 6,100 (1997) **Conscription:** early 1996 government was seeking to reintroduce compulsory military service, which had been suspended under the General Peace Accord **Death penalty:** abolished in 1990 **Defence spend:** (% GDP) 3.9 (1997) **Education spend:** (% GNP) 6.2 (1992) **Health spend:** (% GDP) 4.6 (1990–95)

Economy and resources

Currency: metical **GDP:** (US$) 1.9 billion (1997) **Real GDP growth:** (% change on previous year) 8.5 (1997) **GNP:** 1.7 billion

(1997) **GNP per capita (PPP):** (US$) 520 (1997) **Consumer price inflation:** 7.5% (1997) **Unemployment:** 50% (1990 est) **Foreign debt:** (US$) 5.8 billion (1996) **Major trading partners:** Spain, South Africa, USA, Japan, Italy, India, Zimbabwe, Portugal, France **Resources:** coal, salt, bauxite, graphite; reserves of iron ore, gold, precious and semi-precious stones, marble, natural gas (all largely unexploited in 1996) **Exports:** shrimps and other crustaceans, cashew nuts, raw cotton, sugar, copra, lobsters. Principal market: Spain 17.1% (1996) **Imports:** foodstuffs, capital goods, crude petroleum and petroleum products, machinery and spare parts, chemicals. Principal source: South Africa 54.6% (1996) **Arable land:** 3.8% (1995)

Population and society

Population: 18,880,000 (1998 est) **Population growth rate:** 2.5% (1995–2000); 2.8% (2000–05) **Population density:** (per sq km) 23.8 (1998 est) **Urban population:** (% of total) 37 (1997) **Age distribution:** (% of total population) 0–14 44.9%, 15–64 52.8%, 65+ 2.3% (1998) **Ethnic groups:** the majority belong to local groups, the largest being the Makua-Lomue, who comprise about 38% of the population; the other significant group is the Tsonga (24%) **Language:** Portuguese (official); 16 African languages **Religion:** animist, Roman Catholic, Muslim **Education:** (compulsory years) 7 **Literacy rate:** 64% (men); 37% (women) (1995 est) **Labour force:** 53% of population: 83% agriculture, 8% industry, 9% services (1990) **Life expectancy:** 46 (men); 48 (women) (1995–2000) **Child mortality rate:** (under 5, per 1,000 live births) 163 (1997) **Physicians:** 1 per 36,225 people (1993 est)

Practical information

Visa requirements: UK: visa required. USA: visa required **Embassy in the UK:** 21 Fitzroy Square, London W1P 5HJ. Tel: (0171) 383 3800; fax: (0171) 383 3801 **British embassy:** Caixa Postal 55, Avenida Vladimir I Léuine 310, Maputo. Tel: (1) 420 111/2/5/6/7; fax: (1) 421 666 **Chamber of commerce:** Câmara de Comercio de Mozambique, CP 1836, Rua Mateus Sansão Mutemba 452, Maputo. Tel: (1) 491 970; telex: 6498

Chronology

1st–4th centuries AD: Bantu-speaking peoples settled in Mozambique. **8th–15th century:** Arab gold traders established independent city-states on coast. **1498:** Portuguese navigator Vasco da Gama was the first European visitor; at this time the most important local power was the Maravi kingdom of the Mwene Matapa peoples, who controlled much of the Zambezi basin. **1626:** The Mwene Matapa formally recognized Portuguese sovereignty. Portuguese soldiers set up private agricultural estates and used slave labour to exploit gold and ivory resources. **late 17th century:** Portuguese temporarily pushed south of Zambezi by the ascendant Rozwi kingdom. **1752:** First Portuguese colonial governor appointed; slave trade outlawed. **late 19th century:** Concessions given by Portugal to private companies to develop and administer parts of Mozambique. **1930:** Colonial Act established more centralized Portuguese rule, ending concessions to monopolistic companies and forging closer integration with Lisbon. **1951:** Became an overseas province of Portugal and, economically, a cheap labour reserve for South Africa's mines. **1962:** Frelimo (National Front for the Liberation of Mozambique) established in exile in Tanzania by Marxist guerrillas, including Samora Machel, to fight for independence. **1964:** Fighting broke out between Frelimo forces and Portuguese troops, starting a ten-year liberation war; Portugal despatched 70,000 troops to Mozambique. **1969:** Eduardo Mondlane, leader of Frelimo, was assassinated. **1975:** Following revolution in Portugal, independence achieved as a socialist republic, with Machel as president, Joaquim Chissano as prime minister, and Frelimo as sole legal party; Portuguese settlers left the country. Lourenço Marques renamed Maputo. Key enterprises nationalized. **1977:** Renamo resistance group formed, with covert backing of South Africa. **1979:** Machel encouraged Patriotic Front guerrillas in Rhodesia to accept Lancaster House Agreement, creating Zimbabwe. **1983:** Good relations restored with Western powers. **1984:** Nkomati Accord of nonaggression signed with South Africa. **1986:** Machel killed in air crash near South African border; succeeded by Chissano. **1988:** Tanzanian troops withdrawn from Mozambique. **1989:** Renamo continued attacks on government facilities and civilians. **1990:** One-party rule officially ended, and Frelimo abandoned Marxist–Leninism and embraced market economy. **1992:** Peace accord signed with Renamo. **1993:** Price riots in Maputo as result of implementation of IMF-promoted reforms to restructure the economy devastated by war and drought. **1994:** Demobilization of contending armies completed. Chissano and Frelimo re-elected in first multiparty elections; Renamo (now a political party) agreed to cooperate with government. **1995:** Admitted to Commonwealth.

Myanmar Union of (formerly **Burma,** until 1989)

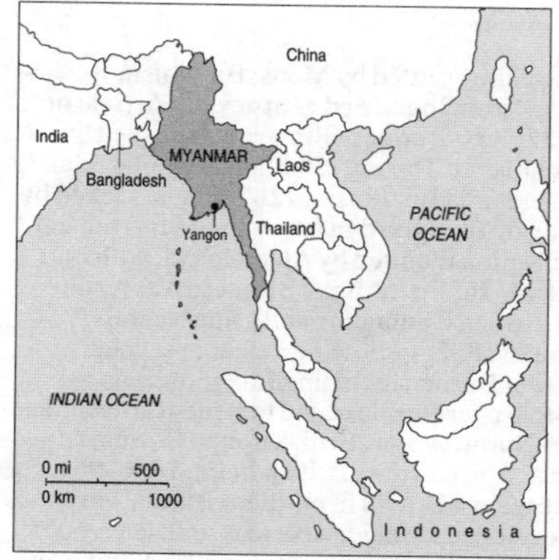

National name: *Thammada Myanmar Naingngandaw* **Area:** 676,577 sq km/261,226 sq mi **Capital:** Yangon (formerly Rangoon) (and chief port) **Major towns/cities:** Mandalay, Mawlamyine, Bago, Bassein, Taunggyi, Sittwe, Manywa

Government

Head of state and government: Than Shwe from 1992 **Political system:** military republic **Administrative divisions:** seven states and seven divisions **Political parties:** National Unity Party (NUP), military-socialist ruling party; National League for Democracy (NLD), pluralist opposition grouping **Armed forces:** 429,000; plus two paramilitary units totalling 85,300 (1997) **Conscription:** military service is voluntary **Death penalty:** retained and used for ordinary crimes **Defence spend:** (% GDP) 7.7 (1997) **Education spend:** (% GNP) 1.3 (1995) **Health spend:** (% GDP) 0.5 (1990–95)

Economy and resources

Currency: kyat **GDP:** (US$) 133.5 billion (1996) **Real GDP growth:** (% change on previous year) 5.7 (1996) **GNP:** 134.1 billion (1996 est) **GNP per capita (PPP):** (US$) 1,280 (1996 est) **Consumer price inflation:** 29.4% (1997) **Unemployment:** 2.1% (1994 est) **Foreign debt:** (US$) 5.18 billion (1996) **Major trading partners:** China, Singapore, India, Japan, Malaysia, Hong Kong **Resources:** natural gas, petroleum, zinc, tin, copper, tungsten, coal, lead, gems, silver, gold **Exports:** teak, rice, pulses and beans, rubber, hardwood, base metals, gems, cement. Principal market: India 16.8% (1997) **Imports:** raw materials, machinery and transport equipment, tools and spares, construction materials, chemicals, consumer goods. Principal source: Singapore 29.5% (1997) **Arable land:** 14.5 (1995)

Population and society

Population: 44,497,000 (1998 est) **Population growth rate:** 1.8% (1995–2000) **Population density:** (per sq km) 71.9 (1998 est) **Urban population:** (% of total) 27 (1997) **Age distribution:** (% of total population) 0–14 36.5%, 15–64 59.3%, 65+ 4.2% (1998) **Ethnic groups:** Burmans, who predominate in the fertile central river valley and southern coastal and delta regions, constitute the ethnic majority, comprising 72% of the total population. Out of more than 100 minority communities, the most important are the Karen (7%), Shan (6%), Indians (6%), Chinese (3%), Kachin (2%), and Chin (2%). The indigenous minority communities, who predominate in mountainous border regions, show considerable hostility towards the culturally and politically dominant Burmans, undermining national unity **Language:** Burmese (official), English

Religion: Hinayāna Buddhist 85%, animist, Christian, Muslim **Education:** (compulsory years) 5 **Literacy rate:** 89% (men); 72% (women) (1995 est) **Labour force:** 68.7% agriculture, 9.8% industry, 21.5% services (1994) **Life expectancy:** 59 (men); 62 (women) (1995–2000) **Child mortality rate:** (under 5, per 1,000 live births) 90 (1997) **Physicians:** 1 per 3,554 people (1994)

Practical information

Visa requirements: UK: visa required. USA: visa required **Embassy in the UK:** 19a Charles Street, Berkeley Square, London W1X 8ER. Tel: (0171) 629 6966; fax: (0171) 629 4169 **British embassy:** PO Box 638, 80 Strand Road, Yangon. Tel: (1) 95300; fax: (1) 89566 **Chamber of commerce:** Myanmar Foreign Trade Bank, PO Box 203, 80–86 Maha Bandoola Garden Street, Yangon. Tel: (1) 83129; fax: (1) 89585

Chronology

3rd century BC: Sittoung valley settled by Mons; Buddhism introduced by missionaries from India. **3rd century AD:** Arrival of Burmans from Tibet. **1057:** First Burmese Empire established by King Anawrahta, who conquered Thaton, established capital inland at Pagan, and adopted Theravāda Buddhism. **1287:** Pagan sacked by Mongols. **1531:** Founding of Toungoo dynasty, which survived until mid-18th century. **1755:** Nation reunited by Alaungpaya, with port of Rangoon as capital. **1824–26:** First Anglo-Burmese war resulted in Arakan coastal strip, between Chittagong and Cape Negrais, being ceded to British India. **1852:** Following defeat in second Anglo-Burmese war, Lower Burma, including Rangoon, was annexed by British. **1886:** Upper Burma ceded to British after defeat of Thibaw in third Anglo-Burmese war; British united Burma, which was administered as a province of British India. **1886–96:** Guerrilla warfare waged against British in northern Burma. **early 20th century:** Burma developed as major rice, teak and, later, oil exporter, drawing in immigrant labourers and traders from India and China. **1937:** Became British crown colony in Commonwealth, with a degree of internal self-government. **1942:** Invaded and occupied by Japan, who installed anti-British nationalist puppet government headed by Ba Maw. **1945:** Liberated from Japanese control by British, assisted by nationalists Aung San and U Nu, formerly ministers in puppet government, who had formed the socialist Anti Fascist People's Freedom League (AFPFL). **1947:** Assassination of Aung San and six members of interim government by political opponents. **1948:** Independence achieved from Britain as Burma, with U Nu as prime minister. Left Commonwealth. Quasi-federal state established. **1958–60:** Administered by emergency government, formed by army chief of staff Gen Ne Win. **1962:** Gen Ne Win reassumed power in left-wing army coup; he proceeded to abolish federal system and follow 'Burmese Way to Socialism', involving sweeping nationalization and international isolation, which crippled the economy. **1973–74:** Adopted presidential-style 'civilian' constitution. **1975:** Opposition National Democratic Front formed by regionally-based minority groups, who mounted guerrilla insurgencies. **1987:** Student demonstrations in Rangoon as food shortages worsened. **1988:** Government resigned after violent student demonstrations and workers' riots. Gen Saw Maung seized power in military coup believed to have been organized by the ousted Ne Win; over 2,000 killed. **1989:** Martial law declared; thousands arrested including advocates of democracy and human rights. Country renamed Myanmar and capital Yangon. **1990:** Landslide general election victory for opposition National League for Democracy (NLD) ignored by military junta; NLD leaders U Nu and Suu Kyi, the daughter of Aung San, placed under house arrest. Breakaway opposition group formed parallel government. **1991:** Martial law and human-rights abuses continued. Government crackdown on Karen ethnic rebels in southeast. Suu Kyi, still imprisoned, awarded Nobel Peace Prize. Pogrom against Muslim community in Arakan province in southwest Myanmar. Western countries imposed sanctions. **1992:** Saw Maung replaced by Than Shwe. Several political prisoners liberated. Martial law lifted, but restrictions on political freedom remained. **1993:** Cease-fire agreed with Kachin rebels in northeast. **1995:** Karen rebels forced to flee to Thailand after further military crackdown. Suu Kyi released from house arrest, but her appointment as NLD leader declared illegal. NLD boycotted constitutional convention. **1996:** Karen rebels agreed to peace talks. Suu Kyi held first party congress since her release; 200 supporters detained by government. Major demonstrations in support of Suu Kyi. **1997:** Admission to Association of South East Asian Nations (ASEAN) granted, despite US sanctions for human-rights abuses. Currency under threat from speculators. **1998:** Japan resumed flow of aid, which had been stopped in 1988. Military junta ignored pro-democracy roadside protests by Aung San Suu Kyi and broke up student demonstrations. Junta leader Lt-Gen Khin Nyunt became chairman of a new political affairs committee. 300 members of the opposition NLD were released from detention.

Namibia **Republic of** (formerly **South West Africa**)

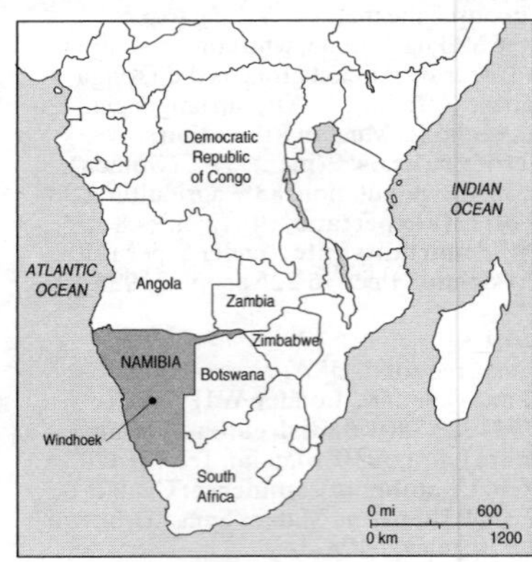

Area: 824,300 sq km/318,262 sq mi **Capital:** Windhoek **Major towns/cities:** Swakopmund, Rehoboth, Rundu **Major ports:** Walvis Bay

Government

Head of state: Sam Nujoma from 1990 **Head of government:** Hage Geingob from 1990 **Political system:** democracy **Administrative divisions:** 13 regions **Political parties:** South West Africa People's Organization (SWAPO), socialist Ovambo-oriented; Democratic Turnhalle Alliance (DTA), moderate, multiracial coalition; United Democratic Front (UDF), disaffected ex-SWAPO members; National Christian Action (ACN), white conservative **Armed forces:** 5,800 (1997) **Conscription:** military service is voluntary **Death penalty:** abolished in 1990 **Defence spend:** (% GDP) 3.5 (1997) **Education spend:** (% GNP) 9.1 (1996) **Health spend:** (% GDP) 3.7 (1990–95)

Economy and resources

Currency: Namibia dollar **GDP:** (US$) 3.4 billion (1997) **Real GDP growth:** (% change on previous year) 4.5 (1997) **GNP:** 3.6 billion (1997) **GNP per capita (PPP):** (US$) 5,440 (1997) **Consumer price inflation:** 10% (1998) **Unemployment:** 38% (1995 est) **Foreign debt:** (US$) 4.7 billion (1993) **Major trading partners:** South Africa, UK, Japan, Germany, France, USA **Resources:** uranium, copper, lead, zinc, silver, tin, gold, salt, semi-precious stones, diamonds (one of the world's leading producers of gem diamonds), hydrocarbons, lithium, manganese, tungsten, cadmium, vanadium **Exports:** diamonds, fish and fish products, live animals and meat, uranium, karakul pelts. Principal market: UK 38% (1996) **Imports:** food and live animals, beverages, tobacco, transport equipment, mineral fuels, chemicals, electrical and other machinery. Principal source: South Africa 87% (1996) **Arable land:** 1% (1995)

Population and society

Population: 1,660,000 (1998 est) **Population growth rate:** 2.4% (1995–2000) **Population density:** (per sq km) 2 (1998 est) **Urban population:** (% of total) 38 (1997) **Age distribution:** (% of total population) 0–14 44.2%, 15–64 51.9%, 65+ 4.0% (1998) **Ethnic groups:** 85% black African, of which 51% belong to the Ovambo tribe; the remainder includes the pastoral Nama and hunter-gatherer groups. There is a 6% white minority **Language:** English (official), Afrikaans, German, indigenous languages **Religion:** mainly Christian (Lutheran, Roman Catholic, Dutch Reformed Church,

Anglican) **Education:** (compulsory years) 7 **Literacy rate:** N/A **Labour force:** 42% of population: 49% agriculture, 15% industry, 36% services (1990) **Life expectancy:** 55 (men); 57 (women) (1995–2000) **Child mortality rate:** (under 5, per 1,000 live births) 98 (1997) **Physicians:** 1 per 4,328 people (1993 est)

Practical information

Visa requirements: UK: visa not required. USA: visa not required **Embassy in the UK:** 6 Chandos Street, London W1M 0LQ. Tel: (0171) 636 6244; fax: (0171) 637 5694 **British embassy:** British High Commission, PO Box 22202, 116 Robert Mugabe Avenue, Windhoek. Tel: (61) 223 022; fax: (61) 228 895 **Chamber of commerce:** Namibia National Chamber of Commerce and Industry, PO Box 9355, Windhoek. Tel: (61) 228 809; fax: (61) 228 009

Chronology

1480s: Coast visited by European explorers. **16th century:** Bantu-speaking Herero migrated into northwest and Ovambo settled in northernmost areas. **1840s:** Rhenish Missionary Society began to spread German influence; Jonkar Afrikaner conquest state dominant in southern Namibia. **1884:** Germany annexed most of the area, calling it South West Africa, with Britain incorporating a small enclave around Walvis Bay in the Cape Colony of South Africa. **1892:** German farmers arrived to settle in the region. **1903–04:** Uprisings by the long-settled Nama (Khoikhoi) and Herero peoples brutally repressed by Germans, with over half the local communities slaughtered. **1908:** Discovery of diamonds led to a larger influx of Europeans. **1915:** German colony invaded and seized by South Africa during World War I and the Ovambo, in the north, were conquered. **1920:** Administered by South Africa, under League of Nations mandate. **1946:** Full incorporation in South Africa refused by United Nations (UN). **1949:** White voters in South West Africa given representation in the South African parliament. **1958:** South West Africa People's Organization (SWAPO) formed to campaign for racial equality and full independence. **1960:** Radical wing of SWAPO, led by Sam Nujoma, forced into exile. **1964:** UN voted to end South Africa's mandate, but South Africa refused to relinquish control or soften its policies towards the economically disenfranchised black majority. **1966:** South Africa's apartheid laws extended to the country; 60% of land was allocated to whites, who formed 10% of the population. **1968:** South West Africa redesignated Namibia by UN; SWAPO, drawing strong support from the Ovambo people of the north, began armed guerrilla struggle against South African rule, establishing People's Liberation Army of Namibia (PLAN). **1971:** Prolonged general strike by black Namibian contract workers. **1973:** UN recognized SWAPO as the 'authentic representative of the Namibian people'. **1975–76:** Establishment of new Marxist regime in independent Angola strengthened position of SWAPO guerrilla movement, but also led to increased military involvement of South Africa in the region. **1978:** UN Security Council Resolution 435 for the granting of full independence accepted by South Africa and then rescinded. **1983:** Direct rule reimposed by Pretoria after the resignation of the Democratic Turnhalle Alliance (DTA), a conservative administration dominated by whites. **1985:** South Africa installed new puppet administration, the Transitional Government of National Unity (TGNU), which tried to reform apartheid system, but was not recognized by UN. **1988:** Peace talks between South Africa, Angola, and Cuba led to agreement on troop withdrawals and full independence for Namibia. **1989:** UN peacekeeping force stationed to oversee free elections to assembly to draft new constitution; SWAPO won the elections. **1990:** Liberal multiparty constitution adopted; independence achieved. Sam Nujoma, SWAPO's former guerrilla leader, elected president. Joined Commonwealth. **1993:** South Africa, with its new multiracial government, relinquished claim to Walvis Bay sovereignty. Namibia dollar launched with South African rand parity. **1994:** SWAPO won assembly elections; Nujoma re-elected president.

Nauru Republic of

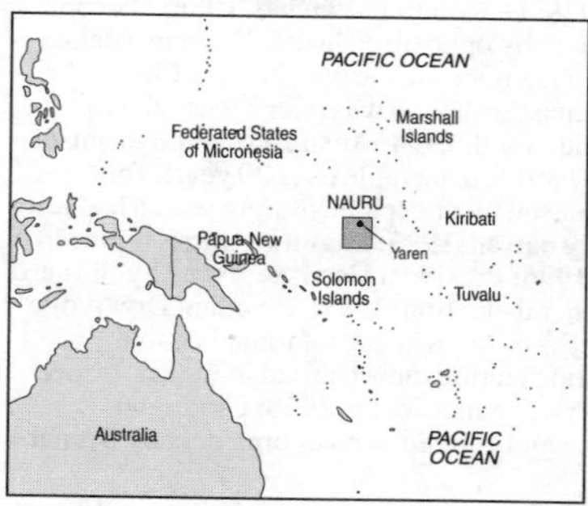

National name: *Naoero* **Area:** 21 sq km/8.1 sq mi **Capital:** (seat of government) Yaren District

Government

Head of state and government: Rene Harris from 1999 **Political system:** liberal democracy **Administrative divisions:** 14 districts **Political parties:** candidates are traditionally elected as independents, grouped into pro- and antigovernment factions; Democratic Party of Nauru (DPN), only formal political party, antigovernment **Armed forces:** no standing army; Australia is responsible for Nauru's defence **Death penalty:** retains the death penalty for ordinary crimes but can be considered abolitionist in practice (no executions since independence)

Economy and resources

Currency: Australian dollar **GDP:** (US$) 368 million (1995) **GNP:** 304 million (1994 est) **GNP per capita (PPP):** (US$) 11,800 (1994 est) **Consumer price inflation:** –3.6% (1993) **Major trading partners:** Australia, New Zealand, Philippines, Japan **Resources:** phosphates **Exports:** phosphates. Principal market: Australia **Imports:** food and live animals, building construction materials, petroleum, machinery, medical supplies. Principal source: Australia

Population and society

Population: 11,000 (1998 est) **Population growth rate:** 1.8% (1995–2025) **Population density:** (per sq km) 500 (1998 est) **Urban population:** (% of total) 100 (1997) **Ethnic groups:** about 87% of European origin (mostly British), about 9% Maori, and about 2% Pacific Islander **Language:** Nauruan (official), English **Religion:** Protestant, Roman Catholic **Education:** (compulsory years) 10 **Literacy rate:** 99% (men); 99% (women) (1994 est) **Life expectancy:** 64 (men); 69 (women) (1996 est) **Child mortality rate:** (under 5, per 1,000 live births) 40 (1994) **Physicians:** 1 per 700 people (1990)

Practical information

Visa requirements: UK: visa required. USA: visa required **Embassy in the UK:** Nauru Government Office, 3 Chesham Street, London SW1X 8ND. Tel: (0171) 235 6911; fax: (0171) 235 7423 **British embassy:** the British Embassy in Suva (see Fiji Islands) deals with enquiries relating to Nauru **Chamber of commerce:** Central Bank of Nauru, PO Box 289, Nauru. Tel: 444 3238; fax: 444 3203

Chronology

1798: British whaler Capt John Fearn first visited Nauru and named it 'Pleasant Island'. **1830s–80s:** The island was a haven for white runaway convicts and deserters. **1888:** Annexed by Germany at the request of German settlers who sought protection from local clan unrest. **1899:** Phosphate deposits discovered; mining began eight years later, with indentured Chinese labourers brought in to work British Australian-owned mines. **1914:** Occupied by Australia on outbreak of World War I. **1920:** Administered by Australia on behalf of itself, New Zealand, and the UK until independence, except 1942–43, when occupied by Japan, and two-thirds of the population were deported briefly to Micronesia. **1951:** Local Government Council set up to replace Council of Chiefs. **1956:** Hammer DeRoburt became head chief of Nauru. **1968:** Independence achieved, with 'special member' British Commonwealth status.

Hammer DeRoburt elected president. **1976:** Bernard Dowiyogo elected president as criticism of DeRoburt's personal style of government mounted. **1978:** DeRoburt re-elected. **1986:** DeRoburt briefly replaced as president by opposition leader Kennan Adeang. **1987:** Adeang established Democratic Party of Nauru. **1989:** DeRoburt replaced by Kenas Aroi, who was later succeeded by Dowiyogo. **1992:** DeRoburt died. **1994:** Australia agreed to out-of-court settlement of A$107 million, payable over 20 years, for environmental damage caused by phosphate mining which had left 80% of land agriculturally barren. **1995:** Lagumot Harris replaced Dowiyogo as president. **1996:** President Harris replaced by Bernard Dowiyogo, following general election. **1997:** President Dowiyogo defeated in no-confidence motion. Kinza Clodumar became president after new general election; new cabinet included former presidents Dowiyogo and Kennan Adeang. **1998:** Clodumar defeated in no-confidence motion; replaced as president by Bernard Dowiyogo.

Nepal Kingdom of

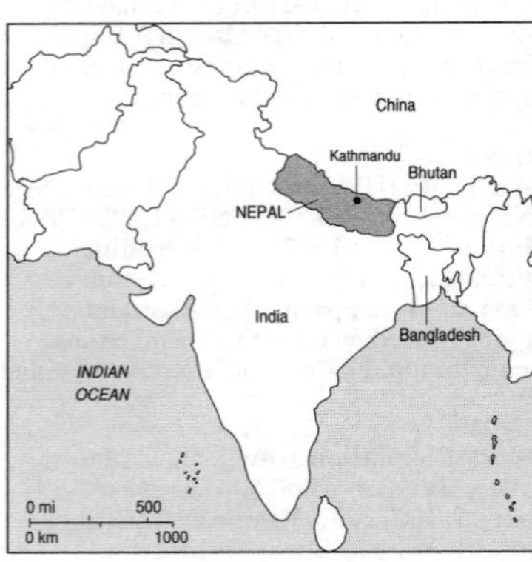

National name: *Nepal Adhirajya* **Area:** 147,181 sq km/56,826 sq mi **Capital:** Kathmandu **Major towns/cities:** Pátan, Moráng, Bhádgáon, Biratnagar, Lalitpur, Bhaktapur, Pokhara

Government

Head of state: King Birendra Bir Bikram Shah Dev from 1972 **Head of government:** Krishna Prasad Bhattarai from 1999 **Political system:** constitutional monarchy **Administrative divisions:** 14 zones **Political parties:** Nepali Congress Party (NCP), left of centre; United Nepal Communist Party (UNCP; Unified Marxist–Leninist), left wing; Rashtriya Prajatantra Party (RPP), monarchist **Armed forces:** 46,000 (1997) **Conscription:** military service is voluntary **Death penalty:** abolished in 1997 **Defence spend:** (% GDP) 0.9 (1997) **Education spend:** (% GNP) 3.1 (1996) **Health spend:** (% GDP) 1.2 (1990–95)

Economy and resources

Currency: Nepalese rupee **GDP:** (US$) 4.9 billion (1997) **Real GDP growth:** (% change on previous year) 6.1 (1996) **GNP:** 4.8 billion (1997) **GNP per capita (PPP):** (US$) 1,090 (1997) **Consumer price inflation:** 9.4% (1996) **Unemployment:** 4.9% (1990) **Foreign debt:** (US$) 2.4 billion (1996) **Major trading partners:** Germany, Thailand, India, Japan, Singapore, USA, Switzerland **Resources:** lignite, talcum, magnesite, limestone, copper, cobalt**Exports:** woollen carpets, clothing, hides and skins, food grains, jute, timber, oil seeds, ghee, potatoes, medicinal herbs, cattle. Principal market: Germany 34% (1997) **Imports:** basic manufactures, machinery and transport equipment, chemicals, pharmaceuticals. Principal source: India 26.9% (1997) **Arable land:** 20.4% (1995)

Population and society

Population: 22,847,000 (1998 est) **Population growth rate:** 2.5% (1995–2000); 2.4% (2000–00) **Population density:** (per sq km) 173.2 (1998 est) **Urban population:** (% of total) 11 (1997) **Age distribution:** (% of total population) 0–14 41.6%, 15–64 55.0%, 65+ 3.3% (1998) **Ethnic groups:** 80% of Indo-Nepalese origin, including the Gurkhas, Paharis, Newars, and Tharus; 20% of Tibeto-Nepalese descent (concentrated in the north and east) **Language:** Nepali (official); 20 dialects spoken **Religion:** Hindu 90%; Buddhist, Muslim, Christian **Education:** (compulsory years) 5 **Literacy rate:** 38% (men); 13% (women) (1995 est) **Labour force:** 47% of population: 93% agriculture, 1% industry, 6% services (1991) **Life expectancy:** 58 (men); 57 (women) (1995–2000) **Child mortality rate:** (under 5, per 1,000 live births) 108 (1997) **Physicians:** 1 per 13,634 people (1993)

Practical information

Visa requirements: UK: visa required. USA: visa required **Embassy in the UK:** 12a Kensington Palace Gardens, London W8 4QV. Tel: (0171) 229 1594; fax: (0171) 792 9861 **British embassy:** PO Box 106, Lainchaur, Kathmandu. Tel: (1) 410 583; fax: (1) 411 789 **Chamber of commerce:** PO Box 198, Chamber Bhavan, Kantipath, Kathmandu. Tel: (1) 222 890; fax: (1) 229 998

Chronology

8th century BC: Kathmandu Valley occupied by Ahirs (shepherd kings), Tibeto-Burman migrants from northern India. *c.* **563 BC:** In Lumbini in far south, Prince Siddhartha Gautama, the historic Buddha, was born. **AD 300:** Licchavis dynasty immigrated from India and introduced caste system. **13th–16th centuries:** Dominated by Malla dynasty, great patrons of the arts. **1768:** Nepal emerged as unified kingdom after ruler of the principality of the Gurkhas in the west, King Prithwi Narayan Shah, conquered Kathmandu Valley. **1792:** Nepal's expansion halted by defeat at the hands of Chinese in Tibet; commercial treaty signed with Britain. **1815–16:** Anglo-Nepali 'Gurkha War'; Nepal became British-dependent buffer state with British resident stationed in Kathmandu. **1846:** Fell under sway of Rana family, who became hereditary chief ministers, dominating powerless monarchy and isolating Nepal from outside world. **1923:** Full independence formally recognized by Britain. **1951:** Monarchy restored to power and Ranas overthrown in 'palace revolution' supported by Nepali Congress Party (NCP). **1959:** Constitution created elected legislature. **1960–61:** Parliament dissolved by King Mahendra; political parties banned after NCP's pro-India socialist leader B P Koirala became prime minister. **1962:** New constitution provided for tiered, traditional system of indirectly elected local councils (*panchayats*) and an appointed prime minister. **1972:** King Mahendra died; succeeded by his son, King Birendra Bikram Shah Dev. **1980:** Constitutional referendum held following popular agitation led by B P Koirala resulted in introduction of direct, but nonparty, elections to National Assembly. **1983:** Overthrow of monarch-supported prime minister by directly elected deputies to National Assembly. **1986:** New assembly elections returned majority opposed to *panchayat* system of partyless government. **1988:** Strict curbs placed on opposition activity; over 100 supporters of banned NCP arrested; censorship imposed. **1989:** Border blockade imposed by India during treaty dispute. **1990:** *Panchayat* system collapsed after mass NCP-led violent prodemocracy demonstrations; new democratic constitution introduced, and ban on political parties lifted. **1991:** Nepali Congress Party, led by Girija Prasad Koirala, won general election. **1992:** Communists led antigovernment demonstrations in Kathmandu and Pátan. **1994:** Koirala's government defeated on no-confidence motion; parliament dissolved. Minority communist government formed under Man Mohan Adhikari. **1995:** Parliament dissolved by King Birendra at Prime Minister Adhikari's request; fresh elections called but Supreme Court ruled the move unconstitutional. Sher Bahadur Deuba (NCP) became prime minister. **1997:** Deuba defeated in vote of no-confidence. New coalition formed, led by right-wing Rastriya Prajatantra Party under Prime Minister Lokendra Bahadur Chand. UCPN successes in local elections. Coalition divided; government defeated on no-confidence vote. Former prime minister Surya Bahadur Thapa returned pending new election. **1998:** Government narrowly survived no-confidence vote. Thapa stood down as prime minister and was replaced by G P Koirala of the NCP.

Netherlands, the Kingdom of (popularly referred to as Holland)

National name: *Koninkrijk der Nederlanden* **Area:** 41,863 sq km/16,163 sq mi **Capital:** Amsterdam **Major towns/cities:** Rotterdam, The Hague (seat of government), Utrecht, Eindhoven,

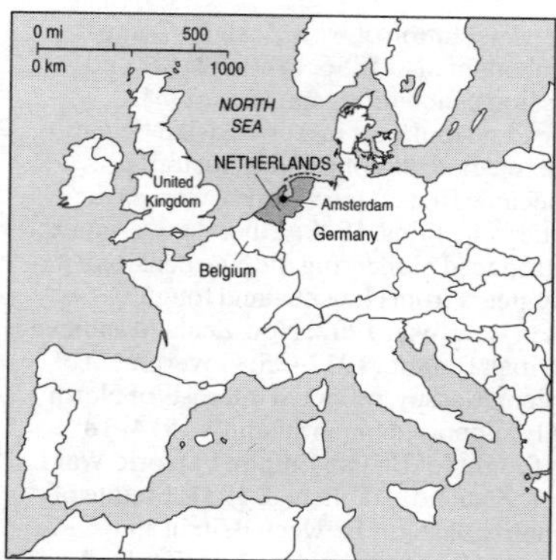

Groningen, Tilburg, Maastricht, Haarlem, Apeldoorn, Nijmegen, Enschede **Major ports:** Rotterdam **Territories:** Aruba, Netherlands Antilles (Caribbean)

Government
Head of state: Queen Beatrix Wilhelmina Armgard from 1980 **Head of government:** Wim Kok from 1994 **Political system:** constitutional monarchy **Administrative divisions:** 12 provinces **Political parties:** Christian Democratic Appeal (CDA), Christian, right of centre; Labour Party (PvdA), democratic socialist, left of centre; People's Party for Freedom and Democracy (VVD), liberal, free enterprise; Democrats 66 (D66), ecologist, centrist; Political Reformed Party (SGP), moderate Calvinist; Evangelical Political Federation (RPF), radical Calvinist; Reformed Political Association (GPV), fundamentalist Calvinist; Green Left, ecologist; General League of the Elderly (AOV), pensioner-oriented **Armed forces:** 57,200 (1997) **Conscription:** military service is voluntary **Death penalty:** abolished in 1982 **Defence spend:** (% GDP) 1.9 (1997) **Education spend:** (% GNP) 5.3 (1995) **Health spend:** (% GDP) 6.7 (1990–95)

Economy and resources
Currency: guilder **GDP:** (US$) 360.5 billion (1997) **Real GDP growth:** (% change on previous year) 3.3 (1997) **GNP:** 402.7 billion (1997) **GNP per capita (PPP):** (US$) 21,340 (1997) **Consumer price inflation:** 2.4% (1998) **Unemployment:** 4% (1998) **Major trading partners:** EU (principally Germany, Benelux, UK, France, and Italy), USA **Resources:** petroleum, natural gas **Exports:** machinery and transport equipment, foodstuffs, live animals, petroleum and petroleum products, natural gas, chemicals, plants and cut flowers, plant-derived products. Principal market: Germany 27.4% (1997) **Imports:** electrical machinery, cars and other vehicles, mineral fuels, metals and metal products, plastics, paper and cardboard, clothing and accessories. Principal source: Germany 20.7% (1997) **Arable land:** 26% (1995)

Population and society
Population: 15,678,000 (1998 est) **Population growth rate:** 0.5% (1995–2000); 0.3% (2000–05) **Population density:** (per sq km) 463.5 (1998 est) **Urban population:** (% of total) 89 (1997) **Age distribution:** (% of total population) 0–14 18.3%, 15–64 68.2%, 65+ 13.5% (1998) **Ethnic groups:** primarily Germanic, with some Gallo-Celtic mixtures; sizeable Indonesian and Surinamese minorities **Language:** Dutch **Religion:** Roman Catholic, Dutch Reformed Church **Education:** (compulsory years) 11 **Literacy rate:** 99% (men); 99% (women) (1995 est) **Labour force:** 48.5% of population: 3.9% agriculture, 22.4% industry, 73.8% services (1996) **Life expectancy:** 75 (men); 81 (women) (1995–2000) **Child mortality rate:** (under 5, per 1,000 live births) 8 (1997) **Physicians:** 1 per 394 people (1994)

Practical information
Visa requirements: UK: visa not required. USA: visa not required **Embassy in the UK:** 38 Hyde Park Gate, London SW7 5DP. Tel: (0171) 584 5040; fax: (0171) 581 3458 **British embassy:** Lange Voorhout 10, 2514 ED The Hague. Tel: (70) 364 5800; fax: (70) 427 0345 **Chamber of commerce:** The Hague Chamber of Commerce and Industry, Konigskade 30, 2596 AA The Hague. Tel: (70) 328 7100; fax: (70) 324 0684

Chronology
55 BC: Julius Caesar brought lands south of River Rhine under Roman rule. **4th century AD:** Region overrun by Franks and Saxons. **7th–8th centuries:** Franks subdued Saxons north of Rhine and imposed Christianity. **843–12th centuries:** Division of Holy Roman Empire: the Netherlands repeatedly partitioned, not falling clearly into either French or German kingdoms. **12th–14th centuries:** Local feudal lords, led by count of Holland and bishop of Utrecht, became practically independent; Dutch towns became prosperous trading centres, usually ruled by small groups of merchants. **15th century:** Low Countries (Holland, Belgium, and Flanders) came under rule of dukes of Burgundy. **1477:** Low Countries passed by marriage to Habsburgs. **1555:** The Netherlands passed to Spain upon division of Habsburg domains. **1568:** Dutch rebelled under leadership of William the Silent, Prince of Orange, and fought a long war of independence. **1579:** Union of Utrecht: seven northern rebel provinces formed United Provinces. **17th century:** 'Golden Age': Dutch led world in trade, art, and science, and founded colonies in East and West Indies, primarily through Dutch East India Company, founded in 1602. **1648:** Treaty of Westphalia: United Provinces finally recognized as independent Dutch Republic. **1652–54:** Commercial and colonial rivalries led to naval war with England. **1652–72:** Johann de Witt ruled Dutch Republic as premier after conflict between republicans and House of Orange. **1665–67:** Second Anglo-Dutch war. **1672–74:** Third Anglo-Dutch war. **1672:** William of Orange became stadholder (ruling as chief magistrate) of the Dutch Republic, an office which became hereditary in the Orange family. **1672–78:** The Netherlands fought to prevent domination by King Louis XIV of France. **1688–97 and 1701–13:** War with France resumed. **18th century:** Exhausted by war, the Netherlands ceased to be a Great Power. **1795:** Revolutionary France conquered the Netherlands and established Batavian Republic. **1806:** Napoleon made his brother Louis king of Holland. **1810:** France annexed the Netherlands. **1815:** Northern and southern Netherlands (Holland and Belgium) unified as Kingdom of the Netherlands under King William I of Orange, who also became grand duke of Luxembourg. **1830:** Southern Netherlands rebelled and declared independence as Belgium. **1848:** Liberal constitution adopted. **1890:** Queen Wilhelmina succeeded to throne; dynastic link with Luxembourg broken. **1894–96:** Dutch suppressed colonial revolt in Java. **1914–18:** The Netherlands neutral during World War I. **1940–45:** Occupied by Germany during World War II. **1948:** The Netherlands formed Benelux customs union with Belgium and Luxembourg; Queen Wilhelmina abdicated in favour of her daughter Juliana. **1949:** Became founding member of North Atlantic Treaty Organization (NATO); most of Dutch East Indies became independent as Indonesia after four years of war. **1953:** Dykes breached by storm; nearly two thousand people and tens of thousands of cattle died in flood. **1954:** Remaining Dutch colonies achieved internal self-government. **1958:** The Netherlands became founding member of European Economic Community (EEC). **1963:** Dutch colony of Western New Guinea ceded to Indonesia. **1975:** Dutch Guiana became independent as Suriname. **1980:** Queen Juliana abdicated in favour of her daughter Beatrix. **1994:** Following inconclusive general election, three-party coalition formed under PvdA leader Wim Kok. **1998:** Gains for Labour in general election. **1999:** Coalition government resigned.

New Zealand Dominion of

Area: 268,680 sq km/103,737 sq mi **Capital:** Wellington (and port) **Major towns/cities:** Auckland, Hamilton, Palmerston North, Christchurch, Dunedin, Napier-Hastings **Major ports:** Auckland **Territories:** Tokelau (three atolls transferred in 1926 from former Gilbert and Ellice Islands colony); Niue Island (one of the Cook Islands, separately administered from 1903: chief town Alafi); Cook Islands are internally self-governing but share common citizenship with New Zealand; Ross Dependency in Antarctica

Government
Head of state: Queen Elizabeth II from 1952, represented by governor general Catherine Tizard from 1990 **Head of government:** Jenny Shipley from 1997 **Political system:** constitutional monarchy **Administrative divisions:** 93 counties, 12

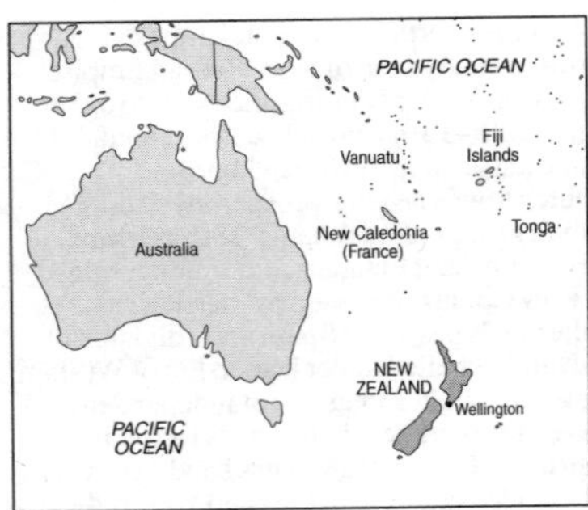

regions, and 6 territorial authorities **Political parties:** Labour Party, moderate, left of centre; New Zealand National Party, free enterprise, centre right; Alliance Party bloc, left of centre, ecologists; New Zealand First Party (NZFP), centrist; United New Zealand Party (UNZ), centrist **Armed forces:** 9,600; around 7,000 reserves (1997) **Conscription:** military service is voluntary **Death penalty:** abolished in 1989 **Defence spend:** (% GDP) 1.6 (1997) **Education spend:** (% GNP) 6.7 (1995) **Health spend:** (% GDP) 5.7 (1990–95)

Economy and resources

Currency: New Zealand dollar **GDP:** (US$) 64.9 billion (1997) **Real GDP growth:** (% change on previous year) 1.9 (1997) **GNP:** 60.5 billion (1997) **GNP per capita (PPP):** (US$) 16,600 (1997) **Consumer price inflation:** 2.0% (1998) **Unemployment:** 7.5% (1998) **Major trading partners:** Australia, USA, Japan, UK **Resources:** coal, clay, limestone, dolomite, natural gas, hydroelectric power, pumice, iron ore, gold, forests **Exports:** meat, dairy products, wool, fish, timber and wood products, fruit and vegetables, aluminium, machinery. Principal market: Australia 20.2% (1997) **Imports:** machinery and mechanical appliances, vehicles and aircraft, petroleum, fertilizer, consumer goods. Principal source: Australia 27.4% (1997) **Arable land:** 5.9% (1995)

Population and society

Population: 3,796,000 (1998 est) **Population growth rate:** 1.1% (1995–2000); 0.8% (2000–05) **Population density:** (per sq km) 13.5 (1998 est) **Urban population:** (% of total) 86 (1997) **Age distribution:** (% of total population) 0–14 23.0%, 15–64 65.4%, 65+ 11.6% (1998) **Ethnic groups:** around 87% of European origin, 9% Maori, 2% Pacific Islander **Language:** English (official), Maori **Religion:** Christian **Education:** (compulsory years) 11 **Literacy rate:** 99% (men); 99% (women) (1995 est) **Labour force:** 49.6% of population: 9.5% agriculture, 24.6% industry, 65.9% services (1996) **Life expectancy:** 75 (men); 80 (women) (1995–2000) **Child mortality rate:** (under 5, per 1,000 live births) 8 (1997) **Physicians:** 1 per 476 people (1996)

Practical information

Visa requirements: UK: visa not required. USA: visa not required **Embassy in the UK:** New Zealand House, 80 Haymarket, London SW1Y 4TQ. Tel: (0171) 930 8422; fax: (0171) 839 4580 **British embassy:** British High Commission, PO Box 1818, 44 Hill Street, Wellington 1. Tel: (4) 472 6049; fax: (4) 471 1974 **Chamber of commerce:** New Zealand Chambers of Commerce and Industry, PO Box 1590, 9th Floor, 109 Featherston Street, Wellington. Tel: (4) 472 2725; fax: (4) 471 1767

Chronology

1642: Dutch explorer Abel Tasman reached New Zealand but indigenous Maoris prevented him from going ashore. **1769:** English explorer James Cook surveyed coastline of islands. **1773 and 1777:** Cook again explored coast. **1815:** First British missionaries arrived in New Zealand. **1826:** New Zealand Company founded in London to establish settlement. **1839:** New Zealand Company relaunched, after initial failure, by Edward Gibbon Wakefield. **1840:** Treaty of Waitangi: Maoris accepted British sovereignty; colonization began and large-scale sheep farming developed. **1845–47:** Maori revolt against loss of land. **1851:** Became separate colony (was originally part of Australian colony of New South Wales). **1852:** Colony procured constitution after dissolution of New Zealand Company; self-government fully implemented in 1856. **1860–72:** Second Maori revolt led to concessions, including representation in parliament. **1891:** New Zealand took part in Australasian Federal Convention in Sydney but rejected idea of joining Australian Commonwealth. **1893:** Became first country to give women the right to vote in parliamentary elections. **1898:** Liberal government under Richard Seddon introduced pioneering old-age pension scheme. **1899–1902:** Volunteers from New Zealand fought alongside imperial forces in Boer War. **1907:** New Zealand achieved dominion status within British Empire. **1912–25:** Government of Reform Party, led by William Massey, reflected interests of North Island farmers and strongly supported imperial unity. **1914–18:** 130,000 New Zealanders fought for British Empire in World War I. **1916:** Labour Party of New Zealand established. **1931:** Statute of Westminster affirmed equality of status between Britain and dominions, effectively granting independence to New Zealand. **1935–49:** Labour governments of Michael Savage and Peter Fraser introduced social reforms and encouraged state intervention in industry. **1936:** Liberal Party merged with Reform Party to create National Party. **1939–45:** New Zealand troops fought in World War II, notably in Crete, North Africa, and Italy. **1947:** Parliament confirmed independence of New Zealand within British Commonwealth. **1951:** New Zealand joined Australia and USA in ANZUS Pacific security treaty. **1965–72:** New Zealand contingent took part in Vietnam War. **1973:** British entry into European Economic Community (EEC) forced New Zealand to seek closer trading relations with Australia. **1985:** Non-nuclear military policy led to disagreements with France and USA. **1986:** USA suspended defence obligations to New Zealand after it banned entry of US warships. **1988:** Free-trade agreement signed with Australia. **1991:** Alliance Party formed to challenge two-party system. **1997:** Bolger replaced as National Party leader and prime minister by Jenny Shipley. **1998:** The government was ordered to return more than more than £2 million worth of land confiscated from its Maori owners more than 30 years earlier.

Nicaragua Republic of

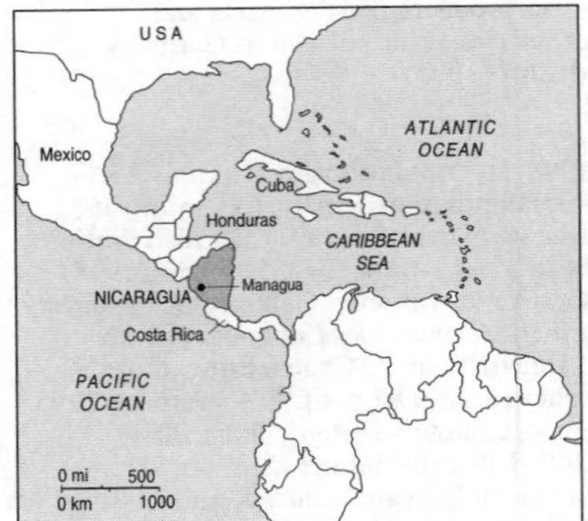

National name: *República de Nicaragua* **Area:** 127,849 sq km/ 49,362 sq mi **Capital:** Managua **Major towns/cities:** León, Chinandega, Masaya, Granada **Major ports:** Corinto, Puerto Cabezas, El Bluff

Government

Head of state and government: Arnoldo Aleman from 1996 **Political system:** emergent democracy **Administrative divisions:** 16 departments **Political parties:** Sandinista National Liberation Front (FSLN), Marxist–Leninist; Opposition Political Alliance (APO, formerly National Opposition Union: UNO), loose US-backed coalition **Armed forces:** 17,000 (1997) **Conscription:** military service is voluntary (since 1990) **Death penalty:** abolished in 1979 **Defence spend:** (% GDP) 1.4 (1997) **Education spend:** (% GNP) 3.6 (1996) **Health spend:** (% GDP) 4.3 (1990–95)

Economy and resources

Currency: cordoba **GDP:** (US$) 2 billion (1997) **Real GDP growth:** (% change on previous year) 4.9 (1997) **GNP:** 1.9 billion (1997) **GNP per capita (PPP):** (US$) 2,370 (1997) **Consumer**

price inflation: 11.0% (1998) **Unemployment:** 15% (1992) **Foreign debt:** (US$) 5.9 billion (1996) **Major trading partners:** USA, Germany, Japan, Canada, Cuba, Costa Rica, Venezuela **Resources:** gold, silver, copper, lead, antimony, zinc, iron, limestone, gypsum, marble, bentonite **Exports:** coffee, meat, cotton, sugar, seafood, bananas, chemical products. Principal market: USA 49.1% (1997) **Imports:** machinery and transport equipment, food and live animals, consumer goods, mineral fuels and lubricants, basic manufactures, chemicals and related products. Principal source: USA 37.2% (1997) **Arable land:** 20.2% (1995)

Population and society

Population: 4,807,000 (1998 est) **Population growth rate:** 2.6% (1995–2000) **Population density:** (per sq km) 38.1 (1998 est) **Urban population:** (% of total) 63 (1997) **Age distribution:** (% of total population) 0–14 44.0%, 15–64 53.3%, 65+ 2.7% (1998) **Ethnic groups:** over 70% of mixed Indian, Spanish, and African origin; about 9% African; 5% Indian **Language:** Spanish (official), Indian, English **Religion:** Roman Catholic 95% **Education:** (compulsory years) 6 **Literacy rate:** 64% (men); 66% (women) (1995 est) **Labour force:** 34% of population: 28% agriculture, 26% industry, 46% services (1990) **Life expectancy:** 66 (men); 71 (women) (1995–2000) **Child mortality rate:** (under 5, per 1,000 live births) 57 (1997) **Physicians:** 1 per 1,566 people (1993)

Practical information

Visa requirements: UK: visa not required for a stay of up to 90 days. USA: visa not required for a stay of up to 90 days **Embassy in the UK:** 2nd Floor, 36 Upper Brook Street, London W1Y 1PE. Tel: (0171) 409 2536; fax: (0171) 409 2593 **British embassy:** Apartado A-169, El Reparto 'Los Robles', Primera Etapa, Entrada principal de la Carretera a Massaya, 4a Casa a Mano Derecha, Managua. Tel: (2) 780 014; fax: (2) 784 085 **Chamber of commerce:** Cámara de Comercio de Nicaragua, Apartado 135, Frente a Lotería Popular, C C Managua JR. Tel: (2) 670 718

Chronology

10th century AD: Indians from Mexico and Mesoamerica migrated to Nicaragua's Pacific lowlands. **1522:** Visited by Spanish explorer Gil Gonzalez de Avila, who named the area Nicaragua after local Indian chief, Nicarao. **1523–24:** Colonized by the Spanish, under Francisco Hernandez de Cordoba, who was attracted by local gold deposits and founded cities of Granada and León. **17th–18th centuries:** British were dominant force on Caribbean side of Nicaragua, while Spain controlled Pacific lowlands. **1821:** Independence achieved from Spain; Nicaragua was initially part of Mexican Empire. **1823:** Became part of United Provinces (Federation) of Central America, also embracing Costa Rica, El Salvador, Guatemala, and Honduras. **1838:** Became fully independent when it seceded from the Federation. **1857–93:** Ruled by succession of Conservative Party governments. **1860:** The British ceded control over Caribbean ('Mosquito') Coast to Nicaragua. **1893:** Liberal Party leader, José Santos Zelaya, deposed Conservative president and established dictatorship which lasted until overthrown by US marines in 1909. **1912–25:** At Nicaraguan government's request, with political situation deteriorating, USA established military bases and stationed marines. **1927–33:** Re-stationed US marines faced opposition from anti-American guerrilla group led by Augusto César Sandino, who was assassinated in 1934 on the orders of the commander of the US-trained National Guard, Gen Anastasio Somoza Garcia. **1937:** Gen Somoza elected president; start of near-dictatorial rule by Somoza family, which amassed huge personal fortune. **1956:** Gen Somoza assassinated and succeeded as president by his elder son, Luis Somoza Debayle. **1961:** Left-wing Sandinista National Liberation Front (FSLN) formed to fight Somoza regime. **1967:** Luis Somoza died and was succeeded as president by his brother Anastasio Somoza Debayle, who headed an even more oppressive regime. **1978:** Nicaraguan Revolution: Pedro Joaquin Chamorro, a popular publisher and leader of anti-Somoza Democratic Liberation Union (UDEL), was assassinated, sparking general strike and mass movement in which moderates joined with FSLN to overthrow Somoza regime. **1979:** Somoza government ousted by FSLN after military offensive. **1980:** Anastasio Somoza assassinated in Paraguay; FSLN junta took power in Managua, headed by Daniel Ortega Saavedra; lands held by Somozas were nationalized and farming cooperatives established. **1982:** Subversive activity against government by right-wing Contra guerrillas promoted by USA and attacking from bases in Honduras. State of emergency declared. **1984:** US troops mined Nicaraguan harbours. Action condemned by World Court in 1986 and $17 billion in reparations ordered. FSLN won assembly elections. **1985:** Denunciation of Sandinista government by US president Ronald Reagan, who vowed to 'remove it' and imposed US trade embargo. **1987:** Central American peace agreement cosigned by Nicaraguan leaders. **1988:** Peace agreement failed. Nicaragua held talks with Contra rebel leaders. Hurricane left 180,000 people homeless. **1989:** Demobilization of rebels and release of former Somozan supporters; cease-fire ended but economy in ruins after Contra war; 60% unemployment. **1990:** FSLN defeated by right-of-centre National Opposition Union (UNO), a US-backed coalition; Violeta Barrios de Chamorro, widow of the murdered Pedro Joaquin Chamorro, elected president. Antigovernment riots. **1992:** Around 16,000 people made homeless by earthquake. **1994:** Peace accord with remaining Contra rebels. **1996:** Right-wing candidate Arnoldo Aleman won presidential elections. **1998:** Daniel Ortega re-elected FSLN leader.

Niger Republic of

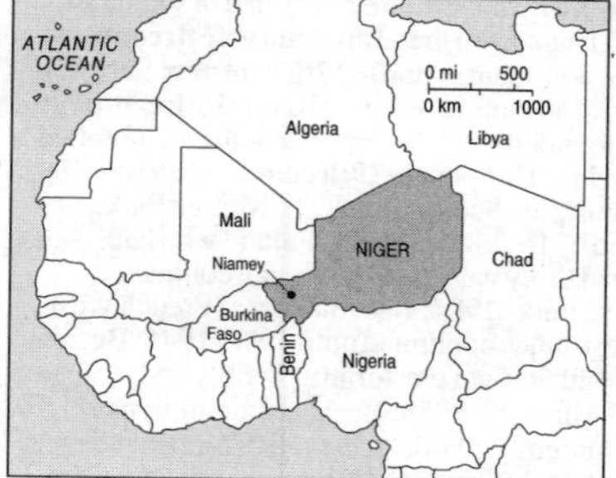

National name: *République du Niger* **Area:** 1,186,408 sq km/458,072 sq mi **Capital:** Niamey **Major towns/cities:** Zinder, Maradi, Tahoua, Agadez, Birui N'Konui

Government

Head of state: Daouda Malam Wanke from 1999 **Head of government:** Ibrahim Hassane Mayaki from 1997 **Political system:** transitional **Administrative divisions:** seven regions and the municipality of Niamey **Political parties:** National Movement for a Development Society (MNSD–Nassara), left of centre; Alliance of the Forces for Change (AFC), left-of-centre coalition; Party for Democracy and Socialism–Tarayya (PNDS–Tarayya), left of centre **Armed forces:** 5,300; plus paramilitary forces of 5,400 (1997) **Conscription:** conscription is selective for two years **Death penalty:** retains the death penalty for ordinary crimes but can be considered abolitionist in practice (last known execution in 1976) **Defence spend:** (% GDP) 1.4 (1997) **Education spend:** (% GNP) 3.1 (1993/94) **Health spend:** (% GDP) 1.6 (1990–95)

Economy and resources

Currency: franc CFA **GDP:** (US$) 1.8 billion (1997) **Real GDP growth:** (% change on previous year) 4.5 (1997 est) **GNP:** 2 billion (1997) **GNP per capita (PPP):** (US$) 920 (1997) **Consumer price inflation:** 3.4% (1997) **Unemployment:** 20.9% (1991) **Foreign debt:** (US$) 1.56 billion (1996) **Major trading partners:** France, Nigeria, Japan, USA, Côte d'Ivoire, Spain **Resources:** uranium (one of world's leading producers), phosphates, gypsum, coal, cassiterite, tin, salt, gold; deposits of other minerals (including petroleum, iron ore, copper, lead, diamonds, and tungsten) have been confirmed **Exports:** uranium ore, live animals, hides and skins, cow-peas, cotton. Principal market: France 41% (1996) **Imports:** machinery and transport equipment, miscellaneous manufactured articles, cereals, chemicals, refined petroleum products. Principal source: France 24% (1996) **Arable land:** 3.9% (1995)

Population and society

Population: 10,078,000 (1998 est) **Population growth rate:** 3.3% (1995–2000); 3.2% (2000–05) **Population density:** (per sq km) 7.6 (1998 est) **Urban population:** (% of total) 19 (1997) **Age distribution:** (% of total population) 0–14 48.1%, 15–64 49.6%, 65+ 2.3% (1998) **Ethnic groups:** three ethnic groups make up over 75% of the population: the Hausa (mainly in central areas and the south), Djerma-Songhai (southwest), and Beriberi-Manga (east); there is also a significant number of the mainly nomadic Fulani people, and the Tuareg in the north **Language:** French (official), Hausa, Djerma, and other minority languages **Religion:** Sunni Muslim; also Christian, and traditional animist beliefs **Education:** (compulsory years) 8 **Literacy rate:** 40% (men); 17% (women) (1995 est) **Labour force:** 49% of population: 90% agriculture, 4% industry, 6% services **Life expectancy:** 47 (men); 50 (women) (1995–2000) **Child mortality rate:** (under 5, per 1,000 live births) 176 (1997) **Physicians:** 1 per 53,986 people (1993 est)

Practical information

Visa requirements: UK: visa required. USA: visa required **Embassy for the UK:** 154 rue du Longchamps, 75116 Paris, France. Tel: (1) 4504 8060; fax: (1) 4504 6226 **British embassy:** Honorary British Vice-Consulate, BP 11168, Niamey. Tel: (227) 732 015/539 **Chamber of commerce:** Chambre de Commerce, d'Agriculture, d'Industrie et d'Artisanat du Niger, BP 209, place de la Concertation, Niamey. Tel: (227) 732 210; telex: 5242

Chronology

10th–13th centuries: Kanem-Bornu Empire flourished in southeast, near Lake Chad, spreading Islam from the 11th century. **15th century:** Tuareg sultanate of Agades dominant in north. **17th century:** Songhai-speaking Djerma established an empire on Niger River. **18th century:** Powerful Gobir kingdom founded by Hausa people, who had migrated from south in 14th century. **late 18th–early 19th centuries:** Visited by European explorers, including the Scottish explorer, Mungo Park; Sultanate of Sokoto formed by Islamic revivalist Fulani, who had defeated the Hausa in a jihad (holy war). **1890s:** French conquered region and ended local slave trade. **1904:** Became part of French West Africa, although Tuareg resistance continued until 1922. **1946:** Became French overseas territory, with its own territorial assembly and representation in French Parliament. **1958:** Became autonomous republic within French community. **1960:** Achieved full independence; Hamani Diori of Niger Progressive Party (NPP) elected president, but maintained close ties with France. **1971:** Uranium production commenced. **1974:** Diori ousted in army coup led by Lt-Col Seyni Kountché after long Sahel drought had led to civil disorder; military government launched drive against corruption. **1977:** Cooperation agreement signed with France. **1984:** Partial privatization of state firms as a result of further drought and increased government indebtedness as world uranium prices slumped. **1987:** Kountché died; replaced by Gen Ali Saibu. **1989:** Ali Saibu elected president without opposition. **1991:** Saibu stripped of executive powers, and transitional government formed amid student and industrial unrest. **1992:** Transitional government collapsed amid economic problems and ethnic unrest among secessionist Tuareg in north. Referendum approved of new multiparty constitution. **1993:** Alliance of the Forces for Change (AFC) left-of-centre coalition won absolute majority in assembly elections. Mahamane Ousmane, a Muslim Hausa, elected president in first free presidential election. **1994:** Peace agreement with northern Tuareg. **1995:** AFC coalition won general election with reduced majority. **1996:** President Ousmane ousted in military coup led by Ibrahim Barre Mainassara. Civilian government restored with Boukary Adji as premier; Mainassara formally elected president. **1999:** President Mainassara assassinated in coup d' etat; Major Daouda Mallam Wanke assumed power.

Nigeria Federal Republic of

Area: 923,773 sq km/356,668 sq mi **Capital:** Abuja **Major towns/cities:** Ibadan, Lagos, Ogbomosho, Kano, Oshogbo, Ilorin,

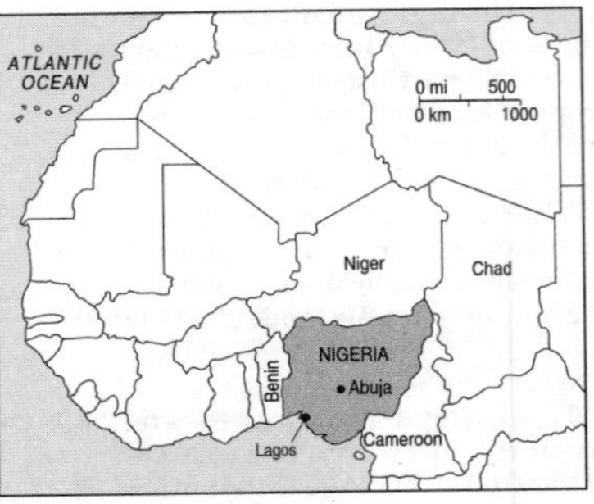

Abeokuta, Zaria, Ouitsha, Iwo, Kaduna **Major ports:** Lagos, Port Harcourt, Warri, Calabar

Government

Head of state and government: Olusegun Obasanjo from 1999 **Political system:** military republic **Administrative divisions:** 30 states and a Federal Capital Territory **Political parties:** Social Democratic Party (SDP), left of centre; National Republican Convention (NRC), right of centre **Armed forces:** 77,000 (1997) **Conscription:** military service is voluntary **Death penalty:** retained and used for ordinary crimes **Defence spend:** (% GDP) 4 (1997) **Education spend:** (% GNP) 1.3 (1993/94) **Health spend:** (% GDP) 0.3 (1990–95)

Economy and resources

Currency: naira **GDP:** (US$) 36.5 billion (1997) **Real GDP growth:** (% change on previous year) 3.4 (1997) **GNP:** 30.7 billion (1997) **GNP per capita (PPP):** (US$) 880 (1997) **Consumer price inflation:** 18% (1998) **Unemployment:** 3.4% (1992) **Foreign debt:** (US$) 31.4 billion (1996) **Major trading partners:** USA, UK, Germany, France, Spain, the Netherlands, Italy **Resources:** petroleum, natural gas, coal, tin, iron ore, uranium, limestone, marble, forest **Exports:** petroleum, cocoa beans, rubber, palm products, urea and ammonia, fish. Principal market: USA 34.6% (1997) **Imports:** machinery and transport equipment, basic manufactures, cereals, chemicals, foodstuffs. Principal source: USA 13.6% (1997) **Arable land:** 33.3% (1995)

Population and society

Population: 106,409,000 (1998 est) **Population growth rate:** 2.8% (1995–2000); 2.7% (2000–05) **Population density:** (per sq km) 121.4 (1998 est) **Urban population:** (% of total) 42 (1997) **Age distribution:** (% of total population) 0–14 44.8%, 15–64 52.3%, 65+ 2.9% (1998) **Ethnic groups:** over 250 tribal groups; major tribes include the Hausa and Fulani in the north, Yoruba in the south, and Ibo in the east **Language:** English (official), Hausa, Ibo, Yoruba **Religion:** Sunni Muslim 50% (in north), Christian 40% (in south), local religions 10% **Education:** (compulsory years) 6 **Literacy rate:** 62% (men); 39% (women) (1995 est) **Labour force:** 40% of population: 43% agriculture, 7% industry, 50% services (1990) **Life expectancy:** 51 (men); 54 (women) (1995–2000) **Child mortality rate:** (under 5, per 1,000 live births) 141 (1997) **Physicians:** 1 per 5,208 people (1993 est)

Practical information

Visa requirements: UK: visa required. USA: visa required **Embassy in the UK:** Nigeria House, 9 Northumberland Avenue, London WC2N 5BX. Tel: (0171) 839 1244; fax: (0171) 839 8746 **British embassy:** British High Commission, Private Mail Bag 12136, 11 Eleke Crescent, Victoria Island, Lagos. Tel: (1) 619 531; fax: (1) 666 909 **Chamber of commerce:** The Nigerian Association of Chambers of Commerce, Industry, Mines and Agriculture; Private Mail Bag 12816; 15a Ikorodu Road, Maryland, Lagos. Tel: (1) 496 4737; telex 21368

Chronology

4th century BC–2nd century AD: Highly organized Nok culture flourished in northern Nigeria. **9th century:** Northeast Nigeria became part of empire of Kanem-Bornu, based around Lake Chad. **11th century:** Creation of Hausa states, including Kano and Katsina. **13th century:** Arab merchants introduced Islam in north. **15th century:** Empire of Benin at its height in south; first contact with European traders. **17th century:** Oyo Empire dominant in southwest; development of slave trade in Niger delta. **1804–17:** Islamic Fulani

(or Sokoto) Empire established in north. **1861:** British traders procured Lagos; spread of Christian missionary activity in south. **1884–1904:** Britain occupied most of Nigeria by stages. **1914:** North and south protectorates united; growth of railway network and trade. **1946:** Nigerians allowed a limited role in decision-making in three regional councils. **1951:** Introduction of elected representation led to formation of three regional political parties. **1954:** New constitution increased powers of regions. **1958:** Oil discovered in southeast. **1960:** Achieved independence from Britain, within Commonwealth. **1963:** Became a republic, with Nnamdi Azikiwe as president. **1966:** Gen Aguiyi-Ironsi of Ibo tribe seized power and imposed unitary government; massacre of Ibo by Hausa in north; Gen Gowon seized power and restored federalism. **1967:** Conflict over oil revenues led to secession of eastern region as independent Ibo state of Biafra; ensuing civil war claimed up to a million lives. **1970:** Surrender of Biafra and end of civil war; development of oil industry financed more effective central government. **1975:** Gowon ousted in military coup; second coup put Gen Olusegun Obasanjo in power. **1979:** Civilian rule restored under President Shehu Shagari. **1983:** Bloodless coup staged by Maj-Gen Muhammadu Buhari. **1985:** Buhari replaced by Maj-Gen Ibrahim Babangida; Islamic northerners dominant in regime. **1992:** Multiparty elections won by Babangida's SDP. **1993:** Moshood Abiola (SDP) won first free presidential election; results suspended. Gen Sani Abacha restored military rule and dissolved political parties. **1995:** Commonwealth membership suspended in protest at human-rights abuses by military regime. **1998:** General Abdulsalam Abubakar took over as president following the death of Abacha. Nigeria's most prominent political prisoner, Moshood Abiola, died suddenly on the eve of his expected release. Move towards political liberalization, with formation of new political parties and release of some dissidents. **1999:** Olusegun Obasanjo elected president. Nigeria's Commonwealth suspension lifted.

Norway Kingdom of

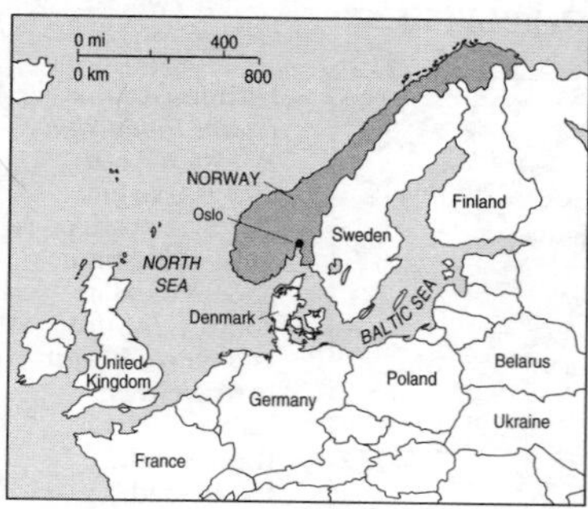

National name: *Kongeriket Norge* **Area:** 387,000 sq km/149,420 sq mi (includes Svalbard and Jan Mayen) **Capital:** Oslo **Major towns/cities:** Bergen, Trondheim, Stavanger, Kristiansand, Drammen **Territories:** dependencies in the Arctic (Svalbard and Jan Mayen) and in Antarctica (Bouvet and Peter I Island, and Queen Maud Land)

Government

Head of state: Harald V from 1991 **Head of government:** Kjell Magne Bondevik from 1997 **Political system:** constitutional monarchy **Administrative divisions:** 19 counties **Political parties:** Norwegian Labour Party (DNA), moderate left of centre; Conservative Party, progressive, right of centre; Christian People's Party (KrF), Christian, centre left; Centre Party (Sp), left of centre, rural-oriented; Progress Party (FrP), right wing, populist **Armed forces:** 33,600; 234,000 reservists (1997) **Conscription:** 12 months, with 4–5 refresher training periods **Death penalty:** abolished in 1979 **Defence spend:** (% GDP) 2.3 (1997) **Education spend:** (% GNP) 7.5 (1996) **Health spend:** (% GDP) 6.6 (1990–95)

Economy and resources

Currency: Norwegian krone **GDP:** (US$) 153.4 billion (1997) **Real GDP growth:** (% change on previous year) 3.9 (1997) **GNP:** 158.9 billion (1997) **GNP per capita (PPP):** (US$) 23,940 (1997) **Consumer price inflation:** 2.2% (1998) **Unemployment:** 4.1% (1997) **Major trading partners:** EU (principally UK and Sweden), USA, Japan **Resources:** petroleum, natural gas, iron ore, iron pyrites, copper, lead, zinc, forests **Exports:** petroleum, natural gas, fish products, non-ferrous metals, wood pulp and paper. Principal market: UK 19.3% (1997) **Imports:** machinery and transport equipment, chemicals, clothing, fuels and lubricants, iron and steel, office machines and computers, telecommunications and sound apparatus and equipment. Principal source: Sweden 15.7% (1997) **Arable land:** 3.2% (1995)

Population and society

Population: 4,419,000 (1998 est) **Population growth rate:** 0.4% (1995–2000) **Population density:** (per sq km) 14.4 (1998 est) **Urban population:** (% of total) 74 (1997) **Age distribution:** (% of total population) 0–14 19.6%, 15–64 64.8%, 65+ 15.7% (1998) **Ethnic groups:** majority of Nordic descent; Saami minority in far north **Language:** Norwegian (official); there are Saami- (Lapp) and Finnish-speaking minorities **Religion:** Evangelical Lutheran (endowed by state) **Education:** (compulsory years) 9 **Literacy rate:** 99% (men); 99% (women) (1995 est) **Labour force:** 50.3% of population: 5.2% agriculture, 23.4% industry, 71.5% services (1995) **Life expectancy:** 75 (men); 81 (women) (1995–2000) **Child mortality rate:** (under 5, per 1,000 live births) 6 (1997) **Physicians:** 1 per 357 people (1996)

Practical information

Visa requirements: UK: visa not required. USA: visa not required **Embassy in the UK:** 25 Belgrave Square, London SW1X 8QD. Tel: (0171) 235 7151; fax: (0171)245 6993 **British embassy:** Thomas Heftyesgate 8, 0244 Oslo 2. Tel: (22) 552 400; fax: (22) 434 005 **Chamber of commerce:** Norwegian Trade Council, Drammensveien 40, 0243 Oslo. Tel: (22) 926 300; fax: (22) 926 400

Chronology

5th century: First small kingdoms established by Goths. *c.* **900:** Harald Fairhair created united Norwegian kingdom; it dissolved after his death. **8th–11th centuries:** Vikings from Norway raided and settled in many parts of Europe. *c.* **1016–28:** Olav II (St Olav) reunited the kingdom and introduced Christianity. **1217–63:** Haakon VI established royal authority over nobles and church and made monarchy hereditary. **1263:** Iceland submitted to authority of king of Norway. **1397:** Union of Kalmar: Norway, Denmark, and Sweden united under a single monarch. **15th century:** Norway, the weakest of the three kingdoms, was increasingly treated as an appendage of Denmark. **1523:** Secession of Sweden further undermined Norway's status. **16th century:** Introduction of sawmill precipitated development of timber industry and growth of export trade. **1661:** Denmark restored formal equality of status to Norway as a twin kingdom. **18th century:** Norwegian merchants profited from foreign wars which increased demand for naval supplies. **1814:** Treaty of Kiel: Denmark ceded Norway (minus Iceland) to Sweden; Norway retained its own parliament but cabinet appointed by king of Sweden. **19th century:** Economic decline followed slump in timber trade due to Canadian competition; expansion of merchant navy and whaling industry. **1837:** Democratic local government introduced. **1884:** Achieved internal self-government when king of Sweden made Norwegian cabinet accountable to Norwegian parliament. **1895:** Start of constitutional dispute over control of foreign policy: Norway's demand for a separate consular service refused by Sweden. **1905:** Union with Sweden dissolved; Norway achieved independence under King Haakon VII. **1907:** Norway became first European country to grant women the right to vote in parliamentary elections. **early 20th century:** Development of industry based on hydroelectric power; long period of Liberal government committed to neutrality and moderate social reform. **1935:** First Labour government took office. **1940–45:** German occupation with Vidkun Quisling as puppet leader. **1945–65:** Labour governments introduced economic planning and permanent price controls. **1949:** Became a founding member of North Atlantic Treaty Organization (NATO). **1952:** Joined Nordic Council. **1957:** Olaf V succeeded his father King Haakon VII. **1960:** Joined European Free Trade Association (EFTA). **1972:** National referendum rejected membership of European Economic Community (EEC).

1975: Export of North Sea oil began. **1981:** Gro Harlem Brundtland (Labour) became Norway's first woman prime minister. **1982:** Kare Willoch formed first Conservative government since 1928. **1986:** Falling oil prices caused recession; Labour re-elected under Brundtland. **1991:** Olaf V succeeded by his son Harald V. **1994:** National referendum rejected membership of European Union (formerly EC). **1996:** Brundtland resigned; succeeded by Thorbjoern Jagland. **1997:** Jagland failed to win decisive majority in general election. Kjell Magne Bondevik (KrF) became prime minister. **1998:** Decline in state of the economy.

Oman Sultanate of

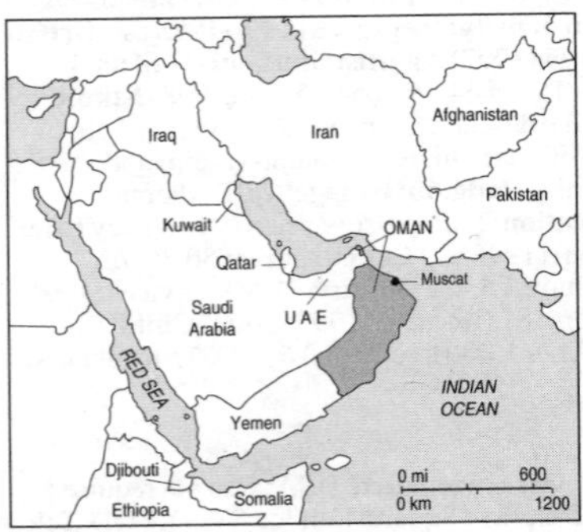

National name: *Saltanat `Uman* **Area:** 272,000 sq km/105,019 sq mi **Capital:** Muscat **Major towns/cities:** Salalah, Ibri, Sohar, Al-Buraimi, Nizwa **Major ports:** Mina Qaboos, Mina Raysut

Government

Head of state and government: Qaboos bin Said from 1970 **Political system:** absolute monarchy **Administrative divisions:** eight regional governates and 59 districts **Political parties:** none **Armed forces:** 43,500 (1997) **Conscription:** military service is voluntary **Death penalty:** retained and used for ordinary crimes **Defence spend:** (% GDP) 10.9 (1997) **Education spend:** (% GNP) 4.6 (1995) **Health spend:** (% GDP) 2.5 (1990–95)

Economy and resources

Currency: Omani rial **GDP:** (US$) 13.7 billion (1995) **Real GDP growth:** (% change on previous year) 6.7 (1996) **GNP:** 10.6 billion (1997) **GNP per capita (PPP):** (US$) 8,690 (1997) **Consumer price inflation:** 1.0% (1998) **Unemployment:** 11.9% (1993) **Foreign debt:** (US$) 3.4 billion (1996) **Major trading partners:** United Arab Emirates, Japan, South Korea, China **Resources:** petroleum, natural gas, copper, chromite, gold, salt, marble, gypsum, limestone **Exports:** petroleum, metals and metal goods, textiles, animals and products. Principal market: Japan 23.3% (1997) **Imports:** machinery and transport equipment, basic manufactures, food and live animals, beverages, tobacco. Principal source: UAE 24.2% (1997) **Arable land:** 0.1% (1995)

Population and society

Population: 2,382,000 (1998 est) **Population growth rate:** 4.2% (1995–2000); 3.7% (2000–05) **Population density:** (per sq km) 11.1 (1998 est) **Urban population:** (% of total) 80 (1997) **Age distribution:** (% of total population) 0–14 40.5%, 15–64 57.1%, 65+ 2.3% (1998) **Ethnic groups:** predominantly Arab, with substantial Iranian, Baluchi, Indo-Pakistani, and East African minorities **Language:** Arabic (official); English, Urdu, other Indian languages **Religion:** Ibadhi Muslim 75%, Sunni Muslim, Shi'ite Muslim, Hindu **Education:** not compulsory **Literacy rate:** 52% (men); 34% (women) (1994 est) **Labour force:** 9.4% agriculture, 27.8% industry, 62.8% services (1993) **Life expectancy:** 69 (men); 73 (women) (1995–2000) **Child mortality rate:** (under 5, per 1,000 live births) 31 (1997) **Physicians:** 1 per 1,265 people (1994)

Practical information

Visa requirements: UK: visa required. USA: visa required **Embassy in the UK:** 167 Queen's Gate, London SW7 5HE. Tel: (0171) 225 0001; fax: (0171) 589 2505 **British embassy:** PO Box 300, 113 Muscat. Tel: (968) 693 077; fax: (968) 693 087 **Chamber of commerce:** Oman Chamber of Commerce and Industry, PO Box 1400, 112 Ruwi. Tel: (968) 707 684; fax: (968) 708 497

Chronology

c. **3000 BC:** Archaeological evidence suggests Oman may have been the semilegendary Magan, a thriving seafaring state at the time of the Sumerian Civilization of Mesopotamia (the Tigris and Euphrates region of Iraq). **9th century BC:** Migration of Arab clans to Oman, notably the Qahtan family from southwest Arabia and the Nizar from northwest Arabia, between whom rivalry has continued. **4th century BC–AD 800:** North Oman under Persian control. **AD 630:** Converted to Islam. **751:** Julanda ibn Masud was elected imam (spiritual leader); Oman remained under imam rule until 1154. **1151:** Dynasty established by Banu Nabhan. **1428:** Dynastic rule came under challenge from the imams. **1507:** Coastal area, including port city of Muscat, fell under Portuguese control. **1650:** Portuguese ousted by Sultan ibn Sayf, a powerful Ya'ariba leader. **early 18th century:** Civil war between the Hinawis (descendents of the Qahtan) and the Ghafiris (descendents of the Nizar). **1749:** Independent Sultanate of Muscat and Oman established by Ahmad ibn Said, founder of the Al Bu Said dynasty that still rules Oman. **first half of 19th century:** Muscat and Oman was most powerful state in Arabia, ruling Zanzibar until 1861, and coastal parts of Persia, Kenya, and Pakistan; came under British protection. **1951:** The Sultanate of Muscat and Oman achieved full independence from Britain. Treaty of Friendship with Britain signed. **1964:** Discovery of oil led to transformation of undeveloped kingdom into modern state. **1970:** After 38 years' rule, Sultan Said bin Taimur replaced in bloodless coup by his son Qaboos bin Said. Name changed to Sultanate of Oman and modernization programme launched. **1975:** Left-wing rebels in Dhofar in the south, who had been supported by South Yemen, defeated with UK military assistance, ending a ten-year insurrection. **1981:** Consultative Council set up; Oman played key role in establishment of six-member Gulf Cooperation Council. **1982:** Memorandum of Understanding with UK signed, providing for regular consultation on international issues. **1991:** Joined US-led coalition opposing Iraq's occupation of Kuwait.

Pakistan Islamic Republic of

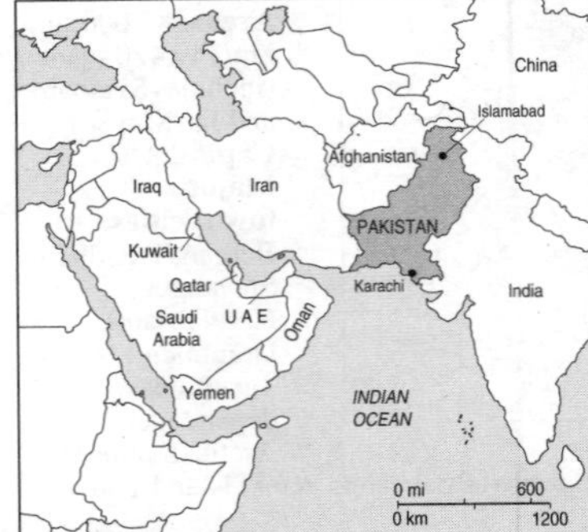

National name: *Islami Jamhuriya e Pakistan* **Area:** 796,100 sq km/ 307,374 sq mi; one-third of Kashmir under Pakistani control **Capital:** Islamabad **Major towns/cities:** Lahore, Rawalpindi, Faisalabad, Karachi, Hyderabad, Multan, Peshawar, Gujranwala, Sialkot, Sargodha, Quetta, Islamabad **Major ports:** Karachi, Port Qasim

Government

Head of state: Rafiq Tarar from 1997 **Head of government:** Nawaz Sharif from 1997 **Political system:** emergent democracy **Administrative divisions:** four provinces, the Federal Capital Territory, and the federally administered tribal areas **Political parties:** Islamic Democratic Alliance (IDA), conservative; Pakistan People's Party (PPP), moderate, Islamic, socialist; Pakistan Muslim League (PML), Islamic conservative (contains pro- and anti-government factions); Pakistan Islamic Front (PIF), Islamic fundamentalist, right wing; Awami National Party (ANP), left wing; National Democratic Alliance (NDA) bloc, left of centre; Mohajir National Movement (MQM), Sind-based *mohajir* settlers (Muslims previously living in India); Movement for Justice, reformative, anti-corruption **Armed**

forces: 587,000; paramilitary forces 247,000 (1997) **Conscription:** military service is voluntary **Death penalty:** retained and used for ordinary crimes **Defence spend:** (% GDP) 5.8 (1997) **Education spend:** (% GNP) 3.0 (1996) **Health spend:** (% GDP) 0.8 (1990–95)

Economy and resources

Currency: Pakistan rupee **GDP:** (US$) 64.3 billion (1997) **Real GDP growth:** (% change on previous year) 3.4 (1997) **GNP:** 67.2 billion (1997) **GNP per capita (PPP):** (US$) 1,590 (1997) **Consumer price inflation:** 11.5% (1998) **Unemployment:** 10% (1991 est) **Foreign debt:** (US$) 29.9 billion (1996) **Major trading partners:** Japan, USA, Germany, UK, Saudi Arabia **Resources:** iron ore, natural gas, limestone, rock salt, gypsum, silica, coal, petroleum, graphite, copper, manganese, chromite **Exports:** cotton, textiles, petroleum and petroleum products, clothing and accessories, leather, rice, food and live animals. Principal market: USA 17.8% (1997) **Imports:** machinery and transport equipment, mineral fuels and lubricants, chemicals and related products, edible oil. Principal source: USA 12% (1997) **Arable land:** 27.3% (1995)

Population and society

Population: 148,166,000 (1998 est) **Population growth rate:** 2.7% (1995–2000); 2.7% (2000–05) **Population density:** (per sq km) 173.5 (1998 est) **Urban population:** (% of total) 36 (1997) **Age distribution:** (% of total population) 0–14 41.8%, 15–64 54.1%, 65+ 4.0% (1998) **Ethnic groups:** four principal, regionally based, antagonistic communities: Punjabis in the Punjab; Sindhis in Sind; Baluchis in Baluchistan; and the Pathans (Pushtans) in the Northwest Frontier Province **Language:** Urdu (official); English, Punjabi, Sindhi, Pashto, Baluchi, other local dialects **Religion:** Sunni Muslim 75%, Shi'ite Muslim 20%; also Hindu, Christian, Parsee, Buddhist **Education:** (years) 5–12 (not compulsory, but free) **Literacy rate:** 47% (men); 21% (women) (1995 est) **Labour force:** 35% of population: 52% agriculture, 19% industry, 30% services (1990) **Life expectancy:** 63 (men); 65 (women) (1995–2000) **Child mortality rate:** (under 5, per 1,000 live births) 99 (1997) **Physicians:** 1 per 1,929 people (1993)

Practical information

Visa requirements: UK: visa required. USA: visa required **Embassy in the UK:** 40 Lowndes Square, London SW1X 9JN. Tel: (0171) 235 2044 **British embassy:** British High Commission, PO Box 1122, Diplomatic Enclave, Ramna 5, Islamabad. Tel: (51) 822 131/5; fax: (51) 823 439 **Chamber of commerce:** Chamber of Commerce and Industry, PO Box 4833, Talpur Road, Karachi. Tel: (21) 241 0814; fax: (21) 242 7315

Chronology

2500–1600 BC The area was the site of the Indus Valley civilization, a sophisticated, city-based ancient culture. **327 BC:** Invaded by Alexander the Great of Macedonia. **1st–2nd centuries:** North Pakistan was the heartland of the Kusana Empire, formed by invaders from Central Asia. **8th century:** First Muslim conquests, in Baluchistan and Sind, followed by increasing immigration by Muslims from the west, from the 10th century. **1206:** Establishment of Delhi Sultanate, stretching from northwest Pakistan and across northern India. **16th century:** Sikh religion developed in Punjab. **16th–17th centuries:** Lahore served intermittently as a capital city for the Mogul Empire, which stretched across the northern half of the Indian subcontinent. **1843–49:** Sind and Punjab annexed by British and incorporated within empire of 'British India'. **late 19th century:** Major canal irrigation projects in West Punjab and the northern Indus Valley drew in settlers from the east, as wheat and cotton production expanded. **1933:** The name 'Pakistan' (Urdu for 'Pure Nation') invented by Choudhary Rahmat Ali, as Muslims within British India began to campaign for the establishment of an independent Muslim territory that would embrace the four provinces of Sind, Baluchistan, Punjab, and the Northwest Frontier. **1940:** The All-India Muslim League (established in 1906), led by Karachi-born Muhammad Ali Jinnah, endorsed the concept of a separate nation for Muslims in the Lahore Resolution. **1947:** Independence achieved from Britain, as dominion within the Commonwealth. Pakistan, which included East Bengal, a Muslim-dominated province more than 1,600 km/1,000 mi from Punjab, was formed following the partition of British India. Large-scale and violent cross-border migrations of Muslims, Hindus, and Sikhs followed, and a brief border war with India over disputed Kashmir. **1948:** Jinnah, the country's first governor general, died. **1956:** Proclaimed a republic. **1958:** Military rule imposed by Gen Ayub Khan. **1965:** Border war with India over disputed territory of Kashmir. **1969:** Power transferred to Gen Yahya Khan following strikes and riots. **1970:** General election produced clear majority in East Pakistan for pro-autonomy Awami League, led by Sheikh Mujibur Rahman, and in West Pakistan for Islamic socialist Pakistan People's Party (PPP), led by Zulfiqar Ali Bhutto. **1971:** East Pakistan secured independence, as Bangladesh, following a civil war in which it received decisive military support from India. Power was transferred from the military to the populist Bhutto in Pakistan. **1977:** Bhutto overthrown in military coup by Gen Zia ul-Haq following months of civil unrest; martial law imposed. **1979:** Bhutto executed for alleged murder; tight political restrictions imposed by Zia regime. **1980:** 3 million refugees fled to Northwest Frontier Province and Baluchistan as a result of Soviet invasion of Afghanistan. **1981:** Broad-based Opposition Movement for the Restoration of Democracy formed. Islamization process pushed forward by government. **1985:** Martial law and ban on political parties lifted. **1986:** Agitation for free elections launched by Benazir Bhutto, the daughter of Zulfiqar Ali Bhutto. **1988:** Islamic legal code, the Shari'a, introduced; Zia killed in military plane crash. Benazir Bhutto became prime minister after the now centrist PPP won the general election. **1989:** Tension with India increased by outbreaks of civil war in Kashmir. Pakistan rejoined the Commonwealth, which it had left in 1972. **1990:** Bhutto dismissed as prime minister by President Ghulam Ishaq Khan on charges of incompetence and corruption. The conservative Islamic Democratic Alliance (IDA), led by Nawaz Sharif, won general election and launched a privatization and economic deregulation programme. **1993:** Khan and Sharif resigned. Benazir Bhutto and PPP re-elected. Farooq Leghari (PPP) elected president. **1994:** Regional sectarian violence between Shia and Sunni Muslims, centred in Karachi. **1996:** Benazir Bhutto dismissed by Leghari amid allegations of corruption. **1997:** Right-of-centre Pakistan Muslim League won in general election, returning Nawaz Sharif to power as prime minister. President Leghari resigned. Rafiq Tarar elected president. **1998:** Antigovernment protests as economy deteriorated. Sharif proposed introducing full Islamic law but met with opposition within parliament. Pakistan conducted its first ever nuclear tests, provoking international condemnation and sanctions by the USA. Benazir Bhutto and her husband charged with corruption. Federal rule imposed on Sindh as a result of escalating violence. $5.5 billion economic bailout package agreed with the IMF and World Bank. **1999:** Benazir Bhutto and her husband found guilty of corruption and sentenced to prison and fined £5.3 million.

Palau Republic of (also known as **Belau**)

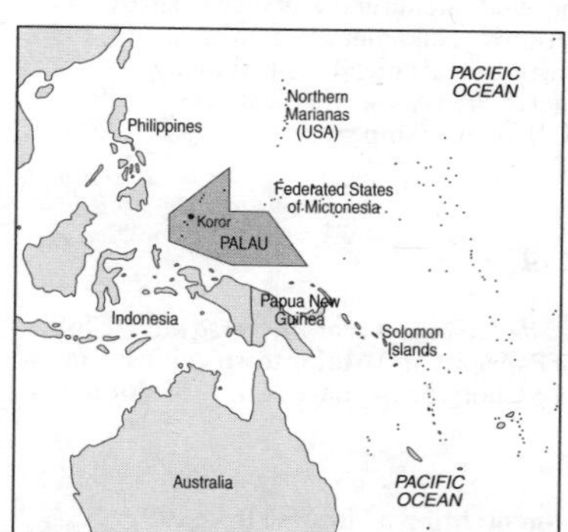

Area: 508 sq km/ 196 sq mi **Capital:** Koror (on Koror Island) **Major towns/cities:** Melekeiok, Garusuun, Malakal

Government

Head of state and government: Kuniwo Nakamura from 1992 **Political system:** liberal democracy **Administrative divisions:** 16 states **Political parties:** there are no formally organized political parties **Armed forces:** no defence forces of its own; under the Compact of Free Association,

the USA is responsible for the defence of Palau; two US military bases operate on the islands **Death penalty:** laws do not provide for the death penalty for any crime

Economy and resources

Currency: US dollar **GDP:** (US$) 109 million (1995 est) **GNP:** N/A **GNP per capita (PPP):** (US$) N/A **Consumer price inflation:** N/A **Unemployment:** 20% (1988 est) **Foreign debt:** (US$) 100 million (1990) **Major trading partners:** USA, UK, Japan **Exports:** copra, coconut oil, handicrafts, trochus, tuna **Imports:** food and live animals, crude materials, mineral fuels, beverages, tobacco, chemicals, basic manufactures, machinery and transport equipment

Population and society

Population: 19,000 (1998 est) **Population growth rate:** 1.7% (1995–2025) **Population density:** (per sq km) 39.5 (1998 est) **Urban population:** (% of total) 72 (1997) **Age distribution:** (% of total population) 0–14 27.4%, 15–64 67.7%, 65+ 4.9% (1998) **Ethnic groups:** predominantly Micronesian **Language:** Palauan and English **Religion:** Christian, principally Roman Catholic **Education:** (compulsory years) 8 **Literacy rate:** 92% (1980) **Life expectancy:** 68 (men); 74 (women) (1994) **Child mortality rate:** (under 5, per 1,000 live births) 35 (1995) **Physicians:** 1 per 1,512 people (1990)

Practical information

Visa requirements: UK: visa not required for a stay of up to 30 days. USA: visa not required for a stay of up to 30 days **Embassy in the UK:** Palau has no diplomatic representation in the UK; the UK Department of Trade and Industry has a Pacific Islands Desk. Tel: (0171) 215 4760; fax: (0171) 215 4398 **British embassy:** the UK has no diplomatic representation in Palau **Chamber of commerce:** Palau Visitors Authority, PO Box 6028, Koror 96940. Tel: (680) 488 2920; fax: (680) 488 2911

Chronology

c. **1000 BC:** Micronesians first settled the islands. **1543:** First visited by Spanish navigator Ruy Lopez de Villalobos. **16th century:** Colonized by Spain. **later 16th century:** Fell under Spanish influence. **1899:** Purchased from Spain by Germany. **1914:** Occupied by Japan at the outbreak of World War I. **1920:** Administered by Japan under League of Nations mandate. **1944:** Occupied by USA after Japanese removed during World War II. **1947:** Became part of United Nations (UN) Pacific Islands Trust Territory, administered by USA. **1981:** Acquired autonomy as the Republic of Belau (Palau) under a constitution which prohibited the entry, storage, or disposal of nuclear or biological weapons. **1982:** Compact of Free Association signed with USA, providing for the right to maintain US military facilities in return for economic aid. However, the compact could not come into force since it contradicted the constitution, which could only be amended by a 75% vote in favour. **1985:** President Haruo Remeliik assassinated; succeeded by Lazarus Salii. **1988:** President Salii committed suicide and was succeeded by Ngiratkel Etpison. **1992:** Kuniwo Nakamura elected president. **1993:** Referendum approved constitutional amendment allowing implementation of Compact of Free Association with USA. **1994:** Independence achieved; UN membership granted.

Panama Republic of

National name: *República de Panamá* **Area:** 77,100 sq km/29,768 sq mi **Capital:** Panamá (or Panama City) **Major towns/cities:** San Miguelito, Colón, David, La Chorrera, Santiago, Chitré **Major ports:** Colón, Cristóbal, Balboa

Government

Head of state and government: Mireya Moscoso from 1999 **Political system:** emergent democracy **Administrative divisions:** nine provinces and one special territory (San Blas) **Political parties:** Democratic Revolutionary Party (PRD), right wing; Arnulfista Party (PA), left of centre; Authentic Liberal Party (PLA), left of centre;

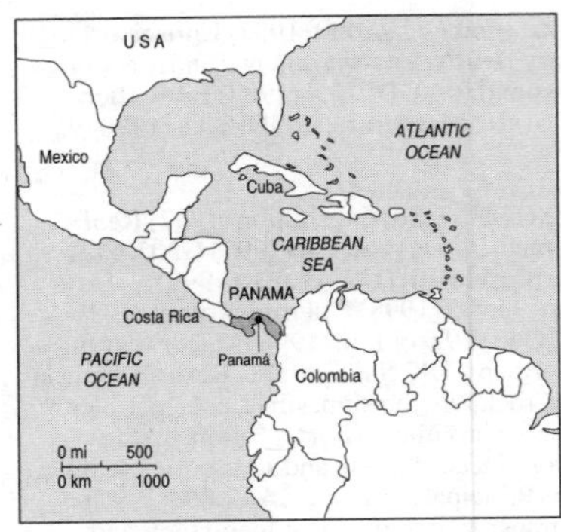

Nationalist Liberal Republican Movement (MOLIRENA), right of centre; Papa Ego Movement (MPE), moderate, centre left **Armed forces:** army abolished by National Assembly (1994); paramilitary forces numbered 11,800 (1997) **Conscription:** military service is voluntary **Death penalty:** laws do not provide for the death penalty for any crime (last known execution in 1903) **Defence spend:** (% GDP) 1.3 (1997) **Education spend:** (% GNP) 5.2 (1995) **Health spend:** (% GDP) 5.4 (1990–95)

Economy and resources

Currency: balboa **GDP:** (US$) 8.7 billion (1997) **Real GDP growth:** (% change on previous year) 4.3 (1997) **GNP (US$):** 8.4 billion (1997) **GNP per capita (PPP):** (US$) 7,070 (1997) **Consumer price inflation:** 1.5% (1998) **Unemployment:** 13.9% (1996) **Foreign debt:** (US$) 7.1 billion (1996) **Major trading partners:** USA, Japan, Costa Rica, Ecuador, Germany, Venezuela, Italy **Resources:** limestone, clay, salt; deposits of coal, copper, and molybdenum have been discovered **Exports:** bananas, shrimps and lobsters, sugar, clothing, coffee. Principal market: USA 46.2% (1997) **Imports:** machinery and transport equipment, petroleum and mineral products, chemicals and chemical products, electrical and electronic equipment, foodstuffs. Principal source: USA 36.9% (1997) **Arable land:** 6.7% (1995)

Population and society

Population: 2,767,000 (1998 est) **Population growth rate:** 1.6% (1995–2000); 1.4% (2000–05) **Population density:** (per sq km) 36 (1998 est) **Urban population:** (% of total) 57 (1997) **Age distribution:** (% of total population) 0–14 32.0%, 15–64 62.4%, 65+ 5.7% (1995) **Ethnic groups:** about 70% mestizos (of Spanish–American and American–Indian descent), 14% West Indian, 10% white American or European, and 6% Indian **Language:** Spanish (official), English **Religion:** Roman Catholic **Education:** (compulsory years) 8 **Literacy rate:** 88% (men); 88% (women) (1995 est) **Labour force:** 39% of population: 26% agriculture, 16% industry, 58% services (1990) **Life expectancy:** 72 (men); 76 (women) (1995–2000) **Child mortality rate:** (under 5, per 1,000 live births) 26 (1997) **Physicians:** 1 per 562 people (1993 est)

Practical information

Visa requirements: UK: visa not required (business visitors need a business visa). USA: visa required **Embassy in the UK:** 48 Park Street, London W1Y 3PD. Tel: (0171) 493 4646; fax: (0171) 493 4333 **British embassy:** Apartado 889, Zona 1, 4th and 5th Floors, Torre Banco Sur, Calle 53 Este, Panama 1. Tel: (2) 690 866; fax: (2) 230 730 **Chamber of commerce:** Cámara de Comercio, Industrias y Agricultura de Panamá, Apartado 74, Edificio Comosa, Avenida Samuel Lewis, Planta Baja, Panamá 1. Tel: (2) 271 233; fax: (2) 274 186

Chronology

1502: Visited by Spanish explorer Rodrigo de Bastidas, at which time it was inhabited by Cuna, Choco, Guaymi, and other Indian groups. **1513:** Spanish conquistador Vasco Núñez de Balboa explored Pacific Ocean from Darien isthmus; he was made governor of Panama (meaning 'abundance of fish'), but was later executed as a result of Spanish court intrigue. **1519:** Spanish city established at Panama, which became part of the Spanish viceroyalty of New Andalucia (later New Granada). **1572–95 and 1668–71:** Spanish settlements sacked by British buccaneers Francis Drake and Henry Morgan. **1821:**

Achieved independence from Spain; joined confederacy of Gran Colombia, which included Colombia, Venezuela, Ecuador, Peru, and Bolivia. **1830:** Gran Colombia split up and Panama became part of Colombia. **1846:** Treaty signed with USA, allowing it to construct a railway across the isthmus. **1880s:** French attempt to build a Panama canal connecting the Atlantic and Pacific Oceans failed as a result of financial difficulties and the death of 22,000 workers from yellow fever and malaria. **1903:** Full independence achieved with US help on separation from Colombia; USA bought rights to build Panama Canal, and were given control of a 10-mile strip, the Canal Zone, in perpetuity. **1914:** Panama Canal opened. **1939:** Panama's status as a US protectorate was terminated by mutual agreement. **1968–81:** Military rule of Gen Omar Torrijos Herrera, leader of the National Guard, who deposed the elected president and launched a costly programme of economic modernization. **1977:** USA–Panama treaties transferred the canal to Panama (effective from 2000), with the USA guaranteeing protection and annual payment. **1984:** Nicolás Ardito Barletta of the right-wing Democratic Revolutionary Party (PRD) elected president by narrow margin. **1985:** Barletta resigned; replaced by Eric Arturo del Valle, to the dissatisfaction of the USA. **1987:** Gen Manuel Noriega (head of the National Guard and effective ruler since 1983) resisted calls for his removal, despite suspension of US military and economic aid. **1988:** Del Valle replaced by Manuel Solis Palma after trying to oust Noriega. Noriega, charged with drug smuggling by the USA, declared a state of emergency after the coup against him failed. **1989:** Assembly elections declared invalid when won by opposition. 'State of war' with USA announced, and US invasion (codenamed 'Operation Just Cause') deposed Noriega; 4,000 Panamanians died in the fighting. Guillermo Endara, who had won earlier elections, was installed as president in December. **1991:** Attempted antigovernment coup foiled. Constitutional reforms approved by assembly, including abolition of standing army; privatization programme introduced. **1992:** Noriega found guilty of drug offences and given 40-year prison sentence in USA. Referendum rejected the proposed constitutional reforms. **1994:** Ernesto Pérez Balladares (PRD) elected president. Constitution amended by assembly; army formally abolished. **1998:** Voters rejected a proposed constitutional change to allow the president to run for a second term. **1999:** Mireya Moscoso was elected first female president.

Papua New Guinea

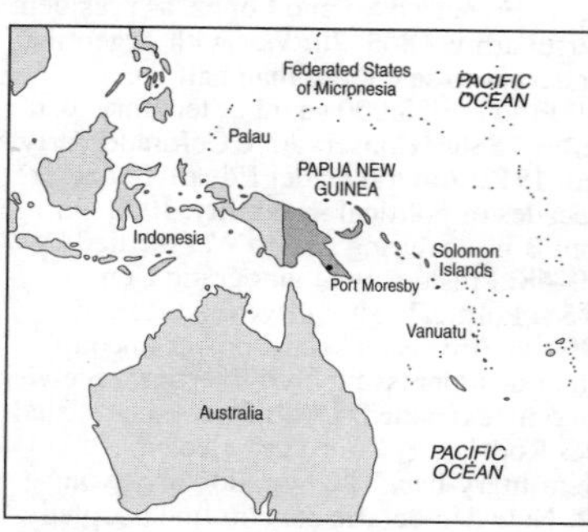

Area: 462,840 sq km/ 178,702 sq mi **Capital:** Port Moresby (on East New Guinea) (also port) **Major towns/cities:** Lae, Madang, Arawa, Wewak, Goroka, Rabaul, Mount Hagen **Major ports:** Rabaul

Government

Head of state: Queen Elizabeth II, represented by governor general Silas Atopare from 1997 **Head of government:** Bill Skate from 1997 **Political system:** liberal democracy **Administrative divisions:** 19 provinces and the National Capital District **Political parties:** Papua New Guinea Party (Pangu Pati: PP), urban- and coastal-oriented nationalist; People's Democratic Movement (PDM), 1985 breakaway from the PP; National Party (NP), highlands-based, conservative; Melanesian Alliance (MA), Bougainville-based, pro-autonomy, left of centre; People's Progress Party (PPP), conservative; People's Action Party (PAP), right of centre **Armed forces:** 4,300 (1997) **Conscription:** military service is voluntary **Death penalty:** retains the death penalty for ordinary crimes but can be considered abolitionist in practice (last execution 1950) **Defence spend:** (% GDP) 1.2 (1997) **Education spend:** (% GNP) 6.3 (1993 est) **Health spend:** (% GDP) 2.8 (1990–95)

Economy and resources

Currency: kina **GDP:** (US$) 5.1 billion (1997) **Real GDP growth:** (% change on previous year) 1.8 (1997) **GNP (US$):** 4.2 billion (1997) **GNP per capita (PPP):** (US$) 2,390 (1997) **Consumer price inflation:** 8.0% (1998) **Foreign debt:** (US$) 2.36 billion (1996) **Major trading partners:** Australia, Japan, USA, Singapore, Germany, South Korea, UK **Resources:** copper, gold, silver; deposits of chromite, cobalt, nickel, quartz; substantial reserves of petroleum and natural gas (petroleum production began in 1992) **Exports:** gold, copper ore and concentrates, crude petroleum, timber, coffee beans, coconut and copra products. Principal market: Australia 31.9% (1997) **Imports:** machinery and transport equipment, manufactured goods, food and live animals, miscellaneous manufactured articles, chemicals, mineral fuels. Principal source: Australia 51% (1997) **Arable land:** 0.1% (1995)

Population and society

Population: 4,600,000 (1998 est) **Population growth rate:** 2.2% (1995–2000); 2.1% (2000–05) **Population density:** (per sq km) 10.2 (1998 est) **Urban population:** (% of total) 17 (1997) **Age distribution:** (% of total population) 0–14 39.7%, 15–64 57.4%, 65+ 3.0% (1998) **Ethnic groups:** mainly Melanesian, particularly in coastal areas; inland (on New Guinea and larger islands), Papuans predominate. On the outer archipelagos and islands, mixed Micronese-Melanesians are found. A small Chinese minority also exists **Language:** English (official); pidgin English, 715 local languages **Religion:** Protestant, Roman Catholic, local faiths **Education:** not compulsory **Literacy rate:** 65% (men); 38% (women) (1995 est) **Labour force:** 49% of population: 79% agriculture, 7% industry, 14% services (1990) **Life expectancy:** 57 (men); 59 (women) (1995–2000) **Child mortality rate:** (under 5, per 1,000 live births) 80 (1997) **Physicians:** 1 per 12,754 people (1993 est)

Practical information

Visa requirements: UK: visa required. USA: visa required **Embassy in the UK:** 14 Waterloo Place, London SW1Y 4AR. Tel: (0171) 930 0922/7; fax: (0171) 930 0828 **British embassy:** British High Commission, PO Box 4778, Kiroki Street, Waigani, Boroko, Port Moresby. Tel: (675) 325 1677; fax: (675) 325 3547 **Chamber of commerce:** Papua New Guinea Chamber of Commerce and Industry, PO Box 1621, Port Moresby. Tel: (675) 213 057; fax: (675) 214 203

Chronology

c. **3000 BC:** New settlement of Austronesian (Melanesian) immigrants. **1526:** Visited by Portuguese navigator Jorge de Menezes, who named the main island the Ilhos dos Papua after the 'frizzled' hair of the inhabitants. **1545:** Spanish navigator Ynigo Ortis de Retez gave the island the name of New Guinea, as a result of a supposed resemblance of the peoples with those of the Guinea coast of Africa. **17th century:** Regularly visited by Dutch merchants. **1828:** Dutch East India Company incorporated western part of New Guinea into Netherlands East Indies (becoming Irian Jaya, in Indonesia). **1884:** Northeast New Guinea annexed by Germany; the southeast was claimed by Britain. **1870s:** Visits by Western missionaries and traders increased. **1890s:** Copra plantations developed in German New Guinea. **1906:** Britain transferred its rights to Australia, which renamed the lands Papua. **1914:** German New Guinea occupied by Australia at outbreak of World War I; from the merged territories Papua New Guinea was formed. **1920–42:** Held as League of Nations mandate by Australia. **1942–45:** Occupied by Japan, who lost 150,000 troops resisting Allied counterattack. **1947:** Held as United Nations Trust Territory by Australia. **1951:** Legislative Council established. **1964:** Elected House of Assembly formed. **1967:** Pangu Party (Pangu Pati; PP) formed to campaign for home rule. **1975:** Independence achieved from Australia, within Commonwealth, with Michael Somare (PP) as prime minister. **1980:** Sir Julius Chan of People's Progress Party (PPP) became prime minister. **1982:** Somare returned to power. **1985:** Somare challenged by deputy prime minister Paias Wingti, who later left the PP and formed the People's Democratic Movement (PDM); he became head of a five-party coalition government. **1988:** Wingti defeated on no-confidence vote; replaced by Rabbie Namaliu (PP), heading coalition government. Joined Solomon

Islands and Vanuatu to form Spearhead Group, aiming to preserve Melanesian cultural traditions. **1989:** State of emergency imposed on copper-rich Bougainville in response to separatist violence. **1990:** Bougainville Revolutionary Army (BRA) issued unilateral declaration of independence. **1991:** Economic boom as gold production doubled. **1992:** Wingti appointed premier, heading a three-party coalition. **1994:** Wingti replaced as premier by Sir Julius Chan. Short-lived peace agreement with BRA. **1996:** Prime minister of Bougainville murdered, jeopardizing peace process. Gerard Sinato elected president of the transitional Bougainville government. **1997:** Army and police mutinied following government's use of mercenaries against secessionist rebels. Bill Skate (PDM) appointed prime minister. Silas Atopare appointed governor general. **1998:** Truce with Bougainville secessionists. At least 1,500 people died and thousands were left homeless when tidal waves destroyed villages on north coast. The PPP left the government, criticizing Skate for mismanaging the economy. **1999:** Bougainville Transitional Government (BTG) replaced by new interim Bougainville Reconciliation Government (BRG), headed by former rebel leader Joseph Kabui and BTG leader Gerard Sinato.

Paraguay

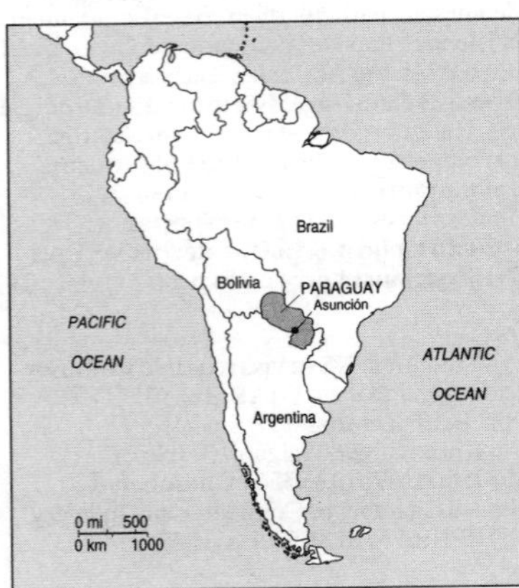

Republic of National name: *República del Paraguay* **Area:** 406,752 sq km/ 157,046 sq mi **Capital:** Asunción (and port) **Major towns/cities:** Ciudad del Este, Pedro Juan Caballero, San Lorenzo, Fernando de la Mora, Lambare, Concepción, Villartica, Encaración **Major ports:** Concepción

Government

Head of state and government: Luis Gonzalez Macchi from 1999 **Political system:** emergent democracy **Administrative divisions:** 17 departments **Political parties:** National Republican Association (Colorado Party), right of centre; Authentic Radical Liberal Party (PLRA), centrist; National Encounter, right of centre; Radical Liberal Party (PLR), centrist; Liberal Party (PL), centrist **Armed forces:** 20,200 (1997) **Conscription:** 12 months (army); 24 months (navy) **Death penalty:** abolished in 1992 **Defence spend:** (% GDP) 1.5 (1997) **Education spend:** (% GNP) 3.9 (1996) **Health spend:** (% GDP) 1.0 (1990–95)

Economy and resources

Currency: guaraní **GDP:** (US$) 10.1billion (1997) **Real GDP growth:** (% change on previous year) 3.0 (1997) **GNP (US$):** 10.2 billion (1997) **GNP per capita (PPP):** (US$) 3,870 (1997) **Consumer price inflation:** 6.2% (1998) **Unemployment:** 9% (1993) **Foreign debt:** (US$) 2.14 billion (1996) **Major trading partners:** Brazil, Argentina, the Netherlands, Japan, USA, France, UK **Resources:** gypsum, kaolin, limestone, salt; deposits (not commercially exploited) of bauxite, iron ore, copper, manganese, uranium; deposits of natural gas discovered in 1994; exploration for petroleum deposits ongoing mid-1990s **Exports:** soya beans (and other oil seeds), cotton, timber and wood manufactures, hides and skins, meat. Principal market: Brazil 38.4% (1997) **Imports:** machinery, vehicles and parts, mineral fuels and lubricants, beverages, tobacco, chemicals, foodstuffs. Principal source: Brazil 31.8% (1997) **Arable land:** 5.5 % (1995)

Population and society

Population: 5,222,000 (1998 est) **Population growth rate:** 2.6% (1995–2000); 2.3% (2000–05) **Population density:** (per sq km) 13.3 (1998 est) **Urban population:** (% of total) 54 (1997) **Age distribution:** (% of total population) 0–14 39.5%, 15–64 55.9%, 65+ 4.6% (1998) **Ethnic groups:** predominantly mixed-race mestizos; less than 5% Spanish or Indian **Language:** Spanish 6% (official), Guaraní 90% **Religion:** Roman Catholic (official religion); Mennonite, Anglican **Education:** (compulsory years) 6 **Literacy rate:** 92% (men); 88% (women) (1995 est) **Labour force:** 45.2% agriculture, 22.5% industry, 32.3% services (1994) **Life expectancy:** 68 (men); 72 (women) (1995–2000) **Child mortality rate:** (under 5, per 1,000 live births) 47 (1997) **Physicians:** 1 per 1,231 people (1993 est)

Practical information

Visa requirements: UK: visa not required. USA: visa not required **Embassy in the UK:** Braemar Lodge, Cornwall Gardens, London SW7 4AQ. Tel: (0171) 937 1253; fax: (0171) 937 5687 **British embassy:** Casilla 404, Calle Presidente Franco 706, Asunción. Tel: (21) 444 472; fax: (21) 446 385 **Chamber of commerce:** Cámara y Bolsa de Comercio, Estrella 540, Asunción. Tel: (21) 493 321; fax: (21) 440 817

Chronology

1526: Visited by Italian navigator Sebastian Cabot, who travelled up Paraná River; at this time the east of the country had long been inhabited by Guaraní-speaking Amerindians, who gave the country its name, which means 'land with an important river'. **1537:** Spanish made an alliance with Guaraní Indians against hostile Chaco Indians, enabling them to colonize interior plains; Asunción founded by Spanish. **1609:** Jesuits arrived from Spain to convert local population to Roman Catholicism and administer the country. **1767:** Jesuit missionaries expelled. **1776:** Formerly part of Spanish Viceroyalty of Peru, which covered much of South America, became part of Viceroyalty of La Plata, with capital at Buenos Aires (Argentina). **1808:** With Spanish monarchy overthrown by Napoleon Bonaparte, La Plata Viceroyalty became autonomous, but Paraguayans revolted against rule from Buenos Aires. **1811:** Independence achieved from Spain. **1814:** Under dictator Gen José Gaspar Rodriguez Francia ('El Supremo'), Paraguay became an isolated state. **1840:** Francia was succeeded by his nephew, Carlos Antonio Lopez, who opened country to foreign trade and whose son, Francisco Solano Lopez, as president from 1862, built up powerful army. **1865–70:** War with Argentina, Brazil, and Uruguay over access to sea; more than half the population died and 150,000 sq km/58,000 sq mi of territory lost; President Lopez killed. **later 1880s:** Conservative Colorado Party and Liberal Party founded. **1912:** Liberal leader Edvard Schaerer came to power, ending decades of political instability. **1932–35:** Territory in west won from Bolivia during Chaco War (settled by arbitration in 1938). **1940–48:** Presidency of autocratic Gen Higinio Morínigo. **1948–54:** Political instability; six different presidents. **1954:** Gen Alfredo Stroessner seized power in coup. He ruled as a ruthless autocrat, suppressing civil liberties; received initial US backing as economy expanded. **1989:** Stroessner ousted in coup led by Gen Andrés Rodríguez. Rodríguez elected president; right-of-centre military-backed Colorado Party won assembly elections. **1992:** New democratic constitution adopted. **1993:** Colorado Party won most seats in first free multiparty elections, but no overall majority; its candidate, Juan Carlos Wasmosy, won first free presidential elections. **1998:** Colorado Party candidate Raul Cubas was elected president. **1999:** President Cubas resigned; replaced by senate leader, Luis Gonzalez Macchi.

Peru Republic of

National name: *República del Perú* **Area:** 1,285,200 sq km/496,216 sq mi **Capital:** Lima **Major towns/cities:** Arequipa, Iquitos, Chiclayo, Trujillo, Cuzco, Piura, Chimbote **Major ports:** Callao, Chimbote, Salaverry

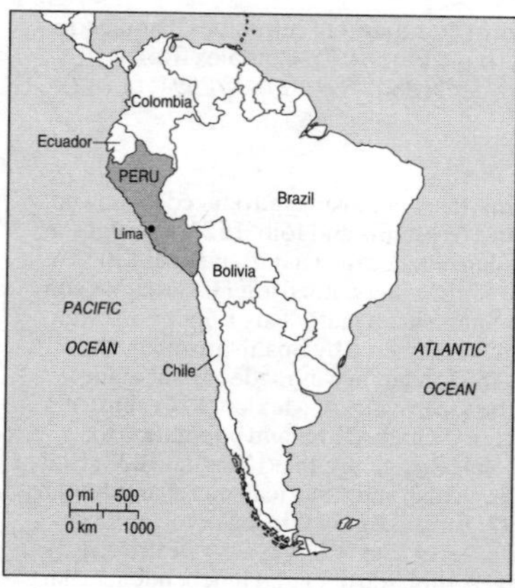

Government

Head of state: Alberto Fujimori from 1990 **Head of government:** Alberto Pandolfi from 1998 **Political system:** democracy **Administrative divisions:** 24 departments and the constitutional province of Callao **Political parties:** American Popular Revolutionary Alliance (APRA), moderate, left wing; United Left (IU), left wing; Change 90 (Cambio 90), centrist; New Majority (Nueva Mayoria), centrist; Popular Christian Party (PPC), right of centre; Liberal Party (PL), right wing **Armed forces:** 125,000; plus paramilitary forces numbering 78,000 (1997) **Conscription:** conscription is selective for two years **Death penalty:** retains the death penalty only for exceptional crimes such as crimes under military law or crimes committed in exceptional circumstances such as wartime (last execution 1979) **Defence spend:** (% GDP) 2.2 (1997) **Education spend:** (% GNP) 2.9 (1996) **Health spend:** (% GDP) 2.6 (1990–95)

Economy and resources

Currency: nuevo sol **GDP:** (US$) 62.4 billion (1997) **Real GDP growth:** (% change on previous year) 6.1 (1997) **GNP (US$):** 60.8 billion (1997) **GNP per capita (PPP):** (US$) 4,390 (1997) **Consumer price inflation:** 8.8% (1998) **Unemployment:** 9.4% (1994 est) **Foreign debt:** (US$) 29.17 billion (1996) **Major trading partners:** USA, Japan, UK, Germany, Italy, China, Argentina, Brazil, Colombia **Resources:** lead, copper, iron, silver, zinc (world's fourth-largest producer), petroleum **Exports:** copper, fishmeal, zinc, gold, refined petroleum products. Principal market: USA 24.9% (1997) **Imports:** machinery and transport equipment, basic foodstuffs, basic manufactures, chemicals, mineral fuels, consumer goods. Principal source: USA 19.1% (1997) **Arable land:** 3% (1995)

Population and society

Population: 24,797,000 (1998 est) **Population growth rate:** 1.7% (1995–2000); 1.7% (2000–05) **Population density:** (per sq km) 20.4 (1998 est) **Urban population:** (% of total) 72 (1997) **Age distribution:** (% of total population) 0–14 35.7%, 15–64 59.8%, 65+ 4.5% (1998) **Ethnic groups:** about 45% South American Indian, 37% mestizo, 15% European, and 3% African **Language:** Spanish, Quechua (both official), Aymara **Religion:** Roman Catholic (state religion) **Education:** (compulsory years) 11 **Literacy rate:** 92% (men); 88% (women) (1995 est) **Labour force:** 33% agriculture, 16.9% industry, 53.1% services (1992) **Life expectancy:** 66 (men); 71 (women) (1995–2000) **Child mortality rate:** (under 5, per 1,000 live births) 60 (1997) **Physicians:** 1 per 939 people (1993 est)

Practical information

Visa requirements: UK: visa not required for a stay of up to 90 days. USA: visa not required for a stay of up to 90 days **Embassy in the UK:** 52 Sloane Street, London SW1X 9SP. Tel: (0171) 235 1917; fax: (0171) 235 4463 **British embassy:** PO Box 854, Natalio Sanchez 125, Edificio El Pacifico, Pisos 11/12, Plaza Washington, Lima 100. Tel: (1) 433 5032; fax: (1) 433 4738 **Chamber of commerce:** Confederación de Cámaras de Comercio y Producción del Perú, Avenida Gregorio Escobedo 398, Lima 11. Tel: (1) 463 3434; fax: (1) 463 2820

Chronology

4000 BC: Evidence of early settled agriculture in Chicama Valley. **AD 700–1100:** Period of Wari Empire, first expansionist militarized empire in Andes. **1200:** Manco Capac became first emperor of South American Indian Quechua-speaking Incas, who established a growing and sophisticated empire centred on the Andean city of Cuzco, and believed their ruler was descended from the Sun. **late 15th century:** At its zenith, Inca Empire stretched from Quito in Ecuador to beyond Santiago in southern Chile. It superseded Chimu civilization, which had flourished in Peru 1250–1470. **1532–33:** Incas defeated by Spanish conquistadores, led by Francisco Pizarro. King Atahualpa killed. Empire came under Spanish rule, as part of Viceroyalty of Peru, with capital in Lima, founded in 1535. **1541:** Pizarro assassinated as rivalries broke out among conquistadores. **1780:** Tupac Amaru, who claimed to be descended from last Inca chieftain, led failed native revolt against Spanish. **1810:** Peru became headquarters for Spanish government as European settlers rebelled elsewhere in Spanish America. **1820–22:** Fight for liberation from Spanish rule led by Gen José de San Martín and Army of Andes which, after freeing Argentina and Chile, invaded southern Peru. **1824:** Became last colony in Central and South America to achieve independence from Spain after attacks from north by Field Marshal Sucre, acting for freedom fighter Simón Bolívar. **1836–39:** Failed attempts at union with Bolivia. **1845–62:** Economic progress under rule of Gen Ramón Castilla. **1849–74:** Around 80,000–100,000 Chinese labourers arrived in Peru to fill menial jobs such as collecting guano. **1866:** Victorious naval war fought with Spain. **1879–83:** Pacific War fought in alliance with Bolivia and Chile over nitrate fields of the Atacama Desert in the south; three provinces along coastal south lost to Chile. **1902:** Boundary dispute with Bolivia settled. **mid-1920s:** After several decades of civilian government, series of right-wing dictatorships held power. **1927:** Boundary dispute with Colombia settled. **1929:** Tacna province, lost to Chile in 1880, was returned. **1941:** Brief war with Ecuador secured Amazonian territory. **1945:** Civilian government, dominated by left-of-centre American Popular Revolutionary Alliance (APRA, formed 1924), came to power after free elections. **1948:** Army coup installed military government led by Gen Manuel Odría, who remained in power until 1956. **1963:** Return to civilian rule, with centrist Fernando Belaúnde Terry as president. **1968:** Return of military government in bloodless coup by Gen Juan Velasco Alvarado, following industrial unrest. Populist land reform programme introduced. **1975:** Velasco replaced, in a bloodless coup, by Gen Morales Bermúdez. **1980:** Return to civilian rule, with Fernando Belaúnde as president; agrarian and industrial reforms pursued. Sendero Luminoso ('Shining Path') Maoist guerrilla group active. **1981:** Boundary dispute with Ecuador renewed. **1985:** Belaúnde succeeded by Social Democrat Alan García Pérez, who launched campaign to remove military and police 'old guard'. **1987:** President García delayed nationalization of Peru's banks after vigorous campaign against the proposal. **1988:** García pressured to seek help from International Monetary Fund (IMF) as economy deteriorated. Sendero Luminoso increased campaign of violence. **1990:** Right-of-centre Alberto Fujimori, the son of Japanese immigrants, defeated ex-communist writer Vargas Llosa in presidential elections. Assassination attempt on president failed. Inflation 400%; privatization programme launched. **1992:** Fujimori allied himself with the army and suspended constitution, provoking international criticism. Sendero Luminoso leader arrested and sentenced to life imprisonment. New single-chamber legislature elected. **1993:** New constitution adopted, enabling Fujimori to seek re-election. **1994:** 6,000 Sendero Luminoso guerrillas surrendered to the authorities. **1995:** Border dispute with Ecuador resolved after armed clashes. Fujimori re-elected. Controversial amnesty granted to those previously convicted of human-rights abuses. **1996:** Prime Minister Dante Cordova resigned in protest against rapid pace of market reform. Hostages held in Japanese embassy by Marxist Tupac Amaru Revolutionary Movement (MRTA) guerrillas. **1997:** Hostage siege ended. **1998:** Javier Valle Riestra appointed prime minister, but resigned two months later. Alberto Pandolfi appointed to succeed him. 157-year-old border dispute settled with Ecuador.

Philippines Republic of the

National name: *Republika ng Pilipinas* **Area:** 300,000 sq km/115,830 sq mi **Capital:** Manila (on Luzon) (and chief port) **Major towns/cities:** Quezon City (on Luzon), Davao, Caloocan, Cebu,

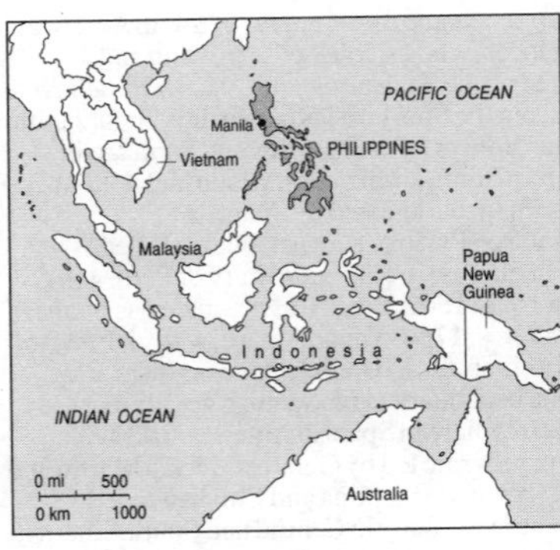

Zamboanga **Major ports:** Cebu, Davao (on Mindanao), Iloilo, Zamboanga (on Mindanao)

Government
Head of state and government: Joseph Ejercito Estrada from 1998 **Political system:** emergent democracy **Administrative divisions:** 15 regions (two of which are autonomous) **Political parties:** Laban ng Demokratikong Pilipino (Democratic Filipino Struggle Party; LDP–DFSP), centrist, liberal-democrat coalition; Lakas ng Edsa (National Union of Christian Democrats; LNE–NUCD), centrist; Liberal Party, centrist; Nationalist Party (Nacionalista), right wing; New Society Movement (NSM; Kilusan Bagong Lipunan), conservative, pro-Marcos; National Democratic Front, left-wing umbrella grouping, including the Communist Party of the Philippines (CPP); Mindanao Alliance, island-based decentralist body **Armed forces:** 110,500 (1995); reserve forces 131,000; paramilitary forces around 42,500 (1997) **Conscription:** military service is voluntary **Death penalty:** retained in law, but considered abolitionist in practice; last execution in 1976 **Defence spend:** (% GDP) 1.7 (1997) **Education spend:** (% GNP) 2.2 (1995) **Health spend:** (% GDP) 1.3 (1990–95)

Economy and resources
Currency: peso **GDP:** (US$) 83.1 billion (1997) **Real GDP growth:** (% change on previous year) 4.3 (1997) **GNP (US$):** 89.3 billion (1997) **GNP per capita (PPP):** (US$) 3,670 (1997) **Consumer price inflation:** 10.1% (1998) **Unemployment:** 8.4% (1995) **Foreign debt:** (US$) 41.2 billion (1996) **Major trading partners:** Japan, USA, Singapore, Taiwan, South Korea, Hong Kong **Resources:** copper ore, gold, silver, chromium, nickel, coal, crude petroleum, natural gas, forests **Exports:** electronic products (notably semiconductors and microcircuits), garments, agricultural products (particularly fruit and seafood), woodcraft and furniture, lumber, chemicals, coconut oil. Principal market: USA 34.9% (1997) **Imports:** machinery and transport equipment, mineral fuels, basic manufactures, food and live animals, textile yarns, base metals, cereals and cereal preparations. Principal source: USA 21.8% (1997) **Arable land:** 18.5% (1995)

Population and society
Population: 72,944,000 (1998 est) **Population growth rate:** 2.0% (1995–2000); 1.8% (2000–05) **Population density:** (per sq km) 260.7 (1998 est) **Urban population:** (% of total) 56 (1997) **Age distribution:** (% of total population) 0–14 37.6%, 15–64 58.8%, 65+ 3.6% (1998) **Ethnic groups:** comprises more than 50 ethnic communities, although 95% of the population is designated 'Filipino', an Indo-Polynesian ethnic grouping **Language:** Tagalog (Filipino, official); English and Spanish; Cebuano, Ilocano, and more than 70 other indigenous languages **Religion:** mainly Roman Catholic; Protestant, Muslim, local religions **Education:** (compulsory years) 6 **Literacy rate:** 90% (men); 89% (women) (1995 est) **Labour force:** 40% of population: 46% agriculture, 15% industry, 39% services (1990) **Life expectancy:** 67 (men); 70 (women) (1995–2000) **Child mortality rate:** (under 5, per 1,000 live births) 42 (1997) **Physicians:** 1 per 853 people (1993)

Practical information
Visa requirements: UK: visa not required for a stay of up to 21 days. USA: visa not required for a stay of up to 21 days **Embassy in the UK:** 9a Palace Green, London W8 4QE. Tel: (0171) 937 1600; fax: (0171) 937 2925 **British embassy:** 15th–17th Floors, LV Locsin Building, 6752 Ayala Avenue, Makati, Metro Manila 1226. Tel: (2) 816 7116; fax: (2) 819 7206 **Chamber of commerce:** Philippine Chamber of Commerce and Industry, Ground Floor, CCP Complex, Roxas Boulevard, Makati, Metro Manila 2801. Tel: (2) 833 8591; fax: (2) 816 1946

Chronology
14th century: Traders from Malay peninsula introduced Islam and created Muslim principalities of Manila and Jolo. **1521:** Portuguese navigator Ferdinand Magellan reached the islands, but was killed in battle with islanders. **1536:** Philippines named after Charles V's son (later Philip II of Spain) by Spanish navigator Ruy López de Villalobos. **1565:** Philippines conquered by Spanish army led by Miguel López de Lagazpi. **1571:** Manila was made capital of the colony, which was part of the viceroyalty of Mexico. **17th century:** Spanish missionaries converted much of lowland population to Roman Catholicism. **1762–63:** British occupied Manila. **1834:** End of Spanish monopoly on trade; British and American merchants bought sugar and tobacco. **1896–97:** Emilio Aguinaldo led revolt against Spanish rule. **1898:** Spanish-American War: US navy destroyed Spanish fleet in Manila Bay; Aguinaldo declared independence, but Spain ceded Philippines to USA. **1898–1901:** Nationalist uprising suppressed by US troops; 200,000 Filipinos killed. **1907:** Americans set up elected legislative assembly. **1916:** Bicameral legislature introduced on US model. **1935:** Philippines gained internal self-government with Manuel Quezon as president. **1942–45:** Occupied by Japan. **1946:** Philippines achieved independence from USA under President Manuel Roxas; USA retained military bases and supplied economic aid. **1957–61:** 'Filipino First' policy introduced by President Carlos García to reduce economic power of Americans and Chinese; official corruption increased. **1965:** Ferdinand Marcos elected president. **1972:** Marcos declared martial law and ended freedom of press; economic development financed by foreign loans, of which large sums were diverted by Marcos for personal use. **1981:** Martial law officially ended but Marcos retained sweeping emergency powers, ostensibly needed to combat long-running Muslim and communist insurgencies. **1983:** Opposition leader Benigno Aquino murdered at Manila airport while surrounded by government troops. **1986:** Marcos falsified election results. Corazon Aquino (widow of Benigno Aquino) used 'people's power' to force Marcos to flee country. **1987:** 'Freedom constitution' adopted; Aquino's People's Power won congressional elections. **1989:** State of emergency declared after sixth coup attempt suppressed with US aid. **1991:** Philippine senate called for withdrawal of US forces; US renewal of Subic Bay naval base lease rejected. **1992:** Fidel Ramos elected to succeed Aquino; 'Rainbow Coalition' government formed. **1995:** Imelda Marcos (widow of Ferdinand Marcos) elected to House of Representatives while on bail from prison on a sentence for corruption. **1996:** LDP withdrew from coalition. Peace agreement between government and Moro National Liberation Front (MNLF) after 25 years of civil unrest on Mindanao. **1997:** Preliminary peace talks between government and Muslim secessionist Moro Islamic Liberation Front (MILF). Major changes in political parties. Supreme Court rejected proposal to allow second presidential term. **1998:** Joseph Estrada, the vice president, inaugurated as president and Gloria Macapagal Arroyo as vice president. Imelda Marcos acquitted of corruption charges. Dispute with China over mineral-rich Spratly Islands resolved with agreement on joint use of the resources.

Poland Republic of

National name: *Rzeczpospolita Polska* **Area:** 312,683 sq km/120,726 sq mi **Capital:** Warsaw **Major towns/cities:** Lódź, Kraków (Cracow), Wroclaw (Breslau), Poznań (Posen), Gdańsk (Danzig), Szczecin (Stettin), Katowice (Kattowitz), Bydgoszcz (Bromberg), Lublin **Major ports:** Gdańsk (Danzig), Szczecin (Stettin), Gdynia (Gdingen)

Government
Head of state: Aleksander Kwaśniewski from 1995 **Head of government:** Jerzy Buzek from 1997 **Political system:** emergent democracy **Administrative divisions:** 49 voivodships (or provinces)

Political parties: Democratic Left Alliance (SLD), reform socialist (ex-communist); Polish Peasant Party (PSL), moderate, agrarian; Freedom Union (UW), moderate, centrist; Labour Union (UP), left wing; Non-Party Bloc in Support of Reforms (BBWR), Christian Democrat, right of centre, pro-Walesa; Confederation for an Independent Poland (KPN), right wing; Solidarity Electoral Action (AWS), Christian, right wing **Armed forces:** 241,800 (1997) **Conscription:** military service is compulsory **Death penalty:** abolished in 1997 **Defence spend:** (% GDP) 2.3 (1997) **Education spend:** (% GNP) 4.6 (1995) **Health spend:** (% GDP) 4.8 (1990–95)

Economy and resources

Currency: zloty **GDP:** (US$) 135.6 billion (1997) **Real GDP growth:** (% change on previous year) 6 (1997) **GNP (US$):** 138.9 billion (1997) **GNP per capita (PPP):** (US$) 6,380 (1997) **Consumer price inflation:** 12.0% (1998) **Unemployment:** 11.5% (1997) **Foreign debt:** (US$) 40.89 billion (1996) **Major trading partners:** Germany, the Netherlands, Russian Federation, Italy, UK, France, USA **Resources:** coal (world's fifth-largest producer), copper, sulphur, silver, petroleum and natural gas reserves **Exports:** machinery and transport equipment, textiles, chemicals, coal, coke, copper, sulphur, steel, food and agricultural products, clothing and leather products, wood and paper products. Principal market: Germany 32.9% (1997) **Imports:** electro-engineering products, fuels and power (notably crude petroleum and natural gas), textiles, food products, iron ore, fertilizers. Principal source: Germany 24.1% (1996) **Arable land:** 46.7% (1995)

Population and society

Population: 38,718,000 (1998 est) **Population growth rate:** 0.1% (1995–2000); 0.3% (2000–05) **Population density:** (per sq km) 126.8 (1998 est) **Urban population:** (% of total) 65 (1997) **Age distribution:** (% of total population) 0–14 20.6%, 15–64 67.6%, 65+ 11.8% (1998) **Ethnic groups:** 98% ethnic Western-Slav ethnic Poles; small ethnic German, Ukrainian, and Belarussian minorities **Language:** Polish **Religion:** Roman Catholic 95% **Education:** (compulsory years) 8 **Literacy rate:** 99% (men); 99% (women) (1995 est) **Labour force:** 44.5% of population: 22.1% agriculture, 31.7% industry, 46.2% services (1996) **Life expectancy:** 67 (men); 76 (women) (1995–2000) **Child mortality rate:** (under 5, per 1,000 live births) 18 (1997) **Physicians:** 1 per 435 people (1995)

Practical information

Visa requirements: UK: visa not required for a stay of up to six months. USA: visa not required **Embassy in the UK:** 47 Portland Place, London W1N 3AG. Tel: (0171) 580 4324/9; fax: (0171) 323 4018 **British embassy:** Aleje Ró 1, 00-556 Warsaw. Tel: (228) 628 1001–5; fax: (228) 217 161 **Chamber of commerce:** Krajowa Izba Gospodarcza (Polish Chamber of Commerce), PO Box 361, Trebacka 4, 00-077 Warsaw. Tel: (22) 260 221; fax: (22) 274 673

Chronology

966: Polish Slavic tribes under Mieszko I, leader of Piast dynasty, adopted Christianity and united region around Poznań to form first Polish state. **1241:** Devastated by Mongols. **13th–14th centuries:** German and Jewish refugees settled among Slav population. **1386:** Jagellonian dynasty came to power: golden age for Polish culture. **1569:** Poland united with Lithuania to become largest state in Europe. **1572:** Jagellonian dynasty became extinct; future kings were elected by nobility and gentry, who formed 10% of the population. **mid-17th century:** Defeat in war against Russia, Sweden, and Brandenburg (in Germany) set in a process of irreversible decline. **1772–95:** Partitioned between Russia, which ruled the northeast; Prussia, the west, including Pomerania; and Austria in the south-centre, including Galicia, where there was greatest autonomy. **1815:** After Congress of Vienna, Russian eastern portion of Poland re-established as kingdom within Russian Empire. **1830 and 1863:** Uprisings against repressive Russian rule. **1892:** Nationalist Polish Socialist Party (PPS) founded. **1918:** Independent Polish republic established after World War I, with Marshal Józef Pilsudski, founder of the PPS, elected president. **1919–21:** Abortive advance into Lithuania and Ukraine. **1926:** Pilsudski seized full power in coup and established autocratic regime. **1935:** On Pilsudski's death, military regime held power under Marshal S migly-Rydz. **1939:** Invaded by Germany; western Poland incorporated into Nazi Reich (state) and the rest became a German colony; 6 million Poles – half of them Jews – were slaughtered in the next five years. **1944–45:** Liberated from Nazi rule by Soviet Union's Red Army; boundaries redrawn westwards at Potsdam Conference. One half of 'old Poland', 180,000 sq km/70,000 sq mi in the east, was lost to the USSR; 100,000 sq km/40,000 sq mi of ex-German territory in Silesia, along the Oder and Neisse rivers, was added, shifting the state 240 km/150 mi westwards; millions of Germans were expelled. **1947:** Communist people's republic proclaimed after manipulated election. **1949:** Joined Comecon. **early 1950s:** Harsh Stalinist rule under communist leader Boleslaw Bierut: nationalization; rural collectivization; persecution of Catholic Church members. **1955:** Joined Warsaw Pact defence organization. **1956:** Poznań strikes and riots. The moderate Wladyslaw Gomulka installed as Polish United Workers' Party (PUWP) leader. **1960s:** Private farming reintroduced and Catholicism tolerated. **1970:** Gomulka replaced by Edward Gierek after Gdań sk riots against food price rises. **1970s:** Poland heavily indebted to foreign creditors after failed attempt to boost economic growth. **1980:** Solidarity, led by Lech Walesa, emerged as free trade union following Gdań sk disturbances. **1981:** Martial law imposed by General Wojciech Jaruzelski, trade-union activity banned, and Solidarity leaders and supporters arrested. **1983:** Martial law ended. **1984:** Amnesty for 35,000 political prisoners. **1988:** Solidarity-led strikes and demonstrations for pay increases. Reform-communist Mieczyslaw Rakowski became prime minister. **1989:** Agreement to relegalize Solidarity, allow opposition parties, and adopt a more democratic constitution, after round-table talks involving Solidarity, the Communist Party, and the Catholic Church. Widespread success for Solidarity in first open elections for 40 years; noncommunist 'grand coalition' government formed, headed by Tadeusz Mazowiecki of Solidarity; economic austerity and free-market restructuring programme began. **1990:** PUWP dissolved and re-formed as Democratic Left Alliance (SLD). Walesa was elected president and Jan Bielecki became prime minister. **1991:** Shock-therapy economic restructuring programme, including large-scale privatization, produced sharp fall in living standards and rise in unemployment rate to 11%. Unpopular Bielecki resigned and, after inconclusive elections, Jan Olszewski formed fragile centre–right coalition government. **1992:** Political instability continued, with Waldemar Pawlak, of centre-left Polish Peasant Party (PSL), and Hanna Suchocka, of centrist Democratic Union, successively replacing Olszewski as prime minister. **1993:** Economy became first in Central Europe to grow since collapse of communism. After new elections, Pawlak formed coalition government with ex-communist SLD, which pledged to continue to build market-based economy and seek early entry into European Union (EU). **1994:** Joined NATO 'partnership for peace' programme; last Russian troops left Poland. **1995:** Ex-communist Józef Oleksy replaced Pawlak as prime minister. Walesa narrowly defeated by Aleksander Kwaśniewski, leader of the SLD, in presidential election. **1996:** Oleksy resigned as prime minister amid allegations of spying for Russia's secret service; replaced by Wlodzimierz Cimoszewicz. **1997:** Speeding-up of structural reform and privatization. New constitution approved. Poland invited to join NATO and begin negotiations to join EU. General election won by Solidarity Electoral Action (AWS). Coalition government formed, led by Jerzy Buzek. **1998:** Full EU membership negotiations

commenced. Government weakened by defections to the opposition. Number of provinces reduced from 49 to 16. **1999:** Poland became full member of NATO.

Portugal Republic of

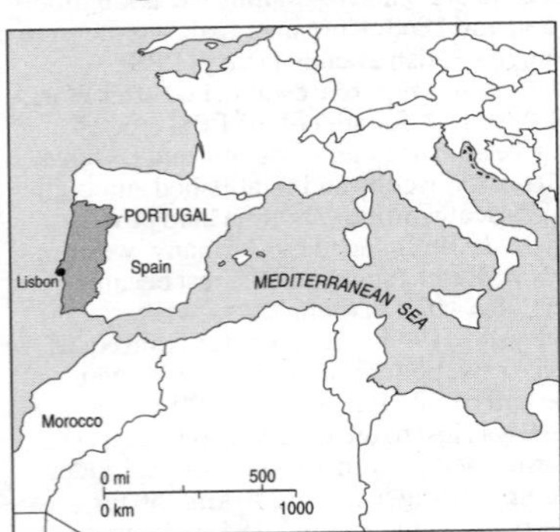

National name: *República Portuguesa* **Area:** 92,000 sq km/35,521 sq mi (including the Azores and Madeira) **Capital:** Lisbon **Major towns/cities:** Porto, Coimbra, Amadora, Setúbal, Guarde, Portalegre **Major ports:** Porto, Setúbal

Government

Head of state: Jorge Sampaio from 1996 **Head of government:** Antonio Guterres from 1995 **Political system:** democracy **Administrative divisions:** 18 districts and two autonomous regions **Political parties:** Social Democratic Party (PSD), moderate left of centre; Socialist Party (PS), centre left; People's Party (PP), right wing, anti-European integration **Armed forces:** 59,300 (1997) **Conscription:** 4–18 months **Death penalty:** abolished in 1976 **Defence spend:** (% GDP) 2.6 (1997) **Education spend:** (% GNP) 5.4 (1995) **Health spend:** (% GDP) 4.5 (1990–95)

Economy and resources

Currency: escudo **GDP:** (US$) 97.5 billion (1997) **Real GDP growth:** (% change on previous year) 3.4 (1997) **GNP (US$):** 103.9 billion (1997) **GNP per capita (PPP):** (US$) 13,840 (1997) **Consumer price inflation:** 2.4% (1998) **Unemployment:** 4.9% (1998) **Major trading partners:** EU (principally Spain, Germany, and France) **Resources:** limestone, granite, marble, iron, tungsten, copper, pyrites, gold, uranium, coal, forests **Exports:** textiles, clothing, footwear, pulp and waste paper, wood and cork manufactures, tinned fish, electrical equipment, wine, refined petroleum. Principal market: Germany 19.8% (1997) **Imports:** foodstuffs, machinery and transport equipment, crude petroleum, natural gas, textile yarn, coal, rubber, plastics, tobacco. Principal source: Spain 23.6% (1997) **Arable land:** 25.2% (1995)

Population and society

Population: 9,869,000 (1998 est) **Population growth rate:** –0.1% (1995–2000); 0% (2000–05) **Population density:** (per sq km) 108.3 (1998 est) **Urban population:** (% of total) 37 (1997) **Age distribution:** (% of total population) 0–14 17.3%, 15–64 67.6%, 65+ 15.1% (1998) **Ethnic groups:** most of the population is descended from Caucasoid peoples who inhabited the whole of the Iberian peninsula in classical and pre-classical times; there are a number of minorities from Portugal's overseas possessions and former possessions **Language:** Portuguese **Religion:** Roman Catholic 97% **Education:** (compulsory years) 9 **Literacy rate:** 89% (men); 81% (women) (1995 est) **Labour force:** 49.2% of population: 12.2% agriculture, 31.4% industry, 56.4% services (1996) **Life expectancy:** 72 (men); 79 (women) (1995–2000) **Child mortality rate:** (under 5, per 1,000 live births) 10 (1997) **Physicians:** 1 per 333 people (1996)

Practical information

Visa requirements: UK: visa not required for a stay of up to three months. USA: visa not required for a stay of up to two months **Embassy in the UK:** 11 Belgrave Square, London SW1X 8PP. Tel: (0171) 235 5331/4; fax: (0171) 245 1287 **British embassy:** Rua de São Bernardo 33, 1200 Lisbon. Tel: (1) 396 1191; fax: (1) 397 6768 **Chamber of commerce:** Confederação do Comércio Português, Rua dos Correeiros 79, 1 º Andar, 1100 Lisbon. Tel: (1) 301 0192; fax: (1) 301 0626

Chronology

2nd century BC: Romans conquered Iberian peninsula. **5th century AD:** Iberia overrun by Vandals and Visigoths after fall of Roman Empire. **711:** Visigoth kingdom overthrown by Muslims invading from North Africa. **997–1064:** Christians resettled northern area, which came under rule of Léon and Castile. **1139:** Afonso I, son of Henry of Burgundy, defeated Muslims; the area became an independent kingdom. **1340:** Final Muslim invasion defeated. **1373:** Anglo-Portuguese alliance signed. **15th century:** Age of exploration: Portuguese mariners surveyed coast of Africa, opened sea route to India (Vasco da Gama), and reached Brazil (Pedro Cabral). **16th century:** 'Golden Age': Portugal flourished as commercial and colonial power. **1580:** Philip II of Spain took throne of Portugal. **1640:** Spanish rule overthrown in bloodless coup; Duke of Braganza proclaimed as King John IV. **1668:** Spain recognized Portuguese independence. **1755:** Lisbon devastated by earthquake. **1755–77:** Politics dominated by chief minister Sebastiao de Carlvalho, Marquis of Pombal, who introduced secular education and promoted trade. **1807:** Napoleonic France invaded Portugal; Portuguese court fled to Brazil. **1807–11:** In the Peninsular War British forces played leading part in liberating Portugal from French. **1820:** Liberal revolution forced King John VI to return from Brazil and accept constitutional government. **1822:** Brazil declared independence; first Portuguese constitution adopted. **1826:** First constitution replaced by more conservative one. **1828:** Dom Miguel blocked succession of his niece, Queen Maria, and declared himself absolute monarch; civil war ensued between liberals and conservatives. **1834:** Queen Maria regained throne with British, French, and Brazilian help; constitutional government restored. **1840s:** Severe disputes between supporters of radical 1822 constitution and more conservative 1826 constitution. **1851:** 'Regeneration' to promote order and economic growth launched by Duke of Saldanha after coup. **late 19th century:** Government faced severe financial difficulties; rise of socialist, anarchist, and republican parties. **1908:** Assassination of King Carlos I. **1910:** Portugal became republic after three-day insurrection forced King Manuel II to flee. **1911:** New regime adopted liberal constitution, but republic proved unstable, violent, and corrupt. **1916–18:** Portugal fought in World War I on Allied side. **1926–51:** Popular military coup installed Gen António de Fragoso Carmona as president. **1928:** António de Oliveira Salazar became finance minister and introduced successful reforms. **1932:** Salazar became prime minister with dictatorial powers. **1933:** Authoritarian 'Estado Novo' ('New State') constitution adopted; living conditions improved, but Salazar resisted political change at home and in colonies. **1949:** Portugal became founding member of North Atlantic Treaty Organization (NATO). **1968:** Salazar retired; succeeded by Marcello Caetano. **1974:** Army seized power to end stalemate situation in African colonial wars; Gen Antó Ribeiro de Spínola became president; succeeded by Gen Francisco da Costa Gomes. **1975:** Portuguese colonies achieved independence; Gomes narrowly averted communist coup. **1976:** First free elections in 50 years resulted in minority government under socialist leader Mario Soares; Gen António Ramahlo Eanes won presidency. **1980:** Francisco Balsemão (PSD) formed centre-party coalition. **1986:** Soares became first civilian president in 60 years; Portugal joined European Community (EC). **1989:** Social Democrat government started to dismantle socialist economy and privatize major industries. **1996:** Jorge Sampaio (PS) elected president.

Qatar State of

National name: *Dawlat Qatar* **Area:** 11,400 sq km/4,401 sq mi **Capital:** Doha (and chief port) **Major towns/cities:** Dukhan, centre of oil production; Halul, terminal for offshore oilfields; Umm Said, Ruwais, Wakra, Al-Khour

Government

Head of state and government: Sheik Hamad bin Khalifa al-Thani from 1995 **Political system:** absolute monarchy **Administrative**

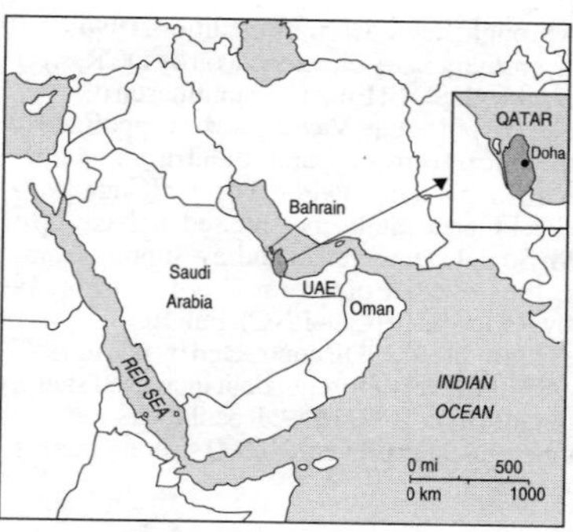

divisions: nine municipalities **Political parties:** none **Armed forces:** 11,800 (1997) **Conscription:** military service is voluntary **Death penalty:** retained and used for ordinary crimes **Defence spend:** (% GDP) 13.7 (1997) **Education spend:** (% GNP) 3.4 (1995) **Health spend:** (% GDP) 3.4 (1995)

Economy and resources

Currency: Qatari riyal **GDP:** (US$) 9 billion (1996) **Real GDP growth:** (% change on previous year) 5.0 (1996 est) **GNP (US$):** 7.4 billion (1997) **GNP per capita (PPP):** (US$) 20,100 (1997 est) **Consumer price inflation:** 2.6% (1998) **Unemployment:** dependent on immigrant workers – shortage of indigenous labour **Foreign debt:** (US$) 6.35 billion (1996) **Major trading partners:** Japan, Italy, USA, UK, Germany, France, Saudi Arabia, Spain **Resources:** petroleum, natural gas, water resources **Exports:** petroleum. Principal market: Japan 49.7% (1997) **Imports:** machinery and transport equipment, basic manufactures, food and live animals, miscellaneous manufactured articles, chemicals. Principal source: UK 25.2% (1997) **Arable land:** 0.7% (1995)

Population and society

Population: 579,000 (1998 est) **Population growth rate:** 1.2% (1995–2025) **Population density:** (per sq km) 63.4 (1998 est) **Urban population:** (% of total) 92 (1997) **Age distribution:** (% of total population) 0–14 27.4%, 15–64 70.6%, 65+ 2.0% (1998) **Ethnic composition:** only about 25% of the population are indigenous Qataris; 40% are Arabs, and the others Pakistanis, Indians, and Iranians **Language:** Arabic (official); English **Religion:** Sunni Muslim **Education:** not compulsory **Literacy rate:** 78% (men); 78% (women) (1995 est) **Labour force:** 57% of population: 3% agriculture, 32% industry, 65% services (1990) **Life expectancy:** 70 (men); 75 (women) (1995–2000) **Child mortality rate:** (under 5, per 1,000 live births) 23 (1997) **Physicians:** 1 per 681 people (1993)

Practical information

Visa requirements: UK: visa not required for a stay of up to 30 days. USA: visa required **Embassy in the UK:** 1 South Audley Street, London W1Y 5DQ. Tel: (0171) 493 2200; fax: (0171) 493 3894 **British embassy:** PO Box 3, Doha. Tel: (974) 421 991; fax: (974) 438 692 **Chamber of commerce:** PO Box 402, Doha. Tel: (974) 425 131; fax: (974) 425 186

Chronology

7th century AD: Islam introduced. **8th century:** Developed into important trading centre during time of Abbasid Empire. **1783:** The al-Khalifa family, who had migrated to northeast Qatar from west and north of the Arabian Peninsula, foiled Persian invasion and moved their headquarters to Bahrain Island, while continuing to rule the area of Qatar. **1867–68:** After the Bahrain-based al-Khalifa had suppressed a revolt by their Qatari subjects, destroying the town of Doha, Britain intervened and installed Muhammad ibn Thani al-Thani, from the leading family of Qatar, as the ruling sheik (or emir). A British Resident was given power to arbitrate disputes with Qatar's neighbours. **1871–1914:** Nominally part of Turkish Ottoman Empire, although in 1893 sheik's forces inflicted a defeat on Ottomans. **1916:** Qatar became British protectorate after treaty signed with Sheik Adbullah al-Thani. **1949:** Oil production began at onshore Dukhan field in west. **1960:** Sheik Ahmad al-Thani became new emir. **1968:** Britain's announcement that it would remove its forces from the Persian Gulf by 1971 led Qatar to make an abortive attempt to arrange a federation of Gulf states. **1970:** Constitution adopted, confirming emirate as absolute monarchy. **1971:** Independence achieved from Britain. **1972:** Emir Sheik Ahmad replaced in bloodless coup by his cousin, the Crown Prince and prime minister Sheik Khalifa ibn Hamad al-Thani. **1991:** Forces joined United Nations coalition in Gulf War against Iraq. **1995:** Sheik Khalifa ousted by his son, Crown Prince Sheik Hamad bin Khalifa al-Thani. **1996:** Announcement of plans to introduce democracy were followed by an assassination attempt on Sheik Hamad.

Romania

National name: *România* **Area:** 237,500 sq km/91,698 sq mi **Capital:** Bucharest **Major towns/cities:** Brasov, Timisoara, Cluj-Napoca, IasI, Constanta, Galati, Craiova, Ploiesti **Major ports:** Galati, Constanta, Brăila

Government

Head of state: Emil Constantinescu from 1996 **Head of government:** Radu Vasile from 1998 **Political system:** emergent democracy **Administrative divisions:** 41 counties **Political parties:** Democratic Convention of Romania (DCR), centre-right coalition; Social Democratic Union (SDU), reformist; Social Democracy Party of Romania (PSDR), social democrat; Romanian National Unity Party (RNUP), Romanian nationalist, right wing, anti-Hungarian; Greater Romania Party (Romania Mare), far right, ultranationalist, anti-Semitic; Democratic Party–National Salvation Front (DP–NSF), promarket; National Salvation Front (NSF), centre left; Hungarian Democratic Union of Romania (HDUR), ethnic Hungarian; Christian Democratic–National Peasants' Party (CD–PNC), centre right, promarket; Socialist Labour Party (SLP), ex-communist **Armed forces:** 227,000 (1997) **Conscription:** military service is compulsory for 12–18 months **Death penalty:** abolished in 1989 **Defence spend:** (% GDP) 2.3 (1997) **Education spend:** (% GNP) 3.6 (1995) **Health spend:** (% GDP) 3.6 (1990–95)

Economy and resources

Currency: leu **GDP:** (US$) 35.2 billion (1997) **Real GDP growth:** (% change on previous year) –2.0 (1997) **GNP (US$):** 32.1 billion (1997) **GNP per capita (PPP):** (US$) 4,290 (1997) **Consumer price inflation:** 46% (1998) **Unemployment:** 6.3% (1996) **Foreign debt:** (US$) 8.3 billion (1996) **Major trading partners:** Germany, Russia, Italy, USA, France, Iran, China, Turkey **Resources:** brown coal, hard coal, iron ore, salt, bauxite, copper, lead, zinc, methane gas, petroleum (reserves expected to be exhausted by mid to late 1990s) **Exports:** base metals and metallic articles, textiles and clothing, machinery and equipment, mineral products, foodstuffs. Principal market: Italy 19.5% (1997) **Imports:** mineral products, machinery and mechanical appliances, textiles, motor cars. Principal source: Germany 16.4% (1997) **Arable land:** 40.5% (1995)

Population and society

Population: 22,474,000 (1998 est) **Population growth rate:** –0.2% (1995–2000); –0.2% (2000–05) **Population density:** (per sq km) 97.2 (1998 est) **Urban population:** (% of total) 57 (1997) **Age distribution:** (% of total population) 0–14 19.0%, 15–64 68.0%, 65+ 13.0% (1998) **Ethnic groups:** 89% non-Slavic ethnic Romanian; substantial Hungarian, German, and Serbian minorities **Language:**

Romanian (official), Hungarian, German **Religion:** mainly Romanian Orthodox **Education:** (compulsory years) 8 **Literacy rate:** 97% (men); 97% (women) (1995 est) **Labour force:** 35.9% agriculture, 35.8% industry, 28.3% services (1993) **Life expectancy:** 66 (men); 73 (women) (1995–2000) **Child mortality rate:** (under 5, per 1,000 live births) 32 (1997) **Physicians:** 1 per 561 people (1995)

Practical information

Visa requirements: UK: visa required. USA: visa not required for a stay of up to 30 days **Embassy in the UK:** Arundel House, 4 Palace Green, London W8 4QD. Tel: (0171) 937 9666/8; fax: (0171) 937 8069 **British embassy:** Strada Jules Michelet 24, 70154 Bucharest. Tel: (1) 312 0305; fax: (1) 312 0229 **Chamber of commerce:** Chamber of Commerce and Industry of Romania, Boulevard Nicolae Balcescu 22, 79502 Bucharest. Tel: (1) 615 4703; fax: (1) 312 2091

Chronology

106: Formed heartland of ancient region of Dacia, which was conquered by Roman Emperor Trajan and became a province of Roman Empire; Christianity introduced. **275:** Taken from Rome by invading Goths, a Germanic people. **4th–10th centuries:** Invaded by successive waves of Huns, Avars, Bulgars, Magyars, and Mongols. *c.* **1000:** Transylvania, in north, became an autonomous province under Hungarian crown. **mid-14th century:** Two Romanian principalities emerged, Wallachia in south, around Bucharest, and Moldova in northeast. **15th–16th centuries:** The formerly autonomous principalities of Wallachia, Moldova, and Transylvania became tributaries to Ottoman Turks, despite peasant uprisings and resistance from Vlad Tepes ('the Impaler'), ruling prince of Wallachia. **late 17th century:** Transylvania conquered by Austrian Habsburgs. **1829:** Wallachia and Moldova brought under tsarist Russian suzerainty. **1859:** Under Prince Alexandru Ion Cuza, Moldova and Wallachia united to form Romanian state. **1878:** Romania's independence recognized by Great Powers in Congress of Berlin. **1881:** Became kingdom under Carol I. **1916–18:** Fought on Triple Entente side (Britain, France, and Russia) during World War I; acquired Transylvania and Bukovina, in north, from dismembered Austro-Hungarian Empire, and Bessarabia, in east, from Russia. This made it largest state in Balkans. **1930:** To counter growing popularity of fascist and antisemitic 'Iron Guard' mass movement, King Carol II abolished democratic institutions and established dictatorship. **1940:** Forced to surrender Bessarabia and northern Bukovina, adjoining Black Sea, to Soviet Union, and northern Transylvania to Hungary; King Carol II abdicated, handing over effective power to Gen Ion Antonescu, who signed Axis Pact with Germany. **1941–44:** Fought on Germany's side against Soviet Union; thousands of Jews massacred. **1944:** Antonescu ousted; Romania joined war against Germany. **1945:** Occupied by Soviet Union; communist-dominated government installed. **1947:** Paris Peace Treaty reclaimed Transylvania for Romania, but lost southern Dobruja to Bulgaria and northern Bukovina and Bessarabia to Soviet Union; King Michael, son of Carol II, abdicated and People's Republic proclaimed. **1948–49:** New Soviet-style constitution; joined Comecon; nationalization and agricultural collectivization. **1955:** Romania joined Warsaw Pact. **1958:** Soviet occupation forces removed. **1965:** Nicolae Ceausescu replaced Gheorghe Gheorghiu-Dej as Romanian Communist Party leader, and pursued foreign policy autonomous of Moscow, refusing to participate in Warsaw Pact manoeuvres. **1975:** Ceausescu made president. **1985–86:** Winters of austerity and power cuts as Ceausescu refused to liberalize the economy. **1987:** Workers' demonstrations against austerity programme brutally crushed at Brasov. **1988–89:** Relations with Hungary deteriorated over 'systematization programme', designed to forcibly resettle ethnic Hungarians in Transylvania. **1989:** Bloody overthrow of Ceausescu regime in 'Christmas Revolution'; Ceausescu and wife tried and executed; estimated 10,000 dead in civil war. Power assumed by NSF, headed by Ion Iliescu. **1990:** Securitate secret police replaced by new Romanian Intelligence Service; Eastern Orthodox Church and private farming re-legalized; systematization programme abandoned. **1991:** Privatization law passed. Prime minister Petre Roman resigned following riots by striking miners; succeeded by Theodor Stolojan heading a new cross-party coalition government. **1992:** NSF split; Iliescu re-elected president; Nicolai Vacaroiu appointed prime minister of minority coalition government. **1994:** Military cooperation pact with Bulgaria. Far-right parties brought into governing coalition. **1996:** Signs of economic growth; parliamentary elections won by DCR, who formed coalition government with SDU; Emil Constantinescu of Democratic Convention elected president; Victor Ciorbea appointed prime minister. **1997:** Economic reform programme and drive against corruption announced. Sharp increase in inflation. Former King Michael returned from exile. Finance minister dismissed in shake-up of economic ministries. **1998:** Social Democrats withdrew support from ruling coalition, criticizing the slow pace of reform. Ciorbea resigned as prime minister, replaced by Radu Vasile (CD–PNC). Full EU membership negotiations commenced. GDP contracted by 6% in 1998, following a 6.6% fall in 1997; the level of foreign debt increased sharply and unemployment rose to more than 10%. **1999:** Roadblocks were imposed by tanks north of Bucharest to prevent 10,000 striking miners entering Bucharest in January.

Russian Federation (formerly to 1991 **Russian Soviet Federal Socialist Republic (RSFSR)**)

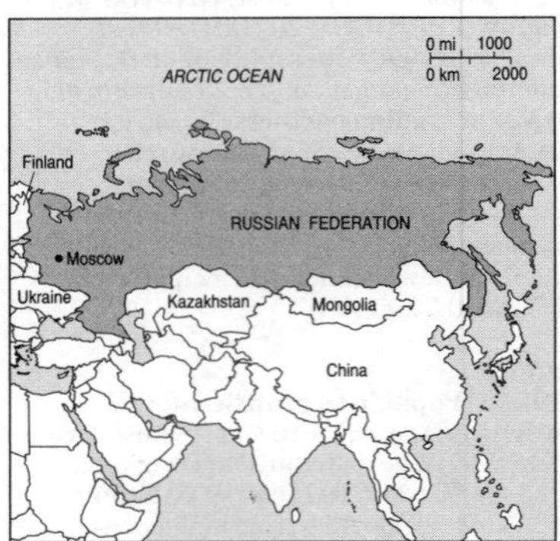

National name: *Rossiskaya Federatsiya* **Area:** 17,075,400 sq km/6,592,811 sq mi **Capital:** Moscow **Major towns/cities:** St Petersburg (Leningrad), Nizhniy Novgorod (Gorky), Rostov-na-Donu, Samara (Kuibyshev), Tver (Kalinin), Volgograd, Vyatka (Kirov), Yekaterinburg (Sverdlovsk), Novosibirsk, Chelyabinsk, Kazan, Omsk, Perm, Ufa

Government

Head of state: Boris Yeltsin from 1991 **Head of government:** Sergei Stepashin from 1999 **Political system:** emergent democracy **Administrative divisions:** 21 republics, 6 territories, 49 provinces, 10 autonomous areas, two cities with federal status, and one autonomous region **Political parties:** Russia is Our Home, centrist; Party of Unity and Accord (PRUA), moderate reformist; Communist Party of the Russian Federation (CPRF), left wing, conservative (ex-communist); Agrarian Party, rural-based, centrist; Liberal Democratic Party, far right, ultranationalist; Congress of Russian Communities, populist, nationalist; Russia's Choice, reformist, centre right; Yabloko, gradualist free market; Russian Social Democratic People's Party (Derzhava), communist-nationalist; Patriotic Popular Union of Russia (PPUR), communist-led; Russian People's Republican Party (RPRP) **Armed forces:** 1,240,000; paramilitary forces of 583,000 (1997) **Conscription:** two years **Death penalty:** retained and used for ordinary crimes **Defence spend:** (% GDP) 5.8 (1997) **Education spend:** (% GNP) 4.1 (1995) **Health spend:** (% GDP) 4.1 (1990–95)

Economy and resources

Currency: rouble **GDP:** (US$) 449.8 billion (1997) **Real GDP growth:** (% change on previous year) 0.2 (1997) **GNP (US$):** 403.5 billion (1997) **GNP per capita (PPP):** (US$) 4,190 (1997) **Consumer price inflation:** 12.0% (1998) **Unemployment:** 9.3% (1996) **Foreign debt:** (US$) 124.8 billion (1996) **Major trading partners:** CIS republics, Germany, UK, China, USA, Japan, Italy **Resources:** petroleum, natural gas, coal, peat, copper (world's fourth-largest producer), iron ore, lead, aluminium, phosphate rock, nickel, manganese, gold, diamonds, platinum, zinc, tin **Exports:** mineral fuels, ferrous and non-ferrous metals and derivatives, precious stones, chemical products, machinery and transport equipment, weapons,

Russia: Republics

Republic	Capital	Area		Population
		sq km	sq mi	(1995)
Adygeya	Maikop	7,600	2,934	451,000
Alania (or North Ossetia)	Vladikavkaz	8,000	3,089	659,000
Altai	Gorno-Altaisk	92,600	35,753	200,000
Bashkortostan	Ufa	143,600	55,444	4,080,000
Buryatia	Ulan-Ude	351,300	135,637	1,053,000
Chechnya	Grozny	16,064	6,202	904,000
Chuvashia	Cheboksary	18,300	7,066	1,361,000
Dagestan	Makhachkala	50,300	19,421	2,067,000
Ingushetia	Nazran	3,236	1,249	280,000[1]
Kabardino-Balkaria	Nalchik	12,500	4,826	790,000
Kalmykia	Elista	76,100	29,382	320,000
Karachai-Cherkessia	Cherkessk	14,100	5,444	436,000
Karelia	Petrozavodsk	172,400	66,564	789,000
Khakassia	Abakan	61,900	23,900	584,000
Komi	Syktyvkar	415,900	160,579	1,202,000
Mari El	Yoshkar-Ola	23,200	8,958	766,000
Mordovia	Saransk	26,200	10,116	959,000
Sakha	Yakutsk	3,103,200	1,198,146	1,036,000
Tatarstan	Kazan	68,000	26,255	3,755,000
Tuva	Kyzyl	170,500	65,830	308,000
Udmurtia	Izhevsk	42,100	16,255	1,641,000

[1] 1996 estimate.

timber and paper products. Principal market: Ukraine 8.3% (1997) **Imports:** machinery and transport equipment, grain and foodstuffs, chemical products, textiles, clothing, footwear, pharmaceuticals, metals. Principal source: Germany 9.7% (1997) **Arable land:** 7.8% (1995)

Population and society

Population: 147,434,000 (1998 est) **Population growth rate:** –0.3% (1995–2000); –0.2% (2000–05) **Population density:** (per sq km) 8.6 (1998 est) **Urban population:** (% of total) 77 (1997) **Age distribution:** (% of total population) 0–14 19.7%, 15–64 67.8%, 65+ 12.5% (1998) **Ethnic groups:** predominantly ethnic Russian (eastern Slav); significant Tatar, Ukranian, Chuvash, Belarussian, Bashkir, and Chechen minorities **Language:** Russian **Religion:** traditionally Russian Orthodox **Education:** (compulsory years) 9 **Literacy rate:** 99% (men); 99% (women) (1995 est) **Labour force:** 52% of population: 14% agriculture, 42% industry, 45% services (1990) **Life expectancy:** 58 (men); 72 (women) (1995–2000) **Child mortality rate:** (under 5, per 1,000 live births) 36 (1997) **Physicians:** 1 per 222 people (1994)

Practical information

Visa requirements: UK: visa required. USA: visa required **Embassy in the UK:** 13 Kensington Palace Gardens, London W8 4QX. Tel: (0171) 229 3628; fax: (0171) 727 8625 **British embassy:** Sofiyskaya Naberezhnaya 14, Moscow 72. Tel: (095) 956 7200; fax: (095) 956 7420 **Chamber of commerce:** Chamber of Commerce and Industry of the Russian Federation, Ulitsa Ilynka 6, 103684 Moscow. Tel: (095) 925 3581

Chronology

9th–10th centuries: Viking chieftains established own rule in Novgorod, Kiev, and other cities. **10th–12th centuries:** Kiev temporarily united Russian peoples into its empire. Christianity introduced from Constantinople 988. **13th century:** Mongols (Golden Horde) overran the southern steppes in 1223, compelling Russian princes to pay tribute. **14th century:** Byelorussia and Ukraine came under Polish rule. **1462–1505:** Ivan the Great, grand duke of Muscovy, threw off Mongol yoke and united lands in northwest. **1547–84:** Ivan the Terrible assumed title of tsar and conquered Kazan and Astrakhan; colonization of Siberia began. **1613:** First Romanov tsar, Michael, elected after period of chaos. **1667:** Following Cossack revolt, eastern Ukraine reunited with Russia. **1682–1725:** Peter the Great modernized the bureaucracy and army; he founded a navy and a new capital, St Petersburg, introduced Western education, and wrested the Baltic seaboard from Sweden. By 1700 colonization of Siberia had reached the Pacific. **1762–96:** Catherine the Great annexed the Crimea and part of Poland and recovered western Ukraine and Byelorussia. **1798–1814:** Russia intervened in Revolutionary and Napoleonic Wars (1798–1801, 1805–07); repelled Napoleon, and took part in his overthrow (1812–14). **1827–29:** Russian attempts to dominate Balkans led to war with Turkey. **1853–56:** Crimean War. **1856–64:** Caucasian War of conquest completed annexation of northern Caucasus, causing more than a million people to emigrate. **1858–60:** Treaties of Aigun 1858 and Peking 1860 imposed on China, annexing territories north of the Amur and east of the Ussuri rivers; Vladivostok founded on Pacific coast. **1861:** Serfdom abolished (on terms unfavourable to peasants). Rapid growth of industry followed, a working-class movement developed, and revolutionary ideas spread, culminating in assassination of Alexander II in 1881. **1877–78:** Russo-Turkish War **1898:** Social Democratic Party founded by Russian Marxists; split into Bolshevik and Menshevik factions in 1903. **1904–05:** Russo-Japanese War caused by Russian expansion in Manchuria. **1905:** A revolution, though suppressed, forced tsar to accept parliament (Duma) with limited powers. **1914:** Russo-Austrian rivalry in Balkans was a major cause of outbreak of World War I; Russia fought in alliance with France and Britain. **1917:** Russian Revolution: tsar abdicated, provisional government established; Bolsheviks seized power under Vladimir Lenin. **1918:** Treaty of Brest-Litovsk ended war with Germany; murder of former tsar; Russian Empire collapsed; Finland, Poland, and Baltic States seceded. **1918–22:** Civil War between Red Army, led by Leon Trotsky, and White Russian forces with foreign support; Red Army ultimately victorious; control regained over Ukraine, Caucasus, and Central Asia. **1922:** Former Russian Empire renamed Union of Soviet Socialist Republics. **1924:** Death of Lenin. **1928:** Joseph Stalin emerged as absolute ruler after ousting Trotsky. **1928–33:** First Five-Year Plan collectivized agriculture by force; millions died in famine. **1936–38:** The Great Terror: Stalin executed his critics and imprisoned millions of people on false charges of treason and sabotage. **1939:** Nazi-Soviet nonaggression pact; USSR invaded eastern Poland and attacked Finland. **1940:** USSR annexed Baltic States. **1941–45:** 'Great Patriotic War' against Germany ended with Soviet domination of eastern Europe and led to 'Cold War' with USA and its allies. **1949:** Council for Mutual Economic Assistance (Comecon) created to supervise trade in Soviet bloc. **1953:** Stalin died; 'collective leadership' in power. **1955:** Warsaw Pact created. **1956:** Nikita Khrushchev made 'secret speech' criticizing Stalin; USSR invaded Hungary. **1957–58:** Khrushchev ousted his rivals and became effective leader, introducing limited reforms. **1960:** Rift between USSR and Communist China. **1962:** Cuban missile crisis: Soviet nuclear missiles installed in Cuba but removed after ultimatum from USA. **1964:** Khrushchev ousted by new 'collective leadership' headed by Leonid Brezhnev and Alexei Kosygin. **1968:** USSR and allies invaded Czechoslovakia. **1970s:** 'Détente' with USA and western Europe. **1979:** USSR invaded Afghanistan; fighting continued until Soviet withdrawal ten years later. **1982:** Brezhnev died; Uri Andropov became leader. **1984:** Andropov died; Konstantin Chernenko became leader. **1985:** Chernenko died; Mikhail Gorbachev became leader and announced wide-ranging reform programme (*perestroika*). **1986:** Chernobyl nuclear disaster. **1988:** Special All-Union Party Congress approved radical constitutional changes and market reforms; start of open nationalist unrest in Caucasus and Baltic republics. **1989:** Multi-candidate elections held in move towards 'socialist democracy'; collapse of Soviet satellite regimes in eastern Europe; end of Cold War. **1990:** Anticommunists and nationalists polled strongly in multiparty local elections; Baltic and Caucasian republics defied central government; Boris Yeltsin became president of Russian Federation and left Communist Party. **1991:** Unsuccessful coup by hardline communists; republics declared independence; dissolution of communist rule in Russian Federation;

USSR replaced by loose Commonwealth of Independent States (CIS). **1992:** Russia assumed former USSR seat on United Nations (UN) Security Council; new constitution devised; end of price controls. **1993:** Power struggle between Yeltsin and Congress of People's Deputies; congress dissolved; attempted coup foiled; new parliament elected. **1994:** Russia joined North Atlantic Treaty Organization (NATO) 'Partnership for Peace'; Russian forces invaded breakaway republic of Chechnya. **1995:** Bloody civil war in Chechnya continued. **1996:** Re-election of President Yeltsin. Peace plan and final withdrawal of Russian troops from Chechnya. **1997:** Peace treaty with Chechnya signed. Yeltsin signed agreement on cooperation with NATO. Russia gained effective admission to G-7 group. **1998:** President Yeltsin sacked government and appointed Sergei Kiriyenko as prime minister. The rouble was heavily devalued. Kiriyenko sacked as prime minister; former communist spy chief, Yevgeny Primakov, became new prime minister, heading a government including prominent figures associated with Soviet state planning, as market-centred reform abandoned. President Yeltsin's health deteriorated. Primakov's cautious economic restructuring programme was approved by the Duma. Yury Luzhkov, the popular mayor of Moscow, formed a new centrist movement, Otechestvo (Fatherland). The USA pledged aid of over 3 million tonnes of grain and meat, after a 5% contraction in GDP in 1998. **1999:** Primakov's government dismissed by President Yeltsin; Sergei Stepashin appointed prime minister.

Rwanda Republic of

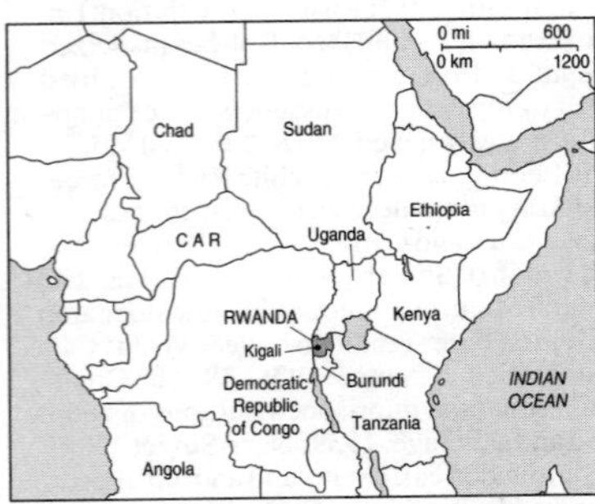

National name: *Republika y'u Rwanda* **Area:** 26,338 sq km/10,169 sq mi **Capital:** Kigali **Major towns/cities:** Butare, Ruhengeri, Gisenyi

Government

Head of state: Pasteur Bizimungu from 1994 **Head of government:** Pierre Celestin Rwigema from 1995 **Political system:** transitional **Administrative divisions:** 10 prefectures **Political parties:** National Revolutionary Development Movement (MRND), nationalist-socialist, Hutu-oriented; Social Democratic Party (PSD), left of centre; Christian Democratic Party (PDC), Christian, centrist; Republican Democratic Movement (MDR), Hutu nationalist; Liberal Party (PL), moderate centrist; Rwanda Patriotic Front (FPR), Tutsi-led but claims to be multiethnic **Armed forces:** 55,000 (1997) **Conscription:** military service is voluntary **Death penalty:** retains the death penalty for ordinary crimes but can be considered abolitionist in practice (last execution 1982) **Defence spend:** (% GDP) 5.5 (1997) **Education spend:** (% GNP) 3.8 (1992); N/A (1993/94) **Health spend:** (% GDP) 1.9 (1990–95)

Economy and resources

Currency: Rwanda franc **GDP:** (US$) 1.7 billion (1997) **Real GDP growth:** (% change on previous year) 13.3 (1996) **GNP (US$):** 1.7 billion (1997) **GNP per capita (PPP):** (US$) 630 (1997) **Consumer price inflation:** 25% (1996) **Foreign debt:** (US$) 1.03 billion (1996) **Major trading partners:** Brazil, Kenya, Belgium, Germany, the Netherlands, South Africa, France, UK **Resources:** cassiterite (a tin-bearing ore), wolframite (a tungsten-bearing ore), natural gas, gold, columbo-tantalite, beryl **Exports:** coffee, tea, tin ores and concentrates, pyrethrum, quinquina. Principal market: Brazil 48.8% (1996) **Imports:** food, clothing, mineral fuels and lubricants, construction materials, transport equipment, machinery, tools, consumer goods. Principal source: Italy 15.1% (1997) **Arable land:** 34.5% (1995)

Population and society

Population: 6,604,000 (1998 est) **Population growth rate:** 7.9% (1995–2000) **Population density:** (per sq km) 318.9 (1998 est) **Urban population:** (% of total) 6 (1997) **Age distribution:** (% of total population) 0–14 44.7%, 15–64 52.5%, 65+ 2.8% (1998) **Ethnic groups:** about 84% belong to the Hutu tribe, most of the remainder being Tutsis; there are also Twa and Pygmy minorities **Language:** Kinyarwanda, French (official); Kiswahili **Religion:** Roman Catholic 54%, animist 23%, Protestant 12%, Muslim 9% **Education:** (compulsory years) 7 **Literacy rate:** 64% (men); 37% (women) (1995 est) **Labour force:** 52% of population: 92% agriculture, 3% industry, 5% services (1990) **Life expectancy:** 41 (men); 43 (women) (1995–2000) **Child mortality rate:** (under 5, per 1,000 live births) 197 (1997) **Physicians:** 1 per 24,967 people (1993 est)

Practical information

Visa requirements: UK: visa required. USA: visa required **Embassy in the UK:** 42 Aylmer Road, London N2. Tel/fax: (0171) 347 6967 **British embassy:** the British Embassy in Kampala (see Uganda) deals with enquiries relating to Rwanda; British Consulate, BP 356, Avenue Paul VI, Kigali. Tel: 75219 or 75905; telex: 509 (a/b 09 RWANDEX RW) **Chamber of commerce:** Chambre de Commerce et de l'Industrie du Rwanda, BP 319, Kigali.

Chronology

10th century onwards: Hutu peoples settled in region formerly inhabited by hunter-gatherer Twa Pygmies, becoming peasant farmers. **14th century onwards:** Majority Hutu community came under dominance of cattle-owning Tutsi peoples, immigrants from the east, who became a semi-aristocracy and established control through land and cattle contracts. **15th century:** Ruganzu Bwimba, a Tutsi leader, founded kingdom near Kigali. **17th century:** Central Rwanda and outlying Hutu communities subdued by Tutsi mwami (king) Ruganzu Ndori. **late 19th century:** Under the great Tutsi king, Kigeri Rwabugiri, a unified state with a centralized military structure was established. **1890:** Known as Ruandi, the Tutsi kingdom, along with neighbouring Burundi, came under nominal German control, as Ruanda-Urundi. **1916:** Occupied by Belgium, during World War I. **1923:** Belgium granted League of Nations mandate to administer Ruanda-Urundi; they were to rule 'indirectly' through Tutsi chiefs. **1959:** Interethnic warfare between Hutu and Tutsi, forcing mwami (king) Kigeri V into exile. **1961:** Republic proclaimed after mwami deposed. **1962:** Independence from Belgium achieved as Rwanda, with Hutu Grégoire Kayibanda as president; many Tutsis left the country. **1963:** 20,000 killed in interethnic clashes, after Tutsis exiled in Burundi had launched a raid. **1973:** Kayibanda ousted in military coup led by Hutu Maj-Gen Juvenal Habyarimana; this was caused by resentment of Tutsis, who held some key government posts. **1981:** Elections created civilian legislation, but dominated by Hutu socialist National Revolutionary Development Movement (MRND), in a one-party state. **1988:** Hutu refugees from Burundi massacres streamed into Rwanda. **1990:** Government attacked by Rwanda Patriotic Front (FPR), a Tutsi refugee military-political organization based in Uganda, which controlled parts of northern Rwanda. **1992:** Peace accord with FPR. **1993:** United Nations mission sent to monitor peace agreement. **1994:** President Habyarimana and Burundian Hutu president Ntaryamira killed in air crash; involvement of FPR suspected. Half a million killed in ensuing civil war, with many Tutsi massacred by Hutu death squads and exodus of 2 million refugees to neighbouring countries. Government fled as FPR forces closed in. French peacekeeping troops established 'safe zone' in southwest. Interim coalition government installed, with moderate Hutu and FPR leader, Pasteur Bizimungu, as president. **1995:** War-crimes tribunal opened. Government human-rights abuses reported. **1996:** Rwanda and Zaire (Democratic Republic of Congo) on brink of war after Tutsi killings of Hutu in Zaire. Massive Hutu refugee crisis narrowly averted as thousands allowed to return to Rwanda. **1997:** Further Tutsi killings by Hutus. **1998:** 378 rebels killed by Rwandan army.

St Kitts and Nevis (or St Christopher and Nevis)
Federation of

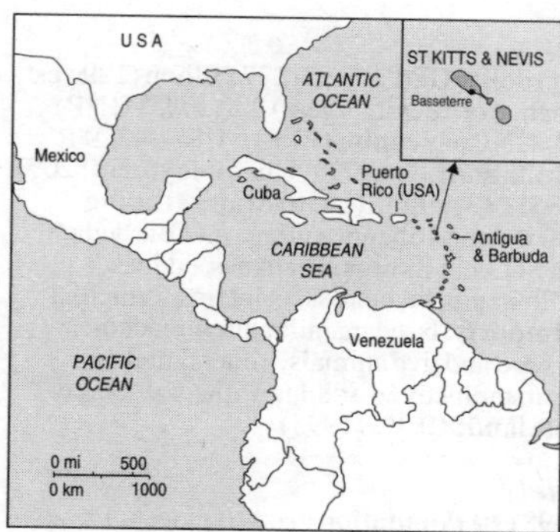

Area: 262 sq km/101 sq mi (St Kitts 168 sq km/65 sq mi, Nevis 93 sq km/36 sq mi) **Capital:** Basseterre (on St Kitts) (and chief port) **Major towns/cities:** Charlestown (largest on Nevis), Newcastle, Sandy Point Town, Dieppe Bay Town

Government
Head of state: Queen Elizabeth II from 1983, represented by governor general Clement Arrindell from 1983 **Head of government:** Denzil Douglas from 1995 **Political system:** federal constitutional monarchy **Administrative divisions:** 14 parishes **Political parties:** People's Action Movement (PAM), centre right; Nevis Reformation Party (NRP), Nevis-separatist, centrist; Labour Party (SKLP), moderate left of centre **Armed forces:** army disbanded in 1981 and absorbed by Volunteer Defence Force; participates in US-sponsored Regional Security System established in 1982 **Death penalty:** retained and used for ordinary crimes **Education spend:** (% GNP) 2.7 (1993) **Health spend:** (% GDP) 3.8 (1998)

Economy and resources
Currency: East Caribbean dollar **GDP:** (US$) 254 million (1997) **Real GDP growth:** (% change on previous year) 2.6 (1997) **GNP (US$):** 252 million (1997) **GNP per capita (PPP):** (US$) 7,730 (1997 est) **Consumer price inflation:** 3% (1996) **Unemployment:** 4.3% (1995 est) **Foreign debt:** (US$) 58 million (1996) **Major trading partners:** USA, UK, Trinidad and Tobago, St Vincent and the Grenadines, Canada, Barbados **Exports:** sugar, manufactures, postage stamps; sugar and sugar products accounted for approximately 40% of export earnings in 1992. Principal market: USA 46.6% (1996) **Imports:** foodstuffs, basic manufactures, machinery, mineral fuels. Principal source: USA 45% (1996) **Arable land:** 22.2% (1995)

Population and society
Population: 39,000 (1998 est) **Population growth rate:** 0.5 (1995–2025) **Population density:** (per sq km) 117.5 (1998 est) **Urban population:** (% of total) 34 (1997) **Age distribution:** (% of total population) 0–14 33.3%, 15–64 60.6%, 65+ 6.2% (1998) **Ethnic groups:** almost entirely of African descent **Language:** English (official) **Religion:** Anglican 36%, Methodist 32%, other Protestant 8%, Roman Catholic 10% **Education:** (compulsory years) 12 **Literacy rate:** 98% (men); 86% (women) (1993 est) **Labour force:** 29.6% agriculture, 24.3% industry, 48.8% services (1985) **Life expectancy:** 66 (men); 72 (women) (1995 est) **Child mortality rate:** (under 5, per 1,000 live births) 40 (1995) **Physicians:** 1 per 2,200 people (1991)

Practical information
Visa requirements: UK: visa not required. USA: visa not required **Embassy in the UK:** High Commission for Eastern Caribbean States, 10 Kensington Court, London W8 5DL. Tel: (0171) 937 9522; fax: (0171) 937 5514 **British embassy:** the British High Commission in St John's (see Antigua and Barbuda) deals with enquiries relating to St Kitts and Nevis **Chamber of commerce:** St Kitts and Nevis Chamber of Industry and Commerce, PO Box 332, South Square Street, Basseterre. Tel: (809) 465 2980; fax: (809) 465 4490

Chronology
1493: Visited by the explorer Christopher Columbus, after whom the main island is named, but for next two centuries the islands were left in the possession of the indigenous Caribs. **1623 and 1628:** St Kitts and Nevis islands successively settled by British as their first Caribbean colony, with 2,000 Caribs brutally massacred in 1626. **1783:** In the Treaty of Versailles France, which had long disputed British possession, rescinded its claims to the islands, on which sugar cane plantations developed, worked by imported African slaves. **1816:** Anguilla was joined politically to the two islands. **1834:** Abolition of slavery. **1871–1956:** Part of the Leeward Islands Federation. **1932:** Centre-left Labour Party founded to campaign for independence. **1937:** Internal self-government granted. **1952:** Universal adult suffrage granted. **1958–62:** Part of the Federation of the West Indies. **1967:** St Kitts, Nevis, and Anguilla achieved internal self-government, within the British Commonwealth, with Robert Bradshaw, Labour Party leader, as prime minister. **1970:** NRP formed, calling for separation for Nevis. **1971:** Anguilla returned to being a British dependency after rebelling against domination by St Kitts. **1978:** Bradshaw died; succeeded by Paul Southwell. **1979:** Southwell died; succeeded by Lee L Moore. **1980:** People's Action Movement (PAM) and NRP centrist coalition government, led by Kennedy Simmonds, formed after inconclusive general election. **1983:** Full independence achieved within the Commonwealth. **1993:** Simmonds continued in office despite criticism of his leadership. Antigovernment demonstrations followed inconclusive general election. **1994:** Three-week state of emergency imposed after violent antigovernment riots by Labour Party supporters in Basseterre. **1995:** Labour Party won general election; Denzil Douglas became prime minister. **1997:** Nevis withdrew from the federation. **1998:** Nevis referendum on secession failed to secure support.

St Lucia

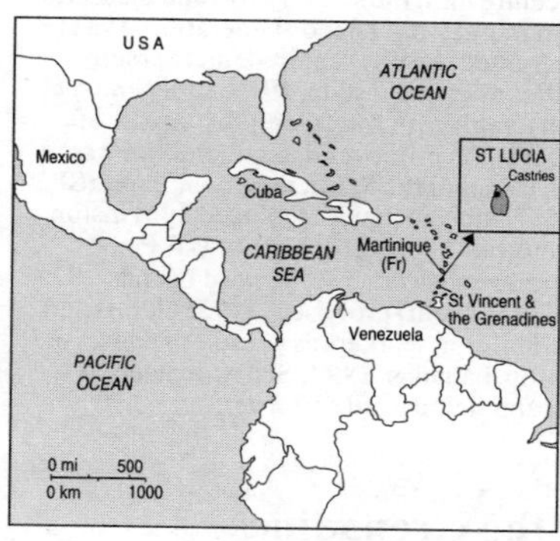

Area: 617 sq km/238 sq mi **Capital:** Castries **Major towns/cities:** Soufrière, Vieux-Fort, Laborie **Major ports:** Vieux-Fort

Government
Head of state: Queen Elizabeth II from 1979, represented by governor general Stanislaus A James from 1992 **Head of government:** Kenny Anthony from 1997 **Political system:** constitutional monarchy **Administrative divisions:** eight regions **Political parties:** United Workers' Party (UWP), moderate left of centre; St Lucia Labour Party (SLP), moderate left of centre; Progressive Labour Party (PLP), moderate left of centre **Armed forces:** none; participates in the US-sponsored Regional Security System established in 1982; police force numbers around 300 **Death penalty:** retained and used for ordinary crimes **Education spend:** (% GNP) 9.9 (1995)

Economy and resources
Currency: East Caribbean dollar **GDP:** (US$) 601 million (1996 est) **Real GDP growth:** (% change on previous year) 2.5 (1997) **GNP (US$):** 576 million (1997) **GNP per capita (PPP):** (US$) 5,030 (1997) **Consumer price inflation:** 3% (1996) **Unemployment:** 20% (1993 est) **Foreign debt:** (US$) 142 million (1996) **Major trading partners:** USA, UK, Trinidad and Tobago (and other CARICOM member states), Japan, Canada, Italy **Resources:** geothermal energy **Exports:** bananas, coconut oil, cocoa beans, copra, beverages, tobacco, miscellaneous articles. Principal market: UK 50% (1995) **Imports:** machinery and transport equipment, foodstuffs, basic manufactures, mineral fuels. Principal source: USA 36% (1995) **Arable land:** 8.2% (1995)

Population and society

Population: 150,000 (1998 est) **Population growth rate:** 1.1% (1995–2025) **Population density:** (per sq km) 249.3 (1998 est) **Urban population:** (% of total) 37 (1997) **Age distribution:** (% of total population) 0–14 34.1%, 15–64 60.5%, 65+ 5.4% (1998) **Ethnic groups:** great majority of African descent **Language:** English; French patois **Religion:** Roman Catholic 90% **Education:** (compulsory years) 10 **Literacy rate:** 82% (men); 79%(women) (1993 est) **Labour force:** 24% agriculture, 13.6% industry, 62.4% services (1991) **Life expectancy:** 68 (men); 75 (women) (1995 est) **Child mortality rate:** (under 5, per 1,000 live births) 22 (1995) **Physicians:** 1 per 2,125 people (1993)

Practical information

Visa requirements: UK: visa not required. USA: visa not required **Embassy in the UK:** High Commission for Eastern Caribbean States, 10 Kensington Court, London W8 5DL. Tel: (0171) 937 9522; fax: (0171) 937 5514 **British embassy:** British High Commission, PO Box 227, Derek Walcott Square, Castries. Tel: (809) 452 2484; fax: (809) 453 1543 **Chamber of commerce:** St Lucia Chamber of Commerce, Industry and Agriculture, PO Box 482, Micond Street, Castries. Tel: (809) 452 3165; fax: (809) 453 6907

Chronology

1502: Sighted by the explorer Christopher Columbus on St Lucia's day but not settled for more than a century due to hostility of the island's Carib Indian inhabitants. **1635:** Settled by French, who brought in slaves to work sugar cane plantations as Carib community was annihilated. **1814:** Ceded to Britain as a crown colony, following Treaty of Paris; black African slaves brought in to work sugar cane plantations. **1834:** Slavery abolished. **1860s:** A major coal warehousing centre until the switch to oil and diesel fuels in 1930s. **1871–1956:** Part of Leeward Islands Federation. **1951:** Universal adult suffrage granted. **1967:** Acquired internal self-government as a West Indies associated state. **1979:** Independence achieved within Commonwealth with John Compton, leader of United Workers' Party (UWP), as prime minister; Compton was replaced by Allan Louisy, leader of the St Lucia Labour Party (SLP), following elections. **1981:** Louisy resigned; replaced by Winston Cenac. **1982:** Compton returned to power at head of UWP government. **1991:** Integration with other Windward Islands (Dominica, Grenada, and St Vincent) proposed. **1993:** Unrest and strikes by farmers and agricultural workers as a result of depressed prices for the chief cash crop, bananas. **1997:** SLP won general election; Kenny Anthony appointed prime minister.

St Vincent and the Grenadines

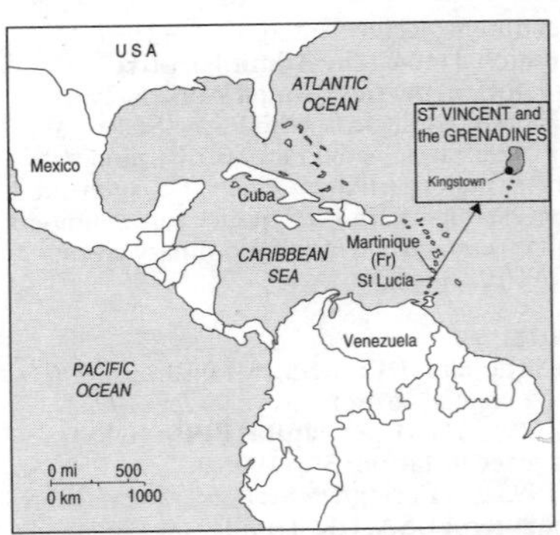

Area: 388 sq km/150 sq mi, including islets of the Northern Grenadines 43 sq km/17 sq mi **Capital:** Kingstown **Major towns/cities:** Georgetown, Châteaubelair, Layon, Baronallie

Government

Head of state: Queen Elizabeth II from 1979, represented by governor general David Jack from 1989 **Head of government:** James Mitchell from 1984 **Political system:** constitutional monarchy **Administrative divisions:** six parishes **Political parties:** New Democratic Party (NDP), right of centre; St Vincent Labour Party (SVLP), moderate left of centre **Armed forces:** none – police force only; participates in the US-sponsored Regional Security System established in 1982 **Death penalty:** retained and used for ordinary crimes **Education spend:** (% GNP) 6.7 (1993/94) **Health spend:** (% GDP) 4.4 (1990)

Economy and resources

Currency: East Caribbean dollar **GDP:** (US$) 277 million (1996 est) **Real GDP growth:** (% change on previous year) 3.8 (1995) **GNP (US$):** 281 million (1997) **GNP per capita (PPP):** (US$) 4,320 (1997) **Consumer price inflation:** 3% (1996) **Unemployment:** 20% (1991) **Foreign debt:** (US$) 213 million (1996) **Major trading partners:** USA, UK, Trinidad and Tobago, Antigua and Barbuda, Barbados, Canada, Japan, St Lucia **Exports:** bananas, eddoes, dasheen, sweet potatoes, flour, ginger, tannias, plantains. Principal market: UK 32% (1994) **Imports:** basic manufactures, machinery and transport equipment, food and live animals, mineral fuels, chemicals, miscellaneous manufactured articles. Principal source: USA 36.1% (1994) **Arable land:** 10.3% (1995)

Population and society

Population: 112,000 (1998 est) **Population growth rate:** 0.9% (1995–2000) **Population density:** (per sq km) 353.4 (1998 est) **Urban population:** (% of total) 51 (1997) **Age distribution:** (% of total population) 0–14 30.6%, 15–64 63.9%, 65+ 5.6% (1998) **Ethnic groups:** largely of African origin; most of the original indigenous Caribs have disappeared **Language:** English; French patois **Religion:** Anglican, Methodist, Roman Catholic **Education:** not compulsory **Literacy rate:** 92% (men); 86% (women) (1993 est) **Labour force:** 25.1% agriculture, 21.1% industry, 53.8% services (1991) **Life expectancy:** 70 (men); 75 (women) (1995 est) **Child mortality rate:** (under 5, per 1,000 live births) 23 (1995) **Physicians:** 1 per 4,037 people (1992)

Practical information

Visa requirements: UK: visa not required. USA: visa not required **Embassy in the UK:** High Commission for East Caribbean States, 10 Kensington Court, London W8 5DL. Tel: (0171) 937 9522; fax: (0171) 937 5514 **British embassy:** British High Commission, PO Box 132, Granby Street, Kingstown. Tel: (809) 457 1701/2; fax: (809) 456 2720 **Chamber of commerce:** St Vincent and the Grenadines Chamber of Industry and Commerce, PO Box 134, Halifax Street, Kingstown. Tel: (809) 457 1464; fax: (809) 456 2944

Chronology

1498: Main island visited by the explorer Christopher Columbus on St Vincent's day. **17th–18th centuries:** Possession disputed by France and Britain, with fierce resistance from the indigenous Carib community. **1783:** Recognized as British crown colony by Treaty of Versailles. **1795–97:** Carib uprising, with French support, resulted in deportation of 5,000 to Belize and Honduras. **1834:** Slavery abolished. **1902:** Over 2,000 killed by the eruption of La Soufrière volcano. **1951:** Universal adult suffrage granted. **1958–62:** Part of West Indies Federation. **1969:** Achieved internal self-government. **1979:** Achieved full independence within Commonwealth, with Milton Cato of centre-left St Vincent Labour Party (SVLP) as prime minister. **1981:** General strike against new industrial-relations legislation at a time of economic recession. **1984:** James Mitchell, of the centre-right New Democratic Party (NDP), replaced Cato as prime minister. **1989:** James Mitchell and the NDP re-elected. **1991:** Integration with other Windward Islands (Dominica, Grenada, and St Lucia) proposed. **1994:** The NDP re-elected. A new opposition left-of-centre party, the United Labour Party (ULP), was formed.

Samoa Independent State of

National name: *Malotutu'atasi o Samoa i Sisifo* **Area:** 2,830 sq km/1,092 sq mi **Capital:** Apia (on Upolu island) (and chief port) **Major towns/cities:** Lalomanu, Falevai, Tuasivi, Falealupo

Government

Head of state: King Malietoa Tanumafili II from 1962 **Head of government:** Tuila'epa Sa'ilele Malielegaoi from 1998 **Political**

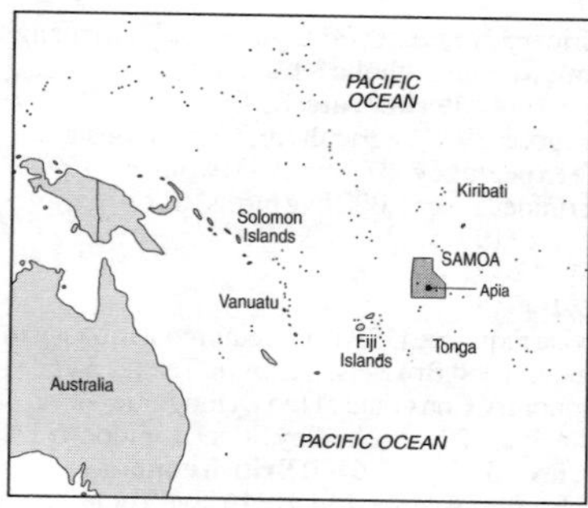

system: liberal democracy **Administrative divisions:** 11 districts **Political parties:** Human Rights Protection Party (HRPP), led by Tofilau Eti Alesana; Samoa Democratic Party (SDP), led by Le Tagaloa Pita; Samoa National Development Party (SNDP), led by Tupuola Taisi Efi and Va'ai Kolone. All 'parties' are personality-based groupings **Armed forces:** no standing defence forces; under Treaty of Friendship signed with New Zealand in 1962, the latter acts as sole agent in Samoa's dealings with other countries and international organizations **Death penalty:** retains the death penalty for ordinary crimes, but can be considered abolitionist in practice **Education spend:** (% GNP) 4.2 (1993/94) **Health spend:** (% GDP) 5.6 (1990)

Economy and resources

Currency: tala, or Samoa dollar **GDP:** (US$) 187 million (1997 est) **Real GDP growth:** (% change on previous year) 3.4 (1997) **GNP (US$):** 199 million (1997) **GNP per capita (PPP):** (US$) 1,570 (1997 est) **Consumer price inflation:** 10% (1997) **Foreign debt:** (US$) 167 million (1996) **Major trading partners:** New Zealand, Australia, Fiji Islands, American Samoa, Japan, USA **Exports:** coconut cream, beer, cigarettes, taro, copra, cocoa, bananas, timber. Principal market: Australia 81.5% (1996) **Imports:** food and live animals, machinery and transport equipment, mineral fuel, clothing and other manufactured goods. Principal source: Australia 33.3% (1996) **Arable land:** 19.4% (1995)

Population and society

Population: 174,000 (1998 est) **Population growth rate:** 1.5% (1995–2000) **Population density:** (per sq km) 78.9 (1998 est) **Urban population:** (% of total) 21 (1997) **Age distribution:** (% of total population) 0–14 39.4%, 15–64 56.5%, 65+ 4.1% (1998) **Ethnic groups:** 90% of Samoan (Polynesian) origin; 10% Euronesian (mixed European and Polynesian) **Language:** English, Samoan (official) **Religion:** Congregationalist; also Roman Catholic, Methodist **Education:** not compulsory **Literacy rate:** 92% (men); 88% (women) (1994 est) **Labour force:** 58% agriculture (1990) **Life expectancy:** 68 (men); 71 (women) (1995–2000) **Child mortality rate:** (under 5, per 1,000 live births) 68 (1997) **Physicians:** 1 per 3,665 people (1992)

Practical information

Visa requirements: UK: visa not required. USA: visa not required **Embassy for the UK:** avenue Franklin D Roosevelt 123, B-1050 Brussels, Belgium. Tel: (2) 660 8454; fax: (2) 675 0336 **British embassy:** Office of the Honorary British Representative, c/o Kruse Va'ai and Barlow, PO Box 2029, Apia. Tel: (685) 21895, fax: (685) 21407 **Chamber of commerce:** c/o Pacific Forum Line, Matantu-tai, PO Box 655, Apia. Tel: (685) 20345

Chronology

c. **1000 BC:** Settled by Polynesians from Tonga. **AD 950–1250:** Ruled by Tongan invaders; the Matai (chiefly) system was developed. **15th century:** United under the Samoan Queen Salamasina. **1722:** Visited by Dutch traders. **1768:** Visted by the French navigator Louis Antoine de Bougainville. **1830:** Christian mission established and islanders were soon converted to Christianity. **1887–89:** Samoan rebellion against German attempt to depose paramount ruler and install its own puppet regime. **1889:** Under the terms of the Act of Berlin, Germany took control of the nine islands of Western Samoa, while the USA was granted American Samoa, and Britain Tonga and the Solomon Islands. **1900s:** More than 2,000 Chinese brought in to work coconut plantations. **1914:** Occupied by New Zealand on the outbreak of World War I. **1918:** Nearly a quarter of the population died in an influenza epidemic. **1920s:** Development of nationalist movement, the Mau, which resorted to civil disobedience. **1920–61:** Administered by New Zealand under League of Nations and, later, United Nations mandate. **1959:** Local government established, headed by chief minister Fiame Mata'afa Mulinu'u. **1961:** Referendum favoured independence. **1962:** Independence achieved within Commonwealth, with Mata'afa as prime minister, a position he retained (apart from a short break 1970–73) until his death in 1975. **1976:** Tupuola Taisi Efi became first nonroyal prime minister. **1982:** Va'ai Kolone, the head of the opposition Human Rights Protection Party (HRPP), became prime minister, but was forced to resign over charges of electoral malpractice. The new HRPP leader, Tofilau Eti Alesana, became prime minister. **1985:** Tofilau Eti Alesana resigned after opposition to budget; head of state invited Va'ai Kolone to lead the government. **1988:** Elections produced hung parliament, with first Tupuola Efi as prime minister and then Tofilau Eti Alesana. **1990:** Universal adult suffrage introduced and power of Matai (elected clan leaders) reduced. **1991:** Fiame Naome became first woman in cabinet; major damage caused by 'Cyclone Val'. **1998:** Name changed officially to 'Samoa'. Tofilau Eti Alesana stepped down, for health reasons, to become senior minister without portfolio and his deputy, Tuila'epa Sa'ilele Malielegaoi, of the HRPP, became the new prime minister.

San Marino Most Serene Republic of

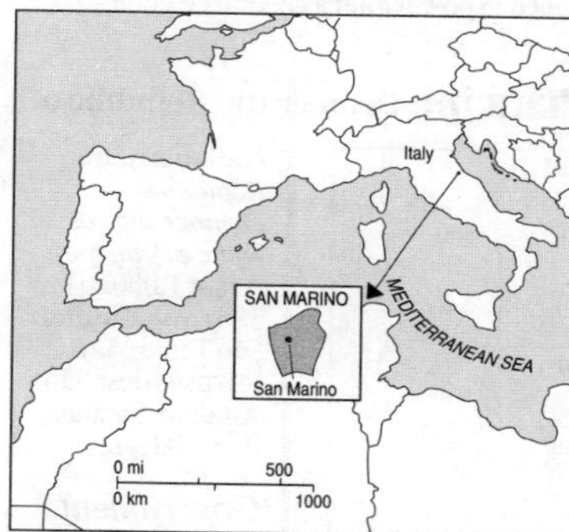

National name: *Serenissima Repubblica di San Marino* **Area:** 61 sq km/24 sq mi **Capital:** San Marino **Major towns/cities:** Serravalle (industrial centre), Faetano, Fiorentino, Monte Giardino

Government

Head of state and government: two captains regent, elected for a six-month period **Political system:** direct democracy **Administrative divisions:** nine districts **Political parties:** San Marino Christian Democrat Party (PDCS), Christian centrist; Progressive Democratic Party (PDP) (formerly the Communist Party: PCS), moderate left wing; Socialist Party (PS), left of centre **Armed forces:** voluntary military forces and a paramilitary gendarmerie **Conscription:** military service is not compulsory, but all citizens between the ages of 15 and 55 may be enlisted in certain circumstances to defend the state **Death penalty:** abolished in 1865

Economy and resources

Currency: Italian lira **GDP:** (US$) 478 million (1995) **Real GDP growth:** (% change on previous year) 3.0 (1995) **GNP (US$):** 470 million (1995 est) **GNP per capita (PPP):** (US$) 20,100 (1995 est) **Consumer price inflation:** 5.3% (1995) **Unemployment:** 4.4% (1996) **Major trading partners:** maintains customs union with Italy (for trade data see Italy) **Resources:** limestone and other building stone **Exports:** wood machinery, chemicals, wine, olive oil, textiles, tiles, ceramics, varnishes, building stone, lime, chestnuts, hides. Principal market: Italy **Imports:** consumer goods, raw materials, energy supply. Principal source: Italy **Arable land:** 16.7% (1995)

Population and society

Population: 26,000 (1998 est) **Population growth rate:** 1.0% (1995–2025) **Population density:** (per sq km) 415 (1998 est) **Urban population:** (% of total) 95 (1997) **Age distribution:** (% of total population) 0–14 16.1%, 15–64 67.3%, 65+ 16.6% (1998) **Ethnic groups:** predominantly Italian **Language:** Italian **Religion:** Roman Catholic 95% **Education:** (compulsory years) 8 **Literacy rate:** 98% (men); 98% (women) (1995 est) **Labour force:** 1.6% agriculture, 43% industry, 55.1% services (1995) **Life expectancy:** 75 (men); 81 (women) (1995 est) **Child mortality rate:** (under 5, per 1,000 live births) 6 (1994) **Physicians:** 1 per 405 people (1990)

Practical information
Visa requirements: UK: visa not required. USA: visa not required **Embassy in the UK:** San Marino has no diplomatic representation in the UK; the UK Department of Trade and Industry has an Italy desk. Tel: (0171) 215 4385; fax (0171) 215 4711 **British embassy:** British Consulate, Lungarno Corsini 2, 50123 Florence, Italy. Tel: (55) 284 133; fax: (55) 219 112

Chronology
c. AD **301:** Founded as a republic (the world's oldest surviving) by St Marinus and a group of Christians who settled there to escape persecution. **12th century:** Self-governing commune. **1600:** Statutes (constitution) provided for a parliamentary form of government, based around the Great and General Council. **1815:** Independent status of the republic recognized by the Congress of Vienna. **1862:** Treaty with Italy signed; independence recognized under Italy's protection. **1945–57:** Communist–Socialist administration in power, eventually ousted in a bloodless 'revolution'. **1957–86:** Governed by a series of left-wing and centre-left coalitions. **1971:** Treaty with Italy renewed. **1986:** Formation of Communist and centre-right Christian Democrat (PDCS) 'grand coalition'. **1992:** Joined the United Nations. PDCS withdrew from 'grand coalition' to form alliance with Socialist Party. **1998:** The ruling PDCS–PSS coalition remained in power after a general election.

São Tomé and Príncipe Democratic Republic of

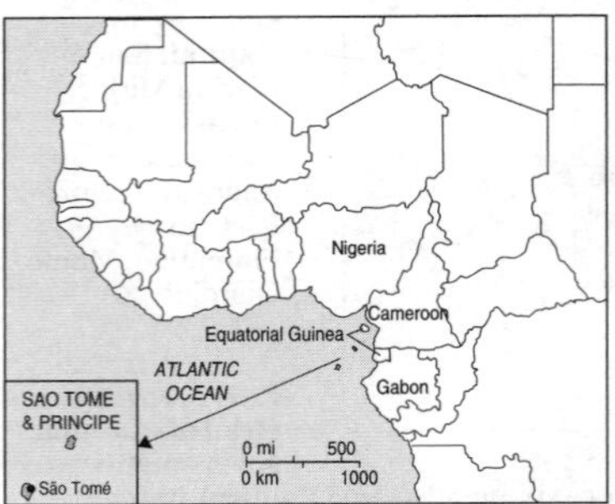

National name: *República Democrática de São Tomé e Príncipe* **Area:** 1,000 sq km/ 386 sq mi **Capital:** São Tomé **Major towns/cities:** São António, Santana, Porto-Alegre

Government
Head of state: Miguel Trovoada from 1991 **Head of government:** Carlos da Graca from 1994 **Political system:** emergent democracy **Administrative divisions:** two provinces **Political parties:** Movement for the Liberation of São Tomé e Príncipe–Social Democratic Party (MLSTP–PSD), nationalist socialist; Democratic Convergence Party–Reflection Group (PCD–GR), moderate left of centre; Independent Democratic Action (ADI), centrist **Armed forces:** no proper army; reorganization of island's armed forces (estimated at 900) and police into two separate police forces (one for public order, the other for criminal investigations) was initiated in 1992 **Death penalty:** abolished in 1990 **Education spend:** (% GNP) 4.3 (1986); N/A (1993/94)

Economy and resources
Currency: dobra **GDP:** (US$) 34 million (1997 est) **Real GDP growth:** (% change on previous year) 1.2 (1996 est) **GNP (US$):** 38 million (1997) **GNP per capita (PPP):** (US$) 860 (1997 est) **Consumer price inflation:** 45% (1997) **Unemployment:** 38% (1995) **Foreign debt:** (US$) 261 million (1996) **Major trading partners:** Portugal, the Netherlands, Germany, Spain, Belgium, France, Japan, Angola **Exports:** cocoa, copra, coffee, bananas, palm oil. Principal market: the Netherlands 63.9% (1996) **Imports:** capital goods, food and live animals (of which 60.7% were donations in 1994), petroleum and petroleum products. Principal source: Portugal 29% (1996) **Arable land:** 2.1% (1995)

Population and society
Population: 141,000 (1998 est) **Population growth rate:** 1.6% (1995–2025) **Population density:** (per sq km) 156.4 (1998 est) **Urban population:** (% of total) 45 (1997) **Age distribution:** (% of total population) 0–14 47.5%, 15–64 48.3%, 65+ 4.1% (1998) **Ethnic groups:** predominantly African **Language:** Portuguese (official); Fang (a Bantu language) **Religion:** Roman Catholic 80%, animist **Education:** (compulsory years) 4 **Literacy rate:** 85% (men); 62% women (1991 est) **Labour force:** 39.9% agriculture, 13.6% industry, 46.5% services (1991) **Life expectancy:** 67 (men); 73 (women) (1994 est) **Child mortality rate:** (under 5, per 1,000 live births) 81 (1995) **Physicians:** 1 per 1,780 people (1992)

Practical information
Visa requirements: UK: visa required. USA: visa required **Embassy in the UK:** 42 avenue Brugmann, 1060 Brussels, Belgium. Tel: (2) 347 5375; fax: (2) 347 5408; Honorary Consulate of the Democratic Republic of São Tomé e Príncipe, 42 North Audley Street, London W1A 4PY. Tel: (0171) 499 1995; fax: (0171) 629 6460 **British embassy:** British Consulate, c/o Hull Blythe (Angola) Ltd, BP 15, São Tomé. Telex: 220 (a/b HBALTD ST) (the British Embassy in Luanda, Angola deals with enquiries relating to São Tomé e Príncipe) **Chamber of commerce:** the British Embassy in Luanda (see Angola) deals with queries relating to São Tomé and Príncipe

Chronology
1471: First visited by the Portuguese, who imported convicts and slaves to work on sugar plantations in the formerly uninhabited islands. **1522:** Became a province of Portugal. **1530:** Slaves successfully revolted, forcing plantation owners to flee to Brazil; thereafter became a key staging post for Congo-Americas slave trade. **19th century:** Forced contract labour used to work coffee and cocoa plantations. **1953:** More than 1,000 striking plantation workers gunned down by Portuguese troops. **1960:** First political party formed, the forerunner of the socialist-nationalist Movement for the Liberation of São Tomé e Príncipe (MLSTP). **1974:** Military coup in Portugal led to strikes, demonstrations, and army mutiny in São Tomé; thousands of Portuguese settlers fled the country. **1975:** Independence achieved, with Manuel Pinto da Costa (MLSTP) as president; close links developed with communist bloc, and plantations nationalized. **1984:** Formally declared a nonaligned state as economy deteriorated. **1988:** Coup attempt against da Costa foiled by Angolan and East European troops. **1990:** Influenced by collapse of communism in Eastern Europe, MLSTP abandoned Marxism; new pluralist constitution approved in referendum. **1991:** In first multiparty elections, the ruling MLSTP lost its majority and the independent Miguel Trovoada, MLSTP prime minister before 1978, was elected president. **1994:** MLSTP returned to power with Carlos da Graca as prime minister. **1995:** Abortive coup by junior army officers. **1998:** MLSTP–PSD won absolute assembly majority.

Saudi Arabia Kingdom of

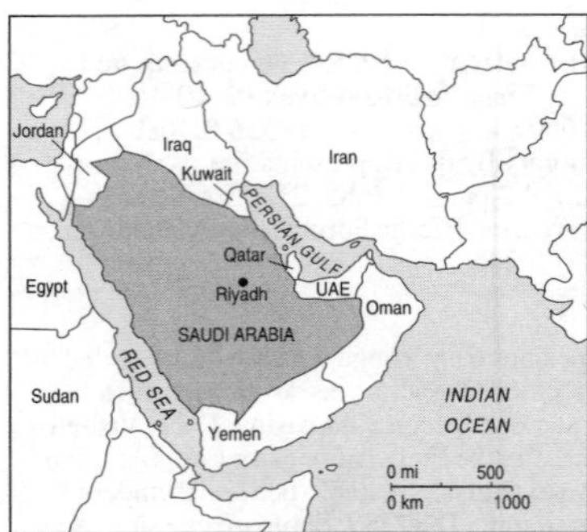

National name: *Mamlaka al-'Arabiya as-Sa'udiya* **Area:** 2,200,518 sq km/849,620 sq mi **Capital:** Riyadh **Major towns/ cities:** Jiddah, Mecca, Medina, Taif, Dammam, Hufuf **Major ports:** Jiddah, Dammam, Jubail, Jizan, Yanbu

Government
Head of state and government: King Fahd Ibn Abdul Aziz from 1996 **Political system:** absolute monarchy **Administrative divisions:** 13 provinces **Political parties:** none **Armed forces:** 162,500; paramilitary forces 15,500 (1997) **Conscription:** military service is voluntary **Death penalty:** retained and used for ordinary crimes **Defence spend:** (% GDP) 12.4 (1997) **Education spend:** (% GNP) 5.5 (1990–95) **Health spend:** (% GDP) 3.1 (1990–95)

Economy and resources

Currency: rial **GDP:** (US$) 145.8 billion (1997) **Real GDP growth:** (% change on previous year) 2.5 (1997) **GNP (US$):** 128.9 billion (1997) **GNP per capita (PPP):** (US$) 10,870 (1997 est) **Consumer price inflation:** 3.6% (1998) **Foreign debt:** US $ 17.8 billion (1996) **Major trading partners:** USA, Japan, Germany, South Korea, France, Italy, Singapore, the Netherlands **Resources:** petroleum, natural gas, iron ore, limestone, gypsum, marble, clay, salt, gold, uranium, copper, fish **Exports:** crude and refined petroleum, petrochemicals, wheat. Principal market: Japan 17% (1997) **Imports:** machinery and transport equipment, foodstuffs, beverages, tobacco, chemicals and chemical products, base metals and metal manufactures, textiles and clothing. Principal source: USA 23.3% (1997) **Arable land:** 1.7% (1995)

Population and society

Population: 20,181,000 (1998 est) **Population growth rate:** 3.4% (1995–2000); 3.1% (2000–05) **Population density:** (per sq km) 9.7 (1998 est) **Urban population:** (% of total) 84 (1997) **Age distribution:** (% of total population) 0–14 43.1%, 15–64 54.5%, 65+ 2.4% (1998) **Ethnic groups:** around 90% Arab; 10% Afro-Asian **Language:** Arabic **Religion:** Sunni Muslim; there is a Shi'ite minority **Literacy rate:** 73% (men); 48% (women) (1995 est) **Labour force:** 34% of population: 19% agriculture, 20% industry, 61% services (1990) **Life expectancy:** 70 (men); 73 (women) (1995–2000) **Child mortality rate:** (under 5, per 1,000 live births) 28 (1997) **Physicians:** 1 per 636 people (1994)

Practical information

Visa requirements: UK: visa required. USA: visa required **Embassy in the UK:** 30 Charles Street, London W1X 7PH. Tel: (0171) 917 3000; fax: (0171) 917 3330 **British embassy:** PO Box 94351, Riyadh 11693. Tel: (1) 488 0077; fax: (1) 488 2373 **Chamber of commerce:** Riyadh Chamber of Commerce and Industry, PO Box 596, Riyadh 11421. Tel: (1) 404 0044; fax: (1) 402 1103

Chronology

622: Muhammad began to unite Arabs in Muslim faith. **7th–8th centuries:** Muslim Empire expanded, ultimately stretching from India to Spain, with Arabia itself being relegated to a subordinate part. **12th century:** Decline of Muslim Empire; Arabia grew isolated and internal divisions multiplied. **13th century:** Mameluke sultans of Egypt became nominal overlords of Hejaz in western Arabia. **1517:** Hejaz became a nominal part of Ottoman Empire after Turks conquered Egypt. **18th century:** Al Saud family united tribes of Nejd in central Arabia in support of the Wahhabi religious movement. *c.* **1830:** The Al Saud established Riyadh as the Wahhabi capital. *c.* **1870:** Turks took effective control of Hejaz and also Hasa on Persian Gulf. **late 19th century:** Rival Wahhabi dynasty of Ibn Rashid became leaders of Nejd. **1902:** Ibn Saud organized Bedouin revolt and regained Riyadh. **1913:** Ibn Saud completed the reconquest of Hasa from Turks. **1915:** Britain recognized Ibn Saud as emir of Nejd and Hasa. **1916–18:** British-backed revolt, under aegis of Sharif Hussein of Mecca, expelled Turks from Arabia. **1919–25:** Ibn Saud fought and defeated Sharif Hussein and took control of Hejaz. **1926:** Proclamation of Ibn Saud as king of Hejaz and Nejd. **1932:** Hejaz and Nejd renamed the United Kingdom of Saudi Arabia. **1933:** Saudi Arabia allowed American-owned Standard Oil Company to prospect for oil, which was discovered in Hasa 1938. **1939–45:** Although officially neutral in World War II, Saudi Arabia received subsidies from USA and Britain. **1940s:** Commercial exploitation of oil began, bringing great prosperity. **1953:** Ibn Saud died; succeeded by his eldest son, Saud. **1964:** King Saud forced to abdicate; succeeded by his brother, Faisal. **1975:** King Faisal assassinated; succeeded by his half-brother, Khalid. **1982:** King Khalid died; succeeded by his brother, Fahd. **1987:** Rioting by Iranian pilgrims caused 400 deaths in Mecca and breach in diplomatic relations with Iran. **1990:** Iraqi troops invaded Kuwait and massed on Saudi Arabian border, prompting King Fahd to call for assistance from US and UK forces. **1991:** Saudi Arabia fought on Allied side against Iraq in Gulf War. **1992:** Under international pressure to move towards democracy, King Fahd formed a 'consultative council' to assist in government of kingdom. **1995:** King Fahd suffered a stroke and transferred power to Crown Prince Abdullah. **1996:** King Fahd resumed power.

Senegal Republic of

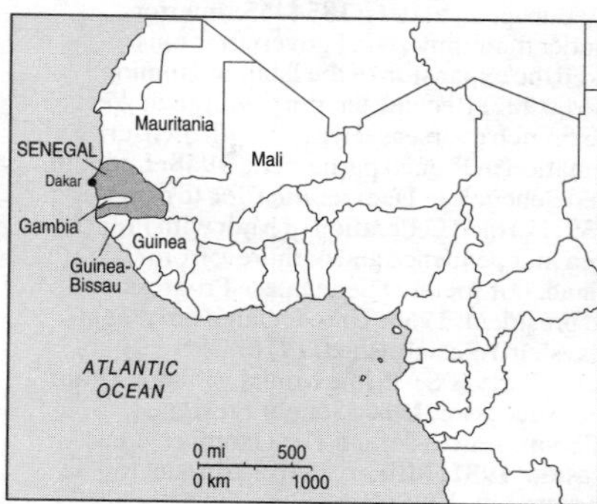

National name: *République du Sénégal* **Area:** 196,200 sq km/ 75,752 sq mi **Capital:** Dakar (and chief port) **Major towns/ cities:** Thiès, Kaolack, Saint-Louis, Ziguinchor, Diourbel

Government

Head of state: Abdou Diouf from 1981 **Head of government:** Mamadou Lamine Loum from 1998 **Political system:** emergent socialist democracy **Administrative divisions:** ten regions **Political parties:** Senegalese Socialist Party (PS), democratic socialist; Senegalese Democratic Party (PDS), centrist **Armed forces:** 13,400 (1997) **Conscription:** military services is by selective conscription for two years **Death penalty:** retains the death penalty for ordinary crimes but can be considered abolitionist in practice (last execution 1967) **Defence spend:** (% GDP) 1.6 (1997) **Education spend:** (% GNP) 3.5 (1995) **Health spend:** (% GDP) 2.5 (1990–95)

Economy and resources

Currency: franc CFA **GDP:** (US$) 4.5 billion (1997) **Real GDP growth:** (% change on previous year) 4.8 (1997 est) **GNP (US$):** 4.9 billion (1997) **GNP per capita (PPP):** (US$) 1,670 (1997) **Consumer price inflation:** 2.0% (1998) **Unemployment:** 10.2% (1993) **Foreign debt:** (US$) 3.89 billion (1996) **Major trading partners:** France, India, Italy, USA, Mali, Côte d'Ivoire, Nigeria, Thailand **Resources:** calcium phosphates, aluminium phosphates, salt, natural gas; offshore deposits of petroleum to be developed **Exports:** fresh and processed fish, refined petroleum products, chemicals, groundnuts and related products, calcium phosphates and related products. Principal market: France 20.3% (1996) **Imports:** food and live animals, machinery and transport equipment, mineral fuels and lubricants (mainly crude petroleum), basic manufactures, chemicals. Principal source: France 35.5% (1996) **Arable land:** 11.7% (1995)

Population and society

Population: 9,003,000 (1998 est) **Population growth rate:** 2.7% (1995–2000) **Population density:** (per sq km) 50.6 (1998 est) **Urban population:** (% of total) 45 (1997) **Age distribution:** (% of total population) 0–14 48.1%, 15–64 49.1%, 65+ 2.8% (1998) **Ethnic groups:** the Wolof group are the most numerous, comprising about 36% of the population; the Fulani comprise about 21%; the Serer 19%; the Diola 7%; and the Mandingo 6% **Language:** French (official); Wolof **Religion:** mainly Sunni Muslim **Education:** (compulsory years) 6 **Literacy rate:** 52% (men); 25% (women) (1995 est) **Labour force:** 45% of population: 77% agriculture, 8% industry, 16% services (1990) **Life expectancy:** 50 (men); 53 (women) (1995–2000) **Child mortality rate:** (under 5, per 1,000 live births) 153 (1997) **Physicians:** 1 per 18,192 people (1993 est)

Practical information

Visa requirements: UK: visa not required. USA: visa not required **Embassy in the UK:** 11 Phillimore Gardens, London W8 7QG. Tel: (0171) 937 0925/6; fax: (0171) 937 8130 **British embassy:** BP 6025, 20 rue du Docteur Guillet, Dakar. Tel: (221) 237 392; fax: (221) 232 766 **Chamber of commerce:** Chambre de Commerce et d'Industrie et d'Agriculture de la Région de Dakar, BP 118, 1 place de l'Indépendence, Dakar. Tel: (221) 237 189; telex: 61112

Chronology

10th–11th centuries: Links established with North Africa; the Tukolor community was converted to Islam. **1445:** First visited by

Portuguese explorers. **1659:** French founded Saint-Louis as a colony. **17th–18th centuries:** Export trades in slaves, gums, ivory, and gold developed by European traders. **1854–65:** Interior occupied by French under their imperialist governor, Louis Faidherbe, who checked the expansion of the Islamic Tukulor Empire; Dakar founded. **1902:** Became territory of French West Africa. **1946:** Became French overseas territory, with own territorial assembly and representation in French parliament. **1948:** Leopold Sedar Senghor founded Senegalese Democratic Bloc to campaign for independence. **1959:** Formed Federation of Mali with French Sudan. **1960:** Achieved independence and withdrew from federation. Senghor, leader of socialist Senegalese Progressive Union (UPS), became president. **1966:** UPS declared only legal party. **1974:** Pluralist system re-established. **1976:** UPS reconstituted as Socialist Party (PS). Prime Minister Abdou Diouf nominated as Senghor's successor. **1980:** Senghor resigned; succeeded by Diouf. Troops sent to defend The Gambia against suspected Libyan invasion. **1981:** Military help again sent to The Gambia to thwart coup attempt. **1982:** Confederation of Senegambia came into effect. **1983:** Diouf re-elected. Post of prime minister abolished. **1989:** Diplomatic links with Mauritania severed after 450 died in violent clashes; over 50,000 people repatriated from both countries. Senegambia federation abandoned. **1992:** Post of prime minister reinstated. Diplomatic links with Mauritania re-established. **1993:** Assembly and presidential elections won by ruling PS. **1998:** PS won the general election despite claims of fraud. Abdou Diouf became 'president for life'. **1999:** A new 60-member Senate was created as Senegal's second legislative chamber.

Seychelles Republic of

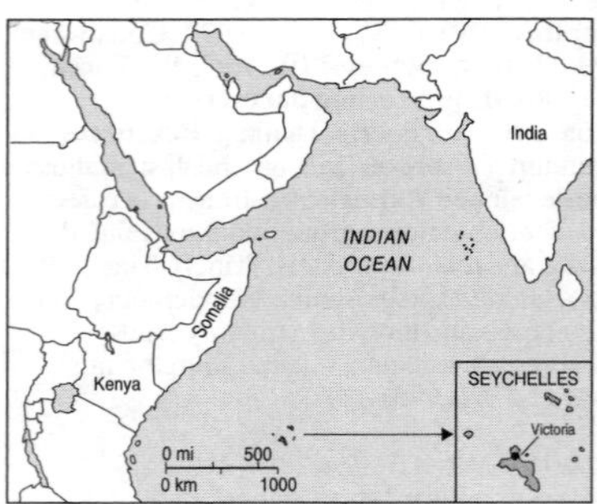

Area: 453 sq km/174 sq mi **Capital:** Victoria (on Mahé island) (and chief port) **Major towns/cities:** Cascade, Port Glaud, Misere

Government

Head of state and government: France-Albert René from 1977 **Political system:** emergent democracy **Administrative divisions:** 23 districts **Political parties:** Seychelles People's Progressive Front (SPPF), nationalist socialist; Democratic Party (DP), left of centre **Armed forces:** 200; 300 paramilitary forces; plus 1,000-strong national guard (1997) **Conscription:** military service is voluntary **Death penalty:** retains death penalty only for exceptional crimes such as crimes under military law or crimes committed in exceptional circumstances such as wartime **Defence spend:** (% GDP) 2.9 (1997) **Education spend:** (% GNP) 7.5 (1995) **Health spend:** (% GDP) 3.8 (1994 est)

Economy and resources

Currency: Seychelles rupee **GDP:** (US$) 536 million (1997 est) **Real GDP growth:** (% change on previous year) 1.3 (1997) **GNP (US$):** 537 million (1997) **GNP per capita (PPP):** (US$) 7,900 (1997 est) **Consumer price inflation:** 0.7% (1997) **Unemployment:** 8.3% (1993) **Foreign debt:** (US$) 148 million (1996) **Major trading partners:** UK, Singapore, Bahrain, South Africa, France, USA, Réunion, Japan **Resources:** guano; natural gas and metal deposits were being explored mid-1990s **Exports:** fresh and frozen fish, canned tuna, shark fins, cinnamon bark, refined petroleum products. Principal market: Yemen 17.2% (1996) **Imports:** machinery and transport equipment, food and live animals, petroleum and petroleum products, chemicals, basic manufactures. Principal source: USA 33.6% (1996) **Arable land:** 2.2% (1995)

Population and society

Population: 76,000 (1998 est) **Population growth rate:** 0.9% (1995–2025) **Population density:** (per sq km) 172.5 (1998 est) **Urban population:** (% of total) 56 (1997) **Age distribution:** (% of total population) 0–14 29.9%, 15–64 63.9%, 65+ 6.3% (1998) **Ethnic groups:** predominantly Creole (of mixed African and European descent); small European minority (mostly French and British) **Language:** creole (Asian, African, European mixture) 95%, English, French (all official) **Religion:** Roman Catholic **Education:** (compulsory years) 9 **Literacy rate:** 86% (men); 82% (women) (1994 est) **Labour force:** 9.9% agriculture, 18.8% industry, 71.3% services (1989) **Life expectancy:** 69 (men); 78 (women) (1994 est) **Child mortality rate:** (under 5, per 1,000 live births) 20 (1995) **Physicians:** 1 per 1,032 people (1993)

Practical information

Visa requirements: UK: visa not required. USA: visa not required **Embassy in the UK:** 2nd Floor, Eros House, 111 Baker Street, London W1M 1FE. Tel: (0171) 224 1660; fax: (0171) 487 5756 **British embassy:** British High Commission, PO Box 161, 3rd Floor, Victoria House, Victoria, Mahé. Tel: (248) 225 225; fax: (248) 225 127 **Chamber of commerce:** Seychelles Chamber of Commerce and Industry, PO Box 443, 38 Premier Building, Victoria, Mahé. Tel: (248) 223 812

Chronology

early 16th century: First sighted by European navigators. **1744:** Became French colony. **1756:** Claimed as French possession and named after an influential French family. **1770s:** French colonists brought African slaves to settle the previously uninhabited islands; plantations established. **1794:** Captured by British during French Revolutionary Wars. **1814:** Ceded by France to Britain; incorporated as dependency of Mauritius. **1835:** Slavery abolished by British, leading to influx of liberated slaves from Mauritius and Chinese and Indian immigrants. **1903:** Became British crown colony, separate from Mauritius. **1963–64:** First political parties formed. **1976:** Independence achieved from Britain as republic within Commonwealth, with a moderate, James Mancham, of the centre-right Seychelles Democratic Party (SDP) as president. **1977:** More radical France-Albert René ousted Mancham in armed bloodless coup and took over presidency; white settlers emigrated. **1979:** Nationalistic socialist Seychelles People's Progressive Front (SPPF) became sole legal party under new constitution; became nonaligned state. **1981:** Attempted coup by South African mercenaries thwarted. **1991:** Multiparty politics promised. **1993:** New multiparty constitution adopted. René defeated Mancham, who had returned from exile, in competitive presidential elections; SPPF won parliamentary elections. **1998:** President René re-elected. SPUP won assembly elections.

Sierra Leone Republic of

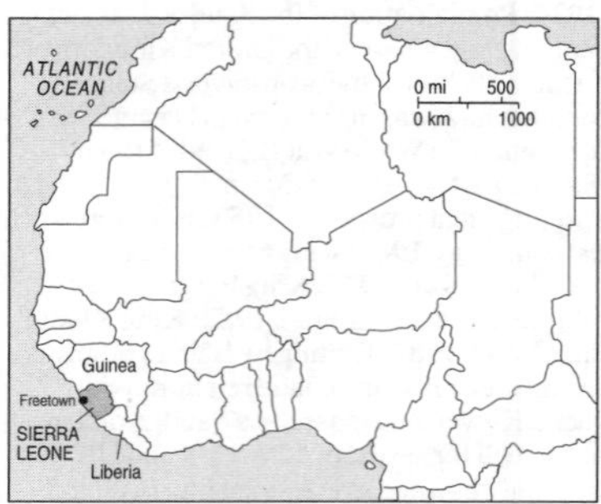

Area: 71,740 sq km/27,698 sq mi **Capital:** Freetown **Major towns/cities:** Koidu, Bo, Kenema, Makeni **Major ports:** Bonthe-Sherbro

Government

Head of state and government: Ahmad Tejan Kabbah from 1998 **Political system:** transitional **Administrative divisions:** four provinces **Political parties:** All People's Congress (APC), moderate socialist; United Front of Political Movements (UNIFORM), centre left. Party political

activity suspended from 1992 **Armed forces:** 15,000 (1997) **Conscription:** military service is voluntary **Death penalty:** retained and used for ordinary crimes **Defence spend:** (% GDP) 6.9 (1997) **Education spend:** (% GNP) 1.4 (1992) **Health spend:** (% GDP) 1.6 (1990–95)

Economy and resources

Currency: leone **GDP:** (US$) 941 million (1995) **Real GDP growth:** (% change on previous year) –3.4 (1997) **GNP (US$):** 0.9 billion (1997) **GNP per capita (PPP):** (US$) 510 (1997) **Consumer price inflation:** 20% (1996) **Unemployment:** 12% (1990) **Foreign debt:** (US$) 1.17 billion (1996) **Major trading partners:** Belgium – Luxembourg, UK, USA, the Netherlands, Nigeria, Germany **Resources:** gold, diamonds, bauxite, rutile (titanium dioxide) **Exports:** rutile, diamonds, bauxite, gold, coffee, cocoa beans. Principal market: Belgium – Luxembourg 48.9% (1997) **Imports:** machinery and transport equipment, food and live animals, basic manufactures, chemicals, miscellaneous manufactured articles. Principal source: UK 16% (1997) **Arable land:** 6.8% (1995)

Population and society

Population: 4,568,000 (1998 est) **Population growth rate:** 3.0% (1995–2000) **Population density:** (per sq km) 70.9 (1998 est) **Urban population:** (% of total) 35 (1997) **Age distribution:** (% of total population) 0–14 45.2%, 15–64 51.7%, 65+ 3.1% (1998) **Ethnic groups:** 18 ethnic groups, 3 of which (the Mende, Tenne, and Limbe) comprise almost 70% of the population **Language:** English (official), Krio (a creole language) **Religion:** animist 52%, Muslim 39%, Protestant 6%, Roman Catholic 2% (1980 est) **Education:** not compulsory **Literacy rate:** 31% (men); 11% (women) (1995 est) **Labour force:** 37% of population: 67% agriculture, 15% industry, 17% services (1990) **Life expectancy:** 36 (men); 39 (women) (1995–2000) **Child mortality rate:** (under 5, per 1,000 live births) 251 (1997) **Physicians:** 1 per 11,619 people (1990)

Practical information

Visa requirements: UK: visa required. USA: visa required **Embassy in the UK:** 33 Portland Place, London W1N 3AG. Tel: (0171) 636 6483/6; fax: (0171) 323 3159 **British embassy:** British High Commission, Standard Chartered Bank Building, Lightfoot-Boston Street, Freetown. Tel: (232) 223 961/5; telex: 3235 (a/b 3235 UKREP SL) **Chamber of commerce:** Sierra Leone Chamber of Commerce, Industry and Agriculture, PO Box 502, 5th Floor, Guma Building, Lamina, Sankoh Street, Freetown. Tel: (232) 226 305; fax: (232) 228 005

Chronology

15th century: Mende, Temne, and Fulani peoples moved from Senegal into region formerly populated by Bulom, Krim, and Gola peoples. The Portuguese, who named the area Serra Lyoa, established a coastal fort, trading manufactured goods for slaves and ivory. **17th century:** English trading posts established on Bund and York islands. **1787–92:** English abolitionists and philanthropists bought land to establish settlement for liberated and runaway African slaves (including 1,000 rescued from Canada), known as Freetown. **1808:** Became a British colony and Freetown a base for British naval operations against slave trade, after parliament declared it illegal. **1896:** Hinterland conquered and declared British protectorate. **1951:** First political party, Sierra Leone People's Party (SLPP), formed by Dr Milton Margai, who became 'leader of government business', in 1953. **1961:** Independence achieved within Commonwealth, with Margai as prime minister. **1964:** Margai died; succeeded by his half-brother, Albert Margai. **1965:** Free-trade area pact signed with Guinea, Liberia, and Ivory Coast. **1967:** Election won by All People's Congress (APC), led by Siaka Stevens, but disputed by army, who set up National Reformation Council and forced governor general to leave the country. **1968:** Army revolt brought back Stevens as prime minister. **1971:** New constitution made Sierra Leone a republic, with Stevens as president. **1978:** New constitution made APC the only legal party. **1985:** Stevens retired; succeeded as president and APC leader by Maj-Gen Joseph Momoh. **1989:** Attempted coup against President Momoh foiled. **1991:** Referendum endorsed multiparty politics and new constitution. Liberian-based rebel group began guerrilla activities. **1992:** President Momoh overthrown by military and party politics suspended as National Provisional Ruling Council established under Capt Valentine Strasser; 500,000 Liberians fled to Sierra Leone as a result of civil war. **1995:** Ban on political parties lifted. Coup attempt foiled. **1996:** Strasser overthrown by deputy, Julius Maada Bio, who was replaced as president by Ahmad Tejan Kabbah after multiparty elections. **1997:** President Kabbah's civilian government ousted in bloody coup. Maj Johnny Paul Koroma seized presidency; Revolutionary Council formed. **1998:** Nigerian-led peacekeeping force drove out Maj Koroma's junta; President Kabbah returned from exile. Execution of former members of military government for treason. **1999:** Cease-fire and peace agreement with rebels.

Singapore Republic of

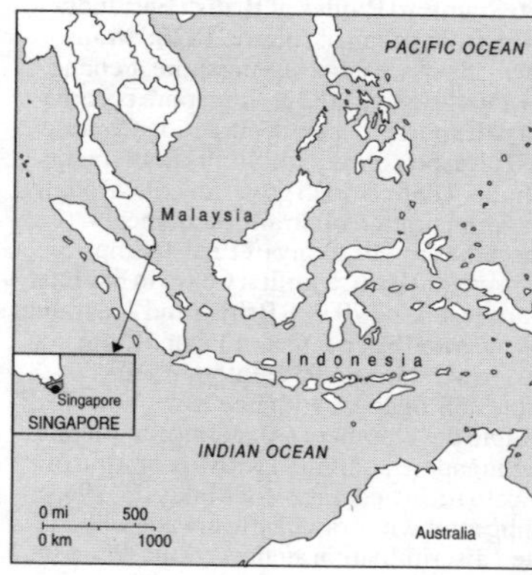

Area: 622 sq km/240 sq mi **Capital:** Singapore City **Major towns/cities:** Jurong, Changi

Government

Head of state: Ong Teng Cheong from 1993 **Head of government:** Goh Chok Tong from 1990 **Political system:** liberal democracy with strict limits on dissent **Administrative divisions:** five districts **Political parties:** People's Action Party (PAP), conservative, free market, multi-ethnic; Workers' Party (WP), socialist; Singapore Democratic Party (SDP), liberal pluralist **Armed forces:** 70,000; 263,800 reservists (1997) **Conscription:** two years **Death penalty:** retained and used for ordinary crimes **Defence spend:** (% GDP) 4.3 (1997) **Education spend:** (% GNP) 3.0 (1995) **Health spend:** (% GDP) 1.3 (1990–95)

Economy and resources

Currency: Singapore dollar **GDP:** (US$) 96.3 billion (1997) **Real GDP growth:** (% change on previous year) 6.7 (1997) **GNP (US$):** 101.8 billion (1997) **GNP per capita (PPP):** (US$) 29,000 (1997) **Consumer price inflation:** 2.4 (1998) **Unemployment:** 3.0% (1996) **Foreign debt:** (US$) 7.2 billion (1996) **Major trading partners:** Japan, USA, Malaysia, Hong Kong, Thailand **Resources:** granite **Exports:** electrical and nonelectrical machinery, transport equipment, petroleum products, chemicals, rubber, foodstuffs, clothing, metal products, iron and steel, orchids and other plants, aquarium fish. Principal market: USA 18.4% (1997) **Imports:** electrical and nonelectrical equipment, crude petroleum, transport equipment, chemicals, food and live animals, textiles, scientific and optical instruments, paper and paper products. Principal source: Japan 17.6% (1997) **Arable land:** 1.6% (1995)

Population and society

Population: 3,476,000 (1998 est) **Population growth rate:** 1.5% (1995–2000) **Population density:** (per sq km) 5,593.5 (1998 est) **Urban population:** (% of total) 100 (1997) **Age distribution:** (% of total population) 0–14 21.4%, 15–64 71.9%, 65+ 6.8% (1998) **Ethnic groups:** 77% of Chinese ethnic descent, predominantly Hokkien, Teochew, and Cantonese; 15% Malay; 7% Indian, chiefly Tamil **Language:** Malay (national tongue), Chinese, Tamil, English

(all official) **Religion:** Buddhist, Taoist, Muslim, Hindu, Christian **Education:** (compulsory years) 6 **Literacy rate:** 93% (men); 79% (women) (1995 est) **Labour force:** 49% of population: 0% agriculture, 36% industry, 64% services (1990) **Life expectancy:** 75 (men); 80 (women) (1995–2000) **Child mortality rate:** (under 5, per 1,000 live births) 6 (1997) **Physicians:** 1 per 709 people (1994)

Practical information

Visa requirements: UK: visa not required. USA: visa not required **Embassy in the UK:** 9 Wilton Crescent, London SW1X 8SA. Tel: (0171) 235 8315; fax: (0171) 245 6583 **British embassy:** British High Commission, Tanglin Road, Singapore 1024. Tel: (65) 473 9333; fax: (65) 475 2320 **Chamber of commerce:** Singapore International Chamber of Commerce, 10-001 John Hancock Tower, 6 Raffles Quay, Singapore 0104. Tel: (65) 224 1255; fax: (65) 224 2785

Chronology

12th century: First trading settlement established on Singapore Island. **14th century:** Settlement destroyed, probably by Javanese Empire of Mahapahit. **1819:** Stamford Raffles of British East India Company obtained Singapore from sultan of Johore. **1826:** Straits Settlements formed from British possessions of Singapore, Penang, and Malacca ruled by governor of Bengal. **1832:** Singapore became capital of Straits Settlements; the port prospered, attracting Chinese and Indian immigrants. **1851:** Responsibility for Straits Settlements fell to governor general of India. **1858:** British government, through the India Office, took over administration of Straits Settlements. **1867:** Straits Settlements became crown colony of British Empire. **1922:** Singapore chosen as principal British military base in Far East. **1942:** Japan captured Singapore, taking 70,000 British and Australian prisoners. **1945:** British rule restored after defeat of Japan. **1946:** Singapore became separate crown colony. **1959:** Internal self-government achieved as State of Singapore with Lee Kuan Yew (PAP) as prime minister. **1960s:** Rapid development as leading commercial and financial centre. **1963:** Singapore combined with Federation of Malaya, Sabah, and Sarawak to form Federation of Malaysia. **1965:** Became independent republic after withdrawing from Federation of Malaysia in protest at alleged discrimination against ethnic Chinese. **1971:** Last remaining British military bases closed. **1984:** Two opposition members elected to national assembly for first time. **1986:** Opposition leader convicted of perjury and prohibited from standing for election. **1988:** Ruling PAP won all but one of available assembly seats; increasingly authoritarian rule. **1990:** Lee Kuan Yew retired from premiership after 31 years; succeeded by Goh Chok Tong. **1992:** Lee Kuan Yew surrendered PAP leadership to Goh Chok Tong. **1993:** Ong Teng Cheong elected president with increased powers. **1996:** Constitutional change introduced, allowing better representation of minority races. **1997:** PAP, led by Prime Minister Goh Chok Tong, won general election. **1998:** Pay cuts introduced as Singapore slipped into recession for the first time in 13 years.

Slovak Republic

National name: *Slovenská Republika* **Area:** 49,035 sq km/ 18,932 sq mi **Capital:** Bratislava **Major towns/cities:** Košice, Nitra, Pre[scaron]ov, Banská Bystrica, Zilina, Trnava

Government

Head of state: Rudolf Schuster from 1999 **Head of government:** Mikulas Dzurinda from 1998 **Political system:** emergent democracy **Administrative divisions:** four regions **Political parties:** Movement for a Democratic Slovakia (MDS), centre left, nationalist-populist; Democratic Union of Slovakia (DUS), centrist; Christian Democratic Movement (KSDH), right of centre; Slovak National Party (SNP), nationalist; Party of the Democratic Left (PDL), reform socialist, (ex-communist); Association of Workers of Slovakia, left wing; Hungarian Coalition, ethnic Hungarian **Armed forces:** 41,200 (1997) **Conscription:** military service is compulsory for 18 months **Death penalty:** abolished in 1990 **Defence spend:** (% GDP) 2.1 (1997) **Education spend:** (% GNP) 4.7 (1996) **Health spend:** (% GDP) 6.0 (1990–95)

Economy and resources

Currency: Slovak koruna (based on Czechoslovak koruna) **GDP:** (US$) 19.5 billion (1997) **Real GDP growth:** (% change on previous year) 5.0 (1997) **GNP (US$):** 19.8 billion (1997) **GNP per capita (PPP):** (US$) 7,850 (1997) **Consumer price inflation:** 10.7% (1998) **Unemployment:** 12.8% (1996) **Foreign debt:** (US$) 7.7 billion (1996) **Major trading partners:** Czech Republic, Germany, Russia, Austria, Hungary, Italy **Resources:** brown coal, lignite, copper, zinc, lead, iron ore, magnesite **Exports:** basic manufactures, machinery and transport equipment, miscellaneous manufactured articles. Principal market: Czech Republic 26.7% (1997) **Imports:** machinery and transport equipment, mineral fuels and lubricants, basic manufactures, chemicals and related products. Principal source: Czech Republic 23% (1997) **Arable land:** 30.8% (1995)

Population and society

Population: 5,377,000 (1998 est) **Population growth rate:** 0.1% (1995–2000) **Population density:** (per sq km) 110 (1998 est) **Urban population:** (% of total) 60 (1997) **Age distribution:** (% of total population) 0–14 20.7%, 15–64 68.0%, 65+ 11.3% (1998) **Ethnic groups:** 87% ethnic Slovak, 11% ethnic Hungarian (Magyar); small Czech, Moravian, Silesian, and Romany communities **Language:** Slovak (official) **Religion:** Roman Catholic (over 50%), Lutheran, Reformist, Orthodox **Education:** (compulsory years) 9 **Literacy rate:** 99% (men); 99% (women) (1995 est) **Labour force:** 12.1% agriculture, 39.8% industry, 48.1% services (1993) **Life expectancy:** 67 (men); 76 (women) (1995–2000) **Child mortality rate:** (under 5, per 1,000 live births) 13 (1997) **Physicians:** 1 per 287 people (1993)

Practical information

Visa requirements: UK: visa not required. USA: visa not required **Embassy in the UK:** 25 Kensington Palace Gardens, London W8 4QY. Tel: (0171) 243 0803; fax: (0171) 727 5824 **British embassy:** Grösslingova 35, 811 09 Bratislava. Tel: (7) 364 420; fax: (7) 364 396 **Chamber of commerce:** Slovak Chamber of Commerce and Industry, Gorkéno 9, 816 03 Bratislava. Tel: (7) 362 787; fax: (7) 362 222

Chronology

9th century: Part of kingdom of Greater Moravia, in Czech lands to west, founded by Slavic Prince Sviatopluk; Christianity adopted. **906:** Came under Magyar (Hungarian) domination and adopted Roman Catholicism. **1526:** Came under Austrian Habsburg rule. **1867:** With creation of dual Austro-Hungarian monarchy, came under separate Hungarian rule; policy of forced Magyarization stimulated a revival of Slovak national consciousness. **1918:** Austro-Hungarian Empire dismembered; Slovaks joined Czechs to form independent state of Czechoslovakia. Slovak-born Tomas Masaryk remained president until 1935, but political and economic power became concentrated in Czech lands. **1939:** Germany annexed Czechoslovakia, which became Axis puppet state under the Slovak autonomist leader Monsignor Jozef Tiso; Jews persecuted. **1944:** Popular revolt against German rule ('Slovak Uprising'). **1945:** Liberated from German rule by Soviet troops; Czechoslovakia re-established. **1948:** Communists assumed power in Czechoslovakia. **1950s:** Heavy industry introduced into previously rural Slovakia; Slovak nationalism and Catholic Church forcibly suppressed. **1968–69:** 'Prague Spring' political reforms introduced by Slovak-born Communist Party leader Alexander Dubček; Warsaw Pact forces invaded Czechoslovakia to stamp out reforms; Slovak Socialist Republic, with autonomy over local affairs, created under

new federal constitution; Slovak-born Gustáv Husák became Communist Party leader in Czechoslovakia. **1989:** Prodemocracy demonstrations in Bratislava; new political parties, including centre-left People Against Violence (PAV), formed and legalized; Communist Party stripped of powers; new government formed, with ex-dissident playwright Václav Havel as president. **1990:** Slovak nationalists polled strongly in multiparty elections, with Vladimir Meciar (PAV) becoming prime minister. **1991:** Increasing Slovak separatism as economy deteriorated. Meciar formed PAV splinter group, Movement for a Democratic Slovakia (HZDS), pledging greater autonomy for Slovakia. Pro-Meciar rallies in Bratislava followed his dismissal. **1992:** Meciar returned to power following electoral victory for HZDS. Slovak parliament's declaration of sovereignty led to Havel's resignation; 'velvet divorce' agreement on separate Czech and Slovak states established a free-trade customs union. **1993:** Entered United Nations and Council of Europe as sovereign state, with Meciar as prime minister and Michal Kovac, formerly of HZDS, as president. **1994:** Joined NATO's 'Partnership for Peace' programme. Meciar ousted on no-confidence vote, but later returned after new elections, heading coalition government that included ultranationalists and socialists. **1995:** Second wave of mass privatization postponed; Slovak made sole official language; Treaty of Friendship and Cooperation signed with Hungary, easing tensions among Hungarian minority community. **1996:** Anti-Meciar coalition formed, the Slovak Democratic Coalition, comprising five opposition parties. **1997:** Referendum on NATO membership and presidential elections declared invalid after confusion over voting papers. **1998:** Presidential powers assumed by Meciar after failure to elect new president. Meciar stepped down as prime minister after opposition SDC polled strongly in general election. New SDC-led coalition formed under Mikulas Dzurinda. The koruna was devalued by 6%.

Slovenia Republic of

National name: *Republika Slovenija* **Area:** 20,251 sq km/7,818 sq mi **Capital:** Ljubljana **Major towns/cities:** Maribor, Kranj, Celji, Velenje, Koper (Capodistria) **Major ports:** Koper

Government

Head of state: Milan Kučan from 1990 **Head of government:** Janez Drnovšek from 1992 **Political system:** emergent democracy **Administrative divisions:** 62 districts **Political parties:** Slovenian Christian Democrats (SKD), right of centre; Slovenian People's Party (SPP), conservative; Liberal Democratic Party of Slovenia (LDS), centrist; Slovenian Nationalist Party (SNS), right-wing nationalist; Democratic Party of Slovenia (LDP), left of centre; United List of Social Democrats (ZLSD) left of centre, ex-communist **Armed forces:** 9,600; plus reserve forces of 53,000 and a paramilitary police force of 4,500 (1997) **Conscription:** military service is compulsory for seven months **Death penalty:** abolished in 1989 **Defence spend:** (% GDP) 1.7% (1997) **Education spend:** (% GNP) 5.8% (1995) **Health spend:** (% GDP) 7.4 (1990–95)

Economy and resources

Currency: tolar **GDP:** (US$) 17.9 billion (1997) **Real GDP growth:** (% change on previous year) 3.3 (1997) **GNP (US$):** 19.3 billion (1997) **GNP per capita (PPP):** (US$) 12,520 (1997) **Consumer price inflation:** 8.0% (1998) **Unemployment:** 14% (1997) **Foreign debt:** (US$) 4.03 million (1996) **Major trading partners:** Germany, Italy, Croatia, France, Austria, former USSR, USA **Resources:** coal, lead, zinc; small reserves/deposits of natural gas, petroleum, salt, uranium **Exports:** raw materials, semi-finished goods, machinery, electric motors, transport equipment, foodstuffs, clothing, pharmaceuticals, cosmetics. Principal market: Germany 29.4% (1997) **Imports:** machinery and transport equipment, raw materials, semi-finished goods, foodstuffs, chemicals, miscellaneous manufactured articles, mineral fuels and lubricants. Principal source: Germany 20.7% (1997) **Arable land:** 11.6% (1995)

Population and society

Population: 1,993,000 (1998 est) **Population growth rate:** –0.1% (1995–2000); –0.1% (2000–05) **Population density:** (per sq km) 97.4 (1998 est) **Urban population:** (% of total) 52 (1997) **Age distribution:** (% of total population) 0–14 16.7%, 15–64 69.9%, 65+ 13.4% (1998) **Ethnic groups:** 98% of Slovene origin, 3% ethnic Croat, 2% Serb **Language:** Slovene, resembling Serbo-Croat, written in Roman characters **Religion:** Roman Catholic **Education:** (compulsory years) 8 **Literacy rate:** 96% (men); 96% (women) (1995 est) **Labour force:** 11.5% agriculture, 42.3% industry, 46.2% services (1994) **Life expectancy:** 70 (men); 78 (women) (1995–2000) **Child mortality rate:** (per 1,000 live births) 11 (1997) **Physicians:** 1 per 481 people (1995)

Practical information

Visa requirements: UK: visa not required. USA: visa not required **Embassy in the UK:** Suite 1, Cavendish Court, 11–15 Wigmore Street, London W1H 9LA. Tel: (0171) 495 7775; fax: (0171) 495 7776 **British embassy:** 4th Floor, Trg Republike 3, 61000 Ljubljana. Tel: (61) 125 7191; fax: (61) 125 0174 **Chamber of commerce:** Chamber of Economy of Slovenia, Slovenska 41, 61000 Ljubljana. Tel: (61) 125 0122; fax: (61) 219 536

Chronology

1st century BC: Came under Roman rule. **AD 395:** In division of Roman Empire, stayed in west, along with Croatia and Bosnia. **6th century:** Settled by the Slovene South Slavs. **7th century:** Adopted Christianity as Roman Catholics. **8th–9th centuries:** Under successive rule of Franks and dukes of Bavaria. **907–55:** Came under Hungarian domination. **1335:** Absorbed in Austro-Hungarian Habsburg Empire, as part of Austrian crownlands of Carniola, Styria, and Carinthia. **1848:** Slovene struggle for independence began. **1918:** On collapse of Habsburg Empire, Slovenia united with Serbia, Croatia, and Montenegro to form the 'Kingdom of Serbs, Croats and Slovenes', under Serbian Karageorgevic dynasty. **1929:** Kingdom became known as Yugoslavia. **1941–45:** Occupied by Nazi Germany and Italy during World War II; anti-Nazi Slovene Liberation Front formed and became allies of Marshal Tito's communist-led Partisans. **1945:** Became constituent republic of Yugoslav Socialist Federal Republic. **mid-1980s:** Slovenian Communist Party liberalized itself and agreed to free elections. Yugoslav counterintelligence (KOV) began repression. **1989:** Constitution changed to allow secession from federation. **1990:** Nationalist Democratic Opposition of Slovenia (DEMOS) coalition secured victory in first multiparty parliamentary elections; Milan Kučan, a reform communist, became president. Sovereignty declared. Independence overwhelmingly approved in referendum. **1991:** Seceded from Yugoslav federation, along with Croatia; 100 killed after Yugoslav federal army intervened; cease-fire brokered by European Community (EC) brought withdrawal of Yugoslav army. **1992:** Janez Drnovšek, a centrist Liberal Democrat, appointed prime minister; independence recognized by EC and USA. Admitted into United Nations. Liberal Democrats and Christian Democrats won assembly elections. **1996:** Governing coalition weakened by withdrawal of ZLSD. LDS failed to win overall majority in assembly elections. **1997:** New government formed by ruling LDS, led by Prime Minister Janez Drnovsek. President Kucan re-elected. European Union agreed to open membership talks with Slovenia.

Solomon Islands

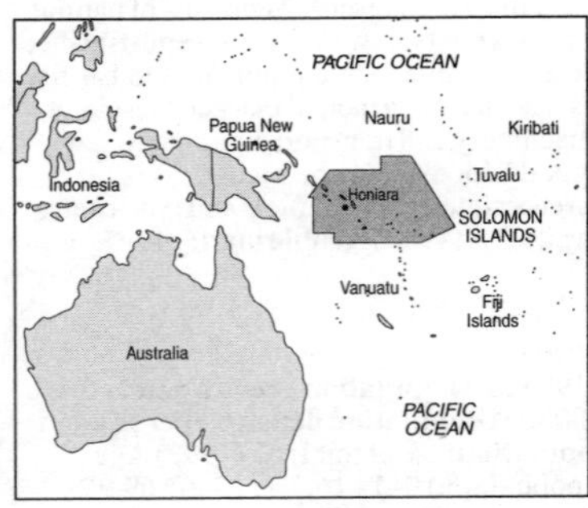

Area: 27,600 sq km/10,656 sq mi **Capital:** Honiara (on Guadalcanal) (and chief port) **Major towns/ cities:** Gizo, Kieta, Auki **Major ports:** Yandina

Government

Head of state: Queen Elizabeth II, represented by governor general Moses Pitakaka from 1994 **Head of government:** Bartholomew Ulufa'alu from 1997 **Political system:** constitutional monarchy **Administrative divisions:** seven provinces and a capital territory **Political parties:** Group for National Unity and Reconciliation (GNUR), centrist coalition; National Coalition Partners (NCP), broad-based coalition; People's Progressive Party (PPP); People's Alliance Party (PAP) **Armed forces:** no standing army; 80-strong marine wing of police force (1995) **Death penalty:** laws do not provide for the death penalty for any crime **Education spend:** (% GNP) 4.2 (1993/94) **Health spend:** (% GDP) 5 (1990)

Economy and resources

Currency: Solomon Island dollar **GDP:** (US$) 400 million (1997 est) **Real GDP growth:** (% change on previous year) 6.0 (1996) **GNP (US$):** 362 million (1997) **GNP per capita (PPP):** (US$) 2,350 (1997 est) **Consumer price inflation:** 8.2% (1997) **Foreign debt:** (US$) 145 million (1996) **Major trading partners:** Australia, Japan, UK, New Zealand, Singapore, South Korea **Resources:** bauxite, phosphates, gold, silver, copper, lead, zinc, cobalt, asbestos, nickel **Exports:** timber, fish products, oil palm products, copra, cocoa, coconut oil. Principal market: Japan 50.5% (1996) **Imports:** rice, machinery and transport equipment, meat preparations, refined sugar, mineral fuels, basic manufactures, construction materials. Principal source: Australia 41.5% (1996) **Arable land:** 1.5% (1995)

Population and society

Population: 417,000 (1998 est) **Population growth rate:** 3.2% (1995–2000); 3.1% (2000–05) **Population density:** (per sq km) 16 (1998 est) **Urban population:** (% of total) 18 (1997) **Age distribution:** (% of total population) 0–14 45.1%, 15–64 51.9%, 65+ 3.0% (1998) **Ethnic groups:** 93% Melanesian, 4% Polynesian, 1.5% Micronesian, 0.7% European, 0.2% Chinese **Language:** English (official); there are some 120 Melanesian dialects spoken by 85% of the population, and Papuan and Polynesian languages **Religion:** Anglican, Roman Catholic, South Sea Evangelical, other Protestant **Education:** not compulsory **Literacy rate:** 60% (men); 60% (women) (1994 est) **Labour force:** 27.4% agriculture, 13.7% industry, 58.9% services (1993) **Life expectancy:** 70 (men); 74 (women) (1995–2000) **Child mortality rate:** (under 5, per 1,000 live births) 27 (1997) **Physicians:** 1 per 5,190 people (1991)

Practical information

Visa requirements: UK: visa not required. USA: visa not required **Embassy for the UK:** BP 3, avenue de l'Yser 13, B-1040 Brussels, Belgium. Tel: (2) 732 7082; fax: (2) 732 6885; Solomon Islands Honorary Consulate, 19 Springfield Road, London SW19 7AL. Tel: (0181) 296 6232; fax: (0181) 946 1744 **British embassy:** British High Commission, PO Box 676, Telekom House, Mendana Avenue, Honiara. Tel: 21705/6; fax: 20765 **Chamber of commerce:** PO Box 64, Honiara. Tel: 22960

Chronology

1568: The islands, rumoured in South America to be the legendary gold-rich 'Islands of Solomon', were first sighted by Spanish navigator Alvaro de Mendana, journeying from Peru. **1595 and 1606:** Unsuccessful Spanish efforts to settle the islands, which had long been peopled by Melanesians. **later 18th century:** Visited again by Europeans. **1840s:** Christian missions established. **1870s:** Development of copra export trade and shipment of islanders to work on sugar cane plantations in Australia and Fiji Islands. **1886:** Northern Solomon Islands became German protectorate. **1893:** Southern Solomon Islands placed under British protection. **1899:** Germany ceded Solomon Islands possessions to Britain in return for British recognition of its claims to Western Samoa. **1900:** Unified British Solomon Islands Protectorate formed and placed under jurisdiction of Western Pacific High Commission (WPHC), with its headquarters in Fiji Islands. **1942–43:** Occupied by Japan. Site of fierce fighting, especially on Guadalcanal, which was recaptured by US forces, with the loss of 21,000 Japanese and 5,000 US troops. **1943–50:** Development of Marching Rule (Ma'asina Ruru) cargo cult populist movement on Malaita island, campaigning for self-rule. **1945:** Headquarters of WPHC moved to Honiara. **1960:** Legislative and executive councils established by constitution. **1974:** Became substantially self-governing, with Solomon Mamaloni of centre-left People's Progressive Party (PPP) as chief minister. **1976:** Became fully self-governing, with Peter Kenilorea of right-of-centre Solomon Islands United Party (SIUPA) as chief minister. **1978:** Independence achieved from Britain within Commonwealth, with Kenilorea as prime minister. **1981:** Mamaloni (PPP) became prime minister, pledging to decentralize power. **1984:** Kenilorea returned to power, heading coalition government. **1986:** Kenilorea resigned after allegations of corruption; replaced by his deputy, Ezekiel Alebua. **1988:** Kenilorea elected deputy prime minister. Joined Vanuatu and Papua New Guinea to form Spearhead Group, aiming to preserve Melanesian cultural traditions. **1989:** Mamaloni, now leader of People's Alliance Party (PAP), appointed prime minister. **1990:** Mamaloni resigned as PAP party leader, but continued as head of a government of national unity, which included Keniloea as foreign minister. **1993:** New Mamaloni-led coalition won largest number of seats in general election, but Francis Billy Hilly, an independent politician, appointed prime minister. **1994:** Billy Hilly resigned; Mamaloni returned to power. **1997:** Bartholomew Ulufa'alu elected prime minister. **1998:** Bartholomew Ulufa'alu's Alliance for Change government narrowly survived a no-confidence vote.

Somalia Somali Democratic Republic

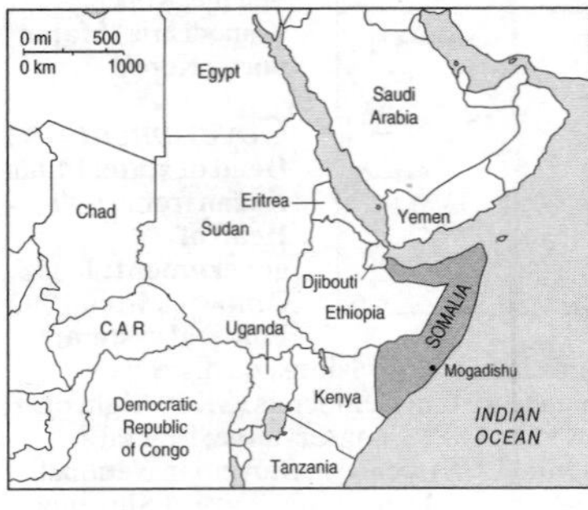

National name: *Jamhuriyadda Dimugradiga ee Soomaliya* **Area:** 637,700 sq km/246,215 sq mi **Capital:** Mogadishu (and port) **Major towns/cities:** Hargeysa, Berbera, Kismayo, Marka **Major ports:** Berbera, Marka, Kismayo

Government

Head of state and government (interim): Hussein Aidid from 1996 **Political system:** transitional **Administrative divisions:** 18 regions **Political parties:** parties are mainly clan-based and include the United Somali Congress (USC), Hawiye clan; Somali Patriotic Movement (SPM), Darod clan; Somali Southern Democratic Front (SSDF), Majertein clan; Somali Democratic Alliance (SDA), Gadabursi clan; United Somali Front (USF), Issa clan; Somali National Movement (SNM) based in self-proclaimed Somaliland Republic **Armed forces:** 225,000 (1997) **Death penalty:** retained and used for ordinary crimes **Defence spend:** (% GDP) 4.8 (1997) **Education spend:** (% GNP) 0.5 (1985); N/A (1993/94) **Health spend:** (% GDP) 0.9 (1990)

Economy and resources

Currency: Somali shilling **GDP:** (US$) 1.2 billion (1995) **Real GDP growth:** (% change on previous year) 0 (1995) **GNP (US$):** N/A **GNP per capita (PPP):** (US$) N/A **Consumer price inflation:** N/A **Foreign debt:** (US$) 2.64 billion (1996) **Major trading partners:** Saudi Arabia, Kenya, Italy, USA, UK, Germany, Ethiopia **Resources:** chromium, coal, salt, tin, zinc, copper, gypsum, manganese, iron ore, uranium, gold, silver; deposits of petroleum and natural gas have been discovered but remain unexploited **Exports:** livestock, skins and hides, bananas, fish and fish products, myrrh. Principal market: Saudi Arabia 54.7% (1996) **Imports:** petroleum, fertilizers, foodstuffs, machinery and parts, manufacturing raw materials. Principal source: Kenya 27.7% (1996) **Arable land:** 1.6% (1995)

Population and society

Population: 9,237,000 (1998 est) **Population growth rate:** 3.9% (1995–2000); 3% (2000–05) **Population density:** (per sq km) 10.9 (1998 est) **Urban population:** (% of total) 27 (1997) **Age distribution:** (% of total population) 0–14 44.2%, 15–64 52.9%, 65+ 2.9% (1998) **Ethnic groups:** 98% indigenous Somali (about 84% Hamitic and 14% Bantu); population is divided into around 100 clans **Language:** Somali, Arabic (both official), Italian, English **Religion:** Sunni Muslim **Education:** (compulsory years) 8 **Literacy rate:** 36% (men); 14% (women) (1995 est) **Labour force:** 44% of population: 75% agriculture, 8% industry, 16% services (1990) **Life expectancy:** 47 (men); 51 (women) (1995–2000) **Child mortality rate:** (under 5, per 1,000 live births) 174 (1997) **Physicians:** 1 per 5,691 people (1990)

Practical information

Visa requirements: UK: visa required. USA: visa required **Embassy in the UK:** no diplomatic representation at present **British embassy:** all staff have been withdrawn for the present; the British Embassy in Addis Ababa (see Ethiopia) deals with enquiries relating to Somalia

Chronology

8th–10th centuries: Arab ancestors of Somali clan families migrated to the region and introduced Sunni Islam; coastal trading cities, including Mogadishu, were formed by Arabian immigrants and developed into sultanates. **11th–14th century:** Southward and westward movement of Somalis and Islamization of Christian Ethiopian interior. **early 16th century:** Portuguese contacts with coastal region. **1820s:** First British contacts with northern Somalia. **1884–87:** British protectorate of Somaliland established in north. **1889:** Italian protectorate of Somalia established in south. **1927:** Italian Somalia became a colony and part of Italian East Africa from 1936. **1941:** Italian Somalia occupied by Britain during World War II. **1943:** Somali Youth League (SYL) formed as nationalist party. **1950:** Italy resumed control over Italian Somalia under UN trusteeship. **1960:** Independence achieved from Italy and Britain as Somalia, with Aden Abdullah Osman as president. **1963:** Border dispute with Kenya; diplomatic relations broken with Britain for five years. **1967:** Dr Abdirashid Ali Shermarke (SYL) became president. **1969:** President Ibrahim Egal assassinated in army coup led by Maj-Gen Muhammad Siad Barre; constitution suspended, political parties banned, Supreme Revolutionary Council set up, and socialist-Islamic state formed. **1972:** 20,000 died in severe drought. **1978:** Defeated in eight-month war with Ethiopia fought on behalf of Somali guerrillas in Ogaden to the southwest. Armed insurrection began in north and hundreds of thousands became refugees. **1979:** New constitution for socialist one-party state dominated by Somali Revolutionary Socialist Party (SRSP). **1982:** Antigovernment Ethiopian-backed Somali National Movement (SNM) formed in north. Oppressive countermeasures by government. **late 1980s:** Guerrilla activity increased in north as civil war intensified. **1991:** Mogadishu captured by rebels; Barre fled; Ali Mahdi Muhammad named president; free elections promised. Secession of northeast Somalia, as Somaliland Republic, announced but not recognized internationally. **1992:** Widespread famine. Western food-aid convoys hijacked by 'warlords'. United Nations peacekeeping troops, led by US Marines, sent in to protect relief operations. **1993:** Leaders of armed factions (excepting Somaliland-based faction) agreed to federal system of government. US-led UN forces destroyed headquarters of warlord Gen Muhammad Farah Aidid after killing of Pakistani peacekeepers. **1994:** Ali Mahdi Muhammad and Aidid signed truce. Majority of Western peacekeeping troops withdrawn, but clan-based fighting continued. **1995:** Last UN peacekeepers withdrawn. **1996:** Aidid killed in renewed faction fighting; his son Hussein Aidid succeeded him, as interim president. **1997:** Peace agreement signed between USC and breakaway USC-SNA. **1998:** Peace plan agreed.

South Africa Republic of

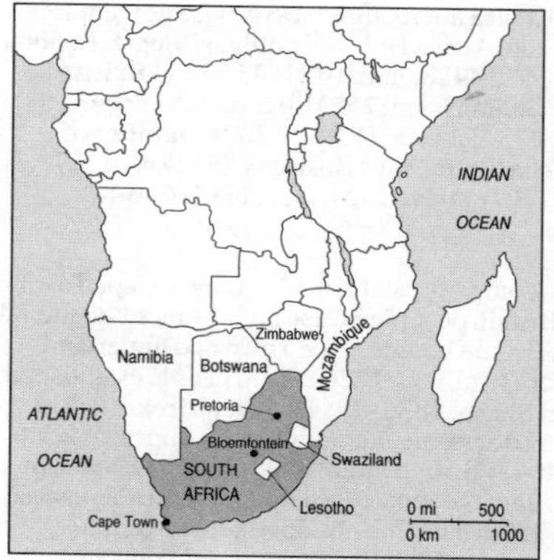

National name: *Republiek van Suid-Afrika* **Area:** 1,222,081 sq km/471,845 sq mi **Capital:** Cape Town (legislative) (and port), Pretoria (administrative), Bloemfontein (judicial) **Major towns/cities:** Johannesburg, Durban, Port Elizabeth, Vereeniging, East London, Pietermaritzburg, Kimberley **Major ports:** Durban, Port Elizabeth, East London **Territories:** Marion Island and Prince Edward Island in the Antarctic

Government

Head of state and government: Thabo Mbeki from 1999 **Political system:** liberal democracy **Administrative divisions:** nine provinces **Political parties:** African National Congress (ANC), left of centre; National Party (NP), right of centre; Inkatha Freedom Party (IFP), centrist, multiracial (formerly Zulu nationalist); Freedom Front (FF), right wing; Democratic Party (DP), moderate, centre left, multiracial; Pan-Africanist Congress (PAC), black, left wing; African Christian Democratic Party (ACDP), Christian, right of centre **Armed forces:** 79,400 (1997) **Conscription:** none **Death penalty:** for exceptional crimes only (from 1995); last execution in 1991 **Defence spend:** (% GDP) 1.8 (1997) **Education spend:** (% GNP) 7.9 (1996) **Health spend:** (% GDP) 3.6 (1990–95)

Economy and resources

Currency: rand **GDP:** (US$) 129.1 billion (1997) **Real GDP growth:** (% change on previous year) 2.0 (1997) **GNP (US$):** 130.2 billion (1997) **GNP per capita (PPP):** (US$) 7,490 (1997) **Consumer price inflation:** 6.5% (1998) **Unemployment:** 29% (early 1995) **Foreign debt:** (US$) 23.6 billion (1996) **Major trading partners:** Germany, Italy, UK, USA, Japan, Switzerland **Resources:** gold (world's largest producer), coal, platinum, iron ore, diamonds, chromium, manganese, limestone, asbestos, fluorspar, uranium, copper, lead, zinc, petroleum, natural gas **Exports:** metals and metal products, gold, precious and semiprecious stones, mineral products and chemicals, natural cultured pearls, machinery and mechanical appliances, wool, maize, fruit, sugar. Principal market: UK 10.1% (1997) **Imports:** machinery and electrical equipment, transport equipment, chemical products, mechanical appliances, textiles and clothing, vegetable products, wood, pulp, paper and paper products. Principal source: Germany 13.7% (1997) **Arable land:** 12.3% (1995)

Population and society

Population: 39,357,000 (1998 est) **Population growth rate:** 2.2% (1995–2000); 2.1% (2000–05) **Population density:** (per sq km) 35.1 (1998 est) **Urban population:** (% of total) 50 (1997) **Age**

distribution: (% of total population) 0–14 34.7%, 15–64 60.8%, 65+ 4.5% (1998) **Ethnic groups:** 77% of the population is black African, 12% white (of European descent), 9% of mixed African–European descent, and 2% Asian **Language:** English and Afrikaans (both official); main African languages: Xhosa, Zulu, and Sesotho (all official) **Religion:** Dutch Reformed Church and other Christian denominations, Hindu, Muslim **Education:** (compulsory years) 10 **Literacy rate:** 81% (men); 81% (women) (1995 est) **Labour force:** 39% of population: 14% agriculture, 32% industry, 55% services (1990) **Life expectancy:** 62 (men); 68 (women) (1995–2000) **Child mortality rate:** (under 5, per 1,000 live births) 68 (1997) **Physicians:** 1 per 1,528 people (1994)

Practical information
Visa requirements: UK: visa not required. USA: visa not required **Embassy in the UK:** South Africa House, Trafalgar Square, London WC2N 5DP. Tel: (0171) 930 4488; fax: (0171) 451 7284 **British embassy:** British High Commission, 255 Hill Street, Arcadia, Pretoria 0002. Tel: (12) 433 121; fax: (12) 433 207 **Chamber of commerce:** South African Chamber of Business, PO Box 91267, Auckland Park 20006. Tel: (11) 482 2524; fax: (11) 726 1344

Chronology
1652: Dutch East India Company established colony at Cape Town as a port of call. **1795:** Britain occupied Cape after France conquered the Netherlands. **1814:** Britain bought Cape Town and hinterland from the Netherlands for £6 million. **1820s:** Zulu people established military kingdom under Shaka. **1836–38:** The Great Trek: 10,000 Dutch settlers (known as Boers, meaning 'farmers') migrated north to escape British rule. **1843:** Britain established colony of Natal on east coast. **1852–54:** Britain recognized Boer republics of Transvaal and Orange Free State. **1872:** The Cape became self-governing colony within British Empire. **1877:** Britain annexed Transvaal. **1879:** Zulu War: Britain destroyed power of Zulus. **1881:** First Boer War: Transvaal Boers defeated British at Majuba Hill and regained independence. **1886:** Disovery of gold on Witwatersrand attracted many migrant miners (uitlanders) to Transvaal, which denied them full citizenship. **1895:** Jameson Raid: uitlanders, backed by Cecil Rhodes, tried to overthrow President Paul Kruger of Transvaal. **1899–1902:** Second South African War (also known as Boer War): dispute over rights of uitlanders led to conflict which ended with British annexation of Boer republics. **1907:** Britain granted internal self-government to Transvaal and Orange Free State on whites-only franchise. **1910:** Cape Colony, Natal, Transvaal, and Orange Free State formed Union of South Africa, with Louis Botha as prime minister. **1912:** Gen Barry Hertzog founded (Boer) Nationalist Party; ANC formed to campaign for rights of black majority. **1914:** Boer revolt in Orange Free State suppressed; South African troops fought for British Empire in World War I. **1919:** Jan Smuts succeeded Botha as premier; South West Africa (Namibia) became South African mandate. **1924:** Hertzog became prime minister, aiming to sharpen racial segregation and loosen ties with British Empire. **1939–45:** Smuts led South Africa into World War II despite neutralism of Hertzog; South African troops fought with Allies in Middle East, East Africa, and Italy. **1948:** Policy of apartheid ('separateness') adopted when National Party (NP) took power under Daniel Malan; continued by his successors Johannes Strijdom 1954–58, Hendrik Verwoerd 1958–66, B J Vorster 1966–78, and P J Botha 1978–89. **1950:** Entire population classified by race; Group Areas Act segregated blacks and whites; ANC responded with campaign of civil disobedience. **1960:** 70 black demonstrators killed at Sharpville; ANC banned. **1961:** South Africa left Commonwealth and became republic. **1964:** ANC leader Nelson Mandela sentenced to life imprisonment. **1967:** Terrorism Act introduced indefinite detention without trial. **1970s:** Over 3 million people forcibly resettled in black 'homelands'. **1976:** Over 600 killed in clashes between black protesters and security forces in Soweto. **1984:** New constitution gave segregated representation to coloureds and Asians, but continued to exclude blacks. **1985:** Growth of violence in black townships led to proclamation of state of emergency. **1986:** USA and Commonwealth imposed limited economic sanctions against South Africa. **1989:** F W de Klerk succeeded P W Botha as president; public facilities desegregated; many ANC activists released. **1990:** Ban on ANC lifted; Mandela released; talks began between government and ANC; daily average of 35 murders; Namibia became independent. **1991:** De Klerk repealed remaining apartheid laws; sanctions lifted; severe fighting between ANC and Zulu Inkatha movement. **1993:** Interim majority rule constitution adopted; de Klerk and Mandela agreed to form government of national unity after free elections. **1994:** ANC victory in first nonracial elections; Mandela became president; Commonwealth membership restored. **1996:** De Klerk withdrew NP from coalition after new constitution failed to provide for power-sharing after 1999. **1997:** New constitution signed by President Mandela. F W de Klerk announced his retirement from politics. Thabo Mbeki succeeded Mandela as ANC president. **1999:** Mandela retired as state president; Thabo Mbeki won presidential election; ANC won assembly majority.

Spain Kingdom of

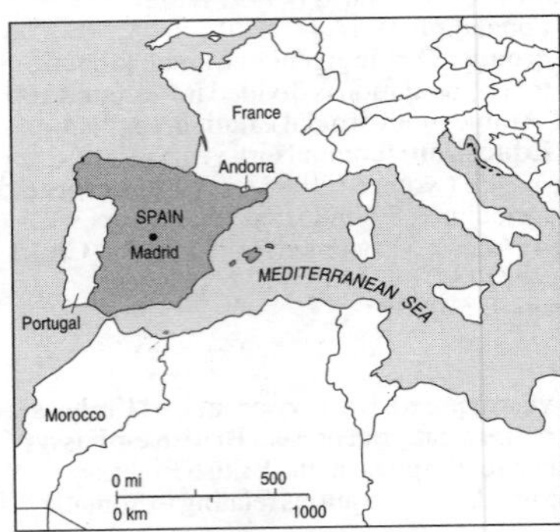

National name: *Reino de España* **Area:** 504,750 sq km/194,883 sq mi **Capital:** Madrid **Major towns/cities:** Barcelona, Valencia, Zaragoza, Seville, Málaga, Bilbao, Las Palmas de Gran Canarias, Murcia, Córdoba, Palma de Mallorca, Granada **Major ports:** Barcelona, Valencia, Cartagena, Málaga, Cádiz, Vigo, Santander, Bilbao **Territories:** Balearic and Canary Islands; in North Africa: Ceuta, Melilla, Alhucemas, Chafarinas Islands, Peñón de Vélez

Government
Head of state: King Juan Carlos I from 1975 **Head of government:** José Maria Aznar from 1996 **Political system:** constitutional monarchy **Administrative divisions:** 17 autonomous regions (contain 50 provinces) **Political parties:** Socialist Workers' Party (PSOE), democratic socialist; Popular Party (PP), centre right **Armed forces:** 197,500 (1997) **Conscription:** nine months **Death penalty:** abolished in 1995 **Defence spend:** (% GDP) 1.4 (1997) **Education spend:** (% GNP) 5.0 (1995) **Health spend:** (% GDP) 6.0 (1990–95)

Economy and resources
Currency: peseta **GDP:** (US$) 531.3 billion (1997) **Real GDP growth:** (% change on previous year) 3.3 (1997) **GNP (US$):** 570.1 billion (1997) **GNP per capita (PPP):** (US$) 15,720 (1997) **Consumer price inflation:** 2.3% (1998) **Unemployment:** 18.8% (1998) **Major trading partners:** EU (principally France, Germany, Italy, and UK), USA, Japan **Resources:** coal, lignite, anthracite, copper, iron, zinc, uranium, potassium salts **Exports:** motor vehicles, machinery and electrical equipment, vegetable products, metals and their manufactures, foodstuffs. Principal market: France 20.1% (1997) **Imports:** machinery and transport equipment, electrical equipment, petroleum and petroleum products, chemicals, consumer goods. Principal source: France 17.4% (1997) **Arable land:** 30.5% (1995)

Population and society
Population: 39,628,000 (1998 est) **Population growth rate:** 0.1% (1995–2000) **Population density:** (per sq km) 78.4 (1998 est) **Urban population:** (% of total) 77 (1997) **Age distribution:** (% of total population) 0–14 15.2%, 15–64 68.5%, 65+ 16.3% (1998) **Ethnic groups:** mostly of Moorish, Roman, and Carthaginian descent **Language:** Spanish (Castilian, official), Basque, Catalan, Galician **Religion:** Roman Catholic **Education:** (compulsory years) 10 **Literacy rate:** 97% (men); 93% (women) (1995 est) **Labour force:**

41.1% of population: 8.7% agriculture, 29.7% industry, 61.6% services (1996) **Life expectancy:** 75 (men); 82 (women) (1995–2000) **Child mortality rate:** (under 5, per 1,000 live births) 9 (1997) **Physicians:** 1 per 238 people (1995)

Practical information

Visa requirements: UK: visa not required. USA: visa not required **Embassy in the UK:** 24 Belgrave Square, London SW1X 8SB. Tel: (0171) 235 5555/6/7; fax: (0171) 235 9905 **British embassy:** Calle de Fernando el Santo 16, 28010 Madrid. Tel: (9) 319 0200, fax: (9) 319 0423 **Chamber of commerce:** Consejo Superior de Cámaras Officiales de Comercio, Industria y Navigación de España, Calle Claudio Coello 19, 1 º, 28001 Madrid. Tel: (9) 575 3400; fax: (9) 435 2392

Chronology

2nd century BC: Roman conquest of the Iberian peninsula, which became the province of Hispania. **5th century AD:** After the fall of the Roman Empire, Iberia was overrun by Vandals and Visigoths. **711:** Muslims invaded from North Africa and overthrew Visigoth kingdom. **9th century:** Christians in northern Spain formed kingdoms of Asturias, Aragón, Navarre, and Léon, and county of Castile. **10th century:** Abd-al-Rahman III established caliphate of Córdoba; Muslim culture at its height in Spain. **1230:** Léon and Castile united under Ferdinand III, who drove the Muslims from most of southern Spain. **14th century:** Spain consisted of Christian kingdoms of Castile, Aragón, and Navarre, and the Muslim emirate of Granada. **1469:** Marriage of Ferdinand of Aragón and Isabella of Castile; kingdoms united on their accession in 1479. **1492:** Conquest of Granada ended Muslim rule in Spain. **1494:** Treaty of Tordesillas; Spain and Portugal divided newly discovered America; Spain became a world power. **1519–56:** Emperor Charles V was both King of Spain and Archduke of Austria; he also ruled Naples, Sicily, and the Low Countries; Habsburgs dominant in Europe. **1555:** Charles V divided his domains between Spain and Austria before retiring; Spain retained the Low Countries and southern Italy as well as South American colonies. **1568:** Dutch rebelled against Spanish rule; Spain recognized independence of Dutch Republic in 1648. **1580:** Philip II of Spain inherited the throne of Portugal, where Spanish rule lasted until 1640. **1588:** Spanish Armada: attempt to invade England defeated. **17th century:** Spanish power declined amid wars, corruption, inflation, and loss of civil and religious freedom. **1701–14:** War of the Spanish Succession: allied powers fought France to prevent Philip of Bourbon inheriting throne of Spain. **1713–14:** Treaties of Utrecht and Rastat: Bourbon dynasty recognized, but Spain lost Gibraltar, southern Italy, and Spanish Netherlands. **1793:** Spain declared war on revolutionary France; reduced to a French client state in 1795. **1808:** Napoleon installed his brother Joseph as King of Spain. **1808–14:** Peninsular War: British forces played a large part in liberating Spain and restoring Bourbon dynasty. **1810–30:** Spain lost control of its South American colonies. **1833–39:** Carlist civil war: Don Carlos (backed by conservatives) unsuccessfully contested the succession of his niece Isabella II (backed by liberals). **1870:** Offer of Spanish throne to Leopold of Hohenzollern-Sigmaringen sparked Franco-Prussian War. **1873–74:** First republic ended by military coup which restored Bourbon dynasty with Alfonso XII. **1898:** Spanish-American War: Spain lost Cuba and Philippines. **1923–30:** Dictatorship of Gen Primo de Rivera with support of Alfonso XIII. **1931:** Proclamation of Second Republic, initially dominated by anticlerical radicals and socialists. **1933:** Moderates and Catholics won elections; insurrection by socialists and Catalans in 1934. **1936:** Left-wing Popular Front narrowly won fresh elections; General Francisco Franco launched military rebellion. **1936–39:** Spanish Civil War: Nationalists (with significant Italian and German support) defeated Republicans (with limited Soviet support); Franco became dictator of nationalist-fascist regime. **1941:** Though officially neutral in World War II, Spain sent 40,000 troops to fight USSR. **1955:** Spain admitted to the United Nations (UN). **1975:** Death of Franco; succeeded by King Juan Carlos I. **1978:** Referendum endorsed democratic constitution. **1982:** Socialists took office under Felipe González; Spain joined the North Atlantic Treaty Organization (NATO); Basque separatist organization (ETA) stepped up terrorist campaign. **1986:** Spain joined the European Economic Community (EEC). **1996:** José Maria Aznar formed a minority PP government. **1997:** 23 Basque nationalist leaders jailed for terrorist activities. **1998:** ETA announced indefinite cease-fire. Government announced that it would begin peace talks.

Spain: Regions

(– = not applicable.)

Region	Capital	Area sq km	Area sq mi	Population (1995)
Andalusia	Seville	87,268	33,694	7,314,600
Aragon	Zaragoza	47,669	18,405	1,205,700
Asturias	Oviedo	10,565	4,079	1,117,400
Balearic Islands	Palma de Mallorca	5,014	1,935	788,000
Basque Country	Vitoria	7,261	2,803	2,130,800
Canary Islands	Las Palmas and Santa Cruz de Tenerife	7,273	2,808	1,631,500
Cantabria	Santander	5,289	2,042	541,900
Castilla–La Mancha	Toledo	79,226	30,589	1,730,700
Castilla–León	Valladolid	94,147	36,350	2,584,400
Catalonia	Barcelona	31,930	12,328	6,226,900
Extremadura	Mérida	41,602	16,063	1,100,500
Galicia	Santiago de Compostela	29,434	11,364	2,825,000
La Rioja	Longroño	5,034	1,944	268,200
Madrid	Madrid	7,995	3,087	5,181,700
Murcia	Murcia[1]	11,317	4,369	1,110,000
Navarra	Pamplona	10,421	4,024	536,200
Valencia	Valencia	23,305	8,998	4,028,800
Ceuta[2]	–	18	7	73,100
Melilla[2]	–	14	5	64,700

[1] Regional parliament is in Cartagena.

[2] Spanish enclave on the north coast of Morocco.

Sri Lanka **Democratic Socialist Republic of** (formerly to 1972 **Ceylon**)

National name: *Sri Lanka Prajathanthrika Samajawadi Janarajaya* **Area:** 65,610 sq km/25,332 sq mi **Capital:** Colombo (and chief port) **Major towns/cities:** Kandy, Dehiwala-Mount Lavinia, Moratuwa, Jaffna, Kotte, Kandy **Major ports:** Jaffna, Galle, Negombo, Trincomalee

Government

Head of state: Chandrika Bandaranaike Kumaratunga from 1994 **Head of government:** Sirimavo Bandaranaike from 1994 **Political system:** liberal democracy **Administrative divisions:** nine provinces, 25 districts **Political parties:** United National Party (UNP), right of centre; Sri Lanka Freedom Party (SLFP), left of centre; Democratic United National Front (DUNF), centre left; Tamil United Liberation Front (TULF), Tamil autonomy (banned from 1983); Eelam People's Revolutionary Liberation Front (EPRLF), Indian-backed Tamil-secessionist 'Tamil Tigers'; People's Liberation Front (JVP), Sinhalese-chauvinist, left wing (banned 1971–77 and 1983–88) **Armed forces:** 117,000 plus paramilitary forces numbering around 110,200 (1997) **Conscription:** military service is voluntary **Death penalty:** retains the death penalty for ordinary crimes but can be considered abolitionist in practice (last execution 1976) **Defence spend:** (% GDP) 6.1 (1997) **Education spend:** (% GNP) 3.4 (1995) **Health spend:** (% GDP) 1.4 (1990–95)

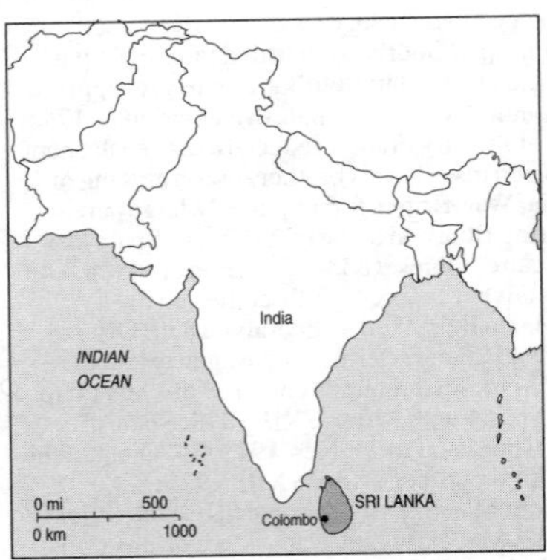

Economy and resources

Currency: Sri Lankan rupee **GDP:** (US$) 15.1 billion (1997) **Real GDP growth:** (% change on previous year) 5.6 (1997) **GNP (US$):** 14.8 billion (1997) **GNP per capita (PPP):** (US$) 2,460 (1997) **Consumer price inflation:** 9% (1998) **Unemployment:** 12.5% (1995) **Foreign debt:** (US$) 7.99 billion (1996) **Major trading partners:** Japan, USA, Germany, UK, India, Malaysia, Singapore, Hong Kong, Taiwan, China, Iran **Resources:** gemstones, graphite, iron ore, monazite, rutile, uranium, iemenite sands, limestone, salt, clay **Exports:** clothing and textiles, tea (world's largest exporter and third-largest producer), precious and semi-precious stones, coconuts and coconut products, rubber. Principal market: USA 35.8% (1997) **Imports:** machinery and transport equipment, petroleum, food and live animals, beverages, construction materials. Principal source: India 9.9% (1997) **Arable land:** 14.1% (1995)

Population and society

Population: 18,455,000 (1998 est) **Population growth rate:** 1.0% (1995–2000) **Population density:** (per sq km) 292.5 (1998 est) **Urban population:** (% of total) 23 (1997) **Age distribution:** (% of total population) 0–14 27.6%, 15–64 66.1%, 65+ 6.3% (1998) **Ethnic groups:** 73% Sinhalese, 19% Tamil, and 7% Moors or Muslims (concentrated in east); the Tamil community is divided between the long-settled 'Sri Lankan Tamils' (11% of the population), who reside in northern and eastern coastal areas, and the more recent immigrant 'Indian Tamils' (8%), who settled in the Kandyan highlands during the 19th and 20th centuries **Language:** Sinhala, Tamil, English **Religion:** Buddhist 69%, Hindu 15%, Muslim 8%, Christian 7% **Education:** (compulsory years) 10 **Literacy rate:** 93% (men); 83% (women) (1995 est) **Labour force:** 42.6% agriculture, 11.7% industry, 45.7% services (1993) **Life expectancy:** 71 (men); 75 (women) (1995–2000) **Child mortality rate:** (under 5, per 1,000 live births) 18 (1997) **Physicians:** 1 per 6,843 people (1993 est)

Practical information

Visa requirements: UK: visa only required by business visitors. USA: visa only required by business visitors **Embassy in the UK:** 13 Hyde Park Gardens, London W2 2LU. Tel: (0171) 262 1841; fax: (0171) 262 7970 **British embassy:** PO Box 1433, 190 Galle Road, Kollupitiya, Colombo 3. Tel: (1) 437 336; fax: (1) 430 308 **Chamber of commerce:** Federation of Chambers of Commerce and Industry of Sri Lanka, 29 Gregory's Road, Colombo 7. Tel: (1) 698 225; fax: (1) 699 530

Chronology

c. **550 BC:** Arrival of the Sinhalese, led by Vijaya, from northern India, displacing long-settled Veddas. **5th century BC:** Sinhalese kingdom of Anuradhapura founded by King Pandukabaya. *c.* **250–210 BC:** Buddhism, brought from India, became established in Sri Lanka. **AD 992:** Downfall of Anuradhapura kingdom, defeated by South Indian Colas. **1070:** Overthrow of Colas by Vijayabahu I and establishment of the Sinhalese kingdom of Polonnaruva, which survived for more than two centuries before a number of regional states arose. **late 15th century:** Kingdom of Kandy established in central highlands. **1505:** Arrival of Portuguese navigator Lorenço de Almeida, attracted by spice trade developed by Arab merchants who had called the island Serendip. **1597–1618:** Portuguese controlled most of Sri Lanka, with the exception of Kandy. **1658:** Dutch conquest of Portuguese territories. **1795–98:** British conquest of Dutch territories. **1802:** Treaty of Amiens recognized island as British colony of Ceylon. **1815:** British won control of Kandy, becoming first European power to rule whole island. **1830s:** Immigration of south Indian Hindu Tamil labourers to work central coffee plantations. **1880s:** Tea and rubber become chief cash crops after blight ended production of coffee. **1919:** Formation of the Ceylon National Congress to campaign for self rule; increasing conflicts between Sinhalese majority community and Tamil minority. **1931:** Universal adult suffrage introduced for elected legislature and executive council in which power was shared with British. **1948:** Ceylon achieved independence from Britain within Commonwealth, with Don Senanayake of conservative United National Party (UNP) as prime minister. **1949:** Indian Tamils disenfranchised. **1952:** Death of Don Senanayake, who was succeeded as prime minister by his son, Dudley. **1956:** Sinhala established as official language; Solomon Bandaranaike became prime minister. **1959:** Bandaranaike assassinated. **1960:** Sirimavo Bandaranaike, the widow of Solomon, won general election and formed SLFP government, which nationalized oil industry. **1965:** General election won by UNP; Dudley Senanayake became prime minister. **1970:** Sirimavo Bandaranaike returned to power as prime minister, leading United Front government. **1971:** Sinhalese Marxist uprising, led by students and People's Liberation Army (JVP). **1972:** Socialist Republic of Sri Lanka proclaimed; Buddhism given 'foremost place' in new state, antagonizing Tamils. **1976:** Tamil United Liberation Front formed to fight for independent Tamil state ('Eelam') in north and east Sri Lanka. **1978:** Presidential constitution adopted by new free-market government headed by Junius Jayawardene of UNP. **1983:** Ethnic riots as Tamil guerrilla violence escalated; state of emergency imposed; more than 1,000 Tamils killed by Sinhalese mobs. **1987:** President Jayawardene and Indian prime minister Rajiv Gandhi signed Colombo Accord aimed at creating new provincial councils, disarming Tamil militants ('Tamil Tigers'), and stationing 7,000-strong Indian Peace Keeping Force. Violence continued despite cease-fire policed by Indian troops. **1988:** Left-wing JVP guerrillas campaigned against Indo-Sri Lankan peace pact. Prime Minister Ranasinghe Premadasa elected president. **1989:** Dingiri Banda Wijetunga became prime minister. Leaders of Tamil Tigers and banned Sinhala extremist JVP assassinated. **1990:** Indian peacekeeping force withdrawn. Violence continued, with death toll exceeding 1,000 per month. **1991:** Defence minister Ranjan Wijeratne assassinated; Sri Lankan army killed 2,552 Tamil Tigers at Elephant Pass in northern Jaffna region. Impeachment motion against President Premadasa failed. A new party, Democratic National United Front (DUNF), formed by former members of UNP. **1992:** Several hundred Tamil Tiger rebels killed in army offensive, code-named 'Strike Force Two'. **1993:** DUNF leader and President Premadasa assassinated by Tamil Tiger terrorists; succeeded by Dingiri Banda Wijetunge. **1994:** UNP narrowly defeated in general election; Chandrika Kumaratunga became prime minister of SLFP-led left-of-centre coalition. Peace talks opened with Tamil Tigers. Kumaratunga elected first female president; her mother, Sirimavo Bandaranaike, became prime minister. **1995:** Renewed bombing campaign by Tamil Tigers. Major offensive drove out Tamil Tigers from Jaffna city. **1996:** State of emergency extended nationwide after Tamils bombed capital. Government forces launched new major offensive against Tamil Tigers. **1997:** Major offensive launched against Tamil separatists. Bomb attack and clashes with Tamil separatists threatened to derail government's peace initiative. **1998:** Tamil Tigers outlawed after bombing of Sri Lanka's holiest Buddhist site. Sept: over 1,300 Sri Lankan soldiers and Tamil Tiger rebels died in renewed fighting in the north. Oct: Tamil Tigers captured the strategic northern town of Kilinochchi, killing more than 600 government troops; government launched new military operation against Tamil Tigers.

Sudan Democratic Republic of

National name: *Jamhuryat es-Sudan* **Area:** 2,505,800 sq km/967,489 sq mi **Capital:** Khartoum **Major towns/cities:** Omdurman, Port Sudan, Juba, Wadi Medani, al-Obeid, Kassala, Atbara, al-Qadarif, Kosti **Major ports:** Port Sudan

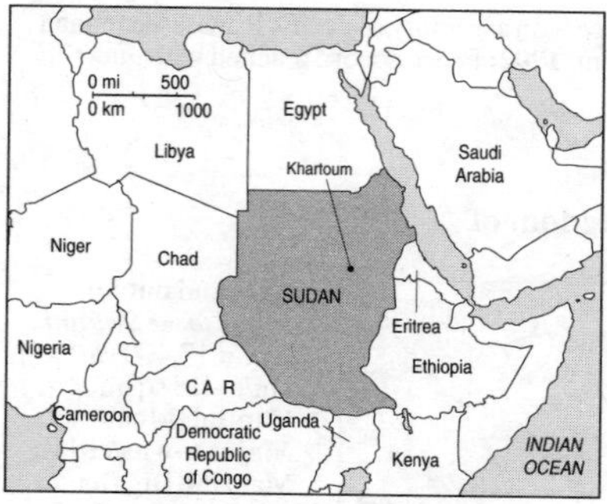

Government

Head of state and government: Gen Omar Hassan Ahmed al-Bashir from 1989 **Political system:** emergent democracy **Administrative divisions:** 26 states **Political parties:** officially banned from 1989, but an influential grouping is the fundamentalist National Islamic Front **Armed forces:** 79,700 (1997) **Conscription:** military service is compulsory for three years **Death penalty:** retained and used for ordinary crimes **Defence spend:** (% GDP) 5.6 (1997) **Education spend:** (% GNP) 4 (1985); N/A (1993/94) **Health spend:** (% GDP) 0.5 (1990)

Economy and resources

Currency: Sudanese dinar **GDP:** (US$) 7 billion (1997 est) **Real GDP growth:** (% change on previous year) 4.5 (1996) **GNP (US$):** 7.8 billion (1997) **GNP per capita (PPP):** (US$) 890 (1997 est) **Consumer price inflation:** 130% (1996) **Unemployment:** 30% (1993 est) **Foreign debt:** (US$) 16.9 billion (1996) **Major trading partners:** Saudi Arabia, Libya, Thailand, Italy, Germany, UK, China, Japan **Resources:** petroleum, marble, mica, chromite, gypsum, gold, graphite, sulphur, iron, manganese, zinc, fluorspar, talc, limestone, dolomite, pumice **Exports:** cotton, sesame seed, gum arabic, sorghum, livestock, hides and skins. Principal market: Saudi Arabia 21.3% (1997) **Imports:** basic manufacture, crude materials (mainly petroleum and petroleum products), foodstuffs, machinery and equipment. Principal source: Libya 16.7% (1997) **Arable land:** 5.4% (1995)

Population and society

Population: 28,292,000 (1998 est) **Population growth rate:** 2.2% (1995–2000) **Population density:** (per sq km) 14.1 (1998 est) **Urban population:** (% of total) 34 (1997) **Age distribution:** (% of total population) 0–14 45.4%, 15–64 52.4%, 65+ 2.2% (1998) **Ethnic groups:** over 50 ethnic groups and almost 600 subgroups; the population is broadly distributed between Arabs in the north and black Africans in the south **Language:** Arabic 51% (official), local languages **Religion:** Sunni Muslim; also animist and Christian **Education:** (compulsory years) 6 **Literacy rate:** 43% (men); 12% (women) (1995 est) **Labour force:** 36% of population: 69% agriculture, 8% industry, 22% services (1990) **Life expectancy:** 54 (men); 56 (women) (1995–2000) **Child mortality rate:** (under 5, per 1,000 live births) 108 (1997) **Physicians:** 1 per 8,979 people (1990)

Practical information

Visa requirements: UK: visa required. USA: visa required **Embassy in the UK:** 3 Cleveland Row, St James Street, London SW1A 1DD. Tel: (0171) 839 8080; fax: (0171) 839 7560 **British embassy:** PO Box 801, Street 10, off Sharia Al Baladiya, Khartoum East. Tel: (11) 770 769; telex: 22189 (a/b PRDRM SD) **Chamber of commerce:** PO Box 81, Khartoum. Tel: (11) 72346

Chronology

c. **600 BC:–AD 350:** Meroê, near Khartoum, was capital of the Nubian Empire, which covered southern Egypt and northern Sudan. **6th century:** Converted to Coptic Christianity. **7th century:** Islam first introduced by Arab invaders, but did not spread widely until the 15th century. **16th–18th centuries:** Arab-African Fur and Fung Empires established in central and northern Sudan. **1820:** Invaded by Muhammad Ali and brought under Egyptian control. **1881–85:** Revolt led to capture of Khartoum by Sheik Muhammad Ahmed, a self-proclaimed Mahdi ('messiah'), and the killing of British general Charles Gordon. **1898:** Anglo-Egyptian offensive led by Lord Kitchener subdued Mahdi revolt at Battle of Omdurman in which 20,000 Sudanese died. **1899:** Sudan administered as Anglo-Egyptian condominium. **1923:** White Flag League formed by Sudanese nationalists in north; British instituted policy of reducing contact between northern and southern Sudan, with the aim that the south would eventually become part of federation of eastern African states. **1955:** Civil war between the dominant Arab Muslim north and black African Christian and animist south broke out. **1956:** Sudan achieved independence from Britain and Egypt as a republic. **1958:** Military coup replaced civilian government with Supreme Council of the Armed Forces. **1964:** Civilian rule reinstated after October Revolution of student demonstrations. **1969:** Coup led by Col Gaafar Mohammed al-Nimeri abolished political institutions and concentrated power in a leftist Revolutionary Command Council. **1971:** Nimeri confirmed as president and the Sudanese Socialist Union (SSU) declared the only legal party by a new constitution. **1972:** Plans to form Federation of Arab Republics, comprising Sudan, Egypt, and Syria, abandoned due to internal opposition. To end 17-year-long civil war, Nimeri agreed to give south greater autonomy. **1974:** National assembly established. **1980:** Country reorganized into six regions, each with own assembly and effective autonomy. **1983:** Shari'a (Islamic law) imposed. Sudan People's Liberation Movement (SPLM) formed in south as civil war broke out again. **1985:** Nimeri deposed in a bloodless coup led by Gen Swar al-Dahab following industrial unrest in north. **1986:** Coalition government formed after general election, with Sadiq al-Mahdi, great-grandson of the Mahdi, as prime minister. **1987:** Civil war with Sudan People's Liberation Army (SPLA); drought and famine in south and refugee influx from Ethiopa and Chad. **1988:** Peace pact signed with SPLA, but fighting continued. **1989:** Al-Mahdi overthrown in coup led by Islamic fundamentalist Gen Omar Hassan Ahmed el-Bashir. All political activity suspended. **1991:** Federal system introduced, with division of country into nine states as civil war continued. **1996:** First presidential and parliamentary elections held since coup of 1989. **1998:** Civil war continued between SPLA and the Islamist government. Famine in south, where millions faced starvation. USA launched missile attack on suspected chemical weapons-producing site in retaliation for bombings of US embassies in Nairobi and Dar es Salaam. SPLA temporary cease-fire. **1999:** Multi-party politics reintroduced.

Suriname Republic of (formerly Dutch Guiana)

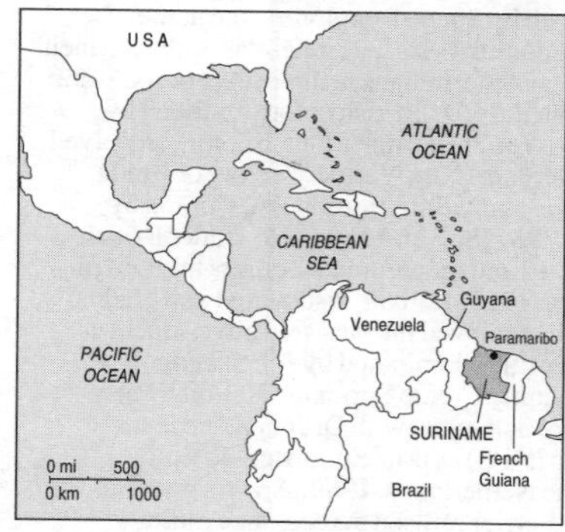

National name: *Republiek Suriname* **Area:** 163,820 sq km/63,250 sq mi **Capital:** Paramaribo **Major towns/cities:** Nieuw Nickerie, Moengo, Pontoetoe, Brokopondo, Nieuw Amsterdam

Government

Head of state: Jules Wijdenbosch from 1996 **Head of government:** Prataapnarain Shawh Radhecheran Radhakishun from 1996 **Political system:** emergent democracy **Administrative divisions:** ten districts **Political parties:** New Front (NF), alliance of four left-of-centre parties: Party for National Unity and Solidarity (KTPI), Suriname National Party (NPS), Progressive Reform Party (VHP), Suriname Labour Party (SPA); National Democratic Party (NDP), left of centre; Democratic Alternative 1991 (DA '91), alliance of three left-of-centre parties **Armed forces:** 1,800 (1997) **Conscription:** military service is voluntary **Death penalty:** retains the death penalty for ordinary crimes but can be considered abolitionist in practice (last execution 1982) **Defence spend:** (% GDP) 4.4 (1997) **Education spend:** (% GNP) 3.5 (1995) **Health spend:** (% GDP) 5.7 (1990)

Economy and resources

Currency: Suriname guilder **GDP:** (US$) 555 million (1997 est) **Real GDP growth:** (% change on previous year) 4.5 (1997) **GNP (US$):** 544 million (1997) **GNP per capita (PPP):** (US$) 2,740 (1997 est) **Consumer price inflation:** 6.0% (1997) **Unemployment:** 16.3% (1993) **Foreign debt:** (US$) 68.2 million (1995) **Major trading partners:** USA, Norway, Trinidad and Tobago, the Netherlands, Netherlands Antilles, Brazil, Japan **Resources:** petroleum, bauxite (one of the world's leading producers), iron ore, copper, manganese, nickel, platinum, gold, kaolin **Exports:** alumina, aluminium, shrimps, bananas, plantains, rice, wood and wood products. Principal market: USA 16.4% (1997) **Imports:** raw materials and semi-manufactured goods, mineral fuels and lubricants, investment goods, foodstuffs, cars and motorcycles, textiles. Principal source: USA 35.4% (1997) **Arable land:** 0.4% (1995)

Population and society

Population: 414,000 (1998 est) **Population growth rate:** 1.2% (1995–2000) **Population density:** (per sq km) 2.7 (1998 est) **Urban population:** (% of total) 51 (1997) **Age distribution:** (% of total population) 0–14 33.3%, 15–64 61.5%, 65+ 5.2% (1998) **Ethnic groups:** a wide ethnic composition, including Creoles, East Indians, Indonesians, Africans, American Indians, Europeans, and Chinese **Language:** Dutch (official), Sranan (creole), English, Hindi, Javanese, Chinese. Spanish is the main working language **Religion:** Christian, Hindu, Muslim **Education:** (compulsory years) 11 **Literacy rate:** 95% (men); 95% (women) (1994 est) **Labour force:** 20% agriculture, 20% industry, 60% services (1992) **Life expectancy:** 69 (men); 74 (women) (1995–2000) **Child mortality rate:** (under 5, per 1,000 live births) 25 (1997) **Physicians:** 1 per 1,605 people (1994)

Practical information

Visa requirements: UK: visa not required. USA: visa required **Embassy for the UK:** Alexander Gogelweg 2, 2517 JH The Hague, The Netherlands. Tel: (70) 365 0844; fax: (70) 361 7445 **British embassy:** British Honorary Consulate, c/o VSH United Buildings, PO Box 1860, Van't Hogerhuysstraat 9–11, Paramaribo. Tel: (597) 472 870; fax: (597) 475 515 **Chamber of commerce:** Suriname Chamber of Commerce and Industry, PO Box 149, Dr J C de Mirandasstraat 10, Paramaribo. Tel: (597) 473 527; fax: (597) 474 779

Chronology

AD **1593:** Visited and claimed by Spanish explorers; the name Suriname derived from the country's earliest inhabitants, the Surinen, who were driven out by other Amerindians in the 16th century. **1602:** Dutch settlements established. **1651:** British colony founded by settlers sent from Barbados. **1667:** Became a Dutch colony, received in exchange for New Amsterdam (New York) by Treaty of Breda. **1682:** Coffee and sugar cane plantations introduced, worked by imported African slaves. **1795–1802 and 1804–16:** Under British rule. **1863:** Slavery abolished and indentured labourers brought in from China, India, and Java. **1915:** Bauxite discovered and gradually became main export. **1954:** Achieved internal self-government as Dutch Guiana. **1958–69:** Politics dominated by Johan Pengel, charismatic leader of the mainly Creole Suriname National Party (NPS). **1975:** Independence achieved, with Dr Johan Ferrier as president and Henck Arron (NPS) as prime minister; 40% of population emigrated to the Netherlands. **1980:** Arron's government overthrown in army coup; Ferrier refused to recognize military regime; appointed Dr Henk Chin A Sen of the Nationalist Republican Party (PNR) to lead civilian administration. Army replaced Ferrier with Dr Chin A Sen. **1982:** Army, led by Lt Col Desi Bouterse, seized power, setting up a Revolutionary People's Front; economic aid from the Netherlands and US cut off after opposition leaders, charged with plotting a coup, were executed. **1985:** Ban on political activities lifted. **1986:** Antigovernment rebels brought economic chaos to Suriname. **1988:** Ramsewak Shankar of the combined opposition parties elected president under new constitution. **1989:** Bouterse rejected peace accord reached by President Shankar with guerrilla insurgents, the Bush Negro (descendents of escaped slaves) maroons, and vowed to continue fighting. **1990:** Shankar deposed in army coup engineered by Bouterse. **1991:** Johan Kraag (NPS) became interim president. New Front opposition alliance won assembly majority. Ronald Venetiaan elected civilian president. **1992:** Peace accord reached with guerrilla groups.

Swaziland Kingdom of

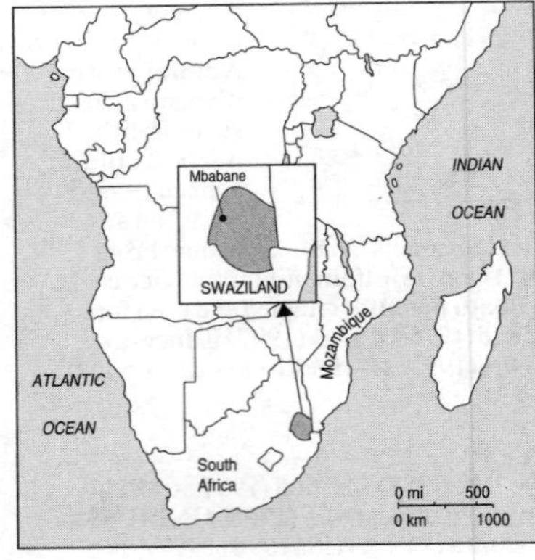

National name: *Umbuso we Swatini* **Area:** 17,400 sq km/6,718 sq mi **Capital:** Mbabane **Major towns/cities:** Manzini, Big Bend, Mhlume, Havelock Mine, Nhlangano

Government

Head of state: King Mswati III from 1986 **Head of government:** Barnabas Sibusiso Dlamini from 1997 **Political system:** transitional absolute monarchy **Administrative divisions:** four regions **Political parties:** Imbokodvo National Movement (INM), nationalist monarchist; Swaziland United Front (SUF), left of centre; Swaziland Progressive Party (SPP), left of centre; People's United Democratic Movement, left of centre **Armed forces:** 127,280 (1995) **Conscription:** military service is compulsory for two years **Death penalty:** retained and used for ordinary crimes **Defence spend:** (% GDP) 2.5 (1993 est) **Education spend:** (% GNP) 7.3 (1996) **Health spend:** (% GDP) 1.1 (1990)

Economy and resources

Currency: lilangeni **GDP:** (US$) 1.2 billion (1997 est) **Real GDP growth:** (% change on previous year) 3.2 (1997) **GNP (US$):** 1.3 billion (1997) **GNP per capita (PPP):** (US$) 3,560 (1997) **Consumer price inflation:** 9.5% (1997) **Unemployment:** 30% (1994 est) **Foreign debt:** (US$) 220 million (1996) **Major trading partners:** South Africa, UK, the Netherlands, Switzerland, France **Resources:** coal, asbestos, diamonds, gold, tin, kaolin, iron ore, talc, pyrophyllite, silica **Exports:** sugar, wood pulp, cotton yarn, canned fruits, asbestos, coal, diamonds, gold. Principal market: South Africa 58.4% (1995) **Imports:** machinery and transport equipment, minerals, fuels and lubricants, manufactured items, food and live animals. Principal source: South Africa 96.3% (1995–96) **Arable land:** 10.9% (1995) **Agricultural products:** sugar cane, cotton, citrus fruits, pineapples, maize, sorghum, tobacco, tomatoes, rice; livestock rearing (cattle and goats); commercial forestry

Population and society

Population: 952,000 (1998 est) **Population growth rate:** 2.8% (1995–2000); 2.6% (2000–05) **Population density:** (per sq km) 56.2 (1998 est) **Urban population:** (% of total) 33 (1997) **Age distribution:** (% of total population) 0–14 46.4%, 15–64 51.1%, 65+ 2.5% (1998) **Ethnic groups:** about 90% indigenous African, comprising the Swazi, Zulu, Tonga, and Shangaan peoples; there are European and Afro-European (Eurafrican) minorities numbering around 22,000 **Language:** Swazi, English (both official) **Religion:** Christian, animist **Education:** (compulsory years) 7 **Literacy rate:** 76% (men); 73% (women) (1995 est) **Labour force:** 34% of population: 39% agriculture, 22% industry, 38% services (1990) **Life expectancy:** 58 (men); 62 (women) (1995–2000) **Child mortality rate:** (under 5, per 1,000 live births) 95 (1997) **Physicians:** 1 per 9,091 people (1991)

Practical information

Visa requirements: UK: visa not required. USA: visa not required **Embassy in the UK:** 20 Buckingham Street, London SW1E 6LB.

Tel: (0171) 630 6611; fax: (0171) 630 6564 **British embassy:** British High Commission, Allister Miller Street, Private Bag, Mbabane. Tel: (268) 42581; fax: (268) 42585 **Chamber of commerce:** Swaziland Chamber of Commerce and Industry, PO Box 72, Mbabane. Tel: (268) 44408; fax: (268) 45442

Chronology

late 16th century: King Ngwane II crossed Lubombo mountains from the east and settled in southeast Swaziland; his successors established a strong centralized Swazi kingdom, dominating the long-settled Nguni and Sothi peoples. **mid-19th century:** Swazi nation was ruled by the warrior King Mswati who, at the height of his power, controlled an area three times the size of the present-day state. **1882:** Gold was discovered in the northwest, attracting European fortune hunters, who coerced Swazi rulers into granting land concessions. **1894:** Came under joint rule of Britain and the Boer republic of Transvaal. **1903:** Following the South African War, Swaziland became a special British protectorate, or High Commission territory, against South Africa's wishes. **1922:** King Sobhuza II succeeded to the Swazi throne. **1968:** Independence achieved within the Commonwealth, as the Kingdom of Swaziland, with King (or Ngwenyama) Sobhuza II as head of state. **1973:** The king suspended the constitution, banned political activity, and assumed absolute powers after the opposition deputies had been elected to parliament. **1977:** King announced substitution of traditional tribal communities (*tinkhundla*) for the parliamentary system, arguing it was more suited to Swazi values. **1982:** King Sobhuza died; his place was taken by one of his wives, Queen Dzeliwe, until his son, Prince Makhosetive, reached the age of 21. **1983:** Queen Dzeliwe ousted by a younger wife, Queen Ntombi, as real power passed to the prime minister, Prince Bhekimpi Dlamini. **1984:** After royal power struggle, it was announced that the crown prince would become king at 18. **1986:** Crown prince formally invested as King Mswati III. **1993:** Direct elections of *tinkhundla* candidates held for the first time; Prince Jameson Mbilini Dlamini appointed premier. **1998:** Prince Dlamini reappointed.

Sweden Kingdom of

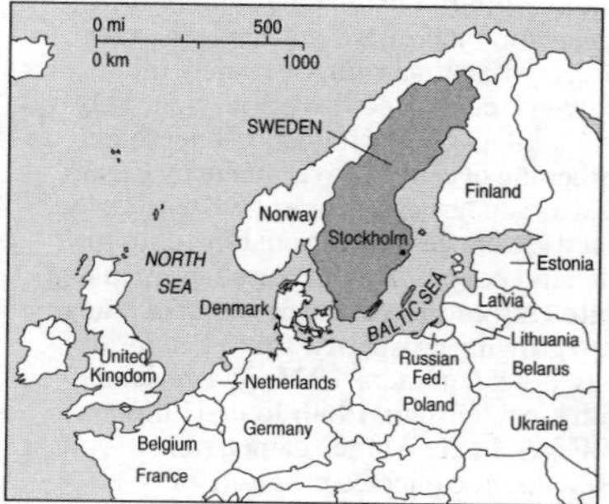

National name: *Konungariket Sverige* **Area:** 450,000 sq km/173,745 sq mi **Capital:** Stockholm (and chief port) **Major towns/cities:** Göteborg, Malmö, Uppsala, Norrköping, Västerås, Linköping, Orebro, Jönköping, Helsingborg, Borås **Major ports:** Helsingborg, Malmö, Göteborg

Government

Head of state: King Carl XVI Gustaf from 1973 **Head of government:** Goran Persson from 1996 **Political system:** constitutional monarchy **Administrative divisions:** 24 counties **Political parties:** Christian Democratic Community Party (KdS), Christian, centrist; Left Party (Vp), European, Marxist; Social Democratic Labour Party (SAP), moderate, left of centre; Moderate Party (M), right of centre; Liberal Party (Fp), centre left; Centre Party (C), centrist; Ecology Party (MpG), ecological; New Democracy (NG), right wing, populist **Armed forces:** 53,400 (1997) **Conscription:** 7–15 months (army and navy); 8–12 months (air force) **Death penalty:** abolished in 1972 **Defence spend:** (% GDP) 2.4 (1997) **Education spend:** (% GNP) 8.0 (1995) **Health spend:** (% GDP) 6.0 (1990–95)

Economy and resources

Currency: Swedish krona **GDP:** (US$) 227.8 billion (1997) **Real GDP growth:** (% change on previous year) 2.6 (1997) **GNP (US$):** 232 billion (1997) **GNP per capita (PPP):** (US$) 19,030 (1997) **Consumer price inflation:** 2.3% (1998) **Unemployment:** 8.2% (1998) **Major trading partners:** Germany, UK, Norway, USA, Denmark, France **Resources:** iron ore, uranium, copper, lead, zinc, silver, hydroelectric power, forests **Exports:** forestry products (wood, pulp, and paper), machinery, motor vehicles, power-generating non-electrical machinery, chemicals, iron and steel. Principal market: Germany 11.3% (1997) **Imports:** machinery and transport equipment, chemicals, mineral fuels and lubricants, textiles, clothing, footwear, food and live animals. Principal source: Germany 19.2% (1997) **Arable land:** 6.7% (1995)

Population and society

Population: 8,875,000 (1998 est) **Population growth rate:** 0.3% (1995–2000); 0.3% (2000–05) **Population density:** (per sq km) 21.6 (1998 est) **Urban population:** (% of total) 83 (1997) **Age distribution:** (% of total population) 0–14 18.7%, 15–64 63.9%, 65+ 17.4% (1998) **Ethnic groups:** predominantly of Teutonic descent, with small Saami (Lapp), Finnish, and German minorities **Language:** Swedish; there are Finnish- and Saami-speaking minorities **Religion:** Evangelical Lutheran (established national church) **Education:** (compulsory years) 9 **Literacy rate:** 99% (men); 99% (women) (1995 est) **Labour force:** 48..4% of population: 2.9% agriculture, 26.1% industry, 71% services (1996) **Life expectancy:** 76 (men); 81 (women) (1995–2000) **Child mortality rate:** (under 5, per 1,000 live births) 6 (1997) **Physicians:** 1 per 323 people (1996)

Practical information

Visa requirements: UK: visa not required. USA: visa not required **Embassy in the UK:** 11 Montagu Place, London W1H 2AL. Tel: (0171) 917 6400; fax: (0171) 724 4174 **British embassy:** PO Box 27819, Skarpögatan 6–8, 115 93 Stockholm. Tel: (8) 671 9000; fax: (8) 662 9989 **Chamber of commerce:** Federation of Swedish Commerce and Trade, PO Box 5512, Grevgatan 34, 114 85 Stockholm. Tel: (8) 666 1100; fax: (8) 662 7457

Chronology

8th century: Kingdom of the Svear, based near Uppsala, extended its rule across much of southern Sweden. **9th–11th centuries:** Swedish Vikings raided and settled along the rivers of Russia. *c.* **1000:** Olaf Skötkonung, king of the Svear, adopted Christianity and united much of Sweden (except south and west coasts, which remained Danish until 17th century). **11th–13th centuries:** Sweden existed as isolated kingdom under the Stenkil, Sverker, and Folkung dynasties; series of crusades incorporated Finland. **1397:** Union of Kalmar: Sweden, Denmark, and Norway united under a single monarch; Sweden effectively ruled by succession of regents. **1448:** Breach with Denmark: Sweden alone elected Charles VIII as king. **1523:** Gustavus Vasa, leader of insurgents, became king of fully independent Sweden. **1527:** Swedish Reformation: Gustavus confiscated Church property and encouraged Lutherans. **1544:** Swedish crown became hereditary in House of Vasa. **1592–1604:** Sigismund Vasa, a Catholic, was king of both Sweden and Poland until ousted from Swedish throne by his Lutheran uncle Charles IX. **17th century:** Sweden, a great military power under Gustavus Adolphus 1611–32, Charles X 1654–60, and Charles XI 1660–97, fought lengthy wars with Denmark, Russia, Poland, and Holy Roman Empire. **1709:** Battle of Poltava: Russians inflicted major defeat on Swedes under Charles XII. **1720:** Limited monarchy established; political power passed to *Riksdag* (parliament) dominated by nobles. **1721:** Great Northern War ended with Sweden losing nearly all its conquests of the previous century. **1741–43:** Sweden defeated in disastrous war with Russia; further conflict 1788–90. **1771–92:** Gustavus III increased royal power and introduced wide-ranging reforms; assassinated at a masked ball. **1809:** Russian invaders annexed Finland; Swedish nobles staged coup and restored powers of Riksdag. **1810:** Napoleonic marshal, Jean-Baptiste Bernadotte, elected crown prince of Sweden, as Charles XIII had no heir. **1812:** Bernadotte allied Sweden with Russia against France. **1814:** Treaty of Kiel: Sweden obtained Norway from Denmark. **1818–44:** Bernadotte reigned in Sweden as Charles XIV John. **1846:** Free enterprise established by abolition of trade guilds and monopolies. **1866:** Series of liberal reforms culminated in new two-chambered *Riksdag* dominated by bureaucrats and farmers. **late 19th century:**

Development of large-scale forestry and iron-ore industry; neutrality adopted in foreign affairs. **1905:** Union with Norway dissolved. **1907:** Adoption of proportional representation and universal suffrage. **1920s:** Economic boom transformed Sweden from an agricultural to an industrial economy. **1932:** Social Democrat government of Per Halbin Hansson introduced radical public-works programme to combat trade slump. **1940–43:** Under duress, neutral Sweden permitted limited transit of German forces through its territory. **1946–69:** Social Democrat government of Tage Erlander developed comprehensive welfare state. **1959:** Sweden joined European Free Trade Association. **1969–76:** Social Democratic Party in power, under Prime Minister Olaf Palme. **1971:** Constitution amended to create single-chamber Riksdag. **1975:** Remaining constitutional powers of monarch removed. **1976–82:** Centre-right government of Thorbjörn Fälldin ended 44 years of Social Democrat dominance. **1982:** Palme regained premiership; assassinated 1986. **1995:** Sweden became a member of European Union. **1998:** Social Democrats (SAP) marginally re-elected in September general election.

Switzerland Swiss Confederation

National name: German *Schweiz,* French *Suisse,* Romansch *Svizra* **Area:** 41,300 sq km/ 15,945 sq mi **Capital:** Bern (Berne) **Major towns/cities:** Zürich, Geneva, Basel, Lausanne, Luzern, St Gallen, Winterthur **Major ports:** river port Basel (on the Rhine)

Government

Head of state and government: Ruth Dreifuss from 1999 **Government:** federal democracy **Administrative divisions:** 20 cantons and six demi-cantons **Political parties:** Radical Democratic Party (FDP/PRD), radical, centre left; Social Democratic Party (SP/PS), moderate, left of centre; Christian Democratic People's Party (CVP/PDC), Christian, moderate, centrist; Swiss People's Party (SVP/UDC), centre left; Liberal Party (LPS/PLS), federalist, right of centre; Green Party (GPS/PES), ecological **Armed forces:** 26,300 (1997) **Conscription:** 17 weeks' recruit training, followed by refresher training of varying length according to age **Death penalty:** abolished in 1992 **Defence spend:** (% GDP) 1.5 (1997) **Education spend:** (% GNP) 5.5 (1995) **Health spend:** (% GDP) 7.2 (1990–95)

Economy and resources

Currency: Swiss franc **GDP:** (US$) 252.1 billion (1997) **Real GDP growth:** (% change on previous year) 0.6 (1997) **GNP (US$):** 313.5 billion (1997) **GNP per capita (PPP):** (US$) 26,320 (1997) **Consumer price inflation:** 1.0% (1998) **Unemployment:** 3.9% (1996) **Major trading partners:** EU (principally Germany, France, Italy, and UK), USA, Japan **Resources:** salt, hydroelectric power, forest **Exports:** machinery and equipment, pharmaceutical and chemical products, foodstuffs, precision instruments, clocks and watches, metal products. Principal market: Germany 23% (1997) **Imports:** machinery, motor vehicles, agricultural and forestry products, construction material, fuels and lubricants, chemicals, textiles and clothing. Principal source: Germany 32% (1997) **Arable land:** 10.1% (1995)

Population and society

Population: 7,299,000 (1998 est) **Population growth rate:** 0.7% (1995–2000); 0.5% (2000–05) **Population density:** (per sq km) 182.6 (1998 est) **Urban population:** (% of total) 62 (1997) **Age distribution:** (% of total population) 0–14 17.3%, 15–64 67.8%, 65+ 14.9% (1998) **Ethnic groups:** majority of Alpine descent; sizeable Nordic element **Language:** German 64%, French 19%, Italian 8%, Romansch 0.6% (all official) **Religion:** Roman Catholic 50%, Protestant 48% **Education:** (compulsory years) 8–9 (depending on canton) **Literacy rate:** 99% (men); 99% (women) (1995 est) **Labour force:** 53.8% of population: 4.5% agriculture, 27.8% industry, 67.7% services (1996) **Life expectancy:** 75 (men); 82 (women) (1995–2000) **Child mortality rate:** (under 5, per 1,000 live births) 7 (1997) **Physicians:** 1 per 322 people (1994)

Practical information

Visa requirements: UK: visa not required. USA: visa not required **Embassy in the UK:** 16–18 Montagu Place, London W1H 2BQ. Tel: (0171) 616 6000; fax: (0171) 724 7001 **British embassy:** Thunstrasse 50, CH-3005 Bern 15. Tel: (31) 352 5021/6; fax: (31) 352 0583 **Chamber of commerce:** Schweizerischer Handels- und Industrie-Verein (Swiss Federation of Commerce and Industry), PO Box 690, Mainaustrasse 49, CH-8034 Zürich. Tel: (1) 382 2323; fax: (1) 382 2332

Chronology

58 BC: Celtic Helvetii tribe submitted to Roman authority after defeat by Julius Caesar. **4th century AD:** Region overrun by Germanic tribes, Burgundians, and Alemannians. **7th century:** Formed part of Frankish kingdom and embraced Christianity. **9th century:** Included in Charlemagne's Holy Roman Empire. **12th century:** Many autonomous feudal holdings developed as power of Holy Roman Empire declined. **13th century:** Habsburgs became dominant as overlords of eastern Switzerland. **1291:** Cantons of Schwyz, Uri, and Lower Unterwalden formed Everlasting League, a loose confederation to resist Habsburg control. **1315:** Battle of Morgarten: Swiss Confederation defeated Habsburgs. **14th century:** Luzern, Zürich, Basel, and other cantons joined Swiss Confederation, which became independent of Habsburgs. **1523–29:** Zürich, Bern, and Basel accepted Reformation but rural cantons remained Roman Catholic. **1648:** Treaty of Westphalia recognized Swiss independence from Holy Roman Empire. **1798:** French invasion established Helvetic Republic, a puppet state with centralized government. **1803:** Napoleon's Act of Mediation restored considerable autonomy to cantons. **1814:** End of French domination; Switzerland reverted to loose confederation of sovereign cantons with a weak federal parliament. **1815:** Great Powers recognized 'Perpetual Neutrality' of Switzerland. **1845:** Seven Catholic cantons founded Sonderbund league to resist any strengthening of central government by Liberals. **1847:** Federal troops defeated Sonderbund in brief civil war. **1848:** New constitution introduced greater centralization; Bern chosen as capital. **1874:** Powers of federal government increased; principle of referendum introduced. **late 19th century:** Development of industry, railways, and tourism led to growing prosperity. **1920:** League of Nations selected Geneva as its headquarters. **1923:** Switzerland formed customs union with Liechtenstein. **1960:** Joined European Free Trade Association (EFTA). **1971:** Women gained right to vote in federal elections. **1986:** Referendum rejected proposal for membership of United Nations (UN). **1992:** Closer ties with European Community (EC) rejected in national referendum. **1996:** Jean-Paul Delamuraz became president. **1997:** Arnold Koller elected president. **1998:** Ruth Dreifuss elected president, the first woman to hold the post in Switzerland.

Syria Syrian Arab Republic

National name: *al-Jamhuriya al-Arabya as-Suriya* **Area:** 185,200 sq km/71,505 sq mi **Capital:** Damascus **Major towns/cities:** Aleppo, Homs, Latakia, Hama **Major ports:** Latakia

Government

Head of state and government: Hafez al-Assad from 1971 **Political system:** socialist republic **Administrative divisions:** 14 administrative districts **Political parties:** National Progressive Front

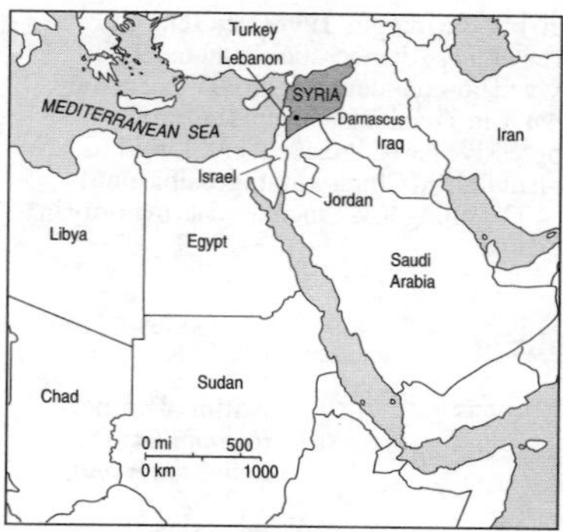

(NPF), pro-Arab, socialist coalition, including the Communist Party of Syria, the Arab Socialist Party, the Arab Socialist Unionist Party, the Syrian Arab Socialist Union Party, the Ba'ath Arab Socialist Party **Armed forces:** 320,000; reserve forces 500,000; paramilitary forces 8,000 (1997) **Conscription:** 30 months **Death penalty:** retained and used for ordinary crimes **Defence spend:** (% GDP) 6.3 (1997) **Education spend:** (% GNP) 4.2 (1996) **Health spend:** (% GDP) 0.4 (1990)

Economy and resources

Currency: Syrian pound **GDP:** (US$) 18.8 billion (1997 est) **Real GDP growth:** (% change on previous year) 3.4 (1997) **GNP (US$):** 17.1 billion (1997) **GNP per capita (PPP):** (US$) 2,990 (1997) **Consumer price inflation:** 18.2% (1998) **Foreign debt:** (US$) 21.4 billion (1996) **Major trading partners:** Germany, Italy, France, Lebanon, Japan, UK, Romania, Belgium **Resources:** petroleum, natural gas, iron ore, phosphates, salt, gypsum, sodium chloride, bitumen **Exports:** crude petroleum, textiles, vegetables, fruit, raw cotton, natural phosphate. Principal market: Italy 17.5% (1997) **Imports:** crude petroleum, wheat, base metals, metal products, foodstuffs, machinery, motor vehicles. Principal source: Ukraine 13.1% (1997) **Arable land:** 27.3% (1995)

Population and society

Population: 15,333,000 (1998 est) **Population growth rate:** 2.5% (1995–2000) **Population density:** (per sq km) 90.6 (1998 est) **Urban population:** (% of total) 53 (1997) **Age distribution:** (% of total population) 0–14 46.1%, 15–64 51.0%, 65+ 2.9% (1998) **Ethnic groups:** predominantly Arab, with many differences in language and regional affiliations **Language:** Arabic 89% (official); Kurdish 6%, Armenian 3% **Religion:** Sunni Muslim 90%; other Islamic sects, Christian **Education:** (compulsory years) 6 **Literacy rate:** 53% (men); 51% (women) (1995 est) **Labour force:** 28% of population: 33% agriculture, 24% industry, 43% services (1990) **Life expectancy:** 67 (men); 71 (women) (1995–2000) **Child mortality rate:** (under 5, per 1,000 live births) 39 (1997) **Physicians:** 1 per 969 people (1994)

Practical information

Visa requirements: UK: visa required. USA: visa required **Embassy in the UK:** 8 Belgrave Square, London SW1X 8PH. Tel: (0171) 245 9012; fax: (0171) 235 4621 **British embassy:** PO Box 37, Quarter Malki, 11 rue Mohammed Kurd Ali, Immeuble Kotob, Damascus. Tel: (11) 712 561/2/3; fax: (11) 713 592 **Chamber of commerce:** Federation of Syrian Chambers of Commerce, PO Box 5909, rue Mousa Ben Nousair, Damascus. Tel: (11) 333 7344; fax: (11) 333127

Chronology

c. **1750 BC:** Syria became part of Babylonian Empire; during the next millennium it was successively conquered by Hittites, Assyrians, Chaldeans, and Persians. **333 BC:** Alexander the Great of Macedonia conquered Persia and Syria. **301 BC:** Seleucus I, one of the generals of Alexander the Great, founded kingdom of Syria, which the Seleucid dynasty ruled for over 200 years. **64 BC:** Syria became part of Roman Empire. **4th century AD:** After division of Roman Empire, Syria came under Byzantine rule. **634:** Arabs conquered most of Syria and introduced Islam. **661–750:** Damascus was capital of Muslim Empire. **1055:** Seljuk Turks overran Syria. **1095–99:** First Crusade established Latin states on Syrian coast. **13th century:** Mameluke sultans of Egypt took control. **1516:** Ottoman Turks conquered Syria. **1831:** Egyptians led by Mehemet Ali drove out Turks. **1840:** Turkish rule restored; Syria opened up to European trade. **late 19th century:** French firms built ports, roads, and railways in Syria. **1916:** Sykes-Picot Agreement: secret Anglo-French deal to partition Turkish Empire allotted Syria to France. **1918:** British expelled Turks with help of Arab revolt. **1919:** Syrian national congress called for independence under Emir Faisal and opposed transfer to French rule. **1920:** Syria became League of Nations protectorate, administered by France. **1925:** People's Party founded to campaign for independence and national unity; insurrection by Druse religious sect against French control. **1936:** France promised independence within three years, but martial law imposed in 1939. **1941:** British forces ousted Vichy French regime in Damascus and occupied Syria in conjunction with Free French. **1944:** Syrian independence proclaimed but French military resisted transfer of power. **1946:** Syria achieved effective independence when French forces withdrew. **1948–49:** Arab–Israeli War: Syria joined unsuccessful invasion of newly independent Israel. **1958:** Syria and Egypt merged to form United Arab Republic (UAR). **1959:** USSR agreed to give financial and technical aid to Syria. **1961:** Syria seceded from UAR. **1964:** Ba'ath Socialist Party established military dictatorship. **1967:** Six-Day War: Syria lost Golan Heights to Israel. **1970–71:** Syria invaded Jordan in support of Palestinian guerrillas. **1970:** Hafez al-Assad staged coup; elected president 1971. **1973:** Yom Kippur War: Syrian attack on Israel repulsed. **1976:** Start of Syrian military intervention in Lebanese civil war. **1978:** Syria opposed peace deal between Egypt and Israel. **1986:** Britain broke off diplomatic relations, accusing Syria of involvement in international terrorism. **1990:** Diplomatic links with Britain restored. **1991:** Syria contributed troops to US-led coalition in Gulf War against Iraq. US Middle East peace plan approved by Assad. **1994:** Israel offered partial withdrawal from Golan Heights in return for peace, but Syria remained sceptical. **1995:** Security framework agreement with Israel.

Taiwan Republic of China

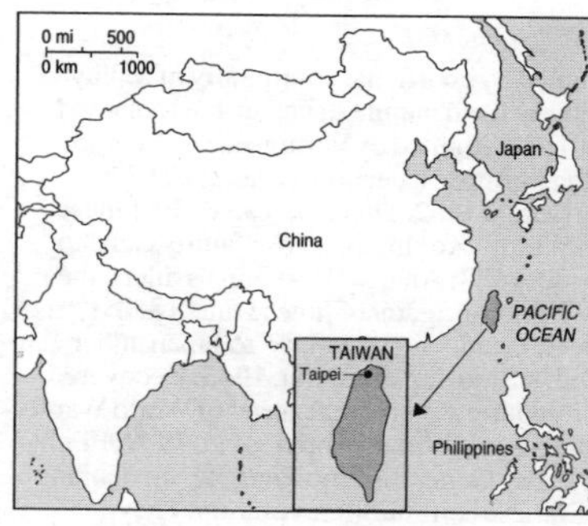

National name: *Chung Hua Min Kuo* **Area:** 36,179 sq km/13,968 sq mi **Capital:** Taipei **Major towns/cities:** Kaohsiung, Taichung, Tainan, Panchiao, Yunlin **Major ports:** Kaohsiung, Keelung

Government

Head of state: Lee Teng-hui from 1988 **Head of government:** Vincent Siew from 1997 **Political system:** emergent democracy **Administrative divisions:** 16 counties, five municipalities, and two special municipalities (Taipei and Kaohsiung) **Political parties:** Nationalist Party of China (Kuomintang: KMT; known as Guomindang outside Taiwan), anticommunist, Chinese nationalist; Democratic Progressive Party (DPP), centrist-pluralist, proself-determination grouping; Workers' Party (Kuntang), left of centre **Armed forces:** 376,000; plus paramilitary forces numbering 26,700 and reserves totalling 1,657,500 (1997) **Conscription:** military service is compulsory for two years **Death penalty:** retained and used for ordinary crimes **Defence spend:** (% GDP) 4.7 (1997) **Education spend:** (% GDP) 2.5 (1994)

Economy and resources

Currency: New Taiwan dollar **GDP:** (US$) 283.4 billion (1997) **Real GDP growth:** (% change on previous year) 6.7 (1997 est) **GNP (US$):** 275 billion (1996) **GNP per capita (PPP):** (US$) 12,340 (1996 est) **Consumer price inflation:** 3.3% (1996) **Unemployment:** 2.7% (1997) **Foreign debt:** (US$) 29.8 billion (1996) **Major trading partners:** USA, Japan, Hong Kong, Germany, Singapore, South

Korea, Australia, China **Resources:** coal, copper, marble, dolomite; small reserves of petroleum and natural gas **Exports:** electronic products, base metals and metal articles, textiles and clothing, machinery, information and communication products, plastic and rubber products, vehicles and transport equipment, footwear, headwear, umbrellas, toys, games, sports equipment. Principal market: USA 26.6% (1998) **Imports:** machinery and transport equipment, basic manufactures, chemicals, base metals and metal articles, minerals, textile products, crude petroleum, plastics, precision instruments, clocks and watches, musical instruments. Principal source: Japan 25.8% (1998) **Arable land:** 24% (1993)

Population and society

Population: 21,908,000 (1998 est) **Population growth rate:** 1.0% (1995–2000) **Population density:** (per sq km) 679.1 (1998 est) **Urban population:** (% of total) 75 (1994) **Age distribution:** (% of total population) 0–14 22.4%, 15–64 69.4%, 65+ 8.2% (1998) **Ethnic groups:** 98% Han Chinese and 2% aboriginal by descent; around 87% are Taiwan-born and 13% are 'mainlanders' **Language:** Mandarin Chinese (official); Taiwan, Hakka dialects **Religion:** officially atheist; Taoist, Confucian, Buddhist, Christian **Education:** (compulsory years) 9 **Literacy rate:** 95% (men); 93% (women) (1995 est) **Labour force:** 10.9% agriculture, 39.2% industry, 49.9% services (1994) **Life expectancy:** 72 (men); 78 (women) (1995) **Child mortality rate:** (per 1,000 live births) 6 (1994) **Physicians:** 1 per 878 people (1995); 3,030 doctors of traditional Chinese medicine (1995)

Practical information

Visa requirements: UK: visa not required for a stay of up to 14 days. USA: visa not required for a stay of up to 14 days **Embassy in the UK:** Taipei Representative Office in the UK, 50 Grosvenor Gardens, London SW1W 0EB. Tel: (0171) 396 9152; fax: (0171) 396 9151 **British embassy:** the UK has no diplomatic representation in Taiwan **Chamber of commerce:** General Chamber of Commerce, 6th Floor, 390 Flushing South Road, Section 1, Taipei. Tel: (2) 701 2671; fax: (2) 755 5493

Chronology

7th century AD: Island occupied by aboriginal community of Malayan descent; immigration of Chinese from mainland began, but remained limited before 15th century. **1517:** Sighted by Portuguese vessels en route to Japan and named Ilha Formosa ('beautiful island'). **1624:** Occupied and controlled by Dutch. **1662:** Dutch defeated by Chinese Ming general, Cheng Ch'eng-kung (Koxinga), whose family came to rule Formosa for a short period. **1683:** Annexed by China's rulers, the Manchu Qing. **1786:** Major rebellion against Chinese rule. **1860:** Ports opened to Western trade. **1895:** Ceded 'in perpetuity' to Japan under Treaty of Shominoseki at end of Sino-Japanese war. **1945:** Recovered by China's Nationalist Guomindang government at end of World War II. **1947:** Rebellion against Chinese rule brutally suppressed. **1949:** Flight of Nationalist government, led by Generalissimo Jiang Jie Shi (Chiang Kai-shek), to Taiwan after Chinese communist revolution. They retained the designation of Republic of China (ROC), claiming to be the legitimate government for all China, and were recognized by USA and United Nations (UN). **1950s onwards:** Rapid economic growth as Taiwan became successful export-orientated Newly Industrializing Country (NIC) and land was redistributed from the gentry 'to-the-tiller'. **1954:** US–Taiwanese mutual defence treaty. **1971:** Expulsion from UN as USA adopted new policy of détente towards communist China. **1972:** Commencement of legislature elections as programme of gradual democratization and Taiwanization launched by mainlander-dominated Guomindang. **1975:** President Jiang Jie Shi died; replaced as Guomindang leader by his son, Jiang Ching-kuo. **1979:** USA severed diplomatic relations and annulled 1954 security pact. **1986:** Centrist Democratic Progressive Party (DPP) formed as opposition to nationalist Guomindang. **1987:** Martial law lifted; opposition parties legalized; press restrictions lifted. **1988:** President Jiang Ching-kuo died; replaced by Taiwanese-born Lee Teng-hui. **1990:** Chinese-born Guomindang members became minority in parliament. **1991:** President Lee Teng-hui declared end to civil war with China. Constitution amended. Guomindang won landslide victory in elections to new National Assembly, the 'superparliament'. **1993:** Cooperation pact with China signed. **1995:** Ruling Guomindang retained majority in working assembly (Legislative Yuan) by slim margin. **1996:** Lee Teng-hui elected president in first-ever Chinese democratic election. **1997:** Government narrowly survived no-confidence motion. Vincent Siew became prime minister. **1998:** Lin Yi-shiung became leader of opposition Democratic Progressive Party. President Lee Teng-hui announced that reunion with mainland China was impossible until Beijing adopted democracy. The ruling KMT increased its majority in parliamentary and local elections.

Tajikistan Republic of

National name: *Respublika i Tojikiston* **Area:** 143,100 sq km/55,250 sq mi **Capital:** Dushanbe **Major towns/ cities:** Khodzhent (formerly Leninabad), Kurgan-Tyube, Kulyab

Government

Head of state: Imamali Rakhmanov from 1994 **Head of government:** Yahya Azimov from 1996 **Political system:** authoritarian nationalist **Administrative divisions:** two provinces and one autonomous region (Gornyi Badakhstan) **Political parties:** Communist Party of Tajikistan (CPT), pro-Rakhmanov; Democratic Party of Tajikistan (DP), anticommunist (banned from 1993); Party of Popular Unity and Justice, anticommunist **Armed forces:** 9,000; paramilitary forces around 1,200 (1997) **Death penalty:** retained and used for ordinary crimes **Defence spend:** (% GDP) 12.1 (1997) **Education spend:** (% GNP) 2.2 (1996) **Health spend:** (% GDP) 6.4 (1990–95)

Economy and resources

Currencies: Tajik and Russian rouble **GDP:** (US$) 1.9 billion (1997 est) **Real GDP growth:** (% change on previous year) 5.0 (1997) **GNP (US$):** 2 billion (1997) **GNP per capita (PPP):** (US$) 930 (1997) **Consumer price inflation:** 40% (1998) **Unemployment:** 2.5% (1996) **Foreign debt:** (US$) 707 million (1996) **Major trading partners:** Uzbekistan, the Netherlands, Switzerland, Russia, UK, Kazakhstan, Ukraine **Resources:** coal, aluminium, lead, zinc, iron, tin, uranium, radium, arsenic, bismuth, gold, mica, asbestos, lapis lazuli; small reserves of petroleum and natural gas **Exports:** aluminium, cotton lint. Principal market: Uzbekistan 36.8% (1997) **Imports:** industrial products and machinery (principally for aluminium plants), unprocessed agricultural products, food and beverages, petroleum and chemical products, consumer goods. Principal source: Netherlands 31.9% (1997) **Arable land:** 5.8% (1995)

Population and society

Population: 6,015,000 (1998 est) **Population growth rate:** 1.9% (1995–2000) **Population density:** (per sq km) 42.1 (1998 est) **Urban population:** (% of total) 33 (1997) **Age distribution:** (% of total population) 0–14 41.4%, 15–64 54.0%, 65+ 4.6% (1998) **Ethnic groups:** 62% ethnic Tajik, 24% Uzbek, 8% ethnic Russian, 1% Tatar, 1% Kyrgyz, and 1% Ukrainian **Language:** Tajik (official), similar to Farsi (Persian) **Religion:** Sunni Muslim **Education:** (compulsory years) 9 **Literacy rate:** 97% (men); 97% (women) (1995 est) **Labour force:** 51.2% agriculture, 18.1% industry, 30.7% services (1993) **Life expectancy:** 64 (men); 70 (women) (1995–2000) **Child mortality rate:** (under 5, per 1,000 live births) 75 (1997) **Physicians:** 1 per 442 people (1994)

Practical information

Visa requirements: UK: visa required. USA: visa required **Embassy**

in the UK: Tajikistan has no diplomatic representation in the UK **British embassy:** the British Embassy in Tashkent (see Uzbekistan) deals with all enquiries relating to Tajikistan **Chamber of commerce:** Chamber of Commerce and Industry, Ulitsa Mazayeva 21, Dushanbe 7340012. Tel: (3772) 279 519

Chronology

c. **330:** Formed an eastern part of empire of Alexander the Great of Macedonia. **8th century:** Tajiks established as distinct ethnic group, with semi-independent territories under the tutelage of the Uzbeks, to the west; spread of Islam. **13th century:** Conquered by Genghis Khan and became part of Mongol Empire. **1860–1900:** Northern Tajikistan came under tsarist Russian rule, while the south was annexed by Emirate of Bukhara, to the west. **1917–18:** Attempts to establish Soviet control after Bolshevik revolution in Russia resisted initially by armed guerrillas (basmachi). **1921:** Became part of Turkestan Soviet Socialist Autonomous Republic. **1924:** Tajik Autonomous Soviet Socialist Republic formed. **1929:** Became constituent republic of Soviet Union (USSR). **1930s:** Stalinist era of collectivization led to widespread repression of Tajiks. **1978:** 13,000 participated in anti-Russian riots. **late 1980s:** Resurgence in Tajik consciousness, stimulated by the *glasnost* initiative of Soviet leader Mikhail Gorbachev. **1989:** Rastokhez ('Revival') Popular Front established and Tajik declared state language. New mosques constructed. **1990:** Violent interethnic Tajik–Armenian clashes in Dushanbe; state of emergency imposed. **1991:** President Kakhar Makhkamov, local communist leader since 1985, forced to resign after supporting failed anti-Gorbachev coup in Moscow. Independence declared. Rakhman Nabiyev, communist leader 1982–85, elected president. Joined new Commonwealth of Independent States (CIS). **1992:** Joined Muslim Economic Cooperation Organization, the Conference on Security and Cooperation in Europe (CSCE; now the Organization on Security and Cooperation in Europe, OSCE), and United Nations. Violent demonstrations by Islamic and prodemocracy groups forced Nabiyev to resign. Civil war between pro- and anti-Nabiyev forces claimed 20,000 lives, made 600,000 refugees, and wrecked the economy. Imamali Rakhmanov, a communist sympathetic to Nabiyev, took over as head of state. **1993:** Government forces regained control of most of the country. CIS peacekeeping forces drafted in to patrol border with Afghanistan, the base of pro-Islamic rebels. **1994:** Cease-fire agreed. Rakhmanov popularly elected president under new constitution. **1995:** Parliamentary elections won by Rakhmanov's supporters. Renewed fighting on Afghan border. **1996:** Pro-Islamic rebels captured towns in southwest. UN-sponsored cease-fire between government and pro-Islamic rebels. **1997:** Four-stage peace plan signed. President Rakhmanov seriously injured by grenade. Peace accord with Islamic rebel group, the United Tajik Opposition (UTO). **1998:** Members of Islamic UTO appointed to government, as part of peace plan. Opposition fighters moved from mountains into UN-monitored camps. Tajikistan joined the CIS Customs Union. The UN military observer mission (UNMOT) suspended its operations, following the killing of four UN workers in July. More than 200 people killed in clashes in Leninabad between the army and rebel forces loyal to the renegade Tajik army commander Col Makhmud Khudoberdiyev; the deputy leader of the Islamic-led UTO, Ali Akbar Turadzhonzada, was appointed first deputy prime minister. Tajikistan joined the CIS.

Tanzania United Republic of

National name: *Jamhuri ya Muungano wa Tanzania* **Area:** 945,000 sq km/364,864 sq mi **Capital:** Dodoma (since 1983) **Major towns/cities:** Zanzibar Town, Mwanza, Tabora, Mbeya, Tanga **Major ports:** (former capital) Dar es Salaam

Government

Head of state: Benjamin Mkapa from 1995 **Head of government:** Cleoopa Msuya from 1994 **Political system:** emergent democracy **Administrative divisions:** 25 administrative regions **Political parties:** Revolutionary Party of Tanzania (CCM), African, socialist; Civic Party (Chama Cha Wananchi), left of centre; Tanzania People's Party (TPP), left of centre; Democratic Party (DP), left of centre; Justice and Development Party, left of centre; Zanzibar United Front

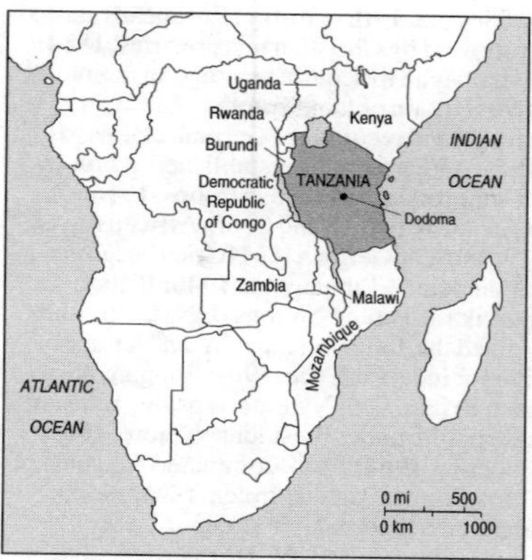

(Kamahuru), Zanzibar-based, centrist **Armed forces:** 34,600; citizen's militia of 80,000 (1997) **Conscription:** two years **Death penalty:** retained and used for ordinary crimes **Defence spend:** (% GDP) 3.4 (1997) **Education spend:** (% GNP) 5.0 (1993/94) **Health spend:** (% GDP) 3.0 (1990–95)

Economy and resources

Currency: Tanzanian shilling **GDP:** (US$) 6.7 billion (1997) **Real GDP growth:** (% change on previous year) 3.1 (1997) **GNP (US$):** 6.6 billion (1997) **GNP per capita (PPP):** (US$) 790 (1997 est) **Consumer price inflation:** 20% (1998) **Foreign debt:** (US$) 7.9 billion (1996) **Major trading partners:** India, UK, Germany, Japan, the Netherlands, Kenya, Malaysia, Rwanda, China **Resources:** diamonds, other gemstones, gold, salt, phosphates, coal, gypsum, tin, kaolin (exploration for petroleum in progress) **Exports:** coffee beans, raw cotton, tobacco, tea, cloves, cashew nuts, minerals, petroleum products. Principal market: India 11.6% (1997) **Imports:** machinery and transport equipment, crude petroleum and petroleum products, construction materials, foodstuffs, consumer goods. Principal source: South Africa 12.8% (1997) **Arable land:** 3.5% (1995)

Population and society

Population: 32,102,000 (1998 est) **Population growth rate:** 2.3% (1995–2000) **Population density:** (per sq km) 34.5 (1998 est) **Urban population:** (% of total) 26 (1997) **Age distribution:** (% of total population) 0–14 44.6%, 15–64 52.5%, 65+ 2.9% (1998) **Ethnic groups:** 99% of the population are Africans, ethnically classified as Bantus, and distributed among over 130 tribes; main tribes are Bantu, Nilotic, Nilo-Hamitic, Khoisan, and Iraqwi **Language:** Kiswahili, English (both official) **Religion:** Muslim, Christian, traditional religions **Education:** (compulsory years) 7 **Literacy rate:** 79% (men); 54% (women) (1995 est) **Labour force:** 52% of population: 84% agriculture, 5% industry, 11% services (1990) **Life expectancy:** 50 (men); 53 (women) (1995–2000) **Child mortality rate:** (under 5, per 1,000 live births) 123 (1997) **Physicians:** 1 per 23,053 people (1991)

Practical information

Visa requirements: UK: visa required. USA: visa required **Embassy in the UK:** 43 Hertford Street, London W1Y 8DB. Tel: (0171) 499 8951; fax: (0171) 499 8954 **British embassy:** British High Commission, PO Box 9200, Hifadhi House, Samora Avenue, Dar es Salaam. Tel: (51) 46300/4; fax: (51) 46301 **Chamber of commerce:** Dar es Salaam Chamber of Commerce, PO Box 41, Kelvin House, Samora Machel Avenue, Dar es Salaam. Tel: (51) 21893

Chronology

8th century: Growth of city states along coast after settlement by Arabs from Oman. **1499:** Portuguese navigator Vasco da Gama visited island of Zanzibar. **16th century:** Portuguese occupied Zanzibar, defeated coastal states, and exerted spasmodic control over them. **1699:** Portuguese ousted from Zanzibar by Arabs of Oman. **18th century:** Sultan of Oman reasserted Arab overlordship of East African coast, which became subordinate to Zanzibar. **1744–1837:** Revolt of ruler of Mombasa against Oman spanned 93 years until final victory of Oman. **1822:** Moresby Treaty: Britain recognized regional dominance of Zanzibar, but protested against slave trade. **1840:** Sultan Seyyid bin Sultan moved his capital from Oman to Zanzibar; trade in slaves and ivory flourished. **1861:** Sultanates of Zanzibar and

Oman separated on death of Seyyid. **19th century:** Europeans started to explore inland, closely followed by Christian missionaries. **1884:** German Colonization Society began to acquire territory on mainland in defiance of Zanzibar. **1890:** Britain obtained protectorate over Zanzibar, abolished slave trade, and recognized German claims to mainland. **1897:** German East Africa formally established as colony. **1905–06:** Maji Maji revolt suppressed by German troops. **1916:** Conquest of German East Africa by British and South African forces, led by Gen Jan Smuts. **1919:** Most of German East Africa became British League of Nations mandate of Tanganyika. **1946:** Britain continued to govern Tanganyika as United Nations (UN) trusteeship. **1954:** Julius Nyerere organized the Tanganyikan African National Union (TANU) to campaign for independence. **1961:** Tanganyika achieved independence from Britain with Nyerere as prime minister. **1962:** Tanganyika became republic under President Nyerere. **1963:** Zanzibar achieved independence. **1964:** Arab-dominated sultanate of Zanzibar overthrown by Afro-Shirazi Party in violent revolution; Zanzibar merged with Tanganyika to form United Republic of Tanzania. **1967:** East African Community (EAC) formed by Tanzania, Kenya, and Uganda; Nyerere pledged to build socialist state. **1977:** Revolutionary Party of Tanzania (CCM) proclaimed as only legal party; EAC dissolved. **1979:** Tanzanian troops intervened in Uganda to help overthrow President Idi Amin. **1985:** Nyerere retired as president; succeeded by Ali Hassan Mwinyi. **1992:** Multiparty politics permitted. **1995:** Benjamin Mkapa of CCM elected president. **1998:** A bomb exploded at the US embassy in Dar es Salaam, killing 6 people and injuring 60; an anti-American Islamic group claimed responsibility. New left-of-centre party formed.

Thailand Kingdom of

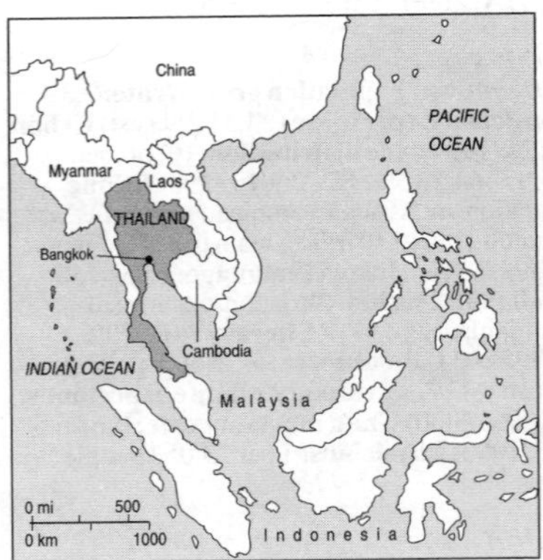

National name: *Prathet Thai* or *Muang Thai* **Area:** 513,115 sq km/198,113 sq mi **Capital:** Bangkok (and chief port) **Major towns/ cities:** Chiangmai, Hat Yai, Khon Kaen, Songkhla, Chon Buri, Nakhon Si Thammarat, Lampang, Phitsannlok, Ratchasima **Major ports:** Nakhon Sawan

Government

Head of state: King Bhumibol Adulyadej from 1946 **Head of government:** Chavalit Yongchaiyudh from 1996 **Political system:** military-controlled emergent democracy **Administrative divisions:** 76 provinces **Political parties:** Democrat Party (DP), centre left; Thai Nation (Chart Thai), right wing, pro-private enterprise; New Aspiration Party (NAP), centrist; Palang Dharma Party (PDP), anti-corruption, Buddhist; Social Action Party (SAP), moderate, conservative; Chart Pattana (National Development), conservative **Armed forces:** 266,000 (1997) **Conscription:** two years **Death penalty:** retained and used for ordinary crimes **Defence spend:** (% GDP) 2.1 (1997) **Education spend:** (% GNP) 4.2 (1995) **Health spend:** (% GDP) 1.4 (1990–95)

Economy and resources

Currency: baht **GDP:** (US$) 157.2 billion (1997) **Real GDP growth:** (% change on previous year) 0.6 (1997) **GNP (US$):** 169.6 billion(1997) **GNP per capita (PPP):** (US$) 6,590 (1997) **Consumer price inflation:** 7.8% (1998) **Unemployment:** 3.2% (1993) **Foreign debt:** (US$) 90.8 billion (1996) **Major trading partners:** Japan, USA, Singapore, Germany, Taiwan, Hong Kong **Resources:** tin ore, lignite, gypsum, antimony, manganese, copper, tungsten, lead, gold, zinc, silver, rubies, sapphires, natural gas, petroleum, fish **Exports:** textiles and clothing, electronic goods, rice, rubber, gemstones, sugar, cassava (tapioca), fish (especially prawns), machinery and manufactures, chemicals. Principal market: USA 19.6% (1997) **Imports:** petroleum and petroleum products, machinery, chemicals, iron and steel, consumer goods. Principal source: Japan 25.6% (1997) **Arable land:** 33.4% (1995)

Population and society

Population: 60,300,000 (1998 est) **Population growth rate:** 0.8% (1995–2000) **Population density:** (per sq km) 117.3 (1998 est) **Urban population:** (% of total) 21% (1997) **Age distribution:** (% of total population) 0–14 24.3%, 15–64 69.6%, 65+ 6.0% (1998) **Ethnic groups:** 75% of the population is of Thai descent; 14% ethnic Chinese, one-third of whom live in Bangkok; Thai Malays constitute the next largest minority, followed by hill tribes; a substantial Kampuchean (Khmer) refugee community resides in border camps **Language:** Thai and Chinese (both official); Lao, Chinese, Malay, Khmer **Religion:** Buddhist **Education:** (compulsory years) 6 **Literacy rate:** 96% (men); 90% (women) (1995 est) **Labour force:** 57% of population: 64% agriculture, 14% industry, 22% services (1990) **Life expectancy:** 66 (men); 72 (women) (1995–2000) **Child mortality rate:** (under 5, per 1,000 live births) 36 (1997) **Physicians:** 1 per 4,416 people (1993 est)

Practical information

Visa requirements: UK: visa not required. USA: visa not required **Embassy in the UK:** 1/3 Yorkshire House, Grosvenor Crescent, London SW1X 7ET. Tel: (0171) 371 7621; fax: (0171) 235 9808 **British embassy:** Wireless Road, Bangkok 10200. Tel: (2) 253 0191; fax: (2) 255 8619 **Chamber of commerce:** 150 Thanon Rajbopit, Bangkok 10200. Tel: (2) 225 0086; fax: (2) 225 3372

Chronology

13th century: Siamese (Thai) people migrated south and settled in valley of Chao Phraya River in Khmer Empire. **1238:** Siamese ousted Khmer governors and formed new kingdom based at Sukhothai. **14th and 15th centuries:** Siamese expanded at expense of declining Khmer Empire. **1350:** Siamese capital moved to Ayatthaya (which also became name of kingdom). **1511:** Portuguese traders first reached Siam. **1569:** Conquest of Ayatthaya by Burmese ended years of rivalry and conflict. **1589:** Siamese regained independence under King Naresuan. **17th century:** Foreign trade under royal monopoly developed with Chinese, Japanese, and Europeans. **1690s:** Siam expelled European military advisers and missionaries and adopted policy of isolation. **1767:** Burmese invaders destroyed city of Ayatthaya, massacred ruling families, and withdrew, leaving Siam in a state of anarchy. **1782:** Reunification of Siam after civil war under Gen Phraya Chakri, who founded new capital at Bangkok and proclaimed himself King Rama I. **1824–51:** King Rama III reopened Siam to European diplomats and missionaries. **1851–68:** King Mongkut employed European advisers to help modernize government, legal system, and army. **1856:** Royal monopoly on foreign trade ended. **1868–1910:** King Chulalongkorn continued modernization and developed railway network using Chinese immigrant labour; Siam became major exporter of rice. **1896:** Anglo-French agreement recognized Siam as independent buffer state between British Burma and French Indo-China. **1932:** Bloodless coup forced King Rama VII to grant a constitution with mixed civilian-military government. **1939:** Siam changed its name to Thailand (briefly reverting to Siam 1945–49). **1941:** Japanese invaded; Thailand became puppet ally of Japan under Field Marshal Phibun Songkhram. **1945:** Japanese withdrawal; Thailand compelled to return territory taken from Laos, Cambodia, and Malaya. **1946:** King Ananda Mahidol assassinated. **1947:** Phibun regained power in military coup, reducing monarch to figurehead; Thailand adopted strongly pro-American foreign policy. **1955:** Political parties and free speech introduced. **1957:** State of emergency declared; Phibun deposed in bloodless coup; military dictatorship continued under Gen Sarit Thanarat (1957–63) and Gen Thanom Kittikachorn (1963–73). **1967–72:** Thai troops fought in alliance with USA in Vietnam War. **1973:** Military government overthrown by student riots. **1974:** Adoption of democratic

constitution, followed by civilian coalition government. **1976:** Military reassumed control in response to mounting strikes and political violence. **1978:** Gen Kriangsak Chomanan introduced constitution with mixed civilian–military government. **1980:** Gen Prem Tinsulanonda assumed power. **1983:** Prem relinquished army office to head civilian government; martial law maintained. **1988:** Chatichai Choonhavan succeeded Prem as prime minister. **1991:** Military coup imposed new military-oriented constitution despite mass protests. **1992:** General election produced five-party coalition; riots forced Prime Minister Suchinda Kraprayoon to flee; Chuan Leekpai formed new coalition government. **1995:** Ruling coalition collapsed; Banharn Silpa-archa appointed premier. **1996:** Banharn resigned; general election resulted in new six-party coalition led by Chavalit Yongchaiyudh. **1997:** Major financial crisis led to floating of currency. Austerity rescue plan agreed with International Monetary Fund (IMF). **1998:** Repatriation of foreign workers commenced, as economy contracted sharply in response to IMF-inspired austerity measures. Economic restructuring plan welcomed by IMF. The opposition Chart Patthana party was brought into the coalition government of Chuan Leekpai, increasing its majority to push through reforms.

Togo Republic of (formerly Togoland)

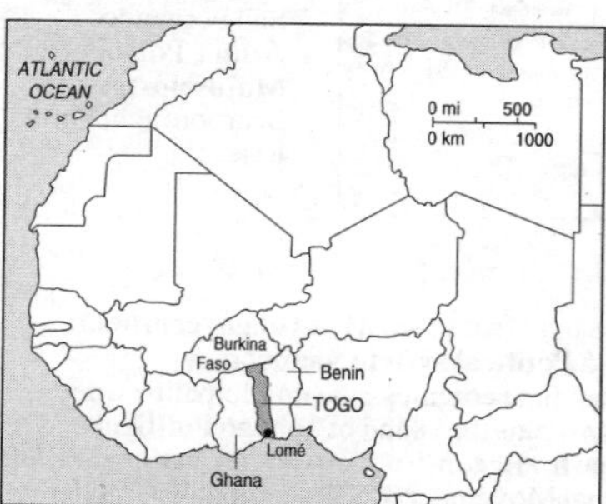

National name: *République Togolaise* **Area:** 56,800 sq km/21,930 sq mi **Capital:** Lomé **Major towns/cities:** Sokodé, Kpalimé, Kara, Atakpamé, Bassar, Tsévié

Government

Head of state: Etienne Gnassingbé Eyadéma from 1967 **Head of government:** Kwasi Klutse from 1996 **Political system:** emergent democracy **Administrative divisions:** five regions **Political parties:** Rally of the Togolese People (RPT), nationalist, centrist; Action Committee for Renewal (CAR), left of centre; Togolese Union for Democracy (UTD), left of centre **Armed forces:** 7,000 (1997) **Conscription:** military service is by selective conscription for two years **Death penalty:** retains the death penalty for ordinary crimes, but can be considered abolitionist in practice **Defence spend:** (% GDP) 2.1 (1997) **Education spend:** (% GNP) 4.7 (1996) **Health spend:** (% GDP) 1.7 (1990–95)

Economy and resources

Currency: franc CFA **GDP:** (US$) 1.3 billion (1997) **Real GDP growth:** (% change on previous year) 5.8 (1997 est) **GNP (US$):** 1.4 billion (1997) **GNP per capita (PPP):** (US$) 1,790 (1997) **Consumer price inflation:** 3.9% (1997 est) **Unemployment:** 2.5% (1989 est) **Foreign debt:** (US$) 1.5 billion (1996) **Major trading partners:** Canada, Ghana, France, Nigeria, Mexico, the Netherlands, Japan, USA, Spain **Resources:** phosphates, limestone, marble, deposits of iron ore, manganese, chromite, peat; exploration for petroleum and uranium was under way in the early 1990s **Exports:** phosphates (mainly calcium phosphates), ginned cotton, green coffee, cocoa beans. Principal market: Canada 7.6% (1997) **Imports:** machinery and transport equipment, cotton yarn and fabrics, cigarettes, antibiotics, food (especially cereals) and live animals, chemicals, refined petroleum products, beverages. Principal source: Ghana 19.1% (1997) **Arable land:** 38% (1995)

Population and society

Population: 4,397,000 (1998 est) **Population growth rate:** 2.7% (1995–2000) **Population density:** (per sq km) 90.2 (1998 est) **Urban population:** (% of total) 32 (1997) **Age distribution:** (% of total population) 0–14 48.3%, 15–64 49.5%, 65+ 2.2% (1998) **Ethnic groups:** predominantly of Sudanese Hamitic origin in the north, and black African in the south; they are distributed among 37 different ethnic groups. There are also European, Syrian, and Lebanese minorities **Language:** French (official), Ewe, Kabre, Gurma **Religion:** animist, Catholic, Muslim, Protestant **Education:** (compulsory years) 6 **Literacy rate:** 56% (men); 31% (women) (1995 est) **Labour force:** 42% of population: 66% agriculture, 10% industry, 24% services (1990) **Life expectancy:** 49 (men); 52 (women) (1995–2000) **Child mortality rate:** (under 5, per 1,000 live births) 130 (1997) **Physicians:** 1 per 11,385 people (1993 est)

Practical information

Visa requirements: UK: visa not required. USA: visa not required **Embassy in the UK:** 8 rue Alfred Roll, 75017 Paris, France. Tel: (1) 4380 1213; fax: (1) 4380 9071 **British embassy:** British Honorary Consulate, BP 20050, British School of Lomé, Lomé. Tel: (228) 264 606; fax: (228) 214 989 **Chamber of commerce:** Chambre de Commerce, d'Agriculture et d'Industrie du Togo, BP 360, angle avenue de la Présidence, Lomé. Tel: (228) 217 065; fax: (228) 214 730

Chronology

15th–17th centuries: Formerly dominated by Kwa peoples in southwest and Gur-speaking Voltaic peoples in north, Ewe clans immigrated from Nigeria and the Ane (Mina) from Ghana and Ivory Coast. **18th century:** Coastal area held by Danes. **1847:** Arrival of German missionaries. **1884–1914:** Togoland was a German protectorate until captured by Anglo-French forces; cocoa and cotton plantations developed, using forced labour. **1922:** Divided between Britain and France under League of Nations mandate. **1946:** Continued under United Nations trusteeship. **1957:** British Togoland, comprising one-third of the area and situated in the west, integrated with Ghana, following a plebiscite. **1960:** French Togoland, situated in the east, achieved independence from France as Republic of Togo with Sylvanus Olympio, leader of United Togolese (UP) party, as head of state. **1963:** Olympio killed in a military coup. His brother-in-law, Nicolas Grunitzky, became president. **1967:** Grunitzky replaced by Lt-Gen Etienne Gnassingbé Eyadéma in bloodless coup; political parties banned. **1969:** Assembly of the Togolese People (RPT) formed by Eyadéma as sole legal political party. **1975:** EEC Lomé convention signed in Lomé, establishing trade links with developing countries. **1977:** Assassination plot against Eyadéma, allegedly involving Olympio family, thwarted. **1979:** Eyadéma returned in election. Further EEC Lomé convention signed. **1986:** Attempted coup failed and situation stabilized with help of French troops. **1990:** Violent antigovernment demonstrations in Lomé suppressed with casualties; Eyadéma relegalized political parties. **1991:** Gilchrist Olympio returned from exile. Eyadéma was forced to call a national conference which limited the president's powers, and elected Joseph Kokou Koffigoh head of interim government. Three attempts by Eyadéma's troops to unseat government failed. **1992:** Strikes in southern Togo; Olympio was attacked by soldiers and fled to France. Overwhelming referendum support for multiparty politics. New constitution adopted. **1993:** Eyadéma won first multiparty presidential elections amid widespread opposition. **1994:** Antigovernment coup foiled. Opposition CAR polled strongly in assembly elections. Eyadéma appointed Edem Kodjo of the minority UTD as prime minister. **1996:** Kwasi Klutse appointed prime minister. **1998:** President Eyadéma re-elected.

Tonga Kingdom of (or Friendly Islands)

National name: *Pule'anga Fakatu'i'o Tonga* **Area:** 750 sq km/290 sq mi **Capital:** Nuku'alofa (on Tongatapu Island) **Major towns/cities:** Pangai, Neiafu

Government

Head of state: King Taufa'ahau Tupou IV from 1965 **Head of government:** Baron Vaea from 1991 **Political system:** constitutional

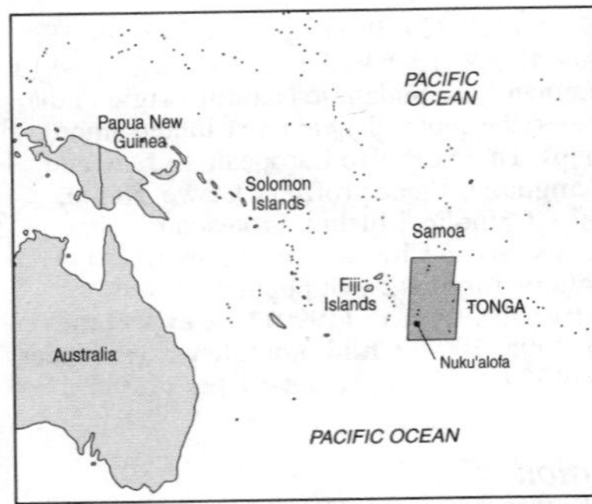

monarchy **Administrative divisions:** five divisions comprising 23 districts **Political parties:** legally none, but one prodemocracy grouping, the People's Party **Armed forces:** 125-strong naval force (1995) **Conscription:** military service is voluntary **Death penalty:** retains the death penalty for ordinary crimes, but can be considered abolitionist in practice (last execution 1982) **Education spend:** (% GNP) 4.8 (1992) **Health spend:** (% GDP) 4.1 (1991 est)

Economy and resources

Currency: Tongan dollar or pa'anga **GDP:** (US$) 194 million (1996) **Real GDP growth:** (% change on previous year) 0 (1997) **GNP (US$):** 179 million (1997) **GNP per capita (PPP):** (US$) 2,630 (1997 est) **Consumer price inflation:** 2.1% (1997) **Unemployment:** 4.2% (1990) **Foreign debt:** (US$) 70 million (1996) **Major trading partners:** New Zealand, Japan, Australia, Fiji Islands, USA, UK **Exports:** vanilla beans, pumpkins, coconut oil and other coconut products, watermelons, knitted clothes, cassava, yams, sweet potatoes, footwear. Principal market: Japan 42.9% (1996) **Imports:** foodstuffs, basic manufactures, machinery and transport equipment, mineral fuels. Principal source: New Zealand 34.2% (1996) **Arable land:** 23.6% (1995)

Population and society

Population: 98,000 (1998 est) **Population growth rate:** 0.4% (1995–2000) **Population density:** (per sq km) 150.9 (1998 est) **Urban population:** (% of total) 44 (1997) **Age distribution:** (% of total population) 0–14 39.6%, 15–64 54.7%, 65+ 5.7% (1992) **Ethnic groups:** 98% of Tongan ethnic origin, a Polynesian group with a small mixture of Melanesian; the remainder is European and part-European **Language:** Tongan (official); English **Religion:** Free Wesleyan Church **Education:** (compulsory years) 8 **Literacy rate:** 95% (men); 89% (women) (1994 est) **Labour force:** 38.1% agriculture, 20.6% industry, 41.3% (1990) **Life expectancy:** 67 (men); 71 (women) (1996 est) **Child mortality rate:** (under 5, per 1,000 live births) 20 (1994) **Physicians:** 1 per 2,325 people (1991)

Practical information

Visa requirements: UK: visa required (issued on arrival). USA: visa required (issued on arrival) **Embassy in the UK:** 36 Molyneux Street, London W1H 6AB. Tel: (0171) 724 5828; fax: (0171) 723 9074 **British embassy:** British High Commission, PO Box 56, Vuna Road, Nuku'alofa. Tel: (676) 21020/1; fax: (676) 24109 **Chamber of commerce:** Office of the Minister of Labour, Commerce and Industries, PO Box 110, Nuku'alofa. Tel/fax: (676) 23688

Chronology

c. **1000 BC:** Settled by Polynesian immigrants from the Fiji Islands. *c.* **AD 950:** The legendary Aho'eitu became the first hereditary Tongan king (Tu'i Tonga). **13th–14th centuries:** Tu'i Tonga kingdom at the height of its power. **1643:** Visited by the Dutch navigator, Abel Tasman. **1773:** Islands visited by British navigator Capt James Cook, who named them the 'Friendly Islands'. **1826:** Methodist mission established. **1831:** Tongan dynasty founded by a Christian convert and chief of Ha'apai, Prince Taufa'ahau Tupou, who became king 14 years later. **1845–93:** Reign of King George Tupou I, during which the country was reunited after half a century of civil war; Christianity was spread and a modern constitution adopted in 1875. **1900:** Friendship ('Protectorate') treaty signed between King George Tupou II and Britain, establishing British control over defence and foreign affairs, but leaving internal political affairs under Tongan control. **1918:** Queen Salote Tupou III ascended the throne. **1965:** Queen Salote died; succeeded by her son, King Taufa'ahau Tupou IV, who had been prime minister since 1949. **1970:** Independence from Britain, but remained within Commonwealth. **1993:** Six prodemocracy candidates elected. Calls for reform of absolutist power. **1996:** Prodemocracy movement led by People's Party won a majority of the 'commoner' seats in legislative assembly. Prodemocracy campaigner Akilisis Pohiva released after a month's imprisonment.

Trinidad and Tobago Republic of

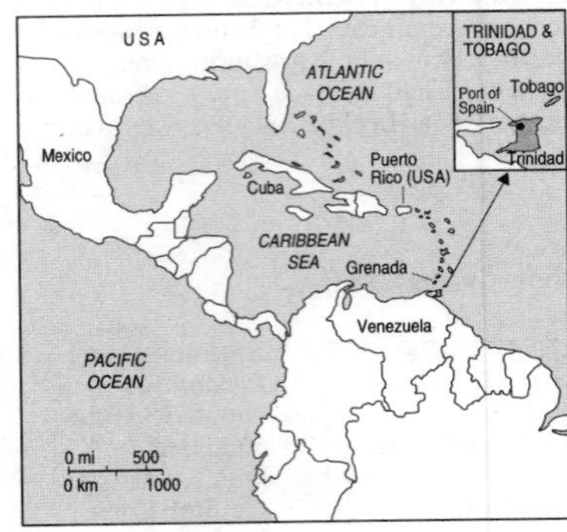

Area: 5,130 sq km/1,980 sq mi including smaller islands (Trinidad 4,828 sq km/1,864 sq mi and Tobago 300 sq km/115 sq mi) **Capital:** Port-of-Spain (and port) **Major towns/cities:** San Fernando, Arima, Point Fortin **Major ports:** Scarborough, Point Lisas

Government

Head of state: Noor Hassanali from 1987 **Head of government:** Basdeo Panday from 1995 **Political system:** democracy **Administrative divisions:** nine counties, two municipalities, and three borough corporations, plus the island of Tobago **Political parties:** National Alliance for Reconstruction (NAR), nationalist, left of centre; People's National Movement (PNM), nationalist, moderate, centrist; United National Congress (UNC), left of centre; Movement for Social Transformation (Motion), left of centre **Armed forces:** 2,100; plus a paramlitary force of 4,800 (1997) **Conscription:** military service is voluntary **Death penalty:** retained and used for ordinary crimes **Defence spend:** (% GDP) 1.4 (1997) **Education spend:** (% GNP) 3.7 (1996) **Health spend:** (% GDP) 2.6 (1990–95)

Economy and resources

Currency: Trinidad and Tobago dollar **GDP:** (US$) 5.8 billion (1997) **Real GDP growth:** (% change on previous year) 3.1 (1997) **GNP (US$):** 5.5 billion (1997) **GNP per capita (PPP):** (US$) 6,410 (1997) **Consumer price inflation:** 4.9% (1998) **Unemployment:** 16.2 (1996 est) **Foreign debt:** (US$) 2.24 billion (1996) **Major trading partners:** USA, Venezuela, UK, Germany, Canada, Barbados, Jamaica, Guyana, Netherlands Antilles **Resources:** petroleum, natural gas, asphalt (world's largest deposits of natural asphalt) **Exports:** mineral fuels and lubricants, chemicals, basic manufactures, food. Principal market: USA 39.7% (1997) **Imports:** machinery and transport equipment, manufactured goods, mineral fuel products, food and live animals, chemicals. Principal source: USA 52.2% (1997) **Arable land:** 14.6% (1995)

Population and society

Population: 1,283,000 (1998 est) **Population growth rate:** 0.8% (1995–2000) **Population density:** (per sq km) 217.6 (1998 est) **Urban population:** (% of total) 73 (1997) **Age distribution:** (% of total population) 0–14 28.1%, 15–64 64.6%, 65+ 7.3% (1998) **Ethnic groups:** the two main ethnic groups are Africans and East Indians; there are also European, Afro-European, and Chinese minorities. The original Carib population has largely disappeared **Language:** English (official); Hindi, French, Spanish **Religion:** Roman Catholic, Anglican, Hindu, Muslim **Education:** (compulsory years) 7 **Literacy rate:** 97% (men); 95% (women) (1995 est)

Labour force: 12.4% agriculture, 25.4% industry, 62.2% services (1994) **Life expectancy:** 72 (men); 76 (women) (1995–2000) **Child mortality rate:** (under 5, per 1,000 live births) 15 (1997) **Physicians:** 1 per 1,113 people (1994)

Practical information

Visa requirements: UK: visa not required for a stay of up to three months. USA: visa not required for a stay of up to three months **Embassy in the UK:** 42 Belgrave Square, London SW1X 8NT. Tel: (0171) 245 9351; fax: (0171) 823 1065 **British embassy:** British High Commission, PO Box 778, 19 Clair Avenue, St Clair, Port of Spain. Tel: (809) 622 2748; fax: (809) 622 4555 **Chamber of commerce:** Trinidad and Tobago Chamber of Industry and Commerce, PO Box 499, Room 950–952, Hilton Hotel, Port of Spain. Tel: (809) 627 4461; fax: (809) 627 4376

Chronology

1498: Visited by the explorer Christopher Columbus, who named Trinidad after the three peaks at its southeastern tip and Tobago after the local form of tobacco pipe. Carib and Arawak Indians comprised the indigenous community. **1532:** Trinidad colonized by Spain. **1630s:** Tobago settled by Dutch, who introduced sugar-cane growing. **1797:** Trinidad captured by Britain and ceded by Spain five years later under Treaty of Amiens. **1814:** Tobago ceded to Britain by France. **1834:** Abolition of slavery resulted in indentured labourers being brought in from India, rather than Africa, to work sugar plantations. **1889:** Trinidad and Tobago amalgamated as British colony. **1956:** The People's National Movement (PNM) founded by Eric Williams, a moderate nationalist. **1958–62:** Part of West Indies Federation. **1959:** Achieved internal self-government, with Williams as chief minister. **1962:** Independence achieved within Commonwealth, with Williams as prime minister. **1970:** Army mutiny and violent Black Power riots directed against minority East Indian population; state of emergency imposed for two years. **1976:** Became a republic, with former governor general Ellis Clarke as president and Williams as prime minister. **1981:** Williams died; succeeded by George Chambers. **1986:** Tobago-based National Alliance for Reconstruction (NAR), headed by Arthur Robinson, won general election. **1987:** Noor Hassanali became president. **1990:** Attempted antigovernment coup by Islamic fundamentalists foiled. **1991:** General election victory for PNM, with Patrick Manning as prime minister. **1995:** United National Congress (UNC), a breakaway from the NAR rooted in the Indian community, and PNM tied in general election; UNC–NAR coalition formed, led by Basdeo Panday.

Tunisia Tunisian Republic

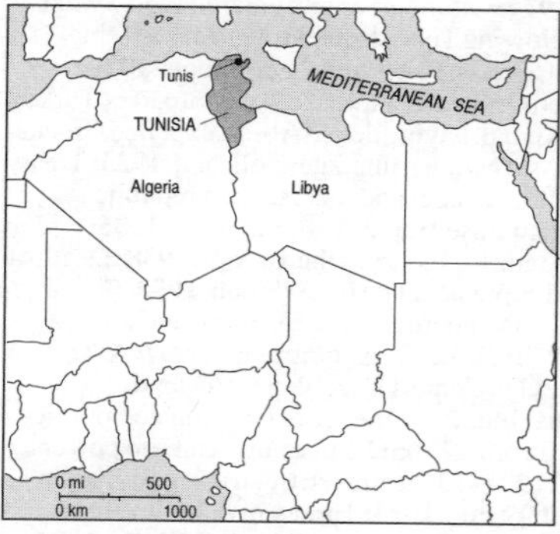

National name: *al-Jumhuriya at-Tunisiya* **Area:** 164,150 sq km/ 63,378 sq mi **Capital:** Tunis (and chief port) **Major towns/cities:** Sfax, Ariana, Bizerte, Djerba, Gabès, Sousse, Kairouan, Bardo, La Goulette **Major ports:** Sfax, Sousse, Bizerte

Government

Head of state: Zine el-Abidine Ben Ali from 1987 **Head of government:** Hamed Karoui from 1989 **Political system:** emergent democracy **Administrative divisions:** 23 governates **Political parties:** Constitutional Democratic Rally (RCD), nationalist, moderate, socialist; Popular Unity Movement (MUP), radical, left of centre; Democratic Socialists Movement (MDS), left of centre; Renovation Movement (MR), reformed communists **Armed forces:** 35,000; plus paramilitary forces numbering 12,000 (1997) **Conscription:** military service is by selective conscription for 12 months **Death penalty:** retained and used for ordinary crimes **Defence spend:** (% GDP) 1.8 (1997) **Education spend:** (% GNP) 6.7 (1996) **Health spend:** (% GDP) 3.0 (1990–95)

Economy and resources

Currency: Tunisian dinar **GDP:** (US$) 19.06 billion (1997) **Real GDP growth:** (% change on previous year) 4.4 (1997) **GNP (US$):** 19.4 billion (1997) **GNP per capita (PPP):** (US$) 4,980 (1997) **Consumer price inflation:** 4.8% (1998) **Unemployment:** 15% (1995 est) **Foreign debt:** (US$) 10.3 billion (1996) **Major trading partners:** France, Italy, Germany, Belgium, USA, Spain, the Netherlands, UK, Libya, Japan **Resources:** petroleum, natural gas, phosphates, iron, zinc, lead, aluminium fluoride, fluorspar, sea salt **Exports:** textiles and clothing, crude petroleum, phosphates and fertilizers, olive oil, fruit, leather and shoes, fishery products, machinery and electrical appliances. Principal market: France 26.1% (1997) **Imports:** machinery, textiles, food (mainly cereals, dairy produce, meat, and sugar) and live animals, petroleum and petroleum products. Principal source: France: 25.3% (1997) **Arable land:** 18.3 (1995)

Population and society

Population: 9,335,000 (1998 est) **Population growth rate:** 1.8% (1995–2000); 1.5% (2000–05) **Population density:** (per sq km) 60.4 (1998 est) **Urban population:** (% of total) 64 (1997) **Age distribution:** (% of total population) 0–14 31.6%, 15–64 62.7%, 65+ 5.7% (1998) **Ethnic groups:** about 10% of the population is Arab; the remainder are of Berber-Arab descent. There are small Jewish and French communities **Language:** Arabic (official); French **Religion:** Sunni Muslim; Jewish, Christian **Education:** (compulsory years) 9 **Literacy rate:** 74% (men); 56% (women) (1995 est) **Labour force:** 21.6% agriculture, 34.4% industry, 44% services (1994) **Life expectancy:** 68 (men); 71 (women) (1995–2000) **Child mortality rate:** (under 5, per 1,000 live births) 46 (1997) **Physicians:** 1 per 1,549 people (1993 est)

Practical information

Visa requirements: UK: visa not required. USA: visa not required **Embassy in the UK:** 29 Prince's Gate, London SW7 1QG. Tel: (0171) 584 8117; fax: (0171) 225 2884 **British embassy:** 5 place de la Victoire, Tunis. Tel: (1) 341 444; fax: (1) 354 877 **Chamber of commerce:** Chambre de Commerce et d'Industrie de Tunis, 1 rue des Entrepreneurs, 1000 Tunis. Tel: (1) 242 872; fax: (1) 354 744

Chronology

814 BC: Phoenician emigrants from Tyre, in Lebanon, founded Carthage, near modern Tunis, as a trading post. By 6th century BC Carthaginian kingdom dominated western Mediterranean. **146 BC:** Carthage destroyed by Punic Wars with Rome, which began 264 BC; Carthage became part of Rome's African province. **AD 533:** Came under control of Byzantine Empire. **7th century:** Invaded by Arabs, who introduced Islam. Succession of Islamic dynasties followed, including Aghlabids (9th century), Fatimids (10th century), and Almohads (12th century). **1574:** Became part of Islamic Turkish Ottoman Empire and a base for 'Barbary Pirates' who operated against European shipping until 19th century. **1705:** Husayn Bey founded local dynasty, which held power under rule of Ottomans. **early 19th century:** Ahmad Bey launched programme of economic modernization, which was to nearly bankrupt the country. **1881:** Became French protectorate, with bey retaining local power. **1920:** Destour (Constitution) Party, named after original Tunisian constitution of 1861, founded to campaign for equal Tunisian participation in French-dominated government. **1934:** Habib Bourguiba founded radical splinter party, the Neo-Destour Party, to spearhead nationalist movement. **1942–43:** Brief German occupation during World War II. **1956:** Independence achieved as monarchy under bey, with Bourguiba as prime minister. **1957:** Bey deposed; Tunisia became one-party republic with Bourguiba as president. **1975:** Bourguiba made president for life. **1979:** Headquarters for Arab League moved to Tunis after Egypt signed

Camp David Accords with Israel. **1981:** Multiparty elections held, as a sign of political liberalization, but were won by Bourguiba's Destourian Socialist Party (DSP). **1982:** Allowed Palestine Liberation Organization (PLO) to use Tunis for its headquarters. **1985:** Diplomatic relations with Libya severed; Israel attacked PLO headquarters. **1987:** Zine el-Abidine Ben Ali, new prime minister, declared Bourguiba (now aged 84) incompetent for government and seized power as president. **1988:** 2,000 political prisoners freed; privatization initiative. Diplomatic relations with Libya restored. DSP renamed RCD. **1990:** Arab League's headquarters returned to Cairo, Egypt. **1991:** Opposition to US actions during Gulf War. Crackdown on religious fundamentalists; Renaissance Party banned. **1992:** Western criticism of human-rights transgressions. **1994:** Ben Ali and RCD re-elected. PLO transferred headquarters to Gaza City in Palestine.

Turkey Republic of

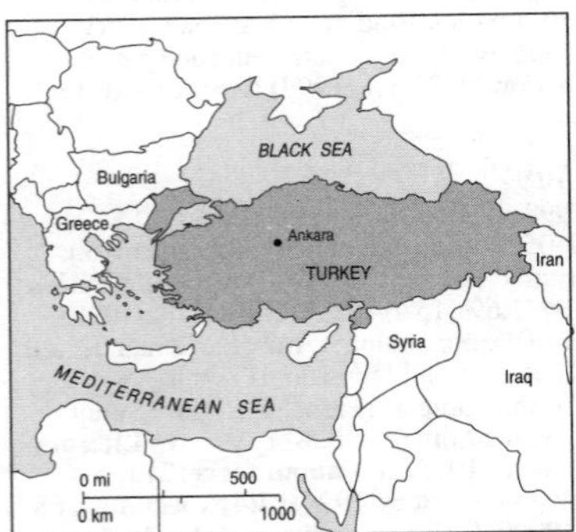

National name: *Türkiye Cumhuriyeti* **Area:** 779,500 sq km/300,964 sq mi **Capital:** Ankara **Major towns/cities:** Istanbul, Izmir, Adana, Bursa, Antakya, Gaziantep, Konya, Mersin, Kayseri, Edirne, Antalya **Major ports:** Istanbul and Izmir

Government

Head of state: Suleiman Demirel from 1993 **Head of government:** Bülent Ecevit from 1999 **Political system:** democracy **Administrative divisions:** 73 provinces **Political parties:** Motherland Party (ANAP), Islamic, nationalist, right of centre; Republican People's Party (CHP), centre left; True Path Party (DYP), centre right, pro-Western; Virtue Party (FP), Islamic fundamentalist; **Armed forces:** 639,000 (1997) **Conscription:** 18 months **Death penalty:** retained for ordinary crimes, but considered abolitionist in practice; last execution in 1984 **Defence spend:** (% GDP) 4.2 (1997) **Education spend:** (% GNP) 3.4 (1995) **Health spend:** (% GDP) 2.7 (1990–95)

Economy and resources

Currency: Turkish lira **GDP:** (US$) 193.8 billion (1997) **Real GDP growth:** (% change on previous year) 5.9 (1997) **GNP (US$):** 199.5 billion (1997) **GNP per capita (PPP):** (US$) 6,430 (1997) **Consumer price inflation:** 83.1% (1998) **Unemployment:** 6.4% (1997) **Foreign debt:** (US$) 79.8 billion (1996) **Major trading partners:** Germany, USA, Italy, France, Saudi Arabia, UK, Russia **Resources:** chromium, copper, mercury, antimony, borax, coal, petroleum, natural gas, iron ore, salt **Exports:** textiles and clothing, agricultural products and foodstuffs (including figs, nuts, and dried fruit), tobacco, leather, glass, refined petroleum and petroleum products. Principal market: Germany 20% (1997) **Imports:** machinery, construction material, motor vehicles, consumer goods, crude petroleum, iron and steel, chemical products, fertilizer, livestock. Principal source: Germany 16.5% (1997) **Arable land:** 32% (1995)

Population and society

Population: 64,479,000 (1998 est) **Population growth rate:** 1.6% (1995–2000); 1.5% (2000–05) **Population density:** (per sq km) 83.8 (1998 est) **Urban population:** (% of total) 72 (1997) **Age distribution:** (% of total population) 0–14 30.9%, 15–64 63.3%, 65+ 5.8% (1998) **Ethnic groups:** over 90% of the population are Turks, although only about 5% are of Turkic or Western Mongoloid descent; most are descended from earlier conquerors, such as the Greeks **Language:** Turkish (official); Kurdish, Arabic **Religion:** Sunni Muslim; Orthodox, Armenian churches **Education:** (compulsory years) 5 **Literacy rate:** 90% (men); 71% (women) (1995 est) **Labour force:** 36.3% of population: 44.9% agriculture, 22% industry, 33.1% services (1996) **Life expectancy:** 67 (men); 72 (women) (1995–2000) **Child mortality rate:** (under 5, per 1,000 live births) 58 (1997) **Physicians:** 1 per 833 people (1995)

Practical information

Visa requirements: UK: visa not required for a stay of up to three months. USA: visa not required for a stay of up to three months **Embassy in the UK:** 43 Belgrave Square, London SW1X 8PA. Tel: (0171) 393 0202; fax: (0171) 393 0066 **British embassy:** Senit Ersan Caddesi 46/A, Cankaya, Ankara. Tel: (312) 468 6230; fax: (312) 468 3214 **Chamber of commerce:** Union of Chambers of Commerce, Industry, Maritime Commerce and Commodity Exchanges of Turkey, Atatürk Bul 149, Bakanhliklar, 06640, Ankara. Tel: (312) 417 7700; fax: (312) 418 3568

Chronology

1st century BC: Asia Minor became part of Roman Empire, later passing to Byzantine Empire. **6th century AD:** Turkic peoples spread from Mongolia into Turkestan, where they adopted Islam. **1055:** Seljuk Turks captured Baghdad; their leader Tughrul took title of sultan. **1071:** Battle of Manzikert: Seljuk Turks defeated Byzantines and conquered Asia Minor. **13th century:** Ottoman Turks, driven west by Mongols, became vassals of Seljuk Turks. *c.* **1299:** Osman I founded small Ottoman kingdom, which quickly displaced Seljuks to include all Asia Minor. **1354:** Ottoman Turks captured Gallipoli and began their conquests in Europe. **1389:** Battle of Kossovo: Turks defeated Serbs to take control of most of Balkan peninsula. **1453:** Constantinople, capital of Byzantine Empire, fell to the Turks; became capital of Ottoman Empire as Istanbul. **16th century:** Ottoman Empire reached its zenith under Suleiman the Magnificent 1520–66; Turks conquered Egypt, Syria, Arabia, Mesopotamia, Tripoli, Cyprus, and most of Hungary. **1683:** Failure of Siege of Vienna marked start of decline of Ottoman Empire. **1699:** Treaty of Karlowitz: Turks forced out of Hungary by Austrians. **1774:** Treaty of Kuchuk Kainarji: Russia drove Turks from Crimea and won the right to intervene on behalf of Christian subjects of the sultan. **19th century:** 'The Eastern Question': Ottoman weakness caused intense rivalry between powers to shape future of Near East. **1821–29:** Greek war of independence: Greeks defeated Turks with help of Russia, Britain, and France. **1854–56:** Crimean War: Britain and France fought to defend Ottoman Empire from further pressure by Russians. **1877–78:** Russo-Turkish War ended with Treaty of Berlin and withdrawal of Turks from Bulgaria. **1908:** Young Turk revolution forced sultan to grant constitution; start of political modernization. **1911–12:** Italo-Turkish War: Turkey lost Tripoli (Libya). **1912–13:** Balkan War: Greece, Serbia, and Bulgaria expelled Turks from Macedonia and Albania. **1914:** Ottoman Empire entered World War I on German side. **1919:** Following Turkish defeat, Mustapha Kemal launched nationalist revolt to resist foreign encroachments. **1920:** Treaty of Sèvres partitioned Ottoman Empire, leaving no part of Turkey fully independent. **1922:** Kemal, having defied Allies, expelled Greeks, French, and Italians from Asia Minor; sultanate abolished. **1923:** Treaty of Lausanne recognized Turkish independence; secular republic established by Kemal, who imposed rapid Westernization. **1935:** Kemal adopted surname Atatürk ('Father of the Turks'). **1938:** Death of Kemal Atatürk; succeeded as president by Ismet Inönü. **1950:** First free elections won by opposition Democratic Party; Adnan Menderes became prime minister. **1952:** Turkey became a member of NATO. **1960:** Military coup led by Gen Cemal Gürsel deposed Menderes, who was executed in 1961. **1961:** Inönü returned as prime minister; politics dominated by the issue of Cyprus. **1965:** Justice Party came to power under Suleyman Demirel. **1971–73:** Prompted by strikes and student unrest, army imposed military rule. **1974:** Turkey invaded northern Cyprus. **1980–83:** Political violence led to further military rule. **1984:** Kurds began guerrilla war in quest for greater autonomy. **1989:** Application to join European Community rejected. **1990–91:** Turkey joined UN coalition against Iraq in Gulf War. **1995:** Turkish offensives against Kurdish bases in northern Iraq; Islamicist Welfare Party won largest number of seats in general election. **1997:** Plans agreed for

curbing of Muslim fundamentalism. Mesut Yilmaz appointed prime minister. Agreement with Greece on peaceful resolution of disputes. **1998:** Islamic Welfare Party (RP) banned by Constitutional Court, and regrouped as Virtue Party (FP). Prime Minister Mesut Yilmaz lost a vote of confidence and was replaced by Yalim Erez. **1999:** Yalim Erez replaced as prime minister by Bülent Ecevit.

Turkmenistan Republic of

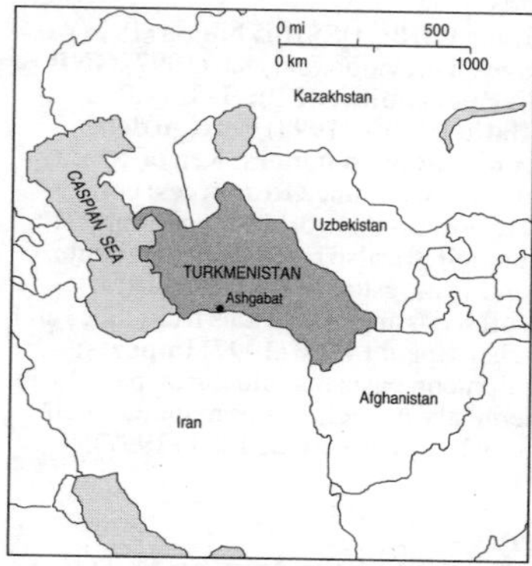

Area: 488,100 sq km/ 188,455 sq mi **Capital:** Ashgabat **Major towns/cities:** Chardzhov, Mary (Merv), Nebit-Dag, Krasnovodsk **Major ports:** Turkmenbashi

Government

Head of state and government: Saparmurad Niyazov from 1991 **Political system:** authoritarian nationalist **Administrative divisions:** five regions **Political parties:** Democratic Party of Turkmenistan, ex-communist, pro-Niyazov; Turkmen Popular Front (Agzybirlik), nationalist **Armed forces:** 18,000 (1997) **Conscription:** military service is compulsory for 18 months **Death penalty:** retained and used for ordinary crimes **Defence spend:** (% GDP) 2.7 (1997) **Education spend:** (% GNP) 7.9 (1993/94) **Health spend:** (% GDP) 2.8 (1990–95)

Economy and resources

Currency: manat **GDP:** (US$) 2.3 billion (1997 est) **Real GDP growth:** (% change on previous year) –15 (1997) **GNP (US$):** 2.9 billion (1997) **GNP per capita (PPP):** (US$) 1,410 (1997) **Consumer price inflation:** 100% (1998) **Unemployment:** 2.5% (1992 est) **Foreign debt:** (US$) 825 million (1996) **Major trading partners:** Ukraine, Russia, Turkey, Iran, USA, Kazakhstan, Tajikistan **Resources:** petroleum, natural gas, coal, sulphur, magnesium, iodine-bromine, sodium sulphate and different types of salt **Exports:** natural gas, cotton yarn, electric energy, petroleum and petroleum products. Principal market: Russia 43.6% (1997) **Imports:** machinery and metalwork, light industrial products, processed food, agricultural products. Principal source: Ukraine 14.9% (1997) **Arable land:** 3% (1995)

Population and society

Population: 4,309,000 (1998 est) **Population growth rate:** 1.9% (1995–2000); 1.9% (2000–05) **Population density:** (per sq km) 8.8 (1998 est) **Urban population:** (% of total) 45 (1997) **Age distribution:** (% of total population) 0–14 38.6%, 15–64 57.3%, 65+ 4.2% (1998) **Ethnic groups:** 72% ethnic Turkmen, 10% ethnic Russian, 9% Uzbek, 3% Kazakh, 1% Ukrainian **Language:** West Turkic, closely related to Turkish **Religion:** Sunni Muslim **Education:** (compulsory years) 9 **Literacy rate:** 98% (1995 est) **Labour force:** 43.4% agriculture, 20.8% industry, 35.8% services (1993) **Life expectancy:** 61 (men); 68 (women) (1995–2000) **Child mortality rate:** (under 5, per 1,000 live births) 74 (1997) **Physicians:** 1 per 311 people (1994)

Practical information

Visa requirements: UK: visa required. USA: visa required **Embassy in the UK:** Turkmenistan has no diplomatic representation in the UK; the Department of Trade and Industry has a desk which deals with enquiries relating to Turkmenistan. Tel: (0171) 215 8427; fax: (0171) 215 4817 **British embassy:** the UK has no diplomatic representation in Turkmenistan **Chamber of commerce:** Commission for International Economic Affairs of the Office of the President of Turkmenistan, Ulitsa Kemine 92, Ashgabat 744000. Tel: (3632) 298 770; fax: (3632) 297 524

Chronology

6th century BC Part of Persian Empire of Cyrus the Great. **4th century BC:** Part of empire of Alexander the Great of Macedonia. **7th century:** Spread of Islam into Transcaspian region, followed by Arab rule from 8th century. **10th–13th centuries:** Immigration from northeast by nomadic Oghuz Seljuk and Mongol tribes, whose Turkic-speaking descendants now dominate the country; conquest by Genghis Khan. **16th century:** Came under dominance of Persia, to the south. **1869–81:** Fell under control of tsarist Russia after 150,000 Turkmen were killed in Battle of Gok Tepe in 1881; became part of Russia's Turkestan Governor-Generalship. **1916:** Turkmen revolted violently against Russian rule; autonomous Transcaspian government formed after Russian Revolution of 1917. **1919:** Brought back under Russian control following invasion by the Soviet Red Army. **1921:** Part of Turkestan Soviet Socialist Autonomous Republic. **1925:** Became constituent republic of USSR. **1920s–30s:** Soviet programme of agricultural collectivization and secularization provoked sporadic guerrilla resistance and popular uprisings. **1960–67:** Lenin Kara-Kum Canal built, leading to dramatic expansion in cotton production in previously semidesert region. **1985:** Saparmurad Niyazov replaced Muhammad Gapusov, local communist leader since 1971, whose regime had been viewed as corrupt. **1989:** Stimulated by *glasnost* initiative of reformist Soviet leader Mikhail Gorbachev, Agzybirlik 'popular front' formed by Turkmen intellectuals. **1990:** Economic and political sovereignty declared. Niyazov elected state president. **1991:** Niyazov initially supported attempted anti-Gorbachev coup in Moscow. Independence was later declared; joined new Commonwealth of Independent States (CIS). **1992:** Joined Muslim Economic Cooperation Organization and United Nations; new constitution adopted. **1993:** New currency, manat, introduced and programme of cautious economic reform introduced, with foreign investment in country's huge oil and gas reserves encouraged; but economy contracted to 1995. **1994:** Nationwide referendum overwhelmingly backed Niyazov's presidency. Ex-communists won most seats in parliamentary elections. **1997:** Private land ownership legalized.

Tuvalu South West Pacific State of (formerly Ellice Islands)

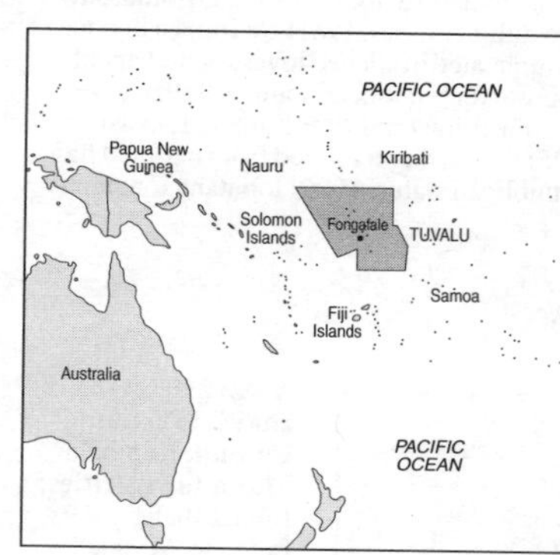

Area: 25 sq km/9.6 sq mi **Capital:** Fongafale (on Funafuti atoll) **Major towns/cities:** Vaitupu, Niutao, Nanumea

Government

Head of state: Queen Elizabeth II from 1978, represented by governor general Tulaga Manuella from 1994 **Head of government:** Ionatana Ionatana from 1999 **Political system:** liberal democracy **Administrative divisions:** one town council and seven island councils **Political parties:** none; members are elected to parliament as independents **Armed forces:** no standing defence force **Death penalty:** laws do not provide for the death penalty for any crime

Economy and resources

Currency: Australian dollar **GDP:** (US$) 8 million (1995 est) **Real GDP growth:** (% change on previous year) N/A **GNP (US$):** N/A **GNP**

per capita (PPP): (US$) N/A **Consumer price inflation:** 3.9 (1985–93) **Foreign debt:** (US$) 6 million (1993) **Major trading partners:** Australia, Fiji Islands, New Zealand, UK **Exports:** copra. Principal market: Australia **Imports:** food and live animals, beverages, tobacco, consumer goods, machinery and transport equipment, mineral fuels. Principal source: Australia

Population and society

Population: 11,000 (1998 est) **Population growth rate:** 0.9% (1995–2025) **Population density:** (per sq km) 401.7 (1998 est) **Urban population:** (% of total) 49 (1997) **Age distribution:** (% of total population) 0–14 35.2%, 15–64 60.0%, 65+ 4.8% (1998) **Ethnic groups:** almost entirely of Polynesian origin, maintaining close ties with Samoans and Tokelauans to the south and east **Language:** Tuvaluan, English **Religion:** Christian (mainly Protestant) **Education:** (compulsory years) 9 **Literacy rate:** N/A **Life expectancy:** 63 (men); 65 (women) (1995) **Child mortality rate:** (under 5, per 1,000 live births) 28 (1994) **Physicians:** 1 per 2,743 people (1990)

Practical information

Visa requirements: UK: visa not required. USA: visa required **Embassy for the UK:** Honorary Consulate General of Tuvalu, Klövensteenweg 115A, 22559 Hamburg, Germany. Tel: (40) 810 580; fax: (40) 811 016 **British embassy:** the British Embassy in Suva (see Fiji Islands) deals with enquiries relating to Tuvalu **Chamber of commerce:** Development Bank of Tuvalu, PO Box 9, Vaiaku, Funafuti. Tel: (688) 20198; telex: 4800

Chronology

c. **300 BC:** First settled by Polynesian peoples. **16th century:** Invaded and occupied by Samoans. **1765:** Islands first reached by Europeans. **1850–75:** Population decimated by European slave traders capturing Tuvaluans to work in South America and by exposure to European diseases. **1856:** The four southern islands, including Funafuti, claimed by USA. **1865:** Christian mission established. **1877:** Came under control of British Western Pacific High Commission (WPHC), with its headquarters in the Fiji Islands. **1892:** Known as the Ellice Islands, they were joined with Gilbert Islands (now Kiribati) to form British protectorate. **1916:** Gilbert and Ellice Islands colony formed. **1942–43:** Became base for US airforce operations when Japan occupied Gilbert Islands during World War II. **1975:** Following referendum, the predominantly Melanesian-peopled Ellice Islands, fearing domination by Micronesian-peopled Gilbert Islands in an independent state, were granted separate status. **1978:** Independence achieved within Commonwealth, with Toaripi Lauti as prime minister; reverted to former name Tuvalu ('eight standing together'). **1979:** The USA signed friendship treaty, relinquishing its claim to the four southern atolls in return for continued access to military bases. **1981:** Dr Tomasi Puapua became premier after Louti implicated in alleged investment scandal. **1986:** Islanders rejected proposal for republican status. **1989:** Bikenibeu Paeniu became prime minister. **1993:** Kamuta Laatasi became prime minister. **1995:** Union flag removed from national flag, presaging move towards republican status. **1999:** Ionatana Ionatana appointed prime minister.

Uganda Republic of

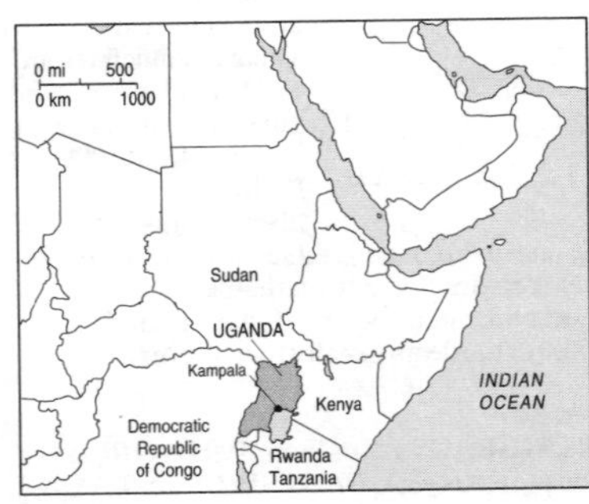

Area: 236,600 sq km/91,351 sq mi **Capital:** Kampala **Major towns/cities:** Jinja, Mbale, Entebbe, Masaka, Bugembe t

Government

Head of state: Yoweri Museveni from 1986 **Head of government:** Apolo Nsibambi from 1999 **Political system:** emergent democracy **Administrative divisions:** 38 districts within four regions **Political parties:** National Resistance Movement (NRM), left of centre; Democratic Party (DP), centre left; Conservative Party (CP), centre right; Uganda People's Congress (UPC), left of centre; Uganda Freedom Movement (UFM), left of centre. From 1986, political parties were forced to suspend activities **Armed forces:** 55,000 (1997) **Conscription:** military service is voluntary **Death penalty:** retained and used for ordinary crimes **Defence spend:** (% GDP) 2.4 (1997) **Education spend:** (% GNP) 1.9 (1993/94) **Health spend:** (% GDP) 1.6 (1990–95)

Economy and resources

Currency: Uganda new shilling **GDP:** (US$) 6.5 billion (1997) **Real GDP growth:** (% change on previous year) 8.0 (1997) **GNP (US$):** 6.6 billion (1997) **GNP per capita (PPP):** (US$) 1,050 (1997) **Consumer price inflation:** 7.0% (1998) **Foreign debt:** (US$) 3.5 billion (1995) **Major trading partners:** Kenya, Spain, UK, Germany, the Netherlands, USA, France **Resources:** copper, apatite, limestone; believed to possess the world's second-largest deposit of gold (hitherto unexploited); also reserves of magnetite, tin, tungsten, beryllium, bismuth, asbestos, graphite **Exports:** coffee, cotton, tea, tobacco, oil seeds and oleaginous fruit; hides and skins, textiles. Principal market: Spain 14.4% (1997) **Imports:** machinery and transport equipment, basic manufactures, petroleum and petroleum products, chemicals, miscellaneous manufactured articles, iron and steel. Principal source: Kenya 31.1% (1997) **Arable land:** 28.3% (1995)

Population and society

Population: 20,554,000 (1998 est) **Population growth rate:** 2.6% (1995–2000) **Population density:** (per sq km) 111 (1998 est) **Urban population:** (% of total) 13 (1997) **Age distribution:** (% of total population) 0–14 51.1%, 15–64 46.7%, 65+ 2.2% (1998) **Ethnic groups:** about 40 different peoples concentrated into four main groups; the Bantu (the most numerous), Eastern Nilotic, Western Nilotic, and Central Sudanic; there are also Rwandan, Sudanese, Zairean, and Kenyan minorities **Language:** English (official), Kiswahili, Bantu and Nilotic languages **Religion:** Christian 50%, animist 40%, Muslim 10% **Education:** not compulsory **Literacy rate:** 62% (men); 45% (women) (1995 est) **Labour force:** 51% of population: 85% agriculture, 5% industry, 11% services (1990) **Life expectancy:** 40 (men); 42 (women) (1995–2000) **Child mortality rate:** (under 5, per 1,000 live births) 180 (1997) **Physicians:** 1 per 22,399 people (1993 est)

Practical information

Visa requirements: UK: visa not required. USA: visa not required **Embassy in the UK:** Uganda House, 58–59 Trafalgar Square, London WC2N 5DX. Tel: (0171) 839 5783; fax: (0171) 839 8925 **British embassy:** British High Commission, PO Box 7070, 101–12 Parliament Avenue, Kampala. Tel: (41) 257 301/4; telex: 61202 (a/b UKREP KAMPALA) **Chamber of commerce:** Uganda Investment Authority, PO Box 7418, Investment Center, Kampala Road, Kampala. Tel: (41) 234 105; fax: (41) 242 903

Chronology

16th century: Bunyoro kingdom founded by immigrants from southeastern Sudan. **17th century:** Rise of kingdom of Buganda people, which became particularly powerful from 17th century. **mid-19th century:** Arabs, trading ivory and slaves, reached Uganda; first visits by European explorers and Christian missionaries. **1885–87:** Uganda Martyrs: Christians persecuted by Buganda ruler, Mwanga. **1890:** Royal Charter granted to British East African Company, a trading company whose agent, Frederick Lugard, concluded treaties with local rulers, including the Buganda and the western states of Ankole and Toro. **1894:** British protectorate established, with Buganda retaining some autonomy under its traditional prince (Kabaka) and other resistance being crushed. **1904:** Cotton growing introduced by Buganda peasants. **1958:** Internal self-government granted. **1962:** Independence achieved from Britain, within Commonwealth, with Milton Obote of Uganda People's Congress (UPC) as prime minister. **1963:** Proclaimed federal republic with King Mutesa II (of Buganda) as president and Obote as prime minister. **1966:** King Mutesa, who opposed creation of one-party state, ousted in coup led by Obote, who ended federal status and became executive president. **1969:** All

opposition parties banned after assassination attempt on Obote; key enterprises nationalized. **1971:** Obote overthrown in army coup led by Maj-Gen Idi Amin Dada; constitution suspended and ruthlessly dictatorial regime established; nearly 49,000 Ugandan Asians expelled; over 300,000 opponents of regime killed. **1976:** Relations with Kenya strained by Amin's claims to parts of Kenya. **1979:** After annexing part of Tanzania, Amin forced to leave country by opponents backed by Tanzanian troops. Provisional government set up with Yusuf Lule as initial president and then Godfrey Binaisa. **1978–79:** Fighting broke out against Tanzanian troops. **1980:** Binaisa overthrown by army. Elections held and Milton Obote returned to power. **1985:** After opposition by pro-Lule National Resistance Army (NRA), and indiscipline in army, Obote ousted by Gen Tito Okello; constitution suspended; power-sharing agreement entered into with NRA leader Yoweri Museveni. **1986:** Museveni became president, heading broad-based coalition government. **1993:** King of Buganda reinstated as formal monarch, in the person of Ronald Muwenda Mutebi II. **1996:** Landslide victory won by Museveni in first direct presidential elections. **1997:** Allied Democratic Forces (ADF) led uprisings by rebels.

Ukraine

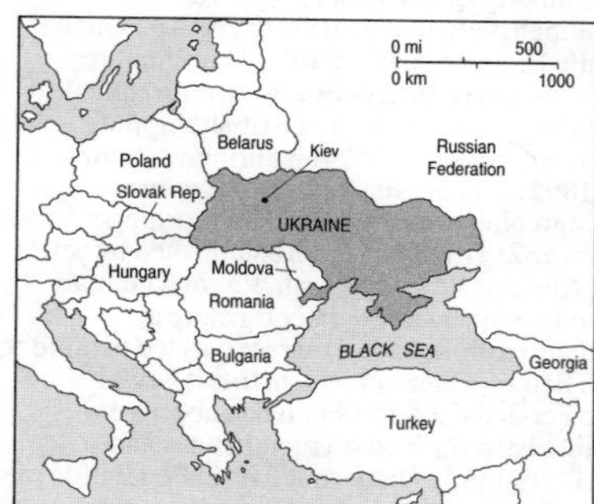

Area: 603,700 sq km/233,088 sq mi **Capital:** Kiev **Major towns/cities:** Kharkov, Donetsk, Dnepropetrovsk, Lugansk (Voroshilovgrad), Lviv (Lvov), Mariupol (Zhdanov), Krivoy Rog, Zaporozhye, Odessa

Government

Head of state: Leonid Kuchma from 1994 **Head of government:** Valery Pustovoitenko from 1997 **Political system:** emergent democracy **Administrative divisions:** 24 provinces and one semi-autonomous region (Crimea) **Political parties:** Ukrainian Communist Party (UCP), left wing, anti-nationalist (banned 1991–93); Peasants' Party of the Ukraine (PPU), conservative agrarian; Ukrainian Socialist Party (SPU), left wing, anti-nationalist; Ukrainian People's Movement (Rukh), Ukrainian Republican Party (URP), Congress of Ukrainian Nationalists (CUN), and Democratic Party of Ukraine (DPU) – all moderate nationalist; Social Democratic Party of Ukraine (SDPU), federalist **Armed forces:** 387,400 (1997) **Conscription:** 18 months (males over 18) **Death penalty:** moratorium placed on executions since 1991 as condition for application to join Council of Europe (joined in 1995). Despite continued demands by Council to uphold moratorium, executions have continued **Defence spend:** (% GDP) 2.7 (1997) **Education spend:** (% GNP) 7.7 (1995) **Health spend:** (% GDP) 5.0 (1990–95)

Economy and resources

Currency: hryvna **GDP:** (US$) 49.7 billion (1997) **Real GDP growth:** (% change on previous year) –5 (1997) **GNP (US$):** 52.4 billion (1997) **GNP per capita (PPP):** (US$) 2,170 (1997) **Consumer price inflation:** 14% (1998) **Unemployment:** 0.6% (1995) **Foreign debt:** (US$) 9.3 billion (1996) **Major trading partners:** Russia, Belarus, China, Moldova, Turkmenistan, USA, Switzerland, Germany **Resources:** coal, iron ore (world's fifth-largest producer), crude oil, natural gas, salt, chemicals, brown coal, alabaster, gypsum **Exports:** grain, coal, oil, various minerals. Principal market: Russia 26.2% (1997) **Imports:** mineral fuels, machine-building components, chemicals and chemical products. Principal source: Russia 45.8% (1997) **Arable land:** 55.2% (1993)

Population and society

Population: 50,861,000 (1998 est) **Population growth rate:** –0.4% (1995–2000) **Population density:** (per sq km) 83 (1998 est) **Urban population:** (% of total) 71 (1997) **Age distribution:** (% of total population) 0–14 19%, 15–64 67%, 65+ 14% (1998) **Ethnic groups:** 73% of the population is of Ukrainian descent; 22% ethnic Russian; 1% Jewish; 1% Belarussian **Language:** Ukrainian (a Slavonic language) **Religion:** traditionally Ukrainian Orthodox; also Ukrainian Catholic **Education:** (compulsory years) 8 (7–15 age limit) **Literacy rate:** 99% (men); 99% (women) (1995 est) **Labour force:** 50% of population: 20% agriculture, 40% industry, 40% services (1990) **Life expectancy:** 64 (men); 74 (women) (1995–2000) **Child mortality rate:** (under 5, per 1,000 live births) 21 (1997) **Physicians:** 1 per 226 people (1994)

Practical information

Visa requirements: UK: visa required. USA: visa required **Embassy in the UK:** 78 Kensington Park Road, London W11 2PL. Tel: (0171) 727 6312; fax: (0171) 792 1708 **British embassy:** vul Desyatinna 9, 252025 Kiev. Tel: (044) 228 0504; fax: (044) 228 3972 **Chamber of commerce:** Chamber of Commerce and Industry, vul Velyka Zhytomyrska 33, 254655 Kiev. Tel: (044) 212 2911; fax: (044) 212 3353

Chronology

9th century: Rus' people established state centred on Kiev and adopted Eastern Orthodox Christianity 988. **1199:** Reunification of southern Rus' lands, after period of fragmentation, under Prince Daniel of Galicia-Volhynia. **13th century:** Mongol-Tatar Golden Horde sacked Kiev and destroyed Rus' state. **14th century:** Poland annexed Galicia; Lithuania absorbed Volhynia and expelled Tatars; Ukraine peasants became serfs of Polish and Lithuanian nobles. **1569:** Poland and Lithuania formed single state; clergy of Ukraine formed Uniate Church, which recognized papal authority but retained Orthodox rites, to avoid Catholic persecution. **16th and 17th centuries:** Runaway serfs known as Cossacks ('outlaws') formed autonomous community in eastern borderlands. **1648:** Cossack revolt led by Gen Bogdan Khmelnitsky drove out Poles from central Ukraine; Khmelnitsky accepted Russian protectorate in 1654. **1660–90:** 'Epoch of Ruins': Ukraine devastated by civil war and invasions by Russians, Poles, and Turks; Poland regained western Ukraine. **1687:** Gen Ivan Mazepa entered into alliance with Sweden in effort to regain Cossack autonomy from Russia. **1709:** Battle of Poltava: Russian victory over Swedes ended hopes of Cossack independence. **1772–95:** Partition of Poland: Austria annexed Galicia, Russian annexations included Volhynia. **1846–47:** Attempt to promote Ukrainian national culture through formation of Cyril and Methodius Society. **1899:** Revolutionary Ukrainian Party founded. **1917:** Revolutionary parliament (Rada), proclaimed Ukrainian autonomy within a federal Russia. **1918:** Ukraine declared full independence; civil war ensued between Rada (backed by Germans) and Reds (backed by Russian Bolsheviks). **1919:** Galicia united with Ukraine; conflict escalated between Ukrainian nationalists, Bolsheviks, anarchists, White Russians, and Poles. **1921:** Treaty of Riga: Russia and Poland partitioned Ukraine. **1921–22:** Several million people perished in famine. **1922:** Ukrainian Soviet Socialist Republic (Ukrainian SSR) became part of Union of Soviet Socialist Republics (USSR). **1932–33:** Enforced collectivization of agriculture caused another catastrophic famine with more than 7.5 million deaths. **1939:** USSR annexed eastern Poland and added Galicia-Volhynia to Ukrainian SSR. **1940:** USSR seized northern Bukhovina from Romania and added it to Ukrainian SSR. **1941–44:** Germany occupied Ukraine; many Ukrainians collaborated; millions of Ukrainians and Ukrainian Jews enslaved and exterminated by Nazis. **1945:** USSR annexed Ruthenia from Czechoslovakia and added it to Ukrainian SSR, which became a nominal member of United Nations (UN). **1946:** Uniate Church forcibly merged with Russian Orthodox Church. **1954:** Crimea transferred from Russian Federation to Ukrainian SSR. **1986:** Major environmental disaster caused by explosion of nuclear reactor at Chernobyl, north of Kiev. **1989:** Rukh (nationalist movement) established as political party; ban on Uniate Church lifted. **1990:** Ukraine declared sovereignty under President Leonid Kravchuk, leader of the CP. **1991:** Ukraine declared independence from USSR; President Kravchuk left CP; Ukraine joined newly formed Commonwealth of Independent States (CIS). **1992:** Crimean sovereignty declared but then rescinded. **1994:** Election gains for radical nationalists in western Ukraine and Russian unionists in eastern Ukraine; Leonid Kuchma succeeded Kravchuk as president. **1996:** New constitution replaced Soviet system, making presidency stronger; remaining nuclear warheads returned to Russia for destruction; new currency introduced. **1997:** New government appointments made to speed economic reform. Treaty of friendship with Russia signed, solving issue of Russian Black Sea fleet. Prime Minister Lazarenko replaced by Valery Pustovoitenko. Loan of $750 million from International Monetary Fund (IMF) approved. Disagreements between president and Supreme Council. **1998:** Communists won largest number of seats in March parliamentary election, but fell short of absolute majority. Three-year $2.2 billion loan agreed by the IMF. The value of the hryvnya fell by over 50% against the US dollar, after being affected by the neighbouring Russian currency crisis. The government survived a no-confidence vote in parliament, tabled by left-wing factions that opposed the government's economic retrenchment program.

United Arab Emirates (UAE) federation of the emirates of Abu Dhabi, Ajman, Dubai, Fujairah, Ras al Khaimah, Sharjah, Umm al Qaiwain

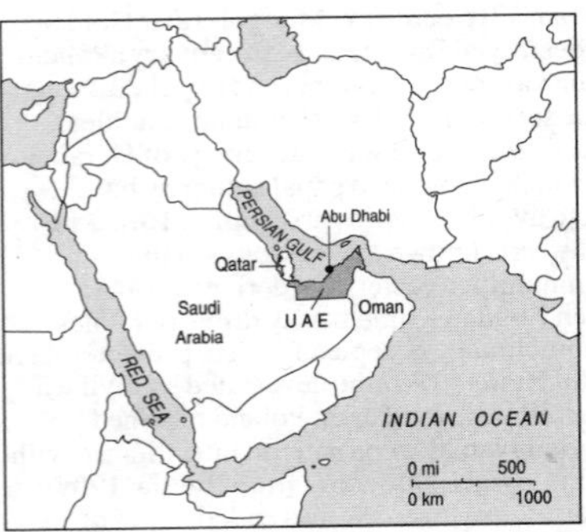

National name: *Ittihad al-Imarat al-Arabiyah* **Area:** 83,657 sq km/ 32,299 sq mi **Capital:** Abu Dhabi **Major towns/ cities:** Dubai, Sharjah, Ras al-Khaimah, Ajman, Fujairah **Major ports:** Dubai

Government

Head of state and government: Sheik Zayed bin Sultan al-Nahayan of Abu Dhabi from 1971 **Supreme council of rulers:** *Abu Dhabi* Sheik Zayed bin Sultan al-Nahayan, president (1966); *Ajman* Sheik Humaid bin Rashid al-Nuami (1981); *Dubai* Sheik Maktoum bin Rashid al-Maktoum (1990); *Fujairah* Sheik Hamad bin Muhammad al-Sharqi (1974); *Ras al Khaimah* Sheik Saqr bin Muhammad al-Quasimi (1948); *Sharjah* Sheik Sultan bin Muhammad al-Quasimi (1972); *Umm al Qaiwain* Sheik Rashid bin Ahmad al-Mu'alla (1981) **Political system:** absolutism **Administrative divisions:** seven emirates **Political parties:** none **Armed forces:** 64,500 (1997) **Conscription:** military service is voluntary **Death penalty:** retained and used for ordinary crimes **Defence spend:** (% GDP) 5.5 (1997) **Education spend:** (% GNP) 1.8 (1995) **Health spend:** (% GDP) 2.0 (1990–95)

Economy and resources

Currency: UAE dirham **GDP:** (US$) 45.1 billion (1997 est) **Real GDP growth:** (% change on previous year) 1.5 (1997) **GNP (US$):** 42.7 billion (1997) **GNP per capita (PPP):** (US$) 21,600 (1997 est) **Consumer price inflation:** 4.7% (1998) **Foreign debt:** (US$) 16.06 billion (1996) **Major trading partners:** Japan, USA, UK, Germany, South Korea, Thailand, Oman, Italy, India, Iran, Singapore **Resources:** petroleum and natural gas **Exports:** crude petroleum, natural gas, re-exports (mainly machinery and transport equipment). Principal market: Japan 36.3% (1997) **Imports:** machinery and transport equipment, food and live animals, fuels and lubricants, chemicals, basic manufactures. Principal source: USA 9.6% (1997) **Arable land:** 0.4% (1995)

Population and society

Population: 2,353,000 (1998 est) **Population growth rate:** 2.0% (1995–2000); 1.8% (2000–05) **Population density:** (per sq km) 27.5 (1998 est) **Urban population:** (% of total) 85 (1997) **Age distribution:** (% of total population) 0–14 31.6%, 15–64 66.5%, 65+ 1.9% (1998) **Ethnic groups:** 75% Iranians, Indians, and Pakistanis; about 25% Arabs **Language:** Arabic (official), Farsi, Hindi, Urdu, English **Religion:** Muslim 96%; Christian, Hindu **Education:** (compulsory years) 6 **Literacy rate:** 78% (men); 78% (women) (1995 est) **Labour force:** 51% of population: 8% agriculture, 27% industry, 65% services (1990); 93% of workforce were non-UAE nationals (1992 est) **Life expectancy:** 74 (men); 77 (women) (1995–2000) **Child mortality rate:** (under 5, per 1,000 live births) 18 (1997) **Physicians:** 1 per 715 people (1993)

Practical information

Visa requirements: UK: visa not required for a stay of up to 30 days. USA: visa required **Embassy in the UK:** 30 Prince's Gate, London SW7 1PT. Tel: (0171) 581 1281; fax: (0171) 581 9616 **British embassy:** PO Box 248, Abu Dhabi. Tel: (2) 326 600; fax: (2) 341 744 **Chamber of commerce:** Dubai Chamber of Commerce and Industry, PO Box 1457, Diera, Dubai. Tel: (4) 221 181; fax: (4) 211 646

Chronology

7th century AD: Islam introduced. **early 16th century:** Portuguese established trading contacts with Persian Gulf states. **18th century:** Rise of trade and seafaring among Qawasim and Bani Yas, respectively in Ras al-Khaimah and Sharjah in north and Abu Dhabi and Dubai in desert of south. Emirates' current ruling families are descended from these peoples. **early 19th century:** Britain signed treaties ('truces') with local rulers, ensuring that British shipping through the Gulf was free from 'pirate' attacks and bringing Emirates under British protection. **1892:** Trucial Sheiks signed Exclusive Agreements with Britain, agreeing not to cede, sell, or mortgage territory to another power. **1952:** Trucial Council established by seven sheikdoms of Abu Dhabi, Ajman, Dubai, Fujairah, Ras al Khaimah, Sharjah, and Umm al Qawain, with a view to later forming a federation. **1958:** Large-scale exploitation of oil reserves led to rapid economic progress. **1968:** Britain's announcement that it would remove its forces from the Persian Gulf by 1971 led to abortive attempt to arrange federation between seven Trucial States and Bahrain and Qatar. **1971:** Bahrain and Qatar ceded from Federation of Arab Emirates, which was dissolved. Six Trucial States formed United Arab Emirates, with ruler of Abu Dhabi, Sheik Zayed, as president. Provisional constitution adopted. **1972:** Seventh state, Ras al Khaimah, joined federation. **1976:** Sheik Zayed threatened to relinquish presidency unless progress towards centralization became more rapid. **1985:** Diplomatic and economic links with Soviet Union and China established. **1987:** Diplomatic relations with Egypt restored. **1990–91:** Iraqi invasion of Kuwait opposed; UAE troops fought as part of United Nations coalition. **1991:** Bank of Commerce and Credit International (BCCI), controlled by Abu Dhabi's ruler, collapsed at cost to the UAE of $10 billion. **1992:** Border dispute with Iran. **1994:** Abu Dhabi agreed to pay BCCI creditors $1.8 billion.

United Kingdom of Great Britain and Northern Ireland (UK)

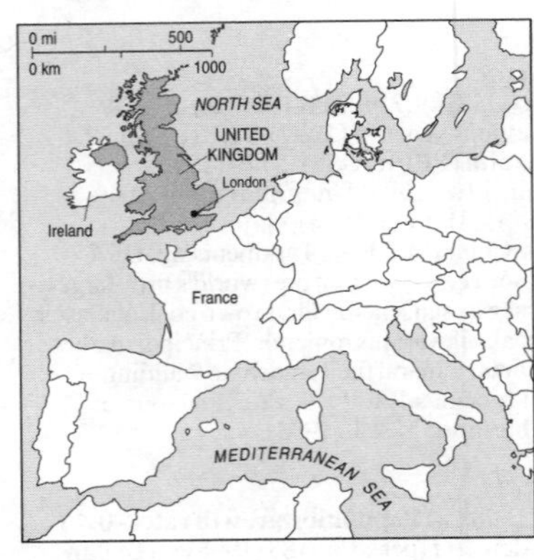

Area: 244,100 sq km/94,247 sq mi **Capital:** London **Major towns/ cities:** Birmingham, Glasgow, Leeds, Sheffield, Liverpool, Manchester, Edinburgh, Bradford, Bristol, Coventry, Belfast, Newcastle upon Tyne, Cardiff **Major ports:** London, Grimsby, Southampton, Liverpool

Territories: Anguilla, Bermuda, British Antarctic Territory, British Indian Ocean Territory, British Virgin Islands, Cayman Islands, Falkland Islands, Gibraltar, Montserrat, Pitcairn Islands, St Helena and Dependencies (Ascension, Tristan da Cunha), Turks and Caicos Islands; the Channel Islands and the Isle of Man are not part of the UK but are direct dependencies of the crown

Government

Head of state: Queen Elizabeth II from 1952 **Head of government:** Tony Blair from 1997 **Political system:** liberal democracy **Administrative divisions:** England: 34 non-metropolitan counties, 46 unitary authorities, 6 metropolitan counties, (with 36 metropolitan boroughs), 32 London boroughs, and the Corporation of London; Scotland: 9 regions, 29 unitary authorities, and 3 island authorities (from 1996); Wales: 9 counties and 22 unitary authorities/county boroughs (from 1996); Northern Ireland: 26 districts within 6 geographical counties **Political parties:** Conservative and Unionist Party, right of centre; Labour Party, moderate left of centre; Social and Liberal Democrats, centre left; Scottish National Party (SNP), Scottish nationalist; Plaid Cymru (Welsh Nationalist Party), Welsh nationalist; Official Ulster Unionist Party (OUP), Democratic Unionist Party (DUP), Ulster People's Unionist Party (UPUP), all Northern Ireland right of centre, in favour of remaining part of United Kingdom; Social Democratic Labour Party (SDLP), Northern Ireland, moderate left of centre; Green Party, ecological **Armed forces:** 213,800 (1997) **Conscription:** military service is voluntary **Death penalty:** abolished for ordinary crimes in 1973; laws provide for the death penalty for exceptional crimes only; last execution in 1964 **Defence spend:** (% GDP) 2.8 (1997) **Education spend:** (% GNP) 5.5 (1995) **Health spend:** (% GDP) 5.8 (1990–95)

Economy and resources

Currency: pound sterling (£) **GDP:** (US$) 1,278.4 billion (1997) **Real GDP growth:** (% change on previous year) 3.4 (1997) **GNP (US$):** 1,220.2 billion (1997) **GNP per capita (PPP):** (US$) 20,520 (1997) **Consumer price inflation:** 3.5% (1998) **Unemployment:** 7.0% (1997) **Major trading partners:** Germany, USA, France, the Netherlands, Japan, Ireland **Resources:** coal, limestone, crude petroleum, natural gas, tin, iron, salt, sand and gravel **Exports:** industrial and electrical machinery, automatic data-processing equipment, motor vehicles, petroleum, chemicals, finished and semi-finished manufactured products, agricultural products and foodstuffs. Principal market: USA 12.1% (1997) **Imports:** industrial and electrical machinery, motor vehicles, food and live animals, petroleum, automatic data processing equipment, consumer goods, textiles, paper, paper board. Principal source: Germany 13.7% (1997) **Arable land:** 24.5% (1995)

Population and society

Population: 58,649,000 (1998 est) **Population growth rate:** 0.1% (1995–2000) **Population density:** (per sq km) 244.1 (1998 est) **Urban population:** (% of total) 89 (1997) **Age distribution:** (% of total population) 0–14 19.3%, 15–64 65.0%, 65+ 15.7% (1998) **Ethnic groups:** 81.5% English; 9.6% Scots; 2.4% Irish; 1.9% Welsh; 2% West Indian, Asian, and African **Language:** English, Welsh, Gaelic **Religion:** Church of England (established Church); other Protestant denominations, Roman Catholic, Muslim, Jewish, Hindu, Sikh **Education:** (compulsory years) 11 **Literacy rate:** 99% (men); 99% (women) (1995 est) **Labour force:** 48.6% of population: 2% agriculture, 27.4% industry, 70.6% services (1996) **Life expectancy:** 75 (men); 80 (women) (1995–2000) **Child mortality rate:** (under 5, per 1,000 live births) 7 (1998) **Physicians:** 1 per 625 people (1994)

Practical information

Visa requirements: USA: visa not required **Chamber of commerce:** Association of British Chambers of Commerce, 9 Tufton Street, London SW1P 3QB. Tel: (0171) 222 1555; fax: (0171) 799 2202

Chronology

c. **400–200 BC:** British Isles conquered by Celts. **55–54 BC:** Romans led by Julius Caesar raided Britain. **AD 43–60:** Romans conquered England and Wales, which formed the province of Britannia; Picts stopped them penetrating further north. **5th–7th centuries:** After Romans withdrew, Anglo-Saxons overran most of England and formed kingdoms, including Wessex, Northumbria, and Mercia; Wales was stronghold of Celts. **500:** The Scots, a Gaelic-speaking tribe from Ireland, settled in the kingdom of Dalriada (Argyll). **5th–6th centuries:** British Isles converted to Christianity. **829:** King Egbert of Wessex accepted as overlord of all England. *c.* **843:** Kenneth McAlpin unified Scots and Picts to become first king of Scotland. **9th–11th centuries:** Vikings raided British Isles, conquering north and east England and northern Scotland. **1066:** Normans led by William I defeated Anglo-Saxons at Battle of Hastings and conquered England. **12th–13th centuries:** Anglo-Norman adventurers conquered much of Ireland, but effective English rule remained limited to area around Dublin. **1215:** King John of England forced to sign Magna Carta, which placed limits on royal powers. **1265:** Simon de Montfort summoned the first English parliament in which the towns were represented. **1284:** Edward I of England invaded Scotland; Scots defeated English at Battle of Stirling Bridge in 1297. **1314:** Robert the Bruce led Scots to victory over English at Battle of Bannockburn; England recognized Scottish independence in 1328. **1455–85:** Wars of the Roses: House of York and House of Lancaster disputed English throne. **1513:** Battle of Flodden: Scots defeated by English; James IV of Scotland killed. **1529:** Henry VIII founded Church of England after break with Rome; Reformation effective in England and Wales, but not in Ireland. **1536–43:** Acts of Union united Wales with England, with one law, one parliament, and one official language. **1541:** Irish parliament recognized Henry VIII of England as king of Ireland. **1557:** First Covenant established Protestant faith in Scotland. **1603:** Union of crowns: James VI of Scotland became James I of England also. **1607:** First successful English colony in Virginia marked start of three centuries of overseas expansion. **1610:** James I established plantation of Ulster in Northern Ireland with Protestant settlers from England and Scotland. **1642–52:** English Civil War between king and Parliament, with Scottish intervention and Irish rebellion, resulted in victory for Parliament. **1649:** Execution of Charles I; Oliver Cromwell appointed Lord Protector in 1653; monarchy restored in 1660. **1689:** 'Glorious Revolution' confirmed power of Parliament; replacement of James II by William III resisted by Scottish Highlanders and Catholic Irish. **1707:** Act of Union between England and Scotland created United Kingdom of Great Britain, governed by a single parliament. **1721–42:** Cabinet government developed under Robert Walpole, in effect the first prime minister. **1745:** 'The Forty-Five': rebellion of Scottish Highlanders in support of Jacobite pretender to throne; defeated 1746. *c.* **1760–1850:** Industrial Revolution: Britain became the first industrial nation in the world. **1775–83:** American Revolution: Britain lost 13 American colonies; empire continued to expand in Canada, India, and Australia. **1793–1815:** Britain at war with revolutionary France, except for 1802–03. **1800:** Act of Union created United Kingdom of Great Britain and Ireland, governed by a single parliament; effective 1801. **1832:** Great Reform Act extended franchise; further extensions in 1867, 1884, 1918, and 1928. **1846:** Repeal of Corn Laws reflected shift of power from landowners to industrialists. **1870:** Home Rule Party formed to campaign for restoration of separate Irish parliament. **1880–90s:** Rapid expansion of British Empire in Africa. **1906–14:** Liberal governments introduced social reforms and curbed power of House of Lords. **1914–18:** United Kingdom played leading part in World War I; British Empire expanded in Middle East. **1919–21:** Anglo-Irish war ended with secession of southern Ireland as Irish Free State; Ulster remained within United Kingdom of Great Britain and Northern Ireland with some powers devolved to Northern Irish parliament. **1924:** First Labour government led by Ramsay MacDonald. **1926:** General Strike arose from coal dispute. Equality of status recognized between United Kingdom and Dominions of British Commonwealth. **1931:** National Government coalition formed to face economic crisis; unemployment reached 3 million. **1939–45:** United Kingdom played a leading part in World War II. **1945:** First Scottish Nationalist MP elected; first Welsh Nationalist MP in 1966. **1945–51:** Labour government of Clement Attlee created welfare state and nationalized major industries. **1947–71:** Decolonization brought about end of British Empire. **1969:** Start of Troubles in Northern Ireland; Northern Irish Parliament suspended in 1972.

1973: UK joined European Economic Community. **1979–90:** Conservative government of Margaret Thatcher pursued radical free-market economic policies. **1982:** Unemployment over 3 million. Falklands War. **1991:** British troops took part in US-led war against Iraq under United Nations umbrella. Severe economic recession and unemployment. **1993:** Peace proposal for Northern Ireland, the Downing Street Declaration, issued jointly with Irish government. **1994:** IRA and Protestant paramilitary declared cease-fire in Northern Ireland. **1996:** IRA renewed bombing campaign in London. **1997:** Labour Party won landslide victory in general election; Tony Blair became prime minister. Blair launched new Anglo-Irish peace initiative. Princess Diana killed in car crash. Meeting between Blair and Sinn Féin leader Gerry Adams; all-party peace talks began in Northern Ireland. Scotland and Wales voted in favour of devolution. **1998:** Historic multiparty agreement (the 'Good Friday Agreement') was reached on the future of Northern Ireland; peace plan approved by referenda in both Northern Ireland and the Irish Republic. UUP leader, David Trimble, elected first minister. **1999:** The Scotttish Parliament and Welsh Assembly opened, with Labour the largest party in both. Talks on Northern Ireland failed to resolve decommissioning issue.

United States of America

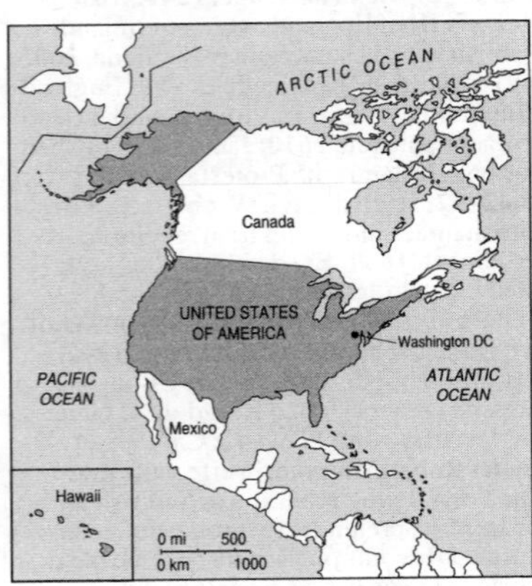

Area: 9,372,615 sq km/3,618,766 sq mi **Capital:** Washington DC **Major towns/cities:** New York, Los Angeles, Chicago, Philadelphia, Detroit, San Francisco, Washington, Dallas, San Diego, San Antonio, Houston, Boston, Baltimore, Phoenix, Indianapolis, Memphis, Honolulu, San José **Territories:** the commonwealths of Puerto Rico and Northern Marianas; Guam, the US Virgin Islands, American Samoa, Wake Island, Midway Islands, and Johnston and Sand Islands

Government

Head of state and government: Bill Clinton from 1993 **Political system:** liberal democracy **Administrative divisions:** 50 states **Political parties:** Democratic Party, liberal centre; Republican Party, centre right **Armed forces:** 1,447,600 (1997) **Conscription:** military service is voluntary **Death penalty:** retained and used for ordinary crimes **Defence spend:** (% GDP) 3.4 (1997) **Education spend:** (% GNP) 5.3 (1995) **Health spend:** (% GDP) 6.6 (1990–95)

Economy and resources

Currency: US dollar **GDP:** (US$) 7,819.3 billion (1997) **Real GDP growth:** (% change on previous year) 3.7 (1997) **GNP (US$):** 7,690.1 billion (1997) **GNP per capita (PPP):** (US$) 28,740 (1997) **Consumer price inflation:** 2.5% (1998) **Unemployment:** 4.5% (1998) **Major trading partners:** Canada, Japan, Mexico, EU (principally UK and Germany), South Korea, China, Taiwan **Resources:** coal, copper (world's second-largest producer), iron, bauxite, mercury, silver, gold, nickel, zinc (world's fifth-largest producer), tungsten, uranium, phosphate, petroleum, natural gas, timber **Exports:** machinery, motor vehicles, agricultural products and foodstuffs, aircraft, weapons, chemicals, electronics. Principal market: Canada 22.3% (1997) **Imports:** machinery and transport equipment, crude and partly refined petroleum, office machinery, textiles and clothing. Principal source: Canada 19.2% (1997) **Arable land:** 20.3% (1995)

Population and society

Population: 274,028,000 (1998 est) **Population growth rate:** 0.8% (1995–2000); 0.8% (2000–05) **Population density:** (per sq km) 29.5 (1998 est) **Urban population:** (% of total) 77 (1997) **Age distribution:** (% of total population) 0–14 21.6%, 15–64 65.7%, 65+ 12.7% (1998) **Ethnic groups:** approximately three-quarters of the population are of European origin, including 29% who trace their descent from Britain and Ireland, 8% from Germany, 5% from Italy, and 3% each from Scandinavia and Poland; 12% are African-Americans, 8% Hispanic, and 3% Asian and Pacific islander; African-Americans form 30% of the population of the states of the 'Deep South', namely Alabama, Georgia, Louisiana, Mississippi, and South Carolina **Language:** English, Spanish **Religion:** Christian 86.5% (Roman Catholic 26%, Baptist 19%, Methodist 8%, Lutheran 5%); Jewish 1.8%; Muslim 0.5%; Buddhist and Hindu less than 0.5% **Education:** (compulsory years) 10 **Literacy rate:** 99% (men); 99% (women) (1995 est) **Labour force:** 51% of population: 2.8% agriculture, 23.8% industry, 73.3% services (1996) **Life expectancy:** 73 (men); 80 (women) (1995–2000) **Child mortality rate:** (under 5, per 1,000 live births) 9 (1997) **Physicians:** 1 per 385 people (1996)

Practical information

Visa requirements: UK: visa not required for a stay of up to 90 days **Embassy in the UK:** 24 Grosvenor Square, London W1A 1AE, Tel: (0171) 499 9000; fax: (0171) 629 9124 **British embassy:** 3100 Massachusetts Avenue, NW, Washington DC 20008. Tel: (202) 462 1340; fax: (202) 898 4255 **Chamber of commerce:** 1615 H Street, NW, Washington DC 20062–0001. Tel: (202) 659 6000; fax: (202) 463 5836

Chronology

c. **15,000 BC:** First evidence of human occupation in North America. **1513:** Ponce de Léon of Spain explored Florida in search of the Fountain of Youth; Francisco Coronado explored southwest region of North America 1540–42. **1565:** Spanish founded St Augustine (Florida), the first permanent European settlement in North America. **1585:** Sir Walter Raleigh tried to establish English colony on Roanoke Island in what he called Virginia. **1607:** English colonists founded Jamestown, Virginia, and began growing tobacco. **1620:** The Pilgrim Fathers founded Plymouth Colony (near Cape Cod); other English Puritans followed them to New England. **1624:** Dutch formed colony of New Netherlands; Swedes formed New Sweden in 1638; both taken by England in 1664. **17th–18th centuries:** Millions of Africans were sold into slavery on American cotton and tobacco plantations. **1733:** Georgia became thirteenth British colony on east coast. **1763:** British victory over France in Seven Years' War secured territory as far west as Mississippi River. **1765:** British first attempted to levy tax in American colonies with Stamp Act; protest forced repeal in 1767. **1773:** 'Boston Tea Party': colonists boarded ships and threw cargoes of tea into sea in protest at import duty. **1774:** British closed Boston harbour and billeted troops in Massachusetts; colonists formed First Continental Congress. **1775:** American Revolution: colonies raised Continental Army led by George Washington to fight against British rule. **1776:** American colonies declared independence; France and Spain supported them in war with Britain. **1781:** Americans defeated British at Battle of Yorktown; rebel states formed loose confederation, codified in Articles of Confederation. **1783:** Treaty of Paris: Britain accepted loss of colonies. **1787:** 'Founding Fathers' devised new constitution for United States of America. **1789:** Washington elected first president of USA. **1791:** Bill of Rights guaranteed individual freedom. **1803:** Louisiana Purchase: France sold former Spanish lands between Mississippi River and Rocky Mountains to USA. **1812–14:** War with Britain arose from dispute over blockade rights during Napoleonic Wars. **1819:** USA bought Florida from Spain. **19th century:** Mass immigration from Europe; settlers moved westwards, crushing Indian resistance and claiming 'manifest destiny' of USA to control North America. By end of century, number of states in the Union had increased from 17 to 45. **1846–48:** Mexican War: Mexico ceded vast territory to USA. **1854:** Kansas–Nebraska Act heightened controversy over slavery in southern states; abolitionists formed Republican Party. **1860:** Abraham Lincoln (Republican) elected

United States of America: States

State	Nickname(s)	Abbreviation	Capital	Area sq km	Area sq mi	Population (1995)	Joined the Union
Alabama	Heart of Dixie/Camellia State	AL	Montgomery	134,700	51,994	4,253,000	1819
Alaska	Mainland State/The Last Frontier	AK	Juneau	1,531,100	591,005	603,600	1959
Arizona	Grand Canyon State/Apache State	AZ	Phoenix	294,100	113,523	4,217,900	1912
Arkansas	Bear State/Land of Opportunity	AR	Little Rock	137,800	53,191	2,483,800	1836
California	Golden State	CA	Sacramento	411,100	158,685	31,589,200	1850
Colorado	Centennial State	CO	Denver	269,700	104,104	3,746,600	1876
Connecticut	Constitution State/Nutmeg State	CT	Hartford	13,000	5018	3,274,700	1788
Delaware	First State/Diamond State	DE	Dover	5,300	2,046	717,200	1787
Florida	Sunshine State/Everglade State	FL	Tallahassee	152,000	58,672	14,165,600	1845
Georgia	Empire State of the South/Peach State	GA	Atlanta	152,600	58,904	7,200,900	1788
Hawaii	Aloha State	HI	Honolulu	16,800	6,485	1,186,800	1959
Idaho	Gem State	ID	Boise	216,500	83,569	1,163,300	1890
Illinois	Inland Empire/Prairie State/Land of Lincoln	IL	Springfield	146,100	56,395	11,829,900	1818
Indiana	Hoosier State	IN	Indianapolis	93,700	36,168	5,803,500	1816
Iowa	Hawkeye State/Corn State	IA	Des Moines	145,800	56,279	2,841,800	1846
Kansas	Sunflower State/Jayhawker State	KS	Topeka	213,200	82,295	2,565,300	1861
Kentucky	Bluegrass State	KY	Frankfort	104,700	40,414	3,860,200	1792
Louisiana	Pelican State/Sugar State/Creole State	LA	Baton Rouge	135,900	52,457	4,342,300	1792
Maine	Pine Tree State	ME	Augusta	86,200	33,273	1,241,400	1812
Maryland	Old Line State/Free State	MD	Annapolis	31,600	12,198	5,042,400	1788
Massachusetts	Bay State/Old Colony	MA	Boston	21,500	8,299	6,073,550	1788
Michigan	Great Lakes State/Wolverine State	MI	Lansing	151,600	58,518	9,549,400	1837
Minnesota	North Star State/Gopher State	MN	St Paul	218,700	84,418	4,609,500	1858
Mississippi	Magnolia State	MS	Jackson	123,600	47,710	2,697,200	1817
Missouri	Show Me State/Bullion State	MO	Jefferson City	180,600	69,712	5,323,500	1821
Montana	Treasure State/Big Sky Country	MT	Helena	381,200	147,143	870,300	1889
Nebraska	Cornhusker State/Beef State	NE	Lincoln	200,400	77,354	1,637,100	1867
Nevada	Sagebrush State/Silver State/Battleborn State	NV	Carson City	286,400	110,550	1,530,100	1864
New Hampshire	Granite State	NH	Concord	24,000	9,264	1,148,300	1788
New Jersey	Garden State	NJ	Trenton	20,200	7,797	7,945,300	1787
New Mexico	Land of Enchantment/Sunshine State	NM	Santa Fé	315,000	121,590	1,685,400	1912
New York	Empire State	NY	Albany	127,200	49,099	18,136,100	1788
North Carolina	Tar Heel State/Old North State	NC	Raleigh	136,400	52,650	7,195,100	1789
North Dakota	Peace Garden State	ND	Bismarck	183,100	70,677	641,400	1889
Ohio	Buckeye State	OH	Columbus	107,100	41,341	11,150,500	1803
Oklahoma	Sooner State	OK	Oklahoma City	181,100	69,905	3,277,700	1907
Oregon	Beaver State/Sunset State	OR	Salem	251,500	97,079	3,140,600	1859
Pennsylvania	Keystone State	PA	Harrisburg	117,400	45,316	12,071,800	1787
Rhode Island	Little Rhody/Ocean State	RI	Providence	3,100	1,197	989,800	1790
South Carolina	Palmetto State	SC	Columbia	80,600	31,112	3,673,300	1788
South Dakota	Coyote State/Mount Rushmore State	SD	Pierre	199,800	77,123	729,000	1889
Tennessee	Volunteer State	TN	Nashville	109,200	42,151	5,256,100	1796
Texas	Lone Star State	TX	Austin	691,200	266,803	18,724,000	1845
Utah	Beehive State/Mormon State	UT	Salt Lake City	219,900	84,881	1,951,400	1896
Vermont	Green Mountain State	VT	Montpelier	24,900	9,611	584,800	1791
Virginia	Old Dominion State/Mother of Presidents	VA	Richmond	105,600	40,762	6,618,400	1788
Washington	Evergreen State/Chinook State	WA	Olympia	176,700	68,206	5,430,900	1889
West Virginia	Mountain State/Panhandle State	WV	Charleston	62,900	24,279	1,828,100	1863
Wisconsin	Badger State/America's Dairyland	WI	Madison	145,500	56,163	5,122,900	1848
Wyoming	Equality State	WY	Cheyenne	253,400	97,812	480,200	1890
District of Columbia (Federal District)	–	DC	Washington	180	69	554,300	est. by Act of Congress 1790–91

president. **1861:** Civil war broke out after 11 southern states, wishing to retain slavery, seceded from USA and formed Confederate States of America under Jefferson Davis. **1865:** USA defeated Confederacy; slavery abolished; President Lincoln assassinated. **1867:** Alaska bought from Russia. **1869:** Railway linked east and west coasts; rapid growth of industry and agriculture 1870–1920 made USA very rich. **1876:** Sioux Indians defeated US troops at Little Big Horn; Indians finally defeated at Wounded Knee in 1890. **1898:** Spanish–American War: USA gained Puerto Rico and Guam; also Philippines (until 1946) and Cuba (until 1901); USA annexed Hawaii. **1913:** 16th amendment to constitution gave federal government power to levy income tax. **1917–18:** USA intervened in World War I; President Woodrow Wilson took leading part in peace negotiations in 1919, but USA rejected membership of League of Nations. **1920:** Women received right to vote; sale of alcohol prohibited, until 1933. **1924:** American Indians made citizens of USA by Congress. **1929:** 'Wall Street Crash': stock market collapse led to Great Depression with 13 million unemployed by 1933. **1933:** President Franklin Roosevelt launched 'New Deal' with public works to alleviate Depression. **1941:** Japanese attacked US fleet at Pearl Harbor, Hawaii; USA declared war on Japan; Germany declared war on USA, which henceforth played a leading part in World War II. **1945:** USA ended war in Pacific by dropping two atomic bombs on Hiroshima and Nagasaki, Japan. **1947:** 'Truman Doctrine' pledged US aid for nations threatened by communism; start of Cold War between USA and USSR. **1950–53:** US forces engaged in Korean War. **1954:** Racial segregation in schools deemed unconstitutional; start of campaign to secure civil rights for black Americans. **1962:** Cuban missile crisis: USA forced USSR to withdraw nuclear weapons from Cuba. **1963:** President Kennedy assassinated. **1964–68:** President Lyndon Johnson introduced 'Great Society' programme of civil-rights and welfare measures. **1961–75:** USA involved in Vietnam War. **1969:** US astronaut Neil Armstrong was first person on Moon. **1974:** 'Watergate' scandal: evidence of domestic political espionage compelled President Richard Nixon to resign. **1979–80:** Iran held US diplomats hostage, humiliating President Jimmy Carter. **1981–89:** Tax-cutting policies of President Ronald Reagan led to large federal budget deficit. **1986:** 'Irangate' scandal: secret US arms sales to Iran illegally funded Contra guerrillas in Nicaragua. **1990:** President George Bush declared end to Cold War. **1991:** Gulf War: USA played leading part in expelling Iraqi forces from Kuwait. **1992:** Democrat Bill Clinton won presidential elections. **1996:** Clinton re-elected. US missile attacks on Iraq in response to Hussein's incursions into Kurdish safe havens. **1997:** Budget agreed between President and Congress. Reform in welfare law brought substantial drop in number of welfare recipients. **1998:** President Clinton testified before a grand jury that he had misled the public about his relationship with White House intern Monica Lewinsky. August: in response to bombings of US embassies in Tanzania and Kenya by an Islamic group, the USA bombed suspected sites in Afghanistan and Sudan. October: House of Representatives voted to impeach President Clinton on the grounds of perjury and obstruction of justice, and a full Senate trial began in January 1999. Clinton's national approval rating remained high, and Democrats made gains in congressional midterm elections. December: USA led air strikes against Iraq following expulsion of UN weapons inspectors by Saddam Hussein. **1999:** Senate voted against impeaching President Clinton. A projected 1999 federal budget surplus of $76 billion announced in President Clinton's annual state-of-the-union address. March: US forces led NATO air strikes against Yugoslavia in protest at Serb violence against ethnic-Albanians in Kosovo.

Uruguay Oriental Republic of

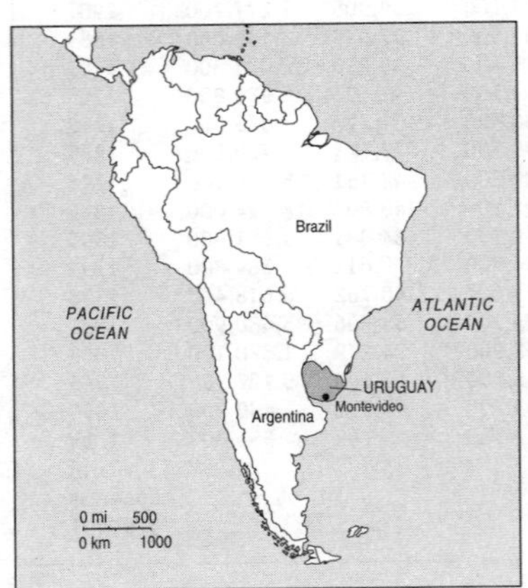

National name: *República Oriental del Uruguay* **Area:** 176,200 sq km/ 68,030 sq mi **Capital:** Montevideo **Major towns/cities:** Salto, Paysandú, Las Piedras

Government

Head of state and government: Julio Maria Sanguinetti from 1994 **Political system:** democracy **Administrative divisions:** 19 departments **Political parties:** Colorado Party (PC), progressive, centre left; National (Blanco) Party (PN), traditionalist, right of centre; New Space (NE), moderate, left wing; Progressive Encounter (EP), left wing **Armed forces:** 25,600 (1997) **Conscription:** military service is voluntary **Death penalty:** abolished in 1907 **Defence spend:** (% GDP) 2.3 (1997) **Education spend:** (% GNP) 3.3 (1996) **Health spend:** (% GDP) 2.0 (1990–95)

Economy and resources

Currency: Uruguayan peso **GDP:** (US$) 20 billion (1997) **Real GDP growth:** (% change on previous year) 4.0 (1997) **GNP (US$):** 19.4 billion (1997) **GNP per capita (PPP):** (US$) 8,460 (1997) **Consumer price inflation:** 13.1% (1998) **Unemployment:** 10.2% (1995) **Foreign debt:** (US$) 5.4 billion (1996) **Major trading partners:** Brazil, Argentina, USA, Italy, Germany, Spain, China **Resources:** small-scale extraction of building materials, industrial minerals, semi-precious stones; gold deposits are being developed **Exports:** textiles, meat (chiefly beef), live animals and by-products (mainly hides and leather products), cereals, footwear. Principal market: Brazil 34.4% (1997) **Imports:** machinery and appliances, transport equipment, chemical products, petroleum and petroleum products, agricultural products. Principal source: Brazil 21.6% (1997) **Arable land:** 7.2% (1995)

Population and society

Population: 3,289,000 (1998 est) **Population growth rate:** 0.6% (1995–2000); 0.6% (2000–05) **Population density:** (per sq km) 18.9 (1998 est) **Urban population:** (% of total) 91 (1997) **Age distribution:** (% of total population) 0–14 24.1%, 15–64 63.0%, 65+ 12.9% (1998) **Ethnic groups:** predominantly of European descent: about 54% Spanish, 22% Italian, with minorities from other European countries **Language:** Spanish (official) **Religion:** mainly Roman Catholic **Education:** (compulsory years) 6 **Literacy rate:** 97% (men); 96% (women) (1995 est) **Labour force:** 15% agriculture, 18% industry, 67% services (1993) **Life expectancy:** 70 (men); 76 (women) (1995–2000) **Child mortality rate:** (under 5, per 1,000 live births) 19 (1997) **Physicians:** 1 per 515 people (1990)

Practical information

Visa requirements: UK: visa not required. USA: visa not required **Embassy in the UK:** 2nd Floor, 140 Brompton Road, London SW3 1HY. Tel: (0171) 584 8192; fax: (0171) 581 9585 **British embassy:** PO Box 16024, Calle Marco Bruto 1073, 1130 Montevideo. Tel: (2) 623 630; fax: (2) 627 815 **Chamber of commerce:** Cámara Nacional de Comercio, Edificio de la Bolsa de Comercio, Misiones 1400, Casilla 1000, 11000 Montevideo. Tel: (2) 961 277; fax: (2) 961 243

Chronology

1516: Río de la Plata visited by Spanish navigator Juan Diaz de Solis, who was killed by native Charrua Amerindians. This discouraged European settlement for more than a century. **1680:** Portuguese from Brazil founded Nova Colonia do Sacramento on Río de la Plata estuary. **1726:** Spanish established fortress at Montevideo and wrested control over Uruguay from Portugal, with much of the Amerindian population being killed. **1776:** Became part of Viceroyalty of La Plata, with capital at Buenos Aires. **1808:** With Spanish monarchy overthrown by Napoleon Bonaparte, La Plata Viceroyalty became autonomous, but Montevideo remained loyal to Spanish Crown and rebelled against Buenos Aires control. **1815:** Dictator José Gervasio Artigas overthrew Spanish and Buenos Aires control. **1820:** Artigas ousted by Brazil, which disputed control of Uruguay with Argentina. **1825:** Independence declared after fight led by Juan Antonio Lavalleja. **1828:** Independence recognized by country's neighbours. **1836:** Civil war between Reds and Whites, after which Colorado and Blanco parties were named. **1840:** Merino sheep introduced by British traders, who later established meat processing factories for export trade. **1865–70:** Fought successfully alongside Argentina and Brazil in war against Paraguay. **1903:** After period of military rule, José Battle y Ordonez, a progressive from centre-left Colorado Party, became president. As president 1903–07 and 1911–15, he gave women the franchise and created an advanced welfare state as a successful ranching economy developed. **1930:** First constitution adopted, but period of military dictatorship followed during Depression period. **1958:** After 93 years out of power, right-of-centre Blanco Party returned to power. **1967:** Colorado Party in power, with Jorge Pacheco Areco as president. Period of labour unrest and urban guerrilla activity by left-wing Tupamaros. **1972:** Juan María Bordaberry Arocena of Colorado Party became president. **1973:** Parliament dissolved and Bordaberry shared power with military dictatorship, which crushed Tupamaros and banned left-wing groups. **1976:** Bordaberry deposed by army; Dr Aparicio Méndez Manfredini became president. **1981:** Gen Grigorio Alvárez Armellino became new military ruler. **1984:**

Violent antigovernment protests after ten years of repressive rule and deteriorating economy. **1985:** Agreement reached between army and political leaders for return to constitutional government and freeing of political prisoners. Colorado Party won general election; Dr Julio María Sanguinetti became president. **1986:** Government of national accord established under President Sanguinetti. **1989:** Luis Alberto Lacalle Herrera of Blanco Party elected president. **1992:** Public voted against privatization in national referendum. **1994:** Colorado candidate Julio Maria Sanguinetti elected president.

Uzbekistan Republic of

National name: *Ozbekistan Respublikasy* **Area:** 447,400 sq km/ 172,741 sq mi **Capital:** Tashkent **Major towns/cities:** Samarkand, Bukhara, Namangan, Andizhan

Government

Head of state: Islam Karimov from 1990 **Head of government:** Otkir Sultonov from 1995 **Political system:** authoritarian nationalist **Administrative divisions:** 12 regions and one autonomous republic (Karakalpakstan) **Political parties:** People's Democratic Party of Uzbekistan (PDP), reform socialist (ex-communist); Fatherland Progress Party (FP; Vatan Taraqioti), pro-private enterprise; Erk (Freedom Democratic Party), mixed economy; Social Democratic Party of Uzbekistan, pro-Islamic; National Revival Democratic Party, centrist, intelligentsia-led **Armed forces:** 70,000 (1997) **Conscription:** military service is compulsory for 18 months **Death penalty:** retained and used for ordinary crimes **Defence spend:** (% GDP) 3.9 (1997) **Education spend:** (% GNP) 8.1 (1996) **Health spend:** (% GDP) 3.5 (1990–95)

Economy and resources

Currency: som **GDP:** (US$) 23.8 billion (1997 est) **Real GDP growth:** (% change on previous year) –1.5 (1997) **GNP (US$):** 23.9 billion (1997) **GNP per capita (PPP):** (US$) 2,450 (1997) **Consumer price inflation:** 57% (1998) **Unemployment:** 0.4% (1996) **Foreign debt:** (US$) 2.3 billion (1996) **Major trading partners:** CIS nations (principally Russia, Tajikistan, and Kazakhstan), Italy, Germany, China, Turkey **Resources:** petroleum, natural gas, coal, gold (world's seventh-largest producer), silver, uranium (world's fourth-largest producer), copper, lead, zinc, tungsten **Exports:** cotton fibre, textiles, machinery, food and energy products, gold. Principal market: Russia 32% (1997) **Imports:** machinery, light industrial goods, food and raw materials. Principal source: Russia 19.9% (1997) **Arable land:** 9.9% (1995)

Population and society

Population: 23,574,000 (1998 est) **Population growth rate:** 1.9% (1995–2000); 1.9% (2000–05) **Population density:** (per sq km) 53.2 (1998 est) **Urban population:** (% of total) 42 (1997) **Age distribution:** (% of total population) 0–14 38.0%, 15–64 57.3%, 65+ 4.7% (1998) **Ethnic groups:** 71% Uzbek, 8% ethnic Russian, 4% Tajik, 3% Kazakh, 2% Tatar **Language:** Uzbek, a Turkic language **Religion:** Sunni Muslim **Education:** (compulsory years) 9 **Literacy rate:** 97% (men); 96% (women) (1995 est) **Labour force:** 43.4% agriculture, 21.3% industry, 35.3% services (1992) **Life expectancy:** 64 (men); 71 (women) (1995–2000) **Child mortality rate:** (under 5, per 1,000 live births) 57 (1997) **Physicians:** 1 per 284 people (1994)

Practical information

Visa requirements: UK: visa required. USA: visa required **Embassy in the UK:** 72 Wigmore Street, London W1H 9DL. Tel: (0171) 935 1899; fax: (0171) 935 9554 **British embassy:** 6 Ulitsa Murtazayeva, Tashkent 700084. Tel: (3712) 345 652; fax: (873) 340 465 **Chamber of commerce:** Tashkent International Business Centre, Ulitsa Pushkina 17, Tashkent. Tel: (3712) 323 231; fax: (3712) 334 414

Chronology

6th century BC: Part of Persian Empire of Cyrus the Great. **4th century BC:** Part of empire of Alexander the Great of Macedonia. **1st century BC:** Samarkand (Maracanda) developed as transit point on strategic Silk Road trading route between China and Europe. **7th century:** City of Tashkent founded; spread of Islam. **12th century:** Tashkent taken by Turks; Khorezem (Khiva), in northwest, became centre of large Central Asian polity, stretching from Caspian Sea to Samarkand in the east. **13th–14th centuries:** Conquered by Genghis Khan and became part of Mongol Empire, with Samarkand serving as capital for Tamerlane. **18th–19th centuries:** Dominated by independent emirates and khanates (chiefdoms) of Bukhara in southwest, Kokand in east, and Samarkand in centre. **1865–67:** Tashkent was taken by Russia and made capital of Governor-Generalship of Turkestan. **1868–76:** Tsarist Russia annexed emirate of Bukhara (1868); and khanates of Samarkand (1868), Khiva (1873), and Kokand (1876). **1917:** Following Bolshevik revolution in Russia, Tashkent soviet ('people's council') established, which deposed the emir of Bukhara and other khans in 1920. **1918–22:** Mosques closed and Muslim clergy persecuted as part of secularization drive by new communist rulers, despite nationalist guerrilla (basmachi) resistance. **1921:** Part of Turkestan Soviet Socialist Autonomous Republic. **1925:** Became constituent republic of USSR. **1930s:** Skilled ethnic Russians immigrated into urban centres as industries developed. **1944:** About 160,000 Meskhetian Turks forcibly transported from their native Georgia to Uzbekistan by Soviet dictator Joseph Stalin. **1950s–80s:** Major irrigation projects stimulated cotton production, but led to desiccation of Aral Sea. **late 1980s:** Upsurge in Islamic consciousness stimulated by *glasnost* initiative of Soviet Union's reformist leader Mikhail Gorbachev. **1989:** Birlik ('Unity'), nationalist movement, formed. Violent attacks on Meskhetian and other minority communities in Ferghana Valley. **1990:** Economic and political sovereignty declared by increasingly nationalist UCP, led by Islam Karimov, who became president. **1991:** Attempted anti-Gorbachev coup by conservatives in Moscow initially supported by President Karimov. Independence declared. Joined new Commonwealth of Independent States (CIS); Karimov directly elected president. **1992:** Violent food riots in Tashkent. Joined Economic Cooperation Organization and United Nations. New constitution adopted. **1993:** Crackdown on Islamic fundamentalists as economy deteriorated. **1994:** Economic, military, and social union formed with Kazakhstan and Kyrgyzstan. Economic integration treaty signed with Russia. Links with Turkey strengthened and foreign inward investment encouraged. **1995:** Ruling PDP (formerly UCP) won general election, from which opposition was banned from participating. Karimov's tenure extended for further five-year term by national plebiscite. **1996:** Agreement with Kazakhstan and Kyrgyzstan to create single economic market. **1998:** A treaty of eternal friendship and a treaty of deepening economic cooperation was signed with Kazakhstan. **1999:** Uzbekistan threatened to end participation in a regional security treaty, accusing Russia of seeking to integrate the former Soviet republics into a superstate.

Vanuatu Republic of

National name: *Ripablik blong Vanuatu* **Area:** 14,800 sq km/5,714 sq mi **Capital:** (and chief port) Port-Vila (on Efate) **Major towns/cities:** Luganville (on Espíritu Santo) **Major ports:** Santo

Government

Head of state: John Bernard Bani from 1999 **Head of government:** Donald Kalpokas from 1998 **Political system:** democracy **Administrative divisions:** six provincial authorities **Political parties:** Union of Moderate Parties (UMP), Francophone centrist; National United Party (NUP), formed by Walter Lini; Vanua'aku Pati (VP), Anglophone centrist; Melanesian Progressive Party (MPP),

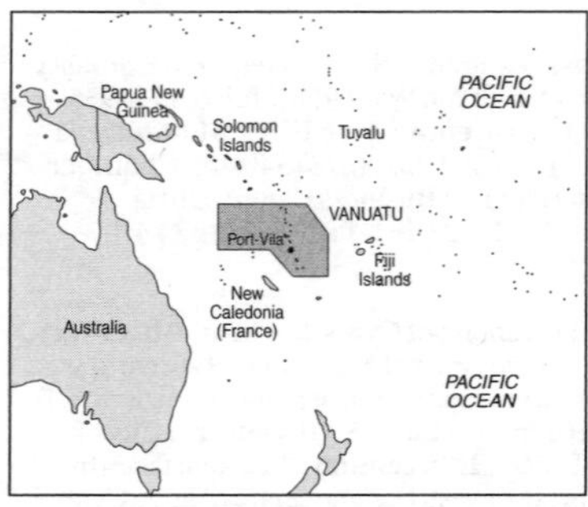

Melanesian centrist; Fren Melanesian Party **Armed forces:** no standing defence force; paramilitary force of around 300; police naval service of around 50 (1995) **Death penalty:** laws do not provide for the death penalty for any crime **Education spend:** (% GNP) 4.9 (1995) **Health spend:** (% GDP) 2.9 (1990)

Economy and resources

Currency: vatu **GDP:** (US$) 250 million (1997 est) **Real GDP growth:** (% change on previous year) 3.0 (1997 est) **GNP (US$):** 233 million (1997) **GNP per capita (PPP):** (US$) 3,020 (1997 est) **Consumer price inflation:** 3.2% (1997) **Foreign debt:** (US$) 47 million (1996) **Major trading partners:** Japan, Australia, the Netherlands, New Zealand, New Caledonia, France **Resources:** manganese; gold, copper, and large deposits of petroleum have been discovered but have hitherto remained unexploited **Exports:** copra, beef, timber, cocoa, shells. Principal market: Japan 27.6% (1996) **Imports:** machinery and transport equipment, food and live animals, basic manufactures, miscellaneous manufactured articles, mineral fuels, chemicals, beverages, tobacco. Principal source: Japan 46.6% (1996) **Arable land:** 1.6% (1995)

Population and society

Population: 182,000 (1998 est) **Population growth rate:** 2.5% (1995–2000) **Population density:** (per sq km) 12.5 (1998 est) **Urban population:** (% of total) 19 (1997) **Age distribution:** (% of total population) 0–14 39.1%, 15–64 57.9%, 65+ 3.0% (1998) **Ethnic groups:** 95% Melanesian, 3% European or mixed European, 2% Vietnamese, Chinese, or other Pacific islanders **Language:** Bislama 82%, English, French (all official) **Religion:** Christian 80%, animist **Education:** (compulsory years) 6 **Literacy rate:** 54% (men); 23% (women) (1995 est) **Labour force:** 68% agriculture, 8% industry, 24% services (1990) **Life expectancy:** 66 (men); 70 (women) (1995–2000) **Child mortality rate:** (under 5, per 1,000 live births) 46 (1997) **Physicians:** 1 per 7,147 people (1990)

Practical information

Visa requirements: UK: visa not required. USA: visa not required **Embassy in the UK:** Vanuatu has no diplomatic representation in the UK; the UK Department of Trade and Industry has a Pacific Islands Desk. Tel: (0171) 215 4985; fax: (0171) 215 4398 **British embassy:** British High Commission, PO Box 567, KPMG House, rue Pasteur, Port-Vila. Tel: (678) 23100; fax: (678) 23651 **Chamber of commerce:** PO Box 189, Port-Vila. Tel/fax: (678) 23255

Chronology

1606: First visited by Portuguese navigator Pedro Fernandez de Queiras, who named the islands Espiritu Santo. **1774:** Visited by British navigator Capt James Cook, who named them the New Hebrides, after the Scottish islands. **1830s:** European merchants attracted to islands by sandalwood trade. Christian missionaries arrived, but many were attacked by the indigenous Melanesians who, in turn, were ravaged by exposure to European diseases. **later 19th century:** Britain and France disputed control; islanders were shipped to Australia, the Fiji Islands, Samoa, and New Caledonia to work as plantation labourers. **1906:** Islands jointly administered by France and Britain as the Condominium of the New Hebrides. **1963:** Indigenous Na-Griamel (NG) political grouping formed on Espíritu Santo to campaign against European acquisition of more than a third of the land area. **1975:** Representative assembly established following pressure from the VP, formed in 1972 by English-speaking Melanesian Protestants. **1978:** Government of national unity formed, with Father Gerard Leymang as chief minister. **1980:** Revolt on the island of Espíritu Santo by French settlers and pro-NG plantation workers delayed independence but it was achieved within the Commonwealth, with George Kalkoa (adopted name Sokomanu) as president and left-of-centre Father Walter Lini (VP) as prime minister. **1988:** Dismissal of Lini by Sokomanu led to Sokomanu's arrest for treason. Lini reinstated. **1989:** Sokomanu succeeded as president by Fred Timakata. **1991:** Lini voted out by party members; replaced by Donald Kalpokas. General election produced coalition government of the Francophone Union of Moderate Parties (UMP) and Lini's new National United Party (NUP) under Maxime Carlot Korman. **1993:** Cyclone caused extensive damage. **1994:** Timakata succeeded as president by Jean Marie Leye. **1995:** Governing UMP–NUP coalition won general election, but Serge Vohor, of VP-dominated Unity Front, became prime minister. **1996:** Vohor briefly replaced by Maxime Carlot Korman, but Vohor returned to power leading new coalition after Carlot government implicated in financial scandal. MFT expelled from governing coalition and replaced by Vanua'aku Party, led by Donald Kalpokas. **1997:** Prime Minister Vohor formed new coalition. Legislature dissolved and new elections called after no-confidence motion against Vohor. **1998:** Two-week state of emergency after rioting in capital. Donald Kalpokas elected prime minister after early election, heading VP–NUP coalition. **1999:** John Bernard Bani elected president.

Vatican City State

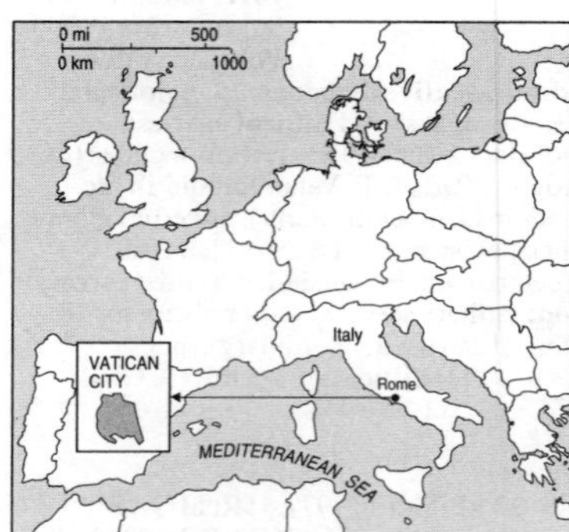

National name: *Stato della Città del Vaticano* **Area:** 0.4 sq km/0.2 sq mi

Government

Head of state: John Paul II from 1978 **Head of government:** Cardinal Sebastiano Baggio **Political system:** absolute Catholicism **Death penalty:** abolished in 1969

Economy and resources

Currency: Vatican City lira; Italian lira **GDP:** see Italy **Real GDP growth:** (% change on previous year) see Italy **GNP (US$):** see Italy **GNP per capita (PPP):** see Italy

Population and society

Population: 480 (1998) **Population density:** (per sq km) 2,273 (1996 est) **Urban population:** (% of total) 100 (1995) **Language:** Latin (official), Italian **Religion:** Roman Catholic **Literacy rate:** see Italy **Life expectancy:** see Italy

Practical information

Visa requirements: see Italy. There is free access to certain areas, including St Peter's Church and Square, the Vatican Museum, and Vatican Gardens; special permission is required to visit all other areas **Embassy in the UK:** Apostolic Nunciature, 54 Parkside, London SW19 5NE. Tel: (0181) 946 1410; fax: (0181) 947 2494 **British embassy:** Via Condotti 91, 00187 Rome. Tel: (6) 678 9462; fax: (6) 994 0684 **Chamber of commerce:** Prefecture of the Economic Affairs of the Holy See, Palazzo delle Congregazioni, Largo del Colonnato 3, 00193 Rome. Tel: (6) 6988 4263; fax: (6) 6988 5011

Chronology

AD 64: Death of St Peter, a Christian martyr who, by legend, was killed in Rome and became regarded as the first bishop of Rome.

The Pope, as head of the Roman Catholic Church, is viewed as the spiritual descendent of St Peter. **756:** The Pope became temporal ruler of the Papal States, which stretched across central Italy, centred around Rome. **11th–13th centuries:** Under Gregory VII and Innocent III the papacy enjoyed its greatest temporal power. **1377:** After seven decades in which the papacy was based in Avignon (France), Rome once again became the headquarters for the Pope, with the Vatican Palace becoming the official residence. **1860:** Umbria, Marche, and much of Emilia Romagna which, along with Lazio formed the Papal States, were annexed by the new unified Italian state. **1870:** First Vatican Council defined as a matter of faith the absolute primacy of the Pope and the infallibility of his pronouncements on 'matters of faith and morals'. **1870–71:** French forces, which had been protecting the Pope, were withdrawn, allowing Italian nationalist forces to capture Rome, which became the capital of Italy; Pope Pius IX retreated into the Vatican Palace, from which no Pope was to emerge until 1929. **1929:** Lateran Agreement, signed by the Italian fascist leader Benito Mussolini and Pope Pius XI, restored full sovereign jurisdiction over the Vatican City State to the bishopric of Rome (Holy See) and declared the new state to be a neutral and inviolable territory. **1947:** New Italian constitution confirmed the sovereignty of the Vatican City State. **1962:** Second Vatican Council called by Pope John XXIII. **1978:** John Paul II became the first non-Italian pope for more than 400 years. **1985:** New concordat signed under which Roman Catholicism ceased to be Italy's state religion. **1992:** Relations with East European states restored.

Venezuela Republic of

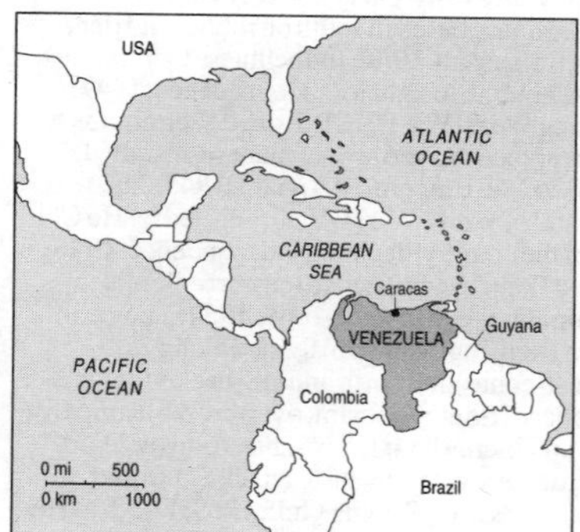

National name: *República de Venezuela* **Area:** 912,100 sq km/ 352,161 sq mi **Capital:** Caracas **Major towns/ cities:** Maracaibo, Maracay, Barquisimeto, Valencia, Ciudad Guayana, San Cristobál **Major ports:** Maracaibo

Government

Head of state and government: Hugo Chavez from 1998 **Political system:** federal democracy **Administrative divisions:** 20 states, two federal territories, one federal district, and 72 federal dependencies **Political parties:** Democratic Action Party (AD), moderate left of centre; Christian Social Party (COPEI), Christian, centre right; National Convergence (CN), broad coalition grouping; Movement towards Socialism (MAS), left of centre; Radical Cause (LCR), left wing **Armed forces:** 56,000 (1997) **Conscription:** military service is by selective conscription for 30 months **Death penalty:** abolished in 1863 **Defence spend:** (% GDP) 1.1 (1997) **Education spend:** (% GNP) 5.2 (1995) **Health spend:** (% GDP) 2.3 (1990–95)

Economy and resources

Currency: bolívar **GDP:** (US$) 87.5 billion (1997) **Real GDP growth:** (% change on previous year) 5.6 (1997) **GNP (US$):** 78.7 billion (1997) **GNP per capita (PPP):** (US$) 8,530 (1997) **Consumer price inflation:** 23.3% (1998) **Unemployment:** 8.7% (1996) **Foreign debt:** (US$) 35.3 billion (1996) **Major trading partners:** USA, Japan, Germany, Italy, the Netherlands, Antilles, Colombia, Brazil **Resources:** petroleum, natural gas, aluminium, iron ore, coal, diamonds, gold, zinc, copper, silver, lead, phosphates, manganese, titanium **Exports:** petroleum and petroleum products, metals (mainly aluminium and iron ore), natural gas, chemicals, basic manufactures, motor vehicles and parts. Principal market: USA 56.7% (1997) **Imports:** machinery and transport equipment, chemicals, food and live animals, basic manufactures, crude materials. Principal source: USA 53.4% (1997) **Arable land:** 3% (1995)

Population and society

Population: 23,242,000 (1998 est) **Population growth rate:** 2.0% (1995–2000); 1.8% (2000–05) **Population density:** (per sq km) 25.9 (1998 est) **Urban population:** (% of total) 87 (1997) **Age distribution:** (% of total population) 0–14 33.8%, 15–64 61.7%, 65+ 4.5% (1998) **Ethnic groups:** 67% mestizos (of Spanish-American and American-Indian descent), 21% Europeans, 10% Africans, 2% Indians **Language:** Spanish (official), Indian languages 2% **Religion:** Roman Catholic **Education:** (compulsory years) 10 **Literacy rate:** 87% (men); 86% (women) (1995 est) **Labour force:** 9.7% agriculture, 26.3% industry, 64% services (1993) **Life expectancy:** 70 (men); 76 (women) (1995–2000) **Child mortality rate:** (under 5, per 1,000 live births) 24 (1997) **Physicians:** 1 per 633 people (1993 est)

Practical information

Visa requirements: UK: visa not required. USA: visa not required **Embassy in the UK:** 1 Cromwell Road, London SW7 2HW. Tel: (0171) 584 4206/7; fax: (0171) 589 8887 **British embassy:** Apartado 1246, Edificio Torre Las Mercedes, 3 °, Avenida la Estancia, Chuao, Caracas 1060. Tel: (2) 993 4111; fax: (2) 993 9989 **Chamber of commerce:** Federación Venezolana de Cámaras y Asociaciones de Comercio y Producción, Apartado 2568, Edificio Fedecámaras, 5 °, Avenida El Empalme, Urb El Bosque, Caracas. Tel: (2) 731 1711; fax: (2) 731 0220

Chronology

1st millenium BC: Beginnings of settled agriculture. AD **1498–99:** Visited by Christopher Columbus and Alonso de Ojeda, at which time the principal indigenous Indian communities were the Caribs, Arawaks, and Chibchas; it was named Venezuela ('little Venice') since the coastal Indians lived in stilted thatched houses. **1521:** Spanish settlement established on the northeast coast and was ruled by Spain from Santo Domingo (Dominican Republic). **1567:** Caracas founded by Diego de Losada. **1739:** Became part of newly created Spanish Viceroyalty of New Granada, with capital at Bogotá (Colombia), but, lacking gold mines, retained great autonomy. **1749:** First rebellion against Spanish colonial rule. **1806:** Rebellion against Spain, led by Francisco Miranda. **1811–12:** First Venezuelan Republic declared by patriots, taking advantage of Napoleon Bonaparte's invasion of Spain, but Spanish Royalist forces re-established their authority. **1813–14:** The Venezuelan, Simón Bolívar, 'El Libertador' (the Liberator), created another briefly independent republic, before being forced to withdraw to Colombia. **1821:** After battle of Carabobo, Venezuelan independence achieved within Republic of Gran Colombia (which also comprised Colombia, Ecuador, and Panama). **1829:** Became separate state of Venezuela after leaving Republic of Gran Colombia. **1830–48:** Gen José Antonio Páez, the first of a series of caudillos (military leaders), established political stability. **1870–88:** Antonio Guzmán Blanco ruled as benevolent liberal–conservative dictator, modernizing infrastructure and developing agriculture (notably coffee) and education. **1899:** International arbitration tribunal found in favour of British Guiana (Guyana) in long-running dispute over border with Venezuela. **1902:** Ports blockaded by British, Italian, and German navies as a result of Venezuela's failure to repay loans. **1908–35:** Harsh rule of dictator Juan Vicente Gómez, during which period Venezuela became world's largest exporter of oil, which had been discovered in 1910. **1947:** First truly democratic elections held, but the new president, Rómulo Gallegos, was removed within eight months by the military in the person of Col Marcos Pérez Jimenez. **1958:** Overthrow of Perez and establishment of an enduring civilian democracy, headed by left-wing Romulo Betancourt of Democratic Action Party (AD). **1964:** Dr Raúl Leoni (AD) became president in first-ever constitutional handover of civilian power. **1969:** Dr Rafael Caldera Rodríguez, of centre-right Christian Social Party (COPEI), became president. **1974:** Carlos Andrés Pérez (AD) became president, with economy remaining

buoyant through oil revenues. Oil and iron industries nationalized. **1979:** Dr Luis Herrera (COPEI) became president. **1984:** Dr Jaime Lusinchi (AD) became president; social pact established between government, trade unions, and business; national debt rescheduled as oil revenues plummetted. **1987:** Widespread social unrest triggered by inflation; student demonstrators shot by police. **1989:** Carlos Andrés Pérez (AD) elected president. Economic austerity programme enforced by a loan of $4.3 billion from International Monetary Fund. Price increases triggered riots known as 'Caracazo'; 300 people killed. Martial law declared. General strike followed. Elections boycotted by opposition groups. **1992:** Attempted antigovernment coups failed, at a cost of 120 lives. **1993:** Pérez resigned, accused of corruption; Ramon José Velasquez succeeded him as interim head of state. Former president Dr Rafael Caldera (COMEI) re-elected. **1996:** Pérez found guilty on corruption charges and imprisoned. **1998:** Hugo Chavez elected president.

Vietnam Socialist Republic of

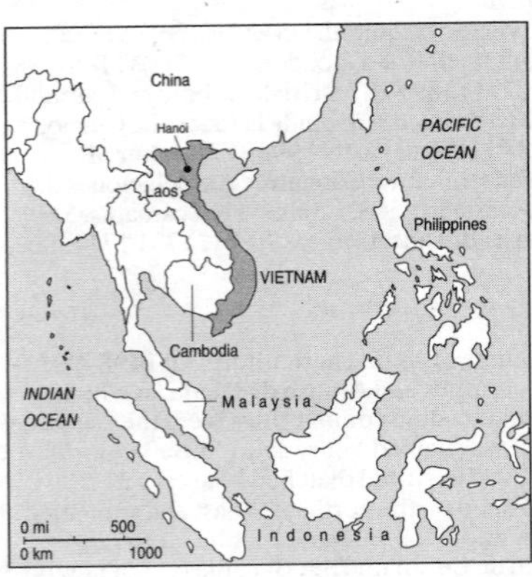

National name: *Công Hòa Xã Hôi Chu Nghia Viêt Nam* **Area:** 329,600 sq km/ 127,258 sq mi **Capital:** Hanoi **Major towns/ cities:** Ho Chi Minh City (formerly Saigon), Haiphong, Da Nang, Can Tho, Nha Trang, Nam Dinh **Major ports:** Ho Chi Minh City (formerly Saigon), Da Nang, Haiphong

Government

Head of state: Tran Duc Luong from 1997 **Head of government:** Phan Van Khai from 1997 **Political system:** communism **Administrative divisions:** 53 provinces within seven regions **Political party:** Communist Party **Armed forces:** 492,000; plus paramilitary forces numbering 65,000 and around 3 million reserves (1997) **Conscription:** military service is compulsory for two years **Death penalty:** retained and used for ordinary crimes **Defence spend:** (% GDP) 4.1 (1997) **Education spend:** (% GNP) 2.7 (1995) **Health spend:** (% GDP) 1.1 (1990–95)

Economy and resources

Currency: dong **GDP:** (US$) 24.9 billion (1997) **Real GDP growth:** (% change on previous year) 8.5 (1997) **GNP (US$):** 24.5 billion (1997) **GNP per capita (PPP):** (US$) 1,670 (1997) **Consumer price inflation:** 11.0% (1998) **Unemployment:** 7% (1994 est) **Foreign debt:** (US$) 26.8 billion (1996) **Major trading partners:** Singapore, Japan, Hong Kong, South Korea, Taiwan, China, Thailand **Resources:** petroleum, coal, tin, zinc, iron, antimony, chromium, phosphate, apatite, bauxite **Exports:** rice (leading exporter), crude petroleum, coal, coffee, marine products, handicrafts, light industrial goods, rubber, nuts, tea, garments, tin. Principal market: Japan 21.3% (1996) **Imports:** petroleum products, machinery and spare parts, steel, artificial fertilizers, basic manufactures, consumer goods. Principal source: Singapore 18.2% (1996) **Arable land:** 16.9% (1995)

Population and society

Population: 77,562,000 (1998 est) **Population growth rate:** 1.8% (1995–2000) **Population density:** (per sq km) 234.3 (1998 est) **Urban population:** (% of total) 20 (1997) **Age distribution:** (% of total population) 0–14 34.6%, 15–64 60.1%, 65+ 5.3% (1998) **Ethnic groups:** 88% Viet (also known as Kinh), 2% Chinese, 2% Khmer, 8% consists of more than 50 minority nationalities, including the Hmong, Meo, Muong, Nung, Tay, Thai, and Tho tribal groups **Language:** Vietnamese (official); French, English, Khmer, Chinese, local languages **Religion:** Taoist, Buddhist, Roman Catholic **Education:** (compulsory years) 5 **Literacy rate:** 92% (men); 84% (women) (1995 est) **Labour force:** 73% agriculture, 13.3% industry, 13.7% services (1994) **Life expectancy:** 65 (men); 70 (women) (1995–2000) **Child mortality rate:** (under 5, per 1,000 live births) 51 (1997) **Physicians:** 1 per 2,279 people (1993 est)

Practical information

Visa requirements: UK: visa required. USA: visa required **Embassy in the UK:** 12–14 Victoria Road, London W8 5RD. Tel: (0171) 937 1912; fax: (0171) 937 6108 **British embassy:** 16 Pho Ly Thuong Kiet, Hanoi. Tel: (4) 252 349; fax: (4) 265 762 **Chamber of commerce:** Vietcochamber (Chamber of Industry and Commerce of Vietnam), 33 Ba Trieu, Hanoi. Tel: (4) 253 023; fax: (4) 256 446

Chronology

300 BC: Rise of Dong Son culture. **111 BC:** Came under Chinese rule. **1st–6th centuries AD:** Southern Mekong delta region controlled by independent Indianized Funan kingdom. **939:** Chinese overthrown by Ngo Quyen at battle of Bach Dang River; first Vietnamese dynasty founded. **11th century:** Theravāda Buddhism promoted. **15th century:** North and South Vietnam united, as kingdom of Champa in the south was destroyed in 1471. **16th century:** Contacts with French missionaries and European traders as political power became decentralized. **early 19th century:** Under Emperor Nguyen Anh authority was briefly recentralized. **1858–84:** Conquered by France and divided into protectorates of Tonkin (North Vietnam) and Annam (South Vietnam). **1887:** Became part of French Indo-China Union, which included Cambodia and Laos. **late 19th–early 20th century:** Development of colonial economy based in south on rubber and rice, drawing migrant labourers from north. **1930:** Indochinese Communist Party (ICP) formed by Ho Chi Minh to fight for independence. **1941:** Occupied by Japanese during World War II; ICP formed Vietminh as guerrilla resistance force designed to overthrow Japanese-installed puppet regime headed by Bao Dai, Emperor of Annam. **1945:** Japanese removed from Vietnam at end of World War II; Vietminh, led by Ho Chi Minh, in control of much of the country, declared independence. **1946:** Vietminh war began against French, who tried to reassert colonial control and set up noncommunist state in south 1949. **1954:** France decisively defeated at Dien Bien Phu. Vietnam divided along 17th parallel between communist-controlled north and US-backed south. **1963:** Ngo Dinh Diem, leader of South Vietnam, overthrown in military coup by Lt-Gen Nguyen Van Thieu. **1964:** US combat troops entered Vietnam War as North Vietnamese army began to attack South and allegedly attacked US destroyers in the Tonkin Gulf. **1969:** Death of Ho Chi Minh, who was succeeded as Communist Party leader by Le Duan. US forces, which numbered 545,000 at their peak, gradually began to be withdrawn from Vietnam as a result of domestic opposition to the rising casualty toll. **1973:** Paris cease-fire agreement provided for withdrawal of US troops and release of US prisoners of war. **1975:** Saigon captured by North Vietnam, violating Paris Agreements. **1976:** Socialist Republic of Vietnam proclaimed. Hundreds of thousands of southerners became political prisoners; many more fled abroad. Collectivization extended to south. **1978:** Diplomatic relations severed with China. Admission into Comecon. Vietnamese invasion of Cambodia. **1979:** Sino-Vietnamese 17-day border war; 700,000 Chinese and middle-class Vietnamese fled abroad as refugee 'boat people'. **1986:** Death of Le Duan and retirement of 'old guard' leaders; pragmatic Nguyen Van Linh became Communist Party leader and encouraged the private sector through *doi moi* ('renovation') initiative. **1987–88:** Over 10,000 political prisoners released. **1989:** Troops fully withdrawn from Cambodia. **1991:** Economic reformer Vo Van Kiet replaced Do Muoi as prime minister. Cambodia peace agreement signed. Relations with China normalized. **1992:** New constitution adopted, guaranteeing economic freedoms. Conservative Le Duc Anh elected president. Relations with South Korea normalized. **1994:** US 30-year-old trade embargo removed. **1995:** Full diplomatic relations re-established with USA. Became full member of ASEAN. **1996:** Economic upturn gained pace. **1997:** Diplomatic

relations with USA restored. Tran Duc Luong and Phan Van Khai elected president and prime minister respectively. Reduction in size of standing army. **1998:** Currency devalued. Corruption charges against a senior communist, Pham The Duyet. New emphasis placed on agricultural development, after export and GDP growth slumped to 3% in 1998. **1999:** Tran Do, a former high ranking communist, was expelled from the Communist Party after urging democratization.

Yemen Republic of

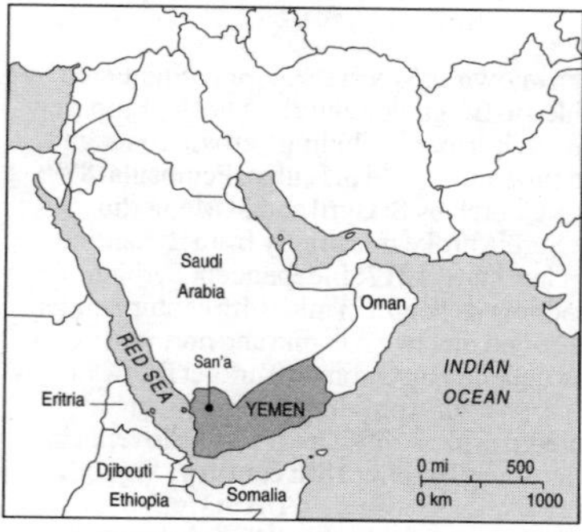

National name: *Jamhuriya al Yamaniya* **Area:** 531,900 sq km/ 205,366 sq mi **Capital:** San'a **Major towns/cities:** Aden, Ta'izz, Al Mukalla, Hodeida, Ibb, Dhamar **Major ports:** Aden

Government

Head of state: Ali Abdullah Saleh from 1990 **Head of government:** Abdul Ali al-Rahman al-Iryani from 1998 **Political system:** emergent democracy **Administrative divisions:** 17 governates **Political parties:** General People's Congress (GPC), left of centre; Yemen Socialist Party (YSP), left wing; Yemen Reform Group (al-Islah), Islamic, right of centre; National Opposition Front, left of centre **Armed forces:** 66,300; plus paramilitary forces numbering at least 80,000 (1997) **Conscription:** military service is compulsory for two years **Death penalty:** retained and used for ordinary crimes **Defence spend:** (% GDP) 7 (1997) **Education spend:** (% GNP) 7.5 (1995) **Health spend:** (% GDP) 1.2 (1990–95)

Economy and resources

Currency: riyal (North); dinar (South), both legal currency throughout the country **GDP:** (US$) 5.4 billion (1997) **Real GDP growth:** (% change on previous year) 3.5 (1997) **GNP (US$):** 4.3 billion (1997) **GNP per capita (PPP):** (US$) 720 (1997) **Consumer price inflation:** 16.5% (1998) **Unemployment:** 36% (1993) **Foreign debt:** (US$) 6.35 billion (1996) **Major trading partners:** China, United Arab Emirates, USA, Saudi Arabia, Japan, France, South Korea, Thailand, Brazil **Resources:** petroleum, natural gas, gypsum, salt; deposits of copper, gold, lead, zinc, molybdenum **Exports:** petroleum and petroleum products, cotton, basic manufactures, clothing, live animals, hides and skins, fish, rice, coffee. Principal market: China 22.8% (1996) **Imports:** textiles and other manufactured consumer goods, petroleum products, sugar, grain, flour, other foodstuffs, cement, machinery, chemicals. Principal source: UAE 8.5% (1996) **Arable land:** 2.7% (1995)

Population and society

Population: 16,887,000 (1998 est) **Population growth rate:** 3.7% (1995–2000); 3.1% (2000–05) **Population density:** (per sq km) 31 (1998 est) **Urban population:** (% of total) 36 (1997) **Age distribution:** (% of total population) 0–14 46.7%, 15–64 50.9%, 65+ 2.4% (1995) **Ethnic groups:** predominantly Arab **Language:** Arabic **Religion:** Sunni Muslim 63%, Shi'ite Muslim 37% **Education:** (compulsory years): 6 (North); 8 (South) **Literacy rate:** 53% (men); 26% (women) (1995 est) **Labour force:** 30% of population: 61% agriculture, 17% industry, 22% services (1990) **Life expectancy:** 57 (men); 58 (women) (1995–2000) **Child mortality rate:** (under 5, per 1,000 live births) 109 (1997) **Physicians:** 1 per 4,498 people (1993 est)

Practical information

Visa requirements: UK: visa required. USA: visa required **Embassy in the UK:** 57 Cromwell Road, London SW7 2ED. Tel: (0171) 584 6607; fax: (0171) 589 3350 **British embassy:** PO Box 1287, 129 Haddah Road, Sana'a. Tel: (1) 215 630; fax: (1) 263 059 **Chamber of commerce:** Federation of Chambers of Commerce, PO Box 16992, Sana'a. Tel: (1) 221 765; telex: 2229

Chronology

1st millenium BC: South Yemen (Aden) divided between economically advanced Qataban and Hadramawt kingdoms. *c.* **5th century BC:** Qataban fell to the Sabaeans (Shebans) of North Yemen (Sana). *c.* **100 BC–AD 525:** All of Yemen became part of Himyarite kingdom. **AD 628:** Islam introduced. **1174–1229:** Under control of Egyptian Ayyubids. **1229–1451:** 'Golden age' for arts and sciences under the Rasulids, who had served as governors of Yemen under the Ayyubids. **1538:** North Yemen came under control of Turkish Ottoman Empire. **1636:** Ottomans left North Yemen and power fell into hands of Yemeni Imams, based on local Zaydi tribes, who also held South Yemen until 1735. **1839:** Aden became a British territory. Port developed into important ship refuelling station after opening of Suez Canal 1869; protectorate was gradually established over 23 Sultanates inland. **1870s:** The Ottomans re-established control over North Yemen. **1918:** North Yemen became independent, with Imam Yahya from Hamid al-Din family as king. **1937:** Aden became British crown colony. **1948:** Imam Yahya assassinated by exiled Free Yemenis nationalist movement, but uprising was crushed by his son, Imam Ahmad. **1959:** Federation of South Arabia formed by Britain between city of Aden and feudal Sultanates (Aden Protectorate). **1962:** Military coup on death of Imam Ahmad; North Yemen declared Yemen Arab Republic (YAR), with Abdullah al-Sallal as president. Civil war broke out between royalists (supported by Saudi Arabia) and republicans (supported by Egypt). **1963:** Armed rebellion by National Liberation Front (NLF) began against British rule in Aden. **1967:** Civil war ended with republicans victorious. Sallal deposed and replaced by Republican Council. The Independent People's Republic of South Yemen formed after British withdrawal from Aden. Many fled to north as repressive communist NLF regime took over in south. **1970:** People's Republic of South Yemen renamed People's Democratic Republic of Yemen. **1971–72:** War between South Yemen and YAR; union agreement brokered by Arab League signed but not kept. **1974:** The pro-Saudi Col Ibrahim al-Hamadi seized power in North Yemen; Military Command Council set up. **1977:** Hamadi assassinated; replaced by Col Ahmed ibn Hussein al-Ghashmi. **1978:** Constituent people's assembly appointed in North Yemen and Military Command Council dissolved. Ghashmi killed by envoy from South Yemen; succeeded by Ali Abdullah Saleh. War broke out again between two Yemens. South Yemen president deposed and executed; Yemen Socialist Party (YSP) formed in south by communists. **1979:** Cease-fire agreed with commitment to future union. **1980:** YSP leader Ali Nasser Muhammad became head of state in South Yemen. **1986:** Civil war in South Yemen; autocratic Ali Nasser dismissed. New administration formed under more moderate Haydar Abu Bakr al-Attas, who was committed to negotiating union with north as a result of deteriorating economy in south. **1989:** Draft multiparty constitution for single Yemen state published. **1990:** Border between two Yemens opened; countries formally united 22 May as Republic of Yemen. **1991:** New constitution approved; Yemen opposed US-led operations against Iraq in Gulf War. **1992:** Anti-government riots. **1993:** Saleh's General People's Congress (GPC) won most seats in general election but no overall majority; five-member presidential council elected, including Saleh as president, YSP leader Ali Salim al-Baidh as vice president, and Bakr al-Attas as prime minister. **1994:** Fighting erupted between northern forces, led by President Saleh, and southern forces, led by Vice President al-Baidh, as southern Yemen announced its secession. Saleh inflicted crushing defeat on al-Baidh and new GPC coalition appointed. **1997:** GPC election victory. Farag Said Ben Ghanem appointed prime minister. **1998:** New government headed by Abdul Ali al-Rahman al-Iryani.

Yugoslavia Federal Republic of

National name: *Federativna Republika Jugoslavija* **Area:** 58,300 sq km/22,509 sq mi **Capital:** Belgrade **Major towns/cities:**

Priština, Novi Sad, Niš, Rijeka, Kragujevac, Podgorica (formerly Titograd), Subotica

Government

Head of state: Slobodan Milošević from 1997 **Head of government:** Momir Bulatović from 1998 **Political system:** socialist pluralist republic **Administrative divisions:** 29 districts **Political parties:** Socialist Party of Serbia (SPS), Serb nationalist, reform socialist (ex-communist); Montenegrin Social Democratic Party (SDPCG), federalist, reform socialist (ex-communist); Serbian Radical Party (SRS), Serb nationalist, extreme right wing; People's Assembly Party, Christian democrat, centrist; Democratic Party (DS), moderate nationalist; Democratic Party of Serbia (DSS), moderate nationalist; Democratic Community of Vojvodina Hungarians (DZVM), ethnic Hungarian; Democratic Party of Albanians/Party of Democratic Action (DPA/PDA), ethnic Albanian; New Socialist Party of Montenegro (NSPM), left of centre **Armed forces:** 114,200 (1997) **Conscription:** military service is compulsory for 12–15 months; voluntary military service for women introduced in 1983 **Death penalty:** retained and used for ordinary crimes **Defence spend:** (% GDP) 7.8 (1997) **Education spend:** (% GNP) 6.1 (1992; former Yugoslavia)

Economy and resources

Currency: new Yugoslav dinar **GDP:** (US$) 17.8 billion (1997) **Real GDP growth:** (% change on previous year) 6.0 (1997) **GNP (US$):** 17.9 billion (1997 est) **GNP per capita (PPP):** (US$) 5,880 (1997 est) **Consumer price inflation:** 23% (1998) **Unemployment:** 26.1% (1996) **Foreign debt:** (US$) 13.45 billion (1996) **Major trading partners:** Germany, Russia, Italy, USA, Macedonia **Resources:** petroleum, natural gas, coal, copper ore, bauxite, iron ore, lead, zinc **Exports:** basic manufactures, machinery and transport equipment, clothing, miscellaneous manufactured articles, food and live animals. Principal market: Italy 11.5% (1997) **Imports:** machinery and transport equipment, electrical goods, agricultural produce, mineral fuels and lubricants, basic manufactures, foodstuffs, chemicals. Principal source: Germany 13.4% (1997) **Arable land:** 36.6% (1995)

Population and society

Population: 10,635,000 (1998 est) **Population growth rate:** 0.5% (1995–2000); 0.4% (2000–05) **Population density:** (per sq km) 85 (1998 est) **Urban population:** (% of total) 57 (1995) **Age distribution:** (% of total population) 0–14 20.6%, 15–64 66.7%, 65+ 12.7% (1998) **Ethnic groups:** according to the 1991 census, 62% of the population of the rump federal republic is ethnic Serb, 17% Albanian, 5% Montenegrin, 3% 'Yugoslav', and 3% Muslim. Serbs predominate in the republic of Serbia, where they form (excluding the autonomous areas of Kosovo and Vojvodina) 85% of the population; in Vojvodina they comprise 55% of the population. Albanians constitute 77% of the population of Kosovo; Montenegrins comprise 69% of the population of the republic of Montenegro; and Muslims predominate in the Sandzak region, which straddles the Serbian and Montenegrin borders. Since 1992 an influx of Serb refugees from Bosnia and Kosovo has increased the proportion of Serbs in Serbia, while many ethnic Hungarians have left Vojvodina, and an estimated 500,000 Albanians have left Kosovo **Language:** Serbo-Croatian; Albanian (in Kosovo) **Religion:** Serbian and Montenegrin Orthodox; Muslim in southern Serbia **Education:** (compulsory years) 8 **Literacy rate:** 97% (men); 88% (women) (1995 est) **Labour force:** 6% agriculture, 41% industry, 53% services (1993 est) **Life expectancy:** 70 (men); 75 (women) (1995–2000) **Child mortality rate:** (per 1,000 live births) 23 (1995) **Physicians:** 1 per 506 people (1993)

Practical information

Visa requirements: UK: visa required. USA: visa required **Embassy in the UK:** 5–7 Lexham Gardens, London W8 5JJ. Tel: (0171) 370 6105; fax: (0171) 370 3838 **British embassy:** Ulica Generala Zdanova 46, 11000 Belgrade. Tel: (1) 645 055; fax: (1) 659 651 **Chamber of commerce:** Chamber of Economy of Serbia, Ulica Generala Zdanova 13–15, 11000 Belgrade. Tel: (1) 340 611; fax: (1) 330 949. Chamber of Economy of Montenegro, Novaka Miloseva 29/II, 81000 Podgorica. Tel: (81) 31071; fax: (81) 34926

Chronology

3rd century BC: Serbia (then known as Moesia Superior) conquered by Romans; empire was extended to Belgrade centuries later by Emperor Augustus. **6th century AD:** Slavic tribes, including Serbs, Croats, and Slovenes, crossed River Danube and settled in Balkan Peninsula. **879:** Serbs converted to Orthodox Church by St Cyril and St Methodius. **mid-10th–11th centuries:** Serbia broke free briefly from Byzantine Empire to establish independent state. **1217:** Independent Serbian kingdom re-established, reaching its height in mid-14th century under Stefan Dushan, when it controlled much of Albania and northern Greece. **1389:** Serbian army defeated by Ottoman Turks at Battle of Kosovo; area became Turkish *pashalik* (province). Montenegro in southwest survived as sovereign principality. Croatia and Slovenia in northwest became part of Habsburg Empire. **18th century:** Vojvodina enjoyed protection from the Austrian Habsburgs. **1815:** Uprisings against Turkish rule secured autonomy for Serbia. **1878:** Independence achieved as Kingdom of Serbia, after Turks defeated by Russians in war over Bulgaria. **1912–13:** During Balkan Wars, Serbia expanded its territory at expense of Turkey and Bulgaria. **1918:** Joined Croatia and Slovenia, formerly under Austrian Habsburg control, to form Kingdom of Serbs, Croats, and Slovenes under Serbian Peter Karageorgević (Peter I); Montenegro's citizens voted to depose their ruler, King Nicholas, and join the union. **1929:** New name of Yugoslavia ('Land of the Southern Slavs') adopted; Serbian-dominated military dictatorship established by King Alexander I as opposition mounted from Croatian federalists. **1934:** Alexander I assassinated by a Macedonian with Croatian terrorist links; his young son Peter II succeeded, with Paul, his uncle, as regent; Nazi Germany and fascist Italy increased their influence. **1941:** Following coup by pro-Allied air-force officers, Nazi Germany invaded. Peter II fled to England. Armed resistance to German rule began, spearheaded by pro-royalist, Serbian-based Chetniks ('Army of the Fatherland'), led by Gen Draza Mihailović, and communist Partisans ('National Liberation Army'), led by Marshal Tito. An estimated 900,000 Yugoslavs died in the war, including more than 400,000 Serbs and 200,000 Croats. **1943:** Provisional government formed by Tito at liberated Jajce in Bosnia. **1945:** Yugoslav Federal People's Republic formed under leadership of Tito; communist constitution introduced. **1948:** Split with Soviet Union after Tito objected to Soviet 'hegemonism'; expelled from Cominform. **1953:** Workers' self-management principle enshrined in constitution and private farming supported; Tito became president. **1961:** Nonaligned movement formed under Yugoslavia's leadership. **1971:** In response to mounting separatist demands in Croatia, new system of collective and rotating leadership introduced. **1980:** Tito died; collective leadership assumed power. **1981–82:** Armed forces suppressed demonstrations in Kosovo province, southern Serbia, by Albanians demanding full republic status. **1986:** Slobodan Milošević, a populist-nationalist hardliner who had the ambition of creating a 'Greater Serbia', became leader of communist party in the Serbian republic. **1988:** Economic difficulties: 1,800 strikes, 250% inflation, 20% unemployment. Ethnic unrest in Montenegro and Vojvodina, and separatist demands in rich northwestern republics of Croatia and Slovenia; 'market socialist' reform package, encouraging private sector, inward investment, and liberalizing prices combined with austerity wage freeze. **1989:** Reformist Croatian Ante Marković became prime minister. Ethnic riots in Kosovo province against Serbian attempt to end autonomous status of Kosovo and Vojvodina; at least 30 were killed and a state of emergency imposed. **1990:** Multiparty systems established in republics; Kosovo and Vojvodina stripped of autonomy. In Croatia, Slovenia, Bosnia, and Macedonia elections bought to power new

non-communist governments seeking a looser confederation. **1991:** Demonstrations against Serbian president Slobodan Milošević in Belgrade crushed violently by riot police and tanks. Slovenia and Croatia declared independence, resulting in clashes between federal and republican armies; Slovenia accepted peace pact sponsored by European Community, but fighting intensified in Croatia, where Serb militias controlled over one-third of the republic; Federal President Stipe Mesic and Prime Minister Marković resigned. **1992:** EC-brokered cease-fire in Croatia; EC and USA recognized Slovenia's and Croatia's independence. Bosnia-Herzegovina and Macedonia declared independence. Bosnia-Herzegovina recognized as independent by EC and USA. New Federal Republic of Yugoslavia (FRY) proclaimed by Serbia and Montenegro but not recognized externally. International sanctions imposed. UN membership suspended. Ethnic Albanians proclaimed new 'Republic of Kosovo', but it was not recognized. **1993:** Pro-Milošević Zoran Lilic became Yugoslav president. Antigovernment rioting in Belgrade. Macedonia recognized as independent under name of Former Yugoslav Republic of Macedonia. Economy severely damaged by international sanctions. **1994:** Border blockade imposed by Yugoslavia against Bosnian Serbs; sanctions eased as a result. **1995:** Serbia played key role in US-brokered Dayton peace accord for Bosnia-Herzegovina and accepted separate existence of Bosnia and Croatia. **1996:** Diplomatic relations restored between Serbia and Croatia. UN sanctions against Serbia lifted. Allies of Pro-Milošević successful in parliamentary elections. Diplomatic relations established with Bosnia-Herzegovina. Mounting opposition to Pro-Milošević's government, following its refusal to accept opposition victories in municipal elections. **1997:** Milošević elected president. Pro-democracy mayor of Belgrade ousted. Validity of Serbian presidential elections continued to be questioned. Anti-Milošević candidate elected president of Montenegro. **1998:** Serb military offensive against ethnic-Albanian separatists in the province of Kosovo led to refugee and humanitarian crisis, with hundreds of people killed and hundreds of thousands displaced. The offensive against Kosovo Liberation Army (KLA) condemned by international community and NATO military intervention threatened. December: Renewed fighting in Kosovo. **1999:** March: NATO launched bombing campaign against the Serbs, following continued violence in Kosovo. April–May: bombing campaign stepped up, while ethnic cleansing of Kosovars by Serbs intensified. Refugee crisis in neighbouring countries worsened as hundreds of thousands of ethnic Albanians fled Kosovo. President Milošević indicted for crimes against humanity by the International War Crimes Tribunal in the Hague. June: Peace agreed on NATO terms. Refugees began to return to Kosovo.

Zambia Republic of (formerly Northern Rhodesia)

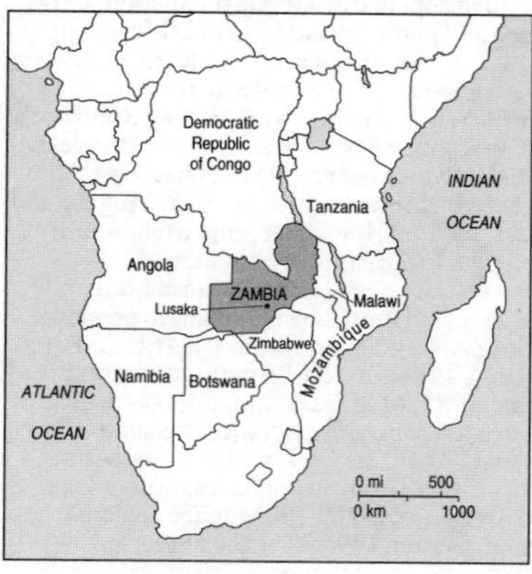

Area: 752,600 sq km/290,578 sq mi **Capital:** Lusaka **Major towns/ cities:** Kitwe, Ndola, Kabwe, Mufulira, Chingola, Luanshya, Livingstone

Government

Head of state and government: Frederick Chiluba from 1991 **Political system:** emergent democracy **Administrative divisions:** nine provinces **Political parties:** United National Independence Party (UNIP), African socialist; Movement for Multiparty Democracy (MMD), moderate, left of centre; Multiracial Party (MRP), moderate, left of centre, multiracial; National Democratic Alliance (NADA), left of centre; Democratic Party (DP), left of centre **Armed forces:** 21,600; plus paramilitary forces of 1,400 (1997) **Conscription:** military service is voluntary **Death penalty:** retained and used for ordinary crimes **Defence spend:** (% GDP) 1.7 (1997) **Education spend:** (% GNP) 1.8 (1995) **Health spend:** (% GDP) 2.4 (1990–95)

Economy and resources

Currency: Zambian kwacha **GDP:** (US$) 4.05 billion (1997) **Real GDP growth:** (% change on previous year) 2.5 (1997) **GNP (US$):** 3.6 billion (1997) **GNP per capita (PPP):** (US$) 890 (1997) **Consumer price inflation:** 28.0% (1998) **Foreign debt:** (US$) 7.1 billion (1996) **Major trading partners:** South Africa, Japan, UK, Thailand, India, Zimbabwe, Saudi Arabia **Resources:** copper (world's fourth-largest producer), cobalt, zinc, lead, coal, gold, emeralds, amethysts and other gemstones, limestone, selenium **Exports:** copper, zinc, lead, cobalt, tobacco. Principal market: Japan 11.6% (1997) **Imports:** machinery and transport equipment, mineral fuels, lubricants, electricity, basic manufactures, chemicals, food and live animals. Principal source: South Africa 48.3% (1997) **Arable land:** 7.1% (1995)

Population and society

Population: 8,781,000 (1998 est) **Population growth rate:** 2.5% (1995–2000); 2.4% (2000–05) **Population density:** (per sq km) 12.8 (1998 est) **Urban population:** (% of total) 44 (1997) **Age distribution:** (% of total population) 0–14 49.2%, 15–64 48.3%, 65+ 2.5% (1998) **Ethnic groups:** over 95% indigenous Africans, belonging to more than 70 different ethnic groups, including the Bantu-Botatwe and the Bemba **Language:** English (official); Bantu languages **Religion:** Christian, animist, Hindu, Muslim **Education:** (compulsory years) 7 **Literacy rate:** 81% (men); 65% (women) (1995 est) **Labour force:** 42% of population: 75% agriculture, 8% industry, 17% services (1990) **Life expectancy:** 42 (men); 44 (women) (1995–2000) **Child mortality rate:** (under 5, per 1,000 live births) 149 (1997) **Physicians:** 1 per 10,917 people (1993 est)

Practical information

Visa requirements: UK: visa not required. USA: visa required **Embassy in the UK:** 2 Palace Gate, London W8 5NG. Tel: (0171) 589 6655; fax: (0171) 581 1353 **British embassy:** British High Commission, PO Box 50050, Independence Avenue, 15101 Ridgeway, Lusaka. Tel: (1) 251 133; fax: (1) 253 798 **Chamber of commerce:** Ministry of Commerce, Trade and Industry, PO Box 31968, Kwacha Annex, Cairo Road, Lusaka. Tel: (1) 228 301; fax: (1) 226 727

Chronology

16th century: Immigration of peoples from Luba and Lunda Empires of Zaire, to the northwest, who set up small kingdoms. **late 18th century:** Visited by Portuguese explorers. **19th century:** Instability with immigration of Ngoni from east, Kololo from west, establishment of Bemba kingdom in north, and slave-trading activities of Portuguese and Arabs from East Africa. **1851:** Visited by British missionary and explorer David Livingstone. **1889:** As Northern Rhodesia, came under administration of British South Africa Company of Cecil Rhodes, and became involved in copper mining, especially from 1920s. **1924:** Became a British protectorate. **1948:** Northern Rhodesia African Congress (NRAC) formed by black Africans to campaign for self-rule. **1953:** Became part of Central African Federation, which included South Rhodesia (Zimbabwe) and Nyasaland (Malawi). **1960:** UNIP formed by Kenneth Kaunda as breakaway from NRAC, as African socialist body to campaign for independence and dissolution of Federation dominated by South Rhodesia's white minority. **1963:** Federation dissolved; internal self-government achieved. **1964:** Independence achieved within Commonwealth as Republic of Zambia with Kaunda of the UNIP as president. **later 1960s:** Key enterprises brought under state control. **1972:** UNIP declared only legal party. **1975:** Opening of Tan-Zam railway from Zambian copperbelt, 322 mi/200 km north of Lusaka, to port of Dar es Salaam in Tanzania. This reduced Zambia's dependence on rail route via Rhodesia for its exports. **1976:** Zambia declared support for Patriotic Front (PF) guerrillas fighting to topple white-dominated regime in Rhodesia

(Zimbabwe). **1980:** Unsuccessful South African-promoted coup against President Kaunda; relations with Zimbabwe improved when PF came to power. **1985:** Kaunda elected chair of African Front Line States. **1991:** New multiparty constitution adopted. MMD won landslide election victory, and its leader Frederick Chiluba became president in what was the first democratic change of government in English-speaking black Africa. **1993:** State of emergency declared after rumours of planned anti-government coup, privatization programme launched. **1996:** Kaunda barred from future elections; President Chiluba re-elected. **1997:** Abortive anti-government coup. **1998:** Former president Kaunda placed under house arrest after alleged involvement in antigovernment coup. Kaunda formally charged but charges subsequently dropped.

Zimbabwe Republic of (formerly Southern Rhodesia)

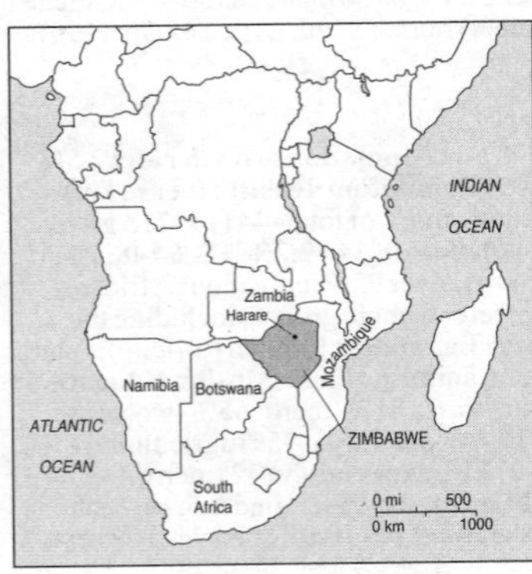

Area: 390,300 sq km/ 150,694 sq mi **Capital:** Harare **Major towns/ cities:** Bulawayo, Gweru, Kwekwe, Mutare, Hwange, Chitungwiza

Government

Head of state and government: Robert Mugabe from 1987 **Political system:** effectively one-party socialist republic **Administrative divisions:** eight provinces and two cities with provincial status **Political parties:** Zimbabwe African National Union–Patriotic Front (ZANU–PF), African socialist; opposition parties exist but none have mounted serious challenge to ruling party **Armed forces:** 39,000; 21,800 paramilitary forces (1997) **Conscription:** military service is voluntary **Death penalty:** retained and used for ordinary crimes **Defence spend:** (% GDP) 4.7 (1997) **Education spend:** (% GNP) 8.5 (1995) **Health spend:** (% GDP) 2.0 (1990–95)

Economy and resources

Currency: Zimbabwe dollar **GDP:** (US$) 8.8 billion (1997 est) **Real GDP growth:** (% change on previous year) 3.3 (1997) **GNP (US$):** 8.6 billion (1997) **GNP per capita (PPP):** (US$) 2,280 (1997) **Consumer price inflation:** 25.0% (1998) **Unemployment:** 44% (1993) **Foreign debt:** (US$) 5 billion (1996) **Major trading partners:** South Africa, UK, Germany, Japan, USA **Resources:** gold, nickel, asbestos, coal, chromium, copper, silver, emeralds, lithium, tin, iron ore, cobalt **Exports:** tobacco, metals and metal alloys, textiles and clothing, cotton lint. Principal market: South Africa 12.1% (1997) **Imports:** machinery and transport equipment, basic manufactures, mineral fuels, chemicals, foodstuffs. Principal source: South Africa 36.6% (1997) **Arable land:** 8% (1995)

Population and society

Population: 11,377,000 (1998 est) **Population growth rate:** 2.1% (1995–2000); 2% (2000–05) **Population density:** (per sq km) 28.6 (1998 est) **Urban population:** (% of total) 34 (1997) **Age distribution:** (% of total population) 0–14 43.8%, 15–64 53.6%, 65+ 2.6% (1998) **Ethnic groups:** four distinct ethnic groups: indigenous Africans, who account for about 95% of the population, Europeans (mainly British), who account for about 3.5%, and Afro-Europeans and Asians, who each comprise about 0.5% **Language:** English (official), Shona, Sindebele **Religion:** Christian, Muslim, Hindu, animist **Education:** (compulsory years) 8 **Literacy rate:** 74% (men); 60% (women) (1995 est) **Labour force:** 46% of population: 68% agriculture, 8% industry, 24% services (1990) **Life expectancy:** 48 (men); 49 (women) (1995–2000) **Child mortality rate:** (under 5, per 1,000 live births) 108 (1997) **Physicians:** 1 per 7,384 people (1993 est)

Practical information

Visa requirements: UK: visa not required. USA: visa not required **Embassy in the UK:** Zimbabwe House, 429 Strand, London WC2R 0SA. Tel: (0171) 836 7755; (0171) 379 1167 **British embassy:** British High Commission, PO Box 4490, Stanley House, Jason Moyo Avenue, Harare. Tel: (4) 793 781; fax: (4) 728 380 **Chamber of commerce:** Zimbabwe National Chambers of Commerce, PO Box 1934, Equity House, Rezende Street, Harare. Tel: (4) 753 444; fax: (4) 753 450

Chronology

13th century: Shona people settled Mashonaland (eastern Zimbabwe), erecting stone buildings (hence name Zimbabwe, 'stone house'). **15th century:** Shona Empire reached its greatest extent. **16th–17th centuries:** Portuguese settlers developed trade with Shona states and achieved influence over kingdom of Mwanamutapa in northern Zimbabwe in 1629. **1837:** Ndebele (or Matabele) people settled in southwest Zimbabwe after being driven north from Transvaal by Boers; Shona defeated by Ndebele led by King Mzilikazi who formed military empire based at Bulawayo. **1870:** King Lobengula succeeded King Mzilikazi. **1889:** Cecil Rhodes' British South Africa Company (BSA Co) obtained exclusive rights to exploit mineral resources in Lobengula's domains. **1890:** Creation of white colony in Mashonaland and founding of Salisbury (Harare) by Leander Starr Jameson, associate of Rhodes. **1893:** Matabele War: Jameson defeated Lobengula; white settlers took control of country. **1895:** Matabeleland, Mashonaland, and Zambia named Rhodesia after Cecil Rhodes. **1896:** Matabele revolt suppressed. **1898:** Southern Rhodesia (Zimbabwe) became British protectorate administered by BSA Co; farming, mining, and railways developed. **1922:** Union with South Africa rejected by referendum among white settlers. **1923:** Southern Rhodesia became self-governing colony; Africans progressively disenfranchised. **1933–53:** Prime Minister Godfrey Huggins (later Lord Malvern) pursued 'White Rhodesia' policy of racial segregation. **1950s:** Immigration doubled white population to around 250,000, while indigenous African population stood at around 6 million. **1953:** Southern Rhodesia formed part of Federation of Rhodesia and Nyasaland. **1961:** Zimbabwe African People's Union (ZAPU) formed with Joshua Nkomo as leader; declared illegal a year later. **1962:** Rhodesia Front party of Winston Field took power in Southern Rhodesia, pledging to preserve white rule. **1963:** Federation of Rhodesia and Nyasaland dissolved as Zambia and Malawi moved towards independence; Zimbabwe African National Union (ZANU) formed, with Robert Mugabe as secretary; declared illegal a year later. **1964:** Ian Smith became prime minister; he rejected British terms for independence which required moves towards black majority rule; Nkomo and Mugabe imprisoned. **1965:** Smith made unilateral declaration of independence (UDI); Britain broke off all relations. **1966–68:** United Nations (UN) imposed economic sanctions on Rhodesia, which still received help from South Africa and Portugal. **1969:** Rhodesia declared itself a republic. **1972:** Britain rejected draft independence agreement as unacceptable to African population. **1974:** Nkomo and Mugabe released and jointly formed Patriotic Front to fight Smith regime in mounting civil war. **1975:** Geneva Conference between British, Smith regime, and African nationalists failed to reach agreement. **1978:** At height of civil war, whites were leaving Rhodesia at rate of 1,000 per month. **1979:** Rhodesia became Zimbabwe-Rhodesia with new 'majority' constitution which nevertheless retained special rights for whites; Bishop Abel Muzorewa became premier; Mugabe and Nkomo rejected settlement; Lancaster House Agreement temporarily restored Rhodesia to British rule. **1980:** Zimbabwe achieved independence from Britain with full transition to African majority rule; Mugabe became prime minister with Rev Canaan Banana as president. **1981:** Rift between Mugabe (ZANU-PF) and Nkomo (ZAPU); Nkomo dismissed from cabinet in 1982. **1984:** ZANU-PF party congress agreed to principle of one-party state. **1987:** Mugabe combined posts of head of state and prime minister as executive president; Nkomo became vice president. **1989:** ZANU-PF and ZAPU formally merged; Zimbabwe Unity Movement founded by Edgar Tekere to oppose one-party state. **1992:** United Party formed to oppose ZANU-PF. Mugabe declared drought and famine a national disaster. **1996:** Mugabe re-elected president. **1998:** Mugabe issued new rules banning strikes and restricting political and public gatherings. Government's radical land distribution plans watered down after pressure from aid donors. Violent antigovernment demonstrations took place in November. **1999:** Scathing report on government by human rights group.

Largest and Smallest Countries

Largest Countries by Area

Rank	Country	Area sq km	Area sq mi
1	Russia	17,075,400	6,592,811
2	Canada	9,970,610	3,849,652
3	China	9,572,900	3,695,942
4	USA	9,372,615	3,618,766
5	Brazil	8,511,965	3,286,469
6	Australia	7,682,300	2,966,136
7	India	3,166,829	1,222,713
8	Argentina	2,780,092	1,073,393
9	Kazakhstan	2,717,300	1,049,150
10	Sudan	2,505,800	967,489
11	Algeria	2,381,741	919,590
12	Congo, Democratic Republic of	2,344,900	905,366
13	Saudi Arabia	2,200,518	849,620
14	Mexico	1,958,201	756,061
15	Indonesia	1,904,569	735,354
16	Libya	1,759,540	679,358
17	Iran	1,648,000	636,292
18	Mongolia	1,565,000	604,246
19	Peru	1,285,200	496,216
20	Chad	1,284,000	495,752

Smallest Countries by Area

Rank	Country	Area sq km	Area sq mi
1	Vatican City State	0.4	0.2
2	San Marino	61	24
3	Liechtenstein	160	62
4	Marshall Islands	181	70
5	St Kitts and Nevis	262	101
6	Maldives	298	115
7	Malta	320	124
8	Grenada	344	133
9	St Vincent and the Grenadines	388	150
10	Barbados	430	166
11	Antigua and Barbuda	440	169
12	Seychelles	453	175
13	Andorra	468	181
14	St Lucia	617	238
15	Singapore	622	240
16	Bahrain	688	266
17	Micronesia	700	270
18	Kiribati	717	277
19	Tonga	750	290
20	Dominica	751	290

Population

Largest Countries by Population Size

Countries with a population of over 100 million, 1998 and 2050.

Rank	Country	Population (millions)	% of world population
1998			
1	China	1,256	21.28
2	India	982	16.64
3	United States	274	4.64
4	Indonesia	206	3.49
5	Brazil	166	2.81
6	Pakistan	148	2.50
7	Russian Federation	147	2.49
8	Japan	126	2.13
9	Bangladesh	125	2.11
10	Nigeria	106	1.79
World total		5,901	
2050 (projected)			
1	India	1,529	17.16
2	China	1,478	16.58
3	United States	349	3.91
4	Pakistan	346	3.88
5	Indonesia	312	3.50
6	Nigeria	244	2.73
7	Brazil	244	2.73
8	Bangladesh	213	2.39
9	Ethiopia	170	1.90
10	Congo, Democratic Republic of	160	1.79
11	Mexico	147	1.65
12	Philippines	131	1.47
13	Vietnam	127	1.42
14	Russian Federation	122	1.42
15	Iran	115	1.29
16	Egypt	115	1.29
17	Japan	105	1.17
18	Turkey	101	1.13
World total		8,909	

Source: United Nations Population Division

Smallest Countries by Population Size

Rank	Country	Population (1998 est)
1	Vatican City State	1,000[1]
2=	Nauru	10,500
	Tuvalu	10,500
4	Palau	18,000
5	San Marino	25,000
6	Liechtenstein	32,000
7	Monaco	32,000
8	St Kitts and Nevis	42,300
9	Marshall Islands	63,000
10	Antigua and Barbuda	64,000
11	Andorra	64,700
12	Dominica	66,000
13	Seychelles	79,000
14	Kiribati	84,000
15	Grenada	96,000
16	Tonga	108,000
17	St Vincent and the Grenadines	120,000
18	Micronesia	130,000
19	São Tomé and Príncipe	150,000
20	St Lucia	152,000
21	Vanuatu	185,000
22	Samoa	225,000

[1] 1996 estimate.

Source: United Nations Population Division

Growth of the World's Largest Cities

Data refer to urban agglomerations. The concept of agglomeration defines the population contained within the contours of contiguous territory inhabited at urban levels of residential density without regard to administrative boundaries.

Rank	City	Population (millions)
1950		
1	New York (NY), USA	12.30
2	London, UK	8.70
3	Tokyo, Japan	6.90
4=	Paris, France	5.40
	Moscow, Russia	5.40
6=	Shanghai, China	5.30
	Essen, Germany	5.30
8	Buenos Aires, Argentina	5.00
9	Chicago (IL), USA	4.90
10	Calcutta, India	4.40
1980		
1	Tokyo, Japan	21.90
2	New York (NY), USA	15.60
3	Mexico City, Mexico	13.90
4	São Paulo, Brazil	12.10
5	Shanghai, China	11.70
6	Osaka, Japan	10.00
7	Buenos Aires, Argentina	9.90
8	Los Angeles (CA), USA	9.50
9=	Calcutta, India	9.00
	Beijing, China	9.00
1995		
1	Tokyo, Japan	26.95
2	Mexico City, Mexico	16.56
3	São Paulo, Brazil	16.53
4	New York (NY), USA	16.33
5	Bombay, India	15.14
6	Shanghai, China	13.58
7	Los Angeles (CA), USA	12.47
8	Buenos Aires, Argentina	11.80
9	Calcutta, India	11.62
10	Seoul, South Korea	11.61
2015 (projected)		
1	Tokyo, Japan	28.90
2	Bombay, India	26.20
3	Lagos, Nigeria	24.60
4	São Paulo, Brazil	20.30
5	Dhaka, Bangladesh	19.50
6	Karachi, Pakistan	19.40
7	Mexico City, Mexico	19.20
8	Shanghai, China	18.00
9	New York (NY), USA	17.60
10	Calcutta, India	17.30

Source: United Nations Population Division

Largest Cities in the World

Urban agglomerations with populations of over 6 million.

1996

Rank	City	Population (millions)
1	Tokyo, Japan	27.2
2	Mexico City, Mexico	16.9
3	São Paulo, Brazil	16.8
4	New York (NY), USA	16.4
5	Bombay, India	15.7
6	Shanghai, China	13.7
7	Los Angeles (CA), USA	12.6
8	Calcutta, India	12.1
9	Buenos Aires, Argentina	11.9
10	Seoul, South Korea	11.8
11	Beijing, China	11.4
12	Lagos, Nigeria	10.9
13	Osaka, Japan	10.6
14=	Delhi, India	10.3
	Rio de Janeiro, Brazil	10.3
16	Karachi, Pakistan	10.1
17	Cairo, Egypt	9.9
18=	Tianjin, China	9.6
	Paris, France	9.6
	Manila, Philippines	9.6
21	Moscow, Russia	9.3
22	Dhaka, Bangladesh	9.0
23	Jakarta, Indonesia	8.8
24	Istanbul, Turkey	8.2
25	London, UK	7.6
26=	Chicago (IL), USA	6.9
	Tehran, Iran	6.9
28	Lima, Peru	6.8
29	Bangkok, Thailand	6.7
30	Essen, Germany	6.5
31	Bogotá, Columbia	6.2
32	Madras, India	6.1

Source: United Nations Population Division

World Population Growth by Major Area

Percentage of world population by area, and total world population.

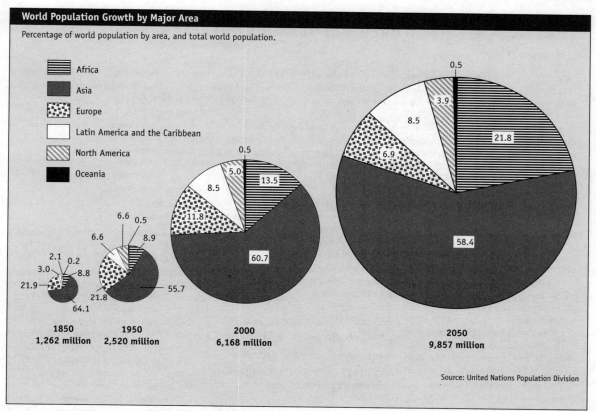

Source: United Nations Population Division

World Population Milestones

World population reached:

Number	*Year*
1 billion	1804
2 billion	1927 (123 years later)
3 billion	1960 (33 years later)
4 billion	1974 (14 years later)
5 billion	1987 (13 years later)
6 billion	1999 (12 years later)
World population may reach:	
7 billion	2013 (14 years later)
8 billion	2028 (15 years later)
9 billion	2054 (26 years later)

Source: United Nations Population Division

Top 10 Contributors to World Population Growth

Sixty percent of the world population increase is contributed by only 10 countries, with 20.6 percent contributed by India and 14.7 percent by China.

1995–2000

Rank	Country	Net addition (in thousands)	Percentage of world population increase
1	India	15,999	20.6
2	China	11,408	14.7
3	Pakistan	4,048	5.2
4	Indonesia	2,929	3.8
5	Nigeria	2,511	3.2
6	USA	2,267	2.9
7	Brazil	2,154	2.8
8	Bangladesh	2,108	2.7
9	Mexico	1,547	2.0
10	Philippines	1,522	2.0
	Total	46,494	59.8
WORLD TOTAL		77,738	100

Source: United Nations Population Division

A World Population Overview

By Nicholas J Ford

Population is essentially the starting point for consideration of humankind's occupation and life experience of, and impact upon, planet Earth. On a global level population change is the product of births (fertility) and deaths (mortality). Within a specified space (such as a single country) total population change must also take account of movements of people in and out (migration). This essay seeks to place some general patterning upon the complex and substantial body of population data, to indicate some of the underlying dynamics, and to identify some of the major impacts of the changes taking place.

The recent historical period from around 1750 to the present has witnessed an unprecedented expansion in human population, culminating in the so-called 'population explosion' of the 20th century. The period 1965–70 was a watershed in which the population growth rate reached an all-time high of 2.1 percent per year. By 1992 the rate of growth had declined to 1.7 percent per year and it is this fundamental change that allows demographers to project a gradual slowing down of population growth in the future, eventually possibly reaching some form of stabilization.

However, it is critical to note that the growth in absolute numbers (estimated at nearly 80 million per year in the late 1990s) is still greater than has ever occurred before. This is due to the phenomenon of 'population momentum' which is carried by the still youthful age structures of the developing world.

The growth in absolute numbers ... is still greater than has ever occurred before.

Divergence in demographic patterns

While the distinction between low (or no) population growth in more developed countries (MDCs) and high population growth in less developed countries (LDCs) persists, a major feature of the past four decades has been the wide divergence in demographic patterns of births and deaths in the developing world. While the detailed pattern is complex, in general terms there has been a rapid fertility decline in east Asia, moderate decline in Latin America and, to a lesser degree, South Asia, and very limited fertility decline in Sub-Saharan Africa. However, there have been recent encouraging indications that a number of (particularly southern) African countries have moved towards fertility decline.

In order to gain a sense of the variations between countries in fertility and mortality it is better to refer to the (total) fertility rates and life expectancy/infant mortality rates, than the crude birth and death rates, which are strongly influenced by age structures.

There has been great interest in the experience of developing countries such as Thailand (fertility rate 1.7 percent) and China (1.8 percent) which have rapidly attained below-replacement levels of fertility. Indeed, that the world as a whole has crossed the watershed beyond increasing rates of growth is a reflection of the contribution of the demographic giant, China, in dealing with its numbers of births. Effective family planning programmes have been at the core of the fertility change in both countries. However, while Thailand has placed especial emphasis on communication and benefited from a conducive sociocultural climate, China has pursued the powerful 'one child' policy.

High levels of fertility are generally associated with high levels of infant mortality (deaths of children before the age of five) and maternal mortality (deaths of women in relation to pregnancy and childbirth). While high levels of fertility partially reflect efforts to replace children who have died or to ensure that at least some children survive, the emphasis on quantity rather than quality in child rearing may well exacerbate infant mortality.

Reproductive health a priority

The 1994 World Population Conference in Cairo emphasized wider 'reproductive health' rather than merely reducing fertility. Part of this emphasis relates to the association of high levels of maternal mortality with high fertility, essentially resulting from too many inadequately spaced births to mothers who are often too young. Deaths in, or related to, childbirth are very rare (and thus eminently preventable) events in Western countries, but, tragically, all too common in the developing world. Reducing maternal deaths requires not only more family planning, but also the range of measures (antenatal, referral, and so on) associated with the international 'safe motherhood' initiative.

The much lower levels of life expectancy (43 for women, 40 for men in Sierra Leone) in the LDCs as compared to the MDCs (83 for women, 77 for men in Japan) primarily reflect the high levels of infant mortality in the poorer countries. However, at least until the advent of AIDS, progress was being made in reducing death rates in many developing countries, and given the sociocultural lag prior to fertility decline, led to very youthful age structures. Thus, while in the LDCs the overwhelming proportion of the dependent population consists of the under-15s, in the MDCs it increasingly consists of the over-65s. Indeed, the progressive ageing of the world's population is inevitable given decreasing birth rates, as well as advances in medical technology which contribute to longer lifespans. The most densely populated countries tend to be small island states, some of which, such as the Maldives, may be threatened by a sea level rise resulting from global warming. In terms of mainland countries the densities are of greatest concern in developing countries such as Bangladesh, rather than industrialized, urban countries, such as the Netherlands or South Korea.

Growth of mega-cities

The pattern of population growth rates ensures that the developing countries contain an increasing proportion of the world's population. This increase in total numbers is accompanied by a growing concentration of population through the process of urbanization, attendant to modernization and development. Along with the virtually universal pattern of rural-urban migra-

tion is the emergence of the mega-cities in the developing world, such as São Paulo, Bombay, and Shanghai. On the one hand, these cities are at the cutting edge of their respective countries' economic development; on the other hand, the sheer scale of in-migration and growth places great pressure on infrastructural capacities, and the related personal dislocations are associated with a range of social problems.

Additionally, such is the scale of human brutality – for example, genocide in Rwanda and the Serbs' 'ethnic cleansing' in the Balkans – that the impacts in human refugee displacements can be clearly identified even at aggregate levels. This forms, however regrettably, a further notable feature of current global population movements.

Population figures help to depict some of human societies' many and varied transformations. The wide-ranging impacts of population trends include the exacerbation of problems of economic development and environmental fragilities in the developing world and the impending problems of socially ageing societies in the developed countries. In all this, perhaps, we should not lose sight of the fact that these aggregate figures of vital statistics are indications of individual life experiences – their varied qualities of life and survival expectancies, bereavements, losses, pleasures, and joys.

Nicholas Ford is senior lecturer in geography at the University of Exeter

Countries with the Fastest- and Slowest-Growing Populations

1995–2000

Rank	Country	Average population growth rate %
Fastest-Growing Populations		
1	Liberia	8.6
2	Rwanda	7.9
3	Afghanistan	5.3
4	Oman	4.2
5	Somalia	3.9
6=	Eritrea	3.7
	Yemen	3.7
8	Saudi Arabia	3.4
9=	Angola	3.3
	Jordan	3.3
	Libya	3.3
	Niger	3.3
13	Ethiopia	3.2
14=	Laos	3.1
	Madagascar	3.1
16=	Kuwait	3.0
	Mali	3.0
	Sierra Leone	3.0

Rank	Country	Average population growth rate %
Slowest-Growing Populations		
1	Latvia	−1.1
2	Estonia	−1.0
3	Hungary	−0.6
4	Bulgaria	−0.5
5	Ukraine	−0.4
6=	Lithuania	−0.3
	Russian Federation	−0.3
8	Romania	−0.2
9=	Belarus	−0.1
	Croatia	−0.1
	Czech Republic	−0.1
	Georgia	−0.1
	Portugal	−0.1
	Slovenia	−0.1
15	Italy	0.0
16=	Kazakhstan	0.1
	Moldova	0.1
	Poland	0.1
	Slovakia	0.1
	Spain	0.1
	United Kingdom	0.1

Source: United Nations Population Fund

Urban Population Growth

Regional totals and selected countries.

	Region/country	Level of urbanization: % of total population in urban settlements			Urban population: Total number in millions			Urban population: % annual growth rate	
		1975	2000	2025	1975	2000	2025	1975–2000	2000–25
Africa	**Total**	25.15	37.30	53.77	104.1	310.1	804.2	4.37	3.81
	Algeria	40.33	59.65	74.05	6.4	18.5	33.6	4.23	2.38
	Angola	17.79	36.17	55.59	1.1	4.7	14.8	5.88	4.56
	Cameroon	26.87	49.33	66.86	2.0	7.5	19.5	5.25	3.81
	Congo, Democratic Republic of	29.50	31.03	49.82	6.8	15.8	52.1	3.35	4.76
	Côte d'Ivoire	32.09	46.95	64.13	2.1	7.8	23.6	5.16	4.40
	Egypt	43.45	46.36	62.20	16.8	32.0	60.5	2.57	2.54
	Ghana	30.06	39.17	57.74	2.9	7.9	21.9	3.93	4.08
	Kenya	12.92	31.76	51.48	1.7	10.3	32.6	7.05	4.59
	Libya	60.95	88.35	92.75	1.5	5.6	11.9	5.32	3.00
	Mozambique	8.62	41.07	61.09	0.9	7.8	21.5	8.62	4.05
	Nigeria	23.38	43.29	61.64	14.6	55.7	146.9	5.34	3.88
	Tanzania	10.08	28.20	48.25	1.6	9.6	30.3	7.17	4.60
Asia	**Total**	24.62	37.68	54.81	592.3	1,407.8	2,718.4	3.46	2.63
	Bangladesh	9.28	21.28	39.99	7.1	28.6	78.4	5.57	4.03
	China	17.25	34.49	54.51	106.0	443.0	831.8	4.07	2.52
	India	21.31	28.56	45.24	132.3	291.9	629.7	3.17	3.08
	Indonesia	19.36	40.34	60.74	26.2	85.8	167.4	4.74	2.67
	Iran	45.82	61.86	74.86	15.3	46.2	92.5	4.42	2.78
	Japan	75.69	78.39	84.86	84.4	99.1	103.2	0.64	0.16
	Korea, South	48.04	86.22	93.70	16.9	40.6	50.9	3.50	0.91
	Pakistan	26.40	37.85	56.73	19.7	61.2	161.6	4.53	3.88
	Philippines	35.56	59.01	74.26	15.3	44.0	77.6	4.23	2.27
	Thailand	15.10	21.90	39.08	6.2	13.5	28.7	3.10	3.01
Europe	**Total**	67.07	75.14	83.22	453.4	548.4	597.6	0.76	0.34
Latin America	**Total**	61.32	76.61	84.67	196.2	401.1	600.9	2.86	1.61
	Argentina	80.73	89.40	93.39	21.0	32.7	43.0	1.77	1.10
	Bolivia	41.51	65.23	78.97	1.9	5.4	10.4	4.05	2.59
	Brazil	61.15	81.21	88.94	66.0	141.9	204.8	3.06	1.47
	Colombia	60.71	75.21	84.14	14.4	28.4	41.5	2.71	1.51
	Mexico	62.76	77.71	85.82	36.9	79.6	117.2	3.07	1.55
	Paraguay	38.98	56.44	71.82	1.0	3.2	6.5	4.44	2.86
	Peru	61.46	74.52	83.54	9.3	19.4	30.6	9.94	1.82
	Venezuela	77.83	94.45	97.17	9.9	22.8	33.8	3.34	1.57
North America	**Total**	73.85	77.44	84.78	176.7	237.2	313.3	1.18	1.11
	Canada	75.61	77.16	83.67	17.5	23.9	32.0	1.24	1.16
	USA	73.65	77.46	84.91	159.0	213.1	281.2	1.17	1.11
Oceania	**Total**	71.78	70.25	74.86	15.4	21.5	30.7	1.34	1.42
	Australia	85.92	84.69	88.59	11.9	16.3	21.8	1.24	1.18
	New Zealand	82.78	87.20	91.64	2.5	3.3	4.0	1.00	0.81
World	**Total**	37.73	47.52	61.07	1,538.3	2,926.4	5,065.3	2.57	2.19
	More developed regions	69.84	76.52	83.98	729.3	904.2	1,040.0	0.86	0.56
	Less developed regions	26.68	40.52	57.05	809.0	2,022.1	4,025.3	3.66	2.75

Source: United Nations Population Division

Median Age of World Population by Major Area

Area	Median age (years) 1950	1998	2050
Africa	18.7	18.3	30.7
Asia	21.9	25.6	39.3
Europe	29.2	37.1	47.4
Latin America and the Caribbean	20.1	23.9	37.8
Northern America	29.8	35.2	42.1
Oceania	27.9	30.7	39.3
Less developed regions	21.3	23.9	36.7
More developed regions	28.6	36.8	45.6
World total	23.5	26.1	37.8

Source: United Nations Population Division

Highest and Lowest Urban Populations

1997

Rank	Country	Population living in urban areas (%)
Highest Urban Population		
1	Vatican City State	100[1]
2	Monaco	100
3	Nauru	100
4	Singapore	100
5	Belgium	97
6	Kuwait	97
7	Andorra	95
8	San Marino	95
9	Iceland	92
10	Qatar	92
11	Bahrain	91
12	Israel	91
13	Uruguay	91
14	Luxembourg	90
15	Malta	90
16	Argentina	89
17	Lebanon	89
18	Netherlands	89
19	UK	89
20	Bahamas	88
Lowest Urban Population		
1	Rwanda	6
2	Bhutan	7
3	Burundi	8
4	Nepal	11
5	Uganda	13
6	Malawi	14
7	Burkina Faso	17
8	Ethiopia	17
9	Papua New Guinea	17
10	Eritrea	18
11	Solomon Islands	18
12	Niger	19
13	Vanuatu	19
14	Bangladesh	20
15	Vietnam	20
16	Afghanistan	21
17	Samoa	21
18	Thailand	21
19	Cambodia	22
20	Laos	22

[1] 1995.

Source: World Health Organization

Highest and Lowest Population Densities

1998

Rank	Country	Population per sq km
Highest Density		
1	Monaco	16,017.5
2	Singapore	5,593.5
3	Vatican City State	2,273.0[1]
4	Malta	1,182.4
5	Bahrain	995.7
6	Maldives	967.4
7	Bangladesh	952.6
8	Taiwan	679.1
9	Mauritius	631.8
10	Barbados	602.4
11	Nauru	500.0
12	Korea, South	472.7
13	Netherlands	463.5
14	San Marino	415.0
15	Tuvalu	401.7
16	St Vincent and the Grenadines	353.4
17	Marshall Islands	348.6
18	Lebanon	342.7
19	Belgium	336.6
20	India	331.0
Lowest Density		
1	Mongolia	1.6
2	Namibia	2.0
3	Australia	2.4
4	Mauritania	2.4
5	Botswana	2.5
6	Iceland	2.7
7	Suriname	2.7
8	Libya	3.0[1]
9	Canada	3.3
10	Guyana	3.6
11	Gabon	4.7
12	Central African Republic	5.4
13	Chad	5.8
14	Kazakhstan	6.2
15	Bolivia	7.2
16	Niger	7.6
17	Congo	7.8
18	Mali	8.3
19	Russia	8.6
20	Angola	8.7

[1] 1996 estimate

Source: US Bureau of the Census

Youngest and Oldest Populations

1998

Rank	Country	% of population
Youngest Populations (aged under 15)		
1	Uganda	51.1
2	Marshall Islands	50.0
3	Zambia	49.2
4	Libya	48.3
5	Togo	48.3
6	Congo	48.2
7	Niger	48.1
8	Senegal	48.1
9	Burkina Faso	48.0
10	Benin	47.9
11	São Tomé and Príncipe	47.5
12	Burundi	47.4
13	Mali	47.4
14	Maldives	47.2
15	Côte d'Ivoire	46.7
16	Yemen	46.7[1]
17	Mauritania	46.5
18	Swaziland	46.4
19	Syria	46.1
20	Ethiopia	46.0
Oldest Populations (aged over 65)		
1	Monaco	19.5
2	Italy	17.6
3	Sweden	17.4
4	Belgium	16.8
5	San Marino	16.6
6	Greece	16.5
7	Spain	16.3
8	Japan	16.0
9	Bulgaria	15.9
10	Germany	15.9
11	France	15.8
12	Norway	15.7
13	UK	15.7
14	Austria	15.5
15	Portugal	15.1
16	Denmark	14.9
17	Latvia	14.9
18	Switzerland	14.9
19	Luxembourg	14.8
20	Croatia	14.7

[1] 1995.

Source: US Bureau of the Census

Numbers and Rates of Abortions Worldwide

Data represent numbers and rates of legally-induced abortions; they are ranked by rate for selected countries. The very high levels of abortion in Russia and Eastern Europe are a legacy of deficiencies in family planning services, which have led to abortions being used as, almost, a routine method of family planning. Clinically-undertaken abortions are a safe procedure in contrast to the many illegal abortions in other countries, especially in the developing world, which contribute substantially to maternal mortality.

1995

Country	Number	Rate (per hundred live births)
Romania	502,840	212.49
Russia	2,766,362	202.28
Latvia	25,933	120.08
Lithuania	31,273	75.94
Hungary	76,957	68.67
Slovak Republic	35,879	58.41
Slovenia	10,791	56.85
Czech Republic[1]	54,836	51.45
Singapore	14,504	29.82
Japan	343,024	28.89
Sweden[1]	32,293	28.76
Croatia	14,282	28.46
Denmark	17,720	25.39
Italy[1]	124,334	23.57
Kyrgyzstan	27,111	23.10
UK	167,297	22.85
USA[1]	1,267,415	21.00
Finland	9,884	15.67
Germany	97,937	12.79
Netherlands	20,933	10.98
Mexico[1]	28,734	0.98
Poland[1]	874	0.84

[1] 1994.

Source: United Nations Department for Economic and Social Information; US Department of Health and Human Services

Births to Teenage Mothers in Developing Countries

Data are for women aged 15–19, showing regional averages and countries with the highest rate of births to teenage mothers. The measure does not indicate the full dimensions of teen pregnancy as only live births are included in the numerator; stillbirths and spontaneous or induced abortions are not reflected.

1995–2000

Region/country	Number of births per 1,000 women aged 15–19
Sub-Saharan Africa	
Average	143
Guinea	229
Angola	212
Somalia	208
Niger	206
Liberia	206
Congo, Dem. Rep. of	206
Sierra Leone	201
Mali	181
Guinea-Bissau	180
Uganda	179
Gabon	175
Chad	173
Ethiopia	168
Malawi	159
Burkina Faso	157
Gambia	153
Senegal	143
Madagascar	142
Cameroon	140
Nigeria	138
Middle East and North Africa	
Average	58
Oman	122
Saudi Arabia	114
Libya	102
Yemen	101
Iran	77
United Arab Emirates	73
Egypt	62
Sudan	52
Iraq	45
Syria	44
Central Asia	
Average	59
Afghanistan	152
Georgia	46
Armenia	41
Kyrgyzstan	40
Uzbekistan	35
Southeast Asia and Pacific	
Average	61
Bangladesh	115
India	109
Pakistan	89
Nepal	89
Bhutan	84
Thailand	70
Indonesia	58
Laos	50
Philippines	40
Mongolia	39
Americas	
Average	70
Nicaragua	133
Honduras	113
Guatemala	111
Venezuela	98
El Salvador	92
Costa Rica	89
Jamaica	88
Dominican Republic	88
Panama	81
Bolivia	79

Source: UNICEF

Births to Teenage Mothers in Developed Countries

Data for women aged 15–19 for selected countries. The measure does not indicate the full dimensions of teen pregnancy as only live births are included in the numerator; stillbirths and spontaneous or induced abortions are not reflected.

1995–2000

Country	Number of births per 1,000 women aged 15–19	Country	Number of births per 1,000 women aged 15–19	Country	Number of births per 1,000 women aged 15–19
USA	60	Bosnia-Herzegovina	29	Ireland	14
Bulgaria	57	Hungary	29	Germany	13
Romania	43	Estonia	27	Finland	11
Macedonia, FYR of	40	Slovenia	27	Spain	10
Russian Federation	39	Poland	25	Sweden	10
Yugoslavia	38	Belarus	24	Belgium	9
Ukraine	36	Canada	24	Denmark	9
Czech Republic	35	Australia	22	France	8
Slovak Republic	35	Lithuania	22	Italy	8
Moldova	32	Portugal	22	Netherlands	7
New Zealand	32	Austria	21	Japan	4
Croatia	31	Israel	19	Switzerland	4
UK	31	Greece	18		
Latvia	30	Norway	16		

Source: UNICEF

Infant Mortality and Female Fertility Rates

Fertility rate is the average number of children per woman; figures show regional average.

1995–2000

Infant mortality rate (per 1,000 births)

Region	Infant mortality rate
Africa	86
Asia	56
Latin America and Caribbean	35
Oceania	24
Europe	12
Northern America	7
World average	57

Fertility rate

Region	Fertility rate
Africa	5.31
Asia	2.65
Latin America and Caribbean	2.65
Oceania	2.46
Northern America	1.93
Europe	1.45
World average	2.79

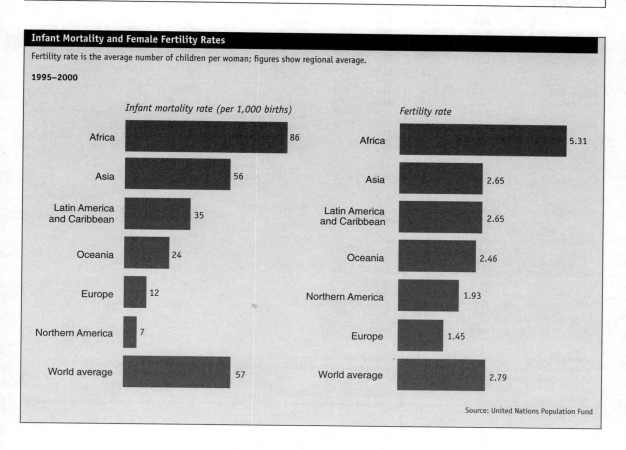

Source: United Nations Population Fund

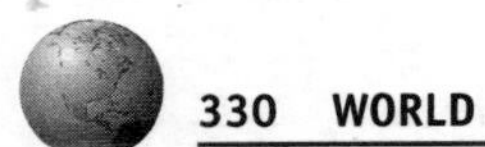

Dependency Ratios Worldwide

Dependency ratio is the ratio of the population under 15 and over 65 to the population aged 15–64.

Region	Age	Dependency ratio 1995	2025	2050
Africa				
Eastern Africa	0–14	91.2	64.5	36.5
	>65	5.5	5.5	9.9
	Total	96.6	70.0	46.4
Northern Africa	0–14	67.9	40.8	32.6
	>65	6.7	10.1	18.9
	Total	74.6	50.9	51.5
Southern Africa	0–14	65.6	43.7	33.4
	>65	7.4	10.0	17.5
	Total	73.0	53.7	50.8
Western Africa	0–14	89.6	65.7	36.7
	>65	5.4	6.1	9.5
	Total	95.1	71.8	46.1
Total	0–14	83.4	59.5	36.0
	>65	6.0	6.9	11.4
	TOTAL	89.4	66.4	47.4
Asia				
Eastern Asia	0–14	37.6	29.6	30.7
	>65	10.0	19.2	30.7
	Total	47.6	48.8	61.4
South-central Asia	0–14	63.3	36.8	30.7
	>65	7.3	10.8	20.6
	Total	70.6	47.6	51.3
Southeast Asia	0–14	57.1	35.1	31.4
	>65	7.0	11.5	22.6
	Total	64.1	46.6	53.9
Western Asia	0–14	65.9	46.2	32.7
	>65	7.6	10.8	17.2
	Total	73.5	57.0	49.9
Total	0–14	51.1	34.6	30.9
	>65	8.5	13.9	23.7
	TOTAL	59.6	48.4	54.7
Europe				
Eastern Europe	0–14	31.4	26.7	30.2
	>65	18.5	26.8	35.3
	Total	49.9	53.5	65.5
Northern Europe	0–14	30.2	29.3	30.7
	>65	23.3	30.8	37.2
	Total	53.5	60.0	67.9
Southern Europe	0–14	25.3	21.6	27.0
	>65	21.3	34.5	54.5
	Total	46.6	56.1	81.5
Western Europe	0–14	26.2	24.4	28.4
	>65	22.1	35.4	47.1
	Total	48.3	59.8	75.5
Total	0–14	28.7	25.5	29.3
	>65	20.6	30.9	41.7
	TOTAL	49.3	56.4	71.0
Latin America and the Caribbean				
Caribbean	0–14	48.3	38.5	32.9
	>65	10.2	16.3	25.0
	Total	58.8	54.9	57.9
Central America	0–14	64.1	37.3	31.8
	>65	7.0	12.1	24.6
	Total	71.1	49.4	56.3
South America	0–14	53.0	34.4	31.3
	>65	8.9	15.5	27.2
	Total	61.8	49.9	58.5
Total	0–14	55.4	35.5	31.6
	>65	8.5	14.6	26.3
	TOTAL	63.9	50.1	57.8
North America				
	0–14	33.5	31.6	31.1
	>65	19.2	29.2	34.6
	TOTAL	52.7	60.7	65.7
Oceania				
Australia and New Zealand	0–14	32.8	30.7	30.9
	>65	17.4	27.0	37.2
	Total	50.2	57.7	68.0
Total	0–14	40.4	34.6	31.6
	>65	14.8	21.3	29.6
	TOTAL	55.2	55.9	61.2
World				
More developed regions[1]	0–14	29.4	27.2	29.9
	>65	20.1	31.4	40.4
	Total	49.5	58.6	70.3
Less developed regions[2]	0–14	57.0	39.7	32.3
	>65	7.7	12.1	20.4
	Total	64.7	51.8	52.8
Least developed countries[3]	0–14	81.9	57.0	35.4
	>65	5.6	6.5	11.5
	Total	87.5	63.5	46.9
Total	0–14	50.9	37.9	32.1
	>65	10.5	14.9	22.7
	TOTAL	61.4	52.8	54.7

[1] More developed regions comprise Northern America, Japan, Europe, and Australia and New Zealand.

[2] Less developed regions comprise all regions of Africa, Asia (excluding Japan), Latin America and the Caribbean, Melanesia, Micronesia, and Polynesia.

[3] Least developed countries according to standard UN designation.

Source: United Nations Population Division

Maternal Deaths per 100,000 Live Births

The data represent numbers of maternal deaths per year in pregnancy and childbirth; they show regional averages, and countries with highest death rates.

1996

Rank	Region/country	Maternal deaths per 100,000 live births
	Sub-Saharan Africa	
	Average	980
1	Sierra Leone	1,800
2=	Somalia	1,600
	Guinea	1,600
4=	Mozambique	1,500
	Chad	1,500
	Middle East and North Africa	
	Average	300
1	Yemen	1,400
2	Sudan	660
3	Morocco	610
4	Iraq	310
5	Lebanon	300
	Central Asia	
	Average	560
1	Afghanistan	1,700
2	Tajikistan	130
3	Kyrgyzstan	110
4	Kazakhstan	80
5	Uzbekistan	55
	Asia and Pacific	
	Average	390
1	Bhutan	1,600
2	Nepal	1,500
3	Papua New Guinea	930
4	Cambodia	900
5	Bangladesh	850
	Americas	
	Average	140
1	Haiti	1,000
2	Bolivia	650
3	El Salvador	300
4	Peru	280
5	Honduras	220
	Europe	
	Average	36
1	Romania	130
2	Russia	75
3	Albania	65
4	Moldova	60
5	Ukraine	50

Source: UNICEF

Maternal Deaths Worldwide

Figures show approximate number of maternal deaths in pregnancy and childbirth.

1996

Rank	Region/country	Number of deaths
1	Asia and Pacific	291,000
2	Sub-Saharan Africa	219,000
3	Middle East and North Africa	35,000
4	Americas	23,000
5	Central Asia	14,000
6	Europe	3,000
	World	585,000

Marriage and Divorce Rates

(– = not applicable.)

Country	Marriages (per thousand people)		Divorces (per thousand people)	
	1986	1996	1986	1996
Austria	6.0	5.2	1.9	2.2
Belgium	5.8	5.0	1.9	2.8
Canada	6.7	5.4[1]	3.0	2.6[1]
Denmark	6.0	6.8	2.8	2.4
Finland	5.2	4.8	2.0	2.7
France	4.8	4.8	2.0	2.0[1]
Germany	6.6	5.2	2.3	2.1[1]
Greece	5.8	4.5	0.9	0.9
Iceland	5.1	4.6[1]	2.0	1.9[1]
Ireland, Republic of	5.2	4.5	–[2]	–[2]
Italy	5.3	4.8	0.3	0.5[1]
Japan	5.9	6.4[1]	1.4	1.6
Luxembourg	5.1	5.1	1.8	2.0
Netherlands	6.0	5.4	2.0	2.3
Norway	4.9	5.0[1]	1.9	2.4[1]
Portugal	6.9	6.4	0.8	1.4[1]
Spain	5.4	5.0	0.5	0.8[1]
Sweden	4.6	3.8	2.3	2.4
Switzerland	6.2	5.7	1.8	2.3
UK	6.9	5.5[1]	3.0	2.9[1]
USA	10.0	8.9[1]	4.8	4.4[1]

[1] 1995.

[2] Divorce was not allowed in the Republic of Ireland until 1997.

Source: *Eurostat Yearbook 1997*, Office for Official Publications of the European Communities © European Communities

Employment

Agricultural and non-Agricultural Employment for Selected Countries

The minimum age for population base varies as follows: USA, France, Sweden, and UK, 16 years; Australia, Canada, Germany, Italy (1996), and Japan, 15 years; and Italy (1990), 14 years. For the USA and Italy the data are not comparable between 1990 and 1996. (N/A = not available.)

Industry			Australia	Canada	France	Germany	Italy	Japan	Sweden	UK	USA
Total Employment (thousands)											
1990	Agriculture, forestry, fishing		440	551	1,248	965	1,879	4,270	178	573	3,394
	Industry[1]	manufacturing	1,170	2,105	4,708	8,839	4,755	15,010	943	5,971[3]	21,346
		Total	1,865	3,117	6,425	10,875	6,842[2]	20,890	1,268	8,128	29,834
	Services		5,554	9,497	14,425	16,112	12,355	36,550	3,056	18,117	85,565
	Total		7,859	13,165	22,098	27,952	21,080	61,710	4,501	26,818	118,793
1996	Agriculture, forestry, fishing		424	565	1,004	N/A	1,392	3,390	131	511	3,570
	Industry[1]	manufacturing	1,120	2,083	N/A	N/A	4,873	14,420	773	5,066	20,518
		Total	1,807	2,969	5,479	N/A	6,471[2]	21,130	1,008	7,006	29,030
	Services		6,113	10,142	15,442	N/A	12,190	39,680	2,868	18,571	94,108
	Total		8,344	13,676	21,925	N/A	20,053	64,200	4,007	26,088	126,708
Percentage Distribution											
1990	Agriculture, forestry, fishing		6	4	6	3	9	7	4	2	3
	Industry[1]	manufacturing	15	16	21	32	23	24	21	22[3]	18
		Total	24	24	29	39	32[2]	34	28	30	25
	Services		71	72	65	58	59	59	68	68	72
	Total		100	100	100	100	100	100	100	100	100
1996	Agriculture, forestry, fishing		5	4	5	N/A	7	5	3	2	3
	Industry[1]	manufacturing	13	15	N/A	N/A	24	23	19	19	16
		Total	22	22	25	N/A	32[2]	33	25	27	23
	Services		73	74	70	N/A	61	62	72	71	74
	Total		100	100	100	N/A	100	100	100	100	100

[1] Includes mining and construction.
[2] Public utilities included in industry.
[3] Includes mining.

Source: US Bureau of Labor Statistics

Civilian Labour Force and Employment for Selected Countries

Data are based on US labour force definitions except that minimum age for population base varies as follows: USA, France, Sweden, and UK, 16 years; Australia, Canada, Japan, the Netherlands, Germany, and Italy (beginning 1994), 15 years; and Italy (prior to 1994) 14 years. (N/A = not available.)

Year	Australia	Canada	France	Germany[1]	Italy	Japan	Netherlands	Sweden	UK	USA
Civilian Labour Force (Millions)										
1980	6.7	12.0	22.9	27.3	21.1	55.7	5.9	4.3	26.5	106.9
1985	7.3	13.1	23.6	28.0	21.8	58.8	6.2	4.4	27.2	115.5
1990	8.4	14.3	24.3	29.4	22.7	63.0	6.7	4.6[2]	28.5	125.8[2]
1994	8.8	14.8	24.8	29.9[3]	22.6[2,3]	65.8	7.2	4.4	28.3	131.1[2]
1995	9.0	14.9	24.9	29.7[3]	22.7[3]	66.0	7.3	4.5	28.5	132.3
1996	9.1	15.1	25.1	29.6[3]	22.8[3]	66.4	7.3	4.5	28.6[3]	133.9
Labour Force Participation Rate (%)[4]										
1980	62.1	64.6	57.5	54.7	48.2	62.6	55.4	66.9	62.5	63.8
1985	61.6	65.8	56.8	54.7	47.2	62.3	55.5	66.9	62.1	64.8
1990	64.6	67.3	56.0	55.3	47.2	62.6	56.3	67.4[3]	63.7	66.5[2]
1994	63.9	65.3	55.5	53.7[2,3]	47.5[2,3]	63.1	59.0	63.8	62.5	66.6[2]
1995	64.6	64.8	55.3	53.2[3]	47.6[3]	62.9	59.3	64.3[3]	62.7[3]	66.6
1996	64.6	64.9	55.5	52.8[3]	47.7[3]	63.0	59.4[3]	64.3[3]	62.7[3]	66.8

(continued)

Civilian Labour Force and Employment for Selected Countries (*continued*)

Year	Australia	Canada	France	Germany[1]	Italy	Japan	Netherlands	Sweden	UK	USA
Civilian Employment (Millions)										
1980	6.3	11.1	21.4	26.5	20.2	54.6	5.5	4.2	24.7	99.3
1985	6.7	11.7	21.2	26.0	20.5	57.3	5.6	4.3	24.3	107.2
1990	7.9	13.2	22.1	28.0	21.1	61.7	6.2	4.5[2]	26.7	118.8[2]
1994	7.9	13.3	21.7	27.9[3]	20.1[2 3]	63.9	6.7	4.0	25.6	123.1[2]
1995	8.2	13.5	21.9	27.8[3]	20.0[3]	63.9	6.8	4.1	26.0	124.9
1996	8.3	13.7	22.0	27.5[3]	20.0[3]	64.2	6.8	4.0	26.3[3]	126.7
Employment–Population Ratio (%)[5]										
1980	58.3	59.7	53.8	53.1	46.1	61.3	52.1	65.6	58.1	59.2
1985	56.5	58.9	50.9	50.7	44.4	60.6	50.1	65.0	55.5	60.1
1990	60.1	61.9	50.9	52.6	43.9	61.3	52.6	66.1[2]	59.6	62.8[2]
1994	57.7	58.5	48.7	50.2[3]	42.1[2 3]	61.3	54.7	57.6	56.5	62.5[2]
1995	59.1	58.6	48.8	49.7[3]	41.8[3]	60.9	55.2[3]	58.4[3]	57.2[3]	62.9
1996	59.1	58.6	48.5	49.0[3]	41.9[3]	60.9	55.6[3]	57.9[3]	57.6[3]	63.2

[1] Former West Germany.
[2] Break in series. Data not comparable with prior years.
[3] Preliminary.
[4] Civilian labour force as a percentage of the civilian working-age population. Germany and Japan include the institutionalized population as part of the working-age population.
[5] Civilian employment as a percentage of the civilian working-age population. Germany and Japan include the institutionalized population as part of the working-age population.

Source: US Bureau of Labor Statistics

Employment by Gender in Selected Countries

(N/A = not available.)

Country	Civilian Employment–Population Ratio[1]							
	Women				Men			
	1980	1990	1995	1996	1980	1990	1995	1996
Australia	41.9	49.3	50.3	50.4	75.1	71.2	68.1	67.9
Canada	46.7	54.0	52.1	52.1	73.1	70.1	65.5	65.2
France	40.3	41.6	41.3	41.1	68.9	61.3	57.3	56.8
Germany	38.9[2]	40.9[3]	N/A	N/A	69.9[2]	65.6[3]	N/A	N/A
Italy	27.9	29.2	28.4[3 4]	28.8[4]	66.0	60.0	56.5[3 4]	56.2[4]
Japan	45.7	48.0	47.7	47.7	77.9	75.4	75.0	74.9
Sweden	58.0	61.8[3]	54.9[4]	54.2[4]	73.6	70.6[3]	62.2[4]	61.8[4]
UK	44.8	49.6	49.6[4]	50.1[4]	72.8	70.3	65.5[4]	65.7[4]
USA	47.7	54.3[3]	55.6[3]	56.0	72.0	72.0[3]	70.8[3]	70.9

[1] Civilian employment as a percentage of the civilian working-age population.
[2] Former West Germany.
[3] Break in series. Data not comparable with prior years.
[4] Preliminary.

Source: US Bureau of Labor Statistics

Female Labour Force Participation Rates for Selected Countries

Data are for female labour force of all ages divided by female population 15–64 years old.
(N/A = not available. In percentages.)

Country	1980	1985	1990	1995
Australia	52.1	54.9	62.9	64.8
Austria	48.7	51.0	55.4	N/A
Belgium	47.0	49.3	52.4	56.1
Canada	59.1	65.1	67.8	67.6
Czech Republic	N/A	N/A	69.1	65.4
Denmark	71.4	74.5	78.5	73.6
Finland	70.1	73.7	72.9	70.3
France	54.4	54.8	57.6	59.5
Germany[1]	52.8	52.9	57.4	61.0
Greece	33.0	41.8	43.6	45.9
Hungary	N/A	N/A	N/A	50.5
Iceland	55.9	66.2	66.0	81.9
Ireland, Republic of	36.3	36.6	38.9	47.6
Italy	39.1	40.5	45.9	42.7
Japan	54.9	57.2	60.4	62.2
Korea, South	N/A	45.3	51.3	53.2
Luxembourg	39.9	43.2	50.7	46.8
Mexico	N/A	N/A	N/A	40.1
Netherlands	35.5	40.9	53.1	57.1
New Zealand	44.5	47.6	62.9	65.8
Norway	62.3	68.0	71.2	72.4
Poland	N/A	N/A	N/A	61.1
Portugal	54.3	56.1	62.9	62.4
Spain	32.2	33.4	41.2	45.1
Sweden	74.1	78.1	80.1	74.5
Switzerland	54.1	56.2	59.6	67.1
Turkey	46.3	36.7	36.7	34.2
UK	58.3	60.6	65.5	66.0
USA	59.7	63.9	68.8	70.7

[1] Prior to 1991 data are for former West Germany.

Source: *Labour Force Statistics*, © OECD

Standardized Unemployment Rates for Selected Countries

Data are annual averages. The standardized unemployment rates shown here are calculated as the number of unemployed persons as a percentage of the civilian labour force. The unemployed are persons of working age who, in the reference period, are without work, available for work, and have taken specific steps to find work.
(N/A = not available.)

Country	1996	1997	1998
Australia	8.6	8.6	N/A
Austria	4.3	4.4	4.4
Belgium	9.7	9.2	8.8
Canada	9.7	9.2	8.3
Denmark	6.8	5.6	5.1
Finland	14.6	12.7	11.4
France	12.4	12.4	11.9
Germany	8.9	9.9	9.4
Ireland, Republic of	11.6	9.9	7.8
Italy	12.0	12.1	N/A
Japan	3.4	3.4	4.1
Luxembourg	3.0	2.8	2.8
Netherlands	6.3	5.2	4.0
New Zealand	6.1	6.6	7.5
Norway	4.9	4.1	N/A
Portugal	7.3	6.8	4.9
Spain	22.2	20.8	18.8
Sweden	9.6	9.9	8.2
Switzerland	3.3	4.2	N/A
UK	8.2	7.0	N/A
USA[1]	5.4	4.9	4.5
European Union	10.6	10.4	9.7
OECD	7.6	7.3	6.9

[1] Revisions to the population estimates. Data from January 1997 are not directly comparable with earlier data.

Source: *Main Economic Indicators*, © OECD 1999

International Political Organizations

Amazon Pact

(Amazon Cooperation Treaty) Agreement to protect and control the industrial or commercial development of the Amazon River region. The pact provides for technical and scientific cooperation in exploiting the natural resources of this ecologically important area.

Date established 1978

Founding members Bolivia, Brazil, Colombia, Ecuador, Guyana, Peru, Suriname, Venezuela

Current members same

Address Tratado de Cooperación Amazónica, Avda Prolongación Primavera 654, Chacarilla, Surco, Lima 33, Peru; phone: (51 14) 499 084; fax: (51 14) 499 718

Andean Community

(Communidad Andino; full name: Junta del Acuerdo di Cartagena [JUNAC]) South American organization aimed at economic and social cooperation between member states. Its ultimate aim is to create a free-trade area.

Date established 1969

Founding members Bolivia, Chile, Colombia, Ecuador, Peru

Current members Bolivia, Colombia, Ecuador, Peru, Venezuela. Observer: 1

Address Av Paseo de la Republica 3895, Lima 21, Peru; phone: (511) 221 3329; fax: (511) 221 2222

Arab League

(League of Arab States) Organization of Arab states established to promote Arab unity, primarily in opposition to Israel.

Date established 1945

Founding members Egypt, Iraq, Lebanon, Saudi Arabia, Syria, Transjordan, Yemen

Current members Algeria, Bahrain, Comoros, Djibouti, Egypt, Iraq, Jordan, Kuwait, Lebanon, Libya, Mauritania, Morocco, Oman, Palestine, Qatar, Saudi Arabia, Somalia, Sudan, Syria, Tunisia, United Arab Emirates, Yemen

Address Arab League Building, Tahrir Square, Cairo, Egypt; phone: (20 2) 575 0511; fax: (20 2) 577 5626

Arab Maghreb Union (AMU)

Association formed to promote cooperation among the Arab states in North Africa. It aims to formulate common policies on military, economic, international, and cultural issues.

Date established 1989

Founding members Algeria, Libya, Mauritania, Morocco, Tunisia

Current members same

Address 26–27 Rue Ogba, Rabat-Agdal, Morocco; phone: (212 7) 777 2668; fax: (212 7) 777 2693

Association of Caribbean States (ACS)

Organization sponsored by the Caribbean Community and Common Market (CARICOM) formed to promote social, political, and economic cooperation in the region, and eventual integration.

Date established 1994

Founding members Antigua and Barbuda, Bahamas, Barbados, Belize, Colombia, Costa Rica, Cuba, Dominica, Dominican Republic, El Salvador, Grenada, Guatemala, Guyana, Haiti, Honduras, Jamaica, Mexico, Nicaragua, Panama, St Kitts and Nevis, St Lucia, St Vincent and the Grenadines, Suriname, Trinidad and Tobago, Venezuela

Current members same. Associate members: 11 dependent territories in the region

Address 11–13 Victoria Avenue, Port of Spain, Trinidad and Tobago; phone: (809) 623 2783; fax: (809) 623 2679

Web site www.acs-aec.org/

Association of South East Asian Nations (ASEAN)

Regional alliance formed to promote peace and economic, social, and cultural development. It took over the nonmilitary role of the Southeast Asia Treaty Organization in 1975.

Date established 1967

Founding members Indonesia, Malaysia, Philippines, Singapore, Thailand

Current members Brunei, Indonesia, Laos, Malaysia, Myanmar, Philippines, Singapore, Thailand, Vietnam

Address ASEAN Secretariat, PO Box 2072, 7-A Jl. Sisingamangaraja, Jakarta, Indonesia; phone: (62 21) 726 2410; fax: (62 21) 739 8234

Web site www.asean.or.id/

Caribbean Community and Common Market (CARICOM)

Organization for economic and foreign policy coordination, and political and cultural unity in the Caribbean region. It replaced the Caribbean Free Trade Association.

Date established 1973

Founding members Barbados, Guyana, Jamaica, Trinidad and Tobago

Current members Antigua and Barbuda, Bahamas (a member of the Community but not of the Common Market), Barbados, Belize, Dominica, Grenada, Guyana, Haiti, Jamaica, Montserrat, St Kitts and Nevis, St Lucia, St Vincent and the Grenadines, Suriname, and Trinidad and Tobago. Associate members: British Virgin Islands, Turks and Caicos Islands. Observers: Dominican Republic, Mexico, Puerto Rico, and Venezuela

Address Bank of Guyana Building, PO Box 10827, Georgetown, Guyana; phone: (592 2) 69281; fax: (592 2) 67816

Web site www.caricom.org/expframe.htm

Commonwealth of Independent States (CIS)

Successor body to the Union of Soviet Socialist Republics, formed to ensure continued cooperation in trade and military policy, and recognition of borders. It has no formal political institutions, and its role is uncertain.

Date established 1991

Founding members Belarus, Russia, Ukraine

Current members Armenia, Azerbaijan, Belarus, Georgia, Kazakhstan, Kyrgyzstan, Moldova, Russia, Tajikistan, Turkmenistan, Ukraine, Uzbekistan

Address 220000 Minsk, Kirava 17, Belarus; phone: (375 172) 293 517; fax: (375 172) 272 339

Cooperation Council for the Arab States of the Gulf

Organization for promoting peace in the Persian Gulf area. It aims to bring about integration, coordination, and cooperation in economic, social, military, and political affairs among Arab Gulf states.

Date established 1982

Founding members Bahrain, Kuwait, Oman, Qatar, Saudi Arabia, United Arab Emirates

Current members same

Address PO Box 7153, Riyadh 11462, Saudi Arabia; phone: (966 482) 7777; fax (966 482) 9089

Council of Europe

Intergovernmental body set up to achieve greater unity between European countries, to facilitate their economic and social progress, and to uphold the principles of parliamentary democracy and respect for human rights.

Date established 1949

Founding members Belgium, Denmark, France, Greece, Republic of Ireland, Italy, Luxembourg, Netherlands, Norway, Sweden, Turkey, UK

Current members Albania, Andorra, Austria, Belgium, Bulgaria, Croatia, Cyprus, Czech Republic, Denmark, Estonia, Finland, France, Germany, Greece, Hungary, Iceland, Republic of Ireland, Italy, Latvia, Liechtenstein, Lithuania, Luxembourg, Former Yugoslav Republic of Macedonia, Malta, Moldova, Netherlands, Norway, Poland, Portugal, Romania, Russia, San Marino, Slovenia, Slovak Republic, Spain, Sweden, Switzerland, Turkey, UK, Ukraine

Address Palais de l'Europe, F-67075 Strasbourg, CEDEX, France; phone: (33 3) 88 41 20 00; fax: (33 3) 88 41 27 81

Web site www.coe.fr/

Council of the Baltic Sea States

Organization founded to foster closer economic and political cooperation between states in the Baltic region.

Date established 1992

Founding members Denmark, Estonia, Finland, Iceland, Germany, Latvia, Lithuania, Norway, Poland, Russia, Sweden, the European Union (EU)

Current members same

Address S–103, 33 Stockholm, Sweden

Web site www.baltinfo.org

Council of the Entente (CE)

(Conseil de l'Entente) Organization of West African states for strengthening economic links and promoting industrial development.

Date established 1959

Founding members Benin, Burkina Faso, Côte d'Ivoire, Niger

Current members Benin, Burkina Faso, Côte d'Ivoire, Niger, Togo

Address Mutual Aid and Loan Guarantee Fund, 01 B.P. 3734, Abidjan 01, Côte d'Ivoire; phone: (225 33) 2835; fax: (225 33) 1149

Group of Seven (G7)

The seven leading industrial nations of the world. The aim of their meetings was initially to coordinate international management of exchange rates. They now meet annually to discuss topical issues rather than to formulate policy. From 1991 Russia participated increasingly in G7 summits; the 1997 and 1998 summits were termed 'The Summit of the Eight', with full Russian participation.

Date established 1975

Founding members Canada, France, West Germany, Italy, Japan, UK, USA

Current members Canada, France, Germany, Italy, Japan, UK, USA

Address no permanent secretariat

International Organization for Migration (IOM)

Intergovernmental body set up to help resettle refugees and displaced persons, and encourage social and economic development through migration. It also aims to advance understanding of migration issues. IOM works closely with the United Nations and the International Catholic Migration Commission.

Date established founded in 1951 as the Intergovernmental Committee for European Migration; became the IOM in 1989

Founding members Australia, Austria, Belgium, Bolivia, Brazil, Canada, West Germany, Greece, Italy, Luxembourg, Netherlands, Switzerland, Turkey, USA

Current members Albania, Angola, Argentina, Armenia, Australia, Austria, Bangladesh, Belgium, Bolivia, Canada, Chile, Colombia, Costa Rica, Croatia, Cyprus, Czech Republic, Denmark, Dominican Republic, Ecuador, Egypt, El Salvador, Finland, France, Germany, Greece, Guatemala, Haiti, Honduras, Hungary, Israel, Italy, Japan, Kenya, South Korea, Luxembourg, Netherlands, Nicaragua, Norway, Pakistan, Panama, Paraguay, Peru, Philippines, Poland, Portugal, Senegal, Slovak Republic, Sri Lanka, Sweden, Switzerland, Tajikistan, Thailand, Uganda, Uruguay, USA, Venezuela, Zambia. Observers: 49

Address 17 Route de Morillons, CP 71, CH-1211 Geneva 19, Switzerland

Web site www.iom.ch/iom/

Nordic Council

Consultative body founded to discuss mutual interests and increase cooperation in the Nordic region.

Date established 1952

Founding members Denmark, Iceland, Norway, Sweden

Current members Denmark, Finland, Iceland, Norway, Sweden; and representatives from the Faroe Islands, the Aland Islands, and Greenland

Address Tyrgatan 7, Box 19506, 10432 Stockholm, Sweden; phone: (46 8) 453 4700; fax: (46 8) 411 7536

North Atlantic Treaty Organization (NATO)

See Also

NATO and European Defence, pp. 639–644.

Military and political association set up to provide for the collective defence of the main western European and North American states against the perceived threat from the USSR. It maintains troops and weapons, including nuclear weapons, in Europe. In 1994 NATO launched a 'Partnership for Peace' programme, inviting ex-Soviet republics and ex-Warsaw Pact countries to take part in a range of military cooperation agreements; by October 1997, 28 countries had joined the Partnership. Poland, Hungary, and the Czech Republic became full members of NATO in April 1999.

Date established 1949

Founding members Belgium, Canada, Denmark, France, Iceland, Italy, Luxembourg, Netherlands, Norway, Portugal, UK, USA

Current members Belgium, Canada, Czech Republic, Denmark, France, Germany, Greece, Hungary, Iceland, Italy, Luxembourg, Netherlands, Norway, Poland, Portugal, Spain, Turkey, UK, USA

Address NATO, 1110 Brussels, Belgium; phone: (32 2) 707 4111; fax: (32 2) 707 4117

Web site www.nato.int/

Organization for Security and Cooperation in Europe (OSCE)

International forum set up to reach agreement in security, economics, science, technology, and human rights. It was originally known (until 1994) as the Conference on Security and Cooperation in Europe (CSCE).

Date established 1972

Founding members Albania, Austria, Belgium, Bulgaria, Canada, Cyprus, Czechoslovakia, Denmark, Finland, France, East Germany, West Germany, Greece, Hungary, Iceland, Republic of Ireland, Italy, Liechtenstein, Luxembourg, Malta, Monaco, Netherlands, Norway, Poland, Portugal, Romania, San Marino, Spain, Sweden, Switzerland, Turkey, UK, USA, USSR, Yugoslavia

Current members Albania, Andorra, Armenia, Austria, Azerbaijan, Belarus, Belgium, Bosnia-Herzegovina, Bulgaria, Canada, Croatia, Cyprus, Czech Republic, Denmark, Estonia, Finland, France, Georgia, Germany, Greece, Hungary, Iceland, Republic of Ireland, Italy, Kazakhstan, Kyrgyzstan, Latvia, Liechtenstein, Lithuania, Luxembourg, Former Yugoslav Republic of Macedonia, Malta, Moldova, Monaco, Netherlands, Norway, Poland, Portugal, Romania, Russia, San Marino, Slovakia, Slovenia, Spain, Sweden, Switzerland, Tajikistan, Turkey, Turkmenistan, UK, Ukraine, USA, Uzbekistan, the Vatican, Yugoslavia (suspended)

Address Kärntnerring 5–7, A-1010, Vienna, Austria; phone: (43 1) 514 360; fax: (43 1) 514 3699

Web site www.osceprag.cz/

Organization of African Unity (OAU)

Association formed to eradicate colonialism and improve economic, cultural, and political cooperation in Africa. It also aims to coordinate military, scientific, and health policies.

Date established 1963

Founding members Cameroon, Central African Republic, Chad, Republic of the Congo, Côte d'Ivoire, Dahomey, Ethiopia, Gabon, Liberia, Madagascar, Mauritania, Niger, Nigeria, Senegal, Sierra Leone, Somalia, Togo, Tunisia, Upper Volta

Current members Algeria, Angola, Benin, Botswana, Burkina Faso, Burundi, Cameroon, Cape Verde, Central African Republic, Chad, Comoros, Democratic Republic of Congo, Republic of the Congo, Côte d'Ivoire, Djibouti, Egypt, Equatorial Guinea, Eritrea, Ethiopia, Gabon, Gambia, Ghana, Guinea, Guinea-Bissau, Kenya, Lesotho, Liberia, Libya, Madagascar, Malawi, Mali, Mauritania, Mauritius, Mozambique, Namibia, Niger, Nigeria, Rwanda, São Tomé and Príncipe, Senegal, Seychelles, Sierra Leone, Somalia, South Africa, Sudan, Swaziland, Tanzania, Togo, Tunisia, Uganda, Zambia, Zimbabwe

Address PO Box 3243, Addis Ababa, Ethiopia; phone: (251 1) 517 7000; fax: (251 1) 513 036

Web site www.oau-oua.org/

Organization of American States (OAS)

Association founded to maintain peace and solidarity within the western hemisphere, also concerned with the social, cultural, and economic development of Latin America.

Date established 1948

Founding members Antigua and Barbuda, Argentina, Bahamas, Barbados, Bolivia, Brazil, Chile, Colombia, Costa Rica, Cuba, Dominica, Dominican Republic, Ecuador, El Salvador, Grenada, Guatemala, Guyana, Haiti, Honduras, Jamaica, Mexico, Nicaragua, Panama, Paraguay, Peru, St Kitts and Nevis, St Lucia, St Vincent and the Grenadines, Suriname, Trinidad and Tobago, Uruguay, USA, Venezuela

Current members Antigua and Barbuda, Argentina, Bahamas, Barbados, Belize, Bolivia, Brazil, Canada, Chile, Colombia, Costa Rica, Cuba, Dominica, Dominican Republic, Ecuador, El Salvador, Grenada, Guatemala, Guyana, Haiti, Honduras, Jamaica, Mexico, Nicaragua, Panama, Paraguay, Peru, St Kitts and Nevis, St Lucia, St Vincent and the Grenadines, Suriname, Trinidad and Tobago, Uruguay, USA, Venezuela. Observers: 40

Address 17th Street and Constitution Avenue NW, Washington DC 20006, USA; phone: (202) 458 3000; fax: (202) 458 3967; e-mail: info@oas.org

Web site www.oas.org/

Organization of the Islamic Conference (OIC)

Association of states in the Middle East, Africa, and Asia, formed to promote Islamic solidarity between member countries, to consolidate economic, social, cultural, and scientific cooperation, and to eliminate racial discrimination.

Date established 1971

Founding members Afghanistan, Algeria, Bahrain, Bangladesh, Benin, Brunei, Burkina Faso, Cameroon, Chad, Comoros, Djibouti, Egypt, Gabon, Gambia, Guinea, Guinea-Bissau, Indonesia, Iran, Iraq, Jordan, Kuwait, Lebanon, Libya, Malaysia, Maldives, Mali, Mauritania, Morocco, Niger, Nigeria, Oman, Pakistan, Palestine, Qatar, Saudi Arabia, Senegal, Sierra Leone, Somalia, Sudan, Syria, Tunisia, Uganda, United Arab Emirates, Zanzibar

Current members Afghanistan, Albania, Algeria, Azerbaijan, Bahrain, Bangladesh, Benin, Brunei, Burkina Faso, Cameroon, Chad, Comoros, Djibouti, Egypt, Gabon, Gambia, Guinea, Guinea-Bissau, Indonesia, Iran, Iraq, Jordan, Kazakhstan, Kuwait, Kyrgyzstan, Lebanon, Libya, Malaysia, Maldives, Mali, Mauritania, Morocco, Mozambique, Niger, Nigeria, Oman, Pakistan, Palestine, Qatar, Saudi Arabia, Senegal, Sierra Leone, Somalia, Sudan, Suriname, Syria, Tajikistan, Tunisia, Turkey, Turkmenistan, Uganda, United Arab Emirates, Yemen. Observers: Central African Republic, Turkish Northern Cyprus, Côte dashingtonIvoire

Address Kilo 6, Mecca Road, PO Box 178, Jeddah 21411, Saudi Arabia; phone: (966 2) 680 0800; fax: (966 2) 687 3568

Schengen Group

Association of states within the European Union that in theory adhere to the ideals of the Schengen Convention, notably the abolition of passport controls at common internal borders and the strengthening of external borders.

Date established 1995

Founding members Belgium, France, Germany, Luxembourg, Netherlands

Current members Austria, Belgium, Germany, Greece, Italy, Luxembourg, Netherlands, Portugal, Spain. Observers: 5

Address c/o Benelux Union Economique, Rue de la Régence 39, B-1000 Brussels, Belgium; phone: (32 2) 519 3811; fax: (32 2) 513 4206

Secretariat of the Pacific Community (SPC)

Organization (known until 1998 as the South Pacific Commission) formed to promote economic and social cooperation between Pacific countries and those with dependencies in the region. A nuclear-free zone in the Pacific is another aim.

Date established 1947

Founding members Australia, France, Netherlands, New Zealand, UK, USA

Current members American Samoa, Australia, Cook Islands, Fiji Islands, France, French Polynesia, Guam, Kiribati, Marshall Islands, Federated States of Micronesia, Nauru, New Caledonia, New Zealand, Niue, Northern Marianas, Palau, Papua New Guinea, Pitcairn Islands, Samoa, Solomon Islands, Tokelau, Tonga, Tuvalu, UK, USA, Vanuatu, Wallis and Futuna

Address B.P. D5, 98848 Noumea Cedex, New Caledonia; phone: (687) 262 000; fax: (687) 263 818; e-mail: spc@spc.org.nc

Web site www.spc.org.nc/

South Asian Association for Regional Cooperation (SAARC)

Organization aiming to promote the welfare and economic, social, and cultural development of the region.

Date established 1985

Founding members Bangladesh, Bhutan, India, Maldives, Nepal, Pakistan, Sri Lanka

Current members same

Address PO Box 4222, Kathmandu, Nepal

Unrepresented Nations' and Peoples' Organization (UNPO)

International association founded to represent ethnic and minority groups unrecognized by the United Nations and to defend the right to self-determination of oppressed peoples around the world.

Date established 1991

Founding members representatives of American Indians, Armenia, Australian Aborigines, the Crimea, Estonia, Georgia, the Greek minority in Albania, the Kurds, the minorities of the Cordillera in the Philippines, the non-Chinese in Taiwan, Tibet, Turkestan, the Volga region, West Irians, West Papuans

Current members 47 ethnic and minority groups, including the above

Address 40A Javastraat, NL-2585 The Hague, The Netherlands; phone: (31 70) 360 3318; fax: (31 70) 360 3346; e-mail: unponl@antenna.nl

Web site www.unpo.org/

Visegrad Group

Association formed to promote cooperation and free trade between the neighbouring member states.

Date established 1991

Founding members Czechoslovakia, Hungary, Poland

Current members Czech Republic, Hungary, Poland, Slovak Republic

Address (no permanent headquarters) c/o Secretary of State, Aleje Ujazdowskie 9, 00-583 Warsaw, Poland

Western European Union (WEU)

Organization set up as a consultative forum for military issues, in close cooperation with NATO. The WEU is the defence component of the European Union and the potential basis of a common European defence policy.

Date established 1954

Founding members Belgium, France, West Germany, Italy, Luxembourg, Netherlands, UK

Current members Belgium, France, Germany, Greece, Italy, Luxembourg, Netherlands, Portugal, Spain, UK

Address Secretariat-General, 4 Rue de la Régence, B-1000 Brussels, Belgium; phone: (32 2) 513 4365; fax: (32 2) 511 3519

The European Union

See Also  **European Union Economy, pp.768–773.**

The European Union (EU) is an organization working towards political and monetary union, a common foreign and security policy, and cooperation on justice and home affairs. The Maastricht Treaty established a single market with free movement of goods and capital in 1993, and a Charter of Social Rights.

In 1997 the European Commission agreed that Estonia, Poland, the Czech Republic, Hungary, Slovenia, and Cyprus, should commence entry talks for the EU's expansion into Central and Eastern Europe. Further negotiations began in April 1998.

In March 1998 the European Commission announced details of the widest ranging shake-up in the 35-year history of its common farm policy, launching a move to phase out price supports, the bedrock of the Common Agricultural Policy (CAP) since its creation in 1962. The new goal was to allow Europe's most efficient farmers, who had been shielded from world trends by artificially high prices, to compete globally for food sales. One of the keystones of the farm policy, a ban on member states subsidizing their own farmers from national coffers, would fall away for the first time. The move appeared to mark the first stage of the dismemberment of the original CAP.

On 1 January 1999 the euro – the world's newest and second most important currency – was successfully launched by the 11 participating countries (all EU members except Denmark, Greece, Sweden, and the UK), with euro notes and coins to begin circulating in 2002.

In March 1999 the Amsterdam Treaty – the EU's new constitution – was ratified by all 15 members and came into effect 1 May 1999. The new treaty amended the 1957 founding treaty of Rome by lifting internal border controls and setting forth additional citizen rights.

Date established 1957 (as the European Economic Community)

Founding members Belgium, France, West Germany, Italy, Luxembourg, Netherlands

Current members Austria, Belgium, Denmark, Finland, France, Germany, Greece, Republic of Ireland, Italy, Luxembourg, Netherlands, Portugal, Spain, Sweden, UK

Address c/o European Commission, Rue de la Loi 200, B-1049 Brussels, Belgium. In the USA: European Union, Delegation of the European Commission to the United States, 2300 M Street NW, Washington, DC 20037; phone: (202) 862 9500; fax: (202) 4291766

Web site www.europa.eu.int/ and www.eurunion.org/

Key Dates in the Growth of the European Union

17 March 1948	Benelux Treaty enters into force.
1948	Creation of the Organization for European Economic Cooperation (OEEC) to administer Marshall Plan aid.
1949	Creation of the Council of Europe based in Strasbourg.
9 May 1950	Schuman Declaration; Robert Schuman proposes pooling Europe's coal and steel industries.
18 April 1951	European Coal and Steel Community (ECSC) Treaty signed.
1952–54	Development and failure of the plan for a European Defence Community (EDC).
25 March 1957	Signing of the Treaties of Rome establishing the European Economic Community (EEC) and European Atomic Energy Community (Euratom).
1967	Merger of the executive institutions of the three European Communities (ESCS, EEC, and Euratom).
1 July 1968	Completion of the Customs Union 18 months early.
1 January 1973	Denmark, Ireland, and the United Kingdom join the European Community (EUR 9).
13 March 1979	European Monetary System (EMS) becomes operative.
1 January 1981	Greece joins the European Community (EUR 10).
29 June 1985	European Council endorses 'White Paper' plan to complete single market by the end of 1992.
1 January 1986	Spain and Portugal join the European Community (EUR 12).
1 July 1987	Single European Act enters into force.
26–27 June 1989	Madrid European Council endorses plan for Economic and Monetary Union.
3 October 1990	Unification of Germany; the states of the former German Democratic Republic enter the European Community.
7 February 1992	Signing of the Maastricht Treaty setting up the European Union.

(continued)

Key Dates in the Growth of the European Union *(continued)*

Date	Event
2 May 1992	European Community and European Free Trade Association (EFTA) agree to form the European Economic Area (EEA).
1 January 1993	European single market is achieved on time.
1 November 1993	Treaty on European Union (Maastricht) enters into force after ratification by the member states.
1 January 1994	Establishment of the European Economic Area.
1 January 1995	Austria, Finland, and Sweden join the European Union (EUR 15).
17 June 1997	Treaty of Amsterdam is concluded.
12 March 1998	European Conference in London launches Europe-wide consultations on issues related to Common Foreign and Security Policy and Justice and Home Affairs.
30–31 March 1998	EU opens membership negotiations with Cyprus, Czech Republic, Estonia, Hungary, Poland, and Slovenia.
2 May 1998	Eleven EU member states qualify to launch the euro on 1 January 1999: Austria, Belgium, Finland, France, Germany, Republic of Ireland, Italy, Luxembourg, the Netherlands, Portugal, and Spain.
1 July 1998	European Central Bank inaugurated in Frankfurt, Germany.
1 January 1999	EMU and euro launched in the 11 qualifying EU countries.
1 May 1999	The Amsterdam Treaty enters into force after ratification by the member states.

European Parliament: Composition by Seats

Although the number of seats allocated to each country takes account of population size, representation is not strictly proportional and favours the smaller countries.

Member state	Number of seats	Member state	Number of seats
Austria	21	Luxembourg	6
Belgium	25	Netherlands	31
Denmark	16	Portugal	25
Finland	16	Spain	64
France	87	Sweden	22
Germany	99	UK	87
Greece	25		
Ireland, Republic of	15		
Italy	87	**Total**	626

European Union: Central Organs

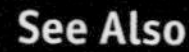

See Also UK Members of the European Parliament, p. 119.

European Commission initiates EU action. Its 20 members (two each from France, Germany, Italy, Spain, and UK; and one each from Austria, Belgium, Denmark, Finland, Greece, Republic of Ireland, Luxembourg, Netherlands, Portugal, and Sweden) are pledged to independence of national interests. Headquarters: Rue de la Loi 200, B-1049 Brussels, Belgium.

Council of Ministers of the European Union makes decisions on the Commission's proposals. Headquarters: Rue de la Loi 200, B-1049 Brussels, Belgium.

Committee of the Regions represents the regions within the EU, with 222 members serving a four-year term. Headquarters: Rue Belliard 79, B-1040 Brussels, Belgium.

Committee of Permanent Representatives (COREPER) consists of permanent officials (one group comprising ambassadors to the EU and one comprising deputy permanent representatives of member states) temporarily seconded by member states to work for the European Commission.

Economic and Social Committee established 1957, a consultative body with 222 members drawn from employers, workers, consumers, and other interest groups within member states. Headquarters: Rue Ravenstein 2, B-1000 Brussels, Belgium.

European Parliament assembly of the EU, directly elected from 1979, which comments on the legislative proposals of the European Commission. Members are elected for a five-year term. The European Parliament has 626 seats, apportioned on the basis of population. It can dismiss the whole Commission and reject the EU budget in its entirety. Full sittings are in Strasbourg, most committees meet in Brussels, and the seat of the secretariat is in Luxembourg. Headquarters: Palais de l'Europe, Avenue Robert Schuman, BP 1024, F-67070 Strasbourg, CEDEX, France.

European Court of Justice established 1957 to safeguard interpretation of the Rome Treaties that form the basis of the EU. It consists of 15 judges and 9 advocates-general drawn from member states for six-year terms. Headquarters: Court of Justice of the European Commission, L-2925 Luxembourg, Luxembourg.

European Union: Selected Specialized Organizations

European Atomic Energy Community (EURATOM) established 1957 to promote cooperation of EU member states in nuclear research and the rapid and large-scale development of nonmilitary nuclear energy. Headquarters: c/o European Commission, Rue de la Loi 200, B-1049 Brussels, Belgium.

European Coal and Steel Community (EDSC) established 1952 to coordinate the coal and steel industries of member countries and eliminate tariffs and other restrictions. Headquarters: Bâtiment Jean Monnet, Rue Alcide de Gasperi, Plateau du Kirchberg, L-3424 Luxembourg, Luxembourg.

European Investment Bank (EIB) established 1957 to provide interest-free, long-term financing of approved capital projects. Headquarters: 100 Boulevard Konrad Adenauer, L-2950 Luxembourg, Luxembourg.

European Monetary System (EMS) established 1979 to promote financial cooperation and monetary stability. Central to the EMS is the Exchange Rate Mechanism (ERM), a voluntary system of semi-fixed exchange rates based on the European currency unit (ECU), planned as a stepping stone towards the introduction of a common currency, the euro. Headquarters: D-2-ecu, Rue de la Loi 200, B-1049 Brussels, Belgium.

Principal EC and EU Treaties and Selected Agreements

Treaty establishing the European Coal and Steel Community (ECSC) Signed in Paris 18 April 1951; entered into force 23 July 1952. Laid the foundation of the European Union. Six countries – Germany, France, Belgium, Luxembourg, Italy, and the Netherlands – agreed to place control of the coal and steel industries under a central authority. As the first European supranational organization, the ECSC was primarily intended to ensure peace in Europe and 'lay the basis for a broader and deeper Community', as stated in the preamble. It is the only one of the three founding treaties with a limited lifespan. It was concluded for 50 years and will expire 2002, after which it will probably be incorporated into the EC Treaty.

Treaty establishing the European Economic Community (EEC) (commonly known as the Treaty of Rome) Signed in Rome 25 March 1957; entered into force 1 January 1958. Created the EEC. New members were added: Denmark, Ireland, and the UK in 1973; Greece in 1981; Spain and Portugal in 1986; Austria, Finland, and Sweden in 1995. The preamble to the EEC Treaty expressed the resolve of the partners to create 'an ever closer union among the peoples of Europe'. Its initial goals of establishing a common market and common agricultural, transport, competition, and economic policies, were gradually followed by new fields of activity such as environment, social, regional, education, and research and technology areas. The Treaties of Rome served to set up a Joint Parliamentary Assembly and a Court common to all three Communities.

The Treaty of Rome was amended in some important respects by the Single European Act, and was extensively remodelled by the Maastricht Treaty and revised by the Amsterdam Treaty.

Treaty establishing the European Atomic Energy Community (EURATOM) Signed in Rome 25 March 1957; entered into force 1 January 1958. Original signatories were Belgium, Germany, France, Italy, Luxembourg, and the Netherlands. The task of this Community is to contribute towards raising the living standards in member states by creating conditions necessary to the establishment and growth of nuclear industries.

Merger Treaty (usually known as the EC treaty) Signed in Brussels 8 April 1965; entered into force 1 July 1967. Brought about the merger of the Council of Ministers of the three Communities and of the High Authority of the ECSC, establishing a single Council and a single Commission of the European Communities.

First Accession Treaty Signed 22 January 1972. Concerned the accession of Denmark, Ireland, and the UK. For the UK, the Treaty entered into force 1 January 1973. From the date of accession the provisions of the original Treaties and the acts adopted by the institutions were made binding on the new member states.

Second Accession Treaty Signed in Athens 28 May 1979; entered into force 1 January 1981. Concerned the accession of Greece. Detailed transitional provisions are set out in the Treaty, most of which deal with agriculture. The Community provisions on free movement of workers did not come into effect until 1 January 1988.

Third Accession Treaty Signed in Lisbon and Madrid 12 January 1985; came into force 1 January 1986. Concerned the accession of Spain and Portugal. Detailed provisions are set out in the Treaty, but most of these interim arrangements were spent by January 1993, and Spanish and Portuguese workers have full free movement rights within the Community.

Single European Act Signed in Luxembourg 17 February 1986, and at the Hague 28 February 1986; entered into force 1 July 1987. Made extensive amendments to the other basic Community legislation, regarding voting procedures in the Council of Ministers and somewhat enlarging the legislative powers of the European Parliament. The main objective was to facilitate the adoption of nearly 300 measures to complete the Community's internal market.

Treaty on European Union (also known as the Maastricht Treaty) Signed in Maastricht 7 February 1992; came into force 1 November 1993. Created the European Union, European citizenship, and endowed the European Parliament with additional powers under a co-decision procedure. A much more thoroughgoing revision of the Treaty of Rome, it comprises two major sets of provisions: those aiming at the establishment of an economic and monetary union (EMU), at the latest by 1 Jan 1999; and those defined as steps towards the achievement of a political union, involving common foreign and defence policies. It renamed the EC to the European Union (EU). The Maastricht Treaty contains a number of fundamental opt-outs such as that granted to the UK under the Social Protocol attached to the Treaty.

The Treaty established three pillars for the European Union:

Pillar 1 incorporates the original three Treaties described above, with amendments. This covers the ongoing process of economic integration to create a single market for the movement of goods, capital, labour, and services. Added to this is a detailed plan for economic and monetary Union and supplementary powers in certain policy areas such as environment, research and technology, education and training.

Pillar 2 gives statutory authority to the Common Foreign and Security Policy (CFSP), and sets out the procedures for policy making and joint action in foreign and security affairs.

Pillar 3 deals with Justice and Home Affairs (JHA), including issues of asylum, immigration, combating drug addiction and fraud on an international scale, judicial cooperation in civil and criminal matters, and customs and police cooperation in areas such as terrorism.

Policy under Pillars 2 and 3 is handled by intergovernmental cooperation, with limitations on the roles of the Commission and Parliament, in comparison with those defined in the founding Treaties.

Treaty of Amsterdam Signed in Amsterdam 2 October 1997; came into force 1 May 1999. Revising the Treaties on which the EU is founded, the Treaty's main objectives are: to reinforce the Parliament's legislative power, strengthen cooperation in foreign and security policy and justice and home affairs, to develop a more coherent EU strategy to boost employment (introducing an Employment Chapter), and to remove remaining barriers to free movement of people across internal borders.

The Treaty reflects the need to make the EU's institutions more efficient in preparation for the next enlargement. It recognizes the fact that many of the potential new members are relatively new democracies with significant ethnic minorities. It therefore includes new Treaty articles making EU membership conditional on upholding the principles of liberty, democracy, respect for human rights, and fundamental freedoms, with the possibility of suspension of right, including voting rights, for any member state which breaches these principles in the treatment of its citizens.

Treaty reforms of institutions aimed at making the EU more effective focus on simplifying decision-making procedures.

– The elected European Parliament (EP) will have increased decision-making powers:
extended co-decision: this means it can adopt decisions jointly with the Council of Ministers or reject proposals, in more areas, including transport policy, research, development aid, Trans-European Networks, and new Treaty areas such as employment policy, public health, the fight against fraud, equal opportunities;
consultation: for unanimous decisions within the Council, the EP may be consulted;
assent: in the case of international agreements, Treaty decisions, and accession of new members.

– The appointment of the Commission President is made subject to the European Parliament's formal approval. The Treaty limits the size of the Parliament to 700 (compared to 626 at present) in anticipation of enlargement.

– The size of the European Commission will be reduced to one commissioner per member state as soon as the Union enlarges (the larger countries currently have two). The Treaty does not change the distribution of voting shares within the Council of Ministers to compensate the larger countries

(a protocol commits the EU to reopen discussions after enlargement takes place).

– Within the Council of Ministers, the Treaty extends the areas where decisions can be taken by a qualified majority, including anti-fraud measures, research, and employment. Unanimity remains the rule, however, in respect of constitutional matters and core sensitive areas such as taxation.

– The Treaty encourages closer ties with the national parliaments. A protocol allows a six week interval between the tabling of any legislative proposal and placing on Council agenda for decision, giving national parliaments a chance to hold a debate at the start of the legislative procedure. New measures to tackle fraud include increased cooperation between the customs authorities of the member states and enabling anti-fraud measures to be taking by majority voting.

Social Charter

In order to take account of the social dimension of the single market, the European Council on 9 December 1989 adopted a Charter of Fundamental Social Rights for Workers – known as the Social Charter – setting out minimum standards in a 47-point list. It covers basic rights for all EU citizens as regards freedom of movement, equal treatment, social protection, and fair wages. Although the Social Charter is not legally binding, the UK voted against it. The Charter was adopted by 11 of the then 12 member states. The Charter's initiatives were based on Articles of the Treaty of Rome, as amended by the Single European Act, which the UK has signed and implemented. Therefore any directive or regulation adopted by the Council of Ministers needs to be implemented by all member states, including the UK.

What is the 'Social Chapter'?

One proposal at the 1991 Intergovernmental Conference (Maastricht) was to replace the existing Social Chapter of the Treaty of Rome with a new Chapter. The UK did not sign the Social Charter in 1989, and, at Maastricht, did not agree to the adoption into the Treaty of the draft Social Chapter. Therefore the other member states adopted a separate Agreement on Social Policy with a text almost identical to the proposed new Social Chapter. The agreement, often referred to as the 'Social Chapter' was appended to a protocol (the 'Social Protocol') which was agreed by all member states. The original chapter of the Treaty of Rome still remains in force.

The Protocol makes clear that any action the other member states take under the Agreement, and any financial consequences, will not apply to the UK. On their accession in 1995, Austria, Finland, and Sweden agreed to accept the Social Protocol and the Agreement on Social Policy. The UK is not party to either the Social Charter or the Social Chapter, though it agreed to the Social Protocol, which allows the other member states to use Community institutions. Measures from the action programme intended to implement the Social Charter apply to the UK if they have been adopted under the Treaty of Rome (as amended), whereas initiatives under the Social Chapter do not, at present.

Legislation introduced under the Treaty of Rome (basis for the Social Charter and Social Action programmes) applies to all 15 member states. For example, the Working Time Directive was introduced through the health and safety provisions in the Treaty of Rome, before the existence of the Social Chapter, and therefore applies to all 15 member states.

Legislation introduced under the Social Chapter – ie, as and when the UK does not wish to participate – is not binding on the UK, at present. So far, only two EU directives have been introduced in this way: the Working Time Directive and the Directive on parental leave agreed in 1996. Numerous UK companies have decided to introduce Works Councils even though they are exempted through the UK opt-out.

Schengen Agreement

Concluded in Schengen, Luxembourg 1990 by Germany, France, Belgium, the Netherlands, and Luxembourg, this agreement is aimed at the gradual removal of controls at internal frontiers between the member states. There is also a further agreement on arrangements for processing asylum applications and cross-border cooperation between police forces. Since 1990 Spain, Portugal, and Italy have joined these arrangements; Austria, Greece, Denmark, Sweden, and Finland are signatories but not the UK and Ireland; whilst Norway and Iceland, who are not EU members, also participate in the Schengen area. The Schengen Agreement was incorporated into the Amsterdam Treaty. This will remove frontier checks between member states as the common area is progressively established.

Voting Procedure in the EU Council of Ministers

The Council of Ministers adopts legislation either by simple majority, qualified majority, or unanimity. In most cases, however, either unanimity or qualified majority is stipulated (by the EC and Euratom Treaties), in order to facilitate Community decision-making and protect the interests of the smaller member states. It eliminates the risk of two of the larger member states constituting a blocking minority. A qualified majority is 62 votes out of a total of 87. A blocking minority is 26 votes.

Qualified Majority Voting System

A weighted voting system gives each member state a vote roughly proportional to its population and economic strength.

Country	Population (1996 est)	Number of votes	Country	Population (1996 est)	Number of votes
France	58,333,000	10	Portugal	9,808,000	5
Germany	81,992,000	10	Austria	8,106,000	4
Italy	57,226,000	10	Sweden	8,819,000	4
UK	58,144,000	10	Denmark	5,237,000	3
Spain	39,674,000	8	Finland	5,126,000	3
Belgium	10,159,000	5	Ireland, Republic of	3,554,000	3
Greece	10,490,000	5	Luxembourg	412,000	2
Netherlands	15,575,000	5			

Presidency of the Council of Ministers

Year	1 January–30 June	1 July–31 December
1998	UK	Austria
1999	Germany	Finland
2000	Portugal	France
2001	Sweden	Belgium
2002	Spain	Denmark
2003	Greece	Italy
2004	Ireland	

What will this mean for the UK?

Because of their common travel area and the fact that they are both islands with common external and internal EU frontiers, a special arrangement has been agreed for the UK and Ireland in this area of cooperation. Both countries will maintain frontier checks at their own borders, although they can participate in individual initiatives taken by the other member states, on asylum or visa policy for example, if they wish to do so. For constitutional reasons there is also a special arrangement for Denmark.

The European Commission: Division of Portfolios 1999–2004

In March 1996 the Commission was hit by a damning report by independent investigators into fraud, nepotism, and mismanagement within the Commission. The Commissioners were collectively accused of having lost control of a bureaucracy that enriched others and of mishandling taxpayers' money, and the

The 20 Proposed Commissioners

Romano Prodi (Italian)	President
Neil Kinnock (British)	Vice-president Administrative Reform
Loyola de Palacio (Spanish)	Vice-president Relations with the European Parliament, Transport and Energy
Mario Monti (Italian)	Competition
Franz Fischler (Austrian)	Agriculture and Fisheries
Erkki Liikanen (Finnish)	Enterprise and Information Society
Frits Bolkestein (Dutch)	Internal Market
Philippe Busquin (Belgian)	Research
Pedro Solbes Mira (Spanish)	Economic and Monetary Affairs
Poul Nielson (Danish)	Development and Humanitarian Aid
Gunter Verheugen (German)	Enlargement
Chris Patten (British)	External Relations
Pascal Lamy (French)	Trade
David Byrne (Irish)	Health and Consumer Protection
Michel Barnier (French)	Regional Policy
Viviane Reding (Luxembourguese)	Education and Culture
Michaele Schreyer (German)	Budget
Margot Wallström (Swedish)	Environment
Antonio Vitorino (Portuguese)	Justice and Home Affairs
Anna Diamantopoulou (Greek)	Employment and Social Affairs

report concluded that it was difficult to find anyone with any sense of responsibility for what had happened. Following the report, and a motion of censure by the European Parliament, all 20 EU commissioners resigned.

Romano Prodi, the former Italian prime minister, was invited to accept the EU presidency, in succession to Jacques Santer. On 9 July 1999 Prodi announced the names and portfolios of the 19 proposed commissioners, and the new Commission was scheduled to take office following approval by the European Parliament in September 1999.

Under the Treaty of Amsterdam, the 19 designated Commissioners were for the first time agreed between the governments of the member states and the incoming president.

The new Commission will include five women, one of them a vice-president, and will seek to promote equal opportunities between men and women throughout its mandate, as well as reflecting the political complexion of the European Parliament. It will be subjected to the highest standards of probity in public life. Each prospective Commissioner has given a personal undertaking that he or she will resign if asked by the President to do so. Prodi underlined his determination to introduce strict rules on conflict of interest for Commissioners once they have left office.

The European Union: Citizenship and Rights

(Information from the European Parliament and European Union.)

Citizens rights

The EU has gradually been conferring on people new rights which can be upheld by national courts and by the European Court of Justice. These rights were written into the EC Treaty at various stages, reflecting the development of Union activities. The Treaty of Rome began by outlawing discrimination based on nationality in matters connected with the free movement of workers. Subsequently three other instruments – the Single Act (1987) and the Maastricht (1992) and Amsterdam (1997) Treaties – added further rights.

According to the EC Treaty, every person holding the nationality of a member state is a citizen of the EU. Nationality is defined according to the national laws of the member state. Citizenship of the EU is complementary to national citizenship and comprises a number of rights and duties in addition to those stemming from citizenship of a member state.

For all citizens of the EU, citizenship implies:

- the right to move and reside freely within the territory of the member states
- the right to vote, and to stand as a candidate in elections to the European Parliament and in municipal elections in the member state in which they reside, under the same conditions as nationals of that state
- the right to diplomatic protection in the territory of a third country (non-EU state) by the diplomatic or consular authorities of another member state, if their own country does not have diplomatic representation there
- the right to petition the European Parliament and the right to apply to the Ombudsman appointed by the European Parliament concerning instances of maladministration in the activities of the Community institutions or bodies, with the exception of the Court of Justice and the Court of First Instance.

The Amsterdam Treaty, which came into force 1 May 1999, builds on this and gives new prominence to the rights of individuals, including:

- a new article permitting the Council to take action by unanimity to combat discrimination based on sex, racial or ethnic origin, religion or belief, disability, age, or sexual orientation
- commitment to eliminate inequalities between men and women, in particular through application of the principle of equal pay for equal work or for work of equal value
- protection against the misuse of personal data held by the Community institutions
- new or strengthened cooperation in areas of particular concern to the Union's citizens: public health, environmental protection and sustainable development, and consumer protection.

Most importantly, the Amsterdam Treaty also takes specific steps to open up the Union's decision-making procedures to closer public scrutiny. Anyone in the EU now has right of access to documents originating from the European Parliament, Council, and Commission, within reasonable limits. Moreover, whenever the Council takes a decision which has legal effect, the voting results will be made public. This will make it much easier for people to see how the decisions which affect them have been taken.

How to get your rights recognized and enforced

If you consider that national, regional, or local authorities have wrongly interpreted your rights under Community law, or that they have discriminated against you or members of your family, you should assert your rights by complaining to the administration concerned. If you are not satisfied with the response, there are other ways to enforce your rights.

You should start by following national procedures. National courts must ensure that rights based on Community law are respected and, where necessary, set aside any measure which infringes it.

In addition, there are also ways of raising your case at Community level. Firstly, you can complain to the European Commission. If the Commission considers your complaint well-founded, it can contact the national authorities concerned to ask for an explanation and to request that the infringement of Community law be terminated. If the Commission is not satisfied with the response of the national authorities, it can open infringement proceedings against the country concerned. This may lead to the case being referred to the European Court of Justice in Luxembourg.

You may also present a petition to the European Parliament (see below) or raise your complaint with a Member of the European Parliament, who can put questions to the Commission and the Council. Their reply to the question must be made public.

You can also contact the European Ombudsman, but only if your complaint concerns maladministration by one of the Community institutions (eg, the European Parliament, the Council, or the European Commission), or by any decentralized body of the Community (eg, the European Training Foundation). Generally speaking, 'maladministration' means administrative irregularities or omissions. The European Ombudsman cannot deal with complaints concerning national or local administrations.

Petitioning European Parliament
The right to petition (added by the Treaty of Maastricht) was introduced to provide European citizens with a new way of sorting out situations which are doing them harm. But petitions are also a valuable source of information for parliamentary business, because they draw Parliament's attention to cases where the principles and rules of European integration are being infringed.

- Any citizen of the Union, and any natural or legal person residing or having its registered office in a member state, may petition Parliament, either individually or in association with others.
- Petitions must concern matters which come within the Community's fields of activity and affect the petitioners directly.
- Petitions must be addressed to the European Parliament.

How to submit your petition

- You should state your name, occupation, nationality, and the place of residence of each petitioner.
- The petition must be written in one of the official languages of the European Union. A petition in another language will not be considered unless the petitioner has attached a translation or a summary of the petition's content in an official EU language, which will serve as the basis for Parliament's work on the petition.

The petition can be submitted in either written or electronic form.

- If you wish to submit a petition in paper form, there is no form to be filled in or standard format to be followed. However, your petition must: bear your name, nationality, occupation, and place of residence (in the case of a group petition, it must bear the name, nationality, occupation, and place of residence of the presenter or, at least, the first signatory); be written clearly and legibly; be signed. Your petition may include annexes, including copies of any supporting documents you may have.
- If you wish to submit a petition via the Internet you should: go to the European Parliament Petition site, www.europarl.eu.int/dg1/en/petition/htm; read the instructions that will appear on the screen; complete the on-screen form. As soon as you have sent your petition you will receive electronic confirmation that it has been received. To enable us to register your petition, you must send us written confirmation. For this purpose simply click on the 'Print' button which will appear once the form has been sent to the European Parliament. Your form will then be displayed on the screen in standard format and can be printed. Then simply send the document by post with all signatures and relevant annexes. When the paper version of your petition has been received it will be officially registered and the consideration procedure will begin.

Admissibility
The Committee on Petitions first decides whether the petition is admissible, by checking that the matter comes within the European Union's fields of activity. If it does not, the committee declares the petition inadmissible and informs petitioners accordingly, giving the reasons and usually suggesting they apply to another authority that can take up the matter.

During the year of operation mid-1997 to mid-1998 the Committee declared 582 petitions admissible and 529 inadmissible.

Examination of petitions
The Committee then asks the Commission to provide information. It sometimes also consults other parliamentary committees and Parliament's Directorate-General for Research. When sufficient information has been collected the petition is put on the agenda for a committee meeting, to which the Commission is also invited. At the meeting the Commission makes an oral statement and comments on its written reply to the issues raised in the petition. Members of the Committee on Petitions then have an opportunity to put questions to the Commission representative.

Further action
This depends on the case:

- If the petition is a special case requiring individual treatment, the Commission contacts the appropriate authorities or puts the case to the permanent representative of the member state concerned, as this approach is likely to settle the matter. In some cases the committee asks the President of Parliament to make representations to the national authorities in person.
- If the petition concerns a matter of general importance, for instance if the Commission finds that Community law has been infringed, the Commission can institute legal proceedings, and this is likely to result in a ruling by the Court of Justice to which the petitioner can then refer.
- If the petition is a political issue, Parliament or the Commission may use it as the basis for a political initiative. Petitions of this kind are dealt with jointly in a report and become part of the political work of Parliament; the individual cases are not taken up. The issues raised in petitions are thus a way of prompting action by Parliament.

In each case the petitioner receives a reply setting out the result of the action taken.

Publication of petitions
Petitions entered in the general register and the main decisions taken on them during the consideration procedure are announced at plenary sittings of the European Parliament. These announcements appear in the minutes of the sitting. The texts of petitions entered in the register and of opinions of the Committee accompanying forwarded petitions are stored in the European Parliament archives, where they may be consulted by any Member of the European Parliament.

The European Union: How Does it Affect Us?

(Information from the European Commission Representation in the UK.)

What has Europe got to do with me?
As a result of the UK's membership of the European Community (or European Union, as it is now officially known), you can now live, work, or study in any of the twelve member states – that is France, Germany, Spain, Portugal, Belgium, Luxembourg, Denmark, Ireland, Greece, the Netherlands, Italy, and the UK. As of 1 January 1994 these opportunities also apply to Iceland, Austria, Finland, Norway, and Sweden who have signed the European Economic Area (EEA) Agreement with the European Union member states. If you have recently crossed the Channel or visited another EC country, you will have noticed that routine passport checks are less frequent and import restrictions on personal goods have been lifted. This means there are no limits on what you can bring back from another member state – including alcohol and tobacco – provided that the goods have been bought, tax paid, for your personal use. These are some of the more visible examples of the benefits of EU membership to ordinary people.

On 1 January 1995, Austria, Finland, and Sweden became members of the EU and parties of the Treaties on which the Union is founded. This means that the provisions of the original Treaties and the acts adopted by the institutions before accession shall be binding on the new member states, subject to temporary derogations and transitional arrangements. They accept the content, principles, and political objectives of the Treaties, including those of the Treaty on European Union. They therefore have to put into effect the measures necessary to comply, from the date of accession, with the provisions of directives and decisions unless a time limit is provided for.

But what if I don't want to go abroad?
If you have no interest in travelling to other EU countries, you might well think the European Union has nothing to do with you. But in fact, almost every aspect of daily life in the UK is affected in some way by the UK's membership of the European Union.

In the home

EC water quality standards ensure that lead, nitrates, and other unwanted residues are kept to safe levels. EC regulations ensure that all electrical appliances are safe. An eco-labelling scheme has been introduced to highlight products which cause least damage to the environment (for example your washing machine). Some products will carry energy consumption ratings. All foodstuffs are labelled with clear price markings, sell-by dates, and lists of ingredients, permitted additives, and nutritional information. Unsafe additives, colourings, or flavourings are banned.

If you have children, their toys must pass EC fire-safety standards to protect them from accidents.

To protect you from unscrupulous door-to-door salesmen, EC rules give you the right to a one week cooling-off period during which you may cancel any contract agreed at home or on the doorstep.

Similarly, if you are been misled by a dishonest advertisement in a magazine or on television, EC rules give you rights to quicker redress when disputes occur.

These rules do not mean that European institutions are trying to standardize all aspects of British life. They simply set out the essential safety, quality, and hygiene standard requirements which should be met before they are placed on the market, for your own protection. It is also important to bear in mind that no major decisions are taken without agreement reached in the Council of Ministers, where all national governments (including the UK) take the decisions affecting us.

In the street

The EC has taken the lead in tightening emissions standards for cars, lorries, and other means of transport. Such environmental action also helps reduce global warming.

In the classroom

Even if you have no interest in foreign travel or learning another language, your children might. A range of EC programmes are in place to encourage language learning, study visits, and exchanges which can lead to job opportunities abroad in the future. Under EC rules, qualifications gained in one country must be recognized in another.

In the town centre

As a direct result of the single market, a wider variety of high-quality produce is available on supermarket shelves than ever before with guaranteed standards of food and product safety.

If you buy a household appliance such as a stereo system, cooker, or fridge, you are protected by EC rules from unfair terms in customer contracts. Credit offers must also be clear and fair and if a product doesn't work or causes injury, EC rules make sure that the producer is liable for any damage caused. If you stop for a snack, EC rules ensure that all food premises and food handling staff meet minimum standards of hygiene and cleanliness.

Managing your money

If you are looking for a mortgage, savings plan, or other financial product, you will soon find more choice in the high street as foreign companies take advantage of the single market to offer their products in the UK. This might enable you to secure a loan at a lower rate of interest than offered by UK institutions, but with the same guarantees.

In the town hall

Like all local authorities in the UK, your local town or county council will be looking to attract funding from one of the Community structural funds to create jobs, boost the local economy, and attract investment. Substantial financial help is also given to the regions, especially run-down areas, to help them face industrial change and restructuring problems. Examples of projects include the construction of industrial sites on formerly derelict land, rejuvenation of inner cities to attract tourists, and initiatives to diversify economies in rural areas. Many councils are also forging closer economic as well as social ties with localities in other EC countries.

In the workplace

If you work in any form of manufacturing or service industry, you may find your business prospects are affected by the need to export products and win contracts in other member states. Until the single market was completed, all sorts of hidden barriers to trade, such as different technical standards, made it difficult to market goods outside the country of origin. Now anything that can be legally marketed and sold in one member state must, in principle, be allowed onto the market of all member states.

On a personal level, EC health and safety rules protect you from hazards in the workplace, such as excessive noise, exposure to dangerous substances, or prolonged work at computer screens. Other rules also ensure that you receive adequate maternity leave and that your conditions of employment are safeguarded if your company is taken over.

You are also protected from sexual discrimination wherever it occurs and EC laws have been passed on equal pay, equal employment rights, and equal social security entitlements between men and women.

On holiday

When booking a holiday, your rights as a consumer have been extended by the package travel directive, which obliges the tour operator to provide clear information, comply with the terms of the contract, and offer a refund or compensation if the service cannot be fully provided. If you buy an air ticket, travel agents are now obliged to inform you of the lowest available fare. To protect your family from health risks caused by dirty water, tough EC standards have been set to ensure high-quality bathing water at beaches and lakes. Should you fall ill abroad, you are entitled to health care and emergency treatment on the same terms as offered to locals. Before you leave the UK, you should obtain an E111 form from any main post office.

But are we still British?

Despite popular rumour, the Community is not looking to interfere in the nooks and crannies of national life in any of the member states. Under the so-called 'subsidiarity principle', joint action is only taken when a problem can be dealt with more effectively at EC level than by national governments alone. This principle was enshrined in EC law by the Maastricht Treaty.

To help clarify the areas in which the Community does and does not play a role in a member state's affairs, the London Office of the European Commission has produced a leaflet entitled 'Do you believe all you read in the newspapers?'. As a citizen of an EU country, you have no fewer national rights, you have simply acquired additional rights as citizens of Europe as well.

So what are these rights?

- The right to set up business in any EU country
- The right to study in any EU country
- The right to the same treatment in terms of employment, healthcare, social security
- The right to consular protection from the embassies of other EU countries, for example if you lose your passport in a non-EU country where your home country is not represented
- The right to complain to your Member of the European Parliament (MEP) or the European Ombudsman about any aspect of EU policy
- The right to vote and stand as a candidate in local and European Parliament elections.

The European Union: Useful Addresses

For information and advice to do with working or studying in another EU country you can dial the freephone number 0800-581591 or visit the Europa Internet site (www.europa.eu.int). You can use the freephone number or the Internet site to obtain Guides on working, living, and studying in an another EU country, as well as consumer issues, travelling, and equal opportunities in the EU. Information and useful addresses relevant to national taxation, voting rights and residence permits in the other member states are contained in factsheets which can be obtained by ringing the freephone number given above.

You can also seek assistance from the embassy or consulate of the country concerned in order to obtain details of relevant national authorities in other member states.

In addition, information on European policies and programmes is available at or through your local library.

Useful addresses Information can be obtained from:

European Commission Offices in the UK Jean Monnet House, 8 Storey's Gate, London SW1P 3AT; phone: (0171) 973 1992; fax: (0171) 973 1900/10; Windsor House, 9/15 Bedford Street, Belfast BT2 7EG; phone: (01232) 240 708; fax: (01232) 248 241; 4 Cathedral Road, Cardiff CF1 9SG; phone: (01222) 371 631; fax: (01222) 395 489; 9 Alva Street, Edinburgh 4PH; phone: (0131) 225 2058; fax: (0131) 226 4105

European Parliament Office in the UK 2 Queen Anne's Gate, London SW1H 9AA; phone: (0171) 227 4300; fax: (0171) 227 4302

European Ombudsman M Jacob Söderman, 1, avenue du Pres R Schuman, BP 403, F-67001 Strasbourg Cedex; phone: (0033) 388 17 40 01; fax: (0033) 388 17 90 62

Citizenship of the EU – voting rights, European elections, civil protection in the EU The Home Office; 50 Queen Anne's Gate, London SW1H 9AT; phone: (0171) 273 3000; fax: (0171) 273 3965

EFTA All queries relating to the exercise of your rights in European Economic Area (EEA) countries which are not members of the European Union (Norway, Iceland, and Liechtenstein) should be addressed to:
EFTA Secretariat; 74 rue de Trèves, B-1040 Brussels; phone: (3 22) 286 1711

The United Nations

The United Nations is an association of states for international peace, security, and cooperation. The UN was established as a successor to the League of Nations, and has played a role in many areas, such as refugees, development assistance, disaster relief, cultural cooperation, and peacekeeping.

The principal institutions are the General Assembly, the Security Council, the Economic and Social Council, and the International Court of Justice.

The UN operates many specialized agencies, involved either in promoting communication between states (such as the International Telecommunication Union, ITU), or concerned with the welfare of states, such as the World Health Organization (WHO), the UN Educational, Scientific and Cultural Organization (UNESCO), and the International Bank for Reconstruction and Development (World Bank). Much of the work of the specialized welfare agencies concerns developing countries, and consists mainly of research and fieldwork. However, they also provide international standards relevant to all countries in their respective fields. Though autonomous, the specialized agencies are related to the UN by special arrangements and work with the UN and each other through the coordinating machinery of the Economic and Social Council.

At a July 1998 UN conference in Rome, a treaty was agreed to set up a permanent international criminal court to try individuals accused of war crimes, genocide, and crimes against humanity.

Date established 1945

Founding members 51 states: Argentina, Australia, Belgium, Bolivia, Brazil, Byelorussian Soviet Socialist Republic, Canada, Chile, China, Colombia, Costa Rica, Cuba, Czechoslovakia, Denmark, Dominican Republic, Ecuador, Egypt, El Salvador, Ethiopia, France, Greece, Guatemala, Haiti, Honduras, India, Iran, Iraq, Lebanon, Liberia, Luxembourg, Mexico, Netherlands, New Zealand, Nicaragua, Norway, Panama, Paraguay, Peru, Philippines, Poland, Saudi Arabia, South Africa, Syria, Turkey, UK, Ukrainian Soviet Socialist Republic, Uruguay, USA, USSR, Venezuela, Yugoslavia

Current members 185 states in 1998

Budget The total operating expenses for the entire UN system – including the World Bank, International Monetary Fund, and all the UN funds, programmes, and specialized agencies – come to $18.2 billion a year.

The budget for the UN's core functions – the Secretariat operations and five regional commissions – is $1.25 billion a year. The UN and its agencies, programmes, and funds – mainly UNICEF, UNDP, UNFPA, WFP, and WHO – have a budget of $4.8 billion a year for economic and social development.

The top seven contributors to the UN are the USA (25%); Japan (17.98%); Germany (9.63%); France (6.49%); Italy (5.39%); the UK (5.07%); and Russia (2.87%). Collectively, they account for more than 72% of the regular UN budget.

The USA owes more in unpaid assessments than any other member state: over $1.6 billion.

Address United Nations, 1 United Nations Plaza, New York, NY 10017, USA; phone: (212) 963 4475

Web site www.un.org/

United Nations Secretaries-General

Term	Secretary-General	Nationality
1946–53	Trygve Lie	Norwegian
1953–61	Dag Hammarskjöld	Swedish
1961–71	U Thant	Burmese
1972–81	Kurt Waldheim	Austrian
1982–92	Javier Pérez de Cuéllar	Peruvian
1992–96	Boutros Boutros-Ghali	Egyptian
1997–	Kofi Annan	Ghanaian

United Nations Charter: Preamble

The Charter of the United Nations (UN) was signed on 26 June 1945 in San Francisco, at the conclusion of the UN Conference on International Organization, and came into force on 24 October 1945. The Statute of the International Court of Justice is an integral part of the charter.

Preamble
We the peoples of the UN determined to save succeeding generations from the scourge of war, which twice in our lifetime has brought untold sorrow to mankind, and to reaffirm faith in fundamental human rights, in the dignity and worth of the human person, in the equal rights of men and women and of nations large and small, and to establish conditions under which justice and respect for the obligations arising from treaties and other sources of international law can be maintained, and to promote social progress and better standards of life in larger freedom, and for these ends to practise tolerance and live together in peace with one another as good neighbours, and to unite our strength to maintain international peace and security, and to ensure, by the acceptance of principles and the institution of methods, that armed force shall not be used, save in the common interest, and to employ international machinery for the promotion of the economic and social advancement of all peoples, have resolved to combine our efforts to accomplish these aims.

Accordingly, our respective governments, through representatives assembled in the city of San Francisco, who have exhibited their full powers found to be in good and due form, have agreed to the present Charter of the United Nations and do hereby establish an international organization to be known as the United Nations.

United Nations: Members and Contributions

Country	Year of admission	Scale of assessments 1999 (%)	Gross contributions for 1999 (US $)
Afghanistan	1946	0.003	36,527
Albania	1955	0.003	36,527
Algeria	1962	0.094	1,144,527
Andorra	1993	0.004	48,703
Angola	1976	0.010	121,758
Antigua and Barbuda	1981	0.002	24,352
Argentina[1]	1945	1.024	12,468,042
Armenia	1992	0.011	133,934
Australia[1]	1945	1.482	18,044,568
Austria	1955	0.941	11,457,449
Azerbaijan	1992	0.022	267,868
Bahamas	1973	0.015	182,637
Bahrain	1971	0.017	206,989
Bangladesh	1974	0.010	121,758
Barbados	1966	0.008	97,406
Belarus[1]	1945	0.082	998,417
Belgium[1]	1945	1.103	13,429,932
Belize	1981	0.001	12,176
Benin	1960	0.002	24,352
Bhutan	1971	0.001	12,176
Bolivia[1]	1945	0.007	85,231
Bosnia-Herzegovina	1992	0.005	60,879
Botswana	1966	0.010	121,758
Brazil[1]	1945	1.470	17,898,459
Brunei	1984	0.020	243,516
Bulgaria	1955	0.019	231,341
Burkina Faso	1960	0.002	24,352
Burundi	1962	0.001	12,176
Cambodia	1955	0.001	12,176
Cameroon	1960	0.013	158,286
Canada[1]	1945	2.754	33,532,214
Cape Verde	1975	0.002	24,352
Central African Republic	1960	0.001	12,176
Chad	1960	0.001	12,176
Chile[1]	1945	0.131	1,595,033
China[1]	1945	0.973	11,847,075
Colombia[1]	1945	0.109	1,327,165
Comoros	1975	0.001	12,176
Congo, Democratic Republic of	1960	0.007	85,231
Congo, Republic of the	1960	0.003	36,527
Costa Rica[1]	1945	0.016	194,813
Côte d'Ivoire	1960	0.009	109,582
Croatia	1992	0.036	438,330
Cuba[1]	1945	0.026	316,571
Cyprus	1960	0.034	413,978
Czech Republic	1993	0.121	1,473,274
Denmark[1]	1945	0.691	8,413,493
Djibouti	1977	0.001	12,176
Dominica	1978	0.001	12,176
Dominican Republic[1]	1945	0.015	182,637
Ecuador[1]	1945	0.020	243,516
Egypt[1]	1945	0.065	791,428
El Salvador[1]	1945	0.012	146,110
Equatorial Guinea	1968	0.001	12,176
Eritrea	1993	0.001	12,176
Estonia	1991	0.015	182,637
Ethiopia[1]	1945	0.006	73,055
Fiji Islands	1970	0.004	48,703
Finland	1955	0.542	6,599,296
France[1]	1945	6.540	79,629,877
Gabon	1960	0.015	182,637
Gambia	1965	0.001	12,176
Georgia	1992	0.019	231,341
Germany[2]	1973/1990	9.808	119,420,464
Ghana	1957	0.007	85,231
Greece[1]	1945	0.351	4,273,713
Grenada	1974	0.001	12,176
Guatemala[1]	1945	0.018	219,165
Guinea	1958	0.003	36,527
Guinea-Bissau	1974	0.001	12,176
Guyana	1966	0.001	12,176
Haiti[1]	1945	0.002	24,352
Honduras[1]	1945	0.003	36,527
Hungary	1955	0.120	1,461,099
Iceland	1946	0.032	389,626
India[1]	1945	0.299	3,640,571
Indonesia	1950	0.184	2,240,351
Iran[1]	1945	0.193	2,349,934
Iraq[1]	1945	0.045	547,912
Ireland, Republic of	1955	0.224	2,727,384
Israel	1949	0.345	4,200,659
Italy	1955	5.432	66,139,066
Jamaica	1962	0.006	73,055
Japan	1956	19.984	243,321,631
Jordan	1955	0.006	73,055
Kazakhstan	1992	0.066	803,604
Kenya	1963	0.007	85,231
Korea, North	1991	0.019	231,341
Korea, South	1991	0.994	12,102,767
Kuwait	1963	0.134	1,631,560
Kyrgyzstan	1992	0.008	97,406
Laos	1955	0.001	12,176
Latvia	1991	0.024	292,220
Lebanon[1]	1945	0.016	194,813
Lesotho	1966	0.002	24,352
Liberia[1]	1945	0.002	24,352
Libya	1955	0.132	1,607,208
Liechtenstein	1990	0.006	73,055
Lithuania	1991	0.022	267,868
Luxembourg[1]	1945	0.068	827,956
Macedonia, Former Yugoslav Republic of	1993	0.004	48,703
Madagascar	1960	0.003	36,527
Malawi	1964	0.002	24,352
Malaysia	1957	0.180	2,191,648
Maldives	1965	0.001	12,176
Mali	1960	0.002	24,352
Malta	1964	0.014	170,461
Marshall Islands	1991	0.001	12,176
Mauritania	1961	0.001	12,176
Mauritius	1968	0.009	109,582
Mexico[1]	1945	0.980	11,932,306
Micronesia	1991	0.001	12,176
Moldova	1992	0.018	219,165
Monaco	1993	0.004	48,703
Mongolia	1961	0.002	24,352
Morocco	1956	0.041	499,209
Mozambique	1975	0.001	12,176
Myanmar	1948	0.008	97,406
Namibia	1990	0.007	85,231
Nepal	1955	0.004	48,703
Netherlands[1]	1945	1.631	19,858,766
New Zealand[1]	1945	0.221	2,690,857
Nicaragua[1]	1945	0.001	12,176
Niger	1960	0.002	24,352
Nigeria	1960	0.040	487,033
Norway[1]	1945	0.610	7,427,251
Oman	1971	0.051	620,967
Pakistan	1947	0.059	718,373
Palau	1994	0.001	12,176
Panama[1]	1945	0.013	158,286
Papua New Guinea	1975	0.007	85,231
Paraguay[1]	1945	0.014	170,461
Peru[1]	1945	0.095	1,156,703
Philippines[1]	1945	0.080	974,066
Poland[1]	1945	0.207	2,520,395
Portugal	1955	0.417	5,077,318
Qatar	1971	0.033	401,802

(continued)

United Nations: Members and Contributions (*continued*)

Country	Year of admission	Scale of assessments 1999 (%)	Gross contributions for 1999 (US $)
Romania	1955	0.067	815,780
Russia[3]	1945	1.487	18,105,447
Rwanda	1962	0.001	12,176
St Kitts and Nevis	1983	0.001	12,176
St Lucia	1979	0.001	12,176
St Vincent and the Grenadines	1980	0.001	12,176
Samoa	1976	0.001	12,176
San Marino	1992	0.002	24,352
São Tomé and Príncipe	1975	0.001	12,176
Saudi Arabia[1]	1945	0.569	6,928,043
Senegal	1960	0.006	73,055
Seychelles	1976	0.002	24,352
Sierra Leone	1961	0.001	12,176
Singapore	1965	0.176	2,142,945
Slovak Republic	1993	0.039	474,857
Slovenia	1992	0.061	742,725
Solomon Islands	1978	0.001	12,176
Somalia	1960	0.001	12,176
South Africa[1]	1945	0.366	4,456,351
Spain	1955	2.589	31,523,204
Sri Lanka	1955	0.012	146,110
Sudan	1956	0.007	85,231
Suriname	1975	0.004	48,703
Swaziland	1968	0.002	24,352
Sweden	1946	1.084	13,198,591
Syria[1]	1945	0.064	779,253
Tajikistan	1992	0.005	60,879
Tanzania	1961	0.003	36,527
Thailand	1946	0.167	2,033,362
Togo	1960	0.001	12,176
Trinidad and Tobago	1962	0.017	206,989
Tunisia	1956	0.028	340,923
Turkey[1]	1945	0.440	5,357,362
Turkmenistan	1992	0.008	97,406
Uganda	1962	0.004	48,703
UK[1]	1945	5.090	61,974,935
Ukraine[1]	1945	0.302	3,677,098
United Arab Emirates	1971	0.178	2,167,296
Uruguay[1]	1945	0.048	584,439
USA[1]	1945	25.000	304,395,555
Uzbekistan	1992	0.037	450,505
Vanuatu	1981	0.001	12,176
Venezuela[1]	1945	0.176	2,142,945
Vietnam	1977	0.007	85,231
Yemen[2]	1947	0.010	121,758
Yugoslavia[4]	1945	0.034	413,978
Zambia	1964	0.002	24,352
Zimbabwe	1980	0.009	109,582
Total		100.00	1,217,582,219

[1] Founder member.
[2] Represented by two countries until unification in 1990.
[3] Became a separate member upon the demise of the USSR which was a founder member in 1945.
[4] Founder member, but suspended from membership in 1993.

Source: UN Secretariat

Principal UN Institutions, Programmes, and Agencies

United Nations: Secretariat

The Secretariat is headed by the secretary general, who has under- and assistant-secretaries general and a large international staff of civil servants with loyalties to the organization and the international community rather than to any government. The secretary general is appointed by the General Assembly on the recommendation of the Security Council for a renewable five-year term.

Secretary-General

Kofi Annan (Ghana)

Economic and Social Affairs

Undersecretaries-General
Policy Coordination and Sustainable Development: Nitin Desai (India)
Development Support and Management Services: Jongjian Jin (China)

Assistant Secretary-General
Advancement of Women: Angela King (Jamaica)

Political, Security, and Humanitarian Affairs

Undersecretaries-General
Humanitarian Affairs: Yasushi Akashi (Japan)
Peacekeeping Operations: Bernard Miyet (France)
Political Affairs: Kieran Prendergast (UK)

Assistant Secretaries-General
Peacekeeping Operations: Hedi Annabi (Tunisia), Manfred Eisele (Germany)
Political Affairs: Alvar de Soto (Peru), Ibrahima Fall (Senegal)

Legal, Administrative Affairs, and Public Information

Undersecretaries-General
Administration and Management: Joseph Connor (USA)
UN Legal Counsel: Hans Corell (Sweden)

Assistant Secretaries-General
UN Controller: Jean-Pierre Halbwachs (Mauritius)
Human Resources: Rafiah Salim (Malaysia)
Public Information: Samir Sanbar (Lebanon)
Conference and Support Services: Benon Sevan (Cyprus)
UN Compensation Commission in connection with Iraq: Jean-Claude Aimé (Haiti)

Secretary-General's Executive Office
Chef de Cabinet and Undersecretary-General: S Iqbal Riza (Pakistan)
External Relations and Assistant Secretary-General: Gillian Sorensen (USA)
Spokesman for the Secretary-General: Fred Eckhard (USA)

United Nations: Security Council

The most powerful body of the UN, responsible for maintaining international peace and security. UN member states undertake to accept and carry out its decisions. Any permanent member of the council can veto a decision. The council may investigate disputes, make recommendations, and call on members to take economic or military measures to enforce its decisions, and if these measures are deemed inadequate it may take military action.

Date established 1945

Founding members China, France, UK, USA, USSR

Current members permanent members: China, France, Russia, UK, USA; rotating members (1996–97): Chile, Egypt, Guinea-Bissau, South Korea, Poland; (1997–98): Costa Rica, Japan, Kenya, Portugal, Sweden; (1999–2000): Argentina, Bahrain, Brazil, Canada, Gabon, Gambia, Malaysia, Namibia, Netherlands, Slovenia

Address United Nations, Room S-3380A, New York, NY 10017, USA

United Nations: General Assembly

The largest decisionmaking body of the UN, consisting of one representative from each of the member states. The General Assembly meets annually. It controls UN finances and approves the budget. Other decisions are not binding; it merely makes recommendations to the Security Council or a member state. It elects the nonpermanent members of the Security Council.

Date established 1945

Current members 185 states

Address United Nations, 1 United Nations Plaza, New York, NY 10017, USA

United Nations: International Court of Justice

The main judicial organ of the UN. Only states, not individuals, can be parties to cases before the court. There is no appeal. Decisions of the court are binding, but states are not obliged to submit cases to it. The court gives advisory opinions at the request of UN bodies.

Date established 1945

Members 15 independent judges, elected by the Security Council and the General Assembly on the basis of their competence in international law and irrespective of their nationalities, except that no two judges can be nationals of the same state

Address Peace Palace, NL-2517 KJ The Hague, The Netherlands

United Nations: Economic and Social Council (ECOSOC)

Organ of the UN that guides and coordinates the General Assembly's economic programme. It initiates studies of international economic, social, cultural, educational, health, and related matters. It also coordinates the activities of the Food and Agriculture Organization.

Date established 1945

Founding members Belgium, Canada, Chile, China, Colombia, Cuba, Czechoslovakia, France, Greece, India, Lebanon, Norway, Peru, UK, Ukrainian Soviet Socialist Republic, USA, USSR, Yugoslavia

Current members 54 members elected for three years, one-third retiring in rotation

Address United Nations, 1 United Nations Plaza, New York, NY 10017, USA

The council includes five regional commissions:

Economic Commission for Africa (ECA) established 1958 to promote and facilitate concerted action for the economic and social development of Africa through research and the coordination of national policies. Headquarters: Africa Hall, PO Box 3001, Addis Ababa, Ethiopia.

Economic and Social Commission for Asia and the Pacific (ESCAP) established 1947 (present name from 1974) to promote regional economic cooperation, poverty alleviation through economic growth and social development, and environmentally sustainable development. Headquarters: UN Building, Rajadamnern Avenue, Bangkok 10200, Thailand.

Economic Commission for Europe (UN/ECE) established 1947 to generate and improve economic relations between member and other countries and to strengthen cooperation between governments, particularly in environment, transport, statistics, trade facilitation, and economic analysis. Headquarters: Palais des Nations, 8–14 Avenue de la Paix, CH-1211 Geneva 10, Switzerland.

Economic Commission for Latin America and the Caribbean (ECLAC) established 1948 to raise the level of economic activity in the region and strengthen the economic relations of member countries with one another and with other countries. Headquarters: Avenida Vitacura 3030, PO Box 179-D, Santiago, Chile.

Economic and Social Commission for Western Asia (ESCWA) established 1973 to raise the level of economic activity in the Middle East and northern Africa, and strengthen the economic relations of member countries with one another and with other countries. Headquarters: PO Box 927115, Amman, Jordan.

United Nations: Selected Programmes and Organs

International Atomic Energy Agency (IAEA) established 1957 to advise and assist member countries in the development and peaceful application of nuclear power, and to guard against its misuse. It is an independent intergovernmental organization under the aegis of the UN. Headquarters: Wagramerstrasse 5, PO Box 100, A-1400 Vienna, Austria.

United Nations Centre for Human Settlements (UNCHS, Habitat) established 1978 to service the intergovernmental Commission on Human Settlements by providing planning, construction, land development, and finance. It is a standing committee under the Economic and Social Council and the General Assembly. Headquarters: 2 United Nations Plaza, Room DC-2-0943, New York, NY 10017, USA.

United Nations Children's Fund (UNICEF) established 1946 to improve the lives of children throughout the world. It carries out programmes in health, nutrition, education, water and sanitation, the environment, women in development, and other areas of importance to children. Headquarters: 3 United Nations Plaza, New York, NY 10017, USA.

United Nations Conference on Trade and Development (UNCTAD) established 1964 to promote international trade, particularly in developing countries. Headquarters: Palais des Nations, 8–14 Avenue de la Paix, CH-1211 Geneva 10, Switzerland.

United Nations Development Fund for Women (UNIFEM) established 1976 to help women achieve equality through economic and social development. It provides direct technical and financial support to women's initiatives. Headquarters: 304 East 45th Street, 6th Floor, New York, NY 10017, USA.

United Nations Development Programme (UNDP) established 1965 to eradicate poverty, especially in the least developed countries, and to achieve sustainable human development, the empowerment of women, and the protection and regeneration of the environment. Headquarters: 1 United Nations Plaza, New York, NY 10017, USA.

United Nations Environment Programme (UNEP) established 1972 to monitor the state of the environment and promote environmentally sound developments throughout the world. Headquarters: PO Box 30552, Nairobi, Kenya.

United Nations High Commissioner for Refugees (UNHCR) established 1951 to help refugees and displaced people worldwide, to give them international protection, and to find solutions to their problems. Headquarters: Centre William Rappard, 154 Rue de Lausanne, CH-1202 Geneva, Switzerland.

United Nations Institute for Training and Research (UNITAR) established 1965 to improve the effectiveness of the UN through training and research. It is a standing committee under the Economic and Social Council and the General Assembly. Headquarters: Palais des Nations, Bureau 1070, 8–14 Avenue de la Paix, CH-1211 Geneva 10, Switzerland.

United Nations Population Fund (UNFPA) established 1972 under the umbrella of UNDP to help countries, at their request, to address issues of reproductive health and population, and to raise awareness of this in all countries. Headquarters: 220 East 42nd Street, New York, NY 10017, USA.

United Nations Research Institute for Social Development (UNRISD) established 1964 to conduct research into problems and policies of social and economic development. It is a standing committee under the Economic and Social Council and the General Assembly. Headquarters: Palais des Nations, Bureau 1070, 8–14 Avenue de la Paix, CH-1211 Geneva 10, Switzerland.

World Food Programme (WFP) established 1963 to improve economic and social development through food aid and to provide emergency relief. It is a standing committee under the Economic and Social Council and the General Assembly. Headquarters: Via Cristoforo Colombo 426, I-00145 Rome, Italy.

United Nations: Specialized Agencies

Food and Agriculture Organization (FAO) established 1945 to coordinate activities to improve food and timber production and levels of nutrition throughout the world. It is also concerned with investment in agriculture and dispersal of emergency food supplies. Headquarters: Viale delle Terme di Caracalla, I-00100 Rome, Italy.

International Civil Aviation Organization (ICAO) established 1947 to promote safety and efficiency in aviation, international facilities, and air law. Headquarters: 999 University Street, Montréal, H3C 5H7, Canada.

International Fund for Agricultural Development (IFAD) established 1977 to provide additional funds for benefiting the poorest in developing countries. Headquarters: Via del Serafico 107, I-00142 Rome, Italy.

International Labour Organization (ILO) established 1919 to formulate standards for labour and social conditions. Headquarters: 4 Route des Morillons, CH-1211 Geneva, Switzerland.

International Maritime Organization (IMO) established 1958 to promote safety at sea, pollution control, and the abolition of restrictive practices. Headquarters: 4 Albert Embankment, London SE1 7SR, UK.

International Monetary Fund (IMF) established 1944 to promote world trade and to smooth loan repayments among member states; the IMF also makes loans to members in balance-of-payments difficulties, on certain conditions. Headquarters: 700 19th Street NW, Washington, DC 20431, USA.

International Telecommunication Union (ITU) established 1934 to promote international regulations for telephone, radio, and telegraph communications, and to allocate radio frequencies. Headquarters: Palais des Nations, 8–14 Avenue de la Paix, CH-1211 Geneva 10, Switzerland.

United Nations Educational, Scientific, and Cultural Organization (UNESCO) established 1946 to promote cooperation among nations through education, science, and culture, and to further respect for justice, the rule of law, and human rights and fundamental freedoms. It pays special attention to women's issues and youth development. Headquarters: 7 Place de Fontenoy, F-75352 Paris 075P, France.

United Nations Industrial Development Organization (UNIDO) established 1966 to promote industrial development and coordination. It acts as the chief coordinating body for industrial activities within the UN system. Headquarters: Vienna International Centre, PO Box 300, A-1400 Vienna, Austria.

Universal Postal Union (UPU) established 1875 to coordinate international collaboration of postal services. It became an agency of the UN in 1947. Headquarters: Bureau International de l'UPU, Weltpoststrasse 4, CH-3000 Bern 15, Switzerland.

World Health Organization (WHO) established 1946 to assist all peoples in attaining the highest possible levels of health, to prevent the spread of diseases, and to eradicate them. It is creating a worldwide early-warning system for infectious diseases. Headquarters: 20 Avenue Appia, CH-1211 Geneva 27, Switzerland.

World Intellectual Property Organization (WIPO) established 1974 to protect copyright, patents, and trademarks in the arts, science, and industry. Headquarters: 34 Chemin des Colombettes, Case Postale 18, CH-1211 Geneva 20, Switzerland.

World Meteorological Organization (WMO) established 1951 to facilitate worldwide cooperation in the creation and maintenance of a network of stations for making meteorological observations and to ensure the rapid exchange of information. Headquarters: Case Postale 2300, 41 Avenue Giuseppe-Motta, CH-1211 Geneva 2, Switzerland.

United Nations: World Bank Group

International Bank for Reconstruction and Development (IBRD, World Bank) established 1945 to promote economic development by lending money to countries in need. The loans are on commercial terms and guaranteed by member states. Headquarters: 1818 H Street NW, Washington, DC 20433, USA.

International Development Association (IDA) established 1960 to meet the need for lending to poor countries on easy terms; administered by the World Bank. Headquarters: 1818 H Street NW, Washington, DC 20433, USA.

International Finance Corporation (IFC) established 1956 to encourage private enterprise in developing countries. It is affiliated to the World Bank. Headquarters: 1850 I Street NW, Washington, DC 20433, USA.

Multilateral Investment Guarantee Agency (MIGA) established 1988 to encourage the flow of private investment to developing member countries. Headquarters: 1818 H Street NW, Washington, DC 20433, USA.

International Human Rights

See Also  The Era of International Criminal Responsibility, p. 504.

Universal Declaration of Human Rights: Preamble

On 10 December 1948 the General Assembly of the United Nations adopted and proclaimed the Universal Declaration of Human Rights. Following this historic act, the Assembly called upon all member countries to publicize the text of the declaration and 'to cause it to be disseminated, displayed, read, and expounded principally in schools and other educational institutions, without distinction based on the political status of countries or territories'.

Preamble

Whereas recognition of the inherent dignity and of the equal and inalienable rights of all members of the human family is the foundation of freedom, justice and peace in the world,

Whereas disregard and contempt for human rights have resulted in barbarous

acts which have outraged the conscience of mankind, and the advent of a world in which human beings shall enjoy freedom of speech and belief and freedom from fear and want has been proclaimed as the highest aspiration of the common people,

Whereas it is essential, if man is not to be compelled to have recourse, as a last resort, to rebellion against tyranny and oppression, that human rights should be protected by the rule of law,

Whereas it is essential to promote the development of friendly relations between nations,

Whereas the peoples of the United Nations have in the Charter reaffirmed their faith in fundamental human rights, in the dignity and worth of the human person and in the equal rights of men and women and have determined to promote social progress and better standards of life in larger freedom,

Whereas member states have pledged themselves to achieve, in cooperation with the United Nations, the promotion of universal respect for and observance of human rights and fundamental freedoms,

Whereas a common understanding of these rights and freedoms is of the greatest importance for the full realization of this pledge,

Now, therefore, the General Assembly proclaims this Universal Declaration of Human Rights as a common standard of achievement for all peoples and all nations, to the end that every individual and every organ of society, keeping this Declaration constantly in mind, shall strive by teaching and education to promote respect for these rights and freedoms and by progressive measures, national and international, to secure their universal and effective recognition and observance, both among the peoples of member states themselves and among the peoples of territories under their jurisdiction.

Universal Declaration of Human Rights: Articles

Article 1
All human beings are born free and equal in dignity and rights. They are endowed with reason and conscience and should act towards one another in a spirit of brotherhood.

Article 2
Everyone is entitled to all the rights and freedoms set forth in this Declaration, without distinction of any kind, such as race, colour, sex, language, religion, political or other opinion, national or social origin, property, birth, or other status. Furthermore, no distinction shall be made on the basis of the political, jurisdictional, or international status of the country or territory to which a person belongs, whether it be independent, trust, non-self-governing, or under any other limitation of sovereignty.

Article 3
Everyone has the right to life, liberty, and security of person.

Article 4
No one shall be held in slavery or servitude; slavery and the slave trade shall be prohibited in all their forms.

Article 5
No one shall be subjected to torture or to cruel, inhuman or degrading treatment or punishment.

Article 6
Everyone has the right to recognition everywhere as a person before the law.

Article 7
All are equal before the law and are entitled without any discrimination to equal protection of the law. All are entitled to equal protection against any discrimination in violation of this Declaration and against any incitement to such discrimination.

Article 8
Everyone has the right to an effective remedy by the competent national tribunals for acts violating the fundamental rights granted him by the constitution or by law.

Article 9
No one shall be subjected to arbitrary arrest, detention, or exile.

Article 10
Everyone is entitled in full equality to a fair and public hearing by an independent and impartial tribunal, in the determination of his rights and obligations and of any criminal charge against him.

Article 11
1. Everyone charged with a penal offence has the right to be presumed innocent until proved guilty according to law in a public trial at which he has had all the guarantees necessary for his defence.
2. No one shall be held guilty of any penal offence on account of any act or omission which did not constitute a penal offence, under national or international law, at the time when it was committed. Nor shall a heavier penalty be imposed than the one that was applicable at the time the penal offence was committed.

Article 12
No one shall be subjected to arbitrary interference with his privacy, family, home, or correspondence, nor to attacks upon his honour and reputation. Everyone has the right to the protection of the law against such interference or attacks.

Article 13
1. Everyone has the right to freedom of movement and residence within the borders of each state.
2. Everyone has the right to leave any country, including his own, and to return to his country.

Article 14
1. Everyone has the right to seek and to enjoy in other countries asylum from persecution.
2. This right may not be invoked in the case of prosecutions genuinely arising from nonpolitical crimes or from acts contrary to the purposes and principles of the United Nations (UN).

Article 15
1. Everyone has the right to a nationality.
2. No one shall be arbitrarily deprived of his nationality nor denied the right to change his nationality.

Article 16
1. Men and women of full age, without any limitation due to race, nationality, or religion, have the right to marry and to found a family. They are entitled to equal rights as to marriage, during marriage, and at its dissolution.
2. Marriage shall be entered into only with the free and full consent of the intending spouses.
3. The family is the natural and fundamental group unit of society and is entitled to protection by society and the state.

Article 17
1. Everyone has the right to own property alone as well as in association with others.
2. No one shall be arbitrarily deprived of his property.

Article 18
Everyone has the right to freedom of thought, conscience, and religion; this right includes freedom to change his religion or belief, and freedom, either alone or in community with others and in public or private, to manifest his religion or belief in teaching, practice, worship, and observance.

Article 19
Everyone has the right to freedom of opinion and expression; this right includes freedom to hold opinions without interference and to seek, receive and impart information and ideas through any media and regardless of frontiers.

Article 20
1. Everyone has the right to freedom of peaceful assembly and association.
2. No one may be compelled to belong to an association.

Article 21
1. Everyone has the right to take part in the government of his country, directly or through freely chosen representatives.
2. Everyone has the right of equal access to public service in his country.
3. The will of the people shall be the basis of the authority of government; this will shall be expressed in periodic and genuine elections which shall be by universal and equal suffrage and shall

be held by secret vote or by equivalent free voting procedures.

Article 22
Everyone, as a member of society, has the right to social security and is entitled to realization, through national effort and international cooperation and in accordance with the organization and resources of each state, of the economic, social, and cultural rights indispensable for his dignity and the free development of his personality.

Article 23
1. Everyone has the right to work, to free choice of employment, to just and favourable conditions of work, and to protection against unemployment.
2. Everyone, without any discrimination, has the right to equal pay for equal work.
3. Everyone who works has the right to just and favourable remuneration ensuring for himself and his family an existence worthy of human dignity, and supplemented, if necessary, by other means of social protection.
4. Everyone has the right to form and to join trade unions for the protection of his interests.

Article 24
Everyone has the right to rest and leisure, including reasonable limitation of working hours and periodic holidays with pay.

Article 25
1. Everyone has the right to a standard of living adequate for the health and well-being of himself and of his family, including food, clothing, housing, and medical care and necessary social services, and the right to security in the event of unemployment, sickness, disability, widowhood, old age, or other lack of livelihood in circumstances beyond his control.
2. Motherhood and childhood are entitled to special care and assistance. All children, whether born in or out of wedlock, shall enjoy the same social protection.

Article 26
1. Everyone has the right to education. Education shall be free, at least in the elementary and fundamental stages. Elementary education shall be compulsory. Technical and professional education shall be made generally available and higher education shall be equally accessible to all on the basis of merit.
2. Education shall be directed to the full development of the human personality and to the strengthening of respect for human rights and fundamental freedoms. It shall promote understanding, tolerance, and friendship among all nations, racial or religious groups, and shall further the activities of the UN for the maintenance of peace.
3. Parents have a prior right to choose the kind of education that shall be given to their children.

Article 27
1. Everyone has the right freely to participate in the cultural life of the community, to enjoy the arts, and to share in scientific advancement and its benefits.
2. Everyone has the right to the protection of the moral and material interests resulting from any scientific, literary, or artistic production of which he is the author.

Article 28
Everyone is entitled to a social and international order in which the rights and freedoms set forth in this Declaration can be fully realized.

Article 29
1. Everyone has duties to the community in which alone the free and full development of his personality is possible.
2. In the exercise of his rights and freedoms, everyone shall be subject only to such limitations as are determined by law solely for the purpose of securing due recognition and respect for the rights and freedoms of others and of meeting the just requirements of morality, public order, and the general welfare in a democratic society.
3. These rights and freedoms may in no case be exercised contrary to the purposes and principles of the UN.

Article 30
Nothing in this Declaration may be interpreted as implying for any state, group or person any right to engage in any activity or to perform any act aimed at the destruction of any of the rights and freedoms set forth herein.

Human Rights and Relief Organizations

ACTIONAID

International charity focusing on long-term development by working with communities in the developing world to strengthen human resources to alleviate poverty and improve quality of life. ACTIONAID operates in 24 countries.

Date established 1972

Membership over 120,000 active supporters (1998)

Funding private donations, child and community sponsorship, contributions from official bodies such as the British government and the European Union, and income from trading, such as the sale of merchandise

Address: Headquarters ACTIONAID UK, Chataway House, Leach Road, Chard, Somerset TA20 1FA, UK; phone: (01460) 62972; fax: (01460) 67191; e-mail: mail@actionaid.org.uk

Address in Ireland ACTIONAID Ireland, Unity Buildings, 16–17 O'Connell Street, Dublin 1, Republic of Ireland; phone: (01353 1) 878 7911; fax: (01353 1) 878 6245

Web site www.actionaid.org/

Amnesty International

Independent, politically-unaligned organization for the protection of human rights worldwide, as set out in the Universal Declaration of Human Rights. Amnesty campaigns for the release of prisoners of conscience; fair trials for political prisoners; and an end to torture, extrajudicial executions, 'disappearances', and the death penalty. It organizes fact-finding missions and human-rights education. Amnesty operates in more than 100 countries.

Date established 1961

Membership more than 1 million (1997)

Funding private donations and membership fees

Addresses in UK Headquarters: International Secretariat, 1 Easton Street, London WC1X 8DJ, UK; phone: (0171) 413 5500; e-mail: amnestyis@amnesty.org; 99–119 Rosebery Avenue, London EC1R 4RE, UK; phone: (0171) 814 6200; fax: (0171) 833 1510; e-mail: info@amnesty. org.uk

Web site www.amnesty.org/

British Helsinki Human Rights Group

Independent nongovernmental organization dedicated to monitoring the progress of democracy and human rights in the OSCE member states.

Date established 1992

Membership 15

Funding private

Human Rights and Human Wrongs

BY STEPHANIE POWELL

Fifty years ago, the world said 'never again' to the atrocities of World War II, the Holocaust, and the violence inflicted on occupied populations by the Germans and the Japanese. The response was the Universal Declaration of Human Rights (UDHR), which sought to 'promote and encourage respect for human rights and for fundamental freedoms for all without distinction as to race, sex, language or religion'. The establishment of human rights as a legitimate concern for all humanity has brought changes to the lives of men, women, and children worldwide. Nelson Mandela, former South African president, said: 'the simple and noble words of the Universal Declaration were a ray of hope at one of our darkest moments'. Yet despite this progress the UDHR has not brought about the end to human rights violations and the global picture continues to be far from dominated by hope.

The changing nature of the world we live in has demanded greater responsibility from governments to provide for the protection of a greater number of rights for a greater number of people. The misery of many vulnerable communities of the world today has illustrated that political and civil rights are indivisible from economic, social and cultural rights. In October 1997, the secretary-general of the United Nations, Kofi Annan, stated: 'Today we know that lasting peace requires a broader vision, encompassing education and literacy, health and nutrition, human rights and fundamental freedoms.'

All over the world governments continue to flout their obligations under refugee law.

Economic issues

The uneven acceleration of globalization has led to economic deprivation for many vulnerable communities, especially women and children. Economic deprivation, which results in the gross inability to satisfy basic human needs, afflicts over 1.3 billion people in the world, who still struggle to survive on less than $1 a day. Economic deprivation in the Russian Federation has forced many women out of the workforce in favour of men. In Pakistan some families are forced to sell their children into low-skilled and low-paid jobs where the risks of injury are often high; for instance, Iqbal Masih was sold to a carpet factory owner at the age of four for a loan of Rs600 ($12). The failure to protect these vulnerable members of society has often led to further human rights abuses, as was shown in the former conflict zone of Rwanda, where many widows faced with denied inheritance rights were forced to find homes for themselves and their families.

Mass human rights violations

The re-emergence of mass persecution based on identity has forced many to relive the nightmare of those who swore 'never again'. The spread of mass human rights violations can in part be attributed to the rise of civil conflict waged on a local, national, and regional level between differing economic, political, ethnic, or religious groups. In the last decade we have seen human rights violations of massive proportions – genocide in Rwanda where up to one million men, women, and children died in the first 100 days of conflict, and mass killings in the Democratic Republic of Congo, Afghanistan, and in the former Yugoslavia, to name but a few. As a result of these conflicts there are over 35 million men, women, and children worldwide who have been driven from their homes, villages, towns, and countries in fear. That is one person in every 115 people in the world or one person every 21 seconds. Over 75 percent of these are women and children. As a result of conflict in Afghanistan there remain over 2.6 million refugees in Pakistan and Iran alone and there are over 1.6 million Palestinians still living in refugee camps in the West Bank and Gaza Strip, some 30 years after the 1967 war.

These conflicts have led to a dramatic rise in the number of civilian casualties of war. It is estimated that over 90 percent of all casualties are civilian casualties which includes more than 2,000 children who are killed, maimed, or disabled each day as a result of conflict. There exists now a very young generation of children who have seen nothing but the perpetuation of violence. In Rwanda eight in ten children have lost a member of their family and one in two children has witnessed massacres. In northern Uganda, the Lord's Resistance Army has systematically abducted between 5,000 and 8,000 children since 1995 to fight their war. In Sierra Leone, the Armed Forces Revolutionary Council and Revolutionary United Front have abducted hundreds of young girls who have been violently raped and forced into sexual slavery. The use of terror and especially rape is rising as a weapon of war, and has been in widespread use in conflicts in Uganda, Sudan, and Kosovo.

Amnesty International

Amnesty International was founded in 1961 to promote the principles enshrined in the Universal Declaration of Human Rights. It was comparatively unknown when it won the Nobel Peace Prize in 1977 but it now has over one million members and supporters in more than 160 countries across the world. It played a vital role in bringing about the 1984 Convention against Torture and it also campaigned for the 1997 treaty banning anti-personnel landmines. Recently it joined 135 other non-governmental organizations (NGOs) who campaigned at the UN conference in Rome in July 1998 that led to the treaty to establish a permanent International Criminal Court (ICC) to try those who commit war crimes and crimes against humanity. Amnesty International, like many other organizations, is guided by a mandate which defines its work. This has been subject to continual developments, especially over the course of the last decade, with the growing need for the protection of whole communities as well as simply individuals. Amnesty International is preparing itself to face new challenges as human rights abuses continue to occur on a massive scale worldwide.

The future

The challenges for the next century will differ greatly from those we have seen until the recent years of this century. Mary Robinson,

UN High Commissioner for Human Rights, has said: 'today's human rights abuses are the causes of tomorrow's conflicts'. Discrimination against women is widespread and the protection of women has been slow – the UN World Conference on Human Rights of 1993 felt it necessary to assert that 'women's rights are human rights'. In Sierra Leone women have suffered at the hands of violent sexual assault and in Afghanistan women are denied the right to work and the right to education. Children have also suffered despite the agreement in 1989 of the UN Convention on the Rights of the Child which has been ratified by every country in the world except Somalia and the USA.

This hostility and indifference on the part of many governments, not only of those that shun the human rights ideal but also of many that claim to uphold it, must be challenged. All over the world governments continue to flout their obligations under refugee law, which puts vulnerable communities at great risk from grave human rights abuses. In 1996, in the face of widespread indifference, hundreds of thousands of Hutu refugees were forced to return to Rwanda from Zaire and Tanzania even though their lives would be in danger – an act known as refoulement. In 1998 refugees who had crossed over into Guinea were not offered sufficient protection in refugee camps and were subject to attacks by armed groups from Sierra Leone who carried out 'operation no living thing' from across the borders. In 1992 the USA intercepted a boat at sea filled with Haitian refugees and summarily returned them without examination of their asylum claims.

International Criminal Court (ICC)

The treaty establishing a permanent International Criminal Court offers a chance to bring to justice those who are responsible for committing crimes against humanity and war crimes; impunity must end and accountability must begin. The establishment of the International Criminal Tribunal for the Former Yugoslavia and the International Criminal Tribunal for Rwanda has marked some progress. In 1998 the Rwanda tribunal addressed the question of rape in war and convicted a man of sexual violence in the Rwandan genocide of 1994. The arrest of General Augusto Pinochet, the former military ruler of Chile, for crimes against humanity and the indictment of President Slobodan Milošević for war crimes continued this process. The permanent International Criminal Court must be seen as a chance to put an end to impunity in all countries of the world.

As Amnesty International has said: 'We must not only accept our own responsibilities but the existence of the responsibilities of others. A permanent International Criminal Court would ensure that those who suffer, do not do so in vain or in silence.'

Stephanie Powell, Amnesty International UK Section

Address British Helsinki Human Rights Group, 22 St Margaret's Road, Oxford, UK; phone: (01865) 510 564; fax: (01865) 510 564; e-mail: bhhrg@bhhrg.org

Web site www.bhhrg.org/

CARE International

Nonprofit, nongovernmental organization aiming to relieve human suffering, to provide economic opportunity, and to build sustained capacity for self-help. CARE International operates in 77 countries.

Date established 1946

Membership not a membership organization

Funding corporate and private donations, government grants, contributions in kind, such as agricultural produce donated by governments

Address: Headquarters Boulevard de Régent 58/10, B-1000 Brussels, Belgium; phone: (32 2) 502 4333; fax: (32 2) 502 8202

Address in UK CARE UK, 36–38 Southampton Street, London WC2E 7AF, UK; phone: (0171) 379 5247; fax: (0171) 379 0543

Web site www.care.org/

Caritas Internationalis (International Confederation of Catholic Organizations for Charitable and Social Action)

Confederation of national Catholic organizations that helps coordinate its members' efforts in emergency aid, rehabilitation, and development, with the objective of spreading charity and social justice worldwide.

Date established 1950

Membership 146 member organizations in 194 countries and territories

Funding membership fees

Address: Headquarters Palazzo San Calisto 16, V-00120 Città del Vaticano, Vatican, Italy; phone: (39 6) 6988 7197; fax: (39 6) 6988 7237; e-mail: ci.comm@caritas.va

Casa Alianza

Nonprofit organization attempting to rehabilitate and protect street children in Guatemala, Honduras, and Mexico. It monitors and cares for children who have been orphaned by civil war, or abused or rejected by their families. Casa Alianza is a subsidiary of the US-based aid organization Covenant House.

Date established 1981

Membership not a membership organization

Address Covenant House Latin America PO Box 2050-1734, San Pedro, San José, Costa Rica; phone: (506) 253 5439; fax: (506) 224 5689; e-mail: bruce@casa-alianza.org

Mailing address SJO 1039, PO Box 025216, Miami, FL 33102-5216, USA

Web site www.casa-alianza.org/

Children's Aid Direct

A UK-based charity which aims to make an immediate and lasting improvement to the lives of children and their carers who are affected by conflict, poverty, or disaster.

Date established 1990

Membership not a membership organization

Funding EU, US and other governments, corporate sponsorship, private donations

Address 12 Portman Road, Reading RG30 1EA, UK; phone: (0118) 958 4000; fax: (0118) 958 8988; e-mail 100523,3025@compuserve.com

Web site www.cad.org.uk

Concern Worldwide

Nongovernmental organization providing relief, assistance, and advancement to people in need in less developed areas of the world. Concern operates in 13 countries throughout Asia, Africa, and Latin America.

Date established 1968

Membership not a membership organization

Funding private donations and co-funding

Address: Headquarters Camden Street, Dublin 2, Ireland; phone: (01353 1) 475 4162; fax: (01353 1) 475 7362; e-mail: cncernd@iol.ie

Address in UK Concern Worldwide UK, 248–250 Lavender Hill, London SW11 1LJ, UK; phone: (0171) 738 1033; fax: (0171) 738 1032; e-mail: concernl.london@btinernet.com

Web site www.irishnet.com/concern.htm

Human Rights Watch

Politically unaligned charity that reports on practices affecting human rights. It documents and publicizes imprisonments, censorship, violation of human-rights laws, and abuses of internationally recognized human rights. It covers more than 70 countries.

Date established 1978 (as Helsinki Watch)

Membership not a membership organization

Funding grants from foundations; private donations

Address: Headquarters 350 Fifth Avenue, New York, NY 10118-3299, USA; phone: (212) 290 4700; fax: (212) 736 1300; e-mail: hrwnyc@hrw.org

Address in UK 33 Islington High Street, London N1 9LH, UK; phone: (0171) 713 1995; fax: (0171) 713 1800; e-mail: hrwatchuk@gn.apc.org

Web site www.hrw.org/

International Committee of the Red Cross (ICRC)

Umbrella body for national Red Cross and Red Crescent societies. It is a neutral, impartial, and independent humanitarian institution. The Red Cross was set up to help all victims of war and internal violence, by providing medical assistance, organizing humanitarian relief, and attempting to ensure implementation of rules restricting armed violence. It also helps victims of natural disasters. The Red Cross operates in more than 50 countries.

Date established 1863

Membership not a membership organization

Funding grants from the states party to the Geneva Convention, and from international organizations such as the European Union, public funds, money from national Red Cross and Red Crescent societies, private donations

Address: Headquarters Public Information Division, 19 Avenue de la Paix, CH 1202 Geneva, Switzerland; phone: (41 22) 734 6001; fax: (41 22) 734 2057; e-mail (press or operational information): press.gva@icrc.org

Web site www.icrc.org/

Médecins Sans Frontières International (MSF)

Nonprofit humanitarian organization offering assistance to populations in distress and to victims of disasters or armed conflict. MSF volunteers provide primary health care, operate emergency nutrition and sanitation programmes, and train local medical staff. MSF observes strict impartiality and neutrality in the name of universal medical ethics and demands full freedom in exercising its functions. MSF is independent of political, religious, or economic influence, and operates in 80 countries.

Date established 1971

Membership not a membership organization

Funding private donations and grants from international organizations and governments

Address: Headquarters 39 Rue de la Tourelle, B-1040, Brussels, Belgium; phone: (32 3) 280 1881; fax: (32 2) 280 0173

Address in UK 124–132 Clerkenwell Road, London EC1R 5DL, UK; phone: (0171) 713 5600; fax: (0171) 713 5004

Web site www.msf.org/ and www.dwb.org/

Minority Rights Group International (MRG)

Educational trust aiming to secure justice for minority or majority groups suffering discrimination; to alert public opinion to violations of human rights; and to foster international understanding of the factors that cause prejudice. The organization has contacts and groups in 25 countries.

Date established 1970

Membership not a membership organization

Funding private donations and the sale of publications

Address 379 Brixton Road, Brixton, London SW9 7DE, UK; phone: (0171) 978 9498; fax: (0171) 738 6265

Oxfam

Charity aiming to put an end to poverty worldwide. It provides assistance for development and relief by working in partnership with local groups, helping poor people to help themselves. Oxfam campaigns internationally, gives poor people channels to voice their concerns, funds long-term projects such as education and training, and provides emergency aid. The organization operates in over 70 countries. Oxfam UK is a member of Oxfam International.

Date established 1942

Membership not a membership organization

Funding donations from individuals, groups, companies, and trusts; grants from the UK Department for International Development, the European Union, United Nations agencies, and governments

Address: Headquarters 274 Banbury Road, Oxford OX2 7DZ, UK; phone: (01865) 311 311; fax: (01865) 313 770; e-mail: oxfam@oxfam.org.uk

Web site www.oxfam.org.uk/

Panos Institute

Organization aiming to provide access to, and freedom of, information on environmental and social development issues, and to help minority and marginal groups to gain access to a wider public and to government and decisionmaking bodies. Panos operates in southern and southeast Asia, and eastern and southern Africa.

Date established 1986

Membership not a membership organization

Address: Headquarters 10 rue de Mail, 75002 Paris, France; phone: (33 1) 4041 0550; fax: (33 1) 4041 0330; e-mail: panos@worldnet.fr

Address in UK Panos London, 9 White Lion Street, London N1 9PD, UK; phone: (0171) 278 1111; fax: (0171) 278 0345; e-mail: panoslondon@gn.apc.org

Web site www.oneworld.org/panos/

Raoul Wallenberg Institute of Human Rights and Humanitarian Law

Charitable trust promoting research, training, and academic education in the fields of human rights and humanitarian law. It organizes programmes in developing countries, especially in Asia and Africa, for government officials, prison administrators, police, judges, and so on; some courses are also held at the University of Lund, Sweden, where the research library is maintained.

Date established 1984

Membership not a membership organization

Funding supported by grants from the Swedish Ministry for Foreign Affairs and the Swedish International Development Cooperation Agency

Address: Headquarters Stora Gråbrödersgatan 17, PO Box 1155, S-221 05 Lund, Sweden; phone: (46) 222 1200; fax: (46) 222 1222

Web site www.ldc.lu.se/raoul/

Save the Children Fund

Charity aiming to achieve lasting benefits for children within the communities in which they live by influencing policy and practice in tackling the underlying causes of poverty. The organization operates in more than 50 countries.

Date established 1919

Membership not a membership organization

Funding government grants, private and corporate donations, shops and trading, donations from sister charities

Address: Headquarters 17 Grove Lane, London SE5 8RD, UK; phone: (0171) 703 5400; fax: (0171) 703 2278; e-mail: info@scflondon.ccmail.compuserve.com

Web site www.oneworld.org/scf/

Survival International

Charity supporting tribal peoples worldwide. It stands for their right to decide their own future and helps them protect their lives, lands, and human rights. It works closely with local indigenous organizations and focuses especially on tribal peoples most recently in contact with the outside world. There were cases in 36 countries worldwide in 1998.

Date established 1969

Membership 18,000 members in 75 countries (1998)

Funding donations from members, private individuals and organizations

Address: Headquarters 11–15 Emerald Street, London WC1N 3QL, UK; phone: (0171) 242 1441; fax: (0171) 242 1771; e-mail: survival@gn.apc.org

Web site www.survival.org.uk/

Voluntary Service Overseas (VSO)

Organization aiming to enable men and women to work alongside people in poorer countries in order to share skills, build capabilities, and promote international understanding and action, in the pursuit of a more equitable world. VSO has recruitment offices in the UK, Canada, and the Netherlands, and operates in 59 countries, with more than 1,950 volunteers overseas in 1997.

Date established 1958

Membership not a membership organization

Funding private donations and foundation grants

Address: Headquarters 317 Putney Bridge Road, London SW15 2PN, UK; phone: (0181) 780 7200; fax: (0181) 780 7300; e-mail: sbernau@vso.org.uk

Web site www.oneworld.org/vso/

WomenAid International

International humanitarian aid and development agency aiming to provide relief and assistance to women and children suffering distress caused by war, disasters or poverty; to empower women through education, training, and provision of credit; and to campaign against violations of women's human rights.

Date established 1988

Membership not a membership organization

Funding various international, national and individual sources

Address 3 Whitehall Court, Whitehall, London SW1A 2EL, UK; phone: (0171) 839 1790; fax: (0171) 839 2929; e-mail: womenaid@womenaid.org

Web site www.womenaid.org/

Refugees

Numbers of Refugees Worldwide

The total number of people of concern to UNHCR rose from 17 million in 1991 to a record 27 million in 1995. In the last three years, however, the number dropped to 22.3 million as of 1 January 1998. Despite the overall fall, this figure still represents one out of every 264 people on earth. They include refugees, returnees, and persons displaced within their own countries. Worldwide, there are an estimated 30 million internally displaced persons (IDPs) and UNHCR assists an estimated 4.5 million of them in various regions. Thus, the total number of people who have been forced to flee their home, whether refugees or IDPs, is around 50 million.

Region	Refugees	Returnees	Asylum seekers and others of concern	Internally displaced people and others of concern	Total of concern to UNHCR (as of 1 Jan 1998)
Africa	3,481,700	2,171,700	37,700	1,694,000	7,385,100
Asia	4,730,300	824,100	15,000	1,889,100	7,458,500
Europe	2,940,700	459,400	267,400	2,389,000	6,056,500
Latin America	83,200	17,800	600	1,700	103,300
North America	688,500	–	626,400	–	1,294,900
Oceania	71,100	–	6,900	–	78,000
Total	11,975,500	3,473,000	954,000	5,973,800	22,376,300

Source: United Nations High Commissioner for Refugees

Destinations of Kosovar Refugees

Destinations of Kosovar refugees evacuated from Macedonia under the UNHCR/IOM Humanitarian Evacuation Program, between 5 April and 3 June 1999.

Receiving Country	Total arrivals	Receiving Country	Total arrivals	Receiving Country	Total arrivals
Australia	2,486	Iceland	70	Slovakia	90
Austria	4,890	Ireland, Republic of	749	Slovenia	483
Belgium	1,223	Israel	206	Spain	1,240
Canada	5,154	Italy	5,829	Sweden	2,768
Croatia	284	Malta	105	Switzerland	1,350
Czech Republic	824	Netherlands	3,681	Turkey	5,581
Denmark	2,168	Norway	6,070	UK	2,459
Finland	958	Poland	1,049	USA	5,370
France	4,756	Portugal	952	**Total**	76,475
Germany	13,639	Romania	41		

Source: United Nations High Commissioner for Refugees

The Kosovo Refugee Crisis: Chronology

1 February 1990 The Yugoslav government sends troops to the Serbian province of Kosovo in an attempt to end clashes between ethnic Albanians and the Serbian authorities.

28 September 1990 The Serbian parliament in Yugoslavia adopts a new constitution, stripping the province of Kosovo of its autonomy.

17 March 1991 Serbia suspends the constitution of Kosovo, and the use of the Albanian language for official purposes is declared illegal.

1 March 1998 Serbia sends troops into Kosovo to flush out ethnic Albanian secessionist paramilitaries. Hundreds of men, women, and children are killed over the next few weeks. The fighting sets off a new wave of displacement.

July 1998 By early July approximately a third of the 200,000 Serbs living in Kosovo have left the province, while ethnic Albanians have returned to fight Serbian forces.

29 July 1998 After four days of fighting, Serb forces overrun Kosovo, routing the Kosovo Liberation Army (KLA). Over 100,000 ethnic Albanians are displaced.

August 1998 United Nations High Commissioner for Refugees (UNHCR)-led multi-agency aid convoys reach more than 250,000 displaced people affected by the conflict in Kosovo.

8 September 1998 Racing against time, international aid agencies ask donors for $54.3 million to avert a humanitarian crisis in the coming winter in Kosovo. An estimated 350,000 Kosovars flee abroad or became internally displaced March–September.

27 October 1998 Yugoslav President Milošević bows to NATO pressure and agrees to a cease-fire and partial pull-out of Yugoslav military and police forces from Kosovo.

October–December 1998 Daily violence undermines fragile truce.

13 November 1998 US special envoy Richard Holbrooke brokers a deal with President Milošević that temporarily suspends the threat of NATO air strikes against Serbia, contingent on Serbia upholding the October ultimatum.

1998 According to UNHCR, more than a quarter of all asylum requests in Europe during this year are made by people from Kosovo.

15 January 1999 The massacre of 45 ethnic Albanians at the village of Racak in Kosovo by Serbian Interior Ministry police shatters the cease-fire agreed in October and renews the threat of NATO bombing. Most of the 2,000 residents of Racak flee their homes by 17 January, heading for the woods or the nearby town of Stimlje.

18 January 1999 The UN High Commissioner for Refugees Sadako Ogata warns that fighting in the Stimlje region has once again forced people to flee into the hills and that children are reported to be dying in the cold. Renewed fighting since Christmas has forced more than 20,000 people to flee at least 23 villages.

23 February 1999 Tentative agreement on substantial autonomy for Kosovo is reached in Rambouillet, France.

3 March 1999 International efforts continue in Kosovo to help 4,000 ethnic Albanians who fled their homes in recent days because of fighting between Serb security forces and KLA rebels. Many mountain villages near to the town of Kacanik and the border town of Jankovic are abandoned by their residents.

22 March 1999 US special envoy Richard Holbrooke warns Milošević of air strikes unless he signs the peace agreement (signed by the Kosovo Albanians 18 March). Milošević refuses.

24 March 1999 NATO launches air war against Yugoslav military targets.

27 March 1999 Thousands of ethnic Albanians – mostly women and children fleeing or expelled from Kosovo – begin flooding into Albania and Macedonia, telling of door-to-door raids, looting, and burning by Serb forces.

April 1999 Tens of thousands of refugees, some packed shoulder to shoulder into trains, pour out of Kosovo, seeking safety in Albania, Macedonia, Montenegro, and Bosnia-Herzegovina.

1 April 1999 The largest daily influx of refugees goes up to 40,000 people, who arrive by train, car, or on foot in Macedonia, coming mostly from the Kosovo capital of Pristina. They tell UNHCR staff that they were

(continued)

The Kosovo Refugee Crisis: Chronology *(continued)*

forced at gunpoint to leave their homes; many were stripped of their identity documents and herded onto overcrowded trains.

6 April 1999 The UNHCR chairs an emergency meeting on Kosovo refugees, calling for an international commitment to ensure the safety of those fleeing the province. More than 400,000 people have fled or were expelled from Kosovo during the past two weeks, in Europe's largest refugee exodus since the war in Bosnia.

15 April 1999 NATO acknowledges mistakenly bombing a refugee convoy of ethnic Albanians under Serb police escort. Yugoslav officials say 75 people died and more than two dozen were injured.

30 April 1999 UNHCR urges non-European countries to take in Kosovo refugees as the refugee crisis in Macedonia worsens.

May 1999 The sweeping ethnic cleansing and expulsions from Kosovo continue. Trains, buses, and tractor wagons from Kosovo continue to offload refugees into neighbouring areas. Although there are no deaths from starvation and no epidemics break out, conditions in the overcrowded refugee camps remain poor, and sanitation facilities are rudimentary.

5 May 1999 Macedonia closes its border for one day, pushing back up to 1,000 refugees, saying it cannot cope with mass arrivals of refugees. Macedonian officials claim the country has taken in too many refugees since NATO began its air campaign in March, expressing fears the refugee influx could upset the country's ethnic balance and aggravate economic problems. The Albanian government says it is willing to take in more people and NATO agrees to build new camps there.

8 May 1999 About 6,000 new refugees cross the border into Albania, the majority coming from western Kosovo. Some of them say that Serb forces shelled their homes and ordered them to leave. The EU's acting commissioner for humanitarian affairs, Emma Bonino, criticizes the international relief effort to help the refugees, saying it lacks coordination.

9 May 1999 Preparations are made to move approximately 60,000 Kosovo refugees sheltering in Macedonia into neighbouring Albania to ease the burden on the Macedonian government.

13 May 1999 Eighty-seven Albanians are killed and more than 100 injured, Yugoslavia says, in a NATO bombing of Korisa, a Kosovo village. NATO says Korisa is a Serb military command post, and suggests Serb forces trapped the refugees next to the target as human shields.

16 May 1999 Aid workers in Macedonia say about 700 refugees enter the country from Kosovo, the largest single influx since the Macedonian government temporarily closed the border 10 days earlier. Refugee organizations say the Yugoslav army seizes up to 150 male refugees as they try to flee to Albania and Bosnia via Montenegro. A UN humanitarian mission arrives in Belgrade to assess the needs of civilians across the country over a 10-day period, particularly in Kosovo. The mission is the first of its kind in Yugoslavia since NATO's bombardment started 24 March.

18 May 1999 Several hundred Kosovo Albanian refugees are allowed to leave Kosovo, a day after Serb military forces turned back their train at the border with Macedonia without explanation, forcing them back into the province.

22 May 1999 The head of NATO's humanitarian force in Albania warns that it could take up to two years to return all refugees to Kosovo. It could take that time to repair the devastation caused by Serb forces. The numbers of internally displaced people meanwhile remains uncertain. The leader of the KLA, Hashim Thaci, who appears in public for the first time in two months, says he believes that 600,000 civilians are now living in the open in Kosovo in extremely difficult conditions.

30 May 1999 About a thousand Kosovo refugees arrive on the Italian coast over a period of 24 hours, ferried there by smugglers.

3 June 1999 Yugoslavia's government accepts a Western-backed peace plan to resolve the Kosovo crisis and allow the return of more than 850,000 ethnic Albanians to the province. Under the peace plan, the UNHCR will take the lead role in the repatriation movement.

4 June 1999 According to UNHCR, the estimated number of refugees and displaced people in the region is 782,100: 69,300 in Montenegro, 247,800 in Macedonia, 443,300 in Albania, and 21,700 in Bosnia-Herzegovina. The number of humanitarian evacuees from Macedonian camps to European countries, Australia, Canada, and the USA totals 76,475. According to unverified Yugoslav government reports, there are 60,000 displaced people from Kosovo who have fled to other parts of Serbia.

9 June 1999 After five days of talks on the Macedonian border, Serbia's top generals sign a military agreement with the NATO commander General Michael Jackson on the immediate Serb withdrawal from the province.

12 June 1999 The first of the NATO peacekeeping troops in Kosovo reach the provincial capital, Pristina. The deployment – one of the biggest military operations in Europe since World War II – is intended to help the hundreds of thousands of Albanian Kosovo refugees return home, though they are warned that the province will have to be made safe. The UNHCR urges caution over how quickly the refugees can return to normal life, and says the entire effort to return refugees depends on the state of the province after the Serb withdrawal and the shape of any political settlement which follows.

Web Sites

ActionAid Home Page

http://www.actionaid.org/

Home page of one of the UK's leading development agencies that includes good resources for teachers.

Amnesty International Online

http://www.amnesty.org/

Home page of the world's foremost human rights organization, with easily accessible information on its structure, current campaigns, and how you can help. There is a library of documents on human rights for every corner of the world.

Baltic Assembly, Baltic Council of Ministers, and Nordic Council

http://www.lrs.lt/baltasm/indexa.htm

Official guide to the regional coordination mechanisms for the Baltic States.

CARE International

http://www.care.org/

Home page of the UK office of CARE International, a confederation of agencies that delivers relief assistance to people in need. The page provides links to all CARE members, and statistics on hunger, poverty, AIDS, the abuse of the environment, children's malnutrition, and illiteracy.

Commonwealth Institute

http://www.commonwealth.org.uk/

Full outline of the role of the Commonwealth Institute. In addition to general information about the Commonwealth and its institutions, there are details of current exhibitions at the Institute. There are also extensive links to embassies, tourist offices, and other institutions in Commonwealth states.

Commonwealth of Independent States (CIS)

http://www.rochester.k12.mn.us/kellogg/rodgers/cis/thecis.htm

Educational site featuring maps and regional guides for the CIS, as well as homework exercises. The history of the area is also analysed in some depth.

Council of Europe

http://www.coe.fr/

Home page of the 50-year-old Strasbourg-based organization charged with strengthening democracy, human rights, and the rule of law among the 40 member states. There is a large documentary archive.

Current Leaders Worldwide

http://web.jet.es/ziaorarr/00now.htm

This site offers a regularly updated resource on current heads of state and government for every country. Other features include 'Political Leaders 1945–99', 'Women World Leaders 1945–99', 'European Governments 1990–99', 'First African Rulers', and 'Political Obituary 1990–99'.

Earthrise

http://earthrise.sdsc.edu/

Earthrise is a growing database of Earth images taken by astronauts from space over the last 15 years. Users can search the image database by keyword, or by clickable topographical and political maps, or just view the highlights.

European and Asian Documents on Fourth World Affairs

http://www.halcyon.com/FWDP/eurasia.html

Extensive text archive on the indigenous people of Europe and Asia maintained by the Fourth World Documentation Project, aimed at educating the international community about the problems that these largely unrecognized national populations face within their states.

European Union

http://europa.eu.int/

Official, multilingual site for the European Union.

G8 Information Center

http://www.g7.utoronto.ca/

Run by the University of Toronto, this site details the economic summits and meetings of the Group of Seven and Group of Eight, and provides copies of relevant documents.

Geographia

http://www.geographia.com/

Excellent site for travellers to explore future destinations. The information is divided into five regional sections, with additional special features on selected locations. The text is supplemented by pictures, videos, and sound clips.

Greatest Places

http://www.greatestplaces.org/

This site takes you on a journey to seven of the most geographically dynamic locations on earth. It features stylish presentation with extensive pictures and cultural commmentary.

Great Globe Gallery

http://hum.amu.edu.pl/~zbzw/glob/glob1.htm

Over 200 globes and maps, showing the earth from all angles, including space shots, political maps, the ancient world, geographical features, and animated spinning globes.

International Committee of the Red Cross

http://www.icrc.org/

Home page of the Red Cross Movement, with frequently updated reports on the charity's operations in more than 50 countries. There is extensive coverage of issues surrounding international humanitarian law, as well as of current Red Cross campaigning issues.

Médecins Sans Frontières (MSF)

http://www.msf.org/

MSF promote access to essential medical aid wherever it is needed, and their Web site attempts to raise awareness of the plight of people in need of treatment. The site also includes a 'Doctor's diary'.

Metropolis – World Association of the Major Metropolises

http://www.metropolis.org/anglais/index.html

Information on the world's major metropolises, providing comparisons of urban strategies and development in the world's leading metropolitan areas. The site includes a directory of member cities and details of the work of Metropolis' four standing commissions.

National Geographic Online

http://www.nationalgeographic.com

Large and lavishly illustrated Web site. Features include the Map Machine Atlas, which allows you to find maps, flags, facts, and profiles for the countries of the world, and discussion forums on a variety of subjects.

Oceania – Documents on Fourth World Affairs

http://www.halcyon.com/FWDP/melpac.html

Extensive text archive on the indigenous people of Oceania. This database aims to increase knowledge and understanding of the problems that these largely unrecognized national populations face within their states. It is maintained by the Fourth World Documentation Project.

Organization for Security and Cooperation in Europe

http://www.osceprag.cz/

Site of the UN organization charged with keeping the peace in Europe. It contains regularly updated information on the work being done around such issues as arms control, election monitoring, and conflict prevention.

Organization of African Unity

http://www.oau-oua.org/

Site of the organization aiming to improve economic, cultural, and political cooperation in Africa. The organization's charter, history, and structures are comprehensively explained. There is frequently updated information on summits, commissions, and job vacancies, in addition to recent press releases.

Organization of American States

http://www.oas.org/

Home page of the alliance of states working towards social and economic development in Latin America. There is an explanation of the organization's structure and its work on issues such as drugs, corruption, poverty, environment, trade, education, democracy, and human rights. Its online magazine (in English and Spanish) may also be accessed.

Our Modern Commonwealth

http://www.rhouse.co.uk/rhouse/rcs/modcom/

General guide to the Commonwealth organized by the Royal Commonwealth Institute. The notes for teachers and worksheets for children are designed to be used by schools in all Commonwealth countries. The material on foods, games, and oral traditions in a large number of countries is interesting and well prepared.

Royal Geographical Society

http://www.rgs.org/

Mine of information for both geographers and non-specialists, including events organized by the RGS, online exhibitions, field expeditions and research projects, publications, and links to other geographical organizations.

Save the Children Fund

http://www.oneworld.org/scf/

Home page of the UK's leading children's charity, with extensive information on its work nationally and in more than 50 other countries. Key topics in international development are presented in a lively manner.

6 Billion Human Beings

http://www.popexpo.net/home.htm

From the Musée de l'Homme in Paris, an interactive site about population growth. It explains the causes for the rapid growth of population over the last 200 years, and why it might stabilize over the next century. You can find out the world's population in the year you were born, and see a ticking counter of the current population as it reaches the six billion mark.

Treaty Establishing the European Community

http://europa.eu.int/abc/obj/treaties/en/entoc05.htm

Complete text of the founding document of the European Economic Community. This is provided by the European Union and includes all associated protocols and documents of ratification.

UNICEF United Nations Children's Fund

http://www.unicef.org/

This is a comprehensive guide to the work of the agency and the tasks it has set itself. As well as providing excellent statistical data and narrative information, there is a section on 'Voices of Youth', with quizzes, discussion forums, and educational activities. UNICEF's annual 'State of the World's Children' report can also be accessed here.

United Nations Educational, Scientific, and Cultural Organization

http://www.unesco.org/

This site details UNESCO's work in 186 countries, the organization's structure and history, its programmes and publications, and current events. There are also links to UNESCO's 60 field offices and information on internships and employment with the agency.

United Nations Environment Programme

http://www.unep.org/

Beginning with an assessment of the state of the global environment, the UNEP site examines environmental issues and the means of addressing them, as well as surveying the problems encountered in different regions and countries.

United Nations Home Page

http://www.un.org/

Official site providing a general overview of the United Nations with news, photographs, key documents, and links to UN departments and information resources.

VolcanoWorld

http://volcano.und.edu

Comprehensive site on volcanoes, with details of the most recent eruptions, currently active volcanoes, a glossary, images and video clips, and even a list of extraterrestrial volcanoes

Voluntary Service Overseas (VSO)

http://www.vso.org.uk/

Opportunities to work as a volunteer in the developing world, as well as information about VSO campaigns, events, and publications. The site includes volunteers reports from all over the globe for those considering applying to the scheme.

Welcome to Oxfam UK and Ireland

http://www.oxfam.org/

Web site of the UK's foremost nongovernmental development and relief agency, giving comprehensive information on Oxfam's work around the world and regular updates of its current campaigns.

WomenAid International

http://www.womenaid.org/

Home page of the organization that seeks to promote women's human rights around the world, through education, training, and provision of credit.

World Factbook

http://www.odci.gov/cia/publications/factbook/

Annual factbook produced by the CIA on countries of the world. It provides exhaustive information on each country, divided into sections on geography, people, government, economy, communications, transportation, and transnational issues. There are also maps and flags.

World Population Estimates

http://www.popin.org/pop1998/

Online edition of the United Nations' '1998 Revision of the World Population Estimates and Projections', which outlines the standard set of population figures used throughout the UN system. The site includes a projected estimate of the world population in 2050, and an assessment of the global demographic impact of HIV/AIDS.

Village

http://www.worldvillage.org/

What if the world were a village inhabited by 1,000 people? This site provides some thought-provoking answers, by scaling down statistics to figures that are easier to comprehend

Education

The Year in Review

8 July 1998 Britain's Higher Education Funding Council issues a report accusing several universities of lowering the standards needed to achieve a degree. The council names 15 universities where standards are said to have dropped.

14 July 1998 Britain's chancellor of the exchequer, Gordon Brown, announces an extra £40 billion for health and education over the next three years.

18 July 1998 The British government announces radical plans for performance-related pay for teachers, claiming that the existing pay structure makes it difficult to recruit and retain talented people in the profession. The proposal is immediately condemned by teaching unions, including The National Union of Teachers, which threaten to strike if the government goes through with its proposal of introducing performance-related pay.

August 1998 A record number of pupils pass their A-levels: 92.5 percent in Wales and 87.8 percent in the rest of the UK. Critics of the exam claim that standards are dropping and A-levels are getting easier.

24 August 1998 In Britain, education minister for Wales Peter Hain announces a plan to encourage schools to hire unemployed people as classroom assistants. The plan is part of the New Deal programme to help the long-term unemployed find work.

27 August 1998 GCSE results reveal a slight increase in pupils achieving C grades and above but a large increase from 81,228 to 123,121 in the number of failures. Critics blame the recent emphasis on school performance league tables, for teaching schools to concentrate on the more able students to improve the overall results of the school, with the low-achievers receiving less attention.

17 September 1998 British higher education minister Baroness Blackstone announces that A-levels will be made easier in 2000 to encourage more pupils to stay at school. She claims that the exams are currently elitist and prevent many young people from working-class families from going to university. A-levels are currently already criticized for being too easy.

18 September 1998 British chief inspector of schools Chris Woodhead receives another five-year contract and a pay rise of 34 percent, angering teachers' unions which contrast it to the 2.5 percent pay rise for teachers.

26 September 1998 The National Union of Teachers, Britain's largest teaching union, threatens to strike, demanding a 10 percent pay rise will be classified as rejecting government plans for performance-related pay.

15 October 1998 Secondary-school students march through Paris, France, protesting against understaffing and poor facilities.

30 October 1998 The British government increases the mark needed to pass National Curriculum reading tests for 7-year-olds. Under the new criteria, 40 percent of 7-year-olds will be classified as unable to read.

November 1998 A US National Institute of Health expert panel on Attention Deficit Hyperactivity Disorder (ADHD) concludes that while Ritalin, a medication for ADHD, improves behaviour, it does not improve academic achievement. In Britain the prescription of Ritalin doubles each year.

Grammar schools threatened *Keri Johnson takes a GCSE woodworking lesson at Queen Mary's High School for Girls in Walsall, which may lose its status as a grammar school following legislation passed in November 1998 which permits local ballots on grammar schools' futures.* Photo: Richard Watt

November 1998 British education secretary David Blunkett presents a Green Paper on the teaching profession that includes plans to offer a fast-track promotion scheme for 1,000 bright graduates a year as part of an initiative to institute performance-related pay for teachers.

25 November 1998 British education secretary David Blunkett announces that the government will spend £1.5 billion to repair school buildings over the next three years.

11 December 1998 Chris Woodhead, the chief inspector of British schools, condemns National Curriculum testing as unreliable.

14 January 1999 The British government announces plans for a scheme costing up to £10 million for special revision classes outside normal school hours to help 11-year-olds pass their exams. Critics of the scheme claim that it is being used by the government to meet ambitious targets of raising test results in maths and English by 2002. Education Secretary David Blunkett promises to resign if the targets are not met.

11 March 1999 Oxford and Cambridge Universities in England launch a campaign to try to change their elitist image by publishing the results of a survey of state school pupils and teachers. According to the results, many state school pupils did not apply to the universities because of the perceived difficulty of getting a place. Last year admissions of students from state schools were 44 percent at Oxford and 46 percent at Cambridge, as compared to 61 percent across all British universities.

13 May 1999 Britain's ruling Labour government announces that it is abandoning much of the National Curriculum, introduced 11 years ago by the Conservatives. Of the original 10 subjects, only English and diluted versions of mathematics and physical education are to be compulsory for students aged 5–16, from September 2000.

21 June 1999 The British government announces that the number of failing schools is decreasing for the first time since 1993, when the Office for Standards in Education (Ofsted) introduced schemes for improvement of sub-standard schools.

World Education

Enrolment Ratios by Level of Education

The data in this table are for the latest year available. Only those countries for which data are available are listed. In some countries a relatively high number of pupils outside the official age range for the respective levels of education attends classes of these levels. Since the enrolment ratio given is for the total enrolment, regardless of age, divided by the population of the official age group, if a country has almost universal education among the school-age population at the first level, the enrolment ratio given will exceed 100. As the school year, in a number of countries, does not coincide with the academic year, the year shown in this table is the one in which the school or academic year starts.
(In percentages. N/A = not available.)

Country	Year	1st level[1]	2nd level[2]	3rd level[3]
Afghanistan	1995	49	22	N/A
Albania	1995	101	35	11.1
Algeria	1996	107	63	12.0[4]
Angola	1991	88	14	0.7
Argentina	1996	113	77	36.2
Armenia	1995	82	79	N/A
Australia	1996	103	153	75.6
Austria	1995	100	103	46.6
Azerbaijan	1996	107	77	17.5
Bahamas	1995	100	86	N/A
Bahrain	1996	106	94	20.2[5]
Bangladesh	1990	69	21	4.4
Barbados	1991	90	85[6]	29.4[5]
Belarus	1996	98	93	44.0
Belgium	1994	103	146	54.4
Belize	1994	121	49	N/A
Benin	1996	76	17	3.1
Bolivia	1990	95	37	22.2
Botswana	1996	112	66	5.8
Brazil	1997	123	45[7]	11.3[7]
Brunei	1996	107	77	6.6
Bulgaria	1996	99	77	41.2
Burkina Faso	1995	40	6[5]	1.0
Burundi	1995	51	7	0.9
Cambodia	1996	131	24	1.4
Cameroon	1994	88	27	N/A
Canada	1995	102[7]	106	90.2
Cape Verde	1993	131	27	N/A
Central African Republic	1991	58	10	1.4
Chad	1996	65	10	0.6[4]
Chile	1996	101	75	30.3
China	1996	120	71	5.7
Colombia	1996	118	72	18.6
Comoros	1995	74	22	0.6
Congo, Democratic Republic of	1994	72	26	2.3
Congo, Republic of the	1995	114	53	N/A
Costa Rica	1996	107	50	31.9[9]
Côte d'Ivoire	1996	71	24	4.5[7]
Croatia	1996	87	82	27.9[4]
Cuba	1996	106	77	12.4
Cyprus	1995	100	97	20.0
Czech Republic	1995	104	99	21.9
Denmark	1995	100	120	45.0
Djibouti	1996	38	14	0.3
Dominican Republic	1994	103	41	N/A
Ecuador	1996	127	54[7]	N/A
Egypt	1996	102	75	20.3[4]
El Salvador	1996	94	33	16.7
Eritrea	1996	54	21	1.0
Estonia	1996	94	104	41.8
Ethiopia	1995	37	11	0.7
Fiji Islands	1992	128	64	11.9[8]
Finland	1995	100	116	70.3
France	1995	106	111	51.0
Gambia	1995	77	25	1.7[7]
Georgia	1996	84	73	39.9
Germany	1995	103	102	44.4
Ghana	1991	76	37	1.4[9]
Greece	1995	94	96	42.5
Guatemala	1996	84	25	8.1[4]
Guinea	1995	48	12	1.2
Guinea-Bissau	1994	64	N/A	N/A
Guyana	1995	95	75	9.7
Haiti	1990	56	22	N/A
Honduras	1994	111	32[5]	10.0
Hong Kong	1995	96	75	21.9[5]
Hungary	1995	104	99	23.8
Iceland	1995	98	104	35.6
India	1996	101	49	6.9
Indonesia	1994	114	48	11.1
Iran	1996	90	74	17.1
Iraq	1995	85	42	11.2
Ireland, Republic of	1995	103	115	38.5
Israel	1995	99	89	41.1
Italy	1995	99	88	41.4
Jamaica	1996	107	64[9]	8.1
Japan	1996	102	99[7]	40.3[7]
Jordan	1992	94	63[6]	24.5[6]
Kazakhstan	1996	96	85	32.7[4]
Kenya	1995	85	24	N/A
Korea, South	1996	94	102	60.3
Kuwait	1996	75	65	25.4[4]
Kyrgyzstan	1995	107	81	12.2
Laos	1996	111	29	2.8
Latvia	1996	96	84	33.3

(continued)

Enrolment Ratios by Level of Education (*continued*)

Country	Year	1st level[1]	2nd level[2]	3rd level[3]
Lebanon	1996	111	82	27.0[4]
Lesotho	1996	97	29	2.4
Libya	1993	110	97[4]	N/A
Lithuania	1996	98	86	31.4
Luxembourg[11]	1994	99	80	N/A
Macedonia, Former Yugoslav Republic of	1996	88	58	18.1
Madagascar	1995	73	13	2.1
Malawi	1995	135	16	0.6
Malaysia	1996	91	58	10.6[7]
Maldives	1997	125	49[5]	N/A
Mali	1996	37	9[7]	N/A
Malta	1996	110	89[4]	21.8[7]
Mauritania	1996	83	16[4]	3.9[4]
Mauritius	1996	107	65	6.5
Mexico	1995	115	61	15.3
Moldova	1996	96	79	26.1
Mongolia	1996	89	56	17.0
Morocco	1996	84	39	11.1[7]
Mozambique	1995	60	7	0.5
Myanmar	1995	100	32	5.4[7]
Namibia	1996	131	61	8.1[4]
Nepal	1994	110	38[5]	5.2[5]
Netherlands	1995	107	137	48.6
New Zealand	1996	103	120	58.5
Nicaragua	1995	110	47	9.4
Niger	1996	29	7	N/A
Nigeria	1994	89	30	4.1[5]
Norway	1995	99	117	58.5
Oman	1996	77	66	6.4
Pakistan	1993	74	26[8]	3.0[8]
Panama	1995	106	68	30.0
Papua New Guinea	1995	80	14	3.2
Paraguay	1996	112	43	11.4
Peru	1995	122	70	31.1[7]
Philippines	1996	117	79	29.7[4]
Poland	1995	96	98	24.7
Portugal	1994	128	106	36.08
Qatar	1995	86	80	27.6
Romania	1996	104	78	22.5
Russia	1994	108	87[5]	42.9
Rwanda	1991	82	11	0.6[6]
Samoa	1997	107	62[10]	N/A
Saudi Arabia	1996	76	61	16.3
Senegal	1996	69	16	3.4[7]
Sierra Leone	1990	50	17	1.3
Singapore	1996	94	72	38.5
Slovak Republic	1996	102	94	22.1
Slovenia	1996	105	93	36.4
Solomon Islands	1994	97	17	N/A
South Africa	1996	116	84	17.3
Spain	1995	105	121	48.6
Sri Lanka	1996	109	75[4]	5.1[4]
Sudan	1996	53	20	N/A
Swaziland	1996	129	52	6.0
Sweden	1995	105	136	46.0
Switzerland	1995	107[5]	91[5]	32.9
Syria	1996	101	42	15.7[7]
Tajikistan	1996	93	76	19.9
Tanzania	1996	66	5	0.5[4]
Thailand	1996	88	57	20.1[4]
Togo	1996	119	27	3.6
Trinidad and Tobago	1995	96	72	7.8
Tunisia	1996	114	66	13.7
Turkey	1994	105	56	18.2
Turkmenistan	1990	N/A	N/A	21.8
Uganda[12]	1995	73	12	1.7
UK	1995	116	133	49.5
Ukraine	1993	87	91	40.6
United Arab Emirates	1996	89	79	11.9
Uruguay	1996	113	85	29.4
USA	1995	102	97	81.0
Uzbekistan	1994	77	93	32.9[13]
Vanuatu	1992	106	20	N/A
Venezuela	1996	91	40	29.0[9]
Vietnam	1995	114	41[7]	4.1
Yemen	1996	70	34	4.2
Yugoslavia	1996	71	64	22.5
Zambia	1995	89	28[7]	2.5[7]
Zimbabwe	1996	113	48	6.5

[1] These figures are for education at the first level, of which the main function is to provide the basic elements of education (for example, at elementary school and primary school).

[2] These figures are for education at the second level, provided at middle school, secondary school, high school, teacher training school at this level, and schools of a vocational or technical nature. This level of education is based upon at least four years' previous instruction at first level and provides general and/or specialized instruction.

[3] These figures are for education at the third level, which is provided at universities, teachers' colleges, and higher professional schools, and which requires, as a minimum condition of entry, the successful completion of education at the second level, or evidence of the attainment of an equivalent level of knowledge.

[4] Figures for 1995.

[5] Figures for 1993.

[6] Figures for 1989.

[7] Figures for 1994.

[8] Figures for 1991.

[9] Figures for 1990.

[10] Figure for 1996.

[11] Some students study in neighbouring countries.

[12] These figures are for government maintained and aided schools.

[13] Figure for 1992.

Source: *UNESCO Statistical Yearbook 1998,* © UNESCO 1998

Countries with the Highest Pupil–Teacher Ratios at First Level of Education

These figures are for education at the first level, of which the main function is to provide the basic elements of education (for example, at elementary school and primary school). Data for each country are for the year in parentheses and are the most recent available.

Rank	Country	Pupils per teacher
1	Central African Republic (1990–91)	77
2=	Congo, Republic of the (1995–96)	70
	Mali (1995)	70
4	Chad (1996–97)	67
5	Bangladesh (1990)	63
6	Malawi (1995–96)	59
7=	Afghanistan (1994)	58
	Mozambique (1995)	58
	Rwanda (1991–92)	58
10	Benin (1996–97)	56
11	Equatorial Guinea (1993–94)	55
12	Gabon (1995–96)	51

Source: *UNESCO Statistical Yearbook 1998,* © UNESCO 1998

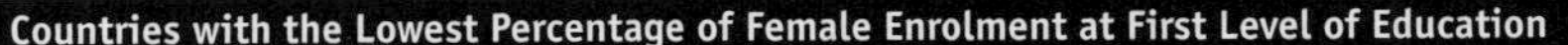

Countries with the Lowest Percentage of Female Enrolment at First Level of Education

These figures are for education at the first level, of which the main function is to provide the basic elements of education (for example, at elementary school and primary school). Data for each country are for the year in parentheses and are the most recent available.

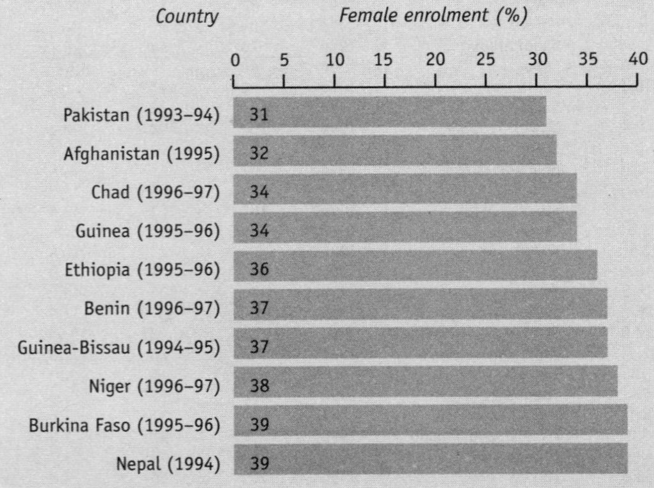

Source: *UNESCO Statistical Yearbook 1998,* © UNESCO 1998

Percentage of Children Attending School Around the World

Figures show the number of children enrolled in primary school as a percentage of the total number of children in the primary school age group. Data are for around 1995.

Region	%
Sub-Saharan Africa	57
South Asia	68
Middle East and North Africa	81
CEE/CIS[1] and Baltics	94
Latin America and Caribbean	92
East Asia and Pacific	96
Industrialized countries average	98

[1] Former USSR.

Source: *State of the World's Children 1999,* © UNICEF and UNESCO 1998

Countries with the Lowest Pupil–Teacher Ratios at First Level of Education

These figures are for education at the first level, of which the main function is to provide the basic elements of education (for example, at elementary school and primary school). Data for each country are for the year in parentheses and are the most recent available.

Rank	Country	Pupils per teacher
1	San Marino (1996–97)	5
2	Qatar (1995–96)	9
3	Denmark (1994–95)	10
4=	Hungary (1994–95)	11
	Italy (1995–96)	11
	Sweden (1994–95)	11
7=	Austria (1995–96)	12
	Belgium (1993–94)	12
	Cuba (1996–97)	12
	Portugal (1993–94)	12
11=	Luxembourg (1990–91	13
	Saudi Arabia (1996–97)	13

Source: *UNESCO Statistical Yearbook 1998,* © UNESCO 1998

Public Expenditure on Education by Region of the World

Data for countries of the former USSR are not included in either the world total or regional totals because there is insufficient information to calculate valid estimates for these countries.

Region	Public expenditure on education ($ thousand millions)				Public expenditure on education (% of GNP)				Public expenditure on education per inhabitant ($)			
	1980	1985	1990	1995	1980	1985	1990	1995	1980	1985	1990	1995
Africa	22.9	22.0	25.7	29.1	5.3	5.7	5.6	5.9	48	40	41	41
America	188.6	249.5	374.9	481.7	4.9	4.9	5.2	5.3	307	375	521	623
Asia	93.8	107.6	199.8	302.1	4.0	3.9	3.7	3.6	37	39	66	93
Europe	200.6	165.8	367.5	492.6	5.1	5.1	5.1	5.4	418	340	741	982
Oceania	10.4	10.6	18.6	24.5	5.6	5.6	5.6	6.0	467	439	715	878
World total	516.4	555.6	986.5	1,329.9	4.8	4.8	4.8	4.9	126	124	202	252

Source: *UNESCO Statistical Yearbook 1997,* © UNESCO 1997

World Illiteracy Rates: Highest 25 Countries

The percentages in this table are all estimates.

1995

Rank	Country	Illiterates (%)
1	Niger	86.4
2	Burkina Faso	80.8
3	Nepal	72.5
4	Mali	69.0
5	Sierra Leone	68.6
6	Afghanistan	68.5
7	Senegal	66.9
8	Burundi	64.7
9	Ethiopia	64.5
10	Guinea	64.1
11	Benin	63.0
12	Mauritania	62.3
13	Pakistan	62.2
14	Bangladesh	61.9
15	Liberia	61.7
16	Gambia	61.4
17=	Côte d'Ivoire	59.9
	Mozambique	59.9
19	Angola	59.0[1]
20	Bhutan	57.8
21	Morocco	56.3
22	Haiti	55.0
23	Madagascar	54.3
24	Sudan	53.9
25	Chad	51.9

[1] This is a 1985 estimate.

Source: *UNESCO Statistical Yearbook 1997,* © UNESCO 1997

Estimated Illiterate Population Around the World

Figures are for people aged 15 and over. (In millions.)

Region	1985			1995			2005		
	Men and women total	Women	Women (% of total)	Men and women total	Women	Women (% of total)	Men and women total	Women	Women (% of total)
More developed regions and countries in transition	22.5	15.6	69.3	12.9	7.9	61.6	8.6	5.0	58.4
Less developed regions	863.3	544.4	63.1	871.8	556.7	63.9	860.9	553.2	64.3
Of which:									
Sub-Saharan Africa	132.0	80.6	61.1	140.5	87.1	62.0	145.4	91.0	62.5
Arab States	59.8	37.1	62.0	65.5	41.2	62.9	69.4	44.1	63.5
Latin America/Caribbean	43.8	24.5	56.0	42.9	23.4	54.7	41.2	21.9	53.3
Eastern Asia/Oceania	258.5	177.8	68.8	209.9	149.5	71.2	152.9	112.7	73.7
Of which:									
China	205.4	141.6	68.9	166.2	119.5	71.9	118.4	89.1	75.3
Southern Asia	370.4	224.3	60.6	415.5	256.1	61.6	456.1	285.0	62.5
Of which:									
India	265.9	164.0	61.7	290.7	182.7	62.8	308.8	196.6	63.7
Least developed countries	144.7	87.0	60.2	165.9	100.8	60.7	188.1	115.1	61.2
World total	885.9	560.1	63.2	884.7	564.7	63.8	869.5	558.2	64.2

Source: *World Education Report,* © UNESCO 1998

Literacy Levels in Selected Developed Countries

In England, about one adult in five is not functionally literate and many more people have problems with numeracy. Some seven million adults in England (one in five adults) if given the alphabetical index of the Yellow Pages, cannot locate the page reference for plumbers. That is an example of functional illiteracy. It means that one in five adults has less literacy than is expected of an 11-year-old child. The data in this table (based on official surveys) are inevitably estimates, and may be a little on the high side: but the order of magnitude is certainly right.

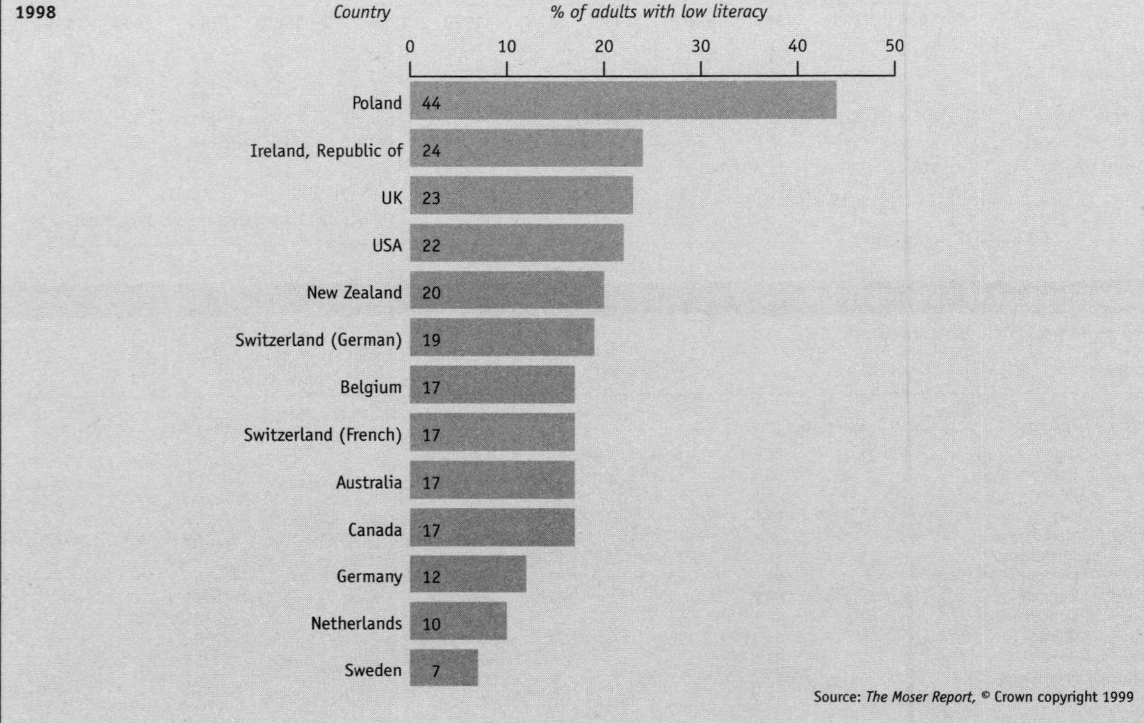

Source: *The Moser Report,* © Crown copyright 1999

Participation in Education of Students Aged 15 and Over, by Age Group, in Selected Countries

The data in this table include apprenticeships in countries such as Austria, Germany, and Switzerland, which operate a dual system. All figures include full-time and part-time students. Enrolment rates are for public and private institutions.
(N/A = not available. N = nil or negligible.)

1996

Country	Minimum leaving age	15–19 (%)	20–29 (%)	30–39 (%)	40 and over (%)
Argentina	14	51.3	16.5	2.7	0.4
Australia	15	82.6	24.5	13.6	5.3
Austria	15	75.7	16.8	2.7	0.3
Belgium	18	92.1	N/A	N/A	N/A
Brazil	14	66.2	16.3	4.1	1.2
Canada	16	78.6	21.4	4.7	1.2
Chile	14	N/A	N/A	N/A	N/A
China	14	N/A	N/A	N/A	N/A
Denmark	16	79.6	26.0	4.9	0.7
Finland	16	81.8	29.6	6.8	1.2
France	16	88.3	19.1	N/A	N/A
Germany	18	87.9	20.5	2.5	0.1
Greece	14.5	72.0	12.0	0.1	0.1
India	14	N/A	N/A	N/A	N/A
Indonesia	15	33.9	7.1	N	N
Ireland, Republic of	15	79.3	14.6	[1]	[1]
Jordan	15	67.3	N/A	N/A	N/A
Korea, South	14	78.3	16.0	0.6	N
Malaysia	16	36.2	6.5	0.2	N
Mexico	15	35.6	8.4	0.5	0.1
Netherlands	18	88.5	23.7	3.8	0.7
New Zealand	16	75.3	19.4	8.1	2.6
Norway	16	83.8	25.2	4.9	1.0
Paraguay	14	N/A	N/A	N/A	N/A
Philippines	12	47.3	21.1	0.6	0.1
Portugal	14	67.5	20.5	3.6	0.5
Russia	15	N/A	N/A	N/A	N/A
Spain	16	73.8	21.8	2.2	0.2
Sweden	16	83.3	23.6	8.9	1.8
Switzerland	15	80.6	15.8	N/A	N/A
Thailand	14	37.2	1.7	N/A	N/A
UK	16	72.1	17.5	8.4	3.3
Uruguay	15	55.3	16.8	3.0	0.3
USA	17	72.9	20.0	5.9	7.7

[1] Data included in another category/column of the table.

Source: *Education at a Glance,* © OECD 1998

UK Schools and Teachers

Pupils Under Five Years of Age in Nursery and Primary Schools in England

As of January for the year shown.

Year	Number of pupils	Percentage of population at previous 31 December: Nursery schools and classes	All pupils under 5	Pupil:teacher ratio
1989	547,564	24	45	23.9
1991	603,586	25	48	24.2
1993	656,711	26	51	24.8
1995	699,844	27	53	25.0
1997	713,509	29	56	24.1
1998	720,478	29	57	24.5

Source: *Statistics of Education: Schools in England 1998,* © Crown copyright 1998

National Curriculum Key Stages

Children's year groups are labelled year 1 to year 11 and within these years learning is divided into four key stages.

Key stage	School year	Age
	reception	4–5
1	year 1	5–6
	year 2	6–7
2	year 3	7–8
	year 4	8–9
	year 5	9–10
	year 6	10–11
3	year 7	11–12
	year 8	12–13
	year 9	13–14
4 (GCSE)	year 10	14–15
	year 11	15–16

Pupils Reaching or Exceeding Expected Standards in Assessments and Tests in England

The government has set targets for 11 year olds. At the end of Key Stage 2, a typical 11 year old is expected to achieve level 4 on the National Curriculum scale. By the year 2002, 75 percent are to attain level 4 in mathematics and 80 percent to attain the same level in English. (In percentages. – = not applicable.)

1997

Assessment/ test	Teacher assessment		Tests	
	Boys	Girls	Boys	Girls
Key Stage 1[1]				
English	75	85	–	–
Mathematics	82	86	82	85
Science	84	86	–	–
Key Stage 2[2]				
English	57	70	57	70
Mathematics	63	65	63	61
Science	68	70	68	69
Key Stage 3[3]				
English	52	70	48	67
Mathematics	62	65	60	60
Science	60	63	61	60

1 Percentage of pupils achieving level 2 or above.
2 Percentage of pupils achieving level 4 or above.
3 Percentage of pupils achieving level 5 or above.

Source: *Social Trends 29,* © Crown copyright 1999

Number of School Pupils by Type of School in the UK

(– = not applicable. N/A = not available.)

School	1970–71	1980–81	1990–91	1995–96	1996–97	1997–98[1]
Public Sector Schools[2]						
Nursery[3]	50,000	89,000	105,000	84,000	110,000	110,000
Primary[3]	5,902,000	5,171,000	4,955,000	5,338,000	5,354,000	5,383,000
Secondary						
modern	1,164,000	233,000	94,000	78,000	63,000	82,000
grammar	673,000	149,000	156,000	189,000	191,000	193,000
comprehensive[4]	1,313,000	3,730,000	2,843,000	3,129,000	3,170,000	3,181,000
other	403,000	434,000	300,000	282,000	288,000	287,000
All public sector schools total	9,507,000	9,806,000	8,453,000	9,099,000	9,174,000	9,236,000
Non-maintained schools total[2]	621,000	619,000	613,000	603,000	609,000	615,000
Special schools total[5]	103,000	148,000	114,000	115,000	116,000	116,000
Pupil referral units total	–	–	–	N/A	8,000	8,000
TOTAL	10,230,000	10,572,000	9,180,000	9,816,000	9,908,000	9,975,000

1 Data for Wales are provisional.
2 Excludes special schools.
3 Nursery classes within primary schools are included in primary schools except for Scotland in 1990–91, in which instance they are included in nursery schools.
4 Excludes sixth form colleges from 1980–81.
5 Includes maintained and non-maintained sectors.

Source: *Social Trends 29,* © Crown copyright 1999

An Overview of the School System in the UK

by Maureen O'Connor

Organization

School education in the UK is a national service locally administered, which means that policies enacted by the national government at Westminster are put into practice by Local Education Authorities (LEAs) in England and Wales, Education Authorities (EAs) in Scotland, and Education and Library Boards in Northern Ireland. These authorities are part of the democratic system of borough and county councils.

Under the Conservative administration (1979–97) some schools were given greater autonomy, but the Labour government is bringing these grant-maintained schools back into a more direct relationship with their LEAs as 'foundation' schools. Funding advantages have been phased out.

State schools have boards of governors drawn from parents, the LEA, and the local community. The governors are responsible for school policy and for overseeing the school's budget. The headteacher is responsible for the day-to-day running of the school, and for discipline.

Seven percent of British children attend fee-paying private schools, which range from famous 'public' schools, such as Eton and Harrow, which are run as non-profitmaking charities, to small private establishments run as businesses. Many private schools have a highly selected intake and are very successful in public examinations.

Growing concern about the performance of schools in some deprived inner-city areas has led the Labour government to set up Education Action Zones. Schools in these areas will be run by partnerships that involve business and industry as well as the LEA. They will be encouraged to innovate and experiment, in an effort to raise standards.

Funding

The main funding for state schools is provided by central government grants to LEAs, with a smaller proportion coming from local taxes. Many schools also raise funds through their parent–teacher associations, and increasingly through sponsorship from business and industry. Individual school budgets are determined by the LEA, but governors have responsibility for allocating funds internally.

Types of school

Schooling in the UK is divided into primary and secondary sectors, with the change of school at age 11 (12 in Scotland). The state system includes a few middle schools taking children from 9 to 13, and private sector secondary schools commonly recruit at 13.

Compulsory schooling begins at five, although an increasing proportion of four-year-olds is being accommodated in primary schools. Nursery education for three- and four-year-olds is not compulsory, but has been expanding in recent years. The Labour government has expanded provision to provide places in either pre-schools or reception classes for all four-year-olds whose parents want it.

The state school system allows some schools to be run in partnership with religious denominations. The majority of these voluntary-aided schools are associated with the Roman Catholic Church or the Church of England. There is a small number of Jewish schools, and approval has recently been given for two Muslim schools to receive government funding.

The vast majority of state secondary schools are comprehensive, which means that they admit children regardless of ability. A few local authorities still maintain selective (grammar) schools, which admit children on the results of an entrance test. The Labour government elected in 1997 is opposed to selection by ability, and has legislated to allow parents of affected children to ballot on whether local grammar schools should remain selective or become comprehensive.

Some other forms of specialization at secondary level were encouraged by the previous, Conservative, government and have been continued by the Labour government. A minority of schools specialize, for example, in technology, languages, or the performing arts. Additional funding is provided for such schools, and admission is by an assessment of aptitude in the specialist subjects, regardless of general academic ability.

When a school is unable to admit all the children who have applied for places, decisions about whether a child can attend a chosen school are usually made on the basis of how close a family lives to the school. There is an appeal system for families who are not satisfied with admissions decisions.

Roughly two percent of children who have serious disabilities or learning difficulties that cannot be catered for in mainstream education are taught in special day or residential schools. Most children with special needs are given additional help within mainstream classrooms. There is a five-stage process of assessing special educational needs and the help children require to enable them to benefit from their education. Children with the most serious difficulties may at the fifth stage of the assessment process be eligible for a statement of special educational needs (SEN) which spells out what help their school – either mainstream or special – must provide. Parents may appeal to an official tribunal if they are not happy with their child's lack of a statement.

Compulsory education ends at the age of 16, and although the majority of young people remain in education after that age, they have the option of moving into different institutions. Young people studying for academic qualifications beyond 16 may take the two-year A level course at their school sixth form or move to a sixth form college. Those seeking vocational courses may opt to switch to a college of further education. A growing number of tertiary colleges offer 16- to 18-year-olds a range of academic and vocational courses in the same institution.

Curriculum

A National Curriculum was established by the Education Reform Act of 1988, under the Conservative government. This act laid down detailed programmes of study for all ten main subjects, as well as eight levels of performance that an average child might be expected to attain between the ages of 5 and 16. Learning is divided into 4 Key Stages for children between 5 and 7, 7 and 11, 11 and 14, and 14 and 16.

As the National Curriculum was put into practice over a five-year period it became apparent that it was extremely onerous

for teachers and pupils, particularly in primary schools. The curriculum was slimmed down after an inquiry conducted by Sir Ron Dearing in 1996, and shortly after taking office in 1997, the Labour government relaxed the requirements for humanities and arts subjects in primary schools, to allow more time to be spent on English, maths, and science. The whole National Curriculum is in the course of being revised for the year 2000. The Labour government has set ambitious targets for achievement in literacy and numeracy extending beyond that year.

Public examinations and testing

British schoolchildren are subjected to more external assessment than any others in the world. Since the introduction of the National Curriculum, pupils have been assessed regularly by a combination of teacher assessment and national tests that are externally marked at the ages of 7, 11, and 14. Public examinations follow at 16 and 18.

From September 1999 there will be a new level of assessment when children start school at five. This 'base-line assessment' conducted in the reception class by teachers will cover six areas: personal and social development; language and literacy; mathematical development; knowledge and under-standing of the world; physical development; and creative development. Schemes are being developed locally but must be accredited by the national body responsible for the implementation of the National Curriculum and assessment regulations. Baseline assessment is closely linked to the government's Desirable Outcomes for Children's Learning on Entering Compulsory Education, which were introduced in 1996. The new assessment is intended to help teachers plan children's work and monitor their progress. It is also anticipated that it will enable progress to be measured when children take their first end of Key Stage tests (SATs) at seven.

There is some debate about the desirability of introducing children under five to the more formal aspects of literacy. The debate has intensified now that 55 percent of four-year-olds are joining primary school reception classes rather than traditional nursery classes or pre-school groups.

The Key Stage tests are related to the attainment targets in the National Curriculum for English and maths at 7, and for English, maths, and science at 11 and 14. Other National Curriculum subjects are not tested. The expectation is that a typical 7-year-old will have reached Level 2, a typical 11-year-old Level 4, and a typical 14-year-old Level 5 or 6. Special arrangements are made to accommodate the minority of children who are unlikely to reach these levels, or who will significantly exceed them. A National Literacy Hour and a National Numeracy Hour have been recommended to primary schools for introduction in 1998 and 1999 as a means of ensuring children reach ambitious government targets of 80 percent at Level 2 in English and 75 percent in maths by 2002.

Results of the Key Stage tests are published annually on an individual school and an LEA basis, and used by government and the media as a basis for comparisons. There is considerable debate about the usefulness of test results as a measure of a school or LEA's performance, given the number of other variables that affect a school.

British children go through a dual system of school-leaving examination. This system consists of GCSE (Standard Grade in Scotland) taken at 16, and A levels taken at 18 (Highers at 17 in Scotland). There is also a parallel system of vocational qualifications. The Scottish school system is in the course of introducing a joint system of academic and vocational qualifications at 17.

It is expected that the majority of children will sit a GCSE examination in most of the ten National Curriculum subjects. Young people intending to study at university usually take three A levels or five Scottish Higher subjects, and entry to a degree course is dependent upon their performance in these exams. Vocational qualifications are also accepted as a qualification for higher education, and are regarded as particularly appropriate for students wanting to study for a vocational diploma or degree course.

Inspection

Schools in England are regularly inspected by the Office for Standards in Education (Ofsted). Ofsted is an independent government department separate from the Department of Education and Employment and headed by Her Majesty's Chief Inspector of Schools. Its main task is to manage a system of regular inspection for all 24,000 schools. (Scotland, Wales, and Northern Ireland have their own systems of inspection.) All state schools, and pre-schools in receipt of public funds, are inspected on a four-year cycle and inspection reports are published.

Inspections are carried out by independent teams of inspectors led by Ofsted-trained Registered Inspectors and including one lay member. Teams will vary in number according to the size of a school but may be as large as 14 for a large secondary school inspection. Inspection contracts are won by competitive tender and inspections are carried out according to a published national framework. Parents are involved in the inspection process by being invited to a pre-inspection meeting and by being sent a summary copy of the inspection report. Inspection covers all aspects of a school's life, from financial management and governance to teaching quality. A school is required to respond to its inspection report by producing an action plan to rectify any areas deemed below standard.

If a school is deemed to be 'failing' it is put under 'special measures' by Ofsted and required to produce and implement a detailed action plan. Inspectors return to assess progress and it is generally expected to improve rapidly if it is to avoid closure. Two years is usually the maximum time allowed to demonstrate clear improvement.

The inspection process is underpinned by Her Majesty's Inspectorate, employed by Ofsted to regulate and monitor the system, and to inspect other aspects of the education system such as independent schools, teacher training, LEAs, and aspects of further education.

Consultation began in autumn 1998 on a new system of school inspection, which would allow for a lighter inspection regime for schools which are recognized to be performing well.

Maureen O'Connor is a writer on education for The Independent *and* Times Educational Supplement

Number of Primary, Secondary, and Special Schools in the UK

(N/A = not available.)

Type of school	1984–85	1986–87	1988–89	1990–91	1992–93	1993–94	1994–95	1995–96	1996–97[1]
Public Sector Mainstream									
Primary									
Total	24,993	24,609	24,344	24,135	23,829	23,673	23,516	23,426	23,306
of which grant maintained	N/A	N/A	N/A	N/A	75	265	415	453	488
Secondary[2]									
Total	5,262	5,091	4,894	4,790	4,648	4,496	4,479	4,462	4,438
of which grant maintained	N/A	N/A	N/A	50	266	564	634	654	664
of which sixth form colleges	N/A	N/A	N/A	N/A	119	N/A	N/A	N/A	N/A
Non-Maintained Mainstream									
Total	2,599	2,544	2,542	2,508	2,476	2,478	2,433	2,436	2,526
of which City Technology Colleges (CTCs)	N/A	N/A	N/A	N/A	14	15	15	15	15
Special									
Total	1,949	1,915	1,873	1,830	1,768	1,742	1,749	1,567	1,532
Maintained									
Total	N/A	N/A	N/A	N/A	N/A	1,670	1,638	1,458	1,432
of which grant maintained	N/A	N/A	N/A	N/A	N/A	N/A	2	9	18
Non-maintained	N/A	N/A	N/A	N/A	N/A	72	111	109	100
Pupil Referral Units									
Total	N/A	N/A	N/A	N/A	N/A	N/A	N/A	287	333

[1] Figures are provisional. They include 1995–96 schools data for Wales.

[2] From 1 April 1993, figures exclude sixth form colleges in England and Wales as these colleges were reclassified as further education colleges.

Source: *Annual Abstract of Statistics 1999,* © Crown copyright 1999

Local Education Authorities in England with the Greatest Number of Small Primary School Classes

The data in this table are for primary schools maintained by the local education authority. As of January 1998.

Rank	Local education authority	Number of classes with 1–20 pupils
1	Hertfordshire	361
2	Essex	337
3	Suffolk	328
4	Cheshire	314
5	Staffordshire	291
6	Norfolk	284
7	Lancashire	282
8	Surrey	263
9	North Yorkshire	252
10	Kent	249
11	Devon	239
12	Hereford and Worcester	219
13	Cumbria	216
14	Birmingham	209

Source: *Statistics of Education: Schools in England 1998,* © Crown copyright 1998

Local Education Authorities in England with the Greatest Number of Large Primary School Classes

The data in this table are for primary schools maintained by the local education authority. As of January 1998.

Rank	Local education authority	Number of classes with 41 or more pupils
1	Manchester	19
2	Derbyshire	18
3	Nottinghamshire	16
4=	Bedfordshire	14
	Dudley	14
	Luton	14
	Staffordshire	14
8	Bolton	11
9	Norfolk	9
10=	Leicester City	8
	North East Lincolnshire	8
	Salford	8
13=	Buckinghamshire	7
	Lancashire	7
15=	Devon	6
	North Lincolnshire	6
	North Yorkshire	6

Source: *Statistics of Education: Schools in England 1998,* © Crown copyright 1998

Local Education Authorities in England with the Greatest Number of Small Secondary School Classes

The data in this table are for secondary schools maintained by the local education authority. As of January 1998.

Rank	Local education authority	Number of classes with 1–20 pupils
1	Kent	2,082
2	Essex	1,628
3	Hertfordshire	1,502
4	Lancashire	1,339
5	Birmingham	1,143
6	Cheshire	1,130
7	Berkshire	1,017
8	Nottinghamshire	1,011
9	Devon	1,006
10	Hampshire	946

Source: *Statistics of Education: Schools in England 1998,* © Crown copyright 1998

Local Education Authorities in England with the Greatest Number of Large Secondary School Classes

The data in this table are for secondary schools maintained by the local education authority. As of January 1998.

Rank	Local education authority	Number of classes with 41 or more pupils
1	Suffolk	28
2	Durham	13
3	Nottinghamshire	12
4	Bedfordshire	11
5=	Hampshire	10
	Hertfordshire	10
7=	Cheshire	8
	Kent	8
	Wirral	8
10	North Tyneside	7
11=	Buckinghamshire	6
	Devon	6
	Hereford and Worcester	6
	Lancashire	6
	Manchester	6
	Norfolk	6
	Northumberland	6
	Westminster	6
18=	Berkshire	5
	Bexley	5
	East Sussex	5
	Lincolnshire	5
	Sefton	5
	Somerset	5
24=	Kirklees	4
	Leicestershire	4
	Shropshire	4
	Staffordshire	4
	Stoke	4
	West Sussex	4

Source: *Statistics of Education: Schools in England 1998,* © Crown copyright 1998

GCE, GCSE, CSE, and SCE Qualifications Obtained by School Pupils in the UK

Data up to 1990–91 relate to school leavers. From 1991–92, data relate to pupils of any age for Great Britain and school leavers for Northern Ireland. From 1992–93 figures exclude sixth form colleges in England, which were reclassified as further education colleges from 1 April 1993. (N/A = not available.)

Qualification	1985–86	1990–91	1993–94	1994–95	1995–96	1996–1997
Male[1]						
Pupils with GCE A level/SCE H grade passes or equivalent						
2 or more A, 3 or more H	66,000	72,000	67,000	67,000	70,000	74,000
1 A, or 2 H	16,000	14,000	23,000	24,000	16,000	17,000
Pupils with GCSE/GCE O level/CSE/SCE O grades alone						
5 or more A–C awards[2]/CSE grade 1	44,000	40,000	133,000	145,000	151,000	152,000
1–4 A–C awards[2]/CSE grade 1[3]	108,000	85,000	135,000	132,000	136,000	132,000
Total school leavers	444,000	338,000	N/A	N/A	N/A	N/A
Female[1]						
Pupils with GCE A level/SCE H grade passes or equivalent						
2 or more A, 3 or more H	61,000	76,000	72,000	73,000	76,000	82,000
1 A, or 2 H	18,000	17,000	27,000	29,000	18,000	18,000
Pupils with GCSE/GCE O level/CSE/SCE O grades alone						
5 or more A–C awards[2]/CSE grade 1	51,000	51,000	155,000	170,000	180,000	181,000
1–4 A–C awards[2]/CSE grade 1[3]	123,000	87,000	137,000	135,000	137,000	132,000
Total school leavers	427,000	323,000	N/A	N/A	N/A	N/A

(continued)

GCE, GCSE, CSE, and SCE Qualifications Obtained by School Pupils in the UK (*continued*)

Qualification	1985–86	1990–91	1993–94	1994–95	1995–96	1996–1997
All						
Pupils with GCE A level/SCE H grade passes or equivalent						
2 or more A, 3 or more H	127,000	148,000	139,000	140,000	145,000	156,000
1 A, or 2 H	34,000	31,000	51,000	53,000	34,000	35,000
Pupils with GCSE/GCE O level/CSE/SCE O grades alone						
5 or more A–C awards[2]/CSE grade 1	95,000	91,000	288,000	315,000	331,000	332,000
1-4 A–C awards[2]/CSE grade 1[3]	231,000	172,000	272,000	267,000	273,000	264,000
Total school leavers	871,000	661,000	N/A	N/A	N/A	N/A
Numbers of pupils who left school in Great Britain with no GCSE/GCE/SCE or CSE qualifications	95,000	49,000	N/A	N/A	N/A	N/A

[1] From 1993–94, male and female figures are estimated for Northern Ireland.
[2] From 1993–94, grades A*–C at GCSE.
[3] Includes pupils with 1 AS level for England and Wales.

Source: *Annual Abstract of Statistics 1999*, © Crown copyright 1999

Number of Pupils Attaining GCSE and A level/AS in Foreign Languages in England

1996–97

GCSE Entries and Passes at A*–C of All Candidates in All Schools and Further Education Sector Colleges

Subject group	Boys		Girls		Total	
	Entries	Passes grades A*–C	Entries	Passes grades A*–C	Entries	Passes grades A*–C
French	147,031	61,658	165,982	91,963	313,013	153,621
German	61,268	28,687	69,419	42,410	130,687	71,097
Spanish	16,270	7,587	24,575	15,126	40,845	22,713
Other modern languages	11,222	7,561	14,770	11,398	25,992	18,959
All subjects[1]	2,524,533	1,216,349	2,561,848	1,446,996	5,086,381	2,663,345

GCE A level/AS Examination Entries and Passes[2] of All 17-Year-Old Pupils[3] in All Schools and of All Candidates in Further Education (FE) Sector Colleges

Subject group	Total 17-year-old pupils in schools				Total candidates in FE colleges			
	A/AS entries		A/AS passes		A/AS entries		A/AS passes	
	Boys	Girls	Boys	Girls	Boys	Girls	Boys	Girls
French	4,903	10,460	4,476	9,573	1,529	4,470	1,245	3,720
German	2,096	4,361	1,923	4,008	748	1,753	615	1,502
Spanish	875	1,933	837	1,765	536	1,303	461	1,136
Other modern languages	746	992	688	944	686	1,249	532	1,041
All subjects	63,190	67,122	60,519	65,002	51,629	70,556	41,697	58,554

[1] Each science double award entry is counted as two entries in the All subjects category.
[2] Each AS entry/pass counts as half an A level.
[3] Those pupils aged 17 at 31 August 1996.

Source: *Statistics of Education: Public Examinations GCSE/GNVQ and GCE in England 1997*, © Crown copyright 1998

School League Tables

BY MAUREEN O'CONNOR

The publication of school examination and test results in England is still controversial. It was introduced by the Conservative government in the early 1990s as part of their drive to impose market forces on the education system. The theory was that if performance became public knowledge, failing schools would either make greater efforts to improve or else parents would abandon them in favour of more successful institutions, and the poor schools would eventually wither and die.

Almost a decade later it is clear that the mountains of information that are now made available to parents about GCSE and A level results, about the SATs tests for 11- and 14-year olds, and about such matters as truancy and rates of improvement, have not affected education in quite the ways anticipated.

There are several reasons for this. The first is simply that the mechanisms of school choice have never allowed a genuine market to work, regardless of whether or not that is desirable. Successful schools often cannot expand because they do not have the space to accommodate more children. Less successful schools continue to attract pupils either because for some families, particularly in rural areas or for those without a car, they are the only practicable choice, or because some parents do not regard academic results as the only mark of a good school.

> *What a school achieves at the end of its educational mission depends very much on what has been put in at the beginning.*

The second reason is that even relatively unsophisticated parents understand what many professionals argued when the tables were introduced: what a school achieves at the end of its educational mission depends very much on what has been put in at the beginning. Statistics that present raw examination results inevitably produce a pecking order that has the most selective schools at the top and those that take in children with the greatest problems at the bottom.

The most blatant example of this emerged during the early days of the tables, when every single school was included. Highly selective independent and state schools, who had carefully chosen their intake for their academic potential, dominated the top end of the tables, while at the bottom languished hundreds of special schools for learning-disabled and very disturbed children who almost inevitably achieved no exam passes at all.

Since then the Department for Education and Employment (DfEE) and the inspectorate, through the Office for Standards in Education (Ofsted), have accepted that if comparisons are to be made and be meaningful, like must be compared with like. Even the newspapers have responded by drawing up leagues of 'best' independent and state schools separately, and distinguishing between private and state grammar schools, which select, and comprehensive schools, which do not.

But problems with the use of raw statistics do not end there. The real difficulty faced by the DfEE, which is still, under the Labour government, committed to the tables as an indication of school quality, and by parents, who may wish to use the tables when choosing schools, is what to make of apparently similar schools that produce dissimilar results.

In a perfect world, every comprehensive school would have a perfectly balanced intake that reflected the abilities and home circumstances of the population at large. In fact only about a quarter of comprehensive schools have a 'balanced' intake. In the real world, intakes reflect the communities the schools serve. A school in a leafy suburb will take in a disproportionate number of children from supportive middle class homes who are very likely to do well in exams. An inner city school will take in a disproportionate number of children who live in poor housing, with single or unemployed parents, who may not speak English at home. For all these reasons, such children are less likely to do well in examinations. As a result, it is fair to conclude that an inner city school that is getting half of its children five good GCSE passes is excelling, while a suburban school with the same results is probably failing miserably.

For years experts have been trying to find ways of indicating how well schools are doing, while taking their intake into account. Given that children are now tested at regular intervals during their school careers, and will soon be assessed when they enter school, it should in theory be easier to assess how much progress they are making between tests. This should allow fairer judgements to be made about whether a school is enabling its pupils to do better than expected – or not.

In 1998 the government proposed measuring pupils' progress between the 14+ SATs and GCSEs at 16, and giving schools a grade from A to D. But ministers dropped the idea when high performing selective schools pointed out that their 'progress' – say from 96% of children gaining five good grades to 97% – could never be as impressive as that of a poorly performing school that might double its progress from 3% to 6%.

Efforts continue to find an acceptable measurement that will give parents an indication of schools' performance irrespective of their intake. In the meantime, all we can be sure of from the reams of data that flow from the DfEE is that performance at GCSE and A Level continues to improve, and the best performing local authorities are actually improving more quickly than the poor performers, so the gap is widening. And in the primary schools, improvement in literacy and numeracy slowed down in 1998.

As far as individual schools are concerned, the data have confirmed what most of us knew already – that some schools produce much better exam results than others. But the reasons for these differences still seem to be much more closely related to the life circumstances and initial abilities of children schools let through their doors than any other factor defined by league tables.

Maureen O'Connor is a writer on education for The Independent *and* Times Educational Supplement

The Best and Worst Performing Local Education Authorities at GCSE

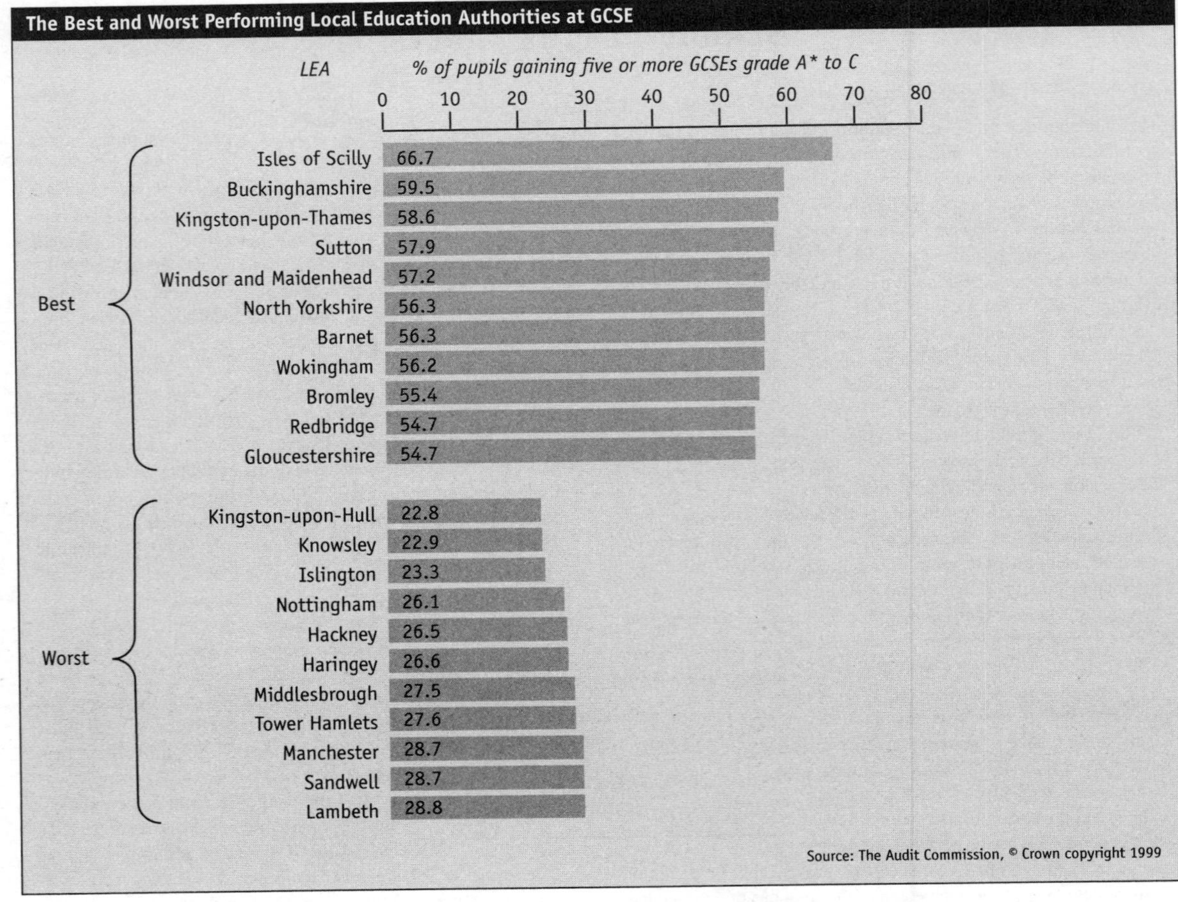

Source: The Audit Commission, © Crown copyright 1999

Pupils with Special Educational Needs in Public Sector and Assisted Schools in England, by Type of School

The data in this table are for full-time and part-time pupils with statements of Special Educational Needs (SEN) as of January for the year shown. (N/A = not available.)

Category	1993	1994	1995	1996	1997	1998
Maintained Schools						
Nursery schools	332	318	416	425	488	440
Primary schools[1 2]	43,464	50,112	55,768	61,698	63,551	67,014
Secondary schools[1 2 3]	41,114	50,142	57,040	65,137	70,080	73,956
Special schools[2 4 5]	82,855	83,673	85,879	87,458	87,330	87,931
Pupil referral units[5]	N/A	N/A	1,325	1,828	1,693	1,798
Other Schools						
Independent schools[6]	5,227	5,458	5,826	5,810	6,461	6,450
Non-maintained special schools[5]	5,037	4,838	5,053	4,992	5,026	4,705
All schools	178,029	194,541	211,307	227,348	234,629	242,294

[1] Includes middle schools as deemed.
[2] Includes grant-maintained schools.
[3] Excludes sixth-form colleges from 1994.
[4] Includes general and special hospital schools.
[5] Excludes dually registered pupils.
[6] Includes direct grant nursery schools and city technology colleges.

Source: *Statistics of Education: Schools in England 1998*, © Crown copyright 1998

Pupil–Teacher Ratios by Type of School in the UK

As of January for the year shown, except for Scotland and Wales where they are as of September.

	1986	1988	1990	1992	1993	1994[1]	1995[1]	1996[1]	1997[1 2]
All Schools or Departments[3 4]									
UK[5]									
England	17.4	17.2	17.0	17.2	17.4	17.7	18.1	18.2	18.3
Wales	18.2	18.0	18.1	18.2	18.2	18.4	18.7	18.7	18.8
Scotland	N/A	15.8	15.3	15.3	15.4	15.5	15.4	15.5	15.8
Northern Ireland	18.5	18.4	18.3	18.3	18.1	17.8	17.3	17.1[6]	16.7
Total	17.4[7]	17.1	16.9	17.1	17.3	17.5	17.8	18.0[6]	18.1
Public Sector Mainstream Schools or Departments									
Nursery	21.7[7]	21.4	21.8	21.6	21.6	21.6	21.9	21.3[6]	21.3
Primary	22.0	21.9	21.7	21.8	21.9	22.2	22.4	22.7[6]	22.8
Secondary	15.7	15.1	14.8	15.2	15.4	15.7	16.0	16.1	16.2
Special Schools[4]									
Total	6.6	6.3	5.8	5.7	5.8	5.9	6.0	6.2	6.2

[1] From 1 April 1993, figures exclude sixth form colleges in England and Wales that were reclassified as further education colleges.
[2] Figures are provisional. They include 1995–96 data for Wales.
[3] From 1980 onwards, figures include non-maintained schools or departments, including independent schools in Scotland.
[4] Up to 1993–94, figures include unqualified teachers for England and Scotland. From 1994–95 figures include qualified teachers only for all countries.
[5] Figures take account of the full-time equivalent of part-time teachers.
[6] Revised figures.
[7] Includes 1984–85 data for Scotland.

Source: *Annual Abstract of Statistics 1999*, © Crown copyright 1999

Numbers of Teachers by Type of School in the UK

Data are for January of each year except in Scotland and Wales, where data are for September.

Type of school	1986	1988	1990	1992	1993	1994[1]	1995[1]	1996[1]	1997[1 2]
Public Sector Mainstream Schools or Departments									
Nursery[3 4]	2,600[5]	2,700	2,700	2,800	2,900	2,800	2,800	2,900	2,900
Primary[3 4]	205,800	210,100	219,000	222,600	224,400	225,500	225,900	227,300	226,900
Secondary[3 4]	260,500	244,900	236,600	232,700	233,600	228,400	228,400	228,200	228,900
Special Schools									
Total[4]	19,600	19,300	19,600	19,600	19,600	19,200	19,200	18,600	18,300
TOTAL[3 6]	540,300	531,100	532,500	534,900	537,800	533,200	532,600	534,000	533,000

[1] From 1 April 1993, figures exclude sixth form colleges in England and Wales as these colleges were reclassified as further education colleges.
[2] Figures are provisional. This column includes 1995–96 data for Wales.
[3] Figures of teachers take account of the full-time equivalent of part-time teachers.
[4] Up to 1993–94, figures include unqualified teachers for England and Scotland. From 1994–95, figures include qualified teachers only for all countries.
[5] Figure includes 1984–85 data for Scotland.
[6] Figures include non-maintained schools or departments, including independent schools in Scotland.

Source: *Annual Abstract of Statistics 1999*, © Crown copyright 1999

Government Spending on Education in the UK

Data are for years ending 31 March. Due to rounding constituent figures may not sum to totals.
(N/A = not available. In millions of pounds.)

Expenditure	1985–86	1986–87	1987–88	1988–89	1989–90	1990–91	1991–92	1992–93[1]	1993–94[2]	1994–95[2]	1995–96[3]
Current Expenditure											
Nursery schools	74	81	4,743	5,259	5,889	6,458	7,247	8,262	8,712	9,094	9,349
Primary schools	3,702	4,157									
Secondary schools	5,061	5,583	5,991	6,437	6,832	7,147	7787	8,347	8,615	8,875	8,987
Special schools	667	727	812	888	1,008	1,121	1,245	1,354	1,420	1,451	1,492
Universities[4]	1,605	1,654	1,824	1,958	2,104	2,265	2,437	3,361	N/A	N/A	N/A
Other higher, further, and adult education[5]	2,475	2,716	2,971	3,277	3,729	4,128	4,454	4,136	N/A	N/A	N/A
Higher Education Funding Council[5] [6]	N/A	N/A	N/A	N/A	N/A	N/A	N/A	N/A	4,908	5,192	5,455
Further Education Funding Council[7]	N/A	N/A	N/A	N/A	N/A	N/A	N/A	N/A	3,072	3,200	3,374
Continuing education	N/A	N/A	N/A	N/A	N/A	N/A	N/A	N/A	380	294	266
Other education expenditure	736	871	900	1,009	1,191	1,325	1,361	1,009	905	963	1,045
Related Current Expenditure											
Training of teachers: residence[8]	19	19	N/A	N/A	N/A	N/A	N/A	N/A	N/A	N/A	N/A
School welfare[9]	37	40	57	70	91	155	214	270	346	359	330
Meals and milk[10]	532	559	547	469	485	506	556	161	149	147	148
Youth service and physical training	239	211	246	277	328	348	360	393	392	401	399
Maintenance grants and allowances to pupils and students[11] [12]	838	806	843	900	934	1,028	1,379	1,705	1,972	2,204	2,180
Transport of pupils	279	290	302	311	335	393	442	417	444	486	506
Miscellaneous expenditure	5	5	6	10	17	2	3	8	10	31	31
Current expenditure total	16,267	17,719	19,240	20,865	22,943	24,876	27,485	29,424	31,325	32,697	33,562
Capital Expenditure											
Nursery schools	8	7	192	246	314	353	376	384	414	517	525
Primary schools	164	180									
Secondary schools	233	187	213	195	397	465	493	518	485	565	574
Special schools	17	23	11	33	38	36	35	32	31	37	51
Universities[4]	140	156	158	172	196	211	231	236	N/A	N/A	N/A
Other higher, further, and adult education[5]	151	152	177	180	248	230	293	285	N/A	N/A	N/A
Higher Education Funding Council[5] [6]	N/A	N/A	N/A	N/A	N/A	N/A	N/A	N/A	406	412	453
Further Education Funding Council[7]	N/A	N/A	N/A	N/A	N/A	N/A	N/A	N/A	194	201	213
Continuing education	N/A	N/A	N/A	N/A	N/A	N/A	N/A	N/A	6	8	10
Other education expenditure	11	10	32	22	41	39	33	25	12	45	25
Related capital expenditure	23	24	21	25	32	26	20	17	23	25	17
Capital expenditure total	737	739	804	873	1,266	1,359	1,481	1,496	1,571	1,810	1,868
VAT refunds to local authorities	284	345	357	399	455	493	584	656	648[13]	886	923
Total Expenditure											
Central government total	2,378	2,567	2,746	3,025	4,337	4,582	4,288	4,722	8,186	9,490	10,234
Local authorities total	14,911	16,235	17,655	19,112	20,325	22,146	25,261	26,853	25,354[13]	25,900	26,118
Total government expenditure on education[14]	17,288	18,803	20,401	22,137	24,664	26,728	29,550	31,576	33,544[13]	35,393	36,352
Total government expenditure as % of GDP[15]	4.78	4.84	4.75	4.62	4.72	4.75	5.01	5.15	5.18	5.16	5.03

[1] Includes 1991–92 data for Wales.
[2] Includes 1993–94 data for Wales.
[3] Provisional data. Includes 1994–95 data for Wales.
[4] Includes expenditure on University departments of Education for England and Wales.
[5] Including tuition fees.
[6] Includes expenditure on Higher Education Institutions in Northern Ireland.
[7] Includes expenditure for Further Education in Northern Ireland.
[8] With effect from 1987–88 included with maintenance grants and allowances.
[9] Expenditure on the school health service is included in the National Health Service.
[10] From 1992–93 expenditure on meals and milk in England has been recharged across other expenditure headings.
[11] From 1986–87, excludes the secondment of teachers on further training.
[12] From 1990–91, includes student loans expenditure.
[13] Revised figure.
[14] Excludes additional adjustment to allow for Capital consumption made for National Accounts purposes amounting to £1,013 million in 1995–96.
[15] GDP includes adjustments to remove the distortion caused by abolition of domestic rates which have led to revisions of the historical series.

Source: *Annual Abstract of Statistics 1999,*

Spending per Pupil on Key Items in LEA-Maintained Schools in England

The expenditure data are drawn from the annual R01 spending returns which local authorities submit to the Department of the Environment, Transport, and Regions (DETR). The pupil data are drawn from the Department of Education and Employment annual Form 7 survey. The real-terms index has been calculated at 1998–99 prices using March 1999 Gross Domestic Product (GDP) deflators, and shows the percentage increase in real-terms spending compared with a base year of 1992–93. Data are for financial year given.

Spending per pupil on:		1993–94	1994–95	1995–96	1996–97	1997–98[1]
Teaching staff	cash (£)	1,290	1,311	1,330	1,342	1,355
	real-terms index	100	100	99	97	95
Support staff	cash (£)	145	162	175	199	212
	real-terms index	100	110	115	127	131
Books and equipment	cash (£)	78	79	78	81	89
	real-terms index	100	100	96	97	104
Repairs and maintenance	cash (£)	79	82	76	77	69
	real-terms index	100	102	92	91	80

[1] Data for 1997–98 are provisional and are based on a combination of actual and estimated expenditure.

Source: *The Government's Expenditure Plans 1999–00 to 2001–02*, Department for Education and Employment and Office for Standards in Education, © Crown copyright 1999

Initial Teacher Training in the UK

This table covers LEA-maintained and grant-maintained schools, and includes data for entrants successfully completing initial teacher training (ITT) courses at universities and other higher education institutions, school centred ITT (SCITT), and Open University (OU) during academic years 1995–96 to 1997–98. The data are arranged by sector and subject specialism. In order to teach in a maintained school, teachers are normally required to have qualified teacher status (QTS). This is normally attained by successfully completing a course of ITT at an accredited institution whose provision meets the Secretary of State's criteria for ITT. In 1993 a new system of SCITT was launched. This is postgraduate training that is designed and delivered by groups of schools. (N = nil or negligible.)

Sector	1995–96	1996–97	1997–98			% increase 1996–97 to 1997–98
			Actual	Target	% difference	
Primary						
Undergraduate	9,240	8,360	7,800	N	N	-6.7
Postgraduate						
school centred ITT	90	170	210	N	N	131.2
Total	5,700	5,450	5,220	N	N	-4.3
TOTAL	14,940	13,810	13,020	12,200	6.7	-5.8
Secondary						
Undergraduate	2,460	2,580	2,650	N	N	2.9
Postgraduate						
school centred ITT	320	370	460	N	N	38.9
Total	13,360	14,260	14,260	N	N	0.0
TOTAL	16,090	16,840	16,910	20,670	-18.2	0.4
Primary and Secondary						
Undergraduate	11,690	10,940	10,460	N	N	-4.4
Postgraduate						
school centred ITT	410	540	670	N	N	68.0
Total	19,330	19,720	19,480	N	N	-1.2
TOTAL	31,020	30,660	29,940	32,870	-8.9	-2.4
Secondary by Subject						
Mathematics	1,890	1,740	1,540	2,370	-35.1	-11.7
English[1]	1,980	2,190	2,260	2,270	-0.7	3.0
Science	2,950	3,080	2,940	3,460	-15.0	-4.5
Languages[2]	1,860	1,810	1,890	2,780	-32.1	4.5
Welsh	60	50	50	80	-38.8	-7.5
Technology[3]	1,950	2,050	2,090	3,380	-38.3	1.8
History	940	1,010	1,040	980	6.4	3.7
Geography	740	900	900	960	-5.8	0.3
Physical education	1,390	1,460	1,730	1,610	7.1	18.6
Art	870	960	960	1,020	-5.7	0.2
Music	590	540	550	650	-16.0	0.6
Religious education	510	670	680	740	-8.8	0.4
Others[4]	380	390	300	370	-18.9	-23.1
Total	16,090	16,840	16,910	20,670	-18.2	0.4

[1] Includes Drama.
[2] Excludes Welsh.
[3] Includes Design and Technology, Engineering, Computer Studies, Business Studies, Commerce, Home Economics, and Needlecraft.
[4] Includes Classics, Economics, other social sciences, and other subjects.

Source: *Statistics of Education: Teachers, England and Wales 1998*, © Crown copyright 1998

Adult Literacy Levels by Gender in the UK

The abilities of working people (aged 16 to 65) were measured on three types of literacy: prose literacy (the ability to understand text), document literacy (the ability to locate and use information in charts and timetables), and quantitative literacy (the ability to perform basic arithmetic operations on numbers embedded in text). Performance on each dimension is grouped into five literacy levels, level 1 being the lowest and level 5 the highest.
(In percentages.)

1996

Type of literacy	Level 1	Level 2	Level 3	Levels 4/5
Men				
Prose	21	30	32	17
Document	20	25	31	24
Quantitative	18	27	30	25
Women				
Prose	22	31	30	16
Document	27	29	30	15
Quantitative	29	29	30	12

Source: *Social Trends 28,* Adult Literacy Survey, © Crown copyright 1998

Highest Qualification Levels Attained, by Gender, in Great Britain

The data in this table are for people of working age (men aged 16 to 64 and women aged 16 to 59).

1997

Qualification level	Women		Men	
	Number	%	Number	%
Higher education	3,200,000	19	3,880,000	21
GCE A level or equivalent	1,957,000	12	2,759,000	15
Recognized trade apprenticeship	613	4	2,762,000	15
GCSE grades A*–C or equivalent	4,601,000	28	3,160,000	17
Qualifications at NVQ level 1 or below	1,329,000	8	931	5
Other qualifications (level unknown)	1,226,000	7	1,694,000	9
No qualifications	3,513,000	21	2,837,000	16
Total[1]	16,539,000	100	18,155,000	100

[1] Includes those whose highest qualification is unknown.

Source: *Equal Opportunities Commission analysis of Labour Force Survey, Spring 1997,* © Crown copyright 1997

Highest Qualification Levels Attained by Gender and Socioeconomic Group in Great Britain

Data are for economically active persons aged 25–69 not in full-time education and are for 1995 and 1996 combined.
(In percentages.)

Highest qualification level attained[1]		Socioeconomic group[2]							
		Professional	Employers and managers	Intermediate non-manual	Junior non-manual	Skilled manual and own account non-professional	Semi-skilled manual and personal service	Unskilled manual	Total
Degree or equivalent	men	65	24	30	12	2	1	1	16
	women	68	22	24	4	4	1	0	11
	Total	66	24	26	5	2	1	0	14
Higher education below degree level	men	17	19	20	13	10	7	2	14
	women	11	19	28	5	4	4	1	11
	Total	16	19	25	6	9	5	1	12
GCE A-level or equivalent[3]	men	7	17	16	24	15	10	7	15
	women	7	13	9	12	10	8	4	10
	Total	7	16	12	14	14	9	5	12
GCSE grades A–C or equivalent[3]	men	5	19	20	29	24	22	20	21
	women	4	23	21	39	28	23	14	27
	Total	5	20	20	37	25	23	16	24
GCSE grades D–G or equivalent/commercial qualifications/ apprenticeship	men	0	5	4	7	14	12	12	9
	women	3	8	7	18	14	12	10	12
	Total	1	6	6	16	14	12	11	10

(continued)

Highest Qualification Levels Attained by Gender and Socioeconomic Group in Great Britain (*continued*)

Highest qualification level attained[1]		Socioeconomic group[2]							
		Professional	Employers and managers	Intermediate non-manual	Junior non-manual	Skilled manual and own account non-professional	Semi-skilled manual and personal service	Unskilled manual	Total
Foreign or other qualifications	men	3	3	3	2	2	3	4	3
	women	7	2	3	2	2	4	2	2
	Total	4	2	3	2	2	3	2	2
No qualifications	men	2	12	7	14	33	45	55	23
	women	0	13	9	21	38	47	69	26
	Total	2	12	8	20	34	46	64	25

[1] Those who never went to school are excluded.
[2] Excludes members of the armed forces, full-time students, and those who had never worked.
[3] Including further-education qualifications.

Source: *Living in Britain 1996: Results from the 1996 General Household Survey*, Office for National Statistics Social Survey Division, © Crown copyright 1998

Level of Education Held by Gender and Ethnic Group in Great Britain

Data are for men aged 16–64 and women aged 16–59, and for combined quarters: Spring 1997 to Winter 1997–98. (In percentages.)

1997–98

	Degree or equivalent	Higher education qualification[1]	GCE A-level or equivalent	GCSE grades A* to C or equivalent	Other qualification	No qualification	All
Men							
Indian/Pakistani/Bangladeshi	18	5	16	14	25	22	100
Black	14	6	22	18	24	16	100
White	14	8	32	18	14	15	100
Other groups[2]	20	5	17	15	27	15	100
Women							
Indian/Pakistani/Bangladeshi	9	5	11	18	25	33	100
Black	9	12	14	27	22	16	100
White	11	9	16	29	15	20	100
Other groups[2]	12	8	15	17	33	15	100

[1] Below degree level.
[2] Includes those who did not state their ethnic group.

Source: *Social Trends 29*, © Crown copyright 1999

The Gender Question: The Performance of Boys and Girls in the UK School System

BY MAUREEN O'CONNOR

In the days when all children in the UK took the eleven-plus examination, which allocated the most successful to grammar schools and the rest to secondary moderns, the results were adjusted to even up the scores for each sex. If this had not been done, far more grammar school places would have been offered to girls than boys.

British children are now some of the most regularly assessed in the world, with National Curriculum Tests at 7, 11, and 14, and public examinations at 16 and 18. As a result it is possible for the monitors of standards – the Quality and Curriculum Authority (QCA), which supervises tests and examinations, and the Office for Standards in Education, which inspects schools in England and Wales – to gain a very clear picture of the relative performance of girls and boys in school. And although the eleven-plus is now a distant memory in most parts of the country, it is clear that gender differences in school performance remain, and in some respects have actually worsened over recent years.

In the primary schools, overall performance has been improving since the introduction of the National Curriculum in 1989 and SATs (standard attainment tests) in English, maths, and science. Girls do particularly well in English, with 83% of seven-year-old girls performing at the 'expected' level, compared to 73% of boys. Throughout their schooling, girls consistently outperform boys in English, often by a significant margin. The gap in favour of girls is less marked in maths and science at seven. By 11, the boys have caught up with the girls in maths and have pulled slightly ahead in science.

By the time pupils take their GCSE examinations at 16 the picture has become more complicated still. Overall, more boys than girls leave school without any qualifications, and girls gain more GCSE passes than boys. But by this stage boys and girls are beginning to take different subjects, so like-with-like comparisons become more difficult. In English and maths, the two subjects most pupils take at GCSE, girls still perform significantly better than boys in English but performance is much the same in maths. In science boys maintain a slight advantage.

At A Level, where the choice of subject is wide and boys and girls tend to opt for different subject areas, comparisons are equally difficult. However, over the last three years, girls have almost eliminated the gap that used to exist between their performance, measured as a total point score, and that of boys. In recent years, subject choices have become more sharply polarized, with girls preferring the humanities and languages, and boys dominating the sciences, computing, and economics.

At university level the picture changes again. Women and men are almost equally represented in higher education, as they have been for 15 years or more, even though participation (the proportion of the total age group going into higher education) has almost doubled during this period. Both boys and girls seem to have been equally motivated towards higher education throughout its expansion in the UK. But in terms of performance at degree level, women's results are clustered around the middle of the degree tables, while men take the majority of first class degrees – and the majority of thirds. And in adult life, of course, men move ahead in the promotion and earnings tables quite sharply.

So what are the reasons for these differences in performance? Research has some of the answers, but by no means all of them, and the subject is complicated by factors other than gender. Social and racial inequalities, teaching and assessment methods, and the expectations of parents, teachers, and society as a whole, may all play their part. Research into the effects of schooling on boys and girls has come up with many clues but no definitive answers. There seems to be little doubt that boys and girls learn in different ways: boys are more assertive in class, girls more attentive; girls learn more effectively by means of sustained tasks, such as essays and projects, while boys succeed through memorizing data and factually based learning; girls favour language activities, boys like maths and science; boys prefer 'sudden death' examinations and do well on multiple choice tests, while girls have an advantage in coursework.

Other factors considered at one time or another to be significant are now regarded as less so. Major studies have shown little difference in the performance of boys and girls in single sex and co-educational schools, if the prior level of attainment of the pupils is taken into account. And it has now been shown that boys perform better at tasks where they are familiar with the context of the problem, either through experience at home or at school. It was previously thought that girls had a particular need for learning in context, while it made little difference to the performance of boys. And there is evidence that in English and maths examiners have taken on board the need to present materials and problems that are not biased in favour of one gender or the other.

Nor is there any evidence of discrimination in tests and exams. When the Associated Examining Board commissioned research on 'blind' marking, using A Level scripts that might be assigned to the wrong sex, the results remained consistent.

The issue of gender in education is immensely complicated by factors external to the schools and colleges. For example, when looking at what the popular press describes as 'the problem with boys', it is difficult to isolate the influence of gender from that of race, family, and social class. Boys are over-represented among children with learning difficulties generally, and with reading difficulties in particular. They also heavily outnumber girls among children with emotional and behavioural difficulties (EBD). White boys are more heavily represented in the first two groups, while black boys predominate among children with EBD. There is something more complicated going on in these boys' lives than can be explained by gender issues alone.

Some of the complications involved are illustrated by the results of the 1990 Youth Cohort Study, which looked at examination scores among white, Asian, and Afro-Carribean boys and girls in three social class groups. Top performers were white girls, followed by Asian and then white boys, all from professional families. Fourth in this particular league table were Asian girls from working-class homes. The lowest scores were obtained by Afro-Carribean boys, and then girls, from working-class families.

Recent years have seen an increase in public concern with children's performance: it is perhaps this concern more than anything that is now persuading schools that differential performance, whatever its causes, is an issue that must be tackled.

Maureen O'Connor is a writer on education for The Independent *and* Times Educational Supplement

Directory of Local Education Authorities in the UK

England

Barking and Dagenham A P Larbalestier, Chief Education Officer, Education Offices, Town Hall, Barking, Essex IG11 7LU; phone: (0181) 592 4500; fax: (0181) 594 9837

Barnet Martyn Kempson, Acting Director of Education Services, LBB Education Services (formerly Friern Barnet Town Hall), Friern Barnet Lane, London N11 3DL; phone: (0181) 359 2000; fax: (0181) 359 3057

Barnsley Derek Dalton, Programme Director of Education and Leisure, Education Offices, Berneslai Close, Barnsley, South Yorkshire S70 2HS; phone: (01226) 770770; fax: (01226) 773599

Bath and North East Somerset Roy Jones, Director of Education, Cultural and Community Service, Bath and North East Somerset Council, PO Box 25, Riverside, Temple Street, Keynsham, Bristol BS31 1LN; phone: (01225) 477000; fax: (01225) 394200

Bedfordshire *(see also Luton)* Paul Brett, Director of Education, Arts and Libraries, County Hall, Cauldwell Street, Bedford MK42 9AP; phone: (01234) 363222; fax: (01234) 228619

Bexley P McGee, Director of Education and Leisure Services, Bexley Council, Hill View, Hill View Drive, Welling, Kent DA16 3RY; phone: (0181) 303 7777; fax: (0181) 319 4302

Birmingham Tim Brighouse, Chief Education Officer, Education Department, Council House Extension, Margaret Street, Birmingham B3 3BU; phone: (0121) 303 2872; fax: (0121) 303 1318

Blackburn with Darwen *(formerly Lancashire)* Mark Pattison, Director of Education and Training, Blackburn with Darwen Borough Council, Town Hall, King William Street, Blackburn, Lancashire BB1 7DY; phone: (01254) 585585; fax: (01254) 698388

Blackpool *(formerly Lancashire)* Dr David Saunders, Director of Education, Blackpool Borough Council, Progress House, Clifton Road, Blackpool FY4 4US; phone: (01253) 476555; fax: (01253) 476504

Bolton Mrs Margaret Blenkinsop, Director of Education and Arts, PO Box 53, Paderborn House, Civic Centre, Bolton, Lancashire BL1 1JW; phone: (01204) 522311; fax: (01204) 365492

Bournemouth *(formerly Dorset)* Kabir Shaikh, Director of Education, Bournemouth Borough Council, Dorset House, 20–22 Christ Church Road, Bournemouth BH1 3NL; phone: (01202) 456219; fax: (01202) 456191

Bracknell Forest *(formerly Berkshire)* Tony Eccleston, Director of Education, Bracknell Forest Council, Edward Elgar House, Skimpedhill Lane, Bracknell RG12 1LY; phone: (01344) 424642; fax: (01344) 354001

Bradford Mrs Diana Cavanagh, Director of Education, Flockton House, Flockton Road, Bradford, West Yorkshire BD4 7RY; phone: (01274) 751840; fax: (01274) 740612

Brent John Simpson, Chief Education Officer, Department of Education, Arts, and Libraries, Brent Council, Chesterfield House, 9 Park Lane, Wembley, Middlesex HA9 7RW; phone: (0181) 937 3190; fax: (0181) 937 3023

Brighton and Hove Mrs Denise Stokoe, Director of Educational Services, Brighton and Hove Council, King's House, Grand Avenue, Hove, East Sussex BN3 2LS; phone: (01273) 290000; fax: (01273) 293456

Bristol Richard Riddell, Director of Education, Bristol City Council, Avon House, The Haymarket, Bristol BS99 7EB; phone: (0117) 922 2000; fax: (0117) 903 7963

Bromley Ken Davis, Director of Education, London Borough of Bromley, Education Department, Bromley Civic Centre, Stockwell Close, Bromley BR1 3UH; phone: (0181) 464 3333; fax: (0181) 313 4049

Buckinghamshire *(see also Milton Keynes)* David McGahey, Chief Education Officer, County Hall, Aylesbury, Buckinghamshire HP20 1UZ; phone: (01296) 395000; fax: (01296) 383367

Bury Harold Williams, Borough Education Officer, Education Department, Athenaeum House, Market Street, Bury, Lancashire BL9 0BN; phone: (0161) 253 5000; fax: (0161) 253 5653

Calderdale Ms Carol White, Director of Education, Education Department, PO Box 33, Northgate House, Nothgate, Halifax, West Yorkshire HX1 1UN; phone: (01422) 357257; fax: (01422) 392515

Cambridgeshire *(see also Peterborough)* Andrew Baxter, Director of Education, Libraries, and Heritage, Castle Court, Shire Hall, Castle Hill, Cambridge CB3 0AP; phone: (01223) 717111; fax: (01223) 717971

Camden Bob Litchfield, Director of Education, London Borough of Camden, Education Department, Crowndale Centre, 218–220 Eversholt Street, London NW1 1BD; phone: (0171) 911 1525; fax: (0171) 911 1536

Cheshire *(see also Halton and Warrington)* David Cracknell, Group Director of Educational Services, County Hall, Chester CH1 1SQ; phone: (01244) 602424; fax: (01244) 603821

Cornwall Jonathan S Harris, Secretary for Education, Education Offices, County Hall, Truro, Cornwall TR1 3BY; phone: (1872) 322000; fax: (01872) 323818

Corporation of London David Smith, City Education Officer, Corporation of London Education Department, PO Box 270, Guildhall, London EC2P 2EJ; phone: (0171) 332 1750; fax: (0171) 332 1621

Coventry Mrs Cathy Goodwin, Chief Education Officer, New Council Offices, Earl Street, Coventry CV1 5RS; phone: (01203) 833333; fax: (01203) 831620

Croydon David Sand, Director of Education, Taberner House, Park Lane, Croydon CR9 1TP; phone: (0181) 686 4433; fax: (0181) 760 0871

Cumbria John Nellist, Director of Education, Education Offices, 5 Portland Square, Carlisle CA1 1PU; phone: (01228) 606060; fax: (01228) 606896

Darlington Geoffrey Pennington, Director of Education, Darlington Borough Council, Town Hall, Darlington DL1 5QT; phone: (01325) 380651; fax: (01325) 382032

Derby, City of Derek D'Hooghe, Director of Education, Derby City Council, 27 St Mary's Gate, Derby DE1 3NN; phone: (01332) 293111; fax: (01332) 716920

Derbyshire *(see also Derby, City of)* Ms Valerie Hannon, Chief Education Officer, County Offices, Matlock, Derbyshire DE4 3AG; phone: (01629) 580000; fax: (01629) 580350

Devon *(see also Plymouth and Torbay)* Tony Smith, Chief Education Officer, County Hall, Exeter EX2 4QG; phone: (01392) 382000; fax: (01392) 382203

Doncaster Matthew Simpson, Director of Education and Leisure Services, PO Box 266, The Council House, Doncaster, South Yorkshire DN1 3AD; phone: (01302) 737222; fax: (01302) 737223

Dorset *(see also Bournemouth and Poole)* Richard Ely, Director of Education, Libraries and Arts, Education Department, County Hall, Colliton Park, Dorchester, Dorset DT1 1XJ; phone: (01305) 251000; fax: (01305) 224499

Dudley Richard P Colligan, Chief Education Officer, Westox House, 1 Trinity Road, Dudley, West Midlands DY1 1JB; phone: (01384) 818181; fax: (01384) 814216

Durham *(see also Darlington)* Keith Mitchell, Director of Education, Education Department, County Hall, Durham DH1 5UJ; phone: (0191) 386 4411; fax: (0191) 386 0487

Ealing Alan Parker, Director of Education, Perceval House, 14–16 Uxbridge Road, Ealing, London W5 2HL; phone: (0181) 579 2424; fax: (0181) 280 1291

East Riding of Yorkshire John Ginnever, Director of Education, Leisure and Libraries, East Riding of Yorkshire Council, County Hall, Beverley, East Riding of Yorkshire HU17 9BA; phone: (01482) 887700; fax: (01482) 884920

East Sussex *(see also Brighton and Hove)* David Mallen, County Education Officer, PO Box 4, County Hall, St Anne's Crescent, Lewes, East Sussex BN7 1SG; phone: (01273) 481000; fax: (01273) 481261

Enfield Ms Liz Graham, Director of Education, Education Department, PO Box 56, Civic Centre, Silver Street, Enfield, Middlesex EN1 3XQ; phone: (0181) 366 6565; fax: (0181) 982 7375

Essex *(see also Southend on Sea and Thurrock)* Paul Lincoln, Director of Learning Services, Education Department, PO Box 47, A Block, County Hall, Victoria Road, Chelmsford CM1 1LD; phone: (01245) 492211; fax: (01245) 492759

Gateshead Brian Edwards, Director of Education, Education Offices, Civic Centre, Regent Street, Gateshead, Tyne and Wear NE8 1HH; phone: (0191) 477 1011; fax: (0191) 490 1168

Gloucestershire Roger Crouch, Chief Education Officer, Shire Hall, Gloucester GL1 2TP; phone: (01452) 425300; fax: (01452) 425496

Greenwich George Gyte, Director of Education, London Borough of Greenwich, 9th Floor, Riverside House, Beresford Street, London SE18 6DE; phone: (0181) 854 8888; fax: (0181) 855 2427

Hackney Ms Elizabeth Reid, Director of Education, Hackney Education Directorate, Edith Cavell House, Enfield Road, London N1 5BA; phone: (0181) 356 5000; fax: (0181) 356 7295

Halton Graham Talbot, Director of Education, Education Department, Halton Borough Council, Grosvenor House, Halton LEA, Runcorn, Cheshire WA7 2GW; phone: (0151) 424 2061; fax: (0151) 471 7321

Hammersmith and Fulham Ms Christine Whatford, Director of Education, London Borough of Hammersmith and Fulham, Town Hall, King Street, London W6 9JU; phone: (0181) 748 3020 (x 3621); fax: (0181) 576 5686

Hampshire *(see also Portsmouth and Southampton)* Andrew Seber, County Education Officer, The Castle, Winchester, Hampshire SO23 8UG; phone: (01962) 841841; fax: (01962) 842355

Haringey Ms Frances Magee, Director of Education Services, London Borough of Haringey, Education Offices, 48 Station Road, Wood Green, London N22 4TY; phone: (0181) 975 9700; fax: (0181) 862 3864

Harrow Paul Osburn, Director of Education, PO Box 22, Civic Centre, Harrow, Middlesex HA1 2UW; phone: (0181) 863 5611; fax: (0181) 427 0810

Hartlepool Jeremy Fitt, Director of Education and Community Services, Hartlepool Council, Civic Centre, Victoria Road, Hartlepool TS24 8AY; phone: (01429) 266522; fax: (01429) 523777

Havering Colin Hardy, Director of Education and Community Services, London Borough of Havering, The Broxhill Centre, Broxhill Road, Harold Hill, Romford RM14 1XN; phone: (01708) 772222; fax: (01708) 773850

Herefordshire *(formerly Hereford and Worcester)* Dr Eddie Oram, Director of Education, Hereford Education and Conference Centre, Herefordshire Council, PO Box 185, Blackfriars Street, Hereford HR4 9ZR; phone: (01432) 260000; fax: (01432) 264348

Hertfordshire Ray Shostack, Director of Education, County Hall, Hertford SG13 8DF; phone: (01992) 555555; fax: (01992) 588674

Hillingdon Graham Moss, Group Director Educational Services, London Borough of Hillingdon, Civic Centre, Uxbridge, Middlesex UB8 1UW; phone: (01895) 250111; fax: (01895) 250878

Hounslow Douglas Trickett, Director of Education, Civic Centre, Lampton Road, Hounslow, Middlesex TW3 4DN; phone: (0181) 862 5352; fax: (0181) 862 5249

Islington Andy Roberts, Director of Education, London Borough of Islington, Laycock Street, London N1 1TH; phone: (0171) 226 1234; fax: (0171) 457 5555

Kensington and Chelsea Roger Wood, Executive Director of Education and Libraries, Royal Borough of Kensington and Chelsea, Town Hall, Hornton Street, London W8 7NX; phone: (0171) 361 3334; fax: (0171) 361 2078

Kent Nick Henwood, Strategic Director of Education and Libraries, Education Department, Sessions House, County Hall, Maidstone, Kent ME14 1XQ; phone: (01622) 671411; fax: (01622) 694091

Kingston upon Hull, City of Miss Joan Taylor, Director of Education, Kingston upon Hull City Council, Essex House, Manor Street, Kingston upon Hull HU1 1YD; phone: (01482) 610610; fax: (01482) 613407

Kingston upon Thames John Braithwaite, Director of Education, Royal Borough of Kingston upon Thames, Guildhall, High Street, Kingston upon Thames, Surrey KT1 1EU; phone: (0181) 546 2121; fax: (0181) 547 5296

Kirklees Gavin Tonkin, Chief Education Officer, Kirklees Metropolitan Council, Oldgate House, 2 Oldgate, Huddersfield HD1 6QW; phone: (01484) 221000; fax: (01484) 225264

Knowsley Peter Wylie, Director of Education, Knowsley Metropolitan Borough Council, Education Office, Huyton Hey Road, Huyton, Merseyside L36 5YH; phone: (0151) 489 6000; fax: (0151) 449 3852

Lambeth Mrs Heather du Quesnay, Director of Education, Lambeth Education Department, London Borough of Lambeth, Blue Star House, 234/244 Stockwell Road, London SW9 9SP; phone: (0171) 926 1000; fax: (0171) 926 2296

Lancashire *(see also Blackpool with Darwen and Blackpool)* Christopher J Trinick, Director of Education and Cultural Studies, Lancashire County Council, PO Box 61, County Hall, Preston PR1 8RJ; phone: (01772) 254868; fax (01772) 261630

Leeds Keith Burton, Director of Education, Leeds Education Department, Selectapost 17, Merrion House, Merrion Centre, Leeds LS2 8DT; phone: (0113) 234 8080; fax: (0113) 234 1394

Leicester City Tom Warren, Director of Education, Leicester City Council, Marlborough House, 38 Welford Road, Leicester LE2 7AA; phone: (0116) 254 9922; fax: (0116) 233 9922

Leicestershire *(see also Leicester City and Rutland)* Ms Jackie Strong, Director of Education, Education Department, County Hall, Glenfield, Leicester LE3 8RF; phone: (0116) 232 3232 fax: (0116) 265 6634

Lewisham Ms Althea Erunshile, Director of Education and Community Services, London Borough of Lewisham, Laurence House, Town Hall, Catford, London SE6 4SW; phone: (0181) 695 6000; fax: (0181) 690 4392

Lincolnshire Norman Riches, Director of Education and Cultural Services, County Offices, Newland, Lincoln LN1 1YQ; phone: (01522) 552222; fax: (01522) 553257

Liverpool M Frank Cogley, Director of Education, Education Offices, 14 Sir Thomas Street, Liverpool L1 6BJ; phone: (0151) 227 3911; fax: (0151) 225 3029

Inner London see separate entries for the former Inner London Education Authority (ILEA) London Boroughs: Camden, Corporation of London (covering the one square mile of the City of London), Greenwich, Hammersmith and Fulham, Hackney, Islington, Kensington and Chelsea, Lambeth, Lewisham, Southwark, Tower Hamlets, Wandsworth, Westminster

Outer London see separate entries for the following London Boroughs: Barking and Dagenham, Barnet, Bexley, Brent, Bromley, Croydon, Ealing, Enfield, Haringey, Harrow, Havering, Hillingdon, Hounslow, Kingston upon Thames, Merton, Newham, Redbridge, Richmond upon Thames, Sutton, Waltham Forest

Luton Tony Dessent, Director of Education, Luton Borough Council, Unity House, 111 Stuart Street, Luton, Bedfordshire LU1 5NP; phone: (01582) 548001; fax: (01582) 548454

Manchester David Johnson, Chief Education Officer, Education Offices, Crown Square, Manchester M60 3BB; phone: (0161) 234 5000; fax: (0161) 234 7147

Medway *(formerly Kent)* Richard Bolsin, Director of Education, Medway Council, Compass Centre, Chatham Maritime, Chatham, Kent ME4 4YN; phone: (01634) 306000; fax: (01634) 890120

Merton Mrs Jenny Cairns, Director of Education, Leisure and Libraries, London Borough of Merton, Crown House, London Road, Morden, Surrey SM4 5DX; phone: (0181) 543 2222; fax: (0181) 545 3443

Middlesbrough Dr Cheryle Berry, Corporate Director of Education and Leisure, Middlesbrough Borough Council, PO Box 191, 2nd Floor, Civic Centre, Middlesbrough TS1 2XS; phone: (01642) 245432; fax: (01642) 262038

Milton Keynes Jill Stansfield, Learning and Development Strategic Director, Milton Keynes Council, Saxon Court, 502 Avebury Boulevard, Milton Keynes MK9 3HS; phone: (01908) 691691; fax: (01908) 253289

Newcastle upon Tyne David Bell, Director of Education and Libraries, Education Offices, Civic Centre, Barras Bridge, Newcastle upon Tyne NE1 8PU; phone: (0191) 232 8520; fax: (0191) 211 4983

Newham Ian Harrison, Director of Education, London Borough of Newham, Education Offices, Broadway House, 322 High Street, Stratford, London E15 1AJ; phone: (0181) 555 5552; fax: (0181) 503 0014

Norfolk Bryan Slater, County Education Officer, County Hall, Martineau Lane, Norwich NR1 2DL; phone: (01603) 222300; fax: (01603) 222119

Northamptonshire Mrs Brenda Bignold, Director of Education and Community Learning, PO Box 149, County Hall, Guildhall Road, Northampton NN1 1AU; phone: (01604) 236236; fax: (01604) 236188

North East Lincolnshire Geoff Hill, Head of Professional Service – Education, North East Lincolnshire Council, Eleanor Street, Grimsby DN32 9DU; phone: (01472) 313131; fax: (01472) 323020

North Lincolnshire Dr Trevor Thomas, Director of Education and Personal Development, North Lincolnshire Council, PO Box 35, Hewson House, Station Road, Brigg DN20 8JX; phone: (01724) 297241; fax: (01724) 297242

North Somerset Alan Moss, Acting Director of Education, North Somerset Council, PO Box 51, Town Hall, Weston-Super-Mare BS23 1ZZ; phone: (01934) 888888; fax: (01934) 888834

North Tyneside Les Walton, Executive Director for Education, Wallsend Town Hall, High Street East, Wallsend, Tyne and Wear NE28 7RU; phone: (0191) 200 5151; fax: (0191) 200 6090

Northumberland Christopher Tipple, Director of Education, Education Department, County Hall, Morpeth, Northumberland NE61 2EF; phone: (01670) 533677; fax: (01670) 533750

North Yorkshire *(see also York)* Miss Cynthia Welbourn, Director of Education, County Hall, Northallerton, North Yorkshire DL7 8AE; phone: (01609) 780780; fax: (01609) 778611

Nottingham, City of *(formerly Nottinghamshire)* Paul Roberts, Director of Education, Nottinghamshire City Council, Sandfield Centre, Sandfield Road, Lenton, Nottingham NG7 1QH; phone: (0115) 915 5555; fax: (0115) 915 0603

Nottinghamshire *(see also Nottingham, City of)* Rob Valentine, Director of Education, Nottinghamshire County Council, County Hall, West Bridgford, Nottingham NG2 7QP; phone: (0115) 982 3823; fax: (0115) 981 2824

Oldham Michael Willis, Director of Education and Leisure Services, Education Department, PO Pox 40, Civic Centre, West Street, Oldham OL1 1XJ; phone: (0161) 911 4260; fax: (0161) 911 3221

Oxfordshire Graham Badman, Chief Education Officer, Education Department, Macclesfield House, New Road, Oxford OX1 1NA; phone: (01865) 792422; fax: (01865) 791637

Peterborough, City of *(formerly Cambridgeshire)* Bill Goodwin, Director of Education, Peterborough City Council, Bayard Place, Broadway, Peterborough PE1 1FB; phone: (01733) 563141; fax: (01733) 748111

Plymouth, City of *(formerly Devon)* Sohail Faruqi, Director of Education, City of Plymouth Council, Civic Centre, Plymouth PL1 2AA; phone: (01752) 307400; fax: (01752) 307403

Poole *(formerly Dorset)* Dr Shirley Goodwin, Policy Director Education, Borough of Poole, Civic Centre, Poole, Dorset BH15 2RU; phone: (01202) 633633; fax: (01202) 633706

Portsmouth John Gaskin, City Education Officer, Portsmouth City Council, Civic Offices, Guildhall Square, Portsmouth PO1 2EA; phone: (01705) 822251; fax: (01705) 834159

Reading Andrew Daykin, Director of Education, Reading Borough Council, Civic Offices, Civic Centre, Reading RG1 7TD; phone: (0118) 939 0900; fax: (0118) 958 9770

Redbridge Don Capper, Director of Education, Education Office, London Borough of Redbridge, Lynton House, 255–259 High Road, Ilford, Essex IG1 1NY; phone: (0181) 478 3020; fax: (0181) 478 9044

Redcar and Cleveland Patrick Scott, Director of Education, Redcar and Cleveland Borough Council, Redcar Council Offices, PO Box 83, Kirkleatham Street, Redcar TS10 1YA; phone: (01642) 444000; fax: (01642) 444122

Richmond upon Thames Vincent McDonnell, Director of Education, London Borough of Richmond upon Thames, Education Department, Regal House, London Road, Twickenham TW1 3QB; phone: (0181) 891 1411; fax: (0181) 891 7714

Rochdale Brian Atkinson, Director of Education, Education Department, PO Box 70, Municipal Offices, Smith Street, Rochdale OL16 1YD; phone: (01706) 647474; fax: (01706) 658560

Rotherham Harry Bower, Director of Education Services, Norfolk House, Walker Place, Rotherham S60 1QT; phone: (01709) 382121; fax: (01709) 372056

Rutland Keith Bartley, Director of Education, Rutland Council, Catmose, Oakham, Rutland LE15 6HP; phone: (01572) 722577; fax: (01572) 758307

St Helens Colin Hilton, Director of Community Education, Community Education and Leisure Services Department, The Rivington Centre, Rivington Road, St Helens, Merseyside WA10 4ND; phone: (01744) 456000; fax: (01744) 455350

Salford David Johnston, Director of Education and Leisure, Education Office, Chapel Street, Salford M3 5LT; phone: (0161) 832 9751/8; fax: (0161) 835 1561

Sandwell Stuart Gallacher, Director of Education and Community Services, Sandwell Metropolitan Borough Council, PO Box 41, Shaftesbury House, 402 High Street, West Bromwich, West Midlands B70 9LT; phone: (0121) 525 7366; fax: (0121) 553 1528

Sefton Brynley Marsh, Director of Education, Sefton Borough Council, Education Department, Town Hall, Bootle, Merseyside L20 7AE; phone: (0151) 933 6003; fax: (0151) 934 3349

Sheffield Jonathon Crossley-Holland, Director of Education, PO Box 67, Leopold Street, Sheffield S1 1RJ; phone: (0114) 272 6444; fax: (0114) 273 6279

Shropshire *(see also Telford and Wrekin)* Ms Carol Adams, Chief Education Officer, The Shirehall, Abbey Foregate, Shrewsbury SY2 6ND; phone: (01743) 251000; fax: (01743) 254415

Slough *(formerly Berkshire)* John Christie, Chief Education Officer, Slough Borough Council, Town Hall, Bath Road, Slough SL1 3UQ; phone: (01753) 552288; fax: (01753) 692499

Solihull David Nixon, Director of Education, Libraries and Arts, PO Box 20, Council House, Solihull, West Midlands B91 3QU; phone: (0121) 704 6000; fax: (0121) 704 6669

Somerset Michael Jennings, Corporate Director of Education, County Hall, Taunton, Somerset TA1 4DY; phone: (01823) 355455; fax: (01823) 355332

Southampton Bob Hogg, Director of Education, Southampton City Council, Civic Centre, Southampton SO14 7LL; phone: (01703) 223855; fax: (01703) 833221

Southend on Sea *(formerly Essex)* Stephen Hay, Director of Education and Libraries Services, Southend on Sea Borough Council, PO Box 6, Civic Centre, Victoria Avenue, Southend on Sea SS2 6ER; phone: (01702) 215000; fax: (01702) 215110

South Gloucestershire Ms Therese Gillespie, Director of Education, South Gloucestershire Offices, Bowling Hill, Chipping Sodbury BS37 6JX; phone: (01454) 863333; fax: (01454) 863263

South Tyneside Ian Reid, Director of Education, Education Department, Town Hall Civic Offices, Westoe Road, South Shields, Tyne and Wear NE33 2RL; phone: (0191) 427 1717; fax: (0191) 427 0584

Southwark Gordon Mott, Director of Education and Library Services, London Borough of Southwark, 1 Bradenham Close (off Albany Road), London SE17 2QA; phone: (0171) 525 5050/5051; fax: (0171) 525 5025

Staffordshire *(see also Stoke-on-Trent)* Dr Philip Hunter, Chief Education Officer, County Buildings, Tipping Street, Stafford ST16 2DH; phone: (01785) 223121; fax: (01785) 278639

Stockport Max Hunt, Chief Education Officer, Education Division, Stopford House, Piccadilly, Stockport SK1 3XE; phone: (0161) 480 4949; fax: (0161) 953 0012

Stockton-on-Tees Stanley Bradford, Chief Education Officer, Stockton-on-Tees Council, PO Box 228, Municipal Buildings, Church Road, Stockton-on-Tees TS18 1XE; phone: (01642) 393939; fax: (01642) 393479

Stoke-on-Trent Nigel Rigby, Director of Education, City of Stoke-on-Trent Council, Swann House, Boothen Road, Stoke-on-Trent ST4 4SY; phone: (01782) 236100; fax: (01782) 236102

Suffolk David Peachey, County Director of Education, Education Department, St Andrew House, County Hall, Ipswich IP4 1LJ; phone: (01473) 584800; fax: (01473) 584624

Sunderland Dr John Williams, Director of Education and Community Services, Education Department, PO Box 101, Town Hall and Civic Centre, Sunderland SR2 7DN; phone: (0191) 553 1000; fax: (0191) 553 1410

Surrey Paul Gray, Director of Education, County Hall, Penrhyn Road, Kingston upon Thames KT1 2DJ; phone: (0181) 541 9501; fax: (0181) 541 9503

Sutton Dr Ian Birnbaum, Director of Education, London Borough of Sutton, The Grove, Carshalton SM5 3AL; phone: (0181) 770 5000; fax: (0181) 770 6548

Swindon Mike Lusty, Chief Education Officer, Swindon Borough Council, Sanford House, Sanford Street, Swindon SN1 2QH; phone: (01793) 463000; fax: (01793) 488597

Tameside Tony Webster, Director of Education, Tameside Metropolitan Borough Council, Education Department, Council Offices, Wellington Road, Ashton under Lyne, Lancashire OL6 6DL; phone: (0161) 342 8355; fax: (0161) 342 3260

Telford and Wrekin *(formerly Shropshire)* Mrs Christine Davis, Corporate Director of Education and Training, Telford and Wrekin Council, PO Box 440, Civic Offices, Telford TF3 4LD; phone: (01952) 202100; fax: (01952) 293946

Thurrock *(formerly Essex)* Raphael Wilkins, Director of Education, Thurrock Council, Civic Offices, New Road, Grays, Essex RM17 6SL; phone: (01375) 652652; fax: (01375) 652792

Torbay *(formerly Devon)* Graham Cane, Director of Education Services, Torbay Borough Council, Oldway Mansion, Paignton, Devon TQ3 2TE; phone: (01803) 208208; fax: (01803) 208225

Tower Hamlets Ms Christine Gilbert, Director of Education and Community Services, London Borough of Tower Hamlets, Education Department, Mulberry Place, 5 Clove Crescent, London E14 2BG; phone: (0171) 364 5000; fax: (0171) 364 4296

Trafford Mrs Kathy August, Director of Education, Arts and Leisure, Trafford Metropolitan Borough Council, PO Box 40, Trafford Town Hall, Talbot Road, Stretford M32 0EL; phone: (0161) 912 3251; fax: (0161) 912 3075

Wakefield John McLeod, Chief Education Officer, Education Department, County Hall, Bond Street, Wakefield, West Yorkshire WF1 2QL; phone: (01924) 306090; fax: (01924) 305632

Walsall Humphrey Smith, Chief Education Services Officer, The Civic Centre, Darwall Street, Walsall, West Midlands WS1 1DQ; phone: (01922) 650000; fax: (01922) 722322

Waltham Forest Andrew Lockhart, Chief Education Officer, London Borough of Waltham Forest, Municipal Offices, High Road, Leyton, London E10 5QJ; phone: (0181) 527 5544; fax: (0181) 556 8720

Wandsworth Paul Robinson, Director of Education, London Borough of Wandsworth, Town Hall, Wandsworth High Street, London SW18 2PU; phone: (0181) 871 8013; fax: (0181) 871 8011

Warrington *(formerly Cheshire)* Malcolm Roxburgh, Director of Education, Education Department, Warrington Borough Council, New Town House, Buttermarket Street, Warrington WA1 2LS; phone: (01925) 444400; fax: (01925) 442705

Warwickshire Eric Wood, County Education Officer, PO Box 24, 22 Northgate Street, Warwick CV34 4SR; phone: (01926) 410410; fax: (01926) 412746

West Berkshire *(formerly Berkshire and Newbury)* Jay Mercer, Corporate Director (Education), West Berkshire Council, Avonbank House, West Street, Newbury RG14 1BZ; phone: (01635) 519723; fax: (01635) 519725

Westminster Deirdre McGrath, Director of Education and Leisure Department, City of Westminster, PO Box 240, Westminster City Hall, Victoria Street, London SW1E 6QP; phone: (0171) 641 6000; fax: (0171) 641 3406

West Sussex Richard Bunker, Director of Education, County Hall, West Street, Chichester, West Sussex PO19 1RF; phone: (01243) 777100; fax: (01243) 777229

Wigan Roy Clark, Director of Education, Education Offices, Gateway House, Standishgate, Wigan WN1 1AE; phone: (01942) 244991; fax: (01942) 828811

Wiltshire *(see also Swindon)* Dr Lindsey Davis, Chief Education Officer, County Hall, Bythesea Road, Trowbridge, Wiltshire BA14 8JB; phone: (01225) 713000; fax: (01225) 713982

Windsor and Maidenhead, Royal Borough of *(formerly Berkshire)* Malcolm Peckham, Director of Education, Royal Borough of Windsor and Maidenhead, Town Hall, St Ives Road, Maidenhead SL6 1RF; phone: (01628) 798888; fax: (01628) 796408

Wirral Christopher Rice, Director of Education, Wirral Metropolitan Borough Council, Hamilton Building, Conway Street, Birkenhead L41 4FD; phone: (0151) 666 2121; fax: (0151) 666 4207

Wokingham *(formerly Berkshire)* Mrs Jacky Griffin, Director of Education and

Cultural Services, Wokingham District Council, Shute End, Wokingham RG40 1NN; phone: (0118) 974 6000; fax: (0118) 974 6103

Wolverhampton Roy Lockwood, Director of Education, Education Department, Civic Centre, St Peter's Square, Wolverhampton WV1 1RR; phone: (01902) 556556; fax: (01902) 554218

Worcestershire Julien Kramer, Director of Education Services, Worcestershire County Council, County Hall, Spetchley Road, Worcester WR5 2NP; phone: (01905) 763763; fax: (01905) 766156

York, City of Mike Peters, Director of Education, City of York Council, 10–12 George Hudson Street, York YO1 6ZG; phone: (01904) 613161; fax: (01904) 554249

The Islands

Guernsey Derek Neale, Director of Education, Education Department, Grange Road, St Peter Port, Guernsey, Channel Islands GY1 1RQ; phone: (01481) 710821; fax: (01481) 714475

Jersey Tom McKeon, Director of Education, Education Department, PO Box 142, St Saviour, Jersey JE4 8QJ; phone: (01534) 509500; fax: (01534) 509800

Isle of Man Ralf Cowin, Director of Education, Education Department, Murray House, Mount Hevelock, Douglas, Isle of Man IM1 2SG; phone: (01624) 685820; fax: (01624) 685834

Isle of Wight Alan Kaye, Director of Education, County Hall, Newport, Isle of Wight PO30 1UD; phone: (01983) 821000; fax: (01983) 826099

Isles of Scilly Philip Hygate, Secretary for Education, Education Department, Town Hall, St Mary's, Isles of Scilly TR21 0LW; phone: (01720) 422537; fax: (01720) 422202

Scotland

Aberdeen J Stodter, Director of Education, Aberdeen City Council, Sumerhill Education Centre, Stronsay Drive, Aberdeen AB15 6JA; phone: (01224) 522000; fax: (01224) 346061

Aberdeenshire M White, Director of Education, Woodhill House, Westburn Road, Aberdeen AB16 5GB; phone: (01224) 665420; fax: (01224) 665445

Angus J Anderson, Director of Education, Angus Council, County Buildings, Market Street, Forfar DD8 3WE; phone: (01307) 461460 (x 3236); fax: (01307) 461848

Argyll and Bute A Morton, Director of Education, Argyll House, Alexandra Parade, Dunoon, Argyll PA23 8AJ; phone: (01369) 704000; fax: (01369) 702614

Clackmannanshire K Bloomer, Director of Education and Community Services, Lime Tree House, Castle Street, Alloa FK10 1EX; phone: (01259) 452435; fax: (01259) 452440

Comhairle nan Eilann Siar N Galbraith, Director of Education and Leisure Services, Sandwick Road, Stornoway, Isle of Lewis HS1 2BW; phone: (01851) 703773 (x 430); fax: (01851) 705796

Dumfries and Galloway F Sanderson, Acting Director of Education, 30 Edinburgh Road, Dumfries DG1 1NW; phone: (01387) 260427; fax: (01387) 260453

Dundee Mrs A Wilson, Director of Education, Tayside House, Crichton Street, Dundee DD1 3RJ; phone: (01387) 260427; fax: (01387) 260453

East Ayrshire J Mulgrew, Director of Education, Council Headquarters, London Road, Kilmarnock KA3 7BU; phone: (01563) 576000; fax: (01563) 576210

East Dunbartonshire I Mills, Director of Education and Leisure Services, Boclair House, 100 Milngavie Road, Bearsden, Glasgow G61 2TQ; phone: (0141) 942 9000; fax: (0141) 942 6814

East Lothian A Blackie, Director of Education and Community Services, Council Buildings, Haddington EH41 3HA; phone: (01620) 827631; fax: (01620) 827291

East Renfrewshire Mrs E Currie, Director of Education, East Renfrewshire Council, Eastwood Park, Rouken Glen Road, Giffnock, Glasgow G46 6UG; phone: (0141) 577 3430; fax: (0141) 577 3405

Edinburgh R Jobson, Director of Education, Council Headquarters, Wellington Court, 10 Waterloo Place, Edinburgh EH1 3EG; phone: (0131) 469 3322; fax: (0131) 469 3320

Falkirk Dr G Young, Director of Education, McLaren House, Marchmont Avenue, Polmont FK2 0NZ; phone: (01324) 506600; fax: (01324) 506664

Fife A McKay, Head of Education, Fife House, North Street, Glenrothes, Fife KY7 5LT; phone: (01592) 414141; fax: (01592) 416411

Glasgow K Corsar, Director of Education, House 1, Charing Cross Complex, 20 India Street, Glasgow G2 4PF; phone: (0141) 287 2000; fax: (0141) 287 6892

Highland B Robertson, Director of Education, Glenurquhart Road, Inverness IV3 5NX; phone: (01463) 702000; fax: (01463) 702828

Inverclyde B McLeary, Director of Education Services, Department of Education Services, 105 Dalrymple Street, Greenock PA15 1HT; phone: (01475) 712824; fax: (01475) 712875

Midlothian D MacKay, Director of Education, Midlothian Council, Fairfield House, 8 Lothian Road, Dalkeith, Midlothian EH22 3ZG; phone: (0131) 271 3718; fax: (0131) 271 3751

Moray K Gavin, Director of Education, High Street, Elgin IV30 1BX; phone: (01343) 563134; fax: (01343) 563416

North Ayrshire J Travers, Director of Education, Cunninghame House, Friars Croft, Irvine KA12 8EE; phone: (01294) 324411; fax: (01294) 324444

North Lanarkshire M O'Neill, Director of Education, Municipal Building, Kildonan Street, Coatbridge ML5 3BT; phone: (01236) 812336; fax: (01236) 812335

Orkney Islands L Manson, Director of Education, School Place, Kirkwall, Orkney KW15 1NY; phone: (01856) 873535 (x 2401); fax: (01856) 870302

Perth and Kinross R McKay, Director of Education, Blackfriars, Perth PH1 5LT; phone: (01738) 476211; fax: (01738) 476210

Renfrewshire Mrs S Rae, Director of Education, Cotton Street, Paisley PA1 1LE; phone: (0141) 842 5663; fax: (0141) 842 5655

Scottish Borders J Christie, Director of Education, Council Headquarters, Newtown St Boswells, Melrose TD6 0SA; phone: (01835) 824000 (x 451); fax: (01835) 825091

Shetlands Islands J Halcrow, Director of Education, Hayfield House, Hayfield Lane, Lerwick ZE1 0QD; phone: (01595) 744000; fax: (01595) 692810

South Ayrshire M McCabe, Director of Educational Services, Wellington Square, Ayr KA7 1DR; phone: (01292) 612201; fax: (01292) 612258

South Lanarkshire Mrs M Allan, Director of Education, Floor 5, Council Offices, Almada Street, Hamilton ML3 0AE; phone: (01698) 454545; fax: (01698) 454465

Stirling G Jeyes, Director of Education, Viewforth, Stirling FK8 2ET; phone: (01786) 443322; fax: (01786) 442782

West Dunbartonshire I McMurdo, Director of Education, Council Offices, Garshake Road, Dumbarton G82 3PU; phone: (01389) 737000; fax: (01389) 737348

West Lothian R Stewart, Corporate Manager of Education Services, Lindsay House, South Bridge Street, Bathgate EH48 1TS; phone: (01506) 776000; fax: (01506) 776378

Wales

Blaenau Gwent B Mawby, Director of Education, Victoria House, Victoria Business Park, Ebbw Vale NP3 6ER; phone: (01495) 350555; fax: (01495) 355495

Bridgend D Matthews, Director of Education and Leisure Services, Education Department, County Council Offices, Sunnyside, Bridgend CF31 4AR; phone: (01656) 642200; fax: (01656) 642646

Caerphilly J N O Harries, Director of Education and Leisure Services, County Offices, Caerphilly Road, Ystrad Mynach, Hengoed CF82 7EP; phone: (01443) 864948; fax: (01443) 816998

Cardiff T Davies, Director of Education, County Hall, Atlantic Wharf, Cardiff CF1 5UW; phone: (01222) 872000; fax: (01222) 872777

Carmarthenshire K P Davies, Director of Education, Pibwrlwyd, Carmarthen SA31 2NH; phone: (01267) 234567; fax: (01267) 221692

Ceredigion R J Williams, Director of Education and Community Services, Education Department, County Offices, Marine Terrace, Aberystwyth SY23 2DE; phone: (01970) 617581; fax: (01970) 615348

Conwy R Elwyn Williams, Director of Education, Education Department, Government Buildings, Dinerth Road, Colwyn Bay LL28 4UL; phone: (01492) 544261 (x 4561); fax: (01492) 541311

Denbighshire E Lewis, Director of Education, Denbighshire County Council, c/o Phase 4 of County Hall, Mold CH7 6GR; phone: (01824) 706777; fax: (01824) 706780

Flintshire K McDonogh, Director of Education, Libraries, and Information, County Hall, Mold CH7 6ND; phone: (01352) 704010; fax: (01352) 754202

Gwynedd D Whittall, Director of Education, Shire Hall Street, Caernarfon LL55 1SH; phone: (01286) 679162; fax: (01286) 677347

Isle of Anglesey R P Jones, Director of Education, Ffordd Glan Hwfa, Llangefni, Ynys Mon LL77 7HY; phone: (01248) 752920; fax: (01248) 752999/750533

Merthyr Tydfil D Jones, Director of Education, Ty Keir Hardie, Riverside Court, Avenue de Clichy, Mertyr Tydfil CF47 8XD; phone: (01685) 724600; fax: (01685) 721965

Monmouthshire D Young, Director of Education, County Hall, Cwmbran NP44 2XH; phone: (01633) 644644; fax: (01633) 644488/ 644525

Neath Port Talbot V Thomas, Director of Education, Civic Centre, Port Talbot SA13 1PJ; phone: (01639) 763333; fax: (01639) 763000

Newport G Bingham, Director of Education, Civic Centre, Newport NP9 4UR; phone: (01633) 232206; fax: (01633) 233376

Pembrokeshire G Davies, Director of Education, Cambria House, PO Box 27, Haverfordwest SA61 1TP; phone: (01437) 764551 (x 5860); fax: (01437) 769557

Powys R J Barker, Director of Education, Llandridnod Wells LD1 5LG; phone: (01597) 826433; fax: (01597) 826475

Rhondda Cynon Taff K Ryley, Director of Education, Education Centre, Grawen Street, Porth CF39 0BU; phone: (01443) 687666; fax: (01443) 680286

Swansea R Parry, Acting Director of Education, County Hall, Swansea SA1 3SN; phone: (01792) 636000; fax: (01792) 636333

Torfaen M de Val, Director of Education, County Hall, Cwmbran NP44 2WN; phone: (01495) 762200; fax: (01495) 648165

Vale of Glamorgan A Davies, Director of Education, Civic Offices, Holton Road, Barry CF63 4RU; phone: (01446) 700111; fax: (01446) 745566

Wrexham T Garner, Director of Education and Leisure Services, Roxburgh House, Hill Street, Wrexham LL11 1SN; phone: (01978) 297471; fax: (01978) 297422

Northern Ireland Education and Library Boards

Belfast David Cargo, Chief Executive of the Education and Library Board, 40 Academy Street, Belfast BT1 2NQ; phone (01232) 564000; fax: (01232) 331714

North-Eastern Gordon Topping, Chief Executive of the Education and Library Board, County Hall, 182 Galgorm Road, Ballymena, Co Antrim BT42 1HN; phone: (01266) 653333; fax: (01266) 46071

South-Eastern Ms Jackie Fitzsimons, Chief Executive of the Education and Library Board, Grahamsbridge Road, Dundonald, Belfast BT16 0HS; phone: (01232) 566200; fax: (01232) 566266/7

Southern Ms Helen McClenaghan, Chief Executive of the Education and Library Board, 3 Charlemont Place, The Mall, Armagh BT61 9AZ; phone: (01861) 512200; fax: (01861) 512490

Western Joseph Martin, Chief Executive of the Education and Library Board, Campsie House, 1 Hospital Road, Omagh, Co Tyrone BT79 0AW; phone: (01662) 411411; fax: (01662) 411400

Source: Welsh Education Office; Northern Ireland Office Education Department; Scottish Office Education Department; Department for Education and Employment,

UK Further and Higher Education

Students in Further and Higher Education Aged 16 and Over in the UK

The data in this table are provisional. The table includes 1994–95 further education data for Wales. Data for higher education include Open University students. Full-time includes sandwich, and for Scotland, short full-time. Part-time comprises both day and evening, including block release (except Scotland) and open/distance learning.
(– = not applicable.)

1996–97

Mode of study	All ages[1]	Age at 31 August 1996[2]						
		16	17	18	19	20	21–24	25 and over
Full-Time Students								
Postgraduate level	138,300	–	100	100	100	800	73,800	58,100
First degree	875,800	400	10,100	132,700	172,300	177,700	262,500	118,800
Other undergraduate[3]	143,700	700	4,300	16,700	23,000	20,500	42,000	35,700
All higher education [4]	1,194,600	1,900	15,600	153,400	201,100	203,400	386,700	230,200
All further education[5]	859,600	244,800	209,400	103,500	41,300	23,700	68,000	157,100
Total FE/HE students	2,054,200	246,700	225,000	256,800	242,500	227,100	454,800	387,300
Part-Time Students								
Postgraduate level	214,400	–	–	100	100	200	27,000	184,700
First degree	174,700	–	100	500	1,500	2,600	22,800	146,000
Other undergraduate[3]	217,000	300	900	2,900	4,300	5,100	31,300	156,400
All higher education[4]	696,900	500	1,300	5,300	9,100	11,300	98,900	550,300
All further education[5]	1,575,700	56,700	63,800	59,000	45,200	38,400	205,300	1,049,500
Total FE/HE students	2,272,500	57,100	65,100	64,300	54,300	49,700	304,100	1,599,900
TOTAL	4,326,700	303,800	290,100	321,100	296,800	276,800	758,900	1,987,200

[1] Includes students aged under 16.
[2] Figures include ages unknown.
[3] Figures exclude nursing and paramedic qualifiers at Department of Health establishments not recorded by HESA.
[4] Data are not available by level for higher education students in further education institutions in England and are included in total higher education figures only.
[5] Excludes approximately 177,000 students in further education institutions in England since the information cannot be broken down in this way. External institutions and specialist designated colleges are also excluded.

Source: *Annual Abstract of Statistics 1999,* © Crown copyright 1999

Loans to Students in the UK

Characteristic	1990–91	1995–96	1996–97	1997–98
Take-up for academic year	180,000	560,000	590,000	615,000
Total value of loans	£70 million	£701 million	£877 million	£941 million
Estimated number of eligible students	643,000	948,800	938,000	937,000
Take-up percentage	28	59	63	66
Size of average loan	£389	£1,252	£1,487	£1,530

Source: Student Loans Company Ltd

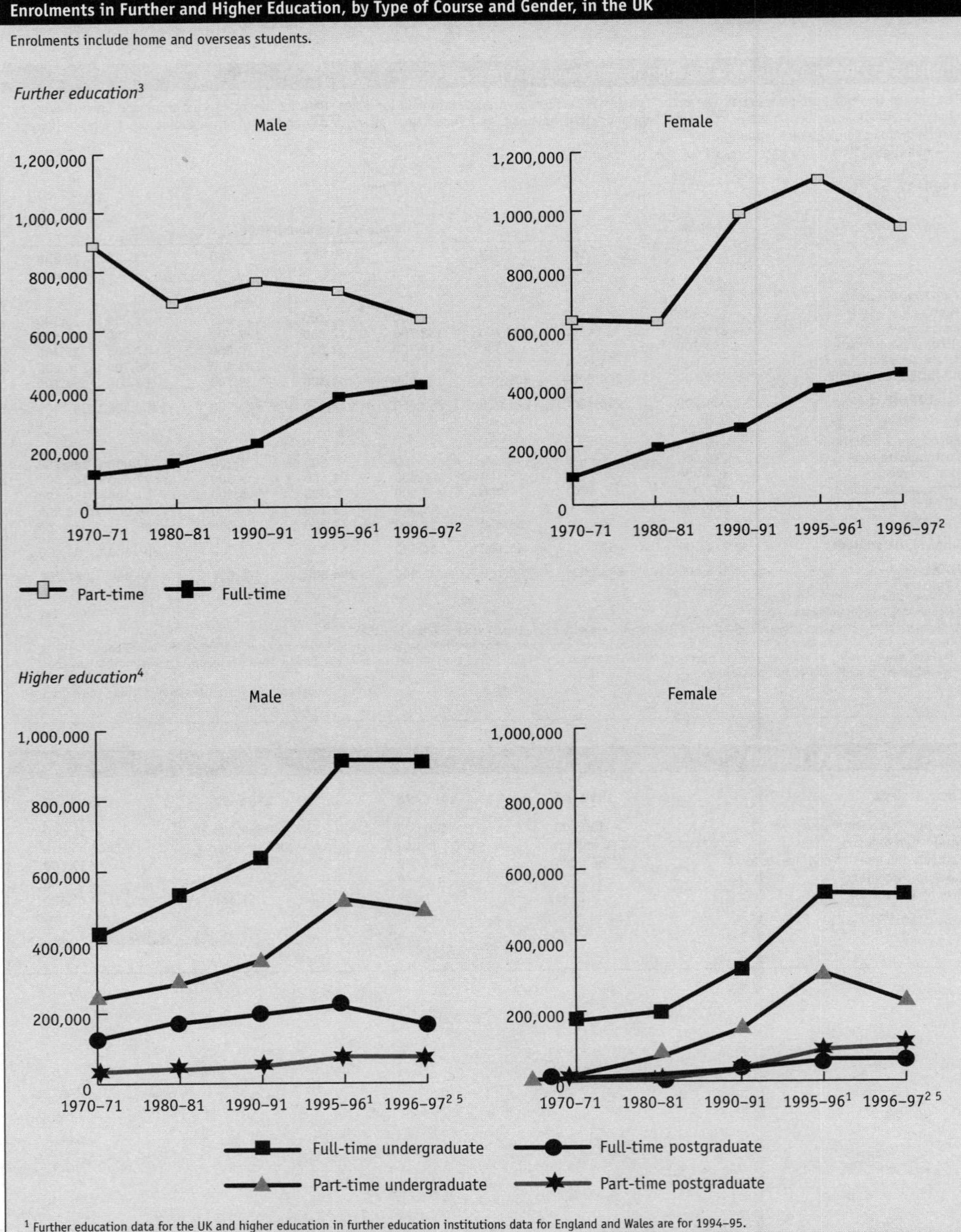

[1] Further education data for the UK and higher education in further education institutions data for England and Wales are for 1994–95.
[2] 1996–97 figures are not directly comparable with other years since those refer to enrolments rather than headcounts. Includes 1994–95 further education data for Wales.
[3] Excludes adult education centres.
[4] Includes Open University.
[5] Data for 1996–97 include students whose level of study is unknown.

Source: *Social Trends 29*, © Crown copyright 1999

Degrees and Diplomas Obtained by Full-Time Students in the UK

The data in this table are for calendar years.
(N/A = not available.)

	1985[1,2]	1986[1]	1987[1]	1988[1]	1989[1]	1990[1]	1991[1]	1992[1]	1993[1]	1994–95[3,4]	1995–96[3,4]	1996–97[3,4]
Degrees												
First degrees: honours												
men	36,119	35,823	35,845	36,735	37,473	38,342	39,360	41,908	43,624	N/A	N/A	N/A
women	26,122	25,988	26,601	27,799	28,578	30,121	31,659	34,423	36,983	N/A	N/A	N/A
First degrees: ordinary[5]												
men	6,057	5,405	5,518	5,520	5,301	4,973	4,879	4,980	4,891	N/A	N/A	N/A
women	3,911	3,696	3,853	3,702	3,601	3,745	3,739	3,582	3,591	N/A	N/A	N/A
First degree totals												
men	N/A	N/A	N/A	N/A	N/A	N/A	N/A	N/A	N/A	104,977	111,050	111,027
women	N/A	N/A	N/A	N/A	N/A	N/A	N/A	N/A	N/A	106,864	115,576	119,388
Higher degrees												
men	16,802	17,354	18,559	19,176	20,424	20,905	22,689	24,929	27,568	19,634[6]	23,743	24,404
women	6,754	7,219	8,008	8,676	9,794	10,419	11,912	14,034	16,374	20,973[6]	25,283	26,743
Total												
men	58,978	58,582	60,059	61,431	63,198	64,202	66,928	71,817	76,101	124,611	133,793	135,431
women	36,787	36,903	38,475	40,177	41,973	44,285	47,310	52,039	56,948	127,837	140,859	146,131
Diplomas and Certificates												
Men	6,447	5,867	6,800	6,659	6,621	6,712	7,914	8,811	9,470	16,606[7]	15,661	15,201
Women	5,751	5,706	6,303	6,611	6,599	7,000	8,997	9,881	11,584	17,199[7]	16,975	19,000

[1] Figures exclude the Open University and former polytechnics and central institutions that obtained university status in 1992.
[2] Figures include Ulster Polytechnic, which merged with the University of Ulster in 1984.
[3] Figures include students in all publicly funded higher education institutions including the Open University and former polytechnics and colleges.
[4] Data are for the academic year, not the calendar year.
[5] Includes some degrees where the class is not recorded.
[6] Figures include all postgraduate qualifications.
[7] Figures include other undergraduate qualifications.

Source: *Annual Abstract of Statistics 1999*, Higher Education Funding Council for England and Higher Education Statistics Agency,

Top 20 Countries with Students in Higher Education in the UK

1996–97

Rank	Country of origin	Post-graduate	First degree	Other under-graduate	Total	Rank	Country of origin	Post-graduate	First degree	Other under-graduate	Total
1	Greece	7,270	13,253	1,214	21,737	11	Japan	2,195	1,458	1,012	4,665
2	Malaysia	4,065	13,450	500	18,015	12	Norway	761	2,273	263	3,297
3	Ireland, Republic of	3,175	8,913	3,484	15,572	13	Cyprus	1,014	1,921	73	3,008
4	Germany	3,845	4,763	3,974	12,582	14	Taiwan	2,042	675	186	2,903
5	France	3,081	5,411	3,609	12,101	15	Netherlands	1,143	1,056	562	2,761
6	USA	3,796	1,250	4,402	9,448	16	Canada	1,908	475	378	2,761
7	Hong Kong	3,189	4,216	362	7,767	17	China	2,235	302	123	2,660
8	Spain	1,571	3,043	2,331	6,945	18	India	1,714	473	115	2,302
9	Singapore	1,579	3,995	72	5,646	19	Sweden	601	1,091	591	2,283
10	Italy	1,934	1,710	1,346	4,990	20	Israel	750	1,341	24	2,115

Source: *Students in Higher Education Institutions, 1996–97*, Higher Education Statistics Agency,

Research Grants and Contracts to Higher Education Institutions in the UK

The financial data in this table relate to the institutions' financial year of 1 August 1996 to 31 July 1997. Research grants and contracts include all income in respect of externally sponsored research carried out by the institution for which directly related expenditure has been incurred. The data are for the 30 higher education institutions receiving the largest grants from the research councils that come under the Office of Science and Technology. These councils include the Biotechnology and Biological Sciences Research Council, the Natural Environment Research Council, the Engineering and Physical Sciences Research Council, the Economic and Social Sciences Research Councils, the Particle Physics and Astronomy Research Council, and the Medical Research Council. The data also include income from the British Academy. Other sources of research grants and contracts include UK based charities, UK industry, health and hospital authorities, UK industry, commerce and public corporations, as well as EU and other overseas sources.

1996–97

Rank	Institution	Research council grant (£)
1	The University of Oxford	107,031,000
2	University College London	97,276,000
3	The University of Cambridge	93,603,000
4	Imperial College of Science, Technology and Medicine	80,174,000
5	The University of Edinburgh	54,660,000
6	The Victoria University of Manchester	50,873,000
7	The University of Leeds	47,768,000
8	The University of Southampton	46,215,000
9	The University of Glasgow	45,132,000
10	The University of Birmingham	44,705,000
11	The University of Bristol	39,711,000
12	The University of Nottingham	39,324,000
13	The University of Sheffield	37,013,000
14	The University of Newcastle-upon-Tyne	35,961,000
15	King's College, London	35,778,000
16	The University of Liverpool	33,355,000
17	Cranfield University	31,024,000
18	Queen Mary and Westfield College	27,656,000
19	United Medical and Dental Schools, Guys and St Thomas's Hospital	27,636,000
20	The University of Leicester	24,652,000
21	The University of Dundee	21,899,000
22	The University of Warwick	21,508,000
23	Royal Postgraduate Medical School	20,169,000
24	The University of York	19,280,000
25	University of Aberdeen	18,520,000
26	The University of Strathclyde	17,988,000
27	The University of Reading	16,577,000
28	Loughborough University	16,181,000
29	University of Wales, Cardiff	15,922,000
30	The University of Manchester Institute of Science and Technology	15,742,000

Source: *Resources of Higher Education Institutions 1996–97*, Higher Education Statistics Agency, © Crown copyright 1998

Full-Time Academic Teaching and Research Staff at Higher Education Institutions in the UK

(– = not applicable. N/A = not available.)

Academic years

	Professors	Readers and senior lecturers	Lecturers and assistant lecturers	Researchers	Other	Total	% annual change
1979–80[1]	4,337	8,734	20,518	N/A	661	34,250	1.6
1980–81[1]	4,382	8,809	20,460	N/A	646	34,297	0.1
1981–82[1]	4,351	8,777	20,045	N/A	562	33,735	−1.6
1982–83[1]	4,017	8,284	18,885	N/A	456	31,642	−6.2
1983–84[1]	3,893	8,145	18,595	N/A	463	31,096	−1.7
1984–85[1 2]	3,807	7,942	18,737	N/A	557	31,043	−0.2
1985–86[1]	3,959	8,025	18,850	N/A	578	31,412	1.2
1986–87[1]	4,070	8,074	18,711	N/A	577	31,432	0.1
1987–88[1]	4,160	8,291	18,268	N/A	542	31,261	−0.5
1988–89[1]	4,093	8,266	17,778	N/A	484	30,621	−2.0
1989–90[1]	4,261	8,618	17,903	N/A	558	31,340	2.3
1990–91[1]	4,520	8,842	17,830	N/A	669	31,861	1.7
1991–92[1]	4,872	9,270	17,824	N/A	672	32,638	2.4
1992–93[1]	5,226	9,650	17,854	N/A	717	33,447	2.5
1993–94[1]	5,545	9,890	18,275	N/A	787	34,497	3.1
1994–95[3]	6,762	16,949	39,295	4,662	4,842	72,510	–
1995–96[3]	7,947	17,457	41,503	5,412	5,582	77,901	7.4
1996–97[3 4]	8,222	17,591	39,820	4,809	5,589	76,031	−2.4

[1] Includes full-time teaching and research staff in posts wholly financed from general university funds but excludes the Open University and the former polytechnics and central institutions who obtained university status in 1992.
[2] Includes Ulster Polytechnic, which merged with the University of Ulster in October 1984.
[3] Includes full-time academic staff of at least 25 percent full-time equivalence who are wholly institutionally financed for all publicly funded higher education institutions (including the Open University and the former polytechnics and colleges).
[4] Due to changes in the definition of the HESA standard staff population for 1996–97, it is not advisable to make direct comparisons with figures for 1994–95 and 1995–96.

Source: *Annual Abstract of Statistics 1999*, Higher Education Funding Council for England and Higher Education Statistics Agency, © Crown copyright 1999

Selected Degree Abbreviations in the UK

BA Bachelor of Arts
BAgr Bachelor of Agriculture
BA(Lan) Bachelor of Languages
BAO Bachelor of Obstetrics
BArch Bachelor of Architecture
BChD Bachelor of Dental Surgery
BCL Bachelor of Civil Law
BCom Bachelor of Commerce
BCommunications Bachelor of Communications
BCS Bachelor of Combined Studies
BD Bachelor of Divinity
BDS Bachelor of Dental Surgery
BEd Bachelor of Education
BEng Bachelor of Engineering
BJur Bachelor of Jurisprudence
BLitt Bachelor of Letters
BMedSci Bachelor of Medical Science
BMet Bachelor of Metallurgy
BMus Bachelor of Music
BPharm Bachelor of Pharmacy
BPhil Bachelor of Philosophy
BSc Bachelor of Science
BSc(Econ) Bachelor of Science in Economics
BscEng Bachelor of Science in Engineering
BscTech Bachelor of Technical Science
BSocSc Bachelor of Social Sciences
BTech Bachelor of Technology
BTh Bachelor of Theology
BVSc Bachelor of Veterinary Science
ChB Bachelor of Surgery
ChM Master of Surgery
DCL Doctor of Civil Law
DD Doctor of Divinity
DDS Doctor of Dental Surgery
DDSc Doctor of Dental Science
DLitt Doctor of Letters
DM Doctor of Medicine
DMus Doctor of Music
DPhil Doctor of Philosophy
DSc Doctor of Science
DT Doctor of Theology
LittD Doctor of Letters
LLB Bachelor of Law
LLD Doctor of Law
LLM Master of Law
MA Master of Arts
MArb Master of Arboriculture
MArch Master of Architecture
MB Bachelor of Medicine
MBA Master of Business Administration
MCh Master of Surgery
MChD Master of Dental Surgery
MChemA Master in Chemical Analysis
MCL Master of Civil Law
MCom Master of Commerce
MD Doctor of Medicine
MDS Master of Dental Surgery
MEcon Master of Economics
MEd Master of Education
MEng Master of Engineering
MLing Master of Languages
MLitt Master of Letters
MMus Master of Music
MPharm Master of Pharmacy
MPhil Master of Philosophy
MPhys Master of Physics
MSc Master of Science
MSc(Econ) Master of Science in Economics
MSW Master in Social Work
MTech Master of Technology
MTh Master of Theology
MVSc Master of Veterinary Science
PhD Doctor of Philosophy

First Destinations of Higher Education Graduates in the UK

This table provides data on all qualifiers by first destination, level of qualification obtained, domicile, and gender.

1996–97

Level of qualification		Employment in the UK	Employment overseas	Undertaking study	Not available for employment, study, or training	Assumed to be unemployed	Others	Total
Postgraduate								
Home	women	14,819	589	976	459	664	112	17,619
	men	12,063	832	1,348	238	701	93	15,275
Overseas	women	679	1,385	614	48	108	3,741	6,575
	men	773	2,908	780	141	123	5,717	10,442
First degree								
Home	women	60,309	2,321	18,447	4,359	5,303	1,246	91,985
	men	51,557	1,955	14,711	3,359	6,600	1,112	79,294
Overseas	women	1,127	1,022	1,688	96	239	5,588	9,760
	men	885	1,408	2,012	150	212	7,764	12,431
Other undergraduate								
Home	women	6,098	51	3,827	227	346	64	10,613
	men	3,389	68	4,514	121	484	95	8,671
Overseas	women	127	27	173	10	17	431	785
	men	48	107	218	7	12	409	801
Total		151,874	12,673	49,308	9,215	14,809	26,372	264,251

Source: *First Destinations of Students Leaving Higher Education Institutions 1996–97*, Higher Education Statistics Agency, © Crown copyright 1998

Employment Destinations of Graduates by Business Sector in the UK

1996–97

Business sector	Postgraduate		First degrees		Other undergraduate		Total
	Women	Men	Women	Men	Women	Men	
Education	10,103	5,640	10,061	3,351	78	76	29,309
Property development, renting, business, and research activities	1,145	2,233	10,087	13,523	305	518	27,811
Health and social work	1,155	577	10,506	4,152	4,030	675	21,095
Manufacturing	641	1,271	5,701	8,002	227	440	16,282
Wholesale and retail trade/repair of motor vehicles, motorcycles, and general and household goods	214	231	7,271	4,902	353	378	13,349
Financial activities	237	518	4,147	4,508	128	140	9,678
Public administration and defence/social security	966	965	3,451	2,949	273	211	8,815
Other community, social, and personal service activities	443	383	3,935	3,376	184	274	8,595
Transport, storage, and communication	153	346	2,605	2,718	131	154	6,107
Hotels and restaurants	38	42	2,306	1,563	227	169	4,345
Construction	24	112	418	1,820	16	122	2,512
Not known	141	188	750	822	69	60	2,030
Electricity, gas, and water supply	56	132	643	713	22	23	1,589
Agriculture and forestry	27	46	280	475	97	192	1,117
Mining and quarrying	44	177	224	533	3	17	998
Private households with employed persons	2	3	160	36	5	6	212
International organizations and bodies	16	26	80	49	1	1	173
Fishing	3	5	5	20	0	1	34
Total	15,408	12,895	62,630	53,512	6,149	3,457	154,051

Source: *First Destinations of Students Leaving Higher Education Institutions 1996–97*, Higher Education Statistics Agency, © Crown copyright 1998

Web Sites

Advisory Centre for Education

http://www.ace-ed.org.uk

The Advisory Centre for Education (ACE) is a charity funded by a variety of organizations, including Local Education Authorities, which runs discussion forums for concerned parents. Parents can submit confidential questions to ACE using a query form.

BBC Education Home Page

http://www.bbc.co.uk/education/

Regularly-updated page containing resources for teachers and schoolchildren. As well as Web pages on a variety of issues related to current BBC programmes, the 'learning station' section of this site has age- and key stage-related games and exercises for both primary and secondary schoolchildren. This site also contains resources for teachers and parents.

Biology for Children

http://www.kapili.com/biology4kids/index.html

Fun, interactive introduction to biology. You can take a quiz to test your knowledge of the basics, take a tour around the site, or search for specific information.

British Council Virtual Education Campus

http://www.britcoun.org/eis/index.htm

Guide to British education provided by the British Council. This site is a good source of information for those wishing to study in Britain or to learn more about the British educational system.

Chemistry for Children

http://www.chem4kids.com/

Fun introduction to chemistry. You can take a quiz to test your knowledge of the basics, take a tour around the site, or search for specific information.

Computer Assisted Learning in Chemistry

http://members.aol.com/ChangChem/

This chemistry site has an extensive range of online activities, some with accompanying downloadable worksheets.

Daily Telegraph Internet for Schools

http://www.internetforschools.co.uk/

The news section from the *Daily Telegraph* includes all of the paper's education news and features for the week, and is a good resource for teachers and parents.

Department for Education and Employment

http://www.dfee.gov.uk/

Official government site which includes contact details of Local Education Authorities in the UK, school and college performance tables, and recent news from the department.

Franklin Institute Science Museum

http://sln.fi.edu/

Virtual museum of science with exhibits especially designed for online presentation. The topics include 'The circle of life', 'A robot zoo', 'The wind', 'The heart', 'Life in nature', and 'Man-made life'.

GCSE English

http://www.gcse.com/recep.htm

As well as revision tips and syllabus details about English GCSE material, this site includes interactive tutorials.

GCSE French Revision

http://www.canonave.ndirect.co.uk/gcse/

Comprehensive French revision pages. The site contains revision material, past papers, and exam questions.

General Music

http://www.talkcity.com/atmusic/GM101/GMindex.shtml

Articles containing audio and graphics on music theory and major periods in music such as the Renaissance and 20th-century music.

Geographical Study Resources

http://freespace.virgin.net/r.cawley/CN/gsr.html

Extensive geographical resource, which includes outline maps in GIF format, and geographical photographs. There is also a guide to writing coursework and essays.

German Language

http://www.rmplc.co.uk/eduweb/sites/haberg/reallyusefulge/default.htm

Interactive exercises in German ranked by level and organized by discussion topic. This site would be suitable for GCSE students as well as those wishing to brush up on their German speaking skills for a holiday.

Gondar Design Science Pages

http://www.purchon.co.uk/science/

The site contains GCSE revision material and tips for physics, chemistry, and biology. Visitors can mail homework questions for additional help, and many of the pages can be downloaded and read offline.

History Channel UK

http://www.thehistorychannel.co.uk/index.htm

History articles targeted at A-level and GCSE students can be accessed at this site, as well as a debate chamber where historical issues can be discussed.

Home Education Advisory Service

http://ourworld.compuserve.com/homepages/home_ed_advisory_srv/

The Home Education Advisory Service is a charity set up by home educators to publicize education options for parents. Their Web site provides useful information for parents interested in educating their children at home, including 'information about parents' legal obligations.

Independent Schools Information Service

http://www.isis.org.uk/

Official site of the organization that represents all of the UK's independent schools. As well as a fully-searchable list of the schools, there is advice on how to choose one for your child, information for non-UK residents and recent press releases of the organization.

Information Technology Revision

http://www.doc.mmu.ac.uk/schools/bramhall/it.htm

Comprehensive reference source for the GCSE IT theory exam. The site covers the key revision areas and skills needed to pass the course.

Learning Through Play

http://www.topmarks.co.uk/parents/words.htm

Contains advice and activities for parents wanting to give their children a headstart at school. The pages have details of activities you can work through with your child at home.

Literacy

http://www.literacytrust.org.uk/Database/index.html

Maintained by the literacy trust, this site contains interesting pages of UK literacy statistics, details of government initiatives, and advice for parents on how to help their children learn to read.

Maths Tuition

http://www.maths-help.co.uk

The site, maintained by a voluntary association of maths teachers, is building up a database of worked problems in the 'knowledge bank', with very clearly explained and presented questions. There is also a maths chat room with scheduled themed sessions.

Maths Tutorials

http://www.gcse.com/Maths/pre.htm

Very focused maths GCSE preparation material, that includes staged interactive tutorials on topics such as negative numbers, probability, and trigonometry.

Montessori Education

http://www.seattleu.edu/~jcm/montessori/menu_link.html

Extensive introduction to the main principles and practices of Montessori education. The site also offers an annotated bibliography, a list of public Montessori schools, and summaries of relevant published research.

National Information Services and Systems

http://www.niss.ac.uk/education/

Education pages of the National Information Services and Systems agency. This site has links to directories, funding, educational resources, and reports and evaluation of higher education institutions.

National Union of Students

http://www.nus.org.uk/

As well as information about the NUS and its current executive, this site features *Student News*, the magazine NUS Network, and articles about student welfare, entertainments, money, media, and the latest on the NUS' fees campaign.

National Year of Reading

http://www.yearofreading.org.uk/

Information about the national year of reading from the UK national literacy trust. The Web site includes a teacher resource centre with practical tips to encourage reading, a searchable index of events, and a database of reviews and comments, to which you are invited to contribute.

NUT Online

http://www.teachers.org.uk

Official site of the National Union of Teachers (NUT). The site contains help for student teachers, discussions of pay and conditions, health and safety articles, and details of NUT policies on important issues.

Ofsted Reports Database

http://www.ofsted.gov.uk/reports/index.htm

Ofsted Reports Database with the full text of reports from Ofsted inspections. Visitors may search by school name, education authority, or postcode. The reports are in PDF format, so you may need to download the Adobe Acrobat Reader – a link to the download site is included.

Online Maths Club

http://nrich.maths.org.uk/

Online maths club developed jointly by the Royal Institution and the University of Cambridge. There are questions (ranked by Key Stage), problems, puzzles and articles, and students are encouraged to send in solutions.

Open University

http://www.open.ac.uk/

Web site from Britain's largest teaching institution (in terms of student numbers). There are examples of the university's distance-learning programmes, an online prospectus, and details of the current crop of BBC weekend programmes, used extensively as part of many of the courses.

Physics Factory – GCSE

http://physics.digiweb.com/gcse.htm

Although aimed at GCSE students, this site would be useful for anyone with an interest in physics.

Qualifications and Curriculum Authority

http://www.qca.org.uk/menu.htm

The Curriculum Authority now has the responsibility of designing and overseeing the National Curriculum. This site offers a clear explanation of the curriculum, as well as details about all the educational qualifications up to A Level, including GCSE, NVQ, and GNVQ.

Schools Online Science Cafe

http://www.shu.ac.uk/schools/sci/sol/experts/exptin.htm

Part of the Schools Online project, this site has suggestions for science experiments, a facility for posting questions to scientists, and a chance to participate in online experiments by submitting your own data.

Schools on the Internet

http://schools.sys.uea.ac.uk/schools/schools.html

Developed from a project run by the School of Information Services, this site provides links to the Web sites of schools, searchable by area.

Student Advice

http://www.studentzone.org.uk/

Maintained for students by the National Information Services and Systems agency, this site contains information about academic resources, grants and scholarships.

Student Loans Company Ltd

http://www.slc.co.uk/

Student Loans Company is wholly owned by the UK government and was formed to administer the student loans scheme. Their site covers details of what loans are available, how interest rates are calculated, and repayments are to be paid.

Student World UK

http://www.student-world.co.uk/main.htm

Resource for students, graduates, and academic staff, with pages on education, finance, jobs, sport, shopping, and culture.

Times Educational Supplement

http://www.tes.co.uk

Online version of the education industry's paper. The site offers a searchable version of the current edition, plus archives and a discussion forum for teachers.

UCAS Home Page

http://www.ucas.ac.uk/

Official site for the organization that handles admissions to universities and colleges in the UK. This site is divided into four sections: a comprehensive search facility for all 'universites, colleges, and courses'; an 'advice centre' with details of how to apply for university electronically; information for higher education staff; and 'studentUK' which includes news, views, and advice for students.

RELIGION AND BELIEF

The Year in Review

8 July 1998 US archaeologists in Aqaba, Jordan, announce the discovery of the world's oldest Christian church, built by the Christian community of Ayla in the late 3rd century.

9 July 1998 Statues of ten 20th-century Christian martyrs are unveiled at Westminster Abbey, London, England.

23 July 1998 The journal *Nature* publishes a survey of leading scientists revealing that only 7 percent believe in God.

5 August 1998 Anglican bishops approve a resolution by a vote of 526–70 that takes a tough stance against homosexuality, at an international church conference in Canterbury, England. The resolution advises against same-sex marriages and the ordination of homosexuals. The resolution is seen as a result of the increasing membership of African and Asian branches of the church, which tend to be more conservative.

6 August 1998 The Polish government refuses to concede to Israeli demands to remove crosses planted by Catholics outside Auschwitz, a Nazi death camp during World War II. The controversy originated when a single cross was erected to commemorate a papal Mass near the camp in 1979. Catholics erected some 50 crucifixes to protest against efforts to remove the cross.

9 October 1998 The National Assembly in Pakistan approves an amendment that makes Islamic law supreme. The amendment is opposed by most opposition political parties, business groups, women's groups, human rights activists, and non-Muslims.

11 October 1998 Pope John Paul II canonizes Edith Stein, a Jewish-born Catholic nun who was killed at Auschwitz during the Holocaust. The pope's action angers many Jewish groups.

15 October 1998 Pope John Paul II issues *Fides et Ratio/Faith and Reason,* an encyclical that he has reportedly worked on for 12 years, in which he emphasizes the importance of a union between religious faith and rational thought.

27 November 1998 Pope John Paul II announces a plan to grant indulgences as part of his celebration of the year 2000 as a 'Holy Year'. Roman Catholics could avoid punishment for their sins by performing charity work and refraining from minor sins.

December 1998 HarperCollins publishes *New Era, New Church,* a handbook for churches to attract larger congregations for the Millennium. In it, George Carey, Archbishop of Canterbury, recommends that churches shorten their services and that Christians should be 'less overtly religious' to gain a wider appeal.

3–14 December 1998 The World Council of Churches meets in Harare, Zimbabwe, marking its 50th anniversary. In a statement issued at the end of the conference, the council calls on donor nations to forgive debt of developing countries by the year 2000, claiming that it is a 'jubilee' year, a year in which, according to the Bible, all debt should be forgiven.

25 December 1998 In his annual Christmas message, Pope John Paul II appeals for the worldwide abolition of capital punishment, as thousands of demonstrators against the death penalty converge on St Peter's Square in the Vatican.

25 December 1998 In his Christmas Day sermon at Canterbury Cathedral, George Carey, Archbishop of Canterbury, says that the word 'insecurity' sums up 1998 for him, lamenting political, economic, and natural disasters of the year.

26 December 1998 Millennium Dome organizers announce that the Dome will include an account of the life of Jesus Christ and have a resident chaplain to offer spiritual guidance and lead visitors in prayer. Plans for the Dome, in Greenwich, London, England, have been criticized for marginalizing Christianity.

29 December 1998 Hindu extremists burn down two Christian churches in the Surat district of Gujarat, India. Some 90 attacks on India's Christians, who comprise 2.5 percent of the population, have been reported in 1998.

January 1999 British rabbis and Catholic leaders at the Vatican agree to form an amicable partnership and accept the legitimacy of each other's beliefs. Until now, relations were hindered by the Catholic belief that the coming of Jesus Christ superseded the Jewish Covenant between God and Abraham.

8 January 1999 Fourteen members of a US doomsday cult, the Concerned Christians, are deported from Israel. They have been accused of planning an apocalyptic shoot-out with police in Jerusalem.

20 January 1999 British church leaders seek assurances that the 'Millennium Moment', including observing a period of silence, lighting candles, and reading a seven-line Millennium resolution, will be fully observed at the Millennium Dome in Greenwich, London, England.

26 January 1999 The Vatican issues an updated version of the rite of exorcism, which has been under revision for ten years. The practice includes chanting, using holy water, and ordering the devil to leave the possessed person, and is little changed from its last update in 1614.

14 February 1999 Orthodox Jews in Jerusalem protest against a series of Supreme Court rulings, such as the end of military exemption for Orthodox teenagers and the integration of formerly Orthodox local religious councils with Conservative and Reform Jews. A group of secular liberal Jews protest against the Orthodox group, which they claim is threatening democracy in Israel.

April 1999 The felony trial begins of US Mormon polygamist leader David Kingston for charges of incest and sexual abuse of a minor. He is accused of making his 16-year-old niece his 15th wife.

25 April 1999 The British government's electoral working party, chaired by Home Office minister George Howarth, recommends that members of the clergy be allowed to stand for Parliament in England and Scotland for the first time in nearly 200 years.

30 April 1999 Henry D'Souza, the archbishop of Calcutta, announces that the Pope has begun the process of canonization of Mother Teresa, waiving the normal mandatory wait of five years after death.

7 May 1999 The Church of England issues a document that proposes guaranteed seats in the House of Lords for Muslims, Sikhs, Hindus, and Jews, as well as other sects of Christianity.

12 June 1999 Maurice Couve de Murville, the Roman Catholic archbishop of Birmingham, England, announces his resignation, thought to be provoked by a legal battle involving the victims of a paedophile priest formerly in his diocese.

17 June 1999 Cardinal Basil Hume, Britain's most senior Catholic cleric, Archbishop of Westminster 1976–99, the first Benedictine monk to be the Archbishop of Westminster since 1850, dies of stomach cancer in London, England, aged 76.

***Cardinal Basil Hume**, Archbishop of Westminster and Britain's most senior Catholic cleric, died on 17 June 1999.* Photo: Richard Watt

24 June 1999 British prime minister Tony Blair, the duchess of Kent, and many other political and religious leaders attend the funeral of Cardinal Basil Hume at Westminster Abbey, London, England.

25 June 1999 The German parliament votes to erect a memorial to Jewish victims of the Holocaust, after more than ten years of debate, in the centre of Berlin. The monument, designed by US architect Peter Eisenman, comprises a labyrinth of 2,700 concrete blocks.

World Religions and Beliefs

Major World Faiths

For religions other than Christianity, the abbreviations CE and BCE have been used for dates instead of AD and BC, in accordance with multi-faith practice.

Baha'i

The Baha'i faith originated in the mid-19th century in the area of present-day Iran. It is based on the belief that the man born as Mirza Husayn Ali in 1817 was the prophet sent by God to the present age. He is now known as Baha'u'llah – 'the Glory of God'.

Baha'is believe that there have been revelations from God appropriate to each era, including the Torah, the New Testament, the Koran, and the words of the Buddha and the Hindu god Krishna. Baha'is maintain that these revelations have been superseded, although not contradicted, by the writings of Baha'u'llah and his successor Abdul Baha. These writings form the main body of Baha'i scripture.

Baha'is believe that humanity is constantly evolving and growing more adult in its understanding and behaviour, and thus gradually becoming capable of forming one world rather than diverse nations, races, and religions. Baha'is also believe in One God, creator of all, and that humanity is a special creation, essentially good.

The Baha'i teachings stress economic justice, equal rights, and education for all, and the breaking down of traditional barriers of race, class, and creed. These are seen as flaws that will disappear as the Baha'i faith becomes universal.

The Baha'i international headquarters is in Haifa, Israel, and includes an International House of Justice in preparation for the time when there will be one world government, guided by the Baha'i faith. The Baha'i community meet in local spiritual assemblies whose structure is democratic and participatory, intended as a model for universal government.

There are 5 million Baha'is worldwide in more than 175 countries, with the largest concentrations in the USA (approximately 300,000) and Africa (approximately 1 million). The claim that the Baha'i sacred texts are the successor to the Koran has led to criticism of Baha'i in many Muslim lands, including Iran, where the faith began. Most Baha'is today are not from Iran.

Buddhism

Buddhists follow the teachings of Siddhartha Gautama, given the title of the Buddha – the 'enlightened' or 'awakened' one. He was born the son of a nobleman in northern India in the 6th century BCE. He grew up in a palace protected from the harsh realities of life, but when he eventually encountered suffering, old age, and death, he left the palace to search for understanding of suffering and the way to end it. When he reached enlightenment, he began to teach the Four Noble Truths:

Suffering exists; There is a reason for suffering; There is a way to end suffering;

The way to end suffering is through the Eightfold Path.

Eightfold Path

1. Right views;
2. Right thoughts;
3. Right speech;
4. Right action;
5. Right livelihood;
6. Right effort;
7. Right mindfulness;
8. Right concentration.

By learning and practising this path one can eventually escape the cycle of birth and death. Buddhists believe that all beings are reborn into many different forms because of the ties of desire. When desire is allowed to cool like a fire going out, the attachment to the cycle of birth and death is loosened. Buddhists try to perfect the qualities of wisdom, compassion, and harmlessness in order to achieve enlightenment, or Buddhahood, leading to the highest peace and freedom, which is nirvana. According to Buddhist tradition, there have been other Buddhas both before and since Siddhartha Gautama.

The teachings of the Buddha were handed down orally and eventually written in the first century BCE in a collection of writings called the *Tripitaka* – 'three baskets'. Different versions survive in Chinese, Tibetan, and Pali (an ancient south Indian language), and they are now translated into hundreds of languages worldwide. There are also important Buddhist scriptures written by later sages and scholars, many of them in the ancient Indian language Sanskrit.

There are three main branches of Buddhism: Theravada, found mainly in southeast Asia, Sri Lanka, and India; Tibetan Mahayana; and Chinese/Japanese Mahayana. There is also a wide variety of new Buddhist movements.

Each branch of Buddhism has its own festivals. The most common is Wesak (May/June), which celebrates the birth, enlightenment, and death of the Buddha, all of which happened on the same day in different years.

It is impossible to estimate the number of Buddhists worldwide, as there is no central organization. The majority of Buddhists live in Asia, although Buddhism is growing rapidly beyond Asia, particularly in the USA and UK. More than 85 percent of the population of Myanmar (Burma) and Thailand are Buddhists, and more than 70 percent in Cambodia, Laos, and Japan. Buddhism is the state religion in Thailand and Bhutan. There is no central authority in Buddhism, each school having its own teachers and spiritual guides, although figures such as the Dalai Lama have raised the worldwide profile of Buddhism and voiced a Buddhist viewpoint on world affairs.

Christianity

Christians believe in one God who created the universe, and created human beings to have a special relationship with him. Through human wilfulness, exemplified in the story of Adam and Eve, this relationship was broken. Christians believe that because of his love for humanity, God took on the form of a man, Jesus, in order to bring them back into a relationship with him. The Gospels relate that Jesus was conceived by a virgin, Mary, through the power of God, and was born as a baby in Bethlehem. Modern scholarship now puts his birth around 4 BC. Christians take their name from the title given to Jesus: 'the Christ', meaning the anointed one of God. After three years of teaching, Jesus was crucified and died, but Christians believe that through the power of God he came to life again. This belief was spread by Jesus's closest followers, the Apostles, and Christianity grew rapidly in the first three centuries AD.

The Christian Bible consists of the Old Testament, originally written in Hebrew (the same book as the Hebrew Bible read by Jews), and the New Testament, originally written in Greek, which contains accounts of the life and teachings of Jesus, and letters from early Christians. The Bible is translated into many different languages.

Major festivals are Christmas (25 December), which celebrates the birth of Jesus, and Easter (March/April), which celebrates his resurrection from death.

There are nearly two billion Christians worldwide, especially in Europe, North and South America, southern Africa and Australasia. Christianity has many different branches, referred to as churches or denominations. Catholicism is the largest with 900 million followers under the leadership of the Pope, who is based in Rome. Other major branches are Orthodox and Protestant. The Orthodox churches are self-governing, each led by a Patriarch. There is a large number of Protestant denominations, each with a different organization and authority. The World Council of Churches provides a forum for dialogue amongst the major Protestant Churches.

Ten Commandments

1. To have no other gods besides Jehovah;
2. To make no idols;
3. Not to misuse the name of God;
4. To keep the sabbath holy;
5. To honour one's parents;
6. Not to commit murder;
7. Not to commit adultery;
8. Not to commit theft;
9. Not to give false evidence;
10. Not to be covetous.

Hinduism

Hinduism encompasses a wide variety of beliefs originating in India, and is regarded by some as not constituting a formal religion at all. No precise dates can be given for its origins, although the Vedas, the earliest texts of Hinduism, arose from a culture that was probably established in India during the second millennium BCE.

Most Hindus believe that God takes many forms and is worshipped by many different names, so the multitude of gods and goddesses in Hindu belief are aspects of the same godhead. God has three main male forms, Brahma the Creator, Vishnu the Preserver, and Shiva the Destroyer. Each of these has a female counterpart: respectively Sarasvati, Lakshmi, and Parvati. God may also come to Earth in human form: the best known of these are Krishna and Rama, both incarnations of Vishnu. Each person and each animal embodies a spark (atman) of the universal soul, which is God. After death the atman is reborn in a new body. Therefore God is in every object in the universe, and everything that exists is part of God.

Hindus believe that every action, good or bad, has an effect (karma) on this life and on future lives. By accumulating positive karma one can eventually break free from the cycles of birth and death to achieve liberation or moksha, which is complete union with God.

There are many sacred books, all written in the ancient Indian language Sanskrit. The oldest are the Vedas, first written in the second millennium BCE, followed by the Upanishads, more philosophical writings. Two great epics, the *Mahābhārata* and the *Rāmayāna*, existed in oral form long before they were written around 2,000 years ago. The *Mahābhārata* contains the best-loved Hindu scripture, the Bhagavad Gita, or 'Song of the Lord', about the god Krishna.

Festivals vary in different parts of India. Two almost universally celebrated festivals are Holi (March/April), a time of games and pranks with several different associated stories, and Divali (October), a new-year festival that celebrates the story of the god Rama and his wife Sita.

There are nearly 750 million Hindus worldwide, almost all living in south Asia. In India there are 650 million Hindus, and other large Hindu communities live in countries where colonial or trading ties encouraged migration from India: the UK, Guyana, Kenya, South Africa, and Indonesia.

Islam

The beliefs of Islam are summed up in the Declaration of Faith: 'There is no god but God, and Muhammad is the Prophet of God'.

Islam means 'peace' or 'submission', and

Five Pillars of Islam

1. Repeating the creed;
2. Daily prayer or salat;
3. Giving alms;
4. Fasting during the month of Ramadan;
5. The hajj, or pilgrimage to Mecca, once in a lifetime.

(continued on p. 399)

Hindu Gods

The Hindu pantheon is dominated by the primary gods Shiva and Vishnu, and, to a lesser extent Brahma, the creator, who control the powers of destruction and preservation. Throughout India, Hinduism is organized around the two main sects, Vaishnavism and Shaivism, whose followers regard either Vishnu or Shiva as the pre-eminent deity. Vishnu is also worshipped in up to 22 earthly incarnations. The best-known deities and their aspects or incarnations are listed below.

Agni god of fire; a three-headed god who rides on a ram
Balarama brother of Krishna
Bhairava incarnation of Shiva
Brahma god of creation
Durga wife of Shiva, the inaccessible
Ganesh elephant-headed son of Shiva
Garuda bird on which Shiva rides
Hanuman monkey god
Indra storm god, bringer of rain
Iswara collectively represented as Trimurti by Brahma, Vishnu, and Shiva; Iswara corresponds to nature and the human soul
Kali goddess of destruction; evil wife of Shiva
Kalkin incarnation of Vishnu as a giant with a horse's head
Kama god of desire and sexual lust
Karaikkal-Ammaiyar mother goddess and teacher, often shown playing the cymbals
Karrttikeya six-headed, twelve-armed god who rides on a peacock
Krishna incarnation of Vishnu which corresponds to the perfect deification of life
Kurma incarnation of Vishnu as a tortoise
Lakshmana half-brother of Rama
Lakshmi (Sri) goddess of wealth and good fortune; wife of Vishnu
Mahadevi Shakti (Mahasakti) supreme goddess; corresponds to the Absolute (Brahman) and facilitates its self-manifestation
Mahishasuramardini consort of Shiva
Matsya incarnation of Vishnu as a fish
Nandin bull vehicle of Shiva
Narada incarnation of Vishnu
Narasimha incarnation of Vishnu as a man-lion
Nataraja aspect of Shiva as the lord of dance and rhythm
Parashurama incarnation of Vishnu
Parvati good wife of Shiva; opposite of Kali
Pidari consort of Shiva
Pushan the enhancer, prosperer, and enlightener
Radha consort of Krishna; represents romantic love
Rama incarnation of Vishnu
Rudra the violent, terrifying aspect of Shiva
Sarasvati mother goddess of art, music, and learning; female counterpart of Brahma
Savitri creator of the true and the just
Shakti female symbol of power or energy
Shani astral god and bringer of ill-luck
Shiva god of creation and destruction; lord of the dance
Shatrughna half brother of Rama
Sita wife of Rama
Skanda formed from the discarded semen of Shiva
Surya sun god; the illuminator
Uma the gracious; ascetic goddess
Vamana incarnation of Vishnu as a dwarf
Varaha incarnation of Vishnu as a boar
Virabhadra incarnation of Shiva
Vishnu god of creation
Yashoda foster mother of Krishna

Islam: Chronology

3rd–6th centuries The eastern Roman Empire and the Persian Sassanians are in continuous conflict for the domination of Syria, Egypt, and Asia Minor.

571 Birth of Muhammad, the prophet of Islam, in Mecca.

6th–7th centuries Islam begins in Arabia, calling for a new way of life based on submission to God. An Islamic state is established that develops further during the formative period of the four Orthodox caliphs or successors to the prophet, Abu Bakr, Umar, Uthman, and Ali. During this period the Persians are defeated (637) and their capital Cteisphon is captured.

8th century Islam expands under the Umayyad and Abbasid dynasties to Spain and Sind; southern France is invaded; Southern Italy is occupied. The early schools of Islamic law continue to develop during this period and Islamic legal doctrine becomes integrated into the legal practices of the courts.

9th century Turkish slave Mamelukes rise to power in Baghdad and a dictatorship is established in Egypt that occupies Syria, in a move towards the fragmentation of the main Islamic state.

10th century The Fatimid Shiite Isma'ili sect conquers Cairo in 969. Al-Azhar University is founded in 972. With the insanity of the Fatimid caliph (who believes himself God) and his death in 1018, a new religion appears in the form of the Druze Shia subsect, comprised of those adherents who believe in the caliph's divinity.

11th century The Abbasid and Fatimid dynasties and the Byzantine empire decline. The central Asian Turkish nomads known as the Seljuks emerges. Islamic law becomes stagnant. The first Christian Crusade captures Muslim-held Jerusalem in 1099.

12th century Muslims are reunited in a jihad or holy war, and recapture Jerusalem under the leadership of Saladin. The Mongols emerge as a new force in the Middle East, seizing Persia and part of Syria.

13th century The Mongols continue their march, sacking Baghdad. With the fall of the city 1258 and the death of the caliph Mustasim, the Abbasid caliphate ends. Only two years later the Mongols are defeated by Qutuz at the decisive Battle of Ayn Jalut on the way to Damascus, ending their expansion towards the heartland of the Muslim world. Thirty years later the Mongol khan converts to Islam. This is followed by the emergence of the first Ottomans in Turkey.

14th century Ottoman Turks invade Bulgarian territory up to the Balkans.

15th century In the Second Battle of Kossova in 1446 Serbia is annexed to Turkey, with Bosnia as its vassal. Muhammad al-Fath conquers Constantinople in 1453. Albania is annexed to the Ottoman Turkish empire. In 1492, Granada, the last Muslim state in Spain, falls to the monarchs of Spain, Ferdinand and Isabella. The Safavid dynasty is founded in Persia.

16th–17th centuries Ottoman power reaches its height during the reign of the Ottoman Suleiman the Magnificent 1520–65. The first unsuccessful Ottoman siege of Vienna is in 1529, and the second in 1683. With the defeat of

(*continued*)

Islam: Chronology (*continued*)

	the Ottomans in the naval battle of Lepanto, their dominance of the Mediterranean ends. The forcible conversion of Muslims to Catholicism begins in Spain.
18th century	In Arabia, Muhammad ibn-Abd-al-Wahab (1703–1792) preaches a return to fundamental Muslim values.
19th century	Muhammad Ali is appointed pasha of Egypt by the Turks in 1805, after subduing the Mamelukes. He occupies Mecca and Taif in 1813 and continues across Arabia, expelling the Saudis from their capital Dariyya in 1818. European powers take control of many territories that previously came under Muslim rule. In 1876 Britain purchases shares in the Suez Canal and becomes involved in Egypt, with military occupation following in 1882. In 1878 Turkey hands Cyprus to Britain and a year later, after the Treaty of Berlin, Turkey loses 80 percent of its European territory.
20th century	European expansion continues in the Middle East. During World War I, the Arabs revolt against Ottoman Turkish rule. In 1921, the British make kings of two sons of the Sharif of Mecca, Abdullah ibn Hussein of Transjordan and Faisal of Iraq. Mustafa Kemal abolishes the Turkish sultanate in 1922 and becomes the first president of Turkey. Reza Shah seizes the government in Persia in 1925. Abdul Aziz Ibn Saud captures Riyadh and Mecca, assuming the title of king in 1926. Hasan al-Banna founds the Muslim Brotherhood in Egypt in 1928. Egyptian president Gamal Abdel Nasser nationalizes the Suez Canal in 1956 and executes Sayyid Qutb, the leader of the Muslim Brotherhood. The secular Pahlavi dynasty in Iran ends in 1979 with the return from exile of Ayatollah Khomeini, who declares Iran an Islamic Republic. The Iraq–Iran War is followed by Saddam Hussein's invasion of Kuwait (1990) and the Gulf War. Revivalist movements arise, calling for a return to fundamental Islamic values; Islamic regimes are established in Iran, Afghanistan, and Sudan.

a Muslim is 'one who submits' (to the will of God). In Islam there is one God (Arabic Allah), who is creator of the universe and the only absolute power. According to Muslim belief, God has sent many prophets, from Adam onwards, to give his message to humanity, but their message was partially lost or misunderstood. The complete message is believed to have been given by the Prophet Muhammad, who lived in Arabia in the 6th century CE. Although this message marked the beginning of a formal religion, Muslims believe that all previous prophets were Muslims, and that Islam is the primordial faith. Muslims regard Muhammad with deep love and respect as God's final prophet, and seek to follow his example, but worship is due only to God.

Muslims believe that the Koran was dictated to the Prophet Muhammad by the angel Jibra'il, a messenger from God, and, because it was committed to memory and written down almost immediately, that it is the final and complete revelation from God. The Koran is believed to have been written by God, in Arabic, before time began. Muslims point to the beauty of the language as evidence of its divine origin, and it is always recited in Arabic.

Muslim festivals are dated according to the lunar calendar. The main festivals are Eid-Lul-Fitr, celebrating the end of the month of fasting, and Eid-ul-Adha, celebrating the obedience of the prophet Ibrahim (Abraham), and the culmination of the annual pilgrimage to Mecca (Arabic Makkah).

There are over a billion Muslims worldwide, especially in the Middle East, North and West Africa, southeastern Europe, Indonesia, and Malaysia. In 19 countries of the Middle East and North Africa, more than 90 percent of the population is Muslim. There are two main branches of Islam: Sunni who make up 80 percent of all Muslims, and Shi'a, who are found mainly in Iran, Iraq, Yemen, and Bahrain. There is no overall world organization of Islam, but several bodies have been set up to promote contact and to give Islam a voice in international affairs. These bodies include the World Muslim Congress, the Muslim World League, and the Organization of the Islamic Conference.

Jainism

The word Jain means follower of the Jinas – 'those who overcome', in the sense of achieving discipline over one's own desires, thoughts, and actions. There were 24 Jinas, also known as Tirthankaras ('bridge-builders'), the last of whom was Mahavira who lived in India in the 5th century BCE. The first is believed to have lived millions of years ago and to have invented human culture. The example of the Jinas helps others to achieve freedom from reincarnation. The belief in non-violence, *ahimsa,* is central to the Jain tradition, and Jains try to avoid violence to life in every form, including animals and plants as well as humans. Jain monks and nuns wear a cloth over the mouth and nose to avoid harming any flying insects, and sweep the ground in front of them to avoid treading on any creature. This central teaching of non-violence has had a powerful effect on Indian culture and thought and was highlighted by the teachings of Mahatma Gandhi.

The main festival is Paryushana (August/September), an eight-day period of confession and fasting.

There are 8 million Jains worldwide, over 98 percent of them in India. The two largest Jain communities outside India are in the UK and the USA.

The Jain tradition is divided into two groups: Svetambaras, who are concentrated in northeast India, and Digambaras, who mainly live in southern India. There are Jain temples in all the main Indian cities.

Judaism

Jews believe in one God, the Creator and Ruler of the universe. They believe that God made a Covenant, or agreement, with Abraham, who is regarded as the father of the Jewish people, and is believed by some scholars to have lived around 1900 BCE. Keeping the law is the Jewish people's part in this Covenant. Jews look forward to the coming of the Messiah, a leader from God, who will bring peace, fruitfulness, and security to the whole world. At the Messiah's coming, the dead will be brought back to life and judged by God.

The Hebrew Bible consists of the Torah (Five Books of Moses), the Prophets, and other writings, including the Psalms. It was originally written in Hebrew, and is still read in Hebrew. The Torah tells the early history of the Jewish people, and contains laws and guidance on one's way of life. Study of the law is an important part of Jewish life. The fifth commandment lays down that no work must be done on the seventh day of the week, the Sabbath, or Shabbat. Since Jewish days are reckoned from nightfall to nightfall, the Sabbath begins as it gets dark on Friday evening, and ends at dusk on Saturday evening. Jewish food laws (called *kashrut*) relate to what is eaten, and how it is slaughtered, prepared, cooked, and eaten. Food is either *kosher* (permitted) or *terefah* (forbidden).

Major festivals are Rosh Hashanah (New Year – September/October), Yom Kippur (the Day of Atonement) which is a major fast within the new-year period, and Pesach (Passover – March/April), which celebrates the escape of the Hebrews from slavery in Egypt.

Jews have no overall religious authority, but questions of belief and practice are debated by Rabbis who are trained in Jewish law and its interpretation. The most traditional form of Judaism is known as Orthodox. Orthodox Jews use only Hebrew in services, and interpret the laws quite strictly. Conservative Judaism, mainly found in the USA, seeks to interpret the law in the light of changing circumstances, while remaining true to tradition. Reform, or Liberal, Judaism arose in the 19th century and observes fewer dietary laws, as well as holding services in the vernacular rather than in Hebrew. Bodies such as the World Jewish Congress, which represents around 70 percent of all Jews, provide a forum for debate and a Jewish voice in world affairs.

There are approximately 12.8 million Jews worldwide, in the sense that a Jew is the child of a Jewish mother, although not all are religious Jews who follow the laws given by God to Moses. Approximately 48 percent live in North America, 30 percent in Israel, and 20 percent in Europe and Russia.

Shintoism

Shinto is the traditional religion of Japan, and means 'the way of the gods'. Shinto religion is closely tied up with the landscape of Japan and with family ancestors. Shinto ceremonies appeal to kami, the mysterious powers of nature, for protection and benevolent treatment. Kami are associated with natural features such as caves, rocks, streams, trees, and particularly mountains. Communal festivals and personal landmarks are celebrated at Shinto shrines, some of which are linked to particular aspects of life such as a trade, or old age.

Major festivals are New Year's Day and the Cherry Blossom Festival in early spring.

It is difficult to estimate numbers of Shinto followers, since the majority of Japanese follow Shinto ceremonies and practices for particular occasions or because of a family tradition, but many combine this with another religion, especially Buddhism. Since Shinto worship is so intimately linked with the land of Japan, it is only found there or in émigré communities.

Sikhism

The Sikh faith began in the Punjab in India in the 15th century. Guru Nanak, the founder of Sikhism, taught this new faith that rejected both Hindu and Muslim religious and social practices of the time. The Punjabi word *Sikh* means 'follower' or 'disciple'. Guru Nanak was succeeded by nine further Gurus, or teachers, each of whom was chosen by his predecessor, and each of whom made a distinctive contribution to the development of the Sikh faith. In 1708 the collection of Sikh writings was instituted as the Guru for all time to come. Sikhs revere their scripture, the Guru Granth Sahib, as they would a living teacher.

The Guru Granth Sahib contains hymns written by some of the Sikh Gurus. These were collected by Guru Arjan, the fifth Guru, who also added hymns and poems written by devout Muslims and Hindus, saying that God's revelation is not confined to Sikhs. This collection was known as the Adi Granth, or 'first book'. Guru Gobind Singh, the tenth Guru, instituted this collection as the Guru for the Sikhs for all time. It is written in Gurmukhi, a form of written Punjabi.

Sikhs believe in one God, described as 'timeless and without form', creator and director of the universe. He cannot be found by religious practices, but makes himself known to those who are ready, as they seek him through prayer and service to others. Sikh teachings emphasize equality, service, and protection of the weak against injustice.

Sikhs wear five distinctive marks of their faith, known as the 'five Ks' because their names in Punjabi all begin with K:

Five Ks

1. Kesh – uncut hair. Devout Sikhs do not cut their hair or beard at any time;
2. Kanga – a comb to keep the hair in place. The hair is also kept tidy under a turban in imitation of the great Sikh Guru, Gobind Singh;
3. Kara – a steel bangle, a complete circle symbolizing one God and one truth;
4. Kirpan – a small sword or dagger, a reminder of the need to fight injustice;
5. Kacchera – short trousers or breeches, indicating readiness to ride into battle.

There are approximately 15 million Sikhs worldwide. Most of them (around 13 million) live in India, mainly in the Punjab in northwest India, but Sikhs have migrated to many parts of the world, and there are sizeable communities in the UK (up to half a million), the USA (over 250,000) and Canada (50,000), and smaller ones in East Africa, Europe, Malaysia, Indonesia, Australia, and New Zealand. The Sikh World Council was formed in 1995 to provide a forum and an international voice for Sikhs.

Taoism

Taoism emerged in China around the first century CE, and is named after the Chinese word *Tao* (Way or Path). The Tao is a natural force, the Way of the Universe, which guides all life. Living in harmony with the Tao brings peace and happiness; struggling against it brings suffering.

The balance of the universe is created by the forces of yin and yang – opposite forces in continual interaction and change, giving order to all life. Yin is heavy, dark, moist, earthy, and is associated with the feminine. Yang is airy, light, dry, hot, heavenly, and associated with the masculine. All forms of life are either predominantly yin or yang, but never exclusively so. The yin/yang symbol represents the two forces in balance, but each containing a speck of the other.

From the 5th to the 3rd century BCE, much was written on the significance of the Tao, most significantly the *Tao Te Ching* of Lao Tzu, the book of the sage Chuang Tzu, and the writings of Kung Fu Tzu (Confucius). They are still influential to this day, but there are also hundreds of other Taoist texts. By the 14th century CE, over 1,440 of these had been collected together to form the Taoist Canon.

Traditional Taoist practices include the exorcism of evil spirits and ghosts, divination in various forms, and the worship of deities, many of whom have specific roles such as help in childbirth or different illnesses. The art of *feng shui,* or geomancy, is also practised in order to build in accordance with the Tao of the landscape.

Major festivals are Chinese New Year (January/February) and the mid-autumn Moon festival.

Because of the repression of religion in China, it is impossible to estimate the number of Taoists. However, the number of male and female Taoist priests in China is growing rapidly, and now stands at around 15,000. New temples are being opened and old ones restored. Taoist traditions are followed by members of Chinese communities throughout the world, and Taoist thought, literature, and philosophy is becoming increasingly popular with non-Chinese followers. The China Taoist Association promotes Taoism in China, although its function is partly political rather than religious.

Important Sites of Pilgrimage in World Religions

For religions other than Christianity, the abbreviations CE and BCE have been used for dates instead of AD and BC, in accordance with multi-faith practice.

Buddhism

Early Buddhist scriptures mention four destinations in Nepal or India that a Buddhist pilgrim might visit – these sites are the Buddha's birthplace at Lumbini in Nepal, Bodh Gaya in India where he found enlightenment, Sarnath where he preached his first sermon, and Kusingara where he died. Relics of the Buddha were housed in specially built structures called stupas. As the traditions of Buddhism have developed and spread, hundreds of sites have become pilgrimage destinations, including temples, stupas, pagodas, mountains, and bodhi-trees (traditionally a religious and spiritual tree).

Important sites include Siripada (Adam's Peak) in Sri Lanka, which attracts not only Buddhists but also Hindu, Muslim, and Christian pilgrims. According to Sri Lankan Buddhist traditions, the Buddha came to Sri Lanka three times during his ministry, and on his third visit he left his footprint on the peak of this mountain. For the Hindu pilgrims the footprint is Krishna's, for the Muslims it is Adam's, and for the Christians it was made by St Thomas. In China there are four main sacred mountains visited by Buddhist pilgrims, and Mount Kailas in western Tibet is an important destination for Tibetan Buddhist pilgrims.

Christianity

Some pilgrimage sites are specific to a local community, and some are associated with the historic area of Palestine, where Jesus lived. This area is now divided between parts of the modern states of Israel, Jordan, and Syria, and is known in Christianity as the Holy Land. The main focus of a pilgrimage to the Holy Land is Jerusalem, where Jesus died and rose again. Other

important sites in the Holy Land are Bethlehem, where Jesus was born, Nazareth where he grew up, and the River Jordan where he was baptized.

Rome is a centre of pilgrimage, particularly for Catholics, as the Vatican is the seat of the papacy, but other Christians visit because of Rome's association with St Peter and St Paul, two of the greatest early Christian leaders.

Santiago de Compostela in northern Spain is believed to be the burial place of St James, one of Jesus' disciples. It was especially popular as a pilgrimage centre in medieval Europe and there are still routes to the shrine from many different countries in Europe. Thousands of pilgrims still walk all or part of the route.

Thousands of people make pilgrimage to Lourdes in France because of a series of visions seen by St Bernadette in 1854, and the healing believed to be associated with the spring of water which arose there.

Hinduism

Pilgrimages are an important part of Hindu devotion, and there are hundreds of pilgrimage sites throughout India. Hindus celebrate many local festivals, often associated with pilgrimage sites or shrines not known outside their own area.

The River Ganges is regarded as holy throughout its length, but particularly at Benares (Varanasi), where pilgrims bathe, and the ashes of the dead are scattered.

Hindus regard the whole range of the Himalayas as sacred, especially Mount Kailas, where it is said that the god Shiva sits in meditation, and where Arjuna (a hero of the *Mahābhārata*) went to visit him.

Vrindavan, on the sacred River Yamuna, is revered as the birthplace of the god Krishna, and attracts pilgrims from all over India and beyond, especially at Janmashtami, the festival celebrating Krishna's birth, when pilgrims travel all round the town to the different temples.

In the town of Puri on the east coast of India, a huge image of the god Vishnu is placed on an enormous wooden chariot called a jagannath and pulled through the

Judaism: Chronology

c. 2000 BCE	Led by Abraham, the ancient Hebrews emigrate from Mesopotamia to Canaan.
18th century BCE –1580 BCE	Some settle on the borders of Egypt and are put to forced labour.
13th century BCE	They are rescued by Moses, who aims at their establishment in Palestine. Moses receives the Ten Commandments from God and brings them to the people. The main invasion of Canaan is led by Joshua in about 1274.
12th–11th centuries BCE	During the period of Judges, ascendancy is established over the Canaanites.
c. 1000 BCE	Complete conquest of Palestine and the union of all Judea is achieved under David, and Jerusalem becomes the capital.
10th century BCE	Solomon succeeds David and enjoys a reputation for great wealth and wisdom, but his lack of a constructive policy leads, after his death, to the secession of the north of Judea (Israel) under Jeroboam, with only the tribe of Judah remaining under the house of David as the southern kingdom of Judah.
9th–8th centuries BCE	Assyria becomes the dominant power in the Middle East. Israel purchases safety by tribute, but the basis of the society is corrupt, and prophets such as Amos, Isaiah, and Micah predict destruction. At the hands of Tiglathpileser and his successor Shalmaneser IV, the northern kingdom (Israel) is made into Assyrian provinces after the fall of Samaria in 721 BCE, although the southern kingdom of Judah is spared as an ally.
586–458 BCE	Nebuchadnezzar takes Jerusalem and carries off the major part of the population to Babylon. Judaism is retained during exile, and is reconstituted by Ezra on the return to Jerusalem.
520 BCE	The Temple, originally built by Solomon, is restored.
c. 444 BCE	Ezra promulgates the legal code that is to govern the future of the Jewish people.
4th–3rd centuries BCE	After the conquest of the Persian Empire by Alexander the Great, the Syrian Seleucid rulers and the Egyptian Ptolemaic dynasty struggle for control of Palestine, which comes under the government of Egypt, although with a large measure of freedom.
2nd century BCE	With the advance of Syrian power, Antiochus IV attempts to intervene in the internal quarrels of the Hebrews, even desecrating the Temple, and a revolt breaks out in 165 BCE led by the Maccabee family.
63 BCE	Judea's near-independence ends when internal dissension causes the Roman general Pompey to intervene, and Roman suzerainty is established.
1st century CE	A revolt leads to the destruction of the Temple (66–70) by the Roman emperor Titus. Judean national sentiment is encouraged by the work of Rabbi Johanan ben Zakkai (c. 20–90), and, following him, the president of the Sanhedrin (supreme court) is recognized as the patriarch of Palestinian Jewry.
2nd–3rd centuries	Greatest of the Sanhedrin presidents is Rabbi Judah Ha-Nasi, who codifies the traditional law in the *Mishnah*. The Palestinian *Talmud* (c. 375) adds the *Gemara* to the *Mishnah*.
4th–5th centuries	The intellectual leadership of Judaism passes to the descendants of the 6th century BCE exiles in Babylonia, who compile the Babylonian *Talmud*.
8th–13th centuries	Judaism enjoys a golden era, producing the philosopher Saadiah, the poet Jehudah Ha-levi (c. 1075–1141), the codifier Moses Maimonides, and others.
14th–17th centuries	Where Christianity becomes the dominant or state religion, the Jews are increasingly segregated from mainstream life and trade by the Inquisition, anti-Semitic legislation, or by expulsion. The Protestant and Islamic states and their colonies allow for refuge. Persecution leads to messianic hopes, strengthened by the 16th-century revival of Kabbalism, culminating in the messianic movement of Shabbatai Sevi in the 17th century.
18th–19th centuries	Outbreaks of persecution increase with the rise of European nationalism. Reform Judaism, a rejection of religious orthodoxy and an attempt to interpret it for modern times, begins in Germany in 1810 and is soon established in England and the USA. In the late 19th century, large numbers of Jews fleeing persecution (pogroms) in Russia and Eastern Europe emigrate to the USA, leading to the development of large Orthodox, Conservative, and Reform communities there. Many become Americanized and lose interest in religion.
20th century	Zionism, a nationalist movement dedicated to achieving a secure homeland where the Jewish people would be free from persecution, is founded in 1896; this leads to the establishment of the state of Israel in 1948. Liberal Judaism (more radical than Reform) develops in the USA. In 1911 the first synagogue in the UK is founded. The Nazi German regime (1933–45) exterminates 6 million European Jews. Hundreds of thousands of survivors take refuge in pre-existing Jewish settlements in what eventually becomes the new state of Israel. Although most Israeli and American Jews are not affiliated with synagogues after the 1950s, they continue to affirm their Jewish heritage. Both Orthodox and Hasidic Judaism, however, flourish in their new homes and grow rapidly in the 1970s and 1980s.

streets for the festival of Ratha Yatra. The large, heavy image gave rise to the word 'juggernaut' to describe a large truck.

Islam

All Muslims who can afford it are expected to perform the *hajj,* or pilgrimage, to Mecca (Arabic Makkah) during the month of pilgrimage at least once in a lifetime; however, the Koran specifically states that one must not put one's own or one's family's health or well-being at risk by going.

Muslims believe that the Ka'ba at Mecca was first built by Adam as a house of worship, and subsequently rebuilt by Ibrahim (Abraham) and his son Isma'il. It is a simple cube-shaped stone building, and has been a religious site since very early times. Every year between two and three million Muslims make their pilgrimage there, and no non-Muslim is allowed to enter the city.

Before entering Mecca the pilgrims set aside their normal clothes and wear a simple white garment as a mark of equality with others and humility before God. Each pilgrim performs seven circuits round the Ka'ba, touching or kissing the black stone in the Ka'ba wall if it is possible to do so in the vast throng of pilgrims. Over six days the pilgrims visit several different sites in and around Mecca, performing special ceremonies at each.

The mosque at Medina, Saudi Arabia, which contains Muhammad's tomb, and the Dome of the Rock in Jerusalem, which is built on the place from which Muhammad began his ascent into heaven, are also important sites of pilgrimage.

Judaism

The land of Israel has a special status for Jews. In the Bible, God promised the land of Canaan to Abraham and his descendants. Although there is no injunction to travel to Israel, many Jews like to visit as often as they can.

In ancient times the Temple in Jerusalem was the place of worship for all Jews, with the presence of God signified by the Ark of the Covenant in the most sacred place inside. The Western Wall in Jerusalem is all that remains of the last great Temple, destroyed in 70 CE. It is a centre of pilgrimage and prayer for Jews from all over the world, both for private prayer, which is said facing the wall, and for public services and bar mitzvahs.

Many Jews also visit Yad Vashem ('a place and a name') in Jerusalem, a memorial to the Jews who died in the Nazi Holocaust.

Shinto

Mountains are especially important because they are homes of the kami (spirits) and of the dead. Mt Fuji is best known and is venerated throughout Japan as a home of the gods and of the departed.

Shinto shrines can be vast complexes or tiny shrines perched beside a rock or surrounding a venerable tree. The most famous Shinto site is at Ise, the shrine of the Sun goddess Amaterasu, who is believed to be the founder of the Japanese imperial family and thus, in effect, the founder of the Japanese.

Sikhism

Guru Ram Das, the fourth Guru of Sikhism, began building the holy city of Amritsar in the Punjab. Here the House of God (Golden Temple) houses the first copy of the Guru Granth Sahib, the Sikh scripture. The city is the spiritual centre of Sikhism.

Anandpur, the site of the founding of the Khalsa, the community of committed Sikhs, is a popular destination, and many items important to Sikh history can be seen in the Gurdwara there.

Other major pilgrimage sites include places of martyrdom, such as the remains of the building at Sarhind in which the two youngest sons of Guru Gobind Singh were immured and killed.

Taoism

The major pilgrimage sites for Taoism are the five Taoist sacred mountains, Hua Shan, Heng Shan, Heng Shan, Tai Shan, and Song Shan, although there are countless smaller ones scattered across China. The Tao (Path) that leads the pilgrim up these mountains passes temples, statues of deities and heroes, and commemorations of myths and legends. The sacred mountains are especially associated with sages and those who achieve immortality through rigorous practices and training.

See Also

Month Equivalents for Gregorian, Jewish, Islamic, and Hindu Calendars, p. 15.

Major Religious Festivals

Festival	Normally held	2000	2001
Theravada Buddhism (Southern Buddhism)[1]			
New Year Festival Images of the Buddha are bathed in scented water and stupas of sand are built on river banks or in temple grounds to be washed away at New Year, symbolizing the clearing away of negative deeds	beginning of Citta	April 2000[2]	April 2001[2]
Vesakha Celebrates the Buddha's birth, enlightenment, and passing into nirvana; processions take place in the temple, bodhi trees are sprinkled with scented water, lanterns are lit, and street stalls are erected	full moon of Vesakha	18 May 2000	7 May 2001
Asalha Commemorates the Buddha's first sermon and marks the beginning of the three-month rainy season, a period of temple retreat known as Vassa	full moon of Asalha	16 July 2000	5 July 2001
Assayuja Celebrates the return of the Buddha from heaven after passing on the teachings to his mother; Assayuja marks the end of Vassa	third full moon of Vassa	October 2000[2]	October 2001[2]
Kattika Commemorates the first Buddhist missionaries who went out to spread the Buddha's teachings; this is also the date for the end of Vassa if the rains continue longer than usual	full moon of Kattika	November 2000[2]	November 2001[2]
Kathina Offerings, especially robes, are presented to the monasteries in elaborate ceremonies	end of Vassa	October/ November 2000[2]	October/ November 2001[2]
Mahayana (East) Buddhism (Eastern Buddhism)[3]			
Birth of the Buddha Images of the Buddha as a child are bathed in scented water or tea, and offerings are made at temples and shrines	eighth day of the fourth lunar month	8 April 2000 (Japan)	8 April 2001 (Japan)

(continued)

Major Religious Festivals (*continued*)

Festival	Normally held	2000	2001
Birth of Kuan Yin The Bodhisattva of Mercy; offerings and prayers are made to her by those who seek help in times of need	19th day of second lunar month	February/ March 2000[2]	February/ March 2001[2]
Enlightenment of Kuan Yin	19th day of sixth lunar month	June/July 2000[2]	June/July 2001[2]
Death of Kuan Yin	19th day of ninth lunar month	September/ October 2000[2]	September/ October 2001[2]
Hungry Ghost Festival Unsettled spirits of the dead are calmed with chanting and offerings to enable them to pass peacefully into the next world	8–15th days of the Chinese seventh lunar month	July/ August 2000[2]	July/ August 2001[2]
O-Bon Families reunite to remember and honour their ancestors; offerings are made to the Buddha and monks visit home shrines to read Buddhist scriptures	13–15 July (Japan)	13–15 July 2000 (Japan)	13–15 July 2001 (Japan)
Mahayana (North) Buddhism (Northern Buddhism)[4]			
Tibetan New Year Houses are cleaned to sweep away any negative aspects from the last year; costumed monks perform new year rituals and chants; people light firecrackers or torches to chase away the spirits	new moon of February	6 February 2000	25 January 2001
Modlam Chenmo The Great Prayer Festival is celebrated with traditional stories, puppet shows, and butter sculptures in the monasteries	8–15th of the first lunar month	February 2000[2]	February 2001[2]
The Buddha's Enlightenment and Passing into Nirvana Pilgrims visit monasteries to make offerings; traditional Chan dancing is performed	15th day of the fourth lunar month	May 2000[2]	May 2001[2]
Guru Rinpoche's Birthday Commemorates the Indian teacher who helped establish Buddhist teachings in Tibet towards the end of the 8th century AD	tenth day of the sixth lunar month	July 2000[2]	July 2001[2]
Chokhor Duchen Celebrates the Buddha's first sermon after his enlightenment	fourth day of the sixth lunar month	July 2000[2]	July 2001[2]
Lhabab Duchen Commemorates the descent of the Buddha from heaven after giving the teachings to his mother	22nd day of the ninth lunar month	October 2000[2]	October 2001[2]
Christianity[5]			
Christmas Day Celebration of the birth of Jesus in Bethlehem; Christians meet for worship, often at midnight, when the events are retold through words, music, drama, and pictures		25 December 2000	25 December 2001
Epiphany Celebrates the arrival of the three wise men from the east who came looking for a newborn king and were led by a bright star to Bethlehem; they brought Jesus gifts of gold, frankincense, and myrrh		6 January 2000	6 January 2001
Ash Wednesday In many churches, people come forward to be marked with ashes, an ancient symbol of sorrow and repentance; Lent is a time of reflection and fasting which recalls the 40 days Jesus spent fasting and praying in the desert	start of Lent (six weeks before Easter)	8 March 2000	28 February 2001
Palm Sunday Christians recall Jesus's entry into Jerusalem during the last week of his life, when he was welcomed by people waving palm fronds; other important days of Holy Week are Maundy Thursday, when Jesus shared the last supper with his disciples, and Good Friday, when he was crucified	start of Holy Week (one week before Easter)	16 April 2000	8 April 2001
Easter Sunday Time of rejoicing that recalls the disciples' discovery that Jesus was alive, and that he had been resurrected; many churches keep a vigil throughout Saturday night so that they can greet Easter Day with services, family meals, and the exchange of flowers and eggs	between 23 March and 24 April in the Roman Catholic and Protestant churches	23 April 2000	15 April 2001
Ascension Day This day commemorates the disciples witnessing Jesus being lifted up to heaven 40 days after Easter Day	40 days after Easter	1 June 2000	24 May 2001
Pentecost or Whitsun When Jesus left his disciples for the last time after his resurrection, he promised them a 'comforter' who would be with them forever; Pentecost celebrates the coming of the Holy Spirit upon the disciples	seventh Sunday after Easter	11 June 2000	3 June 2001
Hinduism			
Mahashivaratri 'Great Night of Shiva' when Shiva, his wife Parvati, and their child Ganesh are honoured; offerings are made to Shiva between midnight and sunrise and the 24-hour fast is broken at dawn	13th or 14th day of dark half of Magh	4 March 2000	21 February 2001

(*continued*)

Major Religious Festivals (*continued*)

Festival	Normally held	2000	2001
Sarasvati Puja Sarasvati, the patron of the arts and learning, is celebrated with music and February/by wearing yellow clothes, symbolizing the warmth of spring	first day of spring season (Phalgun)	February/ March 2000[2]	February/ March 2001[2]
Holi The pranks that Krishna played as a child are celebrated, and the story of Prahalad, a prince who was willing to sacrifice himself for Vishnu, is remembered; offerings are made around bonfires and coloured water or powder is sprayed in high-spirited games	full moon day of Phalgun	21 March 2000	10 March 2001
Rama Naumi Celebrates the birthday of the god Rama, hero of the epic *Rāmayāna* that is recited during the festival; offerings are also made in temples to a statue of the baby Rama	ninth day of the bright half of Caitra	12 April 2000[6]	2 April 2001[6]
Ratha Yatra A statue of Vishnu, also called Jagganath, Lord of the Universe, is placed on a large wooden chariot and pulled through the streets where lamps, flowers, and other offerings are laid in his path	16th day of Asadha	June/July 2000[2]	June/July 2001[2]
Raksha Bandhan Sisters tie rakhis, silk threads decorated with flowers, onto their brothers' wrists as a symbol of protection	full moon day of Sravana	15 August 2000	4 August 2001
Janamashtarni The birth of Krishna is celebrated as an image of the child Krishna is washed with yoghurt, ghee, honey, and milk, and then placed on a swing	eighth day of Bhadrapada	22 August 2000	12 August 2001
Navaratri Dusshera The festival of Dusshera follows immediately after Navaratri; over nine nights different manifestations of the goddess Durga are honoured; in the form of Durga she is the destroyer of evil, as Kali she is the destroyer of time, and as Parvati she is the faithful wife of Shiva; at Dusshera, an effigy of the demon Ravana is burnt to celebrate Durga's power over demons	first ten days of the bright half of Aswin	7 October 2000	26 October 2001
Divali Accounts are settled at this time and worship is given to Lakshmi, goddess of wealth and good fortune; coloured patterns are made on the ground; windows are illuminated with lamps and candles; this festival also celebrates the return of Rama and Sita from exile, a story told in *The Rāmayāna*	13th day of the dark half of Aswin	26 October 2000	14 November 2001
Islam[7] Festival of Ashura Festival commemorating both the escape of the Israelites from Egypt, and also the day Noah's ark touched ground after the flood; in Shi'a Islam, Ashura also celebrates the martyrdom of Ali	10 Muharram	15 April 2000	4 April 2001[6]
Ramadan This month of fasting is one of the Five Pillars of Islam, when adult Muslims refrain from drinking, eating, smoking, and conjugal relations from dawn until dusk	ninth month of the year	27 November 2000	17 November 2001[6]
The Night of Power–Lailat ul Qadr During the last ten days of Ramadan many Muslims spend time praying in the mosque since prayers made on the Night of Power are said to be 'better than a thousand months'	around 27 Ramadan	3 January 2000	3 December 2001[6]
Eid ul-Fitr Important time of communal prayer and celebration when families and friends gather to share special foods and exchange gifts	end of Ramadan, heralded by the sight of a new moon	8 January 2000	16 December 2001[6]
Pilgrimage to Mecca In the Five Pillars of Islam, this is the most important time, but only those who have sufficient finances and are physically able are expected to make the journey	8–13 Dhu al-Hijjah	14–19 March 2000	April 2001[2]
Eid-ul-Adha The willingness of the prophet Ibrahim to sacrifice his son Ishmael is remembered; at God's command a lamb was sacrificed instead, an act commemorated at this time in the sacrifice of a lamb or goat	10 Dhu al-Hijjah	16 March 2000[6]	6 March 2001[6]
Birthday of the Prophet Mohammed (Milad-un-Nabi) The scale of celebrations varies according to country; for example, thousands of pilgrims gather on Lamu island off the coast of Kenya for processions, speeches, and prayers	month of Rabi I	15 June 2000	4 June 2001
Judaism Rosh Hashanah Jewish New Year, a ten-day period of repentance leading up to Yom Kippur	1 Tishri	30 September–1 October 2000	18–19 September 2001
Yom Kippur Day of Atonement, a time when Jews seek forgiveness of those who have been wronged; also the major fast of the year	10 Tishri	9 October 2000	27 September 2001
Succoth Feast of Tabernacles, a time when families build and eat in open-air shelters in commemoration of the temporary desert shelters built by the Israelites during their journey to the Promised Land	15–23 Tishri	14–22 October 2000	2–10 October 2001

(*continued*)

Major Religious Festivals (*continued*)

Festival	Normally held	2000	2001
Simhat Torah End of Succoth and the end of the annual reading of the Torah, which is processed around the synagogue on this day	24 Tishri	22 October 2000	10 October 2001
Hanukkah Dedication of the Temple, a time when the eight-branched Hanukkah candle is lit commemorating the rededication of the Temple in Jerusalem in the 2nd century BCE, when the Temple lamp miraculously stayed alight for ten days, even though there was only enough oil to last one day	25 Kislev–3 Tebet	22 December 2000	30 November 2001
Purim Celebration of the story of Esther who saved her people from destruction at the hands of Haman; the congregation dress in unusual clothes for the synagogue service and boo when Haman's name is read out from the scrolls of Esther	14 Adar	21 March 2000	9 March 2001
Pesach Passover, celebrating God's deliverance of the Israelites from captivity in Egypt; families gather for the first evening of the festival to share the Seder meal, which recalls in words and symbols the departure of the Israelites from Egypt	15–22 Nisan	20–27 April 2000	8–15 April 2001
Shavuot Also known as the Pentecost or the Feast of Weeks, this is both a harvest festival and a thanksgiving for the gift of Torah to Moses on Mount Sinai	6–7 Sivan	9–10 June 2000	28–29 May 2001
Tishah B'Av This date recalls the disasters that have befallen the Jewish people, including the destruction of the first and second temples in Jerusalem; it is also a time to mourn the events of the Holocaust	9 Av	10 August 2000	29 July 2001
Sikhism Baisakhi Commemorates the founding of the Order of the Khalsa in 1699, the community of committed Sikhs who undertake to uphold their faith and defend the weak; it is the usual time for Sikhs to join the Khalsa	13 April (occasionally on the 14 April), first day of the solar month of Baisakh (Sanskrit Vaiśakha)	13 April 2000	April 2001[2]
Martyrdom of the Guru Arjan Dev Time of celebration and sorrow when Sikhs remember those who have suffered for their faith; there is a continuous reading of the Guru Granth Sahib in the gurdwara	fourth Jaistha	5 June 2000	June 2001[2]
Divali Divali lamps are lit at home, and the release from prison of Guru Hargobind is commemorated	second day of Kartik	26 October 2000	October 2001[2]
Guru Nanak's Birthday Colourful street processions are held and hymns honouring Guru Gobind Singh (1469–1539), the founder of the Khalsa, are sung in the gurdwara	full moon day of Kartik	11 November 2000[8]	November 2001[2 8]
Hola Mohalla Falls at the same time as the Hindu festival of Holi; celebrated with games and pranks; sporting contests take place as well as religious congregations, political conferences, pilgrimages, and administration of baptism	starting a day earlier and finishing a day later than Holi; full moon day of Phalgun	20–22 March 2000	9–11 March 2001

[1] Predominant mainly in Sri Lanka and Southeast Asia.
[2] Date unknown.
[3] Predominant mainly in China, Taiwan, Korea, and Japan.
[4] Predominant mainly in Tibet, Nepal, Bhutan, Mongolia, parts of western China, southern Siberia, and northern India.
[5] The calendar reform by pope Gregory XIII in 1582 was rejected by the Orthodox Church. Since 1923, the Orthodox Church has been divided over the calendar. The Greek Church adopted the new calendar except the days that depend on Easter. Others (mostly Slavic) have retained the Julian calendar and therefore remain 13 days behind in their dating (Christmas: 7 January, New Year: 14 January).
[6] Unconfirmed.
[7] The Islamic calendar is entirely lunar, and unlike most other lunar calendars, is not adjusted to keep in step with the solar year. Some dates are therefore approximate and some are not yet known by the relevant authorities; this applies particularly to movable feasts, based on lunar reckonings.
[8] Date in Christian calendar varies from year to year in accordance with traditional dates of the Indian Calendar (Bikrami Sambat); often falls in November.

Books of the Bible

Name of book	Chapters	Date written
Books of the Old Testament		
Genesis	50	mid-8th century BC
Exodus	40	950–586 BC
Leviticus	27	mid-7th century BC
Numbers	36	850–650 BC
Deuteronomy	34	mid-7th century BC
Joshua	24	*c.* 550 BC
Judges	21	*c.* 550 BC
Ruth	4	late 3rd century BC
1 Samuel	31	*c.* 900 BC
2 Samuel	24	*c.* 900 BC
1 Kings	22	550–600 BC
2 Kings	25	550–600 BC
1 Chronicles	29	*c.* 300 BC
2 Chronicles	36	*c.* 300 BC
Ezra	10	*c.* 450 BC
Nehemiah	13	*c.* 450 BC
Esther	10	*c.* 200 BC
Job	42	600–400 BC
Psalms	150	6th–2nd century BC
Proverbs	31	350–150 BC
Ecclesiastes	12	*c.* 200 BC
Song of Solomon	8	3rd century BC
Isaiah	66	late 3rd century BC
Jeremiah	52	604 BC
Lamentations	5	586–536 BC
Ezekiel	48	6th century BC
Daniel	12	*c.* 166 BC
Hosea	14	*c.* 732 BC
Joel	3	*c.* 500 BC
Amos	9	775–750 BC
Obadiah	1	6th–3rd century BC
Jonah	4	600–200 BC
Micah	7	late 3rd century BC
Nahum	3	*c.* 626 BC
Habakkuk	3	*c.* 600 BC
Zephaniah	3	3rd century BC
Haggai	2	*c.* 520 BC
Zechariah	14	*c.* 520 BC
Malachi	4	*c.* 430 BC
Books of the New Testament		
Matthew	28	before AD 70
Mark	16	before AD 70
Luke	24	AD 70–80
John	21	AD 90–100
Acts	28	AD 70–80
Romans	16	AD 55–58
1 Corinthians	16	AD 57
2 Corinthians	13	AD 57
Galatians	6	AD 53
Ephesians	6	AD 140
Philippians	4	AD 63
Colossians	4	AD 140
1 Thessalonians	5	AD 50–54
2 Thessalonians	3	AD 50–54
1 Timothy	6	before AD 64
2 Timothy	4	before AD 64
Titus	3	before AD 64
Philemon	1	AD 60–62
Hebrews	13	AD 80–90
James	5	before AD 52
1 Peter	5	before AD 64
2 Peter	3	before AD 64
1 John	5	AD 90–100
2 John	1	AD 90–100
3 John	1	AD 90–100
Jude	1	AD 75–80
Revelation	22	AD 81–96

Patron Saints

Saint	Occupation
Adam	gardeners
Albert the Great	scientists
Alphonsus Liguori	theologians
Amand	brewers, hotelkeepers
Andrew	fisherfolk
Angelico	artists
Anne	miners
Apollonia	dentists
Augustine	theologians
Barbara	builders, miners
Bernadino (Feltre)	bankers
Bernadino of Siena	advertisers
Camillus de Lellis	nurses
Catherine of Alexandria	librarians, philosophers
Cecilia	musicians, poets, singers
Christopher	motorists, sailors
Cosmas and Damian	barbers, chemists, doctors, surgeons
Crispin and Crispinian	shoemakers
David	poets
Dismas	undertakers
Dominic	astronomers
Dorothy	florists
Eligius	blacksmiths, jewellers, metalworkers
Erasmus	sailors
Fiacre	gardeners, taxi drivers
Florian	firefighters
Francis de Sales	authors, editors, journalists
Francis of Assisi	merchants
Francis of Paola	sailors
Gabriel	messengers, postal workers, radio workers, television workers
Genesius	actors, secretaries
George	soldiers
Gregory	singers
Gregory the Great	musicians, teachers
Homobonus	tailors
Honoratus	bakers
Isidore	farmers
Ivo	lawyers
James	labourers
Jerome	librarians
Joan of Arc	soldiers
John Baptist de la Salle	teachers
John Bosco	labourers
John of God	book trade, nurses, printers
Joseph	carpenters
Joseph (Arimathea)	gravediggers, undertakers
Joseph (Cupertino)	astronauts
Julian the Hospitaler	hotelkeepers
Lawrence	cooks
Leonard	prisoners
Louis	sculptors
Lucy	glassworkers, writers
Luke	artists, butchers, doctors, glassworkers, sculptors, surgeons
Martha	cooks, housewives, servants, waiters
Martin of Tours	soldiers
Matthew	accountants, bookkeepers, tax collectors
Michael	grocers, police
Our Lady of Loreto	aviators
Peter	fisherfolk
Raymond Nonnatus	midwives
Sebastian	athletes, soldiers
Thérèse of Lisieux	florists
Thomas (Apostle)	architects, builders
Thomas Aquinas	philosophers, scholars, students, theologians
Thomas More	lawyers
Vitus	actors, comedians, dancers
Wenceslaus	brewers
Zita	servants

Major Denominations of the Christian Religion

From the beginning of its history, the Christian church has had divisions over teachings or organization. Many smaller divisions died out or were re-united. The Great Schism of 1054 gave rise to the Roman Catholic and the Orthodox churches. The Reformation in the 16th century gave rise to the Protestant denominations which rejected the teaching and authority of the Roman Catholic church. In the following centuries there were further divisions between these denominations, and new Christian groups are still being formed.

Denomination	Organization	Characteristics	Special rites	Orientation
Baptists	self-governing churches; congregational	only adult Christians, capable of own choice, should be baptized	baptism by total immersion	missionary activities; supports separation of church and state
Calvinists	mostly congregational	belief in predestination; Bible as the only source of authority	simple services	individual faith perceived as the only way to salvation
Lutherans	congregational or episcopal	belief in the symbolic presence of Christ in bread and wine offerings; Bible as the only source of authority; no belief in predestination	simple services; infant baptism	personal faith perceived as the only way to salvation; strong theological and ethical background
Methodists	superintendent system and conferences	scripture, tradition, and experience are at the core of the church's practices	forms of worship vary depending on local tradition; infant or adult baptism	extensive missionary activities and social involvement
Orthodox	independent and autonomous national churches governed by synods of bishops; the Patriarch of Constantinople recognized as 'first among equals'	emphasis on Christ's resurrection; belief that the Holy Spirit descends from God the Father only; tradition as a source of authority; rich traditions of worship; veneration of Mary, the mother of God	elaborate liturgy; seven sacraments; veneration of icons	traditional orientation, usually little social involvement
Pentecostal	a wide range of groups; allows for freedom of organization	emphasis on the personal teachings of the Holy Spirit	spirit baptism; healing; adult baptism; ' speaking in tongues'	charismatic
Presbyterians	government by elders (lay people or ordained ministers)	emphasis on self-control and self-discipline; belief in the symbolic presence of Christ in bread and wine offerings	simple services with emphasis on the sermon; infant baptism	strong belief in justice and supremacy of God
Roman Catholics	strict hierarchy with the pope (the Bishop of Rome) as leader	emphasis on teachings of the pope and church authorities; belief in the factual presence of Christ in bread and wine offerings; veneration of Mary, the mother of Jesus Christ	wide range of services focused on the Mass; seven sacraments; rich theological tradition	authority of the church regulates every area of life and belief; controversy over divorce, contraception, and priests' celibacy; since the Second Vatican Council (1962–65) local languages in use

Christianity: Chronology

1st century The Christian church is traditionally said to have originated at Pentecost, and separated from the parent Jewish religion by the declaration of Saints Barnabas and Paul that the distinctive rites of Judaism are not necessary for entry into the Christian church.

3rd century Christians are persecuted under the Roman emperors Septimius Severus, Decius, and Diocletian.

312 Emperor Constantine establishes Christianity as the religion of the Roman Empire.

4th century A settled doctrine of Christian belief evolves, with deviating beliefs condemned as heresies. Questions of discipline threaten disruption within the church; to settle these, Constantine calls the Council of Arles in 314, followed by the councils of Nicaea (325) and Constantinople (381).

5th century Councils of Ephesus (431) and Chalcedon (451). Christianity is carried northwards by such figures as Saints Columba and Augustine.

800 Holy Roman Emperor Charlemagne is crowned by the pope. The church assists the growth of the feudal system of which it forms the apex.

1054 The Eastern Orthodox Church splits from the Roman Catholic Church.

11th–12th centuries Secular and ecclesiastical jurisdiction are often in conflict; for example, Emperor Henry IV and Pope Gregory VII, Henry II of England and his archbishop Becket.

1096–1291 The church supports a series of wars in the Middle East, called the Crusades.

1233 The Inquisition is established to suppress heresy.

14th century Increasing worldliness (against which the foundation of the Dominican and Franciscan monastic orders is a protest) and ecclesiastical abuses leads to dissatisfaction and the appearance of the reformers Wycliffe and Huss.

15th–17th centuries Thousands of women are accused of witchcraft, tortured, and executed.

early 16th century The Renaissance brings a re-examination of Christianity in northern Europe by the humanists Erasmus, More, and Colet.

1517 The German priest Martin Luther becomes leader of

(continued)

Christianity: Chronology (*continued*)

	the Protestant movement and precipitates the Reformation.
1519–64	In Switzerland the Reformation is carried on by Calvin and Zwingli.
1529	Henry VIII renounces papal supremacy and proclaims himself head of the Church of England.
1545–63	The Counter-Reformation is initiated by the Catholic church at the Council of Trent.
1560	The Church of Scotland is established according to Calvin's Presbyterian system.
17th century	Jesuit missionaries establish themselves in China and Japan. Puritans, Quakers, and other sects seeking religious freedom establish themselves in North America.
18th century	During the Age of Reason, Christian dogmas are questioned, and intellectuals begin to examine society in purely secular terms. In England and America, religious revivals occur among the working classes in the form of Methodism and the Great Awakening. In England the Church of England suffers the loss of large numbers of Nonconformists.
19th century	The evolutionary theories of Darwin and the historical criticism of the Bible challeng the Book of Genesis. Missionaries convert people in Africa and Asia, suppressing indigenous faiths and cultures.
1948	The World Council of Churches is founded as part of the ecumenical movement to reunite various Protestant sects and, to some extent, the Protestant churches and the Catholic Church.
1950s–80s	Protestant evangelicism grows rapidly in the USA, spread by television.
1969	A liberation theology of freeing the poor from oppression emerges in South America, and attracts papal disapproval.
1972	The United Reformed Church is formed by the union of the Presbyterian Church in England and the Congregational Church. In the USA, the 1960s–70s sees the growth of cults, some of them nominally Christian, which are a source of social concern.
1980s	The Roman Catholic Church plays a major role in the liberalization of the Polish government; in the USSR the Orthodox Church and other sects are tolerated and even encouraged under Gorbachev.
1988	The Holy Shroud of Turin, claimed by some to be Christ's mortuary cloth, is shown by carbon dating to date from about 1330.
1990s	The Christian church grapples with the question of its attitude to homosexuality; the policy of most churches is to oppose its public acceptance, declaring that homosexual behaviour conflicts with Christian teachings.
1992	After 359 years, the Roman Catholic Church accepts that Galileo is right: the Earth does go round the Sun.

Popes

Name	Date reign began	Name	Date reign began	Name	Date reign began	Name	Date reign began
St Peter	*c.* 42	St Damasus I	366	Theodore I	642	St Adrian III	884
St Linus	*c.* 67	St Siricius	384	St Martin I	649	Stephen V (VI)	885
St Anacletus (Cletus)	*c.* 76	St Anastasius I	399	St Eugene I	654	Formosus	891
St Clement I	*c.* 88	St Innocent I	402	St Vitalian	657	Boniface VI	896
St Evaristus	*c.* 97	St Zosimus	417	Adeodatus II	672	Stephen VI (VII)	896
St Alexander I	*c.* 105	St Boniface I	418	Donus	676	Romanus	897
St Sixtus I	*c.* 115	St Celestine I	422	St Agatho	678	Theodore II	897
St Telesphorus	*c.* 125	St Sixtus III	432	St Leo II	682	John IX	898
St Hyginus	*c.* 136	St Leo I the Great	440	St Benedict II	684	Benedict IV	900
St Pius I	*c.* 140	St Hilary	461	John V	685	Leo V	903
St Anicetus	*c.* 155	St Simplicius	468	Conon	686	Sergius III	904
St Soterus	*c.* 166	St Felix III	483	St Sergius I	687	Anastasius III	911
St Eleutherius	175	St Gelasius I	492	John VI	701	Landus	913
St Victor I	189	Anastasius II	496	John VII	705	John X	914
St Zephyrinus	199	St Symmachus	498	Sisinnius	708	Leo VI	928
St Callistus I	217	St Hormisdas	514	Constantine	708	Stephen VII (VIII)	928
St Urban I	222	St John I	523	St Gregory II	715	John XI	931
St Pontian	230	St Felix IV	526	St Gregory III	731	Leo VII	936
St Anterus	235	Boniface II	530	St Zachary	741	Stephen VII (IX)	939
St Fabius	236	John II	533	Stephen II (III)[1]	752	Marinus II	942
St Cornelius	251	St Agapetus I	535	St Paul I	757	Agapetus II	946
St Lucius I	253	St Silverius	536	Stephen III (IV)	768	John XII	955
St Stephen I	254	Vigilius	537	Adrian I	772	Leo VIII	963
St Sixtus II	257	Pelagius I	556	St Leo III	795	Benedict V	964
St Dionysius	259	John III	561	Stephen IV (V)	816	John XIII	965
St Felix I	269	Benedict I	575	St Paschal I	817	Benedict VI	973
St Eutychian	275	Pelagius II	579	Eugene II	824	Benedict VII	974
St Caius	283	St Gregory (I) the Great	590	Valentine	827	John XIV	983
St Marcellinus	296	Sabinianus	604	Gregory IV	827	John XV	985
St Marcellus I	308	Boniface III	607	Sergius II	844	Gregory V	996
St Eusebius	309	St Boniface IV	608	St Leo IV	847	Sylvester II	999
St Melchiades	311	St Deusdedit (Adeodatus I)	615	Benedict III	855	John XVII	1003
St Sylvester I	314	Boniface V	619	St Nicholas (I) the Great	858	John XVIII	1004
St Marcus	336	Honorius I	625	Adrian II	867	Sergius IV	1009
St Julius I	337	Severinus	640	John VIII	872	Benedict VIII	1012
Liberius	352	John IV	640	Marinus I	882	John XIX	1024

(*continued*)

Popes (*continued*)

Name	Date reign began	Name	Date reign began	Name	Date reign began	Name	Date reign began
Benedict IX[2]	1032	Innocent III	1198	Martin V	1417	Innocent X	1644
Gregory VI	1045	Honorius III	1216	Eugene IV	1431	Alexander VII	1655
Clement II	1046	Gregory IX	1227	Nicholas V	1447	Clement IX	1667
Benedict IX[2]	1047	Celestine IV	1241	Callistus III	1455	Clement X	1670
Damasus II	1048	Innocent IV	1243	Pius II	1458	Innocent XI	1676
St Leo IX	1049	Alexander IV	1254	Paul II	1464	Alexander VIII	1689
Victor II	1055	Urban IV	1261	Sixtus IV	1471	Innocent XII	1691
Stephen IX (X)	1057	Clement IV	1265	Innocent VIII	1484	Clement XI	1700
Nicholas II	1059	Gregory X	1271	Alexander VI	1492	Innocent XIII	1721
Alexander II	1061	Innocent V	1276	Pius III	1503	Benedict XIII	1724
St Gregory VII	1073	Adrian V	1276	Julius II	1503	Clement XII	1730
Victor III	1086	John XXI[3]	1276	Leo X	1513	Benedict XIV	1740
Urban II	1088	Nicholas III	1277	Adrian VI	1522	Clement XIII	1758
Paschal II	1099	Martin IV	1281	Clement VII	1523	Clement XIV	1769
Gelasius II	1118	Honorius IV	1285	Paul III	1534	Pius VI	1775
Callistus II	1119	Nicholas IV	1288	Julius III	1550	Pius VII	1800
Hororius II	1124	St Celestine V	1294	Marcellus II	1555	Leo XII	1823
Innocent II	1130	Boniface VIII	1294	Paul IV	1555	Pius VIII	1829
Celestine II	1143	Benedict XI	1303	Pius IV	1559	Gregory XVI	1831
Lucius II	1144	Clement V	1305	St Pius V	1566	Pius IX	1846
Eugene III	1145	John XXII	1316	Gregory XIII	1572	Leo XIII	1878
Anastasius IV	1153	Benedict XII	1334	Sixtus V	1585	St Pius X	1903
Adrian IV	1154	Clement VI	1342	Urban VII	1590	Benedict XV	1914
Alexander III	1159	Innocent VI	1352	Gregory XIV	1590	Pius XI	1922
Innocent III	1179	Urban V	1362	Innocent IX	1591	Pius XII	1939
Lucius III	1181	Gregory XI	1370	Clement VIII	1592	John XXIII	1958
Urban III	1185	Urban VI	1378	Leo XI	1605	Paul VI	1963
Gregory VIII	1187	Boniface IX	1389	Paul V	1605	John Paul I[4]	1978
Clement III	1187	Innocent VII	1404	Gregory XV	1621	John Paul II	1978
Celestine III	1191	Gregory XII	1406	Urban VIII	1623		

[1] The original Stephen II died before consecration, and was dropped from the list of popes in 1961; Stephen III became Stephen II and the numbers of the other popes named Stephen were also moved up.

[2] Benedict IX was driven from office for scandalous conduct but returned briefly in 1047.

[3] There was no John XX.

[4] John Paul I died after only 33 days as Pontiff.

A Changing Spirituality: The Progress of Religion in the 20th Century

BY CHRISTOPHER PARTRIDGE

The 20th century was a period of considerable change for the world's principal religions. For example, while Christianity has grown in the non-Western world, Western cultures have seen a decline in traditional Christianity. Other faiths too (such as Judaism and Islam) have witnessed an increasing liberalization and felt the impact of secularization. However, this trend has in some cases been matched by a rise in fundamentalist forms of religion across the globe. Particularly in the West there has also been a rise of interest in individuals seeking personal solutions to spiritual questions either in the belief systems of cultures that are not their own or in the increasing variety of 'New Age' and pagan philosophies.

World religions

The 20th century saw the revitalization of certain religions, which were often linked with specific national identities. For example, in the first half of the century, Islam became a unifying force in some countries in their struggle to overthrow colonialism. Sikhism and Hinduism emerged as faiths of major importance: Hindu confidence played an important role in the establishment of an independent India in 1947, and the current conflict in the Punjab also has religious roots.

Buddhism in its various forms experienced a resurgence, as a result of very successful missionary activity. Although

Buddhist nationalism helped secure the independence of Burma and Sri Lanka in 1948, Buddhism suffered greatly under successive communist regimes in the former Soviet Union and elsewhere, particularly with the annexation of Tibet by China in 1950. The Orthodox Church too began to flourish in Russia after decades of repression. Greatly affected in many ways by the Holocaust (which has entered generally into the modern consciousness) and the establishment of the State of Israel on 14 May 1948, Judaism is, at the dawn of the third millennium, a confident faith with a strong sense of identity.

Religious plurality and relativism

Modern methods of communication and the existence of culturally and ethnically diverse societies make it difficult to avoid learning about other religious systems. Although religious plurality is in itself nothing new, our greatly increased awareness of it is. Not only is Western society much more tolerant of the religious beliefs of others, but some individuals, unhappy with the traditional forms of religion in their own culture, have embraced other belief systems, such as Buddhism or Islam.

Although relationships between religions are still competitive rather than cooperative, and despite the growing influence of fundamentalist groups, the 20th century saw the emergence of a commitment to inter-faith dialogue (notably the second World Parliament of Religions, held in 1993). Gradually this dialogue has borne fruit: there are local, national, and international networks to stimulate inter-faith understanding, and adherents of the world's religions are reassessing their attitudes to other faiths more than at any period in history.

'Relativism' argues that no one religion possesses the whole truth.

Although religious plurality is perceived by some as a threat to cultural identity, 'relativism' argues that no one religion possesses the whole truth, indeed, that there are no absolutes. Although there are philosophical problems with relativism, and perceptions of the world vary considerably, relativism grew during the 20th century and is now very popular. Many, implicitly or explicitly, hold that some form of relativism is 'common sense' or even, ironically, a universal truth.

Current trends

There is a continuing tendency in all parts of the world towards secularization, the process by which a society becomes increasingly non-religious. Although some hold that the decline of religion is an inevitable product of a modern education, others argue that religion will always be a human need and a characteristic of human society. Thus, when mainstream religions decline, new forms of religion will emerge to satisfy this need. Despite growing secularization, as noted above, some form of religion/spirituality is still a very important aspect of the lives of many people. This is particularly the case in the non-Western world.

Different religions are seeing the emergence of increasingly vocal and active fundamentalist groups. Fundamentalists feel that the core traditional beliefs of their faith must be defended against what they perceive to be the undermining influences of modernist interpretations and critical scholarship. Some Christians, for example, believing the creation narrative in the Bible to be literally and scientifically true, oppose evolutionary theories of human origins. Fundamentalist movements often have political goals; there are Islamic groups in Egypt, for example, engaged in a struggle to establish an Islamic state with a constitution based on the Koran and a legal system based on the Shari'a (Islamic canon law).

Another notable feature of the world's religious landscape today is the increase in new and alternative forms of religion. As well as groups tracing their origins directly back to one of the major world religions, there has been a proliferation of 'New Age' philosophies that select their beliefs and practices from a variety of sources, from Hinduism to Islamic mysticism, from belief in extraterrestrials to paganism. These forms of spirituality are very much the forms one might expect in late 20th-century consumer culture, with its emphasis on the individual and personal choice.

Faith in the future

It seems likely that both the conservative and liberalizing tendencies in religion will become more pronounced in those societies generally characterized by their opposites: fundamentalism will continue to defend traditional orthodoxy, and liberalism will continue to question dogmatism, strive towards a global understanding, and possibly succumb to relativism.

It also seems likely that the major world religions, particularly those in decline, will be increasingly challenged by the ever-greater variety of new and alternative religions. However, there is much evidence to support the view that religion will continue to be a central characteristic of human nature and society, as it has been from earliest times.

Christopher Partridge is lecturer in theology and religious studies at University College, Chester

Religions in the UK

Dioceses of the Church of England

The addresses given are for the Dean or Provost.

Diocese of Bath and Wells Bishop, The Right Reverend J L Thompson; Dean, The Very Reverend Richard Lewis; The Dean's Lodgings, 25 The Liberty, Wells BA5 2SZ; phone: (01749) 670278; fax: (01749) 679184

Diocese of Birmingham Bishop, The Right Reverend M Santer; Provost, The Very Reverend Peter Berry; Birmingham Cathedral, Colmore Row, Birmingham B3 2Q8; phone: (0121) 236 4333/6323; fax: (0121) 212 0868

Diocese of Blackburn Bishop, The Right Reverend A D Chesters; Provost, The Very Reverend David Frayne; Cathedral Close, Blackburn BB1 5AA; phone: (01254) 51491; fax: (01254) 699963; e-mail: diosec@blackburnce.u–net.com

Diocese of Bradford Bishop, The Right Reverend D J Smith; Provost, The Very Reverend John Richardson; Cathedral Office, 1 Stott Hill, Bradford BD1 4EH; phone: (01274) 777724; fax: (01274) 777730; e-mail: cathedra@legend.co.uk

Diocese of Bristol Bishop, The Right Reverend B Rogerson; Dean, The Very Reverend Robert Grimley; Cathedral Office, Bristol Cathedral, College Green, Bristol BS1 5TJ; phone: (0117) 926 4879; fax: (0117) 925 3678

Diocese of Canterbury Archbishop, The Most Reverend and Right Honourable George L Carey; Dean, The Very Reverend John Simpson; Cathedral House, 11 The Precincts, Canterbury CT1 2EH; phone: (01227) 762862; fax: (01227) 865222

Diocese of Carlisle Bishop, The Right Reverend I Harland; Dean, The Very Reverend Graeme Knowles; The Deanery, The Abbey, Carlisle CA3 8TZ; phone: (01228) 548151; fax: (01228) 547049

Diocese of Chelmsford Bishop, The Right Reverend J F Perry; Provost, The Very Reverend Peter Judd; Cathedral Office, New Street, Chelmsford CM1 1AT; phone: (01245) 294480; fax: (01245) 496802

Diocese of Chester Bishop, The Right Reverend P R Forster; Dean, The Very Reverend Stephen Smalley; Cathedral Office, 12 Abbey Square, Chester CH1 2HU; phone: (01244) 324756; fax: (01244) 341110; e-mail: office@chestercathedral.org.uk; Web site: www.chestercathedral.org.uk

Diocese of Chichester Bishop, The Right Reverend E W Kemp; Dean, The Very Reverend John Treadgold; The Deanery, Chichester PO19 1PX; phone: (01273) 421021; fax: (01273) 421041; e-mail: admin@diochi.org.uk

Diocese of Coventry Bishop, The Right Reverend Colin Bennetts; Provost, The Very Reverend John Fitzmaurice; Pelham Lee House, 7 Priory House, Coventry CV1 5ES; phone: (01203) 227597; fax: (01203) 713271

Diocese of Derby Bishop, The Right Reverend J S Bailey; Provost, The Very Reverend Michael Perham; The Provost's House, 9 Highfield Road, Derby DE22 1GX; phone: (01332) 341201; fax: (01332) 203991

Diocese of Durham Bishop, The Right Reverend A M A Turnbull; Dean, The Very Reverend John Arnold; The Deanery, Durham DH1 3EQ; phone: (0191) 384 7500; fax: (0191) 386 4267

Diocese of Ely Bishop, The Right Reverend S W Sykes; Dean, The Very Reverend Michael Higgins; The Deanery, The College, Ely CB7 4DN; phone: (01353) 667735; fax: (01353) 665658; Web site: www.cathedral.ely.anglican.org

Diocese of Exeter Bishop, to be appointed; Dean, The Very Reverend Keith Jones; Cathedral Office, 1 The Cloisters, Exeter EX1 1HS; phone: (01392) 255573; fax: (01392) 498769; e-mail: admin@exeter-cathedral.org.uk; Web site: www.exeter-cathedral.org.uk

Diocese of Gloucester Bishop, The Right Reverend D E Bentley; Dean, The Very Reverend Nicholas Bury; The Deanery, Miller's Green, Gloucester GL1 2BP; phone: (01452) 524167; fax: (01452) 300469; e-mail: bshpglos@star.co.uk

Diocese of Guildford Bishop, The Right Reverend J W Gladwin; Dean, The Very Reverend Alexander Wedderspoon; Cathedral Office, Guildford Cathedral, Stag Hill, Guildford GU2 5UP; phone: (01483) 565287; fax: (01483) 303350

Diocese of Hereford Bishop, The Right Reverend J K Oliver; Dean, The Very Reverend Robert Willis; Cathedral Office, 5 College Cloisters, Hereford HR1 2NG; phone: (01432) 359880; fax: (01432) 355929

Diocese of Leicester Bishop, The Right Reverend Timothy Stevens; Provost, to be appointed; Cathedral Office, 1 St Martin's East, Leicester LE1 5FX; phone: (0116) 262 5294; fax: (0116) 262 5295; e-mail: cathedral@leicester.anglican.org; Web site: www.cathedral.leicester.anglican.org

(*continued on p. 412*)

Church of England Attendance Figures

Statistics have have been evaluated from the parish returns of membership and finance, and from information obtained from the offices of the diocesan bishops.
(N/A = not available.)

Year	Communicants				Attendances	
	Easter Sunday	Christmas Day	Normal Sunday	Total Sunday communicants per 1,000 population age 15 and over	Normal Sunday	Total Sunday attendances per 1,000 population
1988	1,410,000	1,714,000	725,000	19	1,165,000	24
1989	1,362,000	1,574,000	726,000	19	1,155,000	24
1990	1,376,000	1,556,000	724,000	19	1,143,000	24
1991	1,310,000	1,590,000	719,000	18	1,137,000	24
1992	1,350,000	1,483,000	717,000	18	1,123,000	23
1993	1,317,000	1,481,000	703,000	18	1,090,000	22
1994	1,300,000	1,488,000	693,000	18	1,081,000	22
1996	1,242,000	1,344,000	N/A	N/A	N/A	N/A

Source: *Church Statistics: Some Facts and Figures About the Church of England 1996*, © The Archbishop's Council

Diocese of Lichfield Bishop, The Right Reverend K N Sutton; Dean, The Very Reverend Tom Wright; Chapter Office, 19a The Close, Lichfield WS13 7LD; phone: (01543) 306030; fax: (01543) 416306

Diocese of Lincoln Bishop, The Right Reverend R M Hardy; Dean, The Very Reverend A F Knight; Chapter Office, The Cathedral, Lincoln LN2 1PZ; phone: (01522) 530320; fax: (01522) 511307

Diocese of Liverpool Bishop, The Right Reverend James Jones; Dean, The Very Reverend Derrick Walters; The Cathedral, St James' Mount, Liverpool L1 7AZ; phone: (0151) 709 6271; fax: (0151) 709 1112

Diocese of London Bishop, The Right Reverend R J C Chartres; Dean, The Very Reverend John Moses; Chapter House, St Paul's Churchyard, London EC4M 8AD; phone: (0171) 248 6233; fax: (0171) 248 9721; e-mail: bishop.london@londin.clara.co.uk

Diocese of Manchester Bishop, The Right Reverend C J Mayfield; Dean, The Very Reverend Kenneth Riley; Cathedral Office, The Cathedral, Manchester M3 1SX; phone: (0161) 833 2220; fax: (0161) 839 6226; e-mail: manchester.cathedral@bt.internet.com

Diocese of Newcastle Bishop, The Right Reverend J M Wharton; Provost, The Very Reverend Nicholas Coulton; The Cathedral Office, St Nicholas Churchyard, Newcastle upon Tyne, NE1 1PF; phone: (0191) 232 1939; fax: (0191) 230 0735; e-mail: stnichlas@aol.com

Diocese of Norwich Bishop, The Right Reverend P J Nott; Dean, The Very Reverend Stephen Platten; Cathedral Office, The Close, Norwich NR1 4DH; phone: (01603) 764383; fax: (01603) 766032

Diocese of Oxford Bishop, The Right Reverend R D Harries; Dean, The Very Reverend John Drury; The Deanery, Christ Church, Oxford OX1 1DP; phone: (01865) 276162; fax: (01865) 276238; e-mail: jan.bolongaro@christ-church.ox.ac.uk

Diocese of Peterborough Bishop, The Right Reverend I P M Cundy; Dean, The Very Reverend Michael Bunker; Chapter Office, Minster Precincts, Peterborough PE1 1XS; phone: (01733) 343342; fax: (01733) 552465

Diocese of Portsmouth Bishop, The Right Reverend K W Stevenson; Provost, The Very Reverend Michael Yorke; Cathedral Office, St Thomas's Street, Portsmouth PO1 2HH; phone: (01705) 823300; fax: (01705) 295480

Diocese of Ripon Bishop, to be appointed; Dean, The Very Reverend John Methuen; The Cathedral Office, Ripon Cathedral, Ripon HG4 1QR; phone and fax: (01765) 603462

Diocese of Rochester Bishop, The Right Reverend M J Nazir-Ali; Dean, The Very Reverend Edward Shotter; The Cathedral Office, Garth House, The Precinct, Rochester ME1 1SX; phone: (01634) 843366; fax: (01634) 401410

Diocese of St Albans Bishop, The Right Reverend C W Herbert; Dean, The Very Reverend Christopher Lewis; Cathedral Office, The Chapter House, Sumpter Yard, St Albans AL1 1BY; phone: (01727) 860780; fax: (01727) 850944; e-mail: cathedra@alban.u–net.com; Web site: www.stalbans.gov.uk/diocese/ abbey.htn

Diocese of St Edmundsbury and Ipswich Bishop, The Right Reverend J H R Lewis; Provost, The Very Reverend James Atwell; Cathedral Office, Angel Hill, Bury St Edmunds IP3 1LS; phone: (01284) 754933; fax: (01284) 768655; e-mail: perry@btconnect.com

Diocese of Salisbury Bishop, The Right Reverend D S Stancliffe; Dean, The Very Reverend Derek Watson; The Deanery, 7 The Close, Salisbury SP1 2EF; phone: (01722) 555110; fax: (01722) 555155; e-mail: chapoffice@aol.com

Diocese of Sheffield Bishop, The Right Reverend J Nicholls; Provost, The Very Reverend Michael Sadgrove; Cathedral Office, The Cathedral, Sheffield S1 1HA; phone: (0114) 275 3434; fax: (0114) 278 0244; e-mail: sheffcath@all.com; Web site: www.shef. ac.uk/uni/projects/shefcath

(*continued on p. 413*)

Succession List of the Archbishops of Canterbury

Date elected	Name	Date elected	Name	Date elected	Name	Date elected	Name
597	Augustine	1005	Alphege	1368	William Whittlesey	1747	Thomas Herring
604	Laurentius	1013	Lyfing	1375	Simon Sudbury	1757	Matthew Hutton
619	Mellitus	1020	Ethelnoth	1381	William Courtenay	1758	Thomas Secker
624	Justus	1038	Eadsige	1396	Thomas Arundel	1768	Frederick Cornwallis
627	Honorius	1051	Robert of Jumieges	1398	Roger Walden	1783	John Moore
655	Deusdedit	1052	Stigand	1399	Thomas Arundel[1]	1805	Charles Manners-Sutton
668	Theodore	1070	Lanfranc	1414	Henry Chichele	1828	William Howley
693	Berthwald	1093	Anselm	1443	John Stafford	1848	John Bird Sumner
731	Tatwine	1114	Ralph d'Escures	1452	John Kempe	1862	Charles Thomas Longley
735	Nothelm	1123	William de Corbeil	1454	Thomas Bourchier	1868	Archibald Campbell Tait
740	Cuthbert	1139	Theobald	1486	John Morton	1883	Edward White Benson
761	Bregowine	1162	Thomas à Becket	1501	Henry Deane	1896	Frederick Temple
765	Jaenbert	1174	Richard (of Dover)	1503	William Warham	1903	Randall Thomas Davidson
793	Ethelhard	1184	Baldwin	1533	Thomas Cranmer	1928	William Cosmo Gordon Lang
805	Wulfred	1193	Hubert Walter	1556	Reginald Pole	1942	William Temple
832	Feologeld	1207	Stephen Langton	1559	Matthew Parker	1945	Geoffrey Francis Fisher
833	Ceolnoth	1229	Richard le Grant	1576	Edmund Grindal	1961	Arthur Michael Ramsey
870	Ethelred	1234	Edmund of Abingdon	1583	John Whitgift	1974	Frederick Donald Coggan
890	Plegmund	1245	Boniface of Savoy	1604	Richard Bancroft	1980	Robert Alexander Kennedy Runcie
914	Athelm	1273	Robert Kilwardby	1611	George Abbot	1991–	George Leonard Carey
923	Wulfhelm	1279	John Peckham	1633	William Laud		
942	Oda	1294	Robert Winchelsey	1660	William Juxon		
959	Aelfsige	1313	Walter Reynolds	1663	Gilbert Sheldon		
959	Brithelm	1328	Simon Meopham	1678	William Sancroft		
960	Dunstan	1333	John de Stratford	1691	John Tillotson		
c. 988	Ethelgar	1349	Thomas Bradwardine	1695	Thomas Tenison		
990	Sigeric	1349	Simon Islip	1716	William Wake		
995	Aelfric	1366	Simon Langham	1737	John Potter		

[1] Restored.

Diocese of Sodor and Man Bishop, and Dean, The Very Reverend Nöel Jones; c/o 26 The Fountains, Ballure Promenade, Ramsey, Isle of Man IM8 1NN; phone: (01624) 816545; fax: (01624) 816545

Diocese of Southwark Bishop, The Right Reverend Tom Butler; Provost, The Very Reverend Colin Slee; Cathedral Office, Montague Close, London SE1 9DA; phone: (0171) 407 3708; fax: (0171) 357 7389; e-mail: cathedral@dswark.org.uk; Web site: www. dswark.org

Diocese of Southwell Bishop, The Venerable George Cassidy; Provost, The Very Reverend David Leaning; The Minster Office, Trebeck Hall, Bishop's Drive, Southwell NG25 0JP; phone: (01636) 812649; fax: (01636) 815904; e-mail: pat@southwellminster.prestel.co.uk

Diocese of Truro Bishop, The Right Reverend W Ind; Dean, The Very Reverend Michael Moxon; Cathedral Office, 21 Old Bridge Street, Truro TR1 2AH; phone: (01872) 276782; fax: (01872) 277788; www.truro.anglican.org/cathedral

Diocese of Wakefield Bishop, The Right Reverend N S McCulloch; Provost, The Very Reverend Canon George Nairn-Briggs; Cathedral Office, Northgate, Wakefield WF1 1HG; phone: (01924) 373923; fax: (01924) 215054

Diocese of Winchester Bishop, The Right Reverend M C Scott-Joynt; Dean, The Very Reverend Michael Till; The Deanery, The Close, Winchester SO23 9LS; phone: (01962) 853137; fax: (01962) 841519; e-mail: cathedral.office@dial.pipex.com

Diocese of Worcester Bishop, The Right Reverend Dr P S M Selby; Dean, The Very Reverend Peter Marshall; Cathedral Office, 10a College Green, Worcester WR1 2LH; phone: (01905) 28854; fax: (01905) 611139; e-mail: orcestercathedral@compuserve.com

Diocese of York Archbishop, The Most Reverend and Right Honourable D M Hope; Dean, The Very Reverend Raymond Furnell; The Deanery, York YO1 7JQ; phone: (01904) 623608; fax: (01904) 672002; e-mail: info@yorkminster.org; Web site: www.yorkminster.org

Dioceses of the Church in Wales

Diocese of St Asaph Archbishop, The Most Reverend Alwyn Rice Jones; Esgobty, St Asaph LL17 0TW; phone: (01745) 583503; fax: (01745) 584301

Diocese of Bangor Bishop, to be appointed; Ty'r Esgob, Bangor LL57 2SS; phone: (01248) 362895; 345866

Diocese of St David's Bishop, The Right Reverend D Huw Jones; Llys Esgob Abergwili, Carmarthen SA31 2JG; phone: (01267) 236597; fax: (01267) 237483

Diocese of St Llandaff Bishop, The Right Reverend Dr Barry C Morgan; Llys Esgob, The Cathedral Green, Llandaff, Cardiff CF5 2YG; phone: (01222) 562400; fax: (01222) 577129

Diocese Monmouth Bishop, The Right Reverend Dr Rowan D Williams; Bishopstow, Stow Hill, Newport NP9 4EA; phone: (01633) 263105; fax: (01633) 259946

Diocese of Swansea and Brecon Bishop, The Right Reverend Anthony Edward Pierce; Ely Tower, Brecon LD3 9DE; phone: (01874) 622008; fax: (01874) 622008

Presbyteries of the Church of Scotland

Church Headquarters and Principals

Lord High Commissioner The Lord Macfarlane of Bearsden; **Moderator of the General Assembly** The Right Reverend A McDonald; **Principal Clerk** Reverend F A J Macdonald; **Deputy Clerk** Reverend M A MacLean; **Procurator** A Dunlop; **Law Agent and Solicitor of the Church** Mrs J S Wilson; **Parliamentary Agent** I McCulloch (London); **General Treasurer** D F Ross

Church Office

121 George Street, Edinburgh, EH2 4YN; phone: (0131) 225 5722; fax: (0131) 220 3133

Presbyteries

Edinburgh Reverend W P Graham; **West Lothian** Reverend D Shaw; **Lothian** Reverend J D McCulloch; **Melrose and Peebles** Reverend J M Brown; **Duns** Reverend A C D Cartwright; **Jedburgh** Reverend A D Reid; **Ammandale and Eskdale** Reverend C B Haston; **Dumfries and Kirkcudbright** Reverend G M A Savage; **Wigtown and Stranraer** Reverend D W Dutton; **Ayr** Reverend J Crichton; **Irvine and Kilmarnock** Reverend C G F Brockie; **Ardrossan** Reverend D Broster; **Lanark** Reverend I D Cunningham; **Paisley** Reverend D Kay; **Greenock** Reverend D Mill; **Glasgow** Reverend A Cunningham; **Hamilton** Reverend J H Wilson; **Dumbarton** Reverend D P Munro; **South Argyll** Reverend M A J Gossip; **Dunoon** Reverend R Samuel; **Lorn and Mull** Reverend W T Hogg; **Falkirk** Reverend D E McClements; **Stirling** Reverend B W Dunsmore; **Dunfermline** Reverend W E Farquhar; **Kirkcaldy** Reverend B L Tomlinson; **St Andrews** Reverend J W Patterson; **Dunkeld and Meigle** Reverend A B Reid; **Perth** Reverend M J Ward; **Dundee** Reverend J A Roy; **Angus** Reverend M I Rooney; **Aberdeen** Reverend A M Douglas; **Kincardine and Deeside** Reverend J W S Brown; **Gordon** Reverend I U Thomson; **Buchan** Reverend R Neilson; **Moray** Reverend D J Ferguson; **Abernethy** Reverend J A I MacEwan; **Inverness** Reverend A S Younger; **Lochaber** Reverend A Ramsay; **Ross** Reverend R M MacKinnon; **Sutherland** Reverend J L Goskirk; **Caithness** Reverend M G Mappin; **Lochcarron/Skye** Reverend A I MacArthur; **Uist** Reverend M Smith; **Lewis** Reverend T S Sinclair; **Orkney (Finstown)** Reverend T Hunt; **Shetland (Lerwick)** Reverend N R Whyte; **England (London)** Reverend W A Cairns; **Europe (Portugal)** Reverend J W MacLeod

Membership and Number of Churches and Ministers of the Institutional Churches in the UK

All statistics for 2000 are estimates.

Total Institutional Churches

Year	Membership	Churches	Ministers
1980	6,277,451	29,651	25,283
1985	5,725,071	29,161	24,275
1990	5,408,821	28,874	23,775
1995	5,088,837	28,426	22,172
2000	4,675,256	28,124	21,113

Anglican[1]

Year	Membership	Churches	Ministers
1980	2,179,458	19,399	12,472
1985	1,895,943	19,025	12,158
1990	1,727,977	18,824	12,374
1995	1,785,273	18,674	11,781
2000	1,584,090	18,505	11,407

Roman Catholic

Year	Mass attendance	Churches	Priests
1980	2,457,053	4,160	9,010
1985	2,281,340	4,268	8,517
1990	2,200,844	4,339	8,087
1995	1,915,417	4,286	7,425
2000	1,783,831	4,282	6,974

Orthodox

Year	Membership	Congregations	Priests
1980	203,165	171	168
1985	223,741	200	187
1990	265,968	221	192
1995	288,560	268	214
2000	320,420	296	232

Presbyterian

Year	Membership	Churches	Ministers
1980	1,437,775	5,921	3,633
1985	1,322,047	5,668	3,413
1990	1,214,032	5,490	3,122
1995	1,099,587	5,278	2,752
2000	986,915	5,041	2,500

[1] These figures are for more than just the Church of England, although in 1995 the Church of England membership was 82% of the total.

Source: *UK Christian Handbook: Religious Trends No 1 1998/99* (Christian Research, London), © P W Brierley, Christian Research, London

Membership and Number of Churches and Ministers of the Free Churches in the UK

All statistics for 2000 are estimates.

Total Free Churches

Year	Membership	Churches	Ministers
1980	1,275,895	20,365	10,407
1985	1,256,393	20,339	10,964
1990	1,283,619	20,715	12,842
1995	1,272,481	20,626	13,729
2000	1,267,939	20,524	14,627

Baptist

Year	Membership	Churches	Ministers
1980	239,815	3,317	2,421
1985	243,099	3,348	2,576
1990	230,921	3,588	2,699
1995	223,407	3,448	2,863
2000	220,317	3,427	3,060

Independent[1]

Year	Membership	Churches	Ministers
1980	236,881	4,295	1,277
1985	229,569	4,177	1,261
1990	225,525	4,085	1,248
1995	206,244	3,910	1,250
2000	200,362	3,809	1,240

Methodist

Year	Membership	Churches	Ministers
1980	520,557	8,481	2,414
1985	474,290	7,955	2,298
1990	451,732	7,562	2,337
1995	401,087	7,092	2,161
2000	366,820	6,636	2,130

New Churches

Year	Membership	Congregations	Full-time Leaders
1980	10,137	228	159
1985	35,351	684	476
1990	77,454	1,191	1,195
1995	109,601	1,580	1,555
2000	135,200	1,928	1,877

Pentecostal[2]

Year	Membership	Churches	Ministers
1980	127,068	1,094	2,282
1985	136,669	2,024	2,420
1990	162,499	2,147	3,021
1995	196,531	2,399	3,636
2000	211,476	2,520	3,924

Other Churches[3]

Year	Membership	Churches	Ministers
1980	141,437	2,040	1,854
1985	137,415	2,051	1,933
1990	135,488	2,042	2,342
1995	135,611	2,097	2,264
2000	133,764	2,104	2,396

[1] Total of Brethren, congregational, and other independent churches.
[2] Total of Main Line Afro-Caribbean and Oneness Apostolic Churches.
[3] Total of Central, Holiness, Lutheran, and Overseas Nationals Churches and Denominations.

Source: *UK Christian Handbook: Religious Trends No 1 1998/99* (Christian Research, London), © P W Brierley, Christian Research, London

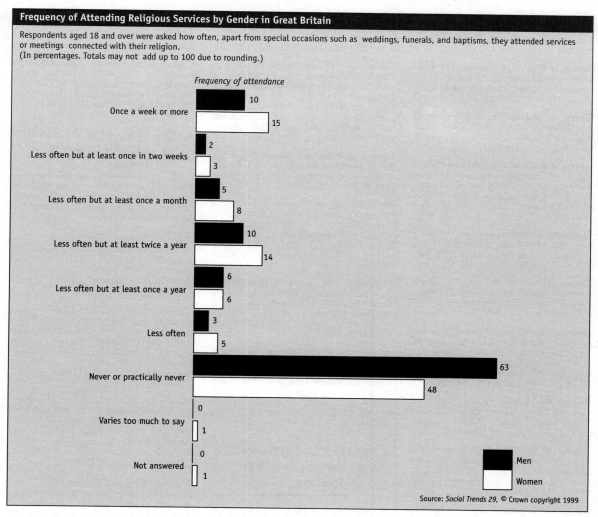

Frequency of Attending Religious Services by Gender in Great Britain

Respondents aged 18 and over were asked how often, apart from special occasions such as weddings, funerals, and baptisms, they attended services or meetings connected with their religion.
(In percentages. Totals may not add up to 100 due to rounding.)

Frequency of attendance	Men	Women
Once a week or more	10	15
Less often but at least once in two weeks	2	3
Less often but at least once a month	5	8
Less often but at least twice a year	10	14
Less often but at least once a year	6	6
Less often	3	5
Never or practically never	63	48
Varies too much to say	0	1
Not answered	0	1

Source: *Social Trends 29,* © Crown copyright 1999

Dioceses of the Church of Ireland

Archbishop of Armagh and Primate of All Ireland
Most Reverend Robert H A Eames

Bishops
Clogher Brian D A Hannon; **Connor** James E Moore; **Derry and Raphoe** James Mehaffey; **Down and Dromore** Harold C Miller; **Kilmore, Elphin, and Ardagh** Michael H G Mayes; **Tuam, Killala, and Achonry** Right Reverend Richard C A Handerson

Archbishop of Dublin, Bishop of Glendalough, and Primate of Ireland
Most Reverend Walton N F Empey

Bishops
Cashel and Ossary John R W Neill; **Cork, Cloyne, and Ross** Right Reverend William P Colton; **Limerick and Killaloe** Edward F Darling; **Meath and Kildare** Most Reverend Richard L Clarke

Dioceses of the Roman Catholic Church in England and Wales

The basic administrative unit of the Catholic Church is the diocese – an area presided over by a bishop, sometimes with auxiliary bishops. In England and Wales there are 22 territorial dioceses, plus two dioceses covering the whole country.

Diocese of Arundel and Brighton Bishop, The Right Reverend Cormac Murphy-O'Connor; Bishop's House, The Upper Drive, Hove, East Sussex BN3 6NE; phone: (01273) 506387; fax: (01273) 501527

Archdiocese of Birmingham Bishop, to be appointed; Auxiliary Bishops, The Right Reverend Philip Pargeter, The Right Reverend Terence Brain; Cathedral House, St Chad's Queensway, Birmingham B4 6EX; phone: (0121) 236 5535; fax: (0121) 233 9266

Diocese of Brentwood Bishop, The Right Reverend Thomas McMahon; Cathedral House, Ingrave Road, Brentwood, Essex CM15 8AT; phone: (01277) 232266; fax: (01277) 261152

Archdiocese of Cardiff Archbishop, The Most Reverend John Aloysius Ward OFMCap.; Archbishop's House, 41–43 Cathedral Road, Cardiff CF1 9HD; phone: (01222) 220411; fax: (01222) 345950

Diocese of Clifton Bishop, The Right Reverend Mervyn Alexander; Egerton Road, Bishopston, Bristol BS7 8HU; phone: (0117) 983 3907

Diocese of East Anglia Bishop, The Right Reverend Peter Smith; The White House, 21 Upgate, Poringland, Norwich NR14 7SH; phone: (01508) 492202; fax: (01508) 495358

Diocese of Hallam The Right Reverend John Rawsthorne; 'Quarters', Carsick Hill Way, Sheffield S10 3LT; phone: (0114) 230 9101; fax: (0114) 230 5722

Diocese of Hexham and Newcastle Bishop, The Right Reverend Michael Ambrose Griffiths OSB; Bishop's House, East Denton Hall, 800 West Road, Newcastle upon Tyne NE5 2BJ; phone: (0191) 228 0003; fax: (0191) 274 0432

Diocese of Lancaster Bishop, The Right Reverend John Brewer; Bishop's House, Cannon Hill, Lancaster LA1 5NG; phone: (01524) 32231; fax: (01524) 849296

Diocese of Leeds Bishop, The Right Reverend David Konstant; 7 St Marks Avenue, Leeds LS2 9BN; phone: (0113) 244 4788; fax: (0113) 244 8084

Archdiocese of Liverpool Bishop, The Most Reverend Patrick Kelly; Auxiliary Bishops, The Right Reverend John Rawsthorne, The Right Reverend Vincent Malone; 152 Brownlow Hill, Liverpool L3 5RQ; phone: (0151) 709 4801; fax: (0151) 708 5167

Diocese of Menevia Bishop, The Right Reverend Daniel Mullins; Curial Office, 79 Walter Road, Swansea SA1 4PS; phone: (01792) 644017; fax: (01792) 458641

Diocese of Middlesbrough Bishop, The Right Reverend John Crowley; 50a The Avenue, Linthorpe, Middlesbrough, Cleveland TS5 6QT; phone: (01642) 850505; fax: (01642) 851404

Diocese of Northampton Bishop, The Right Reverend Patrick Leo McCartie; Bishop's House, Marriott Street, Northampton NN2 6AW; phone: (01604) 715635; fax: (01604) 792186

Diocese of Nottingham Bishop, The Right Reverend James McGuinness; Willson House, Derby Road, Nottingham NG1 5AW; phone: (0115) 953 9800

Diocese of Plymouth Bishop, The Right Reverend Christopher Budd; Bishop's House, 31 Wyndham Street West, Plymouth, Devon PL1 5RZ; phone: (01752) 224414; fax: (01752) 223750

Diocese of Portsmouth Bishop, The Right Reverend Crispian Hollis; Bishop's House, Edinburgh Road, Portsmouth PO1 3HG; phone: (01705) 820894; fax: (01705) 863086

Diocese of Salford The Right Reverend Terence Brain; Cathedral House, 250 Chapel Street, Salford M3 5LL; phone: (0161) 834 9052; fax: (0161) 839 7027

Diocese of Shrewsbury Bishop, The Right Reverend Brian Noble; 2 Park Road South, Birkenhead, Merseyside L43 4UX; phone: (0151) 652 9855; fax: (0151) 653 5172

Archdiocese of Southwark Archbishop, The Most Reverend Michael G Bowen; Area Bishops, The Right Reverend Charles Henderson, The Right Reverend John Jukes, The Right Reverend Howard Tripp; Archbishop's House, 150 St George's Road, Southwark, London SE1 6HX; phone: (0171) 928 5592; fax: (0171) 928 7833

Diocese of Wrexham Bishop, The Right Reverend Edwin Regan; Bishop's House, Sontley Road, Wrexham, LL13 7EW; phone: (01978) 262726; fax: (01978) 354257

Bishopric of the Forces (Covers Her Majesty's Forces across the UK and overseas.) Bishop, The Right Reverend Francis Walmsley; Hampshire House, 62 Peabody Road, Farnborough, Hants GU14 6HA; phone: (01252) 543649; fax: (01252) 543649

Ukrainian Apostolic Exarchate (Serves the Ukrainian Greek Catholic community across the UK.) Bishop, The Right Reverend Michael Kuchmiak CSSR; 22 Binney Street, London W1Y 1YN; phone: (0171) 629 1073

Archdiocese of Westminster Archbishop, to be appointed; Auxiliary Bishops, The Right Reverend James O'Brien, The Right Reverend Vincent Nichols, The Right Reverend Patrick O'Donoghue; Archbishop's House, Ambrosden Avenue, London SW1P 1QJ; phone: (0171) 798 9055; fax: (0171) 798 9077

Dioceses of the Roman Catholic Church for Scotland

Diocese of Aberdeen Bishop, The Right Reverend Mario Joseph Conti; Bishop's House, Queen's Cross, Aberdeen AB15 4XU; phone: (01224) 319154; fax: (01224) 325570

Diocese of Dunkeld Bishop, The Right Reverend Vincent Logan; Bishop's House; 29 Roseangle, Dundee DD1 4LX; phone: (01382) 224327; fax: (01382) 205212

Diocese of Galloway Bishop, The Right Reverend Maurice Taylor; Candida Casa, 8 Corsehill Road, Ayr KA7 2ST; phone and fax: (01292) 266750

Diocese of Glasgow Archbishop, His Eminence Cardinal Thomas Joseph Winning; 40 Newlands Road, Glasgow G43 2JD; phone (Cardinal's office): (0141) 226 5898

Diocese of Motherwell Bishop, The Right Reverend Joseph Devine; 22 Wellhall Road, Hamilton ML3 2BG; phone: (01698) 423058; fax: (01698) 307093

Diocese of Paisley Bishop, The Right Reverend John Aloysius Mone; 107 Corsebar Road, Paisley PA2 9PY; (0141) 889 7200; fax: (0141) 8496053

Diocese of St Andrews and Edinburgh Archbishop, The Most Reverend Keith Patrick O'Brien; St Bennet's, 42 Greenhill Gardens, Edinburgh EH10 4BJ; phone: (0131) 447 3337; fax: (0131) 447 0816

Dioceses of the Roman Catholic Church in Ireland

There is one hierarchy for the whole of Ireland. Several of the dioceses have territory partly in the Republic of Ireland and partly in Northern Ireland.

Apostolic Nuncio to Ireland

The Most Reverend Luciano Storero; The Apostolic Nuncio, The Apostolic Nunciature, 183 Navan Road, Dublin 7, Republic of Ireland; phone: (00353) 8380577; fax: (00353) 8380276

The Most Reverend Archbishops

Armagh Sean Brady; Ara Coeli, Armagh BT61 7QY; phone: (080 1861) 522045; fax: (080 1861) 526182 **Cashel** Dermot Clifford; Archbishop's House, Thurles, County Tipperary, Republic of Ireland; phone: (00353) 504 21512; fax: (00353) 504 22680

Dublin Desmond Connell; Archbishop's House, Drumcondra, Dublin 9, Republic of Ireland; phone: (00353) 1 837 3732; fax: (00353) 1 8373732 **Tuam** Michael Neary; Archbishop's House, Tuam, County Galway, Republic of Ireland; phone: (00353) 93 24166; fax: (00353) 93 28070

The Most Reverend Bishops

Achonry Thomas Flynn; Bishop's House, Ballaghaderreen, County Roscommon, Republic of Ireland; phone: (00353) 907 60021; fax: (00353) 907 60921

Ardagh and Clonmacnois Colm O'Reilly; Bishop's House, St Michael's, Longford, County Longford, Republic of Ireland; phone: (00353) 43 46432; fax: (00353) 43 46833

Clogher Joseph Duffy; Bishop's House, Monaghan, County Monaghan, Republic of Ireland; phone: (00353) 47 81019; fax: (00353) 47 84773

Clonfert John Kirby; Bishop's House, St Brendan's, Coorheen, Loughrea, County Galway, Republic of Ireland; phone: (00353) 91 841560; fax: (00353) 91 841818 **Cloyne** John Magee; Bishop's House, Cobh, County Cork, Republic of Ireland; phone: (00353) 21 811430; fax: (00353) 21 811026

Cork and Ross John Buckley; Diocesan Office, Bishop's House, Redemption Road, Cork, Republic of Ireland; phone: (00353) 21 301717; fax: (00353) 21 301557

Derry Seamus Hegarty; Bishop's House, St Eugene's Cathedral, Derry BT48 9AP; phone: (080 1504) 262302; fax: (080 1504) 371960

Down and Connor Patrick J Walsh; Lisbreen, 73 Somerton Rd, Belfast, County Antrim BT15 4DE; phone: (080 1232) 776185; fax: (080 1232) 779377

Dromore Francis G Brooks; Bishop's House, Violet Hill, Newry, County Down BT 35 6PN; phone: (080 1693) 62444; fax: (080 1693) 60496

Elphin Christopher Jones; St Mary's, Sligo, Republic of Ireland; phone: (00353) 71 62670; fax: (00353) 71 62414

Ferns Brendon Comiskey; Bishop's House, Summerhill, Wexford, County Wexford, Republic of Ireland; phone: (00353) 53 22177; fax: (00353) 53 23436

Galway and Kilmacduagh James McLoughlin; The Cathedral, Galway, Republic of Ireland; phone: (00353) 91 563566; fax: (00353) 91 568333

Kerry William Murphy; Bishop's House, St Brendan's, Killarney, County Kerry, Republic of Ireland; phone: (00353) 64 31168; fax: (00353) 64 31364

Kildare and Leighlin Laurence Ryan; Bishop's House, Carlow, County Carlow, Republic of Ireland; phone: (00353) 503 31102; fax: (00353) 503 32478

Killaloe William Walsh; Bishop's House, Westbourne, Ennis, County Clare, Republic of Ireland; phone: (00353) 65 28638; fax: (00353) 65 42538

Kilmore Thomas Finnegan; Bishop's House, Ballina, County Mayo, Republic of Ireland; phone: (00353) 96 21518; fax: (00353) 96 70344

Limerick Donal Murray; 66 O'Connoll St, Limerick, Republic of Ireland; phone: (00353) 61 315856; fax: (00353) 61 3101816

Meath Michael Smith; Bishop's House, Dublin Rd, Mullingar, County Westmeath, Republic of Ireland; phone: (00353) 44 48841; fax: (00353) 44 43020

Ossory Laurence Forristal; Sion House, Kilkenny, County Killkenny, Republic of Ireland; phone: (00353) 56 62448; fax: (00353) 56 63753

Raphoe Philip Boyce; Ard Adhamhnain, Letterkenny, County Donegal, Republic of Ireland; phone: (00353) 74 21208; fax: (00353) 74 24872

Waterford and Lismore William Lee; Bishop's House, John's Hill, Waterford City, Republic of Ireland; phone: (00353) 51 874463; fax: (00353) 51 852703

Dioceses of the Orthodox Church in the UK

Canonical Orthodox Churches in the UK

Ecumenical Patriarchate of Constantinople

Archdiocese of Thyateira and Great Britain His Eminence Archbishop Gregorios of Thyateira; 5 Craven Hill, London W2 3EN; phone: (0171) 723 4787; fax: (0171) 224 9301 **Assistant Bishops:** The Right Reverend Bishop Aristarchos of Zenoupolis; 59 Selborne Gardens, London NW4 4SH; phone: (0181) 202 4821 or 455 7510

The Right Reverend Bishop Chrysostomos of Kyanea; Greek Orthodox Cathedral of St Andrew, Kentish Town Road, London NW1 9QA; phone: (0171) 703 0137

The Right Reverend Bishop Christophoros of Telmissos; Greek Orthodox Cathedral of St Mary, 305 Camberwell New Road, London SE5 0TF; phone: (0171) 703 0137

The Right Reverend Bishop Kallistos of Diokleia; 15 Staverton Road, Oxford OX2 6XH; phone: (01865) 554023

The Right Reverend Bishop Athanasios of Tropaeou; Greek Orthodox Cathedral of St Mary, Trinity Road, London N22 8LB; phone (0181) 888 2295; fax: (0181) 881 4455

Ukrainian Diocese in Great Britain The Right Reverend Bishop Ioan of Parnassos; 1a Newton Avenue, Acton, London W3 8AJ; phone: (0181) 992 4689

Patriarchate of Antioch

Antiochan Priest for London Father Samir Gholam, 30 Chatsworth Gardens, New Malden, Surrey KT3 6DW; phone: (0181) 942 9676

British Antiochian Orthodox Deanery Father Michael Harper, 1a Selwyn Gardens, Cambridge CB3 9AX; phone: (01223) 327771; fax: (01444) 417871; e-mail: 100307@compuserve.com; Web site: www.antiochianorthodox.co.uk

Russian Orthodox Church, Patriarchate of Moscow

Diocese of Sourozh The Most Reverend Metropolitan Antony of Sourozh; Russian Orthodox Cathedral, 67 Ennismore Gardens, London SW7 1NH; fax only: (0171) 584 9864

Assistant Bishops The Most Reverend Archbishop Anatoly of Kerch; 14a Bloom Park Road, Fulham, London SW6 7BG; phone: (0171) 386 7837

The Right Reverend Bishop Basil of Sergievo; 94a Banbury Road, Oxford OX2 6JT; phone: (01865) 512701

Serbian Orthodox Church, Patriarchate of Serbia

Diocese of Great Britain and Scandinavia

Episcopal Vicar in the UK Protopresbyter-Stavrophore Miklenko Zebic; 131 Cob Lane, Bournville, Birmingham B30 1QE; phone: (0121) 458 5273; fax: (0121) 458 4986

New Gracanica Metropolitanate The Right Reverend Bishop Damaskin of Western Europe; 88 Castle Road, Bedford MK40 3PS; phone: (01234) 340859

Episcopal Vicar in the UK Protopresbyter Nikola Kotur; 29 Brackley Raod, Bedford MK42 9SD; phone: (01234) 273342

Romanian Orthodox Church, Patriarchate of Romania

Representative in the UK Father Sylviu-Petre Pufulete; Romanian House, 250 Clapham Road, London SW9 0PZ; phone: (0171) 735 9515; fax: (0171) 735 9515; e-mail: ppufulete@compuserve.com

Bulgarian Orthodox Church, Patriarchate of Bulgaria

Representative in the UK Father Simeon Iliev; 188 Queen's Gate, London SW7 5HL; phone: (0171) 584 4607

Canonical Oriental Orthodox Churches in the UK

Armenian Orthodox Church, Catholicossate of Etchmiadzin

The Most Reverend Archbishop Yeghishe Gizirian; Armenian Primate of Great Britain, Armenian Vicarage, Iverna Gardens, London W8 6TP; phone: (0171) 937 0152; fax: (0171) 937 9049

Coptic Orthodox Church, Patriarchate of Alexandria

Diocese of Birmingham The Right Reverend Bishop Missaiel; Hill Park House, Lapworth Street, Lapworth, Warwickshire B94 5QS; phone: (01564) 783926

Diocese of Scotland, Ireland, and North East England The Right Reverend Bishop Antony; 40 Kingston Drive, Whitley Bay NE26 1JJ; phone: (0191) 253 5558; fax: (0191) 253 5558

British Orthodox Church The Most Reverend Metropolitan Seraphim; 101 Heathwood Gardens, Charlton, London SE7 8EP; phone: (0181) 843 3090; fax: (0181) 244 7888; e-mail: boc@cwcom.net; Web site: www.uk-christian.net/boc

Eritrean Orthodox Church, Patriarchate of Eritrea

Diocese of Great Britain The Right Reverend Bishop Markos; 11 Anfield Close, Wier Road, London SW12 0NT; phone: (0181) 675 5115

Syrian Orthodox Church

Representative in the UK Father Touma Hazim Dakkama; Antiochian, 5 Canning Road, Croydon CR0 6QA; phone: (0181) 654 7531; fax: (0181) 654 7531

Representative in the UK Father Eldhose Koungampillil; 1 Roslyn Court, Roslyn Avenue, East Barnet, Hertfordshire EN4 8DJ; phone: (0181) 368 2794; fax: (0181) 368 2794

Malankara Orthodox Syrian Church

Representative in the UK Father M S Skariah; Paramula House, 44 Newbury Road, Newbury Park, Ilford, Essex IG2 7HD; phone: (0181) 599 3836

Oriental Orthodox News Service

10 Heathwood Gardens, Charlton, London SE7 8EP; phone: (0181) 843 3090; fax: (0181) 244 7888; e-mail: Orthodox@uk-christian.net; Web site: www.uk-christian.net/oons

The Council of Oriental Orthodox Churches

Secretary: Deacon Aziz M A Nour; 34 Chertsey Road, Church Square, Shepperton, Middlesex TW17 9LF; phone: (0181) 368 8447; fax: (0181) 368 8447

Christian Churches and Religious Groups in the UK

American Church in London Whitefield Memorial Church, 79a Tottenham Court Road, London W1P 9HB; phone: (0171) 580 2791; fax: (0171) 580 5013. Founded 1969

Anglican Catholic Church, Missionary Diocese of UK St Mary's House, 13 Byatt's Grove, Longton, Stoke-on-Trent ST3 2RH; phone: (01782) 330743; fax: (01782) 336361. Founded 1992

Antiochian Orthodox Church 13 Kenwyn Road, Wimbledon, London SW20 8TR; phone: (0181) 879 3046

The Apostolic Church PO Box 389, 24–27 St Helen's Road, Swansea SA1 1ZH; phone: (01792) 473992; fax: (01792) 474087. Founded 1904. 130 churches; 5,500 adherents; 83 ministers

Apostolic Faith Church 95 Fenham Road, Peckham, London SE15 1AE; phone: (0171) 639 9329/8897; fax: (0171) 639 9329. Founded 1906

Armenian Oriental Orthodox Church St Peter's Church, Cranley Gardens, London SW7 3BB; phone: (0171) 373 3565/244 9574

Assemblies of God in Great Britain and Ireland 16 Bridgford Road, West Bridgford, Nottingham NG2 6AF; phone: (0115) 981 1188; fax: (0115) 981 3377. Founded 1924. 653 churches; 75,000 adherents; 880 ministers

Associated Presbyterian Churches PO Box 2, Gairloch IV21 2YA; phone: (01463) 236109. Founded 1989. 20 churches; 1,000 members; 15 ministers

Baptist Union of Great Britain Baptist House, PO Box 44, 129 Broadway, Didcot OX11 8RT; phone: (01235) 512077; fax: (01235) 811537; e-mail: 100442.1750@compuserve.com. Founded 1812. 2,130 churches; 157,000 members; 1,864 pastors

Baptist Union of Ireland 117 Lisburn Road, Belfast BT9 7AF; phone: (01232) 663108; fax: (01232) 663616; e-mail: buofi@aol.com. Founded 1895. 109 churches; 8,454 members; 83 pastors

Baptist Union of Scotland 14 Aytoun Road, Glasgow G41 5RT; phone: (0141) 423 6169; fax: (0141) 424 1422. Founded 1869. 171 churches; 14,328 members; 140 pastors

Baptist Union of Wales Ty Ilston, 94 Mansel Street, Swansea SA1 5TZ; phone: (01792) 655468/469893; fax: (01792) 469489. Founded 1866. 537 churches; 24,178 members; 118 pastors

Belorussian Autocephalic Orthodox Church Holy Mother of God of Zyrovicy Church, Chapel Road, Rainsough, Prestwich, Manchester M22 4JW; phone: (0161) 740 8230. Founded 1948

Born Again Christ Healing Church 77 Beechwood Road, Hornsey, London N8 7NE; phone: (0181) 340 9962. Founded 1979

British Antiochian Orthodox Deanery Stanfords, 27 Muster Green, Haywards Heath RH16 4AL; phone: (01444) 417007; fax: (01444) 417871; e-mail: 100307.540@compuserve.com

British Conference of Mennonites London Mennonite Centre, 14 Shepherds Hill, Highgate, London N6 5AQ; phone: (0181) 340 8775; fax: (0181) 341 6807; e-mail: menno@compuserve.com. Founded 1987

The British Orthodox Church (Coptic Orthodox Patriarchate) Church Secretariat, 10 Heathwood Gardens, Charlton, London SE7 8EP; phone: (0181) 854 3090; fax: (0181) 244 7888; e-mail: seraphim@britorthodox.idiscover.co.uk; Web site: www/uk–christian.net/boc. Founded 1866

Celtic Orthodox Church 33 Brownlow Street, York YO3 7LW; phone: (01904) 626599. Founded 1866

Chinese Church in London 81 Chiltern Street, London W1M 1HT; phone: (0171) 486 0592/0286; fax: (0171) 935 9113; e-mail: admin@ccil.u-net.com. Founded 1951

Christadelphians 404 Shaftmoor Lane, Hall Green, Birmingham B28 8SZ; phone: (0121) 777 6328; fax: (0121) 778 5024. Founded 1864

Christian Brethren 52 Hornsey Lane, London N6 5LU; phone: (0171) 272 0643. Founded 1828

Churches of God, UK 23 Walcott Road, Billinghay, Lincoln LN4 4EG; phone: (01526) 860508; e-mail: coguk@aol.com. Founded 1978

Church in Wales 39 Cathedral Road, Cardiff CF1 9XF; phone: (01222) 231638; fax: (01222) 387835

Church of Christ 64 Grenville Road, Southcourt, Aylesbury HP21 8EZ; phone: (01296) 482875; e-mail: gfisher888@aol.com

The Church of Christ, Scientist (Christian Science Church) 2 Elysium Gate, 126 New Kings Road, London SW6 4LZ; phone: (0171) 371 0600; fax: (0171) 371 9204; Web site: www.tfccs.com. Founded 1895. 200 branches in the UK

Church of England General Synod Church House, Great Smith Street, London SW1P 3NZ; phone: (0171) 222 9011; fax: (0171) 233 2660. (For details concerning the history and membership of the Church of England see relevant tables in this section)

Church of God of Prophecy 6 Beacon Court, Birmingham Road, Great Barr, Birmingham B43 6NN; phone: (0121) 358 2231; fax: (0121) 358 0934. Founded 1953

Church of Ireland Church of Ireland House, Church Avenue, Rathmines, Dublin 6, Ireland; phone: (00353) (1) 497 8422; fax: (1) 497 8821; e-mail: rcbdub@aol.ie

Church of Jesus Christ of Latter-Day Saints (Mormons) Public Affairs, Church Offices, 751 Warwick Road, Solihull B91 3DQ; phone: (0121) 712 1202; fax: (0121) 709 0180; Web site: www.lds.org. Founded 1837. Over 350 congregations; 170,000 members

Church of Scotland 121 George Street, Edinburgh EH2 4YN; phone: (0131) 225 5722; fax: (0131) 220 3113; e-mail: zp80@dial.pipex.com. Founded 1560. 1,600 churches; 700,000 members; 1,200 ministers

Congregational Federation Congregational Centre, 4 Castle Gate, Nottingham NG1 7AS; phone: (0115) 941 3801; fax: (0115) 948 0902. Founded 1972. 313 churches; 11,923 members; 71 ministers

Coptic Orthodox Church Allen Street, Kensington, London W8 6UX; phone: (0171) 603 6701

Coptic Orthodox Church of Scotland Links Street, Kirkcaldy KY1 1QE; phone: (01592) 643333; fax: (01592) 643344; e-mail: vp54@dial.pipex.com. Founded 1977

Cornerstone Central Hall, St Mary Street, Southampton SO14 1NF; phone: (01703) 237700; fax: (01703) 234555; e-mail: cornerstone.communitychurch@dial.pipex.com. Founded 1982

Elim Pentecostal Churches PO Box 38, Cheltenham GL50 3HN; phone: (01242) 519904; fax: (01242) 222279; e-mail: 106000.2410@compuserve.com. Founded 1915. 596 churches; 68,500 adherents; 650 ministers

Evangelical Lutheran Church of England 28 Huntingdon Road, Cambridge; phone: (01223) 355265; fax: (01223) 355265. Founded 1896

Evangelical Presbyterian Church in England and Wales 14 Longshaw Lane, Blackburn BB2 3LU; phone: (01245) 450089; fax: (01245) 260388. Founded 1987

Evangelical Presbyterian Church in Ireland 15 College Square East, Belfast BT1 6DD; phone: (01232) 320529/714820; e-mail: epc@ukonline.co.uk; Web site: web.ukonline.co.uk/epc. Founded 1927

Fellowship of Independent Evangelical Churches (FIEC) 3 Church Road, Croydon CR0 1SG; phone: (0181) 681 7422; fax: (0181) 760 5067. Founded 1922

The Free Church of England St Paul's Rectory, Lowther Road, Fleetwood FY7 7AS; phone: (01253) 873118; fax: (01253) 873118. Founded 1844 (Reformed Episcopal Church of England joined in 1927). 25 churches; 1,500 members; 42 ministers

Free Church of Scotland Free Church Offices, The Mound, Edinburgh EH1 2LS; phone: (0131) 226 5286/4978; fax: (0131) 220 0597; e-mail: freechurch@compuserve.com. Founded 1843. 140 churches; 6,000 members; 110 ministers

Free Presbyterian Church of Scotland 16 Matheson Road, Stornoway HS1 2LA; phone: (01851) 702555. Founded 1893. 50 churches (Scotland); 3,000 members (Scotland), 7,000 (overseas); 26 ministers (Scotland)

Free Presbyterian Church of Ulster Church House, 356 Ravenhill Road, Belfast BT6 8GL; phone: (01232) 457106; address for correspondence: 40 Lombard Avenue, Lisburn BT28 2UP; phone: (01846) 674664. Founded 1851

General Assembly of Unitarian and Free Christian Churches Essex Hall, 1 Essex Street, Strand, London WC2R 3HY; phone: (0171) 240 2384; fax: (0171) 240 3089; e-mail: ga@unitarian.org.uk; Web site: www.unitarian.org.uk. Founded in 1928. 200 congregations; 7,000 members; 150 ministers

The Greater World Christian Spiritualist Association 3 Conway Street, Fitzrovia, London W1P 5HA; phone: (0171) 436 7555; fax: (0171) 580 3485. Founded 1921

Greek Orthodox Archdiocese of Thyateira and Great Britain Thyateira House, 5 Craven Hill, London W2 3EN; phone: (0171) 723 4787; fax: (0171) 224 9301. Founded 1922. 101 churches; 102 priests

Independent Methodist Connexion of Churches Office and Resource Centre, Fleet Street, Pemberton, Wigan WN5 0DS; phone: (01942) 223526; fax: (01942) 227768; e-mail: 106570.2444@compuserve.com. Founded 1805. 100 churches; 3,050 members; 106 ministers

Indian Orthodox (Syrian) Church 44 Newbury Road, Ilford IG2 7HD; phone: (0181) 599 3836. Founded 1975

International Presbyterian Church 53 Drayton Green, Ealing, London W13 0JD; phone: (0181) 997 4706. Founded 1971

Iranian Christian Fellowship 158 Sutton Court Road, Chiswick, London W4 3HR; phone: (0181) 995 4966. Founded 1985

Jehovah's Witnesses Watch Tower House, The Ridgeway, London NW7 1RN; phone: (0181) 906 2211; fax: (0181) 906 3938. Founded 1872. Over 1,400 congregations; 130,000 members

Jesus Fellowship Church (Jesus Army) Nether Heyford, Northampton NN7 3LB; phone: (01327) 349992; fax: (01327) 349997; e-mail: info@jesus.org.uk. Founded 1805. 2,600 members

Kingdom Faith Church Foundry Lane, Horsham RH13 5PX; phone: (01403) 211505; fax: (01403) 211505; e-mail: 106074.700@compuserve.com. Founded 1992

The Liberal Catholic Church 205 Upper Richmond Road, London SW15 6SQ; phone: (0181) 780 5109. Founded 1916

Lutheran Council of Great Britain 5 Kings Croft Road, London NW2 3QE; phone: (0181) 452 9363; fax: (0181) 904 2849. Founded 1948. 100 churches; 27,000 members; 45 ministers

Mar Thoma Syrian Church UK Congregation Mar Thoma Centre, 22 Altmore Avenue, London E6 2BY; phone: (0181) 471 2446. Founded 1957

Methodist Church 25 Marylebone Road, London NW1 5JR; phone: (0171) 486 5502; fax: (0171) 935 1507. Founded 1739; the Wesleyan, Primitive, and United Methodist Churches united in 1932. 6,678 churches; 380,269 members; 3,660 ministers; 12,611 lay preachers

Methodist Church in Ireland 1 Fountainville Avenue, Belfast BT9 6AN; phone: (01232) 324554; fax: (01232) 239467. Founded 1738. 232 churches; 17,636 members; 196 ministers; 316 lay preachers

Moravian Church in Great Britain and Ireland 5 Muswell Hill, London N10 3TH; phone: (0181) 883 3409/1912; fax: (0181) 442 0112. Founded 1737

Mount Zion Pentecostal Apostolic Church 145 Midland Road, Bedford MK40 1DW; phone: (01234) 343609; fax: (01234) 343609. Founded 1965

Multiply Christian Network Jesus Fellowship Central Offices, Nether Heyford, Northampton NN7 3LB; phone: (01327) 349991; fax: (01327) 349997; Web site: www.jesus.org.uk/multiply. Founded 1992

Musama Disco Christo Church 40 Brailsford Road, Tulse Hill, London SW2 2TE; phone: (0181) 671 5099

New Frontiers International 17 Clarendon Villas, Hove BN3 3RE; phone: (01273) 821887; fax: (01273) 770878; e-mail: nfi@compuserve.com; Web site: home.ml.org/nfi. Began in 1980

New Testament Church of God Main House, Overstone Park, Overstone, Northampton NN6 0AD; phone: (01604) 643311/645944; fax: (01604) 790254. Founded 1953. 110 congregations; 20,000 adherents; 7,500 baptized ministers

Old Baptist Union 79 Ainslie Wood Road, Chingford, London E4 9BX; phone: (0181) 529 0783. Founded 1880

Old Roman Catholic Church of Great Britain 11 Calley Close, Tipton DY4 8XY; phone: (0121) 520 0041; fax: (0121) 520 0041. Founded 1908

Orthodox Church in Wales Orthodox Church of the Holy Protection, Blaenau Ffestiniog LL41 4DE; phone: (01766) 831272; fax: (01766) 780932

Pentecostal Revival Church of Christ 220 Ellison Road, Streatham, London SW16 5DJ; phone: (0181) 764 2643. Began in 1973

Pillar of Fire Church 19 Brent Street, Hendon, London NW4 2EU; phone: (0181) 202 3219/7618; fax: (0181) 202 3219. Founded 1915

Pioneer PO Box 79c, Esher KT10 9LP; phone: (01932) 789681; fax: (01932) 789691; e-mail: pioneer_trust@dial.pipex.com. Founded 1982

Plymouth Brethren No 4 c/o 99 Green Lane, Hounslow TW4 6BW; phone: (0181) 577 1603. Founded 1828

The Presbyterian Church in Ireland Church House, Fisherwick Place, Belfast BT1 6DW; phone: (01232) 322284; fax: (01232) 236609; e-mail: clerk@presbyterianireland.org; Web site: www.presbyterianireland.org. Founded 1662; synods united in 1840. 562 congregations; 297,000 members; 400 ministers (all figures for Ireland)

(continued on p. 421)

Major Non-Christian Religions in the UK

All statistics for 2000 are estimates.

Year	Active members	Groups	Leaders
Total Major Religions			
1980	735,735	1,081	2,933
1985	893,154	1,359	3,718
1990	1,066,149	1,601	4,393
1995	1,281,014	2,024	5,028
2000	1,466,265	2,273	5,740
Ahmadiyya Movement[1]			
1980	7,250	35	15[2]
1985	7,500	37	17[2]
1990	7,700	38	18[2]
1995	7,900	40	18[2]
2000	8,125	42	20[2]
Baha'i[3]			
1980	3,000[1]	200[1]	3
1985	4,000[1]	250[1]	4
1990	5,000[4]	320[1]	5
1995	6,000	380	6[1]
2000	7,000	440	7
Buddhist[5]			
1980	17,000	50	210
1985	23,000	92	290
1990	31,500[6,7]	155[8]	350
1995	45,000[9]	180[10]	400[1]
2000	52,400	234	470
Hindu[11]			
1980	120,000	125	120
1985	130,000	130	140
1990	140,000[12]	140	150
1995	155,000[13]	161[13]	150[1]
2000	165,000	169	165
International Society for Krishna Consciousness[1,14]			
1980	300	5	250
1985	350	3	300
1990	425	3	400
1995	600	13	500[15]
2000	670	18	575
Jain			
1980	6,000[1]	8[1]	0
1985	8,000[1]	10[1]	0
1990	10,000[4]	12[1]	0
1995	10,000[16]	15	0
2000	12,000	17	0
Jewish			
1980	110,915[17,18]	321[20]	416[2]
1985	105,455[17,18]	337[1,20]	432[1,2]
1990	101,239[17,18]	356[20]	440[2]
1995	93,684[17,18,19]	365[20]	440[1,2]
2000	88,800[17,18]	383[20]	440[2]
Muslim[21]			
1980	306,000[22]	193[25]	1,540
1985	434,979[22]	314[25]	2,077
1990	495,000[22,23]	350[25,26]	2,500[27]
1995	580,000[22,24]	587[25]	2,900[1]
2000	675,000[22]	660[25]	3,377
Satanist[1,28]			
1980	100	16	5
1985	200	33	8
1990	280	35	10
1995	330	38	14[29]
2000	420	41	16
School of Meditation			
1980	4,820[30]	2	75[2]
1985	6,000[1,30]	2[1]	100[1,2]
1990	7,000[1,30]	2[1]	100[2]
1995	9,000[30]	2[1]	120[2]
2000	11,000[30]	3	130[2]
Sikh[31]			
1980	150,000	105	140[2]
1985	160,000	125	150[2]
1990	250,000	149	180[2]
1995	350,000[32]	202[33]	200[2]
2000	400,000	225	220[2]
Zoroastrian[1,34]			
1980	1,350[1,34]	1[37]	0
1985	1,670[1,34]	1[37]	0
1990	2,000[34,35]	1[37]	0
1995	2,500[36]	1[37]	0
2000	2,850	1[37]	0
Other Religions			
1980	9,000	20	160
1985	12,000	25	200
1990	15,000	30	240
1995	20,000	35	280
2000	23,000	40	320

[1] Estimate.
[2] All male.
[3] *Religions in the UK: A Multi-Faith Directory* (1997) estimates that there are 6,000 Baha'is in the UK, connected to 200 Local Groups (less than 9 adults) and 180 Local Spiritual Assemblies (9 elected adults).
[4] Based on *Religion: Aspects in Britain* (1992), HMSO.
[5] Figures up to 1990 based on surveys of all Buddhist groups 1975, 1980, and 1985.
[6] Including approximately 5,000 Soka Gakkai (Nichiren Shoshu) members, 5,000 lay and 300 ordained members of Friends of the Western Buddhist Order, and 15,000 practitioners of Tibetan Buddhism (so the office of Tibet), given in *Religion Today*, Vol 8, No 2, Spring 1993.
[7] Taken as approximately one-sixth of total European and Asian community in the UK.
[8] M. Baumann in *Journal of Contemporary Religion*, Vol 10 No 1, 1995, states there were 213 Buddhist groups and centres in Great Britain in 1991.
[9] Taken as approximately a third of the estimated community figure of 130,000 given in the 1997 *Religions in the UK: A Multi-Faith Directory*.
[10] Chris Forster in *Planting for a Harvest* (1995) gives a total of 509 groups of 'Buddhist type religions' in 1994, but the 1997 *Religions in the UK: A Multi-Faith Directory* lists only 117 centres, viharas, monasteries, and other publicly accessible buildings.
[11] Active members taken as one-third of the community.
[12] Including perhaps 10,000 followers of Satya Sai Baba (from *The Spirit of Hinduism*, Dr David Burnett (1992).
[13] *Religions in the UK: A Multi-Faith Directory* (1997) lists 161 places of worship and a community figure of 400,000–550,000.
[14] The 'Hare Krishna' movement.
[15] Of which 145 were female.
[16] *Religions in the UK: A Multi-Faith Directory* (1997) gives a community figure of 25–30,000, and lists 3 temples and 12 local groups where worship takes place.
[17] Heads of households, male and female, affiliated to synagogues.
[18] These figures are about one-third of the Jewish community.
[19] Based on a community figure of 300,000.
[20] These congregations use slightly fewer synagogues; in 1983 for example there were 328 congregations but 295 synagogues.
[21] Including non-South Asians.
[22] Taken as 50% of the estimated Muslim community as being the attendance at one of the main Muslim festivals in Great Britain from 'Mosque Attendance', a survey by Dr Jim Holway, reported in the 1987/88 edition of *UK Christian Handbook*.
[23] Community taken as 990,000.
[24] Community taken at 1.16 million. This figure is disputed and estimates range from 1,070,000 (Professor Ceri Peach, 1995), and 1.5 million (Muhammed Anwar, *Muslims in Britain: 1991 Census and Other Statistical Sources*, OSIC Papers No 9 Sept 1993) to 2.5 to 3 million (The Muslim Parliament, 1994).
[25] These are registered mosques but many other buildings are used for worship. For example, in 1985, 612 buildings were used for 926 groups. In 1995, there were about 800 buildings in use, 200 of which were houses.
[26] 1,020 groups meeting.
[27] Of whom 100 were female.
[28] Active members taken as 1% of community. Including members of the Temple of Set, Northern Order of the Prince, Society of the Dark Lily, and Order of the Nine Angels. Country breakdown pro rata to general population.
[29] Of which 7 were female.
[30] Estimates of continuing practitioners, not number enrolling (10,000 per month in October 1972).
[31] All figures based on the Sikh Cultural Society's own estimates.
[32] The Sikh Cultural Society estimated the community to be 500,000. Includes 10,000 Namdhari Sikhs, *Religions in the UK: A Multi-Faith Directory* (1997).
[33] Based on *Religions in the UK: A Multi-Faith Directory* (1997).
[34] These figures are about one-third of the community. Country breakdown pro rata to general population.
[35] From tribute to rock musician Freddie Mercury in the *Independent* of 27 Nov 1991. An article by Harriot Crout-Tree in *Inter-faith Network* on 17 Feb 1992 put the community as 5,000 rather than 6,000.
[36] *Religions in the UK: A Multi-Faith Directory* (1997) gives a community figure of 5–10,000.
[37] Not a Fire Temple but room for worship in Zoroastrian House, London.

Source: *UK Christian Handbook: Religious Trends No 1 1998/99* (Christian Research, London), © P W Brierley, Christian Research, London

Presbyterian Church of Wales (or **Calvinic Methodist Church of Wales**) 53 Richmond Road, Cardiff CF2 3UP; phone: (01222) 494913; fax: (01222) 464293. Founded 1811. 939 churches; 51,720 members; 136 ministers

Protestant Episcopal Reformed Church (The Protestant Evangelical Church of England) Provost Office, 23 Limefield Road, Bolton BL1 6LE; phone: (01204) 491977. Founded in 1922

Reformed Presbyterian Church of Scotland 4 Burn Brae Avenue, Glasgow G61 3ES; phone: (0141) 942 5056. Founded 1743

Reformed Presbyterian Church of Ireland Cameron House, 98 Lisburn Road, Belfast BT9 6AG; phone: (01232) 660689. Founded 1763

Religious Society of Friends (Quakers) in Britain Quaker Communications Department, Friends House, 173–177 Euston Road, London NW1 2BJ; phone: (0171) 663 1000; fax: (0171) 663 1001; Web site: www.quaker.org/BYM. Founded 1652. 500 meeting houses; 27,000 members

Reorganized Church of Jesus Christ of Latter Day Saints British Isles Region, Headquarters, 769 Yardley Wood Road, Billesley, Birmingham B123 0PT; phone: (0121) 444 5243; fax: (0121) 444 5243; Web site: www.rlds.org. Founded 1863

Roman Catholic Bishops' Conference Secretariat 39 Eccleston Square, London SW1V 1BX; phone: (0171) 630 8220. (For details concerning the history and membership of the Roman Catholic Church see relevant tables in this section)

Russian Orthodox Diocese of Sourozh All Saints, Ennismore Gardens, London SW7 1NH; phone: (0171) 584 0096; fax: (0171) 584 9864; e-mail: crow@kbnet.co.uk (Diocesian Secretary). 27 parishes; 26 priests

The Salvation Army UK Territorial Headquarters, 101 Queen Victoria Street, London EC4P 4EP; phone: (0171) 236 5222; fax: (0171) 236 6272; Web site: www.salvationarmy.org.uk. Founded in 1865. 986 worship centres; 65,168 members; 1,732 active officers (figures for the UK and Ireland)

Scottish Congregational Church PO Box 189 Glasgow, G1 2BX; phone: (0141) 332 7667; fax: (0141) 332 8463; e-mail: 1005200.2150@compuserve.com. Founded 1994 (comprises the Congregational Union of Scotland, the Women's Union, and Scottish Congregational College)

Scottish Episcopal Church The Office of the General Synod, 21 Grosvenor Crescent, Edinburgh EH12 5EE; phone: (0131) 225 6357; fax: (0131) 346 7247; e-mail: scot_episc_church@ecunet.org

Serbian Orthodox Church Diocese of Great Britain and Scandinavia, 131 Cob Lane, Birmingham B30 1QE; phone: (0121) 458 5273; fax: (0121) 458 4986. Founded 1952. 33 parishes in the UK

Seventh-Day Adventist Church British Union Conference, Stanborough Park, Watford WD2 6JP; phone: (01923) 672251; fax: (01923) 893212; e-mail: buc@adventist.org.uk; Web site: www.adventist.org.uk. Founded 1878. 238 churches; 18,806 members; 145 ministers (figures for the UK and Ireland)

Union of Welsh Independents/Annibynwr (Welsh Congregational Union) Ty John Penry, 11 St Helen's Road, Swansea SA1 4AL; phone: (01792) 467040/652542; fax: (01792) 650647. Founded 1872. 555 churches; 42,450 members; 150 ministers

United Free Church of Scotland 11 Newton Place, Glasgow G3 7PR; phone: (0141) 332 3435. Founded 1900

United Pentecostal Church of Great Britain and Ireland 41 Bramley Hill, South Croydon CR2 6NW; phone: (0181) 688 5827; fax: (0181) 688 5827. Founded 1958

United Reformed Church in the United Kingdom 86 Tavistock Place, London WC1H 9RT; phone: (0171) 916 2020; fax: (0171) 916 2021; e-mail: agburnham@urc.compulink.co.uk; Web site: www.cix.co.uk/_urc. Founded 1972. 1,752 churches; 250,000 members; 1,100 ministers

Wesleyan Reform Union 123 Queen Street, Sheffield S1 2DU; phone: (0114) 272 1938; fax: (0114) 272 1965. Founded 1849. 115 churches; 2,401 members; 20 ministers; 137 lay preachers

The Worldwide Church of God (UK) Elstree House, Elstree Way, Borehamwood WD6 1LU; phone: (0181) 953 1633; fax: (0181) 207 1216; e-mail: wcgeurope@wcg.org; Web site: www.wcg.org.uk/index.html. Founded 1957

Councils of Churches

Afro-West Indian United Council of Churches The New Testament Church of God, Arcadian Gardens, High Road, London N22 5AA; phone: (0181) 888 9427. Founded 1979. 65 places of worship; 30,000 members; 135 ministers

British Evangelical Council Evershed House, Alma Road, St Albans AL1 3AR; phone: (01727) 855655; e-mail: becoffice@aol.com. Founded 1952

Churches Together in England Inter-Church House, 35 Lower Marsh, London SE1 7RL; phone: (0171) 620 4444; fax: (0171) 928 5771. Founded 1990

Council of African and Afro-Caribbean Churches UK 31 Norton House, Sidney Road, London SW9 0UJ; phone: (0171) 274 5589. Founded 1979. 75 congregations; 17,000 members; 250 ministers

Council of Churches for Britain and Ireland Inter-Church House, 35 Lower Marsh, London SE1 7RL; phone: (0171) 620 4444; fax: (0171) 928 0010. Founded 1990

ENFYS (Covenanted Churches in Wales) Church in Wales Centre, Woodland Place, Penarth CF6 2EX; phone: (01222)705278; fax: (01222) 712413; e-mail: 106074.133@compuserve.com. Founded 1975

Free Church Federal Council 27 Tavistock Square, London WC1H 9HH; phone: (0171) 387 8413; fax: (0171) 383 0150. Founded 1896

International Ministerial Council of Great Britain 55 Tudor Walk, Watford WD2 4NY; phone: (01923) 239266. Founded 1968

Irish Council of Churches Inter-Church Centre, 48 Elmwood Avenue, Belfast BT9 6AZ; phone: (01232) 663145; fax: (01232) 381737; e-mail: icpep@unite.co.uk; Web site: www.niweb.org/icpep. Founded 1922

Joint Council for Anglo-Caribbean Churches 141 Railton Road, London SE24 0LT; phone: (0171) 737 6542

Other Faiths Coalition Evangelical Alliance UK Whitefield House, 186 Kennington Park Road, London SE11 4BT; phone: (0171) 207 2100; fax: (0171) 582 6221; e-mail: members@eauk.org; Web site: www.eauk.org

Women's Inter-Church Consultative Committee The Network Office of the Methodist Church, 25 Marylebone Road, London NW1 5JR; phone: (0171) 486 5502

Buddhist Religious Organizations in the UK

The Buddhist Society 58 Eccleston Square, London SW1V 1PH; phone: (0171) 834 5858. 25,000 members; *c.* 20 temples. Founded 1924

Friends of the Western Buddhist Order (FWBO) 11 Park Road, Moseley, Birmingham B13 8AB. phone: (0121) 449 5279. Founded 1968

International Zen Association UK c/o Bristol Soto Zen Dojo, Gloucester Road, Bishopston, Bristol BS7 8AT; phone: (0117) 942 4347

New Kadampa Tradition Conishead Priory, Ulverston, Cumbria LA12 9QQ; phone: (01229) 584029; fax: (01229) 580080. Founded 1991

Sgi-UK (Soka Gakkai International) Taplow Court, Taplow, Nr Maidenhead, Berkshire SL6 0ER; phone: (01628) 773163; fax: (01628) 773055. Founded 1975

Hindu Religious Organizations in the UK

Arya Pratinidhi Sabha (UK) and Arya Samaj London 69a Argyle Road, London W13 0LY; phone: (0181) 991 1732

Bharatiya Vidya Bhavan Old Church Building, 4a Castletown Road, London W14 9HQ; phone: (0171) 381 3086

Hindu Centre 39 Grafton Terrace, London NW5 4JA; phone: (0171) 485 8200. Founded 1935

International Society for Krishna Consciousness Bhaktivedanta Manor, Hilfield Lane, Aldenham, Watford WD2 8EZ; phone: (01923) 857244; fax: (01923) 852896; e-mail: bhaktivedanta. manor@com.bbt.se. Founded 1969

National Council of Hindu Temples c/o Shree Sanatan Mandir, Weymouth Street, Leicester LE4 6FP; phone: (0116) 266 1402. 150 temples; 360,000 adherents

Swaminarayan Hindu Mission 105–119 Brentfield Road, London NW10 8JB; phone: (0181) 965 2651

Vishwa Hindu Parishad (UK) 48 Wharfedale Gardens, Thornton Heath, Surrey CR7 6LB; phone: (0181) 684 9716

Jewish Religious Organizations in the UK

Office of the Chief Rabbi S Weinberg, Executive Director; 735 High Road, London N12 0US; phone: (0181) 343 6301

Beth Din (Court of the Chief Rabbi) F B Gottlieb, Assistant Registrar; 735 High Road, London N12 0US; phone: (0181) 343 6270

Board of Deputies of British Jews E Tabachnik, President; Commonwealth House, 1–19 New Oxford Street, London WC1A 1NF; phone: (0171) 543 5400

Assembly of Masorti Synagogues H Freedman, Director; 197 Finchley Road, London NW11 0PU; phone: (0181) 201 8772

Federation of Synagogues G Kushner, Administrator; 65 Watford Way, London NW4 3AQ; phone: (0181) 349 4731

Reform Synagogues of Great Britain Rabbi T Bayfield, Chief Executive; The Sternberg Centre for Judaism, 80 East End Road, London N3 2SY; phone: (0181) 349 4731

Spanish and Portuguese Jews' Congregation H Miller, Chief Administrator and Secretary; 2 Ashworth Road, London W9 1JY; phone: (0171) 289 2573

Union of Liberal and Progressive Synagogues R Rosenberg, Director; The Montagu Centre, 21 Maple Street, London W1P 6DS; phone: (0171) 580 1663

Union of Orthodox Hebrew Congregations Rabbi A Klein, Executive Director; 140 Stamford Hill, London N16 6QT; phone: (0181) 802 6226

United Synagogue Head Office J M Lew, Chief Executive; 753 High Road, London N12 0US; phone: (0181) 343 8989

The Chief Rabbinate of Britain

The Chief Rabbinate of Britain has developed from the position of the Rabbi of the Great Synagogue, London. From the early years of the 18th century until recently, he was acknowledged as the spiritual leader of the London Ashkenazi Community and this recognition was also accepted in the provinces and overseas. To conform with constitutional practice, the official designation (1845–1953) was 'Chief Rabbi of the United Hebrew Congregations of the British Commonwealth of Nations' and subsequently 'Chief Rabbi of the United Hebrew Congregations of the Commonwealth'.

Dates of appointment	Name of Chief Rabbi
1709–56	Aaron Hart
1756–64	Hart Lyon
1765–92	David Tevele Schiff
1802–42	Solomon Herschell
1845–90	Nathan Marcus Adler
1891–1911	Hermann Adler
1913–46	Joseph Herman Hertz
1948–65	Israel Brodie
1967–91	Immanuel Jakobovits
1991–	Jonathan Sacks

Muslim Religious Organizations in the UK

Imams and Mosques Council 20–22 Creffield Road, London W5 3RP; phone: (0181) 992 6636. 900 mosques; over 1,000,000 adherents

Islamic Cultural Centre and London Central Mosque 146 Park Road, London NW8 7RG; phone: (0171) 724 3363; fax: (0171) 724 0493. Founded 1944

Islamic Foundation Markfield Conference Centre, Ralby Lane, Markfield, Leicester LE67 9RN; phone: (01530) 244944; fax: (01530) 244946; e-mail: islamicf@islam. demon.co.uk; Web site: www.islamf. demon.co.uk. Founded 1973

The Muslim Educational Trust 130 Stroud Green Road, London N4 3RZ; phone: (0171) 272 8502; fax: (0171) 281 3457. Founded 1966

Muslim World League 46 Goodge Street, London W1P 1FJ; phone: (0171) 636 7568

Union of Muslim Organizations in the UK and Eire 109 Campden Hill Road, London W8 7TL; phone: (0171) 229 0538

Sikh Religious Organizations in the UK

Sikh Missionary Society UK 10 Featherstone Road, Southall UB2 5AA; phone: (0181) 574 1902. 250 gurdwaras; 400,000 adherents

The World Sikh Foundation (Sikh Cultural Society of Great Britain) 33 Wargrave Road, South Harrow HA2 8LL; phone: (0181) 864 9228. Founded 1960

Other Religious Groups in the UK

3HO (Healthy, Happy, Holy) The Lotus Healing Centre, 7 New Court Street, St John's Wood, London NW8 7AA; phone: (0171) 722 5797; fax: (0171) 722 5751. Founded 1975

The Aetherius Society 757 Fulham Road, London SW6 5UU; phone: (0171) 736 4187/731 1094; fax: (0171) 731 1067. Founded 1955

Brahma Kumaris Global Co-operation House, 65 Pound Lane, London NW10 2HH; phone: (0181) 459 1400; fax: (0181) 451 6480. Founded 1937

Church of Scientology Office of Special Affairs, Saint Hill Manor, East Grinstead RH19 4JY; phone: (01342) 318229; fax: (01342) 325474; Web site: www.scientology.org. Founded 1952

Federation of Jain Organizations in the UK 11 Lindsay Drive, Harrow HA3 0TA; phone: (0181) 204 2871

Mahikari Sukio Mahikari, Suffolk Road, South Norwood, London SE25 6ES; phone: (0181) 771 7417; fax: (0181) 771 9441. Founded 1983

National Spiritual Assembly of the Bahá'is of the United Kingdom 27 Rutland Gate, London SW7 1PD; phone: (0171) 584 2566; fax: (0171) 584 9402

The Pagan Federation BM Box 7097, London WC1N 3XX; phone: (01787) 238257; fax: (01787) 238257; e-mail: secretary@paganfed.demon.co.uk; Web site: www.paganfed.demon.co.uk. Founded 1971

The Raelian Movement BCM Minstrel, London WC1N 3XX; phone: (0171) 923 7447. Founded 1975

Sahaja Yoga Life Eternal Trust, 44 Chelsham Road, Clapham, London SW4 6NP. Founded 1972

Solara, Star-Borne Unlimited Holistic Centre, Unit N&M, Royal Albert Walk, Albert Road, Southsea PO4 0JT; phone: (01705) 293668. Founded 1986

The Spiritualist Association of Great Britain 33 Belgrave Square, London SW1X 8QB; phone: (0171) 235 3351; fax: (0171) 245 9706. Founded 1872

The Theosophical Society in England 50 Gloucester Place, London W1H 4EA; phone: (0171) 935 9261; fax: (0171) 935 9543. Founded 1888

United Lodge of Theosophists 62 Queen's Gardens, London W2 3AL; phone: (0171) 723 0688/262 8639. Founded 1925

World Zoroastrian Organization 135 Tennyson Road, South Norwood, London SE25 5NF

Web Sites

About Islam and Muslims

http://www.unn.ac.uk/societies/islamic/

Extensive information about the Islamic faith and culture, including facts about the Koran, and links to newspapers and university sites.

Atheist Express

http://www.hti.net/www/atheism

Site dedicated to atheism, free thought, humanism, ethics, religious criticism, and state–church separation.

Baha'i Faith Page

http://www.bcca.org/~glittle/

Introduction to this religion founded in the 19th century. There is an overview explaining the faith, and a collection of religious writings.

Bhagvat-Gita

http://www.iconsoftec.com/gita/

Fully downloadable text of the most sacred work in the Hindu religion.

Bible Gateway

http://www.gospelcom.net/bible

Full text of six versions of the Bible, including the New International Version, the Revised Standard Version, and the King James Version.

Book of Mormon

http://www.athenet.net/~jlindsay/BOMIntro.shtml

Produced by a self-professed Mormon, this introduction to the Book of Mormon has a link to the complete text, as well as attempts to answer some of the most frequently asked questions about the holy book of The Church of Jesus Christ of Latter-Day Saints.

Brief Introduction to Taoism

http://www.geocities.com/HotSprings/2426/Ttaointro.html

The site includes summaries of the various types of Taoism including philosophical, devotional, magical, and alchemical.

British Humanist Association

http://www.humanism.org.uk/

Explaining and promoting the principles of Humanism, with sections on 'Ceremonies', 'Education', and 'Local Groups'.

Celtic Myth And Lore

http://www.witchhaven.com/shadowdrake/lore.html

Within these pages there is information about the herbology, astronomy, law, stories, and folk practices of the Celtic people.

Chinese Religion

http://birmingham.gov.uk/html/helpline/community/chinese/nereli1.html

All-text site from Birmingham University containing a lot of information about the three main strands of religion in China – Buddhism, Taoism, and Confucianism.

Church of Christ, Scientist (Christian Science)

http://www.religioustolerance.org/cr_sci.htm

Description of the history, beliefs, and attitudes towards healing of the Church of Christ, Scientist.

Church of England

http://www.church-of-england.org/

There is information on the structure of the church, the meaning of being an Anglican, and a guide to prayer. There are links to those dioceses that have web pages of their own and a comprehensive listing of web pages of non-English churches within the Anglican communion.

Classical Mythology Home Page

http://www.princeton.edu/~rhwebb/myth.html

Course materials from the mythology unit of Princeton University's Classics Department.

Confucius

http://sac.uky.edu/~mdtuck0/Resources/Confucius.html

Background information on Confucius and Confucianism as well as images and versions of most of his famous texts on morality.

Development of the Papacy

http://history.idbsu.edu/westciv/papacy/

Part of a larger site on the history of Western civilization maintained by Boise State University, this page provides an introduction to the conflict that existed in the Middle Ages between the church and state.

Fundamentals of Jainism

http://www.angelfire.com/co/jainism/

Comphrehensive introduction to the monastic and ascetic religion of Jainism. Sections include 'Lord Mahavir and Jain religion', 'Path of liberation', 'Jain Gods', and an 'Index of human virtues'.

Gnosticism

http://www.knight.org/advent/cathen/06592a.htm

Extended source of information on the doctrine of salvation by knowledge. The contents include the etymology of the term, gnosticism's extensive pre-Christian roots in a variety of cultural and historical contexts, and its influence on the development of Christianity.

Hinduism Today

http://www.HinduismToday.kauai.hi.us/ashram/

Online magazine produced by Sanatana Dharma's Electronic Ashram. It explores India's ancient spiritual path by providing nine informative sections related to Hinduism.

His Holiness the Dalai Lama

http://www.nalejandria.com/utopia/english/DalaiLama-eng.htm

Profile of Tenzin Gyatso, the 14th incarnation of the Dalai Lama. It traces his childhood, escape from Tibet, and efforts to preserve Tibetan culture in exile.

Holy See (Vatican City)

http://www.vatican.va/

Multilingual, searchable page, with recent news reports and press releases from the Vatican Information Service. It also includes

information about the Vatican museums and their plans for celebrating the year 2000.

Islam at a Glance

http://www.iad.org/books/WAMY1.html

Clear and concise introduction to the key beliefs of Islam. It covers Muhammad, the Koran, prayer, Islam in the modern world, and the Five Pillars of Islam.

Jewish Culture and History

http://www.igc.apc.org/ddickerson/judaica.html

Wide-ranging collection of information on Judaism. The site includes an image gallery of Polish synagogues, links to online Hebrew texts, and an introduction to Judaism.

Koran

http://etext.virginia.edu/koran.html

Full text of the Koran in searchable SGML form, offered by the Electronic Centre at the University of Virginia, USA.

List of Norse Beings

http://www.ugcs.caltech.edu/~cherryne/list.html

Alphabetical listing of all the main Norse Gods and other beings found in Scandinavian mythology.

Manichaeism

http://www.knight.org/advent/cathen/09591a.htm

Extensive discussion of the range of beliefs associated with the Iranian prophet Mani. There is a biography of the founder and the formative influences on his childhood. The syncretic mix of the faith he proclaimed, combining elements of Babylonian folklore, Zoroastrian dualism, Buddhist ethics, and Christianity, is described in detail.

Multifaithnet

http://www.multifaith.org/

Run by the University of Derby, this site gives in-depth descriptions of all the main world religions.

Mysticism in World Religions

http://www.digiserve.com/mystic/

Explores mystical experience in six world religions, by comparing and contrasting quotations from their respective sacred literatures.

Religious Atheism

http://www.hypertext.com/atheisms/

Compilation of non-traditional sources on atheism, including views of the subject according to Christianity, classical atheism, and liberation theology.

Religious Society of Friends

http://www.quaker.org/

Quaker beliefs and ethics are set out here. There is also a detailed history of the faith, and information on Quaker societies throughout the world and their commercial activities.

Salvation Army

http://www.salvationarmy.org/aboutus.htm

International headquarters of the evangelical mission. There is a history of the Salvation Army, an outline of its structure, and details of the various charitable activities it undertakes in more than 100 countries.

Scientology

http://www.religioustolerance.org/scientol.htm

Lengthy and non-partisan explanation of scientology beliefs and practices. There is a biography of L Ron Hubbard, a description of the 'Eight Dynamics', a list of publications, and guide to Internet resources.

Shinto – The Way of the Gods

http://www.trincoll.edu/~tj/tj4.4.96/articles/cover.html

Well arranged guide to Shinto beliefs and practices. The link between Shintoism and Japanese mythology is explained prior to a guide to the main Shinto shrines.

Sikhism Home Page

http://www.sikhs.org/

Brief overview of the main principles of Sikhism. It also follows the development of the religion, explores the philosophy and scriptures connected with Sikhism, and describes the main religious problems, role models, ceremonies, and religious dates in the life of a Sikh.

Sumerian Mythology FAQ

http://pubpages.unh.edu/~cbsiren/sumer-faq.html

Large Web site describing the religious beliefs and mythology of the Sumerian civilization. The site also deals with Sumerian cosmology and the parallels between Sumerian beliefs and the old testament.

Vedas and Upanishads

http://www.san.beck.org/EC7-Vedas.html

Thorough source of information on the Hindu mystical texts. Central Hindu precepts and rituals are explained in the course of summarizing, and providing extracts from, the major Upanishad texts.

Voodoo Information Pages

http://www.arcana.com/shannon/voodoo/

General information on the religion of vodoun, more commonly known as voodoo.

What is Theravada Buddhism?

http://world.std.com/~metta/theravada.html

Full introduction to the school of Buddhism drawing its inspiration from the record of Buddha's teachings known as the Pali Canon. There is a guide for those wishing to learn Pali to deepen understanding of the texts.

'What Sufism Is'

http://www.sufism.org/books/livinex.html

Essay by Kabir Edmund Helminski which describes the nature of the mystical religion of Sufism.

World Council of Churches

http://www.wcc-coe.org/

Large site of the organization bringing together over 300 Christian churches in 120 countries. It contains comprehensive information on the ecumenical movement, evangelism, and the role of Christian churches in development.

World of Hare Krishna

http://pub.intnet.mu/harrish/text/krsna.htm

Guide to the philosophy and religious rituals of Hare Krishna from the International Society for Krishna Consciousness.

World Scripture

http://unification.net/ws/

A good source of scriptural and religious material for scholars and people of all faiths, this site has a comparative anthology of sacred texts containing over 4,000 scriptural passages from 268 sacred texts and 55 oral traditions, organized under 164 different themes.

Worldwide Study Bible

http://ccel.wheaton.edu/wwsb/index.html

Exhaustive guide to the Bible. The full text of all the books of the Old and New Testaments, synopses of important sections, explanations of the significance of many of the most important aspects, and a biblical dictionary are all provided.

Zen Buddhism

http://www.iijnet.or.jp/iriz/irizhtml/irizhome.htm

Largest collection of Buddhist primary text materials on the Internet, together with many examples of Zen art, and information on Zen centres and masters.

Zoroastrianism

http://www.religioustolerance.org/zoroastr.htm

Objective account of the beliefs, history, and practices of the ancient monotheistic faith.

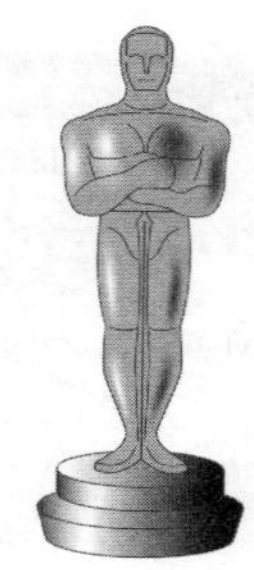

Awards and Prizes

Nobel Prizes

Nobel Prize: Introduction

The Nobel Prizes were first awarded in 1901 under the will of Alfred B Nobel (1833–96), a Swedish chemist, who invented dynamite. The interest on the Nobel endowment fund is divided annually among the persons who have made the greatest contributions in the fields of physics, chemistry, medicine, literature, and world peace. The first four are awarded by academic committees based in Sweden, while the peace prize is awarded by a committee of the Norwegian parliament. A sixth prize, for economics, financed by the Swedish National Bank, was first awarded in 1969. The prizes have a large cash award and are given to organizations – such as the United Nations peacekeeping forces, which received the Nobel Peace Prize in 1988 – as well as to individuals at an awards ceremony held on 10 December each year, the anniversary of Nobel's death.

Nobel Prize for Chemistry

Year	Winner(s)[1]	Awarded for
1989	Sidney Altman (USA) and Thomas Cech (USA)	discovery of catalytic function of RNA
1990	Elias James Corey (USA)	new methods of synthesizing chemical compounds
1991	Richard Ernst (Switzerland)	improvements in the technology of nuclear magnetic resonance (NMR) imaging
1992	Rudolph Marcus (USA)	theoretical discoveries relating to reduction and oxidation reactions
1993	Kary Mullis (USA) Michael Smith (Canada)	invention of the polymerase chain reaction technique for amplifying DNA invention of techniques for splicing foreign genetic segments into an organism's DNA in order to modify the proteins produced
1994	George Olah (USA)	development of technique for examining hydrocarbon molecules
1995	F Sherwood Rowland (USA), Mario Molina (USA), and Paul Crutzen (Netherlands)	explaining the chemical process of the ozone layer

(continued)

Nobel Prize for Chemistry (*continued*)

Year	Winner(s)[1]	Awarded for
1996	Robert Curl Jr (USA), Harold Kroto (UK), and Richard Smalley (USA)	discovery of fullerenes
1997	John Walker (UK), Paul Boyer (USA), and Jens Skou (Denmark)	study of the enzymes involved in the production of adenosine triphospate (ATP), which acts as a store of energy in bodies called mitochondria inside cells
1998	Walter Kohn (USA), John Pople (USA)	research into quantum chemistry

[1] Nationality given is the citizenship of recipient at the time award was made.

Nobel Prize for Economics

Year	Winner(s)[1]	Awarded for
1989	Trygve Haavelmo (Norway)	testing fundamental econometric theories
1990	Harry Markowitz (USA), Merton Miller (USA), and William Sharpe (USA)	pioneering theories on managing investment portfolios and corporate finances
1991	Ronald Coase (USA)	work on value and social problems of companies
1992	Gary Becker (USA)	work linking economic theory to aspects of human behaviour, drawing on other social sciences
1993	Robert Fogel (USA) and Douglass North (USA)	creating a new method of studying economic history (cliometrics)
1994	John Nash (USA), John Harsanyi (USA), and Reinhard Selten (Germany)	work on 'game theory', which investigates decision-making in a competitive environment
1995	Robert Lucas (USA)	developing the 'rational expectations' school, which questions a government's ability to steer the economy
1996	James Mirrlees (UK) and William Vickrey (USA)	fundamental contributions to the economic theory of incentives under assymmetric information
1997	Robert Merton (USA) and Myron Scholes (USA)	pioneering contribution to economic sciences by developing a new method of determining the value of derivatives
1998	Amartya Sen (India)	research into the social and economic causes of famines

[1] Nationality given is the citizenship of recipient at the time award was made.

Nobel Prize for Literature

Year	Winner(s)[1]
1989	Camilo José Cela (Spain)
1990	Octavio Paz (Mexico)
1991	Nadine Gordimer (South Africa)
1992	Derek Walcott (Santa Lucia)
1993	Toni Morrison (USA)
1994	Kenzaburo Oe (Japan)
1995	Seamus Heaney (Ireland)
1996	Wisława Szymborska (Poland)
1997	Dario Fo (Italy)
1998	José Saramago (Portugal)

[1] Nationality given is the citizenship of recipient at the time award was made.

Nobel Prize for Peace

Year	Winner(s)[1]	Awarded for
1989	Dalai Lama (Tibet)	spiritual and exiled temporal leader of Tibet
1990	Mikhail Gorbachev (USSR)	promoting greater openness in the USSR and helping to end the Cold War
1991	Aung San Suu Kyi (Myanmar)	nonviolent campaign for democracy
1992	Rigoberta Menchú (Guatemala)	campaign for indigenous people

(*continued*)

Nobel Prize for Peace (*continued*)

Year	Winner(s)[1]	Awarded for
1993	Nelson Mandela (South Africa) and Frederik Willem de Klerk (South Africa)	work towards dismantling apartheid and negotiating transition to nonracial democracy
1994	Yassir Arafat (Palestine), Yitzhak Rabin (Israel), and Shimon Perez (Israel)	agreement of an accord on Palestinian self-rule
1995	Joseph Rotblat (UK) and the Pugwash Conferences on Science and World Affairs	campaign against nuclear weapons
1996	Carlos Filipe Ximenes Belo (Timorese) and José Ramos-Horta (Timorese)	work towards a just and peaceful solution to the conflict in East Timor
1997	Jody Williams (USA) and the International Campaign to Ban Landmines (ICBL)	campaign for global ban of anti-personnel mines
1998	John Hume (UK) and David Trimble (UK)	efforts to find a peaceful solution to the conflict in Northern Ireland

[1] Nationality given is the citizenship of recipient at the time award was made.

Nobel Prize for Physics

Year	Winner(s)[1]	Awarded for
1989	Norman Ramsey (USA) Hans Dehmelt (USA) and Wolfgang Paul (Germany)	measurement techniques leading to discovery of caesium atomic clock ion-trap method for isolating single atoms
1990	Jerome Friedman (USA), Henry Kendall (USA), and Richard Taylor (Canada)	experiments demonstrating that protons and neutrons are made up of quarks
1991	Pierre-Gilles de Gennes (France)	work on disordered systems including polymers and liquid crystals; development of mathematical methods for studying the behaviour of molecules in a liquid on the verge of solidifying
1992	Georges Charpak (France)	invention and development of detectors used in high-energy physics
1993	Joseph Taylor (USA) and Russell Hulse (USA)	discovery of first binary pulsar (confirming the existence of gravitational waves)
1994	Clifford Shull (USA) and Bertram Brockhouse (Canada)	development of technique known as 'neutron scattering' which led to advances in semiconductor technology
1995	Frederick Reines (USA) Martin Perl (USA)	discovery of the neutrino discovery of the tau lepton
1996	David Lee (USA), Douglas Osheroff (USA), and Robert Richardson (USA)	discovery of superfluidity in helium-3
1997	Claude Cohen-Tannoudji (France), William Phillips (USA), and Steven Chu (USA)	discovery of a way to slow down individual atoms using lasers for study in a near-vacuum
1998	Robert B Laughlin (USA), Horst L Störmer (USA), and Daniel C Tsui (USA)	discovery of a new form of quantum fluid with fractionally charged excitations

[1] Nationality given is the citizenship of recipient at the time award was made.

Nobel Prize for Physiology or Medicine

Year	Winner(s)[1]	Awarded for
1989	Michael Bishop (USA) and Harold Varmus (USA)	discovery of oncogenes, genes carried by viruses that can trigger cancerous growth in normal cells
1990	Joseph Murray (USA) and Donnall Thomas (USA)	pioneering work in organ and cell transplants
1991	Erwin Neher (Germany) and Bert Sakmann (Germany)	discovery of how gatelike structures (ion channels) regulate the flow of ions into and out of cells
1992	Edmond Fisher (USA) and Edwin Krebs (USA)	isolating and describing the action of the enzyme responsible for reversible protein phosphorylation, a major biological control mechanism

(*continued*)

Nobel Prize for Physiology or Medicine (*continued*)

Year	Winner(s)[1]	Awarded for
1993	Phillip Sharp (USA) and Richard Roberts (UK)	discovery of split genes (genes interrupted by nonsense segments of DNA)
1994	Alfred Gilman (USA) and Martin Rodbell (USA)	discovery of a family of proteins (G-proteins) that translate messages – in the form of hormones or other chemical signals – into action inside cells
1995	Edward Lewis (USA), Eric Wieschaus (USA), and Christiane Nüsslein-Volhard (Germany)	discovery of genes which control the early stages of the body's development
1996	Peter Doherty (Australia) and Rolf Zinkernagel (Switzerland)	discovery of how the immune system recognizes virus-infected cells
1997	Stanley Prusiner (USA)	discoveries, including the 'prion' theory, that could lead to new treatments of dementia-related diseases, including Alzheimer's and Parkinson's diseases
1998	Robert Furchgott (USA), Ferid Murad (USA), and Louis Ignarro (USA)	discovery that nitric oxide (NO) acts as a key chemical messenger between cells

[1] Nationality given is the citizenship of recipient at the time award was made.

Film

Academy Awards

The Academy Awards (or 'Oscars') are presented each March for films of the previous year. The awards ceremony is one of the film world's most famous and prestigious.

Year	Best Picture	Best Director	Best Actor	Best Actress	Best Supporting Actor	Best Supporting Actress
1928	*Wings*	Frank Borzage *Seventh Heaven*	Emil Jannings *The Way of All Flesh, The Last Command*	Janet Gaynor *Seventh Heaven, Street Angel, Sunrise*	no award	no award
1929	*The Broadway Melody*	Frank Lloyd *The Divine Lady*	Warner Baxter *In Old Arizona*	Mary Pickford *Coquette*	no award	no award
1930	*All Quiet on the Western Front*	Lewis Milestone *All Quiet on the Western Front*	George Arliss *Disraeli*	Norma Shearer *The Divorcee*	no award	no award
1931	*Cimarron*	Norman Taurog *Skippy*	Lionel Barrymore *A Free Soul*	Marie Dressler *Min and Bill*	no award	no award
1932	*Grand Hotel*	Frank Borzage *Bad Girl*	Fredric March *Dr Jekyll and Mr Hyde* Wallace Beery *The Champ*	Helen Hayes *The Sin of Madelon Claudet*	no award	no award
1933	*Cavalcade*	Frank Lloyd *Cavalcade*	Charles Laughton *The Private Life of Henry VIII*	Katharine Hepburn *Morning Glory*	no award	no award
1934	*It Happened One Night*	Frank Capra *It Happened One Night*	Clark Gable *It Happened One Night*	Claudette Colbert *It Happened One Night*	no award	no award
1935	*Mutiny on the Bounty*	John Ford *The Informer*	Victor McLaglen *The Informer*	Bette Davis *Dangerous*	no award	no award
1936	*The Great Ziegfeld*	Frank Capra *Mr Deeds Goes to Town*	Paul Muni *The Story of Louis Pasteur*	Luise Rainer *The Great Ziegfeld*	Walter Brennan *Come and Get It*	Gale Sondergaard *Anthony Adverse*
1937	*The Life of Emile Zola*	Leo McCarey *The Awful Truth*	Spencer Tracy *Captains Courageous*	Luise Rainer *The Good Earth*	Joseph Schildkraut *The Life of Emile Zola*	Alice Brady *In Old Chicago*
1938	*You Can't Take It With You*	Frank Capra *You Can't Take It With You*	Spencer Tracy *Boys' Town*	Bette Davis *Jezebel*	Walter Brennan *Kentucky*	Fay Bainter *Jezebel*
1939	*Gone With the Wind*	Victor Fleming *Gone With the Wind*	Robert Donat *Goodbye, Mr Chips*	Vivien Leigh *Gone With the Wind*	Thomas Mitchell *Stagecoach*	Hattie McDaniel *Gone With the Wind*
1940	*Rebecca*	John Ford *The Grapes of Wrath*	James Stewart *The Philadelphia Story*	Ginger Rogers *Kitty Foyle*	Walter Brennan *The Westerner*	Jane Darwell *The Grapes of Wrath*
1941	*How Green Was My Valley*	John Ford *How Green Was My Valley*	Gary Cooper *Sergeant York*	Joan Fontaine *Suspicion*	Donald Crisp *How Green Was My Valley*	Mary Astor *The Great Lie*

(continued)

Academy Awards (*continued*)

Year	Best Picture	Best Director	Best Actor	Best Actress	Best Supporting Actor	Best Supporting Actress
1942	*Mrs Miniver*	William Wyler *Mrs Miniver*	James Cagney *Yankee Doodle Dandy*	Greer Garson *Mrs Miniver*	Van Heflin *Johnny Eager*	Teresa Wright *Mrs Miniver*
1943	*Casablanca*	Michael Curtiz *Casablanca*	Paul Lukas *Watch on the Rhine*	Jennifer Jones *The Song of Bernadette*	Charles Coburn *The More the Merrier*	Katina Paxinou *For Whom the Bell Tolls*
1944	*Going My Way*	Leo McCarey *Going My Way*	Bing Crosby *Going My Way*	Ingrid Bergman *Gaslight*	Barry Fitzgerald *Going My Way*	Ethel Barrymore *None But the Lonely Heart*
1945	*The Lost Weekend*	Billy Wilder *The Lost Weekend*	Ray Milland *The Lost Weekend*	Joan Crawford *Mildred Pierce*	James Dunn *A Tree Grows in Brooklyn*	Anne Revere *National Velvet*
1946	*The Best Years of Our Lives*	William Wyler *The Best Years of Our Lives*	Fredric March *The Best Years of Our Lives*	Olivia de Havilland *To Each His Own*	Harold Russell *The Best Years of Our Lives*	Anne Baxter *The Razor's Edge*
1947	*Gentleman's Agreement*	Elia Kazan *Gentleman's Agreement*	Ronald Coleman *A Double Life*	Loretta Young *The Farmer's Daughter*	Edmund Gwenn *Miracle on 34th Street*	Celeste Holm *Gentleman's Agreement*
1948	*Hamlet*	John Huston *Treasure of Sierra Madre*	Laurence Olivier *Hamlet*	Jane Wyman *Johnny Belinda*	Walter Houston *Treasure of Sierra Madre*	Claire Trevor *Key Largo*
1949	*All the King's Men*	Joseph L Mankiewicz *A Letter to Three Wives*	Broderick Crawford *All the King's Men*	Olivia de Havilland *The Heiress*	Dean Jagger *Twelve O'Clock High*	Mercedes McCambridge *All the King's Men*
1950	*All About Eve*	Joseph L Mankiewicz *All About Eve*	José Ferrer *Cyrano de Bergerac*	Judy Holliday *Born Yesterday*	George Sanders *All About Eve*	Josephine Hull *Harvey*
1951	*An American in Paris*	George Stevens *A Place in the Sun*	Humphrey Bogart *The African Queen*	Vivien Leigh *A Streetcar Named Desire*	Karl Malden *A Streetcar Named Desire*	Kim Hunter *A Streetcar Named Desire*
1952	*The Greatest Show on Earth*	John Ford *The Quiet Man*	Gary Cooper *High Noon*	Shirley Booth *Come Back Little Sheba*	Anthony Quinn *Viva Zapata!*	Gloria Grahame *The Bad and the Beautiful*
1953	*From Here to Eternity*	Fred Zinnemann *From Here to Eternity*	William Holden *Stalag 17*	Audrey Hepburn *Roman Holiday*	Frank Sinatra *From Here to Eternity*	Donna Reed *From Here to Eternity*
1954	*On the Waterfront*	Elia Kazan *On the Waterfront*	Marlon Brando *On the Waterfront*	Grace Kelly *The Country Girl*	Edmond O'Brien *The Barefoot Contessa*	Eva Marie Saint *On the Waterfront*
1955	*Marty*	Delbert Mann *Marty*	Ernest Borgnine *Marty*	Anna Magnani *The Rose Tattoo*	Jack Lemmon *Mister Roberts*	Jo Van Fleet *East of Eden*
1956	*Around the World in 80 Days*	George Stevens *Giant*	Yul Brynner *The King and I*	Ingrid Bergman *Anastasia*	Anthony Quinn *Lust for Life*	Dorothy Malone *Written on the Wind*
1957	*The Bridge on the River Kwai*	David Lean *The Bridge on the River Kwai*	Alec Guinness *The Bridge on the River Kwai*	Joanne Woodward *The Three Faces of Eve*	Red Buttons *Sayonara*	Miyoshi Umeki *Sayonara*
1958	*Gigi*	Vincente Minnelli *Gigi*	David Niven *Separate Tables*	Susan Hayward *I Want to Live!*	Burl Ives *The Big Country*	Wendy Hiller *Separate Tables*
1959	*Ben Hur*	William Wyler *Ben Hur*	Charlton Heston *Ben Hur*	Simone Signoret *Room at the Top*	Hugh Griffith *Ben Hur*	Shelley Winters *The Diary of Anne Frank*
1960	*The Apartment*	Billy Wilder *The Apartment*	Burt Lancaster *Elmer Gantry*	Elizabeth Taylor *Butterfield 8*	Peter Ustinov *Spartacus*	Shirley Jones *Elmer Gantry*
1961	*West Side Story*	Robert Wise and Jerome Robbins *West Side Story*	Maximillian Schell *Judgment at Nuremberg*	Sophia Loren *Two Women*	George Chakiris *West Side Story*	Rita Moreno *West Side Story*
1962	*Lawrence of Arabia*	David Lean *Lawrence of Arabia*	Gregory Peck *To Kill a Mockingbird*	Anne Bancroft *The Miracle Worker*	Ed Begley *Sweet Bird of Youth*	Patty Duke *The Miracle Worker*
1963	*Tom Jones*	Tony Richardson *Tom Jones*	Sidney Poitier *Lilies of the Field*	Patricia Neal *Hud*	Melvyn Douglas *Hud*	Margaret Rutherford *The V.I.P.s*
1964	*My Fair Lady*	George Cukor *My Fair Lady*	Rex Harrison *My Fair Lady*	Julie Andrews *Mary Poppins*	Peter Ustinov *Topkapi*	Lila Kedrova *Zorba the Greek*

(*continued*)

Academy Awards (*continued*)

Year	Best Picture	Best Director	Best Actor	Best Actress	Best Supporting Actor	Best Supporting Actress
1965	*The Sound of Music*	Robert Wise *The Sound of Music*	Lee Marvin *Cat Ballou*	Julie Christie *Darling*	Martin Balsam *A Thousand Clowns*	Shelley Winters *A Patch of Blue*
1966	*A Man for All Seasons*	Fred Zinnemann *A Man for All Seasons*	Paul Scofield *A Man for All Seasons*	Elizabeth Taylor *Who's Afraid of Virginia Woolf?*	Walter Matthau *The Fortune Cookie*	Sandy Dennis *Who's Afraid of Virginia Woolf?*
1967	*In the Heat of the Night*	Mike Nichols *The Graduate*	Rod Steiger *In the Heat of the Night*	Katharine Hepburn *Guess Who's Coming to Dinner*	George Kennedy *Cool Hand Luke*	Estelle Parsons *Bonnie and Clyde*
1968	*Oliver!*	Sir Carol Reed *Oliver!*	Cliff Robertson *Charly*	Katharine Hepburn *The Lion in Winter* Barbra Streisand *Funny Girl*	Jack Albertson *The Subject Was Roses*	Ruth Gordon *Rosemary's Baby*
1969	*Midnight Cowboy*	John Schlesinger *Midnight Cowboy*	John Wayne *True Grit*	Maggie Smith *The Prime of Miss Jean Brodie*	Gig Young *They Shoot Horses, Don't They?*	Goldie Hawn *Cactus Flower*
1970	*Patton*	Franklin J Schaffner *Patton*	George C Scott *Patton*	Glenda Jackson *Women in Love*	John Mills *Ryan's Daughter*	Helen Hayes *Airport*
1971	*The French Connection*	William Friedkin *The French Connection*	Gene Hackman *The French Connection*	Jane Fonda *Klute*	Ben Johnson *The Last Picture Show*	Cloris Leachman *The Last Picture Show*
1972	*The Godfather*	Bob Fosse *Cabaret*	Marlon Brando *The Godfather*	Liza Minnelli *Cabaret*	Joel Grey *Cabaret*	Eileen Heckart *Butterflies Are Free*
1973	*The Sting*	George Roy Hill *The Sting*	Jack Lemmon *Save the Tiger*	Glenda Jackson *A Touch of Class*	John Houseman *The Paper Chase*	Tatum O'Neal *Paper Moon*
1974	*The Godfather Part II*	Francis Ford Coppola *The Godfather Part II*	Art Carney *Harry and Tonto*	Ellen Burstyn *Alice Doesn't Live Here Anymore*	Robert De Niro *The Godfather Part II*	Ingrid Bergman *Murder on the Orient Express*
1975	*One Flew Over the Cuckoo's Nest*	Milos Forman *One Flew Over the Cuckoo's Nest*	Jack Nicholson *One Flew Over the Cuckoo's Nest*	Louise Fletcher *One Flew Over the Cuckoo's Nest*	George Burns *The Sunshine Boys*	Lee Grant *Shampoo*
1976	*Rocky*	John G Avildsen *Rocky*	Peter Finch *Network*	Faye Dunaway *Network*	Jason Robards *All the President's Men*	Beatrice Straight *Network*
1977	*Annie Hall*	Woody Allen *Annie Hall*	Richard Dreyfuss *The Goodbye Girl*	Diane Keaton *Annie Hall*	Jason Robards *Julia*	Vanessa Redgrave *Julia*
1978	*The Deer Hunter*	Michael Cimino *The Deer Hunter*	Jon Voight *Coming Home*	Jane Fonda *Coming Home*	Christopher Walken *The Deer Hunter*	Maggie Smith *California Suite*
1979	*Kramer vs Kramer*	Robert Benton *Kramer vs Kramer*	Dustin Hoffman *Kramer vs Kramer*	Sally Field *Norma Rae*	Melvyn Douglas *Being There*	Meryl Streep *Kramer vs Kramer*
1980	*Ordinary People*	Robert Redford *Ordinary People*	Robert De Niro *Raging Bull*	Sissy Spacek *Coal Miner's Daughter*	Timothy Hutton *Ordinary People*	Mary Steenburgen *Melvin and Howard*
1981	*Chariots of Fire*	Warren Beatty *Reds*	Henry Fonda *On Golden Pond*	Katharine Hepburn *On Golden Pond*	John Gielgud *Arthur*	Maureen Stapleton *Reds*
1982	*Gandhi*	Richard Attenborough *Gandhi*	Ben Kingsley *Gandhi*	Meryl Streep *Sophie's Choice*	Louis Gossett Jr *An Officer and a Gentleman*	Jessica Lange *Tootsie*
1983	*Terms of Endearment*	James L Brooks *Terms of Endearment*	Robert Duvall *Tender Mercies*	Shirley Maclaine *Terms of Endearment*	Jack Nicholson *Terms of Endearment*	Linda Hunt *The Year of Living Dangerously*
1984	*Amadeus*	Milos Forman *Amadeus*	F Murray Abraham *Amadeus*	Sally Field *Places in the Heart*	Haing S Ngor *The Killing Fields*	Dame Peggy Ashcroft *A Passage to India*
1985	*Out of Africa*	Sydney Pollack *Out of Africa*	William Hurt *Kiss of the Spider Woman*	Geraldine Page *The Trip to Bountiful*	Don Ameche *Cocoon*	Anjelica Huston *Prizzi's Honor*
1986	*Platoon*	Oliver Stone *Platoon*	Paul Newman *The Color of Money*	Marlee Matlin *Children of a Lesser God*	Michael Caine *Hannah and Her Sisters*	Dianne Wiest *Hannah and Her Sisters*

(*continued*)

Academy Awards (*continued*)

Year	Best Picture	Best Director	Best Actor	Best Actress	Best Supporting Actor	Best Supporting Actress
1987	*The Last Emperor*	Bernardo Bertolucci *The Last Emperor*	Michael Douglas *Wall Street*	Cher *Moonstruck*	Sean Connery *The Untouchables*	Olympia Dukakis *Moonstruck*
1988	*Rain Man*	Barry Levington *Rain Man*	Dustin Hoffman *Rain Man*	Jodie Foster *The Accused*	Kevin Kline *A Fish Called Wanda*	Geena Davis *The Accidental Tourist*
1989	*Driving Miss Daisy*	Oliver Stone *Born on the Fourth of July*	Daniel Day-Lewis *My Left Foot*	Jessica Tandy *Driving Miss Daisy*	Denzel Washington *Glory*	Brenda Fricker *My Left Foot*
1990	*Dances With Wolves*	Kevin Costner *Dances With Wolves*	Jeremy Irons *Reversal of Fortune*	Kathy Bates *Misery*	Joe Pesci *Goodfellas*	Whoopi Goldberg *Ghost*
1991	*The Silence of the Lambs*	Jonathan Demme *The Silence of the Lambs*	Anthony Hopkins *The Silence of the Lambs*	Jodie Foster *The Silence of the Lambs*	Jack Palance *City Slickers*	Mercedes Ruehl *The Fisher King*
1992	*Unforgiven*	Clint Eastwood *Unforgiven*	Al Pacino *Scent of a Woman*	Emma Thompson *Howard's End*	Gene Hackman *Unforgiven*	Marisa Tomei *My Cousin Vinny*
1993	*Schindler's List*	Steven Spielberg *Schindler's List*	Tom Hanks *Philadelphia*	Holly Hunter *The Piano*	Tommy Lee Jones *The Fugitive*	Anna Paquin *The Piano*
1994	*Forrest Gump*	Robert Zemeckis *Forrest Gump*	Tom Hanks *Forrest Gump*	Jessica Lange *Blue Sky*	Martin Landau *Ed Wood*	Dianne Wiest *Bullets Over Broadway*
1995	*Braveheart*	Mel Gibson *Braveheart*	Nicolas Cage *Leaving Las Vegas*	Susan Sarandon *Dead Man Walking*	Kevin Spacey *The Usual Suspects*	Mira Sorvino *Mighty Aphrodite*
1996	*The English Patient*	Anthony Minghella *The English Patient*	Geoffrey Rush *Shine*	Frances McDormand *Fargo*	Cuba Gooding Jr *Jerry Maguire*	Juliette Binoche *The English Patient*
1997	*Titanic*	James Cameron *Titanic*	Jack Nicholson *As Good As It Gets*	Helen Hunt *As Good As It Gets*	Robin Williams *Good Will Hunting*	Kim Basinger *L A Confidential*

1998

Best Picture	*Shakespeare in Love*
Best Director	Steven Spielberg *Saving Private Ryan*
Best Actor	Roberto Benigni *La vita é bella/Life is Beautiful*
Best Actress	Gwyneth Paltrow *Shakespeare in Love*
Best Supporting Actor	James Coburn *Affliction*
Best Supporting Actress	Judi Dench *Shakespeare in Love*
Best Original Screenplay	Marc Norman and Tom Stoppard *Shakespeare in Love*
Best Adapted Screenplay	Bill Condon *Gods and Monsters*
Best Foreign Film	*La vita é bella/Life is Beautiful* (Italy)
Best Cinematography	Janusz Kaminski *Saving Private Ryan*
Best Film Editing	Michael Kahn *Saving Private Ryan*
Best Art Direction	Martin Childs and Jill Quertier *Shakespeare in Love*
Best Costume Design	Sandy Powell *Shakespeare in Love*
Best Dramatic Score	Nicola Piovani *La vita é bella/Life is Beautiful*
Best Comedy/Musical Score	Stephen Warbeck *Shakespeare in Love*
Best Original Song	Stephen Schwartz 'When You Believe' from *The King of Egypt*
Best Makeup	Jenny Shircore *Elizabeth*
Best Sound	Gary Rydstrom, Gary Summers, Andy Nelson, and Ronald Judkins *Saving Private Ryan*
Best Sound Effects Editing	Gary Rydstrom and Richard Hymns *Saving Private Ryan*
Best Visual Effects	Joel Hynek, Nicholas Brooks, Stuart Robertson, and Kevin Mack *What Dreams May Come*
Best Documentary Feature	*The Last Days*
Best Documentary Short Subject	*The Personals: Improvisations on Romance in the Golden Years*
Best Live-Action Short Film	*Valgaften/Election Night*
Best Animated Short Film	*Bunny*
Honorary Award	Elia Kazan
Irving G Thalberg Award	Norman Jewison

BAFTA Awards: Introduction

UK film and television awards, presented annually in March for the previous year. The British Academy of Film and Television Arts was formed in 1959 as a result of the amalgamation of the British Film Academy (founded in 1948) and the Guild of Television Producers (founded in 1954). Film and television awards are presented for both production and performance categories.

BAFTA Film Awards

Film and television awards are presented for both production and performance categories.

1989–98

Year	Best Film
1989	*The Last Emperor* (USA)
1990	*Dead Poets Society* (USA)
1991	*Goodfellas* (USA)
1992	*The Commitments* (UK)
1993	*Howard's End* (UK)
1994	*Schindler's List* (USA)
1995	*Four Weddings and a Funeral* (UK)
1996	*Sense and Sensibility* (UK)
1997	*The English Patient* (USA)
1998	*The Full Monty* (UK)

1999

Best Film	*Shakespeare in Love* (USA/UK)
Best Director	Peter Weir *The Truman Show*
Best Actress	Cate Blanchett *Elizabeth*
Best Actor	Roberto Benigni *La vita é bella/Life is Beautiful*
Best Supporting Actress	Judi Dench *Shakespeare in Love*
Best Supporting Actor	Geoffrey Rush *Shakespeare in Love*
Best Foreign Film	*Central do Brasil/Central Station* (Brazil)
Best Original Screenplay	Andrew Niccol *The Truman Show*
Best Adapted Screenplay	Elaine May *Primary Colors*
The Alexander Korda Award for the Outstanding British Film of the Year	*Elizabeth*
The Orange Audience Award	*Lock, Stock and Two Smoking Barrels*
Music	*Elizabeth*
Newcomer	Richard Kwietniowski, director *Love and Death on Long Island*
Cinematography	Remi Adefarasin *Elizabeth*
Production Design	Dennis Gassner *The Truman Show*
Costume Design	Sandy Powell *Velvet Goldmine*
Short Animated Film	*The Canterbury Tales*
Editing	David Gamble *Shakespeare in Love*
Special Effects	*Saving Private Ryan*
Make-up/Hair	Jenny Shircore *Elizabeth*
Short Film	*Home*

Berlin Film Festival

This international film festival has been held every year in Berlin since 1950.

1999

Award	Winner
Golden Bear (Best Film)	*The Thin Red Line* (USA)
Silver Bear (Jury Grand Prize)	*Mifune's last Chant* (Denmark/Sweden)
Silver Bear for Best Director	Stephen Frears *The Hi-Lo Country* (UK/USA)
Silver Bear for Best Actress	Juliane Köhler and Maria Schrader *Aimée & Jaguar* (Germany)
Silver Bear for Best Actor	Michael Gwisdek *Nachtgestalten/Night Shapes* (Germany)
Silver Bear for Outstanding Single Achievement	Marc Norman and Tom Stoppard for their screenplay for *Shakespeare in Love* (UK)
Silver Bear for Outstanding Artistic Achievements	David Cronenberg *eXistenZ* (Canada/UK)
Silver Bear for Lifetime Achievement	Shirley MacLaine
Silver Bear for Lifetime Contribution to the Art of Cinema	Meryl Streep
The AGIOCA 'Blue Angel' for the best European film on a relevant contemporary issue	Yesim Ustaoglu *Günese Yolculuk/Journey to the Sun* (Turkey/Netherlands/Germany)

Cannes Film Festival

This international film festival is held every May in Cannes, France. The first festival was held in 1947. The main award is the Palme d'Or (known as the Grand Prix prior to 1955) for best film. Awards for supporting performances were introduced in 1979.

1989–98

Year	Palme d'Or for Best Film
1989	*Sex, Lies and Videotape* (USA)
1990	*Wild at Heart* (USA)
1991	*Barton Fink* (USA)
1992	*The Best Intentions* (Sweden)
1993	*The Piano* (New Zealand/Australia); *Farewell, My Concubine* (Hong Kong/China)
1994	*Pulp Fiction* (USA)
1995	*Underground* (Bosnia-Herzegovina)
1996	*Secrets and Lies* (UK)
1997	*The Eel/Unagi* Shohei Imamura (Japan) *The Taste of Cherries* Abbas Kiarostami (Iran)
1998	*Mia Eoniotita Ke Mia Mera/Eternity and A Day* Theo Angelopoulos (Greece)

1999

Award	Winner
Palme d'Or for Best Film	*Rosetta* Luc and Jean-Pierre Dardenne (Belgium)
Grand Jury Prize	*L'humanité* Bruno Dumont (France)
Best Director	Pedro Almodovar *Todo sobre mi madre/All About My Mother* (Spain)
Best Female Performance	Séverine Caneele *L'humanité* (France); Emilie Dequenne *Rosetta* (Belgium)
Best Male Performance	Emmanuel Schotté *L'humanité* (France)
Best Screenplay	Alexandre Sokourov *Moloch* (Germany/Russia)
Jury Prize	*A Carta/The Letter* Manoel de Oliveira (Portugal)
Camera d'Or	*Marana Simhasanam* Murali Nair (India/USA)
Grand Prix Technique de la CST	*The Emperor and the Assassin* Chen Kaige (China)
Palme d'Or for Short Film	*When the Day Breaks* Wendy Tilby and Amanda Forbis (Canada)
Grand Jury Prize for Short Film	*Stop* Rodolphe Marconi (France); *So-Poong* Song Ilgon (South Korea)

Golden Globe Awards for Motion Pictures

The Golden Globe entertainment awards are presented annually in January by the Hollywood Foreign Press Association for motion pictures and television during the previous calendar year.

1998

Award	Winner(s)
Motion Picture (Drama)	*Saving Private Ryan*
Motion Picture (Musical or Comedy)	*Shakespeare in Love*
Actor in a Motion Picture (Drama)	Jim Carrey *The Truman Show*
Actress in a Motion Picture (Drama)	Cate Blanchett *Elizabeth*
Actor in a Motion Picture (Comedy)	Michael Caine *Little Voice*
Actress in a Motion Picture (Comedy)	Gwyneth Paltrow *Shakespeare in Love*
Supporting Actor in a Motion Picture	Ed Harris *The Truman Show*
Supporting Actress in a Motion Picture	Lynn Redgrave *Gods and Monsters*
Director	Steven Spielberg *Saving Private Ryan*
Foreign Language Film	*Central Station* (Brazil)
Screenplay	Marc Norman and Tom Stoppard *Shakespeare in Love*
Original Score	Burkhard Dallwitz (additional music by Philip Glass) *The Truman Show*
Original Song	David Foster 'Prayer'; Carole Bayer Sager 'Quest for Camelot: The Magic Sword'
Cecil B DeMille Award for Lifetime Achievement	Jack Nicholson

London Film Critics' Circle Awards (ALFS)

These awards of the London Film Critics' Circle have been awarded annually since 1980. The Critics' Circle has existed since 1913; its members are the leading critics from Britain's national newspapers and magazines, together with reviewers from television and radio. The ALFS are held in aid of the National Society for the Prevention of Cruelty to Children (NSPCC).

1993–97

Year	Film of the Year
1993	*The Piano* (New Zealand/Australia)
1994	*Schindler's List* (USA)
1995	*Babe* (Australia)
1996	*Fargo* (USA)
1997	*L A Confidential* (USA)

1998

Award	Winner(s)
Director of the Year	Peter Weir *The Truman Show*
Actor of the Year	Jack Nicholson *As Good As it Gets*
Actress of the Year	Cate Blanchett *Elizabeth*
Screenwriter of the Year	Andrew Niccol *The Truman Show* and *Gattaca*
Film of the Year	*Saving Private Ryan* (USA)
British Film of the Year	*Lock, Stock and Two Smoking Barrels*
British Producer of the Year	Alison Owen, Tim Bevan, and Eric Fellner *Elizabeth*
British Director of the Year	John Boorman *The General*
British Screenwriter of the Year	Guy Ritchie *Lock, Stock and Two Smoking Barrels*
British Actor of the Year	Brendan Gleeson *The General*
British Actress of the Year	Helena Bonham Carter *The Wings of the Dove*
British Newcomer of the Year	Peter Mullan *My Name is Joe*
Best British Actor in a Supporting Role	Nigel Hawthorne *The Object of My Affection*
Best British Actress in a Supporting Role	Kate Beckinsale *The Last Days of Disco;* Minnie Driver *Good Will Hunting*
Best Foreign Language Film	*Shall We Dance* (Japan)
The Dilys Powell Award for Outstanding Achievement	Albert Finney; John Hurt
Lifetime Achievement Awards	John Box; John Boorman

Venice Film Festival

International film festival held annually in September, in Venice, Italy.

1998

Award	Winner(s)
Golden Lion for the Best Film	*Così ridevano* Gianni Amelio (Italy)
Silver Lion for the Best Director Emil Kusturica	*Black Cat, White Cat* (Yugoslavia)
Special Prize of the Jury	*Terminus Paradis* Lucian Pintille (Romania)
Volpi Cup for Best Male Lead Performance	Sean Penn *Hurlyburly* (USA)
Volpi Cup for Best Female Lead Performance	Catherine Deneuve *Place Vendôme* (France)
Golden Osella for the Best Screenplay	Eric Rohmer *Conte d'automne* (France)

Television, Radio, and Press

BAFTA Awards: Introduction

UK film and television awards, presented annually in March for the previous year. The British Academy of Film and Television Arts was formed in 1959 as a result of the amalgamation of the British Film Academy (founded in 1948) and the Guild of Television Producers (founded in 1954). Film and television awards are presented for both production and performance categories.

BAFTA Television Awards

Film and television awards are presented for both production and performance categories.

1999

Award	Winner
The Richard Dimbleby Award for Outstanding Personal Contribution to Factual Television	Trevor McDonald
The Dennis Potter Award	David Renwick
The Lew Grade Award for the Most Popular Television Programme	*Goodnight Mr Tom*
The Alan Clarke Award for Outstanding Creative Contribution to Television	Jimmy Mulville; Denise O'Donoghue
Best International (Programme or Series)	*The Larry Sanders Show* (USA)
Best Single Drama	*A Rather English Marriage*
Best Drama Series	*The Cops*
Best Drama Serial	*Our Mutual Friend*
Best Factual Series	*The Human Body*
Best Light Entertainment (programme or series)	*Who Wants to Be A Millionaire?*
Best Comedy	*I'm Alan Partridge*
The Flaherty Documentary Award	*After Lockerbie*
Best Actress	Thora Hird *Talking Heads: Waiting for the Telegram*
Best Actor	Tom Courtenay *A Rather English Marriage*
Best Light Entertainment Performance	Michael Parkinson *Parkinson*
Best Comedy Performance	Dermot Morgan *Father Ted*
Best News and Current Affairs Journalism	*Dispatches: Inside the Animal Liberation Front*
Best Soap	*Eastenders*
Best Comedy (programme or series)	*Father Ted*
The Huw Wheldon Award for the Best Arts Programme or Series	*The Brian Epstein Story*
Best Live Outside Broadcast Coverage	*C4 Racing: Derby Day*
Best Features (programme or series)	*Back to the Floor*
Originality	*The Human Body*
The Academy Fellowship	Morecambe and Wise

British Comedy Awards

These awards are presented annually in December with the Writers' Guild of Great Britain, and are for the best comedy on television, radio, film, and stage.

1998

Award	Winner
Top TV Comedy Actor	Steve Coogan *I'm Alan Partridge*
Top TV Comedy Actress	Emma Chambers *Vicar of Dibley*
Top BBC1 Personality	Harry Enfield *Harry Enfield and Christmas Chums*
Top BBC2, C4 or C5 Comedy Personality	Steve Coogan *I'm Alan Partridge*
Top ITV Personality	Michael Barrymore *My Kind of Music, Strike It Rich*
Top Stand-Up Comedian	Tommy Tiernan
Top TV Comedy Newcomer	Dylan Moran *How Do You Want Me?*
Best New TV Comedy	*The Royle Family*
Best Entertainment Series	*Who Wants To Be A Millionaire?*
Best Comedy Series	*Goodness Gracious Me*
Best TV Sitcom	*I'm Alan Partridge*
Best TV Comedy Drama	*Underworld*
Best Children's Comedy	*Sooty Co*
Best Radio Comedy	*Old Harry's Game*
Cockburn's Best Comedy Film	*Lock, Stock and Two Smoking Barrels*
Writers' Guild of Britain Lifetime Achievement Award	Denis Norden and Frank Muir
Lifetime Achievement Award for Comedy	Thora Hird

Broadcasting Press Guild Television and Radio Awards

These UK media awards were established in 1974 and are presented annually in March for programmes of the previous year.

1998

Award	Winner
Best Entertainment (joint award)	*Cold Feet* (Granada Television for ITV); *Goodness Gracious Me* (BBC2)
Best Documentary Series	*The Life of Birds* (BBC 1)
Best Single Drama	*A Rather English Marriage* (Wall to Wall Productions for BBC 2)
Best Actress	Daniela Nardini *Undercover Heart*
Best Actor	Timothy Spall *Our Mutual Friend* (BBC 2)
Best Single Documentary	*42 Up* (Granada Television for BBC1)
Best Performer (Non-Acting)	Michael Parkinson (BBC 1)
Radio Programme of the Year	*The Food Programme* (BBC Radio 4)
Radio Broadcaster of the Year	John Peel *Home Truths* (BBC Radio 4)
Best Drama Series/Serial	*Our Mutual Friend* (BBC 2)
Writer's Award	Caroline Aherne, Craig Cash, and Henry Normal *The Royle Family* (Granada Television for BBC 2)
Harvey Lee Award for Outstanding Contribution to Broadcasting	*News at Ten* (ITN for ITV)

Royal Television Society Awards

These awards began in 1964 (as the Geoffrey Parr Awards, renamed in 1988) and are presented in recognition of excellence in television for the previous year. The Programme awards are given in March, the Journalism awards in May, and the Sports awards in April.

1998

Award	Winner
Programme	
Situation Comedy and Comedy Drama	*Cold Feet* (Granada Television)
Entertainment	*Who Wants to Be a Millionaire?* (Celador Productions for ITV Network)
Children's Drama	*Microsoap* (BBC Production/Buena Vista Productions for BBC 1)
Children's Factual	*The Fame Game* (BBC Scotland for BBC 1)
Actor Male	Ray Winstone *Our Boy* (Wall to Wall Television for BBC 1)
Actor Female	Thora Hird *Talking Heads: Waiting for the Telegram* (Slow Motion for BBC 2)
Documentary Series	*Windrush* (Pepper Productions for BBC 2)
Single Documentary	*Modern Times: Drinking for England* (Century Films for BBC 2)
Presenter	David Attenborough *Life of Birds* (BBC Production for BBC 1)
Drama Series	*Jonathan Creek*
Single Drama	*A Rather English Marriage* (Wall to Wall Television for BBC 2)
Drama Serial	*A Young Person's Guide to Becoming a Rock Star* (Company TV for Channel Four Television)
Arts	*Close Up: This England* (BBC Production for BBC 2)
Television Performance	Rory Bremner *Rory Bremner. Who Else?* (Vera Productions for Channel Four Television)
Team	*Goodness Gracious Me* (BBC Production for BBC 2)
Documentary Strand	*The Natural World* (BBC Production for BBC 2)
Regional Documentary	*Put to the Test* (Brian Waddell Productions for BBC Northern Ireland)
Regional Programme	*A Light in the Valley* (BBC Wales)
Regional Presenter	Noel Thompson (BBC Northern Ireland)
Features: Daytime	*City Hospital* (Topical Television for BBC 1)
Features: Primetime	*Time Team* (A Videotext/Picture House Production for Channel Four Television)
Network Newcomer Behind the Screen	Damien O'Donnell, director of *Thirty Five Aside* (Clingfilm Productions for BBC 2)
Network Newcomer On Screen	Tony Maudsley *A Life for a Life* (A Celtic/Picture Palace Production for ITV Network)
Writer's Award	Peter Berry *A Life for a Life* (A Celtic/Picture Palace Production for ITV Network)
Special Award	*Father Ted*
Journalism	
News Award, International	*Nine O'Clock News: The Massacre at Drenica* (BBC News)
News Award, Home	*GMTV – Drumcree: Portadown Divided* (GMTV/Reuters)
Regional Daily News Magazine	*London Tonight* (London News network for Carlton Television)
Regional Current Affairs	*Frontline Scotland – The Ghost of Piper Alpha* (BBC Scotland)
Interview of the Year	*Lunchtime News: Dermot Murnaghan Interviews Peter Mandelson* (ITN News on ITV)
Television Journalist of the Year	David Loyn (BBC News)
Young Journalist of the Year	Peter Lane (5 News – ITN))
Current Affairs Award, International	*Correspondent Special: The Serbs' Last Stand* (BBC News)
Current Affairs Award, Home	*Dispatches: Inside the ALF* (Channel Four Television)
Judges' Award	*World in Action* (Granada Television)
Specialist Journalism	*Just Television* (Channel Four Television)
Programme of the Year	*News at Ten* (ITN News on ITV)

(continued)

Royal Television Society Awards (*continued*)

Award	Winner
Sports	
Sports News	*News at Ten: World Cup Trouble* (ITN News on ITV)
Live Outside Broadcast Coverage of the Year	*The First Division Play-Off* (Sky Sports)
Sports Documentary	*The Man Who Jumped to Earth* (BBC Wales for BBC 1)
Regional Sports News	*Meridian Tonight* (Meridian Broadcasting)
Regional Sports Documentary	*Bred For the Red: Home Truths* (BBC Northern Ireland)
Sports Presenter Award	Desmond Lynam (BBC Sport)
Sports Commentator Award	Clive Tyldesley (ITV Sport)
Regional Sports Programme of the Year: Actuality	*Goodwood Historic Racing* (Meridian Broadcasting)
Regional Sports Programme of the Year: Entertainment	*Extreme* (Westcountry Television)
Newcomer	Guy Mowbray (Eurosport)
Sports Pundit	Martin Brundle (MACH 1 for ITV Sport)
Sports Innovation	*Cheltenham: Wire Cam* (Channel Four Television)
Regional Sports Presenter or Commentator	Hazel Irvine (BBC Scotland)
Sports Programme of the Year: Actuality	*World Cup 1998: Argentina v England* (ISN for ITV Sport)
Sports Programme of the Year: Entertainment	*A Question of Sport* (BBC Production for BBC 1)
Television Sports Award of the Year	Sky Sports Football production team
Judges' Award	Jimmy Hill

Emmy Awards: Primetime

These are annual US television awards for primetime programmes. They are announced in September for the previous television season.

1998

Award	Winner(s)
Comedy Series	*Frasier*
Drama Series	*The Practice*
Miniseries	*From the Earth to the Moon*
Made for Television Movie	*Don King: Only in America*
Lead Actor in a Comedy Series	Kelsey Grammer *Frasier*
Lead Actress in a Comedy Series	Helen Hunt *Mad About You*
Lead Actor in a Drama Series	Andre Braugher *Homicide: Life on the Street*
Lead Actress in a Drama Series	Christine Lahti *Chicago Hope*
Supporting Actor in a Comedy Series	David Hyde Pierce *Frasier*
Supporting Actress in a Comedy Series	Lisa Kudrow *Friends*
Supporting Actor in a Drama Series	Gordon Clapp *NYPD Blue*
Supporting Actress in a Drama Series	Camryn Manheim *The Practice*
Lead Actor in a Miniseries or Movie	Gary Sinise *George Wallace*
Lead Actress in a Miniseries or Movie	Ellen Barkin *Before Women Had Wings*
Supporting Actor in a Miniseries or Movie	George C Scott *12 Angry Men*
Supporting Actress in a Miniseries or Movie	Mare Winningham *George Wallace*
Guest Actor in a Comedy Series	Mel Brooks *Mad About You*
Guest Actress in a Comedy Series	Emma Thompson *Ellen*
Guest Actor in a Drama Series	John Larroquette *The Practice*
Guest Actress in a Drama Series	Cloris Leachman *Promised Land*
Directing in a Comedy Series	Todd Holland *The Larry Sanders Show: Flip*
Directing in a Drama Series	Mark Tinker *Brooklyn South (Pilot)* and Paris Barclay *NYPD Blue: Lost Israel, Part 2*
Directing in a Variety or Music Program	Louis J Horvitz *The 70th Annual Academy Awards*
Directing in a Miniseries or Movie	John Frankenheimer *George Wallace*
Writing in a Comedy Series	Peter Tolan and Garry Shandling *The Larry Sanders Show: Flip*
Writing in a Drama Series	Nicholas Wootton, David Milch, and Bill Clark *NYPD Blue: Lost Israel, Part 2*
Writing in a Variety or Music Program	Eddie Feldman (head writer) *Dennis Miller Live*
Writing in a Miniseries or Movie	Kario Salem *Don King: Only in America*
Animated Program (one hour or less)	*The Simpsons: Trash of the Titans*
Classical Music/Dance Program	*Yo-Yo Ma Inspired by Bach*
Children's Program	*Muppets Tonight* and *Nick News Special – What Are You Staring At?*
Non-Fiction Special	*Discovery Sunday – Vietnam POWs: Stories of Survival*
Non-Fiction Series	*The American Experience*
Cinematography for a Series	Constantine Makris *Law & Order: Stalker*
Cinematography for a Miniseries or Special	Eric Van Haren Noman *What the Deaf Man Heard*
Music Composition for a Series (Dramatic Underscore)	Christophe Beck *Buffy the Vampire Slayer: Becoming, Part I*
Music Composition for a Miniseries or Movie (Dramatic Underscore)	Bruce Broughton *Glory & Honor*
Music Direction	Bill Conti *The 70th Annual Academy Awards*
Music and Lyrics	Alf Clausen, Ken Keeler 'You're Checkin' In (A Musical Tribute to the Betty Ford Center)' from *The Simpsons*
Outstanding Commercial	*Think Different* Apple Computer
Variety, Music, or Comedy Series	*Late Show with David Letterman*
Variety, Music, or Comedy Special	*The 1997 Tony Awards*
Performance in a Variety or Music Program	Billy Crystal *The 70th Annual Academy Awards*
Art Direction for a Series	Graeme Murray (production designer), Greg Loewen (art director), Shirley Inget (set decorator) *The X-Files: The Post-Modern Prometheus*

Sony Radio Awards

These UK awards are given in recognition of excellence in radio broadcasting.

1999

Award	Winner	Award	Winner
Gold Award	Zoë Ball	Breakfast Music Award	*The Adam Cole Breakfast Show* (Galaxy 102)
The Event Award	*The Enthronement of 7th Bishop* (BBC Radio Merseyside)	Breakfast Talk/News Award	*5 Live Breakfast* (BBC Radio 5 Live)
The Feature Award – Music	*We Got The Funk* (BBC Radio 1)	Daytime Music Award	*The Mark Radcliffe Show* (BBC Radio 1)
The Feature Award – Speech	*Between the Ears: Out of The Blue* (BBC Radio 3)	Daytime Talk/News Award	*Between Ourselves* (BBC Radio 4)
The Special Interest Music Award	*Shake, Rattle and Roll* (BBC Radio 2)	Drivetime Music Award	*Simon James* (96.3 Aire FM)
Comedy Award	*Old Harry's Game* (BBC Radio 4)	Drivetime Talk/News Award	*Evening Extra: Agreement Day* (BBC Radio Ulster)
The Sports Award	*Metro Sport: Two Wembley Finals* (Metro FM)	Evening/Late Night Music Award	*Pete Tong's Essential Selection* (BBC Radio 1)
The Drama Award	*Bleak House* (BBC Radio 4)	Evening/Late Night Talk/News Award	*Up All Night* (BBC Radio 5 Live)
The Arts Award	*Landscape of Fear* (BBC Radio 4)	Weekend Music Award	*Alan Mann's Afters* (Classic FM)
The Station Branding Award	Classic FM	Weekend Talk/News Award	*Home Truths* (BBC Radio 4)
The Magazine Award	*Home Truths* (BBC Radio 4)	Short Form Award	*Home Truths Inserts* (BBC Radio 4)
The News Award	*Farming Today* (BBC Radio 4)	Competition Award	Radio City's *Live in the Car* (Radio City 96.7)
The Community Award	*Omagh* (BBC Radio Ulster)	Sports Broadcaster Award	*Ian Payne* (BBC Radio 5 Live)
The Talk/News Broadcaster Award	Tim Hubbard (BBC Radio Cornwall)	Music Broadcaster Award	*Mark Lamarr* (BBC Radio 2)
Station of the Year, Local	Moray Firth Radio		
Station of the Year, Regional	Clyde 2		
Station of the Year, UK	BBC Radio 2		

British Press Awards

When first awarded in 1963, these UK press awards were called the Hannen Swaffer National Press Awards; the present name was adopted in 1975. The awards are now sponsored by several major newspaper groups and are widely regarded as the 'Oscars' of the British newspaper industry. The categories of awards vary for each year.

1999

Award	Winner	Award	Winner
National Newspaper of the Year	*The Guardian*	Columnist of the Year	Rebecca Tyrrel *The Sunday Telegraph*
Team Reporting Award	*The Mirror* the Omagh bomb	Critic of the Year	Charles Spencer *The Daily Telegraph*
Scoop of the Year	Michael Sean Gillard, Laurie Flynn *The Guardian*	Young Journalist of the Year	Burhan Wazir *The Observer*
Reporter of the Year	Mazher Mahmood *News of the World*	Cartoonist of the Year	Mac *The Daily Mail*
Specialist Reporter of the Year	Brian Deer *The Sunday Times*	Photographer of the Year	Jeremy Selvyn *Evening Standard*
Foreign Reporter of the Year	John Lichfield *The Independent*	Sports Photographer of the Year	Ian Rutherford *The Scotsman*
Sports Reporter of the Year	Michael Calvin *The Mail on Sunday*	Supplement of the Year	*The Times*
Business Journalist of the Year	Neil Bennett *The Sunday Telegraph*	Financial Journalist of the Year	Alex Brummer *The Guardian*
Feature Writer of the Year	Deborah Ross *The Independent*	On-Line News Service Awards	BBC News Online
		Gold Award	David Chipp former Press Association editor

What the Papers Say Awards

First broadcast in 1956, *What the Papers Say* is the longest running regular weekly programme on British television. Its awards are made in recognition of special achievement in journalism. The awards vary in category from year to year, although most years have included a 'Newspaper of the Year' award. The awards are made in late February for the previous year.

1998

Award	Winner	Award	Winner
Editor of the Year	Simon Kelner *The Independent*	Columnist of the Year	Libby Purves *The Times*
Correspondent of the Year	David McKittrick *The Independent*	Peter Black Award for Broadcasting Writer of the Year	Jaci Stephen *Daily Mail*
Journalist of the Year	Nick Davies *The Guardian*	Gerald Barry Award	Anthony Howard
Front page of the Year	*The Sun*		
Scoop of the Year	*The Guardian*		

BAFTA Interactive Entertainment Awards

1998

Award	Winner
The Best UK Developer Award	RARE
The Berners-Lee Award for Best Personal Contribution by a British Individual	Peter Kindersley
The Comedy Award	Mind Gym (publisher: Marshall Media, developer: NoHo Digital, format: CD-ROM)
The News and Magazine Award	BBC News (publisher: BBC News, developer: BBC, format: Web site)
The Factual Award	RedShift 3 (publisher: DK Interactive Learning, developer: Maris Multimedia Ltd, format: CD-ROM)
The Games Award	GoldenEye 007 (publisher: Nintendo, developer: Rare, format: N64
The Children's Award	Star Wars DroidWorks (publisher: Lucas Learning Ltd, developer: Lucas Learning Ltd, format: CD-ROM)
The Learning Award	Lifting the Weight (publisher: Geese Theatre Co UK, developer: Jubilee Arts Ltd, format: CD-ROM)
The Moving Images Award	The Ceremony of Innocence (publisher: Real World MultiMedia Ltd, developer: Real World MultiMedia Ltd, format: CD-ROM)
The Sound Award	The Ceremony of Innocence (publisher: Real World MultiMedia Ltd, developer: Real World MultiMedia Ltd, format: CD-ROM)
The Interactive Treatment Award	Stage Struck (publisher: National Institute of Dramatic Art (NIDA), developer: Interactive Multimedia Learning Laboratory (IMMLL), University of Wollongong, Australia, format: CD-ROM)
The Design Award	ShiftControl (developer: AudioRom Ltd, format: Enhanced CD)
The Computer Programming Award	Gran Turismo (publisher: SCEE, developer: SCEI, format: PSX)

Literature

Booker Prize

This UK literary prize of £20,000 is awarded annually in October.

Year	Winner	Awarded for
1969	P H Newby	*Something to Answer For*
1970	Bernice Rubens	*The Elected Member*
1971	V S Naipaul	*In a Free State*
1972	John Berger	*G*
1973	J G Farrell	*The Siege of Krishnapur*
1974	Nadine Gordimer	*The Conservationist*
	Stanley Middleton	*Holiday*
1975	Ruth Prawer Jhabvala	*Heat and Dust*
1976	David Storey	*Saville*
1977	Paul Scott	*Staying On*
1978	Iris Murdoch	*The Sea, The Sea*
1979	Penelope Fitzgerald	*Offshore*
1980	William Golding	*Rites of Passage*
1981	Salman Rushdie	*Midnight's Children*
1982	Thomas Keneally	*Schindler's Ark*
1983	J M Coetzee	*The Life and Times of Michael K*
1984	Anita Brookner	*Hotel du Lac*
1985	Keri Hulme	*The Bone People*
1986	Kingsley Amis	*The Old Devils*
1987	Penelope Lively	*Moon Tiger*
1988	Peter Carey	*Oscar and Lucinda*
1989	Kazuo Ishiguro	*The Remains of the Day*
1990	A S Byatt	*Possession*
1991	Ben Okri	*The Famished Road*
1992	Barry Unsworth	*Sacred Hunger*
	Michael Ondaatje	*The English Patient*
1993	Roddy Doyle	*Paddy Clarke Ha Ha Ha*
1994	James Kelman	*How Late It Was, How Late*
1995	Pat Barker	*The Ghost Road*
1996	Graham Swift	*Last Orders*
1997	Arundhati Roy	*The God of Small Things*
1998	Ian McEwan	*Amsterdam*

Whitbread Literary Award Book of the Year

Whitbread, the UK brewing, food, and leisure company, first endowed this literary award in 1971. Winners of five categories (Novel, Biography, Children's Novel, First Novel, and Poetry) are announced in November each year, and the overall winner (The Book of the Year) is awarded the £21,000 prize the following January.

Year	Winner	Awarded for
1987	Christopher Nolan	*Under the Eye of the Clock*
1988	Paul Sayer	*The Comforts of Madness*
1989	Richard Holmes	*Coleridge: Early Visions*
1990	Nicholas Mosley	*Hopeful Monsters*
1991	John Richardson	*A Life of Picasso*
1992	Jeff Torrington	*Swing Hammer Swing!*
1993	Joan Brady	*Theory of War*
1994	William Trevor	*Felicia's Journey*
1995	Kate Atkinson	*Behind the Scenes at the Museum*
1996	Seamus Heaney	*The Spirit Level*
1997	Ted Hughes	*Tales from Ovid*
1998	Ted Hughes	*Birthday Letters*

Betty Trask Award

Awarded annually in June, this UK literary prize was endowed by Betty Trask in 1983 for the first novel of a romantic or traditional nature written by an author under 35. The number of prizes and the values of the prizes vary each year.

Year	Winner	Awarded for
1999	Elliot Perlman	*Three Dollars*

Duff Cooper Memorial Prize

The Duff Cooper Memorial Prize is a UK literary award for a book of history or biography, in memory of Duff Cooper (1890–1954), statesman, diplomat, and author. It was established in 1956 with a cash prize of £2,000 and is awarded annually in February from a trust fund for a book published the previous year.

Year	Winner	Awarded for
1998	Richard Holmes	2-volume biography of Samuel Taylor Coleridge: *Coleridge: Early Visions* and *Coleridge: Darker Reflections*

James Tait Black Memorial Prize

The James Tait Black Memorial Prize was established in 1918. This UK literary award is presented in January or February for the previous year, with a cash prize of £1,500.

1998

Prize	Winner	Awarded for
Fiction	Beryl Bainbridge	*Master Georgie*
Biography	Peter Ackroyd	*The Life of Thomas More*

Mail on Sunday/John Llewellyn Rhys Prize

A UK literary prize inaugurated in memory of the writer, John Llewellyn Rhys. It is awarded to a citizen of the Commonwealth younger than 35 by the time of publication, for the most promising literary work of the previous year. It has been awarded annually in May since 1942. The winner receives a cash prize of £5,000.

Year	Winner	Awarded for
1998	Peter Ho Davies	*The Ugliest House in the World*

Impac Prize

Founded in 1996, and with a cash award of £103,000, this is the world's most valuable book prize for a single work of fiction. The selection process is unique among literary awards in that the winner is chosen from nominations sent in by municipal libraries around the world. The inaugural ceremony took place in Dublin, Ireland in May 1996.

Year	Winner	Awarded for
1999	Andrew Miller	*Ingenious Pain*

Guardian Fiction Prize

This UK literary prize is chosen by the literary editor and book reviewers of *The Guardian* newspaper. The award is for a work of fiction by a British or Commonwealth author.

Year	Winner	Awarded for
1998	Jackie Kay	*Trumpet*

Forward Poetry Prizes

The Forward Poetry Prizes were established in 1992 and are awarded annually in October. Awards for the three categories are £10,000 for Best Collection; £5,000 for Best First Collection; and £1,000 for Best Single Poem.

1998

Category	Winner	Awarded for
Best Collection	Ted Hughes	*Birthday Letters*
Best First Collection	Paul Farley	*The Boy From the Chemist Is Here To See You*
Best Single Poem	Sheenagh Pugh	*Envying Owen Beattie*

Prix Goncourt

Founded in 1903, this French literary award is presented annually in November by the Académie Goncourt for the best French novel of the year. The prize is a nominal 50 FF plus a lifelong annuity of 250 FF per year.

Year	Winner	Awarded for
1984	Marguerite Duras	*L'Amant*
1985	Yann Queffelec	*Les Noces Barbares*
1986	Michel Host	*Valet de Nuit*
1987	Tahir Ben Jelloun	*La Nuit Sacrée*
1988	Erik Orsenna	*L'Exposition Coloniale*
1989	Jean Vautrin	*Un Grand Pas vers le Bon Dieu*
1990	Jean Rouault	*Les Champs d'Honneur*
1991	Pierre Combescot	*Les Filles du Calvaire*
1992	Patrick Chamoisean	*Texaco*
1993	Amin Maalouf	*Le Rocher de Tanios*
1994	Didier van Cauwelaert	*Un Aller Simple*
1995	Andréï Makine	*Le Testament Français*
1996	Pascale Roze	*Le Chasseur Zéro*
1997	Patrick Rambeau	*La Bataille*
1998	Paule Constant	*Confidence pour confidence*

Orange Prize

The Orange Prize is a UK literary prize open only to women, of any nationality. It was established in 1996 with a cash award of £30,000.

Year	Winner	Awarded for
1998	Carol Shields	*Larry's Party*

Smarties Book Prize

The Smarties Book Prize aims to encourage British authors to achieve higher standards of writing for children in three age groups. The prize was established in 1985 and is awarded annually in November.

1998

Category	Winner	Awarded for
9–11 years	J K Rowling	*Harry Potter and the Chamber of Secrets*
6–8 years	Harry Horse	*The Last Gold Diggers*
0–5 years	Sue Heap	*Cowboy Baby*

Somerset Maugham Award

A UK literary award for young British writers to spend on foreign travel; Mr Maugham stressed that originality and promise should be encouraged. The prize (£5,000 to each winner) is awarded annually in June.

1999

Winner	Awarded for
Jonathan Friedland	*Bring Home the Revolution*
Giles Foden	*The Last King of Scotland*
Paul Farley	*The Boy From the Chemist is Here to See You*
Andrea Ashworth	*Once in a House on Fire*

W H Smith Literary Award

The W H Smith Literary Award is given to a Commonwealth or UK citizen for a UK-published book. The award was established in 1959 and is presented each March with a cash prize of £10,000.

Year	Winner	Awarded for
1990	V S Pritchett	*A Careless Widow, and Other Stories*
1991	Derek Walcott	*Omeros*
1992	Thomas Pakenham	*The Scramble for Africa*
1993	Michèle Roberts	*Daughters of the House*
1994	Vikram Seth	*A Suitable Boy*
1995	Alice Monro	*Open Secrets*
1996	Simon Schama	*Landscape and Memory*
1997	Orlando Figes	*A People's Tragedy*
1998	Ted Hughes	*Tales from Ovid*
1999	Beryl Bainbridge	*Master Georgie*

W H Smith's Thumping Good Read Award

UK annual award of £5,000 presented to the best new fiction author of the year. Founded in 1992 by the W H Smith group, the award is judged by a panel of W H Smith customers.

1998

Winner	Awarded for
Douglas Kennedy	*The Big Picture*

Poets Laureate of the UK

The Poet of the British royal household is so called because of the laurel wreath awarded to eminent poets in the Greco-Roman world. There is a stipend of £70 a year, plus £27 in lieu of the traditional butt of sack (cask of wine). The 1999 appointment was, for the first time, on a paid, ten-year tenure, rather than a life appointment.

Appointed	Poet Laureate
1668	John Dryden (1631–1700)
1689	Thomas Shadwell (c 1642–1692)
1692	Nahum Tate (1652–1715)
1715	Nicholas Rowe (1674–1718)
1718	Laurence Eusden (1688–1730)
1730	Colley Cibber (1671–1757)
1757	William Whitehead (1715–1785)
1785	Thomas Warton (1728–1790)
1790	Henry James Pye (1745–1813)
1813	Robert Southey (1774–1843)
1843	William Wordsworth (1770–1850)
1850	Alfred, Lord Tennyson (1809–1892)
1896	Alfred Austin (1835–1913)
1913	Robert Bridges (1844–1930)
1930	John Masefield (1878–1967)
1968	Cecil Day Lewis (1904–1972)
1972	Sir John Betjeman (1906–1984)
1984	Ted Hughes (1930–1998)
1999	Andrew Motion (1952–)

Pulitzer Prizes in Letters: Fiction

The Pulitzer Prizes were endowed by Joseph Pulitzer (1847–1911), the Hungarian-born US newspaper publisher. The prizes have been awarded since 1917 by Columbia University in New York City on the recommendation of the Pulitzer Prize Board.

Year	Winner	Awarded for
1990	Oscar Hijuelos	*The Mambo Kings Play Songs of Love*
1991	John Updike	*Rabbit at Rest*
1992	Jane Smiley	*A Thousand Acres*
1993	Robert Olen Butler	*A Good Scent From a Strange Mountain*
1994	E Annie Proulx	*The Shipping News*
1995	Carol Shields	*The Stone Diaries*
1996	Richard A Ford	*Independence Day*
1997	Steven Millhauser	*Martin Dressler: The Tale of an American Dreamer*
1998	Philip Roth	*American Pastoral*
1999	Michael Cunningham	*The Hours*

Music

Brit Awards

These are among the UK's most prestigious popular music awards. They are run by the British Phonographic Industry; other committee members come from major and independent record companies, publishing and retail sectors, the publicity industry, the media, retailers, promoters, the black music industry, and the Music Publishers' Association.

1993–98

Year	Best Group	Best Newcomer	Best Album	Best Single
1993	Simply Red	Tasmin Archer	Annie Lennox *Diva*	Take That 'Could it be Magic'
1994	Stereo MCs	Gabrielle	Stereo MCs *Connected*	Take That 'Pray'
1995	Blur	Oasis	Blur *Parklife*	Blur 'Parklife'
1996	Oasis	Supergrass	Oasis *(What's the Story) Morning Glory?*	Take That 'Back for Good'
1997	Manic Street Preachers	Kula Shaker	Manic Street Preachers *Everything Must Go*	Spice Girls 'Wannabe'
1998	The Verve	Stereophonics	The Verve *Urban Hymns*	All Saints *Never Ever*

1999

Award	Winner
Best Group	Manic Street Preachers
Best Newcomer	Belle and Sebastian
Best Album	Manic Street Preachers *This Is My Truth, Tell Me Yours*
Best Single	Robbie Williams 'Angels'
Best Male Solo Artist	Robbie Williams
Best Female Solo Artist	Des'ree
Best International Newcomer	Natalie Imbruglia
Best International Group	The Corrs
Best International Male Solo Artist	Beck
Best International Solo Female Artist	Natalie Imbruglia
Best Dance Act	Fatboy Slim
Best Video	Robbie Williams 'Millennium'
Best Soundtrack/Cast Recording	*Titanic*
Outstanding Contribution to British Music	Eurythmics

Eurovision Song Contest

Started in 1956, this European song contest is held annually in May.

1999

Winner	Song
Charlotte Nilsson (Sweden)	'Take Me To Your Heaven'
UK entry (14th place)	
Precious	'Say it Again'

Mercury Music Prize

This annual music prize is one of the UK's most prestigious arts prizes. Established in 1992, it is sponsored by Mercury Communications and supported by both the BPI (British Phonographic Industry) and BARD (British Association of Record Dealers). All ten shortlisted artists are presented with Shortlist Trophies before the overall winner is announced. The winner receives £25,000.

1998

Albums of the Year

Cornershop *When I Was Born For the 7th Time*
Catatonia *International Velvet*
Pulp *This is Hardcore*
Propellerheads *Decksandrumsandrockandroll*
Asian Dub Foundation *Rafi's Revenge*
Massive *Mezzanine*
Eliza Carthy *Red Rice*
Gomez *Bring It On*
4-Hero *Two Pages*
Robbie Williams *Life Through a Lens*
The Verve *Urban Hymns*

Overall Winner

Gomez *Bring It On*

World Music Awards

These awards are presented annually and are chosen by the International Federated Phonograph Industry.

1999

Category	Winner
National Awards	
World's Best-Selling Japanese Artist/Group	B'Z
World's Best-Selling Benelux Artist/Group	Lara Fabian
World's Best-Selling British Artist/Group	Des'ree
World's Best-Selling Canadian Artist/Group	Barenaked Ladies
World's Best-Selling Russian Artist/Group	Philip Kirkorov
World's Best-Selling French Artist/Group	Notre-Dame de Paris
World's Best-Selling German Artist/Group	Modern Talking
World's Best-Selling Irish Artist/Group	The Corrs
World's Best-Selling Italian Artist/Group	883
World's Best-Selling Middle Eastern Artist/Group	Tarkan
World's Best-Selling Swedish Artist/Group	Meja
World's Best-Selling Spanish Artist/Group	Alejandro Sanz
World's Best-Selling Swiss Artist/Group	DJ Bobo
Legend Awards	
Lifelong Contribution to the Music Industry	Cher
Outstanding Contribution to R&B	Janet Jackson
Category Awards	
World's Best-Selling Pop, Dance, R&B, and Rap Male Artist	Will Smith
World's Best-Selling Latin Artist/Group	Ricky Martin
World's Best-Selling R&B, Rap, and New Female Artist	Lauryn Hill

Gramophone Awards

These UK classical music awards have been given since 1977. The awards have various sponsors each year. (– = not applicable.)

1998

Award	Composer	Work	Artist(s)	Conductor	Record label
Baroque Vocal	Monteverdi	*Madrigals, Book 8*	concerto Italiano Alessandrini	–	–
Baroque Non-vocal	Rameau	*Overtures*	Les Talens Lyriques	Rousset	L'Oiseau-Lyre
Chamber	Bartók	*String Quartets*	Takacs Quartet	–	Decca
Choral	Martin/Pizetti	*Mass for double choir/ Messa di Requiem*	Westminster Cathedral Choir	O'Donnell	Hyperion
Concerto	Barber/Walton; Bloch	*Violin Concertos; Baal Shem*	Bell, Baltimore Symphony Orchestra	Zinman	Decca
Contemporary	Birtwistle	*The Mask of Orpheus*	Garrison, Bronder, Rogby, BBC Singers, BBC Symphony Orchestra	Davis, Brabbins	NMC
Early Music	–	*Canciones y Ensaladas*	Clement Jannequin Ensemble	Visse	Harmonia Mundi
Early Opera	Rameau	*Les fetes d'Hebe*	Daneman, Mechaly, Agnew, Les Arts Florissants	Christie	Erato
Editor's Choice Award	Ades	*Living Toys*	various artists	–	EMI
Film Music	various	*The Ladykillers* and other Ealing films	Royal Ballet Sinfonia	Alwyn	Silva
Instrumental	Mompou	*Piano Work*	Hough	–	Hyperion
Music Theatre	Kander and Ebb	*Chicago*	Broadway cast	–	RCA Victor
Opera	Rossini	*Il Turco in Italia*	Pertusi, Bartoli, Corbelli, Vargas, Chorus and Orchestra of La Scala, Milan	Chailly	Decca
Orchestral	Bartók	*The Miraculous Mandarin; Hungarian Sketches; Peasant Songs and Folk Dances*	Hungarian Rad Chorus; Budapest Festival Orchestra	Fischer	Philips
Solo Vocal	Schumann	*Dichterliebe; Liederkreis*	Bostridge	–	EMI
Record of the Year	Martin/Pizetti	*Mass for double choir/ Messa di Requiem*	Westminster Cathedral Choir	O'Donnell	Hyperion
Artist of the Year	Riccardo Chailly	–	–	–	–
Lifetime Achievement	Menahem Pressler	–	–	–	–

MTV Video Music Awards

These awards are announced in September for current year.

1998

Award	Winner
Best Video	Madonna 'Ray of Light'
Best Male Video	Will Smith 'Just the Two of Us'
Best Female Video	Madonna 'Ray of Light'
Best Group Video	Backstreet Boys 'Everybody (Backstreet's Back)'
Best Rap Video	Will Smith 'Gettin' Jiggy With It'
Breakthrough Video	Prodigy 'Smack My Bitch Up'
Best Direction in a Video	Jonas Akerlund, for Madonna's 'Ray of Light'
Best Alternative Music Video	Green Day 'Time of Your Life (Good Riddance)'
Best New Artist in a Video	Natalie Imbruglia 'Torn'
Best Video from a Film	Aerosmith 'I Don't Want to Miss A Thing'
Best R&B Video	Wyclef Jean featuring the Refugee Allstars 'Gone 'Til November'
Best Rock Video	Aerosmith 'Pink'
Best Dance Video	Prodigy 'Smack My Bitch Up'
Best Cinematography	Fiona Apple, director Mark Romanek 'Criminal'
Best Editing	Madonna 'Ray of Light' (director Jonas Akerlund)
Best Choreography	Madonna 'Ray of Light'
Best Special Effects	Madonna 'Frozen' (director Chris Cunningham)
Best Art Direction	Bjork 'Bachelorette' (director Michel Gondry)

Grammy Awards: Introduction

US annual music awards which are for outstanding achievement in the record industry for the previous year. The gold-plated disks are presented by the National Academy of Recording Arts and Sciences. The first Grammy Awards were for records released in 1958.

Grammy Awards

1999 (for releases in 1998)

Category	Winner
Song of the Year	James Horner and Will Jennings, songwriters, Celine Dion 'My Heart Will Go On'
Album of the Year	Lauryn Hill *The Miseducation of Lauryn Hill*
Record of the Year	Celine Dion 'My Heart Will Go On'
New Artist	Lauryn Hill
Female Pop Vocal Performance	Celine Dion 'My Heart Will Go On'
Male Pop Vocal Performance	Eric Clapton 'My Father's Eyes'
Pop Duo or Group Performance	The Brian Setzer Orchestra 'Jump Jive An' Wail'
Rock Song	Alanis Morissette 'Uninvited'
Rock Album	Sheryl Crow *The Globe Sessions*
Female Rock Vocal Performance	Alanis Morissette 'Uninvited'
Male Rock Vocal Performance	Lenny Kravitz 'Fly Away'
Rock Vocal, Duo or Group Performance	Aerosmith 'Pink'
Hard Rock Performance	Jimmy Page and Robert Plant 'Most High'
Metal Performance	Metallica 'Better Than You'
Female R&B Vocal Performance	Lauryn Hill 'Doo Wop (That Thing)'
Male R&B Vocal Performance	Stevie Wonder 'St Louis Blues'
R&B Duo or Group Performance	Brandy & Monica 'The Boy Is Mine'
R&B Song	Lauryn Hill 'Doo Wop (That Thing)'
R&B Album	Lauryn Hill *The Miseducation of Lauryn Hill*
Rap Solo Performance	Will Smith 'Gettin' Jiggy With It'
Rap Duo or Group Performance	Beastie Boys 'Intergalactic'
Rap Album	Jay-Z *Vol 2 Hard Knock Life*
Female Country Vocal Performance	Shania Twain 'You're Still the One'
Male Country Vocal Performance	Vince Gill 'If You Ever Have Forever in Mind'
Country Duo or Group Performance	Dixie Chicks 'There's Your Trouble'
Country Song	Shania Twain 'You're Still The One'
Country Album	Dixie Chicks *Wide Open Spaces*
Jazz Instrumental Solo	Chick Corea and Gary Burton 'Rhumbata'
Individual or Group Jazz Instrumental Performance	Herbie Hancock 'Gershwin's World'
Best Dance Recording	Madonna 'Ray of Light'
Best Pop Album	Madonna *Ray of Light*
Best Alternative Music Performance	Beastie Boys 'Hello Nasty'
Best Country Instrumental Performance	Randy Scruggs and Vince Gill 'A Soldier's Joy'
Best Bluegrass Album	Ricky Skaggs and Kentucky Thunder *Bluegrass Rules!*
Best New Age Album	Clannad *Landmarks*
Best Contemporary Jazz Performance	Pat Metheny Group 'Imaginary Day'
Best Jazz Vocal Performance	Arturo Sandoval 'Hot House'
Best Jazz Vocal Performance	Shirley Horn 'I Remember Miles'
Best Traditional Soul Gospel Album	Cissy Houston *He Leadeth Me*
Best Contemporary Soul Gospel Album	Kirk Franklin *The Nu Nation Project*
Best Latin Pop Performance	Ricky Martin 'Vuelve'
Best Traditional Blues Album	Otis Rush *Any Place I'm Going*
Best Contemporary Blues Album	Keb' Mo' *Slow Down*
Best Traditional Folk Album	The Chieftains with various artists *Long Journey Home*
Best Reggae Album	Sly And Robbie *Friends*
Best World Music Album	Gilberto Gil *Quanta Live*
Best Classical Album	*Barber: Prayers of Kierkegaard/ Vaughan Williams: Dona Nobis Pacem/Bartok: Cantata Profana* Robert Shaw, conductor; James Mallinson, producer; Richard Clement, tenor; Nathan Gunn, baritone; Carmen Pelton, soprano; Atlanta Symphony Orchestra and Chorus
Best Short Form Music Video	Madonna 'Ray of Light'
Best Long Form Music Video	'American masters: Lou Reed: Rock & Roll Heart, Lou Reed'
Lifetime Achievement	Johnny Cash; Mel Tormé; William 'Smokey' Robinson; Otis Redding; Sam Cooke

Grammy Awards: Best Record and Best Album

1958–97

Year	Best Record	Best Album
1961	Henry Mancini 'Moon River'	Judy Garland *Judy at Carnegie Hall*
1962	Tony Bennett 'I Left My Heart in San Francisco'	Vaughn Meader *The First Family*
1963	Henry Mancini 'The Days of Wine and Roses'	Barbra Streisand *The Barbra Streisand Album*
1964	Stan Getz, Astrud Gilberto 'The Girl From Ipanema'	Stan Getz, Astrud Gilberto *Getz/Gilberto*
1965	Herb Alpert 'A Taste of Honey'	Frank Sinatra *September of My Years*
1966	Frank Sinatra 'Strangers in the Night'	Frank Sinatra *A Man and His Music*
1967	5th Dimension 'Up, Up and Away'	The Beatles *Sgt Pepper's Lonely Hearts Club Band*
1968	Simon and Garfunkel 'Mrs Robinson'	Glen Campbell *By the Time I Get to Phoenix*
1969	5th Dimension 'Aquarius/Let the Sunshine In'	Blood, Sweat and Tears *Blood, Sweat and Tears*
1970	Simon and Garfunkel 'Bridge Over Troubled Water'	Simon and Garfunkel *Bridge Over Troubled Water*
1971	Carole King 'It's Too Late'	Carole King *Tapestry*
1972	Roberta Flack 'The First Time Ever I Saw Your Face'	various *The Concert for Bangladesh*
1973	Roberta Flack 'Killing Me Softly With His Song'	Stevie Wonder *Innervisions*
1974	Olivia Newton-John 'I Honestly Love You'	Stevie Wonder *Fulfillingness' First Finale*
1975	Captain and Tennille 'Love Will Keep Us Together'	Paul Simon *Still Crazy After All These Years*
1976	George Benson 'This Masquerade'	Stevie Wonder *Songs in the Key of Life*
1977	Eagles 'Hotel California'	Fleetwood Mac *Rumours*
1978	Billy Joel 'Just the Way You Are'	Bee Gees *Saturday Night Fever*
1979	The Doobie Brothers 'What a Fool Believes'	Billy Joel *52nd Street*
1980	Christopher Cross 'Sailing'	Christopher Cross *Christopher Cross*
1981	Kim Carnes 'Bette Davis Eyes'	John Lennon, Yoko Ono *Double Fantasy*
1982	Toto 'Rosanna'	Toto *Toto IV*
1983	Michael Jackson 'Beat It'	Michael Jackson *Thriller*
1984	Tina Turner 'What's Love Got to Do With It'	Lionel Richie *Can't Slow Down*
1985	USA for Africa 'We Are the World'	Phil Collins *No Jacket Required*
1986	Steve Winwood 'Higher Love'	Paul Simon *Graceland*
1987	Paul Simon 'Graceland'	U2 *The Joshua Tree*
1988	Bobby McFerrin 'Don't Worry, Be Happy'	George Michael *Faith*
1989	Bette Midler 'Wind Beneath My Wings'	Bonnie Raitt *Nick of Time*
1990	Phil Collins 'Another Day in Paradise'	Quincy Jones *Back on the Block*
1991	Natalie Cole, with Nat 'King' Cole 'Unforgettable'	Natalie Cole, with Nat 'King' Cole *Unforgettable*
1992	Eric Clapton 'Tears in Heaven'	Eric Clapton *Unplugged*
1993	Whitney Houston 'I Will Always Love You'	Whitney Houston *The Bodyguard*
1994	Sheryl Crow 'All I Wanna Do'	Tony Bennett *MTV Unplugged*
1995	Seal 'Kiss from a Rose'	Alanis Morissette *Jagged Little Pill*
1996	Eric Clapton 'Change the World'	Celine Dion *Falling into You*
1997	Shawn Colvin 'Sunny Came Home'	Bob Dylan *Time Out of Mind*

Theatre

Evening Standard Drama Awards

These UK annual drama awards are sponsored by the *Evening Standard* newspaper and are awarded in November.

1988–97

Year	Best Play	Best Musical	Best Comedy
1988	*Aristocrats*	no award	*Lettice and Lovage*
1989	*Ghetto*	*Miss Saigon*	*Henceforward*
1990	*Shadowlands*	*Into the Woods*	*Man of the Moment* and *Jeffrey Bernard is Unwell* (joint award)
1991	*Dancing at Lughnasa*	*Carmen Jones*	*Kvetch*
1992	*Angels in America*	*Kiss of the Spider Woman*	*The Rise and Fall of Little Voice*
1993	*Arcadia*	*City of Angels*	*Jamais Vu*
1994	*Three Tall Women*	no award	*My Night With Reg*
1995	*Pentecost*	*Mack and Mabel*	*Dealer's Choice*
1996	*Stanley*	*Passion*	*Art*
1997	*The Invention of Love*	*Lady in the Dark*	*Closer*

1998

Best Play	*Copenhagen* Michael Frayn
Best Musical	*Oklahoma!* Trevor Nunn (director)
Best Actor	Kevin Spacey *The Iceman Cometh*
Best Actress	Sinead Cusack *Our Lady of Sligo*
Best Director	Howard Davies *Flight* and *The Iceman Cometh*
Most Promising Playwright	Mark Ravenhill *Handbag*
Best Stage Designer	Richard Hoover *Handbag*
Theatrical Achievement of the Year	The Almeida Theatre
Special Award	Nicole Kidman (for special and significant contribution to London theatre)

Laurence Olivier Awards

These UK theatre awards are presented annually by the Society of London Theatre.

1999 (for 1998 season)

Award	Winner
Best New Comedy	*Cleo, Camping, Emanuelle and Dick* Terry Johnson
Best Actor	Kevin Spacey *The Iceman Cometh*
Best Actress	Eileen Atkins *The Unexpected Man*
Best Director	Howard Davies *The Iceman Cometh*
Best Actor in a Musical	the cast *Kat and the Kings* (Salie Daniels, Jody Abrahams, Loukmaan Adams, Junaid Booysen, Alistair Izobell, and Mandisa Bardill)
Best Actress in a Musical	Sophie Thompson *Into the Woods*
Best Theatre Choreographer	Susan Stroman *Oklahoma!*
Best New Dance Production	Ballet Frankfurt *Enemy In The Figure,* Sadler's Wells
Special Award for Outstanding Contribution to British Arts	Sir Peter Hall
Outstanding Musical Production	*Oklahoma!*
Best New Opera Production	Welsh National Opera *La Clemenza di Tito* at the Shaftesbury
Best New Musical	*Kat and the Kings*
Best Entertainment	Sean Foley, Hamish McColl, and Josef Houben 'The Right Size' in *Do You Come Here Often?*
Best Supporting Performance	Brendan Coyle *The Weir*
Best Supporting Performance in a Musical	Shuler Hensley *Oklahoma!*
Best Costume Designer	William Dudley *Amadeus* and *The London Cuckolds*
Best Lighting Designer	Hugh Vanstone *The Blue Room* and *The Unexpected Man*
Best Set Designer	Anthony Ward *Oklahoma!*
Outstanding Achievement in Dance	William Forsythe's Sadler's Wells season
Outstanding Achievement in Opera	the Orchestra of the Royal Opera House for *Le Nozze di Figaro, The Bartered Bride,* and *The Golden Cockerel*

Art and Architecture

Turner Prize

Established in 1984 to encourage discussion about new developments in contemporary British art, this prize has often attracted criticism for celebrating what is not traditionally considered to be art. It is open to any British artist under 50 and has a prize of £20,000.

Year	Winner	Year	Winner	Year	Winner
1984	Malcolm Morley	1989	Richard Long	1994	Antony Gormley
1985	Howard Hodgkin	1990	no award	1995	Damien Hirst
1986	Gilbert and George	1991	Anish Kapoor	1996	Douglas Gordon
1987	Richard Deacon	1992	Grenville Davey	1997	Gillian Wearing
1988	Tony Cragg	1993	Rachel Whiteread	1998	Chris Ofili

BP Portrait Award by the National Portrait Gallery

This is an annual art prize of £10,000 and, at the judges' discretion, a commission of £2,000 to paint a well-known person.

Year	Winner	Awarded for
1999	Clive Smith	*Double Single*

Royal Academy Summer Exhibition Awards

UK arts awards held since 1769. Awards vary in amount and are for works in different media.

1999

Award	Amount (£)	Winner
Charles Wollaston Award for the Most Distinguished Work in the Exhibition	25,000	David Hockney for *A Bigger Grand Canyon* (oil)
Diageo Award for First-Time Exhibitor	5,000	Fiona Robertson for *Mr Wheeler Outside the Shop* (oil)
Bovis Europe/*The Architects' Journal* Awards for Architecture	7,250 in total	Grand Award to Foster and Partner for Plenary Building in the Converted Reichstag, Berlin (digital print, ink on film, and photoprint)
Worshipful Company of Chartered Architects (for a measured drawing, or set of drawings, of a work of architecture	1,000	The judges awarded first place to *St Pancras Station* (digital print) by the Rail Link Engineering/Union Railways North team, headed by Adrian Lee, but regrettably were not permitted to award him a prize as an individual. The individual prize was therefore presented to Anton Glikine for *Entrance Hall of Spencer House* (watercolour)
Jack Goldhill Award for Sculpture	8,000 commission for a sculpture	Bryan Kneale for *Mercury One* and *Mercury Two* (stainless steel)
Nordstern Award (for a print in any medium)	1,000	Basil Beattie for *At the Hour of Midnight* (screenprint and woodblock)
Dupree Family Award for a Woman Artist (for a painting or sculpture by a woman artist)	2,500	Rose Wylie for *Henry Δ* (oil)
The Scottish Gallery, Diana King Prize (for a painting)	1,000	Paulo Rego for *Untitled* (oil)

Royal Gold Medallists of Architecture

Instituted by Queen Victoria, the Royal Gold Medal is an international prize awarded annually in March to a distinguished architect, or group of architects, for work of high merit that has in some way promoted the advancement of architecture. In 1999, precedent was broken to award the Royal Gold Medal to a city.

Year	Winner
1848	Charles Robert Cockerell
1849	Luigi Canina
1850	Charles Barry
1851	Thomas L Donaldson
1852	Leo von Klenze
1853	Robert Smirke
1854	Philip Hardwick
1855	Jacques Ignace Hittorff
1856	William Tite
1857	Owen Jones
1858	August Stuler
1859	G Gilbert Scott
1860	Sydney Smirke
1861	J B Lesueur
1862	Robert Willis
1863	Anthony Salvin
1864	E Violet leDuc
1865	James Pennethorne
1866	M Digby Wyatt
1867	Charles Texier
1868	Henry Layard
1869	C R Lepsius
1870	Benjamin Ferrey
1871	James Fergusson
1872	Baron von Schmidt
1873	Thomas Henry Wyatt
1874	George Edmund Street
1875	Edmund Sharpe
1876	Joseph Louis Duc
1877	Charles Barry
1878	Alfred Waterhouse
1879	Marquis de Vogue
1880	John L Pearson
1881	George Godwin
1882	Baron von Ferstel
1883	Fras Cranmer Penrose
1884	William Butterfield
1885	H Schliemann
1886	Charles Gamier
1887	Ewan Christian
1888	Baron von Hansen
1889	Charles T Newton
1890	John Gibson
1891	Arthur Blomfield
1892	Cesar Daly
1893	Richard Morris Hunt
1894	Frederic Leighton
1895	James Brooks
1896	Ernest George
1897	Petrus Josephus Hubertus Cuypers
1898	George Aitchison
1899	George Frederick Bodley
1900	Rodolfo Amadeo Lanciani
1901	no award, owing to the death of Queen Victoria
1902	Thomas Edward Collcutt
1903	Charles Follen McKim
1904	Auguste Choisy
1905	Aston Webb
1906	L Alma-Tadema
1907	John Belcher
1908	Honore Daumet
1909	Arthur John Evans
1910	Thomas Graham Jackson
1911	Wilhelm Dorpfeld
1912	Basil Champneys
1913	Reginald Blomfield
1914	Jean Louis Pascal
1915	Frank Darling
1916	Robert Rowland Anderson
1917	Henri Paul Nenot
1918	Ernest Newton
1919	Leonard Stokes
1920	Charles Louis Girault
1921	Edwin Landseer Lutyens
1922	Thomas Hastings
1923	John James Burnet
1924	no award

(continued)

Royal Gold Medallists of Architecture (*continued*)

Year	Winner
1925	Giles Gilbert Scott
1926	Ragnar Ostberg
1927	Herbert Baker
1928	Guy Dawber
1929	Victor Alexandre Frederic Laloux
1930	Percy Scott Worthington
1931	Edwin Cooper
1932	Hendrik Petrus Berlage
1933	Charles Reed Peers
1934	Henry Vaughan Lanchester
1935	Willem Marinus Dudok
1936	Charles Henry Holden
1937	Raymond Unwin
1938	Ivar Tengborn
1939	Percy Thomas
1940	Charles Francis Annesley Voysey
1941	Frank Lloyd Wright
1942	William Curtis Green
1943	Charles Herbert Reilly
1944	Edward Maufe
1945	Victor Vessnin
1946	Patrick Abercrombie
1947	Albert Edward Richardson
1948	Auguste Perret
1949	Howard Robertson
1950	Eleil Saarinen
1951	Emanuel Vincent Harris
1952	George Grey Wornum
1953	Le Corbusier (C E Jeanneret)
1954	Arthur George Stephenson
1955	John Murray Easton
1956	Walter Adolf Georg Gropius
1957	Hugo Alvar Henrik Aalto
1958	Robert Scholfield Morris
1959	Ludwig Mies van der Rohe
1960	Pier Luigi Nervi
1961	Lewis Mumford
1962	Sven Gottfrid Markelius
1963	William Holford
1964	E Maxwell Fry
1965	Kenzo Tange
1966	Ove Arup
1967	Nikolaus Pevsner
1968	Richard Buckminster Fuller
1969	Jack Antonio Coia
1970	Robert Matthew
1971	Hubert de Cronin Hastings
1972	Louis I Kahn
1973	Leslie Martin
1974	Powell and Moya
1975	Michael Scott
1976	John Summerson
1977	Denys Lasdun
1978	Jom Utzon
1979	The Office of Charles and Ray Earnes
1980	James Stirling
1981	Philip Dowson
1982	Berthold Lubetkin
1983	Norman Foster
1984	Charles Corree
1985	Richard Rogers
1986	Arata Isozaki
1987	Ralph Erskine
1988	Richard Meier
1989	Renzo Piano
1990	Aldo van Eyck
1991	Colin Stansfield Smith
1992	Peter Rice
1993	Giancarlo de Carlo
1994	Michael and Patricia Hopkins
1995	Colin Rowe
1996	Harry Seilder
1997	Tadao Ando
1998	Oscar Neimeyer
1999	Barcelona, its government, its citizens, and design professionals

Source: Royal Institute of British Architects

Stirling Prize

This £20,000 prize is awarded each November by the Royal Institute of British Architects, and the winner is chosen from a regional shortlist.

1998

Winner
American Air Museum in Britain, Imperial War Museum, Duxford Airfield by Foster and Partners

Pritzker Architecture Prize

This US premier architecture award is named for Jay A Pritzker, president of the Hyatt Foundation which sponsors it. The award has been presented annually in April since 1979, with a $100,000 grant.

Year	Winner
1999	Norman Foster, British architect

Religion

Templeton Foundation Prize for Progress in Religion

The Templeton Prize, an award to encourage progress in religion, was established in 1972 by Sir John Templeton, a Tennessee-born British financier and Presbyterian layman. He established the award to redress the fact that no Nobel Prize is granted for religion. Announced in March, it is awarded at Buckingham Palace in London; its value has increased over the years to more than $1 million.

Year	Winner
1973	Mother Teresa of Calcutta, founder of the Missionaries of Charity
1974	Brother Roger, founder and prior of the Taize Community in France
1975	Dr Sarvepalli Radhakrishnan, former president of India and Oxford professor of eastern religions and ethics
1976	H E Leon Joseph Cardinal Suenens, archbishop of Malines-Brussels
1977	Chiara Lubich, founder of the Focolare Movement, Italy
1978	Professor Thomas F Torrance, president of International Academy of Religion and Sciences, Scotland
1979	Nikkyo Niwano, founder of Rissho Kosel Kai and World Conferences on Religion and Peace, Japan
1980	Professor Ralph Wendell Burhoe, founder and editor of *Zygon*, Chicago
1981	Dame Cecily Saunders, originator of Modern Hospice Movement, England
1982	The Reverend Dr Billy Graham, founder, the Billy Graham Evangelistic Association
1983	Aleksandr Solzhenitsyn (USA)
1984	The Reverend Michael Bourdeaux, founder of Keston College, England
1985	Sir Alister Hardy, Oxford, England
1986	The Reverend Dr James McCord, Princeton, New Jersey
1987	The Reverend Professor Stanley L Jaki, Princeton, New Jersey
1988	Dr Inamullah Khan, secretary-general of the World Moslem Congress
1989	The Very Reverend Lord MacLeod of the Iona Community, Scotland, and Professor Carl Friedrich von Weizsäcker of Starnberg, West Germany
1990	Baba Amte, India, and Professor Charles Birch, Sydney, Australia
1991	The Rt. Hon. Lord Jakobovits, Chief Rabbi of Great Britain and the Commonwealth
1992	Dr Kyung-Chik Han, founder of Seoul's Young Nak Presbyterian Church
1993	Charles W Colson, founder, Prison Fellowship, Virginia
1994	Michael Novak, scholar at the American Enterprise Institute, Washington, DC
1995	Dr Paul Davies, professor, University of Adelaide, Australia
1996	Bill Bright, founder of Campus Crusade for Christ, international evangelical ministry
1997	Pandurang Shastri Athavale, Indian spiritual leader
1998	Sir Sigmund Sternberg, Chairman of the Executive Committee of the International Council of Christians and Jews (ICCA)
1999	Ian Barbour, physicist and theologian, advocate for ethics in technology

Mathematics and Science

Fields Medal

This international prize for achievement in the field of mathematics is awarded every four years by the International Mathematical Union.

Year	Winner(s)
1936	Lars Ahlfors (Finland); Jesse Douglas (USA)
1950	Atle Selberg (USA); Laurent Schwartz (France)
1954	Kunihiko Kodaira (USA); Jean-Pierre Serre (France)
1958	Klaus Roth (UK); René Thom (France)
1962	Lars Hörmander (Sweden); John Milnor (USA)
1966	Michael Atiyah (UK); Paul J Cohen (USA); Alexander Grothendieck (France); Stephen Smale (USA)
1970	Alan Baker (UK); Heisuke Hironaka (USA); Sergei Novikov (USSR); John G Thompson (USA)
1974	Enrico Bombieri (Italy); David Mumford (USA)
1978	Pierre Deligne (Belgium); Charles Fefferman (USA); G A Margulis (USSR); Daniel Quillen (USA)
1982	Alain Connes (France); William Thurston (USA); S T Yau (USA)
1986	Simon Donaldson (UK); Gerd Faltings (West Germany); Michael Freedman (USA)
1990	Vladimir Drinfeld (USSR); Vaughan F R Jones (USA); Shigefumi Mori (Japan); Edward Witten (USA)
1994	L J Bourgain (USA/France); P-L Lions (France); J-C Yoccoz (France); E I Zelmanov (USA)
1998	Richard E Borcherds (UK); W Timothy Gowers (UK); Maxim Kontsevich (Russia); Curtis T McMullen (USA)

Enrico Fermi Award

Named in honour of Enrico Fermi, the atomic pioneer, the $100,000 award is given in recognition of outstanding scientific and technical achievement in the field of nuclear energy. The award is announced by the White House.

Year	Winner(s)
1954	Enrico Fermi
1955	no award
1956	John von Neumann
1957	Ernest O Lawrence
1958	Eugene P Wigner
1959	Glenn T Seaborg
1960	no award
1961	Hans A Bethe
1962	Edward Teller
1963	J Robert Oppenheimer
1964	Hyman G Rickover
1965	no award
1966	Otto Hahn, Lise Meitner, and Fritz Strassman
1967	no award
1968	John A Wheeler
1969	Walter H Zinn
1970	Norris E Bradbury
1971	Shields Warren and Stafford L Warren
1972	Manson Benedict
1973	no award
1974	no award
1975	no award
1976	William L Russell
1978	Harold M Agnew and Wolfgang K H Panofsky
1979	no award
1980	Alvin M Weinberg and Rudolf E Peiris
1981	W Bennett Lewis
1982	Herbert Anderson and Seth Neddermeyer
1983	Alexander Hollaender and John Lawrence
1984	Robert R Wilson and Georges Vendryès
1985	Norman C Rasmussen and Marshall N Rosenblath
1986	Ernest D Courant and M Stanley Livingston
1987	Luis W Alvarez and Gerald F Tape
1988	Richard B Setlow and Victor F Weisskopf
1989	no award
1990	George A Cowan and Robley D Evans
1991	no award
1992	Leon M Lederman, Harold Brown, and John S Foster Jr
1993	Freeman J Dyson and Liane B Russell
1994	no award
1995	Ugo Fano and Martin Kamen
1996	Richard Garwin, Mortimer Elkind, and H Rodney Withers
1997	no award
1998	Maurice Goldhaber and Michael E Phelps

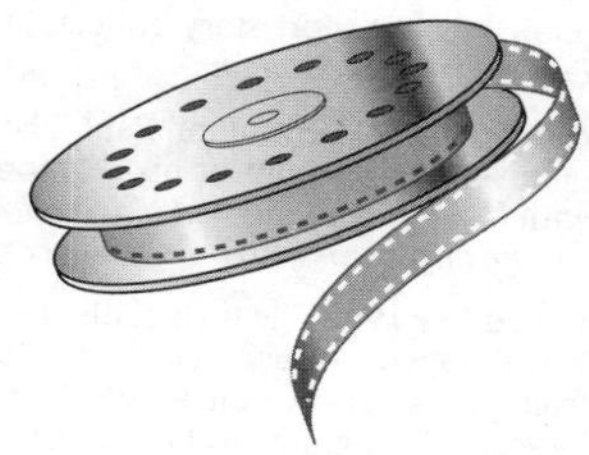

ARTS AND MEDIA

The Year in Review

2 July 1998–4 October 1998 Over 60 paintings by the Russian painter Marc Chagall are shown at the Royal Academy of Art in London.

August 1998 British writer Julian Barnes publishes his novel *England, England.*

30 August 1998 Simon Rattle conducts his final symphony as conductor of the City of Birmingham Symphony Orchestra, in England. His successor is Finnish conductor Sakari Oramo.

September 1998 The shortlist for the Booker Prize for fiction is announced: Beryl Bainbridge, *Master Georgie;* Julian Barnes, *England, England;* Martin Booth, *The Industry of Souls;* Patrick McCabe, *Breakfast on Pluto;* Ian McEwan, *Amsterdam;* and Magnus Mills, *The Restraint of Beasts.*

9 September 1998 The Royal Opera House in London, England, announces that it will close due to serious financial problems, cancelling almost all of its 1999 performances, in an emergency measure to help rescue the debt-ridden company.

13 September 1998 The 50th annual Emmy Awards are held in Los Angeles, California. The National Broadcasting Corporation (NBC) sitcom *Frasier* wins the award for best comedy for the fifth consecutive year. The American Broadcasting Corporation (ABC) programme *The Practice* is named best drama series.

19 September 1998 The opera *A Streetcar Named Desire,* based on the 1947 play by Tennessee Williams, opens at the San Francisco Opera, California, with music by the London Symphony Orchestra conductor laureate André Previn.

22 September 1998 The erotic play *The Blue Room,* adapted from Arthur Schnitzler's *La Ronde* by David Hare, opens at the Donmar Warehouse, London, England, starring Nicole Kidman and Iain Glen.

October 1998 *Time Out* magazine of London, England, names British musician David Bowie the most influential pop star of the last 30 years.

October 1998 British writer Pat Barker publishes her novel *Another World.*

October 1998 The Portuguese writer José Saramago wins the Nobel Prize for Literature. He is the first writer in Portuguese to win the prize.

October 1998 US arts administrator Michael Kaiser becomes director of the Royal Opera House in London, England.

October 1998 US writer Alice Walker publishes her novel *By the Light of My Father's Smile.*

October 1998 US writer Hunter Thompson publishes his novel *The Rum Diary,* which he began nearly 40 years ago.

October 1998 US writer Tom Wolfe publishes his novel *A Man in Full.*

27 October 1998 English novelist Ian McEwan wins the Booker Prize for fiction for his satirical novel *Amsterdam.*

November 1998 British actor Ewan McGregor stars in the play *Little Malcolm and His Struggle Against the*

Eunuchs at the Hampstead Theatre in London, England.

November 1998 The American Air Museum at Duxford, Cambridgeshire, England, designed by British architects Norman Foster and Partners, wins the Royal Institute of British Architects Stirling Prize.

November 1998 The Museum of Scotland, designed by Anglo-Scottish architects Benson and Forsyth, opens in Edinburgh, Scotland.

1 November 1998 A comprehensive exhibition of the work of Jackson Pollock opens at the Museum of Modern Art (MoMA) in New York, USA. The exhibition opens at the Tate Gallery in London, England, in March 1999.

13 November 1998 The MTV annual music awards ceremony is held in Milan, Italy. British pop group the Spice Girls wins awards for best group and best pop act; and British group All Saints wins the award for best breakthrough act.

21 November 1998 Principal conductor designate Kurt Masur conducts his first concert in his new role in the London Philharmonic Orchestra in London, England.

24 November 1998 US chat show host Oprah Winfrey and two partners launch the first cable television station targeted exclusively at a female audience.

30 November 1998 The *Evening Standard* Theatre Awards are held in London, England. Best actor: Kevin Spacey for *The Iceman Cometh;* best director: Howard Davies for *The Iceman Cometh* and *Flight;* best actress: Sinead Cusack for *Our Lady of Sligo;* best play: Michael Frayn for *Copenhagen;* best musical: *Oklahoma!* at the Royal National Theatre; most promising playwright: Mark Ravenhill for *Handbag*. Nicole Kidman receives a special award for her performance in *The Blue Room.* Almeida director Jonathan Kent receives the outstanding achievement award.

December 1998 *Talk on Corners* by the Irish pop group the Corrs is the best-selling album in the UK for 1998.

December 1998 A painting by contemporary British artist Lucian Freud, *Naked Portrait with Reflection,* sells at Sotheby's in London, England for £2.8 million. It is the highest price ever paid for a contemporary work in Europe.

December 1998 British artist Chris Ofili becomes the first painter since 1985 and the first black artist ever to win the Turner Prize. His work incorporates elements of popular culture, and he uses unusual media, such as elephant dung.

December 1998 Cher's single 'Believe' is the best-selling single for 1998 in the UK.

December 1998 US author Alice Munro publishes her short-story collection *The Love of a Good Woman.*

December 1998 US author Paul Theroux publishes an account of his relationship with V S Naipaul, *Sir Vidia's Shadow: A Friendship across Five Continents.*

17 December 1998 The financially troubled Royal Opera House receives a boost from the Arts Council of England, increasing its grant by 11% to £16 million for 1999 and to £20 million for 2000 and 2001.

January 1999 Former South African president F W de Klerk publishes his memoirs, *The Last Trek: A New Beginning,* in which he reveals great animosity between himself and President Nelson Mandela, with whom he shared the Nobel Peace Prize in 1993.

11 January 1999 Ted Hughes posthumously wins the T S Eliot Prize for *Birthday Letters,* a collection about his relationship with Sylvia Plath and the best-selling volume of poetry ever.

23 January 1999–18 April 1999 The exhibition *Monet in the 20th Century,* a collection of 80 paintings by the French impressionist Claude Monet, is held at the Royal Academy, London, England. Tickets cost a record £9 each, and a record 813,000 people visit the exhibition.

24 January 1999 The Golden Globe Awards are held in Los Angeles, California. Best drama: *Saving Private Ryan;* best comedy or musical: *Shakespeare in Love;* best director: Steven Spielberg for *Saving Private Ryan;* best actress, drama: Cate Blanchett for *Elizabeth;* best actor, drama: Jim Carey for *The Truman Show;* best actress, musical or comedy: Gwyneth Paltrow for *Shakespeare in Love;* best actor, musical or comedy: Michael Caine for *Little Voice;* best screenplay: Marc Norman and Tom Stoppard for *Shakespeare in Love.*

26 January 1999 British poet Ted Hughes posthumously wins the Whitbread Book of the Year Award for his collection of poetry *Birthday Letters.* It is the second year in a row that he has won the prize.

28 January 1999 An exhibition of more than 50 paintings by David Hockney opens at the Pompidou Centre in Paris, France.

24 February 1999 The 41st Grammy Awards are held in Los Angeles, California. US vocalist Lauryn Hill wins five awards, more than any other female artist in the history of the awards. Canadian vocalist Celine Dion wins three awards for her song 'My Heart Will Go On' from the 1998 Academy Award-winning film *Titanic.*

March 1999 UK writer John le Carré publishes his novel *Single and Single.*

7 March 1999 Stanley Kubrick, director, producer, screenwriter, and cinematographer, dies (70). His final film, *Eyes Wide Shut,* an erotic psychodrama starring husband and wife Tom Cruise and Nicole Kidman, is scheduled for release on 16 July.

21 March 1999 The 71st annual Academy Awards are held in Los Angeles, California, hosted by US actress and comedian Whoopi Goldberg. The big winners are the romantic comedy *Shakespeare in Love* which wins seven Oscars, and the World War II film *Saving Private Ryan,* which wins five.

April 1999 *The Journals of George Eliot,* edited by Margaret Harris and Judith Johnston, are published for the first time in their entirety.

April 1999 British writer Germaine Greer publishes *The Whole Woman,* a review of the feminist movement over the past 30 years.

April 1999 Indian-born English writer Salman Rushdie publishes his novel *The Ground Beneath Her Feet.*

April 1999 US writer David Guterson publishes his novel *East of the Mountains.*

12 April 1999 British architect Norman Foster, whose firm designed such high-profile buildings as the world's largest airport in Hong Kong, the Great Court for the British Museum in London, England, and a new German Parliament in Berlin, Germany, is named as the 1999 recipient of the prestigious Pritzker Architecture Prize. He will formally receive the award on 7 June 1999 in Berlin.

May 1999 Indian writer Vikram Seth publishes his novel *An Equal Music.*

May 1999 US writer Thomas Harris publishes his novel *Hannibal,* the sequel to *The Silence of the Lambs.*

18 May 1999 The British Museum announces the receipt of its biggest donation in history, £20 million from the Weston foundation for construction of the Great Court, designed by 1999 Pritzker Architecture Prize winner Norman Foster.

18 May 1999 The production *De La Guarda,* performed by a team of 20 Argentine acrobats, opens at the Roundhouse theatre in London, England.

19 May 1999 English poet Andrew Motion succeeds Ted Hughes as UK poet laureate.

19 May 1999 The long-awaited prequel *Star Wars Episode I: The Phantom Menace* opens to great fanfare in the USA, directed by George Lucas and starring Liam Neeson, Ewan McGregor, and Samuel L Jackson. It earns a record-breaking $28.5 million/£17.8 million in its first 24 hours.

23 May 1999 The Cannes Film Festival's Palme d'Or award goes to the little-known Belgian film *Rosetta,* directed by Luc and Jean-Pierre Dardenne and starring Emilie Dequenne.

28 May 1999 Italian artist Leonardo da Vinci's masterpiece *The Last Supper,* completed in 1498, is back in view at the monastery of Santa Maria delle Grazie in Milan, Italy, after a controversial 21-year restoration.

28 May 1999 The follow-up from the writer and producers of *Four Weddings and a Funeral* opens; *Notting Hill* stars Hugh Grant and Julia Roberts.

2 June 1999–26 June 1999 The last paintings of British artist Patrick Heron, who died less than three months before, are exhibited at the Waddington Galleries, London, England.

7 June 1999 British conductor Mark Elder becomes conductor of the Hallé orchestra, Britain's oldest professional orchestra, in Manchester, England.

9 June 1999–5 September 1999 The exhibition of Rembrandt self-portraits *Rembrandt by Himself* is held at the National Gallery, London, England.

12 June 1999 The 14 zones of the Millennium Dome, whose shape and content were heavily debated, are finally named. They are Talk, Learning, Body, Home Planet, Shared Ground, Mind, Journey, Living Island, Self Portrait, Play, Rest, Faith, Money, and Work.

Funding the Arts: Annual Grants from the Arts Councils

1997–98

Region	Total grants (£)
Arts Council of England	123,672,313
Arts Council of Wales	13,182,000
Scottish Arts Council	25,706,000

Source: Data from the Arts Councils of England and Wales, and the Scottish Arts Council

23 June 1999 Simon Rattle, formerly conductor of the City of Birmingham Symphony Orchestra, becomes conductor of the Berlin Philharmonic Orchestra.

Television and Radio

Top 50 Programmes on Terrestrial Television in the UK

1998

Rank	Programme	Channel	Transmission date	Number of viewers
1	*World Cup Argentina–England*	ITV	30 June	23,782,000
2	*World Cup Romania–England*	ITV	22 June	19,480,000
3	*World Cup Colombia–England*	BBC1	26 June	19,131,000
4	*World Cup Post-Match*	ITV	22 June	19,067,000
5	*Coronation Street (Monday)*	ITV	16 November	18,620,000
6	*Coronation Street (Wednesday)*	ITV	18 November	18,524,000
7	*Coronation Street (Sunday)*	ITV	4 January	18,371,000
8	*Coronation Street (Friday)*	ITV	16 January	17,392,000
9	*EastEnders (Tuesday)*	BBC1	29 December	16,907,000
10	*Heartbeat*	ITV	22 February	16,451,000
11	*Celebrity Stars in Their Eyes*	ITV	2 December	16,337,000
12	*EastEnders (Monday)*	BBC1	28 December	15,941,000
13	*EastEnders (Thursday)*	BBC1	3 December	15,758,000
14	*Casualty*	BBC1	28 February	15,741,000
15	*World Cup Brazil–France*	BBC1	12 July	15,647,000
16	*Men Behaving Badly*	BBC1	28 December	15,193,000
17	*Forrest Gump*	BBC1	1 January	15,080,000
18	*EastEnders (Friday)*	BBC1	25 December	15,043,000
19	*World Cup France–Croatia*	BBC1	8 July	14,621,000
20	*World Cup Brazil–Holland*	ITV	7 July	14,095,000
21	*EastEnders (Wednesday)*	BBC1	7 January	14,016,000
22	*Weather*	BBC1	25 December	13,891,000
23	*You've Been Framed*	ITV	13 September	13,859,000
24	*EastEnders (Friday)*	BBC1	9 January	13,811,000
25	*Goodnight Mr Tom*	ITV	25 October	13,811,000
26	*Perfect Day for Christmas*	BBC1	25 December	13,468,000
27	*Birds of a Feather*	BBC1	19 January	13,303,000
28	*World Cup Coronation Street Special*	ITV	12 July	13,279,000
29	*Emmerdale (Tuesday)*	ITV	10 February	13,276,000
30	*National Lottery Live*	BBC1	28 February	13,195,000
31	*National Lottery Draw*	BBC1	8 July	13,037,000

(continued)

Top 50 Programmes on Terrestrial Television in the UK *(continued)*

Rank	Programme	Channel	Transmission date	Number of viewers
32	*The Cruise*	BBC1	13 January	12,863,000
33	*London's Burning*	ITV	11 January	12,823,000
34	*Diana: the Secrets Behind the Crash*	ITV	3 June	12,786,000
35	*News*	BBC1	25 December	12,748,000
36	*World Cup Scotland–Morocco*	BBC1	23 June	12,670,000
37	*Emmerdale (Thursday)*	ITV	7 May	12,634,000
38	*Airline*	ITV	20 March	12,559,000
39	*Emmerdale (Wednesday)*	ITV	14 January	12,522,000
40	*Who Wants to be a Millionaire*	ITV	13 September	12,472,000
41	*Inspector Morse*	ITV	11 November	12,393,000
42	*The Bill*	ITV	30 January	12,338,000
43	*They Think It's All Over*	BBC1	25 December	12,313,000
44	*Dinner Ladies*	BBC1	12 November	12,238,000
45	*Holidays From Hell*	ITV	2 November	12,179,000
46	*World Cup Pre Match*	ITV	30 June	12,135,000
47	*Police, Camera, Action*	ITV	20 January	12,112,000
48	*World Cup Brazil–Scotland*	BBC1	10 June	12,092,000
49	*Before They Were Famous*	BBC1	25 December	11,933,000
50	*Coming Home*	ITV	13 April	11,872,000

Source: Taylor Nelson Sofres TV Research

Top 30 Drama Programmes Shown on Terrestrial Television in the UK

1998

Rank	Programme	Channel	Transmission date	Number of viewers
1	*Coronation Street*	ITV	16 November	18,620,000
2	*Coronation Street*	ITV	18 November	18,524,000
3	*Coronation Street*	ITV	4 January	18,371,000
4	*Coronation Street*	ITV	16 January	17,392,000
5	*EastEnders*	BBC1	29 December	16,907,000
6	*Heartbeat*	ITV	22 February	16,451,000
7	*EastEnders*	BBC1	28 December	15,941,000
8	*EastEnders*	BBC1	3 December	15,758,000
9	*Casualty*	BBC1	28 February	15,741,000
10	*EastEnders*	BBC1	25 December	15,043,000
11	*EastEnders*	BBC1	7 January	14,016,000
12	*EastEnders*	BBC1	9 January	13,811,000
13	*Goodnight Mr Tom*	ITV	25 October	13,811,000
14	*World Cup Coronation Street Special*	ITV	12 July	13,279,000
15	*Emmerdale*	ITV	10 February	13,276,000
16	*London's Burning*	ITV	11 January	12,823,000
17	*Emmerdale*	ITV	7 May	12,634,000
18	*Emmerdale*	ITV	14 January	12,522,000
19	*Inspector Morse*	ITV	11 November	12,393,000
20	*The Bill*	ITV	30 January	12,338,000
21	*Coming Home*	ITV	13 April	11,872,000
22	*Where the Heart is*	ITV	7 June	11,834,000
23	*March in Windy City*	ITV	25 March	11,585,000
24	*Grafters*	ITV	27 October	11,485,000
25	*Taggart*	ITV	1 March	11,413,000
26	*Midsomer Murders*	ITV	22 March	11,364,000
27	*Real Women*	BBC1	26 February	11,069,000
28	*Emmerdale*	ITV	25 December	10,958,000
29	*Jonathan Creek*	BBC1	28 February	10,917,000
30	*Ballykissangel*	BBC1	8 March	10,913,000

Source: Taylor Nelson Sofres TV Research

Top 30 Films Shown on Terrestrial Television in the UK

1998

Rank	Programme	Channel	Transmission date	Number of viewers
1	*Forrest Gump*	BBC1	1 January	15,080,000
2	*Die Hard with a Vengeance*	ITV	13 October	11,582,000
3	*Mrs Brown*	BBC1	27 December	11,532,000
4	*Indiana Jones and the Last Crusade*	BBC1	28 December	10,926,000
5	*Beverly Hills Cop 3*	BBC1	7 March	10,782,000
6	*Jurassic Park*	BBC1	8 February	9,896,000
7	*Speed*	BBC1	22 December	9,803,000
8	*Babe*	BBC1	25 December	9,258,000
9	*Moment of Truth*	ITV	3 October	9,172,000
10	*Waterworld*	BBC1	5 September	9,015,000
11	*The Three Musketeers*	ITV	30 December	8,861,000
12	*Stargate*	BBC1	25 January	8,735,000
13	*Kindergarten Cop*	BBC1	18 January	8,705,000
14	*Seven*	BBC1	11 October	8,701,000
15	*The Bodyguard*	ITV	11 May	8,669,000
16	*Licence to Kill*	ITV	24 August	8,652,000
17	*An Unsuitable Job for a Woman*	ITV	19 February	8,584,000
18	*Home Alone*	ITV	29 December	8,574,000
19	*Philadelphia*	ITV	14 December	8,524,000
20	*Lethal Weapon 3*	ITV	1 June	8,497,000
21	*Robin Hood: Prince of Thieves*	BBC1	22 August	8,394,000
22	*Maverick*	ITV	14 October	8,296,000
23	*Lethal Weapon 2*	ITV	21 January	8,074,000
24	*Cool Runnings*	ITV	3 September	8,061,000
25	*Addams Family Values*	BBC1	15 August	8,029,000
26	*The Naked Gun*	BBC1	10 January	7,996,000
27	*Pretty Woman*	ITV	19 December	7,949,000
28	*Die Hard II*	ITV	18 May	7,792,000
29	*Sleepless in Seattle*	ITV	27 April	7,763,000
30	*Frenchman's Creek*	ITV	20 December	7,411,000

Source: Taylor Nelson Sofres TV Research

Top 30 Light Entertainment Programmes on Terrestrial Television in the UK

1998

Rank	Programme	Channel	Transmission date	Number of viewers
1	*Celebrity Stars in Their Eyes*	ITV	2 December	16,337,000
2	*Men Behaving Badly*	BBC1	28 December	15,193,000
3	*You've Been Framed*	ITV	13 September	13,859,000
4	*Birds of a Feather*	BBC1	19 January	13,303,000
5	*National Lottery Live*	BBC1	28 February	13,195,000
6	*National Lottery Draw*	BBC1	8 July	13,037,000
7	*Who Wants to be a Millionaire*	ITV	13 September	12,472,000
8	*They Think It's All Over*	BBC1	25 December	12,313,000
9	*Dinner Ladies*	BBC1	12 November	12,238,000
10	*Harry Enfield and Chums*	BBC1	28 December	11,786,000
11	*Only Fools and Horses*	BBC1	2 January	11,639,000
12	*Vicar of Dibley*	BBC1	22 January	11,612,000
13	*Men for Sale*	ITV	2 December	11,521,000
14	*Royal Variety Christmas Special*	BBC1	20 December	11,235,000
15	*You've Been Framed Christmas Special*	ITV	25 December	11,190,000
16	*The Kids From It'll be Alright on the Night*	ITV	4 May	11,185,000
17	*National TV Awards*	ITV	28 October	10,903,000
18	*This is Your Life*	BBC1	16 February	10,705,000
19	*Sunday Night at the Palladium*	ITV	15 March	10,622,000
20	*Blind Date*	ITV	17 January	10,490,000
21	*Tarrant on TV*	ITV	25 January	10,368,000
22	*Stars in Their Eyes*	ITV	21 March	10,357,000
23	*French and Saunders Special*	BBC1	26 December	10,305,000
24	*21 Years of It'll be Alright on the Night*	ITV	24 January	10,284,000
25	*Stars in Their Eyes Final*	ITV	13 June	10,150,000
26	*Audience with the Bee Gees*	ITV	7 November	10,115,000
27	*Dennis Norden's 3rd Laughter File*	ITV	5 December	10,003,000
28	*Dennis Norden's Laughter File*	ITV	31 January	9,852,000
29	*Stars in Their Eyes Result*	ITV	13 June	9,742,000
30	*Duck Patrol*	ITV	19 July	9,707,000

Source: Taylor Nelson Sofres TV Research

Top 30 Sports Programmes on Terrestrial Television by Rating in the UK

1998

Rank	Programme	Channel	Transmission date	Number of viewers
1	*World Cup: Argentina–England*	ITV	30 June	23,782,000
2	*World Cup: Romania–England*	ITV	22 June	19,480,000
3	*World Cup: Colombia–England*	BBC1	26 June	19,131,000
4	*World Cup: Post-Match*	ITV	22 June	19,067,000
5	*World Cup: Brazil–France*	BBC1	12 July	15,647,000
6	*World Cup: France–Croatia*	BBC1	8 July	14,621,000
7	*World Cup: Brazil–Holland*	ITV	7 July	14,095,000
8	*World Cup: Scotland–Morocco*	BBC1	23 June	12,670,000
9	*World Cup: Pre-Match*	ITV	30 June	12,135,000
10	*World Cup: Brazil–Scotland*	BBC1	10 June	12,092,000
11	*World Cup: England–Tunisia*	BBC1	15 June	11,432,000
12	*Grand National*	BBC1	4 April	11,390,000
13	*World Cup: Brazil–Chile*	BBC1	27 June	10,632,000
14	*World Cup: Holland–Yugoslavia*	BBC1	29 June	10,546,000
15	*World Cup: Nigeria–Denmark*	ITV	28 June	10,321,000
16	*World Cup: Jamaica–Croatia*	ITV	14 June	10,234,000
17	*Champions' League Football*	ITV	4 March	10,229,000
18	*World Cup: Germany–Croatia*	BBC1	4 July	10,076,000
19	*World Cup: Scotland–Norway*	ITV	16 June	9,996,000
20	*World Cup: Brazil–Morocco*	ITV	16 June	9,897,000
21	*Big Match Champions' League*	ITV	9 December	9,870,000
22	*World Cup: Germany–USA*	BBC1	15 June	9,780,000
23	*World Cup: Italy–Cameroon*	ITV	17 June	9,615,000
24	*The Big Match*	ITV	18 March	9,605,000
25	*World Cup: Morocco–Norway*	ITV	10 June	9,265,000
26	*World Cup: Brazil–Denmark*	ITV	3 July	9,211,000
27	*World Cup: Holland–Belgium*	BBC1	13 June	9,099,000
28	*World Cup: France–Saudi Arabia*	BBC1	18 June	9,061,000
29	*World Cup: Cameroon–Austria*	BBC1	11 June	8,736,000
30	*European Cup Final*	BBC1	13 May	8,728,000

Source: Taylor Nelson Sofres TV Research

Top 20 Programmes Shown on Satellite Television in the UK

1998

Rank	Programme	Channel	Transmission date	Number of viewers
1	*Football*	Sky Sports 2	25 January	2,165,000
2	*Friends*	Sky 1	31 May	2,106,000
3	*Football Special*	Sky Sports 1	16 December	1,949,000
4	*International Football Live*	Sky Sports 2	18 November	1,847,000
5	*Football Review*	Sky Sports 2	11 February	1,819,000
6	*Twister*	Sky Premier	21 March	1,814,000
7	*Caribbean Uncovered*	Sky 1	15 March	1,768,000
8	*The Nutty Professor*	Sky Premier	11 April	1,652,000
9	*Super Sunday Live*	Sky Sports 1	6 December	1,643,000
10	*Independence Day*	Sky Premier	14 February	1,624,000
11	*Eraser*	Sky Premier	28 February	1,608,000
12	*The Simpsons*	Sky 1	31 May	1,549,000
13	*Futbol Mundial*	Sky Sports 2	29 March	1,482,000
14	*Hollywood Sex*	Sky 1	5 April	1,466,000
15	*Greece Uncovered*	Sky 1	23 August	1,414,000
16	*Monday Night Football*	Sky Sports 1	23 February	1,405,000
17	*Football Analysis*	Sky Sports 1	16 December	1,385,000
18	*International Football*	Sky Sports 2	5 September	1,385,000
19	*Mission Impossible*	Sky Premier	17 January	1,347,000
20	*Magic*	Sky 1	3 February	1,294,000

Source: Taylor Nelson Sofres TV Research

Top 20 Sports Programmes Shown on Satellite Television in the UK

1998

Rank	Programme	Channel	Transmission date	Number of viewers
1	*Football*	Sky Sports 2	25 January	2,165,000
2	*Football Special*	Sky Sports 1	16 December	1,949,000
3	*International Football Live*	Sky Sports 2	18 November	1,847,000
4	*Football Review*	Sky Sports 2	11 February	1,819,000
5	*Super Sunday Live*	Sky Sports 1	6 December	1,643,000
6	*Futbol Mundial*	Sky Sports 2	29 March	1,482,000
7	*Monday Night Football*	Sky Sports 1	23 February	1,405,000
8	*Football Analysis*	Sky Sports 1	16 December	1,385,000
9	*International Football*	Sky Sports 2	5 September	1,385,000
10	*Golf*	Sky Sports 2	17 March	1,188,000
11	*Super Sunday Talkback*	Sky Sports 1	6 December	1,095,000
12	*Football Chat*	Sky Sports 2	11 November	990,000
13	*Football League*	Sky Sports 2	25 May	984,000
14	*Monday Football*	Sky Sports 1	28 September	891,000
15	*Football League Review*	Sky Sports 3	7 April	759,000
16	*Super Sunday*	Sky Sports 3	15 March	724,000
17	*Football Intro*	Sky Sports 1	24 September	703,000
18	*Super Sunday Intro*	Sky Sports 1	6 December	632,000
19	*Gillette World Sport*	Sky Sports 2	3 May	609,000
20	*Rugby Union Live*	Sky Sports 2	5 December	566,000

Source: Taylor Nelson Sofres TV Research

Top 20 Films Shown on Satellite Television in the UK

1998

Rank	Programme	Channel	Transmission date	Number of viewers
1	*Twister*	Sky Premier	21 March	1,814,000
2	*The Nutty Professor*	Sky Premier	11 April	1,652,000
3	*Independence Day*	Sky Premier	14 February	1,624,000
4	*Eraser*	Sky Premier	28 February	1,608,000
5	*Mission Impossible*	Sky Premier	17 January	1,347,000
6	*Magic*	Sky 1	3 February	1,294,000
7	*Patriot*	Sky Premier	3 October	1,149,000
8	*Stargate*	Sky 1	8 April	1,056,000
9	*Metro*	Sky Premier	8 August	1,015,000
10	*The Glimmer Man*	Sky Premier	13 June	1,015,000
11	*Stargate*	Sky 1	15 April	1,000,000
12	*Liar Liar*	Sky Premier	14 November	981,000
13	*Ransom*	Sky Premier	25 July	950,000
14	*Last Man Standing*	Sky Premier	24 January	929,000
15	*Dante's Peak*	Sky Premier	26 December	882,000
16	*The Cable Guy*	Sky Moviemax	6 February	881,000
17	*Stargate S G-1*	Sky 1	26 August	855,000
18	*Long Kiss Goodnight*	Sky Premier	30 May	854,000
19	*Daylight*	Sky Premier	12 September	843,000
20	*Hackers*	Sky Premier	31 January	838,000

Source: Taylor Nelson Sofres TV Research

Average Daily Television Usage per Household in the UK

(– = not applicable. In hours.)

Year	Total[1]	ITV	BBC1	BBC2	Channel 4	Channel 5	Other
1969	4.5	2.4	2.1	–	–	–	–
1972	4.8	2.7	1.9	0.3	–	–	–
1976	5.1	2.7	2.1	0.4	–	–	–
1980	5.1	2.5	2.0	0.6	–	–	–
1982	4.9	2.4	1.9	0.6	–	–	–
1986	5.3	2.4	1.9	0.6	0.5	–	–
1990	5.1	2.3	1.9	0.5	0.5	–	–
1995	5.9	2.2	1.9	0.7	0.7	–	–
1998	5.8	1.9	1.7	0.7	0.6	0.3	0.6

[1] Totals may not add due to rounding and the small percentage of other (non-terrestrial) viewing.

Source: Taylor Nelson Sofres TV Research

Average Daily Hours of Viewing by Age and Social Grade in the UK

(In hours.)

Category	1994	1998
Socio-economic group		
adults ABC1	3.2	3.3
adults C2	3.7	3.9
adults DE	4.2	4.6
Age		
4–9	2.6	2.5
10–15	2.7	2.5
16–24	2.8	2.7
25–34	3.5	3.5
35–44	3.4	3.3
45–54	3.6	3.6
55 or over	4.8	4.9
All individuals	3.6	3.6

Source: Taylor Nelson Sofres TV Research

Household Penetration of TV Sets, VCRs, Satellite, and Cable Television in the UK

(– = not applicable.)

Year	All households	TV households	TV households (%)	Receiving colour (%)	2+ TV sets (%)	VCR (%)	Teletext (%)	Satellite households	Cable households
1970	18,364,000	16,895,000	92	2	3	–	–	–	–
1975	19,144,000	18,570,000	97	40	6	–	–	–	–
1980	20,322,000	19,916,000	98	71	19	–	–	–	–
1985	21,242,000	20,605,000	97	86	39	28	12	–	–
1990	22,122,000	21,458,000	97	93	46	61	33	–	–
1995	23,902,000	23,212,000	97	98	55	76	57	–	–
1998	24,539,000	23,804,000	99	99	59	82	70	4,101,000	2,688,000

Source: Taylor Nelson Sofres TV Research

Proportion of Factual Programmes in Peak-Time Television in the UK

(In percentages. – = not applicable.)

Channel	1995–96	1996–97	1997–98
BBC1	49	46	51
BBC2	51	51	50
ITV	28	29	32
Channel 4	52	49	50
Channel 5	–	–	36

Source: *BBC Annual Report 1998, copyright © BBC 1998, with permission*

Proportion of UK-Produced Programmes Shown on Television in the UK

Figures are for peak-time viewing. (– = not applicable.)

Channel	1996–97	1997–98
BBC1	82%	84%
ITV	80%	82%
BBC2	64%	63%
C4	60%	64%
C5	–	46%
All BBC	73%	74%
ITV/C4	70%	73%
All inc C5	–	64%

Source: *BBC Annual Report 1998, copyright © BBC 1998, with permission*

Digital Television and Radio

BY BARRY FOX

UK Developments in Digital TV and Radio

In 1936 Britain pioneered all-electronic TV, with the world's first regular service aimed at home viewers. In 1999 the UK became the test bed for mass-market digital terrestrial TV and radio.

Whereas the USA has seen digital TV as a way of delivering a few channels of high definition (HD) pictures to viewers willing to buy new HD receivers, the UK has adopted a European system which delivers more programmes of standard (analogue PAL system) quality. A set-top box connects the aerial and an ordinary TV set.

BSkyB service

Rupert Murdoch's BSkyB launched a digital satellite service in October 1998, with a unique offer. Anyone who agreed to connect the receiver to a telephone line paid a reduced price for the set-top box and dish aerial. This lets BSkyB's sister company British Interactive Broadcasting offer an online shopping service, called Open, through an ordinary TV.

On Digital

The next month, November 1998, the existing national broadcasters (BBC, ITV, Channels 4 and 5) and new pay broadcaster On Digital, launched a digital terrestrial service. Viewers who signed up to pay for On Digital's pay channels paid a reduced price for the receiver box which connects to an existing TV aerial.

Free receivers

In June 1999 both the rival services raised the stakes by offering free receivers to anyone who signed up for a subscription. Just like the cellphone companies, which have long given away free phones, the broadcasters must now make their money from customer use.

Other digital possibilities

By moving early into digital TV, the UK has given local set-makers a lead over foreign manufacturers. But by waiting a little longer other countries can exploit new twists to the technology. Some will offer terrestrial TV reception on the move, for instance on trains and buses. The Republic of Ireland is trying to make home receivers work like miniature transmitters, so that the viewers can interact, vote, or shop from home without a phone line.

Cheaper digital radio sets

Although the BBC and some British commercial radio stations began broadcasting digital radio in 1995 to encourage manufacturers to make DAB receivers, this happened more slowly than expected. The first consumer DAB car radios came in two parts, one bulky and stored out of sight and one neat in the dashboard, and cost around £1000. The launch of full-scale commercial digital radio and more digital programmes from the BBC, at the end of 1999, should ensure that single-unit car radios, portables, and home hifi DAB receivers become available for a few hundred pounds.

How Digital Television Works

An analogue television station needs up to 8 MHz of frequency space. Two terrestrial transmitters cannot use the same frequency within several hundred kilometres of each other because even weak signals from one will interfere with strong signals from the other. Therefore, each country can only have a few television channels.

A satellite can transmit more channels, but its transmitters cover a wide geographical area. So the satellite usually delivers a handful of channels in different languages to several adjacent countries.

Converting a transmission system from analogue to digital multiplies the number of programme channels it can deliver, by up to ten. The bitstream can be used to carry a few programmes with better-than-analogue picture quality, or many programmes with compromised clarity.

Digital television needs only one-hundredth the transmission power of analogue television. As a result, the digital signals can slot between the analogue frequencies, in the so-called 'taboo' channels which cannot be used for analogue broadcasting because of interference risks. Because the digital terrestrial frequencies are similar to existing analogue frequencies, existing aerials should be able to receive new digital broadcasts.

Once digital television is ubiquitous, broadcasters can plan the end of analogue broadcasting. This will release more frequencies either for digital broadcasting or mobile radio.

Viewers can use a set-top box which converts the digital signals into analogue television, which an existing television set displays. New television sets incorporate the digital circuitry. Most have a wide-format screen, with 16:9 aspect ratio to do justice to movies and

widescreen sports broadcasts. Conventional television sets, with 4:3 screens, may show a slight letterboxing effect, with black borders at the top and bottom of the picture.

National broadcasters will usually 'simulcast' existing 4:3 analogue programmes in digital widescreen, 'free to air'. Extra programmes can be encrypted, and available only if the viewer pays a fee, either by subscription or special event payment. Pay viewing is controlled by a smart card, a credit card with a microchip that slots into the receiver to authorize decoding.

The digital television system for Europe was developed in the 1990s by an independent voluntary industry group, the Digital Video Broadcasting Group (DVB). The DVB's standards were then simply rubber-stamped by Europe's governments and official bodies. Some services have already started.

The impetus for DVB came from the commercial failure of the high-definition television system developed in the 1980s as an official European research project, Eureka 95. High Definition Multiplexed Analogue Components (HD-MAC) was a hybrid system; the transmitted pictures were analogue but they travelled with digitally coded 'helper' signals which a suitable television set could use to make the images much wider and clearer than for conventional television. Although HD-MAC worked, high-definition receivers were prohibitively expensive.

There are three main DVB standards for cable, satellite, and terrestrial broadcasting. All are based on MPEG-2 coding, the digital compression standard set by the Motion Picture Experts Group of the International Electrotechnical Commission (IEC) and the International Standards Organization (ISO). The main differences are in the way the compressed signal is packaged for transmission.

Terrestrial digital television uses a system similar to that developed for digital radio. Instead of transmitting one wide channel, the broadcaster transmits several thousand narrow sub-channels, packed tightly together. The digital code is split into a similar number of streams, so each channel carries fewer bits of code each second, and the bits in each channel are widely spaced apart in time. Unwanted reflections arrive in the gaps and the receiver rejects them.

The European DVB and North American digital terrestrial systems are not compatible. The main difference is that the American system was designed to bridge the gap between televisions and computers, with emphasis on high-definition viewing, whereas the European system is aimed primarily at squeezing more programme channels into available frequency space. The USA and several countries in Europe, including the UK, have digital satellite services. Cable services are converting to digital delivery.

Some observers fear that although the basic systems follow agreed standards, there is room for individual broadcasters to use their own proprietary systems to control pay viewing. This could block the design of a single receiver that works with rival services.

How Digital Radio Works

Conventional radio is broadcast as an analogue signal, using either amplitude modulation (AM) or frequency modulation (FM). The sound suffers interference from other stations and 'multipath' reflections from hills and buildings. If the signal is weak and the receiver is straining to pick it up, the sound is polluted with background hiss.

If analogue sound is converted into digital code before transmission, as long as the signal is strong enough to decode, it is immune from interference and free from hiss. Less transmitter power is needed to cover the same area as an analogue signal. However, if reflections are as strong as the code, the receiver does not work at all. Also, when analogue sound is converted into digits, the raw code takes up more space on the airwaves than the analogue signal.

There is more space in the satellite bands, and some broadcasters and music delivery services have transmitted CD-quality digital sound from space. But the satellite bands are now crowding. Also, the signals can only be received with a dish or plate aerial, mounted in a fixed position.

Digital Audio Broadcasting (DAB) lets a receiver work with a simple rod aerial, even when moving. It also reduces the number of digital bits needed so that the signal takes up less space than an analogue transmission. Although DAB signals can be transmitted from satellites, they will initially come from conventional terrestrial transmitters.

Pan-European Eureka research team number 147 developed a DAB system, and this has been adopted as the standard for Europe. The only difference between countries is in the transmission frequencies to be used; high VHF in some and L band at 1,500 MHz in others.

The Eureka system combines two processes. Analogue sound is first converted into digital code and compressed by a system known as 'Musicam'. When there are two sounds of similar frequency, but different volume level, the 'Musicam' encoder ignores the quieter sound. This can reduce the number of bits by a factor of ten, without the ear noticing.

The bitstream is then split into several hundred parallel channels, so that each carries only slow-moving bits of data. The many channels are broadcast simultaneously on closely neighbouring frequencies. The receiver recombines the channels and rebuilds the sound. Because the bits in each channel are travelling slowly and are quite widely spaced, the receiver can distinguish between wanted signals which arrive direct from the transmitter, and unwanted 'multipath' reflections which arrive later.

The introduction of DAB does not take anything away from existing listeners, but a new radio is needed to listen to new digital broadcasts. These radios will often tune to all possible DAB bands, so that owners can use them anywhere in Europe.

The Eureka system is on offer to other countries; Canada is using it and China is testing. The situation in the USA is still fluid, because rival systems use 'in-band, on-channel' (IBOC) technology. IBOC transmits digital code at very low level, underneath a conventional analogue radio broadcast. So conventional AM and FM radio analogue receivers should continue working as normal, while a new digital radio retrieves the low-level signal and decodes it to deliver high-quality sound.

So new frequencies are not needed for IBOC, but critics say it may be susceptible to 'multipath' reflections and interference. There may be no single agreed standard for the USA, with open market competition left to create a *de facto* standard – like VHS versus Beta home video.

Britain's BBC started regular Eureka DAB transmissions in September 1995, and the commercial stations soon followed, along with most other countries in Europe. At first the only receivers were bulky engineering test prototypes. Compact radios are now starting to appear, with prices falling to consumer levels.

Barry Fox is a freelance journalist specializing in communications technology

Television Companies in the UK

Anglia Television Ltd Anglia House, Norwich NR1 3JG; phone: (01603) 615151; fax: (01603) 763 1032; e-mail: angliatv@angliatv.co.uk; Web site: www.anglia.tv.co.uk

BBC Television Centre, Wood Lane, London W12 7RJ; phone: (0181) 743 8000; fax: (0181) 749 7520; Web site: www.bbc.co.uk

BBC Worldwide Television Woodlands, 80 Wood Lane, London W12 0TT; phone: (0181) 743 5588; fax: (0181) 749 0269; Web site: www.bbc.co.uk

Border Television The Television Centre, Carlisle CA1 3NT; phone: (01228) 541384; fax: (01228) 525101; Web site: www.border-tv.com

Carlton Broadcasting 101 St Martin's Lane, London WC2N 4AZ; phone: (0171) 240 4000; fax: (0171) 240 4171; Web site: www.carltontv.co.uk

Central Broadcasting Central Court, Gas Street, Birmingham B1 2JP; phone: (0121) 643 9898; fax (press office): (0115) 986 3322; Web site: www.carltontv.co.uk

Channel 4 124 Horseferry Road, London SW1P 2TX; phone: (0171) 396 4444; fax (press office): (0171) 306 8366; e-mail: channel4.co.uk; Web site: www.channel4.com

Channel 5 Broadcasting 22 Longacre, London WC2E 9LY; phone: (0171) 550 5555; fax: (0171) 550 5554; Web site: www.channel5.co.uk

Channel Television Television Centre, La Pouquelaye, St Helier, Jersey, Channel Islands JE1 3ZD; phone: (01534) 816816; fax: (01534) 816817; e-mail: newsroom@channeltv.co.uk; Web site: www.channeltelevision.co.uk

GMTV London Television Centre, Upper Ground, London SE1 9TT; phone: (0171) 827 7000; fax (press office): (0171) 827 7009

Grampian Television Queen's Cross, Aberdeen, Grampian AB15 4XJ; phone: (01224) 846846; fax: (01224) 846800; e-mail: gtv@grampiantv.co.uk; Web site: www.grampiantv.co.uk

Granada Television The Television Centre, Quay Street, Manchester M60 9EA; phone: (0161) 832 7211; fax: (0161) 827 2029; Web site: www.granadatv.co.uk

HTV (Cymru) Wales Television Centre, Culverhouse Cross, Cardiff CF5 6XJ; phone: (01222) 590590; fax: (01222) 597183; Web site: www.htv.co.uk

London Weekend Television (LWT) London Television Centre, Upper Ground, London SE1 9LT; phone: (0171) 620 1620; fax: (0171) 261 1290; Web site: www.lwt.co.uk

Meridian Broadcasting Television Centre, Northam, Southampton SO14 0PZ; phone: (01703) 222555; fax: (01703) 335050; Web site: www.meridian.tv.co.uk

Scottish Television Cowcaddens, Glasgow G2 3PR; phone: (0141) 300 3000; fax: (0141) 300 3030; Web site: www.stv.co.uk

Tyne Tees Television The Television Centre, City Road, Newcastle upon Tyne NE1 2AL; phone: (0191) 261 0181; fax: (0191) 261 2302; e-mail: tttv.regional.affairs@gmg.co.uk; Web site: www.tynetees.tv.co.uk

Ulster Television (UTV) Havelock House, Ormeau Road, Belfast BT7 1EB; phone: (01232) 328122; fax: (01232) 246695; e-mail: info@utv.live.com; Web site: www.utvlive.com

Westcountry Television Language Science Park, Western Wood Way, Plymouth PL7 5BG; phone: (01752) 333333; fax: (01752) 333444; e-mail: info@westcountry.co.uk; Web site: www.westcountry.co.uk

Yorkshire Television The Television Centre, Kirkstall Road, Leeds LS3 1JS; phone: (0113) 243 8283; fax: (0113) 244 5107; Web site: www.yorkshiretv.co.uk

Satellite and Cable Television Companies in the UK

Bloomberg International TV Citygate House, 39–45 Finsbury Square, London EC2A 1PQ; phone: (0171) 330 7500; fax: (0171) 392 6000; Web site: www.bloomberg.com/uk

Bravo, Flextech, The Discovery Channel, Trouble, UK Gold, UK Living 160 Great Portland St, London W1N 5TB; phone: (0171) 299 5000; fax: (0171) 299 6000; Web site: www.flextech.co.uk

Carlton Digital, Carlton Food Network 27–35 Mortimer St, London W1N 7RJ; phone: (0171) 725 4600; fax: (0171) 725 4700; Web site: www.carltonselect.co.uk

Channel Broadcasting Cartoon Network 18 Soho Square, London W1V 5FD; phone: (0171) 478 1000; fax: (0171) 478 1010; Web site: www.cartoon-network.co.uk

CNN International CNN House, 19–22 Rathbone Place, London W1P 1DF; phone: (0171) 637 6700; fax: (0171) 637 6738; Web site: www.cnn.com

Disney Channel UK Beaumont House, Kensington Village, Avonmore Road, London W14 8TS; phone: (0181) 222 1300; fax: (0181) 222 1144; Web site: www.disneychannel.co.uk

Eurosport UK 55 Drury Lane, London WC2B 5SQ; phone: (0171) 468 7777; fax: (0171) 468 0023; Web site: www.eurosport.com

Good Life, Granada Plus Granada Sky Broadcasting, Franciscan Court, 16 Hatfields, London SE1 8DJ; phone: (0171) 578 4040; fax: (0171) 578 4035; Web site: www.gsb.co.uk

L!ve TV 24th Floor, One Canada Square, Canary Wharf, London E14 5DJ; phone: (0171) 293 3900; fax: (0171) 293 2151; Web site: www.l!vetv.co.uk

MTV Europe 180 Oxford St, London W1N 0DS; phone: (0171) 284 7777; fax: (0171) 284 7788; Web site: www.mtveurope.com

News 24 Stage 5, BBC TV Centre, Wood Lane, London W12 7RJ; phone: (0181) 743 8000; fax: (0181) 225 8080

Nickleodeon 15–18 Rathbone Place, London W1P 1DF; phone: (0171) 462 1000; fax: (0171) 462 1012; Web site: www.nickleodeon.co.uk

The Sci-Fi Channel 77 Charlotte Street, London W1P 2DD; phone: (0171) 805 6100; fax: (0171) 805 6150; Web site: www.scifi.com

Sky (including the Movie Channel, Sky 1, Sky Movies 1, Sky Movies Gold, Sky Sports (1, 2 and 3), Sky News, National Geographic Channel) BSkyB Ltd, Grant Way, Isleworth, Middlesex TW7 5QD

Top 10 Countries by Number of Television Sets

1996

Rank	Country	TV sets per 1,000 people
1	USA	805
2	Malta	751
3	Monaco	727
4	Canada	714
5	Japan	684
6	El Salvador	675
7	Oman	660
8	Finland	605
9	Denmark	592
10	France	591

Source: *UNESCO Statistical Yearbook 1998,* © UNESCO 1998

BBC World Service Radio Audience Figures

Figures are for an average weekly audience. Figures cover those countries where formal audience data collection is possible. This does not include Myanmar, Iraq, Iran, Cuba, and a number of other countries. Figures include only a proportion of the audience in countries such as Vietnam and Somalia. Audiences to Radio International programmes are also excluded. In 1997–98 BBC World Service had 138 million listeners in total (down from 143 million in 1996–97).

1997–98

% of audience by region	
Southern Asia and Pacific	44
Africa and Middle East	30
Europe	11
Americas	6
Eurasia	9
Total	100

Source: *BBC Annual Report 1998, copyright © BBC 1998, with permission*

National Radio Stations in the UK

BBC Network Radio Broadcasting House, Portland Place, London W1A 1AA; phone (BBC Corporate Press Office): (0171) 576 1865

Radio 1 phone (press office): (0171) 765 4575; Web site: www.bbc.co.uk/radio1

Radio 2 phone (press office): (0171) 765 4330; Web site: www.bbc.co.uk/radio2

Radio 3 phone (press office): (0171) 765 2722; Web site: www.bbc.co.uk/radio3

Radio 4 phone (press office): (0171) 765 5337; Web site: www.bbc.co.uk/radio4

Radio 5 Live phone (press office): (0171) 765 4095; Web site: www.bbc.co.uk/radio5

Classic FM 17 Swallow Place, Oxford Circus, London W1R 7AA; phone: (0171) 343 9000; fax: (0171) 344 2700; Web site: www.classicfm.co.uk

Talk Radio PO Box 1089, London W1A 1PP; phone: (0171) 636 1089; fax: (0171) 636 1053; Web site: www.talk-radio.co.uk

Virgin Radio 1 Golden Square, London W1R 4DJ; phone: (0171) 434 1215; fax: (0171) 434 1197; Web site: www.virginradio.co.uk

Newspapers and Magazines

Newspaper Readership Figures in the UK

Figures are from an unweighted sample of 37,071 adults aged 15 and over. An unweighted sample is 'raw' data which have not been 'weighted' to represent the full population (that is, taking into account age, social grades, and so on). For this survey, the estimated population was 46.14 million and did not include Northern Ireland. Adult coverage is the percentage of the total population aged 15 and over in Great Britain, but not Northern Ireland.

January–December 1998

Newspaper	Adult readers	Adult coverage (%)
National Daily		
The Sun	9,697,000	20.9
The Mirror	6,400,000	13.8
Daily Record	1,823,000	3.9
Daily Mail	5,198,000	11.2
The Express	2,524,000	5.4
The Daily Telegraph	2,348,000	5.1
Daily Star	1,847,000	4.0
The Times	1,843,000	4.0
The Guardian	1,135,000	2.4
The Independent	644,000	1.4
Financial Times	583,000	1.3
Racing Post	285,000	0.6
Any national morning	25,699,000	55.4
National Sunday		
News of the World	11,109,000	23.9
Sunday Mirror	6,354,000	13.7
The Mail on Sunday	5,970,000	12.9
Sunday People	4,344,000	9.4
The Sunday Times	3,466,000	7.5
The Express on Sunday	2,733,000	5.9
The Sunday Telegraph	2,108,000	4.5
Sunday Mail	2,088,000	4.5
The Sunday Post	1,941,000	4.2
The Observer	1,112,000	2.4
Independent on Sunday	790,000	1.7
Sunday Sport	696,000	1.5
Scotland on Sunday	353,000	0.8
Any national Sunday	27,992,000	60.3
Regional Daily		
London Evening Standard	1,016,000	2.2
Liverpool Echo	468,000	1.0
Glasgow Evening Times	360,000	0.8
Newcastle Evening Chronicle	278,000	0.6
The Herald	269,000	0.6
Dundee Courier & Advertiser	257,000	0.6
Leeds Yorkshire Evening Post	254,000	0.5
The Scotsman	216,000	0.5
Yorkshire Post	196,000	0.4
Edinburgh Evening News	183,000	0.4
Dundee Evening Telegraph	95,000	0.2
Any regional morning/evening	12,321,000	26.6
Any regional evening	10,454,000	22.5
Regional Sunday		
Newcastle Sunday Sun	377,000	0.8
Any regional Sunday	787,000	1.7

Source: National Readership Surveys

General Magazine Readership Figures in the UK

Figures are from an unweighted sample of 37,071 adults aged 15 and over. An unweighted sample is 'raw' data which have not been 'weighted' to represent the full population (that is, taking into account age, social grades, and so on). For this survey, the estimated population was 46.4 million and did not include Northern Ireland. Adult coverage is the percentage of the total population aged 15 and over in Great Britain, but not Northern Ireland.

January–December 1998

Periodical	Adult readers	Adult coverage (%)
Weekly		
What's on TV	4,219,000	9.1
Radio Times	3,910,000	8.4
TV Times	3,341,000	7.2
TV Quick	2,140,000	4.6
Auto Trader	2,113,000	4.6
The Big Issue	1,114,000	2.4
Exchange & Mart	1,022,000	2.2
TV & Satellite Week	780,000	1.7
Motorcycle News	558,000	1.2
TES (Times Educational Supplement)	553,000	1.2
Weekly News	505,000	1.1
NME (New Musical Express)	499,000	1.1
Autocar	478,000	1.0
New Scientist	462,000	1.0
Angling Times	448,000	1.0
Match	435,000	0.9
Shoot	416,000	0.9
Time Out	413,000	0.9
Auto Express	413,000	0.9
The Economist	338,000	0.8
Country Life	312,000	0.7
Horse & Hound	289,000	0.6
Amateur Gardening	261,000	0.6
Garden News	260,000	0.6
Angler's Mail	242,000	0.5
Melody Maker	230,000	0.5
Autosport	228,000	0.5
Kerrang!	212,000	0.5
Time	210,000	0.5
The European	123,000	0.3
Amateur Photographer	118,000	0.3
Any general weekly	18,724,000	40.4
Fortnightly		
Smash Hits	867,000	1.9
Private Eye	651,000	1.4
Bike Trader	341,000	0.7
Big!	327,000	0.7
Monthly		
SkyTVguide	5,704,000	12.3
Reader's Digest	4,229,000	9.1
FHM (For Him Magazine)	3,240,000	7.0
Cable Guide	3,240,000	7.0
Loaded	2,191,000	4.7
National Geographic	1,894,000	4.1
BBC Gardener's World	1,700,000	3.7
BBC Top Gear	1,638,000	3.5
Saga Magazine	1,555,000	3.4
Max Power	1,541,000	3.3
What Car?	1,328,000	2.9
Sky	1,033,000	2.2
Maxim	1,002,000	2.2
Classic Cars	926,000	2.0
Men's Health	819,000	1.8
Q	817,000	1.8
Top of the Pops Magazine	803,000	1.7
BBC Match of the Day	788,000	1.7
Golf Monthly	731,000	1.6
GQ	723,000	1.6
FourFourTwo	596,000	1.3
What Hi-Fi?	595,000	1.3
Empire	582,000	1.3
TV Hits	564,000	1.2
Performance Bikes	562,000	1.2
BBC Wildlife	555,000	1.2
Mixmag	541,000	1.2
Fast Car Magazine	535,000	1.2
Superbike	507,000	1.1
Golf World	494,000	1.1
Garden Answers	470,000	1.0
Revs	468,000	1.0
High Life	452,000	1.0
Rugby World	427,000	0.9
Practical Caravan	411,000	0.9
The Garden	403,000	0.9
Flicks	397,000	0.9
Classic and Sportscar	392,000	0.8
Bike	385,000	0.8
Classic Bike	377,000	0.8
Total Football	372,000	0.8
Car/Performance Car	369,000	0.8
Land Rover Owner International	359,000	0.8
Total Sport	322,000	0.7
Esquire	322,000	0.7
Select	317,000	0.7
The Face	312,000	0.7
Choice	297,000	0.6
Fore!	285,000	0.6
Today's Golfer	277,000	0.6
Custom Car	273,000	0.6
Trout & Salmon	270,000	0.6
Practical Classics/Popular Classics	264,000	0.6
Sporting Gun	262,000	0.6
Coarse Angling	261,000	0.6
Practical Photography	258,000	0.6
The Field	250,000	0.5
Ride	249,000	0.5
Your Garden	242,000	0.5
Moneywise	237,000	0.5
Practical Boat Owner	231,000	0.5
Arena	226,000	0.5
BBC Music Magazine	216,000	0.5
The Scot's Magazine	213,000	0.5
Mojo	203,000	0.4
Practical Woodworking	195,000	0.4
Street Machine	189,000	0.4
Fiesta	183,000	0.4
Classic CD	176,000	0.4
Cars/Car Conversions	169,000	0.4
Focus	167,000	0.4
Yachting Monthly	164,000	0.4
Geographical Magazine	160,000	0.3
Yachting World	143,000	0.3
Any general monthly	23,342,000	50.3
Bi-Monthly		
Viz	1,457,000	3.1
The Countryman	187,000	0.4
Quarterly		
AA Magazine	3,789,000	8.2
The Ford Magazine	1,113,000	2.4
Homebase Living	922,000	2.0
Upbeat	371,000	0.8

Source: National Readership Surveys

Women's Magazine Readership Figures in the UK

Figures are from an unweighted sample of 37,071 adults aged 15 and over. An unweighted sample is 'raw' data which have not been 'weighted' to represent the full population (that is, taking into account age, social grades, and so on). For this survey, the estimated population was 46.4 million and did not include Northern Ireland. Adult coverage is the percentage of the total population aged 15 and over in Great Britain, but not Northern Ireland.

January–December 1998

Periodical	Women readers	Women coverage (%)
Weekly		
Take a Break	4,545,000	9.8
Woman's Own	3,007,000	6.5
Bella	2,671,000	5.8
Woman	2,321,000	5.0
Hello!	2,120,000	4.6
Woman's Weekly	2,036,000	4.4
Best	1,868,000	4.0
Chat	1,856,000	4.0
My Weekly	1,229,000	2.6
That's Life	1,142,000	2.5
The People's Friend	1,120,000	2.4
Woman's Realm	889,000	1.9
OK!	665,000	1.4
Eva	567,000	1.2
Now	416,000	0.9
The Lady	189,000	0.4
Any women's weekly	11,430,000	24.6
Fortnightly		
More!	902,000	1.9
Inside Soap	597,000	1.3
Mizz	311,000	0.7
Monthly		
Safeway Magazine	3,369,000	7.3
Sainsbury's Magazine	2,732,000	5.9
The Somerfield Magazine	2,134,000	4.6
Cosmopolitan	2,056,000	4.4
Good Housekeeping	1,995,000	4.3
Marie Claire	1,634,000	3.5
Ideal Home	1,572,000	3.4
Homes & Gardens	1,548,000	3.3
Homes & Ideas	1,475,000	3.2
Prima	1,448,000	3.1
Vogue	1,413,000	3.0
BBC Good Food	1,335,000	2.9
Woman & Home	1,323,000	2.9
House & Garden	1,253,000	2.7
Sugar	1,218,000	2.6
House Beautiful	1,079,000	2.3
Elle	1,012,000	2.2
Family Circle	943,000	2.0
Bliss	938,000	2.0
Candis	853,000	1.8
She	817,000	1.7
Mother & Baby	804,000	1.7
Country Living	780,000	1.7
Just Seventeen	775,000	1.7
Essentials	773,000	1.7
Red	765,000	1.6
Company	730,000	1.6
New Woman	707,000	1.5
BBC Homes & Antiques	657,000	1.4
Country Homes and Interiors	630,000	1.4
Practical Parenting	602,000	1.3
Health & Fitness Magazine	550,000	1.2
Top Santé Health & Beauty	516,000	1.1
'19'	506,000	1.1
Yours	483,000	1.0
Perfect Home	449,000	1.0
Slimming	445,000	1.0
Home & Country	420,000	0.9
Period Living/Traditional Homes	398,000	0.9
Pregnancy & Birth	390,000	0.8
Harpers & Queen	384,000	0.8
Woman's Journal	383,000	0.8
BBC Vegetarian Good Food	371,000	0.8
Looks	342,000	0.7
Inspirations	341,000	0.7
B	335,000	0.7
Vanity Fair	326,000	0.7
Minx	325,000	0.7
Our Baby	295,000	0.6
Parents	291,000	0.6
Elle Decoration	286,000	0.6
Options	275,000	0.6
Babycare & Pregnancy	271,000	0.6
Tatler	268,000	0.6
World of Interiors	257,000	0.6
Here's Health	165,000	0.4
Any women's monthly	18,084,000	39.0
Bi-Monthly		
Weight Watchers	1,206,000	2.6
Hair	1,003,000	2.2
R Conley Diet/Fitness Magazine	536,000	1.2
Slimmer	241,000	0.5
You & Your Wedding	221,000	0.5
Wedding & Home	217,000	0.5
Classic Stitches	197,000	0.4
Brides/Set Up Home	188,000	0.4
Quarterly		
The M&S Magazine	4,514,000	9.7

Source: National Readership Surveys

Top 10 Countries by Number of Daily Newspapers

1996

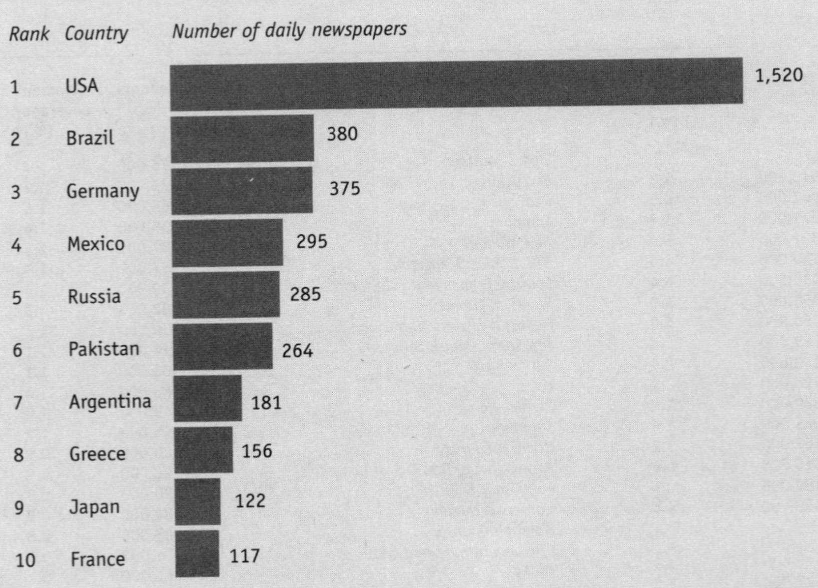

Rank	Country	Number of daily newspapers
1	USA	1,520
2	Brazil	380
3	Germany	375
4	Mexico	295
5	Russia	285
6	Pakistan	264
7	Argentina	181
8	Greece	156
9	Japan	122
10	France	117

Source: *UNESCO Statistical Yearbook 1998*, © UNESCO 1998

Books

Top 10 Best-Selling Hardback Fiction Titles of the Year in the UK

1998

Rank	Title	Author and publisher
1	*Tara Road*	Maeve Binchy (Orion)
2	*The Last Continent*	Terry Pratchett (Doubleday)
3	*Carpe Jugulum*	Terry Pratchett (Doubleday)
4	*The Street Lawyer*	John Grisham (Century)
5	*Rainbow Six*	Tom Clancy (M Joseph)
6	*Point of Origin*	Patricia D Cornwell (Little, Brown)
7	*Charlotte Gray*	Sebastian Faulks (Hutchinson)
8	*Field of 13*	Dick Francis (M Joseph)
9	*About a Boy*	Nick Hornby (Gollancz)
10	*Archangel*	Robert Harris (Hutchinson)

Source: Bookwatch

Top 10 Best-Selling Paperback Fiction Titles of the Year in the UK

1998

Rank	Title	Author and publisher
1	*Captain Corelli's Mandolin*	Louis de Bernières (Vintage)
2	*Bridget Jones's Diary*	Helen Fielding (Picador)
3	*The God of Small Things*	Arundhati Roy (Flamingo)
4	*The Partner*	John Grisham (Arrow)
5	*Enduring Love*	Ian McEwan (Vintage)
6	*Cold Mountain*	Charles Frazier (Sceptre)
7	*Memoirs of a Geisha*	Arthur Golden (Vintage)
8	*Unnatural Exposure*	Patricia D Cornwell (Warner)
9	*Human Croquet*	Kate Atkinson (Black Swan)
10	*Hornet's Nest*	Patricia D Cornwell (Warner)

Source: Bookwatch

Top 10 Best-Selling Hardback Non-Fiction Titles of the Year in the UK

1998

Rank	Title	Author and publisher
1	*Delia's How to Cook: Book 1*	Delia Smith (BBC)
2	*The Life of Birds*	David Attenborough (BBC)
3	*Notes From a Big Country*	Bill Bryson (Doubleday)
4	*The Birthday Letters*	Ted Hughes (Faber)
5	*Meals in Minutes*	Ainsley Harriott (BBC)
6	*Guinness Book of Records 1999*	(Guinness)
7	*Addicted*	Tony Adams with Ian Ridley (CollinsWillow)
8	*The Guv'nor*	Lenny McLean (Blake)
9	*Losing My Virginity*	Richard Branson (Virgin)
10	*Blackadder: The Whole Damn Dynasty*	Richard Curtis and Ben Elton (M Joseph)

Source: Bookwatch

Top 10 Best-Selling Paperback Non-Fiction Titles of the Year in the UK

1998

Rank	Title	Author and publisher
1	*The Little Book of Calm*	Paul Wilson (Penguin)
2	*Angela's Ashes*	Frank McCourt (Flamingo)
3	*Men are from Mars, Women are from Venus*	John Gray (Thorsons)
4	*Notes From a Small Island*	Bill Bryson (Black Swan)
5	*Longitude*	Dava Sobel (4th Estate)
6	*A Walk in the Woods*	Bill Bryson (Black Swan)
7	*Falling Leaves*	Adeline Yen Mah (Penguin)
8	*Complete Theory Test: Cars and Motorcycles*	Driving Standards Agency (TSO)
9	*The Nation's Favourite Poems*	intro. Griff Rhys Jones (BBC)
10	*The Diving Bell and the Butterfly*	Jean-Dominique Bauby (4th Estate)

Source: Bookwatch

Top 10 Best-Selling Children's Hardbacks of the Year in the UK

1998

Rank	Title	Author and publisher
1	*The Beano Annual 1999*	D C Thomson
2	*Harry Potter and the Chamber of Secrets*	J K Rowling (Bloomsbury)
3	*The Dandy Annual 1999*	D C Thomson
4	*Guess How Much I Love You?*	Sam McBratney (Walker)
5	*We're Going on a Bear Hunt*	Michael Rosen (Walker)
6	*The Unofficial World Cup Guide*	Ladybird
7	*Goosebumps: Fright Light*	R L Stine (Scholastic)
8	*The Teletubbies Annual 1999*	World International
9	*Letterland ABC*	Richard Carlisle and Lyn Wendon (HarperCollins)
10	*The Totally Unofficial Spice Girls Annual*	Granddreams

Source: Bookwatch

Top 10 Best-Selling Children's Paperbacks of the Year in the UK

1998

Rank	Title	Author and publisher
1	*The Children's Book of Books 1998*	Random House/Penguin
2	*Harry Potter and the Philosopher's Stone*	J K Rowling (Bloomsbury)
3	*The Lottie Project*	Jacqueline Wilson (Yearling)
4	*Bad Girls*	Jacqueline Wilson (Yearling)
5	*Matilda*	Roald Dahl (Puffin)
6	*Double Act*	Jacqueline Wilson (Yearling)
7	*Northern Lights*	Philip Pullman (Scholastic)
8	*Animal Ark: Dolphin in the Deep*	Lucy Daniels (Hodder)
9	*The Suitcase Kid*	Jacqueline Wilson (Yearling)
10	*The Very Hungry Caterpillar*	Eric Carle (Puffin)

Source: Bookwatch

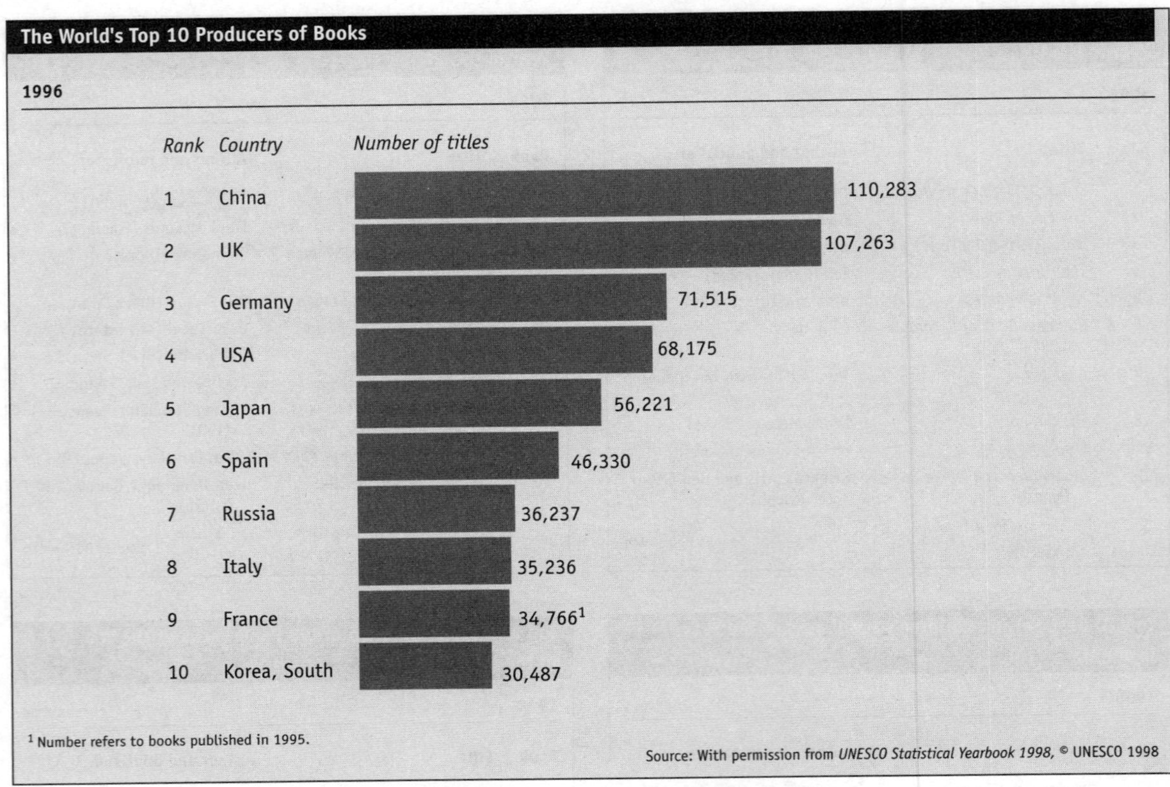

The World's Top 10 Producers of Books
1996
Rank Country Number of titles
1 China 110,283
2 UK 107,263
3 Germany 71,515
4 USA 68,175
5 Japan 56,221
6 Spain 46,330
7 Russia 36,237
8 Italy 35,236
9 France 34,766[1]
10 Korea, South 30,487
[1] Number refers to books published in 1995.
Source: With permission from *UNESCO Statistical Yearbook 1998*, © UNESCO 1998

Some of the World's Most Reprinted Books

All figures are approximate.
(– = not applicable.)

Title	Author	Number of copies
The Bible	Various translations	over 6,000,000,000
Little Red Book	Mao Zedong (Mao Tse Tung) (1893–1976)	over 800,000,000
Eclectic Readers (The McGuffey Readers)	William Holmes McGuffey (1800–1873)	up to 122,000,000
A Grammatical Institute of the English Language (*Webster's Spelling Book*, or *American Spelling Book*)	Noah Webster (1758–1843)	100,000,000
The Guinness Book of Records	–	79,000,000[1]
A Message to Garcia	Elbert Hubbard (1856–1915)	up to 50,000,000
The World Almanac	–	over 40,000,000[1]
The Common Sense Book of Baby and Child Care	Benjamin Spock (1903–1998)	over 39,200,000
The Valley of the Dolls	Jacqueline Susann (*c.* 1926–1974)	30,000,000
In His Steps: What Would Jesus Do?	Charles Monroe Sheldon (1857–1946)	28,500,000

[1] Figures represent aggregate sales of annual publication.

Source: Index Translationem, © UNESCO

Some of the World's Most Translated Authors

(– = not applicable.)

Name	Dates
Various (*The Bible*)	–
Vladimir Ilyich Lenin	1870–1924
Agatha Christie	1890–1976
Jules Verne	1828–1905
William Shakespeare	1564–1616
Enid Blyton	1897–1968
Leo Nikolaievich Tolstoy	1828–1910
Charles Perrault	1628–1703
Georges Simenon	1903–1989
Karl Marx	1818–1883
Fyodor Mikhailovich Dostoyevsky	1821–1881
Barbara Cartland	1901–
Hans Christian Andersen	1805–1875
Jacob and Wilhelm Grimm	1785–1863 and 1786–1859
Konstantin Ustinovich Chernenko	1911–1985
Isaac Asimov	1920–1992
Friedrich Engels	1820–1895
Jack London (John Griffith Chaney)	1876–1916
Arthur Conan Doyle	1859–1930
Mark Twain (Samuel Langhorne Clemens)	1835–1910
Charles Dickens	1812–1870
Robert Louis Stevenson	1850–1894
Walt Disney Productions (collective)	–
Graham Greene	1904–1991
Pope John Paul II (Karol Wojtła)	1920–

Source: Index Translationem, © UNESCO

Libraries

Top 10 Most Borrowed Non-Fiction Titles in the UK

July 1997–June 1998

Rank	Title	Author	Publisher and year of publication
1	*Immediate Action*	Andy McNab	Bantam, 1995
2	*The Complete Theory Test for Cars and Motorcycles*	Driving Standards Agency	HMSO, 1996
3	*Eyewitness Guide: Ancient Egypt*	George Hart	Dorling Kindersley, 1990
4	*Delia Smith's Winter Collection*	Delia Smith (photographs Flo Bayley)	BBC Books, 1995
5	*Menopause*	Miriam Stoppard	Dorling Kindersley, 1994
6	*The Groovy Greeks*	Terry Deary (illustrator Martin Brown)	Hippo, 1996
7	*Wild Swans: Three Daughters of China*	Jung Chang	HarperCollins, 1991
8	*Cruel Kings and Mean Queens*	Terry Deary (illustrator Kate Sheppard)	Andre Deutsch, 1995
9	*The Slimy Stuarts*	Terry Deary (illustrator Martin Brown)	Hippo, 1996
10	*Eyewitness Guide: Ancient Rome*	Simon James	Dorling Kindersley, 1990

Source: Registrar of Public Lending Right

Top 10 Most Borrowed Fiction Titles of the Year in the UK

July 1997–June 1998

Rank	Title	Author	Publisher and year of publication
1	*A Ruthless Need*	Catherine Cookson	Bantam Press, 1995
2	*The Obsession*	Catherine Cookson	Bantam Press, 1995
3	*The Bonny Dawn*	Catherine Cookson	Bantam Press, 1996
4	*The Branded Man*	Catherine Cookson	Bantam Press, 1996
5	*The Bondage of Love*	Catherine Cookson	Bantam Press, 1997
6	*The Year of the Virgins*	Catherine Cookson	Bantam Press, 1993
7	*Justice is a Woman*	Catherine Cookson	Bantam Press, 1994
8	*The Upstart*	Catherine Cookson	Bantam Press, 1996
9	*Malice*	Danielle Steel	Bantam Press, 1996
10	*To The Hilt*	Dick Francis	Michael Joseph, 1996

Source: Registrar of Public Lending Right

Top 20 Most Borrowed Authors in the UK

July 1997–June 1998

Rank	Author
1	Catherine Cookson
2	Danielle Steel
3	Dick Francis
4	Josephine Cox
5	Ruth Rendell
6	Jack Higgins
7	Agatha Christie
8	Emma Blair
9	Terry Pratchett
10	Barbara Taylor Bradford
11	Virginia Andrews
12	Dean R Koontz
13	Rosamunde Pilcher
14	Maeve Binchy
15	Harry Bowling
16	Audrey Howard
17	Bernard Cornwell
18	Ellis Peters
19	Wilbur Smith
20	Mary Higgins Clark

Source: Registrar of Public Lending Right

Top 20 Most Borrowed Classic Authors in the UK

July 1997–June 1998

Rank	Author
1	Beatrix Potter
2	Daphne Du Maurier
3	A A Milne
4	Jane Austen
5	William Shakespeare
6	J R R Tolkien
7	Charles Dickens
8	Thomas Hardy
9	Anthony Trollope
10	E M Forster
11	George Orwell
12	Rudyard Kipling
13	D H Lawrence
14	Arthur Conan Doyle
15	Louisa M Alcott
16	George Eliot
17	Virginia Woolf
18	John Buchan
19	C S Forester
20	Wilkie Collins

Source: Registrar of Public Lending Right

Top 20 Most Borrowed Children's Authors in the UK

July 1997–June 1998

Rank	Author
1	R L Stine
2	Janet and Allan Ahlberg
3	Ann M Martin
4	Roald Dahl
5	Enid Blyton
6	Dick King-Smith
7	John Cunliffe
8	Goscinny
9	Mick Inkpen
10	Eric Hill
11	Shirley Hughes
12	Martin Waddell
13	Nick Butterworth
14	Lucy Daniels
15	Tony Bradman
16	Jacqueline Wilson
17	Jill Murphy
18	Kate William
19	David McKee
20	Colin and Jacqui Hawkins

Source: Registrar of Public Lending Right

Top 10 Most Borrowed Children's Fiction Titles of the Year in the UK

July 1997–June 1998

Rank	Title	Author/illustrator	Publisher and year of publication
1	*Ghost Beach*	R L Stine	Hippo, 1996
2	*Scarecrow Walks at Midnight*	R L Stine	Hippo, 1995
3	*A Quiet Night In*	Jill Murphy	Walker, 1993
4	*A Night in Terror Tower*	R L Stine	Hippo, 1996
5	*It Came from Beneath the Sink!*	R L Stine	Hippo, 1996
6	*My Hairiest Adventure*	R L Stine	Hippo, 1996
7	*The Cuckoo Clock of Doom*	R L Stine	Hippo, 1996
8	*One Day at Horrorland*	R L Stine	Hippo, 1994
9	*Return of the Mummy*	R L Stine	Hippo, 1995
10	*Night of the Living Dummy II*	R L Stine	Hippo, 1996

Source: Registrar of Public Lending Right

Library Loans by Category in the UK

(In percentages.)

Category	1988–89	1996–97	1997–98
Adult Fiction			
General fiction	17.8	21.0	22.1
Historical	3.5	3.1	2.9
Mystery and detection	12.8	12.8	12.8
Horror	0.7	0.5	0.4
Science fiction	0.8	0.1	0.8
War	1.8	1.2	1.3
Humour	0.7	0.3	0.2
Light romance	14.1	10.4	10.6
Westerns	1.2	0.7	0.7
Short stories	0.5	0.3	0.2
Adult fiction total	53.9	50.4	52.0
Adult Non-Fiction			
Science and technology	1.3	1.1	1.0
History	3.5	2.7	2.6
Travel and foreign countries	2.9	2.6	2.4
Social sciences	2.5	2.2	1.9
Religion	0.9	0.8	0.8
Nature and country life	1.5	1.1	1.0
Domestic and leisure	4.7	4.2	4.0
Health	1.7	1.9	1.8
Arts	1.2	1.0	0.9
Biography	2.6	2.6	2.5
Humour	0.7	0.2	0.2
Literature	0.9	0.9	0.7
Adult non-fiction total	24.4	21.3	19.8
Adult total	78.3	71.7	71.8
Children's Books			
Children's fiction	17.5	22.3	22.1
Children's non-fiction	4.2	6.0	6.1
Children's total	21.7	28.3	28.2
All books total	100.0	100.0	100.0

Source: Registrar of Public Lending Right

Copyright Libraries in the UK

Under copyright laws, UK publishers are required to deliver one free copy of every book published (including sheet music and maps) to the British Library. The other copyright libraries have the right to request a free copy of any book within 12 months of its publication.

British Library
Board Headquarters, British Library, 96 Euston Road, London NW1 2DB; phone: (0171) 412 7332 (visitor enquiries), (0171) 412 7000 (switchboard)

Bodleian Library
University of Oxford, Broad Street, Oxford OX1 3BG; phone: (01865) 277000 (enquiries), (01865) 277170 (administration); fax: (01865) 277182; e-mail: enquiries@bodley.ox.ac.uk; Web site: www.bodley.ox.ac.uk

University Library
University of Cambridge, West Road, Cambridge CB3 9DR; phone: (01223) 333000; fax: (01223) 333160; e-mail: library@ula.cam.ac.uk; Web site: www.cam.ac.uk/libraries

National Library of Scotland
George IV Bridge, Edinburgh EH1 1EW; phone: (0131) 226 4531; fax: (0131) 622 4803; e-mail: enquiries@nls.uk; Web site: www.nls.uk

Trinity College Dublin Library
Trinity College Dublin College Street, Dublin 2, Republic of Ireland; phone: (1) 608 1127 (general enquiries), (1) 608 1661 (librarian's office); fax: (1) 671 9003; e-mail: library@tcd.ie; Web site: www.tcd.ie/library/

National Library of Wales: Llyfrgell Genedlaethol Cymru
Aberystwyth, Ceredigion SY23 3BU; phone: (01970) 632800; fax: (01970) 615709; e-mail: holi@llgc.or.uk; Web site: www.llgc.org.uk/

Advertising

Top 20 Advertisers by Spend Across All Media in the UK

Figures include press, television, radio, cinema, and outdoor. Outdoor excludes tobacco advertising and 'moving transport advertising'.

1998

Rank	Company	Amount (£)
1	British Telecommunications plc	138,330,408
2	Procter & Gamble Ltd	121,993,229
3	Dixon's Stores Group Ltd	117,561,857
4	Vauxhall Motors Ltd	95,017,866
5	Ford Motor Company Ltd	93,630,558
6	Renault UK Ltd	79,245,271
7	Kellogg Company of Great Britain Ltd	74,837,927
8	Unilever Elida Fabergé Ltd	68,689,880
9	Golden Ltd	66,806,567
10	Unilever Lever Brothers Ltd	65,039,282
11	Mars Confectionery	58,758,039
12	Procter & Gamble Health and Beauty	57,159,582
13	Van Den Bergh Foods Ltd	54,934,477
14	J Sainsbury plc	50,468,937
15	British Sky Broadcasting Ltd	50,349,233
16	Volkswagen UK Ltd	50,320,156
17	Peugeot Talbot Motor Company plc	50,015,347
18	Rover Group Ltd	48,075,753
19	McDonald's Restaurants Ltd	47,976,704
20	SmithKline Beecham Healthcare plc	46,755,783

Source: AC Nielsen MEAL, 1999

Top 10 Advertising Agencies in the UK

1997

Rank	Agency	Billings (£ millions)
1	Abbott Mead Vickers BBDO	356.00
2=	Ogilvy & Mather	340.00
	Saatchi & Saatchi Advertising	340.00
4	Bates Dorland	307.00
5	J Walter Thompson Company	252.64
6	TBWA GGT Simons Palmer	250.00
7	BMP DDB	246.55
8	Lowe Howard-Spink	230.00
9	Publicis	220.00
10	Leo Burnett Company	217.00

Source: *Advertisers Annual* (Hollis Directories) 0181 977 7711

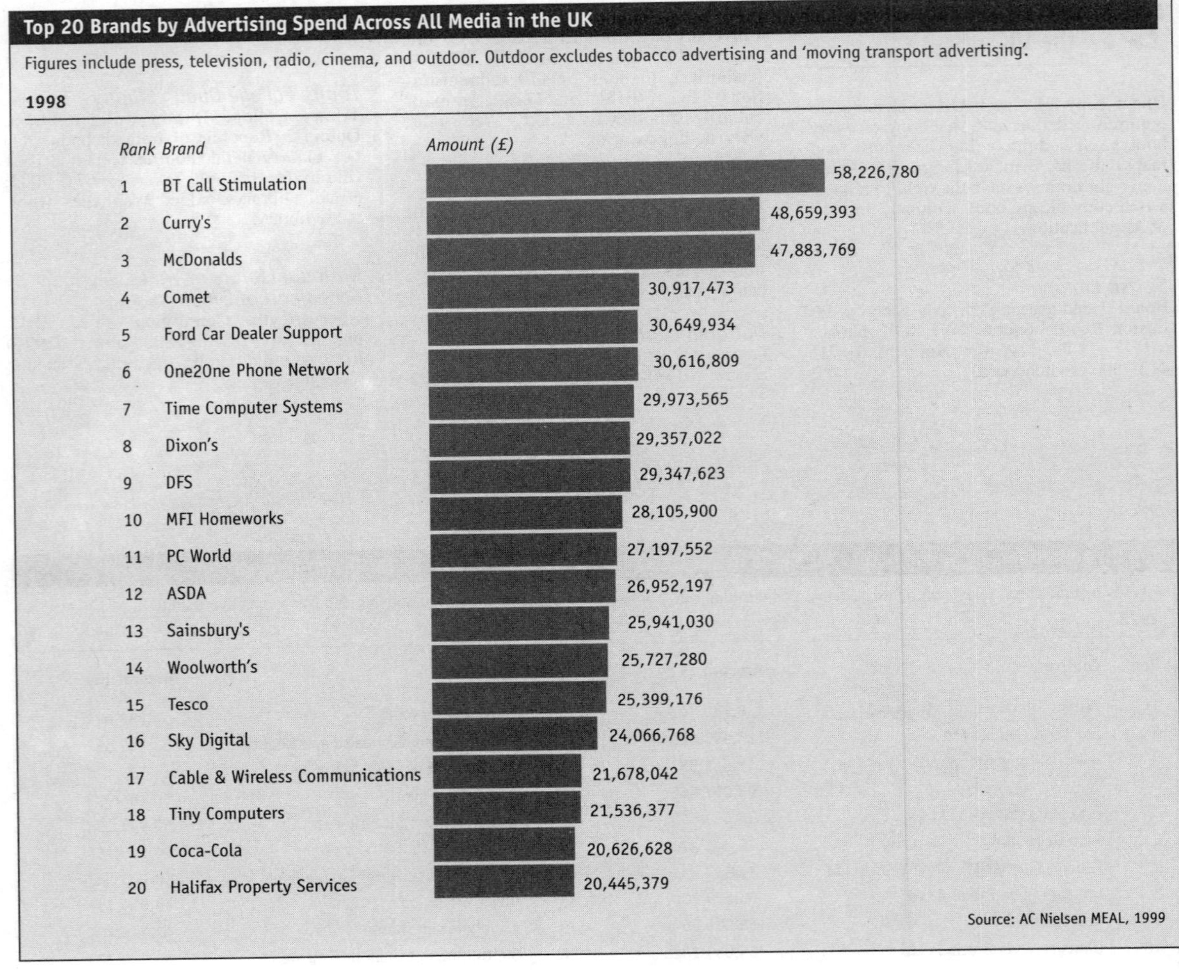

Top 20 Brands by Advertising Spend Across All Media in the UK
Figures include press, television, radio, cinema, and outdoor. Outdoor excludes tobacco advertising and 'moving transport advertising'.
1998
Rank Brand
Amount (£)
1 BT Call Stimulation
58,226,780
2 Curry's
48,659,393
3 McDonalds
47,883,769
4 Comet
30,917,473
5 Ford Car Dealer Support
30,649,934
6 One2One Phone Network
30,616,809
7 Time Computer Systems
29,973,565
8 Dixon's
29,357,022
9 DFS
29,347,623
10 MFI Homeworks
28,105,900
11 PC World
27,197,552
12 ASDA
26,952,197
13 Sainsbury's
25,941,030
14 Woolworth's
25,727,280
15 Tesco
25,399,176
16 Sky Digital
24,066,768
17 Cable & Wireless Communications
21,678,042
18 Tiny Computers
21,536,377
19 Coca-Cola
20,626,628
20 Halifax Property Services
20,445,379
Source: AC Nielsen MEAL, 1999

Films and Videos

30 Notable Films of the Year in the UK

The date is for UK release; year of release in country of origin can be significantly different.

July 1998–June 1999

Beloved (USA) *Director:* Jonathan Demme; *Actors:* Oprah Winfrey, Danny Glover, Thandie Newton

The Big Lebowski (USA) *Director:* Joel Coen and Ethan Coen; *Actors:* Jeff Bridges, John Goodman, Julianne Moore, Steve Buscemi

Le bossu/The Hunchback (France/Italy/Germany) *Director:* Philippe de Broca; *Actors:* Daniel Auteuil, Fabrice Luchini, Vincent Pérez, Maria Gillian

Central do Brasil/Central Station (Brazil/France) *Director:* Walter Salles; *Actors:* Fernanda Montenegro, Marília Pêra, Vinícius de Oliveira

Conte d'automne/An Autumn Tale (France) *Director:* Eric Rohmer; *Actors:* Marie Rivière, Béatrice Romand, Alain Libolt

Elizabeth (India/UK) *Director:* Shekhar Kapur; *Actors:* Cate Blanchett, Geoffrey Rush, Joseph Fiennes, Christopher Eccleston

eXistenZ (USA/France/Canada/UK) *Director:* David Cronenberg; *Actors:* Jennifer Jason Leigh, Jude Law, Willem Dafoe, Ian Holm

Gods and Monsters (USA/UK) *Director:* Bill Condon; *Actors:* Ian McKellen, Brendan Fraser, Lynn Redgrave

Hana-bi/Fireworks (Japan) *Director:* Takeshi Kitano; *Actors:* Takeshi Kitano, Kayoko Kishimoto, Ren Osugi, Susumu Terajima

Hilary and Jackie (UK) *Director:* Anand Tucker; *Actors:* Emily Watson, Rachel Griffiths, James Frain

Idioterne/The Idiots (Denmark) *Director:* Lars Von Trier; *Actors:* Bodil Jørgensen, Jans Albinius, Anne Louise Hassing

The Last Days of Disco (USA) *Director:* Whit Stillman; *Actors:* Chloê Sevigny, Kate Beckinsale, Christopher Eigeman, Matthew Keeslar

Lock, Stock and Two Smoking Barrels (UK) *Director:* Guy Ritchie; *Actors:* Jason Flemyng, Dexter Fletcher, Nick Moran, Vinnie Jones

Mia eonita ke mia mera/Eternity and a Day (France/Greece/Italy) *Director:* Theo Angelopoulos; *Actors:* Bruno Ganz, Isabel Renauld

Notting Hill (UK) *Director:* Roger Michell; *Actors:* Hugh Grant, Julia Roberts

On connaît la chanson/Same Old Song (France) *Director:* Alain Resnais; *Actors:* André Dussollier, Agnès Jaoui, Jean-Pierre Bacri, Sabine Azéme

The Opposite of Sex (USA) *Director:* Don Roos; *Actors:* Christina Ricci, Martin Donovan, Lisa Kudrow, Lyle Lovett

Out of Sight (USA) *Director:* Steven Soderbergh; *Actors:* George Clooney, Jennifer Lopez

Pleasantville (USA) *Director:* Garry Ross; *Actors:* William H Macy, Joan Allen

Saving Private Ryan (USA) *Director:* Steven Spielberg; *Actors:* Tom Hanks, Tom Sizemore, Edward Burns

Shakespeare in Love (USA/UK) *Director:* John Madden; *Actors:* Joseph Fiennes, Gwyneth Paltrow, Judi Dench

Sib/The Apple (Iran/France) *Director:* Samira Makhmalbaf; *Actors:* Ghorban Ali Naderi, Azizeh Mohamadi

Sliding Doors (UK) *Director:* Peter Howitt; *Actors:* Gwyneth Paltrow, John Hannah

Star Wars: Episode I – The Phantom Menace (USA) *Director:* George Lucas; *Actors:* Liam Neeson, Ewan McGregor, Natalie Portman

The Thin Red Line (USA) *Director:* Terence Malick; *Actors:* Sean Penn, Adrian Brody, James Caviezel, Ben Chaplin

The Truman Show (USA) *Director:* Peter Weir; *Actors:* Jim Carey, Ed Harris, Laura Linney

This Year's Love (UK) *Director:* David Kane; *Actors:* Kathy Burke, Ian Hart, Dougray Scott, Catherine McCormack

Todo sobre mi madre/All About My Mother (France/Spain) *Director:* Pedro Almodovar; *Actors:* Cecilia Roth, Eloy Azorín, Marisa Paredes

Velvet Goldmine (UK/USA) *Director:* Todd Haynes; *Actors:* Ewan McGregor, Jonathan Rhys-Meyers, Toni Collette, Christian Bale

La vita è bella/Life is Beautiful (Italy) *Director:* Roberto Benigni; *Actors:* Roberto Benigni, Nicoletta Braschi, Giorgio Cantarini

Top 20 Films at the UK Box Office

This ranking includes films released in the UK between 2 January 1998 and 1 January 1999.

Rank	Title	Distributor	Box office (£)
1	*Titanic*	Twentieth Century Fox	68,971,523
2	*Doctor Dolittle*	Twentieth Century Fox	19,854,598
3	*Saving Private Ryan*	UIP	17,875,260
4	*Armageddon*	Buena Vista	16,506,605
5	*Godzilla*	Columbia Tristar	15,974,736
6	*There's Something About Mary*	Twentieth Century Fox	15,665,386
7	*Sliding Doors*	UIP	12,434,715
8	*Lock, Stock and Two Smoking Barrels*	Polygram	11,520,069
9	*Flubber*	Buena Vista	10,891,774
10	*Lost in Space*	Entertainment	10,664,453
11	*Deep Impact*	UIP	10,199,634
12	*The Truman Show*	UIP	9,929,680
13	*Antz*	UIP	9,672,036
14	*As Good As It Gets*	Columbia Tristar	9,613,181
15	*The Wedding Singer*	Entertainment	9,256,114
16	*Mulan*	Buena Vista	8,902,296
17	*The X-Files Movie*	Twentieth Century Fox	8,426,489
18	*Scream 2*	Buena Vista	8,280,725
19	*Mouse Hunt*	UIP	8,218,817
20	*Good Will Hunting*	Buena Vista	7,806,051

Source: AC Nielsen EDI

Top 10 Retail Videos in the UK

1998

Rank	Title	Distributor
1	*Titanic*	FoxVideo
2	*The Full Monty*	FoxVideo
3	*Matilda*	Columbia Tristar
4	*Men in Black*	Columbia Tristar
5	*Lady & the Tramp*	Walt Disney
6	*Hercules*	Walt Disney
7	*Cats* (cast recording)	PolyGram Video
8	*Flubber*	Walt Disney
9	*Spiceworld–The Movie*	PolyGram Video
10	*Peter Pan*	Walt Disney

Source: Chart Information Network, www.dotmusic.com

Top 10 Video Rentals in the UK

1998

Rank	Title	Distributor
1	*Men in Black*	Columbia Tristar
2	*Face/Off*	Buena Vista
3	*Air Force One*	Buena Vista
4	*Starship Troopers*	Buena Vista
5	*The Fifth Element*	Fox Pathé
6	*The Full Monty*	Fox Pathé
7	*The Lost World – Jurassic Park*	CIC
8	*Devil's Advocate*	Warner
9	*Austin Powers – International Man of Mystery*	Fox Pathé
10	*The Jackal*	CIC

Source: © MRIB

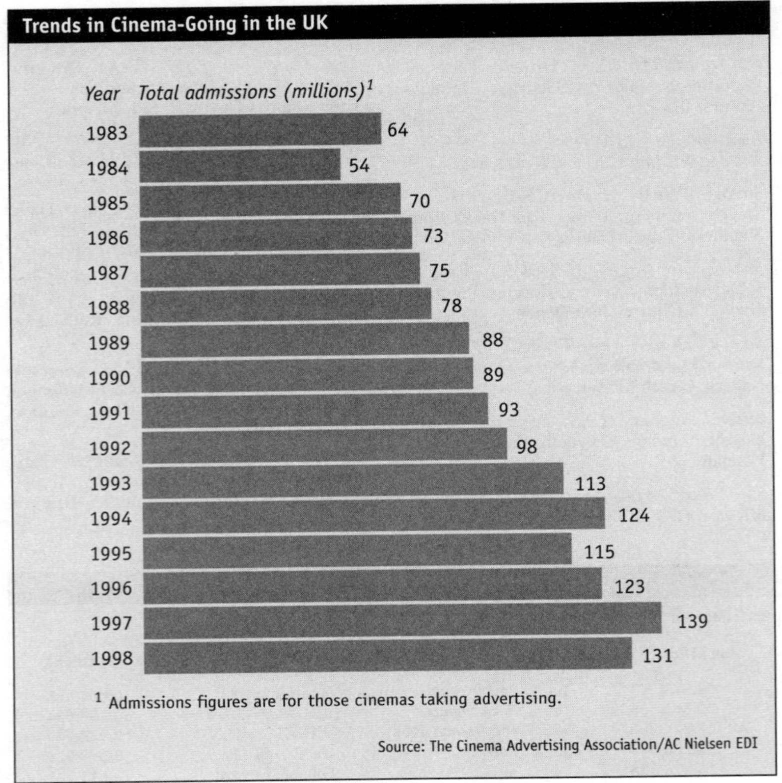

Art

Top 10 Highest Prices Paid for Paintings Sold at Auction

As of 10 March 1999.

Rank	Work	Artist	Place and date of sale	Price ($)
1	*Portrait of Dr Gachet*	Vincent van Gogh	Christie's, New York, 15 May 1990	75,000,000
2	*Au Moulin de la Galette*	Pierre-Auguste Renoir	Sotheby's, New York, 17 May 1990	71,000,000
3	*Portrait de l'artiste sans barbe*	Vincent van Gogh	Christie's, New York, 19 November 1998	65,000,000
4	*Les Noces de Pierette*	Pablo Picasso	Binoche et Godeau, Paris, 30 November 1989	51,671,920
5	*Irises*	Vincent van Gogh	Sotheby's, New York, 11 November 1987	49,000,000
6	*Le Rêve*	Pablo Picasso	Christie's, New York, 10 November 1997	44,000,000
7	*Self Portrait: Yo Picasso*	Pablo Picasso	Sotheby's, New York, 9 May 1989	43,500,000
8	*Au Lapin Agile*	Pablo Picasso	Sotheby's, New York, 15 November 1989	37,000,000
9	*Sunflowers*	Vincent van Gogh	Christie's, London, 30 March 1987	36,225,000
10	*Portrait of Duke Cosimo I de' Medici*[1]	Jacopo Carucci (also known as Pontormo)	Christie's, New York, 31 May 1989	32,000,000

[1] This is the record price for an Old Master.

Source: Art Sales Index Ltd

Top 5 Highest Prices Paid for Paintings at Auction by Living Artists

As of 10 March 1999.

Rank	Work	Artist	Place and date of sale	Price ($)
1	*False Start*	Jasper Johns	Sotheby's, New York, 10 November 1988	15,500,000
2	*Two Flags*	Jasper Johns	Sotheby's, New York, 8 November 1989	11,000,000
3	*Corpse and Mirror*	Jasper Johns	Christie's, New York, 10 November 1997	7,600,000
4	*White Numbers*	Jasper Johns	Christie's, New York, 10 November 1997	7,200,000
5	*Rebus*	Robert Rauschenberg	Sotheby's, New York, 30 April 1991	6,600,000

Source: Art Sales Index Ltd

Top 10 Highest Prices Paid for Sculptures Sold at Auction

As of 10 March 1999.

Rank	Work	Artist	Place and date of sale	Price ($)
1	*Petite Danseuse de Quatorze Ans*	Edgar Degas	Sotheby's, New York, 12 November 1996	10,800,000
2	*The Dancing Faun*	Adriaen de Vries	Sotheby's, London, 7 December 1989	9,796,000
3	*Petite Danseuse de Quatorze Ans* (resold later, see above)	Edgar Degas	Christie's, New York, 14 November 1988	9,250,000
4	*Petite Danseuse de Quatorze Ans* (resold later, see above)	Edgar Degas	Sotheby's, New York, 10 May 1988	9,200,000
5	*La Negresse Blonde*	Constantin Brancusi	Sotheby's, New York, 16 May 1990	8,000,000
6	*La Muse Endormie III*	Constantin Brancusi	Christie's, New York, 14 November 1989	7,500,000
7	*La Forêt-sept figures et une tête*	Alberto Giacometti	Sotheby's, New York, 16 November 1998	6,800,000
8	*Mlle Pogany II*	Constantin Brancusi	Christie's, New York, 14 May 1997	6,400,000
9	*L'Homme Qui Marche I*	Alberto Giacometti	Christie's, London, 28 November 1988	6,358,000
10	*La Muse Endormie II*	Constantin Brancusi	Christie's, New York, 11 November 1997	6,000,000

Source: Art Sales Index Ltd

Top 10 Single-Owner Art Sales

As of 10 March 1999.

Rank	Collection	Place and date of sale	Price (£)
1	The collection of Victor and Sally Ganz	Christie's, New York, 10 November 1997	111,022,783
2	John T Dorrance's collection of oil paintings and watercolours	Sotheby's, New York, 18 October 1989	70,624,937
3	Paintings and watercolours from Madame Bourdon's collection	Christie's, London, 27 November 1989	61,843,177
4	Paintings and sculpture from a European estate	Christie's, New York, 19 November 1998	55,977,579
5	The collection of John and Frances L Loeb	Christie's, New York, 12 May 1997	51,714,727
6	The Reader's Digest collection	Sotheby's, New York, 16 November 1999	47,659,396
7	The collection of Lydia Winston Malbin	Sotheby's, New York, 16 May 1990	39,684,024
8	Jaime Ortiz-Patino's collection of Impressionist paintings	Sotheby's, New York, 9 May 1989	37,834,358
9	Impressionist and modern paintings and sculpture, the Stralem collection	Sotheby's, New York, 8 May 1995	37,703,822
10	Paul Mellon's Impressionist and modern collection	Christie's, New York, 14 November 1989	30,116,131

Source: Art Sales Index Ltd

Top 10 Highest Prices Paid for Books and Manuscripts Sold at Auction

As of 10 March 1999.

Rank	Work	Place and date of sale	Price ($)
1	*The Codex Leicester,* Leonardo da Vinci's autographed manuscript with drawings and diagrams	Christie's, New York, 11 November 1994	30,802,500
2	*The Gospels of Henry the Lion,* 12th-century illuminated manuscript on vellum with 31 full-page miniatures	Sotheby's, London, 6 December 1983	11,000,920
3	Chaucer's *Canterbury Tales* (printed by William Caxton *c.* 1476)	Christie's, London, 8 July 1998	6,890,000
4	*The Northumberland Bestiary* (*c.* 1250–60)	Sotheby's, London, 29 November 1990	5,900,000
5	*The Gutenberg Bible* (1455)	Christie's, New York, 22 October 1987	5,390,000
6	Autographed manuscript of nine symphonies by Wolfgang Amadeus Mozart (*c.* 1773–74)	Sotheby's, London, 22 May 1987	4,316,950
7	John James Audubon's *The Birds of America* (1827–38)	Sotheby's, New York, 6 June 1989	3,960,000
8	The Bible in Hebrew (*c.* 9th–10th century)	Sotheby's, London, 5 December 1989	3,200,000
9	*The Moneypenny Breviary,* illuminated manuscript (*c.* 1490–95)	Sotheby's, London, 19 June 1989	2,800,000
10	*The Hours and Psalter of Elizabeth de Bohun* (*c.* 1340–45)	Sotheby's, London, 21 June 1988	2,530,000

Source: Data from Christie's and Sotheby's

Top 10 Most Popular Art Exhibitions Around the World

Rankings are for total, not daily, attendance figures, and only include exhibitions held outside the UK and for which an entrance fee was levied. Figures are to end December 1998.

1993–98

Rank	Name	Museum and date	Total attendance number
1	Cézanne to Matisse: Paintings from the Barnes Foundation	Musée d'Orsay, Paris (8 September 1993–2 January 1994)	1,500,000
2	Claude Monet: 1840–1926	Art Institute of Chicago (22 July–26 November 1995)	964,895
3	The Origins of Impressionism	Metropolitan Museum of Modern Art, New York (27 September 1994–8 January 1995)	794,108
4	Flemish Artists in Rome: 1508–1608	Palais des Beaux-Arts, Brussels (24 February–21 May 1995)	675,658
5	Treasures from Mount Athos	Museum of Byzantine Culture, Thessaloniki (21 June 1997–30 April 1998)	675,208
6	The Greeks in the West	Palazzo Grassi, Venice (24 May–8 December 1996)	600,000
7	Monet in the 20th Century	Museum of Fine Arts, Boston (20 September–27 December 1998)	565,992
8	Cézanne	Museum of Art, Philadelphia (30 May–1 September 1996)	548,741
9	Picasso: Early Years	National Gallery of Art, Washington (30 March–27 July 1997)	530,911
10	From Monet to Picasso	Palazzo Reale, Milan (15 February–30 June 1996)	530,000

Source: *The Art Newspaper* (London and New York)

Top 10 Most Popular Art Exhibitions in the UK

Rankings are for total, not daily, attendance figures, and include only exhibitions for which an entrance fee was levied. Figures are to end April 1999.

1994–99

Rank	Name	Museum and date	Total attendance number
1	Monet in the 20th Century	Royal Academy, London (23 January–18 April 1999)	>813,000
2	Cézanne	Tate Gallery, London (8 February–28 April 1996)	408,688
3	Picasso: Sculptor-Painter	Tate Gallery, London (16 February–8 May 1994)	296,648
4	Sensation: Young British Artists	Royal Academy, London (18 September–28 December 1997)	285,737
5	Degas: Beyond Impressionism	National Gallery, London (22 May–26 August 1996)	283,000
6	Bonnard	Tate Gallery, London (12 February–17 May 1998)	276,202
7	From Manet to Gaugin: Impressionism and Post-Impressionism from Swiss Private Collections	Royal Academy, London (30 June–8 October 1995)	253,221
8	Africa: The Art of a Continent	Royal Academy, London (4 October 1995–21 January 1996)	250,280
9	The Glory of Venice	Royal Academy, London (15 September–14 December 1994)	230,279
10	Portraits by Ingres: Image of an Epoch	National Gallery, London (27 January–25 April 1999)	199,673

Source: *The Art Newspaper* (London and New York)

Music

Top 40 Singles of the Year in the UK

1998

Rank	Title	Artist (label)
1	'Believe'	Cher (WEA)
2	'My Heart Will Go On'	Celine Dion (Epic)
3	'It's Like That'	Run-DMC, vs Jason Nevins (Sm:)e Communications)
4	'No Matter What'	Boyzone (Polydor)
5	'C'est La Vie'	B'Witched (Epic)
6	'How Do I Live'	Leann Rimes (Curb/The Hit Label)
7	'Chocolate Salty Balls (ps I Love You)'	Chef (Columbia)
8	'Goodbye'	Spice Girls (Virgin)
9	'Ghetto Supastar (That Is What You Are)'	Pras Michel featuring ODB & Mya (Interscope)
10	'Truly Madly Deeply'	Savage Garden (Columbia)
11	'Music Sounds Better with You'	Stardust (Virgin)
12	'Heartbeat/Tragedy'	Steps (Jive)
13	'Viva Forever'	Spice Girls (Virgin)
14	'3 Lions '98'	Baddiel/Skinner/Lightning Seeds (Epic)
15	'Doctor Jones'	Aqua (Universal)
16	'Never Ever'	All Saints (London)
17	'I Don't Want to Miss a Thing'	Aerosmith (Columbia)
18	'The Boy is Mine'	Brandy & Monica (Atlantic)
19	'Feel It'	Tamperer featuring Maya (Pepper)
20	'Brimful of Asha'	Cornershop (Wiiija)
21	'Rollercoaster'	B'Witched (Epic)
22	'Frozen'	Madonna (Maverick)
23	'Horny'	Mousse T vs Hot 'N' Juicy (AM:PM)
24	'Vindaloo'	Fat Les (Telstar)
25	'Angels'	Robbie Williams (Chrysalis)
26	'Dance the Night Away'	Mavericks (MCA Nashville)
27	'Under the Bridge/Lady Marmalade'	All Saints (London)
28	'Freak Me'	Another Level (Northwestside)
29	'Millennium'	Robbie Williams (Chrysalis)
30	'To the Moon and Back'	Savage Garden (Columbia)
31	'One for Sorrow'	Steps (Jive)
32	'Together Again'	Janet Jackson (Virgin)
33	'To You I Belong'	B'Witched (Epic)
34	'Got the Feelin''	Five (RCA)
35	'High'	Lighthouse Family (Wild Card)
36	'Finally Found'	Honeyz (Mercury)
37	'Perfect 10'	Beautiful South (Go! Discs/Mercury)
38	'Sex on the Beach'	T-Spoon (Control)
39	'Save Tonight'	Eagle-Eye Cherry (Polydor)
40	'I Love the Way You Love Me'	Boyzone (Polydor)

Source: Chart Information Network, www.dotmusic.com

Top 40 Albums of the Year in the UK

1998

Rank	Title	Artist (label)
1	*Talk on Corners*	Corrs (Atlantic)
2	*Ladies & Gentlemen – The Best of*	George Michael (Epic)
3	*Where We Belong*	Boyzone (Polydor)
4	*Life Thru a Lens*	Robbie Williams (Chrysalis)
5	*I've Been Expecting You*	Robbie Williams (Chrysalis)
6	*Urban Hymns*	Verve (Hut)
7	*Ray of Light*	Madonna (Maverick)
8	*Let's Talk About Love*	Celine Dion (Epic)
9	*All Saints*	All Saints (London)
10	*Titanic* (soundtrack)	James Horner (Sony Classical)
11	*Postcards from Heaven*	Lighthouse Family (Wild Card)
12	*The Best of*	M People (M People)
13	*Step One*	Steps (Jive)
14	*Quench*	Beautiful South (Go! Discs/Mercury)
15	*Hits*	Phil Collins (Virgin)
16	*Savage Garden*	Savage Garden (Columbia)
17	*One Night Only*	Bee Gees (Polydor)
18	*The Star and the Wiseman – The Best of*	Ladysmith Black Mambazo (PolyGram TV)
19	*Left of the Middle*	Natalie Imbruglia (RCA)
20	*International Velvet*	Catatonia (Blanco y Negro)
21	*The Best of 1980–1990*	U2 (Island)
22	*B'Witched*	B'Witched (Epic)
23	*Blue*	Simply Red (East West)
24	*This is My Truth Tell Me Yours*	Manic Street Preachers (Epic)
25	*Five*	Five (RCA)
26	*The Best of*	James (Fontana)
27	*Spiceworld*	Spice Girls (Virgin)
28	*Voice of an Angel*	Charlotte Church (Sony Classical)
29	*White on Blonde*	Texas (Mercury)
30	*No 1s*	Mariah Carey (Columbia)
31	*Supposed Former Infatuation Junkie*	Alanis Morissette (Maverick)
32	*Believe*	Cher (WEA)
33	*The Best of 1980–1990 B-Sides*	U2 (Island)
34	*Big Willie Style*	Will Smith (Columbia)
35	*The Masterplan*	Oasis (Creation)
36	*Aquarium*	Aqua (Universal)
37	*Songs From Ally McBeal*	Vonda Shepard (Epic)
38	*Trampoline*	Mavericks (MCA Nashville)
39	*Maverick a Strike*	Finley Quaye (Epic)
40	*Mezzanine*	Massive Attack (Virgin)

Source: Chart Information Network, www.dotmusic.com

Top 40 Classical Albums of the Year in the UK

1998

Rank	Title	Artist (label)
1	*Titanic* (soundtrack)	James Horner (Sony Classical)
2	*Voice of an Angel*	Charlotte Church (Sony Classical)
3	*Back to Titanic*	James Horner (Sony Classical)
4	*Most Relaxing Classical Album... Ever!*	Various Artists (Virgin/EMI)
5	*Lesley Garrett*	Lesley Garrett (BBC/BMG Conifer)
6	*Most Relaxing Classical Album...Ever! II*	Various Artists (Virgin/EMI)
7	*Only Classical Album You'll Ever Need*	Various Artists (BMG Conifer)
8	*The 3 Tenors in Paris*	Carreras/Domingo/Pavarotti (Decca)
9	*Simply the Best Classical Anthems*	Various Artists (Warner ESP)
10	*My Secret Passion – The Arias*	Michael Bolton (Sony Classical)
11	*The Greatest Classical Stars on Earth*	Various Artists (Decca)
12	*Brassed Off* (soundtrack)	Grimethorpe Colliery Band (RCA Victor)
13	*A Soprano in Love*	Lesley Garrett (Silva Screen)
14	*Songs of Sanctuary*	Adiemus (Venture)
15	*A Soprano Inspired*	Lesley Garrett (Conifer Classics)
16	*Rutter/Requiem*	King's College Choir/Cleobury (EMI Classics)
17	*Aria – The Opera Album*	Andrea Bocelli (Philips)
18	*The Best Carols in the World... Ever!*	Various Artists(Virgin/EMI)
19	*Worldes Blysse*	Mediaeval Baebes (Venture)
20	*Best Classical Album in the World...Ever!*	Various Artists (Virgin/EMI)
21	*100 Popular Classics*	Various Artists (Marble Arch)
22	*If Ever I Would Leave You*	Bryn Terfel (Deutsche Grammophon)
23	*China Girl – The Classical Album 2*	Vanessa-Mae (EMI Classics)
24	*Desert Island Discs*	Various Artists (BBC Music)
25	*Braveheart* (soundtrack)	London Symphony Orchestra/Horner (Decca)
26	*The Beyondness of Things*	English Co/Barry (Decca)
27	*Agnus Dei II*	Choir of New College, Oxford/Higginbottom (Erato)
28	*Salva Nos*	Mediaeval Baebes (Venture)
29	*Adiemus III – Dances of Time*	Adiemus (Venture)
30	*100 Popular Classics Volume Two*	Various Artists (Pulse)
31	*Best Opera Album in the World ...Ever!*	Various Artists (Virgin)
32	*The Very Best of Gilbert & Sullivan*	D'Oyly Carte Opera Company (Decca)
33	*The Pure Voice Of*	Emma Kirkby (Decca)
34	*The Original Four Seasons*	Vanessa-Mae (EMI)
35	*Opera Hall of Fame*	Various Artists (Classic FM)
36	*Perfect Peace*	Westminster Abbey Choir/Neary (Sony Classical)
37	*Mozart's Adagios*	Various Artists (Decca)
38	*Elgar/Payne/Symphony No 3*	BBC Symphony Orchestra/Davis (NMC)
39	*Agnus Dei*	Choir of New College, Oxford/Higginbottom (Erato)
40	*Paul McCartney's Standing Stone*	London Symphony Orchestra/Foster (EMI Classics)

Source: Chart Information Network, www.dotmusic.com

Selected Symphony and Chamber Orchestras in the UK

Orchestra	Director/conductor
The Academy of Ancient Music	Christopher Hogwood
Academy of London	Richard Stamp
Academy of St Martin in the Fields	Neville Marriner
Ambache Chamber Orchestra	Diana Ambache
BBC Concert Orchestra	Barry Wordsworth
BBC National Orchestra of Wales	Mark Wigglesworth
BBC Philharmonic	Yan Pascal Tortelier
BBC Scottish Symphony Orchestra	Osmo Vänskä
BBC Symphony Orchestra	Andrew Davis
Bournemouth Sinfonietta	Alexander Polianichko
Bournemouth Symphony Orchestra	Yakov Kreizberg
The Brandenburg Consort	Roy Goodman
The Britten Sinfonia	Nicholas Cleobury
CBSO (City of Birmingham Symphony Orchestra)	Sakari Oramo
Charivari Agréable Simfonie	Kah-Ming Ng
City of London Sinfonia	Richard Hickox
City of Oxford Orchestra	Marios Papadopoulos
Corydon Orchestra	Matthew Best
East of England Orchestra	Nicholas Kok
English Camerata	Elizabeth Altman
English Classical Players	Jonathan Brett
English Northern Philharmonia	Richard Mantle
English Sinfonia	Bramwell Tovey
English String Orchestra	William Boughton
English Symphony Orchestra	William Boughton
Fiori Musicali	Penelope Rapson
Guildford Philharmonic Orchestra	En Shao
The Hallé Orchestra	Mark Elder
The Hanover Band	Caroline Brown
The King's Consort	Robert King
London Chamber Orchestra	Christopher Warren-Green
London Handel Orchestra	Denys Darlow
London Jupiter Orchestra	Gregory Rose
London Mozart Players	Matthias Bamert
London Philharmonic Orchestra	Kurt Masur
London Pro Arte Orchestra	Murray Stewart
London Sinfonietta	Markus Stenz
London Symphony Orchestra	Colin Davis
Manchester Camerata	Sachio Fujioka
Mozart Orchestra	Gordon Heard
New London Orchestra	Ronald Corp
New Queen's Hall Orchestra	John Boyden
Northern Sinfonia	Jean-Bernard Pommier
Orchestra da Camera	Kenneth Page
Orchestra of St John's Smith Square	John Lubbock
Orchestra of the Age of Enlightenment	Marshall Marcus
Orchestre Révolutionnaire et Romantique	John Eliot Gardiner
Oxford Orchestra da Camera	Patricia Bavaud
Philharmonia Orchestra	Christoph von Dohnányi
Philomusica of London	David Littaur
The Royal Liverpool Philharmonic Orchestra	Petr Altrichter
Royal Opera House Orchestra	Bernard Haitink
Royal Philharmonic Concert Orchestra	Thomas Siracusa
Royal Scottish National Orchestra	Alexander Lazarev
The Scottish Chamber Orchestra	Joseph Swensen
Sinfonia 21	Dennis Stevenson
Taverner Players	Andrew Parrott
Ulster Orchestra	Michael Henson
Welsh Chamber Orchestra	Anthony Hose
Welsh National Opera Orchestra	Carlo Rizzi
Welsh Philharmonic Orchestra	G J Harries

Selected Symphony Orchestras in Europe

Country	Orchestra	Director/conductor
Austria	Mozarteum Orchester Wiener Philharmoniker Wiener Symphoniker	Hubert Soudant Clemens Hellsberg Rainer Bischof
Belgium	Orchestre National de Belgique	Alain Pierlot
Bulgaria	Bulgarian National Radio Symphony Orchestra	Milen Natchev
Croatia	Dubrovnik Symphony Orchestra	Pero Glavinic
Czech Republic	Czech Philharmonic Orchestra Czech Symphony Orchestra	Ing Jiri Kovár Jiri Kauders
Denmark	Danish National Radio Symphony Orchestra Royal Danish Orchestra	Per Erik Veng Elaine Padmore
Estonia	Estonian National Symphony Orchestra	Ville-Markus Kell
Finland	Finnish Radio Symphony Orchestra	Jukka-Pekka Saraste
France	Orchestre National de France Orchestre Philharmonique de Radio-France	Charles Dutoit Marek Janowski
Germany	Bayerische Staatsorchester Berlin Philharmonic Leipziger Gewandhausorchester Radio-Sinfonie-Orchester Frankfurt	Zubin Mehta Simon Rattle Herbert Blomstedt Hugh Wolff
Hungary	Hungarian National Philharmonic Orchestra	Gilbert Varga
Ireland, Republic of	National Symphony Orchestra of Ireland RTE Concert Orchestra	Alexander Anissimov Proinnsias O Duinn
Italy	Toscanini Symphony Orchestra Orchestra Sinfonica Nazionale della RAI	Patrick Fournillier Sergio Sablich
Latvia	Latvian National Symphony Orchestra	Terje Mikkelsen
Lithuania	Lithuanian National Symphony Orchestra Lithuanian State Symphony Orchestra	Juozas Domarkas Gintaras Rinkevicius
Luxembourg	Orchestre Philharmonique du Luxembourg	Jacques Mauroy
Monaco	Orchestre Philharmonique de Monte-Carlo	James DePreist
Netherlands	Netherlands Philharmonic Orchestra Netherlands Radio Philharmonic Royal Concertgebouw Orchestra	Jan Willem Loot Edo de Waart Riccardo Chailly
Norway	Oslo Philharmonic Orchestra	Trond Okkelmo
Poland	Polish Radio National Symphony Orchestra Warsaw Philharmonic	Antoni Wit Kazimierz Kord
Portugal	Gulbenkian Orchestra Lisbon Metropolitan Orchestra	Muhai Tang Miguel Graça Moura
Russia	Bolshoi Symphony Orchestra Russian National Symphony Orchestra Russian State Philharmonic Orchestra	Mark Ermter Mikhail Pletnev Valery Poliansky
Slovak Republic	Slovak Radio Symphonic Orchestra	R Stankovsky
Slovenia	Slovenian Philharmonic	Boris Sinigoj
Spain	Orquesta Sinfónica de Barcelona i Nacional de Catalunya	Lawrence Foster
Sweden	Swedish Radio Symphony Orchestra	Lennart Stenkvist
Switzerland	Berner Symphonie-Orchester Orchestre de la Suisse Romande Tonhalle-Orchester Zürich	Dmitrij Kitajenko Armin Jordan David Zinman
Ukraine	National Symphony Orchestra of Ukraine Crimea State Symphony Orchestra	Theodore Kuchar Vladimir Nozhov

Some Major Opera Companies in the UK

Company	Director	Company	Director
Central Festival Opera Ltd	Tom Hawkes	New Sussex Opera	David Angus
City of Birmingham Touring Opera	Graham Vick	Northern Opera Ltd	Richard Bloodworth
Dorset Opera	Patrick Shelley	Opera Box Ltd	Fraser Goulding
English Festival Opera	Simon Gray	Opera da Camera	Derek Barnes
English National Opera	Paul Daniel	Opera Europa	John Gibbons
English Touring Opera	Andrew Greenwood	Opera Factory	David Freeman
European Chamber Opera	Stefan Paul Sanchez	Opera North	Richard Mantle
First Act Opera International	Elaine Holden	Opera Northern Ireland	Tim Kerr
Garsington Opera Ltd	Leonard Ingrams	Opera Restor'd	Peter Holman
Glyndebourne Festival Opera	Andrew Davis	Pimlico Opera	Wasfi Kani
Glyndebourne Touring Opera	Louis Langrée	The Royal Opera	Bernard Haitink
London Community Opera	Peter Bridges	Scottish Opera	Richard Armstrong
Music Theatre London	Tony Britten	South Yorkshire Opera Ltd	Nita White
Music Theatre Wales	Michael Rafferty	Surrey Opera	Jonathan Butcher
National Youth Music Theatre	Jeremy James Taylor	Travelling Opera	Peter Knapp
New Chamber Opera	Gary Cooper	Welsh National Opera	Carlo Rizzi

Some Major World Opera Companies

(N/A = not available.)

Country	Company	Director
Argentina	Teatro Colon	Kive Staiff
Australia	Opera Australia	Moffatt Oxenbould
	The State Opera of South Australia	Stephen Phillips
	West Australian Opera	Richard Mills
Austria	Salzburger Landestheater	Lutz Hochstraate
	Wiener Staatsoper	Ioan Holender
	Volksoper Wien	Klaus Bachler
Bulgaria	National Theater Opera de Sofia	Emil Boshnakov
Canada	Calgary Opera	Bob McPee
	L'Opéra de Montréal	Bernard Uzan
	Opéra de Québec	Bernard Labadie
	Opera Ontario	Daniel Lipton
	Vancouver Opera	David Agler
China	Shanghai Opera House	He Zhao-hua
Czech Republic	The National Theatre Opera/Národní Divadlo	Josef Prudek
Denmark	The Royal Danish Opera	Elaine Padmore
Finland	Finnish National Opera	Okko Kamu
France	L'Opéra Comique	Pierre Medecin
	Opéra National de Paris-Bastille	Pierre Bergé
Germany	Bayerische Staatsoper	Zubin Mehta
	Deutsche Oper Berlin	Christian Tuielemann
	Komische Oper	Yakov Kreizberg
	Staatsoper Unter den Linden	Daniel Barenboim
Hungary	The Hungarian State Opera	Géza Oberfrank
Ireland, Republic of	Opera Ireland	Dieter Koegi
Italy	L'Arena di Verona	Renzo Giacchieri
	Teatro Alla Scala	Riccardo Muti
	Teatro di San Carlo	Filippo Zigante
	Teatro Municipale Valli	Bruno Borghi
Japan	Opera Theatre/Konnyakuza	Hikaru Hayashi
Monaco	L'Opéra de Monte-Carlo	John Mordler
Netherlands	De Nederlandse Opera	Pierre Audi
	International Opera Centrum Nederland	Hans Nieuwenhuis
New Zealand	Auckland Opera Company	Stephen Morrison
	National Opera	Patricia Hurley
Norway	Den Norske Opera	Bernt E Bauge
Poland	Grand Theatre/National Opera	Jerzy Bojar
	Warsaw Chamber Opera	Stefan Sutowski
Russia	Mariisky Theatre	Valery Gergyev
Slovak Republic	Slovak National Theatre	Ondrej Lenárd
South Africa	Opera of the Cape Performing Arts	Angelo Gobbato
Sweden	Royal Swedish Opera	Walton Grönroos
	Swedish Folkopera	Claes Fellbom
Switzerland	Grand Théâthre de Genève	Renée Auphan
	Opernhaus Zürich	Franz Welser-Möst
USA	Baltimore Opera Company	William Yannuzzi
	Cleveland Opera	David Bamberger
	The Metropolitan Opera	James Levine

The Royal Opera House: Key Events

7 December 1732	Opening night of the Theatre Royal at Covent Garden, London – the first theatre on the site of the present Royal Opera House. Pantomimes, plays, and opera are all staged here.
19 September 1808	The Theatre Royal is burned down; rebuilding begins immediately.
18 September 1809	The second Theatre Royal reopens, but the 'Old Price' riots soon break out in protest at ticket price increases.
6 April 1847	The music company at the nearby Her Majesty's Theatre in the Haymarket transfers to Covent Garden, which is remodelled and renamed the Royal Italian Opera as a venue for opera and ballet.
5 March 1856	A devastating fire destroys the Royal Italian Opera.
15 May 1858	Opening of the third building on the site; renamed the Royal Opera House in 1892.
1914–18	The house closes for performances during World War I, and is used by the Ministry of Works as a furniture repository.
1940–45	During World War II, the Royal Opera House serves as a Mecca Dance Hall.
1946	The Sadler's Wells Ballet, under the direction of Ninette de Valois, is invited to become the resident ballet company at the Royal Opera House; in 1956 it is renamed the Royal Ballet.
20 February 1946	The Royal Opera House reopens as a government-subsidized classical music and dance venue.
14 January 1947	First performance of the new permanent resident opera company (formed in late 1946); it is renamed the Royal Opera in 1968.
1975	The government purchases land on the north side of Covent Garden to enable major reconstruction of the Royal Opera House.
1985–January 1997	Jeremy Isaacs, former chief executive of Channel 4 television, is general director of the Royal Opera. Financial losses continue to mount throughout the 1980s and 1990s.
1995	The Royal Opera House is awarded £78.5 million from the National Lottery arts fund, to help with the £214 million cost of reconstruction.
January 1997–March 1998	Financial and management crises bring the appointment and swift resignation of two general directors – Genista Macintosh (January–May 1997) and Mary Allen (September 1997–March 1998).
September 1997–December 1999	The Royal Opera House closes for complete reconstruction. Among the major changes, under the supervision of architect Jeremy Dixon, is the building of a second auditorium to increase the 2,250 capacity, the creation of larger public spaces within the complex, and modernization of backstage facilities. During the closure period, the ballet and opera companies go on tour, playing at other houses in London and abroad.
October 1998	US arts administrator Michael Kaiser is appointed general director of the Royal Opera House. In December, the Arts Council of England relieves the opera house's financial difficulties by increasing its grant by 11% to £16 million for 1999 and £20 million for 2000 and 2001.

***Sir Colin Southgate**, chairman of the Royal Opera House, arrives at Covent Garden in September 1998 to announce an 11-month suspension of performances by the cash-strapped organization until the completion of the £200 million rebuilding project.* Photo: Richard Watt

Theatre and Dance

Notable Regional Theatres in the UK

Birmingham Repertory Theatre Centenary Square, Broad Street, Birmingham B1 2EP; phone: (0121) 236 6771; artistic director: Bill Alexander

Theatre Royal King Street, Bristol BS1 4ED; phone: (0117) 949 3993; artistic director: Andy Hay

Chichester Festival Theatre Oaklands Park, Chichester, West Sussex PO19 4AP; phone: (01243) 784437; festival director: Andrew Welch

Belgrade Theatre Belgrade Square, Coventry, Warwickshire CV1 1GS; phone: (01203) 256431; theatre director: Bob Eaton

Derby Playhouse Theatre Walk, Eagle Centre, Derby DE1 2NF; phone: (01332) 363271; artistic director: Mark Clements

Royal Lyceum Theatre Grindlay Street, Edinburgh EH3 9AX; phone: (0131) 229 7404; artistic director: Kenny Ireland

Northcott Theatre Stocker Road, Exeter, Devon EX4 4QB; phone: (01392) 256182; artistic director: Ben Crocker

Citizen's Theatre Gorbals, Glasgow G5 9DS; phone: (0141) 429 5561; artistic director: Giles Havergal

Harrogate Theatre Oxford Street, Harrogate HG1 1QF; phone: (01423) 502710; artistic director: Rob Swain

Hull Truck Theatre Spring Street, Hull HU2 8RW phone: (01482) 224800; artistic director: John Godber

Wolsey Theatre Civic Drive, Ipswich, Suffolk IP1 2AS phone: (01473 218911); artistic director: Andrew Manley

West Yorkshire Playhouse Playhouse Square, Quarry Hill, Leeds LS2 7UP; phone: (0113) 213 7800; artistic director: Jude Kelly

Haymarket Theatre Belgrave Gate, Leicester LE1 3YQ; phone: (0116) 253 0021; artistic director: Paul Kerryson

Royal Exchange Theatre St Ann's Square, Manchester M2 7DH; phone: (0161) 833 9333; artistic directors: Greg Hersov, Braham Murray, Matthew Lloyd

Theatr Clwyd Mold, Flintshire, North Wales CH7 1YA; phone: (01352) 756331; artistic director: Terry Hands

Nottingham Playhouse Wellington Circus, Nottingham NG1 5AF; phone: (0115) 947 4361; artistic director: Giles Croft

Theatre Royal Royal Parade, Plymouth, Devon PL1 2TR; phone: (01752) 668282; chief executive: Adrian Vinken

Stephen Joseph Theatre Westborough, Scarborough YO11 1JW; phone: (01723) 370540; artistic director: Alan Ayckbourn

Crucible Theatre 55 Norfolk Street, Sheffield S1 2AS; phone: (0114) 276 0621; artistic director: Deborah Paige

Theatre Royal St Leonard's Place, York YO1 2HD; phone: (01904) 658162; artistic director: Damian Cruden

Theatres and Theatre-Going in the UK

There are six key organizations representing the people who put on theatre shows in the UK: Theatrical Management Association (TMA), Society of London Theatre (SOLT), Apollo Theatres, Independent Theatre Council (ITC), Little Theatre Guild, and National Operatic and Dramatic Society (NODA).

1998	
Number of performances[1]	104,340
Number of tickets sold	31,597,000
Value of tickets sold (£)[2]	105,600,000
VAT to government on tickets alone (£)[2]	15,800,000
VAT to government on additional sales (eg ice cream, drinks, programmes) (£)[2]	4,000,000
Average ticket price (£)	11.80

[1] Figures are for TMA, SOLT, ITC, and Little Theatre Guild members only.
[2] Figures are for TMA members only.

Source: Theatrical Management Association

Top 10 Longest-Running West End Theatre Productions

As of June 1999.

Rank	Production	Category	Years	Months
1	*The Mousetrap*	whodunnit	46	7
2	*Cats*	musical	18	1
3	*Starlight Express*	musical	15	3
4	*Les Misérables*	musical	13	8
5	*The Phantom of the Opera*	musical	12	8
6	*Blood Brothers*	musical	10	11
7	*The Woman in Black*	thriller	10	4
8	*Miss Saigon*	musical	9	9
9	*Buddy*	musical	9	8
10	*Grease*	musical	5	11

Source: Society of London Theatre

Top 5 Dance Companies by Budget in the UK

1997–98

Rank	Company	Address	Artistic director	Budget
1	The Royal Ballet	Royal Opera House, Covent Garden, London WC2E 9DD; phone: (0171) 240 1200	Anthony Dowell	£6,555,000
2	Birmingham Royal Ballet	Birmingham Hippodrome, Thorp Street, Birmingham B5 4AU; phone: (0121) 622 2555	David Bintley	£5,472,000
3	English National Ballet	Markova House, 39 Jay Mews, London SW7 2ES; phone: (0171) 581 1245	Derek Deane	£3,903,000
4	The Scottish Ballet	261 West Princes Street, Glasgow G4 9EE; phone: (0141) 331 2931	Ken Burke	£2,353,000
5	Rambert Dance Company	94 Chiswick High Road, London W4 1SH; phone: (0181) 995 4246	Christopher Bruce	£1,240,000

Source: Arts Councils of England, Scotland, Wales, and Northern Ireland

Andrew Lloyd Webber Shows Around the World

As of March 1999.

Show	Country/region	City
Aspects of Love	Hungary[1]	Budapest
	Germany[1]	Dresden
Cats	UK	London
	USA	New York (NY)
	USA	National tour
	Germany	Hamburg
	Hungary[1]	Budapest
	Japan	Fukuoka
Jesus Christ Superstar	UK	National tour
Joseph and the Amazing Technicolour Dreamcoat	UK[1]	National tour
	Hungary[1]	Budapest
	Slovak Republic[1]	Bratislava
	Germany	Essen
The Phantom of the Opera	UK	London
	UK	National tour
	USA	New York (NY)
	USA	National tour
	Japan	Tokyo
	Canada	Toronto
	Germany	Hamburg
Starlight Express	UK	London
	Germany	Bochum
Sunset Boulevard	USA	National tour
Whistle Down the Wind	UK	London

[1] Non-replica shows.

Source: Brown Lloyd James

Festivals

Arts Festivals in the UK

England

Aldeburgh Festival of Music and the Arts Festival of opera and classical music, with recitals by leading artists. **Date** June **Address** Aldeburgh Productions, High Street, Aldeburgh, Suffolk IP15 5AX; phone: (01728) 453543; fax: (01728) 452715; e-mail: enquiries@aldeburghfestivals.org **Web site** www.aldeburgh.co.uk

Arundel Festival Festival of jazz and orchestral concerts, as well as drama, street theatre, and family shows. **Date** August–September **Address** The Mary Gate, Arundel, West Sussex BN18 9AT; phone: (01903) 883690; fax: (01903) 884243 **Web site** www.argonet.co.uk/arundel.festival

Bath International Music Festival Wide-ranging music festival, including performances of early, classical, contemporary, jazz, and world music. **Date** May–June **Address** Bath Festivals Box Office, 2 Church Street, Abbey Green, Bath BA1 1NL; phone: (01225) 463362; fax: (01225) 310377

Bath Literature Festival Festival of literature, including appearances by leading literary figures. **Date** February–March **Address** Bath Festivals Box Office, 2 Church Street, Abbey Green, Bath BA1 1NL; phone: (01225) 463362; fax: (01225) 310377

Beverley and East Riding Early Music Festival. Date May **Information** phone: (01904) 645738; fax: (01904) 612631; e-mail: yemf@netcomuk.co.uk

Boxgrove: Music at Boxgrove Series of concerts in Boxgrove's Priory Church, including performances by international artists. **Date** May–June **Address** Music at Boxgrove, PO Box 117, Chichester, West Sussex PO18 0NN; phone: (0118) 981 3190; fax: (0118) 981 0218

Brighton Festival England's largest arts festival, including music recitals and concerts, drama, comedy, and street theatre. **Date** May **Address** 21–22 Old Steine, Brighton, East Sussex BN1 1EL; phone: (01273) 676926; fax: (01273) 622453; e-mail: info@brighton-festival.org.uk **Web site** www.brighton-festival.org.uk

Bury St Edmunds Festival Wide-ranging arts festival featuring international artists. **Date** May **Address** Festival Office, Borough Offices, Angel Hill, Bury St Edmunds, Suffolk IP33 1XB; phone: (01284) 769505; fax: (01284) 757124; e-mail: kevin.appleby@burybo.stedsbc.gov.uk **Web site** www.stedmundsbury.gov.uk/buryfest

Buxton Festival Festival of rarely-performed operas as well as chamber music, jazz, and fringe events. **Date** July **Address** 1 Crescent View, Hall Bank, Buxton, Derbyshire SK17 6EN; phone: (01298) 72190; fax: (01298) 72289

Canterbury Festival Large international festival including concerts in Canterbury Cathedral, drama, dance, and opera, as well as jazz, folk, and cabaret. **Date** October **Address** Festival Office, Christ Church Gate, The Precincts, Canterbury, Kent CT1 2EE; phone: (01227) 452853; fax: (01227) 781830

Chard Festival of Women in Music Festival of music of many styles composed by women. **Date** May **Address** 3 Howards Row, Chard, Somerset TA20 1PH; phone: (01460) 66115; fax: (01460) 66048

Chelmsford Cathedral Festival Ten-day festival of classical music, jazz, and opera, with accompanying exhibitions of the visual arts and many fringe events. **Date** May **Address** Festival Office, Guy Harlings, New Street, Chelmsford CM1 1AT; phone: (01245) 359890; fax: (01245) 280456

Cheltenham Festival of Literature Two-week literary festival including talks and readings by international authors, as well as discussions, street theatre, and workshops. **Date** October **Address** Town Hall, Imperial Square, Cheltenham, Gloucestershire GL50 1QA; phone: (01242) 227979; fax: (01242) 573902; e-mail: townhall@cheltenham.gov.uk **Web site** www.cheltenham.gov.uk

Cheltenham International Festival of Music International festival of contemporary and classical music. **Date** July **Address** Town Hall, Imperial Square, Cheltenham, Gloucestershire GL50 1QA; phone: (01242) 227979; fax: (01242) 573902; e-mail: townhall@cheltenham.gov.uk **Web site** www.cheltenham.gov.uk

Cheltenham International Jazz Festival Weekend programme of jazz, with performances by international artists. **Date** April **Address** Town Hall, Imperial Square, Cheltenham, Gloucestershire GL50 1QA; phone: (01242) 227979; fax: (01242) 573902; e-mail: townhall@cheltenham.gov.uk **Web site** www.cheltenham.gov.uk

Chester Summer Music Festival Two-week music festival including outdoor concerts and performances by leading artists

and orchestras. **Date** July **Address** Festival Office, 8 Abbey Square, Chester CH1 2HU; phone: (01244) 320722; fax: (01244) 341200; e-mail: csmf@dial.pipex.com

Chichester Festivities Programme of events including classical music concerts and jazz. **Date** July **Address** Canon Gate House, South Street, Chichester, West Sussex PO19 1PU; phone: (01243) 785718; fax: (01243) 528356; e-mail: chi.fest@argonet.co.uk **Web site** www.argonet.co.uk/chifest

Dartington International Summer School Five-week programme of concerts, opera, and dance performances, with masterclasses and workshops by an international team of artists. **Date** July–August **Address** Dartington Hall, Totnes, Devon TQ9 6DE; phone: (01803) 867068; fax: (01803) 868108; e-mail: brochure@dissorg.u-net.com **Web site** www.dissorg.u-net.com

Deal Summer Music Festival. Date July–August **Address** Cuilt Brae, Downs Road, East Studdal, Dover, Kent CT15 5DA; phone: (01304) 374529

Dewsbury Festival of Christian Music. Date October **Address** The Minster, Rishworth Road, Dewsbury WF12 8DD; phone: (01924) 457057

Exeter Festival Festival of classical concerts, opera, dance, comedy, and sport. **Date** July **Address** Gerri Bennett, City Centre Marketing Officer, Exeter City Council, Paris Street, Exeter EX1 1NN; phone: (01392) 265118; fax: (01392) 265695; e-mail: gerri.bennett@exeter.gov.uk **Web site** www.exeter.gov.uk

Grassington Festival. Date June–July **Address** Threshfield, Skipton, North Yorkshire BD23 5HR; phone: (01756) 753093; fax: (01756) 753370; e-mail: dawjoy@aol.com **Web site** www.labcenter.co.uk/festival

Guildford Book Festival. Date October **Address** c/o Arts Office, University of Surrey, Guildford GU2 5XH; phone: (01483) 254167; fax: (01483) 300803 **Web site** www.surreyweb.org.uk/

Guildford International Music Festiva.l Date March **Address** c/o Music Department, University of Surrey, Guildford GU2 5XH; phone: (01483) 259690; fax: (01483) 259586; e-mail: P.B.Johnson@surrey.ac.uk **Web site** www.surrey.ac.uk/Music

Harrogate International Festival Wide-ranging arts festival, including jazz, blues, concerts by international symphony orchestras, dance, comedy, street theatre, and fringe events. **Date** July–August **Address** Festival Office, 1 Victoria Avenue, Harrogate, North Yorkshire HG1 1EQ; phone: (01423) 562303; fax: (01423) 521264; e-mail: info@harrogate-festival.org.uk **Web site** www.harrogate-festival.org.uk

Henley Festival Festival of classical and contemporary music, jazz, theatre, and the visual arts, as well as literary events. **Date** July **Address** 14 Friday Street, Henley-on-Thames, Oxfordshire RG9 1AH; phone: (01491) 843404; fax: (01491) 410482; e-mail: info@henley-festival.co.uk **Web site** www.henley-festival.co.uk

Huddersfield Contemporary Music Festival Festival of contemporary music, film, opera, and dance, with performances by leading composers. **Date** November **Address** Department of Music, The University of Huddersfield, Huddersfield HD1 3DH; phone: (01484) 472103; fax: (01484) 425082; e-mail: hcmf@hud.ac.uk **Web site** www.hud.ac.uk/events/hcm/welcome.html

Lake District Summer Music Programme of music events, including morning recitals, masterclasses, and evening concerts by leading artists and emerging young talents. **Date** July–August **Address** LDSM, Stricklandgate House, 92 Stricklandgate, Kendal, Cumbria LA9 4PU; phone: (01539) 733411; fax: (01539) 724441; e-mail: info@ldsm.org.uk **Web site** www.ldsm.org.uk

Ledbury Poetry Festival. Date July **Address** Town Council Offices, Church Street, Ledbury, Herefordshire HR8 1DH; phone: (01531) 634156; fax: (01531) 631193 **Web site** www.ledburypoetfest.org.uk

Leicester International Music Festival. Date June **Address** New Walk Museum, 53 New Walk, Leicester LE1 7EA; phone/fax: (0116) 247 3043

Lichfield International Arts Festival Wide-ranging arts festival featuring international artists, jazz, drama, films, exhibitions, talks, an education programme, medieval market, and fireworks. **Date** July **Address** 7 The Close, Lichfield, Staffordshire WS13 7LD; phone: (01543) 257298; fax: (01543) 415137; e-mail: lichfield. fest@lichfield-art.org.uk **Web site** www. lichfieldfestival.org

London: Bangladesh Festival. Date July **Address** Arts Worldwide, 309A Aberdeen House, 22 Highbury Grove, London N5 2DQ; phone: (0171) 354 3030; fax: (0171) 354 8404; e-mail: artsworldwide@dial.pipex.com

London: BBC Proms World's largest classical music festival with over 70 concerts. **Date** July–September **Information** phone: (0171) 765 5575; e-mail: Proms@bbc.co.uk **Web site** www.bbc.co.uk/proms

London: BOC Covent Garden Festival Three-week festival of opera and music theatre with over 100 performances in a wide variety of venues. **Date** May–June **Address** Unit 47, The Market, The Piazza, Covent Garden, London WC2E 8RF; phone: (0171) 379 0870; fax: (0171) 379 0876; e-mail: cgf@mail.bogo.co.uk **Web site** www.cgf.co.uk

London: City of London Festival Festival of opera, music, theatre, poetry, jazz, and dance, with performances in historic settings throughout the City of London. **Date** June–July **Address** Bishopsgate Hall, 230 Bishopsgate, London EC2M 4HW; phone: (0171) 377 0540; fax: (0171) 377 1972; e-mail: city fest@dircon.co.uk **Web site** www.city-of-london-festival.org.uk

London: Dance Umbrella Five-week programme of contemporary dance events featuring British and international performers. **Date** October–November **Address** 20 Chancellors Street, London W6 9RN; phone: (0181) 741 5881; fax: (0181) 741 7902 **Web site** www.danceumbrella.co.uk

London: Dulwich Festival. Date May **Address** 75 Calton Avenue, London SE21 7DF; phone/fax: (0181) 299 1011 **Web site** www.dulwichin.demon.co.uk/festival/

London: Greenwich and Docklands International Festival Wide-ranging arts festival featuring international theatre, music, dance, and visual arts. **Date** July **Address** 6 College Approach, Greenwich, London SE10 9HY; phone: (0181) 305 1818; fax: (0181) 305 1188; e-mail: greendock@globalnet.co.uk **Web site** www.festival.org

London: Hampstead and Highgate Festival Date June **Address** 60 Ashworth Mansions, London W9 1LW; phone/fax: (0171) 286 8811

London: Islington International Festival Date June **Address** Suite 5, 313–314 Upper Street, London N1 2XQ; phone: (0171) 354 2535; fax: (0171) 354 4282; e-mail: islington.festival@dial.pipex.com **Web site** www.islington-festival.co.uk

London: London International Festival of Theatre (LIFT) Avantgarde theatrical events in a wide range of venues throughout London. **Date** June–July **Address** 19/20 Great Sutton Street, London EC1V 0DR; phone: (0171) 312 1995; fax: (0171) 490 3976; e-mail: lift@easynet.co.uk **Web site** www.lift-info.co.uk

London: Lufthansa Festival of Baroque Music. Date June–July **Address** 200 Broomwood Road, London SW11 6JY; phone: (0171) 222 1061

London: Pride Arts Festival. Date June–July **Information** phone: (0171) 737 5763

London: St Ceciliatide International Festival of Music Festival celebrating Saint Cecilia, patron saint of music, featuring leading artists. **Date** November **Address** Festival Director, Stationers' Hall, Ave Maria Lane, London EC4M 7DD; phone: (01327) 361380; fax: (01327) 361415; e-mail: cecilia@st-ceciliatide.com **Web site** www.st-ceciliatide.com

London: Southwark Festival Festival of contemporary arts, ethnic and classical music, dance, community and culinary events. **Date** October **Address** 16 Winchester Walk, London SE1 9AQ; phone: (0171) 403 7400; fax: (0171) 403 7474; e-mail: swkfest@aol.com

London: Spitalfields Festival Wide-ranging music festival based at Christ Church, Spitalfields, including early, contemporary, and world music, as well as education events. **Date** June **Address** Christ Church, Commercial Street, London E1 6LY; phone: (0171) 377 0287; fax: (0171) 247 0494; e-mail: Spitfest@easynet.co.uk

London: Stoke Newington Midsummer Festival. Date June **Address** Festival Office, 59 Kynaston Road, London N16 0EB; phone/fax: (0171) 923 1599

Ludlow Festival Festival of the arts, ranging from opera, ballet, and jazz, to theatre and children's events. **Date** June–July **Address** Castle Square, Ludlow, Shropshire SY8 1AY; phone: (01584) 872150; fax: (01584) 877673; e-mail: Ludlowfest @aol.com

Manchester: Streets Ahead Festival Free programme of theatre, music, dance, and fireworks. **Date** May **Address** 3 Birch Polygon, Manchester M14 5HX; phone: (0161) 953 4238; fax: (0161) 248 9331; e-mail: mia@mcr1.poptel.org.uk

Newbury International Spring Festival Wide-ranging arts festival including classical and world music, opera, and jazz, as well as family events, film, and visual arts. **Date** May **Address** 1 Bridge Street, Newbury, Berkshire RG14 5BE; phone: (01635) 32421/528766; fax: (01635) 528690

Norfolk and Norwich Festival Britain's oldest city festival, featuring music, theatre, visual arts, dance, opera, comedy, street theatre, and circus. **Date** October **Address** The Ticket Shop, Guildhall, Gaol Hill, Norwich, NR2 1NF; phone: (01603) 764764; fax: (01603) 766699; e-mail: info@nn.fest.eastern-arts.co.uk

Northern Aldborough Festival. Date July **Address** Festival Office, Aldborough Manor, Boroughbridge, Yorkshire YO51 9EP; phone: (01423) 324899; fax: (01423) 323223; e-mail: festival@aldborough.com **Web site** www.aldborough.com/festival

Oldham Walton Festival. Date March **Address** Queen Elizabeth Hall, West Street, Oldham, Lancashire OL1 1UT; phone: (0161) 911 4072

Oundle International Festival and Summer School for Young Organists. Date July **Address** The Old Crown, Glapthorn, Oundle, Peterborough PE8 5BJ; phone: (01832) 272026

Ross-on-Wye International Festival Wide-ranging arts festival including opera and dance, with performances by British and international artists. **Date** August **Address** The Mews, Mitcheldean, Gloucestershire GL17 0SL; phone: (01594) 541070; e-mail: Ross_Festival@compuserve.com **Web site** www.rossfest.wyenet.co.uk

Ryedale Festival Date July **Address** Ryedale Festival Trust, The Old Meeting House, Helmsley, Yorkshire YO62 5DW; phone: (01439) 771518

St Albans International Organ Festival Music festival, including concerts, recitals, talks, and exhibitions, as well as organ competitions. **Date** July **Address** IOFS, PO Box 80, St Albans AL3 4HR; phone/fax: (01727) 844765; e-mail: IOFS@aol.com **Web site** www.stalbans.gov.uk/OrganFestival/

Salisbury Festival Festival of classical concerts, jazz, circus, theatre, visual arts, and children's events. **Date** May–June **Address** 75 New Street, Salisbury SP1 2PH; phone: (01722) 323888; fax: (01722) 410552

Sheffield: Music in the Round May Festival Festival of chamber music, ranging from early to contemporary, performed in the Crucible Studio. **Date** May **Address** Music in the Round, The Workstation, 15 Paternoster Row, Sheffield S1 2BX; phone: (0114) 276 9922; fax: (0114) 221 2183; e-mail: mitr@workstation.org.uk

Solihull Festival. Date May **Address** Lottery Cottage, Hob Lane, Burton Green, Kenilworth CV8 1QA; phone: (01676) 535818

Stour Music. Date June **Address** 2 Rural Terrace, Wye, Ashford, Kent TN25 5AP; phone: (01233) 812267; fax: (01227) 781830

Swaledale Festival. Date May–June **Address** Leyburn Tourist Information Centre, 4 Central Chambers, Railway Street, Leyburn, North Yorkshire, DL8 5AB; phone: (01969) 623069

Thaxted Festival. Date June–July **Address** Clarance House, Thaxted, Essex CM6 2PJ; phone/fax: (01371) 831421

Three Choirs Festival at Worcester Europe's oldest music festival, including major orchestral and choral concerts. **Date** August **Address** Festival Administrator, 5 Deansway, Worcester WR1 2JG; phone: (01905) 212600; fax: (01905) 611139; e-mail: Lucasorg@compuserve.com **Web site** www.3choirs.org

Tyneside: Window on the World International Music Festival Wide-ranging music festival, featuring free performances of world, pop, jazz, blues, and street music from Britain and around the world. **Date** May **Information** phone: (0191) 200 5415; fax: (0191) 200 8910

Warwick and Leamington Festival Classical music and jazz festival featuring performances by international artists. **Date** June–July **Address** Warwick Arts Society, Northgate, Warwick CV34 4JL; phone: (01926) 496277; fax: (01926) 407606 **Web site** welcome.to/warwickarts

Windsor Festival Music festival, including a wide range of concerts including baroque, opera, jazz, and contemporary, performed at Windsor Castle and Eton College. **Date** September–October **Address** 60 Ashworth Mansions, London W9 1LW; phone/fax: (0171) 286 8811

Woking Dance Umbrella International dance festival. **Date** March **Address** 20 Chancellors Street, London W6 9RN; phone: (01483) 761144

York Early Music Festival Festival of early and world music featuring international artists. **Date** July **Address** YEMF, PO Box 226, York YO3 6ZU; phone: (01904) 658338; fax: (01904) 612631; e-mail: yemf@netcomuk.co.uk

Isle of Man

Mananan International Festival. Date June–July **Address** Mananan Festival Office, Erin Arts Centre, Victoria Square, Port Erin, Isle of Man IM9 6LD; phone: (01624) 832662; fax: (01624) 836658; e-mail: erinartscentre@enterprise.net **Web site** www.manxman.co.im/music/mananan

Northern Ireland

Ballymena Arts Festival Wide-ranging festival of classical, jazz, and popular music, dance, theatre, comedy, and visual arts, as well as fringe events and an educational and community programme. **Date** October **Address** Ballymena Borough Council, 'Ardeevin', 80 Galgorm Road, Ballymena, Northern Ireland BT42 1AB; phone: (01266) 660300; fax: (01266) 660400

Belfast Festival at Queen's Wide-ranging arts festival, including international theatre and dance, as well as jazz, classical, folk, and world music. **Date** October–November **Address** Festival House, 25 College Gardens, Belfast BT9 6BS; phone: (01232) 667687; fax: (01232) 663733; e-mail: festival@qub.ac.uk **Web site** www.qub.ac.uk/festival

Scotland

Edinburgh Festival Fringe The largest arts festival in the world. **Date** August **Address** The Fringe Office, 180 High Street, Edinburgh EH1 1QS; phone: (0131) 226 5257; fax: (0131) 220 4205; e-mail: admin@edfringe.com **Web site** www.edfringe.com

Edinburgh International Festival International festival of opera, music, dance, and theatre. **Date** August–September **Address** Edinburgh International Festival, 21 Market Street, Edinburgh EH1 1BW; phone: (0131) 473 2001; e-mail: eif@eif.co.uk **Web site** www.go-edinburgh.co.uk

The Highland Festival. Date May–June **Address** 40 Huntley Street, Inverness IV3 5HR; phone: (01463) 719000 **Web site** www.highlandfestival.demon.co.uk/

Perth Festival of the Arts. Date May **Address** 3–5 High Street, Perth PH1 5JS; phone/fax: (01738) 475295; e-mail: artsfestival@perth.org.uk **Web site** www.perth. org.uk/perth/festival.htm

Wales

Fishguard Music Festival Programme of choral, recital, orchestral music, and jazz, including performances by international artists. **Date** July **Address** Festival Office, Fishguard, Pembrokeshire SA65 9BJ; phone/fax: (01348) 873612

Llangollen International Musical Eisteddfod Six-day festival of music and dance featuring leading international artists. **Date** July **Address** International Eisteddfod Office, Llangollen, North Wales LL20 8NG; phone: (01978) 860236; fax: (01978) 861300; e-mail: @lime.uk.com **Web site** www.lime.uk.com

Presteigne Festival of Music and the Arts. **Date** August **Address** Festival Box Office, Presteigne, Powys LD8 2AA; phone: (01544) 267800; fax: (0171) 435 9166 **Web site** www.cadenza.org/presteigne

Vale of Glamorgan Festival Series of performances of the music of living composers, including specially commissioned new works. **Date** September **Address** St Donats Arts Centre, St Donats Castle, nr Llantwit Major, Vale of Glamorgan CF61 1WF; phone: (01446) 794848; fax: (01446) 794711

Media Groups and Watchdogs

Main Media Groups in the UK

BBC Corporate HQ Broadcasting House, Portland Place, London W1A lAA; phone: (0171) 765 4990; fax: (0171) 637 1630; Web site: www.bbc.co.uk

Capital FM/Capital Gold 30 Leicester Square, London WC2H 7LA; phone: (0171) 766 6000; fax: (0171) 766 6100; Web site: www.capitalradio.co.uk

Carlton Communications 25 Knightsbridge, London SW1X 7RZ; phone: (0171) 663 6363; fax: (0171) 663 6300; Web site: www.carltonplc.co.uk

Daily Mail 2 Derry Street, London W8 5TT; phone: (0171) 938 6000; fax: (0171) 937 3251; Web site: www.dailymail.co.uk

Flextech 160 Great Portland Street, London W1N 5TB; phone: (0171) 299 5000; fax: (0171) 299 6000; Web site: www.flextech.co.uk

Granada Media The London Television Centre, Upper Ground, London SE1 9LT; phone: (0171) 620 1620; fax: (0171) 261 3307; The Television Centre, Quay Street, Manchester M60 9EA; phone: (0161) 832 7211; fax: (0161) 827 2029

Guardian/Observer News Services 119 Farringdon Road, London ECIR 3ER; phone: (0171) 278 2332; fax: (0171) 837 1192; Web site: www.guardian.co.uk

Johnston Press 53 Manor Place, Edinburgh EH3 7EG; phone: (0131) 225 3361; fax: (0131) 225 4580; Web site: www.johnston.co.uk; e-mail: j.brods@johnstonpress.co.uk

Mirror Group 1 Canada Square, Canary Wharf, London E14 5AP; phone: (0171) 510 3000; fax: (0171) 293 3843; Web site: www.independent.co.uk

News International Newspapers Ltd Virginia Street, London E1 9BD; phone: (0171) 782 6000; fax: *Sun* (0171) 782 5605; *News of the World:* (0171) 782 4463; *The Times:* (0171) 782 5988; *The Sunday Times:* (0171) 782 5731; Web sites: *Sun* & *News of the World:* www.lineone.net; *The Times:* www.the_times.co.uk; *The Sunday Times:* www.sunday_times.co.uk

Newsquest Media Group Newspaper House, 33–44 London Road, Morden, Surrey SM4 5BR; phone: (0181) 640 8989; fax: (0181) 646 3997; Web site: www.newsquest.co.uk

Pearson 3 Burlington Gardens, London W1X 1LE; phone: (0171) 411 2000; fax: (0171) 411 2390; Web site: www.pearson.com

Telegraph 1 Canada Square, Canary Wharf, London E14 5DT; phone: (0171) 538 5000; fax: (0171) 538 6242; Web site: www.telegraph.co.uk

Trinity Plc Kings Field Court, Chester Business Park, Chester CH4 9RE; phone: (01244) 687000; fax: (01244) 687100; Web site: www.trinity.plc.uk

United News and Media 245 Blackfriars Road, London SE1 9UY; phone: (0171) 921 5000; fax: (0171) 921 5002; Web site: www.unm.com

Arts and Media Associations and Societies in the UK

(ind = individuals; f = firms; org = organizations; soc = societies; where not specified, figures refer to numbers of individual members; date given is year organization was founded.)

Actors' Equity Association, British (EQUITY) (45,000), Guild House, Upper St Martins Lane, London WC2M 9EG; phone: (0171) 379 6000; 1930

Arts Ltd, National Campaign for the (900 ind; 100 f; 550 org), Francis House, Francis Street, London SW1P 1DE; phone: (0171) 828 4448/630 9766

Arts, Royal Academy of (RA) (85 ind; 71,000 friends of the RA), Burlington House, Piccadilly, London W1V 0DS; phone: (0171) 300 5760/8000; fax: (0171) 300 8001; 1768

Authors' Licensing & Collecting Society (10,000), 14 Holborn, London EC1; phone: (0171) 395 0600; fax: (0171) 395 0660; 1977

Authors, Society of (5,500), 84 Drayton Gardens, London SW10 9SB; phone: (0171) 373 6642; 1884

Broadcasting Entertainment, Cinematograph, & Theatre Union (BECTU) (29,300), 111 Wardour Street, London W1V 4AY; phone: (0171) 437 8506; fax: (0171) 437 8268; 1991

Contemporary Arts, Institute of (ICA) (7,000), 12 Carlton House Terrace, Nash House, The Mall, London SW1Y 5AH; phone: (0171) 930 0493; fax: (0171) 436 7247; 1947

Dancing, Royal Academy of (RAD) (20,000), 36 Battersea Square, London SW11 3RA; phone: (0171) 223 0091; 1920

Decorative and Fine Arts Societies, National Association of (73,000), NADFAS House, 8 Guildford Street, London WC1N 1DT; phone: (0171) 430 0730/242 5044; 1968

Dickens Fellowship (5,500 ind; 5 affiliated societies), 48 Doughty Street, London WC1N 2LF; phone: (0171) 405 2127; 1902

Film and Television Arts, British Academy of (BAFTA) (3,300), 195 Piccadilly, London W1V 0LN; phone: (0171) 734 0022/437 1635; 1963

Film Institute, British (BFI) (41,500 ind; 356 f; 255 film soc), 21 Stephen Street, London W1P 2LN; phone: (0171) 255 1444; fax: (0171) 436 7950; 1933

Fine Arts, Royal Glasgow Institute of the (1,500), 5 Oswald Street, Glasgow G1 4QR; phone: (0141) 248 7411; 1861

Folk Dance and Song Society, English (5,800 ind; 135 clubs; 450 org), Cecil Sharpe House, 2 Regent's Park Road, London NW1 7AY; phone: (0171) 485 2206; 1932

Media Watchdogs in the UK

Agency/programme	Details	Address
Advertising Standards Authority	deals with complaints about advertisements in newspapers and magazines	2 Torrington Place, London WC1E 7HW; phone: (0171) 580 5555; fax: (0171) 323 4339; Web site: www.asa.org.uk
BBC *Feedback*	listener response programme	Feedback, c/o Testbed Productions Limited, 5th Floor, 14–16 Great Portland Street, London W1N 5AB; phone: (0171) 436 0555; fax: (0171) 436 2800; e-mail: feedback@bbc.co.uk
BBC Information Offices	general information: if possible give the programme title, transmission date, and time; a daily summary of comments is seen by senior programme-makers, and written comments will be answered	*TV and radio:* phone: (0870) 0100222 (national rate), open 24 hours; fax: (0181) 749 8258; e-mail: info@bbc.co.uk
BBC *Points of View*	TV programme broadcast weekly, takes complaints and comments to be broadcast about BBC television	Points of View, BBC Television Centre, London W12 7RJ; phone: (0181) 811 1050; e-mail:pov@bbc.co.uk
BBC Programme Complaints Unit	deals with complaints of specific and serious injustice or inaccuracy, or a serious breach of accepted standards in a BBC broadcast	Fraser Steel, Head of the BBC Programme Complaints Unit, BBC Television Centre, London W12 7RJ
BBC Reception Advice	for TV and radio reception advice; Monday–Friday 8 a.m.–7 p.m.	Television Centre, London W12 7RJ; phone: (0870) 010 0123 (national rate); fax: (0181) 576 7466; e-mail: reception@bbc.co.uk
BBC Viewer and Listener Correspondence	deals with all BBC output, and all written comments receive a reply	Viewer and Listener Correspondence, BBC Television Centre, London W12 7RJ
Broadcasting Standards Commission	for complaints about violence, sexual conduct, decency, and taste in TV and radio programmes and advertisements	5 The Sanctuary, London SW1P 3JS; phone: (0171) 233 0544; fax: (0171) 233 0397; e-mail: bsc@bsc.org.uk; Web site: www.bsc.org.uk
Channel 4 *Right to Reply*	takes complaints and suggestions about television programmes for discussion at 6.30 p.m. on Saturdays	Right to Reply, 124 Horseferry Road, London SW1P 2TX; phone: (0171) 306 8582; fax: (0171) 306 8373; e-mail: righttoreply@channel4.co.uk
Independent Television Commission	regulates television advertising and programmes on all commercial channels	33 Foley Street, London W1P 7LB; phone: (0171) 255 3000; fax: (0171) 306 7800; e-mail: publicaffairs@itc.org.uk; Web site: itc.org.uk
Oftel	the watchdog for the telecommunications industry	50 Ludgate Hill, London EC4M 7JJ; phone: (0845) 714 500 or (0171) 634 8700
Press Complaints Commission	self-regulatory body concerned with all editorial material in newspapers and magazines	1 Salisbury Square, London EC4Y 8JB; Helpline: (0171) 353 3732; Scottish helpline: (0131) 220 6652; Text phone: (0171) 583 2264; fax: (0171) 353 8355; e-mail: pcc.org.uk; Web site: www.pcc.org.uk
Press Radio Authority	deals with programmes and advertising on independent (non-BBC) radio	Holbrook House, 14 Great Queen Street, London WC2B 5DG; phone: (0171) 430 2724; fax: (0171) 405 7062; e-mail: info@radioauthority.org.uk; Web site: www.radioauthority.org.uk

Humanist Association, British (3,050 ind; 30 org), 47 Theobalds Road, London WC1X 8SP; phone: (0171) 430 0908; 1963

Jane Austen Society (2,100 ind; 45 libraries), Carton House, Redwood Lane, Medstead, Alton, Hants GU34 5PE; phone: (01705) 475855; fax: (01705) 788842; 1940

Journalists, Chartered Institute of (2,000), 2 Dock Offices, Surrey Quays, Lower Road, London SE16 2XU; phone: (0171) 252 1187; fax: (0171) 232 2302; 1884

Musicians, Incorporated Society of (4,550 ind; 150 f), 10 Stratford Place, London W1N 9AE; phone: (0171) 629 4413; 1882

Operatic & Dramatic Association, National (NODA) (4,500), 1 Crestfield Street, London WC1H 8AU; phone: (0171) 837 5655; 1899

Poetry Society (2,700), 22 Betterton Street, London WC2H 9BU; phone: (0171) 420 9880; 1909

Publishers' Association (180 f), 1 Kingsway, London WC2B 6XF; phone: (0171) 565 7474; fax: (0171) 836 4543; 1896

Publishers' Association, Scottish (68 f), Scottish Book Centre, 137 Dundee Street, Edinburgh EH11 1BG; phone: (0131) 228 6866; fax: (0131) 228 3220; 1974

Songwriters, Composers, and Authors, British Academy of (BASCA) (4,000), The Penthouse, 4 Brook Street, London W1Y 1AA; phone: (0171) 629 0992; fax: (0171) 629 0993; 1947

Television Society, Royal (3,500 ind; 103 f), Holborn Hall, 100 Gray's Inn Road, London WC1X 8AL; phone: (0171) 430 1000; fax: (0171) 430 0924; 1927

Voice of the Listener and Viewer (VLV) (2,530 ind; 40 colleges and university departments; 24 soc), 101 King's Drive, Gravesend, Kent DA12 5BQ; phone: (01474) 352835; fax: (01474) 35112; 1983

Women Writers & Journalists, Society of (500), 110 Whitehall Road, Chingford, London E4 6DW; phone: (0181) 529 0886; 1894

Writers' Guild of Great Britain (2,000), 430 Edgware Road, London W2 1EH; phone: (0171) 723 8074; 1959

Web Sites

American Ballet Theater

http://www.abt.org/

Site of the prestigious US ballet company. There are details of current performances, profiles of dancers and choreographers.

Art Crime

http://museum-security.org/artcrime.html

Latest news about 'cultural property incidents, such as art theft, looting of art in wartime, fire, and forgery'.

Arts Council of England

http://www.artscouncil.org.uk/

Details of the council's work in funding and promoting the arts.

Arts Council of Wales

http://www.ccc-acw.org.uk/

Covering the aims, structure, meetings, and publications of the Welsh arts council.

Ashmolean Museum

http://www.ashmol.ox.ac.uk/

Guide to the museum in Oxford, England. There are full details of permanent collections, exhibitions, and talks.

BalletWeb

http://www.novia.net/~jlw/index.html

Site devoted to classical ballet, with commentary on dance issues and a computer animation illustrating ballet steps.

BBC Symphony Orchestra

http://www.bbc.co.uk/orchestras/so/

Highlights of the current season's performances, as well as a 'Spotlight' on individual musicians in the orchestra.

Bodleian Library, University of Oxford

http://www.bodley.ox.ac.uk/

There is practical information for visitors and readers, and information on a range of online services.

Bolshoi in History

http://www.alincom.com/bolshoi/history/history.htm

Illustrated history of the Bolshoi Theatre in Moscow, Russia.

British Arts Festivals Association

http://www.artsfestivals.co.uk/

A directory of leading professional arts festivals in the UK.

British Library

http://www.bl.uk/

Home page of the British Library. There is extensive information for users of the library's many services.

British Poetry Collection

http://members.tripod.com/the_yellow_jester/index.html

Poetry resource from the British Poetry Collection.

Classic FM

http://www.classicfm.co.uk/

Promoting the station's aim of 'making classical music accessible to as wide an audience as possible'.

Edinburgh Festival Online

http://www.go-edinburgh.co.uk/

The official Edinburgh Festival Web site with full details of all the contributing arts.

English National Ballet

http://www.ballet.org.uk/ballet/cgi-bin/index.cgi

The National Ballet's Web site includes a 'Tour schedule' and 'Company news', as well as the opportunity to contribute to the 'Online think tank' and 'Performance reviews'.

English National Opera

http://www.eno.org/

Details of the company, its current productions, and the low-price ticket scheme 'Enjoy opera for schools'.

Getty

http://www.getty.edu/

Home page of the Getty Institute in California which houses one of the largest art collections in the world.

Glossary of Musical Terms

http://www.hnh.com/mgloss.htm

Online A–Z glossary of musical terms, with links to articles on composers.

Guggenheim Museum Bilbao

http://www.bm30.es/homegug_uk.html

Includes the background to the building of the Guggenheim museum, as well as gallery plans and details of exhibitions.

Louvre Museum and Palace

http://mistral.culture.fr/louvre/louvrea.htm

Guide to the Louvre Museum and Palace, Paris, France, including the historical background to the palace, and floor plans.

MTV UK

http://www.mtv.co.uk/

Pop news, charts, and features, and show infomation for the UK edition of MTV.

Musée d'Orsay

http://www.musee-orsay.fr:8081/ORSAY/orsaygb/HTML.NSF/By+Filename/mosimple+index?OpenDocument

Guide to the museum in Paris, France, and its exhibits.

Museumsworld News

http://www.museumsworld.com/news.htm

Stories from the world of museums, including the latest discoveries and acquisitions, and attempts by some countries to regain treasures 'looted' by others.

National Gallery, London

http://www.nationalgallery.org.uk/

Comprehensive guide to the National Gallery in London, including information about current and future exhibitions.

National Museum of Photography, Film, and Television

http://www.nmsi.ac.uk/nmpft/

Details of collections, events, and forthcoming exhibits at the National Museum of Photography, Film, and Television, in Bradford, England.

NME (New Musical Express)

http://www.nme.com

Weekly guide to the UK rock and pop scene.

Opera for the Culturally Illiterate

http://www.dn.net/schultz/opera.html

Irreverent and entertaining introduction to opera's 'wonderful world of sex, alcohol, and profound carnage' by tenor singer John Schultz.

Place, The

http://www.theplace.org.uk/

Dedicated to contemporary dance, this Web site includes features, listings, reviews, and links to other relevant sites.

Royal Opera House

http://www.royalopera.org/

Web site of Britain's leading opera house. There are sections providing practical information on current performances and bookings.

Royal Philharmonic Orchestra

http://www.rpo.co.uk/

Performance and education are the main themes of this site from the Royal Philharmonic Orchestra.

Scottish Arts Council

http://www.sac.org.uk/

The site showcases Scottish art, with an 'Image of the Month' and 'Poem of the Month'.

Victoria and Albert Museum

http://www.vam.ac.uk/

Guide to the world's largest museum of the decorative arts.

What's On Stage

http://www.whatsonstage.com/

Comprehensive listing of theatre and classical music performances throughout the UK. The site features a searchable database, news, seating plans, and online ticket ordering.

LANGUAGE AND LANGUAGES

Languages of the World

Languages of the World: Introduction

Estimating the number of languages in the world depends on (1) how one defines a 'language', as compared to a component 'dialect', (2) the limited information available about some linguistically complex parts of the world, such as the island of New Guinea, and (3) the uncertain rate at which the languages of small hunting and gathering communities are becoming extinct, as in Amazonia. Defining an individual language very broadly, however, we may set the approximate total of the world's languages at around 5,000, whereas a finer distinction will give us a total of over 13,000.

The principal linguistic question of the year 2000 is how the expansion of major languages, especially English, can be reconciled with the natural linguistic diversity of humankind. The answer can only lie in the development of multilingual education and communication, and in the use of dominant languages as vehicles of understanding among different speech communities rather than of their homogenization. The rate of extinction of languages may not always be as rapid as some linguists have maintained, but it is salutary to recall that massive losses among the world's speech communities have already occurred as a result of the emigration of speakers of European languages during the last half-millennium, primarily to the Americas and Australasia.

Source: David Dalby, *The Linguasphere Register of the World's Languages and Speech Communities* (Linguasphere Press, Hebron, Wales, 1999)

Languages Spoken by More Than 10 Million People

For practical purposes, a distinction is made between 12 *megalanguages*, each comprising more than 100 million voices (or speakers), and 59 *macrolanguages*, each comprising between 10 and 100 million. As world populations rise, more languages reach and pass the total of 10 million voices, but the difficulties involved in estimating totals for each language should not be underestimated.

The following estimates relate not only to the *primary* voices (or 'first language speakers') of each language but also to its *alternate* voices (or 'second language speakers'). The first of these categories includes all who acquire native or 'native-like' competence in a language, usually their 'mother tongue', whereas the category of alternate voices includes those whose speaking of the language in question is influenced by their knowledge of one or more other languages, especially their own mother tongue. Alternate voices are a frequent medium of enrichment for a language, and should not be therefore regarded as 'secondary' in status to primary voices.

In many cases, totals of primary voices alone would have presented a false picture of linguistic reality – only 6 million voices for Swahili, for example (as opposed to 55 million including alternate voices) or only 400 million voices for English (as opposed to around 1,000 million).

Estimates of primary speakers may be based to a large extent on the latest census figures for relevant nation states, updated to allow for population growth, although specific linguistic totals are not available for the majority of countries. The assessment of 'alternate' speakers, on the other hand, must depend on the personal judgement of informed observers, and also on where one draws the line in terms of adequate competence in a language. Many pupils who study a foreign language for several years in school, for example, could not be counted as 'alternate' speakers of that language

in any real sense. If it were possible to measure and count every 'voice' concerned, it would be reasonable to include only those with the ability to 'get by in a language' – to follow the main points of a televised drama or news bulletin, for example, or to ask and reply to straightforward questions about everyday subjects.

Not to be overlooked is the fact that most of the world's principal languages belong to one of a small number of 'chains' of closely related languages. In most cases, such relationships enable speakers of one language to acquire, with relative ease, at least a partial understanding of another language in the same chain.

It is important to observe that the majority (51) of the 71 languages spoken in the world today by more than 10 million each belongs to one of only 12 *chains* of closely related languages. These chains are as follows (with the number of relevant mega- and macrolanguages in brackets):

Continental West Germanic (2), West Iranian (2), Slavic (5), Romance (6), and Indic (11) = 26 from a total of 30 mega- and macrolanguages classified within the Indo-European family

Malayic (2), Transphilippine (2), Turkic (3), Tai (3), Dravidian (4), Bantu (5), and Chinese, or Sinitic (6) = 25 from a total of 42 other mega- and macrolanguages, classified outside the Indo-European family

For certain languages in the following tables, modest allowance is made for voices alternating between languages in the same chain, as in the ability of many Ukrainian and Belarusian voices to adapt themselves to Russian, of Czech and Slovak voices to Polish, or of Portuguese voices to Spanish (although much less in the reverse direction, in each of these cases). A major example is provided by Hindi, reinforced by the popularity of Hindi-speaking films in South Asia. Many millions of voices alternate regularly between Hindi and their own languages in the same Indic chain, often within the same conversation or same sentence.

For the purpose of assessing realistic totals, some pairs of very closely related languages have been treated together as a single unit. Examples from the following tables include Hindi and Urdu, Malay and Indonesian, Serbian and Croatian, Czech and Slovak, and (perhaps controversially) Dutch and Flemish and Afrikaans. This is not to imply that paired languages are the 'same' language but that they are sufficiently close to form an extended transnational speech-community. A similar case might have been made for treating Swedish, Norwegian, and Danish together, providing a combined total of 18 million, although Swedish has been included on its own in the table of macrolanguages (with an increase from 9 million primary voices to 12 million, to allow for the many Danish and Norwegian voices who can also function as alternate voices in Swedish).

Spoken languages, which we are measuring here, must not be confused with corresponding written languages – not only because of varying literacy rates, but also because of the differential distribution of certain writing systems. Croatian and Serbian (formerly treated together as Serbo-Croat) may still be treated as one spoken language but are written in different alphabets (Roman and Cyrillic). In Asia, Hindi and Urdu overlap as spoken languages but are written in different scripts (Devanagari and Perso-Arabic). In contrast, the major Chinese languages (not readily interintelligible when spoken) are the 'same' language in writing, through the use of identical 'meaning-based' characters. For this reason, the estimates below take no account of those able to read a particular language. They therefore exclude the large number of speakers of Japanese and older speakers of Korean, for example, who are able to read Chinese characters without needing to be acquainted with any spoken form of Chinese.

Source: David Dalby, *The Linguasphere Register of the World's Languages and Speech Communities* (Linguasphere Press, Hebron, Wales, 1999)

Megalanguages in the Year 2000: Languages of above 100 Million Voices

Megalanguage describes a language with an estimated total in excess of 100 million primary and *alternate voices.* Of the 12 megalanguages spoken in the world at the end of the 20th century, no less than 8 are classified within the Indo-European language-family. All 12 are national state-languages, and all include a more or less important intercontinental diaspora of speakers.

Although the identity and relative order of these 12 languages is reasonably certain, the figures cited for their estimated number of voices are by their nature only very approximate. The following independent estimates have taken totals from other sources into account, and the demography of the countries involved, although the most difficult estimate is that relating to English. By their nature, in an era of increasing telecommunication and travel, the number of voices for most megalanguages is still expanding throughout the world, and this is particularly true for English. Some estimates in non-English language sources are as low as 500 million, and in some English-language sources as high as 1,500 million or more.

The figure presented here for English, of approximately one billion (1,000 million) primary and alternate voices in the year 2000, is lower than previous estimates, excluding more limited speakers of the language, although it is clear that the demand to learn English and the consequent supply of teaching are increasing rapidly in many parts of the world. It is likely that the total numbers of alternate (especially young) speakers of English are now expanding worldwide at a rate of well above one million a month, having already overtaken the estimated 400 million primary speakers of the language.

That humankind should be seeking and developing a worldwide vehicular language is in keeping with the evolution of our planetary society towards a globalized speech-community. On the other hand, the natural diversity of that community will depend on the development of that language as the 'service-language' of a multilingual society, and **not** as the vehicle of a dominant monolingual culture. This will be measured by the relative position of English in the category of primary speakers, any undue rise in which would indicate a major danger to humankind's linguistic diversity.

An interesting feature of the following table is that Chinese (Putonghua or 'Mandarin') and English appear more or less 'neck and neck' as the planet's two most spoken languages, breaking the barrier of around one billion speakers each at the turn of the millennium. The answer to the question 'which is the world's most widely spoken language?' therefore varies according to the time of day. When the sun is over the western Pacific, the most used language is Chinese. When the sun is over the Atlantic and China sleeps, English takes the lead. In terms of geographical spread, English already occupies an undisputed position in the world, and a steady expansion in its learning and use around the globe will see it taking an increasing lead over all other languages during the early part of the 21st century. Moreover, within a decade or two, it is reasonable to assume that there will be more speakers of English in Asia than in any other continent: India is an increasingly important source of literary creativity in English, and China will not be far behind. Asia will play an important role in helping to ensure that English serves as a transnational auxiliary-language, against a multilingual background.

Modern English (an Indo-European language) does not belong to one of the 12 chains of closely related languages which are identified in the following tables, but it stands in an important relationship with two of them. Its origins as a Continental West Germanic language during the first millennium are reflected in the fact that Old English is today more easily accessible to a speaker of Modern German or Dutch than to a speaker of Modern English. The grammatical system of English has since been simplified and greatly changed, while a major proportion of its present-day vocabulary has been received from French or from other languages of the Romance chain, including Latin itself. English is therefore now best described as a 'Romanized Germanic' language, within the Indo-European family.

In terms of its place in the world, French also is in a category by itself. Measured in terms of primary speakers only, it falls below the level of 100 million speakers and lies in 12th position among the 12 megalanguages. And yet it is the only language that currently provides an alternative to English as a transnational vehicular language around the world, being used as an official or semi-official language in 44 countries in 5 continents.

Source: David Dalby, *The Linguasphere Register of the World's Languages and Speech Communities* (Linguasphere Press, Hebron, Wales, 1999)

Megalanguages in the Year 2000: Languages of above 100 Million Voices

Rank	Languages	Membership of chains of languages)	Primary voices only (millions)	Primary plus alternate voices (millions)	Principal countries
1	Putonghua/ Mandarin	Chinese	800	1,000	China, Taiwan, Thailand, Malaysia, Singapore, Vietnam
2	English		400	1,000	UK, USA, Canada, Republic of Ireland, Australia, New Zealand, South Africa, Botswana, Lesotho, Swaziland, Zimbabwe, Zambia, Malawi, Tanzania, Kenya, Uganda, Rwanda, Somalia, Ethiopia, Cameroon, Nigeria, Ghana, Liberia, Sierra Leone, Gambia, Malta, Israel and Palestine, Jordan, Kuwait, Bahrain, United Arab Emirates, Mauritius, Seychelles, India, Pakistan, Bangladesh, Sri Lanka, Myanmar, Malaysia, Singapore, China (Hong Kong), Papua New Guinea, Philippines, Solomon Islands, Tuvalu, Vanuatu, Samoa, Tonga, Fiji, Kiribati, Micronesia, Nauru, Bahamas, Bermuda, Barbados, Grenada, Jamaica, Trinidad and Tobago, Belize, St Lucia, St Kitts and Nevis, St Vincent, Virgin Islands, Dominica, Puerto Rico, Guyana
3	Hindi and Urdu	Indic	550	900	India, Pakistan, Nepal, Fiji, Mauritius, South Africa, UK
4	Spanish	Romance	400	450	Spain, Mexico, Venezuela, Colombia, Ecuador, Peru, Bolivia, Chile, Argentina, Paraguay, Uruguay, Panama, Costa Rica, Nicaragua, Honduras, El Salvador, Guatemala, Cuba, Dominican Republic, Puerto Rico, Canary Islands, Morocco, Equatorial Guinea, USA
5	Russian	Slavic	170	320	Russia, Ukraine, Kazakhstan, Belarus, Azerbaijan, Georgia, Armenia, Kyrgyzstan, Turkmenistan, Uzbekistan, Tajikistan, Latvia, Estonia, Lithuania, Moldova, Canada, USA
6	Arabic	–	200	250	Saudi Arabia, Yemen, United Arab Emirates, Oman, Kuwait, Bahrain, Qatar, Iraq, Syria, Jordan, Israel and Palestine, Lebanon, Djibouti, Somalia, Sudan, Libya, Tunisia, Mauritania, Algeria, Morocco, Comoros
7	Bengali	Indic	190	250	Bangladesh, India, UK
8	Portuguese	Romance	180	200	Portugal, Brazil, Angola, Cape Verde, Guinea-Bissau, Macau, Mozambique, São Tomé and Príncipe
9	Malay and Indonesian	Malayic	50	160	Indonesia, Malaysia, Singapore
10	Japanese	–	120	130	Japan, USA, Brazil
11	German	Continental West Germanic	100	125	Germany, Austria, Switzerland, France, Italy, Belgium, Luxembourg, Liechtenstein, USA, Canada, Namibia, Kazakhstan, Romania, Russia, Brazil, Argentina
12	French	Romance	90	125	France, Canada, Belgium, Luxembourg, Switzerland, Monaco, St Pierre and Miquelon, Canada, Haiti, Guadeloupe, Martinique, French Guiana, French Polynesia, New Caledonia, Vanuatu, Laos, Cambodia, Vietnam, Réunion, Mauritius, Seychelles, Lebanon, Syria, Tunisia, Algeria, Morocco, Mali, Mauritania, Benin, Burkina Faso, Burundi, Cameroon, Central African Republic, Chad, Comoros, Republic of the Congo, Democratic Republic of Congo, Côte d'Ivoire, Djibouti, Gabon, Guinea, Madagascar, Niger, Rwanda, Senegal, Togo

Source: David Dalby, *The Linguasphere Register of the World's Languages and Speech Communities* (Linguasphere Press, Hebron, Wales, 1999)

Macrolanguages in the Year 2000: Languages of between 10 and 100 Million Voices

Macrolanguage describes a language with an estimated total of between 10 and 100 million primary and alternate voices. Among the following 58 languages estimated to fall within this category, the large majority serve as an educational and often also administrative medium for one or more countries or component federal states. It should be noted that no less than four macrolanguages in the Chinese chain are estimated separately in this table. A large proportion of their component voices now alternate between their own Chinese language and the official national megalanguage or Putonghua ('commonly understood language'). The macrolanguages below that belong to the Indic chain stand in a similar relationship to the Hindi and Urdu megalanguage, although this is not imposed educationally with the same vigour as the national language in China. English has not retreated from the dominant position it occupied in the colonial period in South Asia, and is currently widely studied in English-medium schools frequented by children of the more favoured social classes and castes. Although the political and social situation differs from that in China, it is clear that the return of Hong Kong to China (as a

linguistic 'Trojan horse') has accelerated the demand for English-medium teaching in that country also. The future balance of linguistic diversity in the world will be measured, not only by the degree to which the national and local use of macrolanguages remains unimpaired by the wider use of English and other megalanguages, but also by the degree to which the following languages do not themselves impair the use of less widely spoken languages within their own areas of influence. Figures are estimated totals in round figures.

Source: David Dalby, *The Linguasphere Register of the World's Languages and Speech Communities* (Linguasphere Press, Hebron, Wales, 1999)

Macrolanguages in the Year 2000: Languages of between 10 and 100 Million Voices

Languages	Membership of chains of languages	Primary plus alternate voices (millions)	Principal countries
Panjabi	Indic	85	Pakistan, India, Malaysia, Fiji, UK
Wu	Chinese	85	China
Javanese	–	80	Indonesia
Marathi	Indic	80	India
Korean	–	75	North Korea, South Korea, China, Japan, USA
Vietnamese	–	75	Vietnam, Cambodia, USA
Italian	Romance	70	Italy, Switzerland, USA, Canada, Argentina, Brazil
Yue	Chinese	70	China, Malaysia, Vietnam, Singapore, Indonesia, USA
Tamil	Dravidian	70	India, Sri Lanka, Malaysia, Singapore, Fiji, Mauritius, Trinidad and Tobago
Telugu	(Dravidian)	70	India, Malaysia
Turkish	Turkic	60	Turkey, Bulgaria, Greece, Cyprus, Turkmenistan, Kazakhstan, Uzbekistan, Iran, Azerbaijan, Russia, Germany
Min-nan	Chinese	55	China, Taiwan, Malaysia, Singapore
Swahili	Bantu	55	Tanzania, Kenya, Uganda, Rwanda, Burundi, Democratic Republic of Congo, Somalia, Comoros
Ukrainian	Slavic	47	Ukraine, Russia, Belarus, Poland, USA, Lithuania, Canada, Brazil
Gujarati	Indic	45	India, Uganda, UK
Thai	Tai	45	Thailand
Hausa	–	42	Nigeria, Niger
Kannada	Dravidian	42	India
Persian	West Iranian	40	Iran, Tajikistan, Afghanistan, Pakistan, Iraq
Tagalog	Transphilippine	40	Philippines
Malayalam	Dravidian	39	India
Hakka	Chinese	35	China, Taiwan, Malaysia, Singapore, Indonesia
Burmese	–	33	Burma
Oriya	Indic	33	India
Laotian and Isan	Tai	30	Thailand, Laos
Sundanese	–	30	Indonesia
Dutch, Flemish, and Afrikaans	Continental West Germanic	30	Netherlands, Belgium, Suriname, Netherlands, West Indies, South Africa, Namibia
Romanian and Moldavian	Romance	27	Romania, Moldova
Yoruba	–	26	Nigeria, Benin, Togo
Amharic	–	25	Ethiopia
Pashto	–	25	Afghanistan, Pakistan
Kazakh	Turkic	20	Kazakhstan
Igbo	–	19	Nigeria
Serbian and Croatian	Slavic	19	Serbia, Croatia, Bosnia-Herzegovina
Sindhi	Indic	18	Pakistan, India
Uzbek	Turkic	18	Uzbekistan, Tajikistan, Afghanistan, Kyrgyzstan, Kazakhstan, Turkmenistan
Cebuano	Transphilippine	17	Philippines
Nepali	Indic	17	Nepal, India, Bhutan
Czech and Slovak	Slavic	16	Czech Republic, Slovakia, Ukraine
Fula / Peul	–	16	Nigeria, Guinea, Guinea-Bissau, Senegal, Gambia, Mauritania, Mali, Burkina Faso, Togo, Benin, Niger, Cameroon, Central African Republic, Sudan
Hungarian	–	15	Hungary, Romania, Slovakia, Ukraine, Croatia, Yugoslavia
North and South Kurdish	West Iranian	15	Turkey, Iraq, Iran, Syria
Huang and Buyi	Tai	15	China
Lingala	Bantu	14	Congo, Democratic Republic of Congo
Oromo	–	14	Ethiopia, Kenya
Rwanda and Rundi	Bantu	14	Rwanda, Burundi, Democratic Republic of Congo, Tanzania
Sinhalese	(Indic)	14	Sri Lanka
Bihari and Bhojpuri	Indic	13	Nepal, India, Mauritius
Madurese	Malayic	13	Indonesia
Malagasy	–	13	Madagascar
Mandinka, Bambara, and Jula	–	13	Gambia, Guinea-Bissau, Guinea, Mali, Côte d'Ivoire, Senegal, Burkina Faso, Sierra Leone, Liberia

(*continued*)

Macrolanguages in the Year 2000: Languages of between 10 and 100 Million Voices (*continued*)

Languages	Membership of chains of languages	Primary plus alternate voices (millions)	Principal countries
Greek	–	12	Greece, Cyprus, USA
Min-bei	Chinese	12	China
Sotho and Tswana	Bantu	12	South Africa, Lesotho, Botswana, Namibia, Zimbabwe
Swedish	–	12	Sweden, Finland, Denmark, Norway
Assamese	Indic	11	India, Bhutan, Bangladesh
Catalan	Romance	11	Spain, France, Andorra, Italy (Sardinia)
Zulu, Swazi, and Ndebele	Bantu	11	Zimbabwe, South Africa, Swaziland, Tanzania
Bulgarian and Macedonian	Slavic	10	Bulgaria, Macedonia, Yugoslavia, Albania, Greece, Turkey, Moldova

Source: David Dalby, *The Linguasphere Register of the World's Languages and Speech-Communities* (Linguasphere Press, Hebron, Wales, 1999)

Indo-European Languages: Common Roots

Similarities between six words in Indo-European languages contrasted with their differences from other language groups.

Indo-European languages

English	month	mother	new	night	nose	three
Welsh	mis	mam	newydd	nos	trwyn	tri
Gaelic	mí	máthair	nua	oíche	srón	trí
French	mois	mère	nouveau	nuit	nez	trois
Spanish	mes	madre	nuevo	noche	nariz	tres
Portuguese	mês	mãe	novo	noite	nariz	três
Italian	mese	madre	nuovo	notte	naso	tre
Latin	mensis	mater	novus	nox	nasus	tres
German	Monat	Mutter	neu	Nacht	Nase	drei
Dutch	maand	moeder	nieuw	nacht	neus	drie
Icelandic	mánudur	módir	nýr	nótt	nef	brír
Swedish	månad	moder	ny	natt	näsa	tre
Polish	miesiąc	matka	nowy	noc	nos	trzy
Czech	měsć	matka	nový	noc	nos	tři
Romanian	lună	mamă	nou	noapte	nas	trei
Albanian	muaj	nënë	iri	natë	hundë	tre,tri
Greek	men	meter	neos	nux	rhïs	treis
Russian	mesyats	mat	novy	noch	nos	tri
Lithuanian	menuo	motina	naujas	naktis	nosis	trys
Armenian	amis	mayr	nor	kisher	kit	yerek
Persian	māh	mādar	nau	shab	bini	se
Sanskrit	mās	matar	nava	nakt	nās	trayas

Non-Indo-European languages

Basque	hilabethe	ama	berri	gai	sādār	hirur
Finnish	kuukausi	äiti	uusi	yö	nenä	kolme
Hungarian	hónap	anya	új	éjszaka	orr	három
Turkish	ay	anne	yeni	gece	burun	úç

New Words and Commonly Misspelled Words

Some New Words to Enter the English Language

air rage uncontrolled violent behaviour by airline passengers, often aggravated by an excess of alcohol and involving assaults on the crew and other passengers. The term is adapted from **road rage,** uncontrolled rage among road-users. Other types of 'rage', such as **trolley rage** (in supermarkets) and **golf rage,** are also recorded

attention deficit disorder a behavioural disorder in children, characterized by hyperactivity and an inability to concentrate leading to learning difficulties

body piercing the piercing of parts of the body (other than the ears) so that rings and studs can be inserted in them as a form of personal adornment

challenged used with a preceding word to form a supposedly politically correct (PC) alternative to a term that is regarded as offensive or discriminatory, such as **intellectually challenged** for 'backward' and **vertically challenged** for 'short'; frequently used in a jokey way

charm offensive the use of charm and personal appeal as a means of gaining acceptance for controversial political strategies

dataglove an electronic glove used in computer games and exercises involving virtual reality, in which sensors respond to movements of the hands and fingers and transmit a corresponding input to the screen image

dependency culture a social system in which widespread payment of state benefits is a principal feature, regarded unfavourably as likely to prolong the condition of dependency rather than provide a solution to the underlying problems

DAB digital audio broadcasting, a system of high-quality radio transmission using digitally encoded signals

downsize to reduce the size and scale of a business operation, usually by making redundancies

false memory syndrome the recollection under hypnosis of imaginary childhood traumas, especially of sexual abuse by a near relation

fast track a quick way to get something done, to make progress, or to succeed in life

feel-good factor a feeling of optimism and prosperity in people's financial and material circumstances

feng shui in Chinese philosophy, a system in which natural energies are recognized as having an effect on the physical environment, and are taken into account in determining the location and position of buildings and other features of human existence. These principles are increasingly affecting architectural thinking in Western countries

gay gene a gene which is thought to influence an individual's likelihood of being homosexual

gesture politics political action that seeks to satisfy public opinion in superficial ways

girl power young women as a social and economic force, especially in popular culture

glass ceiling the limit that a person, especially a woman or a member of an ethnic minority, can reach in their career; it is so called because what is on the other side can be seen but can't be reached

helpdesk a department of an organization that answers telephone enquiries from customers, especially in technical matters such as computing

heritage tourism the organization and provision of services for tourists whose main interest is in the history and culture of the places they visit. Other special forms of tourism include **health tourism** (aimed at improving personal health), **nature tourism** (concerned with the study of wildlife), and **urban tourism** (centred on cities)

home shopping a shopping service enabling customers to order goods from their homes by means of telecommunication or computer links to retail outlets. Also known as **online shopping**

hypermedia a combination of **multimedia** and **hypertext**; information presented in a format designed for viewing on the computer screen and which may combine text, graphics, sound, and video, where the components of the presentation may be integrated by means of links or **hyperlinks** to allow the reader to navigate between them; the presentation media include CD-ROM and Internet (HTML) pages

loyalty card an identity card issued to customers by a supermarket or other retail outlet, so that points or credits can be accumulated towards an eventual discount or other benefit

mega- a prefix used to form many compound words denoting great size or scale. Examples are **megabucks** (a lot of money), **megahit** (something highly successful), **megahype** (widespread sales promotion of dubious veracity), **megarich** (very rich), and **megastore** (a large supermarket or other store)

millennium bug a fault in a computer program caused by the coding of dates with only the final two digits of a year, disregarding the first two, and likely to cause difficulties or complete failure when 1999 passes to 2000

nanny state the government regarded as having an excessive or intrusive influence on people's lives

newsgroup a forum for discussion and exchange of information by users of the Internet, especially **Usenet** which comprises thousands of newsgroups dealing with a wide range of topics

out (verb) to expose someone as being homosexual. To **come out** is used of a person who voluntarily admits that they are homosexual

peace dividend the financial benefit resulting from a reduction in military expenditure during a time of international peace

pear-shaped failed or gone seriously wrong

personal space a person's immediate environment, in which they like to conduct activities without the intrusion of others

power dressing dressing in a way that helps to reinforce a person's business position and authority

quality time the free time a person has to enjoy recreational activities or the companionship of others

recreational drug a drug used for enjoyment rather than for medicinal purposes

safe haven a demilitarized area in a war zone that is set aside by international agreement for refugees, especially ethnic minorities and other oppressed people, often maintained by the UN or some other neutral organization

smart drug a drug that is supposed to improve a person's mental powers and enhance perception of their surroundings

soundbite a short extract from a speech or interview, chosen for its effectiveness in making a point and often disregarding the context in which it was originally made

spin doctor a senior marketing or public-relations official who seeks to project a particular image for a party or politician

swipe card a plastic card such as a charge card or credit card with information stored in a magnetic strip on the back, which can be read when it is passed or 'swiped' through an electronic reading device

third wave the present stage of social and cultural existence, regarded in terms of knowledge as disseminated by information technology, and seen in succession to a first wave of agrarian society and a second wave of industrial society

(continued)

Some New Words to enter the English Language (*continued*)

virtual used to denote a transaction or activity done as a simulation of an ordinary-life activity within the context of electronic networks such as the Internet, for example **virtual payment**; it is an extension of the use of **virtual reality**, which denotes the electronic simulation of a person's (real or imagined) immediate environment

voice mail a system for handling and storing verbal messages transmitted over a conventional telephone line, and for providing information and access to the caller

Some Commonly Misspelled Words

accommodation
achieve
acquittal
address
aggressive
amount
anemone
appearance
asphalt
attach
banister
beautiful
beginning
bicycle
biscuit
budgeted
business
cemetery
cigarette
collapsible
committee
competition
conscientious
controversial
definitely
dependant (noun)
dependent (adjective)
describe
desiccate
desperate
detach
diarrhoea
diphtheria
disappear
disappoint
dissect
dissipated
ecstasy
eighth
embarrass
exaggerate
excellent
excitement
exercise
exhilarate
extravagant
February
foreign
friend
fulfil
gauge
gazetteer
government
grammar
guarantee
guard
handkerchief
harass
height
hygiene
hypocrisy
idiosyncrasy
immediately
independent (noun and adjective)
install
instalment
jewellery
league
liaise
library
liquefy
literature
longitude
manoeuvre
Mediterranean
millennium
millionaire
mischievous
mortgage
necessary
neither
niece
noticeable
nuisance
occasion
occurrence
omit
oneself
parallel
paraphernalia
permissible
personnel
Pharaoh
poisonous
possess
potatoes
practice (noun)
practise (verb)
precede
prejudice
privilege
profession
pronunciation
publicly
questionnaire
receive
repellent
seize
separate
sergeant
siege
sieve
sincerely
soldier
solemn
supersede
targeted
terrestrial
tomatoes
tranquillity
traveller
unnecessary
until
unusual
unwieldy
vetoed
vicious
videoed
Wednesday
yield

Sign Language

Language used by deaf people that involves movements of the hands, face, and the upper part of the body, not the voice. Signs do not correspond exactly to words as their meaning depends on the 'speaker's' movements and facial expressions. There are as many sign languages as there are spoken ones. British Sign Language is used by an estimated 50,000 people in Britain.

British Sign Language

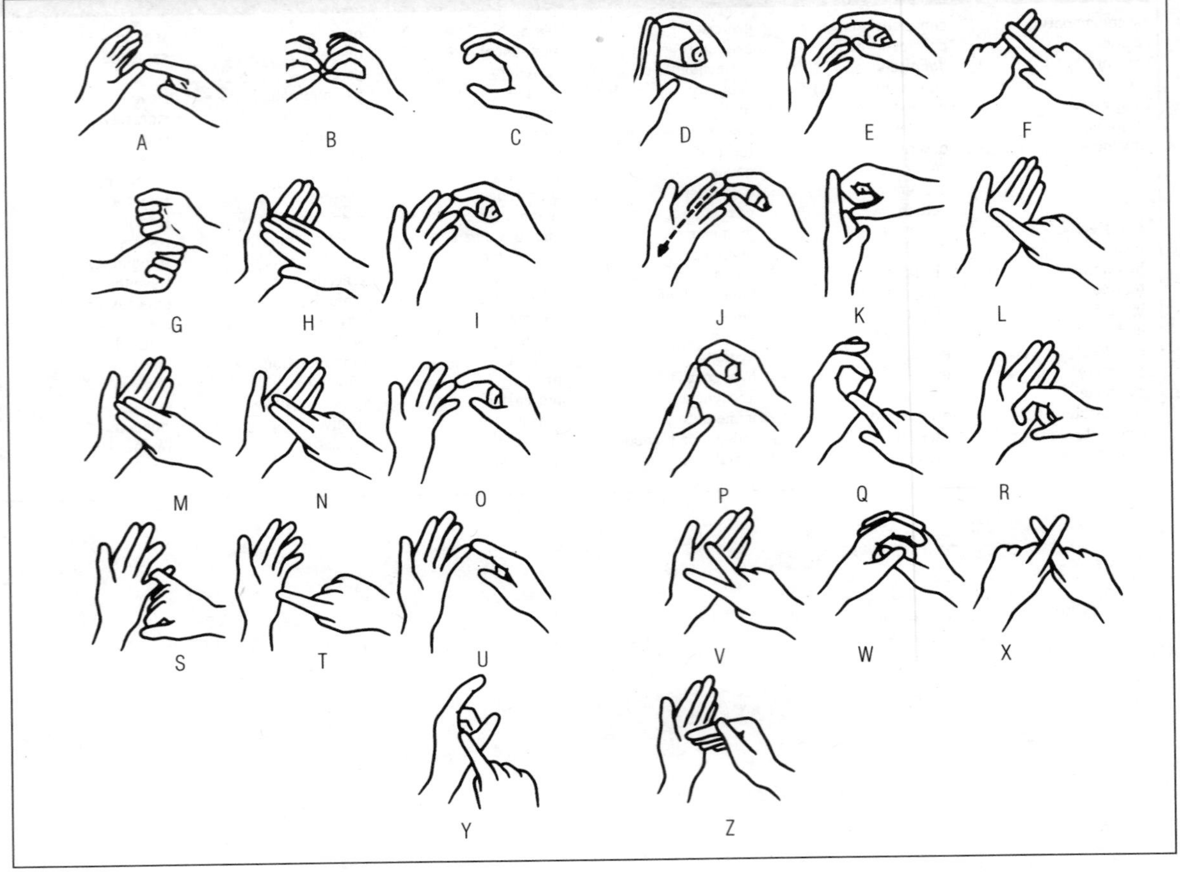

A B C D E F
G H I J K L
M N O P Q R
S T U V W X
Y Z

Web Sites

Acronyms and Abbreviations

http://www.ucc.ie/acronyms/

Immense database of abbreviations, acronyms, and their expanded forms, fully searchable by abbreviation or keyword. It is possible to submit new additions for consideration.

Akkadian Language

http://www.sron.ruu.nl/~jheise/akkadian/index.html

Source of information on the Akkadians and their language. Extensive details on Akkadian phonetics, morphology, paradigms, and dialects (of interest mainly to professional linguists) are accompanied by a good general introduction to Mesopotamia and Assyriology.

Alliterations

http://www.iron.k12.ut.us/schools/cms/resource/ALLIT.HTM

Clear and concise introduction to alliterations for children.

Anagram Insanity

http://anagram.avatartech.com/pages/anagram.html

Anagram-producing page that is basic but effective. Simply key in a string of characters and the server will return an exhaustive list of possible permutations of letters.

Arabic

http://philae.sas.upenn.edu/Arabic/arabic.html

Twelve dialogue lessons from which to learn

Arabic. This site also has a library of Arabic images.

Arabic Writing

http://www.islam.org/Mosque/ihame/Ref3.htm

Informative pages on the history of the Arabic script. There are examples of Arabic writing and colour photographs of various calligraphic styles found in ancient texts.

Bird's Eye View of the Syriac Language and Literature

http://www.geocities.com/Athens/Parthenon/5157/51edip.htm

Profile of this ancient Semitic language spoken over the course of history by Zoroastrians, Buddhists, Jews, Christians, and Muslims. This history of the language and its literature includes details of the Syriac dialects still spoken by Christians in various parts of the Middle East.

Braille and Moon

http://www.rnib.org.uk/braille/welc.htm

Comprehensive information about Braille and Moon from Britain's Royal National Institute for the Blind. You can see how Braille works by typing text and seeing it translated. There is also a good biography of Louis Braille and downloadable Braille and Moon true-type fonts.

Brief History of the English Language

http://www.m-w.com/about/look.htm

Part of a site maintained by Merriam-Webster, this page features a brief history of the English language, showing its evolution through the three periods of Old, Middle, and Modern English.

Chinese Characters

http://zhongwen.com/

Extensive Web site covering the genealogy of Chinese characters. This Web-based etymological dictionary for learning Chinese characters covers over 4,000 characters, including several types of pronunciation for each and a 'family tree' diagram to demonstrate the characters' genealogy.

Cuneiform Writing System

http://www.sron.ruu.nl/~jheise/akkadian/cuneiform.html

Scholarly account of the origin and development of Babylonian and Assyrian cuneiform. There are sections on the origin of this early writing style, as well as detailed examinations of the order, physical appearance, and value of cuneiform signs.

Elements of Style

http://www.columbia.edu/acis/bartleby/strunk/

William Strunk's guide provides a succinct and effective insight into the elementary rules and principles of English grammar.

Esperanto – The International Language

http://esperanto.org/angle/

Thorough official source of information (in many languages) on the international language spoken by two million people. The structure of Esperanto and the history of its development are clearly set out. There is information on national societies and details of Esperanto language courses.

Estonian Language

http://www.ibs.ee/estonian/

Comprehensive guide to the Estonian language. An audio file aids understanding of the alphabet. This site includes a history of the language and an outline of its literature.

Etymological Dictionary of the Gaelic Language

http://www.smo.uhi.ac.uk/gaidhlig/faclair/macbain

E-text of an etymology of Gaelic compiled by Alexander MacBain and published by Gairm Publications, Glasgow.

Euskara – Language of the Basques

http://students.washington.edu/buber/Basque/Euskara/

Thorough introduction to the language of the Basques (a language so complex that a Basque tale relates how the Devil spent seven years trying to learn it, only to give up). There are Basque lessons, an online dictionary, information on software, advice for those learning the language, and a guide to Euskara media.

Finno-Ugrian Languages

http://www.helsinki.fi/hum/sugl/fgr-lang.html

Finnish site exploring the Finno-Ugric (Uralian) language group. There is information on Hungarian, Finnish, and Estonian, and many of the more minor languages in danger of extinction. Lexical and morphological similarities between the languages are examined.

Foundation for Endangered Languages

http://www.bris.ac.uk/Depts/Philosophy/CTLL/FEL/

Bristol University site bringing together the latest information and research on the world's endangered languages. There are online editions of the foundation's newsletter and a large number of contact addresses for scholars and indigenous peoples struggling to preserve their language.

Gaelic and Gaelic Culture

http://sunsite.unc.edu/gaelic/gaelic.html

Dedicated to the Gaelic and Celtic culture and language. This site includes information on the three Gaelic languages; Irish, Manx, and Scottish, along with audioclips giving examples of each.

GCSE French Revision

http://www.canonave.ndirect.co.uk/gcse/

Comprehensive French revision pages. The site contains revision material, past papers, and exam questions.

German Language

http://www.rmplc.co.uk/eduweb/sites/haberg/reallyusefulge/default.htm

Lots of interactive exercises in German ranked by level and organized by discussion topic. This site would be suitable for GCSE students as well as those wishing to brush up on their German speaking skills for a holiday.

Glossary of Rhetorical Terms With Examples

http://www.uky.edu/ArtsSciences/Classics/rhetoric.html

If you are ever confused about how to distinguish synecdoche, litotes, and prolepsis, then this is the site for you.

Hindi Language and Literature

http://www.cs.colostate.edu/~malaiya/hindiint.html

Exploration of Hindi language and culture providing links to information about Hindi-speaking regions, dialects, traditional songs, authors, and poets.

Images of Orality and Literacy in Greek Iconography of the 5th, 4th, and 3rd Centuries BCE

http://ccat.sas.upenn.edu/~awiesner/oralit.html

Important research tool for everybody interested in tracing the history of writing and of the book back to ancient Greece. It involves a collection of images indicative of how the Greeks conceived of the technologies of writing and how they integrated these technologies into their everyday life.

Journal of Pidgin and Creole Languages

http://www.siu.edu/departments/cola/ling/

Results of current research into the theory and description of these languages, supported by an interactive glossary of pidgin and Creole terms and audio samples.

Learn Chinese

http://pasture.ecn.purdue.edu/~agenhtml/agenmc/china/ctutor.html

Audio tutorial of basic Mandarin Chinese. The phrases are presented in both written and audio form and there are over two hundred to choose from.

Linguasphere

http://www.linguasphere.com/

Site of the Linguasphere Observatory, presenting information on the languages of the world and on the Register of the World's Languages and Speech Communities.

Little Venture's Latin Pages

http://www.compassnet.com/mrex/index.html

Online aid to learning or brushing up Latin. Operated by an experienced teacher of the language, this site answers e-mailed grammar and vocabulary inquiries. There is a full list of 'Frequently asked questions' about grammar, a Latin quiz, a fun etymology section, an explanation of the Roman calendar system, and useful links for students or teachers of classics.

Mercator Project

http://www.troc.es/mercator/

Site of the European Union initiative to preserve minority languages and cultures within the EU.

Modern English to Old English Vocabulary

http://www.mun.ca/Ansaxdat/vocab/wordlist.html

Comprehensive online dictionary of modern English words paired with their Old English counterparts.

Mongol Script and Language

http://members.aol.com/yikhmongol/monls.htm

Description of the history of the Mongol script and language. The site includes illustrations of classical Mongolian handwritten script and classical Mongolian printed script.

Noam Chomsky Archive

http://www.worldmedia.com/archive/

Substantial collection of the political work and thought of the US linguist and philosopher Noam Chomsky, with online books, articles, a long archive of his correspondence, an extended list of interviews given by him, and many audio clips.

Peter J Keegan's Maori Language Web Pages

http://webpages.netlink.co.nz/~pkeegan/rauemi/index.html

Introduction to the Maori language. A 'Frequently asked questions' section provides information on the origin and structure of the language, its modern use, and contemporary Maori literature.

Punctuation

http://stipo.larc.nasa.gov/sp7084/sp7084cont.html

Handbook aimed at technical writers and editors, but could help anyone to improve their punctuation. It includes clear information on the correct use of brackets, semicolons, and so on.

Pun Page

http://punpunpun.com/

Page of puns in every shape and form, many of them extremely corny. The site features sections such as 'Pun of the day', 'Longer puns', 'Legal puns', and 'Past puns'.

Roget's Thesaurus

http://humanities.uchicago.edu/forms_unrest/ROGET.html

Online, version of Roget's Thesaurus (last updated in 1991).

Runes, Alphabet of Mystery

http://members.aol.com/cbsunny/index.html

Introduction to the ancient Germanic alphabet, with information on both the alphabet and the stones the letters were traditionally carved upon.

Sapir, Edward

http://kroeber.anthro.mankato.msus.edu/cultural/biography/pqrst/sapir_edward.html

Profile of the German linguist and anthropologist and his pioneering research into Native American languages and the insights derived from it.

Semaphore

http://155.187.10.12/flags/semaphore.html

Diagrams and instructions of how to communicate using this flag signalling system. It includes diagrams of all the letters and numbers and a link to a companion page for the international maritime signal flag system.

Semiotics for Beginners

http://www.aber.ac.uk/~dgc/sem01.html

Clear introduction to the theories and roots of what some theorists have called the 'science of signs'. This site is divided into many sections, that take the visitor through the various forms and applications of this theory, which has become increasingly important in media theory. There is even a useful section on 'DIY semiotic analysis' with hints on how to conduct your own study.

Sign Writing Site

http://www.signwriting.org/

Information about sign language with lessons, dictionaries, stories, and computer programs in sign language. .

Steganography

http://adams.patriot.net/~johnson/html/neil/stegdoc/stegdoc.html

Thorough guide to the technique of camouflaging messages. The contents include the history of steganography, description of various techniques, a guide to available software, and discussions of the implications of steganographic technology.

Traveller's Japanese With Voice

http://www.ntt.co.jp/japan/japanese/

Introduction to Japanese at a level suitable for the business traveller or the occasional visitor to the country.

Welcome to the Walloon Language Page

http://www.wallonie.com/wallang/index.htm

Guide to the history, culture, and language of the Walloons. Presented by a society promoting Walloon culture, the assertion that Walloon is no more than a dialect of French is strongly disputed. In addition to a description of the language, the cultural dangers facing its existence are set out.

Welsh Course

http://www.cs.brown.edu/fun/welsh/home.html

Course on the Welsh language that contains a lexicon and glossary as well as a set of graded lessons.

Wordbot

http://www.cs.washington.edu/homes/kgolden/wordbot.html

Linguistic site that allows you to load pages from the Internet and run them through a variety of filters. These filters can translate foreign language pages into your own language, link words to dictionary definitions, or look up synonyms and antonyms. It's a complicated process, but the results are worth the effort now that more languages are making it onto the Web.

Word Page

http://users.aol.com/jomnet/words.html

This page offers ten different English words per week. All the words are followed by lucid definitions, their origins, words of similar/opposite meaning, and examples of each one in use.

World Wide Words

http://www.quinion.demon.co.uk/words/index.htm

Interesting site listing the latest neologisms (new words) in the English language. Topical words, turns of phrase, and weird words too new to be found in dictionaries are listed and defined.

LAW AND CRIME

The Year in Review

20 July 1998 An inquiry into the murder of black teenager Stephen Lawrence, who was stabbed to death in London, England, on 22 April 1993, concludes that he was killed by racist thugs and that police investigations were incompetent and plagued by racism.

30 July 1998 The court of appeal overturns the guilty verdict on British convict Derek Bentley, who was controversially convicted and hanged in 1953 for the murder of a policeman.

19 August 1998 Irish prime minister Bertie Ahern announces proposals for new legal offences – such as directing an unlawful organization and withholding information – that will make it easier to arrest suspected members of terrorist organizations. The new laws would enable the government to arrest suspected members of the Real IRA, who claimed responsibility for the bomb that killed 28 people in Omagh, County Tyrone, earlier in the month.

29 August 1998 British fugitive Kenneth Noye, who was the target of a two-year manhunt in connection with the road rage murder of Stephen Cameron in May 1996, is arrested near the port of Cadiz, Spain.

2 September 1998 British police officers uncover an international paedophile and pornography network run over the Internet. Police raid 105 separate addresses in Western Europe, the USA, and Australia, arresting around 50 men from 12 countries and recovering more than 100,000 sexually explicit images, some involving children as young as two.

12 October 1998 US student Matthew Shepard dies from his injuries after being lured away from a bar, beaten, tortured, and left tied to a fence near Laramie, Wyoming, four days earlier. The perpetrators, Russell Henderson and Aaron McKinney, are accused of gay-bashing, sparking a heated debate about the failure of the law in several states to protect gays as a minority.

23 October 1998 US obstetrician-gynaecologist Barnett A Slepian is shot dead through the window of his home in Amherst, New York. The murder is linked to four similar attempted killings of doctors in New York and Canada who perform abortions.

28 October 1998 General Pinochet, Chilean dictator 1973–89, wins a high-court battle against his arrest and detention in England, where he went for medical treatment, for torture offences under his regime.

3 November 1998 Patrizia Reggiani, the ex-wife of the late fashion tycoon Maurizio Gucci, is found guilty in a court in Rome, Italy, of orchestrating his murder and is sentenced to 29 years in prison.

20 November 1998 US doctor Jack Kevorkian, known as 'Dr Death', gives fatal injections to Thomas Youk, a terminally ill patient who wants to kill himself, on the CBS programme *60 Minutes*. It is the first time that Kevorkian admits to killing a patient himself rather than assisting in the suicide. The death is treated as a homicide.

25 November 1998 The British law lords rule that Augusto Pinochet, the former dictator of Chile, does not have immunity from arrest in the UK for murder and torture by his government.

27 November 1998 US death row inmate Martin Gurule escapes from prison near Huntsville, Texas. It is the first death row escape in Texas since Bonnie and Clyde broke out a member of their gang in 1934. He is found dead floating in a river near the prison, after a six-day manhunt, apparently drowned.

9 December 1998 British home secretary Jack Straw rules that former Chilean dictator Augusto Pinochet may be extradited to Spain to stand trial for crimes committed during his rule.

10 December 1998 On the 50th anniversary of the United Nations Universal Declaration of Human Rights, a court in the Hague, the Netherlands, sentences Bosnian Croat former paramilitary commander Anto Furundzija to 10 years' imprisonment for standing by and watching one of his men rape and torture a female detainee during an interrogation in 1993. It is the first time that an act of rape is classified as a war crime by the UN tribunal.

17 December 1998 British law lords overturn the judgement to allow the extradition of former Chilean dictator Augusto Pinochet because of the links of one of the judges to Amnesty International. A new appeal is scheduled for January 1999.

12 January 1999 The Police Complaints Authority in London, England, clears all the officers involved in the case of Stephen Lawrence of racism.

15 January 1999 British law lords condemn their colleague Lord Hoffman for failing to declare his association with the human-rights group Amnesty International when he sat on the panel of judges to rule on the extradition of former Chilean dictator Pinochet.

23 February 1999 A jury in Jasper County, Texas, convicts white supremacist John William King of capital murder for killing a black man, James Byrd Jr, by chaining him to the back of his truck and dragging him 5 km/3 mi to his death. King is sentenced to death by lethal injection.

24 February 1999 A panel set up to assess racism in Britain's police forces issues a report that finds racism prevalent in the police force as well as other institutions. The panel was set up in response to controversy over alleged racism in the handling of the Stephen Lawrence case.

24 March 1999 A seven-member committee of the law lords in Britain rules that former Chilean dictator Augusto Pinochet is not immune from arrest and may be extradited to Spain, where he faces charges of torture and murder. The committee was formed to reexamine the case after it was discovered that Lord Hoffmann, a law lord who sat on a previous committee ruling on the case, had a conflict of interest because of his links with the human-rights group Amnesty International.

26 March 1999 A jury in Oakland County, Michigan, convicts US doctor Jack Kevorkian, a crusader for the legalization of physician-assisted suicide, of second-degree murder for killing Thomas Youk (see 20 November). Although Kevorkian claims to have assisted 130 people in committing suicide, by providing a machine that lets the patient administer his or her own lethal injection, this was the first case in which Kevorkian injected the patient himself.

1 April 1999 Anthony Sawoniuk, a former police chief of Domachevo, now in Belarus, is convicted in London, England, of two counts of murder for his participation in Nazi killings of Jews during World War II.

2 April 1999 Computer programmer David Smith is arrested in New Jersey, charged with creating the Melissa virus, which spread via e-mail to more than 100,000 computers worldwide.

5 April 1999 Former Libyan intelligence officers Abdel Basset Ali al-Megrahi and Lamen Khalifa Fhimah, the suspects charged with the bombing of Pan Am Flight 103 over Lockerbie, Scotland in 1988, arrive in the Netherlands to stand trial. The handover results in the automatic end to United Nations sanctions against Libya, whose leader Moamer al-Khaddafi had refused for ten years to release the suspects to stand trial.

7 April 1999 Edgar Pearce, the 'Mardi Gra' bomber, pleads guilty in London, England, to 20 charges related to his bombing campaign against branches of Barclays bank and Sainsbury's supermarket between 1994 and 1998, in which six people were injured.

15 April 1999 British home secretary Jack Straw rules that the extradition case against former Chilean dictator Augusto Pinochet may proceed.

20 April 1999 Eric Harris and Dylan Klebold, two pupils of Columbine High School in Littleton, Colorado, kill 13 people and injure more than 30 others using guns and bombs in a five-hour rampage. They then kill themselves.

7 May 1999 British student Neil Sayers is sentenced to life imprisonment for the murder of his classmate Russell Crookes. Another classmate, Graham Wallis, previously pleaded guilty to the murder and gave evidence against Sayers. Sayers and Wallis stabbed Crookes to death while they were sitting around a campfire near Tonbridge, Kent, then burnt and buried his body. The judge in the case said Sayers and Wallis had been inspired by violent videos, which desensitized them to murder.

11 May 1999 A jury at Newcastle upon Tyne, acquits GP David Moor of the murder of George Liddell, an 85-year-old cancer sufferer in his care. Moor gave his patient a massive overdose of diamorphine to hasten his death.

20 May 1999 A 15-year-old pupil of Heritage High School in Conyers, near Atlanta, Georgia, opens fire with a rifle near the school cafeteria, injuring six students.

20 May 1999 The US government adopts tougher gun control laws, forcing people who wish to buy guns at fairs and pawn shops to wait three days for criminal checks. Vice President Al Gore casts the deciding vote in favour of the new rules after the Senate votes are tied at 50–50. The laws come into force just hours after the aforementioned incident in Georgia.

10 June 1999 The Metropolitan Police in London, England, launch an advertising campaign, featuring a CD and video by rap singer and record producer Charles Bailey, in a drive to recruit more black and Asian officers.

15 June 1999 Charges are brought against 25 prison officers at Wormwood Scrubs prison in London, following allegations of the systematic beating of inmates.

World Law and Crime

Number of Recorded Crimes in Selected Countries

Definitions of offences vary between countries both due to legal differences and statistical recording methods; comparisons may be affected by these differences. (N/A = not available.)

Crime	1997	% change 1996–97
England and Wales		
Homicide	739	9
Violent crime	347,064	1
Theft of a motor vehicle	407,239	–17
Domestic burglary	519,265	–14
Drug trafficking	23,153	5
Northern Ireland		
Homicide	42	8
Violent crime	8,251	–9
Theft of a motor vehicle	8,633	3
Domestic burglary	7,435	–13
Drug trafficking	185	–9
Scotland		
Homicide	95	–30
Violent crime	23,656	–6
Theft of a motor vehicle	28,646	–16
Domestic burglary	36,792	–10
Drug trafficking	8,180	18
Austria		
Homicide	147	–16
Violent crime	46,942	1
Theft of a motor vehicle	3,848	3
Domestic burglary	12,826	–7
Drug trafficking	16,808	13
Australia		
Homicide	360	3
Violent crime	160,574	10
Theft of a motor vehicle	130,406	6
Domestic burglary	284,974	6
Drug trafficking	N/A	N/A
Belgium		
Homicide	145	23
Violent crime	60,605	12
Theft of a motor vehicle	35,242	5
Domestic burglary	143,769	–20
Drug trafficking	11,072	32
Canada		
Homicide	581	–9
Violent crime	296,737	0
Theft of a motor vehicle	177,286	–2
Domestic burglary	233,844	–4
Drug trafficking	16,778	–2
Czech Republic		
Homicide	291	9
Violent crime	23,223	2
Theft of a motor vehicle	29,422	7
Domestic burglary	13,068	–3
Drug trafficking	789	12
Denmark		
Homicide	88	28
Violent crime	13,963	4
Theft of a motor vehicle	41,227	–2
Domestic burglary	111,449	1
Drug trafficking	171	–52
Finland		
Homicide	142	–7
Violent crime	27,797	1
Theft of a motor vehicle	22,015	9
Domestic burglary	10,436	1
Drug trafficking	8,323	6
France		
Homicide	963	–18
Violent crime	189,203	6
Theft of a motor vehicle	417,360	–6
Domestic burglary	213,561	–10
Drug trafficking	86,961	9
Germany		
Homicide	1,178	–6
Violent crime	186,447	4
Theft of a motor vehicle	190,585	–16
Domestic burglary	182,009	–7
Drug trafficking	69,093	5
Greece		
Homicide	203	20
Violent crime	10,733	32
Theft of a motor vehicle	16,555	32
Domestic burglary	44,286	3
Drug trafficking	5,970	40
Hungary		
Homicide	289	7
Violent crime	26,987	9
Theft of a motor vehicle	14,413	–11
Domestic burglary	31,269	4
Drug trafficking	943	114
Ireland, Republic of		
Homicide	38	–10
Violent crime	5,488	–16
Theft of a motor vehicle	13,589	1
Domestic burglary	16,970	–4
Drug trafficking	1,637	71
Italy		
Homicide	928	–8
Violent crime	64,822	5
Theft of a motor vehicle	301,233	–5
Domestic burglary	237,445	3
Drug trafficking	41,420	6
Japan		
Homicide	1,282	5
Violent crime	40,570	8
Theft of a motor vehicle	696,370	1
Domestic burglary	221,678	–1
Drug trafficking	2,359	–12
Netherlands[1]		
Homicide	273	0
Violent crime	66,688	3
Theft of a motor vehicle	36,772	–10
Domestic burglary	103,953	–12
Drug trafficking	6,593	90

(continued)

Number of Recorded Crimes in Selected Countries *(continued)*

Crime	1997	% change 1996–97
New Zealand		
Homicide	89	41
Violent crime	42,191	0
Theft of a motor vehicle	30,776	3
Domestic burglary	49,376	1
Drug trafficking	14,532	15
Norway		
Homicide	38	−12
Violent crime	17,396	−3
Theft of a motor vehicle	20,019	−7
Domestic burglary	16,923	−11
Drug trafficking	34,705	25
Poland		
Homicide	807	−8
Violent crime	66,970	11
Theft of a motor vehicle	56,781	12
Domestic burglary	70,187	6
Drug trafficking	994	101
Portugal		
Homicide	131	13
Violent crime	16,723	8
Theft of a motor vehicle	22,792	14
Domestic burglary	24,202	6
Drug trafficking	3,390	−13
Russia		
Homicide	29,285	0
Violent crime[1]	161,644	−11
Theft of a motor vehicle[1]	41,712	−14
Domestic burglary[1]	17,490	−9
Drug trafficking[1]	96,645	21
South Africa		
Homicide	24,588	−5
Violent crime	645,737	1
Theft of a motor vehicle	100,637	4
Domestic burglary	249,375	1
Drug trafficking	42,805	9
Spain		
Homicide	1,032	7
Violent crime	87,775	1
Theft of a motor vehicle	133,330	17
Domestic burglary	84,430	N/A
Drug trafficking	14,274	−7
Sweden		
Homicide	157	11[1]
Violent crime	68,310	4
Theft of a motor vehicle	78,826	10
Domestic burglary	18,359	9
Drug trafficking	561	−12
Switzerland		
Homicide	87	5
Violent crime	7,385	8
Theft of a motor vehicle	21,534	3
Domestic burglary	82,559	11
Drug trafficking	3,253	29
USA[1]		
Homicide	19,645	−9
Violent crime	1,682,278	−6
Theft of a motor vehicle	1,395,192	−5
Domestic burglary	2,501,524	−4
Drug trafficking	1,506,200	2

[1] 1996 figures and 1995–96 percentage changes.

Source: *Criminal Statistics, England and Wales 1997,* © Crown copyright 1998

Prison Population in Selected Countries

(– = not applicable. N/A = not available.)

Country	1987	1993	1997
England and Wales	47,422	45,633	61,940
Northern Ireland	1,858	1,902	1,581
Scotland	5,446	5,637	6,082
UK total	54,726	53,172	69,603
Australia	11,934	15,003	17,661
Austria	7,419	7,099	6,946
Canada	26,893	31,709	34,166
Czech Republic	28,411	16,567	21,560
Denmark	3,190	3,370	3,170
Finland	4,252	3,432	2,976
France	50,639	51,134	54,442
Germany	51,919	65,838	N/A
Greece	3,809	7,135	5,577
Hungary	22,543	13,196	13,405
Ireland	1,936	2,801	2,424
Italy	34,383	51,231	50,197
Japan	55,210	45,057	50,600
Netherlands	4,909	8,037	11,770
New Zealand	3,117	4,600	5,152
Norway	2,023	2,650	N/A
Portugal	8,424	11,079	14,167
Russia	–	844,870	1,009,863
South Africa	114,098	111,798	134,202
Spain	26,905	46,076	42,756
Sweden	4,776	5,697	5,181
Switzerland	3,449	5,627	5,980
USA	856,906	1,369,185	1,725,842

Source: *Criminal Statistics, England and Wales 1997,* © Crown copyright 1998

Gun-Control in the UK and USA

BY IAN DERBYSHIRE

From the spring of 1996, the debate on gun-control gained international prominence as a result of two horrendous mass killings on opposite sides of the globe.

Dunblane, Scotland

On 13 March, at 9.30 a.m., Thomas Hamilton, a 43-year-old gun-club enthusiast who had been dismissed as a Boy Scout leader as a result of suspicions that he might be a paedophile, entered the grounds of the local elementary school in the small Highlands town of Dunblane, armed with four handguns and wearing a black cap and ear-muffs. In the gymnasium, he went beserk. In four minutes, he fired 105 rounds from two 9 mm Browning semi-automatic pistols. Sixteen children, aged five and six, together with their teacher, were murdered. Twelve others were wounded.

Port Arthur, Australia

On 28 April, Martin Bryant, a 28-year-old loner, opened fire on innocent tourists in the Broad Arrow Cafe in the former penal colony of Port Arthur, Tasmania. Thirty-five people were killed and 18 injured in two minutes of mayhem. The weapons used were semi-automatic rifles, meant for troops and purchased without a gun licence. Such weapons, which had flowed into Australia after the end of the Vietnam War in the 1970s, also featured in Australia's previous worst massacres, in Melbourne (1987) and Sydney (1991), which had caused 22 deaths in total.

Federal, state, and local laws prohibit the purchase and possession of guns by certain 'risky' groups of citizens.

These tragedies were caused by the irrational actions of two unbalanced individuals. However, proponents of stricter gun-control argued that the international evidence of a direct link between levels of gun ownership and gun crime was compelling. For example, in 1995 in the UK, where gun laws were comparatively strict, there were two million legally held firearms among a population of 58 million and only 80 firearm murders. In contrast, in the USA, where control was more lax, there were 220 million weapons (including 70 million handguns) among a population of 260 million and 14,000 firearm deaths. By comparison, the level of non-violent property crime was actually higher in London than in New York City or Los Angeles.

Among developed countries, gun-control laws are tightest in Japan, where handguns may not be kept at home. Illegal possession is punishable by 15 years' imprisonment. There are very few gun deaths in Japan. In contrast, levels of gun ownership and gun violence are much higher in Australia, where, until new federal controls were introduced in May 1996, licensing had been a state-level responsibility. In Switzerland, militia service has spread gun ownership to one-third of all households, and in the more socially-polarized developing states of South Africa and Latin America the situation is even worse. In South Africa the annual murder rate, at 50–55 per 100,000 people, is five times higher than in the USA.

UK gun-control before and after Dunblane

The use of firearms for hunting, clay pigeon shooting, and target practice in gun clubs has long been a popular British minority pastime. In 1987, there were 8,000 gun clubs, 160,000 licensed holders of handguns, and 840,000 licensed holders of shotguns. However, the massacre of 16 people in the small market town of Hungerford by Michael Ryan (a self-styled 'Rambo' who held five licensed firearms) in August 1987 resulted in a partial tightening of the 1968 Firearms Act. Self-loading rifles, though not pistols, were banned, and a general guns amnesty was declared. This resulted in 48,000 weapons being handed in. By 1996, the number of handgun-licence holders in the UK had declined to 57,000, shotgun-licence holders to 723,000, and gun clubs to 2,000.

In the wake of Dunblane, the Conservative government announced a guns amnesty and established an independent inquiry into the gun laws under a senior Scottish judge, Lord Cullen. The opposition parties called for a complete ban on handgun possession. However, Conservative party backbenchers, influenced by the gun lobby, advised against a knee-jerk reaction to the tragedy. Using the incontrovertible argument that 'guns don't kill, people do', they emphasized the impracticality of legislating against the 'lone killer'. In October 1996, the Cullen Inquiry concluded that levels of gun ownership and gun crime were related and recommended that all handguns be stored at gun clubs. The government legislated to restrict licensed ownership of handguns to pistols of up to .22 calibre, which were required to be left in safes at approved gun clubs, rather than kept in homes. This gave the UK one of the world's toughest gun-control laws. At a stroke, it eliminated 90 percent of the country's 200,000 legally-held handguns. However, it was believed that four million firearms were held still held illegally.

The gun-law debate in the USA

Gun culture' is deeply ingrained in the USA and the pro-gun lobby is particularly powerful. As a consequence, gun-control is an emotive political issue and only recently, with the Clinton administration, has a concerted attempt been made to tighten the gun laws.

Guns occupy a central place in American mythology, and their ownership is an important symbol of personal freedom. During the American Revolution, firearms were used by citizens' militias to overthrow British colonial rule, and, during the westward expansion of the American frontier, for protection against Indian and other attacks on property and family. An explicit right to

(continued)

'keep and bear arms' is consequently established in the second amendment to the constitution.

Today, half of all US households possess guns. In rural America, they are used for hunting and sport. In urban America, they are kept for self-defence. Federal, state, and local laws prohibit the purchase and possession of guns by certain 'risky' groups of citizens, including juveniles, minors, and adults with a criminal record or histories of alcohol and drug abuse. However, these laws have proved almost unenforcable since guns can be acquired, illegally but readily, from friends and other family members, from 'street sources', and from burglaries. Consequently, in some inner city areas, surveys have found that more than one-fifth of high school youths are gun owners. Laws that make it illegal either to carry an unlicensed firearm or to discharge a firearm within city limits are also poorly observed.

During the 1980s and early 1990s, levels of violent crime rose sharply in urban America. This was related to widening economic and social divisions and the influx of crack cocaine. However, gun availability contributed to the spiral of violence. By the early 1990s, half a million urban Americans were members of criminal gangs and almost half the deaths of male African-American teenagers were firearms-related. Guns were also widely used by young males for suicides, the rate of which had quadrupled since 1950. They were used in political assassinations and – as in the Hungerford, Dunblane, and Port Arthur incidents – by lone gunmen in massacres at an elementary school in Stockton, California (1989), and a cafe in Killeen, Texas (1991), which together accounted for the loss of 27 lives.

Guns were associated with fanatical religious groups such as David Koresh's Branch Davidian Movement, which perished on 19 April 1993 at Waco, Texas. They were also hoarded by right-wing 'patriot-militias', who, with more than 100,000 members in 30 states, were preparing to wage a violent Second American Revolution in defence of the second amendment.

Despite the breakdown in law and order in urban America, no significant measure of federal gun-control was passed during the 1970s and 1980s. One of the chief reasons for this was the strength of the pro-gun lobby, in particular the National Rifle Association (NRA). Formed in 1871 to promote improved marksmanship, by the 1990s the NRA was one of the country's most powerful pressure groups. It had 3.5 million members (equivalent to 5 percent of US gun owners) and, through its political wing, the Institute for Legislative Action (ILA), 'invested' millions of dollars in support of, chiefly Republican, pro-gun candidates in congressional, state, and presidential elections. It dwarfed its lobbying opponent, the pro-gun-control pressure group, Handgun-control Inc. (established 1974). Another reason for the lack of change was the support of academics who argued that the introduction of further gun-control measures would prove futile, given the circumvention of current laws. Several also provided evidence of the deterrence value of allowing law-abiding citizens to carry concealed handguns, as was permitted in more than 30 states, which had significantly lower rates for violent crimes and murders.

The 'Brady bill'

The November 1992 election as US president of the Democrat Bill Clinton brought into the White House the strongest ever advocate of gun-control. In November 1993 President Clinton signed into law the 'Brady bill'. Named after former President Ronald Reagan's press secretary, James Brady, who had been severely disabled after being shot during a 1981 attempt to assassinate Reagan, the bill imposed a five-day waiting period for handgun purchasers to allow the authorities to carry out criminal record checks. It was the most significant piece of federal gun-control legislation since the 1968 banning of the mail-order sale of rifles and shotguns. Then, in August 1994, a new crime bill banned the sale of 19 types of semi-automatic assault weapons, including AK-47s, which had been used in gang battles and the Stockton massacre.

The impact of these symbolic measures was anticipated to be limited since law enforcement was chiefly a state, rather than federal, responsibility. Nevertheless, during 1995 and 1996 there was a welcome fall in the crime rate across the USA and a decline in the murder rate by 10 percent per annum. This was linked to such factors as reduced use of crack cocaine, tougher parole laws, and new urban policing tactics. In New York, for example, violent crime fell to a 20-year low. Nevertheless, stricter gun-control may have contributed at the margins – between 1994 and 1996 'Brady bill' background checks denied handguns to more than 100,000 would-be purchasers.

The 'Brady bill', though designed as a short-term measure, met judicial challenge from conservatives claiming violation of the 10th amendment. However, since the 19 April 1995 bombing of the Alfred P Murrah federal building in Oklahoma City, which was perpetrated by far-right antigovernment militants and claimed 168 lives, US public opinion has become more inclined towards gun-control. Opinion hardened further following a spate of senseless firearm murders by young students at schools across the USA in 1997, and also in Jonseboro, Arkansas, in March 1998, when two boys, aged 11 and 13, killed four girls and a teacher, and Littleton, Colorado, in April 1999, when two seniors, members of a far-right group, shot dead a teacher and 12 fellow students, before killing themselves. In the wake of such tragedies, the firearms industry has faced a growing number of lawsuits, with cities such as New Orleans claiming damages for the havoc wreaked by their product. Meanwhile, in Richmond, Virginia, an experimental programme launched in February 1997 has prosecuted firearms offences under federal law rather than under less punitive state law. Within a year, murder rates fell by 65 percent, armed robberies by 30 percent, and the number of criminals caught carrying firearms by 60 percent. This suggested a hopeful way forward for other US states.

Ian Derbyshire is a writer on history, politics, and government

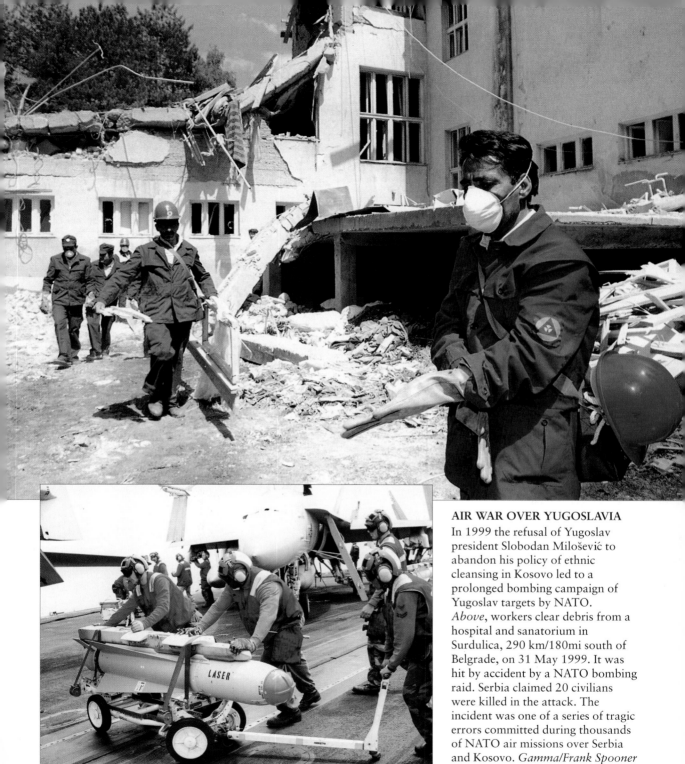

AIR WAR OVER YUGOSLAVIA
In 1999 the refusal of Yugoslav president Slobodan Milošević to abandon his policy of ethnic cleansing in Kosovo led to a prolonged bombing campaign of Yugoslav targets by NATO. *Above*, workers clear debris from a hospital and sanatorium in Surdulica, 290 km/180mi south of Belgrade, on 31 May 1999. It was hit by accident by a NATO bombing raid. Serbia claimed 20 civilians were killed in the attack. The incident was one of a series of tragic errors committed during thousands of NATO air missions over Serbia and Kosovo. *Gamma/Frank Spooner*
Left, munitions experts on the American aircraft carrier *USS Roosevelt* prepare to load a laser-guided 'smart' bomb. *Frederic Castel/Gamma/Frank Spooner*

HUMAN TIDE OF SUFFERING
Two Kosovan Albanian women carry their belongings across the Kosovo-Macedonia border at Blace in early April 1999, during the expulsion by Serb forces of hundreds of thousands of ethnic Albanians from Kosovo. The images of Kosovan refugees without food or shelter provoked horror around the world. *R.Lemoyne/Gamma Liaison*

IMPEACHMENT CRISIS

President Bill Clinton was publicly humiliated in September 1998 when Independent Counsel Kenneth Starr released the much-awaited Starr Report. It documented in explicit detail the sexual relationship between Clinton and Monica Lewinsky and forced the president to admit that he had misled the American people over the affair. Clinton was impeached by the House of Representatives in December 1998 but his presidency survived the Senate trial that followed in January. *Georges de Keerle/Gamma Liaison*

MANDELA STEPS DOWN

Outgoing South African president Nelson Mandela (left) with his successor, Thabo Mbeki, after the presidential swearing-in ceremony in June 1999. Mbeki and the ANC (African National Congress) were the winners in the country's second multi-racial elections since the end of apartheid. The ANC reinforced its hold on power, winning almost 66% of the vote. Mbeki faces impatience from a population still suffering extreme poverty and high crime rates. *Sipa/Rex*

GANDHI DYNASTY CONTINUES

In April 1999 Italian-born Sonia Gandhi, leader of India's Congress Party, came close to creating a minority government after the collapse of the Hindu Nationalist coalition administration of Atal Behari Vajpayee. The suitability of Gandhi – the widow and daughter-in-law respectively of two assassinated Indian prime ministers, Rajiv Gandhi and Indira Gandhi – to be prime minister was questioned by members of her own party because of her European ancestry, but she survived the challenge and intended to fight the Indian general election in September 1999. *Namas Bhojani/Rex*

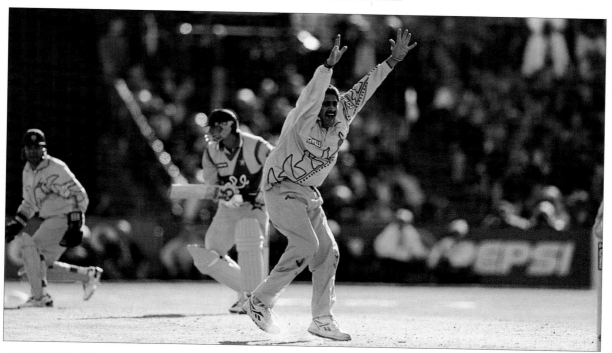

CRICKET CLASH

Anil Kumble of India (right) appeals for the dismissal of Pakistan's Saqlain Mushtaq during India's 47-run Cricket World Cup win on 8 June 1999. Pakistan were bowled out for 180, in reply to India's total of 227 for 6. The World Cup in England in May and June was won by Australia. The India v. Pakistan match, which occurred while the two nations were fighting in the long-disputed border region of Kashmir, was played amid fears that trouble between fanatical supporters might disrupt the game, but these proved unfounded. *Graham Chadwick/Allsport*

NEW CURRENCY FOR EUROPE

Jacques Santer (left), then president of the European Commission and Yves-Thibault de Silguy, then the European Union's commissioner for monetary union, celebrate the launch of the euro in January 1999. The new currency locked together the economies of the 11 nations of the euro zone, but experienced a dramatic decline in value as continental Europe, and Germany in particular, was unable to shake off the effects of recession. The prospect of the euro caused fierce debate in Britain, which chose not to join the euro zone at the first stage. *Gamma*

BACKLASH AGAINST GM CROPS

Greenpeace activists destroy a field of genetically modified maize in France in September 1998. Environmental groups believe that cross-pollination of genetically modified organisms (GMOs) with other crops will lead to irreversible contamination of ecosystems. Health concerns have led to consumer boycotts and legislation forcing the labelling of genetically modified ingredients. *Greenpeace*

DEVOLUTION FOR WALES AND SCOTLAND

The Queen and Prince Philip (pictured), accompanied by the Prince of Wales, attended the opening of the Welsh Assembly on 26 May 1999. Following the elections to the Welsh Assembly, and those for the new Scottish Parliament in Edinburgh, seats were allocated by proportional representation. The results were a minority administration in Wales under First Secretary Alun Michael of Labour, after a surprisingly high showing by Plaid Cymru (the Welsh nationalist party), and a Labour-Liberal Democrat coalition for Scotland. *Ian Jones/Gamma*

NORTHERN IRELAND'S WORST TERRORIST ATTACK

Emergency personnel and soldiers survey the damage in the town of Omagh, Co. Tyrone, Northern Ireland in August 1998, following the worst terrorist attack of the Troubles, in which a car bomb killed 28 people and hospitalized over 100. The bomb was planted by the Real IRA, a splinter group of the Provisional IRA. Misleading warnings led police to evacuate market-day shoppers into, rather than away from, the area of the bomb. *Rex*

ROYAL WEDDING

Prince Edward, seventh in line to the British throne, and Sophie Rhys-Jones leave St George's Chapel at Windsor as the Earl and Countess of Wessex, following their marriage on 19 June 1999. The couple married after a six-year romance, exchanging vows in front of the Rt Rev. Peter Nott, bishop of Norwich. The ceremony was performed before 550 guests, 8,000 members of the public in the grounds of Windsor Castle, and a television audience of around 200 million. *Rex*

CHARLES AND CAMILLA SNAPPED

Prince Charles and Camilla Parker Bowles allowed themselves to be photographed as a couple for the first time on 28 January 1999. The photo opportunity took place on the steps of the Ritz Hotel after the 50th birthday party of Camilla's sister, Annabel Elliott. The relationship between Charles and Camilla was well known, but one objective of the appearance was to prevent members of the paparazzi snatching an exclusive photo of the two together. *Tim Rooke/Rex*

AITKEN JAILED FOR LIES

Former Conservative cabinet minister Jonathan Aitken was jailed in June 1999 for perjury and perverting the course of justice. The offences occurred as he sued *The Guardian* newspaper for libel over accusations concerning his role in international arms sales and a stay at the Ritz Hotel in Paris. Aitken – who after the collapse of the libel action was divorced by his wife and declared bankrupt – was sentenced to 18 months in prison. *Richard Watt*

BUS DRIVER ON BOOKER SHORTLIST

In September 1998, London bus driver Magnus Mills was nominated for the Booker Prize for his debut novel *The Restraint of Beasts*. The £20,000 award for fiction, the most prestigious of its kind in Britain, was won by Ian McEwan for *Amsterdam*. *Richard Watt*

MOURNING THREE ARTISTIC GREATS

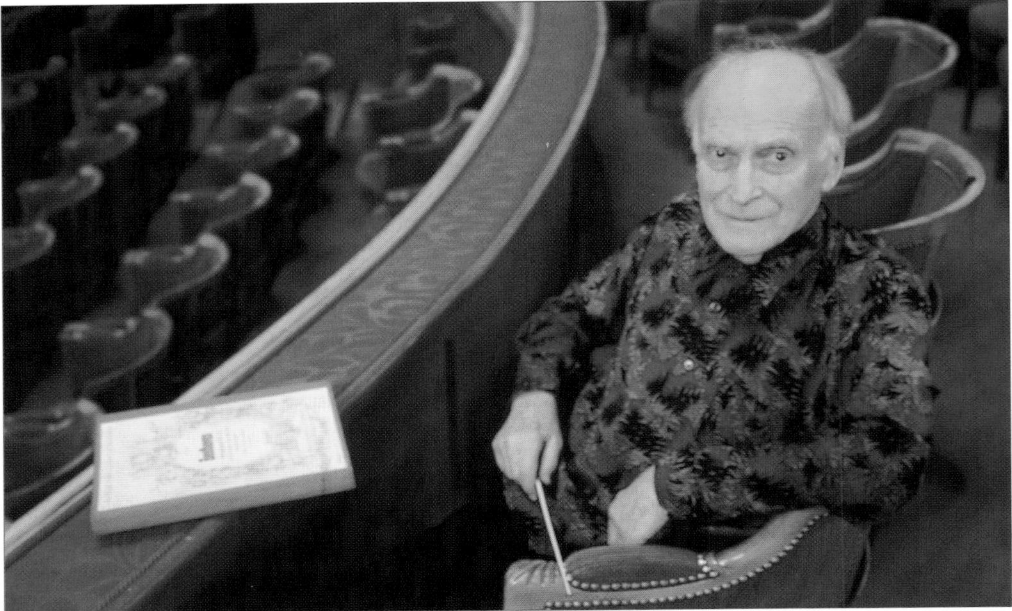

Yehudi Menuhin, who died in March 1999, made his performance debut at the age of 7. As a violinist he was considered one of the foremost interpreters of music in the history of the instrument; he was also highly regarded as a conductor and teacher. *Marc Deville/Gamma*

Dame Iris Murdoch, a professor of philosophy at the University of Oxford for 15 years, was one of the finest novelists of her generation and was known for her incorporation of philosophical thought into her work. She died in February 1999, having published 25 novels since 1954. *Robert Judges/Rex*

Poet Laureate Ted Hughes was best known for the savage imagery of nature in his poetry. He died in October 1998 after 14 years as poet laureate. *Birthday Letters* and *Tales From Ovid* were recent successes. *Rex*

HISTORIC TREBLE FOR MANCHESTER UNITED

David Beckham (left) and Teddy Sheringham of Manchester United hold up the European Cup after their team beat Bayern Munich in the final in Barcelona in May 1999. The German side were leading 1-0 with 90 minutes played, but goals in extra time from Sheringham and Ole Gunnar Solskjaer snatched a 2-1 victory and completed an historic treble: Manchester United, under Alex Ferguson, had already won the English Premiership and the FA Cup before winning European football's most prestigious club competition. *Rex*

THE WORLD: POLITICAL

EUROPE

Abbr.	Nation	Capital city
A.	**Andorra**	Andorra la Vella
AL.	**Albania**	Tiranë
AU.	**Austria**	Vienna
B.	**Belgium**	Brussels
B.H.	**Bosnia-Herzegovina**	Sarajevo
	Bulgaria	Sofia
C.	**Croatia**	Zagreb
CZ.	**Czech Republic**	Prague
D.	**Denmark**	Copenhagen
E.	**Estonia**	Tallinn
H.	**Hungary**	Budapest
LA.	**Latvia**	Riga
L.	**Liechtenstein**	Vaduz
LI.	**Lithuania**	Vilnius
LU.	**Luxembourg**	Luxembourg
MA.	**Macedonia**	Skopje
	Malta	Valletta
M.	**Monaco**	Monaco
MO.	**Moldova**	Chişinău
N.	**Netherlands**	Amsterdam
	Romania	Bucharest
S.	**San Marino**	San Marino
S.R.	**Slovak Republic**	Bratislava
SL.	**Slovenia**	Ljubljana
SW.	**Switzerland**	Bern
V.	**Vatican City**	
Y.	**Yugoslavia**	Belgrade

ASIA

Abbr.	Nation	Capital city
AR.	**Armenia**	Yerevan
AZ.	**Azerbaijan**	Baku
B.	**Bahrain**	Al Manamah
	Brunei	Bandar Seri Begawan
C.	**Cyprus**	Nicosia
G.	**Georgia**	Tbilisi
I.	**Israel**	Jerusalem
	Jordan	Amman
K.	**Kuwait**	Kuwait
L.	**Lebanon**	Beirut
	Maldives	Malé
Q.	**Qatar**	Doha
SI.	**Singapore**	Singapore
	Syria	Damascus
	Tajikistan	Dushanbe
U.A.E.	**United Arab Emirates**	Abu Dhabi

OCEANIA

Nation	Capital city
Fiji Islands	Suva
Kiribati	Bairiki
Marshall Islands	Dalap-Uliga-Da
Micronesia, Federated States of	Kolonia
Nauru	Yaren
Palau	Koror
Samoa	Apia
Solomon Islands	Honiara
Tonga	Nuku'alofa
Tuvalu	Fongafale
Vanuatu	Port-Vila

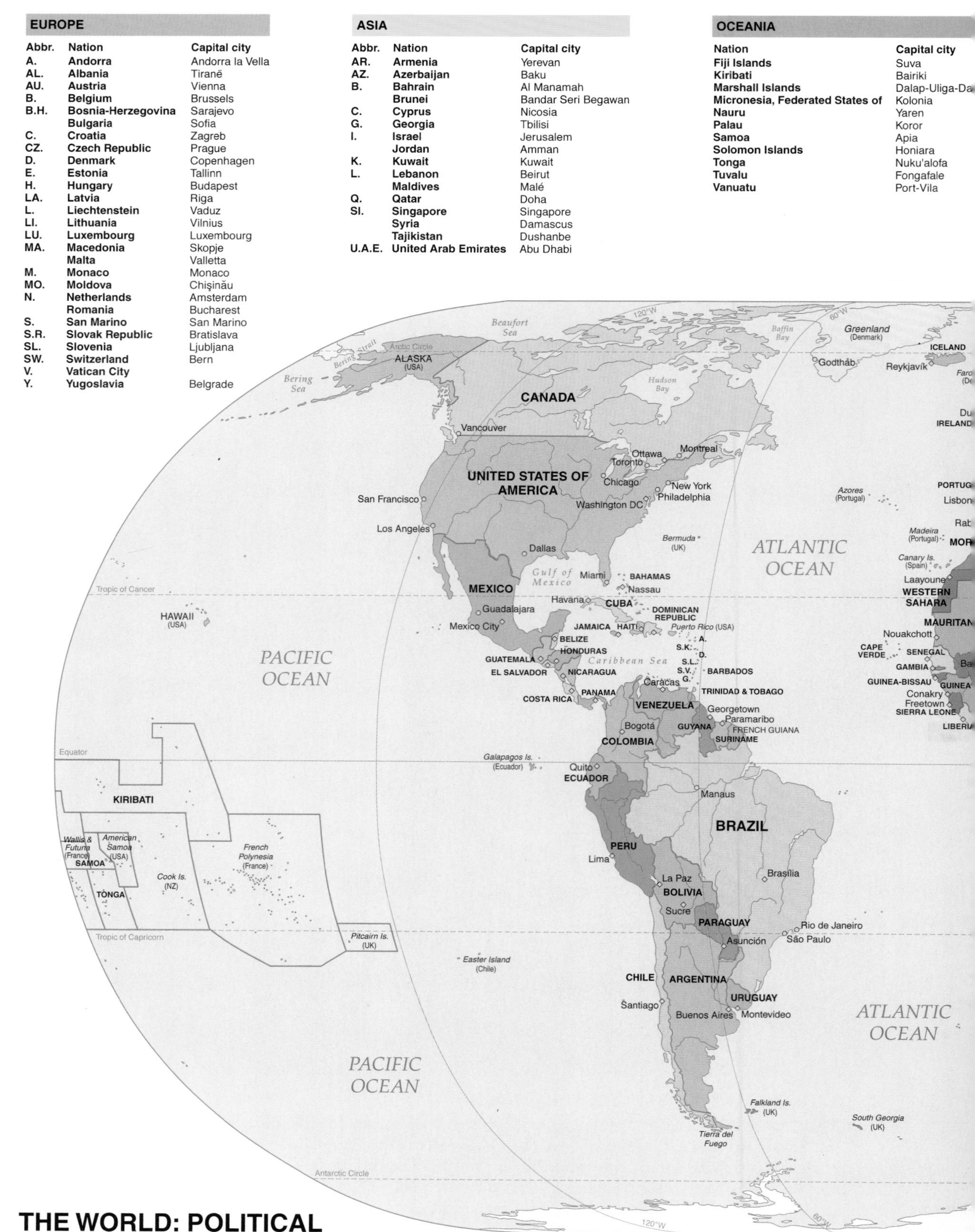

Key

- ◇ capital city
- ○ other major city
- —— international boundary

NORTH AND CENTRAL AMERICA

Abbr.	Nation	Capital city
A.	**Antigua and Barbuda**	St John's
	Barbados	Bridgetown
	Belize	Belmopan
	Costa Rica	San José
D.	**Dominica**	Roseau
	Dominican Republic	Santo Domingo
	El Salvador	San Salvador
G.	**Grenada**	St George's
	Guatemala	Guatemala
	Haiti	Port-au-Prince
	Honduras	Tegucigalpa
	Jamaica	Kingston
	Nicaragua	Managua
	Panama	Panamá
S.K.	**St Kitts and Nevis**	Basseterre
S.L.	**St Lucia**	Castries
S.V.	**St Vincent and the Grenadines**	Kingstown
	Trinidad and Tobago	Port-of-Spain

AFRICA

Abbr.	Nation	Capital city
BE.	**Benin**	Porto Novo
B.F.	**Burkina Faso**	Ouagadougou
B.	**Burundi**	Bujumbura
	Cape Verde	Praia
	Comoros	Moroni
C.I.	**Côte d'Ivoire**	Yamoussoukro
D.	**Djibouti**	Djibouti
E.G.	**Equatorial Guinea**	Malabo
	Eritrea	Asmara
	Gabon	Libreville
	Gambia	Banjul
G.	**Ghana**	Accra
	Guinea-Bissau	Bissau
	Liberia	Monrovia
	Mauritius	Port Louis
R.	**Rwanda**	Kigali
S.T.	**São Tomé and Príncipe**	São Tomé
	Senegal	Dakar
	Seychelles	Victoria
	Swaziland	Mbabane
T.	**Togo**	Lomé

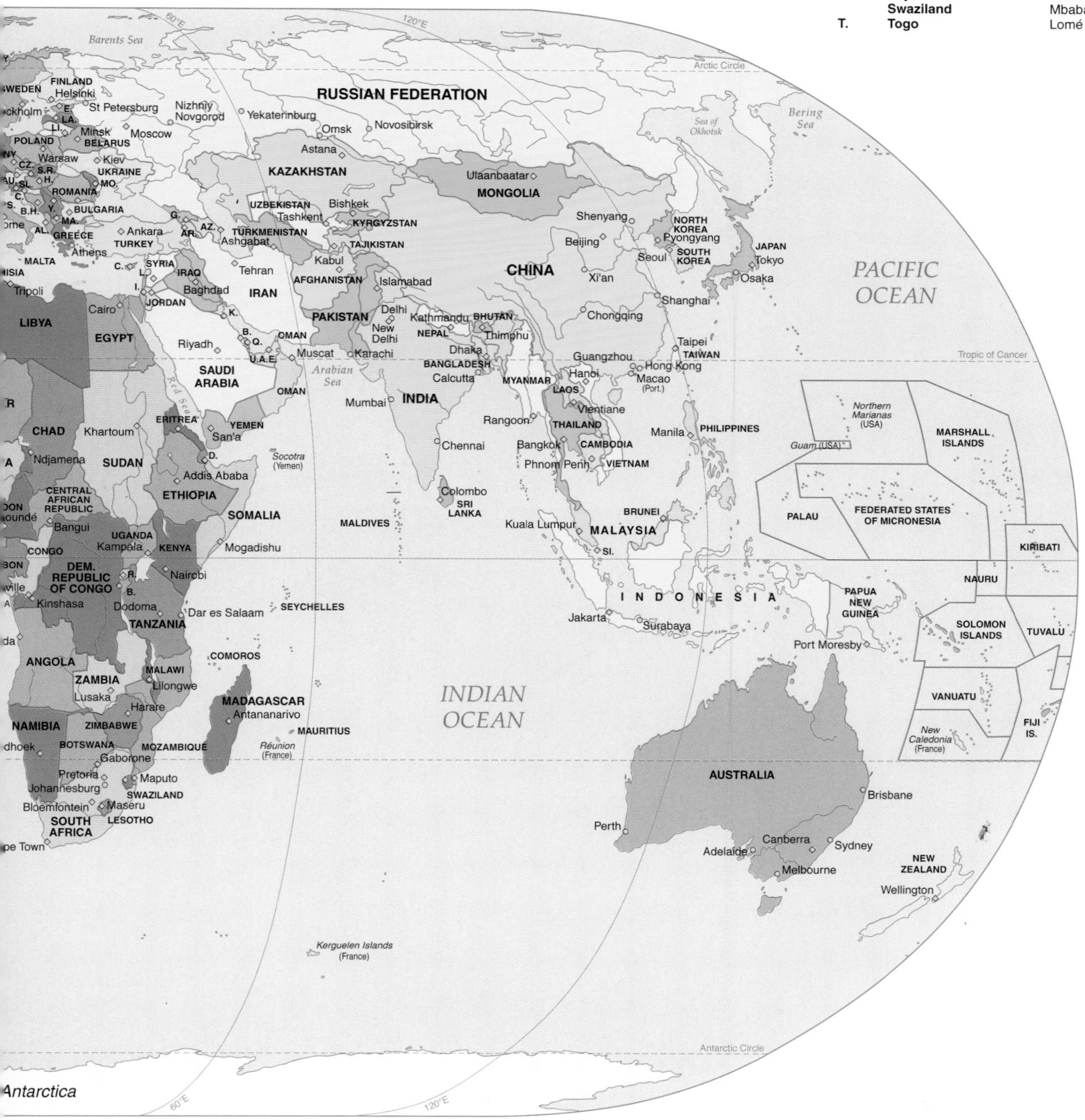

THE WORLD: PHYSICAL

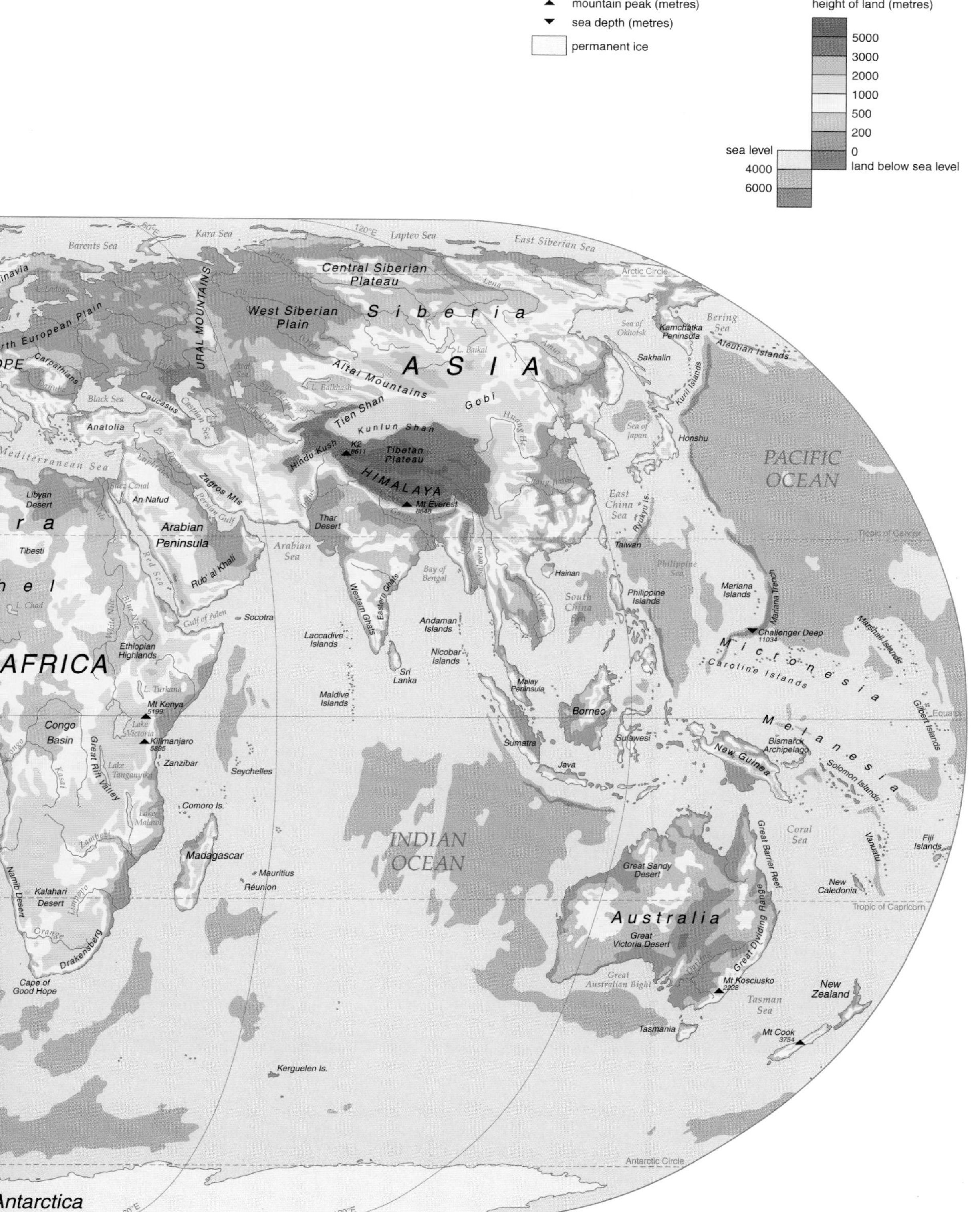

Key
mountain peak (metres)
sea depth (metres)
permanent ice
height of land (metres)
5000
3000
2000
1000
500
200
0
land below sea level
sea level
4000
6000
Kara Sea
Barents Sea
Laptev Sea
East Siberian Sea
Arctic Circle
Central Siberian Plateau
West Siberian Plain
Siberia
URAL MOUNTAINS
North European Plain
Carpathians
Caucasus
Black Sea
Caspian Sea
Aral Sea
L. Balkhash
L. Baikal
Altai Mountains
ASIA
Tien Shan
Gobi
Kunlun Shan
Hindu Kush
K2 8611
Tibetan Plateau
HIMALAYA
Mt Everest 8848
Anatolia
Mediterranean Sea
Libyan Desert
Suez Canal
An Nafud
Zagros Mts
Persian Gulf
Arabian Peninsula
Rub' al Khali
Red Sea
Tibesti
L. Chad
Gulf of Aden
Socotra
Arabian Sea
Thar Desert
Bay of Bengal
Western Ghats
Eastern Ghats
Laccadive Islands
Maldive Islands
Andaman Islands
Nicobar Islands
Sri Lanka
Sea of Okhotsk
Kamchatka Peninsula
Bering Sea
Aleutian Islands
Sakhalin
Kuril Islands
Sea of Japan
Honshu
PACIFIC OCEAN
East China Sea
Ryukyu Is.
Taiwan
Tropic of Cancer
Hainan
South China Sea
Philippine Sea
Philippine Islands
Mariana Islands
Mariana Trench
Challenger Deep 11034
Marshall Islands
Micronesia
Caroline Islands
Malay Peninsula
Borneo
Sumatra
Sulawesi
Java
Gilbert Islands
Equator
Melanesia
Bismarck Archipelago
New Guinea
Solomon Islands
AFRICA
Ethiopian Highlands
L. Turkana
Mt Kenya 5199
Lake Victoria
Kilimanjaro 5895
Zanzibar
Congo Basin
Great Rift Valley
Lake Tanganyika
Seychelles
Comoro Is.
Lake Malawi
Madagascar
Mauritius
Réunion
INDIAN OCEAN
Namib Desert
Kalahari Desert
Limpopo
Orange
Drakensberg
Cape of Good Hope
Tropic of Capricorn
Great Barrier Reef
Coral Sea
Vanuatu
Fiji Islands
New Caledonia
Great Sandy Desert
Australia
Great Victoria Desert
Great Dividing Range
Great Australian Bight
Mt Kosciusko 2228
Tasman Sea
New Zealand
Tasmania
Mt Cook 3754
Kerguelen Is.
Antarctic Circle
Antarctica
60°E
120°E

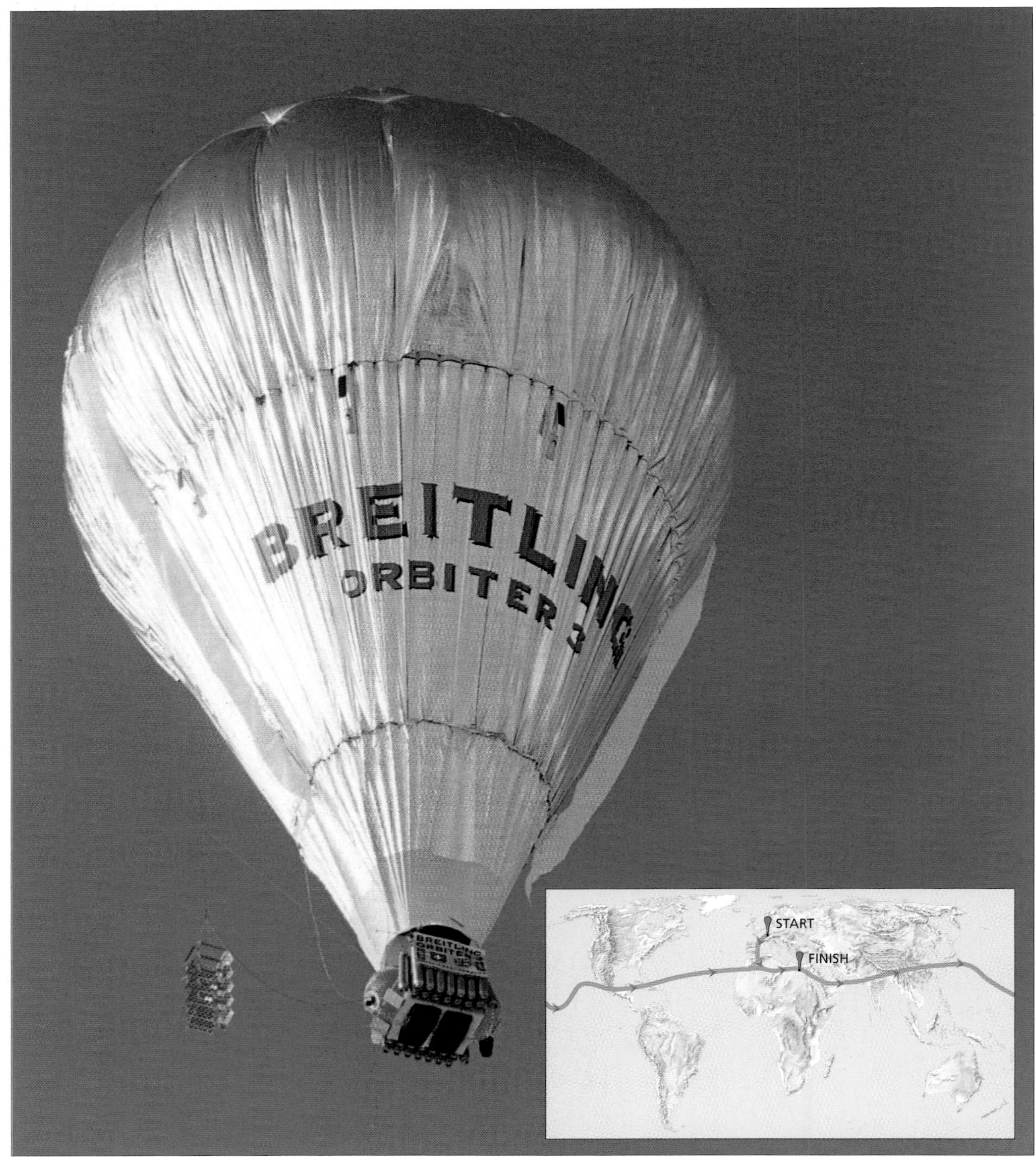

AROUND THE WORLD IN 19 DAYS

The *Breitling Orbiter 3* balloon during its record-breaking flight round the world. Pilots Brian Jones of Britain and Bertrand Piccard of Switzerland became the first to fly non-stop around the world in a balloon when they crossed the line of 9.27 degrees west over Mauritania in West Africa on 20 March 1999, 19 days, 1 hour, and 49 minutes after departing from the Swiss Alps. Sixteen previous attempts at the record had failed. Jones and Piccard had to fly a tightly defined route over Chinese airspace and survive slow winds over the Pacific before they finally touched down in Egypt to celebrate their achievement and a $1 million prize. The map inset shows their route. *Chas Breton/Rex*

Homicide Rates in Selected Cities

Ranked by rate of homicides.

City	Number of homicides 1995–97	Homicides per 100,000 population of the city Average 1995–97
Washington DC	1,057[1]	64.08[1]
Pretoria[2]	1,512	41.13
Moscow[3]	4,723	18.15
Amsterdam	171[4]	7.90[4]
Warsaw[3]	276	5.63
Copenhagen	67	4.55
Belfast	39	4.37
Stockholm	180[4]	4.13[4]
Berlin	396	3.81
Paris	211	3.28
Helsinki	47	2.97
Lisbon	160	2.91
Madrid	253	2.89
Prague	105	2.87
Budapest	160	2.80
Edinburgh	32	2.43[4]
London	491	2.17
Oslo	31	2.08
Ottawa	44	1.87
Brussels	52[1]	1.83[1]
Dublin	58	1.83
Vienna	86	1.80
Wellington	8	1.73
Rome	135	1.70
Athens	47	1.35
Geneva	15	1.23
Tokyo	390	1.10
Canberra	6	0.64

[1] Based on provisional figure for 1997.
[2] Including rural areas.
[3] Including attempts.
[4] 1994–96.

Source: *Criminal Statistics, England and Wales 1997*, © Crown copyright 1998

Countries that Have Abolished the Death Penalty for All Crimes

As of 7 January 1999. (N/A = not available – = not applicable.)

Country	Date of abolition	Date of last execution
Andorra	1990	1943
Angola	1992	N/A
Australia	1985	1967
Austria	1968	1950
Azerbaijan	1998	1993
Belgium	1996	1950
Bulgaria	1998	1989
Cambodia	1989	N/A
Cape Verde	1981	1835
Colombia	1910	1909
Costa Rica	1877	N/A
Croatia	1990	N/A
Czech Republic	1990[1]	N/A
Denmark	1978	1950
Dominican Republic	1966	N/A
Ecuador	1906	N/A
Estonia	1998	1991
Finland	1972	1944
France	1981	1977
Georgia	1997	1994
Germany	1949/1987[2]	1949[2]
Greece	1993	1972
Guinea-Bissau	1993	1986[3]
Haiti	1987	1972[3]
Honduras	1956	1940
Hungary	1990	1988
Iceland	1928	1830
Ireland, Republic of	1990	1954
Italy	1994	1947
Kiribati[4]	N/A	–
Liechtenstein	1987	1785
Luxembourg	1979	1949
Macedonia, Former Yugoslav Republic of	N/A	N/A
Marshall Islands[4]	N/A	–
Mauritius	1995	1987
Micronesia [4]	N/A	–
Moldova	1995	N/A
Monaco	1962	1847
Mozambique	1990	1986
Namibia	1990	1988[3]
Nepal	1997	1979
Netherlands, the	1982	1952
New Zealand	1989	1957
Nicaragua	1979	1930
Norway	1979	1948
Palau	N/A	N/A
Panama	N/A	1903[3]
Poland	1997	1988
Portugal	1976	1849[3]
Romania	1989	1989
San Marino	1865	1468[3]
São Tomé and Príncipe [4]	1990	–
Slovak Republic	1990[1]	N/A
Slovenia	1989	N/A
Solomon Islands [4]	N/A	–
Spain	1995	1975
Sweden	1972	1910
Switzerland	1992	1944
Tuvalu [4]	N/A	–
Uruguay	1907	N/A
Vanuatu [4]	N/A	–
Vatican City State	1969	N/A
Venezuela	1863	N/A

[1] The death penalty was abolished in the Czech and Slovak Federal Republic in 1990. On 1 January 1993 the Czech and Slovak Federal Republic divided into two states, the Czech Republic and the Slovak Republic. The last execution in the Czech and Slovak Federal Republic was in 1988.
[2] The death penalty was abolished in the Federal Republic of Germany (FRG) in 1949 and in the German Democratic Republic (GDR) in 1987. The last execution in the FRG was in 1949; the date of the last execution in the GDR is not known. The FRG and the GDR were unified in October 1990.
[3] Date of last known execution.
[4] No executions since independence.

Source: Amnesty International

THE ERA OF INTERNATIONAL CRIMINAL RESPONSIBILITY

BY DAPO AKANDE

The horrors of World War II, the killing fields of Cambodia, the brutalities of Amin's Uganda, the genocide in Rwanda, and the atrocities of former Yugoslavia are all grim reminders of the fact that the battle to achieve basic, decent, and humane standards of treatment for all human beings is not by any means won. Nevertheless, as we stand at the close of the 20th century we may take some comfort from the fact that international law has made great strides in recognizing and providing for the protection of human rights. This century has seen the adoption of several treaties aimed at protection of human rights, of which best known are the European Convention of Human Rights and the International Covenant on Civil and Political Rights. The emphasis in these treaties focuses on drawing up agreed standards to which states are legally bound to adhere, as well as on setting up mechanisms that would monitor how far states are complying with their obligations. From the legal and political point of view, this has been geared towards setting up systems that would ensure that states respect basic human rights.

International humanitarian law

In parallel with this development of human rights law, since the end of the 19th century there has also been a growing acknowledgement that the ravages of war need to be controlled. The international community has therefore developed legal principles – enshrined in treaties and in customary rules – that seek to control the way in which armed conflicts are fought. This area of law, known as international humanitarian law, has developed principles that seek to control the means and methods of warfare as well as to protect civilian populations, prisoners of war, and other vulnerable communities. As with human rights law, the initial emphasis was on standard-setting as well as on developing means by which the states' compliance could be monitored.

We are now in the age where international law imposes criminal responsibility directly on individuals.

Accountability of individuals

A further development is currently taking place in international law, a development which draws together international human rights law and international humanitarian law in seeking to protect the individual. This, however, goes even further by seeking to protect the individual from abuses committed by other individuals. We are now in the age where international law imposes criminal responsibility directly on individuals.

Historical background

This development is not wholly new. At the end of World War II, the victorious Allied powers set up the Nuremberg and Tokyo War Crimes Tribunals to try the most senior German and Japanese officers and officials accused of crimes against humanity and of violating the laws and customs of war. Following this, various war crimes trials were conducted by the Allied powers in their respective occupied zones of Germany. These trials, despite certain reservations, led to the development of some fundamental and widespread legal principles. Firstly, individuals as well as states are seen as bearing legal responsibility for the commission of atrocities in wartime. As the Nuremberg tribunal stated, crimes against international law are committed by people, not by abstract entities, and only by punishing individuals who commit such crimes can the provisions of international law be enforced. Secondly, it has been accepted that there are certain crimes prohibited by international law that are so serious and so damaging to humanity as a whole that every country has jurisdiction to try the offender as long as it has custody of him. These crimes are regarded as crimes of universal jurisdiction. Finally, appropriately created international tribunals are allowed to exercise jurisdiction over persons who commit some of these serious crimes.

Recent application

The last decade of the 20th century and 1999 in particular have seen remarkable applications of all these principles. The atrocities in the former Yugoslavia in the early 1990s and the feeling that those who committed those atrocities must not go unpunished led to the creation, by the United Nations Security Council, of the International Criminal Tribunal for the Former Yugoslavia. The Security Council has also created the International Criminal Tribunal for Rwanda. Both tribunals have so far had mixed fortunes. They have both indicted the most serious alleged perpetrators of atrocities but failed in their attempts to detain all alleged offenders. Nevertheless, both tribunals have emphasized that international law and the international community must not stand by while the worst elements in humanity are setting about their grizzly tasks.

Significantly, both international criminal tribunals have contributed to the development of a principle that the rank of an individual does not absolve them from international criminal responsibility. If international criminal law is to be effective, it must seek to restrain those who direct criminal acts from the top. Therefore, the law often needs to work against traditional legal deference to the sovereignty of states, especially if their governments are pursuing policies resulting in international crimes. Recent developments have indeed demonstrated that international law, in appropriate circumstances, is able to go right to the top and hold a head of state responsible for international crimes. The statutes setting up both the Rwandan and the Former Yugoslavian war crimes tribunals stated that the official position of any accused person,

whether as head of state or government or as a responsible government official, shall not relieve such person of criminal responsibility nor mitigate punishment. And in 1998, the International Criminal Tribunal for Rwanda convicted and sentenced Jean Kambanda – the prime minister during the 1994 genocide – for his part in the genocide in that country. Likewise, in May 1999, the prosecutor for the International Criminal Tribunal for the former Yugoslavia announced the indictment of Slobodan Miloševć, president of the Federal Republic of Yugoslavia, for war crimes and crimes against humanity committed in Kosovo.

Law as applied to heads of states

It is perhaps not too surprising that an international tribunal set up by a binding decision of the UN Security Council – the international community's repository of peacekeeping powers – is allowed to try the leader of a sovereign country. Whether a court of one country could try the leader – serving or former – of another country was more controversial. International law gives states certain immunities from the jurisdiction of foreign states and this immunity has always been regarded as applying to heads of states. Heads of states could therefore not be sued or prosecuted in a foreign state and even former heads of states continued to be immune from investigation in a foreign court of official acts committed while in office. Therefore, even though international law had developed a principle of universal jurisdiction which allowed any country to try any perpetrator of an international crime, states had never sought to try a serving or former head of state. The Pinochet case in the English courts has, however, clarified (some would say changed) the position. Spain's request for the extradition of the former Chilean head of state from the UK, and the decision of the House of Lords that the extradition should proceed, have further strengthened the principle of individual criminal responsibility for certain international crimes. The House of Lords held that torture (and presumably other international crimes) cannot be part of a head of state's official duties and once that head of state leaves office he/she loses international immunity for such acts. The head of state may therefore be tried in the domestic court of another country for such acts.

International Criminal Court

A further and major advance of the principle of individual criminal responsibility under international law for grave human rights breaches and war crimes was achieved in 1998 when the international community gathered in Rome to draft a statute for a permanent International Criminal Court (ICC). The statute sets up a court which is expected to become operational after 60 countries have ratified the statute, a process which is likely to take well into the first decade of the new millennium. The Rome Statute provides for the trial by the court of war crimes, genocide, crimes against humanity (whether committed in war or in peace time), and of aggression (subject to a definition of aggression being agreed). There are many imperfections in the Rome Statute and it remains to be seen how many states ratify it and when. Nevertheless, what is clear is that we are now in an age where the possibility of individuals being held responsible for their international crimes is far more realistic than at any other time.

Dapo Akande is lecturer in international law at the University of Nottingham

The Death Penalty: Sentences and Executions in 1997

During 1997 at least 2,375 prisoners are known to have been executed in 40 countries and 3,707 sentenced to death in 69 countries. Four countries alone accounted for 84 percent of all executions recorded by Amnesty International (AI) worldwide: China 1,644; Iran 143; Saudi Arabia 122; USA 74. These figures include only cases known to AI; the true figures are certainly higher. AI received reports of hundreds of executions in Iraq but was unable to confirm most of these reports or give an exact figure. Executions are known to have been carried out in the following countries in 1997:

Afghanistan
Bangladesh
Belarus
Burundi
Cameroon
China
Comoros
Congo
Egypt
Guyana
India
Iran
Iraq
Japan
Jordan
Kazakhstan
Korea, South
Kuwait
Kyrgyztan
Lebanon
Libya
Malaysia
Nigeria
Pakistan
Russian Federation (Chechen Republic)
Saudi Arabia
Sierra Leone
Singapore
Somalia
Taiwan
Thailand
Turkmenistan
Ukraine
United Arab Emirates
USA
Uzbekistan
Vietnam
Yemen
Zambia
Zimbabwe
Zimbabwe

Source: Amnesty International

UK Law and Crime

The Police Caution and the Right to Silence

When a suspect is questioned by the police, he or she must first be cautioned. Under the provisions of the Criminal Justice and Public Order Act 1994, the police caution has been amended so that the suspect is now reminded of the right to silence, while at the same time warned that silence may lead to adverse comment by the judge or the prosecution during trial, who may invite the jury to draw adverse inference from silence.

The new caution now reads as follows:

'You do not have to say anything. But it may harm your defence if you do not mention when questioned something which you later rely on in court. Anything you do say may be given in evidence.'

The Code of Practice states that a minor change in the wording so long as the overall meaning is retained is permitted. At the beginning of a police interview at a police station, it is necessary for the interviewing officer to refer the suspect to any significant statement or silence the suspect made in response to questions prior to the interview. The officer should then check that the suspect confirms or denies the prior silence or statement, and whether he or she wishes to add anything.

Where there is a break in questioning, the suspect should be reminded that he or she is still under caution. If the suspect is in any doubt, he or she should be cautioned again before the interview continues.

Police Complaints Authority

The Police Complaints Authority was set up on 29 April 1985 under the provisions of the Police and Criminal Evidence Act 1984, to supervise the investigation of complaints against the police by members of the public. It replaced the Police Complaints Board.

The Authority has three basic functions: to supervise the investigation of the most serious complaints against police officers; to supervise investigations into non-complaint matters voluntarily referred by police forces because of their potential gravity; and to review the outcome of every investigation, whether supervised or not, and to decide whether disciplinary action should be taken against any offence.

The more serious matters investigated by the Authority include the use of firearms by the police; death in police custody or care; cases of corruption; alleged miscarriages of justice; misuse of police records; public order incidents; and child abuse allegations.

The total number of complaints from 1 April 1997 to 31 March 1998 was 18,354; the total number of cases was 9,711.

(Information from the Police Complaints Authority.)

The Lawrence Inquiry: Highlighting Fundamental Prejudices in Society

BY PETER BARTLETT

Systemic racism

On 19 February 1999 Sir William Macpherson delivered the report of the formal inquiry into the police investigation of the murder of black teenager Stephen Lawrence. The report catalogued an array of errors and omissions, and proved that the investigation was handled without sufficient seriousness. It also found that the Metropolitan Police was an institution infused with systemic racism.

The inquiry largely vindicated the concerns of the Lawrence family, and from the perspective of anti-discrimination law it would be difficult not to view the report in positive terms. The concerns of the black community received acknowledgement and affirmation from a pillar of this country's establishment. The UK government responded to the report with proposals for action. While the acknowledgement of problems of racism in the police force must be seen as an important step forward, at the end of the day talk alone is cheap. Issues of racism in police services have been obvious for years to anyone taking trouble to look. Implementation of change and change itself are another matter.

The Macpherson report alone will not automatically trigger the fundamental changes we need. The risk is also that certain broader issues will remain unaddressed. To see the scope of the reforms required, one need only consider another news story that broke on 19 February, the very day the Lawrence Inquiry report topped the headlines. That involved a shooting in a cinema queue in Australia. Since the cinema was in the vicinity of a Vietnamese restaurant, it was uncritically reported that the shooting was thought by the Australian police to be the result of gang wars in that ethnic community. What is extraordinary is not merely the automatic association by the police of minority ethnic groups and crime, in this case on the mere basis of geographic proximity of an ethnic restaurant. Equally startling is that no comment was made in the UK media about this juxtaposition, on a day when the lead story was trumpeting a new challenge to precisely the sort of presumption which the Australian police had apparently adopted so uncritically. Even on that day, the public association of ethnic minorities and crime was so strong, so unchallengeable, that it passed virtually unnoticed.

A couple of hours of race relations training will not necessarily change the mind of a 'seasoned' officer.

Identifying 'most likely' culprits

This is not merely an issue of ethnic stereotyping. Other stereotypes are routinely used by the police, the media, and the public to identify the 'most likely' culprits. To pick another example from the last year's news, it is worth recalling the conviction of Michael Stone – a man with a history of psychiatric problems – for the murder of Lin and Megan Russell. Any critical discussion in the media has focused on the unreliability of his alleged confessions and concerns regarding possible perjury at his trial. Certainly, that was cause for concern – but the grounds for suspicion were equally questionable: Stone was in the vicinity of the murder at the time it was committed, and had mental health problems. The mere whiff of mental disorder, like the taint of colour, is enough to create the perception of criminality.

Certainly, it is appropriate for the affected groups to demand that a professional police force should rise above reasoning based on stereotype. This is nonetheless extremely complex even at its simplest level, in that it requires changes of police culture – a difficult and long-term task. The Lawrence report proposes an array of steps to be taken to accomplish this: measures of public satisfaction, improved documentation of racist incidents and their investigation, and racism awareness training of police. While these may well be appropriate, it is not obvious that they will create a cultural shift in policing. A couple of hours of race relations training will not necessarily change the mind of a 'seasoned' officer. Appointing yet more 'community relations officers' may be appropriate, but will not in itself affect the core problem. Community relations officers are not the people who stop, search, and arrest black people and other minorities in numbers out of all proportion to their presence in the population. That is done by regular police officers, largely insulated from the effects of community relations initiatives. Better recruitment from the minority communities is one strategy to bring about change, but the police culture is a powerful one. The question arises as to whether the new officers will alter the culture, or whether the police culture will alter them.

The Macpherson inquiry *Doreen and Neville Lawrence on 1 October 1998 after Sir Paul Condon, Commissioner of the Metropolitan Police, gave evidence to the Macpherson inquiry into their son's death. Sir Paul apologized for his force's failure to capture the killers of Stephen Lawrence. Doreen Lawrence called for the commissioner to resign. The Macpherson report, officially released on 24 February 1999, was highly critical of the Metropolitan Police and called the organization institutionally racist.* Photo: Richard Watt

Attitudes among the public and media

And how free is the police establishment to change? The population as a whole imports its stereotypes of ethnic behaviour into the arena of law and its enforcement. The attitudes of the police may reinforce or construct public opinion; but they also reflect broader social attitudes. How will the press and the public react, for example, when a murder is committed by a person with a psychiatric history, and the police indicate that they did not use that information to render him a suspect? The public and the media, after all, 'know' (quite wrongly) that people with psychiatric histories are therefore dangerous; to fail to take this into account would be viewed as a paradigm of bad policing. The media would make mincemeat of the officers concerned. Regarding black people, the debate might be somewhat more subtle, but no less critical. For example, was it an option for the Australian police in the case above not to point a finger at the Vietnamese community?

It is difficult to see whether the outcome of the Lawrence inquiry will or can address this underlying problem. The simple truth is that the public, or at least a very powerful proportion of the public, expect, or even demand, that the police rely on the very stereotypes that the Lawrence inquiry challenges. Unless movement is made away from those demands on the police, it is difficult to see how real progress could be made towards the enforcement of law and order that ethnic and other minorities have a right to demand. It is not just police culture that must change but the social culture and way of thinking generally. To address this, Macpherson recommends better education on racial issues. This is no doubt desirable, but hardly a novel suggestion; and the effects of previous programmes are difficult to assess. Certainly, the dominant culture has been remarkably resistant to change. The Lawrence report is a step in the right direction; but continued exposure of these issues and challenge to public attitudes will remain necessary for the foreseeable future.

Peter Bartlett is lecturer in anti-discrimination law at the University of Nottingham

Key Events in the The Stephen Lawrence Inquiry

22 April 1993 Stephen Lawrence, an 18-year-old black student, is murdered in Eltham, southeast London.

29 July 1993 Charges against two youths – Jamie Acourt and David Norris – who first appear in court in June, are dropped; the Crown Prosecution Service concludes there is insufficient evidence to continue with the prosecution.

April 1994 Stephen's parents, Doreen and Neville Lawrence, launch a private prosecution against Neil Acourt, Luke Knight, and Gary Dobson.

April 1996 The Lawrences' private prosecution collapses. Identification evidence relating to the three suspects is ruled inadmissible, leading to acquittal.

10 February 1997 The Coroners Court concludes that Lawrence's death was an 'unlawful killing'. Soon after, the *Daily Mail* publishes front-page pictures of the five suspects – Acourt, Knight, Dobson, Jamie Acourt, and David Norris – calling them murderers.

March 1997 The Police Complaints Authority (PCA) announces it will carry out an internal inquiry into the case.

31 July 1997 Home Secretary Jack Straw announces a public inquiry into Stephen's death, chaired by Sir William Macpherson, 'in order particularly to identify the lessons to be learned for the investigation and prosecution of racially motivated crimes'.

15 December 1997 The PCA report, conducted by Kent police, concludes that the police operation was well-organized and effective and that there was no evidence of racist conduct. It also concludes there were weaknesses and omissions during the investigation and that subsequent attempts to solve the crime had been hampered.

11 March 1998 In advance of the public hearings, Macpherson says the five youths originally arrested must give evidence; if they refuse they will be liable to prosecution.

24 March 1998 Public hearings in the Stephen Lawrence inquiry begin.

27 May 1998 The inquiry hears that Metropolitan Police officers had not followed up leads in the hunt for the murderers; Detective Superintendent Brian Weeden, a senior officer who headed the murder squad for 14 months, admits that he had not understood a basic tenet of criminal law – that he could make early arrests of suspects on the basis of 'reasonable grounds for belief' of involvement.

8 June 1998 Macpherson dismisses the PCA's internal inquiry into the investigation, which concluded it to be satisfactory, as 'indefensible'.

15 June 1998 The inquiry watches a videotape recorded by a secret police camera hidden in the flat of one of the suspects, showing them brandishing knives and expressing violent racist views.

17 June 1998 Ian Johnston, the Assistant Police Commissioner of the Metropolitan Police, publicly apologizes to the parents of Stephen Lawrence for failing to bring their son's killers to justice, and accepts that the internal review of proceedings had been totally discredited.

29 June 1998 Crowd chaos breaks out as the five original suspects arrive to give evidence to the inquiry.

30 June 1998 The five men are pelted with bottles, cans, and stones as they leave the inquiry, after appearing evasive in the giving of evidence. They release a joint statement claiming they were not involved in the murder. Mrs Lawrence calls for Metropolitan Police Commissioner Paul Condon to resign.

1 July 1998 A senior Crown Prosecution Service lawyer accuses the Lawrences of wrecking future prospects of their son's killers being brought to justice.

20 July 1998 The inquiry, having heard 88 witnesses, adjourns until September.

1 October 1998 Condon apologizes to Mr and Mrs Lawrence for the failure of the Metropolitan Police; he repeatedly denies allegations of institutional racism in his force.

13 November 1998 Hearings in the inquiry come to an end in Birmingham.

12 January 1999 The PCA clears all the officers involved in the Stephen Lawrence case of racism.

20 February 1999 Home Secretary Jack Straw obtains an injunction to stop *The Sunday Telegraph* from publishing leaked extracts of the Macpherson report. A senior judge partially overturns the government's ban the next day following pressure from national newspapers.

24 February 1999 The Macpherson report is published. It labels London's police force 'institutionally racist' and condemns officers for 'fundamental errors'. The government praises the report and embraces its 70 recommendations to break down institutionalized racism. Prime Minister Tony Blair promises radical reform in the wake of the report. Condon says he will continue to try to prosecute Stephen's killers. It is discovered that the identities of police informants had been mistakenly left in the appendices of the report, causing distress and further police embarassment.

23 March 1999 Home Secretary Jack Straw unveils new measures to combat racism, setting out the government's point-by-point response to each of the 70 recommendations in the Macpherson report.

8 April 1999 The five men suspected of killing Stephen deny on television any involvement in the killing. Stephen's parents condemn the programme.

21 April 1999 The parents of Stephen Lawrence begin a process of suing the London Metropolitan Police over its handling of the investigation into the murder. They also take out writs against the five men who were the main suspects in the case.

13 May 1999 The Home Secretary tells Parliament that the source of the leak of the inquiry report into the death of Stephen Lawrence in February was likely to have been one of the officials or advisers within the department.

13 July 1999 Detective Inspector Ben Bullock, the only police officer to face severe disciplinary action for the gross mishandling of the 1993 murder investigation, is cleared of almost all charges. The ruling by the police tribunal means no Scotland Yard officer would be punished for the debacle.

Asylum Seekers in the UK

Applications and decisions	1992	1993	1994	1995	1996	1997
Applications Received (Region of Origin)						
Europe	8,435	4,535	5,360	7,050	6,475	9,145
Africa	7,630	10,295	16,960	22,545	11,290	9,515
Asia[1]	8,080	6,695	9,500	12,980	10,035	10,905
Other	465	845	1,010	1,390	1,845	2,935
Total	24,605	22,370	32,830	43,965	29,640	32,500
Median age of applicants	28	28	28	27	28	28
Decisions in Year						
Recognized as a refugee and granted asylum						
Europe	470	345	130	355	1,220	1,870
Africa	225	865	115	80	210	1,460
Asia	420	375	570	845	795	625
Other	5	5	10	10	15	35
Total	1,115	1,590	825	1,295	2,240	3,985
Not recognized as a refugee but granted exceptional leave						
Europe	1,555	915	1,345	800	365	405
Africa	5,820	6,825	1,815	2,475	3,900	1,555
Asia[1]	7,940	3,375	480	1,125	780	1,125
Other	10	10	20	10	5	30
Total	15,325	11,125	3,660	4,410	5,055	3,115
Refused asylum and exceptional leave						
Europe	980	1,155	2,595	3,280	4,910	6,030
Africa	14,550	6,675	7,695	11,155	15,950	11,740
Asia[1]	2,890	2,715	5,660	6,435	10,095	9,770
Other	45	145	555	435	720	1,405
Total	18,465	10,690	16,500	21,300	31,670	28,945
Total number of decisions	34,900	23,405	20,990	27,005	38,960	36,045
Applications withdrawn	1,540	1,925	2,390	2,565	2,925	2,065
Removals and voluntary departures of asylum applicants	1,345	1,820	2,220	3,170	4,810	7,020
Applications outstanding at end of year	49,110	45,805	55,255	69,650	57,405	51,795
Grants of Settlement						
As recognized refugees	1,275	2,845	2,255	675	1,115	2,405
With exceptional leave	500	1,145	1,030	920	3,080	2,425
Total	1,780	3,990	3,285	1,595	4,195	4,830

[1] Including Middle East.

Source: *Home Office Statistical Bulletin,* © Crown copyright 1998

England and Wales

Strength of the Police Service in England and Wales

As of 31 March 1998.

Rank	Strength
Male	
Chief Constables	47
Assistant Chief Constables	135
Superintendents	1,188
Chief Inspectors	1,520
Inspectors	5,732
Sergeants	17,221
Constables	79,349
Total	105,192
Female	
Chief Constables	2
Assistant Chief Constables	8
Superintendents	46
Chief Inspectors	90
Inspectors	320
Sergeants	1,395
Constables	17,745
Total	19,606
TOTAL	124,798
Total officers per 100,000 population	239.9

Source: *Home Office Statistical Bulletin*, © Crown copyright 1998

Number of Recorded Crimes in England and Wales

Offence	1993	1994	1995	1996	1997	% change 1996–97
Violent Crime						
Violence against the person	205,102	218,354	212,588	239,342	253,107	5.8
Sexual offences	31,284	31,971	30,274	31,391	33,514	6.8
Robbery	57,845	60,007	68,074	74,035	64,077	–13.5
Total	294,231	310,332	310,936	344,768	350,698	1.7
Burglary						
Burglary in a dwelling	727,276	678,882	643,645	602,128	520,108	–13.6
Burglary other than in a dwelling	642,308	577,800	595,839	562,455	495,683	–11.9
Total	1,369,584	1,256,682	1,239,484	1,164,583	1,015,791	–12.8
Theft and Handling Stolen Goods						
Theft from the person	47,743	51,119	59,692	59,331	57,859	–2.5
Theft of bicycle	190,685	176,825	169,476	148,970	138,893	–6.8
Theft from shops	275,607	269,017	275,802	282,052	274,077	–2.8
Theft from vehicle	925,819	842,680	813,094	799,552	710,089	–11.2
Theft of motor vehicle	597,519	541,749	508,450	493,489	407,569	–17.4
Other	714,528	683,218	625,595	600,552	577,698	–3.8
Total	2,751,901	2,564,608	2,452,109	2,383,946	2,166,185	–9.1
Fraud and forgery	162,836	145,289	133,016	136,225	135,454	–0.6
Criminal damage	906,746	928,329	913,991	951,274	866,991	–8.9
Other notifiable offences	40,957	47,740	50,705	55,757	60,045	7.7
TOTAL	5,526,255	5,252,980	5,100,241	5,036,553	4,595,164	–8.8

Source: *Notifiable Offences, England and Wales 1997*, © Crown copyright 1998

Number of Crimes Cleared Up in England and Wales

	1988	1990	1992	1993	1994	1995	1996	1997
Method of Clear-Up								
Charge/summons	637,000	687,000	644,000	604,000	604,000	558,000	576,000	579,000
Caution	136,000	151,000	197,000	197,000	187,000	181,000	166,000	173,000
Taken into consideration	212,000	209,000	209,000	183,000	153,000	127,000	132,000	128,000
No Further Action								
Interview of convicted prisoner	188,000	221,000	230,000	221,000	236,000	235,000	211,000	180,000
Other	76,000	111,000	110,000	124,000	151,000	176,000	203,000	198,000
Total[1]	1,249,000	1,379,000	1,390,000	1,329,000	1,331,000	1,277,000	1,288,000	1,258,000

[1] Excluding criminal damage of £20 and under.

Source: *Criminal Statistics, England and Wales 1997*, © Crown copyright 1998

Percentage of Crimes Cleared Up by the Police in England and Wales

Data are in percentages and exclude offences of 'other criminal damage' of £20 and under.

Police force area	1993	1994	1995	1996	1997
Avon and Somerset	17	21	23	24	26
Bedfordshire	21	22	22	33	35
Cambridgeshire	25	25	19	24	27
Cheshire	26	30	31	34	36
Cleveland	27	19	25	24	25
Cumbria	38	37	40	36	40
Derbyshire	21	21	20	21	25
Devon and Cornwall	25	27	27	30	32

(continued)

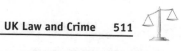

Percentage of Crimes Cleared Up by the Police in England and Wales (*continued*)

Police force area	1993	1994	1995	1996	1997
Dorset	33	30	28	27	29
Durham	30	32	30	30	31
Essex	32	36	33	29	27
Gloucestershire	20	24	27	23	24
Greater Manchester	34	34	24	17	20
Hampshire	26	27	28	28	30
Hertfordshire	21	24	28	30	32
Humberside	16	17	19	20	20
Kent	25	29	26	32	31
Lancashire	35	33	34	33	29
Leicestershire	28	30	29	31	34
Lincolnshire	37	32	39	42	48
London, City of	22	27	23	27	26
Merseyside	39	33	27	29	31
Metropolitan Police	17	23	25	24	26
Norfolk	28	34	31	32	37
Northamptonshire	27	31	28	34	35
Northumbria	20	22	23	24	26
North Yorkshire	30	25	23	25	26
Nottinghamshire	29	28	23	28	28
South Yorkshire	20	24	24	23	29
Staffordshire	29	31	32	34	35
Suffolk	37	35	34	33	37
Surrey	20	30	31	29	33
Sussex	24	24	28	29	26
Thames Valley	21	22	23	25	24
Warwickshire	21	24	25	24	27
West Mercia	29	29	28	26	28
West Midlands	27	25	24	23	24
West Yorkshire	28	20	21	24	27
Wiltshire	35	36	32	29	32
England average	25	26	26	26	28
Dyfed-Powys	50	53	57	58	61
Gwent	45	47	50	50	51
North Wales	36	39	32	33	34
South Wales	28	24	29	32	36
Wales average	34	32	34	37	41

Source: *Criminal Statistics, England and Wales 1997,* © Crown copyright 1998

Notifiable Offences Recorded by the Police in England and Wales

(N = nil or negligible.)

Police force area	1995	1996	1997	% change 1996–97
England				
Avon and Somerset	152,886	156,557	143,128	–9
Bedfordshire	51,104	52,005	47,426	–9
Cambridgeshire	67,652	69,532	60,050	–14
Cheshire	73,202	66,214	60,363	–9
Cleveland	79,719	78,608	64,445	–18
Cumbria	41,230	39,739	35,810	–10
Derbyshire	82,380	78,896	73,792	–6
Devon and Cornwall	102,193	103,121	94,828	–8
Dorset	54,582	49,731	44,104	–11
Durham	57,817	51,849	47,976	–7
Essex	98,097	100,758	90,158	–11
Gloucestershire	55,448	53,675	47,533	–11
Greater Manchester	327,994	327,976	307,403	–6
Hampshire	134,319	135,915	124,306	–9
Hertfordshire	55,891	54,441	50,050	–8
Humberside	128,393	126,932	121,330	–4
Kent	155,251	147,980	122,955	–17
Lancashire	124,921	122,487	119,755	–2
Leicestershire	93,607	94,125	81,259	–14
Lincolnshire	48,015	47,077	43,381	–8
London, City of	5,727	4,831	5,130	6
Merseyside	153,385	145,956	125,979	–14
Metropolitan Police	817,082	841,784	791,732	–6
Norfolk	51,716	55,314	53,332	–4
Northamptonshire	56,524	57,378	54,047	–6
Northumbria	194,141	169,656	140,166	–17
North Yorkshire	63,539	56,919	50,252	–12
Nottinghamshire	151,371	141,307	128,015	–11
South Yorkshire	154,293	151,577	130,690	–14
Staffordshire	91,495	92,155	89,957	–2
Suffolk	38,233	37,094	35,639	–4
Surrey	44,313	42,014	38,440	–9
Sussex	110,300	118,086	111,624	–5
Thames Valley	178,702	172,194	157,423	–9
Warwickshire	38,906	38,926	35,725	–8
West Mercia	80,013	82,254	76,762	–7
West Midlands	318,087	317,892	278,975	–12
West Yorkshire	283,938	268,716	244,142	–9
Wiltshire	36,428	35,911	33,039	–8
Wales				
Dyfed-Powys	19,419	19,072	18,098	–5
Gwent	33,034	44,572	47,268	6
North Wales	41,645	41,024	40,684	–1
South Wales	153,249	141,578	130,886	–8
Total	5,100,241	5,033,828	4,598,327	–9

Source: *Notifiable Offences, England and Wales 1997,* © Crown copyright 1998

Expenditure on the Criminal Justice System in England and Wales

(In millions of current pounds.)

Service	1990–91	1992–93	1993–94	1995–96	1996–97	1997–98
Police	5,976	6,641	6,824	7,015	7,129	7,205
Magistrates' courts	373	403	453	440	340	321
Probation	409	481	530	478	452	437
Prisons	1,807	1,825	1,664	1,753	1,647	1,757
Lord Chancellor's Department[1]	656	801	790	787	1,338	1,275
Crown Prosecution Service	262	313	312	313	307	283

[1] Criminal work only; from 1996–97 includes areas that have not been previously accounted for such as the Duty Solicitors' Scheme.

Source: *Social Trends 29,* © Crown copyright 1999

Murder and Manslaughter Recorded by the Police in England and Wales

Offence	Offences recorded						Offences cleared up 1997[1]	
	1992	1993	1994	1995	1996	1997	Number	% of total
Homicide (murder, manslaughter, infanticide)	687	670	726	745	681	711	650	91
Attempted murder	568	661	651	634	674	655	605	92
Threat or conspiracy to murder	5,487	5,638	6,844	7,044	8,533	9,634	7,721	80
Child destruction[2]	0	3	7	8	2	14	6	43
Causing death by dangerous driving or by careless driving when under the influence of drink and drugs	277	292	278	242	320	290	296	102
Causing death by aggravated vehicle taking[3]	19	17	14	21	34	12	16	133

[1] Offences cleared up in current year may have been initially recorded in an earlier year.

[2] The statutory crime of killing any child capable of being born alive (i.e. after 28 weeks gestation) before it has an existence independent of its mother; it overlaps with the offence of procuring the miscarriage of a viable child.

[3] Offence introduced on 1 April 1992.

Source: *Notifiable Offences, England and Wales, 1997,* © Crown copyright 1998

Racial Incidents in England and Wales

(– = not applicable.)

Police force area	1993–94	1994–95	1995–96	1996–97	1997–98	% change 1996/97–1997/98
England						
Avon and Somerset	159	286	318	310	409	32
Bedfordshire	60	41	43	77	75	–3
Cambridgeshire	100	75	160	141	147	4
Cheshire	98	62	27	92	78	–15
Cleveland	50	62	112	68	76	12
Cumbria	17	24	27	37	46	24
Derbyshire	221	291	192	208	174	–16
Devon and Cornwall	14	44	73	82	90	10
Dorset	25	37	41	67	86	28
Durham	32	26	23	24	37	54
Essex	133	127	178	116	160	38
Gloucestershire	28	37	34	34	32	–6
Greater Manchester	658	637	776	595	624	5
Hampshire	212	210	279	178	219	23
Hertfordshire	117	183	234	295	288	–2
Humberside	79	75	58	55	72	31
Kent	160	173	129	256	276	8
Lancashire	262	222	320	337	311	–8
Leicestershire	315	366	270	299	237	–21
Lincolnshire	4	2	0	7	6	–
London, City of	1	6	2	10	6	–
Merseyside	155	131	130	162	241	49
Metropolitan Police	5,124	5,480	5,011	5,621	5,862	4
Norfolk	33	39	41	56	89	59
Northamptonshire	102	146	214	195	318	63
Northumbria	405	508	475	488	444	–9
North Yorkshire	22	30	37	43	41	–5
Nottinghamshire	264	259	362	330	391	18
South Yorkshire	115	156	194	169	213	26
Staffordshire	117	164	253	225	214	–5
Suffolk	73	73	74	74	54	–27
Surrey	79	39	77	55	45	–18
Sussex	214	247	263	260	298	15
Thames Valley	166	233	266	233	279	20
Warwickshire	87	114	99	66	107	62
West Mercia	100	35	46	64	57	–11
West Midlands	487	375	489	725	632	–13
West Yorkshire	244	254	355	623	644	3
Wiltshire	51	64	37	35	59	69
Wales						
Dyfed-Powys	0	3	23	18	17	–6
Gwent	21	22	32	60	45	–25
North Wales	2	3	5	4	12	–
South Wales	400	517	443	357	367	3
England and Wales total	11,006	11,878	12,222	13,151	13,878	6

Source: *Statistics on Race and the Criminal Justice System,* © Crown copyright 1998

Recent Miscarriages of Justice in the UK

19 October 1989	The alleged terrorists known as the 'Guildford Four' are cleared on appeal of IRA bombing convictions after serving 14 years of their life sentences. They had been convicted following two bomb explosions in separate pubs in Guildford that killed five people in October 1974.
14 March 1991	The 'Birmingham Six' are released after the Court of Appeal quashes their 1974 conviction for IRA pub bombings in Birmingham, after finding that evidence had been fabricated. The six men were each sentenced to 21 life sentences and had spent nearly 17 years in prison.
14 March 1991	The home secretary announces the establishment of a Royal Commission on Criminal Justice charged with examining the effectiveness of the criminal justice system in securing the conviction of the guilty and the acquittal of the innocent.
11 June 1991	The 'Maguire Seven' are acquitted at their hearing before the Court of Appeal. They went on trial in 1976 for providing bombs to the IRA and were sentenced to between 7 and 14 years; one of the seven, Giuseppe Conlon, died in prison.
25 November 1991	Winston Silcott – one of the 'Tottenham Three' – has his conviction quashed, as do Engin Raghip and Mark Braithwaite on 5 December 1991. All three had been convicted of murdering PC Blakelock on the Broadwater Farm Estate in 1985. The Court of Appeal expressed 'profound regret' at their wrongful conviction.
18 February 1992	Stefan Kiszko, who received a life sentence in 1976 for the murder of an 11-year-old girl, has his conviction quashed by the Court of Appeal after the disclosure of fresh evidence showed that he could not have been the killer. Kiszko, who died a year after release, was one of many long-term inmates destined to stay in prison because they refused to admit their guilt and 'address their offending behaviour' – a prerequisite for being granted parole.
12 May 1992	Judith Ward is freed following the Court of Appeal's ruling that her conviction was 'unsafe and unsatisfactory'. She was jailed for life in 1974 for her alleged role in the bombing of a British Army coach on the M62, in which 12 people were killed. Convicted on the basis of an uncorroborated confession, she was later acknowledged to be prone to fantasy.
1993	The detectives at the centre of the Guildford Four case are cleared of fabricating evidence. Prosecutions against police accused of tampering with evidence in the Birmingham Six case are halted.
July 1993	The report of the Royal Commission on Criminal Justice is presented to Parliament. It recommends the establishment of an independent body to consider suspected miscarriages of justice.
1995	The Criminal Appeal Act 1995 is passed, enabling the establishment of the Criminal Cases Review Commission as an executive non-departmental body on 1 January 1997.
21 February 1997	Three people convicted of killing newspaper boy Carl Bridgewater in 1978 – James Robinson, Michael Hickey, and Vincent Hickey – are released. The Court of Appeal quashed their convictions because of tainted police evidence. They had spent 18 years in prison. A fourth man convicted of Bridgewater's murder, Patrick Molloy, died in prison in 1981.
31 March 1997	The Criminal Cases Review Commission begins handling casework.
27 November 1997	Dozens of prisoners in 25 jails across the country and their families go on a 48-hour hunger strike as part of their campaign to prove they are victims of miscarriages of justice. The protest is coordinated by the Action Against Injustice campaign.
24 February 1998	Following a lengthy investigation, the Court of Appeal quashes the conviction of Mahmood Mattan who was hanged for murder in 1952. Mattan was convicted of the murder of Lily Volpert in Swansea 24 July 1952; leave to appeal was refused 19 August, and Mattan was hanged at Cardiff prison 3 September.
12 June 1998	Patrick Nicholls, 70, convicted of the murder of a pensioner in 1977, is formally cleared at a Court of Appeal hearing. New evidence revealed that the 'victim' had died from natural causes. Nicholls, who spent more than 20 years in jail, turned down the chance of parole four times because it would have meant admitting the crime.
28 July 1998	The murder conviction of David Ryan James is quashed by the Court of Appeal. James had been convicted of the murder of his wife in May 1995 and sentenced to life imprisonment.
30 July 1998	The Court of Appeal overturns the guilty verdict on convict Derek Bentley, who was controversially convicted and hanged in 1953 for the murder of PC Sidney Miles in 1952. In pardoning Bentley, the Lord Chief Justice is highly critical of Lord Goddard who had sentenced Bentley to death, claiming Bentley had been denied a fair trial. Derek Bentley was convicted of the murder, even though the fatal shots were fired by accomplice Christopher Craig who, at the age of 16, was too young to receive capital punishment.
August 1998	A former senior prison service official claims that some 1,300 prison inmates are innocent of the crimes for which they were convicted. David Wilson, former governor of Grendon Underwood jail in Buckinghamshire, believes that at least one in 50 inmates is probably innocent.
17 December 1998	Gilbert 'Danny' McNamee, who was found guilty of the IRA's 1982 Hyde Park bombing which killed four members of the Household Cavalry and seven horses, wins his appeal against his conviction. The finding that McNamee's conviction is unsafe is the latest in a line of miscarriages of justice that followed terrorist bombings.
30 April 1999	Since its establishment in 1997, the Criminal Cases Review Commission has received 2,469 cases of alleged miscarriages of justice. Fourteen have been heard by the Court of Appeal (10 quashed; 4 upheld).

Reasons for Not Reporting Violent Crime in England and Wales

(In percentages. N/A = not available.)

Reasons	Violence[1]	Mugging	Domestic	Acquaintance	Stranger
Incident-Related Reasons	39	47	27	41	45
Too trivial/no loss	30	34	13	33	44
Fear of reprisal	10	14	14	9	3
Police-Related Reasons	22	33	16	20	33
Couldn't do anything	13	27	9	11	18
Would not be interested	13	8	9	14	19
Dislike/fear the police	1	1	N/A	1	1
Other Reasons	56	34	73	58	39
Private/dealt with ourselves	41	22	68	38	21
Reported to other authorities	7	N/A	2	12	9
Inconvenient to report	3	4	2	2	4
Other	7	8	3	9	7

[1] Includes wounding, common assault, robbery, and snatch theft.

Source: *The 1998 British Crime Survey, England and Wales,*

Incidence of Violent Crime in England and Wales

Total violent crimes recorded by the police, by police force area per 100,000 population. Violent crimes comprise violence against the person, sexual offences, and robbery.

Police force area	Total violent crime	Police force area	Total violent crime	Police force area	Total violent crime
Metropolitan Police[1]	1,158	West Yorkshire	593	Durham	396
Gwent	1,104	Cambridgeshire	584	Surrey	394
Nottinghamshire	993	Kent	573	North Yorkshire	393
Humberside	875	Lincolnshire	566	Lancashire	390
Greater Manchester	847	Hampshire	554	Essex	382
Avon and Somerset	830	Dyfed-Powys	525	West Mercia	377
Bedfordshire	823	Sussex	514	Dorset	372
Merseyside	784	Devon and Cornwall	502	Gloucestershire	371
Staffordshire	775	Wiltshire	487	Hertfordshire	335
Leicestershire	739	North Wales	483	Warwickshire	327
West Midlands	675	South Yorkshire	472	*England average*	666
South Wales	670	Cheshire	468		
Derbyshire	651	Norfolk	459	*Wales average*	687
Cumbria	644	Northumbria	453		
Northamptonshire	610	Suffolk	452	*England and Wales average*	667
Cleveland	609	Thames Valley	416		

[1] Including City of London.

Source: *Criminal Statistics, England and Wales 1997,*

Complaints against the Police in England and Wales

(– = not applicable.)

Year	Total complaints	Complaints investigated		Withdrawn/not proceeded with		Informally resolved	
1994	36,521	9,590	26%	14,658	40%	12,273	34%
1995–96	35,840	8,653	24%	15,535	43%	11,652	33%
1996–97	36,731	10,820	29%	14,286	39%	11,625	32%
1997–98	35,820	9,832	27%	13,714	38%	12,274	34%

Source: *Police Complaints and Discipline 1998,*

Police Assaulted in the Line of Duty in England and Wales

Degree of injury	1991	1992	1993	1994/95	1995/96	1996/97	1997/98
Fatal	5	0	2	0	1	0	1
Serious	1,275	963	886	684	833	901	837
Other	17,870	17,145	17,062	14,904	14,006	14,587	12,723
Total	19,150	18,108	17,950	15,500	14,840	15,488	13,561

Source: *Report of Her Majesty's Inspectorate of Constabulary,*

Population in Prison Under Sentence in England and Wales

Offence group	1992	1993	1994	1995	1996	1997
Men						
Offences with immediate custodial sentence						
Violence against the person	6,893	7,273	7,715	8,491	9,230	9,836
Rape	1,582	1,593	1,638	1,781	1,926	2,044
Other sexual offences	1,564	1,572	1,629	1,875	2,013	1,929
Burglary	5,349	4,690	5,096	5,896	6,342	7,642
Robbery	4,174	4,856	5,090	5,264	5,591	6,069
Theft and handling	2,910	2,578	3,030	3,450	3,591	3,954
Fraud and forgery	800	826	879	1,071	1,099	1,114
Drugs offences	2,899	2,900	3,186	3,858	5,269	6,309
Motoring offences	967	1,045	1,527	1,660	1,720	1,958
Other offences	2,490	2,448	2,301	2,514	2,952	3,156
Offence not recorded	4,402	1,794	1,869	1,547	1,454	2,599
All offences	34,030	31,375	33,960	37,407	41,187	46,611
In default of payment of a fine	359	522	514	490	136	128
Total	34,389	31,897	34,474	37,897	41,323	46,739
Women						
Offences with immediate custodial sentence						
Violence against the person	184	216	277	290	355	387
Sexual offences	10	15	12	12	12	9
Burglary	51	39	39	57	80	96
Robbery	56	77	95	108	124	154
Theft and handling	190	207	227	279	314	333
Fraud and forgery	53	64	65	96	119	120
Drugs offences	259	308	326	398	486	675
Motoring offences	3	7	20	18	14	27
Other offences	155	118	112	114	150	163
Offence not recorded	191	74	93	84	73	100
All offences	1,152	1,125	1,266	1,482	1,727	2,063
In default of payment of a fine	23	24	23	26	5	3
Total	1,175	1,149	1,289	1,482	1,732	2,066
TOTAL	35,564	33,046	35,763	39,379	43,055	48,805

Source: *The Prison Population in 1997*,

Selected Sex Offences Recorded by the Police in England and Wales

(– = not applicable.)

Offence	**Offences recorded**				**Offences cleared up 1997**	
	1987	**1991**	**1995**	**1997**	**Number**	**%**
Buggery[1]	929	1,127	818	645	606	94
Indecent assault on a male	2,425	3,070	3,150	3,503	3,005	86
Indecency between males	1,127	965	727	520	487	94
Rape						
of a female	2,471	4,045	4,986	6,281	4,946	79
of a male[1]	–	–	150	347	277	80
Indecent assault on a female	13,340	15,792	16,876	18,674	13,314	71
Unlawful sexual intercourse with a girl under 13	312	315	178	148	121	82
Unlawful sexual intercourse with a girl under 16	2,699	1,949	1,260	1,112	1,021	92
Incest	511	389	185	183	173	95
Procuration	175	138	207	131	107	82
Abduction	268	411	364	277	126	45
Bigamy	66	75	86	75	73	97[2]
Gross indecency with a child	831	1,147	1,287	1,269	1,127	89
Total	25,154	29,423	30,274	33,165	25,383	77

[1] The Criminal Justice and Public Order Act 1994 introduced a specific offence of rape of a male. Following this change in legislation, male victims of forced buggery are now classified as male rape.

[2] Based on total of less than 100.

Source: *Criminal Statistics, England and Wales 1997*,

Young Offenders under an Immediate Custodial Sentence in England and Wales

Age and offence group		1991	1992	1993	1994	1995	1996	1997
Men								
Aged under 18	violence against the person	309	385	425	424	546	665	715
	sexual offences	44	35	47	33	46	62	65
	burglary	1,112	1,056	1,070	1,211	1,258	1,284	1,421
	robbery	276	293	330	378	521	704	777
	theft and handling	874	726	1,004	1,192	1,268	1,219	1,230
	fraud and forgery	2	4	4	10	8	14	15
	drugs offences	19	36	32	26	43	63	74
	other offences	545	543	555	625	721	789	857
	offence not recorded	440	266	97	72	94	271	211
	Total	3,621	3,344	3,564	3,971	4,505	5,071	5,365
Aged 18–20	violence against the person	1,261	1,208	1,221	1,378	1,434	1,623	1,834
	sexual offences	130	102	108	81	119	90	108
	burglary	2,730	2,552	2,335	2,535	2,665	2,468	2,495
	robbery	665	731	709	669	726	977	1,019
	theft and handling	2,253	1,737	2,083	2,586	2,737	2,693	2,802
	fraud and forgery	78	45	66	79	72	123	110
	drugs offences	214	299	287	296	391	518	558
	other offences	2,052	1,901	2,098	2,516	2,812	2,833	3,165
	offence not recorded	1,615	911	315	336	219	485	434
	Total	10,998	9,486	9,222	10,476	11,175	11,810	12,525
Total men		14,619	12,830	12,786	14,447	15,680	16,881	17,890
Women								
Aged under 18	violence against the person	13	18	34	54	48	68	83
	sexual offences	1	0	0	0	3	0	0
	burglary	14	8	4	15	21	15	15
	robbery	18	15	22	28	28	40	66
	theft and handling	20	15	20	31	39	43	42
	fraud and forgery	0	2	3	0	0	2	1
	drugs offences	3	4	2	3	4	4	8
	other offences	8	6	15	13	20	31	30
	offence not recorded	20	11	2	5	3	11	7
	Total	97	79	102	149	166	214	252
Aged 18–20	violence against the person	42	41	59	74	67	81	147
	sexual offences	2	2	0	0	1	0	0
	burglary	24	18	35	30	30	34	35
	robbery	23	17	24	30	32	46	45
	theft and handling	76	72	86	113	129	179	166
	fraud and forgery	11	10	13	9	23	23	25
	drugs offences	23	23	24	31	43	58	81
	other offences	43	45	53	56	56	61	89
	offence not recorded	68	37	23	17	17	16	13
	Total	312	265	317	360	398	498	601
Total women		409	344	419	509	564	712	853
TOTAL		15,028	13,174	13,205	14,956	16,244	17,593	18,743

Source: *Prison Statistics, England and Wales 1997*, © Crown copyright 1998

Scotland

Strength of the Police Service in Scotland

Figures exclude support staff. As of 31 March 1998.

Force	Regular police		Special constables	
	Men	Women	Men	Women
Central	606	97	50	22
Dumfries and Galloway	365	73	143	50
Fife	728	127	93	39
Grampian	1,011	191	105	33
Lothian and Borders	2,290	401	148	50
Northern	583	74	359	121
Strathclyde	6,216	1,083	246	73
Tayside	963	180	142	49
Total	12,762	2,226	1,286	437

Source: The Scottish Office, © Crown copyright 1998

Crimes and Offences Recorded by the Police in Scotland

(– = not applicable.)

Category		1993	1994	1995	1996	1997	% change 1996–97
Crimes							
Non-sexual crimes of violence	serious assault	6,527	6,705	6,920	6,988	6,053	–13
	handling offensive weapons	5,152	5,282	6,465	6,822	5,989	–12
	robbery	5,582	5,297	5,330	5,254	4,484	–15
	other	2,143	2,490	2,404	2,473	2,638	7
	Total	19,404	19,774	21,119	21,537	19,164	–11
Crimes of indecency	sexual assault	1,626	1,603	1,638	1,729	1,979	14
	lewd and indecent behaviour	2,721	2,655	2,381	2,465	3,014	22
	other	1,700	1,740	1,528	1,482	2,154	45
	Total	6,047	5,998	5,547	5,676	7,147	26
Crimes of dishonesty	housebreaking	97,829	88,394	74,235	64,470	55,471	–14
	theft by opening lockfast places	84,795	74,862	66,539	60,472	51,131	–15
	theft of a motor vehicle	42,816	41,962	37,514	34,161	28,646	–16
	shoplifting	26,746	26,573	27,952	26,927	26,322	–2
	other theft	93,327	88,900	87,716	82,576	79,612	–4
	fraud	19,125	17,670	17,093	16,081	15,734	–2
	other	10,299	11,985	10,152	10,754	10,291	–4
	Total	374,937	350,346	321,201	295,441	267,207	–10
Fire-raising, vandalism	fire-raising	4,118	3,589	3,299	3,306	2,786	–16
	vandalism, etc	80,076	84,954	83,247	85,719	78,214	–9
	Total	84,194	88,543	86,546	89,025	81,000	–9
Other	crimes against public justice	14,515	16,004	16,359	16,148	16,641	3
	drugs	17,986	19,281	24,773	23,992	29,386	22
	other	164	164	152	137	97	–29
	Total	32,665	35,449	41,284	40,277	46,124	15
Total crimes		517,247	500,110	475,697	451,956	420,642	–7
Offences							
Motor vehicle offences	dangerous and careless driving	19,951	21,088	18,729	17,347	16,319	–6
	drunk driving	10,905	10,835	10,719	11,796	11,208	–5
	speeding	85,398	85,799	85,141	82,355	91,922	12
	unlawful use of vehicle	85,826	88,652	83,416	79,123	79,130	–
	vehicle defect offences	51,387	56,943	56,321	53,451	60,136	13
	other	61,652	67,407	63,175	61,830	72,268	17
	Total	315,119	330,724	317,501	305,902	330,983	8
Other	petty assault	41,339	45,083	46,604	47,605	50,088	5
	breach of the peace	61,370	65,514	66,088	70,830	73,061	3
	drunkenness	10,144	10,289	9,737	9,608	9,697	1
	other	13,740	12,307	11,939	18,043	23,054	28
	Total	126,593	133,193	134,368	146,086	155,900	7
Total offences		441,712	463,917	451,869	451,988	486,883	8
TOTAL		958,959	964,027	927,566	903,944	907,525	0.4

Source: *Recorded Crime in Scotland 1997*, © Crown copyright 1998

Number of Crimes Recorded by the Police by Council and Clear-Up Rates in Scotland

1997

Council	Non-sexual crimes of violence	Crimes of indecency	Crimes of dishonesty	Fire-raising, vandalism, etc	Other crimes	Total crimes	% of crimes cleared up
Aberdeen City	702	569	20,757	3,973	2,458	28,459	36
Aberdeenshire	307	188	5,634	3,143	1,375	10,647	40
Angus	288	143	3,486	1,959	749	6,625	42
Argyll and Bute	240	75	2,485	914	580	4,294	48
Clackmannanshire	113	32	1,448	563	338	2,494	62
Dumfries and Galloway	401	93	4,606	1,647	1,610	8,357	61
Dundee City	753	314	13,192	3,633	1,549	19,441	34
East Ayrshire	364	99	5,306	1,743	812	8,324	38
East Dunbartonshire	293	65	3,861	1,238	452	5,909	28
East Lothian	179	79	2,499	1,150	326	4,233	37
East Renfrewshire	223	35	3,827	824	357	5,266	24
Edinburgh, City of	1,854	747	32,021	8,119	3,662	46,403	34
Eilean Siar[1]	22	13	290	201	109	635	65
Falkirk	339	130	4,963	1,964	1,028	8,424	57
Fife	641	367	14,024	5,187	2,665	22,884	48
Glasgow City	5,655	2,284	55,216	14,566	11,563	89,284	37
Highland	401	154	5,939	2,006	1,971	10,471	67
Inverclyde	471	116	5,749	1,087	1,077	8,500	40
Midlothian	184	72	2,531	1,274	583	4,644	43
Moray	148	114	2,775	1,813	386	5,236	36
North Ayrshire	484	156	5,560	1,736	1,096	9,032	43
North Lanarkshire	1,160	231	15,809	4,976	2,781	24,957	34
Orkney Islands	10	12	158	86	72	338	73
Perth and Kinross	357	98	5,714	1,602	1,002	8,773	41
Renfrewshire	861	164	11,131	3,304	1,374	16,834	29
Scottish Borders	169	109	2,752	1,095	516	4,641	50
Shetland Islands	15	12	417	262	116	822	69
South Ayrshire	345	125	4,957	1,487	916	7,830	49
South Lanarkshire	1,134	208	13,195	3,899	2,093	20,529	34
Stirling	177	73	3,142	783	568	4,743	54
West Dunbartonshire	489	82	6,548	1,890	1,015	10,024	36
West Lothian	385	188	7,215	2,876	925	11,589	32
Total	19,164	7,147	267,207	81,000	46,124	420,642	39

[1] Formerly known as Western Isles.

Source: *Recorded Crime in Scotland 1997*, © Crown copyright 1998

Crimes and Offences Cleared Up by the Police in Scotland

(In percentages.)

Crime/offence category		1993	1994	1995	1996	1997
Non-sexual crimes of violence	serious assault, etc	57	57	54	57	60
	handling an offensive weapon	99	99	99	99	99
	robbery	27	29	29	29	28
	other	83	83	82	84	84
	Total	63	64	65	67	68
Crimes of indecency	sexual assault	63	68	66	69	65
	lewd and indecent behaviour	62	65	67	68	66
	other	97	97	96	98	96
	Total	72	75	74	76	75
Crimes of dishonesty	housebreaking	16	17	17	18	18
	theft by opening lockfast places	12	15	13	15	15
	theft of a motor vehicle	21	24	24	25	26
	shoplifting	77	80	79	78	77
	other theft	17	18	18	19	19
	fraud	75	82	81	79	75
	other	86	84	87	82	88
	Total	25	28	28	30	31

(*continued*)

Crimes and Offences Cleared Up by the Police in Scotland (*continued*)

Crime/offence category		1993	1994	1995	1996	1997
Fire-raising, vandalism, etc	fire-raising	19	19	19	20	19
	vandalism, etc	19	20	21	21	22
	Total	19	20	21	21	22
Other crimes	crimes against public justice	100	100	100	100	100
	drugs	100	100	100	99	100
	other	79	84	80	82	80
	Total	100	100	100	99	100
Miscellaneous offences	petty assault	73	73	74	75	77
	breach of the peace	90	92	93	94	94
	drunkenness	100	100	100	100	100
	other	89	92	95	97	98
	Total	85	86	88	89	90
Total percentage of crimes cleared up		31	34	35	37	39

Source: *Recorded Crime in Scotland, 1997,* © Crown copyright 1998

Outcome of Recorded Crime by Main Penalty in Scotland

Figures for years prior to 1996 incorporate minor revisions to previously published figures.

Penalty	1992	1993	1994	1995	1996
Absolute discharge	967	989	839	939	1,008
Admonition or caution	17,441	16,976	16,243	15,857	15,859
Probation	5,385	5,722	6,145	6,145	6,435
Remit to children's hearing	72	83	124	172	193
Community service order	5,473	5,079	5,320	5,339	5,711
Fine	131,842	116,918	112,748	110,33	105,384
Compensation order	1,575	1,578	1,535	1,527	1,415
Insanity, hospital, guardianship order	133	138	133	136	159
Prison	10,085	10,832	11,583	11,561	12,134
Young offender's institution	4,488	4,461	4,472	4,646	4,744
Detention of child	22	30	36	48	45
Total persons with charge proved	177,483	162,806	159,178	156,707	153,087

Source: *Scottish Abstract of Statistics,* © Crown copyright 1998

Cases of Homicide Recorded in Scotland

Crime and status	1992	1993	1994	1995	1996[1]
Solved cases					
Murder	65	73	62	83	69
Culpable homicide	65	41	42	51	45
Total	130	114	104	134	114
Unsolved cases	1	1	4	1	4
All homicide cases	131	115	108	135	118

[1] The classification as murder or culpable homicide reflects the position as at 30 September 1997 but may change where cases have not been finally disposed of.

Source: The Scottish Office, © Crown copyright 1998

Expenditure on Penal Establishments in Scotland

Figures are for 31 March in year shown. (In thousands of pounds.)

Expenditure	1991–92	1992–93	1993–94	1994–95	1995–96	1996–97	1997–98
Manpower and associated services	124,898	129,597	135,301	140,009	135,941	143,107	137,890
Prisoner and associated costs	8,504	10,274	10,795	11,679	12,373	13,377	16,313
Capital expenditure	13,032	13,681	11,845	15,636	15,377	22,577	22,136
Total gross expenditure	146,434	153,552	157,941	167,324	163,691	179,061	176,339

Source: *Annual Abstract of Statistics 1999,* © Crown copyright 1999

Complaints Cases and Allegations against the Police in Scotland

(N/A = not available.)

	1995–96	1996–97	1997–98
Number of complaint cases			
Outstanding at beginning of year	545	586	579
Received during the year	1,444	1,333	1,321
Disposed of during the year	1,403	1,315	1,263
Standing over at end of year	586	604	637
Number of allegations			
Withdrawn by complainer	93	105	137
Abandoned due to non-cooperation of complainer	29	33	89
Found to be unsubstantiated	580	539	548
Resolved by conciliation or explanation to complainer	124	129	125
Leading to police officers being charged with criminal offences	11	N/A	N/A
Leading to criminal proceedings	29	23	23
Leading to 'No Proceedings' decision by Procurator Fiscal	1,406	1,192	1,089
Leading to criminal convictions	5	0	2
Resulting in disciplinary/ misconduct hearings	9	7	6
Resulting in formal warnings in terms of disciplinary/misconduct regulations	22	20	24
Resulting in corrective advice to officers	138	61	126
Total allegations disposed of during year	2,361	2,113	2,129

Source: *Annual Report of Her Majesty's Chief Inspectorate of Constabulary,*

Average Daily Prison Population and Receptions in Scotland

Components may not add to totals due to rounding. (– = not applicable.)

Category	**1992**	**1993**	**1994**	**1995**	**1996**	**1997**
Average Daily Population						
Men	5,099	5,466	5,408	5,451	5,673	5,900
Women	158	171	177	175	189	184
Total	5,257	5,637	5,585	5,626	5,862	6,084
Analysis by Type of Custody						
Remand	876	948	1,015	998	1,000	947
Persons under sentence						
adult prisoners	3,552	3,795	3,785	3,823	4,026	4,282
young offenders	769	819	720	719	770	787
persons recalled from supervision/licence	32	40	37	44	46	46
others	21	32	28	38	18	19
Total	4,374	4,686	4,570	4,624	4,861	5,134
Persons sentenced by court martial	6	2	1	3	0	1
Civil prisoners	1	1	1	0	1	1
Receptions to Penal Establishments[1]						
Remand						
men	12,722	12,478	13,985	13,377	13,976	13,850
women	824	934	937	876	1,001	976
Total	13,546	13,412	14,922	14,253	14,977	14,826
Persons under sentence						
men	18,856	20,741	19,697	17,737	20,869	21,936
women	1,110	1,416	1,414	1,293	1,286	1,266
Total	19,966	22,157	21,111	19,030	22,155	23,202
imprisoned directly	8,543	9,444	9,349	8,730	10,039	9,698
imprisoned in default of fine	6,603	7,956	7,377	6,299	7,432	8,873
imprisoned in default of compensation order[2]	40	41	26	13	–	–
Persons sentenced to young offenders' institution						
directly	3,041	3,052	2,855	2,772	3,111	2,784
in default of fine	1,736	1,660	1,498	1,210	1,567	1,847
in default of compensation order[2]	2	4	6	4	–	–
Persons recalled from supervision/licence	2	0	0	2	5	0
Persons sentenced by court martial	2	7	5	4	4	4
Civil prisoners	34	37	27	25	32	23

[1] Total receptions cannot be calculated by adding together receptions in each category because there is double counting. This arises because a person received on remand and then under sentence in relation to the same set of charges, is counted in both categories.

[2] From 1996 compensation orders are included in the figures for default of fine.

Source: *Annual Abstract of Statistics 1999,*

Prison Population of Young Offenders in Scotland

Average daily population of under-21 offenders by type and length of sentence.

Type/length of sentence	1992	1993	1994	1995	1996	% change 1995–96[1]
Less than 6 months	240	246	209	249	194	–22
6 months–less than 2 years	303	287	223	227	282	24
2 years–less than 4 years	119	151	160	114	132	16
4 years or over (excluding life)	85	105	103	98	131	34
Life	12	17	15	14	17	21
Section 205 sentences (indeterminate)	7	9	9	14	10	–29
Section 206 sentences (fixed)	4	4	1	2	4	100
Total[2]	769	819	720	719	770	7

[1] Based on rounded figures.
[2] Components may not add to totals due to rounding.

Source: *Scottish Office Statistical Bulletin*,

Northern Ireland

Crimes Recorded and Cleared Up by the Police in Northern Ireland

Crime category	1991	1992	1993	1994	1995	1996	1997
Notifiable crimes recorded	63,492	67,532	66,228	67,886	68,808	68,549	62,222
Number of crimes cleared	22,675	23,253	24,088	24,342	24,838	23,103	19,560
Clear-up rate (%)	36	34	36	36	36	34	31
Percentage of Crimes Recorded that were Cleared Up[1]							
Violence Against the Person							
Murder	60	51	52	58	64	63	65
Manslaughter and infanticide	43	200	160	75	100	125	0
Attempted murder	27	34	35	31	74	49	34
Other violence against the person	66	67	65	69	67	63	60
Sexual Offences							
Rape	80	80	76	69	83	81	79
Attempted rape	97	71	81	73	70	79	88
Incest	84	106	80	71	115	87	100
Indecent assault	83	73	80	82	81	80	82
Other sexual offence	94	90	63	112	82	98	97
Burglary							
Burglary in a dwelling	18	16	15	16	18	17	17
Burglary in a building other than a dwelling	21	19	22	22	19	17	16
Other burglary[2]	54	46	43	43	98	99	97
Robbery							
Armed robbery	18	17	14	18	17	19	22
Hijacking	9	24	13	22	10	5	4
Other robbery	21	19	18	21	27	21	21
Theft							
Theft from the person	24	17	19	16	15	23	19
Theft from dwelling	54	57	66	63	57	54	44
Theft from motor vehicles	12	9	10	8	10	8	7
Shoplifting	92	85	83	86	83	80	74
Theft or unauthorized taking of motor vehicles	29	27	30	19	18	15	14
Other thefts	31	29	31	30	28	26	24
Fraud and Forgery							
Frauds	68	43	64	71	66	66	58
Forgery	52	63	45	38	39	46	39
Criminal Damage							
Arson	20	22	19	20	18	12	14
Explosive offences	33	12	31	26	62	29	24
Other criminal damage[3]	38	41	43	43	39	34	33

(continued)

Crimes Recorded and Cleared Up by the Police in Northern Ireland (*continued*)

Crime category	1991	1992	1993	1994	1995	1996	1997
Offences Against the State							
Offences under the NI Emergency Provisions Act	101	97	95	90	167	84	91
Firearms offences	73	79	66	59	52	66	47
Other offences against the state	67	75	74	86	91	82	81
Other Notifiable Offences							
Drug offences	99	92	91	93	94	97	93
Other notifiable offences	47	58	57	70	74	54	54

[1] Offences cleared up in the current year may have been initially recorded in an earlier year.
[2] From 1995 excludes 'Attempted burglary' which is included in 'Burglary in a dwelling' or 'Burglary in a building other than a dwelling'.
[3] Other criminal damage excludes offences where damage was under £200.

Source: *A Commentary on Northern Ireland Crime Statistics 1997,* © Crown copyright 1998

Notifiable Offences Recorded by the Police in Northern Ireland

Crime category	1991	1992	1993	1994	1995	1996	1997
Violence Against the Person							
Murder	114	108	101	82	22	35	40
Manslaughter and infanticide	7	3	5	4	2	4	2
Attempted murder	360	311	416	255	35	71	116
Other	3,474	3,680	4,075	4,452	5,091	5,530	4,996
Total	3,955	4,102	4,597	4,793	5,150	5,640	5,154
Sexual Offences							
Rape	117	116	151	168	229	264	268
Attempted rape	38	38	42	40	30	28	26
Incest	25	35	20	24	13	15	4
Indecent assault	413	493	597	698	932	991	793
Other	284	291	377	403	475	447	353
Total	877	973	1187	1333	1679	1745	1,444
Burglary							
In a dwelling	7,206	7,461	8,005	9,454	9,774	8,530	7,435
In a building other than a dwelling	8,281	8,677	6,675	6,480	6,499	7,426	6,717
Other[1]	1,076	979	1,055	968	184	158	154
Total	16,563	17,117	15,735	16,902	16,457	16,114	14,306
Robbery							
Armed robbery	686	866	751	657	620	655	621
Hijacking	519	339	365	194	331	439	548
Other	643	646	607	716	588	631	484
Total	1,848	1,851	1,723	1,567	1,539	1,725	1,653
Theft							
From the person	304	242	217	257	330	235	201
In a dwelling	304	356	436	427	618	628	559
From a motor vehicle 7,227	7,117	6,729	6,555	6,715	6,554	5,416	
Shoplifting	3,737	4,549	4,625	4,510	5,410	5,291	4,501
Of, or unauthorized taking of, motor vehicles	8,455	9,376	9,011	8,974	7,794	8,404	8,633
Other	12,006	12,616	12,143	12,510	12,605	11,660	10,233
Total	32,033	34,256	33,161	33,233	33,472	32,772	29,543
Fraud and Forgery							
Frauds	4,533	4,991	4,922	4,127	4,204	3,707	3,461
Forgery	278	495	631	973	680	374	357
Total	4,811	5,486	5,553	5,100	4,884	4,081	3,818
Criminal Damage							
Arson	805	860	901	940	1,132	1,490	1,201
Explosives offences	112	117	88	65	13	7	21
Other[2]	1,477	1,525	1,867	2,072	2,627	3,350	3,470
Total	2,394	2,502	2,856	3,077	3,772	4,847	4,692
Offences Against the State							
Offences under the NI Emergency Provisions Act	151	103	87	106	18	61	32
Firearms offences	114	73	76	98	42	47	55
Other	327	302	273	236	279	292	414
Total	592	478	436	440	339	400	501

(*continued*)

Notifiable Offences Recorded by the Police in Northern Ireland (*continued*)

Crime category	1991	1992	1993	1994	1995	1996	1997
Other							
Drug	287	619	811	1,286	1,426	1,093	998
Other	132	148	169	155	90	132	113
Total	419	767	980	1,441	1,516	1,225	1,111
TOTAL	63,492	67,532	66,228	67,886	68,808	68,549	62,222

[1] From 1995 'other' excludes attempted burglary, which is included in 'burglary in a dwelling' or 'burglary in a building other than a dwelling'.
[2] 'Other criminal damage' excludes offences where damage was under £200.

Source: *A Commentary on Northern Ireland Crime Statistics 1997*, © Crown copyright 1998

Outcome of Recorded Crime in Northern Ireland

Disposal given to those convicted by court.

	1991	1992	1993	1994	1995	1996	1997
Magistrates Court – All Offences							
Prison	960	830	1,027	945	1,046	1,003	989
Young offenders' centre (YOC)	502	588	575	499	483	443	430
Training school	177	120	125	193	169	147	148
Total immediate custody	1,639	1,538	1,727	1,637	1,698	1,593	1,567
Prison suspended	1,379	1,420	1,529	1,558	1,674	1,722	1,506
YOC suspended	432	507	447	447	385	444	461
Attendance centre	90	66	94	89	101	91	66
Probation/supervision	742	849	881	1,017	1,137	1,134	1,155
Community supervision order	547	464	536	551	547	591	561
Fine	19,569	23,418	25,166	24,390	22,726	20,612	21,313
Recognizance	514	713	858	961	1,001	1,203	1,267
Conditional discharge	2,102	1,965	2,021	1,830	1,928	1,679	1,597
Absolute discharge	845	732	690	661	608	509	424
Disqualification	4,211	640	6	6	2	5	2
Other	24	12	7	11	8	10	6
Crown Court – All Offences							
Prison	493	447	555	471	533	469	475
Young offenders' centre (YOC)	125	119	130	87	76	106	111
Training school	13	5	2	5	6	0	4
Total immediate custody	631	571	687	563	615	575	590
Prison suspended	238	249	211	277	265	253	220
YOC suspended	46	63	37	43	63	71	60
Attendance centre	0	0	0	1	0	0	0
Probation/supervision	103	95	73	58	60	49	47
Community Supervision order	89	79	48	59	60	54	37
Fine	23	17	33	23	27	39	40
Recognizance	7	9	5	16	0	7	10
Conditional discharge	53	36	19	15	64	30	31
Absolute discharge	5	8	3	2	1	0	1
Disqualification	6	2	0	0	0	0	0
Other	8	6	6	1	2	3	3

Source: *A Commentary on Northern Ireland Crime Statistics*, © Crown copyright 1998

Juveniles Found Guilty at All Courts in Northern Ireland

Offence	1991	1992	1993	1994	1995	1996	1997
Violence against the person	38	46	43	49	51	75	49
Sexual offences	8	11	7	8	7	4	8
Burglary	194	165	155	180	170	137	124
Robbery	7	8	4	9	22	13	18
Theft	328	247	280	283	345	338	334
Fraud and forgery	10	16	14	14	21	14	11
Criminal damage	92	82	94	117	116	121	136
Offences against the state	5	6	1	8	9	6	10
Other indictable	11	8	2	6	14	24	10
Total indictable[1]	693	589	600	674	755	732	700
Summary[2]	111	113	125	131	180	182	198
Motoring[3]	71	40	44	74	74	58	57
TOTAL[4]	875	742	769	879	1,009	972	955

[1] Excludes indictable motoring offences.
[2] A summary offence is an offence that is triable in a magistrate's court.
[3] Includes indictable motoring offences.
[4] Juveniles are aged 10–16 years inclusive.

Source: *Annual Abstract of Statistics 1999,* © Crown copyright 1999

Complaints Against the Police in Northern Ireland

1997

Offence alleged	Substantiated	Not substantiated	Informally resolved	Withdrawn	Incapable of investigation	Total
Assault	11	775	51	640	603	2,080
Incivility	12	356	297	99	399	1,163
Oppressive conduct/harassment	1	108	157	47	121	434
Irregularity in procedure	9	141	74	44	47	315
Neglect of duty	30	138	134	38	54	394
Unlawful arrest/detention	5	99	4	28	438	574
Irregularity in connection with search of premises	0	32	30	8	37	107
Mishandling of property	0	21	3	9	6	39
Irregularity in relation to evidence/perjury	2	35	0	5	7	49
Traffic offence	1	20	10	5	3	39
Corrupt practice	0	1	0	1	1	3
Discriminatory behaviour	0	0	4	2	6	12
Other	6	113	3	27	75	224
Total	77	1,839	767	953	1,797	5,433

Source: *Annual Report, Chief Constable of Royal Ulster Constabulary 1997/8,* © Crown copyright 1998

Population in Prison Establishments in Northern Ireland

Type of prisoner		1991	1992	1993	1994	1995	1996	1997
Men								
Remand	aged under 21	79	93	96	106	72	69	70
	aged 21 or over	254	307	322	321	240	249	288
	Total	333	400	418	427	312	318	358
Fine defaulter	aged under 21	8	6	7	4	5	5	6
	aged 21 or over	23	27	23	23	23	19	23
	Total	31	33	30	27	28	24	29
Immediate custody	young offenders' centre	141	145	153	133	118	115	104
	young prisoners	116	102	100	91	87	66	57
	adult prisoners	1,136	1,088	1,192	1,179	1,177	1,076	1,044
	Total	1,393	1,335	1,445	1,403	1,382	1,257	1,205

(continued)

Population in Prison Establishments in Northern Ireland (*continued*)

Type of prisoner		1991	1992	1993	1994	1995	1996	1997
Non-criminal		1	1	1	1	5	11	10
Men total		1,758	1,769	1,894	1,858	1,727	1,610	1,602
Women								
Remand	aged under 21	6	6	2	5	2	2	3
	aged 21 or over	10	7	6	7	3	6	5
	Total	16	13	8	12	5	8	8
Fine defaulter	aged under 21	0	0	1	1	0	0	0
	aged 21 or over	1	1	1	2	1	0	1
	Total	1	1	2	3	1	0	1
Immediate custody	young offenders' centre	2	4	3	4	6	4	3
	young prisoners	1	2	3	3	2	1	0
	adult prisoners	18	21	24	19	21	16	18
	Total	21	27	30	26	29	21	21
Non-criminal		0	0	0	0	0	0	0
Women total		38	41	40	41	35	29	30
Both sexes								
Remand		349	413	426	439	317	326	366
Fine defaulter		32	34	32	30	29	24	30
Immediate custody		1,414	1,362	1,475	1,429	1,411	1,278	1,266
Non-criminal		1	1	1	1	5	11	10
TOTAL		1,796	1,810	1,934	1,899	1,762	1,639	1,632

Source: *A Commentary on Northern Ireland Crime Statistics 1997*, © Crown copyright 1998

Royal Ulster Constabulary Staffing Levels

As of 31 December 1997.

Position	Effective strength
Chief constable	1
Deputy chief constable	1
Assistant chief constable	7
Chief superintendent	16
Superintendent	137
Chief inspector	164
Inspector	481
Sergeant	1,393
Constable	6,285
Total	8,485
Full-time reserve	2,982
Part-time reserve	1,324

Source: *Annual Report, Chief Constable of Royal Ulster Constabulary 1997/8*, © Crown copyright 1998

Security Incidents in Northern Ireland

Year	Shootings	Bombings (explosions/ defusings)	Incendiaries (ignitions/ defusings)
1969	73	10	0
1970	213	170	0
1971	1,756	1,515	0
1972	10,631	1,853	0
1973	5,019	1,520	0
1974	3,208	1,113	270
1975	1,803	635	56
1976	1,908	1,192	236
1977	1,081	535	608
1978	755	633	115
1979	728	564	60
1980	642	400	2
1981	1,142	529	49
1982	547	332	36
1983	424	367	43
1984	334	248	10
1985	238	215	36
1986	392	254	21
1987	674	384	9
1988	538	458	8
1989	566	420	7
1990	557	286	33
1991	499	368	237
1992	506	371	126
1993	476	289	61
1994	348	222	115
1995	50	2	10
1996	125	25	4
1997	225	93	9
Total	35,458	15,003	2,161

Source: *Annual Report, Chief Constable of Royal Ulster Constabulary 1997/8*, © Crown copyright 1998

Number of Deaths Due to the Security Situation in Northern Ireland

Year	Royal Ulster Constabulary	Royal Ulster Constabulary Reserves	Army	Ulster Defence Regiment/ Royal Irish Regiment[1]	Civilian	Total
1969	1	0	0	0	13	14
1970	2	0	0	0	23	25
1971	11	0	43	5	115	174
1972	14	3	105	26	322	470
1973	10	3	58	8	173	252
1974	12	3	30	7	168	220
1975	7	4	14	6	216	247
1976	13	10	14	15	245	297
1977	8	6	15	14	69	112
1978	4	6	14	7	50	81
1979	9	5	38	10	51	113
1980	3	6	8	9	50	76
1981	13	8	10	13	57	101
1982	8	4	21	7	57	97
1983	9	9	5	10	44	77
1984	7	2	9	10	36	64
1985	14	9	2	4	26	55
1986	10	2	4	8	37	61
1987	9	7	3	8	68	95
1988	4	2	21	12	55	94
1989	7	2	12	2	39	62
1990	7	5	7	8	49	76
1991	5	1	5	8	75	94
1992	2	1	4	2	76	85
1993	3	3	6	2	70	84
1994	3	0	1	2	56	62
1995	1	0	0	0	8	9
1996	0	0	1	0	14	15
1997	3	1	1	0	17	22
Total	199	102	451	203	2,279	3,234

[1] Figures include Royal Irish Regiment (Home Service Battalions).

Source: *Annual Report, Chief Constable of Royal Ulster Constabulary 1997/8,* © Crown copyright 1998

The UK Legal System and Judiciary

The Law in Britain: Useful Addresses

Lord Advocate's Department 2 Carlton Gardens, London SW1Y 5AA; phone: (0171) 210 1010; Crown Office, 25 Chambers Street, Edinburgh EH1 1LA; phone: (0131) 226 2626; **Lord Chancellor's Department** House of Lords, London SW1A 2AZ; phone: (0171) 210 8500; **Law Officers' Department** 9 Buckingham Gate, London SE1E 6JP; phone: (0171) 828 7155; **The Law Society** 113 Chancery Lane, London WC2A 1PL; phone: (0171) 242 1222; **The Council of Legal Education** 9 Gray's Inn Place, London WC1R 5DX; phone: (0171) 404 5787; **The British Institute of International and Comparative Law** Charles Clore House, 17 Russell Square, London WC1B 5DR; phone: (0171) 636 5802; **The British Council** Bridgewater House, 58 Whitworth Street, Manchester M1 6BB; phone: (0161) 957 7000; **Institute of Advanced Legal Studies** University of London, Charles Clore House, 17 Russell Square, London WC1B 5DR; phone: (0171) 637 1731.

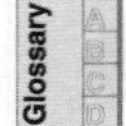

A Glossary of the Law in Britain: Courts, Professionals, and Important Bodies

(– = not applicable.)

Term	Definition	Notes
admiralty court	English court that tries and gives judgement in maritime causes	the court is now incorporated within the Queen's Bench Division of the High Court and deals with such matters as salvage and damages arising from collisions between ships
attorney general	principal law officer of the crown and head of the English Bar	the post is one of great political importance
barrister	a lawyer qualified by study at the Inns of Court to plead for a client in court	barristers also undertake the writing of opinions on the prospects of a case before trial; they act for clients through the intermediary of solicitors
central criminal court	crown court in the City of London, able to try all treasons and serious offences committed in the City or Greater London	–
chambers	in the UK, rented offices used by a group of barristers	chambers in London are usually within the precincts of one of the four law courts
Chancery	a division of the High Court that deals with such matters as the administration of the estates of deceased persons, the execution of trusts, the enforcement of sales of land, and foreclosure of mortgages	–

(continued)

A Glossary of the Law in Britain: Courts, Professionals, and Important Bodies (*continued*)

Term	Definition	Notes
circuit	the geographic district that constitutes a particular area of jurisdiction	in England and Wales the six different centres to which High Court and circuit judges travel to try civil and criminal cases are: Midland and Oxford, Northeastern, Northern, Southeastern, Wales and Chester, and Western
circuit judge	full-time judicial officer; sits as court judge in civil cases and presiding judge in the crown court	circuit judges must have been barristers for ten years or recorders for three years
commissioner for oaths	a person appointed by the Lord Chancellor with power to administer oaths or take affidavits	all practising solicitors have these powers but must not use them in proceedings in which they are acting for any of the parties or in which they have an interest
common law	that part of the English law not embodied in legislation. Consists of rules of law based on common custom and usage and on judicial decisions	English common law became the basis of law in the USA and many other English-speaking countries
coroner	official who investigates the deaths of persons who have died suddenly by acts of violence or under suspicious circumstances, by holding an inquest or ordering a postmortem examination (autopsy)	–
county court	English court of law; exists to try civil cases; presided over by one or more circuit judge	–
Court of Appeal	UK law court comprising a Civil Division and a Criminal Division, set up under the Criminal Appeals Act 1968	the Criminal Division of the Court of Appeal has the power to revise sentences or quash a conviction on the grounds that in all the circumstances of the case the verdict is unsafe or unsatisfactory, or that the judgement of the original trial judge was wrong in law, or that there was a material irregularity during the course of the trial
Court of Arches	in the UK, ecclesiastical court of the archbishop of Canterbury; the presiding judge is the dean of the Arches	–
Court of Protection	in English law, a department of the High Court that deals with the estates of people who are incapable, by reason of mental disorder, of managing their own property and affairs	–
Court of Session	supreme civil court in Scotland, established 1532	the court sits in Edinburgh
Criminal Injuries Compensation Board	UK board established in 1964 to administer financial compensation by the state for victims of crimes of violence	–
crown court	in England and Wales, any of several courts that hear serious criminal cases referred from magistrates' courts after committal proceedings	–
Crown Prosecution Service	body established by the Prosecution of Offences Act 1985, responsible for prosecuting all criminal offences in England and Wales; headed by the Director of Public Prosecutions (DPP)	–
Director of Public Prosecutions	the head of the Crown Prosecution Service (established 1985), responsible for the conduct of all criminal prosecutions in England and Wales	–
ecclesiastical law	in England, the Church of England has special ecclesiastical courts to administer church law	–
European Court of Human Rights	court that hears cases referred from the European Commission of Human Rights, if the Commission has failed to negotiate a friendly settlement in a case where individuals' rights have been violated by a member state, as defined in the 1950 European Convention on Human Rights; the court sits in Strasbourg and comprises one judge for every state that is a party to the 1950 convention	the UK has never incorporated the Human Rights Convention into its laws, which means that a statute that directly contradicts the convention will always prevail over a Strasbourg decision in a British court; in practice, however, the UK has always passed the necessary legislation to make its laws comply with the court's decisions
European Court of Justice	the court of the European Union (EU); it sits in Luxembourg with judges from the member states	–

(*continued*)

Glossary

A Glossary of the Law in Britain: Courts, Professionals, and Important Bodies (*continued*)

Term	Definition	Notes
Faculty of Professional Advocates	organization for Scottish advocates	incorporated in 1532
Inns of Court	four private legal societies in London, England: Lincoln's Inn, Gray's Inn, Inner Temple, and Middle Temple; all barristers (advocates in the English legal system) must belong to one of the Inns of Court	the main function of each Inn is the education, government, and protection of its members; each is under the administration of a body of Benchers (judges and senior barristers)
judge	person invested with power to hear and determine legal disputes	in the UK, judges are chosen from barristers of long standing, but solicitors can be appointed circuit judges; the independence of the higher judiciary is ensured by the principle that they hold their office during good behaviour and not at the pleasure of the crown; they can be removed from office only by a resolution of both houses of Parliament
jury	body of 12 (15 in Scotland) lay people sworn to decide the facts of a case and reach a verdict in a court of law	in England, jurors are selected at random from the electoral roll; certain people are ineligible for jury service (such as lawyers and clerics), and others can be excused (such as members of Parliament and doctors) if the jury cannot reach a unanimous verdict it can give a majority verdict (at least 10 of the 12)
justice of the peace	an unpaid magistrate	–
Land Registry, HM	official body set up in 1925 to register legal rights to land in England and Wales	the records are open to public inspection (since December 1990)
Law Commission	either of two statutory bodies established in 1965 (one for England and Wales and one for Scotland) which consider proposals for law reform and publish their findings	they also keep British law under constant review, systematically developing and reforming it by, for example, the repeal of obsolete and unnecessary enactments
Law Lords	in England, the ten Lords of Appeal who, together with the Lord Chancellor and other peers, make up the House of Lords in its judicial capacity	the House of Lords is the final court of appeal in both criminal and civil cases; Law Lords rank as life peers
Law Society	professional governing body of solicitors in England and Wales	it also functions as a trade union for its members; the society, incorporated in 1831, regulates training, discipline, and standards of professional conduct
Lord Advocate	chief law officer of the crown in Scotland who has ultimate responsibility for criminal prosecutions in Scotland	–
Lord Chancellor	head of the judiciary	a political appointment, the Lord Chancellor is also a member of the cabinet and holds the office of Keeper of the Great Seal
Lord Chief Justice of England	head of the Queen's Bench	ranks second only to the Lord Chancellor
Lord Justice of Appeal	in England and Wales, one of 14 lords justices who form, together with the Lord Chancellor, the Lord Chief Justice of England, the Master of the Rolls, and the president of the Family Division as ex officio members, the penultimate court of appeal (the Court of Appeal) for England and Wales	–
Lord Lieutenant	the sovereign's representative in a county, who recommends magistrates for appointment	it is an unpaid position and the retirement age is 75
magistrate	a person who presides in a magistrates' court: either a justice of the peace or a stipendiary magistrate	–
magistrates' court	in England and Wales, a local law court that mainly deals with minor criminal cases	a magistrates' court consists of between two and seven lay justices of the peace (who are advised on the law by a clerk to the justices), or a single paid lawyer called a stipendiary magistrate
Master of the Rolls	English judge who is the president of the civil division of the Court of Appeal, besides being responsible for Chancery records and for the admission of solicitors	–

(*continued*)

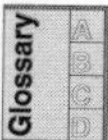

A Glossary of the Law in Britain: Courts, Professionals, and Important Bodies (*continued*)

Term	Definition	Notes
notary public	legal practitioner who attests or certifies deeds and other documents. British diplomatic and consular officials may exercise notarial functions outside the UK	–
Old Bailey	popular term for the Central Criminal Court	–
Police Complaints Authority	an independent group set up under the Police and Criminal Evidence Act 1984 to supervise the investigation of complaints against the police by members of the public	–
probate	formal proof of a will	–
procurator fiscal	officer of a Scottish sheriff's court who (combining the role of public prosecutor and coroner) inquires into suspicious deaths and carries out the preliminary questioning of witnesses to crime	–
Queen's Counsel (QC)	in England, a barrister of senior rank	the title QC is awarded by the Queen on the recommendation of the Lord Chancellor; a QC wears a silk gown, and takes precedence over a junior member of the Bar. When the monarch is a king, the title is King's Council
recorder	in the English legal system, a part-time judge who usually sits in the crown courts in less serious cases but may also sit in the county courts or the High Court	–
royal assent	formal consent given by a British sovereign to the passage of a bill through Parliament	last instance of a royal refusal was the rejection of the Scottish Militia Bill of 1702 by Queen Anne
royal prerogative	powers, immunities, and privileges recognized in common law as belonging to the crown	most prerogative acts in the UK are now performed by the government on behalf of the crown
Serious Fraud Office	set up in 1987 to investigate and prosecute serious or complex criminal fraud cases	–
sheriff	in England and Wales, the crown's chief executive officer in a county for ceremonial purposes; in Scotland, the equivalent of the English county-court judge, but also dealing with criminal cases	–
silk	in UK law, a Queen's Counsel, a senior barrister entitled to wear a silk gown in court	–
slander	spoken defamatory statement	if written, or broadcast on radio or television, it constitutes libel
solicitor	member of one of the two branches of the English legal profession who provides all-round legal services (making wills, winding up estates, conveyancing, divorce, and litigation)	a solicitor cannot appear at High Court level, but must brief a barrister on behalf of his or her client; solicitors may become circuit judges and recorders
Solicitor General	a law officer of the Crown, deputy to the Attorney General, a political appointee with ministerial rank	–
stipendiary magistrate	paid, qualified lawyers, working mainly in London and major cities	–
the Bar	the profession of barristers collectively; to be 'called to the Bar' is to become a barrister	–
Treasury counsel	in the UK, a group of barristers who receive briefs from the DPP to appear for the prosecution in criminal trials at the Central Criminal Court	–
Treasury solicitor	the official representing the crown in matrimonial, probate, and admiralty cases	Queen's Proctor is an obsolete term for treasury solicitor
tribunal	in English law for a body appointed by the government to arbitrate in disputes, or investigate certain matters	tribunals usually consist of a lawyer as chair, sitting with two lay assessors
Writers to the Signet	society of Scottish solicitors	–

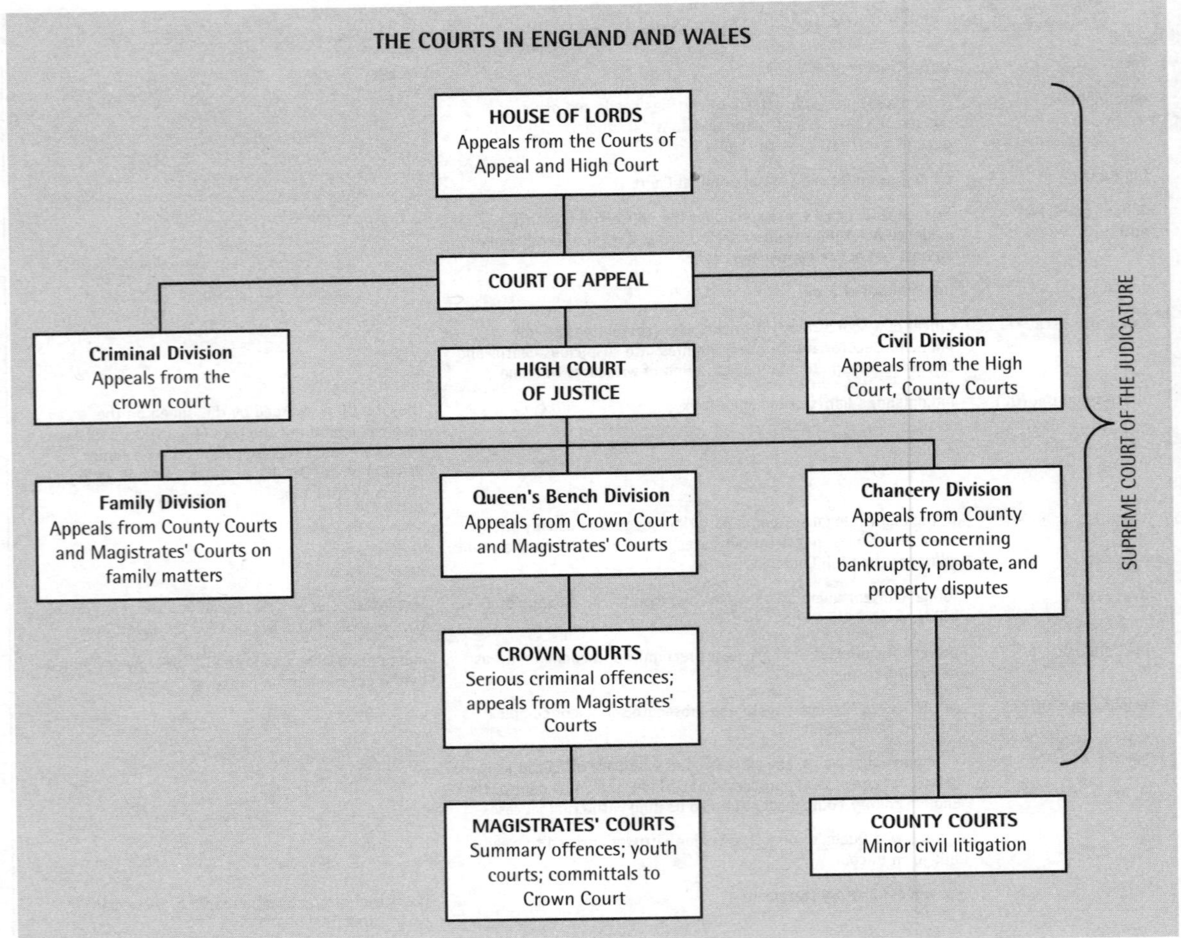

The Law in Britain: The Courts

England and Wales

In England and Wales the court system was reorganized under the Courts Act 1971. The higher courts are:

House of Lords The highest court for the whole of Britain, deals with both civil and criminal appeals.

Court of Appeal This court is divided between criminal and civil appeal courts; it sits in London at the Royal Courts of Justice. The criminal division deals with appeals from the Crown Court and is presided over by the Lord Chief Justice who is the most senior judge in England and Wales. The 25 Lord Justices of Appeal are assisted by High Court judges when required.

High Court of Justice This court deals with important civil cases, it sits at the Royal Courts of Justice and at County Courts around the country; land, patent issues, industrial disputes, property and inheritance matters are dealt with by its Chancery Division. The Queen's Bench Division deals with common law business such as tort and contractual disputes. There is also a Family Division. Appeal is to the Court of Appeal (Civil Division), which also hears appeals from the County Courts and from tribunals.

Crown Courts These courts sit in over ninety permanent centres throughout England and Wales, each centre being designated as first, second or third tier, reflecting the seriousness of the offences tried. Trial of cases is by a jury of 12 people selected at random from the electoral register. They are directed on matters of law by a judge, who may be any one of the 84 High Court Judges, 478 Circuit Judges, 787 Recorders and 454 Assistant Recorders (the latter two being part-time appointments), which handle criminal cases;

County Courts There are 250 county courts which deal with civil matters. Cases are heard before District Judges, who hear uncontested and smaller value claims; higher value claims being dealt with by Circuit Judges. Each court is assigned at least one District and one Circuit Judge.

Magistrates' Courts The lowest tier of criminal court in England and Wales, dealing with about 98 percent of all criminal cases. The 450 courts are funded jointly by local and central government and deal with minor criminal cases and are served by Justices of the Peace or stipendiary (paid) magistrates.

Juvenile Courts These courts are presided over by specially qualified justices. There are also special courts, such as the Restrictive Practices Court and the Employment Appeal Tribunal.

Scotland
The supreme civil court is the House of Lords, below which comes the Court of Session, and then the Sheriff's Court (in some respects similar to the English county court, but with criminal as well as civil jurisdiction). More serious criminal cases are heard by the High Court of Justiciary which also sits as a Court of Criminal Appeal (with no appeal to the Lords). Juries have 15 members, and a verdict of 'not proven' can be given. There is no coroner, inquiries into deaths being undertaken by the procurator fiscal.

Judiciary System: The Lords of Appeal

The House of Lords, Westminster, London SW1A 0PW; phone: (0171) 219 3000.

The Lord High Chancellor of Great Britain The Right Honourable The Lord Irvine of Lairg.

The Lords of Appeal in Ordinary The Right Honourable The Lord Browne-Wilkinson, The Right Honourable The Lord Slynn of Hadley, The Right Honourable The Lord Lloyd of Berwick, The Right Honourable The Lord Nicholls of Birkenhead, The Right Honourable The Lord Steyn, The Right Honourable The Lord Hoffmann, The Right Honourable The Lord Hope of Craighead, The Right Honourable The Lord Clyde, The Right Honourable The Lord Hutton, The Right Honourable The Lord Saville of Newdigate, The Right Honourable The Lord Hobhouse of Woodborough, The Right Honourable The Lord Millett.

Registrar, The Clerk of the Parliaments J M Davies, Esq.

England and Wales

The Supreme Court of Judicature, Court of Appeal

Royal Courts of Justice, The Strand, London WC2A 2LL; phone: (0171) 936 6000 **Civil Appeals Office** Registrar: J D R Adams; phone: (0171) 936 6409 **Criminal Appeal and Courts Martial Appeal Office** Registrar: Master McKenzie (Michael McKenzie); phone: (0171) 936 6190.

The High Court of Justice

Chancery Division
Royal Courts of Justice, The Strand, London WC2A 2LL; phone (0171) 936 6000 **Chancery Chambers** Chief Master: J M Dyson; Court Manager: G C Robinson; phone: (0171) 936 6075 **Bankruptcy and Companies Courts** Chief Registrar: M C B Buckley; Court Manager: M A Brown; phone: (0171) 936 7343 **Restrictive Practices Court** Clerk to the Court: M C B Buckley; Court Manager: M A Brown; phone: (0171) 936 7343.

Queen's Bench Division
Royal Courts of Justice, London WC2A 2LL; phone:(0171) 936 6000 Senior Master and Queen's Rememberance: R L Turner; phone: (0171) 936 6105 **Crown Office** Master of the Crown Office, Queen's Coroner and Attorney: Master McKenzie (Michael McKenzie); phone: (0171) 936 6108.

Family Division
Royal Courts of Justice, The Strand, London WC2A 2LL; phone (0171) 936 6000.

The Crown Prosecution Service

The Crown Prosecution Service (CPS) is responsible for the independent review and conduct of criminal proceedings instituted by police forces in England and Wales.

In April 1999 the CPS was reorganized, moving from 14 to 42 areas that correspond with the police forces of England and Wales (there are 43 police forces in total but the City of London and Metropolitan Police Forces became one CPS area – London).

Each area has its own Chief Crown Prosecutor (CCP) and an area business manager (ABM). The Chief Crown Prosecutor reports to the Director of Public Prosecutions (DPP) and is locally accountable to the public for the way cases are handled. Each area has one or more local branches headed by a Branch Crown Prosecutor; the Branch Crown Prosecutors supervise the management of cases at the local magistrates' courts and the Crown Court.

The restructuring followed the recommendations of the Glidewell Report on the reorganization of the CPS, and aims to make the CPS more accountable to the local population and to enable good working relationships between other agencies in the criminal justice system.

Headquarters 50 Ludgate Hill, London EC4M 7EX; phone: (0171) 796 8000; fax: (0171) 796 8002; public enquiry point: (0171) 796 8500; e-mail (inquiries and comments): inquiries@cps.gov.uk; e-mail (complaints): complaints@cps.gov.uk; Web site: www.cps.gov.uk/

Director of Public Prosecutions (Grade 1) David Calvert-Smith

The Midland and Oxford Circuit

Courts
First Tier Centres Birmingham; Lincoln (Combined Court Centre); Nottingham (Crown Court); Oxford (Combined Court Centre); Stafford (Combined Court Centre); Warwick (Combined Court Centre); **Second Tier Centres** Leicester; Northampton (Combined Court Centre); Shrewsbury; Worcester; **Third Tier Centres** Coventry (Combined Court Centre); Derby (Combined Court Centre); Grimsby (Combined Court Centre); Hereford; Peterborough (Combined Court Centre); Stoke-on-Trent (Combined Court Centre); Wolverhampton (Combined Court Centre).

Offices
Circuit Office The Priory Courts, 33 Bull Street, Birmingham B4 6DW; phone:(0121) 681 3206; fax: (0121) 681 3210; **Circuit Administrator** Peter Handcock; **Birmingham Group** The Priory Courts, 33 Bull Street, Birmingham B4 6DW; phone: (0121) 681 3451; **Group Manager** Keith Dickerson; **Coventry Group** The Priory Courts, 33 Bull Street, Birmingham B4 6DW; phone: (0121) 681 3221; **Group Manager** Donna Ponsonby; **Lincoln Group** 4th Floor, 11–15 Brayford-Wharf East, Lincoln LN5 7BQ; phone: (01522) 544164; **Group Manager** Alan Phillips; **Northampton Group** 2nd Floor, St Katherine's House, St Katherine's Street, Northampton NN1 2TD; phone: (01604) 601636; **Group Manager** Steven Smith; **Nottingham Group** Chaddesden House, 77 Talbot Street, Nottingham NG1 5GN; phone: (0115) 911 1666; **Group Manager** Elizabeth Folman; **Stafford Group** 1st Floor, Combined Court Centre, Victoria Square, Stafford ST16 2QQ; phone: (01785) 255219; **Group Manager** David Bennett; **Presiding Judges** The Honourable Sir Edwin Jowitt; The Honourable Sir Michael Astill.

The North Eastern Circuit

Courts
First Tier Centres Leeds; Newcastle-upon-Tyne; Sheffield; Teesside; **Second Tier Centres** York; Bradford **Third Tier Centres** Doncaster; Durham; Kingston-upon-Hull.

Offices
Circuit Office 17th Floor, West Riding House, Albion Street, Leeds LS1 5AA; phone: (0113) 251 1200; fax: (0113) 251 1247; **Circuit Administrator** P J Farmer; **Bradford Group** The Law Courts, Exchange Square, Drake Street, Bradford BD1 1JA;

phone: (01274) 843553; **Group Manager** F Taylor; **Leeds Group** 1st Floor, Symons House, Belgrave Street, Leeds LS2 8DD; phone: (0113) 245 9611; **Group Manager** P M Norris; **Newcastle-upon-Tyne Group** 4th Foor, Westgate House, Westgate Road, Newcastle-upon-Tyne; phone: (0191) 232 7102; **Group Manager** S Proudlock; **Sheffield Group** Queen Street, Sheffield S1 2ES; phone: (0114) 275 5866; **Group Manager** G Bingham, OBE; **Teesside Group** The Law Courts, Russell Street, Middlesbrough TS1 2EA; phone: (01642) 340000; **Group Manager** Miss E Yates **Presiding Judges** The Honourable Sir Hugh Bennet; The Honourable Sir Anthony Hooper.

The Northern Circuit

Courts
First Tier Centres Carlisle; Liverpool; Manchester (Crown Square); Preston; **Third Tier Centres** Barrow-in-Furness; Bolton; Burnley; Lancaster; Manchester (Minshull Street).

Offices
Circuit Office 15 Quay Street, Manchester M60 9FD; phone: (0161) 833 1004/1005; fax: (0161) 832 8596; **Circuit Administrator** R A Vincent; **Liverpool Group** Group Manager's Office, The Queen Elizabeth II Law Courts, Derby Square, Liverpool L2 1XA; phone: (0151) 330 9602; **Group Manager** Julie Roche **Manchester Central Group** Group Manager's Office, 3rd Floor, 15 Quay Street, Manchester M60 9FD; phone: (0161) 833 1004; **Group Manager** Simon Townley **Outer Manchester Group** Group Manager's Office, 3rd Floor, 15 Quay Street, Manchester M60 9FD; phone: (0161) 833 1004; **Group Manager** Beverley Handcock **Preston Group** Sessions House, Lancaster Road, Preston PR1 2PD; phone: (01772) 821451;

Group Manager Barry Wilson; **Presiding Judges** The Honourable Sir Thayne Forbes (1993); The Honourable Sir Douglas Brown (1989); **Vice Chancellor of the County Palatine of Lancaster** The Honourable Sir William Blackburn .

The South Eastern Circuit

Courts
First Tier Centres Chelmsford; Croydon (Combined Court Centre); Lewes (Combined Court Centre); Norwich (Combined Court Centre); **Second Tier Centres** Central Criminal Court; Ipswich; Luton; Maidstone; Reading; St Albans; **Third Tier Centres** Aylesbury; Basildon (Combined Court Centre); Bury St Edmonds; Cambridge; Canterbury (Combined Court Centre); Chichester (Combined Court Centre); Guildford; King's Lynn; and other Greater London Courts (Croydon, Harrow, Inner London Sessions House, Isleworth, Kingston-upon-Thames, Knightsbridge, Middlesex Guildhall, Snaresbrook, Southwark, Wood Green, Woolwich.

Offices
Circuit Office – London Courts New Cavendish House, 18 Maltravers Street, London WC2R 3EU; phone: (0171) 936 7234; fax: (0171) 936 7230; **Circuit Administrator** R J Clark; **Circuit Office – Provincial Courts** 1st Floor, Steeple House, Chelmsford, Essex CM1 1NH; phone: (01245) 257425; fax: (01245) 491676; **Circuit Administrator** J L Powell **Chelmsford Group** 1st Floor, Steeple House, Chelmsford, Essex CM1 1NH; phone: (01245) 287974; **Group Manager** M Littlewood; **Kingston-upon-Thames Group** Group Manager's Office, 6–8 Penryhn Rd, Kingston-upon-Thames, Surrey KT1 2BB; phone: (0181) 240 2599; **Group Manager** Dave Thompson; **Lewes Group** The Law Courts, 182 High Street, Lewes BN7 1YB; phone: (01273) 485292; **Group Manager** B MacBeth; **Luton Group** 7 George Street, Luton, Bedfordshire LU1 2AA; phone: (01582) 522033; **Group Manager** M McIver; **Maidstone Group** Group Manager's Office, Concorde House, 10–12 London Road, Maidstone, Kent ME16 8QA; phone: (01622) 200120; **Group Manager** Linda Lennon; **Presiding Judges** The Right Honourable Sir William Gage; The Right Honourable Sir Alan Moses.

The Western Circuit

Courts
First Tier Centres Bristol; Exeter (Combined Court Centre); Truro (Combined Court Centre); Winchester (Combined Court Centre); **Second Tier Centres** Gloucester (Combined Court Centre); Plymouth (Combined Court Centre); Weymouth and Dorchester (Combined Court Centre); **Third Tier Centres** Barnstaple; Bournemouth (Combined Court Centre); Newport (Isle of Wight) (Combined Court Centre); Portsmouth (Combined Court Centre); Salisbury (Combined Court Centre); Southampton (Combined Court Centre); Swindon (Combined Court Centre); Taunton (Combined Court Centre).

Offices
Circuit Office Bridge House, Sion Place, Clifton, Bristol BS8 4BN; phone: (0117) 974 3763; fax: (0117) 974 4133; **Circuit Administrator** D Ryan; **Bristol Group** Whitefriars, Southgate, Lewins Mead, Bristol BS1 2NT; phone: (0117) 925 0296; **Group Manager** N Jeffery; **Exeter Group** 5th floor, Northernhay House, Northernhay Place, Exeter EX4 3TH; phone: (01392) 455 900; **Group Manager** D E Gentry; **Winchester Group** South Side Offices, The Law Courts, Winchester, Hants SO23 9EL; phone: (01962) 876004/876005; **Group Manager** A Davison; **Presiding Judges** The Honourable Mr Justice Butterfield, QB; The Honourable Mr Justice Toulson, QB.

The Wales and Chester Circuit

Courts
First Tier Centres Caernarfon; Cardiff; Chester; Mold; Swansea; **Second Tier Centres** Carmarthen; Newport; Welshpool; Merthyr Tydfil; Warrington; **Third Tier Centres** Dolgellau; Haverfordwest; Knutsford.

Offices
Circuit Office 2nd Floor, Churchill House, Churchill Way, Cardiff CF1 4HH; phone: (01222) 415500; fax: (01222) 415511; **Circuit Administrator** Peter Risk; **Cardiff Group** Group Manager's Office, 2nd Floor, Churchill House, Churchill Way, Cardiff CF1 4HH; phone: (01222) 415520; **Group Manager** Mr Graham Pickett; **Mold Group** The Law Courts, County Civic Centre, Mold CH7 1AE; phone: (01352) 754562; **Group Manager** George Kenney; **Swansea Group** 1st Floor, Carvella House, Quay West, Quay Parade, Swansea SA1 1SP; phone: (01792) 510351; **Group Manager** Diane Thomas; **Presiding Judges** The Honourable Mr Justice Connell; The Right Honourable Sir Maurice Kay, QB; The Honourable Mr Justice Jacob; The Honourable Mr Justice Thomas.

Scotland

The Supreme Court of Scotland

The Supreme Courts in Scotland comprise the Court of Session and the High Court of Justiciary.

Court of Session

The Civil Court, comprising the Inner House with its two divisions, and the Outer House. **Address** Parliament House, Parliament Square, Edinburgh EH1 1RQ; phone: (0131) 225 2595.

Addresses

High Court of Justiciary Parliament House, Edinburgh EH1 1RQ; phone: (0131) 225 2595, **Council on Tribunals** Scottish Committee, 44 Palmerston Place, Edinburgh EH12 5BJ; phone: (0131) 220 1236, **Crown Office** 25 Chambers Street, Edinburgh EH1 1LA; phone: (0131) 226 2626, **Faculty of Advocates** Parliament House, Edinburgh EH1 1RF; phone: (0131) 226 5071, **Employment Tribunals (Scotland)** 3rd Floor, Eagle Building, 215 Bothwell Street, Glasgow G2 7TS; phone: (0141) 204 0730, **Lands Tribunal For Scotland** 1 Grosvenor Crescent, Edinburgh EH12 5ER; phone: (0131) 225 7996, **The Law Society of Scotland** Law Society's Hall, 26 Drumsheugh Gardens, Edinburgh EH3 7YR; phone: (0131) 226 7411, **Secretary of Commissions For Scotland** Saughton House, Broomhouse Drive, Edinburgh EH11 3XD; phone: (0131) 244 2691, **Scottish Courts Administration** Hayweight House, 23 Lauriston Street, Edinburgh EH3 9DQ; phone: (0131) 229 9200, **Scottish Land Court:** 1 Grosvenor Crescent, Edinburgh EH12 5ER; phone: (0131) 225 3595, **Sheriff Court of Chancery** 27 Chambers Street, Edinburgh EH1 1LB; phone: (0131) 225 2525, **Transport Tribunal** Parliament House, Edinburgh EH1 1RQ; phone: (0131) 225 2595.

The Sheriff Courts of Scotland

Central Scotland

Sheriff Principal J F Wheatley, QC, **Alloa** Sheriff Court House, Alloa FK10 1HR; phone: (01259) 722734.

Dumfries and Galloway

Sheriff Principal G L Cox, QC, **Dumfries** Sheriff Court House, Dumfries DG1 2AN; phone: (01387) 262334.

Fife

Sheriff Principal J F Wheatley, QC, **Cupar** Sheriff Court House, Cupar KY15 4LX; phone: (01334) 652121.

Grampian

Sheriff Principal D J Risk, QC, **Aberdeen** Sheriff Court House, Aberdeen AB9 1AP; phone: (01224) 648316.

Lothian and Borders

Sheriff Principal C G B Nicholson, QC, **Edinburgh** Sheriff Court House, Edinburgh EH1 2NS; phone: (0131) 225 2525.

Northern

Sheriff Principal D J Risk, QC, **Dingwall** Sheriff Court House, Dingwall IV15 9QX; phone: (01349) 863153.

Strathclyde

Sheriffs Principal E F Bowen, QC (Glasgow and Strathkelvin); B A Kerr, QC (North Strathclyde); G L Cox (South Strathclyde, Dumfries, and Galloway)..

Tayside

Sheriff Principal J F Wheatley, QC, **Arbroath** Sheriff Court House, Arbroath DD11 1HL; phone: (01241) 876600.

Northern Ireland

The Courts of Northern Ireland

The Supreme Court of Judicature comprises the Court of Appeal, the High Court, and the Crown Court. All matters relating to these courts are under the jurisdiction of the UK Parliament.

The Supreme Court

Royal Courts of Justice, Chichester Street, Belfast BT1 3JF; phone: (01232) 235111.

Offices

Queen's Bench, Appeals' and Clerk of the Crown in Northen Ireland Master: J W Wilson, QC; High Court Master: Mrs D M Kennedy **Office of Care and Protection** Master: F B Hall **Bankruptcy and Companies Office** Master: C W G Redpath **Chancery Office** Master: R A Ellison **Probate and Matrimonial Office** Master: Mrs Melody McReynolds **Taxing Office** Master: J C Napier **Court Funds Office** Accountant General: H G Thompson **Official Solicitor** Miss Brenda M Donnelly **Recorders** His Honour Judge Hart, QC; His Honour Judge Burgess; His Honour Judge Martin, QC.

Northern Ireland Court Service

Headquarters: Windsor House, Bedford Street, Belfast BT1 3JF; phone: (01232) 328594.

Civil Proceedings

County Court Actions for Mortgage Possessions in the UK

Data are for local authority and private actions. The figures do not indicate the number of houses repossessed through the courts; not all warrants will have resulted in the issue and execution of warrants of possession. The regional breakdown relates to the location of the court rather than the address of the property. Data exclude Scotland. (N/A = not available.)

Region	1994			1995			1996			1997		
	Actions entered	Suspended orders	Orders made	Actions entered	Suspended orders	Orders made	Actions entered	Suspended orders	Orders made	Actions entered	Suspended orders	Orders made
Northeast	3,200	2,400	1,200	3,300	2,100	1,000	3,500	2,000	1,100	3,000	1,600	1,000
Northwest	9,700	5,400	3,100	10,200	5,500	3,400	9,900	6,300	3,500	8,800	4,500	2,700
Merseyside	2,500	800	600	2,600	1,200	600	2,800	1,400	500	2,100	1,000	600
Yorkshire and the Humber	5,700	7,600	3,200	2,300	7,400	3,600	7,600	3,900	2,600	6,900	3,500	2,300
East Midlands	6,000	3,200	2,400	6,500	3,300	2,100	5,900	3,000	2,000	4,900	2,600	1,700
West Midlands	8,600	4,400	2,600	8,200	4,200	2,400	7,600	3,900	2,100	6,700	3,400	2,000
Eastern	9,300	4,200	3,600	8,500	4,300	3,400	8,300	4,000	3,400	6,700	3,000	2,500
London	15,500	8,400	6,800	12,100	6,700	6,000	11,400	6,400	4,800	9,200	4,700	3,400
Southeast	13,600	7,900	5,600	13,000	7,600	5,300	11,600	6,600	4,000	9,100	5,400	3,100
Southwest	7,400	3,500	2,500	7,100	3,400	2,400	6,300	3,300	2,400	5,700	2,700	1,900
England total	83,500	43,300	30,700	78,900	41,900	28,800	74,900	40,700	26,400	6,310	32,400	21,200
Wales total	4,400	2,300	1,500	5,300	2,700	1,600	4,900	2,700	1,400	3,900	2,400	1,300
Northern Ireland total[1]	1,400	N/A	N/A	1,200	N/A	N/A	1,200	N/A	N/A	1,200	N/A	N/A

[1] Mortgage possession actions are heard in the Chancery Division of the Northern Ireland High Court.

Source: *Regional Trends 33,* © Crown copyright 1998

Bankruptcy Proceedings in England and Wales

Summary of bankruptcy proceedings in the Chancery Division of the High Court.

1997

Nature of proceedings	
Applications filed	
Bankruptcy petitions by creditors	10,709
Bankruptcy petitions by debtors	418
Other applications and summonses	15,339
Total	26,466
Number of appointments before registrars	
Listed	25,132
Unlisted	19,386

Nature of proceedings	
Orders made	
Bankruptcy orders on creditors' petitions	5,658
Bankruptcy orders on debtors' petitions	412
Total	6,070
Withdrawn/dismissed	5,721
Transfers to county courts	4,632
Others	26,021

Source: *Judicial Statistics, England and Wales 1997,* © Crown copyright 1998

Cases Brought to the Employment Appeal Tribunal

The Employment Appeal Tribunal was set up by the Employment Protection Act 1975 and hears appeals on a question of law arising from any decisions of, or any proceeedings before, an industrial tribunal. For example, it deals with unfair dismissal and redundancy matters and allegations of discriminatory acts. It may also hear applications for compensation from persons unreasonably excluded from unions. The Tribunal has wide discretion regarding costs. During 1997, the Tribunal recieved 1,409 cases, a decrease of 4% on the 1996 figure of 1,465. A total of 1,378 cases were disposed of in 1997, 132 fewer than in 1996. The great majority of cases received and dealt with related to claims of unfair dismissal (491 and 597 respectively).

1997

Class	Number of cases received	Cases disposed of				
		By hearing				
		Dismissed	Allowed	Remitted	Withdrawn	Total
EP(C)A 1978[1]						
Unfair dismissal	491	320	24	82	171	597
Interim relief	1	0	0	0	1	1
Redundancy pay	32	21	3	3	6	33
Contract of employment	52	16	5	3	16	40
Trade union activities	11	7	1	0	0	8
Other	88	46	6	9	25	86
Equal Pay Act 1970	5	2	0	1	4	7
Sex Discrimination Act 1975	109	43	4	10	36	93
Race Relations Act 1976	125	68	10	11	29	118
Employment Act 1980	0	0	0	0	0	0
Employment Act 1988	0	0	0	0	0	0
Wages Act 1986	42	31	3	7	15	56
European Communities Act 1972[2]	17	4	3	0	6	13
Jurisdiction/Preliminary	182	61	7	19	30	117
Interlocutories	144	59	41	8	43	151
Reserve Forces Act	0	0	0	0	0	0
Employment Rights Act 1996	110	32	1	1	24	58
Total	1,409	710	108	154	406	1,378

[1] Employment Protection (Consolidation) Act 1978.
[2] Transfers of undertakings.

Source: *Judicial Statistics, England and Wales 1997,* © Crown copyright 1998

Appeals Entered in Apellate Courts in England and Wales

(– = not applicable.)

Nature of court	1938	1958	1968	1978	1988	1990	1995	1996	1997
Judicial Committee of the Privy Council	107	44	37	52	61	52	82	80	73
House of Lords									
from courts in England and Wales	32	29	41	77	75	54	56	49	69
elsewhere	11	23	11	6	15	7	16	16	14
Court of Appeal									
Civil Division	574	668	948	1,401	1,645	1,580	1,853	1,804	1,715
Criminal Division[1]	–	–	6,414	6,099	7,235	6,307	8,187	8,724	8,675
High Court									
Chancery Division	–	27	119	74	111	161	271	283	182
Queen's Bench Division[2]	263	186	394	510	1,800	2,738	4,345	4,572	4,624
Family Division	–	102	263	247	240	235	58	36	36
Total	987	1,079	8,227	84,66	11,182	11,134	14,868	15,564	15,388

[1] Includes applications.
[2] Includes judicial review, appeals by way of case stated, and statutory appeals.

Source: *Judicial Statistics, England and Wales 1997,* © Crown copyright 1998

Matrimonial Suits in England and Wales

Suits	1938	1958	1968	1978	1988	1990	1995	1996	1997
Dissolution of marriage									
Petitions filed	9,970	25,584	54,036	162,450	182,804	191,615	173,966	177,970	163,769
Decrees nisi	7,621	23,456	47,959	151,533	154,788	157,344	155,739	157,588	148,310
Decrees absolute	6,092	22,195	45,036	142,726	152,139	155,239	153,337	155,310	145,886
Nullity of marriage									
Petitions filed	263	655	971	1,117	604	665	881	702	485
Decrees nisi	170	496	819	959	389	430	425	332	248
Decrees absolute	158	459	758	941	494	467	516	669	298
Judicial separation									
Petitions filed	71	158	233	2,611	2,925	2,900	3,349	2,795	1,078
Decrees granted	25	88	105	1,228	1,917	1,794	1,543	1,199	589

Source: *Judicial Statistics, England and Wales 1997,*

Legal Aid

Legal Aid in the UK

The justice system in the United Kingdom provides legal aid to allow people to seek legal advice, assistance, or representation, according to their means. To qualify for free legal aid, a person must be in receipt of income support, or an equivalent level of income. Those who are not entitled to free legal aid as a result of their income, make a contribution towards their legal costs. Any person granted legal aid may be required to repay all or part of it, should they be awarded damages or have their costs paid by a third party. The opponent of a legally aided party may recover costs from the Legal Aid Board in certain circumstances.

In civil law cases legal aid payments are made to lawyers through the Legal Aid Fund, administered by the Legal Aid Board. In Scotland legal aid is administered by the Scottish Legal Aid Board, whilst the Law Society for Northern Ireland performs that role in Northern Ireland.

In criminal proceedings in England, Wales, and Northern Ireland, the court may decide that it is in the interests of justice to grant legal aid. Where a defendant is considered to require financial assistance, this may be provided either in whole or in part. In addition, the Legal Aid Board provides duty solicitors to offer assistance to unrepresented defendants in magistrates' courts. Duty solicitors are available to provide advice and assistance 24 hours a day to suspects questioned by the police at police stations. In Northern Ireland legal aid in criminal cases is provided free of charge.

In Scotland there is a duty solicitor scheme for representing people in custody and at district court, provided free of charge. In summary criminal proceedings an application must be made to the Scottish Legal Aid Board that satisfies the Board that to grant legal aid would be in the interests of justice, and that the defendant could not meet the expenses without undue hardship. For solemn proceedings, the court decides on the applicability of legal aid according to the defendant's circumstances. If a grant of legal aid is made to the defendant in a criminal case, he/she is not required to make a contribution.

Trends in Legal Aid Expenditure

(In millions of pounds, and percentage increases.)

Payment	1992–93	1993–94	1994–95	1995–96	1996–97	1997–98
Gross payments	1,117	1,278	1,383	1,507	1,614	1,670
Recoveries	200	257	298	350	397	436
Net payments	917	1,021	1,085	1,157	1,217	1,235
Net payments in						
matrimonial and family proceedings	272	332	351	374	393	390
other civil proceedings	314	350	379	400	415	403
criminal proceedings	287	291	307	330	355	384
administration	44	47	49	52	54	58
Annual % increase in net payments						
in money terms	20.7	11.3	6.3	6.6	5.2	1.5
in real terms	16.5	9.4	4.0	2.7	3.0	–2.0

Source: *Legal Aid Board Annual Report 1997–98,*

Web Sites

Art Crime

http://museum-security.org/artcrime.html

Latest news about cultural property incidents, such as art theft, looting of art in wartime, fire, and forgery. Contributions to the site are encouraged.

Bentham Archive of British Law

http://www.ndirect.co.uk/~law/bentham.htm

Law resource for research and guidance. The site includes introductions to Roman, property, European, media, and computer law; the full text of recent Acts of Parliament and of the European Union courts; and legal contacts and links.

Bill of Rights

http://earlyamerica.com/earlyamerica/freedom/bill/index.html

Full text of the US Bill of Rights. This site also contains a short background introduction to this significant document.

Code of Hammurabi

http://www.lawresearch.com/v2/codeham.htm

Translation of, and commentary on, the Law Code of Hammurabi, one of the earliest recognized lawcodes of the ancient world.

Court of Justice of the European Communities

http://europa.eu.int/cj/en/index.htm

Official guide to the history and structure of Europe's highest court. Full texts of judgements and lists of cases pending can be accessed. This site gives an indication of the enormous range of issues involved in the interpretation and application of the treaties of the European Union.

Crime Library

http://crimelibrary.com/index.html

Collection of stories and essays about infamous criminals and crimes, divided into 'Classic crime stories', 'Gangsters, outlaws and G-men', 'Serial killers', and 'Terrorists, spies, and assassins'.

Crime Prevention Initiatives

http://www.crime-prevention.org.uk/home_office/guide/

Practical advice on protecting yourself, your family, home, and personal possessions against crime, reproduced from the Home Office publication, Your Practical Guide to Crime Prevention.

Crown Prosecution Service – Working in the Interests of Justice

http://www.cps.gov.uk/

Official site of the body responsible for criminal prosecutions in Britain and Wales. There is practical information for defendants, victims, and witnesses.

Future of Legal Aid in England and Wales

http://www.lovellwhitedurrant.com/NewSite/pr/lit.htm

Detailed examination of Lord Mackay's July 1996 white paper on proposed reforms of the legal aid system.

General Council of the Bar

http://www.barcouncil.org.uk/

Professional body for barristers in England and Wales. The site outlines the role of barristers within the UK legal system, and their education and training, and provides a 'Bar council directory'.

Her Majesty's Prison Risley

http://www.hmp-risley.freeserve.co.uk

Outlines the mission of Her Majesty's Prison Service as a whole, as well as that of Risley prison.

International Law Association (ILA)

http://www.ila-hq.org/

Detailing the ILA's objectives and activities in studying, elucidating, and advancing international law, and promoting the unification of law.

Interpol

http://193.123.144.14/interpol-pr/

International Police Criminal Police Organization Web site, with information on the organization's structure and history, and exhibitions on its work.

Law Commission – Working for Better Law

http://www.gtnet.gov.uk/lawcomm/misc/about.htm#consolidation

Comprehensive information on the role of the Law Commission in England and Wales. There are full details on all the laws currently under review. Recent judgements of the commission can also be easily accessed.

Law Society of England and Wales

http://www.lawsoc.org.uk/

Professional body for solicitors in England and Wales. The Web site contains details about 'Legal education', 'Professional training and accreditation', and 'Law and policy', and incorporates a 'Directory of Members' and 'Gazette', which includes recruitment pages.

Legal Aid (England and Wales)

http://www.open.gov.uk/lab/legal.htm

Covering provision of Legal Aid in England and Wales, with helpful sections such as 'What sort of help do I need?', 'Will I qualify?', and 'Six steps to Legal Aid'.

Medieval Law and Politics

http://www.millersv.edu/~english/homepage/duncan/medfem/law.html

Information on the legal position of medieval women. The issues treated include 'Gender equality', 'Women in the Magna Carta', 'Women and nglish medieval common law', 'Casting spells', and even 'Kissing Cousins'.

Met Police

http://www.met.police.uk/

New Scotland Yard online that includes a complete history of the police in the UK, latest news, recruitment, and information about crime prevention. There is also a 'Youth page' section that includes several 'Streetwise' guides to safety.

Organized Crime

http://www.crime.org/

Crime statistics tutorial, offering guidance on evaluating crime statistics. The site includes analysis of the process of compiling crime statistics and their reliability.

Organized Crime Registry

http://members.tripod.com/~orgcrime/index.htm

Articles, links, and news about organized crime syndicates, including the American mafia, Russian mafia, Japanese yakuza, Triads, South American drug cartels, and other crime syndicates.

Right of Way

http://www.ramblers.org.uk/rightsofway.html

Practical information about rights of way in Britain from Britain's Rambler's Association. The legal status of a right of way, how paths can become rights of way, and the duties and responsibilities of walkers, farmers, and public authorities are clearly spelt out.

Roman Law

http://www.jura.uni-sb.de/Rechtsgeschichte/Ius.Romanum/english.html

Dedicated to collating information on Roman law, including key Latin texts and hyperlinks to other Web sites on the classics.

Scottish Legal Aid Board

http://www.slab.org.uk/

Details on how to obtain legal aid in Scotland, as well as 'News', 'Publications', and 'Statistics' about the use of legal aid.

Stephen Lawrence Inquiry

http://www.official-documents.co.uk/document/cm42/4262/4262.htm

Full text of the report produced by the inquiry into the murder of black British teenager Stephen Lawrence, published by the Stationery Office.

Supreme Court Decisions, 1937–1975

http://www.access.gpo.gov/su_docs/supcrt/index.html

Full text of more than 7,000 US Supreme Court decisions handed down between 1937 and 1975. Cases are accessible by case name, case number, or a keyword search.

Supreme Court Opinion, 1993–1998

http://fedbbs.access.gpo.gov/court01.htm

Decisions and related documents of the Supreme Court handed down since 1993. This page is updated as decisions are made.

United Nations Crime and Justice Information Network

http://www.ifs.univie.ac.at/~uncjin/uncjin.html

Global crime prevention and criminal justice information network on the Web. It provides access to UN documents, links to other UN organizations, and country-specific information including a wide range of area maps.

Web Journal of Current Legal Issues

http://webjcli.ncl.ac.uk/

Bi-monthly electronic legal journal featuring case comments, book reviews, and articles on subjects that include legal education, information technology, law reform, and legal research.

SCIENCE AND TECHNOLOGY

The Year in Review

July 1998 China's Academy of Sciences announces a project to clone the panda by 2003. This involves transferring the nucleus of a panda cell into that of another bear species, with the same species being used as a surrogate mother.

2 July 1998 US scientists report that the spacecraft *Galileo* has discovered 12 different vents on Jupiter's moon Io which spew lava at temperatures greater than those of any planetary body in the solar system – up to 1,175°C/3,100°F. The temperatures are caused by changes in the moon's shape as it orbits Jupiter.

4 July 1998 Astronomers from the University of Hawaii discover the first asteroid entirely within the Earth's orbit; it is 40 m/130 ft in diameter.

4 July 1998 Japan's Institute of Space and Astronautical Science launches *Planet-B,* an uncrewed spacecraft to orbit Mars, from Kagoshima, Japan.

4 July 1998 US ornithologists announce the important discovery of a new species of bird in Ecuador belonging to the genus *Antpitta*.

7 July 1998 A Russian nuclear submarine in the Barents Sea launches a commercial satellite into space. The first launch of its kind, it shows that launches can be made from any latitude and that an increased range of orbit can be achieved.

7 July 1998 Two Japanese satellites, using sensors and lasers, perform the first automatic docking of a space vehicle.

11 July 1998 British astronomers in Hawaii discover what they believe to be a solar system forming around the star Epsilon Eridan, ten light years away.

23 July 1998 Scientists succeed in cloning more than 50 mice at the University of Hawaii, in the first successful cloning of an adult mammal since the creation of the cloned sheep Dolly in 1997.

August 1998 British hotelier Campbell Aird becomes the first person to have a 'bionic arm', a lightweight prosthetic developed by specialists at Princess Margaret Rose Hospital in Edinburgh, Scotland, that has a motorized shoulder, bending elbow, rotating wrist, and contracting fingers.

August 1998 Five new salamander species are discovered in tropical east-central Mexico. The species all belong to the genus *Thorius,* whose members are characterized by their smallness.

September 1998 US computer firm IBM announces that it will release a thumb-nail-sized hard disc drive in 1999. It will hold 340 megabytes.

4 September 1998 US scientist Alan Binder, who is in charge of the uncrewed *Lunar Prospector,* which is orbiting the Moon, reports that there could be as much as 9 billion tonnes/10 billion tons of ice on the Moon.

October 1998 Brain implants are inserted into the motor cortexes of two severely disabled people, by surgeons in Atlanta, Georgia. The implants enable them to control the cursor on a computer just by thinking about moving parts of their body.

October 1998 Dutch researchers discover a large galaxy close to our own. The galaxy is 20 million light years away in the Local Void, an area of space that is generally considered to be nearly empty. It escaped detection due to its faintness.

October 1998 Swiss researchers announce a cheap and efficient solar cell. Based on titanium dioxide, it is twice as efficient as cells currently available commercially.

12 October 1998 The Nobel Prize for Physics is awarded to US professors Daniel Tsui, Horst Stoermer, and Robert Laughlin for their research on electrons.

13 October 1998 British scientist John Pope

and US scientist Walter Kohn share the Nobel Prize for Chemistry for their work in the field of quantum chemistry.

29 October 1998 US astronaut John Glenn (77) becomes the world's oldest active astronaut, when he blasts off on a nine-day mission on the *Discovery* space shuttle. His first trip into space was in 1962, when he was the first American to orbit Earth.

31 October 1998 The Royal Greenwich Observatory, founded in 1675 and Britain's oldest scientific institution, closes its Cambridge site, owing to government budget cuts, and merges with the Royal Observatory, Edinburgh.

November 1998 A significant number of rhinoceros in the Kaziranga National Park in Assam, India, are believed drowned after severe floods. Kaziranga holds 70 percent (1,200) of the world's rhinoceros population.

November 1998 US researchers successfully induce the growth of new hair follicles in adult mice. It is the first time that new hair follicles have been grown in adult skin, leading to the possibility of improved treatment for baldness.

12 November 1998 Scientists from the UK, the USA, France, and Niger find an almost complete skeleton of a long-snouted, fish-eating dinosaur in the Tenere Desert of Niger. The newly discovered species is 11 m/36 ft long and lived 100 million years ago in Africa. It is in the spinosaurids group and has been named *Suchomimus tenerensis*.

20 November 1998 The spacecraft *Zayra,* the first module of the £20 billion Alpha International Space Station set up by a group of 16 countries, is launched from Kazakhstan. The station, which is planned for completion in 2004, will orbit the Earth and will house research laboratories and accommodation for seven scientists.

4 December 1998 The US space shuttle *Endeavour* is launched from Cape Canaveral, Florida, to link up the second component of an international space station to *Zayra,* the first component.

9 December 1998 A team of scientists from Kinki University in Nara, Japan, clone eight calves from an adult cow, in the third instance ever of cloning an adult mammal.

9 December 1998 Palaeontologists from the University of Witwatersrand in Johannesburg, South Africa, discover a skeleton of an australopithecine, an early species of human, in a cave in Sterkfontein, South Africa. The skeleton is estimated to be 3.2–3.6 million years old, making it one of the oldest australopithecines ever found.

10 December 1998 In a joint effort by scientists around the world, the first genetic blueprint for a whole multicellular animal – a nematode worm – is completed. The 97 million-letter code, which is published on the Internet, is for a tiny worm called *C. elegans.* The study began 15 years ago and cost £30 million.

16 December 1998 Scientists at Kyunghee University Hospital in Seoul, South Korea, announce that they have created a human embryo cloned from a female adult, but that they have destroyed it because of the ethical controversy surrounding cloning of humans.

In December 1998 a team of scientists from around the world, led by ***Dr John Sulston*** *(pictured) of the Sanger Centre in Cambridgeshire, announced the completion of a 15-year project to map the entire genetic sequence of the 1 mm-long nematode worm (shown behind him).* Photo: Richard Watt

9 January 1999 Astronomers from San Francisco State University announce the discovery of three more planets orbiting around neighbouring stars, bringing the total number of known planets outside our solar system to 17.

23 January 1999 NASA scientists photograph light emitted by a gamma ray burst for the first time ever.

February 1999 Scientists succeed in slowing down the speed of light from its normal speed of 299,792 km/186,282 mi per second to 61 km/38 mi per hour, opening up potential for the development of high-precision computer and telecommunications technologies, as well as for the advanced study of quantum mechanics.

6 February 1999 NASA launches the uncrewed spacecraft *Stardust* from Cape Canaveral, Florida, to collect samples of dust from the comet Wild-2, in the first mission to collect material from beyond the Moon.

March 1999 Russian scientists at the Institute of Nuclear Research at Dubna create element 114 by colliding isotopes calcium 48 and plutonium 44.

March 1999 Scientists discover a previously undetected fault running under Los Angeles, California, that could potentially cause a major earthquake. The Puente Hills fault extends for 40 km/25 mi.

March 1999 US scientists succeed in transforming a diamond into metal, using a very powerful laser to compress it.

10 March 1999 The US software company Microsoft unveils Venus, whereby people in Shenzhan, China can access the Internet through their TVs.

29 March 1999 A computer virus spreads via e-mail to more than 100,000 computers around the world. Named Melissa, it reportedly spreads more widely and quickly than any previous virus.

April 1999 British public health minister Tessa Jowell announces plans to create an expert panel to review the radiation risks of mobile phones under the guidance of the National Radiological Protection Board.

2 April 1999 British scientists propose to revise the conventions by which fossil species are deemed human, which would mean that *Homo habilis* would no longer be considered human. *Homo ergaster*, which existed some 1.9 million years ago, would replace it as humankind's earliest ancestor.

26 April 1999 The global computer virus Chernobyl, or CIH, which lurked on computers until the thirteenth anniversary of the Chernobyl nuclear disaster, is activated, deleting all files stored on computer hard disks.

10 May 1999 A team of French scientists unearth what is believed to be the world's largest fossil of a land mammal. The fossil, which is 5.5 m/18 ft high and 7 m/23 ft long, is from the Baluchitherium, a 15–20 tonne mammal that looked like a rhinoceros and lived 30 million years ago.

June 1999 US physicists create element 118, which decays into another new element, 116, by bombarding lead with krypton.

1 June 1999 The Russian space agency orders the cosmonauts aboard the *Mir* space station to return to Earth in August, abandoning the problem-ridden space station for good.

11 June 1999 A computer virus called ExploreZip arrives via e-mail in the UK, deleting programs and documents on personal computers.

24 June 1999 British minister for public health Tessa Jowell announces a temporary ban on cloning in the UK, even for medical research. Scientists warn that the ban could impede research into cures for diseases.

The Elements

The Chemical Elements

An element is a substance that cannot be split chemically into simpler substances. The atoms of a particular element all have the same number of protons in their nuclei (their atomic number).
(– = not applicable.)

Name	Symbol	Atomic number	Atomic mass (amu)[1]	Relative density[2]	Melting or fusing point (°C)
Actinium	Ac	89	227[3]	–	–
Aluminium	Al	13	26.9815	2.58	658
Americium	Am	95	243[3]	–	–
Antimony	Sb	51	121.75	6.62	629
Argon	Ar	18	39.948	gas	−188
Arsenic	As	33	74.9216	5.73	volatile, 450
Astatine	At	85	210[3]	–	–
Barium	Ba	56	137.34	3.75	850
Berkelium	Bk	97	249[3]	–	–
Beryllium	Be	4	9.0122	1.93	1,281
Bismuth	Bi	83	208.9806	9.80	268
Bohrium	Bh	107	262[3]	–	–
Boron	B	5	10.81	2.5	2,300
Bromine	Br	35	79.904	3.19	−7.3
Cadmium	Cd	48	112.40	8.64	320
Caesium	Cs	55	132.9055	1.88	26
Calcium	Ca	20	40.08	1.58	851
Californium	Cf	98	251[3]	–	–
Carbon	C	6	12.011	3.52	infusible
Cerium	Ce	58	140.12	6.68	623
Chlorine	Cl	17	35.453	gas	−102
Chromium	Cr	24	51.996	6.5	1,510
Cobalt	Co	27	58.9332	8.6	1,490
Copper	Cu	29	63.546	8.9	1,083
Curium	Cm	96	247[3]	–	–
Dubnium	Db	105	262[3]	–	–
Dysprosium	Dy	66	162.50	–	–
Einsteinium	Es	99	254[3]	–	–
Erbium	Er	68	167.26	4.8	–
Europium	Eu	63	151.96	–	–
Fermium	Fm	100	253[3]	–	–
Fluorine	F	9	18.9984	gas	−223
Francium	Fr	87	223[3]	–	–
Gadolinium	Gd	64	157.25	–	–
Gallium	Ga	31	69.72	5.95	30
Germanium	Ge	32	72.59	5.47	958
Gold	Au	79	196.9665	19.3	1,062
Hafnium	Hf	72	178.49	12.1	2,500
Hassium	Hs	108	265[3]	–	–
Helium	He	2	4.0026	gas	−272
Holmium	Ho	67	164.9303	–	–
Hydrogen	H	1	1.0080	gas	−258
Indium	In	49	114.82	7.4	155
Iodine	I	53	126.9045	4.95	114
Iridium	Ir	77	192.22	22.4	2,375
Iron	Fe	26	55.847	7.86	1,525
Krypton	Kr	36	83.80	gas	−169
Lanthanum	La	57	138.9055	6.1	810
Lawrencium	Lr	103	260[3]	–	–
Lead	Pb	82	207.2	11.37	327
Lithium	Li	3	6.941	0.585	186
Lutetium	Lu	71	174.97	–	–
Magnesium	Mg	12	24.305	1.74	651
Manganese	Mn	25	54.9380	7.39	1,220
Meitnerium	Mt	109	266[3]	–	–
Mendelevium	Md	101	256[3]	–	–
Mercury	Hg	80	200.59	13.596	−38.9
Molybdenum	Mo	42	95.94	10.2	2,500
Neodymium	Nd	60	144.24	6.96	840
Neon	Ne	10	20.179	gas	−248.6
Neptunium	Np	93	237[3]	–	–
Nickel	Ni	28	58.71	8.9	1,452
Niobium	Nb	41	92.9064	8.4	1,950
Nitrogen	N	7	14.0067	gas	−211
Nobelium	No	102	254[3]	–	–
Osmium	Os	76	190.2	22.48	2,700
Oxygen	O	8	15.9994	gas	−227
Palladium	Pd	46	106.4	11.4	1,549
Phosphorus	P	15	30.9738	1.8–2.3	44
Platinum	Pt	78	195.09	21.5	1,755
Plutonium	Pu	94	242[3]	–	–
Polonium	Po	84	210[3]	–	–
Potassium	K	19	39.102	0.87	63
Praseodymium	Pr	59	140.9077	6.48	940
Promethium	Pm	61	145[3]	–	–
Protactinium	Pa	91	231.0359	–	–
Radium	Ra	88	226.0254	6.0	700
Radon	Rn	86	222[3]	gas	−150
Rhenium	Re	75	186.2	21	3,000
Rhodium	Rh	45	102.9055	12.1	1,950
Rubidium	Rb	37	85.4678	1.52	39
Ruthenium	Ru	44	101.07	12.26	2,400
Rutherfordium	Rf	104	262[3]	–	–
Samarium	Sm	62	150.4	7.7	1,350
Scandium	Sc	21	44.9559	–	–
Seaborgium	Sg	106	263[3]	–	–
Selenium	Se	34	78.96	4.5	170–220
Silicon	Si	14	28.086	2.0–2.4	1,370
Silver	Ag	47	107.868	10.5	960
Sodium	Na	11	22.9898	0.978	97
Strontium	Sr	38	87.62	2.54	800
Sulphur	S	16	32.06	2.07	115–119
Tantalum	Ta	73	180.9479	16.6	2,900
Technetium	Tc	43	99[3]	–	–
Tellurium	Te	52	127.60	6.0	446
Terbium	Tb	65	158.9254	–	–
Thallium	Tl	81	204.37	11.85	302
Thorium	Th	90	232.0381	11.00	1,750
Thulium	Tm	69	168.9342	–	–
Tin	Sn	50	118.69	7.3	232
Titanium	Ti	22	47.90	4.54	1,850
Tungsten	W	74	183.85	19.1	2,900–3,000
Ununbium	Uub[4]	112	277[3]	–	–
Ununnilium	Uun[4]	110	269[3]	–	–
Unununium	Uuu[4]	111	272[3]	–	–
Uranium	U	92	238.029	18.7	–
Vanadium	V	23	50.9414	5.5	1,710
Xenon	Xe	54	131.30	gas	−140
Ytterbium	Yb	70	173.04	–	–
Yttrium	Y	39	88.9059	3.8	–
Zinc	Zn	30	65.37	7.12	418
Zirconium	Zr	40	91.22	4.15	2,130

[1] Atomic mass units.
[2] Also known as specific gravity.
[3] The number given is that for the most stable isotope of the element.
[4] Elements as yet unnamed; temporary identification assigned until a name is approved by the International Union for Pure and Applied Chemistry.

element

1 Hydrogen H 1.00794	
1	atomic number
Hydrogen	name
H	symbol
1.00794	relative atomic mass

Key	
■ (shaded)	metals
□ (unshaded)	nonmetals

	I	II							
1	1 Hydrogen **H** 1.00794								
2	3 Lithium **Li** 6.941	4 Beryllium **Be** 9.012							
3	11 Sodium **Na** 22.98977	12 Magnesium **Mg** 24.305							
4	19 Potassium **K** 30.098	20 Calcium **Ca** 40.06	21 Scandium **Sc** 44.9559	22 Titanium **Ti** 47.90	23 Vanadium **V** 50.9414	24 Chromium **Cr** 51.996	25 Manganese **Mn** 54.9380	26 Iron **Fe** 55.847	27 Cobalt **Co** 58.9332
5	37 Rubidium **Rb** 85.4678	38 Strontium **Sr** 87.62	39 Yttrium **Y** 88.9059	40 Zirconium **Zr** 91.22	41 Niobium **Nb** 92.9064	42 Molybdenum **Mo** 95.94	43 Technetium **Tc** 97.9072	44 Ruthenium **Ru** 101.07	45 Rhodium **Rh** 102.9055
6	55 Caesium **Cs** 132.9054	56 Barium **Ba** 137.34	**La**	72 Hafnium **Hf** 178.49	73 Tantalum **Ta** 180.9479	74 Tungsten **W** 183.85	75 Rhenium **Re** 186.207	76 Osmium **Os** 190.2	77 Iridium **Ir** 192.22
7	87 Francium **Fr** 223.0197	88 Radium **Ra** 226.0254	**Ac**	104 Rutherfordium **Rf** 261.109	105 Dubnium **Db** 262.114	106 Seaborgium **Sg** 263.120	107 Bohrium **Bh** 262	108 Hassium **Hs** 265	109 Meitnerium **Mt** 266

Lanthanide series					
57 Lanthanum **La** 138.9055	58 Cerium **Ce** 140.12	59 Praeseodymium **Pr** 140.9077	60 Neodymium **Nd** 144.24	61 Promethium **Pm** 144.9128	62 Samarium **Sm** 150.36

Actinide series					
89 Actinium **Ac** 227.0278	90 Thorium **Th** 232.0381	91 Protactinium **Pa** 231.0359	92 Uranium **U** 238.029	93 Neptunium **Np** 237.0482	94 Plutonium **Pu** 244.0642

Periodic table of the elements *The periodic table of the elements arranges the elements into horizontal rows (called periods) and vertical columns (called groups) according to their atomic numbers. The elements in a group or column all have similar properties – for example, all the elements in the far right-hand column are inert gases.*

			III	IV	V	VI	VII	0
								2 Helium **He** 4002.60
			5 Boron **B** 10.81	6 Carbon **C** 12.011	7 Nitrogen **N** 14.0067	8 Oxygen **O** 15.9994	9 Fluorine **F** 18.99840	10 Neon **Ne** 20.179
			13 Aluminium **Al** 26.98154	14 Silicon **Si** 28.066	15 Phosphorus **P** 30.9738	16 Sulphur **S** 32.06	17 Chlorine **Cl** 35.453	18 Argon **Ar** 39.948
28 Nickel **Ni** 58.70	29 Copper **Cu** 63.546	30 Zinc **Zn** 65.38	31 Gallium **Ga** 69.72	32 Germanium **Ge** 72.59	33 Arsenic **As** 74.9216	34 Selenium **Se** 78.96	35 Bromine **Br** 79.904	36 Krypton **Kr** 83.80
46 Palladium **Pd** 106.4	47 Silver **Ag** 107.868	48 Cadmium **Cd** 112.40	49 Indium **In** 114.82	50 Tin **Sn** 118.69	51 Antimony **Sb** 121.75	52 Tellurium **Te** 127.75	53 Iodine **I** 126.9045	54 Xenon **Xe** 131.30
78 Platinum **Pt** 195.09	79 Gold **Au** 196.9665	80 Mercury **Hg** 200.59	81 Thallium **Tl** 204.37	82 Lead **Pb** 207.37	83 Bismuth **Bi** 207.2	84 Polonium **Po** 210	85 Astatine **At** 211	86 Radon **Rn** 222.0176
110 Ununnilium **Uun** 269	111 Unununium **Uuu** 272	112 Ununbium **Uub** 277						

63 Europium **Eu** 151.96	64 Gadolinium **Gd** 157.25	65 Terbium **Tb** 158.9254	66 Dysprosium **Dy** 162.50	67 Holmium **Ho** 164.9304	68 Erbium **Er** 167.26	69 Thulium **Tm** 168.9342	70 Ytterbium **Yb** 173.04	71 Lutetium **Lu** 174.97
95 Americium **Am** 243.0614	96 Curium **Cm** 247.0703	97 Berkelium **Bk** 247	98 Californium **Cf** 251.0786	99 Einsteinium **Es** 252.0828	100 Fermium **Fm** 257.0951	101 Mendelevium **Md** 258.0986	102 Nobelium **No** 259.1009	103 Lawrencium **Lr** 260.1054

harmful/irritant

radioactive

toxic

explosive

flammable

corrosive

oxidizing/supports fire

biohazardous/infectious

environmentally dangerous

Hazard labels

Common Alloys

Name	Approximate composition	Uses
brass	35–10% zinc, 65–90% copper	decorative metalwork, plumbing fittings, industrial tubing
bronze – common	2% zinc, 6% tin, 92% copper	machinery, decorative work
bronze – aluminium	10% aluminium, 90% copper	machinery castings
bronze – coinage	1% zinc, 4% tin, 95% copper	coins
cast iron	2–4% carbon, 96–98% iron	decorative metalwork, engine blocks, industrial machinery
dentist's amalgam	30% copper, 70% mercury	dental fillings
duralumin	0.5 % magnesium, 0.5% manganese, 5% copper, 95% aluminium	framework of aircraft
gold – coinage	10% copper, 90% gold	coins
gold – dental	14–28% silver, 14–28% copper, 58% gold	dental fillings
lead battery plate	6% antimony, 94% lead	car batteries
manganin	1.5% nickel, 16% manganese, 82.5% copper	resistance wire
nichrome	20% chromium, 80% nickel	heating elements
pewter	20% lead, 80% tin	utensils
silver – coinage	10% copper, 90% silver	coins
solder	50% tin, 50% lead	joining iron surfaces
steel – stainless	8–20% nickel, 10–20% chromium, 60–80% iron	kitchen utensils
steel – armour	1–4% nickel, 0.5–2% chromium, 95–98% iron	armour plating
steel – tool	2–4% chromium, 6–7% molybdenum, 90–95% iron	tools

The Transuranic Elements

A transuranic element is a chemical element with an atomic number of 93 or more – that is, with a greater number of protons in the nucleus than uranium. All transuranic elements are radioactive.
(– = not applicable.)

Atomic number	Name	Symbol	Year discovered	Source of first preparation identified	Isotope	Half-life of first isotope identified
Actinide Series						
93	neptunium	Np	1940	irradiation of uranium-238 with neutrons	Np-239	2.35 days
94	plutonium	Pu	1941	bombardment of uranium-238 with deuterons	Pu-238	86.4 years
95	americium	Am	1944	irradiation of plutonium-239 with neutrons	Am-241	458 years
96	curium	Cm	1944	bombardment of plutonium-239 with helium nuclei	Cm-242	162.5 days
97	berkelium	Bk	1949	bombardment of americium-241 with helium nuclei	Bk-243	4.5 h
98	californium	Cf	1950	bombardment of curium-242 with helium nuclei	Cf-245	44 min
99	einsteinium	Es	1952	irradiation of uranium-238 with neutrons in first thermonuclear explosion	Es-253	20 days
100	fermium	Fm	1953	irradiation of uranium-238 with neutrons in first thermonuclear explosion	Fm-235	20 h
101	mendelevium	Md	1955	bombardment of einsteinium-253 with helium nuclei	Md-256	76 min
102	nobelium	No	1958	bombardment of curium-246 with carbon nuclei	No-255	2.3 sec
103	lawrencium	Lr	1961	bombardment of californium-252 with boron nuclei	Lr-257	4.3 sec
Transactinide Elements						
104	rutherfordium	Rf	1969	bombardment of californium-249 with carbon-12 nuclei	Rf-257	4.7 sec
105	dubnium	Db	1970	bombardment of californium-249 with nitrogen-15 nuclei	Db-260	1.6 sec
106	seaborgium	Sg	1974	bombardment of californium-249 with oxygen-18 nuclei	Sg-263	0.8 sec
107	bohrium	Bh	1976	bombardment of bismuth-204 with nuclei of chromium-54	Bh-262	102 millisec
108	hassium	Hs	1984	bombardment of lead-208 with nuclei of iron-58	Hs-265	1.8 millisec
109	meitnerium	Mt	1982	bombardment of bismuth-209 with nuclei of iron-58	Mt-266	3.4 millisec
110	ununnilium[1]	Uun	1994	bombardment of lead nuclei with nickel nuclei	Uun-269	1.1 millisec
111	unununium[1]	Uuu	1994	bombardment of bismuth-209 with nickel nuclei	Uuu-272	1.5 millisec
112	ununbium[1]	Uub	1996	bombardment of lead nuclei with zinc nuclei	Uub-227	0.24 millisec

[1] Temporary names as proposed by the International Union for Pure and Applied Chemistry.

Discovery of the Elements

(– = not applicable.)

Date	Element (symbol)	Discoverer
Prehistoric knowledge	antimony (Sb)	–
	arsenic (As)	
	bismuth (Bi)	
	carbon (C)	
	copper (Cu)	
	gold (Au)	
	iron (Fe)	
	lead (Pb)	
	mercury (Hg)	
	silver (Ag)	
	sulphur (S)	
	tin (Sn)	
	zinc (Zn)	
1557	platinum (Pt)	Julius Scaliger
1674	phosphorus (P)	Hennig Brand
1730	cobalt (Co)	Georg Brandt
1751	nickel (Ni)	Axel Cronstedt
1755	magnesium (Mg)	Joseph Black (oxide isolated by Humphry Davy in 1808; pure form isolated by Antoine-Alexandre-Brutus Bussy in 1828)
1766	hydrogen (H)	Henry Cavendish
1771	fluorine (F)	Karl Scheele (isolated by Henri Moissan in 1886)
1772	nitrogen (N)	Daniel Rutherford
1774	chlorine (Cl)	Karl Scheele
	manganese (Mn)	Johann Gottlieb Gahn
	oxygen (O)	Joseph Priestley and Karl Scheele, independently of each other
1781	molybdenum (Mo)	named by Karl Scheele (isolated by Peter Jacob Hjelm in 1782)
1782	tellurium (Te)	Franz Müller
1783	tungsten (W)	isolated by Juan José Elhuyar and Fausto Elhuyar
1789	uranium (U)	Martin Klaproth (isolated by Eugène Péligot in 1841)
	zirconium (Zr)	Martin Klaproth
1790	titanium (Ti)	William Gregor
1794	yttrium (Y)	Johan Gadolin
1797	chromium (Cr)	Louis-Nicolas Vauquelin
1798	beryllium (Be)	Louis-Nicolas Vauquelin (isolated by Friedrich Wöhler and Antoine-Alexandre-Brutus Bussy in 1828)
1801	vanadium (V)	Andrés del Rio (disputed), or Nils Sefström in 1830
	niobium (Nb)	Charles Hatchett
1802	tantalum (Ta)	Anders Ekeberg
1804	cerium (Ce)	Jöns Berzelius and Wilhelm Hisinger, and independently by Martin Klaproth
	iridium (Ir)	Smithson Tennant
	osmium (Os)	Smithson Tennant
	palladium (Pd)	William Wollaston
	rhodium (Rh)	William Wollaston
1807	potassium (K)	Humphry Davy
	sodium (Na)	Humphry Davy
1808	barium (Ba)	Humphry Davy
	boron (B)	Humphry Davy, and independently by Joseph Gay-Lussac and Louis-Jacques Thénard
	calcium (Ca)	Humphry Davy
	strontium (Sr)	Humphry Davy
1811	iodine (I)	Bernard Courtois
1817	cadmium (Cd)	Friedrich Strohmeyer
	lithium (Li)	Johan Arfwedson
	selenium (Se)	Jöns Berzelius
1823	silicon (Si)	Jöns Berzelius
1824	aluminium (Al)	Hans Oersted (also attributed to Friedrich Wöhler in 1827)
1826	bromine (Br)	Antoine-Jérôme Balard
1827	ruthenium (Ru)	G W Osann (isolated by Karl Klaus in 1844)
1828	thorium (Th)	Jöns Berzelius
1839	lanthanum (La)	Carl Mosander
1843	erbium (Er)	Carl Mosander
	terbium (Tb)	Carl Mosander
1860	caesium (Cs)	Robert Bunsen and Gustav Kirchhoff
1861	rubidium (Rb)	Robert Bunsen and Gustav Kirchhoff
	thallium (Tl)	William Crookes (isolated by William Crookes and Claude August Lamy, independently of each other in 1862)
1863	indium (In)	Ferdinand Reich and Hieronymus Richter
1868	helium (He)	Pierre Janssen
1875	gallium (Ga)	Paul Lecoq de Boisbaudran
1876	scandium (Sc)	Lars Nilson
1878	ytterbium (Yb)	Jean Charles de Marignac
1879	holmium (Ho)	Per Cleve
	samarium (Sm)	Paul Lecoq de Boisbaudran
	thulium (Tm)	Per Cleve
1885	neodymium (Nd)	Carl von Welsbach
	praseodymium (Pr)	Carl von Welsbach
1886	dysprosium (Dy)	Paul Lecoq de Boisbaudran
	gadolinium (Gd)	Paul Lecoq de Boisbaudran
	germanium (Ge)	Clemens Winkler
1894	argon (Ar)	John Rayleigh and William Ramsay
1898	krypton (Kr)	William Ramsay and Morris Travers
	neon (Ne)	William Ramsay and Morris Travers
	polonium (Po)	Marie and Pierre Curie
	radium (Ra)	Marie Curie
	xenon (Xe)	William Ramsay and Morris Travers
1899	actinium (Ac)	André Debierne
1900	radon (Rn)	Friedrich Dorn
1901	europium (Eu)	Eugène Demarçay
1907	lutetium (Lu)	Georges Urbain and Carl von Welsbach, independently of each other
1913	protactinium (Pa)	Kasimir Fajans and O Göhring
	hafnium (Hf)	Dirk Coster and Georg von Hevesy
1925	rhenium (Re)	Walter Noddack, Ida Tacke, and Otto Berg
1937	technetium (Tc)	Carlo Perrier and Emilio Segrè
1939	francium (Fr)	Marguérite Perey
1940	astatine (At)	Dale R Corson, K R MacKenzie, and Emilio Segrè
	neptunium (Np)	Edwin McMillan and Philip Abelson
	plutonium (Pu)	Glenn Seaborg, Edwin McMillan, Joseph Kennedy, and Arthur Wahl
1944	americium (Am)	Glenn Seaborg, Ralph James, Leon Morgan, and Albert Ghiorso
	curium (Cm)	Glenn Seaborg, Ralph James, and Albert Ghiorso
1945	promethium (Pm)	J A Marinsky, Lawrence Glendenin, and Charles Coryell
1949	berkelium (Bk)	Glenn Seaborg, Stanley Thompson, and Albert Ghiorso
1950	californium (Cf)	Glenn Seaborg, Stanley Thompson, Kenneth Street Jr, and Albert Ghiorso
1952	einsteinium (Es)	Albert Ghiorso and co-workers
1955	fermium (Fm)	Albert Ghiorso and co-workers
	mendelevium (Md)	Albert Ghiorso, Bernard G Harvey, Gregory Choppin, Stanley Thompson, and Glenn Seaborg
1958	nobelium (No)	Albert Ghiorso, Torbjørn Sikkeland, J R Walton, and Glenn Seaborg
1961	lawrencium (Lr)	Albert Ghiorso, Torbjørn Sikkeland, Almon Larsh, and Robert Latimer

(continued)

Discovery of the Elements (*continued*)

Date	Element (symbol)	Discoverer
1967	dubnium (Db)	claimed by Soviet scientist Georgii Flerov and co-workers (disputed by US workers)
1969	rutherfordium (Rf)	claimed by US scientist Albert Ghiorso and co-workers (disputed by Soviet workers)
1970	dubnium (Db)	claimed by Albert Ghiorso and co-workers (disputed by Soviet workers)
1974	seaborgium (Sg)	claimed by Georgii Flerov and co-workers, and independently by Albert Ghiorso and co-workers
1976	bohrium (Bh)	Georgii Flerov and Yuri Oganessian (confirmed by German scientist Peter Armbruster and co-workers)
1982	meitnerium (Mt)	Peter Armbruster and co-workers
1984	hassium (Hs)	Peter Armbruster and co-workers
1994	ununnilium (Uun)	team at GSI heavy-ion cyclotron, Darmstadt, Germany
	unununium (Uuu)	team at GSI heavy-ion cyclotron, Darmstadt, Germany
1996	ununbium (Uub)	team at GSI heavy-ion cyclotron, Darmstadt, Germany

Inventions and Discoveries

Scientific Discoveries

Discovery	Date	Discoverer	Nationality
Absolute zero, concept	1851	William Thomson, 1st Baron Kelvin	Irish
Adrenalin, isolation	1901	Jokichi Takamine	Japanese
Alizarin, synthesized	1869	William Perkin	English
Allotropy (in carbon)	1841	Jöns Jakob Berzelius	Swedish
Alpha particles	1899	Ernest Rutherford	New Zealand-born British
Alternation of generations (ferns and mosses)	1851	Wilhelm Hofmeister	German
Aluminium, extraction by electrolysis of aluminium oxide	1886	Charles Hall, Paul Héroult	US, French
Aluminium, improved isolation	1827	Friedrich Wöhler	German
Anaesthetic, first use (ether)	1842	Crawford Long	US
Anthrax vaccine	1881	Louis Pasteur	French
Antibacterial agent, first specific (Salvarsan for treatment of syphilis)	1910	Paul Ehrlich	German
Antiseptic surgery (using phenol)	1865	Joseph Lister	English
Argon	1892	William Ramsay	Scottish
Asteroid, first (Ceres)	1801	Giuseppe Piazzi	Italian
Atomic theory	1803	John Dalton	English
Australopithecus	1925	Raymond Dart	Australian-born South African
Avogadro's hypothesis	1811	Amedeo Avogadro	Italian
Bacteria, first observation	1683	Anton van Leeuwenhoek	Dutch
Bacteriophages	1916	Felix D'Herelle	Canadian
Bee dance	1919	Karl von Frisch	Austrian
Benzene, isolation	1825	Michael Faraday	English
Benzene, ring structure	1865	Friedrich Kekulé	German
Beta rays	1899	Ernest Rutherford	New Zealand-born British
Big-Bang theory	1948	Ralph Alpher, George Gamow	US
Binary arithmetic	1679	Gottfried Leibniz	German
Binary stars	1802	William Herschel	German-born English
Binomial theorem	1665	Isaac Newton	English
Blood, circulation	1619	William Harvey	English
Blood groups, ABO system	1900	Karl Landsteiner	Austrian-born US
Bode's law	1772	Johann Bode, Johann Titius	German
Bohr atomic model	1913	Niels Bohr	Danish
Boolean algebra	1854	George Boole	English
Boyle's law	1662	Robert Boyle	Irish
Brewster's law	1812	David Brewster	Scottish
Brownian motion	1827	Robert Brown	Scottish
Cadmium	1817	Friedrich Strohmeyer	German
Caesium	1861	Robert Bunsen	German
Carbon dioxide	1755	Joseph Black	Scottish
Charles' law	1787	Jacques Charles	French
Chlorine	1774	Karl Scheele	Swedish
Complex numbers, theory	1746	Jean d'Alembert	French
Conditioning	1902	Ivan Pavlov	Russian
Continental drift	1912	Alfred Wegener	German
Coriolis effect	1834	Gustave-Gaspard Coriolis	French

(*continued*)

Scientific Discoveries (*continued*)

Discovery	Date	Discoverer	Nationality
Cosmic radiation	1911	Victor Hess	Austrian
Decimal fractions	1576	François Viète	French
Dinosaur fossil, first recognized	1822	Mary Ann Mantell	English
Diphtheria bacillus, isolation	1883	Edwin Krebs	US
DNA	1869	Johann Frederick Miescher	Swiss
DNA and RNA	1909	Phoebus Levene	Russian-born US
DNA, double-helix structure	1953	Francis Crick, James Watson	English, US
Doppler effect	1842	Christian Doppler	Austrian
Earth's magnetic pole	1546	Gerardus Mercator	Flemish
Earth's molten core	1916	Albert Michelson	German-born US
Earth's molten core, proof	1906	Richard Oldham	Welsh
Earth's rotation, demonstration	1851	Léon Foucault	French
Eclipse, prediction	585 BC	Thales of Miletus	Greek
Electrolysis, laws	1833	Michael Faraday	English
Electromagnetic induction	1831	Michael Faraday	English
Electromagnetism	1819	Hans Christian Oersted	Danish
Electron	1897	J J Thomson	English
Electroweak unification theory	1967	Sheldon Lee Glashow, Abdus Salam, Steven Weinberg	US, Pakistani, US
Endorphins	1975	John Hughes	US
Enzyme, first animal (pepsin)	1836	Theodor Schwann	German
Enzyme, first (diastase from barley)	1833	Anselme Payen	French
Enzymes, 'lock and key' hypothesis	1899	Emil Fischer	German
Ether, first anaesthetic use	1842	Crawford Long	US
Eustachian tube	1552	Bartolomeo Eustachio	Italian
Evolution by natural selection	1858	Charles Darwin	English
Exclusion principle	1925	Wolfgang Pauli	Austrian-born Swiss
Fallopian tubes	1561	Gabriello Fallopius	Italian
Fluorine, preparation	1886	Henri Moissan	French
Fullerines	1985	Harold Kroto, David Walton	English
Gay-Lussac's law	1808	Joseph-Louis Gay-Lussac	French
Geometry, Euclidean	300 BC	Euclid	Greek
Germanium	1886	Clemens Winkler	German
Germ theory	1861	Louis Pasteur	French
Global temperature and link with atmospheric carbon dioxide	1896	Svante Arrhenius	Swedish
Gravity, laws	1687	Isaac Newton	English
Groups, theory	1829	Evariste Galois	French
Gutenberg discontinuity	1914	Beno Gutenberg	German-born US
Helium, production	1896	William Ramsay	Scottish
Homo erectus	1894	Marie Dubois	Dutch
Homo habilis	1961	Louis Leakey, Mary Leakey	Kenyan/English
Hormones	1902	William Bayliss, Ernest Starling	English
Hubble's law	1929	Edwin Hubble	US
Hydraulics, principles	1642	Blaise Pascal	French
Hydrogen	1766	Henry Cavendish	English
Iapetus	1671	Giovanni Cassini	Italian-born French
Infrared solar rays	1801	William Herschel	German-born English
Insulin, isolation	1921	Frederick Banting, Charles Best	Canadian
Insulin, structure	1969	Dorothy Hodgkin	English
Interference of light	1801	Thomas Young	English
Irrational numbers	450 BC	Hipparcos	Greek
Jupiter's satellites	1610	Galileo	Italian
Kinetic theory of gases	1850	Rudolf Clausius	German
Krypton	1898	William Ramsay, Morris Travers	Scottish, English
Lanthanum	1839	Carl Mosander	Swedish
Lenses, how they work	1039	Ibn al-Haytham Alhazen	Arabic
Light, finite velocity	1675	Ole Römer	Danish
Light, polarization	1678	Christiaan Huygens	Dutch
Linnaean classification system	1735	Linnaeus	Swedish
'Lucy', hominid	1974	Donald Johanson	US
Magnetic dip	1576	Robert Norman	English
Malarial parasite in *Anopheles* mosquito	1897	Ronald Ross	British
Malarial parasite observed	1880	Alphonse Laveran	French
Mars, moons	1877	Asaph Hall	US
Mendelian laws of inheritance	1866	Gregor Mendel	Austrian
Messenger RNA	1960	Sydney Brenner, François Jacob	South African, French
Microorganisms as cause of fermentation	1856	Louis Pasteur	French
Monoclonal antibodies	1975	César Milstein, George Köhler	Argentine-born British, German

(*continued*)

Scientific Discoveries (*continued*)

Discovery	Date	Discoverer	Nationality
Motion, laws	1687	Isaac Newton	English
Natural selection	1859	Charles Darwin	English
Neon	1898	William Ramsay, Morris Travers	Scottish, English
Neptune	1846	Johann Galle	German
Neptunium	1940	Edwin McMillan, Philip Abelson	US
Nerve impulses, electric nature	1771	Luigi Galvani	Italian
Neutron	1932	James Chadwick	English
Nitrogen	1772	Daniel Rutherford	Scottish
Normal distribution curve	1733	Abraham De Moivre	French
Nuclear atom, concept	1911	Ernest Rutherford	New Zealand-born British
Nuclear fission	1938	Otto Hahn, Fritz Strassman	German
Nucleus, plant cell	1831	Robert Brown	Scottish
Ohm's law	1827	Georg Ohm	German
Organic substance, first synthesis (urea)	1828	Friedrich Wöhler	German
Oxygen	1774	Joseph Priestley	English
Oxygen, liquefaction	1894	James Dewar	Scottish
Ozone layer	1913	Charles Fabry	French
Palladium	1803	William Hyde Wollaston	English
Pallas (asteroid)	1802	Heinrich Olbers	German
Pendulum, principle	1581	Galileo	Italian
Penicillin	1928	Alexander Fleming	Scottish
Penicillin, widespread preparation	1940	Ernst Chain, Howard Florey	German, Australian
Pepsin	1836	Theodor Schwann	German
Periodic law for elements	1869	Dmitri Mendeleyev	Russian
Period–luminosity law	1912	Henrietta Swan	US
Phosphorus	1669	Hennig Brand	German
Piezoelectric effect	1880	Pierre Curie	French
Pi meson (particle)	1947	Cecil Powell, Giuseppe Occhialini	English, Italian
Pistils, function	1676	Nehemiah Grew	English
Planetary nebulae	1790	William Herschel	German-born English
Planets, orbiting Sun	1543	Copernicus	Polish
Pluto	1930	Clyde Tombaugh	US
Polarization of light by reflection	1808	Etienne Malus	French
Polio vaccine	1952	Jonas Salk	US
Polonium	1898	Marie and Pierre Curie	French
Positron	1932	Carl Anderson	US
Potassium	1806	Humphry Davy	English
Probability theory	1654	Blaise Pascal, Pierre de Fermat	French
Probability theory, expansion	1812	Pierre Laplace	French
Proton	1914	Ernest Rutherford	New Zealand-born British
Protoplasm	1846	Hugo von Mohl	German
Pulsar	1967	Jocelyn Bell Burnell	Irish
Pythagoras' theorem	550 BC	Pythagoras	Greek
Quantum chromodynamics	1972	Murray Gell-Mann	US
Quantum electrodynamics	1948	Richard Feynman, Seymour Schwinger, Shin'chiro Tomonaga	US, US, Japanese
Quark, first suggested existence	1963	Murray Gell-Mann, George Zweig	US
Quasar	1963	Maarten Schmidt	Dutch-born US
Rabies vaccine	1885	Louis Pasteur	French
Radioactivity	1896	Henri Becquerel	French
Radio emissions, from Milky Way	1931	Karl Jansky	US
Radio waves, production	1887	Heinrich Hertz	German
Radium	1898	Marie and Pierre Curie	French
Radon	1900	Friedrich Dorn	German
Refraction, laws	1621	Willibrord Snell	Dutch
Relativity, general theory	1915	Albert Einstein	German-born US
Relativity, special theory	1905	Albert Einstein	German-born US
Rhesus factor	1940	Karl Landsteiner, Alexander Wiener	Austrian, US
Rubidium	1861	Robert Bunsen	German
Sap circulation	1846	Giovanni Battista Amici	Italian
Sap flow in plants	1733	Stephen Hales	English
Saturn, 18th moon	1990	Mark Showalter	US
Saturn's satellites	1656	Christiaan Huygens	Dutch
Smallpox inoculation	1796	Edward Jenner	English
Sodium	1806	Humphry Davy	English
Stamens, function	1676	Nehemiah Grew	English
Stars, luminosity sequence	1905	Ejnar Hertzsprung	Danish
Stereochemistry, foundation	1848	Louis Pasteur	French

(*continued*)

Scientific Discoveries (*continued*)

Discovery	Date	Discoverer	Nationality
Stratosphere	1902	Léon Teisserenc	French
Sunspots	1611	Galileo, Christoph Scheiner	Italian, German
Superconductivity	1911	Heike Kamerlingh-Onnes	Dutch
Superconductivity, theory	1957	John Bardeen, Leon Cooper, John Schrieffer	US
Thermodynamics, second law	1834	Benoit-Pierre Clapeyron	French
Thermodynamics, third law	1906	Hermann Nernst	German
Thermoelectricity	1821	Thomas Seebeck	German
Thorium-X	1902	Ernest Rutherford, Frederick Soddy	New Zealand-born British, English
Titius–Bode law	1772	Johan Bode, Johann Titius	German
Tranquillizer, first (reserpine)	1956	Robert Woodward	US
Transformer	1831	Michael Faraday	English
Troposphere	1902	Léon Teisserenc	French
Tuberculosis bacillus, isolation	1883	Robert Koch	German
Tuberculosis vaccine	1923	Albert Calmette, Camille Guérin	French
Uranus	1781	William Herschel	German-born English
Urea cycle	1932	Hans Krebs	German
Urease, isolation	1926	James Sumner	US
Urea, synthesis	1828	Friedrich Wöhler	German
Valves, in veins	1603	Geronimo Fabricius	Italian
Van Allen radiation belts	1958	James Van Allen	US
Virus, first identified (tobacco mosaic disease, in tobacco plants)	1898	Martinus Beijerinck	Dutch
Vitamin A, isolation	1913	Elmer McCollum	US
Vitamin A, structure	1931	Paul Karrer	Russian-born Swiss
Vitamin B, composition	1955	Dorothy Hodgkin	English
Vitamin B, isolation	1925	Joseph Goldberger	Austrian-born US
Vitamin C	1928	Charles Glen King, Albert Szent-Györgi	US, Hungarian-born US
Vitamin C, isolation	1932	Charles Glen King	US
Vitamin C, synthesis	1933	Tadeus Reichstein	Polish-born Swiss
Wave mechanics	1926	Erwin Schrödinger	Austrian
Xenon	1898	William Ramsay, Morris Travers	Scottish, English
X-ray crystallography	1912	Max von Laue	German
X-rays	1895	Wilhelm Röntgen	German

Inventions

Invention	Date	Inventor	Nationality
Achromatic lens	1733	Chester Moor Hall	English
Adding machine	1642	Blaise Pascal	French
Aeroplane, powered	1903	Orville and Wilbur Wright	US
Air conditioning	1902	Willis Carrier	US
Air pump	1654	Otto Guericke	German
Airship, first successful	1852	Henri Giffard	French
Airship, rigid	1900	Ferdinand von Zeppelin	German
Amniocentesis test	1952	Douglas Bevis	English
Aqualung	1943	Jacques Cousteau	French
Arc welder	1919	Elihu Thomson	US
Armillary ring	125	Zhang Heng	Chinese
Aspirin	1899	Felix Hoffman	German
Assembly line	1908	Henry Ford	US
Autogiro	1923	Juan de la Cierva	Spanish
Automatic pilot	1912	Elmer Sperry	US
Babbitt metal	1839	Isaac Babbitt	US
Bakelite, first synthetic plastic	1909	Leo Baekeland	US
Ballpoint pen	1938	Lazlo Biró	Hungarian
Barbed wire	1874	Joseph Glidden	US
Bar code system	1970	Monarch Marking, Plessey Telecommunications	US, English
Barometer	1642	Evangelista Torricelli	Italian
Bathysphere	1934	Charles Beebe	US
Bessemer process	1856	Henry Bessemer	British
Bicycle	1839	Kirkpatrick Macmillan	Scottish
Bifocal spectacles	1784	Benjamin Franklin	US
Binary calculator	1938	Konrad Zuse	German
Bottling machine	1895	Michael Owens	US
Braille	1837	Louis Braille	French
Bunsen burner	1850	Robert Bunsen	German
Calculator, pocket	1971	Texas Instruments	US
Camera film (roll)	1888	George Eastman	US
Camera obscura	1560	Battista Porta	Italian
Carbon fibre	1963	Leslie Phillips	English
Carbon-zinc battery	1841	Robert Bunsen	German
Carburettor	1893	Wilhelm Maybach	German
Car, four-wheeled	1887	Gottlieb Daimler	German
Car, petrol-driven	1885	Karl Benz	German
Carpet sweeper	1876	Melville Bissell	US
Cash register	1879	James Ritty	US
Cassette tape	1963	Philips	Dutch
Catapult	c. 400 BC	Dionysius of Syracuse	Greek
Cathode ray oscilloscope	1897	Karl Braun	German
CD-ROM	1984	Sony, Fujitsu, Philips	Japanese, Japanese, Dutch

(*continued*)

Inventions (*continued*)

Invention	Date	Inventor	Nationality
Cellophane	1908	Jacques Brandenberger	Swiss
Celluloid	1869	John Wesley Hyatt	US
Cement, Portland	1824	Joseph Aspidin	English
Centigrade scale	1742	Anders Celsius	Swedish
Chemical symbols	1811	Jöns Jakob Berzelius	Swedish
Chronometer, accurate	1762	John Harrison	English
Cinematograph	1895	Auguste and Louis Lumière	French
Clock, pendulum	1656	Christiaan Huygens	Dutch
Colt revolver	1835	Samuel Colt	US
Compact disc	1972	RCA	US
Compact disc player	1984	Sony, Philips	Japanese, Dutch
Compass, simple	1088	Shen Kua	Chinese
Computer, bubble memory	1967	A H Bobeck and Bell Telephone Laboratories team	US
Computer, first commercially available (UNIVAC 1)	1951	John Mauchly, John Eckert	US
Computerized axial tomography (CAT) scanning	1972	Godfrey Hounsfield	English
Contraceptive pill	1954	Gregory Pincus	US
Cotton gin	1793	Eli Whitney	US
Cream separator	1878	Carl de Laval	Swedish
Crookes tube	1878	William Crookes	English
Cyclotron	1931	Ernest O Lawrence	US
DDT	1940	Paul Müller	Swiss
Diesel engine	1892	Rudolf Diesel	German
Difference engine (early computer)	1822	Charles Babbage	English
Diode valve	1904	Ambrose Fleming	English
Dynamite	1866	Alfred Nobel	Swedish
Dynamo	1831	Michael Faraday	English
Electric cell	1800	Alessandro Volta	Italian
Electric fan	1882	Schuyler Wheeler	US
Electric generator, first commercial	1867	Zénobe Théophile Gramme	French
Electric light bulb	1879	Thomas Edison	US
Electric motor	1821	Michael Faraday	English
Electric motor, alternating current	1888	Nikola Tesla	Croatian-born US
Electrocardiography	1903	Willem Einthoven	Dutch
Electroencephalography	1929	Hans Berger	German
Electromagnet	1824	William Sturgeon	English
Electron microscope	1933	Ernst Ruska	German
Electrophoresis	1930	Arne Tiselius	Swedish
Fahrenheit scale	1714	Gabriel Fahrenheit	Polish-born Dutch
Felt-tip pen	1955	Esterbrook	English
Floppy disk	1970	IBM	US
Flying shuttle	1733	John Kay	English
FORTRAN	1956	John Backus, IBM	US
Fractal images	1962	Benoit Mandelbrot	Polish-born French
Frozen food	1929	Clarence Birdseye	US
Fuel cell	1839	William Grove	Welsh
Galvanometer	1820	Johann Schwiegger	German
Gas mantle	1885	Carl Welsbach	Austrian
Geiger counter	1908	Hans Geiger, Ernest Rutherford	German, New Zealand-born British
Genetic fingerprinting	1985	Alec Jeffreys	British
Glider	1877	Otto Lilienthal	German
Gramophone	1877	Thomas Edison	US
Gramophone (flat discs)	1887	Emile Berliner	German
Gyrocompass	1911	Elmer Sperry	US
Gyroscope	1852	Jean Foucault	French
Heart, artificial	1982	Robert Jarvik	US
Heart-lung machine	1953	John Gibbon	US
Helicopter	1939	Igor Sikorsky	US
Holography	1947	Dennis Gabor	Hungarian-born British
Hovercraft	1955	Christopher Cockerell	English
Hydrogen bomb	1952	US government scientists	US
Hydrometer	1675	Robert Boyle	Irish
Iconoscope	1923	Vladimir Zworykin	Russian-born US
Integrated circuit	1958	Jack Kilby, Texas Instruments	US
Internal-combustion engine, four-stroke	1877	Nikolaus Otto	German
Internal-combustion engine, gas-fuelled	1860	Etienne Lenoir	Belgian
In vitro fertilization	1969	Robert Edwards	Welsh
Jet engine	1930	Frank Whittle	English
Jumbo jet	1969	Joe Sutherland, Boeing team	US
Laser, prototype	1960	Theodore Maiman	US
Lightning rod	1752	Benjamin Franklin	US
Linoleum	1860	Frederick Walton	English
Liquid crystal display (LCD)	1971	Hoffmann-LaRoche Laboratories	Swiss
Lock (canal)	980	Ciao Wei-yo	Chinese
Lock, Yale	1851	Linus Yale	US
Logarithms	1614	John Napier	Scottish
Loom, power	1785	Edmund Cartwright	English
Machine gun	1862	Richard Gatling	US
Magnifying glass	1250	Roger Bacon	English
Map	c. 510 BC	Hecataeus	Greek
Map, star	c. 350 BC	Eudoxus	Greek
Maser	1953	Charles Townes, Arthur Schawlow	US
Mass-spectrograph	1918	Francis Aston	English
Microscope	1590	Zacharias Janssen	Dutch
Miners' safety lamp	1813	Humphry Davy	English
Mohs' scale for mineral hardness	1822	Frederick Mohs	German
Morse code	1838	Samuel Morse	US
Motorcycle	1885	Gottlieb Daimler	German
Neutron bomb	1977	US military	US
Nylon	1934	Wallace Carothers	US
Paper chromatography	1944	Archer Martin, Richard Synge	English
Paper, first	105	Ts'ai Lun	Chinese
Particle accelerator	1932	John Cockcroft, Ernest Walton	English, Irish
Pasteurization (wine)	1864	Louis Pasteur	French
Pen, fountain	1884	Lewis Waterman	US
Photoelectric cell	1904	Johann Elster	German
Photograph, first colour	1881	Frederic Ives	US
Photograph, first (on a metal plate)	1827	Joseph Niepce	French
Piano	1704	Bartelommeo Cristofori	Italian
Planar transistor	1959	Robert Noyce	US
Plastic, first (Parkesine)	1862	Alexander Parkes	English
Plough, cast iron	1785	Robert Ransome	English
Punched-card system for carpet-making loom	1805	Joseph-Marie Jacquard	French
Radar, first practical equipment	1935	Robert Watson-Watt	Scottish
Radio	1901	Guglielmo Marconi	Italian
Radio interferometer	1955	Martin Ryle	English

(*continued*)

Inventions (*continued*)

Invention	Date	Inventor	Nationality
Radio, transistor	1952	Sony	Japanese
Razor, disposable safety	1895	King Gillette	US
Recombinant DNA, technique	1973	Stanley Cohen, Herbert Boyer	US
Refrigerator, domestic	1918	Nathaniel Wales, E J Copeland	US
Richter scale	1935	Charles Richter	US
Road locomotive, steam	1801	Richard Trevithick	English
Road vehicle, first self-propelled (steam)	1769	Nicolas-Joseph Cugnot	French
Rocket, powered by petrol and liquid oxygen	1926	Robert Goddard	US
Rubber, synthetic	1909	Karl Hoffman	German
Scanning tunnelling microscope	1980	Heinrich Rohrer, Gerd Binning	Swiss, German
Seed drill	1701	Jethro Tull	English
Seismograph	1880	John Milne	English
Shrapnel shell	1784	Henry Shrapnel	English
Silicon transistor	1954	Gordon Teal	US
Silk, method of producing artificial	1887	Hilaire, Comte de Chardonnet	French
Spinning frame	1769	Richard Arkwright	English
Spinning jenny	1764	James Hargreaves	English
Spinning mule	1779	Samuel Crompton	English
Stainless steel	1913	Harry Brearley	English
Steam engine	50 BC	Hero of Alexandria	Greek
Steam engine, first successful	1712	Thomas Newcomen	English
Steam engine, improved	1765	James Watt	Scottish
Steam locomotive, first effective	1814	George Stephenson	English
Steam turbine, first practical	1884	Charles Parsons	English
Steel, open-hearth production	1864	William Siemens, Pierre Emile Martin	German, French
Submarine	1620	Cornelius Drebbel	Dutch
Superheterodyne radio receiver	1918	Edwin Armstrong	US
Tank	1914	Ernest Swinton	English
Telephone	1876	Alexander Graham Bell	Scottish-born US
Telescope, binocular	1608	Johann Lippershey	Dutch
Telescope, reflecting	1668	Isaac Newton	English
Television	1926	John Logie Baird	Scottish
Terylene (synthetic fibre)	1941	John Whinfield, J T Dickson	English
Thermometer	1607	Galileo	Italian
Thermometer, alcohol	1730	Réné Antoine Ferchault de Réaumur	French
Thermometer, mercury	1714	Gabriel Fahrenheit	Polish-born Dutch
TNT	1863	J Willbrand	German
Toaster, pop-up	1926	Charles Strite	US
Toilet, flushing	1778	Joseph Bramah	English
Transistor	1948	John Bardeen, Walter Brattain, William Shockley	US
Triode valve	1906	Lee De Forest	US
Tunnel diode	1957	Leo Esaki, Sony	Japanese
Tupperware	1944	Earl Tupper	US
Type, movable earthenware	1045	Pi Shêng	Chinese
Type, movable metal	1440	Johannes Gutenberg	German
Ultrasound, first use in obstetrics	1958	Ian Donald	Scottish
Velcro	1948	Georges de Mestral	Swiss
Video, home	1975	Matsushita, JVC, Sony	Japanese
Viscose	1892	Charles Cross	English
Vulcanization of rubber	1839	Charles Goodyear	US
Wind tunnel	1932	Ford Motor Company	US
Wireless telegraphy	1895	Guglielmo Marconi	Italian
Word processor	1965	IBM	US
Zinc-carbon battery	1868	George Leclanché	French
Zip	1891	Whitcombe Judson	US

Gene Technology

The Human Genome Project

By Tom Wilkie

In the spring of 2000, biologists in the UK and the USA will finish writing what is arguably the most important story in human history. At the dawn of the new millennium, all the secrets of human heredity will be published on the Internet – the results of an international scientific collaboration known as the Human Genome Project.

Simply speaking, the human genome is the collection of all human genes. Its exact composition and sequence has been a challenge for science worldwide; for the past decade in particular, in laboratories around the world scientists have been sifting through human DNA – the chemical messenger of inheritance – to analyse the set of biological instructions for building and maintaining human beings. It is expected that about 90 percent of the first working draft of the human genome will be complete in 2000.

The key to the message of heredity

The instructions for making a human being reside in 80,000 to 100,000 genes (no-one yet knows the exact number). They are encoded in a sequence of about three billion chemical 'letters' that make up the DNA every human being inherits. James Watson and Francis Crick discovered in 1953 that DNA lies coiled as a double helix (resembling a spiral staircase) inside the cells of living organisms. Four different chemicals can act as the 'rungs' winding up inside and linking together the two spirals of the double helix. Their initials form the letters of the genetic code: C; G; A; or T. The

(*continued*)

(continued)

sequence in which these letters are repeated is the key to the message of heredity. And once the sequence is completely decoded, an even greater task will face the scientific community. Researchers will have to work out which parts of the sequence truly are genes, which parts are 'control regions' that determine when a gene is switched on or off, and which parts are simply redundant 'junk'. (Some estimate that as much as 90 percent of human DNA might be meaningless junk.)

Sometimes there are mistakes – mutations and errors as the DNA replicates itself. More than 4,000 disorders known to date result from defects in individual genes; sometimes just one wrong letter out of the three billion is enough to cause a disorder. Most of these genetic disorders cause great suffering and early death. Many of these 'mistakes' go unnoticed, however, as they occur not in the genes themselves but in other parts of the DNA sequence, the 'junk'. Overall, though, one of the greatest hopes for the genome project is that eventually, by understanding what each gene does, we will be able to prevent or alleviate immense human suffering.

Genes active from conception to death

DNA does not act directly: each gene contains a recipe which the body's cells read to make a protein and it is the proteins which do the work of building, repairing, and maintaining the human body. The genes are active throughout life from the moment of conception to death. For example, red cells in our blood have a lifetime of only 120 days and need to be replenished constantly. Several genes act together to provide the instructions for making haemoglobin, the oxygen-carrying molecule that gives blood its characteristic red colour. Haemoglobin is just one of the proteins in red blood cells and the corresponding globin genes are constantly active. Similarly, the enzymes that we need to digest our food are encoded in our DNA and every mealtime the body reads the recipes and starts producing the relevant chemicals as required.

Many diseases may prove to have a genetic component even though they are not inherited.

It is this constant activity of the genes through life that makes the Genome Project so significant. Many diseases may prove to have a genetic component even though they are not inherited. Very few forms of cancer are inherited, for example: most arise from environmental damage sustained long after a child is born and usually after he/she is fully grown. But, by looking at the genes of the very few people who have inherited cancers of some sort, it might be possible to get a clue to what is going wrong not only in the inherited but also in the 'sporadic' cancers. Alternatively, by examining the DNA of tumour cells and comparing it to the DNA sequence of normal cells, researchers may find the damage that allowed the cancer cells to escape the normal constraints on growth. In this way it might be possible to understand precisely what happens, for example, to the cells lining the lungs of a cigarette smoker when they proliferate out of control to form life-threatening tumours. There is also an association between diet and bowel cancer, and DNA analysis might reveal how the environmental damage which results in cancer is caused. Nor are the applications confined to cancer: much of cardiovascular disease too may be further explained using the DNA type of approach.

Private companies have been attracted by the potential profits to be made from understanding human genetic data. In May 1998, Perkin-Elmer, the company manufacturing the automated sequencing machines used in the genome project, announced that it was teaming up with an individual scientist, Dr Craig Venter, to form a company to sequence the human genome privately. This raised the prospect that the human genome might not become public knowledge, but be appropriated as the private intellectual property of the new company, Celera. If the private collaboration should, indeed, succeed in identifying and patenting human genes then this would be the latest in a highly controversial series of attempts to patent and exploit commercially human DNA.

Common heritage for all

This news of the private initiative further galvanized the scientists who felt that the Human Genome Project should be openly published for all, as it forms, almost literally, the common heritage of humankind. Most of the sequencing effort is being carried out at three main centres in the USA and one in the UK. Funded by Federal Government money, the Centre for Genome Research at the Whitehead/Massachusetts Institute of Technology, the Washington University School of Medicine in St Louis, Missouri, and Baylor College of Medicine in Houston, Texas, are expected to complete about 60 percent of the sequence. In the UK, a private charity, the Wellcome Trust, is financing the Sanger Centre at Hinxton, just outside Cambridge, to complete one third of the sequence. An institute run by the US Department of Energy will be responsible for the rest.

When the Genome Project was launched, the completion date was set for 30 September 2006. Now, the long slow slog to sequence the genome has turned into a race. With the announcement in March 1999 that about 90 percent of the first public draft would be available the following year, it looks as if the knowledge of the human heredity will indeed stay in the public domain. But the first draft will not be precise enough to satisfy the scientists, so they intend to spend a further three years going back over their work to checking what they have done and ensure that it is accurate to one part in 100,000.

The Human Genome Project will not, therefore, transform the world overnight. But its impact will grow rather than diminish in the early years of the next century. It is realistic to expect that medicine will be transformed as never before. More far-reaching still will be the changes in humanity's understanding of its biological self and its essential make-up.

Tom Wilkie is head of biomedical ethics at the Wellcome Trust. This article represents the author's personal views and does not reflect in any way the policy or position of the Wellcome Trust.

Genetics: Chronology

1856 Austrian monk and botanist Gregor Mendel begins experiments breeding peas that will lead him to the laws of heredity.

1865 Gregor Mendel publishes a paper in the *Proceedings of the Natural Science Society of Brünn* that outlines the fundamental laws of heredity.

1869 Swiss biochemist Johann Miescher discovers a nitrogen and phosphorous material in cell nuclei that he calls nuclein but which is now known as the genetic material DNA.

1888 Dutch geneticist Hugo Marie de Vries uses the term 'mutation' to describe varieties that arise spontaneously in cultivated primroses.

1902 US geneticist Walter Sutton and German zoologist Theodor Boveri find the chromosomal theory of inheritance when they show that cell division is connected with heredity.

1906 English biologist William Bateson introduces the term 'genetics'.

1910 US geneticist Thomas Hunt Morgan discovers that certain inherited characteristics of the fruit fly *Drosophila melanogaster* are sex linked. He later argues that because all sex-related characteristics are inherited together they are linearly arranged on the X chromosome.

1934 Norwegian biochemist Asbjrn Fölling discovers the genetic metabolic defect phenylketonuria, which can cause retardation; his discovery stimulates research in biochemical genetics and the development of screening tests for carriers of deleterious genes.

1944 The role of deoxyribonucleic acid (DNA) in genetic inheritance is first demonstrated by US bacteriologist Oswald Avery, US biologist Colin MacLeod, and US biologist Maclyn McCarthy; it opens the door to the elucidation of the genetic code.

1945 Working in Japan, US geneticist Samuel G Salmon discovers Norin 10, a semidwarf wheat variety which grows quickly, responds well to fertilizer, does not fall over from the weight of the grains, and, when crossed with disease-resistant strains in the USA, results in a wheat strain that increases wheat harvests by more than 60 percent in India and Pakistan.

25 April 1953 English molecular biologist Francis Crick and US biologist James Watson announce the discovery of the double helix structure of DNA, the basic material of heredity. They also theorize that if the strands are separated then each can form the template for the synthesis of an identical DNA molecule. It is perhaps the most important discovery in biology.

1954 Russian-born US cosmologist George Gamow suggests that the genetic code consists of the order of nucleotide triplets in the DNA molecule.

1958 US geneticists George Beadle, Edward Tatum, and Joshua Lederberg share the Nobel Prize for Physiology or Medicine: Beadle and Tatum for their discovery that genes act by regulating definite chemical events; and Lederberg for his discoveries concerning genetic recombination.

1961 French biochemists François Jacob and Jacques Monod discover messenger ribonucleic acid (mRNA), which transfers genetic information to the ribosomes, where proteins are synthesized.

1967 US scientist Charles Caskey and associates demonstrate that identical forms of messenger RNA produce the same amino acids in a variety of living beings, showing that the genetic code is common to all life forms.

1967 US biochemist Marshall Nirenberg establishes that mammals, amphibians, and bacteria all share a common genetic code.

October 1968 US geneticists Mark Ptashne and Walter Gilbert separately identify the first repressor genes.

1969 US geneticist Jonathan Beckwith and associates at Harvard Medical School isolate a single gene for the first time.

1969 The Nobel Prize for Physiology or Medicine is awarded jointly to US physiologists Max Delbrück, Alfred Hershey, and Salvador Luria for their discoveries concerning the replication mechanism and genetic structure of viruses.

1970 US geneticist Hamilton Smith discovers type II restriction enzyme that breaks the DNA strand at predictable places, making it an invaluable tool in recombinant DNA technology.

1970 US biochemists Howard Temin and David Baltimore separately discover the enzyme reverse transcriptase, which allows some cancer viruses to transfer their RNA to the DNA of their hosts turning them cancerous – a reversal of the common pattern in which genetic information always passes from DNA to RNA.

1972 US microbiologist Daniel Nathans uses a restriction enzyme that splits DNA molecules to produce a genetic map of the monkey virus (SV40), the simplest virus known to produce cancer; it is the first application of these enzymes to an understanding of the molecular basis of cancer.

1972 Venezuelan-born US immunologist Baruj Benacerraf and Hugh O'Neill McDevitt show immune response to be genetically determined.

1973 US biochemists Stanley Cohen and Herbert Boyer develop the technique of recombinant DNA. Strands of DNA are cut by restriction enzymes from one species and then inserted into the DNA of another; this marks the beginning of genetic engineering.

1975 The gel-transfer hybridization technique for the detection of specific DNA sequences is developed; it is a key development in genetic engineering.

1976 US biochemist Herbert Boyer and venture capitalist Robert Swanson found Genentech in San Francisco, California, the world's first genetic engineering company.

28 August 1976 Indian-born US biochemist Har Gobind Khorana and his colleagues announce the construction of the first artificial gene to function naturally when inserted into a bacterial cell. This is a major breakthrough in genetic engineering.

1977 US scientist Herbert Boyer, of the firm Genentech, fuses a segment of human DNA into the bacterium *Escherichia coli* which begins to produce the human protein somatostatin; this is the first commercially produced genetically engineered product.

1980 A new vaccine for the prevention of hepatitis B is tested in the USA. It is the first genetically engineered vaccine and has a success rate of 92 percent. It wins Federal Drug Administration approval in 1986.

16 June 1980 The US Supreme Court rules that a microbe created by genetic engineering can be patented.

1981 The US Food and Drug Administration grants permission to Eli Lilley and Co to market insulin produced by bacteria, the first genetically engineered product to go on sale.

1981 The genetic code for the hepatitis B surface antigen is discovered, creating the possibility of a bioengineered vaccine.

1981 US geneticists Robert Weinberg, Geoffrey Cooper, and Michael Wigler discover that oncogenes (genes that cause cancer) are integrated into the genome of normal cells.

(continued)

Genetics: Chronology (*continued*)

1982	Using genetically engineered bacteria, the Swedish firm Kabivitrum manufactures human growth hormone.
1983	Geneticist James Gusella identifies the gene for Huntington's disease.
1984	British geneticist Alec Jeffreys discovers that a core sequence of DNA is almost unique to each person; this examination of DNA, known as 'genetic fingerprinting', can be used in criminal investigations and to establish family relationships.
1986	The US Department of Agriculture permits the Biological Corporation of Omaha to market a virus produced by genetic engineering; it is the first living genetically altered organism to be sold. The virus is used against a form of swine herpes.
1986	The US Department of Agriculture permits the first outdoor test of genetically altered high-yield plants (tobacco plants).
1987	German-born British geneticist Walter Bodmer and associates announce the discovery of a marker for a gene that causes cancer of the colon.
1987	The first genetically altered bacteria are released into the environment in the USA; they protect crops against frost.
1987	Foxes in Belgium are immunized against rabies by using bait containing a genetically engineered vaccine, dropped from helicopters. The success of the experiment leads to a large-scale vaccination programme.
April 1987	The US Patent and Trademark Office announces its intention to allow the patenting of animals produced by genetic engineering.
10 October 1987	The *New York Times* announces Dr Helen Donis-Keller's mapping of all 23 pairs of human chromosomes, allowing the location of specific genes for the prevention and treatment of genetic disorders.
April 1988	The US Patent and Trademark Office grants Harvard University a patent for a mouse developed by genetic engineering.
1989	Scientists in Britain introduce genetically engineered white blood cells into cancer patients, to attack tumours.
1991	British geneticists Peter Goodfellow and Robin Lovell-Badge discover the gene on the Y chromosome that determines sex.
1992	The US biotechnology company Agracetus patents transgenic cotton, which has had a foreign gene added to it by genetic engineering.
1992	US biologist Philip Leder receives a patent for the first genetically engineered animal, the oncomouse, which is sensitive to carcinogens.
1993	US geneticist Dean Hammer and colleagues at the US National Cancer Institute publish the approximate location of a gene that could predispose human males to homosexuality.
1994	Trials using transfusions of artificial blood begin in the USA. The blood contains genetically engineered haemoglobin.
February 1994	The US Food and Drug Administration approves the use of genetically engineered bovine somatotropin (BST), which increases a cow's milk yield by 10–40 percent. It is banned in Europe.
May 1994	The first genetically engineered food goes on sale in California and Chicago, Illinois. The 'Flavr Savr' tomato is produced by the US biotechnology company Calgene.
1995	A genetically engineered potato is developed that contains the gene for Bt toxin, a natural pesticide produced by a soil bacterium. The potato plant produces Bt within its leaves.
1995	US embryologists Edward Lewis and Eric Wieschaus and German embryologist Christiane Nüsslein-Volhard are jointly awarded the Nobel Prize for Physiology or Medicine for their discoveries concerning the genetic control of early embryonic development.
1995	Australian geneticists produce a genetically engineered variety of cotton that contains a gene from a soil bacteria that kills the cotton bollworm and native budworm.
1995	Trials begin in the USA to treat breast cancer by gene therapy. The women are injected with a virus genetically engineered to destroy their tumours.
April 1995	US surgeons report the successful transplant of genetically altered hearts of pigs into baboons, a notable advance in trans-species operations.
July 1995	The US government approves experimentation of genetically altered animal organs in humans.
August 1995	The US Environmental Protection Agency approves the sale of genetically modified maize, which contains a gene from a soil bacterium that produces a toxin fatal to the European corn borer, a pest that causes approximately $1 billion damages annually.
January 1996	The first genetically engineered salmon are hatched, at Loch Fyne in Scotland. The salmon contain genes from the ocean pout as well as a salmon growth hormone gene that causes them to grow five times as fast as other salmon.
9 May 1996	Scientists at the National Institute of Allergy and Infectious Disease discover a protein, fusin, which allows the HIV virus to fuse with a human immune system cell's outer membrane and inject genetic material. Its presence is necessary for the AIDS virus to enter the cell.
August 1996	US geneticists clone two rhesus monkeys from embryo cells.
27 February 1997	Scottish researcher Ian Wilmut of the Roslin Institute in Edinburgh, Scotland, announces that British geneticists have cloned an adult sheep. A cell was taken from the udder of the mother sheep and its DNA combined with an unfertilized egg that had had its DNA removed. The fused cells were grown in the laboratory and then implanted into the uterus of a surrogate mother sheep. The resulting lamb, Dolly, came from an animal that was six years old. This is the first time cloning has been achieved using cells other than reproductive cells. The news is met with international calls to prevent the cloning of humans.
February 1997	US genetic scientist Don Wolf announces the production of monkeys cloned from embryos. It is a step closer to cloning humans and raises acute philosophical issues.
16 May 1997	US geneticists identify a gene clock in chromosome 5 in mice that regulates the circadian rhythm.
3 June 1997	US geneticist Huntington F Wilard constructs the first artificial human chromosome. He inserts telomeres (which consist of DNA and protein on the tips of chromosomes) and centromeres (specialized regions of DNA within a chromosome) removed from white blood cells into human cancer cells which are then assembled into chromosomes which are about one-tenth the size of normal chromosomes. The artificial chromosome is successfully passed on to all daughter cells.
11 June 1997	English behavioural scientist David Skuse claims that boys and girls differ genetically in the way they acquire social skills. Girls acquire social skills intuitively and are 'pre-programmed', while boys have to be taught. This has important implications for education.

(*continued*)

Genetics: Chronology (*continued*)

August 1997 US geneticist Craig Venter and colleagues publish the genome of the bacterium *Helicobacter pylori*, a bacterium that infects half the world's population and which is the leading cause of stomach ulcers. It is the sixth bacterium to have its genome published, but is the most clinically important. It has 1,603 putative genes, encoded in a single circular chromosome that is 1,667,867 nucleotide base-pairs of DNA long. Complete genomes are increasingly being published as gene-sequencing techniques improve.

18 September 1997 US geneticist Bert Vogelstein and colleagues demonstrate that the p53 gene, which is activated by the presence of carcinogens, induces cells to commit suicide by stimulating them to produce large quantities of poisonous chemicals, called 'reactive oxygen species' (ROS). The cells literally poison themselves. It is perhaps the human body's most effective way of combating cancer. Many cancers consist of cells with a malfunctioning p53 gene.

November 1997 The US Food and Drug Administration (FDA) approves Rituxan, the first anticancer monoclonal antibody made from genetically engineered mouse antibodies. The antibody binds itself to non-Hodgkin's lymphoma (a cancer of the lymph system) cancer cells and triggers the immune system to kill the cells.

October 1998 US scientist French Anderson announces a technique that could cure inherited diseases by inserting a healthy gene to replace a damaged one. He calls for a full debate on the issue of gene therapy, which brings with it the dilemma of whether it is ethical to enable the choice of physical attributes such as eye colour and height.

8 December 1998 The Human Fertilization and Embryology Authority and the Human Genetics Advisory Commission publish a joint report in the UK on cloning. While they oppose cloning for reproductive purposes, they leave the door open for cloning for curing intractable diseases.

10 December 1998 In a joint effort by scientists around the world, the first genetic blueprint for a whole multicellular animal is completed. The 97 million-letter code, which is published on the Internet, is for a tiny worm called *C. elegans*. The study began 15 years ago and cost £30 million.

24 January 1999 US scientist Craig Venter of the Institute for Genomic Research in Maryland announces the possibility of creating a living, replicating organism from an artificial set of genes, at a meeting of the American Association for the Advancement of Science, in Anaheim, California. The experiment is put on hold until the moral question is discussed by religious leaders and ethicists at the University of Pennsylvania.

April 1999 European Union legislation is implemented in the UK, requiring that some foods containing GM protein or DNA be labelled in restaurants and food shops.

18 May 1999 A group of scientists at a specially convened Royal Society meeting finds that the experiments of Hungarian-born doctor Arpad Pusztai on genetically modified foods were 'fundamentally flawed'. In August 1998, Pusztai claimed that his experiments demonstrated that genetically modified potatoes stunted the growth of laboratory rats, strengthening public opinion in the UK against genetically modified foods.

2000 First working draft of the Human Genome Project, which maps the composition and sequence of all human genes, is due to be released.

Genetically Modified Foods

BY TIM ALLMAN

Modifying the genetic composition of crop plants or farm animals by selective breeding has been an important part of agriculture for thousands of years. However, the modern technology of genetic engineering has massively increased the scope for changing the characteristics of crops and livestock.

This direct modification of an organism's genetic material (genome) bypasses conventional breeding methods, producing totally novel genetic combinations which could never occur in nature. Artificial transfer between completely unrelated organisms is possible, because the genetic material in all organisms is made from DNA.

How does it work?

Genetic modification usually involves identifying the genes governing a desirable characteristic in one organism, and inserting them into another in the expectation that the trait will be transferred. For example, a gene from certain bacteria, which causes their production of the toxin Bt, has been inserted into a wide variety of crop plants, including cotton, apple and maize. Transformed plants produce Bt in their tissues, and are therefore less palatable to insect pests.

Once the section of DNA containing the relevant gene has been identified, it is cut from the genome of the donor organism using specific enzymes, creating free fragments of the desired DNA. The standard method for inserting these fragments into another genome, first achieved in 1973, involves using another organism as a vector.

Vectors are able to carry DNA into the host cell, and integrate it into the host's DNA. A bacterial plasmid (circles of DNA independent of the main bacterial chromosome) or a virus can be harnessed as a vector, because either may integrate into a foreign genome during their normal infective process. Therefore, the genetic engineer splices the desired gene into the chosen vector, and allows the modified plasmid or virus to integrate into the host genome, taking the extra gene. The vector is usually 'tagged' with a marker gene, such as one conferring antibiotic resistance, so that successfully transformed cells can be identified.

A newer technique for gene insertion is the use of DNA bullets. Microscopic metal beads can be coated with DNA fragments, and then 'fired' from a miniature gun into the host cell, where the DNA may integrate into the genome. Genes conferring virus resistance have been introduced into rice plants by this method.

(*continued*)

(continued)

Cheaper production and greater yield ...

The dramatic, rapid changes made possible by genetic engineering have a vast range of potential applications in the development of new foodstuffs. Genetically modified (GM) crops may offer farmers greater yields, pest and disease resistance, and tolerance to temperature extremes, drought, or salinity. Plants engineered to be resistant to general herbicides are easier and cheaper to farm, as a whole field can be sprayed with the herbicide, killing all plants except the resistant crop. Agricultural improvements such as these aim for greater efficiency of production, which may be increasingly important as food supplies come under greater pressure due to global population growth.

To the consumer, genetically modified crops can offer enhanced nutritional qualities, such as a lower fat content, or increased levels of vitamins. Improved flavour, appearance, and longer shelf-life are other objectives. There is also the prospect of plants engineered to contain specific ingredients of medical benefit, such as vaccines.

... but at what cost?

However, some scientists have expressed concern about the risks of genetically engineered foodstuffs. There is evidence that GM crops can cross-pollinate with their wild relatives, introducing novel genetic combinations into the wider environment. This may have unknown ecological effects; for instance, some suggest that it could lead to the creation of 'superweeds', where weed plants acquire traits such as herbicide resistance from GM crops, or it could detrimentally affect the life cycles of insect pollinators.

It is still not possible to predict every effect of inserting a gene, nor its long-term stability.

The introduction of GM organisms into the human food chain may also have unpredictable health effects. For example, there are fears that the widespread use of antibiotic-resistant vectors may allow the development of new lines of bacterial pathogens with antibiotic resistance.

Risks such as these illustrate that genetic engineering is often not as precise a technology as may be assumed. Although the ability to isolate and transfer specific genes is an impressive feat, it is still not possible to predict exactly every effect of inserting a gene, nor its long-term stability in the genome. The actual extent of such potential problems should become clearer with time, and after more research.

On the shelves, behind the scenes

There are several GM foodstuffs on the market, ranging from tomatoes to salmon. Not all are sold in all countries; the US currently has the largest number on sale. The most important modified foods are soya and maize. About 30 percent (21 million tonnes) of the 1998 US soya harvest was from modified plants, as was some 20 percent (40 million tonnes) of the total US maize crop. These GM crops are usually mixed with normal crops after harvest for use as ingredients in a wide range of processed foods.

Additionally, GM foods can be found as agents in the food production process, rather than as foodstuffs in their own right. Examples include GM chymosin, used to make vegetarian cheese, and artificial bovine somatotropin (BST), a version of a cattle hormone synthesized by GM bacteria, which can be injected into cows to boost milk yields.

There are a great many more GM crops and types of livestock under development. Research is subject to a variety of legislation, particularly concerning the release of modified organisms into the environment or food chain. For example, only government-licensed trial plots of GM crops are currently permitted in the UK, although commercial-scale growing is likely to be approved in the near future. All foods produced using GM undergo legal scrutiny and testing before approval.

Additionally, EU legislation implemented in the UK in April 1999 requires that some foods containing GM protein or DNA be labelled in restaurants and food shops. However, GM labelling is likely to be a topic of much legal debate, facing problems such as the increasing use of mixed GM/non-GM ingredients (like soya).

Public fears and corporate control

Public opinion on GM foods is mixed, and there is a general uncertainty about the potential impacts of the technology. Some people hold ethical or religious objections to the very idea of manipulating the basis of inheritance, especially where animals are involved. Public concern about possible health risks has made genetic modification an important public health issue in Europe and North America. Resistance to transgenic plants increased in Britain in 1998, leading to activists destroying crops at many separate sites and the formation of numerous local groups to protest against genetic engineering within food and agriculture.

There are also fears about the power of large biotechnology corporations to control agricultural markets. For example, some crops have been engineered to produce sterile seeds, forcing farmers to buy new seed every year; other herbicide-resistant strains are produced by the companies that manufacture the particular herbicide, making farmers dependent on buying more and more of one type of herbicide. This is a particular concern to rural economies in poorer nations, where there is scepticism about the potential of GM to ameliorate the world's food crisis. Such controversies have sparked unrest, such as the burning of GM cotton crops by protesting peasant farmers in India.

It seems certain that GM foods, and modern biotechnology in general, will continue to attract controversy. It remains to be seen to what extent genetic engineering will gain acceptance and become a commonplace technology. It is sure to be the subject of one of the most urgent debates about the relationship between science and society as we enter the 21st century.

Tim Allman is a writer on agriculture and technology

Astronomy

The Planets

(– = not applicable.)

Planet	Main constituents	Atmosphere	Average distance from the Sun km (millions)	mi (millions)	Orbital period (Earth yrs)	Diameter km (thousands)	mi (thousands)	Average density (water = 1 unit)
Mercury	rock, ferrous	–	58	36	0.241	4.88	3.03	5.4
Venus	rock, ferrous	carbon dioxide	108	67	0.615	12.10	7.51	5.2
Earth	rock, ferrous	nitrogen, oxygen	150	93	1.00	12.76	7.92	5.5
Mars	rock	carbon dioxide	228	141	1.88	6.78	4.21	3.9
Jupiter	liquid hydrogen, helium	–	778	483	11.86	142.80	88.73	1.3
Saturn	hydrogen, helium	–	1,427	886	29.46	120.00	74.56	0.7
Uranus	ice, hydrogen, helium	hydrogen, helium	2,870	1,783	84.00	50.80	31.56	1.3
Neptune	ice, hydrogen, helium	hydrogen, helium	4,497	2,794	164.80	48.60	30.20	1.6
Pluto	ice, rock	methane	5,900	3,666	248.50	2.27	1.41	~2

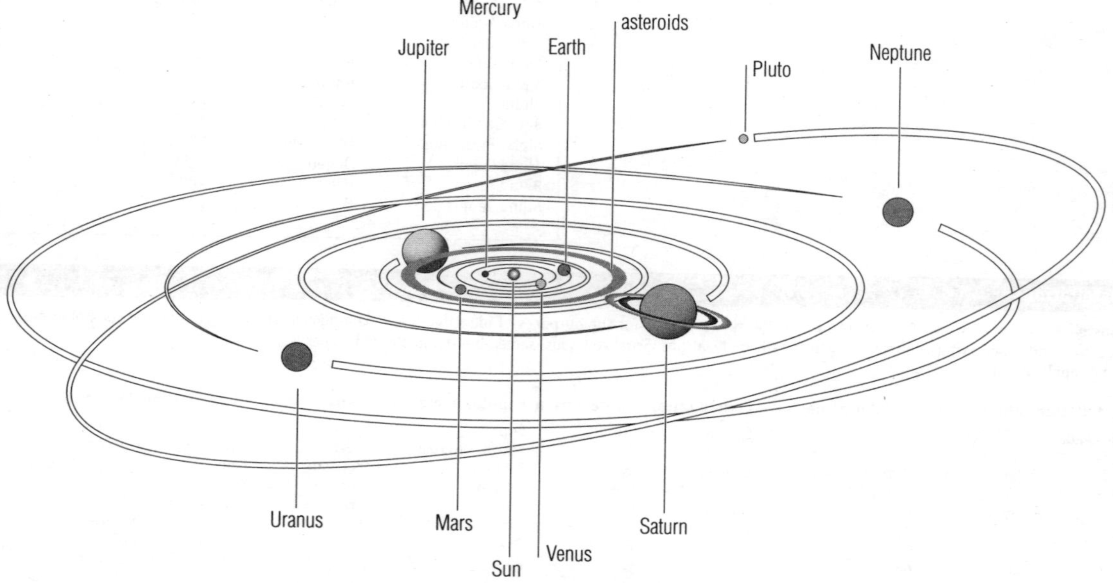

Solar System *The planets in the Solar System are tiny compared to the Sun. If the Sun were the size of a basketball, the planet closest to the Sun, Mercury, would be the size of a mustard seed and would be 15 m/48 ft from the Sun. The most distant planet, Pluto, would be a pinhead 1.6 km/1 mi away from the Sun. The Earth, which is the third planet out from the Sun, would be the size of a pea 32 m/100 ft from the Sun.*

Largest Natural Planetary Satellites

	Planet	Diameter km	mi	Mean distance from centre of primary planet km	mi	Orbital period (Earth days)
Ganymede	Jupiter	5,262	3,300	1,070,000	664,898	7.16
Titan	Saturn	5,150	3,200	1,221,800	759,226	15.95
Callisto	Jupiter	4,800	3,000	1,883,000	1,170,096	16.69
Io	Jupiter	3,630	2,240	421,600	261,982	1.77
Moon	Earth	3,476	2,160	384,400	238,866	27.32
Europa	Jupiter	3,138	1,900	670,900	416,897	3.55
Triton	Neptune	2,700	1,690	354,300	220,162	5.88

The Largest Asteroids

An asteroid is a small body, composed of rock and iron, that orbits the Sun. Most lie in a belt between the orbits of Mars and Jupiter, and are thought to be fragments left over from the formation of the Solar System.

Name	Diameter km	Diameter mi	Average distance from Sun (Earth = 1)	Orbital period (years)
Ceres	940	584	2.77	4.6
Pallas	588	365	2.77	4.6
Vesta	576	358	2.36	3.6
Hygeia	430	267	3.13	5.5
Interamnia	338	210	3.06	5.4
Davida	324	201	3.18	5.7

The Brightest Stars

A star's brightness is referred to as its 'magnitude'. 'Apparent magnitude' is brightness as seen from Earth. 'Absolute magnitude' is measured at a standard distance of 32.6 light years or 10 parsecs from the star.
In October 1997 astronomers at the University of California identified the biggest and brightest star in the universe so far and named it the Pistol Star. The star was detected using NASA's Hubble Space Telescope. Its distance from the Earth is yet to be determined, although its diameter is estimated as 4 light years.

Scientific name	Common name	Distance from Earth (light years)
Alpha Canis Majoris	Sirius	9
Alpha Carinae	Canopus	1,170
Alpha Centauri	Rigil Kent	4
Alpha Boötis	Arcturus	36
Alpha Lyrae	Vega	26
Alpha Aurigae	Capella	42
Beta Orionis	Rigel	910
Alpha Canis Minoris	Procyon	11
Alpha Eridani	Achernar	85
Alpha Orionis	Betelgeuse	310
Beta Centauri	Hadar	460
Alpha Aquilae	Altair	17
Alpha Tauri	Aldebaran	25
Alpha Crucis	Acrux	360
Alpha Scorpii	Antares	330
Alpha Virginis	Spica	260
Beta Geminorum	Pollux	36
Alpha Piscis Austrini	Fomalhaut	22
Alpha Cygni	Deneb	1,830
Beta Crucis	Mimosa	420
Alpha Leonis	Regulus	85

Constellations

A constellation is one of the 88 areas into which the sky is divided for the purposes of identifying and naming celestial objects. The first constellations were simple, arbitrary patterns of stars in which early civilizations visualized gods, sacred beasts, and mythical heroes.
(– = not applicable.)

Constellation	Abbreviation	Popular name
Andromeda	And	–
Antlia	Ant	Airpump
Apus	Aps	Bird of Paradise
Aquarius	Aqr	Water-bearer
Aquila	Aqi	Eagle
Ara	Ara	Altar
Aries	Ari	Ram
Auriga	Aur	Charioteer
Boötes	Boo	Herdsman
Caelum	Cae	Chisel
Camelopardalis	Cam	Giraffe
Cancer	Cnc	Crab
Canes Venatici	CVn	Hunting Dogs
Canis Major	CMa	Great Dog
Canis Minor	CMi	Little Dog
Capricornus	Cap	Sea-goat
Carina	Car	Keel
Cassiopeia	Cas	–
Centaurus	Cen	Centaur
Cepheus	Cep	–
Cetus	Cet	Whale
Chamaeleon	Cha	Chameleon
Circinus	Cir	Compasses
Columba	Col	Dove
Coma Berenices	Com	Berenice's Hair
Corona Australis	CrA	Southern Crown
Corona Borealis	CrB	Northern Crown
Corvus	Crv	Crow
Crater	Crt	Cup
Crux	Cru	Southern Cross
Cygnus	Cyn	Swan
Delphinus	Del	Dolphin
Dorado	Dor	Goldfish
Draco	Dra	Dragon
Equuleus	Equ	Foal
Eridanus	Eri	River
Fornax	For	Furnace
Gemini	Gem	Twins
Grus	Gru	Crane
Hercules	Her	–
Horologium	Hor	Clock
Hydra	Hya	Watersnake
Hydrus	Hyi	Little Snake
Indus	Ind	Indian
Lacerta	Lac	Lizard
Leo	Leo	Lion
Leo Minor	LMi	Little Lion
Lepus	Lep	Hare
Libra	Lib	Balance
Lupus	Lup	Wolf
Lynx	Lyn	–
Lyra	Lyr	Lyre
Mensa	Men	Table
Microscopium	Mic	Microscope
Monoceros	Mon	Unicorn
Musca	Mus	Southern Fly
Norma	Nor	Rule
Octans	Oct	Octant
Ophiuchus	Oph	Serpent-bearer
Orion	Ori	–
Pavo	Pav	Peacock
Pegasus	Peg	Flying Horse
Perseus	Per	–
Phoenix	Phe	Phoenix
Pictor	Pic	Painter
Pisces	Psc	Fishes
Piscis Austrinus	PsA	Southern Fish
Puppis	Pup	Poop
Pyxis	Pyx	Compass
Reticulum	Ret	Net
Sagitta	Sge	Arrow
Sagittarius	Sgr	Archer
Scorpius	Sco	Scorpion
Sculptor	Scl	–
Scutum	Sct	Shield
Serpens	Ser	Serpent
Sextans	Sex	Sextant
Taurus	Tau	Bull
Telescopium	Tel	Telescope
Triangulum	Tri	Triangle
Triangulum Australe	TrA	Southern Triangle
Tucana	Tuc	Toucan
Ursa Major	UMa	Great Bear
Ursa Minor	UMi	Little Bear
Vela	Vel	Sails
Virgo	Vir	Virgin
Volans	Vol	Flying Fish
Vulpecula	Vul	Fox

Some Major Comets

A comet is a small, icy body orbiting the Sun, usually on a highly elliptical path. Comets consist of a central nucleus a few kilometres across, and are often likened to dirty snowballs because they consist mostly of ice mixed with dust.
(– = not applicable.)

Name	First recorded sighting	Orbital period (yrs)	Interesting facts
Halley's comet	240 BC	76	parent of Eta Aquarid and Orionid meteor showers
Comet Tempel-Tuttle	AD 1366	33	parent of Leonid meteors
Biela's comet	1772	6.6	broke in half in 1846; not seen since 1852
Encke's comet	1786	3.3	parent of Taurid meteors
Comet Swift-Tuttle	1862	130	parent of Perseid meteors; reappeared 1992
Comet Ikeya-Seki	1965	880	so-called 'Sun-grazing' comet, passed 500,000 km/300,000 mi above surface of the Sun on 21 October 1965
Comet Kohoutek	1973	–	observed from space by *Skylab* astronauts
Comet West	1975	500,000	nucleus broke into four parts
Comet Bowell	1980	–	ejected from Solar System after close encounter with Jupiter
Comet IRAS-Araki-Alcock	1983	–	passed only 4.5 million km/2.8 million mi from the Earth on 11 May 1983
Comet Austin	1989	–	passed 32 million km/20 million mi from the Earth in 1990
Comet Shoemaker-Levy 9	1993	–	made up of 21 fragments; crashed into Jupiter in July 1994
Comet Hale-Bopp	1995	1,000	spitting out of gas and debris produced a coma, a surrounding hazy cloud of gas and dust, of greater volume than the Sun; the bright coma is due to an outgassing of carbon monoxide; clearly visible with the naked eye in March 1997
Comet Hyakutake	1996	–	passed 15 million km/9.3 million mi from the Earth in 1996

Phases of the Moon 2000

Phases of the Moon shown to the nearest hour with timings given in Greenwich Mean Time (GMT).

New moon

Month	Day	Time
January	6	18:14
February	5	13:03
March	6	05:17
April	4	18:12
May	4	04:12
June	2	12:14
July	1	19:20
July	31	02:25
August	29	10:19
September	27	19:53
October	27	07:58
November	25	23:11
December	25	17:22

First quarter

Month	Day	Time
January	14	13:34
February	12	23:21
March	13	06:59
April	11	13:30
May	10	20:00
June	9	03:29
July	8	12:53
August	7	01:02
September	5	16:27
October	5	10:59
November	4	07:27
December	4	03:55

Full moon

Month	Day	Time
January	21	04:40
February	19	16:27
March	20	04:44
April	18	17:41
May	18	07:34
June	16	22:27
July	16	13:55
August	15	05:13
September	13	19:37
October	13	08:53
November	11	21:15
December	11	09:03

Last quarter

Month	Day	Time
January	28	07:57
February	27	03:53
March	28	00:21
April	26	19:30
May	26	11:55
June	25	01:00
July	24	11:02
August	22	18:51
September	21	01:28
October	20	07:59
November	18	15:24
December	18	00: 41

Astronomical Constants

Constant	Value
Astronomical unit (au)	149,597,870 km
Speed of light in a vacuum (*c*)	299,792.458 km/sec
Solar parallax	8.794148 arc seconds
Mass of the Sun	1.9891×10^{30} kg
Mass of the Earth	5.9742×10^{24} kg
Mass of the Moon	7.3483×10^{22} kg

Constant	Value
Light year (ly)	9.4605×10^{12} km (or 0.30660 pc)
Parsec (pc)	30.857×10^{12} km (or 3.26161 ly)
Obliquity of the elliptic (2000)	23° 26′ 21.448′
General precession (2000)	50.290966 arc seconds/year
Constant of nutation (2000)	9.2025 arc seconds
Constant of aberration (2000)	20.49552 arc seconds

Solar and Lunar Eclipses

This table does not include partial eclipses of the Moon.

Month	Day	Type of eclipse	Duration of maximum eclipse	Region for observation
2000				
January	21	lunar total	4 hr 44 min	the Americas, Europe, Africa, western Asia
February	5	solar partial	12 hr 50 min	Antarctica
July	1	solar partial	19 hr 34 min	southeastern Pacific Ocean
July	16	lunar total	13 hr 56 min	southeastern Asia, Australasia
July	31	solar partial	2 hr 14 min	Arctic regions
December	25	solar partial	17 hr 36 min	USA, eastern Canada, Central America, Caribbean
2001				
January	9	lunar total	20 hr 21 min	Africa, Europe, Asia
June	21	solar total	12 hr 4 min	central and southern Africa
December	14	solar annular	20 hr 52 min	Pacific Ocean
2002				
June	10	solar annular	23 hr 44 min	Pacific Ocean
December	4	solar total	7 hr 31 min	southern Africa, Indian Ocean, Australia
2003				
May	16	lunar total	3 hr 40 min	the Americas, eastern and western Africa
May	31	solar annular	4 hr 8 min	Iceland, Greenland
November	9	lunar total	1 hr 18 min	the Americas, Africa, Europe
November	23	solar total	22 hr 49 min	Antarctica

Space Flight

Successful Satellite Launches

As of January 1999.

Country	Launch site	First success date	Number of successes 1957–98
Russia/CIS	Tyuratam (Baikonur), Kazakhstan	4 October 1957	1,031
	Kapustin Yar, Russia	16 March 1962	83
	Plesetsk, Russia	17 March 1966	1,462
	Svobodny, Russia	8 March 1997	2
USA	Cape Canaveral (Eastern Test Range) and Kennedy Space Center	1 February 1958	590
	Vandenberg AFB (Western Test Range)	28 February 1959	557
	Wallops Island	16 February 1961	35
	US operated air-launch	5 April 1990	21
France	Hammaguir	26 November 1965 (closed since April 1967)	4
USA/Italy	Indian Ocean Platform (San Marco)	26 April 1967	9
Australia/UK	Woomera	29 November 1967 (closed since 1976)	2
Japan	Uchinoura (Kagoshima)	11 February 1970	23
	Tanegashima (Osaki)	9 September 1975	31
France/Europe	Kourou	10 March 1970	119
China	Jiuquan	24 April 1970	23
	Xichang	29 January 1984	25
	Taiyuan	6 September 1988	12
India	Sriharikota	18 July 1980	8
Israel	Palmachim	19 September 1988	3

A Year in Space: 1998–99

By Tim Furniss

1998 ended with a beginning. At last the International Space Station (ISS) (a collaboration between the USA, Russia, Europe, Japan, Canada, and Brazil) project got underway six years late, with a new completion date of 2004. In November, Russia launched the first element, a control module called *Zarya* and the following month, the US space shuttle *Endeavour* was launched to link to *Zarya* a node attachment module called *Unity*. More ISS modules will eventually be able to dock to *Unity*'s several ports. Unfortunately, ISS delays continued, especially with the late delivery of a Russian service module called *Zvezda* which all but stopped the ISS before it had started. *Zvezda* will not now be launched until November 1999 and the first resident crew (two Russians and an American) cannot hope to be on board the ISS until at least March 2000.

In the meantime, however, another US space shuttle, *Discovery*, was launched in May 1999 to equip the ISS with over two tonnes of cargo to make it ready for the first resident crew. *The Discovery* mission was the first by a space shuttle in 1999.

The Russian *Mir* space station programme continued. The final crew was launched to operate on the old space base until possibly August when the station is to be abandoned. Russia says it will be de-orbited in March 2000 if no private funds can be found to keep it operational. Among the last to leave *Mir* will be cosmonaut Sergei Avdeyev, who was launched to *Mir* in August 1998, with over 360 days space experience already under his belt. When he lands, he will become the space record holder with over 700 days of spaceflight.

Failures

The serious launch failures of two US rockets in 1998, followed by the loss of four satellites in four US launches in April–May1999, created great concern about the reliability of US rockets. Disasters included the upper stages of two *Titan 4B* boosters failing, stranding their military payloads. This meant that, counting a failure in 1998, three *Titan 4s* had failed in succession. A *Delta III* failure stranded a civil communications satellite in orbit. The stranding of the *Orion 3* satellite in useless orbit followed the loss of *Galaxy X* last year when the first *Delta III* failed. This has been a major setback to Boeing's plans to operate the *Delta III* commercially. A smaller USA Lockheed *Athena 2* booster also failed to place a commercial remote sensing satellite into orbit and the loss of the *Ikonos 1* craft was a blow to the Space Imaging company led by Lockheed Martin.

At the same time, several communications satellites failed or malfunctioned in orbit, creating concern over quality control. Some of these satellites were USA Motorola Iridium craft launched into a large orbital constellation (fleet of satellites) to provide worldwide mobile cellular phone communications. The Iridium dream faded, however, when a lack of demand and the delayed production of handsets, which were heavier and more expensive than anticipated, created severe financial problems for the company. Despite this, two rival systems, Globalstar and ICO went ahead with plans to launch similar systems. By May 1999 there were already 20 Globalstars in orbit. Twelve of the Globalstars had been launched by a new commercial organization called Starsem, which operates the Russian Soyuz booster with the help of European companies.

Successes

A new satellite launcher, *Sea Launch*, made its debut on 28 March. *Sea Launch* is a Ukrainian *Zenit 2* booster, with a Russian upper stage taken from the Proton launcher. The Sea Launch organization is headed by the US Boeing company. The booster took off from an offshore platform located on the equator in the mid-Pacific Ocean. It placed a demonstration communications satellite to geostationary transfer orbit, the staging post to equatorial geostationary orbit. Launching from the equator gives a booster an advantage and saves fuel, because the rocket flies directly into an equatorial orbit rather than having to make a ‘dog leg’ manoeuvre in flight. The weight saving allows the payload to be heavier.

In March 1999, a potential new low-cost, reusable, single-stage-to-orbit launch vehicle, was unveiled. Called *Roton*, the US privately operated vehicle, which uses a helicopter rotor system for landing, may be launching people into space on brief sightseeing trips within three or four years – demonstration test flight, technology and money permitting.

Continued exploration of the Solar System

NASA continued its assault on Mars with the launch of the Mars Climate Observer (MCO) in December 1998 and the Mars Polar Lander (MPL) in January 1999. MCO is planned to enter Mars orbit in September 1999, while the MPL will touch down near the Martian south pole in December 1999. If the spectacular pictures already being sent back by an earlier spacecraft, the Mars Global Surveyor, are anything to go by, the images returned by the MPL should be exciting.

NASA's attempt to orbit an asteroid did not go as planned in January, however. The Near Earth Asteroid Rendezvous (NEAR) spacecraft made a fly-by but did not orbit due to engine malfunctions; but it is hoped that another attempt to orbit the asteroid Eros can be made by NEAR in May 2000. NASA's *Stardust* spacecraft was launched successfully on 7 February en route for a rendezvous with the comet Wild 2 in January 2004. Using an instrument rather like fly paper, it will collect comet dust and hopefully return it to the Earth for analysis in January 2006. Another NASA spacecraft, called *Deep Space 1*, which was launched in October 1998, became the first craft to operate remotely by using an onboard artificial intelligence system, for a brief period in May 1999. The system, called the Remote Agent, is the forerunner of units that will control spacecraft on voyages deep into the Solar System, just like HAL from the 1968 film *2001: A Space Odyssey*.

Tim Furness is the spaceflight correspondent for Flight International.

Space Probes: Recent Chronology

8 February 1992 *Ulysses* flies past Jupiter at a distance of 380,000 km/236,000 mi from the surface, just inside the orbit of Io and closer than 11 of Jupiter's 16 moons.

10 July 1992 *Giotto* (USA) flies at a speed of 14 kms/8.5 mps to within 200 km/124 mi of comet Grigg-Skellerup, 12 light years (240 million km/150 mi) away from Earth.

25 September 1992 *Mars Observer* (USA) is launched from Cape Canaveral, the first US mission to Mars for 17 years.

10 October 1992 *Pioneer-Venus 1* burns up in the atmosphere of Venus.

21 August 1993 *Mars Observer* disappears three days before it is due to drop into orbit around Mars.

28 August 1993 *Galileo* flies past the asteroid Ida.

December 1995 *Galileo*'s probe enters the atmosphere of Jupiter. It radios information back to the orbiter for 57 min before it is destroyed by atmospheric pressure.

1996 NASA's Near Earth Asteroid Rendezvous (NEAR) is launched to study Eros.

4 July 1997 The US spacecraft *Mars Pathfinder* lands on Mars. Two days later the probe's rover *Sojourner*, a six-wheeled vehicle controlled by an Earth-based operator, begins to explore the area around the spacecraft.

15 October 1997 The *Cassini* space probe to Saturn lifts off. When it reaches Saturn in 2004, it will be the first craft to orbit the planet. On board is the European Space Agency's probe *Huygens*, which will be the first to land on the moon of an outer planet in the solar system when it touches down on the surface of Saturn's largest moon, Titan.

1997 The US space probe *Galileo* begins orbiting Jupiter's moons. It takes photographs of Europa for a potential future landing site, and detects molecules containing carbon and nitrogen on Callisto, suggesting that life once existed there.

1997 The US Near Earth Asteroid Rendezvous (NEAR) spacecraft flies within 1,200 km/746 mi of the asteroid Mathilde, taking high-resolution photographs and revealing a 25-km/15.5-mi crater covering the 53-km/33-mi asteroid.

1997 The US spacecraft *Mars Global Surveyor* goes into orbit around Mars to conduct a detailed photographic survey of the planet, commencing in March 1998, and reports the discovery of bacteria there.

2 July 1998 US scientists report that the spacecraft *Galileo* has discovered 12 different vents on Jupiter's moon Io, which spew lava at temperatures greater than any planetary body in the solar system – up to 1,175°C/3,100°F. The temperatures are caused by changes in the moon's shape as it orbits Jupiter.

7 July 1998 Two Japanese satellites, using sensors and lasers, perform the first automatic docking between space vehicles.

7 July 1998 In the first launch of its kind, a Russian nuclear submarine in the Barents Sea fires a commercial satellite into space. This important innovation will allow launches to be made from any latitude on Earth and will increase the range of satellites' orbits.

1998 The US probe *Lunar Prospector* is launched to go into low orbits around the Moon and transmit data on the composition of its crust, record gamma rays, and map its magnetic field. The satellite detects 11 million tonnes of water on the Moon in the form of ice.

1998 Analysis of high resolution images from the *Galileo* spacecraft suggests that the icy crust of Europa, Jupiter's fourth largest moon, may hide a vast ocean warm enough to support life.

January 1999 As part of the Deep Space 2 mission, the *Mars Polar Lander* craft lifts off to investigate the surface of Mars. It is projected to arrive near the south pole of the planet in December 1999, where it will release twin probes – the first to dig deep beneath the surface of another planet.

7 February 1999 The *Stardust* probe is launched to rendezvous with the comet P/Wild 2 in December 2003 and bring back to Earth material from around it, along with samples of interstellar dust.

May–June 1999 The Venus Multi-Probe mission is launched. Its purpose is to deliver 16 small probes into the atmosphere of Venus to make measurements of temperature and pressure.

August 1999 Researchers into the phenomenon of the solar wind send the *Suess–Urey* (or 'Genesis') probe to collect and return samples.

August–September 1999 After a delayed launch from earlier in the year, the Japanese *Lunar-A* probe is launched to monitor moonquakes and study the interior structure and geothermal properties of the moon.

Recent Crewed Space Flights

Launch date	Spacecraft	Crew	Duration	Remarks
3 February 1995	*Discovery* STS 63	James Wetherbee, Eileen Collins, Michael Foale, Bernard Harris, Janice Ford, Vladimir Titov	8 days 6 hr 28 min	*Spacelab* science rendezvous mission with *Mir* space station and spacewalk – first by British-born astronaut, Foale; Collins first female Shuttle pilot; Titov from Russia
14 March 1995	*Soyuz* TM21	Vladimir Dezhurov, Gennady Strekalov, Norman Thagard	115 days 8 hr 44 min	mission to *Mir 1* with first US astronaut to ride a Russian rocket; record 13 people in space at same time on 14–18 March; crew landed in STS 71
27 June 1995	*Atlantis* STS 71	Robert Gibson, Charles Precourt, Ellen Baker, Bonnie Dundar, Gregory Harbaugh, Anatoli Solovyov, Nikolai Budarin	9 days 19 hr 23 min	100th US crewed flight including Thagard's *Soyuz* TM21 launch; Shuttle/*Mir 1* mission 1; 5 days joined to *Mir*; delivered Solovyov and Budarin and returned with the TM21 crew; first time ten people on board one spacecraft (223 tonnes) in orbit
12 November 1995	*Atlantis* STS 74	Ken Cameron, James Halsall, Jerry Ross, Bill McArthur, Chris Hadfield	8 days 4 hr 30 min	Shuttle/*Mir* mission 2; carried docking module to be left at *Mir;* Hadfield NASA mission specialist from Canada

(continued)

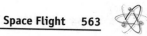

Recent Crewed Space Flights (*continued*)

Launch date	Spacecraft	Crew	Duration	Remarks
22 February 1996	*Columbia* STS 75	Andrew Allen, Scott Horowitz, Maurizio Cheli, Claude Nicollier, Jeff Hoffman, Franklin Chang-Diaz, Umberto Guidoni	15 days 17 hr 40 min	tethered satellite system reflight, satellite lost when tether broke; 12 people, five nations (two from Italy) in space with TM22 and TM23 crews also orbiting
22 March 1996	*Atlantis* STS 76	Kevin Chilton, Richard Searfoss, Ronald Sega, Ric hr Clifford, Linda Godwin, Shannon Lucid	9 days 5 hr 15 min	Shuttle/*Mir* mission 3, delivered Shannon Lucid for extended stay on *Mir;* returned 26 September aboard STS 79; after stay of 188 days, a record for a woman
20 June 1996	*Columbia* STS 78	Tom Henricks, Kevin Kregal, Susan Helms, Charles Brady, Richard Linnehan, Jean-Jaques Favier, Robert Thirsk	16 days 21 hr 47 min	*Spacelab* Life and Microgravity science mission; Favier from France, Thirsk from Canada
17 August 1996	*Soyuz* TM24	Valeri Korzun, Alexander Kaleri, Claudie Andre-Deshays	196 days 16 hr 26 min	new crew for *Mir 1* with Deshays, the first French woman in space, as commercial crew-person on 15-day flight, landing in TM23; Korzun and Kaleri first back-up crew to fly since *Soyuz* 11 in 1971 after prime commander Gennady Manakov hospitalized (if one crew member unable to fly, back-up crew takes over) with heart attack
17 September 1996	*Atlantis* STS 79	William Readdy, Terence Wilcutt, Tom Akers, Jerome Apt, Carl Waltz, John Blaha	10 days 13 hr 18 min	Shuttle/*Mir* mission 4, delivered John Blaha and returned Shannon Lucid from *Mir*
19 November 1996	*Columbia* STS 80	Ken Cockrell, Kent Rominger, Tamara Jernigan, Thomas Jones, Story Musgrave	17 days 15 hr 53 min	Musgrave oldest person in space at 61, flying longest Shuttle mission
12 January 1997	*Atlantis* STS 81	Mike Baker, Brent Jett, John Grunsfield, Jeff Wisoff, Marsha Ivins, Jerry Linenger	10 days 4 hr 55 min	Shuttle/*Mir* mission 5, delivered Jerry Linenger and returned John Blaha from *Mir* after 128 days; Linneger made first US–Russian spacewalk with Tsiblyev, wearing Russian spacesuit
10 February 1997	*Soyuz* TM25	Vasili Tsiblyev, Alexander Lazutkin, Reinhold Ewald	184 days 22 hr 7 min	new crew for *Mir* with German Ewald flying shorter commercial mission; this crew experienced a fire on the space station and a collision with the *Progress* M34 supply ship
11 February 1997	*Discovery* STS 82	Ken Bowersox, Scott Horowitz, Steven Hawley, Mark Lee, Joe Tanner, Greg Harbaugh, Steve Smith	9 days 23 hr 37 min	second mission to service the Hubble Space Telescope; featured five spacewalks
15 May 1997	*Atlantis* STS 84	Charles Precourt, Eileen Collins, Carlos Noregia, Jean Francois Clervoy, Ed Lu, Michael Foale, Yelena Kondakova	9 days 5 hr 19 min	Shuttle/*Mir* mission 6, delivered Michael Foale and returned Jerry Linenger after 132 days; crew the most cosmopolitan in history: Precourt and Collins from USA, Noregia born in Chile, Clervoy from France, Lu born of Chinese parents, Foale British-born, Kondakova from Russia
5 August 1997	*Soyuz* TM26	Anatoli Solovyov, Pavel Vinogradev	197 days 17 hr 31 min in flight	200th launched crewed spaceflight in history; new crew to *Mir* to carry out major repair work to the damaged space station
26 September 1997	*Atlantis* STS 86	James Wetherbee, Mike Bloomfield, Scott Parazinsky, Vladimir Titov, Jean-Loup Chretien, Wendy Lawrence, David Wolf	10 days 19 hr 20 min	Shuttle/*Mir* mission 7, delivered David Wolf and returned Michael Foale after 144 days; featured spacewalk by Parazinsky and Titov – the first Russian to wear US EVA suit
23 January 1998	*Endeavour* STS 89	Terence Willcutt, Joe Frank Edwards, Bonnie Dunbar, Michael Anderson, James Reilly, Andrew Thomas	8 days 19 hr 46 min	Shuttle/*Mir* mission 8, returned David Wolf (with flight time of 127 days) and delivered Andrew Thomas
29 January 1998	*Soyuz* TM27	Talgat Musabeyev, Nikolai Budarin, Leopold Eyharts	205 days 3 hr 36 min	new crew for *Mir* plus French astronaut Eyharts; it was hoped that TM27 would dock while *Endeavour* was still in place, resulting in a record-breaking onboard crew of 13, but the plan was vetoed by French authorities

(*continued*)

Recent Crewed Space Flights (*continued*)

Launch date	Spacecraft	Crew	Duration	Remarks
17 April 1998	*Columbia* STS 90	Rick Searfoss, Scott Altman, Richard Linnehan, Kathryn Hire, Dave Williams, Jay Buckey, Jim Pawelczyk	15 days 21 hr 15 min	final scheduled *Spacelab* mission, carrying out experiments on the neurological effects of microgravity
2 June 1998	*Discovery* STS 91	Charlie Precourt, Dom Gorie, Wendy Lawrence, Franklin Chang-Díaz, Janet Kavandi, Valeri Ryumin	9 days 19 hr 55 min	final Shuttle–*Mir* mission, delivering Russian space chief Ryumin and returning with Andrew Thomas, who had spent 130 days on *Mir*
13 August 1998	*Soyuz* TM28	Gennadi Padalka, Sergei Avdeyev, Yuri Baturin	199 days	delivered new crew for *Mir* (Baturin returned with TM27); on 4 February the crew attempted to unfurl a 25-m/82-ft foil mirror, Znamya 2.5, which would be used to reflect sunlight onto Arctic cities during the dark winter months, but the mirror became entangled and torn and was finally allowed to fall back to Earth
29 October 1998	*Discovery* STS 95	Curt Brown, Steven Lindsey, Stephen Robinson, Scott Parazynski, Pedro Duque, Chiaki Mukai, John Glenn	8 days 21 hr 50 min	US senator Glenn became, at 77, the world's oldest astronaut, returning to space after 36 years to take part in experiments on the process of ageing; the crew also included the first Spanish astronaut, Duque
4 December 1998	*Endeavour* STS 88	Bob Cabana, Rick Stuckow, Jerry Ross, Nancy Currie, Jim Newman, Sergei Krikalyov	11 days 18 hr 14 min	first International Space Station (ISS) assembly mission; the US *Unity* module was attached to the Russian-built *Zarya* control module, already in orbit, to form the foundation for future ISS components
20 February 1999	*Soyuz* TM29	Viktor Afanasyev, Jean-Pierre Haigne, Ivan Bella	in flight	probably the last mission to *Mir;* the crew was expected to remain there until August 1999, when existing funding for the space station runs out (Slovak astronaut Bella returned with TM28)
23 July 1999	*Columbia* STS 93	Eileen Collins, Jeffrey Ashby, Steven Mawley, Catherine Coleman, Michel Tognini	5 days	launched Chandra X-ray observatory; Eileen Collins is the first woman to command a space shuttle flight

The Most Space Flights

As of March 1999.

Number of flights	Name	Country	Number of flights	Name	Country
Men			*Women*		
6	Franklin Chang-Díaz	USA	5	Bonnie Dunbar	USA
	Story Musgrave	USA		Shannon Lucid	USA
	Jerry Ross	USA			
	Gennady Strekalov	USSR/ Russia/ CIS			
	John Young	USA			

The Longest Spacewalks

As of March 1999.

Duration	Name(s)	Country	Mission	Spacecraft	Date
8 hr 29 min	Tom Akers, Rick Hieb, Pierre Thuot	USA	Earth orbit	Space Shuttle *Endeavour* STS 49	13 May 1992
7 hr 54 min	Jeff Hoffman, Story Musgrave	USA	Earth orbit	Space Shuttle *Endeavour* STS 61	12 May 1993
7 hr 45 min	Tom Akers, Kathryn Thornton	USA	Earth orbit	Space Shuttle *Endeavour* STS 49	14 May 1992
7 hr 43 min	Takao Doi, Winston Scott	USA	Earth orbit	Space Shuttle *Columbia* STS 87	24 November 1997
7 hr 37 min	Eugene Cernan, Jack Schmitt	USA	Moon landing	*Apollo 17*	12 December 1972
7 hr 37 min	Jim Newman, Jerry Ross	USA	Earth orbit	Space Shuttle *Endeavour* STS 88	7 December 1998
7 hr 28 min	Gregory Harbaugh, Joe Tanner	USA	Earth orbit	Space Shuttle *Discovery* STS 82	14 February 1997

Selected Forthcoming Missions of the European Space Agency

Proposed date	Mission	Remarks
January 2000	XMM	X-ray multi-mirror mission; a satellite for observations at X-ray wavelengths
2000	Cluster II	four identical satellites designed to provide the first three-dimensional images of events in the Earth's space environment
2001	Integral	international gamma-ray laboratory; a satellite for observations at gamma-ray wavelengths
late 2001	Smart-1	experimental space probe; the first European project to demonstrate solar electric propulsion
2002	Columbus	pressurized laboratory 6.7 m/22 ft long and 4.5 m/15 ft in diameter, to be launched by the Space Shuttle
January 2003	*Rosetta*	space probe to rendezvous with Comet Wirtanen in 2011; *Rosetta* will release two landers which will sample the comet's nucleus
2003	Mars Express	Mars orbiter that will land craft to analyse the surface
2007	FIRST/Planck	far infrared and submillimetric space telescope and cosmic ray observatory combined into one mission

Selected World Space Agencies

Commonwealth of Independent States Some of the countries of the former USSR, particularly Russia, continue to have very active space programmes. Besides Russia, Kazakhstan and the Ukraine are the countries with the most active involvement in space activities. The Russian Space Agency (RKA) was established in 1992. (**Russian Space Agency,** Shchepkin Street 42, 129857 Moscow; phone: +7 095 971 9176; fax: +7 095 975 6936)

Europe Space research and technology in Europe are organized by the European Space Agency (ESA), whose participant countries are Austria, Belgium, Denmark, France, Germany, Ireland, Italy, the Netherlands, Norway, Spain, Sweden, Switzerland, and the UK. It was founded in 1975, with headquarters in Paris. (**European Space Agency,** 8-10 rue Mario-Nikis, 75015 Paris; phone: +33 1 42 73 76 54; fax: +33 1 42 73 75 60)

France France established the French space agency Centre National d'Etudes Spatiales (CNES) in 1961. CNES is responsible for preparing and proposing the long-term objectives of French space activity and for managing the space programmes (both national and international). The government commissioner for CNES is appointed by the Ministry for Research and Space, the authority to which CNES reports. Military programmes are coordinated by the Délégation Générale à l'Armament (DGA) and, more particularly, by the Direction des Missiles et de l'Espace (DME). (**Centre National d'Etudes Spatiales,** 2 place Maurice Quentin, 75039 Paris; phone: +33 1 45 08 75 00; fax: +33 1 45 08 76 76)

Germany Since 1989 German space activities have been coordinated by the Federal Cabinet Committee on Space, chaired by the chancellor. The German space agency, Deutsche Argentur für Raumfahrtangele-genheiten (DARA), was also created in 1989 and concentrates on management tasks related to space technological research and represents Germany on an international level. DARA has represented Germany at ESA since 1989. (**Deutsche Argentur für Raumfahrtangelegenheiten,** Königswinterer Strasse 522-524, 5300 Bonn 3; phone: +49 228 447 0; fax: +49 228 447 700)

Ireland, Republic of Ireland's space activities are coordinated by the Department of Industry and Energy (Direction for Scientific and Technological Affairs). Since 1993 the Forbairt Science and Technology Directorate has been responsible for the formulation of Ireland's space activities, which are focused on the participation in the European Space Agency. (**Forbairt Science and Technology Directorate,** Glasnevin, Dublin 9; phone: +353 1 808 2000; fax: +353 1 808 2587)

Italy The Italian space agency, Agenzia Spaziale Italiana (ASI) was created in 1988. Italian space activities are approved by the International Committee for Economic Planning (CIPE) and coordinated by the Ministry for Scientific and Technological Research (MRST). (**Agenzia Spaziale Italiana,** Via di Villa Patrizi 13, 00161 Rome; phone: +39 6 85 679; fax: +39 6 44 04 212)

UK Funding and implementation of space programmes are ensured by several ministries and institutions, including the Department of Trade and Industry (DTI) and the Ministry of Defence (MOD), and coordinated by the British National Space Centre (BNSC) created in 1985. (**British National Space Centre,** Dean Bradley House, 52 Horseferry Road, London SW1P 2AG; phone: 0171 276 2688; fax: 0171 276 2377)

USA The National Aeronautics and Space Administration (NASA) was established in 1958. It is constitutionally responsible for civil and peaceful activities alone, all military space programmes coming under the aegis of the Department of Defense (DOD). NASA Headquarters exercises management over the Space Flight Centers, Research Centers and other installations that constitute NASA. (**National Aeronautics and Space Administration,** Headquarters, Washington, DC 20546; phone: +1 202 358 0000; fax: +1 202 358 0037)

Computing and Telecommunications

Some Internet Terms

acceptable use set of rules enforced by a service provider or backbone network restricting the use to which their facilities may be put

access provider another term for Internet Service Provider

ack radio-derived term for 'acknowledge', used on the Internet as a brief way of indicating agreement with or receipt of a message or instruction

alt hierarchy 'alternative' set of newsgroups on USENET, set up so that anyone can start a newsgroup on any topic

anonymous remailer service that allows Internet users to post to USENET and send e-mail without revealing their true identity or e-mail address

Archie software tool for locating information on the Internet

bang path list of routing that appears in the header of a message sent across the Internet, showing how it travelled from the sender to its destination

Big Seven hierarchies original seven hierarchies of newsgroups on USENET. They are: **comp.** – computing; **misc.** – miscellaneous; **news.** – newsgroups; **rec.** – recreation; **sci.** – science; **soc.** – social issues; and **talk.** – debate

blocking software any of various software programs that work on the World Wide Web to block access to categories of information considered offensive or dangerous

blue-ribbon campaign campaign for free speech launched to protest against moves towards censorship on the Internet

bookmark facility for marking a specific place in electronic documentation to enable easy return to it. It is used in several types of software, including electronic help files and tutorials. Bookmarks are especially important

on the World Wide Web, where it can be difficult to remember a uniform resource locator (URL) in order to return to it. Most Web browsers therefore have built-in bookmark facilities, whereby the browser stores the URL with the page name attached. To return directly to the site, the user picks the page name from the list of saved bookmarks.

'bot (short for robot) automated piece of software that performs specific tasks on the Internet. 'Bots are commonly found on multi-user dungeons (MUDs) and other multi-user role-playing game sites, where they maintain a constant level of activity even when few human users are logged on

bozo filter facility to eliminate messages from irritating users

browser any program that allows the user to search for and view data; Web browsers allow access to the World Wide Web

bulletin board centre for the electronic storage of messages; bulletin board systems are usually dedicated to specific interest groups, and may carry public and private messages, notices, and programs

cancelbot automated software program that cancels messages on USENET; Cancelbot is activated by the CancelMoose, an anonymous individual who monitors newsgroups for complaints about spamming

chat real-time exchange of messages between users of a particular system. Chat allows people who are geographically far apart to type messages to each other which are sent and received instantly. Users may chat while playing competitive games or while reading messages, as well as joining public or private 'rooms' to talk with a variety of other users.

crawler automated indexing software that scours the Web for new or updated sites

crossposting practice of sending a message to more than one newsgroup on USENET

cybersex online sexual fantasy spun by two or more participants via live, online chat

cyberspace the imaginary, interactive 'worlds' created by networked computers; often used interchangeably with 'virtual world'

cypherpunk passionate believer in the importance of free access to strong encryption on the Internet, in the interests of guarding privacy and free speech

digital city area in cyberspace, either text-based or graphical, that uses the model of a city to make it easy for visitors and residents to find specific types of information

emoticon (contraction of 'emotion' and 'icon') symbol composed of punctuation marks designed to express some form of emotion in the form of a human face. Emoticons were invented by e-mail users to overcome the fact that communication using text only cannot convey nonverbal information (body language or vocal intonation) used in ordinary speech. The following examples should be viewed sideways:

:-) smiling
:-O shouting
:-(glum
8-) wearing glasses and smiling.

e-zine (contraction of **electronic magazine**) periodical sent by e-mail. E-zines can be produced very cheaply as there are no production costs for design and layout, and minimal costs for distribution

FAQ (abbreviation for **frequently asked questions**) file of answers to commonly asked questions on any topic

firewall security system built to block access to a particular computer or network while still allowing some types of data to flow in and out on to the Internet

flame angry public or private electronic mail message used to express disapproval of breaches of netiquette or the voicing of an unpopular opinion

follow-up post publicly posted reply to a USENET message; unlike a personal e-mail reply, follow-up post can be read by anyone

FurryMUCK popular MUD site where the players take on the imaginary shapes and characters of furry, anthropomorphic animals

gateway the point of contact between two wide-area networks

Gopher menu-based server on the Internet that indexes resources and retrieves them according to user choice via any one of several built-in methods such as FTP or Telnet. Gopher servers can also be accessed via the World Wide Web and searched via special servers called Veronicas

Gopherspace name for the knowledge base composed of all the documents indexed on all the Gophers in the world

hit request sent to a file server. Sites on the World Wide Web often measure their popularity in numbers of hits

home page opening page on a particular site on the World Wide Web

hop intermediate stage of the journey taken by a message travelling from one site to another on the Internet

host (or host computer) large computer that supports a number of smaller computers or terminals that are connected to it via a network. Hosts may be mainframe computers that service large number of terminals or green screens, or, for example, Internet hosts that serve Web pages and files to personal computers attached via the Internet.

Acronyms and Abbreviations in Common Use Online

Acronym/ abbreviation	Meaning
AFAICR	As Far As I Can Recall
AFAICT	As Far As I Can Tell
AIUI	As I Understand It
ATM	At The Moment
BTDT	Been There Done That
BTW	By The Way
CUL	See You Later
DQM	Don't Quote Me
DWIM	Do What I Mean
FAQ	Frequently Asked Question
FOAF	Friend Of A Friend
FOC	Free Of Charge
FOCL	Falls Off Chair Laughing
FUD	Fear, Uncertainty, and Doubt
FWIW	For What It's Worth
FYI	For Your Information
IIRC	If I Recall/Remember Correctly
IKWYM	I Know What You Mean
IMO	In My Opinion
IOW	In Other Words
IRL	In Real Life
ISTM	It Seems To Me
ISTR	I Seem To Recall/Remember
IYKWIM	If You Know What I Mean
IYSWIM	If You See What I Mean
LCW	Loud, Confident, and Wrong
LOL	Lots Of Luck/Laughing Out Loud
NAFAIK	Not As Far As I Know
NALOPKT	Not A Lot Of People Know That
NIMBY	Not In My Back Yard
OIC	Oh I See
OLR	Off Line Reader
OTOH	On The Other Hand
OTT	Over The Top
OTTH	On The Third Hand
PIM	Personal Information Manager
PMFJI	Pardon Me For Jumping In
PMJI	Pardon Me Jumping In
POV	Point Of View
ROTFL	Rolling On The Floor Laughing
RSN	Real Soon Now
SO	Significant Other
SOTA	State Of The Art
TIA	Thanks In Anticipation
TIC	Tongue In Cheek
TLA	Three Letter Abbreviation/Acronym
TPTB	The Powers That Be
TTBOMK	To The Best of My Knowledge
TTFN	Ta Ta For Now
TTYL	Talk To You Later
TYVM	Thank You Very Much
UKP	United Kingdom Pounds (sterling)
WRT	With Respect To
WYSIWYG	What You See Is What You Get
YHM	You Have Mail
YKWIM	You Know What I Mean

Number of Hosts on the Internet

Year	Number of hosts
1981	213
1985	1,961
1990	313,000
1991	535,000
1992	992,000
1993	1,776,000
1994	3,212,000
1995	6,642,000
1996	12,881,000
1997	19,540,000
1998	36,739,000

Source: *UK Computer Market 1998*, © Key Note Ltd

HTTP (abbreviation for **Hypertext Transfer Protocol)** protocol used for communications between client (the Web browser) and server on the World Wide Web

hypermedia system that uses links to lead users to related graphics, audio, animation, or video files in the same way that hypertext systems link related pieces of text

in-line graphics images included in Web pages that are displayed automatically by Web browsers without any action required by the user

Internet Relay Chat (IRC) service that allows users connected to the Internet to chat with each other over many channels

Internet Service Provider (ISP) any company that sells dial-up access to the Internet

Jughead (acronym for **Jonzy's Universal Gopher Hierarchy Excavation and Display)** search engine enabling users of the Internet server Gopher to find keywords in Gopherspace directories

killfile file specifying material that you do not wish to see when accessing a newsgroup. By entering names, subjects or phrases into a killfile, users can filter out tedious threads, offensive subject headings, spamming, or contributions from other subscribers

link image or item of text in a World Wide Web document that acts as a route to another Web page or file on the Internet

lurk read a USENET newsgroup without making a contribution

MBONE (contraction of **multicast backbone)** layer of the Internet designed to deliver packets of multimedia data, enabling video and audio communication

MIME (acronym for **Multipurpose Internet Mail Extensions)** standard for transferring multimedia e-mail messages and World Wide Web hypertext documents over the Internet

moderator person or group of people that screens submissions to certain newsgroups and mailing lists before passing them on for wider circulation

MUD (acronym for **multi-user dungeon)** interactive multi-player game, played via the Internet or modem connection to one of the participating computers. MUD players typically have to solve puzzles, avoid traps, fight other participants, and carry out various tasks to achieve their goals

MUSE (abbreviation for **multi-user shared environment)** type of MUD

MUSH (acronym for **multi-user shared hallucination)** a MUD (multi-user dungeon) that can be altered by the players

netiquette behaviour guidelines evolved by users of the Internet including: no messages typed in upper case (considered to be the equivalent of shouting); new users, or new members of a newsgroup, should read the frequently asked questions (FAQ) file before asking a question; and no advertising via USENET newsgroups

net police USENET readers who monitor and 'punish' postings which they find offensive or believe to be in breach of netiquette. Many newsgroups are policed by these self-appointed guardians

network a method of connecting computers so that they can share data and peripheral devices, such as printers. The main types are classified by the pattern of the connections – star or ring network, for example – and by the degree of geographical spread allowed; for example, local area networks (LANs) for communication within a room or building, and wide area networks (WANs) for more remote systems. Internet is the computer network that connects major English-speaking

The World's Top IT Companies by Market Capitalization

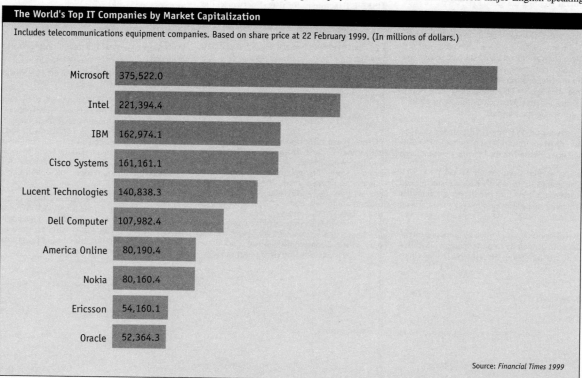

Includes telecommunications equipment companies. Based on share price at 22 February 1999. (In millions of dollars.)

Company	Market capitalization
Microsoft	375,522.0
Intel	221,394.4
IBM	162,974.1
Cisco Systems	161,161.1
Lucent Technologies	140,838.3
Dell Computer	107,982.4
America Online	80,190.4
Nokia	80,160.4
Ericsson	54,160.1
Oracle	52,364.3

Source: *Financial Times 1999*

institutions throughout the world, with around 12 million users.

newbie insulting term for a new user of a USENET newsgroup

newsgroup discussion group on the Internet's USENET. Newsgroups are organized in seven broad categories: **comp.** – computers and programming; **news.** – newsgroups themselves; **rec.** – sports and hobbies; **sci.** – scientific research and ideas; **talk.** – discussion groups; **soc.** – social issues and **misc.** – everything else. In addition, there are alternative hierarchies such as the wide-ranging and anarchic **alt.** (alternative). Within these categories there is a hierarchy of subdivisions

newsreader program that gives access to USENET newsgroups, interpreting the standard commands understood by news servers in a simple, user-friendly interface

news server computer that stores USENET messages for access by users. Most Internet Service Providers (ISPs) offer a news server as part of the service

off-line browser program that downloads and copies Web pages onto a computer so that they can be viewed without being connected to the Internet

off-line reader program that downloads information from newsgroups, FTP servers, or other Internet resources, storing it locally on a hard disk so that it can be read without running up a large phone bill

portal Web site designed to be used as a start-up site for browsing sessions and to provide a gateway to the rest of the Web. To increase their attractiveness, portals expanded rapidly in the late 1990s to offer a wide variety of services such as personalized start-up pages, free e-mail, directories, customized news and weather reports, online calendars, games, and free Web space. The first portals were online services such as America Online, which added gateways to the Internet.

Pretty Good Privacy (PGP) strong encryption program that runs on personal computers and is distributed on the Internet free of charge

proxy server server on the World Wide Web that 'stands in' for another server, storing and forwarding files on behalf of a computer which might be slower or too busy to deal with the request itself

pseudonym name adopted by someone on the Internet, especially to participate in USENET or discussions using IRC (Internet Relay Chat)

signature (or **.sig**) personal information appended to a message by the sender of an e-mail message or USENET posting in order to add a human touch

spamming advertising on the Internet by broadcasting to many or all newsgroups regardless of relevance

spider program that combs the Internet for new documents such as Web pages and FTP files. Spiders start their work by retrieving a document such as a Web page and then following all the links and references contained in it

surfing exploring the Internet. The term is rather misleading: the glitches, delays, and complexities of the system mean the experience is more like wading through mud

sysop (contraction of **system operator**) the operator of a bulletin board system (BBS)

trolling mischievously posting a deliberately erroneous or obtuse message to a newsgroup in order to tempt others to reply – usually in a way that makes them appear gullible, intemperate, or foolish

URL (abbreviation for **Uniform Resource Locator**) series of letters and/or numbers specifying the location of a document on the World Wide Web. Every URL consists of a domain name, a description of the document's location within the host computer, and the name of the document itself, separated by full stops and backslashes

USENET (acronym for **users' network**) the world's largest bulletin board system, which brings together people with common interests to exchange views and information. It consists of e-mail messages and articles organized into newsgroups

vertical spam on USENET, spam which consists of many, often repetitive, messages per day posted to the same newsgroup or small set of newsgroups. The effect is to drown out other, more useful, conversation in the newsgroup

virus a piece of software that can replicate and transfer itself from one computer to another, without the user being aware of it. Some viruses are relatively harmless, but others can damage or destroy data. Viruses are written by anonymous programmers, often maliciously, and are spread on floppy disks, CD-ROMs, and via networks and e-mail (worm). Antivirus software can be used to detect and destroy well-known viruses, but new viruses continually appear and these may bypass existing antivirus programs.

Computers Per Household in Europe and the USA

1996

Country	PC penetration (%)
Netherlands	51.7
Denmark	49.4[1]
USA	45.0[1]
Sweden	37.0
Luxembourg	36.0
UK	36.0
Belgium	32.4
Germany	32.0[1]
Italy	30.2
Austria	26.9
Slovenia	26.6
Portugal	26.1[1]
Finland	23.0
France	23.0
Ireland	22.0
Spain	20.0
Turkey	19.0
Norway	17.0[2]

[1] 1997.
[2] 1994.

wAreZ slang for pirated games or other applications that can be downloaded using FTP

Web authoring tool software for creating Web pages. The basic Web authoring tool is HTML, the source code that determines how a Web page is constructed and how it looks

Web browser client software that allows you to access the World Wide Web

Webmaster system administrator for a server on the World Wide Web

Web page hypertext document on the World Wide Web

webzine magazine published on the World Wide Web, instead of on paper

World Wide Web (WWW) hypertext system for publishing information on the Internet. World Wide Web documents ('Web pages') are text files coded using HTML to include text and graphics, stored on a special computer (a Web server) connected to the Internet. Web pages may also contain Java applets for enhanced animation, video, sound, and interactivity.

worm virus designed to spread from computer to computer across a network. Worms replicate themselves while 'hiding' in a computer's memory, causing systems to crash or slow down, but do not infect other programs or destroy data directly.

Use of Computers at Home and at Work by UK Adults

(– = not applicable.)

1998

Main use for computer	% use Male	Female	Total
Playing games	15	16	15
Educational purposes	9	10	10
Working from home	11	7	9
Using e-mail	5	6	5
Hobbies	6	3	5

Main use for computer	% use Male	Female	Total
Using CD-ROMs	5	3	4
Accessing the Internet	5	4	4
Receiving or sending faxes	5	3	4
None of the above	–	–	11
Do not have a computer	–	–	34

Source: *UK Computer Market 1998*, © Key Note Ltd

Trends in Computer Hardware Sales in the UK

(In millions of pounds at manufacturers' selling prices.)

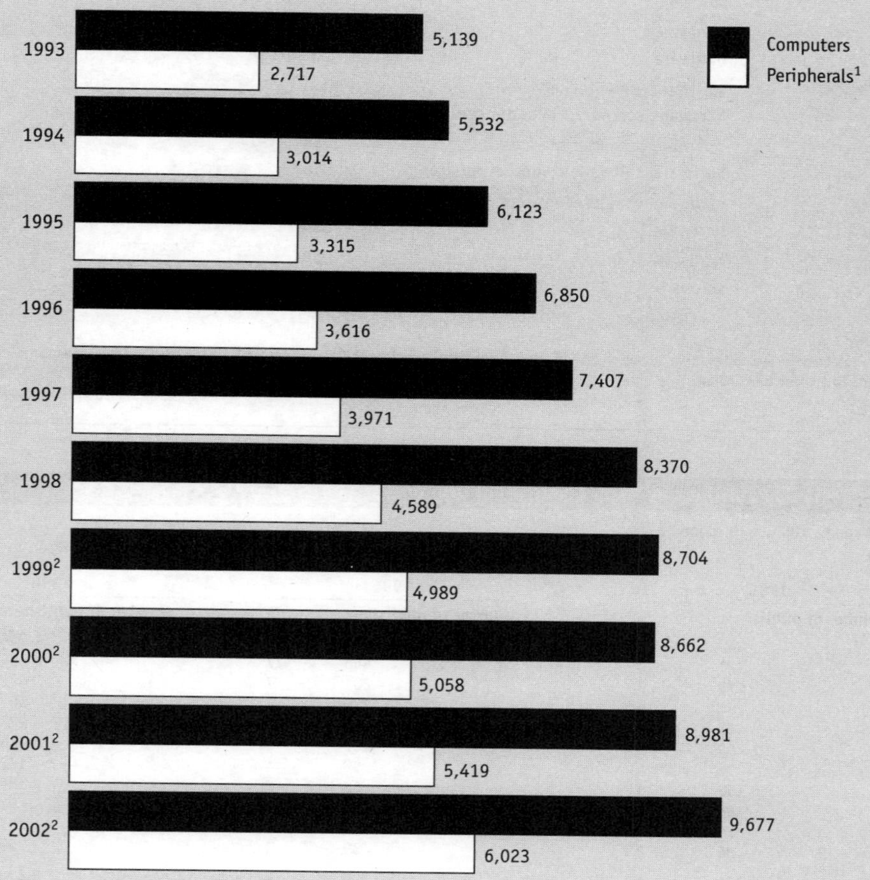

Year	Computers	Peripherals[1]
1993	5,139	2,717
1994	5,532	3,014
1995	6,123	3,315
1996	6,850	3,616
1997	7,407	3,971
1998	8,370	4,589
1999[2]	8,704	4,989
2000[2]	8,662	5,058
2001[2]	8,981	5,419
2002[2]	9,677	6,023

[1] Includes printers, monitors, add-in cards, and data storage devices.

[2] Forecast sales.

Source: *UK Computer Market 1998*, © Key Note Ltd

Top Computer Companies by UK Market Share

1997

Company	Sector strength	Country of origin	Market share (%)[1]
IBM	hardware, computer services	USA	9.8
Compaq Computer/Digital	hardware, software, computer services	USA	6.6
ICL	hardware, software, computer services	Japan	5.0
EDS	software, computer services	USA	3.6
Hewlett-Packard	hardware, software	USA	3.5
Dell Computer	hardware	USA	1.9
Reuters Holdings	software	UK	1.8
Sema	software, computer services	UK/France	1.7
Andersen Consulting	software	USA	1.6
Computer Sciences Corporation	software	USA	1.5
Cap Gemini	software	France	1.3
Toshiba	hardware	Japan	1.2
NEC/Packard Bell	hardware	Japan/USA	1.2
Microsoft	software, computer services	USA	1.2
Bull	hardware, software, computer services	France	1.2
Oracle	software, computer services	USA	1.1
Unisys	hardware, software, computer services	USA	1.0
Siemans Nixdorf	hardware, computer services	Germany	0.9
Seagate Technology	hardware	USA	0.8
3Com	hardware	USA	0.8
Syntegra	software	UK	0.8
Others			51.6

[1] Market share = share in total market less expenditure on personnel and telecommunications charges (i.e. share of the market in which the above companies operate directly). Percentages do not add up to 100 due to rounding.

Source: *UK Computer Market 1998*, © Key Note Ltd

CD-ROM and Multimedia CD Publishers by Major Countries of Origin

Percentages may not add to 100 due to rounding.
(– = not applicable.)

Country/ territory	1995		1996		1999	
	Number of publishers	%	Number of publishers	%	Number of publishers	%
USA	863	46	1,326	49	1,356	36
UK	321	17	465	17	624	16
Germany	173	9	201	7	492	13
France	96	5	175	7	363	10
Australia	42	2	58	2	227	6
Benelux	89	5	107	4	206	5
Canada	74	4	95	4	172	5
Italy	53	3	62	2	129	4
Japan	84	5	124	5	91	2
Spain	25	1	38	1	83	2
Switzerland	36	2	39	1	69	2
Total	1,856	–	2,690	–	3,812	–

Source: Waterlow New Media Information

Telephone Lines Per Person in Selected Countries

1997

Country	Total number of lines (thousands)	Per hundred inhabitants
Sweden	6,010.1	67.93
Luxembourg	279.7	66.87
USA	172,452.5	64.37
Canada	18,459.5	61.52
Germany	45,200	55.07
Singapore	1,684.9	54.29
UK	31,878.0	54.16
Australia	9,350.0[1]	50.45
Japan	60,380.9	47.86
Argentina	6,824.4	19.13
South Africa	4,645.1	10.72
China	70,310.0	5.62
Cambodia	19.0	0.18
Chad	7.5	0.11
Congo, Democratic Republic of	21.0	0.04

[1] Data are for 1998.

Source: International Telecommunication Union

Mobile Phone Ownership in Selected Countries

Country	Cellular mobile subscribers (thousands)		Per hundred inhabitants
	1996	1997	1997
Finland	1,484.0	2,148.1	41.74
Norway	1,261.4	1,676.8	38.07
Sweden	2,492.0	3,169.0	35.82
Japan	26,906.5	38,253.9	30.32
Singapore	430.0	848.6	27.34
Australia	3,815.0	4,893.0	26.40
USA	44,043.0	55,312.3	20.65
UK	7,109.4	8,933.0	15.18
Canada	3,420.3	4,207.0	13.89
Germany	5,512.0	8,170.0	9.95

Source: International Telecommunication Union

Structures

The Top 10 Tallest Buildings in the World

As of January 1999.
(– = not applicable.)

Building/structure	City	Height m	Height ft	Storeys	Year completed
Inhabited Buildings					
Petronas Tower I	Kuala Lumpur, Malaysia	452	1,483	88	1996
Petronas Tower II	Kuala Lumpur, Malaysia	452	1,483	88	1996
Sears Tower[1]	Chicago (IL), USA	443	1,454	110	1973
Jin Mao Building	Shanghai, China	420	1,379	88	1997
One World Trade Center	New York (NY), USA	417	1,368	110	1972
Two World Trade Center	New York (NY), USA	415	1,362	110	1973
Empire State Building	New York (NY), USA	381	1,250	102	1931
Central Plaza	Hong Kong, China	374	1,227	78	1992
Bank of China	Hong Kong, China	369	1,209	70	1989
The Centre	Hong Kong, China	350	1,149	73	1998
Tallest Structures					
Warszawa Radio Maszt[2]	Konstantynów, Poland	646	2,120	–	–
KTHI-TV Mast	Fargo (ND), USA	629	2,063	–	–
KSLA-TV Mast	Shreveport (LA), USA	579	1,898	–	–
CN Tower	Toronto, Ontario, Canada	555	1,822	–	–
Ostankino Tower	Moscow, Russia	537	1,762	–	–
WBIR-TV Mast	Knoxville (TN), USA	533	1,749	–	–
WTVM and WRBL Television Mast	Columbus (GA), USA	533	1,749	–	–
KFVS Television Mast	Cape Girardeau (MO), USA	511	1,676	–	–
WPSD-TV Mast	Paducah (KY), USA	499	1,638	–	–
WGAN Television Mast	Portland (ME), USA	494	1,619	–	–

[1] Height excludes TV antennas.
[2] Collapsed during renovation, August 1991

The Top 10 Tallest Buildings by Continent

As of January 1999.
(– = not available.)

Building	City	Height		Storeys	Year
		m	ft		completed
Asia					
Petronas Tower I	Kuala Lumpur, Malaysia	452	1,483	88	1996
Petronas Tower II	Kuala Lumpur, Malaysia	452	1,483	88	1996
Jin Mao Building	Shanghai, China	420	1,379	88	1997
Central Plaza	Hong Kong, China	374	1,227	78	1992
Bank of China	Hong Kong, China	369	1,209	70	1989
The Centre	Hong Kong, China	350	1,149	73	1998
T&C Tower	Kaohsiung, Taiwan	347	1,140	85	1997
Shun Hing Square	Shenzhen, China	325	1,066	69	1996
Sky Central Plaza	Guangzhou, China	322	1,056	80	1996
Chicago Beach Resort Hotel	Dubai, United Arab Emirates	321	1,053	60	1998
Australia					
Rialto Towers	Melbourne, Australia	242	794	56	1985
MLC Centre	Sydney, Australia	228	748	65	1978
Governor Philip Tower	Sydney, Australia	227	745	54	1993
Bourke Place	Melbourne, Australia	224	735	46	1997
Central Park Tower	Perth, Australia	223	731	52	1993
120 Collins St	Melbourne, Australia	220	722	52	1991
Chifley Tower	Sydney, Australia	215	705	50	1992
BankWest Tower	Perth, Australia	214	702	52	1988
Melbourne Central	Melbourne, Australia	211	692	55	1991
Nauru House	Melbourne, Australia	210	689	53	1977
Europe					
Commerzbank	Frankfurt, Germany	299	981	63	1997
Messeturm	Frankfurt, Germany	256	839	64	1991
1 Canada Square, Canary Wharf	London, UK	244	800	56	1991
MV Lomonosov State University	Moscow, Russia	239	784	39	1953
Palace of Culture and Science	Warsaw, Poland	231	758	42	1955
Tour Maine, Montparnasse	Paris, France	209	686	58	1973
DG Bank	Frankfurt, Germany	208	682	53	1993
Framatome	Paris, France	200	656	44	1975
Ukraine Tower	Moscow, Russia	198	650	34	1961
Tour GAN	Paris, France	188	617	48	1974
North America					
Sears Tower[1]	Chicago (IL), USA	443	1,454	110	1973
One World Trade Center	New York (NY), USA	417	1,368	110	1972
Two World Trade Center	New York (NY), USA	415	1,362	110	1973
Empire State Building	New York (NY), USA	381	1,250	102	1931
Amoco Building	Chicago (IL), USA	346	1,136	80	1973
John Hancock Center	Chicago (IL), USA	344	1,127	100	1968
Chrysler Building	New York (NY), USA	319	1,046	77	1930
NationsBank Tower	Atlanta (GA), USA	312	1,023	55	1992
Library Tower	Los Angeles (CA), USA	310	1,018	75	1990
AT&T Corporate Center	Chicago (IL), USA	306	1,007	60	1989
Rest of the World					
Carlton Centre	Johannesburg, South Africa	222	730	50	1973
Parcque Central Torre Officinas I	Caracas, Venezuela	221	725	56	1978
Parcque Central Torre Officinas II	Caracas, Venezuela	221	725	54	1979
Edifico Italia	São Paulo, Brazil	194	635	45	1965
Colpatria Tower	Bogotá, Colombia	192	630	50	1979
Coltejer	Medellín, Colombia	175	574	37	1972
Las Americas	Bogotá, Colombia	174	571	47	1974
La Nacional	Bogotá, Colombia	171	561	47	–
Palacio Zarzur Kogan	São Paulo, Brazil	170	557	50	1960
Rio Sul Centre	Rio de Janeiro, Brazil	164	538	50	1980

[1] Height excludes TV antennas.

The Longest Bridges by Span in the World

Bridge	Location	Date built/opened	Length m	Length ft
Suspension Spans				
Akashi-Kaikyo	Honshu–Awaji Islands, Japan	1998	1,990	6,529
Store Baelt	Zealand–Funen, Denmark	1998	1,624	5,328
Humber Bridge	Kingston-upon-Hull, UK	1973–81	1,410	4,626
Verrazono Narrows	Brooklyn–Staten Island, New York Harbor (NY), USA	1959–64	1,298	4,260
Golden Gate	San Francisco (CA), USA	1937	1,280	4,200
Mackinac Straits	Michigan (MI), USA	1957	1,158	3,800
Bosporus	Golden Horn, Istanbul, Turkey	1973	1,074	3,524
George Washington	Hudson River, New York (NY), USA	1927–31	1,067	3,500
Ponte 25 Abril (Salazar)	Tagus River, Lisbon, Portugal	1966	1,013	3,323
Firth of Forth (road)	South Queensferry, UK	1958–64	1,006	3,300
Severn Bridge	Beachley, UK	1961–66	988	3,240
Cable-Stayed Spans				
Pont de Normandie	Seine Estuary, France	1995	2,200	7,216
Skarnsundet	near Trondheim, Norway	1991	530	1,740
Cantilever Spans				
Howrah (railroad)	Hooghly River, Calcutta, India	1936–43	988	3,240
Pont de Quebec (railroad)	St Lawrence, Canada	1918	549	1,800
Ravenswood	Ravenswood (WV), USA	1981	525	1,723
Firth of Forth (rail)	South Queensferry, UK	1882–90	521	1,710
Commodore Barry	Chester (PA), USA	1974	494	1,622
Greater New Orleans	Mississippi River (LA), USA	1958	480	1,575
Steel-Arch Spans				
New River Gorge	Fayetteville (WV), USA	1977	518	1,700
Bayonne (Killvan Kull)	New Jersey–Staten Island (NY), USA	1932	504	1,652
Sydney Harbour	Sydney, Australia	1923–32	503	1,500

Notable Railway Bridges in the World

The world's highest railway bridge (above ground) spans the Mala Rijeka Gorge near Kolasin in Yugoslavia. It consists of five steel spans on concrete piers and took 25 years to build. This table shows other bridges that are over 100 m/328 ft above ground level. (N/A = not available.)

Bridge	Railway	Location	Date opened	Height m	Height ft
Mala Rijeka Viaduct	Yugoslav Railways	Kolasin on Belgrade–Bar line	1976	198	650
Vresk	Iranian State	220 km/137 mi from Bandar Shah on Caspian Sea Trans Iranian line	1938	152	500
Fades Viaduct	French National	Clermont-Ferrand–Montluçon line	1909	133	435
Khotur	Iranian State	Khotur River near Khoi	1973	131	430
Victoria Falls	Rhodesia Railways	Livingstone	1904	128	420
Pfaffenberg–Zwenberg	Austrian Federal	Mallnitz–Spittal	1971	120	394
Viaur	French National	Tanus, Rodez–Albi	1902	116	381
Garabit Viaduct	French National	Neussargues–Béziers	1884	112	367
Müngstner	German Federal	Mügsten, over River Wupper	1897	107	350
Rio Grande	Costa Rica	near San José	N/A	105	346
Vance Creek	Simpson Timber Co	Shelton, west of Tacoma (WA), USA	1928	105	346
Tramo Sobre	Former Buenos Aires Great Southern, Argentina	Rio Negro	N/A	104	344
Viaduct No 2	Turkish State	between Konakler and Günaykoy on Izmir–Afyonkarahisar line, 199.3 km/123.8 mi from Izmir	1900	103	338
Faux-Mau-Ti	China	Yunnan section	1910	102	335
Rio Chinipas	Chihuahua–Pacific Mexico	on Ojinago–Topolobampo line	N/A	101	330
Corte	Corsica	Corte	1894	100	328
Lindischgraben	Austrian Federal	Tauern Railway Obervellach–Penk	1977	100	328
Ten Tze	China	Yunnan section	1910	approx. 100	approx. 328

The Highest Dams in the World

This table includes dams registered with the International Commission on Large Dams (ICOLD). Dams registered with ICOLD must be 15 m/ 49 ft in height or more.

Dam	Location	Height above lowest formation	
		m	ft
Rogun	Tajikistan	335	1,099
Nurek	Tajikistan	300	984
Grand Dixence	Switzerland	285	935
Inguri	Georgia	272	892
Vajont	Italy	262	869
Manuel M. Torres	Mexico	261	856
Tehri	India	261	856
Avlvaro Obregon	Mexico	260	853
Mauvoisin	Switzerland	250	820
Alberto Lleras C.	Colombia	243	797
Mica	Canada	243	797
Sayano-Shushenskaya	Russia	242	794
Ertan	China	240	787
La Esmeralda	Colombia	237	778
Kishau	India	236	774
Oroville	USA	235	770
El Cajon	Honduras	234	768
Chirkey	Russia	233	765
Bhakra	India	226	741
Cyprus	USA	226	741

Source: *1998 World Register of Dams,* International Commission on Large Dams

The Longest Railway Tunnels in the World

Tunnel	Location	Year opened	Length	
			km	mi
Seikan	Japan	1985	54	34
Channel Tunnel	UK–France	1994	50	31
Dai-Shimizu	Japan	1979	23	14
Simplon Nos 1 and 2	Switzerland–Italy	1906, 1922	19	12
Kanmon	Japan	1975	19	12
Apennine	Italy	1934	18	11
Rokko	Japan	1972	16	10
Mt MacDonald	Canada	1989	15	9
Gotthard	Switzerland	1882	14	9
Lotschberg	Switzerland	1913	14	9
Hokuriku	Japan	1962	14	9
Mont Canis (Frejus)	France–Italy	1871	13	8
Shin-Shimizu	Japan	1961	13	8
Aki	Japan	1975	13	8
Cascade	USA	1929	13	8
Flathead	USA	1970	13	8
Keijo	Japan	1970	11	7
Lierasen	Norway	1973	11	7
Santa Lucia	Italy	1977	10	6
Arlberg	Austria	1884	10	6
Moffat	USA	1928	10	6
Shimizu	Japan	1931	10	6

The Longest Vehicular Tunnels in the World

Tunnel	Location	Year opened	Length	
			km	mi
Saint Gotthard	Switzerland	1980	16.3	10.1
Arlberg	Austria	1978	14.0	8.7
Fréjus	France–Italy	1980	12.9	8.0
Mont Blanc	France–Italy	1965	11.7	7.3
Gran Sasso	Italy	1976	10.0	6.2
Seelisberg	Switzerland	1979	9.3	5.8
Mount Ena	Japan	1976	8.5	5.3
Rokko 11	Japan	1974	6.9	4.3
San Bernardino	Switzerland	1967	6.6	4.1
Tauren	Austria	1974	6.4	4.0

The Largest Reservoirs by Volume in the World

Reservoir	Location	Year completed	Volume	
			cubic m (millions)	cubic yd (millions)
Kariba	Zambia–Zimbabwe	1959	180,600	236,207
Bratsk	Russia	1964	169,000	221,035
High Aswan	Egypt	1970	162,000	211,880
Akosombo	Ghana	1965	150,000	196,185
Daniel Johnson	Canada	1968	141,851	185,527
Xinfeng	China	1960	138,960	181,746
Guri	Venezuela	1986	135,000	176,567
Bennett W A C	Canada	1967	74,300	97,177
Krasnoyarsk	Russia	1967	73,300	95,869
Zeya	Russia	1978	68,400	89,460
La Grande 2 Barrage	Canada	1978	61,715	80,717
La Grande 3 Barrage	Canada	1981	60,020	78,500
Ust-Ilim	Russia	1977	59,300	77,558
Boguchany[1]	Russia		58,200	76,120
Kuibyshev	Russia	1955	58,000	75,858
Serra de Mesa	Brazil	1998	54,400	71,150
Canapiscau Barrage KA-3	Canada	1980	53,790	70,352
Cahora Bassa	Mozambique	1974	52,000	68,011
Bukhtarma	Kazakhstan	1960	49,800	65,089
Tucuruí	Brazil	1984	49,536	64,788

[1] Under construction.

Source: *1998 World Register of Dams,* International Commission on Large Dams

The Seven Wonders of the World

The canon of seven 'sights' of art and architecture of the Greco-Roman classical world are first recorded in the 2nd century BC. Generally referred to as the Seven Wonders of the ancient world, to distinguish them from more recent wonders, they comprise:

The Pyramids of Egypt, namely, the three pyramids at Gîza, near Cairo. Pyramids were used in ancient Egypt to enclose a royal tomb; for example, the Great Pyramid of Khufu/Cheops at El Gîza, which measures 230 m/755 ft square and 147 m/481 ft high.

The Hanging Gardens of Babylon in the capital of Mesopotamia. According to legend, King Nebuchadnezzar constructed the gardens in the 6th century BC for one of his wives, who was homesick for her birthplace in the Iranian mountains. Archaeological excavations at the site of Babylon, 88 km/55 mi south of Baghdad in modern Iraq, have uncovered a huge substructure that may have supported irrigated gardens on terraces.

The Temple of Artemis at Ephesus is dedicated to the Greek goddess of chastity, the young of all creatures, the Moon, and the hunt (Roman Diana). Artemis is the twin sister of Apollo and was worshipped at cult centres throughout the Greek world, one of the largest of which was at Ephesus.

The Statue of Zeus at Olympia, in gold and ivory, was made by the Greek sculptor Phidias. It was later removed to Constantinople, where it was destroyed in a fire. It is thought that the face of Zeus might probably have served as a model for the face of Christ Pantocrator in the dome of St Sophia there.

The Mausoleum at Halicarnassus, the ancient city in Asia Minor (now Bodrum in Turkey). The tomb of Mausolus was built about 350 BC by his widowed queen Artemisia. Today, little remains at the site of the original monument, although some fragmentary sculptures from it are kept in the British Museum in London.

The Colossus of Rhodes, bronze statue of Apollo erected at the entrance to the harbour at Rhodes 292–280 BC. Said to have been about 30 m/100 ft high, in 224 BC, it fell as a result of an earthquake.

The Lighthouse of Pharos, a gigantic lighthouse at the entrance to the harbour of Alexandria. It was built in the early 3rd century BC by the Macedonian kings of Egypt, Ptolemy I and Ptolemy II, and took its name from the island on which it stood. The lighthouse was repeatedly damaged by earthquakes, and any remains of the ancient structure are now concealed under the medieval fortress of Kait Bey.

Scientific Associations and Societies

Scientific Associations in the UK

Figures refer to numbers of individual members; date given is year organization was founded. (f = firms.)

Astrological Association of Great Britain (1,500), Lee Valley Techno Park, Ashley Road, London N17; phone: (0181) 880 4848; 1958

Astronomical Society, Royal (3,000), Burlington House, Piccadilly, London W1V 0NL; phone: (0171) 734 4582; 1820

Chemical Engineers, Institution of (21,000), Davis Building, 165–189 Railway Terrace, Rugby CV21 3HQ; phone: (0171) 222 2681; 1922

Chemistry, Royal Society of (45,000), Burlington House, Piccadilly, London W1V 0BN; phone: (0171) 437 8656; 1841

Civil Engineers, Institution of (79,756), 1–7 Great George Street, London SW1P 3AA; phone: (0171) 222 7722; 1818

Computer Professionals, Association of (4,000), 204 Barnett Wood Lane, Ashtead KT21 2DB; phone: (01372) 273442; 1994

Computer Society, British (33,000), 1 Sanford Street, Swindon SN1 1HJ; phone: (01793) 417417; 1957

Computer Users' Forum (4,700 ind; 4,300 f), 1 Stuart Road, Thornton Heath CR7 8RA; 1984

Electrical Engineers, Institution of (130,000), Savoy Place, London WC2R 0BL; phone: (0171) 240 1871; fax: (0171) 240 8830; 1871

Electronics & Electrical Incorporated Engineers, Institution of (27,000), Savoy Hill House, Savoy Hill, London WC2R 0BS; phone: (0171) 2401871; 1990

Engineers, Association of Municipal (11,500), c/o The Institution of Civil Engineers, 1 Great George Street, London SW1P 3AA; phone: (0171) 222 7722; 1984

Engineers, Institution of Gas (5,800 ind; 3,588 f), 21 Portland Place, London W1N 3AF; phone: (0171) 636 6603; 1863

Engineers, Institution of Mechanical (77,000), 1 Birdcage Walk, London SW1H 9JJ; phone: (0171) 222 7899; 1847

Engineers, Institution of Structural (23,000), 11 Upper Belgrave Street, London SW1X 8BH; phone: (0171) 235 4535; fax: (0171) 235 4294; 1908

Engineers' & Managers' Association (32,000), Flaxman House, Gogmore Lane, Chertsy KT16 9JS; phone: (01932) 577007; 1913

Forensic Science Society (2,000 ind; 75 f), Clarke House, 18a Mount Parade, Harrogate HG1 1BX; phone: (01423) 506068; 1959

Mathematical Association (6,000 ind; 2,000 schools), 259 London Road, Leicester LE2 3BE; 1872

Mining & Metallurgy, Institution of (4,800), 44 Portland Place, London W1N 4BR; phone: (0171) 580 3802; fax: (0171) 436 5388; 1892

Physics, Institute of (21,000), 76 Portland Place, London W1N 4AA; phone: (0171) 470 4800; fax: (0171) 470 4848; 1970

Plant Engineers, Institution of (6,000), 77 Great Peter Street, London SW1P 2EZ; phone: (0171) 233 2855; 1946

Soil Association (5,000), Organic Food & Farming Centre, 86–88 Colston Street, Bristol BS1 5BB; phone: (0117) 9290661; 1946

Statistical Society, Royal (6,000), 12 Errol Street, London EC1Y 8LX; phone: (0171) 638 8998; fax: (0171) 638 7598; 1834

CAB International

International non-profit organization for scientific research and development. It was established in 1913 as the Imperial Agricultural Bureaux (IAB) and renamed the Commonwealth Agricultural Bureaux in 1948; it became fully international in 1985, with membership open to any country, and was reconstituted CAB International in line with its new status. It has three principal areas of activity: Bioscience, undertaking research and training in biological pest management, biodiversity, biosystematics, and the environment; Information for Development, assisting developing countries to acquire and manage scientific information; and Publishing, producing publications in all fields of agriculture and related fields. **Address** CAB International, Wallingford, Oxon OX10 8DE, UK; phone: +44 (0)1491 832111; fax: +44 (0)1491 833508; e-mail: cabi@cabi.org; Web site: http://www.cabi.org/

Human Genome Mapping Project Resource Centre

British scientific body for the provision of biological and data resources and services to the medical research community working on the Human Genome Programme. Funded by the Medical Reseach Council (MRC), the HGMP–RC is located at the Hinxton Genome Campus, with the Sanger Centre and the European Bioinformatics Institute. It provides access to genomic libraries and updated databases, and has its own, newly formed research division. **Address** UK MRC HGMP Resource Centre, Hinxton, Cambridge CB10 1SB, UK; phone: +44 (0)1223 494500; fax: +44 (0)1223 494512; e-mail: admin@hgmp.mrc.ac.uk; Web site: http://www.hgmp.mrc.ac.uk/

International Centre for Genetic Engineering and Biotechnology

International organization, composed of 41 member states, established to promote the safe use of biotechnology worldwide, with special regard to the needs of the developing world. The two main ICGEB laboratories are located in Trieste, Italy, and in New Delhi, India. It hosts a network of national laboratories in member states. Specific research programmes include the study of human genetic diseases, the genetic manipulation of plants, and the production of novel malaria and hepatitis vaccines. **Address** ICGEB, AREA Science Park, Padriciano 99, 34012 Trieste, Italy; phone: +39 40 37571; fax: +39 40 226555; e-mail: icgeb@icgeb.trieste.it; Web site: http://www.icgeb.trieste.it/

Royal Society, The

British independent academy, founded in 1660, for the promotion of natural and applied sciences. It provides a broad range of services for the scientific community in the national interest and supports international scientific exchange. The Society's publications are essential to its objective for the dissemination of new science, and to this end publications include journals, which provide research findings and authoritative reviews; the RS journal on the history of science; publications of record; reports on scientific studies; submissions to Government; and reports on UK science. **Address** The Royal Society, 6 Carlton House Terrace, London SW1Y 5AG, UK; phone: +44 (0)171 839 5561; fax: +44 (0)171 930 2170; e-mail: ezmb013@mailbox.ulcc.ac.uk; Web site: http://www. royalsoc.ac.uk/

Sanger Centre

British research establishment for the sequencing, mapping, and interpretation of the human genome. It was established in 1992 by the Wellcome Trust and the Medical Research Council (MRC), and is situated at the Hinxton Genome Campus. Renewed funding from the Wellcome Trust enables an increased production rate, and it is estimated that the completion of the entire human genome sequence by an international collaboration, including the Sanger Centre, will be accomplished by 2005. **Address** The Sanger Centre, Wellcome Trust Genome Campus, Hinxton, Cambridge CB10 1SA, UK; phone: +44 (0)1223 834244; fax: +44 (0)1223 494919; Web site: http://www. sanger.ac.uk

Web Sites

Analytical Chemistry Basics

http://www.scimedia.com/chem-ed/analytic/ac-basic.htm

Detailed online course, designed for those at undergraduate level, that provides the user with an introduction to some of the fundamental concepts and methods of analytical chemistry.

Biology Timeline

http://www.zoologie.biologie.de/history.html

Chronology of important developments in the biological sciences. It includes a great range of references to biology in history from hand pollination of date palms in 1800 BC to the Nobel Prize award for the discovery of site-directed mutagenesis in 1993.

Breaking The Genetic Code

http://www.nih.gov/od/museum/neir1.htm

Museum exhibit Web site describing the Nobel prizewinning work of Nirenberg on genetics. The site is broken down into three small pages with links to descriptions of the instruments used in Nirenberg's work.

Brief History of Cosmology

http://www-history.mcs.st-and.ac.uk/~history/HistTopics/Cosmology.html

Based at St Andrews University, Scotland, a site chronicling the history of cosmology from the time of the Babylonians to the Hubble Space Telescope.

Chemistry of the Ozone Layer

http://pooh.chem.wm.edu/chemWWW/courses/chem105/projects/group2/page1.html

Interesting step-by-step introduction to the ozone layer for those wishing to understand the chemistry of ozone depletion, the role of chlorofluorocarbons, the consequences of increased radiation for life on Earth, and actions to tackle the problem. The information may be readily understood by those with a basic knowledge of chemistry.

Dictionary of Cell Biology

http://www.mblab.gla.ac.uk/dictionary/

Searchable database of more than 5,000 terms frequently encountered in reading modern biology literature. The dictionary can be searched as a whole or in sections, such as 'Disease', 'Cytoskeleton', and 'Nucleus, genes, and DNA'.

Dinosaur Controversies

http://www.mov.vic.gov.au/dinosaurs/dinoscontr.stm

Aimed at schoolchildren, this site examines several of the controversies still baffling palaeontologists around the world. Several of the theories about why dinosaurs became extinct are explored here, as well as such questions as 'Did dinosaur parents care for their young?'.

Elementary Science

http://www.lme.mankato.msus.edu/ci/elem.sci.html

Brief biographies of famous scientists, some experiments to do in the home, a featured animal of the month, information on the night sky, and a 'Tell me why' feature. It seems to be an irregularly-updated site, but there are plenty of back issues still available.

Evolutionist, The

http://cpnss.lse.ac.uk/darwin/evo/

Online magazine devoted to evolutionary ideas which includes features, interviews, and comment. It currently includes an article on the recent political interest in Darwinism and a column on the limits of evolutionary theory.

Evolution: Theory and History

http://www.ucmp.berkeley.edu/history/evolution.html

Dedicated to the study of the history and theories associated with evolution, this site explores topics on classification, taxonomy, and dinosaur discoveries, and then looks at the key figures in the field and reviews their contributions.

FAQ on Telescope Buying and Usage

http://www.eyepiece.org/faq/faq.html

Extensive and plain-English guide to buying a telescope. For anybody interested in astronomy and contemplating buying a telescope or setting up an observatory, this is an indispensable source of non-commercial advice. There is a full explanation of jargon used in astronomy and guides to help the amateur astronomer.

Forensic Science Web Page

http://users.aol.com/murrk/index.htm

Aimed at the layperson, this site explains the basics of forensic science. It is broken up into

a series of articles, each explaining a different discipline. Topics covered include firearms and toolmark identification, forensic psychiatry, and crime-scene processing.

Frequently Asked Questions in Mathematics

http://www.cs.unb.ca/~alopez-o/math-faq/mathtext/math-faq.html

Expert answers to frequently asked questions, from 'Why is there no Nobel prize in mathematics?' to 'What is the current status of Fermat's last theorem?'

Galileo Project Information

http://nssdc.gsfc.nasa.gov/planetary/galileo.html

Site dedicated to the Galileo Project and the opportunities it has offered scientists and astronomers to enhance our understanding of the universe. The site includes information about the mission's objectives, scientific results, images, and links to other relevant sites on the Web.

History of Mathematics

http://www-groups.dcs.st-andrews.ac.uk/history/HistTopics/History_overview.html

Overview of the history of mathematics with numerous links to important mathematicians from ancient times to the present day. The site includes sections on the problems of notation and communication, and on brilliant discoveries.

History of Space Exploration

http://www.hawastsoc.org/solar/eng/history.htm

Who was the first woman astronaut? Find out at this site, which also contains information on the history of rocketry and chronologies of exploration by the USA, Russia, Japan, and Europe.

History of the Royal Society

http://www-history.mcs.st-and.ac.uk/~history/Societies/RShistory.html

Web site run by St Andrews University detailing the history of the Royal Society. Biographical details of the founding members are provided, as is information on the main prizes the society awards for scientific achievement.

Human Genome Project Information

http://www.ornl.gov/TechResources/Human_Genome/home.html

US-based site devoted to this mammoth project – with news, progress reports, a molecular genetics primer, and links to other relevant sites.

Hydrology Primer

http://wwwdmorll.er.usgs.gov/~bjsmith/outreach/hydrology.primer.html

Information from the US Geological Survey about all aspects of hydrology. The clickable chapters include facts about surface water and ground water, the work of hydrologists, and careers in hydrology.

Inquirer's Guide to the Universe

http://sln.fi.edu/planets/planets.html

Web site designed for teachers and students, with pages on 'Space science fact' – the universe as humans know it today – and 'Space science fiction' – the universe as humans imagine it might be. Features include planetary fact sheets, information about planets outside the Solar System, virtual trips to black holes and neutron stars, space quotes, and a course in spaceship design.

Learning Centre for Young Astronomers

http://heasarc.gsfc.nasa.gov/docs/StarChild/StarChild.html

Introduction to our universe for young astronomers. The presentation covers a wide range of issues with discussions of quasars, comets, meteoroids, the Milky Way, black holes, the Hubble Space Telescope, space wardrobes, and space probes

Look Inside the Atom

http://www.aip.org/history/electron/jjhome.htm

Part of the American Institute of Physics site, this page examines J J Thomson's 1897 experiments that led to the discovery of a fundamental building block of matter, the electron.

Moon: Home, Sweet Home

http://www.sciam.com/explorations/1998/0316moon/sweet.html

Part of a larger site maintained by Scientific American, this page explores the discovery of ice on the moon and how this discovery may speed plans to build lunar bases and colonies. You will find images and hypertext links to further information. Find out about NASA proposals for moon bases, learn about the Moon Treaty that would regulate development on the moon, and read differing opinions on whether commercial interests should be permitted to exploit the moon's resources.

NASA Home Page

http://www.nasa.gov/

Latest news from NASA, plus the most recent images from the Hubble Space Telescope. This site also contains answers to questions about NASA resources and the space programme, and a gallery of video, audio clips, and still images.

NASA Shuttle Web

http://spaceflight.nasa.gov/shuttle/index.html

Official NASA site for all shuttle missions. There is extensive technical and non-technical information, both textual and graphic. Questions can be sent to shuttle crew members during missions. There is an extensive list of frequently asked questions. There are helpful links to related sites and even a plain-English explanation of NASA's bewildering jargon and acronyms.

Nuclear Energy: Frequently Asked Questions

http://www-formal.stanford.edu/jmc/progress/nuclear-faq.html

Answers to the most commonly asked questions about nuclear energy, particularly with a view to sustaining human progress. It contains many links to related pages and is a personal opinion that openly asks for comment from visitors.

Nuclear Physics

http://www.scri.fsu.edu/~jac/Nuclear/

'Hyper-textbook' of nuclear physics, with an introduction that includes a graphical description of the size and shape of nuclei and their other properties. The site also includes information about the work of nuclear physicists, and the uses and applications of nuclear physics from medicine, through energy, to smoke detectors.

Physics 2000

http://www.colorado.edu/physics/2000/

Fun place to learn about 20th-century physics and familiar high-tech devices. This site is designed to make physics more accessible to people of all ages. The site is divided into three sections: 'What is Physics 2000?', 'Einstein's Legacy', and 'The Atomic Lab'.

Physics Factory – GCSE

http://physics.digiweb.com/gcse.htm

Aimed at GCSE students, this site would be useful for anyone with an interest in physics. As well as regularly changing pages on major topics in physics, there is a screensaver you can download to help you remember the important equations.

Practical Guide to Astronomy

http://www.aardvark.on.ca/space/

Well-illustrated guide to astronomy that contains explanations of many aspects of the subject, including the 'Big Bang' theories of English physicist Stephen Hawking, a list of early astronomers and their key discoveries, and an in-depth look at all the main elements of our Solar System.

Project Skylab

http://www.ksc.nasa.gov/history/skylab/skylab.html

Official NASA archive of the project that launched the USA's first experimental space station in 1973. There are comprehensive details (technical and of general interest) on all the experiments included in the project.

Royal Institution of Great Britain

http://www.ri.ac.uk/

Profile of the history and role of the world's longest established independent research organization. There is information on the structure of the RI, ongoing scientific research, and its extensive programme of activities to educate the public about science.

Royal Society of Chemistry

http://www.rsc.org/

Work of the UK society to promote understanding of chemistry and assist its advancement. There are full details of the society's research work, online and print publications, and comprehensive educational programme. All the resources of the largest UK chemistry library can be searched.

SETI Institute

http://www.seti-inst.edu/

SETI (Search for ExtraTerrestrial Intelligence) Institute conducts research designed to answer the question 'Are we alone in the universe?' This site has information on current and past projects, including their connection with the films Independence Day and Contact. There is also the opportunity to devote some of your own computer's time to 'crunching' the enormous amounts of data the Institute collects and doing a little to help the search.

Solar System

http://www.hawastsoc.org/solar/eng/

Educational tour of the Solar System. It contains information and statistics about the Sun, Earth, planets, moons, asteroids, comets, and meteorites found within the Solar System, supported by images.

Solar System Live

http://www.fourmilab.ch/solar/solar.html

Take a look at the entire Solar System as it might be seen at different times and dates or from different viewpoints.

Space Telescope Electronic Information Service

http://www.stsci.edu/

Home page of the Hubble Space Telescope that includes an archive of past observations, a description of the instruments aboard, and a section for educators, students, and the general public – with pictures, audio clips, and press releases.

Strange Science

http://www.turnpike.net/~mscott/index.htm

Subtitled 'The Rocky Road to Modern Palaeontology and Biology', this site examines some of the medieval discoveries that led to the growth of interest in modern-day science. The site is illustrated with images that clearly show how people's perception of the world differed, and how people made up for gaps in their knowledge with a little imagination!

Tree of Life

http://phylogeny.arizona.edu/tree/phylogeny.html

Project designed to present information about the phylogenetic relationships and characteristics of organisms, illustrating the diversity and unity of living organisms.

Unsolved Mysteries

http://www.pbs.org/wnet/hawking/mysteries/html/myst.html

Part of a larger site on cosmology provided by PBS Online, this page features seven articles that address the most difficult questions regarding the mysteries of our universe. Some of the articles include 'Where does matter come from?', 'Is time travel possible?', 'Where is the missing matter?', 'An inhabited universe?', and 'Is there a theory for everything?'.

Voyager Project Home Page

http://vraptor.jpl.nasa.gov/voyager/voyager.html

Comprehensive information on the Voyager probes and what they have told us about the further reaches of the Solar System. There are details of the organization of the Voyager mission, the systems that are still functioning, and the data they are sending back.

What's New in Mathematics?

http://www.ams.org/new-in-math/

Section of the American Mathematical Society's Web site aimed at the general public, with features on latest developments and buzz words.

World Atom – International Atomic Energy Agency

http://www.iaea.org/

Public information source of the UN agency charged with monitoring and assisting the peaceful uses of nuclear energy. This well organized and easily navigable site is highly informative about the work of the IAEA and the many uses to which nuclear energy is put. The site is regularly updated and has many useful links.

Your Genes, Your Choices: Exploring the Issues Raised by Genetic Research

http://www.ornl.gov/hgmis/publicat/genechoice/index.html

Illustrated electronic book that describes the science of genetic research, as well as the ethical, legal, and social issues that it raises.

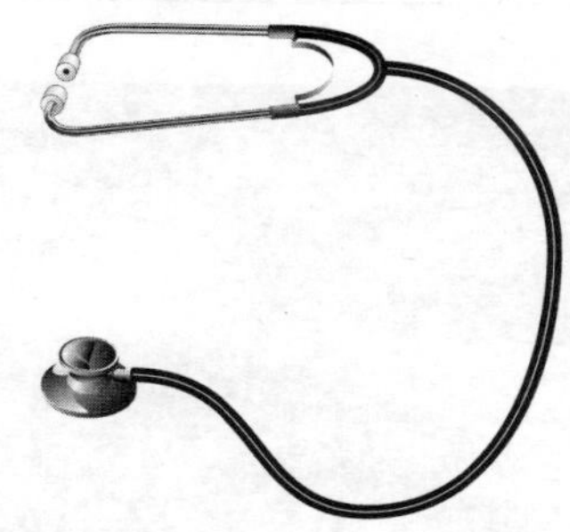

MEDICINE AND HEALTH

The Year in Review

3 July 1998 In England, researchers at the Institute of Animal Health announce the discovery of the gene that gives chickens immunity to salmonella, one of the most intractable health problems in the UK.

4 July 1998 Japanese biotechnicians announce the successful freeze-drying of mouse sperm. The sperm can then be reconstituted and can successfully fertilize eggs. Additionally, the freeze-dried sperm can be kept at room temperature.

8 July 1998 US women claiming to have been injured by silicone breast implants win a $3.2 billion/£2 billion settlement, ending ten years of legal battles and 170,000 lawsuits.

14 July 1998 Britain's chancellor of the exchequer, Gordon Brown, announces an extra £40 billion for health and education over the next three years.

14 July 1998 In Montreal, Canada, UK physician Roy Calne announces that a drug derived from a fungal growth discovered in the soil of Easter Island reduces the risk of rejection among kidney transplant patients by 60 percent, with few side effects. It is the first major transplant advance in 15 years. The drug is called rapamune after the native name for the island.

15 August 1998 An unnamed British couple, both bankers, are reported to be planning to freeze an embryo so that they can postpone parenthood until their late thirties to prevent the interruption of their careers.

24 August 1998 A research team led by Stephen Hecht from the University of Minnesota Cancer Centre in Minneapolis, USA, publishes a report revealing that pregnant smokers transmit a potent cancer-causing chemical to their unborn babies. The scientists detected the tobacco carcinogen NNK in the urine of babies whose mothers smoked during pregnancy.

31 August 1998 A team of international scientists led by François Simon and Françoise Brun-Vezinet of France announce the discovery of a new strain of HIV, the virus that causes AIDS, called YBF30, in a patient who died of AIDS in Cameroon in 1995.

10 September 1998 Scientists from the Imperial College of Science, Technology, and Medicine, in London, England, launch a company, called Bodi Tech, to develop a revolutionary breathalyzer that can diagnose illness and recommend treatment.

14 September 1998 The UK government bans the anti-impotence drug Viagra from prescription by the National Health Service (NHS) days before the drug is officially released in the UK. Health secretary Frank Dobson says the measure is temporary, in

*Prime Minister **Tony Blair** and **Cherie Blair** with Red Cross nurses at a service at Westminster Abbey on 3 July 1998 to mark the 50th anniversary of the formation of the National Health Service.* Photo: Richard Watt

order to assess the costs to the already overstretched health service.

24 September 1998 A multinational team of surgeons performs the world's first hand and arm transplant, using a donated limb, on New Zealand businessman Clint Hallam, in Lyon, France. Hallam, who had lost an arm in a chainsaw accident, received the arm of a Frenchman killed in a road accident.

October 1998 It is revealed that surgeons in Atlanta, Georgia, have inserted brain implants into the motor cortexes of two disabled people. The implants enable them to control a cursor by thinking about moving parts of their bodies.

October 1998 US scientist French Anderson announces a technique that could cure inherited diseases by inserting a healthy gene to replace a damaged one. He calls for a full debate on the issue of gene therapy, which brings with it the dilemma of whether it is ethical to enable the choice of physical attributes such as eye colour and height.

12 October 1998 US scientists Louis Ignarro, Ferid Murad, and Robert Furchgott share the Nobel Prize for Medicine for their work on the pollutant nitric oxide.

30 October 1998 The United Nations launches an anti-malaria programme to educate people about prevention and treatment. The programme will initially focus on Africa, which has the most cases of the disease.

5 November 1998 Two teams of US scientists, from John Hopkins Medical Institutions in Baltimore, Maryland, and the University of Wisconsin in Madison, announce that they have discovered a way to grow cells for any type of human organ in the laboratory and sustain them indefinitely.

11 November 1998 The scientific committee of the House of Lords publishes a report that recommends legalizing cannabis as a prescription for pain relief.

12 November 1998 US scientist Richard Borgens of Purdue University, Indiana, USA, announces that his team of researchers has successfully fused broken spinal cords of animals, offering hope to victims of spinal injury.

23 November 1998 The European Commission ends the ban on the export of British beef imposed in March 1996 after the discovery of the link between BSE and Creutzfeldt-Jakob Disease, a fatal illness affecting humans. The ban formally comes to an end on 1 August 1999.

8 December 1998 The Human Fertilization and Embryology Authority and the Human Genetics Advisory Commission publish a joint report in the UK on cloning. While they oppose cloning for reproductive purposes, they leave the door open for cloning for curing intractable diseases.

January 1999 Scientists report that the source of the HIV virus was an African chimpanzee that developed an immunity to the virus. The virus transferred to humans through the hunters that killed the chimpanzees, which are now on the verge of extinction, for meat. The findings are reported by Beatrice Hahn from the University of Alabama in the USA at the 6th Conference on Retroviruses and Opportunistic Infections.

24 January 1999 US scientist Craig Venter of the Institute for Genomic Research in Maryland, USA, announces the possibility of creating a living, replicating organism from an artificial set of genes, at a meeting of the American Association for the Advancement of Science, in Anaheim, California. An experiment to test this is put on hold until the moral question is discussed by religious leaders and ethicists at the University of Pennsylvania.

February 1999 The number of meningitis cases in the UK reaches its highest in 50 years. Medical experts link the rising number of cases to a new sub-strain of the disease to which the population has low immunity.

1 February 1999 The UK government announces a £1.5 billion pay package for the next ten years for public sector employees, including National Health Service workers, teachers, and members of the armed forces. The plan increases the average salary of newly qualified nurses by up to 12 percent, but angers many teachers whose average increase is 3.5 percent.

10 February 1999 A jury in San Francisco, California, USA, awards $50 million in punitive damages to former smoker Patricia Henley in her lawsuit against tobacco company Philip Morris. The total damages are the largest awarded to date in a smoker's liability suit against a tobacco company.

16 February 1999 UK science minister Lord Sainsbury admits that he owns biotechnology patents as well as shares in his family's supermarket chain. Conservative members of Parliament accuse Sainsbury of a conflict of interest in the controversy over genetically modified foods.

18 February 1999 UK deputy prime minister John Prescott and four other ministers pledge to protect public health when guiding government policy on genetically modified food products. The ministers are responding to widespread public concern about the safety of genetically modified food.

17 March 1999 A US Institute of Medicine panel releases a report on the medical benefits of marijuana, which include relief of the pain and nausea associated with AIDS as well as the muscle spasms associated with multiple sclerosis.

30 March 1999 A jury in Portland, Oregon, USA, awards $81 million in damages to the family of Jesse Williams, a smoker of Marlboro cigarettes who died of lung cancer in 1997, in a lawsuit against Marlboro manufacturer Philip Morris. The award is the largest to date in a smoking-related lawsuit.

May 1999 The United Nations World Health Organization announces that AIDS is now the world's leading infectious killer and the leading cause of death in Africa.

11 May 1999 The World Health Organization publishes its *World Health Report*. According to its figures, depression and related neuropsychiatric conditions are the second greatest cause of death, after heart disease, in the West.

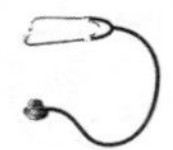

18 May 1999 A group of scientists at a specially convened Royal Society meeting maintain that the experiments of Hungarian-born doctor Arpad Pusztai on genetically modified foods were flawed. Pusztai said in August, 1998, that his experiments showed that genetically modified potatoes stunted the growth of laboratory rats, adding to a furore in the UK about genetically modified foods.

21 May 1999 UK government minister Jack Cunningham announces new measures to boost confidence in genetically modified foods, such as increased monitoring and surveillance to ensure the food does not harm public health. The British Medical Association, as well as consumer and environmental groups, express concerns over labelling and claim that the government measures fail to meet safety concerns.

1 June 1999 Prince Charles attacks the producers of genetically modified crops, describing the technology as unethical, in an article in the UK newspaper, the *Daily Mail*, just after government attempts to reassure the public that the technology is safe.

2 June 1999 European MPs demand a ban on the sale of Belgian chocolates because of fears that they might contain egg products contaminated with dioxin. The move follows a food pollution scandal in Belgium in which chickens and eggs were found to contain dioxins, which have been linked to cancer.

4 June 1999 The UK government orders an emergency measure to seize and destroy all imported meat, dairy products, and eggs from Belgium which may be contaminated by dioxins.

4 June 1999 The US Food Safety and Inspection Service impounds all European imports of pork and poultry in response to a scare over dioxin contamination in Belgian farms.

General Medical Information

First Aid Advice

First aid is the controlled application of tried and tested methods and techniques using the knowledge and resources available at the time of injury or onset of illness until expert help arrives. In other words, the provider of first aid is the casualty's firsthand assistance and, in an emergency situation, this could mean the difference between life and death.

There are hundreds of thousands of personal injury accidents each year. In many cases, first aid knowledge could save lives. At the very least, casualties can be made comfortable and minor injuries attended to before the emergency services arrive. Vital time can be saved, with unnecessary pain and anxiety avoided.

In the UK, the leading first aid organizations are the British Red Cross and St John Ambulance. Both offer training, and first aid courses for children, the general public, and the workforce. Both organizations believe that everyone should obtain at least a basic knowledge of first aid through a two-hour or one-day introductory course.

Authoritative first aid manuals provide good basic guidelines and instructions on how to care for victims of accident, injury, or illness. The British Red Cross supplies the following essential and practical first aid and care guides:

First Aid Manual ISBN: 0 7513 0707 6 £10.99
Practical First Aid ISBN: 0 7513 05646 4 £5.99
First Aid for Children Fast ISBN: 0 7513 0138 8 £8.99
Carer's Handbook ISBN: 0 7513 0464 6 £9.99
The Babysitter's Handbook ISBN: 0 7513 0217 1 £9.99

The Basic Responsible Reactions

In an emergency:

Keep calm Remaining calm while helping the victim will help them to keep calm and cooperate. If the victim becomes anxious or excited the extent of damage from the injury could be increased.

Plan quickly what you need to do Learn basic procedures, or have your first aid manual available, so you can care for the victim.

Send for professional help Reaching help quickly could save a life. Know your local emergency telephone numbers. (999 in the UK or 112 in Ireland or your local emergency telephone number.)

Be an encouragement to the injured person Let the victim know that help is on the way and try to make them as comfortable as possible. Showing care and concern for the victim can give them hope during their circumstances.

Phobias

Fear	Name of phobia
Animals	zoophobia
Bacteria	bacteriophobia, bacillophobia
Beards	pogonophobia
Bees	apiphobia, melissophobia
Being alone	monophobia, autophobia, eremophobia
Being buried alive	taphophobia
Being seen by others	scopophobia
Being touched	haphephobia, aphephobia
Birds	ornithophobia
Blood	h(a)ematophobia, hemophobia
Blushing	ereuthrophobia, erythrophobia
Books	bibliophobia
Cancer	cancerophobia, carcinophobia
Cats	ailurophobia, gatophobia
Chickens	alektorophobia
Childbirth	tocophobia, parturiphobia
Children	paediphobia
Cold	cheimatophobia, frigophobia
Colour	chromatophobia, chromophobia, psychrophobia
Comets	cometophobia
Computers	computerphobia, cyberphobia
Contamination	misophobia, coprophobia
Criticism	enissophobia
Crossing bridges	gephyrophobia
Crossing streets	dromophobia
Crowds	demophobia, ochlophobia
Darkness	achulophobia, nyctophobia, scotophobia
Dawn	eosophobia
Daylight	phengophobia
Death, corpses	necrophobia, thanatophobia
Defecation	rhypophobia
Deformity	dysmorphophobia
Demons	demonophobia
Dirt	mysophobia
Disease	nosophobia, pathophobia
Disorder	ataxiophobia
Dogs	cynophobia
Draughts	anemophobia
Dreams	oneirophobia
Drinking	dipsophobia
Drugs	pharmacophobia
Duration	chronophobia
Dust	amathophobia, koniphobia

(continued)

Phobias (*continued*)

Fear	Name of phobia
Eating	phagophobia
Enclosed spaces	claustrophobia
Everything	pan(t)ophobia
Facial hair	trichopathophobia
Faeces	coprophobia
Failure	kakorrphiaphobia
Fatigue	kopophobia, ponophobia
Fears	phobophobia
Fever	febriphobia
Fire	pyrophobia
Fish	ichthyophobia
Flying, the air	aerophobia
Fog	homichlophobia
Food	sitophobia
Foreign languages	xenoglossophobia
Freedom	eleutherophobia
Fun	cherophobia
Germs	spermophobia, bacillophobia
Ghosts	phasmophobia
Glass	hyalophobia
God	theophobia
Going to bed	clinophobia
Graves	taphophobia
Hair	chaetophobia, trichophobia, hypertrichophobia
Heart conditions	cardiophobia
Heat	thermophobia
Heaven	ouranophobia
Heights	acrophobia, altophobia
Hell	hadephobia, stygiophobia
Home	domatophobia, oikophobia
Horses	hippophobia
Human beings	anthrophobia
Ice, frost	cryophobia
Ideas	ideophobia
Illness	nosemaphobia, nosophobia
Imperfection	atelophobia
Infection	mysophobia
Infinity	apeirophobia
Injustice	dikephobia
Inoculations, injections	trypanophobia
Insanity	lyssophobia, maniaphobia
Insects	entomophobia
Itching	acarophobia, scabiophobia
Jealousy	zelophobia
Knowledge	epistemophobia
Lakes	limnophobia
Large objects	macrophobia
Leaves	phyllophobia
Left side	levophobia
Leprosy	leprophobia
Lice	pediculophobia
Lightning	astraphobia
Machinery	mechanophobia
Many things	polyphobia
Marriage	gamophobia
Meat	carnophobia
Men	androphobia
Metals	metallophobia
Meteors	meteorophobia
Mice	musophobia
Mind	psychophobia
Mirrors	eisoptrophobia, catotrophobia
Money	chrometophobia
Monsters, monstrosities	teratophobia
Motion	kinesophobia, kinetophobia
Music	musicophobia
Names	onomatophobia
Narrowness	anginaphobia
Needles	belonephobia
Night, darkness	achluophobia
Noise	phonophobia
Novelty	cainophobia, cenotophobia, neophobia
Nudity	gymnotophobia
Number 13	triskaidekaphobia, terdekaphobia
Odours	osmophobia
Open spaces	agoraphobia
Pain	algophobia, odynophobia
Parasites	parasitophobia
Physical love	erotophobia
Pins	enetophobia
Places	topophobia
Pleasure	hedonophobia
Pointed instruments	aichmophobia
Poison	toxiphobia, toxophobia, iophobia
Poverty	peniaphobia
Precipices	cremnophobia
Pregnancy	maieusiophobia
Punishment	poinephobia
Rain	ombrophobia
Reptiles	batrachophobia
Responsibility	hypegiaphobia
Ridicule	katagalophobia
Rivers	potamophobia
Robbery	harpaxophobia
Ruin	atephobia
Rust	iophobia
Sacred things	hierophobia
Satan	satanophobia
School	scholionophobia
Sea	thalassophobia
Semen	spermatophobia
Sex	genophobia
Sexual intercourse	coitophobia
Shadows	sciophobia
Sharp objects	belonephobia
Shock	hormephobia
Sin	hamartiophobia
Sinning	peccatophobia
Skin	dermatophobia
Sleep	hypnophobia
Small objects	microphobia
Smell	olfactophobia
Smothering, choking	pnigerophobia
Snakes	ophidiophobia, ophiophobia
Snow	chionophobia
Soiling	rhypophobia
Solitude	eremitophobia, eremophobia
Sound	akousticophobia
Sourness	acerophobia
Speaking aloud	phonophobia
Speed	tachophobia
Spiders	arachn(e)ophobia
Standing	stasiphobia
Standing erect	stasibasiphobia
Stars	siderophobia
Stealing	kleptophobia
Stillness	eremophobia
Stings	cnidophobia
Strangers	xenophobia
Strong light	photophobia
Stuttering	laliophobia, lalophobia
Suffocation	anginophobia
Sun	heliophobia
Symbols	symbolophobia
Taste	geumaphobia
Teeth	odontophobia
Thinking	phronemophobia
Thrown objects	ballistophobia
Thunder	astraphobia, brontophobia, keraunophobia
Touch	aphephobia, haptophobia, haphephobia
Travel	hodophobia
Travelling by train	siderodromophobia
Trees	dendrophobia
Trembling	tremophobia
Vehicles	amaxophobia, ochophobia
Venereal disease	cypridophobia
Void	kenophobia
Vomiting	emetophobia
Walking	basiphobia
Wasps	spheksophobia
Water	hydrophobia, aquaphobia
Weakness	asthenophobia
Wind	ancraophobia
Women	gynophobia
Words	logophobia
Work	ergophobia, ergasiophobia
Worms	helminthophobia
Wounds, injury	traumatophobia
Writing	graphophobia

Compatibility of Blood Groups

Blood group	Antigen on red blood cell	Antibody in plasma	Blood groups that can be received by this individual	Blood groups that can receive donations from this individual
A	A	anti-B	A, O	A, AB
B	B	anti-A	B, O	B, AB
AB	A and B	none	any	AB
O	neither A nor B	anti-A and anti-B	O	any

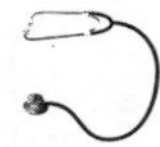

Medical Transplants: Chronology

1682	A Russian doctor uses bone from a dog to repair the skull of an injured nobleman. The graft is reportedly successful, though it angers the Russian Orthodox Church.
1771	Scottish surgeon John Hunter describes his experiments in the transplantation of tissues, including a human tooth into a cock's comb in *Treatise on the Natural History of Human Teeth*.
1905	Corneal grafting, which may restore sight to a diseased or damaged eye, is pioneered.
1950s	Kidneys are first transplanted successfully; kidney transplants are pioneered by British surgeon Roy Calne. Peter Medawar conducts vital research into the body's tolerance of transplanted organs and skin grafts.
1964	Chimpanzee kidneys are transplanted into humans in the USA, but with little success; in the UK a pig's heart valve is transplanted successfully and the operation becomes routine.
1967	South African surgeon Christiaan Barnard performs the first human heart transplant. The 54-year-old patient lives for 18 days.
1969	The world's first heart and lung transplant is performed at the Stanford Medical Center, California, USA.
1970	The first successful nerve transplant is performed in West Germany.
1978	Cyclosporin, an immunosuppressive drug derived from a fungus, revolutionizes transplant surgery by reducing the incidence and severity of rejection of donor organs.
1982	Jarvik 7, an artificial heart made of plastic and aluminium is transplanted; the recipient lives for 112 days.
1986	British surgeons John Wallwork and Roy Calne perform the first triple transplant – heart, lung, and liver – at Papworth Hospital, Cambridge, England.
1987	The world's longest-surviving heart-transplant patient dies in France, 18 years after his operation. A three-year-old girl in the USA receives a new liver, pancreas, small intestine, and parts of the stomach and colon; the first successful five-organ transplant.
1989	Grafts of fetal brain tissue are first used to treat Parkinson's disease.
1990	Nobel Prize for Medicine or Physiology is awarded to two US surgeons, Donnall Thomas and Joseph Murray, for their pioneering work on organ and tissue transplantation.
1995	The first experiments to use genetically altered animal organs in humans are given US government approval July – genetically altered pig livers are attached to the circulatory systems of patients whose livers have failed. An AIDS patient receives a bone marrow transplant from a baboon but the graft fails to take.
1997	Fetal nerve cells from pigs are injected into the brains of Parkinson's patients. In one case the cells survive for seven months.
23 June 1998	Cultured human neural cells are injected into the brain of a stroke victim. This is the first transplant of brain tissue used in stroke treatment and the first use of cultured cells rather than fetal tissue.
24 September 1998	An international team of surgeons in Lyon, France, perform the first hand-and-forearm transplant operation on a man whose arm was amputated 14 years earlier. Although doctors have been able to attach severed limbs for years, they have been unable to successfully move a limb from a dead donor to a living recipient. The first hand transplant from a donor in the USA is performed Jan 1999. The surgical breakthrough raises the ethical question of whether a non-vital body part such as a hand should be transplanted.
5 November 1998	Researchers at John Hopkins University, USA, announce that they have successfully grown human stem cells in a laboratory, a major advance that could one day help organ transplantation, gene therapy, and treatment of various maladies. Stem cells are blank cells that can develop into virtually any kind of cell in the human body.
12 December 1998	A three-year-old Florida boy becomes the first child to get a new heart, both lungs, and a liver in a marathon transplant operation. The surgical procedure, performed at Children's Hospital of Pittsburgh, Pennsylvania, has been performed on a handful of adults, but never before on a child.
14 December 1998	US scientists at Emory University Hospital perform the world's first 'unrelated donor' cord blood transplant in a child with sickle cell anaemia. Researchers say children who might have died from inherited immune disorders or leukaemia may be cured with umbilical cord blood transplants.
30 January 1999	Scientists at Harvard Medical School report that they had managed to grow artificial bladders for transplant into dogs, and that the technology might eventually work for people with bladder disease.

Glossary

Medical Prefixes

a(n)- lacking
ab- away from
abdomin(o)- abdominal
ad- towards, near
andr(o)- male
angi(o)- blood or lymph vessel
ant(i)- against, counteracting
ante- before
arthr(o)- joint
aut(o)- self
bi- twice, two
brachi(o)- arm
brachy- shortness
brady- slowness
bronch(o)- bronchial tube
carcin(o)- cancer
cardi(o)- heart
cerebr(o)- brain
cholecyst- gall bladder
circum- surrounding
colp(o)- vagina
contra- against
crani(o)- skull
cry(o)- cold
crypt- hidden, concealed
cyst(o)- bladder
cyt(o)- cell
dent- tooth
derm- skin
di- double
dys- difficult, painful, abnormal
end(o)- within, inner
enter(o)- intestine
epi- above, upon
ex(o)- outside, outer
extra- outside, beyond
gastr(o)- stomach
gyn- female
haem- blood
hepat(o)- liver
hist(o)- tissue
hyper- above
hypno- sleep
hypo- below
hyster(o)- uterus
immuno- immunity
infra- below
intra- within
laryng(o)- larynx
mal- abnormal, diseased
mast- breast
muco- mucus
my(o)- muscle

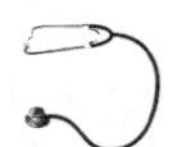

necro- death
neo- new
nephr(o)- kidney
neur(o)- nerve
noct- night
oculo- eye
olig(o)- deficiency, few
ophthalm(o)- eye
oro- mouth
ortho- straight, normal
osteo- bone
ot(o)- ear
paed- children
path(o)- disease
peri- around, enclosing
pharmac(o)- drugs
phleb(o)- vein
phot(o)- light
pneumon- lung
poly- many, excessive
post- after
pre-(pro-) before
ren- kidney
retro- behind
rhin- nose
sclero- thickening
ser(o)- serum
spondyl- vertebra, spine
supra- above
syn- together, union
tachy- fast
tetra- four
therm(o)- heat, temperature
trache(o)- trachea
uni- one
urin- urine, urinary system
utero- uterus
vaso- vessel
vesico- bladder

Medical Suffixes

-aemia condition of blood
-algia pain
-ase enzyme
-blast formative cell
-cele tumour, swelling
-centesis puncture
-cide destructive, killing
-coccus spherical bacterium
-cyte cell
-derm skin
-dynia pain
-ectasis dilation, extension
-ectomy surgical removal of
-facient making, causing
-fuge expelling
-genesis origin, development
-genic causing, produced by
-gram tracing, record
-iasis diseased condition
-iatric practice of healing
-itis inflammation of
-kinesis movement
-lith calculus, stone
-lysis breaking down, dissolution
-malacia softening
-megaly enlargement
-oid likeness, resemblance
-oma tumour
-opia eye defect
-osis disease, condition
-ostomy surgical opening or outlet
-otomy surgical incision into an organ or part
-pathy disease
-penia lack of, deficiency
-pexy surgical fixation
-phage ingesting
-philia affinity for, morbid attraction
-phobia fear
-plasty reconstructive surgery
-plegia paralysis
-pnoea condition of breathing
-poiesis formation
-ptosis prolapse
-scopy visual examination
-stasis stagnation, stoppage of flow
-tome cutting instrument
-uria condition of urine

Medical Abbreviations and Acronyms

A&E accident and emergency department
ABP arterial blood pressure
ADLs activities of daily living
adm. admission
aet. aetiology
AI artificial insemination
AIDS acquired immune deficiency syndrome
ALG antilymphocyte globulin
ALS antilymphocyte serum
ARM artificial rupture of membranes (for delivery)
BCG bacille Calmette-Guérin (TB vaccine)
BMI body mass index
BMR basal metabolic rate
BP blood pressure
BPD bronchopulmonary dysplasia
CA cancer
CABG coronary artery bypass graft
CAPD continuous ambulatory peritoneal dialysis
CAT computerized axial tomography
CCU coronary care unit
CJD Creutzfeldt-Jakob disease
CMV cytomegalovirus
CNS central nervous system
COAD chronic obstructive airways disease
CPAP continuous positive airways pressure
CPR cardiopulmonary resuscitation
CSF cerebrospinal fluid
CT computerized tomography
CV cardiovascular
CVA cardiovascular accident
CVP central venous pressure
CVS chorionic villus sampling
CXR chest X-ray
D&C dilation and curettage
DHA district health authority
DI donor insemination
DIC disseminated intravascular coagulation
disch. discharge
DL danger list
DMD Duchenne's muscular dystrophy
DNA deoxyribonucleic acid
DOA dead on arrival
DPT combined vaccine against diphtheria, pertussis (whooping cough), and tetanus
Dr doctor
DRG diagnostic related group
DTs delirium tremens
DVT deep vein thrombosis
ECG electrocardiogram
ECT electroconvulsive therapy
EEG electroencephalograph
EMG electromyograph
ENT ear, nose, and throat
EPO erythropoietin
ET endotracheal tube (used for patient on ventilator)
GH growth hormone
GIFT gamete intrafallopian transfer
GP general practitioner
GVHD graft-versus-host disease
HBIG hepatitis B immunoglobulin
HCG human chorionic gonadotrophin
HIV human immunodeficiency virus
HLA human leucocyte antigen system
HMO health maintenance organization
HRT hormone replacement therapy
IBS irritable bowel syndrome
ICD international classification of diseases
ICP intracranial pressure
ICU intensive care unit
IHD ischaemic heart disease
IMR infant mortality rate
IMV intermittent mandatory ventilation
IOP intraocular pressure
IPPV intermittent positive pressure ventilation
IQ intelligence quotient
IUD intrauterine device
IV intravenous
IVP intravenous pyelogram
IZS insulin zinc suspension
K&M kaolin and morphine
LBW low birth weight
LP lumbar puncture
LSD lysergic acid diethylamide
MAB monoclonal antibody
MAOI monoamine oxidase inhibitor
MAP mean arterial pressure
MBD minimal brain dysfunction
MD doctor of medicine
ME myalgic encephalomyelitis
MHC major histocompatibility complex
MI myocardial infarction
MLD minimum lethal dose
MMR combined vaccine against measles, mumps, and rubella (German measles)

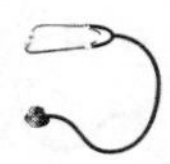

MND motor neurone disease
MO medical officer
MRI magnetic resonance imaging
MRS magnetic resonance spectroscopy
MRSA methicillin-resistant Staphylococcus aureus
MS multiple sclerosis
MSU mid-stream urine specimen
NHS National Health Service (in the UK)
NPO nil per orem (nothing by mouth)
NTD neural tube defect
O&G obstetrics and gynaecology
OA osteoarthritis
OD overdose
OP outpatient
ORT oral rehydration therapy
OT occupational therapy
PA physician's assistant
paed. paediatrics
path. pathology
PCOD polycystic ovary disease
PE pleural effusion
PET positron-emission tomography
PICU paediatric intensive care unit
PID pelvic inflammatory disease
PIH pregnancy-induced hypertension
PKU phenylketonuria
PM postmortem
PMS premenstrual stress disorder
PO per orem (by mouth)
PoP plaster of Paris
pre-op pre-operative
PTA post-traumatic amnesia
RA rheumatoid arthritis
RDS respiratory distress syndrome
REM sleep rapid eye movement sleep
RES reticuloendothelial system
RN registered nurse
RNA ribonucleic acid
RQ respiratory quotient
RSI repetitive strain injury
RSV respiratory syncytial virus
Rx treatment/prescription
SAD seasonal affective disorder
SAH subarachnoid haemorrhage
SIDS sudden infant death syndrome
SLE systemic lupus erythematous
STD sexually transmitted disease
TAB combined vaccine against typhoid, paratyphoid A, and paratyphoid B
TAT thematic apperception test
TATT tired all the time
TB tuberculosis
TENS transcutaneous electrical nerve stimulation
TIA transient ischaemic attack
tPA tissue plasminogen activator (heart drug)
TPR temperature, pulse, and respiration
TS Tourette's syndrome
TSH thyroid-stimulating hormone
Tx transfusion, transplant
URTI upper respiratory tract infection
UTI urinary tract infection
VA visual acuity
VD venereal disease
VF ventricular fibrillation
WHO World Health Organization

Common Allergies

Allergy	Cause	Symptoms/comments
Pollen allergy (hay fever)	mainly grass and tree pollen	allergic rhinitis (running eyes and nose, sneezing, nasal congestion), eczema, urticaria (nettlerash or hives), and asthma; affects about 15% of the UK population
Dust-mite allergy	enzymes in the faeces of mites in house dust, feathers, pillows, and mattresses	symptoms as above; affects about 5% of the UK population
Pet allergy	allergens in the pet's saliva, urine, or skin flakes, carried on its fur	symptoms as above
Mould allergy	spores from moulds growing in damp living spaces and on hay and cereal grain	symptoms as above; often associated with pollen allergies
Bee- and wasp-sting allergy	proteins in the venom	severe and prolonged swelling at the site of the sting, pain, and – in extreme cases – anaphylaxis (respiratory difficulties, a rapid fall in blood pressure, and collapse, followed by loss of consciousness and even death)
Food allergy	most commonly to proteins in dairy foods, eggs, peanuts, true nuts, wheat and soya products, and shellfish, or to chemicals such as monosodium glutamate, tartrazine, sulphur dioxide, and sodium benzoate in food additives	eczema, urticaria, asthma, itching around the mouth, vomiting, diarrhoea, and – in extreme cases – anaphylaxis (see above); food allergy is often confused with food intolerance, which is not caused by the body's immune response but by its inability to digest a particular food (for example, lactose intolerance) or by adverse reactions to druglike chemicals such as caffeine in coffee and amines in chocolate and cheese; peanut allergies affect about 0.5% of the UK population
Drug allergy	most commonly to penicillin and related antibiotics	eczema, urticaria, asthma, dizziness, swelling of the arms and legs, and – in extreme cases – anaphylaxis (see above)

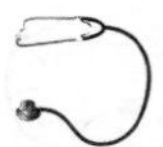

Bones of the Human Body

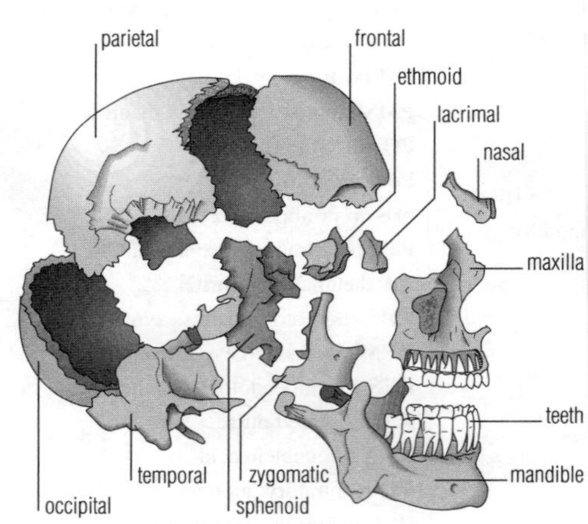

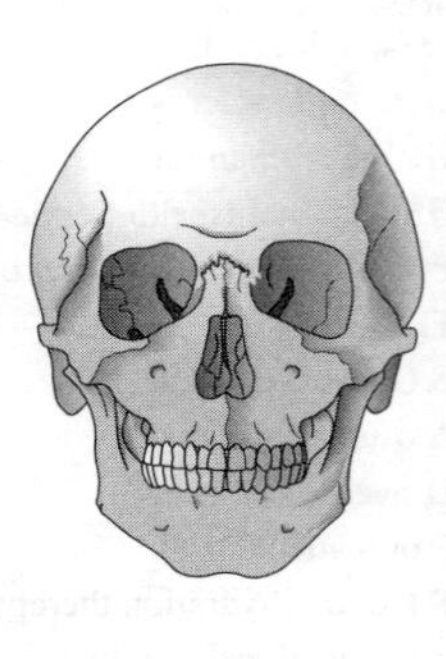

Skull *The skull is a protective box for the brain, eyes, and hearing organs. It is also a framework for the teeth and flesh of the face.*

Bone	Number
Cranium (Skull)	
Occipital	1
Parietal: 1 pair	2
Sphenoid	1
Ethmoid	1
Inferior nasal conchae	2
Frontal: 1 pair, fused	1
Nasal: 1 pair	2
Lacrimal: 1 pair	2
Temporal: 1 pair	2
Maxilla: 1 pair, fused	1
Zygomatic: 1 pair	2
Vomer	1
Palatine: 1 pair	2
Mandible (jawbone): 1 pair, fused	1
Total	21
Ear	
Malleus (hammer)	1
Incus (anvil)	1
Stapes (stirrups)	1
Total (2 x 3)	6
Vertebral Column (Spine)	
Cervical vertebrae	7
Thoracic vertebrae	12
Lumbar vertebrae	5
Sacral vertebrae: 5, fused to form the sacrum	1
Coccygeal vertebrae: between 3 and 5, fused to form the coccyx	1
Total	26
Ribs	
Ribs, 'true': 7 pairs	14
Ribs, 'false': 5 pairs, of which 2 pairs are floating	10
Total	24
Sternum (Breastbone)	
Manubrium	1
Sternebrae	1
Xiphisternum	1
Total	3
Throat	
Hyoid	1
Total	1
Pectoral Girdle	
Clavicle: 1 pair (collar-bone)	2
Scapula (including coracoid): 1 pair (shoulder blade)	2
Total	4

Upper Extremity (Each Arm)	
Forearm	
Humerus	1
Radius	1
Ulna	1
Carpus (Wrist)	
Scaphoid	1
Lunate	1
Triquetral	1
Pisiform	1
Trapezium	1
Trapezoid	1
Capitate	1
Hamate	1
Metacarpals	5
Phalanges (Fingers)	
First digit	2
Second digit	3
Third digit	3
Fourth digit	3
Fifth digit	3
Total (2 x 30)	60
Pelvic Girdle	
Ilium, ischium, and pubis (combined): 1 pair of hip bones, innominate	2
Total	2

Lower Extremity (Each Leg)	
Leg	
Femur (thighbone)	1
Tibia (shinbone)	1
Fibula	1
Patella (kneecap)	1
Tarsus (Ankle)	
Talus	1
Calcaneus	1
Navicular	1
Cuneiform, medial	1
Cuneiform, intermediate	1
Cuneiform, lateral	1
Cuboid	1
Metatarsals (foot bones)	5
Phalanges (Toes)	
First digit	2
Second digit	3
Third digit	3
Fourth digit	3
Fifth digit	3
Total (2 x 30)	60
TOTAL	207

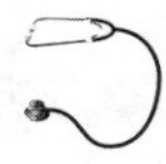

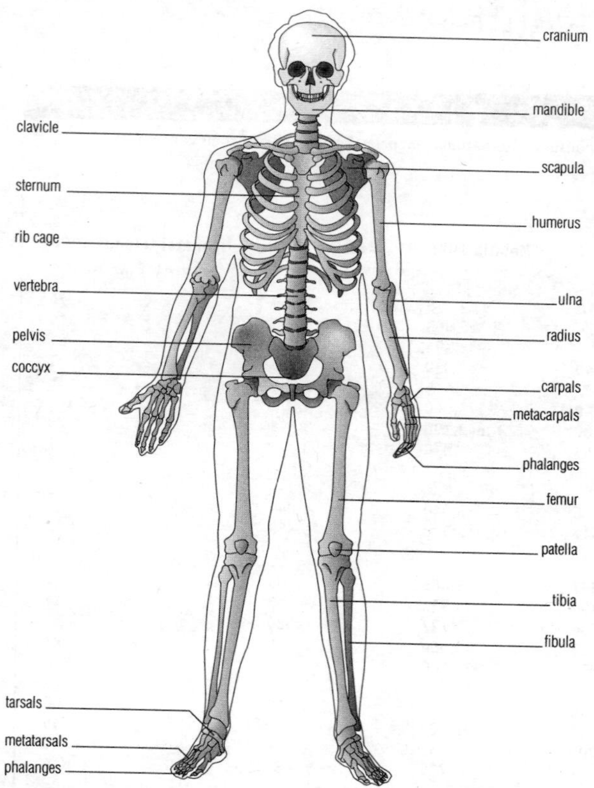

Skeleton
The human skeleton is made up of 207 bones and provides a strong but flexible supportive framework for the body.

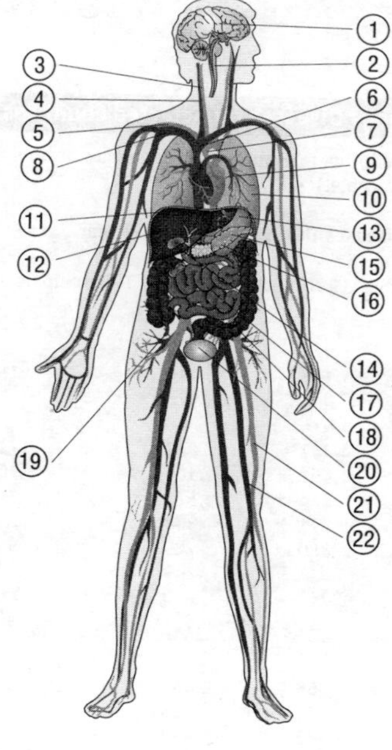

Organs
The adult human body has approximately 650 muscles, 100,000 km/60,000 mi of blood vessels and 13,000 nerve cells.

Human Body: Composition

Chemical element or substance	Body weight (%)	Chemical element or substance	Body weight (%)	Chemical element or substance	Body weight (%)
Pure elements				***Water and solid matter***	
Oxygen	65	Potassium	0.35	Water	60–80
Carbon	18	Sulphur	0.25	Total solid material	20–40
Hydrogen	10	Sodium	0.15	***Organic molecules***	
Nitrogen	3	Chlorine	0.15	Protein	15–20
Calcium	2	Magnesium, iron, manganese, copper, iodine, cobalt, zinc	traces	Lipid	3–20
Phosphorus	1.1			Carbohydrate	1–15
				Other	0–1

World Health

Reported Cases for Infectious Diseases for Selected Countries

Estimates are obtained or derived from relevant WHO programmes or from responsible international agencies for the areas of their concern. (N/A = not available or not applicable.)

Reported Cases of Selected Diseases During the Specified Year

Region/countries	Leprosy 1996	AIDS 1996	Tuberculosis 1996	Malaria 1995	Measles 1996	Neonatal tetanus 1996
Africa						
Algeria	N/A	44	N/A	18	21,003	16
Angola	157	115	15,424	156,603	251	116
Burundi	N/A	576	3,796	932,794	16,099	21
Comoros	N/A	0	140	187,082	0	1
Ethiopia	4,747	832	171,033	N/A	1,586	5
Ghana	1,451	1,166	10,449	1,175,000	34,273	108
Kenya	234	6,520	34,980	4,343,190	3,572	23
Nigeria	6,871	308	24,063	N/A	88,675	1,117
South Africa	280	729	91,578	9,287	6,501	9
Swaziland	N/A	249	3,893	N/A	2,199	1
United Republic of Tanzania	2,747	0	44,416	2,438,040	5,049	19
Zambia	511	4,552	40,417	2,742,118	9,459	15
Americas						
Argentina	565	2,067	13,397	1,065	59	3
Bolivia	32	28	10,194	46,911	7	14
Brazil	39,792	16,469	87,254	565,727	580	51
Colombia	709	1,042	9,702	49,669	160	27
Haiti	72	0	6,632	23,140	1	N/A
Honduras	N/A	797	4,176	59,446	4	4
Mexico	523	4,216	10,852	7,316	180	60
Peru	90	998	41,739	192,629	105	45
Trinidad and Tobago	N/A	412	205	35	0	0
United States of America	157	36,693	21,337	700	489	N/A
Middle East						
Bahrain	N/A	5	156	192	74	0
Cyprus	N/A	4	24	1	55	0
Djibouti	N/A	358	3,071	3,359	410	0
Egypt	1,332	14	12,338	322	4,403	643
Iran	54	35	14,189	67,532	2,329	21
Iraq	N/A	15	29,196	89,984	256	74
Pakistan	1,405	19	4,307	111,836	1,090	2,012
Saudi Arabia	112	100	N/A	18,751	2,407	28
Sudan	2,126	221	20,280	232,177	2,559	40
United Arab Emirates	N/A	0	507	2,914	425	0
Europe						
Azerbaijan	N/A	2	2,480	2,844	151	2
Denmark	N/A	155	484	N/A	118	0
France	N/A	3,684	7,656	977	66,000	0
Germany	N/A	1,169	11,814	N/A	812	0
Italy	N/A	4,891	4,155	N/A	29,099	0
Poland	N/A	96	15,358	N/A	669	N/A
Portugal	1	720	5,248	N/A	111	2
Russian Federation	N/A	46	111,075	N/A	8,184	0
Spain	12	5,678	8,331	N/A	4,457	N/A
Tajikistan	N/A	0	1,647	6,144	21	N/A
Turkey	N/A	37	20,212	82,096	27,171	61
United Kingdom	N/A	1,214	6,238	N/A	2,569	0
South East Asia						
Bangladesh	11,225	0	63,471	152,729	4,929	759
India	415,302	901	1,300,935	2,800,000	47,072	1,313
Indonesia	15,071	32	24,647	1,460,569	15,339	814
Maldives	N/A	2	212	17	0	0
Myanmar	6,935	690	22,201	642,751	1,684	61
Nepal	6,602	37	22,970	9,718	8,513	171

(continued)

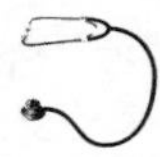

Reported Cases for Infectious Diseases for Selected Countries (*continued*)

Region/countries	Leprosy 1996	AIDS 1996	Tuberculosis 1996	Malaria 1995	Measles 1996	Neonatal tetanus 1996
Sri Lanka	1,528	11	5,439	142,294	158	7
Thailand	1,197	17,942	39,871	82,743	5,677	32
Vietnam	2,883	375	74,711	666,153	5,156	257
Western Pacific						
Australia	N/A	573	N/A	623	N/A	N/A
China	1,845	38	469,358	N/A	68,404	2,543
Japan	N/A	294	42,122	N/A	N/A	N/A
Malaysia	293	300	12,902	59,208	N/A	N/A
Philippines	4,051	51	276,295	366,844	N/A	N/A
Korea, South	39	22	31,134	131	71	0
Samoa	N/A	2	37	N/A	87	0
Solomon Islands	N/A	0	289	118,521	0	1

Source: *The World Health Report 1998*, World Health Organization

Newly Recognized Infectious Diseases

Year of recognition	Agent	Type	Disease/comments
1973	Rotavirus	virus	major cause of infantile diarrhoea worldwide
1975	Parvovirus B19	virus	aplastic crisis in chronic haemolytic anaemia
1976	*Cryptosporidium parvum*	parasite	acute and chronic diarrhoea
1977	Ebola virus	virus	Ebola haemorrhagic fever
1977	*Legionella pneumophila*	bacterium	legionnaires' disease
1977	Hantaan virus	virus	haemorrhagic fever with renal syndrome (HRFS)
1977	*Campylobacter jejuni*	bacterium	enteric pathogen distributed globally
1980	human T-lymphotropic virus 1 (HTLV-1)	virus	T-cell lymphoma-leukaemia
1981	toxin-producing strains of *Staphylococcus aureus*	bacterium	toxic shock syndrome
1982	*Escherichia coli* 0157:H7	bacterium	haemorrhagic colitis; haemolytic uraemic syndrome
1982	HTLV-2	virus	hairy cell leukaemia
1982	*Borrelia burgdorferi*	bacterium	Lyme disease
1983	human immunodeficiency virus (HIV)	virus	acquired immunodeficiency syndrome (AIDS)
1983	*Helicobacter pylori*	bacterium	peptic ulcer disease
1985	*Enterocytozoon bieneusi*	parasite	persistent diarrhoea
1986	*Cyclospora cayetanensis*	parasite	persistent diarrhoea
1986	BSE agent (uncertain)	non-conventional agent	bovine spongiform encephalopathy in cattle and possibly variant Creutzfeldt-Jakob disease (vCJD) in humans
1988	human herpes virus 6 (HHV-6)	virus	exanthem subitum
1988	hepatitis E virus	virus	enterically transmitted non-A, non-B hepatitis
1989	*Ehrlichia chaffeensis*	bacterium	human ehrlichiosis
1989	hepatitis C virus	virus	parenterally transmitted non-A, non-B liver hepatitis
1991	Guanarito virus	virus	Venezuelan haemorrhagic fever
1991	*Encephalitozoon hellem*	parasite	conjunctivitis, disseminated disease
1991	new species of *Babesia*	parasite	atypical babesiosis
1992	*Vibrio cholerae* 0139	bacterium	new strain associated with epidemic cholera
1992	*Bartonella henselae*	bacterium	cat-scratch disease causing flu-like fever; bacillary angiomatosis
1993	Sin Nombre virus	virus	Hantavirus pulmonary syndrome
1993	*Encephalitozoon cuniculi*	parasite	disseminated disease
1994	Sabia virus	virus	Brazilian haemorrhagic fever
1995	human herpes virus 8	virus	associated with Kaposi's sarcoma in AIDS patients
1996	NvCJD	TSE causing agent	New variant Creutzfeldt-Jakob disease
1997	Avian influenza	Type A(9H5N1) virus	Influenza; can cause Reye syndrome

Source: *State of the World's Health*, World Health Organization

Mortality, Morbidity, and Disability for Selected Infectious Diseases in the World

(N/A = not available or not applicable. In thousands.)

1997 Estimates

Disease by main mode of transmission	Deaths	New cases (incidence)	All cases (prevalence)	Persons with severe activity limitation[1]
Person to Person				
Acute lower respiratory infection (ALR)	3,745	395,000	N/A	N/A
Tuberculosis	2,910	7,250	16,300	8,420
Hepatitis B, viral	605	67,730	N/A	N/A
Measles	960	31,075	N/A	N/A
HIV/AIDS	2,300	5,800	30,600	N/A
Whooping cough (pertussis)	410	45,050	N/A	N/A
Meningococcal meningitis	50	N/A	500	60
Poliomyelitis, acute	2	35	N/A	10,600
Leprosy	2	570	1,150	3,000
Gonorrhoea	N/A	62,000	23,000	N/A
Syphilis, venereal	N/A	12,000	28,000	N/A
Chancroid	N/A	2,000	2,000	N/A
Trachoma	N/A	N/A	152,420	5,600
Food-, Water-, and Soil-borne				
Diarrhoea (including dysentery)	2,455	4,000,000[2]	N/A	N/A
Neonatal tetanus	275	415	N/A	N/A
Amoebiasis	70	48,000	N/A	N/A
Hookworm diseases	65	N/A	151,000[3]	N/A
Ascariasis	60	N/A	250,000[4]	N/A
Schistosomiasis	20	N/A	200,000	120,000
Cholera[5]	10	145	N/A	N/A
Trichuriasis	10	N/A	45,530[6]	N/A
Trematode infections (foodborne only)	10	N/A	40,000	N/A
Dracunculiasis (guinea-worm infection)	N/A	70	70	N/A
Insect-borne				
Malaria	1,500-2,700	300,000-500,000	N/A	N/A
Leishmaniasis	80	2,000	12,000	N/A
Onchocerciasis (river blindness)	45	N/A	17,655	770
Chagas' disease (American trypanosomiasis)	45	300	18,000	N/A
Dengue/dengue haemorrhagic fever	140	3,100	N/A	N/A
Sleeping sickness (African trypanosomiasis)	100	150	400	200
Japanese encephalitis	10	45	N/A	N/A
Plague[7]	0.14	2.9	N/A	N/A
Yellow fever	30	200	N/A	N/A
Filariasis (lymphatic)	N/A	N/A	119,100	119,100
Animal-borne				
Rabies (dog-mediated)	60	60	N/A	N/A
Others[8]	740	N/A	N/A	N/A
Total	17,310	N/A	N/A	N/A

[1] Permanent and long-term.
[2] Incidence figure refers to episodes.
[3] Number of infected persons is 1.25 billion.
[4] Number of infected persons is 1.38 billion.
[5] 1996 notifications.
[6] Number of infected persons is 1 billion.
[7] 1995 notifications.
[8] Includes noma and emerging diseases eg influenza, ebola, and lassa.

Source: *The World Health Report 1998,* World Health Organization

Projected Figures for World Deaths by Age Group

	1975–2000		2000–2025	
Age group	Number (thousands)	Percentage of total	Number (thousands)	Percentage of total
0–4	304,970	25	181,024	12
5–19	96,127	8	63,400	4
20–64	349,719	28	422,028	29
65+	482,479	39	787,202	54
Total	1,233,295	100	1,453,654	100

Source: *World Health Report 1998,* World Health Organization

The Leading Causes of Mortality in the World

1997

Rank	Cause	Deaths (thousands)	% of overall deaths
1	Ischaemic heart disease	7,375	13.7
2	Cerebrovascular disease	5,106	9.5
3	Acute lower respiratory infections	3,452	6.4
4	HIV/AIDS	2,285	4.2
5	Chronic obstructive pulmonary disease	2,249	4.2
6	Diarrhoeal diseases	2,219	4.1
7	Perinatal conditions	2,155	4.0
8	Tuberculosis	1,498	2.8
9	Cancer of tranchea/bronchus/lung	1,244	2.3
10	Road traffic accidents	1,717	2.2

Source: *World Health Report 1999,* World Health Organization

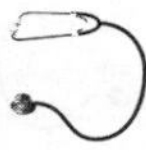

Percentages of Populations with Access to Clean Water and Adequate Sanitation in Selected Countries

(– = not applicable.)

Country	% having access to clean water			% having access to adequate sanitation		
	Total	Urban	Rural	Total	Urban	Rural
South Africa	99	99	53	53	85	12
Bangladesh	97	99	96	48	79	44
Cuba	93	96	85	66	71	51
Iran	90	98	82	81	86	74
Mexico	83	92	57	72	85	32
Brazil	76	88	25	70	80	30
China	67	97	56	24	74	7
Dominican Republic	65	80	–	78	76	83
Turkey	49	63	28	62	83	31
Mongolia	40	73	3	86	99	74
Zambia	27	50	17	64	89	43
Ethiopia	25	91	19	19	97	7
Chad	24	48	17	21	73	7
Eritrea	22	60	8	13	48	–
Afghanistan	12	39	5	8	38	1

Source: UNICEF's *The State of the World's Children 1998*, Oxford University Press 1998

UK Health and Health Care

NHS Reforms

Under the NHS reforms which took effect in April 1999, GP fundholding would be replaced by a system of Primary Care Groups (PCG). Individual GP fundholding practices would no longer purchase care from trusts. Instead, groups of approximately 50 GPs would be organized into local collectives (PCGs) and have responsibility for purchasing health care for around 100,000 patients in their local area. They would be able to buy most hospital and community care for their patients, and would have to decide how to spend local NHS resources in consultation with other health and social services workers.

The government's reforms were outlined in its Health White Paper for England, unveiled in December 1997, which announced a reduction in the number of NHS trusts and health authorities, and a limitation on the internal market system introduced by the Conservatives in 1990. The health secretary claimed the changes would save £1 billion by cutting unnecessary red tape.

PCGs were the government's response to the Conservatives' market-led division of GPs into fundholders and non-fundholders. The 600 PCGs would bring together local health professionals including GPs, managers, and patients. They would make decisions about spending on local health services and each would have a member of the public on its board.

Health minister Alan Milburn averted the threat of industrial action by GPs in June 1998 after agreeing to a package of changes to the government's proposed reforms of the NHS. GPs across the country had expressed increasing disquiet with the government reforms but, after intensive negotiations, said they were satisfied that the proposals to establish a network of PCGs were workable, and the major threats to patient care and GP morale had been addressed.

As no new money had been promised for the NHS, GPs faced the prospect of being blamed by the public for lack of resources. Their biggest fear was that, once operations and drugs had been paid for, there would be nothing left to develop family doctors' surgeries. In June 1998, the health minister personally guaranteed that the level of investment in primary care infrastructure would be maintained and uplifted for inflation.

The Structure of the NHS

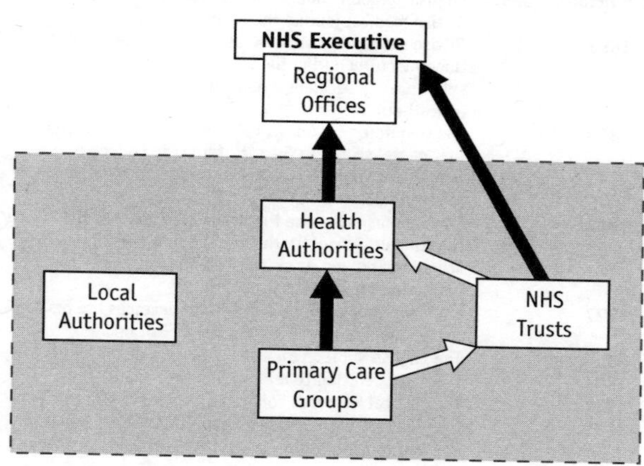

Source: *Britain 1999: The Official Yearbook of the United Kingdom*, © Crown Copyright 1998

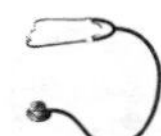

Medicine and Health Care in the UK: Chronology

1518 King Henry VIII founds the Royal College of Physicians at the instigation of his personal physician, Thomas Linacre. It is the first body with the power to license and examine those practising medicine.

1659 Typhoid fever is given a detailed description for the first time by British physician Thomas Willis.

1695 English physician and naturalist Nehemiah Grew isolates magnesium sulphate from Epsom spring water. 'Epsom salts' will become widely used for their purgative properties.

1747 The world's first sexually-transmitted disease clinic is opened at the London Lock Hospital in England.

1761 English naturalist John Hill writes that excessive use of snuff may lead to cancer; this is the first association of tobacco and cancer.

1775 The first evidence that environmental and occupational factors can cause cancer is provided by English surgeon Percivall Pott, who suggests that chimney sweeps' exposure to soot causes cancer of the scrotum and nasal cavity.

1783 English physician Thomas Cawley correctly diagnoses diabetes mellitus by demonstrating the presence of sugar in a patient's urine.

1796 English physician Edward Jenner performs the first vaccination against smallpox.

1819 British surgeon James Blundell makes the first human-to-human blood transfusion. The patient survives for 56 hours.

5 October 1823 English surgeon Thomas Wakley establishes the British medical journal the *Lancet*.

1853 British surgeon John Snow administers chloroform to Queen Victoria during the birth of Prince Leopold. It subsequently becomes a generally accepted anaesthetic.

1858 The Odontological Society of London establishes the first dental school in Great Britain. The College of Dentists of England establishes another school the following year.

1860 English nurse Florence Nightingale establishes the Nightingale School for Nurses. The first nursing school in England, it establishes nursing as a profession for women.

1877 English physician Sophia Jex-Blake becomes the first female medical doctor to practise in Britain.

25 November 1884 The English surgeon Rickman John Godlee performs the first operation to remove a brain tumour.

1911 The Medical Research Council is founded in Britain.

1915 New Zealand-born British surgeon Harold Delf Gillies develops plastic surgery when he treats war casualties at Sidcup, Kent.

1928 Scottish bacteriologist Alexander Fleming discovers penicillin, the first known antibiotic, when he notices that the mould *Penicillium notatum*, which has invaded a culture of staphylococci, inhibits the bacteria's growth.

1948 The NHS (National Health Service) is founded.

1960 British surgeon John Charnley performs a hip replacement operation, using a two-part joint replacement constructed of plastic and cobalt-chrome.

28 March 1974 The National Health Service's family planning service is inaugurated in Britain.

1977 In-vitro fertilization (IVF) is developed by the British gynaecologist and obstetrician Patrick Steptoe.

25 July 1978 Louise Brown is born at Oldham Hospital, London; she is the first 'test tube' baby. Having been unable to remove a blockage from her mother's Fallopian tube, gynaecologist Patrick Steptoe and physiologist Robert Edwards removed an egg from her ovary, fertilized it with her husband's sperm, and re-implanted it in her uterus.

17 December 1986 British surgeons John Wallwork and Roy Calne perform the first triple transplant – heart, lung, and liver – at Papworth Hospital, Cambridge.

1990 The NHS and Community Care Act set up fundholding schemes whereby health authorities and individual GP practices are given annual budgets to purchase healthcare for their patients from healthcare providers; hospitals become NHS trusts, financing their work from contracts to provide services to these fundholders.

1992 The Medical Research Council finds that experiments on human embryos are acceptable for approved research purposes provided that both parents agree.

1997 The British Medical Association updates the Hippocratic Oath. Changes concern issues of modern medical ethics, such as abortion and treating the terminally ill.

1997 The government launches a study to assess the risk of transmission of Creutzfeldt–Jakob disease (CJD) through blood transfusions.

November 1997 The NHS Confederation in the UK reports a growing increase in the number of treatments involving physical manipulation, especially aromatherapy (massage with essential oils), and reflexology (massage of hands and feet). Physiotherapy treatments on the NHS have increased by 26 percent since 1995.

February 1999 The Royal College of Physicians and General Medical Council announce plans to tighten self-regulation and test the competence of consultants, specialists, and other medical practitioners, prompted by an inquiry into the deaths of 29 infants after heart surgery at Bristol Royal Infirmary.

1 April 1999 GP fundholding status is abolished, and all GP practices in England are reorganized into primary care groups (PCGs) of about 50 GPs, which will work with other local health professionals and members of the public to administer the health budget of a local area and commission secondary healthcare; slightly different schemes are introduced in Scotland, Wales, and Northern Ireland.

1 April 1999 The National Institute for Clinical Excellence (NICE) is founded with the aim of providing health professionals with expert advice on the use of new drugs and procedures, and ensuring equality of access to treatment across the country.

13 April 1999 Prime minister Tony Blair announces a pilot scheme to develop 20 walk-in clinics in England – to be located in libraries, pharmacies, and even supermarkets – with the aim of giving patients more convenient access to medical advice.

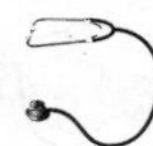

Government Spending on the National Health Service in the UK

Years ending 31 March.
(– = not applicable. In millions of pounds.)

Expenditure	1987–88	1988–89	1989–90	1990–91	1991–92	1992–93	1993–94	1994–95	1995–96	1996–97	1997–98
Current Expenditure											
Central government											
hospitals, Community Health Services,[1] and Family Health Services[2]	18,870	21,110	22,197	25,276	29,061	32,195	35,567	37,698	38,514	39,425	40,993
administration[3]	627	682	855	979	1,119	1,258	–	–	–	–	–
less payments by patients											
hospital services	–106	–347	–407	–510	–540	–505	–368	–111	–42	–42	–48
pharmaceutical services	–256	–202	–242	–247	–270	–297	–324	–342	–383	–376	–396
dental services	–290	–282	–340	–441	–477	–470	–440	–464	–494	–447	–475
ophthalmic services	–1	–	–	–	–	–	–	–	–	–	–
Total	–653	–831	–989	–1,198	–1,287	–1,272	–1,132	–917	–919	–865	–919
Departmental administration	193	206	202	268	293	319	270	256	242	265	245
Other central services	632	604	693	738	865	1,301	1,651	2,304	2,538	3,124	3,242
Total current expenditure	19,669	21,771	22,958	26,063	30,051	33,801	36,356	39,341	40,375	41,949	43,561
Capital Expenditure											
Central government	1,212	1,309	2,071	1,848	1,791	1,612	903	538	316	434	317
Total Expenditure											
Central government	20,881	23,080	25,029	27,911	31,842	35,413	37,259	39,879	40,691	42,383	43,878
Total government expenditure as % of GDP[4]	4.89	4.85	4.84	5.01	5.48	5.84	5.82	5.88	5.70	5.63	5.39

[1] Includes the school health service.
[2] General medical services have been included in the expenditure of the Health Authorities. Therefore, hospitals and Community Health Services and Family Practitioner Services (now Family Health Services) are not identifiable separately.
[3] Administration costs are not separately identifiable from 1993–94.
[4] GDP is adjusted to take account of change from rates to community charge.

Source: *Annual Abstract of Statistics 1999,* © Crown copyright 1999

Employment in the National Health Service in Great Britain

(– = not applicable.)

Health service staff and practitioners	Number of staff (whole-time equivalent)	
	1987	1997
Hospital and Community Health Service Staff		
Medical staff	43,784	61,937
Dental staff	3,168	3,078
Nursing and midwifery staff	489,044	353,933
Professional and technical staff	94,202	107,158
Healthcare assistants	–	19,260
Administrative and clerical staff	136,233	177,957
Ambulance staff	22,523	16,424
Family Health Services Staff		
GPs	29,813	32,477
Dentists	17,083	19,598
Ophthalmic medical practitioners	963	830
Ophthalmic opticians staff	6,281	7,847

Source: *Annual Abstract of Statistics 1999,* © Crown copyright 1999

Staff in the National Health Service in England by Gender and Ethnic Group

Data are correct to September 1997 and include statistics for directly employed personnel only.

Staff description	% of staff						
	Gender		Ethnic group				
	Men	Women	White	Black	Asian	Other	Unkown
All directly employed staff	24.5	75.5	87.2	3.2	3.1	2.5	3.9
Nursing, midwifery, and health-visiting staff	12.2	87.8	86.5	4.1	1.3	2.2	5.9
of which: qualified staff	11.5	88.5	87.5	4.1	1.5	2.3	4.6
Medical and dental staff	67.1	32.9	66.6	3.6	15.8	8.0	6.0
Other direct-care staff	24.0	76.0	88.8	4.8	1.6	2.1	2.7
Administration and estates staff	25.6	74.4	93.6	1.8	1.6	1.2	1.8
Other management and support staff	42.4	57.6	92.4	3.0	0.8	1.9	1.8

Source: *Health and Personal Social Service Statistics for England 1998,*

Health Information Service

The National Health Service provides a freephone Health Information Service for the public. Calls will automatically be routed to a local information centre, providing access to local information as well as details of national organizations and services.

Calls are answered by trained information staff and are in complete confidence. Medical advice and counselling are not provided. Health Information Service centres are open at least from 10.00 a.m. to 5.00 p.m., and in some areas there are longer hours.

Phone the Health Information Service free of charge for information on:

- NHS services
- self-help and support organization
- keeping healthy
- illnesses and treatments
- waiting times
- rights and how to complain

0800 66 55 44 covers England and Wales. In Scotland similar information is provided on 0800 22 44 88.

Details of the Health Information Service and other national helplines are given on the Department of Health web site at: www.open.gov.uk/doh/phone.htm.

National Health Service Hospital Waiting Lists by Region

Data include people waiting for admission as either an in-patient or a day case. As of 30 June 1998. In percentages.

Region	Less than 6 months	6 months, but less than 12	12 months or longer	Total waiting list (thousands)
Northern and Yorkshire	74	24	2	151
North Western	73	22	4	195
Trent	70	24	6	126
West Midlands	77	21	3	119
Anglia and Oxford	70	24	5	133
North Thames	65	26	9	207
South Thames	63	28	9	198
South and West	74	21	4	157
England total	70	24	6	1,288
Wales	N/A	N/A	12	75
Scotland	84	14	1	89
Northern Ireland	60	19	21	47

Source: *Social Trends 29,*

Deaths Analysed by Cause in the UK

The figures relate to the number of deaths registered during each calendar year. However, from 1993 onwards, the figures for England and Wales represent occurrences (see footnote 1). This change has little effect on annual totals. Changes in coding practices for England and Wales, particularly coding of underlying cause of death, from January 1993 have led to some differences in the pattern of cause of death as compared with previous years. (N/A = not available.)

Cause	1991[1]	1992[1]	1993[1]	1994	1995[4]	1996[4]	1997
England and Wales							
Deaths from natural causes[2]							
infectious and parasitic diseases[3]	2,406	2,633	3,257	3,318	3,682	3,636	3,496
intestinal infectious diseases	169	240	194	222	277	339	384
neoplasms	145,355	145,963	142,535	141,747	141,297	139,459	137,618
endocrine, nutritional, and metabolic diseases and immunity disorders	10,538	10,605	7,924	7,430	7,883	7,502	7,383
other metabolic and immunity disorders[3]	1,664	1,747	1,119	1,052	1,138	1,048	1,038
diseases of the blood and blood-forming organs	2,446	2,417	1,974	1,898	1,929	1,986	2,008
mental disorders	13,500	12,950	7,780	8,042	9,149	9,296	9,725
diseases of the nervous system and sense organs	11,889	11,577	9,143	9,010	9,724	9,772	9,772
meningitis	233	208	218	170	209	245	224
diseases of the circulatory system	261,834	254,683	257,989	242,213	243,390	237,669	228,446
diseases of the respiratory system	63,273	60,388	90,981	81,485	91,298	88,630	92,517

(continued)

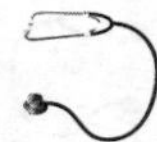

Deaths Analysed by Cause in the UK (*continued*)

Cause	1991[1]	1992[1]	1993[1]	1994	1995[4]	1996[4]	1997
diseases of the digestive system	18,508	18,742	18,399	18,635	19,466	19,946	20,406
diseases of the genito-urinary system	6,464	5,306	6,727	6,812	7,118	6,752	6,757
complications of pregnancy, childbirth, etc	45	45	36	50	45	41	35
diseases of the skin and subcutaneous tissue	930	907	1,019	1,107	1,088	1,075	1,025
diseases of the musculo-skeletal system	5,417	5,376	3,559	3,406	3,646	3,517	3,559
congenital anomalies	1,643	1,565	1,338	1,301	1,290	1,227	1,283
certain conditions originating in the perinatal period	250	242	259	147	148	149	131
signs, symptoms, and ill-defined conditions	5,208	5,278	6,729	7,754	9,783	10,772	12,292
sudden infant death syndrome	912	456	391	371	315	345	327
Total	549,706	538,677	559,649	534,354	550,936	541,429	536,422
Deaths from injury and poisoning[2]							
all accidents	11,049	12,729	10,396	10,219	10,156	10,479	10,661
motor vehicle accidents	4,470	4,114	3,437	3,279	3,123	3,184	3,184
suicide and self-inflicted injury	3,893	3,952	3,719	3,619	3,570	3,445	3,424
all other external causes	2,344	2,294	2,959	2,253	2,323	2,137	2,226
Total	17,286	16,681	17,074	16,091	16,049	16,061	16,311
TOTAL	570,044	555,358	578,799	553,194	569,683	560,135	555,281
Scotland							
Deaths from natural causes[2]							
infectious and parasitic diseases[3]	310	270	340	306	326	493	431
intestinal infectious diseases	14	18	19	19	17	22	19
neoplasms	15,031	15,312	15,619	15,394	15,462	15,419	15,054
endocrine, nutritional, and metabolic diseases and immunity disorders	776	742	775	768	738	722	727
other metabolic and immunity disorders[3]	197	193	215	217	235	140	167
diseases of the blood and blood-forming organs	170	183	173	121	129	180	200
mental disorders	1,110	1,133	1,322	1,306	1,583	1,595	1,611
diseases of the nervous system and sense organs	947	877	879	853	832	852	900
meningitis	26	27	17	24	18	14	17
diseases of the circulatory system	29,166	28,776	29,909	27,138	27,079	26,728	25,911
diseases of the respiratory system	7,068	6,999	8,409	6,981	7,668	7,863	7,891
diseases of the digestive system	2,059	2,122	2,162	2,192	2,252	2,440	2,428
diseases of the genito-urinary system	805	888	857	816	928	839	904
complications of pregnancy, childbirth, etc	9	7	7	9	6	6	4
diseases of the skin and subcutaneous tissue	82	82	100	101	80	75	87
diseases of the musculo-skeletal system	270	306	269	279	303	252	268
congenital anomalies	193	209	216	170	176	192	182
certain conditions originating in the perinatal period	213	216	174	191	178	181	140
signs, symptoms, and ill-defined conditions	300	280	344	311	365	337	383
sudden infant death syndrome	90	64	58	48	48	43	52
Total	58,217	58,098	61,306	56,710	57,864	57,941	56,932
Deaths from injury and poisoning[2]							
all accidents	1,734	1,580	1,469	1,413	1,439	1,497	1,398
motor vehicle accidents	513	468	402	354	422	363	384
suicide and self-inflicted injury	525	569	615	624	623	596	599
all other external causes	273	386	405	335	333	404	376
Total	2,532	2,535	2,489	2,372	2,395	2,497	2,373
TOTAL	61,041	60,937	64,049	59,328	60,500	60,671	59,494
Northern Ireland							
Deaths from natural causes[2]							
infectious and parasitic diseases[3]	44	41	55	39	44	54	61
intestinal infectious diseases	1	N/A	N/A	2	1	1	N/A
neoplasms	3,552	3,621	3,705	3,665	3,585	3,715	3,667
endocrine, nutritional, and metabolic diseases and immunity disorders	38	38	55	47	86	81	106
other metabolic and immunity disorders[3]	23	26	25	20	38	28	17
diseases of the blood and blood-forming organs	31	18	29	29	29	22	20
mental disorders	68	52	56	91	78	100	138
diseases of the nervous system and sense organs	168	181	189	187	224	236	234
meningitis	10	7	15	4	1	7	8
diseases of the circulatory system	6,986	7,112	7,137	7,011	6,929	6,633	6,505
diseases of the respiratory system	2,493	2,423	2,756	2,398	2,656	2,749	2,663
diseases of the digestive system	395	405	445	424	449	483	459
diseases of the genito-urinary system	272	238	261	250	251	254	245

(continued)

Deaths Analysed by Cause in the UK (*continued*)

Cause	1991[1]	1992[1]	1993[1]	1994	1995[4]	1996[4]	1997
complications of pregnancy, childbirth, etc	1	N/A	N/A	N/A	N/A	1	N/A
diseases of the skin and subcutaneous tissue	36	27	33	27	37	29	25
diseases of the musculo-skeletal system	54	43	35	31	40	35	44
congenital anomalies	90	77	116	87	91	72	57
certain conditions originating in the perinatal period	82	63	62	69	93	68	69
signs, symptoms, and ill-defined conditions	40	46	40	44	55	88	92
sudden infant death syndrome	15	11	6	7	9	15	8
Total	14,256	14,303	14,871	14,325	14,516	14,528	14,274
Deaths from injury and poisoning[2]							
all accidents	492	376	391	430	391	402	427
motor vehicle accidents	195	165	152	172	140	121	152
suicide and self-inflicted injury	129	107	129	138	122	124	120
all other external causes	98	98	119	120	150	72	44
Total	719	581	639	688	663	598	591
TOTAL	15,096	14,988	15,633	15,114	15,310	15,218	14,967
UK TOTAL	646,181	631,283	658,481	627,636	641,712	638,896	629,742

[1] On 1 January 1986, a new certificate for deaths within the first 28 days of life was introduced. It is not possible to assign one underlying cause of death from this certificate. The 'cause' figures in this table exclude all deaths at ages under 28 days.
[2] Within certain main categories only selected causes of death are shown.
[3] Deaths assigned to AIDS and AIDS-related diseases are included in immunity disorders for England and Wales up to 1992 and Scotland up to 1995. Northern Ireland has always assigned such deaths to Infectious Diseases. England and Wales adopted this practice from 1993 onwards.
[4] Data for 1995 and 1996 have been amended to show the number of deaths that occurred during the calendar year. Data up to 1992 give the number of deaths that were registered in the calendar year and subsequent years give the number that occurred during the calendar year.

Source: *Annual Abstract of Statistics 1999*, © Crown copyright 1999

Developments in Medical Ethics

BY TOM WILKIE

In May 1999, the UK government announced a comprehensive overhaul of its advisory system for biotechnology, emphasizing the need to receive advice on the ethical and safety aspects of new developments in human genetics and in non-human biotechnology. Two separate commissions were set up: a Human Genetics Commission to cover the ethical, social, and other aspects of human genetics; and an Agricultural and Environmental Biotechnology Commission to cover the uses of biotechnology in agriculture. The move was prompted in part by a massive public reaction to the introduction of genetically modified (GM) foods in supermarkets and the planting of genetically modified crops in the countryside. But it also represented an acknowledgement of the fact that the government had appeared to be caught off-guard by developments in human genetics – most notably cloning.

Hardly a day goes by without newspapers carrying stories reflecting high public sensitivity towards issues in the ethics of conventional medical care and developments at the frontiers of biomedical research. In the same month as the government was reorganizing its advisory machinery, newspapers carried detailed reports of the court case of a doctor accused (and ultimately acquitted) of carrying out a mercy killing. Both issues prompted questions in the media about the power and responsibility of scientists and doctors. This increased concern for ethics has forced responses from government and from the medical profession.

Compulsory courses in ethics and law

British medical students now have to take compulsory courses in medical ethics as part of their professional training. The new undergraduate medical curriculum, agreed by the General Medical Council, stipulates for the first time that students must study ethics and law as applied to medicine and that they must sit examinations in the subject – a powerful stimulus for any student to pay attention in lectures. An agreed core syllabus covering ethics and law as applied to medicine was published in spring 1998.

Such courses in medical ethics come more than 50 years after the Nuremberg 'doctors' trials of 1946 revealed to a horrified world the cruel and abusive Nazi medical experiments. In its concluding judgement, the court enunciated ten principles of ethics to govern research involving human beings. These principles became known as the Nuremberg Code. Its first and most important stipulation was that no one should be expected to take part in medical research unless they had given their prior informed consent. The Nuremberg principles have been used as the basis for other codes over the half century since, the most important being the World Medical Association's Declaration of

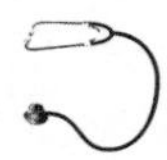

Helsinki – which is now regarded as the fundamental declaration of the ethical duties of doctors and scientists in the conduct of medical research involving humans – and the guidelines set out by the World Health Organization's Council of International Organizations of Medical Science.

Traditionally, British medical students were supposed to learn ethics and the human side of patient care by a process of apprenticeship. The high technology skills of modern scientific medicine could be learned through formal lectures, according to this view, but correct conduct and the bedside manner could be acquired only by observing and following the example of more senior doctors. It was and is a persuasive view, but it no longer appears to be fully adequate in an age of public anxiety about medical ethics.

Medical ethics is nonetheless a comparatively recent concern in both the USA and the UK. For about a decade and a half after the end of World War II, the Nuremberg principles were not seen as really relevant – such codification of research ethics appeared necessary only in the exceptional circumstances of the aberration that was the Nazi political system. However, in the early 1960s details of research abuses were published in both the UK and the USA. The most notable perhaps was the notorious US Tuskegee syphilis study, in which poor African-American men infected with syphilis were denied access to medical treatment over a period of 30 years, even when a complete cure was available, so that researchers could study the progression of the disease.

Pressure for public participation

Since the 1960s, social pressures have grown for public and legal participation in decisions which might once have been left to doctors, such as definitions of life and death in the case of heart transplants and life support machines; abortion and *in vitro* fertilization (IVF); and the research uses of human embryos. The technologies themselves did not necessarily present new dilemmas; rather, there occurred great changes in social attitudes towards what could be considered right and proper to leave to doctors' professional discretion. On the one hand, people feel they should be part of the decision-making process, but on the other also want doctors to believe and to behave in accordance with a duty of care. The changes to the British medical undergraduate curriculum can be seen as recognition of this public dilemma.

Changes are occurring internationally as well. There are controversial proposals to amend the Declaration of Helsinki. In the UK, the British Medical Association has commenced a process of public consultations to establish the climate of medical opinion about revision to the document. The Nuffield Council on Bioethics has also begun to explore the ramifications of international medical research, in particular the highly sensitive issue of medical research involving humans, which is funded by rich developed countries but conducted in poor, underdeveloped countries.

Ban on reproductive cloning continues

Government policies try to catch up with developments in science and technology, attempting to incorporate ethical and medical concerns in their decision-making. In late 1998, two advisory bodies to the UK government published the results of a joint public consultation on the topic of human cloning. The Human Fertilisation and Embryology Authority and the Human Genetics Advisory Commission had embarked on the consultation because of the heated public reaction to the news of the cloning of Dolly the sheep, two years earlier. The joint report concluded that the UK's existing ban on human reproductive cloning – using the technique to bring about the birth of a baby that was the genetic clone of some other person – should be retained. However, it did suggest that another application of the technique might be permissible, whereby normal embryonic development could be interrupted before the 14th day and cloned tissues, rather than a baby, produced as the result. These tissues could have medical uses in transplants and skin grafts. Ironically, one of the bodies responsible for the advice, the Human Genetics Advisory Commission, has since been abolished in the course of the government's reorganization of its advisory systems for the oversight of biotechnology.

What lies ahead?

It remains to be seen whether the new system will reassure the public that the government is in control of the ethical and social implications of advances in biomedicine. As the government is all too well aware, the example of bovine spongiform encephalopathy (BSE)/Creutzfeldt–Jakob disease (CJD) shows what damage can be done if the public loses trust in the regulatory and oversight system. Yet one of the lessons of the public and media outcries in Britain over such inflammatory issues as this, or over GM foods, and Dolly, is that it is very difficult to predict what issues will become matters of public concern. It is not merely a matter of the difficulty in predicting what new developments science will bring, but that social attitudes change. Genetically modified soya was passed for human consumption in Britain in 1994, long before GM foods became an issue of public controversy; old issues which appear to have been settled may suddenly flare up with a change in social sensitivity, while new, apparently controversial technologies may be accepted with little comment. Assisted reproduction, IVF, embryo research, and cloning are likely to continue to be matters of ethical sensitivity. And as genetics seeps more and more into conventional clinical practice, there are likely to be further issues arising there.

Important legal developments may affect doctors and biomedical researchers: the European Directive on Data Privacy could affect the ability of some researchers to get access to patient medical records, while the Directive on Patenting of Biotechnology Inventions may affect the consent that has to be given in the course of research. Finally, although not yet ratified in the UK, the Council of Europe Convention on Human Rights and Biomedicine was adopted in November 1996, and its provisions too could affect the daily practice of medicine and medical research – the only problem being that it is too early to tell quite what effect that will have.

Tom Wilkie is head of biomedical ethics at the Wellcome Trust. This article represents the author's personal views and does not reflect in any way the policy or position of the Wellcome Trust.

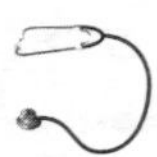

BSE: Chronology

1985 An epidemic of bovine spongiform encephalopathy (BSE or 'mad cow disease') is reported in beef cattle in Britain; it is later traced to cattle feed containing sheep carcasses infected with scrapie.

November 1986 BSE first formally identified by Central Veterinary Laboratory.

15 May 1990 Home-produced beef is banned in UK schools and hospitals as a result of concern about bovine spongiform encephalopathy.

25 March 1996 The European Union bans the export of British beef abroad following anxiety over the potential for transmission of the BSE infection to humans as CJD (Creutzfeldt-Jakob disease).

1 April 1996 The agriculture minister Douglas Hogg proposes a scheme to eradicate BSE in Britain and get the export ban on British beef lifted; 4.6 million cattle over 6 years old would be culled.

1 August 1996 The UK Central Veterinary Laboratory publishes a report indicating that BSE can be transmitted from cow to calf.

2 October 1997 UK scientists Moira Bruce and, independently, John Collinge and their colleagues show that the new variant form of the brain-wasting CJD is the same disease as bovine spongiform encephalopathy in cows.

3 December 1997 Agriculture Secretary Jack Cunningham announces that the government will ban the sale of beef on the bone to help prevent the transmission of BSE to humans.

November 1998 The government announces £120 million emergency aid package for Britain's farmers to compensate for the BSE crisis. Later that month, the European Union partially lifts the ban on the export of British beef pending slaughterhouse inspections.

4 March 1998 EU veterinarians approve the removal of the ban of British beef exports from Northern Ireland. The decision has to be ratified by the EC.

9 March 1998 Public inquiry into the origin and spread of BSE and its human equivalent, CJD, opens in London.

16 March 1998 EU agricultural ministers vote to allow beef from herds in Northern Ireland to be sold abroad again. Northern Ireland becomes the first part of the UK to see the two-year beef ban lifted because it has a computer-based system to keep track of cattle.

17 March 1998 The Agriculture Minister, Jack Cunningham, says the final bill for combating the BSE outbreak would top £4 billion.

December 1998 Phase One (fact finding) hearings of the BSE Inquiry are completed; its report is scheduled to be delivered to Ministers June 1999; this is later postponed to March 2000.

January 1999 Scientists announce they have developed a test for CJD which could show the extent of the disease in the population. The test involves taking tissue from the tonsils and can be conducted on living people. The test also suggests CJD may be more infectious than thought and could be spread through routine surgery.

March 1999 The critical moment when Creutzfeld-Jakob disease or BSE strikes the brain is captured in a test tube for the first time. The breakthrough, by the Medical Research Council's Prion Unit, is a major step forward for the future development of new diagnostic tests and possibly even effective treatments of the disease.

April 1999 The number of people known to have died of the human form of BSE rises to 40. The total number of people who died from CJD in 1998 stands at 16, a sharp increase on previous years. Evidence that the ban was flouted and that contaminated cattle reached the food chain until 1996, means some people may have caught the disease in the 1990s. The government's scientific researchers call for more research to find out if BSE has passed to sheep which were given the same feed as infected cattle.

Suicide Rates by Region, Gender, and Age in England and Wales

Data includes deaths that are undetermined whether accidently or purposely inflicted. (Rate per million population.)

1992–96

Region	Men		Women	
	15–44	45 and over	15–44	45 and over
Northeast	198	192	55	65
Northwest (GOR)	233	176	64	69
Merseyside	208	164	52	53
Yorkshire and the Humber	201	178	53	71
East Midlands	192	171	45	64
West Midlands	181	170	45	63
Eastern	171	175	39	60
London	182	178	56	74
Southeast (GOR)	181	181	48	81
Southwest	196	187	50	76
Wales	247	186	42	62
England and Wales	195	178	50	69

Source: *Social Trends 29*, © Crown copyright 1999

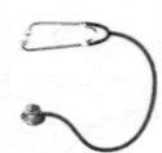

Immunization for Travellers

Details correct as of September 1998. This table is intended to give general advice only. Please take proper medical advice before travelling. (– = not applicable.)

Disease	Immunization	Timing	Reaction	Protection	Duration of protection	Other precautions	Notes
Cholera	2 injections not less than 1 week apart	1 week to 1 month before travel	soreness where injected, fever, headache, fatigue	50–60%	6 months	avoid food or water that may be dirty	low risk in reasonable tourist accommodation; vaccine should not be given to children under 2 months
Hepatitis A	injection of immunoglobulin	just before travel	soreness and swelling where injected, hives in some cases	prevents illness	3 months	see typhoid	–
	vaccine consisting of 2 injections 1 month apart, then a 3rd injection 6–12 months later	2 months before travel	soreness where injected, headache, fatigue	lessens severity	10 years		
Hepatitis B	2 injections of vaccine 1 month apart, then booster 4 months later	last injection 1 month before travel	soreness where injected	80–85%	about 5 years	–	usually only given to those at high risk, such as health workers; part of recommended childhood vaccination series
Malaria	none; take preventative tablets from 1 week before travel to 4 weeks after leaving malaria area	order tablets 2 weeks before travel	–	90%	only while tablets are taken	use anti-mosquito sprays, mosquito nets; keep arms and legs covered after sunset	some anti-malarial drugs are not recommended for pregnant mothers or children under 1 year
Polio	(a) oral vaccine – 3–4 doses (b) injection – 3–4 shots, the best way to be protected is to get 4 doses of polio vaccine immunized adults: 1 booster dose	for travellers who are not up to date, it may be necessary to allow as much as 7 months for the full recommended vaccination schedule, depending on other vaccines that may be necessary for the trip	–	>95%	10 years	–	(a) should not be given to pregnant mothers; (b) recommended only for people 18 years and older who have not yet been vaccinated; should not be given to people who have an allergy problem with the antibiotics neomycin or streptomycin
Rabies	3-dose series of injections, usually given on days 0, 7, and 21 or 28	5 weeks before travel	soreness where injected, headache, abdominal pain, muscle aches, nausea	opinion is divided as to whether vaccine prevents rabies or promotes a faster response to treatment	3 months	avoid bites, scratches, or licks from any animal; wash any bite or scratch with antiseptic or soap as quickly as possible and get immediate medical treatment	–
Tetanus	normally given in childhood with booster every 10 years unimmunized adults: 2 injections 1 month apart then 3rd injection 6 months later	not critical	headache, lethargy in rare cases	>90%	about 10 years	wash any wounds with antiseptic	–

(continued)

Immunization for Travellers (*continued*)

Disease	Immunization	Timing	Reaction	Protection	Duration of protection	Other precautions	Notes
Typhoid	1–2 injections 4–6 weeks apart single injection 4 oral doses, every other day series on days 1, 2, 4, and 6	5–7 weeks before departure 1 year	soreness where injected, nausea, headache (worst in those over 35 and on repeat immunizations) may last 36 hours	70–70%	1–3 years 3 years	avoid food, milk, or water that may be contaminated by sewage or by flies	–
Yellow fever	1 injection	at least 10 days before departure	possible slight headache and low fever 5–10 days later, muscle ache	almost 100%	10 years	as malaria	may only be available from special centres

Cancer

Major Deaths from Cancer in England

Figures are from weighted data where a sample of the population has been used to represent the full population. Percentages do not add up to 100 per cent for each gender due to rounding.

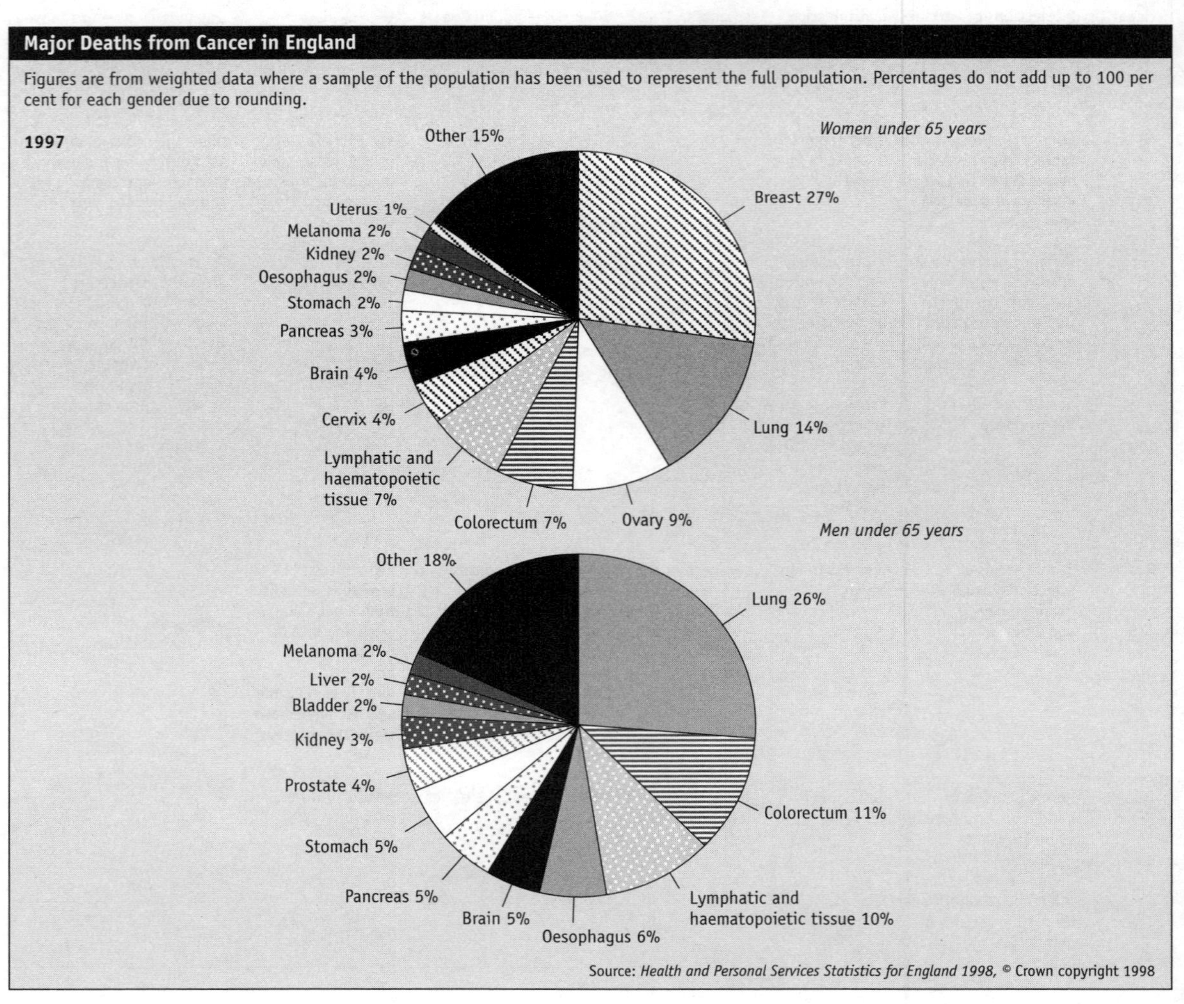

Source: *Health and Personal Services Statistics for England 1998,* © Crown copyright 1998

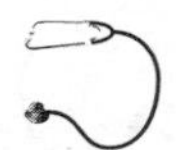

Prevalence of Smoking: Top Countries

Data are for men and women 15 years or older.

1997 Estimates

Male Smoking Prevalence

Rank	Country	Men (% of population)	Women (% of population)
1	Korea, South	68.2	6.7
2	Latvia	67.0	12.0
3	Russian Federation	67.0	30.0
4	Dominican Republic	66.3	13.6
5	Tonga	65.0	14.0
6	Turkey	63.0	24.0
7	China	61.0	7.0
8	Bangladesh	60.0	15.0
9	Fiji	59.3	30.6
10	Japan	59.0	14.8

Female Smoking Prevalence

Rank	Country	Women (% of population)	Men (% of population)
1	Denmark	37.0	37.0
2	Norway	35.5	36.4
3	Czech Republic	31.0	43.0
4	Fiji	30.6	59.3
5 =	Israel	30.0	45.0
	Russian Federation	30.0	67.0
7 =	Canada	29.0	31.0
	Netherlands	29.0	36.0
	Poland	29.0	51.0
10 =	Greece	28.0	46.0
	Iceland	28.0	31.0
	Ireland	28.0	29.0
	Papua New Guinea	28.0	46.0

Source: *Tobacco or Health: A Global Status Report,* World Health Organization 1997

Trends in Smoking in the UK by Age

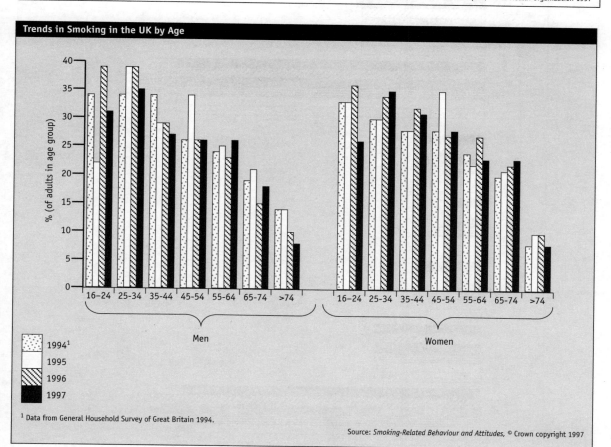

[1] Data from General Household Survey of Great Britain 1994.

Source: *Smoking-Related Behaviour and Attitudes,* © Crown copyright 1997

Cigarette Smoking Trends of Children in England

Data present the prevalence of smoking cigarettes among secondary school children aged 11 to 15 years. (In percentages.)

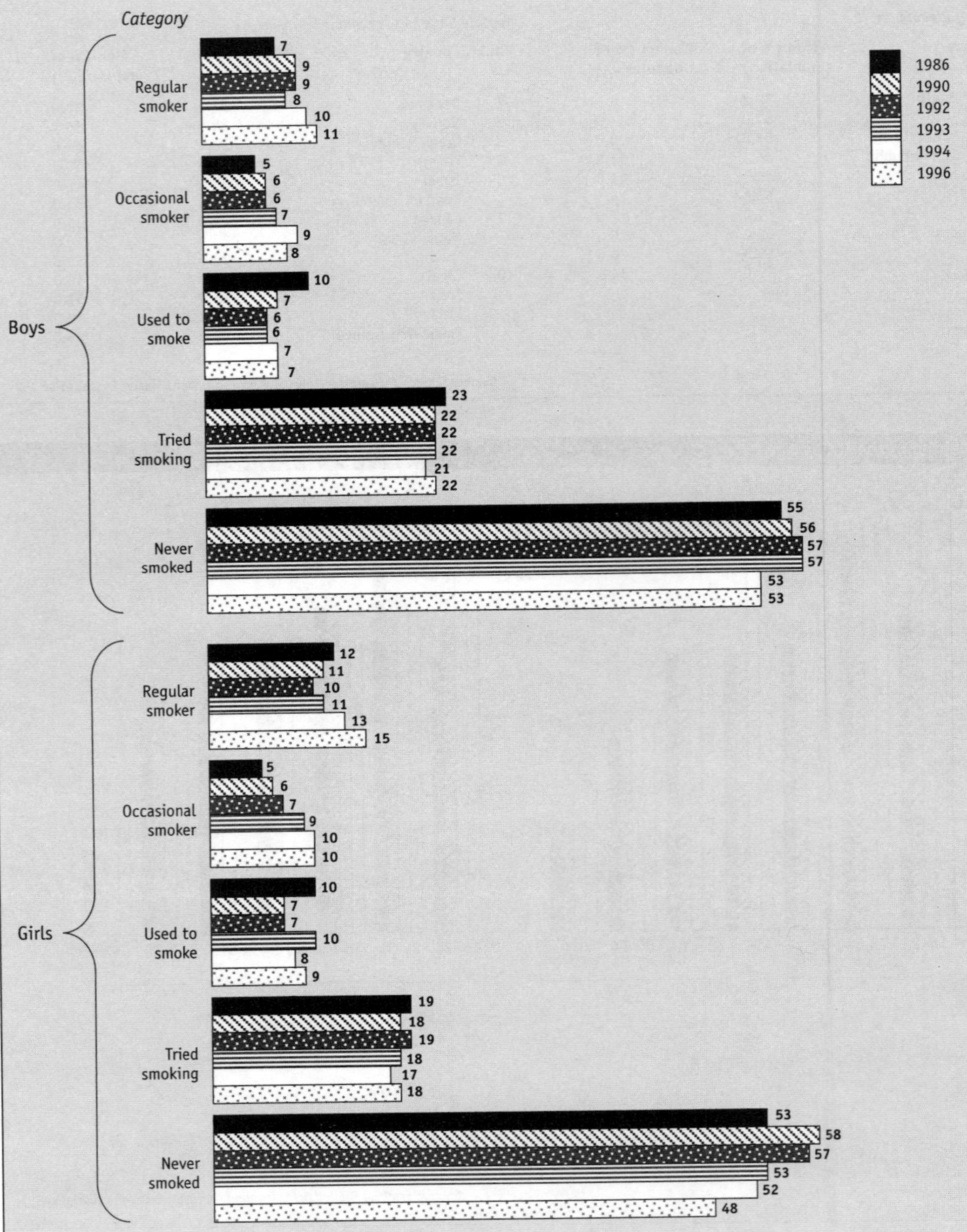

	Category	1986	1990	1992	1993	1994	1996
Boys	Regular smoker	7	9	9	8	10	11
	Occasional smoker	5	6	6	7	9	8
	Used to smoke	10	7	6	6	7	7
	Tried smoking	23	22	22	22	21	22
	Never smoked	55	56	57	57	53	53
Girls	Regular smoker	12	11	10	11	13	15
	Occasional smoker	5	6	7	9	10	10
	Used to smoke	10	7	7	10	8	9
	Tried smoking	19	18	19	18	17	18
	Never smoked	53	58	57	53	52	48

Source: *Health and Personal Services Statistics for England 1998,* © Crown copyright 1998

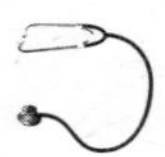

World Mortality from Cancer, and Preventive Measures

1997

Cancers	Deaths	Dietary and lifestyle preventive measures
Trachea, bronchus, and lung	1,050,000	eliminate smoking
Stomach	765,000	increase fruit and vegetable consumption; reduce salt intake
Colon and rectum	525,000	reduce fat and protein consumption; increase vegetable consumption
Liver	505,000	reduce alcohol consumption; vaccinate against hepatitis B
Breast (female)	385,000	reduce fat and animal protein consumption; avoid obesity
Oesophagus	355,000	eliminate smoking; reduce alcohol consumption
Mouth and pharynx	260,000	eliminate smoking; reduce alcohol consumption
Bladder	140,000	eliminate smoking; reduce alcohol consumption

Source: *State of the World 1997*, Worldwatch Institute

AIDS and Other Sexually Transmitted Diseases

New Cases of Sexually Transmitted Diseases in England by Year of Report

(NC = data not collected.)

Disease	Number of cases						
	1977	1987	1993	1994	1995	1996	1997
Syphilis[1]	2,759	589	337	304	132	116	146
Gonorrhoea[2]	58,109	25,254	9,926	9,644	9,938	11,710	12,316
Chlamydia[4]	NC	NC	26,381	27,698	29,213	32,092	38,632
Herpes simplex[4]	NC	NC	14,621	15,347	14,999	15,071	14,993
Genital warts[3]	NC	NC	48,893	49,052	51,166	54,029	58,416
Non-specific genital infection	95,491	131,383	100,795	111,049	104,547	111,315	124,208

[1] Infectious syphilis.
[2] Uncomplicated gonorrhoea.
[3] Uncomplicated chlamydia.
[4] First attacks only.

Source: Communicable Disease Surveillance Centre

Global Summary of the HIV/AIDS Epidemic

Children are below 15 years.

1998

Category	Group	Number (millions)
New HIV infections	adults	5.2
	children	0.59
	Total	5.8
People living with HIV/AIDS	adults	32.2
	children	1.2
	Total	33.4
HIV/AIDS associated deaths	adults	2.0
	children	0.51
	Total	2.5
Cumulative HIV/AIDS deaths[1]	adults	10.7
	children	3.2
	Total	13.9
Cumulative AIDS orphans[1 2]	children	8.2

[1] Up to 1998.
[2] Orphans are defined as HIV-negative children having lost their mother or both parents due to AIDS (end 1997).

Source: United Nations Programme on AIDS, World Health Organization

Estimated Number of Deaths from HIV/AIDS in the World

1997

Region	Estimated deaths
East Asia and Pacific	6,200
Eastern Europe and Central Asia	300
Australia and New Zealand	700
North Africa and Middle East	13,000
Western Europe	15,000
South and Southeast Asia	250,000
North America	29,000
Latin America	81,000
Caribbean	19,000
Sub-Saharan Africa	1,800,000
Total	2,300,000

Source: United Nations Programme on AIDS, World Health Organization

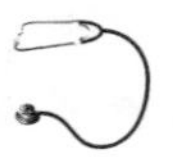

AIDS AND HIV: GLOBAL TRENDS

BY ANNA FARKAS

HIV/AIDS has moved up to fourth place among all causes of deaths worldwide, and has become the number one overall cause of death in Africa, according to the latest World Health Report, released in May 1999 by the World Health Organization (WHO). According to the new report, AIDS is killing more people than any other infectious disease. Heart disease, strokes, and acute respiratory infections – typical causes of death in old age – are the only causes of death to surpass HIV/AIDS. While only small fluctuations in impact have been seen over the years with other causes of death, the AIDS curve is rising sharply.

The epidemic was responsible for one in five deaths in Africa in 1998, approximately 2 million people, according to UNAIDS/WHO estimates. More than 95 percent of all HIV-infected people now live in the developing world, which has likewise experienced 95 percent of all deaths to date from AIDS. These deaths are largely among young adults who would normally be in their peak productive and reproductive years, and the multiple repercussions are reaching crisis levels in some parts of the world. AIDS is making the most destructive impact not only on death rates but on a number of precious development gains bringing deteriorating child survival, crumbling life expectancy, overburdened health care systems, increasing orphanhood, and losses to business in the developing world.

By the end of 1998, an estimated 33.4 million people were living with HIV/AIDS, representing a 10 percent increase compared with 1997. During 1998, 5.8 million people (including 590,000 children) became infected – equivalent to 16,000 new infections per day. Altogether, since the start of the epidemic around two decades ago, HIV has infected more than 47 million people, and has already cost the lives of nearly 14 million adults and children. An estimated 2.5 million of these deaths occurred during 1998, more than ever before in a single year. Approximately one-fifth of these deaths occurred in children, and 45 percent of the adult deaths were in women.

Regional trends

Sub-Saharan Africa remains the hardest-hit region. Four million of the people infected with HIV during 1998 (out of a global total of 5.8 million) live in this region. The estimated 2 million HIV/AIDS deaths in the region during 1998 represent 80 percent of the global total, even though only one-tenth of the world population lives there. It is estimated that by end-1998, there were 21.5 million adults and 1 million children living with HIV/AIDS in Africa. The figure corresponds to approximately 8 percent of Africa's population. The global estimate, by contrast, corresponds to approximately 1.1 percent of the population. At least 95 percent of all AIDS orphans have been African.

Compared to many African countries, Asia still has relatively low prevalence rates, although the absolute numbers of HIV infections is high because of large population sizes. By end-1998 there were an estimated 6.7 million adults and children living with HIV/AIDS in south and southeast Asia, and HIV was clearly beginning to spread in earnest through the vast populations of India and China.

In Latin America, men who have unprotected sex with other men, and injecting drug users who share needles, are the groups mainly affected. While transmission through sex between men and women is on the rise, especially in Brazil, heterosexual HIV spread is especially prominent in the Caribbean.

The spread of HIV is increasing rapidly within the drug-injecting communities of Eastern Europe and Central Asia. The epidemic began in this region in the early 1990s, and it is estimated that by end-1998 there were 270,000 people living there with HIV. Most of the infections are recent, approximately 30 percent having been acquired during 1998.

In North America and Western Europe, new combinations of anti-HIV drugs continue to reduce AIDS deaths significantly. Figures show that in 1997 the death rate for AIDS in the USA was the lowest in a decade – almost two-thirds below what it was two years earlier, before the widespread use of combination therapy. In both regions, however, the number of new HIV infections has remained relatively constant over the past decade. During 1998, nearly 75,000 people became infected with HIV, bringing the total number of North Americans and Western Europeans living with HIV to almost 1.4 million.

Anna Farkas is a freelance researcher and writer

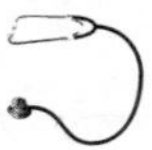

AIDS: Chronology

1977 Two homosexual men in New York are diagnosed as having the rare cancer Kaposi's sarcoma. They are thought to be the first victims of AIDS.

1979 The Center for Disease Control in Atlanta, Georgia, reports the first cases of the disease later known as AIDS.

1981 The Center for Disease Control in Atlanta, Georgia, first conclusively identifies AIDS; doctors realize they have previously seen similar cases among drug users and homosexuals.

1983 US medical researcher Robert Gallo at the US National Cancer Institute, Maryland, and French medical researcher, Luc Montagnier, at the Pasteur Institute in Paris, isolate the virus thought to cause AIDS; it becomes known as the HIV virus (human immunodeficiency virus).

20 March 1987 The AIDS treatment drug AZT is given approval by the US Food and Drug Administration. Treatment costs $10,000 per year per patient. The treatment does not cure the disease but it does relieve some symptoms and extend victims' lives.

31 December 1994 The number of AIDS cases worldwide exceeds 1 million for the first time, when the World Health Organization (WHO) reports that there are 1,025,073 officially reported AIDS cases.

1995 US researchers estimate that HIV reproduces at a rate of a billion viruses a day, even in otherwise healthy individuals, but is held at bay by the immune system producing enough white blood cells to destroy them. Gradually the virus mutates so much that the immune system is overwhelmed and the victim develops AIDS.

9 May 1996 Scientists discover a protein, 'fusin', which allows the HIV virus to fuse with a human immune system cell's outer membrane and inject genetic material. Its presence is necessary for the AIDS virus to enter the cell.

January 1997 The World Health Organization estimates that 22.6 million men, women, and children have to date been infected by HIV, the virus responsible for causing AIDS. Approximately 42 percent of adult sufferers are female, with the proportion of women infected steadily increasing.

February 1997 The Centers for Disease Control and Prevention in Atlanta, Georgia, report that deaths among people with AIDS declined 13 percent during the first six months of 1996 over the same period the year before.

8 May 1997 US AIDS researcher David Ho and colleagues show how aggressive treatment of HIV-1 infection with a cocktail of three antiviral drugs can drive the virus to below the limits of conventional clinical detection within eight weeks.

9 February 1998 US scientist David Ho reports the discovery of the AIDS virus in a 1959 blood sample and suggests that a transfer of the virus from ape to human occurred in the late 1940s or early 1950s.

March 1998 According to a new study, a protein found in the urine of pregnant women could stop the reproduction of HIV, the virus that causes AIDS. The protein is known as human chorionic gonadotropin, or hcg. It also boosts the immune system and, because it is produced by the human body, is non-toxic and has very few side effects.

30 June 1998 Doctors report for the first time the ominous spread of a strain of the AIDS virus that is resistant to protease inhibitors, the medicines that have revolutionized care of the disease.

October 1998 Children born today in 29 sub-Saharan African nations face a life expectancy of just 47 years because of the toll the AIDS pandemic is taking on the region, according to a UN population report.

December 1998 Researchers report they have identified an inherited gene variation that in some patients causes an HIV infection to accelerate rapidly to AIDS. The identification of all the gene variations involved in both the rapid acceleration of HIV and in the slow progress of the disease would help in the design and testing of vaccines.

January 1999 WHO estimates that 33.4 million adults and children are living with AIDS at the end of 1998. Deaths due to HIV/AIDS in 1998 totalled 2.5 million, while the cumulative number of deaths reached 13.9 million.

January 1999 Researchers say they have conclusive evidence that the HIV virus has spread on at least three separate occasions from chimpanzees to humans in Africa. Chimps, which probably carried the virus for hundreds of thousands of years, apparently do not become ill from it. Understanding why, say AIDS experts, could help in a search for a cure and in the development of a vaccine.

February 1999 Thailand gives permission to the US company VaxGen Inc. to begin advance testing of an AIDS vaccine on about 2,500 people. The California-based company has already done preliminary trials of AIDSVAX vaccine on up to 90 Thai drug users. About 30 possible AIDS vaccines are in development, but AIDSVAX is the first to undergo massive testing to determine if it prevents AIDS infection.

16 March 1999 US scientists report they have isolated an enzyme present in tears, which they believe has a powerful anti-HIV effect.

21 April 1999 Hundreds of demonstrators rally in Washington, DC, to protest at policies which they say protect drug companies but make AIDS drugs too expensive for people in Africa.

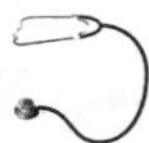

HIV/AIDS: Regional Statistics and Features

December 1998	Epidemic Started	Adults and Children living with HIV/AIDS	Adult Prevalence Rate (%)[1]	HIV-Positive Adults Who Are Women (%)	Main Mode(s) of Transmission For Those Living with HIV/AIDS[2]
Sub-Saharan Africa	Late 1970s–early 1980s	22,500,000	8.0	50	Hetero
South and South-East Asia	Late 1980s	6,700,000	0.69	25	Hetero
Latin America	Late 1970s–early 1980s	1,400,000	0.57	20	MSM, IDU, Hetero
North America	Late 1970s–early 1980s	890,000	0.56	20	MSM, IDU, Hetero
Caribbean	Late 1970s–early 1980s	330,000	1.96	35	Hetero, MSM
Eastern Europe, Central Asia	Early 1980s	270,000	0.14	20	IDU, MSM
East Asia, Pacific	Late 1980s	560,000	0.07	15	IDU, Hetero, MSM
North Africa, Middle East	Late 1980s	210,000	0.13	20	IDU, Hetero
Western Europe	Late 1970s–early 1980s	500,000	0.25	20	MSM, IDU
Australia, New Zealand	Late 1970s–early 1980s	12,000	0.1	5	MSM, IDU

[1] The proportion of adults (15–49 years) living with HIV/AIDS in 1998, using 1997 population figures.
[2] IDU: transmission through injecting drugs; Hetero: heterosexual transmission; MSM: men who have sex with men.

Source: United Nations Programme on AIDS, World Health Organization

AIDS Cases in the UK by Age Group at Diagnosis and Gender

Correct to December 1998.
(– = not applicable.)

Age group	Men		Women	
	Number of cases[1]	% of cases[2]	Number of cases[1]	% of cases[2]
0–14	189	1	169	9
15–24	541	4	156	8
25–34	5,344	38	963	51
35–44	5,008	35	411	22
45–54	2,212	16	119	6
55–64	695	5	42	2
>64	146	1	10	0
Total	14,135	–	1,870	–

[1] Total number of cases from 1982 or earlier to December 1998.
[2] Percentages may not add up to 100 due to rounding.

Source: Communicable Disease Surveillance Centre

HIV Cases by Exposure Category in the UK

Correct to December 1998.

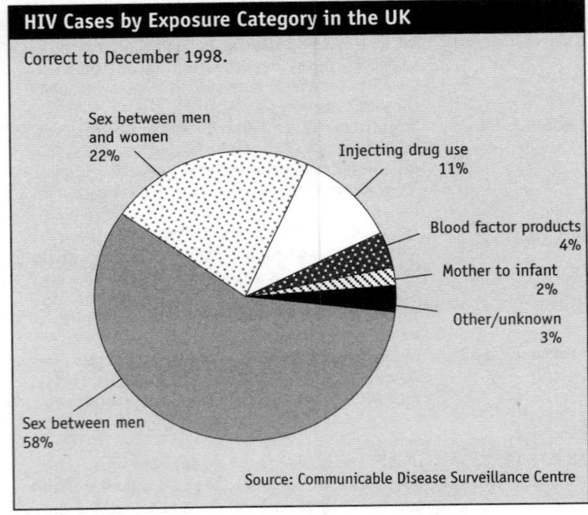

Source: Communicable Disease Surveillance Centre

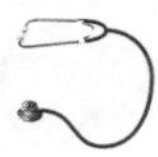

Drug and Alcohol Use and Abuse

Common Drugs Derived from Plants

These plants are poisonous and if swallowed can cause serious illness or unconsciousness. They should only be used if administered by a medically trained professional.

Plant	Drug	Use
Amazonian liana	curare	muscle relaxant
Annual mugwort	artemisinin	antimalarial
Autumn crocus	colchicine	antitumour agent
Coca	cocaine	local anaesthetic
Common thyme	thymol	antifungal
Deadly nightshade (belladonna)	atropine	anticholinergic
Dog button (nux-vomica)	strychnine	central nervous system stimulant
Ergot fungus	ergotamine	analgesic
Foxglove	digitoxin, digitalis	cardiotonic
Indian snakeroot	reserpine	antihypertensive
Meadowsweet	salicylate	analgesic
Mexican yam	diosgenin	birth control pill
Opium poppy	codeine, morphine	analgesic (and antitussive)
Pacific yew	taxol	antitumour agent
Recured thornapple	scopolamine	sedative
Rosy periwinkle	vincristine, vinblastine	antileukaemia
Velvet bean	L-dopa	antiparkinsonian
White willow	salicylic acid	topical analgesic
Yellow cinchona	quinine	antimalarial, antipyretic

Number of New Drug Addicts in the UK

Data are for users presenting to drug misuse services for the first time.

Main drug	Six months ending					
	March 1994	Sept 1995	March 1996	Sept 1996	March 1997	Sept 1997
Heroin	8,546	11,793	12,623	14,334	15,597	12,392
Methadone	3,232	3,469	3,484	3,574	3,704	2,852
Other opiates	574	560	507	493	454	436
Amphetamines	1,786	2,215	2,216	2,248	2,009	1,999
Cannabis	1,205	1,677	1,623	1,533	1,660	1,934
Cocaine	714	1,046	977	870	1,020	925
Benzodiazepines	743	910	717	659	558	598
Ecstasy	175	289	335	268	246	223
Solvents	172	175	176	166	158	148
Other drugs	483	498	368	576	398	412
Not known	234	216	287	158	121	77
Total number of users	17,864	22,848	23,313	24,879	25,925	21,996

Source: *Health and Personal Services Statistics for England 1998,* © Crown copyright 1998

Alcohol Strengths and Recommended Daily Alcohol Intake in the UK

The most recent UK government guidelines on alcohol consumption, published in 1995, advise that drinking up to three to four units a day for men and up to two to three units a day for women poses no significant risk to health, but that regularly consuming at or beyond the maximum level incurs a progressive risk of damage. Women who are or are intending to become pregnant should not drink more than one to two units once or twice a week. Units of alcohol are used to compare the amounts of alcohol in different types of drinks: each contains 10 ml/0.35 fl oz of pure alcohol (ethanol).

Drink	% alcohol by volume (ABV)[1]	Measure constituting one unit
Normal-strength beer, lager, or cider	3.5–4.0	284 ml/$\frac{1}{2}$ pint
Strong beer, lager, or cider	8.0–9.0	$\frac{1}{4}$ of a large, 440 ml/15.5 fl oz can
Low-alcohol beer or lager	1.0	1,136 ml/2 pints
Alcopops	4.7–5.5	$\frac{2}{3}$ of a 330 ml/11.6 fl oz bottle
Wine	8.0–9.0	small glass (125 ml/4.4 fl oz)
Fortified wine, such as sherry or port	15.0–18.0	small glass (50 ml/1.8 fl oz)
Spirits, such as gin, vodka, whisky, rum, or brandy	40.0	single pub measure (25 ml/0.9 fl oz)

[1] The alcohol content of beers and wines can vary greatly – some wines, for example, can be as strong as 13% ABV.

Source: *Sensible Drinking,* © Crown copyright 1995

Commonly Abused Drugs

The two main laws about drugs are the Medicines Act and the Misuse of Drugs Act. The Medicines Act controls the way medicines are made and supplied. The Misuse of Drugs Act bans the nonmedical use of certain drugs. The Misuse of Drugs Act places drugs in different classes – A, B, and C. The penalties for offences involving a drug depend on the class it is in and will also vary according to individual circumstances. Class A drugs carry the highest penalty, class C the lowest. Drug misuse is defined on the illegal use of drugs for nontherapeutic purposes. Under the UK Misuse of Drugs regulations drugs used illegally include: narcotics, such as heroin, morphine, and the synthetic opioids; barbiturates; amphetamines and related substances; benzodiazepine tranquillizers; cocaine, LSD, and cannabis. *Designer drugs,* for example ecstasy, are usually modifications of the amphetamine molecule, altered in order to evade the law as well as for different effects, and may be many times more powerful and dangerous. Crack, a highly toxic derivative of cocaine, became available to drug users in the 1980s. Some athletes misuse drugs such as ephedrine and anabolic steroids. Sources of traditional drugs include the 'Golden Triangle' (where Myanmar, Laos, and Thailand meet), Mexico, Colombia, China, and the Middle East.

This table is intended to give general information only. If required, proper medical or legal advice should be taken from other sources. This table is not intended to condone drug use. The only safe option is not to take drugs.

Name	Source	Forms and appearance	Legal position	Methods of use	Effects of use
Amphetamine (also called speed, uppers, whizz, billy, sulphate)	a totally synthetic product	powder form; tablets and capsules	class B, schedule 2 controlled substance	taken orally in drink or licking off the finger; sniffed; smoked; dissolved in water for injecting	increased energy, strength, concentration, feelings of euphoria and elation; suppression of appetite; reduction in the need for sleep
Anabolic steroids	synthetic products designed to imitate certain natural hormones within the human body	capsules and tablets; liquid	not controlled	injections; also taken orally	increase in body bulk and muscle growth; feelings of stamina and strength
Cannabis (also called dope, grass, hash, ganja, blow, weed)	plants of the genus *Cannabis saliva*	herbal: dried plant material, similar to a coarse cut tobacco (marijuana); resin: blocks of various colours and texture (hashish); oil: extracted from resin, with a distinctive smell	class B, schedule 1 controlled substance	smoked in a variety of ways; can be put into cooking or made into a drink; occasionally eaten on its own	relaxation, feelings of happiness, congeniality, increased concentration, sexual arousal
Cocaine (also called coke, charlie, snow, white lady)	leaves of the coca bush, *Erythroxylum coca*	white crystalline powder; very rarely in paste form	class A, schedule 2 controlled substance	sniffed; injected; smoked (paste)	feelings of energy, strength, exhilaration, confidence; talkativeness
Crack and freebase cocaine (also called rock, wash, cloud nine; base, freebase)	derived from cocaine hydrochloride	crystals (crack cocaine); powder (freebase cocaine)	class A, schedule 2 controlled substances	smoking	elation and euphoria, feelings of power, strength, and well-being
Ecstasy (also called disco burgers, Dennis the Menace, diamonds, New Yorkers, E, Adam, XTC, Fantasy, Doves, rhubarb and custard (red and yellow capsules))	a totally synthetic product	tablets and capsules; rarely, powder; ecstasy is not always available in pure form, which increases the risks	class A, schedule 1	orally; occasionally injections	feelings of euphoria, energy, stamina, sociability, sexual arousal
Gammahydroxybutyrate (GHB) (also called GBH, liquid X)	pre-operation anaesthetic	liquid	controlled by the Medicines Act	orally	relaxation, sleepiness, short-term memory loss; reported sexual arousal
Heroin (also called smack, junk, H, skag, brown, horse, gravy)	from raw opium produced by the opium poppy	powder	class A, schedule 2 controlled substance	smoking; injections; also sniffed or taken orally	feelings of euphoria, inner peace, freedom from fear and deprivation

Adverse effects	Tolerance potential	Habituation potential	Withdrawal effects	Overdose potential
increased blood pressure with risk of stroke; diarrhoea or increased urination; disturbance of sleep patterns; weight loss; depression; paranoia; psychosis	tolerance develops rapidly	physical dependence: rare; psychological dependence: common	mental agitation, depression, panic; no physical symptoms	fatal overdose possible, even at low doses
bone growth abnormalities; hypertension and heart disease; liver and kidney malfunction; hepatitis; sexual abnormalities and impotence; damage to foetal development	tolerance may develop	no physical dependence; profound psychological dependence	sudden collapse of muscle strength and stamina; irritability, violent mood swings	overdose can lead to collapse, convulsions, coma, and death
impaired judgement; loss of short-term memory; dizziness; confusion; anxiety; paranoia; potential for cancer and breathing disorders	tolerance develops rapidly	true physical dependence: rare; psychological dependence: common	disturbed sleep patterns; anxiety, panic	it is not thought possible to overdose fatally
agitation, panic, feelings of being threatened; damage to nasal passages, exhaustion,, weight loss; collapsed veins, ulceration; delusions, violence	tolerance develops rapidly	strong physical and psychological dependence	severe cravings; feelings of anxiety and panic; depression	it is possible to overdose fatally
depression, feelings of being threatened; paranoia, psychosis; violence	some tolerance develops	strong physical and psychological dependence; babies born to pregnant users may also be dependent	severe depression; aggression, panic; risk of suicide	overdose can lead to coma and death
mood swings, nausea and vomiting, overheating, dehydration, convulsions, sudden death	tolerance develops	physical dependence: none; psychological dependence: low	no physical symptoms; irritability, depression	overdose can lead to coma and death
nausea and vomiting; muscle stiffness; disorientation; collapse; risks from mixing with alcohol and unknown concentration of the drug	little tolerance develops	little dependence	few withdrawal symptoms	overdose can lead to convulsions and collapse, and, rarely, death
depressed breathing, severe constipation, nausea, and vomiting; effect on general state of health, lower immunity; vein collapse and ulceration; risk of infection from needles	tolerance develops rapidly	profound physical and psychological dependence	sweating, flu-like symptoms 'going cold turkey'; severe cravings; professional assistance necessary	overdose can lead to coma and death

(*continued*)

Commonly Abused Drugs (*continued*)

Name	Source	Forms and appearance	Legal position	Methods of use	Effects of use
Lysergic acid diethylamide (LSD) (also called acid, trips, tab, blotters, dots)	derived from ergot (a fungus of certain cereal grains)	colourless crystals; for street use, mainly impregnated into squares of blotted paper or into squares of clear gelatine; or into tiny pills	class A, schedule 1 controlled substance	orally (paper squares and pills); under the eyelid (gelatine squares)	hallucinations
Magic (hallucinogenic) mushrooms (also called shrooms, mushies)	natural mushrooms (mainly fly agaric and liberty cap)	several varieties; identification is difficult	possession and eating of fresh mushrooms is not an offence; preparation is[1]	eaten; infused to make a drink	hallucinations; feelings of euphoria, well-being, gaiety
Methadone (also called doll, dolly, red rock, tootsie roll; phy-amps, phy (ampoules))	a totally synthetic product	powder; tablets, ampoules, linctus, mixture	class A, schedule 2 controlled substance	orally; injections	feelings of relaxation, bodily warmth, freedom from pain and worry
Methylamphetamine (also called ice, meth, crystal, glass, ice-cream (crystal form); meth, Methedrine (powder or tablets))	a totally synthetic drug, closely related to amphetamine sulphate	crystals or, less commonly, tablets or powder	class B, schedule 2 controlled substance	burning crystals and inhaling the fumes; drinking, sniffing, licking off the finger (powder and tablets)	feelings of euphoria, great strength and energy, sustained for long periods without rest or food
Nitrites (poppers) (also called nitro, nitrite)	various synthetic volatile chemicals	in small glass bottles under trade names of Liquid Gold, Hi-Tech, Rave, Locker Room, Ram, Rush, etc	controlled by the Medicines Act	inhalation	feelings of excitement and exhilaration; sexual arousal and increased sensitivity of sexual organs
Over-the-counter medicines	range of proprietary medicines	mostly tablets	some are controlled	taken orally; injected	vary
Solvents (also called glue, gas, can, cog (depending on substance and container))	domestic and commercial products	liquid petroleum gases (LPGs): aerosols, camping gas cylinders, lighter gas refills; liquid solvents: fire extinguisher fluid, corrective fluids, certain paints and removers, nail polish and remover, anti-freeze, petrol; solvent-based glues: impact adhesives used for wood, plastic, laminate surfaces, vinyl floor tiles	not controlled	sprayed into the mouth and inhaled (LPGs); sniffing	deep intoxication, hallucinations, excitability
Tranquillizers (also called tranx, barbs, barbies, blockers, tueys, traffic lights, golf balls (tranquillizers); jellies, jelly beans, M&Ms, rugby balls (temazepam in jelly capsules))	pharmaceutical drugs aimed at treating patients with problems of anxiety, insomnia, and depression; based on benzodiazepine or barbiturate	tablets or capsules	benzodiazepine based: class C controlled substances; barbiturate based: class B controlled substances	taken orally or injected	in higher doses: feelings of euphoria, elimination of fear and feeling of deprivation

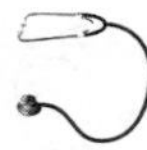

Adverse effects	Tolerance potential	Habituation potential	Withdrawal effects	Overdose potential
risk of accident while hallucinating; flashbacks; risk of developing a latent psychiatric disorder	tolerance develops and disappears rapidly	no physical dependence; some psychological dependence	no physical effect; few psychological effects	there is little danger of fatal overdose
long-term mental problems; risk of poisoning	tolerance develops rapidly	no dependence	few withdrawal effects	little overdose potential
sweating, nausea, itching, tiredness; disruption of menstrual cycle in women	tolerance develops slowly	strong physical and psychological dependence	fever, flu-like symptoms; diarrhoea; aggression	overdose can lead to respiratory depression, collapse, coma, and death
increased blood pressure with risk of stroke and heart failure, diarrhoea or increased urination, severe disturbance of sleep patterns, hallucinations, aggression, psychosis, delusions, paranoia	tolerance develops rapidly	physical dependence: not uncommon; psychological dependence: profound	severe cravings; depression; fear; panic and mental agitation	serious risk of fatal overdose, even at very low levels
nausea and vomiting; headaches and dizziness; skin problems; damage to vision if touches the eyes; poisonous if swallowed	tolerance develops rapidly	no significant physical or psychological dependence	no significant effects	little risk of overdose
vary	tolerance develops quickly	physical and psychological dependence may develop	possible effects	overdose can lead to health disturbances and death
over-stimulation of the heart, and death; asphyxiation from swelling of throat tissues or inhalation of vomit; danger of accidents whilst hallucinating; problems with speech, balance, short-term memory, cognitive skills; possible personality changes	tolerance may develop	no physical dependence; strong psychological dependence	no physical symptoms; anxiety and mood swings	overdose can lead to collapse, coma, and death
violent mood swings, bizarre sexual behaviour, deep depression, disorientation, lethargy	tolerance develops rapidly	profound physical and psychological tolerance	confusion, violent headaches, deep depression; sudden withdrawal may lead to convulsions and death	overdose can lead to convulsions, depression of breathing, collapse, coma, and death (more common for barbiturate-based products; generally increased if combined with alcohol)

[1] Preparation (such as crushing, slicing, drying, etc) is punishable as an offence relating to psilocin and psilocybin – the active ingredients of most hallucinogenic mushrooms, both class A, schedule 1 controlled substances.

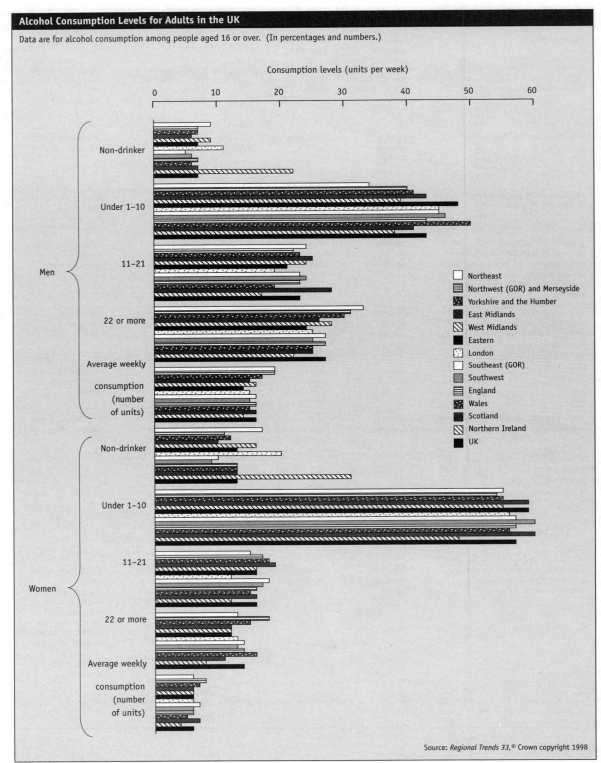

Alcohol Consumption Levels for Adults in the UK

Data are for alcohol consumption among people aged 16 or over. (In percentages and numbers.)

Source: *Regional Trends 33,* © Crown copyright 1998

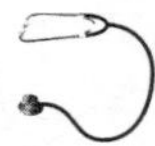

Trends in Alcohol Consumption in the UK

Data are estimated averages of alcohol consumption per person over 15 during the year given. The figures for 1991–97 are not strictly comparable to those for previous years.

Year	Beer	Spirits	Wine	Cider	Total	Year	Beer	Spirits	Wine	Cider	Total
1956	3.86	0.82	0.29	0.10	5.07	1985	4.98	2.13	1.66	0.29	9.05
1960	4.09	0.96	0.42	0.10	5.57	1990	5.02	2.10	1.83	0.33	9.28
1965	4.42	1.07	0.54	0.10	6.13	1995	4.66	1.69	2.03	0.57	8.92
1970	4.96	1.21	0.67	0.15	7.00	1996	5.00	1.70	2.13	0.57	9.40
1975	5.64	1.90	1.07	0.19	8.80	1997	5.10	1.80	2.14	0.56	9.60
1980	5.45	2.24	1.35	0.21	9.25						

Food and Nutrition

Proportion and Number of the World's Undernourished in Developing Countries

Region	% of population undernourished		Number of undernourished (millions)[1]	
	1990–92	1994–96	1990–92	1994–96
Sub-Saharan Africa	40	39	196	210
Near East and North Africa	11	12	34	42
East and Southeast Asia	17	15	289	258
South Asia	21	21	237	254
Latin America and Caribbean	15	13	64	63
Total all developing regions	20	19	822	828

[1] Owing to the ommission of Oceania, numbers do not add up to the total.

Source: *The State of Food and Agriculture 1998,* Food and Agriculture Organization of the United Nations

Body Mass by Gender in England

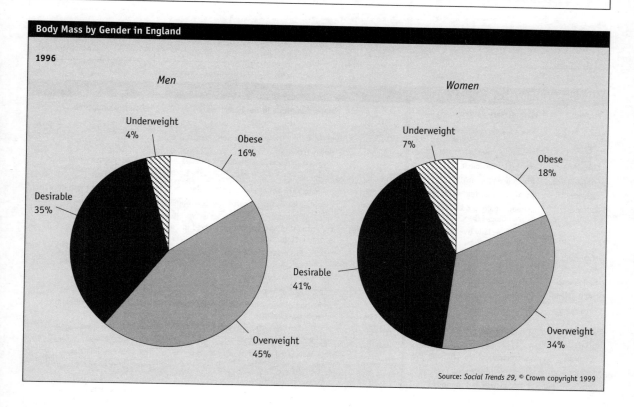

1996

Men

Underweight 4%

Obese 16%

Desirable 35%

Overweight 45%

Women

Underweight 7%

Obese 18%

Desirable 41%

Overweight 34%

Source: *Social Trends 29,* © Crown copyright 1999

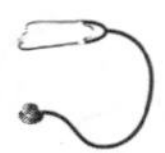

Obesity Trends in England by Age

Obesity – having a high proportion of one's body mass in the form of fat – is commonly measured using the body mass index (BMI), which relates a person's weight in kilograms to their height in metres squared. The UK Department of Health's Health of the Nation programme defines obesity as having a BMI greater than 30, though other thresholds – sometimes differentiating between mild, moderate, and severe obesity – are used elsewhere. Data are percentages of people having a BMI greater than 30 kg/m^2. Figures are from weighted data where a sample of the population has been used to represent the full population.

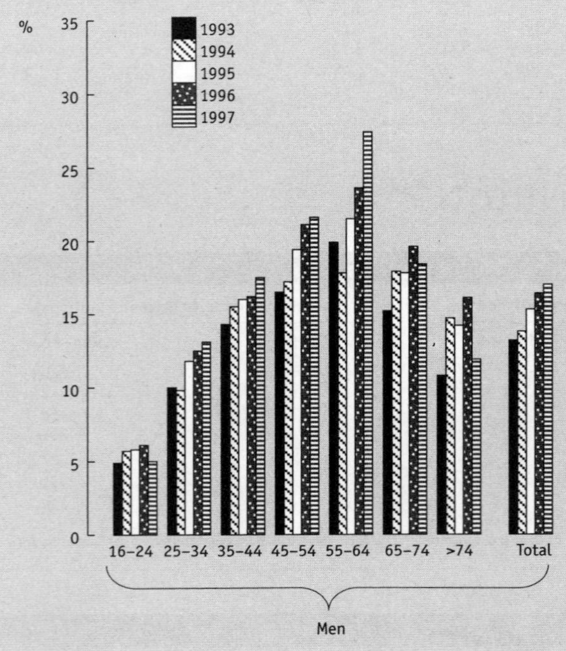

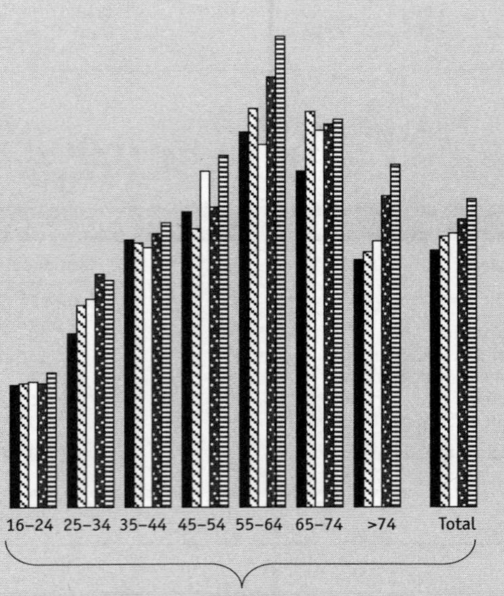

Source: *Health Survey of England 1997*,© Crown copyright 1999

Main Dietary Minerals

Mineral	Main dietary sources	Major functions in the body	Deficiency symptoms
Calcium	milk, cheese, green vegetables, dried legumes	constituent of bones and teeth; essential for nerve transmission, muscle contraction, and blood clotting	tetany
Chromium	vegetable oils, meat	involved in energy metabolism	impaired glucose metabolism
Copper	drinking water, meat	associated with iron metabolism	anaemia
Fluoride	drinking water, tea, seafoods	helps to keep bones and teeth healthy	increased rate of tooth decay
Iodine	seafoods, dairy products, many vegetables, iodized table salt	essential for healthy growth and development	goitre
Iron	meat (especially liver), legumes, green vegetables, whole grains, eggs	constituent of haemoglobin; involved in energy metabolism	anaemia
Magnesium	whole grains, green vegetables	involved in protein synthesis	growth failure, weakness, behavioural disturbances
Manganese	widely distributed in foods	involved in fat synthesis	not known in humans
Molybdenum	legumes, cereals, offal	constituent of some enzymes	not known in humans
Phosphorus	milk, cheese, meat, legumes, cereals	formation of bones and teeth, maintenance of acid–base balance	weakness, demineralization of bone
Potassium	milk, meat, fruits	maintenance of acid–base balance, fluid balance, nerve transmission	muscular weakness, paralysis
Selenium	seafoods, meat, cereals, egg yolk	role associated with that of vitamin E	not known in humans
Sodium	widely distributed in foods	as for potassium	cramp, loss of appetite, apathy
Zinc	widely distributed in foods	involved in digestion	growth failure, underdevelopment of reproductive organs

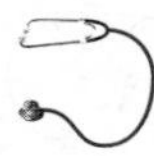

Vitamins

Vitamin	Name	Main dietary sources	Established benefit	Deficiency symptoms
A	retinol	dairy products, egg yolk, liver; also formed in body from ß-carotene,a pigment present in some leafy vegetables	aids growth; prevents night blindness and xerophthalmia (a common cause of blindness among children in developing countries); helps keep the skin and mucous membranes resistant to infection	night blindness; rough skin; impaired bone growth
B_1	thiamin	germ and bran of seeds and grains, yeast	essential for carbohydrate metabolism and health of nervous system	beriberi; Korsakov's syndrome
B_2	riboflavin	eggs, liver, milk, poultry, broccoli, mushrooms	involved in energy metabolism; protects skin, mouth, eyes, eyelids, mucous membranes	inflammation of tongue and lips; sores in corners of the mouth
B_6	pyridoxine/ pantothenic acid/biotin	meat, poultry, fish, fruits, nuts, whole grains, leafy vegetables, yeast extract	important in the regulation of the central nervous system and in protein metabolism; helps prevent anaemia, skin lesions, nerve damage	dermatitis; neurological problems; kidney stones
B_{12}	cyanocobalamin	liver, meat, fish, eggs, dairy products, soybeans	involved in synthesis of nucleic acids, maintenance of myelin sheath around nerve fibres; efficient use of folic acid	anaemia; neurological disturbance
	folic acid	green leafy vegetables, liver, peanuts; cooking and processing can cause serious losses in food	involved in synthesis of nucleic acids; helps protect against cervical dysplasia (precancerous changes in the cells of the uterine cervix)	megaloblastic anaemia
	nicotinic acid (or niacin)	meat, yeast extract, some cereals; also formed in the body from the amino acid tryptophan	maintains the health of the skin, tongue, and digestive system	pellagra
C	ascorbic acid	citrus fruits, green vegetables, tomatoes, potatoes; losses occur during storage and cooking	prevents scurvy, loss of teeth; fights haemorrhage; important in synthesis of collagen (constituent of connective tissue); aids in resistance to some types of virus and bacterial infections	scurvy
D	calciferol, cholecalciferol	liver, fish oil, dairy products, eggs; also produced when skin is exposed to sunlight	promotes growth and mineralization of bone	rickets in children; osteomalacia in adults
E	tocopherol	vegetable oils, eggs, butter, some cereals, nuts	prevents damage to cell membranes	anaemia
K	phytomenadione, menaquinone	green vegetables, cereals, fruits, meat, dairy products	essential for blood clotting	haemorrhagic problems

Nutritive Value of Foods

The energy value of each food is given in kilojoules (kJ) and kilocalories (kcal), and both have been calculated from the protein, fat, and carbohydrate content per 100 g of edible portion.

Food	Energy		Protein (g)	Fat (g)	Saturated fat (g)	Carbohydrate (g)
	kJ	kcal				
Cereal and Cereal Products						
Bread, brown	927	218	8.5	2.0	0.4	44.3
Bread, white	1,002	235	8.4	1.9	0.4	49.3
Flour, plain, white	1,450	341	9.4	1.3	0.2	77.7
Flour, wholemeal	1,318	310	12.7	2.2	0.3	63.9
Oats, porridge, raw	1,587	375	11.2	9.2	1.6	66.0
Rice, brown, boiled	597	141	2.6	1.1	0.3	32.1
Rice, white, boiled	587	138	2.6	1.3	0.3	30.9
Spaghetti, white, boiled	442	104	3.6	0.7	0.1	22.2
Dairy Products						
Butter	3,031	737	0.5	81.7	54.0	0.0
Cheddar cheese	1,708	412	25.5	34.4	21.7	0.1
Cottage cheese	413	98	13.8	3.9	2.4	2.1
Cream, fresh, heavy	1,849	449	1.7	48.0	30.0	2.7
Cream, fresh	817	198	2.6	19.1	11.9	4.1
Eggs, boiled	612	147	12.5	10.8	3.1	0.0

(continued)

Nutritive Value of Foods *(continued)*

Food	Energy kJ	Energy kcal	Protein (g)	Fat (g)	Saturated fat (g)	Carbohydrate (g)
Low-fat spread	1,605	390	5.8	40.5	11.2	0.5
Margarine, polyunsaturated	3,039	739	0.2	81.6	16.2	1.0
Milk, semi-skimmed	195	46	3.3	1.6	1.0	5.0
Milk, skimmed	140	33	3.3	0.1	0.1	5.0
Milk, whole	275	66	3.2	3.9	2.4	4.8
Yoghurt, whole milk, plain	333	79	5.7	3.0	1.7	7.8
Fish						
White fish, steamed, flesh only	417	98	22.8	0.8	0.2	0.0
Shrimps, boiled	451	107	22.6	1.8	0.4	0.0
Fruit						
Apples	199	47	0.4	0.1	0.0	11.8
Apricots	674	158	4.0	0.6	0.0	36.5
Avocados	784	190	1.9	19.5	4.1	1.9
Bananas	403	95	1.2	0.3	0.1	23.2
Cherries	203	48	0.9	0.1	0.0	11.5
Grapefruit	126	30	0.8	0.1	0.0	6.8
Grapes	257	60	0.4	0.1	0.0	15.4
Mangoes	245	57	0.7	0.2	0.1	14.1
Melon	119	28	0.6	0.1	0.0	6.6
Oranges	158	37	1.1	0.1	0.0	8.5
Peaches	142	33	1.0	0.1	0.0	14.0
Pears	169	40	0.3	0.1	0.0	10.0
Plums	155	36	0.6	0.1	0.0	8.8
Raspberries	109	25	1.4	0.3	0.1	4.6
Strawberries	113	27	0.8	0.1	0.0	6.0
Meat						
Beef, lean only, raw	517	123	20.3	4.6	1.9	0.0
Chicken, meat and skin, raw	954	230	17.6	17.7	5.9	0.0
Lamb, lean only, raw	679	162	20.8	8.8	4.2	0.0
Pork, lean only, raw	615	147	20.7	7.1	2.5	0.0
Vegetables						
Aubergine	64	15	0.9	0.4	0.1	2.2
Beetroot	195	46	2.3	0.0	0.0	9.5
Cabbage	109	26	1.7	0.4	0.1	4.1
Celery	32	7	0.5	0.2	0.0	0.9
Courgettes	74	18	1.8	0.4	0.1	1.8
Cucumber	40	10	0.7	0.1	0.0	1.5
Lettuce	59	14	0.8	0.5	0.1	1.7
Mushrooms	55	13	1.8	0.5	0.1	0.4
Onions	150	36	1.2	0.2	0.0	7.9
Parsnips	278	66	1.6	1.2	0.2	12.9
Peas	291	69	6.0	0.9	0.2	9.7
Peppers	65	15	0.8	0.3	0.1	2.6
Potatoes, new, flesh only	298	70	1.7	0.3	0.1	16.1
Potatoes, old, flesh only	318	75	2.1	0.2	0.0	17.2
Spinach	90	21	301	0.8	0.1	0.5
Sweetcorn kernels	519	122	2.9	1.2	0.2	26.6
Sweet potatoes	358	84	1.1	0.3	0.1	20.5
Tofu, soya bean, steamed	304	73	8.1	4.2	0.5	0.7
Watercress	94	22	3.0	1.0	0.3	0.4

Source: *Manual of Nutrition*, © Crown copyright 1995

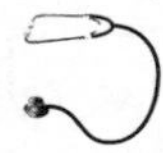

Recommended Daily Intake of Nutrients

(– = not applicable.)

Sex and age		Energy MJ	Energy kcal	Protein (g)	Calcium (mg)	Iron (mg)	Vitamin A (µg)	Thiamine (retinol	Riboflavin (mg)	Niacin (mg)	Vitamin C (mg)	Vitamin D[1] (µg)
Boys												
<1		3.25	780	19	600	6	450	0.3	0.4	5	20	7.5
1		5.00	1,200	30	600	7	300	0.5	0.6	7	20	10
2		5.75	1,400	35	600	7	300	0.6	0.7	8	20	10
3–4		6.50	1,560	39	600	8	300	0.6	0.8	9	20	10
5–6		7.25	1,740	43	600	10	300	0.7	0.9	10	20	–
7–8		8.25	1,980	49	600	10	400	0.8	1.0	11	20	–
9–11		9.50	2,280	56	700	12	575	0.9	1.2	14	25	–
12–14		11.00	2,640	66	700	12	725	1.1	1.4	16	25	–
15–17		12.00	2,880	72	600	12	750	1.2	1.7	19	30	–
Girls												
<1		3.00	720	18	600	6	450	0.3	0.4	5	20	7.5
1		4.50	1,100	27	600	7	300	0.4	0.6	7	20	10
2		5.50	1,300	32	600	7	300	0.5	0.7	8	20	10
3–4		6.25	1,500	37	600	8	300	0.6	0.8	9	20	10
5–6		7.00	1,680	42	600	10	300	0.7	0.9	10	20	–
7–8		8.00	1,900	48	600	10	400	0.8	1.0	11	20	–
9–11		8.50	2,050	51	700	12[2]	575	0.8	1.2	14	25	–
12–14		9.00	2,150	53	700	12[2]	725	0.9	1.4	16	25	–
15–17		9.00	2,150	53	600	12[2]	750	0.9	1.7	19	30	–
Men												
18–34	sedentary	10.50	2,510	62	500	10	750	1.0	1.6	18	30	–
	moderately active	12.00	2,900	72	500	10	750	1.2	1.6	18	30	–
	very active	14.00	3,350	84	500	10	750	1.3	1.6	18	30	–
35–64	sedentary	10.00	2,400	60	500	10	750	1.0	1.6	18	30	–
	moderately active	11.50	2,750	69	500	10	750	1.1	1.6	18	30	–
	very active	14.00	3,350	84	500	10	750	1.3	1.6	18	30	–
65–74		10.00	2,400	60	500	10	750	1.0	1.6	18	30	–
>74		9.00	2,150	54	500	10	750	0.9	1.6	18	30	–
Women												
18–54	most occupations	9.00	2,150	54	500	12[2]	750	0.9	1.3	15	30	–
	very active	10.50	2,500	62	500	12[2]	750	1.0	1.3	15	30	–
Pregnant		10.00	2,400	60	1,200	13	750	1.0	1.6	18	60	10
Lactating		11.50	2,750	69	1,200	15	1,200	1.1	1.8	21	60	10
55–74		8.00	1,900	47	500	10	750	0.8	1.3	15	30	–
>74		7.00	1,680	42	500	10	750	0.7	1.3	15	30	–

[1] Most people who go out in the sun need no dietary source of vitamin D, but children and adolescents in winter, and housebound adults, are recommended to take 10 µg vitamin D daily.

[2] These iron recommendations may not cover heavy menstrual losses.

Rules for Safe Food Production

The World Health Organization (WHO) regards illness due to contaminated food as one of the most widespread health problems in the contemporary world. For infants, immunocompromised people, pregnant women, and the elderly, the consequences of such an illness can be fatal.

WHO data indicate that a small number of factors related to food handling are responsible for a large proportion of food-borne disease episodes everywhere. Common errors include: preparation of food several hours prior to consumption, combined with storage of that food at temperatures that favour growth of bacteria and/or formation of toxins; insufficient cooking or reheating of food and so failing to reduce or eliminate pathogens; cross contamination; handling of the food by people with poor personal hygiene.

The WHO has devised Ten Golden Rules in response to these errors, offering advice that can reduce the risk of food-borne pathogens being able to contaminate, survive, or multiply. By following these basic rules, the risk of food-borne disease will be significantly reduced.

1. Choose foods processed for safety

While many foods, such as fruits and vegetables, are best in their natural state, others simply are not safe unless they have been processed. For example, always buy pasteurized as opposed to unpasteurized milk, and if you have the choice, select fresh or frozen poultry treated with ionizing radiation. When shopping, keep in mind that food processing was invented to improve safety as well as to prolong shelf-life. Certain foods eaten raw, such as lettuce, need thorough washing.

2. Cook food thoroughly

Many raw foods, most notably poultry, meats, eggs, and unpasteurized milk, may be contaminated with disease-causing organisms. Thorough cooking will kill the bacteria, but remember that the temperature of all parts of the food must reach at least 70°C/158°F. If cooked chicken is still raw, put it back in the oven until it is done – all the way through. Frozen meat, fish, and poultry must be thoroughly thawed before cooking.

3. Eat cooked foods immediately

When cooked foods cool to room temperature, microbes begin to proliferate. The longer the wait, the greater the risk. To be on the safe side, eat cooked foods just as soon as they come off the heat.

Food Scares: Chronology

1985	An epidemic of bovine spongiform encephalopathy (BSE), or 'mad cow disease', is reported in beef cattle in Britain; it is later traced to cattle feed containing sheep carcasses infected with scrapie; in following years the consumption of infected beef is linked to CJD (Creutzfeld-Jakob Disease) in humans.
16 December 1988	The junior British health minister Edwina Currie resigns after her claim that most British eggs are infected with salmonella leads to a slump in egg sales.
November 1996	The world's worst outbreak of the lethal food poisoning bug, E.coli 0157, starts in Wishaw, central Scotland. Twenty people die and nearly 500 are sick in the outbreak in 1996 and 1997. Following the tragedy the government sets up a report under Professor Hugh Pennington, which leads to the creation of a Food Safety Agency.
May 1998	It is reported that more people in the UK were poisoned by their food in 1997 than in any other year since records began. Well over a third of all notified cases of poisoning are the result of salmonella infection.
July 1998	Scientists warn that a potentially lethal strain of salmonella has become resistant to some antibiotics. The salmonella strain – which first appeared in the UK in 1990 – is now responsible for 15 percent of all cases.
10 July 1998	A total of 49 people in London suffer a type of food poisoning not seen in Britain for 30 years, after eating mussels. All had eaten mussels originating from the UK. Doctors diagnosed Diarrhetic Shellfish Poisoning (DSP) arising from poisons called phycotoxins produced by small marine organisms.
11 August 1998	The government says milk could possibly carry a bacteria linked to Crohn's Disease, but stresses it is only a small risk and that further investigation is needed.
12 August 1998	The scientist at the centre of controversial claims over the risks of genetically modified (GM) foods, Dr Arpad Pusztai, is effectively forced to retire by the Rowett Research Institute after it accused him of misinterpreting the results of his tests with rats fed on GM potatoes. The tests reportedly showed that the rats suffered damage to their immune systems. He had gone on the ITV *World in Action* programme to raise questions about the safety of GM food in the human diet on the basis of the study.
23 August 1998	Health officials launch an investigation into why 40 mourners were struck down by a suspected food bug after a funeral reception. The Cardiff outbreak is the latest in a stream of food poisonings.
October 1998	At least 91 people fall ill following a salmonella outbreak in London. Public health officials believe the outbreak is linked to chopped liver sold at a delicatessen in Southgate, Enfield.
November 1998	According to a leaked government report, food poisoning affects up to 10 million people in England every year, and cases of poisoning and infection in the UK have been massively underestimated.
January 1999	Official figures on UK food poisoning cases for 1998 show there was a big drop in cases of salmonella, but a large increase in the number of infections caused by another food bug, campylobacter, which is carried by birds and mammals.
12 February 1999	A reports triggers a scare over GM food. The report, published by a group of scientists from 13 different countries, seeks to legitimize the work of Dr Arpad Pusztai. Pusztai was fired by the Rowett Research Institute in 1998 for revealing to the media his findings that rats fed on GM potatoes suffered damage to their vital organs. The UK government now faces calls for an urgent safety review of GM foods as a row brews in the scientific community over the apparent suppression of important research.
March 1999	An outbreak of E.coli food poisoning in Cumbria affects 38 people. Health officials say unpasteurized cheese is the most likely cause of the outbreak.

4. Store cooked foods carefully

If you must prepare foods in advance or want to keep leftovers, be sure to store them under either hot (near or above 60°C/140°F) or cool (near or below 10°C/50°F) conditions. This rule is of vital importance if you plan to store foods for more than four or five hours. Foods for infants should preferably not be stored at all. A common error, responsible for countless cases of food-borne disease, is putting too large a quantity of warm food in the refrigerator. In an overburdened refrigerator, cooked foods cannot cool to the core as quickly as they must. When the centre of food remains warm (above 10°C/50°F) for too long, microbes thrive, quickly proliferating to disease-causing levels.

5. Reheat cooked foods thoroughly

This is your best protection against microbes that may have developed during storage (proper storage slows down microbial growth but does not kill the organisms). Once again, thorough reheating means that all parts of the food must reach at least 70°C/158°F.

6. Avoid contact between raw foods and cooked foods

Safely cooked food can become contaminated through even the slightest contact with raw food. This cross-contamination can be direct, as when raw poultry meat comes into contact with cooked foods. It can also be more subtle. For example, do not prepare a raw chicken and then use the same unwashed cutting board and knife to carve the cooked bird. Doing so can reintroduce the disease-causing organisms.

7. Wash hands repeatedly

Wash hands thoroughly before you start preparing food and after every interruption – especially if you have to change a baby or have been to the toilet. After preparing raw foods such as fish, meat, or poultry, wash again before you start handling other foods. And if you have an infection on your hand, be sure to bandage or cover it before preparing food. Remember too that household pets – dogs, cats, birds, and especially turtles – often harbour dangerous pathogens that can pass from your hands into food.

8. Keep all kitchen surfaces meticulously clean

Since foods are so easily contaminated, any surface used for food preparation must be kept absolutely clean. Think of every food scrap, crumb, or spot as a potential reservoir of germs. Cloths that come into contact with dishes and utensils should be changed frequently and boiled before re-use. Separate cloths for cleaning the floors also require frequent washing.

9. Protect foods from insects, rodents, and other animals

Animals frequently carry pathogenic microorganisms that cause food-borne disease. Storing foods in closed containers is your best protection against contamination against animals.

10. Use safe water

Safe water is just as important for food preparation as for drinking. If you have any doubts about the water supply, boil water before adding it to food or

making ice for drinks. Be especially careful with any water used to prepare an infant's meal.

Source: World Health Organization

Food Standards Agency (FSA)

The creation of the FSA had its beginnings with a government report on an outbreak of E.coli in Scotland at the end of 1996 which caused 20 deaths. The British government announced its plans for a new Food Standards Agency in January 1998, hoping to allay public disquiet which had grown following food scares during 1996–97. The FSA had been an election promise by Labour, and the recent food safety scares over salmonella, E.coli, BSE and GM foods eventually pushed the issue of food safety to the top of the government's agenda. Figures from the Public Health Laboratory showed that 200 people die in England and Wales each year from food poisoning. The FSA, which would take the lead on policy related to food poisoning, was welcomed by health and food organizations alike.

The Draft Food Standards Bill was completed in January 1999, and it was thought that if the legislation could be pushed through in the early part of 1999, the agency could be up and running by early 2000. The government announced plans to charge an annual flat rate of £90 on all food outlets to fund the cost of setting up the agency. However, the plans were under review after the proposed rate provoked a strong protest from retailers and was dubbed a 'poll tax on food'.

According to the Draft Bill, the new agency would help rebuild public confidence in the food industry. The new agency would have a long reach, with powers to trace food hygiene problems all the way back along the food chain. Consumers could expect to receive more and better information about food safety and standards, so that they can make informed choices. The agency would have powers to monitor food law enforcement by local authorities and ensure people can benefit from a more consistent application of the law.

Useful Addresses

Helplines for Health and Related Issues

Source: Department of Health

The National Health Service national phone advice lines include freephone numbers from the Department of Health.

AIDS Helpline phone: (0800) 567123 (24 hours)

Arthritis Care Helpline phone: (0800) 289170 (Monday–Friday 12 noon–4.00 p.m.)

Cancer Helpline helpline of BACUP, a leading organization for people with cancer; phone: (0800) 181199 (9.00 a.m.–7.00 p.m.)

Cerebral Palsy Helpline helpline from Scope for people with cerebral palsy and their carers; phone: (0800) 626216 (Monday–Friday 11.00 a.m.–9.00 p.m., Saturday and Sunday 2.00 p.m.–6.00 p.m.)

Childline helpline for children in danger or distress; phone: (0800) 1111 (24 hours)

Contraception Helpline advice on emergency contraception; phone: (0800) 494847 (24 hours)

Diabetes Careline run by the British Diabetic Association; phone: (0171) 636 6112 (Monday–Friday 9.00 a.m.–5.00 p.m.)

Disability Benefits Enquiry Line phone: (0800) 882200 (Monday–Friday 8.30 a.m.–6.30 p.m., Saturday 9.00 a.m.–1.00 p.m.)

Drinkline national alcohol helpline; phone: (0345) 320202 (Monday–Friday 11.00 a.m.–11.00 p.m.)

Drugs Helpline national drugs helpline; phone: (0800) 776600 (24 hours)

Epilepsy Helpline helpline of the British Epilepsy Association; phone: (0800) 309030 (Monday–Thursday 9.00 a.m.–4.30 p.m., Friday 9.00 a.m.–4.00 p.m.)

Food Safety Helpline phone: (0800) 282407 (Monday–Friday 9.00 a.m.–5.00 p.m.)

Gamblers Anonymous phone: (0114) 262 0026 (24 hours)

Heartline advice relating to all aspects of coronary heart disease and its prevention; phone: (0800) 858585 (Monday–Friday 12 noon–5.00 p.m.)

NHS Health Information Service information on health issues such as illness and disease, self-help groups, and treatments; phone: (0800) 665544 voice and minicom (Monday–Friday 9.00 a.m.–7.00 p.m.)

NSPCC child protection helpline of the National Society for the Prevention of Cruelty to Children; phone: (0800) 800500 (24 hours)

Quitline help for people wanting to stop smoking; phone: (0800) 002200 (24 hours)

Samaritans phone: (0345) 909090 (24 hours)

Saneline for people with mental health problems and their families and carers; phone: (0345) 678000 (24 hours)

Seniorline information line from Help the Aged; phone: (0800) 650065 (Monday–Friday 9.00 a.m.–4.00 p.m.)

Sexwise helpline for young people with concerns over sexual or relationship matters; phone: (0800) 282930 (7.00 p.m.–midnight)

Charitable Societies and Associations for Health and Related Issues

Action for Blind People 14–17 Verney Road, London SE16 3DZ; phone: (0171) 732 8771; fax: (0171) 639 0948; e-mail: info@afbp.org

Action Research Vincent House, Horsham, West Sussex RH12 2DP; phone: (01403) 210406; fax: (01403) 210541

Age Concern England: Astral House, 1268 London Road, London SW16 4ER; phone: (0181) 679 8000; fax: (0181) 679 6069; Northern Ireland: 3 Lower Crescent, Belfast BT7 1NR; phone: (01232) 245729; Scotland: 113 Rose Street, Edinburgh EH2 3DT; phone: (0131) 220 3345; Wales: 1 Cathedral Road, Cardiff CF1 9SD; phone: (01222) 371566

Alcoholics Anonymous PO Box 1, Stonebow House, Stonebow, York YO1 2NJ; phone: (01904) 644026 (administration), (0171) 352 3001 (helpline); fax: (01904) 629091

Alzheimer's Disease Society Gordon House, 10 Greencoat Place, London SW1P 1PH; phone: (0171) 306 0606; fax: (0171) 306 0808; e-mail: 101762.422@compuserve.com

Association for Spina Bifida and Hydrocephalus (ASBAH) 42 Park Road, Peterborough PE1 2UQ; phone: (1733) 555988; fax: (01733) 555985; e-mail: (1734) postmaster@asbah.demon.co.uk

Arthritis Care 18 Stephenson Way, London NW1 2HD; phone: (0171) 916 1500, (0800) 289170 (free helpline); fax: (0171) 916 1505

British Association of Cancer United Patients (BACUP) 3 Bath Place, Rivington Street, London EC2A 3DR; phone: (0171) 696 9003; Cancer Information Service: (0800) 181199 or (0171) 613 2121; fax: (0171) 696 9002

British Association of the Hard of Hearing *see* **Hearing Concern**

British Deaf Association 1–3 Worship Street, London EC2A 2AB; phone: (0171) 588 3520; fax: (0171) 588 3527

British Diabetic Association (BDA) 10 Queen Anne Street, London W1M 0BD; phone: (0171) 323 1531; fax: (0171) 637 3644; e-mail: bda@diabetes.org.uk

British Epilepsy Association (BEA) Anstey House, Hanover Square, Leeds LS3 1BE; phone: (0113) 243 9393, (0800) 309030 (free helpline); fax: (0113) 242 8804; e-mail: epilepsy@bea.org.uk

British Health Care Association 24a Main Street, Garforth, Leeds LS25 1AA; phone: (0113) 232 0903; fax: (0113) 232 0904

British Heart Foundation 14 Fitzhardinge Street, London W1H 4DH; phone: (0171) 935 0185; fax: (0171) 486 5820

British Lung Foundation 78 Hatton Garden, London EC1N 7JR; phone: (0171) 381 5831; fax: (0171) 831 5832

British Migraine Association 178a High Road, Byfleet, West Byfleet, Surrey KT14 7ED; phone: (01932) 352468; fax: (01932) 351257

British Polio Fellowship Ground Floor, Unit A, Eagle Office Centre, The Runway, South Ruislip, Middlesex HA4 6SE; phone: (0181) 842 4999; fax: (0181) 842 0555; e-mail: british.polio@dial.pipex.com

British Red Cross Society 9 Grosvenor Crescent, London SW1X 7EJ; phone: (0171) 235 5454; fax: (0171) 245 6315; e-mail: information@redcross.org.uk

Cancer Research Campaign 10 Cambridge Terrace, London NW1 4JI; phone: (0171) 224 1333; fax: (0171) 487 4310

Chest, Heart and Stroke Association *see* **Stroke Association**

Children's Society Edward Rudolf House, Margery Street, London WC1X 0JL; phone: (0171) 837 4299; fax: (0171) 837 0211; e-mail: communications@the-children's-society.org.uk

Christian Aid PO Box 100, London SE1 7RT; phone: (0171) 620 4444; fax: (0171) 620 0719; e-mail: caid@gn.apc.org

Commonwealth Society for the Deaf (Sound Seekers) 134 Buckingham Palace Road, London SW1W 9SA; phone: (0171) 259 0200; fax: (0171) 259 0300

Cystic Fibrosis Trust Alexandra House, 11 London Road, Bromley, Kent BR1 1B7; phone: (0181) 464 7211; fax: (0181) 313 0472

Downs Syndrome Association 155 Mitcham Road, London SW17 9PG; phone: (0181) 682 4001; fax: (0181) 682 4012

Dyslexia Institute Ltd 133 Gresham Road, Staines, Middlesex TW18 2AJ; phone: (01784) 463851; fax: (01784) 460747

Eating Disorders Association 1st Floor, 103 Prince of Wales Road, Norwich NR1 1DW; phone: (01603) 619090, (01603) 621414 (helpline), (01603) 765050 (youth helpline); fax: (01603) 664915

ENABLE (Scottish Society for the Mentally Handicapped) 6th Floor, 7 Buchanan Street, Glasgow G1 3HL; phone: (0141) 226 4541; fax: (0141) 204 4398

Foundation for the Study of Infant Deaths 14 Halkin Street, London SW1X 7DP; phone: (0171) 235 0965, (0171) 235 1712 (helpline); fax: (0171) 823 1986; e-mail: fsid@dial.pipex.com

Friends of the Elderly and Gentlefolk's Help 42 Ebury Street, London SW1W 0LZ; phone: (0171) 730 8263; fax: (0171) 259 0154

Guide Dogs for the Blind Hillfields, Burghfield Common, Reading, Berks RG7 3YG; phone: (0118) 983 5555; fax: (0118) 983 5433

Haemophilia Society 3rd Floor, Chesterfield House, 385 Euston Road, London NW1 3AU; phone: (0171) 380 0600; fax: (0171) 387 8220; e-mail: info@haemophilia-soc.demon.co.uk

Hearing Concern (British Association for the Hard of Hearing) 7–11 Armstrong Road, London W3 7JL; phone: (0181) 743 1110; fax: (0181) 742 9043

Help the Aged St James's Walk, Clerkenwell Green, London EC1R 0BE; phone: (0171) 253 0253; fax: (0171) 250 4474; e-mail: hta@dial.pipex.com

Imperial Cancer Research Fund PO Box 123, Lincoln's Inn Fields, London WC2A 3PX; phone: (0171) 242 0200; fax: (0171) 269 3100

Leprosy Mission (England and Wales) Goldhay Way, Orton Goldhay, Peterborough PE2 5GZ; phone: (01733) 370505; fax: (01733) 370960; e-mail: TLMEW@cityscape.co.uk

Leukaemia Research Fund 43 Great Ormond Street, London WC1N 3JJ; phone: (0171) 405 0101; fax: (0171) 405 3139; e-mail: info@leukaemia-research.org.uk

Macmillan Cancer Relief Anchor House, 15–19 Brittan Street, London SW3 3TZ; phone: (0171) 351 7811; fax: (0171) 376 8098

Marie Curie Cancer Care 28 Belgrave Square, London SW1X 8QG; phone: (0171) 235 3325; fax: (0171) 823 2380

Maternity Alliance 45 Beech Street, London EC2Y 8AD; phone: (0171) 588 8583; fax: (0171) 588 8584; e-mail: ma@mail.pro-net.co.uk

ME Association 4 Corringham Road, Stanford-le-Hope, Essex SS17 1EF; phone: (01375) 642466

MENCAP (The Royal Society for Mentally Handicapped Children and Adults) 123 Golden Lane, London EC1Y 0RT; phone: (0171) 454 0454; fax: (0171) 608 3254

Mental After Care Association 25 Bedford Square, London WC1B 3HW; phone: (0171) 436 6194; fax: (0171) 637 1980

Migraine Trust 45 Great Ormond Street, London WC1N 3HZ; phone: (0171) 831 4818; fax: (0171) 831 5174

MIND (The National Association for Mental Health) Granta House, 15–19 Broadway, London E15 4BQ; phone: (0181) 519 2122, (0345) 660163 (info line); fax: (0181) 522 1725

Multiple Sclerosis Society of Great Britain and Northern Ireland 25 Effie Road, London SW6 1EE; phone: (0171) 610 7171, (0171) 371 8000 (helpline); fax: (0171) 736 9861; e-mail: info@mssociety.org.uk

National Association for Colitis and Crohn's Disease 4 Beaumont House, Sutton Road, St Albans, Hertfordshire AL1 1AB; phone: (01727) 830038; fax: (01727) 844296; e-mail: nacc@nacc.org.uk

National Association for Maternal and Child Welfare Ltd 1st Floor, 40–42 Osnaburgh Street, London NW1 3ND; phone: (0171) 383 4117; fax: (0171) 383 4115; e-mail: valerie.forebrothernamcw@btinternet.com

National Association for Mental Health *see* **MIND**

National Asthma Campaign Providence House, Providence Place, London N1 0NT; phone: (0171) 226 2260, (0345) 010203 (helpline); fax: (0171) 704 0740

National Childbirth Trust Alexandra House, Oldham Terrace, London W3 6NH; phone: (0181) 992 8637; fax: (0181) 922 5929

National Library for the Blind Far Cromwell Road, Bredbury, Stockport, Cheshire SK6 2SG; phone: (0161) 494 0217; fax: (0161) 406 6728; e-mail: NLBUK@compuserve.com

National Osteoporosis Society PO Box 10, Radstock, Bath, BA3 3YB; phone:

(01761) 471771, (01761) 472721 (helpline); fax: (01761) 471104; e-mail: rosierowe@nos.org.uk

National Schizophrenia Fellowship (NSF) 28 Castle Street, Kingston upon Thames, Surrey, KT1 1SS; phone: (0181) 547 3937, (0181) 974 6814 (advice); fax: (0181) 547 3862; e-mail: nsf@nsf.org.uk

Nutrition Society 10 Cambridge Court, 210 Shepherds Bush Road, London W6 7NJ; phone: (0171) 602 0228; fax: (0171) 602 1756

OPSIS (National Association for the Education, Training and Support of Blind and Partially Sighted People) 16 City Road, London EC1Y 2AA; phone: (0171) 628 1083; fax: (0171) 628 1030

Patients' Association PO box 935, Harrow HA1 3JY; phone: (0181) 423 9111, (0181) 423 8999 (helpline); fax: (0181) 423 9119

Princess Royal Trust for Carers 16 Byward Street, London EC3R 5BA; phone: (0171) 480 7788

Psoriasis Association 7 Milton Street, Northampton NN2 7JG; phone: (01604) 711129; fax: (01604) 792894

QUIT (the society that helps people stop smoking) Victory House, 170 Tottenham Court Road, London W1P 0HA; phone: (0171) 388 5775, (0800) 002200 (free-phone quitline); fax: (0171) 388 5995

RADAR (Royal Association for Disability and Rehabilitation) 12 City Forum, 250 City Road, London EC1V 8AF; phone: (0171) 250 3222; fax: (0171) 250 0212

Red Cross Society *see* **British Red Cross**

Royal Association in Aid of Deaf People 27 Old Oak Road, London W3 7HN; phone: (0181) 743 6187; fax: (0181) 740 6551

Royal Cancer Hospital, Institute of Cancer Research 237 Fulham Road, Chelsea, London SW3 6JB; phone: (0171) 352 8133; fax: (0171) 352 3299

Royal Commonwealth Society for the Blind *see* **Sight Savers International**

Royal London Society for the Blind Dorton House, Seal, Sevenoaks, Kent TN15 0ED; phone: (01732) 761477; fax: (01732) 763363; e-mail: PJTALBOT@compuserve.com

Royal National College for the Blind College Road, Hereford, HR1 1EB; phone: (01432) 265725; fax: (01432) 353478

Royal National Institute for Deaf People 19–23 Featherstone Street, London EC1Y 8SL; phone: (0171) 296 8000; helpline: (0345) 090210; fax: (0171) 296 8199

Royal National Institute for the Blind 224 Great Portland Street, London W1N 6AA; phone: (0171) 388 1266; helpline: (0345) 669999; fax: (0171) 388 2034; e-mail: rnib@rnib.org.uk

Royal School for Deaf Children Victoria Road, Margate, Kent CT9 1NB; phone: (01843) 227561; fax: (01843) 227637

Royal Society for the Prevention of Accidents Edgbaston Park, 353 Bristol Road, Birmingham B5 7ST; phone: (0121) 248 2000; fax: (0121) 248 2001

St John Ambulance 1 Grosvenor Crescent, London SW1X 7EF; phone: (0171) 235 5231; fax: (0171) 235 0796

SANE – The Mental Health Charity 2nd Floor, 199–205 Old Marylebone Road, London NW1 5QP; phone: (0171) 724 6520, (0345) 678000 (helpline); fax: (0171) 724 6502

Sargent Cancer Care for Children 14 Abingdon Road, London W8 6AF; phone: (0171) 565 5100; fax: (0171) 565 5120

Save the Children Fund 17 Grove Lane, London SE5 8RD; phone: (0171) 703 5400; fax: (0171) 703 2278

Scottish Association for Mental Health Cumbrae House, 15 Carlton Court, Glasgow G5 9JP; phone: (0141) 568 7000; fax: (0141) 568 7001

Scottish Society for the Mentally Handicapped *see* **ENABLE**

SENSE (The National Deaf-Blind and Rubella Association) 11–13 Clifton Terrace, London N4 3SR; phone: (0171) 272 7774, (0181) 991 0513 (advice helpline); fax: (0171) 272 6012; e-mail: enquiries@sense.org.uk

Sight Savers International (Royal Commonwealth Society for the Blind) Grosvenor Hall, Bolnore Road, Haywards Heath, West Sussex RH16 4BX; phone: (01444) 446600; fax: (01444) 446688

Stroke Association Stroke House, 123 Whitecross Street, London EC1V 8JJ; phone: (0171) 490 7999; fax: (0171) 490 2686

Terrence Higgins Trust 52–54 Gray's Inn Road, London WC1X 8JU; phone: (0171) 831 0330, (0171) 242 1010 (helpline); fax: (0171) 242 0121; e-mail: info@tht.org.uk

Web Sites

Action on Smoking and Health (ASH)

http://www.ash.org.uk/

ASH, the UK's leading pressure group against smoking, brings news and information of its campaigns plus opportunities to join in.

AIDS and HIV Information

http://www.thebody.com/

AIDS/HIV site offering safe sex and AIDS prevention advice, information about treatments and testing, and health/nutritional guidance for those who have contracted the disease.

Alcohol Concern

http://www.alcoholconcern.org.uk/

Huge resource addressing many of the problems surrounding alcohol abuse.

Allergy Facts

http://www.sig.net/~allergy/facts.html

Basic information about the causes, symptoms, and treatment of allergy attacks.

Alternative and Complementary Medicine Centre

http://www.healthy.net/clinic/therapy/

Guide to a range of disciplines within the field of complementary medicine, which also considers their relationship to mainstream medical treatment.

Ancient Medicine/Medicina Antiqua

http://web1.ea.pvt.k12.pa.us/medant/

This multi-awardwinning site forms a starting point for those wishing to study ancient Greek and Roman medicine.

Animated Medical Graphics

http://www.animatedmedical.com/

Uses animations to explain medical terms and topics to those without a medical background.

Babyworld.Com

http://www.babyworld.co.uk/

Help for all first-time parents that includes an extensive database of possible ailments; it also covers such topics as pregnancy and daily care.

Bovine Spongiform Encephalopathy (BSE)

http://cahpwww.nbc.upenn.edu/bse/bse1.html

Collection of informative articles chronicling the BSE (or 'mad cow') controversy in the UK.

Breast Cancer Awareness

http://avon.avon.com/showpage.asp?thepage=crusade

Promotes awareness of this disease through a library of frequently asked questions.

British Nutrition Society

http://www.nutrition.org.uk/

Offering educational resources for parents, schools and teachers, this site has a wide range of information about the nutritional value of your diet.

Cancer Help UK

http://medweb.bham.ac.uk/cancerhelp/indexy.html

UK cancer information in the form of news, glossaries, treatments, research, and support.

Cancer: The Facts

http://www.icnet.uk/research/factsheet/index.html

Information on cancer from the Imperial Cancer Research Fund. There is a simple explanation of what cancer is, followed by links to sites dealing with bowel, leukaemia, lung, pancreatic, skin, and multiple myeloma cancers, as well as cancers specific to either men or women, or prevalent within families.

Children's Health

http://www.kidshealth.org/

In-depth coverage of children's health issues, including infections, behaviour and emotions, food, and fitness. The site also includes an interactive map of the human body, designed for children to explore.

Fitness Online

http://www.fitnessonline.com/

Guide to getting fit, featuring 'Searchable workouts', and 'Dr Tim' who is available to answer your fitness questions.

Healthy Ideas

http://www.healthyideas.com/

Online magazine that contains news and information about nutrition, natural healing, weight loss and fitness techniques.

Heart: An Online Exploration

http://sln.fi.edu/biosci/heart.html

Explore the heart: discover its complexities, development, and structure; follow the blood on its journey through the blood vessels and learn how to maintain a healthy heart.

Human Anatomy Online

http://www.innerbody.com/indexbody.html

Fun, interactive, and educational site on the human body.

Inner Body

http://www.innerbody.com/

Take a cartoon body apart and zoom in on each part to get a full description of how it works.

Institute for the Study of Drug Dependence (ISDD)

http://www.isdd.co.uk/

Aiming to advance 'knowledge, understanding, and policy-making about drugs', this site from the ISDD contains an online drug encyclopedia and a 'Frequently asked questions' section that tackles many of the main issues.

Internet Drug Index

http://www.rxlist.com/

Online list of prescription and non-prescription drugs, with a search engine to help find specific types or products and access to information about indications and side effects too.

MedicineNet

http://www.medicinenet.com/

Immense US-based site dealing in plain language with all current aspects of medicine.

Mental Health

http://www.mentalhealth.com/

Aiming 'to improve understanding, diagnosis, and treatment of mental illness', this encyclopedia of mental disorders offers information on diagnosing and treating mental health problems.

Multimedia Medical Reference Library

http://www.med-library.com/medlibrary/

Huge medical reference work on the Web, with detailed text, diagrams, and explanations of a great range of ailments.

National Health Service (NHS)

http://www.nhs50.nhs.uk/

Features a detailed history of the NHS, what health services were like before the NHS, and a glimpse into the future.

NHS Story

http://www.nhs50.nhs.uk/nhsstory-index.htm

Written as part of the NHS's 50th birthday celebration, this account conveys the excitement generated in 1948 by the first ever provision of a free comprehensive health service.

Patient Advice

http://www.patient.co.uk/

Excellent site offering advice and help to non-medical people.

Personal and Occupational Stress Management

http://www.stress.org.uk/

Information on what stress is, how to avoid it, and how to deal with it.

Pharmaceutical Information Network

http://pharminfo.com/

Access information about analgesics from this US site, with its substantial drugs databases, related publications, and news.

Plainsense Men's Health

http://www.plainsense.com/Health/Mens/

Covers a wide range of issues specific to male physical and mental health, with practical advice on self-help and treatment options.

Plainsense Women's Health

http://www.plainsense.com/Health/Womens/index.htm

Covers a wide range of issues specific to female physical and mental health, with practical advice on self-help and treatment options.

Suicide Information and Education Center (SIEC)

http://www.siec.ca/

Extensive information on suicide prevention and intervention efforts and trends.

Transplantation and Donation

http://www.transweb.org/index.htm

This site includes information about organ and tissue transplantation and donation, the latest research developments, and answers to commonly asked questions.

Trashed

http://www.trashed.co.uk/index2.html

Health Education Authority site that is designed for young people, offering information about drugs and their effects in a non-judgemental way. For each substance you can access information on its effects, the laws surrounding its use, and how to help people who may be experiencing ill-effects after taking the drug.

United Nations International Drug Control Programme

http://www.undcp.org/undcp.html

Information on the work of the UN agency charged with coordinating international efforts to control the narcotics trade.

Visible Embryo

http://www.visembryo.com/

Learn about the first four weeks of human development.

Visible Human Project

http://www.nlm.nih.gov/research/visible/visible_gallery.html

Sample images from a long-term US project to collect a complete set of anatomically detailed, three-dimensional representations of the human body.

Vitamins and Dietary Supplements

http://www.vitamins.net/cgi-bin/exec/page-display?page=guides/vitamins.html&cart_id=251495198.14786.N001

US-based health site that offers extensive information about the benefits of different vitamins and supplements to your diet.

Wired for Health

http://www.wiredforhealth.gov.uk/mainfram.html

Government health site targeting young people and their teachers, offering well-presented information on how to stay healthy.

World Health Organization

http://www.who.ch/

Overview of the World Health Organization, including its major programmes, and recent world health reports.

You Are What You Eat

http://library.advanced.org/11163/gather/cgi-bin/wookie.cgi/

Interactive exercises included in the site are designed to help visitors learn about their personal eating habits and how to improve them.

Your Body and Nutrition

http://www.ilcnet.com/~nutrition/body.htm

Information and pictures on the way the human body works.

THE MILITARY AND DEFENCE

The Year in Review

6 July 1998 In the largest military operation in Northern Ireland for 30 years, 28,000 British troops and police block the biggest annual Orangemen's parade in its 191-year history when they prevent the 6,000 marchers from returning to Portadown after leaving Drumcree church. The Orangemen vow to remain.

8 July 1998 The British Ministry of Defence announces the sale of £2.3 billion worth of assets to pay for the modernization of the armed forces.

22 July 1998 Iran tests a new medium-range missile capable of hitting Israel; the USA, Israel, and Saudi Arabia protest.

24 July 1998 The British government announces that it will abolish the death penalty for military offences in the armed forces. It was last used in 1920 when Private James Daly was found guilty of mutiny at Jullunder in the Punjab.

28 July 1998 The British Defence and Evaluation Research Agency unveils plans for a revolutionary trimaran hull to replace the long, thin hulls of the Navy's present warships. The new style ships will have a 40% larger deck area than current frigates, and will be capable of speeds up to 40 knots compared to the present 28 knots.

29 July 1998 After four days of fighting, Serb forces overrun the Yugoslav province of Kosovo, routing the Kosovo Liberation Army, who are fighting for Kosovo autonomy. Over 100,000 Albanians are displaced.

20 August 1998 Six US warships and a submarine fire cruise missiles at suspected terrorist facilities in Afghanistan and Sudan, in retaliation for the US embassy bombings in Nairobi, Kenya, and Dar es Salaam, Tanzania, earlier in the month. The targets are a suspected weapons factory in Sudan and the Afghani base of the Saudi millionaire Osmana bin Laden, the prime suspect for the carrying out of the embassy bombings, who escapes unharmed.

25 September 1998 British Armed Forces minister Doug Henderson officially opens a special training centre, attached to the Royal Military College of Science at Shrivenham, Oxfordshire; it is the first facility of its kind in Europe to train military personnel in creating an equal opportunities environment within the forces.

13 October 1998 US special envoy Richard Holbrooke releases details of a peace deal with Yugoslav president Slobodan Milošević to halt the violence in Kosovo, but warns that 'the crisis continues'.

4 November 1998 At an informal defence summit of EU countries in Vienna, Austria, British defence secretary George Robertson calls for a radical overhaul of Europe's military forces in order to effectively handle crises such as the conflict in the Balkans.

12 November 1998 The USA and Britain continue to send military forces and weapons to the Gulf in preparation for air strikes against Iraq. Iraqi president Saddam Hussein continues to refuse to comply with a UN resolution requiring cooperation with weapons inspections.

14 November 1998 Saddam Hussein agrees to compromise with the United Nations, stating that he is now willing to comply with a UN resolution requiring cooperation with weapons inspections. Although UN secretary general Kofi Annan says he is satisfied with Iraq's promise, the USA and UK respond cautiously, still poised for air strikes at any time.

4 December 1998 British prime minister Tony Blair and French president Jacques Chirac sign an agreement in St Malo, France, to create an EU defence policy that gives the European Union the power to operate outside NATO.

5 December 1998 The British Ministry of Defence's quarterly report to the Cabinet Office reveals that nearly 90 percent of the Navy's critical computer systems are still not safeguarded against the millennium bug.

10 December 1998 According to a study by the Royal United Services Institute, the UK has overtaken France to become Europe's second most powerful military force and the fourth most powerful in the world, behind the USA, China, and Russia.

14 December 1998 In a clash between ethnic Albanian guerrillas and Yugoslav soldiers on Kosovo's southern border with Albania, Yugoslav soldiers kill 31 ethnic Albanians and injure 12.

14 December 1998 The British government announces the closure of the Royal Hospital Haslar at Portsmouth, the last military hospital in Britain.

16 December 1998 In Operation Desert Fox, the USA and the UK launch air strikes against Iraq for failing to cooperate with UN weapons inspections.

17 December 1998 The British government announces that it is lifting its 16-year ban on the sale of military equipment to Argentina.

17 December 1998 UK Tornado pilots join US forces in the second night of air strikes against Iraq. The decision of the two countries to take action without approval by the United Nations Security Council divides world opinion, with Russia, China, and France strongly condemning it.

19 December 1998 The USA and the UK launch their fourth and final night of air raids against Iraq in Operation Desert Fox, aimed at degrading Saddam Hussein's capacity to build weapons of mass destruction.

21 December 1998 Iraqi deputy prime minister Tariq Aziz announces that 62 soldiers were killed and 180 were injured in the four nights of UK and US air strikes. Civilian casualties, he said, were much higher. There were no UK or US casualties.

28 December 1998 In renewed tensions nine days after Operation Desert Fox, the Pentagon reports that Iraqi missiles were launched at a group of four US aircraft patrolling the no-fly zone of northern Iraq. The USA retaliates by firing missiles and dropping two bombs over Iraq.

9 January 1999 The Yugoslav army fires on the village of Stari Trg, northwest of the regional capital Pristina, after Kosovo Liberation Army (KLA) guerillas take eight soldiers hostage near the village. Although international monitors are able to broker a temporary peace between the Yugoslav army and separatist guerrillas, Western diplomats report a deteriorating situation that leaves the region on the brink of full-scale war.

17 January 1999 In the worst atrocity since the peace deal established in October 1998, the bodies of 45 ethnic Albanians are discovered outside the village of Recak in Kosovo. The massacre threatens to plunge the region back into full-scale war.

25 January 1999 Iraqi reports claim that US warplane missiles kill 11 and injure 59 people in the southern city of Basra. The Pentagon reports that the missiles were launched after an Iraqi ground radar tracked the planes, which were on routine surveillance flights, and fired on them.

29 January 1999 In a shootout with Serb security forces, 24 ethnic Albanians die in the village of Rugovo, in Kosovo. NATO gives the warring parties a three-week deadline to negotiate a plan for autonomy for the region.

23 February 1999 The British government announces that the Royal Air Force and Royal Navy squadrons of Harrier fighters and bombers will combine to form a single force called Joint Force 2000.

1 March 1999 An international treaty banning the use of antipersonnel land mines, signed by 133 countries, comes into effect, marked by a ceremony at the United Nations headquarters in Geneva, Switzerland.

17 March 1999 US president Bill Clinton withdraws his veto to defence legislation first proposed by former president Ronald Reagan in 1983 to build a missile defence shield against nuclear attack. Clinton dropped his opposition to the 'Star Wars' initiative in the wake of Chinese intelligence gaining access to the designs of US nuclear warheads.

20 March 1999 Serbian forces launch an attack against ethnic Albanians in the central Drenica region of Kosovo, a stronghold of the Kosovo Liberation Army (KLA), which is fighting for independence for the province. The Serbian forces shell and burn villages, and reportedly detain and kill ten men in the village of Srbica. At least 40,000 ethnic Albanians are forced to flee the area.

24 March 1999 NATO launches air strikes against Yugoslavia, starting off a bombing campaign prompted by Serbian president Slobodan Milošević's refusal to sign a peace accord with ethnic Albanians over the area of Kosovo. It is NATO's first assault on a sovereign nation in its 50-year history.

25 March 1999 NATO supreme commander Wesley Clark issues a statement indicating that NATO will continue air strikes until Serbian president Slobodan Milošević's forces are destroyed. Russia and China denounce the NATO air strikes against Yugoslavia, demanding a political rather than military solution to the conflict in Kosovo.

26 March 1999 The United Nations Security Council rejects a Russian-sponsored resolution to suspend the NATO bombing campaign against Serb military forces over the conflict in Kosovo.

11 April 1999 Indian military forces conduct a test launch of a ballistic missile that is capable of carrying a nuclear warhead. Three days later Pakistan conducts two similar launches, renewing international concerns over the possibility of a nuclear arms race in south Asia.

12 April 1999 Foreign ministers from NATO's 19 member countries meet for the first time since bombing began in Kosovo. They pledge to continue the bombing campaign until Yugoslav president Slobodan Milošević withdraws his forces from Kosovo and allows ethnic Albanian refugees to return safely.

12 April 1999 NATO bombers fire missiles at a passenger train as it crosses a bridge in southeastern Serbia, killing at least 10 civilians and injuring 16. NATO says the target was the bridge, which it claims was part of a military supply line.

13 April 1999 NATO forces escalate their air strikes against Serbian military targets in Yugoslavia, in the conflict over the region of Kosovo, after four days of more moderate attacks due to poor visibility.

14 April 1999 NATO fighter jets bomb two ethnic-Albanian refugee columns in western Kosovo, believing them to be a Serbian military convoy. The Serb Information Centre reports that up to 80 people are killed.

21 April 1999 A study by intelligence officials led by Robert Walpole of the US National Intelligence Council reveals that Chinese spies obtained information about US nuclear weapons technologies during the 1980s.

23 April 1999 The heads of 19 NATO countries meet in Washington, DC, for a summit marking the 50th anniversary of the organization. British prime minister Tony Blair announces his resolve to commit ground troops to Yugoslavia in the conflict over the province of Kosovo.

30 April 1999 NATO missiles hit the Yugoslav Army headquarters, the Defence Ministry, and the federal police headquarters in Belgrade. NATO forces also bomb a telecommunications tower, temporarily suspending Serbian state television broadcasts.

May 1999 The Royal Marines announce that women will be allowed to take the green beret commando training course and will be offered places in commando units if they pass. Until now women have been banned from combat roles.

9 May 1999 Nancy Mace becomes the first woman to graduate from the Citadel

military college in South Carolina. Women were first admitted to the Citadel in 1995 by a federal court order, and there are currently 42 women among the college's 1,700 cadets.

9 May 1999 NATO leaders insist that their bombing campaign against Yugoslavia will continue, despite the accidental bombing of the Chinese embassy in Belgrade. The embassy bombing provokes the biggest demonstrations in Beijing since the protests in Tiananmen Square ten years ago.

12 May 1999 The names of 117 agents in Britain's MI6 secret intelligence service, some real and some false, are published on the Internet. The government blames Richard Tomlinson, a former MI6 officer who claims he was sacked unfairly.

13 May 1999 A joint cabinet committee of Labour and Liberal Democrat party members in the UK publishes proposals to increase co-operation in defence between European countries. The agreement calls for European countries to accept greater responsibility for their own defence programmes, without the need for US assistance, and claims that Britain spends a higher proportion of its wealth on defence than any other European country.

13 May 1999 The British government attempts in vain to close down web sites on the Internet identifying 117 people as MI6 secret service officers. One site identifies nine officers named by former MI6 agent Richard Tomlinson, who also suggests that the MI6 is responsible for the death of Diana, Princess of Wales. British foreign secretary Robin Cook blames Tomlinson for the publication of all 117 names, although Tomlinson denies responsibility for the other lists.

17 May 1999 NATO military spokesman Walter Jertz says that NATO air bombing of Serbian military targets in Kosovo is being hampered by the Serb policy of using ethnic Albanian refugees as human shields in target areas.

19 May 1999 NATO claims that hundreds of Serb soldiers have deserted their posts in Kosovo, showing the first signs of flagging morale among Serb forces since NATO bombing began.

25 May 1999 An all-party report from the US Congress claims that Chinese spies have infiltrated US weapons intelligence, stealing data on every major US nuclear warhead in recent years.

26 May 1999 Indian fighter jets bomb mountain peaks in Kashmir, targeting Pakistani guerrillas who have captured key positions in the disputed region. It is India's first bombing of an enemy since 1971, when India and Pakistan went to war.

27 May 1999 The Indian government vows to continue air strikes against Pakistani guerrillas in Kashmir, despite losing two jet fighters and growing Western pressure to maintain their cease-fire.

28 May 1999 Muslim militants shoot down an Indian military helicopter and Indian jets attack guerrilla targets in Kashmir, as the conflict between India and Pakistan over the area of Kashmir escalates.

3 June 1999 Leaders of the European Union nations sign a common defence policy, including the possibility of creating an EU military staff and a military committee based in Brussels, Belgium, with the power to mount peacekeeping operations. NATO secretary-general Javier Solana is appointed head of the common foreign and security policy.

3 June 1999 Yugoslav president Slobodan Milošević formally accepts a peace plan devised by the European Union and Russia, after 72 days of NATO bombing. NATO plans to continue bombing until Serb forces begin to withdraw from the disputed region of Kosovo.

5 June 1999 NATO orders the Serb forces inside Kosovo to leave by three specified routes within seven days and observe a 15-mile buffer zone inside Serbia. Serb military leaders insist that their forces should not pull out until a United Nations Security Council resolution is passed to bring Kfor, the NATO peacekeeping force, under the auspices of the United Nations.

9 June 1999 NATO makes some concessions in its terms for the withdrawal of Yugoslav forces from Kosovo, and (at the Kumanovo air base in Macedonia) Yugoslav military leaders sign the agreement outlining the technicalities of their withdrawal. NATO ceases its bombing campaign; the agreement paves the way to an end to the war in the Balkans.

10 June 1999 As Serb troops start to withdraw from Kosovo, NATO general secretary Javier Solana officially declares an end to the alliance's 78 days of bombing in Yugoslavia, marking an end to the war. NATO makes final preparations for Operation Joint Guardian, the largest peacekeeping force in modern history, which will facilitate the return of up to one million ethnic Albanian refugees to their homes in Kosovo.

11 June 1999 Russian troops are the first to enter Serbia and move toward Kosovo, prompting NATO concerns about possible clashes between Russian and Western troops in the province.

12 June 1999 British, German, French, and US NATO troops enter the province of Kosovo in Yugoslavia and arrive in the capital, Pristina, to liberate the province from Serb forces. British paratroopers encounter 200 Russian troops stationed at Pristina's airport as NATO and Russia enter peace negotiations.

20 June 1999 In a settlement with NATO, the Kosovo Liberation Army agrees to disarm within 90 days, as stipulated by the UN resolution ending the war in the Balkans.

See Also Kosovo in The World Year in Review, pp. 147–51.

World Defence and Weaponry

Biological, Chemical, and Nuclear Warfare

Biological Warfare

The use of living organisms, or of infectious material derived from them, to bring about death or disease in humans, animals, or plants. At least ten countries have this capability.

Biological warfare, together with chemical warfare, was originally prohibited by the Geneva Protocol 1925, to which the United Nations has urged all states to adhere. Nevertheless research in this area continues; the Biological Weapons Convention 1972 permits research for defence purposes but does not define how this differs from offensive weapons development. Advances in genetic engineering make the development of new varieties of potentially offensive biological weapons more likely.

Chemical Warfare

Use in war of gaseous, liquid, or solid substances intended to have a toxic effect on humans, animals, or plants.

Together with biological warfare, it was banned by the Geneva Protocol in 1925, and the United Nations in 1989 also voted for a ban. In June 1990, the USA and USSR agreed bilaterally to reduce their stockpile to 5,000 tonnes each by 2002. The USA began replacing its stocks with new nerve-gas binary weapons. In 1993, over 120 nations, including the USA and Russia, signed a treaty outlawing the manufacture, stockpiling, and use of chemical weapons. However, it was not until 1997 that the Russian parliament ratified the treaty.

Nuclear Warfare

War involving the use of nuclear weapons.

Nuclear-weapons research began in Britain in 1940, but was transferred to the USA after it entered World War II. The research programme, known as the Manhattan Project, was directed by J Robert Oppenheimer. The worldwide total of nuclear weapons in 1990 was about 50,000, and the number of countries possessing nuclear weapons stood officially at five – USA, USSR, UK, France, and China.

Defence Expenditure and Manpower – Global Trends

Figures for the Soviet Union are for 1985 only and for Russia for 1997 only.

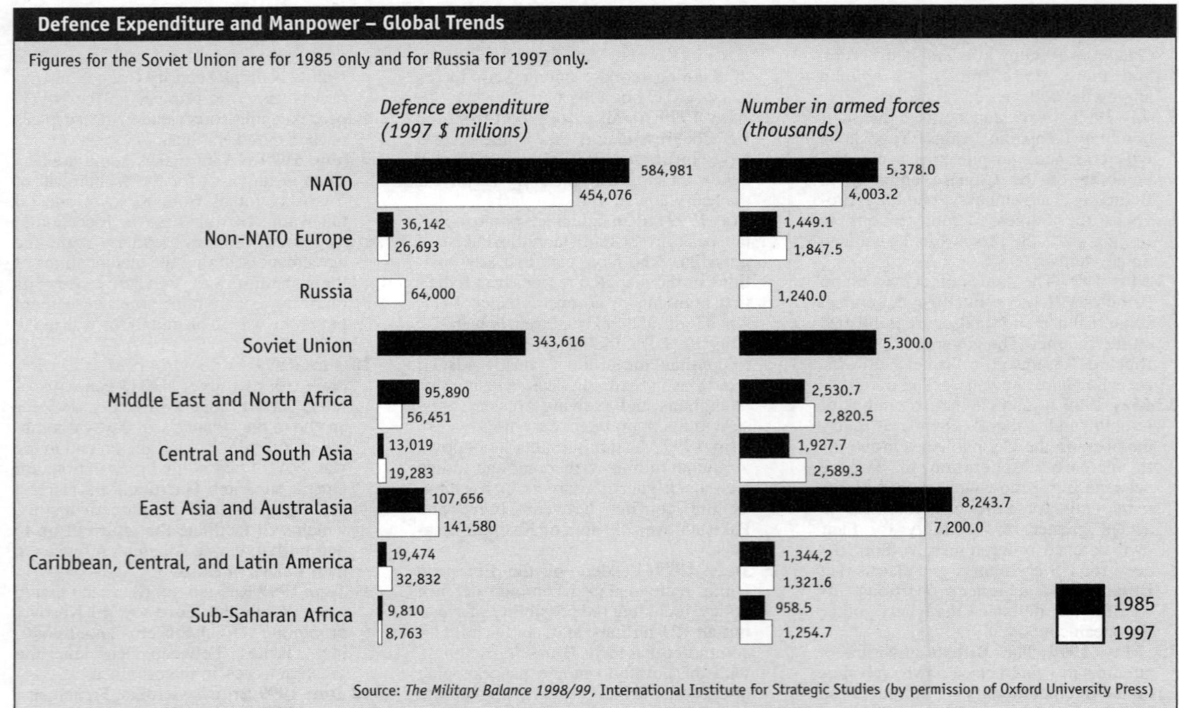

Source: *The Military Balance 1998/99*, International Institute for Strategic Studies (by permission of Oxford University Press)

Defence Research-and-Development Spending for Selected Countries

Includes only countries spending more than $1 million on military R&D. Figures are in millions of constant 1995 dollars.

Country	R&D expenditure	Year
Nuclear Weapon States		
USA	37,000	1996
France	4,900	1996
UK	3,200	1996
Russia	990	1996
China[1]	1,000	1994
Non-Nuclear Weapon and Threshold States		
Germany	2,200	1996
Japan	1,800	1996
Sweden	570	1995
India	510	1994
Korea, South	460	1996
Taiwan	350	1994
Spain	310	1996
Italy	300	1995
Australia	170	1994
South Africa	150	1996
Canada	120	1996
Ukraine	120	1994
Switzerland	100	1995
Netherlands	100	1996
Brazil	78	1996
Norway	71	1996
Finland	25	1996
Poland	24	1996
Czech Republic	15	1996
Argentina	11	1996
Philippines	10	1994
Romania	9.1	1995
Portugal	6.9	1995
Belgium	6.9	1996
Ecuador	6.2	1995
Turkey	5.7	1994
Denmark	5.3	1996
Greece	4.3	1995
New Zealand	3.6	1995
Slovakia	3.1	1996
Hungary	1.7	1994
Luxembourg	1.6	1994

[1] Figure accurate to one significant digit.

Source: Eric Arnett, in *SIPRI Yearbook 1998*, Stockholm International Peace Research Institute (Oxford University Press)

Selected Conventional Weapons Arsenals for Selected Countries

As of January 1998. (N/A = not available.)

Weapon type	Country and weapon strength													
	Brazil	Canada	France	Germany	India	Iraq	Israel	Italy	Nigeria	Poland	Russia	UK	USA	Yugoslavia
Sea Forces														
Tactical submarines	6	3	8	14	19	0	3	8	0	3	72	12	66	4
Carriers	1	0	1	0	1	0	0	1	0	0	1	3	12	0
Cruisers	0	0	1	0	0	0	0	1	0	0	17	0	29	0
Destroyers	0	4	4	3	6	0	0	4	0	1	13	12	57	0
Frigates	18	12	35	12	18	2	0	24	1	1	13	23	40	4
Patrol/coastal	36	14	40	30	49	6	51	17	35	33	124	26	21	34
Mine warfare	6	2	21	38	20	4	0	13	2	24	106[4]	19	26	10
Amphibious[1]	4	0	9	42	10	0	1	3	1	5	27[4]	7	43	20
Support/logistics	25	7	36	42	28	3	0	44	5	12	480[4]	21	99	9
Land Forces														
Main battle tanks	60	114	1,210	2,716	3,414[4]	2,700[4]	4,300	1,299	200	1,727	16,000[4]	484	8,239	785
Armoured reconnaisance vehicles	409	370	1,583	523	100[4]	N/A	400[4]	0	382[4]	510	2,000[4]	462	113	88
Armoured infantry fighting vehicles[2]	0	0	713	2,464	1,350	900[4]	N/A	0	0	1,405	10,344	794	6,720	718
Armoured personnel carriers	803	1,858	3,280	3,455	157	2,000[4]	9,400	2,703	N/A	728[4]	5,245[4]	2,820	17,800	169
Artillery pieces[3]	889[5]	339	1,055	2,040	4,500[6]	1,480[6]	9,690[5]	1,567	800[4]	1,580	16,500[4]	459	7,234	4,453[5]
Anti-tank guided weapons	12	575	2,065	2,367	N/A	N/A	N/A	1,426	0	403	N/A	841	40,077	N/A
Rocket launchers	540	1,151	39,080	0	N/A	N/A	N/A	2,000	N/A	N/A	N/A	0	N/A	3,200
Air defence guns	N/A	34	774	3,058	2,400[4]	6,000[4]	850	275	N/A	1,116	N/A	0	0	1,850
Surface-to-air missiles	2	118	1,071	335	N/A	N/A	N/A	218	64	1,490	4,700[4]	418	1,252	N/A
Air Forces														
Combat aircraft	300	140	566	503	839	316[7]	474	271	91	325	2,174[4]	504	5,292	238
Helicopters	159	165	678	743	314	500[4]	137	482	17	222	2,687[4]	599	5,722	52

[1] Ships specifically employed to disembark troops over unprepared beaches or to support amphibious operations.
[2] Armoured combat vehicles are designed to transport an infantry squad, armed with an integral cannon of at least 20-mm calibre.
[3] Weapons with a calibre of 100mm and above, capable of engaging targets by delivering primarily indirect fire. Includes guns, howitzers, multiple rocket launchers and mortars.
[4] Estimated.
[5] Estimated. Figure includes towed and self-propelled artillery but not multiple rocket launchers for which complete figures are not available.
[6] Does not include mortars, for which figures are not available.
[7] Estimated for bombers, ground attack, and fighter aircraft.

Source: Data from *The Military Balance 1998/99*, International Institute for Strategic Studies

Strategic Nuclear Arsenals

The arsenals of the second-tier powers – UK, France, and China – are in the 260–450 warhead range, many orders of magnitude less than those of the USA and Russia. Plans for British and French nuclear forces are well known, while the size and composition of China's future arsenal is unknown. For the USA and Russia the number of warheads has decreased by one-third from the peak of the late 1980s. As of January 1998. (– = not applicable. ICBM = Inter Continental Ballistic Missile; SLBM= Submarine Launched Ballistic Missile.)

Country	Bombers		ICBMs		SLBMs		Total	
	Deployed weapons	Warheads[1]	Deployed weapons	Warheads[1]	Deployed weapons	Warheads[1]	Deployed weapons	Warheads[1]
USA	92/53[2]	1,800	550	2,000	432	3,456	1,074/1,035	7,256
Russia	70	806	746	3,580	384	1,824	1,200	6,210
	Aircraft							
France	69	65	–	–	64	384	133	449
UK	96	100	–	–	32[3]	160[3]	128	260
			Land-based missiles					
China	150	150	113	233[4]	12	12	175	295

[1] Warheads in stockpile for France, UK, and China.
[2] Hardware configured to carry various combinations of munitions.
[3] Includes SSBNs (Surface to Surface Ballistic Missiles) and SLBMs.
[4] Includes short-range missiles and other tactical weapons.

Source: Robert S Norris and William M Arkin, in *SIPRI Yearbook 1998*, Stockholm International Peace Research Institute (Oxford University Press)

The Leading Suppliers of Major Conventional Weapons

Countries are ranked according to 1993–97 aggregate exports. Figures are trend-indicator values expressed in millions of constant 1990 dollars. (N/A = not available.)

Rank 1993–97	Rank 1992–96	Supplier	1993	1994	1995	1996	1997	1993–97
1	1	USA	12,504	10,434	9,823	9,528	10,840	53,129
2	2	Russia	3,541	1,117	3,218	3,094	3,466	15,246
3	3	UK	1,585	1,506	1,726	1,975	2,631	9,423
4	4	France	898	704	811	2,004	3,343	7,760
5	5	Germany	1,562	2,392	1,255	1,399	569	7,177
6	6	China	1,108	687	887	679	170	3,531
7	7	Netherlands	351	502	381	440	504	2,178
8	8	Italy	353	289	338	393	408	1,781
9	9	Canada	220	365	434	239	81	1,339
10	14	Spain	94	260	120	117	639	1,230
11	11	Israel	186	140	237	260	335	1,158
12	12	Ukraine	127	189	188	192	399	1,095
13	10	Czech Republic	267	377	193	137	19	993
14	13	Sweden	58	59	179	315	273	884
15	24	Moldova	N/A	175	N/A	N/A	392	567
16	16	Korea, North	422	48	48	21	N/A	539
17	17	Uzbekistan	N/A	238	272	N/A	N/A	510
18	19	Belgium	N/A	20	296	69	93	478
19	25	Belarus	N/A	8	24	129	263	424
20	32	Australia	30	24	22	10	318	404

Source: Siemon T Wezeman, Pieter D Wezeman, in *SIPRI Yearbook 1998,* Stockholm International Peace Research Institute (Oxford University Press)

The Leading Recipients of Major Conventional Weapons

Countries are ranked according to 1993–97 aggregate imports. Figures are trend-indicator values expressed in millions of constant 1990 dollars. (N/A = not available.)

Rank 1993–97	Rank 1992–96	Recipient	1993	1994	1995	1996	1997	1993–97
1	1	Saudi Arabia	2,799	1,460	1,259	1,946	2,370	9,834
2	9	Taiwan	907	614	1,138	1,530	4,049	8,283
3	2	Turkey	1,983	1,373	1,253	1,127	1,276	7,012
4	31	Egypt	1,267	1,941	1,680	937	867	6,692
5	6	Korea, South	482	642	1,553	1,591	1,077	5,345
6	8	China	1,097	341	697	1,102	1,816	5,053
7		Japan	1,580	703	1,021	666	584	4,554
8	7	India	582	468	1,062	1,231	1,085	4,428
9	4	Greece	991	1,048	947	248	715	3,949
10	10	Kuwait	650	45	962	1,323	411	3,391
11	14	United Arab Emirates	751	636	475	684	808	3,354
12	13	Thailand	135	835	688	522	1,031	3,211
13	21	Malaysia	17	448	1,143	199	1,346	3,153
14	15	Pakistan	825	719	225	644	572	2,985
15	16	USA	639	504	499	478	656	2,776
16	17	Iran	1,149	295	223	514	11	2,192
17	11	Germany	1,246	649	161	108	N/A	2,164
18	18	Spain	361	625	384	409	316	2,095
19	19	Finland	564	189	155	574	492	1,974
20	22	Indonesia	267	600	359	547	171	1,944

Source: Siemon T Wezeman, Pieter D Wezeman, in *SIPRI Yearbook 1998,* Stockholm International Peace Research Institute (Oxford University Press)

Strategic Defence: The New Star Wars

BY DAVID SHUKMAN

A new word entered the military lexicon on 31 August 1998 and brought with it a wave of near-panic in defence ministries around the world. Taepo-Dong 1 is the code name for a huge rocket that was launched on that date by North Korea. It blasted off into the outer reaches of the atmosphere, passing over Japan and confirming the long-dreaded vision of a rogue nation possessing the means to deliver a nuclear weapon over vast distances, perhaps even as far as the USA. This particular missile, in fact, failed to achieve its mission of placing a satellite in orbit. Nevertheless its political impact was immense: the USA accelerated plans to build a high-tech 'Star Wars' shield against nuclear attack.

Reagan's defence dream

It was the former US president Ronald Reagan who first dreamed of building impregnable fortifications in space to intercept incoming missiles. The Cold War was at its height and the two opposing sides had amassed vast arsenals with which to attack each other. The theory was that if one side attacked, the other would respond in kind and both would be destroyed; hence a so-called nuclear balance was established. Much better, Reagan argued, would be to have a defence system that could simply block the missiles of the USSR and leave American soil untouched. His supporters conjured up images of giant American battlestations in space poised to fire deadly laser beams at the Russian rockets as they rose out of their silos. The term 'Star Wars' was born.

Billions of dollars were spent researching Reagan's Strategic Defence Initiative during the late 1980s. A promotional video showed a child drawing a neat blue line above America protecting it from falling red warheads. But the reality was very different. Some tests of laser weapons which looked dazzlingly effective were later proved to have been faked. Studies found that it would take decades to launch the necessary equipment into space. The likely costs escalated out of control. The USSR repeatedly protested and even the UK, normally a loyal ally, was uneasy. The dream foundered.

Star Wars gave us problems; Son of Star Wars is going to be even worse.

Not until the Gulf War in 1991 was interest in missile defences rekindled. Iraq fired dozens of its Scud missiles at Israel and Saudi Arabia, and the USA found that it had only one weapon, the Patriot interceptor, to provide any sort of protection. The Patriot had been designed to attack enemy aircraft rather than missiles. Last-minute improvements in its software were meant to allow it to take on the Scuds. But such were the difficulties of tracking an approaching missile – at well over supersonic speed – that the Patriots rarely offered more than psychological support to people under attack on the ground.

Theatre High Altitude Air Defence

A new version of the Patriot, the PAC-3, has since been tested, along with other systems including a small laser mounted on a jumbo jet, missile interceptors carried by ships, and a missile known as Theatre High Altitude Air Defence (THAAD). THAAD is meant to rise at great speed to intercept missiles on the edge of the atmosphere. The rationale is that in the Gulf War Patriots attempted to hit incoming Scuds at low altitude with the result that the debris of both missiles would fall intact to the ground – and in Israel the casualty rate per Scud attack actually rose after the USA deployed Patriots there. The THAAD is supposed 'hit-to-kill' on the frontiers of space. But it has worked better on paper than in the air; by May 1999 it had not hit a single target. As yet, no missile defence system can be considered even remotely reliable.

The slow pace of technological advance is due in part to the immense complexity of the challenge – 'hitting a bullet with a bullet', as the Pentagon likes to say. Yet that has not dimmed the interest of politicians in the US Congress. The launch of the Taepo-Dong 1 heightened concern that the USA and its allies were becoming vulnerable to attack by hostile nations. Long-range missiles were suddenly falling into potentially dangerous hands: India, Pakistan, and Iraq are all known to have tested such systems. The Rumsfeld Commission, reporting to the Congress in 1998, concluded that the threat was 'broader, more mature, and evolving more rapidly' than Western intelligence had previously predicted. The Pentagon's Space Command has warned that ballistic missiles have become 'a symbol of strength and prestige', and that there is only limited time before one will be used against the USA.

Countering North Korea's Taepo-Dong 1

The result is that American military scientists are now working on developing a system of interceptors to be fielded by 2005. Gone is the grand Reagan vision of lasers orbiting in space, poised like sentries. Instead, the focus is on satellites that can track incoming missiles and ground-based missiles to intercept them. Yet even this system may never work or prove effective. And in the meantime, there are serious diplomatic ramifications.

The first problem is that back in the Cold War, the USA and the USSR signed the Anti-Ballistic Missile Treaty – an agreement to limit deliberately the number of interceptors each side was allowed. The view then was that war would be less likely if each side knew it could never mount a complete defence. The ABM Treaty of 1972 is still in effect and Russia has warned that the USA risks being in breach if it proceeds with its latest Star Wars plans. Mindful of the need for Russian cooperation in the Balkans, American diplomats are treading warily.

More alarming is the risk of confrontation involving US allies. The North Korean threat is felt most acutely by South Korea and Japan. Taiwan feels similarly affected by China. And all are pressing Washington for help in the form of missile defences. The Pentagon was asked to study the feasibility of offering these countries missile protection using Patriot and THAAD, among other systems. Yet North Korea and China objected, claiming any deployment of this kind would threaten their sovereignty. Such was the diplomatic sensitivity surrounding the Pentagon's report that the authors went to extraordinary lengths to stress that no recommendations for deployment were yet being made.

So Star Wars no longer only concerns Washington and Moscow. The greater the spread of long-range missiles, the stronger the interest in defences against them. The technology is improving but the diplomatic pressures are intensifying. As one US diplomat put it: 'The first Star Wars gave us problems; Son of Star Wars is going to be even worse'.

David Shukman is the BBC World Affairs Correspondent

Largest Arms-Producing Companies

1996

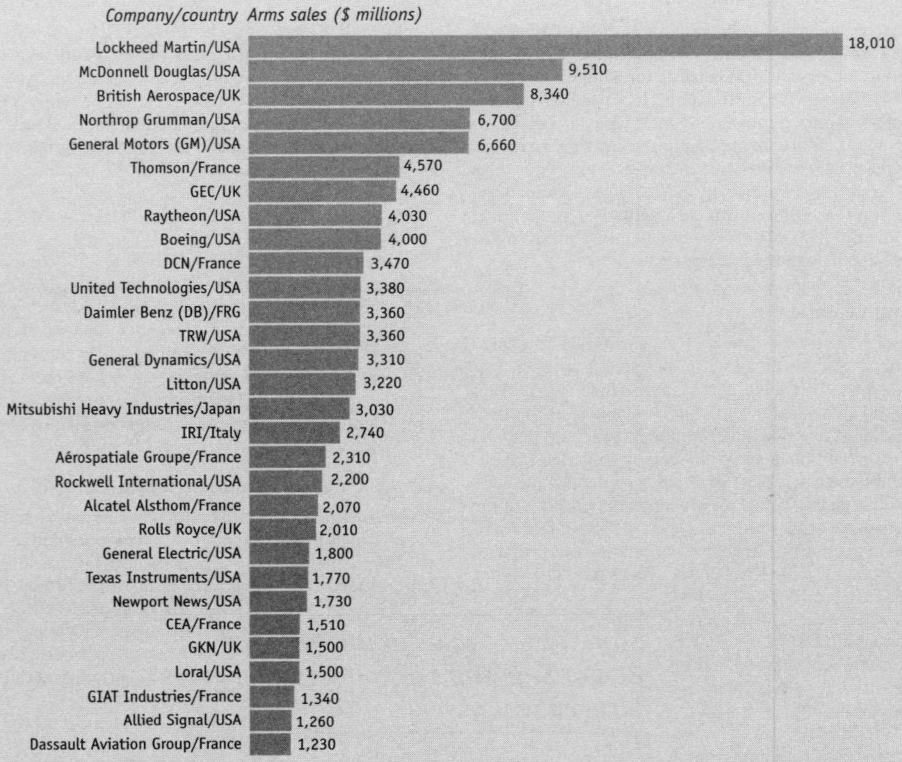

Company/country	*Arms sales ($ millions)*
Lockheed Martin/USA	18,010
McDonnell Douglas/USA	9,510
British Aerospace/UK	8,340
Northrop Grumman/USA	6,700
General Motors (GM)/USA	6,660
Thomson/France	4,570
GEC/UK	4,460
Raytheon/USA	4,030
Boeing/USA	4,000
DCN/France	3,470
United Technologies/USA	3,380
Daimler Benz (DB)/FRG	3,360
TRW/USA	3,360
General Dynamics/USA	3,310
Litton/USA	3,220
Mitsubishi Heavy Industries/Japan	3,030
IRI/Italy	2,740
Aérospatiale Groupe/France	2,310
Rockwell International/USA	2,200
Alcatel Alsthom/France	2,070
Rolls Royce/UK	2,010
General Electric/USA	1,800
Texas Instruments/USA	1,770
Newport News/USA	1,730
CEA/France	1,510
GKN/UK	1,500
Loral/USA	1,500
GIAT Industries/France	1,340
Allied Signal/USA	1,260
Dassault Aviation Group/France	1,230

Source: Elisabeth Sköns, Reinhilde Weidacher, and the SIPRI Arms Industry Network, in *SIPRI Yearbook 1998,* Stockholm International Peace Research Institute (Oxford University Press)

Arms Control Agreements

Treaty	Dates	Parties	Details
Agreements (Nuclear)			
Antarctic Treaty	signed 1 December 1959; entered into force 23 June 1961	37 nations	prohibited any use of Antarctica for military purposes; specifically prohibited nuclear testing and nuclear waste
Partial Test Ban Treaty	signed 5 August 1963; entered into force 10 October 1963	124 nations; an additional 11 nations have signed the treaty, but have not ratified it	prohibited nuclear weapon tests in outer space, in the atmosphere, and underwater
Outer Space Treaty	signed 27 January 1967; entered into force 10 October 1967	98 nations; an additional 28 nations have signed the treaty, but have not ratified it	prohibited nuclear weapons in Earth orbit and outer space
Treaty of Tlatelolco	signed 14 February 1967; entered into force 22 April 1968	31 nations; the USA, the UK, France, Russia, China, and the Netherlands have signed the relevant protocols to the treaty	prohibited nuclear weapons in Latin America and required safeguards on facilities
Non-proliferation Treaty	signed 1 July 1968; entered into force 5 March 1970; renewed indefinitely in 1995	187 nations; all nations that have signed have also formally adopted the treaty; the principal non-signatories are Israel, India, and Pakistan	divided the world into nuclear and non-nuclear weapon states based on status in 1968; obliged non-nuclear states to refrain from acquiring nuclear weapons and to accept International Atomic Energy Agency (IAEA) safeguards on their nuclear energy

(*continued*)

Arms Control Agreements (*continued*)

Treaty	Dates	Parties	Details
			facilities; obliged nuclear states to refrain from providing nuclear weapons to non-nuclear states, to assist in the development of nuclear energy in non-nuclear states, and to work toward global nuclear disarmament
Seabed Arms Control Treaty	signed 11 February 1971; entered into force 18 May 1972	93 nations; an additional 20 nations have signed the treaty, but have not ratified it	prohibited placement of nuclear weapons on the seabed and ocean floor beyond a 19 km/12 mi coastal limit
Accident Measures Agreement	signed and entered into force 30 September 1971	USA and USSR (Russia)	agreed measures to prevent accidental nuclear war, including agreement to notify each other of planned missile launches and the detection of unidentified objects
SALT I – Interim Agreement	signed 26 May 1972; entered into force 3 October 1972	USA and USSR (Russia); USA dropped commitment to agreement in 1986	froze at existing levels the number of strategic ballistic missile launchers on each side; permitted an increase in submarine-launched ballistic missiles (SLBMs) up to an agreed level only with the dismantling or destruction of a corresponding number of older intercontinental ballistic missile (ICBM) or SLBM launchers
ABM Treaty	signed 26 May 1972; entered into force 3 October 1972	USA and USSR (Russia)	prohibited nationwide anti-ballistic missile (ABM) defences, limiting each side to 2 deployment areas (1 to defend the national capital and 1 to defend an ICBM field) of no more than 100 ABM launchers and interceptor missiles each
Prevention of Nuclear War Agreement	signed and entered into force 22 June 1973	USA and USSR (Russia)	agreed to make the removal of the danger of nuclear weapons and their use an 'objective of their policies'; committed to consult with each other in case of danger of nuclear confrontation between them or other countries
ABM Protocol	signed 3 July 1974; entered into force 24 May 1976	USA and USSR (Russia)	limited each side to a single ABM deployment area
Threshold Test Ban Treaty	signed 3 July 1974; entered into force 11 December 1990	USA and USSR (Russia)	limited nuclear tests on each side to a 150 kiloton threshold
Peaceful Nuclear Explosions Treaty	signed 28 May 1976; entered into force 11 December 1990	USA and USSR (Russia)	an agreement not to carry out any underground nuclear explosion for peaceful purposes having a yield exceeding 150 kilotons, or any group explosion having an aggregate yield exceeding 150 kilotons
US–International Atomic Energy Agency Safeguards Agreement	signed 18 November 1977; entered into force 9 December 1980	USA and the IAEA	agreed to apply IAEA safeguards in designated facilities in the USA
SALT II Treaty	signed 18 June 1979	USA and USSR (Russia); USA dropped commitment to the agreement in 1986	never ratified, but both nations pledged to comply with the treaty's provisions; provided for broad limits on strategic offensive nuclear weapons systems, including equal numbers of strategic nuclear delivery vehicles, and restraints on qualitative developments that could threaten future stability; superceded by START in 1991
Convention on the Physical Protection of Nuclear Material	signed 3 March 1980; entered into force 8 February 1987	58 nations; an additional 8 nations have signed the treaty, but have not ratified it	provided for certain levels of physical protection during international transport of nuclear materials
Treaty of Rarotonga	signed 6 April 1985; entered into force 11 December 1986	11 nations are party to the treaty; all 5 declared nuclear weapons states have signed the relevant protocols to the treaty; the USA signed the protocols on 25 March 1996, but has yet to ratify the treaty	established a nuclear-weapons-free zone in the South Pacific
Missile Technology Control Regime	informal association formed in April 1987	28 nations	established export control guidelines and annexed listing nuclear-capable ballistic missile equipment and technologies that would require export licenses
Nuclear Risk Reduction Centres	signed and entered into force 15 September 1987	USA and USSR (Russia)	established centres designed to reduce the risk of nuclear war

(*continued*)

Arms Control Agreements (*continued*)

Treaty	Dates	Parties	Details
Intermediate-Range Nuclear Forces Treaty	signed 8 December 1987; entered into force 1 June 1988	USA and USSR (Russia)	eliminated all US and Soviet ground-launched ballistic and cruise missiles with ranges of 500–5,500 km/ 310–3,418 mi, their launchers, associated support structures, and support equipment
Ballistic Missile Launch Notification Agreement	signed and entered into force 31 May 1988	USA and USSR (Russia)	agreement to notify each other, through nuclear risk reduction centres, no less than 24 hours in advance, of the planned date, launch area, and area of impact for any launch of an ICBM or SLBM
START I Treaty	signed 31 July 1991; entered into force 5 December 1994	USA and USSR (Russia)	Russia formally accepted all of the USSR's arms control treaty obligations after the dissolution of the USSR. Because strategic nuclear weapons affected by the START I Treaty remained on the soil of Ukraine, Kazakhstan, and Belarus after the USSR's demise, an additional agreement was necessary to guarantee their removal; this was assured under the Lisbon protocol of May 1992. START established limits on deployed strategic nuclear weapons, and required the USA and Russia to make phased reductions in their offensive strategic nuclear forces over a 7 year period
START II Treaty	signed 3 January 1993; ratified by USA 26 January 1996	USA and Russia; still awaiting ratification by Russia. Both sides committed to negotiating START III upon Russia's ratification of START II	limited each side to 3,000–3,500 deployed strategic nuclear weapons each by the year 2003; banned multiple-warhead land-based missiles
Treaty of Bangkok	signed 15 December 1995; entered into force 27 March 1977	10 nations; none of the acknowledged nuclear powers have signed the relevant protocols. Brunei, Cambodia, Indonesia, Laos, Malaysia, Myanmar, Singapore, Thailand, and Vietnam have now ratified the treaty; the Philippines have signed but not ratified it	established a nuclear-weapons-free zone in Southeast Asia
Treaty of Pelindaba	signed 11 April 1996; the USA signed on 11 May 1996. Treaty open to signature by all states of Africa. It will enter into force upon the 28th ratification	54 signatories; the 5 acknowledged nuclear weapons states have signed the relevant protocols to the treaty and 6 states have now ratified it	established a nuclear-weapons-free zone in Africa
Comprehensive Test Ban Treaty	signed 24 September 1996	as of January 1998, 150 nations had signed the treaty, but only 13 nations had formally ratified it – to enter into force, the 44 nations that have nuclear electrical-generating and research reactors are required to sign and ratify the treaty; included in the 44 are India, Pakistan, and North Korea, none of which have signed the treaty	banned all explosive nuclear tests
Joint Statement on Parameters on Future Reductions in Nuclear Forces	signed 21 March 1997	USA and Russia	USA and Russia have agreed that negotiations for START III will begin as soon as START II enters into force
Agreements (Non-Nuclear)			
Geneva Protocol	signed 17 June 1925; entered into force 8 February 1928; ratified by USA 22 January 1975	135 nations	prohibited in war the use of asphyxiating or poisonous gas and liquids and all bacteriological (biological) methods of warfare; essentially a 'no first use' agreement, because many signatories ratified it with the reservation that it would cease to be binding if an enemy failed to observe the prohibitions
Biological and Toxic Weapons Convention	signed 10 April 1972; entered into force 26 March 1975	157 nations	prohibited development, production, stockpiling, acquisition, or retention of biological agents not associated with peaceful uses, biological or toxin weapons, and their delivery systems; required destruction or diversion of all prohibited agents to peaceful purposes within 9 months after entry into force; prohibited transfer of, or assistance to manufacture, prohibited agents

(*continued*)

Arms Control Agreements (*continued*)

Treaty	Dates	Parties	Details
Incidents at Sea Agreement	signed and entered into force 25 May 1972	USA and USSR (Russia)	agreement on the prevention of incidents on and over the high seas, including steps to avoid collision and the avoidance of manoeuvres in areas of heavy sea traffic
Environmental Modification Prevention	signed 18 May 1977; entered into force 5 October 1978	67 nations; an additional 17 nations have signed the treaty, but have not ratified it	prohibited deliberate manipulation of natural processes for hostile or other military purposes
Protocol (I) Additional to the 1949 Geneva Convention and Relating to the Protection of Victims of International Conflict	signed 12 December 1977; entered into force 7 December 1978	148 nations; in addition Cambodia acceded to Protocol on 14 January 1998, and UK ratified Protocol on 28 January 1998	Protocol prohibits the use of weapons or means of warfare which cause superfluous injury or unnecessary suffering
Convention on Certain Conventional Weapons (The Inhumane Weapons Convention)	opened for signature 10 April 1981; entered into force 2 December 1983; signed by the USA 2 April 1982 and ratified 24 March 1995	71 nations; 10 nations have signed the convention but not ratified it	banned the use of non-metallic fragmentation weapons and blinding lasers, and imposed restrictions on the use of land mines and incendiary weapons
Australia Group	informal association formed in 1984 in response to chemical weapons use in the Iran–Iraq War	30 nations	established voluntary export controls on certain chemicals
Stockholm Conference	signed and entered into force 19 September 1986	54 nations	established security and confidence-building measures designed to increase openness and predictability with regard to military activities in Europe
US–Soviet Bilateral Memorandum of Understanding	signed and entered into force September 1989	USA and USSR (Russia)	agreement to exchange data on size, composition, and location of chemical weapon stockpiles and storage, production, and destruction facilities, and to conduct reciprocal visits and both routine and challenge inspections
US–Soviet Bilateral Destruction Agreement	signed June 1990; has not yet entered into force	USA and USSR (Russia); currently abandoned by Russia	agreement to stop producing chemical weapons and to reduce their stockpiles to no more than 5,000 agent tons, with destruction to begin by 31 December 1992 and to be completed by 31 December 2002
Conventional Forces in Europe (CFE) Treaty	signed 19 November 1990; entered into force 9 November 1992	30 nations	established limits on the numbers of tanks, armoured combat vehicles, artillery combat aircraft, and helicopters in Europe
Open Skies Treaty	signed 24 March 1992	27 nations; the USA and 21 other nations have ratified the treaty; ratifications by Russia, Belarus, Ukraine, Kyrgyztan, and Georgia are still required for entry into force	permitted unarmed reconnaissance flights designed to promote military transparency and confidence among former NATO and Warsaw Pact adversaries
CFE 1A Treaty	signed 10 July 1992; entered into force 9 November 1992	30 nations	established limits on the number of troops in Europe
Chemical Weapons Convention	opened for signature 13 January 1993; entered into force 29 April 1997	165 nations; 106 signatories have ratified the treaty	prohibited the development, production, acquisition, stockpiling, retention, transfer, and use of chemical weapons – required declaration of chemical weapons or chemical weapon capabilities, including those primarily associated with commercial use; required destruction of declared chemical weapons and associated production facilities; provided for routine inspections of relevant facilities and challenge inspections upon request
Florence Agreement	signed 14 June 1996, entered into force immediately upon signature	Bosnia-Herzegovina, Bosnian Serb Republic, Croatia, Serbia, and Montenegro	the agreement was negotiated under the Dayton Agreement. It set limits on armaments of the warring parties of the conflict in Bosnia-Herzegovina. It covered heavy conventional weapons including main battle tanks, armoured combat vehicles, heavy artillery (75mm and above), combat aircraft, and attack helicopters
Ottawa Treaty	signed 3–4 December 1997	122 countries; 11 countries had ratified the treaty as at 27 April 1998	banned the production, use, and export of anti-personnel mines; also committed signatories to the destruction of stockpiles of mines within four years, and to clearing existing minefields as well as relieving the suffering of the victims of land mines

Arms Embargoes by International Organizations

Data are for 1993–97. (– = not applicable.)

Target	Entry into force[1]	Lifted	Legal basis	Organization
Afghanistan[2]	27 October 1996	–	UNSCR 1076	UN
Afghanistan	1 December 1996	–	–	EU
Bosnia-Herzegovina	–	–	–	EU
China	27 June 1989	–	–	EU
Congo, Democratic Republic of	7 April 1993	–	–	EU
Croatia	–	–	–	EU
Haiti	30 September 1991	15 October 1994	–	OAS
Haiti[3]	13 October 1993	15 October 1994	UNSCR 841	UN
Iraq	6 August 1990	–	UNSCR 661 + 687	UN
Liberia	19 November 1992	–	UNSCR 788	UN
Libya	27 January 1986	–	–	EU
Libya	31 March 1992	–	UNSCR 748 + 883	UN
Myanmar	28 October 1996	–	–	EU
Nigeria[4]	20 November 1995	–	–	EU
Nigeria	24 April 1996	–	–	Commonwealth
Rwanda	17 May 1994	17 August 1995[5]	UNSCR 918	UN
Sierra Leone	8 October 1997	–	UNSCR 1132	UN
Slovenia	–	–	–	EU
Somalia	23 January 1992	–	UNSCR 733	UN
South Africa[6]	4 November 1977	24 May 1994	UNSCR 418	UN
Sudan	15 March 1994	–	–	EU
UNITA (Angola)	25 September 1993	–	UNSCR 864 + 834	UN
Yugoslavia	25 September 1991	1 October 1996	UNSCR 713	UN
Yugoslavia	26 February 1996	–	–	EU

[1] All non-UN embargoes are voluntary.
[2] Voluntary (non-mandatory) embargo.
[3] Originally imposed in June 1993, but temporarily suspended until September 1993.
[4] The embargo does not apply to deliveries under existing contracts.
[5] The arms embargo was suspended on this date and formally ended on 1 September 1996.
[6] A voluntary arms embargo commenced on 7 August 1963 (US Security Council Resolution [UNSCR] 181); a voluntary embargo on equipment and material for arms production on 4 November 1963 (UNSCR 182); and a voluntary embargo on arms imports from South Africa on 13 December 1985 (UNSCR 558).

Source: Siemon T Wezeman and Pieter D Wezeman, in *SIPRI Yearbook 1998,* Stockholm International Peace Research Institute (Oxford University Press)

Major Conflicts and Casualties

Location of Major Armed Conflicts

Conflict locations with at least one major armed conflict in 1997. For abbreviations see page 636.
(N/A = no reliable figures available. – = not applicable.)

Location	Incompatibility[1]	Year formed/ year joined[2]	Warring parties[3]	No of troops in 1997[4]	Total deaths[5] (including 1997)	Deaths in 1997
Europe						
UK	Territory	1969/1969	Govt of UK vs Provisional IRA	214,000 N/A	1,500[6]	3
Middle East						
Iran	Govt	1970/1991	Govt of Iran vs Mujahideen e-Khalq	500,000[7] N/A	N/A	N/A
Iraq	Govt	1980/1991	Govt of Iraq vs SAIRI	350,000–400,000 N/A	N/A	N/A
Israel	Territory	1964/1964	Govt of Israel vs non-PLO groups[8]	170,000–180,000 N/A	> 13,000 (1948–)	100–150 (military) 75–100 (civilians)
Turkey	Territory	1974/1984	Govt of Turkey vs PKK	800,000[9] 6,000–10,000	> 30,000	> 1,000
Asia						
Afghanistan	Govt	1992/1992 1978/1978 1990/1990	Govt of Afghanistan vs Jumbish-i Milli-ye Islami vs Jamiat-i-Islami vs Hezb-i-Wahdat	20,000 N/A N/A N/A	> 20,000[10]	> 2,000
Bangladesh	Territory	1971/1982	Govt of Bangladesh vs JSS/SB	120,000 2,000–5,000	> 3,000–3,500 (1975–)	> 25
Cambodia	Govt	1979/1979	Govt of Cambodia vs PDK	140,000[11] 1,000–4,000	> 25,500[12]	N/A
India	Territory	–/1989 –/1992 1982/1988	Govt of India vs Kashmir insurgents[13] vs BdSF vs ULFA	1,145,000 N/A N/A N/A	> 20,000[14]	> 500
India–Pakistan	Territory	1947/1996	Govt of India vs Govt of Pakistan	1,145,000 587,000	N/A	N/A
Indonesia	Territory	1975/1975	Govt of Indonesia vs Fretilin	310,000 100–200	15,000–16,000 (military)	50–100
Myanmar	Territory	1948/1948	Govt of Myanmar vs KNU	300,000–400,000 2,000–4,000	8,000 (1948–50); 5,000–8,000 (1981–88)	50–200
Philippines	Govt	1968/1968	Govt of the Philippines vs NPA	110,000 N/A	21,000–25,000	< 100
Sri Lanka	Territory	1976/1983	Govt of Sri Lanka vs LTTE	110,000 5,000–8,000	> 40,000	> 4,000
Africa						
Algeria	Govt	1992/1992 1993/1993	Govt of Algeria vs FIS[16] vs GIA	170,000[15] N/A N/A	40,000–80,000	> 3,000
Burundi	Govt	1994/1994	Govt of Burundi vs CNDD	40,000	1,000[17]	800
Congo (Brazzaville)	Govt	/1997	Govt of Congo vs FDU,[18] Angola	10,000 1,500–3,000, 3,500	4,000–7,000	4,000–7,000
Senegal	Territory	1982/1982	Govt of Senegal vs MFDC	13,000 500–1,000	> 1,000	200–500
Sierra Leone	Govt	1991/1991	Govt of Sirerra Leone vs RUF	14,000 3,000–5,000	> 3,000	< 100
Sudan	Govt	1980/1983	Govt of Sudan vs NDA[20]	80,000–100,000 N/A	37,000–40,000 (military)[19] N/A	> 5,000
Uganda	Govt	1993/1994	Govt of Uganda vs LRA	40,000–50,000 1,000–4,000	>1,000	250

(continued)

Location of Major Armed Conflicts (*continued*)

Location	Incompatibility[1]	Year formed/ year joined[2]	Warring parties[3]	No of troops in 1997[4]	Total deaths[5] (including 1997)	Deaths in 1997
Zaire[21]	Govt	1996/1996	Govt of Zaire	28,000	4,000–9,000	> 2,000
			vs ADFL	20,000–40,000		
			vs Rwanda	N/A		
Central and South America						
Colombia	Govt	1949/1978	Govt of Columbia	140,000	N/A[22]	500–1,000
			vs FARC	7,000		
		1965/1978	vs ELN	3,000		
Peru	Govt	1980/1981	Govt of Peru	125,000	> 28,000	50–200
			vs Sendero Luminoso	500–1,500		
		1984/1986	vs MRTA	200		

[1] 'Govt' and 'Territory' refer to contested incompatibilities concerning government (type of political system, a change of central government or in its composition) and territory (control of territory [interstate conflict], secession or autonomy), respectively.
[2] Year formed = year in which the incompatibility was stated. Year joined = year in which use of armed force began or recommenced.
[3] Non-governmental warring parties active during 1997 are listed by the name of the parties using armed force.
[4] Total armed forces of the government warring party, and for non-government parties from the conflict location. For government and non-government parties from outside the location, the figure is for total armed forces within the country that is the location of the armed conflict.
[5] Total battle-related deaths during the conflict.
[6] The total number of deaths in political violence in Northern Ireland is approximately 3,200. The figure given here is an estimate of the deaths incurred between the Government of the UK and the Provisional IRA; the remaining deaths were mainly caused by other paramilitary organizations such as the Ulster Volunteer Force (UVF) and the Ulster Freedom Fighters (UFF).
[7] Including the Revolutionary Guard.
[8] Examples of these groups are Hamas, PFLP–GC (Popular Front for the Liberation of Palestine–General Command), Islamic Jihad, Hizbollah, and Amal.
[9] Including the Gendarmerie/National Guard.
[10] Includes deaths in the fighting since 1992 in which other parties than those listed above also participated.
[11] Including all militias.
[12] Regarding battle-related deaths in 1979–89, ie, not only involving the government and PDK, the only figure available is from official Vietnamese sources, indicating that 25,300 Vietnamese soldiers died in Cambodia. An estimated figure for the period 1979–89, based on various sources, is > 50,000, and for 1989 > 1,000. The figures for 1990, 1991, and 1992 were lower.
[13] Several groups are active, some of the most important being the Jammu and Kashmir Liberation Front (JKLF), the Hizb-e-Mujahideen, and the Harkat-ul-Ansar.
[14] Only the Kashmir conflict.
[15] Including the Gendarmerie and the National Security Forces.
[16] The Islamic Salvation Army (Armée Islamique du Salut, AIS) is considered to be the armed wing of the FIS. There are also several other armed Islamic groups under the FIS military command.
[17] Political violence in Burundi since 1993, involving other groups than the CNDD, has claimed a total of at least 100,000 lives.
[18] Armed action was primarily carried out by the Cobras, the private militia of FDU leader Sassou-Nguesso.
[19] Figure for up to 1991.
[20] The June 1995 Asmara Declaration forms the basis for the political and military activities of the NDA. The NDA is an alliance of several southern and northern opposition organizations, of which the SPLM (Sudan People's Liberation Movement) is the largest, with 30,000–50,000 troops. SPLM leader John Garang is also the leader of the NDA.
[21] After the ADFL victory of May 1997, the name of the country was changed to the Democratic Republic of Congo.
[22] In the past three decades the civil wars of Colombia have claimed a total of some 30,000 lives.

ADFL = Alliance des forces démocratiques pour la libération du Congo-Kinshasa (Alliance of Democratic Forces for the Liberation of Congo-Kinshasa). BdSF = Bodo Security Force. CNDD = Conseil national pour la défense de la démocratie (National Council for the Defence of Democracy). ELN = Ejército de Liberación Nacional (National Liberation Army). FARC = Fuerzas Armadas Revolucionarias Colombianas (Revolutionary Armed Forces of Colombia). FDU = Forces démocratiques unies (United Democratic Forces). FIS = Front Islamique du Salut, Jibhat al-Inqath (Islamic Salvation Front). Fretilin = Frente Revolucionára Timorense de Libertação e Independência (Revolutionary Front for an Independent East Timor). GIA = Groupe Islamique Armé (Armed Islamic Group). JSS/SB = Parbatya Chattagram Jana Sanghati Samiti (Chittagong Hill Tracts People's Coordination Association/Shanti Bahini [Peace Force]). KNU = Karen National Union. LRA = Lord's Resistance Army. LTTE = Liberation Tigers of Tamil Eelam. MFDC = Mouvement des forces démocratiques de la Casamance (Casamance Movement of Democratic Forces). MRTA = Movimiento Revolucionario Tupac Amaru (Tupac Amaru Revolutionary Movement). NDA = National Democratic Alliance. NPA = New People's Army. PDK = Party of Democratic Kampuchea (Khmer Rouge). PKK = Partiya Karkeren Kurdistan, Kurdish Worker's Party, or Apocus. PLO = Palestine Liberation Organization. Provisional IRA = Provisional Irish Republican Army. RUF = Revolutionary United Front. SAIRI = Supreme Assembly for the Islamic Revolution in Iraq. Sendero Luminoso = Shining Path. ULFA = United Liberation Front of Assam.

Source: Margareta Sollenberg, Ramses Amer, Carl Johan Åsberg, Ann-Sofi Jakobsson and Andrés Jato, in *SIPRI Yearbook 1998,* Stockholm International Peace Research Institute (Oxford University Press)

Major Armed Conflicts Worldwide

Data show regional distribution of locations with at least one major armed conflict, for the period 1990–97.

Region	1990	1991	1992	1993	1994	1995	1996	1997
Africa	10	10	7	7	6	6	5	8
Asia	10	8	11	9	9	9	10	9
Central and South America	5	4	3	3	3	3	3	2
Europe	1	2	4	5	4	3	2	1
Middle East	5	5	4	4	5	4	4	4
Total	31	29	29	28	27	25	24	24

Source: Margareta Sollenberg and Peter Wallensteen, Uppsala Conflict Data Project (Uppsala University), in *SIPRI Yearbook 1998,* Stockholm International Peace Research Institute (Oxford University Press)

Fatalities of Armed Conflicts Worldwide Since 1945

(N/A = not available.)

Region/country	Conflict	Year	Deaths
Caribbean and Latin America			
Argentina	armed forces/Peron	1955	4,000
	disappearances	1976–79	15,000
Bolivia	revolution	1952	2,000
Brazil	right-wing terrorism	1980	1,000
Chile	military coup	1973	5,000
	executions	1974	20,000
Columbia	Liberals/government	1949–62	300,000
Costa Rica	National Union/government	1948	2,000
Cuba	Castro/Batista	1958–59	5,000
Dominican Republic	civil war	1965	3,000
Falkland Islands	UK/Argentina	1982	1,000
Guatemala	Conservatives/government	1954	1,000
Honduras	El Salvador/Honduras	1969	5,000
Jamaica	election violence	1980	1,000
Nicaragua	Sandinistas/Samoza	1978–79	50,000
	Contras/Sandinistas	1981–88	30,000
Panama	UK invasion	1989	1,000
Paraguay	Liberals/government	1947	1,000
Peru	Shining Path/government	1981–95	30,000
Regional total			477,000
Middle East and North Africa			
Algeria	civil war	1954–62	100,000
	rebels/government	1962–63	2,000
Egypt	Suez Crisis	1956	4,000
	Six-Day War and border conflict	1967–70	75,000
Iran	Khomeini/Shah	1978–89	1,000
	Iran/Iraq War	1980–88	500,000
Iraq	Shammar tribe/government	1959	2,000
	Kurds/government	1961–70	105,000
Israel	Yom Kippur War	1973	16,000
Jordan	Syria/government	1970	10,000
Kuwait	Iraq/Kuwait/UN	1990–91	20,000
Lebanon	civil war	1958	2,000
	civil war	1975–90	100,000
Morocco	independence	1953–56	3,000
Syria	government/Muslims/ conservatives	1982	20,000
Tunisia	independence	1952–54	3,000
Yemen	Yahya/North Yemen	1948	4,000
	civil war in North Yemen	1962–69	15,000
	civil war in South Yemen	1986–87	11,000
Regional total			993,000
Sub-Saharan Africa			
Angola	independence	1961–75	55,000
	civil war: South Africa and Cuba intervene	1975–91	1,500,000
Burundi	Hutus/government	1972	110,000
Congo, Democratic Republic of	Katanga	1960–65	100,000
Ethiopia	Eritrean revolt	1974–92	75,000
Ghana	Konkomba/Nanumba	1981	1,000
Guinea-Bissau	independence	1962–74	15,000
Kenya	Mau Mau revolt	1954–56	14,000
Liberia	reprisals for putsch	1985–88	5,000
Madagascar	independence	1947–48	15,000
Mozambique	independence	1965–75	30,000
Nigeria	Biafrans/government	1967–70	1,000,000
	Islam/government	1980–81	5,000
	Islam/government	1984	1,000
Rwanda	Tutsi/government	1956–65	105,000
South Africa	political/ethnic violence	1976	1,000
	political/ethnic violence	1983–94	16,000
Sudan	civil war	1963–72	500,000
Uganda	Buganda tribe/government	1966	1,000
	Idi Amin massacres	1971–78	300,000
	Tanzania/Idi Amin	1978–79	3,000
	army/people	1981–87	308,000
Zambia	civil strife	1964	1,000
Zimbabwe	Patriotic Front/Rhodesia	1972–79	12,000
	ethnic and political violence	1983–84	4,000
Regional total			4,177,000
Europe			
Czechoslovakia	Soviet invasion	1968	N/A
Greece	civil war	1945–49	160,000
Hungary	uprising	1956	20,000
Romania	demonstrators/government	1989	1,000
Turkey	terrorism and military coup	1977–80	5,000
Regional total			186,000
Central and South Asia			
Afghanistan	USSR in civil war	1978–92	1,500,000
Bangladesh	civil war	1971	500,000
India	Muslim/Hindu	1946–48	800,000
	Muslim, Pakistan/Kashmir	1947–49	3,000
	India/Hyderabad	1948	2,000
	India/China at border	1962	2,000
	Pakistan/Kasmir	1965	20,000
	Pakistan/India	1971	11,000
Pakistan	Baluchis/government	1973–77	9,000
Sri Lanka	government/Maoists	1971	10,000
Regional total			2,857,000
East Asia			
Cambodia	civil war	1970–75	156,000
	Pol Pot massacre	1975–78	1,000,000
	PDK (Khmer Rouge)	1979–93	65,000
China	Kuomintang/communists	1946–50	1,000,000
	China/Tibet	1950–51	2,000
	government executions	1950–51	1,000,000
	Tibetan revolution	1956–59	100,000
	Cultural Revolution	1967–68	500,000
	government/students	1989–90	3,000
Indonesia	independence	1945–46	5,000
	Moluccans/government	1950	5,000
	Darul Islam/government	1953	1,000
	dissident military/ government	1958–60	30,000
	Putsch including war with Malaysia & UK	1965–66	500,000
Korea	Korean War	1950–53	3,000,000
Korea, South	army suppression	1980	1,000
Laos	Path Lao/government	1960–73	30,000
Malaysia	civil war	1950–60	13,000
Myanmar	Karens/government	1948–51	8,000
	Communists/government	1980	5,000
Philippines	Huks/government	1950–52	9,000
Taiwan	civilian riots/government	1947	20,000
	Taiwan/China	1947	1,000
	China captures Yinkiangshan I	1955	N/A
	civil strife	1954–55	5,000
	China bombards Quemoy-Matsu Islands	1958	N/A
USSR	China attacks USSR border	1969	1,000
Vietnam	independence	1945–54	600,000
	civil war	1960–65	300,000
	South Vietnam/USA/ North Vietnam	1965–75	2,000,000
	China/Vietnam	1979	35,000
	China/Vietnam	1987	1,000
Regional total			10,396,0000

Source: *The Military Balance 1998/99*, International Institute for Strategic Studies (by permission of Oxford University Press)

UK Military Casualties in Conflicts Since 1945

The number of wounded refers to those detained in hospital, and may represent a lower figure than that reported operationally; the number of wounded and killed refers to officers and soldiers in all services. (N/A = not available.)

Conflict/campaign	Number killed	Number wounded	Total
Indonesia (1945–46)	50	N/A	N/A
Palestine (1945–48)	223	478	701
Malaya (1948–61)			
British units	340	613	953
Brigade of Gurkhas	169	308	477
Total	509	921	1,430
Korea (1950–53)	865	2,589	3,454
Egypt (1951–54)	53	N/A	N/A
Kenya (1952)	12	69	81
Cyprus (1955–58)	79	414	493
Egypt (1956)	12	63	75
Borneo and Malaya (1962–66)			
British units	16	36	52
Brigade of Gurkhas	43	87	130
Total	59	123	182
Radfan (1964–67)	24	188	212
Aden (1964–67)	68	322	390
Falklands (1982)	255[1]	777	1,032
Gulf (1991)	42[2]	43	85

[1] Includes five civilians.

[2] Includes nine killed accidentally by US 'friendly fire'.

Military Casualties in World War I

World War I casualty statistics vary greatly from source to source. Official records are often lacking and based on differing criteria and these figures remain open to interpretation and debate. Figures are for 1914–18 and are rounded to the nearest 250. (N/A = not available.)

Country	Mobilized	Deaths (all causes)	Wounded	Total casualties	Prisoners/missing
Allied Powers					
Belgium	207,000	13,750	44,000	57,750	67,750
British Empire[1]					
UK	5,397,000	702,500	1,662,750	2,365,250	170,500
Australia	330,000	59,250	152,250	211,500	4,000
Canada	552,000	56,750	149,750	206,500	3,750
India[2]	1,216,000	64,500	69,250	133,750	11,250
Newfoundland	N/A	1,250	2,250	3,500	250
New Zealand	N/A	16,750	41,250	58,000	500
South Africa	N/A	7,000	12,000	19,000	1,500
Other colonies	N/A	500	750	1,250	N/A
British Empire total	>7,495,000	908,500	2,090,250	2,998,750	191,750
France (including colonial territories)	7,500,000	1,385,250	2,675,000– 4,266,000[3]	4,060,250– 5,651,250	446,250
Greece	230,000	5,000	21,000	26,000	1,000
Italy	5,500,000	460,000	947,000	1,407,000	530,000
Japan	800,000	250	1,000	1,250	0
Montenegro	50,000	3,000	10,000	13,000	7,000
Portugal	100,000	7,250	15,000	22,250	12,250
Romania	750,000	200,000	120,000	320,000	80,000
Russia	12,000,000	1,700,000	4,950,000	6,650,000	2,500,000
Serbia	707,250	127,500	133,250	260,750	153,000
USA	4,272,500	116,750	204,000	320,750	4,500
Central Powers					
Austria-Hungary	6,500,000	1,200,000	3,620,000	4,820,000	2,200,000
Bulgaria	400,000	101,250	152,500	253,750	11,000
Germany	11,000,000	1,718,250	4,234,000	5,952,250	1,073,500
Turkey[4]	1,600,000	>335,750	>400,000	>735,750	>200,000

[1] Figures for the British Empire and constituent countries are for 1914–20.

[2] Includes 4,912 British casualties: British drafts and units serving with the Indian Army.

[3] Official records for the number of French wounded are not available.

[4] There are no official records available for Turkish casualties.

Casualties in World War II

Figures are for 1939–45 and are rounded to the nearest 250. (– = not applicable. N/A = not available.)

Country	Personnel[1]	Military killed	Military wounded	Prisoners of war	Civilian dead
Allied Powers					
Australia	680,000	23,250	39,750	26,250	–
Belgium	800,000	7,750	14,500	N/A	75,000[2]
Brazil	200,000	1,000	4,250	–	–
Canada	780,000	37,500	53,250	9,750	–
China	5,000,000	1,324,500[3]	1,762,000	N/A	N/A[4]
Czechoslovakia	180,000	6,750	8,000	–	310,000[5]
Denmark	15,000	4,250	N/A	–	–
Estonia	–	–	–	–	140,000
France	5,000,000	205,750	390,000	765,000	300,000
Greece	150,000	16,250	50,000	N/A	337,000[6]
India	2,394,000	24,250	64,250	79,500	–
Latvia	–	–	–	–	120,000
Lithuania	–	–	–	–	170,000
Netherlands	500,000	13,750	2,750	N/A	236,250[7]
New Zealand	157,000	12,250	19,250	8,500	–
Norway	25,000	4,750	N/A	N/A	5,500[8]
Poland	1,000,000	320,000	530,000	–	6,028,000[9]
South Africa	140,000	8,750	14,250	14,500	–
UK	4,683,000	264,500	277,000	172,500[10]	60,500
USA	16,353,750	405,500	671,750	105,000	–
USSR	20,000,000	13,600,000	5,000,000	N/A	7,720,000
Yugoslavia	3,741,000	305,000	425,000	–	1,355,000[11]
Axis Powers					
Austria	800,000	380,000	N/A	N/A	145,000[12]
Finland	250,000	79,000	N/A	–	–
Germany	10,000,000	3,300,000	N/A	630,000[13]	3,063,000[14]
Hungary	350,000	147,500	N/A	–	280,000[15]
Italy	4,500,000	262,500	N/A	1,478,000	93,000[16]
Japan	N/A	1,140,500	N/A	11,600[17]	953,000[18]
Romania	600,000	300,000	N/A	N/A	145,000[19]

1 Peak strength of armed forces during World War II.
2 Includes approximately 25,000 Jews.
3 Estimates vary for Chinese military killed.
4 Estimates for Chinese civilian dead vary very widely, from 700,000 to 10,000,000.
5 Includes approximately 250,000 Jews.
6 Includes approximately 260,000 deaths due to starvation.
7 Includes approximately 104,000 Jews, 25,000 civilian underground workers, and 15,000 deaths due to starvation.
8 Includes approximately 2,000 resistance fighters and 750 Norwegians serving in the German army.
9 Includes approximately 3,200,000 Jews.
10 7,250 British prisoners of war died while in German captivity; 12,500 died while in Japanese captivity.
11 Includes approximately 55,000 Jews.
12 Includes approximately 60,000 Jews.
13 Excludes those in the USSR.
14 Includes approximately 170,000 Jews.
15 Includes approximately 200,000 Jews.
16 Includes approximately 8,000 Jews.
17 Excludes those in the USSR.
18 Includes approximately 668,000 killed in air raids on home islands.
19 Includes approximately 60,000 Jews.

NATO and European Defence

NATO International Commands

As of June 1999.

Command	Commander/branch of service
Supreme Allied Commander, Europe (SACEUR)	General Wesley K Clark (US Army)(stepping down in April 2000)
Deputy Supreme Allied Commander, Europe (DSACEUR)	General Sir Rupert Smith (UK Army)
Supreme Allied Commander, Atlantic (SACLANT)	Admiral Harold W Gehman, Jr (US Navy)
Commander-in-Chief, Allied Forces, Southern Europe (AFSOUTH)	Admiral Thomas J Lopez (US Navy)
Commander-in-Chief, Allied Forces, Central Europe (AFCENT)	General Dieter Stöckmann (German Army)
Commander-in-Chief, Allied Forces, Northwestern Europe (AFNORTHWEST)	Air Chief Marshal Sir John Cheshire (UK Royal Air Force)
Chairman, Military Committee (MC)	Admiral Guido Venturoni (Italian Navy)

Defence Spending by NATO Countries

(In millions of dollars at 1995 prices and exchange rates.)

State	Item	1988	1991	1994	1997
North America					
Canada	Personnel	5,019	4,889	4,979	3,821
	Equipment	2,222	1,791	1,685	1,246
USA	Personnel	141,985	135,496	115,513	102,808
	Equipment	93,650	85,626	86,487	65,259
Europe					
Belgium	Personnel	3,915	4,034	3,147	3,021
	Equipment	737	480	354	229
Denmark	Personnel	1,916	1,878	1,849	1,892
	Equipment	476	519	501	475
Germany	Personnel	26,849	29,734	25,479	24,402
	Equipment	10,426	8,195	4,568	4,575
Greece	Personnel	3,108	3,089	3,119	3,547
	Equipment	1,244	974	1,208	1,106
Italy	Personnel	13,101	14,284	13,921	14,935
	Equipment	4,647	3,632	3,289	3,108
Luxembourg	Personnel	99	98	114	118
	Equipment	4	8	3	7
Netherlands	Personnel	5,326	5,168	4,809	4,335
	Equipment	2,001	1,461	1,386	1,466
Norway	Personnel	1,662	1,695	1,356	1,347
	Equipment	685	805	1,107	869
Portugal	Personnel	1,538	1,924	1,955	2,094
	Equipment	244	218	104	411
Spain	Personnel	5,354	5,968	5,526	5,606
	Equipment	2,034	1,190	1,018	1,151
Turkey	Personnel	1,401	2,743	3,280	3,260
	Equipment	886	1,284	1,884	2,432
UK	Personnel	17,322	18,069	15,223	12,610
	Equipment	10,810	8,346	9,156	8,603
NATO Europe	Personnel	81,592	88,684	79,776	77,166
	Equipment	34,193	27,112	24,579	24,434
Total	Personnel	228,596	229,069	200,268	183,795
	Equipment	130,065	114,529	112,751	90,938

Source: Eric Arnett, in *SIPRI Yearbook 1998*, Stockholm International Peace Research Institute (Oxford University Press)

NATO: Chronology

With the collapse of the USSR in 1991, NATO, which had its roots in the Cold War, had to rethink its purpose. Although still a defensive body, NATO in the 1990s has been trying actively to promote peace and stability. In response to the decreased threat, the numbers and readiness of NATO troops have been vastly reduced. This includes a 25% cut in the number of ground combat units and a reduction of over 45% in the peacetime strength of land forces in central Europe. Stockpiles of nuclear weapons are now only one-fifth of their total in 1990.

4 April 1949 The North Atlantic Treaty Organization (NATO) is founded to provide collective defence against the Soviet military presence in Eastern Europe. The treaty is signed in Washington, DC, by the foreign ministers of the USA, Canada, Britain, France, Luxembourg, Belgium, the Netherlands, Italy, Portugal, Denmark, Iceland, and Norway. It comes into effect 24 August.

6 October 1949 US President Harry S Truman signs the Mutual Defense Assistance Act for the provision of military aid to NATO countries.

18 December 1950 NATO foreign ministers, meeting in Brussels, agree to create an integrated defence force under the supreme command of US general Dwight D Eisenhower; they also agree to US use of nuclear weapons to defend NATO countries.

18 February 1952 Greece and Turkey become the 13th and 14th members of NATO.

20 February 1952 A NATO Council, meeting in Lisbon, Portugal, approves the establishment of the proposed European Defence Community; members agree to provide 50 divisions for NATO service by December.

5 May 1955 West Germany becomes the 15th NATO member (the reunited Germany officially accedes 1990).

14 May 1955 The USSR responds to West German troops in NATO by forming the Warsaw Pact, a mutual defence treaty signed by eight Eastern European countries.

28 September 1960 NATO introduces a unified air defence command.

4 December 1962 The Western European Union (WEU) Assembly in Paris, France, calls for a NATO nuclear force.

21 June 1963 France withdraws its naval Atlantic forces from NATO, as it does not want to be part of a joint NATO nuclear force.

1 July 1966 France withdraws from NATO's military structure following a dispute over US involvement in Europe's defence.

16 October 1967 New NATO headquarters officially open in Brussels, Belgium.

14 August 1974 Greece withdraws its armed forces from NATO in protest at NATO's failure to oppose the Turkish 'menace to world peace' following the Turkish invasion of Cyprus.

12 December 1979 NATO decides to deploy Pershing II missiles in Europe if the Soviets refuse to negotiate withdrawal of SS-20 missiles in Eastern Europe.

30 May 1982 Spain becomes the 16th NATO member.

8 December 1987 US President Reagan and Soviet leader Gorbachev sign a treaty eliminating intermediate-range missiles.

19 November 1990 NATO and Warsaw Pact members sign the Conventional Armed Forces in Europe treaty in Paris and publish a Joint Declaration on non-aggression.

1991 The USSR dissolves, as does the Warsaw Pact (formally dissolved 1 July). The Cold War that defined almost half a century is no more, and the sweeping away of the Iron Curtain leaves the NATO allies with no obvious mission.

Autumn 1991 NATO begins to transform its role, aiming to promote peace and stability. A summit in Rome adopts a new strategic concept, and issues a Declaration of Peace and Cooperation, aiming for less reliance on nuclear weapons, and greater involvement in international

(continued)

NATO: Chronology (*continued*)

crisis management. The North Atlantic Cooperation Council (NACC) is created.

17 December 1992 NATO announces its readiness to back future peacekeeping action by the UN in the former Yugoslavia.

10 January 1994 A NATO summit in Brussels, Belgium, launches the 'Partnership for Peace' (PfP) programme, to encourage cooperation with former members of the Warsaw Pact. NATO backs the concept of Combined Joint Task Forces.

9 February 1994 A UN ultimatum, issued through NATO, gives warring factions around the Bosnian capital Sarajevo ten days to withdraw their heavy weapons or face air strikes (the demands are largely met by 17 February).

10 April 1994 NATO carries out air strikes on Serbian posts near the UN 'safe area' of Goradze in Bosnia, but subsequently (17 April) Goradze falls to Serb forces.

21 November 1994 NATO launches air strikes on Serb positions in Bosnia in response to the bombing of the UN safe area of Bihać.

3 June 1995 NATO defence ministers agree the creation of a Mobile Theatre Reserve (known as the 'rapid reaction force') for use in Bosnia, to be operational by mid-July.

30 August 1995 NATO aircraft begin large-scale attacks on Serbian positions in Bosnia; 300 sorties are flown in the first 12 hours, and by 13 September over 800 missions are completed.

14 December 1995 The formal signing of the peace plan for Bosnia-Herzegovina takes place at the Elysée Palace, Paris, France. For the first time ever, NATO organizes a 60,000-strong multinational Implementation Force (IFOR), under a UN mandate, to replace the UN presence and implement the military aspects of the Bosnian peace agreement. The USA supplies one-third of the troops for the mission termed 'Joint Endeavour'.

5 January 1996 Russian Parliament endorses the deployment of Russian forces to Bosnia to join the NATO-led peacekeeping force (IFOR).

2–3 December 1996 The Organization Security Council of Europe summit in Lisbon on European security adopts a Declaration on a Common and Comprehensive Security Model for Europe for the 21st century.

20 December 1996 The Implementation Force (IFOR) completes its work and is replaced by a smaller Stabilization Force (SFOR), which works to lay the basis for the implementation of the Bosnian peace agreement in its entirety.

27 May 1997 In Paris, NATO and Russia sign an historic agreement on their future relations – the Founding Act on Mutual Relations, Cooperation, and Security.

30 May 1997 A NATO–Ukraine Charter is initialled in Sintra, Portugal, where NATO and 'Partnership for Peace' (PfP) countries meet to inaugurate the new Euro-Atlantic Partnership Council (EAPC). The EAPC is a cooperative mechanism which replaces the NACC and builds on the political and military cooperation established under the NACC and PfP.

8 July 1997 At a summit meeting in Madrid, Spain, NATO leaders formally invite the Czech Republic, Hungary, and Poland to join their military alliance in 1999.

29 January 1999 In a shoot-out with Serb security forces, 24 ethnic Albanians die in the village of Rugovo, in Kosovo. NATO gives the warring parties a three-week deadline to negotiate a plan for autonomy for the region.

12 March 1999 The Czech Republic, Hungary, and Poland become members of NATO less than a decade after replacing communist rule with democracy. The allies also give Russia, their former enemy, 'a voice but no veto'.

24 March 1999 NATO launches an air war against Yugoslav military targets. Russia objects to the military action, suspending its cooperation with NATO.

4 April 1999 NATO's 50th anniversary summit faces the alliance's greatest challenge, with more than a million people displaced in Kosovo, fatal mis-strikes by NATO planes, and the stability of neighbouring states in question.

22 May 1999 NATO takes advantage of clear skies to launch its most intensive bombardment against Yugoslavia on its 60th day of conflict. Officials in Washington announce that NATO will give the air war another four weeks to see if it can succeed; if it does not produce results by the time of the G-8 summit late June, it will consider other options – including a ground war.

3 June 1999 Following 72 days of NATO bombing, Slobodan Milošević formally accepts a peace plan devised by Russia and the EU.

5 June 1999 NATO orders Serb forces to leave Kosovo by specified routes within seven days. Serb military leaders state that their forces will leave on condition that the NATO peacekeeping force is brought under the auspices of the UN.

9 June 1999 Following some concessions in NATO's terms for the withdrawal of Serb forces, Serb military leaders sign an agreement to withdraw troops from Kosovo. NATO's bombing campaign comes to an end.

10 June 1999 NATO secretary-general Javier Solana officially declares an end to the alliance's bombing in Yugoslavia. NATO prepares for Operation Joint Guardian which will assist one million ethnic Albanians to return home to Kosovo.

12 June 1999 British, German, French, and US NATO troops enter Pristina, the capital of Kosovo, to liberate the province from Serb forces.

20 June 1999 In a settlement with NATO, the Kosovo Liberation Army agrees to disarm within 90 days.

4 August 1999 George Robertson, currently UK secretary of state for defence, is appointed secretary general of NATO and chairman of the North Atlantic Council, in succession to Javier Solana.

European Defence: Expenditure and Manpower

(– = not applicable.)

Country	Defence expenditure (1997 $ millions)			% of GDP		Numbers in armed forces (thousands)		Estimated reservists (thousands)
	1985	1996	1997	1985	1997	1985	1997	1997
NATO Europe								
Belgium	5,863	4,333	3,769	3.0	1.6	91.6	44.5	144.2
Denmark	2,978	3,152	2,816	2.2	1.7	29.6	32.9	70.5
France	46,522	47,401	41,545	4.0	3.0	464.3	380.8	292.5
Germany	50,220	39,828	33,416	3.2	1.6	478.0	347.1	315.0
Greece	3,317	5,700	5,552	7.0	4.6	201.5	162.3	291.0
Iceland[1]	–	–	–	–	–	–	–	–
Italy	24,471	23,947	21,837	2.3	1.9	385.1	325.2	484.0
Luxembourg	91	145	129	0.9	0.8	0.7	0.8	–
Netherlands	8,470	8,022	6,888	3.1	1.9	105.5	57.2	75.0
Norway	2,948	3,754	3,336	3.1	2.3	37.0	33.6	234.0
Portugal	1,746	2,657	2,559	3.1	2.6	73.0	59.3	210.9
Spain	10,731	8,802	7,671	2.4	1.4	320.0	197.5	431.9
Turkey	3,269	7,674	8,110	4.5	4.2	630.0	639.0	378.7
UK	45,408	35,266	35,736	5.2	2.8	327.1	213.8	320.8
NATO Europe total	206,033	190,681	173,363	3.1	2.2	3,143.4	2,494.0	3,248.5
Non-NATO Europe								
Albania	269	103	94	5.3	6.7	40.4	54.0	155.0
Armenia	–	125	138	–	8.9	60.0	300.0	
Austria	1,839	2,098	1,786	1.2	0.8	54.7	45.5	100.7
Azerbaijan	–	133	146	–	4.0	–	66.7	560.0
Belarus	–	501	381	–	2.9	–	81.8	289.5
Bosnia-Herzegovina	–	255	327	–	5.0	–	40.0	100.0
Bulgaria	2,331	373	339	14.0	3.4	148.5	101.5	303.0
Croatia	–	1,308	1,147	–	5.7	–	58.0	220.0
Cyprus	124	487	505	3.6	5.8	10.0	10.0	88.0
Czech Republic	–	1,176	987	–	2.2	–	61.7	240.0
Czechoslovakia	3,338	–	–	8.2	–	203.3	–	–
Estonia	–	110	119	–	2.5	–	3.5	14.0
Finland	2,139	2,255	1,956	2.8	1.7	36.5	31.0	500.0
FYR (Serbia-Montenegro)[3]	4,759	1,502	1,489	3.8	7.8	241.0	114.2	400.0
FYROM[2]	–	122	132	–	10.2	–	15.4	100.0
Georgia	–	110	109	–	2.9	–	33.2	250.0
Hungary	3,380	713	666	7.2	1.4	106.0	49.1	186.4
Ireland, Republic of	456	757	767	1.8	1.0	13.7	12.7	15.6
Latvia	–	139	156	–	4.6	–	4.5	16.6
Lithuania	–	128	135	–	4.4	–	5.3	11.0
Malta	23	34	31	1.4	0.9	0.8	2.0	–
Moldova	–	48	53	–	4.4	11.0	66.0	
Poland	8,202	3,730	3,073	8.1	2.3	319.0	241.8	406.0
Romania	1,987	762	793	4.5	2.3	189.5	227.0	427.0
Slovakia	–	469	414	–	2.1	–	41.2	20.0
Slovenia	–	231	310	–	1.7	–	9.6	53.0
Sweden	4,564	6,501	5,481	3.3	2.4	65.7	53.4	570.0
Switzerland	2,749	4,672	3,837	2.1	1.5	20.0	26.3	390.0
Ukraine	–	1,286	1,324	–	2.7	–	387.4	1,000.0
Non-NATO Europe total	36,142	30,129	26,693	4.8	3.7	1,449.1	1,847.5	6,781.8
Russia and Soviet Union								
Russia	–	73,990	64,000	–	5.8	–	1,240.0	2,400.0
Soviet Union	343,616	–	–	16.1	–	5,300.0	–	–

[1] Iceland has no defence forces of its own.
[2] FYROM = Former Yugoslav Republic of Macedonia.
[3] FYR = Federal Republic of Yugoslavia.

Source: *The Military Balance 1998/99,* International Institute for Strategic Studies (by permission of Oxford University Press)

NATO'S INTERVENTION IN KOSOVO: A WAR WITHOUT CLEAR GOALS

BY IAN DERBYSHIRE

On 23 March 1999 the patience of NATO's political leaders with Slobodan Milošević, Serbia's capricious strongman president, finally ended. Since coming to power in Serbia in the mid-1980s, Milošević – the communist-nationalist largely responsible for the break-up of the Yugoslav federation in 1990–91 and the puppeteer behind the Bosnian Serb forces during the Bosnian conflict of 1991–95 – had waged a relentless campaign against the political and cultural autonomy of Kosovo, the southern province of Yugoslavia peopled by Albanian Muslims (Kosovars). This campaign had escalated, from 1998, into a relentless process of 'ethnic cleansing', which, by mid-March 1999, had left around 250,000 (or a sixth of the population) homeless.

Milošević's refusal to accept a political settlement for Kosovo, brokered at Rambouillet, near Paris, in February 1999, and his subsequent intensification of repression of the Kosovars were the final straws. On the night of 24 March 1999 large-scale NATO airstrikes were launched, involving satellite-guided cruise missiles and laser-guided bombs despatched by America's stealth F-117s and B-2s, directed against Serbian military and communications targets. Just ten days short of its 50th anniversary, NATO had embarked on a perilous conflict. Furthermore, it was a military intervention with doubtful legality. Directed against a sovereign state engaged in internal repression, it had clear humanitarian motivations, but, technically, breached the UN charter, which permits the use of force in only two circumstances: self-defence against direct attack, or for the maintenance of international peace and security.

Any future operation of this nature must ... clearly operate under UN auspices.

Coming in the wake of recent NATO and US military interventions in Iraq and Bosnia, the action signified a new resolve on behalf of the international community to take a clear stand against dictators engaged in internal repression, and a new faith in the ability of air-based 'smart technology' to achieve military aims at minimal cost of combat lives. However, the intervention in Kosovo was unusually risky. It was directed against a state with a substantial army of 100,000 troops, backed by a further 200,000 reservists and armed police and equipped with effective, though Soviet-era, weapons and air-defence systems. It was situated in a 'tinderbox region' where – notably in neighbouring Albania, Bosnia, and Macedonia – there existed political instability and acute ethnic tensions. And, finally but perhaps most seriously, it was launched without clearly defined and achievable goals.

On 24 March, President Bill Clinton declared that the air raids were designed to deter further Serb attacks on civilians in Kosovo and damage Serbia's capacity to make war. Meanwhile, Javier Solana, NATOs secretary-general, intimated that the West's political aim was to force Serbia to accept the Rambouillet settlement, which had provided for Kosovo's political autonomy within Serbia, policed by a 30,000-strong NATO force and with safeguards for the province's Serb minority. However, the NATO bombing raids failed to achieve the first goal as, during March and April 1999, Serb 'ethnic cleansing' continued, leading to a further mass exodus of hundreds of thousands of Kosovo refugees. This served to increase support for extremists within the Kosovar community, culminating, in late April 1999, in the Kosovo Liberation Army (KLA), led by Hashim Thaci, declaring a provisional independent government, and to the sidelining of Ibrahim Rugova, the moderate political leader of the Kosovar community.

The roots of the conflict: a clash between Serbian Orthodoxy and Islam

Kosovo, a small landlocked and mountainous region of the Balkans, whose population of 1.8 million is 90 percent ethnic Albanian and mainly Muslim, has long been regarded by the Christian Orthodox Serbs as their community's historic homeland, equivalent to 'Jerusalem for the Jews'. The reason for this lies in the history of Kosovo which, until the later Middle Ages, had been a Serb-populated region and had served as the heartland of Serbian kingdoms. The historic rupture occurred in 1389 when Murad I, leader of the Ottoman Turks, defeated the Serbs in the bloody battle of Kosovo. The republic fell under Turkish rule and, as Serbs moved out, so Albanians moved in, with Islam becoming the dominant religion. It remained so during the next five centuries, although Serbian monasteries and churches were maintained in the province.

Serb rule was finally reimposed, through military force, in 1912, and Kosovo became part of the new Yugoslav state in 1918. During the interwar years ethnic Albanian rebellions were suppressed and Serb settlers sent in. However, during World War II, when Kosovo became part of an Italian-controlled Greater Albania, Serbs were again expelled. After the war, Serb hegemony was restored, as a new communist federal republic of Yugoslavia was created. However, under the federation's astute leader, Marshal Tito, Kosovo was conceded significant autonomy, with its own parliament and police.

Kosovo after Tito: repression and rebellion

Following Tito's death in 1980, Kosovo students campaigned for full republic status, but were suppressed and either jailed or sent into exile. Serb repression intensified from 1987 and the coming to power in Serbia of Slobodan Milošević as communist party boss. Kosovo was stripped of its autonomy and direct Serbian rule was imposed over the province in a populist action designed to increase Milošević's domestic standing. In response, Kosovars began to boycott Serbian institutions, setting up their own schools and health care and, under the leadership of Ibrahim Rugova, campaigned for independence, once the old Yugoslavia dissolved in 1991. Rugova chose a course of passive resistance, realizing that the Kosovars lacked the military might to resist a counter-offensive by Serbian forces. However, in 1997, with the breakdown in internal order in neighbouring Albania (following a 'pyramid investment scheme' financial scandal), arms began to flow into landlocked Kosovo and, assisted by funding from Kosovars in Germany and elsewhere, a pro-independence, guerrilla force, the KLA (established in 1993), rose to prominence from February 1998, engaging in clashes with Serbian police.

Support for the KLA increased rapidly, provoking large-scale Serb reprisals from mid-1998 that resulted in more than 200,000 civilians fleeing for their lives. This led to the intervention, under US leadership, of the international community. In October 1998 Milošević, under US pressure, agreed to reduce the number of Serbian troops in Kosovo and to accept the presence of a 'verification force' from the Organization for Security and Cooperation in Europe (OSCE). However, the hoped-for ceasefire failed to hold, with breaches both by the Serbs and the KLA. A final effort to reach a political solution was made at Rambouillet in February 1999, but with the Kosovars and Serbs effectively coerced to attend by the USA, the prospects of an effective solution were always remote.

The Kosovo end-game: resolving the war and achieving a political solution

By day 40 of the conflict, NATO had launched more than 12,000 air-raids, causing extensive physical damage and, through mistakes, claiming the lives of innocent Serb civilians, as well as hitting the Chinese embassy in Belgrade, an error with substantial diplomatic repercussions. However, Slobodan Milošević retained a firm grip on power and, supported by a state-controlled propaganda machine, enjoyed significant popular patriotic support. Meanwhile, influence within the Kosovar community had shifted away from moderates towards hardliners within the KLA.

During the fifth week of virtually incessant bombing there was a marked increase in diplomatic activity with Russian, US, and EU envoys meeting in Moscow. However, pessimism prevailed and the NATO powers announced an increase in the number of troops they were willing to deploy. As diplomacy continued so did the bombing errors, causing acute embarrassment to NATO politicians. Then, in early June, the international war crimes tribunal in The Hague indicted Milošević, meaning that if he stepped outside the Serbian borders he could legitimately be arrested and brought to trial. This development did little to encourage him to reach an understanding with the West. Nevertheless, within a week the international envoys – Victor Chernomyrdin for Russia, Strobe Talbott for the USA, and Martti Ahtisaari for the European Union – announced the securing of a deal with Serbia based on the Rambouillet agreement.

What remained to be determined were the dates for the withdrawal of Serb forces from Kosovo; the precise arrangements for the deployment of NATO troops; and the command structure for the NATO forces. There followed intensive negotiations between NATO and Serb commanders before timetables and routes for withdrawal were accepted. Meanwhile the Russian generals – key players in the unfolding drama but outside NATO – were demanding a greater involvement than had been planned for them, NATO insisting on a single, unified command. There was more than a suspicion that the politicians in Moscow were not in complete control of the actions of their generals on the ground.

Eventually, on 10 June 1999, a military agreement was reached and the Serb withdrawal began. Milošević's propaganda machine sprang into action again, promoting it to the Serbian people as a victory in the face of overwhelming odds. Two days later NATO troops began to move into the province, enthusiastically welcomed by Kosovars, but the twists and turns of the unfolding drama continued. When the overall commander of the NATO forces, Britain's General Sir Michael Jackson, arrived at the airfield of Kosovo's capital, Pristina, he found himself confronted by Russian forces who, apparently without the agreement of the government in Moscow, had rushed there ahead of NATO forces to effect a virtual *fait accompli* of occupation.

By 14 June 1999 the people of Kosovo had been liberated but many unanswered questions remained. What would their future be as long as Milošević was in power? Could fractured relations between Russia and the West be repaired? Would the UN Security Council legitimize the NATO operation as the Western powers hoped? Who would pick up the bill for the enormous repairs to the Serbian infrastructure?

Kosovo was a war without clear goals and, because of that, it is equally unclear whether the eventual outcome was a victory. There are many lessons to be learned, the most important being that any future operation of this nature must be truly international and must clearly operate under UN auspices. Otherwise, however strong the humanitarian motives behind it, it will always be seen by nations not directly involved as a return to the gunboat diplomacy which operated in earlier times.

Ian Derbyshire is a writer on history, politics, and government

See Also  **International Human Rights pp. 349–57, for more on Kosovo refugees.**

Conventional Armed Forces in Europe (CFE)

Data show manpower and Treaty-limited equipment (TLE) current holdings and CFE limits on the forces of the treaty members. Current holdings are derived from data declared as of 1 January 1998.

Country	Manpower		Tanks[1]		Armoured combat vehicles		Artillery		Attack helicopters		Combat aircraft[2]	
	Holding	Limit	Holding	Limit	Holding	Limit	Holding	Limit	Holding	Limit	Holding	Limit
Budapest/Tashkent Group												
Armenia	60,000	60,000	102	220	218	220	225	285	7	50	6	100
Azerbaijan	69,941	70,000	270	220	557	220	301	285	15	50	48	100
Belarus	83,518	100,000	1,778	1,800	2,520	2,600	1,529	1,615	64	80	250	294
Bulgaria	92,955	104,000	1,475	1,475	1,985	2,000	1,744	1,750	43	67	234	235
Czech Republic	58,343	93,333	948	957	1,238	1,367	767	767	36	50	122	230
Georgia	30,000	40,000	79	220	111	220	107	285	3	50	7	100
Hungary	43,286	100,000	835	835	1,316	1,700	840	840	59	108	138	180
Moldova	11,063	20,000	0	210	209	210	154	250	0	50	0	50
Poland	225,690	234,000	1,727	1,730	1,440	2,150	1,580	1,610	105	130	306	460
Romania	219,639	230,000	1,375	1,375	2,095	2,100	1,435	1,475	16	120	362	430
Russia[3]	748,776	1,450,000	5,559	6,400	9,841	11,480	5,999	6,415	805	890	2,868	3,416
Slovak Republic	45,483	46,667	478	478	683	683	382	383	19	25	113	115
Ukraine	335,231	450,000	4,014	4,080	4,902	5,050	3,749	4,040	290	330	966	1,090
North Atlantic Treaty Group												
Belgium	38,873	70,000	155	334	539	1,099	243	320	46	46	137	232
Canada[4]	0	10,660	0	77	0	277	0	38	0	0	0	90
Denmark	30,520	39,000	327	353	286	316	503	553	12	12	77	106
France	285,763	325,000	1,210	1,306	3,672	3,820	1,107	1,292	303	396	619	800
Germany	268,481	345,000	3,135	4,166	2,500	3,446	2,059	2,705	204	306	532	900
Greece	158,621	158,621	1,735	1,735	2,306	2,534	1,887	1,878	20	30	503	650
Italy	250,692	315,000	1,313	1,348	2,924	3,339	1,758	1,955	134	139	542	650
Netherlands	38,288	80,000	697	743	624	1,080	405	607	12	50	180	230
Norway	19,300	32,000	170	170	165	225	216	527	0	0	73	100
Portugal	38,417	75,000	187	300	354	430	340	450	0	26	101	160
Spain	160,372	300,000	688	794	1,187	1,588	1,154	1,310	28	90	198	310
Turkey[3]	527,670	530,000	2,542	2,795	2,529	3,120	2,839	3,523	26	103	388	750
UK	223,322	260,000	505	1,015	2,449	3,176	431	636	271	371	550	900
USA	102,670	250,000	927	4,006	1,809	5,372	497	2,492	138	431	218	784

[1] Includes TLE with land-based maritime forces (Marines, Naval Infantry, etc).
[2] Does not include land-based maritime aircraft, for which a separate limit has been set.
[3] Manpower and TLE are for the Atlantic to the Urals (ATTU) zone only.
[4] Canada has now withdrawn all its TLE from the ATTU.

Source: *The Military Balance 1998/99*, International Institute for Strategic Studies (Oxford University Press)

Peacekeeping

United Nations Peacekeeping Operations

United Nations peacekeeping operations come within the jurisdiction of the Security Council. This table gives operations current as of November 1998. Strength figures include military and civilian police personnel; fatality figures include military, civilian police, civilian international, and local staff. The number of fatalities from 1948 to August 1998 was 1,581. Seventeen UN missions are currently underway, with 14,453 peacekeepers serving in them as of 31 August 1998. The estimated total cost of operations from 1948 to 30 June 1998 was about US $18.3 billion.

Operation	Date of establishment	Area of operation	Fatalities (as of August 1998)	Strength (as of November 1998)	Budget estimate ($ millions)[1]
UNTSO United Nations Truce Supervision Organization	1948	Middle East	38	157	26.4[2]
UNMOGIP United Nations Military Observer Group in India and Pakistan	1949	India and Pakistan	9	45	7.8[2]
UNFICYP United Nations Peacekeeping Force in Cyprus	1964	Cyprus	168	1,306	45.3
UNDOF United Nations Disengagement Observer Force	1974	Syria	39	1,053	35.4
UNIFIL United Nations Interim Force in Lebanon	1978	Lebanon	228	4,528	143.0
UNIKOM United Nations Iraq–Kuwait Observation Mission	1991	Iraq/Kuwait	13	1,099	52.1
MINURSO United Nations Mission for the Referendum in Western Sahara	1991	Western Sahara	8	316	37.3[3]
UNOMIG United Nations Observer Mission in Georgia	1993	Georgia	3	102	19.4
UNMOT United Nations Mission of Observers in Tajikistan	1994	Tajikistan	8	30	8.0

(continued)

United Nations Peacekeeping Operations (*continued*)

Operation	Date of establishment	Area of operation	Fatalities (as of August 1998)	Strength (as of November 1998)	Budget estimate ($ millions)[1]
UNPREDEP United Nations Preventive Deployment Force	1995	Former Yugoslav Republic of Macedonia	4	884	47.9
UNMIBH United Nations Mission in Bosnia-Herzegovina	1995	Bosnia-Herzegovina	6	1,979	190.9
UNMOP United Nations Mission of Observers in Prevlaka	1996	Croatia	0	28[5]	
MONUA United Nations Observer Mission in Angola	1997	Angola	5	1,017	140.8
MIPONUH United Nations Civilian Police Mission in Haiti	1997	Haiti	0	300	14[4]
United Nations Civilian Police Support Group	1998	Croatia	0	396	17.6[5]
MINURCA United Nations Mission in the Central African Republic	1998	Central African Republic	1	1,369	29.1
UNOMSIL United Nations Mission of Observers in Sierra Leone	1998	Sierra Leone	0	61	22.6

[1] 1 July 1998–30 June 1999.
[2] Data for 1998.
[3] 1 November 1998–30 June 1999.
[4] Six-month estimate.
[5] Nine-month estimate. Included in UNMIBH estimate.

Source: UN Department of Public Information

Average Strength and Cost of United Nations Peacekeeping Forces

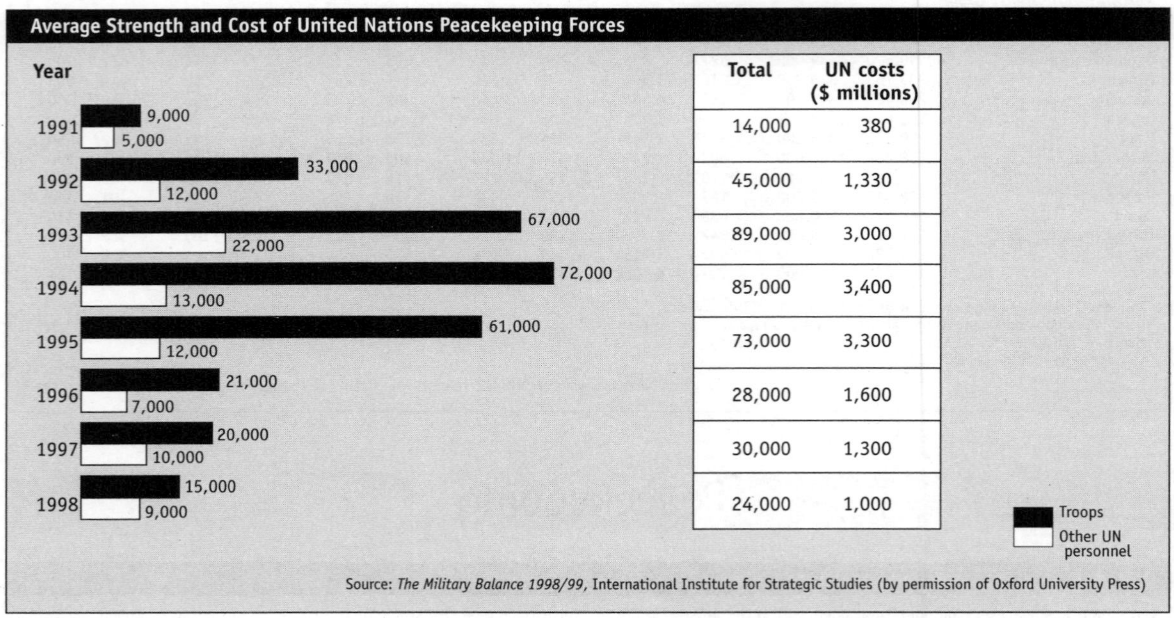

Total	UN costs ($ millions)
14,000	380
45,000	1,330
89,000	3,000
85,000	3,400
73,000	3,300
28,000	1,600
30,000	1,300
24,000	1,000

Source: *The Military Balance 1998/99*, International Institute for Strategic Studies (by permission of Oxford University Press)

Leading Troop Contributions to United Nations Operations

As of 30 June 1998.

Country	Strength	Country	Strength	Country	Strength
Poland	1,048	Norway	729	USA	622
Bangladesh	886	Ireland	726	Fiji Islands	602
Austria	795	Argentina	696	UK	393
Ghana	789	France	677	India	297
Finland	777	Nepal	649	Canada	292

Source: *The Military Balance 1998/99,* International Institute for Strategic Studies (by permission of Oxford University Press)

Selected non-United Nations Peacekeeping Operations

Operation	Date of establishment	Area of operation	Strength	Cost to 1997/8 ($ millions)	Budget 1998/9 ($ millions)
NNSC Neutral Nations Supervisory Commission	1953	North/South Korea	10	45	1
MFO Multinational Force and Observers	1982	Egypt	1,896	1,283	51
MOMEP Military Observer Mission	1995	Ecuador/Peru	35	50	15
SFOR Stablization Force	1996	Bosnia	33,000	5,000	4,000
ECOMOG ECOWAS Ceasefire Monitoring Group	1997	Sierra Leone	4,000	8	8
BELISI Operation Belisi Peace Monitoring Group	1998	Bougainville	250	8	24

Source: *The Military Balance 1998/99,* International Institute for Strategic Studies (by permission of Oxford University Press)

UK Armed Forces and Defence Expenditure

Armed Forces in the UK

General Information

The armed forces of the UK are made up of the Army, the Royal Navy, and the Royal Air Force. The Queen is the commander-in-chief for all branches of the armed forces. The Ministry of Defence (MoD) is concerned with the control, administration, equipment, and support of the armed forces of the Crown. The research, development, production, and purchase of weapons is the concern of the Procurement Executive of the MoD.

The Chief of Staff of the Defence Staff is the professional head of the armed forces and under him each Service's Chief of Staff is responsible for the fighting effectiveness, efficiency, and morale of his Service. They and other senior officers and officials at the head of the department's main functions form the MoD's corporate board, chaired by the Permanent Under-Secretary. The Secretary of State chairs the Defence Council (established 1964) and is responsible to Parliament for the formulation and conduct of defence policy, and the provision of the means to implement it.

The defence and security of the UK are pursued through membership of the European Union (EU), the Western European Union (WEU), the Organization for Security and Cooperation in Europe (OSCE), and the United Nations (UN). The majority of the armed forces are committed to NATO. The UK contributes significantly to the peacekeeping work of the UN both financially and in terms of the deployment of personnel.

All three armed services are professionals, with no conscript element.

Royal Navy

Control of the Royal Navy is vested in the Defence Council and is exercised through the Admiralty Board, chaired by the Secretary of State for Defence. Naval members of the Defence Council are the Chief of Naval Staff (First Sea Lord), responsible for management, planning, fighting efficiency, and operational advice; the combined Second Sea Lord and Commander-in-Chief Naval Home Command, responsible for procurement of ships, their weapons, and equipment; the Chief of Fleet Support, responsible for logistic support, fuels and transport, naval dockyards, and auxiliary services; the Commander-in-Chief Fleet; and the Assistant Chief of Staff, responsible for coordinating advice on certain policy and operational matters.

The principal roles of the Royal Navy are to deploy the national strategic nuclear deterrent, to provide maritime defence of the UK and its dependent territories, to contribute to the maritime elements of NATO forces, and to meet national maritime objectives outside the NATO area. The Commander-in-Chief Fleet, with headquarters at Northwood, is responsible for the command of the fleet, while command of naval establishments in the UK is exercised by the Commander-in-Chief Home Command from Portsmouth.

Royal Marines

The British Corps of Royal Marines was founded in 1664. It is primarily a military force also trained for fighting at sea, and providing commando units, landing craft, crews, and divers. The Royal Marines corps provides a commando brigade comprising three commando groups. Each commando group is approximately 1,000 strong, with artillery, engineering and logistic support, air defence, and three helicopter squadrons. The Royal Marine corps' strength is completed by the Special Boat Squadron and specialist defence units.

Royal Naval Reserve and Royal Marines Reserve

The Royal Naval Reserve (RNR) and the Royal Marines Reserve (RMR) are volunteer forces that provide trained personnel in war to supplement regular forces. The RMR principally provides reinforcement and other specialist tasks with the UK-Netherlands Amphibious Force.

Personnel who have completed service in the Royal Navy and the Royal Marines have a commitment to serve in the Royal Fleet Reserve.

Queen Alexandra's Royal Naval Nursing Service

Nursing sisters were first appointed to naval hospitals in 1884. The Queen Alexandra's Royal Nursing Service (QARNNS) gained its title in 1902. Men were integrated into the Service in 1982; female medical assistants were introduced in 1987. QARNNS ratings, both male and female, enlist on the 'Open Engagement' to complete 22 years of active service with the option to leave at 18 months notice at the completion of a minimum of 2.5 years productive service.

Army

Control of the British Army is vested in the Defence Council and is exercised through the Army Board. The Secretary of State is Chairman of the Army Board. The military members of the Army Board are the Chief of the General Staff, the Adjutant General, the Quartermaster General, the Master General of the Ordnance, the Commander-in-Chief Land Command, and the Assistant Chief of the General Staff.

Women serve throughout the Army in the same regiments and corps as men. There are only a few roles in which they are not employed, such as the Infantry and Royal Armoured Corps.

Territorial Army

The Territorial Army (TA) is a force of volunteer soldiers, created from volunteer regiments (incorporated in 1872) as the Territorial Force in 1908. It was raised and administered by county associations, and intended primarily for home defence. It was renamed Territorial Army in 1922. Merged with the Regular Army in World War II, it was revived in 1947, and replaced by a smaller, more highly trained Territorial and Army Volunteer Reserve, again renamed Territorial Army in 1979. The Army Chief of the General Staff is responsible for the TA.

The role of the TA is to act as a general reserve for the Army, reinforcing it, as required, with individuals, sub-units, and other units, both overseas and in the UK. It also provides the framework and basis for regeneration and reconstruction in the event of unforeseen needs in times of national emergency.

Queen Alexandra's Royal Army Nursing Corps

Founded in 1902 as Queen Alexandra's Imperial Military Nursing Service, the Queen Alexandra's Royal Army Nursing Corps (QARANC) gained its current title in 1949. The Corps has trained nurses and trains and employs health care assistants. Members of the QARANC serve in Ministry of Defence hospital units in the UK and in military hospitals both in the UK and abroad. Service in the Corps was opened to men in 1992.

Royal Air Force

The Royal Air Force (RAF) was formed in 1918 by the merger of the Royal Naval Air Service and the Royal Flying Corps. The RAF is administered by the Air Force Board, which is chaired by the Secretary of State for Defence. Other members of the Board include the Chief of the Air Staff, Air Member for Personnel, Air Member for Logistics, and Air Officer Commanding-in-Chief Strike Command. The RAF is organized into three commands: Strike Command, Personnel and Training Command, and Logistics Command.

Royal Auxiliary Air Force

The Royal Auxiliary Air Force (RAUXAF) was formed in 1924, and merged with the Royal Air Force Volunteer Reserve in 1997. It supports the RAF in air and ground defence of airfields, air movements, maritime air operations, and medical evacuations by air.

Princess Mary's Royal Air Force Nursing Service

The Princess Mary's Royal Air Force Nursing Service (PMRAFNS) offers commissions to Registered General Nurses.

Formation of the UK Armed Forces: Front Line and Support Units

The number of personnel and the amount of equipment in each vessel, regiment, battalion, or squadron vary according to the roles currently assigned. As of 1 April 1998. (N/A = not available.)

Front Line Units			
Royal Navy			
Trident/Polaris submarines		vessels	3
Fleet submarines		vessels	12
Submarines total		vessels	15
Carriers		vessels	3
Assault ships		vessels	2
Destroyers		vessels	12
Frigates		vessels	23
Mine counter measure vessels		vessels	19
Patrol ships and craft		vessels	28
Fixed wing aircraft		squadrons	3
Helicopters		squadrons	12
Royal Marines			
Commandos			3
Army			
Combat arms	armour	regiments	11
	infantry	battalions	40
	special forces	regiments	1
	aviation	regiments	5
Combat support	artillery	regiments	15
	engineers	regiments	10
	signals	regiments	11
Home Service Forces[1]			
Combat arms	infantry	battalions	7
Territorial Army			
Combat arms	armour	regiments	6
	infantry	battalions	33
	special forces	regiments	2
	aviation	regiment	1
Combat support	artillery[2]	regiments	6
	engineers	regiments	9
	signals	regiments	11
Royal Air Force			
Strike/attack		squadrons	6
Offensive support		squadrons	5
Reconnaissance		squadrons	5
Maritime patrol		squadrons	3
Air defence		squadrons	6
Airborne Early Warning		squadrons	2
Air transport, tankers, and helicopters		squadrons	14
Search and Rescue		squadrons	2
RAF regiments	surface to air missiles	squadrons	6
	ground defence	squadrons	5
Royal Auxiliary Air Force	ground defence	squadrons	3
Support Units			
Royal Navy and Royal Fleet Auxiliary Service			
Support ships		vessels	0
Survey ships		vessels	5
Ice patrol ships		vessels	1
Tankers[3]		vessels	9
Fleet replenishment ships[3]		vessels	4
Aviation training ship[3]		vessels	1
Landing ships[3]		vessels	5
Forward repair ships[3]		vessels	1
Royal Marines			
Logistic Unit		regiments	1
Army			
Combat service support	equipment support[4]	battalions	6
	logistics	regiments	24
	field ambulances/ field hospitals	number	12
Territorial Army			
Combat service support	equipment support[4]	battalions	5
	logistics	regiments	N/A
	field ambulances/ field hospitals	number	18
Royal Auxiliary Air Force			
Ground defence		squadrons	3
Offensive support		squadrons	1
Strike/attack		squadrons	1
Air transport, tankers, and helicopters		squadrons	2
Air movements		squadrons	1
Aeromedical/air transportable surgical		squadrons	2
Royal Air Force Reserve			
Meteorological		squadrons	1

[1] Includes Royal Irish Regiment (Home Service) battalions (formed under the Ulster Defence Regiment in 1992) and home defence units raised in the Dependent Territories. Excludes the Home Service Force which was not organized into battalion-size units.
[2] Includes the Honourable Artillery Company.
[3] Ships of the Royal Fleet Auxiliary Service.
[4] The REME Order of Battle did not include regiment or battalion equivalents until 1993.

Source: *UK Defence Statistics 1998*, Defence Analytical Services Agency, © Crown copyright 1998

Armed Forces in Northern Ireland

As of 1 April for the year shown. (N/A = not available.)

		1975	1980	1985	1990	1993	1994	1995	1996	1997	1998
Army [1]											
Major combat units[2]	long tour units	5	6	6	6	6	6	6	6	6	6
	short tour units	10	6	2	4	6	6	5	5	6	6
	Total	15	12	8	10	12	12	11	11	12	12
	Total units serving[3]	50	32	18	25	25	26	22	22	28	N/A
Royal Irish Regiment (Home Service) [4]											
Full-time personnel	male	1,394	2,416	2,552	2,697	2,627	2,621	2,755	2,702	2,515	2,468
	female	12	138	195	242	290	284	301	312	247	233
	Total	1,406	2,554	2,717	2,939	2,917	2,905	3,056	3,014	2,762	2,701
Part-time personnel											
	male	5,708	4,267	3,224	2,819	2,341	2,155	1,943	1,819	1,777	1,750
	female	577	552	508	478	355	330	314	303	229	211
	Total	6,285	4,819	3,732	3,297	2,696	2,485	2,257	2,122	2,006	1,961
Service Personnel Deaths											
Royal Irish Regiment (Home Service)		6	9	4	8	2	2	0	0	0	N/A
	Total	20	17	6	15	8	3	0	1	0	N/A

[1] Includes Royal Marine commandos in the Infantry role, but excludes the battalions of the Royal Irish Regiment (Home Service).

[2] Excludes temporary deployments.

[3] Includes one unit that served two separate tours in Northern Ireland during 1990.

[4] The Royal Irish Regiment was formed on 1 July 1992 by the merger of the Ulster Defence Regiment and the Royal Irish Rangers. The Home Service element of the Royal Irish Regiment corresponds to the former Ulster Defence Regiment. These figures do not include long-term sick.

Source: *UK Defence Statistics 1998,* Defence Analytical Services Agency,

Deployment of UK Military Personnel Overseas

As of 1 April for the year shown. Figures include Service personnel who are on loan to countries in the areas shown and naval services and civilian personnel at sea. All defence attaches and advisers and their staffs are included under 'Other locations' and not identified within specific areas. (– = not applicable.)

Service	1975	1980	1985	1990	1992	1994	1996	1997	1998
Continental Europe									
Naval services	365	413	885	378	857	1,389	394	503	856
Army	58,470	58,782	59,850	56,635	53,602	31,984	26,520	23,189	23,279
Royal Air Force	10,110	11,365	12,194	12,338	9,985	6,787	5,182	4,693	4,982
Civilian	2,512	2,283	1,977	1,984	1,994	1,701	1,344	1,423	1,390
Gibraltar									
Naval services	618	643	733	487	485	420	484	270	247
Army	822	776	771	686	130	147	63	71	103
Royal Air Force	486	404	455	378	374	302	148	135	126
Civilian	318	299	109	108	107	83	73	71	63
Cyprus									
Naval services	14	17	19	6	7	1	3	3	5
Army	3,741	3,253	3,177	2,743	3,430	2,817	2,807	2,898	2,552
Royal Air Force	3,267	1,325	1,539	1,462	1,566	1,457	1,221	1,189	1,117
Civilian	465	370	293	254	278	228	284	289	280
Other Mediterranean, Near East, and Gulf									
Naval services	3,928	2,936	552	1,640	890	1,603	358	354	1,079
Army	282	232	238	152	96	202	216	160	206
Royal Air Force	1,778	76	104	263	131	431	42	39	896
Civilian	172	11	11	7	6	4	7	11	12
Hong Kong									
Naval services	272	326	272	223	220	233	220	223	–
Army	3,434	2,389	1,964	1,624	1,652	1,441	454	807	–
Royal Air Force	562	251	268	265	264	243	211	97	–
Civilian	213	383	298	262	247	122	73	25	–

(continued)

Deployment of UK Military Personnel Overseas (*continued*)

Service	1975	1980	1985	1990	1992	1994	1996	1997	1998
Other Far East									
Naval services	2,734	56	114	1,106	65	328	329	556	195
Army	1,562	199	235	162	145	194	194	370	217
Royal Air Force	1,174	20	9	15	14	11	14	20	29
Civilian	119	27	15	22	22	13	28	27	26
Other Locations									
Naval services	6,418	1,464	2,746	2,343	1,468	979	2,853	2,953	2,839
Army	1,558	1,862	4,406	2,854	1,929	4,922	3,053	3,351	3,453
Royal Air Force	776	770	2,633	1,834	1,877	2,397	2,754	2,593	1,263
Civilian	2,974	2,857	2,752	2,956	2,922	2,690	2,476	2,521	2,638

All Overseas Areas

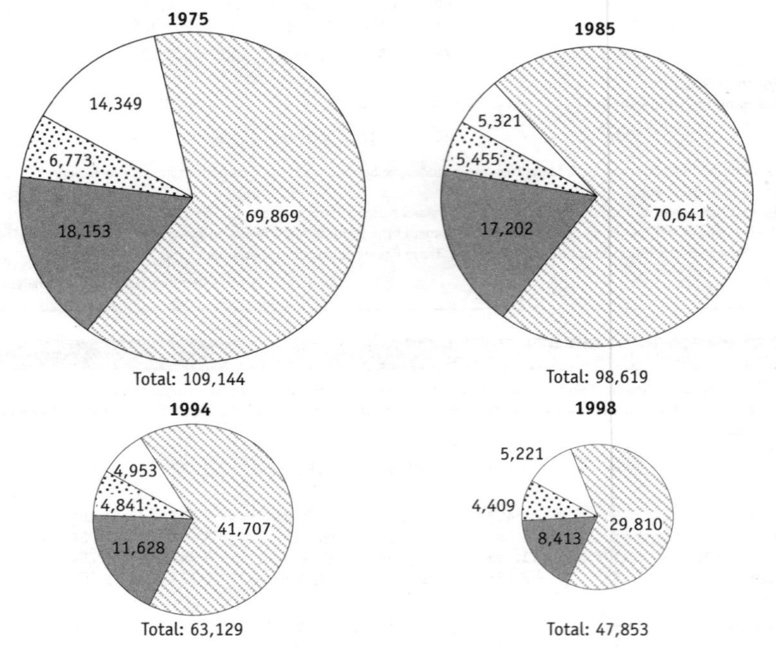

Source: *UK Defence Statistics 1998* Defence Analytical Services Agency, © Crown copyright 1998

Deployment of UK Military Personnel in the UK

Figures show deployment of UK regular forces and Ministry of Defence civilians, including Royal Navy and Royal Marines personnel on board ships in home waters. As of 1 July for the year shown.

Personnel	1980	1985	1990	1993	1994	1995	1996	1997
UK[1]								
Service	238,100	229,600	215,900	204,300	199,500	182,200	177,400	171,600
Civilian	231,200	167,700	135,200	122,000	114,000	108,000	102,600	99,700
Total	496,300	397,200	351,100	326,300	313,500	290,200	280,000	271,300
England								
Service	200,000	193,300	179,600	167,100	162,100	149,400	146,600	142,600
Civilian	196,600	140,400	114,600	102,400	95,000	89,600	85,400	82,000
Total	396,700	333,700	294,200	269,500	257,000	239,000	232,000	224,600
Wales								
Service	6,900	6,300	5,300	5,100	5,500	5,200	4,300	3,300
Civilian	9,500	6,500	5,500	5,000	4,900	4,800	4,700	4,800
Total	16,400	12,800	10,800	10,100	10,400	10,000	9,100	8,200
Scotland								
Service	18,100	20,100	19,300	19,400	18,000	16,900	15,500	13,900
Civilian	21,900	18,100	12,300	11,800	11,200	10,600	9,500	9,800
Total	40,000	38,200	31,600	31,200	29,300	27,500	25,000	23,700
Northern Ireland[2]								
Service	11,900	9,700	11,500	12,500	11,600	9,900	10,500	11,500
Civilian	3,200	2,700	2,700	2,900	2,900	3,000	3,000	3,100
Total	15,100	12,400	14,200	15,400	14,600	12,900	13,500	14,600

[1] The figures for service personnel in England, Scotland, and Wales are obtained from a different source from that used to obtain the UK total; consequently, the sum of the national figures may differ from the UK total.

[2] Includes all personnel serving on emergency tours of duty, but excludes the former Ulster Defence Regiment, now the Home Service element of the Royal Irish Regiment.

Source: *UK Defence Statistics 1998,* Defence Analytical Services Agency, © Crown copyright 1998

UK Defence Expenditure

Figures are VAT-inclusive at current prices and are in millions of pounds, except for percentages. (– = not applicable.)

Type of Expenditure		1985/86	1990/91	1995/96	1996/97	1997/98[1]	1998/99[1]
Expenditure on personnel	of the armed forces	3,510	4,811	6,150	6,223	5,993	6,064
	of the retired armed forces	899	1,406	–	–	–	–
	of civilian staff	1,970	2,594	2,374	2,409	2,286	2,196
	Total	6,379	8,811	8,524	8,633	8,279	8,259
Expenditure on equipment	sea	2,499	2,955	2,110	2,190	2,016	2,351
	land	1,887	1,927	1,576	1,806	1,525	1,702
	air	3,296	3,197	3,356	3,507	4,079	4,394
	other	511	759	1,495	1,597	1,361	1,339
	Total	8,193	8,838	8,537	9,100	8,981	9,785
Other expenditure	works, buildings, and land	1,413	2,067	2,065	1,904	1,212	1,806
	miscellaneous stores and services	1,958	2,582	2,391	2,404	2,650	2,389
	Total	3,371	4,649	4,456	4,308	3,862	4,195
	Total expenditure/budget	18,263	22,207	21,517	22,345	21,835	22,240
	Total expenditure at 1996/97 prices	29,920	27,202	21,517	22,345	21,261	21,045
Percentage of Total Expenditure							
Expenditure on personnel	of the armed forces	19.6	21.6	28.6	28.2	28.4	27.3
	of the retired armed forces	5.0	6.3	–	–	–	–
	of civilian staff	11.0	11.6	11.0	10.9	10.8	9.9
	Total	35.6	39.5	39.6	39.2	39.2	37.1
Expenditure on equipment	sea	13.9	13.3	9.8	9.9	9.5	10.6
	land	10.5	8.6	7.3	8.2	7.2	7.7
	air	18.4	14.3	15.6	15.9	19.3	19.8
	other	2.8	3.4	7.0	7.2	6.5	6.0
	Total	45.6	39.6	39.7	41.3	42.5	44.0
Other expenditure	works, buildings, and land	7.9	9.3	9.6	8.6	5.7	8.1
	miscellaneous stores and services	10.9	11.6	11.1	10.9	12.6	10.7
	Total	18.8	20.9	20.7	19.5	18.3	18.9

[1] Estimate.

Source: Ministry of Defence Resources and Programmes (Finance), *UK Defence Statistics 1998,* Defence Analytical Services Agency, © Crown copyright 1998

UK Armed Forces Weapons Arsenal

Weapon		Number	Weapon		Number
Strategic Weapons			Main battle tanks		484
Strategic submarines[1]		4	Reconnaisance vehicles		462
Conventional Weapons			Armoured infantry fighting vehicles		794
Tactical submarines		12	Armoured personnel carriers		2,820
Carriers		3	Artillery pieces		459
Destroyers		12	Mortars		543
Frigates		23	Anti-tank guided weapons		841
Patrol ships		26	Surface to air missile systems	Army	378
Mine warfare ships		19		RAF	40
Amphibious warfare ships		7	Combat aircraft	RAF	450
Landing/Amphibious craft	Army	16		Fleet Air Arm	54
	Royal Navy	33	Armed helicopters	Army	269
	Royal Marines	27		RAF	162
Support ships		21		Royal Navy	138
				Royal Marines	18
			Training helicopters		12

[1] Each capable of carrying 16 Trident DS missiles carrying 16 Multiple Independently-Targeted Re-entry Vehicles (MIRV).

Source: Data from *The Military Balance 1998/99*, International Institute for Strategic Studies

UK Ministry of Defence Contracts over £100 Million

Data are for 1997–98. (Including suppliers of food, fuels, and services.)

Over £250 million	£100–250 million
British Aerospace Aircraft Group	Annington Recievables Ltd
DERA	Babcock International Group Ltd
Devonport Royal Dockyard Ltd	British Telecom plc
General Electric Co plc	Building and Property Defence Ltd
GEC Alsthom Ltd	ICL plc
GKN plc	John Mowlem and Co
Hunting plc	Matra BAE Dynamics (UK) Ltd
Lockheed Martin Group	Other UK government departments
Rolls Royce plc	Racal Electronics Ltd
Vickers plc	Serco Group plc
	Siemens plc
	Valuation Office Agency

UK Highest-Ranking Officers

UK Chiefs of Staff

Date of appointment given in parentheses.

Chief of the General Staff

Chief of the General Staff General Sir Roger Wheeler, GCB, CBE, ADC (Gen) (1995); **Assistant Chief of the General Staff** Major General M A Willcocks, CB (1992); **Director-General Development and Doctrine** Major General A D Pigott, CBE (1992)

Chief of the Naval Staff

Chief of the Naval Staff and First Sea Lord Admiral Sir Michael Boyce, KCB, OBE, ADC (1998); **Assistant Chief of the Naval Staff** Rear Admiral J Band (1997)

Chief of the Air Staff

Chief of the Air Staff Air Chief Marshal Sir Richard Johns, GCB, CBE, LVO, ADC (1994); **Assistant Chief of the Air Staff** Air Vice-Marshal G E Stirrup, AFC (1998)

Source: Ministry of Defence, © Crown copyright

Defence Council

Date of appointment given in parentheses.

Secretary of State for Defence (Chairman of the Defence Council) The Right Honourable George Robertson MP (1997; until October 1999); **Minister of State for the Armed Forces** The Right Honourable John Spellar MP (1998); **Minister of State for Defence Procurement** Baroness Symons of Vernham Dean; **Parliamentary Under-Secretary of State for Defence** The Right Honourable Peter Kilfoyle MP (1997); **Chief of the Defence Staff** General Sir Charles Guthrie, GCB, LVO, OBE, ADC (Gen); **Permanent Under-Secretary of State** K R Tebbitt, KCB, OBE (1998); **Chief of the Naval Staff and First Sea Lord** Admiral Sir Michael Boyce, KCB, OBE, ADC (1998); **Chief of the General Staff** General Sir Roger Wheeler, GCB, CBE, ADC (Gen) (1997); **Chief of the Air Staff** Air Chief

Marshal Sir Richard Johns, GCB, CBE, LVO, ADC, FRAeS (1997); **Vice Chief of the Defence Staff** Admiral Sir Peter Abbott, KCB (1997); **Chief of Defence Procurement** Vice Admiral Sir Robert Walmsley, KCB (1996); **Chief Scientific Advisor** Professor Sir David Davies, KBE; **Second Permanent Under-secretary of State** Mr Roger Jackling, CB, CBE (1996)

Source: Ministry of Defence, © Crown copyright

The UK Royal Navy: Highest-Ranking Officers

Lord High Admiral of the United Kingdom: HM The Queen

Admirals of the Fleet (Year Appointed)
HRH The Prince Philip, Duke of Edinburgh, KG, KT, OM, GBE, AC, QSO, PC (1953); The Lord Hill-Norton, GCB (1971); Sir Michael Pollock, GCB, LVO, DSC (1974); Sir Edward Ashmore, GCB, DSC (1977); The Lord Lewin, KG, GCB, LVO, DSC (1979); Sir Henry Leach, GCB (1982); Sir Julian Oswald, GCB (1993); Sir Benjamin Bathurst, GCB (1995)

Admirals (Year of Rank)
Sir Michael Boyce, KBC, OBE, ADC (Chief of Naval Staff and First Sea Lord) (1995); Sir Peter Abbott, KCB (Vice-Chief of the Defence Staff; Sir John Brigstocke, KCB, ADC (Commander-in-Chief Naval Home Command and Second Sea Lord); N R Essenhigh (Commander-in-Chief Fleet, Commander-in-Chief Eastern Atlantic Area, and Commander Allied Forces Northwestern Europe

Vice Admirals (Year of Rank)
Sir John Hugh Dunt, KCB (Chief of Fleet Support) (1995); Sir Ian D G Garnett, KCB (Chief of Joint Opperations); F M Malbon (Deputy Commander Fleet) (1999); D A J Blackburn LVO, (Chief of Staff to Commander, Allied Naval Forces Southern Europe); P K Haddacks (UK Military Representative at NATO HQ); A W J West DSC; J H S McAnally, LVO (Commandant, Royal College of Defence Studies)

Source: Ministry of Defence, © Crown copyright

The UK Royal Air Force: Highest-Ranking Officers

Air Commodore-in-Chief: HM The Queen

Marshals of the Royal Air Force (Year Appointed)
HRH The Prince Philip, Duke of Edinburgh, KG, KT, OM, GBE, AC, QSO PC (1953); Sir John Grandy, GCB, GCVO, KBE, DSO (1971); Sir Denis Spotswood, GCB, CBE, DSO, DFC (1974); Sir Michael Beetham, GCB, CBE, DFC, AFC (1982); Sir Keith Williamson, GCB, AFC (1985); The Lord Craig of Radley, GCB, OBE (1988)

Air Chief Marshals (Year of Rank)
Sir Richard Johns, GCB, CBE, LVO, ADC (Chief of the Air Staff) (1994); Sir John Allison, KCB, CBE ADC (Air Officer Commanding-in-Chief, HQ Strike Command and Commander Allied Air Forces Northwestern Europe) (1996); Sir John Cheshire, KBE, CB (Commander-in-Chief Allied Forces Northwestern Europe) (1997)

Air Marshals (Year of Rank)
Sir Peter Squire, KCB, DFC, AFC (Deputy Chief of the Defence Staff (Programmes and Personnel)) (1996); Sir Anthony J C Bagnall, KCB, OBE (Air Member for Personnel and Air Officers, Commander-in-Chief, HQ Personnel and Training Command) (1996); John R Day, OBE (Deputy Chief of the Defence Staff (Commitments)) (1997); Colin G Terry, CB, OBE (Air Officer Commanding-in-Chief Logistics Command, Air Member for Logistics, and Chief Engineer (RAF)) (1997); J A Baird, QHP (Surgeon-General); C C C Coville, CB (Deputy Commander-in-Chief Allied Forces Central Europe); T I Jenner, CB (Chief of Staff and Deputy Commander-in-Chief, HQ Strike Command)

Source: Ministry of Defence, © Crown copyright

The UK Army: Highest-Ranking Officers

HM The Queen

Field Marshals (Year Appointed)
HRH The Prince Philip, Duke of Edinburgh, KG, KT, OM, GBE, AC, QSO (1953); The Lord Carver, GCB, CBE, DSO, MC (1973); Sir Roland Gibbs, GCB, CBE, DSO, MC (1979); The Lord Bramall, KG, GCB, OBE, MC (1982); Sir John Stanier, GCB, MBE, DL (1985); Sir Nigel Bagnall, GCB, CVO, MC, ADC (1988); The Lord Vincent, GBE, KCB, DSO (Colonel Commandant RA) (1991); Sir John Chapple, GCB, CBE, MA (1992); HRH The Duke of Kent, KG, GCMG, GCVO (Colonel-in-Chief Royal Regiment of Fusiliers /Colonel-in-Chief The Devonshire and Dorset Regiment/Colonel Scots Guards) (1993); The Lord Inge, GCB, DL (Colonel Green Howards, Colonel Commandant Army Physical Training Corps) (1994)

Generals (Year of Rank)
Sir Charles Guthrie, GCB, LVO, OBE, ADC (Gen) (Chief of the Defence Staff) (1992); Sir Jeremy MacKenzie, KCB, OBE, ADC (Gen) (Deputy Supreme Allied Commander Europe/Colonel Commandant Adjutant General's Corps, Colonel The Highlanders) (1994); Sir Roger Wheeler, GCB, CBE, ADC (Gen) (Colonel Commandant Intelligence Corps/Colonel Royal Irish Regiment/Chief of the General Staff) (1995); Sir Michael Rose (Hon Colonel Officers Training Corps, Oxford) (1995); Sir Michael Walker, KCB, CMG, CBE, ADC (Colonel The Royal Anglican Regiment/Colonel Commandant AAC/Commander-in-Chief, Land) (1997); Sir Alexander Harley, KBE, CB (Colonel Commandant Royal Artillery/Adjutant-General) (1997); Sir Rupert Smith, KCB, DSO, OBE, QMG (Colonel Commandant Parachute Regiment/Colonel Commandant REME) (D. SACEUR) (1998); Sir Samuel Cowan, KCB, CBE (Colonel Commandant of the Brigade of Gurkhas/Chief of Defence Logistics) (1998)

Source: *The Army List 1998*, © Crown copyright 1999

***UK Chief of Defence Staff General Sir Charles Guthrie** answers questions on the Kosovo crisis at the Ministry of Defence in London. Press briefings occurred daily during the NATO air attacks on Serbian targets in the spring and summer of 1999.* Photo: Richard Watt

UK Central Staffs and Commands

Defence Policy Staff
Deputy Undersecretary of State (Policy) Richard Hatfield, CBE; **Assistant Chief of Defence Staff (Policy)** Major-General C F Drewry, CBE; **Director Defence Policy** John Day; **Director Force Development** Brigadier D W Montgomery; **Director Nuclear Policy** Commodore J M Parkinson, BSC, CEng, MIEE, RN; **Deputy Policy Director** B R Hawtin, CB; **Director North Atlantic and Western Europe** Brigadier A A Milton, OBE; **Director for Central and Eastern Europe** S J Pollard ; **Director Proliferation and Arms Control Secretariat** P W D Hatt; **Head Protocol** Captain M Bickley (RN) (retired)

Defence Programmes and Personnel Staff
Deputy Chief of Defence Staff (Programmes and Personnel) Air Marshal Sir P T Squire, DFC, AFC; **Assistant Chief of Defence Staff (Programmes)** Rear Admiral N R Essenhigh; **Director Programmes** Brigadier F R Dannatt, CBE, MC; **Director**

Navy Plans Commodore R A I McClean, OBE; **Director Army Plans** Brigadier A M D Palmer, CBE; **Director Air Plans** Air Commodore S M Nicholl, CBE, AFC, BA (RAF); **Assistant Chief of Defence Staff (Logistics)** Major General G A Ewer, CBE; **Director Defence Logistics (Programmes)** Colonel C A Hewitt, MBE, CGIA; **Director Defence Logistics (Operations/Policy)** Group Captain D M Wesley, OBE; **Director Defence Logistics (Movements)** Colonel R I Harrison, OBE; **Defence Services Secretary** Rear Admiral R Lees; **Assistant Undersecretary of State (Service Personnel Policy)** P M Aldred, CBE; **Director Service Personnel Policy 1** Brigadier J R Snowdon; **Director Service Personnel Policy 2** Dr N F Price; **Director Service Personnel Policy (Projects)** Air Commodore J C O Luke, CBE, BSc; **Director Service Personnel Policy (Pensions)** J C Robb; **Director Resettlement** Brigadier R C Walker CBE, BSC, FRGS; **Director Reserve Forces and Cadets** Brigadier E L Holmes, CBE, TD

Defence Commitments Staff

Deputy Chief of the Defence Staff (Commitments) Air Marshal J R Day, OBE, BSC, FRAeS (RAF); **Assistant Chief of Defence Staff (Operations)** Rear Admiral S Moore ; **Director Overseas Military Assistance** Commodore J de Halpert (RN); **Director Defence Material Policy** Air Commodore C F Cooper (RAF); **Director Naval Operations** Commodore M D Macpherson, OBE (RN); **Director Military Operations** Brigadier A D Leaky, CBE; **Director Air Operations** Air Commodore P A Crawford, AFC, CSC (RAF); **Director Joint Warfare** Commodore R P Stevens (RN); **Assistant Undersecretary of State, Home and Overseas** Dr E V Buckley

Defence Systems Staff

Deputy Chief of the Defence Staff (Systems) Lieutenant General E F G Burton, OBE; **Director Defence Systems** Air Commodore T W Rimmer, OBE; **Assistant Chief of Defence Staff Operational Requirements (Sea)** Rear Admiral R T R Phillips; **Director Operational Requirements (Sea)** Commodore R G J Ward (RN); **Assistant Chief of Defence Staff Operational Requirements (Land)** Major General P J Russell-Jones, OBE; **Director Operational Requirements (Land)** Brigadier D M O'Callaghan; **Assistant Chief of Defence Staff Operational Requirements (Air)** Air Vice-Marshal C C C Coville, CB, BA, FRAeS (RAF); **Director Operational Requirements (Air)** Air Commodore A A Nicholson, LVO, MA (RAF)

Information and Communication

Director-General Information and Communications Mr A C Sleigh ; **Director Policy (ICS)** Air Commodore R J Holt (RAF); **Director Operational Requirements (ICS)** Commodore S J B Newsom (RN); **Director (DCS)** Air Commodore A M Ferguson

Defence Medical Services Directorate

Surgeon General Surgeon Vice Admiral A L Revell, QHS; **Director Medical Policy** Air Commodore C Sharples, QHP (RAF)

Defence Information Division

Director of Information Strategy and News Oona Muirhead

Defence Scientific Staff

Chief Scientific Adviser Professor Sir David Davis, CBE, FRS, FEng; **Deputy Under Secretary (Science and Technology)** Mr P Ewins; **Assistant Chief Scientific Adviser (Nuclear)** R W Roper; **Deputy Chief Scientist (Systems and Technology)** A F Everett; **Deputy Chief Scientist (Scrutiny and Analysis)** M Earweather; **Director Science (Ballistic Missile Defence)** Dr M Rance

Procurement Executive

Chief of Defence Procurement Vice Admiral Sir Robert Walmsley, KCB, MA, FIEE; **Deputy Chief of Defence Procurement (Operations)/Master General of the Ordnance** Lieutenant General Sir Robert Hayman-Joyce, KCB, CBE, DL; **Director-General Land Systems** Major General D J M Jenkins, CBE; **Director-General Command Information Systems** Dr I Watson; **Director-General Weapons and Electronic Systems** Mr J Allen; **Director General Aircraft Systems 1/Controller Aircraft** Air Vice-Marshall P C Norriss, CB, AFC, MA, FRAeS (RAF); **Director General Aircraft Systems 2** I D Fauset; **Director-General Surface Ships/Acting Controller of the Navy** Rear Admiral P Spencer, MA, MSc; **Director-General Submarines/CSSE** G N Bearen

Second Sea Lord/Commander-in-Chief Naval Home Command

Second Sea Lord and Commander-in-Chief Naval Home Command Admiral Sir John Brigstocke, KCB, ADC; **Chief of Staff to Second Sea Lord and Commander-in-Chief Naval Home Command** Rear Admiral P A Durt; **Flag Officer Training and Recruiting** Rear Admiral J H S McAnally, LVO, MINI, MRIN; **Naval Secretary/ Director-General Naval Manning** Rear Admiral F M Malbon; **Director-General Naval Medical Services** Surgeon Rear Admiral M P W H Paine, QHS, MB, BS, FRCS; **Director-General Naval Chaplaincy Service** Reverend Dr C E Stewart, QHC, BSc, BD, PhD

Naval Support Command

Chief of Fleet Support Vice Admiral J H Dunt; **Director-General Fleet Support (Operations and Plans)** Rear Admiral B B Perowne, OBE; **Director-General Ships** C V Betts; **Director-General Naval Bases and Supply/Chief Executive Naval Bases and Supply Agency** Rear Admiral J A Trewby; **Director-General Aircraft (Navy)** Rear Admiral J A Burch, CBE; **Flag Officer Scotland, Northern England and Northern Ireland** Rear Admiral A M Gregory, OBE

Commander-in-Chief Fleet

Commander-in-Chief Fleet, Eastern Atlantic Area and Commander Naval Forces North Western Europe Admiral Sir Peter Abbott, KCB; **Deputy Commander Fleet/Chief of Staff** Vice Admiral J J Blackham, BA; **Flag Officer Submarines/Chief of Staff (Operations)** Rear Admiral J F Perowne, OBE; **Flag Officer Surface Flotilla** Rear Admiral P M Franklyn, MVO; **Flag Officer Sea Training** Rear Admiral R J Lippett, MBE; **Commander UK Task Group and Commander Anti-Submarine Warfare Striking Force** Rear Admiral A W J West, DSE; **Flag Officer Naval Aviation** Rear Admiral T W Loughran, CB; **Commandant General, Royal Marines** Major General D A S Pennefather, CB, OBE

Quartermaster-General's Department

Quartermaster-General Lieutenant General Sir Sam Cowan, KCB, CBE; **Chief of Staff Headquarters Quartermaster-General** Major General K O'Donoghue, CBE; **Chief Executive of Logistic Information Systems Agency** vacant ; **Director-General Logistic Support (Army)** Major General M S White, CB, CBE; **Director-General Equipment Support (Army)** Major General P V R Besgrove, CBE

Adjutant General's Department

Adjutant General General Sir Alex Harley, KCB, CB; **Chief of Staff** Major General R A Oliver, OBE; **Command Secretary** W A Perry; **Chaplain-General (Army)** The Reverend D V Dobbin, MBE; **Director-General Army Medical Services** Major General W R Short; **Director Army Legal Services** Major General A P V Rogers; **Director-General Army Personnel Centre** Major General D L Burden; **Military Secretary** Major General M I E Scott; **Director-General Individual Training and Chief Executive, Army Individual Training Organization** Major General C L Elliott; **Commandant, Royal Military Academy, Sandhurst** Major General J F Deverell, OBE; **Commandant, Royal Military College of Science** Major General D J M Jenkins, CBE

Commander-in-Chief Land Command

Commander-in-Chief General Sir Michael Walker, KCB, GCB, CBE, ADC; **Deputy Commander-in-Chief/Inspector General Territorial Army** Lieutenant General J F Deverell, OBE ; **Chief of Staff Headquarters** Major General P C C Trousdell; **Deputy Chief of Staff Headquarters (Land)** Major General J D Stoleve, CBE CB, OBE; **Brigadier General Staff Headquarters (Land)** Brigadier J A Thorp, CBE

Strike Command – Command Headquarters

Air Officer Commanding-in-Chief Air Chief Marshal Sir John Allison, KCB, CBE, ADC, FRAeS; **Chief of Staff and Deputy Commander-in-Chief** Air Marshal G A Robertson, CBE, BA, FRAeS, FRSA; **Senior Air Staff Officer and Air Officer Commanding No. 38 Group** Air Vice-

Marshal P O Sturley, MBE, BSc, FRAeS ; **Air Officer Engineering and Supply** Air Vice-Marshal I Brackenbury, OBE, BSc, CEng, FIMechE; **Air Officer Administration and Air Officer Commanding Directly Administered Units** Air Vice-Marshal A J Burton, OBE, BSc, FCIS; **Air Officer Plans** Air Commander N J Sudborough, OBE, MIPD; **Command Secretary** C Wright

Headquarters Logistics Command
Air Officer Commanding-in-Chief, Air Member for Logistics and Chief Engineer (RAF) Air Marshal C G Terry, KBE, CB, BSc (Eng), CEng, FRAeS, FILog, FCGI; **Chief of Staff, Deputy Commander-in-Chief and Air Officer Commanding Directly Administered Units** Air Vice-Marshal M D Pledger, OBE, AFC, BSc, FRAes; **Air Commodore Plans** Air Commodore A J Pye; **Air Commodore Logistics Policy** Air Commodore R Brumpton; **Command Secretary** Mr H Griffiths; **Acting Chief Executive RAF Maintenance Group Defence Agency** Air Commodore K J M Procter, BSc (Eur Ing), CEng, FIEE, FRAeS, FIMgt; **Director-General Support Management (RAF)** Air Vice-Marshal P W Henderson, MBE, BSc, CEng, FRAeS

RAF Personnel and Training Command
Air Member for Personnel and Air Officer Commanding-in-Chief Air Marshal Sir Anthony Bagnall; **Chief of Staff/Air Member for Personnel** Air Vice-Marshal R A Wright, AFC; **Air Officer Administration and Air Officer Commanding Directly Administered Units** Air Commodore O D L Delany, OBE, BA, FBIFM, FIMgt; **Chief Executive Training Group Defence Agency and Air Officer Commanding Training Group** Air Vice-Marshal A J Stables, CBE, FRAeS; **Air Secretary/Chief Executive Personnel Management Agency** Air Vice-Marshal I M Stewert, AFC, LLB; **Director-General Medical Services (RAF)** Air Vice-Marshal C J Sharples, QHP, MSc, FFOM, MRCS (Eng), LRCP, DAvMed, MRAeS; **Director Legal Services (RAF)** Air Vice-Marshal J Weedon, LLB; **Chaplain-in-Chief** The Venerable (Air Vice-Marshal) P R Turner, QHC, MTh, BA, AKC; **Command Secretary** Mrs L D Kyle

Source: *The Army List 1998; The Navy List 1998; The RAF List 1999,* © Crown copyright 1999

UK Service Personnel

Strengths of UK Regular Forces

Figures include trainees. As of 1 April in year given. (N/A = not available.)

Year[1]	TOTAL	Officers			Other ranks		
		Total	Male	Female	Total	Male	Female
All services							
1993	274,849	40,403	37,599	2,804	234,446	218,333	16,113
1994	254,488	37,487	34,749	2,738	217,001	201,977	15,024
1995	233,340	35,545	32,956	2,589	197,795	183,776	14,019
1996	221,870	34,106	31,628	2,478	187,764	174,560	13,204
1997	210,823	32,675	30,295	2,380	178,148	165,697	12,451
1998	210,136	32,625	30,061	2,564	177,511	164,375	13,136
Naval services							
1993	59,357	9,802	9,307	495	49,555	45,564	3,991
1994	55,779	9,182	8,688	494	46,597	42,841	3,756
1995	50,893	8,760	8,287	473	42,133	38,696	3,437
1996	48,307	8,370	7,913	457	39,937	36,763	3,174
1997	44,651	7,810	7,357	453	36,841	34,041	2,800
1998	44,466	7,752	N/A	N/A	36,714	N/A	N/A
Army							
1993	134,583	16,129	14,959	1,170	118,454	112,030	6,424
1994	123,028	14,840	13,669	1,171	108,188	102,307	5,881
1995	111,693	13,956	12,851	1,105	97,737	92,265	5,472
1996	108,840	13,757	12,677	1,080	95,083	89,709	5,374
1997	110,140	13,971	12,831	1,140	96,169	90,074	6,095
1998	109,827	13,898	N/A	N/A	95,929	N/A	N/A
Royal Air Force							
1993	80,909	14,472	13,333	1,139	66,437	60,739	5,698
1994	75,681	13,465	12,392	1,073	62,216	56,829	5,387
1995	70,754	12,829	11,818	1,011	57,925	52,815	5,110
1996	64,723	11,979	11,038	941	52,744	48,088	4,656
1997	56,256	11,010	10,096	914	45,246	41,155	4,091
1998	55,843	10,975	N/A	N/A	44,868	N/A	N/A

Source: *UK Defence Statistics 1998,* Defence Analytical Services Agency, © Crown copyright 1998

Ethnic Composition of UK Regular Forces by Rank

For 'All Services' the ranks are shown in army terms. As of 1 April 1998. (– = not applicable.)

Rank			White		Ethnic minorities		Unknown[1]	
		Total	Number	%	Number	%	Number	%
Naval Services								
Officers	Commander and above	1,438	1,431	99.5	7	0.5	–	–
	Lieutenant Commander and below	6,314	6,250	99.0	64	1.0	–	–
	Total	7,752	7,681	99.1	71	0.9	–	–
Other ranks	Petty Officer and above	13,607	13,504	99.2	103	0.8	–	–
	Leading rate and below	23,107	22,954	99.3	153	0.7	–	–
	Total	36,714	36,458	99.3	256	0.7	–	–
	TOTAL	44,466	44,139	99.3	327	0.7	–	–
Army								
Officers	Lieutenant Colonel and above	2,255	2,231	98.9	24	1.1	–	–
	Major and below	11,643	11,416	98.1	105	0.9	122	1.0
	Total	13,898	13,647	98.2	129	0.9	122	0.9
Other ranks	Sergeant and above	21,982	21,647	98.5	326	1.5	9	0.0
	Corporal and below	73,947	72,931	98.6	691	0.9	325	0.4
	Total	95,929	94,578	98.6	1,017	1.1	334	0.3
	TOTAL	109,827	108,225	98.5	1,146	1.0	456	0.4
Royal Air Force								
Officers	Wing Commander and above	1,568	1,548	98.7	16	1.0	4	0.3
	Squadron Leader and below	9,407	8,973	95.4	107	1.1	327	3.5
	Total	10,975	10,521	95.9	123	1.1	331	3.0
Other ranks	Sergeant and above	12,838	12,652	98.6	179	1.4	7	0.1
	Corporal and below	32,030	31,319	97.8	363	1.1	348	1.1
	Total	44,868	43,971	98.0	542	1.2	355	0.8
	TOTAL	55,843	54,492	97.6	665	1.2	686	1.2
All Services								
Officers	Lieutenant Colonel and above	5,261	5,210	99.0	47	0.9	4	0.1
	Major and below	27,364	26,639	97.4	276	1.0	449	1.6
	Total	32,625	31,849	97.6	323	1.0	453	1.4
Other ranks	Sergeant and above	48,427	47,803	98.7	608	1.3	16	0.0
	Corporal and below	129,084	127,204	98.5	1,207	0.9	673	0.5
	Total	177,511	175,007	98.6	1,815	1.0	689	0.4
	TOTAL	210,136	206,856	98.4	2,138	1.0	1,142	0.5

[1] Ethnic origin not held on the administrative system.

Source: *UK Defence Statistics 1998,* Defence Analytical Services Agency, © Crown copyright 1998

Strength of UK Regular Forces by Gender and Rank

The ranks shown are in army terms. Prior to 1990 the figures relate to 1 January; from 1990 they relate to 1 April.

Rank		1975	1985	1990	1994	1996	1997	1998
Female								
Officers	Major General and above	0	0	0	0	0	0	0
	Brigadier	6	6	7	5	2	2	2
	Colonel	28	23	24	21	19	16	19
	Lieutenant Colonel	62	47	60	88	95	80	89
	Major	336	292	309	399	411	424	441
	Captain	864	936	1,172	1,402	1,265	1,181	1,190
	Lieutenant and below	783	853	965	823	686	677	823
	Total[1]	2,079	2,157	2,537	2,738	2,478	2,380	2,564
Other ranks	Warrant Officer	127	117	144	171	161	174	185
	Staff Sergeant	189	262	361	369	363	372	372
	Sergeant	682	963	1,386	1,396	1,274	1,169	1,187
	Corporal	1,481	2,903	2,979	3,161	2,718	2,357	2,295
	Lance Corporal	860	1,156	1,288	1,282	1,095	1,076	1,174
	Private (including juniors)	9,157	8,843	8,514	8,645	7,593	7,303	7,923
	Total	12,496	14,244	14,672	15,024	13,204	12,451	13,136

(continued)

Strength of UK Regular Forces by Gender and Rank (*continued*)

Rank		1975	1985	1990	1994	1996	1997	1998
Male								
Officers	Major General and above	254	212	203	180	160	149	137
	Brigadier	414	381	381	339	355	347	356
	Colonel	1,587	1,421	1,459	1,272	1,124	1,066	1,070
	Lieutenant Colonel	4,841	4,378	4,556	4,109	3,928	3,785	3,793
	Major	12,457	11,660	11,491	10,311	9,833	9,522	9,511
	Captain	17,336	13,987	13,891	12,992	12,008	11,305	10,994
	Lieutenant and below	8,011	7,947	8,351	5,546	4,220	4,121	4,200
	Total[1]	44,900	39,986	40,332	34,749	31,628	30,295	30,061
Other ranks	Warrant Officer	11,777	11,416	11,407	9,801	8,729	8,614	8,597
	Staff Sergeant	27,102	23,241	22,352	19,317	17,618	16,638	16,469
	Sergeant	37,794	35,042	34,045	28,451	25,563	24,129	23,724
	Corporal	48,645	52,764	52,587	45,152	38,206	34,660	33,343
	Lance Corporal	22,100	22,973	22,553	18,091	15,682	15,292	14,656
	Private (including juniors)	135,628	125,026	105,226	81,165	68,762	66,364	67,586
	Total	283,046	270,462	248,170	201,977	174,506	165,697	164,375

[1] Prior to 1987, professionally qualified female officers serving in the medical, dental, veterinary, and legal specializations are included with the male officer numbers.

Source: *UK Defence Statistics 1998,* Defence Analytical Services Agency, © Crown copyright 1998

Strengths of UK Reserves and Auxiliary Forces

Volunteer reserves and auxiliary forces comprise personnel in civilian occupations who undertake to give a certain amount of their time to train in support of the regular forces. As of 1 April 1998. (– = not applicable.)

Service/force		1985	1990	1995	1996	1997	1998
Regular Reserve	**Total**	205,007	250,008	264,001	264,006	259,005	254,007
Naval Service	Royal Fleet Reserve	11,000	13,006	9,008	10,002	10,000	10,006
	Individuals liable to recall	14,007	13,006	13,005	13,007	14,001	14,002
	Total	25,007	27,002	23,003	23,009	24,001	24,008
Army	Army Reserve	61,009	65,008	53,004	48,005	41,002	36,006
	Individuals liable to recall	88,002	117,007	141,009	147,000	148,009	149,003
	Total	150,002	183,005	195,003	195,005	190,001	186,000
Royal Air Force	Royal Air Force Reserve	2,005	10,001	15,009	16,000	16,003	15,004
	Individuals liable to recall	27,003	30,001	29,006	29,002	29,000	28,005
	Total	29,008	40,001	45,005	45,002	45,004	43,009
Volunteer Reserve	Naval Service	6,003	7,000	3,007	3,005	3,006	3,007
	Army[1]	81,000	81,009	59,009	57,003	57,006	57,000
	Royal Air Force	1,002	1,007	1,003	1,002	1,004	1,006
	Total	88,006	90,006	64,009	62,000	62,005	62,004

[1] Includes the Ulster Defence Regiment prior to 1 July 1992, when it merged with the Royal Irish Rangers and became the Home Service element of the Royal Irish Regiment, part of the Regular Forces. Includes the Home Service Force. Includes non-regular permanent staff.

Source: *UK Defence Statistics 1998,* Defence Analytical Services Agency, © Crown copyright 1998

Relative Ranks in the UK Armed Forces

Royal Navy	Army	Royal Air Force
Admiral of the Fleet	Field Marshal	Marshal of the RAF
Admiral	General	Air Chief Marshal
Vice Admiral	Lieutenant General	Air Marshal
Rear Admiral	Major General	Air Vice Marshal
Commodore	Brigadier	Air Commodore
Captain	Colonel	Group Captain
Commander	Lieutenant Colonel	Wing Commander
Lieutenant Commander	Major	Squadron Leader
Lieutenant	Captain	Flight Lieutenant
Sub Lieutenant	Lieutenant	Flying Officer
Midshipman	Second Lieutenant	Pilot Officer

Source: Ministry of Defence, © Crown copyright

UK Military Orders, Decorations, and Medals in Common Use

(In order of precedence.)

Abbreviation	Order, decoration, or medal
VC	Victoria Cross
GC	George Cross
KG	Knight of the Order of the Garter
KT	Knight of the Order of the Thistle
GCB	Knight Grand Cross or Dame Grand Cross of the Order of the Bath
OM	Member of the Order of Merit
KCB	Knight Commander of the Order of the Bath
CB	Companion of the Order of the Bath
GCMG	Knight Grand Cross or Dame Grand Cross of the Order of St Michael and St George
CMG	Companion of the Order of St Michael and St George
GCVO	Knight Grand Cross or Dame Grand Cross of the Royal Victorian Order
KCVO	Knight Commander of the Royal Victorian Order
DCVO	Dame Commander of the Royal Victorian Order
CVO	Commander of the Royal Victorian Order
GBE	Knight Grand Cross or Dame Grand Cross of the Order of the British Empire
CH	Member of the Order of the Companion of Honour
KBE	Knight Commander of the Order of the British Empire
DBE	Dame Commander of the Order of the British Empire
CBE	Commander of the Order of the British Empire
DSO	Companion of the Distinguished Service Order
LVO	Lieutenant of the Royal Victorian Order
OBE	Officer of the Order of the British Empire
ISO	Companion of the Imperial Service Order (obsolete)
MVO	Member of the Royal Victorian Order
MBE	Member of the Order of the British Empire
CGC	Conspicuous Gallantry Cross
RRC	Member of the Royal Red Cross
DSC	Distinguished Service Cross
MC	Military Cross
DFC	Distinguished Flying Cross
AFC	Air Force Cross
ARRC	Associate of the Royal Red Cross
DCM	Distinguished Conduct Medal (obsolete)
CGM	Conspicuous Gallantry Medal (obsolete)
GM	George Medal
DSM	Distinguished Service Medal (obsolete)
MM	Military Medal (obsolete)
DFM	Distinguished Flying Medal (obsolete)
AFM	Air Force Medal (obsolete)
QGM	Queen's Gallantry Medal
BEM	British Empire Medal (obsolete)
RVM	Royal Victorian Medal
TD	Territorial Decoration or Efficiency Decoration

Source: *The Army List 1998,* © Crown copyright 1999

Military Colleges in the UK

College	Commandant	Address and phone number
Royal College of Defence Studies	Vice Admiral J H S McNally, LVD	Seaford House, 37 Belgrave Square, London SW1X 8NS; (0171) 915 4800
Joint Services Command and Staff College	Commander N R Owen	Bracknell, Berkshire RG12 3DD; (01344) 454593
Royal Naval Military Colleges		
Britannia Royal Naval College	Commodore R A G Clare	Dartmouth, Devon TQ6 0HJ; (01803) 832141
Military Colleges (Army)		
Royal Military College of Science Shrivenham	Major General A S H Irwin, CBE	Swindon, Wiltshire SN6 8LA; (01793) 784455
Royal Military Academy Sandhurst	Major General A G Denaro, CBE	Camberley, Surrey GU15 4PQ; (01276) 63344
Royal Air Force College		
Royal Air Force Staff College	Air Vice Marshal T W Rimmer, OBE	Cranwell, Sleaford, Lincolnshire NG34 8GZ; (01400) 261201

Source: Ministry of Defence, © Crown copyright

Web Sites

A-Bomb WWW Museum

`http://www.csi.ad.jp/ABOMB/index.html`

Commemorative and awareness-raising site of the nuclear catastrophes in Hiroshima and Nagasaki in 1945. A rich display offers scientific data about the bomb, chilling descriptions of the atomic disaster, survivors' narrations, children's memories of the event, a walk through contemporary Hiroshima, and tours around the Peace Memorial Museum and the Peace Park.

Arms Race – How Technology Defined Our Identity

`http://icdweb.cc.purdue.edu/~phealy/arms.html`

Illustrated account of the arms race as part of the Cold War. It contains links expanding on a number of issues raised in the essay, such as the space race and the USA's relations with Cuba and Vietnam.

Atomic Bombings of Hiroshima and Nagasaki

`http://www.yale.edu/lawweb/avalon/abomb/mpmenu.htm`

This page contains the report of the Manhattan Engineer District of the United States Army describing the effects of the atomic bombs dropped on Hiroshima and Nagasaki in August 1945.

Battle of Britain

http://www.geocities.com/Pentagon/4143/

Informative tribute to the Battle of Britain. A history of the battle is included, with further details on many of the key people and technologies. There are also detailed notes on the pilots, the aircraft, and the aircraft losses.

Bosnian Virtual Fieldtrip

http://geog.gmu.edu/gess/jwc/bosnia/bosnia.html

Well-organized virtual visit to war-torn Bosnia. The site is indispensable for those wishing to learn about the history of the region, the war in former Yugoslavia, and the prospects for reconstruction under the Dayton Peace Accord.

British Army

http://www.army.mod.uk/

Home page of the British Army. There is extensive information on the structure of the army, weapons systems, current deployments, and career opportunities.

Chemical and Biological Warfare Chronicle

http://www.stimson.org/cwc/index.html

Features on difficult biological- and chemical-warfare issues, where policy, technology, and politics intersect. It includes information on current treaties as well as maps of biological- and chemical-weapons sites.

Chronicle of the Falkland Islands History and War

http://www.yendor.com/vanished/falklands-war.html

Chronicle of the history of the Falkland Islands, including a detailed account of the 1982 conflict between the UK and Argentina.

Cold War Policies 1945–91

http://ac.acusd.edu/History/20th/coldwar0.html

Illustrations, short features, and notes on the Cold War years from the Yalta Conference to the dissolution of the Soviet Union.

Cyanide Gas

http://www.outbreak.org/cgi-unreg/dynaserve.exe/cb/cyanide.html

Basic medical details on the chemical weapon cyanide gas, including its toxicology, the symptoms it causes, cautions and precautions, first aid therapy for victims of the gas, and a list of neutralization and decontamination methods.

D-Day

http://www.pbs.org/wgbh/pages/amex/dday/index.html

This page tells the story of the allied invasion of Normandy during World War II. This site includes a special feature on the daring paratrooper drop behind enemy lines. You can also read the text of actual newspaper stories covering the invasion and the text of letters written by soldiers at the front.

Desert-Storm.Com

http://www.desert-storm.com/index.html

This site features hoards of information, media clips, and articles, relating to the Gulf War, with special emphasis on the role of the USA.

Federation of American Scientists, Nuclear Resources

http://www.fas.org/nuke/index.html

In-depth site from this US source that covers nuclear forces worldwide. It includes details of the structure, design, and history of nuclear, chemical, and biological weapons; and news and analysis of developments across the globe.

Great War and the Shaping of the 20th Century

http://www.pbs.org/greatwar/

Companion to a co-production of the BBC and US Public Broadcasting Service (PBS), this site is a comprehensive multimedia exploration of the history and effects of World War I.

Gulf War Frontline

http://www2.pbs.org/wgbh/pages/frontline/gulf/index.html

Web site associated with the US–UK co-produced television series, broadcast in 1996. It includes transcripts of interviews with key figures – decision-makers, commanders, and analysts – maps, and a chronology.

HMS Warrior

http://www.wtj.com/artdocs/warrior.htm

This site pays homage to *HMS Warrior*, the world's first ironclad warship, which is currently moored at the Portsmouth Navy Yard in southern England.

Jared's World War II Home Page

http://www.mindspring.com/~jaredd/wwii.htm

Illustrated and informative account of World War II, focusing on the battles and technology used. The descriptions are divided into four sections – 'Important dates during World War II', 'Biographies and pictures', 'Battle descriptions and maps', and 'Aircraft used during the European theatre'.

Kosova

http://albanian.com/main/countries/kosova/index.html

Albanian nationalist perspective on Serbia's troubled province. There is a good description of Kosovo (or Kosova), its economy, places of interest, and the major cities. There is updated news of human rights abuses and demonstrations for an end to Serb rule.

Kosovo and Metohija

http://www.kosovo.com/

Polemical Web site of the Serbian Orthodox Church in the troubled Kosovo region of Yugoslavia. The case that Kosovo is an integral part of Serbia and must remain so is strongly put, with a wealth of historical argument.

Ministry of Defence, United Kingdom

http://www.mod.uk/

Official site of the UK Ministry of Defence, this site gives complete information on the history of the MOD, its ministers and chiefs of staff, its various agencies, and other MOD-related bodies. There are separate pages for each of the armed forces and reserve forces, news and press releases, operations in Kosovo, veterans' service records, contacts, and extensive links to defence ministries in all other countries of the world.

NATO

http://www.nato.int/

The official site of the North Atlantic Treaty Organization. This site includes a guide to NATO's structure and its members and partners; a complete archive of all official documents and both general and specific NATO publications.

Naval Dockyards Society

http://www.canterbury.u-net.com/Dockyards/

Home page of the Naval Dockyards Society. The society is concerned with all aspects of naval dockyards: construction, history, and workforce.

News About Chemical and Biological Agents and Threats

http://www.outbreak.org/cgi-unreg/dynaserve.exe/cb/bionews.html

US-based page on news surrounding the world of chemical and biological weapons.

Nuclear Test Ban Treaty

http://www.ctbt.rnd.doe.gov/ctbt/index.html

US Department of Energy site that explains the efforts to ensure that the signatories remain faithful to the letter of the comprehensive nuclear test ban treaty. There are sections on the various monitoring methods including hydroacoustic, seismic, radio nuclides, and infrasound, as well as onsite inspections.

Patriot Air Defence System

http://imabbs.army.mil/cmh-pg/wwwapena.htm

Comprehensive source of information on the US missile system. It traces the research and development that led to the manufacture and deployment of the system during the Gulf War.

Royal Air Force

http://www.raf.mod.uk/

Well-organized and informative site of the UK's air force. In addition to information for would-be recruits, there is extensive information on the role of the RAF and profiles of all RAF aircraft, weapons systems, and bases.

Royal British Legion

http://www.britishlegion.org.uk/

Site of Britain's leading war veterans' organization. There is comprehensive information about the history of the British Legion, its current activities, and its annual Poppy Appeal. A 'Lost trails' section helps reunite ex-servicemen.

Royal Navy

http://www.royal-navy.mod.uk/

Official guide to the Royal Navy that includes information about the latest training, deployments worldwide, and career opportunities, a history of the navy from its humble beginnings, as well as a 'future' section for each of the four arms of the service.

Special Air Service (SAS)

http://www.ability.org.uk/intro.html

Unofficial information on the elite British Army regiment. Known facts about the SAS are presented, together with information gleaned from the press on their counterinsurgency and anti-terrorist operations. There is also a long listing of books about the SAS.

START II Treaty Fact Sheet

http://www.state.gov/www/regions/nis/russia_start2_treaty.html

Site published by the US Bureau of Public Affairs explaining the START II treaty of 1993 which was designed to further reduce and limit strategic offensive weapons.

Stockholm International Peace Research Institute (SIPRI)

http://www.sipri.se

Research areas include arms transfer and production, military expenditure, military technology, chemical and biological weapons, and European security. As well as details of SIPRI's findings in all these areas, this site includes more general information about the institute's history and structure.

Tear Gases – An Overview of Some Riot Control Agents

http://www.opcw.nl/chemhaz/tear.htm

Detailed description of the chemistry and effects of the most widely used tear gases.

Treaties and Agreements

http://www.acda.gov/treatie2.htm

Text of international treaties provided by the US Arms Control and Disarmament Agency.

United Nations Institute for Disarmament Research

http://www.unog.ch/UNIDIR/webpage.htm

An autonomous institution within the United Nations, researching disarmament, international security, and related issues.

US Army Home Page

http://www.army.mil/

All there is to know about the US Army. The home page offers access to a mass of information.

Vietnam – Stories Since the War

http://www.pbs.org/pov/stories/

Extensive repository of personal narratives about the Vietnam War. Visitors can read or listen to excerpts of the selected stories which are regularly changed. Alternatively, they can search the entire database by specific words or general ideas. If they want to, they can also deposit their own story.

VX Nerve Gas

http://www.outbreak.org/cgi-unreg/dynaserve.exe/cb/vx.html

Basic medical details on the chemical weapon VX gas, including its toxicology, the symptoms it causes, cautions and precautions, first aid therapy for victims of the gas, and a list of neutralization and decontamination methods.

War at Home and Abroad

http://icdweb.cc.purdue.edu/~phealy/mccarthy.html

Illustrated account of the Cold War from the perspective of the USA's home and foreign policy. It contains links expanding on a number of issues raised in the account, such as the Marshall Plan, the Manhattan Project, and Sputnik.

War, Peace, and Security Guide

http://www.cfcsc.dnd.ca/links/index.html

Canadian Forces College guide to armed forces and conflicts worldwide, as well as peace-keeping organizations and treaties. This site includes sections on 'Armed forces of the world', 'Contemporary conflicts', 'International organizations', and 'Peace and disarmament'.

World War I Document Archive

http://www.lib.byu.edu/~rdh/wwi/

Archive of primary documents from World War I, including conventions, treaties, official papers, and memorials and personal reminiscences; plus an image archive, a biographical dictionary, and links to other related resources.

World War II Timeline

http://www.historyplace.com/worldwar2/timeline/ww2time.htm

Large and detailed chronology of World War II, as well as the major interwar events leading up to it. It is divided by year and includes links to subsidiary pages with more details of all major events.

Transport, Travel, and Tourism

The Year in Review

2 July 1998 Hong Kong's Chek Lap Tok Airport, which has the largest passenger terminal in the world, is officially opened. US president Bill Clinton is one of the first to land there. The airport operates in chaos for the first few weeks.

6 July 1998 Hong Kong's Kai Tak Airport, in the centre of the city, closes.

8 July 1998 The European Commission approves a joint venture between British Airways and American Airlines to market their flights between the UK and the USA, on the condition that the airlines surrender a third of their landing slots at the London airports. Critics of the alliance, proposed in 1996, claimed that the combined operations of the two airlines threatened to monopolize the market.

9 July 1998 The British government approves plans to widen the M25 between junctions 12 and 15 to the west of London, England, which would create the nation's first 12-lane motorway.

20 July 1998 British deputy prime minister John Prescott announces government proposals to improve public transport and reduce pollution caused by car emissions. The new legislation would allow local governments to charge tolls on motorways and to charge for parking at places of work. The fees collected would be used to improve public transport, especially coach services.

31 July 1998 The British government shelves more than 100 schemes for widening roads and creating new bypasses, adopting new criteria for road building, including the impact on the environment, safety, jobs, and public transport alternatives.

31 July 1998 The British government announces plans to build a 2 km/1.2 mi tunnel to hide the busy road from London to Exeter next to Stonehenge, to improve the setting of the monument. The plan creates the possibility of closing the A-road past the stones and creating access to the monument by foot using the grassed-over road.

4 August 1998 Australian prime minister John Howard announces that Speedrail, a consortium led by Anglo-French engineering company Alstom SA, has won the bid to build a high-speed rail link between the cities of Canberra and Sydney. The railway would use the same technology as France's TGV. Construction is scheduled to begin in 2000.

14 August 1998 London Transport announces plans to create a £1 billion smartcard system which would enable passengers to travel on the underground, buses, and trains without putting tickets through entry or exit barriers. The system would use sensors to detect the card and deduct the fare.

3 September 1998 A Swissair jet en route from New York, USA, to Geneva, Switzerland, crashes into the Atlantic Ocean off the coast of Nova Scotia, Canada, killing all 229 people on board. The pilot asked to make an emergency landing at Halifax Airport, but the plane nosedived before arriving there. Although the cause of the crash is unknown, the airline rules out terrorism.

15 October 1998 Line 14 of the Paris Métro

opens with fully automated, driverless trains, linking the right and left banks of the Seine river.

30 October 1998 British Airways passenger Steven Hardy attacks and injures flight attendant Fiona Weir on a flight from London Gatwick to Malaga, Spain, creating awareness and concern over the danger of 'air rage' incidents.

November 1998 Leading airlines and travel agents announce plans to work with the International Air Transport Association (IATA) to compile a list of passengers who endanger flights in order to ban them from their businesses. The action is partly in response to the Steven Hardy case.

23 November 1998 A 24-hour strike is called by European rail workers to protest against European Union plans to introduce competition and force state-subsidized monopolies to allow private rivals to use their tracks. Affecting travellers in France, Greece, and Belgium, it is the first cross-European rail strike.

December 1998 Figures from the European Union reveal that 60 of Europe's 74 best-selling cars are more expensive in Britain than any other member nation. Cars sold in Britain are, on average, 35 percent more expensive.

3 December 1998 The British government announces plans to establish a new transport authority for the capital, London, to help combat traffic congestion. The body will have responsibility for major roads, the underground, buses, taxis, and riverboats.

11 December 1998 A Thai Airways airbus crashes into a rubber plantation in Southern Thailand during a severe tropical storm, killing 101 people and injuring more than 40.

10 February 1999 Official figures reveal that the punctuality of privatized British trains has deteriorated further in 1998, with 45 of 77 routes having worse records than in 1997. Punctuality is worse overall than in the last months of British Rail two years previously.

26 February 1999 A new edition of the Highway Code, previously updated six years ago, is published in the UK. Amendments include warnings against using mobile phones, especially hand-held instruments, as well as other electronic equipment which can distract the driver.

15 March 1999 An Amtrak train crashes into a lorry at a railway crossing in Bourbonnais, Illinois, USA, killing 11 passengers and injuring more than 100.

24 March 1999 A fire in a tunnel connecting France and Italy under Mont Blanc kills 40 people.

24 March 1999 The results of a vote by construction engineers around the world on the greatest building achievement of the last century are announced at the Conexpo exhibition in Las Vegas, Nevada, USA. The top-rated construction is the Channel Tunnel.

14 April 1999 The world train speed record is set by a Japanese train that is magnetically levitated above the track, travelling at 552 kph/343 mph, on a test track near Tokyo, Japan.

May 1999 The British government's rail regulatory body reveals that privatized rail companies received nearly a million complaints for the 12 months ending in April, reflecting far greater customer dissatisfaction. Virgin Trains received the most complaints, for its poor record on punctuality.

20 May 1999 The luxury liner *Sun Vista*, carrying more than 1,100 passengers, sinks off the west coast of Malaysia after a fire breaks out in the engine room. All of the passengers are rescued by 14 ships during the 6 hours between the fire beginning and the ship sinking.

6 June 1999 British Airways announces that it is abandoning its £60 million project to respray its jets with 'world images', instead reinstating the traditional union flag.

7 June 1999 British airline Virgin Atlantic announces plans to install 10 full-sized double beds, separated from other passengers by screens, to enable passengers to become legitimate members of the 'Mile High Club'. The company plans to charge £6,600 per couple between London and New York.

15 June 1999 British deputy prime minister John Prescott announces plans to give Railtrack control of the Circle, District, Metropolitan, Hammersmith, City, and East London Underground lines, enabling rail passengers travelling to London to reach the centre without transferring to tube trains.

21 June 1999 The Circle line of the London Underground abruptly closes due to a decaying roof between two stations in west London. It is the first time London Underground has had to close a line. The Circle line is due to reopen in mid-August.

World Aviation

Top Airlines by Number of Passengers

Rankings are for passengers carried on scheduled services.

1998

Rank	International		Domestic		Total	
	Airline	Number of passengers	Airline	Number of passengers	Airline	Number of passengers
1	British Airways	30,092,000	Delta Air Lines	97,948,000	Delta Air Lines	105,305,000
2	Lufthansa	24,752,000	United Airlines	75,302,000	United Airlines	86,800,000
3	Air France	18,190,000	American Airlines	64,151,000	American Airlines	81,453,000
4	American Airlines	17,301,000	US Airways	56,310,000	US Airways	57,990,000
5	KLM	14,920,000	Northwest Airlines	41,921,000	Northwest Airlines	50,489,000

Source: IATA *World Air Transport Statistics 1999*

International Aircraft Registration Prefixes

Most civil aircraft carry one or two letters or a number and a letter to identify their nationality. This nationality mark is painted on both sides of the fuselage or tail. It is also displayed on the underside of the wing. Numbers or letters following the nationality mark on a plane are the registration mark issued to that particular plane in its own country. Each country that belongs to the International Civil Aviation Organization (ICAO) reports its nationality mark to the organization.

Country	ICAO mark
Afghanistan	YA
Albania	ZA
Algeria	7T
Andorra	C3
Angola	D2
Antigua and Barbuda	V2
Argentina	LQ, LV
Armenia	EK
Australia	VH
Austria	OE
Azerbaijan	4K
Bahamas	C6
Bahrain	A9C
Bangladesh	S2, S3
Barbados	8P
Belarus	EW
Belgium	OO
Belize	V3
Benin	TY
Bhutan	A5
Bolivia	CP
Bosnia-Herzegovina	T9
Botswana	A2
Brazil	PP, PT
Brunei	V8
Bulgaria	LZ
Burkina Faso	XT
Burundi	9U
Cambodia	XU
Cameroon	TJ
Canada	C, CF
Cape Verde	D4
Central African Republic	TL
Chad	TT
Chile	CC
China	B
Colombia	HK
Comoros	D6
Congo, Democratic Republic of	9Q, 9T
Congo, Republic of the	TN
Costa Rica	TI
Côte d'Ivoire	TU
Croatia	9A
Cuba	CU
Cyprus	5B
Czech Republic	OK
Denmark	OY
Djibouti	J2
Dominica	J7
Dominican Republic	HI
Ecuador	HC
Egypt	SU
El Salvador	YS
Equatorial Guinea	3C
Eritrea	E3
Estonia	ES
Ethiopia	ET
Fiji Islands	DQ
Finland	OH
France	F
Gabon	TR
Gambia	C5
Georgia	4L
Germany	D
Ghana	9G
Greece	SX
Grenada	J3
Guatemala	TG
Guinea	3X
Guinea-Bissau	J5
Guyana	8R
Haiti	HH
Honduras	HR
Hungary	HA
Iceland	TF
India	VT
Indonesia	PK
Iran	EP
Iraq	YI
Ireland, Republic of	EI
Israel	4X
Italy	I
Jamaica	6Y
Japan	JA
Jordan	JY
Kazakhstan	UN
Kenya	5Y
Kiribati	T3
Korea, North	P
Korea, South	HL
Kuwait	9K
Kyrgyzstan	EX
Laos	RDPL
Latvia	YL
Lebanon	OD
Lesotho	7P
Liberia	EL
Libya	5A
Liechtenstein	HB
Lithuania	LY
Luxembourg	LX
Macedonia, Former Yugoslav Republic of	Z3
Madagascar	5R
Malawi	7Q
Malaysia	9M
Maldives	8Q
Mali	TZ
Malta	9H
Marshall Islands	V7
Mauritania	5T
Mauritius	3B
Mexico	XA, XB, XC
Micronesia	V6
Moldova	ER
Monaco	3A
Mongolia	BNMAU, MONGOL, MT
Morocco	CN
Mozambique	C9
Myanmar	XY, XZ
Namibia	V5
Nauru	C2
Nepal	9N
Netherlands	PH
New Zealand	ZK, ZL, ZM
Nicaragua	YN
Niger	5U
Nigeria	5N
Norway	LN
Oman	A4O
Pakistan	AP
Panama	HP
Papua New Guinea	P2
Paraguay	ZP
Peru	OB
Philippines	RP
Poland	SP
Portugal	CS
Qatar	A7
Romania	YR
Russia	RA
Rwanda	9XR
St Kitts and Nevis	V4
St Lucia	J6
St Vincent and the Grenadines	J8
Samoa	5W
San Marino	T7
São Tomé and Príncipe	S9
Saudi Arabia	HZ
Senegal	6W
Seychelles	S7
Sierra Leone	9L
Singapore	9V
Slovak Republic	OM
Slovenia	S5
Solomon Islands	H4
Somalia	6O
South Africa	ZS, ZT, ZU
Spain	EC
Sri Lanka	4R
Sudan	ST
Suriname	PZ
Swaziland	3D
Sweden	SE
Switzerland	HB
Syria	YK
Taiwan	B
Tajikistan	EY
Tanzania	5H
Thailand	HS
Togo	5V
Tonga	A3
Tunisia	TS
Turkey	TC
Turkmenistan	EZ
Tuvalu	T2
Uganda	5X
UK	G
Ukraine	UR
United Arab Emirates	A6
United Nations	4N
Uruguay	CX
USA	N
Uzbekistan	UK
Vanuatu	YJ
Vatican City State	HV
Venezuela	YV
Vietnam	VN
Yemen	7O
Yugoslavia	YU
Zambia	9J
Zimbabwe	Z

Source: International Civil Aviation Organization

The World's Busiest Airports by Passenger Traffic

The figures are for airports participating in the Airports Council International (ACI) Monthly Airport Traffic Statistics Collection.

1997

Airport	*Number of passengers*
Chicago/O'Hare (IL)	70,385,073
Atlanta (GA)	68,205,769
Dallas/Fort Worth (TX)	60,488,713
Los Angeles (CA)	60,142,588
London/Heathrow	58,142,836
Tokyo/Haneda	49,302,268
San Francisco (CA)	40,493,959
Frankfurt/Main	40,262,691
Seoul/Kimpo	36,757,716
Paris/Charles de Gaulle	35,293,378
Denver (CO)	34,969,021
Miami (FL)	34,533,268
Amsterdam/Schiphol	31,569,977
Detroit (MI)	31,541,650
New York/JFK (NY)	31,355,268
Newark (NJ)	30,915,857
Phoenix (AZ)	30,659,143
Las Vegas (NV)	30,305,822
Minneapolis/St Paul (MN)	30,208,256
Hong Kong/Kai Tak	29,006,565
Houston (TX)	28,705,213
St Louis (MO)	27,661,144
Orlando (FL)	27,305,149
London/Gatwick	26,961,453
Toronto	26,094,527
Tokyo/Narita	25,667,577
Boston (MA)	25,567,888
Singapore	25,174,344
Bangkok	25,124,843
Paris/Orly	25,056,321

Source: Airports Council International, Geneva, Switzerland

The World's Busiest Airports by Cargo Volume

The figures are for airports participating in the Airports Council International (ACI) Monthly Airport Traffic Statistics Collection.

1997

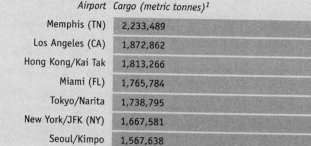

Airport	Cargo (metric tonnes)[1]
Memphis (TN)	2,233,489
Los Angeles (CA)	1,872,862
Hong Kong/Kai Tak	1,813,266
Miami (FL)	1,765,784
Tokyo/Narita	1,738,795
New York/JFK (NY)	1,667,581
Seoul/Kimpo	1,567,638
Frankfurt/Main	1,514,267
Chicago/O'Hare (IL)	1,407,307
Singapore/Changi	1,358,044
Louisville (KY)	1,345,693
London/Heathrow	1,260,068
Anchorage (AK)	1,259,827
Amsterdam/Schiphol	1,207,282
Paris/Charles de Gaulle	1,072,207
Newark (NJ)	1,043,494
Taipei/Chiang Kai Shek	913,520
Atlanta (GA)	864,944
Dayton (OH)	813,180
Dallas/Fort Worth (TX)	810,687
San Francisco (CA)	780,029
Bangkok	771,064
Osaka	744,937
Tokyo/Haneda	696,498
Oakland (CA)	678,083
Indianapolis (IN)	662,923
Brussels	530,718
Sydney	530,601
Toledo (OH)	520,855
Honolulu (HI)	500,830

[1]This includes both loaded and unloaded freight and mail.

Source: Airports Council International, Geneva, Switzerland

Air Distances Between Major World Cities

(In miles.)

City	Bangkok	Beijing	Berlin	Cairo	Cape Town	Caracas	Chicago	Hong Kong	London	Los Angeles	Madrid	Melbourne	Mexico City	Montreal	Moscow	New York	Paris	Rio de Janeiro	Rome	San Francisco	Singapore	Stockholm	Tokyo	Washington, DC
Bangkok		2,046	5,352	4,523	6,300	10,555	8,570	1,077	5,944	7,637	6,337	4,568	9,793	8,338	4,389	8,669	5,877	9,994	5,494	7,931	883	5,089	2,865	8,807
Beijing	2,046		4,584	4,698	8,044	8,950	6,604	1,217	5,074	6,250	5,745	5,643	7,753	6,519	3,607	6,844	5,120	10,768	5,063	5,918	2,771	4,133	1,307	6,942
Berlin	5,352	4,584		1,797	5,961	5,238	4,414	5,443	583	5,782	1,165	9,918	6,056	3,740	1,006	3,979	548	6,209	737	5,672	6,164	528	5,557	4,181
Cairo	4,523	4,698	1,797		4,480	6,342	6,141	5,066	2,185	7,520	2,087	8,675	7,700	5,427	1,803	5,619	1,998	6,143	1,326	7,466	5,137	2,096	5,958	5,822
Cape Town	6,300	8,044	5,961	4,480		6,366	8,491	7,376	5,989	9,969	5,308	6,425	8,519	7,922	6,279	7,803	5,786	3,781	5,231	10,248	6,008	6,423	9,154	7,895
Caracas	10,555	8,950	5,238	6,342	6,366		2,495	10,165	4,655	3,632	4,346	9,717	2,234	2,438	6,177	2,120	4,732	2,804	5,195	3,902	11,402	5,471	8,808	2,047
Chicago	8,570	6,604	4,414	6,141	8,491	2,495		7,797	3,958	1,745	4,189	9,673	1,690	745	4,987	714	4,143	5,282	4,824	1,859	9,372	4,331	6,314	596
Hong Kong	1,077	1,217	5,443	5,066	7,376	10,165	7,797		5,990	7,240	6,558	4,595	8,788	7,736	4,437	8,060	5,990	11,009	5,774	6,905	1,605	5,063	1,791	8,155
London	5,944	5,074	583	2,185	5,989	4,655	3,958	5,990		5,439	785	10,500	5,558	3,254	1,564	3,469	214	5,750	895	5,367	6,747	942	5,959	3,674
Los Angeles	7,637	6,250	5,782	7,520	9,969	3,632	1,745	7,240	5,439		5,848	7,931	1,542	2,427	6,068	2,451	5,601	6,330	6,326	347	8,767	5,454	5,470	2,300
Madrid	6,337	5,745	1,165	2,087	5,308	4,346	4,189	6,558	785	5,848		10,758	5,643	3,448	2,147	3,593	655	5,045	851	5,803	7,080	1,653	6,706	3,792
Melbourne	4,568	5,643	9,918	8,675	6,425	9,717	9,673	4,595	10,500	7,931	10,758		8,426	10,395	8,950	10,359	10,430	8,226	9,929	7,856	3,759	9,630	5,062	10,180
Mexico City	9,793	7,753	6,056	7,700	8,519	2,234	1,690	8,788	5,558	1,542	5,643	8,426		2,317	6,676	2,090	5,725	4,764	6,377	1,887	10,327	6,012	7,035	1,885
Montreal	8,338	6,519	3,740	5,427	7,922	2,438	745	7,736	3,254	2,427	3,448	10,395	2,317		4,401	331	3,432	5,078	4,104	2,543	9,203	3,714	6,471	489
Moscow	4,389	3,607	1,006	1,803	6,279	6,177	4,987	4,437	1,564	6,068	2,147	8,950	6,676	4,401		4,683	1,554	7,170	1,483	5,885	5,228	716	4,660	4,876
New York	8,669	6,844	3,979	5,619	7,803	2,120	714	8,060	3,469	2,451	3,593	10,359	2,090	331	4,683		3,636	4,801	4,293	2,572	9,534	3,986	6,757	205
Paris	5,877	5,120	548	1,998	5,786	4,732	4,143	5,990	214	5,601	655	10,430	5,725	3,432	1,554	3,636		5,684	690	5,577	6,673	1,003	6,053	3,840
Rio de Janeiro	9,994	10,768	6,209	6,143	3,781	2,804	5,282	11,009	5,750	6,330	5,045	8,226	4,764	5,078	7,170	4,801	5,684		5,707	6,613	9,785	6,683	11,532	4,779
Rome	5,494	5,063	737	1,326	5,231	5,195	4,824	5,774	895	6,326	851	9,929	6,377	4,104	1,483	4,293	690	5,707		6,259	6,229	1,245	6,142	4,497
San Francisco	7,931	5,918	5,672	7,466	10,248	3,902	1,859	6,905	5,367	347	5,803	7,856	1,887	2,543	5,885	2,572	5,577	6,613	6,259		8,448	5,399	5,150	2,441
Singapore	883	2,771	6,164	5,137	6,008	11,402	9,372	1,605	6,747	8,767	7,080	3,759	10,327	9,203	5,228	9,534	6,673	9,785	6,229	8,448		5,936	3,300	9,662
Stockholm	5,089	4,133	528	2,096	6,423	5,471	4,331	5,063	942	5,454	1,653	9,630	6,012	3,714	716	3,986	1,003	6,683	1,245	5,399	5,936		5,053	4,183
Tokyo	2,865	1,307	5,557	5,958	9,154	8,808	6,314	1,791	5,959	5,470	6,706	5,062	7,035	6,471	4,660	6,757	6,053	11,532	6,142	5,150	3,300	5,053		6,791
Washington, DC	8,807	6,942	4,181	5,822	7,895	2,047	596	8,155	3,674	2,300	3,792	10,180	1,885	489	4,876	205	3,840	4,779	4,497	2,441	9,662	4,183	6,791	

Recent World Aircraft Disasters

Only disasters in which ten or more persons have died are listed.

Date	Aircraft	Location	Details	Fatalities
1 February 1991	US Boeing 737-300 and Metro SA-227-AC	Los Angeles (CA), USA	collision	34
26 May 1991	Austrian Boeing 767-329ER	Phu Khao Chan, Thailand	crashed in jungle	223
11 July 1991	Nigerian DC8	Jiddah, Saudi Arabia	crashed while landing	261
31 July 1992	Airbus A310-304, Thai Airways Int	Kathmandu, Nepal	crashed on descent	113
31 July 1992	Yakovlev 42D, China General Aviation Corporation	near Nanjing, China	crashed during initial climb	106
28 September 1992	Airbus A300B4-203	Kathmandu, Nepal	crashed on descent	167
24 November 1992	Boeing 737-3Y0, China Southern Airlines	Guilin, China	crashed into mountain on descent	141
22 December 1992	Boeing 727-2L5, Libyan Arab Airlines	Souk al-Sabt, Libya	collided with a MIG-23UB at 1,067 m/3,500 ft and crashed	157
26 April 1994	Chinese A300-600R Airbus	Nagoya, Japan	crashed while landing	264
18 December 1995	Lockheed L-188C Electra, Trans Service Airlift	Kahengula, Angola	crashed after take-off (aircraft over-loaded)	141
20 December 1995	Boeing 757-223, American Airlines	Buga, Colombia	crashed on approach	160
17 July 1996	US Boeing 747	Long Island (NY), USA	crashed after take-off	230
12 November 1996	Saudi Arabian Boeing 747-100 and Kazakh Ilyushin 76TD	Charki Dadri, India	mid-air collision	349
6 August 1997	Korean Boeing 747-300	Guam, Mariana Islands	crashed into mountain	227
26 September 1997	Indonesian Airbus A300B	near Medan, Indonesia	crashed and burst into flames; visibility was reduced due to smog from forest fires	234
10 October 1997	Argentine DC9	near Nuevo Berlin, Uruguay	crashed in swamp land on the banks of the Uruguay River	74
15 December 1997	Tajikistani Tupolev 154B	near Sharjah, United Arab Emirates	crashed and burst into flames while approaching Sharjah	85
17 December 1997	Ukrainian Yakovlev 42	Thessaloniki, Greece	crashed while holding at 10,067 m/35,000 ft near Thessaloniki due to heavy traffic in the area	70
19 December 1997	Indonesian 737	near Palembang, Indonesia	crashed nose-down into the river bed of the River Musi; one of the wings broke off during the plunge	104
13 January 1998	Antonov 24/26, Ariana Afghan Airlines	Khojak Pass area, Pakistan	crashed after fuel exhaustion	51
2 February 1998	DC-9-32 RP-1507, Cebu Pacific Air	near Cagayan de Oro, Philippines	crashed into a volcano (Mt Balatucan)	104
16 February 1998	Airbus A300-600R, China Airlines	Taipei International Airport	crashed in thick fog during a second attempt to land, and burst into flames	205[1]
18 March 1998	Saab 340B, Formosa Airlines	at sea near Hsinchu, Taiwan	crashed into the sea in turbulent weather conditions	13
19 March 1998	727-200, Ariana Afghan Airlines	Charasyab, Afghanistan	crashed into the Sharki Baratayi mountain	45
20 April 1998	727-200, Air France	Bogota, Colombia	crashed into a mountain shortly after take-off	53
30 July 1998	Beech 1900/Cessna, Proteus Air	Lorient, France	mid-air collision	15
24 August 1998	Fokker F27, Myanmar Airways	Manibagi, Myanmar	crashed in bad weather	39
29 August 1998	Tupolev 154M, Cubana	Quito, Ecuador	crashed shortly after take-off	78[1]
2 September 1998	MD11, Swissair	Halifax, Canada	crashed at night into the Atlantic Ocean off Halifax, Nova Scotia	229
25 September 1998	BAe 146-100, Paukn Air	Melilla, Spain	crashed into a mountainous area in Moroccan territory near Melilla, Spain	38
11 December 1998	International A310-200, Thai Airways	Surat Thani, Thailand	crashed on landing	96
24 February 1999	Tupolev 154, China Southwest Airlines	Ruian, China	exploded in mid-air	61

[1] Figures include nine on the ground.

The 10 Worst Aircraft Disasters in Aviation History

Fatalities	Date	Airline(s)	Aircraft	Location
582	27 March 1977	Pan American and KLM (Royal Dutch Airlines)	Two Boeing 747s	Tenerife, Canary Islands
520	12 August 1985	Japan Airlines	Boeing 747	Mount Ogura, Japan
349	12 November 1996	Saudi Arabian Air and Kazak Airlines	Boeing 747 and Ilyushin 76TD	Charki Dadri, India
346	3 March 1974	Turkish Air	DC10	northeast of Paris
329	23 June 1985	Air India	Boeing 747	Republic of Ireland coast, Atlantic Ocean
301	19 August 1980	Saudi Arabian Air	Lockheed L-1011	Riyadh, Saudi Arabia
290	3 July 1988	Iran Air	A300 Airbus	Persian Gulf
275	25 May 1979	American Airlines	DC10	Chicago (IL), USA
270	21 December 1988	Pan American	Boeing 747	Lockerbie, Scotland
269	1 September 1983	Korean Airlines	Boeing 747	near Sakhalin Island, Okhokst Sea

Source: National Transportation Safety Board, US Department of Transportation

Recent International Airline Terrorism

Not every hijacking or bombing can be categorized as a terrorist act. This table excludes hijackings and bombings carried out for ransom or other personal motives rather than for political reasons.

Date	Terrorist act	Airline	Flight	Description
1 March 1988	bombing	BOP Air	Phadabawa–Johannesburg, South Africa	aircraft destroyed in flight; 17 killed
21 December 1988	bombing	Pan American, flight 103	London, UK–New York, USA	aircraft destroyed in flight over Lockerbie, UK; 270 killed
19 September 1989	bombing	Union des Transport	Brazzaville, Congo–Ndjamena, Chad–Paris, France	aircraft destroyed in flight; 171 killed
27 November 1989	bombing	Avianca	Bogota–Cali, Colombia	aircraft destroyed in flight; 107 killed
18 March 1991	bombing	Aeroflot	Moscow–Novokuznetsk, Russia	incendiary device; aircraft landed safely
19 July 1994	bombing	Alas Airline	Colon City–Panama City, Panama	explosion in flight; aircraft crashed over the Santa Rita mountains; 21 killed
3 November 1994	hijacking	Scandinavian Airlines	Bardfoss–Oslo, Norway	80 passengers held hostage; hijacker demanded peace corridor in Bosnia and later surrendered
11 December 1994	bombing	Philippines Airlines 747	Manila, Philippines–Tokyo, Japan	explosion in flight; 1 killed, 10 injured; aircraft landed safely; Abu Sayyaf Group (ASG) responsible
24 December 1994	hijacking; bombing	Air France Airbus 400	Algiers, Algeria–Marseille, France	Algerian hijackers demanded that 2 leaders of Islamic Salvation Front be released; in Marseille police stormed the aircraft and killed all terrorists; dynamite discovered in cabin; 3 hostages had been killed by the terrorists
23 November 1996	hijacking	Ethiopian Airlines	Ethiopia–Kenya	aircraft ran out of fuel on redirected route and crashed near a beach on the Comoros Islands; 125 killed, including the hijackers

UK Aviation

The Top 20 Busiest UK Airports

(N = Nil or negligible.)

1997

Rank by passengers	Airport	Terminal[1] passengers (thousands)	% change from 1996	Cargo volume (tonnes)	Take-offs and landings (thousands)
1	Heathrow	57,808.0	3.7	1,169.5	429.2
2	Gatwick	26,795.5	11.1	269.9	229.3
3	Manchester	15,741.4	8.7	94.3	147.4
4	Glasgow	6,011.7	9.8	11.1	80.1
5	Birmingham	5,904.4	10.3	19.8	79.9
6	Stansted	5,366.6	11.5	130.5	84.4
7	Edinburgh	4,157.8	9.1	8.2	71.7
8	Luton	3,221.3	33.6	23.8	40.3
9	Newcastle	2,592.4	6.6	1.2	42.4
10	Aberdeen	2,568.0	8.0	6.4	86.7
11	Belfast/International	2,459.3	4.6	25.1	35.1
12	Jersey	1,687.1	2.6	5.7	49.8
13	East Midlands	1,878.3	3.1	126.3	41.0
14	Bristol	1,586.4	13.8	0.1	31.6
15	Belfast/City	1,282.4	–5.8	1.3	33.3
16	Leeds/Bradford	1,247.1	18.5	0.4	26.1
17	London City	1,161.1	60.0	N	32.8
18	Cardiff	1,124.1	11.3	0.5	18.2
19	Guernsey	870.7	2.9	5.1	39.6
20	Isle of Man	676.8	11.8	4.5	21.9

[1] Terminal refers to both embarking and disembarking passengers.

Source: *UK Airports: Annual Statements of Movements, Passengers and Cargo 1998*, Civil Aviation Authority

The Top 30 UK International Airline Routes

1998

Rank	Route	Passengers carried
1	Heathrow to New York (JFK)	2,499,820
2	Heathrow to Dublin	1,894,154
3	Heathrow to Paris (Charles de Gaulle)	1,846,290
4	Heathrow to Frankfurt am Main	1,542,553
5	Heathrow to Los Angeles International	1,298,084
6	Heathrow to Chicago	1,152,252
7	Heathrow to Rome (Fiumicino)	1,115,319
8	Stansted to Dublin	1,103,956
9	Heathrow to Brussels	1,064,499
10	Heathrow to San Francisco	1,017,628
11	Heathrow to Toronto	1,005,943
12	Heathrow to Zürich	1,000,927
13	Heathrow to Washington	961,451
14	Heathrow to Milan (Linate)	946,742
15	Heathrow to Hong Kong	928,674
16	Gatwick to Malaga	898,232
17	Heathrow to Munich	860,585
18	Manchester to Palma de Mallorca	850,134
19	Heathrow to Copenhagen	837,695
20	Manchester to Tenerife (Surreira Sofia)	827,339
21	Heathrow to Madrid	822,309
22	Heathrow to Stockholm (Arlonda)	808,885
23	Heathrow to Geneva	801,519
24	Heathrow to New York (Newark)	757,630
25	Heathrow to Boston	754,782
26	Heathrow to Johannesburg	740,638
27	Gatwick to Tenerife (Surreira Sofia)	701,592
28	Gatwick to Palma de Mallorca	699,252
29	Heathrow to Athens	691,360
30	Gatwick to Orlando	680,093

Source: *UK Airports: Annual Statements of Movements, Passengers and Cargo 1998*, Civil Aviation Authority

Total Fleet for UK Airlines

This table shows the number of aircraft in service at the end of each year.
(– = not applicable. N/A = not available.)

Fleet	1987	1988	1989	1990	1991	1992	1993	1994	1995	1996	1997
British Airways[1]	192	200	215	233	233	225	225	227	212	212	226
British Airways (Euro Ops)[2]	40	45	50	40	39	12	15	16	26	28	34
British International Helicopters[3]	29	31	26	27	27	24	25	28	25	21	22
Air Europe	9	14	21	–	–	–	–	–	–	–	–
Air UK	22	21	25	25	29	28	34	36	37	41	39
Bond Helicopters	33	36	35	45	50	45	43	N/A	N/A	N/A	N/A
Bristow Helicopters	62	62	57	65	63	59	56	N/A	N/A	N/A	N/A
Britannia Airways	31	33	40	32	39	33	28	29	29	28	27
British World Airline[4]	16	11	16	17	17	19	20	21	18	17	19
British Midland	17	19	21	29	30	31	34	34	34	34	34
Loganair	16	18	18	17	22	22	24	14	14	13	6
Monarch	8	12	9	17	18	21	16	18	22	24	17
Virgin Atlantic	2	2	4	6	8	8	9	13	12	15	20
Total[5]	615	668	787	690	732	718	728	695	700	722	758

1 Prior to 1988 the data include British Caledonian Airways as well as British Airways and British Airtours.
2 This was formerly Dan Air Services until taken over by British Airways in November 1992.
3 This was formerly British Airways Helicopters until 12 October 1986.
4 This was formerly British Air Ferries until 1993.
5 From 1994 excludes Bond and Bristow Helicopters.

Source: *Transport Statistics Great Britain 1998*, © Crown copyright 1998

Aircraft Near-Miss Incidents in UK Airspace

Aircraft type and risk level	1986	1987	1988	1989	1990	1991	1992	1993	1994	1995	1996
Civil and Military Aircraft											
Risk of collision	21	20	33	30	25	22	25	15	16	17	37
Safety not assured	50	58	59	55	67	70	51	79	62	57	58
Dangerous incidents total	71	78	92	85	92	92	76	94	78	74	95
No risk of collision	104	113	120	118	152	119	141	123	137	134	119
TOTAL	175	191	212	203	244	211	217	217	215	208	214
Commercial Air Transport Aircraft											
Risk of collision	4	2	4	2	6	1	5	3	5	3	7
Safety not assured	8	9	11	9	18	19	11	17	20	21	25
Dangerous incidents total	12	11	15	11	24	20	16	20	25	24	32
No risk of collision	49	44	58	51	78	67	77	56	57	71	76
TOTAL	61	55	73	62	102	87	93	76	82	95	108

Source: *Transport Statistics Great Britain 1998*, © Crown copyright 1998

Shipping

Merchant Fleets of the World

1997

Rank by total ships	Country of registry	Total number of ships	Number of container ships	Number of cruise/ passenger ships	Number of tankers	Number of bulk carriers[1]	Other
1	Panama	3,998	329	54	893	1,086	1,636
2	Russia	1,655	27	10	271	129	1,218
3	Liberia	1,587	153	38	642	461	293
4	China	1,513	97	33	233	345	805
5	Cyprus	1,476	108	18	166	555	629
6	Malta	1,113	28	9	265	337	474
7	Bahamas	954	43	47	241	142	481
8	Greece	874	35	19	266	406	148
9	Singapore	753	114	1	331	126	181
10	Japan	744	37	15	299	182	211
11	Saint Vincent	683	17	1	99	121	445
12	Norway (NIS)[2]	626	5	14	285	102	220
13	Philippines	534	14	6	65	232	217
14	Turkey	516	4	7	74	177	254
15	USA	495	83	15	173	15	209
16	Korea, South	449	65	0	105	124	155
17	Netherlands	445	40	9	71	8	317
18	Indonesia	444	5	9	118	18	294
19	Ukraine	415	11	8	29	21	346
20	Germany	404	180	11	31	1	181
	UK[3]	140	21	20	60	6	33
	World total	26,858	1,936	427	6,384	5,694	12,417

[1] Includes bulk/oil, ore/oil, and ore/bulk/oil carriers.
[2] International Shipping Registry which is an open registry under which the ship flies the flag of the specified nation but is exempt from certain taxation and other regulations.
[3] The UK is ranked 34.

Source: *Statistical Abstract of the United States 1998*, US Department of Transportation 1998

Ports Ranked by Cargo Tonnage in the UK

This table represents all foreign and domestic traffic.
1997

Rank	Port	Traffic (tonnes)	Traffic (%)
1	London	55,692,000	10.0
2	Tees and Hartlepool	51,249,000	9.2
3	Grimsby and Immingham	47,991,000	8.6
4	Forth	43,102,000	7.7
5	Milford Haven	34,518,000	6.2
6	Southampton	33,053,000	5.9
7	Sullom Voe	32,082,000	5.7
8	Liverpool	30,841,000	5.5
9	Felixstowe	28,881,000	5.2
10	Dover	19,073,000	3.4
11	Medway	13,803,000	2.5
12	Port Talbot	13,050,000	2.3
13	Belfast	12,344,000	2.2
14	Orkneys	10,483,000	1.9
15	Hull	10,047,000	1.8
16	Manchester	7,939,000	1.4
17	Rivers Hull and Humber	7,562,000	1.4
18	Clyde	7,494,000	1.3
19	Bristol	7,041,000	1.3
20	Portsmouth	4,543,000	0.8
	All above ports	470,788,000	84.3
	Other major UK ports	51,173,000	9.2
	Other UK ports	36,569,000	6.5
	ALL UK PORTS	558,530,000	100.0

Source: *Maritime Statistics 1997*, © Crown copyright, 1998

The Busiest Rivers and Inland Waterways in the UK

The table shows the volume of goods transported.
(N = nil or negligible. In billions of tonne-kilometres.)

River/waterway	Internal traffic					Seagoing traffic				
	1993	1994	1995	1996	1997[1]	1993	1994	1995	1996	1997[1]
River Thames	0.08	0.10	0.09	0.07	0.07	0.79	0.83	0.70	0.72	0.78
River Medway	N	N	N	N	N	0.05	0.06	0.06	0.04	0.05
River Severn (including Gloucester and Sharpness canal)	N	N	N	N	N	0.01	0.01	0.01	0.01	0.01
River Mersey	0.02	0.01	0.02	0.02	N	0.09	0.09	0.10	0.10	0.10
Manchester Ship Canal	0.02	0.01	0.02	0.01	0.01	0.10	0.10	0.10	0.10	0.10
River Clyde	N	N	N	N	N	0.08	0.09	0.10	0.10	0.10
River Forth	N	N	N	N	N	0.20	0.19	0.19	0.18	0.19
River Humber	0.02	0.02	0.01	0.01	0.01	0.27	0.29	0.31	0.30	0.31
River Ouse	N	N	N	N	N	0.03	0.04	0.04	0.04	0.05
Aire and Calder Navigation	0.03	0.02	0.03	0.02	0.02	N	N	N	N	N
River Trent	0.02	0.02	0.02	0.02	0.01	0.03	0.04	0.04	0.03	0.03
River Orwell	N	N	N	N	N	0.07	0.08	0.06	0.04	0.04
Total	0.18	0.20	0.18	0.16	0.13	1.73	1.81	1.70	1.67	1.76
All waterways total	0.21	0.23	0.20	0.18	0.15	1.79	1.87	1.74	1.71	1.80

[1] The data are preliminary.

Source: *Transport Statistics Great Britain 1998*, © Crown copyright 1998

World Road Transport

Countries that Drive on the Left

Anguilla
Antigua
Australia
Bahamas
Bangladesh
Barbados
Bermuda
Bhutan
Botswana
Brunei
Cook Islands
Cyprus
Dominica
Falkland Islands
Fiji Islands
Grenada
Guyana
Hong Kong
India
Indonesia
Ireland, Republic of
Jamaica
Japan
Kenya
Kiribati
Lesotho
Malawi
Malaysia
Malta
Mauritius
Montserrat
Mozambique
Namibia
Nepal
New Zealand
Norfolk Island
Pakistan
Papua New Guinea
St Kitts and Nevis
St Lucia
St Vincent and the Grenadines
Seychelles
Singapore
Solomon Islands
Somalia
South Africa
Sri Lanka
Suriname
Swaziland
Tanzania
Thailand
Tonga
Trinidad and Tobago
Tuvalu
Uganda
UK (including Guernsey, Jersey, and the Isle of Man)
Virgin Islands (British)
Zambia
Zimbabwe

Motor Vehicle Nationality Abbreviations

Many road vehicles display one or more letters to identify their nationality. These letters are in accordance with the 1968 United Nations (UN) Convention on Road Traffic and the 1949 UN Convention on Road Traffic.

Country	Abbreviation
Aden	ADN
Albania	AL
Alderney	GBA
Algeria	DZ
Andorra	AND
Argentina	RA
Australia	AUS
Austria	A
Bahamas	BS
Bahrain	BRN
Bangladesh	BD
Barbados	BDS
Belarus	SU[1]
Belgium	B
Belize	BH
Benin	DY
Bosnia-Herzegovina	BIH
Botswana	RB
Brazil	BR
Brunei	BRU
Bulgaria	BG
Cambodia	K
Canada	CDN
Central African Republic	RCA
Chile	RCH
China	RC
Congo, Democratic Republic of	ZRE
Congo, Republic of the	RCB
Costa Rica	CR
Côte d'Ivoire	CI
Croatia	HR
Cyprus	CY
Czech Republic	CZ
Denmark	DK
Dominican Republic	DOM
Ecuador	EC
Egypt	ET
Estonia	EST
Faroe Islands	FO
Fiji Islands	FJI
Finland	FIN
France	F
Gambia	WAG
Georgia	GE
Germany	D
Ghana	GH
Gibraltar	GBZ

(continued)

Motor Vehicle Nationality Abbreviations *(continued)*

Country	Abbreviation	Country	Abbreviation	Country	Abbreviation	Country	Abbreviation
Great Britain	GB	Kyrgyzstan	KS	Norway	N	Suriname	SME
Greece	GR	Laos	LAO	Pakistan	PAK	Swaziland	SD
Grenada	WG	Latvia	LV	Papua New Guinea	PNG	Sweden	S
Guatemala	GCA	Lebanon	RL	Paraguay	PY	Switzerland	CH
Guernsey	GBG	Lesotho	LS	Peru	PE	Syria	SYR
Guyana	GUY	Lithuania	LT	Philippines	RP	Tajikistan	TJ
Haiti	RH	Luxembourg	L	Poland	PL	Tanzania	EAT
Hong Kong	HK	Macedonia, Former Yugoslav Republic of	MK	Portugal	P	Thailand	T
Hungary	H	Malawi	MW	Romania	RO	Togo	TG
Iceland	IS	Malaysia	MAL	Russia	RUS	Trinidad and Tobago	TT
India	IND	Mali	RMM	Rwanda	RWA	Tunisia	TN
Indonesia	RI	Malta	M	St Lucia	WL	Turkey	TR
Iran	IR	Mauritius	MS	St Vincent	WV	Turkmenistan	TM
Ireland, Republic of	IRL	Mexico	MEX	Samoa	WS	Uganda	EAU
Isle of Man	GBM	Monaco	MC	San Marino	RSM	Ukraine	UA
Israel	IL	Morocco	MA	Senegal	SN	Uruguay	ROU
Italy	I	Myanmar	BUR	Seychelles	SY	USA	USA
Jamaica	JA	Namibia	NAM	Sierra Leone	WAL	Uzbekistan	UZ
Japan	J	Netherlands	NL	Singapore	SGP	Vatican City State	V
Jersey	GBJ	Netherlands Antilles	NA	Slovak Republic	SK	Venezuela	YV
Jordan	HKJ	New Zealand	NZ	Slovenia	SLO	Yugoslavia	YU
Kazakhstan	KZ	Nicaragua	NIC	South Africa	ZA	Zambia	RNR
Kenya	EAK	Niger	RN	Spain (including African localities and provinces)	E	Zanzibar	EAZ
Korea, South	ROK	Nigeria	WAN	Sri Lanka	CL	Zimbabwe	ZW
Kuwait	KWT						

[1] Belarus has not yet announced its new distinguishing sign. Therefore the sign 'SU' still appears on this list.

Number of Road Accident Deaths for OECD Countries

Countries other than UK are ranked by rate of road deaths (1996) per 100,000 population. (N/A = not available.)

Country	1986	1988	1990	1992	1994	1995	1996	Rate of road deaths in 1996 per 100,000 population[1]
Great Britain	5,382	5,052	5,217	4,229	3,650	3,621	3,598	6.3
Northern Ireland	236	178	185	150	157	144	142	8.5
UK total	5,618	5,230	5,402	4,379	3,807	3,765	3,740	6.4
Other countries								
Portugal	2,577	3,294	3,017	3,084	2,504	2,710	2,730	28.9
Greece	1,669	1,738	1,998	2,103	2,195	2,349	N/A	22.5[2]
Luxembourg	79	84	70	73	74	68	N/A	16.7[2]
USA	46,056	47,087	44,529	39,235	40,716	41,798	41,907	15.8
Czech Republic	915	982	1,307	1,545	1,637	1,588	1,568	15.2
France	11,947	11,497	11,215	9,900	9,019	8,891	8,541	14.7
New Zealand	766	728	729	646	580	581	514	14.1
Spain	7,045	8,252	9,032	7,818	5,615	5,751	5,483	14.0
Belgium	1,951	1,967	1,976	1,672	1,692	1,449	1,356	13.4
Hungary	1,632	1,706	2,532	2,101	1,562	1,589	1,370	13.4
Austria	1,495	1,620	1,558	1,403	1,338	1,210	1,027	12.7
Ireland, Republic of	387	463	478	415	404	437	453	12.4
Italy	7,642	7,494	7,151	8,029	7,104	7,033	6,688	12.3[2]
Australia	2,888	2,887	2,331	1,981	1,937	N/A	1,970	10.8
Germany	10,620	9,862	11,046	10,631	9,814	9,454	8,758	10.7
Canada	4,068	4,154	3,960	3,501	3,260	N/A	3,082	10.3
Denmark	723	713	634	577	546	582	514	9.8
Japan	12,112	13,447	14,595	14,886	12,768	12,670	11,674	9.3
Switzerland	1,003	917	925	834	679	692	616	8.7
Finland	612	653	649	601	480	441	404	7.9
Netherlands	1,527	1,366	1,376	1,285	1,298	1,334	1,180	7.6
Sweden	844	813	772	759	589	572	537	6.1
Norway	452	378	332	325	283	305	255	5.8
Iceland	24	29	24	21	N/A	N/A	10	3.7
Turkey	9,509	8,902	8,212	8,078	N/A	N/A	N/A	N/A

[1] Population taken from the Organization of Economic Cooperation and Development's (OECD's) International Road and Traffic Accidents Database.
[2] 1995 deaths and populations.

Source: *Transport Statistics Great Britain 1998,*

Road Transport Indicators for Selected Countries

1995

Country	Total number				Number per 1,000 persons			
	Cars	Motorcycles and mopeds	Buses	Trucks	Cars	Motorcycles and mopeds	Buses	Trucks[1]
Canada	14,280,000	30,600	65,600	7,250,000	495.5	1.1	2.3	251.6
France	25,100,000	2,990,000[2]	79,000	5,116,000	430.4	51.3	1.4	87.7
Germany	40,499,442	2,304,253	85,434	4,153,086	484.8	27.6	1.0	49.7
Japan	45,000,000	15,340,000	245,000	22,111,000	358.7	122.3	2.0	176.3
Mexico	8,330,000	268,000	131,000	3,501,043[1]	87.0	2.8	1.4	36.6
Sweden	3,630,760	117,387	14,577	307,709[1]	407.9	13.2	1.6	34.6
UK	20,780,000	601,000	107,000	2,624,000	355.3	10.3	1.8	44.9
USA	136,066,045	3,767,029	685,504	64,778,472	517.0	14.3	2.6	246.1

[1] This figure excludes tractor trailers.
[2] This figure is for 1993.

Source: Office of Highway Information Management

UK Road Transport

The Top 20 UK New Car Registrations by Model Range

1998

Rank	Model range	Registrations	Market share (%)
1	Ford Fiesta	116,110	5.17
2	Ford Escort	113,560	5.05
3	Ford Mondeo	99,729	4.44
4	Vauxhall Vectra	92,719	4.13
5	Renault Megane	82,998	3.69
6	Vauxhall Astra	81,494	3.63
7	Vauxhall Corsa	75,673	3.37
8	Peugeot 306	70,169	3.12
9	Rover 200	64,928	2.89
10	Rover 400	57,318	2.55
11	Renault Clio	57,231	2.55
12	Fiat Punto	52,159	2.32
13	Peugeot 106	51,458	2.29
14	Nissan Micra	48,757	2.17
15	Volkswagen Polo	48,402	2.15
16	Peugeot 406	48,242	2.15
17	Volkswagen Golf	42,354	1.88
18	Citroên Saxo	38,916	1.73
19	BMW 3 Series	37,219	1.66
20	Honda Civic	36,791	1.64
Top 20 total		1,316,227	58.57
Market total		2,247,402	100.00

Source: Society of Motor Manufacturers and Traders Ltd

Top 10 Automatic Cars in the UK by Model Range

1998

Rank	Model range	Sales	Market share (%)
1	Mercedes C Class	16,821	5.52
2	Mercedes E Class	14,169	4.65
3	BMW 5 Series	11,027	3.62
4	Vauxhall Vectra	8,816	2.89
5	Vauxhall Omega	8,744	2.87
6	Jaguar V8 XJ Range	8,660	2.84
7	Ford Mondeo	7,577	2.48
8	BMW 3 Series	7,443	2.44
9	Renault Megane	7,166	2.35
10	Nissan Micra	7,105	2.33
Top 10 total		97,528	31.99
Automatics total		304,915	13.57
Market total		2,247,402	100.00

Source: Society of Motor Manufacturers and Traders Ltd

The Top 10 Diesel Cars in the UK by Model Range

1998

Rank	Model range	Sales	Market share (%)
1	Peugeot 306	37,337	10.87
2	Peugeot 406	23,500	6.84
3	Ford Mondeo	19,892	5.79
4	Vauxhall Vectra	15,411	4.49
5	Vauxhall Astra	15,188	4.42
6	Ford Escort	14,860	4.33
7	Volkswagen Passat	13,803	4.02
8	Volkswagen Golf	11,167	3.25
9	Peugeot 106	10,839	3.16
10	Rover 400	10,597	3.09
Top 10 total		172,594	50.26
Diesels total		343,372	15.28
Market total		2,247,402	100.00

Source: Society of Motor Manufacturers and Traders Ltd

Number of Motor Vehicles Registered in the UK for the First Time

Year			All vehicles
1951			413,900
1955			906,500
1960			1,369,400
1965			1,600,700
1970			1,524,900
1975			1,749,900
1980			2,155,800
1985			2,309,300
1990			2,438,700
1991			1,921,500
1992			1,901,800
1993			2,074,000
1994			2,249,000
1995			2,306,500
1996			2,410,100
1997	Private and light goods	2,244,300	
	Goods vehicles	41,800	
	Motor cycles, etc	121,300	
	Public transport vehicles	6,600	
	Special machines and special concessionary	21,700	
	Other vehicles	161,700	
	1997 total		2,597,700

Source: *Transport Statistics Great Britain 1998*, © Crown copyright 1998

The Most Popular Colours of Car in Use in Great Britain

1998

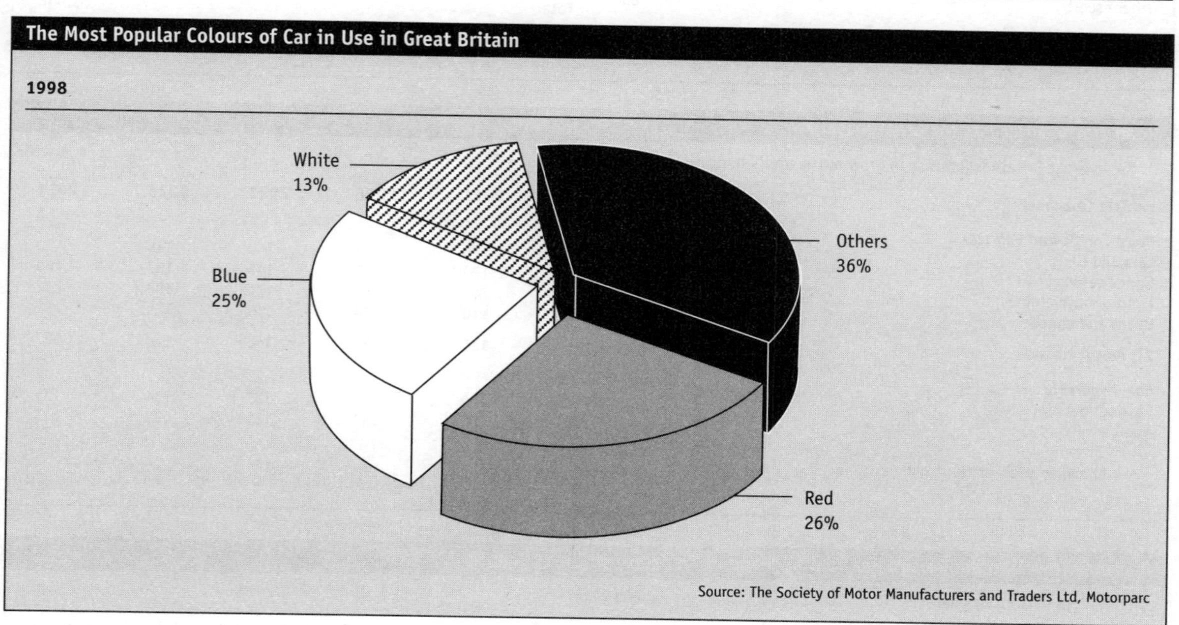

Source: The Society of Motor Manufacturers and Traders Ltd, Motorparc

Seat Belt Laws in the UK

(– = not applicable.)

Vehicle occupants	Front seat	Rear seat	Who is responsible
Driver	seat belt must be worn if available	–	driver
Children aged under 3 years	appropriate child restraint[1] must be used	appropriate child restraint[1] must be used if available	driver
Children aged 3–11 years, and under 1.5 m (approximately 5 ft) in height	appropriate child restraint[1] must be worn if available; if not, adult seat belt must be used	appropriate child restraint[1] must be worn if available; if not, adult seat belt must be worn if available	driver
Children aged 12 or 13 or younger children 1.5 m (approximately 5 ft) or more in height	adult seat belt must be worn if available	adult seat belt must be worn if available	driver
Adult passengers	seat belt must be worn if available	seat belt must be worn if available	passenger

[1] An appropriate child restraint is a baby carrier, child seat harness, or booster seat suitable for the weight of the child using it.

Average Number of Journeys Made per Year per Person in the UK

This table includes journeys under one mile.

Purpose	Number of journeys	Purpose	Number of journeys
Commuting	162	Other personal business	106
Business	37	Visiting friends	185
Education and escorting to education	119	Social/entertainment/holidays/day trips	93
Shopping	222	Other, including just walking	45
Other escort	83	**Total**	1,052

Source: *Transport Statistics Great Britain 1998,* © Crown copyright 1998

Road Traffic Forecasts for Great Britain

Traffic in Great Britain is forecast to grow to the levels indicated 1996 = 100.)

Vehicle forecasts	2001	2006	2011	2016	2021	2026	2031
Road Traffic and Vehicles							
Cars and taxis	107	116	125	133	140	145	150
Goods vehicles[1]	106	114	123	133	145	157	169
Light goods vehicles	112	125	140	156	174	193	212
Buses and coaches	103	106	110	114	119	125	132
All motor traffic	107	116	126	135	143	150	157
Car Ownership							
Cars per person	106	114	120	126	131	134	139
Number of cars	107	116	123	130	135	139	143

[1] Over 3.5 tonnes gross vehicle weight.

Source: *Transport Statistics Great Britain 1998,* © Crown copyright 1998

Distance Travelled per Person per Year by Mode of Transport in Great Britain

(In miles per person per year.)

Mode of travel	1975–76	1985–86	1995–97
Car	3,194	3,796	5,187
Surface rail	284	292	294
Van/lorry	182	228	262
Other local bus	369	258	202
Walking (including short walks)	248	244	195
Private hire bus	149	131	105
Non-local bus	50	109	93
Other public transport including air	17	22	7
London Transport Underground	34	44	51
Buses in London	57	39	50
Taxi/minicab	13	27	43
Other private vehicle	15	33	40
Bicycle	51	44	39
Motorcycle/moped	47	51	30
All modes total	4,710	5,317	6,666

Source: *Transport Statistics Great Britain 1998,* © Crown copyright 1998

Total Road Lengths in the UK

(In kilometres.)

Road type		1986	1988	1990	1992	1994	1996	1997
		Length						
Trunk roads		15,359	15,472	15,666	15,358	15,203	15,540	15,563
Class 1 or principal		34,969	35,041	35,226	35,712	35,867	35,901	35,834
Class 2 or B		29,121	29,681	29,838	30,227	30,347	30,196	30,364
Class 3 or C		80,360	80,165	80,716	81,334	82,105	82,528	82,907
Unclassified		191,267	193,957	196,588	199,679	201,445	204,656	205,199
TOTAL ROADS		351,076	354,315	358,034	362,310	364,966	368,821	369,867
Of which	trunk motorway	2,820	2,891	2,993	3,063	3,092	3,181	3,250
	principal motorway	101	102	77	71	76	45	45
	Total motorway	2,920	2,992	3,070	3,133	3,168	3,226	3,294

Source: *Transport Statistics Great Britain 1998,* © Crown copyright 1998

Principal Motorways in the UK

For roads consisting of motorway and other types of road, the length is given for the motorway part only.

Motorway	Destinations	Length
M1	London–Leeds	304 km/189 mi
M11	London–Cambridge	98 km/61 mi
M18	Rotherham–Goole	56 km/35 mi
M180	Doncaster–Grimsby	82 km/51 mi
M2	Gravesend–Faversham	53 km/33 mi
M20	London–Folkestone	117 km/73 mi
M23	London–Crawley	45 km/28 mi
M25	London orbital	188 km/117 mi
M27	Cadnam–Portsmouth	55 km/34 mi
M3	London–Southampton	129 km/80 mi
M4	London–Llanelli	325 km/202 mi
M40	London–Birmingham	193 km/120 mi
M42	Bromsgrove–Ashby-de-la-Zouch	79 km/49 mi
M5	Birmingham–Exeter	266 km/165 mi
M53	Wallasey–Chester	39 km/24 mi
M54	Wolverhampton–Telford	37 km/23 mi
M55	Preston–Blackpool	29 km/18 mi
M56	Manchester–Chester	39 km/24 mi
M6	Rugby–Carlisle	362 km/225 mi
M74	Glasgow–Abington	103 km/64 mi
M61	Manchester–Preston	50 km/31 mi
M62	Liverpool–Kingston Upon Hull	206 km/128 mi
M63	Salford–Stockport	32 km/20 mi
M65	Bamber Bridge–Colne	45 km/28 mi
M66	Ramsbottom–Stockport	35 km/22 mi
M8	Edinburgh–Greenock	109 km/68 mi
M9	Edinburgh–Dunblane	64 km/40 mi
M90	Rosyth–Perth	48 km/30 mi
A1(M)	London–Newcastle	230 km/143 mi
A74(M)	Gretna–Abington	77 km/48 mi
Northern Ireland		
M1	Belfast–Dungannon	66 km/41 mi
M2	Belfast–Ballymena	42 km/26 mi

Breath Tests Undertaken in Great Britain by Age and Gender

The table shows the percentage of car drivers involved in personal injury accidents who were given breath tests.

1997

Age	Men		Women	
	% tested	% failed	% tested	% failed
Under 17	40.8	12.3	41.4	6.9
17–19	61.9	3.8	50.0	1.0
20–24	57.6	4.6	45.6	1.0
25–29	53.7	3.8	42.8	0.9
30–34	51.1	3.0	41.6	0.9
35–39	52.1	2.9	43.0	1.1
40–49	51.5	2.3	43.4	0.9
50–59	52.7	1.7	44.2	0.8
60–69	51.5	1.1	43.8	0.4
70 and over	50.6	0.9	41.2	0.5
All ages[1]	51.7	2.8	42.7	0.9

[1] Figures include age unknown.

Source: *Social Trends 29,* © Crown copyright 1999

Drink Driving and Breath Tests in Great Britain

The legal alcohol limits in the UK are as follows: 35 microgrammes of alcohol in 100 millilitres of breath, 80 milligrammes of alcohol in 100 millilitres of blood, and 107 milligrammes of alcohol in 100 millilitres of urine.
(N/A = not available.)

Incidents and breath tests	1992	1993	1994	1995	1996	1997
Car drivers involved in injury accidents in Great Britain						
number involved	313,325	312,695	322,813	317,957	330,880	338,741
number breath tested[1]	90,277	88,262	91,879	99,582	133,261	157,299
% of drivers involved tested	29	28	28	31	40	46
number positive	6,892	6,171	6,366	6,637	7,302	7,084
% positive	8	7	7	7	5	5
Motorcycle riders in injury accidents in Great Britain						
number involved	27,631	25,804	25,072	24,162	23,694	25,117
number breath tested[1]	5,773	5,413	5,141	5,702	7,872	9,895
% of drivers involved tested	21	21	21	24	33	39
number positive	555	451	450	438	408	427
% positive	10	8	9	8	5	4
Screening breath tests administered in England and Wales						
number of tests required	531,000	600,000	679,000	703,000	781,000	860,000
proportion positive (%)[1]	17	15	14	13	13	12

[1] Includes refusals.

Source: *Transport Statistics Great Britain 1998,* © Crown copyright 1998

Number of Road Accident Deaths in the UK

Road user type		1987	1997
Pedestrians	Children	264	138
	Adults	1,435	835
	Total pedestrians	1,699	973
Cyclists	Children	79	33
	Adults	201	150
	Total cyclists	280	183

Road user type	1987	1997
Motorcyclists[1] and passengers	723	509
Car drivers and passengers	2,206	1,795
Bus/coach drivers and passengers	15	14
LGV and HGV drivers and passengers	186	109
TOTAL	5,109	3,583
All road users[2]	5,125	3,599

[1] These figures include mopeds and scooters.
[2] These figures include other motor or non-motor road users, and unknown vehicle type and casualty age.

Source: *Transport Statistics Great Britain 1998,* © Crown copyright 1998

Car User Casualties in Great Britain by Age and Gender

Figures are car user casualty rates per 1,000 population.
1997

Age	Men			Women		
	Drivers	Passengers	All car users	Drivers	Passengers	All car users
17–21	7.6	4.4	12.0	5.3	4.7	10.0
22–39	4.4	1.1	5.6	4.1	1.8	5.8
40–59	2.5	0.4	2.9	2.1	1.2	3.3
60 and over	1.6	0.3	1.8	0.6	1.0	1.6
All aged 17 and over[1]	3.4	1.0	4.4	2.6	1.6	4.2

[1] Figures include age unknown.

Source: *Social Trends 29,* © Crown copyright 1999

Rail Transport

Railtrack and the Rail Network in the UK

Under the Conservative government's 1993 Railway Act the old British Rail was split up and sold off. This process was completed by November 1997, by which time British Rail had been divested of all its operating railway functions. The different functions of managing the track, the trains, services, and subsidiary aspects (such as property and policing) are now in a variety of hands.

The British Railways Board (BRB) has retained responsibility for non-operational land, and for the British Transport Police. It also advises the government on railway policy and improving accountability. Railtrack owns the track infrastructure, the stations, and access, and is the front-line provider for the freight and passenger services.

Railtrack runs 14 stations itself, the rest being leased to the 25 Train Operating Companies (TOCs). It also has responsibility for planning and coordinating the train paths and timetables.

The TOCs run the passenger services in specific regions and have to publish a Passengers' Charter to set out the minimum service standards.

The new rail network is accountable to the Office of the Rail Regulator (ORR) and the Office of Passenger Rail Franchising (OPRAF). Set up in 1993, the ORR has a chief executive independent of ministerial control. Its main functions and duties are to issue the licenses to operate trains, networks, and stations; the enforcement of domestic competition in rail services; consumer and passenger protection; and the promotion of the use of passenger and freight services. OPRAF monitors and manages the TOCs with a strong emphasis on protecting passengers' interests and investment in the services. OPRAF is a non-ministerial government department, and works closely with the OPR and with the BRB. The objectives of OPRAF are broadly to increase the number of rail passengers, and promote passenger services by managing the franchises of the train operators. This includes enforcing ticket pricing policy and imposing financial penalties on operators who fail to meet their passenger obligations.

By the end of 1999 the functions of each of these organizations will be subsumed into the Strategic Rail Authority (SRA), which will take over the management of all areas, from franchise licensing to promoting passenger interests.

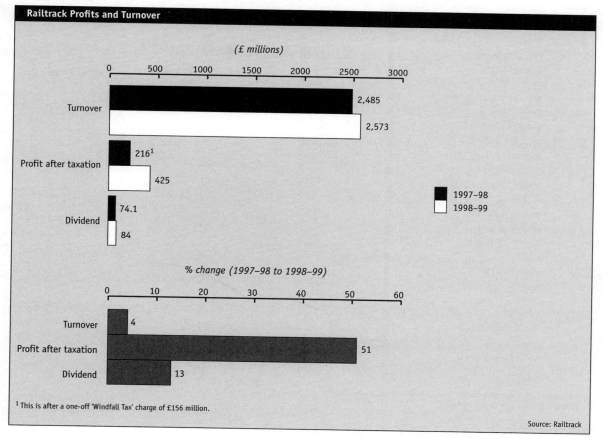

Railtrack Profits and Turnover

(£ millions)

	1997–98	1998–99
Turnover	2,485	2,573
Profit after taxation	216[1]	425
Dividend	74.1	84

% change (1997–98 to 1998–99)

	% change
Turnover	4
Profit after taxation	51
Dividend	13

[1] This is after a one-off 'Windfall Tax' charge of £156 million.

Source: Railtrack

Average Train Fares Paid in the UK

Figures are for pence per mile (ppm).
(N/A = not available.)

Financial year	National average fare paid[1]	% change year on year	% change year on year for all items in the Retail Price Index
1985–86	7.00	N/A	N/A
1990–91	9.80	7.69	6.40
1991–92	10.50	7.14	4.30
1992–93	10.80	2.86	1.30
1993–94	11.50	6.48	2.60
1994–95	12.10	5.22	3.30
1995–96	12.58 (12.71)[2]	3.97	2.40
1996–97	13.01	2.36	2.40
1997–98	13.40	3.00	4.00

[1] Figures from 1985–86 to 1995–96 are from British Rail annual reports; figures thereafter produced by TCI Rail.
[2] Figure is from TCI Rail, post privatization.

Source: The Shadow Strategic Rail Authority (Formerly OPRAF)

Performance of Train Companies in the UK

1998

Overall grade[1]	Subsidy operator	% of trains late	Punctuality grade	% of trains cancelled	Reliability grade	Subsidy (pence per passenger mile)
A	Island Line	5.0	A	0.4	A	63
B	Scotrail	4.1	A	0.6	B	21
	Merseyrail Electrics	4.7	A	0.8	B	37
	Central[2]	6.9	B	0.5	A	23
	Anglia	8.0	B	0.5	A	8
	West Anglia Great Northern	8.8	B	0.9	B	4
	Great Eastern	9.2	B	0.4	A	2
	Gatwick Express	9.9	B	0.4	B	–8
C	LTS Rail	6.0	B	1.5	C	6
	Northern Spirit	6.5	B	1.1	C	24
	Wales & West	8.8	B	1.4	C	13
	Connex South Central	10.0	B	1.1	C	4
	Thameslink	10.1	C	1.5	C	–1
	Midland Mainline	10.2	C	0.2	A	1
	South West Trains	10.5	C	0.6	B	3
	Great North Eastern	11.7	C	0.8	B	2
	Chiltern	13.6	C	0.6	B	6
	Virgin West Coast	14.1	C	0.5	A	3
D	North Western Trains	9.1	B	1.8	D	36
	Cardiff	13.7	C	1.9	D	33
	Great Western	15.5	D	1.0	B	4
	Connex South Eastern	16.2	D	1.3	C	5
	Thames Trains	16.3	D	1.4	C	5
	Virgin CrossCountry	17.7	D	0.7	B	8
E	Silverlink	8.8	B	2.1	E	7

[1] The overall grade is determined by the lower of each company's grades (A to E).
[2] Central's figures exclude 'Centro' services.

Source: The Shadow Strategic Rail Authority (Formerly OPRAF)

National Rail Length and London Underground Statistics in the UK

(N/A = not available.)

Year	Length of National Rail[1] route			Passengers on National Rail[2]		London Underground	
	Total route (km)	Electrified route (km)	Open to passenger traffic (km)	Passenger journeys (millions)	Passenger kilometres (billions)	Passenger journeys (millions)	Passenger kilometres (billions)
1900	29,783	N/A	N/A	N/A	N/A	N/A	N/A
1923	32,462	1,122	N/A	1,772	N/A	N/A	N/A
1946	31,963	N/A	N/A	1,266	47.0	569	N/A
1955	30,676	1,577	23,820	994	32.7	676	5.6
1965	24,011	2,886	17,516	865	30.1	657	4.7
1975	18,118	3,655	14,431	730	30.9	601	4.8
1984/85	16,816	3,798	14,304	701	29.5	672	5.4
1989/90	16,587	4,546	14,318	758	33.3	765	6.0
1990/91	16,584	4,912	14,317	762	33.2	775	6.2
1991/92	16,558	4,886	14,291	741	32.5	751	5.9
1992/93	16,528	4,910	14,317	745	31.7	728	5.8
1993/94	16,536	4,968	14,357	713	30.4	735	5.8
1994/95	16,542	4,970	14,359	702	28.7	764	6.1
1995/96	16,666	5,163	15,002	788	30.0	784	6.3
1996/97	16,666	5,176	15,034	N/A	32.2	772	6.2
1997/98	16,656	5,166	15,024	846	34.2	832	6.5

[1] From 1994/95 route length is for Railtrack.

[2] From 1995/96 passenger traffic is for National Rail and former British Rail Train Operating Companies.

Source: *Transport Statistics Great Britain 1998,* © Crown copyright 1998

Channel Tunnel Traffic to and from Europe

	1994	1995	1996	1997
Passenger vehicles on shuttles[1]	82,000	1,246,000	2,135,000	2,383,000
Freight vehicles on shuttles[1]	65,000	391,000	519,000	268,000
All vehicles on shuttles[1]	147,000	1,637,000	2,654,000	2,651,000
Number of passengers on shuttles and through trains[2]	315,000	7,081,000	12,799,000	14,613,000
Through-train freight (tonnes)	452,000	1,692,000	2,334,000	2,900,000

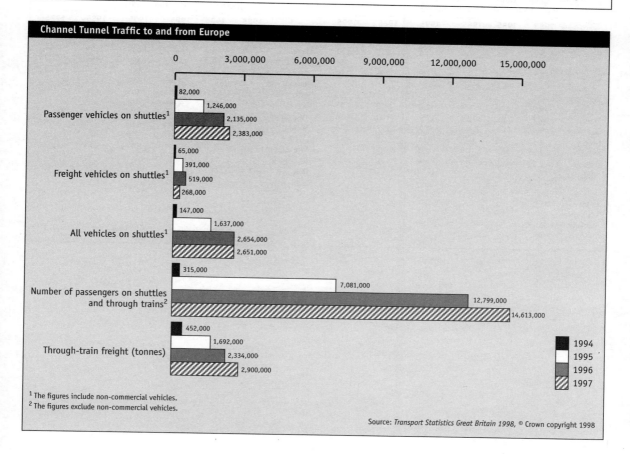

[1] The figures include non-commercial vehicles.

[2] The figures exclude non-commercial vehicles.

Source: *Transport Statistics Great Britain 1998,* © Crown copyright 1998

Train Accidents in the UK

(N/A = not available.)

Type of accident	1987	1988	1989	1990	1991/92	1992/93	1993/94	1994/95	1995/96	1996/97[1]	1997/98
Collisions	290	296	329	290	187	154	135	125	123	120	126
Derailments	193	231	192	183	144	205	113	149	104	119	93
Running into level crossing gates and other obstructions	391	486	510	473	340	532	445	397	488	741	682
Fires	191	229	283	257	225	202	247	217	256	302	344
Damage to drivers' cab windscreens[2]	N/A	N/A	N/A	N/A	N/A	N/A	N/A	N/A	N/A	468	619
Miscellaneous	101	88	120	80	64	59	37	19	18	3	0
Total	1,166	1,330	1,434	1,283	960	1,152	977	907	989	1,753	1,864

[1] New accident reporting regulations (RIDDOR 95) came into force on 1 April 1996.

[2] Category now reportable under RIDDOR 95.

Source: *Transport Statistics Great Britain 1998,* © Crown copyright 1998

International Comparisons of Rail Infrastructures

(N = nil or negligible. N/A = not available.)

Country	Rail network in operation (km thousands)		Of which electrified (km thousands)		Rail network per 1,000 sq km	
	1985	1995	1985	1995	1985	1995
Austria	5.8	5.7	3.1	3.3	68	67
Belgium	3.7	3.4	1.9	2.4	123	111
Croatia	2.4	2.7[1]	0.8	1.0	43	48
Czech Republic	13.1	9.4[1]	3.3	2.6	166	119
Denmark	2.5	2.3	0.1	0.4	57	53
Finland	5.9	5.9	1.4	2.0	18	17
France	34.7	31.9	11.4	13.7	63	58
Germany	45.4	41.7	13.9	17.7	127	116
Greece	2.5	2.5	N/A	N/A	19	19
Hungary	7.8	7.8[1]	1.9	2.3	84	84
Ireland, Republic of	1.9	1.9	N	N	28	28
Italy	16.2	16.0	10.3	9.9[1]	53	53
Japan	21.1	20.3	11.2[2]	11.9[1]	56	54
Luxembourg	0.3	0.3	0.2	0.3	104	106
Netherlands	2.8	2.7	1.8	2.0[1]	70	68
Norway	4.2	3.8[1]	2.4	2.4	13	12
Portugal	3.6	2.9	0.5	0.5	39	30
Slovak Republic	N/A	3.7[1]	N/A	1.4	N/A	75
Spain	12.7	12.3[3]	6.4	6.9[1]	30	25
Sweden	11.3	9.8	7.6	7.2	27	23
Switzerland	5.1	5.1[1]	5.1	5.1[1]	123	124
UK	17.5	16.9	3.8	5.1	70	70
USA	225.4	174.2	1.7	1.7[1]	26	19

[1] 1994 data.

[2] Estimated.

[3] National railways only.

Source: *Transport Statistics Great Britain 1998,* © Crown copyright 1998

Tourism

The UK's Top 20 Fee-Paying Tourist Attractions

(– = not applicable.)

Rank	Attraction	Number of visits 1996	1997
1	Madame Tussaud's, London	2,715,000	2,799,000
2	Alton Towers, Staffordshire	2,749,000	2,702,000
3	Tower of London	2,539,272	2,615,000
4	Natural History Museum, London	1,607,255	1,793,000
5	Chessington World of Adventures, Surrey	1,700,000	1,750,000
6	Canterbury Cathedral	1,700,000	1,613,000
7	Science Museum, London	1,548,286	1,537,000
8	Legoland, Windsor	1,420,511	1,298,000
9	Edinburgh Castle	1,165,132	1,238,000
10	Blackpool Tower, Lancashire	1,200,000	1,200,000
11	Windermere Lake Cruises, Cumbria	1,034,188	1,132,000
12	Windsor Castle, Berkshire	1,215,631	1,130,000
13	Flamingo Land Theme Park, Yorkshire	1,161,000	1,103,000
14	London Zoo	1,002,104	1,098,000
15	Victoria and Albert Museum, London	–	1,041,000
16	Drayton Manor Park, Staffordshire	937,296	1,002,000
17	St Paul's Cathedral, London	1,002,000	965,000
18	Kew Gardens, London	993,527	937,000
19	Roman Baths and Pump Room, Bath	902,186	934,000
20	Thorpe Park, Surrey	1,139,680	912,000

Source: British Tourist Authority and Star UK

Number of International Visitors to the UK by Country of Origin

Country	Number of visitors 1994	1995	1996	1997	% change 1994–97
France	2,762,000	3,184,000	3,690,000	3,586,000	30
USA	2,907,000	3,146,000	3,080,000	3,432,000	18
Germany	2,503,000	2,654,000	2,963,000	2,911,000	16
Ireland, Republic of	1,677,000	1,988,000	2,078,000	2,232,000	33
Netherlands	1,188,000	1,408,000	1,539,000	1,653,000	39
Belgium	975,000	1,296,000	1,554,000	1,345,000	38
Italy	818,000	924,000	924,000	990,000	21
Spain	675,000	772,000	807,000	825,000	22
Australia	552,000	607,000	650,000	684,000	24
Canada	562,000	609,000	595,000	667,000	19
Japan	578,000	619,000	584,000	570,000	−1
Sweden	514,000	552,000	639,000	616,000	20
Switzerland	469,000	541,000	578,000	567,000	21
Norway	334,000	427,000	406,000	453,000	36
Total	16,514,000	18,727,000	20,087,000	20,531,000	24
Other countries	4,280,000	4,810,000	5,076,000	4,984,000	16
WORLD TOTAL	20,794,000	23,537	25,163,000	25,515,000	23

Source: International Passenger Survey, © Key Note Ltd

The UK's Top Free Tourist Attractions

Destinations listed are those attracting 2 million or more people each year.

1997

Albert Dock, Liverpool
Blackpool Pleasure Beach
The British Museum, London
Eastbourne Pier
Magical World of Fantasy Island, Lincolnshire
The National Gallery, London
The Palace Pier, Brighton
Pleasureland Amusement Park, Southport
Strathclyde Country Park
Sutton Park, Sutton Coldfield
Westminster Abbey, London
York Minster

Source: British Tourist Authority and Star UK

World Heritage sites in the UK

There are 17 World Heritage sites in the UK. First determined in 1972 by UNESCO (United Nations Educational, Scientific, and Cultural Organization), World Heritage sites are 'places or buildings of outstanding universal value'. Dates given are the years each site was added to the list.

1986 The Giant's Causeway and Causeway coast
1986 Durham castle and cathedral
1986 Ironbridge Gorge
1986 Studley Royal Park, including the ruins of Fountains Abbey
1986 Stonehenge, Avebury, and associated sites
1986 The castles and town walls of King Edward in Gwynedd
1986 St Kilda, Outer Hebrides
1987 Blenheim Palace
1987 City of Bath
1987 Hadrian's Wall
1987 Palace of Westminster, Abbey of Westminster, and St Margaret's church
1988 Henderson Island (in the South Pacific)
1988 The Tower of London
1988 Canterbury Cathedral, St Augustine's Abbey, and St Martin's Church
1995 Old and New Towns of Edinburgh
1995 Gough Island Wildlife Reserve (in the Atlantic)
1997 Maritime Greenwich

Overseas Visitors to the UK by Age

Age	1995 (%)	1996 (%)	1997 Number	1997 %
15 and under	9.1	8.9	1,867,000	8.0
16–24	15.5	14.5	3,356,000	14.4
25–34	22.0	22.6	5,368,000	23.1
35–44	21.0	21.2	4,956,000	21.3
45–54	19.3	19.5	4,577,000	19.7
55–64	8.6	8.5	2,002,000	8.6
65 and over	4.6	4.9	1,157,000	5.0
Total	100.0	100.0	23,283,000	100.0

Source: International Passenger Survey, © Key Note Ltd

Visits to and Expenditure in the UK by Overseas Residents

	1994	1995	1996	1997	1998[1]	% change 1994–98
Numbers of visits	20,794,000	23,537,000	25,163,000	25,515,000	26,025,000	25.2
Nights spent in the UK (millions)	192	220	220	223	224	16.7
Expenditure in UK (£ millions)	9,786	11,763	12,290	12,244	12,734	30.1
Real expenditure at 1994 prices (£ millions)	9,786	11,488	11,589	11,285	11,379	16.3

[1] 1998 figures are estimates.

Source: International Passenger Survey, © Key Note Ltd

UK Travellers' Favourite Destinations in the UK

1997

Region	Trips (millions)	Nights (millions)	Spending (£ millions)
Cumbria	3.3	11.2	350
Northumbria	3.3	14.9	350
Northwest England	10.0	26.1	1,050
Yorkshire	10.0	33.6	933
Heart of England	16.7	44.8	1,283
East of England	14.5	52.2	1,516
London	14.5	29.8	1,050
West Country	16.7	82.1	2,800
Southern England	12.3	41.0	1,283
Southeast England	11.2	37.3	1,050
England total	111.5	373.1	11,665
Scotland	11.1	48.5	1,690
Wales	10.0	41.8	1,125
Northern Ireland	1.1	5.0	290
TOTAL UK[1]	133.6	473.6	15,075

[1] Total columns may not add up due to rounding.

Source: United Kingdom Tourist Survey, © Key Note Ltd

UK Travellers' Favourite Destinations in the World

Country	Number of travellers 1994	1995	1996	1997	% change 1994–97
France	8,973,000	9,645,000	9,834,000	11,149,000	24.3
Spain	7,676,000	8,239,000	7,545,000	8,281,000	7.9
Ireland, Republic of	2,491,000	2,809,000	3,169,000	3,613,000	45.0
USA	2,472,000	2,657,000	3,079,000	3,028,000	22.5
Germany	1,887,000	1,899,000	1,898,000	2,023,000	7.2
Netherlands	1,399,000	1,364,000	1,532,000	1,756,000	25.5
Italy	1,528,000	1,600,000	1,558,000	1,801,000	17.9
Greece	2,164,000	2,056,000	1,460,000	1,512,000	-30.1
Portugal	1,179,000	1,211,000	1,102,000	1,304,000	10.6
Belgium	959,000	1,077,000	1,421,000	1,419,000	48.0
Turkey	716,000	856,000	1,032,000	998,000	39.4
Cyprus	971,000	669,000	709,000	713,000	-26.6
Austria	587,000	600,000	415,000	425,000	-27.6
Switzerland	570,000	516,000	509,000	580,000	1.8
Total	33,572,000	35,198,000	35,263,000	38,602,000	15.0
Other countries	6,058,000	6,147,000	6,787,000	7,355,000	21.4
WORLD TOTAL	39,630,000	41,345,000	42,050,000	45,957,000	16.0

Source: International Passenger Survey, © Key Note Ltd

The World's Top 10 Tourism Destinations

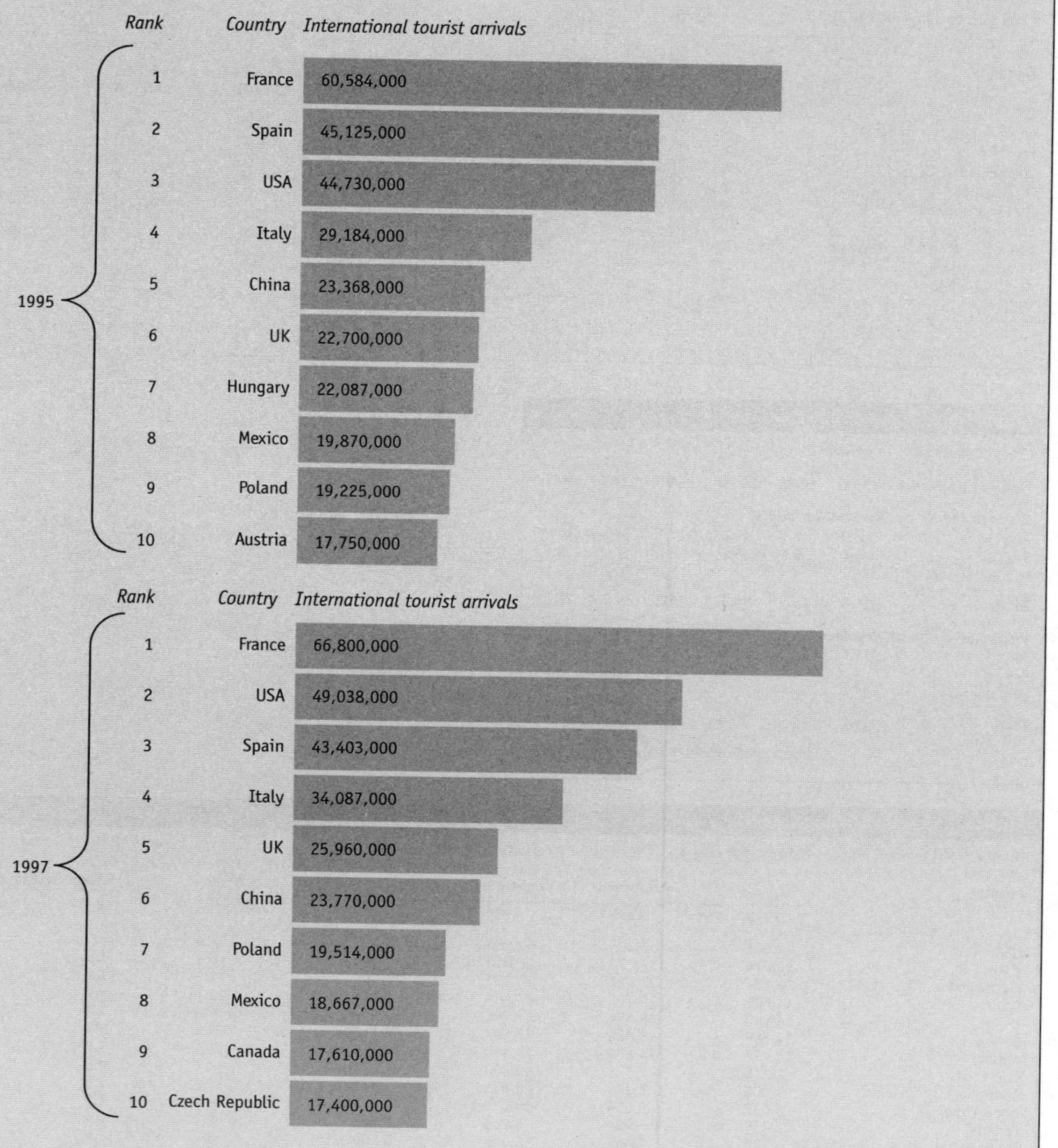

Year	*Rank*	*Country*	*International tourist arrivals*
1995	1	France	60,584,000
	2	Spain	45,125,000
	3	USA	44,730,000
	4	Italy	29,184,000
	5	China	23,368,000
	6	UK	22,700,000
	7	Hungary	22,087,000
	8	Mexico	19,870,000
	9	Poland	19,225,000
	10	Austria	17,750,000

Year	*Rank*	*Country*	*International tourist arrivals*
1997	1	France	66,800,000
	2	USA	49,038,000
	3	Spain	43,403,000
	4	Italy	34,087,000
	5	UK	25,960,000
	6	China	23,770,000
	7	Poland	19,514,000
	8	Mexico	18,667,000
	9	Canada	17,610,000
	10	Czech Republic	17,400,000

Source: World Tourism Organization

Factors Affecting Holiday Choice

Figures are percentages of a weighted sample of 801 UK adults.

1998 (for holidays in 1999)

Factor	All adults	Men	Women	Age				
				16–24	25–34	35–44	45–64	65+
Low air fares	62	59	65	71	63	60	63	56
Family considerations	61	61	61	59	59	72	62	52
Cheap holiday deals	59	58	61	73	68	59	54	48
UK weather	43	44	43	42	36	46	46	46
Personal workload	39	43	36	48	44	51	41	10
Exchange rates	36	35	36	28	26	32	41	45
Economic slow-down/recession	34	34	33	29	27	40	42	25
Interest rates	28	23	33	22	19	31	32	30
Abolition of duty free	19	18	19	28	14	15	19	21
Millennium	17	19	16	32	14	16	17	12

Source: The Gallup Organization, © Key Note Ltd

International Travel to and from the UK

(– = not applicable. In millions.)

Mode of transport	1981	1986	1991	1995	1996	1997
Visits to the UK by Overseas Residents						
Air	6.9	8.9	11.6	15.8	16.3	16.9
Sea	4.6	5.0	5.5	6.0	6.2	5.7
Channel tunnel	–	–	–	1.8	2.7	2.9
Total	11.5	13.9	17.1	23.5	25.2	25.5
Visits Abroad by UK Residents						
Air	11.4	16.4	20.4	28.1	27.9	30.3
Sea	7.7	8.6	10.4	11.3	10.7	11.5
Channel tunnel	–	–	–	1.9	3.5	4.1
Total	19.0	24.9	30.8	41.3	42.1	46.0

Source: *Social Trends 29,* © Crown copyright 1999

Tourism Receipts: Leading Countries

International tourism receipts indicate the revenue generated for a country by international visitors.

Country	Total receipts ($ millions) 1990				% change	% of world total	
	1990	1995	1996	1997	1996–97	1990	1997
USA	43,007	63,395	69,908	75,056	7.4	16.0	16.9
Italy	20,016	27,723	30,018	30,000	–0.1	7.5	6.8
France	20,184	27,527	28,357	27,947	–1.5	7.5	6.3
Spain	18,593	25,701	27,654	27,190	–1.7	6.9	6.1
UK	14,940	18,554	19,296	20,569	6.6	5.6	4.6
Germany	14,288	18,028	17,567	16,418	–6.5	5.3	3.7
Austria	13,417	14,593	13,990	12,393	–11.4	5.0	2.8
China	2,218	8,733	10,200	12,074	18.4	0.8	2.7
Australia	4,088	7,375	8,811	9,324	5.8	1.5	2.1
Hong Kong	5,032	9,604	10,836	9,242	–14.7	1.9	2.1
Canada	6,339	7,994	8,868	8,928	0.7	2.4	2.0
Thailand	4,326	7,664	8,664	8,700	0.4	1.6	2.0
Poland	358	6,600	8,400	8,700	3.6	0.1	2.0
Singapore	4,904	8,378	7,961	7,993	0.4	1.8	1.8
Switzerland	7,411	9,365	8,891	7,960	–10.5	2.8	1.8
Mexico	5,467	6,179	6,934	7,530	8.6	2.0	1.7
Turkey	3,225	4,957	5,962	7,000	17.4	1.2	1.6
Indonesia	2,105	5,228	6,087	6,589	8.3	0.8	1.5
Belgium	3,721	5,719	5,893	5,997	1.8	1.4	1.4
World total	268,310	401,475	433,863	443,770	2.3	100.0	100.0

Source: World Tourism Organization

Ecotourism: Positive Strategy or Marketing Ploy?

BY SUE BERRY

'Ecotourism' is sometimes regarded as a rather nebulous term used to give tourism greater respectability. The Ecotourism Society – an organization for professionals involved in tourism – defines ecotourism as 'responsible travel to natural areas that conserves the environment and sustains the well-being of local people' (Mowforth and Munt, *Tourism and Sustainability*, Routledge, London, 1998). Is this a genuinely attainable goal and deliberate strategy, or just another marketing ploy in an industry that is becoming ever more anxious to be perceived as credible and respectable? Tourism is a very diverse area of business, as it includes the development, management, and marketing not only of tours but also of destinations and travel facilities. It is becoming increasingly harder to monitor the movements and activities of tourists and travellers, as more choose to devise, plan, and undertake trips on their own, without the mediation of an agency or a tour organizer. How, then, in such a vast and diverse sector can responsible travel be encouraged and natural areas protected?

Tourism distribution

In spite of the familiar, alluring advertisements of faraway places beside palm-fringed beaches, reached by sleek aeroplanes, holidays within our own country or quite nearby are still quite popular. This is particularly true of wealthy countries, such as the USA, or regions of a similar scale, such as the European Union (EU). Indeed, in most developed countries, domestic tourists put the most pressure on their own surroundings; international visitors, often receiving adverse press, are in fact in the minority and therefore impact less on the environment. It is in smaller and less affluent regions, especially in South America and in and around the Pacific, that international travellers have a disproportionate effect on the environment.

So how can the ethos that underlies ecotourism reduce the impact of millions of domestic and inbound leisure and business travellers on the environment? Does that ethos even survive intact? Paradoxically, ecotourism has now become one of the most rapidly growing domains of the tourism industry, particularly in its outbound, exploratory sector. It is therefore often identified as a niche marketing slant that is effectively selling unique aspects of our ecosystem to tourists.

Who are the ecotourists?

In practice, most 'ecotourists' are aged between 45 and 64 and fit, roughly speaking, within four categories. The 'hard core', as it were, are the professionals who have a vested interest in the environment, such as scientists and teachers. Dedicated travellers who seek to learn about places and people are the second group. The third group are mainstream tourists who are seeking new experiences and may happen to choose a trip to the Galapagos or to see the gorillas in Rwanda. Finally, there are the 'accidental' ecotourists who happen to include a tour to a natural site within their holiday trip, most of which is actually spent on the beach and by the bar.

Precise figures are not easy to establish, but in the USA, tour operators estimate that between 4 and 6 million Americans now travel overseas annually (and so become international or outbound tourists) for nature-related trips. Popular destinations include Costa Rica and other places with exotic landscapes and wildlife. Within the USA there are an estimated 80 million birdwatchers and scores of enthusiastic scuba- and skin-divers, many of whom have an interest in marine wildlife. This data alone would indicate that there could potentially be a very large market for 'nature-based' holidays and activities.

Profitability

Thus, ecotourism has the potential to make developing and less-known regions more profitable by creating a respectable market niche in them. That could be very positive because visitors bring in money that helps support such areas. Having been there, they may also exert pressure to help gain resources to protect an area and even help by contributing resources themselves. However, it appears that such direct benefits from visitors are limited. Research indicates that international visitors on ecotourism package holidays do not spend much money in the locality they are visiting other than on accommodation and on food. Most also expect comfort and convenience, which puts a lot of pressure on fragile environments. The tourism-carrying capacity of these areas is low and we are exceeding it in many fragile areas.

> *Paradoxically, ecotourism has now become one of the most rapidly growing domains of the tourism industry.*

The problem in attempting to make the impact of tourism more advantageous is that tourism does not function in a vacuum: people travel to work, move goods, live in, and extract a living from, the same environment. We have done so for so long that few places have remained totally unspoilt and 'natural'.

Appreciation

Areas designated as 'protected' achieve that status because governments and other public, charitable, or private bodies have deemed supporting such a venture beneficial and valuable. It is also clear that many people cherish such places, to the extent that the National Trust, for example, now finds that fundraising for the purchase and protection of landscapes that are perceived as natural, distinctive, and high profile (such as Snowdonia in Wales) becomes easier than raising money for the restoration and maintenance of country houses. However, these areas must then earn some income to help pay for their management, for no matter what many visitors may think, all such places have to be managed today in order to cope with the impacts that visitors have, and will have, upon them, and that requires sufficient finance. Many people who go to fragile areas such as Antarctica,

the Lake District in England, or the Yellowstone National Park in the USA, either do not appear to realize that they are wearing away the landscape, or refuse to accept this altogether. However, their impact is far-reaching and includes eroding the footpaths, causing fires, leaving litter that has to be removed, damaging indigenous plants, absorbing space for car parks, to name but a few. Tourism needs to become a vital source of income to offset the wear and tear that visitors cause and also to keep the landscape as we wish to see it.

Potential solutions

If it is possible to awaken the consciences of more of us about the impact we make on the landscape and on the environment in general as we travel, then any emphasis on responsible tourism that helps to reduce the wear and tear on these fragile locations should be encouraged. The tourism industry does use the uniqueness of natural areas as a means of marketing tours such as those to Antarctica and Nepal. The industry can do much to help us consider the environmental implications of our travel by, for example, choosing appropriate approaches to sell such trips. The public sector, as legislators and managers of many fragile areas, can also help by limiting access whenever that is viable. The final test of responsible tourism may be the use of pricing strategies: as the conservation of fragile areas depends on limited access, visitors may find camp sites and other accommodation expensive, seemingly out of proportion to the facilities offered on-site.

Sue Berry is principal lecturer in Tourism Management, University of Brighton

Web Sites

AirSpace

http://www.raes.org.uk/

Online magazine of the Royal Aeronautical Society.

Allstar Network – History of Flight

http://www.allstar.fiu.edu/aero/history1.htm

Three-level guide to the history of aviation beginning with the myths and legends which abounded before flight became a reality.

Allstar Network – Principles of Flight

http://www.allstar.fiu.edu/aero/princ1.htm

Three-level guide to flight and aviation, involving images, explanations, and experiments to demonstrate the physics behind flight.

Automotive Learning Online

http://www.innerbody.com/innerauto/Default.htm

Fun, interactive, and educational site on the automobile. It is a great training resource for engineering minds but also suited to all those who would simply like to know how their car works.

Aviation Enthusiasts' Corner

http://www.brooklyn.cuny.edu/rec/air/air.html

Forum dedicated to furthering interest in aviation-related hobbies. It includes links to museums and displays, features on key events in aviation history, and indexes of aircraft by type and manufacturer.

Canals: Panoramic Photographs, 1851–1991

http://lcweb2.loc.gov/cgi-bin/query/r?ammem/pan:(canal)

Part of the Panoramic Photo Collection of the US Library of Congress, this page features more than 70 photographs of canals, most of which were taken at the turn of the 20th century.

European Railway Server

http://mercurio.iet.unipi.it/home.html

Complete source of information about the railways of Europe. The needs of travellers, railway enthusiasts, and students of public transport are provided for.

EV Information Network

http://www.radix.net/~futurev/

Comprehensive information on electrically powered vehicles (EVs), including electric car events, and details of manufacturers and suppliers.

Helicopter Aviation Home Page

http://www.copters.com/

Contents include a history of the helicopter, technical aerodynamic details of what keeps them in the air, a profile of mechanical components, advice to novice pilots, various helicopter manuals, and images of helicopters.

How Do Planes Fly?

http://observe.ivv.nasa.gov/nasa/exhibits/planes/planes_1a.html

Explanation of the whys and hows connected with the flight of an aeroplane.

International Civil Aviation Organization

http://www.icao.int

Site of the specialized UN agency regulating civil aviation. The role and history of the ICAO are well presented.

National Railway Museum, York

http://www.nmsi.ac.uk/nrm/html/home_pb/menu.htm

Information for railway enthusiasts. In addition to information about the National Railway Museum and its exhibitions, there is news of railway matters from around the world, and a listing of other relevant sites.

Office of Passenger Rail Franchising (OPRAF)

http://www.opraf.gov.uk/

OPRAF is the organization that monitors the 25 passenger train franchises operating on the UK railway network. Its Web site contains relevant documents, news, and a list of 'Frequently asked questions'.

164 Currency Converter

http://www.oanda.com/cgi-bin/ncc

This simple to-use-site allows you to do automatic conversions to and from a wide range of currencies.

Railtrack – The Heart of the Railway

http://www.railtrack.co.uk/home.html

User-friendly Railtrack site which aims to simplify the planning of a railway journey in Britain. Input your destination and time of departure and a timetable appears.

RMS Titanic, Inc

http://www.titanic-online.com/

Official site of RMS Titanic, Inc, the company responsible for recovering artefacts from the shipwreck.

UK Travel Guide

http://www.uktravel.com/index.html

Essential resource for anyone planning to travel in the UK. It includes an A–Z of practical information from accommodation to the weather.

Welcome to IYHF

http://www.iyhf.org/iyhf/ehome.html

Site of the International Youth Hostel Federation. There is general information on the history and structure of the federation and links to national organizations. Reservations in hostels around the world may also be made through this site.

The Environment and Climate

The Year in Review

5 July 1998–25 July 1998 Temperatures in Texas and Oklahoma remain above 38° C/100°F for 20 consecutive days in the worst drought in the area since 1980. Over 100 people die and $4.6 billion/£2.8 billion damage is done to the Texan economy. El Niño is blamed for the high temperatures, which continue into August.

9 July 1998 Friends of the Earth and other environmental advocacy groups in the UK condemn a plan approved by the government to widen the M25 between junctions 12 and 15 to the west of London. They claim that additional road capacity generates more traffic.

17 July 1998 A 10-m/30-ft tidal wave hits the north coast of Papua New Guinea, inundating several villages and killing an estimated 6,000 people. Of the survivors 70 percent are adults; a generation of children is wiped out.

31 July 1998 The British government announces plans to build a 2 km/1.2 mi tunnel to hide part of the busy London to Exeter road next to Stonehenge, with the possibility of closing the road next to Stonehenge and creating a grassy area around the monument. The intention is to protect the monument and other prehistoric earthworks in the World Heritage Site.

26 August 1998 British environmental activist Mathew Williams, aged 11, wins a reprieve against an order to evict him and his mother from their tree house in Epsom, Surrey, England. They are living in the tree as a protest against plans to build an access road for shoppers in a park next to the Epsom town hall.

26 August 1998 Hurricane Bonnie hits Cape Fear, North Carolina, USA, with winds up to 210 kph/130 mph. Half a million people are ordered to evacuate.

September 1998 The Cuban government passes the country's first forest conservation law, to protect and increase its remaining forests, comprising 21 percent of the land. Twenty of Cuba's bird species and more than a hundred of its reptiles and amphibians occur nowhere else in the world.

9 September 1998 Flooding continues to threaten Dhaka, Bangladesh's capital, as thousands of troops and civilians attempt to fortify an embankment protecting the city. The rains, which began on 10 July, are the worst in Bangladesh's history, causing more than 850 deaths and making a quarter of the 124 million population homeless.

25 September 1998 Hurricane Georges, with winds up to 62 kph/100 mph, hits the Florida Keys, in the USA, after ravaging the Caribbean, killing more than 300 people. Eighty thousand people are ordered to evacuate the Keys.

October 1998 A restoration project costing an estimated $7.8 million is planned for the Everglades, Florida, USA, over the next 20 years. It aims to return the area to how it was 50 years ago, before the intervention by the US Army Corps of Engineers. The army built canals and levees and drained marshland for agriculture and building. The project will affect 28,000 sq km/10,800 sq mi of land from Orlando to the Florida Keys.

October 1998 A study in the UK reveals that tritium pollution in the Severn Estuary in 1998 resulted in levels of tritium being hundreds of times higher than would normally be expected. Tritium is discharged into the Severn from a chemical plant in Cardiff.

October 1998 The size of the hole in the ozone layer is measured as three times the size of the USA, bigger than it has ever been before. Its cause may be the adverse effects of El Niño on the climate.

6 October 1998 Ministers of the European Union accept a voluntary agreement by European car manufacturers to cut carbon dioxide emissions from new cars by 25 percent by 2008. Only 3 percent of current new cars would meet the new standard.

November 1998 The Golden Mountains of the Altai range in central Asia are made a World Heritage Site. They cover 1,611,457 hectares and contain rare and endangered species, including snow leopards.

2 November 1998 Britain's Meteorological Office predicts that large areas of the Amazon rainforest will begin to die in around 2050, releasing carbon into the atmosphere and causing global warming to accelerate faster than previously forecasted.

2 November 1998 Tropical storm Mitch rages through Honduras with a death toll of as many as 5,000 people there and more than 7,000 people in total, including victims in neighbouring El Salvador and Nicaragua. In the worst storm to hit Central America this century, floods and landslides cause mass destruction.

2 November 1998–14 November 1998 Delegates from more than 160 countries attend a summit in Buenos Aires, Argentina, to discuss implementing the 1997 Kyoto Protocol to reduce global warming. Participants agree to devise strategies by 2000 for reducing emissions of greenhouse gases.

6 November 1998 Hurricane Mitch continues its path of destruction in Honduras, Guatemala, Nicaragua, and El Salvador, leaving at least 11,000 dead and 2 million homeless.

16 December 1998 A report compiled for a House of Lords select committee concludes that the stored nuclear waste in Britain poses serious dangers, with the risk of fires, explosions, and leaks of radioactive materials.

17 December 1998 The United Nations World Meteorological Organization reports that 1998 is the warmest year ever, with a global average temperature of 14.4°C/58°F. Many scientists blame the greenhouse effect, caused by the burning of industrial gases.

17 December 1998 The Worldwide Fund for Nature warns that Indonesian forest fires are threatening the extinction of orang-utans.

25 January 1999 An earthquake measuring six on the Richter scale hits western Colombia, flattening the city of Armenia. Initial counts estimate more than 1,000 dead.

7 February 1999 A report published by the environmental group Friends of the Earth estimates that British factories spill 10,000 tons of chemicals that can cause cancer into the environment every year. The report names the British company Associated Octel, which makes leaded additives for petrol, as the worst offender.

9 February 1999 Extreme winter weather conditions strike the Alps, with a snowfall of 2 m/7 ft in less than 4 days. In Argentière, France, an avalanche kills at least ten people and injures 27.

24 February 1999 Avalanches in two ski resorts in the Austrian Alps kill 38 people. The avalanches are a result of the region's heaviest snowfall in 50 years.

March 1999 A study published by Swiss chemists reveals that European rain contains high levels of dissolved pesticides which lead to unacceptably high pesticide levels in drinking water.

9 March 1999 British chancellor of the exchequer, Gordon Brown, announces the Labour government's first 'green' tax package, which includes a levy on the use of energy by businesses, designed to reduce the emission of greenhouse gases.

22 March 1999 Britain's Environment Agency publishes a list of the worst polluting British companies. The chemical company ICI, which was fined nearly £400,000 in 1998 for spilling more than 400 tons of chemicals into the environment, is named the worst polluter.

May 1999 The European Union votes to ban white asbestos by 2005.

4 May 1999 The fiercest tornadoes in the USA for more than 10 years strike Oklahoma and Kansas, causing at least 36 deaths and 700 injuries, shattering thousands of homes, and destroying whole neighbourhoods.

7 May 1999 The Green Party, whose primary political agenda is the protection of the environment, has its first British MP when Robin Harper is elected to the Scottish Parliament.

11 June 1999 Environmentalists from Scottish Natural Heritage report that a colony of bottlenose dolphins in Moray Firth could die out within 50 years due to pollution, human disturbance, and changes in the water temperature. The colony attracts a large number of tourists to the Highlands.

23 June 1999 According to the 1999 World Disasters Report, published by the Red Cross, refugees from environmental disasters such as drought, floods, and deforestation totalled 25 million in 1998, outnumbering war refugees for the first time.

Animals and Plants

Classification of Living Things

Classification is the grouping of organisms based on similar traits and evolutionary histories. Taxonomy and systematics are the two sciences that attempt to classify living things. In taxonomy, organisms are generally assigned to groups based on their characteristics. In modern systematics, the placement of organisms into groups is based on evolutionary relationships among organisms. Thus, the groupings are based on evolutionary relatedness or family histories called phylogenies.

The groups into which organisms are classified are called taxa (singular, taxon). The taxon that includes the fewest members is the species, which identifies a single type of organism. Closely related species are placed into a genus (plural, genera). Related genera are placed into families, families into orders, orders into classes, classes into phyla (singular, phylum) or – in the case of plants and fungi – into divisions, and phyla into divisions or kingdoms. The kingdom level, of which five are generally recognized, is the broadest taxonomic group and includes the greatest number of species. The table below provides an example of the classification of an organism representative of the animal kingdom and the plant kingdom.

Taxonomic Groups[1]

Common name	*Kingdom*	*Phylum/division*[2]	*Class*	*Order*	*Family*	*Genus*[3]	*Species*[3]
human	Animalia	Chordata	Mammalia	Primates	Hominoidea	*Homo*	*sapiens*
Douglas fir	Plantae	Tracheophyta	Gymnospermae	Coniferales	Pinaceae	*Pseudotsuga*	*douglasii*

[1] Intermediate taxonomic levels can be created by adding the prefixes 'super-' or 'sub-' to the name of any taxonomic level.
[2] The term division is generally used in place of phylum/phyla for the classification of plants and fungi.
[3] An individual organism is given a two-part name made up of its genus and species names. For example, Douglas fir is correctly known as *Pseudotsuga douglasii*.

The Five Kingdoms of Living Things

Kingdom	Main features of organisms	Number of species
Monera[1]	all are bacteria; single-celled; prokaryotic (lack a membrane-bound nucleus); autotrophic (photosynthesis and chemosynthesis) and heterotrophic; all reproduce asexually, some also reproduce sexually	>10,000
Protista	single-celled or multicelled; eukaryotic (have a membrane-bound nucleus and membrane-bound organelles); autotrophic (photosynthesis in algae and Euglenoids) and heterotrophic; may reproduce asexually or sexually	>100,000
Fungi	single-celled and multicellular; eukaryotic; heterotrophic; form spores at all stages of their life cycle; usually reproduce asexually, many reproduce sexually by conjugation	about 100,000
Plantae	all are multicellular; eukaryotic; most are autotrophic (via photosynthesis); reproduce sexually; in some life cycle includes an alternation of generations (a haploid gametophyte stage and a diploid sporophyte stage)	>250,000
Animalia	all are multicellular; eukaryotic; all are heterotrophic; reproduce sexually; develop from a blastula; most have tissues organized into organs	>1,000,000

[1] The Kingdom Monera is sometimes called the Kingdom Prokaryotae.

Native Species of Animals and Plants in Britain

As of 1997.

Species group	Number of native species
Animals	
Mammals breeding on land	44
Birds	551
Non-marine reptiles	6
Marine reptiles	1
Amphibians	6/7
Freshwater fish	38
Flies	*c.* 6,600
Bees, wasps, ants	542
Beetles	*c.* 4,000
Butterflies, moths	*c.* 2,600
Caddis flies	199
True bugs	540
Grasshoppers, crickets, cockroaches	30
Stoneflies	34
Dragonflies, damselflies	41
Mayflies	48
Spiders, harvestmen, pseudoscorpions	*c.* 687
Larger non-marine crustaceans	*c.* 70
Non-marine molluscs	*c.* 208
Leeches	16
Plants and Other Organisms	
Seed plants	*c.* 2,230
Ferns and related plants	70
Liverworts, mosses	*c.* 1,000
Lichens	>1,700
Stoneworts	30
Fungi	>20,000
Slime moulds	*c.* 350

Source: *Digest of Environmental Statistics No 20, 1998,* © Crown copyright 1998

Plants

Major Divisions in the Plant Kingdom

Phylum	Examples
Bryophyta	mosses, liverworts, hornworts
Psilophyta	whisk ferns
Lycophyta	club mosses
Sphenophyta	horsetails
Filicinophyta	ferns
Cycadophyta	cycads
Ginkgophyta	*Ginkgo*
Coniferophyta	cedar, cypress, juniper, pine, redwood
Anthophyta	flowering plants
Classes of Flowering Plants	
Dicotyledons	magnolia, laurel, water lily, buttercup, poppy, pitcher plant, nettle, walnut, cacti, peonies, violet, begonia, willow, primrose, rose, maple, holly, grape, honeysuckle, African violet, daisy
Monocotyledons	flowering rush, eel grass, lily, iris, banana, orchid, sedge, pineapple, grasses, palms, cat tail

Classification of Carnivorous Plants

Plants that obtain at least some of their nutrition by capturing and digesting prey are called carnivorous plants. Such plants have adaptations that allow them to attract, catch, and break down or digest prey once it is caught. Estimates of the number of species of carnivorous plants number from 450 to more than 600. Generally, these plants are classified into genera based upon the mechanism they have for trapping and capturing their prey. The major genera of these plants are listed in the table.

Common name	Genus	Scientific name	Trapping mechanism
bladderwort	*Utricularia*	*Utricularia vulgaris*	active trap; shows rapid motion during capture
butterwort	*Pinguicula*	*Pinguicula vulgaris*	semi-active trap; two-stage trap in which prey is initially caught in sticky fluid
calf's head pitcher plant	*Darlingtonia*	*Darlingtonia californica*	passive trap; attracts prey with nectar and then drowns prey in fluid contained within plant
flypaper plant	*Byblis*	*Byblis liniflora*	passive trap; attracts prey with nectar and then drowns prey in fluid contained within plant
sundew	*Drosera*	*Drosera linearis*	semi-active trap; two-stage trap in which prey is initially caught in sticky fluid
Venus flytrap	*Dionaea*	*Dionaea muscipula*	active trap; shows rapid motion during capture

Animals

Major Invertebrate and Vertebrate Groups

Phyla are listed in order of the most primitive to the most advanced.

Taxon[1]	Name	Examples
Invertebrates		
P	Porifera	all sponges
P	Cnidaria	corals, sea anemones, *Hydra*, jellyfishes
P	Ctenophora	sea gooseberries, comb jellies
P	Platyhelminthes	flatworms, flukes, tapeworms
P	Nemertina	nemertine worms, ribbon worms
P	Rotifera	rotifers or wheel animals
P	Nematoda	roundworms
P	Ectroprata	ectopracts
P	Mollusca	clams, oysters, snails, slugs, octopuses, squids, cuttlefish
P	Annelida	ringed worms, including lugworms, earthworms, and leeches
P	Arthropoda	(subdivided into classes below)
C	Arachnida	spiders, ticks, scorpions, mites
C	Branchiopoda	water fleas
C	Cirripedia	barnacles
C	Malacostraca	crabs, lobsters, shrimp, woodlice
C	Diplopoda	millipedes
C	Chilopoda	centipedes
C	Insecta	silverfish, dragonflies, mayflies, stoneflies, cockroaches, earwigs, web spinners, termites, booklice, lice, grasshoppers, thrips, lace-wings, scorpion flies, caddis-flies, moths, butterflies, beetles, house flies, fleas, stylopids, ants, bees
P	Echinodermata	sea stars, brittle stars, sea urchins, sand dollars, sea cucumbers
P	Hemichordata	acorn worms, pterobranchs, graptolites
Vertebrates		
C	Agnatha	(jawless fishes) lampreys, hagfishes
C	Chondricthyes	(cartilaginous fishes) dogfishes, sharks, rays, skates
C	Osteichthyes	(bony fishes) sturgeons, eels, herrings, salmon, carps, catfishes, perches, flatfishes including flounder and halibut
C	Amphibia	caecilians, salamanders, newts, toads, frogs
C	Reptilia	turtles, tortoises, tuatara, lizards, snakes, crocodiles
C	Aves	ostriches, rheas, penguins, divers, pelicans, flamingoes, ducks, falcons, pheasants, cranes, gulls, pigeons, parrots, cuckoos, owls, swifts, kingfishers, sparrows
C	Mammalia	platypus, echidnas, kangaroos, opossums, shrews, bats, rats, anteaters, rabbits, dogs, whales, elephants, manatees, horses, tapirs, camels, pigs, lemurs, monkeys, humans

[1] P represents phylum; C represents class.

Classification of Mammals

Order	Number of species	Examples
Leading class: Mammalia		
Subclass: Prototheria (egg-laying mammals)		
Monotremata	3	echidna, platypus
Subclass: Theria		
Infraclass: Metatheria (pouched mammals)		
Marsupiala	266	kangaroo, koala, opossum
Infraclass: Eutheria (placental mammals)		
Rodentia	1,700	rat, mouse, squirrel, porcupine
Chiroptera	970	all bats
Insectivora	378	shrew, hedgehog, mole
Carnivora	230	cat, dog, weasel, bear
Primates	180	lemur, monkey, ape, human
Artiodactyla	145	pig, deer, cattle, camel, giraffe
Cetacea	79	whale, dolphin
Lagomorpha	58	rabbit, hare, pika
Pinnipedia	33	seal, walrus
Edentata	29	anteater, armadillo, sloth
Perissodactyla	16	horse, rhinoceros, tapir
Hyracoidea	11	hyrax
Pholidota	7	pangolin
Sirenia	4	dugong, manatee
Dermoptera	2	flying lemur
Proboscidea	2	elephant
Tubulidentata	1	aardvark

Classification of Major Bird Groups

Orders listed from the most primitive to the most advanced.

Order	Examples
Struthioniformes	ostrich
Rheiformes	rhea
Casuariiformes	cassowary, emu
Apterygiformes	kiwi
Tinamiformes	tinamous
Sphenisciformes	penguin
Gaviiformes	loon
Podicipediformes	grebe
Procellariformes	albatross, petrel, shearwater, storm petrel
Pelecaniformes	pelican, booby, gannet, frigate bird
Ciconiiformes	heron, ibis, stork, spoonbill, flamingo
Anseriformes	duck, goose, swan
Falconiformes	falcon, hawk, eagle, buzzard, vulture
Galliformes	grouse, partridge, pheasant, turkey
Gruiformes	crane, rail, bustard, coot
Charadriiformes	wader, gull, auk, oyster-catcher, plover, puffin, tern
Columbiformes	dove, pigeon, sandgrouse
Psittaciformes	parrot, macaw, parakeet
Cuculiformes	cuckoo, roadrunner
Strigiformes	owl
Caprimulgiformes	nightjar, oilbird
Apodiformes	swift, hummingbird
Coliiformes	mousebird
Trogoniformes	trogon
Coraciiformes	kingfisher, hoopoe
Piciformes	woodpecker, toucan, puffbird
Passeriformes	finch, crow, warbler, sparrow, weaver, jay, lark, blackbird, swallow, mockingbird, wren, thrush

Classification of Fish

Orders listed from the most primitive to the most advanced.

Order	Number of species	Examples
Class Agnatha (jawless fishes)		
Subclass Cyclostomota (scaleless fish with round mouths)		
Petromyzoniformes	30	lamprey
Myxiniformes	30	hagfish
Superclass Pisces (jawed fishes)		
Class Chondrichthyes (cartilaginous fishes)		
Subclass Elasmobranchii (sharks and rays)		
Selachii	>200	shark
Batoidei	>300	skate, ray
Subclass Holocephali (rabbitfishes)		
Chimaeriformes	20	chimaera, rabbitfish
Class Osteichthyes (bony fishes)		
Subclass Sarcopterygii (lobe-finned fishes)		
Coelacanthiformes	1	coelacanth
Ceratodiformes	1	Australian lungfish
Lepidosireniformes	4	South American and African lungfish
Subclass Actinopterygii (ray-finned fishes)		
Polypteriformes	11	bichir, reedfish
Acipensiformes	25	paddlefish, sturgeon
Superorder Teleostei		
Elopiformes	12	bonefish, tarpon, ladyfish
Anguilliformes	>500	eel
Clupeiformes	390	herring, anchovy
Osteoglossiformes	7	arapaima, African butterfly fish
Mormyriformes	150	elephant-trunk fish, featherback
Salmoniformes	160	salmon, trout, smelt, pike
Gonorhynchiformes	15	milkfish
Ostariophsi	6,000	carp, barb, characin, loache, catfish
Myctophiformes	300	deep-sea lantern fish, Bombay duck
Paracathopterygii	853	toadfish, trout-perch, codfish
Atheriniformes	575	flying fish, toothcarp, halfbeak
Gasterosteiformes	150	stickleback, pipefish, seahorse
Pleuronectiformes	402	flatfish, flounder
Tetraodontiformes	250	puffer fish, triggerfish, sunfish
Perciformes	6,500	perch, cichlid, damsel fish, gobie, wrass, parrotfish, gourami, marlin, mackerel, tuna, swordfish, spiny eel, mullet, barracuda, sea bream, croaker, ice fish, butterfish

Classification of Insects

Order	Number of species	Examples
Class insecta		
Subclass Apterygota (wingless insects)		
Collembola[1]	2,000	springtails
Diplura	660	two-pronged bristletails, campodeids, japygids
Protura	120	minute insects living in soil
Thysanura	600	three-pronged bristletails, silverfish
Subclass Pterygota (winged insects or forms secondary wingless), *incorporating two superorders:*		
Superorder Exopterygota *(young resemble adults but have externally-developing wings)*		
Ephemeroptera	2,000	mayflies
Odonata	5,000	dragonflies, damselflies
Grylloblattodea	12	wingless soil-living insects of North America
Plecoptera	3,000	stoneflies
Zoraptera	20	tiny insects living in decaying plants
Isoptera	2,000	termites
Dermaptera	1,500	earwigs
Embioptera	200	web-spinners
Dictyoptera	3,700	cockroaches, praying mantises
Orthoptera	24,000	crickets, grasshoppers, locusts, mantids, roaches
Phasmida	2,500	stick insects, leaf insects
Psocoptera	1,600	booklice, barklice, psocids
Mallophaga	2,500	biting lice, mainly parasitic on birds
Anoplura	250	sucking lice, mainly parasitic on mammals
Hemiptera	39,500	true bugs, including shield- and bedbugs, froghoppers, pond skaters, water boatmen
Homoptera	45,000	aphids, cicadas, hoppers, whiteflies
Thysanoptera	5,000	thrips
Superorder Endopterygota *(young, unlike adults, undergo sudden metamorphosis)*		
Neuroptera	4,500	lacewings, alderflies, snakeflies
Mecoptera	450	scorpion flies
Lepidoptera	138,000	butterflies, moths
Trichoptera	7,000	caddisflies
Diptera	150,000	true flies, including bluebottles, mosquitoes, leatherjackets, midges
Siphonaptera	1,750	fleas
Hymenoptera	130,000	bees, wasps, ants, sawflies, chalcids
Coleoptera	250,000	beetles, including weevils, ladybirds, glow-worms, woodworms, chafers

[1] Some zoologists recognize the Collembola taxon as a class rather than an order.

Animal Lifespans

(N/A = not available.)

Animal	Average longevity (years)	Maximum longevity (years)[1]
Ass	12	35.8
Baboon	20	35.5
Bear (black)	18	36.8
Bear (grizzly)	25	47
Bear (polar)	20	34.7
Beaver	10	20.5
Buffalo (American)	15	N/A
Camel (Bactrian)	12	N/A
Cat (domestic)	12	28
Chimpanzee	40	44.5
Chipmunk	6	8
Cow	15	30
Deer (white-tailed)	8	N/A
Dog (domestic)	12	20
Elephant (African)	60	80
Elephant (Asian)	60	80
Elk	15	26.5
Fox (red)	7	14
Giraffe	25	33.5
Goat (domestic)	8	8
Gorilla	35	50
Guinea pig	4	7.5
Hippopotamus	45	49
Horse	20	46
Kangaroo	12	28
Leopard	12	19.3
Lion	15	25
Monkey (rhesus)	15	N/A
Moose	12	N/A
Mouse (domestic white)	1	3.5
Mouse (meadow)	3	N/A
Opossum (American)	2	8
Pig (domestic)	10	27
Puma	12	19
Rabbit (domestic)	5	13
Rhinoceros (black)	15	N/A
Rhinoceros (white)	20	N/A
Sea lion (California)	12	28
Sheep (domestic)	12	20
Squirrel (grey)	10	N/A
Tiger	16	26.3
Wolf (grey)	12	20
Zebra (Grant's)	15	35

[1] Maximum longevity figures refer to animals in captivity; an animal's potential lifespan is rarely attained in nature.

Average Animal Gestation Periods and Incubation Times

Animal	Gestation[1]/ incubation[2] (days)
Mammals	
Ass	365
Baboon	187
Bear (black)	210
Bear (grizzly)	225
Bear (polar)	240
Beaver	122
Buffalo (American)	270
Camel (Bactrian)	410
Cat (domestic)	58–65
Chimpanzee	230
Chinchilla	110–120
Chipmunk	31
Cow	279–292
Deer (white-tailed)	201
Dog (domestic)	58–70
Elephant (Asian)	645
Elk (Wapiti)	240–250
Fox (red)	52
Giraffe	420–450
Goat (domestic)	145–155
Gorilla	257
Guinea pig	68
Hippopotamus	225–250
Horse	330–342
Kangaroo	42
Leopard	92–95
Lion	108
Llama	330
Mink	40–75
Monkey (rhesus)	164
Moose	240–250
Mouse (domestic white)	19
Mouse (meadow)	21
Muskrat	28–30
Opossum (American)	12–13
Otter	270–300
Pig (domestic)	112–115
Porcupine	112
Puma	90
Rabbit (domestic)	30–35
Raccoon	63
Rhinoceros (black)	450
Seal	330
Sea lion (California)	350
Sheep (domestic)	144–151
Squirrel (grey)	30–40
Tiger	105–113
Whale (sperm)	480–500
Wolf	60–68
Zebra (Grant's)	365
Birds	
Chicken	20–22
Duck	26–28
Finch	11–14
Goose	25–28
Parrot	17–31
Pheasant	24
Pigeon	10–18
Quail	21–23
Swan	33–36
Turkey	28

[1] Mammals.
[2] Birds.

Speeds of Animals

Animal	Speed	
	kph	mph
Cheetah	103	64
Wildebeest	98	61
Lion	81	50
Elk	72	45
Cape hunting dog	72	45
Coyote	69	43
Horse	69	43
Grey fox	68	42
Hyena	64	40
Zebra	64	40
Greyhound	63	39
Whippet	57	35.5
Rabbit (domestic)	56	35
Jackal	56	35
Reindeer	51	32
Giraffe	51	32
White-tailed deer	48	30
Wart hog	48	30
Grizzly bear	48	30
Cat (domestic)	48	30
Human	45	28
Elephant	40	25
Black mamba snake	32	20
Squirrel	19	12
Pig (domestic)	18	11
Chicken	14	9
Giant tortoise	0.27	0.17
Three-toed sloth	0.24	0.15
Garden snail	0.05	0.03

Collective Names for Animals

Animal	Collective name
Ants	colony, swarm, nest
Badgers	cete
Bears	sleuth, sloth
Bees	grist, swarm, hive, nest, colony
Birds	flight, volery, flock
Boars	sounder
Cats	clowder, clutter, litter
Cattle	drove, herd
Chicks	brood, clutch
Clams	bed
Cranes	sedge, siege
Crows	murder
Deer	herd
Dogs	litter, kennel, pack (wild)
Ducks	brace, team, flock
Elephants	herd
Elks	gang
Fishes	school, shoal, draught
Foxes	leash, skulk
Geese	flock, gaggle, skein
Gnats	cloud, horde
Goats	tribe, trip, herd
Goldfinches	chirm, charm
Gorillas	band
Greyhounds	leash
Hares	down, husk
Hawks	cast
Horses	pair, team, herd, stable
Hounds	pack, cry, mute
Kangaroos	mob, troop, herd
Larks	exaltation
Leopards	leap
Lions	pride
Monkeys	troop
Mules	span
Nightingales	watch
Oxen	yoke, drove, herd
Oysters	bed
Partridge	covey
Peacocks	muster, ostentation
Pheasants	nest, nide
Pigs	litter
Plovers	congregation
Quails	bevy, covey
Rhinoceroses	crash
Rooks	parliament
Seals	pod, herd, rookery
Sheep	drove, flock, trip
Swans	bevy, wedge
Swine	drift, sounder
Teals	spring
Termites	colony, nest, swarm
Toads	knot
Turtles	bale, dole, rafter
Vipers	nest
Whales	gam, pod, herd
Wolves	pack

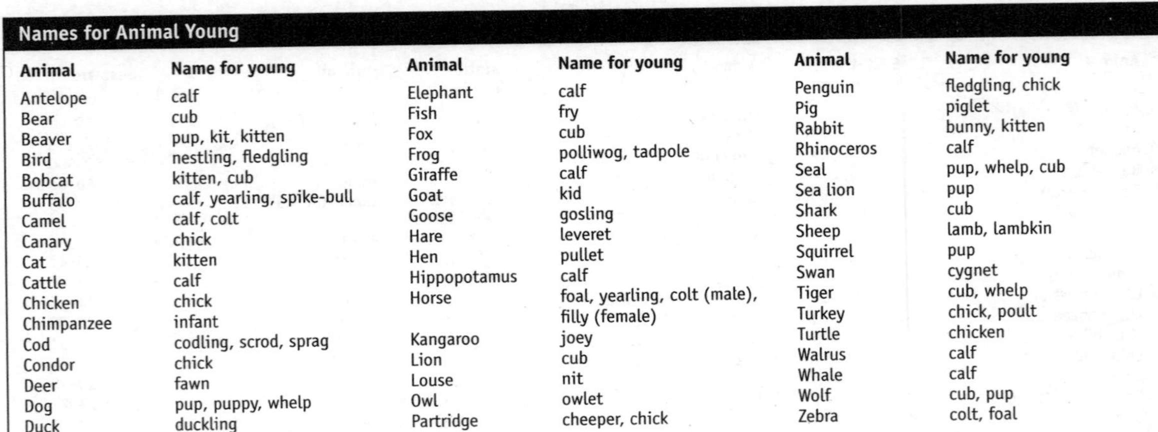

Names for Animal Young

Animal	Name for young	Animal	Name for young	Animal	Name for young
Antelope	calf	Elephant	calf	Penguin	fledgling, chick
Bear	cub	Fish	fry	Pig	piglet
Beaver	pup, kit, kitten	Fox	cub	Rabbit	bunny, kitten
Bird	nestling, fledgling	Frog	polliwog, tadpole	Rhinoceros	calf
Bobcat	kitten, cub	Giraffe	calf	Seal	pup, whelp, cub
Buffalo	calf, yearling, spike-bull	Goat	kid	Sea lion	pup
Camel	calf, colt	Goose	gosling	Shark	cub
Canary	chick	Hare	leveret	Sheep	lamb, lambkin
Cat	kitten	Hen	pullet	Squirrel	pup
Cattle	calf	Hippopotamus	calf	Swan	cygnet
Chicken	chick	Horse	foal, yearling, colt (male), filly (female)	Tiger	cub, whelp
Chimpanzee	infant	Kangaroo	joey	Turkey	chick, poult
Cod	codling, scrod, sprag	Lion	cub	Turtle	chicken
Condor	chick	Louse	nit	Walrus	calf
Deer	fawn	Owl	owlet	Whale	calf
Dog	pup, puppy, whelp	Partridge	cheeper, chick	Wolf	cub, pup
Duck	duckling			Zebra	colt, foal

Dogs Registered with the Kennel Club

Year	Sporting[1]	Non-sporting[2]	Total	Year	Sporting[1]	Non-sporting[2]	Total
1980	90,075	111,545	201,620	1990	131,811	138,958	270,769
1981	75,398	96,960	172,358	1991	126,997	125,527	252,524
1982	75,110	97,410	172,520	1992	121,709	118,448	240,157
1983	78,663	106,236	184,899	1993	119,689	116,204	235,893
1984	77,784	106,259	184,043	1994	125,328	121,379	246,707
1985	84,608	113,682	198,290	1995	136,679	127,412	264,091
1986	83,101	106,315	189,416	1996	144,124	129,217	273,341
1987	79,674	101,762	181,436	1997	142,296	126,194	268,490
1988	75,562	90,988	166,550	1998	141,277	117,469	258,746
1989	135,016	148,899	283,915				

[1] Hounds, gundogs, and terriers.
[2] Toy, utility, and working dogs.

Source: The Kennel Club

Crufts Supreme Champions: Best in Show

(B - bitch. Ch - Champion. D - dog. N - neutered. Sh Ch - Show Champion.)

Year	Dog's name	Breed	Sex	Owner	Breeder
1980	Ch Shargleam Blackcap	Flat coated retriever	D	Miss P Chapman	owner
1981	Ch Astley's Portia of Rua	Irish setter	B	Mrs and Miss Tuite	Mrs M Korbel
1982	Ch Grayco Hazelnut	Toy poodle	B	Mrs L A Howard	owner
1983	Ch Montravia-Kaskarak Hitari	Afghan hound	D	Mrs P Gibbs	Mrs L Race
1984	Ch Saxonsprings Hackensack	Llaso Apso	D	Mrs J Blyth	owner
1985	Ch Montravia Tommy-Gun	Standard poodle	D	Miss M Gibbs	Mrs C Coxall
1986	Ch Ginger Xmas Carol	Airedale terrier	B	Mrs A Livraghi	owner
1987	Ch Viscount Grant	Afghan hound	D	Mr C Amoo	owner
1988	Starlight Express of Valsett	English setter	B	Mr and Mrs J W Watkin	Mrs A R Wick
1989	Ch Potterdale Classic of Moonhill	Bearded collie	B	Mrs B R White	Mr and Mrs M Lewis
1990	Ch Olac Moon Pilot	West Highland white terrier	D	Mr D Tattersall	owner
1991	Sh Ch Raycroft Socialite	Clumber spaniel	D	Mr R Dunne	Mrs R Furness
1992	Ch Penglow Dutch Gold	Whippet	N	Miss Bolton	owner
1993	Sh Ch Dunnaway Debonair	Irish setter	N	Mrs Carrimer	owner
1994	Ch Perston Hit and Miss from Brocalita	Welsh terrier	N	Mrs B Halliwell	owner
1995	Sh Ch Starshell Chicago Bear	Irish setter	N	Miss Rachael Shaw	owner
1996	Sh Ch Canigou Cambrai	Cocker spaniel	N	Ms Tricia Bentley	owner
1997	Ch Ozmilion Mystification	Yorkshire terrier	D	Mr Osman Adam Sameja	owner
1998	Ch Saredon Forever Young	Welsh terrier	D	Mr D Scawthorn and Mrs J Averis	owner
1999	Sh Ch Caspians Intrepid	Irish setter	D	Mrs J Lorrimer	Mr and Mrs M Oakley

Source: The Kennel Club

Endangered Species

Endangered Species

International trade in live plants and animals, and in wildlife products such as skins, horns, shells, and feathers has made some species virtually extinct, and whole ecosystems (for example, coral reefs) are threatened. Wildlife trade is to some extent regulated by CITES (Convention on International Trade in Endangered Species). Species almost eradicated by trade in their products include many of the largest whales, crocodiles, marine turtles, and some wild cats. Until recently, some two million snake skins were exported from India every year. Populations of black rhino and African elephant have collapsed because of hunting for their horns and tusks (ivory), and poaching remains a problem in cases where trade is prohibited.

Species	Observation
plants	a quarter of the world's plants are threatened with extinction by the year 2010
amphibians	worldwide decline in numbers; half of New Zealand's frog species are now extinct; 25% of species threatened with extinction (1996); 38% of US amphibians were endangered (1997)
birds	three-quarters of all bird species are declining; 11% are threatened with extinction (1996)
carnivores	almost all species of cats and bears are declining in numbers
fish	one-third of North American freshwater fish are rare or endangered; half the fish species in Lake Victoria, Africa's largest lake, are close to extinction due to predation by the introduced Nile perch; 33% of species are threatened with extinction (1996)
invertebrates	about 100 species are lost each day due to deforestation; half the freshwater snails in the southeastern USA are now extinct or threatened; 50% of crayfish and 56% of mussel species are endangered in the USA; a quarter of German invertebrates are threatened
mammals	half of Australia's mammals are threatened; 40% of mammals in France, the Netherlands, Germany, and Portugal are threatened; 25% of species are threatened with extinction (1996)
primates	two-thirds of primate species are threatened
reptiles	over 40% of reptile species are threatened; 20% with extinction (1996)

Threatened Animals of the World: Numbers of Species

The table consists of the number of threatened species for each taxonomic class listed.

1996

Class	Extinct species	Species extinct in the wild	Sub-total	Critically endangered species	Endangered species	Vulnerable species[1]	Sub-total	Conservation dependent	Near threatened	Data-deficient[2]
Mammalia (mammals)	86	3	89	169	315	612	1,096	75	598	209
Aves (birds)	104	4	108	168	235	704	1,107	11	875	66
Reptilia (reptiles)	20	1	21	41	59	153	253	1	79	74
Amphibia (amphibians)	5	0	5	18	31	75	124	2	25	42
Cephalaspidomorphi (lampreys)	1	0	1	0	1	2	3	0	5	3
Elasmobranchii (sharks)	0	0	0	1	7	7	15	0	0	2
Actinopterygii (ray-finned fish)	80	11	91	156	125	434	715	12	96	250
Sarcopterygii (lobe-finned fish)	0	0	0	0	1	0	1	0	0	0
Echinoidea (sea urchins)	0	0	0	0	0	0	0	0	1	0
Arachnida (arthropods)	0	0	0	0	1	9	10	0	1	7
Chilopoda (centipedes)	0	0	0	0	0	1	1	0	0	0
Crustacea (crustaceans)	9	1	10	54	73	280	407	9	1	31
Insecta (insects)	72	1	73	44	116	377	537	3	77	40
Merostomata (class of aquatic arthropods)	0	0	0	0	0	0	0	0	1	3
Onychophora (phylum of terrestrial arthropods)	3	0	3	1	3	2	6	0	1	1
Hirudinea (leeches)	0	0	0	0	0	0	0	0	1	0
Oligochaeta (earthworms)	0	0	0	1	0	4	5	0	1	0
Polychaeta (bristleworms)	0	0	0	1	0	0	1	0	0	1
Bivalvia (bivalves)	12	0	12	81	22	11	114	5	62	5
Gastropoda (snails)	216	9	225	176	190	440	806	16	172	541
Enopla (nematodes)	0	0	0	0	0	2	2	0	1	3
Turbellaria (flatworms)	1	0	1	0	0	0	0	0	0	0
Anthozoa (cnidaria)	0	0	0	0	0	2	2	0	0	1

[1] Facing a high risk of extinction in the medium-term future.

[2] Information is inadequate to make a direct or indirect assessment of risk.

Source: World Conservation and Monitoring Centre

Selected Animals on the World Endangered and Threatened Species List

Common name	Scientific name	Range	When listed
Mammals			
armadillo, giant	*Priodontes maximus (= giganteus)*	South America	24 June 1976
bear, brown	*Ursus arctos arctos*	Europe	24 June 1976
bear, brown	*Ursus arctos pruinosus*	Asia	24 June 1976
bear, Mexican grizzly	*Ursus arctos (= U. a. nelsoni)*	North America	2 June 1970
bison, wood	*Bison bison athabascae*	North America	2 June 1970
bobcat	*Felis rufus escuinapae*	North America	24 June 1976
camel, Bactrian	*Camelus bactrianus (= ferus)*	Asia	24 June 1976
cat, leopard	*Felis bengalensis bengalensis*	Asia	24 June 1976
deer, pampas	*Ozotoceros bezoarticus*	South America	24 June 1976
dugong	*Dugong dugon*	Africa	2 December 1970
duiker, Jentink's	*Cephalophus jentinki*	Africa	25 June 1979
eland, western giant	*Taurotragus derbianus derbianus*	Africa	25 June 1979
elephant, African	*Loxodonta africana*	Africa	12 May 1978
elephant, Asian	*Elephas maximus*	Asia	24 June 1974
gazelle, Clark's (Dibatag)	*Ammodorcas clarkei*	Africa	2 June 1970
gorilla	*Gorilla gorilla*	Africa	2 June 1970
kangaroo, Tasmanian forester	*Macropus giganteus tasmaniensis*	Australia	4 June 1973
lemurs	*Lemuridae*	Africa	2 June 1970, 14 June 1976, 24 June 1976
leopard	*Panthera pardus*	Africa, Asia	2 June 1970, 30 March 1972, 28 January 1982
leopard, snow	*Panthera uncia*	Asia	30 March 1972
manatee, Amazonian	*Trichechus inunguis*	South America	2 June 1970
manatee, West African	*Trichechus senegalensis*	Africa	20 July 1979
monkey, black howler	*Alouatta pigra*	North America	19 October 1976
monkey, red-backed squirrel	*Saimiri oerstedii*	South America	2 June 1970
monkey, spider	*Ateles geoffroyi frontatus*	South America	2 June 1970
mouse, Shark Bay	*Pseudomys praeconis*	Australia	2 December 1970
orangutan	*Pongo pygmaeus*	Asia	2 June 1970
panda, giant	*Ailuropoda melanoleuca*	Asia	23 January 1984
rat-kangaroo, Queensland	*Bettongia tropica*	Australia	2 December 1970
rhinoceros, black	*Diceros bicornis*	Africa	14 July 1980
rhinoceros, great Indian	*Rhinoceros unicornis*	Asia	2 December 1970
seal, Saimaa	*Phoca hispida saimensis*	Europe	28 July 1993
sloth, Brazilian three-toed	*Bradypus torquatus*	South America	2 June 1970
tapir, Asian	*Tapirus indicus*	Asia	24 June 1974
tapir, mountain	*Tapirus pinchaque*	South America	2 June 1970
tiger	*Panthera tigris*	Asia	2 June 1970, 30 March 1972
tiger, Tasmanian (thylacine)	*Thylacinus cynocephalus*	Australia	2 June 1970
wallaby, banded hare	*Lagostrophus fasciatus*	Australia	2 December 1970
whale, blue	*Balaenoptera musculus*	Oceanic	2 June 1970
whale, bowhead	*Balaena mysticetus*	Oceanic	2 June 1970
whale, finback	*Balaenoptera physalus*	Oceanic	2 June 1970
whale, humpback	*Megaptera novaeangliae*	Oceanic	2 June 1970
whale, right	*Balaena glacialis* (incl. *australis)*	Oceanic	2 June 1970
whale, sperm	*Physeter macrocephalus (=catodon)*	Oceanic	2 June 1970
wombat, hairy-nosed (Barnard's and Queensland hairy-nosed)	*Lasiorhinus krefftii* (formerly *L. Barnardi* and *L. gillespiei)*	Australia	2 December 1970, 4 June 1973
zebra, Grevy's	*Equus grevyi*	Africa	21 August 1979
zebra, mountain	*Equus zebra zebra*	Africa	24 June 1976, 10 February 1981
Birds			
booby, Abbott's	*Sula abbotti*	Asia	24 June 1976
condor, Andean	*Vultur gryphus*	South America	2 December 1970
crane, hooded	*Grus monacha*	Asia	2 December 1970
crane, Japanese	*Grus japonenis*	Asia	2 June 1970
crane, whooping	*Grus americana*	North America	11 March 1967, and other dates
eagle, harpy	*Harpia harpyja*	South America	24 June 1976
egret, Chinese	*Egretta eulophotes*	Asia	2 June 1970
falcon, American peregrine	*Falco peregrinus anatum*	North America	13 October 1970
hawk, Galapagos	*Buteo galapagoensis*	South America	2 June 1970
ibis, Japanese crested	*Nipponia nippon*	Asia	2 June 1970

(continued)

Selected Animals on the World Endangered and Threatened Species List (*continued*)

Common name	Scientific name	Range	When listed
ibis, northern bald	*Geronticus eremita*	Africa, Asia, Europe	28 September 1990
macaw, glaucous	*Anodorhynchus glaucus*	South America	24 June 1976
macaw, indigo	*Anodorhynchus leari*	South America	24 June 1976
ostrich, Arabian	*Struthio camelus syriacus*	Asia	2 June 1970
ostrich, West African	*Struthio camelus spatzi*	Africa	2 June 1970
parakeet, gold-shouldered (hooded)	*Psephotus chrysopterygius*	Australia	2 June 1970
parakeet, Norfolk Island	*Cyanoramphus novaezelandiae cookii*	Australia	28 September 1990
parrot, ground	*Pezoporus wallicus*	Australia	4 June 1973
parrot, red-capped	*Pionopsitta pileata*	South America	24 June 1976
stork, oriental white	*Ciconia ciconia boyciana*	Asia	2 June 1970
woodpecker, imperial	*Campephilus imperialis*	North America	2 June 1970
woodpecker, Tristam's	*Drycopus javenis richardsi*	Asia	2 June 1970
Reptiles			
alligator, Chinese	*Alligator sinensis*	Asia	24 June 1976
caiman, Apaporis River	*Caiman crocodilus apaporiensis*	South America	24 June 1976
crocodile, African dwarf	*Osteolaemus tetraspis tetraspis*	Africa	24 June 1976
crocodile, African slender-snouted	*Crocodylus cataphractus*	Africa	30 March 1972
crocodile, Morelet's	*Crocodylus moreletii*	South America	2 June 1970
iguana, Barrington land	*Conolophus pallidus*	South America	2 June 1970
lizard, Hierro giant	*Gallotia simonyi simonyi*	Europe	29 February 1984
lizard, Ibiza wall	*Podarcis pityusensis*	Europe	29 February 1984
monitor, Bengal	*Varanus bengalensis*	Asia	24 June 1976
monitor, desert	*Varanus griseus*	Africa	24 June 1976
monitor, yellow	*Varanus flavescens*	Asia	24 June 1976
python, Indian	*Python molurus molurus*	Asia	24 June 1976
tartaruga	*Podocnemis expansa*	South America	2 June 1970
tortoise, Bolson	*Gopherus flavomarginatus*	North America	17 April 1979
tortoise, Galapagos	*Geochelone elephantopus*	South America	2 June 1970
tuatara	*Sphenodon punctatus*	Australia	2 June 1970
turtle, aquatic box	*Terrapene coahuila*	North America	4 June 1973
turtle, green sea	*Chelonia mydas* (incl. *agassizi)*	North America (circumglobal)	28 July 1978
viper, Lar Valley	*Vipera latiffi*	Asia	22 June 1983
Amphibians			
frog, Goliath	*Conraua goliath*	Africa	8 December 1994
frog, Israel painted	*Discoglossus nigriventer*	Europe	2 June 1970
frog, Panamanian golden	*Atelopus varius zeteki*	South America	24 June 1976
frog, Stephen Island	*Leiopelma hamiltoni*	Australia	2 June 1970
salamander, Chinese giant	*Andrias davidianus davidianus*	western China	24 June 1976
salamander, Japanese giant	*Andrias davidianus japonicus*	Japan	24 June 1976
toad, African viviparous	*Nectophrynoides* spp.	Africa	24 June 1976
toad, Cameroon	*Bufo superciliaris*	Africa	24 June 1976
toad, Monte Verde	*Bufo periglenes*	South America	24 June 1976

Source: US Fish and Wildlife Service and World Conservation Monitoring Centre

Some Plants and Animals Removed from the World Endangered and Threatened Species List

Common name	Scientific name	Range	Reason removed from list
dove, Palau	*Gallicolumba canifrons*	West Pacific–Palau Islands	recovered
falcon, Arctic peregrine	*Falco peregrinus tundris*	nests from northern Alaska to Greenland; winters to Central and South America	recovered
fantail, Palau (Old World flycatcher)	*Rhipidura lepida*	West Pacific–Palau Islands	recovered
kangaroo, eastern gray	*Macropus giganteus* (all subspecies except *tasmaniensis*)	Australia	recovered
kangaroo, red	*Macropus rufus*	Australia	recovered
kangaroo, western gray	*Macropus fuliginosus*	Australia	recovered
owl, Palau	*Pyrroglaux podargina*	West Pacific–Palau Islands	recovered
turtle, Indian flap-shelled	*Lissemys punctata punctata*	India, Pakistan, Bangladesh	better data
whale, gray (eastern North Pacific population)	*Eschrichtius robustus*	North Pacific Ocean–coastal and Bering Sea, formerly North Atlantic Ocean	recovered

Source: US Fish and Wildlife Service and World Conservation Monitoring Centre

Some Threatened Plants and Animals Used in the World Wildlife Trade

Common name	Scientific name	Range	Reason threatened
Alligator snapping turtle	*Macroclemys temminckii*	North America	used in canned turtle soup, a delicacy in some countries; also sold as pets
Asian elephant	*Elephas maximus*	Asia	poaching for ivory and other parts of the body is a serious problem which increased sharply in 1995–96
Beluga sturgeon	*Huso huso*	Caspian Sea	caviar is a delicacy in many countries; the long cycle of the fish makes the population vulnerable
Big leaf mahogany	*Swietenia macrophylla king*	Central and South America	mahogany wood is used for furniture in many countries
Black rhino	*Diceros bicornis*	Africa	hunted for their horns, which are used in powdered form in oriental medicine
Bonobo	*Pan paniscus*	Congo, Democratic Republic of	habitat loss and hunting; occasionally hunted for traditional medicinal purposes or magical purposes; specific body parts are thought to enhance strength and sexual vigour
Chimpanzee	*Pan tryglodytes*	Equatorial Africa	habitat loss, hunting of adults for bushmeat, capture of infants to supply the pet trade and entertainment industry, and the international biomedical trade
Giant panda	*Ailuropoda melanaleca*	China	destruction of the bamboo forests, the natural habitat for pandas, makes the population more vulnerable; as does poaching and demand as zoo animals
Goldenseal	*Hydrastis canadensis*	North America	used in herbal medicine as a natural antibiotic; demand has increased as herbal medicine becomes more widespread
Green-cheeked parrot	*Amazona viridiginohs*	Mexico	hunted and captured for pet trade; many birds die in transit
Hawksbill turtle	*Eretmochelys imbricata*	tropical seas	the shell is used as tortoiseshell, although under an official ban in most places; the slow reproductive cycle of the turtle makes the population more vulnerable
Mako shark	*Isurus oxyrinchus*	Atlantic, Pacific, and Indian Oceans	shark meat is a delicacy in some countries; the slow reproductive cycle makes the population more vulnerable
Tiger	*Panthera tigris*	Asia	destruction of jungle; hunted for bones and other parts for use in oriental medicine

Native Wildlife Species at Risk in Britain

In Great Britain there are just over 28,500 native species of invertebrates of which 15,000 have been assessed, 38 species of freshwater fish, 2,300 species of seed plants, ferns and related plants, and over 23,000 species of liverworts, mosses, lichens, stoneworts, fungi, and slime moulds. It is believed that a total of 155 native animal species and 107 native plant species have become extinct in Great Britain since 1900; these are included in the 'threatened' category in the table.
As of 1997. (– = not applicable.)

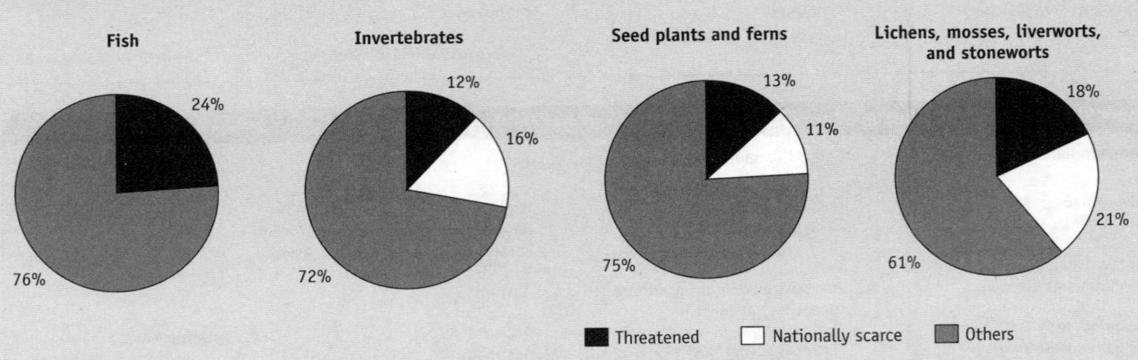

Source: *The Environment in Your Pocket 1998*, © Crown copyright 1998

World Climate and Weather

World Weather Records

As of April 1998.
(N/A = not available.)

Record	Location	Details
Highest amount of rainfall in the northern hemisphere in 24 hours	Paishih, Taiuan	124 cm/49 in
Highest amount of rainfall in 24 hours (not induced by the presence of mountains)	Dharampuri, India	99 cm/39 in
Highest amount of rainfall in 24 hours	Cilaos, La Reunion Island	188 cm/74 in
Highest amount of rainfall over 5 days	Cilaos, La Reunion Island	386 cm/152 in
Highest amount of rainfall in 12 hours	Belouve, La Reunion Island	135 cm/53 in
Highest amount of rainfall in 20 minutes	Curtea-de-Arge, Romania	21 cm/8.1 in
Highest yearly number of days of rainfall	Bahia Felix, Chile	325 days
Longest period without rainfall	Arica, Chile	14 years
Highest yearly average period of thunderstorms	Kampala, Uganda	242 days per year
Highest sustained yearly average period of thunderstorms	Bogor, Indonesia	322 days per year from 1916 to 1919
Longest snowfall	Bessans, France	19 hours with 173 cm/68 in of snow
Highest yearly average rainfall in Africa	Debundscha, Cameroon	1,029 cm/405 in (with an average variability of 191 cm/75 in)
Lowest yearly average rainfall in Africa	Wadt Halfa, Sudan	3 mm/0.1 in
Lowest yearly average rainfall in Asia	Aden, South Yemen	5 cm/1.8 in
Highest yearly average rainfall in Europe	Crkvice, Bosnia-Herzegovina	465 cm/183 in
Lowest yearly average rainfall in Europe	Astrakhan, Russia	16 cm/6.4 in
Highest amount of rainfall in Australia in 24 hours	Crohamhurst, Queensland	91 cm/36 in
Highest yearly average rainfall in Australia	Bellenden Ker, Queensland	864 cm/340 in
Lowest yearly average rainfall in Australia	Mulka, South Australia	10 cm/4.1 in
Highest yearly average rainfall in South America	Quibdo, Colombia	899 cm/354 in
Lowest yearly average rainfall in South America	Arica, Chile	0.7 mm/0.03 in
Highest yearly average rainfall in North America	Henderson Lake, British Columbia, Canada	650 cm/256 in
Lowest yearly average rainfall in North America	Bataques, Mexico	3 cm/1.2 in
Highest temperature ever recorded in the world	El Aiziza, Libya	58°C/136°F
Lowest temperature ever recorded in the world	Vostok, Antarctica	–53.8°C/–129°F
Highest yearly average temperature in world	Dallol, Ethiopia	34°C/94°F
Highest yearly average temperature range	Eastern Sayan Region, Russia	through 63°C/146°F
Highest average temperature sustained over a long period	Marble Head, Australia	38°C/100°F for 162 consecutive days
Highest temperature in Antarctica	Vanda Station, South Coast	near 15°C/59°F
Lowest temperature in Antarctica	Vostok	–53.8°C/–129°F
Lowest temperature in Africa	Ifrane, Morocco	–24°C/–11°F
Highest temperature in Asia	Tirat Tsvi, Israel	54°C/129°F
Highest temperature in Australia	Cloncurry, Queensland	53°C/128°F
Lowest temperature in Australia	Charlotte Press, New South Wales	–23°C/–9.4°F
Highest temperature in Europe	Seville, Spain	50°C/122°F
Lowest temperature in Europe	Ust 'Shchugor, USSR	–55°C/–67°F
Lowest temperature in Greenland	Northice	–66°C/–87°F
Lowest temperature in North America (excluding Greenland)	Snag, Yukon Territory, Canada	–63°C/–81°F
Lowest temperature in northern hemisphere	Verkhoyansk, Oimekon, USSR	–68°C/–90°F
Highest temperature in South America	Rivadavia, Argentina	49°C/120°F
Lowest temperature in South America	Sarmiento, Argentina	–33°C/–27°F
Highest temperature in western hemisphere	Death Valley (CA)	57°C/134°F
Highest peak wind	Thule Air Base, Greenland	333 kph/207 mph
Highest average wind speed in 24 h	Port Martin, Antarctica	173 kph/108 mph
Highest peak wind gust	Mt Washington (NH)	372 kph/231 mph
Highest monthly average wind speed	Port Martin, Antarctica	104 kph/65 mph

Average Monthly High and Low Temperatures for Major Cities of the World (Adelaide – Kinshasa)

Data is given in °C. To convert from °C to °F, use the equation F = (C × 180/100) + 32. Data as of January 1997.

City	January		February		March		April		May		June	
	°C max	°C min	°C max	°C min	°C max	°C min	°C max	°C min	°C max	°C min	°C max	°C min
Adelaide, Australia	30	16	30	17	27	15	23	13	19	10	16	8
Algiers, Algeria	15	9	16	9	17	11	20	13	23	15	26	18
Almaty, Kazakhstan	−5	−14	−3	−13	4	−6	13	3	20	10	24	14
Ankara, Turkey	4	−4	6	−3	11	−1	17	4	23	9	26	12
Asunción, Paraguay	35	22	34	22	33	21	29	18	25	14	22	12
Athens, Greece	13	6	14	7	16	8	20	11	25	16	30	20
Balboa Heights, Panama[1]	31	22	32	22	32	22	31	23	30	23	31	23
Bangkok, Thailand	32	20	33	22	34	24	35	25	34	26	33	24
Barcelona, Spain	13	6	14	7	16	9	18	11	21	14	25	18
Beijing, China	1	−10	4	−8	11	−1	21	7	27	13	31	18
Belfast, Northern Ireland	6	2	7	2	9	3	12	4	15	6	18	9
Belgrade, Yugoslavia	3	−3	5	−2	11	2	18	7	23	12	26	15
Berlin, Germany	2	−3	3	−3	8	0	13	4	19	8	22	12
Bogotá, Colombia	19	9	20	9	19	10	19	11	19	11	18	11
Bombay, India	28	19	28	19	30	22	32	24	33	27	32	26
Brussels, Belgium	4	−1	7	0	10	2	14	5	18	8	22	11
Bucharest, Romania	1	−7	4	−5	10	−1	18	5	23	10	27	14
Budapest, Hungary	1	−4	4	−2	10	2	17	7	22	11	26	15
Buenos Aires, Argentina	29	17	28	17	26	16	22	12	18	8	14	5
Cairo, Egypt	18	8	21	9	24	11	28	14	33	17	35	20
Cape Town, South Africa	26	16	26	16	25	14	22	12	19	9	18	8
Caracas, Venezuela	24	13	25	13	26	14	27	16	27	17	26	17
Copenhagen, Denmark	2	−2	2	−3	5	−1	10	3	16	8	19	11
Dakar, Senegal	26	18	27	17	27	18	27	18	29	20	31	23
De Bilt, Netherlands[1]	4	−1	5	−1	10	1	13	4	18	8	21	11
Delhi, India	21	7	24	9	31	14	36	20	41	26	39	28
Detroit, USA	−1	−7	0	−8	6	−3	13	3	19	9	25	14
Djibouti, Djibouti	29	23	29	24	31	25	32	26	34	28	37	30
Dublin, Republic of Ireland	8	1	8	2	10	3	13	4	15	6	18	9
Edinburgh, Scotland	6	1	6	1	8	2	11	4	14	6	17	9
Frankfurt, Germany	3	−2	5	−1	11	2	16	6	20	9	23	13
Guatemala City, Guatemala	23	12	25	12	27	14	28	14	29	16	27	16
Havana, Cuba	26	18	26	18	27	19	29	21	30	22	31	23
Helsinki, Finland	−3	−9	−4	−10	0	−7	6	−1	14	4	19	9
Hong Kong, China	18	13	17	13	19	16	24	19	28	23	29	26
Istanbul, Turkey	8	3	9	2	11	3	16	7	21	12	25	16
Jakarta, Indonesia	29	23	29	23	30	23	31	24	31	24	31	23
Jerusalem, Israel	13	5	13	6	18	8	23	10	27	14	29	16
Johannesburg, South Africa	26	14	25	14	24	13	22	10	19	6	17	4
Kabul, Afghanistan	2	−8	4	−6	12	1	19	6	26	11	31	13
Karachi, Pakistan	25	13	26	14	29	19	32	23	34	26	34	28
Katmandu, Nepal	18	2	19	4	25	7	28	12	30	16	29	19
Kiev, Ukraine	−4	−10	−2	−8	3	−4	14	5	21	11	24	14
Kinshasa, Democratic Republic of Congo	31	21	31	22	32	22	32	22	31	22	29	19

(continued)

Average Monthly High and Low Temperatures for Major Cities of the World (Adelaide – Kinshasa) (*continued*)

City	July		August		September		October		November		December	
	°C max	°C min	°C max	°C min	°C max	°C min	°C max	°C min	°C max	°C min	°C max	°C min
Adelaide, Australia	15	7	17	8	19	9	23	11	26	13	28	15
Algiers, Algeria	28	21	29	22	27	21	23	17	19	13	16	11
Almaty, Kazakhstan	27	16	27	14	22	8	13	2	4	−5	−2	−9
Ankara, Turkey	30	15	31	15	26	11	21	7	14	3	6	−2
Asunción, Paraguay	23	12	26	14	28	14	30	17	32	18	34	21
Athens, Greece	33	23	33	23	29	19	24	15	19	12	15	8
Balboa Heights, Panama[1]	31	23	30	23	29	23	29	23	29	23	31	23
Bangkok, Thailand	32	24	32	24	32	24	31	24	34	22	31	20
Barcelona, Spain	28	21	28	21	25	19	21	15	16	11	13	8
Beijing, China	31	21	30	20	26	14	20	6	9	−2	3	−8
Belfast, Northern Ireland	18	11	18	11	16	9	13	7	9	4	7	3
Belgrade, Yugoslavia	28	17	28	17	24	13	18	8	11	4	5	0
Berlin, Germany	24	14	23	13	20	10	13	6	7	2	3	−1
Bogotá, Colombia	18	10	18	10	19	9	19	10	19	10	19	9
Bombay, India	29	25	29	25	29	24	32	24	32	23	31	21
Brussels, Belgium	23	12	22	12	21	11	15	7	9	3	6	0
Bucharest, Romania	30	16	30	15	25	11	18	6	10	2	4	−3
Budapest, Hungary	28	16	27	16	23	12	16	7	8	3	4	−1
Buenos Aires, Argentina	14	6	16	6	18	8	21	10	24	13	28	16
Cairo, Egypt	36	21	35	22	32	20	30	18	26	14	20	10
Cape Town, South Africa	17	7	18	8	18	9	21	11	23	13	24	14
Caracas, Venezuela	26	16	26	16	27	16	26	16	25	16	26	14
Copenhagen, Denmark	22	14	21	14	18	11	12	7	7	3	4	1
Dakar, Senegal	31	24	31	24	32	24	32	24	30	23	27	19
De Bilt, Netherlands[1]	22	13	22	13	19	10	14	7	9	3	5	1
Delhi, India	36	27	34	26	34	24	34	18	29	11	23	8
Detroit, USA	28	17	27	17	23	13	16	7	8	1	2	−4
Djibouti, Djibouti	41	31	39	29	36	29	33	27	31	25	29	23
Dublin, Republic of Ireland	20	11	19	11	17	9	14	6	10	4	8	3
Edinburgh, Scotland	18	11	18	11	16	9	12	7	9	4	7	2
Frankfurt, Germany	25	15	24	14	21	11	14	7	8	3	4	0
Guatemala City, Guatemala	26	16	26	16	26	16	24	16	23	14	22	13
Havana, Cuba	32	24	32	24	31	24	29	23	27	21	26	19
Helsinki, Finland	22	13	20	12	15	8	8	3	3	−1	−1	−5
Hong Kong, China	31	26	31	26	29	25	27	23	23	18	20	15
Istanbul, Turkey	28	18	28	19	24	16	20	13	15	9	11	5
Jakarta, Indonesia	31	23	31	23	31	23	31	23	30	23	29	23
Jerusalem, Israel	31	17	31	18	29	17	27	15	21	12	15	7
Johannesburg, South Africa	17	4	20	6	23	9	25	12	25	13	26	14
Kabul, Afghanistan	33	16	33	15	29	11	23	6	17	1	8	−3
Karachi, Pakistan	33	27	31	26	31	25	33	22	31	18	27	14
Katmandu, Nepal	29	20	28	20	28	19	27	13	23	7	19	3
Kiev, Ukraine	25	15	24	14	20	10	13	6	6	0	−1	−6
Kinshasa, Democratic Republic of Congo	27	18	29	18	31	20	31	21	31	22	30	21

Average Monthly High and Low Temperatures for Major Cities of the World (Lagos – Zürich)

City	January		February		March		April		May		June	
	°C max	°C min	°C max	°C min	°C max	°C min	°C max	°C min	°C max	°C min	°C max	°C min
Lagos, Nigeria	31	23	32	25	32	26	32	25	31	24	29	23
La Paz, Bolivia	17	6	17	6	18	6	18	4	18	3	17	1
Lhasa, Tibet	7	−10	9	−7	12	−2	16	1	19	5	24	9
Lima, Peru	28	19	28	19	28	19	27	17	23	16	20	14
Lisbon, Portugal	14	8	15	8	17	10	20	12	21	13	25	15
London, UK	6	2	7	2	10	3	13	6	17	8	20	12
Los Angeles, USA	18	8	19	8	19	9	21	10	22	12	24	13
Madrid, Spain	9	2	11	2	15	5	18	7	21	10	27	15
Manila, Philippines	30	21	31	21	33	22	34	23	34	24	33	24
Melbourne, Australia	26	14	26	14	24	13	20	11	17	8	14	7
Mexico City, Mexico	19	6	21	6	24	8	25	11	26	12	24	13
Milan, Italy	5	0	8	2	13	6	18	10	23	14	27	17
Montevideo, Uruguay	28	17	28	16	26	15	22	12	18	9	15	6
Moscow, Russia	−9	−16	−6	−14	0	−8	10	1	19	8	21	11
Nagasaki, Japan	9	2	10	2	14	5	19	10	23	14	26	18
Nairobi, Kenya	25	12	26	13	25	14	22	13	21	12	21	11
New York City, USA	3	−4	3	−4	7	−1	14	6	20	12	25	16
Oslo, Norway	−2	−7	−1	−7	4	−4	10	1	16	6	20	10
Ottawa, Canada	−6	−16	−6	−16	1	−9	11	−1	19	7	24	12
Paris, France	6	1	7	1	12	4	16	6	20	10	23	13
Prague, Czech Republic	0	−5	1	−4	7	−1	12	3	18	8	21	11
Quito, Ecuador	22	8	22	8	22	8	21	8	21	8	22	7
Reykjavik, Iceland	2	−2	3	−2	4	−1	6	1	10	4	12	7
Rio de Janeiro, Brazil	29	23	29	23	28	22	27	21	25	19	24	18
Riyadh, Saudi Arabia	21	8	23	9	28	13	32	18	38	22	42	25
Rome, Italy	11	5	13	5	15	7	19	10	23	13	28	17
St Petersburg, Russia	−7	−13	−5	−12	0	−8	8	0	15	6	20	11
Santiago, Chile	29	12	29	11	27	9	23	7	18	5	14	3
Seoul, South Korea	0	−9	3	−7	8	−2	17	5	22	11	27	16
Shanghai, China	8	1	8	1	13	4	19	10	25	15	28	19
Singapore, Singapore	30	23	31	23	31	24	31	24	32	24	31	24
Sofia, Bulgaria	2	−4	4	−3	10	1	16	5	21	10	24	14
Stockholm, Sweden	−1	−5	−1	−5	3	−4	8	1	14	6	19	11
Sydney, Australia	26	18	26	18	24	17	22	14	19	11	16	9
Tehran, Iran	7	−3	10	0	15	4	22	9	28	14	34	19
Tokyo, Japan	8	−2	9	−1	12	2	17	8	22	12	24	17
Toronto, Canada	−1	−9	−1	−9	3	−5	10	1	17	7	23	12
Tripoli, Libya	16	8	17	9	19	11	22	14	24	16	27	19
Vancouver, Canada	5	0	7	1	10	3	14	4	18	8	21	11
Vienna, Austria	1	−4	3	−3	8	−1	15	6	19	10	23	14
Warsaw, Poland	0	−6	0	−6	6	−2	12	3	20	9	23	12
Washington DC, USA	6	−3	7	−2	12	2	18	7	24	12	28	17
Wellington, New Zealand	21	13	21	13	19	12	17	11	14	8	13	7
Zürich, Switzerland	2	−3	5	−2	10	1	15	4	19	8	23	12

(continued)

Average Monthly High and Low Temperatures for Major Cities of the World (Lagos – Zürich) (*continued*)

City	July		August		September		October		November		December	
	°C max	°C min	°C max	°C min	°C max	°C min	°C max	°C min	°C max	°C min	°C max	°C min
Lagos, Nigeria	28	23	28	23	28	23	29	23	31	24	31	24
La Paz, Bolivia	17	1	17	2	18	3	19	4	19	6	18	6
Lhasa, Tibet	23	9	22	9	21	7	17	1	13	–5	9	–9
Lima, Peru	19	14	19	13	20	14	22	14	23	16	26	16
Lisbon, Portugal	27	17	28	17	26	17	22	14	17	11	15	9
London, UK	22	14	21	13	19	11	14	8	10	5	7	4
Los Angeles, USA	27	16	28	16	27	14	24	12	23	10	19	8
Madrid, Spain	31	17	30	17	25	14	19	10	13	5	9	2
Manila, Philippines	31	24	31	24	31	24	31	23	31	22	30	21
Melbourne, Australia	13	6	15	6	17	8	19	9	20	11	24	12
Mexico City, Mexico	23	12	23	12	23	12	21	10	20	8	19	6
Milan, Italy	29	20	28	19	24	16	17	11	10	6	6	2
Montevideo, Uruguay	14	6	15	6	17	8	20	9	23	12	26	15
Moscow, Russia	23	13	22	12	16	7	9	3	2	–3	–5	–10
Nagasaki, Japan	29	23	31	23	27	20	22	14	17	1	12	4
Nairobi, Kenya	21	11	24	11	24	13	23	13	23	13	23	13
New York City, USA	28	19	27	19	26	16	21	9	11	3	5	–2
Oslo, Norway	22	13	21	12	16	8	9	3	3	–1	0	–4
Ottawa, Canada	27	14	25	13	20	9	12	3	4	–3	–4	–13
Paris, France	25	15	24	14	21	12	16	8	10	5	7	2
Prague, Czech Republic	23	13	22	13	18	9	12	5	5	1	1	–3
Quito, Ecuador	22	7	23	7	23	7	22	8	22	7	22	8
Reykjavik, Iceland	14	9	14	8	11	6	7	3	4	0	2	–2
Rio de Janeiro, Brazil	24	17	24	18	24	18	25	19	26	20	28	22
Riyadh, Saudi Arabia	42	26	42	24	39	22	34	16	29	13	21	9
Rome, Italy	30	20	30	20	26	17	22	13	16	9	13	6
St Petersburg, Russia	21	13	20	13	15	9	9	4	2	–2	–3	–8
Santiago, Chile	15	3	17	4	19	6	22	7	26	9	28	11
Seoul, South Korea	29	31	31	22	26	15	19	7	11	0	3	–7
Shanghai, China	32	23	32	23	28	19	23	14	17	7	12	2
Singapore, Singapore	31	24	31	24	31	24	31	23	31	23	31	23
Sofia, Bulgaria	27	16	26	15	22	11	17	8	9	3	4	–2
Stockholm, Sweden	22	14	20	13	15	9	9	5	5	1	2	–2
Sydney, Australia	16	8	17	9	19	11	22	13	23	16	25	17
Tehran, Iran	37	22	36	22	32	18	24	12	17	6	11	1
Tokyo, Japan	28	21	30	22	26	19	21	13	16	6	11	1
Toronto, Canada	26	15	25	14	21	11	13	4	6	–1	1	–6
Tripoli, Libya	29	22	30	22	29	22	27	18	23	14	18	9
Vancouver, Canada	23	12	23	12	18	9	14	7	9	4	6	2
Vienna, Austria	25	15	24	15	20	11	14	7	7	3	3	–1
Warsaw, Poland	24	15	23	14	19	10	13	5	6	1	2	–3
Washington DC, USA	31	20	29	19	26	15	19	9	13	3	7	–2
Wellington, New Zealand	12	6	12	6	14	8	16	9	17	10	19	112
Zürich, Switzerland	25	14	24	13	20	11	14	6	7	2	3	–2

[1] Locations of weather stations providing data.

Average Monthly Rainfall for Major Cities of the World

In millimetres. Data as of January 1997.

City	January	February	March	April	May	June	July	August	September	October	November	December
Adelaide, Australia	20	18	25	46	69	76	66	66	53	43	28	25
Algiers, Algeria	112	84	74	41	46	15	0	5	41	79	130	137
Almaty, Kazakhstan	33	23	96	102	94	66	36	31	25	51	48	33
Ankara, Turkey	33	31	33	33	48	25	15	10	18	23	31	48
Asunción, Paraguay	140	130	109	132	117	69	56	38	79	140	150	158
Athens, Greece	62	37	37	23	23	14	6	7	15	51	56	71
Balboa Heights, Panama[1]	25	10	18	74	203	213	180	201	208	257	259	122
Bangkok, Thailand	8	20	86	58	198	160	160	175	305	206	66	5
Barcelona, Spain	31	39	48	43	54	37	27	46	76	86	52	45
Beijing, China	4	5	8	17	35	78	243	141	58	16	11	3
Belfast, Northern Ireland	80	52	50	48	52	68	94	77	80	83	72	90
Belgrade, Yugoslavia	47	46	46	54	74	96	61	55	50	55	61	55
Berlin, Germany	46	40	33	42	49	65	73	69	48	4.9	46	43
Bogotá, Colombia	58	66	102	147	114	61	51	56	61	160	119	66
Bombay, India	2.5	2.5	2.5	0	18	485	617	340	264	64	13	2.5
Brussels, Belgium	66	61	53	60	55	76	95	80	63	83	75	88
Bucharest, Romania	48	26	28	59	77	121	53	45	45	29	36	27
Budapest, Hungary	37	44	38	45	72	69	56	47	33	57	70	46
Buenos Aires, Argentina	79	71	109	89	76	61	56	61	79	86	84	99
Cairo, Egypt	5	5	5	3	3	0	0	0	0	0	3	5
Cape Town, South Africa	15	8	18	48	79	84	89	66	43	31	18	10
Caracas, Venezuela	23	10	15	33	79	102	109	109	107	109	94	46
Copenhagen, Denmark	49	39	32	38	43	47	71	66	62	59	48	49
Dakar, Senegal	0	0	0	0	0	18	89	254	132	38	3	8
De Bilt, Netherlands[1]	68	53	44	49	52	58	77	87	72	72	70	64
Delhi, India	23	18	13	8	13	74	180	173	117	10	3	10
Detroit, USA	53	53	64	64	84	91	84	69	71	61	61	58
Djibouti, Djibouti	10	13	25	13	5	0	3	8	8	10	23	13
Dublin, Republic of Ireland	67	55	51	45	60	57	70	74	72	70	67	74
Edinburgh, Scotland	57	39	39	39	54	47	83	77	57	65	62	54
Frankfurt, Germany	58	44	38	44	55	73	70	76	57	52	55	54
Guatemala City, Guatemala	8	3	13	31	152	274	203	198	231	173	23	8
Havana, Cuba	71	46	46	58	119	165	125	135	150	173	79	58
Helsinki, Finland	56	42	36	44	41	51	68	72	71	73	68	66
Hong Kong, China	33	46	74	137	292	394	381	367	257	114	43	31
Istanbul, Turkey	109	92	72	46	38	34	34	30	58	81	103	119
Jakarta, Indonesia	300	300	211	147	114	97	64	43	66	112	142	203
Jerusalem, Israel	132	132	64	28	3	0	0	0	0	13	71	86
Johannesburg, South Africa	114	109	89	38	25	8	8	8	23	56	107	125
Kabul, Afghanistan	31	36	94	3.7	102	5	3	3	0	15	20	10
Karachi, Pakistan	13	10	8	0.3	3	18	81	41	13	0	3	5
Katmandu, Nepal	15	41	23	0.9	122	246	373	345	155	38	8	3
Kiev, Ukraine	46	37	40	1.6	38	35	64	39	36	24	43	52
Kinshasa, Democratic Republic of Congo	5	84	178	158	137	114	132	165	183	218	198	84
Lagos, Nigeria	28	46	102	150	269	460	279	64	140	206	69	25
La Paz, Bolivia	114	107	66	33	13	8	10	13	28	41	48	94
Lhasa, Tibet	0	13	8	5	25	64	122	89	66	13	3	0

(continued)

Average Monthly Rainfall for Major Cities of the World (*continued*)

City	January	February	March	April	May	June	July	August	September	October	November	December
Lima, Peru	3	0	0	0	5	5	8	8	8	3	3	0
Lisbon, Portugal	111	76	109	54	44	16	3	4	33	62	93	103
London, UK	54	40	37	37	46	45	57	59	49	57	64	48
Los Angeles, USA	79	76	71	25	10	3	0	0	5	15	31	66
Madrid, Spain	39	34	43	48	47	27	11	15	32	53	47	48
Manila, Philippines	23	13	18	33	130	254	432	422	356	193	145	66
Melbourne, Australia	48	46	56	58	53	53	48	48	58	66	58	58
Mexico City, Mexico	13	5	10	20	53	119	170	152	130	51	18	8
Milan, Italy	44	60	77	94	76	118	64	91	69	125	122	77
Montevideo, Uruguay	74	66	99	99	84	81	74	79	76	66	74	79
Moscow, Russia	39	38	36	37	53	58	88	71	58	45	47	54
Nagasaki, Japan	71	84	125	185	170	312	257	175	249	114	94	81
Nairobi, Kenya	38	64	125	211	158	46	15	23	31	53	109	86
New York City, USA	94	97	91	81	81	84	107	109	86	89	76	91
Oslo, Norway	49	35	26	43	44	70	82	95	81	74	68	63
Ottawa, Canada	74	56	71	69	64	89	86	66	81	74	76	66
Paris, France	56	46	35	42	57	54	59	64	55	50	51	50
Prague, Czech Republic	18	18	18	27	48	54	68	55	31	33	20	21
Quito, Ecuador	99	112	142	175	137	43	20	31	69	112	97	79
Reykjavik, Iceland	89	64	62	56	42	42	50	56	67	94	78	79
Rio de Janeiro, Brazil	125	122	130	107	79	53	41	43	66	79	104	137
Riyadh, Saudi Arabia	3	20	23	25	10	0	0	0	0	0	0	0
Rome, Italy	71	62	57	51	46	37	15	21	63	99	129	93
St Petersburg, Russia	35	30	31	36	45	50	72	78	64	76	46	40
Santiago, Chile	3	3	5	13	64	84	76	56	31	15	8	5
Seoul, South Korea	31	20	38	76	81	130	376	267	119	41	46	25
Shanghai, China	48	58	84	94	94	180	147	142	130	71	51	36
Singapore, Singapore	252	173	193	188	173	173	170	196	178	208	254	257
Sofia, Bulgaria	36	28	41	61	87	73	68	64	41	65	48	49
Stockholm, Sweden	43	35	25	31	34	45	61	76	60	48	53	48
Sydney, Australia	89	102	127	135	127	117	117	76	74	71	74	74
Tehran, Iran	46	38	46	36	13	3	3	3	3	8	20	31
Tokyo, Japan	48	74	107	135	147	165	142	152	234	208	97	56
Toronto, Canada	69	61	66	64	74	69	74	69	74	61	71	66
Tripoli, Libya	81	46	28	10	5	3	0	0	10	41	66	94
Vancouver, Canada	218	147	127	84	71	64	31	43	91	147	211	224
Vienna, Austria	39	44	44	45	70	67	84	72	42	56	52	45
Warsaw, Poland	27	32	27	37	46	69	96	65	43	38	31	44
Washington DC, USA	86	76	91	84	94	99	112	109	94	74	66	79
Wellington, New Zealand	81	81	81	97	117	117	137	117	97	102	89	89
Zürich, Switzerland	74	69	64	76	101	129	136	124	102	77	73	64

[1] Locations of weather stations providing data.

The World's Climates

Despite the complexity of climatic patterns produced by altitude, proximity to the oceans and aspect in relation to prevailing winds the world climates may be categorized. Broadly similar climates are found in different parts of the world in the same latitude and in similar positions on each continent.

Tropical Climates

These are grouped into two types: The equatorial climates are found within about 5° of latitude north and south of the equator, and the weather is hot and wet throughout the year. The hot tropical climates with a distinct wet and dry season are found roughly between 5° and 15° north and south of the equator. Parts of south and southeast Asia have a very clear division between the wet and dry seasons and are called *tropical monsoon climates*.

Dry Climates

There are three types of dry climate: Hot deserts with little rain at any season and no real cold weather, although the temperature drops sharply at night. The Sahara desert and much of the Arabian peninsula are the best examples of this type of climate. The second type is tropical steppe or semi-desert with a short rainy season during which the rains are unreliable and vary much from place to place. Examples are found in the drier parts of India and the Sahel region of Africa. The third type is deserts with a distinctly cold season which occur in higher latitudes in the interior of large continents. The best examples are parts of central Asia and western China.

Warm Temperate Climates

These fall into two groups: Rain occurs at all seasons, but summer is the wettest time of the year and temperatures then are warm to hot. Winters are mild with occasional cold spells. Much of eastern China and the southeastern states of the USA are in this category. Winters are generally mild and wet; summers are warm or hot with little or no rain. This type of climate is often called *Mediterranean* because of its wide extent around that sea. It also occurs in smaller areas elsewhere, for example central Chile, California and Western Australia.

Cold Temperate Climates

These are categorized into two types: The cool temperate oceanic type of climate. Rain occurs in all months and there are rarely great extremes of heat or cold. This climate is found in much of northwest Europe, New Zealand, and coastal British Columbia. The second type is cold continental climates with a warm summer and a cold winter. Much of eastern and central Europe and eastern central Canada and the USA have this type of climate.

Sub-Arctic or Tundra Climates

The winters are long and very cold. Summers are short, but during the long days temperatures sometimes rise surprisingly high. This type of climate occurs in central and northern Canada and much of northern and central Siberia.

Arctic or Icecap Climates

In all months temperatures are near or below freezing point. Greenland and the Antarctic continents are the best examples of this type but it also occurs on some islands within the Arctic and Antarctic circles, such as South Georgia and Spitzbergen.

Climates of High Mountains and Plateaux

Where land rises above or near the permanent snow line in any latitude, the climate resembles that of the Sub-Arctic and Arctic. The best examples are Tibet and the great mountain ranges of the Himalayas. In Africa only the isolated peaks of Mount Kenya and Kilimanjaro and the Ruwenzori range are high enough to carry permanent snow. Similar mountain climates are more extensive in North and South America.

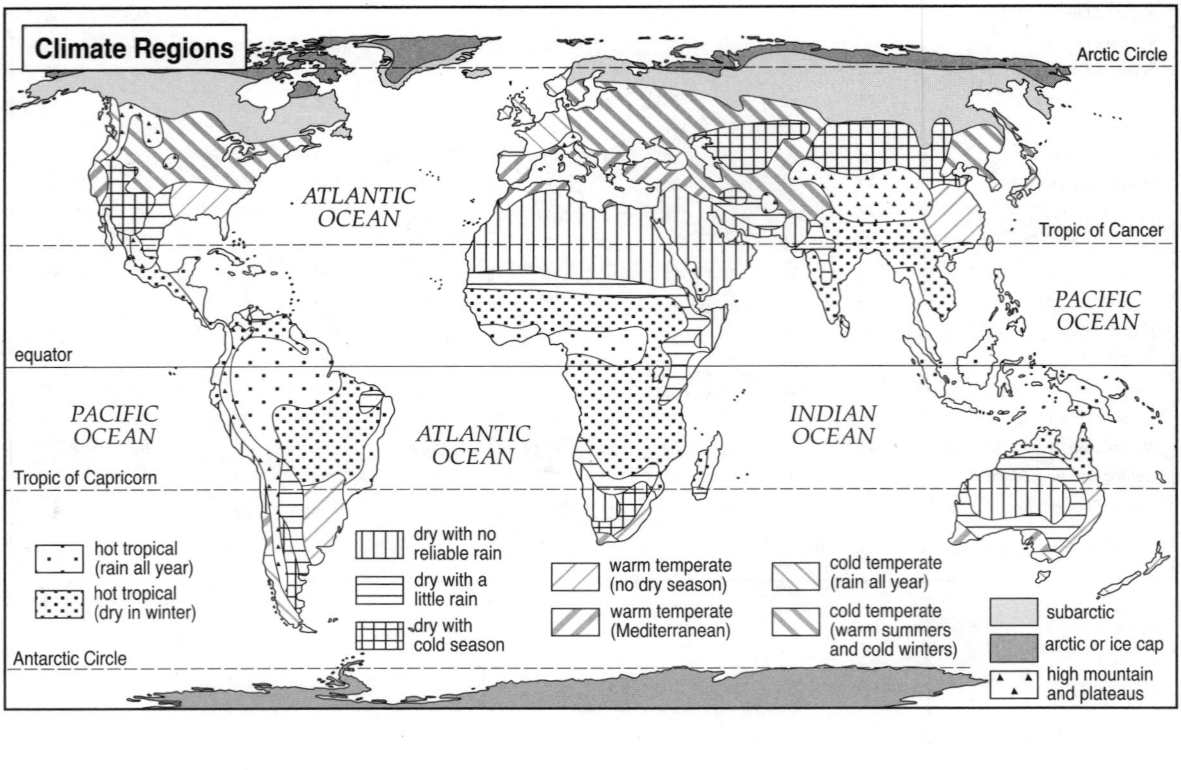

Climate Regions

Retired Hurricane and Tropical Storm Names

The names used for tropical storms and hurricanes are reused on a four- or six-year cycle, depending upon the part of the world in which the storm strikes. However, the names of tropical storms and hurricanes that cause severe damage or result in great loss of life are retired and not used again. Storm names that have been retired appear in the table with the year of their retirement. The table covers Atlantic storms only.

Name	Year	Name	Year	Name	Year	Name	Year
Agnes	1972	Caro	1954	Eloise	1975	Hugo	1989
Alicia	1983	Celia	1970	Fifi	1974	Inez	1966
Allen	1980	Cesar	1996	Flora	1963	Ione	1955
Andrew	1992	Cleo	1964	Fran	1996	Janet	1955
Anita	1977	Connie	1955	Frederic	1979	Joan	1988
Audrey	1957	David	1979	Gilbert	1988	Klaus	1990
Betsy	1965	Diana	1990	Gloria	1985	Luis	1995
Beulah	1967	Diane	1955	Gracie	1959	Marilyn	1995
Bob	1991	Dona	1960	Hattie	1961	Opal	1995
Camille	1969	Dora	1964	Hazel	1954	Roxanne	1995
Carla	1961	Edna	1954	Hilda	1964		
Carmen	1974	Elena	1985	Hortense	1996		

Major Floods and Tsunamis of the Late 20th Century

A tsunami is an ocean wave generated by vertical movements of the sea floor resulting from earthquakes or volcanic activity. As of January 1999.

Year	Event	Location	Number of deaths
1981	floods	northern China	550
1982	floods	Peru	600
	floods	Guangdong, China	430
	floods	El Salvador/Guatemala	>1,300
1983	tsunami	Japan/South Korea	107
1984	floods	South Korea	>200
1987	floods	northern Bangladesh	>1,000
1988	floods	Brazil	289
	floods	Bangladesh	>1,300
1990	tsunami	Bangladesh	370
	floods	Mexico	85
	floods	Tanzania	283
1991	floods	Afghanistan	1,367
	floods	Bangladesh	150,450
	floods	Benin	30
	floods	Chad	39
	floods/storm	Chile	
	floods	China	6,728
	floods	India	2,024
	floods	Malawi	1,172
	floods	Peru	40
	floods/typhoon	Philippines	8,890
	floods	Romania	138
	floods	South Korea	54
	floods	Sudan	2,000
	floods	Turkey	30
	floods	Texas, USA	33
	floods	Vietnam	136
1992	floods	Afghanistan	450
	floods	Argentina	104
	floods	Chile	41
	floods	China	197
	floods	India	551
	floods	Pakistan	1,446
	floods	Vietnam	55
1993	floods	Indonesia	18
	floods	midwestern USA	48
1994	floods	Moldova	47
	floods	southern China	1,400
	floods	India	>600
	floods	Vietnam	>175
	floods	northern Italy	>60
1995	floods	Benin	10
	floods	Bangladesh	>200
	floods	Somalia	20
	floods	northwestern Europe	40
	floods	Hunan Province, China	1,200
	floods	southwestern Morocco	136
	floods	Pakistan	>120
	floods	South Africa	147
	floods	Vietnam	85
1996	floods	southern and western India	>300
	floods	Tuscany, Italy	30
	floods	North and South Korea	86
	floods	Pyrenees, France/Spain	84
	floods	Yemen	324
	floods	central and southern China	2,300
1997	floods	west coast, USA	36
	floods	Sikkim, India	>50
	floods	Germany/Poland/Czech Republic	>100
	floods	Somalia	>1,700
	floods	eastern Uganda	>30
	floods	Spain and Portugal	70
1998	tsunami	Papua New Guinea	>1,700
	floods/mudslides	southern Italy	118
	floods	western Pakistan	>300
	floods	western Ukraine	17
	floods	Bangladesh	>400
	floods	northern India	>1,300
	floods	central, southeast, north, and northeast China	>3,650
	floods	Nepal	>250
	floods	South Korea	>195
	floods	Slovak Republic/Poland	>34
	floods	Kyrgyzstan/Uzbekistan border	>200
1998–99 (25 December–6 January)	floods	Sri Lanka	>5 (approximately 155,000 affected and 15,000 families initially displaced)

Ultraviolet Index

The Ultraviolet (UV) Index is a measurement used to forecast the potential strength of the sun's rays during specific periods.
There are four types of UV radiation (see table below), each having different wavelengths. Specifically, the UV Index measures UV-B radiation, the most dangerous and damaging type of ultraviolet radiation because it is not blocked by the earth's ozone layer. Using these measurements, a forecast can be made indicating the potential danger resulting from exposure to UV radiation for peak hours of sunlight.

Wavelengths of UV Radiation by Type

UV category	*Wavelengths (nm)*
UV-A	320–400
UV-B	280–320
UV-C	200–280
UV-D	<200

The UVI uses a scale of 0–10+ to indicate the potential danger of the sun's rays on a given day. The index is issued on a daily basis. From the index, an estimate can be made of how long (in minutes) an individual can be exposed to the sun's rays before damage to exposed skin may result. These values are presented in the following table.

Ultraviolet Index and Skin Damage Estimates

UVI	*Exposure level*	*Minutes before skin damage*
0–2	minimal	>60
3–4	low	45
5–6	moderate	30
7–9	high	15
>10	very high	<10

Global Warming: Chronology

1967	US scientists Syukuvo Manabe and R T Wetherald warn that the increase in carbon dioxide in the atmosphere, produced by human activities, is causing a 'greenhouse effect', which will raise atmospheric temperatures and cause a rise in sea levels.
1980	A ten-year World Climate Research Programme is launched to study and predict climate changes and human influence on climate change.
1989	The warmest year on record worldwide; environmentalists suggest this is due to the 'greenhouse effect'.
3 June 1992	The United Nations Conference on Environment and Development is held in Rio de Janeiro, Brazil, attended by delegates from 178 countries, most of whom sign binding conventions to combat global warming.
1993	An ice core drilled in Greenland, providing evidence of climate change over 250,000 years, suggests that sudden fluctuations have been common and that the recent stable climate is unusual.
1995	The Prince Gustav Ice Shelf and the northern Larsen Ice Shelf in Antarctica begin to disintegrate as a result of global warming.
11 December 1997	Delegates at the Kyoto, Japan, conference on global warming agree to cut emissions of greenhouse gases by 5.2 percent from 1990 levels during the years 2008 and 2012.
17 April 1998	An iceberg 40 km/25 mi long and 4.8 km/3 mi wide breaks off from the Larson B Ice Shelf in Antarctica
17 December 1998	The United Nations World Meteorological Organization reports that 1998 is the warmest year on record, with a global average temperature of 14.4°C/58°F.

Major Hurricanes, Typhoons, Cyclones, and other Storms since 1995

As of end January 1999.

Date	Event/name	Location	Estimated number of deaths
23 January 1995	snowstorms	Kashmir, India	>200
5–7 September 1995	hurricane, *Luis*	Caribbean	14
2–3 November 1995	typhoon, *Angela*	Philippines	722
13 May 1996	tornado	Bangladesh	>600
27–28 July 1996	hurricane, *César*	Panama/El Salvador/Costa Rica	50
31 July–1 August 1996	typhoon, *Herb*	Taiwan	400
5–6 September 1996	hurricane, *Fran*	North Carolina and Virginia, USA	36
4 November 1996	cyclone	Andhra Pradesh, India	>1,000
4–5 January 1997	storms	Brazil	68
19 May 1997	cyclone	Bangladesh	112
27 September 1997	cyclone	Bangladesh	>47
9 October 1997	hurricane, *Pauline*/floods	Pacific coast of Mexico	128
2–3 November 1997	typhoon, *Linda*	southern Vietnam/Thailand	3,500
23 February 1998	tornadoes	central Florida, USA	38
8 April 1998	tornadoes	Alabama, Georgia, Mississippi, USA	>41
15 September–1 October 1998	hurricane, *Georges*	Caribbean	602
17 September–27 October 1998	three typhoons, *Vickie, Zeb,* and *Babs*	Philippines	>1,000
19 October–26 November 1998	three tropical storms, *Chip, Dawn,* and *Elvis*	central Vietnam	>265
22 October–5 November 1998	hurricane, *Mitch*	Central America and the Caribbean	>10,500
10–15 December 1998	typhoon, *Faith*	central Vietnam/Philippines	>45
15–19 January 1999	cyclone, *Dani*	Vanuatu/Fiji	>10

UK Climate and Weather

Weather in the UK

The climate of Britain is notoriously variable and changeable from day to day. Weather is generally cool to mild with frequent cloud and rain but occasional settled spells of weather occur at all seasons.

The frequent changes of weather affect all parts of the country in very much the same way; there are no great differences from one part of the country to another.

While the south is usually a little warmer than the north and the west wetter than the east, the continual changes of British weather mean that, on occasions, these differences may be reversed. Extremes of weather are rare in Britain but they do occur. For example, in December 1981 and January 1982, parts of southern and central England experienced for a few days lower temperatures than central Europe and Moscow! During the long spells of hot, sunny weather in the summers of 1975 and 1976, parts of Britain were drier and warmer than many places in the western Mediterranean.

The greatest extremes of weather and climate in Britain occur in the mountains of Scotland, Wales, and northern England. Here at altitudes exceeding 600 m/2,000 ft conditions are wet and cloudy for much of the year with annual rainfall exceeding 1,500 mm/60 in and in places reaching as much as 5,000 mm/200 in. These are among the wettest places in Europe. Winter conditions may be severe with very strong winds, driving rain, or blizzards.

Virtually all permanent settlement in Britain lies below 300 m/1,000 ft and at these levels weather conditions are usually much more congenial. As a general rule the western side of Britain is cloudier, wetter, and milder in winter, with cooler summers than the eastern side of the country. See tables for **Oban** on the west coast of Scotland, for **Belfast** in Northern Ireland, and for **Cardiff** and **Aberystwyth**, both in Wales.

The eastern side of Britain is drier the year round, with a tendency for summer rain to be heavier than that of winter. The east is a little colder in winter and warmer in summer. See the tables for **London** in southeastern England, **York** in northeastern England, and **Edinburgh** in eastern Scotland.

Much of central England, see table for **Birmingham**, has very similar weather to that of the east and south of the country.

The table for **Plymouth** shows that southwestern England shares the greater summer warmth of southern England but experiences rather milder and wetter winters than the east of the country.

The average number of hours of sunshine is greatest in the south and southeast of England and least in the north and west. Western Scotland, Wales, and Northern Ireland have rather less sunshine than most of England. In Britain daily sunshine hours range from between one and two in midwinter to between five and seven in midsummer.

Winter sunshine is much reduced in Britain because of frequent fogs and low cloud. This is a consequence of winds from the Atlantic and seas surrounding Britain, which bring high humidity. For the same reason, British mountain areas are particularly cloudy and wet.

The chief differences of weather and climate in Britain can be summed up by saying that Scotland is rarely much colder than England despite its more northerly latitude. Summers in Scotland, however, are usually shorter and rather cooler. Wales, western Scotland, and Northern Ireland are wetter the year round than most of England. Northwestern England and the Lake District are, however, particularly wet and cloudy.

Current Weather Statistics for England and Wales

January 1998–March 1999.

June and July 1998 were the second wettest combination of months in Scotland since the Scottish composite rainfall series started in 1869 (the wettest is noted as being 1938). Several months in the year were notably warmer than average: January (+1.4°C), February (+3.5°C), March (+2.2°C), and May (+1.9°C). The 13th of February was the warmest February day on record, with a temperature of 19.6°C recorded at Barbourne, Worcestershire. It was the wettest year since 1990 (at Heathrow, London, it was the wettest year since 1974), the eighth warmest year this century, and the dullest since 1993. Figures in parentheses show relative difference to the average figures taken from the period 1961–1990.

Month	Average rainfall (mm/in)	Average temperature (°C/°F)	Average sunshine (hours per day)	Remarks
1998				
January	109/4.2 (124%)	5.3/41.54 (+1.5°C)	2.0 (120%)	wettest month since 1995, the warmest January since 1993 and the sunniest since 1994
February	18.4/0.7 (29%)	7.2/44.96 (+3.4°C)	3.1 (131%)	mildest February since 1990 and the second mildest since 1869, breaking many temperature records on the 13th; the eighth sunniest February since records began 1909
March	84.4/3.3 (117%)	8.0/46.4 (+2.3°C)	2.4 (69%)	wettest March since 1994
April	134.4/5.2 (222%)	7.7/45.86 (−0.2°C)	4.6 (94%)	wettest April since 1818 and the coldest since 1989
May	25.4/4.9 (40%)	13.1/55.58 (+1.9°C)	6.8 (110%)	warmest May since 1992 and the driest since 1991
June	125.1/4.9 (192%)	14.1/57.38 (−0.1°C)	5.1 (80%)	the fourth wettest June this century
July	52.8/2.0 (85%)	15.7/60.26 (−0.4°C)	4.9 (82%)	dullest and wettest July since 1998 and the coldest and wettest since 1993
August	47.1/1.8 (62%)	15.9/60.62 (+0.1°C)	6.2 (109%)	coolest and driest August since 1994 and driest since 1995
September	87/3.4 (113%)	14.7/58.46 (+1.1°C)	4.4 (97%)	among the warmest Septembers since 1961; the eighth warmest this century
October	135/5.3 (163%)	10.8/51.44 (+0.2°C)	3.2 (104%)	wettest October since 1987 and the dullest since 1992
November	80/3.1 (90%)	6.2/43.16 (−0.4°C)	2.7 (123%)	driest November since 1993
December	84/3.3 (89%)	5.3/41.54 (−0.6°C)	1.5 (92%)	a nearly average December
1999				
January	1174.6 (135%)	5.2/41.36 (+1.4°C)	2.1 (127%)	sunniest January since 1991
February	47/1.8 (74%)	4.9/40.82 (+1.1°C)	3.0 (123%)	tenth sunniest February since current series began 1961
March	59/2.3 (82%)	6.8/44.24 (+1.1°C)	3.2 (92%)	third mild March in a row

UK Weather Records

Record	Location	Details	Date
Highest temperature	Tonbridge, Kent	38.1°C/100.6°F	22 July 1868
Lowest temperature	Braemar, Grampian	–27.8°C/–82.0°F	11 February 1895
Greatest temperature range in a single day	Tummel Bridge, Tayside	from –7°C/19.4°F to 22°C/71.6°F (a range of 29°C/55.2°F)	9 May 1978
Highest amount of rainfall in 24 hours	Martinstown, Dorset	280 mm/11 in	18 July 1955
Highest yearly average rainfall	Sprinkling Tarn, Cumbria	6,528 mm/257 in	1954
Fastest gust of wind	Cairn Gorm station, Highland	150 knots/173 mph	20 March 1986
Highest number of days with gale in a year	Lerwick, Shetlands	86 days	1949
Heaviest hailstone	Horsham, Sussex	141 g/5 oz; with diameters of up to 6 cm/2.4 in	1958
Highest average summer temperature (June, July, August)	UK	June: 17°C/62.6°F, July: 18.7°C/65.7°F, August: 17.6°C/63.7°F	1976

Weather in the UK: Aberystwyth, Wales

	Sunshine	Temperatures								Precipitation and humidity		Wet days
	average hours per day	Average daily minimum		Average daily maximum		Highest recorded		Lowest recorded		Average monthly precipitation		more than 0.25 mm/ 0.01 in
		°C	°F	°C	°F	°C	°F	°C	°F	mm	in	
January	2	2	36	7	44	14	57	–11	12	97	3.8	21
February	3	2	35	7	44	15	59	–9	16	72	2.8	17
March	4	3	38	9	49	20	68	–7	20	60	2.4	16
April	5	5	41	11	52	23	73	–3	27	56	2.2	16
May	6	7	45	15	58	26	78	–1	30	65	2.6	16
June	7	10	50	17	62	31	87	4	39	76	3.0	16
July	5	12	54	18	64	31	88	6	43	99	3.9	19
August	5	12	54	18	65	29	85	5	41	93	3.7	18
September	4	11	51	16	62	26	78	2	36	108	4.3	19
October	3	8	46	13	56	25	77	–2	28	118	4.7	20
November	2	5	41	10	50	17	63	–3	27	111	4.4	20
December	2	4	38	8	47	15	59	–6	22	96	3.8	22

Weather in the UK: Belfast, Northern Ireland

	Sunshine	Temperatures								Precipitation and humidity				Wet days
	average hours per day	Average daily minimum		Average daily maximum		Highest recorded		Lowest recorded		Relative 08:30	Relative 14:30	Average monthly precipitation		more than 0.25 mm/ 0.01 in
		°C	°F	°C	°F	°C	°F	°C	°F	%	%	mm	in	
January	1	2	35	6	43	13	56	–13	9	92	87	80	3.2	20
February	2	2	35	7	44	14	57	–12	11	91	80	52	2.1	17
March	3	3	37	9	49	19	67	–12	10	88	74	50	2.0	16
April	5	4	39	12	53	21	69	–4	24	83	69	48	1.9	16
May	6	6	43	15	59	26	79	–3	26	79	66	52	2.1	15
June	6	9	49	18	64	28	83	–1	31	80	71	68	2.7	16
July	4	11	52	18	65	29	85	4	39	84	73	94	3.7	19
August	4	11	51	18	65	28	82	1	34	87	75	77	3.0	17
September	4	9	49	16	61	26	78	–2	28	89	78	80	3.2	18
October	3	7	44	13	55	21	70	–4	24	91	80	83	3.3	19
November	2	4	39	9	48	16	61	–6	21	92	85	72	2.8	19
December	1	3	37	7	44	14	58	–11	13	92	89	90	3.5	21

Weather in the UK: Birmingham, England

	Sunshine average hours per day	Temperatures: Average daily minimum °C	Average daily minimum °F	Average daily maximum °C	Average daily maximum °F	Highest recorded °C	Highest recorded °F	Lowest recorded °C	Lowest recorded °F	Precipitation and humidity: Relative 08:30 %	Relative 14:30 %	Average monthly precipitation mm	Average monthly precipitation in	Wet days more than 0.25 mm/ 0.01 in
January	1	2	35	5	42	13	56	−12	11	89	82	74	3.0	17
February	2	2	35	6	43	16	60	−9	16	89	76	54	2.1	15
March	3	3	37	9	48	21	69	−7	19	85	68	50	2.0	13
April	5	5	40	12	54	24	75	−2	29	75	58	53	2.1	13
May	5	7	45	16	60	29	85	−1	30	74	58	64	2.5	14
June	6	10	51	19	66	31	87	3	37	74	59	50	2.0	13
July	5	12	54	20	68	32	90	6	43	75	62	69	2.7	15
August	5	12	54	20	68	33	91	6	43	80	64	69	2.7	14
September	4	10	51	17	63	27	81	3	37	84	67	61	2.4	14
October	3	7	45	13	55	25	77	−2	28	88	73	69	2.7	15
November	2	5	40	9	48	19	67	−4	24	90	80	84	3.3	17
December	1	3	37	6	44	14	58	−6	21	90	84	67	2.6	18

Weather in the UK: Cardiff, Wales

	Sunshine average hours per day	Temperatures: Average daily minimum °C	Average daily minimum °F	Average daily maximum °C	Average daily maximum °F	Highest recorded °C	Highest recorded °F	Lowest recorded °C	Lowest recorded °F	Precipitation and humidity: Relative humidity 09:00 %	Average monthly precipitation mm	Average monthly precipitation in	Wet days more than 0.25 mm/ 0.01 in
January	2	2	35	7	45	15	59	−17	2	89	108	4.3	18
Febryary	3	2	35	7	45	16	61	−9	15	87	72	2.8	14
March	4	3	38	10	50	20	68	−8	18	82	63	2.5	13
April	5	5	41	13	56	24	75	−3	27	74	65	2.6	13
May	6	8	46	16	61	29	84	−1	31	74	76	3.0	13
June	7	11	51	19	68	31	87	4	39	73	63	2.5	13
July	6	12	54	20	69	31	88	7	44	76	89	3.5	14
August	6	13	55	21	69	33	91	6	43	78	97	3.8	15
September	5	11	51	18	64	28	83	2	35	81	99	3.9	16
October	3	8	46	14	58	25	77	−3	26	85	109	4.3	16
November	2	5	41	10	51	18	65	−3	26	88	116	4.7	17
December	2	3	37	8	46	15	59	−7	19	89	108	4.3	18

Weather in the UK: Edinburgh, Scotland

	Sunshine average hours per day	Temperatures: Average daily minimum °C	Average daily minimum °F	Average daily maximum °C	Average daily maximum °F	Highest recorded °C	Highest recorded °F	Lowest recorded °C	Lowest recorded °F	Precipitation and humidity: Relative humidity 09:00 %	Average monthly precipitation mm	Average monthly precipitation in	Wet days more than 0.25 mm/ 0.01 in
January	2	1	34	6	42	14	57	−8	17	84	57	2.2	17
February	3	1	34	6	43	14	58	−9	15	83	39	1.5	15
March	4	2	36	8	46	20	68	−6	21	81	39	1.5	15
April	5	4	39	11	51	22	72	−4	25	75	39	1.5	14
May	6	6	43	14	56	24	76	−1	31	76	54	2.1	14
June	6	9	49	17	62	28	83	3	37	75	47	1.9	15
July	5	11	52	18	65	28	83	6	42	78	83	3.3	17
August	4	11	52	18	64	28	82	4	40	80	77	3.0	16
September	4	9	49	16	60	25	77	1	33	80	57	2.2	16
October	3	7	44	12	54	20	68	−2	28	82	65	2.6	17
November	2	4	39	9	48	19	67	−4	24	83	62	2.4	17
December	1	2	36	7	44	14	58	−7	20	84	57	2.2	18

Weather in the UK: London, England

	Sunshine average hours per day	Temperatures: Average daily minimum °C	Average daily minimum °F	Average daily maximum °C	Average daily maximum °F	Highest recorded °C	Highest recorded °F	Lowest recorded °C	Lowest recorded °F	Precipitation and humidity: Relative humidity % 08:30	Relative humidity % 14:30	Average monthly precipitation mm	Average monthly precipitation in	Wet days more than 0.25 mm/ 0.01 in
January	1	2	36	6	43	14	58	−10	15	86	77	54	2.1	15
February	2	2	36	7	44	16	61	−9	15	85	72	40	1.6	13
March	4	3	38	10	50	21	71	−8	18	81	64	37	1.5	11
April	5	6	42	13	56	26	78	−2	28	71	56	37	1.5	12
May	6	8	47	17	62	30	86	−1	30	70	57	46	1.8	12
June	7	12	53	20	69	33	91	5	41	70	58	45	1.8	11
July	6	14	56	22	71	34	93	7	45	71	59	57	2.2	12
August	6	13	56	21	71	33	92	6	43	76	62	59	2.3	11
September	5	11	52	19	65	30	86	3	37	80	65	49	1.9	13
October	3	8	46	14	58	26	78	−4	26	85	70	57	2.2	13
November	2	5	42	10	50	19	66	−5	23	85	78	64	2.5	15
December	1	4	38	7	45	15	59	−7	19	87	81	48	1.9	15

Weather in the UK: Oban, Scotland

	Sunshine average hours per day	Temperatures: Average daily minimum °C	Average daily minimum °F	Average daily maximum °C	Average daily maximum °F	Highest recorded °C	Highest recorded °F	Lowest recorded °C	Lowest recorded °F	Precipitation and humidity: Average monthly precipitation mm	Average monthly precipitation in	Wet days more than 0.25 mm/ 0.01 in
January	1	2	35	6	43	13	56	−8	17	146	5.8	20
February	2	1	35	7	44	13	55	−7	20	109	4.3	17
March	3	3	37	9	48	19	67	−6	22	83	3.3	15
April	5	4	40	11	52	21	69	−2	29	90	3.5	17
May	7	7	44	14	58	26	78	−4	25	72	2.8	16
June	6	9	49	16	61	29	84	3	37	87	3.4	16
July	4	11	51	17	63	29	85	5	41	120	4.7	20
August	4	11	51	17	63	27	81	3	38	116	4.6	19
September	4	9	49	15	60	24	75	1	33	141	5.6	19
October	2	7	44	12	54	22	72	−5	23	169	6.7	21
November	1	4	40	9	49	16	60	−5	23	146	5.8	20
December	1	3	37	7	45	14	58	−6	21	172	6.8	22

Weather in the UK: Plymouth, England

	Sunshine average hours per day	Temperatures: Average daily minimum °C	Average daily minimum °F	Average daily maximum °C	Average daily maximum °F	Highest recorded °C	Highest recorded °F	Lowest recorded °C	Lowest recorded °F	Precipitation and humidity: Relative humidity % 08:30	Relative humidity % 14:30	Average monthly precipitation mm	Average monthly precipitation in	Wet days more than 0.25 mm/ 0.01 in
January	2	4	39	8	47	14	57	−9	16	89	81	99	3.9	19
February	3	4	38	8	47	15	59	−8	17	88	78	74	2.9	15
March	4	5	40	10	50	19	67	−5	23	86	74	69	2.7	14
April	6	6	43	12	54	22	72	−2	29	78	69	53	2.1	12
May	7	8	47	15	59	26	79	−1	31	77	71	63	2.5	12
June	7	11	52	18	64	28	82	2	35	80	73	53	2.1	12
July	6	13	55	19	66	29	84	7	45	81	74	70	2.8	14
August	6	13	55	19	67	31	88	4	39	83	75	77	3.0	14
September	5	12	53	18	64	27	81	3	37	86	75	78	3.1	15
October	4	9	49	15	58	23	74	−2	29	88	77	91	3.6	16
November	2	7	44	11	52	17	63	−4	25	88	79	113	4.5	17
December	2	5	41	9	49	14	58	−5	23	89	82	110	4.3	18

Weather in the UK: York, England

	Sunshine	Temperatures								Precipitation and humidity			Wet days
	average hours per day	Average daily minimum		Average daily maximum		Highest recorded		Lowest recorded		Relative humidity 09.00	Average monthly precipitation		more than 0.25 mm/ 0.01 in
		°C	°F	°C	°F	°C	°F	°C	°F	%	mm	in	
January	1	1	33	6	43	15	59	−14	7	89	59	2.3	17
February	2	1	34	7	44	17	62	−10	14	87	46	1.8	15
March	3	2	36	10	49	21	70	−13	9	81	37	1.5	13
April	5	4	40	13	55	24	75	−3	27	73	41	1.6	13
May	6	7	44	16	61	29	85	−1	30	71	50	2.0	13
June	6	10	50	19	67	32	90	2	36	71	50	2.0	14
July	6	12	54	21	70	31	88	5	41	74	62	2.4	15
August	5	12	53	21	69	33	92	4	39	77	68	2.7	14
September	4	10	50	18	64	29	84	−1	31	80	55	2.2	14
October	3	7	44	14	57	26	78	−4	24	85	56	2.2	15
November	2	4	39	10	49	19	66	−7	20	88	65	2.6	17
December	1	2	36	7	45	16	60	−8	18	88	50	2.0	17

The Worst Storms, Floods, and Hurricanes in the UK

Date	Location	Details
26–27 November 1703	southwest England	one of the worst storms in British history (called The Great Storm); it occurred before records were kept, but sources show that 125 people were killed on land and 8,000 at sea
16 January 1841	River Till	following heavy snow in the first week of 1841, the temperature rose to 5°C/41°F and meltwater burst the banks of the River Till
29 December 1897	Tay Bridge	part of the bridge collapsed during gale force winds, causing a train to plunge into the water below, drowning 75 people
26 August 1912	Norwich	torrential rain amounting to the equivalent of 3 months' rainfall in a single day caused severe flooding, damaging or destroying about 3,650 buildings
29 May 1920	Louth	thunderstorms, where 115 mm/4.5 in of rain fell in 2.5 hours, caused severe flooding and devastated the town
28 January 1927	Glasgow	gale force winds caused extensive damage and 11 people were killed and over 100 injured
6 January 1928	London	torrential rain and meltwater from snow caused widespread flooding of the Thames and its tributaries; 14 people were drowned in the basements of their houses
21 May 1950	Berkshire	tornado with a wind speed of up to 370 kph/230 mph blazed a trail of destruction for nearly 161 km/100 mi in approximately 4 hours
15 August 1952	Lynmouth	torrential rainfall measuring 386 mm/15.2 in in 12 hours on Exmoor caused flood water to flow down the River Lyn and devastate Lynmouth; 34 people were killed
1–7 December 1952	London	anticyclone prevented the passage of clean air clearing fog over London; it is believed that up to 4,000 deaths in 1952 were a direct result of the black smoke from chimneys, or 'smog', which had settled in the air
4 November 1957	Hatfield	gale force winds caused damage to 26 houses
16 February 1962	Sheffield	severe gale with gusts of up to 154 kph/96 mph caused extensive damage to buildings; a crane was uprooted and crashed onto the new technical college and 100,000 homes were damaged, including 100 beyond repair
21 July 1965	Wisley	tornado lasting about 10 minutes caused destruction 10–30 m/32–98 ft-wide for a distance of 3 km/2 mi
1 November 1965	Ferrybridge	gusting winds caused three cooling towers to collapse
27 December 1965	Sea Gem Oil Rig	high winds created waves 6 m/20 ft high, and caused oil rig to collapse; nine people died
24 June 1967	Mossdale	heavy rains filled the caves, drowning six people inside
15 January 1968	Glasgow	gale force winds gusting up to 161 km/100 mph caused extensive damage; over 100,000 homes were damaged
16 September 1968	River Mole	150–200 mm/5.9–7.9 in of rainfall over 3 days caused the River Mole to burst its banks
21 November 1971	Cairngorms	snow blizzard caused deaths of six members of a school party on a climbing expedition
16 October 1987	south England	the worst storm since 1703, causing extensive damage to tree areas and a total of 17 deaths
24 December 1997	Scotland and northwest England	widespread winds and severe gales seriously damaged many buildings, uprooted thousands of trees, and resulted in six deaths; electricity supply was disrupted for up to four days and Blackpool pier was breached
10 April 1998	eastern and central England	the worst flooding in 50 years, resulting in five deaths and estimated damage of up to £500 million
21 October–2 November 1998	Wales and west England	torrential rain and flooding submerged huge areas under several feet of water, caused over £100 million damage and claimed four lives; Manchester suffered its wettest October since records began in 1942 and Worcestershire suffered its worst floods for more than 30 years

World Pollution

The World's Worst-Polluted Cities

A report published by the Washington-based World Resources Institute in January 1999 lists the ten cities in the world with the worst air pollution, finding that nine out of the ten were in China. The fifth-worst city is in India. Ranked number one is Lanzhou, in Gansu Province, North West China. This is a region that has a large petrochemical industry and oil refineries.

According to World Health Organization (WHO) guidelines, the maximum permissible amount of total suspended particulates (TSPs) is 90 micrograms per cubic litre of air. Lanzhou has more than 700. The next worst ranked city is Jilin, which has almost 700, while Taiyun – ranked number three – has nearly 600. The remaining seven cities listed in the report, in order of descending TSP levels, are Jiaozuo, Rajkot in India, Wanxian, Urumqi, Yichang, Hanzhong, and Anyang.

The study, funded by the WHO, the US Environmental Protection Agency, and other groups, found that millions of children risked disease and death because they lived in these badly polluted cities. Children are more at risk because they breathe faster and because their lungs are still developing. The problem is that these cities have rapidly growing economies, but lack the more modern and cleaner technology that developed countries benefit from.

Air Pollution in the World's Megacities

This table provides indications of air pollution in 14 of the world's megacities (urban areas with more than 10 million people by the year 2000). Total suspended particulates refer to smoke, soot, dust, and liquid droplets from combustion that are in the air. They indicate the quality of the air a population is breathing. As of the most official available data, 1995. Reliable figures are not available for other megacities such as New York (USA), Los Angeles (California, USA), Buenos Aires (Brazil), London (England), Karachi (Venezuela), and Cairo (Egypt).

Rank	City	Total suspended particulates (micrograms per cubic metre)	Rank	City	Total suspended particulates (micrograms per cubic metre)
1	Delhi	415	8	Bangkok	223
2	Beijing	377	9	Manila	200
3	Calcutta	375	10	Rio de Janeiro	139
4	Mexico City	279	11	Moscow	100
5	Jakarta	271	12	São Paulo	86
6	Shanghai	246	13	Seoul	84
7	Bombay	240	14	Tokyo	49

Source: *World Development Indicators 1998,* IBRD/World Bank 1998

The Greenhouse Effect

This is the phenomenon of the Earth's atmosphere by which solar radiation, trapped by the Earth and re-emitted from the surface as infrared radiation, is prevented from escaping by various gases in the air. Greenhouse gases trap heat because they readily absorb infrared radiation. The result is a rise in the Earth's temperature (global warming). The main greenhouse gases are carbon dioxide, methane, and chlorofluorocarbons (CFCs) as well as water vapour. Fossil-fuel consumption and forest fires are the principal causes of carbon dioxide build-up; methane is a byproduct of agriculture (rice, cattle, sheep). Dubbed the 'greenhouse effect' by Swedish scientist Svante Arrhenius, it was first predicted in 1827 by French mathematician Joseph Fourier.

The United Nations Environment Programme estimates that by 2025, average world temperatures will have risen by 1.5°C/2.7°F with a consequent rise of 20 cm/7.9 in in sea level. Low-lying areas and entire countries would be threatened by flooding and crops would be affected by the change in climate. However, predictions about global warming and its possible climatic effects are tentative and often conflict with each other.

At the 1992 Earth Summit it was agreed that by 2000 countries would stabilize carbon dioxide emissions at 1990 levels, but to halt the acceleration of global warming, emissions would probably need to be cut by 60 percent. Any increases in carbon dioxide emissions are expected to come from transport. The Berlin Mandate, agreed unanimously at the climate conference in Berlin in 1995, committed industrial nations to the continuing reduction of greenhouse gas emissions after 2000, when the existing pact to stabilize emissions runs out. The stabilization of carbon dioxide emissions at 1990 levels by 2000 will not be achieved by a number of developed countries, including Spain, Australia, and the USA, according to 1997 estimates. Australia is in favour of different targets for different nations, and refused to sign a communiqué at the South Pacific Forum meeting in the Cook Islands in 1997 which insisted on legally binding reductions in greenhouse gas emissions.

Air Pollution: Major Pollutants

Air pollution is contamination of the atmosphere caused by the discharge, accidental or deliberate, of a wide range of toxic airborne substances. Often the amount of the released substance is relatively high in a certain locality, so the harmful effects become more noticeable. The cost of preventing any discharge of pollutants into the air is prohibitive, so attempts are more usually made to reduce the amount of discharge gradually and to disperse it as quickly as possible by using a very tall chimney, or by intermittent release.

Possibly the world's worst ever human-made air pollution disaster occurred in Indonesia in September 1997. It was caused by forest clearance fires. Smoke pollution in the city of Palangkaraya reached 7.5 mg per cu m (nearly 3 mg more than in the London smog of 1952). The pollutants spread to Malaysia and other countries of the region. The 1997 Kyoto protocol committed the industrialized nations of the world to cutting their levels of harmful gas emissions to 5.2% by 2012. Europe is expected to take the biggest cut of 8%, the USA 7%, and Japan 6%. The agreement covers Russia and eastern Europe as well.

Pollutant	Sources	Effects
Sulphur dioxide (SO_2)	oil, coal combustion in power stations	acid rain formed, which damages plants, trees, buildings, and lakes
Oxides of nitrogen (NO, NO_2)	high-temperature combustion in cars, and to some extent power stations	acid rain formed
Lead compounds	from leaded petrol used by cars	nerve poison
Carbon dioxide (CO_2)	oil, coal, petrol, diesel combustion	greenhouse effect
Carbon monoxide (CO)	limited combustion of oil, coal, petrol, diesel fuels	poisonous, leads to photochemical smog in some areas
Nuclear waste	nuclear power plants, nuclear weapon testing, war	radioactivity, contamination of locality, cancers, mutations, death

Nuclear Waste for Selected Countries

The table presents the annual spent fuel in nuclear power plants of selected OECD countries, and includes projections up to 2010 (as made in 1997). Spent fuel arisings are one part of the radioactive waste generated at various stages of the nuclear fuel cycle (uranium mining and milling, fuel enrichment, reactor operation, spent fuel reprocessing). Radioactive waste also arises from decontamination and decommissioning of nuclear facilities, and from other activities using isotopes, such as scientific research and medical activities. Data in the table do not represent all radioactive waste generated; amounts of spent fuel arisings depend on the share of nuclear electricity in the energy supply and on the nuclear plant technologies adopted. The impact of nuclear waste on humans and the environment depends on the level of radioactivity and on the conditions under which the waste is handled, treated, stored, and disposed of.
(N/A = not available. N = nil or negligible.)

Rank (1996 figures)	Country	Spent fuel (tonnes of heavy metal)					
		1982	1992	1996	2000	2005	2010
1	USA	1,100	2,300	2,300	2,200	2,000	1,900
2	Canada	856	1,690	1,690	1,782	1,798	1,798
3	France	375	1,050	1,200	1,210	1,210	1,210
4	UK	900	997	1,023	1,258	397	204
5	Japan	510	869	980	940	1,040	1,380
6	Germany	270	500	450	420	400	400
7	Korea	N/A	261	254	650	750	850
8	Sweden	100	250	230	230	230	200
9	Spain	60	168	160	158	155	159
10	Belgium	44	102	137	110	110	110
11	Finland	62	60	68	76	76	76
12	Switzerland	60	85	64	64	64	64
13	Hungary	N/A	N/A	55	53	53	53
14	Czech Republic	N/A	N/A	45	43	85	85
15	Mexico	N	N	39	30	28	23
16	Netherlands	16	15	14	12	N	N
17	Turkey	N	N	N	N	29	58

Source: *OECD Environmental Data 1997*, © OECD 1997

Major Oilspills Throughout the World

As of January 1997.

Date	Location	Description	Amount: tonnes	Amount: millions of gallons
March 1967	off Cornwall, England	grounding of *Torrey Canyon*	118,000	35.4
June 1968	off South Africa	hull failure of *World Glory*	37,000	11.0
December 1972	Gulf of Oman	collision of *Sea Star* with another ship	103,500	31.0
May 1976	La Caruña, Spain	grounding of the *Urquioia*	60–70,000	18.0–21.0
December 1976	Nantucket (MA), USA	grounding of *Argo Merchant*	25,000	7.5
February 1977	mid-Pacific	*Haiwaiian Patriot* develops leak and catches fire	100,000	30.0
April 1977	North Sea	blow-out of well in *Ekofisk* oil field	270,000	81.0
March 1978	Portsall, Brittany, France	grounding of the *Amoco Cadiz*	226,000	68.0
June 1979	Gulf of Mexico	blow-out of well in *Ixtoc 1* oil field	600,000	180.0
July 1979	off Tobago, Caribbean	collision of the *Atlantic Empress* and *Aegean Captain*	370,000	111.0
February 1983	Persian Gulf	blow-out of well in *Nowruz* oil field	600,000	180.0
August 1983	off Cape Town, South Africa	fire on board the *Castillo de Beliver*	250,000	75.0
September 1985	Delaware River (DE), USA	grounding of *Grand Eagle*	1,500	0.5
January 1988	Floreffe (PA), USA	collapsing of *Ashland* oil storage tank	2,400–2,500	0.7–0.8
March 1989	Prince William Sound, off Alaskan Coast	grounding of *Exxon Valdez*	37,000	11.0
June 1989	Canary Islands	fire on board the *Kharg 5*	65,000	19.5
January 1991	Sea Island Terminal of Persian Gulf	deliberate release of oil by Iraqi troops at end of Persian Gulf War	799,120	240.0
January 1993	Shetland Islands, Scotland	grounding of *Braer*	130,000	39.0
August 1993	Tampa Bay (FL), USA	collision of two barges and a Philippine freighter	984	0.3
January 1996	Pembrokeshire coastline of Wales, British Isles	grounding of *Sea Empress*	>100,000	19.0
January 1996	south shore of Rhode Island (RI), USA	grounding of the tugboat *Scandia* and *North Cape* tanker it was towing	1,000	0.3

Household Waste Generated in Selected Countries

As of 1995 or latest available year.

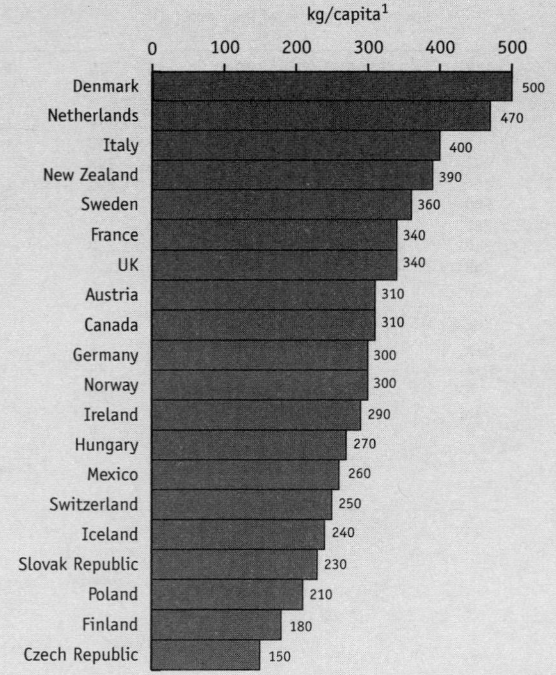

Rank (by amount per capita)	Country	Household waste generated (thousands of tonnes)
1	Denmark	2,610
2	Netherlands	7,319
3	Italy	23,000
4	New Zealand	1,400
5	Sweden	3,200
6=	France	20,000
	UK	20,000
8=	Austria	2,509
	Canada	8,925
10=	Germany	24,203
	Norway	1,262
12	Ireland	1,026
13	Hungary	2,787
14	Mexico	24,408
15	Switzerland	1,770
16	Iceland	65
17	Slovak Republic	1,215
18	Poland	7,958
19	Finland	900
20	Czech Republic	1,593

[1] National definitions may differ. Values per capita are rounded.

Source: *OECD Environmental Data 1997*, © OECD 1997

Some Ozone Destroyers

A Class I substance is any chemical with an ozone-depleting potential (ODP) of 0.2 or greater. Class II substances include all of the hydrochlorofluorocarbons (HCFCs).
(– = not applicable.)

Substance	Chemical name	ODP[1]	GWP[2]
Class I Ozone-Depleting Substances			
Group I			
CFC-11	trichlorofluoromethane	1.0	4,000
CFC-12	dichlorodifluoromethane	1.0	8,500
CFC-113	1,1,1-trichlorotrifluoroethane	0.8	5,000
	1,1,2-trichlorotrifluoroethane	0.8	–
CFC-114	dichlorotetrafluoroethane	1.0	9,300
CFC-115	monochloropentafluoroethane	0.6	9,300
Group II			
Halon 1211	bromochlorodifluoromethane	3.0	–
Halon 1301	bromotrifluoromethane	10.0	5,600
Halon 2402	dibromotetrafluoroethane	6.0	–
Group III			
CFC-13	chlorotrifluoromethane	1.0	11,700
CFC-111	pentachlorofluoroethane	1.0	–
CFC-112	tetrachlorodifluoroethane	1.0	–
CFC-211	heptachlorofluoropropane	1.0	–
CFC-212	hexachlorodifluoropropane	1.0	–
CFC-213	pentachlorotrifluoropropane	1.0	–
CFC-214	tetrachlorotetrafluoropropane	1.0	–
CFC-215	trichloropentafluoropropane	1.0	–
CFC-216	dichlorohexafluoropropane	1.0	–
CFC-217	chloroheptafluoropropane	1.0	–
Group IV			
CC14	carbon tetrachloride	1.1	1,400
Group V			
Methyl chloroform	1,1,1-trichloroethane	0.1	110
Group VI			
CH_3Br	methyl bromide	0.7	–
Selected Class II[3] Ozone-depleting Substances			
HCFC-22	chlorodifluoromethane	0.05	1,700
HCFC-123	2,2-dichloro-1,1,1-trifluoroethane	0.02	93
HCFC-124	2-chloro-1,1,1,2-tetrafluoroethane	0.02	480
HCFC-141b	1,1-dichloro-1-fluoroethane	0.1	630
HCFC-142b	1-chloro-1,1-difluoroethane	0.06	2,000

[1] ODP (ozone depletion potential) is a ratio of a chemical's impact on ozone compared with the impact of a similar mass of CFC-11.
[2] GWP (global warming potential) represents a ratio of the warming caused by a substance to the warming caused by the same mass of carbon dioxide (CO_2).
[3] Although all HCFCs are included in Class II, only commonly used HCFCs are listed.

Source: Stratospheric Protection Division of the US Environmental Protection Agency

Recycling Rates in Industrialized Countries

This table refers to municipal waste, waste handled by scrapping industry, and other waste from economic activities. Material that is collected for recycling by private sources is also included. Recycling is defined as any reuse of material in a production process that diverts it from the waste stream, except reuse as fuel. 'Recycling rates' are the amounts recycled relative to apparent consumption (economic notion of domestic production of the respective material + imports – exports). It should be noted that definitions may vary from one country to another. In particular, total amounts of waste produced, rather than apparent consumption, may be used in some areas to derive recycling rates.
(N/A = not available.)

Country	Percentage of apparent consumption			
	Paper and cardboard		Glass	
	1990	1995	1990	1995
Austria	37	65	60[1]	76
Belgium	14[2]	12	39[2]	67
Canada	28	N/A	17[3]	N/A
Denmark	44	35[1]	35	63
Finland	41	57	36	50
France	34	38	29	50
Germany	44	67	54	75
Greece	28	19	15	20[4]
Iceland	10	N/A	70	N/A
Ireland	11[2]	12	23	39
Italy	27	29	48	53
Japan	50	N/A	48	N/A
Korea, South	44	53	46	57
Mexico	2[1]	2	4[1]	4
Netherlands	50	2	41	4
Norway	25	41	22[1]	75
Portugal	41	37	27	42
Spain	51	52	27	32
Sweden	43	54	44[1]	61
Switzerland	49	61	65	85
Turkey	27	34	31	12
UK	35	35	21	27
USA	29	35[5]	20	23[5]

[1] Data are for 1991. [2] Data are for 1987.
[3] Data are for 1992. [4] Data are for 1993.
[5] Data are for 1994.

Source: *OECD Environmental Data 1997*,

UK Pollution

Air Pollution in the UK: Selected Pollutants and Cities

Air pollution levels vary with a number of factors, such as time of day, season of the year, location in the UK, whether you are in an urban or rural environment etc, hence summarizing pollution levels is difficult and often misleading. However, in order to give a brief summary of the measurements from automatic networks, and some idea of the sorts of levels measured in UK cities, this table gives annual means for 1996 for five pollutants: Carbon monoxide (CO) – The sites with the highest annual means are measuring close to roads, since road traffic is one of the major sources of carbon monoxide.

Particulates (PM_{10}) – there is a wide gradient in the concentrations of PM_{10} in the UK, from the SE (higher levels) to the NW (lower levels). Local effects from transport and industrial emissions increase PM_{10} concentrations.

Sulphur Dioxide (SO_2) – Sulphur dioxide annual means are highest in areas where coal is used as a fuel, or where the site is influenced by a major power point source, such as a nuclear power station.

Nitrogen Dioxide (NO_2) – Nitrogen dioxide means are highest in sites measuring close to roads, and lowest in rural areas.

Ozone (O_3) – Ozone annual means are actually higher in rural locations than in cities. This is because ozone is 'scavenged' in urban areas – reaction with emissions from motor vehicles leads to rapid, local removal from the atmosphere.
(N/A = not available.)

1996

City/site	Annual mean				
	CO (ppm)	PM_{10} (μg m^{-3})	SO_2 (ppb)	NO_2 (ppb)	O_3 (ppb)
Belfast	0.5	24	20	20	17
Birmingham	0.5	24	7	22	16
Bristol	1.3	25	5	28	17
Cardiff	0.5	25	5	21	16
Edinburgh	0.5	19	4	25	16
Exeter	1.7	N/A	3	N/A	N/A
Glasgow	0.7	22	4	26	N/A
Leamington Spa	0.3	20	3	21	N/A
Leeds	0.7	27	6	27	14
Leicester	0.5	22	5	22	16
Liverpool	0.4	25	10	25	16
London[1]	0.7	24	6	26	14
Manchester	0.4	26	8	24	12
Middlesbrough	0.4	21	5	16	21
Newcastle	0.5	24	6	21	17
Nottingham	0.8	24	6	28	N/A
Oxford	1.4	N/A	10	N/A	N/A
Sheffield	0.5	28	9	26	16
Southampton	0.7	23	4	24	15
Swansea	0.5	23	7	23	18
Wolverhampton	0.6	26	6	21	17

[1] Data for London are averages derived from statistics from several different Network stations. The top station/site in London for each type of pollutant is as follows: CO Cromwell Road – 1.4 ppm; PM_{10} Bloomsbury – 30 μg m^{-3}; SO_2 Cromwell Road – 9 ppb; NO_2 Bloomsbury – 36 ppb; O_3 Brent – 18 ppb.

The Top Worst Polluting Companies in Britain

In 1998 British companies were fined a total of £2 million for pollution offences. The government's Environment Agency is calling on the courts to impose stiffer penalties in a bid to reduce pollution. Some specific examples of the pollution incidents in this year are given in the table footnotes.

Ranking	Company	Fines levied in pounds
1	ICI Chemicals	382,500[1]
2	Tyseley Waste Disposal Ltd	95,500
3	London Waste Ltd	38,500[2]
4	Wessex Water Ltd	36,500
5	Alco Waste Management	30,000
6	Anglian Water Services Ltd	24,250
7	EOM Construction Ltd	21,000
8=	Shell (UK) Ltd	20,000[3]
	BNFL	20,000[4]
10=	Celtic Energy	18,000
	European Vinyls Corporation Ltd	18,000

[1] A £300,000 fine was incurred in March 1998 for polluting groundwater with almost 150 tonnes of choloroform in April 1997. The company was also fined for releasing a metal-cleaning chemical that evaporated into the air and entered a nearby canal, and for a discharge at a site at Cleveland that sprayed across marshland and killed birds, fish and vegetation.

[2] The company was fined £95,000 after the disappearance of radioactive material during demolition work at an incinerator plant in Birmingham.

[3] Shell UK was fined £20,000 for polluting the Manchester Ship Canal with the equivalent of 10,500 household buckets of refined oil from the Stanlow Manufacturing Complex in Ellesmere Port.

[4] BNFL was fined £20,000 because of a discharge from a site in Preston into the River Ribble in 1997.

Source: The Environment Agency, © Crown copyright 1999

Quality of Seaside Bathing Waters in the UK

In order to comply with an EC Bathing Water Directive (76/160/EEC), at least 95 percent of samples taken during the bathing season must have no more than 10,000 coliform bacteria in total per 100 ml and no more than 2,000 faecal coliform bacteria per ml.

Region/country	Identified bathing waters		Number complying		% complying	
	1993	1997	1993	1997	1993	1997
Anglian	33	35	28	35	85	100
Northumbrian[1]	34	34	25	32	74	94
North West	33	34	13	17	39	50
Southern	67	75	58	67	87	89
South West[1]	133	137	107	125	80	91
Thames	3	3	3	3	100	100
Welsh	51	64	42	60	82	94
Wessex[1]	42	43	35	39	83	91
Yorkshire[1]	22	22	21	19	95	86
England and Wales total	418	447	332	397	79	89
Scotland	23	23	18	18	78	78
Northern Ireland	16	16	15	14	94	88
UK total	457	486	365	429	80	88

[1] In 1993, Northumbrian and Yorkshire were amalgamated into one region, now called North East; and Wessex and South West were amalgamated into one region, now called South West. Results for the old regions are given for comparison.

Source: *Digest of Environmental Statistics No. 20 1998,*

Quality of Waters in Rivers and Canals in the UK

The table indicates the lengths of rivers and canals in General Quality Assessment chemical grades. A contains 80 percent dissolved oxygen, B 70 percent, C 60 percent, D 50 percent, E 20 percent, and F contains no measurable amount of dissolved oxygen. (N = nil or negligible.)

1994–96 (1995 for Scotland)

Region/country	Length (km)[1]							% of total	
	Good		Fair		Poor	Bad	Total	Good or fair	Poor or bad
	A	B	C	D	E	F			
Anglian	280	1,520	1,490	910	590	30	4,810	87	13
Midlands	840	2,210	2,070	870	670	60	6,720	89	11
North East[2]	1,830	1,870	1,090	690	790	140	6,410	86	14
North West	1,160	1,860	1,200	620	750	160	5,750	84	16
Southern	320	890	580	220	200	10	2,220	90	10
South West	2,450	2,190	940	270	200	20	6,070	96	4
Thames	500	1,360	1,020	580	330	10	3,800	91	9
Welsh	3,680	930	260	80	80	N	5,040	98	2
England and Wales	11,070	12,840	8,640	4,230	3,600	420	40,800	90	10
Northern Ireland	180	870	630	390	270	20	2,360	88	12

	Unpolluted	Fairly good	Poor	Grossly polluted	Total	% of total: Unpolluted or fairly good	% of total: Poor or grossly polluted
Scotland	48,890	1,090	220	60	50,260	99	1

[1] Lengths are rounded to the nearest 10 km and may not sum to totals.

[2] In 1993, Northumbrian and Yorkshire were amalgamated into one region, now called North East.

Source: *Digest of Environmental Statistics No. 20 1998,*

Water Pollution Incidents in the UK

The table shows data for substantiated water pollution incidents by type of pollutant. There were a total of 35,290 reported water pollution incidents during 1996 in England, Wales, and Northern Ireland; of these 22,213 were substantiated. A similar breakdown of incidents by type of pollutant is not available for Scotland.
(– = not applicable.)

1996

Region/country	Organic wastes	Fuels and oil	Sewage	Chemicals	Other	Total	%
Anglian	189	763	555	239	671	2,417	10
Midlands	436	1,258	991	446	1,174	4,305	17
North East	150	562	761	199	471	2,143	9
North West	341	588	843	308	738	2,818	11
Southern	66	443	346	102	232	1,189	5
South West	549	768	666	193	866	3,042	12
Thames	86	817	428	153	475	1,959	8
Welsh	312	388	688	197	700	2,285	9
England and Wales	2,129	5,587	5,278	1,837	5,327	20,158	81
Scotland	–	–	–	–	–	2,878	11
Northern Ireland	512	375	556	152	460	2,055	8
UK total[1]	2,641	5,962	5,834	1,989	5,787	25,091	100
%[2]	11.9	26.8	26.3	8.9	26.1	100.0	–

[1] Totals for the breakdown by type of pollutant do not include Scotland.
[2] Percentages by type of pollutant are based on the totals for England, Wales, and Northern Ireland, as a similar breakdown of incidents is not available for Scotland.

Source: *Digest of Environmental Statistics No. 20 1998,* © Crown copyright 1998

Emissions in the UK

(In thousands of tonnes.)

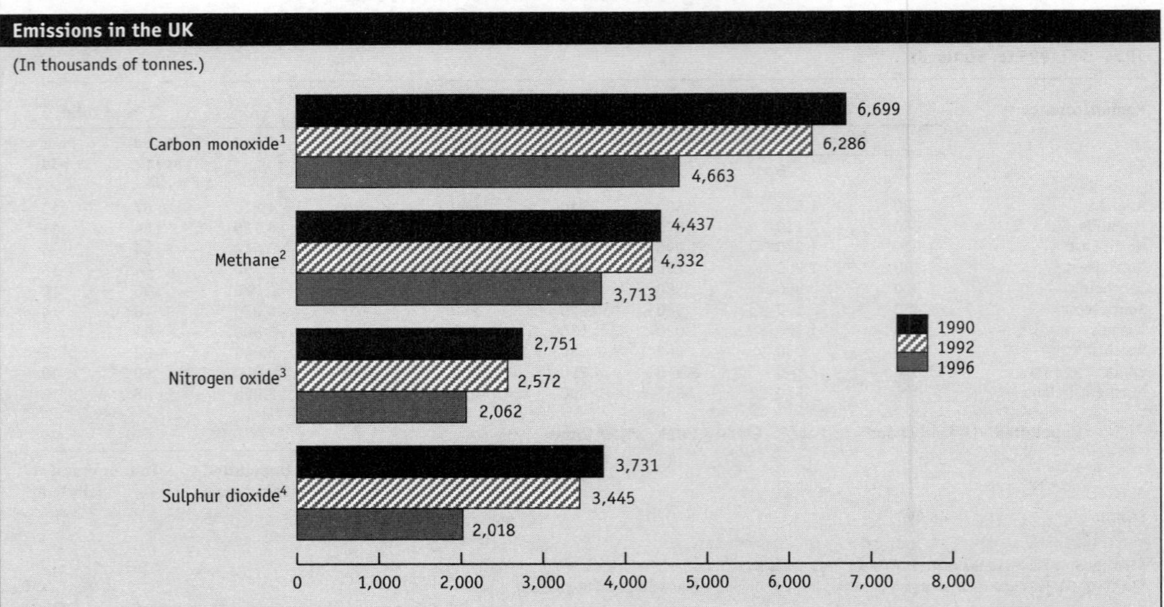

[1] Colourless, odourless gas formed when carbon is oxidized in a limited supply of air. It is a poisonous constituent of car exhaust fumes, forming a stable compound with haemoglobin in the blood, thus preventing the haemoglobin from transporting oxygen to the body tissues. The main source in the UK is road transport (3,299,000 tonnes in 1996).
[2] Colourless, odourless, and lighter than air, it burns with a bluish flame and explodes when mixed with air or oxygen. It is the chief constituent of natural gas and also occurs in the explosive firedamp of coal mines. The main source in the UK is landfill sites (1,720,000 tonnes in 1996).
[3] Gas compound that contains only nitrogen and oxygen. Nitrogen monoxide and nitrogen dioxide contribute to air pollution. The main sources in the UK are road transport (966,000 tonnes in 1996) and power stations (449,000 tonnes in 1996).
[4] Pungent gas produced by burning sulphur in air or oxygen. It is widely used for disinfecting food vessels and equipment, and as a preservative in some food products. It occurs in industrial flue gases and is a major cause of acid rain. The main source in the UK is power stations (1,318,000 tonnes in 1996).

Source: *Digest of Environmental Statistics No. 20 1998,* © Crown copyright 1998

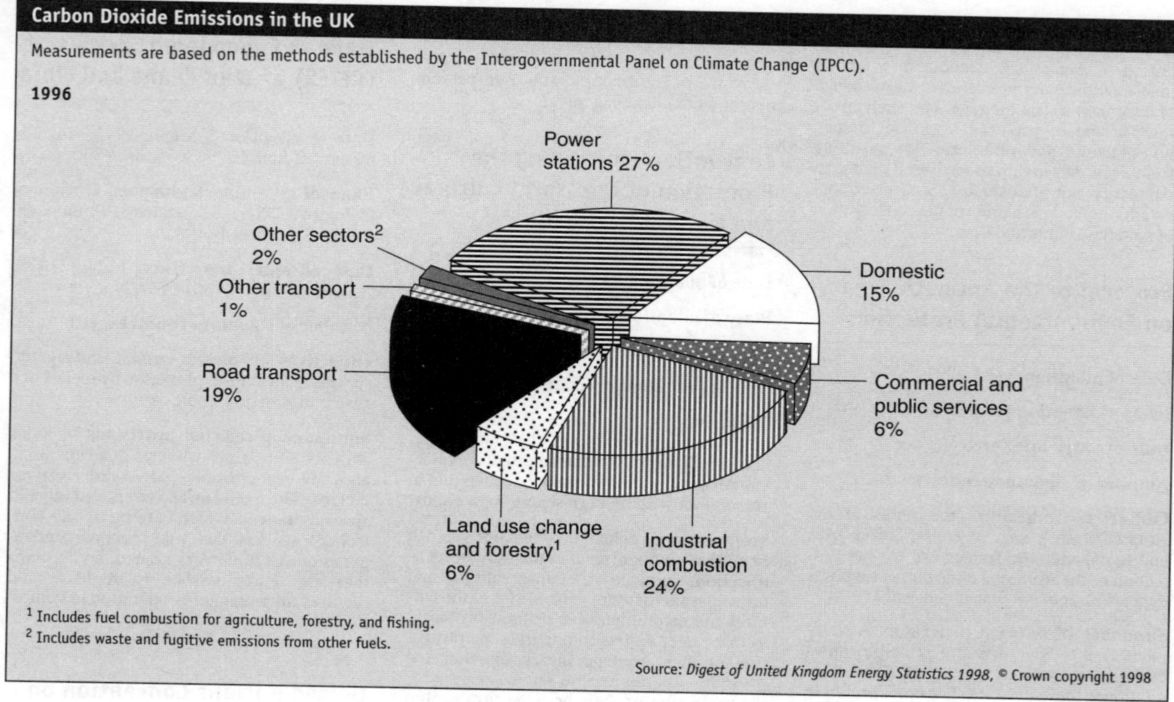

International Environmental Agreements

International Convention for the Regulation of Whaling

Date of adoption 2 December 1946; Amendment: 19 November 1956

Place of adoption Washington, District of Columbia, USA

Date of entry into force 10 November 1948; Amendment: 4 May 1959

Number of signatory countries 49

Objectives To protect all species of whales from overfishing and safeguard for future generations the great natural resources represented by whale stocks. To establish a system of international regulation for the whale fisheries to ensure proper conservation and development of whale stocks.

Summary of selected provisions Establishment of an International Whaling Commission (IWC) to encourage research and investigation, to collect and analyse statistical information, and to appraise and disseminate information concerning whaling and whale stocks. The IWC meets annually to adopt regulations for the conservation and utilization of whale stocks, dealing with protected and unprotected species, size limits for species, maximum catches for any one season, types of gear and apparatus to be used, contracting Governments to take measures to enforce these regulations, and to report any infraction to them to the IWC.

International Plant Protection Convention

Date of adoption 6 December 1951; Amendment: November 1979

Place of adoption Rome, Italy

Date of entry into force 3 April 1952; Amendment: 4 April 1991

Number of signatory countries 97

Objectives To maintain and increase international cooperation in controlling pests and diseases of plants and plant products, and in preventing their introduction and spread across national boundaries.

Summary of selected provisions Parties undertake to adopt the legislative, technical and administrative measures specified in the Convention; specific and regional agreements to be made in conjunction with the Food and Agriculture Organization (FAO) of the United Nations; each Party to set up an official plant protection organization to inspect areas under cultivation and consignments of plants in international traffic for existence or outbreak of plant pests or diseases, and to carry out research in the field of plant protection; Parties to regulate very strictly the import and export of plants and plant products, by means, where necessary, of prohibitions, inspections, and destruction of consignments.

The Antarctic Treaty

Date of adoption 1 December 1959

Place of adoption Washington, District of Columbia, USA

Date of entry into force 23 June 1961

Number of signatory countries 40

Objectives To ensure that Antarctica is used for peaceful purposes, for international cooperation in scientific research, and does not become the scene or object of international discord.

Summary of selected provisions No military bases, military manoeuvres, or weapon testing in Antarctica; freedom of scientific investigation and cooperation in the exchange of information regarding plans for such investigation and of personnel engaged in such investigation, and of information resulting from such investigation; territorial claims in Antarctica not affected by the Convention; detailed agreed measures for the conservation of Antarctic fauna and flora.

Protocol to the Antarctic Treaty on Environmental Protection

Date of adoption 3 Oct 1991

Place of adoption Madrid, Spain

Date of entry into force Not yet

Number of signatory countries 34

Objectives To reaffirm the status of the Antarctica as a special conservation area, and to enhance the framework for the protection of the Antarctic environment with its dependent and associated ecosystems.

Summary of selected provisions A statement of the environmental principles governing the conduct of States Parties in relation to the Antarctica. The basic principle is to protect the Antarctic environment and dependent and associated ecosystems as well as the intrinsic value of the Antarctica with its aesthetic values, as well as its status as a place of research; prohibition of mineral resource enterprises in the Antarctic Treaty area, save for purposes of scientific research; requirement of environmental impact assessment in the Antarctic Treaty area in respect of activities that are likely to entail significant adverse environmental consequences. The Protocol has the following annexes environment: impact assessment; conservation of Antarctic fauna and flora; waste disposal and waste management; prevention of marine pollution.

Convention on Wetlands of International Importance

Date of adoption 2 February 1971

Place of adoption Ramsar, Iran

Date of entry into force 21 December 1975

Number of signatory countries 62

Objectives To stem the progressive encroachment on and loss of wetlands now and in the future, recognizing the fundamental ecological functions of wetlands and their economic, cultural, scientific, and recreational value.

Summary of selected provisions Parties to designate at least one national wetland for inclusion in a 'List of Wetlands of International Importance'; Parties to establish wetland nature reserves, cooperate in the exchange of information, and train personnel for wetland management.

Convention Concerning the Protection of the World Cultural and Natural Heritage

Date of adoption 23 November 1972

Place of adoption Paris, France

Date of entry into force 17 December 1975

Number of signatory countries 127

Objectives To establish an effective system of collective protection of the cultural and natural heritage of outstanding universal value, organized on a permanent basis and in accordance with modern scientific methods.

Summary of selected provisions Each State Party recognizes that the duty of identification, protection, conservation, and transmission to future generations of the cultural and natural heritage belongs primarily to that State; Parties to integrate the protection of their heritage into comprehensive planning programmes, to set up services for the protection of their heritage, to develop scientific and technical studies, and to take necessary legal, scientific, administrative and financial steps to protect their heritage. A World Heritage Committee established, to which each Party will submit an inventory of its national heritage and which will publish a 'World Heritage List' and a 'List of World Heritage in Danger'; establishment of a World Heritage Fund, financed by the Parties and other interested bodies.

Convention on the Conservation of Migratory Species of Wild Animals

Date of adoption 23 June 1979

Place of adoption Bonn, Germany

Date of entry into force 1 November 1983

Number of signatory countries 39

Objective To protect those species of wild animals that migrate across or outside national boundaries.

Summary of selected provisions Listing of endangered migratory species; international agreements dealing with those aspects of the conservation and management of the migratory species concerned which serve to achieve the object of protection; establishment of a scientific council to provide advice on scientific matters.

Convention on International Trade in Endangered Species (CITES) of Wild Fauna and Flora

Date of adoption 3 March 1973; Amendments: 22 June 1979; 30 April 1983

Place of adoption Washington, District of Columbia, USA; Amendments: Bonn, Germany; Gaborone, Botswana

Date of entry into force 1 July 1975; Amendments: 13 April 1987; Not yet

Number of signatory countries 110

Objectives To protect certain endangered species from over-exploitation by means of a system of import/export permits.

Summary of selected provisions Includes animals and plants whether dead or alive, and any recognizable parts or derivatives thereof. The Convention covers endangered species, trade in which is to be tightly controlled; species that may become endangered unless trade is regulated; and species that any Party wishes to regulate and requires international cooperation to control trade.

United Nations Convention on the Law of the Sea

Date of adoption 10 December 1982

Place of adoption Montego Bay, Jamaica

Date of entry into force Not yet

Number of signatory countries 160

Objective To set up a comprehensive new legal regime for the sea and oceans and, as far as environmental provisions are concerned, to establish material rules concerning environmental standards as well as enforcement provisions dealing with pollution of the marine environment.

Summary of selected provisions Definition of the territorial sea and the contiguous zone; land-locked States to enjoy the right of access to and from the sea and freedom of transit; the sea bed and ocean floor and its subsoil are beyond the limits of national jurisdiction and its resources to be the common heritage of mankind. International rules and national legislation to be developed for the prevention, reduction, and control of pollution of the marine environment, and provisions set out concerning enforcement and responsibility and liability; rules set out to govern marine scientific research, the development and transfer of marine technology and the settlement of disputes.

The Vienna Convention on the Protection of the Ozone Layer

Date of adoption 22 March 1985

Place of adoption Vienna, Austria

Date of entry into force 22 September 1988

Number of signatory countries 169

Objectives To protect the ozone layer and encourage governments to cooperate in developing scientific understanding of atmospheric processes.

Summary of selected provisions Agreement on specific measures to be taken to tackle ozone depletion, and on protocols that established specific controls.

Montreal Protocol on Substances that Deplete the Ozone Layer

Date of adoption 16 September 1987

Place of adoption Montreal, Canada

Date of entry into force 1 January 1989

Number of signatory countries 168

Objectives To reduce and eventually eliminate the emissions of man-made ozone-depleting substances.

Summary of selected provisions Reductions in emissions of man-made ozone-depleting substances through controls on their production and supply. Stipulation of a 50 percent reduction in CFC consumption by 1999. The Montreal Protocol on Substances that Deplete the Ozone Layer has been amended four times so far. Its control provisions were strengthened through four adjustments to the Protocol adopted in London 1990 (came into force 10 September 1992; ratified by 127 countries), Copenhagen 1992 (came into force 14 June 1994; ratified by 87 countries), and Montreal 1997 (not yet in force; ratified by 10 countries as of 15 March 1999). Under the Protocol and its amendments, Parties agreed to: phase out production and consumption of CFCs, carbon tetrachloride, methyl chloroform, and HBFCs by 1996; phase out production and consumption of halons by 1994; phase out production and consumption of HCFCs by 2030 and of methyl bromide by 2005.

Within the Protocol and its amendments, special dispensations are given for essential uses and, in the case of methyl bromide, quarantine applications. A certain amount of production is also permitted to meet the needs of developing countries which have a 10-year grace period for compliance. There is no agreement on HFCs which are seen as long-term substitutes in some applications, which is significant as these are also greenhouse gases.

Basel Convention on the Control of Transboundary Movements of Hazardous Wastes and Their Disposal

Date of adoption 1989

Place of adoption Basel, Switzerland

Date of entry into force 5 May 1992

Number of signatory countries 121

Objectives To minimize hazardous waste generation, regulate the transboundary movement of hazardous wastes, and provide obligations to its Parties to ensure that such wastes are managed and disposed of in an environmentally sound manner.

Summary of selected provisions Reduction of transboundary movements of hazardous watses to a minimum consistent with their environmentally sound management; to control the transboundary movement of hazardous wastes, monitor and prevent illegal traffic, provide assistance for the environmentally sound management of hazardous wastes; to promote cooperation between Parties in the field and develop technical guidelines for the management of hazardous wastes.

Convention on Biological Diversity

Date of adoption 22 May 1992

Place of adoption Nairobi, Kenya

Date of entry into force 29 December 1993

Number of signatory countries 175

Objectives The conservation of biological diversity, the sustainable use of its components, and the fair and equitable sharing of benefits arising from the use of genetic resources.

Summary of selected provisions To promote scientific and technical cooperation, access to financial and genetic resources, and the transfer of ecologically sound technologies. Parties will develop national strategies or programmes for the conservation and sustainable use of biological diversity; identify and monitor components of biological diversity important for its conservation and sustainable use; and establish a system of protected areas to conserve biological diversity. The Convention is the first global, comprehensive agreement to address all aspects of biological diversity genetic resources, species and ecosystems.

UN Framework Convention on Climate Change (UNFCCC)

Also known as the Earth Summit or Rio Summit.

Date of adoption 14 June 1992

Place of adoption Rio de Janeiro, Brazil

Date of entry into force 15 March 1993

Number of signatory countries 176

Objectives Stabilization of greenhouse gas concentrations in the atmosphere at a level that would prevent dangerous anthropogenic interference with the climate system. Achievement of such a level within a timeframe sufficient to allow ecosystems to adapt naturally to climate change, to ensure that food production is not threatened, and to enable economic development to proceed in a sustainable manner.

Summary of selected provisions Developed countries to commit to stabilizing their emissions of carbon dioxide and other greenhouse gases at 1990 levels by 2000. To promote sustainable management, and promote and cooperate in the development, applications, and diffusion of technologies, practices and processes that control, reduce or prevent emissions of greenhouse gases not controlled by the Montreal Protocol. Parties to make available to the Conference, and periodically update, national inventories of anthropogenic emissions by sources. Take climate change considerations into account, to the extent feasible, in their relevant social, economic, and environmental policies and actions. Promote and cooperate in scientific, technological, and other research related to the climate system. Commitments for developing countries are less – relating mostly to reporting requirements and development of national programmes – because of their lesser contribution to the problem to date and their lower levels of development.
At the first meeting of the Conference Parties in Berlin 1994, it was agreed that existing commitments were inadequate and negotiations to come up with a new agreement were initiated, culminating in the 'Kyoto Protocol' in December 1997. The 'Kyoto Protocol' sets out for the first time legally-binding emission targets for developed countries. These vary from country to country but, if achieved, are expected to result in an overall reduction in greenhouse gas emissions by an overall 8 percent by 2010 compared with 1990 levels. However, many other issues still remain unclear under the Protocol, and will be subject to further negotiations. As of 15 March 1999, the Protocol had been signed by 84 countries and was not yet in force.

Conventions under Preparation, Brokered by United Nations Environmental Programme (UNEP)

As of 15 March 1999.

- Convention on Trade in Dangerous Chemicals and Pesticides (PIC)
- Convention on Persistent Organic Pollutants (POPs)

Natural Disasters

Major Late 20th-Century Earthquakes

As of 1 February 1999.
(N/A = not available.)

Date	Location	Magnitude (Richter scale)	Estimated number of deaths
10 October 1980	northern Algeria	7.7	3,000
23 November 1980	southern Italy	7.2	4,800
13 December 1982	northern Yemen	6.0	1,600
30 October 1983	eastern Turkey	6.9	1,300
19, 21 September 1985	Mexico City, Mexico	8.1	5,000[1]
20 August 1988	Nepal/India	6.9	1,000
6 November 1988	southwestern China	7.6	1,000
7 December 1988	Armenia, USSR	6.8	25,000
17 October 1989	San Francisco (CA), USA	7.1	62
20–21 June 1990	northwestern Iran	7.7	50,000
16 July 1990	Luzon, Philippines	7.7	1,660
1 February 1991	Afghanistan/Pakistan	6.8	1,000
April 1991	northern Georgia	7.2	>100
20 October 1991	Uttar Pradesh, India	6.1	1,500
13, 15 March 1992	Erzincan, Turkey	6.7	2,000
12 December 1992	Flores Island, Indonesia	7.5	2,500
12 July 1993	western coast of Hokkaido, Japan	7.8	200
29 September 1993	Maharashtra, India	6.3	9,800
13–16 October 1993	Papua New Guinea	6.8	>60
6 June 1994	Cauca, Colombia	6.8	1,000
19 August 1994	northern Algeria	5.6	200
16 January 1995	Kobe, Japan	7.2	5,500
14 June 1995	Sakhalin Island, Russia	7.6	2,000
2 October 1995	southwestern Turkey	6.0	84
7 October 1995	Sumatra, Indonesia	7.0	>70
9 October 1995	Mexico	7.6	>66
3 February 1996	Yunnan Province, China	7.0	>250
17 February 1996	Irian Jaya, Indonesia	7.5	108
28 March 1996	Ecuador	5.7	21
4, 28 February 1997	Ardabil, Iran	N/A	>1,000
28 February 1997	Baluchistan Province, Pakistan	7.3	>100
10 May 1997	northeastern Iran (Khorasah Province)	7.1	>1,600
22 May 1997	India	6.0	>40
26 September 1997	central Italy	5.8	>11
28 September 1997	Sulawesi, Indonesia	6.0	>20
14 October 1997	north of Santiago, Chile	6.8	>10
21 November 1997	Chittagong, Bangladesh	6.0	17
11 January 1998	northeastern China	6.2	>47
4 February 1998	Takhar province, Afghanistan	6.1	>3,800
30 May 1998	north-east Afghanistan	6.9	4,000
27 June 1998	southern Turkey	6.2	145
19 November 1998	southwestern China	5.6 and 6.2	5
29 November 1998	Molluccas, Indonesia	6.5	>50
25 January 1999	western Colombia	5.8	>935

[1] Some estimates put the death toll as high as 20,000.

Most Destructive Earthquakes in the World

(N/A = not available.)

Date	Location	Estimated number of deaths	Magnitude (Richter scale)
23 January 1556	Shaanxi, China	830,000	N/A
11 October 1737	Calcutta, India	300,000	N/A
27 July 1976	Tangshan, China	255,000[1]	8.0
9 August 1138	Aleppo, Syria	230,000	N/A
22 May 1927	near Xining, China	200,000	8.3
22 December 856	Damghan, Iran	200,000	N/A
16 December 1920	Gansu, China	200,000	8.6
23 March 893	Ardabil, Iran	150,000	N/A
1 September 1923	Kwanto, Japan	143,000	8.3
30 December 1730	Hokkaido, Japan	137,000	N/A
September 1290	Chihli, China	100,000	N/A
November 1667	Caucasia, Russia	80,000	N/A
18 November 1727	Tabriz, Iran	77,000	N/A
28 December 1908	Messina, Italy	70,000–100,000	7.5
1 November 1755	Lisbon, Portugal	70,000	8.7
25 December 1932	Gansu, China	70,000	7.6
31 May 1970	northern Peru	66,000	7.8
1268	Cilicia, Asia Minor	60,000	N/A
11 January 1693	Sicily, Italy	60,000	N/A
4 February 1783	Calabria, Italy	50,000	N/A
20 June 1990	Iran	50,000	7.7
30 May 1935	Quetta, India	30,000–60,000	7.5

[1] This is the official casualty figure; the estimated death toll is as high as 750,000.

Major Volcanic Eruptions in the 20th Century

Volcano	Location	Year	Estimated number of deaths
Santa María	Guatemala	1902	1,000
Pelée	Martinique	1902	28,000
Taal	Philippines	1911	1,400
Kelut	Java, Indonesia	1919	5,500
Vulcan	Papua New Guinea	1937	500
Lamington	Papua New Guinea	1951	3,000
St Helens	USA	1980	57
El Chichon	Mexico	1982	1,880
Nevado del Ruiz	Colombia	1985	23,000
Lake Nyos	Cameroon	1986	1,700
Pinatubo	Luzon, Philippines	1991	639
Unzen	Japan	1991	39
Mayon	Philippines	1993	70
Loki[1]	Iceland	1996	0
Soufriere	Montserrat	1997	23
Merapi	Java, Indonesia	1998	38

[1] The eruption caused severe flooding, and melted enough ice to create a huge sub-glacial lake.

Conservation

Freshwater Resources and Withdrawals

Continent	Annual internal renewable water resources[1]			Annual withdrawals		
	Total (cubic km)	1998 per capita (cubic metres)	Year of data	Total (cubic km)	% of water resources[1]	Per capita (cubic metres)
Africa	3,996.0	5,133	1995	145.14	4	202
Asia	13,206.7	3,680	1987	1,633.85	12	542
Europe	6,234.6	8,547	1995	455.29	7	625
Central America	1,056.7	8,084	1987	96.01	9	916
North America	5,308.6	17,458	1991	512.43	10	1,798
Oceania	1,614.3	54,795	1995	16.73	1	591
South America	9,526.0	28,702	1995	106.21	1	335
World total	41,022.0	6,918	1987	3,240.00	8	645

[1] Annual internal renewable water resources usually include river flows from other countries.

Source: *World Resources 1998–99*, World Resources Institute

Water-Scarce Countries

In 1990 quantities of renewable fresh water qualified 20 nations as water-scarce, 15 of them with rapidly growing populations. By 2025 between 10 and 15 nations will be added to this category. Between 1990 and 2025 the number of people living in countries in which renewable water is a scarce resource will rise from 131 million to somewhere between 817 million (under the UN's low projection of population growth) and 1.079 billion (under the high projection). In this case, the difference between the high and low projections – 262 million – is precisely the number of people living in water-scarce countries in 1990. For several countries varying population scenarios could mark the difference between potentially manageable water stress and outright water scarcity in 2025. In 1990 Peru, for example, had 1,856 cubic metres of renewable water per person per year. Under almost any conditions, that figure will plunge, but the rate of population growth could determine whether Peru crosses into water scarcity or hovers in water stress in 2025. Similar possibilities face Tanzania, Zimbabwe, and Cyprus. For Sri Lanka, Mozambique, and Mauritania, the population trajectory will determine whether the threshold is crossed from relative water abundance to water stress. The following table shows countries experiencing water scarcity in 1955, 1990, and 2025 (projected), based on availability of less than 1,000 cubic metres of renewable water per person per year.

Water-scarce countries in 1955	Countries added to scarcity category by 1990	Countries added to scarcity category by 2025 under all UN population growth projections	Countries added to scarcity category by 2025 only if they follow UN medium or high projections
Malta	Qatar	Libya	Cyprus
Djibouti	Saudi Arabia	Oman	Zimbabwe
Barbados	United Arab Emirates	Egypt	Tanzania
Singapore	Yemen	Comoros	Peru
Bahrain	Israel	South Africa	
Kuwait	Tunisia	Syria	
Jordan	Cape Verde	Iran	
	Kenya	Ethiopia	
	Burundi	Haiti	
	Algeria		
	Rwanda		
	Malawi		
	Somalia		

Source: *Sustaining Water*, Population Action International

World Forest Ecosystems

1996

Continent/region	Closed Forests				
	Land area (thousand ha)	Original forest as a % of land area[1]	Forest as a % of original forest		% frontier forests threatened[3]
			Current forests[2]	Frontier forests[3]	
Africa	2,963,468	22.9	33.9	7.8	76.8
Asia	3,085,414	49.1	28.2	5.3	63.1
Europe	2,260,320	72.7	58.4	21.3	18.7
Central America	264,835	67.2	54.5	9.7	87.0
North America	1,838,009	59.7	77.3	34.1	26.2
South America	1,752,925	55.6	69.1	45.6	54.0
Oceania	849,135	16.9	64.9	22.3	76.3
World total	13,048,300	47.7	53.4	21.7	39.5

Continent/region	Forest Ecosystems							
	Mangroves		Tropical forests		Non-tropical forests		Sparse trees and parkland	
	Area (thousand ha)	% protected	Area (thousand ha)	% protected	Area (thousand ha)	% protected	Area (thousand ha)	% protected
Africa	3, 801	1.4	448,197	9.1	8,249	2.0	69,710	11.3
Asia	4,033	26.5	210,720	16.4	145,101	5.1	42,384	7.0
Europe	0	0	0	0	1,019,178	2.9	10,350	1.0
Central America	1,679	14.9	71,893	12.3	21,293	3.1	26	0
North America	199	60.0	443	6.7	683,700	8.9	148,827	5.7
South America	2,929	32.1	620,514	12.2	39,291	15.7	168,216	2.4
Oceania	5,466	6.6	53,560	9.1	27,088	18.7	102,126	6.1
World total	16,945	13.3	1,407,649	11.7	1,823,787	6.0	541,616	5.5

[1] Original forest is that estimated to have covered the planet 8,000 years ago given current climate conditions.
[2] Includes frontier and non-frontier forests.
[3] Frontier forests are large, relatively undisturbed forest ecosystems.

Source: *World Resources 1998–99: A Guide to the Global Environment*, World Resources Institute

Deforestation of Tropical and Temperate Forests Worldwide

(In hectares.)

Region	Forest area		Total change 1990–95	Annual change	Annual change (%)
	1990	1995			
Africa	538,978,000	520,237,000	–18,741,000	–3,748,000	–0.7
Asia	490,812,000	474,172,000	–16,640,000	–3,328,000	–0.7
Europe[1]	144,044,000	145,988,000	1,944,000	389,000	0.3
Former USSR[1]	813,381,000	816,167,000	2,786,000	557,000	0.1
North and Central America	537,898,000	536,529,000	–1,369,000	–274,000	–0.1
Oceania	91,149,000	90,695,000	–454,000	–91,000	–0.1
South America	894,466,000	870,594,000	–23,872,000	–4,774,000	–0.5

[1] No tropical forests exist in these regions, thus totals represent only temperate forests.

Source: *State of the World's Forests 1997*, Food and Agriculture Organization of the United Nations

Afforestation

This involves the planting of trees in areas that have not previously held forests. (**Reafforestation** is the planting of trees in deforested areas.) Trees may be planted (1) to provide timber and wood pulp; (2) to provide firewood in countries where this is an energy source; (3) to bind soil together and prevent soil erosion; and (4) to act as windbreaks. Afforestation is a controversial issue because while many ancient woodlands of mixed trees are being lost, the new plantations consist almost exclusively of conifers. It is claimed that such plantations acidify the soil and conflict with the interests of biodiversity (they replace more ancient and ecologically valuable species and do not sustain wildlife).

Deforestation

This involves the destruction of forest for timber, fuel, charcoal burning, and clearing for agriculture and extractive industries, such as mining, without planting new trees to replace those lost (reafforestation) or working on a cycle that allows the natural forest to regenerate. Deforestation causes fertile soil to be blown away or washed into rivers, leading to soil erosion, drought, flooding, and loss of wildlife. It may also increase the carbon dioxide content of the atmosphere and intensify the greenhouse effect, because there are fewer trees absorbing carbon dioxide from the air for photosynthesis. Many people are concerned about the rate of deforestation as great damage is being done to the habitats of plants and animals. Deforestation ultimately leads to famine, and is thought to be partially responsible for the flooding of lowland areas – for example, in Bangladesh – because trees help to slow down water movement.

Countries Losing Greatest Areas of Forest

1990–95

Rank	Country	Area of lost forest (hectares)
1	Brazil	2,554,000
2	Indonesia	1,084,000
3	Congo, Democratic Republic of	740,000
4	Bolivia	581,000
5	Mexico	508,000
6	Venezuela	503,000
7	Malaysia	400,000
8	Myanmar	387,000
9	Sudan	353,000
10	Thailand	329,000
11	Paraguay	327,000
12	Tanzania	323,000
13	Zambia	264,000
14=	Colombia	262,000
	Philippines	262,000
16	Angola	237,000
17	Peru	217,000
18	Ecuador	189,000
19	Cambodia	164,000
20	Nicaragua	151,000
21	Laos	148,000
22	Vietnam	135,000
23	Papua New Guinea	133,000
24	Madagascar	130,000
25	Cameroon	129,000
26	Central African Republic	128,000
27	Nigeria	121,000
28	Afghanistan	118,000
29	Ghana	117,000
30	Mozambique	1116,000
31	Guinea-Bissau	114,000
32	Honduras	102,000
33	Chad	94,000
34	Gabon	91,000
35	Argentina	89,000
36	Hong Kong, China	87,000
37	Guatemala	82,000
38	Guinea	75,000
39	Botswana	71,000
40	Panama	64,000

Source: *State of the World's Forests 1997,* Food and Agriculture Organization of the United Nations

The Top 30 Countries with the Fastest Forest Depletion Rates

1990–95

Rank	Country	Average (annual loss) (%)	Rank	Country	Average (annual loss) (%)
1	Lebanon	7.8	16=	Jordan	2.5
2	Jamaica	7.2		Nicaragua	2.5
3	Afghanistan	6.8	18	Malaysia	2.4
4	Comoros	5.6	19	Honduras	2.3
5	Virgin Islands (British)	4.4	20	Syria	2.2
6	St Lucia	3.6	21	Panama	2.1
7	Philippines	3.5	22	Guatemala	2.0
8	Haiti	3.4	23=	Iran	1.7
9	El Salvador	3.3		Guadeloupe	1.7
10=	Costa Rica	3.0	25=	Cambodia	1.6
	Sierra Leone	3.0		Dominican Republic	1.6
12	Pakistan	2.9		Malawi	1.6
13=	Thailand	2.6	28	Trinidad and Tobago	1.5
	Bahamas	2.6	29=	Myanmar	1.4
	Paraguay	2.6		Vietnam	1.4

Source: *State of the World's Forests 1997,* Food and Agriculture Organization of the United Nations

Land and Protected Areas

The Top 25 Countries with the Greatest Protected Land Area

The International Union for the Conservation of Nature and Natural Resources (IUCN) identifies a protected area as an area of land and/or sea dedicated to the protection and maintenance of biological diversity and natural and associated cultural resources that are managed through legal or other effective means. The main purpose of management of a region or area as a protected area are: for scientific research; wilderness protection; preservation of species and genetic diversity; maintenance of environmental services; protection of specific natural and cultural features; tourism and recreation; education; sustainable use of resources from natural ecosystems; and maintenance of cultural and traditional attributes. The number of protected areas in the UK is 191 and the total area protected is 51,280 sq km (19,799 sq mi). This represents 20.94 percent of the total land area.

1996

	Country	Area		Number of protected areas	Area protected		Land area protected (%)
		sq km	sq mi		sq km	sq mi	
1	USA	9,368,900	3,618,770	1,494	1,042,380	402,463	11.12
2	Greenland	2,186,000	844,014	2	982,500	379,344	44.95
3	Australia	7,682,300	2,966,136	892	935,455	361,180	12.18
4	Canada	9,970,610	3,849,674	640	825,455	318,708	8.32
5	Russia	17,075,500	6,591,100	199	655,368	253,038	3.84
6	China	9,596,960	3,599,975	463	580,666	224,195	6.05
7	Brazil	8,511,965	3,285,618	273	321,898	124,285	3.78
8	Venezuela	912,100	352,162	100	263,223	101,631	28.86
9	Indonesia	1,191,443	740,905	175	185,653	71,680	9.67
10	India	3,166,829	1,222,396	374	143,507	55,408	4.53
11	Tanzania	945,000	364,865	30	138,900	53,629	14.78
12	Chile	756,950	292,257	66	137,251	52,992	18.26
13	Algeria	2,381,741	919,352	19	119,192	46,020	5.00
14	Chad	1,284,000	495,624	9	114,940	44,378	8.95
15	Ecuador	461,475	178,176	15	111,139	42,910	24.08
16	Botswana	582,000	225,000	9	106,633	41,171	18.54
17	Nambia	824,300	318,262	12	102,178	39,451	12.40
18	Congo, Democratic Republic of	2,344,900	905,366	8	99,166	38,288	4.23
19	Mexico	1,958,201	756,198	65	97,287	37,563	4.93
20	Sudan	2,505,815	967,489	16	93,825	36,226	3.74
21	Colombia	1,141,748	440,715	79	93,580	36,131	8.22
22	Bolivia	1,098,581	424,052	25	92,330	35,649	8.40
23	Germany	357,041	137,853	504	91,957	35,505	25.77
24	Niger	1,186,408	457,953	5	84,162	32,495	7.09
25	Iran	1,648,000	636,128	68	82,996	32,045	5.04

Source: US Fish and Wildlife Service

The Top 20 Countries with the Greatest Percentage of Protected Land Area

1996

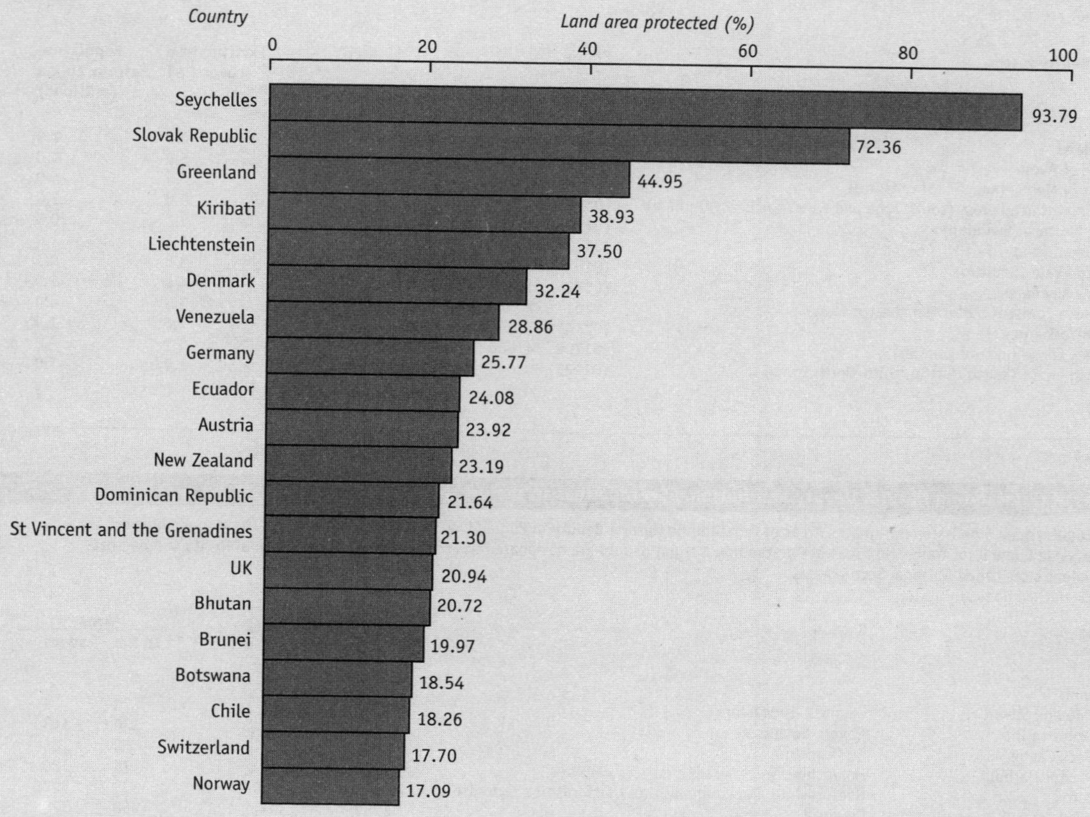

Country	Land area protected (%)
Seychelles	93.79
Slovak Republic	72.36
Greenland	44.95
Kiribati	38.93
Liechtenstein	37.50
Denmark	32.24
Venezuela	28.86
Germany	25.77
Ecuador	24.08
Austria	23.92
New Zealand	23.19
Dominican Republic	21.64
St Vincent and the Grenadines	21.30
UK	20.94
Bhutan	20.72
Brunei	19.97
Botswana	18.54
Chile	18.26
Switzerland	17.70
Norway	17.09

Source: US Fish and Wildlife Service

Protected Areas in the UK

As of March 1997.

Type of site[1]	Number of sites	Area (sq km)
National nature reserves	362	2,070
Local nature reserves (Great Britain only)	629	330
Sites of special scientific interest (SSSIs) (Great Britain only)	6,264	20,840
Areas of special scientific interest (ASSIs) (Northern Ireland)	147	820
Statutory marine nature reserves	3	196
Areas protected by international agreements		
Candidate special areas of conservation (SACs)	255	13,320
Special protection areas (SPAs)	150	5,760
Ramsar sites	111	4,180

[1] Some sites may be included in more than one category.

Source: *The Official Yearbook of the United Kingdom*, © Crown copyright 1998

Community Forests in England

Most countries in Europe have 20–25 percent of their landscape under trees. England has just 7.5 percent. The aim, in association with the Forestry Commission, is to double the figure to 15 percent by the year 2050.
(– = not applicable.)

Community forest	Phone	Area		Existing tree cover (%)	Population within 20 km (millions)
		sq km	sq mi		
Cleveland	(01642) 300716	255	98	6.9	1.0
Forest of Avon	(0117) 953 2141	573	221	5.9	1.0
Forest of Mercia (south Staffordshire)	(01543) 505488	210	81	6.4	4.0
The Great North Forest (south Tyne and Wear/northeast Durham)	(0191) 460 6200	160	62	8.0	1.0
Great Western (Swindon)	(01793) 466324	390	151	3.0	0.3
The Greenwood	(01234) 767037	414	160	11.3	1.0
Marston Vale (Bedford)	(01623) 758231	158	61	3.6	0.5
The Mersey Forest	(01925) 816217	925	357	4.0	5.0
Red Rose Forest (Greater Manchester West)	(0161) 872 1660	760	293	3.9	4.0
South Yorkshire	(0114) 257 1199	395	153	7.6	1.9
Thames Chase (east of London)	(01708) 641880	98	38	9.7	3.0
Watling Chase (south Hertfordshire/North London)	(01923) 852641	163	63	7.9	3.0
Total	–	4,497	1,736	–	25.7

Areas of Outstanding Natural Beauty and National Scenic Areas in the UK

The Countryside Commission designates Areas of Outstanding Natural Beauty in England. In Wales, similar areas are the responsibility of the Countryside Council for Wales. No Areas of Outstanding Natural Beauty are designated in Scotland; the Scottish Natural Heritage recognizes equivalent sites called National Scenic Areas.
(N/A = not available.)

Name	Region	Established (year)	Area	
			sq km	sq mi
England				
Arnside and Silverdale	Cumbria, Lancashire	1972	75	29
Blackdown Hills	Devon, Somerset	1991	370	143
Cannock Castle	Staffordshire	1958	68	26
Chichester Harbour	Hampshire, West Sussex	1964	74	29
Chilterns	Bedfordshire, Buckinghamshire, Hertfordshire, Oxfordshire	1965; extended 1990	833	322
Cornwall	Cornwall	1959; Camel estuary 1983	958	370
Cotswolds	south Gloucestershire, Bath and North East Somerset, Gloucestershire, Oxfordshire, Wiltshire, Warwickshire, Worcestershire	1966	2,038	787
Cranborne Chase and West Wiltshire Downs	Dorset, Hampshire, Somerset, Wiltshire	1983	983	379
Dedham Vale	Essex, Suffolk	1970; extended 1978, 1991	90	35
Dorset	Dorset, Somerset	1959	1,129	436
East Devon	Devon	1963	268	103
East Hampshire	Hampshire	1962	383	148
Forest of Bowland	Lancashire, North Yorkshire	1964	802	310
High Weald	Sussex, Kent, Surrey	1983	1,460	564
Howardian Hills	North Yorkshire	1987	204	79
Isle of Wight	Isle of Wight	1963	189	73
Isles of Scilly	Isles of Scilly	1976	16	6
Kent Downs	Bromley, Kent	1968	878	339
Lincolnshire Wolds	Northeast Lincolnshire	1973	558	215
Malvern Hills	Gloucestershire, Herefordshire, and Worcestershire	1959	105	40
Mendip Hills	North West Somerset, Bath and North East Somerset	1972	198	76
Nidderdale	North Yorkshire	1994	603	233
Norfolk Coast	Norfolk	1968	451	174
North Devon	Devon	1960	171	66
North Pennines	Cumbria, Durham, Northumberland	1988	1,983	766
Northumberland Coast	Northumberland	1958	135	52
North Wessex Downs	Berkshire, Hampshire, Oxfordshire, Wiltshire	1972	1,730	668
Quantock Hills	Somerset	1957	99	38
Shropshire Hills	Shropshire	1959	804	310
Solway Coast	Cumbria	1964	115	44

(continued)

Areas of Outstanding Natural Beauty and National Scenic Areas in the UK (*continued*)

Name	Region	Established (year)	Area	
			sq km	sq mi
South Devon	Devon	1960	337	130
South Hampshire Coast	Hampshire	1967	77	30
Suffolk Coast and Heaths	Suffolk	1970	403	156
Surrey Hills	Surrey	1958	419	162
Sussex Downs	Sussex	1966	983	379
Tamar Valley	Devon, Cornwall	1995	195	115
Wye Valley (England)	Gloucestershire, Herefordshire, and Worcestershire	1971	209	126
Wales				
Anglesey	Anglesey	1967	221	85
Clwydian Range	Denbighshire, Flintshire	1985	157	60
Gower	Swansea	1956	189	73
Llyn	Gwynedd	1957	161	62
Scotland				
Assynt-Coigach	Highland	N/A	902	348
Ben Nevis and Glen Coe	Highland, Argyll and Bute, Perth and Kinross	N/A	1,016	392
Cairngorm Mountains	Highland, Aberdeenshire, Moray	N/A	672	259
Cuillin Hills	Highland	N/A	219	85
Deeside and Lochnagar	Aberdeenshire, Angus	N/A	400	154
Dornoch Firth	Highland	N/A	75	29
East Stewartry Coast	Dumfries and Galloway	N/A	45	17
Eildon and Leaderfoot	Scottish Borders	N/A	36	14
Fleet Valley	Dumfries and Galloway	N/A	53	20
Glen Affric	Highland	N/A	193	75
Glen Strathfarrar	Highland	N/A	38	15
Hoy and West Mainland	Orkney Islands	N/A	148	57
Jura	Argyll and Bute	N/A	218	84
Kintail	Highland	N/A	155	60
Knapdale	Argyll and Bute	N/A	198	76
Knoydart	Highland	N/A	395	153
Kyle of Tongue	Highland	N/A	185	71
Kyles of Bute	Argyll and Bute	N/A	44	17
Lochna Keal, Mull	Argyll and Bute	N/A	127	49
Loch Lomond	Argyll and Bute, Stirling, West Dunbartonshire	N/A	274	106
Loch Rannoch and Glen Lyon	Perth and Kinross, Stirling	N/A	484	187
Loch Shiel	Highland	N/A	134	52
Loch Tummel	Perth and Kinross	N/A	92	36
Lynn of Lorn	Argyll and Bute	N/A	48	19
Morar, Moidart, and Ardnamurchan	Highland	N/A	135	52
Ninth estuary	Dumfries and Galloway	N/A	93	36
North Arran	North Ayrshire	N/A	238	92
North-West Sutherland	Highland	N/A	205	79
River Earn	Perth and Kinross	N/A	30	12
River Tay	Perth and Kinross	N/A	56	22
St Kilda	Western Isles	N/A	9	3
Scarra, Lunga, and the Garvellachs	Argyll and Bute	N/A	19	7
Shetland	Shetland Islands	N/A	116	45
Small Isles	Highland	N/A	155	60
South Lewis, Harris, and North Uist	Western Isles	N/A	1,096	423
South Uist Machair	Western Isles	N/A	61	24
The Trossachs	Stirling	N/A	46	18
Trotternish	Highland	N/A	50	19
Upper Tweeddale	Scottish Borders	N/A	105	41
Wester Ross	Highland	N/A	1,453	561
Northern Ireland				
Antrim Coast and Glens	Co. Antrim	1988	706	273
Causeway Coast	Co. Antrim	1989	42	16
Lagan Valley	Co. Down	1965	21	8
Lecale Coast	Co. Down	1967	31	12
Mourne	Co. Down	1986	570	220
North Derry	Co. Londonderry	1966	130	50
Ring of Gullion	Co. Armagh	1991	154	59
Sperrin	Co. Tyrone, Co. Londonderry	1968	1,010	390
Strangford Lough	Co. Down	1972	186	72

National Parks in England and Wales

The Countryside Commission is responsible for designating areas in England and Wales as National Parks, and advises Government on policy towards them. There are seven National Parks in England which, together with The Broads, are managed by a special Authority and cover 7.6 percent (9,934 sq km/3,836 mi) of England.

Name	Region	Established (year)	Area sq km	Area sq mi	Natural features	Activities
England						
The Broads[1]	between Norwich and Great Yarmouth, Norfolk	1989	303	117	fens, waterways, marshes, woodlands	walking, sailing, fishing, birdwatching
Dartmoor	Devon	1951	954	368	boggy plateaux, rocky land, river valleys; prehistoric remains	walking, fishing, riding
Exmoor	Somerset and Devon	1954	693	268	moorlands, cliffs; prehistoric remains	walking, riding, cycling, fishing
Lake District	Cumbria	1951	2,292	885	lakes, mountains, moorlands, fells	walking, climbing, sailing
The New Forest[2]	Hampshire	1990	376	117	forest, woodlands, heathlands	walking, riding, cycling
Northumberland	Northumberland	1956	1,049	405	grass moorlands, deep burn valleys, hills, mountains; Roman antiquities	walking, rock-climbing, canoeing, riding
North York Moors	North Yorkshire, Redcar, Cleveland	1952	1,436	554	open heather moorlands; unique wildlife	walking, riding
Peak District	Derbyshire, Staffordshire, South Yorkshire, Cheshire, west Yorkshire, Greater Manchester	1951	1,438	555	dales, hills, peat moorlands	walking, rock-climbing
Yorkshire Dales	North Yorkshire, Cumbria	1954	1,769	683	limestone cliffs, gorges, and pavements; valleys, waterfalls, caves	walking, caving
Wales						
Breacon Beacons	Powys, Carmarthenshire, Rhondda, Cynon, Taff, Merthyr Tydfil, Blaneau, Gwent, Monmouthshire	1957	1,351	522	mountains, valleys	walking, riding
Pembrokeshire Coast	Pembrokeshire	1952 and 1995	584	225	cliffs, moorlands; includes Skomer Islands	walking, birdwatching, marine life watching
Snowdonia	Gwynedd, Conwy	1951	2,142	827	deep valleys, rugged mountains	hill walking, rock-climbing, riding

[1] The Broads are considered to have equivalent status to National Parks due to Statutory designation.

[2] The New Forest does not enjoy Statutory designation, despite planning protection that recognizes its high landscape qualities. Therefore the area does not have equivalent administration or funding to a National Park. 1990 is the date of the establishment of the New Forest Committee.

Heritage Coasts in England

England has many popular coastal resorts but 32 percent (1,027 km/638 mi) of scenic English coastline is conserved as Heritage Coasts. These special coastlines are managed so that their natural beauty is conserved and, where appropriate, the accessibility for visitors is improved. The first Heritage Coast to be defined was the famous white chalk cliffs of Beachy Head in Sussex.
(– = not applicable.)

Coast	Defined[1] (year)	Length km	Length mi	Location
Dover-Folkestone[2]	1975	7	4	Kent
East Devon	1984	27	17	Devon
Exmoor	1991	45	28	Devon/Somerset
Flamborough Headland	1989	19	12	East Riding of Yorkshire/North Yorkshire
Godrevy-Portreath	1986	9	6	Cornwall
Gribbin Head-Polperro	1986	24	15	Cornwall
Hamstead	1988	11	7	Isle of Wight
Hartland (Cornwall only)	1986	11	7	Cornwall
Hartland (Devon)	1990	37	23	Devon
Isles of Scilly	1974	64	40	Isles of Scilly
Lundy	1990	14	9	Devon
North Devon	1992	32	20	Devon
North Norfolk	1975	64	40	Norfolk
North Northumberland	1992	110	68	Northumberland
North Yorkshire and Cleveland	1981	57	35	north Yorkshire/Redcar and Cleveland
Pentire Point-Widemouth	1986	52	32	Cornwall
Penwith	1986	54	34	Cornwall
Purbeck	1981	50	31	Dorset
Rame Head	1986	8	5	Cornwall
St Agnes	1986	11	7	Cornwall

(*continued*)

Heritage Coasts in England (continued)

Coast	Defined[1] (year)	Length km	Length mi	Location
St Bees Head	1992	6	4	Cumbria
South Devon	1986	75	47	Devon
South Foreland[2]	1975	7	4	Kent
Spurn	1988	18	11	East Riding of Yorkshire
Suffolk	1979	57	35	Suffolk
Sussex	1973	13	8	Sussex
Tennyson	1988	34	21	Isle of Wight
The Lizard	1986	27	17	Cornwall
The Roseland	1986	53	33	Cornwall
Trevose Head	1986	4	2	Cornwall
West Dorset	1984	41	25	Dorset
Total	–	1,041	647	–

[1] Date of completion definition.
[2] Coastal frontage only defined.

National Trails in England

The first National Trail was the 412 km/256 mi Pennine Way opened in 1965. The longest is the 962 km/598 mi South West Coast Path which meanders through Somerset, Devon, Cornwall, and Dorset. The latest is Thames Path (344 km/214 mi) which was opened in July 1997. It is unique in that it follows the course of a river – the Thames – from its source in Gloucestershire to its end at the Thames Barrier in London. (– = not applicable.)

National Trail	Opened (year)	Length km	Length mi	Location
Cleveland Way	1969	176	109	north Yorkshire/Redcar and Cleveland; 44 km/27 mi of the trail is open to both horse riders and cyclists, while 3.4 km/2.1 mi is open to motorized vehicles
North Downs Way	1978	246	153	Surrey/Kent; 122 km/76 mi of the trail is open to both horse riders and cyclists, while 74 km/46 mi is open to motorized vehicles
Offa's Dyke Path	1971	285	177	Gloucestershire/Herefordshire/Shropshire (includes 198 km/123 mi in Wales); 22 km/14 mi of the trail is open to horse riders, 49 km/30 mi to cyclists, and 57 km/35 mi to motorized vehicles
Peddars Way/Norfolk Coast Path	1986	150	93	Norfolk/Suffolk; 70 km/43 mi of the trail is open to horse riders, cyclists, and motorized vehicles
Pennine Way	1965	412	256	Derby/north Yorkshire/Kirklees/Calderdale/Bradford/Rochdale/Oldham/Durham/Cumbria/Northumberland (includes 16 km/10 mi in Scotland); 83 km/52 mi of the trail is open to both horse riders and cyclists, while 38 km/24 mi is open to motorized vehicles
Ridgeway	1973	137	85	Wiltshire/Oxfordshire/Berkshire/Buckinghamshire/Hertfordshire; 101 km/63 mi of the trail is open to both horse riders and cyclists, while 83 km/52 mi is open to motorized vehicles
South Downs Way	1972	171	106	Hampshire/west and east Sussex; 171 km/106 mi of the trail is open to both horse riders and cyclists, while 25 km/16 mi is open to motorized vehicles
South West Coast Path	1973–78	962	598	Somerset/Devon/Cornwall/Dorset; 35 km/22 mi of the trail is open to cyclists, while 45 km/28 mi is open to motorized vehicles
Thames Path	1997	344	214	Gloucestershire/Wiltshire/Oxfordshire/Berkshire/Buckinghamshire/Surrey/Greater London; 14 km/9 mi of the trail is open to horse riders, 16 km/10 mi to cyclists, and 0.6 km/0.4 mi to motorized vehicles
Wolds Way	1982	130	81	East Riding of Yorkshire/north Yorkshire; 44 km/27 mi of the trail is open to both horse riders and cyclists, while 20 km/12 mi is open to motorized vehicles
TOTAL	–	3,013	1,872	–

Environmental Groups and Initiatives

The Atmospheric Research and Information Centre

Organization that aims to research into urban air quality and to increase awareness of acid rain and the greenhouse effect through education and public information.

Date established 1984

Address c/o The Manchester Metropolitan University, Department of Environmental and Geographical Sciences, Chester Street, Manchester M1 5GD; phone: (0161) 247 1590/1/2/3; fax: (0161) 247 6332; e-mail: aric@mmu.ac.uk

Web site www.doc.mmu.ac.uk/aric/arichome.html

British Hydropower Association

Association that aims to protect and promote the use of water to generate energy. It is believed that it is in the nation's and the world's interest to extend the use of water power and to save fossil fuels. The association is affiliated with the European Small Hydro-Power Association and the Association of Independent Electricity Producers.

Date established 1996

Address 60 Bramhall Lane South, Bramhall, Stockport, Cheshire SK7 2DU; phone: (0161) 440 9196; fax: (0161) 440 9273; e-mail: weal@mcmail.com

Web site www.bwea.com/bhaindex.htm

British Trust for Conservation Volunteers

Major practical conservation organization and the largest in the UK. It has numerous affiliations including BCTV Enterprises, the National Trust, Green Alliance, Groundwork, Wildlife Link, and the Environmental Council.

Date established 1959

Membership 8,728

Address 36 St Mary's Street, Wallingford, Oxfordshire OX10 0EU; phone: (01491) 839766; fax: (01491) 839646; e-mail: information@btcv.org.uk

Web site www.btcv.org.uk

British Wind Energy Association

Organization that aims to promote excellence in wind energy research, development, and deployment. It is affiliated with the European Wind Energy Association, Eurosolar, AEP, and the Irish Wind Energy Association.

Date established 1977

Membership *c.* 900

Address 26 Spring Street, London W2 1JA, UK; phone: (0171) 402 7102; fax: (0171) 402 7107; e-mail: bwea@gn.apc.org

Web site www.bwea.com

Butterfly Conservation

Organization formed for the purpose of the conservation of butterflies and their habitats by owning, managing, and advising on habitat management and reserves. It is affiliated with English Nature, JCCBI, and Wildlife Link.

Date established 1968

Membership 10,000

Address PO Box 222, Dedham, Colchester, Essex CO7 6EY; phone: (01206) 322342; fax: (01206) 322739; e-mail: butterfly@cix.compulink.co.uk

Centre for Alternative Technology

Organization set up to invesigate, use, demonstrate, and promote environmentally and socially appropriate technologies for energy generation and conservation, food production, and building design.

Date established 1974

Membership 3,500

Address Machynlleth, Powys SY20 9AZ; phone: (01654) 702400; fax: (01654) 702782; e-mail: help@catinfo.demon.co.uk

Web site www.cat.org.uk

Conservation International

Organization established in order to conserve the Earth's living natural heritage and global biodiversity, and to demonstrate, through science, economics, policy, and community involvement, that human societies can live in harmony with nature. The organization has members in 22 countries.

Date established 1987

Membership 40,000

Address 2501 M Street NW, Suite 200, Washington, DC 20037; phone: (202) 4295660; fax: (202) 8870192; e-mail: newmember@conservation.org

Web site www.conservation.org/

Countryside Commission

Organization working to conserve the natural beauty of the English countryside. An advisory and promotional body, rather than an executive one, the Commission owns no land and manages no facilities but achieves its objectives through collaboration with other organizations. It has seven regional offices.

Date established 1968

Address John Dower House, Crescent Place, Cheltenham, Gloucestershire GL50 3RA; phone: (01242) 521381; fax: (01242) 584270; e-mail: info@countryside.gov.uk

Web site www.countryside.gov.uk

The Earth Council

Organization that aims to support and empower people in building a more secure, equitable, and sustainable future, to promote awareness and support, encourage public participation, and build bridges of understanding between citizens and government. Funding comes through the Earth Council Foundation's sponsoring institutions, foundations, corporations, and individuals.

Date established 1992

Membership covers 22 countries

Address Deputy Executive Director, Apartado 2323-1002, San José, Costa Rica; phone: (506) 2561611; fax: (506) 2552197; e-mail: eci@terra.ecouncil.ac.cr

Web site www.ecouncil.ac.cr

Earthwatch

Charity organization that aims to build a sustainable world through active partnership between scientists and citizens, by gathering data and communicating information to empower people and governments to act wisely as global citizens. It is funded through membership dues and donor organizations and individuals. The organization has members in over 118 countries.

Date established 1971

Membership 70,000

Address Earthwatch Europe, Belsyre Court, 57 Woodstock Road, Oxford, OX2 6HJ, UK; phone: (44 1865) 311600; fax: (44 1865) 311383; e-mail: info@uk.earthwatch.org

Web site www.sitka.demon.co.uk/ewis.htm

Energy and Environmental Programme

Part of the Royal Institute of International Affairs (RIIA), the Programme researches and publishes reports on strategic and economic planning.

Date established 1985

Membership 5,000 (RIIA)

Address Chatham House, 10 St James's Square, London SW1Y 4LE; phone: (0171) 957 5711; fax: (0171) 957 5710; e-mail: eep-admin@riia.org

Web site www.riia.org/Research/eep/eep.html

Friends of the Earth

Charity organization that aims to protect the planet from environmental degradation, to preserve biological, cultural, and ethnic diversity, and to empower citizens to have an influential voice in decisions affecting the quality of their environment and their lives. It is funded through membership dues, donations, and subsidies.

Date established 1969

Membership 35,000

Address: Headquarters Friends of the Earth International, PO Box 19199, NL-1000 GD, Amsterdam; phone: (31 20) 622-1369; fax: (31 20) 639-2181; e-mail: foeint@antenna.nl

Address in UK Friends of the Earth, 26–28 Underwood Street, London, N1 7JQ; phone: (0171) 490 1555; fax: (0171) 490 0881; e-mail: foe@foe.org

Web site www.foe.org; www.foe.co.uk

Green Alliance

Organization that works on environmental policy and politics. Its main activities fall into three areas; greening government, greening

business and finance, and greening science. It is affiliated with the European Environment Bureau, Wildlife Link, and the National Council for Voluntary Organizations.

Date established 1978

Membership 380

Address 49 Wellington Street, London WC2E 7BN; phone: (0171) 836 0341; fax: (0171) 240 9205; e-mail: gralliance@gn.apc.org

Greenpeace International

Independent organization that aims to protect biodiversity in all its forms, to prevent pollution and abuse of the Earth's ocean, land, air, and fresh water, to end all nuclear threats, and to promote peace, global disarmament, and non-violence. It is funded through donations, voluntary contributions from the public, and sales of merchandise. Greenpeace does not accept funds from business interests or governments. The organization has offices in 30 countries.

Date established 1971

Membership 4,500,000

Address: Headquarters Keizersgracht 176, NL-1016 DW, Amsterdam, The Netherlands; phone: (31 20) 523 6222; fax: (31 20) 523 6200; e-mail: greenpeace.international@greenz.dat.de

Address in UK Canonbury Villas, London N1 2PN; phone: (0171) 865 8100; fax: (0171) 865 8200

Web site www.greenpeace.org

Institute of Terrestrial Ecology

Organization that undertakes specialist ecological research in all aspects of the terrestrial environment and seeks to understand the ecology of species and of human-made communities. The Institute is part of the National Environment Research Council and has six research stations based in the UK.

Date established 1973

Address Monk's Wood, Abbots Ripton, Huntingdon, Cambridgeshire PE17 2LS; phone: (01487) 773381; fax: (01487) 773590; e-mail: eic@itc.ac.uk

Web site www.nmw.ac.uk/ite

Institute of Wastes Management

Organization that aims to advance the scientific, technical, and professional aspects of waste management for the safeguarding of the environment.

Date established 1898

Address 9 Saxon Court, St Peter's Gardens, Northampton, Northamptonshire NN1 1SX; phone: (01604) 20426; fax: (01604) 21339; e-mail: membership@iwm.co.uk,education@iwm.co.uk

Web site www.iwm.co.uk

International Energy Agency (IEA)

Autonomous agency linked with the OECD that aims to foster cooperation among participating countries to increase energy security through diversification of energy supply, more efficient and cleaner use of energy, energy conservation, and the development of alternative energy sources. The governments of the 23 OECD member states form the membership of the International Energy Agency.

Date established 1974

Membership governments of 23 OECD countries

Address: Headquarters 9 rue de la Fédération, 75739 Paris Cedex 15, France; phone: (33 1) 40576554; fax: (33 1) 40576559

Web site www.iea.org/

International Wildlife Coalition (home of Whale Adoption Project)

Organization that aims to preserve wildlife all over the world.

Date established 1983

Membership *c.*150,000 individual members in five countries

Address 141A High Street, Edenbridge, Kent TN8 5AX; phone: (01732) 866955; fax: (01792) 866955; e-mail: iwcuk@iwcmail.demon.co.uk

Web site www.webcom.com/iwcwww/

Marine Conservation Society

Organization that aims to protect the marine environment for both wildlife and future generations by promoting its sustainable and environmentally sensitive management.

Date established 1983

Address 9 Gloucester Road, Ross on Wye, Hereford HR9 5BU; phone: (01989) 566017; fax: (01989) 567815; e-mail: mcsuk@wcmail.com

Web site www.mcsuk.mcmail.com

National Association for Environmental Education

Association set up to promote and encourage environmental education through all levels of the education system.

Date established 1960

Membership 1,500

Address Wolverhampton University, Walsall Campus, Gorway Road, Walsall WS1 3BD; phone: (01922) 31200; fax: (01922) 31200

New Economics Foundation

Organization that aims to build a just and sustainable economy, with ideas and action that put people and the environment first. The Foundation has close links with Friends of the Earth, GreenNet, and the Centre for Employment Initiatives.

Date established 1986

Membership 1,700

Address Cinnamon House, 6–8 Cole Street, London SE1 4YH; phone: (0171) 377 5696; fax: (0171) 407 6473; e-mail: info@neweconomics.org.uk

Web site www.neweconomics.org.uk

Population Action International

Organization that aims to advance policies and programs that slow the world's population growth in order that the quality of life for all people can be enhanced.

Date established 1965

Address 1120 19th Street NW, Suite 550, Washington, DC 20036, USA; phone: (202) 659 1833; fax: (202) 293 1795; e-mail: pai@popact.org

Web site www.populationaction.org/

Rainforest Action Network (RAN)

Non-profit volunteer and member-based organization that aims to protect tropical rainforests and support the rights of indigenous peoples. It is financed by membership dues, foundation grants and donations, and special events.

Date established 1985

Membership 30,000 individual and 150 organizations and groups, covering 74 countries and territories

Address 221 Pine Street, Suite 500, San Francisco, CA 94104, USA; phone: (415) 3984404; fax: (415) 3982732; e-mail: rainforest@ran.org

Web site www.ran.org/ran/

Royal Society for the Protection of Birds (RSPB)

Organization acting for the protection of wild birds and their habitats. This includes the buying of land to create new nature reserves and protecting existing bird sites from any type of environmental encroachment.

Date established 1889

Membership 967,000

Address The Lodge, Sandy, Bedfordshire SG19 2DL; phone: (01767) 680551; fax: (01767) 692365

Trees for Life

Charity organization that aims to help people in Third World countries become self-sufficient by providing funding, planning, management, materials, and information on the planting, cultivation, and harvest of food-bearing trees. It is funded by membership dues and donations.

Date established 1984

Membership 5,000

Address 3006 W St Louis, Wichita, KS 67203; phone: (316) 945-6929; fax: (316) 263-5293; e-mail: info@treesforlife.org

Web site www.treesforlife.org

Waste Management Information Bureau

The UK's national referral centre for advice and information on waste management.

Date established 1973

Address National Environmental Technology Centre, AEA Technology Environment, F6 Culham, Abingdon, Oxfordshire OX14 3ED; phone: (01235) 463162; fax: (01235) 463004; e-mail: wmib@aeat.co.uk

Web site www.aeat.co.uk

Waste Watch

Organization that aims to promote recycling and waste reduction, with particular reference to the interests of the voluntary sector.

Date established 1987

Membership 200

Address Gresham House, 24 Holborn Viaduct, London EC1A 2BN; phone: (0171) 248 1818; Wasteline: (0171) 248 0242; fax: (0171) 248 1404

The Wildfowl and Wetlands Trust

Organization that aims to promote the conservation of wildfowl and their wetland habitats through research, conservation, and education programmes. The Trust's Mission Statement is to save wetlands for wildlife and people.

Membership 70,000

Date established 1946

Address Slimbridge, Gloucestershire GL2 7BT; phone: (01453) 890333 ext 279; fax: (01453) 890827

World Conservation Union

Organization that aims to influence, encourage, and assist societies throughout the world to conserve the integrity and diversity of nature, and to ensure that any use of natural resources is equitable and ecologically sustainable.

Date established 1948

Membership 74 governments and more than 700 NGOs

Address: Headquarters Rue Mauverney 28, CH-1196 Gland, Switzerland; phone: (41) 22 999 00 01; fax: (41) 22 999 00 02; e-mail: mail@hq.iucn.org

Address in UK World Conservation Monitoring Centre, 219 Huntingdon Road, Cambridge, CB3 0DL; phone: (01223) 277314; fax: (01223) 277136; e-mail: info@wcmc.org.uk

Web site w3.iprolink.ch/iucnlib/; www.wcmc.org.uk

World Society for the Protection of Animals (WSPA)

Organization that aims to end the exploitation of animals through practical projects, educational campaigns, and representations at government level. WSPA policy states that it aims to 'encourage respect for animals, and responsible stewardship and laws and enforcement structures to provide legal protection for animals'. It is a charity that relies on member societies, individual membership dues, donations, and bequests. It accepts no financial aid from governments. It has a network of 350 member societies in more than 70 countries.

Date established 1981 (previously active in another name for over 40 years)

Membership 250,000

Address: Eastern Hemisphere Head-quarters 2 Langley Lane, London, SW8 1TJ, UK; phone: (0171) 793 0540; fax: (0171) 793 0208; e-mail: wspa@wspa.org. uk

Address: Western Hemisphere Headquarters PO Box 190, 29 Perkins Street, Boston, MA 02130; phone: (617) 522-7000; fax: (617) 522-7077; e-mail: wspa@world.std.com

Web site www.wspa.org.uk

World Wide Fund for Nature (WWF)

International organization that aims to protect the biological resources upon which human well-being depends and to preserve endangered and threatened species of wildlife and plants as well as habitats and natural areas of the world. It is funded through membership dues, legacies, bequests, corporate subscriptions, governments and aid agencies, foundation grants, and other earned income.

Date established 1961

Membership 1.2 million

Address: Headquarters WWF International (World Wide Fund for Nature), Avenue du Mont-Blanc, CH-1196 Gland, Switzerland; phone: (41 22) 3649111; fax: (41 22) 3645358

Address in UK WWF-UK, Panda House, Weyside Park, Godalming, Surrey GU7 1XR; phone: (01483) 426444; fax: (01483) 426409; e-mail: www-uk@wwf-uk.org

Web site www.panda.org

Web Sites

About the National Trust

http://www.nationaltrust.org.uk/aboutnt.htm

Information about the charity, supported by 2.4 million members, entrusted with the care of large parts of the British countryside and many historic buildings.

Amazon Interactive

http://www.eduweb.com/amazon.html

Interactive guide to the Amazon River, specifically focusing on the part that runs through Ecuador but covering all aspects of the river.

Bathing Water Quality

http://www.environment-agency.gov.uk/gui/dataset1/1frame.htm

Regularly updated guide to the state of Britain's beaches provided by the Environment Agency. A searchable beach-by-beach index reports the number of faecal coliforms and salmonella colonies on every British beach and tells you what levels are acceptable by European Union standards.

Biodiversity: Measuring the Variety of Nature

http://www.nhm.ac.uk/science/projects/worldmap/

Exhibition on biodiversity and conservation from the Natural History Museum in London, with sections on 'Biodiversity value', 'Rarity and endemism', and 'Conservation priority and gap analysis'.

Biomass

http://www.nrel.gov/research/industrial_tech/biomass.html

Information on biomass from the US Department of Energy. A graph supports the textual explanation of the fact that the world is only using 7 percent of annual biomass production.

Biosphere 2 Centre

http://www.bio2.edu/

All about the Biosphere 2 project in Oracle, Arizona, including a virtual tour of the site. There are full details of the research programmes being conducted on the 'seven wilderness ecosystems' contained within the dome. The site also contains tailored educational resources for schoolchildren.

British Trust for Conservation Volunteers (BTCV)

http://www.btcv.org/

BTCV is the largest organization in the UK promoting practical conservation work by volunteers. Their Web site details 'Conservation opportunities' – volunteering, holidays, training, and employment – as well as information about 'BTCV enterprises' and links to other environmental resources.

British Wind Energy Association

http://www.bwea.com/

Promoting the use of wind power as a clean, sustainable source of energy, this site includes a list of wind farms throughout the UK, as well as a detailed selection of fact sheets about related issues.

Centre for Alternative Technology

http://www.cat.org.uk/

Dedicated to the Centre For Alternative Technology in Wales, this includes a virtual tour of the site, pictures, and maps. It also includes a quiz, a question forum, and an extensive list of educational resources.

Conservation International

http://www.conservation.org/

Non-profit-making organization which uses science, economics, policy, and community involvement to promote biodiversity conservation worldwide.

Countryside Commission

http://www.countryside.gov.uk/

Guide to the work of the Commission and to the attractions of the British countryside. There is information on all of Britain's national parks and officially-designated areas of outstanding beauty.

Earth Council

http://www.ecouncil.ac.cr/

Details the aims and activities of the Earth Council, a non-governmental organization promoting the implementation of the Earth Summit agreements.

Earthwatch Institute

http://www.earthwatch.org/

Earthwatch Institute promotes conservation through scientific field research, creating partnerships between scientists, educators, and the public. Members have the opportunity to work with distinguished researchers in a range of different fields; the site includes details of how to join, as well as news of current expeditions and research progress.

Endangered Species

http://endangeredspecie.com/

Claiming to offer 'The rarest info around', this site is packed with photos and information about endangered species and extinction rates.

English Heritage

http://www.english-heritage.org.uk/dminterface/dmindex.asp

Site of the public body charged with protecting England's historic environment. The role and structure of English Heritage are described, together with publications and education activities. A clickable map accesses information on historic properties.

English Nature – Facts and Figures

http://www.english-nature.org.uk/facts.htm

Outline of the role of the government agency charged with conserving wildlife and natural features in England.

Environmental Education Network

http://envirolink.org/enviroed/

Collaborative effort to place environmental information on the Internet.

Friends of the Earth Home Page

http://www.foe.co.uk/

Appeal for raised awareness of environmental issues with masses of information and tips for action from Friends of the Earth. The site hosts lengthy accounts of several campaigns undertaken by FoE and maintains an archive of press releases on some of the most controversial environmental problems encountered last year around the world.

Global Climate Change Information Programme (GCCIP)

http://www.doc.mmu.ac.uk/aric/gcciphm.html

Established in October 1991, the GCCIP provides an information link between scientists (both natural and social), politicians, economists, and the general public, on the subjects of climate change and air quality.

Global Warming

http://pooh.chem.wm.edu/chemWWW/courses/chem105/projects/group1/page1.html

Step-by-step explanation of the chemistry behind global warming. There is information about the causes of global warming, the environmental effects, and the social and economic consequences. The views of those who challenge the assertion that the world is warming up are also presented.

Met. Office Home Page

http://www.meto.govt.uk/

Authoritative account of global warming issues such as the ozone problem, El Niño (and the less known La Niña) the tropical cyclones, and forecasting methods. Scientific explanations alternate with images and film clips in an educational site which especially targets teachers and their students.

National Grid Four Seasons

http://www.4seasons.org.uk/mainmenu.htm

A range of environmental resources for schools, including detailed descriptions of projects, all clearly explained and well-illustrated.

National Wind Technology Centre

http://www.nrel.gov/wind/

Source of information on the importance of tapping wind power and how to do it. This US Department of Energy site has reports on the latest research. For children there is a wind energy quiz and details of educational materials.

Nature Explorer

http://www.naturegrid.org.uk/explorer/index.html

Wealth of information about water creatures. The presentation is fun and interactive, including a 'Virtual pond dip'.

Paul Ehrlich and the Population Bomb

http://www.pbs.org/kqed/population_bomb/

Companion to a US Public Broadcasting Service (PBS) television programme, this site details US biologist Paul Ehrlich's crusade to warn and inform people that over-consumption of resources, environmental destruction, and unchecked population growth will destroy the Earth's ability to sustain life.

Rachel Carson Homestead

http://www.rachelcarson.org/

Information on the life and legacy of the pioneering ecologist from the trust preserving Carson's childhood home. There is a biography of Carson, details of books by and about Carson, and full details of the work of the conservation organizations continuing her work.

Recycle City

http://www.epa.gov/recyclecity/

Child-friendly site of the US Environmental Protection Agency designed to help people to live more ecologically. The site includes games and activities to encourage children to think about waste disposal issues.

Royal Society for the Protection of Birds

http://www.rspb.co.uk/

Europe's largest wildlife conservation charity provides online news and local contact details, as well as a vast amount of information on birds and bird-watching in the UK, with descriptions, sketches and photographs of every common UK bird.

Royal Society for the Prevention of Cruelty to Animals

http://www.rspca.co.uk/

Great site for animal lovers, featuring a selection of interactive quizzes and puzzles for children, as well as information about how to deal with animal problems you may have.

Sea Empress Oil Spill

http://www.swan.ac.uk/biosci/empress/empress.htm

Overview of the Sea Empress oil spill on the coast of South Wales in February 1996. The site contains scientific information about the spill including its effect on the mammals, birds, and fish in the region.

6 Billion Human Beings

http://www.popexpo.net/home.htm

From the 'Musée de l'Homme' in Paris, France, a bilingual site about population growth. It includes pages examining why the number of people has grown so rapidly over the last 250 years, and whether the rapid growth rate will change. It also includes a page letting you see how many people were alive when you were born and a continually ticking counter of the current world population.

Solar Power in the UK

http://www.greenpeace.org.uk/solar/index.html

Greenpeace site campaigning for greater use of solar power. According to this environmental group, solar panels installed on buildings in the UK have the potential to provide as much electricity as we currently use per year in the UK.

State of the Environment

http://www.environment-agency.gov.uk/state_of_enviro/index3+.html

Britain's Environment Agency's page on the environment, with access to data collected and studied by the Agency on the topics of 'Bathing water quality', 'River habitats', and 'River gauging stations'.

Sustainable Development

http://iisd1.iisd.ca/

Tackles a complex issue from many different points of view. There are sections on trade and key topics such as forests and oceans. The site also reports on global initiatives to encourage sustainability.

UNFPA – United Nations Population Fund

http://www.unfpa.org/

Provides news and information on its work assisting developing countries, as well as a section of reports on the state of the world population, and information on the agency's activities, publications, and conferences.

United Nations Educational, Scientific, and Cultural Organization

http://www.unesco.org/

Well-organized site detailing UNESCO's work in 186 countries with access to reports from around the world. The structure of UNESCO and its history are explained.

Virtual Earthquake

http://vquake.calstatela.edu/edesktop/VirtApps/VirtualEarthQuake/VQuakeIntro.html

US-based site that allows you to simulate an earthquake to learn how they are measured and how they effect the environment.

Volcanoes

http://www.learner.org/exhibits/volcanoes/

Attractive site that contains detailed information about volcanic activity, supported by video clips and other interactive tasks.

What's it like where you live?

http://www.mobot.org/MBGnet/index2.htm

Aimed at younger children, this imaginative site has sections on different ecosystems from around the world, and includes related activities.

Worldwide Fund for Nature

http://www.panda.org/

Online base of the international wildlife charity. As well as giving information about current campaigns and encouraging you to join, there is a wealth of well-presented information here about the natural world, including quizzes, interactive maps, and a regularly updated news section.

Economy and Business

The Year in Review

7 July 1998 The London Stock Exchange and the German stock exchange, Deutsche Börse, agree to create a pan-European stock exchange, with a capital of £2,000 billion.

23 July 1998 German car manufacturer Volkswagen AG announces plans to acquire the Italian sports car company Lamborghini SpA.

23 July 1998 Members of Nationwide, the UK's largest building society, vote by a narrow margin against conversion into a publicly traded bank.

26 July 1998 The USA's and UK's largest telecommunications companies, AT&T Corp and British Telecommunications plc, announce a joint venture to provide telecommunications services to multinational corporations.

28 July 1998 German car manufacturer BMW announces the acquisition of the Rolls-Royce brand name for £40 million. BMW will take control of Rolls-Royce cars, currently owned by Volkswagen AG, from 2003.

28 July 1998 US telecommunications firm Bell Atlantic Corporation, the largest local telephone service provider in the USA, announces a proposed $53 billion merger with GTE Corp. The deal would create a company that controls 63 million telephone lines or one-third of all local telephone links.

11 August 1998 British Petroleum plc announces a proposed $48.2 billion merger with its US oil industry competitor Amoco Corp, which would be the largest oil industry merger ever.

12 August 1998 Credit Suisse and UBS AG, Switzerland's two largest banks, agree to pay $1.25 billion to Holocaust survivors and their heirs who had lost assets deposited in accounts before and during World War II.

12 August 1998 The British government announces that the country's unemployment rate has fallen to 4.7 percent in July, its lowest rate since 1980.

18 August 1998 The Russian government devalues the rouble in an effort to stabilize the country's foundering economy. Russian president Boris Yeltsin's economics advisor, Aleksander Livshits, resigns, and the Russian stock market is periodically suspended.

19 August 1998 Italy's largest insurance company, Assicurazioni Generali SpA, agrees to pay $100 million to the victims of the Holocaust and their heirs who had life insurance policies confiscated by the Nazis during World War II. Several other European insurance firms follow suit a few days later, agreeing to compensate Holocaust victims for lost policies.

27 August 1998 The Russian government's decision to stop propping up the ailing rouble leads to uncertainty about the future of President Boris Yeltsin and the entire reform process, causing global stock markets to plummet.

4 September 1998 The Japanese manufacturer of semi-conductors, Fujitsu, announces the closure of its factory in Newton Aycliffe, County Durham, England, with the loss of 600 jobs, in another casualty of the economic crisis in the Far East.

14 September 1998 Finance ministers from the Group of Seven (Canada, France, Germany, Italy, Japan, the UK, and the USA), the world's leading industrial countries, plan to lower interest rates in an attempt to revive failing economies throughout the world.

14 September 1998 Winning a bidding war against rival telecommunications firms British Telecommunications plc (BT) and GTE Corp, WorldCom announces its merger with MCI Communications Corp in a deal worth an estimated $40 billion, in the largest US telecommunications merger ever.

21 September 1998 Five airlines – American Airlines, British Airways, Canadian Airlines, Cathay Pacific, and Qantas Airways – announce plans of a joint marketing venture called Oneworld, in which the airlines would coordinate flights and link frequent-flier programmes.

25 September 1998 A two-year study commissioned by the British government says that large supermarkets are squeezing out small grocers and decreasing employment in small English towns.

30 September 1998 US president Clinton announces that the federal budget for the 1998 fiscal year has resulted in a surplus for the first time since 1969.

8 October 1998 The Bank of England lowers interest rates for the first time in two years in an effort to protect the British economy from the international financial crisis.

14 October 1998 Indian economist and academic Amartya Sen, head of Trinity College, Cambridge, wins the 1998 Nobel Prize in Economics for his research into welfare economics and the distribution of income in poor countries.

15 October 1998 Governor of the Bank of England Eddie George presents evidence to a Treasury committee that businesses and homeowners are likely to suffer higher bank charges to help banks recoup huge losses suffered on the international stock market. His comments coincide with a survey of businesses that shows a recession in manufacturing and a slump in the service industry.

30 October 1998 The G7 countries announce an action plan to boost and restore confidence in failing economies worldwide. The plan features a contingency fund of $90 million from the International Monetary Fund for economies in danger of collapse.

5 November 1998 The Bank of England cuts interest rates for borrowers by half a point to 6.75 percent, the biggest cut in five years, in reaction to the UK's declining economy and the threat of recession.

12 November 1998 US car manufacturer Chrysler Corp and German car manufacturer Daimler-Benz AG merge to form DaimlerChrysler AG, in a deal valued at $38.3 billion.

13 November 1998 The International Monetary Fund (IMF) announces an aid package of $42 billion to save Brazil's economy, which is on the verge of collapse as a result of the world economic crisis sparked off in Asia.

17 November 1998 US Federal Reserve chairman Alan Greenspan announces a cut in interest rates for the third time in seven weeks, responding to fears of a stock market crash and recession.

19 November 1998 British home secretary Jack Straw announces plans for a crackdown on tax evasion in Jersey, Guernsey, and the Isle of Man.

23 November 1998 British engineering companies Siebe plc and BTR plc announce plans to merge, creating the world's largest manufacturer of industrial control and automation systems.

24 November 1998 America Online (AOL), the largest Internet service provider in the USA, announces plans to acquire the software company Netscape Communications Corp, the manufacturer of Netscape Navigator, the best-selling brand of Web browser.

27 November 1998 Barclays plc chief executive Martin Taylor unexpectedly resigns, reportedly because of controversy over his proposal to split the bank into a retail and an investment arm.

30 November 1998 Deutsche Bank announces its acquisition of Bankers Trust of America, creating the biggest financial institution in the world but resulting in the loss of 5,500 jobs in London and New York.

December 1998 The British Petroleum plc/ Amoco Corp merger comes into effect.

1 December 1998 US energy company Exxon Corporation announces a plan to buy Mobil Corporation for $75.3 billion. The deal, between the two largest US energy companies in the USA, is the largest merger in history to date.

3 December 1998 Eleven European countries cut their interest rates to 3 percent in preparation for the launch of the euro in January 1999.

8 December 1998 AT&T, the largest telecommunications firm in the USA, announces plans to acquire the global data network of International Business Machines (IBM) for $5 billion.

31 December 1998 The European Commission announces the official conversion rates between the euro and the national currencies of the 11 countries joining the single European currency.

January 1999 The new UK minimum wage of £3.60 per hour, announced in June 1998, comes into effect.

January 1999 Britain has its highest monthly trade deficit ever, £2.83 billion. The strength of the pound and the economic crisis in Asia are blamed.

1 January 1999 The single European currency, the euro, is launched in 11 participating EU countries: Austria, Belgium, Finland, France, Germany, Ireland, Italy, Luxembourg, the Netherlands, Portugal, and Spain.

11 January 1999 Tobacco companies Rothmans and British American Tobacco (BAT) announce a merger in an effort to compete against the number one tobacco seller Philip Morris.

12 January 1999 The Brazilian real is devalued in an effort to prop up the ailing economy, causing the world stock market to plummet.

15 January 1999 Vodafone, the UK's largest mobile-phone company, announces plans to acquire the US mobile-phone company AirTouch Communications Inc, which would make the combined firm, Vodafone AirTouch plc, the largest mobile-phone company in the world, with 23 million customers.

19 January 1999 British Aerospace plc announces plans to acquire British defence-contracting firm Marconi Electronic Systems from Britain's General Electric Co.

21 January 1999 The USA's four largest tobacco companies announce plans to establish a $5.15 billion fund to support tobacco farmers who will have a reduced market after the companies' settlements of lawsuits from smokers.

28 January 1999 Internet search engine Yahoo! Inc announces plans to acquire GeoCities Inc, another US Internet company, for $5 billion. Yahoo was the second most visited site and GeoCities the third on the Web in 1998.

28 January 1999 The US company Ford, the world's second-largest car manufacturer, buys Volvo for £3.9 billion.

1 February 1999 French bank Société Générale announces plans to acquire Paribas, a competitor, for 100 billion francs. The merged bank would be the largest in France and the third largest in Europe.

4 February 1999 Deutsche Bank AG, Germany's largest bank, confirms that it helped finance the building of Auschwitz, a concentration camp in Poland, during World War II.

8 February 1999 British hotel and casino company Ladbroke, which owns all of the Hilton hotels outside the USA, announces plans to acquire rival company Stakis for £1.16 billion.

17 February 1999 The British government announces that 1,305,300 people were seeking unemployment benefit in January, the lowest number since 1980.

23 February 1999 Prime Minister Tony Blair announces a draft timetable for adopting the euro, starting with a cabinet vote on whether or not the government favours becoming part of the single European currency. Tory party leader William Hague, who is against adopting the euro, criticizes the plan.

1 March 1999 The owners of Canary Wharf announce plans to sell shares of the property to the public, in an effort to recover losses following its filing for bankruptcy in 1992.

29 March 1999 The Dow Jones Industrial Average closes above 10,000 for the first time ever.

1 April 1999 British oil company BP Amoco plc, created in December 1998 by the merger of British Petroleum and Amoco Corp, announces plans to acquire US oil producer Atlantic Richfield Co (ARCO) in a deal worth around $25.7 billion. The merged company would be the largest oil producer in Britain and the USA.

1 April 1999 Internet search engine Yahoo! Inc announces that it plans to buy broadcast.com, Inc, the leading Internet video and audio broadcaster, in a deal valued at $5.7 billion.

8 April 1999 The European Central Bank cuts interest rates for the euro for the first time. The Bank of England also cuts the pound's interest rate, to 5.25 percent, its lowest level since 1994.

9 April 1999 The US government announces plans to impose 100 percent tariffs on a number of European products in retaliation for EU restrictions on the import of bananas from Latin America.

16 April 1999 The retail firm Kingfisher plc announces its plan to purchase the Asda supermarket chain for £5.8 billion, which would make Kingfisher the largest retailer in the UK.

26 April 1999 Representatives from the major industrialized nations attend a Group of Seven (G7) meeting in Washington, DC. The group announces renewed confidence in the global economy after a two-year international financial crisis that nearly caused the economies of several countries to collapse.

24 May 1999 The British Office of National Statistics reports zero economic growth for the first quarter of 1999. It is the first time since 1992 that quarterly growth is stagnant. The previous year's high interest rates and the strength of the pound are blamed.

25 May 1999 British Airways chief executive Bob Ayling confirms a 61 percent loss in company profits, from £580 million to £225 million in 12 months, the worst since the recession of the early 1990s.

June 1999 Students at 100 universities across the USA stage sit-ins to protest against the universities' buying of sportswear made by Nike, which uses workers in sweatshops in developing countries.

2 June 1999 The Bank of Scotland plans to cancel its deal with US televangelist Pat Robertson after he said that Scotland was overrun by gays whose influence was a frightening prospect. The bank had planned to market a British-style telephone bank to the 55 million viewers of Robertson's Christian Broadcasting Network.

10 June 1999 The Bank of England cuts the base interest rate to its lowest level since 1977, by a quarter-point to 5 percent.

11 June 1999 British chancellor Gordon Brown denounces the burden of debt for developing countries and pledges a $50 billion reduction from Britain, with further reductions to follow.

14 June 1999 US company Wal-Mart, the world's largest retailer, acquires the British supermarket chain Asda for £7 billion.

17 June 1999 The German-owned British car manufacturer Rover begins selling the Rover 75, the company's first new design of car since it was taken over by BMW in 1994.

18 June 1999 The Group of Seven (G7) industrialized nations unveils a $100 billion package of debt relief for developing countries, at the end of a three-day economic summit in Cologne, Germany.

19 June 1999 The average rate of interest for mortgages in the UK is 5.53 percent, the lowest rate for 30 years. The Council of Mortgage Lenders predicts the largest number of home buyers this year since the late 1980s.

21 June 1999 The Bank of England announces a new design for the £20 note that includes advanced anti-forgery production techniques. The note, whose design was last updated in 1993, is the most popular among counterfeiters.

23 June 1999 German chancellor Gerhard Schroeder announces plans for radical spending cuts totalling £10 billion for next year and a reduction of taxes for businesses. Pension and welfare schemes will take large budget cuts.

24 June 1999 US media group Gannett, owner of the national newspaper *USA Today*, announces an offer to buy Newsquest, England's largest publisher of regional newspapers, for £904 million.

28 June 1999 More than 40 leaders of European Union and South American countries meet for an economic summit in Rio de Janeiro, Brazil, where they agree to launch free-trade negotiations between the two continents.

29 June 1999 A British government task force led by architect Lord Rogers, designer of the Millennium Dome, publishes a report on how to stem the flow of people moving out of cities into the countryside. Under the proposal, businesses and individuals would be offered lower tax rates for city properties.

World Economy Overview

Countries with the Highest and Lowest GDP

(In millions of dollars.)

1997

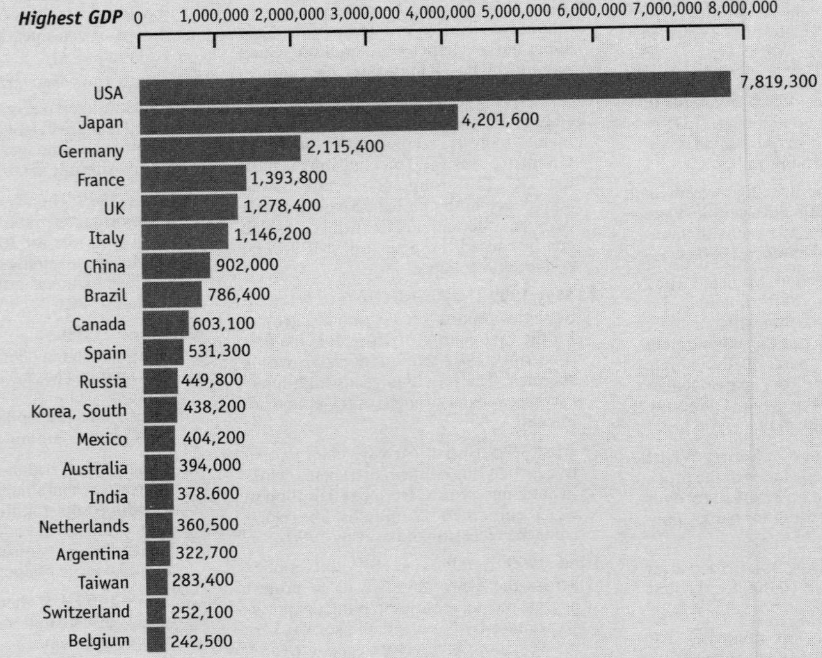

Highest GDP

USA	7,819,300
Japan	4,201,600
Germany	2,115,400
France	1,393,800
UK	1,278,400
Italy	1,146,200
China	902,000
Brazil	786,400
Canada	603,100
Spain	531,300
Russia	449,800
Korea, South	438,200
Mexico	404,200
Australia	394,000
India	378.600
Netherlands	360,500
Argentina	322,700
Taiwan	283,400
Switzerland	252,100
Belgium	242,500

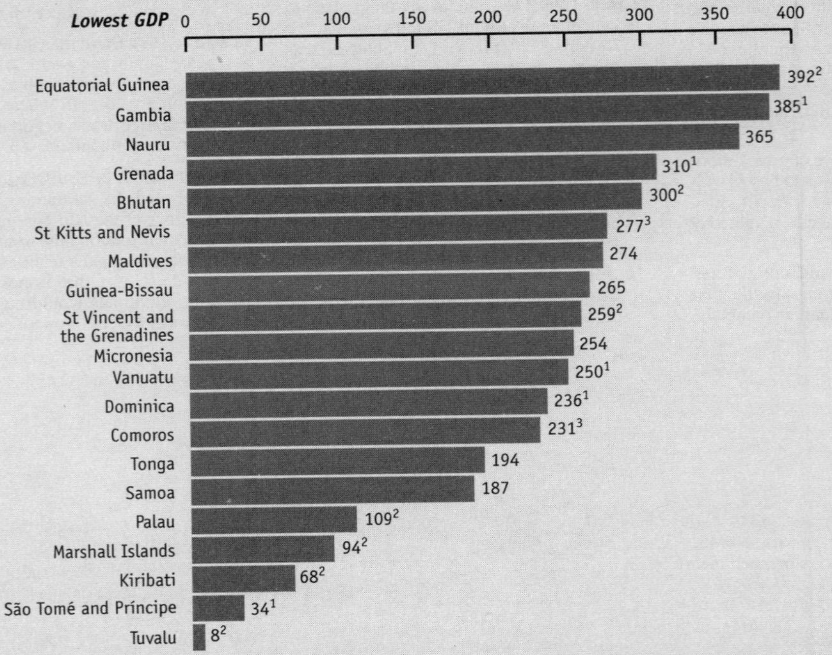

Lowest GDP

Equatorial Guinea	392[2]
Gambia	385[1]
Nauru	365
Grenada	310[1]
Bhutan	300[2]
St Kitts and Nevis	277[3]
Maldives	274
Guinea-Bissau	265
St Vincent and the Grenadines	259[2]
Micronesia	254
Vanuatu	250[1]
Dominica	236[1]
Comoros	231[3]
Tonga	194
Samoa	187
Palau	109[2]
Marshall Islands	94[2]
Kiribati	68[2]
São Tomé and Príncipe	34[1]
Tuvalu	8[2]

[1] 1997 estimate.
[2] 1995 estimate.
[3] 1996 estimate.

Living in a Global Economy

By Peter Robinson

The 'global economy' is now a familiar term in the developed world. Some see it as a wholly positive and liberating phenomenon, breaking down barriers between nations; others perceive in it a threat to the independence of governments and individuals.

What is the global economy?

For some, the global economy means Western market capitalism, now the world's dominant organizing economic principle following reforms in countries such as China and the collapse of the Soviet bloc. In this economic model, firms supply consumers in the marketplace; the state is confined to regulating this activity and providing those services the market cannot efficiently provide. For others, the term global economy also implies a greater role for international flows of trade, investment, and finance. The downside of the resulting interdependence between countries is that the consequences of an economic crisis are quickly felt elsewhere.

In addition to concerns about the cultural imperialism associated with Western capitalism, there are also vital economic issues. Multinational companies are in a position to exploit workforces or the environment in developing countries, and can threaten to pull out of those countries whose governments do not follow their preferred economic or environmental policies. Similarly, international financial institutions can penalize developing countries by withdrawing or withholding funds. There is a real worry that these unelected bodies can coerce elected governments.

Why do we have a global economy?

The idea that countries concentrate on producing only those goods and services that they could produce relatively efficiently, and trade them for goods and services that they could only produce less efficiently, with the result that everyone might be better off, is a 19th-century concept. Without international trade, a vast number of foodstuffs and raw materials would not be available in the UK. In practice most trade, especially that between industrialized countries, is now in the same products (cars, for example). As consumers grow richer, international trade facilitates the wider choice of goods and services expected.

Closing the gap between relatively rich and relatively poor countries remains perhaps the greatest challenge.

There are significant advantages to an international economy, although these do not imply that it is problem-free. Countries are able to invest (for example, in transport infrastructure) by borrowing from institutions in other countries; higher yields may be achieved by lending abroad than by lending domestically. By importing expertise from abroad, a country can benefit its workers and its consumers.

Is the global economy new?

A global economy was already in existence at the beginning of the 20th century: by 1913 the UK was exporting a significantly greater proportion of its factory output than in the 1990s, and providing the greater proportion of the world's investment funding; UK firms had establishments on all continents. A number of Western countries (together with their then colonies) were integrated into a world economy similar to today's, with extensive flows of trade and capital. World War I and the Great Depression of the inter-war years shattered this first global economy. The global effects of the US depression throughout the 1930s demonstrate that vulnerability to outside economic events is nothing new. Since 1945, nothing in our experience has come close to this economic meltdown.

International economic organizations

Since 1945, the global economy has been rebuilt by international agencies, attaining only comparatively recently the levels of integration reached before World War I. Two key economic institutions established by the victorious Western powers (primarily the USA and the UK), following a meeting in the USA in 1944, were the International Monetary Fund (IMF) and what became known as the World Bank (International Bank for Reconstruction and Development). The IMF offers advice and loans to countries facing financial problems; the World Bank lends or gives funds to countries to foster long-term economic development. Both organizations now deal mainly with developing countries, though originally they also interacted with the Western economies.

The IMF is the more controversial of the two institutions, as its loans come with advice or conditions attached, which, many critics argue, force governments to introduce policies that hurt the vulnerable; the IMF argues that it is the governments' own policies that are at fault. However, individual governments in developed countries also frequently offer financial aid to developing countries with advice and conditions attached.

There are several more recently formed economic institutions. The World Trade Organization (WTO) is the successor of the General Agreement on Tariffs and Trade (GATT), which played a major role in dismantling national barriers to international trade (set up in part in the wake of the Great Depression). The original purpose of the Organization for Economic Cooperation and Development (OECD) was to disperse funds made available by the USA to help rebuild European economies after World War II; it now acts as a forum for debate for most of the richest countries on issues such as unemployment and taxation. The G7 ('group of seven') countries are the world's largest and richest (the USA, Japan, Germany, France, the UK, Italy, and Canada), and have been meeting regularly since the 1970s to discuss the global economy. More recently, Russia has been invited to attend these meetings, and the group became known as G8.

All of these economic organizations are dominated by the rich developed countries that lead the international economy, and many developing countries feel excluded as a result. By virtue of their huge populations, China and Brazil have economies which are now bigger than Canada's and are certainly more important than Russia's.

Regionalization

In addition to globalization, countries in particular regions are coming closer together. The best known regional grouping is the European Union (EU), which certainly has a greater impact on the lives of those living in its 15 member states than any international institution; the countries of North America and of the Asia-Pacific region have also fostered new links in their areas. The issue facing many individual countries is the effect that joining or staying out of these arrangements may have on their independence.

The future of the global economy

Several questions remain about the course of the international economy at the start of the third millennium. Will regional coalitions of countries become the main players, or will international institutions retain their importance? How should these institutions be overhauled to make them more relevant and more responsive to the needs of developing countries? While the global economy has brought a wide choice of more competitively priced goods and services for many, for others the benefits may seem less obvious, and closing the gap between relatively rich and relatively poor countries remains perhaps the greatest challenge of all.

Peter Robinson is senior economist at the Institute for Public Policy Research, London

Countries with the Fastest and Slowest Economic Growth

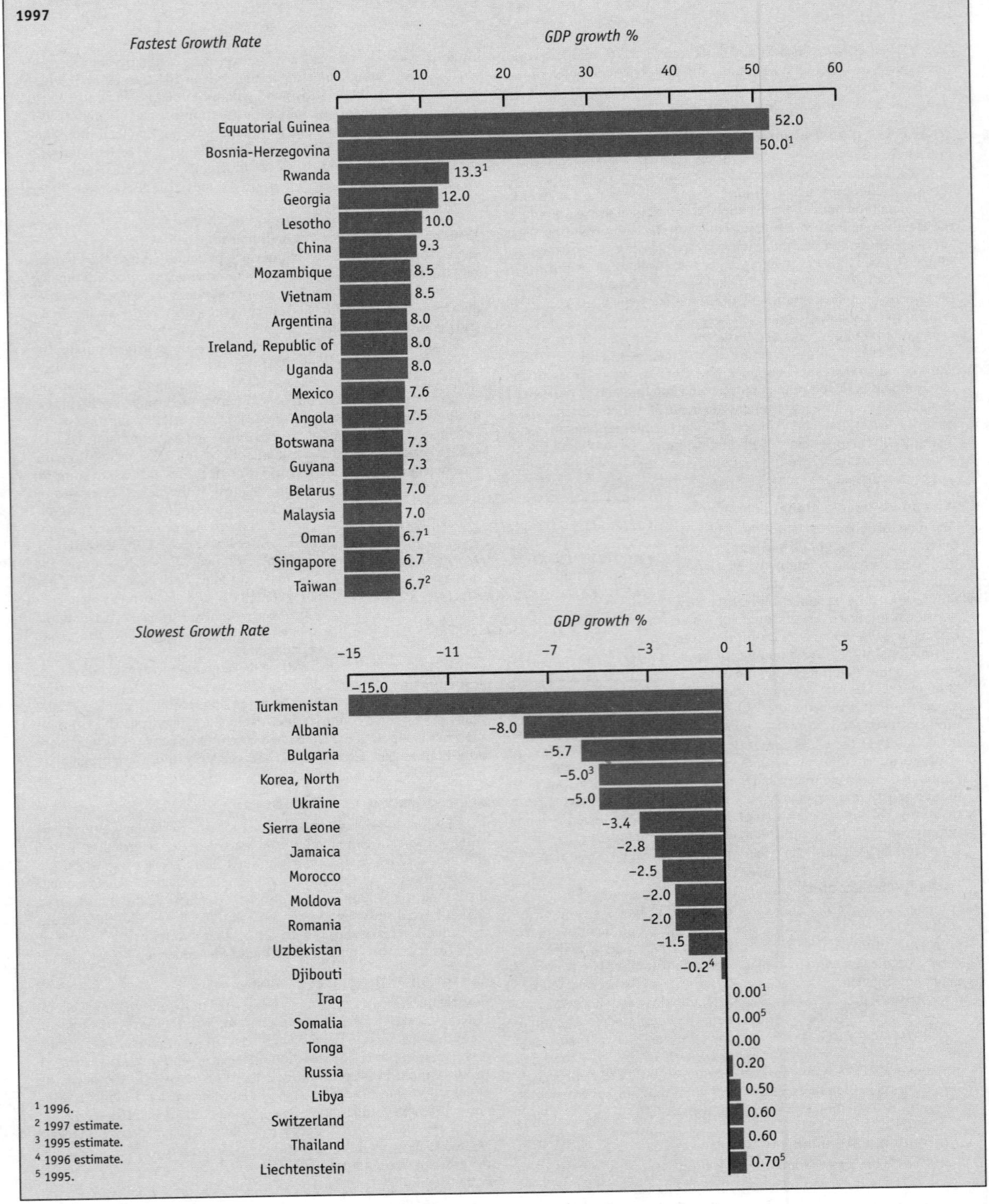

1997

Fastest Growth Rate

Country	GDP growth %
Equatorial Guinea	52.0
Bosnia-Herzegovina	50.0[1]
Rwanda	13.3[1]
Georgia	12.0
Lesotho	10.0
China	9.3
Mozambique	8.5
Vietnam	8.5
Argentina	8.0
Ireland, Republic of	8.0
Uganda	8.0
Mexico	7.6
Angola	7.5
Botswana	7.3
Guyana	7.3
Belarus	7.0
Malaysia	7.0
Oman	6.7[1]
Singapore	6.7
Taiwan	6.7[2]

Slowest Growth Rate

Country	GDP growth %
Turkmenistan	−15.0
Albania	−8.0
Bulgaria	−5.7
Korea, North	−5.0[3]
Ukraine	−5.0
Sierra Leone	−3.4
Jamaica	−2.8
Morocco	−2.5
Moldova	−2.0
Romania	−2.0
Uzbekistan	−1.5
Djibouti	−0.2[4]
Iraq	0.00[1]
Somalia	0.00[5]
Tonga	0.00
Russia	0.20
Libya	0.50
Switzerland	0.60
Thailand	0.60
Liechtenstein	0.70[5]

[1] 1996.
[2] 1997 estimate.
[3] 1995 estimate.
[4] 1996 estimate.
[5] 1995.

World Debt and the Jubilee 2000 Campaign

BY ANNA FARKAS

Jubilee 2000 is an international umbrella organization active in over 40 countries which advocates a debt-free start to the millennium for the world's poorest countries. The highly visible Jubilee 2000 Campaign brings together a broad coalition of faith-based organizations, non-governmental organizations, trade unions, press, and general public, and has attracted the support of some leading religious, sports, and entertainment personalities. It currently has campaigns organized in most countries of the Organization for Economic Cooperation and Development (OECD), as well as in Africa and Latin America. Despite the broad-based nature of this coalition, Jubilee 2000 is unified in its objective for debt cancellation, while accepting that there will always be differences between individual campaigns and individuals within campaigns. Jubilee 2000 does not prescribe for individual countries how debt settlements should be worked out, believing that this should be resolved between the individual debtor country and creditors, with civil society involvement.

The key features which characterize the campaign include:

- The demand that unpayable debts be forgiven. This could range from an outright cancellation of all debts to a limitation of the debt service burden to a small fraction of budgetary and/or export revenues (for example, between three and five percent). The Biblical notion of Jubilee 'seeks to re-establish justice between debtors and creditors'.
- The need to establish an arbitration process that would give debtors a greater say in the negotiations (internationalization of Chapter 9 of US bankruptcy law).
- The acceleration of debt relief, with the year 2000 being symbolic of a new 'debt-free start'.

There have been many different Jubilee 2000 declarations, including the Accra Declaration of 19 April 1998, and a Jubilee Call for debt cancellation and economic justice, adopted at the first Jubilee 2000 international conference in Rome, on 17 November 1998, and the Tegucigalpa Declaration of 27 January 1999.

The burden of debt falls on those least able to pay – the poorest countries in the world where the bulk of the population has an income of less than $1 per day. This is considered by many commentators to be immoral and/or unjust. A further rationale given by religious groups is the call for debt relief related to the Jubilee year 2000 and the call for the forgiveness of debts before the new millennium. In particular, policy makers are requested to 'heed the Biblical call to 'proclaim Jubilee' by the year 2000'. Various groups have been calling for a shortening of the waiting period, particularly in cases where countries are emerging from a post-conflict and post-catastrophe situation such as Hurricane Mitch. It is argued that early debt relief could play a significant role in helping these countries overcome the devastation and begin the enormous task of rebuilding basic infrastructures.

According to the Jubilee 2000, debt should be forgiven because it perpetuates the dependency of the poorest countries; the campaign describes this dependency as 'chains of debt' and uses an image of chain links as its official logo. The Jubilee 2000 lobby has run an increasingly vociferous campaign since 1996, and in June 1999 organized a series of events throughout the UK in which tens of thousands of supporters joined hands to form human chains to put pressure on the world's richest nations to cancel Third World debt prior to a scheduled meeting of G7 finance ministers in Frankfurt, Germany. The ministers agreed on 12 June on a plan to write off $50 billion/£32 billion of debts owed by the poorest countries. In the face of mounting pressure from debt campaigners, they also decided to reduce Overseas Development Agency loans by a further £20 billion. The finance ministers pledged to contribute to a Millennium Trust Fund, announced by British chancellor of the exchequer Gordon Brown earlier in June, with an initial contribution of $100 million. The Millennium Trust Fund was being built up by the World Bank to reduce the interest payments that the world's poorest countries were paying on their debts to the richest governments. They also agreed in principle that IMF gold should be sold off to help pay for the reduction in debt.

Third World debt is a problem that has been with us since at least 1982, when Mexico warned its bankers that it would not be able to pay its debt, sending shock waves around the international banking industry. A spreading international financial crisis, dragging down banks around the world, was a real risk, so through much of the 1980s and 1990s there were strenuous efforts, led mostly by the USA, to sort out these problems, with some success. Since 1996, the group of debt-burdened countries, known as the highly indebted poor countries (HIPCs), has been the focus of a lot of attention at the International Monetary Fund (IMF) and the World Bank, and among the big economic powers, leading to agreement on stage one of the debt reduction initiative for these countries. Britain has been pushing this effort from the start. Groups like Jubilee 2000 are partly responsible for the current growing momentum behind the initiative, with the urgent aim of giving more debt relief, to more countries, more quickly.

Anna Farkas is a freelance researcher and writer

Countries with the Highest and Lowest Foreign Debt

(In millions of dollars.)

1996

Highest Foreign Debt		*Lowest Foreign Debt*	
Brazil	177,800	Slovenia	4.03
Mexico	157,100	Tuvalu	6.0[1]
Indonesia	129,030	Kiribati	21.0[1]
China	128,800	Eritrea	46.0
Russia	124,800	Vanuatu	47.0
Iraq	100,400	St Kitts and Nevis	58.0
Korea, South	95,500	Suriname	68.2[2]
Argentina	91,200	Tonga	70.0
Thailand	90,800	Bhutan	87.0
India	89,800	Palau	100.0[3]

[1] 1993.
[2] 1995.
[3] 1990.

Countries with the Highest and Lowest Consumer Price Inflation

Country	Inflation rate (%)	Year	Country	Inflation rate (%)	Year
Highest Inflation			*Lowest Inflation*		
Angola	1,200.0	1998	Seychelles	0.7	1997
Congo, Republic of the	659.0	1996	Bahrain	0.8	1998
Iraq	200.0	1997	Belize	0.8	1997
Chad	152.0	1997	Liechtenstein	0.8	1996
Sudan	130.0	1996	Oman	1.0	1998
Belarus	127.0	1998	Switzerland	1.0	1998
Liberia	100.0	1996	Japan	1.1	1998
Turkmenistan	100.0	1998	Dominica	1.5	1997
Turkey	83.1	1998	Finland	1.5	1998
Uzbekistan	57.0	1998	Panama	1.5	1998
Romania	46.0	1998	Austria	1.6	1998
Mongolia	45.8	1996	France	1.6	1998
São Tomé and Príncipe	45.0	1997	Luxembourg	1.6	1998
Bosnia-Herzegovina	40.0	1998	Bahamas	1.7	1997
Guinea-Bissau	40.0	1996	Australia	1.8	1998
Tajikistan	40.0	1998	Argentina	1.9	1998
Jamaica	34.7	1998	Germany	1.9	1998
Bulgaria	32.0	1998	New Zealand	2.0	1998
Libya	30.0	1998	Senegal	2.0	1998
Myanmar	29.4	1997	Tonga	2.1	1997

Annual Percent Change in Consumer Prices, Selected Countries

Figures are percentage change from previous year. (N/A = not available. – = not applicable.)

Country	1992	1993	1994	1995	1996	1997
Argentina	24.9	10.6	4.2	3.4	0.2	0.5
Australia	1.0	1.8	1.9	4.6	2.6	0.3
Belgium	2.4	2.8	2.4	1.5	2.1	1.6
Brazil	1,009.0	2,148.0	2,076.0	66.0	15.8	6.9
Canada	1.5	1.8	0.2	2.2	1.6	1.6
Chile	15.4	12.7	11.4	8.2	7.4	6.1
Colombia	27.0	22.6	23.8	21.0	20.2	18.5
France	2.4	2.1	1.7	1.8	2.0	1.2
Germany	4.0	5.0	2.7	1.8	1.5	1.8
India	11.8	6.4	10.2	10.2	9.0	7.2
Indonesia	7.5	9.7	9.6	9.0	6.6	11.6
Iran	25.6	21.2	31.5	49.6	28.9	17.2
Israel	11.9	10.9	12.3	10.0	11.3	9.0
Italy	5.1	4.5	4.0	5.2	4.0	2.0
Japan	1.7	1.3	0.7	–0.1	0.1	1.7
Korea, South	6.2	4.8	6.2	4.5	4.9	4.4
Malaysia	4.8	3.5	3.7	5.3	3.5	2.7
Mexico	15.5	9.8	7.0	35.0	34.4	20.6
Netherlands	1.4	2.1	1.8	2.8	3.6	3.3
Nigeria	44.6	57.2	57.0	72.8	29.3	8.2
Norway	2.3	2.3	1.4	2.5	1.3	2.6
Pakistan	9.5	10.0	12.4	12.3	10.4	11.4
Philippines	8.9	7.6	9.1	8.1	8.4	5.1
Romania	211.0	255.0	137.0	32.0	N/A	N/A
Russia	N/A	N/A	307.4	197.4	47.6	14.6
South Africa	13.9	9.7	9.0	8.6	7.4	8.5
Spain	5.9	4.6	4.7	4.7	3.6	2.0
Sweden	2.3	4.6	2.2	2.5	0.5	0.5
Switzerland	4.1	3.3	0.8	1.8	0.8	0.5
Turkey	70.1	66.1	106.3	88.1	80.3	85.7
UK	3.7	1.6	2.5	3.4	2.4	3.1
USA	3.0	3.0	2.6	2.8	2.9	2.3
Venezuela	31.4	38.1	60.8	59.9	99.9	50.0

Source: © International Monetary Fund

The Top 50 Companies in the World

Rank 1998	Rank 1997	Company	Country	Market capitalization ($ millions)
1	3	Microsoft	USA	271,854.4
2	1	General Electric	USA	258,871.3
3	4	Exxon	USA	172,212.5
4	2	Royal Dutch/Shell	Netherlands/UK	164,156.5
5	8	Merck	USA	154,752.7
6	22	Pfizer	USA	148,074.0
7	6	Intel	USA	144,060.0
8	5	Coca-Cola	USA	142,164.3
9	18	Wal-Mart Stores	USA	123,062.0
10	11	IBM	USA	121,183.6
11	7	NTT	Japan	117,652.1
12	12	Philip Morris	USA	112,436.5
13	10	Novartis Ag	Switzerland	108,474.8
14	21	Johnson & Johnson	USA	105,241.9
15	20	Glaxo Wellcome	UK	105,190.8
16	19	Bristol Myers Squibb	USA	103,325.4
17	26	AT&T	USA	102,480.0
18	17	Roche	Switzerland	102,006.9
19	51	Cisco Systems	USA	96,587.1
20	13	Procter & Gamble	USA	95,126.9
21	45	Lucent Technologies	USA	90,985.0
22	16	British Petroleum	UK	88,618.7
23	28 =	Lilly (Eli)	USA	86,246.5
24		MCI Worldcom	USA	86,214.0
25	64	BT	UK	86,134.4
26	9	Toyota Motor	Japan	85,910.8
27	44	Deutsche Telekom	Germany	83,724.1
28	89	Dell Computer	USA	83,634.0
29	23	American International Group	USA	82,293.9
30	35	SBC Communications	USA	81,529.7
31	41	Nestlé	Switzerland	77,489.9
32	72	Schering-Plough	USA	76,106.6
33	29	Bell Atlantic	USA	75,246.4
34	36	Allianz	Germany	74,382.6
35	58	Bellsouth	USA	74,196.5
36	37	Berkshire Hathaway -CI A	USA	73,963.6
37	55	American Home Products	USA	69,200.2
38	33	Unilever Plc/NV	Netherlands/UK	67,214.5
39	49	Fannie Mae	USA	66,434.5
40	50	Abbott Laboratories	USA	66,137.0
41	27	Du Pont (E I) De Nemours	USA	63,631.1
42	77	Warner-Lambert	USA	61,855.3
43	43	SmithKline Beecham	UK	60,665.5
44	25	Lloyds TSB Group	UK	60,214.8
45	32 =	Mobil	USA	59,355.0
46		France Telecom	France	58,128.3
47	70	Home Depot	USA	58,076.9
48	42	Ford Motor	USA	57,387.0
49	39	Chevron	USA	55,012.4
50	24	Hewlett-Packard	USA	54,902.4

Source: *FT500, Financial Times Surveys,* © *Financial Times* 1999

The Top 25 Banking Companies in the World

Data are based on total at year-end 1998.

Rank	Company	Country	Market capitalization ($ millions)
1	Citigroup Inc	USA	114,876.3
2	BankAmerica Corporation	USA	106,759.7
3	Lloyds TSB Group	UK	77,640.8
4	Fannie Mae	USA	77,375.9
5	HSBC Holdings	UK	70,165.3
6	UBS AG	Switzerland	66,022.3
7	Wells Fargo	USA	63,473.2
8	Bank One Corporation	USA	61,038.6
9	Chase Manhattan Corporation	USA	60,896.5
10	Bank of Tokyo-Mitsubishi, Japan	Japan	47,685.8
11	American Express	USA	47,384.5
12	Freddie Mac	USA	43,994.3
13	Morgan Stanley Dean Witter & Co	USA	42,277.9
14	Credit Suisse Group	Switzerland	41,721.5
15	Halifax	UK	34,836.4
16	National Westminster Bank	UK	32,861.7
17	Barclays	UK	32,696.8
18	Banco Bilbao Vizcaya	Spain	31,950.8
19	Sumitomo Bank	Japan	31,762.4
20	Deutsche Bank	Germany	31,255.2
21	Bayerische Hypotheken und Vereinsbank	Germany	30,723.7
22	Abbey National	UK	30,409.6
23	Bank of New York	USA	30,331.4
24	ABN Amro Holding	Netherlands	30,216.5
25	Associates First Capital Corporation	USA	29,823.8

Source: *FT500, Financial Times Survey,* © *Financial Times* 1999

Gold Reserves, Industrial Countries

(– = not applicable. In millions of fine troy ounces.)

Country	1990	1992	1994	1996	1997
Europe					
Austria	20.39	19.93	18.34	10.75	7.87
Belgium	30.23	25.04	25.04	15.32	15.32
Denmark	1.65	1.66	1.63	1.66	1.69
Finland	2.00	2.00	2.00	1.60	1.60
France	81.85	81.85	81.85	81.85	81.89
Germany	95.18	95.18	95.18	95.18	95.18
Greece	3.40	3.43	3.45	3.47	3.64
Iceland	0.05	0.05	0.05	0.05	0.05
Ireland, Republic of	0.36	0.36	0.36	0.36	0.36
Italy	66.67	66.67	66.67	66.67	66.67
Luxembourg	0.34	0.34	0.31	0.31	0.31
Netherlands	43.94	43.94	34.77	34.77	27.07
Norway	1.18	1.18	1.18	1.18	1.18
Portugal	15.83	16.06	16.07	16.07	16.07
Spain	15.61	15.62	15.62	15.63	15.63
Sweden	6.07	6.07	6.07	4.70	4.72
Switzerland	83.28	83.28	83.28	83.28	83.28
UK	18.94	18.61	18.44	18.43	18.42
North America					
USA	261.91	261.84	261.73	261.66	261.64
Canada	14.76	9.94	3.89	3.09	3.09
Pacific					
Australia	7.93	7.93	7.90	7.90	2.56
Japan	24.23	24.23	24.23	24.23	24.23
New Zealand	–	–	–	–	–
Industrial countries total	795.81	785.24	768.05	748.16	732.47
WORLD TOTAL	939.01	927.55	917.98	907.55	890.57

Source: *International Financial Statistics Yearbook 1998,* International Monetary Fund

World Share Prices Comparison

Indices on the basis of 1990 = 100.

Country	1996	1997	1998
Canada	154	189	198
Mexico	554.8	779.2	744.0
USA	195	249	300
Australia	152	171	179
Japan	74	64	54
Korea	111.4	87.4	54.7
New Zealand	140	152	130
Austria	67.3	76.1	85.8

Country	1996	1997	1998
Belgium	132	177	245
Denmark	117	166	191
Finland	153	240	340
France	118	152	198
Germany	115.6	158.4	202.4
Greece	93	146	216
Ireland, Republic of	160	214	304
Italy	96	131	210

Country	1996	1997	1998
Netherlands	200.7	302.3	381.7
Norway	143	206	201
Portugal	127	200	316
Spain	137	210	308
Sweden	182.7	263.3	305.2
Switzerland	213	300	400
Turkey	1,752	5,268	8,022
UK	167	189	222

Source: *Main Economic Indicators,* © OECD 1999

The Global Economic Crisis 1997–99

July 1997	The Philippines peso falls nearly 10 percent against the dollar, followed by the Malaysian ringgit and the Indonesian rupiah. Regional stock markets plunge.
July 1997	South Korea's Kia Group, the country's third largest car maker and the country's eighth largest 'chaebol' conglomerate, is put under the control of a government-organized alliance of banks. Kia is the fourth of South Korea's top 30 chaebols to collapse, or nearly collapse, in 1997.
2 July 1997	Thailand is forced to abandon its fixed exchange rate for the baht against the US dollar. The baht plunges more than 20 percent immediately and continues to slide. Currency speculators and investors begin pulling out of the whole region. At the end of the month, Thailand finally asks for help from the International Monetary Fund (IMF).
August 1997	Indonesia abandons its fixed exchange rate for the rupiah against the dollar.
August 1997	The IMF approves a $17 billion rescue package for Thailand.
August 1997	Asian stock markets plunge again. Hong Kong is affected for the first time and its stock market falls 17 percent in five days.
10 September 1997	Brazil's financial markets see a record drop.
9 October 1997	Indonesia asks for help from the IMF and a $23 billion rescue package is assembled.
22 October 1997	Hong Kong's stock market crashes 40 percent during the month. But Hong Kong's monetary authority is able to counter heavy selling of the Hong Kong dollar and maintain its exchange rate with the US dollar. On 24 October it recovers to rise 7 percent.
27 October 1997	Fears of an Asian recession hit Wall Street and the Dow Jones index makes its biggest drop in history – 554 points – triggering the first ever automatic trading cut-off.
November 1997	The Malaysian government announces the creation of a National Economic Action Council, chaired by the prime minister, to rescue the economy from crisis.
November 1997	Thailand's government resigns.
17 November 1997	Hokkaido Takushoku, Japan's tenth-largest commercial bank, ceases operations.
22 November 1997	South Korea asks for help from the IMF, indicating it needs $20 billion.
24 November 1997	Japan's fourth-largest securities house, Yamaichi, collapses with debts estimated at Y3,200 billion/$25 billion, becoming Japan's biggest-ever corporate failure. The failure of the 100-year-old company causes concern about the health of Japanese business.
25 November 1997	Leaders of the Asia-Pacific Economic Cooperation (APEC) issue a bulletin at the close of their annual trade meeting in Vancouver, Canada, in which they outline plans for reducing tariffs and liberalizing trade restrictions in an effort to stabilize the floundering Southeast Asian economies. They also agreed that the IMF would be in charge of the bailout.
1 January 1998	In an attempt to bolster its ailing economy Russia replaces its currency, the rouble. Each of the new coins, called the 'new rouble', is worth 1,000 old roubles and the move is expected to help curb runaway inflation.
6 April 1998	In the USA, where the effects of the 'Asian flu' remain minimal, the Dow Jones Industrial Index soars to above 9,000 points for the first time.
8 April 1998	The South Korean government sells $4 billion worth of government bonds to international investors. Analysts view the high demand for the bonds as increased confidence in the South Korean economy after the country's financial crisis in 1997.
May 1998	The Indonesian capital is engulfed by rioting; a besieged President Suharto steps down, ending his 32-year rule.
9 July 1998	The World Bank approves two loans worth around $700 million to help Thailand overcome the impact of Asia's economic crisis.
18 August 1998	The Russian government devalues the rouble in an effort to stabilize the country's foundering economy. President Yeltsin's economics advisor, Aleksander Livshits, resigns, and the Russian stock market is periodically suspended.
27 August 1998	The Russian government's decision to stop propping up the ailing rouble leads to uncertainty about the future of President Yeltsin and the entire reform process, causing global stock markets to plummet.
31 August 1998	World share markets teeter on the edge following a near-record 500-point plunge on Wall Street. Fears over the economic problems in Russia and Asia, and concerns about Latin America, lead to a selling spree by investors in New York.
August–September 1998	International investors turn timid in other emerging markets, such as Brazil and Russia, fearing the problems in Asia could spread. About $30 billion of funds flee Brazil amid a dramatic loss in confidence, prompting fears of a financial collapse for the world's eighth-largest economy.
10 September 1998	Brazilian markets, caving in under the international financial crisis and the government's failure over the past four years to make crucial changes, career towards record losses, with recent emergency measures proving futile to end the slide in investor confidence.
September–October 1998	Fears of international economic turmoil begin to grow in the USA and Europe.
30 September 1998	The US Federal Reserve cuts interest rates by a quarter of a percentage point in an attempt to keep the financial turmoil afflicting much of the world from derailing the US economy.
1 October 1998	In an unusually pessimistic report, the IMF says that it now expects the Russian economy to contract by 6 percent during 1998–99, and Japan to sink to its deepest recession since the end of World War II.
8 October 1998	The Bank of England lowers interest rates for the first time in two years in an effort to protect the British economy from the international financial crisis.
28 October 1998	The Brazilian government introduces a three-year, $80 billion package of spending cuts and tax increases in an effort to restore the country's flagging credibility in world markets and prepare the way for a rescue plan led by the IMF.
30 October 1998	The Group of Seven (G7) countries announce an action plan to boost and restore confidence in failing economies worldwide. The plan features a contingency fund of $90 million from the IMF for economies in danger of collapse.
4 November 1998	The Russian government says for the first time that it will not pay its foreign debt the following year, and will renegotiate the loans.
11 November 1998	The United Nations Conference on Trade and Development (UNCTAD) says that despite east Asia's economic crisis, the region saw inward investment rise the previous year by 8 percent. In the five nations most affected by the crisis – Indonesia, South Korea, Malaysia, the Philippines, and Thailand – investment flows remained stable.
13 November 1998	After months of negotiations, the IMF and more than 15 other nations announce a package of loans to

(*continued*)

The Global Economic Crisis 1997–99 *(continued)*

Brazil totalling $41.5 billion to stabilize the country's economy.

17 November 1998 US Federal Reserve chairman Alan Greenspan announces a cut in interest rates for the third time in seven weeks, responding to fears of a stock market crash and recession.

3 December 1998 The IMF approves an immediate $5.3 billion emergency payment for Brazil to rescue its economy.

10 December 1998 The Bank of England cuts interest rates for the third month in a row in a continuing response to the weakening world economy.

12 January 1999 The Brazilian real is devalued in an effort to prop up the country's ailing economy, causing the world stock market to plummet.

22 January 1999 The world's leading stock markets tumble amid worries over Brazil's economic problems and their possible impact on the rest of Latin America. Brazil's central bank intervenes in currency markets for the first time since the currency was allowed to float freely, in an attempt to stabilize the real.

18 May 1999 The Organization for Economic Cooperation and Development, in its latest assessment of the global economy, says confidence has returned to financial markets.

25 April 1999 According to the IMF, the financial crisis which rocked economies across the world for almost two years appears to be over. However, the social effects of economic downturn and rising unemployment will continue to be felt for some time.

3 June 1999 Top officials from across east and southeast Asia – gathered at a conference in Tokyo – say they believe Asia is recovering from its two-year economic crisis, but cooperation is needed to prevent a recurrence.

The Dow Jones World Index by Country and Industry

Indexes based on 30 June 1982 = 100 for USA; 31 December 1991 = 100 for world. Based on share prices denominated in US dollars. Stocks in countries that impose significant restrictions on foreign ownership are included in the world index in the same proportion that shares are available to foreign investors.
(As of 31 December.)

By Country

Country		1995	1996	1997
Americas	USA	581.43	700.56	922.35
	Canada	108.25	135.41	190.22
	Mexico	77.96	94.31	375.72
	Total	143.61	173.40	227.09
Asia/Pacific	Australia	127.90	148.78	156.23
	Hong Kong	223.67	299.50	223.42
	Indonesia	172.48	187.42	145.78
	Japan	114.08	95.63	73.63
	Malaysia	223.08	265.49	114.64
	New Zealand	176.17	203.35	155.58
	Singapore	195.91	199.84	127.74
	Thailand	196.76	126.66	59.94
	Total	119.80	108.93	77.93
Europe	Austria	101.29	110.00	126.68
	Belgium	142.56	158.64	210.25
	Denmark	112.42	137.26	213.02
	Finland	202.88	280.72	411.28
	France	120.03	142.38	182.44
	Germany	138.24	161.41	232.98
	Ireland, Republic of	152.83	196.04	274.91
	Italy	103.51	113.62	223.02
	Netherlands	167.30	207.58	316.06
	Norway	129.21	159.87	209.76
	Spain	114.31	149.44	286.63
	Sweden	163.14	213.88	341.28
	Switzerland	232.62	236.03	352.50
	UK	124.49	152.02	198.16
	Total	136.54	162.41	191.64
	TOTAL	133.46	147.57	166.63

By Industry

Industry	1995	1996	1997
Basic materials	130.91	136.62	119.65
Conglomerate	146.57	171.32	169.13
Consumer, cyclical	135.13	148.64	160.15
Consumer, noncyclical	130.19	152.04	188.21
Energy	132.32	163.27	188.61
Financial services	134.62	142.64	168.20
Industrial	118.38	122.31	117.79
Technology	168.07	197.94	242.59
Utilities	118.44	123.90	152.77

Source: Dow Jones and Co, Inc, New York 1998,

Stock Markets: Market Capitalization and Value of Shares Traded by Country

Market capitalization is defined as the total amount of the various securities (bonds, debentures, and stock) issued by corporations. (N/A = not available. In millions of dollars.)

Country	Market capitalization[1]				Value of shares traded[2]		
	1990	1995	1996	1997	1990	1995	1996
Argentina	3,268	37,783	44,679	59,252	852	4,594	4,382
Australia	107,611	245,218	311,988	696,656	39,333	97,884	145,482
Austria	11,476	32,513	33,953	35,724	18,609	25,759	20,528
Belgium	65,449	104,960	119,831	136,965	6,425	15,249	26,120
Brazil	16,354	147,636	216,990	255,478	5,598	79,186	112,108
Canada	241,920	366,344	486,268	567,635	71,278	183,686	265,360
Chile	13,645	73,860	65,940	72,046	783	11,072	8,460
China	N/A	42,055	113,755	206,366	N/A	49,774	256,008
Colombia	1,416	17,893	17,137	19,529	71	1,254	1,360
Czech Republic	N/A	15,664	18,077	12,786	N/A	3,630	8,431
Denmark	39,063	56,223	71,688	93,766	11,105	25,942	34,667
Finland	22,721	44,138	63,078	73,322	3,933	19,006	22,422
France	314,384	522,053	591,123	674,368	116,893	364,550	277,100
Germany	355,073	577,365	670,997	825,233	501,805	573,549	768,745
Greece	15,228	17,060	24,178	34,164	3,924	6,091	8,283
Hong Kong	83,397	303,705	449,381	413,323	34,633	106,888	166,419
India	38,567	127,199	122,605	128,466	21,918	13,738	109,448
Indonesia	8,081	66,585	91,016	29,105	3,992	14,403	32,142
Italy	148,766	209,522	258,160	344,665	42,566	86,904	102,351
Japan	2,917,679	3,667,292	3,088,850	2,216,699	1,602,388	1,231,552	1,251,998
Korea, South	110,594	181,955	138,817	41,881	75,949	185,197	177,266
Luxembourg	10,456	30,443	32,692	33,892	87	205	534
Malaysia	48,611	222,729	307,179	93,608	10,871	76,822	173,568
Mexico	32,725	90,694	106,540	156,595	12,212	34,377	43,040
Netherlands	119,825	356,481	378,721	468,736	40,199	248,606	339,500
New Zealand	8,835	31,950	38,288	90,483	1,933	8,407	9,871
Norway	26,130	44,587	57,423	66,503	13,996	24,420	35,882
Pakistan	2,850	9,286	10,639	10,966	231	3,210	6,054
Peru	812	11,795	12,291	17,586	99	3,935	3,805
Philippines	5,927	58,859	80,649	31,361	1,216	14,727	25,519
Portugal	9,201	18,362	24,660	38,954	1,687	4,233	7,147
South Africa	137,540	280,526	241,571	232,069	8,158	17,048	27,202
Spain	111,404	197,788	242,779	290,383	40,967	59,791	249,128
Sweden	92,102	178,049	247,217	272,730	15,718	93,197	136,898
Switzerland	160,044	433,621	402,104	575,338	N/A	310,928	392,783
Taiwan	100,710	187,206	273,608	287,813	715,005	383,099	470,193
Thailand	23,896	141,507	99,828	23,538	22,894	57,000	44,365
Turkey	19,065	20,772	30,020	61,090	5,841	51,392	36,831
UK	848,866	1,407,737	1,740,246	1,996,225	278,740	510,131	578,471
USA	3,059,434	6,857,622	8,484,433	11,308,779	1,815,476	5,108,591	7,121,487
Venezuela	8,361	3,655	10,055	14,581	2,232	510	1,275

[1] Year-end total market values of listed domestic companies.
[2] Annual turnover of listed company shares.

Source: *Emerging Stock Markets Factbook,* International Finance Corporation

World Trade and Aid

Net Flow of Financial Resources to Developing Countries of the World

Net flow covers loans, grants, and grant-like flows minus amortization on loans. Military flows are excluded. Developing countries cover countries designated by the Development Assistance Committee (DAC) as developing. Official development assistance covers all flows to developing countries and multilateral institutions provided by official agencies, including state and local governments, or by their executive agencies, which are administered with the promotion of economic development and welfare of developing countries as their main objective and whose financial terms are intended to be concessional in character with a grant element of at least 25 percent. Other official flows cover export credits and portfolio investment from the official sector.

(N/A = not available. In billions of dollars.)

Origin and type of resource	1980	1990	1995
DAC Countries[1]			
Official development assistance	27.3	53.0	58.9
Other official flows	5.3	8.6	9.8
Private flows at market terms	40.4	9.8	92.0
Private voluntary agencies	2.4	5.1	6.0
Total	75.4	76.4	166.7
Total Net Flow to Developing Countries, by DAC Country[1]			
Australia	0.9	1.5	2.5
Austria	0.3	0.6	0.9
Belgium	2.9	0.1	−0.2
Canada	3.2	3.5	4.7
Denmark	0.8	1.1	1.8
Finland	0.2	1.0	0.6
France	11.6	5.7	12.8
Germany[2]	10.6	13.6	21.2
Ireland, Republic of	[3]	0.2	0.2
Italy	4.0	3.2	2.8
Japan	6.8	17.2	42.3
Luxembourg	N/A	N/A	0.1
Netherlands	2.4	4.0	6.8
New Zealand	0.1	0.1	0.2
Norway	0.9	1.2	1.5
Portugal	N/A	0.3	0.3
Spain	N/A	1.0	1.6
Sweden	1.9	2.8	2.2
Switzerland	2.7	3.4	0.9
UK	12.2	6.5	15.5
USA	13.9	11.1	47.8
Total	75.4	76.4	166.7

[1] Includes flows to OPEC countries: Algeria, Ecuador, Gabon, Iran, Iraq, Kuwait, Libya, Nigeria, Qatar, Saudi Arabia, United Arab Emirates, and Venezuela. Country totals may not add to DAC total because debt forgiveness of non-official development assistance claims is not included in DAC totals.

[2] Former West Germany.

[3] Less than $50 million.

Source: *Statistical Abstract of the United States 1998*

Free Trade: from GATT to WTO

30 October 1947 Twenty-three countries sign the General Agreement on Tariffs and Trade (GATT). The first round of trade negotiations result in 45,000 tariff concessions affecting one-fifth of total world trade.

1 January 1949 GATT enters into force.

26 May 1956 Another trade round is completed, producing some $2.5 billion worth of tariff reductions.

1960–62 The fifth GATT round yields tariff concessions worth $4.9 billion of world trade and involves negotiations related to the creation of the European Economic Community (EEC).

1964–67 The Kennedy Round achieves tariff cuts worth $40 billion of world trade.

1973–79 The seventh GATT round, launched in Tokyo, Japan, reaches agreement to start reducing not only tariffs but trade barriers as well; tariff reductions worth more than $300 billion are achieved.

1986–94 GATT trade ministers launch the Uruguay Round, embarking on the most ambitious and far-reaching trade round so far.

1994 Ministers meet for the last time under GATT auspices at Marrakesh, Morocco, to establish the World Trade Organization (WTO) and sign other agreements.

1 January 1995 The World Trade Organization comes into force. The main differences between WTO and GATT are that GATT was a provisional legal agreement, whereas WTO is an organization with permanent agreements. GATT had only contracting parties and dealt exclusively with trade in goods; WTO has members and covers services and intellectual property as well.

1999 At a time when global economic growth is slowing and the 134-member WTO needs to focus on defending free trade, it faces splits in its membership, trade wars between the USA and other members, and a weakened credibility due to lack of compliance (notably by the EU) to its rulings.

November 1999 The crucial Seattle summit is due to begin, intended to be the launchpad for the first global trade negotiations since the Uruguay Round ended in 1994. Dubbed the millennium round, the talks are expected to last three years.

Leading Exporters and Importers of Commercial Services

(N/A = not available.)

1997

Exporters

Rank	Country	Value ($ billions)	Share (%)	Annual change (%)
1	USA	229.9	17.5	7
2	UK	85.5	6.5	12
3	France	80.3	6.1	–3
4	Germany	75.4	5.7	–4
5	Italy	71.7	5.5	4
6	Japan	68.1	5.2	3
7	Netherlands	48.5	3.7	–1
8	Spain	43.6	3.3	–1
9	Hong Kong	37.3	2.8	0
10	Belgium/Luxembourg	34.0	2.6	–2
11	Singapore	30.4	2.3	2
12	Canada	29.3	2.2	2
13	Austria	28.5	2.2	N/A
14	Switzerland	25.6	2.0	–2
15	Korea, South	25.4	1.9	12
16	China	24.5	1.9	19
17	Turkey	19.2	1.5	49
18	Australia	18.2	1.4	1
19	Sweden	17.6	1.3	5
20	Taipei, Chinese	17.0	1.3	5
21	Denmark	16.5	1.3	N/A
22	Thailand	15.8	1.2	–5
23	Philippines	15.1	1.2	17
24	Malaysia	14.5	1.1	4
25	Norway	14.3	1.1	2
26	Russia	13.5	1.0	4
27	Mexico	11.2	0.9	5
28	Poland	10.1	0.8	N/A
29	Egypt	9.7	0.7	6
30	Greece	9.4	0.7	N/A
31	India	8.8	0.7	N/A
32	Israel	8.3	0.6	5
33	Brazil	7.9	0.6	37
34	Portugal	7.5	0.6	–8
35	Czech Republic	7.0	0.5	–13
36	Finland	6.8	0.5	–6
37	Indonesia	6.8	0.5	5
38	Ireland, Republic of	6.0	0.5	8
39	Ukraine	4.9	0.4	3
40	South Africa	4.9	0.4	11
	Total	1,204.2	91.8	3
WORLD TOTAL		1,310.0	100.0	3

Importers

Rank	Country	Value ($ billions)	Share (%)	Annual change (%)
1	USA	150.1	11.6	7
2	Japan	122.1	9.4	–5
3	Germany	120.1	9.3	–5
4	Italy	70.1	5.4	5
5	UK	68.6	5.3	9
6	France	62.1	4.8	–5
7	Netherlands	43.8	3.4	–2
8	Canada	35.9	2.8	1
9	Belgium/Luxembourg	32.1	2.5	–3
10	China	30.1	2.3	34
11	Korea, South	29.0	2.2	0
12	Austria	27.4	2.1	–10
13	Spain	24.3	1.9	1
14	Taipei, Chinese	24.1	1.9	2
15	Hong Kong	22.7	1.8	6
16	Sweden	19.5	1.5	4
17	Singapore	19.4	1.5	1
18	Brazil	19.0	1.5	36
19	Russia	18.7	1.4	0
20	Australia	18.2	1.4	0
21	Thailand	17.2	1.3	–11
22	Malaysia	16.8	1.3	0
23	Indonesia	16.1	1.2	9
24	Ireland, Republic of	15.0	1.2	12
25	Denmark	14.7	1.1	N/A
26	Norway	14.5	1.1	8
27	Switzerland	14.1	1.1	–8
28	Philippines	14.1	1.1	50
29	Saudi Arabia	13.9	1.1	11
30	Mexico	11.5	0.9	16
31	India	11.0	0.9	N/A
32	Israel	10.9	0.8	5
33	Turkey	8.1	0.6	34
34	Finland	8.1	0.6	–6
35	Egypt	7.2	0.6	52
36	Poland	6.5	0.5	N/A
37	Portugal	6.1	0.5	–6
38	South Africa	6.0	0.5	4
39	Argentina	6.0	0.5	12
40	Czech Republic	5.3	0.4	–14
	Total	1,175.2	90.7	2
WORLD TOTAL		1,295.0	100.0	2

Source: World Trade Organization 1998

Leading Exporters and Importers of Merchandise

1997

Exporters

Rank	Country	Value ($ billions)	Share (%)	Annual change (%)
1	USA	688.7	12.6	10
2	Germany	511.7	9.4	−2
3	Japan	421.0	7.7	2
4	France	289.5	5.3	0
5	UK	281.6	5.2	8
6	Italy	238.2	4.4	−5
7	Canada	214.4	3.9	6
8	Netherlands	193.8	3.5	−5
9	Hong Kong	188.2	3.4	4
10	China	182.7	3.3	21
11	Belgium/Luxembourg	168.2	3.1	−1
12	Korea, South	136.2	2.5	5
13	Singapore	125.0	2.3	0
14	Taipei, Chinese	121.9	2.2	5
15	Mexico	110.4	2.0	15
16	Spain	104.3	1.9	2
17	Sweden	82.7	1.5	−3
18	Malaysia	78.4	1.4	1
19	Switzerland	76.2	1.4	−6
20	Russia[1]	66.3	1.2	−4
21	Australia	62.9	1.2	4
22	Austria	58.6	1.1	1
23	Thailand	57.4	1.1	3
24	Indonesia	53.5	1.0	7
25	Ireland, Republic of	53.1	1.0	9
26	Brazil	53.0	1.0	11
27	Saudi Arabia[2]	52.8	1.0	−7
28	Denmark	48.9	0.9	−4
29	Norway	47.7	0.9	−2
30	Finland	40.8	0.7	1
31	India	33.9	0.6	3
32	South Africa	30.3	0.6	6
33	Turkey	26.2	0.5	14
34	Poland	25.8	0.5	5
35	Argentina	25.5	0.5	7
36	Philippines	25.3	0.5	24
37	United Arab Emirates[2]	25.0	0.5	−4
38	Portugal	23.2	0.4	−6
39	Venezuela	23.1	0.4	0
40	Czech Republic	22.8	0.4	4
41	Israel	22.5	0.4	9
42	Hungary	19.1	0.3	22
43	Iran[2]	17.7	0.3	−6
44	Chile	16.9	0.3	10
45	Kuwait	14.8	0.3	0
46	Nigeria[2]	14.5	0.3	1
47	New Zealand	14.1	0.3	−3
48	Algeria[2]	12.7	0.2	10
49	Colombia	11.5	0.2	9
50	Greece	10.8	0.2	−9
	Total[3]	5,223.7	95.6	
WORLD TOTAL[3]		5,460.0	100.0	3

Importers

Rank	Country	Value ($ billions)	Share (%)	Annual change (%)
1	USA	899.0	16.0	9
2	Germany	411.5	7.8	−4
3	Japan	338.8	6.0	−3
4	UK	308.2	5.5	7
5	France	268.4	4.8	−5
6	Hong Kong	213.3	3.8	6
7	Italy	208.1	3.7	0
8	Canada	200.9	3.6	15
9	Netherlands	177.2	3.1	−4
10	Belgium/Luxembourg	155.8	2.8	−3
11	Korea, South	144.6	2.6	−4
12	China	142.4	2.5	3
13	Singapore	132.4	2.4	1
14	Spain	122.7	2.2	1
15	Mexico	113.3	2.0	24
16	Taipei, Chinese	113.2	2.0	12
17	Malaysia	79.0	1.4	1
18	Switzerland	76.0	1.3	−4
19	Australia	65.9	1.2	1
20	Sweden	65.4	1.2	−2
21	Brazil	65.0	1.2	14
22	Austria	64.8	1.2	−4
23	Thailand	63.6	1.1	−13
24	Russia[1]	48.8	0.9	13
25	Turkey	48.6	0.9	13
26	Denmark	44.6	0.8	−1
27	Poland	42.3	0.8	14
28	Indonesia	42.0	0.7	−2
29	India	40.4	0.7	8
30	Ireland, Republic of	39.2	0.7	9
31	Philippines	38.0	0.7	11
32	Norway	35.5	0.6	0
33	Portugal	33.6	0.6	−5
34	South Africa	32.9	0.6	9
35	Israel	30.8	0.5	−3
36	Finland	30.7	0.5	0
37	Argentina	30.3	0.5	28
38	United Arab Emirates[2]	27.8	0.5	7
39	Saudi Arabia	27.3	0.5	−2
40	Czech Republic	27.2	0.5	−2
41	Greece	25.2	0.4	−11
42	Hungary	21.2	0.4	17
43	Chile	19.9	0.4	11
44	Colombia	15.4	0.3	12
45	New Zealand	14.5	0.3	−1
46	Iran[2]	13.8	0.2	7
47	Egypt	13.2	0.2	1
48	Pakistan	11.6	0.2	−4
49	Venezuela[2]	11.5	0.2	16
50	Vietnam[2]	11.3	0.2	1
	Total[3]	5,237.0	93.0	
WORLD TOTAL[3]		56,300	100.0	3

[1] Excludes trade with the Baltic States and the CIS. Including trade with these states would lift Russian exports and imports to $87 billion and $68 billion respectively.
[2] Estimates.
[3] Includes significant re-exports or imports for re-export.

Source: World Trade Organization 1998

Merchandise Trade Balance for Selected Countries

(N/A = not available. In millions of dollars.)

Country	1995	1996	1997
Industrial Countries			
Australia	-4,223	-635	1,807
Austria	-7,203	-7,786	-4,043
Belgium/Luxembourg	9,463	8,516	8,343
Canada	25,429	30,720	17,556
Denmark	6,820	7,532	N/A
Finland	12,346	11,082	11,590
France	10,998	14,936	28,069
Germany	65,110	71,215	74,701
Greece	-14,425	-15,505	N/A
Iceland	206	N/A	N/A
Ireland, Republic of	13,5571	15,754	18,646
Italy	44,759	60,862	46,785
Japan	131,787	83,561	101,600
Netherlands	22,102	21,777	17,752
New Zealand	895	492	387
Norway	8,571	12,923	11,062
Portugal	-8,910	-9,340	-9,551
Spain	-18,244	-16,027	-13,347
Sweden	15,978	18,636	17,921
Switzerland	3,223	1,836	N/A
UK	18,310	19,611	20,544
USA	-171,690	-189,253	-197,001
Developing Countries			
Africa			
Botswana	581	791	N/A
Burundi	-63	-60	-11
Congo, Republic of the	516	194	941
Côte d'Ivoire	1,345	1,860	N/A
Ethiopia	-714	-797	N/A
Ghana	-257	-366	N/A
Mauritius	-241	-328	-458
Morocco	-2,397	-2,111	N/A
Nigeria	2,125	8,482	N/A
Seychelles	-161	-185	-188
South Africa	1,715	2,330	1,992
Tanzania	-657	-449	-449
Tunisia	-1,989	-1,804	N/A
Uganda	-367	-348	-467
Africa total	1,200	13,227	13,111
Asia			
Bangladesh	-2,324	-2,251	N/A
Cambodia	-332	-428	-328
China	18,050	19,535	46,222
India	-6,719	-9,462	N/A
Indonesia	6,533	5,948	10,090
Korea	-4,444	-14,965	-3,179
Nepal	-961	-1,106	-1,308
Pakistan	-2,878	N/A	N/A
Philippines	-8,944	-11,342	-11,127
Singapore	977	2,224	1,145
Sri Lanka	-985	-800	-628
Thailand	-7,969	-9,488	-1,564
Asia total	-17,989	-24,796	20,540
Europe			
Albania	-475	-678	-535
Bulgaria	121	188	395
Croatia	-2,126	-2,497	-5,225
Czech Republic	-3,685	-5,877	-4,639
Hungary	-2,433	-2,652	N/A
Lithuania	-698	-896	-1,147
Poland	-1,646	-7,287	N/A
Russia	20,807	23,078	17,326
Slovak Republic	-229	-2,283	-1,481
Slovenia	-954	-882	-772
Turkey	-13,212	-10,582	-15,466
Europe total	-14,317	-25,823	-33,436
Middle East			
Egypt	-7,597	-8,390	N/A
Iran	5,586	7,402	N/A
Israel	-7,688	-7,969	N/A
Jordan	-1,518	-2,001	N/A
Kuwait	5,582	6,964	6,296
Saudi Arabia	24,390	35,370	33,530
Syrian Arab Republic	-143	-338	454
Middle East total	24,607	39,396	36,566
Western Hemisphere			
Argentina	2,238	1,622	-3,195
Bahamas	-931	-1,014	-1,038
Bolivia	-182	-189	N/A
Brazil	-3,157	N/A	N/A
Chile	1,368	-1,094	-1,296
Dominican Republic	-1,492	-1,765	N/A
Ecuador	354	1,220	598
El Salvador	-1,523	-1,197	-1,107
Guatemala	-875	-643	N/A
Haiti	-429	-416	N/A
Jamaica	-825	-994	-1,110
Mexico	7,089	6,531	N/A
Nicaragua	-335	-360	-742
Panama	-575	-630	N/A
Peru	-2,170	-2,000	N/A
Uruguay	-563	-687	-723
Venezuela	7,013	13,756	11,592
Western hemisphere total	-1,407	552	-21,298
Industrial countries total	128,239	101,711	103,201
Developing countries total	-7,907	2,557	15,483
ALL COUNTRIES TOTAL	120,331	104,267	118,684

Source: *International Financial Statistics Yearbook 1998,* © International Monetary Fund

Recent World Trade Wars: Chronology

1989 The European Union (EU) bans hormone-treated beef; the USA promises to export only 'hormone-free' beef to Europe.

1993 The EU introduces a new banana import policy which protects former colonies of Britain and France by waiving trade tariffs on their banana trade with Europe and giving them guaranteed quotas. The Latin American growers face tariffs on their exports to the EU and receive no quota guarantees.

26 May 1993 A GATT arbitration rules that EU import restrictions on bananas unfairly limit Latin American imports.

25 March 1996 The EU bans the export of British beef abroad following anxiety over the potential for transmission of the BSE infection to humans as CJD (Creutzfeldt-Jakob disease).

21 May 1996 Britain begins a policy of non-cooperation with its European partners in response to the EU ban on British beef exports, disrupting the running of the EU and the Intergovermental Conference to plan the future development of Europe.

21 June 1996 At an EU summit in Florence, Italy, a deal is made for the lifting of the export ban on British beef (involving the slaughter of 147,000 at-risk cattle); in return, Britain ends its obstruction of EU business.

16 March 1998 EU agriculture ministers approve plans to export beef from Northern Ireland. This will be the first export of beef from the UK since the ban was imposed in March 1996.

23 November 1998 The EU votes to end the ban of the exports of British beef; the ban formally comes to an end on 1 August 1999.

December 1998 The Clinton administration warns Europe that it is preparing to retaliate in the 'banana war', publishing a list of goods that would be doubled in price for a total of $520 million – the amount US banana companies (including Dole Food Company and Chiquita Brands) say they've lost because of EU restrictions.

January 1999 Official figures show that Japan's trade surplus surged by 40 percent in 1998 to a new record, sparking fears of a new trade war with the USA. The USA says Japan must cut back its steel exports or face trade sanctions for 'dumping' – selling steel for less than it costs to produce it. Thanks to the devaluation of Asian currencies, Japanese steel exports to the USA surged by 400 percent in 1998.

1 January 1999 The EU introduces reforms to its banana import rules after the World Trade Organization (WTO) rules that its import rules broke international trading rules designed to offer a level playing field to exporters. However, the USA says the EU's reforms are token, do not go far enough, and that Latin American producers are still missing out because the rules are still being flouted.

3 March 1999 The USA announces that it is applying to the WTO to enforce trade sanctions which would amount to 100 percent taxes on $520 million in EU goods. The argument centres on the preferential treatment the EU gives to banana producers from former colonies at the expense of Latin American growers and the US backers.

At the same time, the USA heats up another politically contentious trade dispute with Europe – the 'hush kit' war – threatening to ban Concorde from landing in the USA in retaliation for a European ruling that would ban many older US aeroplanes from landing in Europe. The European Parliament had recently passed legislation banning the takeoff or landing of older aeroplanes even if their engines had been retrofitted with devices called 'hush kits', because they still make more noise than newer planes. US officials say the EU's restriction is designed to promote the sale of new engines and aircraft made by European manufacturers.

6 April 1999 The USA claims victory in the banana dispute with the EU, after a WTO arbitration panel agrees with the USA that new EU banana import rules violate international trade. But the panel significantly lowers the extent of sanctions sought by the USA in the case. It is the first time the WTO approves a set of sanctions imposed by one member on another.

9 April 1999 The USA issues a final target list that will impose 100 percent punitive tariffs on $191 million of European imports to retaliate in the trade war over bananas. The final list excludes a number of products that had been on the original target list, including Italian pecorino cheese, Scottish cashmere sweaters, and British sweet biscuits.

24 April 1999 The USA and Europe appear to be squaring up for another trade war, this time over genetically-modified (GM) foods. In Europe, where there is widespread public concern over the safety of GM foods, commercially grown GM crops are banned. At WTO talks in Seattle, the US Agriculture Under-secretary warns that the USA will take action if Europe continues to drag its feet in approving new GM crops and food.

28 April 1999 The EU announces a total ban on US beef imports on health grounds. The ban is to come into force on 15 June and includes beef that was being sold as 'hormone-free'. The widening of the trade embargo, ordered by the EU's standing veterinary committee, followed scientific tests that showed that 12 percent of supposedly hormone-free US beef contained hormone residues.

30 April 1999 The USA goes on the trade warpath, announcing that it is filing seven complaints with the WTO – against India, Canada, Argentina, and two each against the EU and South Korea. The seven complaints, which concern manufacturing, agriculture, intellectual property rights, and government procurement, are outlined in the annual report by the US trade representative to Congress.

13 May 1999 Europe braces itself for an extension of its trade war with the USA after the European Commission's decision to defy a WTO ruling that it must lift its decade-old ban on hormone-treated beef.

14 May 1999 The US government says it will impose punitive tariffs of $202 million on European goods, as a retaliatory move in the growing trade war over hormone-treated beef. The USA says that Europe must comply with the WTO ruling and accept imports of US beef. The EU will, under WTO rules, seek arbitration on the amount of sanctions the USA can impose.

3 June 1999 The WTO approves the US request to impose sanctions on the EU in response to its ban on hormone-treated beef. But the WTO also agrees to a European request for a neutral arbitration panel to study the amount due to the USA and Canada. The implementation of sanctions is delayed until the panel reports back.

1 August 1999 The European Union's ban on British beef formally comes to an end.

World Energy and Minerals

Energy Consumption and Production Worldwide

(– = not applicable. N/A = not available. † = less than 5 trillion British thermal units (Btu), 500 barrels per day, or 500,000 short tons.)

Country	Primary energy consumed				Primary energy produced					
	Total (quadrillion Btu[1])		Per capita (million Btu)		Dry natural gas (quadrillion Btu)		Crude pretroleum (1,000 barrels per day)		Coal (million short tons)	
	1990	1996	1990	1996	1990	1996	1990	1996	1990	1996
Algeria	1.1	1.4	45	47	1.90	2.56	1,175	1,242	†	†
Argentina	1.8	2.6	57	74	0.59	1.11	483	756	†	†
Australia	3.7	4.1	217	223	0.76	1.12	575	570	226	274
Austria	1.2	1.3	154	158	0.05	0.06	22	21	3	1
Bahrain	0.3	0.3	532	517	0.21	0.26	42	35	N/A	N/A
Bangladesh	0.3	0.4	2	3	0.15	0.25	1	1	N/A	N/A
Belarus	–	1.0	–	100	–	0.01	–	36	–	N/A
Belgium	2.2	2.5	216	247	†	†	N/A	N/A	3	1
Brazil	5.7	7.2	39	46	0.11	0.24	631	795	5	5
Bulgaria	1.3	1.0	141	115	0	†	4	1	35	32
Canada	10.9	12.2	392	407	3.90	5.97	1,553	1,837	75	84
Chile	0.6	0.8	43	55	0.07	0.06	20	9	2	1
China	27.0	37.0	23	30	0.56	0.78	2,774	3,131	1,190	1,550
Colombia	1.0	1.3	30	36	0.14	0.17	440	623	23	33
Congo, Democratic Republic of	N/A	N/A	3	2	N/A	N/A	29	30	†	†
Cuba	0.5	0.4	46	37	†	†	14	30	N/A	N/A
Czech Republic	–	2.3	–	227	–	0.01	–	4	–	77
Denmark	0.8	0.9	156	173	0.12	0.25	121	208	N/A	N/A
Ecuador	N/A	N/A	25	29	0.01	0.01	285	396	N/A	N/A
Egypt	1.4	1.6	27	27	0.30	0.50	873	922	N/A	N/A
Finland	1.1	1.1	229	208	N/A	N/A	N/A	N/A	N/A	N/A
France	8.8	9.9	156	169	0.11	0.10	61	43	15	10
Germany	–	14.4	–	176	–	0.70	–	60	–	264
Greece	1.1	1.2	103	112	0.01	†	15	8	57	66
Hong Kong	0.5	0.6	85	97	N/A	N/A	N/A	N/A	N/A	N/A
Hungary	1.3	1.1	120	112	0.15	0.16	40	32	19	17
India	7.7	11.6	9	12	0.41	0.80	660	651	233	311
Indonesia	2.2	3.5	12	18	1.53	2.65	1,462	1,547	12	53
Iran	3.1	4.0	57	66	0.88	1.45	3,088	3,686	1	1
Iraq	0.9	1.2	51	58	0.15	0.12	2,040	579	N/A	N/A
Ireland, Republic of	0.4	0.5	105	127	0.08	0.10	N/A	N/A	†	†
Israel	0.5	0.6	96	112	†	†	†	†	N/A	N/A
Italy	7.0	7.6	122	131	0.63	0.72	87	101	1	†
Japan	18.1	21.4	147	170	0.08	0.09	11	12	11	7
Korea, North	2.1	2.2	103	96	N/A	N/A	N/A	N/A	71	81
Korea, South	3.7	7.2	86	157	N/A	N/A	N/A	N/A	19	5
Kuwait	0.5	0.5	208	319	0.19	0.22	1,175	2,062	N/A	N/A
Libya	0.5	0.6	123	102	0.23	0.24	1,375	1,401	N/A	N/A
Malaysia	1.0	1.7	55	81	0.68	1.36	619	695	†	†
Mexico	4.9	5.6	57	58	0.96	1.08	2,553	2,855	7	10

(continued)

Energy Consumption and Production Worldwide (*continued*)

Country	Primary energy consumed				Primary energy produced					
	Total (quadrillion Btu[1])		Per capita (million Btu)		Dry natural gas (quadrillion Btu)		Crude pretroleum (1,000 barrels per day)		Coal (million short tons)	
	1990	1996	1990	1996	1990	1996	1990	1996	1990	1996
Morocco	0.3	0.4	13	14	†	†	†	†	1	1
Myanmar	N/A	N/A	2	2	0.04	0.06	13	15	†	†
Netherlands	3.4	3.8	225	242	2.41	3.01	70	56	N/A	N/A
New Zealand	0.7	0.9	218	247	0.17	0.20	40	37	3	4
Nigeria	0.7	0.9	6	7	0.14	0.19	1,810	2,188	†	†
Norway	1.6	1.7	373	397	1.06	1.61	1,704	3,104	†	†
Pakistan	1.2	1.7	10	13	0.45	0.65	62	55	3	4
Peru	N/A	N/A	18	21	0.02	0.03	129	120	†	†
Philippines	0.7	1.0	12	14	0	†	5	2	1	2
Poland	3.9	3.8	103	98	0.12	0.13	2	5	237	219
Portugal	0.7	0.9	75	87	N/A	N/A	N/A	N/A	†	†
Romania	2.9	2.1	124	93	1.07	0.67	163	135	42	45
Russia	–	26.0	–	176	–	19.35	–	5,850	–	302
Saudi Arabia	3.2	4.0	212	214	1.13	1.53	6,410	8,218	N/A	N/A
Serbia	–	0.5	–	51	–	0.02	–	22	–	43
South Africa	3.4	4.3	91	100	0	0.07	N/A	N/A	193	227
Spain	3.9	4.5	101	115	0.06	0.02	16	15	40	33
Sweden	2.2	2.3	252	255	N/A	N/A	†	†	†	†
Switzerland	1.2	1.2	174	172	†	0	N/A	N/A	N/A	N/A
Syria	0.6	0.7	50	45	0.11	0.10	388	604	N/A	N/A
Taiwan	2.0	3.1	100	145	0.08	0.04	3	1	1	†
Tajikistan	N/A	N/A	–	30	–	†	–	2	–	†
Thailand	1.3	2.3	22	39	0.21	0.43	44	61	14	21
Trinidad and Tobago	N/A	N/A	185	284	0.18	0.32	150	130	N/A	N/A
Tunisia	N/A	N/A	25	27	0.01	0.03	93	87	N/A	N/A
Turkey	2.0	2.7	35	43	0.01	0.01	73	67	52	63
UK	9.5	10.1	165	171	1.92	3.34	1,820	2,568	106	56
Ukraine	–	6.3	–	122	–	0.59	–	66	–	77
United Arab Emirates	1.2	1.8	640	793	0.82	1.34	2,117	2,278	N/A	N/A
USA	84.2	93.4	337	352	18.36	19.54	7,355	6,465	1,029	1,064
Venezuela	2.1	2.6	108	117	0.91	1.06	2,137	3,053	2	4
Vietnam	0.3	0.5	4	6	†	0.03	50	175	5	9
World total	344.0	375.1	65	65	72.53	81.90	60,566	64,054	5,356	5,185

Source: *Statistical Abstract of the United States 1998*

Crude Oil Production Worldwide

Data are for production of crude oil and natural gas liquids (NGL). (In thousands of metric tons.)

Country/region	1993	1994	1995	1996	1997
OECD					
North America					
Canada	88,375	92,371	96,270	99,687	103,074
Mexico	158,176	158,104	153,555	160,776	168,376
USA	389,039	379,526	375,554	373,501	370,074
Total	635,590	630,001	625,379	633,964	641,524
Europe					
Austria	1,195	1,147	1,079	989	995
Czech Republic	111	128	146	152	163
Denmark	8,265	9,118	9,170	10,121	11,360
France	3,205	3,229	2,913	2,513	2,139
Germany	3,064	2,938	2,926	2,874	2,799
Greece	562	531	457	514	465
Hungary	2,041	1,955	2,302	2,119	2,172
Italy	4,640	4,895	5,236	5,452	6,006
Netherlands	3,248	4,323	3,479	3,103	2,925
Norway	114,471	128,514	138,500	156,804	155,549
Poland	235	284	292	317	250
Spain	1,102	948	783	512	371
Turkey	3,892	3,696	3,516	3,500	3,449
UK	100,089	126,939	130,324	129,838	128,212
Total	246,120	288,650	301,127	318,808	316,855
Pacific					
Australia	26,654	25,067	26,870	26,366	27,025
Japan	744	710	704	683	684
New Zealand	2,026	1,955	1,668	2,177	2,840
Total	29,424	27,732	29,242	29,226	30,549
OECD TOTAL	911,134	946,383	955,748	981,998	988,928
Non-OECD					
Latin America					
Argentina	31,999	35,573	38,616	41,951	44,515
Bolivia	1,312	1,510	1,693	1,736	1,985
Brazil	33,484	34,786	35,727	40,378	43,148
Chile	866	860	732	575	670
Colombia	23,764	23,731	30,433	32,641	33,811
Cuba	1,106	1,426	1,643	1,649	1,758
Ecuador	18,104	19,974	20,160	20,096	19,647
Guatemala	337	366	468	730	1,323
Peru	6,295	6,345	6,072	6,000	5,862
Trinidad and Tobago	6,720	7,098	7,136	7,073	7,206
Venezuela	113,268	128,460	150,775	156,978	168,989
Other	334	334	338	338	349
Total	237,589	260,463	293,793	310,145	329,263
Europe					
Albania	568	535	522	489	386
Bulgaria	43	36	43	32	50
Romania	6,931	6,974	6,951	6,852	6,730
Slovak Republic	69	70	76	72	54
Former Yugoslavia	3,289	2,902	2,829	2,563	2,616
Total	10,900	10,517	10,421	10,008	9,836
Former USSR					
Azerbaijan	10,295	9,563	9,162	9,100	9,022
Belarus	2,005	2,000	1,932	1,860	1,795
Georgia	100	74	47	128	299
Kazakhstan	23,000	20,279	20,450	22,975	26,436
Kyrgyzstan	88	88	89	100	50
Lithuania	73	93	128	155	155
Russia	351,496	315,767	305,107	301,214	303,424
Tajikistan	51	33	25	21	20
Turkmenistan	5,154	3,360	3,500	4,100	4,458
Ukraine	4,248	4,200	4,058	4,102	3,371
Uzbekistan	3,944	5,500	7,456	7,496	6,884
Total	400,454	360,957	351,954	351,251	355,914
Africa					
Algeria	56,110	55,369	55,719	58,722	60,909
Angola/Cabinda	24,189	24,237	25,437	34,689	35,632
Benin	302	310	228	193	150
Cameroon	6,421	6,267	5,495	5,325	5,976
Congo, Democratic Republic of	1,280	1,345	1,371	1,371	1,279
Congo, Republic of the	9,408	9,562	9,275	10,370	12,253
Egypt	47,527	46,497	46,734	45,174	43,733
Gabon	15,583	17,214	18,246	18,549	18,577
Ghana	12	304	304	355	250
Côte d'Ivoire	N/A	N/A	307	788	749
Libya	66,976	67,780	70,376	70,105	71,818
Morocco	10	8	5	5	5
Nigeria	96,509	96,217	97,541	98,651	103,924
South Africa	393	393	393	393	391
Sudan	N/A	N/A	N/A	102	499
Tunisia	5,020	4,450	4,352	4,291	4,078
Other	222	243	251	251	250
Total	329,962	330,196	336,034	349,334	360,473
Middle East					
Bahrain	2,440	2,421	2,375	2,329	2,168
Iran	182,870	180,950	182,919	183,802	181,764
Iraq	23,648	26,006	27,185	28,540	56,689
Israel	28	25	28	25	25
Jordan	1	2	2	2	2
Kuwait	96,539	105,162	106,556	106,758	108,178
Oman	39,067	40,629	42,788	44,328	44,785
Qatar	21,398	20,744	20,856	21,336	27,040
Saudi Arabia	433,794	428,721	430,844	432,231	438,996
Syria	26,767	29,000	31,329	30,745	29,658
United Arab Emirates	108,490	116,520	115,481	118,769	120,168
Yemen	11,048	17,138	17,472	17,631	16,787
Total	946,090	967,318	977,835	986,496	1,026,260
Asia					
Bangladesh	124	105	10	10	7
Brunei	9,178	9,459	9,578	9,354	9,407
India	28,951	33,213	37,180	34,142	34,719
Indonesia	76,129	76,268	75,517	77,043	75,023
Malaysia	33,543	35,469	36,637	35,078	35,915
Myanmar	675	681	474	402	411
Pakistan	3,013	2,813	2,755	2,947	2,669
Philippines	500	300	191	135	599
Chinese Taipei	56	59	53	51	50
Thailand	4,536	4,291	4,173	5,205	4,105
Vietnam	6,312	7,259	8,502	9,586	8,829
Other	5,400	5,500	6,500	6,500	4,892
Total	168,417	175,417	181,570	180,453	176,626
China	145,174	146,082	150,044	157,334	160,158
NON-OECD TOTAL	2,238,586	2,250,950	2,301,651	2,345,021	2,418,530
WORLD TOTAL	3,149,720	3,197,333	3,257,399	3,327,019	3,407,458

Source: *Oil Information 1997,* © OECD/International Energy Agency 1998

Electricity Production in OECD Countries

In gigawatt hours (GWh). A gigawatt is one thousand million watts, and a gigawatt hour means that a power station produces one thousand million watts of electrical power in one hour.

Country/region	1992	1993	1994	1995	1996
Australia	159,649	163,747	167,517	173,384	177,320
Austria	52,126	52,638	53,261	56,587	54,835
Belgium	72,277	70,856	72,251	74,430	76,149
Canada	521,020	527,793	557,045	562,145	570,662
Czech Republic	59,131	58,881	58,705	60,847	64,257
Denmark	30,862	33,744	40,097	36,787	53,551
Finland	57,722	61,078	65,630	63,896	69,372
France	463,461	472,665	476,907	493,900	513,139
Germany	537,453	526,197	528,641	537,045	555,325
Greece	37,275	38,305	40,549	41,457	42,461
Hungary	31,685	32,915	33,515	34,017	35,089
Iceland	4,546	4,727	4,780	4,981	5,123
Ireland, Republic of	16,031	16,430	17,140	17,895	19,201
Italy	226,319	222,865	231,877	241,542	244,491
Japan	895,265	906,705	964,328	989,880	1,012,147
Korea	130,962	144,437	183,329	203,547	225,846
Luxembourg	1,199	1,068	1,191	1,237	1,314[1]
Mexico	130,239	136,106	147,393	152,548	162,526
Netherlands	77,285	76,994	79,647	80,971	85,045
New Zealand	31,973	33,873	35,270	35,507	36,150
Norway	117,506	120,095	113,213	123,011	104,756
Poland	132,750	133,867	135,347	139,006	143,173
Portugal	30,088	31,206	31,382	33,265	34,521
Spain	158,670	156,808	161,857	167,084	174,435[1]
Sweden	146,444	145,811	143,039	148,350	139,686
Switzerland	59,126	61,267	66,453	63,080	56,888
Turkey	67,342	73,808	78,321	86,247	94,862
UK	320,963	323,307	325,739	334,438	347,855
USA	3,291,867	3,411,280	3,473,435	3,582,114	3,677,812
OECD North America	3,943,126	4,075,179	4,177,873	4,296,807	4,411,000
OECD Pacific	1,217,849	1,248,762	1,350,444	1,402,318	1,451,463
OECD Europe	2,700,261	2,715,532	2,759,542	2,840,073	2,915,528
OECD TOTAL	7,861,236	8,039,473	8,287,859	8,539,198	8,777,991
EU Total	2,228,175	2,229,972	2,269,208	2,328,884	2,411,380

[1] Estimate.

Source: *Energy Statistics of OECD Countries 1995–96*, © OECD International Energy Agency 1998

Nuclear Electricity Production in OECD countries

(– = not applicable. In gigawatt hours.)

Country/region	1989	1991	1993	1995	1996
Australia	–	–	–	–	–
Austria	–	–	–	–	–
Belgium	41,217	42,861	41,927	41,356	43,336
Canada	79,872	84,929	94,823	97,844	92,767
Czech Republic	12,418	12,132	12,627	12,230	12,850
Denmark	–	–	–	–	–
Finland	19,090	19,511	19,928	19,216	19,476
France	303,931	331,340	368,188	377,231	397,340
Germany	161,671	147,229	153,276	153,091	160,016
Greece	–	–	–	–	–
Hungary	13,891	13,726	13,796	14,026	14,180
Iceland	–	–	–	–	–
Ireland, Republic of	–	–	–	–	–
Italy	–	–	–	–	–
Japan	182,869	213,460	249,256	291,254	302,200
Korea	47,365	56,311	58,138	67,029	73,924
Luxembourg	–	–	–	–	–
Mexico	372	4,242	4,931	8,443	7,878
Netherlands	4,019	3,329	3,948	4,018	4,160
New Zealand	–	–	–	–	–
Norway	–	–	–	–	–
Poland	–	–	–	–	–
Portugal	–	–	–	–	–
Spain	56,126	55,578	56,060	55,455	56,330
Sweden	65,603	76,761	61,395	69,935	73,274
Switzerland	22,836	22,953	23,351	24,895	25,142
Turkey	–	–	–	–	–
UK	71,734	70,543	89,362	88,964	94,671
USA	561,165	649,399	646,987	713,806	715,212
OECD North America	641,409	738,570	746,741	820,093	815,857
OECD Pacific	230,234	269,771	307,394	358,283	376,124
OECD Europe	772,536	795,963	843,858	860,417	900,775
OECD TOTAL	1,644,179	1,804,304	1,897,993	2,038,793	2,092,756
EU total	723,391	747,152	794,084	809,266	848,603

Source: *Energy Statistics of OECD Countries 1995–96*, © OECD International Energy Agency 1998

World Production of Major Mineral Commodities

(N/A = not available.)

Commodity	Units	1990	1995	1996	1997[1]	Leading producers, 1996
Mineral Fuels						
Coal	million short tons	5,356	5,144	5,185	N/A	China, USA, India
Dry natural gas	trillion cubic feet	73.6	77.9	82.0	N/A	Russia, USA, Canada
Natural gas plant liquids[2]	million barrels[3]	1,691	2,002	2,037	N/A	USA, Saudi Arabia, Canada
Petroleum, crude	million barrels[3]	22,107	22,751	23,380	N/A	Saudi Arabia, USA, Russia
Non-Metallic Minerals						
Cement, hydraulic	million metric tons	1,160	1,444	1,485	1,500	China, Japan, USA
Diamond, gem and industrial	million carats	111	113	117	118	Australia, Russia, Democratic Republic of Congo
Nitrogen in ammonia	million metric tons	97.5	96.1	97.5	96.0	China, USA, India
Phosphate rock	million metric tons	162	130	133	136	USA, China, Morocco
Potash, marketable	million metric tons	27.5	24.7	23.9	23.5	Canada, Germany, Belarus
Salt	million metric tons	183	192	192	192	USA, China, Canada
Sulphur, elemental basis	million metric tons	57.8	53.2	52.2	54.0	USA, Canada, China

(continued)

World Production of Major Mineral Commodities (*continued*)

Commodity	Units	1990	1995	1996	1997[1]	Leading producers, 1996
Metals						
Aluminium[4]	million metric tons	19.3	19.9	20.7	21.2	USA, Russia, Canada
Bauxite, gross weight	million metric tons	113.0	107.0	114.0	115.0	Australia, Guinea, Jamaica
Chromite, gross weight[2]	thousand metric tons	13,200	14,300	12,200	12,000	South Africa, Turkey, India
Copper, metal content[5]	thousand metric tons	8,950	10,100	11,000	11,300	Chile, USA, Canada
Gold, metal content	metric tons	2,180	2,220	2,250	2,300	South Africa, USA, Australia
Iron ore, gross weight[6]	million metric tons	983	1,030	1,020	1,030	China, Brazil, Australia
Lead, metal content[5]	thousand metric tons	3,370	2,780	2,920	2,900	Australia, China, USA
Manganese ore, gross weight	million metric tons	26.1	23.0	22.3	N/A	China, South Africa, Ukraine
Nickel, metal content[5]	thousand metric tons	974	1,030	1,080	1,080	Russia, Canada, New Caledonia (France)
Steel, crude	million metric tons	771	755	758	773	European Union, Japan, China
Tin, metal content[5]	thousand metric tons	221	195	196	201	China, Indonesia, Peru
Zinc, metal content[5]	thousand metric tons	7,150	7,240	7,440	7,800	Canada , Australia, China

[1] 1997 data are preliminary.
[2] Excludes China.
[3] Barrels hold 42 gallons.
[4] Unalloyed ingot metal.
[5] Mine output.
[6] Includes iron ore concentrates and iron ore agglomerates.

Source: *Statistical Abstract of the United States 1998*

World Industry

Countries with the Highest and Lowest Industrial Output

1990–96

High growth: Country	Average annual % growth	Low growth: Country	Average annual % growth
China	17.3	Armenia	–28.7
Papua New Guinea	13.6	Moldova	–23.7
Vietnam	13.3	Kyrgyzstan	–21.7
Lesotho	12.5	Latvia	–20.2
Uganda	12.2	Ukraine	–20.0
Laos	12.1	Congo, Democratic Republic of	–15.9
Cambodia	11.3	Kazakhstan	–15.7
Malaysia	11.2	Rwanda	–14.9
Jordan	10.9	Haiti	–13.7
Myanmar	10.7	Estonia	–11.6

Source: *World Development Indicators 1998,* The World Bank

Index of Industrial Production of OECD Countries

Industrial production index measures output in the manufacturing, mining, and electric and gas utilities industries. (N/A = not available.)

Country	Index (1990 = 100)								Annual % change				
	1980	1985	1992	1993	1994	1995	1996	1997	1992–93	1993–94	1994–95	1995–96	1996–97
Australia	76.6	84.9	98.3	100.1	107.1	107.6	110.4	112.1	2.8	5.9	0.5	2.6	1.5
Austria	76.0	82.9	100.7	99.2	103.2	108.3	109.6	N/A	−1.5	4.0	4.9	1.2	N/A
Belgium	82.1	85.5	98.0	92.9	94.6	100.7	101.6	106.0	−5.2	1.8	6.4	0.9	4.3
Canada[1]	81.4	93.9	97.2	102.1	108.3	112.7	114.4	120.1	5.0	6.1	4.1	1.5	5.0
Czech Republic	N/A	N/A	71.8	68.1	69.5	75.6	77.0	80.5	−5.2	2.1	8.8	1.9	4.5
Finland	75.3	87.8	92.2	97.2	108.3	117.1	121.0	131.8	5.4	11.4	8.1	3.3	8.9
France	89.2	89.2	97.6	93.9	97.6	99.6	99.8	103.6	−3.8	3.9	2.0	0.2	3.8
Germany[2]	83.0	85.6	100.9	93.6	96.9	98.9	99.3	103.3	−7.2	3.5	2.1	0.4	4.0
Greece	90.9	97.4	98.0	95.2	96.4	98.2	99.3	100.6	−2.9	1.3	1.9	1.1	1.3
Hungary	102.9	112.6	73.8	76.6	84.0	87.9	90.9	100.9	3.8	9.7	4.6	3.4	11.0
Ireland, Republic of	54.2	69.5	112.7	119.0	133.2	158.3	170.9	197.1	5.6	11.9	18.8	8.0	15.3
Italy	87.5	84.8	97.8	95.7	101.7	107.9	104.8	107.7	−2.1	6.3	6.1	−2.9	2.8
Japan	67.3	79.8	96.0	92.0	93.1	96.2	98.5	101.9	−4.2	1.2	3.3	2.4	3.5
Korea, South	33.1	54.5	116.0	121.1	134.5	150.5	161.6	172.6	4.4	11.1	11.9	7.4	6.8
Luxembourg	69.7	84.7	99.5	95.2	100.9	102.3	100.4	107.4	−4.3	6.0	1.4	−1.9	7.0
Mexico[3]	84.0	88.8	107.9	108.2	113.4	104.5	115.2	125.9	0.3	4.8	−7.8	10.2	9.3
Netherlands	86.8	91.7	101.5	100.3	104.6	106.7	111.2	113.4	−1.2	4.3	2.0	4.2	2.0
Norway	58.3	79.0	108.3	112.2	120.0	127.2	134.1	138.6	3.6	7.0	6.0	5.4	3.4
Poland	N/A	122.4	87.4	91.6	103.6	114.3	125.0	139.1	4.8	13.1	10.3	9.4	11.3
Portugal	62.8	73.9	97.7	95.2	95.0	99.4	100.8	103.3	−2.6	−0.2	4.6	1.4	2.5
Spain	83.0	85.7	96.3	91.8	98.6	103.3	102.0	109.1	−4.7	7.4	4.8	−1.3	7.0
Sweden[4]	83.0	91.5	93.8	94.3	105.5	117.8	120.5	129.4	0.5	11.9	11.7	2.3	7.4
Switzerland	82.0	85.0	99.0	97.0	102.0	104.0	103.0	109.0	−2.0	5.2	2.0	−1.0	5.8
UK	81.6	88.2	101.1	98.4	103.4	105.9	107.3	N/A	2.2	5.1	2.4	1.3	N/A
USA	80.5	89.0	101.1	104.7	110.3	115.8	119.8	125.8	3.6	5.3	5.0	3.5	5.0
OECD total	79.3	86.3	99.3	98.7	103.2	107.0	109.3	114.2	−0.6	4.6	3.7	2.1	4.5

[1] Gross domestic product in industry at factor cost and 1986 prices.
[2] 1980–90 former West Germany; later data use 1990 annual average data for West Germany as base year.
[3] Includes construction.
[4] Mining and manufacturing.

Source: *Statistical Abstract of the United States 1998*

Leading Producers of Selected Commodities

1996

World leading countries		Leading developing countries	
Country or area	Share (%)[1]	Country or area	Share (%)[2]
Food Products			
USA	24.0	Brazil	13.5
Japan	14.9	Argentina	9.6
Germany (western part)	6.6	India	6.7
France	6.6	Korea, South	6.3
UK	4.8	Mexico	6.1
Italy	3.9	Indonesia	5.8
Spain	3.1	Philippines	4.6
Brazil	2.8	Turkey	4.0
Canada	2.7	China (Taiwan province)	3.8
Netherlands	2.0	Thailand	3.3
Argentina	2.0	Chile	2.8
Australia	1.6	Peru	2.1
Belgium	1.5	Egypt	1.9
India	1.4	Colombia	1.7
Korea, South	1.3	Iran	1.6
Total	79.2	**Total**	73.8
Textiles			
USA	20.2	India	17.0
Italy	11.4	China (Taiwan province)	8.9
Japan	10.7	Brazil	8.9
India	5.7	Turkey	8.5
Germany (western part)	4.6	Korea, South	7.4
France	4.3	Iran	4.3
UK	3.0	Pakistan	4.1
China (Taiwan province)	3.0	Indonesia	4.0
Brazil	3.0	China (Hong Kong SAR)	3.2
Turkey	2.8	Argentina	3.1
Korea, South	2.5	Mexico	2.9
Spain	2.3	Peru	2.3
Canada	1.5	Colombia	1.9
Iran	1.4	Egypt	1.8
Pakistan	1.4	Malaysia	1.2
Total	77.8	**Total**	79.5
Wearing Apparel			
USA	24.1	Brazil	12.8
Japan	13.8	China (Hong Kong SAR)	10.5
Italy	10.5	Korea, South	8.5
France	4.4	Indonesia	7.0
UK	4.2	Turkey	4.6
Brazil	3.5	Argentina	4.2
Germany (western part)	3.4	China (Taiwan province)	2.7
China (Hong Kong SAR)	2.9	Tunisia	2.7
Spain	2.7	India	2.5
Canada	2.3	Philippines	2.2
Korea, South	2.3	Mexico	1.9
Indonesia	1.9	Morocco	1.7
Portugal	1.3	Iraq	1.6
Turkey	1.3	Sri Lanka	1.4
Argentina	1.1	Malaysia	1.2
Total	79.7	**Total**	65.5

World leading countries		Leading developing countries	
Country or area	Share (%)[1]	Country or area	Share (%)[2]
Leather and Fur Products			
Italy	18.4	Argentina	17.0
Japan	11.2	Brazil	12.6
USA	10.6	Mexico	10.8
France	6.8	Korea, South	8.0
Argentina	5.7	India	6.2
Spain	4.7	Bangladesh	5.0
Brazil	4.2	China (Taiwan province)	3.5
Germany (western part)	3.9	Uruguay	2.6
Mexico	3.6	Indonesia	2.3
UK	3.4	Paraguay	1.7
Korea, South	2.7	Morocco	1.4
India	2.1	Turkey	1.2
Bangladesh	1.7	Iran	1.2
Portugal	1.3	Tunisia	1.1
China (Taiwan province)	1.2	Chile	1.1
Total	81.5	**Total**	75.7
Footwear			
Italy	24.3	Brazil	26.3
Brazil	8.6	Argentina	12.2
USA	7.8	Mexico	6.5
Japan	6.2	Indonesia	6.2
France	6.0	China (Taiwan province)	5.8
UK	4.6	India	3.3
Spain	4.1	Korea, South	3.0
Argentina	4.0	Tunisia	2.4
Portugal	3.2	Iraq	2.3
Germany (western part)	3.1	Chile	2.1
Mexico	2.1	Turkey	1.6
Indonesia	2.0	Colombia	1.5
China (Taiwan province)	1.9	Iran	1.4
South Africa	1.4	Venezuela	1.4
Austria	1.3	Morocco	1.0
Total	80.6	**Total**	77.0
Industrial Chemicals			
USA	24.7	China (Taiwan province)	14.5
Japan	15.3	Brazil	12.4
Germany (western part)	12.9	Korea, South	12.1
France	5.0	Mexico	12.0
UK	4.8	India	10.8
Italy	4.1	Saudi Arabia	7.2
Netherlands	3.0	Turkey	4.0
China (Taiwan province)	2.7	Malaysia	3.0
Brazil	2.3	Argentina	3.0
Korea, South	2.3	Indonesia	2.4
Mexico	2.3	Venezuela	1.9
Belgium	2.1	Pakistan	1.7
India	2.0	Singapore	1.6
Spain	1.8	Colombia	1.1
Canada	1.7	Philippines	0.9
Total	87.0	**Total**	88.6

(continued)

Leading Producers of Selected Commodities (*continued*)

World leading countries: Country or area	Share (%)[1]	Leading developing countries: Country or area	Share (%)[2]
Other Chemicals			
USA	26.1	Korea, South	14.8
Japan	17.8	Brazil	12.9
Germany (western part)	9.2	Argentina	10.4
France	5.4	India	10.1
UK	5.3	Mexico	10.1
Switzerland	3.8	Turkey	5.2
Spain	2.9	China (Taiwan province)	4.2
Italy	2.6	Philippines	3.3
Korea, South	2.6	Thailand	2.6
Brazil	2.2	Chile	2.4
Canada	2.1	Peru	2.0
Argentina	1.8	Indonesia	1.9
India	1.7	Singapore	1.7
Mexico	1.7	Colombia	1.5
Ireland, Republic of	1.3	Venezuela	1.4
Total	86.5	**Total**	84.5
Iron and Steel			
Japan	22.0	India	18.5
USA	15.2	Korea, South	16.1
Germany (western part)	7.8	Brazil	12.3
Italy	7.7	China (Taiwan province)	10.7
India	4.7	Mexico	10.6
France	4.3	Indonesia	6.8
Korea, South	4.1	Turkey	4.4
UK	3.3	Argentina	2.4
Brazil	3.1	Venezuela	2.0
Spain	2.8	Malaysia	1.4
China (Taiwan province)	2.7	Philippines	1.2
Mexico	2.7	Chile	1.0
Canada	1.8	Peru	0.9
Indonesia	1.7	Egypt	0.8
Austria	1.5	Colombia	0.8
Total	85.4	**Total**	89.9
Metal Products			
USA	23.3	Korea, South	16.9
Japan	20.6	China (Taiwan province)	12.0
Germany (western part)	13.3	Brazil	11.4
France	6.5	Mexico	7.3
Italy	4.5	Argentina	6.7
UK	3.7	India	4.9
Spain	2.4	Malaysia	4.3
Canada	1.9	Turkey	3.4
Korea, South	1.9	Singapore	3.3
Austria	1.5	Chile	2.1
Sweden	1.4	Indonesia	1.9
China (Taiwan province)	1.4	Iran	1.9
Netherlands	1.3	Peru	1.7
Brazil	1.3	China (Hong Kong SAR)	1.7
Australia	1.3	Syria	1.2
Total	86.3	**Total**	80.7
Non-Electrical Machinery			
USA	38.5	Korea, South	19.4
Japan	17.5	Brazil	17.9
Germany (western part)	10.3	India	12.8
Italy	7.7	Singapore	9.4
UK	4.4	China (Taiwan province)	7.9
France	3.6	Turkey	5.7
Canada	1.8	Argentina	5.1
Korea, South	1.4	Mexico	4.1
Spain	1.3	Iran	2.7
Brazil	1.3	Malaysia	2.5
India	0.9	China (Hong Kong SAR)	1.9
Netherlands	0.9	Chile	0.9
Finland	0.9	Philippines	0.5
Singapore	0.7	Venezuela	0.4
Sweden	0.7	Egypt	0.4
Total	91.9	**Total**	91.6
Electrical Machinery			
USA	27.0	Korea, South	23.2
Japan	24.6	China (Taiwan province)	22.0
Germany (western part)	11.8	Brazil	13.4
France	4.7	India	6.9
Italy	4.2	Malaysia	6.4
UK	3.1	Mexico	4.6
Korea, South	3.1	Singapore	4.4
China (Taiwan province)	2.9	Turkey	3.5
Brazil	1.8	Argentina	2.7
Spain	1.5	Philippines	1.9
Netherlands	1.3	China (Hong Kong SAR)	1.6
Sweden	1.2	Iran	0.8
Austria	1.2	Indonesia	0.8
Canada	1.1	Algeria	0.4
India	1.9	Peru	0.4
Total	90.4	**Total**	93.0

[1] In world total value added (excluding eastern Europe and the former USSR) at constant 1990 prices.
[2] In total value added of developing countries at constant 1990 prices.

Source: *International Yearbook of Industrial Statistics 1999*, United Nations Industrial Development Organization (UNIDO), and Edward Elgar Publishing Ltd

Motor Vehicle Production in Selected Countries

(N/A = not available. – = not applicable.)

Country	Passenger cars				Commercial vehicles			
	1991	1993	1995	1997	1991	1993	1995	1997
Austria	13,682	40,777	59,196	97,774	22,545	7,886	9,174	10,215
Belgium	253,491	374,424	385,894	355,779	101,587	68,519	103,637	96,334
France[1]	3,187,634	2,836,280	3,050,929	2,258,782	423,001	319,437	423,776	312,360
Germany	4,676,666	3,794,491	4,360,235	4,677,974	357,784	237,309	307,129	344,906
Italy	1,632,904	1,117,053	1,422,359	1,562,865	245,385	160,389	244,911	253,645
Netherlands	84,709	80,246	100,434	197,225	13,915	6,262	17,629	20,428
Spain	1,773,752	1,505,949	1,958,789	2,010,267	307,959	261,691	374,998	551,810
Sweden	269,431	279,002	387,659	375,705	75,259	58,384	102,483	104,034
UK	1,236,900	1,375,524	1,532,084	1,698,015	217,141	193,467	233,001	237,703
EU total	13,129,169	11,403,746	13,257,579	13,234,386	1764,576	1,313,344	1,816,738	1,931,435
Argentina	114,113	286,964	226,656	366,140	24,845	55,380	58,779	79,729
Australia	278,421	285,076	293,631	301,280	14,904	19,393	25,405	N/A
Brazil	705,363	1,100,309	1,302,742	1,679,566	254,750	291,057	332,799	387,886
Canada	1,059,607	1,352,834	1,336,725	1,372,111	827,965	893,368	1,070,430	1,197,561
Czech Republic and Slovak Republic	172,726	222,670	228,068	398,079	33,891	14,408	13,477	15,745
Hungary	N/A	N/A	36,453	63,540	5,001	3,200	1,212	N/A
India	209,344	243,869	393,495	486,132	145,689	127,761	242,521	260,019
Japan	9,753,069	8,493,943	7,610,533	8,491,440	3,492,363	2,733,602	2,585,003	2,483,647
Korea, South	1,158,245	1,592,669	2,003,146	2,308,476	339,573	457,389	523,254	509,799
Poland	167,000	334,000	391,929	520,208	22,000	18,000	10,644	62,134
Romania	73,836	82,000	70,973	109,189	18,603	17,771	21,209	20,529
Russia[2]	1,185,389	1,090,587	880,539	969,317	750,093	553,534	199,044	99,015[3]
Turkey	195,574	348,095	233,412	242,780	46,264	72,580	49,028	101,572
USA	5,438,579	5,980,981	6,350,433	5,927,281	3,371,942	4,883,157	5,634,724	6,191,888
Yugoslavia	213,327	7,359	7,502	–	26,264	954	1,809	–
TOTAL	33,853,762	32,825,102	34,623,816	36,469,925	11,138,723	11,454,898	12,586,076	13,340,959

[1] France has changed its way of reporting production statistics. Previously non-countable units already included in other overseas markets were in the totals. Historical information is not yet available.
[2] Includes Russia, Belarus, Ukraine, Latvia, and Armenia. Data for 1997 exclude those produced in Ukraine.
[3] Russian figures for 1997 are for the first six months only.

Source: *Motor Industry of Great Britain 1998 World Automotive Statistics*, Society of Motor Manufacturers and Traders Ltd

World Agriculture

Global Food Production

(In millions of metric tons.)

Commodity	1990	1991	1992	1993	1994	1995	1996	1997[1]
Grains								
Wheat	588.0	543.0	562.3	559.3	524.6	537.5	582.4	609.8
Coarse grains (including corn)	828.6	810.3	871.8	799.5	873.6	801.9	908.1	898.9
Rice, milled	352.0	354.7	355.7	355.5	364.5	371.2	379.9	381.4
Total	1,768.6	1,708.0	1,789.8	1,714.3	1,762.7	1,710.6	1,870.4	1,890.1
Oils	58.3	61.0	61.7	63.7	70.1	73.0	74.9	77.2
Soybeans	104.2	107.4	117.4	117.8	137.7	125.0	131.6	152.2
Rapeseed	25.1	28.3	25.3	26.8	30.4	34.5	31.4	33.7
Pulses	58.4	53.4	51.0	55.7	57.2	55.3	55.3	57.7
Vegetables and melons	461.4	462.4	478.6	509.5	532.9	559.9	589.1	595.6
Fruits	352.2	350.8	379.0	384.7	390.4	404.9	426.7	429.4
Nuts	4.6	4.8	5.0	5.0	5.3	4.9	5.1	5.2
Red meat	116.0	117.8	118.6	117.7	119.9	124.4	128.6	130.2
Poultry	37.4	38.9	40.6	42.2	44.8	48.4	51.1	53.4
Milk	441.3	428.4	423.7	393.5	383.7	380.8	379.8	381.3

[1] Preliminary.

Source: *Statistical Abstract of the United States 1998*

Leading Producers of Fruit in the World

Figures exclude melons. (In tonnes.)

Country	1995	1996	1997
China	44,138,000	48,792,000	52,406,000
Brazil	33,684,000	35,870,000	37,765,000
India	36,126,000	37,130,000	37,130,000
USA	29,301,000	28,791,000	31,887,000
Italy	16,261,000	18,268,000	15,656,000
Spain	11,522,000	12,907,000	14,010,000
Mexico	11,676,000	12,418,000	12,616,000
France	11,252,000	11,798,000	10,193,000
Iran	9,635,000	10,110,000	10,001,000
Uganda	9,640,000	9,781,000	9,941,000

Source: *FAO Production Yearbook 1997*, Food and Agriculture Organization of the United Nations

Leading Producers of Meat in the World

(In tonnes.)

Country	1995	1996	1997
China	52,299,800	58,168,800	63,975,000
USA	33,902,000	34,563,510	34,718,000
Brazil	10,086,890	10,964,890	11,222,000
France	6,312,493	6,325,500	6,321,000
Germany	5,742,749	5,840,349	5,881,000
Russia	5,748,200	5,272,000	4,800,000
India	4,272,429	4,294,579	4,553,000
Italy	3,982,803	4,071,782	4,018,000
Spain	3,991,801	3,800,313	3,986,000
Mexico	3,799,026	3,682,136	3,902,000

Source: *FAO Production Yearbook 1997*, Food and Agriculture Organization of the United Nations

Leading Producers of Rice in the World

(In tonnes.)

Country	1995	1996	1997
China	185,226,000	188,000,000	198,471,000
India	119,442,000	120,012,000	123,012,000
Indonesia	49,744,140	51,165,000	50,632,000
Bangladesh	26,398,500	28,008,000	28,183,000
Vietnam	24,963,700	26,300,000	26,397,000
Thailand	21,130,000	21,800,000	21,280,000
Myanmar	19,568,450	20,865,000	18,900,000
Japan	13,435,000	13,000,000	12,531,000
Philippines	10,540,650	11,283,570	11,269,000
Brazil	11,225,990	10,035,400	9,334,000

Source: *FAO Production Yearbook 1997*, Food and Agriculture Organization of United Nations

Leading Producers of Vegetables in the World

Figures include melons. (In tonnes.)

Country	1995	1996	1997
China	204,465,000	227,138,000	236,938,000
India	54,059,000	54,967,000	54,967,000
USA	34,633,000	35,204,000	34,965,000
Turkey	21,848,000	22,149,000	21,026,000
Italy	13,798,000	15,217,000	14,056,000
Japan	13,636,000	13,683,000	13,755,000
Russia	11,551,000	11,099,000	11,591,000
Egypt	10,237,000	11,695,000	11,505,000
Korea, South	11,423,000	10,693,000	11,241,000
Spain	10,280,000	11,163,000	10,650,000

Source: *FAO Production Yearbook 1997*, Food and Agriculture Organization of United Nations

Leading Producers of Wheat in the World

(In tonnes.)

Country	1995	1996	1997
China	102,207,000	109,000,000	122,600,000
India	65,767,000	62,620,000	69,000,000
USA	59,400,000	62,099,000	68,761,000
Russia	30,117,600	34,900,000	44,180,000
France	30,879,000	35,946,000	33,928,000
Canada	25,017,000	30,495,000	24,270,000
Germany	17,816,000	18,921,700	19,867,000
Turkey	18,015,000	18,515,000	18,650,000
Australia	17,262,700	23,497,000	18,554,000
Ukraine	16,273,000	13,547,999	17,377,000

Source: *FAO Production Yearbook 1997*, Food and Agriculture Organization of the United Nations

Fishing Catches by Country

The data indicate annual catches in all regions. (In thousands of tonnes live weight. – = not applicable.)

Country/region	1990	1993	1994	1995
European Union				
Austria	5	5	5	4
Belgium	42	37	36	36
Denmark	1,511	1,527	1,880	2,034
Finland	129	140	156	159
France	761	713	738	680
Germany	391	294	269	303
Greece	148	201	225	198
Italy	530	558	554	615
Ireland, Republic of	216	275	298	387
Luxembourg	–	–	–	–
Netherlands	361	420	384	441
Portugal	326	270	250	263
Spain	1,142	1,132	1,219	1,214
Sweden	254	345	390	408
UK	813	872	917	943
EU total	6,629	6,788	7,320	7,704
Iceland	1,522	1,727	1,571	1,614
Norway	1,603	2,392	2,334	2,525
European Economic Area total	9,754	10,908	11,225	11,844
Switzerland	4	3	3	3
USA	5,797	5,988	6,035	5,704
Canada	1,671	1,188	1,103	872
Japan	11,125	8,769	8,175	7,477

Source: *Eurostat Yearbook 1997*, Office for Official Publications of the European Community

The European Economy

Main European Union Trading Partners: Exports

Rank	Partner	Value (billion ECU)					% of trade share				
		1993	1994	1995	1996	1997	1993	1994	1995	1996	1997
	Extra EU-15[1]	471.4	523.6	572.8	625.1	720.4	100.0	100.0	100.0	100.0	100.0
1	USA	91.5	103.7	103.3	114.4	141.2	19.4	19.8	18.0	18.3	19.6
2	Switzerland	42.7	46.8	51.0	51.4	53.2	9.1	8.9	8.9	8.2	7.4
3	Japan	24.7	29.1	32.9	35.7	36.1	5.2	5.6	5.7	5.7	5.0
4	Russia	12.7	14.4	16.1	19.1	25.5	2.7	2.7	2.8	3.1	3.5
5	Poland	11.1	12.3	15.3	19.9	25.1	2.4	2.4	2.7	3.2	3.5
6	Norway	14.3	16.5	17.3	19.7	23.3	3.0	3.2	3.0	3.2	3.2
7	Turkey	12.4	9.3	13.4	18.2	22.3	2.6	1.8	2.3	2.9	3.1
8	Hong Kong	12.0	13.9	15.8	17.5	20.4	2.5	2.7	2.8	2.8	2.8
9	China	12.4	14.0	14.7	14.7	16.5	2.6	2.7	2.6	2.4	2.3
10	Czech Republic	7.1	9.2	11.7	14.0	15.8	1.5	1.8	2.0	2.2	2.2
11	Brazil	5.7	7.5	11.4	11.7	14.8	1.2	1.4	2.0	1.9	2.1
12	Korea, South	8.4	10.9	12.3	14.3	14.5	1.8	2.1	2.2	2.3	2.0
13	Canada	9.5	10.6	10.3	10.7	14.1	2.0	2.0	1.8	1.7	2.0
14	Hungary	6.4	8.1	8.7	10.0	13.6	1.4	1.5	1.5	1.6	1.9
15	Singapore	8.3	9.7	10.9	12.3	13.5	1.8	1.9	1.9	2.0	1.9
16	Saudi Arabia	10.1	9.3	8.6	10.3	13.2	2.1	1.8	1.5	1.7	1.8
17	Australia	7.9	9.7	10.5	11.5	13.1	1.7	1.8	1.8	1.8	1.8
18	Taiwan	7.6	8.7	10.1	9.9	12.7	1.6	1.7	1.8	1.6	1.8
19	Israel	8.0	9.4	9.7	10.4	11.5	1.7	1.8	1.7	1.7	1.6
20	India	6.5	7.5	9.4	9.9	10.3	1.4	1.4	1.6	1.6	1.4

[1] Total trade with partners outside the EU.

Source: *External and Intra-European Trade, Monthly Statistics 11/1998,* Eurostat, Office for Official Publications of the European Communities

European Union Main Trading Partners: Imports

Rank	Partner	Value (billion ECU)					% of trade share				
		1993	1994	1995	1996	1997	1993	1994	1995	1996	1997
	Extra EU-15[1]	470.2	518.5	545.1	581.5	670.5	100.0	100.0	100.0	100.0	100.0
1	USA	90.6	100.0	103.6	112.8	137.7	19.3	19.3	19.0	19.4	20.5
2	Japan	52.2	53.8	54.3	52.5	59.6	11.1	10.4	10.0	9.0	8.9
3	Switzerland	38.4	41.8	43.2	42.7	45.1	8.2	8.1	7.9	7.3	6.7
4	China	21.1	24.6	26.3	30.0	37.4	4.5	4.7	4.8	5.2	5.6
5	Norway	21.0	23.7	25.5	30.6	33.7	4.5	4.6	4.7	5.3	5.0
6	Russia	17.1	21.5	21.5	23.3	26.9	3.6	4.1	3.9	4.0	4.0
7	Taiwan	10.4	10.3	11.8	12.9	15.7	2.2	2.0	2.2	2.2	2.3
8	Poland	8.5	10.1	12.3	12.3	14.2	1.8	2.0	2.2	2.1	2.1
9	Korea, South	8.3	9.1	10.9	11.1	13.0	1.8	1.8	2.0	1.9	1.9
10	Brazil	8.5	10.9	10.8	10.4	12.6	1.8	2.1	2.0	1.8	1.9
11	Canada	8.3	9.8	11.7	11.5	12.5	1.8	1.9	2.1	2.0	1.9
12	Turkey	6.8	7.9	9.2	10.2	11.9	1.5	1.5	1.7	1.8	1.8
13	Czech Republic	5.6	7.4	9.0	9.8	11.7	1.2	1.4	1.7	1.7	1.8
14	Hungary	4.9	6.1	7.6	8.8	11.6	1.0	1.2	1.4	1.5	1.7
15	Singapore	6.8	8.2	8.8	9.3	11.2	1.4	1.6	1.6	1.6	1.7
16	Saudi Arabia	9.8	9.2	8.8	10.1	10.9	2.1	1.8	1.6	1.7	1.6
17	Malaysia	6.6	7.9	9.2	9.4	10.8	1.4	1.5	1.7	1.6	1.6
18	India	6.2	7.2	7.8	8.6	9.5	1.3	1.4	1.4	1.5	1.4
19	South Africa	8.8	6.9	7.8	8.2	9.1	1.9	1.3	1.4	1.4	1.4
20	Thailand	5.8	6.6	6.6	7.5	8.6	1.2	1.3	1.2	1.3	1.3

[1] Total trade with partners outside the EU.

Source: *External and Intra-European Trade, Monthly Statistics 11/1998,* Eurostat, Office for Official Publications of the European Communities

The Top 25 Companies in Europe

Market capitalization is the market value of a company's issued share capital, i.e. the quoted price of its shares multiplied by the number of shares issued.

1998

Rank	Company	Country	Market capitalization ($ millions)
1	Royal Dutch/Shell	Netherlands/UK	164,156.5
2	Novartis	Switzerland	108,474.8
3	Glaxo Wellcome	UK	105,190.8
4	Roche	Switzerland	102,006.9
5	British Petroleum	UK	88,618.7
6	BT (British Telecom)	UK	86,134.4
7	Deutsche Telekom	Germany	83,724.1
8	Nestlé	Switzerland	77,489.9
9	Allianz	Germany	74,382.6
10	Unilever plc/NV	Netherlands/UK	67,214.5
11	SmithKline Beecham	UK	60,665.5
12	Lloyds TSB Group	UK	60,214.8
13	France Telecom	France	58,128.3
14	HSBC Holdings	UK	48,430.8
15	Daimler-Benz	Germany	48,326.1
16	Eni	Italy	48,184.6
17	Nokia	Finland	46,926.4
18	Aegon	Netherlands	45,311.2
19	ING Groep	Netherlands	41,668.4
20	Münchener Rückvers	Germany	41,350.0
21	UBS	Switzerland	41,319.7
22	Zürich Financial Services	Switzerland/UK	38,900.0
23	TIM	Italy	38,011.4
24	Ericsson(Lm)Tel	Sweden	37,008.9
25	Telefonica	Spain	36,747.2

Source: *FT500, FT Surveys,* © *Financial Times* 1999

The Top 20 Banks in Europe

This table is ranked by market capitalization. Market capitalization is the market value of a company's issued share capital, that is the quoted price of its shares multiplied by the number of shares issued.

1998

Rank	Bank	Country	Market capitalization ($ millions)
1	Lloyds TSB Group	UK	60,214.8
2	HSBC Holdings	UK	48,430.8
3	UBS AG	Switzerland	41,319.7
4	Halifax	UK	31,370.8
5	Credit Suisse Group	Switzerland	29,136.8
6	Bayerische Hypotheken & Vereinsbank	Germany	28,639.5
7	Deutsche Bank	Germany	27,796.2
8	Barclays	UK	24,275.6
9	Abbey National	UK	24,116.9
10	ABN Amro	Netherlands	23,892.6
11	National Westminster Bank	UK	22,632.0
12	Banco Bilbao Vizcaya	Spain	21,482.1
13	Dresdner Bank	Germany	20,414.3
14	KBC Bankverzekering	Belgium	18,774.9
15	Banco Santander	Spain	17,782.8
16	Almanij	Belgium	14,340.3
17	Commerzbank	Germany	12,662.4
18	Allied Irish Banks	Ireland, Republic of	12,424.2
19	Credito Italiano	Italy	11,708.7
20	Bank of Scotland	UK	11,636.1

Source: *FT500, FT Surveys,* © *Financial Times* 1999

Harmonized Consumer Price Index for EU Countries

Country	1995	1996	1997	1997						1998								
				July	Aug	Sep	Oct	Nov	Dec	Jan	Feb	March	April	May	June	July	Aug	Sep
Belgium	98.3	100.0	101.5	101.8	101.6	101.7	101.8	101.9	101.7	101.8	102.0	101.8	102.4	102.9	102.8	103.0	102.6	102.5
Denmark	98.0	100.0	101.9	101.9	102.1	102.5	102.4	102.5	102.3	102.4	102.8	103.0	103.2	103.7	103.7	103.3	103.2	103.6
Germany	98.8	100.0	101.5	101.9	102.0	101.7	101.6	101.5	101.7	101.7	102.0	101.7	102.0	102.5	102.6	102.8	102.7	102.3
Greece	92.7	100.0	105.4	104.3	104.5	106.3	106.8	107.3	108.1	107.1	106.5	109.2	111.0	111.4	111.7	109.3	109.4	111.6
Spain	96.6	100.0	101.9	101.6	102.1	102.6	102.6	102.7	103.0	103.2	102.9	103.0	103.2	103.4	103.4	103.9	104.2	104.2
France	98.0	100.0	101.3	101.1	101.4	101.6	101.5	101.7	101.7	101.3	101.7	101.9	102.1	102.2	102.3	101.9	102.0	102.1
Ireland, Republic of	97.9	100.0	101.2	101.2	100.9	101.4	101.5	101.9	102.2	101.5	102.0	102.5	103.1	103.5	104.0	103.7	103.9	104.2
Italy	96.2	100.0	101.9	101.9	101.9	102.0	102.4	102.7	102.8	103.1	103.4	103.6	103.8	103.9	104.0	104.0	104.1	104.1
Luxembourg	98.8	100.0	101.4	101.3	101.5	101.8	102.0	102.1	102.1	102.2	102.1	102.2	102.0	102.3	102.3	102.5	102.5	102.5
Netherlands	98.6	100.0	101.9	101.4	101.8	102.9	103.0	103.0	102.6	102.0	102.7	103.8	104.2	104.0	103.5	103.2	103.2	104.2
Austria	98.3	100.0	101.2	101.1	101.2	101.1	101.2	101.5	101.7	101.8	102.1	102.2	102.3	102.1	101.9	101.9	101.9	101.7
Portugal	97.2	100.0	101.9	101.8	102.3	102.2	102.1	102.6	102.8	102.7	102.5	102.8	103.6	104.3	104.5	104.7	104.6	104.4
Finland	98.9	100.0	101.2	101.4	101.6	101.7	101.9	101.8	101.8	101.9	101.9	102.1	102.6	102.8	103.0	102.5	102.7	103.1
Sweden	99.2	100.0	101.9	101.6	101.7	103.0	103.1	102.9	102.9	102.5	102.4	102.7	103.1	103.4	103.2	102.9	102.3	102.9
UK	97.6	100.0	101.8	101.6	102.2	102.5	102.6	102.6	102.8	102.1	102.4	102.7	103.3	103.8	103.7	103.1	103.5	104.0
EU average	97.7	100.0	101.7	101.7	101.9	102.1	102.2	102.3	102.4	102.2	102.5	102.6	103.0	103.3	103.3	103.2	103.2	103.3

Source: *Eurostat Yearbook 1998,* Office for Official Publications of the European Communities

EUROPE 1998–99: A DEFINING YEAR

BY SEAN RICKARD

The year from May 1998, which started with so much promise – it will go down as one of the European Community's defining periods – drew to a close this summer in an atmosphere of disappointment and lost opportunities. History will remember this time in European affairs primarily for the launch of the single currency, but it was also a year of mixed economic success and a lack of clear leadership.

Meeting EMU convergence criteria

In May 1998 the European Union leaders formalized the creation of the euro monetary zone, made up of Austria, Belgium, Finland, France, Germany, the Republic of Ireland, Italy, Luxembourg, the Netherlands, Portugal, and Spain. In the event it was not the outer, periphery, Mediterranean nations that struggled to meet the convergence criteria for European Monetary Union (EMU) but embarrassingly the Germans, who had been so forceful in limiting the scope for political manipulation of the criteria. The financial markets shrugged off the sceptics' criticism: all 11 founders had demonstrated an impressive degree of determination and the currencies now locked together began to appreciate in the run-up to the launch of the euro in January 1999.

But convergence had not come without cost. In reducing inflation and government deficits to meet the criteria, economic growth across the prospective euro zone had slowed, thereby adding to already high levels of unemployment.

Were it not for the launch of the euro ... many of these developments would not have attracted adverse publicity.

Reforming agricultural and regional policies

Despite these observations, by the time the EU leaders met for their June 1998 summit they were assured of the euro's successful launch and felt confident enough to set an ambitious nine-month deadline for reforming the Community's agricultural and regional policies in order to prepare for the admission of Estonia, Poland, the Czech Republic, Hungary, Slovenia, and Cyprus in the early years of the new millennium.

The reforms were necessary because the applicant nations are all relatively poor by EU standards – GDP per capita being on average about half that for the EU as a whole. As poor nations they rely more heavily on agriculture for employment than the EU overall, and would contribute relatively little to the EU budget. If the Common Agricultural Policy (CAP) and regional policies remained unchanged the existing members of the EU would have to make large net payments to the newcomers. The solution to this dilemma was circulated in a Commission document entitled 'Agenda 2000'. In essence it proposed a reform of the CAP that would provide annual compensation payment to EU farmers in return for lowering their prices. As the applicants were not going to suffer any price cuts there was no question of compensation. Similarly, the complex regional structural policies that had been instrumental in helping to make a success of previous enlargements of the EU were to be reduced in scope and eligibility for funds made more rigorous. To add to the EU's difficulties the Germans, who contributed a massive 30 percent of the EU budget, were themselves now feeling the fiscal pressures of reunification and were demanding a more equitable sharing of the costs of running the EU.

By the autumn of 1998 GDP for the soon-to-be euro zone was growing at an annual rate of more than 3 percent. Despite, or because of, concerns and doubts regarding global market conditions following the dramatic setback to Asian growth, global investors pushed European stockmarkets upwards and also purchased the currencies of the new euro zone, pushing them to a high value against the dollar. In November the EU commenced ministerial-level negotiations with the five central European applicants and Cyprus. Officially 2002 remained the accession date but the negotiations were proceeding slowly and the likely date for entry was in danger of slipping.

Birth of the euro zone

By November, however, world attention was focusing on the impending launch of the euro, which started trading on 4 January 1999. On that day the euro zone, the world's second largest economy after the USA and the world's largest trading bloc, was born. With the arrival of the euro the eleven founder members ceded control of monetary policy to the European Central Bank (ECB). The Maastricht Treaty established the ECB as a highly independent central bank with the overriding objective of achieving price stability. The severe limits placed on the ECB's freedom of action were devised to convince doubting global financiers that the euro would be a sound currency untainted by political interference. Fiscal policy remained devolved but in truth the stability pact – embodied in the Amsterdam Treaty – left very little room for member state macroeconomic policies to deviate from tight fiscal stances. The constraints placed on the ECB and the macroeconomic policy in general for the euro zone were the price demanded by the Germans, in particular by Chancellor Kohl's redoubtable finance minister, Theo Waigel, for giving up the Deutschmark.

But by the launch of the euro the political landscape had changed. A new German government, which leaned more towards the old fiscal orthodoxy, was now in power and within days of the euro's launch Germany's new finance minister, Oskar Lafontaine, was extolling the virtue of increased government expenditure and exhorting the ECB to cut interest rates. The new German government was much more in tune with the French socialist government. The danger with this development was that the ensuing demands for more public expenditure and greater policy co-ordination between governments and the ECB came at the wrong time for the euro. The euro's overriding need was to build credibility – yet the new EU leaders were tending to undermine confidence.

(continued)

Growth forecasts revised down

The financial markets' reappraisal of the euro was also prompted by new reports from the Commission that revised downwards its forecasts for economic growth. The 'engine of Europe', the German economy, was faltering. Germany, it was becoming clear, was suffering more than had been anticipated from the slowdown in Asian growth and the collapse of the Russian economy owing to the loss of traditional export markets in these regions. As Germany slowed down, other nations were continuing to recover and on the euro zone's periphery smaller economies were growing much faster.

This was not the way it was supposed to be. EMU was supposed to aid economic convergence, and should eventually do so, but in the months following the launch of the euro, the markets appeared to lose some confidence in the ECB's ability to accommodate a euro zone with a sluggish core and a booming periphery with a single rate of interest. The markets' fear that this situation could put new strains on the 'stability pact' appeared confirmed when EU finance ministers gave Italy permission to loosen its tight fiscal stance previously agreed.

Were it not for the launch of the euro, upon which unrealistic expectations were heaped, many of these events would not have attracted adverse publicity. A falling currency and some loosening of fiscal policy are precisely the policies needed to generate recovery. The problem is that the European Union is having to address these issues whilst still in the stage of establishing the euro's credibility. Euro zone governments are now learning that this will take some years of fiscal constraint and ECB independence.

EU enlargement delayed

A disappointing year was added to by the outcome of the 'Agenda 2000' reforms. After 19 months of discussion the heads of governments at their Berlin Summit finally reached agreement in the early hours of 26 March. But the agreement was only achieved by weakening significant aspects of the Agenda 2000 reforms. An important opportunity to put in place necessary reforms had been missed. The CAP will continue to account for the lion's share of the EU's budget and regional policy reform has been curtailed. Just when the Community was going to need enhanced regional policies to help integrate the poorer members from the East, it lacked the political will to secure additional funds for the purpose. As a result, EU enlargement will now be delayed, possibly until 2005, and meanwhile the euro zone awaits German recovery.

Sean Rickard is lecturer at Cranfield Management School

Social Protection in the European Union

1995

Category	Austria	Belgium	Denmark	Finland	France	Germany	Ireland, Republic of	Italy	Luxembourg	Netherlands	Portugal	Spain	Sweden	UK	EU-14 average[1]
% Total Expenditure															
Sickness	3.9	4.6	3.5	4.0	3.0	6.9	5.6	0.9	2.9	7.1	2.9	5.5	4.9	3.7	4.6
Health	20.9	19.6	13.8	16.7	24.4	22.9	28.3	19.6	20.6	20.4	26.3	23.7	16.5	21.2	21.8
Disability	7.5	6.1	10.3	14.4	5.6	6.7	4.5	6.9	12.7	14.7	10.7	7.5	12.1	11.4	8.0
Old-age and survivors	46.7	39.8	36.6	31.8	40.7	40.8	24.9	62.7	43.2	35.5	38.6	44.1	36.6	38.0	42.4
Family and children	11.0	7.7	12.0	12.9	8.5	7.2	11.2	3.4	12.8	4.4	5.1	1.8	11.2	8.7	7.3
Unemployment	5.4	13.4	14.3	13.9	7.8	8.8	16.6	2.1	2.9	9.6	4.9	13.9	11.0	5.7	8.1
Housing	0.3	0.0	2.4	1.5	3.0	0.6	2.9	0.0	0.2	1.0	0.0	0.4	3.4	6.8	1.9
Social exclusion	1.1	2.5	4.3	2.0	1.6	2.1	1.8	0.0	1.4	2.2	0.4	0.4	3.0	1.0	1.6
Administration	2.0	4.5	2.8	2.8	3.8	3.7	4.1	3.1	2.8	3.8	4.8	2.5	1.4	3.5	3.4
Other	1.3	1.8	0.0	0.0	1.5	0.2	0.1	1.5	0.6	1.3	6.3	0.3	0.0	0.0	0.8
Total	100.0	100.0	100.0	100.0	100.0	100.0	100.0	100.0	100.0	100.0	100.0	100.0	100.0	100.0	100.0
% GDP															
Sickness	1.2	1.4	1.2	1.3	0.9	2.0	1.1	0.2	0.7	2.2	0.6	1.2	1.7	1.0	1.3
Health	6.2	5.8	4.8	5.5	7.5	6.7	5.6	4.8	5.2	6.4	5.4	5.2	5.9	5.8	6.2
Disability	2.2	1.8	3.5	4.7	1.7	2.0	0.9	1.7	3.2	4.7	2.2	1.6	4.3	3.1	2.3
Old-age and survivors	13.9	11.8	12.6	10.4	12.5	12.0	5.0	15.4	10.9	11.2	8.0	9.6	13.0	10.4	12.1
Family and children	3.3	2.3	4.1	4.2	2.6	2.1	2.2	0.8	3.2	1.4	1.1	0.4	4.0	2.4	2.1
Unemployment	1.6	4.0	4.9	4.6	2.4	2.6	3.3	0.5	0.7	3.0	1.0	3.0	3.9	1.5	2.3
Housing	0.1	0.0	0.8	0.5	0.9	0.2	0.6	0.0	0.0	0.3	0.0	0.1	1.2	1.9	0.6
Social exclusion	0.3	0.7	1.5	0.7	0.5	0.6	0.4	0.0	0.4	0.7	0.1	0.1	1.1	0.3	0.5
Administration	0.6	1.3	1.0	0.9	1.2	1.1	0.8	0.8	0.7	1.2	1.0	0.6	0.5	1.0	1.0
Other	0.4	0.5	0.0	0.0	0.5	0.1	0.0	0.4	0.1	0.4	1.3	0.1	0.0	0.0	0.2
Total	29.7	29.7	34.3	32.8	30.6	29.4	19.9	24.6	25.3	31.6	20.7	21.8	35.6	27.3	28.5

[1] EU-14 excludes Greece for which there is no breakdown by function.

Source: *Eurostat Yearbook 1997*, Office for Official Publications of the European Communities

Number of Hours Worked Per Week in the European Union

Number of hours usually worked per week by full-time employees.
(N/A = not available.)

Country	1986	1987	1988	1989	1990	1991	1992	1993	1994	1995	1996
Austria	40.8	40.6	40.4	40.3	40.1	40.1	40.1	40.1	40.2	39.3	40.0
Belgium	38.3	38.0	38.0	38.1	38.0	38.0	38.2	38.0	38.2	38.4	38.3
Denmark	40.6	39.8	39.8	39.1	39.0	38.4	38.8	38.8	39.1	39.0	38.7
Finland	N/A	N/A	N/A	38.5	38.4	38.3	38.3	38.3	38.4	38.6	38.7
France	39.5	39.8	39.9	39.9	39.6	39.7	39.7	39.8	39.9	39.9	39.8
Germany	40.8	40.7	40.5	40.3	39.9	39.8	39.7	39.5	39.5	39.7	40.0
Greece	40.3	40.3	40.4	40.0	40.2	40.3	40.5	40.6	40.5	40.3	40.4
Ireland, Republic of	40.6	40.5	40.5	40.5	40.4	40.4	40.4	40.1	40.0	40.2	40.4
Italy	38.7	38.7	38.6	38.6	38.6	38.7	38.5	38.5	38.5	38.4	38.6
Luxembourg	39.8	39.8	39.8	39.9	39.9	39.8	39.7	39.8	39.8	39.5	39.5
Netherlands	N/A	39.4	39.2	39.1	39.0	38.9	39.4	39.4	39.5	39.5	39.4
Portugal	42.3	42.3	42.3	42.0	41.9	41.5	41.3	41.2	41.2	41.2	41.2
Spain	N/A	41.1	40.9	40.7	40.7	40.5	40.6	40.6	40.5	40.7	40.6
Sweden	N/A	40.7	40.7	40.7	40.7	40.7	40.7	40.7	40.7	40.0	40.0
UK	43.2	43.2	43.7	43.6	43.7	43.4	43.4	43.4	43.7	43.9	43.9
EU average	N/A	40.6	40.7	40.6	40.4	40.3	40.3	40.2	40.3	40.3	40.4

Source: *Eurostat Yearbook 1997*, Office for Official Publications of the European Communities

Euro Conversion Rates for Participating Currencies

The conversion rates for the euro for the 11 participating currencies came into effect on 1 January 1999 as follows:

Currency	Units of national currency for 1 euro
Austrian schilling	13.7603
Belgian franc	40.3399
Deutschmark	1.95583
Dutch guilder	2.20371
Finnish markka	5.94573
French franc	6.55957
Irish punt	0.787564
Italian lira	1,936.27
Luxembourg franc	40.3399
Portuguese escudo	200.482
Spanish peseta	166.386

Source: European Central Bank

Exchange Rates for the Euro and Other Major Currencies

As of March 1999.

Currency	1999		
	January	February	March
Australian dollar	1.839	1.751	1.726
Canadian dollar	1.765	1.679	1.651
Danish krone	7.44	7.44	7.43
Greek drachma	323.6	322.0	322.5
Hong Kong dollar	8.99	8.68	8.43
Japanese yen	131.3	130.8	130.2
Korean won	1,362.5	1,330.2	1,336.2
Mexican peso	11.83	11.21	10.60
New Zealand dollar	2.159	2.062	2.045
Norwegian krone	8.65	8.65	8.51
Singapore dollar	1.950	1.905	1.881
Swedish krona	9.08	8.88	8.94
Swiss franc	1.605	1.598	1.595
Taiwan dollar	37.43	36.41	36.04
UK pound	0.703	0.689	0.671
US dollar	1.161	1.121	1.088

Source: European Central Bank

The Road to the Euro: Chronology

25 March 1957 The Treaties of Rome are signed, establishing the European Economic Community (EEC), and creating the Monetary Committee and the European Investment Bank.

1–2 December 1969 Summit in The Hague, the Netherlands, requests a report, under Pierre Werner (who later led the Christian Social Party in Luxembourg 1979–84), on the possibilities of developing the Community into an economic and monetary union (EMU), stipulating 1980 as target date for launch.

22 March 1971 The Council adopts the Werner Plan to strengthen coordination of economic policies. EEC Member States commit themselves to harmonize their budgetary policies and reduce the margins of fluctuation between their currencies.

10 April 1972 The six EEC countries agree to limit the margin of fluctuation between their currencies to 2.25 percent; they are soon joined by sterling, the Irish punt, and Danish and Norwegian kroner.

6–7 July 1978 The European Council meeting in Bremen, Germany, agrees the French-German proposal to launch the European Monetary System (EMS).

13 March 1979 The European Monetary System comes into force and the Exchange Rate Mechanism (ERM) is set up with eight participating member states (the UK stays outside) required to maintain their currencies within 2.25 percent fluctuation margins. The Spanish peseta, Italian lira, Portuguese escudo, and sterling are allowed a 'broad band' of 6 percent. The European currency unit (ECU) as a weighted average of all European currencies is introduced.

(continued)

The Road to the Euro: Chronology (*continued*)

10 June 1985 Committee of Governors of Central Banks of Member States adopts measures designed to strengthen EMS.

10 June 1987 The Single European Act comes into force. It formalizes the single market programme.

27–28 June 1988 European Council in Hanover, Germany appoints a committee (chaired by the president of the European Commission, Jacques Delors) to outline 'concrete stages' leading to economic and monetary union.

19 June 1989 Spanish peseta joins ERM on with 6 percent fluctuation bands.

26–27 June 1989 Madrid European Council decides to liberalize capital movements in Europe. Heads of state or government approve the Delors Report, and decide to begin the first stage of EMU 1 July 1990.

1 July 1990 The first phase of EMU comes into force. It involves the removal of most of the remaining restrictions on capital movements, more intensive cooperation between central banks, and increased coordination of economic policies.

6 October 1990 The UK joins ERM with 6 percent bands, at 2.95 Deutschmarks per pound sterling.

9–10 December 1991 A summit of European Community heads of government in Maastricht, the Netherlands, reaches agreement on a draft treaty on European union – known as the Maastricht Treaty – which calls for closer economic and political union. Britain obtains the right to abstain from social legislation and a single currency. The treaty requires completion of EMU and the introduction of the single European currency, the ecu, by 1999 at the latest.

4 April 1992 Portuguese escudo joins ERM with 6 percent bands.

16–17 September 1992 Speculators attack the weaker ERM currencies; sterling, the lira, and the peseta all fall below their ERM floors. 'Black Wednesday' in the UK; sterling is withdrawn from the ERM and allowed to 'float', and the base rate returns to 12 percent (cut to 9 percent on 22 September). The Italian lira is suspended from the ERM and the Spanish peseta is devalued by 5 percent.

1 January 1993 The single market establishing the free movement of capital enters into force.

2 August 1993 Following speculative pressure on currencies in the ERM, the French franc dips below the ERM floor and currencies are allowed to fluctuate within a broad band of 15 percent on either side of central rates.

1 November 1993 The Treaty on European Union enters into force.

1 January 1994 Stage II of EMU begins and the European Monetary Institute (EMI) is established. Final deadline of 1 January 1999 is agreed for the beginning of Stage III of EMU, regardless of the number of member states qualifying and of the general economic climate.

31 May 1995 The European Commission adopts a Green Paper on 'Practical Arrangements for the Introduction of the Single Currency'.

15–16 December 1995 The European Council meeting in Madrid, Spain names the European currency unit 'euro' and confirms the EMI plan envisaging conversion to the euro over a four-year timetable, with its introduction on 1 January 1999.

October 1996 Finnish markka joins ERM with 15 percent fluctuation band. The Italian lira re-enters ERM in November.

13 December 1996 A European Council meeting summit in Dublin, Ireland, makes significant progress towards the introduction of a single currency.

January 1997 EMI specifies regulatory and organizational framework for the European Central Bank and the European System of Banks.

17 June 1997 The draft Amsterdam Treaty is agreed, including resolution on ERM II. Unemployment is a large issue in the talks.

27 October 1997 In a speech before Parliament, British chancellor of the exchequer Gordon Brown says that the government does not plan to join the economic and monetary union (EMU) until at least 2002.

25 March 1998 The European Commission officially recommends that all 11 applicant EU countries – Austria,Belgium, Finland, France, Germany, Ireland, Italy, Luxembourg, the Netherlands, Portugal, and Spain – qualify for monetary union. Of the other four EU countries, Greece would not meet the economic criteria in time, and Britain, Denmark, and Sweden had already chosen not to participate in EMU from the outset.

2 May 1998 EMU commences, six months ahead of schedule. European Union heads of state formalize the creation of the euro zone and confirm the 11 countries that qualify for EMU, fix bilateral conversion rates, and agree to maintain their economies in line with the Maastricht convergence criteria. A compromise is reached over a long-standing dispute over who will head the new European Central Bank (ECB): Wim Duisenberg of the Netherlands is appointed to the bank's presidency for the full eight years, but will voluntarily bow to the French candidate, Jean-Claude Trichet, halfway through the term, in 2002.

July 1998 London and Frankfurt stock exchanges agree a strategic alliance, laying the foundations for a pan-European stock exchange.

3 December 1998 Euroland central banks (except Italy) cut their interest rates to 3 percent, in preparation for the launch of the euro. European central bank governors fix euro conversion rates.

1 January 1999 The single European currency, the euro, is launched in 11 participating EU countries. It performs strongly when trading begins on 4 January, but subsequently falters.

The next steps

1 January 1999 –1 January 2002 Changeover to the euro by the banking and finance industry to take place.

1 January 2002 European System of Central Banks (ESCB) to start circulation of euro banknotes; member states to start circulation of euro coins and complete the changeover to the euro in public administration.

1 July 2002 Member states and the ESCB will cancel the legal-tender status of national banknotes and coins.

Economic Organizations

African Development Bank (ADB)

Bank founded in 1964 by the Organization of African Unity to promote and finance economic development across the African continent. Its regional members are: Algeria, Angola, Benin, Botswana, Burkina Faso, Burundi, Cameroon, Cape Verde, Central African Republic, Chad, Comoros, Congo, Côte d'Ivoire, Democratic Republic of Congo, Djibouti, Egypt, Equatorial Guinea, Eritrea, Ethiopia, Gabon, Gambia, Ghana, Guinea, Guinea Bissau, Kenya, Lesotho, Liberia, Libya, Madagascar, Malawi, Mali, Mauritania, Mauritius, Morocco, Mozambique, Namibia, Niger, Nigeria, Rwanda, São Tomé and Príncipe, Senegal, Seychelles, Sierra Leone, Somalia, South Africa, Sudan, Swaziland, Tanzania, Togo, Tunisia, Uganda, Zambia, Zimbabwe. Non-regional members are: Argentina, Austria, Belgium, Brazil, Canada, China, Denmark, Finland, France, Germany, India, Italy, Japan, Korea, Kuwait, Netherlands, Norway, Portugal, Saudi Arabia, Spain, Sweden, Switzerland, UK, USA. Address: Rue Joseph Anoma 01 BP 1387, Abidjan 01, Côte d'Ivoire; phone: (225) 204444; fax: (225) 204909; Web site: www.afdb.org/

Arab Monetary Fund (AMF)

Money reserve established in 1976 by 20 Arab states to provide a mechanism for promoting greater stability in exchange rates and to coordinate Arab economic and monetary policies. It operates mainly by regulating petrodollars within the Arab community to make member countries less dependent on the West for the handling of their surplus money. Its members are: Algeria, Bahrain, Djibouti, Egypt, Iraq, Jordan, Kuwait, Lebanon, Libya, Mauritania, Morocco, Oman, Palestine, Qatar, Saudi Arabia, Somalia, Sudan, Syria, Tunisia, United Arab Emirates, Yemen, and the Palestine Liberation Organization. Address: PO Box 2818, Abu Dhabi, United Arab Emirates; phone: (971 2) 215000; fax: (971 2) 326454; Web site: www.imf.org/external/np/sec/decdo/amf.htm

Asian Development Bank (ADB)

Bank founded in 1966 to stimulate growth in Asia and the Far East by administering direct loans and technical assistance. Its regional members are: Afghanistan, Australia, Bangladesh, Bhutan, Cambodia, China, Cook Islands, Fiji Islands, Hong Kong (China), India, Indonesia, Japan, Kazakhstan, Kiribati, Krygyzstan, Laos, Malaysia, Maldives, Marshall Islands, Micronesia, Mongolia, Myanmar, Nauru, Nepal, New Zealand, Pakistan, Papua New Guinea, Philippines, Samoa, Singapore, Solomon Islands, South Korea, Sri Lanka, Tajikistan, Taipei (China), Thailand, Tonga, Tuvalu, Uzbekistan, Vanuatu, Vietnam. Its non-regional members are: Austria, Belgium, Canada, Denmark, Finland, France, Germany, Italy, Netherlands, Norway, Spain, Sweden, Switzerland, Turkey, UK, USA. Address: PO Box 789, 0980 Manila, Philippines; phone (632) 632 4444; fax: (632) 636 2444; Web site: www.adb.org/mainpage.asp

Asia-Pacific Economic Cooperation (APEC)

Trade group of Pacific Asian countries, formed in 1989 to promote multilateral trade and economic cooperation between member states. Its members are Australia, Brunei, Canada, Chile, China, Hong Kong, Indonesia, Japan, Malaysia, Mexico, New Zealand, Papua New Guinea, Peru, the Philippines, Singapore, South Korea, Thailand, Taiwan, and the USA. Address: Ministry of Trade and Industry, 100 High Street 09-01, The Treasury, Singapore 179434; phone: (65) 332 7249; fax: (65) 334 8135; Web site: www.apecsec.org.sg

Bank for International Settlements (BIS)

Organization established in 1930 whose function is to promote cooperation between central banks and to facilitate international financial settlements; it is also a centre for economic and monetary research. Central banks of the main trading states are members, each providing a director to the board, which meets at least ten times a year. The Bank was largely superseded by the International Monetary Fund. Its liaising role among central banks is its primary function today. Address: Centralbahnplatz 2, CH-4002 Basle, Switzerland; phone: (41 61) 280 8080; fax: (41 61) 280 9100; Web site: www.bis.org/

Colombo Plan

Plan for cooperative economic and social development in Asia and the Pacific, established in 1950. Its member countries are Afghanistan, Australia, Bangladesh, Bhutan, Cambodia, Fiji Islands, India, Indonesia, Iran, Japan, South Korea, Laos, Malaysia, the Maldives, Myanmar, Nepal, New Zealand, Pakistan, Papua New Guinea, the Philippines, Singapore, Sri Lanka, Thailand, and the USA. Address: 12 Melbourne Avenue, PO Box 596, Colombo 4, Sri Lanka; phone: (94 1) 581813; fax: (94 1) 581754; Web site: www.tcol.co.uk/comorg/colplan.htm

Communauté Economique des Etats de l'Afrique Centrale (CEEAC)/Economic Community of Central African States

Organization formed in 1983 to foster economic cooperation between member states, which are Burundi, Cameroon, the Central African Republic, Chad, the Republic of the Congo, Equatorial Guinea, Gabon, Rwanda, São Tomé and Príncipe, and the Democratic Republic of Congo (formerly Zaire). Angola has observer status. The Community's headquarters are in Libreville, Gabon.

Communauté Economique des Etats de l'Afrique de l'Ouest/Economic Community of West African States (ECOWAS)

Organization promoting economic cooperation and development, established in 1975 by the Treaty of Lagos. Its members are Benin, Burkina Faso, Cape Verde, Côte d'Ivoire, the Gambia, Ghana, Guinea, Guinea-Bissau, Liberia, Mali, Mauritania, Niger, Nigeria, Senegal, Sierra Leone, and Togo. Address: 60 Yakubu Gowon Crescent, Abuja, Nigeria; phone (9) 234 7647; fax: (9) 234 7646.

Economic Cooperation Organization (ECO)

Islamic regional grouping formed in 1985 by Iran, Pakistan, and Turkey to reduce customs tariffs and promote commerce, with the aim of eventual customs union. In 1992 the newly independent republics of Azerbaijan, Kyrgyzstan, Tajikistan, Turkmenistan, and Uzbekistan were admitted into the ECO. Address: 1 Golbou Street, Kamranieh, Tehran, Iran; phone: (21) 283 1731; fax: (21) 283 1732; e-mail: eco.org@neda.net.

European Bank for Reconstruction and Development (EBRD)

International bank established in 1991, with an initial capital of 10 billion European Currency Units (ECUs), to assist the economic reconstruction of Central and Eastern Europe. The Bank aims to help Central and Eastern European countries to implement structural and sectoral economic reform, including demonopolization, decentralization, and privatization. The EBRD has 60 members: 58 countries, including 26

countries in Central and Eastern Europe and the Commonwealth of Independent States, the European Union, and the European Investment Bank. Each member appoints a Governor and an alternate. The Board of Governors delegates power to a Board of Directors, responsible for the direction of the general operations of the Bank. The president is elected by the Board of Governors. The Bank's headquarters are in London, UK. Address: 1 Exchange Square, London EC2A 2JN, UK; phone: (0171) 338 6000; fax: (0171) 338 6100; Web site: www.ebrd.com/

European Free Trade Association (EFTA)

Organization established in 1960 consisting of Iceland, Norway, Switzerland, and Liechtenstein (from 1991), previously a nonvoting associate member. There are no import duties between members. Of the original EFTA members, the UK and Denmark left in 1972 to join the European Community (EC), as did Portugal in 1985; Austria, Finland, and Sweden joined the EC's successor, the European Union, in 1995. In 1973 the EC signed agreements with EFTA members, setting up a free-trade area of over 300 million consumers. Trade between the two groups amounted to over half of total EFTA trade. A further pact signed in 1991 between the EC and EFTA provided for a European Economic Area (EEA), allowing EFTA greater access to the EC market by ending many restrictions. The EEA came into effect in January 1994. Address: 9–11 rue de Varembé, 1211 Geneva 20, Switzerland; phone: (41 22) 749 1111; fax: (41 22) 733 9291; Web site: www.efta.int/structure/main/index.html

Inter-American Development Bank (IDB)

Bank founded in 1959, at the instigation of the Organization of American States, to finance economic and social development, particularly in the less wealthy regions of the Americas. Its 46 members include the states of Central and Southern America, the Caribbean, and the USA, as well as Austria, Belgium, Canada, Denmark, Finland, France, Germany, Israel, Italy, Japan, the Netherlands, Norway, Portugal, Spain, Sweden, Switzerland, and the UK. Address: 1300 New York Avenue, NW, Washington DC 20577, USA; phone: (202) 623 1000; Web site: www.iabd.org/

International Monetary Fund (IMF)

Specialized agency of the United Nations with its headquarters in Washington, DC, established under the 1944 Bretton Woods agreement and operational since 1947. It seeks to promote international monetary cooperation and the growth of world trade, and to smooth multilateral payment arrangements among member states. IMF standby loans are available to members in balance-of-payments difficulties (the amount being governed by the member's quota), usually on the basis that the country must agree to take certain corrective measures. The IMF also operates other drawing facilities, including several designed to provide preferential credit to developing countries with liquidity problems. Having previously operated in US dollars linked to gold, since 1972 the IMF has used the special drawing right (SDR) as its standard unit of account, valued in terms of a weighted 'basket' of currencies. Since 1971, IMF rules have been progressively adapted to floating exchange rates. Address (headquarters): 700 19th Street, NW, Washington DC 20431; phone: (202) 623 7000; fax: (202) 623 4661; Web site: www.imf.org

Asociación Latino-Americana de Integración (ALADI)/Latin American Integration Association (LAIA)

Organization established to create a common market in Latin America. To promote trade, it applies tariff reductions preferentially on the basis of the different stages of economic development that individual member countries have reached. Formed in 1980 to replace the Latin American Free Trade Association, it has 11 members: Argentina, Bolivia, Brazil, Chile, Colombia, Ecuador, Mexico, Paraguay, Peru, Uruguay, and Venezuela. Address: Cebollati 1461, Montevideo, Uruguay; phone: (598) 401 7278; fax: (598) 409 4372; Web site: www.aladi.org

Mercado Comun del Cono Sur (Mercosur)/Southern Cone Common Market

Free-trade organization, founded in 1991 on the signing of the Asunción Treaty by Argentina, Brazil, Paraguay, and Uruguay, and formally inaugurated on 1 January 1995. With a GNP of $800,000 million and a population of more than 190 million, Mercosur constitutes the world's fourth-largest free-trade bloc after the European Economic Area, the North American Free Trade Area, and the Asia-Pacific Economic Cooperation. Mercosur's headquarters are in Montevideo, Uruguay. Web site: www.mercosur.com

North American Free Trade Agreement (NAFTA)

Trade agreement between the USA, Canada, and Mexico, agreed in August 1992 and effective from January 1994. The first trade pact of its kind to link two highly-industrialized countries to a developing one, it created a free market of 360 million people, with a total GDP of $6.45 trillion. Tariffs were to be progressively eliminated over a 10–15 year period and investment into low-wage Mexico by Canada and the USA progressively increased. Chile was invited to join in 1994, but its entry was delayed. Address: for information contact The Trade Development Center, phone: 1-800-872 8723; Web site: www.itaiep.doc.gov/nafta/nafta2.htm

Organization for Economic Cooperation and Development (OECD)

International organization of 30 industrialized countries that provides a forum for discussion and coordination of member states' economic and social policies. Founded in 1961, the OECD superseded the Organization for European Economic Cooperation, which had been established in 1948 to implement the Marshall Plan. The Commission of the European Union also participates in the OECD's work. The OECD's subsidiary bodies include the International Energy Agency which was set up in 1974 in the face of a world oil crisis. The scope of the OECD also includes development aid. Members are: Australia, Austria, Belgium, Canada, the Czech Republic, Denmark, Finland, France, Germany, Greece, Iceland, the Republic of Ireland, Italy, Japan, Luxembourg, Mexico, the Netherlands, New Zealand, Norway, Portugal, Spain, Sweden, Switzerland, Turkey, the UK, and the USA; Hungary, Poland, and the Slovak Republic joined in 1996, and South Korea in 1997. The headquarters are in Paris, France. Address (headquarters): 2, rue André-Pascal, 75775 Paris Cedex 16, France; Web site: www.oecd.org/

Organization of Arab Petroleum Exporting Countries (OAPEC)

Body established in 1968 to safeguard the interests of its members and encourage economic cooperation within the petroleum industry. Its members are Algeria, Bahrain, Egypt, Iraq, Kuwait, Libya, Qatar, Saudi Arabia, Syria, and the United Arab Emirates. Address: PO Box 20501, Safat 13066, Kuwait City, Kuwait; phone: (965) 484 4500; fax: (965) 481 5747; Web site: www.kuwait.net/~oapec/

Organization of Petroleum Exporting Countries (OPEC)

Body established in 1960 to coordinate price and supply policies of oil-producing states. Its concerted action in raising prices in the 1970s triggered worldwide recession but also lessened demand so that its influence was reduced by the mid-1980s. OPEC members in 1998 were: Algeria, Indonesia, Iran, Iraq, Kuwait, Libya, Nigeria, Qatar, Saudi Arabia, the United Arab Emirates, and Venezuela.

Address: Obere Donaustrasse 93, A-1020 Vienna, Austria; phone: (43 1) 211 120; fax: (43 1) 2149 827; Web site: www.opec.org

Common Market for Eastern and Southern African Countries (COMESA)

Organization established in 1981 as the Preferential Trade Area of Eastern and Southern African States (PTA) with the objective of increasing economic and commercial cooperation between member states, harmonizing tariffs, and reducing trade barriers. The PTA developed into a common market in 1993. Its members are: Angola, Burundi, Comoros, Democratic Republic of Congo, Eritrea, Ethiopia, Kenya, Lesotho, Madagascar, Malawi, Mauritius, Mozambique, Namibia, Rwanda, Sudan, Swaziland, Tanzania, Uganda, Zambia, and Zimbabwe. Address: COMESA Centre, Ben Bella Road, PO Box 30051, Lusaka, Zambia; phone: (260 1) 229726; fax: (260 1) 225107; Web site: www.comesa.org

Southern African Development Community (SADC)

Formerly (to 1992) Southern African Development Coordination Conference (SADCC). Established in April 1980, SADCC's original aim was to promote regional independence from the economic dominance of the Republic of South Africa. With the adoption of the new name, the organization recast its objective as increased regional coordination and cooperation for mutual benefit. The community comprises 14 member states. Address: Private Bag 0095, Gaborone, Botswana; phone: (267) 351863; fax: (267) 372848; Web site: www.mbendi.co.za/orsodc.htm

South Asian Association for Regional Cooperation (SAARC)

Organization established in 1985 by India, Pakistan, Bangladesh, Nepal, Sri Lanka, Bhutan, and the Maldives to cover agriculture, telecommunications, health, population, sports, art, and culture. In 1993 a preferential trade agreement was adopted to reduce tariffs on intra-regional trade. SAARC's headquarters are in Kathmandu, Nepal. Web site: www.positiveindia.com/saarc.html

World Bank

Popular name for the International Bank for Reconstruction and Development (IBRD), a specialized agency of the United Nations that borrows in the commercial market and lends on commercial terms. It was established in 1945 under the 1944 Bretton Woods agreement, which also created the International Monetary Fund. The International Development Association is an arm of the World Bank. Control of the bank is vested in a board of executives representing national governments, whose votes are apportioned according to the amount they have funded the bank. Thus, the USA has nearly 20 percent of the vote and always appoints the board's president. The World Bank is based in Washington DC. Web site: www.worldbank.org

World Trade Organization (WTO)

World trade monitoring body established in January 1995, on approval of the Final Act of the Uruguay round of the General Agreement on Tariffs and Trade (GATT). Under the Final Act, the WTO, a permanent trading body with a status commensurate with that of the International Monetary Fund or the World Bank, effectively replaced GATT. The WTO monitors agreements to reduce barriers to trade, such as tariffs, subsidies, quotas, and regulations which discriminate against imported products. All members of GATT were automatically to become members of the WTO on their parliaments' ratification of the Uruguay round; new members, without exception, would have to meet the criteria established by the Uruguay round. Address: 154 rue de la Lausanne, 1211 Geneva 21, Switzerland; Web site: www.wto.org

UK Economy Overview

Balance of Payments of the UK

(In millions of pounds.)

	1988	1989	1990	1991	1992	1993	1994	1995	1996	1997
Trade in goods and services										
goods	−21,553	−24,724	−18,707	−10,223	−13,050	−13,319	−11,091	−11,724	−13,086	−11,792
services	4,330	3,917	4,010	4,471	5,674	6,623	6,528	8,915	8,897	11,160
net	−17,223	−20,807	−14,697	−5,752	−7,376	−6,696	−4,563	−2,809	−4,189	−632
Income										
compensation of employees	−64	−138	−110	−63	−49	35	−170	−296	93	83
investment income	1,355	74	−448	−1,890	2,164	650	7,940	6,272	8,018	12,085
net	1,291	−64	−558	−1,953	2,115	685	7,770	5,976	8,111	12,168
Current transfers										
central government	2,934	2,869	2,299	3,528	748	1,150	213	50	1,698	1,287
other sectors	−4,539	−5,489	−6,557	−4,197	−5,569	−5,757	−4,878	−6,962	−6,220	−4,817
net	−1,605	−2,620	−4,258	−669	−4,821	−4,607	−4,665	−6,912	−4,522	−3,530
Current account balance	−17,537	−23,491	−19,513	−8,374	−10,082	−10,618	−1,458	−3,745	−600	8,006
Capital account balance	235	270	497	290	421	309	33	534	736	262
Financial account										
direct investment	−8,859	−2,891	7,978	27	−1,848	−7,569	−16,105	−15,229	−5,954	−13,087
portfolio investment	18,501	−20,656	−2,501	−21,374	−19,312	−61,157	55,020	−2,109	−15,626	−22,368
other investment	8,254	37,131	12,128	34,016	25,469	78,695	−44,988	18,075	22,851	24,986
reserve assets	−2,761	5,440	−76	−2,679	1,407	−698	−1,045	200	510	2,357
Financial account balance	15,135	19,024	17,529	9,990	5,716	9,271	−7,118	937	1,781	−8,112
Net errors and omissions	2,167	4,197	1,487	−1,906	3,945	1,038	8,543	2,274	−1,917	−156

Source: *United Kingdom Balance of Payments. The Pink Book 1998,* © Crown copyright 1998

Government Income and Expenditure in the UK

(– = not applicable. In millions of pounds.)

Item	1990	1991	1992	1993	1994	1995	1996	1997
Resources								
Balance of primary incomes, gross	60,617	71,766	71,480	72,628	77,415	80,532	85,518	93,736
Current taxes								
current taxes on income	79,903	81,428	80,222	78,275	85,344	95,045	99,292	107,390
other current taxes	13,231	10,496	10,299	10,551	11,140	11,937	12,795	13,696
Total	93,134	91,924	90,521	88,826	96,484	106,982	112,087	121,086
Social contributions								
employers' actual social contributions	21,251	22,573	23,185	24,615	25,000	26,141	27,580	29,633
employees' actual social contributions	15,276	16,029	16,525	17,235	19,649	21,091	21,700	23,827
actual social contributions by self- and non-employed persons	1,177	1,206	1,281	1,472	1,469	1,541	1,771	1,433
Actual social contributions total	37,704	39,808	40,991	43,322	46,118	48,773	51,051	54,893
imputed social contributions	3,966	4,943	5,426	5,397	5,419	5,279	5,300	5,587
Social contributions total	41,670	44,751	46,417	48,719	51,537	54,052	56,351	60,480
Other current transfers								
non-life insurance claims	314	382	408	361	340	377	371	352
current transfers within general goverment	39,290	48,859	54,527	55,891	57,736	58,587	59,458	60,064
current international cooperation	1,752	4,616	1,907	2,558	1,752	1,233	2,424	1,739
current international cooperation from institutions of the EC	1,714	2,506	1,898	2,558	1,752	1,233	2,424	1,739
miscellaneous current transfers from sectors other than general government	222	353	178	296	420	469	429	496
Total other current transfers								
from general government	39,290	48,859	54,527	55,891	57,736	58,587	59,458	60,064
from other sectors	2,288	5,351	2,493	3,215	2,512	2,079	3,224	2,587
Total	41,578	54,210	57,020	59,106	60,248	60,666	62,682	62,651
RESOURCES TOTAL	236,999	262,651	265,438	269,279	285,684	302,232	316,638	337,953
Uses								
Social benefits other than social transfers in kind	65,999	81,753	94,766	102,585	106,187	109,877	112,568	115,791
Other current transfers								
net non-life insurance premiums	314	382	408	361	340	377	371	352
current transfers within general government	39,290	48,859	54,527	55,891	57,736	58,587	59,458	60,064
current international cooperation	1,374	1,677	1,931	1,774	1,825	2,018	1,598	1,544
current international cooperation to institutions of the EC	–	–	–	2	7	8	8	31
miscellaneous current transfers to sectors other than general government	4,561	4,965	5,096	9,055	10,760	11,369	13,386	14,347
GNP based fourth own resource	1	813	914	1,558	2,071	1,826	2,454	2,458
Total other current transfers								
from general government	39,290	48,859	54,527	55,891	57,736	58,587	59,458	60,064
from other sectors	6,249	7,024	7,435	11,190	12,925	13,764	15,355	16,243
Total	45,539	55,883	61,962	67,081	70,661	72,351	74,813	76,307
Disposable income, gross	125,461	125,015	108,710	99,613	108,836	120,004	129,257	145,855
USES TOTAL	236,999	262,651	265,438	269,279	285,684	302,232	316,638	337,953
After deduction of fixed capital consumption	–8,253	–8,203	–7,756	–7,576	–7,711	–8,368	–8,952	–9,522
Disposable income, net	117,208	116,812	100,954	92,037	101,125	111,636	120,305	136,333

Source: *United Kingdom National Accounts 1998*, © Crown copyright 1998

Government Expenditure as a Percentage of GDP in the UK

(– = not applicable.)

Category	1987–88	1989–90	1991–92	1992–93	1993–94	1994–95	1995–96	1996–97	1997–98 (est)
Defence[1]	4.4	4.0	3.9	3.8	3.6	3.3	3.0	2.8	2.7
International development assistance and other international services	0.5	0.5	0.5	0.6	0.5	0.5	0.5	0.4	0.4
Agriculture, fisheries, food, and forestry	0.6	0.4	0.5	0.5	0.6	0.5	0.6	0.8	0.7
Trade, industry, energy, employment, and training	1.6	1.6	1.7	1.7	1.7	1.5	1.4	1.2	1.1
Transport	1.3	1.3	1.6	1.8	1.6	1.5	1.2	1.2	1.1
Housing	1.0	1.0	1.0	1.0	0.8	0.8	0.7	0.5	0.4
Other environmental services	1.3	1.3	1.4	1.5	1.3	1.4	1.4	1.3	1.2
Law, order, and protective services	1.9	2.0	2.2	2.3	2.3	2.3	2.2	2.2	2.1
Education	4.8	4.8	5.0	5.2	5.2	5.2	5.0	4.9	4.6
Culture, media, and sport	0.4	0.4	0.4	0.4	0.4	0.4	0.4	0.4	0.3
Health and personal social services	5.7	5.7	6.4	6.7	6.7	6.8	6.8	6.7	6.7
Social security	11.4	10.2	12.1	13.1	13.6	13.1	13.1	12.9	12.4
Central administration and associated expenditure[2]	1.3	1.3	0.8	1.1	1.1	0.9	1.2	0.9	0.8
Total expenditure on services	36.1	34.5	37.7	39.7	39.5	38.2	37.5	36.2	34.6
General government net debt interest	2.8	2.3	1.9	2.1	2.3	2.6	2.8	2.9	3.0
Other accounting adjustments	1.5	1.5	1.4	1.6	1.6	1.9	2.0	1.9	1.9
Allowance for shortfall	–	–	–	–	–	–	–	–0.1	–0.2
General government interest and dividend receipts	1.4	1.4	1.0	0.9	0.8	0.8	0.8	0.7	0.6
National Lottery	–	–	–	–	–	–	–	–	0.1
Privatization proceeds	–1.2	–0.8	–1.4	–1.3	–0.9	–0.9	–0.3	–0.6	–0.2
General government expenditure	40.6	38.9	40.6	42.9	43.2	42.5	42.7	41.1	39.8

1 The items for defence for 1990–91 and 1991–92 are net of other governments' contributions to the cost of the Gulf conflict. Figures for 1996–97 and 1997–98 include receipts from the sale of Ministry of Defence married quarters.
2 Includes contributions to the European Communities and activities required for the general maintenance of government such as tax collection and the registration of population.

Source: *Public Expenditure: Statistical Analyses 1998–99*,

National and Domestic Product of the UK

Main aggregates	1990	1991	1992	1993	1994	1995	1996	1997
Indices (1995 = 100)								
Values at current prices								
gross domestic product at current market prices ('money GDP')[1]	77.8	81.8	85.1	89.5	94.9	100.0	105.9	112.5
gross value added at current basic prices	78.8	82.3	85.8	90.2	95.3	100.0	106.1	112.2
Values at 1995 prices								
gross domestic product at 1995 market prices	92.4	91.0	91.1	93.2	97.3	100.0	102.6	106.1
gross value added at 1995 basic prices	92.0	90.9	91.1	93.2	97.4	100.0	102.5	106.0
gross national disposable income at 1995 market prices[1]	92.0	91.4	91.9	93.9	98.6	100.0	103.4	108.5
Prices								
implied deflator of gross domestic product at market prices[1]	84.2	89.9	93.5	96.1	97.5	100.0	103.3	106.1
Values at Current Prices (£ millions)								
Gross measures, before deduction of fixed capital consumption at current market prices								
gross domestic product at current market prices	554,486	582,946	606,582	637,817	676,036	712,548	754,601	801,972
employment, property, and entrepreneurial income from abroad	–558	–1,953	2,115	685	7,770	5,976	8,111	12,168
subsidies (receipts) less taxes (payments) on production from/to abroad	–5,138	–3,512	–4,253	–4,510	–3,063	–4,927	–3,888	–2,605
gross national income at current market prices	548,790	577,481	604,444	633,992	680,743	713,597	758,824	811,535
current transfers from abroad	889	2,849	–562	–98	–1,605	–1,987	–636	–924
gross national disposable income at current market prices	549,679	580,330	603,882	633,894	679,138	711,610	758,188	810,611

(continued)

National and Domestic Product of the UK (*continued*)

Main aggregates	1990	1991	1992	1993	1994	1995	1996	1997
Values at 1995 Prices (£ millions)								
Gross measures, before deduction of fixed capital consumption at 1995 market prices								
gross domestic product at 1995 market prices	658,480	648,639	648,975	664,018	693,177	712,548	730,767	756,144
terms of trade effect	2,245	4,284	7,303	8,058	4,836	–	2,182	8,550
real gross domestic income	660,726	652,922	656,278	672,076	698,013	712,548	732,949	764,694
real employment, property, and entrepreneurial income from the rest of the world	–684	–2,207	2,288	721	8,024	5,976	7,884	11,601
subsidies (receipts) less taxes (payments) on production from/to abroad	–6,720	–3,580	–4,097	–4,795	–2,896	–4,927	–4,649	–3,334
gross national income at 1995 market prices	653,322	647,135	654,469	668,002	703,141	713,582	736,184	772,963
real current transfers from the rest of the world (receipts less payments)	1,040	3,206	–620	–102	–1,662	–1,987	–622	–886
gross national disposable income at 1995 market prices	654,408	650,425	653,865	667,926	701,479	711,610	735,562	772,075

[1] Expenditure based, 'total home costs per unit of output'.

Source: *Annual Abstract of Statistics 1999*, © Crown copyright 1999

Reserve Assets of the UK

(In millions of pounds. N/A = not available; – = not applicable.)

Year	Net debits								Gross assets						
				Level of reserves					Foreign exchange holdings by instrument						
									Currency and deposits			Securities			
	Drawings on (+) or in addition to (–) official reserves	Revaluation and other changes	Changes in level[1]	Total	Gold	IMF special drawing rights	Position in the IMF[2]	Foreign exchange holdings	Total	with MAs	with banks	Total	Bonds and notes	Money market instruments	Other claims
1992	1,407	–5,273	–3,869	27,494	3,149	356	1,325	–	–	–	–	22,513	22,513	–	–
1993	–698	–849	–1,549	29,043	3,084	195	1,265	–	–	–	–	23,407	23,407	–	–
1994	–1,046	2,027	984	28,059	3,397	297	1,212	–	–	–	–	24,577	24,577	–	–
1995	200	–3,900	–3,702	31,761	4,610	267	1,615	25,269	5,714	3,473	2,241	19,554	16,986	2,568	–
1996	509	3,923	4,432	27,329	4,006	209	1,430	21,684	5,919	2,858	3,061	15,765	14,059	1,706	–
1997	2,361	2,100	4,480	22,849	3,218	286	1,793	17,552	5,949	3,015	2,934	11,603	10,640	963	–
1998	163	N/A	N/A	23,347	N/A	N/A	N/A	N/A	N/A	N/A	N/A	N/A	N/A	N/A	N/A

[1] The difference between the December 1998 and January 1999 level of reserves will be at least partly due to the effect of a partial revaluation arising from the process of euro conversion.

[2] Figure includes the UK contribution to the General Arrangements to Borrow.

Source: *Financial Statistics*, No. 442, February 1999, © Crown copyright 1999

Public Expenditure on Overseas Aid in the UK

(In millions of pounds.)

Expenditure	1989	1990	1991	1992	1993	1994	1995	1996
Bilateral								
Project aid								
Department for International Development, excluding Aid and Trade Provision	178.0	225.6	146.6	129.4	95.0	114.8	107.7	106.9
Aid and Trade Provision (ATP)	51.7	74.3	113.0	77.2	68.9	82.9	49.0	60.4
Commonwealth Development Corporation	150.7	136.8	159.7	168.4	217.8	227.8	273.9	225.4
Total	380.5	436.8	419.3	375.0	381.7	425.4	430.6	392.7
Non-project aid	275.9	151.3	256.2	309.5	210.2	370.9	257.1	256.8
Technical cooperation	407.2	425.6	528.9	528.5	530.1	544.1	618.9	665.5
Administrative costs	65.7	56.1	57.0	61.7	66.6	71.3	74.1	90.4
Bilateral total	1,129.2	1,069.8	1,261.5	1,274.6	1,188.6	1,411.8	1,380.7	1,405.5
Multilateral								
European Community	305.3	312.7	437.7	482.9	584.9	593.5	542.8	598.9
World Bank Group	208.2	185.2	224.5	236.2	279.8	278.1	257.7	264.6
UN agencies	89.5	86.0	116.2	125.0	107.6	103.2	121.6	134.2
Other multilateral	75.3	74.6	63.5	105.4	113.0	104.4	25.7	56.5
Multilateral total	678.3	658.5	842.0	949.5	1,085.3	1,079.3	947.8	1,054.3
TOTAL	1,807.5	1,728.3	2,103.4	2,224.1	2,274.0	2,491.1	2,328.5	2,459.7

Source: *Annual Abstract of Statistics 1998,*

Retail Prices Index: Rates of Change in the UK

Item	% change on the previous year					
	1992	1993	1994	1995	1996	1997
Housing	−0.7	−5.4	3.3	6.7	1.3	6.5
Food	2.1	1.8	1.0	3.9	3.2	0.1
Motoring expenditure	6.8	4.3	3.5	1.8	3.0	5.3
Alcohol	6.4	4.5	2.5	3.8	2.9	2.8
Household goods	3.3	1.2	0.3	3.7	3.3	1.2
Leisure services	8.1	4.5	3.7	3.2	3.6	4.9
Clothing and footwear	0.3	0.8	0.5	0.2	−0.7	0.8
Household services	5.8	3.6	0.1	−0.3	0.1	1.8
Catering	6.3	5.2	4.2	4.3	4.0	3.8
Leisure goods	2.6	1.4	−0.6	−0.1	1.6	0.2
Fuel and light	2.2	−1.3	4.4	2.1	0.2	3.1
Personal goods and services	6.6	4.0	3.7	3.2	3.7	3.6
Tobacco	11.0	8.5	7.5	6.7	6.7	7.4
Fares and other travel	6.2	5.2	2.6	2.5	3.0	3.4
Total	3.7	1.6	2.4	3.5	2.4	3.1
All items except housing	4.7	3.1	2.3	2.7	2.7	2.4
All items except mortgage interest payments	4.7	3.0	2.3	2.9	3.0	2.8

Source: *Social Trends 29,*

UK budget *Chancellor of the Exchequer Gordon Brown before the March 1999 budget. Among new measures introduced was a 10 pence rate of income tax.* Photo: Sean Aidan

Retail Prices Index Summary in the UK

(– = not applicable.)

Period	Annual average	January	June	December
January 1962 = 100				
1962	101.6	100.0	102.9	102.3
1963	103.6	102.7	103.9	104.2
1964	107.0	104.7	107.4	109.2
1965	112.1	109.5	112.7	114.1
1966	116.5	114.3	117.1	118.3
1967	119.4	118.5	119.9	121.2
1968	125.0	121.6	125.4	128.4
1969	131.8	129.1	132.1	134.4
1970	140.2	135.5	139.9	145.0
1971	153.4	147.0	154.3	158.1
1972	164.3	159.0	163.7	170.2
1973	179.4	171.3	178.9	188.2
1974	–	191.8	–	–

Period	Annual average	January	June	December
January 1974 = 100				
1974	108.5	100.0	108.7	116.9
1975	134.8	119.9	137.1	146.0
1976	157.1	147.9	156.0	168.0
1977	182.0	172.4	183.6	188.4
1978	197.1	189.5	197.2	204.2
1979	223.5	207.2	219.6	239.4
1980	263.7	245.3	265.7	275.6
1981	295.0	277.3	295.8	308.8
1982	320.4	310.6	322.9	325.5
1983	335.1	325.9	334.7	342.8
1984	351.8	342.6	351.9	358.5
1985	373.2	359.8	376.4	378.9
1986	385.9	379.7	385.8	393.0
1987	–	394.5	–	–

Period	Annual average	January	June	December
January 1987 = 100				
1987	101.9	100.0	101.9	103.3
1988	106.9	103.3	106.6	110.3
1989	115.2	111.0	115.4	118.8
1990	126.1	119.5	126.7	129.9
1991	133.5	130.2	134.1	135.7
1992	138.5	135.6	139.3	139.2
1993	140.7	137.9	141.0	141.9
1994	144.1	141.3	144.7	146.0
1995	149.1	146.0	149.8	150.7
1996	152.7	150.2	153.0	154.4
1997	157.5	154.4	157.5	160.0
1998	162.9	159.5	163.4	164.4

Source: *Annual Abstract of Statistics 1999,* © Crown copyright 1999

Household Consumer Expenditure by Commodity in the UK

(In millions of pounds at 1995 prices.)

Commodity	1990	1991	1992	1993	1994	1995	1996	1997
Durable Goods								
Cars, motorcycles, and other vehicles	22,425	18,598	17,397	19,016	20,334	20,749	22,673	24,729
Other durable goods	15,968	15,894	16,980	17,196	18,249	18,747	20,028	22,413
Total	38,101	34,436	34,474	36,221	38,583	39,496	42,701	47,142
Non-Durable Goods								
Food (household expenditure)	47,055	47,114	47,664	48,282	48,931	49,274	50,931	51,768
Alcohol and tobacco	41,654	40,258	38,415	37,861	38,441	37,456	38,007	38,342
Clothing and footwear	22,105	22,502	23,683	24,875	26,928	28,347	29,773	31,339
Energy products	27,389	28,281	27,961	28,123	27,754	27,118	28,210	27,573
Other goods	47,995	47,567	47,817	49,035	50,119	51,947	55,419	60,688
Total	184,983	184,760	185,041	187,926	192,173	194,142	202,340	209,710
Services								
Rental and water charges	56,127	56,743	57,191	58,015	58,862	59,798	60,344	60,974
Catering	39,539	36,806	36,279	37,539	37,319	37,727	39,704	40,582
Transport and communication	36,320	35,121	35,704	38,473	40,011	41,360	42,188	43,520
Financial services	16,603	16,477	16,202	17,168	16,397	16,784	18,034	19,469
Other services	45,577	44,808	44,736	45,183	46,008	48,602	48,863	49,991
Total	194,093	189,592	189,729	196,363	198,597	204,271	209,133	214,536

Source: *United Kingdom National Accounts. The Blue Book 1998,* © Crown copyright 1998

Purchasing Power of the Pound within the UK

To find the purchasing power of the pound in 1993, given that it was 100 pence in 1980, select the column headed 1980 and look at the 1993 row. The result is 48 pence, which means the pound could purchase in 1993 less than half of what it could in 1980. These figures are calculated by taking the inverse ratio of the respective annual averages of the Retail Prices Index. In pence.

Year	1980	1981	1982	1983	1984	1985	1986	1987	1988	1989	1990	1991	1992	1993	1994	1995	1996	1997
1980	100	112	122	127	133	142	146	152	160	172	189	200	207	210	216	223	228	236
1981	89	100	109	114	119	127	131	136	143	154	169	179	185	188	193	199	204	211
1982	82	92	100	105	110	116	120	125	132	142	155	164	171	173	177	184	188	194
1983	79	88	96	100	105	111	115	120	126	136	148	157	163	166	170	176	180	185
1984	75	84	91	95	100	106	110	114	120	129	141	150	155	158	162	167	171	177
1985	71	79	86	90	94	100	103	108	113	122	133	141	146	149	152	158	161	166
1986	68	76	83	87	91	97	100	104	109	118	129	136	142	144	147	152	156	161
1987	66	73	80	83	88	93	96	100	105	113	124	131	136	138	141	146	150	155
1988	63	70	76	79	83	88	92	95	100	108	118	125	130	132	135	139	143	147
1989	58	65	71	74	77	82	85	88	93	100	109	116	120	122	125	129	133	137
1990	53	59	64	67	71	75	78	81	85	91	100	106	110	112	114	118	121	125
1991	50	56	61	64	67	71	73	76	80	86	94	100	104	105	108	112	114	118
1992	48	54	59	61	64	68	71	74	77	83	91	96	100	102	104	108	110	114
1993	48	53	58	60	63	67	70	72	76	82	90	95	98	100	102	106	109	112
1994	46	52	56	59	62	66	68	71	74	80	88	93	96	98	100	103	106	109
1995	45	50	54	57	60	63	66	68	72	77	85	90	93	94	97	100	102	106
1996	44	49	53	56	58	62	64	67	70	75	83	87	91	92	94	98	100	103
1997	42	47	52	54	57	60	62	65	68	73	80	85	88	89	92	95	97	100

Source: *Annual Abstract of Statistics 1999*, © Crown copyright 1999

See Also  **Working Hours Needed to Buy Selected Commodities, p. 854.**

UK Public Spending

Government and Other Public Sector Expenditure on Housing in the UK

(N = nil or negligible. Years ending 31 March. In millions of pounds.)

Type of expenditure	1988–89	1989–90	1990–91	1991–92	1992–93	1993–94	1994–95	1995–96	1996–97	1997–98
Government Expenditure										
Current expenditure										
central government housing subsidies										
to local authorities	603	714	1,273	1,144	992	874	814	687	717	706
to public corporations	304	285	284	260	208	214	228	228	236	231
to housing associations	43	53	67	40	135	180	207	235	215	200
grants to housing associations	8	7	85	117	59	13	3	1	1	N
local authorities housing subsidies	554	487	3	N	1	N	N	3	1	1
administration	250	249	320	373	394	364	405	402	425	449
Total	1,763	1,794	2,032	1,934	1,789	1,645	1,657	1,556	1,595	1,587
Capital expenditure										
investment in housing by local authorities	79	1,387	1,322	822	913	780	842	1,009	710	849
capital grants to housing associations	956	552	1,495	2,045	2,583	2,136	1,774	1,329	1,407	985
improvement grants	809	886	862	1,150	1,240	1,287	1,105	843	918	1,240
net lending for house purchase	−148	−259	−596	−782	−211	−402	−141	−136	−719	−894
capital grants to public corporations	65	241	774	482	631	439	387	837	386	400
net lending to public corporations	855	672	176	−104	39	34	10	7	−1	−57
Total	2,616	3,479	4,033	3,613	5,195	4,274	3,977	3,889	2,701	2,682

(continued)

Government and Other Public Sector Expenditure on Housing in the UK *(continued)*

Type of expenditure	1988–89	1989–90	1990–91	1991–92	1992–93	1993–94	1994–95	1995–96	1996–97	1997–98
Total expenditure										
central government	3,023	2,547	3,835	3,697	4,595	3,839	3,409	3,313	2,376	1,811
local authorities	1,356	2,726	2,230	1,850	2,389	2,080	2,225	2,132	1,920	2,427
Total government expenditure	4,379	5,273	6,065	5,547	6,984	5,919	5,634	5,445	4,296	4,269
Public Corporations' Capital Expenditure										
Investment in housing	285	451	519	673	549	568	560	580	556	450
Net lending to private sector	−8	−2	−3	−4	3	1	−1	−5	−5	−4
Total	277	449	516	669	552	569	559	575	551	446
Total public sector expenditure[1]	3,736	4,809	5,631	5,838	6,866	6,015	5,796	5,176	4,462	4,372
Total public sector expenditure as % of GDP[2]	0.78	0.92	1.00	0.99	1.12	0.93	0.85	0.72	0.58	0.54

[1] Total government expenditure less grants and loans to public corporations, plus public corporations' capital expenditure.
[2] GDP is adjusted to take account of change from rates to community charge.

Source: *Annual Abstract of Statistics 1999,* © Crown copyright 1999

Government Expenditure on Social Security Benefits in the UK

(– = not applicable. Years ending 31 March. In millions of pounds.)

Government current expenditure	1990–91	1991–92	1992–93	1993–94	1994–95	1995–96	1996–97	1997–98
National insurance fund retirement pensions	22,725	25,691	27,076	28,481	28,925	30,158	32,218	33,885
lump sums to pensioners	114	114	115	122	123	124	129	118
widows' and guardians' allowances	893	884	1,014	1,041	1,034	1,018	974	992
unemployment benefit	892	1,627	1,761	1,623	1,277	1,099	588	–
jobseeker's allowance[1]	–	–	–	–	–	–	314	379
sickness benefit	222	278	365	294	426	12	–	–
invalidity benefit	4,544	5,461	6,198	7,146	8,042	271	–	–
incapacity benefit[2]	–	–	–	–	–	7,615	7,667	7,472
maternity benefit	35	40	42	32	17	28	31	36
death grant	–	–	–	–	–	–	–	–
disablement benefit	526	–	–	–	–	–	–	–
industrial death benefit	62	–	–	–	–	–	–	–
statutory sick pay	966	725	688	688	24	24	28	28
statutory maternity pay	344	396	416	440	498	480	492	508
payments in lieu of benefits foregone	–	–	–	–	–	–	–	–
Total	31,323	35,216	37,675	39,867	40,366	40,829	42,442	43,418
Maternity fund	–	–	–	–	–	–	–	–
Redundancy fund	130	276	321	110	208	128	108	88
Social fund	123	130	175	189	183	216	204	168
Non-contributory benefits								
war pensions	688	844	976	913	1,083	1,247	1,352	1,284
family benefits								
child benefit	4,840	5,433	5,950	6,347	6,294	6,332	6,635	7,098
one parent benefit	227	249	275	282	289	310	317	9
family credit	466	626	929	1,208	1,441	1,739	2,084	2,338
family income supplement	–	–	–	–	–	–	–	–
maternity grants	–	–	–	–	–	–	–	–
income support/supplementary benefits								
supplementary pensions	–	–	–	–	–	–	–	–
supplementary allowances	–	–	–	–	–	–	–	–
income support	9,106	12,325	15,578	16,997	16,387	16,650	14,438	11,999
other								
old persons' pensions	38	36	36	36	35	36	30	29
lump sums to pensioners	8	11	13	14	13	15	15	17
attendance allowance	1,698	1,706	1,553	1,795	1,963	2,194	2,393	2,640
invalid care allowance	229	285	345	442	526	617	736	745
mobility allowance	895	1,063	68	–	–	–	–	–
disability living allowance	–	–	1,973	2,772	3,125	3,802	4,498	5,018
disability working allowance	–	–	3	7	11	19	34	44

(continued)

Government Expenditure on Social Security Benefits in the UK (*continued*)

Government current expenditure	1990–91	1991–92	1992–93	1993–94	1994–95	1995–96	1996–97	1997–98
severe disablement allowance	407	596	640	703	776	820	906	1,007
industrial injury benefits	142	655	668	687	706	731	744	754
retail price index adjustment	–	–	–	–	–	–	–	–
housing benefit	4,735	6,053	7,670	9,163	10,345	10,868	10,764	9,466
Administration	3,206	3,617	3,998	4,273	4,190	4,076	3,998	4,170
Total government expenditure	58,261	69,121	78,846	85,805	87,941	90,629	91,698	90,292
Total government expenditure as % of GDP[3]	10.47	11.89	12.99	13.40	12.96	12.54	12.00	11.10

[1] Jobseeker's allowance was introduced in October 1996 to replace unemployment benefit and income support for the unemployed.
[2] Sickness benefit and invalidity benefit were replaced by a single incapacity benefit in 1995.
[3] GDP is adjusted to take account of the change from rates to community charge.

Source: *Annual Abstract of Statistics 1999*, © Crown copyright 1999

Government Expenditure on Welfare Services in the UK

(N = nil or negligible. Years ending 31 March. Does not include school meals and milk. In millions of pounds.)

Item	1987–88	1988–89	1989–90	1990–91	1991–92	1992–93	1993–94	1994–95	1995–96	1996–97	1997–98
Personal social services											
central government current expenditure	126	127	143	163	190	202	216	197	140	101	73
local authorities current expenditure: running expenses	3,537	3,971	4,395	5,022	5,725	6,122	7,113	8,400	9,531	9,996	10,484
capital expenditure	133	163	213	227	200	189	190	235	229	221	213
Total	3,909	4,346	4,877	5,626	4,732	6,513	7,519	8,832	9,900	10,318	10,770
Welfare foods service											
central government current expenditure on welfare foods (including administration)	124	105	108	120	142	171	182	185	228	264	306
less receipts from the public	N	N	N	–1	–1	–1	–1	–1	–1	–1	–1
Total	124	105	108	119	141	170	181	184	227	263	305
Total government expenditure	4,033	4,451	4,985	5,745	4,873	6,683	7,700	9,016	10,127	10,581	11,075
Total government expenditure as % of GDP[1]	0.94	0.93	0.95	1.02	0.83	1.09	1.19	1.31	1.40	1.38	1.36

[1]GDP is adjusted to take account of change from rates of community charge.

Source: *Annual Abstract of Statistics 1999*, © Crown copyright 1999

Benefit Expenditure by Recipient Group in the UK

(In millions of pounds.)

Recipient	1992–93	1993–94	1994–95	1995–96	1996–97	1997–98 (est)	1998–99 (plans)
Cash Terms							
Elderly people	34,140	36,570	37,360	38,800	40,980	42,820	45,070
Long-term sick and disabled	14,800	17,810	19,660	21,080	22,550	23,230	24,860
Short-term sick	1,320	1,290	710	950	990	1,170	1,230
Family	13,890	15,150	16,090	17,210	18,160	18,670	19,580
Unemployed people	9,350	9,770	9,150	8,650	7,570	6,150	5,420
Widows and others	1,810	1,830	1,870	2,060	2,020	2,070	2,120
Total	75,310	82,420	84,850	88,750	92,270	94,110	98,280

(*continued*)

Benefit Expenditure by Recipient Group in the UK (*continued*)

(In millions of pounds.)

Recipient	1992–93	1993–94	1994–95	1995–96	1996–97	1997–98 (est)	1998–99 (plans)
Real Terms							
Elderly people	38,750	40,320	40,590	41,020	42,090	42,820	43,800
Long-term sick and disabled	16,800	19,640	21,360	22,290	23,160	23,230	24,160
Short-term sick	1,500	1,430	780	1,010	1,010	1,170	1,190
Family	15,760	16,700	17,480	18,190	18,650	18,670	19,030
Unemployed people	10,610	10,770	9,940	9,140	7,770	6,150	5,270
Widows and others	2,050	2,020	2,030	2,170	2,070	2,070	2,060
Total	85,470	90,890	92,180	93,820	94,760	94,110	95,510

Source: *The Government's Expenditure Plans 1998/99,* © Crown copyright 1998

Child Benefit in the UK

Number of families and children receiving allowances. Data are for 31 December of each year.

Type of family		1983	1988	1992	1993	1994	1995	1996
Families with	1 child	2,905,000	2,878,000	2,906,000	2,920,000	2,941,000	2,970,000	2,983,000
	2 children	2,904,000	2,714,000	2,752,000	2,772,000	2,781,000	2,783,000	2,794,000
	3 children	878,000	839,000	894,000	908,000	920,000	928,000	929,000
	4 children	205,000	205,000	226,000	231,000	228,000	231,000	236,000
	5 children	48,000	48,000	55,000	57,000	60,000	60,000	59,000
	6 or more children	19,000	21,000	24,000	24,000	24,000	24,000	23,000
Total		6,958,000	6,706,000	6,857,000	6,913,000	6,955,000	6,996,000	7,024,000
Children attracting benefit total		12,526,000	12,021,000	12,425,000	12,555,000	12,632,000	12,698,000	12,745,000

Source: *Social Security Statistics 1998,* © Crown copyright 1998

Awards of Family Credit in the UK

As of 30 November 1997.

Type of family		Average amount (£ per week)	Number of families receiving family credit: All amounts	Under £30.00	£30.00–39.99	£40.00–49.99	£50.00–59.99	£60.00–69.99	£70.00–79.99	£80.00 and over
All families	with 1 child	48.58	290,100	57,400	31,400	34,800	98,700	38,100	27,100	2,600
	with 2 children	58.34	272,200	44,300	23,600	25,700	26,200	29,600	76,100	46,700
	with 3 children	69.02	134,900	17,500	9,400	11,100	10,600	11,600	11,700	63,100
	with 4 or more children	88.51	68,600	5,900	3,000	3,900	4,400	4,100	4,400	42,900
	all children	59.22	765,800	125,100	67,400	75,500	139,900	83,300	119,300	155,300
Couples	with 1 child	44.20	99,000	29,100	13,100	11,200	21,800	9,200	13,500	1,100
	with 2 children	54.16	148,600	32,700	15,900	15,500	13,700	13,200	30,300	27,300
	with 3 children	64.69	93,800	15,600	8,200	9,000	7,700	8,300	7,400	37,700
	with 4 or more children	86.65	57,000	5,600	2,900	3,600	4,000	3,600	3,800	33,600
	all children	58.81	398,400	83,000	40,000	39,400	47,200	34,300	54,900	99,700
Lone parents	with 1 child	50.84	191,100	28,300	18,400	23,600	76,900	28,900	13,600	1,500
	with 2 children	63.37	123,500	11,600	7,700	10,200	12,500	16,400	45,800	19,400
	with 3 children	78.88	41,200	1,900	1,200	2,000	3,000	3,200	4,300	25,500
	with 4 or more children	97.65	11,600	300	200	300	400	500	700	9,300
	all children	59.67	367,400	42,100	27,400	36,100	92,700	49,000	64,400	55,600

Source: *Social Security Statistics 1998,* © Crown copyright 1998

Number of Recipients of Social Security Benefits in the UK

(– = not applicable. N = nil or negligible.)

Benefit	1988	1989	1990	1991	1992	1993	1994	1995	1996	1997
Unemployment benefit	630,200	380,800	331,400	569,500	685,200	671,900	553,500	426,500	397,800	N
Jobseeker's allowance[1]	–	–	–	–	–	–	–	–	–	1,520,700
Sickness and invalidity benefit	1,278,000	1,394,700	1,515,600	1,479,500	1,646,300	1,805,000	1,893,900	1,987,700	N	N
Incapacity benefit[2 3]	–	–	–	–	–	–	–	–	1,910,000	1,772,700
Attendance allowance	742,000	795,000	871,000	957,000	1,092,000	945,000	1,018,000	1,109,000	1,161,000	1,229,000
Mobility allowance	525,000	570,000	615,000	659,000	718,000	N	N	N	N	N
Disability living allowance	N	N	N	N	N	1,187,000	1,376,000	1,579,000	1,786,000	1,963,000
Guardians' allowance	2,600	1,900	2,000	2,200	2,100	2,200	2,300	2,300	2,300	2,400
Widows' benefits	388,000	371,000	365,200	362,300	351,000	345,300	335,000	323,100	311,600	284,600
National Insurance retirement pensions										
males	3,479,100	3,481,700	3,553,900	3,512,800	3,613,700	3,623,600	3,657,500	3,728,700	3,836,600	3,926,700
females	6,523,500	6,520,400	6,625,700	6,515,300	6,683,000	6,680,000	6,727,100	6,777,200	6,948,500	6,983,200
Total	100,001,600	10,002,200	10,179,600	10,028,100	10,296,800	10,303,600	10,384,700	10,505,900	10,785,100	10,909,900
Non-contributory retirement pensions										
males	6,000	6,700	6,700	6,100	6,100	6,100	6,100	6,500	6,100	5,900
females	32,600	31,500	29,400	25,300	25,700	24,900	24,100	24,500	23,500	22,500
Total	39,300	38,200	36,000	31,400	31,800	31,000	30,200	31,000	29,600	28,300
Industrial injuries disablement pensions assessments	189,000	193,000	196,900	200,200	204,300	212,400	232,800[4]	235,200	248,900	271,700[4]
Reduced earnings allowance/ retirement allowance assessments	150,500	154,900	160,000	163,700	159,700	156,000	156,900[4]	152,000	154,900	158,500[4]
Child benefit										
families receiving benefit	6,923,000	6,695,000	6,949,500	7,024,400	7,078,300	7,136,400	7,179,900	7,222,200	7,251,600	7,195,700
Family credit[5]	313,100	311,900	331,700	360,400	404,600[4]	505,700[4]	564,500[4]	630,900[4]	716,300[4]	801,500[4]
Income support[6]	4,536,000	4,350,000	4,376,000	4,683,000	5,292,900	5,858,400	5,897,600	5,896,500	5,778,300	4,329,400
Housing benefit and council tax benefit										
rent rebate	3,132,000	2,971,500	2,928,100	2,944,000	3,033,900	3,052,500	3,016,100	3,075,200	2,898,300	2,792,200
rent allowance[7]	968,700	958,100	1,067,200	1,082,400	1,291,600	1,480,500	1,633,900	1,793,100	1,877,500	1,846,900
rate rebate	5,225,400	4,299,800	–	–	–	–	–	–	–	–
community charge benefit	–	N	6,518,400	6,290,700	6,563,900	–	–	–	–	–
community charge rebate	–	876,100	–	–	–	–	–	–	–	–
council tax benefit[8]	–	–	–	–	–	5,251,200	5,496,600	5,623,800	5,614,200	5,497,900
War pensions	258,300	252,200	248,000	249,600	260,100	292,900	309,200	315,400	327,500	320,700

[1] Jobseeker's allowance was introduced on 7 October 1996, replacing unemployment benefit.
[2] Incapacity benefit replaced sickness benefit and invalidity benefit from 13 April 1995.
[3] Incapacity benefit figures are taken at the last day in February.
[4] Includes an allowance for late returns.
[5] Family income supplement was replaced by family credit from April 1988.
[6] From April 1988 supplementary benefit was repalced by income support. From 9 October 1996 income support for the unemployed was replaced by income-based jobseeker's allowance. Figures in this table up to and including 1996 include unemployed income support claimants. Figures from 1997 exclude unemployed who will be counted in the jobseeker's allowance claims.
[7] Rent allowance figures include housing association tenants.
[8] Community charge benefit was replaced by council tax benefit in April 1993.

Source: *Annual Abstract of Statistics 1999*, © Crown copyright 1999

Income Support: Average Weekly Amounts of Benefit in the UK

(Figures are for May of each year. In pounds per week.)

Recipient	1992	1993	1994	1995	1996	1997
All income support	51.77	54.75	56.16	56.29	57.26	58.03
Aged 60 and over	40.79	43.59	42.45	41.18	41.69	42.24
Disabled	48.08	53.12	57.56	59.73	61.07	62.42
Lone parent	67.59	70.31	74.93	76.63	78.19	79.21
Other	67.60	70.73	68.44	64.92	63.59	63.24

Source: *Social Security Statistics 1998,* © Crown copyright 1998

National Insurance Fund of the UK

The National Insurance Fund is a social-security scheme that provides child allowances, maternity benefits, and payments to the unemployed, sick, and retired, and also covers medical treatment. It is paid for by weekly or monthly contributions from employees and employers. (N/A = not available. Years ending 31 March. In millions of pounds.)

	1990–91	1991–92	1992–93	1993–94	1994–95	1995–96	1996–97
Receipts							
Opening balance	10,579.7	12,161.2	8,637.6	3,577.7	4,672.3	7,042.1	8,044.9
Contributions	31,480.9	33,156.7	34,331.7	N/A	38,712.2	40,874.6	42,806.4
Grant from consolidated fund	N/A	N/A	N/A	7,785.0	6,445.0	3,680.0	1,951.5
Compensation for statutory sick pay/statutory maternity pay	N/A	1,089.8	1,124.5	1,158.3	563.4	474.7	541.8
Consolidated fund supplement	N/A	N/A	N/A	N/A	N/A	N/A	N/A
Reimbursement for industrial injury benefit payments	436.5	N/A	N/A	N/A	N/A	N/A	N/A
Transfers from Great Britain	225.0	125.0	40.0	40.0	145.0	125.0	75.0
Income from investments	1,022.5	1,160.0	970.9	488.5	365.1	459.2	488.7
Other receipts	944.7	19.4	24.8	42.0	60.6	76.5	85.1
Redundancy receipts[1]	2.0	19.1	27.0	25.7	25.3	23.9	26.2
Total receipts	44,691.3	47,731.2	45,156.4	48,990.0	50,989.0	52,756.0	54,019.7
Expenditure							
Unemployment	899.0	1,641.9	1,800.6	1,689.6	1,330.9	1,131.3	605.1
Sickness	227.0	286.5	378.1	378.4	350.7	14.7	N/A
Invalidity	4,613.0	5,701.2	6,452.7	7,341.2	8,009.3	599.8	N/A
Incapacity	N/A	N/A	N/A	N/A	N/A	7,622.9	7,992.7
Maternity	34.6	32.1	32.7	34.2	28.2	29.9	34.3
Widows' pensions	920.7	1,044.7	1,044.4	1,076.0	1,057.4	1,050.7	1,016.8
Guardians' allowances[2] and child's special allowance	1.6	1.6	2.1	1.1	1.1	1.8	1.6
Retirement pensions[3]	23,305.4	28,605.0	29,995.4	31,720.9	31,366.9	32,616.6	34,735.7
Disablement[4]	419.8	N/A	N/A	N/A	N/A	N/A	N/A
Death	47.9	N/A	N/A	N/A	N/A	N/A	N/A
Pensioners' lump sum payments	118.3	117.2	118.0	125.1	126.3	127.2	131.6
Other benefits	3.2	N/A	N/A	N/A	N/A	N/A	N/A
Total benefits	30,590.4	37,430.2	39,824.0	N/A	42,270.8	35,575.1	44,517.9
Other payments	9.6	9.7	10.5	35.0	8.9	14.2	17.4
Administration	1,056.8	1,243.5	1,379.2	1,604.5	1,323.6	1,218.8	1,065.3
Transfers to Northern Ireland	225.0	125.0	40.0	40.0	145.0	125.0	75.0
Redundancy payments	N/A	285.3	325.0	271.6	198.5	155.1	133.6
Total expenditure	31,881.8	39,093.6	41,578.7	44,317.7	43,946.9	37,088.1	45,809.2
Accumulated funds	12,530.6	8,637.6	3,577.7	4,672.3	7,042.1	8,044.9	8,065.9

[1] The assets of the redundancy fund became those of the National Insurance fund on 31 January 1991.

[2] Includes figures of child's special allowance for Northern Ireland.

[3] Includes figures for personal pensions.

[4] From 1 April 1990, industrial injury benefits are no longer paid for out of the National Insurance fund; this amount is reimbursement for expenditure incurred by the fund for the period 1 April 1990 to 31 December 1990.

Source: *Annual Abstract of Statistics 1999,* © Crown copyright 1999

Financing Requirements of Nationalized Industries in the UK

'Financing requirements' excludes central government grants and subsidies that are generally available to the private sector; these grants and subsidies are treated as contributing to internal resources and are included in central government's own expenditure.
(– = not applicable. In millions of pounds.)

Industry		1996–97	1997–98 (est)	1998–99 (plans)
Department of Trade and Industry	British Coal[1]	41	59	19
	British Nuclear Fuels	–149	138	179
	British Shipbuilders	–1	–26	–
	Nuclear Electric[2]	–	–	–
	Post Office	–285	–313	–335
	Total	–394	–141	–137
Department of Environment, Transport, and the Regions	National Railways	–1,061	70	158
	Union Railways	12	–	–
	European Passenger Services	15	–	–
	Civil Aviation Authority	–13	–34	–40
	London Transport	917	609	523
	Total	–131	644	642
Scotland	Highlands and Islands Airports	7	7	9
	Scottish Nuclear	–	–	–
	Caledonian MacBrayne	10	18	17
	Scottish Transport Group	–	–	–
	Total	18	26	26
TOTAL EXTERNAL FINANCE		–507	528	531

[1] Figures for 1995–96 onwards largely reflect departmental costs of meeting coal-related liabilities.
[2] British Nuclear Electric and Magnox Electric merged on 30 January 1998.

Source: *Public Expenditure: Statistical Analyses 1998–99*, © Crown copyright 1998

Debt of the Public Sector in the UK

Data show nominal amount outstanding as of 31 March in each year.
(N = nil or negligible. N/A = not available. In millions of pounds.)

Item	1988	1989	1990	1991	1992	1993	1994	1995	1996	1997
Central Government										
Sterling national debt										
sterling debt	192,705	192,048	186,246	190,462	205,360	228,949	288,999	331,047	372,842	404,283
less official holdings	19,364	30,147	32,293	34,646	33,644	22,039	31,207	42,043	45,654	49,292
Foreign currency national debt										
foreign currency debt	4,725	5,272	6,675	8,268	9,399	20,178	18,308	18,488	18,329	15,626
less official holdings	N	N	221	371	752	1,285	1,447	1,575	1,540	1,285
Total market holdings of national debt	178,066	167,173	160,407	163,713	180,363	225,803	274,653	305,917	343,977	369,332
Other liabilities										
net indebtedness to Banking Department	583	969	1,451	1,223	1,258	437	729	869	N	1,149
deposits with National Savings Bank ordinary account	1,657	1,632	1,555	1,474	1,435	1,438	1,444	1,446	1,432	1,419
liability to trustee savings banks	N	N	N	N	N	N	N	N	N	N
accrued interest on national savings	6,109	5,440	4,647	3,897	3,525	3,478	3,103	3,316	3,517	3,422
notes and coin in circulation	16,105	16,907	17,678	18,670	17,582	18,520	21,447	21,771	23,427	25,638
Northern Ireland government debt	168	165	172	155	150	154	128	127	114	109
public corporations' balances with the Paymaster General	79	77	44	41	25	52	124	224	199	264
borrowing from UK banks	N	N	N	N	N	44	28	40	46	51
Other sectors										
local authorities	120	147	181	150	94	81	124	149	153	155
public corporations	1,893	2,227	2,015	2,218	1,508	2,454	3,056	4,460	6,936	8,699
domestic private sector	174,990	162,242	156,178	158,270	168,058	199,393	240,214	272,867	306,932	332,317
overseas	25,764	27,747	27,580	28,535	34,678	47,998	58,262	56,234	58,691	60,213
Total held by other sectors	202,767	192,363	185,954	189,173	204,338	249,926	301,656	333,710	372,712	401,384

(continued)

Debt of the Public Sector in the UK (*continued*)

Item	1988	1989	1990	1991	1992	1993	1994	1995	1996	1997
Local Authorities										
Sterling debt	46,989	50,101	50,986	53,751	54,382	48,976	49,403	49,460	49,868	51,037
Foreign currency debt	768	742	733	642	599	621	536	470	384	262
Other sectors										
central government	39,677	44,404	47,124	48,814	49,173	41,527	40,977	40,707	41,266	42,555
public corporations	965	960	821	1,513	1,483	1,585	1,620	1,586	890	805
domestic private sector	6,264	4,692	3,081	3,399	3,638	5,783	6,501	6,779	7,209	6,997
overseas	851	787	693	667	687	702	841	858	887	942
Total held by other sectors	47,757	50,843	51,719	54,393	54,981	49,597	49,939	49,930	50,252	51,299
Public Corporations										
Sterling debt	23,397	19,580	13,340	9,279	10,719	15,618	23,354	26,542	26,350	26,665
Foreign currency debt	3,001	2,276	1,421	1,160	790	576	513	373	245	124
Other sectors										
central government	22,182	18,598	12,787	8,842	10,312	15,227	22,951	26,278	25,980	26,295
public corporations	291	247	36	26	29	11	69	3	N	1
domestic private sector	1,026	769	566	460	414	396	340	261	370	369
overseas	2,899	2,242	1,372	1,111	754	560	507	373	245	124
Total held by other sectors	26,398	21,856	14,761	10,439	11,509	16,194	23,867	26,915	26,595	26,789
Public Sector Debt Held Outside the Public Sector										
Sterling debt held by										
domestic private sector	179,450	166,460	158,322	160,667	170,897	198,113	243,506	277,331	312,135	336,630
overseas	23,850	23,729	22,540	22,088	27,295	36,629	45,249	42,285	44,785	49,621
Foreign currency debt held by										
domestic private sector	2,830	1,243	1,503	1,462	1,213	7,459	3,549	2,576	2,376	3,053
overseas	5,664	7,047	7,105	8,225	8,824	12,631	14,361	15,180	15,038	11,658
Total	211,794	198,479	189,479	192,442	208,229	254,832	306,665	337,372	374,334	400,962
Debt Excluded from Public Sector Borrowing Requirement Financing										
Central government	569	697	776	877	1,006	1,263	1,608	1,834	1,870	2,066
Contingent Liabilities of Central Government										
Export credit guarantees	36,128	36,552	40,106	41,818	38,291	29,350	32,964	34,081	35,943	34,817
Assistance to industry, guaranteed loans	1,788	1,947	2,468	2,420	1,978	1,668	1,442	1,427	1,248	1,080
Overseas development, guaranteed loans	5	5	4	5	4	4	4	4	3	1
National heritage acts, guaranteed loans	881	1,172	1,629	2,043	2,696	2,030	2,733	3,059	2,198	2,233
Other identified	65	23	19	21	16	16	20	18	17	17
Total	38,867	39,699	44,226	46,307	42,985	33,068	37,163	38,589	39,409	38,148
% of total debt held outside the public sector	76.5	74.9	75.1	75.8	76.9	80.7	81.7	82.2	83.3	83.6
Debt held outside the public sector as a % of GDP	48.7	41.0	36.0	34.6	35.8	42.0	47.9	49.7	52.5	53.3
Debt held overseas as a % of debt held outside the public sector	13.9	15.5	15.6	15.8	17.3	19.3	19.4	17.0	16.0	15.3
Debt held overseas as a % of GDP	6.8	6.4	5.6	5.4	6.2	8.1	9.3	8.5	8.4	8.1
Foreign currency debt as a % of debt held outside the public sector	4.0	4.2	4.5	5.0	4.8	7.9	5.8	5.3	4.7	3.7

Source: *Annual Abstract of Statistics 1999*,

See Also 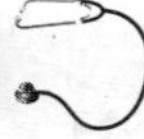 **Government Spending on the National Health Service in the UK, p. 593.**

See Also  **UK Defence Expenditure, p. 651.**

See Also  **Government Spending in Education in the UK, p. 376.**

See Also  **Taxation, pp. 842–850; Mortgage and Finance Information, pp. 850–852.**

UK Industry and Business

Summary of Industrial Production by Sector in the UK

(N = nil or negligible. N/A = not available. In millions of pounds.)

Category	Year	Estimates for all firms							
		Gross output (production)[1]	Gross value added	Stocks and work in progress: At end of year	Stocks and work in progress: Change during year	Capital expenditure less disposals	Wages and salaries	Average number of persons employed[2]	Gross value added per person employed (£)
Main production and construction	1994	506,477.7	163,110.6	N/A	N/A	20,809.9	83,607.6	5,507.8	29,615
	1995	N/A	176,754.7	72,058.7	N/A	23,798.6	76,335.9	5,667.2	31,189
	1996	576,309.5	185,760.7	68,398.2	N/A	23,672.2	88,606.3	5,470.0	33,960
Production industries	1994	435,895.6	143,203.5	52,940.7	3,170.4	19,560.0	70,847.0	4,608.6	31,073
	1995	473,200.5	152,601.4	58,212.2	4,888.6	22,499.1	72,291.5	4,655.7	32,777
	1996	494,056.1	159,731.8	55,475.4	-5.6	22,485.7	74,137.1	4,454.1	35,862
Mining and quarrying of energy producing materials	1994	2,006.0	752.5	372.1	-78.3	72.9	339.0	14.1	53,408
	1995	2,447.6	888.2	364.8	-101.1	92.4	401.3	17.0	52,305
	1996	2,250.8	949.6	369.4	-12.3	157.1	443.0	18.8	50,460
except energy producing materials	1994	3,142.0	1,059.3	190.5	-5.6	198.9	504.8	31.2	33,949
	1995	3,195.3	1,366.2	201.4	16.9	205.6	494.1	30.9	44,268
	1996	3,726.4	1,637.2	249.4	24.1	316.6	575.4	36.1	45,363
Total	1994	5,147.9	1,811.8	562.6	-83.9	271.8	843.8	45.3	40,003
	1995	5,643.0	2,254.4	566.2	-84.1	298.0	895.4	47.8	47,120
	1996	5,977.2	2,586.8	618.8	11.9	473.7	1,018.4	54.9	47,110
Manufacturing of food, beverages, and tobacco	1994	68,474.0	17,608.9	6,253.9	269.3	2,290.3	7,509.1	562.9	31,283
	1995	72,609.9	17,640.0	6,765.6	377.2	2,444.2	7,366.7	533.1	33,092
	1996	75,880.6	19,345.2	6,984.5	501.9	2,346.5	7,529.3	498.0	38,845
of textiles and textile products	1994	15,912.9	6,163.8	2,914.6	424.8	470.5	3,638.6	370.9	16,616
	1995	16,982.8	6,374.2	2,869.8	197.4	467.0	3,720.5	380.1	16,768
	1996	17,306.4	6,803.5	2,786.1	15.3	575.3	3,872.0	356.6	19,077
of leather and leather products	1994	2,747.4	976.0	473.9	51.9	65.6	592.8	59.0	16,547
	1995	2,292.3	788.5	358.3	24.9	60.5	568.6	54.7	14,425
	1996	2,355.8	886.5	382.3	3.4	48.9	425.5	39.6	22,407
of wood and wood products	1994	5,533.2	1,598.5	682.4	82.2	130.6	1,041.5	83.2	19,205
	1995	5,777.1	1,814.1	713.5	14.1	158.3	1,094.9	87.4	20,758
	1996	5,601.0	1,799.9	629.6	-6.7	170.1	1,080.1	87.0	20,696
of pulp, paper, and paper products; publishing and printing	1994	35,611.0	14,802.5	2,735.5	332.5	1,761.4	8,033.7	471.9	31,366
	1995	39,119.0	16,236.2	3,150.9	437.3	2,121.0	8,056.6	481.8	33,697
	1996	40,630.4	16,678.0	2,828.3	-194.1	1,784.9	8,690.4	467.8	35,649
of coke, refined petroleum products, and nuclear fuel	1994	21,864.2	2,270.2	1,092.6	25.7	580.1	675.3	28.0	81,202
	1995	22,422.6	2,912.2	1,220.0	227.3	752.2	670.3	27.2	107,044
	1996	25,984.9	2,558.5	1,128.3	-121.3	716.8	714.3	27.9	91,756
of chemicals, chemical products, and man-made fibres	1994	40,575.8	13,510.8	5,111.0	259.1	1,888.9	5,339.5	271.1	49,843
	1995	44,721.5	15,411.9	5,808.8	447.2	2,285.9	5,735.7	281.7	54,707
	1996	45,588.4	15,440.3	5,717.1	264.8	2,758.2	5,702.1	267.1	57,810

(continued)

Summary of Industrial Production by Sector in the UK (*continued*)

Category	Year	Estimates for all firms: Gross output (production)[1]	Gross value added	Stocks and work in progress: At end of year	Stocks and work in progress: Change during year	Capital expenditure less disposals	Wages and salaries	Average number of persons employed[2]	Gross value added per person employed (£)
of rubber and plastic products	1994	16,681.9	6,382.2	1,670.5	167.9	764.8	3,444.6	239.4	26,660
	1995	18,102.5	6,553.9	1,820.2	171.2	952.7	3,613.0	248.0	26,427
	1996	19,175.5	7,122.8	1,891.7	27.5	983.8	3,836.8	250.0	28.496
of other non-metalic mineral products	1994	10,699.1	4,533.4	1,343.5	97.9	423.2	2,280.6	159.8	28,366
	1995	11,855.6	4,976.9	1,462.0	121.4	607.6	2,437.5	167.1	29,776
	1996	11,349.0	4,976.5	1,437.3	94.3	671.9	2,374.3	156.8	31,732
of basic iron and non-ferro alloys	1994	38,171.4	13,612.0	4,204.0	257.2	1,128.8	8,131.3	541.9	25,118
	1995	43,489.1	15,889.6	4,711.8	515.9	1,369.6	8,647.9	582.8	27,263
	1996	43,725.9	15,344.2	4,452.6	7.7	1,572.2	8,860.9	551.8	27,806
of machinery and equipment not elsewhere specified	1994	28,808.0	10,553.3	4,940.5	161.4	873.1	6,570.6	403.4	26,163
	1995	33,839.5	12,014.6	5,661.6	376.1	1,080.1	6,993.0	423.1	28,397
	1996	34,700.4	12,478.2	5,198.5	69.0	1,177.8	6,993.3	400.2	31,177
of electrical and optical equipment	1994	45,490.6	15,745.2	6,958.1	575.3	1,793.3	8,623.2	544.3	28,926
	1995	50,427.2	16,717.5	7,373.7	733.2	2,370.1	8,472.2	537.5	31,102
	1996	54,777.8	17,480.6	6,975.1	–213.2	2,193.6	8,977.3	533.0	32,797
of transport equipment	1994	45,485.8	13,617.6	10,716.8	1,082.0	1,512.2	7,240.4	408.2	33,360
	1995	47,033.2	13,425.3	12,335.0	1,305.9	2,303.0	7,418.3	408.3	32,885
	1996	51,840.5	14,833.4	11,493.3	–432.7	2,414.9	7,867.0	406.3	36,512
not elsewhere classified	1994	12,495.7	4,366.8	1,543.4	128.4	328.4	2,778.7	222.4	19,634
	1995	13,514.3	4,631.2	1,704.2	125.5	433.5	2,722.9	220.8	20,976
	1996	13,882.5	5,151.1	1,607.9	74.3	421.8	2,829.9	214.0	24,074
Manufacturing total	1994	388,551.0	125,741.1	50,640.6	3,915.7	14,011.3	65,899.7	4,366.5	28,797
	1995	422,186.5	135,386.1	55,955.3	5,074.5	17,405.7	67,518.0	4,433.6	30,536
	1996	442,799.0	140,898.9	53,512.6	90.2	17,836.7	69,783.1	4,256.1	33,106
Electricity, gas, and water supply	1994	42,196.6	15,650.6	1,737.5	–661.4	5,276.9	4,103.4	196.8	79,517
	1995	45,371.0	15,14,960.9	1,690.7	–101.8	4,795.5	3,878.1	174.3	85,841
	1996	45,279.9	16,246.1	1,344.0	–107.7	4,175.3	3,335.5	143.2	113,483
Construction	1994	70,582.1	19,907.0	N/A	N/A	1,249.9	12,760.6	899.2	22,139
	1995	N/A	24,153.3	13,846.6	N/A	1,299.5	4,044.4	1,011.5	23,879
	1996	82,253.4	26,028.8	12,922.8	435.9	1,186.5	14,469.3	1,015.9	25,621

[1] Figures for gross output include a substantial amount of duplication represented by the total value of partly manufactured goods sold by one industrial establishment to another. The extent of duplication varies from one census industry to another.

[2] The figures include working proprietors but exclude outworkers.

Source: *Annual Abstract of Statistics 1999,* © Crown copyright 1999

Retail Businesses in the UK

Figures include retail outlets and retail turnover of sales by mail-order, party-plan, automatic vending machines, market stalls, roadside pitches, and door-to-door.
(N = nil or negligible.)

1996

Retail business		Number of businesses	Number of outlets	Total turnover (£ millions)[1 2]	VAT in total turnover (£ millions)
Non-specialized stores					
retail sales	mainly food, drinks, or tobacco	22,157	37,556	71,968	4,815
	other	15,402	21,953	17,687	2,386
	Total	37,559	59,508	89,656	7,201
Specialized stores					
retail sales of food, drinks, or tobacco	fruit and vegetables	6,841	8,979	1,279	21
	meat and meat products	10,662	12,459	2,464	7
	fish	1,997	2,551	245	1
	bread, cakes, flour, or sugar confectionery	4,931	9,506	1,463	55
	alcoholic and other drinks	6,313	11,172	3,773	534
	tobacco products	17,127	18,537	3,940	389
	other	10,450	10,931	1,400	61
	Total	58,321	74,134	14,565	1,069
retail sales of pharmarceutical and medical goods, cosmetics, and toilet articles	dispensing chemists	6,643	11,537	6,043	373
	medical and orthopaedic goods	194	514	128	12
	cosmetics and toilet articles	484	1,738	1,203	167
	Total	7,321	13,789	7,375	551
other sales of new goods	textiles	1,592	3,019	847	115
	clothing	15,274	33,133	24,398	2,598
	footwear and leather goods	6,265	13,865	3,783	379
	furniture, lighting, and household articles	9,941	14,616	6,764	1,003
	electrical household appliances, radio and television goods	7,447	13,245	8,280	1,204
	hardware, paints, and glass	6,124	8,231	6,345	936
	books, newspapers, and stationery	9,590	16,650	4,542	310
	floor coverings	1,988	3,016	1,463	218
	photographic, optical, and precision equipment, office supplies and equipment (including computers, etc)	5,330	8,513	3,047	367
	other	26,739	39,505	11,019	1,400
	Total	90,291	153,795	70,488	8,530
retail sales of second-hand goods		5,146	7,013	1,511	87
retail sales not in stores	mail order houses	2,102	3,053	7,199	963
	stalls and markets	1,031	2,961	301	14
	other	3,188	3,720	1,704	204
	Total	6,321	9,734	9,204	1,181
repair of personal and household goods		2,005	2,649	438	61
TOTAL RETAIL BUSINESSES		206,964	320,622	193,236	18,681

[1] Inclusive of VAT.
[2] Includes retail hire from non-hire retail businesses.

Source: *Annual Abstract of Statistics 1999,*

Construction: Value of New Orders Obtained by Contractors in Great Britain

(In millions of pounds.)

Item			1990	1992	1994	1996	1997
New housing	public housing		683	1,246	1,386	1,073	995
	private housing[1]		4,855	4,016	5,721	5,416	6,253
	Total		5,538	5,263	7,106	6,487	7,248
Infrastructure	water		321	669	412	640	733
	sewerage		491	469	389	481	656
	electricity		187	281	170	294	382
	roads		1,425	1,322	1,356	1,710	928
	gas, communications, air		391	554	494	745	693
	railways		160	200	412	524	416
	harbours		216	252	218	270	182
	Total	public	2,029	1,690	2,211	1,671	1,352
		private	1,161	2,056	1,240	2,993	2,639
	Total		3,190	3,746	3,451	4,664	3,991
Other public non-housing	factories		149	128	111	91	72
	warehouses		14	54	38	14	27
	oil, steel, coal		81	47	12	4	4
	schools and colleges		527	584	658	707	749
	universities		146	203	376	355	273
	health		663	644	752	681	491
	offices		570	499	469	379	391
	entertainment		283	189	308	259	342
	garages		56	28	49	28	34
	shops		24	23	14	12	35
	agriculture		5	14	22	8	33
	other		601	351	844	419	441
	Total		3,117	2,763	3,654	2,956	2,894
Private industrial[1]	factories		2,094	1,006	1,451	1,603	2,184
	warehouses		648	426	498	663	901
	oil, steel, coal		108	72	51	71	64
	Total		2,850	1,503	1,999	2,337	3,149
Private commercial[1]	schools, universities		169	121	115	156	189
	health		271	193	255	277	356
	offices		4,215	1,691	1,777	2,169	2,506
	entertainment		1,195	747	928	1,407	1,847
	garages		364	234	300	265	344
	shops		1,345	1,034	1,453	1,795	1,937
	agriculture		127	94	120	123	148
	other		109	103	127	198	198
	Total		7,796	4,218	5,075	6,390	7,525
TOTAL			22,491	17,493	21,285	22,834	24,806

[1] Figures for private sector include work to be carried out by contractors on their own initiative for sale.

Source: *Annual Abstract of Statistics 1999,* © Crown copyright 1999

Motor Vehicle Production in the UK

(N/A = not available.)

Motor vehicle			1988	1990	1992	1994	1995	1996	1997
Passenger cars	< 1,001 cc		129,446	93,039	22,037	98,178	95,198	108,645	119,894
	1,001 cc–1,600 cc		764,289	809,219	793,307	729,397	814,873	845,084	829,086
	1,601 cc–2,800 cc		260,231	325,116	437,951	573,357	528,444	635,861	653,154
	> 2,800 cc		72,869	68,236	38,585	65,891	93,569	96,544	95,881
	Total		1,226,835	1,295,610	1,291,880	1,466,823	1,532,084	1,686,134	1,698,015
Commercial vehicles	light commercial vehicles		250,053	230,510	216,477	197,285	199,346	205,372	210,942
	trucks	< 7.5 tonnes	19,732	10,515	9,558	8,154	9,523	9,812	7,026
		> 7.5 tonnes	24,887	13,674	11,113	10,016	11,717	9,229	7,158
	motive units for articulated vehicles		6,171	3,327	2,788	2,794	3,476	208	N/A
	buses, coaches, and minibuses		16,500	12,320	8,517	9,566	8,939	9,254	7,653
	Total		317,343	270,346	248,453	227,815	233,001	238,314	237,703

Source: *Annual Abstract of Statistics 1999,* © Crown copyright 1999

UK Agriculture

Agricultural Land Use in the UK

The data in this table cover all holdings (including minor holdings) in England, Wales, and Northern Ireland but exclude minor holdings in Scotland. (Area given is that at the annual June agricultural census. In hectares. N/A = not available.)

Land use	1986	1987	1988	1989	1990	1991	1992	1993	1994	1995	1996	1997
Agricultural area												
crops	5,240,000	5,272,000	5,255,000	5,138,000	5,013,000	4,956,000	4,981,000	4,519,000	4,469,000	4,544,000	4,721,000	4,990,000
bare fallow	48,000	42,000	58,000	65,000	64,000	64,000	53,000	47,000	44,000	40,000	35,000	29,000
Total	18,670,000	18,672,000	18,634,000	18,580,000	18,563,000	18,498,000	18,511,000	18,530,000	18,503,000	18,406,000	18,401,000	18,653,000
Tillage												
all grass under 5 years old	1,721,000	1,690,000	1,613,000	1,538,000	1,582,000	1,586,000	1,562,000	1,561,000	1,436,000	1,387,000	1,376,000	1,405,000
Total	5,288,000	5,314,000	5,313,000	5,203,000	5,077,000	5,020,000	5,033,000	4,566,000	4,513,000	4,584,000	4,756,000	5,020,000
Arable land												
all grass 5 years old and over	5,075,000	5,107,000	5,159,000	5,239,000	5,272,000	5,261,000	5,213,000	5,209,000	5,322,000	5,309,000	5,289,000	5,282,000
Total	7,008,000	7,003,000	6,926,000	6,741,000	6,659,000	6,605,000	6,595,000	6,127,000	5,949,000	5,971,000	6,133,000	6,425,000
Tillage and grass												
sole right rough grazing	4,826,000	4,790,000	4,763,000	4,739,000	4,715,000	4,685,000	4,680,000	4,611,000	4,551,000	4,516,000	4,489,000	4,657,000
set aside[1]	N/A	N/A	N/A	N/A	72,000	97,000	160,000	677,000	728,000	633,000	509,000	306,000
all other land on agricultural holdings, including woodland	544,000	555,000	571,000	624,000	609,000	616,000	632,000	678,000	708,000	729,000	745,000	763,000
Total	12,083,000	12,110,000	12,085,000	11,980,000	11,931,000	11,866,000	11,808,000	11,335,000	11,271,000	11,280,000	11,241,000	11,706,000
Land on agricultural holdings												
common rough grazing	1,216,000	1,216,000	1,216,000	1,236,000	1,236,000	1,233,000	1,230,000	1,229,000	1,246,000	1,248,000	1,237,000	1,221,000
Total	17,454,000	17,456,000	17,419,000	17,344,000	17,327,000	17,264,000	17,281,000	17,301,000	17,258,000	17,158,000	17,164,000	17,432,000
Crops												
Cereals												
wheat	1,997,000	1,994,000	1,886,000	2,083,000	2,013,000	1,980,000	2,067,000	1,759,000	1,811,000	1,859,000	1,976,000	2,036,000
barley	1,917,000	1,831,000	1,879,000	1,652,000	1,516,000	1,393,000	1,297,000	1,164,000	1,106,000	1,192,000	1,267,000	1,359,000
oats	97,000	99,000	120,000	118,000	106,000	103,000	100,000	92,000	109,000	112,000	96,000	100,000
mixed corn	7,000	6,000	5,000	5,000	4,000	4,000	4,000	3,000	3,000	3,000	3,000	2,000
rye[2]	7,000	7,000	7,000	7,000	8,000	9,000	8,000	6,000	7,000	8,000	8,000	9,000
triticale[3]	N/A	N/A	N/A	8,000	9,000	11,000	11,000	7,000	6,000	7,000	7,000	8,000
Total	4,025,000	3,936,000	3,898,000	3,874,000	3,657,000	3,500,000	3,487,000	3,031,000	3,042,000	3,180,000	3,357,000	3,514,000
Other arable crops (excluding potatoes)												
oilseed rape	299,000	388,000	347,000	321,000	390,000	440,000	421,000	377,000	404,000	354,000	356,000	445,000
sugar beet not for stock feeding[2]	205,000	203,000	201,000	197,000	194,000	196,000	197,000	197,000	195,000	196,000	199,000	196,000
hops[4]	4,000	4,000	4,000	4,000	4,000	4,000	4,000	3,000	3,000	3,000	3,000	3,000
peas for harvesting dry and field beans	150,000	208,000	260,000	215,000	216,000	203,000	208,000	244,000	228,000	195,000	178,000	197,000
linseed[5]	N/A	N/A	N/A	17,000	34,000	92,000	144,000	150,000	58,000	54,000	49,000	73,000
others	165,000	156,000	156,000	128,000	133,000	142,000	143,000	159,000	187,000	204,000	217,000	211,000
Total	824,000	958,000	968,000	882,000	971,000	1,076,000	1,117,000	1,130,000	1,076,000	1,005,000	1,003,000	1,126,000
CROPS TOTAL	5,240,000	5,272,000	5,255,000	5,138,000	5,013,000	4,956,000	4,981,000	4,519,000	4,469,000	4,544,000	4,721,000	4,990,000
Potatoes	177,000	178,000	180,000	174,000	177,000	176,000	180,000	170,000	164,000	171,000	177,000	166,000
Horticultural	214,000	200,000	209,000	208,000	208,000	204,000	197,000	187,000	189,000	187,000	189,000	185,000
Vegetables grown in the open	146,000	132,000	141,000	141,000	142,000	139,000	135,000	126,000	127,000	130,000	132,000	126,000
Orchard fruit	38,000	38,000	37,000	36,000	34,000	34,000	33,000	32,000	32,000	28,000	28,000	30,000
Soft fruit	15,000	15,000	15,000	15,000	15,000	15,000	14,000	13,000	13,000	12,000	12,000	11,000
Ornamentals[6]	12,000	12,000	13,000	14,000	14,000	14,000	14,000	14,000	14,000	15,000	14,000	14,000
Glasshouse crops	2,000	2,000	2,000	2,000	2,000	2,000	2,000	2,000	2,000	2,000	2,000	2,000

[1] Figures are for England only in 1990 and 1991, and Great Britain only in 1992.
[2] Figures are for England and Wales only.
[3] Figures are for Great Britain only.
[4] Figures are for England and Wales only for 1989 and England only from 1990.
[5] Figures are for England and Wales only from 1989 to 1991, and for Great Britain only in 1992.
[6] Includes non-commercial orchards.

Source: *Annual Abstract of Statistics 1999,*

Agricultural Outputs, Inputs, Net Products, and Incomes in the UK

Figures are given in calendar years. 1997 figures are provisional.
(N = nil or negligible. In millions of pounds.)

1996–97

Category		England and Wales		Scotland		Northern Ireland	
		1996	1997	1996	1997	1996	1997
Outputs[1]							
1	Total cereals	2,698	2,297	361	288	22	20
2	Total other crops	991	947	52	67	2	2
3	Total potatoes	419	266	110	69	16	13
4	Total horticulture	1,888	1,781	89	92	57	56
5	Total livestock[2 3]	4,739	4,208	996	972	661	610
6	Total livestock products	3,311	2,997	339	307	392	351
7	Own account capital formation: livestock	–90	22	–4	–6	11	19
8	Total output (1+2+3+4+5+6+7)	13,955	12,516	1,944	1,790	1,160	1,071
9	Other direct receipts[3 4]	650	531	100	79	94	49
10	Total receipts (8+9)	14,606	13,047	2,043	1,869	1,254	1,120
11	Total value of physical increase in output stocks	81	18	–25	–7	–11	–12
12	Gross output (10+11)	14,687	13,065	2,018	1,862	1,243	1,108
Inputs							
13	Total expenditure[2]	6,772	6,487	976	939	685	659
14	Value of physical increase in input stock[5]	–10	–27	N	4	N	N
15	Gross input (13–14)	6,782	6,514	976	935	686	659
16	Gross product (12–15)	7,905	6,552	1,042	928	557	449
17	Total depreciation	1,547	1,575	224	222	169	170
18	Net product (16–17)	6,358	4,976	818	705	389	279
19	Interest[6]	423	476	86	94	37	44
20	Net rent	141	160	15	15	N	N
21	Income from agriculture of total labour (18–19–20)	5,794	4,341	717	596	352	235
22	Labour: hired[7 8]	1,476	1,552	214	224	34	33
23	Total income from farming (21–22)	4,318	2,789	503	372	319	203
24	Labour: family, partners, and directors[9 10]	891	942	76	83	71	63
25	Farming income[10] (23–24)	3,427	1,847	427	289	247	140

1 Output is net of VAT collected on the sale of non-edible products. Figures for total output include subsidies but not 'other direct receipts'.
2 In this table, total livestock includes sale of store between England, Wales, and Scotland. Similarly, total expenditure includes the purchases of such stock. The sum of the four countries will therefore not match the UK total for some items.
3 Compensation payments to farmers paid for the Over Thirty Months Scheme and the Calf Processing Aid Scheme are included in 'other direct receipts'.
4 These receipts include compensation for set-aside land and milk quota cuts.
5 Input stocks comprise fertilizers and purchased feed.
6 Figures include interest charges on loans for current farming purposes and buildings and works, less interest on money held on short term deposit.
7 Includes employers' national insurance contributions, perks, and other payments (including the payment by farmers of rates on farm cottages occupied by farm workers and of their council tax).
8 Excludes the value of work done by farm labour on own account capital formation in buildings and works.
9 The estimate in respect of family workers, non-principal partners, and directors (and their spouses) is calculated on the basis of the earnings of hired labour.
10 Income is calculated as the return to farmers (and their spouses) for their labour, management skills, and own capital invested after providing for depreciation.

Source: *Farm Incomes in the United Kingdom 1996/97*, © Crown copyright 1998

Number and Size of Farms in the UK

As of June 1997.

Number and area of holdings	Hectares													
	<2	2–<5	5–<10	10–<20	20–<30	30–<40	40–<50	50–<100	100–<200	200–<300	300–<500	500–<700	700 and over	Total[1]
England														
number of holdings	10,707	12,568	18,573	20,696	13,152	10,159	8,503	24,425	16,366	4,850	3,161	879	738	144,777
%	7.4	8.7	12.8	14.3	9.1	7.0	5.9	16.9	11.3	3.3	2.2	0.6	0.5	100.0
area of holdings (ha)	9,789	41,985	136,077	298,156	324,628	352,844	379,513	1,744,532	2,272,425	1,168,446	1,194,385	511,383	789,153	9,223,317
%	0.1	0.5	1.5	3.2	3.5	3.8	4.1	18.9	24.6	12.7	12.9	5.5	8.6	100.0
Scotland[2]														
number of holdings	1,959	3,556	2,939	3,461	2,335	1,839	1,672	5,849	4,862	1,651	1,131	471	1,163	32,888
%	6.0	10.8	8.9	10.5	7.1	5.6	5.1	17.8	14.8	5.0	3.4	1.4	3.5	100.0
area of holdings (ha)	2,355	11,673	21,176	49,872	57,594	64,017	74,724	423,478	676,867	398,462	430,778	276,405	2,705,750	5,193,149
%	0.0	0.2	0.4	1.0	1.1	1.2	1.4	8.2	13.0	7.7	8.3	5.3	52.1	100.00
Wales														
number of holdings	815	1,721	3,795	4,650	3,104	2,469	2,090	5,532	2,779	552	303	67	60	27,937
%	2.9	6.2	13.6	16.6	11.1	8.8	7.5	19.8	9.9	2.0	1.1	0.2	0.2	100.0
area of holdings (ha)	768	5,933	28,355	67,399	76,522	85,760	93,410	390,216	375,384	133,227	115,323	39,090	66,060	1,477,447
%	0.1	0.4	1.9	4.6	5.2	5.8	6.3	26.4	25.4	9.0	7.8	2.6	4.5	100.0
Northern Ireland														
number of holdings	1,039	2,380	4,550	7,211	4,932	3,367	2,333	4,710	1,328	177	71	11	9	32,118
%	3.2	7.4	14.2	22.5	15.4	10.5	7.3	14.7	4.1	0.6	0.2	0.0	0.0	100.0
area of holdings (ha)	833	8,362	33,762	105,245	121,453	116,467	103,829	321,202	174,002	41,852	25,958	6,329	9,569	1,068,862
%	0.1	0.8	3.2	9.8	11.4	10.9	9.7	30.1	16.3	3.9	2.4	0.6	0.9	100.0
Total UK														
number of holdings	14,520	20,225	29,857	36,018	23,523	17,834	14,598	40,516	25,335	7,230	4,666	1,428	1,970	237,720
%	6.1	8.5	12.6	15.2	9.9	7.5	6.1	17.0	10.7	3.0	2.0	0.6	0.8	100.0
area of holdings (ha)	13,744	67,954	219,369	520,672	580,196	619,088	651,476	2,879,428	3,498,678	1,741,987	1,766,443	833,207	3,570,533	16,962,776
%	0.1	0.4	1.3	3.1	3.4	3.6	3.8	17.0	20.6	10.3	10.4	4.9	21.0	100.0

[1] Totals may not necessarily agree with the sum of their components, due to rounding.

[2] Figures for Scotland include 40 holdings with zero area which are sheep stock clubs.

Source: *The Digest of Agricultural Census Statistics*, © Crown copyright 1998

Fishing Fleet of the UK

Prior to 1990 the figures refer to vessels that were active; after 1990 the figures refer to vessels in the registered fleet for which the data are currently under review.
(– = not applicable. N/A = not available.)

Fleet by size and segment	1992	1993	1994	1995	1996	1997
By size (metres)						
10 and under	7,376	7,666	7,194	6,319	5,606	5,474
>10						
10.00–12.19	1,450	1,361	1,167	1,016	800	732
12.20–17.00	787	751	680	622	540	523
17.01–18.29	232	220	193	187	164	162
18.30–24.38	697	657	610	574	509	471
24.39–30.48	200	210	211	212	223	227
30.49–36.58	120	124	126	127	114	104
>36.58	117	119	116	117	117	119
Total >10m	3,603	3,442	3,103	2,855	2,467	2,338
Total UK fleet (excluding islands)	10,979	11,108	10,297	9,174	8,073	7,812

(continued)

Fishing Fleet of the UK (*continued*)

Fleet by size and segment	1992	1993	1994	1995	1996	1997
By segment						
pelagic gears	76	69	68	67	58	49
beam trawls	227	240	212	220	215	153
demersal trawls	1,039	988	854	856	N/A	N/A
nephrop trawls	566	560	593	528	411	N/A
seines	255	203	197	165	N/A	N/A
demersal trawls and seines	N/A	N/A	N/A	N/A	1,040	N/A
demersal, seines, and nephrops	N/A	N/A	N/A	N/A	N/A	1,428
lines and nets	339	329	300	267	224	214
shellfish: mobile	214	181	206	194	265	227
shellfish: fixed	306	312	305	283	339	352
distant water	16	14	13	12	15	13
under 10 metres	7,831	8,128	7,607	6,757	6,091	6,022
non-active/non-TAC[1]	692	668	472	371	–	–
other: mussel dredgers	N/A	N/A	N/A	N/A	N/A	3
Total UK fleet[2]	11,561	11,692	10,827	9,720	8,658	8,461

[1] TAC = Total Allowable Catch; this is for fish species for which there are quotas.
[2] The UK figures here include Channel Islands and Isle of Man.

Source: *Annual Abstract of Statistics 1999,* © Crown copyright 1999

Forestry in the UK

(Years ending 31 March. Area: thousands of hectares; volume: millions of cubic metres.)

Item	1987–88	1988–89	1989–90	1990–91	1991–92	1992–93	1993–94	1994–95	1995–96	1996–97	1997–98
Forest Area[1]											
Great Britain	2,285	2,307	2,326	2,336	2,350	2,361	2,377	2,390	2,405	2,423	2,440
Northern Ireland	72	73	74	75	77	77	78	79	80	81	81
Total UK	2,357	2,380	2,400	2,411	2,427	2,438	2,455	2,469	2,485	2,504	2,521
Forestry Commission (Great Britain)											
Productive woodland	888	888	864[5]	859	855	845	827	815	804	795	785
Net disposals of forestry land[2]	4.7	2.5	4.5	0.8	4.2	6.5	14.1	9.6	8.2	9.6	10.3
New planting[3]	5.0	4.1	4.1	3.5	3.0	2.4	1.4	0.9	0.4	0.5	0.1
Restocking[3]	8.1	8.5	7.9	7.6	8.3	8.5	7.9	7.9	7.5	7.9	7.8
Volume of timber removed[4]	3.4	3.6	3.5	3.4	3.9	4.1	4.3	4.3	4.2	4.7	4.7
Total estates	1,148	1,143	1,140	1,133	1,128	1,115	1,100	1,089	1,080	1,073	1,062
Private Forestry (Great Britain)											
Productive woodland	1,227	1,231	1,266	1,281	1,298	1,317	1,344	1,367	1,392	1,417	1,444
New planting[3]	24.0	25.4	15.6	15.5	14.3	15.5	16.1	18.5	15.3	16.4	16.2
Restocking[3]	5.0	4.9	6.3	7.2	7.9	8.1	8.5	6.2	5.8	6.6	5.6
Volume of timber removed[4]	2.8	3.2	3.6	3.3	3.1	2.9	3.0	3.8	4.2	4.0	4.4
State Afforestation in Northern Ireland											
Land under plantation	58.4	58.3	58.5	58.8	60.6	60.8	60.8	61.0	61.0	60.9	61.0
Plantable land acquired during year	0.4	0.4	0.6	0.4	0.3	0.4	0.4	0.1	0.1	0.1	0.1
Total area planted during year	1.0	1.0	1.0	1.0	0.9	0.9	0.8	0.8	0.8	0.6	0.7
Total estates	74.1	74.3	74.6	74.8	75.1	75.2	75.5	75.5	75.3	75.5	75.5

[1] Includes unproductive woodland.
[2] Data represent disposals less acquisitions, for plantations and plantable land.
[3] New planting is planting on ground not previously carrying forest; restocking is replacing trees after felling.
[4] Figures represent standing volume overbark; private forestry figures are for calendar years ending the previous December.
[5] The apparent decrease in 1989–90 is mainly the result of the reclassification of certain woodland types within the Forestry Commission.

Source: *Annual Abstract of Statistics 1999,* © Crown copyright 1999

UK Energy

Electricity Distributed by Regional Company in the UK

1997

Region	Area (sq km)	Number of customers	Customer density (number per sq km)	Electricity distributed (gigawatt hours)
Eastern	20,300	3,167,000	156	31,916
East Midlands	16,000	2,300,000	144	25,553
London	665	1,954,000	2,938	21,444
Manweb	12.200	1,357,000	111	18,353
Midlands	13,300	2,220,000	165	25,555
Northern	14,400	1,455,000	101	15,739
Northern Ireland	13,506	663,000	49	6,930
Norweb	12,500	2,176,000	174	23,254
Scottish Hydro-Electric	54,390	630,000	12	8,004
Scottish Power	22,950	1,800,000	78	21,688
Seeboard	8,200	1,985,000	242	18,582
Southern	16,900	2,599,000	154	28,663
Swalec	11,800	960,000	81	11,872
South Western	14,400	1,297,000	90	13,778
Yorkshire	10,700	2,048,000	191	23,580
Total	242,211	26,611,000	110	294,645

Source: *Digest of United Kingdom Energy Statistics 1998,* © Crown copyright 1998

Electricity Generation, Supply, and Consumption in the UK

(– = not applicable. N/A = not available. N = nil or negligible. In gigawatt hours.)

Category		1988	1990	1992	1994	1996	1997
Electricity Generated							
Major power producers[1]							
conventional steam stations		222,887	230,376	217,228	174,943	160,565	133,132
combined cycle gas turbine stations		N/A	N/A	2,991	36,971	65,880	86,974
nuclear stations		58,867	61,306	73,269	88,282	91,040	98,146
gas turbines and oil engines		464	432	358	244	226	459
hydro-electric stations	natural flow	4,171	4,393	4,591	4,317	2,801	3,337
	pumped storage	2,121	1,982	1,697	1,463	1,556	1,486
renewables other than hydro[2]		1	4	45	506	588	609
Total		288,511	298,495	300,177	306,726	326,287	324,143
Other generators[3]							
conventional steam stations[4]		14,294	15,014	15,049	14,866	17,200	16,304
combined cycle gas turbine stations		N/A	292	409	902	1,232	1,500
nuclear stations[5]		4,589	4,441	3,538	4,338	3,631	–
hydro-electric stations (natural flow)		762	814	840	777	560	790
renewables other than hydro[2]		659	683	1,028	1,707	2,107	2,605
Total		20,314	21,244	20,864	18,252	21,099	21,999
All generating companies							
conventional steam stations		237,181	245,390	232,277	189,809	177,765	149,436
combined cycle gas turbine stations		N/A	292	3,400	37,873	67,112	88,474
nuclear stations		63,456	65,749	76,807	88,282	94,671	98,146
gas turbines and oil engines		464	432	358	244	226	459
hydro-electric stations	natural flow	4,933	5,207	5,431	5,094	3,361	4,127
	pumped storage	2,121	1,982	1,697	1,463	1,556	1,486
renewables other than hydro[2]		670	687	1,073	2,213	2,695	3,214
Total		308,825	319,739	321,043	325,397	347,386	345,342
Electricity used on works							
major generating companies[1]		18,694	17,891	18,485	15,921	16,064	15,404
other generators[3]		1,532	1,720	1,752	1,583	1,664	956
Total		20,226	19,611	20,237	17,504	17,728	16,369

(continued)

Electricity Generation, Supply, and Consumption in the UK (*continued*)

Category		1988	1990	1992	1994	1996	1997
Electricity Supplied (Gross)							
Major power producers[1]							
conventional steam stations		211,502	218,957	205,897	167,289	153,170	127,075
combined cycle gas turbine stations		N/A	N/A	2,964	36,315	65,604	86,609
nuclear stations		55,642	58,664	69,135	79,962	85,820	89,341
gas turbines and oil engines		430	403	311	233	216	436
hydro-electric stations	natural flow	4,160	4,384	4,579	4,265	2,763	3,299
	pumped storage	2,025	1,892	1,635	1,417	1,507	1,439
renewables other than hydro[2]		1	3	37	455	533	540
Total		269,817	280,604	281,692	290,030	309,612	308,739
Other generators[3]							
conventional steam stations[4]		13,442	14,082	14,033	14,183	16,340	15,583
combined cycle gas turbine stations		N/A	280	394	866	1,180	1,425
nuclear stations[5]		3,942	3,700	2,866	3,550	2,949[5]	
hydro-electric stations (natural flow)		669	806	832	769	554	751
renewables other than hydro[2]		643	656	987	1,639	1,954	2,475
Total		18,782	19,524	19,112	17,457	20,028	20,234
All generating companies							
conventional steam stations[4]		224,944	233,039	219,930	182,066	169,510	142,658
combined cycle gas turbine stations		N/A	280	3,358	37,681	66,784	88,034
nuclear stations		55,642	58,664	69,135	79,962	85,820	89,341
gas turbines and oil engines		430	403	311	233	216	436
hydro-electric stations	natural flow	4,914	5,190	5,411	5,034	3,317	4,050
	pumped storage	2,025	1,892	1,635	1,417	1,507	1,439
renewables other than hydro[2]		644	659	1,024	2,094	2,487	3,015
Total		288,599	300,128	300,804	307,893	329,641	328,973
Electricity used in pumping	major power producers[1]	2,888	2,626	2,257	2,051	2,430	2,477
Electricity supplied (net)	major power producers[1]	266,929	277,978	279,435	287,979	307,181	306,262
	other generators[3]	18,782	19,524	19,112	17,457	20,028	20,234
Generation and supply total		265,711	297,502	298,547	305,842	327,209	326,496
Net imports		12,830	11,990	16,694	16,887	16,677	16,575
Electricity available		298,540	309,408	315,241	322,729	343,866	343,071
Losses in transmission, etc		24,036	24,988	23,788	30,947	29,601	25,585
Electricity consumption							
Fuel industries		9,163	9,986	9,984	7,518	8,629	8,235
Final users							
industrial sector		97,143	100,643	95,277	95,067	103,129	104,743
domestic sector		92,362	93,793	99,482	101,407	107,513	104,455
other sectors		75,837	79,997	86,711	87,790	95,014	100,053
Total		265,342	274,434	281,468	284,264	305,656	309,251
Consumption total		274,505	284,420	291,453	291,782	314,285	317,486

[1] Represents generating companies corresponding to the old public sector supply system, i.e. National Power, PowerGen, Nuclear Electric, First Hydro Ltd, Scottish Power, Scottish Hydro-Electric, Scottish Nuclear, Premier Power Ltd, Coolkeeragh Power Ltd, Midland Power (UK) Ltd, South Western Electricity, NIGEN, and new independent generators, i.e. Teeside Power Ltd, Lakeland Power Ltd, Corby Power Ltd, Peterborough Power Ltd, Regional Power Ltd, Fibropower Ltd, Fibrogen Ltd, Fellside Heat and Power Ltd, Kead by Generation Ltd, Barking Power Ltd, Elm Energy and Recycling (UK) Ltd, South East London Combined Heat and Power Ltd, Derwent Cogeneration Ltd, Medway Power Ltd.

[2] Includes wind and biofuels.

[3] Represents larger establishments in the industrial and transport sectors generating one gigawatt-hour or more a year. Reactors operated by the United Kingdom Atomic Energy Authority and by British Nuclear Fuels plc are included.

[4] For other generators, conventional steam stations cover all types of station not separately listed.

[5] Nuclear generators are included under 'major power producers' only from 1997.

Source: *Annual Abstract of Statistics 1999*, © Crown copyright 1999

Nuclear Power Plants in the UK

(Magnox – named after the magnesium oxide casing surrounding the uranium fuel rod. PWR – pressure water reactor; AGR – advanced gas reactor.)

Station name	Company	Fuel	Installed capacity (megawatts)	Year of commission
Hinkley Point B	Nuclear Electric	AGR	1,275	1978
Torness	Scottish Nuclear	AGR	1,250	1988
Heysham 2	Nuclear Electric	AGR	1,320	1989
Sizewell B	Nuclear Electric	PWR	1,200	1994
Hunterston B	Scottish Nuclear	AGR	1,150	1976
Heysham 1	Nuclear Electric	AGR	1,150	1989
Hartlepool	Nuclear Electric	AGR	1,200	1989
Dungeness B	Nuclear Electric	AGR	1,112	1985
Wylfa	Magnox Electric	Magnox	1,050	1971
Hinkley Point A	Magnox Electric	Magnox	475	1965
Dungeness A	Magnox Electric	Magnox	445	1965
Oldbury	Magnox Electric	Magnox	440	1967
Sizewell A	Magnox Electric	Magnox	430	1966
Brodwell	Magnox Electric	Magnox	240	1962
Calder Hall	British Nuclear Fuels	Magnox	192	1956
Chapelcross	British Nuclear Fuels	Magnox	196	1959

Source: *Energy Report: Transforming Markets 1998,*

Renewable Energy Utilization in the UK

Data include some waste of fossil fuel origin. (In thousands of tonnes of oil equivalent.)

Source	1993	1995	1997
Used to Generate Electricity[1]			
Onshore wind	18,800	33,600	57,200
Hydro			
small scale	13,600	14,300	13,600
large scale[2]	356,200	401,700	341,200
Biofuels			
landfill gas	146,600	185,500	288,600
sewage sludge digestion[3]	123,800	120,200	131,300
municipal solid waste combustion[4]	189,000	315,300	413,100
other[5]	59,000	133,200	137,500
Total biofuels	518,400	754,2000	970,400
TOTAL	907,100	1,203,800	1,382,500
Used to Generate Heat			
Active solar heating[6]	7,500	8,200	9,000
Biofuels			
landfill gas	15,000	20,300	20,100
sewage sludge digestion[3]	34,000	53,300	60,200
wood combustion (domestic)[7]	204,200	204,200	204,200
wood combustion (industrial)[7]	236,800	498,100	506,100
straw combustion[8]	71,700	71,700	71,700
municipal solid waste combustion[4]	44,800	42,300	13,900
other[9]	37,300	46,000	43,700
Total biofuels	643,700	935,800	919,900
Geothermal aquifiers	800	800	800
TOTAL	652,000	944,900	929,700
Total Use of Renewable Sources			
Active solar heating[6]	7,500	8,200	9,000
Onshore wind	18,700	33,600	57,200
Hydro			
small scale	13,600	14,300	13,600
large scale[2]	356,200	401,700	341,200
Biofuels			
landfill gas	161,600	205,800	308,700
sewage sludge digestion[3]	157,800	173,500	191,500
wood combustion (domestic)[7]	204,200	204,200	204,200
wood combustion (industrial)[7]	236,800	498,100	506,100
straw combustion[8]	71,700	71,700	71,700
municipal solid waste combustion[4]	233,800	357,600	427,000
other[5 9]	96,200	179,200	181,200
Total biofuels	1,162,100	1,690,100	1,890,300
Geothermal aquifiers	800	800	800
TOTAL	1,559,100	2,148,700	2,312,200

[1] For wind and hydro, the figures represent the energy content of the electricity supplied, but for biofuels the figures represent the energy content of the fuel used.
[2] Excluding pumped storage stations.
[3] No estimate is made for digestors where gas is used to heat the sludge.
[4] Includes combustion of refuse-derived fuel pellets.
[5] Includes electricity from farm waste digestion, poultry litter combustion, and waste tyre combustion.
[6] Figures are based on a survey carried out in 1994.
[7] Figures are an approximate estimate of domestic combustion based on a survey carried out in 1989; a moisture content of five percent is assumed. Industrial wood combustion is included under 'other'.
[8] An approximate estimate based on a limited survey carried out in 1994 and on information collected in 1990.
[9] Includes heat from industrial wood waste combustion, waste tyre combustion, hospital waste combustion, general industrial waste combustion, and farm waste digestion.

Source: *Digest of United Kingdom Energy Statistics 1998,*

Total Inland Energy Consumption in the UK

(In millions of tonnes of oil equivalent.)

Category	1990	1992	1994	1996	1997
Inland Energy Consumption of Primary Fuels and Equivalents[1]					
Coal[2]	67.4	63.6	52.5	46.9	42.0
Petroleum[3]	78.3	78.3	77.6	78.2	75.5
Primary electricity[4]	17.7	20.4	23.1	23.9	24.8
Natural gas[5]	51.4	55.6	66.1	83.9	84.5
Less energy used by fuel producers and losses in conversion and distribution	67.6	66.8	66.2	70.9	69.0
Total consumption by final users[1]	**146.4**	**150.0**	**153.2**	**162.0**	**157.9**
Total internal energy consumption[1]	**214.9**	**217.8**	**219.4**	**233.0**	**226.9**
Final Energy Consumption by Type of Fuel					
Coal (direct use)	8.1	8.1	6.9	5.0	4.6
Coke and breeze	4.3	3.9	3.8	4.0	3.9
Other solid fuel[6]	1.2	1.1	1.5	1.4	1.3
Coke oven gas	0.6	0.5	0.6	0.6	0.7
Natural gas (direct use)[5]	46.1	48.7	50.2	57.7	54.5
Electricity	23.6	24.2	24.4	26.3	26.6
Petroleum (direct use)[6]	63.3	64.6	66.8	66.9	66.3
Final Energy Consumption by Class of Consumer					
Agriculture	1.3	1.4	1.4	1.4	1.3
Iron and steel industry	6.9	6.5	7.7	8.0	7.9
Other industries	30.9	29.1	30.7	30.2	31.2
Railways[7]	1.0	1.0	0.7	0.6	0.5
Road transport	38.8	39.4	39.7	40.8	41.3
Water transport	1.4	1.4	1.3	1.3	1.2
Air transport	7.3	7.4	8.1	8.9	9.3
Domestic	40.8	44.0	44.0	48.1	44.8
Public administration	7.7	9.1	8.3	9.0	8.6
Commercial and other services[8]	10.3	10.5	11.0	12.1	12.2

[1] Includes, from 1988, small amounts of primary heat sources (solar, geothermal, etc). Up to 1988 includes natural gas used for non-energy purposes (e.g. petrochemicals).
[2] Includes net trade and stock change in other solid fuels. Includes, from 1988, solid renewable sources (wood, waste, etc).
[3] Figures give refinery throughput of crude oil, plus net foreign trade and stock change in petroleum products. Petroleum products not used as fuels (chemical feedstock, industrial and white spirits, lubricants, bitumen, and wax) are excluded.
[4] Primary electricity comprises nuclear, natural flow hydro, net imports of electricity, and, from 1988, generation of wind stations.
[5] Natural gas includes colliery methane, non-energy use of natural gas up to 1988, and, from 1988, landfill gas and sewage gas.
[6] Includes products such as briquettes, ovoids, Phurnacite, and Coalite, and, from 1988, wood, waste, and other materials used for heat generation.
[7] Figures include fuel used at transport premises from 1990.
[8] Figures include fuel used at transport premises prior to1990.

Source: *Annual Abstract of Statistics 1999,* © Crown copyright 1999

UK Trade

Goods Transport in Great Britain

(N/A = not available.)

Item		1987	1988	1989	1990	1991	1992	1993	1994	1995	1996	1997
In billion tonne km												
Road		113.3	130.2	137.8	136.3	130.0	126.5	134.5	143.7	149.6	153.9	157.1
Rail		17.5	18.1	16.7	16.0	15.3	15.5	13.8	13.0	13.3	15.1	16.9
Water[1]	coastwise oil[2]	31.4	34.2	34.1	32.1	31.2	29.4	28.9	28.9	31.4	38.7	33.8
	other	22.7	25.1	23.8	23.6	26.5	25.5	22.3	23.3	21.2	17.4	14.4
Pipelines		10.5	11.1	9.8	11.0	11.1	11.0	11.6	12.0	11.1	11.6	11.2
Total		195.2	218.8	222.8	218.8	214.1	208.3	210.9	220.8	226.6	236.7	233.4
In million tonnes												
Road		1,542	1,758	1,812	1,749	1,600	1,555	1,615	1,689	1,701	1,730	1,740
Rail		144	150	143	138	136	122	103	97	101	102	105
Water[1]	coastwise oil[2]	43	47	46	44	44	43	42	43	47	54	52
	other	99	109	109	108	100	97	92	97	98	88	91
Pipelines		83	99	93	121[6]	105	106	125	161	168	157	148
Total		1,909	2,163	2,206	2,163	1,984	1,923	1,984	2,087	2,115	2,131	2,136

[1] Water figures are provisional for 1997.
[2] Oil comprises crude oil and all petroleum products. 'Coastwise' includes all sea traffic within the UK, Isle of Man, and Channel Islands. 'Other' means coastwise plus inland waterway traffic and one-port traffic (one-port traffic is largely crude oil direct from rigs).

Source: *Annual Abstract of Statistics 1999,* © Crown copyright 1999

Imports and Exports by Commodity of the UK

(In millions of pounds.)

Category		1990	1992	1994	1996	1997
Import of Goods						
Food and live animals	meat and meat preparations	1,890	2,030	1,976	2,663	2,331
	dairy products and eggs	916	1,113	1,144	1,246	1,144
	cereals and animal feeding stuffs	1,411	1,722	1,777	2,020	2,089
	vegetables and fruit	2,966	3,118	3,484	4,408	4,094
	Total	10,411	11,402	12,385	14,835	13,997
Beverages and tobacco	beverages	1,531	1,563	1,882	2,316	2,438
	tobacco	377	462	382	626	571
	Total	1,908	2,027	2,262	2,945	3,012
Crude materials	wood, lumber, and cork	1,408	1,026	1,406	1,288	1,338
	pulp and waste paper	779	630	642	713	628
	textile fibres	549	480	633	691	645
	metal ores	1,478	1,164	1,165	1,619	1,624
	Total	5,721	4,667	5,547	6,357	6,186
Fuels	petroleum and petroleum products	6,286	5,325	4,843	5,730	5,206
	coal, gas, and electricity	1,581	1,689	1,311	1,310	1,322
	Total	7,866	7,018	6,154	7,040	6,526
Animal and vegetable oils and fats	**Total**	377	421	539	731	647
Chemicals	organic chemicals	2,630	2,794	3,544	4,890	4,634
	inorganic chemicals	964	952	1,105	1,288	1,158
	plastics	3,228	3,038	3,775	4,478	4,292
	Total	10,833	11,618	14,623	18,746	18,017
Manufactures classified chiefly by material	wood and cork manufactures	951	847	1,039	1,121	1,129
	paper and paperboard manufactures	4,017	3,804	4,287	5,113	4,676
	textile manufactures	3,938	3,943	4,551	5,255	5,179
	iron and steel	2,688	2,515	2,975	3,716	3,432
	non-ferrous metals	3,004	2,592	3,032	3,860	3,756
	metal manufactures	2,592	2,579	2,925	3,625	3,700
	Total	21,903	20,671	24,551	29,611	28,843
Machinery and transport equipment	mechanical machinery	12,068	11,665	13,432	17,116	17,612
	electrical machinery	18,451	20,129	26,942	36,741	37,272
	road vehicles	12,597	12,120	16,287	20,851	22,222
	other transport equipment	4,052	3,410	4,279	3,723	5,654
	Total	47,164	47,319	60,931	78,426	82,759
Miscellaneous manufactures	clothing and footwear	5,074	5,629	6,368	8,097	8,814
	scientific and photographic	4,073	4,258	4,989	6,240	6,304
	Total	18,171	19,051	21,915	25,864	27,471
Other commodities and transactions	**Total**	1,740	1,679	991	1,613	1,630
IMPORTS TOTAL		126,090	125,867	149,890	182,151	189,079
Export of Goods						
Food and live animals	meat and meat preparations	613	829	1,237	1,099	932
	dairy products and eggs	461	535	697	745	746
	cereals and animal feeding stuffs	1,302	1,543	1,528	2,044	1,811
	vegetables and fruit	265	333	399	480	457
	Total	4,344	5,292	6,352	7,117	6,609
Beverages and tobacco	beverages	2,116	2,448	2,876	3,183	3,334
	tobacco	656	971	871	1,213	1,228
	Total	2,774	3,417	3,745	4,399	4,562
Crude materials	wood, lumber, and cork	27	25	45	52	52
	pulp and waste paper	52	39	50	56	64
	textile fibres	496	489	574	620	572
	metal ores	634	459	666	668	644
	Total	2,163	1,880	2,405	2,626	2,509
Fuels	petroleum and petroleum products	7,544	6,665	8,520	10,424	9,649
	coal, gas, and electricity	326	308	416	661	779
	Total	7,867	6,970	8,936	11,085	10,429

(continued)

Imports and Exports by Commodity of the UK (*continued*)

Category		1990	1992	1994	1996	1997
Animal and vegetable oils and fats	**Total**	88	87	171	209	265
Chemicals	organic chemicals	3,353	3,701	4,749	5,234	5,010
	inorganic chemicals	954	1,185	1,125	1,210	1,192
	plastics	2,123	2,139	2,811	3,348	3,194
	Total	13,183	14,977	18,859	22,504	22,015
Manufactures classified chiefly by material	wood and cork manufactures	116	131	172	229	250
	paper and paperboard manufactures	1,539	1,734	2,056	2,381	2,307
	textile manufactures	2,448	2,457	2,966	3,527	3,448
	iron and steel	3,035	3,006	3,676	4,130	3,663
	non-ferrous metals	2,192	1,751	2,235	2,723	2,790
	metal manufactures	2,117	2,212	2,654	3,415	3,404
	Total	15,824	15,485	19,635	23,495	22,794
Machinery and transport equipment	mechanical machinery	14,423	14,263	16,446	21,005	22,784
	electrical machinery	15,196	16,429	25,151	33,725	34,691
	road vehicles	7,300	8,895	9,736	14,609	15,008
	other transport equipment	4,935	4,837	4,849	5,492	7,421
	Total	41,852	44,422	56,176	74,824	79,899
Miscellaneous manufactures	clothing and footwear	1,973	2,426	3,219	4,029	3,900
	scientific and photographic	4,112	4,459	5,402	6,749	7,108
	Total	13,313	13,925	17,463	21,380	21,898
Other commodities and transactions	**Total**	2,299	2,070	1,460	1,940	1,943
EXPORTS TOTAL		103,691	108,509	135,189	169,569	172,908

Source: *Annual Abstract of Statistics 1999*, © Crown copyright 1999

Imports and Exports of Manufactured Goods of the UK

(In millions of pounds. N.e.c. = not elsewhere classified.)

Item	Imports[1]			Exports[2]		
	1995	1996	1997	1995	1996	1997
Food products and beverages	12,631	13,510	12,866	9,106	9,011	8,877
Tobacco products	222	241	207	1,127	1,201	1,206
Textiles	5,286	5,722	5,744	3,448	3,660	3,512
Wearing apparel; dressing and dyeing of fur	4,386	5,171	5,447	2,534	2,779	2,579
Tanning and dressing of leather; luggage, handbags, saddlery, harness, and footwear	2,184	2,564	2,635	953	1,089	1,055
Wood and products of wood and cork, except furniture; articles of straw and plaiting materials	2,211	2,294	2,354	242	291	297
Pulp and paper products; publishing, and printing	6,281	5,715	5,161	2,430	2,431	2,361
Publishing, printing, and reproduction of recorded media	1,453	1,438	1,486	2,436	2,498	2,394
Coke, petroleum products, and nuclear fuel	1,753	2,132	1,904	2,974	3,574	4,116
Chemicals and chemical products	18,374	19,042	18,292	21,925	23,230	22,487
Rubber and plastic products	4,545	4,713	4,530	3,889	4,191	4,051
Other non-mineral products	1,779	1,904	1,846	1,986	2,151	2,103
Basic metals	8,485	8,578	7,975	8,091	7,557	7,092
Fabricated metal products, except machinery	3,414	3,675	3,657	3,206	3,517	3,522
Machinery and equipment n.e.c.	14,212	14,984	15,111	16,250	17,902	18,102
Office machinery and computers	12,401	12,875	13,775	11,799	12,279	12,966
Electrical machinery and apparatus n.e.c.	6,497	6,918	7,022	5,657	6,447	6,579
Radio and television equipment	12,000	15,179	14,247	12,228	13,310	12,849
Medical and precision instruments	5,175	5,944	5,855	5,470	6,139	6,510
Motor vehicles, trailers, and similar vehicles	19,167	21,785	22,495	13,380	16,191	16,544
Other transport equipment	5,041	6,238	8,621	6,946	8,527	11,433
Furniture; manufacturing n.e.c.	4,753	5,464	6,079	3,427	3,786	3,933

[1] Calculated on a cost, insurance, and freight basis.
[2] Calculated on a free on board basis.

Source: *Business Monitor MQ10*, © Crown copyright 1998

Imports and Exports of the UK and Main Trading Partners

(N/A = not available. In millions of pounds.)

	Imports to the UK				Exports from the UK			
Country/region	1992	1994	1996	1997	1992	1994	1996	1997
European Union total	72,022	83,627	101,846	101,012	65,610	77,297	97,445	95,949
Germany	19,153	22,194	27,660	25,916	15,337	17,441	21,080	20,659
France	12,305	15,223	18,135	17,942	11,608	13,728	17,397	16,583
Italy	6,808	7,609	8,964	9,652	6,196	6,873	8,169	8,205
Netherlands	9,969	10,214	12,628	12,462	8,573	9,653	13,718	13,909
Belgium and Luxembourg	5,771	7,193	8,761	9,155	5,761	7,397	8,668	8,446
Denmark	2,397	2,203	2,397	2,342	1,573	1,830	2,254	2,091
Republic of Ireland	5,095	5,985	7,368	7,470	5,788	7,204	8,816	9,348
Greece	372	358	399	409	777	938	1,166	1,050
Portugal	1,177	1,305	1,690	1,781	1,176	1,269	1,707	1,746
Spain	3,039	3,735	5,131	5,160	4,552	5,161	6,842	6,739
Sweden	3,300	4,260	4,852	4,742	2,459	3,423	4,496	4,448
Finland	1,687	2,306	2,688	2,572	1,007	1,323	1,845	1,567
Austria	949	1,042	1,173	1,409	803	1,057	1,287	1,158
Other Western Europe total	8,602	9,657	11,829	11,341	4,318	5,727	7,383	7,995
Norway	3885	3,823	4,982	4,926	1,421	2,035	2,066	2,658
Switzerland	3,919	4,818	5,403	4,896	1,845	2,460	3,206	3,010
Turkey	456	630	933	1,044	691	815	1,566	1,769
Iceland	241	240	269	244	93	110	155	159
North America total	15,872	19,937	25,743	28,065	14,262	19,525	22,436	23,975
USA	13,715	17,729	22,809	25,029	12,231	16,909	19,831	20,993
Canada	1,898	1,883	2,485	2,556	1,584	1,917	1,975	2,155
Mexico	154	241	334	383	292	390	319	431
Other OECD countries total	10,442	12,593	14,355	15,192	5,493	7,664	10,922	10,774
Japan	7,444	8,832	8,992	9,433	2,233	3,000	4,265	4,182
Australia	1,014	1,064	1,296	1,370	1,377	1,928	2,464	2,456
South Korea	932	1,097	2,039	2,240	660	972	1,303	1,222
Poland	356	546	601	620	606	701	1,353	1,354
New Zealand	429	542	632	580	263	416	473	410
Czech Republic	148	278	374	465	188	374	715	709
Oil exporting countries total	3,078	3,267	3,750	3,971	6,014	5,738	8,095	9,788
Saudi Arabia	964	812	753	997	1,966	1,519	2,484	3,801
Kuwait	128	239	181	201	263	314	580	504
Indonesia	538	783	981	1,031	314	366	830	702
Iran	163	134	119	37	583	290	398	404
Nigeria	166	124	296	123	622	459	433	426
Rest of the world total	15,549	20,385	28,213	29,216	12,534	18,701	22,660	24,003
Eastern Europe	1,022	1,767	2,535	2,776	747	1,485	2,272	2,680
Other America	2,226	2,470	3,167	3,070	1,469	2,378	2,677	3,193
China	953	1,642	2,202	2,495	428	846	739	922
Hong Kong	2,398	3,083	4,074	4,344	1,612	2,297	2,926	3,214
India	864	1,291	1,612	1,622	946	1,312	1,706	1,576
Israel	486	572	832	881	587	1,034	1,267	1,179
Malaysia	1,104	1,204	2,381	2,020	636	1,311	1,160	1,205
Pakistan	273	360	391	380	312	354	344	269
Philippines	241	245	896	761	204	356	397	601
Singapore	1,193	1,896	2,573	2,715	1,147	1,769	2,144	2,041
South Africa	866	971	1,222	1,392	1,079	1,415	1,880	1,636
Taiwan	1,395	1,583	2,090	2,344	559	736	941	1,034
Thailand	643	914	1,189	1,222	475	749	974	862

Source: *Annual Abstract of Statistics 1999,* © Crown copyright 1999

Visible Trade of the UK

A country's **balance of trade** is its visible exports (goods) minus visible imports. It is a component of the current account on the balance of payments. The **balance of payments** is an account of a country's debit and credit transactions with other countries. Items are divided into the **current account,** which includes both visible trade (imports and exports of goods) and invisible trade (services such as transport, tourism, interest, and dividends); and the **capital account,** which includes investment in and out of the country, international grants, and loans. Deficits or surpluses on these accounts are brought into balance by buying and selling reserves of foreign currencies.

Trade	1990	1992	1994	1995	1996	1997
Value (£ millions)						
Exports of goods	102,313	107,863	135,260	153,725	167,403	171,798
Imports of goods	121,020	120,913	146,351	165,449	180,489	183,590
Balance on trade in goods	–18,707	–13,050	–11,091	–11,724	–13,086	–11,792
Price Index Numbers (1995 = 100)						
Exports of goods	81.7	84.5	96.9	100.0	100.8	95.2
Imports of goods	81.2	82.9	94.3	100.0	100.1	93.8
Terms of trade[1]	100.6	101.9	102.8	100.0	100.7	101.5
Volume Index Numbers (1995 = 100)						
Exports of goods	77.2	79.9	91.3	100.0	107.7	116.5
Imports of goods	86.5	87.3	94.6	100.0	109.1	119.0

[1] Terms of trade are the export price index as a percentage of the import price index.

Source: *Annual Abstract of Statistics 1999,* © Crown copyright 1999

UK Investment and Banking

Investment of Overseas Companies in the UK

Data show net investment analysed by area and main country; includes unremitted profits. Unremitted profits are profits that are not repatriated for the UK home company.
(N = nil or negligible. A minus sign indicates a net disinvestment overseas, that is a decrease in the amount due to the investor's home country. In millions of pounds.)

Country/region	1993	1994	1995	1996	1997
Europe					
EU					
Austria	13	60	21	20	18
Belgium and Luxembourg	–427	357	520	6	769
Denmark	97	76	68	151	229
Finland	–42	32	–36	2	154
France	–37	310	1,004	1,321	2,693
Germany	656	71	2,090	835	1,170
Greece	N	N	N	N	N
Ireland, Republic of	49	224	–35	221	1,138
Italy	80	177	328	–184	–32
Netherlands	1,244	1,915	–633	2,610	992
Portugal	N	N	N	N	N
Spain	14	21	17	66	71
Sweden	–56	119	184	–379	129
Total	1,589	3,367	3,555	4,673	7,330
EFTA					
Norway	49	–131	124	1,060	–71
Switzerland	501	–44	912	1,151	1,321
Total	550	–176	1,036	2,211	1,258

Country/region	1993	1994	1995	1996	1997
Other European countries					
Russia[1]	49	0	19	61	19
UK offshore islands[2]	–	–	–	–	–26
Total	64	–125	36	47	24
Europe total	2,202	3,065	4,626	6,931	8,612

Country/region	1993	1994	1995	1996	1997
America					
Canada	33	–246	–438	444	475
USA	5,142	2,138	9,293	6,742	10,708
America total	5,175	1,891	8,853	7,481	N/A
Asia					
Near and Middle East countries	115	78	58	64	103
Other Asian countries					
Hong Kong	106	45	–124	10	6
Japan	277	4	–379	209	350
Singapore	14	2	40	1	17
South Korea	43	2	85	–8	–78
Total	456	110	–248	348	327
Asia total	570	186	–189	412	430
Australasia and Oceania					
Australia	995	260	–708	1,096	1,219
New Zealand	0	127	60	–104	–7
Australasia and Oceania total	995	387	–647	992	1,211
Africa					
South Africa	58	50	125	109	149
Africa total	111	63	117	118	161
OECD total	8,636	5,346	12,511	15,235	21,250
Central and eastern Europe total	0	–141	15	–19	13
WORLD TOTAL	9,871	6,046	12,654	15,662	21,751

[1] Prior to 1995 Russia covers other former USSR countries, the Baltic States, and Albania.
[2] The UK offshore islands consist of the Channel Islands and the Isle of Man, excluded from the definition of the economic territory of the UK from 1997.

Source: *Business Monitor,* © Crown copyright 1998

Investment Overseas by UK Companies

Data show net investment analysed by area and main country; includes unremitted profits. Unremitted profits are profits that are not repatriated for the UK home company. (A minus sign indicates a net disinvestment overseas, that is a decrease in the amount due to the UK. NA = not available. In millions of pounds.)

Country	1993	1994	1995	1996	1997
Europe					
EU					
Austria	13	102	90	102	10
Belgium and Luxembourg	160	132	438	991	1,521
Denmark	237	64	416	−176	118
Finland	10	26	112	28	−5
France	471	423	1,515	2,375	1,520
Germany	1,333	1,261	1,478	1,184	1,273
Greece	44	84	163	106	303
Ireland, Republic of	1,082	100	776	755	398
Italy	282	298	406	421	442
Country	**1993**	**1994**	**1995**	**1996**	**1997**
Netherlands	2,436	4,615	2,953	6,577	8,544
Portugal	25	169	159	56	86
Spain	−31	460	431	735	911
Sweden	84	546	522	277	370
Total	6,146	8,278	9,457	13,432	15,489
EFTA					
Norway	92	662	−255	96	1,999
Switzerland	−177	−16	−338	−110	320
Total	−84	645	−594	−12	2,320
Other European countries					
Russia[1]	11	115	39	132	456
UK offshore islands[2]	N/A	N/A	N/A	N/A	−864
Total	110	317	322	−97	1,927
Europe total	6,171	9,241	9,184	13,321	19,735
America					
Bermuda	586	349	291	142	−44
Brazil	38	291	473	692	355
Canada	5	−4	244	−159	779
Chile	101	76	220	89	156
Colombia	−245	204	123	100	242
Mexico	44	42	79	110	762
Panama	−100	94	75	103	599
USA	7,975	6,549	11,840	1,837	11,288
America total	8,673	8,464	13,460	3,277	14,711

Country	1993	1994	1995	1996	1997
Asia					
Near and Middle East countries					
Gulf Arabian countries	−236	250	116	30	280
Total	−239	253	154	28	373
Other Asian countries					
Hong Kong	456	128	734	730	−348
India	139	87	61	110	182
Country	**1993**	**1994**	**1995**	**1996**	**1997**
Indonesia	69	92	−28	155	80
Japan	−49	245	169	378	384
Malaysia	363	286	28	184	755
Singapore	528	590	−48	535	329
South Korea	44	27	47	32	16
Thailand	103	177	245	194	106
Total	1,834	1,796	1,503	2,794	2,117
Asia total	1,596	2,049	1,657	2,823	2,490
Australasia and Oceania					
Australia	655	625	2,258	1,472	1,240
New Zealand	71	264	67	244	257
Australasia and Oceania total	658	959	2,596	1,843	1,336
Africa					
Kenya	33	9	67	24	61
Nigeria	347	−197	−271	−94	234
South Africa	314	170	466	−25	401
Zimbabwe	36	28	16	25	7
Africa total	262	327	707	561	684
OECD total	14,864	16,880	23,686	17,545	32,743
Central and Eastern Europe total	41	168	194	201	1,695
WORLD TOTAL	17,358	21,040	27,604	21,823	38,957

[1] Prior to 1995 Russia covers other former USSR countries, the Baltic States, and Albania.
[2] The UK offshore islands consist of the Channel Islands and the Isle of Man, excluded from the definition of the economic territory of the UK from 1997.

Source: *Overseas Direct Investment 1997*, © Crown copyright 1998

The Top 10 Largest Banks in the UK

This table is ranked by market capitalization. Market capitalization is the market value of a company's issued share capital, that is the quoted price of its shares multiplied by the number of shares issued.
As of 22 January 1999.

1998

Rank	Bank	Market capitalization (£ millions)
1	Lloyds TSB Group	60,214.8
2	HSBC Holdings	48,430.8
3	Halifax	31,370.8
4	Barclays	24,275.6
5	Abbey National	24,116.9
6	National Westminster Bank	22,632.0
7	Bank of Scotland	11,636.1
8	Royal Bank of Scotland Group	9,861.8
9	Woolwich	9,293.8
10	Alliance & Leicester	8,558.6

Source: *FT500, FT Surveys*, © *Financial Times* 1999

Assets and Liabilities of the Bank of England

(In millions of pounds.)

Year	Issue Department					Banking Department							
	Liabilities		Assets			Liabilities				Assets			
	Notes in circulation	Notes in Department	Government Banking	Other securities	Total securities	Public	Bankers' deposits	Reserves deposits accounts	Total and other	Government securities	Advances and other accounts	Premises, equipment, and other securities	Notes and coin
1989	16,849	11	13,946	2,914	5,398	69	1,750	3,565	5,398	1,354	726	3,307	11
1990	17,283	7	14,672	2,618	8,613	44	1,842	6,713	8,615	1,432	2,146	5,030	7
1991	17,466	4	11,791	5,679	5,825	104	1,813	3,894	5,825	1,346	2,443	2,031	5
1992	17,542	8	7,808	9,742	5,623	97	1,553	3,959	5,623	1,237	3,935	443	8
1993	18,218	12	6,816	11,414	11,095	6,205	1,700	3,175	11,095	1,174	9,411	498	12
1994	20,055	5	11,468	8,592	6,192	938	1,855	3,385	6,192	1,050	4,696	441	5
1995	21,262	7	14,552	6,717	7,114	1,159	2,001	3,941	7,114	1,090	5,499	518	7
1996	22,407	12	16,524	5,896	6,229	1,001	2,021	3,193	6,229	1,232	2,339	2,646	12
1997	23,715	5	16,416	7,304	7,221	1,192	2,800	3,214	7,221	1,373	5,388	455	5

Source: *Annual Abstract of Statistics 1999,*

Assets and Liabilities of Banks in the UK

UK banks comprise offices in Great Britain and Northern Ireland of authorized institutions under the Banking Act 1987, together with certain institutions in the Channel Islands and Isle of Man, the Banking Department of the Bank of England, and, from 1993, in accordance with the Second Banking Co-Ordination Directive, UK branches of 'European Authorized Institutions' entitled to accept deposits in the UK and covered by the UK's Deposits Protection Scheme. Inter-bank items are netted with the resulting differences allocated to appropriate sectors, and adjustments (to deposits and loans) are made to allow for transit items. Figures for other currencies are affected by changes in exchange rates. Figures given are for the end of the year. (In millions of pounds.)

Assets and liabilities		1992	1993	1994	1995	1996	1997
Assets							
Lending to public sector	sterling	14,358	17,708	25,887	34,791	29,941	27,262
	other currencies	5,438	5,903	1,732	1,595	2,614	4,664
Lending to private sector[1]	sterling	415,805	426,836	438,096	493,367	547,734	731,971
	other currencies	69,481	76,949	83,432	110,002	134,330	140,876
Lending to non-resident sector	sterling	52,294	62,760	62,690	66,424	77,076	118,863
	other currencies	596,308	620,690	674,564	774,480	754,729	919,563
	Total	1,153,685	1,210,846	1,286,401	1,480,658	1,546,424	1,943,199
Liabilities							
Public sector deposits	sterling	14,996	18,563	13,005	17,105	17,661	20,338
	other currencies	391	344	340	585	628	248
Private sector deposits[1]	sterling	329,451	346,044	356,489	412,559	468,037	610,759
	other currencies	53,253	58,517	70,241	94,313	112,865	102,677
Non-resident sector deposits	sterling	76,470	77,992	84,022	92,065	90,192	145,325
	other currencies	601,738	624,564	668,458	760,891	741,376	900,989
Non-deposit liabilities (net)		77,385	84,823	93,796	103,141	115,664	162,862
	Total	1,153,685	1,210,846	1,286,401	1,480,658	1,546,424	1,943,199

[1] Revised rules on netting of customers' credit balances against their borrowing increased the UK private sector's outstanding balances of deposits and borrowing by £2.5 billion at end-December 1993. Re-netting during 1994 amounted to £1.7 billion.

Source: *Annual Abstract of Statistics 1999,*

Base Interest Rates of Selected Banks in the UK

Percentage rates operative between the dates shown. The base rate is the rate of interest which forms the basis for the charges for bank loans and overdrafts, or deposit rates.

Date of change		New rate	Date of change		New rate	Date of change		New rate
1990	8 October	14.00		19 October	8.00		31 October	6.00
1991	13 February	13.50		13 November	7.00	1997	6 May	6.25
	27 February	13.00	1993	26 January	6.00		6 June	6.25–6.50
	22 March	12.50		23 November	5.50		9 June	6.50
	12 April	12.00	1994	8 February	5.25		10 July	6.75
	24 May	11.50		12 September	5.75		7 August	7.00
	12 July	11.00		7 December	6.25		6 November	7.25
	4 September	10.50	1995	2 February	6.25–6.75	1998	4 June	7.50
1992	5 May	10.00		3 February	6.75		8 October	7.25
	16 September	12.00		13 December	6.50		5 November	6.75
	17 September	10.00–12.00	1996	18 January	6.25		10 December	6.25
	18 September	10.00		8 March	6.00	1999	7 January	6.00
	22 September	9.00		6 June	5.75		4 February	5.50
	16 October	8.00–9.00		30 October	5.75–6.00		8 April	5.25
							10 June	5.00

Source: *Financial Statistics February 1999,* © Crown copyright 1999

Building Societies in the UK

The figures for each year relate to accounting years ending on dates between 1 February of that year and 31 January of the following year. (N/A = not available.)

Building societies		1988[1]	1990	1992	1994	1996[2]	1997[2]
Societies on register (number)		130	117	105	96	88	82
Share investors (number)		43,816,000	36,948,000	37,533,000	38,150,000	37,768,000	19,234
Depositors (number)		4,306,000	4,299,000	3,879,000	5,369,000	6,718,000	882
Borrowers (number)		7,369,000	6,724,000	7,005,000	7,222,000	6,586,000	2,703,000
Liabilities (£ millions)	shares	149,791.1	160,538.2	187,108.4	201,812.2	196,546.4	90,092.8
	deposits and loans	26,528.5	40,695.5	57,067.5	69,925.2	73,919.1	31,033.7
	taxation and other	2,953.4	3,768.8	2,559.5	2,939.2	3,727.4	1,338.8
	general reserves	8,466.0	10,206.1	12,634.4	16,312.3	17,940.3	7,331.2
	other capital	1,105.1	1,639.7	3,144.7	4,125.7	4,762.3	1,643.9
Assets (£ millions)	mortgages	153,015.4	175,745.4	210,994.5	240,297.2	241,472.9	107,531.5
	investments	20,964.9	35,050.9	42,909.1	50,786.7	51,016.7	21,869.8
	cash	11,748.1	6,052.0	8,610.1	4,030.7	4,405.9	2,039.1
	other	3,115.7					
	Total	188,844.2	216,848.3	262,514.5	295,114.6	296,895.5	131,440.4

Transactions		1988[1]	1990[3]	1992[3]	1994[3]	1996[2]	1997[2]
Shares (£ millions)	received	111,716.9	N/A	N/A	N/A	N/A	N/A
	interest thereon	9,852.6	N/A	N/A	N/A	N/A	N/A
	withdrawn (including interest)	100,991.8	N/A	N/A	N/A	N/A	N/A
Deposits (£ millions)	received	58,637.2	N/A	N/A	N/A	N/A	N/A
	interest thereon	2,170.0	N/A	N/A	N/A	N/A	N/A
	withdrawn (including interest)	54,924.7	N/A	N/A	N/A	N/A	N/A
Mortgages (£ millions)	advances	47,374.9	43,081.0	34,989.0	34,829.0	38,488.0	28,771.7
	repayments of principal	25,002.8	N/A	N/A	N/A	N/A	N/A
	interest[4]	15,965.1	N/A	N/A	N/A	N/A	N/A
Management expenses (£ millions)		2,074.7	2.363.0	2,723.7	3,136.7	3,555.3	2,270.5
Rate of interest (%[5])	paid on shares	7.04	N/A	N/A	N/A	N/A	N/A
	paid on deposits	9.21	N/A	N/A	N/A	N/A	N/A
	received on mortgage advances	11.25	N/A	N/A	N/A	N/A	N/A

1 1988 and subsequent years include Northern Ireland societies, responsibility for which was acquired under the Building Societies Act 1986.
2 The societies which have converted to the banking sector, namely Cheltenham and Gloucester (August 1995), National and Provincial (August 1996), Alliance and Leicester (April 1997), Halifax (June 1997), Woolwich (July 1997), Bristol and West (July 1997), and Northern Rock (October 1997) have been included in flow figures (using flows up to the date of conversion), but have been excluded from end year balances.
3 Apart from mortgage advances and management expenses no new data are available for 1990 onwards. This is due to procedural changes.
4 Includes amounts recoverable from HM Government under Option Mortgage Scheme and Mortgage Interest Relief at Source (MIRAS).
5 Based on the mean of the amounts outstanding at the end of previous and the current year.

Source: *Annual Abstract of Statistics 1999,* © Crown copyright 1999

Capital Issues and Redemptions of Borrowers in the UK

The table gives data on the value of securities issued to raise cash for companies. Redemptions cover 'partial redemptions' on instruments (where a bond, for example, pays out before reaching maturity) and payments on maturity.
(N/A = not available. N = nil or negligible. LSE = London Stock Exchange. USM = Unlisted Securities Market. In millions of pounds.)

	Net issues of share and loan capital						Ordinary shares					
	Of which[1]			Comprising			Gross issues			Net issues		
Year	Total on LSE	Listed on USM	Listed	Local authorities and public cororations	Industrial and commercial companies	Financial institutions	Total	Of which: rights issues	Redemptions	Total	Of which[1] Listed on LSE	Listed on USM
1992	14,088	2,535	149	1	8,453	5,634	6,253	3,200	29	6,224	5,951	138
1993	29,933	9,723	248	−1	16,680	13,254	16,672	10,918	N	16,672	16,321	234
1994	25,241	8,246	507	N	13,467	11,774	14,619	4,958	2	14,617	13,751	505
1995	15,462	14,151	247	N	15,903	−441	9,813	4,524	36	9,777	5,687	250
1996	24,231	N/A	N/A	N	13,201	11,030	10,673	3,884	400	10,273	N/A	N/A
1997	23,622	N/A	N/A	N	16,941	6,681	8,614	2,112	N	8,614	N/A	N/A
1998	19,504	N/A	N/A	N	13,348	6,156	4,383	1,412	N	4,383	N/A	N/A

[1] Ceased to be compiled as from February 1996.

Source: *Financial Statistics March 1999*, © Crown copyright 1999

Currency in the UK

The monetary unit in use in the UK is **Pound Sterling** (£). The unit is divided into 100 **Pence** (p).

Notes

UK notes are issued by the Bank of England in the following denominations: £5, £10, £20, and £50. Series D £10 note was withdrawn on 20 May 1994. Series E £50 note came into circulation on 20 April 1994.

Coins

Coins in general circulation are: nickel brass £1, cupro-nickel 5p, 10p, 20p and 50p, and bronze 1p and 2p. 1p and 2p coins are (from September 1992) issued in copper-plated steel. A bi-colour £2 coin was issued into general circulation on 15 June 1998. Another legal tender is a nickel brass £2 coin. It was, however, issued as a commemorative coin and as such is not intended for general circulation.

Coins that remain a legal tender and can sometimes be found in circulation are silver or cupro-nickel crowns dating from 1816 onwards. These had been equivalent to 25p; in 1990 the face value of the crown changed from 25p to £5.

Gold coins dating from 1838 onwards in denominations of £1, £2, £5, and 10 shilling (=50p) are legal tender but only at face value. Gold coins introduced in October 1987 as Britannia Gold Bullion Coins, in denominations of £100, £50, £20, and £10, are not found in general circulation.

Most Active Stocks in the UK

1997

Rank	Company	Turnover value (£ millions)	Shares traded (millions)
1	HSBC Holdings	48,267.4	2,888.1
2	British Telecommunications	39,977.4	9,228.9
3	Shell Transport and Trading	25,879.0	4,242.8
4	British Petroleum Company	25,247.0	3,033.2
5	Glaxo Wellcome	24,313.1	1,961.6
6	Lloyds TSB Group	20,788.2	3,344.6
7	SmithKline Beecham	19,761.5	2,269.5
8	Barclays plc	19,462.1	1,555.8
9	National Westminster Bank	15,448.4	1,881.2
10	BAT Industries	14,764.4	2,700.2

Source: *London Stock Exchange Fact File (1999)*,
© London Stock Exchange Limited. Reproduced with permission.

Average *Financial Times*/Stock Exchange (FTSE) Actuaries Share Indices

FTSE Actuaries share indices		1993	1994	1995	1996	1997
FTSE 100[1]	January	2,790.29	3,431.29	3,028.27	3,715.78	4,166.48
	February	2,840.17	3,396.40	3,051.68	3,738.08	4,316.57
	March	2,897.07	3,206.10	3,078.24	3,697.50	4,349.78
	April	2,837.45	3,130.94	3,198.38	3,792.32	4,312.51
	May	2,830.13	3,089.23	3,288.31	3,758.41	4,622.62
	June	2,874.70	2,980.32	3,351.55	3,734.02	4,649.40
	July	2,850.73	3,036.57	3,426.50	3,707.21	4,843.16
	August	3,019.28	3,178.50	3,486.95	3,841.75	4,945.56
	September	3,028.12	3,098.35	3,534.27	3,927.10	5,010.35
	October	3,125.15	3,046.77	3,531.80	4,020.99	5,145.13
	November	3,111.59	3,086.85	3,580.31	3,969.54	4,846.24
	December	3,313.68	3,026.62	3,650.05	4,038.89	5,087.53
FT Non-Financials[1]	January	1,496.94	1,818.98	1,631.29	1,919.36	2,104.75
	February	1,522.74	1,818.96	1,631.03	1,941.86	2,150.64
	March	1,552.97	1,745.46	1,631.47	1,953.49	2,178.24
	April	1,522.32	1,708.89	1,690.67	2,021.61	2,149.68
	May	1,522.69	1,690.44	1,738.74	2,013.00	2,219.45
	June	1,539.22	1,618.42	1,767.52	1,999.60	2,231.81
	July	1,521.63	1,642.28	1,806.86	1,958.89	2,284.21
	August	1,614.52	1,726.77	1,846.24	2,002.27	2,326.86
	September	1,623.43	1,680.38	1,868.17	2,043.06	2,369.90
	October	1,653.67	1,639.72	1,851.30	2,069.12	2,439.08
	November	1,643.34	1,654.73	1,854.75	2,040.44	2,332.02
	December	1,733.10	1,622.39	1,879.54	2,056.24	2,401.00
Financials[1]	January	1,718.78	2,619.71	2,084.15	2,916.24	3,674.44
	February	1,822.76	2,607.79	2,125.71	2,942.72	3,919.61
	March	1,888.45	2,324.02	2,170.51	2,837.38	3,876.31
	April	1,901.37	2,240.03	2,264.66	2,866.93	3,825.30
	May	1,926.91	2,164.18	2,350.00	2,898.78	4,331.40
	June	2,011.94	2,111.15	2,411.52	2,867.16	4,281.17
	July	2,065.80	2,129.92	2,466.78	2,886.69	4,468.02
	August	2,175.74	2,197.58	2,526.20	3,078.43	4,647.61
	September	2,174.42	2,181.71	2,599.72	3,149.04	4,634.33
	October	2,310.58	2,137.44	2,691.46	3,292.82	4,787.52
	November	2,289.99	2,188.27	2,805.33	3,300.68	4,407.61
	December	2,502.99	2,134.40	2,879.80	3,418.82	4,756.91
Investment Trusts[1]	January	2,064.63	3,058.15	2,609.12	3,079.31	3,198.05
	February	2,217.35	3,056.69	2,604.17	3,142.90	3,328.88
	March	2,244.24	2,901.35	2,583.43	3,106.91	3,340.35
	April	2,225.74	2,844.45	2,648.57	3,216.41	3,234.90
	May	2,256.79	2,812.57	2,762.00	3,237.58	3,377.50
	June	2,330.08	2,709.20	2,791.09	3,170.26	3,422.71
	July	2,372.09	2,725.64	2,874.20	3,075.76	3,453.98
	August	2,563.16	2,882.04	2,938.91	3,147.91	3,512.81
	September	2,549.64	2,831.12	2,969.59	3,182.58	3,493.30
	October	2,663.51	2,732.79	2,924.52	3,204.46	3,534.96
	November	2,669.09	2,732.46	2,932.60	3,137.47	3,275.77
	December	2,880.07	2,686.29	2,998.07	3,129.25	3,370.41
FTSE All Share[1]	January	1,351.60	1,710.35	1,501.87	1,818.72	2,041.99
	February	1,384.99	1,709.09	1,506.17	1,839.78	2,105.82
	March	1,415.40	1,619.80	1,511.04	1,836.04	2,121.89
	April	1,393.70	1,582.06	1,566.98	1,892.47	2,092.74
	May	1,397.10	1,559.27	1,614.69	1,889.96	2,203.40
	June	1,419.94	1,497.44	1,643.59	1,875.05	2,207.24
	July	1,413.38	1,517.70	1,680.80	1,844.67	2,269.94
	August	1,498.55	1,591.47	1,718.13	1,899.46	2,324.27
	September	1,505.06	1,554.01	1,743.26	1,938.37	2,357.80
	October	1,544.80	1,516.65	1,739.84	1,973.94	2,422.75
	November	1,535.11	1,533.46	1,755.17	1,951.91	2,293.45
	December	1,628.88	1,502.42	1,783.30	1,976.41	2,388.17

[1] Working day average.

Source: *Annual Abstract of Statistics 1999*, © Crown copyright 1999

Average Rates on Representative British Government Stocks

Data show working day average.

Rate	1993	1994	1995	1996	1997
5-year conventional rate					
January	6.88	5.76	8.61	6.78	7.19
February	6.72	6.05	8.52	7.02	6.86
March	6.62	6.72	8.44	7.56	7.08
April	6.91	7.33	8.26	7.43	7.30
May	7.10	7.74	7.96	7.61	6.98
June	7.01	8.22	7.79	7.52	7.01
July	6.70	8.06	7.90	7.35	7.09
August	6.35	8.31	7.69	7.21	7.02
September	6.34	8.61	7.45	7.20	6.78
October	6.17	8.57	7.54	7.01	6.59
November	6.09	8.44	7.16	7.22	6.79
December	5.66	8.49	6.83	7.26	6.60
10-year conventional rate					
January	8.22	6.23	8.66	7.42	7.53
February	7.91	6.61	8.59	7.75	7.17
March	7.66	7.29	8.53	8.05	7.41
April	7.82	7.68	8.39	8.05	7.60
May	8.06	8.13	8.12	8.08	7.13
June	7.87	8.54	8.08	8.04	7.10
July	7.49	8.37	8.23	7.91	7.01
August	6.98	8.52	8.10	7.81	7.05
September	6.90	8.80	7.92	7.80	6.77
October	6.81	8.70	8.08	7.51	6.47
November	6.77	8.57	7.75	7.56	6.59
December	6.29	8.53	7.45	7.54	6.34
20-year conventional rate					
January	8.74	6.53	8.45	7.73	7.71
February	8.44	6.88	8.43	8.04	7.35
March	8.19	7.49	8.40	8.28	7.58
April	8.42	7.81	8.30	8.26	7.74
May	8.58	8.18	8.09	8.31	7.21
June	8.36	8.48	8.08	8.31	7.15
July	7.98	8.35	8.30	8.21	6.93
August	7.46	8.46	8.19	8.12	6.98
September	7.31	8.65	8.06	8.11	6.74
October	7.18	8.56	8.26	7.84	6.45
November	7.12	8.46	7.93	7.77	6.50
December	6.57	8.39	7.70	7.67	6.32
10-year index-linked rate					
January	3.60	2.70	3.89	3.42	3.44
February	3.23	2.81	3.87	3.57	3.23
March	3.07	3.07	3.86	3.70	3.41
April	3.11	3.25	3.79	3.66	3.55
May	3.30	3.51	3.58	3.74	3.52
June	3.31	3.78	3.58	3.80	3.62
July	3.22	3.85	3.61	3.82	3.68
August	3.16	3.82	3.52	3.59	3.59
September	3.09	3.85	3.46	3.57	3.47
October	3.03	3.84	3.65	3.41	3.17
November	2.96	3.84	3.54	3.42	3.23
December	2.75	3.85	3.45	3.41	3.01
20-year index-linked rate					
January	3.84	2.96	3.91	3.58	3.62
February	3.64	3.11	3.89	3.70	3.43
March	3.50	3.35	3.89	3.82	3.55
April	3.51	3.45	3.81	3.77	3.65
May	3.62	3.64	3.64	3.84	3.61
June	3.57	3.88	3.67	3.88	3.65
July	3.48	3.90	3.71	3.72	3.68
August	3.32	3.83	3.62	3.75	3.54
September	3.22	3.87	3.60	3.74	3.43
October	3.15	3.86	3.74	3.60	3.17
November	3.14	3.85	3.62	3.59	3.16
December	2.98	3.86	3.55	3.58	3.02

Source: *Annual Abstract of Statistics 1999*, © Crown copyright 1999

Share Ownership in the UK

(For the end of the given year. In billions of pounds.)

Share ownership	1990	1991	1992	1993	1994	1997
Insurance companies[1]	91.0	110.2	119.8	159.8	167.2	298.8
Pension funds[1]	140.4	165.7	199.5	251.5	211.8	279.8
Individuals	90.5	105.3	125.4	141.1	154.6	208.8
Unit trusts	27.3	30.4	38.0	52.7	51.8	85.2
Other financial institutions	3.0	4.4	2.7	4.5	9.8	25.9
Charities, etc	8.2	12.8	11.2	12.5	9.9	24.3
Investments trusts	6.9	7.8	12.8	19.8	15.0	24.2
Private non-financial companies	12.7	17.6	11.3	11.7	8.7	14.8
Public sector	9.0	6.8	11.3	10.2	5.8	1.1
Banks	3.2	1.1	3.0	4.7	3.0	0.8
Rest of the world	52.7	68.1	80.7	130.2	124.3	304.2
Total	444.9	530.2	615.7	798.7	761.9	1,267.9

[1] Data for pension funds and insurance companies were partially estimated in 1992 and 1993.

Source: *Share Ownership,* © Crown copyright 1998

UK Companies

Major Companies by Industry Group in the UK

Rank	Company	Sales (£ millions)
Agriculture, Forestry, and Fishing		
1	Associated Co-Operative Creameries Ltd	601.98
2 =	Grampian Country Food Group Ltd	469.03
	Grampian Foods Ltd	469.03
4	Bernard Matthews plc	371.81
5	Marshall Food Group Ltd	232.81
6	Lawrie Group plc	232.46
7	Linton Park plc	185.04
8	Sovereign Food Group Ltd	164.69
9	Moy Park Ltd	140.77
10	F W Baker Ltd	139.53
Mining		
1	The British Petroleum Co plc	43,460.00
2	Shell UK Ltd	7,463.00
3	BG plc	5,351.00
4	Esso UK plc	4,766.60
5	Rio Tinto plc	4,711.00
6	Conoco (UK) Ltd	3,039.30
7	AMEC plc	2,774.30
8	BP Oil UK Ltd	2,705.00
9	Total Oil Holdings Ltd	2,420.02
10	BP Exploration Operating Co Ltd	2,121.36
Construction		
1	BICC plc	4,139.00
2	Kvaerner plc	3,702.10
3	Tarmac plc	2,773.10
4	Balfour Beatty Ltd	2,047.80
5	John Laing plc	1,402.40
6	John Mowlem and Co plc	1,400.00
7	Taylor Woodrow plc	1,295.70
8	George Wimpey plc	1,223.40
9	Tarmac Construction Ltd	1,096.67
10	Laing Construction plc	1,094.70
Manufacturing of Food and Related Products		
1	Unilever plc	29,766.00
2	Diageo plc	17,698.00
3	Grand Metropolitan plc	8,174.00
4	Bass plc	5,254.00
5	Wittington Investments Ltd	5,235.00
6	Associated British Foods plc	5,203.00
7	Tomkins plc	4,588.80
8	Tate and Lyle plc	4,352.60
9	Cadbury Schweppes plc	4,220.00
10	Scottish and Newcastle plc	3,352.30
Transportation, Communication, Power Generation and Distribution, and Other Services		
1	British Telecommunications plc	15,640.00
2	British Airways plc	8,359.00
3	Firstgroup plc	7,950.00
4	Centrica plc	7,842.00
5	Cable and Wireless plc	7,001.00
6	British Gas Trading Ltd	6,813.75
7	The Post Office	6,370.00
8	Peninsular and Oriental Steam Navigation Co	5,917.60
9	National Power plc	3,354.00
10	Scottish Power plc	3,128.20
Wholesale Trade Durable Goods		
1	BTR plc	8,091.00
2	Wolseley plc	4,601.90
3	Compaq Computer Group Ltd	2,889.76
4	Honda Motor Europe Ltd	2,809.10
5	Sony United Kingdom Ltd	2,213.15
6	Mercedes-Benz (United Kingdom) Ltd	1,812.39
7	Amalgamated Metal Corporation plc	1,765.25
8	Littlewoods Home Shopping Group Ltd	1,533.59
9	Meyer International plc	1,254.10
10	Computacenter plc	1,133.52

(continued)

Major Companies by Industry Group in the UK (*continued*)

Rank	Company	Sales (£ millions)
Wholesale Trade Non-Durable Goods		
1	Booker plc	5,265.00
2	ABF Investments plc	5,203.00
3	Hillsdown Holdings plc	3,094.10
4	Itochu Europe plc	3,010.44
5	Booker Belmont Wholesale Ltd	2,377.35
6	Palmer and Harvey McLane (Holdings) Ltd	2,375.03
7	Palmer and Harvey McLane Ltd	2,306.74
8	Elementis plc	1,919.20
9	Bunzl plc	1,753.20
10	AAH Pharmaceuticals Ltd	1,650.87
Retail Trade		
1	Tesco plc	16,452.00
2	Tesco Stores Ltd	12,973.00
3	Sainsbury's Supermarkets Ltd	10,836.00
4	Marks & Spencer plc	8,243.00
5	Asda Group plc	7,619.20
6=	Safeway plc	6,978.70
	Safeway Stores plc	6,978.70
8	Asda Stores plc	6,883.43
9	Kingfisher plc	6,409.40
10	Allied Domecq plc	4,449.00
Financial and Investment Services		
1	J Sainsbury plc	14,500.00
2	The Standard Life Assurance Co	9,803.80
3	The Boots Co plc	5,021.90
4	Lucasvarity plc	4,681.00
5	Guardian Royal Exchange plc	3,243.00
6	The Energy Group Ltd	2,519.00
7	The Equitable Life Assurance Society	2,385.50
8	Bunge Corporation Ltd	2,081.27
9	Scottish Widows Fund and Life Assurance Society	1,936.56
10	Hoops Ltd	1,630.75
Other Services		
1	WPP Group plc	7,287.30
2	Inchcape plc	5,931.40
3	Camelot Group plc	5,513.70
4	Cordiant Communications Group plc	4,206.20
5	Granada Group plc	4,091.00
6	Ladbroke Group plc	3,816.20
7	Aegis Group plc	3,652.50
8	Rentokil Initial plc	2,812.10
9	ICL plc	2,477.10
10	The Rank Group plc	2,012.00

[1] Sales figures are not available; companies are ranked on number of employees.

Source: *Key British Enterprises, British Business Rankings 1999*, Dun and Bradstreet 1999

The Top 25 Companies in the UK

Market capitalization is the market value of a company's issued share capital, that is the quoted price of its shares multiplied by the number of shares issued. As of 28 January 1999.

1998

Rank	Company	Market capitalization (£ millions)
1	Glaxo Wellcome	62,546.5
2	British Petroleum	52,692.7
3	BT (British Telecom)	51,215.5
4	SmithKline Beecham	36,071.7
5	Lloyds TSB	35,803.7
6	Shell Transport & Trading	35,423.8
7	HSBC Holdings	28,797.0
8	Vodafone	21,129.4
9	Diageo	20,103.3
10	Zeneca	19,752.9
11	Halifax	18,653.1
12	Prudential Corporation	16,715.1
13	Unilever	16,417.6
14	BG (British Gas)	16,179.0
15	Barclays	14,434.3
16	Abbey National	14,339.9
17	Cable & Wireless	13,484.1
18	National Westminster Bank	13,457.0
19	Marks & Spencer	12,941.2
20	CGU	11,923.8
21	General Electric Company	11,727.3
22	Tesco	11,052.6
23	Sainsbury, J	10,773.8
24	Rentokil Initial	10,393.0
25	Allied Zurich	9,455.3

Source: *FT500, FT Surveys*, © *Financial Times* 1999

Fastest-Growing Companies in Great Britain

Ranked by growth of turnover.

1998–99

Rank	Company	Business activity	Turnover (£ millions)	Profit (£ millions)	Profit (%)	Profit growth (%)	Turnover growth (%)
1	Posthouse Hotels Ltd	hoteliers	430,201,000	42,853,000	9.96	601	1,579
2	The Global Travel Group plc	travel agency franchising company	14,735,670	48,097	0.33	74	1,450
3	Action	holding company	172,095,000	5,084,000	2.95	637	1,432
4	D P Mann Ltd	insurance underwriters	14,595,108	7,343,426	50.31	799	1,287
5	Virgin Management Ltd	transportation services	397,198,000	13,541,000	3.41	233	765
6	Market Link Publishing plc	magazine and periodical publishers	4,956,106	763,331	15.40	311	664
7	Electronique Group Ltd	holding company – electrical components manufacturing companies	14,678,000	8,000	0.05	104	491
8	Incepta Group plc	financial and corporate communications group	88,171,000	5,611,000	6.36	248	424
9	NCR (UK) Group Ltd	holding company	559,433,000	39,178,000	7.00	154	419
10	UPM-Kymmene Ltd	paper wholesalers	437,132,000	2,083,000	0.48	291	383
11	Banks Hoggins O'Shea	advertising agents	28,462,348	678,737	2.38	26	317
12	Blane Leisure Ltd T/A Sports Division	sports wear and goods retailers	231,422,000	21,743,000	9.40	188	309
13	Roach Bridge Holdings plc	holding company	3,461,897	25,126	0.73	777	306
14	Morelock Signs Ltd	road signs manufacturers	4,417,829	60,315	1.37	5	303
15	Polestar Petty Ltd	intermediate holding company – printers	4,244,000	7,200,000	169.65	30	299
16	Avicore Ltd	holding company	17,755,000	2,456,000	13.83	264	283
17	Jordec Group plc	holding company	27,497,000	506,000	1.84	182	263
18	Planet Online Ltd	Internet access provider	24,729,026	535,503	2.17	170	252
19	Baan UK Ltd	computer software marketers	25,825,851	3,595,227	13.92	389	236
20	Solent & Pratt (Engineering) Ltd	butterfly valves manufacturers	5,380,374	783,501	14.56	604	235
21	Flights Travel Group Ltd	travel agents, holiday company, and conference organizers	13,173,742	273,435	2.08	328	228
22	Vocalis Group plc	holding company	6,232,000	72,000	1.16	104	211
23	J L A Group Ltd	holding company	13,684,367	897,549	6.56	78	189
24	Shotton Paper Co plc	newsprint manufacturers	182,981,000	34,804,000	19.02	113	184
25	Progressive Computer Recruitment Ltd	employment agency	31,009,286	2,784,870	8.98	659	177

Source: Reproduced from *National Star Performers* with the permission of the publisher, Commerce Publications Ltd, tel (01908) 614477

Major Take-Overs, Mergers, and Significant Bids in the UK

1 January 1998–30 April 1999

Companies	Value ($ billions)	Date reported
Glaxo Wellcome/SmithKline Beecham[1]	100	31 January 1998
Zeneca/Astra	43	6 April 1998
Halifax/Barclays[1]	40	29 November 1998
BP/Amoco	30	31 December 1998
BPAmoco/Atlantic Richfield	27	2 April 1999
GEC/Lockheed	25	27 December 1998
Asda/Kingfisher[1]	17	17 April 1999
British Aerospace/GEC Marconi	16	19 January 1999
British Aerospace/DASA (Defence Analytical Services Agency)[1]	14	12 December 1998
Commerical Union/General Accident (new company = CGU)	14	26 February 1998
National Power/United Utilities[1]	12.5	11 February 1999
Somerfield/Booker	11	18 August 1998
PowerGen/Houston Industries[1]	10	2 August 1998

[1] Called off.

Major Foreign Acquisitions of UK Companies

Major acquisitions with a bid value over £1 billion, January 1998 to April 1999.

Acquirer	Target	Value (£ billions)	Date reported
Texas Utilities (USA)	Energy Group	4.45	1 May 1998
TRW (USA)	Lucas Varity	4.0	30 January 1999
Axa (France)	Guardian Royal Exchange	3.3	2 February 1999
AMP (Australia)	NPI	2.7	21 December 1998
Owens Illinois (USA)	BTR (glass, plastics, bottling)	2.2	3 March 1998
Electricité de France (France)	London Electricity	1.9	1 December 1998
AKZO (Netherlands)	Courtaulds	1.83	3 June 1998
Huntsman (USA)	ICI (polyurethane, tioxide, petrochemicals)	1.7	16 April 1999
CIBA Speciality Chemicals (Switzerland)	Allied Colloids	1.42	22 January 1998
DuPont (USA)	ICI (Polymer)	1.4	3 January 1998
Enron (USA)	Wessex Water	1.36	25 July 1998
Marsh McLennan (USA)	Sedgwick	1.25	26 August 1998
Coca Cola (USA)	Cadbury Schweppes (non-US soft drinks)	1.2	12 December 1998

Company Insolvencies by Industry in England and Wales

Industry		1993	1994	1995	1996	1997
Agriculture and horticulture		157	166	99	89	51
Manufacturing	food, drink, and tobacco	213	142	130	163	93
	chemicals	91	108	69	65	31
	metals and engineering	1,381	932	681	658	591
	textiles and clothing	917	736	567	568	596
	timber and furniture	333	252	267	249	181
	paper, printing, and publishing	777	579	452	438	364
	other	878	859	681	599	613
	Total	4,590	3,608	2,847	2,740	2,469
Construction and transport	construction	3,189	2,401	1,844	1,610	1,419
	transport and communication	1,082	774	706	682	540
	Total	4,271	3,175	2,550	2,292	1,959
Wholesaling	food, drink, and tobacco	231	244	205	183	158
	motor vehicles	142	112	83	95	41
	other	639	638	678	429	340
	Total	1,012	994	966	707	539
Retailing	food, drink, and tobacco	388	299	246	236	219
	motor vehicles and filling stations	229	226	195	227	132
	other	1,388	1,186	1,127	956	891
	Total	2,055	1,711	1,568	1,419	1,242
Services	financial institutions	421	259	198	222	111
	business services	2,415	1,807	1,525	1,500	1,528
	hotels and catering	912	777	692	708	609
	Total	3,748	2,843	2,415	2,430	2,248
Other		4,925	4,231	4,091	3,784	4,102
TOTAL		20,708	16,728	14,536	13,461	12,610

Source: *Annual Abstract of Statistics 1999,*

Business Registrations and Deregistrations in the UK

Figures show enterprises registered for VAT. An enterprise is defined as a legal unit, person, or group of people producing goods or services under their own control and with their own legal identity. A branch or office of a larger organization is not in itself an enterprise. There may be one or more VAT units within an enterprise.

Region	1995						1996					
	Registrations	Deregistrations	Net change	Registration rates (%)[1]	Deregistration rates (%)[1]	End-year stock	Registrations	Deregistrations	Net change	Registration rates (%)[1]	Deregistration rates (%)[1]	End-year stock
England												
Northeast	4,100	5,100	−1,000	9.4	11.6	42,500	4,100	4,300	−200	9.6	10.2	42,200
Northwest	13,500	15,500	−2,000	9.8	11.3	135,500	13,700	13,700	0	10.1	10.1	135,500
Merseyside	2,400	2,900	−500	10.9	13.0	21,900	2,800	2,500	300	12.7	11.4	22,200
Yorkshire and the Humber	11,100	13,200	−2,100	9.2	11.0	118,400	11,300	11,500	−200	9.6	9.7	118,200
East Midlands	10,700	11,400	−700	9.7	10.3	110,000	10,800	11,100	−300	9.9	10.1	109,700
West Midlands	13,300	14,700	−1,300	9.7	10.7	135,200	13,300	13,300	0	9.8	9.8	135,200
Eastern	16,000	16,500	−500	10.2	10.5	156,900	16,100	15,000	1,100	10.3	9.6	158,000
London	32,700	29,100	3,500	13.5	12.0	245,100	34,100	26,700	7,400	13.9	10.9	252,400
Southeast	26,500	27,100	−600	11.0	11.2	240,400	27,100	24,800	2,300	11.3	10.3	242,700
Southwest	13,000	15,500	−2,600	8.6	10.3	147,600	13,800	13,800	0	9.4	9.3	147,600
Total	143,200	151,000	−7,800	10.5	11.1	1,353,300	147,100	136,600	10,500	10.9	10.1	1,363,800
Wales	6,000	7,100	−1,200	7.8	9.2	76,100	6,100	6,500	−400	8.0	8.6	75,700
Scotland	11,200	12,000	−800	9.4	10.1	117,800	11,300	10,900	400	9.6	9.3	118,100
Northern Ireland	3,600	3,100	500	6.9	6.0	52,900	3,700	2,900	800	7.0	5.4	53,700
TOTAL UK	164,000	173,200	−9,300	10.2	10.8	1,600,100	168,200	157,000	11,200	10.5	9.8	1,611,300

[1] Registrations and deregistrations during the year as a percentage of the stock figure at the end of the previous year.

Source: *Regional Trends 33*, © Crown copyright 1998

Companies Spending the Most on Research and Development in the UK

Total expenditure on scientific research and development in 1996 was £14,340 million – 1.94 percent of GDP (compared to 2.04 percent in 1995). Expenditure on civil research and development was £12,254 million in 1996, the rest going to defence projects. Research and development spending includes spending overseas.

1996

Rank	Company	Annual investment (£ millions)	As % of sales	Rank	Company	Annual investment (£ millions)	As % of sales
1	Glaxo Wellcome	1,148	14	6	Shell	403	1
2	SmithKline Beecham	841	11	7	Ford Motors	338	5
3	Zeneca	653	13	8	Pfizer	312	99[1]
4	Unilever	546	2	9	BT	291	2
5	General Electric	458	7	10	British Aerospace	301	4

[1] Pfizer's UK sales have been low, but much of their research and development is in Britain.

Source: *Britain 1999: The Official Yearbook of the United Kingdom*, © Crown copyright 1998

Wealthiest Executives in the UK

(N/A = not available.)

Director	Company	Financial year ending	Pay (£)	% change
Top Ten Pay Increases for Directors of Publicly Quoted Companies				
Don Tidey	Associated British Foods	September 1997	2,200,000	+801.6
Roderick Kent	Close Brothers	July 1997	3,591,000	+669.0
Peter Stone	Close Brothers	July 1997	2,350,000	+545.6
Peter Winkworth	Close Brothers	July 1997	1,608,000	+341.8
Denis Mulhall	Berisford	September 1997	631,183	+204.1
Hugh Collum	SmithKline Beecham	December 1997	2,266,000	+199.7
David Webster	Safeway	March 1998	1,446,000	+189.8
Colin Smith	Safeway	March 1998	1,387,000	+163.2
Peter Wood	Royal Bank of Scotland	September 1997	1,248,000	+149.6
Kevin Doyle	Wassall	December 1997	927,000	+141.4

(*continued*)

Wealthiest Executives in the UK (*continued*)

Director	Company	Financial year ending	Pay (£)	% change
Directors of Publicly Quoted Companies (£1 Million or More a Year)				
Sam Chisholm	British Sky Broadcasting	June 1997	6,807,640	+78.1
Roderick Kent	Close Brothers	July 1997	3,591,000	+669.0
David Chance	British Sky Broadcasting	June 1997	3,035,059	+15.4
Martin Sorrell	WPP	December 1997	2,568,000	+3.9
Jim Fifield	EMI	March 1998	2,513,900	−35.1
Charles Brady	AMVESCAP	December 1997	2,485,000	+27.2
Jan Leschly	SmithKline Beecham	December 1997	2,410,000	+15.0
Peter Stone	Close Brothers	July 1997	2,350,000	+545.6
Hugh Collum	SmithKline Beecham	December 1997	2,266,000	+199.7
Lawrence Fish	Royal Bank of Scotland	September 1997	2,249,000	−12.5
Top Paid Private Company Directors				
Bernie Ecclestone	Formula One promotions	December 1996	43,930,000	+6.6
John Madejski	Hurst Publishing	March 1997	8,550,363	+95.2
Highest paid	Deutsche Morgan Grenfell	December 1996	7,141,684	N/A
Richardson brother	Spirepoint	December 1996	7,009,846	+290.4
Richardson brother	Spirepoint	December 1996	7,005,000	N/A
Edwin Healey	Stadium City	September 1997	5,278,832	+60.8
Cameron Mackintosh	Cameron Mackintosh	March 1997	5,192,465	−7.5
Terry Crawley	Crawley Futures	June 1997	5,157,068	−37.2
Highest paid	Morgan Grenfell	December 1996	4,421,455	N/A
Paul Gibbons	Hurst Publishing	March 1997	4,260,000	N/A
The Celebrity Top Ten				
Phil Collins	Philip Collins	December 1996	11,812,084	+34.5
Sting	Steerpike/Steerpike Overseas	July 1996	9,843,000	−4.0
Paul McCartney	Apple/MPL	January and December 1997	6,111,798	−16.5
George Harrison	Apple	January 1997	5,742,530	+41.7
Yoko Ono	Apple	January 1997	5,742,530	+41.7
Ringo Starr	Apple	January 1997	5,592,530	+43.3
Mark Knopfler	Chariscourt	March 1997	1,774,843	+4.8
Peter Gabriel	Peter Gabriel	December 1996	1,370,000	N/A
Eric Clapton	Marshbrook	September 1997	1,232,000	−43.1
Ian Anderson	Ian Anderson Group	December 1996	834,000	−60.9

Source: *Labour Research Magazine,* September 1998

Web Sites

APEC Secretariat Web Site

http://www.apecsec.org.sg/

Complete overview of the history and reponsibilities of Asia-Pacific Economic Cooperation (APEC).

Bank for International Settlements

http://www.bis.org/

Full source of official information on this international bank and its role to promote cooperation among central banks.

Bank of England – Banknote Printing

http://www.bankofengland.co.uk/print.htm#top

This easily-navigable site is well linked and contains details of the origins of money and the complex printing process involved in the manufacture of new notes.

Budget

http://www.hm-treasury.gov.uk/pub/html/budget.html

Frequently updated information on the UK's budget from the Treasury. There is an index of official press releases relating to the budget.

Business Ethics Magazine Online

http://condor.depaul.edu/ethics/bizethics.html

Online version of a print magazine which combines two aspects often thought not to sit well together: business and ethics.

Capitalism.org

http://www.capitalism.org/home.htm

Philosophical, economic, and political examination of capitalism. This site includes a 'Capitalism tour', a multimedia introduction to capitalism, and an online version of Capitalism Magazine.

Confederation of British Industry

http://www.cbi.org.uk/home.html

Representing over 250,000 public and private sector companies, the CBI Web site has sections on 'News', 'CBI at work', and 'Business services'.

Cooperative Principles and History

http://www.wisc.edu/uwcc/prin.html

Clear exposition of the definition, values, principles, identity, and history of the cooperative movement, by the University of Wisconsin Center for Cooperatives.

Dow Jones Indexes

http://indexes.dowjones.com/

Latest readings from the Dow Jones Index, 'the Markets' Measure'. The various indexes

are backed up with explanations of the methodology used to compile them, and archives of previous readings.

European Bank for Reconstruction and Development

http://www.ebrd.com/

Explanation of the role and structure of the London-based group that finances 'the economic transition in Central and Eastern Europe and the CIS'. The text is heavy-going and aimed at economists interested in developments in central Europe and the former USSR, or countries wishing to find about the mechanisms of obtaining economic support.

European Free Trade Association

http://www.imf.org/external/np/sec/decdo/efta.htm

Introduction to the group of European states that are not levying import duties on each other.

Federal Budget of the USA

http://www.access.gpo.gov/omb/index.html

Download entire federal budget documents or search for individual sections.

Federal Reserve Board

http://www.bog.frb.fed.us

Description of the complex functioning of the US central banking system.

Grameen Bank

http://www.citechco.net/grameen/bank/

Information about the pioneering work of the Grameen Bank, which extends credit without collateral to the poor of Bangladesh.

History of Money from Ancient Times to the Present Day

http://www.ex.ac.uk/~RDavies/arian/llyfr.html

Online version of a book about the history of money. It begins with a 'Comparative history of money' and ends with 'Third World money and debt in the 20th century'.

International Monetary Fund

http://www.imf.org/external/index.htm

Explanation of this organization's role in promoting international monetary cooperation and assisting states with balance-of-payments difficulties.

London Stock Exchange

http://www.londonstockex.co.uk/

London Stock Exchange Web site that tells you how the exchange and its markets work.

OECD – Organization for Economic Cooperation and Development

http://www.oecd.org

Regularly updated site with information on the role, structure, and history of this organization.

164 Currency Converter

http://www.oanda.com/cgi-bin/ncc

Simple to use and effective site allowing you to do automatic conversions to and from a wide range of currencies, from the Afghani to the złoty. You can select the amount to convert and also the date of the exchange rate you want to use.

Reserve Bank of Australia

http://www.rba.gov.au/about/ab_ind.html

Home page of Australia's central bank.

Secrets of Making Money

http://www.pbs.org/wgbh/nova/moolah/

Companion to a US Public Broadcasting Service (PBS) television programme, this page investigates the science and art of minting money.

Stockmarket – the UK's Personal Finance Web Site

http://www.moneyworld.co.uk/stocks/index.html

Constantly updated financial information from the leading stock exchanges. You can follow the fortunes of the FTSE and the Dow and the latest currency fluctuations. If your investments plummet there are links to a number of financial advisors.

United Nations Department of Economic and Social Affairs – Statistics Division

http://www.un.org/Depts/unsd/

Detailed, worldwide economic data, regularly updated and supported by sections on 'Statistical Methods' and 'Sources and References'.

US Securities and Exchange Commission

http://www.sec.gov/

Information on the US agency charged with the regulation of securities and financial markets.

World Bank Home Page

http://www.worldbank.org/

Easy-to-use site that explains the workings of the organization.

World Economic Forum

http://www.weforum.org/

Independent international organization constituting a global partnership of business, political, and intellectual leaders, focusing on global economic development.

World Trade Organization

http://www.wto.org/wto/index.htm

Extensive information on the functions of the United Nations agency charged with administering international trade agreements. The contents are in English, French, and Spanish, and the full text of many international agreements is included.

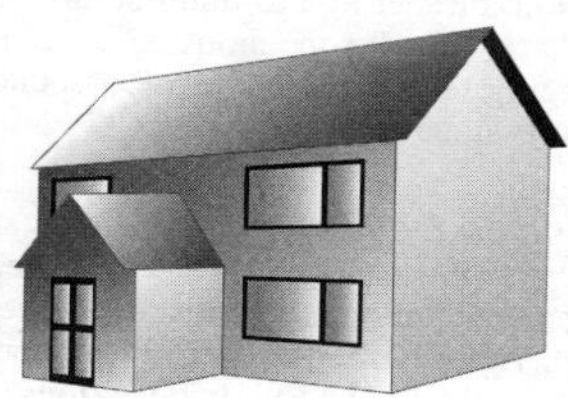

The Consumer and Citizenship

Consumer Information

Guide for Consumers in the UK

In General

Before you buy, ask yourself:

- Is it what I am looking for?
- Can I afford it?
- Is this the best place to buy it?
- Can I take it back if I do not like it?
- How will I pay for it?
- Have I seen what other shops have to offer?
- Does the trader have a good reputation for treating customers fairly?

Statutory Rights

As a customer purchasing goods, you have certain statutory rights, whether what you are buying is new or second-hand. Under the Sale and Supply of Goods Act 1994, goods must: fit any description given, whether on a label, packaging, in an advertisement, or anywhere else; be in good condition, free from any minor or major faults, and capable of doing the job expected of them for a reasonable length of time; be fit for the purpose for which they are intended: if you have told a retailer that you need the goods for a specific purpose, they must be fit for that purpose as well as for general use; correspond with any samples you have been shown.

If goods fail to meet the above criteria, you are legally entitled to reject them and to receive your money back, in cash. It is illegal for a retailer or supplier to insist on providing a credit note or a replacement instead of a cash repayment, unless you agree to accept it. You have a 'reasonable' time in which to reject goods that fail to meet with the above requirements, if you do not reject goods in such time you may only be able to insist on having an item repaired at no cost. Current legislation does not specify the length of 'reasonable' time, but it can be as little as a few days.

Under hire purchase or conditional sale agreement terms, you have the same basic rights as if you had paid cash, but your contract is with the finance company, not the retailer. If, however, the goods are faulty, your rights last for the length of time of the hire purchase agreement, not just for a 'reasonable' length of time.

Guarantees and Warranties

Guarantees provide you with additional rights over and above your statutory rights. A guarantee does not take away or replace your statutory rights. Guarantees are required by law to state that your 'statutory rights are not affected'.

Traditional guarantees – those provided by manufacturers with their new products – are often subject to conditions of use. They

promise to repair any faults that occur due to defects from the manufacture of an item, during a specified period. These guarantees are dependent on the proper use, servicing, maintenance, and so on, of a product. It is not a legal requirement for manufacturers to provide a guarantee with their products.

Guarantees are also sometimes given with second-hand goods, but may only be a verbal statement by the seller, or be written on the receipt. If something goes wrong with a second-hand product, there is no legal way to enforce a verbal or even a written guarantee, but you could sue for breach of contract under civil law. It is not a criminal offence to renege on a verbal agreement.

When you purchase goods from a retailer, you may be offered an extended warranty. Warranties usually have to be purchased from a specialist insurance or warranty company; they are sold to you in addition to the goods you purchase and, as with guarantees, have terms and conditions with which you must comply in order to obtain any benefit from them. They tend to cover problems with goods, such as the failure of components within the period of the warranty, and do not cover failures due to general wear and tear. Insurance-backed warranties can mean that you have to pay the trader to carry out repairs and then claim the cost back from the insurers.

Guarantees usually last for one year, during which time the manufacturer of a product is legally obliged to repair any faults that are due to manufacturing or material defects. If faults occur very soon after purchasing an item, you can claim your money back, under your statutory rights, without having to have the item repaired under guarantee.

Make sure, where there is a registration card for return to the manufacturer, that the seller has filled in details of the purchase; the registration may not be valid without this having been done. For the guarantee to be effective you may need to ensure that you return the registration card to a stated address. Make sure you retain the documentation that is supplied with the goods and tells you how to make a claim under your guarantee. It is important to note that a guarantee or warranty is only as good as the company that issues it; if the company stops trading, the guarantee or warranty is worthless.

Trade Associations

Trade associations and professional bodies can develop and enforce their own codes of conduct, or practice guidelines, for their members. If a trader, for example a builder, carries out unsatisfactory work, he or she can be reported to the trade association of which he or she is a member. If traders are found to be in breach of their trade association's code of conduct, they can be excluded from the association. However, membership of a trade association is not always a guarantee of quality; not all trade associations regulate their members. It is always advisable to check the membership status of a trader and to find out any benefits there may be in choosing a supplier belonging to a particular trade association or professional body.

Buying on Credit

Most people at some time will enter an agreement to purchase goods or services on credit. Before entering a credit agreement you should take the following actions:

Work out what the total cost of the loan will be.

Shop around for credit: how much will a loan cost to repay each month and for how long? Check also the annual percentage rate of charge (normally referred to as APR). Generally speaking, the lower the APR the better the deal. Some traders offer interest-free credit (0% APR) but you will need to take care that you are not paying higher amounts in other ways; for example, it may be a higher cash price than you would pay for the same goods elsewhere.

Make absolutely sure you have read and understood all credit agreements before signing them. If there is anything you do not understand, ask.

Make sure you can afford to pay back the loan and the interest – and still have enough to cover all your other commitments. Check whether the loan has a variable rate of interest. If it has, your repayments can go up as well as down.

Make sure you can really afford the purchase. If you are refused credit you have certain rights. You have the right to know the name and address of the credit reference agency that the lender contacted for details about you; the right to see any information held about you by that agency; and the right to correct any inaccurate information. Some loans are only given if they are secured on your home. These loans are not available if you rent. A secured loan gives security to the lender, not to you. If you cannot keep up with the repayments, the lender can sell your home to cover any loss. You might get a lower rate of interest with a secured loan, but you could have a lot at stake.

Right to Cancel a Credit Deal

If you change your mind and want to cancel a credit deal, you should be able to do so if:

the deal was made within the last few days; you talked to the lender or supplier in person (not on the telephone); when you signed the credit agreement you were not on the lender's or supplier's business premises, including an exhibition stand (agreements signed in shops, etc are not normally cancellable, but agreements signed at home usually are).

When you sign, you should always be given a copy of the credit agreement, which sets out your cancellation rights. You should also receive, by post, a second copy or a notice of your cancellation rights.

If you change your mind, and the lender has not yet signed the agreement, you have the right to withdraw from a credit deal.

Credit Brokers' Fees

If you use a credit broker to get a loan, including a mortgage or a loan secured on your home, you will probably be charged a fee for the service. Make sure you know what this fee will be before you commit yourself. If, however, you do not enter into an agreement within six months of being introduced to a possible lender, the broker can only charge a fee or commission of £3, and if you have already paid more you can recover the excess. Similarly, other fees, such as a survey fee, or insurance premium paid to a credit broker in connection with a loan that you do not eventually take up, are also refundable to you for credit agreements up to £25,000.

Shopping by Mail, Telephone, and Television

Before you send any money, take note of these points:

If ordering by mail, check that the newspaper, magazine, or catalogue is up-to-date.

If you buy through a newspaper, magazine, or television advertisement, check whether you are covered by a protection scheme. If you are not, and you pay in advance, you could lose your money if the trader goes out of business.

Try to avoid sending cash by post. Use credit cards, cheques, or postal orders, and make sure you retain cheque stubs or counterfoils as a record of payment. If you have to send cash, use registered post.

Be careful when giving out your credit card details. Make sure that you know who the trader is, and that you have a business address of the trader before giving the information.

Keep a copy or record of your order and note the date it was sent or placed.

Keep a copy of the advertisement. If this isn't possible, keep a note of the advertiser's name and address, where and when the advertisement appeared and any other details. Make sure there is a full postal address given for the trader – be wary of dealing with any company which only has a post office box number.

If you intend to purchase a product based on a telephone call from a company, make sure you have asked for the company's name, address, and telephone number, as well as the name of the sales representative who contacted you, before you consider the offer and decide whether to call and place your order.

If you are joining a book or record club, make sure you know what commitment you are making and the cancellation terms. Find out exactly what you have to buy and over how long a period in order to qualify for any introductory offer.

Before buying a product from a television shopping programme, check the cost of the same item sold by shops and mail order catalogues.

Paying by Credit

You have some extra protection if you buy the goods with a credit card. This

protection applies to goods costing £100 or more for one item, even if you only pay a deposit. If you have a claim against the seller because, for example, the goods are not what you asked for or are faulty, you may also have a claim against the credit card company. This claim could be useful if the seller were to go out of business.

Untrue Claims

It is a criminal offence for a trader to say or write something untrue about what is being offered for sale. If, when you have bought the goods, you feel that you have been seriously misled, tell your local Trading Standards or Consumer Protection Department, which may decide to prosecute the trader. If the trader is convicted, a claim for compensation may be considered in court, except in Northern Ireland, where you would have to sue separately.

Delivery

If you insist on, or are given, a delivery date when you send for the goods, and this date is not met, you can cancel your order and ask for your money back. Even if no definite date is given, goods should be delivered within a reasonable time, usually 28 days, or as specified in the advertisement or by the telephone sales representative. If they are not delivered within such a time, contact the seller to say that if the goods have not arrived by a certain date (for example, within two weeks) you will not accept them and will ask for your money back. But if you agree to give the seller extra time (for example, another month), you cannot change your mind and try to cancel your order before that extra time is up.

Unsolicited Goods

If you receive goods you have not ordered, you do not have to accept them. If you do nothing and do not hear any more from the trader for six months, the goods will become yours. Or you can write to the trader saying that the goods were 'unsolicited' (unasked for). If the trader does not then collect them within 30 days, the goods are yours. You must, of course, allow unsolicited goods to be collected, provided that the trader comes to collect them at a reasonable time after prior notice. You must also take care of the goods until they are collected.

Price

Make sure you know all the conditions regarding price. You may have agreed to pay any increase which takes place between ordering and delivery, or perhaps you will have agreed a fixed price. Be sure you know whether there are extra charges for postage and packing, and if so, what they are.

Unfair Contract Terms

If you have entered into a contract on the trader's standard terms of business, the law says that certain types of terms which act against the consumer's interest may be unfair and unenforceable. If you think a term is unfair, you may wish to seek advice from your local Trading Standards service or Citizens' Advice Bureau. You can also write to the Director General of Fair Trading. He can take court action to stop the use of an unfair term in future contracts. He cannot, however, get involved with individual cases.

Counterfeit Products

An increasing range of products are being copied and sold, including video and audio tapes, 'designer' clothes, perfume, cosmetics, toys, computer software, etc. The practice of counterfeiting is illegal and it infringes on the intellectual property rights of those who own the copyright, designs, patents, and trade marks of these products. The production, distribution, and sale of fake goods purporting to be original is viewed very seriously by Trading Standards Departments; counterfeit goods can be seized and those responsible prosecuted, resulting in large fines and prison sentences.

To control counterfeiting, UK trade marks, copyright, and trade descriptions legislation is provided for under the Trades Descriptions Act of 1968 and specifies the following:

A trade mark can be a name, logo, word, or signature that connects a person/company to a product; therefore, they have the right to use the mark; copyright provides rights to the creator of literary, dramatic, musical, or artistic work; a trade description can be applied to anything that a person is likely to think applies to the goods and which conduces to a belief in the authenticity of a product's origin or the quality of an item.

Under UK trade descriptions legislation it is therefore illegal to: apply a registered trade mark to goods or packaging without the consent or licence of the trade mark owner; infringe copyright by copying work without the authorization or licence of the copyright owner; apply any kind of identity to products or packaging which is likely to mislead a consumer as to the origin of manufacture or the identity of the producer.

Source: Office of Fair Trading, © Crown copyright 1998

Consumer Complaints in the UK

When you complain, get your facts right and always keep calm. You are probably more likely to get matters resolved if you do not lose your temper.

Goods

Return to the shop as soon as possible with your receipt or proof of purchase (bank or credit card statement showing the amount paid through your account); explain the problem and what you expect to be done, setting a deadline; if the outcome is not satisfactory, put your complaint in writing; address your letter to the customer services manager, chairman, or, where the shop is part of a chain, the head office; if the problem is still not resolved, get further advice and/or consider going to court.

Services

Complain verbally to the supplier and provide an opportunity for the supplier to resolve the problem; complain in writing if the matter is not resolved and provide a deadline for it to be corrected; consider withholding payment until the problem is resolved, but beware: check the small print of any contract you have signed and obtain further advice before refusing to pay, especially if you have a credit agreement. Note: if you continue to pay for a service you are not happy with under a credit agreement, you still have legal redress against the lender for providing an unsatisfactory service; keep a diary of events, notes of telephone calls, and copies of any relevant documentation, such as letters. Also take photographs where necessary. These records will all help in case you have to bring legal action to resolve the matter; consider obtaining an expert opinion to support your complaint.

Complaints over the Phone

Make a note beforehand of what you want to say; have receipts and any other documents handy; note the name of the person you speak to; write down the date and time of the call and what was said; follow up your call with a letter, particularly if the complaint is a serious one.

Complaints in Writing

Type your letter if possible; if your letter is handwritten, make sure it is clear and legible; include your name, address, and home and work telephone numbers; keep your letter brief, polite, and to the point, avoid repetition and personal remarks; describe the item or service; say where and when you bought the item, or when the service was done, and how much it cost; explain what is wrong, any action you have already taken, to whom you spoke, and what happened; say what you want done to remedy the situation – for example, a refund or repair, or the job done again without charge; set a deadline by which you want a response from the other party; use special delivery so you can check that your letter has been delivered; keep copies of any letters you send; do not send original documents, such as receipts and guarantees – send copies instead; be persistent: if you fail to get what you want at your first attempt, write another letter of complaint setting out your dissatisfaction.

Model Complaint Letter

[Your name and address]
[Date]

[Name of person, if known, or 'Customer Services Manager' or 'Chairman']
[The person's title, if name is known]
[Company name] [Full address, including postal code]

Dear [Person's surname, if known, or 'Dear Sir or Madam']

Re: [Order, account, or reference number]

On [full date], I [ordered, bought, rented, leased, had repaired, sought a service] [a name of the product with its serial and/or model number or service performed] at/from [company, location, catalogue, and other important details relevant to the transaction] price [£...].

Unfortunately, your product [does not correspond with its description, was damaged in transit, showed serious defects, etc.] [or the service was inadequate]. I am disappointed because [describe why the product or service was faulty or inadequate, misrepresented, and so on, or why you believe the billing was incorrect].

To resolve this problem, I would appreciate your [state the specific action you want: reimbursement, charge-card credit, replacement, repair, exchange, the service done or improved, etc.] within [... days]. Enclosed are copies of my records (include copies, not originals, of any relevant documents].

I look forward to [your reply, your cheque for £..., receiving a replacement, etc.]. I will wait until [date] before seeking help from [my local trading standards or consumer protection department]. Please contact me at the above address or by telephone at [give home and work numbers with their area codes].

Yours sincerely/faithfully
[Your name]
Enclosure(s)
cc: [Name(s) of any person(s) to whom you are sending a copy of this letter]

Taking Further Action

If you are struggling to get a complaint addressed satisfactorily, you can take further action. Just telling a trader who is being unhelpful or obstructive that you will go to court could be enough to get your complaint resolved. If you do have to take legal action, it can be much easier than it sounds and could well be worth the effort.

Before going to arbitration or to court, you may wish to seek an impartial opinion on the merits of your case. This opinion is best obtained from a solicitor. Some solicitors work in law centres or advice agencies that offer free advice. Many solicitors in private practice offer a low-cost initial interview. Your local Citizens' Advice Bureau can help you find such a solicitor.

Conciliation and Arbitration

If the trader is a member of a trade association, there may be a conciliation or arbitration scheme you can use. Some associations have both. Such schemes are informal and generally inexpensive. However, arbitration may not necessarily be cheaper than going to court under the small claims procedure. Check what fees you will be expected to pay if you lose the case.

You have to choose between court and arbitration – you cannot do both. If you do not like an arbitrator's decision, you cannot then go to court (except in special circumstances). Under the Consumer Arbitration Agreements Act 1996, a clause in a contract which says that you have to go to arbitration cannot bind you as long as the value of your dispute is not greater than the small claims limit.

Going to Court

If, after trying to resolve your complaint by telephone and in writing, you remain unsatisfied, you can take further action by going to court. If the threat of court action is not sufficient to make a trader/service provider address your problem seriously, you can proceed with legal action and go to court to sue for the return of your money or for compensation. In England and Wales, a claim of £3,000 or less can be dealt with as a 'small claim'; in Northern Ireland, the limit is £1,000; in Scotland, small claims of up to £750 can be taken to the Sheriff Court. You do not require the services of a solicitor to pursue a small claim, and even if your opponent employs the services of one, you are not liable for their legal costs if you lose the case (unless you are found to have made an unreasonable claim, caused unnecessary expense costs, or do not attend a hearing).

The necessary forms for filing a small claim are available from County Court offices (Sheriff Court in Scotland). The court will then serve the summons and advise you on what to do next. There are court fees which are payable by your opponent if you win your case. Outside Scotland, the fees are 10 pence for every £1 claimed, with a minimum fee of £10 and a maximum of £65 for claims of £1,000–3,000. In Scotland the fees are £6 for claims up to £50 and £32 for claims of £50–750.

Major Consumer Organizations

Citizens' Advice Bureaux (CAB) CABs provide a wide range of advice and can help resolve many consumer problems, including complaints about goods and services. Details on contacting your nearest branch can be found in the telephone book under Citizens' Advice Bureaux.

Trading Standards departments Trading Standards (or consumer protection) departments have the powers to investigate complaints about goods and services and can advise on everyday consumer issues. Details on contacting your local Trading Standards department can be found in the telephone book under Trading Standards Service. In Northern Ireland, contact the trading standards branch of the Department of Economic Development.

Office of Fair Trading The Office of Fair Trading is a non-ministerial government department responsible for a wide range of issues of fair trading in the UK. It has powers to protect consumers in the following ways: identifying and correcting trading practices which are against the consumer's interests; regulating the provision of consumer credit; investigating and acting to prevent anti-competitive practices; encouraging competitive behaviour.

Utilities regulators If you have a complaint about utilities services, that is gas, electricity, water, or telephones, you can take the matter to the relevant regulatory body if your problem is not resolved by the company. Each of the four utilities has a regulator that can help solve consumer problems: OFFER, Office of Electricity Regulation; OFWAT, Office of Water Services; OFTEL, Office of Telecommunications; Gas Consumers' Council. Contact information for these bodies can be found in the telephone book.

The Ombudsmen Ombudsmen exist to deal with complaints from citizens about certain public bodies or private sector services. There are 23 recognized Ombudsman schemes, most of which are established by statute. The schemes vary in the procedures they use and the powers that they have.

Using the services of an Ombudsman is a last resort. The party against which a complaint is being made must first be given reasonable time to resolve the complaint; indeed, many organizations have their own complaints procedures, which normally resolve problems satisfactorily. It is only if and when a complaint has not been resolved by going through the normal channels that an Ombudsman will consider it.

Ombudsmen schemes include: The Health Service Ombudsman; Police Complaints Authority; The Legal Services Ombudsman; Broadcasting Standards Commission; The Independent Housing Ombudsman; The Parliamentary Ombudsman. There are also Ombudsmen schemes for banking, pensions, and investments.

Other organizations Other organizations from which help and advice can be obtained include environmental health departments (for advice on health matters) law centres, and trade associations. Contact information for many consumer organizations can be found here, or consult your telephone book.

Source: Office of Fair Trading, © Crown copyright 1999

Directory of Consumer Bodies in the UK

Arbitration

Chartered Institute of Arbitrators Apartment 24, 324 Angel Gate, City Road, London EC1V 2RS; phone: (0171) 837 4483; fax: (0171) 837 4185; e-mail: 71411.2735@compuserve.com

Scottish Council for Arbitration 27 Melville Street, Edinburgh EH3 7JF; phone: (0131) 220 4776; fax: (0131) 226 2501

Ombudsmen

Banking Ombudsman 70 Grays Inn Road, London WC1X 8NB; phone: (0171) 404

9944; fax: (0171) 405 5052; e-mail: banking.ombudsman@obo.org.uk

Building Societies Ombudsman Millbank Tower, Millbank, London SW1P 4XS; phone: (0171) 931 0044; fax: (0171) 233 9836; e-mail: blgsocombudsman@easynet.co.uk

Ombudsman for Estate Agents Beckett House, 4 Bridge Street, Salisbury, Wiltshire SP1 2LX; phone: (01722) 333306; fax: (01722) 332296; Web site: www.oea.co.uk

The Funeral Ombudsman 26–30 Bedford Row, London WC1R 4HE; phone: (0171) 430 1112; fax: (0171) 430 1012; e-mail: fos@dircon.co.uk

The Insurance Ombudsman Scheme Bureau City Gate One, 135 Park Street, London SE1 9EA; phone: (08456) 006666; fax: (0171) 902 8197; e-mail: complaint@theiob.org.uk

Legal Services Ombudsman 22 Oxford Court, Oxford Street, Manchester M2 3WQ; phone: (0161) 236 9532; fax: (0161) 236 2651; e-mail: enquires.olso@gtnet.gov.uk

Pensions Ombudsman 11 Belgrave Road, London SW1V 1RB; phone: (0171) 834 9144; fax: (0171) 821 0065; e-mail: pensions.ombudman@iclweb.com

Personal Investment Authority Ombudsman Hertsmere House, Hertsmere Road, London E14 4AB; phone: (0171) 216 0016; fax: (0171) 712 8742

Doorstep and Party Plan Selling

Direct Selling Association Ltd 29 Floral Street, London WC2E 9DP; phone: (0171) 497 1234; fax: (0171) 497 3144; e-mail: ukdsa@global.net.co.uk

Electrical Goods

The Association of Manufacturers of Domestic Electrical Appliances Rapier House, 40–46 Lambs Conduit Street, London WC1N 3NW; phone: (0171) 405 0666; fax: (0171) 405 6609; e-mail: lynn:owen@amdea.org.uk

The Radio, Electrical, and Television Retailers' Association Ltd RETRA House, St John's Terrace, 1 Ampthill Street, Bedford MK42 9EY; phone: (01234) 269110; fax: (01234) 269609; e-mail: retra@retra.co.uk

Furniture

Qualitas National Conciliation Service Chief Conciliation Officer, Maxwell Street, Stevenage, Herts SG1 2EW; phone: (01438) 316100; fax: (01438) 777780

Holidays

Air Travel Organizer's Licence (ATOL) Civil Aviation Authority, CAA House, 45–59 Kingsway, London WC2B 6TE; phone: (0171) 832 5620/6600; fax: (0171) 832 6692; Web site: www.caa.co.uk

Association of British Travel Agents (ABTA) 68–71 Newman Street, London W1P 4AH; phone: (0171) 637 2444; fax: (0171) 307 1992

Association of Independent Tour Operators (AITO) 133a St Margarets Road, Twickenham, Middlesex TW1 1RG; phone: (0181) 744 9280; fax: (0181) 744 3187; e-mail: aito@martex.co.uk

The Timeshare Council 23 Buckingham Gate, London SW1E 6LB; phone: (0171) 821 8845; fax: (0171) 828 0739

Home Maintenance and Improvements

Glass and Glazing Federation 44–48 Borough High Street, London SE1 1XB; phone: (0171) 403 7177; fax: (0171) 357 7458

Mail Order

Direct Marketing Association Haymarket House, 1 Oxendon Street, London SW1Y 4EE; phone: (0171) 321 2525; fax: (0171) 321 0191; e-mail: dma@dma.org.uk

Mailing/Telephone Preference Service FREEPOST 22, London W1E 7EZ; phone: (0171) 766 4410; fax: (0171) 976 1886; e-mail: mps@dma.org.uk

Mail Order Protection Scheme 16 Tooks Court, London EC4A 1LB; phone: (0171) 269 0520; fax: (0171) 404 0106; Web site: www.mops.org.uk

Mail Order Traders' Association 40 Waterloo Road, Birkdale, Southport PR8 2NG; phone: (01704) 563787; fax: (01704 551247; e-mail: malcolmlandau@compuserve.com

Telephone Preference Services BT: phone: (0800) 398893; Cable & Wireless: phone: (0500) 730730; Mercury: phone (0500) 398893. For general public to stop receiving cold calls. Customers of other companies should call the customer services number on their bill.

Motor Trade

Complaints about Used Cars, Repairs, and Servicing in England, Wales, and Northern Ireland

The National Conciliation Service, Retail Motor Industry Federation 9 North Street, Rugby CV21 2AB; phone: (01788) 538316; fax: (01788) 538337

Complaints about Cars Still Under a Manufacturer's Warranty

The Customer's Relation Adviser, Society of Motor Manufacturers and Traders Forbes House, Halkin Street, London SW1X 7DS; phone: (0171) 235 7000; fax: (0171) 235 7112; Web site: www.smmt.co.uk

Complaints about Car Body Repair

The Conciliation Service, The Vehicle Builders' and Repairers' Association Belmont House, 102 Finkle Lane, Gildersome, Leeds LS27 7TW; phone: (0113) 253 8333; fax: (0113) 238 0496

Complaints about Used Cars, Repairs, and Servicing in Scotland

Customer Complaints Service, Scottish Motor Trade 3 Palmerston Place, Edinburgh EH12 5AF; phone: (0131) 225 3643; fax: (0131) 220 0446

Vehicle Checks

Equifax HPI Autodata Dolphin House, New Street, Salisbury, Wiltshire SP1 1TB; phone: (01722) 422422

Small Claims Procedure

Court Service Customer Services Unit Southside, 105 Victoria Street, London SW1E 6QT; phone: (0171) 210 1689; fax: (0171) 210 1797; e-mail: cust.ser.cs@gtnet.gov.uk

Scottish Courts Service Hayweight House, 23 Lauriston House, Edinburgh EH3 9DQ; phone: (0131) 229 9200; fax: (0131) 221 6890; e-mail: enquiries@scotcourts.gov.uk

General Consumer and Advisory Bodies

Advice Services Alliance (ASA) Universal House, 2nd Floor, 88–94 Wentworth Street, London E1 7SA; phone: (0171) 236 6022; fax: (0171) 248 3367

Citizens' Advice Scotland (CAS) 26 George Square, Edinburgh EH8 9LD; phone: (0131) 667 0156; fax: (0131) 668 4359

Consumers' Association (CA) 2 Marylebone Road, London NW1 4DF; phone: (0171) 830 6000; fax: (0171) 830 7600; e-mail: editor@which.co.uk

Department of Trade and Industry (DTI) Consumer Affairs Enquiry Unit DTI, 1 Victoria Street, London SW1H 0ET; phone: (0171) 215 5000; Web site: www.dti. gov.uk

Federation of Independent Advice Centres (FIAC) 4 Deans Court, St Paul's Churchyard, London EC4V 5AA; phone: (0171) 489 1800; fax: (0171) 489 1804

General Consumer Council for Northern Ireland (GCCNI) Elizabeth House, 116 Holywood Road, Belfast BT4 1NY; phone: (01232) 672488; fax: (01232) 657701; e-mail: gcc@nics.gov.uk

Institute of Trading Standards Administration 3–5 Hadleigh Business Centre, 351 London Road, Hadleigh, Essex SS7 2BT; phone: (01702) 559922; fax: (01702) 551161; e-mail: institute@itsa. org.uk

Law Centres Federation Duchess House, 18–19 Warren Street, London W1P 5DB;

phone: (0171) 387 8570; fax: (0171) 387 8368; e-mail: info@lawcentres.org.uk

National Association of Citizens' Advice Bureaux (NACAB) Myddleton House, 115–123 Pentonville Road, London N1 9LZ; phone: (0171) 833 2181; fax: (0171) 833 4360; e-mail: consultancy@nacab. org.uk

National Consumer Council (NCC) 20 Grosvenor Gardens, London SW1W 0DH; phone: (0171) 730 3469; fax: (0171) 730 0191; e-mail: info@ncc.org.uk

National Federation of Consumer Groups 527 Leeds Road, Scholes, Leeds LS15 4RD; phone: (0113) 264 8341

Office of Fair Trading (OFT) Head Office, Field House, 15–25 Bream Buildings, London EC4A 1PR; phone: (0171) 211 8000; fax: (0171) 211 8800

OFT Consumer Information Line (0345) 224499 (local call rates apply on BT lines within the UK)

Scottish Consumer Council (SCC) Royal Exchange House, 100 Queen Street, Glasgow G1 3DN; phone: (0141) 226 5261; fax: (0141) 221 0731; e-mail: scc@ scotconsumer.org.uk

Welsh Consumer Council (WCC)/ Cyngor Defnyddwyr Cymru (CDC) Castle Buildings, Womanby Street, Cardiff CF1 2BN; phone: (01222) 255454

See Also  **Legal Aid, p.536.**

Forms of Address

Forms of Address in the UK

Two dashes indicate first name and surname; one dash indicates surname or place; C– indicates first name only. Honourable is abbreviated to Hon. Formal ceremonial styles for closing letters are provided where appropriate. Spoken address is provided where a special style is followed, and only in selected instances. For the royal family, it is more normal practice to address letters to the private secretary, lady-in-waiting, or equerry of the relevant member of the family. Both formal and social forms of address are given for the peerage, where usage differs in some cases. In general, the social form is now generally preferred to the formal. For formal forms of address used for official documents and on very formal occasions, as well as for more detailed information on forms of address, see Debrett's *Correct Form* and Black's *Titles and Forms of Address*.

Addressee	Address	Salutation
Government Officers		
Cabinet minister	The Right Hon – –	Dear Minister
Member of Parliament	– –, Esq, adding MP after title or name and honours	Dear Minister
Minister of the Crown	if a Privy Counsellor, see relevant section below; otherwise, Member of Parliament or grade of peerage below	Dear Secretary of State, or Dear Minister if the matters concerns the department
Prime Minister	The Right Hon – –	Dear (Mr) Prime Minister
Privy Counsellor	The Right Hon – –, if not a peer; The Right Hon, the Earl of –, PC (PC after all orders and decorations)	according to rank
Secretary of State	The Right Hon – –, MP, Secretary of State for –, or The Secretary of State for –; otherwise according to rank	Dear Secretary of State
Diplomatic Officials		
Ambassador	His/Her Excellency the Ambassador of –, or HM Ambassador to –	Your Excellency; close letter: I have the honour to be, Sir/Madam (or according to rank), Your Excellency's obedient servant; spoken address: Your Excellency at least once, and then Sir or Madam by name
Consul	– –, Esq, HM Consul-General (Consul, or Vice-Consul, as the case may be)	Sir
Governor of a country	His Excellency (preceding all ranks and titles); if knighted: His Excellency Mr – –	according to rank; close letter: have the honour to be, Sir (or My Lord, if a peer), Your Excellency's obedient servant; spoken address: Your Excellency
Governor-General	His Excellency (preceding all ranks and titles) followed by ordinary designation, Governor-General of –. (The Governor-General of Canada has the rank of Right Hon, which he retains for life)	as for Governor
Governor-General's wife	the style Her Excellency is confined to wives of Governor-Generals of Commonwealth countries within the country administered by her husband	
High Commissioner	His Excellency (preceding all ranks and titles) the High Commissioner of –	as for Ambassador
Lieutenant-Governor	Isle of Man, Jersey, and Guernsey	as for Governor

(continued)

Forms of Address in the UK (*continued*)

Addressee	Address	Salutation
Civic Titles		
Lady Mayoress	as for Lord Mayor's wife	
Lord Mayor	the Lord Mayors of London, York, Belfast, Cardiff, Dublin, and also Sydney, Melbourne, Adelaide, Brisbane, and Hobart are styled: The Right Hon the Lord Mayor of –. Other Lord Mayors are styled: The Right Worshipful the Lord Mayor of –	My Lord Mayor, or Dear Lord Mayor
Lord Mayor's wife	The Lady Mayoress of –	
Mayor	The Right Worshipful the Mayor of – (if mayor of a city); The Worshipful the Mayor of – (if mayor of a borough or town mayor)	My Lady Mayoress
Lord Provost	the Lord Provosts of Edinburgh and Glasgow are styled: The Right Hon the Lord Provost; the Lord Provosts of Perth, Aberdeen, and Dundee are styled: The Lord Provost of –	Dear Mr Mayor (may be used for a man or woman); Mr Mayor, or Sir/Madam My Lord Provost
Provost	The Provost of –	
Aldermen	Mr/Miss/Mrs Alderman –	Dear Lord Provost
Councillor	Councillor –; Miss/Mrs Councillor –	Dear Sir; Dear Alderman; Dear Alderman – Dear Councillor; Dear Councillor –; Dear Miss/Mrs Councillor –; never Mr Councillor
The Bench		
Judge of City of London Court	as for Circuit Judge	
Judge, Circuit	His or Her Honour Judge –; if a Knight, His Honour Judge Sir – –	Dear Sir or Madam; spoken address: when on the bench, Your Honour; otherwise Sir
Judge of High Court (men)	The Hon Mr Justice –	Dear Sir; spoken address: when on the bench, My Lord or Your Lordship; otherwise Sir
Judge of High Court (women)	The Hon Mrs (or Miss) Justice –	Dear Madam; spoken address: when on the bench, My Lady or Your Ladyship; otherwise Madam
Justice of the Peace	as for Esquire (see peerage)	spoken address: when on the bench, Your Worship; otherwise as for Esquire
Lord Advocate	The Right Hon the Lord Advocate, or The Right Hon – –	as for Esquire (see Peerage)
Lord Chancellor	The Right Hon the Lord High Chancellor	as for peer, according to rank (see Peerage)
Lord Chief Justice	The Lord Chief Justice of England or The Right Hon Lord –, Lord Chief Justice of England	Dear Lord Chief Justice
Lord Justice Clerk and Lord Justice General	The Right Hon the Justice Clerk, and The Right Hon the Lord Justice General	My Lord, Dear Lord Justice General/Clerk, or Dear Lord –
Lord Justice of Appeal	The Right Hon Lord Justice –, or The Right Hon Sir – –	as for Judge of High Court
Lord of Appeal-in-Ordinary	as for Baron (see peerage)	
Lord of Session, Scottish	The Hon Lord/Lady –	My Lord/Lady/Madam, or Dear Lord/Lady/Madam –
Lord of Session's wife or widow	Lady –	as for a Baron's wife (see Peerage)
Master of the Rolls	The Right Hon the Master of the Rolls, or The Right Hon –, according to rank	Dear Sir; spoken address: when on the bench, My Lord or Your Lordship; otherwise Sir
Queen's Counsel	– – Esq, QC	as for Esquire (see Peerage)
Sheriff	Sheriff Principal –	Dear Sheriff
Peerage and Other Titles		
Baron	The Right Hon Lord – (formal), The Lord – (social)	The Lord – (formal), Dear Lord – (social); spoken address: Lord –
Baroness in her own right	The Right Hon the Baroness – (formal), The Baroness – (social)	My Lady (formal), Dear Lady – (social); spoken address: Lady –
Baron's wife	The Right Hon Lady – (formal), The Lady – (social)	as for Baroness in her own right
Baron's children	The Hon – –	Dear Mr/Miss/Madam –
Baronet	Sir – –, Bt	Dear Sir (formal), Dear Sir C– (social); spoken address: Sir C–
Baronet's wife	Lady –	Dear Madam (formal), Dear Lady – (social); spoken address: Lady –

(*continued*)

Forms of Address in the UK (*continued*)

Addressee	Address	Salutation
Countess	The Right Hon the Countess of –	as for Baroness in her own right
Courtesy titles	while his father is alive, the heir apparent to a Duke, Earl, or Marquess takes the highest of his father's other titles as a courtesy title; these courtesy titles are not preceded by The Most Hon or The Right Hon; in correspondence the title is not preceded by The	
Dames of Orders of Chivalry	Dame – –, followed by appropriate post-nominal letters	Dear Madam (formal), Dear Dame C– (social); spoken address: Dame C–
Duchess	Her Grace the Duchess of – (formal), The Duchess of – (social)	Dear Madam (formal), Dear Duchess (social); spoken address: Duchess
Duke	His Grace the Duke of – (formal), The Duke of – (social)	My Lord Duke (formal), Dear Duke (social); spoken address: Your Grace (formal), Duke (social)
Duke's daughter	Lady – – (formal), Dear Madam (social)	Dear Lady C–; spoken address: Lady C–
Duke's eldest son	see Courtesy titles	
Duke's younger son	Lord – –	My Lord (formal); Dear Lord C– (social); spoken address: My Lord (formal), Lord C– (social)
Earl	The Right Hon the Earl of – (formal), The Earl of – (social)	My Lord (formal), Dear Lord – (social); spoken address: My Lord (formal), Lord – (social)
Earl's daughter	as for Duke's daughter	
Earl's eldest son	see Courtesy titles	
Earl's wife	The Right Hon the Countess of – (formal), The Countess of – (social)	Madam (formal), Lady – (social); spoken address: Madam (formal), Lady – (social)
Earl's younger son	The Hon – –	as for Baron's children
Esquire	– – Esq	Sir; spoken address: Sir
Knight Bachelor	Sir – –	Dear Sir (formal), Dear Sir C– (social); spoken address: Sir C–
Knight's wife	as for a Baronet's wife	as for Knight Bachelor
Knight of an Order of Chivalry	Sir – –, followed by appropriate post-nominal letters	
Life Peer	as for Baron	
Life Peeress	as for Baroness in her own right	
Life Peer's children	as for Baron's children	
Life Peer's wife	as for Baron's wife	
Marchioness	The Most Hon the Marchioness of – (formal), The Marchioness of – (social)	as for Baroness
Marquess	The Most Hon the Marquess of – (formal), The Marquess of – (social)	My Lord (formal), Dear Lord – (social); spoken address: My Lord (formal), Lord – (social)
Marquess's daughter	Lady – –	as for Duke's daughter
Marquess's eldest son	see Courtesy titles	
Marquess's younger son	Lord – –	as for Duke's younger son
Master	The Master of –; the title is used in Scottish peerage by the heir apparent or presumptive of a peer; heirs apparent of the senior grades of the peerage usually use a courtesy title	Dear Sir (formal), Dear Master of – (social); spoken address: Master, or Sir (formal), Master, or Mr – (social)
Master's wife	according to her husband's rank	
Prince	His Royal Highness the Duke of –, if a duke; His Royal Highness the Prince C–, if the son of a sovereign; otherwise His Royal Highness Prince C–	Sir; close letter: I have the honour to be, Your Royal Highness's most humble and obedient servant; spoken address: Your Royal Highness
Princess	Her Royal Highness the Duchess of –, if the wife of a Royal duke; Her Royal Highness The Princess C–; otherwise Her Royal Highness the Princess C–	Madam; close letter: I have the honour to be, Madam, Your Royal Highness's most humble and obedient servant; spoken address: Your Royal Highness
Queen Mother	Her Gracious Majesty Queen Elizabeth The Queen Mother, for state and formal documents; otherwise Her Majesty Queen – The Queen Mother	as for Queen Regent
Queen Regent	The Queen's Most Excellent Majesty, for state and formal documents; otherwise Her Majesty The Queen	Madam, May it please your Majesty; close letter: I have the honour to remain Madam, or, Majesty's most humble and obedient servant; spoken address: Your Majesty

(continued)

Forms of Address in the UK (*continued*)

Addressee	Address	Salutation
Viscount	The Right Hon the Viscount – (formal), The Viscount – (social)	My Lord (formal), Dear Lord – (social); spoken address: Lord –
Viscount's wife	The Right Hon the Viscountess – (formal), The Viscountess – (social)	Madam (formal), Dear Lady – (social); spoken address: Lady –
Viscount's children	as for Baron's children	
Widow and Divorcee	widows and divorcees keep their husbands' titles until remarriage; the wife of the holder of a peerage becomes a dowager on the death of her husband or on the marriage of the new peer if unmarried at the time of succession; she is addressed as The Dowager Lady; the same title can be held by more than one person, hence the term is used less frequently today, and an alternative form, eg, The Right Hon C–, Countess of – is used, distinction being made by the use of the first name; the ex-wives of Marquesses and below are not styled The Most Hon or The Right Hon	
Clerical Titles		
Archbishop (Anglican)	Most Reverend the Lord Archbishop of –; (the Archbishops of Canterbury and York are Privy Counsellors, and should be addressed as The Most Reverend and Right Hon the Lord Archbishop of –)	Your Grace (more formal), Dear Archbishop, or My Lord Archbishop; spoken address: Your Grace
Archbishop (Roman Catholic)	His Grace the Archbishop of –	My Lord Archbishop; spoken address: Your Grace
Archdeacon	The Venerable the Archdeacon of –	Dear Archdeacon, Dear Mr Archdeacon, or Venerable Sir; spoken address: Archdeacon
Bishop (Anglican)	The Right Reverend the Lord Bishop of –; (the Bishop of London is a Privy Counsellor and should be addressed as The Right Reverend and Right Hon the Lord Bishop of London; the Bishop of Meath is styled The Most Reverend)	Dear Bishop or My Lord; spoken address: Bishop
Bishop (Episcopal Church in Scotland)	The Right Reverend – –, Bishop of –	as for Anglican bishop
Bishop (Roman Catholic)	His Lordship the Bishop of –, or The Right Reverend – –, Bishop of –; in Ireland, The Most Reverend is used instead of The Right Reverend	My Lord, or My Lord Bishop; spoken address: My Lord, or My Lord Bishop
Canon (Anglican)	The Reverend Canon – –	Dear Canon, or Dear Canon –; spoken address: Canon, or Canon –
Canon (Roman Catholic)	The Very Reverend Canon – –	Very Reverend Sir; spoken address: Canon –
Cardinal	His Eminence Cardinal –; if an archbishop, His Eminence the Cardinal Archbishop of –	Your Eminence, My Lord Cardinal, or Dear Cardinal –; spoken address: Your Eminence
Dean and priest	The Reverend – –	Dear Mr/Mrs/Miss/Ms – (or Father – if a male priest prefers, or if Roman Catholic)
Monsignor	The Very Reverend Monsignor – –	Reverend Sir or Dear Monsignor; spoken address: Monsignor –
Pope	His Holiness the Pope	Your Holiness or Most Holy Father; close letter: if Roman Catholic: I have the honour to be Your Holiness's most devoted and obedient child (or, most humble child); if not Roman Catholic: I have the honour to be (or remain) Your Holiness's obedient servant; spoken address: Your Holiness
Prebendary (Anglican)	The Very Reverend Prebendary – –	Dear Prebendary, or Dear Prebendary –; spoken address: Prebendary, or Prebendary –
Prebendary (Roman Catholic)	The Very Reverend Prebendary – –	Very Reverend Sir; spoken address: Prebendary –
Rabbi	Rabbi – –; with a doctorate, Rabbi Doctor – –	Dear Sir, Dear Rabbi, or Dear Doctor; spoken address: Rabbi –, or Doctor –
Armed Forces	professional rank always precedes any other rank or title, for example, Admiral the Right Hon the Earl of, Air Marshal Sir –; officers below the rank of Rear-Admiral and Marshall of the Royal Air Force are entitled to RN and RAF respectively after their name; officers in the women's services add WRNS, WRAF, or WRAC	
Academic		
Chancellor of University	The Chancellor of the University of –	Dear Sir/Madam, My Lord (if a peer), or Dear Chancellor
Dean, Director, Master, Mistress, President, Principal, Provost, Rector, and Warden of university college	The Dean/Director, etc, of – College, University of –, or title/status – – (position) of – College, University of –	as for Chancellor, substituting relevant position

(*continued*)

Forms of Address in the UK (*continued*)

Addressee	Address	Salutation
High Steward	The High Steward of the University of –	Dear High Steward
Professor	Professor – –; if in holy orders, The Reverend Professor	Dear Sir/Madam, or Dear Professor; spoken address: according to rank
Vice-Chancellor	The Vice-Chancellor of the University of –; The Reverend the Vice-Chancellor of Oxford, and The Right Worshipful the Vice-Chancellor of the University of Cambridge	Dear Vice-Chancellor

Postal Information

Summary of First and Second Class Mail in the UK

As of April 1999.

First Class costs 26p up to 60 g, and 39p up to 100 g. Rates continue to increase according to weight up to 1 kg, which costs £2.75; each extra 250 g above 1 kg costs 70p.

Second Class costs 20p up to 60 g, and 31p up to 100 g. Rates continue to increase according to weight up to 750 g, which costs £1.55 and is the maximum weight that can be sent by Second Class.

Summary of Royal Mail Domestic Services in the UK

As of April 1999.

Sending Mail

First Class costs from 26p, and is usually delivered the next working day after posting. A certificate of posting is available free on request, and compensation for a lost item is either the market value of the item or up to £26, whichever is lower.

Second Class costs from 20p, and is usually delivered within 3 working days after posting. A certificate of posting is available free on request, and compensation for a lost item is either the market value of the item or up to £26, whichever is lower.

Recorded costs 60p plus the first or second class postage, and is delivered within the usual first or second class period. A certificate of posting is available free on request, and compensation for a lost item is either the market value of the item or up to £26, whichever is lower.

Special Delivery costs from £3.20, and delivery to 99 percent of UK addresses is guaranteed by 12.00 p.m. on the next working day. Proof of posting and delivery is provided; standard compensation is £250 for loss of, or damage to, an item; a Consequential Loss service is available at extra cost.

Receiving Mail

Callers Service allows you to collect items from your local delivery office before the delivery round begins and costs 26p per collection.

Keepsafe Royal Mail stores your mail while you are away from 1 day to 2 months and delivers it on your return. It costs £5–£15.

Poste Restante allows you to select a Post Office from which to collect your mail while travelling in the UK. There is a maximum duration of 3 months in any town, and there is no charge.

Private Box (PO Box) provides you with an alternative address and holds your mail for collection from your local delivery office. There is no maximum duration, and the cost is £42 for 6 months and £52 for 1 year.

Redirection (personal mail) Royal Mail forwards your personal mail to a new permanent or temporary address, either in the UK or abroad. There is a maximum duration of 2 years, and the cost (per surname) ranges from £6 for 1 month to £30 for 1 year (redirection within the UK) and £12 for 1 month to £60 for 1 year (abroad).

Redirection (business mail) Royal Mail forwards your business mail to a new permanent or temporary address, either in the UK or abroad. There is a maximum duration of 2 years, and the cost (per business name) ranges from £12 for 1 month to £60 for 1 year.

Summary of International Letter Rates from the UK

As of April 1999.

Surface mail and postcards outside Europe only items up to 20 g cost 31p, up to 60 g cost 52p; and up to 100 g cost 75p. Rates increase with each extra 50 g up to 500 g, which costs £3.18; thereafter rates increase with each extra 500 g up to a maximum of 2 kg, which costs £12.21.

Airmail Europe items up to 20 g cost 30p. Items over 20 g are charged at the same rate for both areas, and rates increase with each extra 20 g up to 500 g, which costs £3.33; thereafter rates increase with each extra 500 g up to a maximum of 2 kg, which costs £13.08.

Airmail zone 1 items up to 10 g cost 43p, and 63p up to 20 g. Rates increase with each extra 20 g up to 500 g, which costs £8.66; thereafter rates increase with each extra 500 g up to a maximum of 2 kg, which costs £33.41.

Airmail zone 2 items up to 10 g cost 43p, and 63p up to 20 g. Rates increase with each extra 20 g up to 500 g, which costs £11.17; thereafter rates increase with each extra 500 g up to a maximum of 2 kg, which costs £44.17.

Summary of International Small Packets Service from the UK

As of April 1999.

The International Small Packets service is for sending gifts or goods worldwide. Items intended for this service should be marked 'Small Packet', and those sent by Airmail should be marked 'Par Avion – By Airmail'. It is permissible to include a letter in the Small Packet if it relates to the contents. Delivery times are normally the same as for letters. Small Packets sent to countries in the Commonwealth of Independent States must be unsealed and the contents must not include any correspondence or be worth over £19.

Customs declarations are obligatory for all Small Packets unless they are sent within the European Union. The required declaration varies according to the value of the Packet's contents; information is available from a Post Office.

Rates

Surface mail costs 50p up to 100 g. Rates increase by 16–17p per extra 50 g up to 500 g, which costs £1.84, and thereafter by 17p

per extra 20 g up to a maximum of 2 kg, which costs £6.91.

Airmail Europe costs 75p up to 100 g. Rates increase by 7–8p per extra 20 g up to 500 g, which costs £2.22, and thereafter by 8p per extra 20 g up to a maximum of 2 kg, which costs £8.22.

Airmail zone 1 costs £1.06 up to 100 g. Rates increase by 15–16p per extra 20 g up to 500 g, which costs £4.19, and thereafter by 16p per extra 20 g up to a maximum of 2 kg, which costs £16.19.

Airmail zone 2 costs £1.18 up to 100 g. Rates increase by 18–19p per extra 20 g up to 500 g, which costs £4.95, and thereafter by 19p per extra 20 g up to a maximum of 2 kg, which costs £19.20; for Papua New Guinea the maximum is 500 g.

Add-On Services

International Recorded costs £2.50 plus the normal postage rate. Advice of delivery is available for an extra 40p, and compensation for a lost item is up to £28.

International Registered is available in two price brackets: £3.00 plus the normal postage rate, with advice of delivery available for an extra 40p, and compensation for a lost item up to £500; and £4.00 plus the normal postage rate, with advice of delivery available for an extra 40p, and compensation for a lost item up to £1,000.

Swiftair costs £2.70 plus the airmail postage rate, and ensures that items arrive at least one day in advance of normal Airmail.

Summary of Royal Mail Special International Services from the UK

As of April 1999.

International Recorded costs £2.50 plus Airmail postage. Advice of delivery (a copy of the signature taken on delivery) is available for an extra 40p, and compensation for a lost item is up to £28. Items must have an International Recorded label, available from a Post Office.

International Registered is for items of monetary value, and costs £3.00 plus Airmail postage for compensation cover up to £500, and £4.00 plus Airmail postage for compensation cover up to £2,200. Advice of delivery (a copy of the signature taken on delivery) is available for an extra 40p. Items must have an International Registered label attached, with 'Insured for xxx pounds' written in ink above the address. Secure sealing is advisable, and for some countries a signed customs declaration is required. The maximum weight is 2 kg.

Swiftair is for packages that require priority handling, so that they are sent on the first available flight to their destination countries. It is not a guaranteed courier service. It costs £2.70 per item plus Airmail postage. Items must have a Swiftair label attached, available from a Post Office. The maximum weight for letters and Small Packages is 2 kg, and for books and pamphlets 5 kg. Swiftair is available from the UK to most destinations worldwide.

Swiftair Plus Recorded combines Swiftair with International Recorded, and costs £3.30 plus Airmail postage. Advice of delivery is available for an extra 40p. The maximum weight is 2 kg for letters and Small Packets, and 5 kg for books and pamphlets.

Swiftair Plus Registered combines Swiftair with International Registered, and costs £3.80 for compensation cover up to £500 and £4.50 for compensation cover up to £2,200. Advice of delivery is available for an extra 40p. The maximum weight is 2 kg.

Summary of International Printed Papers Service from the UK

As of April 1999.

The International Printed Papers service is for sending printed material (such as books, newspapers, pamphlets) other than personalised material (such as personal correspondence). Items intended for this service should be marked 'Printed Papers', and those sent by Airmail should be marked 'Par Avion – By Airmail'. Delivery times are normally the same as for letters.

Customs labels are not usually obligatory. For items just containing books, a Customs declaration is required for the following countries: Algeria; Dominican Republic. For all Printed Papers items a Customs declaration is required for the following countries: Bangladesh; Djibouti; India; Japan; Zimbabwe. For Venezuela, please consult a Post Office. Customs labels are available from a Post Office.

Rates

Surface mail costs 50p up to 20 g. Rates increase by 16–17p per extra 50 g up to 500 g, which costs £1.84, and thereafter by 17p per extra 20 g up to a maximum of 2 kg for printed material other than books and pamphlets, which costs £6.91; and a maximum of 5 kg for books and pamphlets (2 kg for books and pamphlets sent to Canada).

Airmail Europe costs 61p up to 100 g. Rates increase by 6–7p per extra 20 g up to 500 g, which costs £1.86, and thereafter by 7p per extra 20 g up to a maximum of 2 kg for printed material other than books and pamphlets, which costs £7.11; and a maximum of 5 kg for books and pamphlets.

Airmail zone 1 costs £1.06 up to 100 g. Rates increase by 15–16p per extra 20 g up to 500 g, which costs £4.19, and thereafter by 16p per extra 20 g up to a maximum of 2 kg for printed material other than books and pamphlets, which costs £16.19; and a maximum of 5 kg for books and pamphlets (2 kg for books and pamphlets sent to Canada or Cambodia).

Airmail zone 2 costs £1.18 up to 100 g. Rates increase by 18–19p per extra 20 g up to 500 g, which costs £4.95, and thereafter by 19p per extra 20 g up to a maximum of 2 kg for printed material other than books and pamphlets, which costs £19.20; and a maximum of 5 kg for books and pamphlets.

Add-On Services

International Recorded costs £2.50 plus the normal postage rate. Advice of delivery is available for an extra 40p, and compensation for a lost item is up to £28.

Swiftair costs £2.70 plus the airmail postage rate, and is for express delivery of items.

Summary of International Delivery Times from the UK

As of April 1999.

Surface mail delivery times noted by Royal Mail are 2 weeks within Western Europe (all European countries not part of the former USSR or Eastern Europe); 4 weeks to other parts of Europe; and up to 8–12 weeks for places outside Europe.

Airmail delivery times are 3 days within Western Europe; 5–7 days to Eastern Europe; 4–8 days outside Europe.

Airmail distinctions outside Europe are categorized as either Zone 1 or Zone 2. The Post Office supplies full lists of the zones into which individual countries fall.

Telephone Information

Public Telecommunications Operators in the UK

The UK was one of the first countries in the world to break up telecommunications and postal services within its state-owned monopoly and allow competition by issuing licences to new Public Telecommunications Operators (PTOs) of fixed networks and mobile networks.

Two events in 1981 heralded the beginning of deregulation and increased competition in the UK telecommunications industry: the government sold shares in Cable, and postal and telecommunications services, which had both been run by the Post Office, were separated and British Telecommunications plc (BT) was formed.

Privatization of BT took place in stages, beginning in 1984 when the Government sold 51 percent of its shares in BT to the public. In the same year, BT lost its monopoly on telecommunications provision and services in the UK when Mercury Communications was granted an operator's licence. The introduction of Vodafone and Cellnet cellular radio networks in 1985 provided the BT and Mercury duopoly with some competition, encouraging the development of new markets. Cable television operators were also granted licences to provide telecommunications services, but only as agents for BT and Mercury.

The BT/Mercury duopoly on fixed services continued until 1991 when the Government decided to accept applications for licences from new operators. Vodafone and Cellnet were issued with licences to provide fixed services, and cable television networks were allowed to offer services in their own right.

Restrictions on the use of leased lines for the provision of international services were lifted in 1991. Further competition was encouraged with the creation of International Simple Resale (ISR). This system allows operators of international leased lines to interconnect with public networks between designated countries and re-sell their services to both residential and business customers.

In 1996, the Department of Trade and Industry removed the BT/Mercury duopoly on the provision of international telecommunications services and opened the telecommunications industry to full competition.

Data from Oftel

BT General Services in the UK

Service		Details	Contact (service is free unless stated otherwise)
Customer services	residential customers	to enquire about any BT service or product, to change your phone book entry, or to make a complaint; 8 a.m. to 6 p.m., Monday to Saturday	from a BT line: 150; from a mobile phone or non-BT line: 0800 800150
	business customers	Sales Office: to make an enquiry about a BT product or service; Service Centre: to make an after-sales enquiry, to change your phone book entry or to make a complaint; 8 a.m. to 6 p.m., Monday to Saturday	from a BT line: 152; from a mobile phone or non-BT line: 0800 800152
	general enquiries	to enquire about BT media relations, schools liaison, building services, land planning, wayleaves (concerning access to properties for building work, etc), or personnel; 8 a.m. to 6 p.m., Monday to Friday	from any line: 0800 309409; from a mobile phone or non-BT line: 0800 309409
Fault reporting	residential customers	24 hours a day, 7 days a week	from a BT line: 151; from a mobile phone or non-BT line: 0800 800151
	business customers	24 hours a day, 7 days a week	from any line: 0800 800154; from a mobile phone: 0800 800154
Bill enquiries	residential customers	8 a.m. to 6 p.m., Monday to Saturday	from a BT line: 150; from a mobile phone or non-BT line: 0800 800150
	business customers	8 a.m. to 6 p.m., Monday to Saturday	from any line: 0800 800156; from a mobile phone: 0800 800156
Making a complaint		contact customer services (see above) for complaints about any BT services	contact customer services (see above)
Operator services		for help making a call, 24 hours a day, 7 days a week	local and national calls, and calls to the Republic of Ireland: 100; international calls: 155
Directory enquiries		for help finding a number or code, 24 hours a day, 7 days a week	local and national numbers and numbers for the Republic of Ireland: 192[1]; international numbers: 153[1]; for those who cannot hold, handle, or read *The Phone Book*, contact 195 for free directory enquiry service

(continued)

BT General Services in the UK (*continued*)		
Service	**Details**	**Contact (service is free unless stated otherwise)**
Customers with special needs	details of BT services for customers with special needs, including people with impaired hearing, speech difficulties, restricted vision, and limited mobility, can be found in *The Phone Book*	
Malicious calls	customer services will provide simple advice on the most suitable action to take	150
	adviceline: BT provides information on how to deal with unwanted phone calls and what BT can offer to help tackle the problem, 24 hours a day, 7 days a week	0800 666700
	specialist bureau: specially trained investigators will help tackle the problem. In extreme cases, they can work with the police to trace calls	0800 661441

[1] Unless calls are made from a public payphone, users are charged 21p (excluding VAT) per use for directory enquiries services for both residential and business lines.

Data from British Telecommunications plc

Operator-Connected Calls in the UK

Help Making Calls

The Operator can provide help in making calls, 24 hours a day, 7 days a week. For help making local and national calls and calls to the Republic of Ireland, call free on 100. For help with international calls, call free on 155.

The operator can help with the following services: calls to someone else in the UK; calls to someone abroad; calls from abroad; calls to or from a ship; reverse charges (collect): the operator can arrange a phone call from you if the recipient agrees to accept the cost of the call and vice versa, both within the UK and internationally.

Alarm Calls

The Operator can arrange for you to be called at a set time. Users of this service will be charged £2.70.

Telemessages

The Operator can arrange for a message given over the phone to be delivered by post the next day. Telemessages within the UK cost £8.99 for 50 words. For special occasions, such as weddings or birthdays, a telemessage card with up to 50 words can be sent for £9.99. For more information, contact Freefone: 0800 190190.

Emergency Telephone Numbers in the UK

For emergency services in the UK: Fire, Police, Ambulance, Coastguard (sea and cliff rescue), Mountain Rescue, and Cave Rescue, dial: 999. 112 can also be dialled as an alternative.

The operator asks callers which emergency service they require and then connects the caller to the service. Callers should tell the emergency service: where the trouble is; what the trouble is; where the caller is, and the number of the telephone they are using.

Textphone users should contact Typetalk's emergency relay service on: 0800 112999 text.

It is against the law to make false calls to the emergency services. Callers making false calls can be traced immediately to the telephone that they are calling from.

Citizenship and Immigration

Customs Allowances of the UK

If travellers are entering the UK from another European Union (EU) country, they no longer need to go through the red ('something to declare') or green ('nothing to declare') channels at Customs. EU travellers usually go through a separate exit, sometimes called the blue channel, and do not have to pass through Customs at all.

While travellers may not see any Customs officers on arrival in the UK, it is important to remember that Customs do carry out selective checks to look for prohibited and restricted goods.

The EU countries are: Austria, Belgium, Denmark, Finland, France, Germany, Greece, the Republic of Ireland, Italy, Luxembourg, the Netherlands, Portugal, Spain (but not the Canary Islands), Sweden, and the UK (but not the Channel Islands).

Prohibited and Restricted Goods

Certain goods are restricted or banned completely from being brought into the UK from any country. Restricted goods are those which cannot be imported into the UK without an appropriate authority, such as a licence. Within the EU, these restrictions may vary slightly. Travellers are advised to contact the Customs departments of the countries they are leaving to enquire whether particular goods are banned or restricted in the UK. The table below provides examples of banned and restricted goods from outside the EU, together with contact details for enquiries.

Goods Bought in the EU – Duty-Free and Tax-Free Goods

Travellers to EU countries can purchase goods in the quantities shown below from duty-free and tax-free shops. Under EU law, it is illegal for these shops to sell you more, in total, than these quantities. However, these quantities can be purchased on each journey to an EU country and brought back into the UK as long as they are for personal use.

The duty-free and tax-free goods are: 200 cigarettes or 100 cigarillos or 50 cigars or 250 g of tobacco; 2 litres of still table wine; 1 litre of spirits or strong liqueurs over 22 percent volume or 2 litres of fortified wine, sparkling wine, or other liqueurs; 60 cc/ml of perfume; 250 cc/ml of toilet water; £75 worth of all other goods including souvenirs and gifts.

Note: people aged under 17 do not have a tobacco or alcohol allowance; they are not allowed to bring tobacco or alcohol into the country.

Duty-Paid and Tax-Paid Goods

If goods are bought within the EU and have had the duty or tax paid on them, the allowances are different. The law states that these allowances are a guide; it is permitted to bring more than the below allowances into the country, but if more than the following levels are brought into the UK, Customs officers must completely satisfied that the goods are for personal use and not for resale: 800 cigarettes; 400 cigarillos; 200 cigars; 1 kg of smoking tobacco; 10 litres of spirits; 20 litres of fortified wine (such as port or sherry); 90 litres of wine (of which not more than 60 litres can be sparkling wine); 110 litres of beer.

(*continued on p. 832*)

Prohibited and Restricted Goods

(– = not applicable.)

Type of goods	Details	Contact for further information
Prohibited (Banned) Goods		
Unlicensed drugs	such as heroin, morphine, cocaine, cannabis, amphetamines, barbiturates, and LSD	–
Offensive weapons	such as flick knives, swordsticks, knuckledusters, and some martial arts equipment	–
Obscene material	such as pornographic material in the form of books, magazines, films, video tapes, laser discs, and computer software, and indecent or obscene material featuring children	
Counterfeit and copied goods	such as watches, clothes, and CDs. Also any fake goods with false marks of their origin, e.g. fake designer labels on clothes	–
Restricted Goods		
Firearms, explosives, and ammunition	including electric shock devices (such as stunguns) and gas canisters	Excise and Inland Customs Advice Centre (see below)
Dogs, cats, and other animals	including rabbits, gerbils, rats, and mice; a British import (rabies) licence is vital	Ministry of Agriculture, Fisheries and Food: (0181) 330 4411
Live birds	including family pets, unless they are covered by a British health import licence	Ministry of Agriculture, Fisheries and Food: (0181) 330 4411
Endangered species	including birds and plants, whether alive or dead. Also goods, such as fur, ivory, or leather, that have been taken from endangered species	Department of the Environment: (0117) 987 8202
Meat and poultry	including most products made from them, such as bacon, ham, sausages, paté, eggs, milk, and cream; 1 kg of meat per person is allowed as long as it is fully cooled and in airtight containers	Ministry of Agriculture, Fisheries and Food: (0181) 330 4411
Certain plants and their produce	including trees, shrubs, potatoes, certain fruit, bulbs, and seeds	Ministry of Agriculture, Fisheries and Food: (01904) 455195
Radio transmitters	such as CB radios that are not approved for use in the UK	Radio Communications Agency: (0171) 211 0211

Note: these quantities include anything bought duty- or tax-free. Personal use includes gifts (i.e. goods bought for others are included in your personal allowance). The selling on of duty-free or duty-paid goods can be a criminal offence. Anyone caught committing such an offence can face the seizure of their goods and up to seven years in prison. If an individual is being paid for buying alcohol or tobacco for somebody else (including receiving only travel expenses), Customs must be contacted and arrangements made to pay any duty and tax owed.

Goods Bought Outside the EU

Travellers arriving in the UK from a country that is not part of the EU must go through customs; through the red channel if they have something to declare; through the green channel if they are confident that they have no more than the Customs allowances and are not carrying any prohibited, restricted, or commercial goods.

For travellers arriving from outside the EU, the following allowances apply: 200 cigarettes or 100 cigarillos or 50 cigars or 250 g of tobacco; 2 litres of still table wine; 1 litre of spirits or strong liqueurs over 22 percent volume or 2 litres of fortified wine, sparkling wine, or other liqueurs; 60 cc/ml of perfume; 250 cc/ml of toilet water; £145 worth of all other goods including souvenirs and gifts.

Note: people aged under 17 do not have a tobacco or alcohol allowance, they are not allowed to bring tobacco or alcohol into the country.

Money

There are no legal limits to the amount of money that travellers can bring into the UK from either within or outside the EU. However, if a traveller is found be in possession of more than £10,000 sterling in cash or items transferable to cash, such as traveller's cheques or share certificates, they will be challenged to explain why and to provide proof of their explanation.

Further Information

For further information about UK Customs rules and allowances, contact one of the Excise and Inland Customs Advice Centres below:

Belfast Custom House, Queens Square, Belfast BT1 3ET; phone: (01232) 562600; fax: (01232) 562971; open: 9.00 a.m.–5.00 p.m.

Birmingham Two Broadway, Broad Street, Five Ways, Birmingham B15 1BG; phone: (0121) 697 4295; fax: (0121) 697 4130; open: 9.00 a.m.–4.00 p.m.

Cardiff Portcullis House, 21 Cowbridge Road East, Cardiff CF1 9SS; phone: (01222) 386200; fax: (01222) 386222; open: 9.00 a.m.–4.30 p.m.

Cheadle Boundary House, Cheadle Point, Cheadle, Cheshire SK8 2JZ; phone: (0161) 912 7997; fax: (0161) 912 7399; open: 9.00 a.m.–4.30 p.m.

Dundee Caledonian House, Greenmarket, Dundee DD1 1HD; phone: (0345) 442266; fax: (01382) 313247; open: 9.00 a.m.–4.00 p.m.

Glasgow Portcullis House, 21 India Street, Glasgow G2 4PZ; phone: (0345) 442266; fax: (0141) 308 3416; open: 9.00 a.m.–4.30 p.m.

Ipswich Haven House, 17 Lower Brook Street, Ipswich, Suffolk IP4 1DN; phone: (01473) 235951; fax: (01473) 235921; open: 9.00 a.m.–4.30 p.m.

London Central Berkeley House, 304 Regents Park Road, Finchley, London N3 2JY; phone: (0171) 865 4400; fax: (0181) 346 9154; open: 9.00 a.m.–4.30 p.m.

London South Dorset House, Stamford Street, London SE1 9PY; phone: (0171) 202 4227; fax: (0171) 202 4216; open: 9.00 a.m.–5.00 p.m.; non-UK phone: (44) 171 202 4227; non-UK fax: (44) 171 202 4216

Newcastle-upon-Tyne Custom House, 39 Quayside, Newcastle-upon-Tyne NE1 3ES; phone: (0191) 201 1719; fax: (0191) 201 1594; open: 9.00 a.m.– 4.00 p.m.

Nottingham Bowman House, 100–102 Talbot Street, Nottingham NG1 5NG;

phone: (0115) 971 2107; fax: (0115) 971 2219; open: 9.00 a.m.–4.00 p.m.

Plymouth Crownhill Court, Tailyour Road, Crownhill, Plymouth PL6 5BZ; phone: (01752) 777123; fax: (01752) 765807; open: 10.00 a.m.–4.00 p.m.

Reading Eldon Court, 75 London Road, Reading RG1 5BS; phone: (0118) 964 4355; fax: (0118) 964 4206; open: 9.00 a.m.–5.00 p.m.

Redhill Warwick House, 67 Station Road, Redhill, Surrey RH1 1QU; phone: (08450) 199199; fax: (01737) 734600; open: 9.00 a.m.–5.00 p.m.

Southampton Custom House, Orchard Place, Southampton SO14 3NS; phone: (01703) 827068; fax: (01703) 827048; open: 9.00 a.m.–5.00 p.m.

Contact details can also be found in the phone book under Customs and Excise.

For advice on Air Passenger Duty, please contact the Excise and Inland Customs Advice Centre office: 1 Park Road, Uxbridge, Middx UB8 1PW; phone: (0189) 584 2226; fax: (0189) 581 4305 (not open to the public)

Web site: www.open.gov.uk/customs

Source: HM Customs and Excise, © Crown copyright 1999

Passport Regulations and Requirements of the UK

Eligibility for a UK Passport

As of 1 January 1983, under the British Nationality Act 1981, UK passports are issued to: British citizens; British subjects; British Dependent Territories citizens; British Overseas citizens; British Protected Persons; British Nationals (Overseas). British Nationals (Overseas) passports can be acquired only by people with a connection to Hong Kong.

The most usual ways to qualify as one of the above (excluding British Nationals (Overseas)), are: by birth in the UK or a British Colony; by naturalization in the UK or a British Colony; by registration as a citizen of the UK and Colonies; by legitimate descent from a father to whom one of the above applies.

Women who marry UK citizens do not automatically acquire British nationality by marriage (see 'Immigration Rules of the UK'). Anyone who is unsure about their eligibility to hold a UK passport should contact a Passport Office for advice (see below). While the holder of a UK passport can generally travel anywhere in the world, travellers are not exempt from immigration rules in other countries. Nor are they exempt from obtaining any necessary visas.

Passport Applications

UK passports are issued in the UK by the six Regional Passport Offices of the United Kingdom Passport Agency, an Executive Agency of the Home Office. Passport application forms can be obtained from the Regional Passport Offices (see below), main Post Offices, Lloyds Bank, and ARTAC WorldChoice Travel Agents. Until recently, three types of passport were available in the UK: the standard ten-year passport, the British Visitor's Passport, valid for travel to EU countries for one year, and the Collective Passport, valid for a single journey for sponsored parties of young people under the age of 18. The British Visitor's Passport has been abolished, and the standard ten-year passport is now required to travel abroad. The Collective Passport is still available. The following table gives details of the current types of passports available, together with information on validity, postal application fees, and the forms required to make applications. (Fees are current as of 22 March 1999.)

Notes

Family passports have now been discontinued, but existing ones may still be used until they expire. Applications that are made in person to Passport Offices will incur a handling charge of £10 per application in addition to the fees listed above. Personal applications do not guarantee a priority service. Women who are getting married and want to change their names on their passports in time for their honeymoon can do so by requesting special forms PD1 and PD2. Applications must not be made more than three months before the wedding. For further information, contact a Passport Office (see table). It should be noted that some countries will not grant visas on these passports. Travellers are advised to contact the Embassy or High Commission of the country concerned for further information. Married women can also amend their passport details after their marriage to show their new name, if applicable, using Form C. If a passport is lost or stolen, an application for a replacement can be made using Forms A or B. Details of the lost passport will need to be given and photographs, relevant documents, and the usual fee will have to be submitted. Initially, a replacement passport, valid for one year, might be issued, to enable enquiries about the lost passport to be made.

Since October 1998, all children who were not *already* included on a valid 10-year passport now need to hold their own passport if they are to travel abroad. It is no longer possible to add or re-include children on British passports. This includes newborn babies and all children up to the age of 16. Children aged 16 and over already have to hold their own passports and are unaffected by these changes.

Completing Passport Applications

Instructions for completing applications are provided on the forms. Original documents proving status and eligibility for a UK passport must be sent with an application; copies are not acceptable. The type of documents required with an application are detailed on application forms and vary according to the type of application. Documents to be produced may include any of the following: birth certificate; marriage certificate; proof of a name change; adoption certificate; divorce decree; old passport; registration document; naturalization document.

(*continued on p. 834*)

UK Passports

Type of passport	Validity/details	Application fee (£)	Application form required
New Passports			
Standard passport (32 pages)	normally valid for 10 years	21	Form A
Large standard passport (48 pages)	for persons who travel widely, valid for 10 years	31	Form A
Standard passport for minors under 16	valid initially for 5 years	11	Form B
Collective passports	valid on a single journey for organized trips for school children or young people under the age of 18	40	contact Passport Office for application form
Additions/Amendments to Existing Passports			
Standard passport	if replacing and surrendering a ten-year passport	11	Form R
Standard passport	to make changes or add children to a UK passport	11	Form C
Standard passport for minors under 16	to extend a passport (total possible life is ten years)	no fee[1]/11[2]	Form D

[1] For passports issued before 28 March 1998.
[2] For passports issued after 28 March 1998.

Where photographic evidence of identity is required with a passport application, two identical copies of a recent photograph should be included. These should be unmounted, printed on normal thin photographic paper, and should measure 45 mm x 35 mm/1.77 in x 1.38 in. The photograph should show the full face, without a hat, and should be taken against a light background. One copy of the photograph must be signed by someone else to confirm the identity of the applicant. This person must be one of the following: Member of Parliament; Justice of the Peace; Minister of Religion; professionally qualified person (for example, doctor, lawyer, teacher, etc); Local Councillor; Bank Officer; Civil Servant; Police Officer; or someone of similar standing who has known you for at least two years, and who is either a British citizen, British Dependent Territories citizen, British National (Overseas), British Overseas citizen, British Subject, or a citizen of a Commonwealth country. A relative cannot countersign a passport application.

Passport applications should be made at least one month before the passport is needed. The time of year that an application is made can affect the speed with which it is processed. The UK Passport Agency explains in its leaflet *Answers to Questions People Ask Us* (included with all passport application forms) that passports can be issued within two weeks between the months of September and December. Between January and August, applications can take up to four weeks to be processed. If a passport is needed more quickly than in two to four weeks, it is possible to process properly completed applications if they are submitted together with a photocopy of proof of travel, for example, a flight ticket. It is not normally possible to obtain a passport on the day of application. However, in cases of emergency, travellers are advised to contact a Passport Office for advice (see below).

Regional Passport Offices and Areas Covered

(Minicom numbers are for the deaf and hard of hearing.)

Liverpool Passport Office 5th Floor, India Buildings, Water Street, Liverpool L2 0QZ; phone: (0870) 521 0410; minicom: (0151) 236 6292

Areas covered by the Liverpool Passport Office:

Cheshire; Cleveland; Cumbria; Derbyshire; Durham; Greater Manchester; Humberside; Lancashire; Merseyside; Northumberland; North Yorkshire; South Yorkshire; Staffordshire; Tyne and Wear; West Yorkshire

London Passport Office Clive House, 70 Petty France, London SW1H 9HD; phone: (0870) 521 0410; minicom: (0171) 271 8808

The London Office only deals with personal callers. Postal applications from residents of Greater London should be sent to the Glasgow Passport Office.

Newport Passport Office Olympia House, Upper Dock Street, Newport, Gwent NP9 1XA; phone: (0870) 521 0410; minicom: (01633) 473701

Areas covered by the Newport Passport Office:

Avon; Berkshire; Cornwall; Clwyd; Devon; Dorset; Dyfed; East Sussex; Gloucestershire; Gwent; Gwynedd; Hampshire; Hereford; Isle of Wight; Mid Glamorgan; Oxfordshire; Powys; Shropshire; Somerset; South Glamorgan; Surrey (less London Boroughs); West Glamorgan; West Sussex; Wiltshire

Peterborough Passport Office Aragon Court, Northminster Road, Peterborough PE1 1QG; phone: (0870) 521 0410; minicom: (01733) 555688

Areas covered by the Peterborough Passport Office:

Bedfordshire; Buckinghamshire; Cambridgeshire; Essex (less London Boroughs); Hertfordshire (less London Boroughs); Kent (less London Boroughs); Leicestershire; Lincolnshire; Norfolk; Northamptonshire; Nottinghamshire; Suffolk; Warwickshire; West Midlands

Belfast Passport Office Hampton House, 47–53 High Street, Belfast BT1 2QS; phone: (0870) 521 0410; minicom: (01232) 330214

The Belfast Passport Office deals with all applications in Northern Ireland.

Glasgow Passport Office 3 Northgate, 96 Milton Street, Cowcaddens, Glasgow G4 0BT; phone: (0870) 521 0410; minicom: (0141) 332 4621

The Glasgow Passport Office deals with all applications in Scotland and those from Greater London.

Source: The UK Passport Agency, © Crown copyright 1997; with Helicon updates

Visa Requirements for Travel to and from the UK

(See also 'Visiting and Immigration to the UK', p. 835.)

Foreign Visitors Travelling to the UK

All overseas nationals wishing to enter the UK must satisfy immigration officers on arrival in this country that they meet the requirements of UK immigration law. Where necessary, people must have a valid entry clearance (visa or entry certificate) before arriving in the UK. Nationals of the countries or territories listed below must have a valid UK visa each time they enter the country:

Afghanistan; Albania; Algeria; Angola; Armenia; Azerbaijan; Bahrain; Bangladesh; Belarus; Benin; Bhutan; Bosnia-Herzegovina; Bulgaria; Burkina Faso; Burundi; Cambodia; Cameroon; Cape Verde; Central African Republic; Chad; China; Colombia; Comoros; Congo, Democratic Republic of; Congo, Republic of the; Côte d'Ivoire; Cuba; Cyprus, Turkish Republic of Northern; Djibouti; Dominican Republic; Ecuador; Egypt; Equatorial Guinea; Eritrea; Ethiopia; Fiji Islands; Gabon; Gambia; Georgia; Ghana; Guinea; Guinea-Bissau; Guyana; Haiti; India; Indonesia; Iran; Iraq; Jordan; Kazakhstan; Kenya; Kyrgyzstan; Korea, North; Kuwait; Laos; Lebanon; Liberia; Libya; Macedonia, Former Yugoslav Republic of; Madagascar; Maldives; Mali; Mauritania; Mauritius; Moldova; Mongolia; Morocco; Mozambique; Myanmar; Nepal; Niger; Nigeria; Oman; Pakistan; Papua New Guinea; Peru; Philippines; Qatar; Romania; Russia; Rwanda; São Tomé and Príncipe; Saudi Arabia; Senegal; Sierra Leone; Slovak Republic; Somalia; Sri Lanka; Sudan; Suriname; Syria; Taiwan; Tajikistan; Tanzania; Thailand; Togo; Tunisia; Turkey; Turkmenistan; Uganda; Ukraine; United Arab Emirates; Uzbekistan; Vietnam; Yemen; Yugoslavia (documents issued by former SFR of Yugoslavia or by present Yugoslav authorities); Zambia

Nationals of any country not listed above do not need a UK visa for a visit or to study in the UK. However, an entry clearance must be obtained if they wish to do one of the following: settle in the UK; work in the UK (unless a work permit is held); set up business in the UK; live in the UK as a person of independent means; accompany or join someone going to the UK for any of the above purposes.

Applicants for entry clearance to the UK must fill in all necessary official forms. These forms are available from British Missions in foreign countries offering entry clearance services. Applicants should check with their nearest British Mission for information and advice.

For more information about British immigration and visa requirements, see the Internet Service of the Foreign and Commonwealth Office: www.fco.gov.uk/visa/ or contact the Immigration and Nationalisation Directorate (IND) at: Lunar House, 40 Wellesley Road, Croydon, Surrey CR9 2BY; phone: (0181) 686 0688 (general enquiries).

Alternatively, contact the Immigration Advisory Service (IAS). The IAS is an independent charity that gives free and confidential advice, assistance and representation to anyone applying for an entry clearance to the UK. Their address is: County House, 190 Great Dover Street, London SE1 4YB; phone: (0171) 357 6917; duty office 24 hrs: (0181) 814 1559; fax: (0171) 378 0665.

British Nationals Travelling Overseas

British nationals wishing to travel abroad should enquire about any visa requirements at the Embassy, High Commission, or consulate of the country they plan to visit. Tourists can check with their travel agents. Business and tourist visa requirements in foreign countries change constantly, sometimes at short notice.

They also vary according to the length of stay and purpose of the visit.

There are some countries to which UK nationals are advised against travelling (as at March 1999).

The Travel Advice Unit of the Foreign and Commonwealth Office advises against all travel to the following destinations:

Afghanistan, Algeria, Burundi, the Democratic Republic of Congo, the Republic of the Congo, Chechen Republic (Russian Federation), Eritrea, Iraq, Jammu and Kashmir (India), Sierra Leone, Somalia, north and east Sri Lanka, Sudan, Tajikistan, Western Sahara, Yemen, Federal Republic of Yugoslavia (FRY) (Kosovo).

Unless on essential business, the Travel Advice Unit advises against travel to the following destinations:

northeast Albania, Angola, Central African Republic, the Democratic Republic of Congo (Kinshasa), Djibouti, Ethiopia, Guinea-Bissau, Liberia, Montserrat, Rwanda, south eastern Turkey, Federal Republic of Yugoslavia (FRY) (Serbia and Montenegro).

Travellers wanting up-to-date information or advice from the Foreign and Commonwealth Office about travelling abroad can use the Internet Service of the Foreign and Commonwealth Office – www.fco.gov.uk/visa/ – or contact the British Embassy of the country to which they wish to travel.

Source: Foreign and Commonwealth Office; Home Office Immigration and Nationality Directorate, © Crown copyright 1997; with Helicon updates

Visiting and Immigration to the UK

(See also 'Visa Requirements for Travel to and from the UK', p. 834.)

General Information

People wishing to visit the UK must be able to prove that they wish to visit the country for no more than six months, that they plan to leave the UK at the end of their visit, and that they have enough funds to finance their visit without applying for social security benefits. Multiple-entry visas (valid for two years) can be applied for by frequent business visitors.

People wishing to visit the UK on business can do so if they satisfy the criteria above, with an additional proviso that they live and work abroad and do not intend to move their business base to this country, or plan to take employment, produce goods, or provide services in the UK.

There is no strict limit to the number of visits to the UK. However, a visitor is not normally expected to spend more than six months out of any twelve month period in the country.

Students

People who wish to come to the UK to study must show that they have been accepted for a course of study at a publicly funded institution of further or higher education, a bona fide private education institution, or an independent fee-paying school.

They must also show that they will be undertaking an appropriate educational course, such as a recognised full-time degree course, a weekday course with a minimum of 15 hours' organised daytime study per week, or a full-time course of study at an independent fee-paying school.

Students must be able to meet the costs of their course and maintain and accommodate themselves (and any dependants) without working or applying for benefits. Students must be intending to leave the UK on completion of their studies.

Au Pairs

An au pair placement is an arrangement whereby a single person aged between 17 and 27 comes to the UK to study English and live as a member of an English-speaking family. The au pair helps in the home for a maximum of five hours a day with a minimum of two full days off each week. In return, the au pair receives a reasonable allowance and the use of his or her own room. An au pair placement is for a maximum of two years.

The following countries are included in the au pair scheme:

Andorra; Bosnia-Herzegovina; Croatia; Cyprus; Czech Republic; Faroe Islands; Greenland; Hungary; Macedonia, Former Yugoslav Republic of; Malta; Monaco; San Marino; Slovak Republic; Slovenia; Switzerland; Turkey.

Nationals of the European Economic Area (EEA) can enter the UK to work or study without any formalities (see details on the European Economic Area below).

Visas have to be obtained by nationals of the following countries applying to work in the UK as an au pair: Bosnia-Herzegovina; Macedonia, Former Yugoslav Republic of; Turkey.

Anyone who wishes to come to the UK as an au pair must show that they want to enter the country having arranged an au pair placement and that: they are not married; they have no dependants; they do not intend to stay in the UK for more than two years as an au pair; they are able to maintain and accommodate themselves without applying for benefits; they intend to leave the country on completion of their stay as an au pair.

Permission to extend a stay in the UK for more than the normal two-year period will only be granted to someone who entered the UK as an au pair; permission will not be granted to anyone who did not enter the UK as an au pair.

Working Holidaymakers

In the UK, there is a working holidaymaker scheme. This is an arrangement whereby a single person aged between 17 and 27 comes to the UK for an extended holiday (maximum two years) before settling down in their own country. Part-time or casual employment is allowed as part of the conditions of being in the UK as a working holidaymaker.

Working holidaymakers must show that they: are a Commonwealth citizen, British Dependent Territories citizen, or British Overseas citizen; are seeking entry for an extended holiday; are unmarried or married to a person who at the same time qualifies for entry as a working holidaymaker, and that they intend to take a holiday together; do not have any dependent children who are five years of age or over, or who will reach five years of age before they complete their holiday; only intend to take employment that will be incidental (casual or part-time) to their holiday; are able to support and accommodate themselves without applying for benefits; have the means to pay for their onward journey; intend to leave the UK on completion of their holiday.

Spouses and Fiancé(e)s

A person's spouse or fiancé(e) can apply to join or accompany the person in the UK so long as the person is lawfully living in the UK themselves. Alternatively, they must be returning to settle in the UK on the same occasion as their spouse or fiancé(e).

Spouses must show that they: are lawfully married; intend to live together permanently; have met each other; can support themselves and any dependants without applying for benefits; have adequate accommodation where they and their dependants can live without applying for benefits; are not under the age of 16.

On arrival in the UK, a spouse will be given permission to stay and work for 12 months. Near the end of the 12 months, if the couple are still married and intend to live together, the spouse may apply to remain here permanently.

Fiancé(e)s must show that they: plan to marry within a reasonable time (usually six months); both plan to live together permanently after they are married; have met each other; have somewhere to live until they are married, without needing to apply for benefits; are able to support themselves and any dependants without applying for benefits.

A fiancé(e) will be given permission to stay in the UK for six months without permission to work. Once married, the fiance(e) can apply to stay. If granted, permission will be given to stay and work for 12 months after which time an application to stay in the UK permanently can be made.

Children

To qualify to bring children to the UK, the parents must show that they: are present and settled in the UK, meaning that they live here lawfully, with no time limit on their stay; have adequate accommodation in which the family can all live without applying for benefits; are the child's parent (this includes the stepfather/mother of a child whose father/mother is dead, both the father and mother of an illegitimate child, and an adoptive parent in certain defined circumstances).

For children to qualify to join their parents in the UK, children must show that they: are not leading a life independent of their parents, are not married, or have not formed an independent family unit; are less than 18 years old.

Children cannot normally come to live in the UK if one parent lives abroad, unless the parent here has had sole responsibility for the child's upbringing, or there are serious and compelling reasons which make it undesirable not to allow the child to come here.

Provided that the parents of children are settled in the UK, or that the person applying for children to be allowed into the country has sole responsibility for the children, children will normally be allowed to remain permanently in the UK from the date of their arrival.

If children are accompanying a spouse into the country, they will normally be given permission to remain in the country for one year, the same period as the spouse. If the spouse is given permission to remain in the country permanently, the children will normally also be allowed to remain permanently in the country.

Adopted Children

Different rules apply to the admission of adopted children into the UK. For information, contact the Immigration and Nationality Directorate of the Home Office: (0181) 686 0688.

Right of Abode in the UK (British Citizenship)

The right of abode means that a person is entirely free from UK immigration control; they do not need to obtain the permission of an immigration officer to enter the UK; and they may live and work without restriction.

To apply for or to obtain further information about British citizenship contact: Nationality Directorate, 3rd Floor, India Buildings, Water Street, Liverpool L2 0QN; phone: (0151) 237 5200.

Relatives

Immigration rules in the UK allow for the admission of widowed mothers and fathers aged 65 or over and the parents or grandparents travelling together, of whom at least one is aged 65 or over. In certain circumstances sons, daughters, sisters, brothers, uncles, and aunts over the age of 18, and also parents and grandparents under 65 may be granted entrance to the UK.

People who would like relatives to join them in the UK must be lawfully living in the country with no time limit on their stay. They must be able to show that they have sufficient funds to support and accommodate their relatives without applying for benefits, and that their relatives are: wholly or mainly financially dependent on them; without other close relatives to turn to for financial support.

Children over 18, sisters, brothers, aunts, uncles, and other parents and grandparents may come if they meet the requirements set out above, and if they can show that they live alone in 'exceptional circumstances'.

Nationals of the European Economic Area (EEA)

If you are a national of one of the following countries, you are a national of the EEA:

Austria; Belgium; Denmark; Finland; France; Germany; Greece; Iceland; Ireland, Republic of; Italy; Liechtenstein; Luxembourg; Netherlands; Norway; Portugal; Spain; Sweden

Note: Iceland, Liechtenstein, and Norway are not members of the European Union (EU). However, under the European Economic Area Agreement, nationals of these countries have the same rights as EU citizens.

European Community law grants EEA nationals a right to live and work in the UK. This right is called a right of residence.

EEA nationals have a right of residence in the UK if they are working in the UK, or if they are not working in the UK, but have enough funds to support themselves throughout their stay in the country without needing assistance through applying for benefits. Family members of EEA nationals in the UK have the same rights to live and work here.

Further information about rights of residence of EEA nationals and their family members can be obtained by writing to: EC Group, European Directorate, Immigration and Nationality Directorate, Room 1204, Apollo House, 36 Wellesley Road, Croydon CR9 3RR.

Further Information

For further information about immigration rules on the above and other categories of immigrants to the UK, contact the Immigration and Nationality Directorate (IND) at: Immigration and Nationality Directorate, Lunar House, 40 Wellesley Road, Croydon, Surrey CR9 2BY.

The IND's Telephone Enquiry Bureau (TEB) deals with general enquiries: (08706) 067 766.

The TEB is open from 9 a.m. to 4.45 p.m., Monday to Wednesday, 10 a.m. to 4.45 p.m. Thursday, and from 9 a.m. to 4.30 p.m. on Fridays.

In addition, there are a number of public recorded-information lines: overseas visitors call: (0181) 760 1600; overseas students call: (0181) 760 1622; work-permit holders call: (0181) 760 1644; au pairs call: (0181) 760 1666.

There are also regional offices which deal with personal enquiries only:

Belfast Belfast Immigration Office, Olive Tree House, Fountain Street, Belfast BT1 5EA; phone: (01232) 322547; open: Tuesday to Thursday 2.00 p.m.–4.00 p.m.

Birmingham Birmingham Public Enquiry Office, Dominion Court, 41 Station Road, Solihull B91 3RT; phone: (0121) 606 7345; open: Monday to Friday 9.00 a.m.–3.00 p.m.

Glasgow Glasgow Immigration Office, Dumbarton Court Argyll Avenue, Glasgow Airport, Paisley PA3 2TD; phone: (0141) 887 2255; open: Monday to Friday 9.30 a.m.–12.30 p.m. and 2.00 p.m–4.00 p.m.

Liverpool Liverpool Immigration Office, Graeme House, Derby Square, Liverpool L2 7SF; phone: (0151) 236 4909; open: Monday to Friday 9.00 a.m.–12.00 p.m.

Source: Home Office Immigration and Nationality Directorate, © Crown copyright 1997; with Helicon updates

Birth, Marriage, and Death

See Also 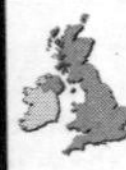 Population and Demography, pp. 124–29.

Birth, Marriage, and Death Registration and Records in the UK

Births

In England, Wales, and Northern Ireland, a child's birth must be registered within six weeks of the event. In Scotland, a birth must be registered within three weeks. If the parents are married, either parent should go to their district Registrar of Births, Deaths, and Marriages and provide details of the child and of both parents. It is not a requirement to provide proof of the birth. If the parents are not married, both parents must visit the Registrar if they wish both their details to appear on the birth certificate. Otherwise, only the mother's details will be entered on the certificate. Alternatively, the father can send a sworn testimonial stating that he is the father of the child.

Marriages

Marriages are registered at the time of the event, and a certificate is given to the couple getting married.

Deaths

A death must be registered with the local Registrar of Births, Marriages, and Deaths within five days of the event. When registering a death, the registrar will require the following information about the deceased: full name (including maiden name if applicable) and home address; full details of date and place of birth, and sex; date of birth of surviving husband or wife, if applicable; occupation of the deceased; date and place of death.

The registrar will also need the following documents: a doctor's certificate of cause of death; the deceased's NHS card; details of any state benefits the deceased was receiving; war pension order book, if applicable.

Whoever goes to register a death with the registrar must also supply their own details. Certificates registering the death and allowing a burial are then issued.

How to Obtain a Copy of a Birth, Death, or Marriage Certificate

Copies of birth, marriage, and death certificates can be obtained from the Register Office in the area where the event took place. This can be done by post or in person. If you don't know where the event occurred, you can obtain copies of certificates by searching the indexes to records held at the Family Records Centre. All the indexes to births, deaths, and marriages from 1837 in England and Wales are held at the Centre and are available for public searches.

The address of the Family Records Centre is: 1 Myddleton Place, London EC1R 1UW.

Obtaining a copy of a certificate from the Family Records Centre can be done in one of four ways:

In person The Family Records Centre is open Monday–Friday, between 8.30 a.m. and 4.30 p.m. (except for public holidays), and you can search the indexes of records held there. If you make your application in person, there are two services available: a 24-hour priority service allows you to collect a certificate one clear working day after the day of application; alternatively, you can collect the certificate on the fourth working day. Otherwise, it will be posted to you within four working days.

By post You can make an order for certificates by post. Again, there are two services available: a priority service, through which your order will be posted to you within two working days, and a standard service, through which the order will be posted within 22 working days. If you can provide the volume reference number for the certificate from the General Register Office index, your order will be posted to you within ten working days.

By telephone Certificates can be ordered by telephone at the following number: (0151) 471 4800. Telephone orders must be paid for by credit or debit card when the order is placed. Again, there are priority and standard services, and dispatch times are the same as orders by post.

By fax Orders can also be made by fax on (01704) 550013. You must quote your credit or debit card details.

For an application form and a list of fees, contact: General Register Office, PO Box 2, Merseyside PR8 2JD; phone: (0151) 471 4800.

Many public libraries and local public record offices keep microfilm copies of the indexes that are available for public use.

Source: Office of National Statistics, © Crown copyright 1998

Births in the UK

Dates are annual averages or for calendar years and figures have been rounded. (N/A = not available.)

Year(s)	Live births			Sex ratio[1]	Rates		Total period fertility rate[4]	Stillbirths[5]	Stillbirth rate[5]
	Male	Female	Total		Crude birth rate[2]	General fertility rate[3]			
1900–02	558,000	537,000	1,095,000	1,037	28.6	115.1	N/A	N/A	N/A
1910–12	528,000	508,000	1,037,000	1,039	24.6	99.4	N/A	N/A	N/A
1920–22	522,000	496,000	1,018,000	1,052	23.1	93.0	N/A	N/A	N/A
1930–32	383,000	367,000	750,000	1,046	16.3	66.5	N/A	N/A	N/A
1940–42	372,000	351,000	723,000	1,062	15.0	N/A	1.89	26,000	N/A
1950–52	413,000	390,000	803,000	1,061	16.0	73.7	2.21	18,000	N/A
1960–62	487,000	459,000	946,000	1,063	17.9	90.3	2.80	18,000	N/A
1970–72	453,000	427,000	880,000	1,064	15.8	82.5	2.36	12,000	13
1980–82	377,000	358,000	735,000	1,053	13.0	62.5	1.83	5,000	7
1981	375,000	356,000	731,000	1,053	13.0	62.1	1.81	5,000	7
1982	369,000	350,000	719,000	1,054	12.8	60.6	1.78	5,000	6
1983	371,000	351,000	721,000	1,058	12.8	60.2	1.77	4,000	6
1984	373,000	356,000	730,000	1,049	12.9	60.3	1.77	4,000	6
1985	385,000	366,000	751,000	1,053	13.3	61.4	1.80	4,000	6
1986	387,000	368,000	755,000	1,053	13.3	61.1	1.78	4,000	5
1987	398,000	378,000	776,000	1,053	13.6	62.3	1.82	4,000	5
1988	403,000	384,000	788,000	1,049	13.8	63.2	1.84	4,000	5
1989	398,000	379,000	777,000	1,051	13.6	62.4	1.81	4,000	5
1990	409,000	390,000	799,000	1,049	13.9	64.2	1.84	4,000	5
1991	406,000	386,000	793,000	1,052	13.7	63.6	1.82	4,000	5
1992	400,000	380,000	781,000	1,052	13.5	63.4	1.80	3,000	4
1993	391,000	371,000	762,000	1,054	13.1	62.4	1.76	4,000	6
1994	385,000	365,000	751,000	1,054	12.9	61.6	1.74	4,000	6
1995	375,000	357,000	732,000	1,052	12.5	60.1	1.71	4,000	6
1996	376,000	357,000	733,000	1,055	12.5	60.1	1.72	4,000	6
1997	372,000	354,000	726,000	1,051	12.3	59.5	1.72	4,000	5

[1] Sex ratio is the number of male births per 1,000 female births.

[2] Rate per 1,000 population (male and female).

[3] Rate per 1,000 women aged 15–44.

[4] Total period fertility rate is the average number of children which would be born per woman if women experienced the age-specific fertility rates of the period in question throughout their child-bearing life span. Figures for the years 1970–72 and earlier are estimates.

[5] Figures given are based on stillbirths of 28 or more completed weeks of gestation. On 1 October 1992, the legal definition of a stillbirth was altered to include babies born dead between 24 and 27 completed weeks' gestation. Between 1 October and 31 December 1992 in the UK, there were 258 babies born dead between 24 and 27 completed weeks' gestation (216 in England and Wales, 35 in Scotland, and 7 in Northern Ireland). If these babies were included in the stillbirth figures given, the UK stillbirth rates would be 5. Stillbirth rate = number of stillbirths ÷ by total births (stillbirths + total live births) × 1,000.

Source: *Annual Abstract of Statistics 1999*, © Crown copyright 1999

Top 50 Boys' and Girls' Names in the UK

(– = no change.)

1998

Rank	Boys	Increase/ decrease on previous year	Girls	Increase/ decrease on previous year	Rank	Boys	Increase/ decrease on previous year	Girls	Increase/ decrease on previous year
1	Jack	–	Chloe	–	26	Kieran	(+1)	Sarah	(–5)
2	Thomas	(+1)	Emily	–	27	Jacob	(+3)	Holly	–
3	James	(–1)	Megan	(+2)	28	Ben	(+1)	Caitlin	(+19)
4	Daniel	–	Jessica	–	29	Cameron	(+6)	Rachel	(–1)
5	Joshua	–	Sophie	(–2)	30	Aaron	(+2)	Elizabeth	–
6	Matthew	–	Charlotte	(+3)	31	Bradley	(–3)	Amber	(+9)
7	Samuel	–	Hannah	(–1)	32	Christopher	(–6)	Paige	–
8	Callum	(+7)	Lauren	–	33	Charlie	(+6)	Georgina	–
9	Joseph	(–1)	Rebecca	(–2)	34	Mohammed	(–1)	Danielle	–
10	Jordan	–	Lucy	(+2)	35	Jamie	(–4)	Nicole	(+3)
11	Connor	(+1)	Amy	–	36	Brandon	(+4)	Grace	(+6)
12	Ryan	(–3)	Georgia	(–2)	37	Robert	(–3)	Natasha	(+4)
13	Luke	(–2)	Katie	(+2)	38	Kyle	–	Ella	(+6)
14	William	(+5)	Bethany	–	39	David	(–3)	Chelsea	(–5)
15	Harry	(+2)	Emma	(–2)	40	Andrew	(–3)	Leah	(–4)
16	Benjamin	(–2)	Olivia	(+2)	41	Charles	(+3)	Anna	(–2)
17	George	(+1)	Courtney	(+3)	42	Reece	(–1)	Victoria	(–7)
18	Lewis	(+3)	Shannon	(–2)	43	Edward	–	Phoebe	new entry
19	Alexander	(–3)	Eleanor	–	44	Owen	new entry	Zoe	(–13)
20	Oliver	(+4)	Jade	(+4)	45	Alex	(–3)	Samantha	(–8)
21	Adam	(–1)	Abigail	(+2)	46	Dylan	new entry	Alexandra	(–3)
22	Jake	–	Ellie	(+4)	47	Ethan	new entry	Jasmine	(+1)
23	Liam	(–10)	Molly	(–1)	48	Jonathan	(–3)	Amelia	new entry
24	Michael	(–1)	Laura	(–7)	49	Sam	(–2)	Louise	(–4)
25	Nathan	–	Alice	–	50	Max	new entry	Lydia	new entry

Source: Office of National Statistics, © Crown copyright 1999

Marriage Laws and Procedure in the UK

(This article includes some information on Guernsey, Jersey, and the Isle of Man. Please note that these territories are not part of the UK, but are British Crown Dependencies.)

Minimum Age and Parental Consent

The minimum legal age for getting married throughout the UK is 16. In England, Wales, Northern Ireland, Guernsey, and the Isle of Man, the written consent of parents or legal guardians is required if you are under 18 years of age. In Jersey, parental consent is required if you under 20 years of age. In Scotland, no parental consent is required.

Marriage in England and Wales

As long as the legal requirements are met, anyone from anywhere in the world can get married in England or Wales, either by civil or religious ceremony. Marriages in England and Wales must take place between 8 a.m. and 6 p.m. Most ceremonies, civil or religious, are governed by the opening times of register offices and the times of church services.

Civil marriage Marriage at a register office or other licensed venue (see below) can take place anywhere in England or Wales and does not have to be the place of residence of one or both of the people wishing to marry. If you wish to marry by civil ceremony you should contact the Superintendent Registrar of the district in which you wish to get married to discuss any arrangements that must be made. Details of your nearest register office can be found in your local telephone directory under 'Registration of Births, Deaths, and Marriages'. To start civil marriage proceedings, you must 'give notice' at your local register office. This can be done in one of three ways and up to 12 months before your marriage:

Marriage by Certificate without Licence. This is the most common form of notice. After 21 days of giving notice, you will be issued with a certificate of marriage to enable you to get married. You must both meet a seven day residency requirement when you give notice. You must get married within 12 months of the date of entry in the notice book.

Marriage by Certificate and Licence. This allows couples to marry more quickly, but it is more expensive. One whole day after giving notice, the Superintendent Registrar will issue a certificate of marriage. One of you must meet a 15-day residency requirement when you give notice. Your marriage must then take place within 12 months of the date of entry in the notice book.

Marriage by Registrar General's Licence. This licence is available for couples where one partner cannot attend a place where marriages can be legally solemnized. This situation would apply to those who are seriously ill at home or in hospital, or those who are in prison. The marriage can take place at any time and at any place, as long as it is within three months of the date of entry in the notice book (one month for the seriously ill). No residency requirement needs to be fulfilled.

Civil marriage: at a licensed venue Since April 1995, it has been possible to arrange for a civil marriage ceremony to take place at a specially licensed venue. As at July 1999, there were over 2,700 approved premises such as hotels, stately homes, and castles licensed for civil ceremonies. No religious content is allowed at all, but in addition to the statutory declaratory and contracting words that you are required to say in a civil ceremony, it is also possible to have your own choice of vows and promises and to include readings, poems, and live music. The legal requirements for getting married at such a venue are the same as those for getting married by civil ceremony at a register office, but with the additional requirement of arranging for the attendance of a Superintendent Registrar at the venue. You do not have to give formal notice of your marriage to the Superintendent Registrar of the registration district in which the venue is situated. However, once you have chosen your venue and made a provisional booking, you should contact the local Superintendent Registrar as his or her attendance is required to solemnize the marriage.

You can obtain a full list of the addresses and telephone numbers of approved premises by sending a cheque or postal order for £5.00, made payable to 'Office for National Statistics', to:

Local Services Office for National Statistics, Smedley Hydro, Trafalgar Road, Southport PR8 2HH; phone: (0151) 471 4458 (major credit cards accepted).

Civil marriage: further information For more information on legal civil marriage issues in England and Wales, you can contact the Marriages Section of the Registrar General for England and Wales by telephoning: (01704) 569824. Alternatively you can write to the Marriages Section at the same address as the Office for National Statistics (above).

Religious marriage You don't have to be regular churchgoer to be married in the Church of England or the Church in Wales. If you wish to be married in either Church, you should visit the minister of the church in which you want to get married to discuss your plans. There are four ways of getting married in accordance with the procedures of the Church of England:

Publication of banns. This simply means announcing aloud your intention to marry. It is the traditional and most popular method, used by most couples, and is equivalent to the civil method of getting married by certificate. Church congregations are invited to register objections, if they have any. Couples are usually required to be in attendance on at least one of the three occasions when banns are read. If couples live in different parishes, the banns are read in both parishes. *Marriage by common licence*. This is equivalent in timing to the civil method of getting married by certificate and licence. Banns are not required to be published. The bishop of the diocese in which you wish to marry approves the application to marry, and one whole day's notice is required before the ceremony can take place. To be married by common licence, one of the couple must have lived in the parish during the fifteen days before the application for the licence. One of the couple must also have been baptized. A common licence lasts for three months from the date of issue.

Marriage by special licence. Approved by the Archbishop of Canterbury, a special licence allows couples to get married in a church of a parish where neither live. If granted, you can get married at any time within three months without meeting any residence requirement. For more information on getting married by special licence, you should contact the Registrar of Court Faculties: The Sanctuary, London SW1P 3JT; phone: (020) 7222 5381.

Marriage by Superintendent Registrar's Certificate without Licence. This is a rarely used method of getting married in church, as ministers will prefer you to marry by either publication of banns or by common licence.

Religious marriage: further information If you would like more information about getting married in a church of the Church of England or Church in Wales, you should either see your minister, or you can contact the Enquiry Centre of the General Synod of the Church of England. The address is: Church House, Great Smith Street, London SW1P 3NZ; phone: (020) 7222 5381

Religious marriage: Roman Catholic marriages The legal requirements that have to be fulfilled for a Roman Catholic wedding are the same that apply to civil marriages. However, if the church is in a different registration district and you cannot prove the church is your normal place of worship, you will be required to give notice in the registration district in which the church is situated after having met the necessary residency requirement.

For more information, you should talk to your priest or contact either of the following organizations: Marriage Care, 1 Blythe Mews, Blythe Road, London W14 0NW; phone: (020) 7371 1341; The Catholic Enquiry Office, The Chase Centre, 114 West Heath Road, London NW3 7TX; phone: (020) 8458 3316; fax: (020) 8905 5780.

Cost of marriage By civil ceremony: from April 1999, for a civil ceremony where you both live in the same registration district, giving notice costs £23. If you live in different districts you each have to pay £23 when giving notice. The registrar's attendance fee for solemnizing your marriage at a register office is £32. If you are getting married by a superintendent registrar's certificate and licence, an additional £46.50 is payable. Each extract of your marriage entry in the register of marriages (your marriage certificate) costs £3.50 (£6.50 if purchased at a later date). Therefore, the minimum you can pay for a civil ceremony (by certificate without licence) at a register office, where you both live in the same registration district, is £58.50 (including a marriage certificate).

If you are getting married at a licensed venue (an approved premise), an additional fee is payable for the registrar to attend and solemnize your marriage. This fee is set by your local authority and you should expect to pay between £100–200 (varies depending upon the day of the week).

By religious ceremony: the fee payable for a religious marriage is not fixed and is decided by the religious celebrant solemnizing your marriage. The fees for getting married in the Church of England or Church in Wales also depend upon the method used, that is whether by banns, common licence, or special licence. However, you should expect to pay between £200–300 but this will vary depending upon whether you have bells, an organist, a choir, and heating, which are all extra. There may also be an additional fee if you wish to have your service videoed.

If your religious celebrant is not authorized to solemnize marriages and you have to get married at a register office beforehand, you will also have to pay the appropriate civil ceremony fees. If a superintendent registrar needs to attend your religious ceremony, a further attendance fee will be payable.

Marriage in Scotland

Civil marriage A civil marriage can only be solemnized in a register office by a Registrar or an Assistant Registrar who has been authorized by the Registrar General. In Scotland, there are no time-of-day restrictions for marriage ceremonies, although ceremonies are restricted to the opening times of register offices. Some remote Scottish communities have their own Parlour Registrars, who are authorized to perform civil marriages in their home. These marriages can take place at any time, at the discretion of the Parlour Registrar.

Religious marriage Religious ceremonies can take place at any time and in any place in Scotland, as long as an authorized celebrant can attend and officiate, and there are two witnesses present. Scottish churches make no provision for marriage by the publication of banns.

Residency requirements Scotland is the only country in the UK where there is no residency requirement to be fulfilled. Instead, at least one of the couple must visit the Registrar from the district in which the marriage is to take place during the seven days before the date of the wedding. In the case of civil marriages, this is to make arrangements with the Registrar; in the case of religious marriages, it is to collect the marriage schedule.

Giving notice Couples must both submit a marriage notice to the Registrar for the district in which they intend to marry during the three months before the wedding date, and not later than 15 days before the date.

The marriage schedule No marriage can take place in Scotland without a marriage schedule (the licence to marry), which must be presented to the person performing the ceremony before it commences.

Marriage at Gretna Green Possibly the world's most famous wedding venue, Gretna Green is a small town in Dumfriesshire. In 1998, it was host to more than 5,500 weddings, about 19 percent of all weddings held in Scotland. The minimum age for getting married in Scotland has been 16, without parental consent, since the eighteenth century. Once the first stage-coach stop over the English/Scottish border, Gretna Green became the place for young English couples wishing to elope and marry without their parents' consent.

Cost of marriage From April 1999, the cost of giving notice to get married by either civil or religious ceremony is £12. For the solemnization of a civil marriage, the fee is £45. For Saturday afternoon ceremonies, there is sometimes a surcharge which can be in the region of £50. The marriage certificate will cost £8.

The cost of marriage by religious ceremony is not fixed and is decided by the religious celebrant solemnizing the marriage. Couples should speak to the minister in charge of their chosen venue to discuss fees.

Further information For further information and advice about getting married in Scotland and to obtain a list of all register offices in Scotland, contact the General Register Office: Marriages Section, New Register House, Edinburgh EH1 3YT; phone: (0131) 314 4447; e-mail: marriage@gro-scotland.gov.uk.

Marriage in Northern Ireland

Civil marriage Civil marriages can take place in Northern Ireland by either a registrar's certificate or by a registrar's licence. The marriage of house-bound or detained persons can only take place on the authority of a licence issued by the Registrar General.

Civil marriage: by certificate A registrar's certificate authorizes you to marry in a register office, church, or other registered building, providing at least one of you resides in the district in which you wish to marry. A certificate allowing the marriage to take place is issued 21 days after notice of intent to marry is given. You must both meet a seven-day residency requirement when you give notice.

Civil marriage: by licence A registrar's licence allows you to get married a little quicker: seven days after giving notice. One of you must meet a 15-day residency requirement when you give notice.

Civil marriage: by Registrar General's licence This licence allows you to marry if one of you is either house-bound or detained as a prisoner. A Registrar General's licence cannot be issued for a marriage between two people of the Roman Catholic, Jewish, or Quaker religions.

Religious marriage Church of Ireland: marriage according to the rites and ceremonies of the Church of Ireland can take place by the publications of banns, licence, special licence, or a registrar's certificate.

Provided that one or both people are members of the Church of Ireland, or other Protestant Episcopal Church, a licence is available from a Church of Ireland licensing minister. Names and addresses of licensing ministers can be obtained from any member of the Church of Ireland clergy.

Special licences may be granted by a bishop of the Church of Ireland, provided that one or both of you are members of that Church or other Protestant Episcopal Church. The marriage may then take place at any time and in any place within the diocese of the bishop granting the licence.

To obtain a registrar's certificate to authorize your marriage, one or both of you must belong to the Church of Ireland.

Marriage by any of these means can be advised on by your minister.

Presbyterian Church Marriages: the governing bodies of the Presbyterian Church in Northern Ireland are the General Assembly of the Presbyterian Church in Ireland, the Remonstrant Synod of Ulster (non-subscribing), the Presbytery of Antrim, and the Reformed Presbyterian Synod of Ireland. Marriages according to the disciplines of these bodies can take place by licence, special licence, or publication of banns. You should discuss with your Presbyterian minister which method would be most suitable, according to your circumstances.

Roman Catholic Church: where both of you are Roman Catholics, the marriage procedure is governed by the laws of the Roman Catholic Church. Information and guidance on your marriage should be obtained from a member of the Roman Catholic clergy.

According to the Irish Marriage Acts, marriage in a Roman Catholic church can also take place by licence or registrar's certificate. These methods apply where one of you is not a Roman Catholic.

Religious marriage: other Church marriages Marriages according to the customs of other religious bodies can take place in Northern Ireland by registrar's licence (except for Jews and Quakers), by registrar's certificate, or by special licence. Information about these marriages can be obtained from the registrar in the district in which you wish to marry.

Cost of marriage If your marriage is on the authority of a licence issued by a licensing minister of the Church of Ireland or Presbyterian Church, there is no charge for giving notice. However, the licence will cost between £13 and £15 depending upon region.

From November 1998, to give notice to marry by licence or certificate issued by a Registrar of Marriages costs £8.50. A registrar's certificate costs £5.50; a registrar's licence costs £10.50. The solemnization of your marriage in the presence of a registrar will cost £12.50.

For ceremonies taking place in a church, the celebrant will charge a fee for the church service. These fees are set by the relevant church authorities. Couples should consult their church minister for information.

Further information For information about getting married in Northern Ireland, contact the registrar of marriages in the registration district in which you wish to get married. Alternatively, contact the General Register Office:

Oxford House, 49–55 Chichester Road, Belfast BT1 4HL; phone: (028) 9025 2000.

Other Religions and Interfaith Marriages

For information and advice about Jewish weddings, contact the Jewish Marriage Council: 23 Ravenhurst Avenue, London NW4 4EE; phone: (020) 8203 6311; e-mail: jmc@dircon.co.uk

For information about Quaker marriages, contact the Religious Society of Friends: 173–177 Euston Road, London NW1 2BJ; phone: (020) 7663 1000.

For advice when partners are practising members of different Churches, contact: Association of Interchurch Families, 35–41 Lower Marsh, London SE1 7RL; phone: (020) 7620 4444; fax: (020) 7928 0010.

Documents Required for Marriage

To be married in the UK you must produce your birth certificate. If you have been married before, you must produce your decree absolute of divorce (dissolution or annulment papers in Northern Ireland) or, if you are widowed, the death certificate of your former spouse.

If you are travelling to the UK to get married, you will have to produce your passport and travel documents to prove your identity and that you have met the necessary residency requirements.

For marriages in Scotland and Northern Ireland you must obtain from your own country's marriage authority a certificate stating that there is no impediment to marry, i.e. that you are both free to marry.

For further information, contact the registrar of the registration district in which you wish to get married.

Same-Sex Marriages in the UK

It is not possible for gay and lesbian couples to have a legally solemnized marriage. UK marriage laws prohibit people of the same sex at birth from marrying.

Marriage Prohibitions (forbidden degrees of relationship)

A man may not marry his: mother (including step-mother, former step-mother, mother-in-law, former mother-in-law, adoptive mother or former adoptive mother); daughter (including step-daughter, former step-daughter, daughter-in-law, former daughter-in-law, adoptive daughter or former adoptive daughter); sister (including half-sister or step-sister); father's mother (grandmother); mother's mother (grandmother); father's father's former wife (step-grandmother); mother's father's former wife (step-grandmother); son's daughter (granddaughter); daughter's daughter (granddaughter); wife's son's daughter (step-granddaughter); wife's daughter's daughter (step-granddaughter); son's son's wife (grandson's wife); daughter's son's wife (grandson's wife); father's sister (aunt); mother's sister (aunt); brother's daughter (niece); sister's daughter (niece).

A woman may not marry her: father (including step-father, former step-father, father-in-law, former father-in-law, adoptive father or former adoptive father); son (including step-son, former step-son, son-in-law, former son-in-law, adoptive son or former adoptive son); brother (including half-brother or step-brother); father's father (grandfather); mother's father (grandfather); mother's mother's former husband (step-grandfather); father's mother's former husband (step-grandfather); son's son (grandson); daughter's son (grandson); husband's daughter's son (step grandson); husband's son's son (step grandson); son's daughter's husband (granddaughter's husband); daughter's daughter's husband (granddaughter's husband); father's brother (uncle); mother's brother (uncle); brother's son (nephew); sister's son (nephew).

In Scotland, a man may not marry his great-grandmother or great-granddaughter and a woman may not marry her great-grandfather or great-granddaughter.

Exceptions for step-relatives and relatives-in-law: In England, Scotland, and Wales (not Northern Ireland, Isle of Man, Guernsey, or Jersey), the Marriage Act of 1986 allows for the following relatives to marry:

Step-relatives can marry provided they are at least 21 years of age. The younger of

the couple must not ever have lived in the same house as the older of the couple before the age of 18, nor must they ever have been treated as the child of the older person's family.

Although a man may marry his sister-in-law and a woman may marry her brother-in-law, other relatives-in-law may marry provided they are at least 21 years of age and the family members involved in creating the in-law relationship are both dead. For example, if a man wishes to marry his daughter-in-law, both his son and his son's mother must be dead. In England and Wales, marriages under this Act are not permitted with the calling of banns but can take place in a church on the authority of a licence issued by a superintendent registrar.

Marriage of cousins: It is not illegal to marry a cousin. However, cousins who wish to marry should visit their GP to ensure there are no factors in their family health records that might make a decision to have children inadvisable on medical grounds.

Source: The Wedding Guide UK (www.wedding-guide.co.uk)

Marriages in the UK

Category	1985	1990	1991	1992	1993	1994	1995	1996[1]
Men								
under 21	30,243	15,930	13,271	11,031	8,767	7,091	6,302	5,497
21–24	123,242	92,270	79,877	74,458	65,129	56,877	48,432	42,488
25–29	109,896	122,800	115,637	118,255	114,101	111,108	105,218	101,647
30–34	47,594	56,966	56,970	62,470	63,848	65,490	68,245	69,867
35–44	46,265	49,984	48,147	51,125	50,553	51,310	53,350	56,513
45–54	19,652	21,996	20,915	23,290	23,841	24,136	24,786	26,252
55 and over	16,225	15,464	14,922	15,384	15,369	15,220	14,918	15,250
Women								
under 21	82,209	45,626	38,305	32,618	26,839	22,903	20,643	18,485
21–24	137,437	119,037	105,505	102,494	93,125	84,171	75,071	66,191
25–29	80,105	103,209	99,851	105,223	104,517	102,803	100,644	99,651
30–34	33,424	42,794	43,617	48,514	49,546	52,359	54,819	57,752
35–44	35,380	38,983	37,582	40,075	40,090	41,213	43,115	45,969
45–54	14,892	16,825	16,473	18,504	18,800	19,280	19,720	21,025
55 and over	9,670	8,936	8,406	8,585	8,691	8,503	8,239	8,441
Total	393,117	375,410	349,739	356,013	341,608	331,232	322,251	317,514
Persons marrying per 1,000 resident population	13.9	13.1	12.1	12.3	11.7	11.3	11.0	10.8
Previous Marital Status								
Bachelors	291,171	276,512	256,538	258,567	245,996	236,619	227,717	221,826
Divorced men	88,981	88,199	83,069	87,419	85,824	85,261	85,743	87,113
Widowers	12,965	10,699	10,132	10,027	9,788	9,352	8,791	8,575
Spinsters	296,797	279,442	259,084	260,252	248,063	237,241	228,462	221,697
Divorced women	83,921	85,608	81,224	86,361	84,268	85,220	85,396	87,618
Widows	12,399	10,360	9,431	9,400	9,277	8,771	8,393	8,199
First marriage for both partners	256,594	240,729	222,369	222,142	210,567	200,910	192,078	185,293
First marriage for one partner only	74,780	74,496	70,884	74,535	72,925	72,040	72,023	72,937
Remarriage for both partners	61,743	60,185	56,486	59,336	58,116	58,282	58,150	59,284

[1] Provisional. Later figures not available.

Source: *Annual Abstract of Statistics 1999,* © Crown copyright 1999

Divorce Laws and Procedure in the UK

According to UK divorce law, there is essentially one basis for divorce: that a marriage has 'irretrievably broken down'. To satisfy a court that a marriage has reached this condition, one or more of the following five grounds must be proved: A spouse has committed adultery. It is no longer necessary to name a third party in this case. If no third party is named, a defendant can admit to adultery on a form called an 'Acknowledgement of Service'. If a defendant will not admit to adultery, other forms of proof may be necessary to satisfy a court that adultery has been committed.

The couple have been living apart for two years or more, and both agree to a divorce.

The couple have lived apart for five years, and one partner wants a divorce.

One partner deserted the marriage more than two years before. (Note: desertion is not the same as agreed separation.)

One partner has behaved in such a way that the other partner can no longer be expected to tolerate living with them. 'Unreasonable behaviour' covers a very broad range of acts: physical and/or verbal abuse, drunkenness, public humiliation, mental cruelty, financial irresponsibility, excessive jealousy, and even excessive DIY, and failure to help with household work.

It is not possible to get divorced unless you have been married for at least one year. The legal procedure for obtaining a divorce in England begins with issuing a divorce petition to any divorce county court, or, in London, the Principle Registry. In Scotland, divorces are generally conducted in the Sheriff Court. Less commonly, they can also be issued in the Court of Session in Edinburgh, Scotland's supreme court. In Northern Ireland, the majority of divorces are issued in the High Court, although it is possible to seek divorce through the county courts.

After a divorce petition is successful, a Decree Nisi is granted, and a further six or more weeks after this, a Decree Absolute, which finalizes the dissolution of the marriage.

It is not a legal requirement to employ the services of a solicitor when you wish to get divorced. A free booklet on obtaining an undefended divorce, 'DIY Divorce', can be obtained from any county court. Professional advice is recommended, however. The advice of a professional can help determine whether there are grounds for a divorce. Legal advice can also be essential in guiding couples through the legal processes involved in divorce, as well as settling matters such as financial support for children. It is not recommended that you pursue a divorce without professional advice if children are involved, and/or extra financial settlement is being sought.

Common-Law Marriage

Contrary to popular and widespread belief, there is no such thing as common-law marriage. It is often believed that if man and a woman live together, after a certain length of time they acquire similar rights to an actual wife or husband. Where cohabiting couples (both heterosexual or same-sex partnerships) end their relationship, the law in the UK is not the same as for married couples. Property rights are unaffected between unmarried couples, i.e. the distinction between 'his', 'hers', and 'theirs' remains the same as beforehand when a relationship breaks down; each is entitled to keep their own property. The position for married couples is that the courts can divide all property whichever way they think best, regardless of who actually owns it.

If a couple live together, and they have children, the situation can become more complex if the relationship fails. An unmarried mother has legal responsibility for her children; an unmarried father has to ask the courts to give him joint responsibility. However, whether the father has joint responsibility or not, he is still responsible for maintaining his children, and this responsibility can be enforced.

Arrangements for Children

The Children Act resulted in a change in the arrangements for children of divorced parents. Parents are now encouraged to agree access and living arrangements without the need for the courts to step in. If this attempt fails, the courts will intervene to make a decision on behalf of the children; the Children Act requires that courts put the good of the children first. Children now have the right to have their wishes heard when decisions are made about them.

In 1993 a system for child maintenance was introduced in England, Wales, Scotland, and Northern Ireland. A government agency called the Child Support Agency (CSA) operates the scheme. Under the Child Support Act, 1991, child support maintenance is an amount of money that absent parents pay regularly as a contribution to the financial support of their children. Absent parents must now, by law, support their children, whether the couple are married, divorced, separated, formerly lived together, or had a child during a very brief relationship. The courts no longer decide on the financial contributions that absent parents must make towards their children; the CSA has been given these decision-making powers. The amount that absent parents pay is calculated by the CSA; the agency also assesses and reviews the amounts of child support maintenance needed. The CSA is empowered to collect money from an absent parent and pass it on to the guardian parent.

The Child Support Agency can be contacted at the following address: PO Box 55, Brierley Hill, West Midlands DY5 1YL; National Enquiry Line: (0345) 133133.

Counselling

The National Marriage Guidance Council (Relate), Herbert Gray College, Little Church Street, Rugby, Warwickshire CV21 3AP; phone: (01788) 573241; fax: (01788) 535007.

Relate provides help with marital and relationship problems. There are over 130 branches nationwide. For your nearest branch, look in your local telephone directory.

Marriage Care, Clitherow House, 1 Blythe Mews, Blythe Road, London W14 0NW; phone: (0171) 371 1341; fax: (0171) 371 4921. Relationship counselling service for the Roman Catholic community.

Divorces in England and Wales, and Scotland

(N/A = not available.)

Item	1985	1990	1991	1992	1993	1994	1995	1996	1997
England and Wales									
Decrees absolute, granted[1] (rate per 1,000 married couples[1])	13.4	13.0	13.5	13.7	13.9	13.4	13.1	13.8	N/A
Total[1]	160,300	153,386	158,745	160,385	165,018	158,175	155,499	157,107	N/A
Duration of marriage (years)									
0–4	45,776	36,299	37,779	36,898	37,252	35,695	34,507	34,924	N/A
5–9	41,537	42,061	42,735	43,745	46,536	44,769	44,304	44,609	N/A
10–14	27,087	27,310	28,791	29,285	30,156	28,073	27,365	27,332	N/A
15–19	18,460	19,819	20,127	20,160	20,233	19,200	18,943	19,321	N/A
20 and over	26,427	27,881	29,294	30,290	30,836	30,431	30,370	30,912	N/A
Not stated	13	16	19	7	5	7	10	9	N/A
Age of wife at marriage (years)									
16–19	52,858	41,116	40,594	39,731	38,810	34,068	31,319	29,927	N/A
20–24	69,663	71,489	74,050	74,698	76,580	73,287	71,355	71,123	N/A
25–29	18,689	21,701	24,025	25,172	27,177	28,358	29,439	31,396	N/A
30–34	8,544	8,909	9,608	9,939	10,593	11,007	11,585	12,335	N/A
35–39	4,612	4,880	5,024	5,200	5,673	5,615	5,800	6,051	N/A
40–44	2,609	2,598	2,727	2,872	3,091	3,064	3,121	3,254	N/A
45 and over	3,325	2,693	2,717	2,766	2,819	2,769	2,870	3,021	N/A
Age of wife at divorce (years)									
16–24	26,170	15,454	14,960	13,482	12,924	10,956	9,783	8,615	N/A
25–29	35,680	35,121	35,582	34,853	35,362	32,608	30,563	30,075	N/A
30–34	28,668	31,295	33,195	34,901	36,300	35,848	35,538	36,274	N/A
35–39	26,554	24,421	25,661	26,577	28,162	27,195	27,550	28,727	N/A
40–44	17,767	21,263	21,979	21,783	21,891	20,765	20,739	20,774	N/A
45 and over	25,448	25,816	27,349	28,782	30,374	30,796	31,316	32,633	N/A
Not stated	13	16	19	7	5	7	10	9	N/A
Divorces involving no children[2]	51,912	47,119	48,115	46,979	47,652	48,286	48,560	48,800	N/A
Divorces involving 1 or more children[2]	108,388	106,267	110,630	113,406	117,366	109,889	106,939	108,307	N/A
Scotland									
Decrees absolute, granted[3 4] (rate per 1,000 married couples[5])	11.1	10.5	10.6	10.8	11.1	11.5	10.8	10.9	11.0
Total[1]	13,371	12,272	12,399	12,479	12,787	13,133	12,249	12,308[6]	12,222

(continued)

Divorces in England and Wales, and Scotland (*continued*)

Item	1985	1990	1991	1992	1993	1994	1995	1996	1997
Duration of marriage (years)									
0–4	2,364	2,208	2,142	2,085	2,092	2,095	1,908	1,914	1,793
5–9	3,882	3,546	3,508	3,610	3,722	3,790	3,399	3,432	3,224
10–14	2,684	2,361	2,484	2,454	2,539	2,592	2,407	2,310	2,385
15–19	1,868	1,617	1,718	1,675	1,745	1,786	1,698	1,709	1,804
20 and over	2,573	2,540	2,547	2,655	2,689	2,870	2,837	2,934	3,016
Age of wife at marriage (years)									
16–20	7,143	5,600	5,592	5,378	5,406	5,306	4,600	4,420	4,142
21–24	3,914	4,185	4,147	4,198	4,252	4,532	4,336	4,341	4,321
25–29	1,246	1,377	1,545	1,685	1,812	1,926	1,887	1,933	2,151
30–34	461	497	514	575	612	628	654	697	791
35–39	247	275	249	301	312	329	338	393	360
40–44	143	139	148	138	152	163	196	234	199
45 and over	170	159	142	153	164	166	166	198	173
Not stated	49	40	62	51	77	83	72	92	85
Age of wife at divorce (years)									
16–24	1,881	1,199	1,038	963	844	767	622	583	426
25–29	3,152	2,938	2,932	2,807	2,775	2,750	2,353	2,269	2,021
30–34	2,628	2,611	2,741	2,785	3,037	3,045	2,747	2,708	2,736
35–39	2,183	1,891	2,037	2,092	2,212	2,390	2,290	2,307	2,469
40–44	1,440	1,614	1,665	1,685	1,771	1,788	1,734	1,761	1,819
45 and over	2,040	1,979	1,924	2,096	2,071	2,310	2,431	2,587	2,667
Age not stated	49	40	62	51	77	83	72	93	84
Actions involving no children[7]	6,040	6,555	6,521	6,927	6,951	7,390	7,515	N/A	N/A
Actions involving 1 or more children[7]	7,331	5,717	5,878	5,552	5,836	5,743	4,734	N/A	N/A

[1] Data include decrees of divorce and of nullity.
[2] Children of the family as defined by the Matrimonial Causes Act, 1973.
[3] For divorces under pre-1976 legislation, these figures relate only to persons who were married in Scotland, and obtained their decree of divorce from the Court of Session. Also with effect from 1 May 1984, the jurisdiction of the Sheriff Courts was extended to include divorce.
[4] With effect from 1984, these statistics have been collected on the basis of divorces granted only, and any difference in the number of divorces brought and granted relates to nullity of marriages.
[5] Rates are calculated using the average of the estimated married male and female populations.
[6] Includes 9 cases where the duration of marriage was not recorded.
[7] These actions relate to all persons divorced or separated in Scotland, irrespective of the country of marriage.

Source: *Annual Abstract of Statistics 1999*, © Crown copyright 1999

See Also 

Death Rates per 1,000 Population in the UK p. 125.

Taxation

Estimated Average Incomes of Households Before and After Tax in the UK

Original income is the total income in cash and kind of household before the deduction of taxes or the addition of state benefits. The addition of cash benefits (retirement pensions, child benefit, etc) and the deduction of income tax, council tax, water charges, domestic rates, and employees' National Insurance contributions give disposable income. By further allowing for taxes paid on goods and services purchased, such as value added tax (VAT), an estimate of 'post-tax' income is derived.

1996–97 Households	Non-retired households						All households				
	Retired households[1]	One adult	Two or more adults	One adult	Two adults	Three or more adults	One adult with children[2]	Two adults with one child[2]	Two adults with two children[2]	Two adults with three or more children[2]	Three or more adults with children[2]
Number of households in population (thousands)	3,422	2,869	3,481	5,165	2,091	1,281	1,822	2,221	1,018	883	24,253
Average per Household (£ per Year)											
Original income	3,029	8,369	13,030	26,248	33,383	5,479	25,268	27,627	22,552	29,504	18,494
Disposable income	6,767	12,817	11,596	21,778	28,876	9,828	21,316	23,238	21,712	26,749	17,397
Post-tax income	5,649	10,022	9,408	17,682	22,470	7,521	17,114	18,733	17,187	20,375	13,897

[1] A retired household is defined as one where the combined income of retired members amounts to at least half the total gross income of the household, where a retired person is defined as anyone who describes themselves as 'retired' or anyone over the minimum National Insurance pension age describing themselves as 'unoccupied' or 'sick or injured but not intending to seek work'.
[2] Children are defined as persons aged under 16 or aged between 16 and 18, unmarried and receiving non-advanced further education.

Source: *Annual Abstract of Statistics 1999*, © Crown copyright 1999

Average Council Tax by Region of England, Scotland, and Wales

Council Tax assessment is performed in the following way: having taken into account its budgeted expenditure and precepts levelled by County Councils, the billing authority (that is, the District Council) then deducts whatever income it derives from the Business Rate, Rate Support Grant, and any other items of income; the amount then remaining is that raised by the Council Tax. This is divided among the number of houses in the District. The amount actually payable per house is adjusted by the proportions listed in the Bands A–H. Amounts shown below for Council Tax are headline Council Tax for the area of each billing authority for Band D, 2 adults, before transitional relief and benefit. The ratios of other bands are: A 6/9, B 7/9, C 8/9, E 11/9, F 13/9, G 15/9, and H 18/9. The revenue raised in these proportions has to equal the total sum required to meet that needed from the Council Tax. Averages are calculated by dividing the sum of the tax requirement for each area by the tax base for the area. The tax base is calculated by weighting each dwelling on the valuation list to take account of exemptions, discounts, and disabled relief, and the valuation bands it falls into. It therefore represents the number of Band D equivalent (fully chargeable) dwellings. The table reflects the implementation of the local government reorganization up to 1 April 1997.
(UA = Unitary Authority.)

Band	England	Scotland	Wales
A	up to £40,000	up to £27,000	up to £30,000
B	£40,001–£52,000	£27,001–£35,000	£30,001–£39,000
C	£52,001–£68,000	£35,001–£45,000	£39,001–£51,000
D	£68,001–£88,000	£45,001–£58,000	£51,001–£66,000
E	£88,001–£120,000	£58,001–£80,000	£66,001–£90,000
F	£120,001–£160,000	£80,001–£106,000	£90,001–£120,000
G	£160,001–£320,000	£106,001–£212,000	£120,001–£240,000
H	£320,001 or over	£212,001 or over	£240,001 or over

Region	Council tax (£) April 1997
England	
Northeast	
Former County of Cleveland	
Hartlepool UA	886
Middlesbrough UA	712
Redcar and Cleveland UA	942
Stockton-on-Tees UA	801
Darlington UA	598
Durham	779
Northumberland	736
Tyne and Wear	791
Area average	782
Northwest and Merseyside	
Northwest	
Cheshire	710
Cumbria	759
Greater Manchester	794
Lancashire	763
Northwest average	766
Merseyside	930
Area average	798
Yorkshire and the Humber	
Former County of Humberside	
East Riding of Yorkshire UA	782
Kingston-upon-Hull UA	683
North East Lincolnshire UA	788
North Lincolnshire UA	932
Former County of North Yorkshire	
York UA	605
North Yorkshire County	626
South Yorkshire	716
West Yorkshire	713
Area average	710
East Midlands	
Derby UA	672
Derbyshire County	734
Leicester UA	610
Rutland UA	793
Leicestershire County	704
Lincolnshire	658
Northamptonshire	659
Nottinghamshire	769
Area average	705
West Midlands	
Hereford and Worcester	615
Shropshire	666
Stoke-on-Trent UA	645
Staffordshire County	632
Warwickshire	713
West Midlands (Met County)	762
Area average	701
Eastern	
Bedfordshire County	764
Cambridgeshire	590
Essex	645
Hertfordshire	628
Luton UA	602
Norfolk	620
Suffolk	651
Area average	639
London	651
Southeast	
Berkshire	641
Brighton and Hove UA	599
Buckinghamshire County	639
East Sussex County	691
Former County of Hampshire	
Hampshire County	659
Portsmouth UA	603
Southampton UA	603
Isle of Wight UA	675
Kent	631
Milton Keynes UA	634
Oxfordshire	635
Surrey	627
West Sussex	652
Area average	640
Southwest	
Former County of Avon	
Bath and South East Somerset UA	708
Bristol UA	915
North Somerset	625
South Gloucestershire UA	690
Cornwall and the Isles of Scilly	647
Devon	629
Former County of Dorset	
Bournemouth UA	612
Dorset County	705
Poole	610
Gloucestershire	642
Somerset	658
Swindon UA	606
Wiltshire County	650
Area average	667
England average	688
Scotland	
Aberdeen City	712
Aberdeenshire	643
Angus	679
Argyll and Bute	801
Clackmannanshire	753
Dumfries and Galloway	714
Dundee City	920
East Ayrshire	779
East Dunbartonshire	771
East Lothian	724
East Renfrewshire	682
Edinburgh, City of	837
Eilean Siar (Western Isles)	599
Falkirk	680
Fife	747
Glasgow City	982
Highland	719
Inverclyde	831
Midlothian	858
Moray	652
North Ayrshire	718
North Lanarkshire	787
Orkney Islands	515
Perthshire and Kinross	732
Renfrewshire	783
Scottish Borders, The	612
Shetland Islands	486
South Ayrshire	765
South Lanarkshire	793
Stirling	776
West Dunbartonshire	978
West Lothian	792
Scotland average	783
Wales	
Blaenau Gwent	492
Bridgend	539
Caerphilly	519
Cardiff	486
Carmarthenshire	557
Ceredigion	562
Conwy	403
Denbighshire	529
Flintshire	511
Gwynedd	515
Isle of Anglesey	424
Merthyr Tydfil	569
Monmouthshire	403
Neath Port Talbot	621
Newport	413
Pembrokeshire	451
Powys	426
Rhondda, Cynon, Taff	560
Swansea	478
Torfaen	483
The Vale of Glamorgan	443
Wrexham	528
Wales average	496

Source: *Regional Trends 33*, © Crown copyright 1998

Income Tax in the UK

Taxes on individual incomes are generally progressive in that larger incomes are subject to a greater amount of tax. Income tax is imposed for the year of assessment beginning on 6 April. In the budget of March 1999, the government announced a new starting rate of tax of 10 percent for the first £1,500 of taxable income. The basic rate of tax was reduced from 23 percent to 22 percent with effect from 6 April 2000. The higher rate of tax remains at 40 percent.

Allowances and reliefs reduce an individual's income tax liability. All taxpayers are entitled to a personal allowance against income from all sources. In addition, there is a married couple's allowance, which may be allocated to either partner, or they may receive half each. Tax relief for the married couple's allowance has been reduced from a flat rate of 15 percent to 10 percent from 6 April 1999. It is due to be phased out completely from 6 April 2000. The Working Families Tax Credit has been increased by £2.50 and the tax credit for children under 11 years has been increased by £4.70 from October 1999. From 6 April 2000 there is a further increase of £1.10 above indexation in the credit for children under 11 years. A tax credit of up to 8 percent per week (£4,160 per year at 10 percent) will be introduced from 6 April 2001 for families with children; the credit will be tapered away from families where one or both parents are higher rate taxpayers.

Among the most important reliefs is that for mortgage interest payments on borrowing for house purchase up to a limit of £30,000. Relief, which is (from April 1999) 10 percent, is usually given 'at source', that is, repayments that the borrower makes to the lender are reduced to take account of tax relief and the tax refund is passed directly by the tax authorities to the lender rather than to the individual borrower. Relief on mortgage interest repayments has been removed with effect from 6 April 2000. Mortgage interest relief for those aged 65 and over who take out a loan to buy a life annuity (a home income plan) ended with effect from 9 March 1999, but existing loans continue to qualify for relief for the remainder of the loan period. Employees' contributions to their pension schemes also qualify for tax relief.

In general, income tax is charged on all income that originates in the UK – although some forms of income are exempt, such as child benefit – and on all income arising abroad of people resident in the UK. The UK has entered into agreements with many countries to provide relief from double taxation; where such agreements are not in force, unilateral relief is often allowed. British residents working abroad for the whole year may benefit from 100 percent tax relief. The 1998 budget included a measure whereby the 'foreign earnings deduction' was eliminated for all but seafarers with effect from 6 April 1998.

Most wage and salary earners pay their income tax under the Pay-As-You-Earn (PAYE) system whereby tax is deducted and accounted for to the Inland Revenue by the employer, in a way that enables most employees to pay the correct amount of tax during the year.

A new self-assessment system for collecting personal taxation has been introduced. The first 'new style' tax returns were sent out in April 1997 to around 8 million people who regularly complete a tax return – primarily higher-rate taxpayers, the self-employed, and those receiving investment income (particularly where this is paid without tax being deducted). Taxpayers are now able to calculate their own tax liability, although they can choose to have the calculations done by the Inland Revenue. There is a new legal requirement to keep records of income and capital gains from all sources.

Source: *Britain 1999: The Official Yearbook of the United Kingdom*, © Crown copyright 1998; with Helicon updates

Rates of Income Tax in the UK

(– = not applicable.)

Tax year	Taxable income	Lower rate	Basic rate	Higher rate	Additional rate applicable to trusts[2]	Rate applicable to trusts[2]
1991–92	bands of taxable income[1] (£)	–	1–23,700	over 23,700	–	–
	rate of tax (%)	–	25	40	10	–
1992–93	bands of taxable income[1] (£)	1–2,000	2,001–23,700	over 23,700	–	–
	rate of tax (%)	20	25	40	10	–
1993–94	bands of taxable income[1] (£)	1–2,500	2,501–23,700	over 23,700	–	–
	rate of tax (%)	20	25[3]	40	–	35
1994–95	bands of taxable income[1] (£)	1–3,000	3,001–23,700	over 23,700	–	–
	rate of tax (%)	20	25[3]	40	–	35
1995–96	bands of taxable income[1] (£)	1–3,200	3,201–24,300	over 24,300	–	–
	rate of tax (%)	20	25[3]	40	–	35
1996–97	bands of taxable income[1] (£)	1–3,900	3,901–25,500	over 25,500	–	–
	rate of tax (%)	20	24[4]	40	–	34
1997–98	bands of taxable income[1] (£)	1–4,100	4,101–26,100	over 26,100	–	–
	rate of tax (%)	20	23[4]	40	–	34
1998–99	bands of taxable income[1] (£)	1–4,300	4,301–27,100	over 27,100	–	–
	rate of tax (%)	20	23[4]	40	–	33
1999–2000	bands of taxable income[1] (£)	1–1,500	1,501–28,000	over 28,000	–	–
	rate of tax (%)	10	23[4]	40	–	33
2000–01	bands of taxable income[1] (£)	1–1,530	1,531–28,500	over 28,500	–	–
	rate of tax (%)	10	22[4]	40	–	–

[1] Taxable income is defined as gross income for income tax purposes less any allowances and reliefs available at the taxpayer's marginal rate.
[2] Applies to the income of discretionary and accumulation trusts. Prior to 1993–94 trusts paid tax at the basic rate, with an additional rate of 10 percent.
[3] The basic rate of tax on dividend income is 20 percent.
[4] The basic rate of tax on savings income is 20 percent.

Source: Board of Inland Revenue, © Crown copyright 1999; with Helicon updates

Income Tax Personal Allowances and Reliefs in the UK

(In pounds, unless otherwise indicated.)

Allowances and reliefs	1991–92	1995–96	1996–97	1997–98	1998–99	1999–2000
Personal allowance[1]	3,295	3,525	3,765	4,045	4,195	4,335
Married couple's allowance[2]	1,720	1,720	1,790	1,830	1,900	1,970
Age allowance[3]						
personal (aged 65–74)	4,020	4,630	4,910	5,220	5,410	5,720
personal (aged 75 or over)	4,180	4,800	5,090	5,400	5,600	5,980
married couple's (either partner between 65–74 but neither partner 75 or over)	2,355	2,995	3,115	3,185	3,305	5,125
married couple's (either partner 75 or over)	2,395	3,035	3,155	3,225	3,345	5,195
income limit	13,500	14,600	15,200	15,600	16,200	16,800
marginal fraction	$\frac{1}{2}$	$\frac{1}{2}$	$\frac{1}{2}$	$\frac{1}{2}$	$\frac{1}{2}$	$\frac{1}{2}$
Additional personal allowance[4]	1,720	1,720	1,790	1,830	1,900	1,970
Widow's bereavement allowance[5]	1,720	1,720	1,790	1,830	1,900	1,970
Blind person's allowance[6]						
single, or married (one spouse blind)	1,080	1,200	1,250	1,280	1,330	1,380
married (both spouses blind)	2,160	2,400	2,500	2,560	2,660	2,760
Life assurance relief (% of gross premium)[7]	12.5% or 0	12.5% or 0	12.5% or 0	12.5% or 0	12.5% or 0	12.5% or 0

[1] Every individual taxpayer is entitled to a personal allowance. The personal allowance is an amount you can receive without having to pay any tax, and can be set against any type of income. Where an individual's total income is less than the allowance, their tax liability is reduced to nil. However, any unused part of the personal allowance cannot be transferred to any other person.

[2] In the year of marriage the allowance is reduced by one twelfth for each complete month (beginning on the sixth day of each calendar month) prior to the date of marriage. The married couple's allowance, and allowances linked to it, that is, the additional personal allowance and the widow's bereavement allowance, are restricted to 20 percent in 1994–95 and 15 percent from 1995–96. In 1998–99 the maximum value of the allowance was £1,900×15 percent = £285. From April 1999 this is restricted to a flat rate of 10 percent; the maximum value of the allowance is £1,970×10 percent = £197. It is due to be phased out completely from 6 April 2000.

[3] The amount of the personal allowance depends on the age of the individual taxpayer. The amount of the married couple's allowance depends on the age of the elder of the husband or wife. The maximum value of these age-related allowances will be given provided the individual taxpayer's total income is below the income limit shown. For incomes in excess of the limit, the allowance is reduced by £1 for each additional £2 of income until the basic levels of the personal and married couple's allowances are reached.

[4] The additional personal allowance may be claimed by a single person who has a child resident with him or her during the year (or by a married man with children if his wife is totally incapacitated).

[5] Widow's bereavement allowance is due to a widow in the year of her husband's death and in the following year provided the widow has not remarried before the beginning of that year.

[6] You can claim the blind person's allowance if you are registered as blind with a local authority in England or Wales, or live in Scotland or Northern Ireland, and are unable to perform any work in which eyesight is essential. Surplus blind person's allowance may be transferred to a husband or wife.

[7] From 1984–85 life assurance premium relief is confined to policies made before 14 March 1984.

Source: *Inland Revenue Statistics 1997,* © Crown copyright 1997; with Helicon updates

National Insurance Contributions in the UK

Entitlement to National Insurance benefits such as Retirement Pension, Incapacity Benefit, contributory Jobseeker's Allowance, Maternity Allowance, and Widow's Benefit, is dependent upon the payment of contributions. There are five classes of National Insurance contributions. The rates given below are effective from April 1999 to April 2000.

Class 1

Class 1 contributions are paid by employers and their employees. Employees who earn less than £66 a week do not pay Class 1 contributions. For earnings above £66 per week the rate of contributions is 10 percent up to the upper earnings limit of £500 per week. Employees who are contracted out of SERPS pay a lower rate of 8.4 percent. The employer pays contributions at the rate of 12.2 percent for all earnings above £83 per week. For employees who are contracted out of SERPS the employer pays 9.2 percent up to the upper earnings limit of £500 per week, and 12.2 percent for earnings above £500 per week.

Class 1A

Class 1A contributions are paid by employers who provide their employees with fuel and/or a car for private use. A Class 1A contribution is payable on the cash equivalent of the benefit provided.

Class 2

Class 2 contributions are paid by the self-employed. These contributions are at a flat rate of £6.55 a week. The self-employed may claim exemption from Class 2 contributions if their profits are expected to be below £3,770 for the 1999–2000 tax year. Self-employed people are not eligible for unemployment and industrial injuries benefits.

Class 3

Class 3 contributions are paid voluntarily to safeguard rights to some benefits and for pension purposes. Contributions are at a flat rate of £6.55 a week.

Class 4

Class 4 contributions are paid by self-employed people on their taxable profits between £7,540 and £26,000 a year (in addition to their Class 2 contribution). Class 4 contributions are payable at the rate of 6 percent.

Employees who work after pensionable age (60 for women and 65 for men) do not pay contributions but the employer continues to be liable. Self-employed people over pensionable age do not pay contributions.

Source: *Britain 1999: The Official Yearbook of the United Kingdom,* © Crown copyright 1998; with Helicon updates

Rates of Capital Gains Tax in the UK

Capital gains tax (CGT) is payable by individuals and trusts on gains realized from the disposal of assets. It is payable on the amount by which total chargeable gains for a year exceed the exempt amount (£7,100 for individuals and £3,550 for trusts in

Rates of Capital Gains Tax in the UK

Tax year	Annual exempt amount (£)	
	Individuals	Trusts
1980–81 and 1981–82	3,000	1,500
1982–83	5,000	2,500
1983–84	5,300	2,650
1984–85	5,600	2,800
1985–86	5,900	2,950
1986–87	6,300	3,150
1987–88	6,600	3,300
1988–89 to 1990–91	5,000	2,500
1991–92	5,500	2,750
1992–93 to 1994–95	5,800	2,900
1995–96	6,000	3,000
1996–97	6,300	3,150
1997–98	6,500	3,250
1998–99	6,800	3,400
1999–2000	7,100	3,550

Source: *Inland Revenue Statistics 1997,* and *Britain 1998: An Official Handbook,* © Crown copyright 1997; with Helicon updates

1999–2000). For individuals, CGT had been calculated at income tax rates from 1988–89 to 1998–99, as if the amount were additional taxable income, while there are special rates for trusts. From 6 April 1999 CGT is charged at 20 percent or 40 percent depending on the overall level of the individual's income and gains to bring it into line with the rates of income tax payable on savings income. Only gains arising since 1982 are subject to tax. Indexation relief is given to take account of the effects of inflation. Gains on some types of asset are exempt from CGT. These include the principal private residence, government securities, certain corporate bonds, and gains on shares and corporate bonds owned under Personal Equity Plans (PEPs). For companies, capital gains are charged to corporation tax, although there is no annual exempt amount.

The table gives the annual amount exempt from tax. The rate of tax chargeable on the excess of gains over the annual exempt amount was 30 percent from 1980–81 to 1987–88. Thereafter the rate has been the same as income tax.

Source: *Inland Revenue Statistics 1997* and *Britain 1998: An Official Handbook,* © Crown copyright 1997; with Helicon updates

Rates of Stamp Duty in the UK

Certain kinds of transfer are subject to stamp duty. Transfers of shares attract duty at 0.5 percent of the cost, while certain instruments, such as declarations of trust, have small fixed duties of 50p or £1, though in practice (from 1 October 1999) Stamp Duty is collected in multiples of £5. Transfers by gift and transfers to charities are exempt. The March 1999 budget raised the rate of stamp duty on the transfers of property (except shares) over £250,000. Duty is now payable at 1 percent of the total price above £60,000, 2.5 percent for property above £250,000, and 3.5 percent for property where the price exceeds £500,000.

Source: *Inland Revenue Statistics 1997* and *Britain 1999: The Official Yearbook of the United Kingdom,* © Crown copyright 1997 and 1998; with Helicon updates

Rates of Stamp Duty in the UK

(– = not applicable. In pounds.)

Commencing date	Threshold and rates of stamp duty							
	Nil rate	0.5%	1%	1.5%	2%	2.5%	3%	3.5%
	Considerations up to	Considerations exceeding						
22 March 1982	25,000	25,000	30,000	35,000	40,000	–	–	–
13 March 1984	30,000	–	30,000	–	–	–	–	–
20 December 1991	250,000	–	250,000	–	–	–	–	–
20 August 1992	30,000	–	30,000	–	–	–	–	–
16 March 1993	60,000	–	60,000	–	–	–	–	–
8 July 1997	60,000	–	60,000	250,000	500,000	–	–	–
24 March 1998	60,000	–	60,000	–	250,000	–	500,000	–
16 March 1999	60,000	–	60,000	–	–	250,000	–	500,000

Source: *Inland Revenue Statistics 1997,* and *Britain 1999: The Official Yearbook of the United Kingdom,* © Crown copyright 1997 and 1998; with Helicon updates

Rates of Inheritance Tax/Capital Transfer Tax in the UK

Inheritance tax is essentially charged on estates at the time of death and on gifts made within seven years of death; most other lifetime transfers are not taxed. There are several important exemptions. Generally, transfers between spouses are exempt, and gifts and bequests to British charities, major political parties, and heritage bodies are also normally exempt. In general, business assets and farmland are exempt from inheritance tax, so that most family businesses can be passed on without a tax charge. Tax is charged at a single rate of 40 percent above a threshold, currently £231,000. Only about 2 percent of estates a year become liable for an inheritance tax bill.
The table gives the lower limit of the slice of chargeable capital/transfer.
(– = not applicable. In pounds unless otherwise indicated.)

	Threshold above which tax is charged														
Rates of tax (%)	15 March 1983–12 March 1984	13 March 1984–5 April 1985	6 April 1985–17 April 1986	18 March 1986–16 March 1987	17 March 1987–14 March 1988	15 March 1988–5 April 1989	6 April 1989–5 April 1990	6 April 1990–5 April 1991	6 April 1991–9 March 1992	10 March 1992–5 April 1995	6 April 1995–5 April 1996	6 April 1996–5 April 1997	6 April 1997–5 April 1998	6 April 1998–5 April 1999	From 6 April 1999
On Transfers on Death															
30	60,000	64,000	67,000	71,000	90,000	–	–	–	–	–	–	–	–	–	–
35	80,000	85,000	89,000	95,000	–	–	–	–	–	–	–	–	–	–	–
40	110,000	116,000	122,000	129,000	140,000	110,000	118,000	128,000	140,000	150,000	154,000	200,000	215,000	223,000	231,000
45	140,000	148,000	155,000	164,000	–	–	–	–	–	–	–	–	–	–	–
50	175,000	185,000	194,000	206,000	220,000	–	–	–	–	–	–	–	–	–	–
55	220,000	232,000	243,000	257,000	–	–	–	–	–	–	–	–	–	–	–
60	270,000	285,000	299,000	317,000	330,000	–	–	–	–	–	–	–	–	–	–
65	700,000	–	–	–	–	–	–	–	–	–	–	–	–	–	–
70	1,325,000	–	–	–	–	–	–	–	–	–	–	–	–	–	–
75	2,650,000	–	–	–	–	–	–	–	–	–	–	–	–	–	–
Lifetime Transfers															
15.0	60,000	64,000	67,000	71,000	90,000	–	–	–	–	–	–	–	–	–	–
17.5	80,000	85,000	89,000	95,000	–	–	–	–	–	–	–	–	–	–	–
20.0	110,000	116,000	122,000	129,000	140,000	110,000	118,000	128,000	140,000	150,000	154,000	200,000	215,000	223,000	231,000
22.5	140,000	148,000	155,000	164,000	–	–	–	–	–	–	–	–	–	–	–
25.0	175,000	185,000	194,000	206,000	220,000	–	–	–	–	–	–	–	–	–	–
27.5	–	232,000	243,000	257,000	–	–	–	–	–	–	–	–	–	–	–
30.0	220,000	285,000	299,000	317,000	330,000	–	–	–	–	–	–	–	–	–	–
35.0	270,000	–	–	–	–	–	–	–	–	–	–	–	–	–	–
40.0	700,000	–	–	–	–	–	–	–	–	–	–	–	–	–	–
42.5	–	–	–	–	–	–	–	–	–	–	–	–	–	–	–
45.0	1,325,000	–	–	–	–	–	–	–	–	–	–	–	–	–	–
50.0	2,650,000	–	–	–	–	–	–	–	–	–	–	–	–	–	–

Source: *Inland Revenue Statistics 1997* and *Britain 1998: An Official Handbook*, © Crown copyright 1997; with Helicon updates

Value Added Tax in the UK

Value Added Tax (VAT) is a broadly based expenditure tax, with a standard rate of 17.5 percent and a reduced rate of 5 percent on domestic fuel and power. It is collected at each stage in the production and distribution of goods and services by taxable persons. The final tax is payable by the consumer.

The annual level of turnover above which traders must register for VAT is £51,000. Certain goods and services are relieved from VAT, either by being charged at a zero rate or by being exempt.

Zero Rating

Under zero rating, a taxable person does not charge tax to a customer but reclaims any input tax paid to suppliers. Among the main categories where zero-rating applies are: goods exported to other countries; most food; water and sewerage for non-business use; domestic and international passenger transport; books, newspapers, and periodicals; construction of new residential buildings; young children's clothing and footwear; drugs and medicines supplied on prescription; specified aids for handicapped people; and certain supplies by or to charities.

Exemptions

For exempt goods or services, a taxable person does not charge any output tax but is not entitled to reclaim the input tax. The main categories where exemption applies are: many supplies of land and buildings; insurance and other financial services; postal services; betting; gaming (with certain important exceptions); lotteries; much education and training; and health and welfare.

Source: *Britain 1999: The Official Yearbook of the United Kingdom,* © Crown copyright 1998; with Helicon updates

Rates of Corporation Tax in the UK

The rates of company tax in the UK are lower than in most other industrialized countries. Companies pay corporation tax on their income and capital gains after deduction of certain allowances and reliefs. A company that distributes profits to its shareholders is required to pay advance corporation tax (ACT) on these distributions to the Inland Revenue. ACT is set against the company's liability to corporation tax, subject to a limit. In the budget of March 1998 the government announced the abolition of advance corporation tax from April 1998, and its intention to introduce a new instalment system for the payment of large companies' corporation tax. Shareholders (except pension schemes and companies) resident in the UK receiving distributions from UK-resident companies are treated as having some or all their liability to income tax satisfied for such income.

The main rate of corporation tax has been reduced from 31 percent to 30 percent from April 1999, and the reduced rate for smaller companies (those with profits below £300,000 a year) has been reduced from 21 percent to 20 percent. Relief is allowed for companies with profits between £300,000 and £1.5 million, so that the company's overall rate is between the main rate and the small companies' rate. From April 2000 there is a new 10 percent rate of corporation tax for profits up to £10,000; this is due to benefit companies with profits up to £50,000. The government announced in the budget of March 1999 its intention to introduce tax credits for research and development spending by small and medium-sized companies. Some capital expenditure may qualify for relief in the form of capital allowances. Examples include expenditure on machinery and plant, industrial buildings, agricultural buildings, and scientific research. Expenditure on machinery or plant by small or medium-sized businesses qualifies for a first-year allowance. This was introduced in 1997 and set at the rate of 50 percent if the expenditure was incurred in the year to July. This scheme was extended from 1 July 1999 to 1 July 2000 at the rate of 40 percent.

Source: *Inland Revenue Statistics 1997* and *Britain 1999: The Official Yearbook of the United Kingdom,* © Crown copyright 1997 and 1998; with Helicon updates

Rates of Corporation Tax in the UK

(– = not applicable.)

Financial year commencing 1 April	Full rate (%)	Advance rate on distributions	Capital gains relief (general[1])	Small companies				Cooperative and building societies rate rate (%[2])
				Rate (%)	Range of profit for		Marginal relief fraction	
					Lower relief (£)	Upper relief (£)		
1980	52	3/7	11/26	40	80,000	200,000	2/25	40
1981	52	3/7	11/26	40	90,000	225,000	2/25	40
1982	52	3/7	11/26	38	100,000	500,000	7/200	40
1983	50	3/7	2/5	30	100,000	500,000	1/20	40
1984	45	3/7	1/3	30	100,000	500,000	3/80	40
1985	40	3/7	1/4	30	100,000	500,000	1/40	–
1986	35	29/71	1/7	29	100,000	500,000	3/200	–
1987	35	27/73	–	27	100,000	500,000	1/50	–
1988	35	25/75	–	25	100,000	500,000	1/40	–
1989	35	25/75	–	25	150,000	750,000	1/40	–
1990	34	25/75	–	25	200,000	1,000,000	9/400	–
1991	33	25/75	–	25	250,000	1,250,000	1/50	–
1992	33	25/75	–	25	250,000	1,250,000	1/50	–
1993	33	9/31	–	25	250,000	1,250,000	1/50	–
1994	33	20/80	–	25	300,000	1,500,000	1/50	–
1995	33	20/80	–	25	300,000	1,500,000	1/50	–

(*continued*)

Rates of Corporation Tax in the UK (*continued*)

Financial year commencing 1 April	Full rate (%)	Advance rate on distributions	Capital gains relief (general[1])	Small companies				Cooperative and building societies rate rate (%[2])
				Rate (%)	Range of profit for		Marginal relief fraction	
					Lower relief (£)	Upper relief (£)		
1996	33	$\frac{20}{80}$	–	24	300,000	1,500,000	$\frac{9}{400}$	–
1997	31	$\frac{20}{80}$	–	21	300,000	1,500,000	$\frac{1}{40}$	–
1998	31	$\frac{20}{80}$	–	21	300,000	1,500,000	$\frac{1}{40}$	–
1999	30	–[3]	–	20	300,000	1,500,000	$\frac{1}{40}$	–

[1] Chargeable gains realized after 16 March 1987 are taxed at the same rate as income.
[2] Normal corporation tax rates apply from 1985 after abolition of the special rate.
[3] Abolished April 1999.

Source: *Inland Revenue Statistics 1997*, and *Britain 1999: The Official Yearbook of the United Kingdom*, © Crown copyright 1997 and 1998; with Helicon updates

Mortgage and Finance Information

Types of Mortgages in the UK

Outlined below are the most popular types of mortgage taken out by borrowers in the UK. However, other types of mortgage can sometimes be made available to borrowers, and anyone needing more information on finding a mortgage to suit their financial circumstances should visit a mortgage lender for advice.

Repayment Mortgage

The repayment mortgage provides for regular monthly repayments of the amount borrowed, over the whole term of the mortgage (usually 25 years). Monthly repayments are made up of interest on the loan and repayments on the capital amount. During the first few years, most of each monthly repayment goes towards paying the interest on the loan. As the mortgage term reduces, the capital payments increase, and the interest payments reduce. Relief on mortgage interest repayments will be removed from 6 April 2000. Mortgage interest relief for those aged 65 and over who take out a loan to buy a life annuity (a home income plan) ended with effect from 9 March 1999, but existing loans qualify for relief for the remainder of the loan period.

Most repayment mortgages are taken out on a variable rate of interest. That is, monthly payments vary according to changes in general interest rates. Some lenders, however, adjust mortgage repayments on an annual basis, taking into account the previous year's interest rates. Borrowers on a variable rate mortgage do have options for altering their repayments in some cases. For example, if interest rates increase, borrowers may be given an option not to increase their payments. This depends on the length of the term and the amount outstanding. Failure to increase repayments in line with current interest rates can result in not paying enough to meet interest charges on the loan. Conversely, when interest rates decease, borrowers can opt not to reduce their monthly payments and thereby reduce the term of their mortgage.

Endowment Mortgage

An endowment policy is one of a variety of investment-linked mortgages available to home buyers. Investment-linked mortgages allow for interest payments on a loan to be paid and leave the capital sum borrowed unpaid. The borrower makes an investment over the term of the loan which, when matured, is used to repay the capital at the end of the term. With an endowment policy, borrowers pay a monthly premium into an endowment insurance policy, commonly a with-profits or unit-linked policy. On a with-profits policy, profit bonuses are normally added each year. These bonuses cannot be removed or reduced. Over the term of the policy it may be possible to increase the amount insured so that when the time comes to pay off the capital on the loan, there may be more money in the policy than required. With a unit-linked policy, the premiums are paid into investments such as stocks and shares. The potential benefits of investing premiums into these investments are clear, but it is important to remember that investing in this way can be risky. Most insurers conduct regular reviews of the performance of unit trusts in order to monitor whether the projected maturity will be sufficient to cover the loan.

Another form of endowment policy, known as a unitized policy, is a combination of the with-profits and the unit-linked policies. Part of the premium is invested in a with-profits endowment and the rest is invested in stocks and shares.

Endowment-linked mortgages may have an additional benefit of providing for a loan to be paid off in full in the event of the death of the borrower. Some policies may, however, require additional life cover.

Unlike the repayment mortgage, endowment mortgages do not usually offer a facility to extend the term of a mortgage if interest rates increase; higher payments need to be met in full. It is also important to note that endowment policies have a low surrender value in the early years of a policy. However, most mortgages do not run to their full term, i.e. they are paid off when home owners sell and move home. In such cases, an existing endowment policy can usually be used to secure a new mortgage.

Personal Equity Plan (PEP)

Personal Equity Plan (PEP) mortgage – PEPs have been replaced by Individual Savings Accounts (ISAs). These mortgages are designed to repay your loan at the end of an agreed term. You make monthly payments to the lender and invest an agreed sum with your ISA provider. At the end of the term the investment should repay the amount borrowed and provide a tax-free surplus.

Pension-Linked Mortgage

For the self-employed or holders of personal pensions, a loan can be linked to a pension plan. The borrower pays interest on the loan to the lender and pays contributions to their pension fund. At the end of the term of the loan, part of the proceeds of the pension fund are used to pay off the mortgage. For those eligible for tax relief on pension contributions and interest payments, this can be an attractive option. However, it is important to remember that this sort of mortgage will reduce the amount of pension available to the borrower when they retire.

Fixed Rate Mortgage

Many lenders offer mortgages with fixed interest rates over a period of years, generally between one and five years. After the term

Annual Repayments on a £30,000 Mortgage over 25 Years

Calculations for a repayment mortgage, assuming no change in the interest rate payable or in the applicable MIRAS percentage rate of 15 percent. Based on a mortgage at 7 percent (5.95 percent after MIRAS has been deducted). As from 6 April 2000, the MIRAS scheme is to be abolished. (In pounds.)

Year	Constant net annual repayment	Principal	Interest	Balance at end of year	Year	Constant net annual repayment	Principal	Interest	Balance at end of year
1	2,335.66	550.66	1,785.00	29,449.34	14	2,335.66	1,167.34	1,168.32	18,468.28
2	2,335.66	583.43	1,752.23	28,865.91	15	2,335.66	1,236.80	1,098.86	17,231.48
3	2,335.66	618.14	1,717.52	28,247.77	16	2,335.66	1,310.39	1,025.27	15,921.09
4	2,335.66	654.92	1,680.74	27,592.85	17	2,335.66	1,388.36	947.31	14,532.73
5	2,335.66	693.89	1,641.78	26,898.96	18	2,335.66	1,470.97	864.70	13,061.77
6	2,335.66	735.18	1,600.49	26,163.78	19	2,335.66	1,558.49	777.17	11,503.28
7	2,335.66	778.92	1,556.74	25,384.86	20	2,335.66	1,651.22	684.45	9,852.06
8	2,335.66	825.26	1,510.40	24,559.60	21	2,335.66	1,749.47	586.19	8,102.60
9	2,335.66	874.37	1,461.29	23,685.23	22	2,335.66	1,853.56	482.10	6,249.04
10	2,335.66	926.39	1,409.28	22,758.84	23	2,335.66	1,963.85	371.82	4,285.19
11	2,335.66	981.51	1,354.15	21,777.33	24	2,335.66	2,080.69	254.97	2,204.50
12	2,335.66	1,039.91	1,295.75	20,737.41	25	2,335.73	2,204.50	131.16	0
13	2,335.66	1,101.79	1,233.88	19,635.63					
					Total	58,391.57	30,000.00	28,391.57	0

Source: Council of Mortgage Lenders

of the fixed rate, the interest reverts to current rates, or a new fixed rate term can be taken out on the loan. The advantage of fixed interest payments is that monthly mortgage repayments are guaranteed and borrowers can budget for their mortgage payments for a definite period. On the other hand, while fixed interest rates will protect the borrower from increases in general interest rates, borrowers may also find themselves paying more if rates decrease. There can also be high financial penalties for redeeming a fixed interest rate mortgage early.

Discount Rate Mortgage

A popular option for first time buyers, the discount rate mortgage offers a loan with interest at a discounted rate, generally for the first year or two of the loan. The rate is discounted by 1 percent or more and can make a big difference to mortgage payments. Borrowers should remember, though, that once the term of the discounted rate is over, the mortgage payments will revert to the current interest rate; the difference between repayments on a discounted rate mortgage and current rates over two years can be quite considerable. As with the fixed rate mortgage, borrowers can be subject to financial penalties if they redeem a discount rate mortgage early.

Capped Rate Mortgage

Capped interest on a mortgage means that, for a certain period, borrowers can arrange for maximum and minimum interest rates to be charged on a loan. Capped rate mortgages benefit borrowers when interest rates are high, because interest payments on their loan will not exceed the capped rate. However, if interest rates decrease, the minimum rate of interest set on the loan may be higher than the general rate of interest.

Monthly Repayments on a £30,000 Mortgage at Various Rates

Calculations for a repayment mortgage, assuming no change in the applicable percentage rate of 15 percent (the Mortgage Interest Relief at Source (MIRAS) rate). Mortgage rate figures in parentheses are net values (that is, the figure after MIRAS has been deducted). As from 6 April 2000, the MIRAS scheme is to be abolished.
(In pounds unless otherwise indicated.)

Mortgage rate (%)	20 year term	25 year term	30 year term	Mortgage rate (%)	20 year term	25 year term	30 year term
5.00 (4.25)	188.05	164.29	149.00	10.00 (8.50)	264.18	244.28	232.63
5.50 (4.67)	195.12	171.65	156.65	10.50 (8.92)	272.40	252.97	241.72
6.00 (5.10)	202.31	179.16	164.49	11.00 (9.35)	280.73	261.77	250.93
6.50 (5.52)	209.63	186.83	172.49	11.50 (9.77)	289.15	270.67	260.23
7.00 (5.95)	217.08	194.64	180.65	12.00 (10.20)	297.67	279.67	269.63
7.50 (6.37)	224.64	202.59	188.97	12.50 (10.62)	306.27	288.76	279.12
8.00 (6.80)	232.33	210.68	197.43	13.00 (11.05)	314.97	297.93	288.69
8.50 (7.22)	240.12	218.89	206.04	13.50 (11.47)	323.74	307.20	298.34
9.00 (7.65)	248.03	227.24	214.78	14.00 (11.90)	332.60	316.54	308.06
9.50 (8.07)	256.05	235.70	223.64				

Source: Council of Mortgage Lenders

Average House Prices at Mortgage Completion in the UK

(– = not applicable. N/A = not available. In pounds.)

1997

Region	First-time buyers	Other	All buyers	Percentage increase 1996–97
Northeast	36,600	70,100	52,800	4
Northwest	45,100	81,500	63,500	11
Merseyside	42,900	81,000	60,700	4
Yorkshire and the Humber	43,000	76,900	60,000	7
East Midlands	44,300	78,200	61,900	5
West Midlands	46,300	86,500	67,800	5
Eastern	57,100	99,600	81,400	11
London	74,000	137,400	105,800	13
Southeast	64,200	114,500	94,800	8
Southwest	53,200	86,300	73,000	7

Region	First-time buyers	Other	All buyers	Percentage increase 1996–97
England total	54,800	98,900	78,800	9
Wales total	42,000	75,200	58,400	6
Scotland total	38,800	78,500	57,900	2
Northern Ireland total	40,000	69,800	53,300	12
UK TOTAL	52,500	96,200	75,900	8

Source: *Social Trends 29,* Department of the Environment, Transport, and the Regions, © Crown copyright 1999

Individual Insolvencies in the UK

Figures are the number of individual insolvencies in each year.
(N/A = not available.)

Type of insolvency	1987	1988	1989	1990	1991	1992	1993	1994	1995	1996	1997
England and Wales											
Bankruptcies[1 2]	6,994	7,717	8,138	12,058	22,632	32,106	31,016	25,634	21,933	21,803	19,892
Individual voluntary arrangements[3]	404	779	1,224	1,927	3,002	4,686	5,679	5,103	4,384	4,466	4,545
Deeds of arrangement	29	11	3	2	6	2	8	2	2	2	4
Total	7,427	8,507	9,365	13,987	25,640	36,794	36,703	30,739	26,319	26,271	24,441
Scotland											
Sequestrations[4]	808	1,401	2,301	4,350	7,665	10,845	6,828	2,182	2,188	2,503	2,502
Northern Ireland											
Bankruptcies[5 6]	134	164	238	286	367	406	474	438	399	415	393
Individual voluntary arrangements[7]	N/A	N/A	N/A	N/A	2	42	67	84	64	101	84
Total	134	164	238	286	369	448	541	522	463	516	477

[1] Comprise receiving and administration orders under the Bankruptcy Act, 1914, and bankruptcy orders under the Insolvency Act, 1986.
[2] Orders later consolidated or rescinded are included in these figures.
[3] Introduced under the Insolvency Act, 1986.
[4] Sequestrations awarded but not brought into operation are included in these figures.
[5] Comprise bankruptcy adjudication orders, arrangement protection orders, and orders for the administration of estates of deceased insolvents.
[6] Orders later set aside or dismissed are included in these figures.
[7] Introduced under the insolvency Northern Ireland order, 1989.

Source: *Annual Abstract of Statistics 1999,* Department of Trade and Industry, © Crown copyright 1999

Compound Interest

This table assumes that interest is calculated annually and takes no account of taxation.

Value of £100 after:	Interest rate											
	4%	5%	6%	7%	8%	9%	10%	11%	12%	13%	14%	15%
3 months	101.0	101.3	101.5	101.8	102.0	102.3	102.5	102.8	103.0	103.3	103.5	103.8
6 months	102.0	102.5	103.0	103.5	104.0	104.5	105.0	105.5	106.0	106.5	107.0	107.5
1 year	104.0	105.0	106.0	107.0	108.0	109.0	110.0	111.0	112.0	113.0	114.0	115.0
2 years	108.2	110.3	112.4	114.5	116.6	118.8	121.0	123.2	125.4	127.7	130.0	132.3
3 years	112.5	115.8	119.1	122.5	126.0	129.5	133.1	136.8	140.5	144.3	148.2	152.1
4 years	117.0	121.6	126.2	131.1	136.0	141.2	146.4	151.8	157.4	163.0	168.9	174.9
5 years	121.7	127.6	133.8	140.3	146.9	153.9	161.1	168.5	176.2	184.2	192.5	201.1
6 years	126.5	134.0	141.9	150.1	158.7	167.7	177.2	187.0	197.4	208.2	219.5	231.3
7 years	131.6	140.7	150.4	160.6	171.4	182.8	194.9	207.6	221.1	235.3	250.2	266.0
8 years	136.9	147.7	159.4	171.8	185.1	199.3	214.4	230.5	247.6	265.8	285.3	305.9
9 years	142.3	155.1	168.9	183.8	199.9	217.2	235.8	255.8	277.3	300.4	325.2	351.8
10 years	148.0	162.9	179.1	196.7	215.9	236.7	259.4	283.9	310.6	339.5	370.7	404.6
15 years	180.1	207.9	239.7	275.9	317.2	364.2	417.7	478.5	547.4	625.4	713.8	813.7
20 years	219.1	265.3	320.7	387.0	466.1	560.4	672.7	806.2	964.6	1,152.3	1,374.3	1,636.7
25 years	266.6	338.6	429.2	542.7	684.8	862.3	1,083.5	1,358.5	1,700.0	2,123.1	2,646.2	3,291.9

Consumer Expenditure

Households and their Expenditure in the UK

Category	1990	1991	1992	1993	1994–95	1995–96	1996–97	1997–98
Number of households supplying data	7,046	7,056	7,418	6,979	6,853	6,797	6,415	6,409
Total number of persons supplying data	17,437	17,089	18,174	17,291	16,617	16,586	15,732	15,430
Total number of adults supplying data[1]	12,939	12,934	13,563	12,792	12,365	12,219	11,495	11,429
Household Percentage Distribution by Tenure								
Rented unfurnished	29.2	27.7	28.4	27.9	27.5	28.9	27.9	28.9
Rented furnished	3.4	3.3	3.8	3.7	3.9	3.7	4.5	3.0
Rent-free	1.3	2.0	2.0	1.5	1.3	1.2	1.7	1.5
Owner-occupied	66.1	67.0	65.8	66.9	67.4	66.1	65.9	66.7
Average Number of Persons per Household								
All persons	2.475	2.422	2.450	2.478	2.425	2.440	2.452	2.408
Males	1.193	1.169	1.182	1.201	1.162	1.172	1.178	1.152
Females	1.281	1.253	1.268	1.276	1.263	1.268	1.275	1.256
Adults[1]								
persons under 65	1.459	1.455	1.460	1.466	1.444	1.433	1.436	1.436
persons 65 and over	0.378	0.378	0.369	0.367	0.360	0.365	0.356	0.348
Total	1.836	1.833	1.828	1.833	1.804	1.798	1.792	1.783
Children[1]								
children under 2	0.075	0.077	0.071	0.076	0.073	0.076	0.079	0.069
children 2 and under 5	0.119	0.112	0.111	0.123	0.113	0.108	0.116	0.113
children 5 and under 18	0.444	0.400	0.439	0.446	0.435	0.458	0.465	0.442
Total	0.638	0.589	0.621	0.645	0.621	0.642	0.660	0.624
Persons economically active	1.195	1.171	1.169	1.153	1.150	1.134	1.161	1.141
Persons not economically active								
men 65 and over, women 60 and over	0.405	0.408	0.399	0.400	0.391	0.390	0.378	0.375
others	0.875	0.843	0.882	0.925	0.883	0.915	0.913	0.892
Total	1.280	1.251	1.281	1.324	1.275	1.306	1.292	1.266
Average Weekly Household Expenditure on Commodities and Services (£)[4]								
Housing[2,3]	44.42	50.24	47.36	44.85	46.42	48.25	49.10	51.53
Fuel and power	11.11	12.25	13.02	13.24	12.95	12.92	13.35	12.66
Food	44.81	46.13	47.66	49.96	50.43	52.88	55.15	55.92
Alcoholic drink	10.01	10.83	11.06	11.95	12.32	11.41	12.41	13.33
Tobacco	4.82	5.15	5.38	5.59	5.61	5.81	6.07	6.12
Clothing and footwear	16.03	15.80	16.39	17.40	17.13	17.15	18.27	19.96
Household goods[3]	20.00	20.13	21.90	23.05	22.66	23.45	26.74	26.90
Household services[3]	12.28	13.00	13.40	15.44	15.08	15.13	16.36	17.89
Personal goods and services	9.47	9.47	10.18	11.04	10.78	11.55	11.64	12.54
Motoring expenditure	33.83	34.12	35.66	36.28	36.17	36.99	41.20	46.63
Fares and other travel costs	6.19	5.58	7.20	6.95	6.64	6.17	7.45	8.12
Leisure goods	11.28	12.06	13.32	13.26	13.89	13.23	15.17	16.35
Leisure services[3]	21.54	22.20	27.56	25.56	31.20	32.05	33.95	38.81
Miscellaneous	1.37	1.59	1.75	2.10	2.30	2.37	2.21	2.02
Total	247.16	259.04	271.83	276.68	289.86	2.89	309.07	328.78
Expenditure on Commodity or Service as a Percentage of Total Expenditure[4]								
Housing[2,3]	18.0	19.4	17.4	16.2	16.4	16.6	15.9	15.7
Fuel and power	4.5	4.7	4.8	4.8	4.6	4.5	4.3	3.9
Food	18.1	17.8	17.5	18.1	17.8	18.2	17.8	17.0
Alcoholic drink	4.1	4.2	4.1	4.3	4.3	3.9	4.0	4.1
Tobacco	2.0	2.0	2.0	2.0	2.0	2.0	2.0	1.9
Clothing and footwear	6.5	6.1	6.0	6.3	6.0	5.9	5.9	6.1
Household goods[3]	8.1	7.8	8.1	8.3	8.0	8.1	8.7	8.2
Household services[3]	5.0	5.0	4.9	5.6	5.3	5.2	5.3	5.4
Personal goods and services	3.8	3.8	3.7	4.0	3.8	4.0	3.8	3.8

(continued)

Households and their Expenditure in the UK (*continued*)

Category	1990	1991	1992	1993	1994–95	1995–96	1996–97	1997–98
Motoring expenditure	13.7	13.2	13.1	13.1	12.8	12.8	13.3	14.2
Fares and other travel costs	2.5	2.2	2.6	2.5	2.3	2.1	2.4	2.5
Leisure goods	4.6	4.7	4.9	4.8	4.9	4.7	4.9	5.0
Leisure services[3]	8.7	8.6	10.1	9.2	11.0	11.1	11.0	11.8
Miscellaneous	0.6	0.6	0.6	0.8	0.8	0.8	0.7	0.6

[1] Adults = all persons 18 and over and married persons under 18; children = all unmarried persons under 18.

[2] Until 1992 excludes mortgage payments but includes imputed rent of owner-occupancy and of rent-free occupancy. Imputed expenditure is the weekly equivalent of the rateable value which is adjusted to allow for general increases in rents since date of valuation. 1985 assessments of rateable values in Scotland were used from 1 April 1985 in the calculation of imputed income and housing expenditure of owner-occupiers and those living rent-free. In 1992 values of income and expenditure pertaining to households in owner-occupied and rent-free housing were no longer imputed. From 1992 onwards the interest element of mortgage payments is recorded as part of housing expenditure.

[3] Expenditure on certain items was recorded on a retrospective basis from 1989 and 1990.

[4] A new classification system for expenditure was introduced in April 1994. There have been some minor adjustments to the coverage of the following expenditure groups: leisire goods and services, motoring expenditure and fares, household goods and services, personal goods and services. As a result, figures for these expenditure groups, and for total expenditure, are not directly comparable with figures for earlier years.

Source: *Annual Abstract of Statistics 1999, Family Expenditure Survey,* © Crown copyright 1999

Working Hours Needed to Buy Selected Commodities in the UK

Figures indicate the length of time necessary for a person on average hourly adult earnings for all industries and services to work so that his/her net income pays for various goods. The earnings figures are based on full-time employees on adult rates whose pay was not affected for the survey period by absence. Net income also includes child benefit payments.

Commodity	Married couple with husband only working[1]		Working single mother with child	
	1971	1998	1971	1998
800 g white sliced wrapped bread	9 min	4 min	14 min	5 min
1 pint milk	5 min	3 min	8 min	3 min
Dozen eggs, first quality, size 2	21 min	11 min	32 min	14 min
1 kg potatoes	4 min	6 min	6 min	7 min
1 kg cod fillets	1 hr 1 min	48 min	1 hr 30 min	59 min
1 kg rump steak	1 hr 54 min	1 hr 5 min	2 hr 49 min	1 hr 19 min
1 pint of beer (bitter)	14 min	13 min	20 min	15 min
20 cigarettes (king size filter)	22 min	24 min	33 min	29 min
Road fund tax	40 hr 1 min	18 hr 25 min	59 hr 54 min	22 hr 31 min
First class stamp	3 min	2 min	4 min	2 min

[1] Married man with non-earning wife and two children under 11.

Source: Office for National Statistics; Inland Revenue; DVLA; Postal Museum, © Crown copyright 1999

Electronic Commerce

BY PAUL BRAY

The Internet has the potential to cause the biggest revolution in world commerce since the invention of money. There may be half a billion companies out there, trying to sell us everything from cars to garden gnomes. Beside the Net, the advent of the credit card, the supermarket, and the single European currency may be no more than footnotes on the balance sheet of history.

It is difficult not to lapse into hyperbole when discussing Internet commerce. Sober-suited business analysts publish outlandish predictions. Mighty corporations jostle for our attention on the World Wide Web with animated gimmicks and unbeatable offers. Politicians hold high-level pow-wows and pretend to understand it all (though really they are trying to work out how to tax it).

Buying on the Internet

Three or four years ago the Internet was all promise and hot air. Early attempts at virtual shopping malls attracted much interest from the chattering classes, but sold virtually nothing. The few enterprising souls who did try to buy online were often disappointed, finding that choice was limited, or that they had to log off and place their orders by phone or fax.

More recently, things appeared to be looking up. Virtual bookstores opened, offering lower prices and more stock than conventional shops; they even claimed to get to know their customers and lead them to titles which they thought would interest them. Personal computer makers allowed people to design their own

PC online and have it delivered to their door within days. Banks let customers check account balances and transfer funds from the comfort of their home PCs.

But it emerged that the bookshops made no profits, and that many PC buyers were window-shopping on the Net but ordering by phone. And the queues at the banks got little shorter, since only a minority of customers had logged on to virtual branches.

According to research firm IDC, British consumers spent just £300 million pounds on the Net in 1998, with business-to-business sales accounting for another £550 million. The most popular purchases included computer equipment and software, travel items like air tickets, and books and CDs. Consumer sales are projected to rise to £6.5 billion by 2002, and business sales to £23 billion. This sounds impressive, but it would only represent about 3% of the UK's gross domestic product (GDP).

None of this is very surprising. Telephones had been around for generations before they carried significant amounts of trade. Hole-in-the-wall cash machines were largely ignored for a decade, until customers came to trust them. It would be naive to expect people suddenly to part with billions of pounds via a medium many of them had never even heard of five years ago.

Pros and cons

The potential drawbacks of buying and selling on the Net are obvious to all but its most die-hard adherents. Customers cannot handle the goods, as in a shop. They must pay for the privilege, in telephone and other charges, unlike a catalogue. They may have to trust that a company they have never heard of, possibly overseas, will supply the goods they have ordered, within reasonable time, and in good condition; that it will offer after-sales support if necessary, or take goods back if unwanted or damaged; and that it will take good care of their credit card number, not misusing it or allowing it to be intercepted by fraudsters.

We shall all become the targets of 'micromarketing' campaigns – a carefully personalized mix of offers.

And yet Net commerce makes good economic sense. From the seller's point of view, it incurs a fraction of the cost of maintaining and stocking conventional retail outlets (a tenth, say some analysts). It allows them to sell to markets, overseas or within their own countries, which they would otherwise lack the resources to reach. It offers the chance to establish personal relationships with customers – with the individual's consent, of course – which would be much more difficult in a big store.

Customers can shop, bank, or renew their insurance from home or office, at any hour of the day or night. They can compare prices and garner product information without tramping from shop to shop. They can consult impartial consumer advice, from magazines, user groups, and the like. And they can often benefit from lower prices and wider choice, as Net traders strive to differentiate themselves from more established competitors, and intermediaries like eBay and Priceline run online auctions or invite consumers to name their own price.

Concerns about security are understandable, but largely unfounded. Quoting your credit card number online should be no more risky than giving it over the telephone, or handing your card to a waiter in a restaurant. UK consumer credit laws also apply online, so holders of personal credit cards are given some protection by the credit card company if the goods are faulty or fail to arrive, as long as the transaction is worth over £100 and takes place in the UK.

It is important that the vendor uses an appropriate 'encryption' (encoding) standard, and no-one should buy online without ensuring that this is the case – for example by checking that the vendor uses the Secure Electronic Transactions (SET) system, or a secure intermediary like Netbanx, or that it displays the logo of an independent vetting service such as WebTrust. For small transactions, 'electronic cash' is being developed, which can be downloaded via the Net from the user's bank account, stored on their PC or a smartcard, and 'spent' at merchants' Web sites. The technology is there, and could be implemented as soon as the market demands it.

Even the weekly trudge round the supermarket can be replaced by Internet ordering. At selected Tesco stores, customers can send in their shopping list via the Net and have the goods delivered for a £5 charge. More than 100 stores throughout the UK should be online by February 2000. Sainsbury's will deliver Internet orders within Greater London. And Safeway is piloting a scheme giving customers handheld computers to send in their orders by wireless link, then collect the shopping at their local store.

Future possibilities

Net commerce is not just about physical goods. In fact, as a virtual medium it is better suited to 'virtual' products, like insurance policies, share trading, or information services – not to mention pornography, which has been one of the early success stories of Net commerce. Airlines can sell 'tickets' without issuing pieces of paper, by instead giving the passenger an authorization code which can be quoted at the check-in. Music publishers can sell tracks or whole albums without manufacturing CDs, by allowing customers to download them from Web sites for a fee.

Nor is the Web just about consumer sales. Large corporations like General Electric are already making big savings in time and money, by procuring raw materials, manufactured goods, and services via the Web – either seeking out the best deals around the world, or inviting tenders.

Internet commerce will have a profound effect on us all. Some of us will lose our jobs or see our shareholdings dwindle as some firms miss the electronic boat. Others will strike it rich as startup businesses can compete on equal terms with multinationals. Some will see our lifestyles change as we have access to an undreamed-of variety of goods and services. We shall all become the targets of 'micromarketing' campaigns – a carefully personalized mix of offers and e-mails designed to appeal to our individual tastes, as revealed by our previous purchases or even the products we have glanced at on the vendor's Web site.

Nobody knows when Internet commerce will hit the big time – three years, five years, ten years maybe. But when it does, the impetus of a market with limited costs and limitless reach – what *Business Week* magazine described as 'frictionless capitalism' – will be almost impossible to stop.

Paul Bray is a freelance journalist specializing in technology

The National Lottery

The National Lottery: Introduction

Parliament

In 1993, the National Lottery Act was passed by parliament, enabling a national lottery to be set up in the UK. Eight consortia submitted bids to run the UK lottery. The license was awarded to the Camelot consortium by Sir Peter Davies of the lottery regulatory body OFLOT (now the National Lottery Commission). The license is up for review in 2001 and Camelot is expected to put in a bid. Parliament also decided the five 'good causes' to benefit from the lottery. These are: arts, sport, heritage, charities, and the 'millennium'.

Government

In the year to end March 1998, the Government received a total of £661.7 million in lottery duty. See *How the Income is Distributed* table for the full breakdown of how the money is divided up.

National Lottery Commission (OFLOT)

The National Lottery Act 1998 brought in the new commission, including members with expertise in consumers' views, business, the lottery market, and lottery distribution. The status of the Commission is as a non-departmental Government Body (as of 1 April 1999). The Commission's principal duties are to protect the interests of National Lottery players and ensure that the lottery is run fairly and properly. It is also a legal objective to maximize the money raised for good causes. The Commission will select the next operator when the current license expires in September 2001. The 1998 legislation also gives the Commission powers to impose financial penalties for breaches of the current license.

Camelot

Set-up Camelot is made up of five shareholders: Cadbury Schweppes – consumer product marketing; De La Rue – security printing; ICL – computer systems, field service, and retailer training; Racal – data communication; GTECH – lottery systems worldwide.

Camelot's profit after tax for the year to March 1998 was £54.2 million. Camelot returns more money to Good Causes, in money and percentage revenue, than any other lottery in the world. The profit is expected to remain under 1 percent of sales during the period of the license. Under the terms of the license, as sales increase, a higher percentage of earnings go to the Good Causes, and a smaller percentage to Camelot to cover operating costs.

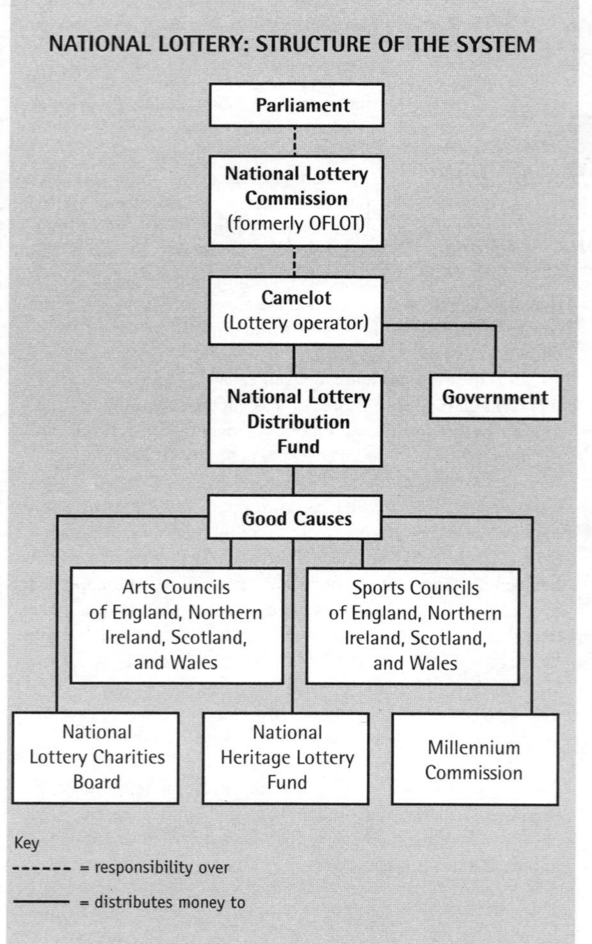

National Lottery Ticket Sales

Camelot's assessment of total yearly sales of tickets and Instants is as follows:

Year	Sales (£ millions)
1995[1]	1,190.7
1996	5,217.0
1997	4,723.0
1998	5,513.7

[1] Part year.

Source: *Camelot Annual Review 1998*; Camelot Group plc

National Lottery: How the Income is Distributed

This table shows the average distribution anticipated by Camelot over the seven-year period of their National Lottery licence.

Recipient	%
Prize fund	50
Good Causes	28
The Government: lottery duty, tax, and VAT	12
Retail commission	5
Operating costs	4
Profit to Camelot	1

Source: Camelot Group plc

Retailers

Retailers are selected on the basis of: prime location, with preferably in excess of 500 adult customers a day, quality of premises, long opening hours, and easy access from residential and work areas. Kiosks are also placed in public areas such as railway stations and shopping centres. There are over 36,000 National Lottery retailers of which 24,000 are online. 68.87 percent of retailers are independently owned. The average weekly lottery sales for an online independent retailer is £2,259. Retailers earn 5 percent commission on all sales and 1 percent commission on all prizes paid out between £10–200. In the year to end March 1998 retailer commission totalled £281.7 million.

Household Participation in the National Lottery by Social Class in the UK

In the two-week diary-keeping period following interview between January and March each year for Saturday draw, and between February and March for Wednesday draw. (In percentages.)

Social group	Saturday draw			Wednesday draw	
	1995	1997	1998	1997	1998
Professional	63	54	43	21	23
Managerial and technical	70	62	58	33	36
Skilled non-manual	82	67	58	31	38
Skilled manual	89	80	75	47	50
Partly skilled	75	69	66	40	43
Unskilled	79	68	64	29	45
Economically inactive	62	52	55	29	33
Average	72	62	61	33	38

Source: *Social Trends 29*, © Crown copyright 1999

National Lottery Distribution Fund (NLDF)

Camelot is legally obliged to maximize the funds raised by the National Lottery for the Good Causes. Camelot is not responsible for the distribution of funds to the Good Causes which are distributed by the NLDF. Camelot aims to raise £10 billion for the Good Causes by 2001.

Good Causes

These receive weekly funds from the NLDF. For the year ended March 1998 these totalled £1,566.8 million. Each of the five Good Causes has a specific agenda to promote:

The Arts Councils of England, Northern Ireland, Scotland, and Wales To help people to take part in and enjoy the broadest range of arts activities, helping young people to develop their talent, as well as capital projects.

The Millennium Commission To fund millennium projects that make a substantial contribution to their community, as well as promoting a nationwide programme of events in the year 2000.

National Heritage Lottery Fund To safeguard and enhance the heritage of the United Kingdom.

National Lottery Charities Board Gives grants to help those at the greatest disadvantage and to improve the quality of life in the community. The first three programmes focused on poverty, community involvement, and health and social research.

The Sports Councils of England, Northern Ireland, Scotland, and Wales To help people across the UK enjoy sports of all kinds. They give awards to initiatives as well as individuals.

Each of the 11 grant-making bodies has its own application and decision-making procedure.

In addition to the five Good Causes, two new bodies have been set up:

New Opportunities Fund A non-departmental public body sponsored by the Department for Culture, Media, and Sports. This was created by the National Lottery Act 1998 and is responsible for distributing National Lottery grants throughout the UK, for health, education, and environment initiatives. The initiatives are determined by Government after consultation. An initial £1 billion was given to fund three grant programmes: healthy living centres; out of school hours childcare and out of school hours learning; and ICT training for teachers, school librarians, and librarians' activities.

National Endowment for Science, Technology and the Arts (NESTA) This was set up by the Government as part of the National Lottery Act 1998, and is due for full launch at the end of July 1999. It has a one-off grant of £200 million from the lottery to be used as an endowment. The interest from this capital, an estimated £12 million per year, will be given out as grants to relevant organizations. Unlike other grant-giving bodies, NESTA's primary activity will be the support of individuals, rather than organizations.

Top 10 Awards from the National Lottery Distribution Fund

As of 31 March 1999.

Rank	Recipient	Project name	Award amount (£)	Award date	Distributing body
1	English National Stadium Trust	English National Stadium, Wembley	120,000,000	17 October 1997	The English Sports Council
2	Royal Opera House Covent Garden Ltd	Restoration, refurbishment, and extension of Royal Opera House	55,000,000	17 July 1995	Arts Council of England
3=	Tate Gallery	Tate Gallery of Modern Art, Bankside	50,000,000	18 October 1995	Millennium Commission
	The Earth Centre Millennium Partnership	The Earth Centre, Doncaster	50,000,000	20 September 1995	Millennium Commission
	Birmingham City Council	Digbeth Millennium Campus	50,000,000	16 October 1996	Millennium Commission
6	Welsh Rugby Union and South Glamorgan	Welsh National Stadium	46,000,000	23 February 1996	Millennium Commission
7	The Ulster Museum and Sheridan Group	The Odyssey Project	45,000,000	11 June 1997	Millennium Commission
8	Sustrans	National Cycle Network	43,500,000	6 September 1995	Millennium Commission
9	Bristol 2000 Ltd	Bristol 2000	41,300,000	16 May 1996	Millennium Commission
10	Salford City Council	Creation of The Lowry Centre	41,000,000	21 February 1996	Arts Council of England

Source: National Lottery Commission, © Crown copyright 1999

National Lottery Winners and Prizes

As of 30 March 1999.

Total number of winners	332,593,096
Total number of millionaires created	763
Total number of tickets worth more than one million	887
Biggest win on a single ticket	£22,590,829[1]
Biggest jackpot prize[2]	£42,008,610[3]

1 To 10 June 1995.
2 To 31 March 1998.
3 Shared by three tickets.

Source: *Camelot Annual Review 1998*, Camelot Group plc

National Lottery Totals

As of 30 March 1999.
(In pounds.)

Total	Amount (£)
Sales since launch	>21.8 billion
Amount passed to Good Causes[1]	>6.5 billion
Paid to lottery retailers in sales commission	>1.1 billion
Paid to the Government in lottery duty	>2.6 billion
Online and Instants Prizes allocated	10.4 billion
Unclaimed prizes gone to Good Causes from the online game	>195.6 million
Camelot's charitable donations	12 million[2]
Cumulative profit after tax	187 million[2]

1 Includes unclaimed prizes and contribution from Instants.
2 To 12 September 1998.

Source: Camelot Group plc

Web Sites

British Immigration and Visa Requirements

http://193.114.50.10/travel/visa.asp

Clear explanation of UK entry requirements.

British Official Publications: Library and Information Resources

http://www-sul.stanford.edu/depts/jonsson/brit.html

Comprehensive set of resources available for viewing UK government documents.

Budget

http://www.hm-treasury.gov.uk/pub/html/budget.html

Frequently updated information on Britain's Budget from the Treasury.

CA Net

http://www.dss.gov.uk/ca/index.htm

Guide to Britain's national insurance system.

Citizen's Charter Unit

http://www.open.gov.uk/charter/ccuhome.htm

This official explanation of the work of the Unit explains the various charters, provides discussion documents, explains how to complain about government services, and invites public feedback.

Consumer Reports

http://www.consumerreports.org/

Online consumer magazine featuring articles and test results.

Consumer World

http://www.consumerworld.org/

A non-commercial resource for consumers.

Licensing Agency

http://www.cla.co.uk/

UK Reproduction Rights Organization Web site. The organization provides online documentation about the UK copyright laws.

Her Majesty's Customs and Excise

http://www.hmce.gov.uk/

Information for businesses and the public about UK Customs regulations and allowances.

HM Land Registry

http://www.open.gov.uk/landreg/home.htm

Explanation of the role of the land registration agency for England and Wales.

HSE – Health and Safety Executive

http://www.open.gov.uk/hse/hsehome.htm

Explanation of HSE's role in protecting the health of the British workforce.

Inland Revenue and National Insurance Contributions Office

http://www.inlandrevenue.gov.uk

The site contains detailed information about individual and business tax.

Mortgages Online

http://www.mortgages-online.co.uk

Independent mortgage advice online.

Office of Fair Trading

http://www.oft.gov.uk/

Site of the agency charged with protecting consumers and enforcing UK competition policy.

Oftel

http://www.oftel.gov.uk/

Comprehensive details of the watchdog agency overseeing Britain's telecommunications industry.

OFWAT – Office of Water Services

http://www.open.gov.uk/ofwat/index.htm

Description of the role of the agency charged with monitoring and regulating the supply of water in the UK.

Patent Office – Home Page

http://www.patent.gov.uk/

Guide around the notions surrounding rights and intellectual property.

Royal Mail

http://www.royalmail.co.uk

Official and comprehensive coverage of postal services in the UK.

Source, The

http://www.statistics.gov.uk/

UK government service Web site that provides easy access to statistics, including demographics.

Trading Standards Central

http://www.tradingstandards.gov.uk/index.htm

The site includes sections on 'Safety warnings', 'For business', 'For consumers', 'For schools', 'Legislation', and 'Europe'.

UK Passport Agency

http://www.open.gov.uk/ukpass/ukpass.htm

Comprehensive information on who is eligible to get a passport and how to obtain or renew one.

UK PAYE Tax Calculator

http://listen.to/taxman

A quick, unofficial calculator to work out your personal tax liability.

Welsh Consumer Council

http://www.wales.consumer.org.uk/index.english.htm

National consumer body for Wales.

PEOPLE

People in the News

Family Matters

UK foster parents, Jeff and Jenny Bramley, go on the run with five-year-old Jade and three-year-old Hannah Bennett on **13 September 1998,** after Cambridgeshire's social services department refuse them permission to adopt the half-sisters who have been in their care for six months. On **14 January 1999** an open letter from Cambridgeshire's head of social services offers to let the courts decide on the future of the children.

Diane Blood gives birth to a son, Liam, on **11 December 1998** having fought a long legal battle to use the frozen sperm of her late husband Stephen, who died in February 1995.

British prime minister Tony Blair faces controversy after allowing his children to miss the beginning of the **January 1999** school term owing to a New Year break in the Seychelles. Education secretary David Blunkett had recently announced plans to clamp down on term-time absenteeism caused by parents' holiday arrangements.

Scary Spice Girl Melanie Gulzar Brown gives birth to a daughter, Phoenix Chi, at London's Portland Hospital, on **19 February 1999.**

Identical twins Ermelinda and Nuccia Nicotra, aged 40, give birth at exactly the same time – to a boy and a girl respectively – in Catania, Sicily, at 3.35 p.m. on **22 February 1999.**

Posh Spice Girl Victoria Adams gives birth to a son, Brooklyn Joseph Beckham, on **4 March 1999;** he is named after the New York suburb in which the pregnancy was confirmed. Proud father Manchester United midfielder David Beckham has 'Brooklyn' tattooed on his back and embroidered on his football boots.

Condomi's vegan-friendly condoms are launched in mid-**April 1999;** the milk protein casein, normally used in production, has been replaced by cocoa powder.

Bechet Dumaine Allen, daughter of Woody Allen and Soon-Yi Previn, the adopted daughter of his former partner Mia Farrow, makes her first public appearance in Central Park, New York in **April 1999.**

A report in **May 1999** by a team of doctors in Modena, Italy, suggests that between 5 p.m. and 5.30 p.m. the average man is 35 percent more potent than he is at 7 a.m., making it the optimum time to conceive.

Nicola Pridham enters the record books when she gives birth in **May 1999** to her 20th child.

In China, a newborn baby survives a fall through the open squat toilet of a high-speed train as it leaves the southern city of Guangzhou in **May 1999.** The mother, Yang Zhua, let the baby slip after giving birth prematurely.

Estelle and Pierre-Alain Renaudin are denied the right to call their son the biblical Zébulon in **May 1999** by a judge in Besançon, France. He feels that the name, the French counterpart of Zebedee in the children's animation *The Magic Roundabout,* would 'due to its televisual connotations...provoke sarcasm and mockery.'

A primary school teacher in Lanarkshire, Scotland, is convicted of assault in **May 1999** for smacking his eight-year-old daughter on her bare bottom in a health centre waiting room after she refused to have a tooth out.

Jack and Zena Briggs seek the intervention of the UK Home Office on **26 May 1999,** after being on the run for six years. They have been hounded by bounty hunters and death threats from Zena's family following her rejection of an arranged marriage with a cousin in Pakistan and marriage to a white man.

Leading Mormon David Kingston of Salt Lake City, Utah, USA, is found guilty in **June 1999** of incest and unlawful sex with his 15th wife, who is also his 16-year-old niece, focusing attention on the fundamentalist Mormon practice of polygamy.

Romance

Shane and Donna McLaughlin have a memorable wedding day in **August 1998** when 22 police are called in to separate an all-out fight between the 70 guests at their reception in Horfield, near Bristol, England. Order is restored by spraying CS gas and charging the mob in riot gear.

Carla Germaine and Greg Cordell marry on **25 January 1999,** 30 seconds after they first met through a competition on Birmingham's BRMB radio station. Their prizes include a free honeymoon in the Bahamas, a year's free use of a motor car, and 12 months' rent-free accommodation. On **14 April 1999** it is announced that the couple have split.

Prince Charles and his previously under-cover consort Camilla Parker-Bowles make their first public appearance together as they leave a 50th birthday party at the Ritz in London, England, on **28 January 1999.**

Pop icons BBC radio and TV presenter Zoë Ball, and DJ and musician Norman Cook (Fatboy Slim) announce their engagement after a Valentine's Day proposal in **February 1999.**

More than one in five people in the UK said they had sex at work according to a *Guardian* poll in **April 1999.** Desktops were the most popular venue, the next most popular being the boss's office.

Triathlon competitors Mike Gambril and Barbara Cole are married while taking part in the 19th London Marathon on **18 April 1999.** The bride wears a Lycra gown, and the bridegroom a lightweight top hat and tails.

Eighty-seven percent of women still believe in a 'Mr Right' according to a survey published in the **May 1999** edition of UK *Elle* magazine.

James Major, son of former UK prime minister John Major, weds former TV quiz show hostess Emma Noble in the Crypt Chapel of the House of Commons on **28 May 1999.** Rights to their wedding photos are sold to *Hello!* for a reported £400,000.

A ban on kissing in public parks in Caracas, Venezuela, issued in 1997 by former mayor and Miss Universe Irene Saez to clean up the look of the city, is lifted on **2 June 1999.**

At their wedding service in St George's chapel in Windsor, England, on **19 June 1999,** Sophie Rhys-Jones promises to obey her husband Prince Edward.

Endings

Rock superstar Mick Jagger contests former Texan supermodel Jerry Hall's petition for divorce in **January 1999,** on the grounds that their Hindu wedding ceremony in Bali in 1990 was not legal. The couple have been together for 21 years and have four children.

The UK magazine *Chat,* holds a competition in **February 1999,** promising £500 towards solicitors' fees for the reader who sends in the best reason for wanting a divorce.

England footballer Paul Gascoigne agrees to a settlement with his former wife Sheryl in **February 1999,** worth over £1 million. The couple were divorced in August 1998 on the grounds of the Middlesbrough midfielder's unreasonable behaviour.

Australian cancer sufferer June Burns pleads for her right to die in the first of a series of four commercials commissioned by the New South Wales branch of the Voluntary Euthanasia Society. The advertisements, approved for broadcast on Australian television from **15 March 1999,** were branded as a macabre stunt by pro-life organizations.

Pamela Anderson, former *Baywatch* babe and the subject of the Internet's favourite video-clip, has her breast implants removed in **April 1999,** as she wants her body to go back to its natural state.

Retired US pathologist Jack Kevorkian, an advocate of euthanasia and assisted suicide, who had filmed himself giving a lethal injection to a dying man, is convicted of second degree murder and jailed for 10–25 years on **13 April 1999.** He had earned the nickname Dr Death for helping at least 130 people end their lives since 1990.

The frozen corpse of English mountaineer George Mallory is found on Everest on **1 May 1999;** he had disappeared on 8 June 1924. It was hoped that film contained in his primitive Kodak camera would establish whether he was the first to reach the summit, but this is not retrieved.

Radio presenter Anne Diamond and her husband of 10 years, Mike Hollingworth, are divorced on **4 May 1999** following the highly publicized breakdown of their marriage.

Julia Clark, 49, has a half million pound divorce settlement from her millionaire octogenarian husband cut to £175,000 by UK Appeal Court judges in **May 1999,** on the grounds that she had abused him, refused to consummate the marriage, and siphoned off his wealth for herself and her 34-year-old lover.

A GP in Newcastle upon Tyne, England, Dave Moor, is cleared of murdering terminally ill George Liddell, aged 85, on **11 May 1999,** after being accused of injecting him with lethal dose of diamorphine. The case highlights issues concerning euthanasia in the UK.

In the Limelight

The amateur rock group Alive, a teenage band from Rochdale and Bury, are booked to perform for Prince Charles' 50th birthday on **13 November 1998** after offering their services to Buckingham Palace.

Nejla Kanteper, aged 14 years, sets fire to herself at a rally in **February 1999** outside the Greek Embassy in London to show support for the Kurd leader Abdullah Ocalan.

Californian Patricia Henley, aged 53, who suffers from inoperable lung cancer, is awarded more than $51 million punitive damages against Philip Morris, maker of Marlboro cigarettes on **11 February 1999.** She claims that she had become hooked on nicotine before health warnings were issued, and pledged to donate any money received to the education of youngsters on smoking issues.

Barbie, the world's best-selling doll, celebrates her 40th birthday in **March 1999** with a new dress encrusted with 160 diamonds and jewellery accessories in 18 carat white gold made by the diamond company De Beers. It is estimated to be worth £50,000.

In **April 1999** it is reported that Earl Spencer's funeral oration for his sister, Diana, Princess of Wales, is to be included in a school textbook as an example of effective use of English.

Multiple sclerosis sufferer Zoe Kiplowitz crosses the finishing line of the London Marathon on **20 April 1999** amidst rush hour traffic, having completed the course in 30 hours.

The sight of US film star Julia Roberts' unshaven armpits at the London premier of her film *Notting Hill* in **May 1999** provides many media images and much discussion in the press.

Open University beat Oriel College, Oxford, in the **May 1999** final of the BBC's *University Challenge.* Quizmaster Jeremy Paxman later berates the winning team for their use of 'professional quiz player' Lance Haward, who had notched up over 30 appearances on other quiz shows, including *Mastermind,* and had joined an Open University course to qualify for the Challenge.

US actress Sarah Michell Gellar, star of TV's *Buffy the Vampire Slayer,* is voted the world's sexiest female in the UK magazine *FHM* poll in **May 1999.** In the same month singer Robbie Williams is voted the sexiest man of the century by readers of UK *Company* magazine.

In **May 1999,** Prince William becomes the secretary of the agricultural society at his school, Eton College.

Record Breakers

French-born American Ben Lecomte begins a world record swim across the Atlantic from Hyannis, Massachusetts, USA, on **16 July 1998,** reaching Quiberon, France, on **September 25 1998.** The 5,900 km/3,700 mi journey is achieved with the aid of a large double-footed flipper, and raises £100,000 for a Scottish-based cancer charity.

Geoff Smith of Mansfield, Nottingham, England, begins his bid to beat the world record for being buried alive on **29 August 1998,** emerging successfully 147 days later on **17 January 1999.** He intended to regain

the record for his mother, whose 101 days of interment in 1968 had been beaten in 1981, but later learns that the *Guinness Book of Records* had removed the category for safety reasons.

Four teams of windsurfers make the first crossing of the Atlantic by board from St John's in Newfoundland, Canada, to Weymouth, Dorset, England, in **September 1998.**

Nepalese climber Kaji Sherpa achieves the quickest climb of Everest in **October 1998,** taking 20 hours 24 minutes to reach the summit from base camp without supplementary oxygen. He is sponsored by a Danish brewing company.

Bungy-jumper A J Hackett leaps from Auckland's Sky Tower in New Zealand, freefalling the 180 m/594 ft at 130 km/80 mi per hour, to create a new record for jumping from a man-made structure on **5 October 1998.**

Malaysian Mahaguru Sani, a former zoo keeper, claims the world record for the longest period surrounded by poisonous snakes on **13 March 1999,** having survived 35 days closeted with 250 king cobras. The feat was condemned by Friends of the Earth.

The Breitling Orbiter 3 balloon, manned by Swiss psychiatrist Bertrand Piccard and Briton Brian Jones, achieves the non-stop round-the-world ballooning record on **20 March 1999,** having completed the 41,600 km/26,000 mi from Switzerland to Mauritania in 19 days.

Disabled Londoner Andrew Halsey, a sufferer of epileptic seizures, sets off in **May 1999** to row non-stop across the Pacific from San Diego, USA, to Sydney, Australia, in an attempt to become the first to row unsupported from west to east. His bullet-shaped vessel, the *Brittany Rose,* carried him across the Atlantic in 1997.

New York resident Michael Hebranko is admitted to hospital on **7 June 1999** to undergo treatment for obesity. Unable to fit his 495 kg/78 st 8 lb frame through the front door, he is forklifted through a dismantled window on to a stretcher normally used to transport small whales. Ten years previously Hebranko had achieved a record weight loss of 318 kg/50 st to reach 89 kg/ 14 st, and was listed in the *Guinness Book of Records.*

Red Faces

BBC *Blue Peter* presenter Richard Bacon is sacked from the long-running children's TV show in **October 1998** after he admitted taking cocaine. The BBC later denies that it would be scrapping the *Blue Peter Annual,* which includes a photograph of Bacon in a greenhouse under the caption 'Pot it!'.

US film star Tom Cruise is turned away from a branch of Blockbuster Video in Hertfordshire, England, in **October 1998** because he cannot supply the two forms of ID necessary to join, even though his face appears on numerous video jackets in the store.

Thames Valley police are forced to close the Newbury bypass on **10 January 1999** when 250 environmentalists commemorate the eviction of protesters from the route of the controversial roadway in 1996; banners are flown, and hedgehogs, bike lanes, and warning signs drawn in the fast lane.

Ron Roberts flies from Australia to Britain for his mother's funeral in **January 1999,** only to be told she is still alive following an error of identification with another Mrs Roberts, deceased, at the Royal Liverpool University Hospital.

Chief Inspector of Schools in the UK, Chris Woodhead's remarks in **January 1999** about relationships between teachers and sixth-formers being 'educative' raises an outcry, and causes further embarrassment in **March 1999** after his ex-wife accuses him of beginning an affair with his 17-year-old former pupil, Amanda Johnston, while he was a teacher at the Gordano School.

David Howard, a white assistant to the mayor of Washington DC, USA, resigns amid allegations that he had used the word 'nigger' in a conversation with a black colleague on **15 January 1999.** The latter took Howard's phrase, 'I will have to be niggardly with this fund,' as being racially abusive.

England coach Glen Hoddle is sacked by the Football Association on **2 February 1999** following remarks which suggest that he believes disabled people are paying for indiscretions committed in previous lives, and his refusal to disassociate himself from faith healer Eileen Drewery.

Japan's minister of justice, Shozaburo Nakamura, hands in his notice on **10 March 1999,** after allowing Arnold Schwarzenegger entry into the country without a passport the previous October and mislaying his letter of explanation; the minister admits to being a fan of the actor. Schwarzenegger had reported his American passport stolen.

Prince Charles' visit of reconciliation to Buenos Aires in **March 1999** sparks off an international diplomatic incident when he expresses the hope, 'that the people of modern democratic Argentina ...will be able to live amicably alongside the people of another modern, if rather smaller democracy lying a few hundred miles off your coast.' Vice-president Carlos Ruckauf declares that Britain had 'stolen the Falklands', and the Union Jack is burnt on the streets.

Passengers of a British Airways flight from San Francisco in **April 1999,** who are wrongly told that they are about to crash into the sea, later receive a box of Belgian chocolates and an apology.

Tom Parker-Bowles, 24 year-old son of Camilla and godson of Prince Charles, is quoted by undercover journalists at the Cannes Film Festival in **May 1999** as having admitted to using cocaine.

Laurence Dallaglio resigns as England's rugby captain on **24 May 1999,** the eve of England's tour to Australia, after the *News of the World* published extracts from a taped interview, alleging that he had used and sold drugs. Dallaglio denies ever having dealt in drugs.

David Yelland, editor of *The Sun,* apologises to Prince Edward's fiancee, Sophie Rhys-Jones, and Buckingham Palace on **27 May 1999** after publishing an 11-year-old photo of Sophie topless with broadcaster Chris Tarrant, which had been supplied by their former colleague Kara Noble.

US tabloid photographer Eric Ford is sentenced in **May 1999** to six months in a halfway house, fined $3,000, and ordered to carry out 150 hours of community service work for tapping Nicole Kidman and Tom Cruise's phone and selling recordings of their conversations to the press during February 1998.

Esther Kelbie of Dundee, Scotland, makes British legal history in **June 1999** by becoming the first officially registered nuisance neighbour.

The Duke of Edinburgh affronts members of the British Deaf Association during celebrations in Cardiff marking the opening of the Welsh assembly on **26 May 1999.** When a leader tried to introduce him to a group of deaf youngsters, who were standing near the loudspeakers of a Caribbean steel band, he commented, 'Deaf? If you are near there, no wonder you are deaf', and walked on.

Rich Pickings

Millard Drexler of the Gap clothing chain is ranked America's top-earning executive in **January 1999,** having amassed $482 million in salary, bonuses, and stock options, closely followed by Timothy Koogle of the Yahoo! internet company with $476 million. The analysis conducted for *USA Today* includes unrealized gains on options.

English Formula One driver Damon Hill, racing for Jordan, is ranked number one in the pay line for British sport in **January 1999,** with earnings in 1998 of £6.9 million. However, his projected earnings for 1999 of £8.5 million place him in second place behind boxer Lennox Lewis, whose earnings are forecast at £23.1 million.

The Internazionale and Brazil striker Ronaldo is top of the season's football pay league, earning about £5.7 million on and off the field. Manchester United's David Beckham emerges in **April 1999** as the second highest paid footballer in the world, with earnings of just over £3 million.

A list of the thousand richest in Britain published by *The Sunday Times* on **11 April 1999** is headed by Hans Rausing, whose father patented the milk carton, with £3.4 billion, followed by Lord Sainsbury of Turville, with £3.1 billion, and financier George Soros, around £2 billion. Aristocrats make up less than a third of the list for the first time. The richest woman is Lady Grantchester who, with £1.5 billion, is reportedly six times wealthier than the Queen.

Michael Eisner, head of Disney, sees his bonus shrink from $9.9 million (£6 million) last year to $5 million after an unsuccessful year end, it is announced in **April 1999.** However, his salary went to $764,423 from $750,000 and he exercised stock options worth $569.8 million, making him America's richest employee. He also signed a contract guaranteeing another $700 million if Disney's share prices rise 10 percent over 10 years.

Ninety British multimillionaires aged 30 or under are identified by an *Observer* investigation in **April 1999.** Aristocratic heirs ranked highest, with the Earl of Burlington, aged 30, topping the list with an anticipated inheritance of £750 million. Leading the business roll was Tahir Mohsan of Time Computer Systems, who was valued at £27 million, followed by internet services provider Jason Drummond, with £24 million. Only two of the top ten young entrepreneurs operated outside the IT industry. Spice Girl Victoria Adams was the richest young entertainer with an estimated personal wealth of £24 million.

The Hinduja brothers, leaders of a global trading, oil, and banking family, are ranked as Britain's richest Asians by *Eastern Eye* in **April 1999.** Srichand and Gopi are declared worth £1.3 billion and £1.2 billion respectively.

Alex Ferguson of Manchester United becomes the highest-paid manager in the history of British football following a pay settlement on **4 May 1999.**

Prince Charles is ranked the sixth richest individual European royal by *EuroBusiness,* in **June 1999,** with an estimated fortune of £299 million, £6.5 million more than his mother, Queen Elizabeth II. Buckingham Palace dismisses the estimates as 'overblown'.

UK top management receive an average 9 percent increase in salaries over last year's average £546,000 salary, excluding share options, according to a Monks Partnership listing issued in **June 1999.** After allowing for inflation this was three-and-a-half times more than the percentage pay rise for the average British employee.

New Directions

English television broadcaster and producer Janet Street-Porter is appointed general secretary of the Ramblers' Association in **November 1998.**

The vicar of a church in Macclesfield, Cheshire, enrols on a circus skills course in **April 1999** so that he can liven up his sermons.

Prince Andrew launches the Royal family's on-line magazine at a Buckingham Palace Road internet café on **7 April 1999.** The site includes a gold state coach to print, cut out, and keep.

Disillusioned with the beef industry, a farmer in Telford, Shropshire, gives up cattle rearing and buys 100 parrots for breeding, it is reported in **May 1999.**

Musician Paul McCartney launches the first public exhibition of his artwork at The Art Forum in Siegen, near Cologne, Germany, on **1 May 1999.** He began painting seriously in the 1980s.

London Underground reports that recordings of a Marilyn Monroe soundalike will begin to replace current on-train announcements from **May 1999.** Research has shown that passengers favour her breathy, seductive tones.

Artist Damien Hirst announces in **June 1999** that he will be providing a specially commissioned spot painting for calibration purposes during the *Beagle 2* landing on Mars, part of Europe's Mars Express mission in June 2003.

In **June 1999,** The Vatican permits nuns in cloistered orders to surf the Web and have mobile telephones although television and radio access remain restricted to religious broadcasting.

Obituaries in Brief

Deaths: July–December 1998

Abdoulkarim Mohamed Taki, 63, politician, president of the Comoros Islands 1996–98; 6 November

Abdul-Rahman, Aisha, 85, Egyptian leading Islamic female scholar and writer; 1 December

Abiola Moshood Kashimawoo Olawale, 60, Nigerian politician, leader of the opposition, won the 1993 elections annulled by his rival General Abacha; 2 July

Acklin Barbara, 54, US singer, famous for 'Am I the Same Girl' (1968) and albums *Someone Else's Arms* (1970), *I Did It* (1971), and *I Call It Trouble;* 27 November

Adams Johnny (Laten John), 66, US blues and soul singer of international recognition; 14 September

Addison John Mervyn, 68, English composer of film, ballet, theatre, and concert music; 7 December

Agate John, 79, English geriatrician who developed and championed new techniques of rehabilitation for elderly patients; 31 October

Ajit (Hamid Ali Khan), 76, Indian actor famous for his roles as a villain; 21 October

Albright William Hugh, 53, US composer, organist, and teacher, known mostly for his compositions for piano and organ; 17 September

Allen William Alexander, 84, Canadian-born architect active in the UK who worked on a wide range of projects including the Gulbenkian Museum, Lisbon, Portugal; 14 December

Alphonso Roland, 67, US saxophonist, composer, and arranger, a founding member of the Skatalites; 20 November

Ambler Eric, 89, English writer famous for his thrillers; 23 October

Anselm Aleksei Andreevich, 64, Russian theoretical physicist known for his work on the Higgs particles and on the CP violation; 23 August

Arzubide Germán List, 100, Mexican poet, writer, and revolutionary, author of *El movimiento estridentista* (1926); 19 October

Autry Orvon Gene, 91, US actor known for his roles in westerns; 2 October

Barer Marshall Louis, 75, US lyricist, librettist, singer, songwriter, and director; 25 August

Barnes Binnie (Gertrude Maude), 95, English-born US actress, known for her role in *The Private Life Of Henry VIII* and for her philanthropy; 27 July

Barriteau Carl, 84, British clarinet and saxophone player, born in Trinidad, later Australian citizen, associated with the style of Artie Shaw, member of Cyril Stapleton's band in 1951; 24 August

Bartok Eva Martha (born Szoke), 82, Hungarian-born British actress, famous for *The Crimson Pirate* and *Blood and Black Lace;* 1 August

Bates Clayton 'Peg Legs', 92, US tap dancer who, despite having only one leg, developed a career that spanned over six decades; 6 December

Béchervaise John Mayston, 88, Australian polar explorer and author who popularized Australia's involvement in the Antarctic programme; 13 July

Bennett Charles Moihi Te Arawaka, 85, Maori soldier, diplomat, and civil servant active in New Zealand, who distinguished himself promoting the rights of the Maori people; 26 November

Beriosova Svetlana, 66, Russian ballerina born in modern-day Lithuania, active in England, principal dancer of the Sadler's Wells Theatre Ballet and the Royal Ballet; 10 November

Bingham Alfred Mitchell, 93, US writer, politician, and lawyer, author of *Violence & Democracy* (1970) and a liberal; 2 November

Blanchflower Jackie (John), 65, British footballer, survivor of Manchester United's plane crash in Munich in 1958; 2 September

Bogatyrev Alexander Yurievich, 49, Russian dancer born in modern-day Estonia, principal dancer and then acting artistic director of the Moscow Bolshoi Ballet 1995–97; 11 October

Boon Ronnie (Ronald) Winston, 89, Welsh sportsman, rugby player, cricketer, and athlete, a physical education teacher; 3 August

Boswell Eve (Eva Keleti), 74, Hungarian-born pop singer, active mainly in the 1950s, versatile and popular performer; 13 August

Bowden Ray (Edwin Raymond), 89, English footballer who won six England caps 1934–36; 23 September

Boyd-Carpenter John Archibald, 90, English politician, minister of transport and civil aviation 1954–55, minister of pensions and national insurance 1955–62, paymaster general 1962–64; 11 July

Bradley Thomas, 80, US police officer and politician, campaigner for racial equality, black liberal mayor of Los Angeles from 1973; 29 September

Brossa Joan, 79, Spanish Catalan poet, member of the avant-garde and a surrealist, author of 'object poems'; 30 December

Bryden Beryl, 78, English jazz singer, washboard player, and photographer; 14 July

Cairncross Alexander Kirkland, Scottish economist, chancellor of Glasgow University 1972–96, and economic adviser to the government; 21 October

Calamai Clara, 89 (or 83), Italian actress, first to appear topless in an Italian film (1941); 21 September

Carmichael Stokely (Kwame Ture), 57, Trinidad-born US radical political activist, author of *Black Power* (1967); 15 November. (See full obituary p. 876.)

Carpenter Edward Frederick, 87, English priest, Dean of Westminster 1974–85; 26 August

Carter Betty (Lillie Mae Jones), 69, US jazz singer with a distinctive style, and a popular teacher; 26 September

César real name César Baldaccini, 77, French sculptor, a member of the avant-garde New Realism movement, famous for his 'squash-and-melt' approach; 6 December

Chadwick John, 78, English classical scholar who, together with Michael Ventris, deciphered the Linear B script; 24 November

Chino Wendell, 74, US activist and minister of the Dutch Reformed Church, noted for his championing of the rights of American Indian peoples; 4 November

Clancy Paddy, 76, Irish singer, a founding member of the Irish folk group the Clancy Brothers; 11 November

Clark Dane (Bernard Zanville), 85, US actor known for his portrayals of intense, rebel, or dissatisfied personalities; 11 September

Clements-Mann Mary Lou, 51, US epidemiologist, professor at the John Hopkins University 1985–98 and director of the John Hopkins Center for Immunisation Research; died in a plane crash with husband Jonathan **Mann;** 2 September

Clifford Clark McAdams, 91, US lawyer and presidential adviser, associated with Harry Truman and John F Kennedy; 10 October

Clifford Judith Gay (Gay Allis Rose Clifford), English scholar, writer, and poet; 22 July

Clifford Ruth, 98, US actress, best known for her role in *Butterfly* (1924); 30 November

Collingwood Vera (Vera Ester Maria Fratoni), 77, Italian-born photographer active in England, known for her photographs of National Trust properties and stately homes; 1 September

Connell Philip Henry, 77, English psychiatrist who specialized in working with children and young people, investigated drug dependencies, and was involved in medical management; 26 July

Cotes Peter (born Sydney Arthur Rembrandt Boulting), 86, English actor, producer, and director; 10 November

Crewe Quentin Hugh Dodds, 72, English journalist, traveller, and writer; 14 November

Cristòfol Leandre, *c.* 90, Spanish carpenter and sculptor, famous for his surrealist, abstract, and *arte povera* structures; 19 August

Crowson John Lamar, 72, US pianist and teacher, famous for his performances of chamber music; 25 August

Deems Barrett, 84, US drummer and band-leader, known as 'the fastest drummer in the world', associated with Louis Armstrong's All Stars; 15 September

Delamuraz Jean-Pascal, 62, Swiss politician, twice president of Switzerland; 4 October

Denevi Marco, 76, Argentinian writer , author of 'Ceremonia secreta/Secret Ceremony' (1960), *Un pequeño café/A Small Café* (1967), *El jardín de las delicias/Garden of Delights* (1992); 12 December

Denison John Michael Terence Wellesley, 82, English actor particularly noted for his stage performances in the 1960s; 22 July

Denning Richard, Jr (born Ludwig Albert Heindrich Denninger), 84, US actor who starred in *Beyond the Blue Horizon* (1942) and appeared in B thrillers and westerns; 11 October

Douglas Carolyn Maynard (born Williamson), 58, Welsh family therapist, founder (in 1982) and co-director of Exploring Parenthood; 3 September

Driftwood Jimmy (James Corbett Morris), 91, US songwriter, singer, teacher, and conservationist; 12 July

Drury Allen Stuart, 80, US political journalist and novelist, famous for his *Advise and Consent* (1959); 2 September

Dudintsev Vladimir, 79, writer born in the Ukraine and active in Russia, famous for his anti-totalitarian *Not By Bread Alone* (1956) and *White Coats;* 23 July

Dumont Louis, 87, French anthropologist born in Greece, known in particular for his contribution to the history and anthropology of India; 19 November

Dunnett Alastair MacTavish, 89, Scottish journalist, editor of *The Scotsman* 1956–72; 2 September

Dutton Geoffrey Piers Henry, 76, Australian author of poetry, novels, and literary criticism; 17 September

Edwards Penny (Millicent Maxine), US actress, star of B westerns; 26 August

Elliott Margaret Mary, 77, historian of science, fellow of the Royal Society and the British Academy; 7 November

English Donald, 68, English Methodist minister and teacher, committed to working with other churches; 28 August

Farlow Tal (Talmadge) Holt, 77, US jazz guitarist and gifted technician of the instrument, member of the Norvo's trio; 25 July

Feathers Charlie Arthur, 66, US singer and guitarist, eccentric rockabilly performer; 29 August

Feibusch Hans Nathan, 99, German-born English painter and muralist, famous for his church works; 18 July

Fell Norman, 74, US actor known for his character roles; 14 December

Ferragamo Fiamma, 57, Italian designer and businesswoman, famous for her designs of shoes and accessories; 28 September

Feuillère Edwige Caroline (born Cunati), 91, French actress, one of the most memorable character actresses of the 20th century; 14 November

Fiorentino Sergio, 70, Italian pianist and acclaimed teacher; 22 August

Flowers Tommy (Thomas Harold), 92, English engineer, leader of the team that constructed Colossus at Bletchley Park, the first electronic programmable computer used for codebreaking during World War II; 28 October

Forest Jean-Claude, 68, French cartoonist, creator of *Barbarella;* 30 December

Forster Jackie (Jacqueline Moir Mackenzie), 81, gay rights activist, founder of the magazine *Sappho* in 1972, editor, and broadcaster; 10 October

Fougeron André Alfred, 84, French artist, the most prominent socialist realist painter in the history of French art; 10 September

Fowlie Wallace, 89, US literary scholar; 16 August

Foxx Charlie (Charles), 58, US singer, guitarist, and songwriter, famous for his rhythm 'n' blues duo with his sister Inez; 18 September

Freeman Ralph Anthony, 52, English civil and structural engineer, constructor of the Britannia Rail Bridge in north Wales, the Avonmouth Bridge, the Ting Kau Bridge, Hong Kong, and numerous other projects in the UK and abroad; 15 July

Freeman Ralph, 87, English civil engineer, associated with the international civil engineering consultancy Freeman, Fox & Partners; 24 August

Friers Rowel Boyd, 78, British artist and cartoonist active in Northern Ireland, author of politically-charged satirical drawings and cartoons in the British and Irish press; 21 September

Frost Eunice Ellen, 83, English publisher involved with Penguin Books; 12 August

Fuhrop Roland Walter (known as **Tiny Rowland**), 80, British businessman and entrepreneur of Dutch-German origin, born in India; 24 July. (See full obituary p. 889.)

Gable Christopher Michael, 58, English dancer, actor, and choreographer, founder and artistic director of the Central School of Ballet 1982–98 and artistic director of the Northern Ballet Theatre 1987–98; 23 October

Gaddis William, 75, US writer famous for his 'postmodern' novel *The Recognition* (1955), creator of language experiments, whose works carried a powerful political message; 16 December

Gallie Walter Boyce, 85, English philosopher and academic teacher, known for 'Essentially Contested Concepts'; 31 August

Gandar Laurence Owen Vine, 83, South African journalist and press editor who influenced the political profile of the country's press; 15 November

Garro Elena, 69, Mexican writer and committed social activist, former wife of Octavio Paz; 22 August

Gatsonides Maurice, 87, Dutch rally driver born in Java, inventor of the timing device to curb speeding and the Gatso flash camera for the same purpose; 29 November

Gertler André, 90, Hungarian-born violinist and teacher, leader of the Gertler Quartet 1931–51; 23 July

Giant Haystacks real name Martin Ruane, 52, English wrestler of great skill and charisma; 29 November

Godden Margaret Rumer, 90, English writer, best known for *Black Narcissus* (1938), *The River* (1946), and *The Greengage Summer* (1958); 8 November. (See full obituary p. 879.)

Goldman James, 71, US playwright, screenwriter, and novelist, author of *A Lion in Winter,* filmed in 1968; 28 October

Golovine Serge, 73, dancer and teacher of Breton and Russian origin, born in Monaco, famous for the diversity of his roles; 31 July

Gonella Nat (Nathaniel) Charles, 90, English trumpeter, band-leader, and vocalist; 6 August

Goring Marius, 86, English actor, manager, and director, campaigner for the rights of actors; 30 September

Goulding Cathal, 75, Irish political activist, one-time IRA chief of staff and leader of the Official IRA; 26 December

Grade Lew (Louis Winogradsky), 91, Ukrainian-born British dancer, theatrical agent, television executive, businessman, film producer, and theatre owner, chairman and managing director of ITC Entertainment 1958–82, chairman for life 1995–98; 13 December. (See full obituary p. 879.)

Grant Ian Dawson, 73, English architect and interior designer, creator of, or consultant for, numerous interiors in central London; 27 August

Green David, 86, UK architect specializing, with Herbert Tayler, in rural housing; 3 October

Green Julien (Julian) Hartridge, 97, US writer born and active in France whose works reflect a dychotomy between spiritual purity and physical passion; 13 August

Griffith-Joyner (Delorez) Florence, 39, flamboyant US athlete known as 'Flo-Jo', record-breaking 100 and 200 metres sprinter; 21 September

Grillmeier Alois, 88, German priest and Jesuit theologian, a member of the Sacred College of Cardinals; 13 September

Grisey Gérard, 52, French composer influenced by African and Oriental music, teacher of composition, professor of orchestration and composition at the Conservatoire de Paris 1987–98; 11 November

Haggart Bob (Robert Sherwood), 84, US bassist, band-leader, and composer, a member of the Crosby band and leader of the Lawson-Haggart Jazz Band; 2 December

Hajdari Azem, 35, Albanian student leader and opposition politician, assassinated in Tirana outside his Democratic Party (DP) headquarters; 12 September

Haksar Parmeshwar Narain, 85, Indian diplomat and political advisor, principal secretary to Indira Ghandi 1967–73 and chief negotiator between India, Pakistan, and Bangladesh 1972–73; 25 November

Hanson John (John Wats), 76, British actor and singer born in Canada, known as 'the last of the matinee idols', famous for *The Desert Song;* 3 December

Häring, Bernhard, German theologian and Redemptorist priest, chair in moral theology at the Pontifical Lateran University, Rome, Italy, 1957–87; 3 July

Harmsworth, Vere Harold Esmond, Viscout Rothermere, 73, English newspaper proprietor, chairman of the *Daily Mail* and General Trust plc 1978–98; 1 September. (See full obituary p. 888.)

Hatfield (William Rukard) Hurd, 80, US actor best known for his role in *The Picture of Dorian Gray;* 25 December

Hayes Patricia, 88, English actress known for her comedy roles and impersonations; 19 September

Heino Viljo Akseli, 84, Finnish athlete, long-distance runner known as one of the 'flying Finns'; 15 September

Henriques Pauline Clothilde, 84, Jamaican-born British actress, the first black actress to appear on British television (1946), also famous for her counselling work with teenagers; 1 November

Herbert Zbigniew, 74, Polish poet whose works reflected the richness of culture and tradition as well as the autonomy and integrity of an individual; 28 July

Hervey Irene (Irene Herwick), 88, US actress popular in the 1930s and 1940s, mother of actor Jack Jones; 20 December

Hickson Joan, 92, English actress famous for her role as Mrs Marple; 17 October. (See full obituary p. 881.)

Higginbotham A(loysius) Leon, US lawyer, champion of racial integration and human and civil rights; 14 December

Higgins Dick (Richard), 60, US artist, writer, composer, and publisher, one of the leading figures in the 1960s avantgarde; 25 October

Hoban Lillian (born Aberman), 73, US illustrator of children's books; 17 July

Hobson Valerie Babette Louise, 81, British actress, wife of the politician John Profumo, campaigner for the mentally disabled; 13 November

Hodgkin Alan Lloyd, 85, English experimental biologist, best known for his research in the excitation and conduction in nerve fibres and in the mechanics of vision, who in 1963 shared the Nobel prize with Andrew Huxley; 20 December

Hoff Chet (Chester), 107, US baseball player; 17 September

Holm Anne (Anne Lise Elfe), 76, Danish writer, author of the famous book for children *I am David;* 27 December

Hopkins John Richard, 67, English writer who worked in the UK and in the USA, creator of television programmes such as *Z Cars* and *Smiley's People;* 23 July

Howard James Griffiths, English biomedical scientist who specialized in immunology; 6 October

Hughes Ted (Edward James), 68, English poet, author of *Tales from Ovid* (1997) and *Birthday Letters* (1998), Poet Laureate 1984–98; 28 October. (See full obituary p. 882.)

Hunt Henry Cecil John, 88, British mountaineer, leader of the 1952–53 Mount Everest expedition; 7 November

Ireland Derek, 49, English yoga practitioner and teacher who introduced to Europe the *astanga vinyasa* (aerobic yoga); 24 September

Ireland Jimmy (James Cecil Hardin), 94, Scottish rugby player, sports activist, and referee; 25 October

Jenkins Megs (Muguette Mary), 81, English actress popular for her stage, television, and radio character roles; 5 October

Jennings Margaret (Margaret Mabel Gladys Allan), 89, English racing and rally driver, successful in the 1930s; 21 September

John Rosamund (Nora Rosamund Jones), 85, English actress, most popular in the 1940s; 27 October

Johnson Ian, 79, Australian cricketer and captain who led the 1956 touring team; 9 October

Jones Horace Charles, 92, Welsh writer known for his provocative and critical works; 12 September

Kaiser Thomas Reeve,74, Australian space physicist who developed pioneering research in the ionisation trails of meteors; 2 July

Kane Bob (Robert Kahn), 83, US cartoonist, creator of Batman; 3 November

Karelli Zoe (Chrysoula Pentziki), 96, Greek poet, essayist, and playwright, one of the country's foremost literary figures; 16 July

Karmann Wilhelm, 83, German car manufacturer who specialized in convertibles and sports cars; 25 October

Kemmer Nicholas, 87, Russian-born British particle physicist also engaged in mathematical physics; 21 October

Kinskey Leonid, 95, US actor of Russian origin, known for his versatile character roles; 8 September

Kirkland Kenny (Kenneth David), 43, US pianist, performer of classical music and, later, jazz, who worked with Wynton Marsalis 1981–85; *c.* 12 November

Kitwood Thomas Marris, 51, English psychogerontologist who worked on Alzheimer's disease and dementia; 1 November

Koppel Herman David, 89, Danish composer, pianist, and teacher, one of Denmark's most prominent musicians; 14 July

Kurosawa Akira, 88, Japanese film director who combined motifs of Samurai history and tradition with Western archetypes; 6 September. (See full obituary p. 885.)

Kurti Nicholas, 90, Hungarian-born British physicist, participant in the UK Atomic Bomb Project 1940–45; 24 November

Lane David William Stennis Stuart, 76, English politician, the first chairman of the Commission for Racial Equality 1977–82; 16 November

Lewis Janet, 99, US poet and writer whose works are full of wisdom and empathy; 1 December

Lewis Shari (born Hurwitz), 65, US puppeteer, actress, ventriloquist, and conductor, famous for her television work for children; 2 August

Leyton Paul Henry, 84, English engineer and restaurateur, chief rocket development engineer for Saunders Roe 1956–59 and engineering director for Black & Decker 1959–61; 4 November

Lickley Robert Lang, 86, Scottish aeronautical engineer active in the UK and in the USA, who developed a model of a rotary-wing aircraft capable of vertical take-off and landing; 7 July

Lighthill Michael James, 74, English mathematician known for his work in aeronautical research, control systems, waves, and biological mechanics; 17 July

Littleton John, 68, US singer, performer of popular spiritual and liturgical music; 24 August

Lloyd George Walter Selvyn, 85, English composer, author of *Symphonic Mass* (1983) and *Litany* (1995); 3 July

McDade Butch (David Hugh), 52, US drummer, singer, and songwriter, member of the Amazing Rhythm Aces; 29 November

McDonald Dick (Richard), 89, US restaurateur who, with his brother Mac (Maurice) conceived the idea, and owned the first outlet, of the fast food chain McDonald's; 14 July

McDowall Roddy (Roderick Andrew Anthony Jude), 70, US actor remembered for his child roles in films such as *Lassie Comes Home* (1943); 3 October

MacGibbon Margot, 92, Australian-born violinist, co-founder of the Lasserson Memorial Competition in 1979; 4 September

MacLean Bryan, 52, US guitarist, singer, and songwriter in the psychedelic band Love; 25 December

McLean Francis Charles, 94, British soldier and broadcasting engineer, BBC director of engineering 1963–68; 19 December

Machlis Joseph, 92, US Latvian-born musicologist and writer, author of *The Enjoyment of Music* (1955); 17 October

Malacki Wladimir (Jean Malaquais), *c.* 90, Polish-born writer active in France, the USA, and Switzerland, author of *Les Javanais* (1938, new edition 1995); 22 December

Mann Jonathan, 51, US epidemiologist, involved in international projects and director of the François-Xavier Bagnoud Center for Health and Human Rights 1993–98; died in a plane crash with wife, Mary Lou **Clements-Mann;** 2 September

Manners David (Rauff de Ryther Duan Acklom), 96, Canadian actor active in the USA, famous for his roles in horror movies such as *Dracula, The Mummy,* and *The Black Cat;* 23 December

Manuguerra Matteo, 73, French opera singer famous for his baritone roles in Verdi's operas; 30 July

Marais Jean Alfred Villain-, 84, French actress most famous for her roles in films directed by Jean Cocteau; 8 November

Marasco Robert, 62, US playwright, author of *Child's Play* (1970); 6 December

Marion Alain, 59, French flautist associated with Pierre Boulez's L'Ensemble InterContemporain, and a celebrated teacher; 16 August

Marsden Beatrice (Betty), 79, UK actress and comedienne, famous for her impersonations; 18 July

Marsden Charles David, 60, clinical neurologist active in the UK and in the USA, who founded the Parkinson's Disease Society Brain Bank; 29 September

Marshall Everett G, 88, US actor whose diverse career spanned seven decades; 24 August

Martin William McChesney, 91, US banker, stockbroker, and public servant, associated with Truman's presidency; 27 July

Massey Andrew Christopher, 55, English soldier, commanding officer of the SAS 1984–87, deputy director of Special Forces 1990–91, operational commander of the UK special Forces for Operation Granby during the Gulf War; 19 August

Medrano Jérôme, 91, French circus owner and entrepreneur; 14 November

Miller Sigmund, 87, Austrian writer involved in entertainment and, later, in scientific reference literature; 5 August

Minetti Bernhard, 93, German character actor known for his theatrical peformances; 12 October

Misraki (Misrachi) Paul, 90, French songwriter and author born in Constantinople (modern Istanbul, Turkey) who wrote over 180 songs, 145 film scores, and a study *Pour comprende Teilhard;* 30 October

Monteverdi Peter Rosolino, 64, Swiss car designer and manufacturer, creator of a car museum in his former factory; 4 July

Moore Archie (Archibald Lee Wright), 84, US boxer, world light-heavyweight champion 1952–62; 9 December

Moore John Darrel, 64, US singer, member of the soul group The Drifters; 30 December

Morissean-Leroy Felix, *c.* 86, US poet and playwright, champion of the Creole language; 5 September

Moro Peter, 87, German architect active in the UK; 10 October

Moss Jeffrey, *c.* 56, US songwriter, composer, lyricist, poet, and writer, involved in children's television shows such as *Captain Kangaroo* and *Sesame Street;* 25 September

Munari Bruno, 90, Italian versatile artist, inventor, designer, teacher, and writer, co-founder of the MAC movement; 29 September

Murray Andrew James Jowett, 81, English journalist, painter, and etcher, known for his images of London; 11 October

Napier Priscilla (Priscilla Hayter), 90, English writer, author of books on the Napier family and others, such as *A Late Beginner;* 10 October

Newton Leslie Gordon, 90, English journalist, editor of the *Financial Times* 1950–72, director 1967–72; 31 August

Nightingale Michael David, 70, English banker and antiquary, best known as a conservationist; 2 September

Nkosi West, 58, South African musician, songwriter, and record producer, important in the development of the style of South African popular music; 15 October

Nock Pio (Pius), 77, Swiss circus artist, high-wire performer, and clown; 4 December

Nutting Jack, 74, English metallurgist and academic specializing in industrial metals and alloys; 8 July

Oda Mikio, 93, Japanese athlete and sports administrator, the pioneer champion of Japanese athletics; 2 December

O'Driscoll, Martha, 76, US actress, star of numerous B movies; 3 November

Ordóñez Antonio, 66, Spanish matador, friend of Ernest Hemingway and Orson Welles; 19 December

Oxlee Keith, 63, South African rugby player and chemical salesman, remembered for championing South African rugby internationally in the late 1950s; 31 August

Page Eugene, 57, US arranger, pianist, and composer of film music, associated with Barry White, composer of hits such as 'Endless Love', 'Tonight I Celebrate My Love', 'The Greatest Love of All'; 24 August

Pakula Alan Jay, 70, US film director, producer, and writer, famous for such successes as *To Kill a Mockingbird* (1962), *All the President's Men* (1976), *Presumed Innocent* (1990), and *Pelican Brief* (1993); 19 November

Panton Verner, 72, Danish furniture and interior designer, creator of visually striking pieces in unconventional colours; 5 September

Paor Liam de, 72, Irish archaeologist, historian, and political scientist, committed to the Gaelic heritage and a celebrated political dissident; 13 August

Pena Arlindo Chenda Isaac, 42, known as 'Ben Ben', general and guerrilla leader, former chief-of-staff of the Angolan rebel movement UNITA; 19 October

Phillips Ron (Ivor Ronald), 63, Guyana-born champion of black self-awareness and identity, charismatic orator and activist, active in the UK as well as in the USA; 31 October

Philpott Trevor, 74, English journalist, creator of *Tonight* and *The Philpott file;* 29 July

Pires José Cardoso, Portuguese writer, author of *Balada da Praia dos Caes/Ballada of Dog's beach* (1982); 26 October

Platt Kenneth, 77, English comedian and broadcaster, presenter of *Spot the Tune* and star of *The Good Old Days* (1969); 2 October

Pollard Sidney (Siegfried Pollak), 73, Austrian-born British economic and social historian, university lecturer and author, notably of *The Development of the British Economy;* 22 November

Postel Jon (Jonathan Bruce), 55, US computer scientists, one of the 'fathers of the Internet'; 16 October

Powell Roy Colin, 33, English rugby league player for Leeds; 27 December

Prescott Alan, 61, English rugby league player, famous for his determination and courage; 20 September

Prey Hermann, 69, German singer, one of the most distinguished lyric baritones; 23 July

Quilliot Roger, 73, French politician, writer, and teacher, for over 20 years mayor of Clermont-Ferrand; 17 July

Radford Courtenay Arthur Ralegh, English internationally-oriented archaeologist who worked on a variety of subjects from ancient Roman remains to more recent Balkan art; 27 December

Ramirez de León Ricardo (Rolando Morán) , 67, Guatemalan guerrilla fighter and politician, co-founder of the Guatemalan Army of the Poor (EGP) and leader of the Guatemalan National Revolutionary Unity (URNG); 10 September

Rees Roberts Peter William, 75, English artist, known for his murals and for his work for the national press; 22 October

Reichmann Eva Gabriele (born Jungmann), 101, Silesian-born writer, historian, and community leader settled in England, celebrated campaigner for German-Jewish reconciliation and Jewish-Christian cooperation; 15 September

Reines Frederick, 80, US physicist, specialist in neutrino physics; 26 August

Richards Gordon, 68, English racehorse trainer famous for training two winners of the Grand National; 29 September

Robbins Jerome (Jerome Rabinowitz), 79, US ballet dancer, choreographer, and director, associated with the New York City Ballet; 29 July

Roberts John Eric, 91, English medical physicist; 14 October

Rogers Roy (born Leonard Franklin Slye), 85, US actor, singer, and producer, famous for his westerns; 6 July

Roth Alfred, 95, Swiss architect, exponent of the functionalist style; 20 October

Rothermere Viscount Vere Harold Esmond see **Harmsworth**. (See also full obituary p. 888.)

Rouve Pierre (Peter Christoff Ouvaliev), 83, Bulgarian art critic, broadcaster, and film director, active in the UK; 11 December

Ruane Martin: see **Giant Haystacks**

Ruiz Frankie (José Antonio), 40, US singer of Puerto Rican origin, known as 'El Papa de la Salsa'; 9 August

Ryan Chico (David-Allen), 50, US singer and bass-player, member of Sha Na Na; 26 July

Rybakov Anatoli (Anatoli Naumovich Aronov), 87, Ukrainian-born writer famous for *Deti Arbata/Children of the Arbat* (1966) and *Tridtsat' pyat' i drugie gody/Thirty-Five and Other Years* (translated as *Fear* 1992); 23 December

Sainsbury Alan John, 96, supermarket owner and politician, chairman of J Sainsbury 1956–67 and president 1967–98; 21 October. (See full obituary p. 890.)

Samuelson Michael Edward Wylie, 47, English film producer and director, owner of Michael Samuelson Lighting Ltd, also a philanthropist, involved in the Variety Club; 26 August

Sandler Joseph John, British psychoanalyst born in South Africa, a creative psychoanalytic theoretician, editor of the *International Journal of Psychoanalysis;* 6 October

Sargent Patrick Nigel, 41, English potter famous for his idiosyncratic and provocative works; 4 September

Sata Ineko, 94, Japanese writer and champion of women's rights; 12 October

Saura Antonio, 76, Spanish avant-garde artist, founder and director of the El Paso movement, creator of *Hiroshima Mon Amour* (1963); 22 July

Searle Vera Maud (born Palmer), 97, English athlete and sport administrator, a world class sprinter; 12 September

Secchiaroli Tazio, 73, Italian photographer who worked with Federico Fellini; 24 July

Seymour-Smith, Janet (born de Glanville), 68, English classical scholar and translator, author of *The Greek Myths* (1955) and *Robert Graves* (1982; revised 1995); 2 September

Seymour-Smith Martin, English poet and writer, biographer, critic, and author of reference works; 1 July

Shankland William, 91, Australian rugby league player and golfer who competed successfully in both disciplines; 8 September

Shelest Alla Yakovlevna, 79, Russian dancer, ballerina of the Kirov Ballet in the 1940s and 1950s; 7 December

Shepard Alan Bartlett, 74, US astronaut, the first American in space; 21 July

Silk Dennis, 69, English-born poet, one of the most significant literary figures of modern Israel; 3 July

Silva Minnette de, 80, Sri Lankan architect whose work was influenced by Le Corbusier and modernist architecture; 24 November

Smith Iain Crichton, 70, Scottish poet; 15 October

Soper Donald Oliver, 95, English minister of the Methodist church, chairman of the Shelter organization 1974–78; 22 December

Speight Johnny, 76, English playwright and scriptwriter, creator of *Till Death Us Do Part;* 6 July. (See full obituary p. 891.)

Spivakovsky Tossy, 91, Ukrainian-born US violinist known for his bowing technique and his knowledge of performance practice; 20 July

Stagerup Henrik, Danish novelist and film director, author of *The Seducer: It Is Hard to Die in Dieppe* (1985) and *Brother Jacob* (1991); 3 July

Starovoitova Galina Vasilievna, 52, Russian politician, parliamentary deputy 1990–93 and 1995–98, a champion of democracy, assassinated in St Petersburg; 20 November. (See full obituary p. 892.)

Sumner John Daniel, 73, US singer and leader of the Stamps Quartet, inducted into the Gospel Hall of Fame in 1983 as an individual and in 1998 with the Stamps; 15 November

Sutherland Stuart, 71, English experimental psychologist and author of *Breakdown, Dictionary of Psychology,* and *Irrationality: The Enemy Within;* 8 November

Taylor Don (Donald Ritchie), 78, US actor, director, and writer, who starred in *Father of the Bride* and directed *Escape from the Planet of the Apes* and *Damien – Omen II;* 28 December

Thompson Kay, 85, US actress, comedienne, and author of children's books; 2 July

Thornton Barbara, 48, US singer and musicologist, member of the Sequentia; 8 November

Thorogood Peter, 51, English developmental biologist who developed extensive research into the development of cranio-facial features in the embryo and foetus and into birth defects; 25 August

Tiny Rowland see Roland Walter **Fuhrop**

Turney Catherine, *c.* 92, US screenwriter for Warner and Paramount; 9 September

Udall Morris King, 76, US politician, Democrat, whose career in the House of Representatives spanned 30 years; 12 December

ul Haq Mahbub, 64, Pakistani economist, planning and finance minister 1982–88, special adviser to the United Nations (UN) Development Programme Administration 1989–96; 16 July

Van Elps George Abel, 85, US guitarist who also starred in *Pete Kely's Blues;* 29 November

Vieru Anatol, Romanian composer, conductor, and teacher whose music was influenced both by the Romanian folklore and by modernist trends in European art; 8 October

Wallace George Corley, 79, US lawyer and politician, four times governor of Alabama, white supremacist and segregationist; 13 September

Ward Frank Clifford, 84, English artist and teacher, known for his war-time sketches; 13 October

Waters Benjamin, 96, US saxophonist, 'world's most modern saxophone player over 90' (French Ministry of Culture, in an accolade); 11 August

Waterson Lal (Elaine), 55, English singer and songwriter involved in the English folk music revival; 4 September

Weidman Jerome, 85, US novelist, screenwriter, and playwright, known for *I Can Get It For You Wholesale* (1937); 6 October

Wells Robert (real name Robert Levinson), US lyricist, composer, writer, and producer of television shows; 23 September

West Dorothy, 91, US writer and editor, involved in the Harlem Renaissance of the 1930 and famous for her two main works, *The Living Is Easy* (1948) and *The Wedding* (1995); 16 August

Whitehead Oothout Zabriskie, 87, US actor and writer, famous for his roles in *The Grapes of Wrath* (1940) and *The Man Who Shot Liberty Valance* (1962); 29 July

Wichterle Otto, 84, Czech chemist who developed the hydrophilic soft contact lens; 18 August

Wicksteed Ivan Benedict, 84, English motorcyclist; 22 October

Winter Vincent, 50, Scottish actor famous for his roles in Disney films, winner of the Academy Award for an 'outstanding juvenile performance' in *The Kidnappers* (1953); 2 November

Wrede Casper Gustaf Kenneth,70, Finnish theatre director, co-creator of the Royal Exchange Theatre Company in Manchester, England; 28 September

Wright Douglas Vivian Parson, 84, English cricketer with a high strike rate, who achieved 108 wickets in 34 Tests at an average of 39; 16 November

Wynd Oswald Morris (Gavin Black), 85, Scottish writer born in Japan, famous for his thrillers; 21 July

Yang Shangkun *c.* 91, Chinese revolutionary and politician, state president 1988–93, associated with the Tiananmen Square massacre of 1989; 14 September

Young Frederick Archibald, 96, English cameraman; 1 December

Young Robert George, 91, US actor, star of the award-winning radio series *Father Knows Best* 1949–61; 21 July

Youshkevitch Nina, 77, US Ukrainian-born ballet dancer and teacher, protégé of Bronislava Nijinska; 3 November

Zeri Federico, 77, Italian art historian and critic, who specialized mostly in the 14th–16th-century art; 4 October

Zhivkov Todor Hristo, 87, Bulgarian communist politician, prime minister 1962–71 and head of state 1971–89; 5 August

Deaths: January–June 1999

Abdul Aziz Abdulah Bin Baz 87, the Grand Mufti of Saudi Arabia and leader of the Council of Ulema (Islamic scholars) from 1962; 13 May

Abraham Edward Penley, 85, English chemist, best known for isolating penicillin and his other work on antibiotics; 8 May

Ackles David Thomas, 62, US singer and songwriter who achieved recognition with albums *David Ackles* (1969), *Subway to the Country* (1970), and *American Gothic* (1972); 2 March

Aigner Lucien (Ladislas), 97, Hungarian-born photographer and photojournalist active in Europe and in the USA, later involved in the Hungarian section of the Voice of America; 29 March

Alcantara Dolores Jimenez, 89, Spanish singer known as 'La Nina de La Puebla'; 14 June

Allen Jim, English scriptwriter and playwright involved in social and political issues; 24 June

Allen Richard, 66, English abstract painter, designer, printmaker, teacher, and art consultant; 9 February

Alley Ronald Edgar, 73, English art historian who was a leading force at the Tate Gallery, London, from the 1950s, and in the years 1965–86 was Keeper of the Modern Collection there; 25 April

Alyn Kirk (John Feggo), 88, US actor, the first to portray Superman on screen; 14 March

Atwood John Leland, 94, US aeronautic engineer whose career spanned 50 years, designer of the Mustang, the Twin Mustang, the Sabre, and the X-15 aircrafts; 5 March. (See full obituary p. 874.)

Avallone Michael Angelo, 74, US writer of popular fiction – horrors, crime, gothic, romance, spy, etc; 26 February

Bailey Robin,79, English actor best known for his television performances, especially in comedies; 14 January

Baillie Ross, 21, Scottish hurdler whose sudden death ended a promising career; 18 June

Ballantine Bill (William Oliver), 88, US circus performer, clown, artist, and writer; 14 May

Barbezat Marc, 85, French editor and publisher renowned for his uncompromising attitude and for publishing lesser-known as well as famous authors; 26 April

Barr Robert, 89, Scottish war correspondent who was a member of General D Eisenhower's staff, and later television scriptwriter; 30 January

Bart Lionel, 68, English composer and lyricist, author of well-known musicals such as *Oliver!* and *Blitz!;* 3 April

Barzin Leon, 98, Belgian-born US conductor and teacher who worked both in the USA and in Europe; 29 April

Bellon Loleh (Marie-Laure), 74, French actress and playwright whose stage career spanned four post-war decades; 22 May

Beloff Max, 85, English historian, political scientist, and politician of Russian origin who discussed the history and structure of governments and the merits of the UK's membership of the European Union; 22 March. (See full obituary p. 874.)

Bender Adolf Eric, 80, UK food scientist and nutritionist, expert on protein nutrition and food toxicology; 21 February

Benjamin Rose Elisabeth, 90, English architect, one of the first women in the profession, whose designs were full of simplicity and proportion; 29 March

Bidder Muriel Joyce, 93, English sculptor who worked with various materials for about 60 years; 26 February

Bird Vere Cornwall, Antiguan politician, champion of Antigua's independence, and prime minister of Antigua and Barbuda 1981–94; 28 June

Blacker Harry, 89, English illustrator and cartoonist known as 'Nero'; 27 June

Blades James, 97, English percussionist, teacher, and author; 19 May

Blakeley Mary, 88, English nurse who promoted the nursing profession nationally and abroad; 3 May

Bogarde Dirk (Derek Jules Ulric Niven van den), 78, actor; 8 May. (See full obituary p. 875.)

Bonner Neville Thomas, 76, Australian politician, the first Aborigine in Australia's federal parliament; 5 February

Borland Adrian, 41, English singer, guitarist, and songwriter, frontman of the Sound; 26 April

Borradaile Osmond, 100, Canadian photographer and cinematographer, best known for his work on *Elephant Boy* (1937) and *Scott of the Antarctic;* 24 March

Bottini Reginald Norman, 82, English trade union leader, general secretary of the National Union of Agricultural and Allied Workers 1970–78; 5 May

Bowling Henry John, 67, English writer famous for his 'Cockney sagas'; 5 February

Box Betty Evelyn, 78, English film producer respected for her talent, dedication, and diligence; 15 January

Boxcar Willie (Lecil Travis Martin), 67, US country singer and songwriter; 12 April

Boyd Arthur Merric Bloomfield, 78, Australian painter regarded as the leading artist of his generation, who explored mythical, mystical, and Biblical themes; 24 April

Bramall Ernest Ashley, 83, English Labour politician, dedicated to education issues; 10 February

Brandon-Jones John, 90, English anti-modernist architect, teacher, and conservationist; 1 May

Branford Henrietta Diana Primrose, 53, English writer well known for her children's books; 23 April

Bridgwater Emmy Frith, 92, English surrealist painter; 13 March

Brilliant Fredda, 96, Polish-born US sculptor and actress known for her larger-than-lifesize sculptures; 25 May

Brooke Hillary (Beatrice Peterson), 85, US actress known for her supporting roles in Hollywood B movies; 25 May

Brooking Dorothea Smith (born Wright), 82, English television director and producer, best known for her adaptations of Edith Nesbit's children's stories; 23 March

Brough Peter Royce, 83, English ventriloquist, star, with his dummy Archie, of *Educating Archie;* 3 June

Broughton James Richard, 85, US highly regarded poet, playwright, and film-

maker, associated with San Francisco; 17 May

Brown Charles, 76, US blues musician, posthumously inducted into the Rock and Roll Hall of Fame; 21 January

Brown Vanessa (Smylla Brind), 71, Austrian-born US actress and, in later life, journalist and writer; 21 May

Brox Bobbe (Josephine Brock), 98, US singer, the last surviving member of the singing trio Brox Sisters; 2 May

Butler George, 94, English artist, best known for his watercolours; 19 April

Byard Jaki (John A), 76, US jazz pianist, instrumentalist, composer, and teacher, shot in New York; 11 February

Calhoun Rory (Francis Timothy McCown), 76, US actor who appeared in a number of low-budget westerns; 28 April

Callahan Harry Morey, 86, US photographer and teacher, a leading force in US photography in the 1950s and 1960s; 15 March

Casares Adolfo Bioy, 84, Argentinean writer, winner of the Cervantes Prize in 1990, co-author and friend of Jorge Luis Borges; 8 March

Cato Bob, 76, artist, photographer, and designer, author of *Joyce Images* (1994), who epitomised the golden era of Manhattan art directors; 19 March

Cawley Robert Hugh, 74, English psychiatrist, supporter of combining psychotherapy and drug therapy; 21 April

Cockerell Christopher Sydney, 88, English designer and inventor who pioneered the hovercraft; 1 June

Cody Iron Eyes: see **Iron Eyes Cody**

Cole Walter Vivian, 85, English potter famous for his tin-glazed earthenware; 19 January

Cooper Joan Davies, 84, English pioneer of social work with children; 15 January

Corby Ellen (Ellen Hansen), 85, US actress best known for her role as Grandmother Walton in *The Waltons;* 14 April

Curran Joan, born Strothers, 82, Welsh-born physicist and charity worker, founder of the Scottish Society for the Parents of Mentally Handicapped Children (Enable) and the Lady Curran Endowment Fund; 10 February

Dagley Norman, 69, English billiards player, English amateur champion 1965–84, UK and European champion in 1987, twice world amateur champion; 15 January

Dance Stanley Frank, 88, UK author and record producer, active in the USA, expert on jazz; 23 February

Dando Jill Wendy, 37, English television presenter of popular programmes such as *Crimewatch* and *Holiday,* shot outside her home; 26 April

Darré Jeanne-Marie, 93, French virtuoso pianist famous for her performances of Romantic music; 26 January

Daube David, 90, German scholar active in the UK and USA, who specialized in Roman law and Jewish studies; 24 February

Davies Charles Alfred, 75, English theologian who left the Roman Catholic priesthood in 1966 and subsequently taught extensively in Canada; 28 January

Debré Olivier, 79, French abstract painter; 1 June

Delf Vera (Vera Eleanor Hart), 94, English painter, campaigner, and protester; 26 February

Denning Alfred Thompson, 100, English judge, OM 1997; 5 March. (See full obituary p. 876.)

Devigny André, 82, French soldier and general, hero of the French Resistance during World War II; 12 February

DiMaggio Joe (Joseph Paul), 84, US baseball player of great talent and charisma who became a symbol of his generation; 8 March. (See full obituary p. 877.)

Dias Gomes Alfredo de Freitas, 76, Brazilian writer best known for his play *O pagador do promesas/The Keeper of Vows* (1959); 18 May

Domerque Faith, 73, US actress who appeared in a number of science fiction and fantasy films, protegée of Howard Hughes; 4 April

Donnellan Philip, 75, English pioneer of television documentaries; 15 February

Douglas Robert (Robert Douglas Finlayson), 89, English-born actor of film and stage, active in the USA; 18 January

Dunstan Donald Allan, 73, Australian politician, prime minister of the Labor government in South Australia 1970–79

Durr Virginia Heard, born Foster, 95, US campaigner for civil rights, especially in southern states; 24 February

Eccles David McAdam, 94, English politician, champion of investment in education; 24 February

Edwards Gwilym Meredith, 81, Welsh character actor; 8 February

Ehrlichman John Daniel, 73, US lawyer and government official, involved in the Watergate affair and Richard Nixon's impeachment proceedings; 14 February. (See full obituary p. 877.)

Einaudi Giulio, 87, Italian left-wing publisher, translator, and writer; 5 April

Eissler Kurt Robert, 90, Austrian psychoanalyst, follower of Sigmund Freud, active in Vienna and then in the USA; 17 February

Elion Gertrude Belle, 81, US biochemist who shared the Nobel Prize for Physiology or Medicine in 1988 with George Herbert Hitchings and Sir James Whyte Black; 21 February. (See full obituary p. 878.)

Elson Rebecca Anne Wood, 39, Canadian astronomer and poet, best known for her work on globular clusters; 19 May

Englund Sven Einar, 83, Finnish composer, teacher, and pianist, best known for his symphonies; 27 June

Evans Thomas Godfrey, 78, English cricketer of great talent and charisma; 3 May. (See full obituary p. 878.)

Everett Francine (Franceine Everette), 79, US actress and musical performer, famous for her appearance in *Dirty Gertie from Harlem, USA* (1946); 27 May

Eyck Aldo van, 80, Dutch innovative architect, recipient of the Fritz Schumacher Prize in 1992 and the Wolf Prize in 1998; 14 January

Falk Lee (Leon), 94, US writer and producer, creator of Mandrake the Magician; 13 March

Fatafehi Tu'ipelehake 77, Tonga politician, governor of Vava'u 1949–51 and prime minister of Tonga 1965–91; 10 April

Fairgrieve Thomas Russell, 74, Scottish businessman and politician, champion of the country's devolution, chairman of the Scottish Conservative Party 1975–80; 17 February

Feast Fred, 69, English actor, best known for his role as Fred Gee in *Coronation Street;* 25 June

Feininger Andreas, 92, French-born photographer, member of the Bauhaus, then active in the USA; 18 February

Fifield Elaine, 68, Australian ballet dancer who was also active in England; 11 May

Figueroa John Joseph Maria, 78, Jamaican poet and educationalist, promoter of the Caribbean literary legacy; 5 March

Fish Hugh, 76, English chemist and water and environmental manager, credited with the initiative to clean up the River Thames; 27 May

Fitzgerald Joan, 76, wife of the Irish politician and prime minister (1981–82 and 1982–87) Garret Fitzgerald; 12 June

Fleet Edgar Augustus, 67, English singer and choral director who specialized in early church music; 10 April

Ford Charles Edmund, 86, English mammalian cytogeneticist best renowned for his work on aberrant chromosome numbers and their links with certain illnesses and syndromes; 7 January

Fox Jeremy Dacre, 72, English barrister active in the James Hanratty A6 murder case for over three decades; 26 May

Foyle Christina Agnes Lilian, 88, English bookseller, daughter of William Foyle, one of the founders of the London bookshop in Charing Cross Road; 8 June

Fraenkel-Conrat Heinz, 88, German-born US biochemist who reconstituted a live virus; 10 April

Francescato Ivan, 31, Italian rugby player, one of six rugby-playing brothers; 18 January

Freaky Tah (Raymond Rodgers), 27, US rapper and songwriter, member of the Lost Boyz; 29 March

Fredericks Bill (William), 57, US singer, vocalist of the Drifters; 28 April

French Leslie Richard, 94, English actor and director, best known for his Shakespearean performances; 21 January

Fulson Lowell, 77, influential US blues singer, guitarist, and songwriter; 6 March

Gay John (Hans Gohler), 89, German-born photographer active in England, famous for his photographs of railway stations; 24 January

Gillinson-Schein Regina Rebecca, 90, Swiss-born cellist of Russian origin, best known for her performances of chamber music; 7 April

Gipps Ruth Dorothy Louisa, 78, English composer, conductor, and teacher, founder of the London Repertoire Orchestra (LRO); 23 February

Gold Ernest, 77, Austrian-born composer best known for his film music for movies such as *Judgment at Nuremberg* (1961) or *A Child is Waiting* (1963); 17 March

Golding John, 67, English trade union activist and Labour politician, MP 1969–86, who championed the cause of the working people throughout his career; 20 January

Goldwater John Leonard, 82, US publisher best known for Archie Andrews comic books; 26 February

Goodchild Jon, English graphic designer who worked for *Oz;* 4 June

Goodman Robert Howard, 71, British architect, chief architect (1971–78) and director of development (1978–85) in the Department of Health; 22 April

Govan Jock (Thomas), 76, Scottish footballer and mining engineer; 19 February

Goytisolo José Agustín, 70, Spanish poet, a passionate opponent of Franco; 19 March

Green Sid (Sidney Charles), 71, English comedy scriptwriter associated with Richard Hills, his co-author, and with Morecambe and Wise; 15 March

Gregory Gerald, 65, US singer and songwriter known as 'Bounce' Gregory; 12 February

Gretton Rob (Robert Leo), 46, English music manager involved with Joy Division and New Order; 15 May

Grillo Joann, 65, US singer (mezzo-soprano), famous for her operatic performances; 1 February

Grotowski Jerzy, 65, Polish avant-garde theatre director and theoretician, also active in the USA and Italy, author of the classic *Towards a Poor Theatre* and leader of the experimental Laboratory Theatre in Wrocław, Poland; 14 January. (See full obituary p. 880.)

Guayasamín Oswaldo Aparicio Calero, 79, Ecuadorian artist regarded as the leading painter and sculptor of his generation; 10 March

Guthrie Gwen, 49, US soul singer and songwriter; 3 February

Haddy Anne, 71, Australian actress, best known as Helen Daniels in the soap opera *Neighbours;* 6 June

Hall Huntz (Henry Richard Hall), 79, US character actor best remembered for his performance in *Dead End;* 30 January

Hanuman Guru, 98, Indian wrestler, champion of free-style wrestling; 24 May

Hartmann, Erich, 76, German photographer, famous for his work for the *Fortune* magazine and for the book *In the Camps* (1995); 4 February

Hawkins Desmond, 90, English broadcaster specializing in natural history programmes for the BBC, active also as literary critic and writer; 6 May

Hawkins Sheila, 93, Australian-born illustrator of children's books, active in the UK; 10 January

Heron Patrick, 79, English painter and critic, regarded as one of the most outstanding artists of his generation; 19 March. (See full obituary p. 880.)

Herzberg Gerhard, 94, German molecular physicist active in Canada, winner of the 1971 Nobel Prize for Chemistry for his research on free radicals; 3 March. (See full obituary p. 881.)

Higashiyama Shinkichi 'Kaii', 91, Japanese painter and writer whose art reflected the symbolism of Japanese scenery; 6 May

Hilton William Samuel, 73, English Labour politician and industrialist active in the building industry; 12 June

Hirt Alois Maxwell, 76, US jazz trumpeter and bandleader, owner of the 'Al Hirt' club in New Orleans; 27 April

Hull Rod, 63, English television entertainer best known for his act with Emu, a puppet bird; 17 March

Hume (George) Basil, 76, archbishop of Westminster and leader of the Roman Catholic Church in the UK 1976–99; 17 June. (See full obituary p. 882.)

Hunt Kevan, 61, English industrial relations manager, head of industrial relations at the National Coal Board 1982–84, executive director of Industrial Relations 1988–91, chairman of the British Coal Enterprise 1993–96; 17 March

Hussein Kamal el-Din, 78, Egyptian politician, vice-president 1960–64; 19 June

Hussein ibn Talal, 63, king of Jordan from 1952; 7 February. (See full obituary p. 883.)

Ibraimov Jumabek Ibraimovich, 55, Kyrgyz politician, prime minister of Kyrgyzstan from December 1998; 4 April

Iron Eyes Cody, *c.* 91, US American Indian actor of Cherokee origin, involved in the Keep America Beautiful movement and protector of the image of North American Indians; 4 January

Irving Bob (Robert), 50, English rugby league player, an outstanding second-row forward of his generation; 18 April

Isa bin Salman al-Khalifa, 65, ruler of Bahrain from 1961, emir from 1971; 6 March

Itokawa Hideo, 86, Japanese aeronautical engineer and rocket scientist; 21 February

Janes Alfred George, 87, Welsh-born artist active in England, most notably at the Croydon School of Art; 3 February

Jefferys Margot, born Davies, 82, English medical sociologist who helped establish medical sociology as an academic discipline; 3 March

Jones Henry Burk, 86, US character actor who appeared on Broadway and contributed to numerous television programmes and films; 17 May

Jones R Gerallt (Robert Gerallt Hamlet), 64, Welsh writer and educationalist, promoter of the Welsh language and heritage in literature, media, and cultural undertakings; 9 January

Kalman Tibor, 49, Hungarian-born designer and editor active in the USA, editor of the Benetton magazine *Colors;* 2 May

Kane Sarah, 28, English playwright, author of *Cleansed* (1997) and *Crave* (1998); 19 February

Kanin Garson (Gershon Labe), 86, US scriptwriter, playwright, and director, who created the classic Broadway comedy *Born Yesterday;* 13 March

Kapp Yvonne, 96, English-born writer, researcher, and activist, author of *Eleanor Marx* (1972–76); 22 June

Karekin I (Neshan Sarkissian), 66, Syrian-born priest, head of the Armenian Apostolic Church, Catholicos of All Armenians (1995–99); 29 June

Karpati Rudolf, 78, Hungarian musicologist and sabre fencer; 1 February.

Keller Andräs (Andrew), 73, Hungarian-born polymer scientist active in the UK, Fellow of the Royal Society from 1972 and member of Academia Europea from 1994; 7 February

Kelley Jackson DeForest, 79, US actor best known for his performance as Leonard 'Bones' McCoy in *Star Trek;* 11 June

Kendall Henry Way 72, US physicist, winner of the Nobel Prize in Physics (with Richard E Taylor and Jerome I Friedman) in 1990 for his work on quarks; 15 February

Kiley, Richard Paul, 75, US actor famous for his performances in musicals; 5 March

Killanin Michael Morris, 84, Irish sports administrator, member of the International Olympic Committee (IOC) 1952–80, president 1972–80, whose varied career led him through journalism and the military to film production; 25 April

Kirwan Archibal Laurence Patrick, 93, Irish-born archaeologist and geographer, director and secretary of the Royal Geographical Society 1945–75; 16 April

Kline Herbert, 89, US documentary film-maker and left-wing activist; 5 February

Knox Buddy Wayne, 65, US singer and songwriter; 14 February

Koenigsberger Otto Heinrich Gustav, 90, German-born architect, urban planner, and Egyptologist, active in India and the UK, specialist in the sociology, economics, and political implications of human settlements; 3 January

Kubrick, Stanley, 70, US film director, 7 March. (See full obituary p. 884.)

Kulik Buzz (Seymour), 77, US director of films and television programmes such as *Brian's Song;* 13 January

Lecoq Jacques, 77, French actor, most influential as a charismatic teacher; 19 January

Lee Dorothy (Marjorie Elizabeth Millsap), 88, US actress and musical performer popular in the 1930s; 24 June

Leontief, Wassily, 92, US Russian-born economist whose research concentrated on input-output analysis and raw data, contributor to the US economic planning; 5 February

Lewin Terence Thornton, 78, English naval officer, Admiral of the Fleet; 23 January

Liebermann Rolf, 88, Swiss composer, music critic, and broadcaster, reformer and administrator of the Paris Opéra 1973–80; 2 January

Lini Walter Hadye, 57, Vanuatu priest and politician, prime minister 1980–91 and deputy prime minister 1998; 21 February

Liston Melba Doretta, 73, US jazz trombonist, best known for her work as arranger and composer; 23 April

Long Joan Dorothy Boundy, 73, Australian screenwriter and film producer, the first chairperson of the National Film and Sound Archive in 1984; 2 January

Lortel Lucille (Louise Wadler), 98, US actress and theatre producer, known as 'Queen of Off-Broadway'; 4 April

Lustig Jo (Joseph George), 73, US manager, press agent, and producer, active in the USA and in the UK; 29 May

Lutyens Mary, 90, English writer and expert on the Indian philosopher Krishnamurti; 9 April

McClelland James Robert, 83, Australian judge, politician, author, and newspaper columnist who led the investigation over British nuclear tests in Australia; 16 January

McComb David, 36, Australian rock singer, songwriter, and guitarist, member of the Triffids; 1 February

McCrea William Hunter, 94, Irish-born mathematician and astrophysicist, an instrumental figure in British astronomy who worked on cosmological models, cosmical gas dynamics, and other topics including pure mathematics; 25 April

McGahey Michael, 73, English miner and trade union activist, vice-president of the National Union of Mineworkers 1974–87; 30 January. (See full obituary p. 885.)

McKenzie Donald Francis, 67, bibliographer and academic, born in New Zealand and active in England, mostly at the University of Oxford; 22 March

Machin Arnold, 87, English sculptor, best known for his portraits of Queen Elizabeth II on British coins (1964–85) and stamps (since 1967); 9 March

Macura Vladimír, 53, Czech writer and translator of Estonian literature; 17 April

Magin Milosz (Milosz), 69, Polish-born composer and pianist resident in Paris, founder of the Milosz Magin International Piano Competition in 1985; 4 March

Mainassara Ibrahim Baré, 50, soldier and politician, president of Niger 1996–99, assassinated in Niamey; 9 April

Major Theodore, 90, English artist whose work reflected his Lancastrian roots and uncompromising social-political views; 17 January

Maraj James Ajodhya, 68, Trinidad-born educationalist and diplomat, the first president of the Commonwealth of Learning 1988–95; 3 April

March Elspeth Mackenzie, 86, English actress educated at the Central School of Speech and Drama, known for her appearances in stage comedies; 29 April

Martin, Charlie (John Christopher), 72, English nuclear weapon designer, pioneer of pulse power, who was also active in the UK Atomic Energy Authority; 22 March

Mason Philip, 92, English colonial civil servant, politician, and writer, director of the Institute of Race Relations 1958–69; 25 January

Matthews Tanya (Tatiana Svetlova Borissova), 85, Russian journalist settled in England who later worked for four decades for the BBC African Service in Tunisia; 3 March

Mellon Paul, 91, US philanthropist, art collector, and racehorse breeder; 2 February

Menuhin Yehudi, 82, US-born violinist and conductor active in the UK; 12 March. (See full obituary p. 886.)

Meric Rosalie de, 82, English artist and teacher, whose work contains elements of the supernatural; 2 April

Merryfield Buster, 78, English actor, best known for his role as Uncle Albert in *Only Fools and Horses;* 23 June

Mitchison Naomi Margaret (born Haldane), 101, Scottish writer, traveller, and social activist, author of historical novels such as *Corn King and Spring Queen* (1931) and *The Blood of the Martyrs* (1939); 11 January

Monck John Goldman, 91, English film-maker and farmer, known for *Man of Aran* (1934) and *King Solomon's Mines* (1937); 8 May

Moore Brian, 77, Irish novelist active in the USA whose novels carried incisive moral message, known for *The Colour of Blood* (1987) and *Lies of Silence* (1990); 11 January

Morris Johnny (Ernest John), 82, British television entertainer and broadcaster, best known for the programme *Animal Magic;* 6 May

Mosley Bryan, 67, English actor, famous as Alf Roberts in *Coronation Street;* 9 February

Murdoch (Jean) Iris, 79, Irish-born English writer; 8 February. (See full obituary p. 886.)

Musin Ilya Aleksandrovich, 95, Russian conductor and teacher at the Leningrad Conservatoire of Music; 6 June

Narducci Pietro Antonio (Pietro Carmella), 84, Italian-born reclusive artist instrumental in the development of the US art; 1 March

Nedwell Robin, 52, English actor famous for his performance in *Doctor in the House;* 1 February

Negri Richard, 71, English theatre designer, best known for his work at the Royal Exchange in Manchester as well as at the Old Vic and the Royal Shakespeare Company; 17 April

Newley George Anthony, 67, English actor, singer, composer, and writer; 14 April

Nimmo Derek Robert, 68, English actor, producer, and author, famous for his contributions to television and radio comedy; 24 February. Successful also in the USA, who with Leslie Bricusse, wrote hits such as, 'What kind of fool am I'?

Normanville Peter Bernard Augustin de, 76, English film-maker specializing in scientific documentaries; 7 March

Nutting Harold Anthony, 79, English conservative politician whose career effectively ended after the Suez crisis; 23 February

O'Hara Brian, 58, English singer and guitarist, member of the Fourmost; 17 June

Oliveira João Carlos de, 45, Brazilian triple-jumper; 30 May

O'Neill Jeremiah Michael, 77, Irish playwright and novelist, landlord at the Duke of Wellington, a theatre pub in Islington; 21 May

Opoku Ware II of Ashanti (Jacob Matthew Poku – Barima Kwaku Adusei), 79, barrister, born in Ghana, and ruler of the Ashanti people – the 15th Asantehene – from 1970; 26 February

Osmond Andrew Philip Kingsford, 61, English writer associated with *Private Eye,* known mainly for his political thrillers; 15 April

Ottaway James, 90, English actor known for his performances in the West End and, from the 1960s, on television; 16 June

Pablo Augustus (Horace Swaby), 46, Jamaican melodica and keyboard player, representative of the instrumental variation of reggae known as the dub sound; 18 May

Papadopoulos Georgios, 80, Greek soldier and politician, head of the military junta who assumed power between 1967 and 1973; 27 June

Paris Henri d'Orléans, comte de Paris, 90, great-great-grandson of King Louis-Philippe, and head of the royal house of France who hoped for, but never achieved, political power; 19 June

Parsons Terry (Terence), 63, Welsh snooker player, five times Welsh amateur champion and the world amateur champion in 1982; 8 May

Paton Thomas Angus Lyall, 93, British civil engineer involved in projects that included government contracts and overseas assignments; 7 April

Patten Tom, British marine scientist with a long-standing career at the Heriot-Watt University, Edinburgh, Scotland; 10 April

Pearcey Eilean Blake, 97, Australian-born artist active in England, who specialized in drawings of dancers; 1 February

Peck Robert, 53, English actor best known for his television drama performances, as in *Edge of Darkness* (1985); 4 April

Peters Jim (James), 80, English runner known for his determination, the first man to run the marathon in a time under 2 hours 20 minutes; 9 January

Petrucciani Michel, 36, French jazz pianist settled in the USA, who overcame his handicap (*osteogenesis imperfecta* – 'glass bones disease') to become a celebrated and award-winning performer; 6 January

Peynet Raymond, 90, French artist and designer, creator of *Les Amoreux de Peynet;* 14 January

Phillips, Lord of Ellesmere David Chilton, 74, English biophysicist, pioneer of structural biology, also active in politics; 22 February

Pierce Charles, 73, US actor and impersonator of female performers, notably Bette Davis and Mae West; 31 May

Pierre José, 72, French writer of works on Surrealism and surrealistic novels; 7 April

Pillai Thakazhi Sivasankara, 79, Indian writer, author of novels in Malayalam with a strong social slant; 11 April

Pleeth William, 80, English cellist best know for his teaching achievements; 6 April

Prince Lincoln (Lincoln Thompson), 49, Jamaican reggae singer; 14 January

Pritchard Barry, 54, English singer and guitarist, member of the Fortunes; 11 January

Purbrook Colin Thomas, influential English jazz pianist, arranger, bandleader, and composer; 5 February

Quarry Jerry, 53, US boxer turned professional in 1965 who fought Muhammad Ali twice and at the end of his life suffered acute pugillistic dementia; 3 January

Quintero Jose Benjamin, 74, Panama-born theatre director active in the USA, especially associated with productions of plays by Eugene O'Neill; 26 February

Ramsey Alf (Alfred Ernest), 79, English footballer and football manager, 32 times capped for England 1948–53, England's manager 1963–74; 28 April. (See full obituary p. 887.)

Reading Charles, 88, English actor, theatre director, designer, and writer, best known for his post-war accomplishments at the Palladium; 17 May

Red Norvo (Kenneth Norville), 91, US innovative jazz instrumentalist – xylophonist, vibraharpist, and bandleader; 6 April

Reed Robert Oliver, 61, English actor of great presence and charisma; 2 May. (See full obituary p. 888.)

Rees Ioan Bowen, 70, Welsh solicitor, local government officer, and writer, secretary and chief executive of the Gwynedd County Council 1974–91; 4 May

Rehman Indrani, born Bjapai, 68, Indian classical dancer and teacher who brought her art to Western audiences; 5 February

Rhodes James Robert Vidal, 66, English historian, biographer, and politician; 20 May

Robens Alfred, Baron Robens of Woldingham, 98, English trade unionist and industrialist, chair of the National Coal Board 1961–71; 27 June

Roberts Bobby (Robert Otto Fossett), 86, English circus performer and circus owner (with his brother Tommy); 5 April

Robinson Elizabeth, 87, US athlete, the first woman to win an athletic gold medal in Olympic history in the 100 metres final in Amsterdam in 1928; 18 May

Roché Mary Elizabeth, 79, US jazz singer associated with the Duke Ellington band; 16 February

Rogers Charles 'Buddy', 94, US actor and musician, husband of Mary Pickford; 21 April

Rose Jim (Eliot Joseph Benn), 89, English publisher, journalist, and writer involved in race relations; 20 May

Rossington Norman, 70, English comic actor; 21 May

Russell Ray Robert, 74, US writer of gothic, disturbing novels and short stories; 15 March

Ryan Marion (Marion Sapherson), 65, English pop singer most famous for her work in the 1950s and for regular appearances in the television quiz *Spot the Tune;* 15 January

Rylands George Humphrey Wolferstan, 96, English actor, theatre director, and scholar; 16 January

Sacher Paul, 93, Swiss conductor and musicologist, founder of the Basel Chamber Orchestra and of the Paul Sacher Foundation; 26 May

Salant Walter S, 87, US economist who popularized Keynesian thinking in the USA, presidential and NATO adviser; 30 April

Sarazen Gene (Eugene Saraceni), 97, US golf player, the first to win the four major professional championships – the Masters, the US Open, the Open, and the US PGA; 13 May

Savery Constance Winifred, 101, prolific English children's writer; 2 March

Sawtelle Charles, 53, US bluegrass guitarist; 20 March

Sayão Bidú, 96, Brazilian-born coloratura soprano active in the USA; 12 March

Sayyid Muhammad bin Sayyid Muhammad Sadiq al-Sadr, 55, Iraqi ayatollah, religious scholar, jurist, and prolific author, assassinated in Najaf; 19 February

Schawlow Arthur Leonard, 77, US physicist, winner of the 1981 Nobel Prize for Physics for his research in laser spectroscopy (with Nicolaas Bloembergen and Kai M Siegbahn); 28 April. (See full obituary p. 890.)

Schnabel Stefan, German actor who worked extensively with Orson Welles and whose films include *The Iron Curtain* (1948); 11 March

Schoon Marius, 61, South-African political and racial activist, opponent of apartheid,

poet, and teacher; 7 February

Seaborg Glenn Theodore, 86, US chemist, Nobel Prize winner (with Edwin McMillan) in 1951, who discovered plutonium; 25 February. (See full obituary p. 891.)

Seale Douglas, 85, English actor and theatre director active both in the UK and the USA; 13 June

Seidner David, 42, US photographer and writer, known for his portraits and idiosyncratic style; 6 June

Sellers 'Brother' John, 74, US gospel and jazz singer; 27 March

Shapley Olive Mary, 88, English broadcaster and producer of radio documentaries; 13 March

Shaw Sam, 87, US photographer and film producer famous for his iconic photographs of Marilyn Monroe and Marlon Brando; 5 April

Shute Charles Cameron Donald, 81, English histologist and Egyptologist, who, with Peter Lewis, mapped the cholinergic pathways in the brain; 2 January

Silva Raúl Henriquez, 91, Chilean priest, politically active bishop of Santiago 1961–83, cardinal from 1962; 9 April

Silverstein Shel (Shelby), 66, US singer, songwriter, poet, cartoonist, and composer, known for his wry humour; 10 May

Singh Raghubir, 56, Indian photographer who captured the essence of life in different regions of his country; 18 April

Siskel Eugene Kal, 52, US film critic, journalist, and broadcaster; 20 February

Sneh Simha, 90, Polish-born author, the last Argentinean writer in Yiddish; 4 April

Soldati Mario, 92, Italian novelist and film director, author of *Le Lettere di Capri/ The Capri Letters* (1954); 19 June

Sommer Frederich, 94, US photographer renowned for his abstract, surreal works; 23 January

Speer Brock, 78, US white gospel singer and backing vocalist for Elvis Presley; 29 March

Spence Alexander Lee ('Skip'), 52, Canadian-born singer, songwriter, drummer, and guitarist, member of Jefferson Airplane and Moby Grape; 16 April

Spoerry Anne, 80, French physician and aviator, famous for her work in Kenya with the Flying Doctor Service; 2 February

Springfield Dusty (Mary Isabel Catherine Bernadette O'Brien), 59, UK singer who epitomised the sound and style of 1960s pop music; 2 March. (See full obituary p. 892.)

Stader Maria (Maria Molnár), 87, Hungarian-born Swiss concert singer, also known for her opera and oratorio recordings; 27 April

Stanky Eddie (Edward Raymond), 81, US baseball player, nicknamed 'The Brat'; 6 June

Stanton Eric (Ernest Stanzone), 72, US illustrator known for his powerful, fetishistic images; 31 March

Steinberg Saul, 84, Romanian-born US artist, known for the cartoons he contributed to the *New Yorker;* 12 May

Stone Jesse, 97, US rock musician, famous for 'Shake, Rattle and Roll'; 1 April

Stone Lawrence, 79, English historian, author of *The Crisis of the Aristocracy 1558–1641* (1965); 16 June

Stoph Willi, 84, German politician instrumental in the creation of the German Democratic Republic, head of state 1973–76; 13 April

Strasberg Susan, 60, US actress, daughter of Lee Strasberg, who appeared both on stage and in films, as in Roger Corman's *The Trip* (1967); 21 January

Sutch Screaming Lord (David Edward), 58, Monster Raving Loony Party candidate for 35 years and musician; 16 June. (See full obituary p. 893.)

Sweeney Edmund ('Birdy'), 67, Northern Irish character actor, well known for his role in the series *Ballykissangel*; 11 May

Sweet Darrell, 51, English drummer and songwriter associated with the group Nazareth; 30 April

Tait Margaret, 80, Scottish filmmaker and writer, well known for *Rose Street* (1956); 16 April

Tapscott Horace, 64, US composer, trombonist, and bandleader, active mostly in Los Angeles; 27 February

Thomas Amos Leon, 61, US jazz singer and percussionist associated with Santana and with the saxophonist Pharoah Sanders; 8 May

Thomas Robert John Roydon, 72, Welsh sculptor known for portraying eminent men and women of Wales; 11 May

Thorp Roderick Mayne, 62, US writer, author of *Nothing Lasts Forever* (1979), later filmed as *Die Hard* (1988); 28 April

Tilberis Liz (Elizabeth Jane), English fashion designer who became editor-in-chief of both *Vogue* and *Harper's Bazaar*; 21 April. (See full obituary p. 893.)

Tormé Mel (Melvin Howard Torme), 73, US singer and songwriter, also active as composer, pianist, drummer, arranger, and actor; 5 June

Torrance Robert William, 75, English physiologist and academic whose work focussed on arterial chemoreceptors of the carotid bodies; 8 January

Trainer Patrick Joseph, 89, Scottish trade union activist and local government officer, councillor for the Glasgow City Council 1962–90; 6 June

Trickett Mabel Rachel, 77, English historian and novelist, principal of St Hugh's College, Oxford (1973–91); 24 June

Troup Robert Williams, 80, US songwriter, pianist, and vocalist, famous for 'Route 66'; 7 February

Troutman Roger, 58, US singer, songwriter, instrumentalist, and producer, lead singer and instrumentalist of Zapp, shot in Dayton, Ohio; 25 April

Trussardi Nicola, 56, Italian luxury fashion designer, art promoter, and businessman; 14 April

Tuohy John Francis, 73, English novelist and author of short stories, lecturer in Poland, Brazil, and Japan; 11 April

Turowicz Jerzy, 86, leading Polish Catholic journalist, chief editor of *Tygodnik Powszechny/Universal Weekly* 1945–53 and 1956–99; 27 January

Vigoreux Joseph Evenor Paul, 96, British metrologist born in Mauritius, influential in the formulation of the International System of Metric Units (the SI); 15 April

Viollet Dennis Sydney, 65, English footballer who played for Manchester United (1949–62) and was twice capped by England (1961–62); 6 March

Waddell Alexander Nicol Anton, 85, British colonial administrator who held posts in the Solomon Islands, Borneo, the Gambia, Sierra Leone, and Sarawak, and later in the former Gilbert Islands (Kiribati); 14 June

Ware Peter John Wallace, 70, English architect active mostly in the West Country; 17 March

Washbrook Cyril, 84, English cricketer best known for his opening partnership for England with Len Hutton; 27 April

Watson Bobs (Robert Ball), 68, US child actor, later pastor in the Methodist Church; 26 June

Weinreb Ben (Benjamin), 87, English bookseller, co-author of the *London Encyclopaedia,* and historian of architecture; 3 April

Wellburn Alan Richard, 58, English plant biochemist, expert on climate change and on the effects of pollution and acid rain on the environment; 8 May

Wences known as 'Señor Wences' (Wenceslao Moreno), 103, Spanish-born US ventriloquist, also active in Paris, France; 20 April

West Louis Jolyon, 74, US psychiatrist renowned for his research into extreme experiences such as substance and sexual abuse, sleep deprivation, effects of war and torture, pain, and dreams and hypnosis; 2 January

Westoll Tim (James), 80, English ornithologist and public servant active mostly in Cumbria; 7 February

Whiston Peter Rice, 86, Scottish architect and teacher; 24 January

White Joan, 89, English actress born in Egypt, also active in the USA, best known for her roles in 'high' comedies; 8 June

Whitelaw Willie (William Stephen Ian), British Conservative polition, who was at the forefront of British politics for many years; 31 June. (See full obituary p. 893.)

Whyte William Hollingsworth, 81, US urbanologist, planner, and writer, author of the influential *The Organization Man;* 12 January

Wiik Bjørn Hârvard, 62, Norwegian physicist active mostly in Germany, designer of the electron-proton collider 'Hera', member of several international advisory bodies; 26 February

Williams Joe (Joseph Goreed), 80, US jazz singer associated with Count Basie's band; 29 March

Wilson Laura Emma Elizabeth, 98, Australian-born English ballet dancer, member of Diaghilev's Ballets Russes, and later a distinguished ballet teacher; 14 May

Wisdom John Minor, 93, US judge, enforcer of the rules of desegregation in the 5th Circuit Court of Appeal jurisdiction – the Deep South; 15 May

Wise Ernie (Ernest Wiseman), 73, English comedian, member of the comedy duo Morecambe and Wise; 21 March. (See full obituary p. 894.)

Wrigley William, Jr, 66, US chewing gum producer; 8 March

Young 'Mighty' Joe, 71, US blues guitarist and singer; 24 March

Yu Qiuli 84, Chinese politician, deputy prime minister 1975–82 and deputy secretary-general of the Military Commission 1982–87; 3 February

Zanetti José Vela, 85, Spanish painter and mural artist, best known for his mural *La lucha del hombre por la paz/Mankind's Struggle for Peace* (1953) for the United Nations headquarters, New York, USA; 4 January

Zoll Paul Maurice, 87, US cardiologist, who invented and developed the cardiac pacemaker, cardiac defibrillator, and cardiac monitoring; 5 January. (See full obituary p. 894.)

Full Obituaries

Denis Derbyshire (DD); Anna Farkas (AF); Richard Martin (RM); Dan McCausland (DM); Sue Purkis (SP); Ben Ramos (BR); Helen Rappaport (HR); Catherine Thompson (CT).

Atwood, John Leland

(1906–1999)

John Leland Atwood will be remembered as a US aircraft designer and executive who was involved in the production of some of the most important military planes in aviation history. Born just a year after the Wright brothers first flew, he played major roles in the creation of the P-51 Mustang (considered by many the finest piston-engined fighter ever), one of the best jet fighters, the rocket-powered X-15, and craft that ventured into space as North American Aviation (NAA) was transformed from modest beginnings into a giant of the defence and aerospace industry.

Atwood, known to all as Lee, gained his undergraduate degree from Hardin-Simmons University and earned a master's degree in engineering from the University of Texas in 1928 before starting work for the Army, which then controlled all military aircraft. He subsequently spent four years with Douglas Aircraft before joining General Aviation, a subsidiary of car giant General Motors. Federal legislation forced General Aviation to become independent and the business changed its name to North American Aviation.

The company's early successes were the Texan trainer aircraft, known as the Harvard by British pilots, and Atwood's creation – the B-25 Mitchell bomber, famous for the carrier-launched Doolittle raids on Tokyo. The British were desperate for fighters in early 1940 and approached NAA to build P-40 Warhawk fighters under licence from rival corporation, Curtiss. Atwood, who had by then moved into management, convinced the Purchasing Commission that they should instead take a chance on a new fighter that had yet to be designed. They did and in just 102 days the P-51 Mustang was born. A talented team at NAA, including designer Edgar Schmued, produced a plane with an extremely clean shape, a laminar flow wing, and a radical radiator mounted in the rear fuselage.

Test pilot Ronald Harker convinced the British Air Ministry to replace the Mustang's inadequate Allison engine with the Rolls-Royce Merlin and the result was spectacular. Top speed rose to 440 mph, high-altitude performance was transformed, and with external drop tanks the Mustang became the first Allied fighter able to escort bombers to Berlin, allowing the US Army Air Force to resume daylight bombing raids over Germany. In all, 15,586 Mustangs were built and some were still in use as a ground attack role in the Korean War.

In that conflict the NAA's XP-86 Sabre was the only American fighter that could compete with the Soviet MiG-15. Atwood used captured German research on swept back wings to give the Sabre world-record performance. The next NAA jet, the Super Sabre, was capable of supersonic speed in level flight, again a record for a Western fighter.

With Atwood at the controls, NAA played a key part in landing men on the moon by building the Apollo space capsules but the achievement was marred by the death of three astronauts in a fire on the ground in 1967. Atwood admitted to a congressional hearing that such an emergency had not been considered and NAA's reputation was damaged by revelations of shoddy work. Three years earlier he had also faced harsh questioning over links between political power brokers and lobbyists and favours given to them.

NAA merged with Rockwell-Standard in 1967 and Atwood served as chief executive of the new company. Neil Armstrong stepped on to the lunar surface in 1969, a year before Atwood's retirement, and Atwood was given NASA's Public Service Award. He remained active in the aerospace world, corresponding with fellow plane enthusiasts, giving talks around the world, and writing for aviation publications. He died in Santa Monica on 5 March 1999 aged 94. DM

Beloff, Max

Baron Beloff of Wolvercote
(1913–1999)

British historian, political writer, and politician. Although a brilliant scholar and prolific historian, he will probably be best remembered by the general public as a political commentator with extreme views about the demise of the British Empire and the adverse consequences of European Union (EU) membership. He himself would certainly see his greatest achievement as the foundation of the independent University College at Buckingham in 1974.

In his youth Beloff was a committed Liberal, with a strong radical outlook, but in the early 1970s he became concerned about what he saw as the Liberal drift to the left, and particularly the Liberal Party's support for comprehensive education, and was attracted to the radical Conservatism of Margaret Thatcher. His support for Conservative policies was not, however, unquestioning and when he entered the House of Lords in 1981 he was not averse to making trenchant criticisms of the party which had put him there as a life peer. His friends and former colleagues have generally remembered him as a kind and considerate man but in later life he had a reputation

for extreme, and often quite unpredictable, views on social and political developments.

The son of Jewish immigrants who had fled the Russian communist revolution, he was born in London and attended St Paul's School before going to Corpus Christi College, Oxford, where he obtained a First in Modern History. Although his academic career later widened considerably, history remained his greatest strength and interest.

After a period as research fellow at Corpus Christi, in 1939 he was appointed assistant lecturer in history at Manchester University and, with the outbreak of war, joined the army but was soon released on health grounds . In 1946 he was made reader in comparative study of institutions at the newly-created Nuffield College, Oxford, broadening his academic interests into American institutions and Soviet foreign policy. He published well-received books in these two areas, to be followed in the 1950s by many others in a similar direction. In 1947 he was made a Fellow of Nuffield College and ten years later became Gladstone Professor of Government and Public Administration and a fellow of All Souls.

Meanwhile, he had been active in founding the independent University College at Buckingham, a unique seat of higher learning in Britain in that it relied entirely on private finance rather than government funding, and in 1974 became its first principal, a post which he held until 1979. He was delighted when, four years later, the college was granted its university charter.

Well-regarded by Prime Minister Margaret Thatcher, Beloff was knighted in 1980 and made a life peer in the following year. As in everything he did, he was an assiduous attendee at the Lords, which provided him with a platform for his trenchant speeches, reflecting his often dogmatic views. At first his vigorous style drew good audiences but his fellow peers grew tired of his approach to many of the topics under debate. His opposition to European involvement, at the expense of maintaining and developing Britain's Commonwealth links, became increasingly tedious. In domestic matters he often appeared equally dogmatic. For example, he called for a public inquiry into the funding of the Economic and Social Research Council because it had made a grant to the Industrial Relations Institute at Warwick University, which he claimed to be 'notoriously biased'. Later he argued that the grant to the Royal Shakespeare Company should be cut because, in his view, the theatre performed Shakespeare so badly.

He clearly admired Margaret Thatcher and was appalled when Oxford University voted not to award her an honorary degree, but his admiration did not deter him from disagreeing with her from time to time, particularly when she argued that universities should be more 'useful'. He was even said to have lectured to her on maintaining the independence of institutions of higher education on occasions when they met.

He had a rewarding private life, having married in 1938 and made Wolvercote, from where he derived his title, his home. He and his wife had two sons, one of whom became president of Trinity College, Oxford.

As Beloff grew older, he became increasingly extreme in his views but, his academic achievements and his contribution to the world of learning should not be underestimated. He died in London on 22 March 1999 at the age of 85. DD

Bogarde, Dirk

stage name of Derek Niven van den Bogaerde
(1921–1999)

It took a long time for the English actor Dirk Bogarde to shrug off the matinee-idol reputation foisted upon him during his years as a Rank contract player in the 1950s. The son of a proud and austere half-Dutch father, who was art critic of *The Times,* Derek Gontron Jules Gaspard Ulric Niven van den Bogaerde was not the kind to invite willingly the adoration of teenage female fans nor the promotion of himself as the pretty boy of British cinema.

Bogarde was born on 28 March 1921. After a desultory schooling he studied commerical art at Chelsea Polytechnic and took to the stage, soon to have his acting ambitions interrupted by the war, during which he distinguished himself as a major in British intelligence. After being demobbed in 1946, Bogarde was quickly discovered by the British film industry and offered his first film, *Esther Waters,* in 1947. He soon made his mark, in an unlikely menacing role, in *The Blue Lamp* (1949). Such was the popularity of Bogarde's first few films, in particular as the hapless Dr Simon Sparrow in the *Doctor in the House* series, that for the next 14 years he found himself unwillingly chained to the treadmill of over 36 films for Rank, playing a series of suave or occasionally diffident romantic heroes. Whilst he displayed notable romantic charisma in leading roles, as the consumptive painter in *The Doctor's Dilemma* (1959), as Liszt in *Song Without End* (1960, made during a brief foray into the, for him, loathsome world of Hollywood) or as Sidney Carton in Dickens's *Tale of Two Cities* (1958), he found little personal satisfaction in it all.

The opportunity to turn his popular reputation on its head by accepting a trio of uncommercial black-and-white films in the 1960s: *Victim* (1961), *The Servant* (1963), and *Accident* (1967) was the catalyst Bogarde needed as a creative artist; in all of them he unequivocally demonstrated that he was no mere pin-up but an actor to be taken seriously. He relished the challenge in *The Servant* of playing (against type, and with a north-country accent to boot) the part of an evil and manipulative, working-class manservant, and in *Victim,* he made the brave decision to perform in one of the first films to deal openly with homosexuality. And Bogarde continued to prove that he was better than the box office fodder he had previously graced, by turning in fine performances in *King and Country* (1964), *Darling,* (1966) and *The Fixer* (1968).

However, the increasing domination of the 'kitchen-sink' genre of British realist cinema of the 1960s soon left Bogarde artistically stranded. His box-office career seemed in decline until he reinvented himself on the Continent, where he made the transition into the kind of beautiful, languidly decadent arthouse cinema that better suited his perfectionism and fastidious talent. It brought work with directors such as Luchino Visconti with whom he created *The Damned* (1969) and probably his most enduring role as Von Aschenbach in *Death in Venice* (1973); he also worked with Alain Resnais (*Providence,* 1977), Liliana Cavani (*The Night Porter,* 1973) and Rainer W Fassbinder (*Despair,* 1978). Here Bogarde was allowed to develop his talent for conveying inner turmoil seething under the surface of controlled detachment. Such films, however, were not without their detractors, who claimed they indulged Bogarde's tendency toward mannerism and archness, and he occasionally miscalculated in his over-reverential approach to material that was at times questionable – such as in the portentous and misguided *The Night Porter* with its risible and contrived sado-erotic undercurrents.

Having turned his back on Britain artistically, in the 1970s Bogarde decamped to a farmhouse in Provence, where he lived with his manager and companion Tony Forwood until Forwood's death in 1988. It was also at this time, with the encouragement of publisher Norah Smallwood, that he began writing, publishing *A Postillion Struck by Lightning* (1977), the first of a series of seven beautifully crafted but strangely guarded memoirs, beginning with an idyllic reflection on a happy childhood in rural Sussex. He later graduated to fiction with his first novel *A Gentle Occupation* (1980) and several others based on his wartime and acting experiences; for him literary acclaim as a writer was a much greater prize than any accolades as an actor. He later also took on book reviewing, with marked success.

With the long illness and eventual death of Forwood in 1988 Bogarde incurred heavy medical expenses, and reluctantly sold up in France and returned to England, eventually withdrawing to a flat in Chelsea. He became an increasingly reclusive and melancholic figure after the loss of Forwood, his companion of 40 years, and gave a moving account of his irreparable pain in *A Short Walk from Harrods* (1993). He was briefly lured back to the cinema in two French films, *Daddy Nostalgie* (1990) and *These Foolish Things* (1992), the latter year being finally awarded a knighthood.

The subject of Bogarde's private life was one on which he remained notoriously tight-lipped. Whilst he is known to have had relationships with women, he resisted responding to the inevitable suggestions of homosexuality which regularly resurfaced during his career, and in particular in the light of his role in *Accident* as a homosexual barrister. He was rigorous also in destroying all letters and diaries relating to his private life after he had drawn on them for each volume of memoirs. Determined to project his own, highly controlled public persona and let no stranger ever see into the window of his soul, Bogarde once acerbically put down the intrusive questioning of Russell Harty during a 1986 TV interview with the words 'I'm still in the shell, and you're not going to crack it, ducky'. And indeed the shell was never ever cracked – the performances consummate, well crafted, and detailed though they might be never quite convince beyond the level of technique. For here was an artist who never ever revealed himself, not even in his most intimate work on camera, and whose final and bitter message to a home country – that he felt had always undervalued him – was that he did not wish to be remembered: 'no funeral, no memorial service, just forget me'. He died on 8 May 1999 at the age of 78. HR

Carmichael, Stokely

former name of Kwame Ture
(1941–1999)

Black firebrand and orator who coined the term 'Black Power' and preached militancy and separatism. He reacted to the brutal violence unleashed on civil right protesters in the 1960s American South by refusing to turn the other cheek and instead, with rising stridency, called for the use of violence and for self-reliance. His increasing radicalism split the civil rights movement and eventually left him a marginalised figure in exile in Africa.

Born in Port of Spain, Trinidad, on 29 June 1941, he was the son of a carpenter and a ship's stewardess. His parents moved to New York City when he was two and he lived with his grandmother until he joined them in Harlem nine years later. Despite a self-described youth of petty crime as the only black member of the Morris Park Dukes gang in the East Bronx, he won entry to the well-regarded Bronx High School of Science and from there went to the all-black Howard University in Washington, DC. As a student he joined in the struggle to force the desegregation of the South and in 1961 he took part in the Congress for Racial Equality's Freedom Rides, challenging the segregation practised on buses. Carmichael joined the Student Non-Violent Co-ordinating Committee (SNCC) in 1964, following graduation from Howard, and his charisma, charm, and self-confidence propelled him up the ranks of the group. He marshalled a successful voter registration programme in Lowndes County, Alabama, and formed the all-black Lowndes County Freedom Organisation, choosing as its logo the black panther, which was to become the symbol of black militancy. Exposure to the violence against civil rights activists, black and white, shocked him and his reaction was to reject the orthodoxy of non-violence advocated by leaders such as Martin Luther King. In May 1966, already on the radical fringe, he manoeuvred his election as chairman of the SNCC, forcing out the moderate John Lewis, a former friend. The following month he used the phrase 'Black Power' in a speech in Greenwood, Mississippi, after the wounding of James Meredith, the first black student at the University of Mississippi, while on a protest march.

Taken up as a war cry by young blacks across America, the rallying call of 'Black Power' was criticized by other black leaders and raised racial tensions, alienating many liberal whites who had supported the civil rights movement. Carmichael was expelled from the SNCC in 1967 and made honorary prime minister of the extremist Black Panther Party formed by Bobby Seale and Huey P Newton. He nevertheless continued to move further from the mainstream and, by the time he moved to Africa in the spring of 1969, he had even denounced the Panthers for enlisting support from whites.

He spent the last 30 years of his life in Guinea espousing the pan-African dogma of the All African People's Revolutionary Party to the diminishing numbers who would listen. He called himself Kwame Ture after Ghanaian Kwame Nkrumah and Guinean Séou Touré, two leading proponents of pan-African action. Although he continued to speak around the world, his influence was waning rapidly. At different times he was banned from the UK and Trinidad due to his advocacy of violence – he advised Brixton rioters to get hold of grenades – and he alienated many in later years by his anti-Zionism, praise for Hitler, and dismissal of the role of women. The years eroded his reputation considerably, especially in comparison to the mark left on history by Malcolm X, whose mantle he adopted after the 'Black Power' speech, and Martin Luther King. Both his marriages were dissolved. He died in Conakry, Guinea, on 15 November 1998 of prostate cancer at the age of 57, blaming his demise on the forces of US imperialism. DM

Denning, Alfred Thompson

Baron Denning of Whitchurch
(1899–1999)

Widely regarded as one of the greatest judges of the present century, Lord Denning will always be remembered as the champion of the common man, who saw his priority as dispensing justice rather than merely adhering to the letter of the law. He took the view that people would better respect the law if they believed it to be fair and just. Thus throughout his career as a judge, fairness became his major priority, and his success in this respect was demonstrated by the legislative changes which were made following some of his judgements. During law vacations he travelled the world, preaching his gospel of justice to a wide range of audiences. In so doing, he became particularly popular with young people who hitherto had regarded law and lawyers as rigid and remote: out of touch with the real world as they saw it.

Despite this, it has been said that there were flaws in his judgement in his later life. In his 83rd year, in his book *What Next in the Law?*, he questioned the wisdom of selecting black jurors in a particular case, prompting the two jurors concerned to threaten legal action. Nine years later, nearly a decade after his retirement, he was reported in *The Spectator* as saying that had the death penalty been in force at the time of the conviction of the Guildford Four 'they'd have probably hanged the right men', and that if the Birmingham Six had been hanged all the campaigns to have them released would have been avoided. These instances must, however, be regarded as aberrations, at odds with the overall attitude and behaviour of a man dedicated to securing what he saw as a just result in every case in which he was involved. For example, he was particularly concerned about the plight of wives deserted by their husbands and his judgements were eventually enshrined in the Matrimonial Causes Act, 1967.

He came particularly to the notice of the general public when in 1963 Prime Minister Harold Macmillan asked him to conduct an inquiry into the security risks arising from the resignation of the secretary of state for war, John Profumo, after the revelations of his affair with Christine Keeler. He always expressed himself in simple, straightforward English and the *Denning Report* was a classic of its kind, with chapter headings such as 'Christine tells her story' and 'The man in the mask' making it an instant best-seller. He became an overnight celebrity, appearing on television chat shows and having T-shirts emblazoned with his name.

More important, however, was the respect with which Denning continued to be held by his fellow lawyers. They appreciated the clarity of his mind, the wealth of knowledge he had accumulated over the years, and his ability to distinguish the essential justice needed in a judgement over and above the strict niceties of the written law. On the occasion of his retirement in July 1982 the Lord Chief Justice's Court was full to overflowing. The Lord Chancellor, Lord Hailsham, described him as a legend in his own lifetime.

Alfred Thompson Denning, called Tom from an early age, was the fourth of five sons of a draper in Whitchurch, Hampshire. There must have been some particular quality in the Denning genes because one of his brothers entered the army and rose to the rank of lieutentant-general and another became a vice-admiral in the navy. Tom attended elementary school in Whitchurch and then Andover grammar school before serving on the Western Front in World War I. After the war he read mathematics at Magdalen College, Oxford, gaining first class honours. He then taught briefly at Winchester College before returning to Magdalen, this time to study law. Again, he came out with a First. Having failed the All Souls Prize Fellowship examination he came top in the Bar exams and was called to the Bar, at Lincoln's Inn, in 1923. He practised in London and on the Western Circuit, making a comfortable living, until 1938 when he was made a KC. In 1944 he was

appointed a high court judge in the Probate, Divorce, and Admiralty Division, being transferred a year later to the King's Bench Division as a trial judge. It was here that he established a reputation for clarity and fairness in pension appeals and matrimonial cases. In 1948 he moved to the Court of Appeal and nine years later became a Lord of Appeal, with the title Baron Denning of Whitchurch. His progression continued, becoming Master of the Rolls, the country's senior civil judge, in 1962, a position he held until his retirement.

After his retirement he continued to debate in the House of Lords but was not particularly enamoured with it, saying that it was rather like heaven: a place you would like to go to but not while there was still any life in you. He was awarded the Order of Merit in 1997.

After living for some time in Sussex, in 1963 he returned to Whitchurch where he lived happily with his second wife, his first having died prematurely. Tom Denning never lost his country roots and retained his delightful Hampshire burr. He was indeed a legend in his own lifetime: a man of the people and a judge for the people. He died at Winchester, Hampshire, on 3 March 1999 at the age of 100. DD

DiMaggio, Joe (Joseph Paul)

(1914–1999)

US baseball player. Nicknamed 'Joltin' Joe' or the 'Yankee Clipper', he was one of baseball's greatest players, and one of the USA's most cherished sporting heroes. Graceful and athletic, he was perhaps the cleanest and most consistent hitter baseball has ever seen. Naturally talented, supremely self-confident, yet honest and unassuming, his popularity among baseball fans transcended team loyalties. His brief marriage to Marilyn Monroe in 1954 added to his fame, but by this time his exploits on the baseball field had already made him a revered national institution. In thirteen seasons in the major leagues between his debut in 1936 and his retirement in 1951, he had helped the New York Yankees to win the World Series on nine occasions. In 1941 he had set one of baseball's best known and most long-established records when he hit safety in 56 straight games, an achievement which has never been equalled, and which instantly became part of US sporting legend.

Joseph Paul DiMaggio, Jr, was born on 25 November 1914 in Martinez, near San Francisco, California. The eighth of nine children, two of his brothers, Vince and Dom, also became major league baseball players. His parents had emigrated from Sicily, and in California his father became a crab fisherman. A star player at San Francisco Junior High School, in 1932, aged only 17, Joe Jr signed for the San Francisco Seals of the Pacific Coast League. His talents were immediately apparent and it was not long before several major league teams were vying for his signature. In 1934 he was bought by the New York Yankees, though it was agreed that he would stay with the Seals for two years to develop his skills. When he finally arrived in New York in 1936 it was as the most heralded newcomer to the major leagues since Ty Cobb in 1905. Despite this heavy burden of expectation the rookie centrefielder did not disappoint. He averaged .321 hits in a season in which the Yankees won their first World Series in four years. Crowds were impressed by his smooth but powerful hitting, and by his brilliant, almost nonchalant fielding. In both 1939, when he achieved a career best hitting mark of .381, and in 1940 when he hit .352, he won the American League batting title. His famous 56 game hitting streak began on 15 May 1941. When it ended on 17 July he had exceeded the previous record set in 1897, by 12 games.

In 1943 he volunteered for the military service and served until 1945 as a physical training instructor. This meant he missed the Yankees' 1943 World Series success, but he returned for the 1946 season. In 1949 he became baseball's first ever $100,000 a year player. Any doubts about whether he was worth such a colossal amount were soon dispelled when he came back from a two-month injury layoff to face a formidable Boston Red Sox team in the contest for the American League championship. DiMaggio hit four home runs in three games, to lead the Yankees into the World Series contest where they overcame the Brooklyn Dodgers.

Increasingly troubled by injury, in December 1951 he announced his retirement. In his 13 seasons in the Major League he had hit 1,390 runs, including 361 home runs, at an average of .325. As well as his two batting titles he was named the American League's Most Valuable Player in 1939, 1941, and 1947. And throughout his major league career he never failed to make the All-Star team.

DiMaggio had married Dorothy Arnold, a Hollywood starlet, in 1939. They had a son, Joe DiMaggio III, but they divorced five years later. In 1952, he was introduced to Marilyn Monroe, who was just starting to make her name as a film star. Encouraged by her studio who saw the publicity value of her associating with someone as famous and revered as DiMaggio, they began seeing each other. In January 1954, in one of the celebrity events of the decade, they were married. The relationship, however, was doomed from the start. DiMaggio, despite his fame, was essentially a private man, and loathed the brash, artificial Hollywood lifestyle. He soon grew jealous of all the attention she received, and after just nine months their marriage was dissolved. Any bitterness they had between them was short-lived, and to the end he remained her protector. Shortly before her death in 1962 there were rumours that they might get back together again. DiMaggio himself organized her funeral, and for the rest of his life he sent two roses to her grave three times a week.

In retirement DiMaggio remained highly marketable and was in demand from businesses to endorse and promote their products. Indeed in the 1950s he found new fame, if that were possible, as television's Mr Coffee. He accumulated a not inconsiderable fortune, much of which he spent on charitable and philanthropic projects such as the Joe DiMaggio Children's Hospital, in his adopted home of Hollywood, Florida. In later life he was seen less and less in public, although every year he would return to Yankee Stadium to pitch the ceremonial first ball of the season.

He died at Hollywood, Florida, on 8 March 1999. BR

Ehrlichman, John (Daniel)

(1925–1999)

US politician, Watergate conspirator, and Nixon confidant. Jailed for 18 months for his role in the break-ins and attempted cover-up that caused the fall of President Richard Nixon, he was a key member of the White House's inner circle. Ehrlichman and his colleague H R Haldeman shared the president's paranoia and were nicknamed the 'Berlin Wall' by the press for the way they sealed off Nixon from the outside world. Ehrlichman formed a secret band of agents to perform dirty tricks on behalf of the president and the leak-plugging of the 'plumbers' led to disgrace for Nixon and prison for himself. In later life, he voiced regret for his actions and, speaking from experience, warned against making moral judgements to anyone else. His motivation seems to have been a fierce and genuine desire to serve his president. Ehrlichman had become White House chief advisor on domestic policy in 1969, after a spell as counsel, but his involvement in Watergate completely overshadowed the promise, energy, and sharp mind noted by political observers at the time.

He was born on 20 March 1925, in Tacoma, Washington, and flew in 26 bombing raids over Germany while serving in the United States Army Air Force. He returned to the USA and graduated from UCLA, then gained a law degree from Stanford, and was a planning law expert with his own firm in Seattle when Haldeman, a contemporary at UCLA, recruited him into politics. Ehrlichman worked on the Nixon campaign for the presidency in 1960 and for the governorship of California in 1962 before Nixon took the White House in 1968.

The arrest of five 'plumbers' during a break-in lit the fuse that ruined Ehrlichman and Nixon. The agents, operating under the direction of 'Creep', the Committee to Re-Elect the President, were trying to repair a bug in the headquarters of the Democratic National Committee in the Watergate Hotel in Washington, DC. The White House was seeking to glean intelligence on the Democrats in the run-up to the 1972 elections. Nixon was determined to exploit every avenue in order to secure four more years in office.

Equally explosive had been an earlier burglary of the offices of Dr Lewis Fielding in September 1971. Fielding was the Beverley Hills psychiatrist of whistle blower Dr Daniel Ellsberg, who had leaked the 'Pentagon Papers' to the press. The secret documents, which sparked a First Amendment battle between the government and *The New York Times* and the *Washington Post,* detailed the truth of American involvement in the Vietnam War.

As the scale of White House wrongdoing was teased into the open gradually by *The Washington Post* and congressional hearings, Ehrlichman argued that a confession was the best strategy. Once deception was decided upon, however, he became a central and willing figure in the attempts to mislead the nation and to protect the president. On 30 April 1973, Nixon forced Ehrlichman and Haldeman to resign, and sacked counsel John Dean in a vain effort to save his own position. Teetering on the brink of impeachment, Nixon announced his own resignation on 9 August 1974 and handed the presidency to Gerald Ford. Ehrlichman, Haldeman, and former Attorney General John N Mitchell were convicted in January 1975 on charges related to the Watergate scandal. Ehrlichman served 18 months for conspiracy, perjury, and obstruction of justice, and settled in New Mexico after his release from Stafford Federal Prison in Arizona.

Disbarred, he wrote a number of books based on his experience of political life and an account of the Nixon years, *Witness to Power* (1982). He also worked on radio and television. In recent years he resurrected his legal career and was involved in a law firm dealing in issues surrounding hazardous waste. Ehrlichman died in Atlanta on 14 February 1999, having suffered from diabetes for about a year. DM

Elion, Gertrude Belle

(1918–1999)

US biochemist who developed several drugs and shared the Nobel Prize for Physiology or Medicine in 1988 with her colleague George Herbert Hitchings (1905–98) and Scottish pharmacologist Sir James Whyte Black (1924–). She was the first woman to be inducted in the National Inventors' Hall of Fame in 1991. She was also named in the Engineering and Science Hall of Fame and received the National Medal for Science. In addition, she won the Higuchi Memorial Award in 1995. Her name is on over 40 patents.

Gertrude Elion was born in New York City to Lithuanian and Russian parents and was educated at Hunter College, graduating with a BA in chemistry in 1937. While studying at night school for her Masters degree in chemistry she worked as a lab assistant, a food analyst, and a school teacher. Her ambition from a young age had been to find a cure for cancer, an aim influenced by the deaths of her grandfather and mother from cancer during her teenage years.

World War II opened up laboratory jobs for women, and after completing her Masters degree in 1941, Elion worked as a biochemist in the Wellcome Research Laboratories in Tuckahoe, New York. It was there that she began her long association with George Herbert Hitchings, becoming his research associate in 1944. They were pioneers of pharmaceutical research, developing drugs to treat previously incurable diseases. She later became senior research chemist in the company and from 1967 to 1983 was head of experimental therapy. After retiring from Burroughs Wellcome in 1983 she was research emeritus at Glaxo Wellcome until her death.

With Hitchings, Elion worked on the development of a drug that would stop the growth of bacteria or tumour cells by synthesizing compounds to inhibit DNA synthesis, and prevent the replication of unwanted cells. Elion started work on purines (which are important constituents of DNA) and the synthesis of nucleic acids. During this time she had to choose between continuing this work and a doctorate she had started at Brooklyn Polytechnic Institute. She chose to continue in her job and although she never finished her doctorate she was rewarded later by several honorary doctorates for her research, and by 25 honorary degrees.

At a time when most other researchers were testing randomly selected molecules for efficacy, Elion and Hitchings were using their knowledge of nucleic acid structure to target systematically specific molecules. Their methods revolutionized the pharmacological research and caused them to be singularly prolific in their discovery of new drugs.

In 1950 they produced pyrimethamine, which was found to be 2,000 times more toxic to the malarial parasite than to the human host and was thus very effective in contemporary malarial treatment.

In the early 1950s, Elion and Hitchings' research into the chemistry of purines and pyramidines led to the development of drugs called purine antimetabolites; two of these were successful in treating leukaemia in rodents. One of these, 6-mercaptopurine (6MP), was tested on terminally ill children and found to produce complete remission in one in three patients, although this was sometimes temporary. This opened up whole new areas of research and 6MP is still used in combination with other drugs to treat children with acute leukaemia, with success in around 80 percent of cases.

From the study of 6MP, Elion developed the antibiotic trimethroprim in 1956 and the drug azathioprene in 1957, used to block the immune response which caused the rejection of transplanted kidneys. Azathioprene is also used to treat autoimmune diseases including rheumatoid arthritis and systemic lupus. With her colleagues she also synthesized allopurinol which inhibits the formation of uric acid and is used to treat gout and other diseases related to the over-production of uric acid.

In 1970 Elion and her team synthesized acyclovir which has been in use since 1981 and is very effective in the treatment of herpes virus in its various forms, including shingles (caused by varicella-zoster), and life-threatening herpes encephalitis. This preceded the successful development of AZT, the first AIDS drug, by researchers at Burroughs Wellcome who had been trained by Hitchings and Elion. When Elion was awarded her Nobel prize, the Nobel committee commented that really she and Hitchings deserved a prize for each of the drugs they had discovered.

Following her retirement from Burroughs Wellcome in 1983, Elion took up honorary lectureships, served on many advisory boards and shared her experience with medical research students. She also worked with the World Health Organization and the American Cancer Society. She died in North Carolina on 21 February 1999, aged 81. CT

Evans, (Thomas) Godfrey

(1920–1999)

English cricketer, one of the most popular players of the postwar period. The English public's enthusiasm for the cricket was never higher than immediately after World War II. The England Test team was studded with stars: Denis Compton, the swashbuckling genius, Len Hutton, the imperious master batsman, and Alec Bedser, the lethally accurate seam bowler. And behind the stumps was Godfrey Evans, the showman. Flamboyant, animated, boundlessly energetic, and always highly competitive, he was popular with team-mates and spectators alike. Remarkably agile given his stocky build, he was renowned for his diving catches, and lightning-quick leg side stumpings. He stood up to all but the fastest bowlers. In particular, he formed a fruitful partnership with Alec Bedser, and his intimidating presence behind the stumps contributed greatly to the Surrey bowler's ability to dominate opposing batsmen. Evans's qualities were ably summed up by Don Bradman in his 1959 book *The Art of Cricket:* 'Godfrey Evans displayed more agility than anyone I can remember and he also possessed astonishing energy. In fact his whole effervescent personality, his infectious humour and obvious enjoyment of the task, must have been a great inspiration to many England teams'.

Evans was not the sort of wicket-keeper interested in averages and records, yet statistically alone he is one of the game's greats. He was the first keeper to make 200 dismissals in Test cricket, and his career total of 219 dismissals, 173 of them caught and 46 stumped, set in 91 Tests between 1946 and 1959 was a world record until the mid 1970s.

A hard-hitting, right-handed batsman, he scored 2,439 Test runs, including two centuries, at an average of 20.69. He was the first wicket-keeper to achieve the double of 200 dismissals and 2,000 runs. For a player who liked to score his runs quickly it is remarkable that in a 1948–49 match against Australia at Adelaide he set a new Test record for slow scoring by going 97 minutes without getting a run. However, in occupying the crease for so long he helped to save England from defeat, and Evans was above all a team man. More characteristic though was his innings against India at Lord's in 1952, when he scored 98 runs before lunch.

Thomas Godfrey Evans was born on 18 August, 1920 in Finchley, London. Brought up in Kent, he captained his Canterbury school at football and hockey as well as

cricket. He joined the playing staff at Kent County Cricket Club at the age of 16. At the time he also showed promise as a boxer; however, Kent insisted that he gave up the sport in case he damaged his eyes. In 1939 he made his first class debut, and might have claimed a regular place if war had not intervened. However, he excelled in wartime service matches, and when first class cricket was resumed in 1946 he was immediately installed as Kent's first choice wicket-keeper. In August 1946 he was called up by England for the last Test of the series against India. Evans was given little chance to impress in a rain-interrupted match but for the next 13 years he would be an almost permanent fixture of the England side. He went on four England tours to Australia and twice toured the West Indies and South Africa. Among the high points of his career was the 1953 home series against Australia when England regained the Ashes for the first time since before the war. In 1954 he broke the record for the most dismissals by a wicket-keeper in Test cricket when he surpassed Bert Oldfield's mark of 154, which had stood since 1936.

Evans played his last Test against India at Lord's in 1959. England won the match but he had had a poor game by his standards and was dropped. He immediately announced his retirement from international cricket though he continued to play county cricket for another ten years, and helped to nurture the talent of Kent's talented young wicket-keeper, Alan Knott. He retired from the first class game with a career total of 1,066 dismissals, 816 of which were caught and 250 stumped. He had scored nearly 15,000 runs.

In retirement he pursued a number of commercial ventures but he always stayed close to the game, his ebullient personality and natural bonhomie ensuring that he remained one of cricket's best-loved characters. He died at Northampton on 3 May 1999. BR

Godden, (Margaret) Rumer

(1907–1998)

The English writer Rumer Godden, who died not long after publishing her last novel (at the age of 90), turned a life, that began in ex-patriot privilege and included periods of emotional and physical deprivation, into the stuff of memorable stories. She held that such experiences fuelled her writing – 'I'm a great believer in the garrett'.

Many of Godden's 24 novels are set in the exotic milieu of India, where she grew up (in what is now Bangladesh), the ugly duckling of four daughters of a British steamship company owner. The best-known of these, her 1938 novel *Black Narcissus,* which was filmed in 1946, is a haunting story about Anglican nuns struggling to maintain an isolated convent in the Himalayas in an atmosphere of escalating emotional strain and repressed passions that finally unhinges one of them.

Godden was born in Eastbourne, Sussex. Her idyllic childhood in India was interrupted in 1920 by a period in a succession of much-loathed boarding schools in England. Returning to India in 1924 she fell back on her training in ballet and shocked Anglo-Indian society by opening a multi-racial dance school in Calcutta. It was the first of many independent stands Godden took in her refusal to kowtow to what she saw as narrow and outmoded convention and in her desire to get closer to the Indian people and learn more about Hinduism.

Godden's life was thrown into crisis in 1934 when, after an affair with an English stockbroker, Laurence Sinclair Foster, she found herself pregnant and obliged to marry a man with whom she had little rapport. Her baby died soon after being born. By the outbreak of war, with two small daughters, her husband away in the army, and a pile of his unpaid debts, Godden went to live in a remote part of Kashmir, where, in a simple cottage without running water or electricity, she supported her children through her writing.

Godden had begun dabbling with poetry as a child, but it was not until 1935 that she had published her first book, for children, *Chinese Puzzle.* Whilst she later produced some fine children's fiction, including the prize-winning *The Diddakoi* (1972), it was her third, adult novel that would become a best seller and establish her international reputation. The film version of *Black Narcissus,* with its surprisingly erotic undercurrents, became an arthouse classic and something of a cult film. Directed by Michael Powell and Emeric Pressburger and with Academy Award-winning cinematography by Jack Cardiff, the film helped ensure the book's enduring popularity and its continuing availability in print. Godden, however, remained unimpressed with the film, which for her turned a story grounded in her own real experience of India into artistic fantasy and emotional melodrama. She described it as 'phoney' and an 'abomination', a result, as she saw it, of its not being shot on location in the Himalayas but recreated in a garden in Surrey, with the legendary mountain range mocked up by swathes of muslin draped around poles.

At the end of the war, after nearly being killed by her deranged Indian cook, who laced her dahl curry with ground glass, marijuana, and opium, Godden returned to England. She remarried in 1949. James Haynes Dixon was a devoted and self-effacing man whose quiet adoration, she admitted, was not reciprocated by her, but who loyally supported her through the writing of many more novels. She often took a young person as her subject in her adult novels, with the focus on childhood rites of passage and the predatory role grown-ups often take in the child's transition to adulthood. Other novels such as *The River* (1946) and *Greengage Summer* (1958) were successfully filmed (with Godden taking much greater pleasure working with French director Jean Renoir on the 1951 film adaptation of her study of Indian village life, *The River),* but there were many other memorable works of fiction, including *Kingfishers Catch Fire* (1953), *In This House of Brede* (1969), *The Peacock Spring* (1975, dramatized by BBC TV in 1995), *Coromandel Sea Change* (1990), and *Pippa Passes* (1994).

An independent spirit, Godden freely admitted that her true male ideal was a fictional one – Jane Austen's Mr Darcy. Once smitten, she read the novel more than a dozen times, and admitted in later life that she had loved Darcy 'far better than my own husbands'. Such an observation would seem to summarize a long, disciplined, and at times solitary life driven by a highly fertile imagination. Certainly that undimmed imagination had provided the background, right to the end, for a rich creative career, producing poetry, translations, a much-admired biography of Hans Christian Andersen (1955), several volumes of memoirs, and an autobiography *A Time to Dance, No Time to Weep* (1987). It had also, no doubt, left its mark upon a personal life tinged with disappointment and the self-imposed loneliness of the writer. In 1968 Rumer Godden became a Roman Catholic and through her new-found faith gained a degree of spiritual solace in relation to both her life and work, averring that the writer 'is simply an instrument through which the wind blows and I believe it is the Holy Spirit that makes the artist creative'. She died at the age of 90 on 8 November. HR

Grade, Lew

Lord Grade of Elstree
(1906–1998)

Lew Grade often affectionately, if not enviously, nick-named Sir Low Greed, was the nearest Britain has come to having a home-grown movie mogul. The face certainly had exactly the right belligerent look, especially with a fat Monte Cristo cigar rammed in the side of the mouth, and Grade was in many ways the archetypal larger-than-life show-biz personality, possessed of the irrepressible energy of a man who made things happen, always sticking to his own simple philosophy of giving the public what he was damned sure they wanted and which he would give them in his own inimitable way.

Like many other of his Jewish contemporaries who escaped life in the villages of Eastern Europe and emigrated in hope of a better life, he made good in an industry that would be dominated by hard-working and visionary Eastern European Jews – particularly in Hollywood. In 1912 the Winogradsky family left Ukraine and came to England, where they settled in the Jewish East End of London. Here Lew took up the family trade of tailoring at the age of 14. Even at this age there was already something of the showman in him, which found its outlet in dance, and he became a champion tap dancer, winning the 'world solo Charleston championship' in 1926. During a ten-year career as a professional dancer around the variety halls, and even at the Moulin Rouge in Paris, he changed his name to Grade. But not content with having his own career, Grade soon began fostering the careers of other performers and in 1943, deciding he had a flair for discovering new talent, he became a theatrical agent with his brother Leslie and founded the Grade Organization.

It was inevitable that a man of Grade's abilities would be quick to home in on the potential of commercial television during its infancy in the 1950s, when Grade sunk practically everything he had in shares in ATV (Associated Television). From here he dominated British commercial television for the next 20 years, bringing the public programmes such as the soap opera *Crossroads* (which ran for 24 years), *Danger Man, The Prisoner, The Saint, Thunderbirds, Sunday Night at the London Palladium* (which from 1955 to 1967 held the prime slot of weekend viewing), and finally, one of his biggest worldwide hits, *The Muppet Show,* which sold in 112 countries. Ultimately he even achieved a level of 'artistic' credibility and international critical acclaim with the 1977 mini-series *Jesus of Nazareth,* starring Robert Powell. But Grade never actively sought validation in the field of 'arts' programming, since he considered art and entertainment two separate fields, commenting once on a TV arts programme that it 'must be culture: it certainly isn't entertainment'.

By this time Grade, and his two brothers, Leslie and Bernard (later Lord Delfont) had between them come to dominate popular entertainment in Britain (it was Grade's brother, Bernard, who owned the London Palladium). But Grade, a compulsive workaholic, had no thoughts of retiring (or for that matter holidays, which he hated), and when he gave up his chairmanship of ATV in 1976, he did not take a rest but dived into a new and much bigger fishpond – motion pictures. Here, unfortunately, the Midas touch failed him somewhat; films such as *Voyage of the Damned* (1976), *The Boys From Brazil* (1978), and *Sophie's Choice* (1982) were never a big pull on audiences. His big money-spinner in the cinema was undoubtedly the hugely popular *Pink Panther* films starring Peter Sellers as the comic French detective Inspector Clouseau, although the 1973 horror film *The Exorcist* has since developed a cult following. Meanwhile, those who resented Grade's domination of the industry and his ruthlessness in business dealings enjoyed their moment of *schadenfreude* when his ambitious 1980 big-budget film *Raise the Titanic* bombed at the box office, taking only $7 million after costing $40 million to make. As Grade himself good-humouredly remarked – 'It would have been cheaper to lower the Atlantic'.

Loved or not, Grade was generally respected for his energy and generosity; he did a lot for the British film and TV industry in selling his product and the skills of British actors and technicians abroad, particularly in the previously resistant US market. His efforts in this respect were rewarded with a knighthood in 1969 and in 1976 he became a life peer. Grade retained his energy for life right to his dying day. He remained unshakeably convinced of the virtues of his own products and in a quip to rival the classic *non sequiturs* of his US equivalent Sam Goldwyn, he once said 'All my shows are great. Some of them are bad, but they're all great'. Grade died on 13 November at the age of 91. HR

Grotowski, Jerzy

(1933–1999)

Polish theatrical visionary, revolutionary director, and champion of 'poor' theatre, which dismissed customary scenic trappings. Hailed as a genius when he brought the raw energy of his emotionally charged productions to New York in 1969, he influenced a generation of acolytes despite protesting against what he considered excessive adulation. His concept of drama stripped to its essence inspired theatrical troupes in the image of the Polish Laboratory Theatre, with which he carried out his early work.

Born in Rzeszów, Poland, he was brought up by his mother after his father left. He attended the State Theatre School in Cracow between 1951 and 1959. He then spent time in Moscow and China to further his education, having been blocked from studying in the West. He returned to Poland in 1957 and founded his own group in Opole in 1959. The Theatre of 13 Rows, the name indicating the importance he placed on audience proximity, became the Laboratory Theatre and moved to the city of Wrocław.

As a director he stripped away the props of traditional or 'rich' theatre – scenery, lighting, and music – and concluded that only the reaction of the spectator to the actor was necessary. In pioneering versions of Marlowe's *Dr Faustus* (1963) and Pedro Calderón de la Barca's *The Constant Prince* (1965), his 'poor' theatre productions breached the emotional distance between actor and audience, invading the comfort zone of the watchers through extreme performances. Howls, savage cries, contortions, and unnatural movement were common in Grotowski's plays but beneath the apparent chaos on stage lay enormous discipline. No deception was permitted to dilute the dynamics of conflict set up with the audience. The members of the Laboratory Theatre followed a strict training schedule and had to dedicate themselves totally to the poor theatre. It was far removed from traditional drama.

The Laboratory Theatre performed in the West for the first time in 1966 and Grotowski's reputation grew with the publication of his book *Towards a Poor Theatre* two years later. His influence exploded in 1969 with a series of productions in New York City. Grotowski rejected the traditional arena of the theatre and the setting was tailored for each production, always remaining intimate. Capacity was limited to 100 for *Akropolis* and *The Constant Prince* at the Washington Square Methodist Church but the scale of the audiences bore no relation to the impact the revolutionary plays had on the world of avant-garde theatre. The likes of André Gregory, Peter Brook, and Joseph Chaikin were all influenced by the work of the impeccably turned-out Pole. Companies such as the Performance Group and the Living Theatre attempted to live by his ideals of the stage as a way of life and similar ensembles emerged all over the world.

Grotowski, however, was far from happy with the chorus of praise that greeted his arrival in the USA. In 1970 he sought to clarify the nature of his approach with a series of seminars in New York entitled 'Misconceptions in the United States about the Grotowski Method'. He spent increasing amounts of time in the West, especially Italy, and in the 1980s taught at Columbia University in New York and the University of California at Irvine. He was granted a MacArthur award to support his work but moved away from plays and turned his attention to 'events'. Eventually he settled in Italy and created a theatre centre in Pontedera where he focused on creating a physical vocabulary of genuine emotion, drawn from the rituals of world religions, to replace theatrical symbolism. Grotowski died on 14 January 1999 in Pontedera, having suffered from leukaemia for many years. DM

Heron, Patrick

(1920–1999)

English painter and writer-critic, who became widely regarded as the UK's foremost abstract artist. A persistent non-conformist, he had a inventive and unpredictable creative career. His painting and writing celebrated the power of modern art, challenging the English tradition of narrative, figurative work. The rock at the centre of the St Ives group, he drew inspiration from the Cornish landscape and his acknowledged masters, Braque, Matisse, and Bonnard, melding Cubist space with Fauvist colour.

Heron was born in Headingley, Yorkshire, on 30 January 1920, and suffered asthma from early childhood. His creativeness was nurtured in an environment of unorthodox socialism by his parents, Tom and Eulalie, who were active pacifists of high cultural and spiritual awareness and early on became aware of their son's vocation as an artist. He always regarded his first works, signed and dated from the age of 5, as an integral part of his lifelong artistic development. The ideals of his parents were a continuing inspiration throughout his life, animating the intensity of his ethical and political personality. A socialist and pacifist, he was a founding member of the Campaign for Nuclear Disarmament (CND) and frank in his intense dislike of the Conservative governments of the 1980s and 1990s; he refused a knighthood offered by Margaret Thatcher. He was also an ardent conservationist, campaigning successfully for the preservation of the Zennor headlands and moors of Cornwall.

Heron first moved to the southwest when his father set up Crysede Silks in St Ives in 1925, and he retained lasting memories of a landscape suffused with light and colour. The winter of 1927–28 was spent at Eagles Nest, a house on the promontory above Zennor, owned by Hugh Arnold-Forster, who was creating an extraordinary garden with specimens from southern hemisphere highlands; it was to become Heron's permanent home and inspiration after 1956.

In 1929 the Herons relocated to Welwyn Garden City, Hertfordshire, where his father established Cresta Silks. Heron produced his first design for the company in 1934, a print after Matisse, and was to become Cresta's principal designer after World War II. He attended St George's School, Harpenden, and the Slade School of Art, although the latter left him uninspired. With the outbreak of war, he followed his father's example by registering as a conscientious objector, and endured three years of heavy agricultural labour although he was eligible for exemption as an asthmatic. Declared unfit after a bout of pneumonia, he was taken on as a journeyman at the St Ives Pottery by Bernard Leach, whose 'power to materialise a concept' greatly influenced Heron's creative philosophy.

In 1945 he married Delia Reiss whom he had met at school in 1929 and would regard as his 'best and most essential critic'. They lived in Holland Park, London, but spent every summer in St Ives with their two daughters. During this period he began work as a writer and critic, contributing a series of authoritative essays on artists such as Nicholson, Klee, and Picasso to *The New English Weekly.* From 1947 to 1954 he produced reviews for the *New Statesman* and *Nation,* and he became London correspondent for *Arts (New York)* from 1955 to 1958. *The Changing Forms of Art,* a collection of his writings and lectures which became a standard text, was published in 1955.

His articles attacked the 'cultural imperialism' of American art in the mid-1960s and debated issues concerning art education, such as the merger of the English art schools with the polytechnics in the early 1970s. In later years he produced essays on Bonnard, Picasso, and Matisse, and published *Painter as Critic* in 1998. He was an articulate writer, his subtle analytical abilities, particularly of the plastic qualities of painting and nuances of style, stemming from close introspection of his own artistic development.

Heron insisted that the material reality of the painting was the prime statement: 'Space in colour is the subject of my painting. After all, what you see consists of one thing only, colour'. He rarely worked from the motif, considering memory to be a crucial element in the invention of images, as it recorded the impact of a form on the receiving imagination rather than simply noting its appearance. Even his portraiture, which included studies of T S Eliot and A S Byatt, was completed without the sitter. He also condemned art of the 1990s, which he saw as created purely through concept rather than visual response.

Throughout the 1940s and 1950s he drew inspiration from the modern French masters, Braque, Matisse, Bonnard, and Cézanne, frequently applying colour directly from the tube. In the early 1950s he advanced to more complex subjects such as *Christmas Eve, 1951* shown at the Festival of Britain. However, the Braque-influenced linear figuration of his post-war work decreased after the purchase, in April 1956, of Eagles Nest on Zennor Moor, acknowledged as 'very nearly the greatest passion' of his life. His paintings in these new surroundings became full of non-figurative forms, moving towards abstraction with tachiste 'garden paintings'.

In the late 1950s he became increasingly interested in the work of American Expressionists such as Mark Rothko, although he insisted that his 'horizon' and 'stripe' paintings of 1957–58 anticipated and influenced developments in American art rather than derived from it. His investigation of gentler forms in the 1960s – soft-edge abstract 'direction of colour' paintings executed in vibrant colours – was replaced by his 'wobbly hard-edge' compositions of the 1970s, although the sudden death of his wife in 1979 rendered him unable to paint for several months. His work was given fresh impetus by a visit to Australia as artist in residence at the Art Gallery of New South Wales, Sydney (1989–90), sparking the creation of the *Sydney Garden,* and *Big Paintings* (1994). He also designed stained glass for the Tate Gallery, St Ives, and banners for the Tate Gallery bookshop and the Chelsea and Westminster Hospital.

Heron won the Grand Prize at the John Moores Liverpool Exhibition in 1959 and was awarded the Silver Medal at the Sao Paolo VII Biennal in 1965. In 1977 he was appointed CBE. A successful retrospective of his work was held at the Tate Gallery, London, in 1998, and in June 1999 the Wadsworth Galleries, London, presented a memorial exhibition of his last project, 43 small gouaches. Heron died in Zennor, Cornwall, on 19 March 1999. SP

Herzberg, Gerhard

(1904–1999)

German-born Canadian physicist who used spectroscopy to determine the electronic structure and geometry of molecules, especially free radicals (atoms or groups of atoms that possess a free, unbonded electron), using spectroscopy. He received many honours for his work, including the 1971 Nobel Prize for Chemistry.

Herzberg was born on 25 December 1904 in Hamburg, where he had his early education. He then studied at the Technische Universität in Darmstadt, from which he gained his doctorate in 1928, and carried out postdoctoral work at the universities of Göttingen (1928–29) and Bristol (1929–30). On returning to Germany in 1930 he became a Privatdozent (an unsalaried lecturer) at the Darmstadt Technische Universität but in 1935, with the rise to power of Adolf Hitler, he fled to Canada after being told he could no longer teach, as his wife, Luise Oettinger, was of Jewish origin. In Canada, he became Research Professor of Physics at the University of Saskatchewan, Saskatoon, from 1935 to 1945. He spent the period from 1945 to 1948 in the USA as professor of spectroscopy at the Yerkes Observatory (part of the University of Chicago) in Wisconsin, then returned to Canada. From 1949 until his retirement in 1969 he was director of the division of pure physics for the National Research Council in Ottawa – a laboratory generally acknowledged as being one of the world's leading centres for molecular spectroscopy. He was Distinguished Research Scientist 1969–95 (Emeritus). He was also awarded Canada's CC (1968) and PC (1992).

Herzberg's most important work concerned the application of spectroscopy to elucidate the properties and structure of molecules. Depending on the conditions, molecules absorb or emit electromagnetic radiation (much of it in the visible part of the spectrum) of discrete wavelengths. Moreover, the radiation spectrum is directly dependent on the electronic and geometric structure of an atom or molecule and therefore provides detailed information about molecular energies, rotations, vibrations, and electronic configurations. Herzberg, studying common molecules such as hydrogen, oxygen, nitrogen, and carbon monoxide, discovered new lines in the spectrum of molecular oxygen; now called Herzberg bands, these spectral lines have been useful in analysing the upper atmosphere. He also elucidated the geometric structure of molecular oxygen, carbon monoxide, hydrogen cyanide, and acetylene (ethyne); discovered the new molecules phosphorus nitride and phosphorus carbide; proved the existence of the methyl and methylene free radicals; and demonstrated that both neutrons and protons are part of the nucleus. His research in the field of molecular spectroscopy not only provided experimental results of fundamental importance to physical chemistry and quantum mechanics but also helped to stimulate further research into the chemical reactions of gases.

In addition, Herzberg developed certain aspects of astronomy. He interpreted the spectral lines of stars and comets, finding in the latter a rare form of carbon. He also showed that hydrogen exists in the atmospheres of some planets, and identified the spectra of certain free radicals in interstellar gas.

Herzberg's publications include his monumental review of spectroscopy *Spectra of Diatomic Molecules* (second edition; 1950) which continues to be used in laboratories today; and the trilogy of monographs *Molecular Spectra and Molecular Structure* (I–III; 1939–66), also still in regular use. Herzberg died in Ottawa, Ontario, on 3 March 1999. CT

Hickson, Joan

(1906–1998)

Among her numerous roles, Joan Hickson was best known to the UK public as Agatha Christie's genteel home counties detective, Miss Marple. Yet it was not until she was 78 that Hickson took on this role, in a BBC TV series that lasted until 1992.

Hickson's longevity in the acting profession typified her attitude to her work, born of the now-lost tradition of the theatrical 'trooper'. The acting profession held no mystery for her, and her attitude to it was as brisk and no-nonsense as many of the roles she played. During a 60-year career she quietly and professionally turned her hand to whatever was asked of her, commenting that the great advantage of her profession was that you need never retire. In Hickson's case, the older she became, the more she was in demand.

As a character actress, Hickson never had to suffer humiliating competition for glamour roles. She worked solidly from her first acting engagement in provincial rep in 1927, having trained at the more salubrious venue of RADA, at a time when the acting profession was still considered somewhat risqué for nice young women such as herself. Whilst quickly making her mark in the West End, she also found her niche in films from the 1930s, in a string of supporting roles, many of them comic or eccentric, but in all cases imbued with her own particular skill for observing human idiosyncrasies. She rapidly cornered the market for somewhat imperious, toffee-nosed, middle-class ladies, but she could also turn her hand to characters that were more plain and homely, or even grotesque. Although Margaret Rutherford became the first to define Miss Marple in the cinema, adding a batty element to her portrayal in film versions of the early 1960s, it was Hickson who was Agatha Christie's own preferred choice for the role, as indicated in a letter to Hickson as early as 1945, and to which Hickson reacted with characteristic modesty.

Hickson continued to appear on the British stage into the 1970s, most notably in *A Day in the Death of Joe Egg* (1969) and Alan Ayckbourn's *Bedroom Farce* (1977) – travelling to Broadway with both productions. Her film career – spanning over 100 films – petered off at around the same time, after memorable cameos in *Doctor in the House* (1954), *Heavens Above!* (1963) and several of the Carry-On films. From this point on her TV work grew. Off-stage, Hickson remained a suburban housewife, to the end dismissing her acting talents as 'superficial' and merely a matter of instinct. Instinct or not, her television incarnation of Miss Marple remains definitive. With her polite, restrained demeanour, her neat tweeds and twin sets, Hickson's Miss Marple lived in a Britain long since lost: where little old ladies could ride their bicycles in safety, take afternoon tea in their chintzy cottages and look out over their well-manicured, chocolate-box village greens. The image had enormous appeal to audiences. There was something supremely comforting in Miss Marple and her nice orderly world, as represented by Hickson; a reminder of those halcyon days when nothing ever seemed to change. Hickson died on 17 October at the age of 92. HR

Hughes, Ted (Edward James)

(1930–1998)

The death of one of the great British poets of the second half of this century came as as much of a shock to his many admirers as had the moving and revealing publication, only 10 months previously, of his last published work – *Birthday Letters* – which was the long awaited poetic response to his tormented relationship with his first wife, the poet Sylvia Plath.

Ted Hughes was a massive and magnetic presence in British poetry, who became the inspiration to several generations of younger poets and writers. A strong and dignified personality, he retained his composure and his silence throughout a long and sustained attack from feminists, who had taken it upon themselves to condemn him for supposedly having driven their icon, the brilliant but unstable Plath, to suicide. For 30 years or more Hughes's life seemed blighted by this fateful relationship, until he settled the score, by publishing – unannounced – the compelling and eloquent verse narrative *Birthday Letters*.

Hughes was born, the son of a carpenter, in West Yorkshire. His early life amid the wild and rugged surroundings of the Yorkshire landscape instilled in him a powerful obsession with the primal forces of nature and wildlife that began as a childish compulsion to catch and kill small creatures. He likened this enduring obsession with the very fact of living, as 'an extension of your whole organism into the whole environment that's created you – that's created *us*. We're just the animal tip of it. And so to be still actively engaged in the system of interaction that created us – is like keeping contact with your own organs in your own body'. In adult life, it became the focal point of much of his most popular and visceral poetry.

In 1951 Hughes went to Cambridge to study English, but changed to anthropology, although poetry was by now the dominating force in his creative life. As with the lives of many great poets, however, Hughes's was hijacked by tragic destiny, in the form of his relationship with the US poet Sylvia Plath, whom he met in the autumn of 1955. Plath captivated Hughes with her intellectual brilliance and quicksilver personality and within four months they were married. At first they appeared to be living the idyllic life of two like minds, living for and sharing poetry in a mutually supportive creative relationship; both poets did much to promote each other's careers and on more than one occasion Hughes himself remarked that of the two of them, his wife was the better poet. However, cracks in the relationship soon developed. Plath had already attempted suicide on one occasion, before meeting Hughes, and once again became caught up with her own inner demons. Ironically, it is Hughes who helped put her in touch with her own poetic self, but it was a poetic self of such emotional intensity and destructiveness that it culminated in her suicide in February 1963. A year before, Hughes had left Plath for another woman, Assia Wevill, but that relationship too seemed blighted, in part by Plath's haunting presence and the speculation in the literary industry that Plath's death had spawned. Within six years of Plath's death, Assia Wevill also committed suicide, further fuelling Hughes's demonization by feminists for his treatment of the women in his life.

In the meantime, Hughes had stamped his mark on English poetry with his first and probably most popular collection, *The Hawk in the Rain* in 1957, which contained the often-quoted and much admired poem, 'The Thought-Fox'. He followed this collection with other equally successful ones: *Lupercal* (1960); *Wodwo* (1967); and *Crow* (1972); as well as several children's books such as *The Iron Man* (1968) – all of which continued to demonstrate his fascination with the primeval forces of nature and with the dark, primitive power of the world humankind inhabits. After a few disappointing collections Hughes's poetic talents revived with the publication in 1979 of *Moortown*, born of a now more contented existence with his second wife, Carol, and a life farming in Devon and pursuing his favourite pastime of fishing for trout in the River Torridge.

In 1984 Hughes succeeded John Betjeman as poet laureate and in the last few years of his life produced some of his most stunning and consummate work, with fine versions of Ovid's *Metamorphoses*, Racine's *Phèdre* and garnering a clutch of awards for *Tales from Ovid* (1997) and *Birthday Letters*. The timing of *Birthday Letters* was brilliant – whether or not it was accidental or the result of intimations of imminent death and the compulsion to finally unburden himself of his side of the Plath story, the book silenced many of Hughes's critics and its publication became even more poignant, if not tragic, in the light of his death, from cancer, not long after. In characteristically quiet and dignified fashion, at the end Hughes did not attempt to play the martyr or use his terminal illness as a means of exploiting the sympathy vote, but kept it a secret. Only 12 days before his death he travelled to Buckingham Palace to receive the Order of Merit from the Queen. Hughes died on 28 October at the age of 68. HR

Hume, (George) Basil

(1923–1999)

A remarkably popular archbishop of Westminster and one of the most admired public figures in Britain, Cardinal Hume succeeded in strengthening the reputation of the Catholic Church in England and Wales, and in making it more fashionable than it has been since the Reformation. Although he shepherded a flock of just 4.6 million, Hume's simplicity and humility, together with his ability to cut through convoluted moral arguments and get to the nub of the matter, made his a voice heard beyond his own church. One of Cardinal Hume's main achievements was in building bridges with the Church of England. During his time at Westminster, the Queen attended her first Catholic service, Cardinal Hume spoke at the Anglican's General Synod, and he persuaded Pope John Paul II to visit Britain in 1982 – a public relations coup that was well received by both Catholics and Anglicans.

In February 1976 Basil Hume – then a relatively obscure Benedictine abbot – was plucked from Ampleforth Abbey and private school in North Yorkshire, to become the new Archbishop of Westminster. He was the first monk to hold this office. At the time he admitted his surprise and unease, and said that he was 'shattered' when he got the news.

His election as cardinal in May 1976 was totally unexpected, the favourite successor and obvious candidate in informed circles being Monsignor Derek Worlock, then bishop of Portsmouth and later archbishop of Liverpool. Basil Hume's appointment was considered a daring choice, one that represented a deliberate break with tradition. Although half-French and half-Scottish, Hume came across as the epitome of an English gentleman, while his tastes also led him to a lifelong passion with squash and Newcastle United Football Club.

He quickly developed exceptional diplomatic skills, successfully unifying the Catholic Church in England by reconciling opposing conservative and liberal factions, especially after the Second Vatican Council (1962–65). His appealing spirituality, sincerity, and deftly considered public statements and opinions won him respect from many outside the Catholic Church, who came to see him as one of Britain's chief moral leaders. The Queen, the Church of England's supreme governor, reputedly thought of Basil Hume as 'my cardinal', and chose him to become one of the 24 members of the Order of Merit in 1999. He was the first Catholic bishop to receive this honour.

George (later Basil) Hume was born in Newcastle upon Tyne, the son of a Protestant physician and a French Catholic mother. His early faith was influenced by the Benedictine monastery at his Catholic private school in Ampleforth, North Yorkshire. At 18, he entered the monastery at Ampleforth as a Benedictine novice, taking the name Basil, and was ordained as a priest in 1950. He then studied at the school's sister college, Benet's Hall, Oxford, and at Fribourg University, Switzerland. He was senior master in modern languages at Ampleforth from 1952 and worked as a housemaster from 1955 at his old school, St Bede's, until 1963, when he was elected abbot of the Ampleforth Community. The contemplative, monastic life came to an abrupt end with his appointment as archbishop, and later cardinal, in 1976. His inauguration service was followed by an ecumenical service at Westminster Abbey. It was the first time in four centuries that the Anglican Abbey had resounded to Catholic plainsong, and provided a foretaste of things to come.

The cardinal had a close relationship with the Pope, to whom he remained steadfastly loyal, despite having a more liberal outlook than the pontiff himself. A firm supporter of the Vatican's line on priestly celibacy, women priests, homosexuality, contraception, and abortion, he was also known for his distaste at society's 'obsession with sex'. Yet, Cardinal Hume came through as less rigidly conservative than the Pope on many sensitive issues, never losing sight of human frailties, and always encouraging people from where they were to make progress towards the Church's ideals while still upholding the church's teaching. The cardinal surprised some more dogmatic Christians in 1993 when he affirmed the dignity of homosexuals, telling them 'not to develop a sense of guilt or think of themselves as unpleasing to God. On the contrary, they are precious to God'. This did not, however, prevent him from suspending the listing of Quest, an association of homosexual Catholics, from the new edition of the annual Catholic Directory, when it advocated same-sex relationships.

The toughest test of his leadership came in 1992 when the Church of England voted for the ordination of women. Despite his increasingly close dialogue with Canterbury, the Anglicans' acceptance of women priests stood in the way of church unity. Thousands of Anglo-Catholics turned to Rome, and Rome agreed to accept Anglican clergymen who were already married. About 300 Anglican clergy became Roman Catholics, but on Rome's terms: any hoped-for special concessions for converts – such as Anglican-rite liturgies and a dispensation allowing married priests to run parishes – were resisted. The cardinal made it clear that would-be converts could not expect to accept Catholic doctrine in part, but would have to embrace it in its entirety. He summed up his stance by telling those considering conversion that 'there is no question of becoming Catholic à la carte. You have to take the set menu – or move to another restaurant'.

He sparked controversy in 1998 when he called for an end to the 'hype' surrounding Diana, Princess of Wales, saying she had been 'by no means a saint'. However, his requiem Mass for Diana, and another for Mother Teresa, a week later, touched and moved not only the thousands who crowded Westminster Cathedral but millions of others who watched on television or listened on the radio. He always placed the highest emphasis on spirituality, and initiated a programme of spiritual renewal for the diocese and established a Centre for Spirituality in 1995.

Basil Hume emphasized the Church's role in fighting for social justice and his efforts on behalf of the Guildford Four and the Maguire Seven, wrongfully convicted as IRA bombers, helped lead to the quashing of their convictions in 1989. Touched by their plight after meeting one of the Maguire Seven in prison, Cardinal Hume took up their case. He was joined in 1986 by Lord Scarman and Lord Devlin, two law lords, and Merlyn Rees and Roy Jenkins, two former home secretaries. Together this 'Deputation' put a strong case to the home secretary for the cases to be referred to the Court of Appeal. Moved by the sight of the homeless people in the streets around Westminster Cathedral, Hume founded the Cardinal Hume Centre for young people at risk, and in December 1990 opened the cathedral hall to be used as a night shelter. The hall continued to be used in this way until 1992, when an alternative, permanent shelter was opened. The cardinal visited Ethiopia during the famine of 1984 and was deeply affected by the suffering he saw. He sought support for the Catholic Fund for Overseas Development, and tried to press the Foreign Office both to increase emergency aid as well as, from 1985, consider cancelling the debts of the world's poorest countries. He spoke out on many other issues including nuclear weapons, the arms trade, abortion, embryology, and euthanasia, and always strongly supported marriage and family values, human rights, and racial justice.

During Hume's time at Westminster, church attendance among Roman Catholics declined, as did those of other Christian denominations, but in the Diocese of Westminster about 600 new adult converts were brought in yearly. The Roman Catholic Church also saw a number of prominent people join its ranks, notably the Duchess of Kent. The cardinal, though, warned against triumphalism over this issue. When he became archbishop the diocese had a debt of over £6 million, which doubled over the next ten years. Displaying great industriousness, Hume managed, with the help of his administrators, to eliminate the debt. He reorganized the pastoral structure of the Diocese of Westminster, and focused his efforts on saving those institutions that were most financially troubled. The Cathedral Choir School, threatened with closure on his arrival, became one of his priorities. His support was rewarded when the Choir won two internationally renowned awards. Cardinal Hume also did much to strengthen ecumenical and interfaith links, acting as president of the Council of Churches in Britain and Ireland, now CTBI, and of Churches Together in England. He maintained strong relationships with the Jewish community and developed links with the Orthodox Church, encouraging inter-faith dialogue by contributing to the formation in 1997 of the Three Faiths Forum, which brought together Muslims, Christians, and Jews.

He also wrote several books, among them *Searching for God* (1977), a collection of short talks to the assembly of monks at Ampleforth; *To Be a Pilgrim* (1984), his most widely-read work; and *The Mystery of the Cross* (1998), a collection of meditations.

The cardinal was keen to retire in 1998, expressing a desire to end his days in his old monastery, but the Pope ordered him to retain his position. In April 1999 Hume revealed that he was dying of cancer, and it was only with great effort that he was able to go to Buckingham Palace to receive his honour of the Order of Merit. Widely respected for his deep spirituality, ecumenical views, and anti-dogmatic manner, Cardinal Hume came to occupy a special place in the nation's affections. The cardinal faced his final illness with a serene dignity. He died in London on 17 June 1999, aged 76. AF

Hussein ibn Talal

King of Jordan
(1935–1999)

Hussein ibn Talal was king of Jordan from 1952 to 1999. A member of the ancient Hashemite dynasty, he came to the throne of Jordan at the age of 17 so that although he died at the relatively early age of 63, after a long battle with cancer, he was, at his death, the longest-serving head of state in the Middle East. He succeeded his father, King Talal, who had been incapacitated through mental illness after less than two years in power. The young Hussein was already acutely aware of the violence which could erupt around him, having closely witnessed the assassination of his grandfather, King Abdullah, a year earlier.

The kingdom he inherited was a comparatively new creation, having been part of Palestine, and under British control, by virtue of a League of Nations mandate, until 1923 and subsequently still governed by Britain, as Trans-Jordan, until it secured complete independence in 1946. In 1948 the British mandate to govern Palestine expired and Jewish leaders claimed it for a new state of Israel. Fighting broke out between Arabs and Jews, and as a result King Abdullah occupied the West Bank area to add to the new state of Jordan. Three years later he was assassinated.

The young king found himself torn between often conflicting loyalties. On the one hand, he was a member of the ancient Hashemite dynasty and, as such, an obvious symbol of leadership in the Arab world. On the other hand, he had enjoyed a thoroughly English upbringing, at a major public school and then a British military college, and the Jordanian army, which had been established by the British as the Arab Legion, and was still commanded by a British officer, Sir John Bagot Glubb, known as 'Glubb Pasha'. His subjects and Arab neighbours were suspicious of his British links and in 1956, in an attempt to assuage their misgivings, he summarily dismissed Glubb Pasha and replaced him with a Jordanian.

When his cousin King Faisal II of Iraq was overthrown in 1958 he was viewed by the West as their most reliable ally in the Middle East, but he kept his close association with Iraq until it was ended in 1968 by the formation of a Revolutionary Command in Baghdad under Saddam Hussein, leaving Jordan relatively isolated. Egypt had now acquired a new leader, Gamal Nasser, who had grandiose territorial ambitions and, although Hussein distrusted him, he made the mistake of joining Egypt and Syria in 1967 in the Six-Day War against Israel, resulting in Jordan's loss of the West Bank and East Jerusalem.

Meanwhile King Hussein's claim to lead the Arab cause was disputed by the formation, in 1964, of the Palestine Liberation Organization (PLO) which began carrying out raids into Israel. Initially Hussein refused to accept the legitimacy of the PLO and his attempt to control the PLO guerrillas provoked a civil war in Jordan, in September 1970, the king only being saved by the loyalty of his Bedouin regiments. The young king was enjoying a knife-edge existence, positively embracing the Arab cause but dependent on the material and political support of the West. In 1974 Hussein suffered a serious political setback when the Arab League decided to recognize the PLO as the sole representative of the Palestinian people, a decision which the king saw as a serious slight on his leadership. Nevertheless he survived this setback as he had many others.

Nasser died suddenly in 1970 and was succeeded by Anwar Sadat, a much more rational and reasonable leader. Hussein became a major moderating influence in Middle East politics and established a successful working relationship with the PLO leader, Yassir Arafat. Although he had approved secret talks with Israeli representatives, in 1979 he joined the Arab world in opposing Egypt's peace treaty with Israel, mainly because it involved Israel's retention of control of the West Bank. His knife-edge existence continued when, with the approval of the West, he encouraged Saddam Hussein to go to war against Iran and then apparently supported Iraq's invasion of Kuwait.

In 1994, following successful US-inspired negotiations between the PLO and Israel, he signed a peace agreement with Israel, ending a 46-year-old 'state of war' between the two countries. Thereafter Hussein put his full weight behind the Middle East peace process and evidence of the value his friends and allies attributed to his efforts was the fact that more than 50 heads of state or government attended his funeral in Amman. US president Bill Clinton said: 'When peace finally comes to the Middle East his name will be inscribed upon it', while UK Prime Minister Tony Blair described him as 'a remarkable man of rare vision, integrity, and courage'.

King Hussein was educated at Harrow public school and the Royal Military Academy at Sandhurst. He had had four wives. In 1955 he married Princess Dina, a graduate of Girton College, Cambridge, but the marriage was soon dissolved and in 1961 an Englishwoman, who was given the title of Princess Muna, became his second wife. She was mother of his son and heir, Abdullah. In 1972 Hussein divorced Princess Muna and married Alia Baha Eddin Toukan but five years later she was killed in a helicopter crash. In 1978 he entered into his last marriage to Lisa Halabi, an American with Lebanese roots, who took the title Queen Noor. Hussein died in his home country after long periods of medical treatment in the USA, on 7 February 1999, at the age of 63. DD

Kubrick, Stanley

(1928–1999)

The enormous cult status of film director Stanley Kubrick was built on an opus of only 13 films made during a 45-year career. By the time he died, suddenly, only days after finally finishing the characteristically meticulous editing of his latest film, *Eyes Wide Shut,* he had ensured, deliberately or not, that the film world would be on tenterhooks to see the final, long-awaited statement of one of its acknowledged but most controversial masters.

Kubrick was born on 26 July 1928 in New York's Bronx and became interested in photography in his teens, selling his first photograph to *Look* magazine when he was 16. He worked for the magazine for the next five years whilst developing his real passion for film. In 1951 he financed his own first film, a short documentary entitled *Day of the Fight* and raised the finance for two further low-budget films – *Fear and Desire* (1953) and *Killer's Kiss* (1955). In 1956 United Artists provided the backing for his first commercial work, the film noir-inspired *The Killing.* But it was not until *Paths of Glory* (1957), his passionate statement on the hypocrisy of the French military leadership during World War I, that Kubrick's gifts achieved wider critical notice. On the strength of this film, which had starred Kirk Douglas, he was asked by Douglas himself to take over the direction of the Hollywood epic *Spartacus* in 1960. But Kubrick found the experience an uncomfortable one, manifesting a patent dislike of having to share editorial control and kowtow to studios and big stars. In his desire to retain total artistic autonomy he turned his back on Hollywood, although such became his reputation that the big studios, perhaps out of a baffled sense of awe at Kubrick's status, still seemed prepared to stump up the money to make his increasingly expensive films with their inordinately protracted production schedules.

In 1962 Kubrick settled in England, where he made *Lolita,* a critical and box office failure which could not capture the subtleties and eloquence of Nabokov's original novel and which, because of its paedophilic element, invited the kind of controversy that would dog the remainder of his cinematic career. Two years later – thanks to the brilliant black comedy of Peter Sellers's performances in three different roles – Kubrick produced *Dr Strangelove*, a savage Cold War satire, and a work that many critics consider was never transcended by his later, big-budget films. Whilst *Strangelove* became a cult film in its own right, it was, however, Kubrick's sci-fi extravaganza *2001: A Space Odyssey,* released in 1969, that brought his work to a mass cinema audience. It was certainly one of the first films to be carried as much by its eclectic and unsettling choice of soundtrack music as by its special effects, and with its psychedelic imagery it inspired many imitators. The critics, however, were divided by the film, and the poles of opinion over Kubrick's work have widened ever since. For the devotees the films are a profound metaphor for the times, the work of a deeply pessimistic and troubled cinematic auteur of genius who ranks alongside Orson Welles. Others find Kubrick's opus obsessed with technique at the expense of narrative. It is precisely this emphasis on the perfection of the visual element that for them reveals a coldness at the heart of Kubrick's work that reflects the misanthropy of the director himself.

The critical debate was further inflamed with the release of the futuristic *A Clockwork Orange* in 1971, again with a highly subversive choice of musical soundtrack. Its depiction of mindless violence and rape reportedly inspired copycat acts of rape and thuggery and a distraught Kubrick, angry that his directorial intentions had been misinterpreted and misrepresented by the press, withdrew the film from circulation, thus ensuring its inevitable and continuing cult status as cinematic forbidden fruit. It was four years before Kubrick's fans found themselves flummoxed by another

change in genre, this time to the vacuous beauty of his enormously long picaresque film *Barry Lyndon* (based on Thackeray's novel), although its exquisite cinematography (interior scenes were shot almost entirely by candlelight), costumes, and art direction brought much-deserved Oscars.

By now Kubrick had established himself in splendid isolation in a mansion in Hertfordshire, refusing to grant interviews or to make films outside the UK because of his fear of flying. Inexorably his reputation for being the Howard Hughes of the film world grew as he became increasingly reclusive and obsessive. His choice of a disturbing horror story for his 1980 film *The Shining*, featuring the grand guignol performance of a maniacal Jack Nicolson, led to accusations of artistic over-indulgence, although his return to a discourse on the savagery of war in his 1987 film *Full Metal Jacket* went some way to redeeming his reputation.

Kubrick's fans might well have wondered whether they would ever see another film from him when rumours began circulating in 1996 that he was planning to film an adaptation by the British screenwriter Frederick Raphael of an erotic story by Arthur Schnitzler. The levels of secrecy surrounding the project reached epic proportions before and during its ardouous 19-month shoot, which was funded to the tune of £40 million by an ever-loyal Warner Brothers. During the shooting Kubrick insisted on endless retakes (which during his career had been known to reach as many as 100), and their commitment to the film completely monopolized the lives of his two lead actors, Tom Cruise and Nicole Kidman, for more than a year. By the strangest of ironies Kubrick died in his sleep on 7 March 1999 shortly after finishing the film – the timing of his death suggesting that perhaps he had finally said all he wanted to say as an artist and that the ennervating process of doing so in his own exhaustive way had finally worn him out. HR

Kurosawa, Akira

(1910–1998)

Japanese film director, whose career spanned more than 50 years, embracing screenwriting, editing, producing, and acting assignments as well as the directorial role for which he earned a place in the pantheon of leading 20th-century filmmakers. Justly recognized as one of the most influential figures ever to have worked not only in Japanese, but also world, cinema, Kurosawa was responsible for the direction of such screen classics as *Rashomon/In the Woods* (1950), *Ikiru/To Live* (1952), *Sichinin no samurai/Seven Samurai* (1954), *Yojimbo/The Bodyguard* (1961), and *Ran/Chaos* (1985). These works ranged from small-scale, introspective, philosophical, sentimental studies of humanity, to sweeping, Western-influenced, melodramatic, violent epics exploring Japanese history and the Samurai tradition.

Akira Kurosawa was born on 23 March 1910 in Ohi-machi, Tokyo, the youngest of Isamu and Shima Kurosawa's eight children. From an early age he displayed a talent for art, a discipline he studied in his teens. The pinnacle of his accomplishment in this field was reached when his painting *Seibutsu* was accepted for the Nika Exhibition in 1928. Unable to gain a place at art college, however, he turned to filmmaking in his mid-twenties, working as an assistant director for a prestigious Japanese production company, Photo Chemical Laboratories (later better known as Toho Studios).

After seven years of working as an assistant, Kurosawa was handed his first opportunity to direct a film himself with *Sugata Sanshiro/Judo Saga* (1943), which he also wrote. Ten additional films followed, including *Ichiban utsukushiki/The Most Beautiful* (1944), *Zoku sugata shanshiro/Judo Saga II* (1945), and *Yoidore tenshi/Drunken Angel* (1948), before he achieved international recognition and worldwide critical acclaim with *Rashomon*. A formal and philosophical *tour de force*, the film questions the nature of reality, jumping back and forth in time as it explores the account of a woman's violation and murder in feudal Japan from four varying perspectives. Kurosawa's arrival on the world stage was signalled by the film's triumph at the Venice Film festival; it would also receive a special Academy Award as Best Foreign Picture.

Where *Rashomon* was imbued with a sense of Eastern mysticism, Kurosawa's next international hit, *Seven Samurai*, with its Western-style structure, signalled the director's fascination with Western society and its culture. Indeed, one of Kurosawa's great achievements in the 1950s was to develop a style of filmmaking that dismantled boundaries, with the filmmaker clearly borrowing from both Eastern and Western traditions, and melding together elements of high and popular culture. Western literature, in particular, became a source of great inspiration for him, with his filmography including adaptations of Dashiell Hammett's crime novel *Red Harvest* (the model for *Yojimbo*), Dostoyevsky's *The Idiot* (*Hakuchi*, 1951), Gorky's *The Lower Depths* (*Donzoko*, 1957), and Shakespeare's tragic plays, *Macbeth* and *King Lear*, which served as the inspiration for the Samurai films *Kumonosu jo/Throne of Blood* (1957) and *Ran* respectively.

Of course, it was not all one-way traffic. Kurosawa's own films would exert a great influence on Western cinema too, especially on that hitherto uniquely American genre, the western. *Seven Samurai*, for example, would be adapted by Hollywood into the star-laden *The Magnificent Seven*, while Sergio Leone's first spaghetti western collaboration with Clint Eastwood, *A Fistful of Dollars*, was not only modelled on *Yojimbo*, but at times seemed a shot-by-shot duplicate of it. Even 1990s Depression-set gangster films like *Miller's Crossing* and *Last Man Standing*, which return to Hammett's source material, at times evidence a visual, structural, and thematic indebtedness to the Japanese director's original film. Kurosawa's masterful storytelling would also receive the Hollywood treatment in *Outrage*, a 1964 adaptation of *Rashomon*. In his later life Kurosawa would enjoy fruitful friendships with such American film industry luminaries as Martin Scorsese, who features as Vincent van Gogh in his *Yume/Akira Kurosawa's Dreams* (1990), and Steven Spielberg; George Lucas would even confess that his blockbuster *Star Wars*, which gave birth to one of the most phenomenal franchises in film history, was indebted to Kurosawa's *Kakushi toride no san akunin/The Hidden Fortress* (1958).

Celebrated in the West for his mastery of composition and movement, for the powerful performances he attained from his actors, and for his humanist sensibilities, Kurosawa was nevertheless not so highly acclaimed in the country of his birth. The low point came in the early 1970s when, following increasing difficulties in finding financing for his projects and the failure of his most recent film, *Dodesukaden/Clickety-Clack* (1970), he made a suicide attempt. 1974's *Dersu Uzala*, shot in the USSR, would see a return to form and won him new plaudits. From this point his output became increasingly intermittent, but well-received: *Kagemusha/The Shadow Warrior* and *Ran* were visually spectacular Samurai epics, whereas his later works, *Yume* and *Hachigatsu no kyoshikyoku/Rhapsody in August* (1991) were smaller scale, personal works. In 1993 he filmed *Madadayo/Not Yet*, his last directorial work.

Akira Kurosawa died on 6 September 1998, having bridged a gap between Eastern and Western cinematic traditions, and leaving behind a unique cinematic legacy. RM

McGahey, Mick

(1925–1999)

Michael (Mick) McGahey was a miner and communist trade unionist. Known to his friends as Michael and to his enemies as 'Red Mick', McGahey, like his father, James, who helped to found the Communist Party of Great Britain, was proud of his political stance, calling himself a 'devout communist'. He became a part-time union official at the age of 18, at the same time putting in a three-day week in the pits, where he had started as a boy four years earlier. As an active unionist he did much to improve the miners' lot, being instrumental in the introduction of pithead baths and other work facilities.

A natural intellectual and avid reader, his talents were soon recognized by the National Union of Mineworkers (NUM) hierarchy and he was encouraged to progress within the union. He became an area president and in 1971 unsuccessfully challenged Joe Gormley for the national presidency. However, when Gormley retired in 1973 the union rules prevented him from fighting the election because of his age, and he became deputy to the new leader, Arthur Scargill.

In 1974 the union faced a major challenge from the Conservative government of Edward Heath, the prime minister singling out McGahey as one of the communists bent on bringing down the government. The subsequent general election which Heath lost did nothing to improve McGahey's standing among the Conservatives but increased his reputation among those to the left of the outgoing government. The challenge the union faced ten years later was a much different proposition. Margaret Thatcher had learnt much from the demise of her predecessor and was determined not to commit his fatal error. Because the miners' strike had been called without first holding a ballot, its critics could claim that it was unconstitutional. It can be speculated that, if McGahey had been president and not number two in the union, he might have had a ballot, because he was a strong believer in the democratic process, but Scargill preferred not to and eventually Mrs Thatcher won the day.

Apart from his intellectual qualities, McGahey was an extremely kind man. For example, he declined to write his memoirs, in which he might have referred critically to former colleagues while they were still alive. At the same time in his work he was an extremely tough negotiator, respected on both sides of the negotiating table. His other great quality was his loyalty, particularly to his union. This loyalty was so strong that, although at times he had fundamental differences with Scargill, he refused to criticise him in public.

Born in Shotts, Lanarkshire, he moved with his family as a child to Cambuslang, near Glasgow. His parents were, on the surface, dissimilar but in reality shared the same outlook. James McGahey was an overt communist, born in Lanarkshire, while his mother was a devout Irish-born Catholic. She persuaded Michael to sing in her local school choir but he took a very relaxed view about religion, being more convinced about the soundness of his father's communism than her Catholicism. He was largely self-educated, having left school at 14, but his wide reading enabled him in his impressive speeches to draw examples from sources as diverse as William Shakespeare and Karl Marx. He was a tough man, both mentally and physically, but suffered for most of his life from chronic emphysema, which eventually killed him. A genuine working-class hero, he died in Edinburgh on 30 January 1999, at the age of 73. DD

Menuhin, Yehudi

Lord Menuhin of Stoke d'Abernon
(1916–1999)

The prodigious musical talents of Yehudi Menuhin spanned a career that lasted more than 70 years, during which time he lent his supreme artistry to the great violin concertos of Elgar, Bach, Beethoven, Bartók, and Mendelssohn, and worked with legendary conductors – Furtwängler, Toscanini, Boult, and Walter. But despite such a superlative musical pedigree, Menuhin's mission was never purely an esoteric one of art for art's sake. A deeply spiritual and humane man, he sought to bring the healing powers of music to a troubled world. In the course of his rich and active life, he embraced numerous moral and political causes and spoke out in many countries against abuses of human rights. His discovery of the soothing spirituality of Indian mysticism, and with it the practice of yoga and dietary asceticism, occasionally left him open to parody as something of an eccentric, but he demonstrated genuine and passionate concerns that in many cases were ahead of his time.

Menuhin came from a great line of 20th-century Jewish musical talents that sprang out of the ghettos of Eastern Europe and the immigrant tenement blocks of the New World. He was born in New York, the son of Russian-Jewish immigrants, and grew up in San Francisco, where he first took up the violin at the tender age of four. Having revealed a precocious musical talent, he was nurtured by dedicated parents, whose sacrifice for the sake of their son's art affected the life of the whole of the family. Together with his sisters Yaltah and Hepzibah, Menuhin was educated at home and all three children developed their musical talents to the exclusion of the mundane childhood pursuits of climbing trees and riding bicycles. Having made his musical debut in 1924, Menuhin and his family followed his violin teacher back to New York, before travelling to Europe, where Menuhin studied with the Romanian violinist Georges Enescu. Throughout, it was Menuhin's mother Marutha who drove his talent, organized his life, and later even selected a wife for him.

At the age of ten, now back in New York again, Menuhin astonished the music world by performing Beethoven's challenging *Violin Concerto* at the Carnegie Hall. In 1929, his playing enhanced by a priceless Stradivarius violin bought for him by an admiring American philanthropist, Menuhin made his debut in Berlin. Here he was famously congratulated by none other than Albert Einstein, who having heard Menuhin's performance declared 'Now I know there is a God in Heaven'. In July 1932 Menuhin was honoured – when still only 16 – with being asked to record Edward Elgar's *Violin Concerto*. After the recording at London's Abbey Road studios, Elgar (who had in fact written the work for Fritz Kreisler) commended Menuhin as 'the most wonderful artist I have ever heard'. Soon Menuhin was undertaking a gruelling world tour which took him to 73 cities. Right up until his death he would travel and perform tirelessly, and constantly extended his repertoire. He played over 500 concerts for Allied troops during the war and after the liberation of Belsen in 1945 performed for the exhausted survivors of the camp. But he was equally ready later in his life to play to dispossessed Palestinians in Israel, and he was one of the first Jewish performers after the war to play German music with a German orchestra, in the face of considerable hostility from his fellow Jews.

After the failure of his first brief marriage to an Australian heiress, Menuhin remarried in 1947. His second wife, a dancer, Diana Gould, would remain a dominant influence for the rest of his life and, like Menuhin's mother before her, she dedicated herself to supporting his genius. In 1963 Menuhin fulfilled a personal musical ambition when he set up the Menuhin School of Music in Surrey to foster musical talent in the UK. With its emphasis on the stringed instruments, one of the first talents to emerge from the school was Nigel Kennedy, who himself went on to become one of the great interpreters of Elgar's *Violin Concerto*.

Menuhin's musical career meanwhile continued to burgeon. During the war he had developed a close working relationship with the Hungarian composer Béla Bartók and premiered various of his violin works including the *Solo Sonata* (1947), which Bartók had written specially for him. From the mid-1950s he took up conducting, became involved in numerous musical festivals such as those in Gstaad and Bath, and gave continuing support and encouragement to contemporary composers such as Britten, Maxwell Davies, Oliver Knussen, and Walton. All this was complemented by work for UNESCO and a growing interest in humanitarian concerns and green issues as the patron of innumerable organizations.

By the end of his very fulfilled life, Menuhin probably more than any other 20th-century performer had popularized the great violin concertos of the classical repertoire and had brought his charismatic presence to a wide audience who, whether or not aware of the technicalities of performance, were beguiled by Menuhin's modesty and charm. For Menuhin was never elitist in his art, but was always ready to experiment and explore new musical forms – such as in his improvised sessions with the jazz violinist Stephan Grapelli and his collaboration with the Indian sitar player Ravi Shankar.

Menuhin settled in London in 1959 and was made a KBE in 1965. He took British citizenship in 1985 and was made a life peer in 1993. Whilst musical purists might contend that Menuhin never equalled the technical ability and restraint of his contemporaries – the great violin virtuosos David Oistrakh and Yasha Heifitz or his own mentor Fritz Kreisler – it was precisely Menuhin's charismatic personality and occasional loss of control in 'too passionate playing' (as he himself described it) that gave richness and individuality to his performances. Menuhin's name became synonymous with all that was good and humane in music, precisely those qualities that transcend the divide between cultures and creeds and break down the barriers of ignorance and prejudice. He died on 12 March at the age of 82. HR

Murdoch, (Jean) Iris

(1919–1999)

The final few years of Dame Iris Murdoch's life were consumed by the cruel progression of Alzheimer's disease, which inexorably reduced a once pre-eminent philosopher and novelist of outstanding inventiveness and intellectual powers to a quivering and bewildered child. The real tragedy for those who knew her and admired Murdoch's work was,

as her devoted husband John Bayley so plaintively put it, that, 'She does not know that she has written 27 remarkable novels, as well as her books on philosophy; received honorary doctorates from the major universities; become a Dame of the British Empire'. A pitiless disease had wiped clean a great intellect that had dominated British writing for more than 40 years.

Irish Murdoch was born in Dublin and gained a first class degree in Greats at Somerville College, Oxford. She worked briefly as a civil servant and then for the United Nations Relief and Rehabilitation Administration (1944–46), during which time she travelled in Europe and, already interested in the work of the French existentialists, met the French novelist and philosopher Jean Paul Sartre. She returned to college, this time Newnham, Cambridge, to study philosophy, which she then taught at Oxford, becoming a fellow of St Anne's College (1948–63). In 1956 she married the literary critic and Oxford don John Bayley and together the couple settled into the quiet academic life, living for many years in absent-minded chaos (neither of them was houseproud) in Steeple Aston, north of Oxford.

Iris Murdoch's familiar figure around the quadrangles of Oxford's colleges was the personification of the blue-stocking in its blend of earnestness and incipient eccentricity: 'A tousled heel-less ladder-stockinged little lady – crackling with intelligence.' as George Lyttelton described her; and there was indeed an air of intellectual challenge in the somewhat pugnacious face with its large, watchful, questioning eyes. She was hugely popular with students and fellow dons, who since her death have spoken of her warmth and open-heartedness, her almost childlike goodness and moral strength, and her generosity (material as well as spiritual, for she gave many of her royalties away).

Initially pursuing her interest in metaphysics and the work of the postwar existentialists, Murdoch's first published book was *Sartre, Romantic Rationalist* (1953). But she soon moved from the rarified world of philosophy into fiction; her first novel, *Under the Net* (1954) displayed great promise and was a considerable critical success. Novels such as *The Bell* (1958), *A Severed Head* (1961), and *An Unofficial Rose* (1962) established Murdoch's international reputation. In these and other fine fiction – *The Black Prince* (1973), the Booker Prize-winner *The Sea, The Sea* (1978) – Murdoch's philosophical preoccupations spill over into her narrative, which often describes in macabre and gothic style the destructive powers of passion and the unpredictable ways of love and its ramifications: adultery, infidelity, and even incest. At the heart of such narratives lie Murdoch's own deeply held religious and moral concerns reflected in a juxtaposition of the inherent conflict between good and evil, the sacred and the profane. Her vivid and complex plots are laced with philosophical allusion and symbolism, with many of her frequently intellectual and middle-class professional characters finding themselves embroiled in the black humour of life's absurdities.

Many critics perceive a change in direction, if not a positive downturn in Murdoch's writing from the late 1970s, and novels such as *The Good Apprentice* (1985), *The Message to the Planet* (1989), *The Green Knight* (1993), and her last novel, *Jackson's Dilemma* (1995), manifest a more realistic mode of story telling, which Murdoch acknowledged as being inspired by the Russian school of the 'quasi-documentary' novel. She herself felt that these excelled over her earlier fiction, but this change in narrative style produced much more ponderous books, often over 500 pages long, which some critics felt suffered from a lack of judicious editing. Despite gathering accusations of repetition, excessive description, and literary self-indulgence, Murdoch doggedly refused to allow her work to be edited – and by that she meant not at all, for not even a comma was changed. Whilst the lapses in her later work are unlikely to damage her standing as one of the leading female writers of the postwar period – in the eyes of many on a par with literary greats such as Henry James, Proust, George Eliot, and Tolstoy (in Russia in particular she is revered as the leading exponent of the contemporary British novel) – Murdoch remained determinedly modest about her literary achievements, insisting that she was not among the greats but only in 'the second league' of writers.

Murdoch continued to pursue her interest in philosophy throughout her career, publishing *The Sovereignty of Good* (1970), a study of Plato entitled *Fire and Sun* (1977), and, most recently, *Metaphysics as a Guide to Morals* (1993). A quiet, private person who was as uninterested in fame as she was in criticism ('A bad review is even less important than whether it is raining in Patagonia'), she was made a Dame of the British Empire in 1987. But in 1995 the onset of Alzheimer's disease brought a falling away of her powers. Murdoch was left rudderless by her increasing inability to write, which for someone who had produced a new novel almost every year, and who began writing her next within hours of finishing the previous one, seemed unbearably tragic.

In 1996 it was formally announced that she had Alzheimer's; her husband of 45 years, John Bayley, described her progressive loss of memory as 'rather like falling from stair to stair in a series of bumps', but he remained a devoted carer and only relinquished the task in the final two weeks of her life, when she went into an Oxford hospice to die a peaceful death at the age of 79. In 1998, Bayley published an uplifting testament to their happy marriage and a moving account of the dark and bewildering world in which Iris Murdoch increasingly found herself, that will no doubt become a classic account of Alzheimer's in its own right. Murdoch died on 8 February at the age of 79. HR

Ramsey, Alf(red) Ernest

(1920–1999)

English football manager who led England to victory in the 1966 World Cup. This achievement, which none of his successors has been able to match, guaranteed him a place among the immortals of English sport. England's success owed much to Ramsey's tactical acumen, his dogged determination, his coolness under pressure, his powers of motivation, and perhaps above all, his ability to command the loyalty and respect of his players. Notwithstanding the brilliant individual contributions of players like Geoff Hurst, Bobby Moore, and Bobby Charlton, it was the camaraderie, the indomitable team spirit nurtured by Ramsey, that made the difference.

Although he was adored and respected by his players few people knew him well. Taciturn, unemotional, he was socially ill at ease, and appeared to lack warmth. However, he had great integrity, which he maintained through the highs and lows of his career. He did not bask in the glory of England's World Cup triumph, neither did he seek public sympathy when he was sacked in 1974.

Alfred Ernest Ramsey was born in Dagenham, Essex, on 22 January 1920. As a youth he was a promising footballer, but when he left school he pursued a career as a grocer. If it had not been for the war he probably would have been lost to the game. However, after joining the Duke of Cornwall's Light Infantry he became involved in services football, and in 1942 he signed for Portsmouth Football Club as an amateur. He moved to Southampton in 1943, signing professional forms a year later. Playing at right back, he was a good passer of the ball, cool under pressure, his tactical awareness and positional sense making up for his lack of height and pace. Such was his progress that in 1948 he made his England debut. Transferred the following year to Tottenham Hotspur, he helped the north London side achieve the rare feat of winning the Second and First Division titles in successive seasons. In 1950 he travelled with England to Brazil for the World Cup and was in the team that lost 1–0 to the USA in what is still one of the biggest upsets in English football history. He won a total of 32 caps before losing his place for good after another historic England defeat, the humiliating 6–3 thrashing by Hungary at Wembley in 1953.

He went on to captain Tottenham before being appointed manager of Ipswich Town in 1955. The small East Anglian club had just been relegated from the Second Division, and Ramsey had scant resources to improve the side. However, in only his second season in charge he led them to the Third Divison (South) championship. Then in 1960–61 they won the Second Division title. Few people believed that Ramsey's team of journeyman footballers would survive even a season in the top division. Remarkably, they won the championship, and thus Ramsey emulated as a manager what he had achieved as a player by winning the Second and First titles in consecutive years.

When Walter Winterbottom stepped down as England manager in January 1963, Ramsey was appointed in his place. Unlike his predecessor, he was able to insist on being given control over of all aspects of team selection and preparation. His reign as England manager began inauspiciously with a 5–2 defeat against France. Ramsey however, far from being worried, boldly asserted that England would win the next World Cup.

England's performances in the years leading up to the 1966 World Cup were satisfactory. Ramsey created a solid team, founded on defence, but few believed that England were capable of fulfilling his promise despite the advantage of playing on home soil. When the tournament started, England progressed competently through to the group stage, but Ramsey was widely criticised in the press for the generally lacklustre quality of his team's play. Ramsey characteristically refused to accept that there was anything wrong but he decided to change the team's formation. Going against traditional football wisdom he dispensed with his wingers and instead packed the midfield. This change was greeted with widespread scepticism, but when England progressed through the quarter and semi-finals and then went on to defeat West Germany 4–2 in the final it was hailed as a masterstroke. England's hat-trick hero, Geoff Hurst, had been a controversial choice for the final, as Ramsey had been under pressure to restore the prolific scoring Jimmy Greaves to the side. Once again, Ramsey's judgement was spot on.

The 1966 World Cup was the highpoint of his time as England manager. England finished a disappointing third in the 1968 European Championships. When they lost 3–2 to West Germany in the quarter-finals of the 1970 World Cup some blamed Ramsey for substituting the ageing Bobby Charlton when England were 2–0 up. Defeat by West Germany in the quarter-finals of the 1972 European Championships further weakened his position. When England failed to qualify for the next World Cup finals his days as England manager were numbered and in May 1974 he was sacked. He had won 69 of 113 games in charge of England and lost only 17.

Ramsey had never enjoyed a good relationship with his employers, the Football Association, and had resented the paltry financial reward he and his players received for winning the World Cup. Nevertheless, given his unmatched wealth of experience, it was surprising that they never consulted him again on any matter.

He retired from football after his dismissal, but returned in 1977 for a brief spell as a caretaker manager of Birmingham City, and then in 1980 when he worked as technical director to the Greek club Panathanaikos. Thereafter he was rarely seen in public, and lived quietly with his wife in their home near Ipswich.

Ramsey was knighted in 1967 for services to football. He died at Ipswich on 28 April 1999. BR

Reed, (Robert) Oliver

(1938–1999)

Witnessing the inexorable slide of Oliver Reed, a promising and magnetic personality in the British film industry, down the slippery slope of alcoholism into self-parody might lead one to imagine that drink was the one big problem in his life. It was the demon drink, one might argue, that denied him the kind of acting career his talent deserved. Reed, however, saw things otherwise. He had no regrets about his legendary drinking, or about his bad behaviour when in his cups: drinking was a way of life, and he took the greatest of pleasure in it: 'I like the effect drink has on me', he once said, 'What's the point of being sober?'

Having opted for an acting career almost by default, as did several of his British acting contemporaries who found themselves similarly stranded after two years of National Service in the 1950s, it was the acting that would fund Oliver Reed's long and expensive love affair with booze. Here was an actor who never would claim drink was a refuge from the pressures of stardom, or thwarted ambition, or the artistic stresses and strains of being an actor. And if, somewhere along the way, a few good films resulted, then all well and good. No doubt if Reed had taken a more reverential attitude towards his profession and towards cinema as art he might have made more of himself in a career during which he made over 53 films, but the truth is, he had already turned in his best performances by 1970.

Reed's reputation as a tearaway began early; it is claimed he was expelled from 15 different schools (although he himself denied this), but no doubt his academic failures were due in part to his being dyslexic. A desultory string of jobs, as a bouncer in a Soho strip club, a fairground boxer, and even a mortuary attendant, were followed by National Service, after which Reed, eschewing the traditional route of drama school, decided on a career in films. He started out as an extra and graduated to bit parts in the late 1950s. His natural animal magnetism and physicality soon found their niche in a Hammer Horror, *The Curse of the Werewolf* (1961). This opened the door to a string of roles as the smouldering 'baddy' in films such as Joseph Losey's *The Damned* (1963) and Norman Panama's *The Trap* (1966). But Reed also had a talent for comedy that many, including his later co-star Glenda Jackson, felt was never really tapped by the industry, and which he demonstrated in 'Swinging London' films of the sixties such as *The Jokers* and *I'll Never Forget What's-'Is-Name* (both 1967).

In 1968, Reed was cast in probably his most memorable role – as a cruel and sinister Bill Sykes in the film version of Lionel Bart's musical *Oliver!,* which was directed by his uncle, Carol Reed. Film buffs might suggest that Reed's real success lay in the 'arthouse' integrity of Ken Russell's 1969 adaptation of D H Lawrence's *Women in Love,* in which he gave a fine performance as the tortured Gerald and in which he and Alan Bates famously created the first full frontal male nude scene (the fireside wrestling match) passed by the British censors. Reed followed this with another powerful performance in Russell's albeit camp and rococo saga of medieval witch-hunting, *The Devils* in 1971. But it was at this point that his career began to dip, with fewer good films such as *The Three Musketeers* (1973) or *Castaway* (1986) among the dross of cameo parts in quickly forgotten potboilers.

But the quality of the work mattered not one jot to Reed. The film roles – good or bad – funded the lifestyle and he increasingly played to the gallery in this respect, indulging in predictably notorious drunken antics, which reached their nadir/apogee (depending on which way one views it) with leery, inebriated appearances on TV chat shows such as *Parkinson* and *After Dark.* Ironically, it was probably on these occasions that he delivered his most famous and much-loved performances – as a professional drunk and rebel-rouser, intent on shocking a prurient audience that expected nothing less of him. As he himself observed: 'Even if I wanted to make myself seem like a normal human being I couldn't because that's not what people want me to be'. On the film set, however, his professionalism and discipline were impeccable.

Reed was briefly married to the actress Kate Byrne, and later, away from the public eye, lived happily with his second wife Josephine, whom he married in 1985. People said the marriage could not possibly work because of Reed's drinking and her youth (she was 27 years younger); but it proved a surprisingly happy and stable partnership and with Josephine's support, and happily settled in Churchtown, County Cork, Reed even occasionally gave up drinking. No doubt such respites for his overloaded liver bought him a few extra years of life.

Reed died, on 2 May after collapsing during a drinking binge in a bar in Malta, whilst on location filming *The Gladiators* for Steven Spielberg. Despite his bibulous reputation he had never been out of work as an actor. The great roles and the Oscars may have passed him by, but as a modern-day Rabelaisian bon-viveur, Oliver Reed lived his life the way he wanted. In his will, he ensured that funds were provided for the quiet little village of Churchtown to give him the best of all possible Irish wakes. HR

Rothermere, Viscount

Vere Harold Esmond Harmsworth, 3rd Viscount Rothermere

(1925–1998)

English press baron, saviour of the *Mail* newspaper group, and aristocrat. Vere Harold Esmond Harmsworth gained his title and place in the boardroom through an accident of birth but it was his ability and success that earned him the respect of Fleet Street. He transformed the *Daily Mail* into the paper of Middle England, in the process redefining the landscape of British newspapers. Under his stewardship *The Daily Mail,*

Mail on Sunday, and the *Evening Standard* all became leaders in their sectors.

Although his destiny was always to inherit his father's newspapers, he demonstrated little promise in an unhappy youth devoid of real achievement. His mother and father split up when he was young and he lived at Claridge's hotel with his mother. His education at Eton was disturbed by World War II, and he spent a spell at Kent School in Connecticut after his evacuation. He did not go to university and served as a private during his National Service, having failed to win a commission, but later he credited his time in the ranks for giving him insight into the life and aspirations of ordinary people. Certainly, few other aspects of his life gave him such an opportunity, and he defined himself as a nobleman.

The grandson of the 1st Viscount Rothermere and great-nephew of Viscount Northcliffe, who had both run the Associated Newspapers empire he inherited, Rothermere maintained homes in London, Sussex, New York, France, and the Caribbean. The 2nd Viscount Rothermere, his father, gave him £2.75 million when he married in 1957. Rothermere began his working life in Canada with Anglo-Canadian Paper Mills. He returned to Britain to work in the family business but began with lowly positions before he was handed the reins of a far from healthy Associated group in 1970. During his years in the lower reaches of the newspaper world he developed a friendship with David English, an editor on the *Daily Sketch,* which was to be vital in his later successes. English, who was knighted in 1982, was won back from the *Express* group in 1971 and became the editorial force behind the *Mail* newspapers. The *Daily Mail* trailed its rival *The Express* by a large margin and discussions had taken place over a merger between the two. Rothermere took another course that maintained independence but was full of risk. He closed the *Daily Sketch,* cutting large numbers of staff in the process, appointed David English as editor of the *Mail,* and changed the format of the paper from a broadsheet to a tabloid in May 1971. Despite initial circulation losses, this proved to be a masterstroke and the remodelled paper placed itself in the newspaper market between the broadsheets and the traditional tabloids. It successfully attracted women through its 'Femail' section and general approach, gained readers, and rapidly overtook the declining *Express.*

In 1976 Rothermere failed in a bid for *The Observer* and four years later, Rupert Murdoch outmanoeuvred him for control of *Times* newspapers when the Thomson Organisation sold. Having been unable to buy a Sunday paper, Rothermere set to creating his own and personally oversaw the development of *The Mail on Sunday,* which was financed by the sale of his oil interests in the North Sea. The new title was launched in May 1982 to complete the Associated stable. Rothermere kept his nerve in the face of significant early losses and the paper finally became a great success.

Turning his attention to the London market, Rothermere merged his unprofitable *Evening News* with the *Evening Standard* in return for a 50% share of the latter. Vitally, he negotiated a first refusal on the other half if owners, Trafalgar House, wanted to sell. That happened in 1987, and by insisting on exercising his purchase rights Rothermere acquired a monopoly in the capital. That dominance was challenged by Robert Maxwell, owner of the Mirror Group, who launched the *London Daily News* to oppose the *Evening Standard.* The *Evening News* was resurrected to muddy the waters and in combination with Associated's dominance of the street sellers it was enough, to Rothermere's great delight, to force Maxwell to bow out after four months.

By his death, the unpromising circumstances he had inherited had been reversed: *The Express* group's titles were sickly and their *Mail* rivals were doing well. The effort required to achieve business success, however, contributed to the breakdown of Rothermere's marriage to Patricia Brooks, an actress once voted one of the ten most beautiful women in London. They had married in 1957, after Rothermere had ignored the attempts of her first husband, Christopher Brooks, to keep him away. Patricia Brooks' entertaining and love of fun earned her the nickname 'Bubbles' and her parties gave Rothermere a far higher profile on the London scene than before. They had two daughters and a son, Jonathan Harmsworth, who became the 4th Viscount Rothermere, but although they remained married until her death in 1992 of an accidental overdose of sleeping pills, they rarely lived together after the early years. While his wife remained based in London, Rothermere moved – in part to escape high taxation – to his Paris flat. After 1978 he shared his life outside the UK with his Korean lover, Maiko Joeong-shun Lee, and he married the former model, 25 years his junior, in 1993.

Rothermere's unconventional lifestyle, which included study of the paranormal and Buddhism, was in marked contrast to the crusading middle-class morality of his papers. He rarely imposed his own opinions on his papers and, as the owner of the staunchly right-of-centre *Daily Mail,* sat on the government benches in the House of Lords after Labour's election victory in 1997. He even expressed the view that the monarchy had run its course in a characteristically mischievous interview given shortly before his death. He died in London, on 3 September, of a heart attack at the age of 73. DM

Rowland, Tiny

adopted name of Roland Walter Fuhrop
(1917–1998)

Tiny Rowland will be remembered as a tough business tycoon, outsider, and significant force in African affairs. Rowland built the London & Rhodesia Mining and Land Company (Lonhro) into an international conglomerate, in doing so amassing a personal fortune and a reputation for unconventional methods and ruthlessness. He rose from disadvantaged beginnings to acquire considerable powers in the politics of Africa through the influence of the company he ran in his own singular style. His success made him a hero to investors but his enemies – such as Harrods owner Mohamed al-Fayed – faced in him an implacable foe.

Rowland was born Roland Walter Fuhrop on 27 November 1917 to German parents in a British internment camp in India. His early life was studded with contradictions before he made the provident decision to move to southern Africa under a new name in 1947. After his family moved back to Germany, for instance, he both enrolled in the Hitler Youth and was jailed for two months in 1939 for contact with opponents of the Nazis. He changed his name, formalizing his nickname of Tiny and adding his middle initial into his first name to create a surname, and made his way to the UK with his parents who were again interned when World War II began. Rowland, however, served in the British army before the authorities learnt that his two brothers were in the German forces. His mother died in a camp on the Isle of Man, which no doubt contributed to his bitterness towards the British establishment.

Rowland left menial jobs as a porter and a waiter for the lure of Southern Rhodesia in 1947, prospering as he acquired farms and a range of interests including the franchise for Mercedes cars. His businesses were swapped for shares that would become his fortune when he was recruited to become the joint managing director of the struggling London & Rhodesia Mining and Land Company (Lonrho) in 1961. Rapid expansion under Rowland's direction – without much consultation with the board of directors – was accompanied by financial instability and an investigation into fraud in South African operations. Sir Basil Smallpiece later became chairman of the Lonrho board and sought to impose more traditional methods on Rowland's managing style. The conflict climaxed in May 1973 when shareholders at a packed meeting rejected Smallpiece's City-supported bid to remove Rowland and instead voted the chairman off the board. Nevertheless, the subsequent government probe of Lonrho prompted Prime Minister Edward Heath to label Rowland the 'unacceptable face of capitalism'.

That verdict did little to slow the corporation's continued expansion and by the late 1980s the group ran 600 companies with revenues of $8 billion. Holdings in scores of countries ranged from mining interests and plantations to hotels, car franchises, and newspapers, but the focus remained in Africa. Rowland cemented his influence through constant travel across the region and judicious gifts to leaders and, when prudent, opposition leaders. Success did little to mellow the Lonhro boss and he continued to bridle against the views of the establishment. The distaste was largely returned.

Rowland's venom for those who crossed him was most famously highlighted in the vicious feud with al-Fayed, which was conducted through the pages of Rowland's own newspaper, *The Observer* (which he owned from 1981 to 1993), and the rest of Fleet

Street. Lonhro started to accumulate shares in Scottish & Universal Trusts in 1977 as a way of gaining control over Harrods. The subsequent contest was going Lonhro's way until an adverse government ruling halted its progress. The Scottish & Universal shares and control of Harrods ended up in the hands of the Fayed brothers in much disputed circumstances, much to Rowland's fury. Other subjects of his wrath, however, fared much worse than the Fayeds: the Australian magnate Alan Bond was ruined when his financial weaknesses were exposed by Rowland in 1990.

His business battles were conducted in public but apart from some basic facts his personal life remained private. He had homes in Buckinghamshire and London, collected African art and Siamese cats, but the perfectly dressed millionaire (his fortune is estimated to have peaked at £200 million) avoided any ostentatious spending of his wealth.

This outsider finally fell for the most common and least personal reason in business: poor results. He was replaced at Lonrho in 1995 following four years of low corporate profits and continuing disapproval from investors. He died on 24 July 1998 at the age of 80. DM

Sainsbury, Alan

Baron Sainsbury of Drury Lane
(1902–1998)

British grocer who introduced the supermarket to the British consumer. Mr Alan, as he was called, guided the Sainsbury's family business during massive change and expansion, revolutionizing British shopping in the process. He also sought to promote the welfare state and a fair society through corporate practice, work in the House of Lords, and charitable giving.

The first Sainsbury's store was opened in London in 1869 by his grandparents, John James and Mary Ann Sainsbury, with backing of just £100. Alan's father, John Benjamin Sainsbury, oversaw the company's expansion across southern England, and his mother, Mabel Van den Bergh, came from a Dutch Jewish family that had accumulated a fortune based on margarine business. School days at Haileybury found him an outsider despite the family's wealth. After expressing an interest in becoming a social worker and a spell working in the East End – a distinct contrast to his privileged upbringing in Hampstead – he was persuaded to join the family business. He began as a worker on the shop floor in Boscombe in Devon, where he was taught the basics of the grocery business by his uncles. A series of higher-powered positions followed, with the directorship of the company in 1933. Sainsbury became joint general manager with his younger brother Robert in 1938, following their father's ill health. Robert controlled Sainsbury's administrative and financial matters while Alan focused on trading developments.

They kept going through the difficulties of the war and the restrictions of rationing, bomb damage, and the dislocation of business. The company gained a reputation for fairness and Sainsbury saw it as his duty to serve on a number of committees of the Ministry of Food. That work for the government was to bear fruit for Sainsbury's in 1949 when Sainsbury was given a diplomatic passport to travel to the USA to research the potential of frozen foods. During his time in the USA his imagination was fired by the supermarkets he saw there. He pitched the concept enthusiastically to a sceptical board on his return and the shoppers in the Croydon store were selected to be guinea pigs for Sainsbury's supermarket experiment in 1950.

The old order of shop assistants behind a counter, fetching and packing the goods requested by the customer and often arranging their delivery, was swept away. Not everyone was pleased by the move from traditional service to self-reliance. One of the new store's first customers reportedly threw his shopping basket at Sainsbury in disgust. The protests were in vain, however, as the Croydon store generated huge revenues and was a great success. Rationing and shortages initially slowed the spread of supermarkets but over the next three decades the old stores were replaced with self-service supermarkets at an increasing rate and the last of the counter shops closed in 1982. Competitors also saw the potential of the new style of shopping and quickly became disciples of the supermarket.

Sainsbury's also led the way with innovations such as own-brand lines, frozen foods, and a greater selection of fruit and vegetables. With the supermarket aisle and the increased range of goods on offer came the need to catch the shopper's eye. Sainsbury insisted on simple striking designs for Sainsbury's own brands and from 1967 promoted his philosophy of good food at low prices with television advertising.

Alan ran Sainsbury's with his brother until 1962 when they oversaw the transfer of responsibility to their sons and nephews. He succeeded his father as chairman in 1956, retiring in 1967, and maintained a close interest in the business in later years as life president of Sainsbury's. He was made Baron Sainsbury of Drury Lane in 1962, choosing for his title the street which had been home to the first Sainsbury's.

He took his duty to society very seriously, defending consumer rights as a working peer, and waged a fierce battle against the trading stamps offered by his rivals in the 1960s. They were, he believed, a false saving which exploited the public and resulted in higher prices. He also contributed to many committees connected to the food industry and sat on an array of boards. Politically, he changed his initial alliance with the Liberal Party (he had unsuccessfully stood for the House of Commons as a candidate for the Liberals in the Sudbury constituency in the elections of 1929, 1931, and 1935) when he joined the Labour Party in 1945. He sat on the Labour benches until 1981 when he gave his backing to the nascent Social Democratic Party (SDP).

Despite a family fortune that rose to an estimated £2.5 billion, and a chauffeured Rolls Royce, Sainsbury eschewed most luxuries and instead gave generously to charities, including the Pestalozzi Children's Village Trust, of which he was president. He died, aged 96, in Toppesfield, Essex, on 21 October 1998, by which time Sainsbury's supermarkets carried 23,000 items and generated annual sales of £11 billion. DM

Schawlow, Arthur Leonard

(1921–1999)

US physicist who worked in laser spectroscopy and is generally considered, with US physicist Charles Townes, to be co-inventor of the laser. Schawlow used the laser as a tool to study atomic spectra and their associated energy levels. He derived improved values for atomic constants such as the Rydberg constant. In 1981 he was awarded the Nobel Prize for Physics, which he shared with the Dutch-born US physicist Nicolaas Bloembergen (1920–) and Swedish physicist Kai Siegbahn (1918–).

Schawlow was born in Mount Vernon, New York, USA, on 5 May 1921. He was awarded a scholarship to read mathematics and physics at the University of Toronto, Canada, receiving his doctorate in 1949. During World War II, he taught on military courses and worked on microwave antenna. He met Charles Townes in Columbia in 1949 when he gained a fellowship to study applications of microwave spectroscopy in organic chemistry. Not only was his collaboration with Townes long and fruitful but he was also to marry Townes's sister, Aurelia.

Schawlow joined the Bell Telephone Laboratories, New Jersey, USA, in 1951. Townes had been working on the maser (a device that amplifies microwave radiation; maser is an acronym of 'microwave amplification by stimulated emission of radiation') and although Schawlow did not work on masers himself he did wonder if the maser principle could be applied to shorter wavelengths or higher frequencies. Townes had been thinking along the same lines and the two collaborated. They also collaborated on the book *Microwave Spectroscopy* (1955). They selected potassium to work with as it emits visible light and its optical characteristics were well documented. From experiments with potassium they produced a theoretical paper on 'optical masers' entitled 'Optical and Infrared Masers' (1958). The first laser was built by US physicist Theodore Maiman in 1960. Ironically Maiman used ruby, a material that Schawlow had experimented with only briefly. Schawlow then replicated Maiman's laser and published a detailed report on laser experimentation.

In 1961 he left Bell Telephone Laboratories to become J G Jackson–C J Wood Professor of Physics at Stanford University, California, a post he retained until he retired in 1991. He was president of the American Physical Society and the Optical Society of America and the Laser Institute of America named its highest award the Arthur Schawlow medal, the first of which was presented to him in 1982.

Schawlow was also involved in research into autism. His only son is autistic and lives in a centre in California that bears his father's name. Schawlow died in Palo Alto, California, on 28 April 1999, aged 77. CT

Seaborg, Glenn (Theodore)

(1912–1999)

US physical chemist Glenn Seaborg is best known for his discovery of plutonium in 1941 and for his researches on the synthetic transuranic elements. He was involved in the synthesis of ten artificial elements and for this work he shared the 1951 Nobel Prize for Chemistry with his co-worker Edwin McMillan (1907–1991).

Seaborg was born in Ishpeming, Michigan, on 19 April 1912 into a Swedish immigrant family; his father was a machinist. Seaborg spoke Swedish before speaking English. When he was ten years old the family moved to Los Angeles, where he graduated from High School in 1929. He went to study literature at the University of California but changed to science and graduated in 1934. He then went on to study at Berkeley under Gilbert Lewis, gaining his PhD in 1937 and spending a further two years as one of Lewis' research associates; he became an instructor in 1939. During part of World War II Seaborg was a section chief at the metallurgical laboratory at Chicago University, where much of the early work on the atomic bomb was carried out. He married Helen Griggs, with whom he was to have five children, in 1942.

After the war, in 1945, he was appointed professor of chemistry and director of nuclear chemical research at the Lawrence Radiation Laboratory at Berkeley, becoming associate director of the laboratory from 1954 to 1961 and chancellor of the campus from 1958 to 1961. In 1961 he was made chairman of the US Atomic Energy Commission and held the appointment for ten years. He returned to the Lawrence Radiation Laboratory in 1971 to resume his post as associate director (until 1975) and to become University Professor of Chemistry, a post he held until his death.

The transuranic elements, on which Seaborg's work was mainly focused, are all those that lie beyond uranium in the periodic table, that is, all elements of atomic number higher than 92. They constitute the majority of the actinides (elements 89 to 103), so called by analogy with the lanthanides or rare earths. They are all radioactive and none occurs to any appreciable extent in nature; they are synthesized by transmutation reactions. In the 1940s and 1950s, Seaborg was involved in the identification of ten new transuranic elements: plutonium (atomic number 94), americium (95), curium (96), berkelium (97), californium (98), einsteinium (99), fermium (100), mendelevium (101), nobelium (102), and (in 1974) unnilhexium (106). In 1997, unnilhexium was officially named seaborgium (symbol Sg) in his honour. This decision was fairly controversial at the time as no element had been named after a living scientist.

Seaborg and his collaborators discovered plutonium in 1940 by bombarding uranium with deuterons in the Berkeley 152-cm/60-in cyclotron. The first isotope found had a mass of 238, and the more important (because it is fissionable) plutonium-239 was discovered in 1941 (by neutron bombardment of U-238). In 1944 helium bombardment of Pu-239 yielded Cm-242, the first isotope of curium. Americium, as Am-241, was identified by Seaborg and others at the Metallurgical Laboratory in 1944–1945. Helium bombardment of Am-241 at Berkeley produced berkelium (as Bk-249) at the end of 1949, and three months later the minute amount of Cm-242 available was also bombarded with helium to form californium-245. Einsteinium was identified in the debris from the 'Mike' nuclear explosion staged by the Los Alamos Scientific Laboratory in November 1952, where it arose from the radioactive decay of heavy uranium isotopes. Another decay product, fermium-255, was discovered in January 1953. Helium bombardment was again used in early 1955 to create mendelevium-256 out of Es-253. Nobelium, element 102, was discovered in spring 1957 at the Nobel Institute of Physics in Stockholm. The transactinide element seaborgium, element 106, was created in 1974 by a Berkeley team led by Albert Ghiorso by bombarding californium-249 with oxygen nuclei.

Seaborg was always very concerned with the safety aspects of the new elements he discovered and established many safety procedures to protect himself and fellow researchers that have become widely adopted as standard laboratory practice. Despite this awareness of danger he was always keen to stress that: 'People must understand that science is inherently neither a potential for good nor for evil. It is a potential to be harnessed by man to do his bidding' (Associated Press interview with Alton Blakeslee, 29 September 1964). As Chairman of the Atomic Energy Commission, Seaborg encouraged the rapid growth of the US nuclear power industry and worked hard to dispel public misunderstanding of the dangers of the industry. Many of the isotopes he discovered have also found other uses in industry and in medicine.

Seaborg's publications include *The Chemistry of the Actinide Elements* (with Joseph Katz; 1958), *The Transuranium Elements* (1958), *Men and the Atom* (with William A Corliss; 1971), and *Nuclear Milestones* (1972).

In addition to the Nobel prize, Seaborg was also awarded the Enrico Fermi Award (awarded by the US Atomic Energy Commission) in 1957; the Priestley Medal of the American Chemical Society in 1979; the Henry De Wolf Smyth Award of the American Nuclear Society in 1982; and the Actinide Award in 1984.

Seaborg died in Lafayette, California, on 25 February 1999, aged 86. CT

Speight, Johnny

(1922–1998)

English playwright and scriptwriter, celebrated for his creation of the foul-mouthed, working-class, right-wing, bigot Alf Garnett in the controversial BBC television sitcom *Till Death Us Do Part* (1965–74). Heralding the advent of alternative television comedy, the series was shocking and irreverent, unique in the strength of its language, its assault on such formerly sacred subjects as religion and royalty, and its blatant exposition of all the worst traits ascribed to the English national character.

Speight was born the son of a docker in London on 2 June 1922, in a Canning Town slum. Following a poor education, aimed at turning out factory workers rather than screenwriters, he left school at 14 with little ability in the niceties of spelling and grammar. World War II enabled him to escape Canning Town, which he once likened to prison, and having learned to play the drums in the army, he joined a jazz band when the war finished.

He attributed his inspiration to become a comic writer to Bernard Shaw, whom he had originally assumed to be a stand-up comedian until chancing upon one of the playwright's books. After showing his first scripts to Frankie Howerd, Speight was introduced to Eric Sykes, and joined a clique of aspiring writers, including Spike Milligan, which later formalised as Associated London Scripts. Graduating from link gags for Edmundo Ros's South American music broadcasts, Speight wrote for such rising stars as Morecambe and Wise and Peter Sellers. However, the first true evidence of Speight's reprobate brand of humour appeared with his sketches for ATV's *The Arthur Haynes Show* (1960–66), featuring Haynes as a rude, disreputable tramp thwarting officialdom.

Turning to playwriting, Speight created the heavily censored *The Knacker's Yard* (1962), the award-winning *If There Weren't Any Blacks You'd Have to Invent Them,* and various television plays, including *The Compartment* (1962), *The Playmates,* and *The Salesman* in 1965.

Till Death Us Do Part first emerged as a one-off sitcom commissioned by Dennis Main Wilson for the BBC's *Comedy Playhouse* collection. Warren Mitchell starred as Alf Ramsey, the surname Garnett being adopted in the subsequent series which began in 1966 with the episode *Arguments, Arguments.* The Garnett family – including Alf's recalcitrant wife Else (Dandy Nichols), dubbed 'you silly old moo'; his lively daughter Rita (Una Stubbs); and her left-wing, 'scouse git' boyfriend Mike (Anthony Booth) – grabbed the nation's attention on an unprecedented scale. Damned by moral watchdogs of the Swinging Sixties such as Mary Whitehouse, and applauded by journalists for its ground-breaking brilliance, the series earned Screenwriters' Guild Awards in 1966, 1967, and 1968, and sold around the world, as well as being remade in the USA as *All in the Family.* Film versions appeared in 1968 and in 1972 with *The Alf Garnett Saga.*

Less successful was his sitcom *Curry and Chips* (1969) for London Weekend, a study on racism starring Eric Sykes and a blacked-up Spike Milligan, which was scrapped after six episodes. *Till Death Us Do Part,* however, continued until 1974, and rights to the original were bought by ATV and shown as *Till Death* (1981). Returning to the Garnetts, Speight began the BBC's *In Sickness and in Health* (1985–86), initially written around a wheelchair-bound Dandy Nichols. Other television work included *Spooner's Patch* (1979–82) and *The Nineteenth Hole* (1989).

Speight's autobiography *For Richer, For Poorer* was published in 1991, and he also wrote the comic *It Stands to Reason* (1973) and *The Thoughts of Chairman Alf* (1973). He died in Chorleywood, Hertfordshire, on 6 July 1998. SP

Springfield, Dusty

stage name of Mary Isabel Catherine Bernadette O'Brien
(1939–1998)

Dusty Springfield, the closest Britain ever came in the 1960s to producing a 'black' soul singer (Cliff Richard dubbed her the 'white negress') was one of those iconic performers whose manner of delivering a song became emblematic, just as her true persona remained carefully concealed behind a highly cosmetic image – of Barbie-doll blonde, rigidly coiffed hair and heavily blackened eyes. Such was her own identification with and security within the contrived public image that she would never go out without it.

Mary Isabel Catherine Bernadette O'Brien was born on 16 April 1939 in Hampstead to Irish Catholic parents. She performed briefly with a syrupy girl trio, the Lana Sisters, after completing her convent education, before joining up with her brother Tom on the folk circuit in 1960 and forming The Springfields with Tim Field.

In those days a neatly suburban and unremarkable Dusty Springfield in huge flouncy skirts appeared on British TV performing hits such as 'Island of Dreams' (1962) and 'Say I Won't Be There' (1963), whilst 'Silver Threads and Golden Needles' was an enormous hit for the Springfields in the USA. Whilst the image was clean-cut, the voice that Dusty Springfield projected had a richness and husky sophistication that seemed to merit better material than middle-of-the-road folk material, and she soon proved that she was someone who could handle a real song. When the Springfields disbanded in 1963, Dusty proceeded to make big dramatic ballads her forte, as one of the great sixties pop divas. The voice brought her a string of Top Ten hits: 'I Only Want to Be With You', 'You Don't Have to Say You Love Me', 'I Just don't Know What to do with Myself' (her No1 million-seller in 1966), 'Some of Your Loving'. There were also a very successful BBC television show, numerous awards in pop music polls as Best Female Vocalist, and that much coveted breakthrough for any British artist – musical recognition in the USA, as the first female singer to achieve a US Top Ten Hit in the pop era.

At times, accusations of being 'difficult' to work with were made. Despite her success, Springfield was a woman whose shyness and insecurity could manifest itself in self-loathing and unpredictable behaviour. She was also tormented by the search for perfectionism in her work and exercised close artistic control over everything she chose to record. A case in point was her foray into black soul and R & B in Memphis in 1968, which produced the album she was most proud of (*Dusty in Memphis)* and the hit single 'Son of a Preacher Man' (a song originally written for Aretha Franklin).

But in 1970, with 16 hits and five best-selling albums behind her, Springfield's career had peaked and despite her careful choice of consistently good material, her torch-song vocal style fitted less and less into the increasingly progressive musical climate. And every now and then talk surfaced with rumours of bisexuality. Disillusioned, she disappeared to the USA, where, with a houseful of cats, she lived through several artistically desolate years during which she was dogged by ill health and insecurity problems leading to increasing dependency on drink and drugs, so much so that she later admitted that 'in seven months I was a brain-scrambled wreck'.

The occasional recording or attempted British comeback failed dismally, until she was rediscovered by Neil Tennant and Chris Lowe of The Pet Shop Boys in 1987, who persuaded her to record 'What Have I Done to Deserve This', a No 2 hit in the UK, and another successful collaboration, 'Nothing Has Been Proved', in 1989.

In 1994 Springfield returned to England, but not long afterwards breast cancer was diagnosed and, despite a period of remission, it came back to kill her on 2 March 1998 – only a few days after she was awarded the OBE for her services to music.

Whilst Springfield's great years were undoubtedly those between 1965 and 1968, when she demonstrated her versatility with Tamla Motown soul hits, rhythm and blues numbers, as well as pop ballads by Bacharach and David songs ('The Look of Love', 'Wishin' and Hopin''), it was ultimately that inimitable husky, expressive voice rather than the material itself that ensured that her classic pop recordings will be endlessly revived. HR

Starovoitova, Galina Vasilievna

(1946–1998)

In the history of Russian politics since the turn of the century – and even more so since the days of entrenched Soviet rule, which never once saw a female member of the Politburo – outstanding women politicians have been extremely few and far between. That Russia's finest, most outspoken and most committed reformist female politician (probably since Alexandra Kollontai) could be gunned to death outside her own home is the most chilling indicator yet of the rapid decline into chaos of Russian society since the collapse of the Soviet Union.

Galina Starovoitova grew up in the Urals and studied social psychology and anthropology in Leningrad. A highly intelligent and gifted woman, she could no doubt have lived out her working life in the relatively safe academic world of the Soviet Academy of Sciences, where she worked for 17 years. Her move into politics was however a natural progression, stemming in part from her dogged political independence and passionate belief in democracy (she never joined the Communist Party) and her work as an ethnographer, which had led her to take an interest in Soviet minority groups and to support their right to self-determination. Starovoitova had taken a particular interest in the bitter struggle of Armenians in the enclave of Nagorno-Karabakh in Azerbaijan to gain autonomy, and as a result of her support for this cause she was elected to the Congress of People's Deputies in 1989 as the representative of an Armenian constituency. Once inside Congress, she continued to pursue her support for minority interests as a member of its human rights commission.

In 1990 Starovoitova was elected to the Russian parliament as an independent candidate representing a constituency in the recently renamed St Petersburg and aligning herself with other independents in Boris Yeltsin's Inter-Regional Group of People's Deputies. After the failed coup of August 1991 and the departure of Gorbachev, Starovoitova worked closely with Boris Yeltsin on nationality issues but was later sacked for criticizing government policy over ethnic clashes in the North Caucasus. She was politically sidelined for the next three years – taking a strong moral line on the invasion of Chechnya, over which she fell out with Yeltsin – and spent her time working and lecturing in the USA and the UK, where, thanks to her superb English, she fast developed a reputation as one of the foremost media pundits on the Russian political scene. Late in 1995, she returned to Russia to take up a seat in the State Duma, again representing a St Petersburg constituency. By now Russian politics had become fractured into a discordant, multi-party system, with even the democratic group succumbing to bitter infighting. Starovoitova stood apart from this and continued to build a solid political reputation, with her social concerns remaining uppermost; she now began to speak out against the growing nationalist domination of the Duma and the ominous revival in Russia of anti-Semitism and fascism.

At the time of her death Starovoitova was talking of running for governor of the Leningrad region and of her intentions to stand in the presidential elections in 2000, both of which had offered hope to many Russians who had become resigned and cynical about Russia's political future. It is a damning indictment of the current state of Russian politics that even Starovoitova's son could look upon her death as 'utterly predictable' in the light of her outspoken condemnation of right-wing extremism and her recent voiced intention of revealing to the Duma the contents of a dossier she had been compiling on the

alleged corruption of senior Communist politicians.

Whilst public opinion in Russia has become inured, if not indifferent to the frequent occurrence of Mafia-linked assassinations in the world of Russian commerce, business, and even the media, the shock of Starovoitova's murder was profound; so much so that St Petersburg witnessed a mass gathering of mourners wishing to pay their last respects of a type that had not been seen since the deaths of Soviet presidents. But of course, this time there was one important difference: there was no obligation for the 20,000 or more people who patiently stood in line in the freezing cold to pay their respects to be there, as there had been under Communism. Ordinary people had felt compelled to express their despair at the loss of a woman whom Boris Yeltsin described as 'a passionate tribune of democracy'. Her death, if nothing else, had served as an all too painful reminder to this beleaguered nation that the fragile, new-found freedoms of the post-Soviet era would cost it dear. She died on 20 November at the age of 52. HR

Sutch, Screaming Lord

adopted name of David Edward Sutch
(1940–1999)

The appearance of the irrepressible Monster Raving Loony Party candidate Screaming Lord Sutch at British elections over the last 35 years was, one might say, for all its absurdity the ultimate manifestation of all that was good, and fair, and terribly British about a democratic parliamentary system which, true to the spirit of tolerance and even-handedness, welcomed all-comers to the political podium. To many, Sutch was the epitome of incoherent craziness, but somewhere, underneath all the glitz, the gigantic rosettes, and the silly hats, there was a serious edge to what he wanted to say about freedom of expression; and he provided a refreshing injection of satire into the sober business of British politics.

For Sutch, electioneering was an extension of his flamboyant pop career after a penurious childhood growing up in Kilburn with his widowed mother. In the late 1950s he began singing in a Soho coffee bar; but unlike his contemporaries Cliff Richard and Adam Faith, there were no neatly quiffed hairstyles or shiny suits for him. Instead he evolved a long-haired caveman style that was loud and anarchic, a fusion of gothic horror and comedic Neanderthal aggression (as testified by songs, such as 'All Black and Hairy') that drew its inspiration from the slapstick of music hall that he had loved as a child and the voodoo rhythm and blues of the American deep south. And the music itself was not without value; if nothing else for providing a showcase, through Sutch's backing group The Raving Savages, for the embryonic talents of several musicians who later went on to form much more successful groups (the Yardbirds, Deep Purple, and the Jimi Hendrix Experience, for example).

Sutch patently never fitted into the mould of sixties Beatlemania, nor was he ever in the league of heavy metal bands, but instead remained a fringe performer, happy to turn up and perform wherever the fans were. With his leopardskin outfits and top hat, he became a cult figure with rockers, who made albums such as *Hands of Jack the Ripper* a hit for him in the 1970s, although his singles never made it into the Top 10.

In 1963 Sutch turned his irreverent attention to politics and stood as the National Teenage party candidate at a by-election in Stratford-upon-Avon. Realizing he could reach a far wider audience by inviting tut-tut-ting controversy with his mainly silly (turning the European butter mountain into a ski slope) but occasionally serious (introducing the vote at 18, abolition of the 11-plus) ideas on political reform, Sutch became a regular feature of by-elections for the next 35 years. Thus he entered history and the *Guinness Book of Records* for managing to lose his deposit in 40 by-elections; the Loony Party remained constantly on the brink of financial collapse. Claiming to have cemented his nickname 'Lord' Sutch by deed poll, he continued to make intermittent appearances on the pub circuit with The Raving Savages and remained unrepentant about his much-maligned antics, releasing a single 'I'm Still Raving' in 1995. But following the death of his mother in 1997 he suffered from depression and, on 16 June 1999, he hanged himself at his suburban semi in Harrow at the age of 58. From their modest HQ of the Golden Lion Hotel in Devon, the members of the Loony Party have since announced their intention to keep the party going, whilst even Downing Street acknowledged Sutch's 'unique contribution' to politics in Britain. HR

Tilberis, Liz (Elizabeth Jane)

(1947–1999)

English fashion editor who rose through the ranks of British *Vogue* from fashion assistant in 1970 to editor-in-chief (1987–92), and became editor-in-chief of *Harper's Bazaar,* New York (1992–99), dramatically reversing its declining fortunes. Considered one of the magazine industry's great 20th-century talents, she pursued a vision of democratic accessible fashion with great panache, sweeping away snobbery and promoting the marriage of couture fantasy and affordable chic.

As a pivotal figure of two of the world's most influential fashion publishing houses, she was respected for her formidable determination and energy, but also admired for her open friendliness, and for the poise with which she faced a six-year battle with ovarian cancer, described in her autobiography *No Time To Die* (1999). Unstinting in her efforts to inform and fundraise, she became president of the Ovarian Cancer Research Fund in 1997.

Tilberis was born in Alderley Edge, Cheshire, on 7 September 1947. Expelled from her first fashion course at Leicester Polytechnic for entertaining a man in her room, she pleaded for a place at the Jacob Kramer Art College, Leeds, winning over the interviewing tutor Andrew Tilberis with her enthusiasm; they were to marry in 1971. Her association with *Vogue* began when she was runner-up in an essay-writing competition. Rewarded with an internship, she was initiated into the world of the photoshoot, absorbing every facet with dedication. She was appointed fashion assistant (1970–73), fashion editor (1973–85), executive fashion editor (1985–86), and fashion director (1986–87). In 1987, on the verge of moving to New York with Ralph Lauren's design team, she was offered the editorship of *Vogue;* she celebrated with a family supper of fish and chips and champagne.

During her time with *Vogue,* Tilberis subverted the elitist, using unlikely sources of fashion material and, with inventive flair, vital, barefaced models; she also promoted the combination of glamour, fantasy, and real-life scenes and props. She introduced the work of photographer Bruce Weber, persuaded Diana, Princess of Wales, to pose for the 1990 cover shot by Arthur Elgort that redefined her image as a modern princess, and, in 1991, marked *Vogue*'s 75th anniversary with a collection specially created by the world's top designers, snapped by its foremost photographers.

Robust in behaviour and appearance, with a dress size she acknowledged as virtually criminal in the fashion world, Tilberis teased fashion's pretension but staunchly defended its life-enhancing exuberance. A team-player who refused to take credit alone, she pursued an open-door policy which admitted only talent and high aspirations; a colleague described her as 'an iron fist in a velvet glove'.

However, in England Tilberis felt undervalued as 'just' the editor of a fashion magazine, and in 1992 she accepted editorial control of *Harper's Bazaar* in New York. Vowing to take Manhattan, within two years she had transformed the ailing magazine into a cool confection of fantasy and understated glamour, completely outmanoeuvring its competitor, American *Vogue.* She was nicknamed 'Million Dollar Liz'.

In December 1993, she hosted a celebration of *Bazaar*'s fashion awards, including the presentation of two Ellies (the industry's equivalent of the Oscars), aware that she would be facing surgery for ovarian cancer the following day. *No Time To Die,* a candid account of her illness, is also a humorous, self-deprecating profile of her career, and a testimony to her close family ties, the misery of unsuccessful fertility treatment being swept away by the adoption of her two sons, Robert in 1981 and Christopher in 1985. For Tilberis, fashion was always a hugely joyful element of life but never its total sum. She died in New York on 21 April 1999. SP

Whitelaw, Willie (William Stephen Ian)

Viscount Whitelaw of Penrith
(1918–1999)

British Conservative politician. Although born in Nairn, northeast Scotland, Whitelaw's upbringing and education at Winchester and Trinity College, Cambridge, where he read history and law, produced the image of a well-bred, landed English gentleman. Charm was probably his most notable attribute as well as the ability to get on with anyone, regardless of their background, religion, or political views. It was this natural courteousness which carried him to the forefront of British politics and won him the confidence of a succession of leaders of his party. Often regarded by the general public as a rather bumbling, old-fashioned figure, he was much more astute than he appeared and might well have been Conservative leader and prime minister if his innate loyalty and decency had not inhibited his political ambitions. He once admitted that he deliberately cultivated the impression of being less bright than he really was.

To whatever he turned his hand, Whitelaw distinguished himself. Serving throughout World War II in the Scots Guards, he was awarded the military cross for bravery. After the war he initially tended his large land holdings but was later persuaded to enter the political arena. After two unsuccessful attempts, he was elected to the House of Commons, representing Penrith and the Borders, in 1955. He soon became a significant figure within the Conservative Party, later winning the trust and respect of two very different prime ministers, Edward Heath and Margaret Thatcher.

The Conservatives were out of power between 1964 and 1970, and during this period Whitelaw's talents were recognized by the new Tory leader, Sir Alec Douglas-Home, who made him opposition chief whip. The Conservatives returned to power, under Edward Heath, in 1970, and Whitelaw immediately joined the cabinet. At first he was leader of the Commons and then, from 1972, secretary of state for Northern Ireland. He was moved to the department for employment in 1974 and soon afterwards Heath was confronted by a national miners' strike. Although Whitelaw advised against it, the prime minister decided to challenge the unions by calling an early general election, which he lost. Opposition to Heath began to build up within the party and when he put himself forward for re-election in 1975 there were several possible serious challengers, one of the front runners being William Whitelaw. Immensely loyal to his friends and colleagues, he chose not to contest the first round of the leadership elections, allowing an unexpected candidate, the former education secretary, Margaret Thatcher, a clear first-round win. Whitelaw decided to enter the second round but by then it was too late and Mrs Thatcher had a decisive victory.

When the Conservatives returned to power in 1979, Prime Minister Thatcher made him home secretary, and recognized his contribution to the party by naming him her deputy. There followed an unusual relationship between the two politicians: in public Whitelaw was completely loyal, as he had been to Mrs Thatcher's predecessors, but privately he was critical of her confrontational style and right-wing politics. In 1983 he left the Commons arena, accepting an hereditary peerage, but continued to be an influential figure within the party.

Willie Whitelaw has been credited with a number of notable quotations. During the 1970 general election campaign he accused the Labour leader, Harold Wilson, and his followers of 'going up and down the country stirring up apathy' and in 1972, when he first arrived in Belfast as the newly appointed Northern Ireland secretary and was asked complicated questions about Irish history, he said: 'I always think it is entirely wrong to prejudge the past.' Probably the most famous quotation about Whitelaw himself was by Margaret Thatcher who, appreciating the enormous contribution he had made to her government and the party, said: 'Every prime minister needs a Willie.'

History is likely to view him as a substantial and influential figure, avoiding the highest political office more by choice than circumstance. Viscount Whitelaw died peacefully in his sleep on 31 June 1999. DD

Wise, Ernie

stage name of Ernest Wiseman
(1925–1999)

Such was the popularity of Britain's most-loved comic duo, Morecambe and Wise, that it might all too easily be assumed that Ernie Wise's career really began in 1961 when the nation first began welcoming *The Morecambe and Wise Show* into their living rooms and then their hearts. But this is to deny a long apprenticeship that Ernie Wise served in the hard slog of clubs and music halls, and a 20-year association with Eric Morecambe that preceded their much praised and legendary television partnership, sadly cut short by Eric's death in 1984.

Morecambe and Wise's first TV series for ITV established their brand of comedy as a benchmark for British comedy and they proved an extremely hard act to follow.

Ernest Wiseman (as he then was), came from a working class background in Leeds, Yorkshire. Born on 27 November 1925, he sang at his father's knee in the clubs as a small boy, when they appeared together as 'Bert Carson and His Little Wonder'. Wise seemed to have a great solo career in prospect when he was labelled 'Britain's answer to Mickey Rooney' in the late 1930s, but then, in 1939, he met Eric Morecambe when Eric auditioned for a children's talent show, *Youth Takes a Bow,* in which Ernie was touring. Their double act germinated in 1941 when they were both still only 17, but war intervened and they temporarily went their separate ways. Eric and Ernie rediscovered each other in 1946 at a dismal variety circus in Surrey, where Eric uncharacteristically found himself playing the straight man to Ernie's comedian in 1947. Likened to Stan Laurel and Oliver Hardy, and influenced by Abbott and Costello, their act remained very much grounded in music hall tradition as they began to garner attention in the late 1950s, with appearances on radio and on the north-country club circuit.

In 1961 they made the breakthrough into television with a series on ITV, but it was in their BBC years, from 1968, that they earned audiences of as many as 29 million (for their 1977 *Christmas Show)*, and that elevated Eric and Ernie to the status of icons of the essential fabric of British popular culture. With Ernie's talent for song and dance, musical numbers became an integral part of the TV show, supported by the brilliant script writing of Sid Green and Dick Hills up to 1968 and Eddie Braben in later years. Like all straight men, Ernie Wise was frequently undervalued. Eric the gawky, seemingly undisciplined and irrepressible clown devoured attention, whilst 'Little Ern' with the 'short, fat, hairy legs' was the rock on which Eric's pratfalls depended for effect. To some it seemed a thankless task, constantly playing the role of foil for Eric's insults and parody, and Ernie Wise hated being described merely as Eric's 'stooge'. His talent lay in setting himself up with an array of absurd literary and personal pretensions that Eric would then proceed to demolish with playful glee, most notably belittling the plays 'wot he [Ernie] wrote' and making constant fun of Ernie's non-existent toupée. Ernie remained gracious in his acceptance of the greater appeal of Eric's wildly flamboyant humour and his ability effortlessly to create moments of great comic pathos. He seemed happy to accept that his own talent was as a 'song-and-dance man', which the format of their TV shows was increasingly tailored to exploit. During the 1970s the *Morecambe and Wise Christmas Show* became the essential element of peak-time festive viewing, and thespians and TV personalities such as Glenda Jackson, André Previn, Peter Cushing, Angela Rippon, Vanessa Redgrave, and Shirley Bassey all took manifest delight in appearing in Ernie's 'plays' and the set-piece musical numbers on the show. However, in 1978, after Eric and Ernie were lured back to ITV, the quality of the shows became patchy and by now Eric's heart trouble was taking its toll.

When Eric died in 1984, Ernie, like all theatrical troupers, soldiered on, but without Eric he was artistically rudderless and could not find a niche for his comedic talents. After a few years appearing in cabaret, pantomime, a farce on the West End stage, and as a panellist on TV shows such as *What's My Line?,* Ernie retired in 1996. Of his long association with Eric Morecambe he once remarked 'We were ordained for each other. It was like a marriage'. He died on 21 March 1999, having outlived Eric Morecambe for 15 years. HR

Zoll, Paul Maurice

(1911–1999)

US cardiologist who invented the heart pacemaker, cardiac defibrillator, and cardiac monitor, and hence saved and improved the life of millions worldwide. Zoll was awarded the Albert Lasker award in 1973 and many believe he merited a Nobel prize for any one of his three major inventions.

Zoll was born in Boston, Massachusetts, on 15 July 1911 and educated at Harvard College, graduating in 1932 and then gaining an MD from Harvard Medical School in 1936. He was assistant in medicine at the Beth Israel Hospital, Boston, 1939–54; Head of Cardiac Clinic 1947–58, and Physician 1954–93. He was associate editor on the American Heart Association journal *Circulation* 1956–65, and was professor of medicine at Harvard Medical School 1941–65.

As a research fellow in the early 1940s, Zoll studied the relationship between cardiac arrest and the blockage of the coronary artery by injecting dye into the heart. This work formed the basis of modern-day coronary angiography (a technique for X-raying major blood vessels by injecting a radiopaque dye into the bloodstream so that the blood vessel is silhouetted on the X-ray film).

During World War II, Zoll worked as an army medical officer in the UK. It was here that he first observed the excitability of the heart. During operations to remove shell fragments from close to the heart, Zoll observed that the heart would beat every time it was touched by forceps. Later this observation reoccurred to him, after he lost a patient who died as a result of her heart intermittently arresting. Zoll realized that if the heart could have been artificially stimulated, the patient's life would have been prolonged. His first research into regulating heartbeat was noninvasive, using electrical pacing through the chest. His success led to a race to devise the first implantable heart pacemaker, and Zoll's group was the first actually to implant pacemakers, in 1960.

Zoll had also turned his attention to treating the chaotic heartbeat (ventricular fibrillation) that is found after a heart attack. In 1956 he was the first to apply an electric shock to the chest to control the heart beat (cardiac defibrillation). Now defibrillators are standard not only in hospitals, but also in emergency vehicles, and even on commercial airlines.

Zoll also pioneered cardiac monitoring using an oscilloscope with audio alarms and such monitoring is now straightforward throughout hospitals, as even during straightforward operations the heartbeat is monitored. Zoll's discoveries spread quickly worldwide mainly due to his refusal to take out patents on his work. He died in Newton, Massachusetts, on 5 January 1999, aged 87. CT

The World's Royal Families

Living Members of the World's Royal Families

Name	Date of birth	Relationship to monarch
Belgium		
Albert II	1934	king
Paola Ruffo de Calabria	1937	wife
Philippe[1]	1960	son
Astrid	1962	daughter
Laurent	1963	son
Denmark		
Margrethe II	1940	queen
Henry de Laborde de Montpezat	1934	husband
Frederik[1]	1968	son
Joachim	1969	son
Japan		
Akihito	1933	emperor
Michiko	1934	wife
Hiro (Naruhito)[1]	1960	son
Aya (Fumihito)	1965	son
Nori (Sayako)	1969	daughter
Jordan		
Abdullah	1962	king
Rania	1970	wife
Hamzah[1]	1980	brother
Muna	–[2]	mother
Muhammad	1940	uncle
Hassan	1947	uncle
Basma	1950	aunt
Dina	–[2]	stepmother
Noor	1951	stepmother
Alia	1956	sister
Faisal	1963	brother
Aisha	1968	sister
Zein	1968	sister
Haya	1974	sister
Ali	1975	brother
Hashem	1981	brother
Iman	1983	sister
Raiya	1986	sister
Liechtenstein		
Johann Adam	1945	prince
Marie Aglae Kinsky	1940	wife
Alois Philippe[1]	1968	son
Maximillian	1969	son
Constantine	1972	son
Tatiana	1973	daughter
Philipp	1946	brother
Nikolaus	1947	brother
Nora	1950	sister
Luxembourg		
Jean	1921	grand duke
Josephine of Belgium	1927	wife
Marie-Astrid	1954	daughter
Henri[1]	1955	son
Jean	1957	son
Margaretha	1957	daughter
Guillaume	1963	son
William John	1981	grandson
Mary Christine	1983	granddaughter
Felix	1984	grandson
Louis	1986	grandson
Monaco		
Rainier III	1923	prince
Caroline	1957	daughter
Albert[1]	1958	son
Stephanie	1965	daughter
Netherlands		
Beatrix	1938	queen
Juliana	1909	mother
Claus von Amsberg	1926	husband
Willem-Alexander[1]	1967	son
Johan Friso	1968	son
Constantine	1969	son
Irene	1939	sister
Margriet	1943	sister
Christina	1947	sister
Norway		
Harald V	1937	king
Sonja Haraldsen	1937	wife
Marthan Louise	1971	daughter

(continued)

Living Members of the World's Royal Families (*continued*)

Name	Date of birth	Relationship to monarch
Haakon Magnus[1]	1973	son
Ragnhild	1930	sister
Astrid	1932	sister
Spain		
Juan Carlos I	1938	king
Sofia of Greece	1938	wife
Elena	1963	daughter
Christina	1965	daughter
Felipe[1]	1968	son
Sweden		
Carl XVI Gustaf	1946	king
Silvia Sommerlath	1944	wife
Victoria[1]	1977	daughter
Carl Philip	1979	son
Madeleine	1982	daughter
Margaretha	1934	sister
Birgitta	1937	sister
Désirée	1938	sister
Christina	1953	sister
Thailand		
Bhumibol Adulyadej (Rama IX)	1927	king
Mom Rajwong Sirikit Kitayakorn	1932	wife
Ubol Ratana	1951	daughter
Vajiralongkorn[1]	1952	son
Sirimdhorn	1955	daughter
Chulabhorn	1957	daughter
Tonga		
Taufa'ahau Tupou IV	1918	king
Ma'Ataha	1926	wife
Tupouto'A[1]	1948	son
Pilolevu	1951	daughter
Fatafehi	1954	son
Aho'Eitu	1959	son
United Kingdom		
Elizabeth II	1926	queen
Elizabeth Bowes-Lyon	1900	mother
Philip of Greece	1921	husband
Charles[1]	1948	son
Anne	1950	daughter
Andrew	1960	son
Edward	1964	son
Peter	1977	grandson
Zara	1981	granddaughter
William	1982	grandson
Harry	1984	grandson
Beatrice	1988	granddaughter
Eugenie	1990	granddaughter
Margaret Rose	1930	sister

[1] This member of each family is the heir to the throne.
[2] Year of birth not published.

European Rulers and Political Leaders

Belgian Monarchs from 1831

Reign	Name
1831–65	Leopold I
1865–1909	Leopold II
1909–14	Albert I
1914–18	German occupation
1918–34	Albert I
1934–40	Leopold III
1940–44	German occupation
1944–50 (regent)	Prince Charles
1950–51	Leopold III
1951–93	Baudouin

Belgian Prime Ministers from 1944

Term	Name	Party
1944–45	Hubert Pierlot	Catholic Party
1945–46	Achille van Acker	Socialist Party
1946	Paul-Henri Spaak	Socialist Party
1946	Achille van Acker	Socialist Party
1946–47	Camille Huysmans	Socialist Party
1947–49	Paul-Henri Spaak	Socialist Party
1949–50	Gaston Eyskens	Christian Social Party
1950	Jean Duvieusart	Christian Social Party
1950–52	Joseph Pholien	Christian Social Party
1952–54	Jean van Houtte	Christian Social Party
1954–58	Achille van Acker	Socialist Party
1958–61	Gaston Eyskens	Christian Social Party
1961–65	Théodore Lefèvre	Christian Social Party
1965–66	Pierre Harmel	Christian Social Party
1966–68	Paul van den Boeynants	Christian Social Party
1968–72	Gaston Eyskens	Christian Social Party
1972–74	Edmond Leburton	Socialist Party
1974–78	Léo Tindemans	Christian Social Party
1978–79	Paul van den Boeynants	Christian Social Party
1979–81	Wilfried Martens	Christian People's Party
1981	Mark Eyskens	Christian People's Party
1981–92	Wilfried Martens	Christian People's Party
1992–99	Jean-Luc Dehaene	Christian People's Party
1999–	Guy Verhofstadt	(Flemish) Liberal

Danish Monarchs from 1848

Reign	Name
House of Oldenburg	
1848–63	Frederick VII
Line of Glücksburg	
1863–1906	Christian IX
1906–12	Frederick VIII
1912–47	Christian X
1947–72	Frederick IX
1972–	Margrethe II

Danish Prime Ministers from 1945

Term	Name	Party
1945	Vilhelm Buhl	Social Democratic Party
1945–47	Knud Kristensen	Agrarian Party
1947–50	Hans Hedtoft	Social Democratic Party
1950–53	Erik Eriksen	Agrarian Party
1953–55	Hans Hedtoft	Social Democratic Party
1955–60	Hans Hansen	Social Democratic Party
1960–62	Viggo Kampmann	Social Democratic Party
1962–68	Jens-Otto Krag	Social Democratic Party
1968–71	Hilmar Baunsgaard	Radical Party
1971–72	Jens-Otto Krag	Social Democratic Party
1972–73	Anker Jøgensen	Social Democratic Party
1973–75	Poul Hartling	Liberal Party
1975–82	Anker Jøgensen	Social Democratic Party
1982–93	Poul Schlüter	Conservative Party
1993–	Poul Nyrup Rasmussen	Social Democratic Party

Dutch Monarchs from 1806

Reign	Name
1806–10	Lodewijk I
1810	Lodewijk II
1810–13	French annexation
1813–15	Provisional government
1815–40	Willem I
1840–49	Willem II
1849–90	Willem III
1890–1940	Wilhelmina
1940–45	German occupation
1945–48	Wilhelmina
1948–80	Juliana
1980–	Beatrix

Dutch Prime Ministers from 1945

Term	Name	Party
1945	Pieter Gerbrandy	Anti-Revolutionary Party
1945–46	Willem Schermerhorn	Socialist Party
1946–48	Louis Beel	Catholic Party
1948–58	Willem Drees	Socialist Party
1958–59	Louis Beel	Catholic Party
1959–63	Jan de Quay	Catholic Party
1963–65	Victor Marijnen	Catholic Party
1965–66	Joseph Cals	Catholic Party
1966–67	Jelle Zijlstra	Anti-Revolutionary Party
1967–71	Petrus de Jong	Catholic Party
1971–73	Barend Biesheuvel	Anti-Revolutionary Party
1973–77	Johannes (Joop) den Uyl	Labour Party
1977–82	Andreas van Agt	Christian Democratic Appeal Party
1982–94	Rudolphus (Ruud) Lubbers	Christian Democratic Appeal Party
1994–	Wim Kok	Labour Party

Sovereigns of England and the United Kingdom from 899

Reign	Name	Relationship
West Saxon Kings		
899–924	Edward the Elder	son of Alfred the Great
924–39	Athelstan	son of Edward the Elder
939–46	Edmund	half-brother of Athelstan
946–55	Edred	brother of Edmund
955–59	Edwy	son of Edmund
959–75	Edgar	brother of Edwy
975–78	Edward the Martyr	son of Edgar
978–1016	Ethelred (II) the Unready	son of Edgar
1016	Edmund Ironside	son of Ethelred (II) the Unready
Danish Kings		
1016–35	Canute	son of Sweyn I of Denmark who conquered England in 1013
1035–40	Harold I	son of Canute
1040–42	Hardicanute	son of Canute
West Saxon Kings (restored)		
1042–66	Edward the Confessor	son of Ethelred (II) the Unready
1066	Harold II	son of Godwin
Norman Kings		
1066–87	William I	illegitimate son of Duke Robert the Devil
1087–1100	William II	son of William I
1100–35	Henry I	son of William I
1135–54	Stephen	grandson of William II
House of Plantagenet		
1154–89	Henry II	son of Matilda (daughter of Henry I)
1189–99	Richard I	son of Henry II
1199–1216	John	son of Henry II
1216–72	Henry III	son of John
1272–1307	Edward I	son of Henry III
1307–27	Edward II	son of Edward I
1327–77	Edward III	son of Edward II
1377–99	Richard II	son of the Black Prince
House of Lancaster		
1399–1413	Henry IV	son of John of Gaunt
1413–22	Henry V	son of Henry IV
1422–61, 1470–71	Henry VI	son of Henry V
House of York		
1461–70, 1471–83	Edward IV	son of Richard, Duke of York
1483	Edward V	son of Edward IV
1483–85	Richard III	brother of Edward IV

(continued)

Soverigns of England and the United Kingdom from 899 (*continued*)

Reign	Name	Relationship
House of Tudor		
1485–1509	Henry VII	son of Edmund Tudor, Earl of Richmond
1509–47	Henry VIII	son of Henry VII
1547–53	Edward VI	son of Henry VIII
1553–58	Mary I	daughter of Henry VIII
1558–1603	Elizabeth I	daughter of Henry VIII
House of Stuart		
1603–25	James I	great-grandson of Margaret (daughter of Henry VII)
1625–49	Charles I	son of James I
1649–60	the Commonwealth	
House of Stuart (restored)		
1660–85	Charles II	son of Charles I
1685–88	James II	son of Charles I
1689–1702	William III and Mary	son of Mary (daughter of Charles I); daughter of James II
1702–14	Anne	daughter of James II
House of Hanover		
1714–27	George I	son of Sophia (granddaughter of James I)
1727–60	George II	son of George I
1760–1820	George III	son of Frederick (son of George II)
1820–30	George IV (regent 1811–20)	son of George III
1830–37	William IV	son of George III
1837–1901	Victoria	daughter of Edward (son of George III)
House of Saxe-Coburg		
1901–10	Edward VII	son of Victoria
House of Windsor		
1910–36	George V	son of Edward VII
1936	Edward VIII	son of George V
1936–52	George VI	son of George V
1952–	Elizabeth II	daughter of George VI

French Rulers 751–1958

Date of accession	Name
751	Pepin III/Childerich III
752	Pepin III
768	Charlemagne/Carloman
814	Louis I
840	Lothair I
843	Charles (II) the Bald
877	Louis II
879	Louis III
884	Charles (III) the Fat
888	Odo
893	Charles (III) the Simple
922	Robert I
923	Rudolf
936	Louis IV
954	Lothair II
986	Louis V
987	Hugues Capet
996	Robert II
1031	Henri I
1060	Philippe I
1108	Louis VI
1137	Louis VII
1180	Philippe II
1223	Louis VIII
1226	Louis IX
1270	Philippe III
1285	Philippe IV
1314	Louis X
1316	Jean I
1328	Philippe V
1322	Charles IV
1328	Philippe VI
1350	Jean II
1356	Charles V
1380	Charles VI
1422	Charles VII
1461	Louis XI
1483	Charles VIII
1498	Louis XII
1515	François I
1547	Henri II
1559	François II
1560	Charles IX
1574	Henri III
1574	Henri IV
1610	Louis XIII
1643	Louis XIV
1715	Louis XV
1774	Louis XVI
1792	National Convention
1795	Directory (five members)
1799	First Consul Napoléon Bonaparte
1804	Emperor Napoléon I
1814	King Louis XVIII
1815	Emperor Napoléon I
1815	King Louis XVIII
1824	Charles X
1830	Louis XIX
1830	Henri V
1830	Louis-Philippe
1848	President of the National Assembly Philippe Buchez
1848	Minister of War Louis Cavaignac
1848	President Louis Napoléon Bonaparte
1852	Emperor Napoléon III
1871	President Adolphe Thiers
1873	Patrice MacMahon
1879	Jules Grevy
1887	François Sadui-Carnot
1894	Jean Casimir-Périer
1895	François Faure
1899	Emile Loubet
1913	Armand Fallières
1913	Raymond Poincaré
1920	Paul Deschanel
1920	Alexandre Millerand
1924	Gaston Doumergue
1931	Paul Doumer
1932	Albert Le Brun
1940	Vichy government Philippe Pétain
1944	provisional government
1947	President Vincent Auriol
1954	René Coty

French Presidents and Prime Ministers from 1959 (the Fifth Republic)

Term	Name	Party
Presidents		
1959–69	General Charles de Gaulle	Gaullist
1969–74	Georges Pompidou	Gaullist
1974–81	Valéry Giscard d'Estaing	Republican/Union of French Democracy
1981–95	François Mitterand	Socialist
1995–	Jacques Chirac	Neo-Gaullist RPR
Prime Ministers		
1959–62	Michel Debré	Gaullist
1962–68	Georges Pompidou	Gaullist
1968–69	Maurice Couve de Murville	Gaullist
1969–72	Jacques Chaban-Delmas	Gaullist
1972–74	Pierre Messmer	Gaullist
1974–76	Jacques Chirac	Gaullist
1976–81	Raymond Barre	Union of French Democracy
1981–84	Pierre Mauroy	Socialist
1984–86	Laurent Fabius	Socialist
1986–88	Jacques Chirac	Neo-Gaullist RPR
1988–91	Michel Rocard	Socialist
1991–92	Edith Cresson	Socialist
1992–93	Pierre Bérégovoy	Socialist
1993–95	Edouard Balladur	Neo-Gaullist RPR
1995–97	Alain Juppé	Neo-Gaullist RPR
1997–	Lionel Jospin	Socialist

German Political Leaders from 1949

Term	Name	Party
Federal Republic of Germany		
Chancellors		
1949–63	Konrad Adenauer	Christian Democrat
1963–66	Ludwig Erhard	Christian Democrat
1966–69	Kurt Kiesinger	Christian Democrat
1969–74	Willy Brandt	Social Democrat
1974–82	Helmut Schmidt	Social Democrat
1982–98[1]	Helmut Kohl	Christian Democrat
Democratic Republic of Germany		
Communist Party leaders		
1949–50	Wilhelm Pieck	
1950–71	Walter Ulbricht	
1971–89	Erich Honecker	
1989	Egon Krenz	
Prime Ministers		
1989–90	Hans Modrow	
1990–91	Lothar de Maizière	
Germany		
Chancellors		
1998–	Gerhard Schroeder	Social Democrat

[1] The official reunification of the two countries, with Kohl as chancellor, took place in 1990.

Holy Roman Emperors

Reign	Name
Carolingian Kings and Emperors	
800–14	Charlemagne (Charles the Great)
814–40	Louis the Pious
840–55	Lothair I
855–75	Louis II
875–77	Charles (II) the Bald
881–87	Charles (III) the Fat
891–94	Guido of Spoleto
892–98	Lambert of Spoleto (co-emperor)
896–901	Arnulf (rival)
901–05	Louis III of Provence
905–24	Berengar
911–18	Conrad (I) of Franconia (rival)
Saxon Kings and Emperors	
918–36	Henry I the Fowler
936–73	Otto (I) the Great
973–83	Otto II
983–1002	Otto III
1002–24	Henry (II) the Saint
Franconian (Salian) Emperors	
1024–39	Conrad II
1039–56	Henry (III) the Black
1056–1106	Henry IV
1077–80	Rudolf of Swabia (rival)
1081–93	Hermann of Luxembourg (rival)
1093–1101	Conrad of Franconia (rival)
1106–25	Henry V
1126–37	Lothair II
Hohenstaufen Kings and Emperors	
1138–52	Conrad III
1152–90	Frederick Barbarossa
1190–97	Henry VI
1198–1215	Otto IV
1198–1208	Philip of Swabia (rival)
1215–50	Frederick II
1246–47	Henry Raspe of Thuringia (rival)
1247–56	William of Holland (rival)
1250–54	Conrad IV
1254–73	no ruler (the Great Interregnum)
Rulers from Various Noble Families	
1257–72	Richard of Cornwall (rival)
1257–73	Alfonso X of Castile (rival)
1273–91	Rudolf I, Habsburg
1292–98	Adolf I of Nassau
1298–1308	Albert I, Habsburg
1308–13	Henry VII, Luxembourg
1314–47	Louis IV of Bavaria
1314–25	Frederick of Habsburg (co-regent)
1347–78	Charles IV, Luxembourg
1378–1400	Wenceslas of Bohemia
1400	Frederick III of Brunswick
1400–10	Rupert of the Palatinate
1411–37	Sigismund, Luxembourg
Habsburg Emperors	
1438–39	Albert II
1440–93	Frederick III
1493–1519	Maximilian I
1519–56	Charles V
1556–64	Ferdinand I
1564–76	Maximilian II
1576–1612	Rudolf II
1612–19	Matthias
1619–37	Ferdinand II
1637–57	Ferdinand III
1658–1705	Leopold I
1705–11	Joseph I
1711–40	Charles VI
1742–45	Charles VII of Bavaria
Habsburg-Lorraine Emperors	
1745–65	Francis I of Lorraine
1765–90	Joseph II
1790–92	Leopold II
1792–1806	Francis II

House of Habsburg 1804–1916

Reign	Name
Emperors of Austria	
1804–35	Francis (Franz) I (of Austria) and II (as Holy Roman emperor until 1806)
1835–48	Ferdinand I
Emperors of Austria–Hungary	
1848–1916	Franz Josef
1916–18	Charles (Karl Franz Josef)

Italian Kings from 1861

Reign	Name
1861–78	Victor Emmanuel II
1878–1900	Umberto I
1900–46	Victor Emmanuel III
1946	Umberto II (abdicated)

Irish Prime Ministers from 1922

Term	Name	Party
1922	Michael Collins	Sinn Féin
1922–32	William T Cosgrave	Fine Gael
1932–48	Eamon de Valera	Fianna Fáil
1948–51	John A Costello	Fine Gael
1951–54	Eamon de Valera	Fianna Fáil
1954–57	John A Costello	Fine Gael
1957–59	Eamon de Valera	Fianna Fáil
1959–66	Sean Lemass	Fianna Fáil
1966–73	Jack Lynch	Fianna Fáil
1973–77	Liam Cosgrave	Fine Gael
1977–79	Jack Lynch	Fianna Fáil
1979–81	Charles Haughey	Fianna Fáil
1981–82	Garrett Fitzgerald	Fine Gael
1982	Charles Haughey	Fianna Fáil
1982–87	Garrett Fitzgerald	Fine Gael
1987–92	Charles Haughey	Fianna Fáil
1992–94	Albert Reynolds	Fianna Fáil
1994–97	John Bruton	Fine Gael
1997–	Patrick 'Bertie' Ahern	Fianna Fáil

Italian Prime Ministers from 1945

Term	Name	Party
1945–53	Alcide de Gasperi	Christian Democratic Party
1953–54	Giuseppe Pella	Christian Democratic Party
1954	Amintore Fanfani	Christian Democratic Party
1954–55	Mario Scelba	Christian Democratic Party
1955–57	Antonio Segni	Christian Democratic Party
1957–58	Adone Zoli	Christian Democratic Party
1958–59	Amintore Fanfani	Christian Democratic Party
1959–60	Antonio Segni	Christian Democratic Party
1960	Fernando Tambroni	Christian Democratic Party
1960–63	Amintore Fanfani	Christian Democratic Party
1963	Giovanni Leone	Christian Democratic Party
1963–68	Aldo Moro	Christian Democratic Party
1968	Giovanni Leone	Christian Democratic Party
1968–70	Mariano Rumor	Christian Democratic Party
1970–72	Emilio Colombo	Christian Democratic Party
1972–73	Giulio Andreotti	Christian Democratic Party
1973–74	Mariano Rumor	Christian Democratic Party
1974–76	Aldo Moro	Christian Democratic Party
1976–79	Giulio Andreotti	Christian Democratic Party
1979–80	Francesco Cossiga	Christian Democratic Party
1980–81	Arnaldo Forlani	Christian Democratic Party
1981–82	Giovanni Spadolini	Republican Party
1982–83	Amintore Fanfani	Christian Democratic Party
1983–87	Benedetto (Bettino) Craxi	Socialist Party
1987	Amintore Fanfani	Christian Democratic Party
1987–88	Giovanni Goria	Christian Democratic Party
1988–89	Ciriaco de Mita	Christian Democratic Party
1989–92	Giulio Andreotti	Christian Democratic Party
1992–93	Giuliano Amato	Socialist Party
1993–94	Carlo Azeglio Ciampi	Christian Democratic Party
1994–95	Silvio Berlusconi	Freedom Alliance
1995–96	Lamberto Dini	independent
1996–98	Romano Prodi	Olive Tree Alliance
1998–	Massimo D'Alema	Democrats of the Left

Norwegian Prime Ministers from 1945

Term	Name	Party
1945–51	Einar Gerhardsen	Labour Party
1951–55	Oscar Torp	Labour Party
1955–63	Einar Gerhardsen	Labour Party
1963	John Lyng	Conservative Party
1963–65	Einar Gerhardsen	Labour Party
1965–71	Per Borten	Centre Party
1971–72	Trygve Bratteli	Labour Party
1972–73	Lars Korvald	Christian People's Party
1973–76	Trygve Bratteli	Labour Party
1976–81	Odvar Nordli	Labour Party
1981	Gro Harlem Brundtland	Labour Party
1981–86	Kaare Willoch	Conservative Party
1986–89	Gro Harlem Brundtland	Labour Party
1989–90	Jan Syse	Conservative Party
1990–96	Gro Harlem Brundtland	Labour Party
1996–97	Thorbjoern Jagland	Labour Party
1997–	Kjell Magne Bondevik	Christian People's Party

Norwegian Monarchs from 1905

Reign	Name	Reign	Name
1905–40	Haakon VII (exiled)	1957–91	Olaf V
1940–45	German occupation	1991–	Harald V
1945–57	Haakon VII (restored)		

Polish Political Leaders from 1945

Term	Name	Party
Communist Party Leaders[1]		
1945–48	Władysław Gomułka	
1948–56	Bolesław Bierut	
1956	Edward Ochab	
1956–70	Władysław Gomułka	
1970–80	Edward Gierek	
1980–81	Stanisław Kania	
1981–89	Wojciech Jaruzelski	
Presidents		
1989–90	Wojciech Jaruzelski	
1990–95	Lech Wałesa	Solidarity/independent
1995–	Aleksander Kwaśniewski	Democratic Left Alliance

[1]From 1945–90 the political leaders were the Communist Party leaders.

Roman Emperors 27 BC–337 AD

Reign	Name
Julio-Claudian Emperors	
27 BC–AD 14	Augustus
14–37	Tiberius I
37–41	Caligula (Gaius Caesar)
41–54	Claudius I
54–68	Nero
Civil Wars	
68–69	Galba
69	Otho
69	Vitellius
Flavian Emperors	
69–79	Vespasian
79–81	Titus
81–96	Domitian
96–98	Nerva
98–117	Trajan
117–38	Hadrian
Antonine Emperors	
138–61[1]	Antoninus Pius
161–69[1]	Lucius Verus
Despotic Emperors	
161–80	Marcus Aurelius
180–92[2]	Commodus
193	Pertinax
193	Didius Julianus
The Severi	
193–211	Septimus Severus
193–97	Clodius Albinus
193–94	Pescennius Niger
211–217	Caracalla
209–12	Geta
217–18	Macrinus
218	Diadumenianus
218–22	Elagabalus
222–35	Alexander Severus
The Soldier Emperors	
235–38	Maximinus
238	Gordian I
238	Gordian II
238	Balbinus
238	Pupienus
238–44	Gordian III
244–49	Philip (I) the Arab
249–51	Trajan Decius
251–53	Trebonianus Gallus
251–53	Volusianus
253–60	Valerian
253–68	Gallienus
268–70	Claudius II
270	Quintillus
270–75	Aurelian
275–76	Tacitus
276	Florianus
276–82	Probus
282–83	Carus
283–85	Carinus
283–84	Numerianus
284–305	Diocletian[3]
286–305	Maximianus
293–306	Constantius I
293–311	Galerius
305–337	Constantine I

[1] Divided voluntarily between two brothers.

[2] Between 180 and 284 there was a succession of emperors placed on the throne by their respective armies or factions. Therefore, dates of emperors' reigns in this period often overlap.

[3] The end of Diocletian's reign marked the split of the Roman empire. Whereas Diocletian retained supreme power, Maximianus ruled Italy and Africa, Constantius I ruled Gaul and Spain, and Galerius ruled Thrace.

Russian Tsars from 1547

Reign	Name
House of Rurik	
1547–84	Ivan the Terrible
1584–98	Theodore (Fyodor) I
1598	Irina
House of Godunov	
1598–1605	Boris Godunov
1605	Theodore (Fyodor) II
Usurpers	
1605–06	Dimitri III
1606–10	Basil IV
1610–13	Interregnum
House of Romanov	
1613–45	Michael Romanov
1645–76	Alexis
1676–82	Theodore III
1682–96	Peter (I) the Great and Ivan V (brothers)
1689–1721	Peter I, as tsar
1721–25	Peter I, as emperor
1725–27	Catherine I
1727–30	Peter II
1730–40	Anna Ivanovna
1740–41	Ivan VI
1741–62	Elizabeth
1762	Peter III
1762–96	Catherine (II) the Great
1796–1801	Paul
1801–25	Alexander I
1825–55	Nicholas I
1855–81	Alexander II
1881–94	Alexander III
1894–1917	Nicholas II

Scottish Monarchs 1005–1603

This table covers the period from the unification of Scotland to the union of the crowns of Scotland and England.

Reign	Name
Celtic Kings	
1005–34	Malcolm II
1034–40	Duncan I
1040–57	Macbeth
1057–93	Malcolm III Canmore
1093–94	Donald III Donalbane
1094	Duncan II
1094–97	Donald III (restored)
1097–1107	Edgar
1107–24	Alexander I
1124–53	David I
1153–65	Malcolm IV
1165–1214	William the Lion
1214–49	Alexander II
1249–86	Alexander III
1286–90	Margaret of Norway
English Domination	
1292–96	John Baliol
1296–1306	annexed to England
House of Bruce	
1306–29	Robert I the Bruce
1329–71	David II
House of Stuart	
1371–90	Robert II
1390–1406	Robert III
1406–37	James I
1437–60	James II
1460–88	James III
1488–1513	James IV
1513–42	James V
1542–67	Mary
1567–1625	James VI[1]

[1] After the union of crowns in 1603, he became James I of England.

Spanish Presidents, Chiefs of State, and Prime Ministers from 1931

Term	Name	Party
Presidents		
1931–36	Niceto Alcala Zamora	Liberal Republicans
1936	Diego Martinez y Barro	Radical Party
1936–39	Manuel Azaña y Diéz	Left Republican Party
Chiefs of State		
1939–75	Francisco Franco y Bahamonde	National Movement/Falange
Prime Ministers		
1931–33	Manuel Azaña y Diéz	Left Republican Party
1933	Alejandro Lerroux y García	Radical Republican Party
1933	Diego Martínez y Barro	Radical Republican Party
1933–34	Alejandro Lerroux y García	Radical Republican Party
1934	Ricardo Samper Ibañez	Radical Republican Party–Valencian branch
1934–35	Alejandro Lerroux y García	Radical Republican Party
1935	Joaquín Chapaprieta y Terragosa	independent
1935–36	Manuel Portela Valladares	Radical Republican Party
1936	Manuel Azaña y Diéz	Left Republican Party
1936	Santiago Cásares Quiroga	Left Republican Party
1936	José Giral y Pereira	Left Republican Party
1936–37	Francisco Largo Caballero	Socialist Party
1937–39	Juan Negrin	Socialist Party
1939–73	Francisco Franco Bahamonde	National Movement
1973	Luis Carrero Blanco	National Movement
1973–74	Torcuato Fernández Miranda	National Movement
1974–76	Carlos Arias Navarro	National Movement
1976–81	Adolfo Suárez González	Union of the Democratic Centre
1981–82	Leopoldo Calvo-Sotelo y Bustelo	Union of the Democratic Centre
1982–96	Felipe González Márquez	Socialist Workers' Party
1996–	José María Aznar	Popular Party

Soviet and Russian Presidents and Communist Party Leaders

Term	Name
USSR	
Communist Party Leaders	
1917–22	Vladimir Ilich Lenin
1922–53	Joseph Stalin
1953–64	Nikita Khrushchev
1964–82	Leonid Brezhnev
1982–84	Yuri Andropov
1984–85	Konstantin Chernenko
1985–91	Mikhail Gorbachev
Presidents	
1917–22	Vladimir Ilich Lenin[1]
1919–46	Mikhail Kalinin[2]
1946–53	Nikolai Shvernik
1953–60	Marshal Kliment Voroshilov
1960–64	Leonid Brezhnev
1964–65	Anastas Mikoyan
1965–77	Nikolai Podgorny
1977–82	Leonid Brezhnev
1982–83	Valery Kuznetsov (acting)
1983–84	Yuri Andropov
1984	Valery Kuznetsov (acting)
1984–85	Konstantin Chernenko
1985	Valery Kuznetsov (acting)
1985–88	Andrei Gromyko
1988–91	Mikhail Gorbachev
Russia	
Presidents	
1991–	Boris Yeltsin

[1] In 1917 Lenin was elected chairman of the Council of People's Commissars, that is, head of government. He held that post until 1922.
[2] In 1919, Kalinin became head of state (president of the Central Executive Committee of the Soviet government until 1937; president of the Presidium of the Supreme Soviet until 1946.)

Spanish Monarchs from 1516

Reign	Name
House of Habsburg	
1516–56	Charles I
1556–98	Philip II
1598–1621	Philip III
1621–65	Philip IV
1665–1700	Charles II
House of Bourbon	
1700–46	Philip V
1746–59	Ferdinand VI
1759–88	Charles III
1788–1808	Charles IV
1808	Ferdinand VII (deposed)
1808–13	Joseph Napoleon[1]
1813–33	Ferdinand VII (restored)
1833–68	Isabel II
1868–70	provisional government
1870–73	Amadeus I[2] (abdicated)
1873–74	first republic
1874–86	Alfonso XII
1886–1931	Alfonso XIII (deposed)
1975–	Juan Carlos

[1] House of Bonaparte.
[2] House of Savoy.

Swedish Monarchs from 950

Period	Name
c. 950–c. 95	Erik VIII
c. 995–c. 1022	Olof
c. 1022–c. 50	Anund Jakob
c. 1050–c. 60	Edmund
c. 1060–c. 80	Stenkil
c. 1080–c. 1110	Inge I/Halsten
c. 1110–c. 18	Filip
c. 1118–c. 22	Inge II
c. 1130–c. 56	Sverker I
c. 1150–c. 60	Erik IX Jerdvardsson
c. 1161–c. 67	Carl VII Sverkersson
c. 1167–c. 96	Knut I Eriksson
c. 1196–c. 1208	Sverker II Carlsson
c. 1208–c. 16	Erik X Eriksson
c. 1216–c. 22	Johan I Sverkersson
c. 1222–c. 29	Erik XI Eriksson
c. 1229–c. 34	Knut II
1234–50	Erik XI Eriksson
1250–75	Valdemar
1275–90	Magnus I Laduläs
1290–1318	Birgir Magnusson
1319–56	Magnus II Eriksson
1356–59	Magnus II Eriksson/Eric XII
1359–62	Magnus II Eriksson
1362–64	Magnus II Eriksson/Haakon
1364–89	Albrekt
1389–97	Margrethe
1397–1434	Erik XIII
1434–36	Regent: Engelbrekt Engelbrektsson
1436–40	Regent: Carl Knutsson
1441–48	Christoffer
1448–57	Carl VIII Knutsson
1457–64	Christian I
1464–65	Carl VIII Knutsson
1465–67	Interregnum
1467–70	Carl VIII Knutsson
1470–97	Sten Sture the Elder (regent)
1497–1501	Johan II
1501–03	Sten Sture the Elder (regent)
1503–12	Svante Sture (regent)
1512–20	Sten Sture the Younger (regent)
1520–23	Christian II
1523–60	Gustaf I
1560–68	Erik XIV
1568–92	Johan III
1592–99	Sigismund
1599–1604	Carl IX (viceroy)
1604–1611	Carl IX (king)
1611–32	Gustaf II Adolf
1632–54	Christina
1654–60	Carl X Gustaf
1660–97	Carl XI
1697–1718	Carl XII
1718–20	Ulrica Eleonora
1720–51	Fredrik
1751–71	Adolf Fredrik
1771–92	Gustaf III
1792–1809	Gustaf IV Adolf
1809–18	Carl XIII
1818–44	Carl XIV Johan
1844–59	Oscar I
1859–72	Carl XV
1872–1907	Oscar II
1907–50	Gustaf V
1950–73	Gustaf VI Adolf
1973–	Carl XVI Gustaf

Swedish Prime Ministers from 1946

Term	Name	Party
1946–69	Tage Erlander	Social Democratic Labour Party
1969–76	Olof Palme	Social Democratic Labour Party
1976–78	Thorbjörn Fälldin	Centre Party
1978–79	Ola Ullsten	Liberal Party
1979–82	Thorbjörn Fälldin	Centre Party
1982–86	Olof Palme	Social Democratic Labour Party
1986–91	Ingvar Carlsson	Social Democratic Labour Party
1991–94	Carl Bildt	Moderate Party
1994–96	Ingvar Carlsson	Social Democratic Labour Party
1996–	Göran Persson	Social Democratic Labour Party

Rulers and Political Leaders of the Americas

Argentine Presidents from 1944

Term	Name	Party
1944–46	Edelmiro Farrell	military
1946–55	Juan Perón	Justice Front of Liberation
1955	Eduardo Lonardi	military
1955–58	Pedro Aramburu	military
1958–62	Arturo Frondizi	Civic Radical Union-Intransigent
1962–63	José Guido	acting: independent
1963–66	Arturo Illía	Civic Radical Union of the People
1966–70	Juan Onganía	military
1970–71	Roberto Levingston	military
1971–73	Alejandro Lanusse	military
1973	Héctor Cámpora	Justice Front of Liberation
1973	Raúl Lastiri	acting: independent
1973–74	Juan Perón	Justice Front of Liberation
1974–76	Maria Estela de Perón	Justice Front of Liberation
1976–81	Jorge Videla	military
1981	Roberto Viola	military
1981–82	Leopoldo Galtieri	military
1982	Alfredo Saint-Jean	acting: military
1982–83	Reynaldo Bignone	military
1983–89	Raúl Alfonsín	Civic Radical Union
1989–	Carlos Saúl Menem	Justice Party

Aztec Emperors *c.* 1372–1521

Reign[1]	Name
c. 1372–c. 91	Acamapichtli (chieftain at Tenochtitlán; traditional founder of Aztec royal house)
c. 1391–c. 1416	Huitzilihuitl (son)
c. 1416–c. 27	Chimalpopoca (son)
c. 1427–c. 40	Itzcoatl (son of Acamapichtli)
c. 1440–c. 68	(Huehue) Motecuhzoma
c. 1468–81	Axayacatl (grandson of Itzcoatl)
1481–86	Tizoc (brother)
1486–1502	Ahuitzotl (brother)
1502–20	Motecuhzoma Xocoyotl (son of Axayacatl); known as Montezuma II
1520	Cuitlahuac (brother)
1520–21	Cuauhtemoc (son of Ahuitzotl)

[1] Dates before 1468 are approximate.

Brazilian Presidents from 1945

Term	Name	Party
1945–46	José Linhares	independent
1946–51	Eurico Dutra	Social Democratic Party
1951–54	Getúlio Vargas	Brazil Labour Party
1954–55	João Café	Social Progressive Party
1955	Carlos da Luz	independent
1955–56	Nereu Ramos	independent
1956–61	Juscelino Kubitschek	Social Democratic Party
1961	Jânio Quadros	Christian Democratic Party/Democratic National Union
1961–64	João Goulart	Brazil Labour Party
1964	Ranieri Mazzili	independent
1964–67	Humberto Branco	military
1967–69	Arthur da Costa e Silva	military
1969–74	Emilio Medici	military
1974–79	Ernesto Geisel	military
1979–85	João Figueiredo	military
1985–89	José Sarney	Social Democratic Party
1989–92	Fernando Collor de Mello	National Reconstruction Party
1992–94	Itamar Franco	National Reconstruction Party
1995–	Fernando Henrique Cardoso	Social Democratic Party

Inca Emperors *c.* 1200–1572

Reign	Name
The Kingdom of Cuzco	
c. 1200–1400	Manco Capac[1]
	Sinchi Roca[1]
	Lloque Yupanqui[1]
	Mayta Capac[1]
	Capac Yupanqui[2]
	Inca Roca[2]
	Yahuar Huacadc[2]
until 1438	Viracocha Inca
The Empire	
1438–71	Pachacuti
1471–93	Topa Inca
1493–1528	Huayna Capac
1528–32	Huascar
1532–33	Atahualpa
The Vilcabamba State	
1533	Topa Hualpa
1533–45	Manco Inca
1545–60	Sayri Tupac
1560–71	Titu Cusi Yupanqui
1571–72	Tupac Amaru

[1] This is a mythical figure.
[2] The dates of his reign are unknown.

Mexican Prime Ministers from 1946

Term	Name	Party
1946–52	Miguel Alemán Valdés	Institutional Revolutionary Party
1952–58	Adolfo Ruiz Cortines	Institutional Revolutionary Party
1958–64	Adolfo López Mateos	Institutional Revolutionary Party
1964–70	Gustavo Díaz Ordaz	Institutional Revolutionary Party
1970–76	Luís Echeverría Alvarez	Institutional Revolutionary Party
1976–82	José López Portillo y Pacheco	Institutional Revolutionary Party
1982–88	Miguel de la Madrid Hurtado	Institutional Revolutionary Party
1988–94	Carlos Salinas de Gortari	Institutional Revolutionary Party
1994–	Ernesto Zedillo Ponce de Léon	Institutional Revolutionary Party

Canadian Prime Ministers from 1867

Term	Name	Party
1867–73	John A Macdonald	Conservative
1873–78	Alexander Mackenzie	Liberal
1878–91	John A Macdonald	Conservative
1891–92	John J Abbott	Conservative
1892–94	John S D Thompson	Conservative
1894–96	Mackenzie Bowell	Conservative
1896	Charles Tupper	Conservative
1896–1911	Wilfred Laurier	Liberal
1911–20	Robert L Borden	Conservative
1920–21	Arthur Meighen	Conservative
1921–26	William L M King	Liberal
1926	Arthur Meighen	Conservative
1926–30	William L M King	Liberal
1930–35	Richard B Bennett	Conservative
1935–48	William L M King	Liberal
1948–57	Louis S St Laurent	Liberal
1957–63	John G Diefenbaker	Conservative
1963–68	Lester B Pearson	Liberal
1968–79	Pierre E Trudeau	Liberal
1979–80	Joseph Clark	Progressive Conservative
1980–84	Pierre E Trudeau	Liberal
1984	John Turner	Liberal
1984–93	Brian Mulroney	Progressive Conservative
1993	Kim Campbell	Progressive Conservative
1993–	Jean Chretien	Liberal

Leaders of South American Wars of Liberation

Leader	Lifespan	Details
Artigas, José Gervasio	1764–1850	Uruguayan independence leader from 1811 and national hero
Bolívar, Simón	1783–1830	born in Caracas, Venezuela, into a wealthy Creole[1] landowning family; he became president of Venezuela in 1817 and of Colombia in 1819; known as 'the Liberator'
Boyer, Jean-Pierre	1776–1850	Haitian mulatto[2] leader who left the regular army to join the revolutionary forces and became president (1818–43)
Christophe, Henry	1767–1820	Grenada-born Haitian revolutionary leader, from 1793, who became president of the black-led north in 1807 and ruled from 1811 as King Henry I
Dessalines, Jean-Jacques	1758–1806	Haitian revolutionary leader of African slave descent who took over the liberation struggle against the French after the arrest of Toussaint L'Ouverture in 1802, securing independence in 1804
Flores, Juan José	1800–1864	Ecuadoran freedom fighter and first president; the illegitimate son of a Spanish merchant, he fought in the royalist army until 1817, when, on being taken prisoner, he joined Bolívar's patriot forces
Lavalleja, Juan Antonio	1784–1853	Uruguayan soldier and independence leader from 1811 and loyal follower of Artigas
Miranda, Francisca de	1750–1816	born in Caracas, Venezuela, of Creole parents, he lived in exile in London, before leading a revolt against the Spanish in Venezuela in 1810; he capitulated to the royalists in 1812 and was disowned by fellow freedom fighters, including Bolívar, and died in a prison in Cadiz, Spain
O'Higgins, Bernardo	1778–1842	illegitimate son of an Irish-born viceroy of Chile and Peru, with San Martin he played a key role in the liberation of Chile between 1810 and 1818 and became head of the new government
Páez, José Antonio	1790–1873	Venezuelan military leader of the llaneros (plains people) who joined Bolívar's forces in 1818; he became president in 1831 and remained dominant until 1848
Pedro I	1826–1831	son of King John VI of Portugal, he became prince-regent of Brazil on his father's return to Portugal in 1821; a liberal, he declared Brazil's independence in 1822 and was crowned king in 1826, abdicating in 1831
Rivera, José Fructuoso	1784–1854	Uruguayan independence leader, a follower of Artigas and the country's first president
San Martín, General José de	1778–1850	Argentinian-born leader of the Army of the Andes, which secured the independence of Chile in 1818 and Peru in 1821
Santander, Francisco de Paula	1792–1840	Colombian general and political leader who was left by Bolívar to organize newly liberated New Granada from 1819
Sucre, General Antonio José de	1795–1830	Venezuelan-born general in Bolívar's army who liberated Quito in 1822 and secured Bolivia's independence in 1824
Toussaint L'Ouverture, Dominique	1743–1803	Haitian revolutionary leader of African slave descent who led the revolt against French rule in 1800, but was captured and died in prison in France

[1] Creole = Spaniard born in America.
[2] Mulatto = of mixed European and African blood.

US Presidents

Year elected/ took office		President	Party	Losing candidate(s)	Party
1789	1	George Washington	Federalist	no opponent	
1792		re-elected		no opponent	
1796	2	John Adams	Federalist	Thomas Jefferson	Democrat–Republican
1800	3	Thomas Jefferson	Democrat–Republican	Aaron Burr	Democrat–Republican
1804		re-elected		Charles Pinckney	Federalist
1808	4	James Madison	Democrat–Republican	Charles Pinckney	Federalist
1812		re-elected		DeWitt Clinton	Federalist
1816	5	James Monroe	Democrat–Republican	Rufus King	Federalist
1820		re-elected		John Quincy Adams	Democrat–Republican
1824	6	John Quincy Adams	Democrat–Republican	Andrew Jackson	Democrat–Republican
				Henry Clay	Democrat–Republican
				William H Crawford	Democrat–Republican
1828	7	Andrew Jackson	Democrat	John Quincy Adams	National Republican
1832		re-elected		Henry Clay	National Republican
1836	8	Martin Van Buren	Democrat	William Henry Harrison	Whig
1840	9	William Henry Harrison	Whig	Martin Van Buren	Democrat
1841	10	John Tyler[1]	Whig		
1844	11	James K Polk	Democrat	Henry Clay	Whig
1848	12	Zachary Taylor	Whig	Lewis Cass	Democrat
1850	13	Millard Fillmore[2]	Whig		
1852	14	Franklin Pierce	Democrat	Winfield Scott	Whig
1856	15	James Buchanan	Democrat	John C Fremont	Republican

(continued)

US Presidents (*continued*)

Year elected/ took office		President	Party	Losing candidate(s)	Party
1860	16	Abraham Lincoln	Republican	Stephen Douglas	Democrat
				John Breckinridge	Democrat
				John Bell	Constitutional Union
1864		re-elected		George McClellan	Democrat
1865	17	Andrew Johnson[3]	Democrat		
1868	18	Ulysses S Grant	Republican	Horatio Seymour	Democrat
1872		re-elected		Horace Greeley	Democrat–Liberal Republican
1876	19	Rutherford B Hayes	Republican	Samuel Tilden	Democrat
1880	20	James A Garfield	Republican	Winfield Hancock	Democrat
1881	21	Chester A Arthur[4]	Republican		
1884	22	Grover Cleveland	Democrat	James Blaine	Republican
1888	23	Benjamin Harrison	Republican	Grover Cleveland	Democrat
1892	24	Grover Cleveland	Democrat	Benjamin Harrison	Republican
				James Weaver	People's
1896	25	William McKinley	Republican	William J Bryan	Democrat–People's
1900		re-elected		William J Bryan	Democrat
1901	26	Theodore Roosevelt[5]	Republican		
1904		re-elected		Alton B Parker	Democrat
1908	27	William Howard Taft	Republican	William J Bryan	Democrat
1912	28	Woodrow Wilson	Democrat	Theodore Roosevelt	Progressive
				William Howard Taft	Republican
1916		re-elected		Charles E Hughes	Republican
1920	29	Warren G Harding	Republican	James M Cox	Democrat
1923	30	Calvin Coolidge[6]	Republican		
1924		re-elected		John W Davis	Democrat
				Robert M LaFollette	Progressive
1928	31	Herbert Hoover	Republican	Alfred E Smith	Democrat
1932	32	Franklin D Roosevelt	Democrat	Herbert C Hoover	Republican
				Norman Thomas	Socialist
1936		re-elected		Alfred Landon	Republican
1940		re-elected		Wendell Willkie	Republican
1944		re-elected		Thomas E Dewey	Republican
1945	33	Harry S Truman[7]	Democrat		
1948		re-elected		Thomas E Dewey	Republican
				J Strom Thurmond	States' Rights
				Henry A Wallace	Progressive
1952	34	Dwight D Eisenhower	Republican	Adlai E Stevenson	Democrat
1956		re-elected		Adlai E Stevenson	Democrat
1960	35	John F Kennedy	Democrat	Richard M Nixon	Republican
1963	36	Lyndon B Johnson[8]	Democrat		
1964		re-elected		Barry M Goldwater	Republican
1968	37	Richard M Nixon	Republican	Hubert H Humphrey	Democrat
				George C Wallace	American Independent
1972		re-elected		George S McGovern	Democrat
1974	38	Gerald R Ford[9]	Republican		
1976	39	James Earl Carter	Democrat	Gerald R Ford	Republican
1980	40	Ronald Reagan	Republican	James Earl Carter	Democrat
				John B Anderson	Independent
1984		re-elected		Walter Mondale	Democrat
1988	41	George Bush	Republican	Michael Dukakis	Democrat
1992	42	Bill Clinton	Democrat	Ross Perot	Independent
				George Bush	Republican
1996		re-elected		Bob Dole	Republican
				Ross Perot	Reform

[1] Became president on death of Harrison.
[2] Became president on death of Taylor.
[3] Became president on assassination of Lincoln.
[4] Became president on assassination of Garfield.
[5] Became president on assassination of McKinley.
[6] Became president on death of Harding.
[7] Became president on death of F D Roosevelt.
[8] Became president on assassination of Kennedy.
[9] Became president on resignation of Nixon.

Middle Eastern Rulers and Political Leaders

Egyptian Dynasties

Period	Name	Description
Early Dynastic Period		
c. 3100–*c.* 2905 BC	First Dynastic Period	Thinite
c. 2905–*c.* 2755 BC	Second Dynasty	Thinite
Old Kingdom		
c. 2755–*c.* 2680 BC	Third Dynasty	Memphite
c. 2680–*c.* 2544 BC	Fourth Dynasty	Memphite
c. 2544–*c.* 2407 BC	Fifth Dynasty	Memphite
c. 2407–*c.* 2255 BC	Sixth Dynasty	Memphite
First Intermediate Period		
c. 2255–*c.* 2235 BC	Seventh–Eighth Dynasties	Memphite
c. 2235–*c.* 2035 BC	Ninth–Tenth Dynasties	Heracleopolitan
Middle Kingdom		
c. 2134–*c.* 1991 BC	Eleventh Dynasty	Theban
c. 1991–*c.* 1786 BC	Twelfth Dynasty	Theban
Second Intermediate Period		
c. 1786–*c.* 1668 BC	Thirteenth Dynasty	Theban
c. 1720–*c.* 1665 BC	Fourteenth Dynasty	Xoite
c. 1668–*c.* 1560 BC	Fifteenth Dynasty	Hyksos
c. 1665–*c.* 1565 BC	Sixteenth Dynasty	Hyksos
c. 1668–*c.* 1570 BC	Seventeenth Dynasty	Theban
New Kingdom		
c. 1570–*c.* 1293 BC	Eighteenth Dynasty	Theban
c. 1293–*c.* 1185 BC	Nineteenth Dynasty	Theban
c. 1185–*c.* 1070 BC	Twentieth Dynasty	Theban
Third Intermediate Period		
c. 1070–*c.* 946 BC	Twenty-first Dynasty	Theban
c. 946–*c.* 712 BC	Twenty-second Dynasty	Bubastite
c. 828–*c.* 720 BC	Twenty-third Dynasty	Tanite
c. 740–*c.* 712 BC	Twenty-fourth Dynasty	Saite
c. 767–*c.* 656 BC	Twenty-fifth Dynasty	Nubian
Saite Period		
c. 664–*c.* 525 BC	Twenty-sixth Dynasty	Nubian
Later Dynastic Period		
c. 525–*c.* 405 BC	Twenty-seventh Dynasty	Persian Kings
c. 405–*c.* 399 BC	Twenty-eighth Dynasty	Saite
c. 399–*c.* 380 BC	Twenty-ninth Dynasty	Mendesian
c. 380–*c.* 343 BC	Thirtieth Dynasty	Sebennytic
c. 343–332 BC	Thirty-first Dynasty	Persian Kings
Conquest of Egypt by Alexander the Great		
332–323 BC	Alexander the Great	
Ptolemaic Period		
323–30 BC	Ptolemaic Dynasty	Ptolemies
Conquest of Egypt by Octavian (Augustus) in 30 BC		

Israeli Prime Ministers from 1948

Term	Name	Party
1948–53	David Ben-Gurion	Mapai
1953–55	M Sharett	Mapai
1955–63	David Ben-Gurion	Mapai
1963–69	Levi Eshkol	Mapai/ Labour
1969–74	Golda Meir	Labour
1974–77	Yitzhak Rabin	Labour
1977–83	Menachem Begin	Likud
1983–84	Yitzhak Shamir	Likud
1984–86	Shimon Peres	Labour
1986–92	Yitzhak Shamir	Likud
1992–95	Yitzhak Rabin	Labour
1995–96	Shimon Peres	Labour
1996–99	Binjamin Netanyahu	Likud
1999–	Ehud Barak	Labour

Ottoman Emperors 1280–1922

Reign	Name
1280–*c.* 1326	Osman I
1324–62	Orhan
1362–89	Murad I
1389–1402	Bayezid(I) the Thunderbolt
1402–03	Isa
1402–11	Suleiman
1409–13	Mesa
1413–21	Mehmed I
1421–44	Murad II
1444–46	Mehmed (II) the Conqueror
1446–51	Murad II
1451–81	Mehmed (II) the Conqueror
1481–1512	Bayezid II
1512–20	Selim (I) the Grim
1520–66	Suleiman (I) the Magnificent
1566–74	Selim (II) the Sot
1574–95	Murad III
1595–1603	Mehmed III
1603–17	Ahmed I
1617–18	Mustafa I
1618–22	Osman II
1622–23	Mustafa I
1623–40	Murad IV
1640–48	Ibrahim
1648–87	Mehmed IV
1687–91	Suleiman II
1691–95	Ahmed II
1695–1703	Mustafa II
1703–30	Ahmed III
1730–54	Mahmud I
1754–57	Osman III
1757–74	Mustafa III
1774–89	Abdulhamid I
1789–1807	Selim III
1807–08	Mustafa IV
1808–39	Mahmud II
1839–61	Abdulmecid I
1861–76	Abdulaziz
1876	Murad V
1876–1909	Abdulhamid II
1909–18	Mehmed V
1918–22	Mehmed VI

African Rulers and Political Leaders

Kenyan Presidents from 1963

Term	Name	Party
1963–78	Jomo Kenyatta	Kenya African National Union (KANU)
1978–	Daniel arap Moi	KANU

South African Prime Ministers and Presidents from 1910

Term	Name
Prime Ministers	
1910–19	L Botha
1919–24	Jan Smuts
1924–39	James Hertzog
1939–48	Jan Smuts
1948–54	Daniel Malan
1954–58	J Strijdon
1958–66	Hendrik Verwoerd
1966–78	Balthazar Johannes Vorster
1978–84	Pieter Botha
Presidents[1]	
1984–89	Pieter Botha
1989–94	F W de Klerk
1994–99	Nelson Mandela
1999–	Thabo Mbeki

[1] The post of prime minister was abolished in 1984 and combined with that of president.

Nigerian Leaders from 1960

Term	Name	Party
Governor-Generals		
1960	James Robertson	independent
1960–63	Nnamdi Azikiwe	Nigerian National Democratic Party
Presidents[1]		
1963–66	Nnamdi Azikiwe	Nigerian National Democratic Party
1966	Johnson Aguiyi-Ironsi	military
1966–75	Colonel Yakubu Gowon	military
1975–76	Murtala Mohammed	military
1976–79	General Olusegun Obasanjo	military
1979–83	Shehu Shagari	National Party of Nigeria
1983–85	Major General Mohammed Buhari	military
1985–93	Major General Ibrahim Babangida	military
1993	Ernest Shonekan	independent
1993–98	General Sani Abacha	military
1998–99	General Abdusalam Abubakar	military
1999–	Olusegun Obasanjo	People's Democratic Party

[1] Heads of state from January 1966 until October 1979 and from December 1983 did not officially use the title of president.

Asian Rulers and Political Leaders

Chinese Dynasties

Period	Dynasty	Major events
c. 2205–*c.* 1776 BC	Hsia[1]	agriculture; use of bronze; first writing
c. 1776–*c.* 1027 BC	Shang or Yin	first major dynasty; first Chinese calendar
c. 1027–*c.* 256 BC	Zhou	developed society using money, iron, and written laws; age of Confucius
221–206 BC	Qin	unification after period of Warring States; building of Great Wall begun; roads built
206 BC–AD 220	Han	first centralized and effectively administered empire; introduction of Buddhism
220–265	Wei, Shu, Wu (Three Kingdoms)	division into three parts; prolonged fighting (Three Kingdoms) and eventual victory of Wei over Shu and Wu; Confucianism superseded by Buddhism and Taoism
265–317	Tsin	beginning of Hun invasions in the north
581–618	Sui	reunification; barbarian invasions stopped; Great Wall refortified
618–907	T'ang	centralized government; empire greatly extended; period of excellence in sculpture, painting, and poetry
907–960	Wu Tai (Five Dynasties)	economic depression and loss of territory in northern China, central Asia, and Korea; first use of paper money
960–1279	Song	period of calm and creativity; printing developed (movable type); central government restored; northern and western frontiers neglected and Mongol incursions begun
1279–1368	Yüan	beginning of Mongol rule in China, under Kublai Khan; Marco Polo visited China; dynasty brought to an end by widespread revolts, centred in Mongolia
1368–1644	Ming	Mongols driven out by native Chinese, Mongolia captured by 2nd Ming emperor; period of architectural development; Beijing flourished as new capital
1644–1912	Qing (Manchu)	China once again under non-Chinese rule, the Qing conquered by nomads from Manchuria; trade with the West; culture flourished, but conservatism eventually led to the dynasty's overthrow by nationalistic revolutionaries led by Sun Yatsen

[1] This dynasty is also known as Xia. It was a legendary and historically doubtful dynasty.

Chinese Prime Ministers and Communist Party Leaders

Term	Name
Prime Ministers	
1949–76	Zhou Enlai
1976–80	Hua Guofeng
1980–87	Zhao Ziyang
1987–98	Li Peng
1998–	Zhu Rongji
Communist Party Leaders	
1935–76	Mao Zedong
1976–81	Hua Guofeng
1981–87	Hu Yaobang
1987–89	Zhao Ziyang
1989–	Jiang Zemin

Indian Prime Ministers

Term	Name	Party
1947–64	Jawaharlal Nehru	Congress
1964–66	Lal Bahadur Shastri	Congress
1966–77	Indira Gandhi	Congress (I)
1977–79	Morarji Desai	Janata
1979–80	Charan Singh	Janata/Lok Dal
1980–84	Indira Gandhi	Congress (I)
1984–89	Rajiv Gandhi	Congress (I)
1989–90	Viswanath Pratap Singh	Janata Dal
1990–91	Chandra Shekhar	Janata Dal (Socialist)
1991–96	P V Narasimha Rao	Congress (I)
1996	Atal Behari Vaj Payee	Bharatiya Janata Party
1996–97	H D Deve Gowda	Janata Dal
1997–98	Inder Kumar Gujral	Janata Dal
1998–	Atal Bihari Vaijpayee	Bharatiya Janata Party

Indian Dynasties and Rulers

Only major dynasties and the most important rulers are included. The dates given for dynasties and rulers cover periods of their importance.

Reign	Name
Saisunaga Dynasty (Magadhan ascendancy, northern India) 7th–4th centuries BC	
c. 543–c. 491 BC	Bimbisara (Srenika)
c. 491–c. 461 BC	Ajashatru (Kunika)
Nandas[1] 4th century BC	
c. 362–c. 334 BC	Mahapadma and eight sons
Mauryan Empire (India, except the area south of Karnataka) 4th–2nd centuries BC	
c. 321–c. 298 BC	Chandragupta Maurya
c. 298–c. 272 BC	Bindusara Amitraghata
c. 272–c. 232 BC	Asoka (-vardhana)
c. 232–c. 185 BC	later Mauryas
Shungas (Ganges Valley and part of central India) 2nd–1st centuries BC	
c. 185–c. 173 BC	Pushyamitra (Pushpamitra)
Indo-Greeks (northwest India) 2nd–1st centuries BC	
c. 180–c. 165 BC	Demetrius II
c. 155–c. 130 BC	Menander (Milinda)
Kanvas (northern India) c. 73–28 BC	
Satavahanas (north Deccan) 1st century BC–3rd century AD	
c. AD 120	Gautamiputra Satakarni
c. 130	Vashishthiputra Satakarni
c. 170–c. 200	Yajna Sri
Shakas (western India) 1st century BC–3rd century AD	
Kushanas (northern India and Central Asia) 1st century BC–3rd century AD	
c. 48–c. 78	Kadphises I
c. 78–c. 100	Kadphises II
c. 120–c. 162	Kanishka
c. 162–c. 182	Huvishka
c. 182–c. 220	Vasudeva
Guptas (northern India) 4th–6th centuries	
320–30	Chandragupta I
330–75	Samadragupta
375–415	Chandragupta II Vikramaditya
415–54	Kumaragupta I
454–67	Skandagupta
467–99	Buddhagupta
Hunas (northwest India and Central Asia) 5th–6th centuries	
Maukharis 6th–7th centuries	
Later Guptas of Magadha 6th–7th centuries	
Harsha 7th century	
606–47	Harshavardana
Pallavas (Tamil Nadu) c. 300–888	
630–68	Narasimhavaraman
730–96	Nandivarman II
Chalukyas of Vatapi (west and central Deccan) c. 556–757	
610–43	Pukaleshin II
Pandyas of Madurai (Tamil Nadu) 7th–10th centuries	
768–815	Varuguna I
815–62	Shrimara Shrivallabha
862–67	Varuguna II
Eastern Chalukyas of Vengi (Andhra Pradesh) c. 630–970	
Palas (Bengal and Bihar) c. 750–1100	
c. 750	Gopala
770–813	Dharmapala
813–55	Devapala
1005–55	Mahipala
Rashtrakutras (west and central Deccan) c. 753–973	
780–93	Dhruva
793–833	Govinda III
814–78	Amoghavarsha
878–914	Krishna II
914–72	Indra II
972–86	Krishna III
Pratiharas (west India and upper Ganges Valley) c. 773–1019	
773–93	Vatsaraja
793–833	Nagabhata
836–85	Bhoja
c. 908–42	Mahipala
Cholas of Thanjavur (Tamil Nadu) c. 850–1278	
984–1014	Rajaraja I
1014–44	Rajendra
1070–1118	Kulottunga I
Chandellas (Bundelkhand) c. 900–1203	
Kalachuris of Tripuri (Madhya Pradesh) c. 950–1195	
Chahamanis (east Rajasthan) c. 973–1192	
Chalukyas of Kalyani (west and central Deccan) 973–1189	
992–1008	Satyashraya
1043–68	Someshvara I
1076–1126	Vikramaditya VI
1181–89	Someshvara IV
Chaulukyas (Gujarat) c. 974–1238	
Gahadavalas (Qanauj) c. 974–1060	
Hoysalas of Dvarasamudra (central and south Deccan) c. 1110–1327	
Senas (Bengal) c. 1118–1199	
1158–69	Vallala Sena
Yadavas of Devagiri (north Deccan) c. 1190–1294	
Kakatiyas of Warangal (Andhra Pradesh) c. 1197–1323	
Sultans of Delhi 1206–1526	
1206–90	Slave Kings
1290–1320	Khaljis
1320–1413	Tughluqids
1414–51	Sayyids
1451–1526	Lodis
Sultans of Bengal 1336–1576	
1345–1414	line of Ilyas Shah
1414–36	line of Raja Ganesha
1437–87	line of Ilyas Shah (restored)
1487–94	line of Habashis
1494–1532	line of Sayyid Husain Shah

(continued)

Indian Dynasties and Rulers (*continued*)

Reign	Name
Sultans of Kashmir 1346–1589	
1346–1526	line of Shah Mirza Swati
Sultans of Gujarat 1391–1583	
1391–1411	Zafar Khan Muzaffar I
1411–42	Ahmad I
1458–1511	Mahmud I Begra
1511–26	Muzaffar II
Sharqi Sultans of Jaunpur 1394–1479	
Sultans of Malva 1401–1531	
Bahmanid Sultans of the Deccan and their successors 1347–1527	
Imadshahis of Berar 1484–1572	
Nizamshahis of Ahmadnagar 1490–1595	
Baridishahis of Bidar 1492–c. 1609	
Adilshahis of Bijapur 1489–1686	
Qutbshahis of Golconda 1512–1687	
Faruqi Sultans of Khandesh 1370–1601	
Pandyas of Madurai (Tamil Nadu) 1216–1327	
Rulers of Vijayanagar Empire 1336–1646	
1336–54	Harihara I
1354–77	Bukka I
1377–*c.* 1404	Harihara II
c. 1404–06	Bukka I
1406–22	Devaraya I
1422–25	Vira Vijaya
1425–47	Devaraya II
1447–65	Mallikarjuna
1465–85	Virupaksa
1485–86	Praudhadevaraya
c. 1486–92	Saluva Narasimha
c. 1492–1503	Immadi Narasimha
1503–09	Vira Narasimha
1509–30	Krishnadevaraya
c. 1530–42	Achyuta
1542–*c.* 70	Sadashiva
c. 1570–73	Tirumala
c. 1573–85	Rauga I
1585	Venkata I
1642–46	Ranga II
Chatrapati Bhonsles 1674–1707	
1674–80	Shivaji I
1680–89	Sambhaji
1689–1700	Rajaram
1700–07	Tara Bai
Mogul Emperors 1526–1858	
Great Moguls 1526–1707	
1526–30	Babur (Zahiruddin Muhammad)
1530–56	Humayun (Nasiruddin Muhammad)[2]
1556–1605	Akbar (Jalaluddin Muhammad)
1605–27	Jahangir (Nuruddin)
1627–28	Dewar Baksh
1628–58	Shah Jahan (Shihabuddin; dethroned)
1658–1707	Aurangzeb (Muhiyuddin)
Lesser Moguls 1707–1858	
1707–07	Azam Shah
1707–12	Shah Alam I (Muhammad Mu'azzam)
1712–12	Azim-ush Shan
1712–13	Jahandar Shah (Muhammad Muizzuddin)
1713–19	Farrukh Siyar (Jalaluddin Muhammad)
1719	Rafi ud-Darayat (Shamsuddin)
1719	Rafi ud-Daula Shah Jahan II
1719	Nikusiyar
1719–48	Muhammad Shah (Nasiruddin)
1748–54	Ahmad Shah Bahadur (Abu al-Nasir Muhammad)
1754–60	Alamgir II (Muhammad Azizuddin)
1760	Shah Jahan III
1760–1806	Shah Alam II (Jalaluddin Ali Jauhar; deposed briefly in 1788)
1806–37	Akbar Shah II (Muhiyuddin)
1837–58	Bahadur Shah II (Abul al-Zafar Muhammad Sirajuddin; banished)

[1] Low-caste Hindus, hostile to Brahmans and Kashatniyas; they were destroyed by Chandragupta Maurya.
[2] Humayun was defeated in 1540 and expelled from India until 1555, leaving northern India under the control of Sher Shah Suri (died 1545), Islam Shah, and Sikander Shah.

Japanese Emperors

Japanese chronology does not always match the emperor's reign dates. Rather, it is marked by occurrences, such as significant political events, military gains, and natural disasters.
(Date in parentheses = date of enthronement, when later than date of accession.)

Reign dates[1]		Name
Probable	Traditional	
Legendary and Yamato Period 40 BC–592 AD		
40–10 BC	660–585 BC	Jimmu
10 BC–AD 20	581–49 BC	Suizei
20–50	549–11 BC	Annei
50–80	510–477 BC	Itoku
80–110	475–393 BC	Kōshō
110–40	392–291 BC	Kōan
140–70	290–15 BC	Kōrei
170–200	214–158 BC	Kōgen
200–30	157–98 BC	Kaika
230–58	97–30 BC	Sujin
259–90	29 BC–70 AD	Suinin
291–323	71–130	Keikō
323–56	131–90	Seimu
356–62	192–200	Chūai
363–80	201–269	Jingū Kōgō (regent)
380–95	270–310	Ōjin
395–428	313–99	Nintoku
428–33	400–05	Richū
433–38	406–10	Hanzei
438–55	412–53	Ingyō
455–57	454–56	Ankō
457–90	457–79	Yūryaku
490–95	480–84	Seinei
495–98	485–87	Kenzō
498–504	488–98	Ninken
504–10	499–506	Buretsu
510–34	507–31	Keitai
534–36	531–35	Ankan
536–39	535–39	Senka
539–71		Kimmei
572–85		Bidatsu
585–87		Yomei
587–92		Sushun
Asuka Period 592–710		
593–628		Suiko (empress)
629–41		Jomei
642–45		Kōgyoku (empress)
645–54		Kōtoku
655–61		Saimei (empress)

(continued)

Japanese Emperors (*continued*)

Reign dates[1] Probable	Traditional	Name
661–72	(668)	Tenji
672		Kōbun
672–86	(673)	Temmu
686–97	(690)	Jitō (empress)
697–707		Mommu
Nara Period 710–794		
707–15		Gemmei (empress)
715–24		Genshō (empress)
724–49		Shōmu
749–58		Kōken (empress)
758–64		Junnin
764–70		Shōtoku (empress)
770–81		Kōnin
Heian Period 794–1192		
781–806		Kammu
806–09		Heizei
809–23		Saga
823–33		Junna
833–50		Nimmyō
850–58		Montoku
858–76		Seiwa
876–84		Yōzei
884–87		Kōkō
887–97		Uda
897–930		Daigo
930–46		Suzaku
946–67		Murakami
967–69		Reizei
969–84		En'yū
984–86		Kazan
986–1011		Ichijō
1011–16		Sanjō
1016–36		Go-Ichijō
1036–45		Go-Suzaku
1045–68		Go-Reizei
1068–73		Go-Sanjō
1073–87		Shirakawa (1086–1129 cloistered rule)
1087–1107		Horikawa
1107–23	(1108)	Toba (1129–56 cloistered rule)
1123–42		Sutoku
1142–55		Konoe
1155–58		Go-Shirakawa (1158–92 cloistered rule)
1158–65	(1159)	Nijō
1165–68		Rokujō
1168–80		Takakura
1180–85		Antoku
Kamakura Period 1192–1333		
1183–98	(1184)	Go-Toba
1198–1210		Tsuchimikado
1210–21	(1211	Juntoku
1221		Chūkyō
1221–32	(1222)	Go-Horikawa
1232–42	(1233)	Shijō
1242–46		Go-Saga
1246–60		Go-Fukakusa
1260–74		Kameyama
1274–87		Go-Uda
1287–98		Fushimi
1298–1301		Go-Fushimi
1301–08		Go-Nijo
1308–18		Hanazono
Namboku Period 1334–92[2]		
The Southern Court		
1318–39		Go-Daigo
1339–68		Go-Murakami
1368–83		Chōkei
1383–92		Go-Kameyama
The Northern Court		
1331–33	(1332)	Kōgon
1336–48	(1338)	Kōmyō
1348–51	(1350)	Sukō
1351–71	(1354)	Go-Kōgon
1371–82	(1375)	Go-En'yū
Muromachi Period 1392–1573[3]		
1382–1412	(1392)	Go-Komatsu
1412–28	(1415)	Shōkō
1428–64	(1430)	Go-Hanazono
1464–1500	(1466)	Go-Tsuchimikado
1500–26	(1521)	Go-Kashiwabara
1526–57	(1536)	Go-Nara
Momoyama Period 1573–1603		
1557–86	(1560)	Ōgimachi
Edo Period 1603–1867		
1586–1611	(1587)	Go-Yōzei
1611–29		Go-Mizunoo
1629–43	(1630)	Meishō (empress)
1643–54		Go-Kōmyō
1655–63	(1656)	Gosai
1663–87		Reigen
1687–1709		Higashiyama
1709–35	(1710)	Nakamikado
1735–47		Sakuramachi
1747–62		Momozono
1762–71	(1763)	Go-Sakuramachi (empress)
1771–79		Go-Momozono
1780–1817		Kōkaku
1817–46		Ninkō
1846–67	(1847)	Kōmei
Meiji Period 1868–1912		
1867–1912	(1868)	Meiji (Mutsuhito)
Taisho Period 1912–26		
1912–26	(1915)	Taisho (Yoshihito)
Showa Period 1926–89		
1926–89	(1928)	Showa (Hirohito)
1989–		Heisei Akihito

[1] Reign dates for the first 28 emperors are the subject of some doubt and speculation. The traditional view, upon which the National Calendar is based, places the accession of Jimmu at 660 BC. Modern research approximates the date to be much later at *c.* 40 BC. Both probable and traditional dates are given until 539.
[2] Although the Southern Court was set up in exile, it retained the imperial regalia and is considered to be the legitimate line.
[3] The Muromachi Period begins with the unification of the Southern and Northern Courts in 1392.

Japanese Prime Ministers from 1945

Term	Name	Party
1945–46	Kijurō Shidehara	coalition
1946–47	Shigeru Yoshida	Liberal
1947–48	Tetsu Katayama	coalition
1948	Hitoshi Ashida	Democratic
1948–54	Shigeru Yoshida	Liberal
1954–56	Ichirō Hatoyama	Liberal[1]
1956–57	Tanzan Ishibashi	LDP
1957–60	Nobusuke Kishi	LDP
1960–64	Hayato Ikeda	LDP
1964–72	Eisaku Satō	LDP
1972–74	Kakuei Tanaka	LDP
1974–76	Takeo Miki	LDP
1976–78	Takeo Fukuda	LDP
1978–80	Masayoshi Ohira	LDP
1980–82	Zenkō Suzuki	LDP
1982–87	Yasuhiro Nakasone	LDP
1987–89	Noboru Takeshita	LDP
1989	Sōsuke Uno	LDP
1989–91	Toshiki Kaifu	LDP
1991–93	Kiichi Miyazawa	LDP
1993–94	Morohiro Hosokawa	JNP-led coalition
1994	Tsutoma Hata	Shinseito-led coalition
1994–96	Tomiichi Murayama	SDPJ-led coalition
1996–98	Ryutaro Hashimoto	LDP
1998–	Keizo Obuchi	LDP

[1]The conservative parties merged in 1955 to form the Liberal Democratic Party (LDP, Jiyū-Minshūtō).

Australasian Rulers and Political Leaders

Australian Prime Ministers from 1901

Term	Name	Party
1901–03	Edmund Barton	Protectionist
1903–04	Alfred Deakin	Protectionist
1904	John Watson	Labor
1904–05	George Reid	Free Trade–Protectionist coalition
1905–08	Alfred Deakin	Protectionist
1908–09	Andrew Fisher	Labor
1909–10	Alfred Deakin	Fusion
1910–13	Andrew Fisher	Labor
1913–14	Joseph Cook	Liberal
1914–15	Andrew Fisher	Labor
1915–23	William Hughes	Labor (National Labor from 1917)
1923–29	Stanley Bruce	National–Country Coalition
1929–32	James Scullin	Labor
1932–39	Joseph Lyons	United Australia–Country coalition
1939	Earle Page	United Australia–Country coalition
1939–41	Robert Menzies	United Australia
1941	Arthur Fadden	Country–United Australia coalition
1941–45	John Curtin	Labor
1945	Francis Forde	Labor
1945–49	Joseph Chifley	Labor
1949–66	Robert Menzies	Liberal–Country coalition
1966–67	Harold Holt	Liberal–Country coalition
1967–68	John McEwen	Liberal–Country coalition
1968–71	John Gorton	Liberal–Country coalition
1971–72	William McMahon	Liberal–Country coalition
1972–75	Gough Whitlam	Labor
1975–83	Malcolm Fraser	Liberal–National coalition
1983–91	Robert Hawke	Labor
1991–96	Paul Keating	Labor
1996–	John Howard	Liberal–National coalition

New Zealand Prime Ministers from 1891

Term	Name	Party
1891–93	John Ballance	Liberal
1893–1906	Richard Seddon	Liberal
1906	William Hall-Jones	Liberal
1906–12	Joseph Ward	Liberal
1912	Thomas MacKenzie	Liberal
1912–25	William Massey	Reform
1925–28	Joseph Coates	Reform
1928–30	Joseph Ward	United
1930–35	George Forbes	United
1935–40	Michael Savage	Labour
1940–49	Peter Fraser	Labour
1949–57	Sidney Holland	National
1957	Keith Holyoake	National
1957–60	Walter Nash	Labour
1960–72	Keith Holyoake	National
1972	John Marshall	National
1972–74	Norman Kirk	Labour
1974–75	Wallace Rowling	Labour
1975–84	Robert Muldoon	National
1984–89	David Lange	Labour
1989–90	Geoffrey Palmer	Labour
1990–97	Jim Bolger	National
1997–	Jenny Shipley	National

Other Political Leaders

Other Political Leaders

See individual country listings for leaders not included here.

Alia Ramiz (1925–) Albanian communist politician who was head of state (1982–92)

Allende (Gossens) Salvador (1908–1973) president of Chile who was overthrown in 1973 by an army coup backed by the CIA

Amin (Dada) Idi (1925–) Ugandan president (1971–79) who exercised a reign of terror over his people

Annan Kofi (1938–) Ghanaian secretary-general of the United Nations from 1997

Antall József (1932–1993) Hungary's first post-communist prime minister (1990–93)

Aquino (Maria) Corazon ('Cory') (born Cojuangco) (1933–) president of the Philippines (1986–92) following ousting of Ferdinand Marcos

Arafat Yassir (born Muhammed Abed Ar'ouf Arafat) (1929–) chairman of Palestine Liberation Organization from 1969 and Palestine Authority from 1996

Aristide Jean-Bertrand (1953–) president of Haiti (December 1990–October 1991 and October 1994–December 1995)

Arzu Alvaro Irigoyen (1947–) president of Guatemala from 1996

Assad Hafez al (1930–) president of Syria from 1971

Atatürk Mustafa Kemal (adopted name of Mustafa Kemal Pasha) (1881–1938) first president of Turkey from 1923

Aung San (1916–1947) Burmese (Myanman) politician who helped lead Burma's fight for independence from the UK

Banda Hastings Kamuzu (1905–1997) president of Malawi (1966–94)

Bandaranaike Sirimavo (born Ratwatte) (1916–) Sri Lankan politician who was the world's first female prime minister (1960–65, 1970–77 and from 1994)

Banzer Suárez Hugo (1926–) president of Bolivia (1971–78 and from 1997)

Barrios de Chamorro Violeta (*c.* 1939–) president of Nicaragua (1990–96) whose election ended Sandinista rule

Batista Fulgencio (1901–1973) Cuban dictator who was overthrown by Fidel Castro in 1959

Ben Ali Zine el Abidine (1936–) president of Tunisia from 1987

Ben Bella Muhammed Ahmed (1916–) first prime minister of independent Algeria (1962–63) and president (1963–65)

Beneš Edvard (1884–1948) president of Czechoslovakia (1935–48)

Berisha Sali (1941–) president of Albania (1992–97)

Bhumibol Adulyadej (1927–) king of Thailand from 1946 who helped overthrow the military government in 1973

Bhutto Benazir (1953–) prime minister of Pakistan (1988–90 and 1993–96)

Bhutto Zulfikar Ali (1928–1979) prime minister of Pakistan overthrown in 1977 during an army coup led by General Zia ul-Haq

Birendra Bir Bikram Shah Dev (1945–) king of Nepal from 1972

Bismarck Otto Eduard Leopold von (1815–1898) chancellor of the German Empire (1871–90)

Biya Paul (1933–) president of Cameroon from 1982

Bokassa Jean-Bedel (1921–96) self-proclaimed emperor of the Central African Republic (1977–79)

Bolkiah Hassanal (1946–) Sultan of Brunei from 1967

Bondevik Kjell Magne (1947–) prime minister of Norway from 1997

Bourguiba Habib ben Ali (1903–) first president of Tunisia (1957–87)

Boutros-Ghali Boutros (1922–) Egyptian diplomat who was United Nations secretary general (1992–96)

Burnham (Linden) Forbes Sampson (1923–1985) prime minister of Guyana (1964–80)

Buthelezi Mangosuthu Gatsha, Chief (1928–) South African Zulu leader and politician

Castro Fidel (1927–) prime minister of Cuba (1959–76) and president from 1976

Cavaco Silva Anibal (1939–) prime minister of Portugal (1985–95) who led Portugal into the European Community in 1985

Ceauşescu Nicolae (1918–1989) president of Romania (1967–89) who was overthrown in a bloody coup in December 1989

Charles (Mary) Eugenia (1919–) prime minister of Dominica (1980–95) who was the first female minister in the Caribbean

Chernomyrdin Viktor (1938–) prime minister of Russia (1992–98)

Chiluba Frederick (1943–) president of Zambia from 1991

Chissano Joaquim (1939–) Mozambique nationalist, president from 1986, who won the first free presidential elections in 1994

Clerides Glafkos John (1919–) president of Cyprus from 1993

Constantinescu Emil (1939–) president of Romania from 1996

Cosgrave William Thomas (1880–1965) Irish head of state (1922–32)

Craig James, 1st Viscount Craigavon (1871–1940) first prime minister of Northern Ireland (1921–40)

Craxi Bettino (Benedetto) (1934–) prime minister of Italy (1983–87)

Delors Jacques Lucien Jean (1925–) French politician and president of the European Commission (1985–94)

Deng Xiaoping or **Teng Hsiao-ping** (1904–1997) Chinese political leader who introduced an economic modernization programme in the 1970s

Denktaş Rauf R (1924–) Turkish-Cypriot politician and president of Northern Cyprus from 1983

Diem Ngo Dinh (1901–1963) prime minister of South Vietnam (1954–55) and president (1955–63)

Dini Lamberto (1932–) prime minister of Italy (1995–96)

Diouf Abdou (1935–) president of Senegal from 1980

Dos Santos Jose Eduardo (1942–) president of Angola from 1979 who negotiated the withdrawal of South African and Cuban forces from Angola

Duan Le (1908–1986) North Vietnamese leader who succeeded Ho Chi Minh

Duarte José Napoleon (1925–1990) president of El Salvador (1980–82 and 1984–88)

Dubček Alexander (1921–1992) Czechoslovak leader whose liberalization policies led to the Soviet invasion of Czechoslovakia in 1968

Duvalier François (1907–1971) president of Haiti (1957–71)

Fahd (Ibn Abdul Aziz) (1923–) king of Saudi Arabia from 1982

Faisal Ibn Abd al-Aziz (1905–1975) king of Saudi Arabia from 1964 who undertook modernization of his country

Flores Facussé Carlos (1950–) president of Honduras from 1998

Franz Ferdinand or **Francis Ferdinand** (1863–1914) Archduke of Austria whose assassination precipitated World War I

Franz Josef or **Francis Joseph** (1830–1916) emperor of Austria–Hungary from 1848 whose attack on Serbia hastened World War I

(continued)

Other Political Leaders (*continued*)

Fujimori Alberto (1938–) president of Peru from 1990

Fulbright J William (1905–1995) US senator (1945–75) who opposed US involvement in the Vietnam war

Gaviria (Trujillo) Cesar (1947–) president of Colombia (1990–94)

Geingob Hage Gottfried (1941–) first prime minister of an independent Namibia from 1990

Gingrich Newt(on) Leroy (1943–) US politician and speaker of the US House of Representatives (1995–98)

Goebbels (Paul) Josef (1897–1945) German Nazi minister of propaganda from 1933

Goh Chok Tong (1941–) prime minister of Singapore from 1990

Gore Al(bert) (1948–) US vice president from 1993

Gramsci Antonio (1891–1937) Italian Marxist who helped to found the Italian Communist Party in 1921

Haig Alexander M (1924–) US general and politician, NATO commander (1974–79), secretary of state (1981–82)

Haile Selassie Ras Tafari Makonnen (1892–1975) emperor of Ethiopia (1930–74)

Hamilton Alexander (1757–1804) US politician who influenced the adoption of a US constitution with a strong central government

Hammarskjöld Dag (Hjalmar Agne Carl) (1905–1961) Swedish secretary general of the United Nations (1953–61)

Hasina Wazed Sheik (1947–) prime minister of Bangladesh from 1996

Hassan II (1929–1999) king of Morocco from 1961

Havel Václav (1936–) president of Czechoslovakia (1989–92) and president of Czech Republic from 1993

Hekmatyar Gulbuddin (1949–) prime minister of Afghanistan (1993–94 and 1996)

Hess (Walter Richard) Rudolf (1894–1987) German deputy Führer to Adolf Hitler (1933–39)

Hindenburg Paul Ludwig Hans Anton von Beneckendorf und (1847–1934) president of Germany (1925–33)

Hitler Adolf (1889–1945) Austrian-born German dictator (1933–45)

Ho Chi Minh (adopted name of Nguyen Tat Thanh) (1890–1969) North Vietnamese communist politician, premier, and president (1954–69)

Horn Gyula (1932–) prime minister of Hungary (1994–98)

Hoxha Enver (1908–1985) prime minister of Albania (1944–54) who was the founder of the Albanian Communist Party in 1941

Hull Cordell (1871–1955) US secretary of state (1933–44) who helped to lay the foundation for the United Nations

Hun Sen (1950–) prime minister of Cambodia (1985–93) and single effective leader from July 1997

Hussein Saddam (1937–) leader of Iraq from 1968

Hussein ibn Talal (1935–1999) king of Jordan from 1952

Ibn Saud Abdul Aziz (*c.* 1880–1953) first king of Saudi Arabia from 1932

Iliescu Ion (1930–) president of Romania (1990–96)

Itagaki Taisuke (1837–1919) Japanese political leader who founded Japan's first political party

Itō Hirobumi Prince (1841–1909) Japanese politician who helped draft the Meiji constitution of 1889

Izetbegović Alija (1925–) president of Bosnia-Herzegovina from 1990

Jagan Janet (1920–) president of Guyana from 1997

Jayawardene Junius Richard (1906–96) first president of Sri Lanka (1978–88)

Jiang Jie Shi or **Chiang Kai-shek** (1887–1975) president of China (1928–31 and 1943–49) and president of Taiwan from 1949

Jiang Qing or **Chiang Ching** (1914–1991) Chinese minister for culture who played a key role in the 1966–76 Cultural Revolution

Jinnah Muhammad Ali (1876–1948) first governor general of Pakistan from 1947

Kabbah Ahmad Tejan (1932–) president of Sierra Leone from 1997

Kabila Laurent-Desiré (1939–) president of the Democratic Republic of Congo from 1997

Karadzic Radovan (1945–) leader of the unofficial government of the Bosnian Serbs (1992–96)

Karamanlis Konstantinos (1907–1998) Greek prime minister (1955–58, 1961–63) and president (1980–85)

Kaunda Kenneth David (1924–) first president of independent Zambia (1964–91)

Kelly Petra (1947–1992) German politician who founded the German Green Party in 1972

Kerekou Mathieu Ahmed (1933–) president of Benin (1972–91 and from 1996)

Khaddhafi or **Gaddafi** or **Qaddafi** Moamer al (1942–) Libyan leader since 1969

Khama Seretse (1921–1980) first president of Botswana (1966–80)

Khatami Seyyed Muhammad (1943–) president of Iran from 1997

Khomeini Ayatollah Ruhollah (1900–1989) Iranian Shi'ite leader who established a fundamentalist Islamic republic

Kim Dae Jung (1924–) president of South Korea from 1998

Kim Il Sung (1912–1994) prime minister of North Korea (1948–72) and president (1972–94)

Kim Jong Il (1942–) North Korean national leader from 1994

Kim Young Sam (1927–) president of South Korea (1993–97)

Kissinger Henry Alfred (1923–) German-born US diplomat who negotiated US withdrawal from Vietnam in 1973

Klaus Vaclav (1941–) prime minister of the Czech Republic (1993–97)

Konare Alpha Omar (1946–) president of Mali from 1992

Kravchuk Leonid (1934–) president of the Ukraine (1990–94)

Kruger (Stephanus Johannes) Paul(us) (1825–1904) president of the Transvaal (1883–1900) whose policies precipitated the Boer War

Kuchma Leonid (1938–) president of the Ukraine from 1994

Kwaśniewski Aleksander (1954–) president of Poland since 1995

Kyprianou Spyros (1932–) Cypriot president (1977–88)

Landsbergis Vytautas (1932–) president of Lithuania (1990–93) who drafted the Republic's declaration of independence from the USSR

Lee Kuan Yew (1923–) first prime minister of Singapore (1959–90)

Lee Teng Hui (1923–) president of Taiwan since 1988

Lodge Henry Cabot, II (1902–1985) US ambassador to South Vietnam (1963–64 and 1965–67)

McAleese Mary (1951–) president of Republic of Ireland from 1997

McCarthy Joe (Joseph Raymond) (1908–1957) US senator (1946–57) who conducted congressional search for suspected communist infiltration in the USA

McNamara Robert Strange (1916–) US secretary of defense (1961–68) who supported US military involvement in South Vietnam

Mahathir bin Mohamed (1925–) prime minister of Malaysia since 1981

Mandela Nelson Rolihlahla (1918–) president of South Africa (1994–1999)

Manley Michael Norman (1924–1997) prime minister of Jamaica (1972–80 and 1989–92)

Marcos Ferdinand Edralin (1917–1989) president of the Philippines (1965–86)

Marcos Imelda Romualdez (1930–) Filipino politician and wife of Ferdinand Marcos

(*continued*)

Other Political Leaders (*continued*)

Masaryk Tomaš Garrigue (1850–1937) first president of the Czechoslovak Republic (1918–35)

Masire Quett Ketumile Joni (1925–) president of Botswana (1980–98)

Mbeki Thabo (1942–) president of South Africa from 1999

Meciar Vladimir (1942–) prime minister of the Slovak Republic (January 1993–March 1994 and from October 1994)

Milošević Slobodan (1941–) president of Serbia (1986–97) and president of Yugoslavia from 1997

Mitsotakis Constantine (1918–) prime minister of Greece (1990–93)

Mkapa Benjamin William (1938–) president of Tanzania since 1995

Mobutu Sese Seko (1930–1997) president of Zaire (1965–97)

Molotov Vyacheslav Mikhailovich (assumed name of Vyacheslav Mikhailovich Skriabin) (1890–1986) Soviet foreign minister (1939–49 and 1953–56)

Mubarak Hosni (1928–) president of Egypt from 1981

Mugabe Robert Gabriel (1925–) prime minister of Zimbabwe from 1980 and president from 1987

Muluzi Bakili (1943–) president of Malawi since 1994

Museveni Yoweri Kaguta (1945–) president of Uganda from 1986

Mussolini Benito Amilcare Andrea (1883–1945) Italian dictator (1925–43)

Muzorewa Abel Tendekayi (1925–) prime minister of Rhodesia/Zimbabwe (1979–80)

Mwinyi Ali Hassan (1925–) president of Tanzania (1985–95)

Nahayan Sheik Sultan bin Zayed al- (1918–) emir of Abu Dhabi from 1969

Nasser Gamal Abdel (1918–1971) president of Egypt (1956–70) who was an early leader of the non-aligned movement

Nazarbayev Nursultan (1940–) president of Kazakhstan from 1990

Nguyen Van Thieu (1923–) South Vietnamese president (1967–75)

Nkomo Joshua (1917–) vice president of Zimbabwe from 1988

Nkrumah Kwame (1909–1972) first president of Ghana (1960–66)

Noriega Manuel Antonio Morena (1940–) Panamanian military ruler (1983–89)

Nu U (Thakin) (1907–1995) prime minister of Burma (1947–62)

Nujoma Sam (1929–) first president of Namibia from 1990

Nyerere Julius Kambarage (1922–) first president of Tanzania (1964–85)

Obote (Apollo) Milton (1924–) president of Uganda (1966–71 and 1980–85)

Ortega Saavedra Daniel (1945–) Nicaraguan head of state (1984–90)

Pahlavi Muhammad Reza Shah (1918–1980) shah of Iran (1941–79)

Papandreou Andreas (1919–1996) prime minister of Greece (1981–89 and 1993–96)

Park Chung Hee (1917–1979) president of South Korea (1963–79)

Paz (Estenssoro) Victor (1907–) president of Bolivia (1952–56, 1960–64, and 1985–89) and founder of the Movimiento Nacionalista Revolucionario

Pérez de Cuéllar Javier (1920–) Peruvian diplomat who was secretary general of the United Nations (1982–91)

Persson Goran (1949–) prime minister of Sweden from 1996

Pindling Lynden Oscar (1930–) first black prime minister of the Bahamas (1967–92)

Pinochet (Ugarte) Augusto (1915–) military ruler of Chile (1973–89)

Pol Pot (also known as Saloth Sar) (*c.* 1928–1998) leader of Khmer Rouge government in Cambodia (1975–79)

Prasad Rajendra (1884–1963) India's first president after independence (1950–62)

Preval Rene (1943–) president of Haiti from 1996

Qaboos bin Said (1940–) sultan of Oman from 1970

Rabuka Sitiveni (1948–) prime minister of Fiji Islands (1992–99)

Rafsanjani Ali Akbar Hashemi (1934–) president of Iran (1989–97)

Rahman Tunku (Prince) Abdul (1903–1990) first prime minister of independent Malaya (1957–63) and of Malaysia (1963–70)

Ramos Fidel (Eddie) (1928–) president of the Philippines (1992–98)

Rawlings Jerry (1947–) president of Ghana from 1981

René France-Albert (1935–) first prime minister of independent Seychelles and president from 1977

Rhee Syngman (1875–1965) president of South Korea (1948–60)

Robinson Mary (1944–) president of Republic of Ireland (1990–97)

Roh Tae-woo (1932–) South Korean president (1988–93)

Rusk Dean (1909–1994) US secretary of state (1961–69) who favoured US military involvement in South Vietnam

Sabah Sheik Jabir al-Ahmad al-Jabir al- (1928–) emir of Kuwait from 1977

Sadat (Muhammad) Anwar (1918–1981) president of Egypt from 1970 who signed the Camp David Agreements

Santer Jacques (1937–) president of the European Commission 1995–99

Sassau-Nguesso Denis (1943–) president of the Republic of the Congo (1979–92 and from 1997)

Savimbi Jonas Malheiro (1934–) Angolan revolutionary and founder of UNITA (National Union for the Total Independence of Angola)

Senghor Leopold Sedar (1906–) first president of independent Senegal (1960–80)

Shevardnadze Edvard Amvrosievich (1928–) Soviet foreign minister (1985–91) and president of Georgia from 1992

Sihanouk Norodom (1922–) king of Cambodia (1941–55 and from 1993)

Simitis Costas (1936–) prime minister of Greece from 1996

Smith Ian (Douglas) (1919–) founder of the Rhodesian Front in 1962 and prime minister of Rhodesia (1964–79)

Soares Mario Alberto Nobre Lopes (1924–) president of Portugal (1986–96)

Somoza García Anastasio (1896–1956) president of Nicaragua (1937–47 and 1950–56)

Suharto (1921–) president of Indonesia (1967–98)

Sukarno Achmed (1901–1970) first president of Indonesia (1945–67)

Suu Kyi Aung San (1945–) Myanman (Burmese) opposition leader who won the Nobel Prize for Peace (1991)

Tito Marshal (adopted name of Josip Broz) (1892–1980) prime minister of Yugoslavia (1945–53) and president (1953–80)

Tudjman Franjo (1922–) president of Croatia from 1990

Vieira João Bernardo (1939–) president of Guinea-Bissau (1980–99)

Weizmann Chaim Azriel (1874–1952) first president of Israel (1948–52)

Weizsäcker Richard Baron von (1920–) president of Germany (1984–94)

Yilmaz A Mesut (1947–) prime minister of Turkey (1991, 1996, and from 1997)

Zahir Shah Muhammad (1914–) king of Afghanistan (1933–73)

Zeroual Lamine (1941–) president of Algeria from 1994

Zhelev Zhelyu (1935–) president of Bulgaria (1990–96)

SPORTS

The Year in Review

1 July 1998 In the USA, the Players Association of the National Basketball Association (NBA) imposes a lockout that forbids contact between teams and players in any dispute over pay.

3 July 1998 The British powerboat *Adventurer* lands in Gibraltar after voyaging around the world in 74 days, 20 hours, and 58 minutes, breaking the 38-year-old record by 8 days.

4–5 July 1998 US tennis player Pete Sampras wins the men's singles title at the All England Tennis Championship at Wimbledon, for the fifth time, tying the record for the most Wimbledon men's titles in the Open era with Swedish tennis player Bjorn Borg. Sampras defeats Goran Ivanisevic of Croatia 6–7, 7–6, 6–4, 3–6, 6–2 in the final. Czech tennis player Jana Novotna defeats Nathalie Tauziat of France 6–4, 7–6 to win the women's title.

7 July 1998 The American League defeats the National League 13–8 to win Major League Baseball's All-Star Game at Coors Field, Denver, Colorado, USA.

12 July 1998 France wins the football World Cup defeating Brazil 3–0. The following day 500,000 people fill the Champs Elysées to celebrate the victory.

12 July 1998 German racing car driver Michael Schumacher wins the British Grand Prix at Silverstone, England.

19 July 1998 US golfer Mark O'Meara wins the British Open golf tournament at the Royal Birkdale Golf Club in Southport, England. The English amateur Justin Rose finishes joint fourth, the best position by an amateur since Frank Stranahan in 1953.

21 July 1998 British financial journalist Brian Milton lands in Surrey, England, after circumnavigating the globe in a microlight in 120 days, beating the 175-day record set in 1924 for the round-the-world flight in an open-cockpit, single-engine aircraft.

2 August 1998 Italian cyclist Marco Pantani, riding for the Mercatone Uno team, wins the Tour de France cycling race, from Dublin, Ireland, to Paris, France. The tour, however, is tainted by allegations that several participants are taking performance-enhancing drugs.

6 August 1998 The International Swimming Federation bans Irish swimmer Michelle Smith de Bruin from competition for four years for allegedly manipulating her urine sample from a random drug test with alcohol. De Bruin won three gold medals at the 1996 Olympics in Atlanta, Georgia, USA.

9 August 1998 Arsenal beats Manchester United 3–0 in the Football Association Charity Shield at Wembley Stadium, London.

9 August 1998 Yugoslavia defeats Russia 64–62 to win the men's world basketball championships in Athens, Greece.

10 August 1998 The England cricket team beats South Africa by 23 runs at Leeds, in the final day of the fifth Test to win the series 2–1.

16 August 1998 Fijian golfer Vijay Singh wins the US PGA golf title, at the Sahalee Country Club in Seattle, Washington, USA.

16 August 1998 German racing driver Michael Schumacher, driving a Ferrari, wins the Hungarian Grand Prix Formula 1 motor race in Budapest, Hungary.

20 August 1998 British runner Darren Campbell wins the gold medal in the 100 metres at the European Championships in athletics at Budapest, Hungary, taking 0.04 seconds off Linford Christie's championship record.

21 August 1998 Trinidad and Tobago footballer Dwight Yorke leaves Aston Villa for Manchester United in a £12.6 million transfer deal, Manchester United's largest deal ever.

23 August 1998 Britain leaves the European Championships in Athletics at Budapest, Hungary, with nine gold medals, the highest number that year.

27 August 1998 Former Chelsea manager Ruud Gullit replaces Kenny Dalglish as manager of Newcastle United football team, in Newcastle, England, becoming the highest-paid manager in the Premier League, with a contract worth about £1 million per year.

30 August 1998 British footballer Michael Owen scores a hat-trick in the first half of the Premiership league match in which his team, Liverpool, beats Newcastle United 4–1 at St James's Park.

30 August 1998 English racing driver Damon Hill wins the Belgian Grand Prix, beating fellow Jordan driver Ralf Schumacher of Germany by 0.932 seconds.

31 August 1998 On the final day of a one-off Test between England and Sri Lanka at the Oval, London, Sri Lanka's Muttiah Muralitharan takes 9-65 in England's second innings to help Sri Lanka achieve its first Test victory in England.

5 September 1998 The England football team loses to Sweden 2–1 in a European Championship qualifier in Stockholm, Sweden.

7 September 1998 US baseball player Mark McGwire ('Big Mac') hits his 61st home run of the season, tying the all-time record, at Busch stadium in St Louis, Missouri, USA.

8 September 1998 The board of the Manchester United football club accepts a £625 million bid from media mogul Rupert Murdoch's BSkyB television company. The controversial deal, the most lucrative takeover of a football club in the world, is examined by the Office of Fair Trading for a possible breach of competition law.

11 September 1998 The Commonwealth Games open in Kuala Lumpur, Malaysia.

12–13 September 1998 Australian tennis player Patrick Rafter wins the men's singles title and US tennis player Lindsay Davenport wins the women's singles title in the US Open tennis tournament in Flushing Meadow, New York, USA.

13 September 1998 German racing driver Michael Schumacher wins the Italian Grand Prix at Monza.

20 September 1998 Brazilian runner Ronaldo de Costa breaks the world marathon record by 45 seconds, completing the Berlin Marathon in 2 hours 6 minutes 5 seconds.

25 September 1998 French swimmer Benoit Lecomte becomes the first person to swim across the Atlantic Ocean, after a 72-day journey from Hyannis, Massachusetts, USA, to the coast of Brittany, France.

27 September 1998 US baseball player Mark McGwire ('Big Mac') hits two home runs on the last day of the regular season, bringing his season total to 70 home runs, a world record.

10 October 1998 The England football team draws against Bulgaria 0–0 in a European Championship qualifier at Wembley Stadium, London.

14 October 1998 The England football team defeats Luxembourg 3–0 in a European Championship qualifier in Luxembourg.

17 October 1998 Nepali mountain guide Kaji Sherpa breaks the world record for climbing Mount Everest, with a time of 20 hours and 24 minutes.

21 October 1998 The New York Yankees defeat the San Diego Padres 3–0 in San Diego, California, USA, to clinch Major League baseball's 94th World Series by four games to nil.

31 October 1998 English boxer Naseem Hamed defeats Ireland's Wayne McCullough in Atlantic City, New Jersey, USA, to retain his World Boxing Organization world featherweight championship title.

1 November 1998 Finnish racing driver Mika Hakkinen, in a McLaren Mercedes, wins the Formula 1 world championship with his victory at the Japanese Grand Prix in Suzuka.

8 November 1998 British tennis player Greg Rusedski defeats Pete Sampras of the USA 6–4, 7–6, 6–3 to win the Paris Open in France.

14 November 1998 In a rugby union World Cup qualifier at Huddersfield, England, England beats the Netherlands with a record score of 112–0.

20 November 1998–24 November 1998 The first Ashes Test match, in Brisbane, Australia, is abandoned as a draw owing to poor light and rain. The weather saves England from probable defeat.

22 November 1998 England defeats Italy 23–15 at Huddersfield, England, in a rugby union World Cup qualifier.

22 November 1998 England, represented by golfers Nick Faldo and David Carter, wins its first World Cup of Golf championship, at the Gulf Harbour Country Club in Whangaparaoa, New Zealand.

25 November 1998 The Arsenal football team loses 1–0 to Lens at Wembley Stadium, London, and so does not reach the knock-out stages of the European Champions League.

28 November 1998 The England rugby team loses 12–11 to Australia at Twickenham, London, in front of a crowd of 75,000 people.

29 November 1998 Alex Corretja beats fellow Spaniard Carlos Moya in the ATP World Tennis Championship final, in Hanover, Germany. England's Tim Henman reaches the semi finals.

29 November 1998 John Higgins of Scotland beats Matthew Stevens of Wales 10–6 to win the UK snooker championship at the International Centre in Bournemouth, England.

30 November 1998 In the second Ashes Test, England loses to Australia by seven wickets at the Waca Cricket Ground, Perth, Australia.

5 December 1998 The England rugby team beats South Africa 13–7 at Twickenham, London, ending the Springboks' 17-win run.

6 December 1998 The Swedish tennis team defeats Italy 4–1 to win the Davis Cup in Milan, Italy.

15 December 1998 Football Association executive Graham Kelly resigns after allegations that he was involved in a payment of a £3.2 million loan to the Football Assiciation of Wales in return for the support of the Welsh Association in helping the FA chairman Keith Wiseman to a become a vice-president of FIFA.

15 December 1998 The England cricket team loses to Australia by 201 runs in the third Ashes Test at the Adelaide Oval, Australia.

January 1999 In the USA, the National Basketball Association (NBA) negotiates a settlement with players after six months of strikes. A series of 52 games is planned to begin in February.

13 January 1999 Chicago Bulls player Michael Jordan announces his retirement from basketball.

16 January 1999 US boxer Mike Tyson knocks out South African François Botha in the fifth round to win a heavyweight fight in Las Vegas, Nevada, USA. It is Tyson's first fight since his ban for biting off the ear of heavyweight champion Evander Holyfield.

19 January 1999 Finnish representative to the International Olympic Committee (IOC) Pirjo Haggman resigns after accusations that her former husband got jobs through the Olympic bidding committees of Salt Lake City, Utah, USA, and Toronto, Canada.

22 January 1999 Libyan representative to the International Olympic Committee (IOC) Bashir Mohamed Attarabulsi resigns after accusations that his son received scholarships to universities in Utah, USA, paid for by the Salt Lake City, Utah, bid committee for the 2002 winter games.

24 January 1999 The International Olympic Committee (IOC) Executive board announces that six members should be expelled in the continuing scandal over the Salt Lake City, Utah, bid for the 2002 winter games. It is alleged that the members, from Ecuador, Kenya, Sudan, Chile, Mali, and the Republic of the Congo, took gifts from Salt Lake City's Olympic bid committee. The IOC also announces major anticorruption reforms, including a change in the way cities bid to host the games.

31 January 1999 In their second consecutive Super Bowl victory, the Denver Broncos beats the Atlanta Falcons 34–19 to win the 33rd Super Bowl in Miami, Florida, USA, before a crowd of 74,803.

3 February 1999 The Football Association sacks England football coach Glenn Hoddle for Hoddle's alleged remarks in an interview with *The Times* that disabled people might be paying for sins committed in a previous life.

6 February 1999 US heavyweight boxer Mike Tyson begins a one-year prison sentence for a road-rage attack in August 1998.

17 February 1999 The Football Association appoints Kevin Keegan, head coach of Fulham Football Club, as manager of the England national team. He replaces Glenn Hoddle, who was sacked two weeks earlier for comments he made to the press about disabled people.

1 March 1999 A panel appointed by the US Olympic Committee releases a report that criticizes the International Olympic Committee for a history of 'improper gift-giving' and recommends radical reforms. The panel was appointed to investigate charges that members of the Salt Lake City, Utah, bid committee bribed members of the International Olympic Committee to vote for Salt Lake City as the site for the 2002 Winter Games.

7 March 1999 British motor racing driver Eddie Irvine wins the Australian Grand Prix, driving a Ferrari, in Melbourne, Australia.

13 March 1999 British heavyweight boxer Lennox Lewis fights his US rival Evander Holyfield for the undisputed heavyweight title of the world, at Madison Square Garden, New York, New York, in front of a crowd of 21,000. The match ends in a draw, causing an international outcry from many who believed that Lewis had clearly outboxed Holyfield.

17 March 1999 The International Olympic Committee, meeting in Lausanne, Switzerland, votes to expel six members who had allegedly accepted bribes to vote for Salt Lake City as the site of the 2002 Winter Olympic Games.

20 March 1999 Swiss balloonist Bertrand Piccard and British balloonist Brian Jones complete the first-ever nonstop round-the-world balloon trip. The *Breitling Orbiter 3* completes the circumnavigation in 19 days, 1 hour, 49 minutes.

28 March 1999 US tennis player Venus Williams defeats her younger sister Serena Williams to win the Lipton Championships in Key Biscayne, Florida. It is the first time since 1884 that sisters have played each other in the final of a major international tennis tournament.

3 April 1999 Cambridge wins the Oxford and Cambridge University Boat Race for the seventh consecutive year.

11 April 1999 Finnish motor racing driver Mika Hakkinen wins the Brazilian Grand Prix, driving a McLaren Mercedes, in Sao Paulo, Brazil.

11 April 1999 Spanish golfer José Maria Olazábal wins the 63rd US Masters golf tournament, in Augusta, Georgia, USA.

11 April 1999 Wales defeats England 32–31 in a Rugby Union Five Nations match at Wembley Stadium, London. This means that Scotland wins the 1999 Five Nations Championship.

18 April 1999 A record 31,582 runners start the 19th annual London Marathon, raising an estimated £15 million for charity. Abdelkader El Mouaziz of Morocco wins the men's race in 2 hours 7 minutes 57 seconds. Joyce Chepchumba wins the women's race in 2 hours 23 minutes 22 seconds.

May 1999 Officials at the British High Commissions in India, Pakistan, Bangladesh, and Sri Lanka test cricket fans applying for visas to travel to England for the World Cup on their knowledge of their country's cricket team as a prerequisite for entry into the UK. The policy, which is used for Asians but not South African, Australian, and New Zealand cricket fans, is criticized as being racist.

2 May 1999 German motor racing driver Michael Schumacher, driving a Ferrari, wins the San Marino Grand Prix in Imola, Italy.

3 May 1999 Scottish snooker player Stephen Hendry defeats Mark Williams of Wales 18–11 in the final to win the Embassy World Championships in snooker, at the Crucible Theatre in Sheffield, England, making him the first player to win the championship seven times.

14 May 1999 England defeats Sri Lanka by 8 wickets in the opening match of the cricket World Cup, at Lord's cricket ground, London.

15 May 1999 Wasps defeat Newcastle 29–19 in a rugby union match to win the Tetley's Bitter Cup at Twickenham, London.

16 May 1999 German motor racing driver Michael Schumacher, driving a Ferrari, wins the Monaco Grand Prix in Monte Carlo.

16 May 1999 Manchester United beats Tottenham Hotspur 2–1 at Old Trafford to clinch their fifth Premiership title in seven years.

17 May 1999 Manchester United captain Roy Keane is arrested in a Manchester bar less than 24 hours after his team wins football's Premiership title. Two women accused him of becoming violent and physically attacking them.

22 May 1999 Manchester United beats Newcastle United 2–0 to win the Football Association (FA) Cup at Wembley

Stadium, London, adding to their Premiership title.

22 May 1999 South Africa defeats England by 122 runs in a World Cup cricket match at The Oval cricket ground, London, England.

23 May 1999 The UK Sunday tabloid newspaper *News of the World* publishes an article in which an undercover reporter claims that England rugby union captain Lawrence Dallaglio told her that he took cocaine and ecstasy to celebrate a British Lions victory in 1997 and that he used to be a drug dealer.

24 May 1999 Lawrence Dallaglio resigns his position as England rugby union team captain after the Sunday tabloid newspaper *News of the World* publishes allegations of his using and dealing illegal drugs. He denies the allegations, however, claiming he was part of an elaborate set-up by the newspaper.

26 May 1999 Manchester United football club beats Bayern Munich 2–1, scoring both goals during three minutes of injury time, to win the European Cup final, at the Nou Camp stadium in Barcelona, Spain, becoming the first English side to win the treble.

29 May 1999 India defeats England by 63 runs in a World Cup cricket match at Edgbaston, knocking England out of the World Cup competition.

30 May 1999 Finnish motor racing driver Mika Hakkinen, driving a McLaren Mercedes, wins the Spanish Grand Prix in Barcelona, Spain.

30 May 1999 Manchester City defeats Gillingham on penalties 3–1 after a 2–2 draw to win the Football League second division play-off final at Wembley Stadium, London.

31 May 1999 Scottish golfer Colin Montgomerie wins the Volvo PGA Championship at Wentworth, Surrey.

31 May 1999 Watford defeats Bolton Wanderers 2–0 at Wembley Stadium, London, to win the Football League first division play-off final.

6 June 1999 German tennis player Steffi Graf defeats Martina Hingis of Switzerland 4–6, 7–5, 6–2 to win the French Open women's final in Paris.

6 June 1999 Northern Ireland golfer Darren Clarke wins the English Open golf championship.

6 June 1999 US tennis player Andre Agassi beats Andrei Medvedev of Ukraine 1–6, 2–6, 6–4, 6–3, 6–4 to win the French Open in Paris. He becomes one of only five men to have won all four grand slam titles.

9 June 1999 In football's European Championship qualifying games, England and Bulgaria draw 1–1 in Sofia; Denmark defeats Wales 2–0 in Liverpool; and the Czech Republic defeats Scotland 3–2 in Prague.

11 June 1999 Ian McGeechan, a former Northampton and British Lions rugby union coach, succeeds Jim Telfer as coach of the Scotland national team.

11 June 1999 Scottish football manager Alex Ferguson receives a knighthood for his success as the manager of Manchester United, which in 1999 won the FA Cup, the Premier League, and the European Cup.

11 June 1999 Scottish football player and manager Kenny Dalglish returns to Celtic as director of football, bringing John Barnes with him as head coach.

11 June 1999 Scottish former motor racing driver Jackie Stewart sells his Formula 1 racing team to car manufacturer Ford for £50 million.

13 June 1999 Finnish motor racing driver Mika Hakkinen, driving a McLaren Mercedes, wins the Canadian Grand Prix in Montreal.

16 June 1999 The British former Grand Prix world champion Damon Hill announces that he will retire from motor racing at the end of the season.

16 June 1999 US sprinter Maurice Greene sets a new world record for the 100 metres, at 9.79 seconds in Athens, Greece.

17 June 1999 Australia ties with South Africa in the World Cup cricket semi finals. Australia go through to the final.

19 June 1999 In rugby union matches, England defeats Queensland 39–14 in Brisbane, Australia; and Australia defeats Ireland 32–26 in Perth, Australia.

20 June 1999 Australia defeats Pakistan by 8 wickets to win the World Cup cricket final at Lord's, London, England.

22 June 1999 In one of the biggest upsets in the history of tennis at Wimbledon, Australian unknown Jelena Dokic, ranked 122 in the world, beats top seed Martina Hingis of Switzerland 6–2, 6–0.

22 June 1999 US golfer Payne Stewart wins the US Open golf tournament at Pinehurst, North Carolina, USA.

23 June 1999 Nasser Hussain becomes the England cricket captain, taking over from Alec Stewart.

26 June 1999 Australia defeats England 22–15 in a rugby union match in Sydney, Australia.

26 June 1999 In a rugby union match to mark the opening of the Millennium Stadium, Cardiff, Wales defeats world champions South Africa 29–19.

26 June 1999 The San Antonio Spurs defeat the New York Knicks 78–77 to win the National Basketball Association (NBA) finals 4–1.

27 June 1999 German racing driver, Heinz-Harald Frentzen, driving for the Jordan team, wins the French Grand Prix at Magny-Cours.

29 June 1999 Manchester United propose to withdraw from the Football Association (FA) Cup, angering many sponsors and supporters. The FA offered the club the chance to withdraw from the competition in return for participating in a new 8-team world club tournament in Brazil in January 2000.

30 June 1999 English tennis player Tim Henman defeats US tennis player Jim Courier 4–6, 7–5, 7–5, 6–7, 9–7 to reach the quarter finals at Wimbledon, London. At 4 hours, 30 minutes, it was the second-longest match in Wimbledon history.

4 July 1999 US tennis scores an Independence-day double when the Wimbledon men's singles and women's singles titles are both won by US players, Pete Sampras and Lindsay Davenport. Sampras's win over Andre Agassi (also US) in straight sets gives him the Wimbledon title for the sixth time in seven years. Shortly after Lindsay Davenport beats seven-times Wimbledon winner Steffi Graf (Germany) in straight sets, Graf announces her retirement from Wimbledon.

The Sporting Year

Calendar of Sporting Events October 1999–October 2000

(– = not applicable; tbd = to be decided.)

Date	Sport	Fixture	Location
1999			
October			
1 October–6 November	rugby union	World Cup	UK and France
3	horse racing	Prix de l'Arc de Triomphe	Longchamp, Paris
9	rugby league	Super League Championship grand final	Old Trafford, Manchester
14–17	golf	World Matchplay Championship	Wentworth, Surrey
16	baseball	start of World Series	–
November			
6	rugby union	World Cup final	Millennium Stadium, Cardiff
21–23	motor racing	Network Q RAC Rally	UK
25–29	cricket	South Africa versus England First Test	Johannesburg
30 November –5 December	squash	World Open	Cairo
December			
3–5	tennis	Davis Cup final	tbd
7	rugby union	Cambridge University versus Oxford University	Twickenham, London
9–13	cricket	South Africa versus England Second Test	Port Elizabeth
16–20	show jumping	Olympia International Show Jumping	Olympia, London
26–30	cricket	South Africa versus England Third Test	Durban
2000			
January			
2–6	cricket	South Africa versus England Fourth Test	Cape Town
5–14	football	FIFA World Club Championship	Brazil
8–16	darts	BDO World Professional Championshps	Frimley Green, Surrey
9	basketball	National Cup final	Sheffield Arena
14–18	cricket	South Africa versus England Fifth Test	Centurion
17–30	tennis	Australian Open	Melbourne
30	American football	Super Bowl XXXIV	Atlanta, Georgia
February			
5	rugby union	Wales versus France (Six Nations)	Millennium Stadium, Cardiff
5	rugby union	England versus Ireland (Six Nations)	Twickenham, London
5	rugby union	Italy versus Scotland (Six Nations)	Rome
19	rugby union	France versus England (Six Nations)	Stade de France, St-Denis
19	rugby union	Ireland versus Scotland (Six Nations)	Lansdowne Road, Dublin
19	rugby union	Wales versus Italy (Six Nations)	Millennium Stadium, Cardiff
27	football	Worthington Cup final	Wembley Stadium, London
March			
4	rugby union	England versus Wales (Six Nations)	Twickenham, London
4	rugby union	Scotland versus France (Six Nations)	Murrayfield, Edinburgh
4	rugby union	Ireland versus Italy (Six Nations)	Lansdowne Road, Dublin
8–12	badminton	Yonex All-England Championships	National Indoor Arena, Birmingham
14–16	horse racing	Cheltenham National Hunt Festival	Cheltenham
18	rugby union	Wales versus Scotland (Six Nations)	Millennium Stadium, Cardiff
18	basketball	Uniball Trophy final	National Indoor Arena, Birmingham
18	rugby union	Italy versus England (Six Nations)	Rome
18–19	athletics	IAAF World Cross-Country Championships	Vilamoura
19	football	Scottish League Cup final	Hampden Park, Glasgow
19	rugby union	France versus Ireland (Six Nations)	Stade de France, St-Denis
31 March–15 April	bowls	World Outdoor Championships	Johannesburg
April			
1	rugby union	Ireland versus Wales (Six Nations)Dublin	Lansdowne Road,
1	rugby union	France versus Italy (Six Nations)	Stade de France, St-Denis
1–2	ice hockey	Sekonda Superleague finals	tbd
2	rugby union	Scotland versus England (Six Nations)	Murrayfield, Edinburgh
3–9	golf	US Masters	Augusta National Club, Georgia
8	horse racing	Grand National	Aintree, Liverpool
15 April–1 May	snooker	Embassy World Championships	Crucible Theatre, Sheffield
16	athletics	London Marathon	London
16	football	Autowindscreens Cup final	Wembley Stadium, London
29	rugby league	Challenge Cup final	Murrayfield, Edinburgh
May			
4–7	three-day eventing	Badminton Horse Trials	Badminton House, Gloucestershire
6	basketball	Budweiser League, Championship play-off finals	Wembley Arena, London
6[1]	horse racing	2000 Guineas	Newmarket, Suffolk
7[1]	horse racing	1000 Guineas	Newmarket, Suffolk
7	hockey	EHA Cup finals (men's and women's)	Milton Keynes

(continued)

Calendar of Sporting Events October 1999–October 2000 (*continued*)

Date	Sport	Fixture	Location
13	rugby union	Tetley's Bitter Cup final	Twickenham, London
13[1]	rugby union	SWALEC Cup final	Millennium Stadium, Cardiff
14	football	FA Carling Premiership final day of the season	–
17	football	UEFA Cup final	tbd
20	football	FA Cup final	Wembley Stadium, London
24	football	European Champions' League final	tbd
27	football	Scottish Cup final	Hampden Park, Glasgow
29 May–11 June	tennis	French Open	Roland Garros, Paris
June			
9	horse racing	The Oaks	Epsom
10	horse racing	The Derby	Epsom
10 June–7 July	football	European Championships	Belgium and Netherlands
12–18	golf	US Open	Pebble Beach, California
17–18	motor racing	Le Mans 24-Hour Race	Sarthe
20–23	horse racing	Royal Ascot	Ascot
24[1]	greyhound racing	Greyhound Derby final	Wimbledon, London
26 June – 9 July	tennis	The All-England Championships	Wimbledon, London
28 June–2 July	rowing	Henley Royal Regatta	Henley
July			
1–23	cycling	Tour de France	France
7	football	European Championships final	Feyenoord Stadion, Rotterdam
16[1]	motor racing	British Grand Prix	Silverstone, Northamptonshire
20–23	golf	British Open	St Andrews, Scotland
29 July – 5 August	sailing	Cowes Week	Cowes, Isle of Wight
August			
1–5	horse racing	Glorious Goodwood	Goodwood, West Sussex
11–13	athletics	Great Britain Olympic Trials incorporating the AAA Championships	tbd
28 August – 3 September	cycling	PruTour of Britain	UK
28 August – 10 September	tennis	US Open	Flushing Meadow, New York
September			
9	horse racing	St Leger	Doncaster
15 September –1 October		Olympic Games	Sydney
October			
1	horse racing	Prix de l'Arc de Triomphe	Longchamp, Paris
6–8	golf	Solheim Cup Europe versus USA	Loch Lomond, Scotland
18–29	Paralympic Games		Sydney
28 October – 25 November	rugby league	World Cup	UK, Republic of Ireland, France

[1] Provisional date.

BBC Sports Personality of the Year

First presented in 1954. The most prestigious award for British sportsmen and sportswomen, it is based on the votes of television viewers.

Year	Winner	Sport
1989	Nick Faldo	golf
1990	Paul Gascoigne	football
1991	Liz McColgan	athletics
1992	Nigel Mansell	motor racing
1993	Linford Christie	athletics
1994	Damon Hill	motor racing
1995	Jonathan Edwards	athletics
1996	Damon Hill	motor racing
1997	Greg Rusedski	tennis
1998	Michael Owen	football

Sports Organizations

English County Cricket Clubs

Derbyshire County Cricket Club County Cricket Ground, Nottingham Road, Derby DE2 6DA; phone: (01332) 383211

Durham County Cricket Club County Ground, Riverside, Chester-le-Street, County Durham DH3 3QR; phone: (0191) 387 1717

Essex County Cricket Club County Ground, New Writtle Street, Chelmsford CM2 0PG; phone: (01245) 252420

Glamorgan County Cricket Club Sofia Gardens, Cardiff CF1 9XR; phone: (01222) 343478

Gloucestershire County Cricket Club Phoenix County Ground, Nevil Road, Bristol BS7 9EJ; phone: (0117) 910 8000

Hampshire County Cricket Club County Ground, Northlands Road, Southampton SO15 2UE; phone: (01703) 333788

Kent County Cricket Club St Lawrence Ground, Old Dover Road, Canterbury CT1 3NZ; phone: (01227) 456886

Lancashire County Cricket Club Old Trafford, Manchester M16 0PX; phone: (0161) 282 4021

Leicestershire County Cricket Club County Ground, Grace Road, Leicester LE2 8AD; phone: (0116) 283 2128

Middlesex County Cricket Club Lord's Cricket Ground, London NW8 8QN; phone: (0171) 289 1300

Northamptonshire County Cricket Club County Ground, Wantage Road, Northampton NN1 4TJ; phone: (01604) 514455

Nottinghamshire County Cricket Club Trent Bridge, Nottingham NG2 6AG; phone: (0115) 982 1525

Somerset County Cricket Club County Ground, St James's Street, Taunton TA1 1JT; phone: (01823) 272946

Surrey County Cricket Club Kennington Oval, London SE11 5SS; phone: (0171) 582 6660

Sussex County Cricket Club County Ground, Eaton Road, Hove BN3 3AN; phone: (01273) 827100

Warwickshire County Cricket Club County Ground, Edgbaston, Birmingham B5 7QU; phone: (0121) 446 4422

Worcestershire County Cricket Club County Ground, New Road, Worcester WR2 4QQ; phone: (01905) 748474

Yorkshire County Cricket Club Headingley Cricket Ground, Leeds LS6 3BU; phone: (0113) 278 7394

English and Scottish Football Clubs

FA Carling Premiership Clubs

Arsenal Arsenal Stadium, Avenell Road, Highbury, London N5 1BU; phone: (0171) 704 4000

Aston Villa Villa Park, Trinity Road, Birmingham B6 6HE; phone: (0121) 327 2299

Bradford City The Pulse Stadium at Valley Parade, Bradford BD8 7DY; phone: (01274) 773355

Chelsea Stamford Bridge, Fulham Road, London SW6 1HS; phone: (0171) 385 5545

Coventry City Highfield Road Stadium, King Richard Street, Coventry CV2 4FW; phone: (01203) 234000

Derby County Pride Park Stadium, Derby DE24 8XL; phone: (01332) 667503

Everton Goodison Park, Liverpool L4 4EL; phone: (0151) 330 2200

Leeds United Elland Road, Leeds LS11 0ES; phone: (0113) 226 6000

Leicester City City Stadium, Filbert Street, Leicester LE2 7FL; phone: (0116) 291 5000

Liverpool Anfield Road, Liverpool L4 0TH; phone: (0151) 263 2361

Manchester United Sir Matt Busby Way, Old Trafford, Manchester M16 0RA; phone: (0161) 872 1661

Middlesbrough Cellnet Riverside Stadium, Middlesborough, Cleveland TS3 6RS; phone: (01642) 877700

Newcastle United St James's Park, Newcastle-upon-Tyne NE1 4ST; phone: (0191) 201 8400

Sheffield Wednesday Hillsborough, Sheffield S6 1SW; phone: (0114) 221 2121

Southampton The Dell, Milton Road, Southampton SO15 2XH; phone: (01703) 220505

Sunderland Stadium of Light, Sunderland, Tyne-and-Wear SR2 1SU phone: (0191) 551 5000

Tottenham Hotspur 748 High Road, Tottenham, London N17 0AP; phone: (0181) 365 5000

Watford Vicarage Road Stadium, Watford WD1 8ER; phone: (01923) 496000

West Ham United Boleyn Ground, Green Street, Upton Park, London E13 9AZ; phone: (0181) 548 2748

Wimbledon Selhurst Park, South Norwood, London SE25 6PY; phone: (0181) 771 2233

Nationwide Football League Division One Clubs

Barnsley Oakwell Ground, Grove Street, Barnsley, South Yorkshire S71 1ET; phone: (01226) 211211

Birmingham City St Andrews, Birmingham B9 4NH; phone: (0121) 772 0101

Blackburn Rovers Ewood Park, Blackburn BB2 4JF; phone: (01254) 698888

Bolton Wanderers The Reebok Stadium, Mansell Way, Horwich; phone: (01204) 673673

Charlton Athletic The Valley, Floyd Road, Charlton, London SE7 8BL; phone: (0181) 333 4000

Crewe Alexandra Gresty Road, Crewe CW2 6EB; phone: (01270) 213014

Crystal Palace Selhurst Park, South Norwood, London SE25 6PU; phone: (0181) 768 6000

Fulham Craven Cottage, Stevenage Road, London SW6 6HH; phone: (0171) 384 4700

Grimsby Town Blundell Park, Cleethorpes DN35 7YP; phone: (01472) 697111

Huddersfield Town The Alfred McAlpine Stadium, Leeds Road, Huddersfield HD1 6PX; phone: (01484) 484100

Ipswich Town Portman Road, Ipswich IP1 2DA; phone: (01473) 400500

Manchester City Maine Road, Moss Side, Manchester M14 7WN; phone (0161) 224 5000

Norwich City Carrow Road, Norwich NR1 1JE; phone: (01603) 760760

Nottingham Forest City Ground, Nottingham NG2 5FJ; phone: (0115) 982 4444

Portsmouth Fratton Park, Portsmouth PO4 8RA; phone: (01705) 731204

Port Vale Vale Park, Burslem, Stoke-on-Trent ST6 1AW; phone: (01782) 814134

Queens Park Rangers Loftus Road, South Africa Road, London W12 7PA; phone: (0181) 743 0262

Sheffield United Bramall Lane Ground, Sheffield S2 4SU; phone: (0114) 221 5757

Stockport County Edgeley Park, Hardcastle Road, Stockport, Cheshire SK3 9DD; phone: (0161) 286 8888

Swindon Town County Ground, Swindon, Wiltshire SN1 2ED; phone: (01793) 430430

Tranmere Rovers Prenton Park, Prenton Road West, Birkenhead L42 9PN; phone: (0151) 608 4194

Walsall Bescot Stadium, Bescot Crescent, Walsall WS1 4SA; phone: (01922) 622791

West Bromwich Albion The Hawthorns, West Bromwich B71 4LF; phone: (0121) 525 8888

Wolverhampton Wanderers Molineux, Wolverhampton WV1 4QR; phone: (01902) 655000

Scottish Premier Division Clubs

Aberdeen Pittodrie Stadium, Pittodrie Street, Aberdeen AB2 1QH; phone: (01224) 632328

Dundee Dens Park, Sandeman Street, Dundee DD3 7JS; phone: (01382) 826104

Dundee United Tannadice Park, Tannadice Street, Dundee DD3 7JW; phone: (01382) 833166

Glasgow Celtic Celtic Park, 95 Kerrydale Street, Glasgow G40 3RE; phone: (0141) 556 2611

Glasgow Rangers Ibrox Stadium, Edminston Drive, Glasgow G51 2XD; phone: (0141) 427 8500

Heart of Midlothian Tynecastle Park, Gorgie Road, Edinburgh EH11 2NL; phone: (0131) 337 6132

Hibernian Easter Road Stadium, Albion Road, Edinburgh EH7 5QG; phone: (0131) 661 2159

Kilmarnock Rugby Park, Kilmarnock KA1 2DP; phone: (01563) 525184

Motherwell Fir Park, Motherwell ML1 2QN; phone: (01698) 333333

St Johnstone McDiarmid Park, Crieff Road, Perth PH1 2SJ; phone: (01738) 626961

English Rugby Union Clubs

Allied Dunbar Premiership Division One Clubs

Bath The Recreation Ground, Bath BA2 6PW; phone: (01225) 325200

Bedford Goldington Road, Bedford MK42 3DN; phone: (01234) 347980

Bristol Memorial Ground, Filton Avenue, Horfield, Bristol BS7 0AQ; phone: (0117) 908500

Gloucester Kingsholm, Kingsholm Road, Gloucester GL1 3AX; phone: (01452) 381087

Leicester Welford Road Ground, Aylestone Road, Leicester LE2 7LF; phone: (0116) 2541607

London Irish[1] The Avenue, Sunbury-on-Thames, Middlesex TW16 5EQ; phone: (01932) 783034

London Scottish[1] Stoop Memorial Ground, Craneford Way, Twickenham TW2 7SX; phone: (0181) 410 6000

NEC Harlequins of London The Stoop Memorial Ground, Twickenham TW2 7SQ; phone: (0181) 410 6000

Newcastle Falcons Kingston Park, Brunton Road, Kenton Bank Foot, Newcastle NE13 8AF; phone: (0191) 214 0422

Northampton Franklins' Gardens, Weedon Road, Northampton NN5 5BG; phone: (01604) 751543

Richmond[1] Merevale House, Richmond, Surrey TW5 2RG; phone: (0181) 332 7112

Sale Heywood Road, Brooklands, Sale, Cheshire M33 3WB; phone: (0161) 973 6348

Saracens Vicarage Road Stadium, Watford WD1 8ER; phone: (01923) 496200

Wasps Loftus Road Stadium, South Africa Road, London W12 7PA; phone: (0181) 743 0262

[1] London Irish, London Scottish, and Richmond have agreed to merge. The name of the new club had not been decided at the time of going to press.

Welsh Rugby Union Clubs

Bridgend Brewery Field, Tondu Road, Bridgend, Mid Glamorgan CF31 4JE; phone: (01656) 652707

Caerphilly Virginia Park, Virginia View, Caerphilly, Mid Glamorgan CF83 3JA; phone: (01222) 865077

Cardiff Cardiff Arms Park, Westgate Street, Cardiff CF1 1JA phone: (01222) 302000

Dunvant Club House, Broadacre, Killay, Swansea, West Glamorgan SA2 7RU; phone: (01792) 207291

Ebbw Vale Eugene Cross Park, Pontygof, Ebbw Vale, Gwent NP23 5AZ; phone: (01495) 352861

Llanelli Stradey Park, Llanelli, Dyfed, SA15 4BT; phone: (01554) 774060

Neath The Gnoll, Gnoll Park Road, Neath, West Glamorgan SA11 3BU; phone: (01639) 769660

Newport Rodney Road, Newport, Gwent NP19 0UU; phone: (01633) 670690

Pontypridd Club House, Sardis Road, Pontypridd, Mid Glamorgan CF37 1 HA; phone: (01443) 405006

Swansea St Helen's Ground, Bryn Road, Swansea, West Glamorgan SA2 0AR; phone: (01792) 466593

Scottish Rugby Union Clubs

Boroughmuir Meggetland, Colinton Road, Edinburgh EH14 1AS; phone: (0131) 443 7571

Currie Malleny Park, Balerno, Edinburgh EH14 5HA; phone: (0131) 449 2432

Edinburgh Academicals Raeburn Place, Stockbridge, Edinburgh EH4 1HQ; phone: (0131) 332 1070

Hawick Mansfield Park, Mansfield, Hawick; phone: (01450) 370687

Heriot's FP Goldenacre, Bangholm Terrace, Edinburgh EH3 5QN; phone: (0131) 552 5925

Jed-Forest Riverside Park, Jedburgh TD8 6UE; phone: (01835) 862855

Melrose The Greenyards, Melrose, Roxburghshire TD6 9SA; phone: (01896) 822993

Stirling County Bridgehaugh, Causewayhead Road, Stirling SK9 5EG; phone: (01786) 478866

Watsonians Myreside, Myreside Road, Edinburgh EH10 5DB; phone: (0131) 447 5200

West of Scotland Burnbrae, Glasgow Road, Milngavie, Glasgow G62 6HX; phone: (0141) 956 3116/2891

Rugby League Super League Clubs

Bradford Bulls Odsal Stadium, Bradford BD6 1BS; phone: (01274) 733899

Castleford Tigers Wheldon Road, Castleford WF10 2SD; phone: (01977) 552674

Gateshead Thunder Department of Leisure Services, Civic Centre, Regent Street, Gateshead NE8 1HH; phone: (0191) 477 9158

Halifax Blue Sox The Pavilion, Thrum Hall HX1 4TL; phone: (01422) 250600

Huddersfield Giants Alfred McAlpine Stadium, Kirklees Way, Huddersfield HD1 6PZ; phone: (01484) 530710

Hull Sharks The Boulevard, Airlie Street, Hull; phone: (01482) 327200

Leeds Rhinos Headingley, St Michael's Lane, Leeds LS6 3BR; phone: (0113) 278 6181

London Broncos The Stoop Memorial Ground, Twickenham, Middlesex TW8 7SX; phone: (0181) 410 5000

St Helens Knowsley Road, St Helens, Merseyside, WA10 4AD; phone: (01744) 23697

Salford Reds The Willows, Willows Road, Weaste, Salford M5 2ST; phone: (0161) 737 6363

Sheffield Eagles 824 Attercliffe Road, Sheffield S9 3RS; phone: (0114) 261 0326

Wakefield Trinity Belle Vue, Doncaster Road, Wakefield, West Yorkshire WF1 5HL; phone: (01924) 211611

Warrington Wolves Wilderspool Stadium, Wilderspool Causeway, Warrington, WA4 6PY; phone: (01925) 635338

Wigan Warriors The Pavilion, Central Park, Wigan WN1 1XF; phone: (01942) 231321

Sports Organizations in the UK

Sports Councils

Central Council of Physical Recreation Francis House, Francis Street, London SW1P 1DE; phone: (0171) 828 3163

Sport England 16 Upper Woburn Place, London WC1H 0QP; phone: (0171) 273 1500

Scottish Sports Council Caledonia House, South Gyle, Edinburgh EH12 9DQ; phone: (0131) 317 7200

Sports Council for Northern Ireland House of Sport, Upper Malone Road, Belfast BT9 5LA; phone: (01232) 381222

Sports Council for Wales Sophia Gardens, Cardiff CF1 9SW; phone: (01222) 300500

UK Sports Council Walkden House, 3–10 Melton Street, London NW1 2EB; phone: (0171) 380 8000

American Football

World League of American Football 26A Albemarle Street, London W1X 3FA; phone: (0171) 355 1995

Angling

National Federation of Anglers Halliday House, Eggington Junction, Near Hitton, Derbyshire DE65 6GU; phone: (01283) 734735

Archery

Grand National Archery Society National Agricultural Centre, Seventh Street, Stoneleigh, Kenilworth, Warwickshire CV8 2LG; phone: (01203) 696631

Athletics

UK Athletics 30a Harborne Road, Birmingham B15 3AA; phone: (0121) 456 5098

Badminton

Badminton Association of England Ltd National Badminton Centre, Bradwell Road, Loughton Lodge, Milton Keynes MK8 9LA; phone: (01908) 268400

Scottish Badminton Union Cockburn Centre, 40 Bogmoor Place, Glasgow G51 4 TQ; phone: (0141) 445 1218

Welsh Badminton Union Fourth Floor, 3 Westgate Street, Cardiff CF1 1ND; phone: (01222) 222082

Baseball

British Baseball Federation PO Box 45, Hessle, East Yorks, HU13 0YQ; phone: (01482) 643551

Basketball

Basketball Association of Wales Connies House, Rhymney River Bridge Road, Cardiff CF3 7YZ; phone: (01222) 454395

English Basketball Association 48 Bradford Road, Stanningley, Leeds LS28 6DF; phone: (0113) 236 1166

Scottish Basketball Association Caledonia House, South Gyle, Edinburgh EH12 9DQ; phone: (0131) 317 7260

Billiards and Snooker

World Professional Billiards and Snooker Association 27 Oakfield Road, Clifton, Bristol BS28 2AT; phone: (0117) 974 4491

Bobsleigh

British Bobsleigh Association The Chestnuts, 85 High Street, Codford, Warminster, Wiltshire BA12 0ND; phone: (01985) 850064

Bowls

British Isles Bowling Council 28 Woodford Park, Lurgan, County Armargh BT66 7HA; phone: (01762) 322036

British Isles Indoor Bowls Council 9 Highlight Lane, Barry CF62 8AA; phone: (01446) 733978

British Isles Women's Bowling Council 2 Case Gardens, Seaton, Devon EX12 2AP; phone: (01297) 21317

British Isles Women's Indoor Bowls Council 3 Scirocco Close, Moulton Park, Northampton NN3 6AP; phone: (01604) 494163

English Bowling Association Lyndhurst Road, Worthing, West Sussex BN11 2AZ; phone: (01903) 820222

English Indoor Bowling Association David Cornwell House, Bowling Green, Leicester Road, Melton Mowbray, Leicestershire LE13 0DA; phone: (01664) 481900

Boxing

Amateur Boxing Association of England Ltd Crystal Palace National Sports Centre, London SE19 2BB; phone: (0181) 778 0251

British Amateur Boxing Association High Street, Lochee, Dundee DD2 2AY; phone: (01382) 611412

British Boxing Board of Control Ltd Jack Petersen House, 52A Borough High Street, London SE1 1XY; phone: (0171) 403 5879

Canoeing

British Canoe Union John Dudderidge House, Adbolton Lane, West Bridgford, Nottingham NG2 5AS; phone: (0115) 982 1100

Chess

British Chess Federation 9A Grand Parade, St Leonards-on-Sea, East Sussex TN38 0DD; phone: (01424) 442500

Cricket

England and Wales Cricket Board Lord's, London NW8 8QN; phone: (0171) 432 1200

MCC Lord's, London NW8 8QN; phone: (0171) 289 1611

Women's Cricket Association c/o Warwickshire CCC, Edgbaston, Birmingham B5 7QX; phone: (0121) 440 0567

Croquet

Croquet Association c/o The Hurlingham Club, Ranelagh Gardens, London SW6 3PR; phone: (0171) 736 3148

Cycling

British Cycling Federation National Cycling Centre, Stuart Street, Manchester M11 4DQ; phone: (0161) 230 2301

Road Time Trials Council 77 Arlington Drive, Penninfton Leigh, Lancashire WN7 3QP; phone: (01942) 603976

Darts

Britsh Darts Organization 2 Pages Lane, Muswell Hill, London N10 1PS; phone: (0181) 883 5544

Diving

Great Britain Diving Federation PO Box 222, Batley, West Yorkshire WT17 8XD; phone: (01924) 422322

Equestrianism

British Equestrian Federation British Equestrian Centre, Stoneleigh Park, Kenilworth, Warks CV8 2LR; phone: (01203) 698871

British Horse Trials Association British Equestrian Centre, Stoneleigh Park, Kenilworth, Warwickshire CV8 2LR; phone: (01203) 696697

Fencing

British Fencing Association 1 Baron's Gate, 33–35 Rothschild Road, London W4 5HT; phone: (0181) 742 3032

Football, Association

The Football Association 16 Lancaster Gate, London W2 3LW; phone: (0171) 262 4542

Football Association of Ireland 80 Merrion Square South, Dublin 2; phone: (00535) 1 676 6864

Football Association of Wales Plymouth Chambers, 3 Westgate Street, Cardiff CF1 1DD; phone: (01222) 372325

The Football League Ltd 319 Clifton Drive South, Lytham St Annes, Lancashire FY8 1JG; phone: (01253) 729421

The Football Supporters' Association PO Box 11, Liverpool L26 1XP; phone: (0151) 709 2594

Irish Football Association 20 Windsor Avenue, Belfast BT9 6EE; phone: (01232) 669458

Irish Football League 96 University Street, Belfast BT7 1HE; phone: (01232) 242888

Scottish Football Association 6 Park Gardens, Glasgow G3 7YF; phone: (0141) 332 6372

Scottish Football League 188 West Regent Street, Glasgow G2 4RY; phone: (0141) 248 3844

Women's Football Association 16 Lancaster Gate, London W2 3LW; phone: (0171) 262 4542

General

British Olympic Association No. 1 Wandsworth Plain, London SW18 1EH; phone: (0181) 871 2677

British Paralympic Association Delta Point Room 13A, 35 Wellesley Road, Croydon CR9 2YZ; phone: (0181) 666 4556

Commonwealth Games Federation Walkden House, 3–10 Melton Street, London NW1 2EB; phone: (0171) 383 5596

Gliding

British Gliding Association Kimberley House, 47 Vaughan Way, Leicester LE1 4SE; phone: (0116) 253 1051

Golf

Royal and Ancient Golf Club of St Andrews Golf Place, St Andrews, Fife KY16 9JD; phone: (01334) 472112

European Golf Tour Wentworth Drive, Virginia Water, Surrey GU25 4LX; phone: (01344) 842881

Women's European Tour The Tytherington Club, Dorchester Way, Tytherington, Macclesfield, Cheshire SK10 2JP; phone: (01625) 611444

Greyhound Racing

National Greyhound Racing Club Ltd Twyman House, 16 Bonny Street, London NW1 9QD; phone: (0171) 267 9256

Gymnastics

British Amateur Gymnastics Association Registered Office, Ford Hall, Lilleshall National Sports Centre Newport, Shropshire TF10 9NB; phone: (01952) 820330

Hockey

The Hockey Association The Stadium, Silbury Boulevard, Milton Keynes MK9 1NR; phone: (01908) 689290

Horse Racing

British Horse Racing Board 42 Portman Square, London W1H 0EN; phone: (0171) 396 0011

The Jockey Club 42 Portman Square, London W1H 0EN; phone: (0171) 486 4921

Ice Hockey

Ice Hockey UK The Galleries of Justice Shire Hall, High Pavement, Lace Market, Nottingham NG1 1HN; phone: (0115) 915 9204

Ice Skating

National Ice Skating Association of the UK Ltd 15–27 Gee Street, London EC1V 3RE; phone: (0171) 273 3824

Judo

British Judo Association 7A Rutland Street, Leicester LE1 1RB; phone: (0116) 255 9669

Lacrosse

English Lacrosse Association 4 Western Court, Bromley Street, Digbeth, Birmingham B9 4AN; phone: (0121) 773 4422

Martial Arts

Martial Arts Development Commission PO Box 381, Erith, Kent DA8 1TF; phone: (01322) 430441

English Karate Governing Body 12 Princes Avenue, Woodford Green, Essex IG8 0LN; phone: (0181) 599 0711

Modern Pentathlon

Modern Pentathlon Association of Great Britain 8 The Commons, Shaftsbury, Dorset SP7 8JU; phone: (01747) 855833

Motor Sports

Auto-Cycle Union ACU House, Wood Street, Rugby, Warwickshire CV21 2YX; phone: (01788) 540519

RAC Motor Sports Association Ltd Motorsports House, Riverside Park, Colnbrook, Slough SL3 0HG; phone: (01753) 681736

Mountaineering

British Mountaineering Council 177–179 Burton Road, West Didsbury, Manchester M20 2BB; phone: (0161) 445 4747

Netball

All England Netball Association Ltd Netball House, 9 Paynes Park, Hitchin, Hertfordshire SG5 1EH; phone: (01462) 442344

Northern Ireland Netball Association House of Sport, Upper Malone Road, Belfast BT9 5LA; phone: (01232) 381222

Scottish Netball Association 24 Ainslie Road, Hillington Business Park, Hillington, Glasgow G5S 4RC; phone: (0141) 570 4016

Welsh Netball Association 50 Cathedral Road, Cardiff CF1 9LE; phone: (01222) 237048

Orienteering

British Orienteering Federation Riversdale, Dale Road North, Darley Dale, Matlock, Derbyshire DE4 2HX; phone: (01629) 734042

Polo

The Hurlingham Polo Association Winterlake, Kirtlington, Kidlington, Oxfordshire OX5 3HG; phone: (01869) 350044

Rackets and Real Tennis

Tennis and Rackets Association c/o The Queen's Club, Palliser Road, London W14 9EQ; phone: (0171) 386 3447/8

Rifle Shooting

National Rifle Association Bisley Camp, Brookwood, Woking, Surrey GU24 0PR; phone: (01483) 797777

Rowing

Amateur Rowing Association Ltd The Priory, 6 Lower Mall, London W6 9DJ; phone: (0181) 748 3632

Henley Royal Regatta Regatta Headquarters, Henley-on-Thames, Oxfordshire RG9 2LY; phone: (01491) 572153

Scottish Amateur Rowing Association 18 Daniel McLauchlin Place, Kirkintilloch, Glasgow G66 2LH; phone: (0141) 775 0522

Welsh Amateur Rowing Association Monmouth School, Monmouth NP5 3NP; phone: (01600) 713143

Rugby League

The Rugby Football League Red Hall, Red Hall Lane, Leeds LS17 8NB; phone: (0113) 232 9111

Rugby Union

Irish Rugby Football Union 62 Lansdowne Road, Ballsbridge, Dublin 4, Republic of Ireland; phone: (00 353) 1668 4601

Rugby Football Union Twickenham TW1 1DZ; phone: (0181) 892 2000

Scottish Rugby Union Murrayfield, Edinburgh EH12 5PJ; phone: (0131) 346 5000

Welsh Rugby Union PO Box 22, Hodge House, St Mary Street, Cardiff CF1 1DY; phone: (01222) 390111

Skiing

British Ski Federation 258 Main Street,

East Calder, Livingstone, West Lothian EH53 0EE; phone: (01506) 884343

Speedway
Speedway Control Board Ltd ACU Headquarters, Wood Street, Rugby, Warwickshire CV21 2YX; phone: (01788) 540096

Squash Rackets
Squash Rackets Association PO Box 1106, London W3 0ZD; phone: (0181)746 1616

Swimming
Amateur Swimming Association of Great Britain Harold Fern House, Derby Square, Loughborough, Leicestershire LEH OAL; phone: (01509) 618700

Table Tennis
English Table Tennis Association Queensbury House, Havelock Road, Hastings, East Sussex TN34 1HF; phone: (01424) 722525

Tennis
All England Lawn Tennis and Croquet Club Church Road, Wimbledon, London SW19 5AE; phone: (0181) 944 1066

Lawn Tennis Association The Queen's Club, London W14 9EG; phone: (0171) 381 7000

Trampolining
British Trampoline Federation Ltd 146 College Road, Harrow HA1 1BH; phone: (0181) 863 7278

Volleyball
British Volleyball Federation 27 South Road, West Bridgford, Nottingham NG2 7AG; phone: (0115) 945 6324

Water Skiing
British Water Ski Federation 390 City Road, London EC1V 2QA; phone: (0171) 833 2855

Weight Lifting
British Amateur Weightlifters Association Iffley Turn, Oxford OX4 4DU; phone: (01865) 200339

Wrestling
British Amateur Wrestling Association 41 Great Clowes Street, Salford, Manchester M7 9RQ; phone: (0161) 832 9209

Yachting
Royal Yachting Association RYA House, Romsey Road, Eastleigh, Hampshire SO50 9YA; phone: (01703) 627400

Major International Sports Organizations

International dialling codes are given for organizations not based in the UK or USA.

Athletics
International Amateur Athletic Federation (IAAF) 17 Rue Princesse Florestine, BP 359, MC 9800, Monaco; phone: (33) 93 30 70 70

Boxing
International Boxing Federation (IBF) 134 Evergreen Place, 9th Floor, East Orange, NJ 07018, USA; phone: (201) 4140300

World Boxing Association (WBA) Centro Comercial Cuidad Turmero, Local no. 21, Piso no. 2, Calle Petion Cruce Con Urdaneta, Turmero, 2115 Estado Aragua, Venezuela; phone: (58) 44631584

World Boxing Council (WBC) Genova 33-503, Col. Juarez, Delegacion Cuauhternac, Mexico 06600, DF Mexico; phone: (52) 5 5336546

World Boxing Organization (WBO) Borinquen St no. 57, Santa Rita, San Juan, Puerto Rico 00925; phone: (809) 765 7542

Football, Association
Federation Internationale de Football Associations (FIFA) PO Box 85, Hitzigweg 11, Zurich 8030, Switzerland; phone: (41) 1 384 9595

Union of European Football Associations (UEFA) Chemin de la Redoute 54, Case Postale 303 CH-1260, Nyon, Switzerland; phone: (41) 22 994 4444

Golf
Royal and Ancient Golf Club of St Andrews St Andrews, Fife KY16 9JD; phone: (01334) 472112

Motor Racing
Federation Internationale de Sport Automobile (FISA – Formula One) 8 Bis rue Boissy d'Anglais, 75008 Paris, France; phone: (33) 1 4312 4455

Olympics
International Olympic Committee (IOC) Chateau de Vidy, CH-1007 Lausanne, Switzerland; phone: (41) 21 621 6111

Skiing
Federation Internationale de Ski (FIS) (International Ski Federation), Oberhofen 3653, Switzerland; phone: (41) 33 44 6161

Swimming
Federation Internationale de Natation Amateur (FINA) (International Amateur Swimming Federation), Avenue de Beaumont 9, 1012 Lausanne, Switzerland; phone: (41) 21 312 6602

Tennis
International Tennis Federation Bank Lane, Roehampton, London W15 5XZ; phone: (0181) 878 6464

Summer Olympic Games

Summer Olympic Games Venues

(– = not applicable.)

Year	Olympiad	Venue
1896	I	Athens, Greece
1900	II	Paris, France
1904	III	St Louis, USA
1906	–	Athens, Greece[1]
1908	IV	London, Great Britain
1912	V	Stockholm, Sweden
1916	VI	Berlin, Germany[2]
1920	VII	Antwerp, Belgium
1924	VIII	Paris, France
1928	IX	Amsterdam, Netherlands
1932	X	Los Angeles, USA
1936	XI	Berlin, Germany
1940	XII	Tokyo, Japan[3]
1944	XIII	London, Great Britain[3]
1948	XIV	London, Great Britain
1952	XV	Helsinki, Finland
1956	XVI	Melbourne, Australia[4]
1960	XVII	Rome, Italy
1964	XVIII	Tokyo, Japan
1968	XIX	Mexico City, Mexico
1972	XX	Munich, West Germany
1976	XXI	Montreal, Canada
1980	XXII	Moscow, USSR
1984	XXIII	Los Angeles, USA
1988	XXIV	Seoul, South Korea
1992	XXV	Barcelona, Spain
1996	XXVI	Atlanta, USA
2000	XXVII	Sydney, Australia
2004	XXVIII	Athens, Greece

[1] The 1906 Intercalated (or Interim) Games at Athens are not regarded as official by the International Olympic Committee but the results are included in most Olympic record books.
[2] Cancelled because of World War I.
[3] Cancelled because of World War II.
[4] Equestrian events held in Stockholm, Sweden.

Archery: Olympic Gold Medallists

1996

Category	Archer	Country	Category	Archer	Country
Men			***Women***		
Individual	Justin Huish	USA	Individual	Kim Kyung-Wook	South Korea
Team		USA	Team		South Korea

Men's Athletics: Olympic Gold Medallists

The year in which an event was first introduced to the Olympics is in parentheses after the event name.

Year	Name	Country	Result
100 m (1896)			
1980	Allan Wells	Great Britain	10.25
1984	Carl Lewis	USA	9.99
1988	Carl Lewis	USA	9.92
1992	Linford Christie	Great Britain	9.96
1996	Donovan Bailey	Canada	9.84
200 m (1900)			
1980	Pietro Mennea	Italy	20.19
1984	Carl Lewis	USA	19.80
1988	Joe DeLoach	USA	19.75
1992	Mike Marsh	USA	20.01
1996	Michael Johnson	USA	19.32
400 m (1896)			
1980	Viktor Markin	USSR	44.60
1984	Alonzo Babers	USA	44.27
1988	Steve Lewis	USA	43.87
1992	Quincy Watts	USA	43.50
1996	Michael Johnson	USA	43.49
800 m (1896)			
1980	Steve Ovett	Great Britain	1:45.40
1984	Joaquim Cruz	Brazil	1:43.00
1988	Paul Ereng	Kenya	1:43.45
1992	William Tanui	Kenya	1:43.66
1996	Vebjörn Rodal	Norway	1:42.58
1,500 m (1896)			
1980	Sebastian Coe	Great Britain	3:38.40
1984	Sebastian Coe	Great Britain	3:32.53
1988	Peter Rono	Kenya	3:35.96
1992	Fermin Cacho	Spain	3:40.12
1996	Noureddine Morceli	Algeria	3:35.78
5,000 m (1912)			
1980	Miruts Yifter	Ethiopia	13:21.00
1984	Saïd Aouita	Morocco	13:05.59
1988	John Ngugi	Kenya	13:11.70
1992	Dieter Baumann	Germany	13:12.52
1996	Venuste Niyongabo	Burundi	13:07.96
10,000 m (1912)			
1980	Miruts Yifter	Ethiopia	27:42.70
1984	Alberto Cova	Italy	27:47.54
1988	Brahim Boutayeb	Morocco	27:21.46
1992	Khalid Skah	Morocco	27:46.70
1996	Haile Gebrselassie	Ethiopia	27:07.34
Marathon (1896)			
1980	Waldemar Cierpinski	East Germany	2h 11:03.00
1984	Carlos Lopes	Portugal	2h 09:21.00
1988	Gelindo Bordin	Italy	2h 10:32.00
1992	Hwang Young-cho	South Korea	2h 13:23.00
1996	Josia Thugwane	South Africa	2h 12:36.00
110 m Hurdles (1896)			
1980	Thomas Munkelt	East Germany	13.39
1984	Roger Kingdom	USA	13.20
1988	Roger Kingdom	USA	12.98
1992	Mark McKoy	Canada	13.12
1996	Allen Johnson	USA	12.95
400 m Hurdles (1900)			
1980	Volker Beck	East Germany	48.70
1984	Edwin Moses	USA	47.75
1988	Andre Phillips	USA	47.19
1992	Kevin Young	USA	46.78
1996	Derrick Adkins	USA	47.54
20 km Walk (1956)			
1980	Maurizio Damilano	Italy	1h 23:35.50
1984	Ernesto Canto	Mexico	1h 23:13.00
1988	Josef Pribilinec	Czechoslovakia	1h 19:57.00
1992	Daniel Plaza	Spain	1h 21:45.00
1996	Jefferson Perez	Ecuador	1h 20:07.00
50 km Walk (1932)			
1980	Hartwig Gauder	East Germany	3h 49:24.00
1984	Raul Gonzalez	Mexico	3h 47:26.00
1988	Vyacheslav Ivanenko	USSR	3h 38:29.00
1992	Andrei Perlov	USSR	3h 50:13.00
1996	Robert Korzeniowski	Poland	3h 43:30.00
3,000 m Steeplechase (1900)[1]			
1980	Bronisław Malinowski	Poland	8:09.70
1984	Julius Korir	Kenya	8:11.80
1988	Julius Kariuki	Kenya	8:05.51
1992	Matthew Birir	Kenya	8:08.84
1996	Joseph Keter	Kenya	8:07.12
High Jump (1896)			
1980	Gerd Wessig	East Germany	2.36 m/7 ft 8$\frac{3}{4}$ in
1984	Dietmar Mögenburg	West Germany	2.35 m/7 ft 8$\frac{1}{2}$ in
1988	Gennady Avdeyenko	USSR	2.38 m/7 ft 9$\frac{1}{2}$ in
1992	Javier Sotomayor	Cuba	2.34 m/7 ft 8 in
1996	Charles Austin	USA	2.39 m/7 ft 10 in
Pole Vault (1896)			
1980	Władisław Kozakiewicz	Poland	5.78 m/18 fr 11$\frac{1}{2}$ in
1984	Pierre Quinon	France	5.75 m/18 ft 10$\frac{1}{4}$ in
1988	Sergei Bubka	USSR	5.90 m/19 ft 4$\frac{1}{4}$ in
1992	Maksim Tarassov	Unified Team[2]	5.80 m/19 ft $\frac{1}{4}$ in
1996	Jean Galfione	France	5.92 m/19 ft 5 in
Long Jump (1896)			
1980	Lutz Dombrowski	East Germany	8.54 m/28 ft $\frac{1}{4}$ in
1984	Carl Lewis	USA	8.54 m/28 ft $\frac{1}{4}$ in
1988	Carl Lewis	USA	8.72 m/28 ft 7$\frac{1}{4}$ in
1992	Carl Lewis	USA	8.67 m/28 ft 5$\frac{1}{2}$ in
1996	Carl Lewis	USA	8.50m/27 ft 10$\frac{3}{4}$ in

(continued)

Men's Athletics: Olympic Gold Medallists (*continued*)

Year	Name	Country	Result
Triple Jump (1896)			
1980	Jaak Udmäe	USSR	17.35 m/56 ft 11¼ in
1984	Al Joyner	USA	17.26 m/56 ft 7½ in
1988	Khristo Markov	Bulgaria	17.61 m/57 ft 9¼ in
1992	Mike Conley	USA	18.17 m/57 ft 10¼ in
1996	Kenny Harrison	USA	18.09 m/59 ft 4¼ in
Shot Put (1896)			
1980	Vladimir Kiselyev	USSR	21.35 m/70 ft ½ in
1984	Alessandro Andrei	Italy	21.26 m/69 ft 9 in
1988	Ulf Timmermann	East Germany	22.47 m/73 ft 8¾ in
1992	Mike Stulce	USA	21.70 m/71 ft 2¼ in
1996	Randy Barnes	USA	21.62 m/70 ft 11¼ in
Discus (1896)			
1980	Viktor Rashchupkin	USSR	66.64 m/218 ft 8 in
1984	Rolf Danneburg	West Germany	66.60 m/218 ft 6 in
1988	Jürgen Schult	East Germany	68.82 m/225 ft 9¼ in
1992	Romas Ubartas	Lithuania	65.12 m/213 ft 7¾ in
1996	Lars Reidel	Germany	69.40 m/227 ft 8 in
Hammer (1900)			
1980	Yuri Sedykh	USSR	81.80 m/268 ft 4½ in
1984	Juha Tiainen	Finland	78.08 m/256 ft 2 in
1988	Sergei Litvinov	USSR	84.80 m/278 ft 2½ in
1992	Andrei Abduvaliyev	Unified Team[2]	82.54 m/270 ft 9½ in
1996	Balazs Kiss	Hungary	81.24 m/266 ft 6 in
Javelin (1908)			
1980	Dainis Kula	USSR	91.20 m/299 ft 2⅜ in
1984	Arto Härkonen	Finland	86.76 m/284 ft 8 in
1988	Tapio Korjus	Finland	84.28 m/276 ft 6 in
1992	Jan Zelezny	Czechoslovakia	89.66 m/294 ft 2 in
1996	Jan Zelezny	Czech Republic	88.16 m/289 ft 3 in
Decathlon (1904)			
1980	Daley Thompson	Great Britain	8,495 points
1984	Daley Thompson	Great Britain	8,798 points
1988	Christian Schenk	East Germany	8,488[3] points
1992	Robert Zmelic	Czechoslovakia	8,611 points
1996	Dan O'Brien	USA	8,824 points
4 × 100 m Relay (1912)			
1980		USSR	38.26
1984		USA	37.83
1988		USSR	38.19
1992		USA	37.40
1996		Canada	37.69
4 × 400 m Relay (1908)			
1980		USSR	3:01:10
1984		USA	2:57:91
1988		USA	2:56:16
1992		USA	2:55:16
1996		USA	2:55:74

[1] Run as 2,500 m in 1900, 2,590 m in 1904, and 3,200 m in 1908.
[2] Commonwealth of Independent States plus Georgia.
[3] New points systems were introduced before the 1964 and 1988 Games.

Women's Athletics: Olympic Gold Medallists

The year in which an event was first introduced to the Olympics is in parentheses after the event name.

Year	Name	Country	Result
100 m (1928)			
1980	Lyudmila Kondratyeva	USSR	11.06
1984	Evelyn Ashford	USA	10.97
1988	Florence Griffith-Joyner	USA	10.54
1992	Gail Devers	USA	10.82
1996	Gail Devers	USA	10.94
200 m (1948)			
1980	Bärbel Wöckel[1]	East Germany	22.03
1984	Valerie Brisco-Hooks	USA	21.81
1988	Florence Griffith-Joyner	USA	21.34
1992	Gwen Torrence	USA	21.81
1996	Marie-José Pérec	France	22.12
400 m (1964)			
1980	Marita Koch	East Germany	48.88
1984	Valerie Brisco-Hooks	USA	48.83
1988	Olga Brzygina	USSR	48.65
1992	Marie-José Pérec	France	48.83
1996	Marie-José Pérec	France	48.25
800 m (1928)			
1980	Nadyezda Olizarenko	USSR	1:53.42
1984	Doina Melinte	Romania	1:57.60
1988	Sigrun Wodars	East Germany	1:56.10
1992	Ellen van Langen	Netherlands	1:55.54
1996	Svetlana Masterkova	Russia	1:57.73
1,500 m (1972)			
1980	Tatyana Kazankina	USSR	3:56.60
1984	Gabriella Dorio	Italy	4:03.25
1988	Paula Ivan	Romania	3:53.96
1992	Hassiba Boulmerka	Algeria	3:55.30
1996	Svetlana Masterkova	Russia	4:00.83
3,000 m[2] (1984)			
1984	Maricica Puica	Romania	8:35.96
1988	Tatyana Samolenko	USSR	8:26.53
1992	Yelena Romanova	Unified Team[3]	8:46.04
5,000 m (1996)			
1996	Wang Junxia	China	14:59.88
10,000 m (1988)			
1988	Olga Bondarenko	USSR	31:05.21
1992	Derartu Tulu	Ethiopia	31:06.02
1996	Fernanda Ribeiro	Portugal	31:01.63
Marathon (1984)			
1984	Joan Benoit	USA	2h 24:52
1988	Rosa Mota	Portugal	2h 25:40
1992	Valentina Yegorova	Unified Team[3]	2h 32:41
1996	Fatuma Roba	Ethiopia	2h 26:05
100 m Hurdles (1932)[4]			
1980	Vera Komisova	USSR	12.56
1984	Benita Fitzgerald-Brown	USA	12.84

(*continued*)

Women's Athletics: Olympic Gold Medallists (*continued*)

Year	Name	Country	Result
1988	Yordanka Donkova	Bulgaria	12.38
1992	Paraskevi Patoulidou	Greece	12.64
1996	Lyudmila Engquist	Sweden	12.58
400 m Hurdles (1984)			
1984	Nawal El Moutawakel	Morocco	54.61
1988	Debra Flintoff-King	Australia	53.17
1992	Sally Gunnell	Great Britain	53.23
1996	Deon Hemmings	Jamaica	52.82
10 km Walk (1992)			
1992	Chen Yueling	China	44:32
1996	Yelena Nikolayeva	Russia	41:49
Triple Jump (1996)			
1996	Inessa Kravets	Ukraine	15.33 m/50 ft $3\frac{1}{2}$ in
High Jump (1928)			
1980	Sara Simeoni	Italy	1.97 m/6 ft $5\frac{1}{2}$ in
1984	Ulrike Meyfarth	West Germany	2.02 m/6 ft $7\frac{1}{2}$ in
1988	Louise Ritter	USA	2.03 m/6 ft 8 in
1992	Heike Henkel	Germany	2.02 m/6 ft $7\frac{1}{2}$ in
1996	Stefka Kostadinova	Bulgaria	2.05 m/6 ft $8\frac{3}{4}$ in
Long Jump (1948)			
1980	Tatyana Kolpakova	USSR	7.06 m/23 ft 2 in
1984	Anisoara Stanciu	Romania	6.96 m/22 ft 10 in
1988	Jackie Joyner-Kersee	USA	7.40 m/24 ft $3\frac{1}{2}$ in
1992	Heike Drechsler	Germany	7.14 m/23 ft $5\frac{1}{4}$ in
1996	Chioma Ajunwa	Nigeria	7.12 m/23 ft $4\frac{1}{2}$ in
Shot Put (1948)			
1980	Ilona Slupianek	East Germany	22.41 m/73 ft $6\frac{1}{4}$ in
1984	Claudia Losch	West Germany	20.48 m/67 ft $2\frac{1}{4}$ in
1988	Natalya Lisovskaya	USSR	22.24 m/72 ft $11\frac{1}{2}$ in
1992	Svetlana Krivelyova	Unified Team[3]	21.06 m/69 ft $1\frac{1}{2}$ in
1996	Astrid Kumbernuss	Germany	20.56 m/67 ft $5\frac{1}{2}$ in
Discus (1928)			
1980	Evelin Jahl[5]	East Germany	69.96 m/229 ft 6 in
1984	Ria Stalman	Netherlands	65.36 m/214 ft 5 in
1988	Martina Hellmann	East Germany	72.30 m/237 ft $2\frac{1}{4}$ in
1992	Maritza Marten	Cuba	70.06 m/222 ft 10 in
1996	Ilke Wyludda	Germany	69.66 m/228 ft 6 in
Javelin (1932)			
1980	Maria Colon	Cuba	68.40 m/224 ft 5 in
1984	Tessa Sanderson	Great Britain	69.56 m/228 ft 2 in
1988	Petra Felke	East Germany	74.68 m/245 ft 0 in
1992	Silke Renk	Germany	68.34 m/224 ft $2\frac{1}{2}$ in
1996	Heli Ratanen	Finland	67.94 m/222 ft 11 in
Pentathlon[6] (1964)			
1980	Nadyezda Tkachenko	USSR	5,083 points
Heptathlon (1984)			
1984	Glynis Nunn	Australia	6,390 points
1988	Jackie Joyner-Kersee	USA	7,291 points
1992	Jackie Joyner-Kersee	USA	7,044 points
1996	Ghada Shouaa	Syria	6,780 points
4 × 100 m Relay (1928)			
1980		East Germany	41.60
1984		USA	41.65
1988		USA	41.98
1992		USA	42.11
1996		USA	41.95
4 × 400 m Relay (1972)			
1980		USSR	3:20.20
1984		USA	3:18.29
1988		USSR	2:15.18
1992		Unified Team[3]	3:20.20
1996		USA	3:20.91

[1] Born Eckert.
[2] Replaced by 5,000 metres in 1996.
[3] Commonwealth of Independent States plus Georgia.
[4] 80 m from 1932 to 1968. 100 m since 1972.
[5] Born Schlaak.
[6] Replaced by heptathlon in 1984.

Badminton: Olympic Gold Medallists

1996

Category	Name	Country
Men's singles	Poul-Erik Hoyer-Larsen	Denmark
Men's doubles	Rexy Mainaky and Ricky Subagja	Indonesia
Women's singles	Bang Soo-hyun	Korea, South
Women's doubles	Ge Fei and Gu Jun	China
Mixed doubles	Kim Dong-moon and Gil Young-ah	Korea, South

Baseball: Olympic Medallists

Baseball was introduced as a medal sport in 1992.

Year	Gold	Silver	Bronze
1992	Cuba	Taiwan	Japan
1996	Cuba	Japan	USA

Basketball: Olympic Medallists

Basketball was introduced as a medal sport for men in 1936 and for women in 1976.

Year	Gold	Silver	Bronze
Men			
1980	Yugoslavia	Italy	USSR
1984	USA	Spain	Yugoslavia
1988	USSR	Yugoslavia	USA
1992	USA	Croatia	Lithuania
1996	USA	Yugoslavia	Lithuania
Women			
1980	USSR	Bulgaria	Yugoslavia
1984	USA	Korea, South	China
1988	USA	Yugoslavia	USSR
1992	Unified Team[1]	China	USA
1996	USA	Brazil	Australia

[1] Commonwealth of Independent States plus Georgia.

Beach Volleyball: Olympic Medallists

Beach volleyball was introduced to the Olympics in 1996.

Year	Gold		Silver		Bronze	
	Name	Country	Name	Country	Name	Country
Men						
1996	Karch Kiraly and Kent Steffes	USA	Mike Dodd and Mike Whitmarsh	USA	John Child and Mark Heese	Canada
Women						
1996	Sandra Pires and Jackie Silva	Brazil	Monica Rodrigues and Adriana Samuel	Brazil	Natalie Cook and Kerri Ann Pottharst	Australia

Boxing: Olympic Gold Medallists

1996

Name	Country
Super Heavyweight *(Over 91 kg/201 lb)* Vladimir Klichko	Ukraine
Heavyweight *(Since 1984 up to 91 kg/200.5 lb)* Felix Savon	Cuba
Light Heavyweight *(Since 1952 up to 81 kg/178.5 lb)* Vasili Jirov	Kyrgyzstan
Middleweight *(Since 1952 up to 75 kg/165 lb)* Ariel Hernández	Cuba
Light Middleweight *(Up to 71 kg/157 lb)* David Reid	USA
Welterweight *(Since 1948 up to 67 kg/148 lb)* Oleg Saitov	Russia
Light Welterweight *(Up to 63.5 kg/140 lb)* Hector Vinent	Cuba
Lightweight *(Since 1952 up to 60 kg/132 lb)* Hocine Soltani	Algeria
Featherweight *(Since 1952 up to 57 kg/126 lb)* Somluck Kamsing	Thailand
Bantamweight *(Since 1948 up to 54 kg/119 lb)* István Kovacs	Hungary
Flyweight *(Since 1948 up to 51 kg/112 lb)* Maikro Romero	Cuba
Light Flyweight *(Up to 48 kg/105.8 lb)* Daniel Bojilov	Bulgaria

Canoe/Kayak: Olympic Gold Medallists

1996

Category	Name	Country
Men		
Kayak sprint 500 m singles	Antonio Rossi	Italy
Kayak sprint 1,000 m singles	Knut Holmann	Norway
Kayak sprint 500 m pairs	Kay Bluhm and Torsten Gutsche	Germany
Kayak sprint 1,000 m pairs	Antonio Rossi and Daniele Scarpa	Italy
Kayak sprint 1,000 m fours		Germany
Kayak slalom singles	Oliver Fix	Germany
Canoe sprint 500 m singles	Martin Doktor	Czech Republic
Canoe sprint 1,000 m singles	Martin Doktor	Czech Republic
Canoe sprint 500 m pairs	Csaba Horvath and György Kolonics	Hungary
Canoe sprint 1,000 m pairs	Andreas Dittmer and Gunar Kirchbach	Germany
Canoe slalom singles	Michal Martikan	Slovak Republic
Canoe slalom pairs	Frank Adisson and Wilfrid Forgues	France
Women		
Kayak sprint 500 m singles	Rita Koban	Hungary
Kayak sprint 1,000 m pairs	Angneta Andersson and Susanne Gunnarsson	Sweden
Kayak sprint 1,000 m fours		Germany
Kayak slalom singles	Stepanka Hilgertová	Czech Republic

Cycling: Olympic Gold Medallists

1996

Category	Name	Country
Men		
Road		
Individual road race (225 km)	Pascal Richard	Switzerland
Individual time trial (52 km)	Miguel Indurain	Spain
Track		
1 km time trial	Florian Rousseau	France
Individual match sprint	Jens Fiedler	Germany
4,000 m individual pursuit	Andrea Collinelli	Italy
4,000 m team pursuit	France	
Individual points race (40 km)	Silvio Martinello	Italy
Cross-Country		
Mountain bike (47.7 km)	Bart Jan Brentjens	Netherlands

Category	Name	Country
Women		
Road		
Individual road race (106 km)	Jeannie Longo-Ciprelli	France
Individual time trial (26 km)	Zulfia Zabirova	Russia
Track		
Individual match sprint	Felicia Ballanger	France
3,000 m individual pursuit	Antonella Belluti	Italy
Individual points race (25 km)	Nathalie Even-Lancien	France
Cross-Country		
Mountain bike (32 km)	Paola Pezzo	Italy

Diving: Olympic Gold Medallists

1996

Category	Name	Country	Category	Name	Country
Men			***Women***		
Springboard diving	Ni Xiong	China	Springboard diving	Fu Mingxia	China
Platform diving	Dimitri Sautin	Russia	Platform diving	Fu Mingxia	China

Fencing: Olympic Gold Medallists

Olympic gold medallists automatically become world champions.

1996

Category	Name	Country	Category	Name	Country
Men			***Women***		
Foil	Alessandro Puccini	Italy	Foil	Laura Badea	Romania
Epée	Aleksandr Beketov	Russia	Epée	Laura Flessel	France
Sabre	Stanislav Pozdniakov	Russia	Team foil		Italy
Team foil		Russia	Team epée		France
Team epée		Italy			
Team sabre		Russia			

Gymnastics: Olympic Gold Medallists

1996

Category	Name	Country	Category	Name	Country
Men			***Women***		
Team		Russia	Team		USA
Individual combined exercises	Li Xiaoshuang	China	Individual combined exercises	Lilia Podkopayeva	Ukraine
Floor	Ionnis Melissanidis	Greece	Floor	Lilia Podkopayeva	Ukraine
Pommel	Li Donghua	Switzerland	Vault	Simona Amanar	Romania
Rings	Yuri Chechi	Italy	Asymmetric bars	Svetlana Chorkina	Russia
Vault	Alexei Nemov	Russia	Beam	Shannon Miller	USA
Parallel bars	Rustam Sharipov	Ukraine	Rhythmic Gymnastics		
High bar	Andreas Wecker	Germany	Group		Spain

Men's Gymnastics: Individual Olympic Gold Medallists

Introduced as a medal sport in 1900.

Year	Name	Country
1980	Aleksandr Ditiatin	USSR
1984	Koji Gushiken	Japan
1988	Vladimir Artemov	USSR
1992	Vitali Shcherbo	Unified Team[1]
1996	Li Xiaoshuang	China

[1] Commonwealth of Independent States plus Georgia.

Women's Gymnastics: Individual Olympic Gold Medallists

Introduced as a medal sport in 1952.

Year	Name	Country
1980	Elena Davidova	USSR
1984	Mary Lou Retton	USA
1988	Elena Chouchounova	USSR
1992	Tatiana Gutsu	Unified Team[1]
1996	Lilia Podkopaieva	Ukraine

[1] Commonwealth of Independent States plus Georgia.

Handball: Olympic Gold Medallists

Handball was introduced in 1936 as an 11-a-side outdoor game. It was reintroduced in 1972 as a 7-a-side indoor game. It was first played by women as an Olympic sport in 1976.

Year	Country	Year	Country
Men		***Women***	
1980	East Germany	1980	USSR
1984	Yugoslavia	1984	Yugoslavia
1988	USSR	1988	South Korea
1992	Unified Team[1]	1992	South Korea
1996	Croatia	1996	Denmark

[1] Commonwealth of Independent States plus Georgia.

Hockey: Olympic Medallists

Introduced for men in 1908 and for women in 1980.

Year	Gold	Silver	Bronze
Men			
1980	India	Spain	USSR
1984	Pakistan	West Germany	Great Britain
1988	Great Britain	West Germany	Netherlands
1992	Germany	Australia	Pakistan
1996	Netherlands	Spain	Australia
Women			
1980	Zimbabwe	Czechoslovakia	USSR
1984	Netherlands	West Germany	USA
1988	Australia	South Korea	Netherlands
1992	Spain	Germany	Great Britain
1996	Australia	South Korea	Netherlands

Judo: Olympic Gold Medallists

1996

Category	Name	Country
Men		
60 kg/132 lb	Tadahiro Nomura	Japan
65 kg/143 lb	Udo Quellmalz	Germany
71 kg/157 lb	Kenzo Nakamura	Japan
78 kg/172 lb	Djamel Bouras	France
86 kg/190 lb	Jeon Ki-young	Korea, South
95 kg/209 lb	Pawél Nastula	Poland
>95 kg/>209 lb	David Douillet	France
Women		
48 kg/106 lb	Kye Sun-hi	Korea, North
52 kg/115 lb	Marie-Claire Restoux	France
56 kg/123 lb	Driulis Gonzalez	Cuba
61 kg/134 lb	Yuko Emoto	Japan
66 kg/146 lb	Cho Min-sun	Korea, South
72 kg/159 lb	Ulla Werbrouck	Belgium
>72 kg/>159 lb	Sun Fuming	China

Shooting: Olympic Gold Medallists

1996

Category	Name	Country
Men		
25 m rapid pistol	Ralf Schumann	Germany
50 m free pistol	Boris Kokorev	Russia
10 m air pistol	Roberto di Donna	Italy
10 m air rifle	Artem Khadzhibekov	Russia
50 m free rifle 3 positions	Jean-Pierre Amat	France
50 m free rifle prone	Christian Klees	Germany
10 m running target	Yang Ling	China
Skeet	Ennio Falco	Italy
Trap	Michael Diamond	Australia
Double trap	Russell Mark	Australia
Women		
25 m sport pistol	Li Duihon	China
10 m air pistol	Olga Klochneva	Russia
10 m air rifle	Renata Mauer	Poland
50 m rifle 3 positions	Aleksandra Ivosev	Yugoslavia
Double trap	Kim Rhode	USA

Men's Swimming: Olympic Gold Medallists

1996

Category	Name	Country	Time
50 m freestyle	Aleksandr Popov	Russia	22.13
100 m freestyle	Aleksandr Popov	Russia	48.74
200 m freestyle	Danyon Loader	New Zealand	1:47.63
400 m freestyle	Danyon Loader	New Zealand	3:47.97
1,500 m freestyle	Kieren Perkins	Australia	14:56.40
100 m breaststroke	Fred Deburghgraeve	Belgium	1:00.65
200 m breaststroke	Norbert Rozsa	Hungary	2:12.57
100 m backstroke	Jeff Rouse	USA	54.10
200 m backstroke	Brad Bridgewater	USA	1:58.54
100 m butterfly	Denis Pankratov	Russia	52.27
200 m butterfly	Denis Pankratov	Russia	1:56.51
200 m individual medley	Attila Czene	Hungary	1:59.91
400 m individual medley	Tom Dolan	USA	4:14.90
4 × 100 m freestyle relay		USA	3:15.41
4 × 200 m freestyle relay		USA	7:14.84
4 × 100 m medley relay		USA	3:34.84

Modern Pentathlon: Olympic Gold Medallists

Introduced in 1952.
(– = not applicable.)

Year	Country	Year	Country
1980	USSR	1992	Poland
1984	Italy	1996[1]	–
1988	Hungary		

[1] Event not held in 1996.

Rowing: Olympic Gold Medallists

1996

Category	Name	Country
Men		
Single sculls	Xeno Müller	Switzerland
Double sculls	Davide Tizzano and Agostino Abbagnale	Italy
Lightweight double sculls	Markus Gier and Michael Gier	Switzerland
Quad sculls		Germany
Coxless pairs	Steve Redgrave and Matthew Pinsent	Great Britain
Coxless fours		Australia
Lightweight coxless fours		Denmark
Eights		Netherlands
Women		
Single sculls	Yekaterina Khodotovich	Belarus
Double sculls	Marnie McBean and Kathleen Heddle	Canada
Lightweight double sculls	Constanta Burcica and Camelia Macoviciuc	Romania
Quad sculls		Germany
Coxless pairs	Megan Still and Kathy Slatter	Australia
Eights		Romania

Softball: Olympic Medallists (Women)

Softball was introduced as a medal sport for women in 1996.

Year	Gold	Silver	Bronze
1996	USA	China	Australia

Women's Swimming: Olympic Gold Medallists

1996

Category	Name	Country	Time
50 m freestyle	Amy Van Dyken	USA	24.87
100 m freestyle	Le Jingyi	China	54.50
200 m freestyle	Claudia Poll	Costa Rica	1:58.16
400 m freestyle	Michelle Smith	Ireland, Republic of	4:07.25
800 m freestyle	Brooke Bennett	USA	8:27.89
100 m breaststroke	Penny Heyns	South Africa	1:07.73
200 m breaststroke	Penny Heyns	South Africa	2:25.41
100 m backstroke	Beth Botsford	USA	1:01.19
200 m backstroke	Krisztina Egerszegi	Hungary	2:07.83
100 m butterfly	Amy Van Dyken	USA	59.13
200 m butterfly	Susan O'Neill	Australia	2:07.76
200 m individual medley	Michelle Smith	Ireland, Republic of	2:13.93
400 m individual medley	Michelle Smith	Ireland, Republic of	4:39.29
4 × 100 m freestyle relay		USA	3:39.29
4 × 200 m freestyle relay		USA	7:59.87
4 × 100 m medley relay		USA	4:02.88

Table Tennis: Olympic Gold Medallists

1996

Category	Name	Country
Men		
Singles	Liu Guoliang	China
Doubles	Kong Linghui and Liu Guoliang	China
Women		
Singles	Deng Yaping	China
Doubles	Deng Yaping and Qiao Hong	China

Volleyball: Olympic Medallists

Year	Gold	Silver	Bronze
Men			
1980	USSR	Bulgaria	Romania
1984	USA	Brazil	Italy
1988	USA	USSR	Argentina
1992	Brazil	Netherlands	USA
1996	Netherlands	Italy	Yugoslavia
Women			
1980	USSR	East Gemany	Bulgaria
1984	China	USA	Japan
1988	USSR	Peru	China
1992	Cuba	Unified Team[1]	USA
1996	Cuba	China	Brazil

[1] Commonwealth of Independent States plus Georgia.

Tennis: Olympic Gold Medallists

Tennis was reintroduced as a medal sport in 1988 after an absence of 64 years.

1996

Category	Name	Country
Men		
Singles	Andre Agassi	USA
Doubles	Todd Woodbridge and Mark Woodforde	Australia
Women		
Singles	Lindsay Davenport	USA
Doubles	Gigi Fernandez and Mary Joe Fernandez	USA

Water Polo: Olympic Gold Medallists

Year	Country	Year	Country
1980	USSR	1992	Italy
1984	Yugoslavia	1996	Spain
1988	Yugoslavia		

Weightlifting: Olympic Gold Medallists

1996

Category	Name	Country	Weight
54 kg/119 lb	Halil Mutlu	Turkey	287.5 kg/632.5 lb
59 kg/130 lb	Tang Ningsheng	China	307.5 kg/677.75 lb
64 kg/141 lb	Naim Suleymanoglu	Turkey	335.0 kg/738.50 lb
70 kg/154 lb	Zhan Xugang	China	357.5 kg/786.5 lb
76 kg/168 lb	Pablo Lara	Cuba	367.5 kg/807.5 lb
83 kg/183 lb	Pyrros Dimas	Greece	392.5 kg/863.5 lb
91 kg/201 lb	Aleksei Petrov	Russia	402.5 kg/885.5 lb
99 kg/201 lb	Akakide Kakhiashvilis	Greece	420.0 kg/925.75 lb
108 kg/238 lb	Timor Taimazov	Ukraine	430.0 kg/946 lb
>108 kg/ >238 lb	Andrei Chermerkin	Russia	457.5 kg/1,008 lb

Wrestling: Olympic Gold Medallists

1996

Category	Name	Country
Greco-Roman		
Light flyweight 48 kg/105.8 lb	Sim Kwon Ho	Korea, South
Flyweight 52 kg/114.5 lb	Armen Nazarian	Armenia
Bantamweight 57 kg/125.5 lb	Iuri Melnichenko	Kazakhstan
Featherweight 62 kg/136.5 lb	Włodzimierz Zawadzki	Poland
Lightweight 68 kg/149.5 lb	Ryszard Wolny	Poland
Welterweight 74 kg/163 lb	Feliberto Ascuy Aguilera	Cuba
Middleweight 82 kg/180.5 lb	Hamza Yerlikiya	Turkey
Light heavyweight 90 kg/198 lb	Viacheslav Oleinik	Ukraine
Heavyweight 100 kg/220 lb	Andrzej Wroński	Poland
Super heavyweight 130 kg/286 lb	Aleksandr Karelin	Russia
Freestyle		
Light flyweight 48 kg/105.8 lb	Kim Il	Korea, North
Flyweight 52 kg/114.5 lb	Valentin Jordanov	Bulgaria
Bantamweight 57 kg/125.5 lb	Kendall Cross	USA
Featherweight 62 kg/136.5 lb	Tom Brands	USA
Lightweight 68 kg/149.5 lb	Vadim Bogiev	Russia
Welterweight 74 kg/163 lb	Buvaisa Saitiev	Russia
Middleweight 82 kg/180.5 lb	Khadzhimurad Magomedov	Russia
Light heavyweight 90 kg/198 lb	Rasull Khadem Azghadi	Iran
Heavyweight 100 kg/220 lb	Kurt Angle	USA

Yachting: Olympic Gold Medallists

1996

Category	Name	Country/territory
Open		
Laser	Robert Scheidt	Brazil
Tornado	Jose Luis Ballester and Fernando Leon	Spain
Star	Torben Grael and Marcelo Ferreira	Brazil
Soling		Germany
Men		
Finn	Mateusz Kusznierewicz	Poland
Mistral	Nikolaos Kaklamanakis	Greece
470	Yevhen Braslavets and Iho Matviyenko	Ukraine
Women		
Europe	Kristine Roug	Denmark
Mistral	Lee Lai-Shan	Hong Kong
470	Begona Via Dufresne and Theresa Zabell	Spain

Winter Olympic Games

Winter Olympic Games Venues

Year	Venue
1924	Chamonix, France
1928	St Moritz, Switzerland
1932	Lake Placid, New York, USA
1936	Garmisch-Partenkirchen, Germany
1948	St Moritz, Switzerland
1952	Oslo, Norway
1956	Cortina d'Ampezzo, Italy
1960	Squaw Valley, Colorado, USA
1964	Innsbruck, Austria
1968	Grenoble, France
1972	Sapporo, Japan
1976	Innsbruck, Austria
1980	Lake Placid, New York, USA
1984	Sarajevo, Yugoslavia
1988	Calgary, Alberta, Canada
1992	Albertville, France
1994	Lillehammer, Norway
1998	Nagano, Japan
2002	Salt Lake City, Utah, USA
2006	Turin, Italy

Olympic Alpine Skiing Gold Medallists

1998

Category	Name	Country
Men		
Alpine combination (downhill and slalom)	Mario Reiter	Austria
Downhill	Jean Luc-Crétier	France
Giant slalom	Hermann Maier	Austria
Slalom	Hans-Petter Buraas	Norway
Super giant slalom	Hermann Maier	Austria
Women		
Alpine combination (downhill and slalom)	Katja Seizinger	Germany
Downhill	Katja Seizinger	Germany
Giant slalom	Deborah Compagnoni	Italy
Slalom	Hilde Gerg	Germany
Super giant slalom	Picabo Street	USA

Commonwealth Games

Commonwealth Games Final Medal Table

1998

Country	Gold	Silver	Bronze	Total
Australia	80	61	58	199
England	36	47	53	136
Canada	30	31	38	99
Malaysia	10	14	12	36
South Africa	9	11	14	34
New Zealand	8	7	20	35
India	7	10	8	25
Kenya	7	5	4	16
Jamaica	4	2	0	6
Wales	3	4	8	15
Scotland	3	2	7	12
Nauru	3	0	0	3
Northern Ireland	2	1	2	5
Zimbabwe	2	0	3	5
Ghana	1	1	3	5
Cyprus	1	1	1	3
Mauritius	1	1	1	3
Tanzania	1	1	1	3
Trinidad and Tobago	1	1	1	3
Bahamas	1	1	0	2
Mozambique	1	1	0	2
Barbados	1	0	2	3
Lesotho	1	0	0	1
Cameroon	0	3	3	6
Namibia	0	2	1	3
Seychelles	0	2	0	2
Sri Lanka	0	1	1	2
Bermuda	0	1	0	1
Fiji	0	1	0	1
Isle of Man	0	1	0	1
Pakistan	0	1	0	1
Papua New Guinea	0	0	1	1
Uganda	0	0	1	1
Zambia	0	0	1	1

Commonwealth Games Venues

These games were inaugurated in 1930 as the British Empire Games, became the British Empire and Commonwealth Games in 1954, and the British Commonwealth Games in 1970.

Year	Venue	Year	Venue
1930	Hamilton, Canada	1974	Christchurch, New Zealand
1934	London, England		
1938	Sydney, Australia	1978	Edmonton, Canada
1950	Auckland, New Zealand	1982	Brisbane, Australia
1954	Vancouver, Canada	1986	Edinburgh, Scotland
1958	Cardiff, Wales	1990	Auckland, New Zealand
1962	Perth, Australia	1994	Victoria, Canada
1966	Kingston, Jamaica	1998	Kuala Lumpur, Malaysia
1970	Edinburgh, Scotland	2002	Manchester, England
		2006	Melbourne, Australia

Men's Athletics: Commonwealth Gold Medallists

1998

Event	Winner	Country	Result
100 m	Ato Boldon	Trinidad and Tobago	9.88
200 m	Julian Golding	England	20.18
400 m	Iwan Thomas	Wales	44.52
800 m	Japheth Kimutai	Kenya	1:43.82
1,500 m	Laban Rotich	Kenya	3:39.49
5,000 m	Daniel Komen	Kenya	13:22.57
10,000 m	Simon Maina	Kenya	28:10.00
Marathon	Thabiso Moqhabi	Lesotho	2 h 19:15
110 m hurdles	Tony Jarrett	England	13.47
400 m hurdles	Dinsdale Morgan	Jamaica	48.28
3,000 m steeplechase	John Kosgei	Kenya	8:15.34
20 km walk	Nick A'Hern	Australia	1 h 24:59
50 km walk	Govindasamy Saravanan	Malaysia	4 h 10:05
4 × 100 m relay		England	38.20
4 × 400 m relay		Jamaica	2:59.03
High jump	Dalton Grant	England	2.31 m
Pole vault	Riaan Botha	South Africa	5.60 m
Long jump	Peter Burge	Australia	8.22 m
Triple jump	Onochie Achike	England	17.10 m
Shot put	Burger Lambrechts	South Africa	20.01
Discus	Robert Weir	England	64.42
Hammer	Stuart Rendell	Australia	74.71
Javelin	Marius Corbett	South Africa	88.75
Decathlon	Jagan Hames	Australia	8,490 pts

Boxing: Commonwealth Gold Medallists

1998

Event	Winner	Country
Light flyweight (up to 48kg)	Sapok Biki	Malaysia
Flyweight (up to51kg)	Richard Sunee	Mauritius
Bantamweight (up to 54kg)	Michael Yomba	Tanzania
Featherweight (up to 57kg)	Alex Arthur	Scotland
Lightweight (up to 60kg)	Raymond Nahr	Ghana
Light welterweight (up to 63.5kg)	Michael Strange	Canada
Welterweight (up to 67kg)	Jeremy Molitor	Canada
Light middleweight (up to 71kg)	Chris Bessey	England
Middleweight (up to 75kg)	John Pearce	England
Light heavyweight (up to 81kg)	Courtney Fry	England
Heavyweight (up to 91kg)	Mark Simmons	Canada
Super heavyweight (over 91 kg)	Audley Harrison	England

Women's Athletics: Commonwealth Gold Medallists

1998

Event	Winner	Country	Result
100 m	Chandra Sturrup	Bahamas	11.06
200 m	Nova Peris-Kneebone	Australia	22.77
400 m	Sandie Richards	Jamaica	50.17
800 m	Maria Mutola	Mozambique	1:57.60
1,500 m	Jackline Maranga	Kenya	4:05.27
5,000 m	Kate Anderson	Australia	15:52.74
10,000 m	Esther Wanjiru	Kenya	33:40.13
Marathon	Heather Turland	Australia	2 h 41:24
100 m hurdles	Gillian Russell	Jamaica	12.70
400 m hurdles	Andrea Blackett	Barbados	53.91
10 km walk	Jane Saville	Australia	43:57
4 × 100 m relay		Australia	43.39
4 × 400 m relay		Australia	3:27.28
High jump	Hestrie Storbeck	South Africa	1.91 m
Pole vault	Emma George	Australia	4.20 m
Long jump	Joanne Wise	England	6.63 m
Triple jump	Ashia Hansen	England	14.32 m
Shot put	Judith Oakes	England	18.83 m
Discus	Beatrice Faumuina	New Zealand	65.92 m
Hammer	Deborah Sosimenko	Australia	66.56 m
Javelin	Louise McPaul	Australia	66.96 m
Hepathlon	Denise Lewis	England	6,513 pts

Badminton: Commonwealth Gold Medallists

1998

Event	Winner	Country
Men		
Singles	Wong Choong Hann	Malaysia
Doubles	Lee Wan Wah and Choong Tan Fook	Malaysia
Team		India
Women		
Singles	Kelly Morgan	Wales
Doubles	Joanne Goode and Donna Kellogg	England
Mixed doubles	Simon Archer and Joanne Goode	England
Team		England

Cricket: Commonwealth Medallists

1998

Medal	Country
Gold	South Africa
Silver	Australia
Bronze	New Zealand

Cycling: Commonwealth Gold Medallists

1998

Event	Winner	Country
Men		
Sprint	Darryn Hill	Australia
1,000 m time trial	Shane Kelly	Australia
4,000 m individual pursuit	Bradley McGee	Australia
4,000 m team pursuit		Australia
20 km scratch race	Michael Rogers	Australia
40 km points race	Glen Thompson	New Zealand
42 km road individual time trial	Eric Wohlberg	Canada
184 km road race	Jay Sweet	Australia
Women		
Sprint	Tanya Dubnicoff	Canada
3,000 m individual pursuit	Sarah Ullmer	New Zealand
24 km points race	Alayna Burns	Australia
28 km road individual time trial	Anna Wilson	Australia
92 km road race	Lyne Bessette	Canada

Artistic Gymnastics: Commonwealth Gold Medallists

1998

Event	Winner	Country
Men		
Individual	Andrei Kravtsov	Australia
Floor	Andrei Kravtsov	Australia
Pommel horse	Andrei Kravtsov	Australia
Rings	Pavel Mamine	Australia
Vault	Simon Hutcheon	South Africa
Parallel bars	Andrei Kravtsov	Australia
Horizontal bar	Alexander Jeltkov	Canada
Team		England
Women		
Individual all-around	Zeena McLaughlin	Australia
Floor	Annika Reeder	England
Beam	Trudy McIntosh	Australia
Vault	Lisa Mason	England
Assymetric bars	Lisa Skinner	Australia
Team		Australia

Rhythmic Gymnastics: Commonwealth Gold Medallists

1998

Event	Winner	Country
Individual all-around	Erika-Leigh Stirton	Canada
Hoop	Erika-Leigh Stirton	Canada
Rope	Erika-Leigh Stirton	Canada
Clubs	Erika-Leigh Stirton	Canada
Ribbon	Erika-Leigh Stirton	Canada
Team		Malaysia

Men's Diving: Commonwealth Medallists

1998

Event	Winner	Country
Platform diving	Alexander Despatie	Canada
1 m springboard diving	Evan Stewart	Zimbabwe
3 m springboard diving	Shannon Roy	Australia

Women's Diving: Commonwealth Medallists

1998

Event	Winner	Country
Platform diving	Vyninka Arlow	Australia
1 m springboard diving	Chantelle Michell	Australia
3 m springboard diving	Eryn Bulmer	Canada

Hockey: Commonwealth Medallists

1998

Medal	Country	Medal	Country
Men		***Women***	
Gold	Australia	Gold	Australia
Silver	Malaysia	Silver	England
Bronze	England	Bronze	New Zealand

Lawn Bowls: Commonwealth Medallists

1998

Medal	Country	Medal	Country
Men		***Women***	
Gold	Australia	Gold	Australia
Silver	Malaysia	Silver	England
Bronze	England	Bronze	New Zealand

Netball: Commonwealth Medallists

1998

Medal	Country
Gold	Australia
Silver	New Zealand
Bronze	England

Rugby Sevens: Commonwealth Medallists

Medal	Country
Gold	New Zealand
Silver	Fiji
Bronze	Australia

Shooting: Commonwealth Gold Medallists

1998

Event	Winner	Country
Men		
Air pistol, individual	Michael Gault	England
Air pistol, pairs	Michael Gault and Nick Baxter	England
Air rifle, individual	Chris Hector	England
Air rifle, pairs	Nigel Wallace and Chris Hector	England
Free pistol, individual	Michael Gault	England
Free pistol, pairs	Michael Gault and Nick Baxter	England
Centre-fire pistol, individual	Jaspal Rana	India
Centre-fire pistol, pairs	Ahsok Pandit and Jaspal Rana	India
Rapid-fire pistol, individual	Metodi Igorov	Canada
Rapid-fire pistol, pairs	Patrick Murray and Michelangelo Guistiniano	Australia
Small-bore rifle (prone), individual	John Paton	Canada
Small-bore rifle (prone), pairs	Michael Thiele and Gavin van Rhyn	South Africa
Small-bore rifle (3 positions), individual	Timothy Lowndes	Australia
Small-bore rifle (3 positions), pairs	Wayne Sorensen and Michel Dion	Canada
Trap, individual	Michael Diamond	Australia
Trap, pairs	Mansher Singh and Manavjit Singh	India
Skeet, individual	Desmond Davies	Wales
Skeet, pairs	Antonis Nicolaides and Costis Stratis	Cyprus
Women		
Air pistol, individual	Annemarie Forder	Australia
Air pistol, pairs	Annemarie Forder and Christine Trefy	Australia
Air rifle, individual	Nurul Baharin	Malaysia
Air rifle, pairs	Christina Ashcroft and Sharon Bowes	Canada
Sport pistol, individual	Christine Trefry	Australia
Sport pistol, pairs	Christine Trefry and Annette Woodward	Australia
Sport rifle (prone), individual	Roopa Unikrishnan	India
Sport rifle (prone), pairs	Kim Frazer and Carrie Quigley	Australia
Sport rifle (3 positions), individual	Susan McCready	Australia
Sport rifle (3 positions), pairs	Christina Ashcroft and Sharon Bowes	Canada
Open		
Full-bore rifle, individual	Desmond Davies	Canada
Full-bore rifle, pairs	David Calvert and Martin Millar	Northern Ireland

Squash: Commonwealth Gold Medallists

1998

Event	Winner	Country
Men		
Singles	Peter Nicol	Scotland
Doubles	Paul Johnson and Mark Chaloner	England
Women		
Singles	Michelle Martin	Australia
Doubles	Sue Wright and Cassie Jackman	England
Mixed doubles	Craig Rowland and Michelle Martin	Australia

Men's Swimming: Commonwealth Medallists

1998

Event	Winner	Country	Result
50 m freestyle	Mark Foster	England	22.58
100 m freestyle	Michael Klim	Australia	49.43
200 m freestyle	Ian Thorpe	Australia	1:46.70
400 m freestyle	Ian Thorpe	Australia	3:44.35
1500 m freestyle	Grant Hackett	Australia	14:50.92
100 m breaststroke	Simon Cowley	Australia	1:02.00
200 m breaststroke	Simon Cowley	Australia	2:13.13
100 m backstroke	Mark Versfeld	Canada	55.52
200 m backstroke	Mark Versfeld	Canada	1:59.67
100 m butterfly	Geoff Huegill	Australia	52.81
200 m butterfly	James Hickman	England	1:57.11
200 m individual medley	Matthew Dunn	Australia	2:00.26
400 m individual medley	Trent Steed	Australia	4:19.89
4 × 100 m freestyle relay		Australia	3:17.83
4 × 200 m freestyle relay		Australia	7:11.86
4 × 100 m medley relay		Australia	3:38.52

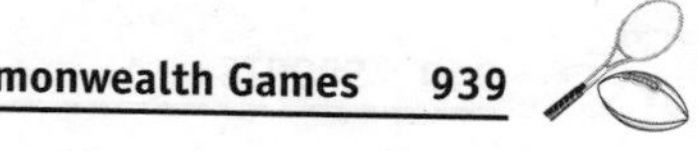

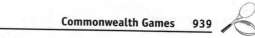

Women's Swimming: Commonwealth Medallists

1998

Event	Winner	Country	Result
50 m freestyle	Susan Rolph	England	25.82
100 m freestyle	Susan Rolph	England	55.17
200 m freestyle	Susie O'Neill	Australia	2:00.24
400 m freestyle	Susie O'Neill	Australia	4:12.56
800 m freestyle	Rachel Harris	Australia	8:42.23
100 m breaststroke	Helen Denman	Australia	1:08.71
200 m breaststroke	Samantha Riley	Australia	2:27.30
100 m backstroke	Giaan Rooney	Australia	1:02.43
200 m backstroke	Katy Sexton	England	2:13.18
100 m butterfly	Petria Thomas	Australia	59.42
200 m butterfly	Susie O'Neill	Australia	2:06.60
200 m individual medley	Marianne Limpert	Australia	2:15.05
400 m individual medley	Joanne Malar	Canada	4:43.74
4 × 100 m freestyle relay		Australia	3:42.61
4 × 200 m freestyle relay		Australia	8:03.73
4 × 100 m medley relay		Australia	4:06.36
Synchronized, solo	Valerie Hould-Marchand	Canada	
Synchronized, duet		Canada	

Ten-Pin Bowling: Commonwealth Medallists

1998

Event	Winner	Country
Men		
Singles	Kenny Ang	Malaysia
Doubles	Kenny Ang and Ben Heng	Malaysia
Women		
Singles	Cara Honeychurch	Australia
Doubles	Cara Honeychurch and Maxine Nable	Australia
Mixed doubles	Frank Ryan and Cara Honeychurch	Australia

Weightlifting: Commonwealth Gold Medallists

1998

Event	Winner	Country
Up to 56kg		
Snatch	Mehmet Yagci	Australia
Clean and jerk	Dharmaraj Wilson	India
Combined	Arumugum Pandian	India
Up to 62 kg		
Snatch	Marcus Stephen	Nauru
Clean and jerk	Marcus Stephen	Nauru
Combined	Marcus Stephen	Nauru
Up to 69 kg		
Snatch	Sebastien Grouix	Canada
Clean and jerk	Muhamad Hamidon	Malaysia
Combined	Sebastien Grouix	Canada
Up to 77 kg		
Snatch	Satheesha Rai	India
Clean and jerk	Damian Brown	Australia
Combined	Damian Brown	Australia
Up to 85 kg		
Snatch	Stephen Ward	England
Clean and jerk	Leon Griffin	England
Combined	Leon Griffin	England
Up to 95 kg		
Snatch	Kiril Kounev	Australia
Clean and jerk	Kiril Kounev	Australia
Combined	Kirl Kounev	Australia
Up to 105 kg		
Snatch	Akos Sandor	Canada
Clean and jerk	Akos Sandor	Canada
Combined	Akos Sandor	Canada
Over 105 kg		
Snatch	Darren Liddel	New Zealand
Clean and jerk	Darren Liddel	New Zealand
Combined	Darren Liddel	New Zealand

American Football

World Bowl Winners

Year	Winners	Losers	Score
1991	London Monarchs	Barcelona Dragons	21–0
1995	Frankfurt Galaxy	Amsterdam Admirals	26–22
1996	Scottish Claymores	Frankfurt Galaxy	32–27
1997	Barcelona Dragons	Rhein Fire	38–24
1999	Frankfurt Galaxy	Barcelona Dragons	38–24

Super Bowl Results

Super Bowl	Year	Result	Venue	Attendance
XIV	1980	Pittsburgh Steelers 31, Los Angeles Rams 19	Pasadena	103,985
XV	1981	Oakland Raiders 27, Philadelphia Eagles 10	New Orleans	76,135
XVI	1982	San Francisco 49ers 26, Cincinnati Bengals 21	Pontiac	81,270
XVII	1983	Washington Redskins 27, Miami Dolphins 17	Pasadena	103,667
XVIII	1984	Los Angeles Raiders 38, Washington Redskins 9	Tampa	72,920
XIX	1985	San Francisco 38, Miami Dolphins 16	Stanford	84,059
XX	1986	Chicago Bears 46, New England Patriots 10	New Orleans	73,818
XXI	1987	New York Giants 39, Denver Broncos 20	Pasadena	101,063
XXII	1988	Washington Redskins 42, Denver Broncos 10	San Diego	73,302
XXIII	1989	San Francisco 49ers 20, Cincinnati Bengals 16	Miami	75,179
XXIV	1990	San Francisco 49ers 55, Denver Broncos 10	New Orleans	72,919
XXV	1991	New York Giants 20, Buffalo Bills 19	Tampa	73,813
XXVI	1992	Washington Redskins 37, Buffalo Bills 24	Minneapolis	63,130
XXVII	1993	Dallas Cowboys 52, Buffalo Bills 17	Pasadena	102,000
XXVIII	1994	Dallas Cowboys 30, Buffalo Bills 13	Atlanta	72,817
XXIX	1995	San Francisco 49ers 49, San Diego 26	Miami	74,107
XXX	1996	Dallas Cowboys 27, Pittsburgh Steelers 17	Tempe (AZ)	76,347
XXXI	1997	Green Bay Packers 35, New England Patriots 21	New Orleans	72,301
XXXII	1998	Denver Broncos 31, Green Bay Packers 24	San Diego	68,912
XXXIII	1999	Denver Broncos 34, Atlanta Falcons 19	Miami	74,803

Angling

World Individual Freshwater Champions

Year	Name	Country
1994	Bob Nudd	England
1995	Paul Jean	France
1996	Alan Scotthorne	England
1997	Alan Scotthorne	England
1998	Alan Scotthorne	England

World Team Freshwater Champions

Year	Country	Year	Country
1989	Wales	1994	England
1990	France	1995	France
1991	England	1996	Italy
1992	Italy	1997	Italy
1993	Italy	1998	England

UK Fishing Records (Selected)

Records are for fish caught on rod and line in waters of England, Scotland, Wales, Northern Ireland, and the Channel Islands. As of April 1999. (drms = drams; 1 ounce = 16 drams.)

Species	Weight					Captor/location	Year
	Imperial			Metric			
	lb	oz	drms	kg	g		
Freshwater Fish							
Coarse Fish							
Bream (Common, Bronze), *Abramis brama*	16	9	0	7	512	M McKeown, Syndicate water, South of England	1991
Carp, *Cyprinus carpio*	56	6	0	25	571	K Cumir, Wraysbury, Berkshire, England	1998
Catifsh (Wels), *Silurus glanis*	62	0	0	28	123	R Garner, Withy Pool, Henlow, Bedfordshire, England	1997
Chub, *Leuciscus cephalus*	8	10	0	3	912	P Smith, River Tees, Blackwell, County Durham, England	1994
Eel, *Anguilla anguilla*	11	2	0	5	046	S Terry, Kingfisher Lake, Near Ringwood, Hampshire, England	1978
Perch, *Perca fluviatilis*	5	9	0	2	523	J Shayler, private lake, Kent, England	1985
Pike, *Esox lucius*	46	13	0	21	234	R Lewis, Llangdegfedd, Wales	1992
Roach, *Rutilus rutilus*	4	3	0	1	899	R N Clarke, Dorset Stour, England	1990
Rudd, *Scardinius erythrophtalmus*	4	8	0	2	041	Reverend E C Alston, Thetford, Norfolk, England	1933
Tench, *Tinca tinca*	14	7	0	6	548	G Beaven, private water, Hertfordshire, England	1993
Game Fish							
Salmon, Atlantic, *Salmo salar* (natural)	64	0	0	29	029	Miss G W Ballatine, River Tay, Scotland	1922
Trout, American Brook (Brook Char), *Salvelinus fontinalis* (cultivated)	6	0	0	2	721	D Caisley, Fontburn Reservoir, Yorkshire, England	1996
Trout, Brown, *Salmo trutta* (natural)	25	2	0	11	396	A Finlay, Loch Awe, Argyllshire, Scotland	1996
Trout, Brown, *Salmo trutta* (cultivated)	21	3	7	9	623	S Collyer, Dever Springs Trout Fishery, Hampshire, England	1993
Trout, Rainbow, *Oncorhynchus mykiss* (cultivated)	36	14	8	16	740	C White, Dever Springs Fishery, Hampshire, England	1995
Trout, Rainbow, *Oncorhynchus mykiss* (resident)	24	1	4	10	921	J Hammond, Hanningfield Reservoir, Essex, England	1998
Trout, Sea, *Salmo trutta* (natural)	28	5	4	12	850	J Farrent, Calshot Spit, River Test, Hants, England	1992
Sea Fish[1]							
Angler Fish, *Lophius piscatorius*	94	12	4	42	985	S M A Neill, Belfast Lough, Northern Ireland	1985
Bass, *Dicentrarchus labrax*	19	9	2	8	876	P McEwan, off Reculvers, Herne Bay, Kent, England	1987
Brill, *Scophthalmus rhombus*	16	0	0	7	257	A H Fisher, Isle of Man	1950
Catfish, *Anarhichas lupus*	26	4	0	11	906	S P Ward, 5 miles out from Whitby, Yorkshire, England	1989
Cod, *Gadus morhua*	58	6	0	26	478	N Cook, North Sea off Whitby, North Yorkshire, England	1992
Conger, *Conger conger*	112	8	0	51	030	N Basil, wreck off Dartmouth, South Devon; also D Mash, from wreck, South East Plymouth, Devon, England	1992
Dab, *Limanda limanda*	2	12	4	1	254	R Islip, Gairloch, Wester Ross, Scotland	1975
Haddock, *Melanogrammus aeglefinus*	13	11	4	6	215	G Bones, off Falmouth, Cornwall	1978
Hake, *Merluccius merluccius*	25	12	14	11	706	R Roberts, Loch Etive, Scotland	1997
Halibut, *Hippoglossus hippoglossus*	234	0	0	106	136	C Booth, Dunnet Head, off Scrabster, Scotland	1979
Herring, *Clupea harengus*	1	1	0	0	481	B Barden, off Bexhill-on-Sea, Sussex, England	1973
John Dory (St Peter's Fish), *Zeus faber*	11	14	0	5	386	J Johnson, off Newhaven, East Sussex, England	1977
Ling, *Molva molva*	59	8	0	26	987	J Webster, off Bridlington, Yorkshire, England	1989
Mackerel, *Scomber scombrus*	6	2	7	2	790	W J Chapple, 1.5 miles off Penberth Cove, Cornwall, England	1984
Monkfish, *Squatina squatina*	66	0	0	29	936	C G Chalk, Shoreham, Sussex, England	1965
Mullet, Red, *Mullus surmuletus*	3	15	0	1	786	A Wright, Longy Bay, Alderney, Channel Islands	1996
Ray, Electric, *Torpedo nobiliana*	96	1	0	43	571	N J Cowley, off Dodman Point, Cornwall, England	1975
Ray, Sting, *Dasyatis pastinaca*	72	2	0	32	715	P Burgess, River Blackwater, Essex, England	1996
Shark, Blue, *Prionace glauca*	218	0	0	98	878	N Sutcliffe, Looe, Cornwall, England	1959
Shark, Mako, *Isurus oxyrinchus*	500	0	0	226	786	Mrs J M Yallop, off Eddystone Lighthouse, English Channel	1971
Shark, Porbeagle, *Lamna nasus*	507	0	0	230	0	C Bennett, Dunnet Head, Scotland	1993
Shark, Thresher, *Alopias vulpinus*	323	0	0	146	504	S Mills, 6 miles south Nab Tower, off Portsmouth, Hampshire, England	1982
Skate, Common, *Raja batis*	227	0	0	102	961	R Banks, 8 miles off Tobermory, Inner Hebrides, Scotland	1986
Sole, *Solea solea*	4	1	12	2	119	M Eppelein, Great Bank, off Channel Islands	1993

[1] Sea fish records are boat-caught unless otherwise stated.

Source: British Record Fish Committee

Australian Football

Australian Football League Champions

Year	Team	Year	Team	Year	Team	Year	Team
1980	Richmond	1985	Essendon	1990	Collingwood	1995	Carlton Blues
1981	Carlton	1986	Hawthorn	1991	Hawthorn	1996	North Melbourne
1982	Carlton	1987	Carlton	1992	West Coast	1997	Adelaide
1983	Hawthorn	1988	Hawthorn	1993	Essendon	1998	Adelaide
1984	Essendon	1989	Hawthorn	1994	West Coast		

Athletics

Men's Outdoor Athletics World Records

As of 30 June 1999.

Category	Record	Name(s)	Country	Date	Location
100 m	9.79[1]	Maurice Greene	USA	16 June 1999	Athens, Greece
200 m	19.32	Michael Johnson	USA	1 August 1996	Atlanta (GA), USA
400 m	43.29	Butch Reynolds	USA	17 August 1988	Zurich, Switzerland
800 m	1:41.11	Wilson Kipketer	Denmark	24 August 1997	Cologne, Germany
1,000 m	2:12.18	Sebastian Coe	Great Britain	11 July 1981	Oslo, Norway
1,500 m	3:26.00	Hicham El Guerrouj	Morocco	17 July 1998	Rome, Italy
Mile	3:43.13[1]	Hicham El Guerrouj	Morocco	7 July 1999	Rome, Italy
2,000 m	4:47.88	Noureddine Morceli	Algeria	3 July 1995	Paris, France
3,000 m	7:20.67	Daniel Komen	Kenya	1 September 1996	Rieti, Italy
5,000 m	12:39.36	Haile Gebrselassie	Ethiopia	13 June 1998	Helsinki, Finland
10,000 m	26:22.75	Haile Gebrselassie	Ethiopia	1 June 1998	Hengelo, Netherlands
20,000 m	56:55.60	Arturo Barrios	Mexico	30 March 1991	La Flèche, France
25,000 m	1h 13:55.80	Toshihiko Seko	Japan	22 March 1981	Christchurch, New Zealand
3,000 m steeplechase	7:55.72	Bernard Barmasai	Kenya	24 August 1997	Cologne, Germany
Half marathon	59:17[2]	Paul Tergat	Kenya	4 April 1998	Milan, Italy
Marathon	2h 6:05[2]	Ronaldo da Costa	Brazil	20 September 1998	Berlin, Germany
110 m hurdles	12.91	Colin Jackson	Great Britain	20 August 1993	Stuttgart, Germany
400 m hurdles	46.78	Kevin Young	USA	6 August 1992	Barcelona, Spain
4 × 100m relay	37.40	Marsh, Burrell, Mitchell, Lewis	USA	8 August 1992	Barcelona, Spain
		Drummond, Cason, Mitchell, Burrell	USA	21 August 1993	Stuttgart, Germany
4 × 200 m relay	1:18.68	Marsh, Burrell, Heard, Lewis	USA	17 April 1994	Walnut (CA), USA
4 × 400 m relay	2:54.29	Valmon, Watts, Reynolds, Johnson	USA	22 August 1993	Stuttgart, Germany
4 × 800 m relay	7:03.89	Elliott, Cook, Cram, Coe	Great Britain	30 August 1982	London, UK
High jump	2.45 m/8 ft $\frac{1}{2}$ in	Javier Sotomayor	Cuba	27 July 1993	Salamanca, Spain
Long jump	8.95 m/29 ft $4\frac{1}{2}$ in	Mike Powell	USA	30 August 1991	Tokyo, Japan
Triple jump	18.29 m/60 ft $\frac{1}{4}$ in	Jonathan Edwards	Great Britain	7 August 1995	Gothenburg, Sweden
Pole vault	6.14 m/20 ft $1\frac{3}{4}$ in	Sergei Bubka	Ukraine	31 July 1994	Sestriere, Italy
Shot put	23.12 m/75 ft $10\frac{1}{4}$ in	Randy Barnes	USA	20 May 1990	Los Angeles (CA), USA
Discus	74.08 m/243 ft	Jürgen Schult	East Germany	6 June 1986	Neubrandenburg, Germany
Javelin	98.48 m/323 ft 1 in	Ján Zelezny	Czech Republic	25 May 1996	Jena, Germany
Hammer	86.74 m/284 ft 7 in	Yuri Sedykh	USSR	30 August 1986	Stuttgart, Germany
Decathlon	8,894 pts[1]	Tomas Dvorak	Czech Republic	4 July 1999	Prague, Czech Republic
20 km walk	1h 17:25.6	Bernardo Segura	Mexico	7 May 1994	Bergen, Norway
30 km walk	2h 01:44.1	Maurizio Damilano	Italy	3 October 1992	Cuneo, Italy
50 km walk	3h 40:57.9	Thierry Toutain	France	29 September 1996	Héricourt, France

[1] Awaiting ratification.
[2] World best performance.

Women's Outdoor Athletics World Records

As of 20 March 1999.

Category	Record	Name	Country	Date	Location
100 m	10.49	Florence Griffith-Joyner	USA	16 July 1988	Indianapolis (IN), USA
200 m	21.34	Florence Griffith-Joyner	USA	29 September 1988	Seoul, South Korea
400 m	47.60	Marita Koch	East Germany	6 October 1985	Canberra, Australia
800 m	1:53.28	Jarmila Kratochvílová	Czechoslovakia	26 July 1983	Munich, West Germany
1,000 m	2:28.98	Svetlana Masterkova	Russia	23 August 1996	Brussels, Belgium
1,500 m	3:50.46	Qu Yunxia	China	11 September 1993	Beijing, China
Mile	4:12.56	Svetlana Masterkova	Russia	14 August 1996	Zurich, Switzerland
2,000 m	5:25.36	Sonia O'Sullivan	Ireland, Republic of	9 July 1994	Edinburgh, UK
3,000 m	8:06.11	Wang Junxia	China	13 September 1993	Beijing, China
5,000 m	14:28.09	Jiang Bo	China	23 October 1997	Shanghai, China
10,000 m	29:31.78	Wang Junxia	China	8 September 1993	Beijing, China
Half marathon	1h 06:43[1]	Masako Chika	Japan	19 April 1997	Tokyo, Japan
Marathon	2h 20:47.00[2]	Tegla Loroupe	Ethiopia	19 April 1998	Rotterdam, Netherlands
100 m hurdles	12.21	Yordanka Donkova	Bulgaria	21 August 1988	Bulgaria
400 m hurdles	52.61	Kim Batten	USA	11 August 1995	Gothenburg, Sweden
4 × 100 m relay	41.37	Gladisch, Rieger, Auerswald, Göhr	East Germany	6 October 1985	Canberra, Australia
4 × 200 m relay	1:28.15	Göhr, Müller, Wöckel, Koch	East Germany	9 August 1980	Jena, East Germany
4 × 400 m relay	3:15.17	Ledovskaya, Nazarova, Pinigina, Bryzgina	USSR	1 October 1988	Seoul, South Korea
4 × 800 m relay	7:50.17	Olizarenko, Gurina, Borisova, Podyalovskaya	USSR	5 August 1984	Moscow, Russia
High jump	2.09 m/6 ft 10¼ in	Stefka Kostadinova	Bulgaria	30 August 1987	Rome, Italy
Long jump	7.52 m/24 ft 8¼ in	Galina Chistyakova	USSR	11 June 1988	Leningrad, Russia
Triple jump	15.50 m/50 ft 10¼ in	Inessa Kravets	Ukraine	10 August 1995	Gothenburg, Sweden
Pole vault	4.60 m/15 ft 1 in[1]	Emma George	Australia	20 February 1999	Sydney, Australia
Shot put	22.64 m/74 ft 3 in	Natalya Lisovskaya	USSR	7 June 1987	Moscow, Russia
Discus	76.80 m/252 ft	Gabriele Reinsch	East Germany	9 July 1988	Neubrandenburg, East Germany
Hammer	73.14 m/239 ft 11 in	Michaela Melinte	Romania	16 July 1998	Poiana Brasov, Romania
Javelin	80.00 m/262 ft 5 in	Petra Felke	East Germany	9 September 1988	Potsdam, Germany
Heptathlon	7,291 pts	Jackie Joyner-Kersee	USA	23–24 September 1988	Seoul, South Korea
5 km walk	20:13.26	Kerry Saxby-Junna	Australia	25 February 1996	Hobart, Australia
10 km walk	41:56.23	Nadezhda Ryashkina	USSR	24 July 1990	Seattle (WA), USA

[1] World best performance.

[2] Awaiting ratification.

Men's Athletics: European Championships Gold Medallists

First held in 1934. The 1998 championships were held in Budapest, Hungary, 18–23 August.

1998

Event	Winner	Country	Result
100 m	Darren Campbell	Great Britain	10.04
200 m	Doug Walker	Great Britain	20.53
400 m	Iwan Thomas	Great Britain	44.52
800 m	Nils Schumann	Germany	1:44.89
1,500 m	Reyes Estevez	Spain	3:41.31
5,000 m	Isaac Viciosa	Spain	13:37.46
10,000 m	Antonio Pinto	Portugal	27:48.62
Marathon	Stefano Baldini	Italy	2 h 12:01
110 m hurdles	Colin Jackson	Great Britain	13.02
400 m hurdles	Pawel Januszewski	Poland	48.17
3,000 m steeplechase	Damian Kallabis	Germany	8:13.10
20 km walk	Ilya Markov	Russia	1 h 21:10
50 km walk	Robert Korzeniowski	Poland	3 h 43:51
4 × 100 m relay		Great Britain	38.52
4 × 400 m relay		Great Britain	2:58.68
High jump	Artur Partyka	Poland	2.34 m
Pole vault	Maksim Tarasov	Russia	5.81 m
Long jump	Kiril Sosunov	Russia	8.28 m
Triple jump	Jonathan Edwards	Great Britain	17.99 m
Shot put	Aleksandr Bagach	Ukraine	21.17 m
Discus	Lars Riedel	Germany	67.07 m
Hammer	Tibor Gecsek	Hungary	82.87 m
Javelin	Steve Backley	Great Britain	89.72 m
Decathlon	Erki Nool	Estonia	8,667 points

Women's Athletics: European Championships Gold Medallists

First held in 1938. The 1998 championships were held in Budapest, Hungary, 18–23 August.

1998

Event	Winner	Country	Result
100 m	Christine Arron	France	10.73
200 m	Irina Privalova	Russia	22.62
400 m	Grit Breuer	Germany	49.93
800 m	Yelena Afanasyeva	Russia	1:58.50
1,500 m	Svetlana Masterkova	Russia	4:11.91
5,000 m	Sonia O'Sullivan	Ireland	15:06.50
10,000 m	Sonia O'Sullivan	Ireland	31:29.33
Marathon	Manuela Machado	Portugal	2 h 27:10
100 m hurdles	Svetla Dimitrova	Bulgaria	12.56
400 m hurdles	Ionela Tirlea	Romania	53.37
10 km walk	Annarita Sidoti	Italy	42:49
4 × 100 m relay		France	42.59
4 × 400 m relay		Germany	3:23.03
High jump	Monica Iagar-Dinesco	Romania	1.97 m
Pole vault	Anzhela Balakhonova	Ukraine	4.31 m
Long jump	Heike Drechsler	Germany	7.16 m
Triple jump	Olga Vasdeki	Greece	14.55 m
Shot put	Vita Pavlysh	Ukraine	21.69 m
Discus	Franka Dietzsch	Germany	67.49 m
Hammer	Michaela Melinte	Romania	71.17 m
Javelin	Tanja Damaske	Germany	69.10 m
Heptathlon	Denise Lewis	Great Britain	6,559 points

International Amateur Athletic Federation (IAAF) World Indoor Championships, Gold Medallists

First held in 1985. Staged every two years. The 1999 championships were held in Maebashi, Japan.

1999

Category	Name	Country	Result
Men			
60 m	Maurice Greene	USA	6.42
200 m	Frankie Fredericks	Namibia	20.10
400 m	Jamie Baulch	Great Britain	45.73
800 m	Johan Botha	South Africa	1:45.47
1,500 m	Haile Gebrselassie	Ethiopia	3:33.77
3,000 m	Haile Gebrselassie	Ethiopia	7:53.57
60 m hurdles	Colin Jackson	Great Britain	7.38
4 × 400 m relay		USA	3:02.83[1]
High jump	Javier Sotomayor	Cuba	2.36 m/7ft 9 in
Pole vault	Jean Galfione	France	6.00 m/19 ft 8 in
Long jump	Iván Pedroso	Cuba	8.62 m/28 ft 3 in
Triple jump	Charles Michael Friedek	Germany	17.18 m/56 ft 4 in
Shot put	Aleksandr Bagach	Ukraine	21.41 m/70 ft 3 in
Heptathlon	Sebastian Chmara	Poland	6,386 points
Women			
60 m	Ekaterini Thanou	Greece	6.96
200 m	Ionela Tirlea	Romania	22.39
400 m	Grit Breuer	Germany	50.80
800 m	Ludmila Formanova	Czech Republic	1:56.90
1,500 m	Gabriela Szabo	Romania	4:03.23
3,000 m	Gabriela Szabo	Romania	8:36.42
60 m hurdles	Olga Shishigina	Kazakhstan	7.86
4 × 400 m relay		Russia	3:24.25[1]
High jump	Khristina Kalcheva	Bulgaria	1.99 m/6 ft 6 in
Pole vault	Nastja Ryshich	Germany	4.50 m/14 ft 9 in
Long jump	Tatyana Kotova	Russia	6.86 m/22 ft 6 in
Triple jump	Ashia Hansen	Great Britain	15.02 m/49 ft 3 in
Shot put	Vita Pavlysh	Ukraine	21.43 m/70 ft 4 in
Pentathlon	Le Shundra Nathan	USA	4,753 points

[1] New world record.

International Amateur Athletic Federation (IAAF) World Cross-Country Championships

This championship is run over 12 km. In 1998 a new short course race run over 4 km was introduced.

Year	Name	Country
Men's Individual		
1995	Paul Tergat	Kenya
1996	Paul Tergat	Kenya
1997	Paul Tergat	Kenya
1998[1]	Paul Tergat	Kenya
1998[2]	John Kibowen	Kenya
1999[1]	Paul Tergat	Kenya
1999[2]	Benjamin Limo	Kenya
Women's Individual		
1995	Derartu Tulu	Ethiopia
1996	Gete Wami	Ethiopia
1997	Derartu Tulu	Ethiopia
1998[1]	Sonia O'Sullivan	Ireland, Republic of
1998[2]	Sonia O'Sullivan	Ireland, Republic of
1999[1]	Jackline Maranga	Kenya
1999[2]	Gete Wami	Ethiopia
Men's Team		
1995		Kenya
1996		Kenya
1997		Kenya
1998[1]		Kenya
1998[2]		Kenya
1999[1]		Kenya
1999[2]		Kenya
Women's Team		
1995		Kenya
1996		Kenya
1997		Kenya
1998[1]		Kenya
1998[2]		Morocco
1999[1]		France
1999[2]		Ethiopia

[1] Long course.
[2] Short course.

London Marathon Winners

This event was first held in 1981, it is now sponsored by Flora.

Year	Name	Country	Time
Men			
1995	Dionicio Ceron	Mexico	2h 8:30
1996	Dionicio Ceron	Mexico	2h 10:00
1997	Antonio Pinto	Portugal	2h 7:55
1998	Abel Anton	Spain	2h 7:57
1999	Abdelkader El Mouaziz	Morocco	2h 7:57
Women			
1995	Małgorzata Sobańska	Poland	2h 27:43
1996	Liz McColgan	Great Britain	2h 27:54
1997	Joyce Chepchumba	Kenya	2h 25:51
1998	Catherina McKiernan	Ireland, Republic of	2h 26:26
1999	Joyce Chepchumba	Kenya	2h 23:22

Badminton

Yonex All-England Badminton Championships

These championships were first held in 1899. The 1999 championships were held at Birmingham, 9–14 March.

1999

Event	Name	Country
Mixed doubles	Simon Archer/Jo Goode	England
Men		
Singles	Peter Gade Christensen	Denmark
Doubles	Tony Gunawan/Candra Wijaya	Indonesia
Women		
Singles	Ye Zhaoying	China
Doubles	Chung Jae-Hee/Ra Kyung-Min	Korea, South

World Badminton Championships

The Thomas and Uber Cups were last held in 1998 (even years). The other events were last held in 1997 (odd years).

Event	Name	Country
1998 Team Championships		
Thomas Cup (men's)		Indonesia
Uber Cup (women's)		China
1999 World Championships		
Men's singles	Sun Jun	China
Women's singles	Camilla Martin	Denmark
Men's doubles	Kim Dong-Moon/Ha Tae-Kwon	Korea, South
Women's doubles	Ge Fei/Gu Yun	China
Mixed doubles	Kim Dong-Moon/Ra Kyung-Min	Korea, South

Baseball

World Series

Since 1993. (AL = American League; NL = National League.)

Year	Winner	Loser	Score
1993	Toronto Blue Jays, AL	Philadelphia Phillies, NL	4–2
1994	no World Series[1]		
1995	Atlanta Braves, NL	Cleveland Indians, AL	4–2
1996	New York Yankees, AL	Atlanta Braves, NL	4–2
1997	Florida Marlins, NL	Cleveland Indians, AL	4–3
1998	New York Yankees, AL	San Diego Padres, NL	4–0

[1] Owing to a players' strike.

Basketball

World Champions

The world championship was first held in 1950 for men and 1953 for women. It is contested every four years.

Men

Year	Country	Year	Country
1963	Brazil	1982	USSR
1967	USSR	1986	USA
1970	Yugoslavia	1990	Yugoslavia
1974	USSR	1994	USA
1978	Yugoslavia	1998	Yugoslavia

Women

Year	Country	Year	Country
1964	USSR	1983	USSR
1967	USSR	1986	USA
1971	USSR	1990	USA
1975	USSR	1994	Brazil
1979	USA	1998	USA

British Basketball Champions (Men)

1998–99

Event	Champions/result
Budweiser League	Sheffield Sharks
Budweiser League Championship final	London Towers 82 Thames Valley Tigers 71
Uniball Trophy final	Manchester Giants 90 Derby Storm 69
National Cup final	Sheffield Sharks 67 Greater London Leopards 65
National Basketball League Division One	Solent Stars
National Basketball League Division One Championship final	Plymouth Raiders 76 Teesside Mohawks 66
National Basketball League Division Two	Birmingham Bullets B
National Trophy final	Teesside Mohawks 66 Plymouth Raiders 65
Scottish League	Glasgow Sports Division
Scottish Cup	St Mirren 70 Edinburgh 62

British Basketball Champions (Women)

1998–99

Event	Champions/result
National Basketball League Division One	Sheffield Hatters
National Basketball League Division One Championship final	Sheffield Hatters 63 Thames Valley Lady Tigers 60
National Basketball League Division Two	Plymouth Ladies
National Cup	Sheffield Hatters 75 Birmingham Quality Cats 47
Scottish League	Polonia Phoenix
Scottish Cup	Glasgow Sports Division 69 Dalkeith Saints 66

British Basketball: The Budweiser League Final Table

1998–99

Position	Team	Played	Won	Lost	Points
1	Sheffield Sharks[1 2]	36	31	5	62
2	Manchester Giants[1]	36	30	6	60
3	Thames Valley Tigers[1]	36	24	12	48
4	London Towers[1]	36	22	14	44
5	Newcastle Eagles[1]	36	21	15	42
6	Derby Storm[1]	36	21	15	42
7	Birmingham Bullets[1]	36	21	15	42
8	Great London Leopards[1]	36	19	17	38
9	Edinburgh Rocks	36	12	24	24
10	Milton Keynes Lions	36	10	26	20
11	Chester Jets	36	10	26	20
12	Leicester Riders	36	9	27	18
13	Worthing Bears	36	4	32	8

[1] Qualified for Budweiser Championships.
[2] League champions.

British Basketball: The Budweiser League Play-Off Results

The top eight teams in the Budweiser League qualify for the Championships.

1999

Winner	Loser	Score
Quarter Finals Series Results (best of three)		
Manchester Giants	Birmingham Bullets	2–1
Sheffield Sharks	Greater London Leopards	2–1
London Towers	Newcastle Eagles	2–1
Thames Valley Tigers	Derby Storm	2–0
Semi Finals		
London Towers	Sheffield Sharks	85–78
Thames Valley Tigers	Manchester Giants	79–76
Third Place Play-Off		
Sheffield Sharks	Manchester Giants	98–88
Final		
London Towers	Thames Valley Tigers	82–71

National Basketball Association Champions (USA)

The National Basketball Association (NBA) Championship has been held since 1947.

Year	Winner	Runner up	Series
1980	Los Angeles Lakers	Philadelphia 76ers	4–2
1981	Boston Celtics	Houston Rockets	4–2
1982	Los Angeles Lakers	Philadelphia 76ers	4–2
1983	Philadelphia 76ers	Los Angeles Lakers	4–0
1984	Boston Celtics	Los Angeles Lakers	4–3
1985	Los Angeles Lakers	Boston Celtics	4–2
1986	Boston Celtics	Houston Rockets	4–2
1987	Los Angeles Lakers	Boston Celtics	4–2
1988	Los Angeles Lakers	Detroit Pistons	4–3
1989	Detroit Pistons	Los Angeles Lakers	4–0
1990	Detroit Pistons	Portland Trail Blazers	4–1
1991	Chicago Bulls	Los Angeles Lakers	4–1
1992	Chicago Bulls	Portland Trail Blazers	4–2
1993	Chicago Bulls	Phoenix Suns	4–2
1994	Houston Rockets	New York Knicks	4–3
1995	Houston Rockets	Orlando Magic	4–0
1996	Chicago Bulls	Seattle SuperSonics	4–2
1997	Chicago Bulls	Utah Jazz	4–2
1998	Chicago Bulls	Utah Jazz	4–2
1999	San Antonio Spurs	New York Knicks	4–1

Billiards

World Professional Billiards Championship

The championship was instituted in 1870 on a challenge basis and restored as an annual tournament in 1980.

Year	Name	Country
1993	Geet Sethi	India
1994	Peter Gilchrist	England
1995	Geet Sethi	India
1996	Mike Russell	England
1997	not held	
1998	Geet Sethi	India

Bowls

World Outdoor Bowls Championship

The championship was first held in 1966 for men and in 1969 for women.

Year	Name	Country
Men		
1980	David Bryant	England
1984	Peter Belliss	New Zealand
1988	David Bryant	England
1992	Tony Allcock	England
1996	Tony Allcock	England
Women		
1981	Norma Shaw	England
1985	Merle Richardson	Australia
1988	Janet Ackland	Wales
1992	Margaret Johnston	Ireland, Republic of
1996	Carmelita Anderson	Norfolk Island

World Indoor Bowls Championship

The championship was first held in 1979 for men and in 1988 for women.

Year	Name	Country
Men		
1995	Andy Thomson	England
1996	David Gourlay Jr	Scotland
1997	Hugh Duff	Scotland
1998	Paul Foster	Scotland
1999	Alex Marshall	Scotland
Women		
1995	Joyce Lindores	Scotland
1996	Sandy Hazell	England
1997	Norma Shaw	England
1998	Caroline McAllister	Scotland
1999	Caroline McAllister	Scotland

Boxing

Sanctioning Bodies in World Boxing

The major sanctioning bodies in world boxing are:

World Boxing Association (WBA) formed as the National Boxing Association (NBA) in the USA in 1920; it changed its name to WBA in 1962

World Boxing Council (WBC) formed in Mexico City in 1963

International Boxing Federation (IBF) formed as a breakaway from the WBA in 1983

The World Boxing Organization (WBO) founded in 1988

Current World Professional Boxing Champions

World Boxing Association (WBA)

Heavyweight (>86.2 kg/>190 lb)	Evander Holyfield (USA)
Cruiserweight (86.2 kg/190 lb)	Fabrice Tiozzo (France)
Light heavyweight (79.4 kg/175 lb)	Roy Jones Jr (USA)
Super middleweight (76.2 kg/168 lb)	Byron Mitchell (USA)
Middleweight (72.6 kg/160 lb)	William Joppy (USA)
Super welterweight (69.9 kg/154 lb)	David Reid (USA)
Welterweight (66.7 kg/147 lb)	James Page (USA)
Junior welterweight (63.5 kg/140 lb)	Sharmba Mitchell (USA)
Lightweight (61.2 kg/135 lb)	Julien Lorcy (France)
Junior lightweight (59 kg/130 lb)	Takanori Hatekeyama (Japan)
Featherweight (57.2 kg/126 lb)	Freddie Norwood (USA)
Junior featherweight (55.3 kg/122 lb)	Nestor Garza (Mexico)
Bantamweight (53.5 kg/118 lb)	Johnny Tapia (USA)
Junior bantamweight (52.2 kg/115 lb)	Jesus Rojas (Venezuela)
Flyweight (50.8 kg/112 lb)	Leo Gamez (Venezuela)
Junior flyweight (49 kg/108 lb)	Pichitnoi Choi Siriwat (Thailand)
Strawweight (47.6 kg/105 lb)	Ricardo Lopez (Mexico)

World Boxing Council (WBC)

Heavyweight (>86.2 kg/>190 lb)	Lennox Lewis (UK)
Cruiserweight (86.2 kg/190 lb)	Juan Carlos Gomez (Cuba)
Light heavyweight (79.4 kg/175 lb)	Roy Jones Jr (USA)
Super middleweight (76.2 kg/168 lb)	Richie Woodhall (UK)
Middleweight (72.6 kg/160 lb)	Keith Holmes (USA)
Super welterweight (69.9 kg/154 lb)	Javier Castillejo (Spain)
Welterweight (66.7 kg/147 lb)	Oscar De La Hoya (USA)
Junior welterweight (63.5 kg/140 lb)	Kostya Tszyu (Russia)
Lightweight (61.2 kg/135 lb)	Steve Johnston (USA)
Junior lightweight (59 kg/130 lb)	Floyd Mayweather (USA)
Featherweight (57.2 kg/126 lb)	Cesar Soto (Mexico)
Junior featherweight (55.3 kg/122 lb)	Erik Morales (Mexico)
Bantamweight (53.5 kg/118 lb)	Veeraphol Sahaprom (Thailand)
Junior bantamweight (52.2 kg/115 lb)	Injoo Choo (South Korea)
Flyweight (50.8 kg/112 lb)	Manny Pacquiao (Philippines)
Junior flyweight (49 kg/108 lb)	Saman Sorjaturong (Thailand)
Strawweight (47.6 kg/105 lb)	Ricardo Lopez (Mexico)

International Boxing Federation (IBF)

Heavyweight (>86.2 kg/>190 lb)	Evander Holyfield (USA)
Cruiserweight (86.2 kg/190 lb)	Vassily Jirov (Kazakhstan)
Light heavyweight (79.4 kg/175 lb)	Roy Jones Jr. (USA)
Super middleweight (76.2 kg/168 lb)	Sven Ottke (Germany)
Middleweight (72.6 kg /160 lb)	Bernard Hopkins (USA)
Super welterweight (69.9 kg/154 lb)	Fernando Vargas (USA)
Welterweight (66.7 kg/147 lb)	Felix Trinidad (Puerto Rico)
Junior welterweight (63.5 kg/140 lb)	Terronn Millett (USA)
Lightweight (61.2 kg/135 lb)	vacant
Junior lightweight (59 kg/130 lb)	Roberto Garcia (USA)
Featherweight (57.2 kg/126 lb)	Manuel Medina (Mexico)
Junior featherweight (55.3 kg/122 lb)	Lehlohonolo Ledwaba (South Africa)
Bantamweight (53.5 kg/118 lb)	Tim Austin (USA)
Junior bantamweight (52.2 kg/115 lb)	Mark Johnson (USA)
Flyweight (50.8 kg/112 lb)	Irene Pacheco (Venezuela)
Junior flyweight (49 kg/108 lb)	Will Grigsby (USA)
Strawweight (47.6 kg/105 lb)	Zolani Petelo (South Africa)

World Boxing Organization (WBO)

Heavyweight (>86.2 kg/>190 lb)	Vitali Klitschko (Ukraine)
Cruiserweight (86.2 kg/190 lb)	Johnny Nelson (UK)
Light heavyweight (79.4 kg/175 lb)	Darius Michalczewski (Germany)
Super middleweight (76.2 kg/168 lb)	Joe Calzaghe (UK)
Middleweight (72.6 kg/160 lb)	Bert Schenk (Germany)
Super welterweight (69.9 kg/154 lb)	Harry Simon (Namibia)
Welterweight (66.7 kg/147 lb)	Ahmed Kotiev (Russia)
Junior welterweight (63.5 kg/140 lb)	Randall Bailey (USA)
Lightweight (61.2 kg/135 lb)	Artur Grigorian (Germany)
Junior lightweight (59 kg/130 lb)	Anatoly Alexandrov (Kazakhstan)
Featherweight (57.2 kg/126 lb)	Naseem Hamed (UK)
Junior featherweight (55.3 kg/122 lb)	Marco Antonio Barrera (Mexico)
Bantamweight (53.5 kg/118 lb)	Eliecer Julio (Colombia)
Junior bantamweight (52.2 kg/115 lb)	Victor Godoi (Argentina)
Flyweight (50.8 kg/112 lb)	Jose Lopez Bueno (Spain)
Junior flyweight (49 kg/108 lb)	Jorge Arce (Mexico)
Strawweight (47.6 kg/105 lb)	Kermin Guardia (Colombia)

World Heavyweight Champions

Present weight limit: over 86.2 kg/190 lb. Fighters are US nationals unless otherwise stated.

Year	Name
Champions 1882–1978	
1882–92	John L Sullivan[1]
1892–97	James J Corbett
1897–99	Bob Fitzsimmons (UK)
1899–1904	James J Jeffries[2]
1905–06	Marvin Hart
1906–08	Tommy Burns (Canada)
1908–15	Jack Johnson
1915–19	Jess Willard
1919–26	Jack Dempsey
1926–28	Gene Tunney[2]
1928–30	vacant
1930–32	Max Schmeling (Germany)
1932–33	Jack Sharkey
1933–34	Primo Carnera (Italy)
1934–35	Max Baer
1935–37	James J Braddock
1937–49	Joe Louis[2]
1949–51	Ezzard Charles
1951–52	Jersey Joe Walcott
1952–56	Rocky Marciano[2]
1956–59	Floyd Patterson
1959–60	Ingemar Johansson (Sweden)
1960–62	Floyd Patterson
1962–64	Sonny Liston
1964–67	Cassius Clay (Muhammad Ali)[2 3]
1965–67	Ernie Terrell (WBA title)[4]
1968–70	Joe Frazier (New York title)
1968–70	Jimmy Ellis (WBA title)
1970–73	Joe Frazier
1973–74	George Foreman
1974–78	Muhammad Ali
1978	Leon Spinks[5]
WBA Champions (Since 1978)	
1978	Leon Spinks
1978–79	Muhammad Ali[2]
1979–80	John Tate
1980–82	Mike Weaver
1982–83	Michael Dokes
1983–84	Gerrie Coetzee (South Africa)
1984–85	Greg Page
1985–86	Tony Tubbs
1986	Tim Witherspoon
1986–87	James 'Bonecrusher' Smith
1987–90	Mike Tyson (& WBC, IBF)
1990	James 'Buster' Douglas (& WBC, IBF)
1990–92	Evander Holyfield (& WBC, IBF)
1992–93	Riddick Bowe (& IBF, WBC)[6]
1993–94	Evander Holyfield (& IBF)
1994	Michael Moorer (& IBF)
1994–95	George Foreman (& IBF)[2]
1995–96	Bruce Seldon
1996	Mike Tyson
1996–	Evander Holyfield (& IBF)
WBC Champions (Since 1978)	
1978	Ken Norton
1978–83	Larry Holmes[7]
1984	Tim Witherspoon
1984–86	Pinklon Thomas
1986	Trevor Berbick (Canada)
1986–90	Mike Tyson (& WBA, IBF 1987–90)
1990	James 'Buster' Douglas (& WBA, IBF)
1990–92	Evander Holyfield (& WBA, IBF)
1992	Riddick Bowe (& IBF, WBC)[6]
1992–94	Lennox Lewis (UK)
1994–95	Oliver McCall
1995–96	Frank Bruno (UK)
1996	Mike Tyson[2]
1997–	Lennox Lewis (UK)
IBF Champions (Since 1983)	
1983–85	Larry Holmes
1985–87	Michael Spinks[2]
1987	Tony Tucker
1987–90	Mike Tyson (& WBA, WBC)
1990	James 'Buster' Douglas (& WBA, WBC)
1990–92	Evander Holyfield (& WBA, WBC)
1992–93	Riddick Bowe (& IBF, WBC)[6]
1993–94	Evander Holyfield (& WBA)
1994	Michael Moorer (& WBA)
1994–95	George Foreman (& WBA)[2]
1996	Michael Moorer
1997–	Evander Holyfield (& WBA)

[1] Sullivan was the last of the bareknuckle world champions.
[2] Relinquished or stripped of title, or retired as champion.
[3] Clay changed his name to Muhammad Ali after becoming world champion.
[4] The WBA withdrew recognition of Ali after he signed for a return match with Liston in 1964. Ernie Terrell won the vacant WBA title in 1965. However, Ali remained the widely accepted champion and two years later defeated Terrell to regain the undisputed title.
[5] Spinks was stripped of his WBC title in March 1978 and remained WBA champion until losing to Ali in September 1978.
[6] Bowe relinquished his WBC title in December 1992.
[7] Holmes relinquished his WBC title in December 1983 to become the newly formed IBF's first champion.

Current British Professional Boxing Champions

As of 1 June 1999.

Weight	Name
Heavyweight (over 86.2 kg/190 lb)	Julius Francis
Cruiserweight (limit 86.2 kg/190 lb)	vacant
Light heavyweight (limit 79.4 kg/175 lb)	Clinton Woods
Super middleweight (limit 76.2 kg/168 lb)	David Starie
Middleweight (limit 72.6 kg/160 lb)	Howard Eastman
Light middleweight (limit 69.9 kg/154 lb)	Ensley Bingham
Welterweight (limit 66.7 kg/147 lb)	Derek Roche
Light welterweight (limit 63.5 kg/140 lb)	Jason Rowland
Lightweight (limit 61.2 kg/135 lb)	Bobby Vanzie
Super featherweight (limit 59 kg/130 lb)	Charles Shepherd
Featherweight (limit 57.2 kg/126 lb)	Jon Jo Irwin
Super bantamweight (limit 55.3 kg/122 lb)	Drew Docherty
Bantamweight (limit 53.5 kg/118 lb)	Paul Lloyd
Flyweight (limit 50.8 kg/112 lb)	Keith Knox

Chess

World Chess Champions

The first recognized world chess championship-title match took place in 1886 between Wilhelm Steinitz and Johannes Zuckertort. However, the winner of that match, Steinitz, had been widely regarded as the world champion since 1866. The Fédération Internationale de Échecs (FIDE) took over control of the world championship in 1948 and remained the sole governing body until 1993, when the breakaway Professional Chess Association (PCA), led by the world champion Garry Kasparov, organized a rival championship, which Kasparov himself won. Since then there have been two world champions, Kasparov and Anatoly Karpov, who, after Kasparov had been stripped of his title, won a play-off for the FIDE title. However, it is Kasparov who is widely regarded as the true world champion.

Dates	Name	Country
1866–94	Wilhelm Steinitz	Austria
1894–21	Emanuel Lasker	Germany
1921–27	José Raul Capablanca	Cuba
1927–35	Alexander Alekhine	Russia[1]
1935–37	Max Euwe	Netherlands
1937–46	Alexander Alekhine	Russia[1]
1948–56	Mikhail Botvinnik	USSR[2]
1957–58	Vassily Smyslov	USSR
1958–60	Mikhail Botvinnik	USSR
1960–61	Mikhail Tal	USSR
1961–63	Mikhail Botvinnik	USSR
1963–69	Tigran Petrosian	USSR
1969–72	Boris Spassky	USSR
1972–75	Bobby Fischer	USA
1975–85	Anatoly Karpov	USSR
1985–	Garry Kasparov	USSR/Azerbaijan[3 4]
1993–	Anatoly Karpov	Russia[5]

[1] Alekhine became a French citizen in 1927.
[2] Botvinnik won a five-man tournament organized by FIDE to determine a successor to Alekhine, who had died in 1946.
[3] Kasparov is an Azerbaijani but has represented Russia internationally at chess.
[4] FIDE world champion 1985–93; PCA world champion since 1993.
[5] FIDE world champion.

Cricket

1999 Cricket World Cup

World Cup Group A Final Table

1999

Team	Played	Won	Lost	Tied	No result	Run rate	Points
South Africa[1]	5	4	1	0	0	+0.86	8
India[1]	5	3	2	0	0	+1.28	6
Zimbabwe[1]	5	3	2	0	0	+0.02	6
England	5	3	2	0	0	–0.33	6
Sri Lanka	5	2	3	0	0	–0.81	4
Kenya	5	0	5	0	0	–1.20	0

[1] Qualified for the Super Six stage.

World Cup Group B Final Table

1999

Team	Played	Won	Lost	Tied	No result	Run rate	Points
Pakistan[1]	5	4	1	0	0	+0.53	8
Australia[1]	5	3	2	0	0	+0.73	6
New Zealand[1]	5	3	2	0	0	+0.58	6
West Indies	5	3	2	0	0	+0.50	6
Bangladesh	5	2	3	0	0	–0.54	4
Scotland	5	0	5	0	0	–1.93	0

[1] Qualified for the Super Six Stage.

World Cup Group A Results

1999

Date	Location	Result
14 May	Lord's	England (207) defeated Sri Lanka (204) by 8 wickets
15 May	Hove	South Africa (254–6) defeated India (253–5) by 4 wickets
15 May	Taunton	Zimbabwe (231–5) defeated Kenya (229–7) by 5 wickets
18 May	Canterbury	England (204–1) defeated Kenya (203) by 9 wickets
19 May	Northampton	South Africa (199–9) defeated Sri Lanka (110) by 89 runs
19 May	Leicester	Zimbabwe (252–9) defeated India (249) by 3 runs
22 May	The Oval	South Africa (225–7) defeated England (103) by 122 runs
22 May	Worcester	Sri Lanka (198–6) defeated Zimbabwe (197–9) by 4 wickets
23 May	Bristol	India (329–2) defeated Kenya (235–7) by 94 runs
25 May	Nottingham	England (168–3) defeated Zimbabwe (167–8) by 7 wickets
26 May	Taunton	India (373–6) defeated Sri Lanka (216) by 157 runs
26 May	Amstelveen	South Africa (153–3) defeated Kenya (152) by 7 wickets
29 May	Chelmsford	Zimbabwe (233–6) defeated South Africa (185) by 48 runs
29–30 May	Birmingham	India (232–8) defeated England (169) by 63 runs
30 May	Southampton	Sri Lanka (275–6) defeated Kenya (230–6) by 45 runs

The Cricket World Cup 1999

BY BEN RAMOS

The seventh cricket World Cup was won by Australia who defeated Pakistan by eight wickets in the final at Lord's on 20 June. In doing so Australia became only the second side after the West Indies to win the event twice, having previously won it in 1987. Pakistan, after winning the toss, were bowled out for 132 in just 39 overs. A revitalized Shane Warne, with figures of 4–33 was Pakistan's chief tormentor. In reply, Australia needed only 20.1 of the allotted 50 overs to pass Pakistan's total. If the match was an anti-climax for the 30,000 crowd, and for the estimated worldwide television audience of 500 million, it was hard not to admire the ruthless professionalism of Steve Waugh's team. Tough and uncompromising, Australia were clearly determined to avoid a repeat of the last World Cup final in 1995 when they were humbled by Sri Lanka, and, from the moment Australia's fast bowler Glenn McGrath broke through in the fifth over to when Darren Lehmann hit the winning runs, they did not loosen their grip on the match. But if Australia were worthy winners, Pakistan did not deserve to suffer such a humiliating defeat. Their richly talented team, ably captained by Wasim Akram, and their exuberant supporters had done much to give credibility to the World Cup's billing as a 'Carnival of Cricket'.

Finals of major tournaments have a tendency to fall short of expectations, and this was always likely to be the case in this one after the magnificent semi-final between Australia and South Africa at Edgbaston on 17 June, a contest described by Steve Waugh as the best game of cricket he had ever played in. A match of pulsating excitement and brilliant cricket ended in high farce when Allan Donald, South Africa's last man, was run-out on the fourth ball of the final over after a mix-up with Lance Klusener, when needing only one run for victory. The tied result meant that Australia progressed to the final by virtue of their win over South Africa in the Super Six round (another match South Africa should have won). That it was Klusener who should have called the fateful run was the game's final dramatic twist. The tournament's outstanding player, he had brought South Africa to the brink of victory with 31 runs from only 16 deliveries. It would have been of little consolation to him when he was later named player of the series.

Until that match there had been a sense of disappointment that only three of the 39 matches played had had close finishes. But while the dramatic Edgbaston semi-final is likely to monopolize many people's memories of the 1999 World Cup it would be wrong to say that the tournament lacked excitement or atmosphere. It is doubtful whether more noise has been generated by a crowd at a cricket match in England than during India's contest with Pakistan at Old Trafford. Already the fiercest rivals in world cricket, the teams played against the background of growing political and military tension between the two countries over disputed territory in Kashmir. And there were some notable giant-killing acts, such as Bangladesh's 62-run defeat of Pakistan at Northampton. Other moments which will remain long in the memory include Steve Waugh's match-winning 120 not out in the Super Six match against South Africa. And there was Rahul Dravid and Saurav Ganguly's mammoth 318 partnership for India against Sri Lanka at Taunton, a record stand for any wicket in a One-Day International.

England, the tournament hosts, were eliminated at the first group stage, a failure which cost Alec Stewart the England captaincy. It had been thought that with home advantage England had a good chance of winning the World Cup for the first time, however, the team's limp performances merely re-emphasized England's eclipse as a force in world cricket.

Ben Ramos is a freelance writer

World Cup Group B Results

1999

Date	Venue	Result
16 May	Worcester	Australia (182–4) defeated Scotland (181–7) by 6 wickets
16 May	Bristol	Pakistan (229–8) defeated West Indies (202) by 27 runs
17 May	Chelmsford	New Zealand (117–4) defeated Bangladesh (116) by 6 wickets
20 May	Cardiff	New Zealand (214–5) defeated Australia (213) by 5 wickets
20 May	Chester-le-Street	Pakistan (261–6) defeated Scotland (167) by 94 runs
21 May	Dublin	West Indies (183–3) defeated Bangladesh (182) by 7 wickets
23 May	Leeds	Pakistan (275–8) defeated Australia (265) by 10 runs
24 May	Edinburgh	Bangladesh (185–9) defeated Scotland (163) by 22 runs
24 May	Southampton	West Indies (158–3) defeated New Zealand (156) by 7 wickets
27 May	Leicester	West Indies (70–2) defeated Scotland (68) by 8 wickets
27 May	Chester-le-Street	Australia (181–3) defeated Bangladesh (178–7) by 7 wickets
28 May	Derby	Pakistan (269–8) defeated New Zealand (208–8) by 61 runs
30 May	Manchester	Australia (111–4) defeated West Indies (110) by 6 wickets
31 May	Edinburgh	New Zealand (123–4) defeated Scotland (121) by 6 wickets

World Cup Super Six Results

1999

Date	Venue	Result
4 June	The Oval	Australia (282–6) defeated India (205) by 77 runs
5 June	Nottingham	South Africa (221–7) defeated Pakistan (220–7) by 3 wickets
6–7 June	Leeds	New Zealand (70–3) versus Zimbabwe (175) no result
8 June	Manchester	India (227–6) defeated Pakistan (180) by 47 runs
9 June	Lord's	Australia (303–4) defeated Zimbabwe (259–6) by 44 runs
10 June	Birmingham	South Africa (287–5) defeated New Zealand (213–8) by 74 runs
11 June	The Oval	Pakistan (271–9) defeated Zimbabwe (123) by 148 runs
12 June	Nottingham	New Zealand (253–5) defeated India (251–6) by 5 wickets
13 June	Leeds	Australia (272–5) defeated South Africa (271–7) by 5 wickets

World Cup Super Six Final Table

1999

Team	Played	Won	Lost	Tied	No result	Run rate	Points
Pakistan	5	3	2	0	0	+0.65	6
Australia	5	3	2	0	0	+0.36	6
South Africa	5	3	2	0	0	+0.17	6
New Zealand	5	2	2	0	1	–0.52	5
Zimbabwe	5	2	2	0	1	–0.79	5
India	5	1	4	0	0	–0.15	2

World Cup Semi Finals

1999

Date	Venue	Result
16 June	Manchester	Pakistan (242–1) defeated New Zealand (241–7) by 9 wickets
17 June	Birmingham	Australia (213) tied with South Africa[1] (213)

[1] Australia go through to the final by virtue of their victory over South Africa in the Super Six stage.

World Cup Final

The World Cup Final was held at Lord's on 20 June 1999. Pakistan won the toss and elected to bat. The Umpires were David Shepherd (England) and Steve Bucknor (West Indies). **Result** Australia won by 8 wickets; **Man of the Match** Shane Warne (Australia); **Man of the Series** Lance Klusener (South Africa)
(– = not applicable.)

1999

Pakistan		**Runs**
Saeed Anwar	b Fleming	15
Wajahatullah Wasti	c M Waugh b McGrath	1
Abdul Razzaq	c S Waugh b Moody	17
Ijaz Ahmed	b Warne	22
Inzamam-ul-Haq	c Gilchrist b Reiffel	15
Moin Khan[1]	c Gilchrist b Warne	6
Shahid Afridi	lbw b Warne	13
Azhar Mahmood	c and b Moody	8
Wasim Akram[2]	c S Waugh b Warne	8
Saqlain Mushtaq	c Ponting b McGrath	0
Shoaib Akhtar	not out	2
Extras (leg byes: 10; wides: 13; no balls: 2)		25
Total	all out, 39 overs	132
Fall of wickets	1–21, 2–21, 3–68, 4–77, 5–91, 6–104, 7–113, 8–129, 9–129, 10–132	
Bowling	McGrath 9–3–13–2; Fleming 6–0–30–1; Reiffel 10–1–29–1; Moody 5–0–17–2; Warne 9–1–33–4	

Australia		**Runs**
Mark Waugh	not out	37
Adam Gilchrist[1]	c Inzamam-ul-Haq b Saqlain Mushtaq	54
Ricky Ponting	c Moin Khan b Wasim Akram	24
Darren Lehmann	not out	13
Steve Waugh[2]	did not bat	–
Michael Bevan	did not bat	–
Tom Moody	did not bat	–
Shane Warne	did not bat	–
Paul Reiffel	did not bat	–
Damien Fleming	did not bat	–
Glenn McGrath	did not bat	–
Extras (leg byes: 1; wides: 1; no balls: 3)		5
Total	2 wickets, 20.1 overs	133
Fall of wickets	1–75, 2–112	
Bowling	Wasim Akram: 8–1–41–1; Shoaib Akhtar: 4–0–37–0; Abdul Razzaq: 2–0–13–0; Azhar Mahmood: 2–0–20–0; Saqlain Mushtaq: 4.1–0–21–1	

[1] Wicket-keeper.
[2] Captain.

World Cup Leading Averages

1999

Batting

Player (country)	**Matches**	**Innings**	**Not outs**	**Runs**	**Highest score**	**Average**
Lance Klusener (South Africa)	9	8	6	281	52 not out	140.50
Tom Moody (Australia)	7	5	4	117	56 not out	117.00
Ridley Jacobs (West Indies)	5	4	2	205	80 not out	102.50
Steve Waugh (Australia)	10	8	3	398	120 not out	79.60
Roger Twose (New Zealand)	9	9	5	318	80 not out	79.50
Minhajul Abedin (Bangladesh)	4	4	2	140	68 not out	70.00
Shivnarine Chanderpaul (West Indies)	5	4	2	134	77	67.00
Rahul Dravid (India)	8	8	1	461	145	65.85
Nasser Hussain (England)	5	5	2	194	88 not out	64.66
Gavin Hamilton (Scotland)	5	5	1	217	76	54.25

Bowling[1]	**Matches**	**Overs**	**Maidens**	**Runs**	**Wickets**	**Best bowling**	**Average**
Courtney Walsh (West Indies)	5	47	8	108	11	4–25	9.81
Reon King (West Indies)	5	31.3	4	95	8	3–30	11.87
Curtly Ambrose (West Indies)	4	40	5	94	7	3–31	13.42
Geoff Allott (New Zealand)	9	87.4	7	325	20	4–37	16.25
Darren Gough (England)	5	48.4	4	192	11	4–34	17.45
Mervyn Dillon (West Indies)	4	36.5	2	140	8	4–46	17.50
Alan Mullally (England)	5	50	6	176	10	4–37	17.60
Shane Warne (Australia)	10	94.2	13	361	20	4–29	18.05
Mark Ealham (England)	5	50	5	191	10	2–28	19.10
Robin Singh (India)	6	32.3	1	153	8	5–31	19.12

[1] Qualification 30 overs.

World Cup Winners

This competition was first held in 1975.

Year	Winner	Runner-up	Location
1975	West Indies	Australia	England
1979	West Indies	England	England
1983	India	West Indies	England
1987	Australia	England	India
1992	Pakistan	England	Australia
1996	Sri Lanka	Australia	India, Pakistan, and Sri Lanka
1999	Australia	Pakistan	UK

World Cup Highs

1999

High	Score	Match/player
Highest team score	373–6	India versus Sri Lanka
Lowest team score	68	Scotland versus West Indies
Highest individual score	183	Saurav Ganguly (India) versus Sri Lanka
Best partnership	318	Saurav Ganguly and Rahul Dravid (India) versus Sri Lanka
Best bowling	5–14	Glenn McGrath (Australia) versus West Indies
Leading run maker	461	Rahul Dravid (India)
Leading wicket takers	20	Geoff Allott (New Zealand) and Shane Warne (Australia)

Test Cricket

England versus Australia: 1998–99 Test Series Results

Australia won the five-match Test series 3–1 to retain the Ashes.

First Test
Brisbane, 20–24 November 1998
Match drawn. Australia 485 (Healy 134, S Waugh 112; Mullally 5–105) and 237 for 3 declared (Slater 113), England 375 (Butcher 116; McGrath 6–85).

Second Test
Perth, 28–30 November, 1998
Australia won by 7 wickets. England 112 (Fleming 5–46) and 191 (Gillespie 5–88), Australia 240 and 64–3.

Third Test
Adelaide, 11–15 December, 1998
Australia won by 205 runs. Australia 392 (Langer 179 not out) and 278–5 declared (Slater 103), England 227 and 237.

Fourth Test
Melbourne, 26–29 December, 1998
England won by 12 runs. England 270 (Stewart 107) and 244, Australia 340 (S Waugh 122 not out; Gough 5–96) and 162 (Headley 6–60).

Fifth Test
Sydney, 2–5 January 1999
Australia won by 98 runs. Australia 322 (M Waugh 121) and 184 (Slater 123; Such 5–81), England 220 (MacGill 5–57) and 188 (MacGill 7–50).

England versus New Zealand: 1999 Test Series Results

First Test
Edgbaston, 1–3 July 1999
England won by 7 wickets. New Zealand 226 (Parore 73) and 107 (Caddick 5–32), England 126 and 211/3 (Tudor 99).

Second Test
Lord's, 22–25 July 1999
New Zealand won by 9 wickets. England 186 (Hussain 61; Cairns 6–77) and 229, New Zealand 358 (Horne 100) and 60/1.

Third Test
Old Trafford, 5–9 August 1999
Match drawn. England 199 (Ramprakash 69 not out) and 181/2, New Zealand 496/9 declared (McMillan 107 not out, Astle 101).

Test Cricket: Team-by-Team Summary of Results

As of 1 May 1999.
(– = not applicable.)

Team	Tests	Won	Lost	Drawn	Tied
Australia	593	250	167	174	2
England	757	255	218	284	–
South Africa	233	64	90	79	–
West Indies	352	134	91	126	1
New Zealand	267	40	109	118	–
India	325	60	107	157	1
Pakistan	258	74	59	125	–
Sri Lanka	90	14	38	38	–
Zimbabwe	33	3	15	15	–

Test Cricket: England Record

As of 1 May 1999.

Opponent	Tests	Won	Lost	Drawn
Australia	296	93	117	86
India	84	32	14	38
New Zealand	78	36	4	38
Pakistan	55	14	9	32
South Africa	115	49	21	45
Sri Lanka	6	3	2	1
West Indies	121	28	51	42
Zimbabwe	2	0	0	2
Total	757	255	218	284

Test Cricket: Highest Individual Innings, Batting

As of 8 January 1999.

Score	Batsman (team)	Opponents	Venue	Season
375	Brian Lara[1] (West Indies)	England	St John's	1993–94
365[2]	Gary Sobers (West Indies)	Pakistan	Kingston	1957–58
364	Len Hutton (England)	Australia	The Oval	1938
340	Sanath Jayasuriya[1] (Sri Lanka)	India	Colombo	1997–98
337	Hanif Mohammad (Pakistan)	West Indies	Bridgetown	1957–58
336[2]	Walter Hammond (England)	New Zealand	Auckland	1932–33
334[2]	Mark Taylor (Australia)	Pakistan	Peshawar	1998–99
334	Don Bradman (Australia)	England	Headingley	1930
333	Graham Gooch (England)	India	Lord's	1990
325	Andrew Sandham (England)	West Indies	Kingston	1929–30

[1] Current player.

[2] Not out.

Test Cricket: Most Wickets in an Innings, Bowling

As of 20 June 1999.

Best bowling	Bowler (team)	Opponents	Venue	Season
10–53	Jim Laker (England)	Australia	Manchester	1956
10–74	Anil Kumble[1] (India)	Pakistan	Delhi	1998–99
9–28	George Lohmann (England)	South Africa	Johannesburg	1895–96
9–37	Jim Laker (England)	Australia	Manchester	1956
9–52	Richard Hadlee (New Zealand)	Australia	Brisbane	1985–86
9–56	Abdul Qadir (Pakistan)	England	Lahore	1987–88
9–57	Devon Malcolm[1] (England)	South Africa	The Oval	1994
9–65	Muttiah Muralitharan[1] (Sri Lanka)	England	The Oval	1998
9–69	Jasubhai Patel (India)	Australia	Kanpur	1959–60
9–83	Kapil Dev (India)	West Indies	Ahmedabad	1983–84
9–86	Sarfraz Nawaz (Pakistan)	Australia	Melbourne	1978–79

[1] Current player.

Test Cricket: Leading Career Run Makers

As of 20 June 1999.

Batsman	Team	Tests	Innings	Not out	Runs	Average
Allan Border	Australia	156	265	44	11,174	50.56
Sunil Gavaskar	India	125	214	16	10,122	51.12
Graham Gooch	England	118	215	6	8,900	42.58
Javed Miandad	Pakistan	124	189	21	8,832	52.57
Viv Richards	West Indies	121	182	12	8,540	50.23
David Gower	England	117	204	18	8,231	44.25
Geoff Boycott	England	108	193	23	8,114	47.72
Gary Sobers	West Indies	93	160	21	8,032	57.78
Colin Cowdrey	England	114	188	15	7,624	44.06
Steve Waugh[1]	Australia	115	185	35	7,622	50.81
Gordon Greenidge	West Indies	108	185	16	7,558	44.72
Mark Taylor	Australia	104	186	13	7,525	43.49
Clive Lloyd	West Indies	110	175	14	7,515	46.67

[1] Current player.

Test Cricket: Leading Career Wicket Takers

As of 20 June 1999.

Bowler	Team	Tests	Wickets	Runs	Average
Kapil Dev	India	131	434	12,867	29.64
Richard Hadlee	New Zealand	86	431	9,612	22.30
Courtney Walsh[1]	West Indies	110	423	9,612	25.11
Ian Botham	England	102	383	10,878	28.40
Wasim Akram[1]	Pakistan	88	378	8,574	22.68
Malcolm Marshall	West Indies	81	376	7,876	20.94
Curtly Ambrose[1]	West Indies	88	369	7,865	21.31
Imran Khan	Pakistan	88	362	8,258	22.81
Dennis Lillee	Australia	70	355	8,493	23.92
Bob Willis	England	90	325	8,190	25.20
Shane Warne[1]	Australia	71	317	8,134	25.65
Lance Gibbs	West Indies	79	309	8,989	29.09

[1] Current player.

One-Day Internationals

One-Day Internationals: Leading Career Run Makers

As of 22 June 1999.

Name	Matches	Innings	Not outs	Runs	Highest score	Average
Mohammad Azharuddin (India)[1]	323	297	53	9,110	153 not out	37.33
Desmond Haynes (West Indies)	238	237	28	8,648	152 not out	41.37
Aravinda de Silva (Sri Lanka)[1]	259	252	25	8,093	145	35.65
Sachin Tendulkar (India)[1]	218	211	21	8,054	143	42.38
Arjuna Ranatunga (Sri Lanka)[1]	269	255	47	7,454	131 not out	35.83
Javed Miandad (Pakistan)	233	218	41	7,381	119 not out	41.70
Saleem Malik (Pakistan)[1]	283	256	38	7,169	102	32.88
Viv Richards (West Indies)	187	167	24	6,721	189 not out	47.00
Mark Waugh (Australia)[1]	191	186	14	6,636	130	38.58
Saeed Anwar (Pakistan)[1]	180	178	15	6,540	194	40.12

[1] Current player.

One-Day Internationals: Leading Career Wicket Takers

Bowler	Matches	Overs	Wickets	Runs	Average
Wasim Akram (Pakistan)[1]	275	2,357.3	386	9,057	23.46
Waqar Younis (Pakistan)[1]	173	1,435	285	6,581	23.09
Kapil Dev (India)	225	1,867	253	6,945	25.30
Javagal Srinath (India)[1]	232	1,474.1	232	6,431	27.71
Anil Kumble (Inida)[1]	174	1,570.3	232	6,449	27.79
Curtly Ambrose (West Indies)[1]	165	1,470.5	220	5,210	23.68
Courtney Walsh (West Indies)[1]	193	1,699.3	217	6,526	30.07
Allan Donald (South Africa)[1]	121	1,073	206	4,336	21.04
Saqlain Mushtaq (Pakistan)[1]	108	939.5	204	4,012	24.71
Craig McDermott (Australia)	138	1,243.3	203	5,018	24.71

[1] Current player.

County Cricket

Britannic Assurance County Championship Final Table

The previous year's positions are shown in brackets.

1998

Position	Team	Played	Won	Lost	Drawn	Bonus points[1] Batting[2]	Bonus points[1] Bowling[3]	Points
1	Leicestershire (10)	17	11	0	6	47	51	292
2	Lancashire (11)	17	11	1	5	30	56	277
3	Yorkshire (6)	17	9	3	5	47	63	269
4	Gloucestershire (7)	17	11	5	1	23	65	267
5	Surrey (8)	17	10	5	2	38	57	261
6	Hampshire (14)	17	6	5	6	27	61	202
7	Sussex (14)	17	6	7	4	30	63	201
8	Warwickshire (4)	17	6	8	3	35	60	200
9	Somerset (12)	17	6	7	4	30	54	192
10	Derbyshire (16)	17	6	7	4	28	55	191
11	Kent (2)	17	5	5	7	18	59	178
12	Worcestershire (3)	17	4	6	7	32	59	176
13	Glamorgan (1)	17	4	6	7	36	55	176
14	Durham (17)	17	3	9	5	30	65	158
15	Northamptonshire (15)	17	4	5	8	31	52	146
16	Nottinghamshire (13)	17	3	10	4	20	60	140
17	Middlesex (4)	17	2	9	6	28	52	130
18	Essex (8)	17	2	11	4	16	58	118

[1] Accrued in the first 100 overs of the first 2 innings.
[2] 1 point for every 50 runs above 150 (maximum 4 points).
[3] 1 point for every 2 wickets above and including 3 wickets fallen.

Final First Class Batting Averages

To qualify for inclusion, a player must participate in a minimum of eight matches.

1998

Name	Team	Matches	Innings	Not out	Runs	Highest score	Average	100s	50s
John Crawley	Lancashire	18	28	3	1,851	239	74.04	8	5
Hansie Cronje	South Africa	11	12	2	704	195	70.40	2	4
Daryll Cullinan	South Africa	12	17	4	900	200[1]	69.23	2	6
Gary Kirsten	South Africa	12	19	5	892	210	63.71	4	2
Justin Langer	Middlesex	15	28	5	1,448	233[1]	62.95	4	6
Ben Smith	Leicestershire	19	24	4	1,240	204	62.00	4	4
Darren Lehmann	Yorkshire	10	16	0	969	200	60.56	3	4
Mal Loye	Northamptonshire	15	22	2	1,198	322[1]	59.90	4	4
Aftab Habib	Leicestershire	19	22	5	952	198	56.00	3	3
Jacques Kallis	South Africa	10	14	3	612	132	55.63	2	3

[1] Not out.

Final First Class Bowling Averages

To qualify for inclusion, a player must take a minimum of 20 wickets.

1998

Name	Team	Overs	Maidens	Runs	Wickets	Average	Best bowling figures
Muttiah Muralitharan	Sri Lanka	226.3	77	463	34	13.61	9–65
Vince Wells	Leicestershire	199.1	66	514	36	14.27	5–18
Craig White	Yorkshire	147.1	36	391	25	15.64	8–55
Courtney Walsh	Gloucestershire	633	164	1,835	106	17.31	6–36
Saqlain Mushtaq	Surrey	475	136	1,119	63	17.76	8–65
Alan Mullally	Leicestershire	448.4	156	1,128	60	18.80	7–55
Matthew Bulbeck	Somerset	154.4	28	609	32	19.03	4–40
Tim Munton	Warwickshire	278.5	71	708	37	19.13	7–66
David Leatherdale	Worcestershire	111.4	22	416	21	19.80	5–20
Andy Caddick	Somerset	687.2	156	2,082	105	19.82	8–64

English County Championship Winners

The championship was sponsored by Schweppes, 1977–83. Since 1984 it has been sponsored by Britannic Assurance. Counties winning most championships: Yorkshire, 30 (including one shared); Surrey, 16 (including one shared); Middlesex, 12 (including two shared); Lancashire, 8 (including one shared).

Year	Team	Year	Team	Year	Team	Year	Team
1946	Yorkshire	1958	Surrey	1972	Warwickshire	1986	Essex
1947	Middlesex	1959	Yorkshire	1973	Hampshire	1987	Nottinghamshire
1948	Glamorgan	1960	Yorkshire	1974	Worcestershire	1988	Worcestershire
1949	Middlesex/Yorkshire (shared)	1961	Hampshire	1975	Leicestershire	1989	Worcestershire
		1962	Yorkshire	1976	Middlesex	1990	Middlesex
1950	Lancashire/Surrey (shared)	1963	Yorkshire	1977	Kent/Middlesex (shared)	1991	Essex
		1964	Worcestershire	1978	Kent	1992	Essex
1951	Warwickshire	1965	Worcestershire	1979	Essex	1993	Middlesex
1952	Surrey	1966	Yorkshire	1980	Middlesex	1994	Warwickshire
1953	Surrey	1967	Yorkshire	1981	Nottinghamshire	1995	Warwickshire
1954	Surrey	1968	Yorkshire	1982	Middlesex	1996	Leicestershire
1955	Surrey	1969	Glamorgan	1983	Essex	1997	Glamorgan
1956	Surrey	1970	Kent	1984	Essex	1998	Leicestershire
1957	Surrey	1971	Surrey	1985	Middlesex		

AXA (Sunday) League Final Table

The league's matches were played on Sundays and each innings consisted of a maximum of 40 overs. The previous year's positions are shown in brackets.

Position	Team	Games played	Wins	Losses	Ties	No result	Net run rate[1]	Points
1	Lancashire (3)	17	12	2	0	3	12.18	54
2	Warwickshire (1)	17	9	5	0	3	4.23	42
3	Essex (7)	17	9	5	1	2	1.27	42
4	Leicestershire (4)	17	9	6	0	2	15.13	40
5	Kent (2)	17	8	6	0	3	1.19	38
6	Gloucestershire (11)	17	7	6	0	4	–1.65	36
7	Worcestershire (8)	17	7	6	1	3	–4.60	36
8	Hampshire (15)	17	8	8	0	1	0.95	34
9	Yorkshire (10)	17	8	8	0	1	–2.47	34
10	Glamorgan 13)	17	7	8	0	2	–0.25	32
11	Nottinghamshire (12)	17	7	8	1	1	–0.67	32
12	Middlesex (16)	17	7	8	0	2	–4.90	32
13	Northamptonshire (9)	17	6	7	1	3	2.80	32
14	Somerset (6)	17	6	8	1	2	–0.10	30
15	Derbyshire (14)	17	6	8	0	3	–5.10	30
16	Sussex (18)	17	6	9	0	2	–1.84	28
17	Durham (17)	17	4	9	1	3	–7.89	24
18	Surrey (5)	17	3	12	0	2	–8.17	16

[1] Total runs scored times 100 divided by balls received, minus the run rate of the opposing side.

AXA (Sunday) League Winners

This 40-over-a-side Sunday league tournament was first held in 1969. It has been sponsored by John Player, 1969–86, Refuge Assurance, 1987–91, and AXA Equity and Law from 1992.

Year	Team	Year	Team	Year	Team	Year	Team
1980	Warwickshire	1985	Essex	1990	Derbyshire	1995	Kent
1981	Essex	1986	Hampshire	1991	Nottinghamshire	1996	Surrey
1982	Sussex	1987	Worcestershire	1992	Middlesex	1997	Warwickshire
1983	Yorkshire	1988	Worcestershire	1993	Glamorgan	1998	Lancashire
1984	Essex	1989	Lancashire	1994	Warwickshire		

Nat West Trophy Winners

This trophy competition was the first one-day county cricket tournament and was first held in 1963 as a 65-over (60 overs from 1964) -a-side knockout competition. It has been sponsored by Gillette, 1963–80, and National Westminster Bank (since 1981). All finals are played at Lord's. Most wins: Lancashire, 6; Warwickshire, 5; Sussex, Middlesex, 4.

Year	Team	Year	Team	Year	Team	Year	Team
1980	Middlesex	1985	Essex	1990	Lancashire	1995	Warwickshire
1981	Derbyshire	1986	Sussex	1991	Hampshire	1996	Lancashire
1982	Surrey	1987	Nottinghamshire	1992	Northamptonshire	1997	Essex
1983	Somerset	1988	Middlesex	1993	Warwickshire	1998	Lancashire
1984	Middlesex	1989	Warwickshire	1994	Worcestershire		

Benson and Hedges Cup Winners

This one-day 55-overs-a-side competition was first held in 1972. All finals are played at Lord's.

Year	Team	Year	Team	Year	Team	Year	Team
1980	Northamptonshire	1985	Leicestershire	1990	Lancashire	1995	Lancashire
1981	Somerset	1986	Middlesex	1991	Worcestershire	1996	Lancashire
1982	Somerset	1987	Yorkshire	1992	Hampshire	1997	Surrey
1983	Middlesex	1988	Hampshire	1993	Derbyshire	1998	Essex
1984	Lancashire	1989	Nottinghamshire	1994	Warwickshire		

English Minor Counties Cricket Championship

This competition was first contested in 1895.

Year	Team	Year	Team	Year	Team	Year	Team	Year	Team
1989	Oxfordshire	1991	Staffordshire	1993	Staffordshire	1995	Devon	1997	Devon
1990	Hertfordshire	1992	Staffordshire	1994	Devon	1996	Devon	1998	Staffordshire

Curling

Curling World Champions

This championship was first held in 1959 for men and in 1979 for women.

Year	Country	Year	Country
Men		*Women*	
1995	Canada	1995	Sweden
1996	Canada	1996	Canada
1997	Sweden	1997	Canada
1998	Canada	1998	Sweden
1999	Scotland	1999	Sweden

Cycling

Tour de France Winners

First held 1903.

Year	Name	Country	Year	Name	Country	Year	Name	Country
1979	Bernard Hinault	France	1987	Stephen Roche	Ireland, Republic of	1994	Miguel Induráin	Spain
1980	Joop Zoetemelk	Netherlands	1988	Pedro Delgado	Spain	1995	Miguel Induráin	Spain
1981	Bernard Hinault	France	1989	Greg LeMond	USA	1996	Bjarne Riis	Denmark
1982	Bernard Hinault	France	1990	Greg LeMond	USA	1997	Jan Ullrich	Germany
1983	Laurent Fignon	France	1991	Miguel Induráin	Spain	1998	Marco Pantani	Italy
1984	Laurent Fignon	France	1992	Miguel Induráin	Spain	1999	Lance Armstrong	USA
1985	Bernard Hinault	France	1993	Miguel Induráin	Spain			
1986	Greg LeMond	USA						

Tour of Britain Winners

The Tour of Britain, formerly the Milk Race, was first held in 1951. Following an absence of three years, it was revived in 1998 as the PruTour of Britain.

Year	Name	Country	Year	Name	Country
1990	Shane Sutton	Australia	1995	no race	
1991	Chris Walker	UK	1996	no race	
1992	Conor Henry	UK	1997	no race	
1993	Chris Lillywhite	UK	1998	Stuart O'Grady	Australia
1994	Maurizio Fondriest	Italy	1999	Marc Wauters	Belgium

Cycling World Champions and Major Tour Winners

1998

Category	Name	Country	Category	Name	Country
Men			***Women***		
Road			*Road*		
Giro d'Italia	Marco Pantani	Italy	Tour de France	Edita Pucinskaite	Lithuania
Vuelta a España	Abraham Olano	Spain	World Road Race Championship	Diana Ziliute	Lithuania
World Cup	Michele Bartoli	Italy	Time trial	Leontien Van Moorsel	Netherlands
World Road Race Championship	Oscar Camenzind	Switzerland	*Mountain Biking*		
Time trial	Abraham Olano	Spain	Cross country	Laurence Leboucher	France
Off-Road			Downhill	Anne-Caroline Chausson	France
Cyclo-cross	Mario de Clercq	Belgium			
Mountain biking: cross country	Christophe Dupouey	France	*Track*		
Mountain biking: downhill	Nicolas Vouillez	France	Points race	Teodora Ruano-Sanchon	Spain
Track					
1 km time trial	Arnaud Tournant	France	Sprint	Felicia Ballanger	France
Keirin	Jens Fiedler	Germany	500 m time trial	Felicia Ballanger	France
Madison		Belgium	Individual pursuit	Lucy Tyler-Sharman	Australia
Olympic sprint		France			
Individual pursuit	Phillipe Ermenault	France			
Sprint	Florian Rousseau	France			
Points race	Juan Llaneras	Spain			
Team pursuit		Ukraine			

Darts

World Professional Darts Champions

Year	Name	Country
1990	Phil Taylor	England
1991	Dennis Priestley	England
1992	Phil Taylor	England
1993	John Lowe	England
1994	John Part	Canada
1995	Richie Burnett	Wales
1996	Steve Beaton	England
1997	Les Wallace	Scotland
1998	Raymond Barneveld	Netherlands
1999	Raymond Barneveld	Netherlands

World Darts Council Champions

The World Darts Council Championships were first held in 1994.

Year	Name	Country
1994	Dennis Priestley	England
1995	Phil Taylor	England
1996	Phil Taylor	England
1997	Phil Taylor	England
1998	Phil Taylor	England
1999	Phil Taylor	England

Equestrianism

Show Jumping World Champions

This championship was first held in 1953.

Year	Name	Country
1982	Norbert Koof	West Germany
1986	Gail Greenhough	Canada
1990	Eric Navet	France
1994	Franke Sloothaak	Germany
1998	Rodrigo Pessoa	Brazil

Show Jumping: Volvo World Cup Champions

This championship was established by the Fédération Equestre Internationale (FEI) in 1979. Riders compete in a series of mostly indoor events, beginning in October and culminating in a final in April of the following year.

Year	Name	Country
1995	Nick Skelton	Great Britain
1996	Hugo Simon	Austria
1997	Hugo Simon	Austria
1998	Jos Lansink	Netherlands
1999	Rodrigo Pessoa	Brazil

British Show Jumping Championship

This championship first took place in 1961. It is held at Hickstead, Sussex, as part of the British Show Jumping Derby, and is now sponsored by Peugeot.

Year	Name	Country
1994	Captain John Ledingham	Ireland, Republic of
1995	Captain John Ledingham	Ireland, Republic of
1996	Nelson Pessoa	Brazil
1997	John Popely	Great Britain
1998	Michael Whitaker	Great Britain

Three-Day Eventing: World Champions

This championship was first held in 1966.

Year	Name	Country
1982	Lucinda Green[1]	Great Britain
1986	Virginia Leng[2]	Great Britain
1990	Blyth Tait	New Zealand
1994	Vaughan Jefferis	New Zealand
1998	Blyth Tait	New Zealand

[1] Born Prior-Palmer.
[2] Born Holgate.

Three-Day Eventing: Badminton Horse Trials

This competition first took place in 1949. It is held at Badminton House, Gloucestershire, and is now sponsored by Mitsubishi Motors.

Year	Name	Country
1995	Bruce Davidson	USA
1996	Mark Todd	New Zealand
1997	David O'Connor	USA
1998	Chris Bartle	Great Britain
1999	Ian Stark	Great Britain

Fencing

World Fencing Champions

These championships were held in Le Chaux-de-Fronds, Switzerland, 5–11 October.

1998

Category	Name	Country
Men		
Épée	Hugues Obry	France
Foil	Sergei Golubitsky	Ukraine
Sabre	Luigi Tarantino	Italy
Team épée		Hungary
Team foil		Poland
Team sabre		Hungary

Category	Name	Country
Women		
Épée	Donna Saworsky	Canada
Foil	Sabine Bau	Germany
Team épée		France
Team foil		Italy

Football

International Football

World Cup Finals

This tournament was not held in 1942 or 1946.

Year	Winner	Runner-up	Score	Venue
1930	Uruguay	Argentina	4–2	Uruguay
1934	Italy	Czechoslovakia	2–1	Italy
1938	Italy	Hungary	4–2	France
1950	Uruguay	Brazil	2–1	Brazil
1954	West Germany	Hungary	3–2	Switzerland
1958	Brazil	Sweden	5–2	Sweden
1962	Brazil	Czechoslovakia	3–1	Chile
1966	England	West Germany	4–2	England
1970	Brazil	Italy	4–1	Mexico
1974	West Germany	Holland	2–1	West Germany
1978	Argentina	Holland	3–1	Argentina
1982	Italy	West Germany	3–1	Spain
1986	Argentina	West Germany	3–2	Mexico
1990	West Germany	Argentina	1–0	Italy
1994	Brazil[1]	Italy	0–0	USA
1998	France	Brazil	3–0	France

[1] Brazil won 3–2 on penalties.

European Championship Winners

The championship was instituted in 1958, with the first final in 1960; it is contested every four years.

Year	Winner	Runner-up	Score	Location
1960	USSR	Yugoslavia	2–1[1]	France
1964	Spain	USSR	2–1	Spain
1968	Italy	Yugoslavia	1–1[1]	Italy
1968	Italy	Yugoslavia	2–0	Italy
1972	West Germany	USSR	3–0	Belgium
1976	Czechoslovakia	West Germany	2–2[2]	Yugoslavia
1980	West Germany	Belgium	2–1	Italy
1984	France	Spain	2–0	France
1988	Netherlands	USSR	2–0	West Germany
1992	Denmark	Germany	2–0	Sweden
1996	Germany	Czech Republic	2–1[1]	England

[1] After extra time.
[2] Czechoslovakia won 5–4 on penalties.

Fédération Internationale de Football Association (FIFA) Women's World Cup

This cup was inaugurated in 1991.

Year	Winner	Runner-up	Score	Venue
1991	USA	Norway	2–1	China
1995	Norway	Germany	2–0	Sweden
1999	USA	China	0–0[1]	USA

[1] USA won 5–4 on penalties after extra time.

International Results

All European Championships (Euro 2000) qualifying matches unless otherwise stated.

Date	Teams		Score	Location
5 September 1998	Lithuania	Scotland	0–0	Vilnius
5 September 1998	Turkey	Northern Ireland	3–0	Istanbul
5 September 1998	Ireland, Republic of	Croatia	2–0	Dublin
5 September 1998	Sweden	England	2–1	Stockholm
9 September 1998	Wales	Italy	0–2	Liverpool
10 October 1998	Denmark	Wales	1–2	Copenhagen
10 October 1998	England	Bulgaria	0–0	Wembley
10 October 1998	Northern Ireland	Finland	1–0	Belfast
10 October 1998	Scotland	Estonia	3–2	Edinburgh
14 October 1998	Luxembourg	England	0–3	Luxembourg
14 October 1998	Ireland, Republic of	Malta	5–0	Dublin
14 October 1998	Scotland	Faroe Islands	2–1	Aberdeen
14 October 1998	Wales	Belarus	3–2	Cardiff
18 November 1998	England	Czech Republic	2–0[1]	Wembley
18 November 1998	Northern Ireland	Moldova	2–2	Belfast
18 November 1998	Yugoslavia	Ireland, Republic of	1–0	Belgrade
10 February 1999	England	France	0–2[1]	Wembley
10 February 1999	Ireland, Republic of	Paraguay	2–0[1]	Dublin
27 March 1999	England	Poland	3–1	Wembley
27 March 1999	Northern Ireland	Germany	0–3	Belfast
31 March 1999	Moldova	Northern Ireland	0–0	Kishinev
31 March 1999	Scotland	Czech Republic	1–2	Glasgow
31 March 1999	Switzerland	Wales	2–0	Zurich
27 April 1999	Northern Ireland	Canada	1–1[1]	Belfast
28 April 1999	Germany	Scotland	0–1[1]	Bremen
28 April 1999	Hungary	England	1–1[1]	Budapest
28 April 1999	Ireland, Republic of	Sweden	2–0[1]	Dublin
29 May 1999	Ireland, Republic of	Northern Ireland	0–1[1]	Dublin
5 June 1999	England	Sweden	0–0	Wembley
5 June 1999	Faroe Islands	Scotland	1–1	Toftir
5 June 1999	Italy	Wales	4–0	Bologna
9 June 1999	Bulgaria	England	1–1	Sofia
9 June 1999	Czech Republic	Scotland	2–3	Prague
9 June 1999	Ireland, Republic of	Macedonia	1–0	Dublin
9 June 1999	Wales	Denmark	0–2	Liverpool

[1] Friendly match.

European Football

European Cup Champions' League

(Key: P = played; W = won; D = drawn; L = lost; F = goals for; A = goals against; Pt = points.)

1998–1999

Group Stage

Team	P	W	D	L	F	A	Pt
Group A							
Olympiakos (Greece)	6	3	2	1	8	6	11
Croatia Zagreb (Croatia)	6	2	2	2	5	7	8
FC Porto (Portugal)	6	2	1	3	11	9	7
Ajax Amsterdam (Netherlands)	6	2	1	3	4	6	7
Group B							
Juventus (Italy)	6	1	5	0	7	5	8
Galatasaray (Turkey)	6	2	2	2	8	8	8
Rosenborg (Norway)	6	2	2	2	7	8	8
Athletic Bilbao (Spain)	6	1	3	2	5	6	6
Group C							
Inter Milan (Italy)	6	4	1	1	9	5	13
Real Madrid (Spain)[1]	6	4	0	2	17	8	12
Spartak Moscow (Russia)	6	2	2	2	7	6	8
Sturm Graz (Austria)	6	0	1	5	2	16	1
Group D							
Bayern Munich (Germany)	6	3	2	1	9	6	11
Manchester United (England)[1]	6	2	4	0	20	11	10
Barcelona (Spain)	6	2	2	2	11	9	8
Brondby (Denmark)	6	1	0	5	4	8	3
Group E							
Dynamo Kiev (Ukraine)	6	3	2	1	11	7	11
Lens (France)	6	2	2	2	5	6	8
Arsenal (England)[2]	6	2	2	2	8	8	8
Panathinaikos (Greece)	6	2	0	4	6	9	6
Group F							
Kaiserslautern (Germany)	6	4	1	1	12	6	13
Benfica (Portugal)	6	2	2	2	8	9	8
PSV Eindhoven (Netherlands)	6	2	1	3	10	11	7
HJK Helsinki (Finland)	6	1	2	3	8	12	5

Quarter Finals

Winner	Loser	Scores (home score given first)		Aggregate
Bayern Munich	Kaiserslautern	2–0	0–4	6–0
Juventus	Olympiakos	2–1	1–1	3–2
Manchester United	Inter Milan	2–0	1–1	3–1
Dynamo Kiev	Real Madrid	1–1	2–0	3–1

Semi Finals

Winner	Loser	Scores (home score given first)		Aggregate
Bayern Munich	Dynamo Kiev	3–3	1–0	4–3
Manchester United	Juventus	1–1	2–3	4–3

Final

26 May 1999, Nou Camp Stadium, Barcelona. Attendance: 90,000

Winner	Loser	Score
Manchester United (Sheringham 90 minutes) (Solskjaer 90 minutes)	Bayern Munich (Basler 6 minutes)	2–1

Teams: Manchester United Schmeichel, G Neville, Stam, Johnsen, Irwin, Giggs, Beckham, Butt, Blomqvist (Sheringham 66 minutes), Yorke, Cole (Solksjaer 80 minutes) **Bayern Munich** Kahn, Matthäus (Fink 80 minutes), Linke, Kuffour, Babbel, Effenberg, Jeremies, Tarnat, Basler (Salihamidzic 89 minutes), Jancker, Zickler (Scholl 70 minutes)

[1] Qualified for quarter finals as one of the two best runners-up. Manchester United's results: (Manchester United score given first) Manchester United versus Barcelona (home) 3–3; Manchester United versus Bayern Munich (away) 2–2; Manchester United versus Brondby (away) 6–2; Manchester United versus Brondby (home) 5–0; Manchester United versus Barcelona (away) 3–3; Manchester United versus Bayern Munich (home) 1–1.

[2] Arsenal's results: (Arsenal score given first) Arsenal versus Lens (away) 1–1; Arsenal versus Panathinaikos (home) 2–1; Arsenal versus Dynamo Kiev (home) 1–1; Arsenal versus Dynamo Kiev (away) 1–3; Arsenal versus Lens (home) 0–1; Arsenal versus Panathinaikos (home) 3–1.

European Cup Winners' Cup

This cup was awarded to the winners of a competition between winners of the domestic knock-out cup competitions of each European country. The competition was first held in 1961. It was discontinued after the 1998–99 competition. From the 1999–2000 season domestic cup winners will play in the UEFA Cup. The 1999 final between Lazio (Italy) and Real Mallorca (Spain) took place at Villa Park, Birmingham on 19 May. Lazio's Nedved scored the winner after Mallorca's Dani had equalized Vieri's opening goal for the Italians.

Year	Team	Country
1990	Sampdoria	Italy
1991	Manchester United	England
1992	Werder Bremen	Germany
1993	Parma	Italy
1994	Arsenal	England
1995	Real Zaragoza	Spain
1996	Paris St Germain	France
1997	Barcelona	Spain
1998	Chelsea	England
1999	Lazio	Italy

Union of European Football Associations (UEFA) Cup Winners

This cup was established in 1955 as the International Industries Fairs Inter-Cities Cup. It was renamed the European Fairs Cup in 1966 and took on its present name in 1971. Most wins: Inter Milan, 5; Juventus, Barcelona, 3. The 1999 final took place at Luzhniki stadium in Moscow, Russia, on 12 May between Parma (Italy) and Olympique Marseille (France) in front of 61,000 spectators. Parma won the match 3–0, with goals from Crespo, Varoli, and Chiesa.

Year	Team	Country
1990	Juventus	Italy
1991	Inter Milan	Italy
1992	Ajax	Holland
1993	Juventus	Italy
1994	Inter Milan	Italy
1995	Parma	Italy
1996	Bayern Munich	Germany
1997	Schalke	Germany
1998	Inter Milan	Italy
1999	Parma	Italy

European Champions' Cup Winners

This championship was played entirely on a knock-out basis until 1992, when a Champions' League of two divisions replaced the quarter- and semi-final stages. In 1995 the League was increased to four groups of four teams who compete for places in the quarter-finals, which are played on a knock-out format. In 1996 the runners-up as well as the champion clubs of the leading European leagues were allowed to take part in the competition. Most wins: Real Madrid 7; AC Milan, 5; Ajax Amsterdam, Bayern Munich, Liverpool, 4.

Year	Winners	Runners-up	Score
1956	Real Madrid	Stade de Reims	4–3
1957	Real Madrid	Fiorentina	2–0
1958	Real Madrid	AC Milan	3–2[1]
1959	Real Madrid	Stade de Reims	2–0
1960	Real Madrid	Eintracht Frankfurt	7–3
1961	Benfica	Barcelona	3–2
1962	Benfica	Real Madrid	5–3
1963	AC Milan	Benfica	2–1
1964	Internazionale	Real Madrid	3–1
1965	Internazionale	Benfica	1–0
1966	Real Madrid	Partizan Belgrade	2–1
1967	Glasgow Celtic	Internazionale	2–1
1968	Manchester United	Benfica	4–1[1]
1969	AC Milan	Ajax Amsterdam	4–1
1970	Feyenoord	Glasgow Celtic	2–1[1]
1971	Ajax Amsterdam	Panathinaikos	2–0
1972	Ajax Amsterdam	Inter Milan	2–0
1973	Ajax Amsterdam	Juventus	1–0
1974	Bayern Munich	Atletico Madrid	1–1
Replay	Bayern Munich	Atletico Madrid	4–0
1975	Bayern Munich	Leeds United	2–0
1976	Bayern Munich	St Etienne	1–0
1977	Liverpool	Borussia Mönchengladbach	3–1
1978	Liverpool	Club Brugge	1–0
1979	Nottingham Forest	Malmö	1–0
1980	Nottingham Forest	Hamburg	1–0
1981	Liverpool	Real Madrid	1–0
1982	Aston Villa	Bayern Munich	1–0
1983	Hamburg	Juventus	1–0
1984	Liverpool	Roma	1–1[1 2]
1985	Juventus	Liverpool	1–0
1986	Steaua Bucharest	Barcelona	0–0[1 3]
1987	Porto	Bayern Munich	2–1
1988	PSV Eindhoven	Benfica	0–0[4]
1989	AC Milan	Steaua Bucharest	4–0
1990	AC Milan	Benfica	1–0
1991	Red Star Belgrade	Olympique Marseille	0–0[5]
1992	Barcelona	Sampdoria	1–0[1]
1993	Olympique Marseille	AC Milan	1–0[6]
1994	AC Milan	Barcelona	4–0
1995	Ajax Amsterdam	AC Milan	1–0
1996	Juventus	Ajax Amsterdam	1–1[7]
1997	Borussia Dortmund	Juventus	3–1
1998	Real Madrid	Juventus	1–0
1999	Manchester United	Bayern Munich	2–1

[1] After extra time.
[2] Liverpool won 4–2 on penalties.
[3] Steaua won 2–0 on penalties.
[4] PSV won 6–5 on penalties.
[5] Red Star Belgrade won 5–3 on penalties.
[6] Replay.
[7] Juventus won 4–2 on penalties.

European Leagues, Selected Champions

1998–99

Country	Team
Austria	Sturm Graz
Belgium	RC Genk
Bulgaria	Litex
Croatia	Croatia Zagreb
Czech Republic	Sparta Prague
Denmark	AAB Aalborg
France	Bordeaux
Germany	Bayern Munich
Greece	Olympiakos
Hungary	MTK Hungaria
Italy	AC Milan
Northern Ireland	Glentoran
Poland	Wisla Kraków
Portugal	FC Porto
Republic of Ireland	Saint Patrick's Athletic
Romania	Rapid Bucharest
Spain	Barcelona
Switzerland	Servette FC
Netherlands	Feyenoord
Turkey	Galatasaray
Wales	Barry Town
Yugoslavia	Partizan Belgrade

European Footballer of the Year

Year	Player	Club	Country of origin
1989	Marco Van Basten	AC Milan	Netherlands
1990	Lothar Matthäus	Inter Milan	Germany
1991	Jean-Pierre Papin	Marseille	France
1992	Marco Van Basten	AC Milan	Netherlands
1993	Roberto Baggio	Juventus	Italy
1994	Hristo Stoichkov	Barcelona	Bulgaria
1995	George Weah	AC Milan	Liberia
1996	Matthias Sammer	Borussia Dortmund	Germany
1997	Ronaldo	Inter Milan	Brazil
1998	Zinedine Zidane	Juventus	France

FIFA World Player of the Year

This award was first presented in 1991. It is sponsored by FIFA, the European Sports Management Association, and Adidas, and is selected by national team coaches.

Year	Player	Team	Country of origin
1991	Lothar Matthäus	Inter Milan	Germany
1992	Marco Van Basten	AC Milan	Netherlands
1993	Roberto Baggio	Juventus	Italy
1994	Romario	Barcelona	Brazil
1995	George Weah	AC Milan	Liberia
1996	Ronaldo	Barcelona	Brazil
1997	Ronaldo	Inter Milan	Brazil
1998	Zinedine Zidane	Juventus	France

English Football

FA Carling Premiership Final Table

(Key: P = played; W = won; D = drawn; L = lost; F = goals for; A = goals against; Pt = points; GD = goal difference.)

1998–99

Position	Team	Home						Away						
		P	W	D	L	F	A	W	D	L	F	A	Pt	GD
1	Manchester United	38	14	4	1	45	18	8	9	2	35	19	79	43
2	Arsenal	38	14	5	0	34	5	8	7	4	25	12	78	42
3	Chelsea	38	12	6	1	29	13	8	9	2	28	17	75	27
4	Leeds United	38	12	5	2	32	9	6	8	5	30	25	67	28
5	West Ham United	38	11	3	5	32	26	5	6	8	14	27	57	–7
6	Aston Villa	38	10	3	6	33	28	5	7	7	18	18	55	5
7	Liverpool	38	10	5	4	44	24	5	4	10	24	25	54	19
8	Derby County	38	8	7	4	22	19	5	6	8	18	26	52	–5
9	Middlesbrough	38	7	9	3	25	18	5	6	8	23	36	51	–6
10	Leicester City	38	7	6	6	25	25	5	7	7	15	21	49	–6
11	Tottenham Hotspur	38	7	7	5	28	26	4	7	8	19	24	47	–3
12	Sheffield Wednesday	38	7	5	7	20	15	6	2	11	21	27	46	–1
13	Newcastle United	38	7	6	6	26	25	4	7	8	22	29	46	–6
14	Everton	38	6	8	5	22	12	5	2	12	20	35	43	–5
15	Coventry City	38	8	6	5	26	21	3	3	13	13	30	42	–12
16	Wimbledon	38	7	7	5	22	21	3	5	11	18	42	42	–23
17	Southampton	38	9	4	6	29	26	2	4	13	8	38	41	–27
18	Charlton Athletic[1]	38	4	7	8	20	20	4	5	10	21	36	36	–15
19	Blackburn Rovers[1]	38	6	5	8	21	24	1	9	9	17	28	35	–14
20	Nottingham Forest[1]	38	3	7	9	18	31	4	2	13	17	38	30	–34

[1] Relegated.

FA Carling Premiership Results

(– = not applicable.)

1998–99

Home team	Away team									
	Arsenal	Aston Villa	Blackburn Rovers	Charlton Athletic	Chelsea	Coventry City	Derby County	Everton	Leeds United	Leicester City
Arsenal	–	1–0	1–0	0–0	1–0	2–0	1–0	1–0	3–1	5–0
Aston Villa	3–2	–	1–3	3–4	0–3	1–4	1–0	3–0	1–2	1–1
Blackburn Rovers	1–2	2–1	–	1–0	3–4	1–2	0–0	1–2	1–0	1–0
Charlton Athletic	0–1	0–1	0–0	–	0–1	1–1	1–2	1–2	1–1	0–0
Chelsea	0–0	2–1	1–1	2–1	–	2–1	2–1	3–1	1–0	2–2
Coventry City	0–1	1–2	1–1	2–1	2–1	–	1–1	3–0	2–2	1–1
Derby County	0–0	2–1	1–0	0–2	2–2	0–0	–	2–1	2–2	2–0
Everton	0–2	0–0	0–0	4–1	0–0	2–0	0–0	–	0–0	0–0
Leeds United	1–0	0–0	1–0	4–1	0–0	2–0	4–1	1–0	–	0–1
Leicester City	1–1	2–2	1–1	1–1	2–4	1–0	1–2	2–0	1–2	–
Liverpool	0–0	0–1	2–0	3–3	1–1	2–0	1–2	3–2	1–3	0–1
Manchester United	1–1	2–1	3–2	4–1	1–1	2–0	1–0	3–1	3–2	2–2
Middlesbrough	1–6	0–0	2–1	2–0	0–0	2–0	1–1	2–2	0–0	0–0
Newcastle United	1–1	2–1	1–1	0–0	0–1	4–1	2–1	1–3	0–3	1–0
Nottingham Forest	0–1	2–2	2–2	0–1	1–3	1–0	2–2	0–2	1–1	1–0
Sheffield Wednesday	1–0	0–1	3–0	3–0	0–0	1–2	0–1	0–0	0–2	0–1
Southampton	0–0	1–4	3–3	3–1	0–2	2–1	0–1	2–0	3–0	2–1
Tottenham Hotspur	1–3	1–0	2–1	2–2	2–2	0–0	1–1	4–1	3–3	0–2
West Ham	0–4	0–0	2–0	0–1	1–1	2–0	5–1	2–1	1–5	3–2
Wimbledon	1–0	0–0	1–1	2–1	1–2	2–1	2–1	1–2	1–1	0–1

(continued)

FA Carling Premiership Results (*continued*)

Home team	Away team: Liverpool	Manchester United	Middles-brough	Newcastle United	Nottingham Forest	Sheffield Wednesday	Southampton	Tottenham Hotspur	West Ham United	Wimbledon
Arsenal	0–0	3–0	1–1	3–0	2–1	3–0	1–1	0–0	1–0	5–1
Aston Villa	2–4	1–1	3–1	1–0	2–0	2–1	3–0	3–2	0–0	2–0
Blackburn Rovers	1–3	0–0	0–0	0–0	1–2	1–4	0–2	1–1	3–0	3–1
Charlton Athletic	1–0	0–1	1–1	2–2	0–0	0–1	5–0	1–4	4–2	2–0
Chelsea	2–1	0–0	2–0	1–1	2–1	1–1	1–0	2–0	0–1	3–0
Coventry City	2–1	0–1	1–2	1–5	4–0	1–0	1–0	1–1	0–0	2–1
Derby County	3–2	1–1	2–1	3–4	1–0	1–0	0–0	0–1	0–2	0–0
Everton	0–0	1–4	5–0	1–0	0–1	1–2	1–0	0–1	6–0	1–1
Leeds United	0–0	1–1	2–0	0–1	3–1	2–1	3–0	2–0	4–0	2–2
Leicester City	1–0	2–6	0–1	2–0	3–1	0–2	2–0	2–1	0–0	1–1
Liverpool	–	2–2	3–1	4–2	5–1	2–0	7–1	3–2	2–2	3–0
Manchester United	2–0	–	2–3	0–0	3–0	3–0	2–1	2–1	4–1	5–1
Middlesbrough	1–3	0–1	–	2–2	1–1	4–0	3–0	0–0	1–0	3–1
Newcastle United	1–4	1–2	1–1	–	2–0	1–1	4–0	1–1	0–3	3–1
Nottingham Forest	2–2	1–8	1–2	1–2	–	2–0	1–1	0–1	0–0	0–1
Sheffield Wednesday	1–0	3–1	3–1	1–1	3–2	–	0–0	0–0	0–1	1–2
Southampton	1–2	0–3	3–3	2–1	1–2	1–0	–	1–1	1–0	3–1
Tottenham Hotspur	2–1	2–2	0–3	2–0	2–0	0–3	3–0	–	1–2	0–0
West Ham	2–1	0–0	4–0	2–0	2–1	0–4	1–0	2–1	–	3–4
Wimbledon	1–0	1–1	2–2	1–1	1–3	2–1	0–2	3–1	0–0	–

Nationwide League Division One Final Table

Promotion play-offs: Semi-finals over two legs played home and away. Watford 1 Birmingham City 0; Birmingham City 1 Watford 0. (Aggregate score 1–1 after extra time. Watford wins 7–6 on penalties.) Bolton Wanderers 1 Ipswich Town 0; Ipswich Town 4 Bolton Wanderers 3. (Aggregate score 4–4 after extra time. Bolton Wanderers win on away goals.) Final (Wembley Stadium 31 May 1999) Bolton Wanderers 0 Watford 2. Watford wins promotion to the Premiership. (Key: P = played; W = won; D = drawn; L = lost; F = goals for; A = goals against; Pt = points; Gls = goals scored.)

1998–99

Position	Team	P	Home W	Home D	Home L	Home F	Home A	Away W	Away D	Away L	Away F	Away A	Pt	Gls
1	Sunderland[1]	46	19	3	1	50	10	12	9	2	41	18	105	91
2	Bradford City[2]	46	15	4	4	48	20	11	5	7	34	27	87	82
3	Ipswich Town	46	16	1	6	37	15	10	7	6	32	17	86	69
4	Birmingham City	46	12	7	4	32	15	11	5	7	34	22	81	66
5	Watford[3]	46	12	8	3	30	19	9	6	8	35	37	77	65
6	Bolton Wanderers	46	13	6	4	44	25	7	10	6	34	34	76	78
7	Wolverhampton Wanderers	46	11	10	2	37	19	8	6	9	27	24	73	64
8	Sheffield United	46	12	6	5	42	29	6	7	10	29	37	67	71
9	Norwich City	46	7	12	4	34	28	8	5	10	28	33	62	62
10	Huddersfield Town	46	11	9	3	38	23	4	7	12	24	48	61	62
11	Grimsby Town	46	11	6	6	25	18	6	4	13	15	34	61	40
12	West Bromwich Albion	46	12	4	7	43	33	4	7	12	26	43	59	69
13	Barnsley	46	7	9	7	35	30	7	8	8	24	26	59	59
14	Crystal Palace	46	11	10	2	43	26	3	6	14	15	45	58	58
15	Tranmere Rovers	46	8	7	8	37	30	4	13	6	26	31	56	63
16	Stockport County	46	7	9	7	24	21	5	8	10	25	39	53	49
17	Swindon Town	46	7	8	8	40	44	6	3	14	19	37	50	59
18	Crewe Alexandra	46	7	6	10	27	35	5	6	12	27	43	48	54
19	Portsmouth	46	10	5	8	34	26	1	9	13	23	47	47	57
20	Queens Park Rangers	46	9	7	7	34	22	3	4	16	18	39	47	52
21	Port Vale	46	10	3	10	22	28	3	5	15	23	47	47	45
22	Bury[4]	46	9	7	7	24	27	1	10	12	11	33	47	35
23	Oxford United[4]	46	7	8	8	31	30	3	6	14	17	41	44	48
24	Bristol City[4]	46	7	8	8	35	36	2	7	14	22	44	42	57

[1] Promoted as champions.
[2] Promoted as runners-up.
[3] Promoted after play-offs.
[4] Relegated.

Nationwide League Division Two Final Table

Promotion play-offs: Semi-finals over two legs played home and away. Preston North End 1 Gillingham 1; Gillingham 1 Preston North End 0; Gillingham wins 2–1 on aggregate. Wigan Athletic 1 Manchester City 1; Manchester City 1 Wigan Athletic 0; Manchester City wins 2–1 on aggregate. Final (Wembley Stadium 30 May 1999) Gillingham 2 Manchester City 2 (after extra time); Manchester City wins 3–1 on penalties and is promoted to Division One. (Key: P = played; W = won; D = drawn; L = lost; F = goals for; A = goals against; Pt = points; Gls = goals scored.)

1998–99

Position	Team		Home					Away						
		P	W	D	L	F	A	W	D	L	F	A	Pt	Gls
1	Fulham[1]	46	19	3	1	50	12	12	5	6	29	20	101	79
2	Walsall[2]	46	13	7	3	37	23	13	2	8	26	24	87	63
3	Manchester City[3]	46	13	6	4	38	14	9	10	4	31	19	82	69
4	Gillingham	46	15	5	3	45	17	7	9	7	30	27	80	75
5	Preston North End	46	12	6	5	46	23	10	7	6	32	27	79	78
6	Wigan Athletic	46	14	5	4	44	17	8	5	10	31	31	76	75
7	Bournemouth	46	14	7	2	37	11	7	6	10	26	30	76	63
8	Stoke City	46	10	4	9	32	32	11	2	10	27	31	69	59
9	Chesterfield	46	14	5	4	34	16	3	8	12	12	28	64	46
10	Millwall	46	9	8	6	33	24	8	3	12	19	35	62	52
11	Reading	46	10	6	7	29	26	6	7	10	25	37	61	54
12	Luton Town	46	10	4	9	25	26	6	6	11	26	34	58	51
13	Bristol Rovers	46	8	9	6	35	28	5	8	10	30	28	56	65
14	Blackpool	46	7	8	8	24	24	7	6	10	20	30	56	44
15	Burnley	46	8	7	8	23	33	5	9	9	31	40	55	54
16	Notts County	46	8	6	9	29	27	6	6	11	23	34	54	52
17	Wrexham	46	8	6	9	21	28	5	8	10	22	34	53	43
18	Colchester United	46	9	7	7	25	30	3	9	11	27	40	52	52
19	Wycombe Wanderers	46	8	5	10	31	26	5	7	11	21	32	51	52
20	Oldham Athletic	46	8	4	11	26	31	6	5	12	22	35	51	48
21	York City[4]	46	6	8	9	28	33	7	3	13	28	47	50	56
22	Northampton Town[4]	46	4	12	7	26	31	6	6	11	17	26	48	43
23	Lincoln City[4]	46	9	4	10	27	27	4	3	16	15	47	46	42
24	Macclesfield Town[4]	46	7	4	12	24	30	4	6	13	19	33	43	43

[1] Promoted as champions.
[2] Promoted as runners up.
[3] Promoted after play-offs.
[4] Relegated.

Nationwide League Division Three Final Table

Promotion play-offs: Semi-finals over two legs played home and away. Leyton Orient 0 Rotherham 0; Rotherham 0 Leyton Orient 0; aggregate score 0–0 after extra time, Leyton Orient wins 4– 2 on penalties. Swansea City 1 Scunthorpe United 0; Scunthorpe United 3 Swansea City 1; after extra time Scunthorpe United wins 3– 2 on aggregate. Final (Wembley Stadium 29 May 1999) Leyton Orient 0 Scunthorpe United 1. (Key: P = played; W = won; D = drawn; L = lost; F = goals for; A = goals against; Pt = points; Gls = goals scored.)

1998–99

Position	Team		Home					Away						
		P	W	D	L	F	A	W	D	L	F	A	Pt	Gls
1	Brentford[1]	46	16	5	2	45	18	10	2	11	34	38	85	79
2	Cambridge United[2]	46	13	6	4	41	21	10	6	7	37	27	81	78
3	Cardiff City[2]	46	13	7	3	35	17	9	7	7	25	22	80	60
4	Scunthorpe United[3]	46	14	3	6	42	28	8	5	10	27	30	74	69
5	Rotherham United	46	11	8	4	41	26	9	5	9	38	35	73	79
6	Leyton Orient	46	12	6	5	40	30	7	9	7	28	29	72	68
7	Swansea City	46	11	9	3	33	19	8	5	10	23	29	71	56
8	Mansfield Town	46	15	2	6	38	18	4	8	11	22	40	67	60
9	Peterborough United	46	11	4	8	41	29	7	8	8	31	27	66	72
10	Halifax Town	46	10	8	5	33	25	7	7	9	25	31	66	58
11	Darlington	46	10	6	7	41	24	8	5	10	28	34	65	69
12	Exeter City	46	13	5	5	32	18	4	7	12	15	32	63	47
13	Plymouth Argyle	46	11	6	6	32	19	6	4	13	26	35	61	58
14	Chester City	46	6	12	5	28	30	7	6	10	29	36	57	57
15	Shrewsbury Town	46	11	6	6	36	29	3	8	12	16	34	56	52
16	Barnet	46	10	5	8	30	31	4	8	11	24	40	55	54
17	Brighton and Hove Albion	46	8	3	12	25	35	8	4	11	24	31	55	49
18	Southend United	46	8	6	9	24	21	6	6	11	28	37	54	52
19	Rochdale	46	9	8	6	22	21	4	7	12	20	34	54	42
20	Torquay United	46	9	9	5	29	20	3	8	12	18	38	53	47
21	Hull City	46	8	5	10	25	28	6	6	11	19	34	53	44
22	Hartlepool United	46	8	7	8	33	27	5	5	13	19	38	51	52
23	Carlisle United	46	8	8	7	25	21	3	8	12	18	32	49	43
24	Scarborough[4]	46	8	3	12	30	39	6	3	14	20	38	48	50

[1] Promoted as champions.
[2] Promoted.
[3] Promoted after play-offs.
[4] Relegated to Nationwide Conference.

Nationwide Conference Final Table

This was formerly the Vauxhall Conference. (Key: P = played; W = won; D = drawn; L = lost; F = goals for; A = goals against; Pt = points; GD = goal difference.)

1998–99

Position	Team	P	Home					Away					Pt	GD
			W	D	L	F	A	W	D	L	F	A		
1	Cheltenham[1]	42	11	9	1	35	14	11	5	5	36	22	80	35
2	Kettering Town	42	11	5	5	31	16	11	5	5	27	21	76	21
3	Hayes	42	12	3	6	34	25	10	5	6	29	25	74	13
4	Rushden & Diamonds	42	11	4	6	41	22	9	8	4	30	20	72	29
5	Yeovil	42	8	4	9	35	32	12	7	2	33	22	71	14
6	Stevenage Borough	42	9	9	3	37	23	8	8	5	25	22	68	17
7	Northwich Victoria	42	11	3	7	29	21	8	6	7	31	30	66	9
8	Kingstonian	42	9	7	5	25	19	8	6	7	25	30	64	1
9	Woking	42	9	5	7	27	20	9	4	8	24	25	63	6
10	Hednesford Town	42	9	8	4	30	24	6	8	7	19	20	61	5
11	Dover Athletic	42	7	9	5	27	21	8	4	9	27	27	58	6
12	Forest Green Rovers	42	9	5	7	28	22	6	8	7	27	28	58	5
13	Hereford United	42	9	5	7	25	17	6	5	10	24	29	55	3
14	Morecambe	42	9	5	7	31	29	6	3	12	29	47	53	−16
15	Kidderminster Harriers	42	9	4	8	32	22	5	5	11	24	30	51	4
16	Doncaster Rovers	42	7	5	9	26	26	5	7	9	25	29	48	−4
17	Telford United	42	7	8	6	24	24	3	8	10	20	36	46	−16
18	Southport	42	6	9	6	29	28	4	6	11	18	31	45	−12
19	Barrow	42	7	5	9	17	23	4	5	12	23	40	43	−23
20	Welling United[2]	42	4	7	10	18	30	5	7	9	26	35	41	−21
21	Leek Town[2]	42	5	5	11	34	42	3	3	15	14	34	32	−28
22	Farnborough Town[2]	42	6	5	10	29	48	1	6	14	12	41	32	−48

[1] Promoted to Nationwide League Division Three.
[2] Relegated.

FA Challenge Cup Results

1998–99

Home	Away	Score
Third Round		
Aston Villa	Hull City	3–0
Blackburn Rovers	Charlton Athletic	2–0
Bolton Wanderers	Wolverhampton Wanderers	1–2
Bournemouth	West Bromwich Albion	1–0
Bradford City	Grimsby Town	2–1
Bristol City	Everton	0–2
Bury	Stockport County	0–3
Cardiff City	Yeovil Town	1–1
Yeovil Town	Cardiff City[1,2]	1–2
Coventry City	Macclesfield Town	7–0
Crewe Alexandra	Oxford United	1–3
Leicester City	Birmingham City	4–2
Lincoln City	Sunderland	0–1
Manchester United	Middlesbrough	3–1
Newcastle United	Crystal Palace	2–1
Nottingham Forest	Portsmouth	0–1
Oldham Athletic	Chelsea	0–2
Port Vale	Liverpool	0–3
Plymouth Argyle	Derby County	0–3
Preston North End	Arsenal	2–4
Queens Park Rangers	Huddersfield Town	0–1
Rotherham United	Bristol Rovers	0–1
Rushden & Diamonds	Leeds United	0–0
Leeds United	Rushden & Diamonds[2]	3–1
Sheffield United	Notts County	1–1
Notts County	Sheffield United[1,2]	3–4
Sheffield Wednesday	Norwich City	4–1
Southampton	Fulham	1–1
Fulham	Southampton[2]	1–0
Southport	Leyton Orient	0–2
Swindon Town	Barnsley	0–0
Barnsley	Swindon Town[2]	3–1
Tottenham Hotspur	Watford	5–2
Tranmere Rovers	Ipswich Town	0–1
West Ham United	Swansea City	1–1
Swansea City	West Ham United[2]	1–0
Wimbledon	Manchester City	1–0
Wrexham	Scunthorpe United	4–3

(continued)

FA Challenge Cup Results (*continued*)

Home	Away	Score
Fourth Round		
Aston Villa	Fulham	0–2
Barnsley	Bournemouth	3–1
Blackburn Rovers	Sunderland	1–0
Bristol Rovers	Leyton Orient	3–0
Everton	Ipswich Town	1–0
Leicester City	Coventry	0–3
Manchester United	Liverpool	2–1
Newcastle United	Bradford City	3–0
Oxford United	Chelsea	1–1
Chelsea	Oxford United[2]	4–2
Portsmouth	Leeds United	1–5
Sheffield Wednesday	Stockport County	2–0
Sheffield United	Cardiff City	4–1
Swansea City	Derby County	0–1
Wimbledon	Tottenham Hotspur	1–1
Tottenham Hotspur	Wimbledon[2]	3–0
Wolverhampton Wanderers	Arsenal	1–2
Wrexham	Huddersfield Town	1–1
Huddersfield Town	Wrexham[2]	2–1
Fifth Round		
Arsenal	Sheffield United	2–1
Arsenal	Sheffield United[2]	2–1
Barnsley	Bristol Rovers	4–1
Everton	Coventry City	2–1
Huddersfield Town	Derby County	2–2
Derby County	Huddersfield Town[2]	3–1
Leeds United	Tottenham Hotspur	1–1
Tottenham Hotspur	Leeds United[2]	2–0
Manchester United	Fulham	1–0
Newcastle United	Blackburn Rovers	0–0
Blackburn Rovers	Newcastle United[2]	0–1
Sheffield Wednesday	Chelsea	0–1
Quarter Finals		
Arsenal	Derby County	1–0
Barnsley	Tottenham Hotspur	0–1
Manchester United	Chelsea	0–0
Chelsea	Manchester United[2]	0–2
Newcastle United	Everton	4–1
Semi Finals		
Arsenal	Manchester United (at Villa Park)[1]	0–0
Arsenal	Manchester United (at Villa Park)[1 2]	1–2
Newcastle United	Tottenham Hotspur (at Old Trafford)[1]	4–1
Final (Wembley Stadium, 22 May 1999)		
Attendance: 79,101		
Manchester United (Sheringham 11 minutes) (Scholes 52 minutes)	Newcastle United	2–0

Teams: Manchester United Schmeichel, G Neville, Johnsen, P Neville, May, Beckham, Scholes (Stam 77 minutes), Keane (Sheringham 8 minutes), Giggs, Cole (Yorke 60 minutes), Solksjaer **Newcastle United** Harper, Griffin, Charvet, Dabizas, Domi, Lee, Hamann (Ferguson 45 minutes), Speed, Solano (Maric 68 minutes), Ketsbaia (Glass 79 minutes), Shearer.

Man of the Match: Sheringham

[1] After extra time.
[2] Replay.

FA Challenge Cup Winners

All finals have been played at Wembley Stadium since 1923, except for the 1970 Chelsea versus Leeds replay, which was played at Old Trafford.

Year	Winners	Runners-up	Score
1872	Wanderers	Royal Engineers	1–0
1873	Wanderers	Oxford University	2–0
1874	Oxford University	Royal Engineers	2–0
1875	Royal Engineers	Old Etonians	1–1[1]
replay	Royal Engineers	Old Etonians	2–0
1876	Wanderers	Old Etonians	1–1
replay	Wanderers	Old Etonians	3–0
1877	Wanderers	Oxford University	2–1[1]
1878	Wanderers	Royal Engineers	3–1
1879	Old Etonians	Clapham Rovers	1–0
1880	Clapham Rovers	Oxford University	1–0
1881	Old Carthusians	Old Etonians	3–0
1882	Old Etonians	Blackburn Rovers	1–0
1883	Blackburn Olympic	Old Etonians	2–1
1884	Blackburn Rovers	Queen's Park	2–1
1885	Blackburn Rovers	Queen's Park	2–0
1886	Blackburn Rovers	West Bromwich Albion	0–0
replay	Blackburn Rovers	West Bromwich Albion	2–0
1887	Aston Villa	West Bromwich Albion	2–0
1888	West Bromwich Albion	Preston North End	2–1
1889	Preston North End	Wolverhampton Wanderers	3–0
1890	Blackburn Rovers	Sheffield Wednesday	6–1
1891	Blackburn Rovers	Notts County	3–1
1892	West Bromwich Albion	Aston Villa	3–0
1893	Wolverhampton Wanderers	Everton	1–0
1894	Notts County	Bolton Wanderers	4–1
1895	Aston Villa	West Bromwich Albion	1–0
1896	Sheffield Wednesday	Wolverhampton Wanderers	2–1
1897	Aston Villa	Everton	3–2
1898	Nottingham Forest	Derby County	3–1
1899	Sheffield United	Derby County	4–1
1900	Bury	Southampton	4–0
1901	Tottenham Hotspur	Sheffield United	2–2
replay	Tottenham Hotspur	Sheffield United	3–1
1902	Sheffield United	Southampton	1–1
replay	Sheffield United	Southampton	2–1
1903	Bury	Derby County	6–0
1904	Manchester City	Bolton Wanderers	1–0
1905	Aston Villa	Newcastle United	2–0
1906	Everton	Newcastle United	1–0
1907	Sheffield Wednesday	Everton	2–1
1908	Wolverhampton Wanderers	Newcastle United	3–1
1909	Manchester United	Bristol City	1–0
1910	Newcastle United	Barnsley	1–1
replay	Newcastle United	Barnsley	2–0
1911	Bradford City	Newcastle United	0–0
replay	Bradford City	Newcastle United	1–0
1912	Barnsley	West Bromwich Albion	0–0
replay	Barnsley	West Bromwich Albion	1–0[1]
1913	Aston Villa	Sunderland	1–0
1914	Burnley	Liverpool	1–0
1915	Sheffield United	Chelsea	3–0
1916–19	not held		

(*continued*)

FA Challenge Cup Winners (*continued*)

Year	Winners	Runners-up	Score
1920	Aston Villa	Huddersfield Town	1–0[1]
1921	Tottenham Hotspur	Wolverhampton Wanderers	1–0
1922	Huddersfield Town	Preston North End	1–0
1923	Bolton Wanderers	West Ham United	2–0
1924	Newcastle United	Aston Villa	2–0
1925	Sheffield United	Cardiff City	1–0
1926	Bolton Wanderers	Manchester City	1–0
1927	Cardiff City	Arsenal	1–0
1928	Blackburn Rovers	Huddersfield Town	3–1
1929	Bolton Wanderers	Portsmouth	2–0
1930	Arsenal	Huddersfield Town	2–0
1931	West Bromwich Albion	Birmingham City	2–1
1932	Newcastle United	Arsenal	2–1
1933	Everton	Manchester City	3–0
1934	Manchester City	Portsmouth	2–1
1935	Sheffield Wednesday	West Bromwich Albion	4–2
1936	Arsenal	Sheffield United	1–0
1937	Sunderland	Preston North End	3–1
1938	Preston North End	Huddersfield Town	1–0[1]
1939	Portsmouth	Wolverhampton Wanderers	4–2
1940–45	not held		
1946	Derby County	Charlton Athletic	4–1[1]
1947	Charlton Athletic	Burnley	1–0[1]
1948	Manchester United	Blackpool	4–2
1949	Wolverhampton Wanderers	Leicester City	3–1
1950	Arsenal	Liverpool	2–0
1951	Newcastle United	Blackpool	2–0
1952	Newcastle United	Arsenal	1–0
1953	Blackpool	Bolton Wanderers	4–3
1954	West Bromwich Albion	Preston North End	3–2
1955	Newcastle United	Manchester City	3–1
1956	Manchester City	Birmingham City	3–1
1957	Aston Villa	Manchester United	2–1
1958	Bolton Wanderers	Manchester United	2–0
1959	Nottingham Forest	Luton Town	2–1
1960	Wolverhampton Wanderers	Blackburn Rovers	3–0
1961	Tottenham Hotspur	Leicester City	2–0
1962	Tottenham Hotspur	Burnley	3–1
1963	Manchester United	Leicester City	3–1
1964	West Ham United	Preston North End	3–2
1965	Liverpool	Leeds United	2–1[1]
1966	Everton	Sheffield Wednesday	3–2
1967	Tottenham Hotspur	Chelsea	2–1
1968	West Bromwich Albion	Everton	1–0[1]
1969	Manchester City	Leicester City	1–0
1970	Chelsea	Leeds United	2–2[1]
replay	Chelsea	Leeds United	2–1[1]
1971	Arsenal	Liverpool	2–1[1]
1972	Leeds United	Arsenal	1–0
1973	Sunderland	Leeds United	1–0
1974	Liverpool	Newcastle United	3–0
1975	West Ham United	Fulham	2–0
1976	Southampton	Manchester United	1–0
1977	Manchester United	Liverpool	2–1
1978	Ipswich Town	Arsenal	1–0
1979	Arsenal	Manchester United	3–2
1980	West Ham United	Arsenal	1–0
1981	Tottenham Hotspur	Manchester City	1–1[1]
replay	Tottenham Hotspur	Manchester City	3–2
1982	Tottenham Hotspur	Queens Park Rangers	1–1[1]
replay	Tottenham Hotspur	Queens Park Rangers	1–0
1983	Manchester United	Brighton & Hove Albion	2–2[1]
replay	Manchester United	Brighton & Hove Albion	4–0
1984	Everton	Watford	2–0
1985	Manchester United	Everton	1–0
1986	Liverpool	Everton	3–1
1987	Coventry City	Tottenham Hotspur	3–2
1988	Wimbledon	Liverpool	1–0
1989	Liverpool	Everton	3–2
1990	Manchester United	Crystal Palace	3–3[1]
replay	Manchester United	Crystal Palace	1–0
1991	Tottenham Hotspur	Nottingham Forest	2–1[1]
1992	Liverpool	Sunderland	2–0
1993	Arsenal	Sheffield Wednesday	1–1[1]
replay	Arsenal	Sheffield Wednesday	2–1[1]
1994	Manchester United	Chelsea	4–0
1995	Everton	Manchester United	1–0
1996	Manchester United	Liverpool	1–0
1997	Chelsea	Middlesbrough	2–0
1998	Arsenal	Newcastle United	2–0
1999	Manchester United	Newcastle United	2–0

[1] After extra time.

English Football: League Cup Winners

This competition was first held in 1960–61. It has been known as the Milk Cup, 1982–86, the Littlewoods Cup, 1987–90, the Rumbelows Cup, 1991–92, the Coca-Cola Cup, 1993–98, and from 1999 as the Worthington Cup.

Year	Winner	Runner-up	Score
1990	Nottingham Forest	Oldham Athletic	1–0
1991	Sheffield Wednesday	Manchester United	1–0
1992	Manchester United	Nottingham Forest	1–0
1993	Arsenal	Sheffield Wednesday	2–1
1994	Aston Villa	Manchester United	3–1
1995	Liverpool	Bolton Wanderers	2–1
1996	Aston Villa	Leeds United	3–0
1997	Leicester City	Middlesbrough	1–1[1]
replay	Leicester City	Middlesbrough	1–0[1]
1998	Chelsea	Middlesbrough	2–0[1]
1999	Tottenham Hotspur	Leicester City	1–0

[1] After extra time.

English Football: League Champions

The championship was organized by the Football League from its inception in 1888 until 1992, when the 22 First Division clubs formed the Premier League under the auspices of the Football Association.

Year	Winners	Year	Winners	Year	Winners
1888–89	Preston North End	1925–26	Huddersfield Town	1965–66	Liverpool
1889–90	Preston North End	1926–27	Newcastle United	1966–67	Manchester United
1890–91	Everton	1927–28	Everton	1967–68	Manchester City
1891–92	Sunderland	1928–29	Sheffield Wednesday	1968–69	Leeds United
1892–93	Sunderland	1929–30	Sheffield Wednesday	1969–70	Everton
1893–94	Aston Villa	1930–31	Arsenal	1970–71	Arsenal
1894–95	Sunderland	1931–32	Everton	1971–72	Derby County
1895–96	Aston Villa	1932–33	Arsenal	1972–73	Liverpool
1896–97	Aston Villa	1933–34	Arsenal	1973–74	Leeds United
1897–98	Sheffield United	1934–35	Arsenal	1974–75	Derby County
1898–99	Aston Villa	1935–36	Sunderland	1975–76	Liverpool
1899–1900	Aston Villa	1936–37	Manchester City	1976–77	Liverpool
1900–01	Liverpool	1937–38	Arsenal	1977–78	Nottingham Forest
1901–02	Sunderland	1938–39	Everton	1978–79	Liverpool
1902–03	Sheffield Wednesday	1940–45	not held	1979–80	Liverpool
1903–04	Sheffield Wednesday	1946–47	Liverpool	1980–81	Aston Villa
1904–05	Newcastle United	1947–48	Arsenal	1981–82	Liverpool
1905–06	Liverpool	1948–49	Portsmouth	1982–83	Liverpool
1906–07	Newcastle United	1949–50	Portsmouth	1983–84	Liverpool
1907–08	Manchester United	1950–51	Tottenham Hotspur	1984–85	Everton
1908–09	Newcastle United	1951–52	Manchester United	1985–86	Liverpool
1909–10	Aston Villa	1952–53	Arsenal	1986–87	Everton
1910–11	Manchester United	1953–54	Wolverhampton Wanderers	1987–88	Liverpool
1911–12	Blackburn Rovers	1954–55	Chelsea	1988–89	Arsenal
1912–13	Sunderland	1955–56	Manchester United	1989–90	Liverpool
1913–14	Blackburn Rovers	1956–57	Manchester United	1990–91	Arsenal
1914–15	Everton	1957–58	Wolverhampton Wanderers	1991–92	Leeds United
1916–18	not held	1958–59	Wolverhampton Wanderers	1992–93	Manchester United
1919–20	West Bromwich Albion	1959–60	Burnley	1993–94	Manchester United
1920–21	Burnley	1960–61	Tottenham Hotspur	1994–95	Blackburn Rovers
1921–22	Liverpool	1961–62	Ipswich Town	1995–96	Manchester United
1922–23	Liverpool	1962–63	Everton	1996–97	Manchester United
1923–24	Huddersfield Town	1963–64	Liverpool	1997–98	Arsenal
1924–25	Huddersfield Town	1964–65	Manchester United	1998–99	Manchester United

AutoWindscreens Cup Final

The final took place at Wembley Stadium on 18 April 1999 in front of 55,349 spectators. The winning goal was scored by Rogers in injury time.

1999

Winner	Runner-up	Score
Wigan Athletic	Millwall	1–0

FA Carling Premiership Leading Scorers

1998–99

Position	Player	Team	Goals scored			
			League competitions	Domestic cup competitions	European	Total
1	Dwight Yorke	Manchester United	18	3	8	29
2	Andy Cole	Manchester United	17	2	5	24
3	Michael Owen	Liverpool	18	3	2	23
4	Alan Shearer	Newcastle United	14	6	1	21
5	Jimmy Floyd Hasselbaink	Leeds United	18	1	1	20
6=	Nicolas Anelka	Arsenal	17	0	1	18
	Hamilton Ricard	Middlesbrough	15	3	0	18
	Robbie Fowler	Liverpool	14	2	2	18
	Ole Gunnar Solskjaer	Manchester United	12	4	2	18

Nationwide League Division One Leading Scorers

1998–99

Position	Player	Team	Goals scored		
			League	Domestic cup competitions	Total
1	Lee Hughes	West Bromwich Albion	31	1	32
2	Marcus Stewart	Huddersfield Town	22	4	26
3=	Lee Mills	Bradford City	24	1	25
	Kevin Phillips	Sunderland	23	2	25
5=	Iwan Roberts	Norwich City	19	4	23
	Ade Akinbiyi	Bristol City	19	4	23
7=	Niall Quinn	Sunderland	18	3	21
	Dean Windass	Bradford City	18	3	21[1]
9	Iffy Onuora	Swindon Town	20	0	20

[1] Includes 18 goals for Oxford United.

Nationwide League Division Two Leading Scorers

1998–99

Position	Player	Team	Goals scored		
			League	Domestic cup competitions	Total
1	Jamie Cureton	Bristol Rovers	25	4	29
2	Stuart Barlow	Wigan Athletic	19	7	26
3	Mark Stein	Bournemouth	15	10	25
4=	Andy Payton	Burnley	20	3	23
	Jason Roberts	Bristol Rovers	16	7	23
6	Carl Asaba	Gillingham	20	2	22[1]
7=	Shaun Goater	Manchester City	18	3	21
	Kurt Nogan	Preston North End	18	3	21
9	Andy Rammell	Walsall	18	2	20

[1] Includes one goal for Reading.

Nationwide League Division Three Leading Scorers

1998–99

Position	Player	Team	Goals scored		
			League	Domestic cup competitions	Total
1	Marco Gabbiadini	Darlington	24	1	25
2	Lloyd Owusu	Brentford	22	3	25
3	Jamie Forrester	Scunthorpe United	20	3	23
4	Scott Partridge	Brentford	20	2	22[1]
5	Martin Butler	Cambridge United	17	4	21
6=	Lee Peacock	Mansfield Town	17	2	19
	John Taylor	Cambridge United	17	2	19
8	Kevin Nugent	Cardiff City	15	3	18

[1] Includes 15 goals for Torquay United.

English Football: Top 10 Transfers Involving British Clubs

April 1998–March 1999

Rank	Name	From	To	Fee (£ millions)	Date
1	Dwight Yorke	Aston Villa	Manchester United	12.6	20 August 1998
2	Jaap Stam	PSV Eindhoven	Manchester United	10.75	1 July 1998
3=	Kevin Davies	Southampton	Blackburn Rovers	7.5	1 June 1998
	John Hartson	West Ham United	Wimbledon	7.5	14 January 1999
5	Duncan Ferguson	Everton	Newcastle United	7	24 November 1998
6	Paul Merson	Middlesbrough	Aston Villa	6.75	8 September 1998
7	Dion Dublin	Coventry City	Aston Villa	5.75	5 November 1998
8=	Andrei Kanchelskis	Fiorentina	Rangers	5.5	15 July 1998
	Steve Stone	Nottingham Forest	Aston Villa	5.5	11 March 1999
10	Pierluigi Casiraghi	Lazio	Chelsea	5.4	29 May 1999

English Writers' Association Footballer of the Year

Year	Player	Team
1980	Terry McDermott	Liverpool
1981	Frans Thijssen	Ipswich Town
1982	Steve Perryman	Tottenham Hotspur
1983	Kenny Dalglish	Liverpool
1984	Ian Rush	Liverpool
1985	Neville Southall	Everton
1986	Gary Lineker	Everton
1987	Clive Allen	Tottenham Hotspur
1988	John Barnes	Liverpool
1989	Steve Nicol	Liverpool
1990	John Barnes	Liverpool
1991	Gordon Strachan	Leeds United
1992	Gary Lineker	Tottenham Hotspur
1993	Chris Waddle	Sheffield Wednesday
1994	Alan Shearer	Blackburn Rovers
1995	Jürgen Klinsmann	Tottenham Hotspur
1996	Eric Cantona	Manchester United
1997	Gianfranco Zola	Chelsea
1998	Dennis Bergkamp	Arsenal
1999	David Ginola	Tottenham Hotspur

Scottish Football

Scottish Premier League Results

(– = not applicable.)

1998–99

Home team	Away team									
	Aberdeen		Celtic		Dundee		Dundee United		Dunfermline	
Aberdeen	–	–	3–2	1–5	2–2	1–2	0–3	0–4	2–1	3–1
Celtic	2–0	3–2	–	–	6–1	5–0	2–1	2–1	5–0	5–0
Dundee	0–2	1–2	1–1	0–3	–	–	2–2	1–3	1–0	3–1
Dundee United	1–0	3–0	1–1	–	0–1	0–2	–	–	1–1	1–1
Dunfermline	1–1	1–2	2–2	1–2	2–0	2–0	2–1	2–2	–	–
Hearts	2–0	0–2	2–1	2–4	0–2	1–2	0–1	4–1	2–1	2–0
Kilmarnock	4–0	4–2	2–0	0–0	2–1	0–0	2–0	2–0	0–0	0–0
Motherwell	2–2	1–1	1–2	1–7	2–1	1–2	1–0	2–0	0–0	1–1
Rangers	2–1	3–1	0–0	2–2	1–0	6–1	2–1	0–1	1–1	1–0
St Johnstone	2–0	4–1	2–1	1–0	1–1	1–0	1–3	1–0	1–1	1–1

(continued)

Scottish Premier League Results (*continued*)

Home team	Away team: Hearts		Kilmarnock		Motherwell		Rangers		St Johnstone	
Aberdeen	2–0	–	0–1	2–1	1–1	1–1	1–1	2–4	0–1	1–0
Celtic	1–1	3–0	1–1	1–0	2–0	1–0	5–1	0–3	0–1	5–0
Dundee	1–0	2–0	1–1	2–1	1–0	1–0	0–4	1–1	1–1	0–1
Dundee United	0–0	1–3	0–2	0–0	2–2	0–3	0–0	1–2	1–1	0–1
Dunfermline	1–1	0–0	0–3	0–6	1–1	–	0–2	0–3	1–1	1–0
Hearts	–	–	2–1	2–2	3–0	0–2	2–1	2–3	1–1	0–2
Kilmarnock	3–0	1–0	–	–	0–0	0–1	1–3	0–5	2–2	1–1
Motherwell	3–2	0–4	0–0	1–2	–	–	1–0	1–5	1–0	1–2
Rangers	3–0	0–0	1–0	–	2–0	2–1	–	–	4–0	1–0
St Johnstone	1–1	0–0	0–0	0–1	5–0	0–0	0–7	3–1	–	–

Scottish Football: Premier League Final Table

This was formerly the Bell's Scottish Premier Division. The team finishing bottom is automatically relegated. (Key: P = played; W = won; D = drawn; L = lost; F = goals for; A = goals against; Pt = points; GD = goal difference.)

1998–99

Position	Team	P	Home W	Home D	Home L	Home F	Home A	Away W	Away D	Away L	Away F	Away A	Pt	GD
1	Rangers	36	12	5	1	32	11	11	3	4	46	20	77	47
2	Celtic	36	14	2	2	49	12	7	6	5	35	23	71	49
3	St Johnstone	36	8	7	3	24	18	7	5	6	15	20	57	1
4	Kilmarnock	36	8	7	3	24	15	6	7	5	23	14	56	18
5	Dundee	36	7	4	7	18	23	6	3	9	18	33	46	−20
6	Heart of Midlothian	36	8	2	8	27	26	3	7	8	17	24	42	−6
7	Motherwell	36	6	5	7	20	31	4	6	8	15	23	41	−19
8	Aberdeen	36	6	4	8	24	35	4	3	11	19	36	37	−28
9	Dundee United	36	2	8	8	13	22	6	2	10	24	26	34	−11
10	Dunfermline Athletic	36	4	7	7	18	29	0	9	9	10	30	28	−31

Scottish Division One Final Table

The team finishing top is automatically promoted. The bottom two teams are automatically relegated to Division Two. (Key: P = played; W = won; D = drawn; L = lost; F = goals for; A = goals against; Pt = points; GD = goal difference.)

1998–99

Position	Team	P	Home W	Home D	Home L	Home F	Home A	Away W	Away D	Away L	Away F	Away A	Pt	GD
1	Hibernian	36	16	1	1	45	13	12	4	2	39	20	89	51
2	Falkirk	36	9	5	4	28	18	11	1	6	32	20	66	22
3	Ayr United	36	8	4	6	38	23	11	1	6	28	19	62	24
4	Airdrie	36	6	2	10	17	29	12	3	3	25	14	59	−1
5	St Mirren	36	10	2	6	26	25	4	8	6	16	18	52	−1
6	Greenock Morton	36	5	5	8	20	24	9	2	7	25	17	49	4
7	Clydebank	36	5	6	7	17	18	6	7	5	19	20	46	−2
8	Raith Rovers	36	5	5	8	19	27	3	6	9	18	30	35	−20
9	Hamilton Academicals	36	3	5	10	13	26	3	5	10	17	36	28	−32
10	Stranraer	36	2	2	14	14	31	3	0	15	15	43	17	−45

Scottish Division Two Final Table

The teams finishing first and second are automatically promoted. The bottom two teams are automatically relegated to the Third Division. (Key: P = played; W = won; D = drawn; L = lost; F = goals for; A = goals against; Pt = points; GD = goal difference.)

1998–99

Position	Team		Home					Away						
		P	W	D	L	F	A	W	D	L	F	A	Pt	GD
1	Livingston	36	13	4	1	32	12	9	7	2	34	23	77	31
2	Inverness Caledonian Thistle	36	14	4	0	44	20	7	5	6	36	28	72	32
3	Clyde	36	10	4	4	28	16	5	4	9	18	26	53	4
4	Queen of the South	36	7	8	3	26	17	6	1	11	24	28	48	5
5	Alloa Athletic	36	8	3	7	41	30	5	4	9	24	26	46	9
6	Stirling Albion	36	7	3	8	27	28	5	5	8	23	35	44	–13
7	Arbroath	36	7	4	7	19	25	5	4	9	18	27	44	–15
8	Partick Thistle	36	7	4	7	18	19	5	3	10	18	26	43	–9
9	East Fife	36	7	3	8	22	31	5	3	10	20	33	42	–22
10	Forfar Athletic	36	6	3	9	31	34	2	4	12	17	36	31	–22

Scottish Division Three Final Table

The teams finishing first and second are automatically promoted. (Key: P = played; W = won; D = drawn; L = lost; F = goals for; A = goals against; Pt = points; GD = goal difference.)

1998–99

Position	Team		Home					Away						
		P	W	D	L	F	A	W	D	L	F	A	Pt	GD
1	Ross County	36	12	1	5	39	16	12	4	2	48	26	77	45
2	Stenhousemuir	36	9	2	7	34	26	10	5	3	28	16	64	20
3	Brechin City	36	7	6	5	21	19	10	2	6	26	24	59	4
4	Dumbarton	36	6	5	7	25	21	10	4	4	28	19	57	13
5	Berwick Rangers	36	7	3	8	28	27	5	11	2	25	22	50	4
6	Queen's Park	36	6	7	5	22	21	5	4	9	19	25	44	–5
7	Albion Rovers	36	5	4	9	22	36	7	4	7	21	27	44	–20
8	East Stirling	36	4	10	4	27	22	5	3	10	23	26	40	2
9	Cowdenbeath	36	5	2	11	19	30	3	5	10	15	35	31	–31
10	Montrose	36	5	4	9	26	31	3	2	13	16	43	30	–32

Scottish League Champions

Year	Team
1890–91	Dumbarton and Rangers (shared)
1891–92	Dumbarton
1892–93	Celtic
1893–94	Celtic
1894–95	Hearts
1895–96	Celtic
1896–97	Hearts
1897–98	Celtic
1898–99	Rangers
1899–1900	Rangers
1900–01	Rangers
1901–02	Rangers
1902–03	Hibernian
1903–04	Third Lanark
1904–05	Celtic
1905–06	Celtic
1906–07	Celtic
1907–08	Celtic
1908–09	Celtic
1909–10	Celtic
1910–11	Rangers
1911–12	Rangers
1912–13	Rangers
1913–14	Celtic
1914–15	Celtic
1915–16	Celtic
1916–17	Celtic
1917–18	Rangers
1918–19	Celtic
1919–20	Rangers
1920–21	Rangers
1921–22	Celtic
1922–23	Rangers
1923–24	Rangers
1924–25	Rangers
1925–26	Celtic
1926–27	Rangers
1927–28	Rangers
1928–29	Rangers
1929–30	Rangers
1930–31	Rangers
1931–32	Motherwell
1932–33	Rangers
1933–34	Rangers
1934–35	Rangers
1935–36	Celtic
1936–37	Rangers
1937–38	Celtic
1938–39	Rangers
1940–45	not held
1946–47	Rangers
1947–48	Hibernian
1948–49	Rangers
1949–50	Rangers
1950–51	Hibernian
1951–52	Hibernian
1952–53	Rangers
1953–54	Celtic
1954–55	Aberdeen
1955–56	Rangers
1956–57	Rangers
1957–58	Hearts
1958–59	Rangers
1959–60	Hearts
1960–61	Rangers
1961–62	Dundee
1962–63	Rangers
1963–64	Rangers
1964–65	Kilmarnock
1965–66	Celtic
1966–67	Celtic
1967–68	Celtic
1968–69	Celtic
1969–70	Celtic
1970–71	Celtic
1971–72	Celtic
1972–73	Celtic
1973–74	Celtic
1974–75	Rangers
1975–76	Rangers
1976–77	Celtic
1977–78	Rangers
1978–79	Celtic
1979–80	Aberdeen
1980–81	Celtic
1981–82	Celtic
1982–83	Dundee United
1983–84	Aberdeen
1984–85	Aberdeen
1985–86	Celtic
1986–87	Rangers
1987–88	Celtic
1988–89	Rangers
1989–90	Rangers
1990–91	Rangers
1991–92	Rangers
1992–93	Rangers
1993–94	Rangers
1994–95	Rangers
1995–96	Rangers
1996–97	Rangers
1997–98	Celtic
1998–99	Rangers

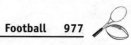

Scottish FA Cup Winners

First final held in 1874.

Year	Team	Year	Team	Year	Team
1980	Celtic	1987	St Mirren	1994	Dundee United
1981	Rangers	1988	Celtic	1995	Celtic
1982	Aberdeen	1989	Celtic	1996	Rangers
1983	Aberdeen	1990	Aberdeen	1997	Kilmarnock
1984	Aberdeen	1991	Motherwell	1998	Hearts
1985	Celtic	1992	Rangers	1999	Rangers
1986	Aberdeen	1993	Rangers		

Scottish FA Cup Results

1998–99

Home	Away	Score
Third Round		
Aberdeen	Livingston	0–1
Ayr United	Kilmarnock	3–0
Brechin City	Albion Rovers	1–1
Albion Rovers	Brechin City	3–1[1]
Celtic	Aidrieonians	3–1
Clydebank	Ross County	1–1
Ross County	Clydebank	2–3[1 2]
Falkirk	Huntly	3–0
Greenock Morton	Dundee	2–1
Hibernian	Stirling Albion	1–1
Stirling Albion	Hibernian	2–1[1]
Motherwell	Heart of Midlothian	3–1
Patrick Thistle	Dunfermline Athletic	1–2
Queen's Park	Dundee United	0–0
Dundee United	Queen's Park	1–0[1]
Raith Rovers	Clyde	0–4
Rangers	Stenhousemuir	2–0
St Johnstone	Forfar Athletic	1–0
St Mirren	Hamilton Academicals	1–1
Hamilton Academicals	St Mirren	1–0[1]
Stranraer	East Stirling	1–0
Fourth Round		
Ayr United	Albion Rovers	1–0
Celtic	Dunfermline Athletic	4–0
Clydebank	Dundee United	2–2
Dundee United	Clydebank	3–0[1]
Greenock Morton	Clyde	6–1
Hamilton Academicals	Rangers	0–6
Livingston	St Johnstone	1–1
Motherwell	Stirling Albion	2–0
Stranraer	Falkirk	1–2
Quarter Finals		
Ayr United	Dundee United	0–0
Dundee United	Ayr United	2–1[1]
Greenock Morton	Celtic	0–3
Motherwell	St Johnstone	0–2
Rangers	Falkirk	2–1
Semi Finals		
St Johnstone	Rangers	0–4
Celtic	Dundee United	2–0

Final (29 May, 1999)

Attendance: 52,000

Home	Away	Score
Celtic	Rangers (Wallace, 48 minutes)	0–1

Teams: Celtic Gould, Boyd, Mahe (O'Donnell 77 minutes), Stubbs, Larsson, Wieghorst, Lambert, Annoni (Johnson 61 minutes), Blinker, Moravcik, Mjallby **Rangers** Klos, Porrini (Kanchelskis 77 minutes), Hendry, Amoruso, Vidmar, McCann (Ferguson 67 minutes), McInnes, Van Bronckhorst, Wallace, Amato (Wilson 90 minutes), Albertz

[1] Replay.
[2] After extra time.

Scottish League Cup Recent Winners

Year	Winners	Year	Winners	Year	Winners
1988–89	Rangers	1992–93	Rangers	1996–97	Rangers
1989–90	Aberdeen	1993–94	Rangers	1997–98	Celtic
1990–91	Rangers	1994–95	Raith Rovers	1998–99	Rangers
1991–92	Hibernian	1995–96	Aberdeen		

Scottish Premier League Leading Scorers

1998–99

Name	Team	Goals scored			
		League	Domestic cup competitions	European competitions	Total
Henrik Larsson	Celtic	29	5	4	38
Rod Wallace	Rangers	18	4	3	25
Billy Dodds	Dundee United	14	4	0	18
Jorg Albertz	Rangers	10	4	4	18
Jonatan Johansson	Rangers	8	4	5	17
Eion Jess	Aberdeen	14	0	0	14
Robert Winters	Aberdeen	13	0	0	13
Neil McCann	Rangers	8	3	1	12[1]
Gary McSwegan	Hearts	11	1	0	12[2]

[1] Includes four goals for Hearts.
[2] Includes four goals for Dundee United.

Scottish Football: Scottish Divisions One, Two, and Three Leading Scorers

1998–99

Name	Team	Goals scored		
		League	Domestic cup competitions	Total
Alexander Bone	Stirling Albion	21	2	23
Scott McLean	Inverness Caledonian Thistle	19	1	20
Glynn Hurst	Ayr United	18	2	20
Patrick Flannery	Dumbarton	18	1	19
Andy Walker	Ayr United	15	4	19
Steven Ferguson	Ross County	17	0	17
Marino Keith	Falkirk	16	1	17
Martin Cameron	Alloa Athletic	15	2	17
John Dickson	Brechin City	15	2	17

Gaelic Football

The All-Ireland Gaelic Football Championship

Since 1990.

Year	Team	Year	Team	Year	Team	Year	Team	Year	Team
1990	Cork	1992	Donegal	1994	Down	1996	Meath	1998	Galway
1991	Down	1993	Derry	1995	Dublin	1997	Kerry		

Golf

British Open Golf Championship Winners

The competition was played over 36 holes between 1860 and 1891; since 1892 it has been played over 72 holes.

Year	Name	Country	Location	Score
1946	Sam Snead	USA	St Andrews	290
1947	Fred Daly	UK	Hoylake	293
1948	Henry Cotton	UK	Muirfield	284
1949	Bobby Locke	South Africa	Sandwich	283[1]
1950	Bobby Locke	South Africa	Troon	279
1951	Max Faulkner	UK	Portrush	285
1952	Bobby Locke	South Africa	Royal Lytham	287
1953	Ben Hogan	USA	Carnoustie	282
1954	Peter Thomson	Australia	Royal Birkdale	283
1955	Peter Thomson	Australia	St Andrews	281
1956	Peter Thomson	Australia	Hoylake	286
1957	Bobby Locke	South Africa	St Andrews	279
1958	Peter Thomson	Australia	Royal Lytham	278[1]
1959	Gary Player	South Africa	Muirfield	284
1960	Kel Nagle	Australia	St Andrews	278
1961	Arnold Palmer	USA	Royal Birkdale	284
1962	Arnold Palmer	USA	Troon	276
1963	Bob Charles	New Zealand	Royal Lytham	277[1]
1964	Tony Lema	USA	St Andrews	279
1965	Peter Thomson	Australia	Royal Birkdale	285
1966	Jack Nicklaus	USA	Muirfield	282
1967	Roberto de Vincenzo	Argentina	Hoylake	278
1968	Gary Player	South Africa	Carnoustie	289
1969	Tony Jacklin	UK	Royal Lytham	280
1970	Jack Nicklaus	USA	St Andrews	283[1]
1971	Lee Trevino	USA	Royal Birkdale	278
1972	Lee Trevino	USA	Muirfield	278
1973	Tom Weiskopf	USA	Troon	276
1974	Gary Player	South Africa	Royal Lytham	282
1975	Tom Watson	USA	Carnoustie	279[1]
1976	Johnny Miller	USA	Royal Birkdale	279
1977	Tom Watson	USA	Turnberry	268
1978	Jack Nicklaus	USA	St Andrews	281
1979	Seve Ballesteros	Spain	Royal Lytham	283
1980	Tom Watson	USA	Muirfield	271
1981	Bill Rogers	USA	Sandwich	276
1982	Tom Watson	USA	Troon	284
1983	Tom Watson	USA	Royal Birkdale	275
1984	Seve Ballesteros	Spain	St Andrews	276
1985	Sandy Lyle	UK	Sandwich	282
1986	Greg Norman	Australia	Turnberry	280
1987	Nick Faldo	UK	Muirfield	279
1988	Seve Ballesteros	Spain	Royal Lytham	273
1989	Mark Calcavecchia	USA	Troon	275[1]
1990	Nick Faldo	UK	St Andrews	270
1991	Ian Baker-Finch	Australia	Royal Birkdale	272
1992	Nick Faldo	UK	Muirfield	272
1993	Greg Norman	Australia	Sandwich	267
1994	Nick Price	Zimbabwe	Turnberry	268
1995	John Daly	USA	St Andrews	282[1]
1996	Tom Lehman	USA	Royal Lytham	271
1997	Justin Leonard	USA	Troon	272
1998	Mark O'Meara	USA	Royal Birkdale	280[1]
1999	Paul Lawrie	UK	Carnoustie	290[1]

[1] Won after play-off.

US Masters Golf Winners

This competition has been held annually at the Augusta National course, Georgia, USA, since 1934.

Year	Name	Country	Score
1990	Nick Faldo	UK	278[1]
1991	Ian Woosnam	UK	277
1992	Fred Couples	USA	275
1993	Bernhard Langer	Germany	277
1994	José-Maria Olazábal	Spain	279
1995	Ben Crenshaw	USA	274
1996	Nick Faldo	UK	276
1997	Tiger Woods	USA	270
1998	Mark O'Meara	USA	279
1999	José Maria Olazábal	Spain	279

[1] Won after play-off.

Men's US Open Golf Championship Winners

Year	Name	Country	Location	Score
1990	Hale Irwin	USA	Medinah (IL)	280[1]
1991	Payne Stewart	USA	Hazeltine (MN)	282[1]
1992	Tom Kite	USA	Monterey (CA)	285
1993	Lee Janzen	USA	Baltusrol (NJ)	272
1994	Ernie Els	South Africa	Oakmont (PA)	279
1995	Corey Pavin	USA	Shinnecock Hills (NY)	280
1996	Steve Jones	USA	Oakland Hills (MI)	278
1997	Ernie Els	South Africa	Congressional (MI)	276
1998	Lee Janzen	USA	Olympic Club (CA)	280
1999	Payne Stewart	USA	Pinehurst (NC)	279

[1] Score after play-off.

US Professional Golf Association (US PGA) Championship Winners

This competition was first held in 1916. It was contested as a matchplay between 1916 and 1957, and has been contested as strokeplay since 1958. Players are of US nationality unless otherwise stated.

Year	Name	Score
1989	Payne Stewart	276
1990	Wayne Grady (Australia)	282
1991	John Daly	276
1992	Nick Price (Zimbabwe)	278
1993	Paul Azinger	272[1]
1994	Nick Price (Zimbabwe)	269
1995	Steve Elkington (Australia)	267
1996	Mark Brooks	277[1]
1997	Davis Love III	269
1998	Vijay Singh (Fiji)	271
1999	Tiger Woods	277

[1] Score after play-off.

Ryder Cup Winners

This competition is a biennial team event, inaugurated in 1927 between professional golfers of the USA and the UK. From 1973 to 1977, the event was between the USA and a combined UK and Republic of Ireland team. Since 1979, it has been between the USA and Europe. Locations are in the USA unless otherwise stated.

Year	Winner	Score	Location
1979	USA	17–11	Greenbrier (WV), USA
1981	USA	18.5–9.5	Walton Heath, Surrey, England
1983	USA	14.5–13.5	PGA National GC (FL), USA
1985	Europe	16.5–11.5	The Belfry, Sutton Coldfield, England
1987	Europe	15–13	Muirfield Village GC (OH), USA
1989	tie	14–14	The Belfry, Sutton Coldfield, England
1991	USA	14.5–13.5	Ocean Course (SC), USA
1993	USA	15–13	The Belfry, Sutton Coldfield, England
1995	Europe	14.5–13.5	Oak Hill CC (NY), USA
1997	Europe	14.5–13.5	Valderrama, Andalucia, Spain

World Golf Matchplay Champions

This competition has been held annually at Wentworth, Surrey, England, since 1964. Since 1992, it has been sponsored by Toyota.

Year	Name	Country
1994	Ernie Els	South Africa
1995	Ernie Els	South Africa
1996	Ernie Els	South Africa
1997	Vijay Singh	Fiji
1998	Mark O'Meara	USA

European Professional Golfers' Association: Harry Vardon Trophy Winners

This trophy has been awarded since 1937 to the leader of the European PGA Order of Merit. Most wins: Severiano Ballesteros, 6; Colin Montgomerie, 5; Peter Oosterhuis, 4.

Year	Name	Country
1994	Colin Montgomerie	UK
1995	Colin Montgomerie	UK
1996	Colin Montgomerie	UK
1997	Colin Montgomerie	UK
1998	Colin Montgomerie	UK

British Amateur Golf Championship Winners

This championship was first held in 1885. Winners are from the UK or the Republic of Ireland unless otherwise stated.

Year	Name
1990	Rolf Muntz (Netherlands)
1991	Gary Wolstenholme
1992	Stephen Dundas
1993	Iain Pyman
1994	Lee James
1995	Gordon Sherry
1996	Warren Bladon
1997	Craig Watson
1998	Sergio Garcia (Spain)
1999	Graeme Storm

Walker Cup Winners

This team competition has been held every two years since 1922 (except 1940–45) between the amateur golfers of the USA and those of the UK and the Republic of Ireland.

Year	Winners	Score
1989	UK and Republic of Ireland	12.5–11.5
1991	USA	14–10
1993	USA	19–5
1995	UK and Republic of Irelandf	14–10
1997	USA	18–6

British Women's Open Golf Championship Winners

This championship has been held as a strokeplay event since 1976. It is now sponsored by Weetabix.

Year	Name	Country
1994	Liselotte Neumann	Sweden
1995	Karrie Webb	Australia
1996	Emilee Klein	USA
1997	Karrie Webb	Australia
1998	Sherri Steinhauer	USA
1999	Sherri Steinhauer	USA

Solheim Cup Winners

This is a biennial team competition between the women professional golfers of the USA and Europe. It was first held in 1990.

Year	Winner	Score	Location
1990	USA	11.5–4.5	Orlando (FL), USA
1992	Europe	11.5–6.5	Dalmahoy, Scotland
1994	USA	13–7	Greenbrier (WV), USA
1996	USA	17–11	Chepstow, Wales
1998	USA	16–12	Muirfield Village (OH), USA

Gymnastics

Gymnastics World Championships: Overall Individual Winners

These championships were first held in 1903 for men and in 1934 for women. They are contested every two years.

Year	Name	Country
Men		
1989	Igor Korobichensky	USSR
1991	Gregori Misutin	USSR
1993	Vitaly Scherbo	Belarus
1995	Li Xiaoshuang	China
1997	Ivan Ivankov	Belarus

Year	Name	Country
Women		
1989	Svetlana Boginskaya	USSR
1991	Kim Zmeskal	USA
1993	Shannon Miller	USA
1995	Lilia Pôdkopaeva	Ukraine
1997	Svetlana Khorkina	Russia

Hockey

Men's Hockey World Cup

This championship was inaugurated in 1971 by the Fédération Internationale de Hockey (FIH).

Year	Country
1982	Pakistan
1986	Australia
1990	Netherlands
1994	Pakistan
1998	Netherlands

Women's Hockey World Cup

This championship was inaugurated in 1974 by the Fédération Internationale de Hockey (FIH).

Year	Country
1983	Netherlands
1986	Netherlands
1990	Netherlands
1994	Australia
1998	Australia

English National Hockey League: Premier Division Final Table (Men)

1998–99

Position	Team	Played	Won	Drawn	Lost	Goals for	Goals against	Points
1	Cannock[1 2]	22	16	4	2	87	37	52
2	Southgate[2]	22	15	2	5	62	50	47
3	Reading[2]	22	13	4	5	77	49	43
4	Canterbury[2]	22	13	3	6	87	60	42
5	Beeston	22	11	5	6	61	46	38
6	Teddington	22	11	3	8	67	54	36
7	Old Loughtonians	22	9	3	10	76	77	30
8	Guildford	22	9	3	10	71	91	30
9	Bournville	22	6	6	10	50	68	24
10	Hounslow[3]	22	3	6	13	38	63	15
11	East Grinstead[4]	22	2	3	17	52	87	9
12	Brookland[4]	22	2	2	18	42	88	8

[1] Champions.
[2] Qualified for Premiership Tournament.
[3] Relegated after losing a play-off with Division One champions Surbiton.
[4] Relegated to Division One.

English National Hockey League: Premiership Tournament Play-Offs (Men)

Play-Offs, Reading, 17–18 April 1999

Winner	Loser
Reading 8	Canterbury 2
Cannock 1	Southgate 0
Reading 4	Southgate 2

Final, Milton Keynes, 3 May 1999

Cannock 3[1]	Reading 3[1]

[1]After extra time Cannock won 4–3 on penalty strokes.

English National Hockey League: Premiership Tournament Play-Offs (Women)

Play-Offs, Reading, 17–18 April 1999

Winner	Loser
Clifton 2	Hightown 1
Slough 2	Ipswich 1
Slough 4	Clifton 2

Final, Milton Keynes, 3 May 1999

Slough 4	Clifton 2

English National Hockey League: Premier Division Final Table (Women)

The championship was decided for the first time by an end of season Premiership tournament contested by the teams finishing in the top four league positions.

1998–99

Position	Team	Played	Won	Drawn	Lost	Goals for	Goals against	Points
1	Slough[1 2]	14	10	2	2	53	25	32
2	Ipswich[2]	14	9	2	3	36	20	29
3	Hightown[2]	14	5	8	1	28	22	23
4	Clifton[2]	14	7	2	5	27	21	23
5	Olton	14	4	5	5	27	34	17
6	Leicester	14	4	2	8	26	34	14
7	Sutton Coldfield	14	3	1	10	19	38	10
8	Doncaster[3]	14	2	2	10	23	45	8

[1] Champions.
[2] Qualify for Premiership Tournament.
[3] Doncaster retain their Premier Division status after defeating Division One side Aldridge in a play-off.

Horse Racing

Flat Racing

The Derby

This race was first held in 1780 and is held at Epsom over 1 mile and 4 furlongs. Since 1984 it has been sponsored by Ever Ready. Colts carry 9 stone; fillies 8 stone 9 lb. Most wins for a jockey: Lester Piggott, 9; Jem Robinson, 6, Steve Donoghue, 6.

Year	Horse	Jockey	Year	Horse	Jockey
1960	St Paddy	Lester Piggott	1980	Henbit	Willie Carson
1961	Psidium	Roger Poincelet	1981	Shergar	Walter Swinburn
1962	Larkspur	Neville Sellwood	1982	Golden Fleece	Pat Eddery
1963	Relko	Yves Saint-Martin	1983	Teenoso	Lester Piggott
1964	Santa Claus	Scobie Breasley	1984	Secreto	Christy Roche
1965	Sea Bird II	Pat Glennon	1985	Slip Anchor	Steve Cauthen
1966	Charlottown	Scobie Breasley	1986	Shahrastani	Walter Swinburn
1967	Royal Palace	George Moore	1987	Reference Point	Steve Cauthen
1968	Sir Ivor	Lester Piggott	1988	Kahyashi	Ray Cochrane
1969	Blakeney	Ernie Johnson	1989	Nashwan	Willie Carson
1970	Nijinsky	Lester Piggott	1990	Quest For Fame	Pat Eddery
1971	Mill Reef	Geoff Lewis	1991	Generous	Alan Munro
1972	Roberto	Lester Piggott	1992	Dr Devious	John Reid
1973	Morston	Eddie Hide	1993	Commander in Chief	Michael Kinane
1974	Snow Knight	Brian Taylor	1994	Erhaab	Willie Carson
1975	Grundy	Pat Eddery	1995	Lammtarra	Walter Swinburn
1976	Empery	Lester Piggott	1996	Shaamit	Michael Hills
1977	The Minstrel	Lester Piggott	1997	Benny The Dip	Willie Ryan
1978	Shirley Heights	Greville Starkey	1998	High-Rise	Olivier Peslier
1979	Troy	Willie Carson	1999	Oath	Kieren Fallon

1,000 Guineas

This race was first held in 1814 and is run over 1 mile at Newmarket. The race is for 3-year-old fillies only, who each carry 9 stone.

Year	Horse	Jockey
1995	Harayir	Richard Hills
1996	Bosra Sham	Pat Eddery
1997	Sleepytime	Kieren Fallon
1998	Cape Verdi	Frankie Dettori
1999	Wince	Kieren Fallon

2,000 Guineas

This race was first held in 1809 and is run over 1 mile at Newmarket. It is for 3-year-olds only; colts carry 9 stone, fillies 8 stone 9 lb.

Year	Horse	Jockey
1995	Pennekamp	Thierry Jarnet
1996	Mark of Esteem	Frankie Dettori
1997	Entrepreneur	Michael Kinane
1998	King of Kings	Michael Kinane
1999	Island Sands	Frankie Dettori

The Oaks

This race was first held in 1779 and is run over 1 mile 4 furlongs at Epsom in Surrey. The Oaks is for 3-year-old fillies only, who each carry 9 stone.

Year	Horse	Jockey
1995	Moonshell	Frankie Dettori
1996	Lady Carla	Pat Eddery
1997	Reams of Verse	Kieren Fallon
1998	Shahtoush	Michael Kinane
1999	Ramruma	Kieren Fallon

The St Leger

This is the oldest English classic race and was first held in 1776. It is run over 1 mile 6 furlongs 132 yards at Doncaster. It is for three-year-olds; colts carry 9 stone, fillies 8 stone 9 lbs.

Year	Horse	Jockey
1994	Moonax	Pat Eddery
1995	Classic Cliché	Frankie Dettori
1996	Shantou	Frankie Dettori
1997	Silver Patriarch	Pat Eddery
1998	Nedawi	John Reid

Prix de l'Arc de Triomphe

This race was first held in 1920 and is run over 2,400 m at Longchamp in Paris, France.

Year	Horse	Jockey
1994	Carnegie	Thierry Jarnet
1995	Lammtarra	Frankie Dettori
1996	Helissio	Olivier Peslier
1997	Peintre Celebre	Olivier Peslier
1998	Sagamix	Olivier Peslier

Champion Jockeys

Year	Jockey	Number of winners
1994	Frankie Dettori	233
1995	Frankie Dettori	211
1996	Pat Eddery	186
1997	Kieren Fallon	196
1998	Kieren Fallon	202

National Hunt Racing

The Grand National

This race has been run at Aintree, Liverpool since 1839 with the exception of the war years (1916–18) when it was held at Gatwick, Surrey. The race is a handicap steeplechase and the current course takes in 30 fences and is run over 4 miles 4 furlongs. Most wins for a horse: Red Rum, 3. Most wins for a jockey: George Stevens, 5; Tom Oliver, 4.
(– = not applicable.)

Year	Horse	Jockey
1946	Lovely Cottage	Captain Bobby Petre
1947	Caughoo	Eddie Dempsey
1948	Sheila's Cottage	Arthur Thompson
1949	Russian Hero	Leo McMorrow
1950	Freebooter	Jimmy Power
1951	Nickel Coin	Johnny Bullock
1952	Teal	Arthur Thompson
1953	Early Mist	Bryan Marshall
1954	Royal Tan	Bryan Marshall
1955	Quare Times	Pat Taaffe
1956	E.S.B	Dave Dick
1957	Sundew	Fred Winter
1958	Mr What	Arthur Freeman
1959	Oxo	Michael Scudamore
1960	Merryman II	Gerry Scott
1961	Nicolaus Silver	Bobby Beasley
1962	Kilmore	Fred Winter
1963	Ayala	Pat Buckley
1964	Team Spirit	Willie Robinson
1965	Jay Trump	Mr Tommy Smith
1966	Anglo	Tim Norman
1967	Foinavon	John Buckingham

(continued)

The Grand National (*continued*)

Year	Horse	Jockey
1968	Red Alligator	Brian Fletcher
1969	Highland Wedding	Eddie Harty
1970	Gay Trip	Pat Taaffe
1971	Specify	John Cook
1972	Well To Do	Graham Thorner
1973	Red Rum	Brian Fletcher
1974	Red Rum	Brian Fletcher
1975	L'Escargot	Tommy Carberry
1976	Rag Trade	John Burke
1977	Red Rum	Tommy Stack
1978	Lucius	Bob Davies
1979	Rubstic	Maurice Barnes
1980	Ben Nevis	Mr Charlie Fenwick
1981	Aldaniti	Bob Champion
1982	Grittar	Mr Dick Saunders
1983	Corbiére	Ben de Haan
1984	Hallo Dandy	Neale Doughty
1985	Last Suspect	Hywel Davies
1986	West Tip	Richard Dunwoody
1987	Maori Venture	Steve Knight
1988	Rhyme N' Reason	Brendan Powell
1989	Little Polvier	Jimmy Frost
1990	Mr Frisk	Mr Marcus Armytage
1991	Seagram	Nigel Hawke
1992	Party Politics	Carl Llewellyn
1993[1]	–	–
1994	Miinnehoma	Richard Dunwoody
1995	Royal Athlete	Jason Titley
1996	Rough Quest	Mick Fitzgerald
1997[2]	Lord Gyllene	Tony Dobbin
1998	Earth Summit	Carl Llewellyn
1999	Bobbyjo	Paul Carberry

[1] Race void after a false start.
[2] Held on the Monday following a bomb scare at the Saturday meeting.

Tote Cheltenham Gold Cup Chase

This race was first run in 1924; it is held annually at Prestbury Park, Cheltenham, during the Cheltenham Spring Festival. Current distance is 3 miles, 2 furlongs and about 110 yards. Most wins for a horse: Golden Miller, 4; Cottage Rake, Arkle, 3. Most wins for a jockey: Pat Taafe, 4.

Year	Horse	Jockey
1995	Master Oats	Norman Williamson
1996	Imperial Call	Conor O'Dwyer
1997	Mr Mulligan	Tony McCoy
1998	Cool Dawn	Richard Thornton
1999	See More Business	Mick Fitzgerald

The Smurfit Champion Hurdle Challenge Trophy

This race was first run in 1927, and is held annually at Prestbury Park, Cheltenham, during the Cheltenham Spring Festival; current distance is 2 miles 110 yards.

Year	Horse	Jockey
1995	Alderbrook	Norman Williamson
1996	Collier Bay	Graham Bradley
1997	Make A Stand	Tony McCoy
1998	Istabraq	Charlie Swan
1999	Istabraq	Charlie Swan

National Hunt Racing: Other Selected Winners

1998–99

Race	Date	Racecourse	Horse	Jockey
Murphy's Gold Cup	14 November 1998	Cheltenham	Cyfor Malta	Tony McCoy
Hennessy Gold Cup	28 November 1998	Newbury	Teeton Mill	Norman Williamson
Tripleprint Gold Cup	12 December 1998	Cheltenham	Northern Starlight	Tony McCoy
King George VI Chase	26 December 1998	Kempton Park	Teeton Mill	Norman Williamson
Queen Mother Champion Chase	17 March 1999	Cheltenham	Call Equiname	Mick Fitzgerald
Irish Grand National	5 April 1999	Fairyhouse	Glebe Lad	Tom Rudd
Scottish Grand National	17 April 1999	Ayr	Young Kenny	Brendan Powell
Whitbread Gold Cup	24 April 1999	Sandown	Eulogy	Barry Fenton

National Hunt Racing: Champion Jockeys

Year	Jockey	Number of winners
1993–94	Richard Dunwoody	198
1994–95	Richard Dunwoody	160
1995–96	Tony McCoy	175
1996–97	Tony McCoy	190
1997–98	Tony McCoy	253
1998–99	Tony McCoy	186

Hurling

All-Ireland Hurling Champions

This championship was first held in 1887.

Year	Team	Year	Team
1994	Offaly	1997	Clare
1995	Clare	1998	Offaly
1996	Wexford		

Ice Hockey

Ice Hockey: World Championship Winners

Since 1990.

Year	Country	Year	Country
1990	USSR	1995	Finland
1991	Sweden	1996	Czech Republic
1992	Sweden	1997	Canada
1993	Russia	1998	Sweden
1994	Canada	1999	Czech Republic

Ice Hockey: British Sekonda Superleague Final Table

Scoring: win = 2 points; tie = 1 point; overtime loss = losing team receives 1 point.

1998–99

Position	Team	Played	Won	Tied	Lost	Overtime losses	Goals for	Goals against	Points
1	Manchester Storm	42	30	1	7	4	155	86	65
2	Cardiff Devils	42	27	0	10	5	144	102	59
3	Nottingham Panthers	42	25	1	14	2	140	134	53
4	Bracknell Bees	42	19	2	17	4	144	149	44
5	Ayr Scottish Eagles	42	18	3	18	3	136	140	42
6	Sheffield Steelers	42	17	4	19	2	135	141	40
7	Newcastle Cobras	42	14	2	24	2	117	150	32
8	London Knights	42	10	3	25	4	114	183	27

Ice Hockey: British Sekonda Superleague Play-Offs

The top two teams in each group qualify for the Championship semi-finals.

1998–99

Position	Team	Played	Wins	Ties	Losses	Overtime losses	Goals for	Goals againts	Points
Group A Final Standings									
1	Manchester Storm	6	5	0	1	0	22	9	10
2	Bracknell Bees	6	5	0	1	0	25	19	10
3	Sheffield Steelers	6	2	0	4	0	20	23	4
4	London Knights	6	0	0	5	1	14	30	1
Group B Final Standings									
1	Nottingham Panthers	6	5	0	1	0	20	16	10
2	Cardiff Devils	6	3	1	2	0	20	16	7
3	Ayr Scottish Eagles	6	2	1	3	0	21	20	5
4	Newcastle Cobras	6	1	0	3	2	14	23	4

Ice Hockey: British Sekonda Superleague Finals

1999

Winner	Loser
Semi Finals	
Cardiff Devils 5	Manchester Storm 0
Nottingham Panthers 4	Bracknell Bees 2
Final	
Cardiff Devils 2	Nottingham Panthers 1

Ice Hockey: National Hockey League (NHL): Stanley Cup Winners

Since 1990.

Year	Team
1990	Edmonton Oilers
1991	Pittsburgh Penguins
1992	Pittsburgh Penguins
1993	Montreal Canadiens
1994	New York Rangers
1995	New Jersey Devils
1996	Colorado Avalanche
1997	Detroit Red Wings
1998	Detroit Red Wings
1999	Dallas Stars

Ice Hockey: National Hockey League (NHL) Stanley Cup Finals

Dallas Stars win the series 4–2. (OT = overtime; 3OT = triple overtime.)

1999

Game	Dates	Home team	Away team
Game 1	8 June	Dallas Stars 2	Buffalo Sabres 3 (OT)
Game 2	10 June	Dallas Stars 4	Buffalo Sabres 2
Game 3	12 June	Buffalo Sabres 1	Dallas Stars 2
Game 4	15 June	Buffalo Sabres 2	Dallas Stars 1
Game 5	17 June	Dallas Stars 2	Buffalo Sabres 0
Game 6	19 June	Buffalo Sabres 1	Dallas Stars 2 (3OT)

Motor Racing

Formula 1 Grand Prix Winners

Final table 1st: Mika Hakkinen (Finland), 100 points; 2nd: Michael Schumacher (Germany), 86 points; 3rd: David Coulthard (UK), 56 points; 4th: Eddie Irvine (UK) 47 points; 5th Jacques Villeneuve (Canada) 21 points; 6th Damon Hill (UK) 20 points.

1998

Date	Grand Prix	Venue	Name	Country	Car
8 March	Australian	Melbourne	Mika Hakkinen	Finland	McLaren-Mercedes
29 March	Brazilian	Sao Paulo	Mika Hakkinen	Finland	McLaren-Mercedes
12 April	Argentinian	Buenos Aires	Michael Schumacher	Germany	Ferrari
26 April	San Marino	Imola	David Coulthard	UK	McLaren-Mercedes
10 May	Spanish	Barcelona	Mika Hakkinen	Finland	McLaren-Mercedes
24 May	Monaco	Monte Carlo	Mika Hakkinen	Finland	McLaren-Mercedes
7 June	Canadian	Montreal	Michael Schumacher	Germany	Ferrari
28 June	French	Magny-Cours	Michael Schumacher	Germany	Ferrari
12 July	British	Silverstone	Michael Schumacher	Germany	Ferrari
26 July	Austrian	Zeltweg	Mika Hakkinen	Finland	McLaren-Mercedes
2 August	German	Hockenheim	Mika Hakkinen	Finland	McLaren-Mercedes
16 August	Hungarian	Budapest	Michael Schumacher	Germany	Ferrari
30 August	Belgian	Spa-Francorchamps	Damon Hill	UK	Jordan-Mugen Honda
13 September	Italian	Monza	Michael Schumacher	Germany	Ferrari
27 September	Luxembourg	Nurburgring	Mika Hakkinen	Finland	McLaren-Mercedes
1 November	Japanese	Suzuka	Mika Hakkinen	Finland	McLaren-Mercedes

Formula 1 World Drivers' Championship Winners

This championship was inaugurated in 1950.

Year	Name	Country	Car
1950	Giuseppe Farina	Italy	Alfa Romeo
1951	Juan Manuel Fangio	Argentina	Alfa Romeo
1952	Alberto Ascari	Italy	Ferrari
1953	Alberto Ascari	Italy	Ferrari
1954	Juan Manuel Fangio	Argentina	Maserati-Mercedes
1955	Juan Manuel Fangio	Argentina	Mercedes-Benz
1956	Juan Manuel Fangio	Argentina	Lancia-Ferrari
1957	Juan Manuel Fangio	Argentina	Maserati
1958	Mike Hawthorn	Great Britain	Ferrari
1959	Jack Brabham	Australia	Cooper-Climax
1960	Jack Brabham	Australia	Cooper-Climax
1961	Phil Hill	USA	Ferrari
1962	Graham Hill	Great Britain	BRM
1963	Jim Clark	Great Britain	Lotus-Climax
1964	John Surtees	Great Britain	Ferrari
1965	Jim Clark	Great Britain	Lotus-Climax
1966	Jack Brabham	Australia	Brabham-Repco
1967	Denny Hulme	New Zealand	Brabham-Repco
1968	Graham Hill	Great Britain	Lotus-Ford
1969	Jackie Stewart	Great Britain	Matra-Ford
1970	Jochen Rindt	Austria	Lotus-Ford
1971	Jackie Stewart	Great Britain	Tyrrell-Ford
1972	Emerson Fittipaldi	Brazil	Lotus-Ford
1973	Jackie Stewart	Great Britain	Tyrrell-Ford
1974	Emerson Fittipaldi	Brazil	McLaren-Ford

Year	Name	Country	Car
1975	Niki Lauda	Austria	Ferrari
1976	James Hunt	Great Britain	McLaren-Ford
1977	Niki Lauda	Austria	Ferrari
1978	Mario Andretti	USA	Lotus-Ford
1979	Jody Scheckter	South Africa	Ferrari
1980	Alan Jones	Australia	Williams-Ford
1981	Nelson Piquet	Brazil	Brabham-Ford
1982	Keke Rosberg	Finland	Williams-Ford
1983	Nelson Piquet	Brazil	Brabham-BMW
1984	Niki Lauda	Austria	McLaren-TAG
1985	Alain Prost	France	McLaren-TAG
1986	Alain Prost	France	McLaren-TAG
1987	Nelson Piquet	Brazil	Williams-Honda
1988	Ayrton Senna	Brazil	McLaren-Honda
1989	Alain Prost	France	McLaren-Honda
1990	Ayrton Senna	Brazil	McLaren-Honda
1991	Ayrton Senna	Brazil	McLaren-Honda
1992	Nigel Mansell	Great Britain	Williams-Renault
1993	Alain Prost	France	Williams-Renault
1994	Michael Schumacher	Germany	Benetton-Ford
1995	Michael Schumacher	Germany	Benetton-Renault
1996	Damon Hill	Great Britain	Williams-Renault
1997	Jacques Villeneuve	France	Williams-Renault
1998	Mika Hakkinen	Finland	McLaren-Mercedes

Formula 1 World Constructors' Championship Winners

This championship was inaugurated in 1958.

Year	Constructor	Year	Constructor	Year	Constructor	Year	Constructor
1979	Ferrari	1984	McLaren-TAG	1989	McLaren-Honda	1994	Williams-Renault
1980	Williams-Ford	1985	McLaren-TAG	1990	McLaren-Honda	1995	Williams-Renault
1981	Williams-Ford	1986	Williams-Honda	1991	McLaren-Honda	1996	Williams-Renault
1982	Ferrari	1987	Williams-Honda	1992	Williams-Renault	1997	Williams-Renault
1983	Ferrari	1988	McLaren-Honda	1993	Williams-Renault	1998	McLaren-Mercedes

RAC Rally Winners

This race was formerly known as the RAC International Rally of Great Britain. It was first held in 1927, though not recognized as an international event by the Fédération Internationale de l'Automobile (FIA) until 1951. Sponsored by Network Q since 1993.

Year	Name	Country	Car
1994	Colin McRae	UK	Subaru Impreza
1995	Colin McRae	UK	Subaru Impreza
1996	Armin Schwarz	Germany	Toyota Celica
1997	Colin McRae	UK	Subaru Impreza
1998	Richard Burns	UK	Mitsubishi Lancer

World Rally Champions

A manufacturers' world championship was established in 1968. The FIA Cup for Drivers, a championship for drivers, was inaugurated in 1977 and two years later became the official world drivers' championship.

Year	Name	Country	Car
1994	Didier Auriol	France	Toyota Celica
1995	Colin McRae	UK	Subaru Impreza
1996	Tommi Mäkinen	Finland	Mitsubishi Lancer
1997	Tommi Mäkinen	Finland	Mitsubishi Lancer
1998	Tommi Mäkinen	Finland	Mitsubishi Lancer

Le Mans 24-Hour Race Champions

This race was first held in 1923.

Year	Names	Car
1995	Yannick Dalmas, J J Lehto, Masanori Sekiya	McLaren
1996	Davy Jones, Manuel Reuter, Alexander Wurz	Porsche
1997	Michele Alboreto, Stefan Johansson, Tom Kristensen	Porsche
1998	Allan McNish, Stephane Ortelli, Laurent Aiello	Porsche
1999	Yannick Dalmas, Pierluigi Martini, Joachim Winkelhock	BMW

Motorcycle Racing

500cc World Road Racing Champions

The championship was inaugurated in 1949.

Year	Name	Country	Manufacturer
1994	Michael Doohan	Australia	Honda
1995	Michael Doohan	Australia	Honda
1996	Michael Doohan	Australia	Honda
1997	Michael Doohan	Australia	Honda
1998	Michael Doohan	Australia	Honda

World Superbike Champions

This event was first held in 1988.

Year	Name	Country	Manufacturer
1994	Carl Fogarty	UK	Ducati
1995	Carl Fogarty	UK	Ducati
1996	Troy Corser	Australia	Ducati
1997	John Kocinski	USA	Honda
1998	Carl Fogarty	UK	Ducati

Isle of Man Tourist Trophy Senior TT

This road race was first held in 1907.

Year	Name	Country	Manufacturer
1995	Joey Dunlop	UK	Honda
1996	Phillip McCallen	UK	Honda
1997	Phillip McCallen	UK	Honda
1998	Ian Simpson	UK	Honda
1999	David Jefferies	UK	Yamaha

Motorcycle Racing World Champions

1998

Road Racing			
125cc	Kazuto Sakata	Japan	Aprilia
250 cc	Loris Capirossi	Italy	Aprilia
500 cc	Michael Doohan	Australia	Honda
Superbike	Carl Fogarty	UK	Ducati
Endurance	Doug Polen and Christian Lavieille	USA and France	Honda
Sidecar (World Cup)	Steve Webster and David James	UK	LCR Honda
Motocross			
125cc	Alessio Chiodi	Italy	Husqvarna
250cc	Sebastian Tortelli	France	Kawasaki
500cc	Joel Smets	Belgium	Husaberg
Sidecar	Kristers Sergis and Artis Rasmanis	Latvia	BSU
Trials	Doug Lampkin	UK	Beta

Netball

Netball World Championship

This championship was first held in 1963 and is held every four years.

Year	Country
1979	Australia, New Zealand, and Trinidad and Tobago
1983	Australia
1987	New Zealand
1991	Australia
1995	Australia

Rowing

World Rowing Championship

These championships were held in Cologne, Germany, 6–13 September.

1998

Category	Name	Country
Men		
Single sculls	Rob Waddell	New Zealand
Double sculls	Stephan Volkert and Andreas Hajek	Germany
Quad sculls		Italy
Lightweight single sculls	Stefano Basalini	Italy
Lightweight double sculls	Tomasz Kucharski and Robert Sycz	Poland
Lightweight quad sculls		Italy
Coxless pairs	Robert Sens and Detlef Kirchhoff	Germany
Coxed pairs	Nick Green, James Tomkins and Brett Hayman	Australia
Coxless fours		Great Britain
Coxed fours		Australia
Eights		USA
Lightweight coxless pairs	Vincent Montabonel and Jean-Christophe Bette	France
Lightweight coxless fours		Denmark
Lightweight eights		Germany
Women		
Single sculls	Irina Fedotova	Russia
Double sculls	Miriam Batten and Gillian Lindsay	Great Britain
Quad sculls		Germany
Lightweight single sculls	Pia Vogel	Switzerland
Lightweight double sculls	Christine Collins and Sarah Garner	USA
Lightweight quad sculls		Germany
Coxless pairs	Emma Robinson and Alison Korn	Canada
Coxless fours		Great Britain
Eights		Romania
Lightweight coxless pairs	Juliet Machan and Jo Nitsch	Great Britain

Henley Royal Regatta

Since 1995.

Year	Name	Country
Diamond Challenge Sculls[1]		
1995	Juri Jaanson	Estonia
1996	Merlin Vervoorn	Netherlands
1997	Greg Searle	UK
1998	Jamie Koven	USA
1999	Marcel Hacker	USA
Grand Challenge Cup[2]		
1995	San Diego	USA
1996	Imperial College and Queen's Tower	UK
1997	Australian Institute of Sport and NSW Institute of Sport	Australia
1998	RC Hansa Dortmund and Berliner RC	Germany
1999	RC Hansa Dortmund and Berliner RC	Germany

[1] First held in 1884.

[2] For eights; first held in 1839.

The Boat Race

This race was first held in 1829. It is rowed annually by crews from Oxford and Cambridge Universities, between Putney and Mortlake on the River Thames. Cambridge currently lead Oxford by 76 wins to 68. The 1877 race ended in a dead heat.

Year	Team	Year	Team
1990	Oxford	1995	Cambridge
1991	Oxford	1996	Cambridge
1992	Oxford	1997	Cambridge
1993	Cambridge	1998	Cambridge
1994	Cambridge	1999	Cambridge

Rugby League

World Cup Winners

Inaugurated in 1954.

Year	Team	Year	Team
1954	Great Britain	1972	Great Britain
1957	Australia	1975	Australia
1960	Great Britain	1977	Australia
		1988	Australia
1968	Australia	1992	Australia
1970	Australia	1995	Australia

International Results (Selected)

1998

Date	Result	Venue
Great Britain versus New Zealand Lincoln Test Series		
31 October (1st Test)	Great Britain 16–New Zealand 22	McAlpine Stadium, Huddersfield
7 November (2nd Test)	Great Britain 16–New Zealand 36	Reebok Stadium, Bolton
14 November (3rd Test)	Great Britain 23–New Zealand 23	Vicarage Road, Watford
New Zealand wins the series 2–0		

Challenge Cup Winners Since 1980

Year	Team	Year	Team	Year	Team	Year	Team
1980	Hull Kingston Rovers	1985	Wigan	1990	Wigan	1995	Wigan
1981	Widnes	1986	Castleford	1991	Wigan	1996	St Helens
1982	Hull	1987	Halifax	1992	Wigan	1997	St Helens
1983	Featherstone Rovers	1988	Wigan	1993	Wigan	1998	Sheffield Eagles
1984	Widnes	1989	Wigan	1994	Wigan	1999	Leeds Rhinos

JJB Sports Super League Final Table

1998

Team	Played	Won	Drawn	Lost	Points for	Points against	League points
Wigan Warriors[1]	23	21	0	2	762	222	42
Leeds Rhinos[1]	23	19	0	4	662	369	38
Halifax Blue Sox[1]	23	18	0	5	658	390	36
St Helens[1]	23	14	1	8	673	459	29
Bradford Bulls[1]	23	12	0	11	498	450	24
Castleford Tigers	23	10	1	12	446	522	21
London Broncos	23	10	0	13	415	476	20
Sheffield Eagles	23	8	2	13	495	541	18
Hull Sharks	23	8	0	15	421	574	16
Warrington Wolves	23	7	1	15	411	645	15
Salford Reds	23	6	1	16	319	575	13
Huddersfield Giants	23	2	0	21	288	825	4

[1] Qualified for play-offs.

JJB Sports Super League Play-Offs: Results

Wigan Warriors were crowned Super League champions after defeating Leeds Rhinos 10–4 in the inaugural Grand Final at Old Trafford on 24 October .

1998

Team	Points	Team	Points	Location
St Helens	46	Bradford	24	Knowsley Road, St Helens
Leeds Rhinos	13	Halifax Blue Sox	6	Headingley, Leeds
Halifax Blue Sox	30	St Helens	37	The Shay, Halifax
Wigan Warriors	17	Leeds Rhinos	4	Central Park, Wigan
Leeds Rhinos	44	St Helens	16	Headingley, Leeds
Grand Final				
Wigan Warriors	10	Leeds Rhinos	4	Old Trafford, Manchester (attendance: 43,553)

League Championship: Recent Winners

Inaugurated in 1895–96. From 1907 to 1973 the championship was decided by a play-off. From 1974 to 1996 the championship title was awarded to the team finishing top of Division One. In 1996 a new Super League was introduced (currently sponsored by JJB Sports).

Year	Team
Division One	
1980	Bradford Northern
1981	Bradford Northern
1982	Leigh
1983	Hull
1984	Hull Kingston Rovers
1985	Hull Kingston Rovers
1986	Halifax
1987	Wigan
1988	Widnes
1989	Widnes
1990	Wigan
1991	Wigan
1992	Wigan
1993	Wigan
1994	Wigan
1995	Wigan
1996	Wigan
Super League	
1996	St Helens
1997	Bradford Bulls
1998	Wigan Warrriors

Rugby Union

International

World Cup

This competition, for the William Webb Ellis Trophy, was first held in 1987.

Year	Country
1987	New Zealand
1991	Australia
1995	South Africa

International Five Nations Championship Winners

This championship was instituted in 1884 and is now a tournament between England, France, Ireland, Scotland, and Wales. The Grand Slam is achieved by teams winning all four games. The Triple Crown is achieved by beating the other three 'home nations', and does not apply to France. Italy will join the championship in 2000.
Most outright championship wins: Wales, England, 22. Most Grand Slams: England, 11. Most Triple Crowns: England, 21.

Year	Team	Year	Team	Year	Team
1990	Scotland[1 2]	1994	Wales	1998	France[1 3]
1991	England[1 2]	1995	England[1 2]	1999	Scotland
1992	England[1 2]	1996	England[2]		
1993	France	1997	France[1 3]		

[1] Grand Slam winners.
[2] Also won the Triple Crown.
[3] England won the Triple Crown.

International Five Nations Championship Results

1999

Date	Home team	Away team	Result	Location
6 February	Ireland	France	9–10	Lansdowne Road, Dublin
6 February	Scotland	Wales	33–20	Murrayfield, Edinburgh
20 February	England	Scotland	24–21	Twickenham, London
20 February	Wales	Ireland	23–29	Wembley Stadium, London
6 March	Ireland	England	15–27	Lansdowne Road, Dublin
6 March	France	Wales	33–34	Stade de France, St-Denis
20 March	England	France	21–10	Twickenham, London
20 March	Scotland	Ireland	30–13	Murrayfield, Edinburgh
10 April	France	Scotland	22–36	Stade de France, St-Denis
11 April	Wales	England	32–31	Wembley Stadium, London

International Five Nations Championship Final Table

1999

Position	Team	Played	Won	Drawn	Lost	Points for	Points against	Points
1	Scotland	4	3	0	1	120	79	6
2	England	4	3	0	1	103	78	6
3	Wales	4	2	0	2	109	126	4
4	Ireland	4	1	0	3	66	90	2
5	France	4	1	0	3	75	100	2

Rugby Union: International Results

As of 20 June 1999.

1998–99

Date	Result	Date	Result
14 November 1998	Wales 20–South Africa 28	18 November 1998	Romania 27–Georgia 23[1]
14 November 1998	England 110–Holland 0[1]	21 November 1998	Scotland 10–South Africa 35
14 November 1998	Ireland 70–Georgia 0[1]	21 November 1998	Wales 43–Argentina 30
18 November 1998	Italy 67–Holland 7[1]	21 November 1998	Ireland 53–Romania 35[1]

(continued)

Rugby Union: International Results (*continued*)

Date	Result	Date	Result
22 November 1998	France 21–Australia 32	5 June 1999	Argentina 26–Wales 36
22 November 1998	England 23–Italy 15[1]	12 June 1999	South Africa 74–Italy 3
28 November 1998	England 11–Australia 12	12 June 1999	Argentina 16–Wales 23[2]
28 November 1998	Ireland 13–South Africa 27	12 June 1999	Australia 46–Ireland 10
28 November 1998	Scotland 85–Portugal 11[1]	12 June 1999	Samoa 22–France 39
2 December 1998	Spain 21–Portugal 17[1]	16 June 1999	Tonga 20–France 16
5 December 1998	England 13–South Africa 7	18 June 1999	New Zealand 71–Samoa 13
5 December 1998	Scotland 85–Spain 3[1]	19 June 1999	Australia 32–Ireland 26[3]
6 March 1999	Scotland 30–Italy 12	26 June 1999	Australia 22–England 15
20 March 1999	Italy 21–Wales 60	26 June 1999	New Zealand 54–France 7
10 April 1999	Ireland 39–Italy 30	26 June 1999	Wales 29–South Africa 19

[1] World Cup qualifier.
[2] Wales wins the two-match series 2–0.
[3] Australia wins the two-match series 2–0.

International Club Competitions

Rugby Union: European Cup Winners

This European club competition was first held in 1995–96.

Year	Winner	Runner-up	Score	Location
1996	Toulouse (France)	Cardiff (Wales)	21–18	Cardiff
1997	Brive (France)	Leicester (England)	28–9	Cardiff
1998	Bath (England)	Brive (France)	19–18	Bordeaux
1999	Ulster (Ireland)	Colomiers (France)	21–6	Dublin

Rugby Union: Super 12

This tournament for club teams from Australia, New Zealand, and South Africa was first held in 1996.

Year	Team
1996	Auckland Blues
1997	Auckland Blues
1998	Canterbury Crusaders
1999	Canterbury Crusaders

English Rugby Union

English League Champions

This championship was first held 1987–88. It was known as the Courage League Division One 1996–97 and has since been known as the Dunbar Premiership Division One since 1997–98.

Year	Team	Year	Team
1988	Leicester	1994	Bath
1989	Bath	1995	Leicester
1990	Wasps	1996	Bath
1991	Bath	1997	Wasps
1992	Bath	1998	Newcastle
1993	Bath	1999	Leicester

Tetley's Bitter Cup

This English club knockout tournament has been sponsored by John Player and Pilkington, and is now sponsored by Tetley Bitter. It was first held in 1971–72.

Year	Team	Year	Team
1990	Bath	1995	Bath
1991	Harlequins	1996	Bath
1992	Bath	1997	Leicester
1993	Leicester	1998	Saracens
1994	Bath	1999	Wasps

County Championship

This championship was first held in 1888.

Year	Team	Year	Team	Year	Team	Year	Team	Year	Team
1990	Lancashire	1992	Lancashire	1994	Yorkshire	1996	Gloucestershire	1998	Cheshire
1991	Cornwall	1993	Lancashire	1995	Warwickshire	1997	Cumbria	1999	Cornwall

Allied Dunbar Premiership Final Tables

(Key: P = played; W = won; D = drawn; L = lost; F = points for; A = points against; Pt = League points.)

1998–99

Division One

Position	Team	P	W	D	L	F	A	Pt
1	Leicester	26	22	0	4	771	423	44
2	Northampton	26	19	0	7	754	556	38
3	Saracens	26	16	1	9	748	583	33
4	Harlequins	26	16	1	9	690	653	33
5	Wasps	26	15	1	10	717	506	31
6	Bath	26	15	0	11	698	574	30
7	London Irish	26	15	0	11	703	607	30
8	Newcastle	26	14	0	12	719	639	28
9	Richmond[1]	26	11	2	13	720	715	22
10	Gloucester	26	9	1	16	554	643	19
11	Sale	26	9	1	16	604	731	19
12	London Scottish	26	8	0	18	491	734	16
13	Bedford[2]	26	6	0	20	541	840	12
14	West Hartlepool[3]	26	3	1	22	501	1,007	7

Division Two

Position	Team	P	W	D	L	F	A	Pt
1	Bristol[4]	26	22	0	4	848	418	44
2	Rotherham[5]	26	22	0	4	756	336	44
3	Worcester[1]	26	18	0	8	716	409	34
4	London Welsh	26	17	0	9	662	552	34
5	Exeter	26	14	1	11	591	598	29
6	Leeds[6]	26	16	0	10	713	367	28
7	Coventry	26	14	0	12	652	560	28
8	Orrell	26	12	0	14	566	483	24
9	Waterloo	26	12	0	14	419	634	24
10	Moseley	26	10	0	16	498	633	20
11	Rugby	26	9	0	17	425	660	18
12	Wakefield	26	6	0	20	469	812	12
13	Blackheath[6]	26	5	0	21	419	842	10
14	Fylde[6]	26	4	1	21	375	805	9

[1] Deducted two points.
[2] Retained Division One status after winning promotion/relegation play-off against Rotherham.
[3] Relegated.
[4] Promoted to Allied Dunbar Premiership Division One.
[5] Lost promotion/relegation play-off against Bedford.
[6] Deducted four points.

Scottish Rugby Union

Tennent's Velvet Premiership Division One Final Table

(Key: P = played; W = won; D = drawn; L = lost; F = points for; A = points against; B = bonus points; Pt = total points.)

1998–99

Position	Team	P	W	D	L	F	A	B	Pt
1	Heriot's F P	18	14	0	4	620	335	13	69
2	Melrose	18	13	0	5	491	311	11	63
3	Glasgow Hawks	18	13	1	4	437	280	7	61
4	Currie	18	12	0	6	434	351	8	56
5	Hawick	18	9	0	9	338	465	5	41
6	Watsonians	18	7	2	9	396	434	6	38
7	Jed-Forest	18	7	2	9	356	452	3	35
8	West of Scotland	18	6	0	12	355	428	10	34
9	Boroughmuir	18	6	0	12	382	464	10	34
10	Stirling County[1]	18	0	1	17	300	668	6	8

[1] Relegated.

Tennent's Velvet Cup

This Scottish knockout tournament was first held in 1996.

Year	Team
1996	Hawick
1997	Melrose
1998	Glasgow Hawks
1999	Gala

Scottish Club Champions

This championship was first held in 1974; formerly known as the McEwan's League Division One, it became the Tennent's Premiership Division One in 1995–96, and the Tennent's Velvet Premiership Division One in 1998–99.

Year	Team	Year	Team	Year	Team	Year	Team	Year	Team
1990	Melrose	1992	Melrose	1994	Melrose	1996	Melrose	1998	Watsonians
1991	Boroughmuir	1993	Melrose	1995	Stirling County	1997	Melrose	1999	Heriot's FP

Welsh Rugby Union

Welsh League Premier Division Final Table

1998–99

Position	Team	Played	Won	Drawn	Lost	Points for	Points against	Tries	Bonus points	League points
1	Llanelli	19	14	1	4	727	319	97	17	60
2	Pontypridd	19	12	0	7	624	427	67	10	46
3	Neath	20	12	0	8	568	491	68	8	44
4	Ebbw Vale	20	12	1	7	541	468	58	7	44
5	Caerphilly	19	9	2	8	521	536	59	5	34
6	Bridgend	19	8	2	9	467	568	53	4	30
7	Newport	19	5	0	14	470	574	59	8	23
8	Aberavon	19	2	0	17	365	900	47	3	9

Welsh League Premier Division

This championship was first held in 1990–91.

Year	Team	Year	Team
1991	Neath	1996	Neath
1992	Swansea	1997	Pontypridd
1993	Llanelli	1998	Swansea
1994	Swansea	1999	Llanelli
1995	Cardiff		

SWALEC Welsh Cup

This club knockout tournament was formerly known as the Schweppes Welsh Cup. It was first held in 1971–72.

Year	Team	Year	Team
1990	Neath	1995	Swansea
1991	Llanelli	1996	Pontypridd
1992	Llanelli	1997	Cardiff
1993	Llanelli	1998	Llanelli
1994	Cardiff	1999	Swansea

Irish Rugby Union

All-Ireland Championship

This championship was first held in 1990–91.

Year	Team
1991	Cork Constitution
1992	Garryowen
1993	Young Munster
1994	Garryowen
1995	Shannon
1996	Shannon
1997	Shannon
1998	Shannon
1999	Cork Constitution

Allied Irish Bank League Division One Final Table

(Key: P = played; W = won; D = drawn; L = lost; F = points for; A = points against; Pt = League points.)

1998–99

Position	Team	P	W	D	L	F	A	Pt
1	Garryowen[1,2]	11	8	0	3	236	140	16
2	Cork Constitution[2]	11	8	0	3	265	170	16
3	Buccaneers[2]	11	8	0	3	196	202	16
4	St Mary's[2]	11	7	0	4	215	177	14
5	Lansdowne	11	7	0	4	189	177	14
6	Shannon	11	6	0	5	224	164	12
7	Young Munster	11	4	1	6	134	135	9
8	Terenure	11	4	1	6	174	193	9
9	Ballymena	11	4	0	7	190	223	8
10	Clontarf	11	4	0	7	198	246	8
11	Blackrock College[3]	11	4	0	7	183	232	8
12	Galwegians[3]	11	1	0	10	118	263	2

[1] Champions.
[2] Qualified for play-offs.
[3] Relegated.

Shinty

Camanachd Cup

Year	Team
1995	Kingussie
1996	Oban Camanachd
1997	Kingussie
1998	Kingussie
1999	Kingussie

Skating

World Figure Skating Champions

This championship was first held in 1896.

Year	Name	Country
Men		
1995	Elvis Stojko	Canada
1996	Todd Eldredge	USA
1997	Elvis Stojko	Canada
1998	Alexei Yagudin	Russia
1999	Alexei Yagudin	Russia
Women		
1995	Lu Chen	China
1996	Michelle Kwan	USA
1997	Tara Lipinski	USA
1998	Michelle Kwan	USA
1999	Maria Butyrskaya	Russia
Pairs		
1995	Rene Novotny and Radka Kovarikova	Czech Republic
1996	Andrei Bushkov and Marina Eltsova	Russia
1997	Yevgeny Platov and Mandy Wotzel	Russia
1998	Anton Sikharudlidze and Elena Berezhnaya	Russia
1999	Anton Sikharudlidze and Elena Berezhnaya	Russia
Ice Dance		
1995	Oksana Gritschuk and Yevgeny Platov	Russia
1996	Oksana Gritschuk and Yevgeny Platov	Russia
1997	Oksana Gritschuk and Yevgeny Platov	Russia
1998	Angelika Krylova and Oleg Ovsyannikov	Russia
1999	Angelika Krylova and Oleg Ovsyannikov	Russia

Skiing

Alpine World Championships

Inaugurated in 1931. Now held every two years. The 1999 championships were held at Vail, Colorado, 1–14 February.

1999

Category	Name	Country
Men		
Downhill	Hermann Maier	Austria
Slalom	Kalle Palander	Finland
Giant slalom	Lasse Kjus	Norway
Super giant slalom	Hermann Maier/Lasse Kjus	Austria/Norway (shared)
Combination	Kjetil Andre Aamodt	Norway
Women		
Downhill	Renate Goetschl	Austria
Slalom	Zalle Steggall	Australia
Giant slalom	Alexandra Meissnitzer	Austria
Super giant slalom	Alexandra Meissnitzer	Austria
Combination	Pernilla Wiberg	Sweden

Alpine World Cup

Annual series of events, first held in 1967.

1998–99

Category	Name	Country
Men		
Downhill	Lasse Kjus	Norway
Slalom	Thomas Stangassinger	Austria
Giant slalom	Michael Von Grünigen	Switzerland
Super giant slalom	Hermann Maier	Austria
Overall	Lasse Kjus	Norway
Women		
Downhill	Renate Goetschl	Austria
Slalom	Sabine Egger	Austria
Giant slalom	Alexandra Meissnitzer	Austria
Super giant slalom	Alexandra Meissnitzer	Austria
Overall	Alexandra Meissnitzer	Austria

Snooker

World Professional Snooker Championship

This championship was first held in 1926–27. Between 1952 and 1957, the professional players staged a match-play championship for the world title following a disagreement with the game's governing body at that time, the Billiards Association and Control Club. Between 1964 and 1968, the championship was organized on a challenge basis before becoming a knockout tournament in 1969. Since 1977 all finals have been held at the Crucible Theatre, Sheffield. It has been sponsored by Embassy since 1976.

Year	Name	Country	Year	Name	Country
1980	Cliff Thorburn	Canada	1991	John Parrott	England
1981	Steve Davis	England	1992	Stephen Hendry	Scotland
1982	Alex Higgins	Northern Ireland	1993	Stephen Hendry	Scotland
1983	Steve Davis	England	1994	Stephen Hendry	Scotland
1984	Steve Davis	England	1995	Stephen Hendry	Scotland
1985	Dennis Taylor	Northern Ireland	1996	Stephen Hendry	Scotland
1986	Joe Johnson	England	1997	Ken Doherty	Ireland, Republic of
1987	Steve Davis	England			
1988	Steve Davis	England	1998	John Higgins	Scotland
1989	Steve Davis	England	1999	Stephen Hendry	Scotland
1990	Stephen Hendry	Scotland			

World Amateur Snooker Championship

This championship was first held in 1963.

Year	Name	Country/ territory
1994	Mohammad Yusuf	Pakistan
1995	Sakchai Sim-Ngam	Thailand
1996	Stuart Bingham	England
1997	Marco Fu	Hong Kong
1998	Luke Simmonds	England

Speedway

British Elite League Final Table

1998

Team	Played	Won	Drew	Lost	Points for	Points against	Points	Bonus points	Total
Ipswich	32	26	1	5	1,653.5	1,211.5	53	16	69
Belle Vue	32	20	0	12	1,524.5	1,353.5	40	12	52
Coventry	32	18	1	13	1,474	1,401	37	11	48
Swindon	32	15	1	16	1,429	1,450	31	7	38
Eastbourne	32	15	0	17	1,430	1,449	30	7	37
Wolverhampton	32	14	1	17	1,421	1,444	29	8	37
Oxford	32	13	2	17	1,388	1,490	28	5	33
Poole	32	11	1	20	1,348	1,529	23	5	28
King's Lynn	32	8	1	23	1,270	1,610	17	1	18

World Speedway Champions

Since 1989.

Year	Name	Country
1989	Hans Nielsen	Denmark
1990	Per Jonsson	Sweden
1991	Jan Pedersen	Denmark
1992	Gary Havelock	England
1993	Sam Ermolenko	USA
1994	Tony Rickardsson	Sweden
1995	Hans Nielsen	Denmark
1996	Billy Hamill	USA
1997	Greg Hancock	USA
1998	Tony Rickardsson	Sweden

Squash

World Open Squash Champions

This competition was first held in 1976.

Year	Name	Country	Year	Name	Country
Men			*Women*		
1994	Jansher Khan	Pakistan	1994	Michelle Martin	Australia
1995	Jansher Khan	Pakistan	1995	Michelle Martin	Australia
1996	Jansher Khan	Pakistan	1996	Sarah Fitz-Gerald	Australia
1997	Rodney Eyles	Australia	1997	Sarah Fitz-Gerald	Australia
1998	Jonathan Power	Canada	1998	Sarah Fitz-Gerald	Australia

Swimming

Long Course World Records

As of 19 July 1999.

Category	Time	Name	Country	Date	Location
Men					
50 m freestyle	0:21.81	Tom Jager	USA	24 March 1990	Nashville (TN), USA
100 m freestyle	0:48.21	Aleksandr Popov	Russia	18 June 1994	Monte Carlo
200 m freestyle	1:46.67	Grant Hackett	Australia	23 March 1999	Brisbane, Australia
400 m freestyle	3:43.80	Kieren Perkins	Australia	9 September 1994	Rome, Italy
800 m freestyle	7:46.00	Kieren Perkins	Australia	24 August 1994	Victoria, Canada
1,500 m freestyle	14:41.66	Kieren Perkins	Australia	24 August 1994	Victoria, Canada
100 m backstroke	0:53.86	Jeff Rouse	USA	31 July 1992	Barcelona, Spain
200 m backstroke	1:56.57	M Lopez-Zubero	Spain	23 November 1991	Tuscaloosa (AL), USA
100 m breaststroke	1:00.60	Fred Deburghgraeve	Belgium	20 July 1996	Atlanta (GA), USA
200 m breaststroke	2:10:16	Mike Barrowman	USA	29 July 1992	Barcelona, Spain
100 m butterfly	0:52.15	Michael Klim	Australia	9 October 1997	Brisbane, Australia
200 m butterfly	1:55.22	Denis Pankratov	Russia	14 June 1995	Canet de Rousillon, France
200 m individual medley	1:58.16	Jani Sievinen	Finland	11 September 1994	Rome, Italy
400 m individual medley	4:12.30	Tom Dolan	USA	6 September 1994	Rome, Italy
4 × 100 m freestyle relay	3:15.11		USA	12 August 1995	Atlanta (GA), USA
4 × 200 m freestyle relay	7:11.86		Australia	13 September 1998	Kuala Lumpar, Malaysia
4 × 100 m medley relay	3:34.84		USA	26 July 1996	Atlanta (GA), USA
Women					
50 m freestyle	0:24.51	Jingyi Le	China	11 September 1994	Rome, Italy
100 m freestyle	0:54.01	Jingyi Le	China	5 September 1994	Rome, Italy
200 m freestyle	1:56.78	Franziska Van Almsick	Germany	6 September 1994	Rome, Italy
400 m freestyle	4:03.85	Janet Evans	USA	22 September 1988	Seoul, South Korea
800 m freestyle	8:16.22	Janet Evans	USA	20 August 1989	Tokyo, Japan
1,500 m freestyle	15:52.10	Janet Evans	USA	26 March 1988	Orlando (FL), USA
100 m backstroke	1:00.16	Cihong He	China	10 September 1994	Rome, Italy
200 m backstroke	2:06.62	Kristina Egerszegi	Hungary	25 August 1991	Athens, Greece
100 m breaststroke	1:06.95[1]	Penelope Heyns	South Africa	18 July 1999	Los Angeles, USA
200 m breaststroke	2:24.51[1]	Penelope Heyns	South Africa	17 July 1999	Los Angeles, USA
100 m butterfly	0:57.93	Mary T Meagher	USA	16 August 1981	Brown Deer (WI), USA
200 m butterfly	2:05.96	Mary T Meagher	USA	13 August 1981	Brown Deer (WI), USA
200 m individual medley	2:09.72	Yanyan Wu	China	17 October 1997	Shanghai, China
400 m individual medley	4:34.79	Yan Chen	China	17 October 1997	Shanghai, China
4 × 100 m freestyle relay	3:37.91		China	7 September 1994	Rome, Italy
4 × 200 m freestyle relay	7:55.47		East Germany	18 August 1987	Strasbourg, France
4 × 100 m medley relay	4:01.67		China	10 September 1994	Rome, Italy

[1] Awaiting ratification.

Tennis

Wimbledon Men's Singles Champions Since 1946

Inaugurated in 1877. Wimbledon became an open Championship in 1968.

Year	Name	Country
1946	Yvon Petra	France
1947	Jack Kramer	USA
1948	Bob Falkenburg	USA
1949	Ted Schroeder	USA
1950	Budge Patty	USA
1951	Dick Savitt	USA
1952	Frank Sedgman	Australia
1953	Vic Seixas	USA
1954	Jaroslav Drobny	Egypt
1955	Tony Trabert	USA
1956	Lew Hoad	Australia
1957	Lew Hoad	Australia
1958	Ashley Cooper	Australia
1959	Alex Olmedo	USA
1960	Neale Fraser	Australia
1961	Rod Laver	Australia
1962	Rod Laver	Australia
1963	Chuck McKinley	USA
1964	Roy Emerson	Australia
1965	Roy Emerson	Australia
1966	Manuel Santana	Spain
1967	John Newcombe	Australia
1968	Rod Laver	Australia
1969	Rod Laver	Australia
1970	John Newcombe	Australia
1971	John Newcombe	Australia
1972	Stan Smith	USA
1973	Jan Kodes	Czechoslovakia
1974	Jimmy Connors	USA
1975	Arthur Ashe	USA
1976	Bjorn Borg	Sweden
1977	Bjorn Borg	Sweden
1978	Bjorn Borg	Sweden
1979	Bjorn Borg	Sweden
1980	Bjorn Borg	Sweden
1981	John McEnroe	USA
1982	Jimmy Connors	USA
1983	John McEnroe	USA
1984	John McEnroe	USA
1985	Boris Becker	West Germany
1986	Boris Becker	West Germany
1987	Pat Cash	Australia
1988	Stefan Edberg	Sweden
1989	Boris Becker	West Germany
1990	Stefan Edberg	Sweden
1991	Michael Stich	Germany
1992	Andre Agassi	USA
1993	Pete Sampras	USA
1994	Pete Sampras	USA
1995	Pete Sampras	USA
1996	Richard Krajicek	Netherlands
1997	Pete Sampras	USA
1998	Pete Sampras	USA
1999	Pete Sampras	USA

Wimbledon Women's Singles Champions Since 1946

Inaugurated in 1884. Wimbledon became an open championship in 1968.

Year	Name	Country	Year	Name	Country	Year	Name	Country
1946	Pauline Betz	USA	1966	Billie Jean King	USA	1986	Martina Navratilova	USA
1947	Margaret Osborne	USA	1967	Billie Jean King	USA	1987	Martina Navratilova	USA
1948	Louise Brough	USA	1968	Billie Jean King	USA	1988	Steffi Graf	West Germany
1949	Louise Brough	USA	1969	Ann Jones	UK	1989	Steffi Graf	West Germany
1950	Louise Brough	USA	1970	Margaret Court[1]	Australia	1990	Martina Navratilova	USA
1951	Doris Hart	USA	1971	Evonne Goolagong	Australia	1991	Steffi Graf	Germany
1952	Maureen Connolly	USA	1972	Billie Jean King	USA	1992	Steffi Graf	Germany
1953	Maureen Connolly	USA	1973	Billie Jean King	USA	1993	Steffi Graf	Germany
1954	Maureen Connolly	USA	1974	Chris Evert	USA	1994	Conchita Martinez	Spain
1955	Louise Brough	USA	1975	Billie Jean King	USA	1995	Steffi Graf	Germany
1956	Shirley Fry	USA	1976	Chris Evert	USA	1996	Steffi Graf	Germany
1957	Althea Gibson	USA	1977	Virginia Wade	UK	1997	Martina Hingis	Switzerland
1958	Althea Gibson	USA	1978	Martina Navratilova	Czechoslovakia	1998	Jana Novotna	Czech Republic
1959	Maria Bueno	Brazil	1979	Martina Navratilova	Czechoslovakia	1999	Lindsay Davenport	USA
1960	Maria Bueno	Brazil	1980	Evonne Cawley[2]	Australia			
1961	Angela Mortimer	UK	1981	Chris Evert Lloyd[3]	USA			
1962	Karen Susman	USA	1982	Martina Navratilova	USA			
1963	Margaret Smith	Australia	1983	Martina Navratilova	USA			
1964	Maria Bueno	Brazil	1984	Martina Navratilova	USA			
1965	Margaret Smith	Australia	1985	Martina Navratilova	USA			

[1] Born Smith.
[2] Born Goolagong.
[3] Born Evert.

Wimbledon All-England Championships Final Results

1999

Category	Winner	Runners-up	Score
Men's singles	Pete Sampras (USA)	Andre Agassi (USA)	6-3, 6-4, 7-5
Women's singles	Lindsay Davenport (USA)	Steffi Graf (Germany)	6-4, 7-5
Men's doubles	Mahesh Bhupathi and Leander Paes (India)	Paul Haarhuis (Netherlands) and Jered Palmer (USA)	6-7, 6-3, 6-4, 7-6
Women's doubles	Lindsay Davenport and Korina Morariu (USA)	Mariaan de Swardt (South Africa) and Elena Tatarkova (Ukraine)	6-4, 6-4
Mixed doubles	Leander Paes (India) and Lisa Raymond (USA)	Jonas Bjorkman (Sweden) and Anna Kournikova (Russia)	6-4, 3-6, 6-3

US Open Singles Champions

The men's championship was first held in 1881 and the women's in 1887. In 1968 and 1969, there was a separate Open Champion of professional players. In 1970, the championship became the US Open.

Year	Name	Year	Name
Men		*Women*	
1989	Boris Becker (West Germany)	1989	Steffi Graf (West Germany)
1990	Pete Sampras (USA)	1990	Gabriela Sabatini (Argentina)
1991	Stefan Edberg (Sweden)	1991	Monica Seles (Yugoslavia)
1992	Stefan Edberg (Sweden)	1992	Monica Seles (Yugoslavia)
1993	Pete Sampras (USA)	1993	Steffi Graf (Germany)
1994	Andre Agassi (USA)	1994	Arantxa Sanchez Vicario (Spain)
1995	Pete Sampras (USA)	1995	Steffi Graf (Germany)
1996	Pete Sampras (USA)	1996	Steffi Graf (Germany)
1997	Patrick Rafter (Australia)	1997	Martina Hingis (Switzerland)
1998	Patrick Rafter (Australia)	1998	Lindsay Davenport (USA)

French Open Singles Champions

This competition became an open championship in 1968.

Year	Name	Country
Men		
1990	Andrés Gómez	Ecuador
1991	Jim Courier	USA
1992	Jim Courier	USA
1993	Sergi Bruguera	Spain
1994	Sergi Bruguera	Spain
1995	Thomas Muster	Austria
1996	Yevgeny Kafelnikov	Russia
1997	Gustavo Kuerten	Brazil
1998	Carlos Moya	Spain
1999	Andre Agassi	USA
Women		
1990	Monica Seles	Yugoslavia
1991	Monica Seles	Yugoslavia
1992	Monica Seles	Yugoslavia
1993	Steffi Graf	Germany
1994	Arantxa Sanchez Vicario	Spain
1995	Steffi Graf	Germany
1996	Steffi Graf	Germany
1997	Iva Majoli	Croatia
1998	Arantxa Sanchez Vicario	Spain
1999	Steffi Graf	Germany

Australian Open Singles Champions

This competition became an open championship in 1969.

Year	Name	Country
Men		
1990	Ivan Lendl	Czech Republic
1991	Boris Becker	Germany
1992	Jim Courier	USA
1993	Jim Courier	USA
1994	Pete Sampras	USA
1995	Andre Agassi	USA
1996	Boris Becker	Germany
1997	Pete Sampras	USA
1998	Petr Korda	Czech Republic
1999	Yevgeny Kafelnikov	Russia
Women		
1990	Steffi Graf	West Germany
1991	Monica Seles	Yugoslavia
1992	Monica Seles	Yugoslavia
1993	Monica Seles	Yugoslavia
1994	Steffi Graf	Germany
1995	Mary Pierce	France
1996	Monica Seles	USA
1997	Martina Hingis	Switzerland
1998	Martina Hingis	Switzerland
1999	Martina Hingis	Switzerland

Davis Cup Winners

This international men's team competition was first held in 1900. Until 1972 the winner was decided in a Challenge Round in which the holders of the trophy met the winners of a knockout competition. Since then, the competition has been played entirely on a knockout basis.

Year	Winner	Runner-up	Score
1989	West Germany	Sweden	3–2
1990	USA	Australia	3–2
1991	France	USA	3–1
1992	USA	Switzerland	3–1
1993	Germany	Australia	4–1
1994	Sweden	Russia	4–1
1995	USA	Russia	3–2
1996	France	Sweden	3–2
1997	Sweden	USA	5–0
1998	Sweden	Italy	4–1

Fed Cup Winners

This international women's team competition was first held in 1963 and was known as the Federation Cup until 1995. Most wins: USA, 15; Australia, 7; Czechoslovakia and Spain, 5 each.

Year	Country	Year	Country	Year	Country
1989	USA	1993	Spain	1997	France
1990	USA	1994	Spain	1998	Spain
1991	Spain	1995	Spain		
1992	Germany	1996	USA		

Volleyball

Volleyball World Champions

The men's championship was first held in 1949; the women's championship was first held in 1952.

Year	Country	Year	Country
Men		***Women***	
1982	USSR	1982	China
1986	USA	1986	China
1990	Italy	1990	USSR
1994	Italy	1994	Cuba
1998	Italy	1998	Cuba

Water Skiing

Water Skiing World Championship

This championship was first held in 1949.

Year	Name	Country
Men		
1989	Patrice Martin	France
1991	Patrice Martin	France
1993	Patrice Martin	France
1995	Patrice Martin	France
1997	Patrice Martin	France

Year	Name	Country
Women		
1989	Deena Maple[1]	USA
1991	Karen Neville	USA
1993	Natalya Rumyantseva	Russia
1995	Judy Messer	Canada
1997	Elena Milakova	Russia

[1] Born Brush.

Yachting

Admiral's Cup Winners

Year	Country
1969	USA
1971	UK
1973	West Germany
1975	UK
1977	UK
1979	Australia
1981	UK
1983	West Germany
1985	West Germany
1987	New Zealand
1989	UK
1991	France
1993	Germany
1995	Italy
1997	USA
1999	The Netherlands

America's Cup Winners

In 1851 the US schooner *America* of the New York Yacht Club received a 'hundred guinea cup' from the Royal Yacht Squadron for winning a race around the Isle of Wight, England, against 15 British yachts. Renamed the America's Cup it was offered as a challenge trophy by the New York Yacht Club, with the first challenge taking place in 1870. The yachts are from the USA unless otherwise stated.

Year	Winning yacht	Winning skipper	Series	Challenger
1958	*Columbia*	Briggs Cunningham	4-0	*Sceptre* (England)
1962	*Weatherly*	Emil Mosbacher Jr	4-1	*Gretel* (Australia)
1964	*Constellation*	Bob Bavier Jr	4-0	*Sovereign* (England)
1967	*Intrepid*	Emil Mosbacher Jr	4-0	*Dame Pattie* (Australia)
1970	*Intrepid*	Bill Ficker	4-1	*Gretel II* (Australia)
1974	*Courageous*	Ted Hood	4-0	*Southern Cross* (Australia)
1977	*Courageous*	Ted Turner	4-0	*Australia* (Australia)
1980	*Freedom*	Dennis Conner	4-1	*Australia* (Australia)
1983	*Australia II* (Australia)	John Bertrand	4-3	*Liberty*
1987	*Stars & Stripes*	Dennis Conner	4-0	*Kookaburra III* (Australia)
1988	*Stars & Stripes*	Dennis Conner	2-0	*New Zealand* (New Zealand)
1992	*America*	Bill Koch	4-1	*Il Moro di Venezia* (Italy)
1995	*Black Magic* (New Zealand)	Russell Coutts	5-0	*Young America*

Web Sites

Archery Index

http://www.rmplc.co.uk/eduweb/sites/splomas/myarch/archy1.html#British

Home page maintained by a British archery enthusiast, with links to many related topics.

Badminton Home Page

http://huizen.dds.nl/~anita/badmint.html

Rules of badminton, strategies for playing, and ways of organizing tournaments.

British Athletics Federation

http://www.british-athletics.co.uk/

Includes a UK athletic club directory and tips on training and coaching.

British Water Skiing In Cyberspace

http://www.u-net.com/waterski/

British water skiing's home page, run by the British Water Skiing Association.

Canoeing

http://www.canoeing.co.uk/home.html

Centralized UK-based resource for canoeists.

Climbing Archive

http://www.dtek.chalmers.se/Climbing/index.html

Climbing dictionary, a guide to rating systems for climbs, trip reports, techniques and training, and a trivia quiz.

CricInfo: The Home of Cricket on the Internet

http://www-uk.cricket.org/

The site includes reports on recent and live test matches, and details of the domestic seasons throughout the cricket-playing world.

England 2006

http://www.fa2006.org/

The reasons why the Football Association believes the 2000 World Cup should be held in Britain, and the latest news of the campaign are reported here.

English Basketball Association

http://www.basketballengland.org.uk/

The official Web site of the English Basketball Association. This Web site includes an events calendar, and articles from Zone Press, the official publication of the Association.

Football Unlimited

http://www.footballunlimited.co.uk/

Football database from *The Guardian*. This site contains the breaking football stories from all divisions, and also includes full statistics for each club.

GolfWeb

http://www.golfweb.com/

This site includes news, a library section, and an interactive search facility of over 14,000 courses worldwide.

History of the Olympic Games

http://devlab.dartmouth.edu/olympic/history/

This site describes the birth, development, and significance of the Olympic Games in ancient times.

Horse News

http://www.horsenews.com/

Equestrian Times Web site which offers news and photos from the worlds of show jumping, dressage, and three-day eventing.

Ice Skating International Online

http://www1.crl.com/~iceskate/

Online magazine that contains details of many international competitions.

International Amateur Athletics Federation

http://www.iaaf.org/

Wealth of authoritative information about athletics, with pages on each of the events.

International Sailing Federation

http://sailing.org/

The site includes information on international competitions, news and articles, and weather reports.

Internet Squash Federation

http://www.squash.org/

Information about clubs, training, doping policy, hardware, history, newsletters, player profiles, and rules.

Lord's – The Home of Cricket

http://www.lords.org/

Official site of the world's foremost cricket ground. In addition to information about the ground, there is constantly updated cricket news.

Motor Racing Regulations

http://www.fia.com/homepage/regle-a.htm

Rules, regulations, and results of international motor racing from the Fédération Internationale de l'Automobile (FIA).

Official Site of the Championships – Wimbledon

http://www.wimbledon.org/

Official site of one of the world's most prestigious tennis tournaments. There is a comprehensive history of the championship, and during Wimbledon fortnight there is a constantly updated news service.

Rowing FAQ

http://riceinfo.rice.edu/~hofer/Rowingfaq.html

Various classes of boats, races and regulations, and rowing terminology are clearly explained. There is also advice on technique.

Schneid's Volleyball Page

http://www.xnet.com/~schneid/vball.shtml

Guide designed for both coach and player, including ways to improve your game and answers to 'frequently asked questions'.

Ski Club of Great Britain

http://www.skiclub.co.uk/

Official Ski Club of Great Britain Web site which features snow reports, articles, and resort reviews.

Sport of Gymnastics

http://www.usa-gymnastics.org/gymnastics/

Basic guide to gymnastics from USA Gymnastics Online.

Table Tennis FAQ

http://peacock.tnjc.edu.tw/ADD/sport/faq.html

Comprehensive list of answers to common questions about table tennis.

Tennis

http://www.cse.unsw.edu.au/~s2213093/tennis.html

This site includes current world ratings of the top male and female pros and a complete list of winners of the four major Grand Slam events since 1980.

10 Tenths Motor Sport

http://www.ten-tenths.com/

Motor Sport Web site which covers all aspects of UK motor sports from Indy to Touring, and Karting to Speedway.

Tour de France

http://www.letour.fr/

Official site of the Tour de France that includes accounts of past tours and a guide to next year's event. Some pages are only available in French.

Triathlete's Web

http://w3.one.net/~triweb/triweb.html

The 'Essentials' section contains answers to frequently asked questions, and this site also includes articles on such topics as safe cycling.

UK Karting

http://www.karting.co.uk/

Comprehensive source of information about the karting scene in the UK.

Water Polo

http://www.ausport.gov.au/wpolo/wposp.html

Australian Sports Commission's description of the game's history, rules, and tactics.

Welcome to the Real Tennis Web Site

http://www.real-tennis.com/

Comprehensive information on the history, rules, and world of real tennis.

Windsurfer

http://www.windsurfer.com/

'How to' guide to windsurfing for the beginner or the professional.

Winning Post

http://www.winning-post.com/

National Hunt racing site with reviews and previews of all the major races.

Women's Sports Federation

http://www.wsf.org.uk/

The Women's Sports Foundation was set up 'to pursue and promote equity for women in and through sport'.

World Snooker Association

http://www.wpbsa.com/

The Web site features news, explanations of the rules of snooker, world rankings, and a tournament calendar.

INDEX